# FIRST CENSUS
# OF THE UNITED STATES
# 1790

# CONNECTICUT

**Southern Historical Press, Inc.**
**Greenville, South Carolina**

This volume was reproduced
from a personal copy located in
the Publishers private library

Please direct all correspondence and book orders to:
**SOUTHERN HISTORICAL PRESS, Inc.**
**1071 Park West Blvd.**
**Greenville, SC 29611**

Copyright 1908 by: Government Printing Office
Washington, D.C.
ISBN #978-1-63914-689-5
*Printed in the United States of America*

DEPARTMENT OF COMMERCE AND LABOR
BUREAU OF THE CENSUS
S. N. D. NORTH, DIRECTOR

---

# HEADS OF FAMILIES

AT THE FIRST CENSUS OF THE

UNITED STATES TAKEN

IN THE YEAR

1790

## CONNECTICUT

WASHINGTON
GOVERNMENT PRINTING OFFICE
1908

# HEADS OF FAMILIES AT THE FIRST CENSUS
## 1790

INTRODUCTION.

The First Census of the United States (1790) comprised an enumeration of the inhabitants of the present states of Connecticut, Delaware, Georgia, Kentucky, Maine, Maryland, Massachusetts, New Hampshire, New Jersey, New York, North Carolina, Pennsylvania, Rhode Island, South Carolina, Tennessee, Vermont, and Virginia.

A complete set of the schedules for each state, with a summary for the counties, and in many cases for towns, was filed in the State Department, but unfortunately they are not now complete, the returns for the states of Delaware, Georgia, Kentucky, New Jersey, Tennessee, and Virginia having been destroyed when the British burned the Capitol at Washington during the War of 1812. For several of the states for which schedules are lacking it is probable that the Director of the Census could obtain lists which would present the names of most of the heads of families at the date of the First Census. In Virginia, state enumerations were made in 1782, 1783, 1784, and 1785, but the lists on file in the State Library include the names for only 39 of the 78 counties into which the state was divided.

The schedules of 1790 form a unique inheritance for the Nation, since they represent for each of the states concerned a complete list of the heads of families in the United States at the time of the adoption of the Constitution. The framers were the statesmen and leaders of thought, but those whose names appear upon the schedules of the First Census were in general the plain citizens who by their conduct in war and peace made the Constitution possible and by their intelligence and self-restraint put it into successful operation.

The total population of the United States in 1790, exclusive of slaves, as derived from the schedules was 3,231,533. The only names appearing upon the schedules, however, were those of heads of families, and as at that period the families averaged 6 persons, the total number was approximately 540,000, or slightly more than half a million. The number of names which is now lacking because of the destruction of the schedules is approximately 140,000, thus leaving schedules containing about 400,000 names.

The information contained in the published report of the First Census of the United States, a small volume of 56 pages, was not uniform for the several states and territories. For New England and one or two of the other states the population was presented by counties and towns; that of New Jersey appeared partly by counties and towns and partly by counties only; in other cases the returns were given by counties only. Thus the complete transcript of the names of heads of families, with accompanying information, presents for the first time detailed information as to the number of inhabitants—males, females, etc.—for each minor civil division in all those states for which such information was not originally published.

In response to repeated requests from patriotic societies and persons interested in genealogy, or desirous of studying the early history of the United States, Congress added to the sundry civil appropriation bill for the fiscal year 1907 the following paragraph:

The Director of the Census is hereby authorized and directed to publish, in a permanent form, by counties and minor civil divisions, the names of the heads of families returned at the First Census of the United States in seventeen hundred and ninety; and the Director of the Census is authorized, in his discretion, to sell said publications, the proceeds thereof to be covered into the Treasury of the United States, to be deposited to the credit of miscellaneous receipts on account of "Proceeds of sales of Government property:"

*Provided*, That no expense shall be incurred hereunder additional to appropriations for the Census Office for printing therefor made for the fiscal year nineteen hundred and seven; and the Director of the Census is hereby directed to report to Congress at its next session the cost incurred hereunder and the price fixed for said publications and the total received therefor.

The amount of money appropriated by Congress for the Census printing for the fiscal year mentioned was unfortunately not sufficient to meet the current requirement of the Office and to publish the transcription of the First Census, and no provision was made in the sundry civil appropriation bill for 1908 for the continuance of authority to publish these important records. Resources, however, were available for printing a small section of the work, and the schedules of New Hampshire, Vermont, and Maryland accordingly were published.

The urgent deficiency bill, approved February 15, 1908, contained the following provision:

> That the Director of the Census is hereby authorized and directed to expend so much of the appropriation for printing for the Department of Commerce and Labor allotted by law to the Census Office for the fiscal year ending June thirtieth, nineteen hundred and eight, as may be necessary to continue and complete the publication of the names of the heads of families returned at the First Census of the United States, as authorized by the sundry civil appropriation act approved June thirtieth, nineteen hundred and six.

In accordance with the authority given in the paragraph quoted above, the names returned at the First Census in the states of Connecticut, Maine, Massachusetts, New York, North Carolina, Pennsylvania, Rhode Island, and South Carolina have been published, thus completing the roster of the heads of families in 1790 so far as they can be shown from the records of the Census Office. As the Federal census schedules of the state of Virginia for 1790 are missing, the lists of the state enumerations made in 1782, 1783, 1784, and 1785 have been substituted and, while not complete, they will, undoubtedly, prove of great value.

### THE FIRST CENSUS.

The First Census act was passed at the second session of the First Congress, and was signed by President Washington on March 1, 1790. The task of making the first enumeration of inhabitants was placed upon the President. Under this law the marshals of the several judicial districts were required to ascertain the number of inhabitants within their respective districts, omitting Indians not taxed, and distinguishing free persons (including those bound to service for a term of years) from all others; the sex and color of free persons; and the number of free males 16 years of age and over.

The object of the inquiry last mentioned was, undoubtedly, to obtain definite knowledge as to the military and industrial strength of the country. This fact possesses special interest, because the Constitution directs merely an enumeration of inhabitants. Thus the demand for increasingly extensive information, which has been so marked a characteristic of census legislation, began with the First Congress that dealt with the subject.

The method followed by the President in putting into operation the First Census law, although the object of extended investigation, is not definitely known. It is supposed that the President or the Secretary of State dispatched copies of the law, and perhaps of instructions also, to the marshals. There is, however, some ground for disputing this conclusion. At least one of the reports in the census volume of 1790 was furnished by a governor. This, together with the fact that there is no record of correspondence with the marshals on the subject of the census, but that there is a record of such correspondence with the governors, makes very strong the inference that the marshals received their instructions through the governors of the states. This inference is strengthened by the fact that in 1790 the state of Massachusetts furnished the printed blanks, and also by the fact that the law relating to the Second Census specifically charged the Secretary of State to superintend the enumeration and to communicate directly with the marshals.

By the terms of the First Census law nine months were allowed in which to complete the enumeration. The census taking was supervised by the marshals of the several judicial districts, who employed assistant marshals to act as enumerators. There were 17 marshals. The records showing the number of assistant marshals employed in 1790, 1800, and 1810 were destroyed by fire, but the number employed in 1790 has been estimated at 650.

The schedules which these officials prepared consist of lists of names of heads of families; each name appears in a stub, or first column, which is followed by five columns, giving details of the family. These columns are headed as follows:

> Free white males of 16 years and upward, including heads of families.
> Free white males under 16 years.
> Free white females, including heads of families.
> All other free persons.
> Slaves.

The assistant marshals made two copies of the returns; in accordance with the law one copy was posted in the immediate neighborhood for the information of the public, and the other was transmitted to the marshal in charge, to be forwarded to the President. The schedules were turned over by the President to the Secretary of State. Little or no tabulation was required, and the report of the First Census, as also the reports of the Second, Third, and Fourth, was produced without the employment of any clerical force, the summaries being transmitted directly to the printer. The total population as returned in 1790 was 3,929,214, and the entire cost of the census was $44,377.

A summary of the results of the First Census, not including the returns for South Carolina, was transmitted to Congress by President Washington on October 27, 1791. The legal period for enumeration, nine months, had been extended, the longest time consumed being eighteen months in South Carolina. The report of October 27 was printed in full, and published in what is now a very rare little volume; afterwards the report for South Carolina was "tipped in." To contain the results of the Twelfth Census, ten large quarto volumes, comprising in all 10,400 pages, were required. No illustration of the expansion of census inquiry can be more striking.

The original schedules of the First Census are now contained in 26 bound volumes, preserved in the Census Office. For the most part the headings of the schedules were written in by hand. Indeed, up to and including 1820, the assistant marshals generally used for the schedules such paper as they happened to have, ruling it, writing in the headings, and binding the sheets together themselves. In some cases merchants' account paper was used, and now and then the schedules were bound in wall paper.

As a consequence of requiring marshals to supply their own blanks, the volumes containing the schedules vary in size from about 7 inches long, 3 inches wide, and ½ inch thick to 21 inches long, 14 inches wide, and 6 inches thick. Some of the sheets in these volumes are only 4 inches long, but a few are 3 feet in length, necessitating several folds. In some cases leaves burned at the edges have been covered with transparent silk to preserve them.

### THE UNITED STATES IN 1790.

In March, 1790, the Union consisted of twelve states—Rhode Island, the last of the original thirteen to enter the Union, being admitted May 29 of the same year. Vermont, the first addition, was admitted in the following year, before the results of the First Census were announced. Maine was a part of Massachusetts, Kentucky was a part of Virginia, and the present states of Alabama and Mississippi were parts of Georgia. The present states of Ohio, Indiana, Illinois, Michigan, and Wisconsin, with part of Minnesota, were known as the Northwest Territory, and the present state of Tennessee, then a part of North Carolina, was soon to be organized as the Southwest Territory.

The United States was bounded on the west by the Mississippi river, beyond which stretched that vast and unexplored wilderness belonging to the Spanish King, which was afterwards ceded to the United States by France as the Louisiana Purchase, and now comprises the great and populous states of South Dakota, Iowa, Nebraska, Missouri, Kansas, Arkansas, and Oklahoma, and portions of Minnesota, North Dakota, Montana, Wyoming, Colorado, New Mexico, Texas, and Louisiana. The Louisiana Purchase was not consummated for more than a decade after the First Census was taken. On the south was another Spanish colony known as the Floridas. The greater part of Texas, then a part of the colony of Mexico, belonged to Spain; and California, Nevada, Utah, Arizona, and a portion of New Mexico, also the property of Spain, although penetrated here and there by venturesome explorers and missionaries, were, for the most part, an undiscovered wilderness.

The gross area of the United States was 827,844 square miles, but the settled area was only 239,935 square miles, or about 29 per cent of the total. Though the area covered by the enumeration in 1790 seems very small when compared with the present area of the United States, the difficulties which confronted the census taker were vastly greater than in 1900. In many localities there were no roads, and where these did exist they were poor and frequently impassable; bridges were almost unknown. Transportation was entirely by horseback, stage, or private coach. A journey as long as that from New York to Washington was a serious undertaking, requiring eight days under the most favorable conditions. Western New York was a wilderness, Elmira and Binghamton being but detached hamlets. The territory west of the Allegheny mountains, with the exception of a portion of Kentucky, was unsettled and scarcely penetrated. Detroit and Vincennes were too small and isolated to merit consideration. Philadelphia was the capital of the United States. Washington was a mere Government project, not even named, but known as the Federal City. Indeed, by the spring of 1793, only one wall of the White House had been constructed, and the site for the Capitol had been merely surveyed. New York city in 1790 possessed a population of only 33,131, although it was the largest city in the United States; Philadelphia was second, with 28,522; and Boston third, with 18,320. Mails were transported in very irregular fashion, and correspondence was expensive and uncertain.

There were, moreover, other difficulties which were of serious moment in 1790, but which long ago ceased to be problems in census taking. The inhabitants, having no experience with census taking, imagined that some scheme for increasing taxation was involved, and were inclined to be cautious lest they should reveal too much of their own affairs. There was also opposition to enumeration on religious grounds, a count of inhabitants being regarded by many as a cause for divine displeasure. The boundaries of towns and other minor divisions, and even those of counties, were in many cases unknown or not defined at all. The hitherto semi-independent states had been under the control of the Federal Government for so short a time that the different sections had not yet been welded into an harmonious nationality in which the Federal authority should be unquestioned and instructions promptly and fully obeyed.

# AN ACT PROVIDING FOR THE ENUMERATION OF THE INHABITANTS OF THE UNITED STATES

### APPROVED MARCH 1, 1790

SECTION 1. Be it enacted by the Senate and House of Representatives of the United States of America in Congress assembled, That the marshals of the several districts of the United States shall be, and they are hereby authorized and required to cause the number of the inhabitants within their respective districts to be taken; omitting in such enumeration Indians not taxed, and distinguishing free persons, including those bound to service for a term of years, from all others; distinguishing also the sexes and colours of free persons, and the free males of sixteen years and upwards from those under that age; for effecting which purpose the marshals shall have power to appoint as many assistants within their respective districts as to them shall appear necessary; assigning to each assistant a certain division of his district, which division shall consist of one or more counties, cities, towns, townships, hundreds or parishes, or of a territory plainly and distinctly bounded by water courses, mountains, or public roads. The marshals and their assistants shall respectively take an oath or affirmation, before some judge or justice of the peace, resident within their respective districts, previous to their entering on the discharge of the duties by this act required. The oath or affirmation of the marshal shall be, "I, A. B., Marshal of the district of ———, do solemnly swear (or affirm) that I will well and truly cause to be made a just and perfect enumeration and description of all persons resident within my district, and return the same to the President of the United States, agreeably to the directions of an act of Congress, intituled 'An act providing for the enumeration of the inhabitants of the United States,' according to the best of my ability." The oath or affirmation of an assistant shall be "I, A. B., do solemnly swear (or affirm) that I will make a just and perfect enumeration and description of all persons resident within the division assigned to me by the marshal of the district of ———, and make due return thereof to the said marshal, agreeably to the directions of an act of Congress, intituled 'An act providing for the enumeration of the inhabitants of the United States,' according to the best of my ability." The enumeration shall commence on the first Monday in August next, and shall close within nine calendar months thereafter. The several assistants shall, within the said nine months, transmit to the marshals by whom they shall be respectively appointed, accurate returns of all persons, except Indians not taxed, within their respective divisions, which returns shall be made in a schedule, distinguishing the several families by the names of their master, mistress, steward, overseer, or other principal person therein, in manner following, that is to say:

The number of persons within my division, consisting of ———, appears in a schedule hereto annexed, subscribed by me this ——— day of ———, 179–. A. B. *Assistant to the marshal of* ———.

*Schedule of the whole number of persons within the division allotted to A. B.*

| Names of heads of families. | Free white males of 16 years and upwards, including heads of families. | Free white males under 16 years. | Free white females, including heads of families. | All other free persons. | Slaves. |
|---|---|---|---|---|---|
| | | | | | |

SECTION 2. And be it further enacted, That every assistant failing to make return, or making a false return of the enumeration to the marshal, within the time by this act limited, shall forfeit the sum of two hundred dollars.

SECTION 3. And be it further enacted, That the marshals shall file the several returns aforesaid, with the clerks of their respective district courts, who are hereby directed to receive and carefully preserve the same: And the marshals respectively shall, on or before the first day of September, one thousand seven hundred and ninety-one, transmit to the President of the United States, the aggregate amount of each description of persons within their respective districts. And every marshal failing to file the returns of his assistants, or any of them, with the clerks of their respective district courts, or failing to return the aggregate amount of each description of persons in their respective districts, as the same shall appear from said returns, to the President of the United States within the time limited by this act, shall, for every such offense, forfeit the sum of eight hundred dollars; all which forfeitures shall be recoverable in the courts of the districts where the offenses shall be committed, or in the circuit courts to be held within the same, by action of debt, information or indictment; the one-half thereof to the use of the United States, and the other half to the informer; but where the prosecution shall be first instituted on the behalf of the United States, the whole shall accrue to their use. And for the more effectual discovery of offenses, the judges of the several district courts, at their next sessions, to be held after the expiration of the time allowed for making the returns of the enumeration hereby directed, to the President of the United States, shall give this act in charge to the grand juries, in their respective courts, and shall cause the returns of the several assistants to be laid before them for their inspection.

SECTION 4. And be it further enacted, That every assistant shall receive at the rate of one dollar for every one hundred and fifty persons by him returned, where such persons reside in the country; and where such persons reside in a city, or town, containing more than five thousand persons, such assistants shall receive at the rate of one dollar for every three hundred persons; but where, from the dispersed situation of the inhabitants in some divisions, one dollar for every one hundred and fifty persons shall be insufficient, the marshals, with the approbation of the judges of their respective districts, may make such further allowance to the assistants in such divisions as shall be deemed an adequate compensation, provided the same does not exceed one dollar for every fifty persons by them returned. The several marshals shall receive as follows: The marshal of the district of Maine, two hundred dollars; the marshal of the district of New Hampshire, two hundred dollars; the marshal of the district of Massachusetts, three hundred dollars; the marshal of the district of Connecticut, two hundred dollars; the marshal of the district of New York, three hundred dollars; the marshal of the district of New Jersey, two hundred dollars; the marshal of the district of Pennsylvania, three hundred dollars; the marshal of the district of Delaware, one hundred dollars; the marshal of the district of Maryland, three hundred dollars; the marshal of the district of Virginia, five hundred dollars; the marshal of the district of Kentucky, two hundred and fifty dollars; the marshal of the district of North Carolina, three hundred and fifty dollars; the marshal of the district of South Carolina, three hundred dollars; the marshal of the district of Georgia, two hundred and fifty dollars. And to obviate all doubts which may arise respecting the persons to be returned, and the manner of making the returns.

SECTION 5. Be it enacted, That every person whose usual place of abode shall be in any family on the aforesaid first Monday in August next, shall be returned as of such family; the name of every person, who shall be an inhabitant of any district, but without a settled place of residence, shall be inserted in the column of the aforesaid schedule, which is allotted for the heads of families, in that division where he or she shall be on the said first Monday in August next, and every person occasionally absent at the time of the enumeration, as belonging to that place in which he usually resides in the United States.

SECTION 6. And be it further enacted, That each and every person more than 16 years of age, whether heads of families or not, belonging to any family within any division of a district made or established within the United States, shall be, and hereby is, obliged to render to such assistant of the division, a true account, if required, to the best of his or her knowledge, of all and every person belonging to such family, respectively, according to the several descriptions aforesaid, on pain of forfeiting twenty dollars, to be sued for and recovered by such assistant, the one-half for his own use, and the other half for the use of the United States.

SECTION 7. And be it further enacted, That each assistant shall, previous to making his return to the marshal, cause a correct copy, signed by himself, of the schedule containing the number of inhabitants within his division, to be set up at two of the most public places within the same, there to remain for the inspection of all concerned; for each of which copies the said assistant shall be entitled to receive two dollars, provided proof of a copy of the schedule having been so set up and suffered to remain, shall be transmitted to the marshal, with the return of the number of persons; and in case any assistant shall fail to make such proof to the marshal, he shall forfeit the compensation by this act allowed him.

Approved March 1, 1790.

## FIRST CENSUS OF THE UNITED STATES.

*Population of the United States as returned at the First Census, by states: 1790.*

| DISTRICT. | Free white males of 16 years and upward, including heads of families. | Free white males under 16 years. | Free white females, including heads of families. | All other free persons. | Slaves. | Total. |
|---|---|---|---|---|---|---|
| Vermont | 22,435 | 22,328 | 40,505 | 255 | [1] 16 | [2] 85,539 |
| New Hampshire | 36,086 | 34,851 | 70,160 | 630 | 158 | 141,885 |
| Maine | 24,384 | 24,748 | 46,870 | 538 | None. | 96,540 |
| Massachusetts | 95,453 | 87,289 | 190,582 | 5,463 | None. | 378,787 |
| Rhode Island | 16,019 | 15,799 | 32,652 | 3,407 | 948 | 68,825 |
| Connecticut | 60,523 | 54,403 | 117,448 | 2,808 | 2,764 | 237,946 |
| New York | 83,700 | 78,122 | 152,320 | 4,654 | 21,324 | 340,120 |
| New Jersey | 45,251 | 41,416 | 83,287 | 2,762 | 11,423 | 184,139 |
| Pennsylvania | 110,788 | 106,948 | 206,363 | 6,537 | 3,737 | 434,373 |
| Delaware | 11,783 | 12,143 | 22,384 | 3,899 | 8,887 | [3] 59,094 |
| Maryland | 55,915 | 51,339 | 101,395 | 8,043 | 103,036 | 319,728 |
| Virginia | 110,936 | 116,135 | 215,046 | 12,866 | 292,627 | 747,610 |
| Kentucky | 15,154 | 17,057 | 28,922 | 114 | 12,430 | 73,677 |
| North Carolina | 69,988 | 77,506 | 140,710 | 4,975 | 100,572 | 393,751 |
| South Carolina | 35,576 | 37,722 | 66,880 | 1,801 | 107,094 | 249,073 |
| Georgia | 13,103 | 14,044 | 25,739 | 398 | 29,264 | 82,548 |
| Total number of inhabitants of the United States exclusive of S. Western and N. territory | 807,094 | 791,850 | 1,541,263 | 59,150 | 694,280 | 3,893,635 |

| | Free white males of 21 years and upward. | Free males under 21 years of age. | Free white females. | All other persons. | Slaves. | Total. |
|---|---|---|---|---|---|---|
| S. W. territory | 6,271 | 10,277 | 15,365 | 361 | 3,417 | 35,691 |
| N. " | | | | | | |

[1] The census of 1790, published in 1791, reports 16 slaves in Vermont. Subsequently, and up to 1860, the number is given as 17. An examination of the original manuscript returns shows that there never were any slaves in Vermont. The original error occurred in preparing the results for publication, when 16 persons, returned as "Free colored," were classified as "Slave."

[2] Corrected figures are 85,425, or 114 less than figures published in 1790, due to an error of addition in the returns for each of the towns of Fairfield, Milton, Shelburne, and Williston, in the county of Chittenden; Brookfield, Newbury, Randolph, and Strafford, in the county of Orange; Castleton, Clarendon, Hubbardton, Poultney, Rutland, Shrewsbury, and Wallingford, in the county of Rutland; Dummerston, Guilford, Halifax, and Westminster, in the county of Windham; and Woodstock, in the county of Windsor.

[3] Corrected figures are 59,096, or 2 more than figures published in 1790, due to error in addition.

# HEADS OF FAMILIES—CONNECTICUT.

*Summary of population, by counties and towns: 1790.*

## FAIRFIELD COUNTY.

| TOWN. | Number of heads of families. | Free white males of 16 years and upward, including heads of families. | Free white males under 16 years. | Free white females, including heads of families. | All other free persons. | Slaves. | Total. |
|---|---|---|---|---|---|---|---|
| Brookfield | 189 | 267 | 219 | 522 | 7 | 3 | 1,018 |
| Danbury | 563 | 780 | 704 | 1,503 | 20 | 23 | 3,030 |
| Fairfield | 707 | 1,027 | 896 | 1,869 | 14 | 203 | 4,009 |
| Greenwich | 527 | 801 | 638 | 1,572 | 32 | 89 | 3,132 |
| Huntington | 476 | 671 | 625 | 1,278 | 48 | 120 | 2,742 |
| New Fairfield | 277 | 401 | 404 | 755 | 4 | 9 | 1,573 |
| Newtown | 445 | 723 | 635 | 1,342 | 10 | 64 | 2,774 |
| Norwalk } Stamford | 1,629 | 2,196 | 2,160 | 4,253 | 88 | 113 | 8,810 |
| Reading | 264 | 392 | 327 | 735 | 17 | 32 | 1,503 |
| Ridgefield | 351 | 488 | 461 | 989 | 4 | 5 | 1,947 |
| Stratford | 548 | 822 | 726 | 1,536 | 59 | 98 | 3,241 |
| Weston | 437 | 619 | 603 | 1,187 | 24 | 36 | 2,469 |
| Total | 6,413 | 9,187 | 8,398 | 17,541 | 327 | 795 | 36,248 |

## HARTFORD COUNTY.

| TOWN. | Number of heads of families. | Free white males of 16 years and upward. | Free white males under 16 years. | Free white females. | All other free persons. | Slaves. | Total. |
|---|---|---|---|---|---|---|---|
| Berlin | 452 | 631 | 561 | 1,258 | 11 | 4 | 2,465 |
| Bristol | 440 | 595 | 612 | 1,236 | 16 | 3 | 2,462 |
| East Hartford | 473 | 790 | 670 | 1,519 | 7 | 30 | 3,016 |
| East Windsor | 481 | 715 | 563 | 1,281 | 33 | 8 | 2,600 |
| Enfield | 317 | 478 | 382 | 927 | | 13 | 1,800 |
| Farmington | 439 | 679 | 673 | 1,302 | 34 | 8 | 2,696 |
| Glastenbury | 468 | 639 | 672 | 1,323 | 71 | 27 | 2,732 |
| Granby | 489 | 674 | 669 | 1,226 | 21 | 5 | 2,595 |
| Hartford | 664 | 1,057 | 858 | 2,033 | 94 | 48 | 4,090 |
| Simsbury | 424 | 657 | 649 | 1,256 | 12 | 2 | 2,576 |
| Southington | 389 | 540 | 504 | 1,038 | 16 | 12 | 2,110 |
| Suffield | 407 | 639 | 592 | 1,181 | 27 | 28 | 2,467 |
| Wethersfield | 685 | 950 | 816 | 1,924 | 52 | 64 | 3,806 |
| Windsor | 456 | 738 | 619 | 1,310 | 36 | 11 | 2,714 |
| Total | 6,584 | 9,782 | 8,840 | 18,814 | 430 | 263 | 38,129 |

## LITCHFIELD COUNTY.

| TOWN. | Number of heads of families. | Free white males of 16 years and upward. | Free white males under 16 years. | Free white females. | All other free persons. | Slaves. | Total. |
|---|---|---|---|---|---|---|---|
| Bethlem | 178 | 275 | 243 | 534 | | 4 | 1,056 |
| Cornwall | 256 | 396 | 318 | 710 | 27 | 19 | 1,470 |
| Harwinton | 230 | 354 | 334 | 673 | | 6 | 1,367 |
| Kent | 215 | 348 | 317 | 635 | 11 | 7 | 1,318 |
| Litchfield | 3,361 | 5,206 | 4,931 | 9,912 | 199 | 94 | 20,342 |
| New Milford | 555 | 849 | 728 | 1,523 | 41 | 26 | 3,167 |
| Southbury | 308 | 485 | 369 | 842 | 19 | 23 | 1,738 |
| Warren | 146 | 199 | 207 | 373 | 5 | 6 | 790 |
| Washington | 268 | 442 | 399 | 818 | 11 | 5 | 1,675 |
| Watertown | 573 | 801 | 779 | 1,562 | 3 | 25 | 3,170 |
| Woodbury | 476 | 686 | 624 | 1,327 | 7 | 18 | 2,662 |
| Total | 6,566 | 10,041 | 9,249 | 18,909 | 323 | 233 | 38,755 |

## MIDDLESEX COUNTY.

| TOWN. | Number of heads of families. | Free white males of 16 years and upward. | Free white males under 16 years. | Free white females. | All other free persons. | Slaves. | Total. |
|---|---|---|---|---|---|---|---|
| Chatham | 563 | 812 | 730 | 1,648 | 21 | 19 | 3,230 |
| East Haddam | 472 | 702 | 592 | 1,400 | 35 | 20 | 2,749 |
| Haddam | 356 | 576 | 474 | 1,142 | 2 | 1 | 2,195 |
| Killingworth | 390 | 586 | 454 | 1,094 | 11 | 11 | 2,156 |
| Middletown | 944 | 1,240 | 1,266 | 2,684 | 56 | 129 | 5,375 |
| Saybrook | 559 | 819 | 696 | 1,663 | 19 | 36 | 3,233 |
| Total | 3,284 | 4,735 | 4,212 | 9,631 | 144 | 216 | 18,938 |

## NEW HAVEN COUNTY.

| TOWN. | Number of heads of families. | Free white males of 16 years and upward. | Free white males under 16 years. | Free white females. | All other free persons. | Slaves. | Total. |
|---|---|---|---|---|---|---|---|
| Branford | 384 | 565 | 504 | 1,108 | 36 | 54 | 2,267 |
| Cheshire | 440 | 592 | 507 | 1,192 | 31 | 15 | 2,337 |
| Derby | 553 | 751 | 727 | 1,414 | 52 | 50 | 2,994 |
| Durham | 209 | 315 | 214 | 526 | 7 | 9 | 1,071 |
| East Haven | 169 | 234 | 225 | 524 | 7 | 35 | 1,025 |
| Guilford | 728 | 951 | 714 | 1,732 | 22 | 41 | 3,460 |
| Hamden | 291 | 374 | 322 | 718 | 4 | 4 | 1,422 |
| Milford | 446 | 536 | 442 | 988 | 69 | 63 | 2,098 |
| New Haven city | 918 | 1,125 | 928 | 2,234 | 121 | 76 | 4,484 |
| North Haven | 238 | 320 | 275 | 626 | 8 | 7 | 1,236 |
| Wallingford | 656 | 846 | 784 | 1,667 | 26 | 52 | 3,375 |
| Waterbury | 552 | 734 | 717 | 1,460 | 14 | 12 | 2,937 |
| Woodbridge | 414 | 513 | 499 | 1,069 | 28 | 15 | 2,124 |
| Total | 5,998 | 7,856 | 6,858 | 15,258 | 425 | 433 | 30,830 |

*Summary of population, by counties and towns: 1790—Continued.*

## NEW LONDON COUNTY.

| TOWN. | Number of heads of families. | Free white males of 16 years and upward. | Free white males under 16 years. | Free white females. | All other free persons. | Slaves. | Total. |
|---|---|---|---|---|---|---|---|
| Not returned by towns | 5,692 | 8,224 | 7,183 | 16,478 | 729 | 586 | 33,200 |

## TOLLAND COUNTY.

| TOWN. | Number of heads of families. | Free white males of 16 years and upward. | Free white males under 16 years. | Free white females. | All other free persons. | Slaves. | Total. |
|---|---|---|---|---|---|---|---|
| Bolton | 228 | 317 | 322 | 648 | 4 | 2 | 1,293 |
| Coventry | 336 | 512 | 515 | 1,079 | 17 | 7 | 2,130 |
| Ellington | 171 | 285 | 220 | 534 | 15 | 2 | 1,056 |
| Hebron | 345 | 611 | 516 | 1,064 | 23 | 20 | 2,234 |
| Somers | 200 | 224 | 301 | 595 | 2 | 5 | 1,127 |
| Stafford | 315 | 476 | 445 | 956 | 4 | 4 | 1,885 |
| Tolland | 236 | 386 | 422 | 713 | 12 | 5 | 1,538 |
| Union | 100 | 150 | 162 | 318 | | 1 | 631 |
| Willington | 208 | 302 | 289 | 603 | 17 | 1 | 1,212 |
| Total | 2,139 | 3,263 | 3,192 | 6,510 | 94 | 47 | 13,106 |

## WINDHAM COUNTY.

| TOWN. | Number of heads of families. | Free white males of 16 years and upward. | Free white males under 16 years. | Free white females. | All other free persons. | Slaves. | Total. |
|---|---|---|---|---|---|---|---|
| Ashford | 393 | 661 | 644 | 1,250 | 21 | 7 | 2,583 |
| Brooklyne | 177 | 352 | 302 | 633 | 30 | 11 | 1,328 |
| Canterbury | 288 | 501 | 387 | 975 | 16 | 2 | 1,881 |
| Hampton | 201 | 338 | 303 | 680 | 10 | 1 | 1,332 |
| Killingley | 326 | 543 | 544 | 1,050 | 20 | 9 | 2,166 |
| Lebanon | 574 | 1,042 | 932 | 2,089 | 53 | 50 | 4,166 |
| Mansfield | 394 | 689 | 611 | 1,319 | 9 | 7 | 2,635 |
| Plainfield | 238 | 466 | 356 | 821 | 60 | 10 | 1,713 |
| Pomfret | 244 | 463 | 376 | 890 | 20 | 19 | 1,768 |
| Thompson | 333 | 562 | 555 | 1,138 | 5 | 7 | 2,267 |
| Voluntown | 290 | 487 | 435 | 915 | 14 | 21 | 1,872 |
| Windham | 414 | 670 | 580 | 1,424 | 63 | 28 | 2,765 |
| Woodstock | 330 | 666 | 526 | 1,222 | 19 | 12 | 2,445 |
| Total | 4,202 | 7,440 | 6,551 | 14,406 | 340 | 184 | 28,921 |

*Assistant marshals for the state: 1790.*

| DISTRICT. | NAME. |
|---|---|
| Fairfield county (part of).—Brookfield, Danbury, Fairfield, Huntington, and New Fairfield towns. | Daniel Bradley. |
| Fairfield county (part of).—Greenwich, Norwalk, and Stamford towns. | David Maltbie. |
| Fairfield county (part of).—Newtown, Reading, Stratford, and Weston towns. | Sam¹ B. Sherwood. |
| Fairfield county (part of).—Ridgefield town. | John Keeler. |
| Hartford county.—Berlin, Bristol, East Hartford, East Windsor, Enfield, Farmington, Glastenbury, Granby, Hartford, Simsbury, Southington, Suffield, Wethersfield, and Windsor towns. | John Dodd. |
| Litchfield county (part of).—Bethlem, Cornwall, Harwinton, Kent, New Milford, Southbury, Warren, Washington, Watertown, and Woodbury towns. | David Judson. |
| Litchfield county (part of).—Litchfield town. | Sam¹ Marsh. |
| Middlesex county.—Chatham, East Haddam, Haddam, Killingworth, Middletown, and Saybrook towns. | Sam¹ Canfield. |
| New Haven county.—Branford, Cheshire, Derby, Durham, East Haven, Guilford, Hamden, Milford, North Haven, Wallingford, Waterbury, and Woodbridge towns, and New Haven city. | John Rutherford Throop. |
| New London county.—Entire county. | Joshua Huntington. |
| Tolland county.—Bolton, Coventry, Ellington, Hebron, Somers, Stafford, Tolland, Union, and Willington towns. | Wm Williams. |
| Windham county.—Ashford, Brooklyne, Canterbury, Hampton, Killingley, Lebanon, Mansfield, Plainfield, Pomfret, Thompson, Voluntown, Windham, and Woodstock towns. | Eben^r Gray. |

## FAIRFIELD COUNTY.[1]

| NAME OF HEAD OF FAMILY. | Free white males of 16 years and upward, including heads of families. | Free white males under 16 years. | Free white females, including heads of families. | All other free persons. | Slaves. | NAME OF HEAD OF FAMILY. | Free white males of 16 years and upward, including heads of families. | Free white males under 16 years. | Free white females, including heads of families. | All other free persons. | Slaves. | NAME OF HEAD OF FAMILY. | Free white males of 16 years and upward, including heads of families. | Free white males under 16 years. | Free white females, including heads of families. | All other free persons. | Slaves. |
|---|---|---|---|---|---|---|---|---|---|---|---|---|---|---|---|---|---|
| **BROOKFIELD TOWN.** | | | | | | **BROOKFIELD TOWN—continued.** | | | | | | **BROOKFIELD TOWN—continued.** | | | | | |
| Stephens, Hezekiah, Jr. | 2 | 2 | 2 | | | Smith, Joseph | 1 | 4 | 3 | | | Northrop, Andrew | 1 | 3 | 3 | | |
| Morehouse, John | 1 | 1 | 2 | | | Sherman, Rufus | 1 | 1 | 2 | | | Picket, Thomas | 2 | | 3 | | |
| Frank, Robin | | | | 7 | | Bulkley, Luther | 1 | | 2 | | 1 | Platt, Nathan | 1 | 2 | 1 | | |
| Wakeley, Lemwell | 4 | 1 | 5 | | | Towner, Nathanel | 2 | 1 | 3 | | | Brooks, Thomas, Jr. | 1 | 1 | 3 | | |
| Rugles, Eden | 1 | | 1 | | | Wheeler, Amos | 2 | 3 | 3 | | | **DANBURY TOWN.** | | | | | |
| Buckingham, Curtis | 1 | | 1 | | | Lockwood, Isaac | 1 | 1 | 5 | | | | | | | | |
| Osborn, Israel | 1 | | 1 | | | Northrop, Isaac | 1 | 1 | 3 | | | Wood, James | 1 | 3 | 4 | | |
| Stephens, Hezekiah | 1 | 1 | 2 | | | Murrin, Samuel | 2 | | 1 | | | Olmsted, Daniel | 1 | | 2 | | |
| Brush, Joseph | 1 | 1 | 1 | | | Murrin, Andrew | 1 | 1 | 1 | | | Barnum, Josiah | 1 | | 4 | | |
| Starr, Giddeon | 1 | | 2 | | | Peck, David | 1 | 3 | 3 | | | Griffin, Catherine | | 2 | 2 | | |
| Chase, Isaac | 1 | 1 | 4 | | | Peck, Miel | 3 | 1 | 5 | | | Sanford, Joel | 1 | 1 | 1 | | |
| Hull, Abraham | 1 | | 1 | | | Camp, Nathan | 2 | 1 | 3 | | | Knapp, John | 1 | | 1 | | |
| Wileman, Lebeus | 1 | 1 | 2 | | | Bunnel, Job | 1 | 3 | 4 | | | Dightman, Thaddeus | 2 | 2 | 2 | | |
| Starr, Joseph | 2 | | 3 | | | Hawley, Nehemiah | 2 | 1 | 2 | | | Wood, Samuel | 3 | 2 | 4 | | |
| Wileman, Richard | 1 | 2 | 3 | | | Hawley, Jedidah | | 2 | 1 | | | Washburn, Joseph | 1 | 2 | 3 | | |
| Gregory, John, Jr. | 1 | 1 | 3 | | | Dunnen, Joseph | 1 | 1 | 2 | | | Clark, Mary | | | 1 | | 2 |
| Stephens, John | 1 | 1 | 3 | | | Hawley, Sarah | | | 2 | | 2 | Wood, Daniel | 1 | | 3 | | |
| Gregory, John | 2 | | 5 | | | Cole, Elezer | 1 | | 1 | | | Wood, Daniel, Jr. | 1 | 3 | 3 | | |
| Dunnen, Nathan | 2 | | 2 | | | Dunnen, Woolcott | 1 | 2 | 2 | | | Chapman, Joshua | 1 | 1 | 1 | | |
| Dunnen, Jeremiah | 1 | 1 | 4 | | | Bennet, John | 2 | 1 | 2 | | | Wood, Nathan | 2 | 1 | 5 | | |
| Starr, Zarr | 1 | 1 | 1 | | | Cox, William | 1 | 3 | 4 | | | Barnum, John | 1 | | 2 | | |
| Sturdevant, John | 1 | | 1 | | | Dunnen, Reubin | 1 | 3 | 4 | | | Dightman, Thomas | 1 | | 1 | | |
| Sturdevant, Timothy | 2 | 4 | 3 | | | Keeler, John, Jr. | 1 | 2 | 5 | | | Barnum, Noah | 1 | 2 | 2 | | |
| Barnum, Ebenezer | 1 | | 1 | | | Dunnen, Giddeon | 1 | 3 | 4 | | | Peck, Abijah | 1 | 1 | 2 | | |
| Dunnen, John | 1 | | 2 | | | Dunnen, Eli | 1 | | 1 | | | Benedict, Michael | 1 | | 1 | | |
| Penny, Jane | | | 1 | | | Dunnen, Luther | 1 | 2 | 2 | | | Barnum, Eliphilet | 1 | 2 | 4 | | |
| Starr, John | 1 | | 2 | | | Dunnen, Jered | 1 | 1 | 1 | | | Andrews, Hannah | 1 | | 1 | | |
| Hamblen, William | 1 | | 1 | | | Booth, Abel | 2 | 1 | 4 | | | Andrews, Samuel | 1 | 2 | 1 | | |
| Patch, Thompson | 1 | 6 | 2 | | | Booth, Philo | 2 | | 1 | | | Stringham, Peter | 1 | | 3 | | |
| Anderson, Daniel | 1 | | 5 | | | Jackson, Gershom | 2 | 2 | 6 | | | Benedict, Peter | 1 | 2 | 4 | | |
| Lobden, Daniel | 1 | 2 | 1 | | | Jackson, Ephraim | 1 | 2 | 4 | | | Hawley, Closen | 1 | 1 | 5 | | |
| Lobden, John | 1 | 1 | 4 | | | Tredway, John | 2 | | 5 | | | Brown, James | 1 | 1 | 4 | | |
| Clark, Oliver | 2 | | 2 | | | French, Samuel | 1 | 1 | 2 | | | Taylor, Major | 2 | 2 | 5 | | 1 |
| Starr, James | 2 | | 3 | | | Gun, Joseph | 1 | | 1 | | | Benedict, Eliakam | 2 | 2 | 2 | | |
| Brister, Isarel | 2 | | 2 | | | Davis, George | 1 | | 1 | | | Bennedict, Mary | | 1 | 1 | | |
| Lobden, Lewis | 1 | | 6 | | | Wakelin, James | 1 | | 2 | | | Hoyt, Comfort | 1 | 3 | 3 | | |
| Gray, Hezekiah | 1 | | 1 | | | Botchford, James | 1 | 2 | 2 | | | McClane, John | 3 | 1 | 7 | | 1 |
| Barnum, Isaac | 2 | | 2 | | | Hurd, Jabesh | 1 | | 3 | | | Clark, James | 7 | 3 | 6 | | |
| Veal, John | 1 | 2 | 3 | | | Hurd, Abel | 2 | | 8 | | | Seib, James | 1 | | 2 | | |
| Barnum, Ezbon | 1 | 2 | 5 | | | Northrop, Enos | 2 | 1 | 2 | | | Rider, John | 2 | 2 | 2 | | |
| Osborn, David | 2 | 1 | 2 | | | Sherman, Zadock | 3 | 2 | 4 | | | Foot, Eli | 1 | 1 | 2 | | |
| Barlow, Nehemiah | 3 | 1 | 3 | | | Smith, Ebenezer | 3 | 1 | 3 | | | Douglass, Nathan | 3 | 1 | 1 | | |
| Bennet, David | 1 | 2 | 2 | | | Smith, Sherman | 2 | 2 | 3 | | | Jarvis, Stephen | 2 | | 2 | | |
| Burrit, Franses | 1 | 1 | 2 | | | Smith, Joseph, 3d | 1 | 2 | 3 | | | White, Joseph M | 7 | 3 | 4 | | 1 |
| Osborn, James | 2 | 1 | 2 | | | Smith, Richard | 1 | 1 | 5 | | | Whiting, Frederick S. | 2 | 2 | 1 | | 1 |
| Camp, Abraham | 1 | | 1 | | | Blackman, Ebenezer | 1 | | 2 | | | Wood, John | 2 | | 1 | | |
| Camp, Levi | | 1 | 2 | | | Blackman, Niram | 1 | 1 | 1 | | | Starr, Thomas | 1 | 2 | 1 | | |
| Hubbell, Coleman | 1 | 3 | 2 | | | Blackman, Philo | 1 | 1 | 1 | | | Wood, David | 1 | 2 | 4 | | |
| Noble, Elethan | 2 | 4 | 3 | | | Hawse, James | 1 | | 1 | | | Church, Daniel | 1 | | 1 | | |
| Noble, Jesse | 2 | 2 | 5 | | | Bostwick, Levi | 3 | 5 | 4 | | | Benedict, Joshua | 1 | 1 | 6 | | |
| Smith, Jehiel | 1 | | 1 | | | Taylor, Andrew | 1 | 1 | 2 | | | Mygatt, Eli | 3 | 2 | 6 | | 1 |
| Palmer, Amme | 2 | 1 | 1 | | | Northrop, Ezra | 2 | 2 | 4 | | | Ames, Everit | 1 | 1 | 3 | | |
| Bostwick, Benjamin | 4 | | 7 | | | Dunnen, John, Jr. | 2 | 3 | 3 | | | Foot, Patience | | 1 | 3 | | |
| Tomlinson, Joseph | 3 | 2 | 3 | | | Stephens, Daniel | 1 | 2 | 2 | | | Clark, Joseph | 3 | 2 | 2 | | |
| Rugles, Samuel | 2 | 3 | 6 | | | Northrop, Mary | | | 1 | | | Smith, Josiah | 2 | | 1 | | |
| Rugles, Joseph | 4 | | 2 | | | Peck, John | 1 | 2 | 3 | | | Peck, Eliakam | 4 | 1 | 2 | | |
| Knowls, Elezer | 1 | 1 | 4 | | | Sherman, Samuel | 1 | 1 | 4 | | | Hodges, Ezra | 1 | 2 | 4 | | |
| Rudles, Timothy | 4 | 2 | 3 | | | Jackson, David | 1 | 4 | 6 | | | Hambleton, Paul | 1 | 3 | 5 | | |
| Like, Andrew | 3 | 1 | 3 | | | Jackson, Daniel | 1 | 4 | 5 | | | Knapp, John | 1 | 1 | 1 | | |
| Beeman, Josiah | 1 | 1 | 4 | | | Brooks, Thomas | 2 | | 1 | | | Hambleton, John | 1 | 3 | 3 | | |
| Bawlden, Tibbals | 3 | 2 | 4 | | | Northrop, Wait | 1 | | 1 | | | Maxfield, Joseph | 1 | | 1 | | |
| Rugles, Abijah | 4 | 1 | 6 | | | Northrop, Anne | 1 | | 1 | | | Porter, Joshua | 1 | 1 | 5 | | |
| Rugles, Benjamin | 1 | 1 | 3 | | | Hawley, Isaac | 2 | 1 | 4 | | | Seger, Daniel | 1 | 3 | 1 | | |
| Bawlden, Thaddeus | 4 | 1 | 5 | | | Dunnen, Liverius | 2 | 2 | 1 | | | Hoyt, Thaddeus | 1 | | 4 | | |
| Warner, Martin | 3 | | 5 | | | Northrop, Joshua, Jr. | 1 | | 3 | | | Morehouse, Thaddeus | 1 | | 2 | | |
| Warner, Solomon | 2 | | 4 | | | Northrop, Joshua | 1 | | 2 | | | Comstolk, Stephen | 2 | 2 | 5 | | |
| Warner, Rugles | 1 | 1 | 3 | | | Northrop, Asa | 1 | 1 | 2 | | | Picket, David | 1 | | 1 | | |
| Summers, Mark | 1 | 1 | 3 | | | French, Wells | 1 | | 1 | | | Bass, Newcomb | 1 | 3 | 2 | | |
| Hamblen, Elisha | 1 | 3 | 3 | | | Judson, Joel | 1 | 1 | 4 | | | Starr, Ethel | 1 | 1 | 1 | | |
| Keeler, David | 1 | 1 | 2 | | | Carman, John | 1 | 1 | 3 | | | Starr, Nathanel | 4 | 1 | 4 | | |
| Keeler, John | 1 | | 1 | | | Wood, Preserve | 1 | | 2 | | | Wileman, Timothy | 2 | 1 | 5 | | |
| Keeler, Elisha | 1 | | 1 | | | Northrop, Drake | 1 | 1 | 1 | | | Brush, Stephen | 1 | 1 | 1 | | |
| Keeler, Nathan | 1 | 3 | 5 | | | Knapp, Fransis | 1 | 1 | 1 | | | Wileman, Ezekiel | 2 | 1 | 1 | | |
| Nearing, Henery | 1 | 5 | 2 | | | Gun, Abel | 1 | 2 | 5 | | | Cornwell, John | 1 | | 1 | | |
| Smith, Ralph | 1 | 2 | 3 | | | Brown, Samuel | 2 | 3 | 3 | | | Cornwell, Nathan | 1 | 2 | 1 | | |
| Nichols, William | 1 | | 3 | | | Peck, Hennery | 3 | | 2 | | | Steward, James | 2 | 2 | 6 | | |
| Rood, John | 1 | 1 | 3 | | | Northrop, David | 2 | 1 | 2 | | | Steward, Alexander | 2 | 1 | 2 | | |
| Keeler, Sarah | | | 2 | | | Stephens, Joshua | 1 | | 2 | | | Hoyt, Eli | 4 | 2 | 2 | | |
| Hamblen, David | 1 | | 1 | | | Hallebert, David | 1 | 2 | 3 | | | Hoyt, David | 1 | | 2 | | |
| Murry, Benjamin | 1 | 2 | 1 | | | Stephens, Josiah | 1 | | 3 | | | Hoyt, Ager | 1 | 1 | 1 | | |
| Mallet, Edmon | 1 | 3 | 3 | | | Stephens, Ager | 1 | 1 | 2 | | | Hubbell, Ezra | 2 | 1 | 2 | | |
| Murrin, Nathan | 1 | 1 | 6 | | | Stephens, Eden | 1 | | 4 | | | Nichols, Ebenezer | 1 | 2 | 1 | | |
| Wheeler, Daniel | 1 | 3 | 2 | | | Dibble, Ezra | 1 | 1 | 3 | | | Wileman, Isaac | 1 | 2 | 3 | | |
| Murrin, Isaac | 3 | 3 | 5 | | | Dibble, Levi | 1 | | 1 | | | Benedict, Abraham | 1 | | 1 | | |
| Starr, Elijah | 1 | 1 | 6 | | | Dibble, Ezra, Jr. | 1 | 1 | 2 | | | Benedict, Abraham, Jr. | 1 | 2 | 2 | | |
| Rugles, Bostwick | 1 | | 4 | | | Smith, Joseph | 2 | 1 | 2 | | | Gregory, Thomas | 1 | 2 | 3 | | |
| Rugles, Ashbell | 1 | | 1 | | | Smith, Eli | 1 | 1 | 2 | | | Wileman, Noah | 1 | | 1 | | |
| Murrin, Levi | 2 | | 3 | | | Smith, Amos | 2 | 1 | 3 | | | Wileman, Isaac, Jr. | 1 | 1 | 3 | | |
| Hawley, Liverius | 1 | | 3 | | | Smith, Zalmon | 1 | | 1 | | | Wileman, David | 1 | 1 | 1 | | |
| Nearnin, John H. | 1 | 3 | 1 | | | Smith, Amos, Jr. | 1 | 2 | 1 | | | Patch, Quint | 1 | 1 | 2 | | |
| Nearnin, Joseph | 1 | 3 | 3 | | | Smith, Abel | 1 | 3 | 3 | | | Patch, Ezra | 1 | 3 | 1 | | |
| Murrin, Samuel, Jr. | 2 | 1 | 1 | | | Gray, Isaac | 2 | 2 | 3 | | | | | | | | |
| Smith, David | 1 | | 1 | | | | | | | | | | | | | | |

[1] No attempt has been made in this publication to correct mistakes in spelling made by the deputy marshals, but the names have been reproduced as they appear upon the census schedules.

# HEADS OF FAMILIES—CONNECTICUT.

## FAIRFIELD COUNTY—Continued.

### DANBURY TOWN—con.

| NAME OF HEAD OF FAMILY. | Free white males of 16 years and upward, including heads of families. | Free white males under 16 years. | Free white females, including heads of families. | All other free persons. | Slaves. |
|---|---|---|---|---|---|
| Starr, Thomas, Jnr | 1 | | 1 | | |
| Bowton, Daniel | 1 | 2 | 3 | | |
| Judd, Abner | 1 | 1 | 2 | | |
| Judd, Thomas, 1 | 1 | | 1 | | |
| Coles, Levi | 2 | 1 | 2 | | |
| Nichols, Samuel | 2 | 1 | 2 | | |
| Dibble, Elisha | 2 | | 2 | | |
| Judd, Thomas, 2 | 2 | 1 | 3 | | |
| Hoyt, Jonathan | 2 | | 1 | | |
| Picket, Ebenezer | 1 | 3 | 6 | | |
| Hoyt, Enos | 1 | 1 | 1 | | |
| Bowton, Eli | 1 | 2 | 3 | | |
| Mygatt, Philo | 1 | | 4 | | |
| Dibble, Tar | 1 | 1 | 2 | | |
| Hoyt, Daniel | 1 | | 3 | | |
| Daley, Benjamin | 1 | 1 | 1 | | |
| White, Thomas P | 2 | 5 | 3 | | 1 |
| Knapp, Joshua | 2 | | 2 | | |
| Knapp, Daniel | 1 | 2 | 4 | | |
| Judd, Jacob | 2 | 3 | 4 | | |
| Hambleton, Silas | 1 | | 2 | | |
| Hoyt, Drake, Jnr | 1 | | 1 | | |
| Patch, William | 1 | 2 | 3 | | |
| Wileman, Joseph | 2 | 1 | 2 | | |
| Shute, Richard | 2 | 1 | 5 | | |
| Hoyt, Justus | 1 | 2 | 6 | | |
| Hoyt, Noah | 4 | 4 | 3 | | |
| Stephens, Forward | 1 | | 4 | | |
| Stephens, Ezra, Jnr | 1 | 1 | 7 | | |
| Stephens, Ezra | 1 | 1 | 3 | | |
| Stephens, Samuel | 1 | 4 | 3 | | |
| Peck, Levi | 2 | 4 | 3 | | |
| Peck, Ezra | 1 | 2 | 1 | | |
| Hays, James | 3 | 1 | 3 | | |
| Hambleton, Joseph | 1 | 1 | 1 | | |
| Hambleton, Eliakam | 1 | | 1 | | |
| Nash, Nathanel | 1 | 3 | 2 | | |
| Knapp, David | 1 | 1 | 2 | | |
| Hoyt, Daniel D | 1 | | 3 | | |
| Lenslee, Lemuel | 1 | 2 | 3 | | |
| Lenslee, James | 1 | 2 | 3 | | |
| Lindslee, Mathew | 2 | | 2 | | |
| Barnum, Judah | 1 | 1 | 3 | | |
| Barnum, Seth | 1 | 6 | 2 | | |
| Barnum, Joseph | 2 | | 2 | | |
| Barnum, Joseph, Jnr | 1 | 2 | 1 | | |
| Barnum, Gabriel | 1 | 1 | 4 | | |
| Hoyt, Nathan | 1 | 3 | 3 | | |
| Hoyt, Starr | 1 | 1 | 4 | | |
| Wilks, Mathew | 1 | 1 | 2 | | |
| Barnum, John, Jnr | 1 | 3 | 3 | | |
| Barnum, Olive | | | 3 | | |
| Hoyt, John | 2 | 1 | 3 | | |
| Barnum, Jesby | 1 | | 2 | | |
| Hoyt, Daniel | 1 | | 3 | | |
| Bennedict, Elezer | 1 | 1 | 1 | | |
| Hawkins, William | 1 | 4 | 3 | | |
| Wilks, Mathew, Jnr | 1 | | 3 | | |
| Knapp, Elnathan | 3 | | 3 | | |
| Knapp, Elnathan, Jnr | 1 | | 2 | | |
| Benedict, Timothy | 1 | | 4 | | |
| Roberts, William | 2 | 1 | 3 | | |
| Barnum, Abijah, Jnr | 1 | 1 | 1 | | |
| Knapp, James | 2 | | 2 | | |
| Picket, Ebenezer, Jnr | 1 | | 1 | | |
| Bouton, Mathew | 2 | | 4 | | |
| Benedict, David | 1 | | 3 | | |
| Boughton, Thomas | 1 | 1 | 1 | | |
| Pierce, Joshua | 1 | 1 | 3 | | |
| Weed, Throm | 1 | 1 | 3 | | |
| Stone, Oliver | 1 | 2 | 2 | | |
| Barnum, Nathanel | 3 | | 2 | | |
| Finch, Nathanel | 1 | 1 | 4 | | |
| Hoyt, Eleazer | 1 | 1 | 3 | | |
| Sturges, Moris S | 1 | | 3 | | |
| Barnum, Abijah | 2 | 2 | 3 | | |
| Benedict, Asa | 1 | 4 | 3 | | |
| Benedict, Samuel, 1st | 1 | 1 | 1 | | |
| Benedict, Elijah | 1 | 3 | 1 | | |
| Benedict, Asor | 1 | 2 | 7 | | |
| Weed, Samuel | 1 | | 1 | | |
| Benedict, Samuel, 2d | 1 | | 2 | | |
| Weed, Azer | 1 | 3 | 2 | | |
| Barber, Benjamin | 2 | | 1 | | |
| Pierce, David | 2 | 2 | 2 | | |
| Weed, David | 1 | 1 | 3 | | |
| Knapp, Henery | 1 | 2 | 5 | | |
| Gregory, Nathanel | 2 | 2 | 4 | | |
| Gregory, John | 2 | 1 | 3 | | |
| Gregory, Samuel | 1 | 3 | 2 | | |
| Combs, John | 1 | 1 | 6 | | |
| Boughton, Joseph | 1 | 1 | 2 | | |
| Weed, Ebenezer | 1 | | 2 | | |
| Cook, Thomas | 1 | 1 | 1 | | |
| Presbrey, Joseph | 1 | | 1 | | |
| Vinen, Josiah | 1 | | 1 | | |
| Gorham, Benjamin | 1 | 1 | 6 | | |
| Peck, John | 1 | 1 | 4 | | |
| Husted, Andrew | 1 | 3 | 5 | | |
| Bennedict, Ephraim | 1 | 1 | 2 | | |
| Barnum, Ezra | 1 | | 1 | | |
| Ludeman, John | 1 | | 1 | | |
| Trobridge, Isaac | 2 | 1 | 1 | | |
| Barnum, Samuel | 1 | | 1 | | |
| Boughton, David, Jnr | 4 | 1 | 2 | | |
| Boughton, Abijah | 1 | | 2 | | |
| Bowton, David | 4 | | 2 | | |
| Foot, John | 3 | 3 | 4 | | |
| Bishop, Nathan | 1 | 1 | 2 | | |
| Moss, Amasa | 1 | 1 | 4 | | |
| Cook, Samuel | 1 | | 4 | | |
| Van Doosen, John | 1 | | 1 | | |
| Hoyt, Elijah | 1 | 3 | 6 | | |
| Cook, Joseph P | 3 | 1 | 4 | | |
| Phillips, Samuel H | 1 | 2 | 1 | 1 | |
| White, Ebenezer R | 3 | 4 | 7 | 1 | |
| Cook, Joseph P., Jr | 3 | 1 | 2 | 1 | |
| Gregory, Ebenezer | 3 | | 2 | | |
| Benedict, Noble | 3 | 1 | 2 | | |
| Peck, Abijah | 3 | | 1 | | |
| Heneries, Elizabeth | | | 1 | | |
| Barnum, Eleazer | 1 | 3 | 5 | | |
| Church, Elizabeth | 1 | | 2 | | |
| Barnum, Stephen | 2 | 3 | 3 | | |
| Barnum, Olive | | | 2 | | |
| Barnum, Justus | 3 | 2 | 4 | | |
| Agens, Andrew | 1 | 2 | 4 | | |
| Brown, James | 1 | 1 | 4 | | |
| Joyce, John | 2 | 3 | 3 | | |
| Barnum, Benjamin, 1st | 1 | | 2 | | |
| Ambler, Stephen | 1 | 1 | 3 | | |
| Combs, William | 1 | 2 | 5 | | |
| Hawley, John | 1 | 3 | 2 | | |
| Barnum, Benjamin, 2d | 2 | 1 | 2 | | |
| Hubbell, Noah | 1 | | 1 | | |
| Roberts, Zelotus | 1 | 5 | 2 | | |
| Porter, John | 1 | | 2 | | |
| Porter, Manoah | 1 | 1 | 2 | | |
| Green, Orastus | 1 | 1 | 2 | | |
| Gregory, Nathan | 1 | | 3 | | |
| Bartram, John | 1 | 1 | 1 | | |
| Curtis, Samuel | 2 | | 1 | | |
| Curtis, Stephen | 1 | | 1 | | |
| Cummins, Asa | 2 | 1 | 5 | | |
| Cato (Negro) | | | | 2 | |
| Weed, Asa | 1 | 5 | 1 | | |
| Castle, Peter | 1 | 1 | 2 | | |
| Weed, Jonas | 1 | | 2 | | |
| Weed, Ephraim | 1 | | 2 | | |
| Seger, Eli | 1 | 2 | 4 | | |
| Stephens, Eliphilet | 2 | 2 | 5 | | |
| Stephens, Jonathan | 1 | 2 | 5 | | |
| Stephens, Thomas, 1st | 2 | | 2 | | |
| Stephens, Thomas, 2 | 1 | 1 | 3 | | |
| Stephens, James | 2 | 2 | 6 | | |
| Burrit, Philip | 1 | 6 | 3 | | |
| Benedict, Theofelus | 1 | 2 | 3 | | |
| Foster, Jesse | 2 | 1 | 5 | | |
| De Forest, Elihue | 1 | 1 | 2 | | |
| Taylor, Theofelus | 1 | 1 | 4 | | |
| Taylor, John | 1 | 1 | 3 | | |
| Taylor, Jonathan | 2 | 3 | 3 | | |
| Bawlden, Samuel | 1 | 3 | 4 | | |
| Bawlden, Calep | 1 | | 1 | | |
| Taylor, Zalmon | 2 | 2 | 2 | | |
| Benedict, Jonas | 2 | 3 | 5 | | |
| Whitney, Nathan | 1 | 2 | 1 | | |
| Benedict, Lemwell | 2 | 1 | 4 | | |
| Benedict, Stephen B | | | 2 | | |
| Benedict, Ebenezer | 1 | 2 | 2 | | |
| Benedict, Abigail | | | 2 | | |
| Benedict, Nathan | 1 | 2 | 4 | | |
| Taylor, Elezer | 2 | 2 | 5 | | |
| Benedict, Thomas | 2 | 2 | 5 | | |
| Welimar, Thomas | 2 | 1 | 2 | | |
| Knapp, Noah | 1 | | 2 | | |
| William, Daniel | 4 | 1 | 4 | | |
| Stone, Anne | | 1 | 3 | | |
| Bishop, Jonathan A | 1 | | 3 | | |
| Scofield, Enos | 1 | | 3 | | |
| Celogg, Eliphilet | 3 | | 5 | | |
| Peck, Stephen | 1 | 3 | 3 | | |
| Rayment, Isaac | 1 | 1 | 2 | | |
| Crary, James | 1 | 3 | 2 | | |
| Phelmer, John | 1 | | 3 | | |
| Brunson, Ezra | 1 | | 4 | | |
| Bettes, James | 1 | 1 | 1 | | |
| Bettey, Daniel | 1 | | 1 | | |
| Brunson, Thaddeus | 2 | | 2 | | |
| Brunson, Amos | 1 | | 1 | | |
| Curtis, Stephen | 2 | 2 | 3 | | |
| Platt, Joseph | 2 | | 6 | | |
| Peck, Eliphilet | 1 | | 1 | | |
| Wood, John | 1 | | 4 | | |
| Dean, John | 1 | 1 | 1 | | |
| Osborn, Joseph | 1 | 2 | 1 | | |
| Silik, James | 1 | 2 | 3 | | |
| Dightman, Daniel | 1 | 1 | 1 | | |
| Silik, Benjamin | 1 | 2 | 5 | | |
| Silik, Nathanel | 1 | 2 | 1 | | |
| Osborn, David | 1 | | 3 | | |
| Whitlock, Samuel | 3 | 2 | 4 | | |
| Sturges, Joseph | 1 | 1 | 7 | | |
| Knapp, Bracy | 2 | 2 | 5 | | |
| Heacock, Samuel | 1 | 1 | 3 | | |
| Benedict, Daniel | 1 | | 5 | | |
| Ambler, Peter | 4 | 2 | 5 | | |
| Brooks, William | 1 | | 1 | | |
| Stalker, Anne | | 1 | 3 | | |
| Crowfoot, Ezra | 1 | 1 | 3 | | |
| Mills, John | 1 | 1 | 3 | | |
| Scofield, Stephen | 1 | 4 | 2 | | |
| Crowfoot, Joseph | 2 | 1 | 4 | | |
| Crowfoot, Seth | 1 | 3 | 4 | | |
| Shove, Seth | 2 | | 3 | | |
| Shove, Levi | 1 | 1 | 5 | | |
| Stone, Elizabeth | | 1 | 3 | | |
| Monson, Levi | 1 | 1 | 4 | | |
| Washburn, Ephraim | 3 | 1 | 3 | | |
| Ambler, John | 1 | 1 | 2 | | |
| Wileman, Samuel | 2 | | 2 | | |
| Jube (Negro) | | | | 6 | |
| Convass, Demor | 2 | 2 | 1 | | |
| Wileman, Samuel, Jur | 1 | 1 | 1 | | |
| Moris, Shadrack | 2 | 1 | 3 | | |
| Shove, Daniel, Jur | 2 | 2 | 5 | | |
| Shove, Daniel | 1 | | 3 | | |
| Stone, Levi | 2 | 2 | 4 | | |
| Fieldin, James | 2 | 2 | 5 | | |
| Gregory, Monson | 1 | 2 | 2 | | |
| Cosher, Benjamin | 5 | 3 | 4 | | |
| Tweedy, Samuel | 2 | 2 | 2 | | |
| Ambler, Squire | 4 | | 2 | | |
| Wileman, Abraham | 2 | 1 | 3 | | |
| Benedict, Ezra | 1 | 2 | 3 | | |
| Cheehan, Nathanel | 2 | | 3 | | |
| Hambleton, Joseph | 3 | | 3 | | |
| Bennedict, Calep, Jur | 1 | 2 | 2 | | |
| Benedict, Calep | 2 | 1 | 2 | | |
| Morris, Ephraim | 1 | | 2 | | |
| Morris, Samuel | 3 | 2 | 4 | | |
| Hoyt, Daniel | 1 | 3 | 4 | | |
| Starr, Rachel | 1 | | 2 | | 2 |
| Forgerson, John | 1 | 1 | 1 | | |
| Carington, Daniel N | 2 | 1 | 5 | | |
| Washburn, Edman | 2 | | 2 | | |
| Curtis, Reubin | 1 | 5 | 4 | | |
| Smith, Samuel | 1 | 1 | 1 | | |
| Benedict, Zadock | 3 | | 3 | | |
| Tucker, Thomas | 3 | 2 | 3 | | |
| Knapp, Benjamin | 4 | 1 | 5 | | |
| Starr, Jabes | 1 | 2 | 3 | | |
| Comstalk, Daniel | 2 | | 2 | | |
| Porter, John | 2 | 3 | 1 | | |
| Osborn, Levi | 2 | 2 | 2 | | |
| Trobridge, John | 2 | 4 | 4 | 1 | 2 |
| Burr, Oliver | 4 | 3 | 7 | | |
| Langin, Timothy | 1 | | 2 | | |
| Bennedict, Ashel | 1 | | 2 | | |
| Church, Winter | 3 | 2 | 3 | | |
| Gregory, Nathan | 2 | 1 | 1 | | |
| Gregory, Ezra | 2 | | 2 | | |
| Gregory, Mathew | 1 | 1 | 2 | | |
| Stephens, Elijah | 1 | | 1 | | |
| Weed, John | 1 | 1 | 4 | | |
| Starr, Rebekah | | | 1 | | |
| Starr, Calep | 4 | 5 | 3 | | |
| Finch, Peluk | 1 | 2 | 2 | | |
| Finch, Jacob | 2 | 1 | 2 | | |
| Phillips, Abiel | 2 | 2 | 2 | | |
| Manson, Eber | 1 | | 2 | | |
| Loveless, Richard | 1 | 2 | 4 | | |
| Gregory, Deborah | | | 3 | | |
| Benedict, Joseph | 1 | 2 | 5 | | |
| Bennedict, Ebenezer, Jur | 1 | 1 | 2 | | |
| Benedict, Ebenezer | 1 | | 2 | | |
| Taylor, Timothy, Jur | 2 | 1 | 3 | | |
| Whitlesey, Elisha | 1 | 1 | 2 | | |

# FIRST CENSUS OF THE UNITED STATES.

## FAIRFIELD COUNTY—Continued.

| NAME OF HEAD OF FAMILY. | Free white males of 16 years and upward, including heads of families. | Free white males under 16 years. | Free white females, including heads of families. | All other free persons. | Slaves. |
|---|---|---|---|---|---|
| **DANBURY TOWN—con.** | | | | | |
| Mygatt, Comfort | 3 | | 5 | | |
| Starr, Ezra | 1 | 2 | 5 | | 3 |
| Jackson, Robert | 1 | 2 | 2 | | |
| White, Fairchild | 1 | 1 | 1 | | |
| Barnum, Eunice | | 1 | 2 | | |
| Hoyt, Comfort | 2 | | 1 | | |
| Glover, Christopher | 2 | 5 | 3 | | |
| Bennedict, Thaddeus | 1 | | 2 | | |
| Curtis, Asa | 1 | 5 | 3 | | |
| Cato (Negro) | | | | 5 | |
| Brewer, John | 1 | 4 | 4 | | |
| Starr, Jonathan | 2 | | 5 | | |
| Zimri (Negro) | | | | 5 | |
| Taylor, Joseph | 1 | | | | 1 |
| Bennedict, Comfort | 1 | 3 | 2 | | |
| Bennedict, Jonah | 1 | 2 | 2 | | |
| Griffin, William | 1 | 1 | 2 | | |
| Flin, Thomas | 1 | 1 | 2 | | |
| Andress, Eliakam | 1 | 2 | 1 | | |
| Sperry, Benjamin | 1 | | 2 | | |
| Hoyt, Amos | 3 | 1 | 2 | | |
| Osborn, Daniel | 2 | 1 | 2 | | |
| Dibble, Daniel | 2 | | 1 | | |
| Dibble, Ezra | 1 | | 3 | | 1 |
| Daw, Isaac | 3 | | 2 | | |
| Taylor, Gilead | 2 | 1 | 3 | | |
| Osborn, Moses | 1 | | 2 | | |
| Nikerson, Hannah | 1 | | 2 | | |
| Taylor, Lemwell | 1 | 1 | 3 | | |
| Dibble, Nehemiah | 5 | 2 | 3 | | |
| Judd, Daniel | 2 | 2 | 4 | | |
| Judd, Elihue | 1 | 2 | 2 | | |
| Gray, Justus | 1 | 1 | 4 | | |
| Taylor, Eliakam | 1 | 1 | 2 | | |
| Griffin, Jonathan | 1 | 1 | 3 | | |
| Hall, David | 1 | 1 | 2 | | |
| Judd, David | 1 | 3 | 6 | | |
| Starr, Nathan | 1 | | 3 | | |
| Starr, Josiah | 1 | 1 | 2 | | 2 |
| Starr, Eliakam | 1 | | 5 | | 1 |
| Starr, Zadock | 2 | 1 | 5 | | |
| Starr, Mathew | 1 | 2 | 5 | | |
| Wheeler, Philip | 2 | 1 | 3 | | |
| Hays, Peter | 1 | 2 | 3 | | |
| Trobridge, Stephen | 1 | | 3 | | |
| Bennedict, Joseph | 1 | | 3 | | |
| Bennedict, Levi | 1 | 3 | 3 | | |
| Bennedict, Seth | 1 | | 3 | | |
| Andress, Robert, Jr | 1 | 5 | 1 | | |
| Henery, Obediah | 2 | 1 | 3 | | |
| Scogel, James | 1 | 1 | 2 | | |
| Standley, Joseph | 1 | | 2 | | |
| Rockwell, Mercy | | | 1 | | |
| Andress, Robert | 1 | | 4 | | |
| Trobridge, James | 2 | 2 | 3 | | |
| Bennedict, John | 1 | | 1 | | |
| Bennedict, John, Jur | 1 | 2 | 1 | | |
| Taylor, Thomas | 2 | 1 | 2 | | |
| Heacock, Daniel | 2 | 2 | 3 | | |
| Mathews, John | 1 | 4 | 2 | | |
| Heacock, Benjamin | 2 | 2 | 5 | | |
| Comstalk, Mercy | | 1 | 4 | | |
| Hoyt, James | 1 | 3 | 6 | | |
| Barnum, Levi | 1 | | 6 | | |
| Bennedict, Isaac | 1 | | 1 | | |
| Stove, Samuel | 1 | 3 | 3 | | |
| Bunnel, Gershom | 1 | 1 | 1 | | |
| Bartram, James | 2 | 1 | 5 | | |
| Burchard, Elijah | 1 | | 2 | | |
| Canfield, Samuel | 1 | 5 | 3 | | |
| Peck, Joseph | 1 | 1 | 1 | | 1 |
| Barnum, Daniel | 1 | 2 | 2 | | |
| Bennedict, William | 1 | | 6 | | |
| Holcomb, Luther | 2 | 5 | 2 | | |
| Taylor, Samuel | 1 | | 2 | | |
| Taylor, Eli | 2 | 1 | 3 | | |
| Bennedict, Nathanel | 2 | 2 | 2 | | |
| Taylor, Thomas | 2 | 3 | 3 | | |
| Silliman, Ebenezer | 1 | 1 | 3 | | |
| Barnum, Lazerus | 1 | 3 | 2 | | |
| Andress, John, Jur | 1 | | 1 | | |
| Andress, Eden | 1 | 1 | 2 | | |
| Andress, John | 1 | | 2 | | |
| Taylor, Jabes | 2 | | 1 | | |
| Hubbell, Silevant | 1 | 1 | 2 | | |
| Ferry, Eliphilet | 1 | 2 | 5 | | |
| Roberts, Luke | 2 | 3 | 4 | | |
| Taylor, Noah | 2 | | 5 | | |
| Starr, Samuel | 1 | 2 | 5 | | |
| Taylor, John, Jur | 3 | 2 | 4 | | |
| Peck, Benjamin | 1 | | 2 | | |
| Hoyt, Samuel | 1 | | 1 | | |
| Hoyt, Asa | 1 | 1 | 2 | | |
| Peck, Calvin | 1 | 1 | 3 | | |
| Hoyt, Jesse | 1 | 3 | 1 | | |
| **DANBURY TOWN—con.** | | | | | |
| Taylor, Silas | 1 | 2 | 3 | | |
| Peck, Eliphilet | 1 | 3 | 2 | | |
| Peck, Jesse | 1 | 2 | 1 | | |
| Judd, Samuel | 1 | | 1 | | |
| Judd, Ebenezer | 1 | | 1 | | |
| Thompson, James | 1 | 3 | 2 | | |
| Whitlock, Hezekiah | 2 | | 4 | | |
| Williams, Benjamin | 1 | | 3 | | |
| Whitlock, Seth | 1 | | 2 | | |
| Whitlock, John | 2 | | 2 | | |
| Whitlock, Ebenezer | 1 | | 4 | | |
| Whitlock, Nehemiah | 2 | 1 | 4 | | |
| Whitlock, Squire | 1 | | 2 | | |
| Hoyt, Joshua | 2 | 1 | 4 | | |
| Ferrys, Joshua | 1 | | 2 | | |
| Ferrys, Sarah | | | 2 | | |
| Wakely, John | 1 | 2 | 4 | | |
| Wileman, John | 1 | 2 | 2 | | |
| Weed, Jonas, Jur | 1 | 2 | 2 | | |
| Weed, Jonas | 2 | 1 | 1 | | |
| Crawfoot, Samuel | 1 | 1 | 1 | | |
| Crowfoot, Sealee | 1 | | 1 | | |
| Crawfoot, Samuel, Jur | 1 | | 1 | | |
| Platt, Ebenezer | 1 | | 4 | | |
| Sealee, James | 1 | 1 | 1 | | |
| Bennedict, Oliver | 1 | 1 | 2 | | |
| Bennedict, Ira | 1 | | 1 | | |
| Hoyt, Samuel | 1 | 1 | 7 | | |
| Benedict, Eliakam | 1 | | 1 | | |
| Bennedict, Benjamin | 1 | | 1 | | |
| Taylor, Eliad | 1 | 1 | 3 | | |
| Elmer, Hezekiah | 1 | 4 | 3 | | |
| Judd, Abigail | | | 5 | | |
| Heacock, Ebenezer | 2 | 1 | 3 | | |
| Lacy, Abel | 1 | 1 | 2 | | |
| Baley, Benjamin | 1 | 2 | 2 | | |
| Baley, Ebenezer | 1 | 1 | 4 | | |
| Taylor, Phineus | 1 | | 3 | | |
| Taylor, Nathan | 1 | | 3 | | |
| Baley, Samuel | 2 | 1 | 1 | | |
| Baley, Benona | 1 | | 3 | | |
| Taylor, Timothy | 1 | 3 | 4 | | |
| Taylor, Joshua | 1 | 2 | 2 | | |
| Taylor, Jabes, Jur | 1 | 2 | 4 | | |
| Taylor, Jonathan | 1 | 3 | 4 | | |
| Taylor, Ebenezer | 1 | 2 | 4 | | |
| Crawfoot, Daniel | 1 | 1 | 5 | | |
| Beebe, Edmond | 1 | 1 | 2 | | |
| Barnum, Elijah | 1 | | 3 | | |
| Barnum, Ephraim | 1 | | 3 | | |
| Bennedict, Benajah | 3 | 2 | 4 | | |
| Hoyt, Benjamin | 1 | 1 | 3 | | |
| Barnum, Abel | 1 | 2 | 1 | | |
| Barnum, David | 2 | 3 | 3 | | |
| Ferry, Benjamin | 1 | 1 | 4 | | |
| Barnum, Mathew, Jur | 1 | 1 | 3 | | |
| Dibble, Thomas | 1 | 1 | 4 | | |
| Dibble, Jeddediah H | 1 | | 1 | | |
| Dibble, Samuel | 2 | 1 | 7 | | |
| Starr, Thaddeus | 1 | 1 | 3 | | |
| Benedict, Hezekiah | 1 | | 3 | | |
| Bennedict, James | 2 | 1 | 3 | | |
| Bennedict, Asel | 2 | 1 | 2 | | |
| Bennedict, David, Jur | 1 | 1 | 3 | | |
| Millson, Daniel | 1 | | 3 | | |
| Lacy, Aaron | 2 | | 2 | | |
| Bennedict, Nathanel | 1 | | 1 | | |
| Veal, Moses | 1 | 2 | 3 | | |
| Beebe, Joseph | 1 | 1 | 1 | | |
| Beebe, Joseph, Jur | 1 | 2 | 4 | | 1 |
| Bennedict, Jonathan | 1 | 4 | 4 | | |
| Bennedict, Lemuel | 2 | | 2 | | |
| Bennedict, Samuel | 1 | | 1 | | |
| Picket, Hannah | 2 | 2 | 4 | | |
| Dibble, Nathan | 1 | | 4 | | 1 |
| Bennedict, Eleazer | 1 | 2 | 2 | | |
| Starr, Jonathan | 1 | 1 | 1 | | |
| Dibble, Eli | 1 | 1 | 5 | | |
| Barnum, John | 1 | 2 | 4 | | |
| Bennedict, Thomas | 1 | | 3 | | |
| Bennedict, Thomas | 1 | | 1 | | |
| Wood, Elijah | 1 | 3 | 3 | | |
| Crawfoot, Mathew | 1 | 1 | 4 | | |
| Crowfoot, Levi | 1 | | 2 | | |
| Starr, Joseph | 2 | 1 | 2 | | |
| Starr, Joseph, Jur | 3 | 2 | 2 | | |
| Crawfoot, Josiah | 1 | | 2 | | |
| Beebee, Ethel | 1 | | 1 | | |
| Beebe, Lemuel | 1 | | 2 | | |
| Beebe, David | 1 | | 5 | | |
| Beebe, Lemuel, Jur | | 2 | 3 | | |
| Barnum, Ephraim | 1 | 4 | 4 | | |
| Barnum, Mathew | 2 | | 7 | | |
| Barnum, Joseph | 1 | 2 | 1 | | |
| Jennings, Burrit | 1 | | 1 | | |
| **DANBURY TOWN—con.** | | | | | |
| Hoyt, Nathanel | 2 | 4 | 5 | | |
| Maxfield, Eber | 1 | 1 | 1 | | |
| Hoyt, Thomas | 2 | 1 | 2 | | |
| Williams, Thaddeus | 1 | 4 | 4 | | |
| Hoyt, Eleazer | 1 | | 1 | | |
| Judd, Benjamin | 1 | 1 | 1 | | |
| Weed, Solomon | 2 | 3 | 2 | | |
| Bennedict, Hezekiah, Jur | 1 | 4 | 3 | | |
| Williams, Hezekiah | 1 | 4 | 4 | | |
| Beardslee, Daniel | 1 | 1 | 2 | | |
| **FAIRFIELD TOWN.** | | | | | |
| Burr, David | 1 | | 2 | | |
| Burr, David, Jnr | 1 | 3 | 3 | | |
| Sherwood, Daniel | 1 | 3 | 3 | | |
| Redfield, James, Jnr | 1 | 1 | 3 | | |
| Bulkley, Abigail | | 1 | 2 | | |
| Oysterbanks, David | 2 | 2 | 1 | | |
| Mills, Joseph | 1 | 3 | 2 | | |
| Chapman, James | 2 | 2 | 4 | | 1 |
| Oysterbanks, Isaac | 1 | 1 | 3 | | |
| Sherwood, Moses | 2 | 1 | 3 | | 6 |
| Craft, David | 2 | 2 | 1 | | |
| Hide, Joseph | 2 | | 2 | | 4 |
| Hide, John, Jnr | 1 | | 4 | | |
| Adams, Nathaniel | 1 | 2 | 5 | | 2 |
| Oysterbanks, Joshua | 1 | | 4 | | |
| Redfield, Ebenezer | 1 | 1 | 2 | | |
| Batterson, John | | 1 | 1 | | |
| Allan, Moses | 2 | 1 | 1 | | |
| Raymong, Elijah | 1 | 3 | 2 | | |
| Nichols, Moses | 2 | 1 | 2 | | |
| Davis, Thomas | 1 | 1 | 2 | | |
| Darrow, Daniel | 1 | | 2 | | |
| Beers, David, Jnr | 1 | 3 | 1 | | |
| Meeker, Seth, Jnr | 1 | 1 | 3 | | |
| Raymong, David | 2 | | 4 | | |
| Sherwood, Daniel | 2 | 1 | 2 | | |
| Sturgis, Andrew | 1 | 1 | 1 | | 2 |
| Batterson, Jorge, Jnr | 1 | 1 | 5 | | |
| Gray, Giddeon | 1 | 1 | 4 | | |
| Ogden, John | 1 | 1 | 1 | | |
| Burr, Eunice | 1 | | 4 | | |
| Wynkoop, Grisel | 1 | 1 | 3 | | |
| Chapman, Sarah | 1 | | 3 | | |
| Chapman, John | 1 | | 1 | | |
| Chapman, Albert | 2 | 3 | 2 | | 1 |
| Couch, Josiah | 2 | 1 | 3 | | |
| Gorham, Ebenezer | 1 | 2 | 3 | | |
| Lockwood, Stephen | 1 | 2 | 5 | | |
| Hurlbutt, Giddeon | 1 | 5 | 1 | | |
| Bennet, Thomas | 1 | | 1 | | |
| Persall, John | 1 | 1 | 2 | | |
| Persall, Samuel | 2 | 1 | 2 | | 4 |
| Persall, Samuel, Jnr | 1 | 1 | 2 | | |
| Bennet, Deliverance | 1 | 2 | 4 | | |
| Hanford, Joseph | 2 | 2 | 4 | | |
| Bennet, Hayns | 1 | 1 | 2 | | |
| Hanford, John | 1 | | 2 | | |
| Godfry, Mary | | 1 | 3 | | |
| Jesop, Ebenezer, Jnr | 1 | | 2 | | |
| Hanford, Betty | | | 1 | | |
| Clift, William | 1 | | 1 | | |
| Wood, Samuel | 2 | 1 | 4 | | |
| Baker, Ebenezer | 3 | 3 | 4 | | |
| Couch, Nehemiah | 2 | 1 | 3 | | |
| Adams, Stephen | 1 | 2 | 1 | | |
| Cable, Thomas | 3 | 1 | 3 | | |
| Judah, David | 1 | 3 | 4 | | |
| Smith, Samuel | 1 | 3 | 5 | | |
| Gray, Solomon | 3 | 1 | 2 | | |
| Allen, Gabriel | 1 | 3 | 5 | | |
| Johnson, Nathanel | 1 | | 1 | | |
| Elwood, Richard | 2 | 2 | 2 | | |
| Batterson, John, Jnr | 1 | 1 | 1 | | |
| Squire, Seth | 1 | 1 | 2 | | |
| Elwood, Hezekiah | 2 | | 4 | | |
| Elwood, Nathan | 1 | 2 | 2 | | |
| Green, Samuel | 1 | | 3 | | |
| Batterson, James, Jnr | 1 | | 1 | | |
| Allen, Gershom | 1 | | 2 | | |
| Brothington, Daniel | 1 | 1 | 5 | | |
| Disbrow, Justis | 1 | 3 | 5 | | |
| Sherwood, Asahel | 2 | 3 | 1 | | |
| Batterson, James | 1 | | 1 | | |
| Frasier, Daniel | 1 | 1 | 1 | | |
| Burr, Daniel | 3 | 1 | 3 | | |
| Ogden, Ebenezer | 1 | 1 | 4 | | |
| Hide, John | 2 | 1 | 5 | | 6 |
| Gorham, Joseph, Jnr | 1 | 3 | 3 | | |
| Mills, Daniel | 1 | 2 | 6 | | |
| Cooley, Hezekiah | 1 | 1 | 4 | | |
| Goodsell, John | 1 | 2 | 5 | | |
| Hanford, Jorge | 1 | 1 | 2 | | |

# HEADS OF FAMILIES—CONNECTICUT.

## FAIRFIELD COUNTY—Continued.

### FAIRFIELD TOWN—con.

| NAME OF HEAD OF FAMILY. | Free white males of 16 years and upward, including heads of families. | Free white males under 16 years. | Free white females, including heads of families. | All other free persons. | Slaves. |
|---|---|---|---|---|---|
| Meeker, Benjamin | 2 | 3 | 5 | | |
| Meeker, Seth | 1 | | 3 | | |
| Meeker, Joseph | 3 | 1 | 2 | | |
| Sherwood, David | 3 | 1 | 3 | | |
| Hull, Daniel | 3 | 1 | 7 | | |
| Philips, Thomas | 1 | 1 | 3 | | |
| Alvord, John | 4 | 4 | 3 | | |
| Osborn, Levi | 1 | 2 | 1 | | |
| Bradley, Daniel | 2 | 2 | 4 | | |
| Jennings, Aaron | 1 | 4 | 2 | | |
| Row, Ebenezer, Jnr | 1 | | 4 | | |
| Row, Ebenezer | 4 | | 5 | | |
| Wakeman, Giddeon | 4 | 1 | 4 | | 1 |
| Burr, Talcott | 2 | 1 | 4 | | 1 |
| Taylor, Samuel | 4 | 1 | 2 | | |
| Andrews, John | 1 | 1 | 3 | | |
| Cooley, John | 1 | 1 | 1 | | |
| Wicks, Nathaniel | 1 | | 2 | | |
| Disbrow, Isaac | 1 | | 2 | | |
| Guire, Stephen | 3 | 3 | 1 | | |
| Raymong, William | 1 | | 2 | | |
| Philips, John | 1 | 2 | 4 | | |
| Couch, Giddeon | 1 | 3 | 2 | | |
| Nash, Thomas | 1 | 3 | 2 | | 5 |
| Nash, Thomas, Jnr | 1 | 1 | 1 | | |
| Allen, Eliphlet | 1 | 1 | 1 | | |
| Morehouse, John | 1 | | 2 | | |
| Wakeman, Joseph | 1 | 1 | 3 | | 3 |
| Jerod, John | 1 | 3 | 3 | | |
| Hanford, Hayns | 1 | | 2 | | |
| Allen, John | 1 | | 1 | | |
| Bennet, William | 1 | 2 | 2 | | |
| Mosher, George | 1 | 1 | 5 | | |
| Disbrow, Jason | 2 | 1 | 2 | | |
| Bennet, Joseph | 1 | 3 | 4 | | 1 |
| Bennet, Nathan | 1 | 1 | 3 | | |
| Allen, Benjamin | 2 | 2 | 4 | | |
| Bennet, Daniel | 2 | 2 | 4 | | |
| Allen, Ebenezer | 2 | 3 | 2 | | |
| Allen, Stephen | 1 | 1 | 1 | | |
| Thorp, William | 1 | | 3 | | |
| Bennet, Moses | 2 | | 4 | | |
| Disbrow, Levi | 1 | 1 | 3 | | |
| Bennet, James | 2 | 3 | 2 | | |
| Thorp, Stephen | 2 | | 4 | | |
| Disbrow, Joshua | 1 | 4 | 2 | | |
| Disbrow, John | 1 | 3 | 1 | | |
| Gray, William | 2 | | 4 | | |
| Bennet, Jabez | 2 | 1 | 3 | | |
| Bennet, Jesse | 1 | 1 | | | |
| Hill, Thomas | 1 | 1 | 4 | | |
| Ripley, Hezekiel | 2 | 1 | 3 | | 1 |
| Cable, George | 2 | | 4 | | |
| Disbrow, Thaddeus | 1 | 1 | 6 | | 2 |
| Disbrow, Asahel | 1 | 5 | 6 | | 1 |
| Disbrow, Jabez | 1 | 3 | 3 | | |
| Disbrow, Elias | 1 | 2 | 4 | | |
| Stratton, Cornelius | 1 | 2 | 3 | | |
| Godfry, Stephen | 2 | | 3 | | |
| Godfry, Ebenezer | 2 | 1 | 1 | | |
| Elwood, Abraham | 1 | 1 | 1 | | |
| Elwood, Abijah | 1 | 1 | 1 | | |
| Couch, Joshua | 1 | | 5 | | |
| Allen, Elethan | 1 | 1 | 3 | | |
| Allen, William | 1 | | 3 | | |
| Burrit, Wakeman | 2 | 2 | 5 | | |
| Chapman, Daniel | 1 | 1 | 2 | | |
| Chapman, Denne | 2 | | 3 | | |
| Chapman, Lovel | 1 | 2 | 1 | | |
| Banks, Talcott | 1 | 2 | 4 | | |
| Godfry, Nathan | 1 | 1 | 2 | | 1 |
| Patterson, John | 1 | 1 | 2 | | |
| Raymong, William, Jnr | 1 | 2 | 2 | | |
| Andrews, Thomas | 1 | 3 | 1 | | |
| Couch, Simon | 1 | 3 | 2 | | 2 |
| Davis, John | 2 | 3 | 2 | | |
| Jesop, Ebenezer | 1 | 1 | 4 | | 5 |
| Poor, Jonathan | 1 | | 2 | | |
| Batterson, William | 1 | 2 | 8 | | |
| Morehouse, Samuel | 1 | 3 | 2 | | |
| Morehouse, Ebenezer | 3 | 3 | 2 | | |
| Morehouse, Abraham | 1 | 2 | 3 | | |
| Morehouse, Eunice | | | 2 | | |
| Batterson, George | 3 | | 3 | | |
| Morehouse, Groman | 1 | | 5 | | |
| Whitehead, Jehiel | 3 | | 4 | | |
| Jennings, David | 1 | 4 | 4 | | |
| Burr, John | 1 | 3 | 5 | | |
| Bulkley, Peter | 2 | | 2 | | |
| Bulkley, Abraham | 1 | 2 | 3 | | |
| Godfry, Jonathan | 1 | 1 | 1 | | |
| King, Richard | 1 | | 2 | | |
| Jennings, Joshua | 5 | 2 | 4 | | |
| Osborn, Abigail | | | 2 | | 1 |
| Osborn, Ebenezer | 2 | 1 | 4 | | |
| Stratton, Joseph | 2 | 3 | 3 | | |
| Bradley, Nathan | 2 | 3 | 6 | | |

### FAIRFIELD TOWN—con.

| NAME OF HEAD OF FAMILY. | Free white males of 16 years and upward, including heads of families. | Free white males under 16 years. | Free white females, including heads of families. | All other free persons. | Slaves. |
|---|---|---|---|---|---|
| Ogden, Samuel | 1 | 2 | 1 | | |
| Ogden, Hezekiah | 1 | 1 | 3 | | |
| Banks, Jonathan | 3 | 3 | 3 | | |
| Blackman, John | 1 | 2 | 5 | | |
| Perry, Joseph | 1 | 2 | 1 | | |
| Murrin, Meeker | 1 | 1 | 2 | | |
| Murrin, Abijah | 2 | | 4 | | |
| Burr, George | 1 | | 4 | | |
| Perry, Nathan | 2 | 3 | 4 | | |
| Couch, Abraham | 1 | 1 | 3 | | |
| Smith, Peter | 1 | 5 | 2 | | |
| Smith, Samuel | 1 | 4 | 1 | | |
| Thorp, Gershom | 1 | 3 | 1 | | |
| Lion, Joseph, Jnr | 1 | 1 | 1 | | |
| Banks, Gershom, Jnr | 1 | 3 | 4 | | |
| Banks, Benjamin, Jnr | 1 | 1 | 8 | | |
| Banks, Samuel | 1 | | 3 | | |
| Banks, Gershom | 2 | | 2 | | |
| Whitney, Samuel | 1 | | 2 | | |
| Whitney, Josiah | 1 | 1 | | | |
| Hubbard, Sarah | | | | 4 | |
| Bradley, Frances | | | 4 | | |
| Banks, Daniel | 2 | | 2 | | |
| Thorp, Jehiel | 1 | 3 | 2 | | |
| Thorp, Ruel | 1 | 2 | 4 | | |
| Holt, Daniel | 1 | 2 | 1 | | |
| Gray, Siliman | 2 | 1 | 1 | | |
| Banks, Nathan | 1 | 2 | 2 | | |
| Banks, Elizabeth | | | 1 | | 1 |
| Parrit, David | 1 | 1 | 1 | | |
| Sherwood, Noah | 1 | | 1 | | |
| Banks, Moses | 1 | 3 | 4 | | |
| Goodsell, Lewis | 1 | 2 | 3 | | |
| Banks, Sarah | | | 4 | | |
| Goodsell, James | 1 | 3 | 3 | | |
| Smith, Daniel | 1 | | 1 | | |
| Smith, Ebenezer | 1 | 1 | 2 | | |
| Sherwood, Jehiel | 2 | 3 | 5 | | |
| Sherwood, Squire | 1 | 2 | 5 | | |
| Whitney, Samuel | 2 | 2 | 5 | | |
| Banks, John | 2 | | 3 | | |
| Sherwood, Joseph | 2 | 1 | 5 | | |
| Sherwood, Elihue | 3 | 1 | 5 | | |
| Hubbell, John | 1 | | 2 | | |
| Bradley, Adad | 1 | 2 | 1 | | |
| Nichols, Ephraim | 2 | 3 | 2 | | |
| Bradley, Albin | 1 | | 2 | | |
| Bradley, Seth | 2 | 3 | 2 | | 4 |
| Rogers, David | 4 | 4 | 2 | | 2 |
| Wakeman, John | 4 | 1 | 2 | | |
| Goodsell, David | 1 | | 3 | | |
| Bradley, John | 2 | | 2 | | 2 |
| Oysterbanks, David, Jnr | 1 | | 1 | | |
| Bradley, Abel | 2 | 2 | 5 | | 1 |
| Banks, Isaac | 1 | | 2 | | |
| Sherwood, Gershom | 1 | | 2 | | |
| Goodsell, Thomas | 2 | 1 | 2 | | |
| Ogden, Moses | 2 | 2 | 2 | | |
| Lion, Joseph | 1 | | 3 | | |
| Putnam, Aaron | 1 | 3 | 3 | | |
| Banks, Elijah | 1 | 1 | 3 | | |
| Murrin, Ebenezer | 1 | | 1 | | |
| Bradley, Elisha | 3 | 2 | 5 | | |
| Mitchel, John | 1 | 1 | 2 | | |
| Smith, Benjamin | 2 | | 2 | | |
| Bradley, Samuel | 2 | 1 | 5 | | 4 |
| Bradley, Hezekiah | 4 | 1 | 7 | | |
| Bradley, Walter | 2 | 2 | 2 | | 1 |
| Bulkley, Joseph | 2 | | 3 | | |
| Bradley, Zalmon | 2 | | 6 | | 2 |
| Jennings, Joel | 1 | | 6 | | |
| Jennings, John | 2 | 2 | 2 | | 1 |
| Bradley, David | 1 | | 3 | | |
| Downs, Abel | 1 | 1 | 1 | | |
| Brown, Samuel | 1 | 1 | 3 | | |
| Downs, Chauncy | 1 | 4 | 3 | | |
| Price, Zalmon | 2 | | 1 | | |
| Gray, Nehemiah | 2 | 3 | 4 | | |
| Lion, Seth | 2 | 1 | 2 | | |
| Downs, Joseph | 1 | 1 | 2 | | |
| Downs, John | 1 | | 1 | | |
| Price, David | 1 | | 3 | | 1 |
| Gray, Joseph | 1 | | 1 | | |
| Downs, Mary | | 2 | 2 | | |
| Price, Hezekiah | 1 | 2 | 2 | | |
| Wakeman, Thaddeus | 2 | 2 | 3 | | |
| Williams, Huldah | 1 | 1 | 1 | | |
| Williams, William | 1 | 3 | 2 | | |
| Wakeman, Abel | 1 | | 2 | | |
| Wakeman, Gershom | 3 | | 2 | | 1 |
| Hubble, David | 4 | 3 | 1 | | 1 |
| Dwight, Timothy | 3 | 9 | 5 | 1 | 1 |
| Bawlden, Dudley | 2 | 2 | 2 | | |
| Middlebrook, Sylvanus | 2 | 6 | 2 | | |
| Betts, Moses | 2 | 2 | 2 | | |
| Grant, Darius | 1 | | 1 | | |
| Sherwood, Samuel, 1st | 1 | 1 | 3 | | |

### FAIRFIELD TOWN—con.

| NAME OF HEAD OF FAMILY. | Free white males of 16 years and upward, including heads of families. | Free white males under 16 years. | Free white females, including heads of families. | All other free persons. | Slaves. |
|---|---|---|---|---|---|
| Sherwood, Albert | 4 | | 4 | | |
| Redfield, James | 2 | | 2 | | |
| White, Jacob | 3 | | 2 | | |
| Middlebrook, Oliver | 1 | 2 | 5 | | |
| Bradley, Peter | 1 | 5 | 3 | | |
| Bradley, Mable | | | 3 | | |
| Bradley, Joseph | 2 | 1 | 4 | | |
| Hubbell, Gershom | 2 | 3 | 2 | | |
| Sherwood, Ralph | 2 | | 2 | | |
| Lion, Jesse | 1 | 1 | 2 | | |
| Burr, Jesse | 1 | 2 | 2 | | |
| Sherwood, Increase | 1 | | 4 | | |
| Bradley, Elethan | 2 | 1 | 4 | | |
| Bulkley, Turney | 1 | 1 | 6 | | |
| Bulkley, Daniel | 1 | | 3 | | |
| Meeker, Daniel | 2 | 2 | 4 | | |
| Dimon, Samuel | 1 | 1 | 2 | | |
| Polley, John | 1 | 3 | 1 | | |
| Bradley, Nathan | 2 | 2 | 11 | | |
| Perry, Thomas | 1 | 1 | 4 | | |
| Wakeman, Ebenezer | 3 | 2 | 2 | | |
| Williams, David | 1 | | 3 | | |
| Wheeler, Daniel | 3 | 3 | 5 | | |
| Burr, Ebenezer, 3d | 1 | 2 | 1 | | |
| Burr, Timothy | 1 | | 1 | | |
| Burr, Zalmon | 1 | | 2 | | |
| Wakeman, William | 5 | 1 | 3 | | |
| Burr, Ebenezer | 1 | 3 | 2 | | |
| Nichols, Jesse | 1 | 2 | 2 | | |
| Hill, William | 2 | | 2 | | |
| Nichols, Ebenezer | 2 | 2 | 2 | | |
| Nichols, David | 2 | 6 | 4 | | |
| Wakeman, Epaphras | 2 | 2 | 5 | | |
| Hill, Eliphilet | 1 | | 1 | | |
| Burr, Joseph | 1 | | 1 | | |
| Burr, Increase | 2 | 1 | 2 | | |
| Hawley, Catherin | | 1 | 3 | | |
| Wakeman, Moses | 1 | | 2 | | |
| Whitehead, Jeremiah | 1 | | 2 | | |
| Wakeman, Liman | 1 | 2 | 2 | | 1 |
| Whitehead, David | 1 | 1 | 2 | | |
| Scudder, Roberd | 1 | 1 | 1 | | |
| Jennings, Edmond | 2 | 5 | 4 | | |
| Jennings, Enoch | 1 | | 1 | | |
| Bulkley, Nathan | 1 | 2 | 3 | | |
| Bulkley, Peter | 1 | | 3 | | |
| Henneries, Samuel | 1 | 3 | 6 | | |
| Henneries, Abner | 1 | 3 | 4 | | |
| Willson, Jesse | 1 | 1 | 1 | | |
| Jennings, Gershom | 2 | 2 | 3 | | |
| Wakeman, Eli | 1 | 1 | 1 | | 1 |
| Wakeman, John, 3d | 1 | | 4 | | |
| Adams, Ephraim | 2 | 2 | 6 | | |
| Jennings, William | 1 | 1 | 3 | | |
| Lion, Jese | 1 | 2 | 1 | | |
| Gould, Samuel | 1 | | 1 | | |
| Willson, Robert | 1 | 3 | 5 | | |
| Meeker, Stephen | 1 | | 1 | | |
| Parret, John | 1 | | 5 | | |
| Davis, Jabez | 2 | | 1 | | |
| Wilson, Samuel | 2 | 2 | 3 | | |
| Staples, John | 2 | 1 | 2 | | |
| Waley, Aaron | 1 | | 2 | | |
| Waley, Hezekiah | 1 | 1 | 2 | | |
| Gould, Stephen | 1 | | 3 | | |
| Gould, Dimon | 1 | | 3 | | |
| Hull, Stephen | 1 | | 1 | | |
| Jennings, Thaddeus | 1 | 1 | 3 | | |
| Gould, Echobod | 1 | 3 | 2 | | |
| Gould, Jesse | 1 | 4 | 2 | | |
| Gould, David | 2 | | 2 | | 2 |
| Gould, Nathan | 5 | | 1 | | |
| Lion, Wakeman | 1 | 1 | 1 | | |
| Lion, Eliphlet | 1 | | 2 | | |
| Gould, Samuel | 3 | 1 | 2 | | |
| Burr, Samuel | 1 | 2 | 6 | | |
| Webb, Isaac | 3 | 1 | 7 | | |
| Hill, Ebenezer | 6 | 2 | 4 | | |
| Hill, Joseph | 2 | | | | 3 |
| Wheeler, Thomas, Jnr | 2 | 1 | 2 | | |
| Wheeler, Nathan | 1 | 3 | 3 | | |
| Burr, Edmon | 2 | 2 | 1 | | |
| Hull, Ezekiel | 3 | 1 | 2 | | 3 |
| Goodsell, Epaphras | 2 | 3 | 2 | | |
| Burr, Bud | 1 | | 2 | | 1 |
| Sherwood, John | 2 | | 2 | | |
| Sherwood, Eliphilet | 1 | 2 | 4 | | |
| Sherwood, John, Jnr | 1 | | 5 | | |
| Middlebrook, Jonathan | 2 | | 2 | | 1 |
| Banks, Nehemiah, Jnr | 1 | 5 | 3 | | |
| Banks, Nehemiah | 1 | | 2 | | 1 |
| Hull, Eliphilet | 1 | 1 | 5 | | |
| Sherwood, Daniel | 4 | 2 | 3 | | 1 |
| Banks, Joseph | 1 | 3 | 2 | | |
| Hull, John | 4 | 1 | 3 | | |
| Fry, Thomas | 1 | | 2 | | |
| Banks, David | 1 | | 2 | | 1 |

# FIRST CENSUS OF THE UNITED STATES.

## FAIRFIELD COUNTY—Continued.

| NAME OF HEAD OF FAMILY. | Free white males of 16 years and upward, including heads of families. | Free white males under 16 years. | Free white females, including heads of families. | All other free persons. | Slaves. | NAME OF HEAD OF FAMILY. | Free white males of 16 years and upward, including heads of families. | Free white males under 16 years. | Free white females, including heads of families. | All other free persons. | Slaves. | NAME OF HEAD OF FAMILY. | Free white males of 16 years and upward, including heads of families. | Free white males under 16 years. | Free white females, including heads of families. | All other free persons. | Slaves. |
|---|---|---|---|---|---|---|---|---|---|---|---|---|---|---|---|---|---|
| **FAIRFIELD TOWN—con.** | | | | | | **FAIRFIELD TOWN—con.** | | | | | | **FAIRFIELD TOWN—con.** | | | | | |
| Rayment, Daniel | 1 | | 4 | | | Allen, David | 4 | 3 | 3 | | | Sherwood, Samuel, 2d | 1 | 2 | 4 | | |
| Bulkley, Gershom | 5 | 4 | 3 | | | Bennedict, Jesse | 1 | 1 | 2 | | | Morehouse, Isaac | 1 | 2 | 5 | | |
| Osborn, Abel | 1 | | 2 | | | Penfield, Samuel | 2 | 1 | 3 | | 1 | Morehouse, Elijah | 1 | | 1 | | |
| Sherwood, Sarah | | | 1 | | | Elwood, Thomas | 1 | 1 | 4 | | | Jennings, Zacherius | 1 | | 1 | | |
| Gould, Luther | 3 | 1 | 2 | | | Bulkley, Hannah | 4 | 1 | 6 | | 3 | Morehouse, Abraham | 1 | 3 | 3 | | |
| Bulkley, Gershom, 2d | 3 | 5 | 5 | | | Hubbard, Justin | 2 | 1 | 6 | | | Wilson, John, Jnr | 1 | | 1 | | |
| Wynkoop, James | 1 | | 2 | | | Bulkley, Nathan | 2 | | 3 | 1 | 8 | Morehouse, Seth | 2 | 4 | 4 | | |
| Osborn, Daniel | 2 | 1 | 3 | | | Hull, David | 1 | | 2 | | 1 | Wilson, Nathaniel | 2 | | 1 | | 3 |
| Osborn, John | 1 | 2 | 4 | | | Palmitter, Geaner | | | 1 | | | Willson, Isaac | 1 | | 2 | | |
| Osborn, Howes | 1 | | 2 | | | Fowler, Stephen | 1 | | 4 | | | Hays, Nehemiah | 1 | | 1 | | |
| Osborn, Stephen | 1 | 2 | 3 | | 1 | Silliman, William | 1 | | 2 | | | Willson, John | 2 | | 3 | | |
| Bulkley, James, Jnr | 1 | | | | | White, Right | 1 | 2 | 3 | | | Lion, Calep | 3 | | 4 | | |
| Sheffield, Paul | 2 | 1 | 2 | | | Jennings, Moses | 2 | 1 | 3 | | | Jennings, David | 3 | 1 | 2 | | |
| Burr, Wakeman | 1 | 1 | 4 | | | Bibbins, Israel | 2 | 2 | 5 | | | Morehouse, Peter | 1 | 3 | 4 | | |
| Bulkley, Elihue | 1 | 2 | 2 | | | Bulkley, Deborah | 1 | | 2 | | | Meeker, Abigail | | | 2 | | |
| Jennings, Nathanel | 1 | 4 | 1 | | | Burr, Samuel, 3d | 2 | 2 | 5 | | | Meeker, Thankfull | 2 | | 1 | 5 | |
| Hubbell, Lidea | 1 | 1 | 2 | | | Burr, Samuel, 1st | 2 | | 4 | | 1 | Jennings, Liman | 1 | 3 | 5 | | |
| Sherwood, Abel | 1 | 1 | 1 | | | Fourge, Sarah | 1 | | 1 | | 2 | Willson, Jonathan | 2 | | 1 | | |
| Pike, William | 1 | 4 | 3 | | 2 | Burr, Isaac | 1 | 1 | 2 | | 1 | Ogden, Bethuel | 2 | | 2 | | |
| Thorp, Eliphilet | 4 | 1 | 3 | | 1 | Hubbell, Jabez | 1 | | 2 | | | Burr, William | 1 | | 4 | | |
| Cannon, Samuel | 2 | 1 | 2 | | | Hubbell, Isaac | 3 | 4 | 3 | | 4 | Smedley, James | 2 | 1 | 4 | | 2 |
| Perry, Miah | 2 | | 2 | | | Abel, Elijah | 1 | | 3 | | | Jennings, Jeremiah | 3 | 2 | 2 | | |
| Sturges, Solomon | 1 | 1 | 3 | | | Bulkley, Ebenezer | 2 | | 1 | | | Squire, Ebenezer | 1 | 1 | 5 | | |
| Sturges, Ebenezer | 1 | 2 | 2 | | 1 | Turney, Isaac | 3 | 4 | 5 | | | Jennings, Peter | 1 | 1 | 4 | | |
| Whitney, Peter | 1 | 1 | 2 | | | Squire, Samuel | 1 | | 5 | | 1 | Osborn, Daniel | 1 | | 1 | | |
| Haleburd, Hosea | 1 | | 4 | | | Squire, George | 1 | 2 | 5 | | | Allen, George | 2 | 1 | 3 | | |
| Swords, Frances D | 3 | | 1 | | | Nichols, Paul | 3 | 2 | 6 | | | Staples, Thomas | 1 | 1 | 1 | | |
| Roberson, William | 1 | | 2 | | | Hill, Joseph | 1 | 1 | 4 | | | Jennings, Isaac | 1 | 2 | 5 | | 2 |
| Roberson, John | 1 | 6 | 2 | | | Squire, William | 1 | 1 | 2 | | | Burr, Peter | 1 | 1 | 6 | | 1 |
| Wicks, Alexander | 2 | 1 | 2 | | | Burt, Richard | 1 | | 1 | | | Mallery, Levi | 1 | 1 | 4 | | |
| Perry, Jonathan | 1 | 1 | 2 | | | Penfield, James, Jnr | 1 | | 3 | | | Anebal, Antoni | 1 | | 1 | | |
| Perry, Jabez | 1 | 2 | 2 | | | Penfield, James | 3 | | 5 | | | Phipeny, Nehemiah | 2 | 1 | 4 | | |
| Squire, Daniel | 2 | 3 | 4 | | | Burr, Nehemiah | 3 | 1 | 3 | | | Pierson, John | 1 | | 2 | | |
| Bulkley, Joseph | 1 | 5 | 4 | | | Squire, John | 2 | 1 | 2 | | | Smith, Joseph | 2 | 3 | 2 | | |
| Smith, Elnathan | 1 | | 2 | | | Holeburton, Thomas | 1 | 2 | 3 | | | Jennings, Peter | 1 | | 2 | | |
| Perry, Peter | 3 | 2 | 6 | | | Siliman, Christian | | | 3 | | | Wakeman, Andrew | 2 | | 3 | | 2 |
| Godfry, John | 1 | 1 | 1 | | | Squire, David | 2 | 5 | 3 | | | Burr, Nathan | | 1 | 4 | | |
| Godfry, Hannah | 3 | | 2 | | | Wheeler, Rebeckah | | | 3 | | | Burr, Hezekiah | 1 | 2 | 1 | | |
| Osborn, David | 2 | 2 | 1 | | | Chancy, Woolcott | 1 | 1 | 4 | | | Burr, Ebenezer, 2d | 1 | | 3 | | 1 |
| Spragg, Joseph | 1 | | 2 | | | Stone, Leman | 2 | 1 | 3 | | | Silliman, Job | | | | 6 | |
| Squire, Benjamin | 1 | | | | | Bartram, Mary | 3 | | 3 | | | Osborn, Gershom | 1 | 2 | 2 | | |
| Perry, John | 2 | | 2 | | | Sturges, Barlow | 1 | 1 | 1 | | | Silliman, Mary | | 2 | 2 | | 7 |
| Osborn, Ebenezer, Jnr | 2 | 1 | 3 | | | Parret, Abraham | 2 | 2 | 4 | | | Noyse, Joseph | | 3 | 1 | | |
| Perry, Ebenezer | 2 | | 2 | | | Wheeler, Ichaburd | 3 | | 1 | | | Eliot, Andrew | 1 | 2 | 5 | | 3 |
| Perry, Nathanel, Jnr | 2 | | 2 | | | Wheeler, David | 1 | | 2 | | | Knapp, John, Jnr | 1 | 1 | 5 | | |
| Beers, Nathan | 1 | | 1 | | | Wheeler, Chancy | 1 | | 4 | | | Silliman, Gould | 1 | | 1 | | |
| Beers, Nathan, Jnr | | 3 | 4 | | | Adams, Stephen | 1 | 1 | 3 | | 1 | Silliman, Ebenezer | 2 | | 4 | | |
| Beers, Samuel, Jnr | 2 | 2 | 1 | | | Turney, Asa | 1 | 1 | 2 | | | McRay, James | | 2 | 3 | | |
| Barlow, David | 1 | | 3 | | 2 | Staples, Thomas | 1 | 1 | 2 | | | Morehouse, Abijah | 1 | 5 | 3 | | |
| Barlow, Daniel | 1 | 1 | 2 | | | Turney, Aaron | 1 | 2 | 2 | | | Davis, Joshua | | | 3 | | |
| Thorp, Jabez | 2 | | 2 | | 1 | Squire, Joseph | 1 | 4 | 4 | | | Patchen, Josiah | 1 | 1 | 4 | | |
| Sturges, Dimon | 1 | 2 | 3 | | | Warson, John | 1 | 3 | 4 | | 1 | Morehouse, William | 1 | 3 | 6 | | |
| Sturges, Eward | 1 | 1 | 1 | | | Gould, Elizabeth | 1 | 2 | 2 | | | Morehouse, Uriah | 2 | 1 | 1 | | |
| Parsons, Nathan | 1 | | 3 | | | Buttonton, Walter | 1 | 5 | 3 | | | Patchen, David | 1 | 1 | 2 | | |
| Beers, Reubin | 2 | 1 | | | | Buttonton, William | 1 | | 1 | | | Knapp, James | 3 | 1 | 2 | | |
| Beers, David | 3 | 1 | 1 | | | Williams, John | 2 | 1 | 2 | | | Knapp, John | 2 | | 2 | | |
| Beers, David, Jnr | 1 | 1 | 3 | | | Turney, Abel | 1 | 1 | 2 | | | Meeker, Liman | 1 | | 2 | | |
| Beers, Joseph, Jnr | 1 | 1 | 3 | | | Carson, Walter | 1 | 1 | 1 | | | Meeker, Justus | 1 | | 1 | | |
| Beers, Joseph | 2 | | 1 | | | Turney, Abiah | 1 | | 1 | | | Vaune, Olive | 1 | | 4 | | |
| Beers, Samuel | 1 | 1 | 1 | | | Hays, Nathan | 1 | | 1 | | | Knapp, Benjamin | 1 | 2 | 3 | | |
| Sturges, Abigail | 2 | 2 | 4 | | 1 | Turney, Peter | 1 | | 3 | | | Hawley, Silas | 1 | | 2 | | |
| Bulkley, Joseph, 2d | 1 | 2 | 3 | | | Burr, Charles | 3 | 3 | 5 | | | Nichols, John | 2 | 3 | 6 | | |
| Barlow, Edmon | 1 | 3 | 3 | | | Lewis, Jonathan | 1 | | 2 | | 3 | Hubbell, Richard | 2 | 3 | 4 | | 3 |
| Sturges, Hezekiah | 2 | | 2 | | 4 | Gould, Talcott | 1 | | 3 | | | Shelton, Philo | 2 | 2 | 3 | | 1 |
| Redfield, Lucretia | | 1 | 2 | | | Gould, Isaac | 1 | 1 | 1 | | | Burr, Aaron | 2 | | 2 | | |
| Bulkley, Josiah | 2 | 2 | 4 | | | Nichols, Squire | 1 | | 1 | | | Burr, Osias | 3 | 4 | 5 | | |
| Sturges, William | 1 | 2 | 2 | | | Dimon, Daniel | 3 | 1 | 5 | | | Hubbell, Joel | 1 | 1 | 1 | | |
| Sturges, Hezekiah, Jnr | 2 | | 2 | | | Ogden, David | 1 | 1 | 3 | | | Meeker, Peter | 1 | | 2 | | |
| Trubey, Answell | 1 | 3 | 5 | | | Sherwood, Zalmon | 1 | 1 | 2 | | | Burr, John, Jnr | 1 | 3 | 3 | | |
| Bulkley, Andrew | 1 | | 2 | | | Ogden, Sturges | 1 | 1 | 2 | | | Tredwell, David | 1 | 2 | 4 | | |
| Sturges, Benjamin | 2 | | 3 | | | Ogden, Jean | | | 1 | | | Wheeler, Hezekiah | 1 | | 2 | | |
| Sturges, Jonathan | 4 | 1 | 6 | | 3 | Sherwood, Benjamin | 2 | | 1 | | | Wheeler, Willson | | 1 | 4 | | |
| Sturges, Seth | 4 | 3 | 1 | | | Sherwood, Seth | 3 | 5 | 7 | | 1 | Odle, Sarah | | | 1 | | |
| Darrow, Benjamin | 1 | | 2 | | | Stratton, Samuel | 1 | 3 | 4 | | | Wakelin, Abel | 1 | 2 | 2 | | |
| Roberson, John, Jnr | 1 | | 2 | | | Stratton, John | 1 | 1 | 2 | | | Warden, William, Jnr | 1 | 3 | 2 | | |
| Rollins, Aaron | 1 | | 3 | | | Jennings, Noah | 1 | 3 | 3 | | | Wheeler, Timothy | 2 | | 2 | | |
| Osborn, Mable | | | 3 | | 1 | Bennet, Stephen | 1 | 2 | 5 | | | Mallet, Lewis | 1 | 1 | 6 | | |
| Jennings, David | 1 | 1 | 5 | | | Sealee, Ezra | 2 | 3 | 3 | | | Wheeler, Benjamin | 1 | | 1 | | |
| Lewis, Lothrop | 1 | 1 | 3 | | 3 | Meeker, Ichobud | 1 | 6 | 3 | | | Porter, John | 2 | 3 | 2 | | |
| Bruster, Calep | 1 | 2 | 3 | | | Hall, Ichobud | 1 | 1 | 2 | | | Wheeler, Samuel | 1 | | 2 | | |
| Wakeman, Ebenezer | 2 | 2 | 2 | | 2 | Odle, Nehemiah S | 1 | 1 | 2 | | | Odle, Isaac | 1 | 2 | 4 | | |
| Burr, David, 3d | 3 | | 2 | | 3 | Sisco, Hannah | 1 | | 2 | | | Bennet, Joseph W | 1 | | 2 | | |
| Rowland, Andrew | 3 | 2 | 2 | | 2 | Bennet, Thaddeus | 1 | 3 | 2 | | | Beerdslee, John | 1 | | 2 | | |
| Nichols, Hezekiah | 3 | 2 | 3 | 1 | | Tredwell, Abel | 2 | 1 | 3 | | | Hall, Joseph | 2 | | 4 | | |
| Smedley, Samuel | 1 | | 1 | | | Hall, William | 2 | 1 | 3 | | | Hall, John | | | 2 | | |
| Rowland, Abigail | 1 | | 3 | | | Hodgden, David | 2 | 2 | 3 | | | Cable, Samuel | 3 | | 3 | | |
| Spalden, Rowland | 1 | | 3 | | | Hall, Ebenezer | | | 2 | | | Duncomb, John | 1 | 3 | 4 | | |
| Runnels, Anne | | 1 | 3 | | | Cary, William | 1 | | 1 | | | Holeburton, William | 1 | 2 | 5 | | |
| Jennings, Nathan | 1 | | 3 | | | Patchen, James | | | 2 | | | Ross, Robert | 1 | 1 | 1 | | |
| Dimon, William | 1 | 2 | 4 | | | Patchen, Woolcott | 1 | | 4 | | | Fairweather, Benjamin | | | | | |
| Woodhull, Abraham C | 1 | | 3 | | | Morehouse, David | 1 | | 2 | | | Strong, Joseph | 2 | 1 | 6 | | |
| Sturges, Abigail | | | 2 | | | Hall, Liman | 1 | | 1 | | | Brothwell, Thomas | | | | | |
| Burr, Thaddeus | 1 | | 2 | 1 | 5 | Hall, James | 1 | | 2 | | 2 | Hull, William | 1 | 1 | 1 | | |
| Burr, Gershom | 1 | | 2 | | 2 | Squire, Samuel, Jnr | 2 | 1 | 6 | | | Hubbell, Aaron | 1 | | 3 | | |
| Malbey, Jonathan | 2 | 1 | 6 | | 1 | Hubbell, Abel | 2 | 1 | 5 | | | Buttonton, Nehemiah | 1 | | 1 | | |

# HEADS OF FAMILIES—CONNECTICUT.

## FAIRFIELD COUNTY—Continued.

| NAME OF HEAD OF FAMILY. | Free white males of 16 years and upward, including heads of families. | Free white males under 16 years. | Free white females, including heads of families. | All other free persons. | Slaves. |
|---|---|---|---|---|---|
| **FAIRFIELD TOWN—con.** | | | | | |
| Burr, Jesse, 2d | 1 | 3 | 4 | | |
| Burr, Elijah | 1 | 3 | 2 | | |
| Patchen, Elijah | 1 | 5 | 2 | | |
| Hubbell, Giddeon | 1 | 1 | 3 | | |
| Hubbell, Daniel | 3 | | 4 | | |
| Sherwood, Zachariah | 1 | | 2 | | |
| Meeker, John | 1 | | 1 | | |
| Sealee, Deborah | | 4 | 5 | | |
| Meeker, David | 1 | | 1 | | |
| Brothwell, Joseph | 1 | | 2 | | |
| Sealee, Seth | 2 | 1 | 5 | | |
| Meeker, Hezekiah | 1 | 2 | 4 | | |
| Cable, Rebekah | | | 1 | | |
| Taylor, Anne | 1 | | 5 | | |
| Jackson, Nathan | 2 | | 2 | | |
| Hall, Benjamin | 2 | | 2 | | |
| Lacy, Daniel | 2 | 4 | 3 | | |
| Lacy, Margeret | | | 2 | | |
| Lacy, John | 1 | | 1 | | |
| Brothwell, Benjamin | 1 | 1 | 3 | | |
| Lacy, David | 1 | 2 | 3 | | |
| Bangs, Lemwell | 1 | 4 | 3 | | |
| Fowler, Nehemiah | 1 | 2 | 4 | | |
| Willson, Nathanel, Junr | 1 | 1 | 3 | | 1 |
| Silliman, Seth | 2 | | 3 | | |
| Silliman, Samuel | 2 | | 1 | | |
| Knapp, Ebenezer | 2 | 1 | 5 | | |
| Knapp, Daniel | 2 | | | | |
| Willson, Amos | 2 | 3 | 4 | | |
| Willson, Silliman | 1 | | 2 | | |
| Adams, Stephen | 2 | | 2 | | 1 |
| Adams, Nathan | 1 | | 3 | | 1 |
| Jennings, Mathew | 1 | 1 | 2 | | 6 |
| Hays, William | 1 | | 1 | | |
| Hays, Joseph | 2 | 1 | 3 | | |
| Jennings, Ezra | 2 | 8 | 3 | | |
| Willson, Daniel | 3 | 2 | 3 | | 1 |
| Willson, Ann | 1 | | 3 | | |
| Hallins, Abigail | | | 4 | | |
| Jennings, Abel | 4 | | 5 | | |
| Jennings, Robert | 1 | 1 | 1 | | |
| Hull, Jeddediah | 2 | 1 | 2 | | |
| Sherwood, Reubin | 1 | 2 | 3 | | |
| Sherwood, Sarah | 1 | | 1 | | |
| Sherwood, Benjamin, Junr | 1 | 2 | 3 | | |
| Bulkley, William | 2 | 1 | 4 | | |
| Bulkley, James | 1 | 1 | 3 | | |
| Robins, Ephraim | 1 | 2 | 1 | | 1 |
| Banks, Ebenezer | 2 | 1 | 5 | | 2 |
| **GREENWICH TOWN.** | | | | | |
| Hendric, William | 1 | 3 | 5 | | |
| Jezup, Jonathan | 5 | 2 | 4 | | |
| Peck, Moses | 2 | 1 | 1 | | |
| Lockwood, Noah | 1 | 2 | 1 | | |
| Husted, Joseph | 1 | 6 | 2 | | |
| Adams, Joseph | 1 | 2 | 2 | | |
| Waring, Henry | 1 | 4 | 3 | | |
| Morris, Revd Robert | 1 | | 1 | | |
| Lockwood, Philip | 1 | 3 | 5 | | |
| Lockwood, Samuel | 2 | 2 | 4 | | |
| Lockwood, Andrew | 1 | | 2 | | |
| Lockwood, Edward | 1 | 2 | 3 | | |
| Lockwood, Gilbert | 2 | 1 | 3 | | |
| Bay, Thomas | 1 | 1 | 4 | | 2 |
| Ferris, Samuel | 3 | 2 | 1 | | |
| Jezup, Ebenezer | 1 | | 2 | | |
| Knapp, Charles | 1 | | 5 | | |
| Knapp, Timothy | 3 | 1 | 5 | | |
| Lockwood, Mary (Wd) | | 2 | 2 | | |
| Palmer, Stephen | 2 | 4 | 3 | | |
| Lockwood, Enos | 3 | | 2 | | |
| Ferris, Jeremiah | 2 | 1 | 5 | | |
| Joyce, Sarah (Wd) | | | 5 | | 1 |
| Ferris, Nathel, Junr | 1 | 3 | 6 | | |
| Lockwood, Caleb | 2 | 4 | 4 | | |
| Lockwood, Joseph | 2 | | 2 | | |
| Parrot, John | 1 | 1 | 1 | | |
| Lockwood, Jonathan, 3d | 1 | | 2 | | |
| Lockwood, John | 2 | 1 | 2 | | |
| Lockwood, George | 2 | 4 | 2 | | |
| Sackett, Nathel | 2 | 1 | 3 | | |
| Hobby, Thomas | 1 | 1 | 4 | | |
| Hobby, Jabez Mead | 1 | | 4 | | |
| Hobby, Charles | 1 | 2 | 2 | | |
| Rundle, Timothy | 2 | 2 | 3 | | |
| Peck, Joseph | 4 | 1 | 5 | | |
| Johnson, Henry | 4 | 2 | 4 | | |
| Rundle, Amy (Wd) | 1 | 2 | 2 | | |
| Peck, Isaac | 1 | 2 | 3 | | |
| Whiting, Samuel | 2 | 2 | 2 | | |
| Peck, Jeremiah | 1 | | 2 | | |
| **GREENWICH TOWN—con.** | | | | | |
| Lockwood, Jonathan | 1 | | 2 | | |
| Lockwood, Abraham | 2 | 1 | 3 | | |
| Lockwood, Frederick | 1 | 2 | 2 | | |
| Peck, Samuel | 4 | | 1 | | |
| Peck, Ebenezer | 2 | 2 | 6 | | |
| Guernsey, Samuel | 1 | | 2 | | |
| Knapp, Enos | 3 | 1 | 3 | | |
| Rundle, Jeremiah | 1 | | 1 | | |
| Jezup, Silvanus | 1 | 1 | 2 | | |
| Selleck, Joseph | 1 | | 2 | | |
| Peck, George | 3 | | 3 | | |
| Ferris, Stephen | 1 | 2 | 3 | | |
| Lockwood, Stephen | 1 | 1 | 2 | | |
| Peck, Roberts | 2 | 2 | 2 | | |
| Whelpley, Abigail | | | 2 | | |
| Adams, John | 1 | 3 | 2 | | |
| Ferris, Jeduthan | 4 | 3 | 5 | | |
| Ferris, Samuel | 4 | 1 | 2 | | |
| Knapp, Jeremiah | 2 | 2 | 4 | | |
| Reynolds, Samuel | 1 | 1 | 3 | | |
| Sherwood, Nathan | 1 | 2 | 1 | | |
| Palmer, B. (Wd) | 1 | | 5 | | |
| Goff, Peter | 1 | 2 | 2 | | |
| Reynolds, Briggs | 2 | 3 | 4 | | |
| Lane, John | 1 | 1 | 4 | | |
| Whelpley, Anne (Wd) | | 1 | 4 | | |
| Titus, Daniel | 1 | 2 | 4 | | |
| Titus, Samuel | 2 | | 3 | | |
| Knapp, David | 1 | 1 | 1 | | |
| Knapp, Samuel | 1 | | 2 | | |
| Ash, Samuel | 1 | 4 | 4 | 1 | |
| Dayton, Abraham | 1 | 2 | 3 | | |
| Palmer, John | 3 | | 3 | | |
| Simmons, Timothy (negro) | | | | 6 | |
| Weed, David | 1 | 1 | 3 | | |
| Davis, Stephen | 1 | 1 | 5 | | |
| Palmer, Smith | 2 | 2 | 1 | | |
| Edgerly, John | 1 | 2 | 2 | | |
| Knapp, William | 1 | 1 | 4 | 1 | |
| Reynolds, Daniel | 3 | | 3 | | |
| Whelpley, Ebenezer | 1 | 1 | 2 | | |
| Howe, Jonathan | 2 | | 1 | | |
| Johnson, Thomas | 2 | 4 | 4 | | |
| Johnson, William | 1 | 2 | 4 | | |
| Pomroy, Joel | 2 | 1 | 3 | | |
| Wilmot, Frank | 1 | 1 | 2 | | |
| Ritch, John | 1 | | 2 | | |
| Ritch, Lemuel | 1 | | 3 | | |
| Ferris, Park | 2 | 1 | 2 | | |
| Ferris, Shubeal | 1 | | 2 | | |
| Ferris, Moses | 2 | | 2 | | |
| Ferris, David, Jr | 1 | 2 | 2 | | |
| Miller, John | 1 | 2 | 3 | | |
| Mead, Edward | 1 | | 1 | | |
| Selleck, Silvanus | 1 | 2 | 4 | | |
| Mead, Stephen | 2 | | 2 | | |
| Morrel, Jacob | 2 | 4 | 1 | | |
| Titus, William | 1 | 1 | 1 | | |
| Peck, Nathaniel | 1 | 1 | 7 | | |
| Ferris, David | 2 | | 5 | | |
| Bush, Joseph | 1 | | 3 | | |
| Mead, Nehemiah | 3 | | 3 | | |
| Hubble, Jehiel | 1 | 2 | 2 | | |
| Hitchcock, Joseph | 1 | 2 | 1 | | |
| Fletcher, M. (Wd) | 1 | | 1 | | |
| Tenpany, Michael C | 1 | 1 | 3 | | |
| Wilmot, Samuel | 1 | | 2 | | |
| Holly, Lois (Wd) | 1 | 3 | 4 | | |
| Sacket, George | 3 | | 3 | | |
| Mead, Jeremiah, Junr | 2 | 2 | 2 | | |
| Hitchcock, Thomas | 1 | 1 | 4 | | |
| Deforest, Samuel | 1 | 1 | 3 | | |
| Peck, Isaac, 3d | 1 | | 1 | | |
| Mead, Israel | 1 | 1 | 1 | | |
| Marshall, Andrew | 3 | 1 | 5 | | |
| Marshall, Ezra | 1 | 3 | 4 | | |
| Knapp, Gilbert | 2 | | 2 | | |
| Marshall, Isaac | 2 | | 9 | | |
| Holmes, Benjamin | 2 | 2 | 2 | | |
| Mead, Andrew | 2 | | 2 | | 1 |
| Hobby, Benjamin | 2 | | 2 | | 2 |
| Hobby, Ebenezer | 2 | 3 | 2 | 1 | 2 |
| Brown, Bazaleel | 2 | | 1 | | |
| Hubby, Benjamin, Jr | 1 | | 2 | | |
| Mead, Titus | 5 | 1 | 3 | | 1 |
| Mead, Jabez | 2 | | 2 | | |
| Mead, Titus, Junr | 1 | 1 | 3 | | |
| Hobby, Joseph | 2 | 2 | 3 | | |
| Hobby, Mills | 2 | 1 | 4 | | 1 |
| Mead, Elkanah | 2 | 1 | 2 | | 1 |
| Knapp, Eben | 2 | 3 | 4 | | |
| Mead, Jonah | 2 | 3 | 4 | | 1 |
| Rundle, Solomon | 2 | 3 | 3 | | |
| Hobby, Abraham | 1 | 1 | 4 | | |
| **GREENWICH TOWN—con.** | | | | | |
| Close, Gilbert | 1 | 1 | 1 | | |
| Hobby, Joseph, Junr | 1 | 3 | 6 | | 2 |
| Rundle, Reuben | 2 | 1 | 1 | | |
| Rundle, Samuel | 1 | | 4 | | |
| Reynolds, Horton | 2 | 2 | 4 | | |
| Mead, Nathel, 3d | 3 | 2 | 5 | | |
| Mead, Joshua | 3 | 2 | 4 | 1 | 1 |
| Knapp, Joshua, Jr | 3 | 1 | 4 | | |
| Lyon, Caleb | 1 | 1 | 4 | | |
| Lyon, Job | 3 | | 3 | | |
| Rundle, Elizabeth (Wd) | | 1 | 2 | | |
| Brown, Sherman | 3 | 1 | 3 | | |
| Rundle, Nathaniel | 2 | 1 | 3 | | |
| Knapp, Phebe (Wd) | 1 | 2 | 4 | | |
| Brown, Josiah | 1 | | 3 | | |
| Brown, Levi | 1 | 1 | 1 | | |
| Ritch, Mary (Wd) | | | 2 | | |
| Close, Jonathan | 1 | 1 | 1 | | |
| Ritch, Thomas | 1 | 2 | 4 | | |
| Ritch, James | 1 | 1 | 2 | | |
| Ferris, Oliver | 1 | 1 | 5 | | |
| Lyon, Daniel, 3d | 2 | | 6 | | |
| Marshall, Thomas | 1 | 1 | 4 | | |
| Reynolds, Joseph | 2 | 1 | 2 | | 1 |
| Lockwood, Anny (Wd) | 1 | | 1 | | |
| Davis, Isaac | 1 | | 2 | | |
| Reynolds, Ellihu | 1 | 2 | 1 | | |
| Jezup, Elizabeth (Wd) | 1 | 1 | 1 | | |
| Mosier, James | 1 | 2 | 5 | | |
| Palmer, Elliot | 1 | 1 | 1 | | |
| Palmer, Denham | 2 | 4 | 1 | | |
| Studwell, Deborah (Wd) | 2 | 1 | 2 | | |
| Studwell, Anthony | 2 | 3 | 3 | | |
| Reynolds, Nathaniel | 3 | 1 | 2 | | |
| Mead, Abel | 1 | 1 | 6 | | |
| Reynolds, Philo | 1 | | 2 | | |
| Reynolds, Ezekiel | 2 | 1 | 4 | | |
| Reynolds, Nathel, Jr | 2 | 3 | 3 | | |
| Lockwood, Thaddeus | 2 | 2 | 5 | | |
| Lockwood, Nathan | 2 | 1 | 2 | | |
| Ferris, Nathaniel | 3 | 2 | 6 | | |
| Ingersol, Nathaniel | 3 | | 5 | | |
| Knapp, Amy (Wd) | | | 3 | | |
| Knapp, Rachel (Wd) | | | 1 | | |
| Bush, William | 1 | 1 | 2 | | 1 |
| Denton, Humphry | 5 | | 3 | | |
| Mead, Amos | 3 | | 2 | 2 | 4 |
| Sacket, Justice | 2 | 3 | 3 | | 1 |
| Seymore, Samuel | 1 | 1 | 2 | | |
| Mead, Jared | 3 | 1 | 6 | 1 | 4 |
| Hobby, John | 3 | 2 | 5 | | 1 |
| Hobby, Thomas, Junr | 2 | 5 | 4 | | |
| Holmes, Stephen | 2 | | 4 | | |
| Holmes, Isaac | 1 | | | | |
| Hayes, Abraham | 1 | | 2 | | |
| Weed, Isaac | 1 | 1 | 2 | | |
| Wilson, Benjamin | 1 | 1 | 3 | | |
| Mead, Nehemiah, Jr | 2 | 3 | 3 | | |
| Mead, Joseph | 1 | 2 | 3 | | |
| Mead, Nathaniel, Junr | 2 | 2 | 3 | | |
| Mead, Smith | 1 | 4 | 1 | | |
| Lewis, Revd Isaac | 4 | 1 | 4 | | 1 |
| Mead, Henry | 3 | 1 | 5 | | |
| Mead, Matthew | 2 | 2 | 6 | | |
| Wilson, Nehemiah, Junr | 1 | | 3 | | |
| Addington, John | 2 | 1 | 3 | | |
| Avery, John | 1 | 1 | 2 | | |
| Simmons Isaac | 1 | | 2 | | |
| Mead, John | 2 | 2 | 3 | 2 | 1 |
| Town, Jonathan | 1 | 1 | 5 | | |
| Townsend, Coles | 1 | 1 | 5 | | |
| Banks, James | 2 | 1 | 6 | | |
| Lyon, Gilbert | 3 | 1 | 3 | | |
| Lyon, Daniel | 1 | 1 | 4 | | |
| Banks, Joseph | 1 | 2 | 3 | | |
| Brundage, Joseph | 2 | | 1 | | |
| Lyon, David | 1 | 3 | | | |
| Wilson, Solomon | 3 | | 3 | | |
| Lyon, James | 2 | 1 | | | |
| Lyon, Benjamin | 1 | | 3 | | |
| Lyon, James, 3d | 1 | 4 | 3 | 1 | 1 |
| Lyon, Stephen | 1 | | 2 | | |
| Lyon, Shubeal | 1 | 2 | 4 | | |
| Lyon, James, Junr | 1 | 2 | 4 | | |
| Merrit, Abraham | 1 | 2 | 3 | | |
| Taylor, Zebediah | 1 | 1 | 2 | | |
| Lyon, James, Junr | 1 | 2 | 5 | | |
| Merrit, Jesse | 1 | 1 | 1 | | |
| Merrit, Abraham | 1 | 1 | 3 | | |
| Merrit, Solomon | 3 | | 3 | | |
| Mosier, Daniel | 1 | | 2 | | |
| Bacon, Ephraim | 5 | 1 | 4 | | |
| Lyon, Gilbert, Junr | 1 | | 2 | | |
| Sherwood, Daniel | 1 | 4 | 5 | | |
| Bearmore, Nathanel | 1 | | 2 | | |

# FIRST CENSUS OF THE UNITED STATES.

## FAIRFIELD COUNTY—Continued.

| NAME OF HEAD OF FAMILY. | Free white males of 16 years and upward, including heads of families. | Free white males under 16 years. | Free white females, including heads of families. | All other free persons. | Slaves. |
|---|---|---|---|---|---|
| **GREENWICH TOWN—con.** | | | | | |
| Lyon, Daniel | 1 | 1 | 4 | 1 | |
| Darrow, Sarah (W^d) | | | 2 | | |
| Jordon, W^m | 1 | | 3 | | |
| Merritt, Eben | 1 | 2 | 2 | | |
| Wilson, Amos | 1 | | 1 | | |
| Merrit, Nathan | 2 | | 4 | | 1 |
| Rathburn, Susannah | | | 1 | | |
| Sherwood, Jabez | 1 | | 3 | | |
| Wilson, Nehemiah | 1 | 3 | 3 | | 1 |
| Vanziekland, Minna | 2 | 2 | 3 | | |
| Anderson, Jeremiah | 1 | 1 | 1 | | 1 |
| Merrit, Jonathan | 1 | | 1 | | |
| Anderson, Joseph | 1 | 3 | 1 | | |
| Strang, Jared | 2 | 1 | 2 | | |
| Anderson, Isaac | 1 | 3 | 6 | | |
| Reynolds, Nathan | 2 | | 2 | | |
| Merrit, Adam | 1 | 2 | 1 | | |
| Lewis, Isaac | 1 | 1 | 2 | | |
| Brundage, Sarah | | | 2 | | |
| Eden, David | 2 | | 1 | | |
| Sutton, William | 1 | 2 | 2 | | |
| Carrihart, Hacaliah | 1 | 1 | 2 | | |
| Wilson, Jotham | 2 | 1 | 1 | 1 | 1 |
| Purdy, Daniel | 1 | 2 | 4 | | |
| Anderson, Stephen | 1 | 1 | 2 | | |
| Anderson, William | 2 | | 4 | | |
| Maynerd, Elisha | 1 | 1 | 2 | | |
| Horton, Timothy | 1 | 1 | 3 | | |
| Pine, Samuel | 1 | 2 | 2 | | 1 |
| Green, Caleb | 1 | 2 | 4 | | |
| Field, Aaron | 2 | 2 | 3 | | |
| Cunningham, Abigail | | 1 | 3 | | |
| Clapp, Thomas | 3 | 1 | 4 | | |
| Pughby, Samuel | 1 | 2 | 5 | | 1 |
| Field, Uriah | 6 | 3 | 8 | 1 | |
| Clapp, Phebe (W^d) | 2 | 2 | 4 | | |
| Nutt, Robert | 1 | 1 | 5 | | |
| Jeffery (Black) | | | | 2 | |
| Conklin, Mary (W^d) | | | 3 | | |
| Bush, David | 2 | 2 | 6 | 1 | 8 |
| Peck, Ephraim | 1 | 1 | 4 | | |
| Mesnard, John | 2 | | 3 | | |
| Studwell, Sarah (W^d) | | 1 | 2 | | |
| Fairchild, Ezekiel | 1 | 2 | 2 | | |
| Studwell, Gabriel | 1 | 2 | 3 | | |
| Smith, Isaac | 1 | 3 | 3 | | |
| Knapp, Israel | 3 | 2 | 7 | 1 | 3 |
| Close, Hannah (W^d) | 1 | | 4 | | |
| Fitch, Col. Jabez | 1 | 1 | 5 | | 1 |
| Grigg, Henry | 1 | 1 | 3 | | |
| Grigg, Alexander | 1 | | 4 | | |
| Mead, Abraham | 3 | 2 | 4 | | |
| Davis, Elisha | 1 | | 5 | | |
| Davis, Stephen, Jr | 1 | | 2 | | |
| Howard, Daniel | 1 | | 5 | | |
| Close, Elihu | 1 | 2 | 1 | | |
| Reynolds, Ezra | 1 | 2 | 4 | | |
| Mead, Abigail (W^d) | 2 | 3 | 3 | | |
| Holmes, Reuben | 3 | | 3 | | |
| Mead, Ebenezer | 2 | 2 | 6 | | |
| Lyon, Noah | 1 | 3 | 2 | | |
| Darrow, James | 1 | | 3 | | |
| Betts, Sarah (W^d) | | 1 | 4 | | |
| Marshall, Gilbert | 1 | 3 | 5 | | |
| Studwell, Henry | 1 | | 4 | | |
| Wood, David | 4 | 1 | 5 | | |
| Ferris, Jabez | 3 | 1 | 3 | | |
| Husted, Jared | 1 | | 2 | | |
| Ferris, Solomon, Jun^r | 2 | 1 | 3 | | |
| Norcott, Dennis | 1 | 1 | 3 | | |
| Johnson, Samuel | 1 | 1 | 4 | | |
| Burley, Sarah (W^d) | | | 6 | | |
| Burley, Silas | 1 | 1 | 4 | | |
| Palmer, John W | 1 | 6 | 3 | | |
| Palmer, Messenger | 1 | 1 | 1 | 1 | 2 |
| Palmer, Seth | 2 | | 2 | | |
| Quintard, Isaac | 1 | 1 | 2 | | |
| Sackett, Peter | 1 | 1 | 3 | | |
| Bush, Samuel | 1 | | 3 | | 4 |
| Banks, Elizabeth (W^d) | | 1 | 4 | | 1 |
| Banks, Daniel | 1 | | 4 | | |
| Banks, Benjamin | 1 | 2 | 4 | | |
| Banks, Joshua | 1 | 1 | 3 | | |
| Mead, Benjamin | 2 | 1 | 3 | | 1 |
| Mead, David | 2 | 1 | 1 | | |
| Mead, Whitman | 1 | | 3 | 1 | |
| Rowel, Valentine | 1 | | 3 | | |
| Dayton, Amos | 1 | 1 | 3 | | |
| Rowel, W^m | 1 | 2 | 6 | | |
| Mead, Jehiel | 3 | | 3 | | |
| Mead, Eliphalet, Jun^r | 2 | | 1 | | |
| Mead, Henry, Jun^r | 1 | | 2 | | |
| Mead, Silas | 4 | | 2 | | |
| Mead, Calvin | 2 | 1 | 2 | | |
| Cornwall, John | 1 | 2 | 4 | | |
| Nash, Francis | 5 | | 3 | | |
| **GREENWICH TOWN—con.** | | | | | |
| Dun, Michael | 2 | | 1 | | |
| Reynolds, Israel | 2 | 2 | 5 | | |
| Ireland, Job | 1 | 1 | 2 | | |
| Tomkins, Oliver | 1 | 3 | 3 | | |
| Ireland, Abraham | 1 | 2 | 3 | | |
| Stokam, Reuben | 1 | 3 | 3 | | |
| Bard, Alexander | 1 | 1 | 2 | | |
| Sherwood, Nehemiah, Jr | 1 | | 2 | | |
| Cherry, Poll | | 1 | 2 | | |
| Jermain, Elizabeth | | 1 | 1 | | |
| Mead, John, Jun^r | 1 | 1 | 6 | | |
| Hayes, Abraham, Jr | 1 | 2 | 7 | | |
| Mead, Zacheus | 1 | 1 | 5 | | |
| Wix, John | 1 | 3 | 5 | | |
| Mead, Abigail (W^d) | | | 1 | | |
| Mead, Jonathan | 1 | 1 | 2 | | |
| Mead, Peter | 2 | 2 | 4 | 1 | |
| Husted, Abraham | 4 | 3 | 2 | | 1 |
| Avery, Peter | 2 | 3 | 4 | | |
| Palmer, Samuel, Jr | 4 | 2 | 3 | | |
| Rundle, Amy (W^d) | | | 4 | | |
| Palmer, Samuel | 5 | | 4 | | |
| Rundle, Phinehas | 1 | 2 | 3 | | |
| Rundle, Samuel | 2 | 1 | 3 | | |
| Hibbard, Nathaniel | 3 | | 3 | | |
| Finch, Nathaniel | 3 | | 3 | | |
| Brown, David | 2 | 2 | 8 | | |
| MCaul, Angus | 4 | 2 | 3 | | |
| Marshall, Henry | 3 | 3 | 3 | | |
| Peck, Theophilus | 2 | | 3 | | |
| Peck, Gilbert | 2 | | 3 | | |
| Husted, Moses, Jr | 1 | | 2 | | 7 |
| Howe, Isaac | 1 | 1 | 9 | | |
| Peck, Abraham | 1 | 1 | 5 | 1 | |
| Peck, Israel | 2 | 2 | 2 | | |
| Peck, Samuel, Jr | 2 | 2 | 5 | | |
| Peck, Isaac | 1 | | 1 | | 1 |
| Knapp, Jonas | 2 | 2 | 3 | | |
| Mead, Nathaniel | 3 | | 3 | 1 | 2 |
| Beard, Robert | 2 | 1 | 2 | | |
| Hibbard, Jonathan | 1 | 3 | 3 | | |
| Lyon, Caleb, Jun^r | 3 | 6 | 4 | | |
| Mead, Jasper | 1 | 3 | 2 | | |
| Purdy, Ruth (W^d) | 1 | 1 | 2 | | |
| Belcher, Elisha | 2 | | 5 | | 1 |
| Knapp, Jonah | 2 | 4 | 5 | | |
| Lockwood, Israel | 1 | 3 | 1 | 3 | |
| Ferris, Ashford | 2 | 2 | 2 | 1 | |
| Knapp, Jonathan | 1 | 4 | 5 | | 1 |
| Hobby, Seymore | 1 | 1 | 3 | | |
| Holmes, Jabez | 1 | 1 | 3 | | |
| Knapp, Shubeal | 2 | 2 | 3 | | |
| Knapp, Joshua, 3^d | 1 | 1 | 3 | | |
| Knapp, Joshua | 1 | 2 | 5 | | 1 |
| Green, Charles | 1 | | 2 | 1 | |
| Husted, Nathan | 1 | 1 | 4 | | |
| Worden, Roger | 1 | 1 | 3 | | |
| Mills, Amos | 4 | 1 | 2 | | |
| Reynolds, Elizabeth (W^d) | | | 2 | | |
| Southerland, Roger | | | 3 | | |
| Lockwood, Nathaniel | 1 | 1 | 3 | | |
| Rundle, Rachel (W^d) | | | 3 | | |
| Close, Odel, Jun^r | 2 | 2 | 1 | | |
| Finch, Jonathan | 2 | 2 | 7 | | |
| Brush, Benjamin | 1 | 2 | 3 | 1 | 1 |
| Brown, Nehemiah | 3 | | 2 | 1 | |
| Brown, Major | 1 | 1 | 4 | 1 | |
| Brown, Roger | 1 | 2 | 4 | 1 | |
| Holmes, Ebenezer | 1 | 2 | 7 | | |
| Mead, Jesse | 1 | 1 | 5 | | |
| Mead, Zebediah | 2 | | 4 | | |
| Clapp, Benjamin | 2 | 2 | 3 | | |
| Clapp, Joseph | 2 | 1 | 2 | | |
| Clapp, James | 2 | 2 | 1 | | |
| Vanevert, Abraham | 1 | 2 | 2 | | |
| Wood, Mary | | | 3 | | |
| Sherwood, Gilbert | 2 | | 3 | | |
| Brown, Laurence | 1 | 1 | 2 | | |
| Brundage, Gabriel | 3 | 2 | 2 | | |
| Fairchild, Oliver | 1 | 2 | 2 | | |
| Sutton, Benjamin | 1 | 3 | 3 | | |
| Purdy, Nathan | 1 | | 2 | | |
| Merrit, Nehemiah | 1 | 1 | 2 | | |
| Harmony, Nicholas | 1 | 3 | 3 | | |
| Purdy, Elizabeth (W^d) | | | 1 | | |
| Sherwood, Oliver | 2 | 1 | 1 | | |
| Peck, David | 1 | 2 | 6 | | |
| Sherwood, Elnathan | 1 | 1 | 5 | | |
| Simmons, Jemimah (W^d) | | | 1 | | 2 |
| Peck, Gideon | 1 | | 2 | | |
| Merrit, Nathan, Jun^r | 1 | 3 | 2 | | 3 |
| Green, John | 2 | 2 | 2 | 1 | 1 |
| Miller, Andrew | 2 | 2 | 3 | 1 | |
| Merrit, Nathaniel | 1 | 1 | 3 | | |
| **GREENWICH TOWN—con.** | | | | | |
| Wilson, Daniel | 1 | 2 | 2 | | |
| Gunn, William | 1 | | 2 | | |
| Coe, Jonathan | 1 | | 1 | | 1 |
| Coe, Reuben | 1 | 3 | 2 | | |
| Green, James | 3 | 1 | 4 | | |
| Wilson, David | 1 | 3 | 4 | | |
| Lewis, Daniel | 1 | 4 | 4 | | |
| Wilson, Uriah | 1 | | 2 | | |
| Wilson, Joseph | 1 | 2 | 3 | | |
| Peck, Solomon | 1 | | 1 | | |
| Knapp, Uriah | 5 | 2 | 4 | | |
| Armer, Abigail (W^d) | | 1 | 2 | | |
| Lockwood, Samuel, Jr | 1 | 1 | 4 | | |
| Brown, James | 2 | 3 | 3 | | |
| Lockwood, Amos | 1 | | 2 | | |
| Lockwood, Stephen | 1 | 1 | 3 | | |
| Reynolds, Joseph | 1 | 1 | 2 | | |
| Reynolds, Benjamin | 2 | 2 | 4 | | |
| Reynolds, Joannah (W^d) | | | 3 | | |
| Palmer, Winas | 2 | 1 | 3 | | |
| Palmer, Jonathan | 1 | | 1 | | |
| Mills, Samuel | 3 | 1 | 7 | | 1 |
| Mead, Ruth (W^d) | 2 | 1 | 2 | | |
| Mead, Daniel | 1 | 2 | 1 | | |
| Mead, Jotham | 1 | 1 | 3 | | |
| Mead, Enos | 1 | 3 | 2 | | |
| Close, Abraham | 1 | 3 | 3 | | |
| Close, Joseph | 4 | 1 | 4 | | |
| Knapp, Hannah (W^d) | | | 2 | | |
| Finch, William | 1 | 3 | 3 | | |
| Knapp, Anne (W^d) | | | 4 | | |
| Finch, Timothy | 3 | 3 | 3 | | |
| Finch, William N | 1 | 1 | 3 | | |
| Londen, John | 1 | 2 | 7 | | |
| Husted, Peter | 4 | 3 | 4 | | |
| Husted, Moses | 1 | | 1 | | |
| Numan, Platt | 2 | 1 | 3 | | |
| Dota, William | 1 | | 1 | | |
| Peck, Benjamin | 2 | 3 | 2 | | |
| Close, Odel | 3 | 2 | 4 | | |
| Mead, Sibela (W^d) | 1 | | 1 | 1 | |
| Reynolds, Ambrose | 1 | 2 | 2 | | |
| Brown, Peter | 1 | | 1 | | |
| Knapp, Joseph | 1 | 2 | 3 | | |
| Minor, John | 1 | 2 | 2 | | |
| Howe, Ebenezer | 1 | 3 | 4 | | |
| Palmer, Gideon | 1 | 4 | 2 | | |
| Croney, Elizabeth | | 1 | 2 | | |
| Finny, Solomon | 1 | 1 | 1 | | |
| Palmer, Enos | 1 | | 1 | | |
| Palmer, Titus | 1 | 1 | 1 | | |
| Palmer, Israel | 1 | 1 | 2 | | |
| Clason, Isaac | 1 | | 3 | | |
| Mosier, Henry | 1 | | 2 | | |
| Reynolds, Jonathan | 1 | 2 | 4 | | |
| Mead, Shadrach | 1 | | 2 | | |
| Peck, Samuel, 3^d | 1 | | 2 | | |
| Johnson, James | 1 | 2 | 5 | | |
| Sherwood, James | 1 | | 5 | | |
| Lyon, Amos | 1 | 2 | 5 | | |
| Finch, Timothy, Jr | 1 | | 4 | | |
| Ferris, Joseph, Jun^r | 1 | 3 | 2 | | |
| Ferris, Thomas | 1 | | 3 | | |
| Ferris, Timothy | 1 | 3 | 2 | | |
| Palmer, Levi | 2 | 1 | 2 | | |
| Ferris, Josiah | 3 | 5 | 4 | | |
| Blakely, Obidiah | 1 | 2 | 3 | | |
| Husted, Benjamin | 2 | 3 | 6 | | |
| Fisk, William | 3 | 5 | 4 | | |
| Close, Benjamin | 1 | 2 | 2 | | |
| Whelpley, Isaac | 1 | | 5 | | |
| Gerrineau, Peter | 1 | | 1 | | |
| Stockwell, Robert | | 1 | 1 | | |
| Lockwood, Sarah | | 2 | 1 | | |
| Rundle, Charles | 1 | 3 | 1 | | |
| Lockwood, Shubeal | 3 | | 2 | | |
| Finch, Ezekiel | 1 | | 1 | | |
| Finch, Isaac | 1 | 1 | 2 | | |
| Brush, Shubeal | 3 | 4 | 3 | | |
| Lockwood, Gershom | 1 | 1 | 1 | | |
| Wood, Lemuel | 1 | | 3 | | |
| Suard, Rev^d William | 3 | 1 | 4 | | 1 |
| Peck, Aaron | 2 | | 5 | | |
| Hobby, David | 1 | 6 | 3 | | |
| Hobby, Jonathan | 1 | | 3 | | |
| Howe, Silvanus | 1 | 2 | 3 | | |
| Brush, James | 3 | | 4 | | |
| M^cKay, John | 3 | 1 | 5 | | |
| Ferris, Joseph | 1 | | 1 | | |
| Finch, Jonathan, Jr | 4 | 1 | 1 | | |
| Ingersoll, Simon | 2 | 2 | 1 | | |
| Ingersoll, Elizabeth (W^d) | | | 3 | | |
| Ferris, Solomon | 1 | 2 | 3 | | |

# HEADS OF FAMILIES—CONNECTICUT.

## FAIRFIELD COUNTY—Continued.

| NAME OF HEAD OF FAMILY. | Free white males of 16 years and upward, including heads of families. | Free white males under 16 years. | Free white females, including heads of families. | All other free persons. | Slaves. | NAME OF HEAD OF FAMILY. | Free white males of 16 years and upward, including heads of families. | Free white males under 16 years. | Free white females, including heads of families. | All other free persons. | Slaves. | NAME OF HEAD OF FAMILY. | Free white males of 16 years and upward, including heads of families. | Free white males under 16 years. | Free white females, including heads of families. | All other free persons. | Slaves. |
|---|---|---|---|---|---|---|---|---|---|---|---|---|---|---|---|---|---|
| GREENWICH TOWN—con. | | | | | | HUNTINGTON TOWN—continued. | | | | | | HUNTINGTON TOWN—continued. | | | | | |
| Hubbard, William | 3 | 1 | 3 | | | Sherman, Philo | 2 | 1 | 3 | | | Lewis, Birdsley | 1 | 1 | 5 | | |
| Hubbord, Daniel | 1 | | 1 | | | Hubbell, Jeremiah | 2 | 1 | 3 | | | Lewis, Everit | 1 | 2 | 2 | | |
| Hubbord, Henry | 4 | 3 | 6 | | | Sherwood, Ephraim | 1 | 1 | 2 | | | Beardslee, Thaddeus | 3 | 1 | 6 | | |
| Mead, Edmond | 4 | 5 | 4 | | | Curtis, Jonathan | 1 | 4 | 3 | | | Edwards, William | 3 | 1 | 2 | | |
| Banks, David | 1 | 2 | 5 | | | Curtis, Abel | 2 | 3 | 4 | | | Beardslee, George | 2 | 1 | 2 | | |
| Lockwood, Jonathan, Jr | 1 | 3 | 6 | | | Porter, Nathanel | 2 | | 2 | | 1 | Mitchel, Zacheriah | 1 | 1 | 2 | | |
| Ferris, Mary (Wd) | 1 | 1 | 3 | | | Hawley, Israel | 1 | 3 | 5 | | | Beardslee, William | 2 | 1 | 1 | | |
| Buxton, Dorras (Wd) | | | 4 | | | Hawley, Ephraim | 1 | 4 | 2 | | | Beardslee, Isaac | 2 | | 2 | | |
| Mead, Prudence (Wd) | 2 | | 2 | | | Northrop, Isaiah | 2 | 3 | 5 | | | Shelton, Benjamin | 1 | 2 | 1 | | |
| Mead, Jeremiah | 4 | | 3 | | | Hawley, Elias | 1 | 3 | 5 | | 1 | Shelton, Daniel | 2 | 2 | 2 | | 5 |
| Parsons, Sarah (Wd) | | 1 | 3 | | | Curtis, Andrew | 1 | | 6 | | 1 | Nichols, David | 2 | | 3 | | 1 |
| Gibbs, Hannah | | | 2 | | | Beardslee, Daniel | 1 | 1 | 2 | | 1 | Nichols, Tiles | 1 | 1 | 2 | | |
| Ferris, Joseph | 1 | | 1 | | | Payn, Urana | 1 | | 2 | | | Nichols, Nathan | 2 | 2 | 3 | | |
| | | | | | | Booth, Nathan | 2 | | 1 | | 2 | Nichols, James | 3 | 2 | 2 | | |
| HUNTINGTON TOWN. | | | | | | Downs, John | 1 | | 6 | | | Lewis, Abel | 1 | 1 | 3 | | |
| Beardslee, Hennery | 2 | 2 | 2 | | | Booth, Lewis | 1 | 2 | 1 | | | Thompson, Samuel | 1 | 1 | 3 | | |
| Davis, Benjamin | 1 | 1 | 1 | | | Hurd, Nehemiah | 2 | | 1 | | | Judson, Lemwell | 2 | | 1 | | |
| Hambleton, Alexander | 2 | 3 | 2 | | | Hurd, Abraham | 1 | | 1 | | | Judson, Lewis | 2 | | 1 | | |
| Wakelin, Isaac | 1 | 4 | 5 | | | Beardslee, Lewis | 2 | | 2 | | | Thompson, Elihue | 1 | 1 | 2 | | |
| Bennet, Daniel | 1 | 3 | 5 | | | Wakeley, Samuel, Jr | 1 | 3 | 1 | | | Thompson, Jonathan | 2 | | 2 | | |
| Hubbell, Mathew | 2 | 1 | 4 | | | Hurd, Ebenezer | 3 | 1 | 4 | | | Chitester, Moses | 2 | 3 | 5 | | |
| Hubbell, Giddeon | 1 | 1 | 3 | | | Curtis, James | 2 | 1 | 1 | | | Bennet, Silas | 1 | 1 | 1 | | |
| Sherman, Walker | 1 | | 2 | | | Hawley, Giddeon | 1 | 4 | 5 | | | Clark, George | 1 | 2 | 3 | | |
| Watkins, William | 1 | 4 | 2 | | | Curtis, Robert | 1 | 1 | 2 | | | Thompson, David | 1 | 2 | 1 | | |
| French, Jeriel | 2 | | 2 | | | Beardslee, Josiah | 1 | 3 | 2 | | | Beardslee, Benjamin, Jur | | 3 | 1 | | |
| Hays, Stephen | 1 | 2 | 2 | | | Booth, Samuel | 2 | 2 | 5 | | | Beardslee, Benjamin | 3 | 1 | 3 | | 1 |
| Winton, David, Jur | 1 | 1 | 4 | | | Booth, Nathan, Jur | 2 | 2 | 4 | | | Beard, David, Jur | 1 | | 1 | | 1 |
| Burr, Hosea | 2 | 1 | 4 | | | Henman, Samuel | 1 | 1 | 1 | | | Clark, John | 1 | | 1 | | |
| Beardslee, Eli | 1 | | 3 | | | Curtis, Elijah | 1 | | 1 | | | Beardslee, Thomas | 1 | 4 | 4 | | |
| Winton, David | 2 | 1 | 2 | | | Booth, Silas | 1 | 1 | 4 | | | Beard, David | 2 | 2 | 1 | | |
| Winton, Samuel | 1 | 2 | 3 | | | Hurd, Mead | 1 | 1 | 1 | | | Buckingham, Enoch | 3 | 3 | 4 | | |
| Bundy, Ebenezer | 1 | 1 | 3 | | | Judson, Ezekiel | 1 | 5 | 4 | | | Frasier, William | 1 | 1 | 5 | | |
| Beers, Lewis | 1 | 1 | 1 | | | French, Ebenezer | 2 | 2 | 6 | | 2 | Beardslee, Jered | 3 | 3 | 5 | | |
| Tyrel, John | 1 | 2 | 4 | | | French, Othenial | 1 | 3 | 3 | | | Wooster, Ephraim | 2 | 3 | 6 | | |
| Beach, Hezekiah | 1 | 2 | 6 | | | Judson, John | 1 | | 2 | | | Hawley, Walleson | 2 | 1 | 3 | | 1 |
| Burr, Jehue | 1 | 4 | 2 | | | Judson, John, 3d | 2 | 2 | 3 | | | Beard, Charles | 2 | | 3 | | |
| Nichols, Philip | 1 | 1 | 1 | | | Beach, John | 1 | 1 | 1 | | | Pool, John | | 2 | 3 | | |
| Middleton, Peter | | | | 3 | | Slane, Charles | 3 | | 3 | 1 | | Lewis, Nathanel | 1 | 2 | 4 | | 1 |
| Dimon, Nimrod | | | | 4 | | Judson, Ephraim | 3 | 1 | 3 | | | Davison, Zacherius | 2 | 3 | 2 | | |
| Tredwell, Cato | | | | 4 | | Beardslee, Israel | 2 | | 3 | | | Hawley, Joseph | 1 | 4 | 4 | | |
| Watkins, Hezekiah | 1 | | 1 | | | Farnum, Peter | 2 | 1 | 4 | | | Thompson, Abraham | 1 | 3 | 1 | | |
| Watkins, Abijah | 1 | | 1 | | | Daton, Benjamin | 1 | 4 | 3 | | | Loreing, Joseph | 1 | | 2 | | |
| Prindle, Isaac | 2 | 1 | 4 | | | Dunnen, Isaac | 1 | 2 | 3 | | | Judson, Jonathan | 1 | 2 | 2 | | |
| Hubbell, David | 1 | 1 | 5 | | | Twiner, George | 1 | 1 | 2 | | | Blackman, Ruth | | 1 | 2 | | |
| Lenenworth, Daniel | 3 | | 1 | | | Lewis, Walker | 1 | 1 | 5 | 1 | 1 | Judd, Balmerin | 2 | 3 | 4 | | |
| Hubbell, William | 1 | 2 | 2 | | | Lewis, Ebenezer | 2 | 1 | 3 | | 1 | Beardslee, Lemwell | 1 | 2 | 4 | | |
| Tyrel, Amos | 1 | 1 | 3 | | | Beardslee, Elisha | 3 | 4 | 2 | | | Judson, Nathanel | 2 | 4 | 2 | | |
| Silliman, Data | 1 | 3 | 5 | | | Barlow, Samuel | 2 | 4 | 6 | | | Gilbert, John | 1 | 3 | 4 | | |
| Beers, Archebus | 1 | | 3 | | | French, James | 1 | 1 | 3 | | | De Forest, Hezekiah | 1 | 2 | 4 | | |
| Rowel, Jacob | 1 | 1 | 5 | | | Reels, John | 1 | 1 | 1 | 2 | | Mills, Jedediah | 1 | | 1 | | |
| Beers, Nathanel | 1 | | 2 | | | French, Abner | 1 | 1 | 2 | | | Lewis, Ebenezer | 1 | 1 | 3 | | |
| Blackman, Timothy | 2 | | 2 | | | Lewis, Wells | 3 | 2 | 3 | | | Lewis, Sarah | | | 2 | | |
| Beardslee, Aaron | 1 | 1 | 2 | | | Beach, Ebenezer | 1 | 3 | 2 | | 2 | Clark, Abraham E | 1 | | 2 | | 1 |
| Blackman, Asahel | 1 | 1 | 1 | | | Hawley, Charrity | | 2 | 1 | | | Clark, Blagg | 2 | 2 | 4 | | |
| Pane, Samuel | 1 | 2 | 4 | | | Beardslee, Joshua | 1 | 2 | 4 | | | Clark, Nathan | 2 | | 2 | | |
| Burrit, John | 2 | 4 | 5 | | | Lewis, Fredrick | 1 | 2 | 3 | | | Clark, Samuel | 2 | 2 | 3 | | 1 |
| Pane, David | 1 | 2 | 3 | | | Hawley, Ruth | | | 1 | | | Newton, David | 2 | 2 | 3 | | 1 |
| Beardslee, Elizabeth | | 2 | 3 | | | Cole, Hezekiah | 2 | 1 | 4 | | | De Forest, Othenial | 3 | 2 | 3 | | |
| Burr, James | 3 | 1 | 6 | | | Rexford, Elisha | 1 | | 4 | | 2 | Mills, Isaac | 1 | | 1 | | |
| Vanostran, Aaron | 2 | 3 | 4 | | | Lewis, Samuel | 4 | | 3 | | | Benton, Sealey | 1 | 2 | 2 | | |
| Niles, William | 1 | 2 | 3 | | | DeForest, Nehemiah | 2 | 2 | 5 | | 2 | Marks, Mordica | 1 | 2 | 2 | | 1 |
| Sears, Elijah | 1 | 1 | 3 | | | Moss, Lewis | 2 | | 2 | | | Eli, David | 1 | 3 | 4 | | |
| Sears, Gershom | 1 | 1 | 2 | | | Moss, Joseph | 1 | | 2 | | 1 | Mills, Elisha | 1 | 1 | 3 | 1 | |
| Curtis, Isaac | 1 | 3 | 6 | | | Tuday, Huldah | | | 2 | | | Yates, John | 3 | 1 | 2 | | |
| Mand, Dependence | 2 | 1 | 3 | | | Curtis, Ezra | 2 | 2 | 7 | | | Beardslee, Stephen | 2 | 2 | 3 | | |
| Albin, John | 1 | 2 | 1 | | | Smith, Heber | 1 | 1 | 2 | | | Lapener, Antony | 1 | 2 | 2 | | |
| Mallet, Philo | 1 | 3 | 3 | | | Barnum, Eunice | | 1 | 3 | | | Thompson, Nathan | 1 | | 1 | | |
| Hawley, Jonathan | 2 | 1 | 2 | | 2 | Moss, Daniel | 2 | 2 | 4 | | | Hide, Eliakam | 1 | | 1 | | |
| Hawley, Abel | 1 | 2 | 4 | | | Beardslee, Philo | 1 | | 2 | | | Hawley, Job | 1 | 1 | 2 | | |
| Hawley, Anne | | 2 | 2 | | | Healey, George | 2 | 2 | 2 | | | Rines, Daniel | 1 | 3 | 3 | | |
| Hawley, Elijah | 2 | 1 | 2 | | | Beers, Barnabus | 1 | | 1 | | | Lester, John | 1 | 3 | 1 | | |
| Jackson, William | 1 | | 6 | | | Nichols, Elethan | 1 | 1 | 2 | | | Bawlden, Elias | 1 | | 2 | | |
| Larkin, Joshua | 1 | 2 | 6 | | | Hurd, Philo | 1 | 3 | 2 | | | Hide, Elisha | 4 | | 3 | | 2 |
| Wakelin, Samuel | 2 | | 1 | | | Osborn, Daniel | 1 | 2 | 2 | | | Shelton, Andrew | 2 | 4 | 5 | | |
| Dascomb, John | 1 | 2 | 3 | | | Clark, Hezekiah | 1 | | 2 | | | Blackman, Eli | 1 | | 2 | | |
| Nichols, Benjamin | 1 | | 4 | | | Johnson, Ephraim | 4 | 4 | 4 | | | Perry, David | 1 | 1 | 2 | | |
| Bradford, Hennery | 3 | 1 | 4 | | | Coban, Daniel | 1 | 1 | 3 | | | Sealee, Giddeon | 1 | | 2 | | |
| Nichols, Joseph | 1 | 1 | 1 | | | Johnson, Ebenezer | 1 | 3 | 5 | | | Wheeler, David B | 1 | | 2 | | |
| Edwards, Ager | 2 | 1 | 2 | | | Nichols, Mansfield | 2 | | 2 | | | Wheeler, Elene | | 2 | 3 | | |
| Sears, Bartholomew | 1 | | 1 | | | Judson, Phineus | 1 | | 4 | | | Shelton, Zacheriah | 1 | 2 | 1 | | |
| Sears, Richard | 1 | | 1 | | | Munrow, John | 1 | 3 | 1 | | | Hide, Samuel | 1 | 2 | 2 | | |
| French, Jehiel | 3 | 2 | 1 | | | Clark, Elisha | 3 | 6 | 3 | | | Kelogg, Martin | 1 | | 1 | | |
| Corney, Allen | 1 | 1 | 2 | | | DeForest, Samuel | 1 | 2 | 2 | | | Gilbert, Elihue | 1 | 2 | 4 | 5 | |
| Odle, John | 2 | 1 | 2 | | | Henman, Nathan | 2 | | 2 | | | Shelton, Samuel | 1 | 1 | 2 | | |
| Odle, Aaron | 1 | 1 | 2 | 1 | | Lewis, Thomas | 3 | 1 | 1 | | | Lewis, Zacheriah | 2 | | 3 | | 2 |
| Hawley, Thomas | 2 | 2 | 3 | | 2 | Booth, Nathanel | 1 | 1 | 4 | | | Hawley, Elijah | 2 | 1 | 6 | | |
| Man, Richard | 1 | | 2 | | | Fairchild, John | 3 | | 2 | | | Shelton, Jeremiah | 1 | | 2 | | 1 |
| Elmer, Elijah | 1 | 3 | 2 | | | Fairchild, Joseph, Jur | 1 | | 2 | | | Clark, Sarah | | | | | |
| Curtis, Timothy | 1 | 3 | 5 | | | Dunnen, Abraham | 2 | 2 | 3 | | | Booth, Ashbell | 1 | 3 | 4 | | |
| Sanders, Aaron | 1 | 1 | 1 | | | Barlow, Samuel | 1 | | 3 | | | Babbet, Stephen | 2 | | 2 | | |
| Sherman, Nathanel | 3 | 1 | 3 | | | Malery, Calep | 1 | | 2 | | | Gilbert, Obediah | | 1 | 5 | | |
| Sherman, Phineus | 4 | | 6 | | | Mallery, Gideon | 1 | 2 | 2 | | | Curtis, James | 1 | 2 | 4 | | |
| Sherman, Nathanel, Jur | 1 | 3 | 2 | | | Mannon, Samuel | 1 | | 2 | | | Judson, James | | 4 | 1 | | |
| Picksley, David | 1 | 3 | 3 | | | Summers, Zacheriah S | 1 | 1 | 1 | | | Carpenter, William | 2 | | 1 | | |

## FIRST CENSUS OF THE UNITED STATES.

### FAIRFIELD COUNTY—Continued.

#### HUNTINGTON TOWN—continued.

| NAME OF HEAD OF FAMILY. | Free white males of 16 years and upward, including heads of families. | Free white males under 16 years. | Free white females, including heads of families. | All other free persons. | Slaves. |
|---|---|---|---|---|---|
| Bailey, Hezekiah | 3 |  | 2 |  |  |
| Hurd, Samuel | 2 |  | 2 | 1 |  |
| Moss, John | 1 |  | 3 |  |  |
| Wheeler, Nathan | 1 | 1 | 3 |  | 1 |
| Moss, Elihue | 1 | 1 | 6 |  | 1 |
| Scott, William | 1 | 2 | 3 |  |  |
| Moss, Elizabeth |  | 3 | 2 |  |  |
| Booth, Isaac | 1 | 5 | 1 |  |  |
| Cable, Abner | 1 | 2 | 2 |  |  |
| Clark, Nathan, 3d | 2 | 1 | 1 |  |  |
| Hurd, Elethan | 1 | 2 | 5 |  | 1 |
| Wheeler, Anne | 2 |  | 2 |  |  |
| Lattin, David | 1 | 1 | 5 |  |  |
| Blackman, Ephraim | 1 | 4 | 3 |  |  |
| Jurden, David | 1 |  | 1 |  |  |
| Smith, Eli | 2 | 2 | 3 |  | 1 |
| Beardslee, Eliot | 1 | 1 | 1 |  | 1 |
| Mathews, Giddeon | 1 | 1 | 3 |  |  |
| Dick, Betty |  | 2 | 3 |  |  |
| Beardslee, Zeph |  |  |  | 3 |  |
| George, Amos | 1 | 1 | 4 |  |  |
| Hawley, Anne |  |  | 4 |  |  |
| Moss, William | 1 | 1 | 3 |  |  |
| Hawley, John | 1 |  | 1 |  |  |
| Beardslee, John | 1 | 3 | 2 |  | 1 |
| Beardslee, Daniel | 1 |  | 1 |  |  |
| Raymong, David | 1 | 1 | 1 |  |  |
| Bostwick, Elethan H | 1 | 2 | 3 |  | 1 |
| Pulford, Lewis | 1 |  | 2 |  |  |
| Hurd, David | 1 |  | 4 |  |  |
| Hawley, Milton | 3 | 1 | 3 |  |  |
| Mitchel, John | 2 |  | 5 |  |  |
| Lattin, Thomas | 3 | 1 | 5 |  | 1 |
| Judson, Samuel | 2 |  | 2 |  |  |
| Basset, Hennery |  |  |  | 3 |  |
| Laberee, James | 2 |  | 2 |  |  |
| Laberee, Bennedict | 1 |  | 1 |  |  |
| Blackman, Samuel | 3 |  | 4 |  |  |
| Wells, Joana | 2 | 2 | 5 |  | 2 |
| Clark, James | 2 |  | 5 |  |  |
| Clark, Nathan, 2d | 1 | 2 | 3 |  | 1 |
| Blackman, David | 1 | 2 | 4 |  |  |
| Willcox, John | 2 | 1 | 6 |  | 2 |
| Willcox, David | 1 | 1 | 5 |  |  |
| Hays, Elizabeth | 1 | 2 | 4 |  |  |
| Judson, Isaac | 3 |  | 3 |  |  |
| Willcox, Timothy | 2 |  | 2 |  | 3 |
| Basset, John | 1 | 2 | 8 |  |  |
| Wells, Zalmon | 1 |  | 1 |  | 1 |
| Curtis, Elijah | 1 | 2 | 4 |  |  |
| Piercy, Nathanel | 1 |  | 1 |  |  |
| Beardslee, Hall | 1 |  | 2 | 3 |  |
| Curtis, Silas | 3 | 1 | 5 |  |  |
| McKune, James | 2 | 1 | 3 |  |  |
| Anebal, Ebenezer | 1 | 1 | 2 |  |  |
| Beardslee, Moses | 1 | 1 | 3 |  |  |
| Beardslee, Samuel | 3 | 1 | 6 |  | 1 |
| Goodluck, London |  |  |  | 2 |  |
| Raymong, Jesse |  |  | 2 |  |  |
| Jurden, Edmon | 2 | 2 | 4 |  |  |
| Sherman, Vincen | 2 | 1 | 4 |  |  |
| Curtis, Hennery | 1 | 2 | 3 |  | 1 |
| Curtis, Elihue | 2 | 3 | 4 |  |  |
| Wetmore, Josiah | 1 |  | 1 |  |  |
| Hick, John | 1 |  | 2 |  |  |
| Tomlinson, Ager | 1 | 2 | 4 |  | 1 |
| Shelton, Daniel | 3 |  | 2 |  | 8 |
| French, Joseph | 1 | 3 | 2 |  |  |
| Shelton, Thaddeus | 1 | 1 | 3 |  | 1 |
| Fanton, Jonathan | 1 | 1 | 2 |  |  |
| Nodine, Fredrick | 1 | 3 | 2 |  |  |
| Hays, Jesse | 1 | 1 | 3 |  |  |
| Wheeler, Elisha | 2 |  | 1 |  |  |
| Hibbard, Peter | 1 |  | 2 |  |  |
| Beardslee, Abijah | 2 | 2 | 2 |  |  |
| Hubbell, Elisha | 1 | 5 | 3 |  |  |
| Hull, Samuel | 1 |  | 1 |  |  |
| Hubbell, Giddeon | 3 | 3 | 4 |  |  |
| Wheeler, Calep | 2 | 2 | 3 |  |  |
| Wheeler, Elene |  |  | 1 |  |  |
| Hubbell, Timothy | 2 | 1 | 3 |  |  |
| Hubbell, John | 2 | 3 | 7 |  |  |
| Hubbell, Mathew | 1 |  | 1 | 4 |  |
| Levensworth, Giddeon | 2 | 1 | 5 |  |  |
| Sissen, William | 1 | 2 | 4 |  |  |
| Curtis, Stiles | 1 |  | 4 |  |  |
| Levensworth, Edmon | 2 |  | 6 | 1 |  |
| Patterson, Samuel | 1 | 3 | 3 |  |  |
| Beardslee, David | 1 | 1 | 2 |  |  |
| Sander, John M | 2 | 2 | 4 |  |  |
| Mills, James | 1 | 2 | 4 |  |  |
| Patterson, Mark | 1 |  | 4 |  |  |
| Patterson, James | 1 | 1 | 1 |  |  |
| Platt, Moses | 1 | 4 | 7 |  | 1 |
| Blackman, William | 2 | 1 | 3 |  |  |
| Hamblin, Cornelius | 2 | 1 | 2 |  |  |
| Hubbell, David, 2d | 1 |  | 2 |  |  |
| Ransley, William | 1 | 1 | 1 |  |  |
| Blackman, Joel | 3 |  | 1 |  | 1 |
| Birdslee, Joseph | 3 | 2 | 3 |  | 3 |
| Hawley, David | 1 |  | 1 |  | 5 |
| Judson, Ager, Jur | 3 | 3 | 4 | 1 | 5 |
| Judson, Ager | 2 |  | 1 |  | 6 |
| Beardslee, Calep | 2 | 1 | 3 |  |  |
| Shelton, Elisha | 1 | 3 | 4 |  | 1 |
| Lake, Jabes | 3 | 1 | 3 |  |  |
| Downs, Joseph | 1 | 2 | 1 |  |  |
| Judson, Silas | 1 | 3 | 4 |  |  |
| Tomlinson, Beach | 1 | 2 | 3 |  | 2 |
| Wheeler, John | 1 | 3 | 1 |  |  |
| Wheeler, Moses | 2 | 4 | 2 |  |  |
| Summers, Luke | 2 | 4 | 5 |  |  |
| Hill, Isaac | 1 | 1 | 2 |  |  |
| Hill, Mary |  |  | 2 |  |  |
| Mallery, Benajah | 1 | 2 | 2 |  |  |
| Beardslee, Joseph | 2 | 2 | 3 |  |  |
| Sealee, Liman | 1 | 1 | 1 |  |  |
| Gilbert, Joel | 1 | 1 | 2 |  |  |
| Gilbert, Ager | 1 | 1 | 3 |  |  |
| Gilbert, Lemwell | 1 | 1 | 4 |  |  |
| Beardslee, Samuel | 1 | 1 | 3 |  |  |
| Gilbert, Abraham | 2 | 2 | 2 |  |  |
| Gilbert, Thomas | 1 | 1 | 4 |  |  |
| Judson, John | 2 |  | 3 |  |  |
| Curtis, Temperance |  |  |  | 2 |  |
| Beers, Tine |  | 1 |  | 1 |  |
| Fulford, Edmon | 1 | 1 | 1 |  |  |
| Garlic, Hennery | 2 | 2 | 2 |  |  |
| French, Jonas | 1 | 5 | 2 |  |  |
| French, Jonathan | 1 |  | 1 |  |  |
| Lewis, Beach | 2 |  | 3 |  |  |
| Curtis, Ephraim | 2 | 2 | 2 |  |  |
| Wheeler, Moses | 1 | 3 | 5 |  |  |
| Curtis, Levi | 1 | 1 | 2 |  |  |
| Ellis, Timothy | 1 | 2 | 4 |  |  |
| Shelton, Ager | 2 | 1 | 4 |  | 4 |
| Perry, James | 1 | 1 | 2 |  |  |
| Brown, Ruth |  | 1 | 2 |  |  |
| Perry, Abner | 2 |  | 3 |  |  |
| Perry, Abner, Jur | 1 |  | 3 |  |  |
| Curtis, William | 1 | 2 | 6 |  |  |
| Calkin, Israel | 1 |  | 3 |  |  |
| Curtis, Elethan | 2 |  | 2 |  | 2 |
| Shelton, James | 1 |  | 2 | 1 |  |
| Dart, Job | 1 | 5 | 3 |  |  |
| Perry, Elijah | 1 |  | 2 |  |  |
| Perry, Abijah | 1 | 1 | 2 |  |  |
| Perry, Joseph | 1 | 1 | 2 |  |  |
| Bennet, Daniel | 4 | 1 | 4 |  |  |
| Shelton, William | 2 | 3 | 3 |  | 2 |
| Shelton, Sealee | 1 | 1 | 2 |  |  |
| Hull, Joseph | 3 | 4 | 1 |  |  |
| Clark, Hezekiah | 1 | 1 | 2 |  |  |
| Jellet, Canfield | 2 | 1 | 2 |  |  |
| Clark, George | 2 | 1 | 2 |  |  |
| Davis, William | 1 | 2 | 4 |  |  |
| Moor, Robert | 2 | 3 | 5 |  | 2 |
| Mills, Samuel | 1 | 1 | 1 |  | 1 |
| Beers, Joseph | 1 | 2 | 2 |  |  |
| Chatfield, Lemuel | 3 | 2 | 1 |  |  |
| Wakelee, Josiah S | 1 | 2 | 2 |  |  |
| Nanneistran, Charles | 3 |  | 3 |  |  |
| Hall, George | 1 | 2 | 3 |  |  |
| Shelton, Joane |  |  | 1 | 2 |  |
| Wakelin, David | 1 | 2 | 3 |  |  |
| Shelton, Abijah | 1 | 1 | 2 |  | 2 |
| Shelton, Abijah, 2d | 1 | 2 | 1 |  |  |
| Wakelee, James | 4 | 3 | 4 |  | 3 |
| Shelton, Noah |  |  |  | 3 |  |
| Stephens, Eliphilet | 1 |  | 4 |  |  |
| Brown, Elisha | 1 | 2 | 3 |  |  |
| Beardslee, Joseph | 1 |  | 1 |  |  |
| Beardslee, Zepheniah | 1 | 3 | 3 |  |  |
| Blackman, Samuel | 1 | 3 | 2 |  |  |
| Wooster, Joseph L | 2 |  | 2 |  | 1 |
| Tomlinson, Curtis | 4 | 2 | 4 |  | 4 |
| Blackman, Ager | 1 | 2 | 2 |  |  |
| Lewis, Elijah | 1 |  | 2 |  |  |
| Umphrevile, Patty | 2 | 1 | 2 |  |  |
| Smith, Joseph | 1 | 2 | 1 |  |  |
| Smith, Nathan | 2 |  | 4 |  |  |
| Bennet, Nathan | 1 | 3 | 5 |  | 1 |
| Beard, Samuel | 2 |  | 5 |  |  |
| Shelton, Eunice | 1 | 1 | 2 |  |  |
| Howse, Zacheriah | 1 | 3 | 2 |  |  |
| Beard, Joel | 1 | 2 | 1 |  |  |
| Wells, Robert | 1 | 3 | 3 |  |  |
| Wells, Giddeon | 2 | 1 | 2 |  | 1 |
| Wells, Daniel | 2 |  | 2 |  |  |
| Wells, Abner | 1 | 2 | 2 |  |  |
| Cosher, Enoch | 1 | 3 | 2 |  |  |
| Blackman, David | 1 | 2 | 1 |  |  |
| Wooster, John | 3 |  | 1 |  |  |
| Clenton, Antine | 1 |  | 2 |  |  |
| Willcox, James | 2 |  | 3 |  |  |
| Blackman, Jonas | 4 |  | 2 |  |  |
| Birdsey, John | 1 |  | 2 |  |  |
| Smith, Zalmon | 2 | 1 | 2 |  |  |
| Sweetlove, Elis | 1 | 1 | 2 |  |  |
| Harrop, Joseph | 1 |  | 1 |  |  |
| Blacklidge, George |  |  |  | 7 |  |
| Carsey, Devonshier |  |  |  | 5 |  |
| Lewis, Floria |  |  |  | 3 |  |
| Blacklidge, Pamey | 1 | 1 | 1 |  |  |
| De Forest, Nehemiah | 1 | 1 | 4 |  |  |
| Vanorstrain, Aaron | 1 | 1 | 3 |  |  |
| French, John | 1 |  | 1 |  |  |
| Fairchild, Joseph | 2 |  | 4 |  |  |

#### NEW FAIRFIELD TOWN.

| NAME OF HEAD OF FAMILY. | Free white males of 16 years and upward, including heads of families. | Free white males under 16 years. | Free white females, including heads of families. | All other free persons. | Slaves. |
|---|---|---|---|---|---|
| Hallebert, John | 3 |  | 2 |  |  |
| Smith, Joseph | 1 | 1 | 6 |  |  |
| Smith, Cornal | 1 | 3 | 3 |  |  |
| Trobridge, Seth | 2 |  | 1 |  |  |
| Rogers, Medad | 1 | 1 | 2 |  |  |
| Beardslee, John | 2 | 2 | 3 |  |  |
| Lacy, Anne |  |  | 4 |  |  |
| Lacy, Chancy | 1 | 1 | 1 |  |  |
| Bass, Joseph | 1 | 1 | 6 |  |  |
| Fairchild, Enoch | 2 | 1 | 4 |  |  |
| Beers, Noah | 1 | 2 | 1 |  |  |
| Fairchild, Alexander | 2 |  | 1 |  |  |
| Stephens, Eli | 1 | 4 | 2 |  |  |
| Hoyt, Walter | 1 |  | 2 |  |  |
| Scofield, James | 1 | 4 | 4 |  |  |
| Beardslee, Josiah | 2 | 3 | 4 |  |  |
| Beardslee, Nathan S | 1 |  | 1 |  |  |
| Stephens, Benjamin | 2 |  | 2 |  |  |
| Beardslee, Giddeon, Jur | 2 | 2 | 2 |  |  |
| Trobridge, John | 1 | 1 | 3 |  |  |
| Beardslee, Phineus | 3 | 1 | 2 |  |  |
| Beardslee, Obediah | 1 |  | 2 |  |  |
| Beardslee, Elijah | 1 | 4 | 2 |  |  |
| Beardslee, Zalmon | 1 | 2 | 2 |  |  |
| Beardslee, Giddeon | 2 |  | 1 |  |  |
| Knapp, Oliver | 1 | 2 | 3 |  |  |
| Knapp, Moses | 1 | 2 | 5 |  |  |
| Bass, Thomas | 3 |  | 2 |  |  |
| Spencer, Samuel | 2 | 1 | 3 |  |  |
| Knapp, James | 1 | 1 | 2 |  |  |
| Penfield, Peter | 2 | 3 | 1 |  |  |
| Penfield, Lewis | 1 | 1 | 1 |  |  |
| Bass, John | 2 | 1 | 2 |  |  |
| Man, Jabez | 1 |  | 5 |  |  |
| Barnum, Zadock | 2 | 3 | 7 |  |  |
| Barnum, Abel | 3 | 1 | 4 |  |  |
| Wanzer, Nicholas | 3 | 4 | 3 |  |  |
| Barlow, David | 2 | 2 | 2 |  | 1 |
| Wanzer, Moses | 1 | 4 | 3 |  |  |
| Allen, John | 3 |  |  |  | 1 |
| Hallester, Giddeon | 1 | 3 | 2 |  |  |
| Sutlow, Richard | 2 | 2 | 4 |  |  |
| Towner, Zacheus | 2 |  | 2 |  |  |
| Carpenter, Benedict | 3 |  | 2 |  |  |
| Vaune, William | 1 | 1 | 2 |  |  |
| Wanzer, Ebenezer | 2 | 2 | 3 |  |  |
| Vaune, Benjamin | 1 | 2 | 2 |  |  |
| Page, Abel | 1 | 4 | 3 |  |  |
| Leach, Echabod | 1 | 1 | 3 |  |  |
| Hevelan, Thomas | 2 | 1 | 2 |  |  |
| Eastman, Joseph | 2 | 1 | 1 |  |  |
| Wanzer, Abraham | 1 | 2 | 4 |  |  |
| Leach, Mary | 1 | 1 | 2 |  |  |
| Platt, David | 1 | 3 | 3 |  |  |
| Conger, Ephraim | 1 |  | 1 |  |  |
| French, William | 1 | 2 | 2 |  |  |
| Hubbell, Ephraim | 1 | 1 | 2 |  | 1 |
| Hubbell, Amos | 1 | 2 | 5 |  |  |
| Bennedict, Elezer | 1 | 1 | 2 |  |  |
| Osborn, John | 1 | 4 | 3 |  |  |
| Hatch, John | 2 | 1 | 4 |  |  |
| Cowdry, John | 1 |  | 2 |  | 1 |
| Phelps, Joseph | 1 | 5 | 2 |  |  |
| Sherwood, Nathan | 1 | 4 | 3 |  |  |
| Sherwood, Ebenezer | 1 | 2 | 1 |  |  |
| Hatch, Hennery | 1 | 1 | 2 |  |  |
| Bennedict, John | 1 | 1 | 4 |  |  |
| Bartum, Noah | 1 | 2 | 4 |  |  |
| Bartrum, Isaac | 1 | 2 | 2 |  |  |
| Prindle, Amos | 1 |  | 2 |  |  |
| Leach, Daniel | 2 | 1 | 4 |  |  |
| Richerson, Samuel | 1 |  | 1 | 3 |  |
| Gregory, James | 1 | 3 | 3 |  |  |

# HEADS OF FAMILIES—CONNECTICUT.

## FAIRFIELD COUNTY—Continued.

| NAME OF HEAD OF FAMILY. | Free white males of 16 years and upward, including heads of families. | Free white males under 16 years. | Free white females, including heads of families. | All other free persons. | Slaves. |
|---|---|---|---|---|---|
| **NEW FAIRFIELD TOWN—continued.** | | | | | |
| Hallester, Jonathan | 1 | 1 | | | |
| Northrop, Abraham | 2 | 1 | 1 | | |
| Northrop, Isaac | 1 | 1 | 2 | | |
| Craw, Reubin | 1 | 2 | 3 | | |
| Gorham, Meeker | 1 | 2 | 2 | | |
| Lewis, Abraham | 1 | 2 | 3 | | |
| Towner, Dan | 3 | | 2 | | |
| Prindle, Aaron | 2 | 1 | 2 | | |
| Buck, Josiah | 1 | 1 | 5 | | |
| Higgins, George | 1 | 2 | 4 | | |
| Merchant, John | 1 | 1 | 1 | | |
| Northrop, David | 2 | | 4 | | |
| Hungerford, Ezra | 1 | 3 | 3 | | |
| Potter, Milton | 1 | 2 | 1 | | |
| Wright, Abel | 1 | | 2 | | |
| Steward, Sylvanus | 1 | 1 | 2 | | |
| Barns, James | 1 | 1 | 6 | | |
| Howse, Edmon | 2 | 1 | 2 | | |
| Phelps, William | 2 | | 1 | | |
| Carpenter, Barnard | 1 | | 1 | | |
| Carpenter, Isaiah | 1 | 1 | 1 | | |
| Potter, James | 3 | 3 | 4 | | |
| Hill, Jonathan | 1 | | 4 | | |
| Carpenter, Barnee | 2 | 1 | 2 | | |
| Picket, Benjamin | 2 | 1 | 2 | | |
| Picket, Polly I. | | 1 | 1 | | |
| Bennet, Benjamin, Jur | 1 | 2 | 3 | | |
| Yates, Paul | 1 | | 1 | | |
| Waring, Samuel | 1 | 3 | 1 | | |
| Bennet, Benjamin | 1 | | 1 | | |
| Bennet, Daniel N. | 1 | 2 | 4 | | |
| Hungerford, Mary | 1 | | 1 | | |
| Dutton, Joel | 1 | 4 | 1 | | |
| Hungerford, Uriah | 1 | 1 | 5 | | |
| Giddeons, Jonathan | 2 | 3 | 5 | | |
| Tibbets, Obediah | 1 | 5 | 3 | | |
| Graves, Ezra | 1 | 2 | 2 | | |
| Graves, Jedediah | 2 | | 1 | | |
| Page, Jonathan | 2 | 2 | 3 | | |
| Barns, Stephen | 3 | 4 | 5 | | |
| Morehouse, John | 3 | 4 | 2 | | |
| Barns, William | 2 | 1 | 6 | | |
| Giddeons, Joseph | 3 | | 2 | | |
| Seman, Abraham | 1 | 1 | 4 | | |
| Giddeons, William | 3 | 4 | 3 | | |
| Babcock, Isaiah | 3 | 3 | 3 | | |
| Bostwick, William | 1 | 1 | 1 | | |
| Burley, Ebenezer | 1 | | 2 | | |
| Butts, Isaac | 1 | 3 | 4 | | |
| Woodrough, Asa | 1 | 1 | 3 | | |
| Tupper, Charles | 1 | 4 | 3 | | |
| Nichols, Robert | 1 | 2 | 3 | | |
| Morehouse, Hezekiah | 1 | | 3 | | |
| Sealee, Abel | 3 | 1 | 6 | | |
| Briggs, Zepheniah | 1 | 3 | 6 | | |
| Foster, Asa | 1 | 1 | 4 | | |
| Kerbey, Robert | 1 | | 1 | | |
| Bradley, Ephraim | 3 | 1 | 3 | 1 | |
| Hungerford, Isaiah | 1 | 4 | 3 | | |
| Hallebert, Job | 1 | 1 | 1 | | |
| Waring, Major | 1 | 2 | 2 | | |
| Sealee, Bradley | 3 | 1 | 3 | 1 | |
| Stewart, Elihue | 1 | 3 | 1 | | |
| Stewart, Alexander | 3 | 1 | 2 | | |
| Hungerford, Josiah | 4 | 2 | 5 | | |
| Northrop, Amos | 1 | 2 | 2 | | |
| Stewart, Alexander, Jur | 2 | 5 | 3 | | |
| Sanders, William | 2 | 2 | 3 | | |
| Page, Samuel | 1 | | 7 | | |
| Pane, Aaron | 3 | | 2 | | |
| Draper, Giddeon | 1 | | 1 | | |
| Giddeons, Zebulon | 1 | 3 | 1 | | |
| Buck, Daniel | 1 | 2 | 1 | | |
| Holmes, Thatford | 1 | 1 | 2 | | |
| Wane, Russel | 2 | | 3 | | |
| Sherman, Jesse | 1 | | 1 | | |
| Acorns, Daniel | 2 | 1 | 5 | | |
| Wing, Thomas | 3 | 3 | 6 | | |
| Bowdish, William | 1 | | 2 | | |
| Hubbell, Eleazer | 2 | 3 | 4 | 1 | |
| Penfield, John | 1 | 5 | 6 | | |
| Wakeman, Seth | 1 | 2 | 2 | | |
| Wakeman, Giddeon | 1 | 1 | 2 | | |
| Pepper, Setz | 1 | 1 | 3 | | |
| Pepper, Dan | 1 | 2 | 4 | | |
| Leach, Amos | 1 | | 3 | | |
| Goud, William | 1 | | 4 | | |
| Sturdefant, John | 1 | 2 | 5 | | |
| Sturdefant, Jonathan | 1 | | 2 | | |
| Ackley, David | 2 | | 4 | | |
| Bronson, Alford | 1 | 1 | 2 | | |
| Cosher, Abel | 1 | 3 | 5 | | |
| Osborn, Aaron | 1 | | 3 | | |
| Uvit, John | 1 | 3 | 1 | | |
| Woodard, Asa | 1 | 2 | 4 | | |
| **NEW FAIRFIELD TOWN—continued.** | | | | | |
| Mosher, James | 1 | | 4 | | |
| Hubbell, Giddeon | 1 | | 3 | | |
| Osborn, Jonathan | 2 | 3 | 4 | | |
| Osborn, Reubin | 2 | 2 | 3 | | |
| Conger, Joel | 1 | 3 | 4 | | |
| Wileman, Paul | 1 | 3 | 2 | | |
| Pepper, Stephen | 2 | 2 | 4 | | |
| Pepper, Stephen, Jur | 1 | 1 | 5 | | |
| Stephenson, Stephen | 1 | 3 | 3 | | |
| Wanzer, Eliud | 2 | | 3 | | |
| Rinevault, William | 2 | 1 | 4 | | |
| Wanzer, Husted | 1 | 2 | 3 | | |
| Buck, Abner | 1 | 2 | 1 | | |
| Hawley, Isaac | 1 | | 1 | | |
| Barnum, David | 1 | 3 | 2 | | |
| Chase, Giddeon | 1 | | 2 | | |
| Hevelan, Nathanel | 1 | 1 | 1 | | |
| Stedwell, Roger | 1 | | 3 | | |
| Stedwell, Gilbert | 1 | | 3 | | |
| Brush, Thomas | 1 | 4 | 6 | | |
| Heveland, Roger | 2 | 2 | 3 | | |
| Heveland, Isaac | 1 | 4 | 1 | | |
| Wakeman, Jeremiah | 1 | | 5 | | |
| Bradley, Jonathan | 1 | 1 | 2 | | |
| Hall, John | 1 | 3 | 3 | | |
| Hendrick, John | 2 | 1 | 3 | | |
| Hubbell, Giddeon | 1 | 2 | 2 | | |
| Wakeman, David | 1 | | 2 | | |
| Hubbell, Barrack | 2 | | 2 | | |
| Driskill, Timothy | 1 | 2 | 2 | | |
| Gray, Joseph | 1 | 2 | 3 | | |
| Rion, Jeremiah | 1 | 1 | 5 | | |
| Cole, Hyman | 1 | | 1 | | |
| Stephens, Joseph | 1 | | 1 | | |
| Setle, Thomas | 1 | | 1 | | |
| Barnum, David | 3 | 1 | 3 | | |
| Carlee, John | 1 | | 2 | | |
| Day, Jonathan | 1 | | 2 | | |
| Gorham, Echabod | 2 | | 2 | | |
| Barnum, Stephen | 1 | 1 | 2 | | |
| Ball, Wait | 1 | 2 | 6 | | |
| Hodge, Abel | 1 | 1 | 2 | | |
| Hodges, Thaddeus | 1 | 1 | 1 | | |
| Pardy, Stephen | 1 | 2 | 2 | | |
| Pardy, Asher | 1 | 1 | 2 | | |
| Sherwood, Abel | 1 | 4 | 3 | | |
| Perry, Elisha | 2 | | 3 | | |
| Hodge, Thomas | 1 | 3 | 2 | | |
| Gray, Elias | 2 | 2 | 5 | | |
| Gray, Moses | 4 | 2 | 2 | | |
| Hendrick, Samuel | 1 | | 1 | | |
| Stephens, Israel | 1 | 4 | 1 | | |
| Oakley, Jeremiah | 1 | 1 | 2 | | |
| Oakley, Gilbert | 1 | | 2 | | |
| Brush, Thomas, 2d | 2 | 1 | 2 | | |
| Brush, Jonas | 1 | 3 | 4 | | |
| Wakeman, William | 1 | 3 | 3 | | |
| Beardslee, David | 1 | 2 | 3 | | |
| Brush, Amos | 1 | 2 | 2 | | |
| Beardslee, Nehemiah | 2 | | 5 | | |
| Bates, Isaac | 1 | | 1 | | |
| Fairchild, Andrew | 2 | | 2 | | |
| Rundle, William | 2 | | 7 | | |
| Nash, Eliakam | 3 | | 3 | | |
| Rundle, Experience | | | 1 | | |
| Cleaveland, John | 1 | 4 | 2 | | |
| Barnum, Timothy | 1 | | 2 | | |
| Barnum, Samuel | 1 | | 2 | | |
| Barnum, Timothy, Jr | 1 | 2 | 2 | | |
| Wheeler, Jedediah | 2 | | 3 | | |
| Wheeler, Samuel | 2 | 3 | 7 | | |
| Hendrick, Benjamin | 2 | | 1 | | |
| Hendrick, Samuel | 1 | | 1 | | |
| Hendrick, James | 2 | | 1 | | |
| Disbrow, Joseph | 1 | 1 | 4 | 1 | |
| Disbrow, Hennery | 1 | 1 | 3 | | |
| Fealds, William | 4 | | 1 | | |
| Allen, Giddeon | 2 | | 3 | | |
| Wheeler, James | 1 | 3 | 2 | | |
| Wheeler, Nehemiah | 1 | 2 | 1 | | |
| Wheeler, Enoch | 1 | | 5 | | |
| Scribner, Osias | 1 | 3 | 3 | | |
| Brush, Zacheus | 1 | 1 | 1 | 1 | |
| Ball, Eliphilet | 1 | 2 | 2 | | |
| Hambleton, John | 1 | | 2 | | |
| Disbrow, Asahel | 1 | 4 | 5 | | |
| Dixon, George | 1 | | 4 | | |
| Fuller, Joseph | 1 | 1 | 1 | | |
| Brown, Charles | 1 | | 1 | | |
| Hibbard, Elisha | 1 | 1 | 5 | | |
| Hibbard, Nathanel | 1 | | 2 | | |
| Hoyt, Moses | 3 | 1 | 3 | | |
| Osborn, Elezer | 3 | 2 | 7 | | |
| Hall, Seth | 2 | | 2 | | |
| Taylor, Benjamin | 1 | | 3 | | |
| **NEW FAIRFIELD TOWN—continued.** | | | | | |
| Taylor, Thofelus | 1 | 1 | 2 | | |
| Bulkley, Jonathan | 1 | 3 | 5 | | |
| Bass, Benjamin | 2 | | 2 | | |
| Bass, Joseph | 1 | 2 | 3 | | |
| Stephens, Ebenezer | 4 | | 3 | | |
| Brush, Stephen | 2 | 1 | 1 | | |
| Bass, Elijah | 1 | | 5 | | |
| Stephens, Reubin | 1 | 2 | 2 | | |
| Stephens, Daniel | 1 | 3 | 3 | | |
| Kelogg, Martin, Jur | 1 | 2 | 2 | | |
| Keelogg, Martin | 2 | 1 | 2 | | 1 |
| Stephens, Amos | 2 | 1 | 3 | | |
| Gregory, Ralph | 1 | 2 | 3 | | |
| **NEWTOWN TOWN.** | | | | | |
| Tomlinson, Henery | 1 | 2 | 3 | | 1 |
| Tomlinson, Josiah | 1 | 3 | 2 | | 3 |
| Sharp, Jesse | 1 | 2 | 5 | | |
| Sharp, Eliakim | 1 | 1 | 6 | | |
| Wetmore, James | 1 | 1 | 3 | | |
| Clark, Zachariah | 5 | 4 | | | 1 |
| Curtis, Benjamin | 1 | 3 | 5 | | |
| Curtis, Nehemiah | 2 | | 5 | | 2 |
| Beardsley, Josiah | 3 | 1 | 1 | | |
| Beardsley, Samuel | 1 | | 3 | | |
| Wadeling, Esther | | | 1 | | |
| Shermon, Filo | 2 | 2 | 4 | | |
| Shermon, Lymon | 1 | 2 | 2 | | |
| Beardsley, Elias | 3 | 2 | 2 | | |
| Hurd, Nirum | 3 | 1 | 4 | | |
| Beardsley, Jonathan | 3 | 2 | 2 | | |
| Hurd, John | 2 | 5 | 6 | | |
| Peck, Ephraim | 2 | 2 | 1 | | |
| Chambers, Asa | 1 | 1 | 4 | | |
| Williams, Amos | 1 | | 3 | | |
| Bennitt, Abel | 2 | 1 | 5 | | 1 |
| Platt, Josiah | 3 | 1 | 6 | | |
| Bennitt, Amos | 1 | 1 | 4 | | |
| Bennitt Richard | 1 | 2 | 4 | | |
| Bennett James | 2 | 1 | 2 | | 1 |
| Bennett, Thomas | 3 | 4 | 3 | | 1 |
| Masters, James | 1 | 2 | 2 | | |
| Sanford, Thomas | 2 | 3 | 5 | | |
| Beardsley, Abigail (Wid.) | 1 | 1 | 7 | | |
| Curtis, Filo | 1 | 3 | 4 | | |
| Curtis, Abijah | 4 | 2 | 2 | | 3 |
| Blackman, Edward | 1 | 1 | 2 | | |
| Hubbill, Lewis | 1 | 4 | 4 | | |
| Hubbill, John | 2 | | 3 | | |
| Allen, William | 2 | 4 | 4 | | |
| Murrey, Pattern | 2 | | 3 | | |
| Beach, John, Junr | 1 | 3 | 4 | | 1 |
| Hubbill, Comfort | 2 | 2 | 4 | | |
| Hubbill, Enoch | 1 | 1 | 3 | | |
| Sanford, William | 1 | | 3 | | |
| Botchford, Joseph | 2 | 2 | 4 | | |
| Bochford, Abraham | 4 | | 4 | | |
| Sanford, Hezekiah | 2 | 3 | 5 | | |
| Baldwin, Isaac | 2 | | 4 | | |
| Sanford, John, Junr | 2 | 2 | 3 | | |
| Booth, Asael | 2 | 2 | 6 | | |
| Booth, Olive (Wid.) | 3 | | 4 | | |
| Crowfoot, Stephen | 2 | 1 | 6 | | |
| Cogswell, Asael | 1 | | 1 | | 2 |
| Sanford, James | 2 | | 7 | | |
| Sanford, Samuel | 4 | | 8 | | |
| Shermon, Lewis | 1 | 2 | 6 | | |
| Baldwin, John | 1 | 2 | 2 | | |
| Booth, Jonathan | 1 | 3 | 6 | | 1 |
| Brau, Hanah (Wid.) | 2 | 1 | 2 | | |
| Booth, David | 3 | | 4 | | 1 |
| Bennett, Caleb | 1 | 2 | 2 | | |
| Booth, Abiel | 1 | 2 | 2 | | |
| Booth, Daniel | 2 | 3 | 6 | | |
| Chandler, John | 5 | | 7 | | 1 |
| Edmonds, William | 1 | | 2 | | |
| Curtis, Josiah | 2 | 4 | 7 | | 2 |
| Bochford, John | 2 | 1 | 2 | | 1 |
| Jerrold, Jabez | 2 | 4 | 3 | | |
| Sherman, Ephraim | 2 | 5 | 5 | | |
| Curtis, Matthew | 3 | 1 | 3 | | |
| Farmon, Jeabud | 2 | 3 | 4 | 1 | |
| Lyon, Betty | 1 | | 2 | | |
| Bochford, Elijah | 1 | 3 | 5 | | |
| Fairchild, William A | 1 | 1 | 3 | | |
| Bochford, Jabez | 2 | 1 | 3 | | 1 |
| Bochford, Abel | 3 | 1 | 5 | 2 | |
| Finney, Elded | 2 | 4 | 4 | | |
| Gregory, Aaron M | 1 | 2 | 4 | | |
| Farmon, Henery | 1 | | 4 | | |
| Booth, Phebe (Wid.) | | | 2 | | 2 |
| Booth, Ezra | 3 | 3 | 4 | | |
| Burrill, Stephen | 1 | 1 | 2 | | 1 |

# FIRST CENSUS OF THE UNITED STATES.

## FAIRFIELD COUNTY—Continued.

| NAME OF HEAD OF FAMILY. | Free white males of 16 years and upward, including heads of families. | Free white males under 16 years. | Free white females, including heads of families. | All other free persons. | Slaves. | NAME OF HEAD OF FAMILY. | Free white males of 16 years and upward, including heads of families. | Free white males under 16 years. | Free white females, including heads of families. | All other free persons. | Slaves. | NAME OF HEAD OF FAMILY. | Free white males of 16 years and upward, including heads of families. | Free white males under 16 years. | Free white females, including heads of families. | All other free persons. | Slaves. |
|---|---|---|---|---|---|---|---|---|---|---|---|---|---|---|---|---|---|
| NEWTOWN TOWN—con. | | | | | | NEWTOWN TOWN—con. | | | | | | NEWTOWN TOWN—con. | | | | | |
| Perry, Rev<sup>d</sup> Filo | 1 | 2 | 3 | | | Beach, Lazarus | 1 | 1 | 4 | | | Fulford, Oliver | 2 | 6 | 2 | | |
| Baldwin, Abraham | 1 | | 3 | | 1 | Morgin, Hezekiah | 2 | 2 | 4 | | | Booth, James | 1 | 1 | 2 | | |
| Beers, David | 1 | 4 | 4 | | | Underhill, John | 2 | 2 | 3 | | | Booth, Hezekiah | 2 | | 3 | | 1 |
| Hull, Eliphalit | 1 | 1 | 4 | | | Basset, John | 3 | 2 | 6 | | | Glover, Daniel | 1 | 1 | 6 | | 4 |
| Burch, William | 2 | | 1 | | | Crowfoot, John | 1 | 1 | 2 | | | Glover, James | 4 | | 2 | | 2 |
| Wallis, Jacob | 1 | 2 | 3 | | | Taylor, Ebenezer | 5 | | 1 | | 7 | Sanford, Jonas | 2 | 2 | 6 | | |
| Shepherd, John | 2 | 2 | 2 | | | Platt, Jesse | 3 | 2 | 1 | | | Sanford, Jonathan | 2 | | 8 | | |
| Thomas, James | 1 | | 3 | | | Platt, Timothy | 4 | | 3 | | | Sanford, Soloman | 2 | 1 | 3 | | |
| Bochford, Joel | 1 | 1 | 3 | | | Farmer, Filo | 1 | | 4 | | | Prindle, Samuel | 2 | | 4 | | |
| Foot, Peter | 2 | 1 | 3 | | | Towsie, Zalmon | 1 | 1 | 2 | | | Glover, John | 3 | 1 | 3 | | 3 |
| Griffin, Abner | 2 | 1 | 5 | | | Towsie, Filo | 1 | | 3 | | 1 | Osborn, Edward | 1 | 1 | 2 | | |
| Griffin, Amos | 2 | 2 | 3 | | | Crowfoot, Daniel | 1 | 2 | 3 | | | Sherborn, Benjamin | 1 | 1 | 1 | | |
| Foot, Edward | 2 | 5 | 6 | | | Crowfoot, Isaac | 1 | 1 | 1 | | | Lattain, Jacob | 2 | 2 | 4 | | |
| Deforest, Alexander | 1 | 1 | 2 | | | Crowfoot, John | 1 | | 1 | | 1 | Lattain, Benjamin | 2 | | 4 | | |
| Shepherd, Stephen | 1 | 2 | 2 | | | Crowfoot, Elihu | 1 | 1 | 2 | | 1 | Lattain, Luke | 2 | | 9 | | |
| Shermon, Ebenezer | 1 | 2 | 5 | | | Crowfoot, Molly (Wid.) | 1 | | 1 | | | Morris, Amos | 2 | 1 | 2 | | |
| Tuttle, Daniel | 2 | 1 | 4 | | | Roberts, Thomas | 3 | 1 | 3 | | | Morris, Daniel | 1 | 4 | 3 | | |
| Kimble, Fitch | 1 | 1 | 3 | | | Shepherd, James | 3 | 1 | 4 | | | Peck, Joshua | 1 | 1 | 4 | | |
| Burch, William | 1 | | 1 | | | Stilson, Israel | 2 | 1 | 6 | | | Judson, Elijah | 2 | 2 | 3 | | |
| Hull, John | 3 | | 5 | | | Fairchild, Apheus | 2 | 3 | 3 | | | Peck, Eli | 2 | 1 | 4 | | |
| Shepherd, David | 2 | 4 | 7 | | | Fairchild, John | 1 | 1 | 6 | | | Malery, Mary (Wid.) | | | 3 | | |
| Northrop, Ruth (Wid.) | 1 | | 1 | | | Shepherd, Merrit | 1 | 1 | 1 | | | Malery, Thomas | 1 | 1 | 2 | | |
| Prindle, Lazarus | 2 | | 2 | | | King, David | 3 | 1 | 8 | | | Lattain, Joseph | 2 | 3 | 4 | | |
| Prindle, Philimon | 1 | 1 | 1 | | | Shepherd, Moses | 1 | 2 | 8 | | | Shermon, Lymon | 1 | 1 | 3 | | |
| Prindle, Joseph | 2 | | 1 | | 1 | Fairchild, Ager | 2 | | 1 | | | Shermon, Filo | 1 | 2 | 4 | | |
| Prindle, Jonas | 1 | | 2 | | | Mills, Andrew | 1 | 1 | 2 | | | Curtis, Zalmon | 1 | 2 | 2 | | |
| Parmely, Noah | 1 | 3 | | | | Rample, George | 1 | 1 | 3 | | | Shermon, Elijah | 2 | 1 | 2 | | |
| Prindle, Sirus | 1 | 1 | 3 | | | Fairchild, Jonathan | 1 | 1 | 1 | | | Shermon, Ezra | 1 | 5 | 1 | | |
| Prindle, Abiel | 1 | 1 | 5 | | | Fairchild, Peter | 1 | 2 | 2 | | | Shermon, John | 2 | 2 | 2 | | |
| Stilson, Benjamin | 2 | | 2 | | | Fairchild, Silus | 2 | 1 | 4 | | | Squire, William | 1 | 2 | 3 | | |
| Northop, Lawrence | 1 | | | | | Wheeler, Joseph | 1 | 2 | 2 | | | Cato (Negro) | | | | 6 | |
| Northrop, Nathan<sup>el</sup> | 1 | 3 | 2 | | 1 | Hubbill, Jepthan | 2 | 1 | 4 | | | Beardsley, Abigail | 2 | 1 | 7 | | |
| Ferris, Abel | 3 | | 3 | | | Prindle, Abijah | 1 | 1 | 4 | | | Hurd, Finious | 2 | 3 | 4 | | |
| Northrop, Peter | 1 | 2 | 3 | | | Wheeler, David | 1 | 1 | 2 | | | Beers, Eben | 5 | 4 | 5 | | 1 |
| Northrop, George | 1 | 2 | 1 | | | Fairchild, Seth | 3 | 1 | 3 | | | Johnson, Enoch | 2 | 2 | 4 | | |
| Northrop, Gideon | 1 | 2 | 2 | | | Weed, Solomon | 2 | 3 | 2 | | | Beers, Finious | 1 | 2 | 2 | | |
| Jellet, Abraham | 2 | 2 | 5 | | | Wheeler, Ann (Wid.) | 1 | | 1 | | | Warner, Molly | | | 3 | | |
| Jellet, Moses | 1 | 2 | 1 | | | Wheeler, Jerusha (Wid.) | | | 2 | | | Ferris, Zacheriah | 1 | | 2 | | |
| Shepherd, George | 2 | 4 | 6 | | | Fairchild, Filo | 1 | 1 | 2 | | | Walker, John | 2 | 3 | 1 | | |
| Shepherd, Amos | 2 | 3 | 4 | | | Fairchild, James | 1 | 2 | 3 | | | Warner, Noadoc | 1 | 1 | 5 | | |
| Burchin, William | 1 | | 1 | | | Shermon, Seth | 1 | 2 | 3 | | | Shermon, Nathan | 3 | | 3 | | |
| Jellet, John | 1 | 2 | 2 | | | Shermon, David | 2 | 1 | 3 | | | Beach, John | 1 | | 4 | | 2 |
| Glover, Elias | 1 | 3 | 5 | | | Foot, Joseph | 1 | 2 | 6 | | | Glover, Zalmon | 2 | 2 | 2 | | |
| Shepherd, Abraham | 2 | 5 | 3 | | | Fairchild, Zadoc | 1 | 4 | 3 | | | Hull, Elijah | 2 | 1 | 6 | | |
| Northrop, Nehemiah | 2 | 1 | 5 | | | Fairchild, Clemon | 1 | | 1 | | | Wells, Isaac | 2 | 3 | 1 | | |
| Northrop, Abel | 3 | 1 | 2 | | | Fairchild, Eben<sup>r</sup> | 2 | | 2 | | | Foot, Filo | 1 | | 3 | | |
| Northrop, William | 2 | | 2 | | | Foot, George | 2 | 1 | 2 | | | Hurd, Amos | 6 | 1 | 5 | | |
| Foot, Daniel | 1 | | 2 | | | Fairchild, Josiah | 1 | 5 | 2 | | 1 | Foot, Peter | 2 | 3 | 5 | | |
| Brister, Joseph | 1 | 1 | 1 | | | Winton, Daniel | 1 | | | | | Glover, Henery | 3 | | 4 | | |
| Washburn, Zebee | 2 | 2 | 1 | | | Summers, John | 2 | | 5 | | | Hurd, Curtis | 1 | 1 | 5 | | |
| Stilson, Jonathan | 1 | | 1 | | | Winton, Lockwood | 1 | 1 | 2 | | | Bochford, Moses | 2 | 3 | 4 | | |
| Ferris, Peter | 2 | | 2 | | | Sanford, Nathan<sup>el</sup> | 2 | 2 | 6 | | | Bochford, Jerid | 3 | 1 | 3 | | |
| Ferris, Samuel | 1 | 1 | 6 | | | Foot, Jehiel | 1 | 2 | 1 | | | Stilson, Nehemiah | 1 | 1 | 6 | | |
| Northrop, John | 2 | | 2 | | | Summers, Robert | 3 | | 1 | | | Taylor, Stephen | 1 | 2 | 1 | | |
| Betts, Abner | 1 | 2 | 2 | | | Mills, Stephen | 1 | | 2 | | | Foot, George | 2 | 3 | 2 | | |
| Beers, Truman | 1 | 1 | 3 | | | Daton, Hezekiah | 1 | 2 | 6 | | | Taylor, Nicholas | 1 | 2 | 2 | | |
| Beers, Sarah (Wid.) | 2 | 1 | 3 | | | Blackman, Josiah | 2 | 2 | 5 | | | Judson, Sarah | | | 2 | | |
| Beers, Oliver | 1 | 1 | 6 | | | Blackman, Joseph | 2 | | 3 | | | Malery, Ebenezer | 2 | 2 | 3 | | |
| Beers, John | 2 | 2 | 2 | | | Blackman, John | 2 | | 1 | | | Curtis, Stiles | 1 | 1 | 2 | | |
| Beers, Andrew | 1 | 2 | 4 | | | Camp, Hezekiah | 1 | | 2 | | | Judson, Abel | 3 | 5 | 5 | | |
| Basset, Joel | 1 | 1 | 1 | | | Camp, Julius | 1 | 1 | 3 | | 1 | Judson, Nathan<sup>el</sup> | 1 | 8 | 3 | | |
| Ferris, Joseph | 3 | | 2 | | | Bochford, Clemon | 1 | 1 | 5 | | | Curtis, Gold | 2 | 2 | 4 | | 1 |
| Nichols, Richard | 2 | | 2 | 2 | | Bochford, Gideon | 1 | 5 | 4 | | | Tousey, Oliver | 2 | | 4 | | |
| Beers, Elias | 1 | | 1 | | | Bochford, Theopholus | | | | | | Peck, Levi | 2 | 1 | 2 | | |
| Tousey, John | 1 | | 1 | | | Blackman, Reuben | 1 | 2 | 3 | | | Peck, Henery | 3 | 1 | 2 | | |
| Baldwin, Clark | 1 | 3 | 4 | | | Shermon, Lemuel | 3 | 1 | 5 | | | Meeker, David | 2 | | 2 | | |
| Baldwin, Sweeten | 1 | 2 | 2 | | | Baldwin, Amos | 1 | 2 | 1 | | | Glover, Solimon | 1 | 2 | 7 | | 1 |
| Norton, Filo | 4 | 3 | 2 | | | Bochford, Gideon | 4 | 2 | 5 | | 1 | Peck, Shadrack | 1 | 2 | 2 | | |
| Peck, Isaac | 1 | 3 | 4 | | | Bennett, Abraham | 2 | 1 | 4 | | | Boscon, Patience | | 1 | 3 | | |
| Peck, Elizabeth (Wid.) | | 1 | 5 | | | Parcks, Michael | 1 | 2 | 3 | | | Prindle, Jonathan | 3 | 1 | 4 | | |
| Williams, John | 1 | 2 | 2 | | | Glover, Benjamin | 2 | | 3 | | | Towsie, Isaac | 2 | 1 | 2 | | |
| Sharp, Thomas | 1 | 3 | 5 | | | Lacy, Sarah (Wid.) | | | 2 | | | Towsie, Zalmon | 3 | 1 | 4 | | |
| Griffin, Reubin | 1 | 1 | 2 | | | Bancraft, Oliver | | 2 | 2 | | | Heard, Oliver C | 3 | | 2 | | |
| Griffin, Joseph | 2 | 2 | 3 | | | Elwood, Rion | 1 | 8 | 2 | | | Peck, Moses | 2 | | 5 | | |
| French, Gamaliel | 1 | | 3 | | | Turrel, Jared | 3 | 2 | 4 | | | Nichols, Sarah | 1 | 3 | 3 | | 1 |
| Tredwell, Timothy | 1 | | 2 | | | Chambers, Thomas | 2 | 1 | 2 | | | Nichols, Elijah | 2 | | 1 | | 2 |
| Johnson, John | 2 | 4 | 4 | | | Curtis, Nirum | 1 | | 1 | | | Shermon, Jotham | | 1 | 2 | | |
| Stilson, Jacob | 3 | | 2 | | | Burritt, Amos | 1 | 1 | 6 | | | Hinman, Mary | | | 2 | | |
| Towsie, Donald | 1 | 1 | 2 | | | Hall, William | 4 | 1 | 4 | | | Booth, Reuben | 2 | 1 | 2 | | 2 |
| Johnson, Abel | 1 | 2 | 3 | | | Peck, Samuel | 3 | 2 | 4 | | | Mogenot, John | 1 | 2 | 2 | | |
| Gray, Seth | 1 | 1 | 3 | | | Bobbit, Samuel | 1 | 2 | 2 | | | Strong, Nehemiah | 1 | | 2 | | 1 |
| Chapman, Collins | 1 | 1 | 1 | | | Norton, Nathan | 2 | 3 | 2 | | | Johnson, Joel | 2 | 1 | 3 | | |
| Peck, Matthew | 2 | 3 | 5 | | | Mills, Daniel | 1 | 1 | 1 | | | Pringle, Ephraim | 1 | | 2 | | |
| Lekes, Ephraim | 2 | | 2 | | | Wheeler, Joseph | 2 | | 1 | | | Whiting, Samuel | 2 | 3 | 4 | | |
| Bescoro, Nathan | 1 | 1 | 3 | | | Wheeler, Bennett | | 1 | 3 | | | Burritt, William | 3 | 1 | 2 | | |
| Prindle, Daniel | 3 | 1 | 5 | | | Wheeler, Eli | 1 | 1 | 4 | | | Hinman, David | 1 | 1 | 4 | | |
| Gilbert, Stephen | 2 | 1 | 3 | | | Peck, Ezra | 1 | | | | | Stilson, Bailey | 1 | 1 | 3 | | |
| Dimon, Gold | 1 | | | | | Peck, Sarah (Wid.) | | 1 | 3 | | | Shepherd, Gideon | 1 | 2 | 6 | | |
| Rowland, Jabez | 2 | 3 | 5 | | | Peck, Heth | 1 | 1 | 2 | | | Perry, Bennitt | 1 | 3 | 4 | | |
| Raymond, Justin | 2 | | 4 | | | Peck, Heth, Jun<sup>r</sup> | 2 | 1 | 2 | | | Gilbert, John | 1 | | 2 | | |
| Tumey, John | 1 | | 2 | | | Peck, Nathaniel | 2 | | 1 | | | Baldwin, Caleb | 3 | 1 | 1 | | 1 |
| Platt, Jarvis | 2 | 1 | 4 | | | Burritt, Rebeckah (Wid.) | | | 1 | | | Baldwin, David | 1 | 2 | 3 | | 1 |
| Lacy, Richard | 3 | | 3 | | | Wheeler, Thomas | 2 | 1 | 5 | | 1 | Beers, Sirus | 3 | 1 | 1 | | |
| Platt, Justin | 1 | 1 | 2 | | | | | | | | | Bagger, John | 1 | 3 | 2 | | |
| Gilbert, Seth | 3 | 5 | 2 | | | | | | | | | Biscow, Sarah (Wid.) | 1 | 2 | 2 | | 1 |

# HEADS OF FAMILIES—CONNECTICUT.

## FAIRFIELD COUNTY—Continued.

| NAME OF HEAD OF FAMILY. | Free white males of 16 years and upward, including heads of families. | Free white males under 16 years. | Free white females, including heads of families. | All other free persons. | Slaves. | NAME OF HEAD OF FAMILY. | Free white males of 16 years and upward, including heads of families. | Free white males under 16 years. | Free white females, including heads of families. | All other free persons. | Slaves. | NAME OF HEAD OF FAMILY. | Free white males of 16 years and upward, including heads of families. | Free white males under 16 years. | Free white females, including heads of families. | All other free persons. | Slaves. |
|---|---|---|---|---|---|---|---|---|---|---|---|---|---|---|---|---|---|
| **NEWTOWN TOWN—con.** | | | | | | **NORWALK AND STAMFORD TOWNS—con.** | | | | | | **NORWALK AND STAMFORD TOWNS—con.** | | | | | |
| Beers, Daniel | 1 | | 1 | | | Hoyt, Timothy | 1 | 7 | 3 | | | Gregory, Samuel | 1 | | 1 | | |
| Perry, Ezra | 2 | 1 | 2 | | | Coza (Negro) | | | | 2 | | Gregory, John | 2 | 1 | 6 | | |
| Lee, Stephen | 1 | | 1 | | | Anne (Negro) | | | | 2 | | Beers, Samuel | 1 | 1 | 3 | | |
| Beers, Samuel | 2 | 2 | 4 | | | Warson, Robert | 3 | 1 | 7 | | | Cowley, James | 2 | 2 | 2 | | |
| Beers, Simeon | 1 | 2 | 4 | | | Syphax (Negro) | | | | 6 | | Rogers, Lemuel | 1 | | 1 | | |
| Stilson, Abel | 1 | 1 | 3 | | | Comestock, David, Ju$^r$ | 1 | 2 | 4 | 1 | | Camp, Isaac | 2 | 2 | 6 | | |
| Stilson, Vincent | 2 | 1 | 3 | | | Church, Ebenezer | 5 | 1 | 3 | | 2 | Camp, Isaac, Jun$^r$ | 1 | 1 | 1 | | |
| Peck, Ebenezer | 4 | | 1 | | | Fitch, Thomas, Esq$^r$ | 6 | | 3 | 2 | 2 | Jackson, Rachel (W$^d$) | | | 3 | | |
| Ferris, Nathan | 1 | 2 | 2 | | | Marvin, Samuel | 3 | | 2 | | | Harris, William | 1 | 1 | 3 | | |
| Stilson, Elnathan | 1 | | 2 | | | Rogers, Mary (W$^d$) | | | 5 | | | Finch, Ruth | | | 1 | | |
| Baldwin, Abigail | 1 | | 4 | | | Gregory, Samuel | 1 | | 2 | | | Phillo, John | 1 | 1 | 1 | | |
| Skidmore, Daniel | 1 | 1 | 4 | | | Hanford, Daniel | 1 | 2 | 4 | | | Phillo, Isaac | 1 | 1 | 2 | | |
| Turrel, George | 1 | 1 | 5 | | | Fitch, Timothy | 2 | 2 | 5 | | | Olmsted, Reuben | 1 | 2 | 2 | | |
| Hurd, Ammon | 2 | 5 | 4 | | | Saunders, Jabez | 2 | 1 | 3 | | | Stuart, Albert | 1 | 3 | 1 | | |
| Upum, Wate | 2 | | 3 | 1 | | Wilson, Nathan | 1 | 1 | 4 | | | Olmsted, Silvanus | 1 | | 2 | | |
| Peck, Nathan | 1 | 4 | 2 | | | Smith, Hutton | 2 | 4 | 4 | | | Grumman, John | 2 | | 2 | | |
| Peck, Enoch | 4 | 3 | 4 | | | Hyatt, Isaac | 1 | 2 | 3 | | | Grumman, Jeremiah | 2 | 1 | 2 | | |
| Peck, David | 2 | 1 | 2 | | | Lockwood, Thomas | 1 | | 2 | | | Grumman, Ezra | 2 | 2 | 2 | | |
| Peck, John | 2 | 1 | 4 | | | Betts, Mary (W$^d$) | 1 | | 2 | | | Richard, Stephen | 1 | | 1 | | |
| Biscow, John | 1 | 4 | 4 | | | Hendrick, Nathan | 1 | 3 | 2 | | | Grumman, Nehemiah | 1 | | 2 | | |
| Peck, Jabez | 2 | 1 | 4 | | | Hyatt, Daniel | 1 | 1 | 1 | | | Abbott, Jedediah | 1 | 2 | 3 | | |
| Peck, Isarel | 1 | 2 | 2 | | | Raymond, Josiah | 2 | 3 | 4 | | 6 | Betts, Abijah | 2 | 1 | 4 | | |
| Peck, Joseph | 2 | 5 | 3 | | | Smith, James | 2 | 2 | 1 | | | Hyatt, Elvin | 1 | 2 | 2 | | |
| Stilson, Thomas | 1 | | 2 | | | Raymond, Abigail (w$^d$) | | | 1 | | | Grumman, Isaac | 1 | 2 | 3 | | |
| Whiting, James | 1 | 3 | 5 | | | S$^t$ John, W$^m$, Jun$^r$ | 1 | 2 | 4 | | 1 | Birrchard, Daniel | 2 | 1 | 3 | | |
| Peck, Asher | 1 | 4 | 6 | | | Smith, Hannah (W$^d$) | | | 1 | | | Whitlock, Abel | 1 | | 2 | | |
| Peck, Livenus | 1 | 2 | 2 | | | Mallory, Polly (W$^d$) | 1 | 1 | 3 | | | Church, Daniel | 2 | 3 | 4 | | |
| Peck, Enos | 1 | 3 | 4 | | | Fitch, Haynes | 3 | 6 | 3 | | | Lambart, David | 1 | 3 | 5 | | |
| Nichols, Peter | 3 | 1 | 3 | | 1 | Fitch, Rebecca (W$^d$) | | 1 | 2 | | | Betts, Thaddeus | 2 | 1 | 6 | | |
| Nichols, Lemuel | 1 | 1 | 4 | | | Waters, Robert | 2 | | 1 | | | Abbott, Seth | 2 | 2 | 6 | | |
| Nichols, Philo | 1 | 1 | 1 | | | Pope, Charles | 1 | | 1 | | | Jarvis, Jesse | 1 | | 3 | | |
| Judson, John | 3 | | 9 | | | Hanford, Hezekiah | 1 | 1 | 3 | | | Stuard, Simon | 1 | 3 | 3 | | |
| Starling, David | 2 | 1 | 1 | | | Hanford, Hezekiah, Jun$^r$ | 1 | 4 | 2 | | | Abbott, Ebenezer | 3 | 3 | 4 | 2 | 3 |
| Starlin, Jacob | 1 | | 2 | | | Fitch, James | 2 | 1 | 2 | | | Gayler, Elizabeth (W$^d$) | 1 | 1 | 2 | | |
| Sherwood, Justin | 1 | 2 | 1 | | | Fitch, James, Jun$^r$ | 1 | 1 | 2 | | | Betts, Benjamin | 2 | | 4 | | |
| Stilson, Aaron | 1 | 2 | 4 | | | Hyatt, Mary (W$^d$) | | | 1 | | | Paching, Ebenezer | 1 | 5 | 3 | | |
| Sherwood, Eben | 3 | | 3 | | | Gregory, Abraham | 3 | 2 | 3 | | | Rockwell, Joseph | 1 | | | | |
| Taylor, Phineus | 3 | 1 | 3 | | | Gregory, Seely | 1 | 1 | 3 | | | Whitlock, Mary (W$^d$) | 3 | 1 | 2 | | |
| Taylor, Phineus, Jr | 1 | | 3 | | | Gregory, Ebenezer | 1 | | 3 | | | Dunning, Richard | 1 | 2 | 2 | | |
| Summers, Gershom | 3 | 1 | 3 | | | Mallory, Cap$^t$ Nathan | 2 | | 3 | | | Raymond, Asahel | 2 | 2 | 3 | | |
| Burr, Noah | 2 | 2 | 1 | | | Smith, Sarah (W$^d$) | | | 4 | | | Betts, Abigail (W$^d$) | 2 | | 2 | | |
| Sherwood, Daniel | 1 | 1 | 3 | | | Bessy, Bridget (W$^d$) | | | 1 | | | Betts, Daniel | 1 | 2 | 1 | | |
| Foot, Daniel | 1 | 1 | 3 | | | Eversley, John | 3 | | 2 | | | Betts, Jesse | 1 | | 2 | | |
| Shepherd, Simeon | 2 | 3 | 3 | | | Burnet, Rev$^d$ Matthias | 1 | 2 | 3 | | 2 | Raymond, Clapp | 1 | 1 | 2 | | |
| Hurd, Jonathan | 1 | 1 | 4 | | | Bennedict, Elizabeth (W$^d$) | | | 1 | | | Raymond, Clapp, Jr | 1 | 3 | 2 | | |
| Tousey, Abel | 1 | 2 | 3 | 1 | | Hall, Hannah | | | 2 | | | Belding, Samuel | 1 | 4 | 1 | | 2 |
| Tousey, Rebecka (Wid.) | 1 | 1 | 3 | | | Bartram, Job | 1 | 2 | 4 | | 1 | Betts, Moses | 1 | 2 | 4 | | |
| Gray, William | 1 | 1 | 6 | | | Scudder, Elizabeth (W$^d$) | | | 1 | | | Sevans, David | 1 | | 2 | | |
| Dimon, Gold | 1 | 2 | 5 | | | Pomp (Negro) | | | | 3 | | Deforest, Lemuel | 2 | 1 | 2 | | |
| Willisson, John | 1 | 2 | 2 | | | Mentor | | | | 4 | | Ogden, Jesse | 2 | 3 | 2 | | |
| Blackman, Treuman | 1 | 2 | 3 | | | Peter (Negro) | | | | 3 | | Cole, Asa | 1 | | 5 | | |
| Blackman, John, Jun$^r$ | 2 | 4 | 5 | | | Ann (Negro) | | | | 3 | | Rockwell, Joseph, Jr | 1 | 3 | 1 | | |
| Hawley, Benjamin | 1 | 1 | 1 | | | Grumman, Thomas | 2 | | 4 | | | Wix, Stephen | 1 | 2 | 1 | | |
| Hatcher, Joshua | 1 | 1 | 4 | | | Lockwood, John | 3 | | 3 | | | Starling, Samuel, Jr | 1 | 4 | 3 | | |
| Shermon, Matthew | 1 | | 5 | | | S$^t$ John, William | 1 | 4 | 3 | 1 | 2 | Hecock, Beth$^l$ | 1 | | | | |
| Hatch, Joseph | 1 | 1 | 6 | | | Belding, Thomas | 2 | | 1 | 1 | 1 | Hecock, Nathan$^{el}$ | 3 | 2 | 5 | | |
| Camp, Joel | 4 | 2 | 2 | | | Betts, John | 1 | 2 | 4 | | | Raymond, Seth | 2 | 1 | 7 | | |
| Blackman, James | 3 | 1 | 2 | | | Lockwood, Ebenezer | 3 | 5 | 3 | | | Hendrick, Deodate | 1 | 1 | 1 | | |
| Trowbridge, Samuel | 1 | | 2 | | | Jarvis, Stephen | 1 | | 2 | | | Betts, Elijah | | 1 | 4 | | |
| Fairchild, Ranson | 1 | 2 | 1 | | | Oglesby, Rev$^d$ Geo | 1 | 1 | 4 | | 1 | Chitester, Abraham | 2 | 3 | 2 | | |
| Turney, John | 1 | 3 | 2 | | | James, Hezekiah | 3 | 4 | 4 | | | Patrick, Abraham | 1 | 3 | 2 | | |
| Turney, Nathan | 2 | | 2 | | | Lockwood, Hezekiah | 1 | 2 | 4 | | | Fox, Jonathan | 1 | 5 | 2 | | |
| Hawley, Joseph | 1 | | 2 | | | Fairchild, Samuel | 1 | | 2 | | | Betts, Stephen | 3 | 1 | 2 | | |
| Hawley, William | 2 | 1 | 3 | | | Knight, Doct$^r$ Jonath$^n$ | 1 | 2 | 4 | | | Raymond, Seth | 1 | 1 | 7 | | |
| Colson, Joseph | 1 | 1 | 2 | | | Betts, Thomas | 1 | 1 | 3 | | | Raymond, Benjamin | 1 | | | | |
| Hawley, Jotham | 1 | 2 | 1 | | | Bennedict, William | 2 | | 2 | | | Hubble, Thaddeus | 1 | 1 | 2 | | |
| Hawley, Abel | 2 | | 3 | | | Canon, James | 1 | | 2 | | | Hubbell, Zadoch | 1 | 1 | 5 | | |
| Baldwin, Mathew | 1 | 2 | 5 | | | Betts, Hezekiah | 3 | 1 | 3 | | | Hubble, Nathan | 2 | 1 | 3 | | |
| Lake, John | 1 | 2 | 2 | | | Marvin, Seth | 1 | 1 | 1 | | | Marvin, Matthew | 3 | 2 | 2 | 1 | 1 |
| Wheeler, Stephen | 1 | 2 | 2 | | | Lockwood, Eliphalet | 3 | 2 | 3 | | | Wescots, John | 1 | 1 | 1 | | |
| Hennerics, Ellis | 1 | | 3 | | | Rogers, Uriah | 1 | | 5 | | | Osborn, Jacob | 2 | 2 | 2 | | |
| Skidmore, Ephraim | 2 | 4 | 5 | | | Beers, Nathaniel | 3 | 2 | 5 | | | Cannon, John, Jun$^r$ | 1 | 3 | 4 | | 2 |
| Skidmore, Amos | 1 | 2 | 1 | | | Camp, Richard | 1 | 3 | 5 | | | Gilbert, Nathan | 3 | | 4 | 1 | |
| Skidmore, Abel | 1 | 3 | 3 | | | Hanford, Jedediah | 2 | | 3 | | | Hecock, Noah | 2 | 1 | 2 | | |
| Skidmore, John | 2 | 1 | 2 | | | S$^t$ John, John | 1 | 1 | 5 | | | Starling, Daniel | 1 | | 2 | | |
| Lake, Peter | 1 | 2 | 3 | | | Smith, Jeremiah | 1 | 1 | 4 | | | Starling, William | 1 | | 2 | | |
| Lake, David | 1 | 1 | 5 | | | Whitehead, Sibbely | | | 1 | | | Starling, William, Jr | 1 | 5 | 4 | | |
| Smith, John | 1 | | 1 | | | S$^t$ John, Josiah | 2 | | 5 | | | Hollibert, Joseph | 1 | 3 | 5 | | |
| Turril, Amos | 3 | 1 | 5 | | | S$^t$ John, Stephen | 2 | 1 | 1 | | | Dikeman, Levi | 1 | 4 | 5 | | |
| Foot, Elisha | 2 | 2 | 2 | | | Hendrick, Peter | 1 | 1 | 3 | | | Betts, Reuben | 2 | 3 | 5 | | |
| Turril, Roger | 3 | 1 | 3 | | | Demmon, Nathaniel | 5 | 1 | 5 | | | Mead, John Betts | 1 | | 1 | | |
| Booth, Abraham | 1 | 1 | 2 | | | Lockwood, Matthew | 1 | | 1 | | | Stuart, Samuel | 1 | 2 | 6 | | |
| Turrel, Ruben | 2 | 1 | 2 | | | Thallter, Thaddeus B | 1 | | 2 | | | Williams, John | 1 | | 2 | | |
| **NORWALK AND STAMFORD TOWNS.** | | | | | | Betts, Elijah | 1 | | 1 | | | Marvin, Samuel, 3$^d$ | 1 | 1 | | | |
| | | | | | | Betts, Isaac | 1 | | 2 | | | Cole, Thomas | 1 | 4 | 2 | | |
| | | | | | | Betts, Isaac, Jun | 1 | 1 | 3 | | | Cole, Jonathan | 1 | 1 | 2 | | |
| Mott, Reuben | 3 | | 3 | | | Evcret, Richard | 1 | 1 | 3 | | | Nichols, James | 1 | 4 | 3 | | |
| Keeler, Anne (W$^d$) | | | 3 | | | Patrick, Ellen (W$^d$) | | | 4 | | | Starling, Samuel | 1 | | 2 | | |
| Rose (Negro) | | | | 2 | | Camp, Jonathan | 3 | 1 | 4 | | | Belding, Asa | 2 | 4 | 2 | | |
| Harry (Negro) | | | | 4 | | Scribner, Stephen | 2 | 2 | 3 | | | Belding, David | 2 | | 4 | | |
| Jackson, Daniel | 1 | 3 | 1 | | | Betty, James | 1 | 2 | 4 | | | S$^t$ John, Amy (W$^d$) | 1 | 3 | 3 | | |
| Keeler, Nathaniel | 2 | 2 | 2 | | | Gregory, Silas | 1 | 1 | 2 | | | Morgan, John | 1 | 2 | 2 | 1 | |
| Seymore, Jonathan | 1 | 1 | 2 | | | Gregory, Denton | 1 | | 1 | | | Keeler, Philip | 1 | 2 | 2 | | |
| Mott, William | 1 | 2 | 5 | | | Gregory, Stephen | 3 | 1 | 3 | | | Nash, Ebenezer | 1 | 3 | 3 | | |
| | | | | | | | | | | | | Davis, James | 2 | 2 | 3 | | |

# FIRST CENSUS OF THE UNITED STATES.

## FAIRFIELD COUNTY—Continued.

| NAME OF HEAD OF FAMILY. | Free white males of 16 years and upward, including heads of families. | Free white males under 16 years. | Free white females, including heads of families. | All other free persons. | Slaves. | NAME OF HEAD OF FAMILY. | Free white males of 16 years and upward, including heads of families. | Free white males under 16 years. | Free white females, including heads of families. | All other free persons. | Slaves. | NAME OF HEAD OF FAMILY. | Free white males of 16 years and upward, including heads of families. | Free white males under 16 years. | Free white females, including heads of families. | All other free persons. | Slaves. |
|---|---|---|---|---|---|---|---|---|---|---|---|---|---|---|---|---|---|
| **NORWALK AND STAMFORD TOWNS—con.** | | | | | | **NORWALK AND STAMFORD TOWNS—con.** | | | | | | **NORWALK AND STAMFORD TOWNS—con.** | | | | | |
| Scott, Wm, Junr | 2 | 2 | 3 | | | Husted Thaddeus | 1 | 2 | 3 | | | Seymore, Seth | 1 | 2 | 1 | | |
| Bennett, Nathan | 1 | 6 | 2 | | | Sturges, Aquilla | 1 | | 4 | | | Brooks, Lemuel | 2 | 3 | 5 | | |
| Abbott, James | 1 | 1 | 3 | | | Seymore, Ezra | 2 | 2 | 7 | | | Brooks, Lemuel, Junr | 1 | | 1 | | 1 |
| Sanford, Nathan | 1 | 1 | 3 | | | Seymore, Thomas | 2 | | 1 | | | Brown, Jedediah | 2 | 1 | 6 | | |
| Denton, Benjamin | 1 | | 5 | | | Hanford, Abraham | 1 | 4 | 3 | | | Quintard, Peter | 1 | 1 | 2 | | |
| Smith, Eliakim | 1 | | 2 | | | Jarvis, John | 1 | 1 | 3 | | | Russique, Mary | | | 2 | | |
| Keeler, Isaac | 1 | | 2 | | | Bolt, William | 3 | 1 | 4 | | | Raymond, Uriah | 2 | 3 | 3 | | |
| Keeler, Elijah | 1 | 1 | 3 | | | Reed, William | 1 | | 1 | | | Evertson, Evert | 1 | | 2 | | |
| Birchard, Jesse | 1 | 1 | 4 | | | Reed, William, Junr | 2 | 3 | 2 | | | Garner, William | 1 | 1 | 1 | | |
| Rogers, John | 1 | 3 | 1 | | | Kellagg, Isaac | 2 | 1 | 3 | | | Smith, Eliakim | 2 | 4 | 2 | | |
| Beers, Moses, Junr | 1 | 1 | 1 | | | Waring, Eunice (Wd) | | 3 | 2 | | | Hoyt, Job | 1 | 2 | 2 | | |
| Scott, William | 3 | 1 | 1 | | | Hanford, Alexander | 1 | 2 | 1 | | | Weed, Scudder | 1 | 3 | 3 | | |
| Scott, John | 1 | | 1 | | | Reed, Abigail | | | 1 | | | Bloomer, William | 1 | 3 | 3 | | |
| Scott, Aaron | 1 | 1 | 1 | | | Reed, Thaddeus | 2 | 1 | 1 | | | Scott, Eleazer | 1 | 2 | 4 | | |
| Seymore, Abijah | 1 | 2 | 2 | | | Reed, John | 2 | 2 | 3 | | | Pickett, Ezra | 2 | 1 | 2 | | |
| Mead, Jeremiah | 2 | | 3 | | | Hayes, John | 2 | | 1 | | | Hoyt, Nathan | 1 | | 1 | | |
| Keeler, Timothy | 1 | 1 | 2 | | | Smith, Noah | 1 | | 1 | | | Hoyt, Henry | 1 | 1 | 3 | | |
| Keeler, Nathan | 1 | 3 | 5 | | | Waring, Jesse | 1 | 3 | 2 | | | Hoyt, Asa | 2 | 3 | 4 | | |
| Ayres, Benjamin | 2 | 2 | 1 | | | Whitmore, Solomon | 1 | | 2 | | | Raymond, Nathel, Jr | 2 | 6 | 3 | | |
| Mead, Thaddeus | 2 | 2 | 2 | | | Younges, Richard | 1 | 3 | 4 | | | Raymond, Eliakim | 1 | | 2 | | |
| Beers, Moses | 2 | | 2 | | | Reed, Capt Eli | 1 | 1 | 2 | | | Whitney, Lois (Wd) | | | 3 | | |
| Keeler, Samuel | 3 | 3 | 4 | | | Brown, Jesse | 1 | 1 | 2 | | | Gibbs, Samuel | 1 | 4 | 3 | | |
| Mead, Azor | 1 | 1 | 2 | | | Reed, Jesse | 1 | 4 | 2 | | | Raymond, Naphtha | 1 | 1 | | | |
| Keeler, Elizabeth | | | 1 | | | Nash, David | 2 | 2 | 2 | | | Raymond, George | 1 | | 2 | | |
| Wescott, Elijah | 1 | 2 | 3 | | | Street, Nathaniel | 2 | 2 | 4 | | | Quintard, James | 4 | 3 | 2 | | |
| Mead, Matthew | 4 | 2 | 4 | | | Selleck, Nathaniel | 1 | 2 | 4 | | | Hoyt, Isaac | 1 | 1 | 5 | | |
| Comestock, Samuel | 2 | 1 | 3 | | | Bishop, Jacob | 1 | 3 | 4 | | | Raymond, Nathaniel | 1 | 2 | 4 | | |
| Bigsby, Gracy (Wd) | | | 1 | | | Hanford, Levi | 1 | 3 | 3 | | | Seymore, William | 1 | 1 | 1 | | |
| Thomas, Gregory | 1 | | 2 | | | Bennedict, Caleb | 1 | 4 | 3 | 2 | 2 | Raymond, Simon | 1 | | 2 | | |
| Baker, James | 1 | 4 | 4 | | | St. John, David | 2 | 2 | 4 | | | Hoyt, Sarah (Wd) | 1 | | 2 | | |
| Olmsted, James | 1 | 1 | 6 | | | Weed, Abraham | 1 | 1 | 2 | | | Raymond, Hezekiah | 2 | 4 | 2 | | |
| Whitlock, Daniel | 1 | | 1 | | | Boutain, Eleazer | 1 | | 2 | | | Raymond, Aaron | 1 | | 4 | | |
| Whitlock, Daniel, Jr | 2 | 1 | 6 | | | Boutain, Eleazer, Junr | 1 | 2 | 2 | | | Raymond, Moses | 1 | 1 | 7 | | |
| Olmsted, Samuel | 1 | 3 | 3 | | | Gray, Hannah (Wd) | 1 | | 2 | | | Woods, Stephen | 1 | 2 | 3 | | |
| Whitlock, David | 1 | 1 | 4 | | | St. John, Selleck | 1 | | 2 | | | Woods, Sarah (Wd) | | | 1 | | |
| St John, John | 3 | 2 | 2 | | | Silliman, Samuel C. | 1 | 1 | 1 | 1 | | Boutain, William | 2 | 2 | 6 | | |
| Nichols, Nehemiah | 1 | | 1 | | | Boutain, David | 1 | 3 | 2 | | | Boutain, Joshua | 1 | 1 | 4 | | |
| Scofield, Peter | 1 | 2 | 6 | | | Ambler, Mercy | | | 1 | | | Boutain, Sarah (Wd) | | | 1 | | |
| St John, Isaac | 3 | 1 | 3 | | | Silliman, Doctr Joseph | 1 | 2 | 3 | | | Hoyt, Thomas | 1 | 3 | 3 | | |
| St John, Silas | 1 | 1 | 4 | | | Mitchel, Revd Justice | 1 | 3 | 5 | | | Hoyt, Sarah (Wd) | | | 4 | | |
| Morgan, James | 3 | 3 | 3 | | | Comestock, Aaron | 1 | 3 | 3 | | | Raymond, Samuel | 1 | 5 | 6 | | |
| Betts, Matthew | 1 | | 1 | | | St John, Justice | 1 | 1 | 3 | | | Jones, Elijah | 1 | 3 | 5 | | |
| Tuttle, Enoch | 1 | 1 | 4 | | | Comestock, Enoch | 3 | 1 | 2 | | | Hoyt, John | 1 | 1 | 3 | | |
| Gates, Samuel, Jr | 1 | 3 | 2 | | | Comestock, Moses | 1 | 3 | 6 | | | Briggsby, John | 1 | 1 | | | |
| Gates, Moses | 1 | 1 | 2 | | | Kellagg, Nathan | 1 | 4 | 5 | | | Briggsby, Moses | 1 | | 2 | | |
| Gates, Samuel | 2 | | 3 | | | Seymore, John | 2 | 1 | 2 | | | Briggsby, Joseph | 1 | | 1 | | |
| Nichols, Enos | 1 | 2 | 2 | | | Smith, Doctr David | 1 | 1 | 2 | | | Saunders, Holmes | 1 | 1 | 1 | | |
| Lyon, Palatia | 1 | 1 | 2 | | | June, Jabez | | | 2 | | | Hoyt, Mary (Wd) | | 1 | 2 | | |
| Nichols, Jonathan | 1 | 2 | 4 | | | Tuttle, Abigail (Wd) | 2 | | 3 | | | Hoyt, Moses | 1 | | 2 | | |
| Boutain, Seth | 1 | 1 | 3 | | | Tuttle, Ebenezer | 1 | | 2 | | | Marvin, Hercules | 1 | 1 | 2 | | |
| St. John, Ezra | 1 | | 1 | | | Tuttle, Levi | 1 | 1 | 5 | | | Briggsby, Hopkins | 1 | | 2 | | |
| St John, Jonathan | 1 | 4 | 1 | | | Bennedict, Isaac | 2 | 3 | 4 | | | Briggsby, Hopkins | 1 | 3 | 2 | | |
| Gregory, Isaac | 1 | | 2 | | | Betts, Stephen | 1 | 2 | 3 | 1 | 1 | Waring, Joseph, Jr | 2 | 1 | 3 | | |
| Gregory, Isaac, Jr | 1 | 2 | 1 | | | Raymond, Ebenezer | 2 | | 2 | | | Bessy, Peleg | 1 | 1 | 4 | | |
| Jackson, Nathan | 2 | 1 | 1 | | | Raymond, John | 1 | 3 | 5 | | | Brown, Nathan | 2 | | 1 | | |
| Mead, Joseph | 2 | 1 | 1 | | | Tuttle, Eli | 1 | | 6 | | | Boutain, Zarius | 2 | 1 | 2 | | |
| Bennit, David | 1 | 1 | 5 | | | Lockwood, Samuel | 1 | 4 | 4 | | | Boutain, Samuel | 1 | | 3 | | |
| Gunn, Aaron | 1 | | 1 | | | Lockwood, Ephraim | 3 | 4 | 4 | | | Knapp, Caleb | 1 | 1 | 3 | | |
| Black, Step (negro) | | | | 1 | | Kellagg, Samuel | 4 | 1 | 4 | | | Raymond, Paul | 1 | 1 | 5 | | |
| Batterson, James | 1 | 1 | 1 | | | Elles, Jeremiah | 1 | 1 | 6 | | | Raymond, Edward | 1 | 2 | 3 | | |
| Olmsted, Joseph | 2 | 1 | 4 | | | Lockwood, Jacob | 3 | 5 | 4 | | | Raymond, Gershom | 1 | | 5 | | |
| Webster, Thomas | 1 | 1 | 1 | | | Waring, Solomon | 1 | 2 | 4 | | | Raymond, Gershom, Jr | 1 | 2 | 2 | | |
| Olmsted, Lydia (Wd) | | | 2 | 3 | | Green, Caleb | 1 | 2 | 2 | | | Smith, Noah | 1 | | 2 | | |
| Olmsted, David | 1 | 2 | 1 | | | Slason, Stephen | 1 | 2 | 5 | | | Morehouse, Sarah (Wd) | | | 3 | | |
| Olmsted, Nathan | 2 | 2 | 4 | | | Reynolds, Isaac | 3 | 4 | 4 | | | Abbott, Eunice | | | 1 | | |
| Olmsted, James | 3 | 3 | 3 | | | Bennedict, Thaddeus | 1 | 4 | 1 | | | Abbott, John | 2 | 1 | 2 | | |
| Thomas, Joseph | 1 | 2 | 1 | | | Hoyt, Jonathan | 1 | 2 | 6 | | | Abbott, Aaron | 1 | | 1 | | |
| Scribner, Uriah | 1 | | 4 | | | Raymond, David | 1 | 2 | 3 | | | Acorn, Thomas | 1 | 3 | 3 | | |
| Nichols, Enoch | 1 | | 3 | | | Marvin, Benjamin | 1 | 2 | 3 | | | Green, Daniel | 1 | 2 | 3 | | |
| Jackson, Mary (Wd) | | | 1 | | | Duran, Joseph | 1 | | 4 | | | Betts, Burrell | 2 | 1 | 4 | | |
| Nichols, Jeremiah | 1 | | 4 | | | Seymore, Samuel | 2 | 1 | 4 | | | Odel, Nathaniel | 1 | 2 | 5 | | |
| Russique, Nathan | 1 | | 1 | | | Reed, Benjamin | 1 | 2 | 4 | | | Mead, Abijah | 1 | | 2 | | |
| Batterson, Pawel | 1 | | 2 | | | Burral, Samuel | 4 | 2 | 1 | | 1 | Mead, Mehitable (Wd) | 1 | | 2 | | |
| Stuart, Thaddeus | 1 | 1 | 1 | | | Belding, John | 3 | 1 | 2 | | 2 | Mead, David | 1 | | 2 | | |
| Nash, William | 1 | 2 | 4 | | | Keeler, Isaac | 1 | 3 | 2 | | | Burkout, Peter | 1 | 1 | 2 | | |
| Buttersworth, John | 1 | 1 | 2 | | | Fairweather, Hanford | 1 | 3 | 3 | | | Chapman, Robert | 1 | | 2 | | |
| Smith, Henry | 1 | 2 | 2 | | | Bennedict, Thomas | 2 | | 2 | | 3 | Keeler, Stephen | 1 | 1 | 5 | | |
| Sterling, Thaddeus | 2 | 1 | 6 | | | Grummon, Samuel, Jr | 5 | 2 | 1 | | 1 | Stone, Onely | 1 | 1 | 5 | | |
| Elies, John | 1 | 3 | 2 | | | Lockwood, John | 1 | 1 | 3 | | | Nash, Edward | 1 | | 1 | | |
| Hanford, Theophilus | 2 | | 1 | | | Kellagg, John | 1 | | 3 | | | Tuttle, Nathan | 1 | 1 | 1 | | |
| Selleck, Uriah | 1 | | 2 | | | Seymore, Phebe (Wd) | | 2 | 2 | | | Tuttle, Nathan, Jr | 2 | | 1 | | |
| Hanford, Timothy | 1 | 1 | 2 | | | Saunders, John, Senr | 1 | 1 | 1 | 1 | | Greenslit, Titus | 1 | | | | |
| Kellagg, Jonathan | 2 | | 4 | | | Finch, Dan | 1 | | 3 | | | Richard, Abigail (Wd) | | | 5 | | |
| Johnson, Moses | 1 | 3 | 3 | | | Phillips, Ebenezer | 1 | | 3 | | 1 | Richard, Gershom | 1 | 2 | 2 | | |
| Stone, Elizabeth (Wd) | | | 1 | | | White, Peter | 2 | 1 | 2 | | | Waring, Eliakim | 3 | 2 | 1 | | |
| Hoyt, Justice | 2 | 2 | 4 | | | White, Samuel | 2 | 2 | 4 | | | Richards, Nathan | 2 | 3 | 3 | | |
| Hanford, Levi | 2 | 1 | 2 | | | Seymore, Anne (Wd) | | | 2 | | | Richards, Rebecca (Wd) | | 1 | 2 | | |
| Hanford, Mary (wd) | 1 | 1 | 3 | | | Bennedict, Nathaniel | 3 | | 2 | 3 | 3 | Neptune | | | | 5 | |
| Hanford, Eliphalet | 1 | 1 | 1 | | | Seymore, David | 1 | 1 | 2 | | | Price, David | 1 | 1 | 2 | | |
| Hanford, Ebenezer, Junr | 1 | 3 | 2 | | | Seymore, John | 1 | 2 | 2 | | | Nash, Nathan | 3 | 4 | 3 | | 2 |
| Hanford, Ebenezer | 1 | | 1 | | | Seymore, James | 2 | 2 | 6 | | | Tayler, Paul | 1 | 2 | 6 | | |
| Hanford, Samuel | 1 | | | | | Seymore, Rebecca (Wd) | 1 | | 3 | | | Waring, Deborah (Wd) | | | 2 | | |
| Hanford, Moses | 2 | 3 | 5 | | 1 | Renton, James | 1 | | 2 | | | Blackley, Admer | 2 | 2 | 4 | | |
| Hanford, Samuel, Junr | 2 | 2 | 2 | | | Bennedict, Nathaniel, J | 2 | 4 | 4 | | | Tuttle, Jesse | 2 | | 1 | | |
| Hanford, Mary (Wd) | | | 1 | | | Smith, Daniel | 1 | | 6 | | | Arnold, Jacob | 1 | 3 | 1 | | |

# HEADS OF FAMILIES—CONNECTICUT.

## FAIRFIELD COUNTY—Continued.

### NORWALK AND STAMFORD TOWNS—con.

| NAME OF HEAD OF FAMILY. | Free white males of 16 years and upward, including heads of families. | Free white males under 16 years. | Free white females, including heads of families. | All other free persons. | Slaves. |
|---|---|---|---|---|---|
| Parks, James | 1 | 3 | 2 | | |
| Kellagg, Enos | 2 | 1 | 6 | | |
| Kellagg, Stephen | 2 | 3 | 4 | | |
| Kellagg, Epenetus | 2 | 3 | 6 | | |
| Saunders, John | 1 | 2 | 4 | | |
| Fairweather, Thomas | 2 | 1 | 2 | | |
| Kellagg, James | 3 | 3 | 4 | | |
| Bennedict, Thomas, 2nd | 1 | 1 | 3 | | |
| Fitch, John | 3 | 2 | 8 | | |
| Fitch, Theophilus | 1 | 3 | 4 | | |
| Fitch, Bushnel | 1 | | 1 | | |
| Fitch, Stephen | 1 | 3 | 2 | | 1 |
| Smith, Peter | 1 | 1 | 2 | | |
| Elles, Moses C | 2 | 3 | 5 | | |
| Carter, Samuel | 1 | 1 | 1 | | |
| Carter, John | 1 | 1 | 4 | | 1 |
| Warley, Mary (Wd) | | | 3 | | |
| Fitch, Abijah | 2 | | 3 | | |
| Hoyt, John, Junr | 1 | | | | |
| Elles, Jeremiah B | 4 | 2 | 6 | | |
| Selleck, Jacob | 2 | 1 | 5 | | |
| Carter, Ebenezer | 1 | 1 | 1 | | |
| Bennedict, Nehemiah | 1 | | | | |
| Selleck, Thaddeus | 1 | | 1 | | |
| Hoyt, David | 1 | 1 | 3 | | |
| Finch, Seth | 1 | | 2 | | |
| St John, Anna | 1 | 1 | 3 | | |
| Auction, Thomas | 1 | | 3 | | |
| Hoyt, John | 1 | 4 | 6 | | |
| Hoyt, Timothy | 2 | 2 | 8 | | |
| Bennedict, Hezekiah | 2 | 2 | 5 | | |
| Bennedict, James | 2 | 2 | 4 | | |
| Bennedict, Ezra | 1 | 2 | 7 | | |
| Bennedict, James, Jr | 1 | | 1 | | |
| Bennedict, Nehemiah, Jr | 1 | 1 | 2 | | |
| Bennedict, John | 2 | 1 | 4 | | |
| Gildersleeve, Finch | 1 | 1 | 3 | | |
| St John, Caleb | 1 | 1 | 2 | | 2 |
| St John, Hezekiah | 1 | 2 | 9 | | |
| Fitch, Joseph | 1 | 2 | 2 | | |
| Hoyt, Matthew | 1 | 3 | 4 | | |
| Lockwood, James | 2 | 2 | 4 | | |
| Smith, Samuel | 1 | | 3 | | 1 |
| Bennedict, Samuel | 1 | | 4 | | |
| Bennedict, Stephen | 2 | 1 | 3 | | |
| Tuttle, David | 2 | 1 | 1 | | |
| Keeler, David | 1 | | 3 | | |
| Hayes, Eunice (Wd) | 1 | 1 | 2 | | |
| Smith, Phinehas | 2 | 2 | 3 | | |
| Smith, Samuel, Junr | 1 | 4 | 4 | | |
| Ressique, James | 2 | | 1 | | |
| Keeler, Daniel | 1 | 1 | 2 | | |
| Keeler, Isaac | 2 | 1 | 3 | | |
| Comstock, Abijah | 2 | 1 | 2 | | |
| Raymond, Comfort | 1 | | 2 | | |
| Croford, Samuel | 1 | 1 | 4 | | |
| St John, Matthew, Junr | 1 | 1 | 4 | | |
| Hoyt, Thaddeus | 2 | 1 | 2 | | |
| Croford, Ebenezer | 1 | 1 | 4 | | |
| Holly, John | 1 | | | | |
| Betts, Ruth (Wd) | | 2 | | | |
| Richards, James, Junr | 1 | 1 | 4 | | |
| Abbott, Jonathan | 1 | 1 | 3 | | |
| Richards, Edmond | 1 | 2 | 5 | | |
| Richards, Jesse | 1 | 1 | 3 | | |
| Richards, James | 2 | 2 | 5 | | |
| Clinton, Allen | 1 | | 2 | | |
| Hoyt, William | 1 | 4 | 3 | | |
| Deforest, Isaac | 1 | 2 | 3 | | |
| Keeler, Phinehas | 2 | 1 | 3 | | |
| Deforest, Sarah (Wd) | 1 | 2 | 5 | | |
| Keeler, Stephen | 1 | 2 | 7 | | |
| Dunnin, David | 1 | 4 | 3 | | |
| Gregory, Ezra | 2 | 3 | 5 | | |
| Hecock, Ebenezer | 1 | | 5 | | |
| Nichols, Jonathan | 1 | 1 | 2 | | |
| Joseph | 1 | 2 | 6 | | |
| Baxto, Reuben | 1 | 3 | 2 | | |
| Evans, Joseph | 1 | 2 | 4 | | |
| Abbott, Enoch | 1 | 2 | 5 | | |
| Betts, Silas | 1 | | 5 | | |
| Fitch, Seymore | 1 | 2 | 3 | | |
| Raymond, Wm | 2 | 1 | 2 | | |
| Comstock, Thomas | 2 | 2 | 6 | | |
| Arnolds, Isaac | 1 | | 3 | | |
| Arnold, Isaac, Junr | 1 | 1 | 2 | | |
| Croford, Joseph | 1 | 2 | 2 | | |
| Hait, Elijah, Junr | 3 | 1 | 5 | | |
| Birchard, Jemima (Wd) | 2 | | 2 | | |
| Birchard, James | 1 | | 3 | | |
| St John, Benona | 2 | 3 | 3 | | |
| St John, Peter | 3 | 2 | 5 | | |
| St John, Nehemiah | 3 | 1 | 2 | | |
| St John, Stephen, Junr | 1 | 2 | 2 | | |
| St John, Daniel | 4 | | 3 | | |

| NAME OF HEAD OF FAMILY. | Free white males of 16 years and upward, including heads of families. | Free white males under 16 years. | Free white females, including heads of families. | All other free persons. | Slaves. |
|---|---|---|---|---|---|
| Whitney, David | 2 | 1 | 2 | | |
| Comstock, Caleb | 2 | 2 | 3 | | |
| Beers, Ezekiel | 2 | | 2 | | |
| St John, Nehemiah, Jr | 1 | | 6 | | |
| Platt, John | 3 | 2 | 6 | | |
| Comstock, Sarah | 2 | 1 | 4 | | 1 |
| Comstock, David | 1 | 2 | 3 | | 1 |
| Comstock, Abijah, Jr | 2 | 1 | 3 | | |
| St John, Matthias | 2 | 1 | 4 | | |
| Clinton, Joseph | 2 | | 1 | | |
| Hunte, William | 1 | | 1 | | |
| Hodge, Job | 1 | 2 | 2 | | |
| Robertson, Mercy | | | 2 | | |
| Hoyt, Stephen | 1 | 2 | 2 | | |
| St John, Phinehas | 1 | 1 | 3 | | |
| Brown, Jonathan | 1 | 2 | 7 | | |
| Waring, Joseph | 1 | 1 | 3 | | |
| James (Negro) | | | | 5 | 2 |
| Raymond, Jesse | 1 | | 2 | | |
| Hanford, Nehemiah | 3 | 2 | 7 | | |
| Waring, Enoch | 1 | 1 | 5 | | |
| Raymond, Esther (Wd) | | | 1 | | |
| Raymond, Abraham | 1 | | 1 | | |
| Hoyt, Water | 1 | 2 | 1 | | |
| Chitester, Henry | 1 | 1 | 2 | | |
| Chitester, Sarah (Wd) | | | 1 | | |
| Marvin, Majr Ozias | 2 | 4 | 3 | | 1 |
| Wentworth, Edward | 3 | 3 | 5 | | |
| Selleck, James | 4 | 3 | 5 | | 2 |
| Betts, Samuel | 1 | 3 | 1 | | |
| Raymond, Wm | 1 | 1 | 8 | | |
| Hoyt, Daniel | 1 | 2 | 5 | | |
| Gregory, Jabez | 2 | 1 | 1 | | 1 |
| Betts, William M | 1 | 2 | 1 | | |
| Jarvis, William | 1 | | 1 | | |
| Isaacs, Isaac | 1 | 2 | 2 | | 1 |
| Reed, Matthew | 3 | 2 | 4 | | |
| Keeler, Samuel | 1 | 3 | 2 | | |
| Sherman, Taylor | 1 | 2 | 2 | | |
| Hoyt, Gould | 4 | 3 | 2 | | 2 |
| Rogers, Hezekiah | 1 | 1 | 3 | | 1 |
| Rogers, Joseph | 1 | 2 | 2 | 1 | |
| Coneklin, John | 1 | | 2 | | |
| Adams, Aaron | 1 | 3 | | | |
| Adams, Mary (Wd) | 1 | | 2 | | |
| Hanford, Eleazer, Junr | 1 | 2 | 3 | | |
| Taylor, Abijah | 2 | 5 | 1 | 1 | |
| Hollibert, James | 3 | 3 | 2 | | |
| Betts, Jeremiah | 1 | 2 | 2 | | |
| Nash, Aaron | 1 | 1 | 1 | | |
| Burrel, Samuel, Jr | 1 | | 4 | | |
| Ketchum, Isaac | 1 | 2 | 4 | | 1 |
| Finny, Elisha | 1 | 1 | 2 | | |
| Taylor, Marthy (Wd) | 1 | 1 | 5 | | |
| Patrick, Samuel | 1 | 1 | 3 | | |
| Olmsted, Jesse | 1 | | 2 | | |
| Keeler, James | 1 | 2 | 2 | | |
| Rockwell, John | 2 | 3 | 3 | | |
| Keeler, Jeremiah | 1 | | 1 | | |
| Keeler, Aaron | 1 | 1 | 2 | | |
| Keeler, Thaddeus | 1 | 2 | 2 | | |
| Middlebrook, Samuel | 5 | 4 | 4 | | |
| Morehouse, Jared | 1 | | 2 | | |
| Middlebrook, Somers | 1 | 4 | 2 | | |
| Richard, John | 2 | | 1 | | |
| Gregory, Silas | 1 | 1 | 2 | | |
| Gregory, Daniel | 3 | 3 | 3 | | |
| Gregory, Aaron | 2 | 3 | 3 | | |
| Gregory, Ebenezer | 2 | 1 | 2 | | |
| Gregory, Isaiah | 1 | 1 | 6 | | |
| Middlebrook, Jonathan | 1 | 1 | 1 | | |
| Comestock, Nathan | 1 | | 2 | | |
| Comstock, Strong | 2 | 4 | 2 | | |
| Dunning, Aaron | 1 | | 2 | | |
| Dunning, Daniel | 1 | | 1 | | |
| Nichols, Thaddeus | 2 | 1 | 3 | | |
| Deforest, Ebenezer | 1 | | 1 | | |
| Dunning, Moses | 2 | 2 | 2 | | |
| Stuart, Isaac | 1 | 2 | 4 | | |
| Turrell, Nathaniel | 2 | 2 | 3 | | |
| Waistcott, Jeremiah | 3 | | 1 | | |
| Wescott, David | 3 | | 3 | | |
| Gregory, Dolly (Wd) | 1 | 2 | 4 | 1 | |
| Gregory, Moses | 1 | 1 | 2 | | |
| Gregory, Thomas | 2 | | 2 | | |
| Gregory, Jeheel | | 1 | 1 | | |
| Rockwell, Clapp | 2 | 2 | 3 | | |
| Gregory, Nathan | 1 | | 2 | | |
| Gregory, Ebenezer, Junr | 1 | | 2 | | |
| James, Peter | 4 | 2 | 2 | | |
| Breto, Isaac | 1 | | 2 | | |
| Stuard, Sarah | | | 1 | | |
| Betts, Stephen 3d | 1 | | 2 | | |
| Whitlock, Hezekiah | 3 | 2 | 3 | | |
| Keeler, Justice | 2 | 1 | 4 | | |

| NAME OF HEAD OF FAMILY. | Free white males of 16 years and upward, including heads of families. | Free white males under 16 years. | Free white females, including heads of families. | All other free persons. | Slaves. |
|---|---|---|---|---|---|
| Newel, Frances | 1 | 1 | 2 | | |
| Stuart, Sarah (Wd) | | | 1 | | |
| Gregory, Rebecca (Wd) | | | 2 | | |
| Jackson, Hannah | | | 1 | | |
| Buttersby, Wm | 1 | 4 | 3 | | |
| St John, Jesse | 1 | | 1 | | |
| St John, Nathan | 1 | 1 | 2 | | |
| Lockwood, Sarah (Wd) | | 3 | 1 | | |
| Betts, Peter, Junr | 1 | 2 | 1 | | |
| Betts, Samuel | 1 | 1 | 1 | | |
| Marvin, David | 1 | 2 | 3 | | |
| Bennedict, Mary (Wd) | | 1 | | | |
| Keeler, Seth | 2 | | 2 | | |
| Hoyt, Jesse | 1 | | 2 | | |
| Holmes, Isaac | 2 | 3 | 4 | | |
| Selleck, Isaac | 1 | | 2 | | |
| Hyat, Samuel | 1 | 2 | 2 | | |
| Hoyt, Nehemiah | 1 | 2 | 5 | | |
| Keeler, Luke | 1 | 1 | 2 | | |
| Keeler, Aaron | 1 | 3 | 1 | | |
| Betts, Daniel | 1 | 2 | 2 | | |
| Cannon, John | 3 | 1 | 2 | | 1 |
| Thatcher, Josiah, Jur | 1 | 2 | 2 | | |
| St John, Anna (Wd) | 2 | | 2 | | 1 |
| Ritch, John | 1 | 3 | 1 | | |
| Downs, Woolcot | 1 | | 3 | | |
| Bellknapp, Abel | 2 | 4 | 3 | | |
| Jarvis, Henry | 1 | 3 | 3 | | |
| Hanford, Hannah (Wd) | | | 1 | | |
| Bolt, John | 3 | 2 | 2 | | |
| Jennings, Jacob | 2 | 1 | 7 | | |
| Betts, Peter | 3 | 3 | 2 | | |
| Bennedict, Jesse | 2 | 1 | 4 | | |
| Hill, Esther (Wd) | | | 2 | | |
| Hyatt, John | 2 | | 1 | | |
| Lockwood, Martha (Wd) | | 3 | 3 | | |
| Jarvis, Samuel (Comp) | 1 | 1 | 2 | | |
| Whitney, Abraham | 2 | | 3 | | |
| Whitney, Timothy | 1 | 3 | 5 | | |
| Lockwood, Stephen | 3 | 3 | 3 | | |
| Finch, William | 1 | 1 | 2 | | |
| Lockwood, Joseph | 2 | 3 | 3 | | |
| Keeler, Thomas | 2 | 4 | 3 | | |
| Jennings, Seth | 1 | | 2 | | |
| Kellagg, Jarvis | 2 | | 6 | | |
| Gregory, Abijah | 3 | 1 | 3 | | |
| Gregory, Moses | 1 | 1 | 2 | | |
| Hyatt, Abraham | 1 | 3 | 3 | | |
| Hanford, John | 1 | 3 | 6 | | |
| Hanford, Uriah | 1 | 1 | 3 | | |
| Betts, Seth | 2 | 1 | 4 | | |
| Leonard, Timothy | 1 | 1 | 2 | | |
| Lorain, David | 1 | 2 | 2 | | |
| Squeer, Seely | 1 | 6 | 1 | | |
| Griffith, Wm | 2 | | 2 | | |
| Abbott, Stephen | 1 | 1 | 3 | | |
| Wright, Obadiah | 1 | 3 | 7 | | |
| Bennet, Moses | 1 | 5 | 4 | | |
| Dickenson, Deborah (Wd) | | | 3 | | |
| Wright, Dennis | 2 | 1 | 3 | | |
| Nash, Daniel | 2 | 2 | 3 | | 1 |
| Marvin, Barna | 2 | 2 | 3 | | 1 |
| Hanford, Ozias | 2 | | 2 | | |
| Craft, Stephen | 1 | 3 | 5 | | |
| Lockwood, Gershom | 1 | 3 | 4 | | |
| Gorham, Samuel | 1 | 3 | 2 | | |
| Couch, David | 1 | | 4 | | |
| Morehouse, Solomon | 3 | 2 | 3 | | |
| Finch, John | 2 | | 4 | | |
| Cable, Benjamin | 1 | | 1 | | |
| Cable, Gershom | 1 | | 4 | | |
| Taylor, Levi | 3 | 3 | 3 | | |
| Taylor, Gamaliel | 1 | 1 | 3 | | |
| Toby, Samuel | 1 | 2 | 3 | | |
| Scribner, Levi | 1 | 3 | 3 | | |
| Nash, Micajah | 1 | | 1 | | |
| Scribner, Abraham | 2 | 1 | 1 | | |
| Marvin, Ozias, Junr | 1 | 1 | 6 | | |
| Hyatt, Thomas | 1 | | 2 | | |
| Platt, Samuel | 1 | 4 | 2 | | |
| Platt, Jabez | 1 | 1 | 3 | | |
| Platt, Joseph | 1 | 1 | 2 | | |
| Marvin, Stephen | 1 | 1 | 6 | | |
| Scribner, Enoch | 2 | 3 | 8 | | |
| Scribner, Matthew | 1 | 1 | 2 | | |
| Scribner, Thomas | 1 | 1 | 3 | | |
| Tillet, James | 1 | 2 | 3 | | |
| McNab, Alexander | 2 | 2 | 3 | | |
| Cable, Martha (Wd) | | | 2 | | |
| Saunders, Thomas | 1 | | 1 | | |
| Ketchum, Peter | 2 | 1 | 1 | | |
| Beers, Nathan | 3 | | 1 | | |
| Blacksly, Benjamin | 1 | 1 | 1 | | |
| Stuart, Justice | 1 | | 1 | | |

# FIRST CENSUS OF THE UNITED STATES.

## FAIRFIELD COUNTY—Continued.

| NAME OF HEAD OF FAMILY. | Free white males of 16 years and upward, including heads of families. | Free white males under 16 years. | Free white females, including heads of families. | All other free persons. | Slaves. | NAME OF HEAD OF FAMILY. | Free white males of 16 years and upward, including heads of families. | Free white males under 16 years. | Free white females, including heads of families. | All other free persons. | Slaves. | NAME OF HEAD OF FAMILY. | Free white males of 16 years and upward, including heads of families. | Free white males under 16 years. | Free white females, including heads of families. | All other free persons. | Slaves. |
|---|---|---|---|---|---|---|---|---|---|---|---|---|---|---|---|---|---|
| **NORWALK AND STAMFORD TOWNS—con.** | | | | | | **NORWALK AND STAMFORD TOWNS—con.** | | | | | | **NORWALK AND STAMFORD TOWNS—con.** | | | | | |
| Archer, John | 1 | 2 | 4 | | | Tuttle, Peter | 1 | 2 | 5 | | | Peck, Darius | 1 | 1 | 1 | | |
| Smith, John | 2 | | 4 | | | Hanford, Eleazer | 1 | | 2 | | | Dibble, George | 3 | 3 | 9 | | |
| Barnes, John | 2 | | 1 | | | Hanford, Stephen | 2 | 4 | 5 | | | Hart, Joel | 1 | | 1 | | |
| Barnes, John, Junr | 1 | | 2 | | | Adams, Peter | 1 | 1 | 2 | | | Nichols, James | 2 | | 2 | | |
| Nash, John | 3 | 2 | 4 | | | Bennedict, Eli | 1 | | 2 | | | Nichols, Moses | 1 | 1 | 2 | | |
| Patrick, John | 2 | 1 | 3 | | | Wilson, Charles | 1 | | 2 | | | Knapp, Nathan | 2 | 2 | 3 | | |
| Patrick, Noah | 1 | 1 | 2 | | | Webb, Samuel | 1 | 4 | 3 | | | Selleck, Stephen | 1 | 2 | 1 | | |
| Olmsted, Darius | 2 | 3 | 3 | | | DMill, Anthony | 1 | | | | | Smith, Jesse | 1 | 1 | 2 | | |
| Scribner, Ezra | 1 | | 2 | | | DMill, Joseph | 1 | | 1 | | 1 | Smith, Abraham | | | | | |
| Nash, Samuel | 1 | 3 | 4 | | | Maltbie, David | 2 | 1 | 1 | | | Finchly, George | | | 2 | | |
| Olmsted, Nathaniel | 2 | 1 | 2 | | | Hoyt, Samuel, 4th | 1 | 1 | 4 | | | Lockwood, Isaac | 3 | 2 | 5 | | |
| Taylor, John | 1 | 1 | 1 | | | Holly, David | 1 | 1 | 2 | | | Lockwood, Edmond | 3 | 1 | 3 | | |
| Couch, Rachel (Wd) | | | 1 | | | Smith, Ezekiel | 2 | 2 | 4 | | | Silleck, Peter, Junr | 2 | 3 | 2 | | |
| Bennet, Andrew | 1 | | 3 | | | Smith, Martha (Wd) | | | 2 | | | Knapp, James | 3 | | 2 | | |
| Dikeman, John, Jr | 1 | 2 | 1 | | | Judson, John | 3 | 3 | 5 | | | Mead, Reuben, Junr | 1 | 1 | 2 | | |
| Dikeman, Daniel | 1 | 1 | 1 | | | Weed, Smith | 2 | 2 | 5 | | | Mead, Ezra | 1 | | 1 | | |
| Cable, Ebenezer | 1 | 1 | 1 | | | Dibble, Revd Ebenezer | 1 | | 2 | | 2 | Whitney, Daniel | 1 | | 1 | | |
| Sturges, Eliphalet | 1 | 1 | 2 | | | Arnold, Mary (Wd) | | | 5 | | | Palmer, Jeremiah | 1 | 2 | 5 | | |
| Whitlock, Thomas | 1 | 3 | 2 | | | Fifer, Simon | 1 | 1 | 1 | | | Betts, Peter | 1 | 1 | 3 | | |
| Downs, William | 2 | 1 | 3 | | | Webb, Samuel, Jr | 2 | 3 | 3 | | | Lockwood, Daniel | 3 | | 3 | | |
| Sturges, Elias | 1 | 2 | 2 | | | Webb, David | 3 | 1 | 2 | | 1 | Clason, Stephen | 2 | 2 | 2 | | |
| Jezup, Blackledge | 1 | 4 | 5 | 1 | 3 | Davenport, John Junr | 2 | 2 | 7 | | 6 | Clason, Samuel | 1 | 1 | 6 | | |
| Morehouse, David | 1 | 2 | 5 | | | Weed, Eliphalet | 2 | | 2 | | | Clason, Enoch | 1 | | 2 | | |
| Green, William | 1 | 3 | 2 | | | Munday, Sarah | 1 | 1 | 2 | | | Wardwell, Jacob | 2 | 2 | 4 | | |
| Betts, Enoch | 3 | 3 | 4 | | | Hoyt, John, Junr | 3 | 2 | 4 | | | Knapp, Charles | 2 | | 3 | | |
| Jezup, Joseph | 1 | 2 | 2 | | | Davenport, Silas | 4 | 2 | 4 | | | White, Jacob, Junr | 1 | | 2 | | |
| Batterson, Stephen | 1 | 1 | 2 | | | Hutton, Samuel | 5 | | 4 | | | Thomson, John | 1 | 1 | 3 | | |
| Patching, Abigail (Wd) | | | 2 | | | Davenport, James, Esqr | 3 | | 3 | 1 | 10 | Brown, Rebecca, 2d (Wd) | | | 2 | | |
| Hendrick, Nathaniel | 3 | | 1 | | | Weed, Thaddeus | | | 2 | | | Hoyt, Nathaniel | 2 | | 1 | | |
| Bennet, Silas | 1 | | 5 | | | Wedd, Ebenezer, Junr | 2 | 3 | 6 | | | Knapp, James, Jr | 1 | 3 | 2 | | |
| Patching, Daniel | 2 | | 2 | | | Hoyt, William | 2 | 1 | 1 | | | Hait, Samuel, 3d | 1 | 4 | 4 | | |
| Bennet, Ebenezer | 1 | 4 | 5 | | | Ferris, Revd Ebenezer | 1 | 2 | 3 | 1 | | Bell, Abraham | 3 | 1 | 3 | | |
| Bedient, Mordecai | 1 | 2 | 2 | | | Numan, Stephen | 4 | 3 | 4 | | | Dillabrose, Martin | 1 | | 2 | | |
| Gilbert, Benjamin | 2 | 1 | 3 | | | Seymore, Daniel | 2 | 1 | 2 | | | Hait, Joseph, Junr | 1 | 2 | 3 | | |
| Hecock, Thomas | 1 | 1 | 1 | | | Holly, Nathan | 1 | | 1 | | | Weed, Aaron | 5 | | 3 | | |
| Hollibert, John | 3 | 1 | 2 | | | Brown, Enos | 1 | 1 | 1 | | | Weed, James, 3d | 1 | | 2 | | |
| Williams, Jacob | 1 | 2 | 1 | | | Brown, Joseph | 4 | 2 | 3 | | | Webb, William | 1 | 2 | 2 | | |
| Williams, Nathan | 2 | 2 | 2 | | | Wilson, Elizabeth (Wd) | 1 | | 3 | | | Waterbury, Nathaniel | 1 | | 1 | | |
| Hollibert, Daniel | 2 | 2 | 6 | | | Baul, Doctr J | 1 | 2 | 1 | | 1 | Waterbury, Jonathan | 1 | 1 | 4 | | |
| Guyer, Luke | 1 | | 1 | | | Holly, John W | 5 | 2 | 1 | 1 | 1 | Hoit, Mary | | | 1 | | |
| Stuart, John | 2 | 3 | 2 | | | Bishop, Alexander | 3 | 4 | 4 | | | Mather, Noyes | 1 | 3 | 3 | | |
| Hollibert, Stephen | 2 | | 1 | | | Holly, Numan | 1 | 2 | 3 | | | Hoyt, Samuel, 5th | 2 | 2 | 3 | | |
| Bedient, Jesse | 1 | 1 | 1 | | | Bishop, Silas | 3 | 1 | 4 | | | Waring, Thaddeus | 2 | 3 | 4 | | |
| Bedient, John | 1 | 1 | 2 | | | Webb, Epenetus, 3d | 1 | 1 | 1 | | | Weed, John | 2 | 1 | 4 | | |
| Knapp, Epenetus | 1 | 2 | 4 | | | Skelding, John | 2 | 1 | 1 | | | Clock, Jonas | 2 | 2 | 3 | | 1 |
| Morehouse, Samuel | 1 | 2 | 2 | | | Skelding, James | 2 | 2 | 2 | | | Weed, Hezekiah | 1 | 5 | 1 | | |
| Bedient, William | 1 | 4 | 7 | | | Lockwood, Jared | 1 | 2 | 2 | | | Brookes, Anna (Wd) | | | 1 | 1 | 1 |
| Jezup, Blacklege, Junr | 1 | | 3 | | | Wooster, Mary (Wd) | | | 1 | | | Waterbury, David, Jr | 2 | 1 | 4 | | |
| Wright, Henry | 2 | 1 | 1 | | | Smith, Abigail | | | 5 | | | Waterbury, Phinehas | 3 | 4 | 4 | | |
| Hyatt, Stephen | 1 | 1 | 5 | | | Hubbard, Mary (Wd) | | | 1 | | 2 | Waterbury, Jemimah (Wd) | | | 2 | | |
| Fitch, Joseph P | 1 | 1 | 1 | | | Jarvis, Martha (Wd) | 1 | | 2 | | | Bishop, Jonathan | 2 | 1 | 3 | | |
| St John, Capt John | 1 | 5 | 3 | | | Quintard, Isaac | 1 | | 1 | 1 | | Bishop, Samuel | 1 | | 2 | | |
| Olmsted, Samuel | 2 | 2 | 4 | | | Quintard, Peter | 4 | | 3 | | 2 | Smith, Jesse, Junr | 1 | 1 | 4 | | |
| Fitch, Samuel, Junr | 1 | 2 | 2 | | | Jarvis, James | 7 | 2 | 4 | 1 | 2 | Youngs, Abraham | 1 | 1 | 1 | | |
| Stuart, Simeon | 2 | 2 | 3 | | | Webb, Charles, Esqr | 2 | | 2 | | | Weed, Nathan | 1 | 2 | 2 | 1 | 2 |
| Fitch, Samuel | 2 | | 4 | | | Fitch, William | 2 | 2 | 4 | 1 | 2 | Weed, Nathan, Junr | 1 | | 4 | | |
| Fitch, Elijah | 2 | 1 | 3 | | | Nichols, James, Jr | 1 | 2 | 2 | | | Starr, Capt Nathanel | 3 | 3 | 4 | | |
| Hanford, Phineas, Junr | 1 | 3 | 3 | | | Guensey, Ezra | 1 | 1 | 2 | | | Wooster, Ebenezer | 1 | 2 | 1 | | |
| Stuart, Benjamin | 2 | 1 | 1 | | | Hoyt, Hannah (Wd) | | | 2 | | | Lockwood, Charles | 1 | | 1 | | |
| Olmsted, Reuben | 1 | | 1 | | | Gilman, Evans | 1 | 1 | 1 | | | Clock, Martin | 2 | | 4 | | |
| Leemmis, George | 1 | 2 | 2 | | | Avery, Revd John | 1 | 5 | 2 | | | Clock, Martin, Jr | 1 | | 1 | | |
| Murray, Daniel | 1 | 2 | 1 | | | Judson, Joseph | 1 | | 1 | | | Beachgood, John | 2 | 1 | 2 | | |
| Olmsted, Catharine (Wd) | | | 3 | | | Crauford, Thomas | 1 | | 3 | | | Brown, James | 2 | | 2 | | |
| Olmsted, Samuel | 2 | 2 | 5 | | | Jagger, Joannah | | | 1 | | | Hait, Josiah | 2 | 1 | 2 | | |
| Olmsted, James | 1 | | 2 | | | Mills, Alexander | 1 | 1 | 1 | | | Mather, Joseph | 1 | 2 | 5 | | |
| Fitch, William | 2 | 3 | 1 | | | Mills, George | 1 | | 1 | | | Mentor, Thomas | 1 | 1 | 2 | | |
| Patrick, Ellen (Wd) | | | 1 | | | Lockwood, Eliphalet | 1 | | 1 | | | Waring, Nathan | 1 | | 4 | | |
| Stuart, Ephraim | 1 | 1 | 3 | | | Webb, Elizabeth, Jr (Wd) | | | 2 | | | Waring, Elizabeth (Wd) | | | 3 | | |
| Finch, Ichabod | 1 | 3 | 2 | | | Toun, William | 1 | | 3 | | | Dixson, John | 1 | 1 | 4 | | |
| Patrick, Asa | 1 | | 2 | | | Hecock, Samuel | 1 | 4 | 2 | | | Webb, Epenetus, Junr | 2 | 1 | 2 | | |
| Waterbury, Cloe (Wd) | | 2 | 3 | | | Smith, Peter | 1 | 1 | 1 | | | Marshall, Polly | 1 | | 1 | | |
| Waterbury, Thaddeus | 1 | | 3 | | | Dascomb, Wm | 1 | 2 | 3 | | | Waterbury, Janus | 1 | 3 | 3 | | |
| Olmsted, James, 2d | 1 | | 1 | | | Webb, Jared | 1 | 1 | 1 | | | Holly, Martha (Wd) | | | 2 | | |
| Phillo, James | 1 | 1 | 5 | | | Guernsey, Zacheus | 1 | | 1 | | | Bunnel, Hannah | | | 2 | | |
| Olmsted, Phebe (Wd) | | 1 | 4 | | | Scofield, Nathaniel | 1 | | 1 | | | Waterbury, John 4th | 2 | | 1 | | 1 |
| Phillo, Benjamin | 2 | 2 | 2 | | | Smith, Ethan | 1 | 2 | 3 | | | Kenworthy, Thomas | 1 | | 1 | | |
| Tuttle, Edmond | 1 | 1 | 2 | | | Jones, Benjamin | 1 | | | | | Waterbury, Elizabeth | | | 1 | | |
| Lockwood, Daniel | 1 | 1 | 2 | | | Jones, Capt Ebenezer | 1 | 2 | 4 | | | Webb, Sarah (Wd) | | | 2 | | |
| Hanford, Levi | 1 | | 2 | | | Webb, Epenetus | 2 | 1 | 3 | | | Bishop, Abijah | 1 | 2 | 4 | | |
| Carver, Melzer | 1 | 4 | 3 | | | Webb, Elizabeth (Wd) | | | 4 | | | Knapp, Daniel | 1 | 1 | 2 | | |
| Gregory, Josiah | 2 | | 2 | | | Smith, Ezra | 3 | 1 | 1 | | | Whitney, Daniel, Junr | 1 | 3 | 3 | | |
| Taylor, Jonathan | 2 | | 3 | | | Smith, Martha (Wd) | | | 2 | | | Whitney, Jonathan | 4 | 3 | 4 | | |
| Burrell, Sarah | | | 1 | | | Whitney, Justice | 1 | 2 | 1 | | | Scofield, Elisha | 1 | 1 | 4 | | |
| Mills, John | 4 | | 2 | | | Jones, Lewis | 1 | 1 | 1 | | | Green, Abraham | 1 | | 2 | | |
| Finch, John, Junr | 1 | 1 | 2 | | | Webb, Seth | 1 | | 1 | | | Green, Mercy (Wd) | | | 3 | | |
| Beers, James | 1 | 3 | 2 | | | Webb, Ebenezer, Jr | | 2 | 2 | | | Scofield, James | 4 | 2 | 2 | | |
| Morehouse, Michael | 1 | 1 | 2 | | | Knapp, Silvanus | 2 | 2 | 4 | | | Green, Amos | 1 | | 1 | | |
| Morehouse, Stephen | 1 | | 2 | | | Selleck, Peter | 2 | 1 | 1 | | | Smith, Samuel | 1 | | 1 | | |
| Smith, Eunice (Wd) | 2 | 2 | 4 | | | Smith, Mary (Wd) | 1 | 1 | 2 | | | Smith, Martha (Wd) | 2 | 3 | 4 | | |
| Sturges, Daniel | 1 | 2 | 3 | | | Lockwood, Jacob | 2 | | 1 | | | Smith, John | 1 | 3 | 4 | | |
| Gillet, William | 2 | 4 | 3 | | | Hobby, Henry | 1 | 4 | 4 | | | Fountain, Moses | 1 | | 1 | | |
| Beers, Elnathan | 1 | 1 | 2 | | | Finch, Ezekiel | 1 | 4 | 7 | | | Bates, Nehemiah | 1 | | 3 | | |
| Smith, Joseph | 1 | | 3 | | | Brush, Benjamin | 2 | 2 | 2 | | | Clason, Solomon | 1 | 1 | 1 | | |
| Chapman, Doctr Joseph | 3 | 2 | 7 | | 1 | Banks, Samuel | 2 | | 2 | | | Smith, Whitman | 1 | | | | |

# HEADS OF FAMILIES—CONNECTICUT.

## FAIRFIELD COUNTY—Continued.

| NAME OF HEAD OF FAMILY. | Free white males of 16 years and upward, including heads of families. | Free white males under 16 years. | Free white females, including heads of families. | All other free persons. | Slaves. |
|---|---|---|---|---|---|
| **NORWALK AND STAMFORD TOWNS—con.** | | | | | |
| Clason, Seth | 1 | | 1 | | |
| Smith, Jabez | 1 | 3 | 4 | | |
| Weed, Mercy (W d) | | | 4 | | |
| Nichols, Daniel, Jun r | 1 | 2 | 2 | | |
| Lounsbury, Monmouth | 2 | 1 | 9 | | |
| Smith, Solomon | 1 | | 2 | | |
| June, Nathanel | 1 | 3 | 4 | | |
| Davis, Abraham | 1 | 1 | 3 | | |
| Reynolds, Richardson | 1 | | 1 | | |
| Lockwood, Jonathan | 1 | | 1 | | |
| Lockwood, Jonathan, Jr | 1 | 2 | 2 | | |
| Austin, Isaiah | 1 | 2 | 1 | | |
| Smith, Joshua | 1 | | 2 | | |
| Smith, Mary (W d) | | 1 | 4 | | |
| Longwell, Stephen | 1 | 1 | 3 | | |
| Stevens, James | 1 | 3 | 1 | | |
| Austin, Samuel | 1 | | 2 | | |
| Shelp, Joseph | 2 | | 1 | | |
| Smith, Charles | 4 | | 2 | | |
| Hoyt, Ruth (W d) | | | 2 | | |
| Knapp, Samuel | 2 | 1 | 5 | | |
| Comestock, Elizabeth (W d) | | 2 | 1 | | |
| Hait, Jesse | 1 | 1 | 2 | | |
| Hait, Jonathan, 3 d | 1 | 1 | 1 | | |
| Hait, Jonathan, Jr | 2 | | 3 | | |
| Mitchel, David | 1 | 1 | 2 | | |
| Numan, Benjamin | 3 | | 3 | | |
| Hait, Seth | 1 | | 2 | | |
| Wheaton, Samuel | 1 | 3 | 3 | | |
| Numan, Israel | 1 | 1 | 5 | | |
| Numan, Clark | 1 | | 1 | | |
| Gale, W m | 2 | 2 | 2 | | |
| Numan, Samuel | 1 | | 2 | | |
| Numan, Nathaniel | 2 | 1 | 1 | | |
| Carrigal, Henry | 1 | 2 | 3 | | |
| Dunn, Reuben | 1 | 3 | 4 | | |
| June, Silas | 1 | 1 | 5 | | |
| Smith, John, Jun r | 1 | 2 | 1 | | |
| Smith, Eben | 1 | | 2 | | |
| Smith, Molly (W d) | 3 | | 2 | | |
| Smith, Stephen | 2 | 1 | 7 | | |
| Briggs, Ezra | 1 | 1 | 2 | | |
| Briggs, Hannah (W d) | | | 2 | | |
| Lockwood, Thaddeus | 2 | 1 | 1 | | |
| Briggs Hannah, Jr (W d) | | 1 | 2 | | |
| Smith, Nathanel | 2 | | 4 | | |
| Smith, Daniel | 2 | 1 | 3 | | |
| Briggs, Caleb | 1 | 4 | 4 | | |
| June, Ezra | 2 | | 4 | | |
| June, Thomas | 2 | | 2 | | |
| Briggs, Stephen | 2 | 2 | 3 | | |
| Ferris, Jonah | 2 | 1 | 4 | | |
| Smith, Isaac | 1 | 3 | 4 | | |
| Smith, Hannah (W d) | | | 1 | | |
| Smith, David, 3 d | 3 | | 3 | | |
| June, Abner | 2 | | 5 | | |
| Gale, Isaac | 1 | 3 | 3 | | |
| Numan, David | 1 | 1 | 1 | | |
| Numan, Nehemiah | 1 | | 2 | | |
| Smith, Nehemiah | 2 | 1 | 8 | | |
| Smith, David, Jun r | 1 | 1 | 1 | | |
| Smith, Nath el, Jun r | 2 | 2 | 3 | | |
| Hoyt, Frederick | 1 | 1 | 4 | | |
| Hoyt, David | 1 | 1 | 3 | | |
| Todd, John | 5 | | 1 | | |
| Sibley, Richard | 1 | 1 | 2 | | |
| Numan, Ezra | 2 | | 2 | | |
| Waring, Hezron | 1 | 2 | 2 | | |
| Scofield, James, Jun r | 1 | 3 | 2 | | |
| Whelpley, Amos | 1 | | 2 | | |
| Tredwell, Samuel | 1 | 1 | 2 | | |
| Smith, Amos | 2 | 1 | 4 | | |
| Mills, Nath el | 1 | | 2 | | |
| Ingersol, Elizabeth (W d) | | | 2 | 4 | |
| Stuard, Aaron | 1 | 2 | 2 | | |
| Lockwood, Gershom | 1 | 3 | 1 | | |
| Waring, Linas | 1 | | 2 | | |
| Rockwell, Stephen | 1 | | 2 | | |
| White, Jacob | 1 | | 1 | | |
| White, William | 1 | 3 | 3 | | |
| Waring, Jonathan | 2 | 1 | 2 | | |
| Waring, Jesse | 1 | 4 | 5 | | |
| Waring, Joseph | 2 | | 7 | | |
| Waring, Noah | 1 | | 4 | | |
| Holly, Stephen, Jr | 1 | 1 | 3 | | |
| Lounsbury, Jacob | 1 | 4 | 3 | | |
| Webb, Benjamin | 1 | | 2 | | |
| Webb, Nathaniel, jr | 1 | | 5 | | |
| Scofield, Billy | 1 | 3 | 2 | | |
| Holly, Abraham | 2 | 1 | 5 | | |
| Holly, Stephen | 2 | 3 | 3 | | |
| Webb, Ebenezer | 1 | 2 | 6 | | |
| June, Abisha | | 1 | 2 | | |
| Youngs, Clemence | 1 | | 3 | | |
| Youngs, Benjamin | 1 | 4 | 3 | | |
| Lounsbury, David | 2 | 1 | 3 | | |
| Sherwood, Mathew | 2 | | 3 | | |
| Waters, Jacob | 1 | 2 | 1 | | |
| Austin, Charles | 1 | 2 | 3 | | |
| Lounsbury, Nath el, Jr | 1 | 3 | 3 | | |
| Lounsbury, Nath el | 1 | | 1 | | |
| Galer, Reuben | 1 | 2 | 3 | | |
| June, William | 2 | 3 | 3 | | |
| Ferris, Ransford A | 2 | 2 | 5 | | |
| June, Israel, Jr | 2 | 3 | 2 | | |
| Lounsbury, Michael | 1 | 4 | 4 | | |
| Smith, David | 3 | 1 | 3 | | |
| June, Joshua | 1 | 2 | 3 | | |
| Nichols, Robert | 3 | 1 | 3 | | |
| Smith, Joseph | 3 | | 4 | | |
| Smith, Josiah | 2 | | 3 | | |
| Smith, Gould | 1 | 4 | 4 | | |
| Scofield, Nath el, Jun r | 1 | 1 | 3 | | |
| Mead, Reuben | 2 | | 6 | | |
| Weeks, Henry | 1 | 3 | 3 | | |
| Knapp, Peter | 1 | 3 | 5 | | |
| Knapp, Jacob | 1 | 1 | 3 | | |
| Hoyt, Thaddeus | 4 | 2 | 6 | | |
| Wix, Bartholomew | 3 | | 3 | | |
| Knapp, Nathaniel | 2 | | 2 | | |
| Blanchard, Jacob | 1 | 4 | 2 | | |
| Smith, Austin | 1 | | 2 | | |
| Smith, Austin, Jun r | 2 | 3 | 3 | | |
| Scofield, Abraham, Jr | 1 | 2 | 2 | | |
| Webb, Nathaniel 3 d | 1 | 2 | 3 | | |
| Webb, Nath el | 1 | 1 | 2 | | |
| Webb, Elisha | 1 | 2 | 3 | | |
| Donald, Lewis M | 3 | | 2 | | |
| Lockwood, Nathaniel | 1 | | 2 | | |
| Waterbury, David | 2 | | 3 | | |
| Hoyt, Silas | 3 | 2 | 5 | | |
| Hoyt, Josep, 3 d | 1 | 1 | 2 | | |
| Wilson, Mary (W d) | | | 3 | | |
| Brown, Mercy | | | 2 | | |
| Scofield, Gideon | 2 | | 1 | | |
| Scofield, Israel | 1 | | 3 | | |
| Knapp, Usial | 1 | 1 | 1 | | |
| Blanchard, William | 2 | | 2 | | |
| Hait, Isaac | 2 | 1 | 3 | | |
| Ambler, Jacob | 1 | 3 | 1 | | |
| Scofield, Jonas | 1 | | 3 | | |
| Waterbury, Enos | 2 | 1 | 4 | | |
| Lewis, Jonathan | 1 | 1 | 4 | | |
| Scofield, James, 3 d | 1 | | 2 | | |
| Ambler, Joshua | 1 | | 1 | | |
| Weed, Ebenezer P | 1 | 3 | 3 | | |
| S t John, Hannah (W d) | 2 | | 3 | | |
| Weed, Peter | 1 | | 4 | | |
| Ingersol, Mary (W d) | | | 3 | | |
| Smith, Gabriel | 1 | 2 | 4 | | |
| Lounsbury, Gideon | 2 | | 2 | | |
| Knapp, John | 1 | 1 | 1 | | |
| Hait, Elijah | 1 | 3 | 3 | | |
| Scofield, Jacob, Jr | 1 | 2 | 2 | | |
| Scofield, Silvanus, Jun r | 2 | 2 | 5 | | |
| Scofield, Epenetus | 1 | 2 | 4 | | |
| Pardy, John | 3 | 2 | 4 | | |
| Scofield, Daniel | 1 | 2 | 2 | | |
| Scofield, Nathan | 2 | 2 | 5 | | |
| Weed, Enos | 2 | | 3 | | |
| Mead, Eber | 1 | 1 | 2 | | |
| Scofield, Samuel, Jr | 2 | | 2 | | |
| Dogharty, Andrew | 1 | | 3 | | |
| Lockwood, Titus | 1 | 4 | 2 | | |
| Knapp, William | 1 | 2 | 5 | | |
| Scofield, Jonathan H | 1 | 1 | 2 | | |
| Buxton, James | 3 | 4 | 5 | | |
| Buxton, Samuel | 1 | 2 | 3 | | |
| Lounsbury, Enos | 1 | 3 | 1 | | |
| Lounsbury, Nathan | 1 | | 2 | | |
| Ambler, Joseph | 2 | 1 | 2 | | |
| Scofield, John | 1 | 5 | 3 | | |
| Lockwood, Elizabeth (W d) | | | 2 | | |
| Lockwood, Josiah | 1 | 1 | 1 | | |
| Lockwood, Hannah (W d) | | 1 | 1 | | |
| Hawley, Elijah | | | 3 | | |
| Jones, Ebenezer, Jun r | 1 | | 1 | | |
| Lockwood, Freelove (W d) | | | 2 | | |
| Weed, Miles | 3 | | 3 | | |
| Mead, Sarah (W d) | | | 2 | | |
| Lockwood, Reuben | 1 | 3 | 5 | | |
| Dibble, Solomon | 1 | | 5 | | |
| Buxton, John | 2 | 1 | 2 | | |
| Buxton, Peter | 1 | 2 | 1 | | |
| Lounsbury, Elijah | 1 | 1 | 1 | | |
| Lounsbury, John | 2 | 1 | 3 | | |
| Dean, Ebenezer | 2 | | 2 | | |
| Weed, Jonathan, Jun r | 1 | 1 | 1 | | |
| Buxton, Mercy (W d) | | | 3 | | |
| Ayres, Bradley | 1 | 1 | 4 | | |
| Scofield, Abraham | 3 | 1 | 6 | | |
| Dan, Squire | 2 | 2 | 5 | | |
| Scofield, Silvanus | 1 | | 1 | | |
| Scofield, Sarah (W d) | 1 | 1 | 3 | | |
| Scofield, Josiah | 2 | | 1 | | |
| Scofield, Weed | 1 | 1 | 2 | | |
| Weed, Asahel | 1 | 1 | 4 | | |
| Lockwood, David, Jun r | 1 | | 7 | | |
| Scofield, Seth | 1 | 3 | 2 | | |
| Scofield, Seeley | 1 | 2 | 1 | | |
| Weed, Samuel | 1 | | 4 | | |
| Curtis, Jeremiah | 2 | 2 | 3 | | |
| Deal, George | 1 | | 1 | | |
| Lounsbury, James | 1 | 2 | 2 | | |
| Scofield, Josiah W | 1 | | 2 | | |
| Seely, John | 1 | | 3 | | |
| Seely, Obadiah | 1 | 2 | 3 | | |
| June, Israel | 1 | 2 | 3 | | |
| Jones, Enos | 1 | | 1 | | |
| Defres, Reuben | 1 | 1 | 6 | | |
| June, Joel | 1 | 2 | 1 | | |
| Jones, Josiah | 1 | 2 | 4 | | |
| Reynolds, Peroz | 1 | 1 | 2 | | |
| Hait, Jonas | 4 | 1 | 3 | | |
| Hoyt, Epenetus | 1 | | 1 | | |
| Hoyt, Joseph, 4 th | 1 | | 1 | | |
| Holt, Nezer | 1 | 1 | 3 | | |
| Hoit, Deodate | 1 | 2 | 1 | | |
| Weed, Amos, Jun r | 1 | 1 | 4 | | |
| Weed, Amos | 1 | | 1 | | |
| Weed, Benjamin, Jr | 1 | | 5 | | |
| Weed, Jesse | 1 | | 4 | | |
| Weed, Israel | 2 | 1 | 5 | | |
| Weed, Israel, Jun r | 2 | 2 | 4 | | |
| Weed, Ananias | 1 | 3 | 3 | | |
| Shepherd, Rev d John | 1 | 2 | 4 | | 1 |
| Bishop, Stephen | 1 | | 1 | | |
| Bishop, Stephen, Jun r | 1 | 2 | 2 | | |
| Weed, Jonathan | 2 | 2 | 4 | | |
| Weed, Seth, Jun r | 2 | | 5 | | |
| Husted, Thaddeus | 2 | 2 | 4 | | |
| Husted, Zebulon | 1 | | 2 | | |
| Weed, Jabez | 1 | 3 | 6 | | |
| Weed, Gideon | 1 | | 1 | | |
| Weed, Abisha | 1 | 1 | 2 | | |
| Weed, Benjamin | 1 | 1 | 4 | | |
| Hoyt, James | 1 | 1 | 1 | | |
| Provost, Samuel | 1 | | 1 | | |
| Scofield, Samuel, 3 d | 1 | 1 | 3 | | |
| Laurence, Timothy | 2 | 1 | 5 | | |
| Hoyt, Elizabeth (W d) | 1 | | 2 | | |
| Jones, Ephraim | 1 | 1 | 4 | | |
| Davenport, John | 4 | 2 | 6 | | |
| Scofield, Nezer | 1 | 6 | 4 | | |
| Hoyt, Jesse, Jun r | 1 | 1 | 2 | | |
| Scofield, Samuel | 2 | 2 | 1 | | |
| Scofield, David | 1 | 1 | 1 | | |
| Curtis, Rebecca (W d) | | | 3 | | |
| Scofield, Reuben | 3 | 3 | 3 | | |
| Scofield, Peter | 2 | 1 | 4 | | |
| Scofield, Jacob | 1 | 1 | 4 | | |
| Scofield, Stephen | 1 | | 4 | | |
| Scofield, Benjamin | 2 | 5 | 3 | | |
| Scofield, Joseph, Jun r | 2 | 1 | 5 | | |
| Scofield, Warren | 1 | 1 | 2 | | |
| Scofield, Josiah | 1 | | 1 | | |
| Scofield, Thaddeus | 1 | 1 | 2 | | |
| Ayres, John | 1 | | 2 | | |
| Scofield, Edward | 1 | 1 | 2 | | |
| Slason, Thomas | 1 | 3 | 4 | | |
| Ferris, James | 1 | 3 | 2 | | |
| Scofield, Uriah | 1 | 3 | 2 | | |
| Brown, Nath el | 2 | | 2 | | |
| Scofield, Elias | 1 | | 2 | | |
| Hoyt, Josiah | 1 | | 2 | | |
| Finch, Hannah (W d) | | | 3 | | |
| Lockwood, Abigail (W d) | | | 3 | | |
| Wilmoth, Zopher | 1 | 1 | 2 | | |
| Holly, Francis | 2 | | 5 | | |
| Curtis, Timothy | 1 | | 2 | | |
| Curtis, Jonathan | 1 | | 2 | | |
| Bell, Noah | 2 | 3 | 4 | | |
| Bell, Stephen | 1 | 2 | 2 | | |
| Chapman, William E | 2 | 2 | 6 | | |
| Finch, Nathaniel | 2 | 1 | 5 | | |
| Bell, Joannah (W d) | | | 1 | | |
| Bush, Samuel | | | | 4 | |
| Jezup, Samuel | 1 | 4 | 4 | | |
| Jeffery, Samuel | 1 | 1 | 4 | | |
| Tryon, Samuel | 1 | 4 | 4 | | |

# FIRST CENSUS OF THE UNITED STATES.

## FAIRFIELD COUNTY—Continued.

### NORWALK AND STAMFORD TOWNS—con.

| NAME OF HEAD OF FAMILY. | Free white males of 16 years and upward, including heads of families. | Free white males under 16 years. | Free white females, including heads of families. | All other free persons. | Slaves. |
|---|---|---|---|---|---|
| Hait, Nathan | 1 | | 4 | | |
| Hait, Peter | 4 | | 3 | | |
| Hait, David | 1 | 2 | 4 | | |
| Hoyt, John | 3 | 1 | 2 | | |
| Scofield, Hait | 1 | 2 | 2 | | |
| Holly, Increas | 2 | | 4 | | |
| Holly, Enoch | 1 | | 2 | | |
| Hull, Esther (W d) | | 1 | 1 | | |
| Scofield, Jacob, 3d | 1 | 1 | 2 | | |
| Holly, John | 1 | | 5 | | |
| Holly, John, Junr | 1 | | 2 | | |
| Crissy, Jesse | 1 | 1 | 1 | | |
| Hait, Uriah | 1 | 1 | 5 | | |
| Hait, Samuel, Junr | 1 | | 2 | | |
| Hoyt, Joseph | 1 | 2 | 3 | | |
| Hoyt, Warren | 1 | | 1 | | |
| Crissy, Abraham | 1 | | 2 | | |
| Crissy, Nathaniel | 1 | | 2 | | |
| Crissy, William | 1 | 2 | 4 | | |
| Crissy, Samuel | 1 | | 3 | | |
| Crissy, Mary (W d) | 1 | 1 | 3 | | |
| Seely, Abijah | 2 | 1 | 5 | | |
| Seely, Abijah, Junr | 1 | | 1 | | |
| Leeds, Gideon | 1 | 1 | 3 | | |
| Seely, Samuel | 1 | 1 | 3 | | |
| Stevens, David | 1 | 1 | 2 | | |
| Seymore, Jared | 2 | 1 | 2 | | |
| Finch, Titus | 2 | 2 | 3 | | |
| Bishop, Peter | 1 | 2 | 3 | | |
| Weed, Wm | 3 | 2 | 2 | | |
| Davenport, Deodate | 3 | | 9 | | |
| Davenport, Deodate | 1 | 1 | 1 | | |
| Ayres, Jonathan | 1 | 5 | 5 | | |
| Nichols, Daniel | 1 | | 3 | | |
| Young, Robert | 1 | 2 | 2 | 1 | |
| Webb, David, Junr | 1 | 3 | 1 | | |
| Young, Samuel | 1 | 3 | 2 | | |
| Stevens, Henry | 1 | 1 | 3 | | |
| Weed, Ezra | 1 | 2 | 4 | | |
| Jones, Samuel | 1 | 1 | 2 | | |
| Stevens, Jonathan | 1 | 2 | 5 | | |
| Weed, Ebenezer | 2 | | 2 | | |
| Hunt, John | 3 | | 3 | | |
| Brown, Abigail (W d) | | 1 | 2 | | |
| Knapp, Hezekiah | 2 | 2 | 4 | | |
| Hoyt, Jacob | 1 | 1 | 1 | | |
| Hoyt, John, 3d | 1 | | 1 | | |
| Brown, Isaac | 1 | 1 | 5 | | 2 |
| Brown, Jonathan | 1 | | 2 | | |
| Tryon, Benjamin | 2 | 3 | 3 | | |
| Grey, Joseph | 1 | 1 | 5 | | |
| Smith, Reuben | 2 | 1 | 3 | | |
| Waters, Elisha | 1 | 1 | 1 | | |
| Leeds, Carey | 1 | 1 | 3 | | |
| Scofield, Gilbert | 1 | | 3 | | |
| Crissy, Nathel, Jur | 1 | 2 | 2 | | |
| Young, Mary (W d) | | | 2 | | |
| Chittester, Abraham | 2 | | 1 | | |
| Waring, Martha (W d) | | 1 | 1 | | |
| Chittester, Nathan | 1 | | 2 | | |
| Stevens, Hannah (W d) | | | 3 | | |
| Meaker, David | 1 | | 1 | | |
| Stevens, Solomon | 1 | 2 | 4 | | |
| Wilkes, Augustus | 1 | | 1 | | |
| Stevens, Abner | 3 | | 2 | | |
| Allen, John | 1 | 1 | 2 | | |
| Slason, Israel | 1 | | 6 | | |
| Slason, David | 1 | 2 | 4 | | |
| Slason, Jonathan, Junr | 1 | 2 | 1 | | |
| Stevens, Reuben | 2 | 2 | 4 | | |
| Stevens, Daniel | 1 | | 1 | | |
| Slason, Jonathan | 2 | 2 | 4 | | |
| Jones, Thomas | 1 | 2 | 2 | | |
| Jones, Samuel, Junr | 1 | 1 | 1 | | |
| Stevens, Abraham | 1 | 4 | 4 | | |
| Stevens, Amos | 3 | 6 | 2 | | |
| Stevens, John | 2 | | 3 | | |
| Brister, Soloman | 1 | 2 | 3 | | |
| Jones, Reuben | 1 | 2 | 4 | | |
| Lockwood, David | 1 | 3 | 2 | | |
| Waters, John | 1 | 1 | 2 | | |
| Stevens, Jacob | 2 | 4 | 3 | | |
| Stevens, Amos, Junr | 1 | 1 | 1 | | |
| Raymond, Luke | 3 | 1 | 4 | | |
| Stevens, Seth | 1 | | 1 | | |
| Stevens, Isaac | 1 | 1 | 2 | | |
| Scofield, Selleck | 1 | | 1 | | |
| Howard, Sarah | | 1 | 3 | | |
| Dan, Nathaniel | 1 | | | | |
| Hoyt, Waterbury | 1 | | 1 | | |
| Dan, Nathan | 1 | 3 | 2 | | |
| Weed, Jonas, 3d | 1 | 4 | 2 | | |
| Howes, Noah | 1 | 3 | 1 | | |
| Raymond, Lemuel | 1 | 2 | 1 | | |
| Bebee, Lydia (W d) | | | 4 | | |
| Chittester, David | 1 | 3 | 2 | | |
| Penoyre, Martha (W d) | 3 | 1 | 1 | | |
| Penayre, Amos | 2 | 1 | 3 | | |
| Howes, Prince, Junr | 2 | | 3 | | |
| Reed, Timothy | 3 | 3 | 5 | | |
| Penoyre, Gould S | 2 | 3 | 7 | | |
| Coggswell, Dunlap | 2 | 5 | 2 | | |
| Howes, Prince | 1 | | 1 | | |
| Lockwood, Elnathan | 1 | 1 | 4 | | |
| Bishop, Parsons | 1 | | 3 | | |
| Weed, Charles | 3 | 1 | 3 | | |
| Weed, Abraham | 1 | | 2 | | |
| Comestock, Enoch | 2 | 2 | 4 | | |
| Weed, Peter | 1 | 2 | 6 | | |
| Weed, Enos | 1 | | 1 | | |
| Weed, Daniel | 1 | 1 | 2 | | |
| Weed, James | 1 | 1 | 4 | | |
| Weed, Josiah | 2 | 1 | 5 | | |
| Weed, Jonathan, 3d | 1 | | 1 | | |
| Weed, Hannah | | | 2 | | |
| Weed, Seth | 2 | | 2 | | |
| Boutain, Daniel | 2 | 4 | 2 | | |
| Tucker, Isaac | 1 | 1 | 2 | | |
| Peter (Negro) | | | | 4 | |
| Stevens, Joseph | 3 | 3 | 2 | | |
| Stevens, Joseph, Jr | 1 | 1 | 2 | | |
| Talmage, Seymore | 1 | 5 | 2 | | |
| Talmage, James | 1 | | 1 | | |
| Talmage, Jonathan | 1 | 2 | 2 | | |
| Talmage, Bethiah (W d) | | | 3 | | |
| Smith, Joseph, Junr | 2 | 1 | 8 | | |
| Wright, Dennis | 1 | 2 | 3 | | |
| Jarvis, Catharine | | | 4 | | |
| Jones, Asa | 1 | | 4 | | |
| Weed, Stephen | 1 | 2 | 2 | | |
| Stevens, Obadiah | 3 | 3 | 4 | | |
| Stevens, Sarah (W d) | | 1 | 5 | | |
| Stevens, Admer | 1 | 1 | 1 | | |
| Weed, Joel | 1 | 5 | 1 | | |
| Hoyt, Nathaniel, Junr | 3 | 1 | 4 | | |
| Waterbury, Nathaniel | 2 | 1 | 2 | | |
| Hoyt, Jonathan | 3 | 1 | 2 | | |
| Hoyt, Samuel | 1 | 1 | | | |
| Hoyt, Hanford | 2 | | 4 | | |
| Husted, Jonathan | 2 | 3 | 3 | | |
| Holmes, John | 1 | 1 | 7 | | |
| Waterbury, Wm | 1 | 3 | 3 | | |
| Leeds, Mary (W d) | 3 | | 3 | | |
| Leeds, Abraham | 1 | 2 | 2 | | |
| Leeds, Elizabeth (W d) | 1 | | 1 | | |
| Waterbury, Rebecca (W d) | | | 2 | | |
| Wilmot, Joseph | 1 | 5 | 2 | | |
| Sherwood, Stephen | 2 | | 2 | | |
| Waterbury, Jacob | 1 | | 2 | | |
| Waterbury, Martha (W d) | | | 3 | | |
| Waterbury, John, Junr | 1 | 3 | 6 | | |
| Bates, Gershom | 2 | 3 | 5 | | |
| Brown, Francis | 1 | 1 | 2 | | |
| Waterbury, Thankful (W d) | | | 3 | | |
| Weed, Silvanus | 1 | 1 | 3 | | |
| Packeton, Dennis | 1 | 2 | 1 | | |
| Selleck, Gershom | 1 | 2 | 2 | | |
| Waterbury, John | 2 | | 2 | | |
| Seely, Jonas | 1 | 1 | 1 | | |
| Leeds, Elisha | 2 | | 2 | | |
| Seely, Silvanus | 1 | | 1 | | |
| Seely, Silvanus, Junr | 1 | 4 | 2 | | |
| Bennedict, Caleb | 2 | 4 | 2 | | |
| Seely, Nathan | 1 | 3 | 2 | | |
| Suard, Samuel | 1 | | 2 | | |
| Seely, Eliphalet | 2 | 2 | 2 | | |
| Seely, Joseph | 3 | 5 | 3 | | |
| Seely, Ebenezer | 1 | 4 | 2 | | |
| Bates, John, Junr | 3 | | 4 | | |
| Bates, Charles | 2 | 2 | 4 | | |
| Bates, Mary (W d) | 1 | | 4 | | |
| Weed, Gideon, Junr | 1 | 1 | 1 | | |
| Hait, Frederick, Junr | | | | | |
| Hayt, Ezra | 1 | | 1 | | |
| Weed, James, Jar | 1 | 2 | 1 | | |
| Weed, Henry | 1 | | 1 | | |
| Weed, Mary (W d) | | | 7 | 1 | |
| Brown, Rebecca (W d) | 4 | | 2 | | |
| Slason, Jacob | 3 | 1 | 2 | | |
| Slason, Zepheniah | 2 | 3 | 2 | | |
| Weed, Gideon | 4 | 4 | 5 | | |
| Andres, Jeremiah | 2 | | 4 | | |
| Andres, John | 2 | 2 | 4 | | 1 |
| Bishop, Caty (W d) | | 1 | 2 | | |
| Johnson, Elizabeth | | | 2 | | |
| Wyatt, Sarah (W d) | | 1 | 1 | | |
| Little, Ebenezer | 1 | | 1 | | |
| Waterbury, Ebenezer | 2 | | 4 | | |
| Weed, Deodate | 1 | 2 | 1 | | |
| Weed, Jonas, 4th | 2 | | 4 | | |
| Slason, Abraham | 1 | | 1 | | |
| Weed, Jonas | 1 | | | | |
| Bell, Thaddeus, Jr | 1 | 1 | 4 | | |
| Slason, Gershom | 1 | 2 | 1 | | |
| Slason, Deliverance | 1 | 2 | 1 | | |
| Dibble, Anne (W d) | | | 3 | | |
| Bell, John | 2 | 2 | 3 | | |
| Bell, Jonathan | 2 | 4 | 3 | | |
| Holly, Abraham, Junr | 1 | 3 | 3 | | |
| Waterbury, James | 1 | | 2 | | |
| Weed, Mary, Junr (W d) | 1 | 1 | 2 | | |
| Bell, John, Junr | 1 | | 3 | | |
| Bell, Thaddeus | 2 | 1 | 3 | | |
| Weed, Jonas, Junr | 1 | 3 | 3 | | |
| Howe, Jacob | 2 | 2 | 4 | | |
| Scofield, John, 5th | 1 | | 1 | | |
| Howe, Ebenezer | 1 | | 5 | | |
| Howe, Nathan | 1 | 2 | 1 | | |
| Slason, Charles | 1 | 1 | 2 | | |
| Howe, David | 1 | | 1 | | |
| Howe, Bowers | 1 | 2 | 3 | | |
| Platt, Joseph Y | 1 | 3 | 2 | | |
| Dibble, John | 2 | 1 | 3 | | |
| Shaw, James | 2 | 2 | 3 | | |
| Weed, Sarah (W d) | | | 1 | | |
| Walmsbey, William | 1 | | 3 | | |
| Weed, Benjamin, 3d | 1 | | 4 | | |
| Morehouse, Joshua | 1 | | 2 | | |
| Weed, John, Junr | 1 | 2 | 2 | | |
| Seely, Esther (W d) | | 1 | 2 | | |
| Clock, John | 2 | 1 | 3 | | |
| Clock, Sarah (W d) | | | 3 | | |
| Clock, Comfort (W d) | 1 | | 1 | | |
| Clock, Abraham | 1 | 1 | 3 | | |
| Younges, Samuel | 1 | | 4 | | |
| Clock, Nathaniel | 3 | 1 | 6 | | |
| Gotham, Daniel | 2 | 5 | 2 | 2 | |
| Selleck, Mary (W d) | | | 1 | 1 | 2 |
| Selleck, Samuel | 2 | 1 | 6 | | |
| Penoyre, Isaac | 1 | 6 | 2 | | |
| Penoyre, Samuel | 1 | 1 | 4 | | |
| Fancher, David | 1 | | 3 | | |
| Little, John | 2 | 1 | 2 | | |
| Wilson, John | 1 | 1 | 2 | 1 | 2 |
| Gorham, Hannah (W d) | | | 2 | | |
| Selleck, Simeon | 1 | 1 | 4 | | |
| Roberts, Amos | 1 | 2 | 4 | | |
| Selleck, Nathan | 1 | 1 | 2 | | |
| Seely, Wix | 1 | 2 | 2 | | |
| Selleck, Edward | 1 | 1 | 4 | | |
| Selleck, Daniel | 2 | 1 | 5 | | |
| Lockwood, Daniel, Jr | 2 | 3 | 3 | | |
| Betts, Benjamin | 2 | 3 | 2 | | |
| Selleck, Seymore | 1 | 2 | 3 | | |
| Selleck, Stephen, Jr | 1 | 3 | 3 | | |
| Sudmore, Joseph | 1 | 2 | 3 | | |
| Raymond, Stephen | 2 | 1 | 5 | | |
| Mills, Ezra | 2 | 5 | 1 | | |
| Scofield, Silvanus | 1 | 2 | 2 | | |
| Provost, Thomas | 1 | 1 | 2 | | |
| Petten, Samuel | 3 | 2 | 1 | | |
| Fancher, Silvanus, Jr | 1 | 1 | 1 | | |
| Ambler, Isaac | 2 | | | | |
| Waterbury, Hannah (W d) | 1 | | 1 | | 1 |
| Waring, Samuel | 1 | 1 | 4 | | |
| Waring, Mary (W d) | 1 | | 1 | | |
| Waring, Sally (W d) | | 2 | 4 | | |
| Waterbury, Wm, Jr | 1 | 1 | 2 | | |
| Waring, Silvanus | 2 | | 1 | | |
| Hait, Nathaniel, 3d | 1 | 3 | 2 | | |
| Street, Joseph | 1 | | | | |
| Nich (Negro) | | | | 2 | |
| Jack (Negro) | | | | 3 | |
| Bates, William | 1 | 3 | 1 | | |
| Whitney, Henry | 1 | 1 | 2 | | |
| Whitney, Charles | 1 | 2 | 2 | | |
| Matthias, Bethial (W d) | | | | | |
| Whitney, Eliasaph | 2 | 1 | 3 | | |
| Bates, David | 1 | 1 | 3 | | |
| Bates, Jerom | 1 | 3 | 2 | | |
| Mather, Revd Moses | 2 | | 2 | | |
| Hait, Elizabeth (W d) | | 1 | 1 | | |
| Scofield, Josiah, Junr | 2 | | 5 | | |
| Scofield, Gershom | 1 | 3 | 5 | | |
| Whiting, Samuel | 1 | | 2 | | |
| Scofield, Joseph | 2 | 1 | 3 | | |
| Scofield, Henry | 1 | | 2 | | |
| Howe, Sarah (W d) | | | 2 | | |
| Fancher, Silvanus | 1 | | 3 | | |
| Fancher, David, Junr | 1 | | 1 | | |

# HEADS OF FAMILIES—CONNECTICUT.

## FAIRFIELD COUNTY—Continued.

| NAME OF HEAD OF FAMILY. | Free white males of 16 years and upward, including heads of families. | Free white males under 16 years. | Free white females, including heads of families. | All other free persons. | Slaves. | NAME OF HEAD OF FAMILY. | Free white males of 16 years and upward, including heads of families. | Free white males under 16 years. | Free white females, including heads of families. | All other free persons. | Slaves. | NAME OF HEAD OF FAMILY. | Free white males of 16 years and upward, including heads of families. | Free white males under 16 years. | Free white females, including heads of families. | All other free persons. | Slaves. |
|---|---|---|---|---|---|---|---|---|---|---|---|---|---|---|---|---|---|
| **NORWALK AND STAMFORD TOWNS—con.** | | | | | | **READING TOWN—con.** | | | | | | **READING TOWN—con.** | | | | | |
| Selleck, Jesse | 2 | 1 | 2 | | 2 | Roberts, Philip | | | 4 | | 3 | Starr, David | 2 | 3 | 4 | | |
| Morehouse, Gershom | 1 | | 5 | | | Betts, Stephen | 2 | 1 | 4 | | 3 | Starr, David, Junr | 1 | | 2 | | |
| Knapp, Nathan, Junr | 1 | 1 | 2 | | | Napp, David | 1 | | 3 | | | Sanford, Peter | 2 | | 4 | | |
| Bates, Jonathan | 2 | 2 | 3 | | | Hull, Seth | 5 | | 5 | | | Crowfoot, Uriah | 2 | | 3 | | |
| Bates, John | 2 | 1 | 4 | | | Perry, Elihu | 1 | 2 | 4 | | | Sanford, Eli | 2 | | 2 | | |
| Street, David | 2 | 1 | 3 | | | Whitlock, Ephraim | 1 | 2 | 2 | | | Sanford, Sarah | | | 3 | | |
| Reed, Jonathan | 1 | | 1 | | | Gray, James | 1 | | 4 | | | Sanford, Ezra | 2 | 1 | 3 | | |
| Mather, Samuel | 1 | 1 | 1 | | | Napp, Rebecka | | 1 | 2 | | | Smith, Reubin | 1 | 1 | 4 | | |
| Gray, Daniel | 1 | 1 | 2 | | | Bloidell, Thomas | 1 | 3 | 3 | | | Burr, Elijah | 2 | 1 | 4 | | |
| Bates, James | 1 | | 1 | 1 | | Squire, Seth | 1 | | 3 | | | Coley, Jesse | 1 | 1 | 2 | | |
| Waterbury, Benjamin | 3 | | 3 | | | Devern, John | 1 | | 1 | | | Jackson, David | 2 | 4 | 5 | | |
| Mosier, Rachel (Wd) | | | 2 | | | Crowfoot, Israel | 2 | 3 | 2 | | | Couch, Elijah | 3 | 4 | 3 | | |
| Little, James | 4 | 2 | 3 | | | Beardsley, Jesse | 2 | 1 | 1 | | | Couch, John | 2 | 2 | 3 | | |
| Wardwell, Abigail (Wd) | 1 | | 3 | | | Couch, Simon | 1 | 1 | 2 | 1 | 3 | Burr, Charles | 1 | | 2 | | |
| Waterbury, Deodate | 1 | 1 | 1 | | | Glover, Lemuel | 1 | | 1 | | | Sanford, Elnathan | 1 | | 1 | | |
| Waterbury, Epenetus | 1 | 2 | 2 | | | Drew, John | 2 | 1 | 2 | | | Sebens, Josiah | 1 | 1 | 2 | | |
| Reed, Nathan | 1 | 2 | 3 | | | Whitlock, Justus | 1 | 1 | 1 | | | Burr, Nathan | 1 | 2 | 5 | | |
| Selleck, Wray | 1 | 4 | 4 | | | Whitlock, Nathaniel | 1 | | 2 | | | Olmstord, Grace | 1 | 1 | 5 | | |
| Boutain, Nathan | 1 | 1 | 2 | | | Fiarchild, Andrew | 3 | | 2 | 2 | | Peet, John | 1 | 6 | 2 | | |
| Weed, Mary (Wd) | | | 1 | | | Drew, John | 2 | 6 | 2 | | | Burr, Abel | 1 | | 1 | 1 | |
| Belding, Benjamin | 1 | 2 | 1 | 1 | 2 | Morehouse, John | 1 | 1 | 2 | | | Burr, Seth | 1 | 1 | 1 | | |
| Waterbury, David, 3d | 2 | | 3 | | | MᴿRow, David | 3 | 1 | 3 | | | Hull, Sirenus | 1 | 1 | 2 | | |
| | | | | | | Drew, Isaac | 1 | 3 | 5 | | | Hull, Chapman | 1 | | 1 | 1 | |
| **READING TOWN.** | | | | | | Drew, Peter | 1 | 2 | 2 | | | Lator, Preserv'd | 2 | | 7 | | |
| Dimon, Thomas | 2 | | 1 | | | Judd, Elijah | 1 | 1 | 4 | | | Bennitt, Shubel | 2 | | 3 | | |
| Sanford, Hezekiah | 1 | 2 | 2 | | 1 | Lyon, Lemuel | 1 | 2 | 2 | | | Platt, Isaac | 1 | | 2 | | |
| Gray, John | 3 | | 3 | | | Manchant, Enoch | 1 | | 1 | | | Platt, Philip | 1 | | 2 | | |
| Andrews, Ebenezer | 1 | 1 | 1 | | | Star, Eward | 2 | 1 | 4 | | | Banks, Seth | 2 | | 3 | | |
| Stratton, Stephen | 2 | 5 | 1 | | | Couch, Stephen | 2 | 2 | 4 | | | Laton, Abraham | 1 | 1 | 3 | | |
| Andrews, Sarah | | | 3 | | | Lyon, Grace | | 1 | 4 | | | Burr, Ezekiel | 1 | 2 | 2 | | |
| Andrews, Seth | 1 | 1 | 2 | | | Sanford, Aaron | 2 | 2 | 3 | | 1 | Banks, Thadeus | 2 | 2 | 4 | | |
| Hull, John | 1 | 2 | 2 | | | Bartrum, Paul | 2 | | 3 | | | Sanford, Biah | 1 | 2 | 3 | | |
| Gorham, Isaac | 1 | | 2 | 1 | 7 | Platt, Isaac | 1 | 1 | 4 | | | Burr, Joel | 1 | | 2 | | |
| Gorham, Isaac, Junr | 1 | 1 | 4 | | | Hawley, Joseph | 2 | 2 | 2 | | 1 | Bouton, David | 2 | 1 | 2 | | |
| Thorp, Lyman | 1 | 1 | 1 | | | Hawley, William | 3 | | 1 | 1 | 1 | Couch, Thomas | 1 | 4 | 3 | | |
| Fairchild, Abraham | 2 | | 2 | | | Marchant, Chaney | 2 | 3 | 4 | | | Green, Joseph | 1 | 3 | 2 | | |
| Fairchild, Stephen | 1 | 3 | 1 | | | Marchant, Elenar | 1 | | 3 | | | Gray, Gilead | 1 | 4 | 1 | | |
| Fairchild, Samuel | 1 | | 2 | | | Platt, Jonas | 1 | 1 | 3 | | | Bento, Silus | 2 | 1 | 4 | | |
| Fairchild, John | 1 | 2 | 1 | | | Morehouse, Gershom | 1 | 1 | 3 | | | Coley, Gershom | 2 | 1 | 2 | | |
| Sanford, Oliver | 3 | 3 | 6 | | | Abbet, Thadeus | 2 | | 2 | | | Smith, Lewis | 1 | 1 | 1 | | |
| Morgan, Nathanel | 1 | 2 | 3 | | | Jarvis, Samuel | 1 | 5 | 3 | | 1 | Jackson, Ezekiel | 1 | 2 | 3 | | |
| Godfry, Samuel | 1 | | 1 | | | Rogers, James | 2 | 1 | 6 | | 1 | Parsons, Abijah | 1 | | 4 | | |
| Morgan, Joseph | 1 | 3 | 4 | | | Platt, Jonas, Junr | 1 | 1 | 1 | | | Davis, John | 2 | 1 | 3 | | |
| Banks, Jesse | 2 | | 3 | | | Morehouse, Aaron | 1 | 1 | 3 | | 1 | Hillard, Jacy | 2 | | 3 | | |
| Banks, Jesse, Junr | 1 | | 1 | | | Sanford, Hezekiah | 5 | | 3 | | 2 | Meeker, Igaci | 1 | | 2 | | |
| Banks, Joseph | 2 | | 2 | | | Starr, Levi | 1 | 1 | 1 | | | Hull, Nehemiah | 1 | 1 | 2 | | |
| Gorham, Jaber | 1 | | 4 | | | Bartlett, Daniel | 1 | 4 | 3 | | | Perry, Daniel | 3 | 2 | 3 | | |
| Platt, Zebulon | 2 | 1 | 3 | | | Bartrum, Daniel | 1 | 4 | 3 | | | Burr, Stephen | 1 | | 2 | | |
| Platt, Hezekiah | 3 | | 4 | | | Read, Eli | 1 | | 3 | | 1 | Rumsey, Ephraim | 1 | 2 | 4 | | |
| Lyon, Daniel | 2 | | 2 | | | Read, Zalmon | 1 | 3 | 2 | | | Bennitt, Miles | 1 | 1 | 3 | | |
| Lyon, Nathan | 1 | 2 | 3 | | | Read, Hezekiah | 3 | 1 | 7 | | | Meeker, Seth | 2 | 1 | 7 | | |
| Beers, Gershom | 1 | 2 | 1 | | | Lynes, John | 1 | 2 | 3 | | | Meeker, Elonyer | 1 | 1 | 2 | | |
| Platt, Mary | | | 1 | | | White, Charles | 1 | 3 | 4 | | | Dikeman, Frederick | 1 | 2 | 6 | | |
| Malery, Jonathan | 2 | 3 | 4 | | | Rowland, Israel | 1 | 1 | 2 | | | Byington, John | 1 | | 1 | | |
| Lyon, Arel | 2 | 2 | 3 | | | Rowland, Thomas | 1 | | 2 | | | Bennit, Daniel | 2 | 1 | 2 | | |
| Lyon, Andrew | 1 | | 2 | | | Evans, Daniel | 1 | 1 | 4 | | | Perry, John | 1 | 1 | 3 | | |
| Whitlock, Nathan | 1 | 1 | 4 | | | Hamlinton, Benjamin | 3 | 2 | 7 | | | Sherwood, Isaac | 3 | 2 | 3 | | |
| Merit, Ebenezer | 1 | 1 | 3 | | | Read, John | 1 | 4 | 2 | | 1 | Sturges, Ebenezer | 1 | 3 | 1 | | |
| Burr, Joseph | 2 | 1 | 2 | | | Hall, Ebenezer | 1 | | 3 | | | Sturges, Perry | 1 | 3 | 3 | | |
| Hill, Andrew | 2 | | 3 | | | Adams, Joseph | 3 | 1 | 3 | | | Perry, Thadeus | 1 | 3 | 4 | | |
| Hill, Daniel | 2 | 1 | 3 | | | Munson, Theophelus | 2 | 2 | 3 | | | Sturges, Benjamin | 1 | | 2 | | 1 |
| Crowfoot, James | 1 | 1 | 4 | | | Stoe, Robert | 1 | 3 | 4 | | | Backsster, Arline | 1 | 2 | 1 | | |
| Lyon, Filo | 2 | 2 | 1 | | | Morehouse, Elijah | 1 | 2 | 2 | | | Guire, John | 1 | | 3 | | |
| Bulkley, Peter, Junr | 1 | | 1 | | | Bartrum, David | 2 | | 6 | | | Morehouse, Beebe | 1 | 2 | 3 | | |
| Bulkley, Aaron | 2 | 1 | 7 | | | Gold, Samuel | 2 | | 4 | | | Guire, Thadius | 1 | 1 | 3 | | |
| Hill, Aliel | 1 | 1 | 2 | | | Banks, Hyat | 1 | 4 | 1 | | | Parsons, Jonathan | 1 | 2 | 3 | | |
| Meeker, Ephraim | 1 | | 1 | | | Patchon, Arael | 2 | | 1 | | | Lee, Silus | 1 | 2 | 3 | | |
| Malery, John | 1 | | 3 | | | Adams, Abraham | 1 | 2 | 6 | | | Lee, Enos | 1 | 3 | 1 | | |
| Meeker, Ogden | 1 | 1 | 1 | | | Griffin, Joseph | 2 | 1 | 3 | | | Malery, Daniel | 2 | 1 | 3 | | |
| Mungo, Simeon | 1 | | 3 | | | Winecoop, John | 1 | 1 | 2 | | | Malery, Samuel | 1 | 2 | 2 | | |
| Heron, William | 2 | 1 | 7 | | 1 | Persons, Timothy | 1 | 1 | 3 | | | Hilliard, Thurstain | 1 | | 1 | | |
| Meeker, Jonathan | 3 | | 3 | | | Persons, Daniel | 1 | 2 | 3 | | | Smith, Joel | 2 | 1 | 2 | | |
| Hill, David | 1 | 1 | 6 | | | Mead, Jeremiah | 2 | 1 | 1 | | | Andrews, Francis | 1 | 2 | 3 | | |
| Hill, Ezekiel | 2 | 2 | 5 | | | Benedict, Thadeus | 2 | 4 | 2 | | 2 | Bradley, Elijah | 2 | 1 | 2 | | |
| Starr, Thomas | 1 | | 1 | | | Bartlett, Nathaniel | 2 | | 5 | | | Jackson, Stephen | 1 | 1 | 2 | | |
| Beech, Lazarus | 2 | | 3 | 1 | | Gray, Stephen | 2 | | 2 | | | Guire, Samuel | 1 | | 2 | | |
| Wheeler, Ephraim | 2 | | 2 | | | Sanford, Lemuel | 2 | 3 | 1 | 5 | | Mead, Uriah | 1 | 1 | 3 | | |
| Marwell, Edward | 1 | 1 | 4 | | | Fitch, Arael | 2 | | 5 | 1 | | Hull, David | 1 | | 1 | | |
| Wheeler, Seth | 1 | 1 | 2 | | | Hull, John | 2 | 1 | 3 | | | Barlow, Gershom | 1 | | 3 | | 1 |
| Morgin, Abijah | 1 | 1 | 4 | | | Couch, John | 1 | | 3 | | | Smith, Elieaser | 1 | 2 | 2 | | |
| Dickerson, Zadoc | 1 | 1 | 2 | | | Byington, John | 1 | 1 | 2 | | | Bates, Justus | 2 | | 2 | | |
| Wheeler, Enos | 3 | | 4 | | | Salmon, Asael | 3 | 1 | 2 | | | Lee, Enos | 3 | 1 | 5 | | |
| Wheeler, John | 2 | | 5 | | 1 | Smith, Samuel | 4 | 1 | 3 | 1 | | Lord, Gold | 1 | | 2 | | |
| Sanford, John | 1 | | | | | Hull, Zalmon | 2 | 3 | 4 | | | Malery, Nathan | 2 | | 2 | | |
| Hill, Daniel | 1 | 1 | 2 | | | Meeker, Isaac | 1 | 1 | 2 | | | Malery, Nathan | 1 | 3 | 2 | | |
| Sanford, James | 2 | 3 | 2 | | | Napp, David | 2 | 2 | 3 | | | Mead, Elias | 1 | 2 | 2 | | |
| Jacson, Aaron | 1 | | 1 | | | Napp, Jonathan | 2 | 2 | 3 | | | Sanford, Ezekiel | 3 | 2 | 7 | | |
| Finne, Jesse | 2 | 1 | 2 | | | Lyon, Ezra | 1 | 1 | 2 | | | Coley, Samuel | 2 | | 4 | | |
| Crofoot, David | 2 | 1 | 4 | | | Parsons, Elijah | 1 | | 1 | | | Coley, Onisimus | 3 | | 5 | | |
| Leach, John | 1 | 2 | 3 | | | Hull, Peter | 1 | 1 | 4 | | | Darling, Benjamin | 1 | 2 | 3 | | 1 |
| Morehouse, Daniel | 2 | | 2 | | | Frost, Joseph | 3 | 1 | 4 | | | Sherwood, John | 2 | 2 | 4 | | |
| Freeman, Thomas | | | | 2 | | Sanford, Seth | 2 | | 2 | | | Starr, Mijah | 2 | 3 | 4 | | |
| Bulkley, Peter | 1 | 4 | 6 | | | Sanford, Ebenezer | 1 | 1 | 2 | | | Morgen, Joseph | 1 | 1 | 3 | | |
| Morehouse, David | 1 | 2 | 3 | | | Sanford, Elias | 1 | | 2 | | | Wakeman, Timothy | 2 | 3 | 5 | | |
| | | | | | | Barlow, Aaron | 4 | 6 | 6 | 1 | 1 | Wakeman, Jabez | 2 | 4 | 1 | | |

# FIRST CENSUS OF THE UNITED STATES.

## FAIRFIELD COUNTY—Continued.

| NAME OF HEAD OF FAMILY. | Free white males of 16 years and upward, including heads of families. | Free white males under 16 years. | Free white females, including heads of families. | All other free persons. | Slaves. | NAME OF HEAD OF FAMILY. | Free white males of 16 years and upward, including heads of families. | Free white males under 16 years. | Free white females, including heads of families. | All other free persons. | Slaves. | NAME OF HEAD OF FAMILY. | Free white males of 16 years and upward, including heads of families. | Free white males under 16 years. | Free white females, including heads of families. | All other free persons. | Slaves. |
|---|---|---|---|---|---|---|---|---|---|---|---|---|---|---|---|---|---|
| **READING TOWN—con.** | | | | | | **RIDGEFIELD TOWN—con.** | | | | | | **RIDGEFIELD TOWN—con.** | | | | | |
| Gray, Justus | 1 | 1 | 5 | | | Wilson, Ezekiel | 3 | | 2 | | | Gates, Noah | 1 | 2 | 2 | | |
| Couch, Simon | 1 | 4 | 4 | | | Smith, Benjamin | 2 | 3 | 5 | | | Jackson, John | 1 | 2 | 3 | | |
| Gray, Joel | 1 | | 2 | | | Wilson, Jeremiah | 1 | | 1 | | 1 | Price, Hurd | 1 | 1 | 2 | | |
| Guire, Mathew | 2 | | 2 | | | Lobdell, Caleb | 1 | | 1 | | | Jackson, Daniel | 1 | 1 | 4 | | |
| **RIDGEFIELD TOWN.** | | | | | | Lobdell, Phillip | 1 | 2 | 1 | | | Bowton, Roger | 1 | 2 | 2 | | |
| | | | | | | Lobdell, Josiah | 1 | 2 | 1 | | | Price, Ebenezer | 1 | | 1 | | |
| Bradley, Philip B., Esqr | 2 | 2 | 5 | | | Smith, Sarah, 3d (Ww) | | 1 | 1 | | | Edmond, Robert | 3 | 1 | 2 | | |
| Keeler, Mathew | 2 | 1 | 2 | | | Dauchey, Nathan | 3 | 1 | 5 | | | Riggs, Joseph | 1 | | 3 | | |
| Seymour, Matthew | 1 | | 2 | 1 | 1 | Keeler, Paul | 1 | 2 | 5 | 1 | | Smith, James | 1 | | 4 | | |
| Keeler, Matthew, Junr | 1 | 2 | 2 | | | Sturgis, Thaddeus | 1 | 1 | 5 | | | Munro, Joseph | 1 | 3 | 1 | | |
| Keeler, John | 3 | | 4 | | | Mills, Denton | 1 | | 1 | | | Lee, Seth | 1 | | 3 | | |
| Waterous, John | 3 | 2 | 4 | | | Mead, Ezra | 2 | 4 | 2 | | | Lee, John | 2 | 2 | 3 | | |
| Jones, Ebenezer | 2 | | 3 | | | Smith, Thomas | 2 | | 1 | | | Lee, Elijah | 1 | 3 | 1 | | |
| Jones, Ebenezer, 2d | 1 | 1 | 1 | | | Smith, Hezekiah, 2d | 1 | 4 | 1 | | | Lee, Daniel | 2 | 3 | 5 | | |
| Rockwell, Thaddeus | 2 | 2 | 7 | | | Perry, David | 1 | 4 | 3 | | | Lee, Elias | 1 | 1 | 1 | | |
| Rockwell, James | 1 | 3 | 5 | | | Dauchey, Philip | 1 | | 3 | | | Williams, Solomon | 1 | 1 | 3 | | |
| Resiguie, James | 2 | 2 | 4 | | | Sherwood, Benjamin | 1 | 5 | 5 | | | Gregory, Zaccheus | 1 | | 1 | | |
| Resiguie, Jacob | 2 | | 2 | | | Smith, Clemence | 2 | 1 | 2 | | | Cain, Hugh | 1 | | 1 | | |
| Resiguie, Jacob, 2d | 1 | 1 | 2 | | | Smith, Ebenezer | 1 | 1 | 2 | | | Banks, David | 1 | | 3 | | |
| Scribner, Rachel | | 1 | 2 | | | Smith, Stephen | 2 | 1 | 1 | | 1 | Bears, Nathan | 1 | | 3 | | |
| Olmsted, Samuel | 1 | 3 | 5 | | | Smith, Thaddeus | 2 | 1 | 2 | | | Olmsted, David, 2d | 1 | 2 | 6 | | |
| Olmsted, James | 1 | 3 | 3 | | | Stebbins, Joseph | 1 | 1 | 5 | | | Hull, Silas | 3 | 1 | 3 | | |
| Keeler, Jeremiah | 1 | | | | | Bennit, Josiah | 1 | 1 | 2 | | | Keeler, Jabez | 1 | 5 | 3 | | |
| Seymour, Thomas, 2d | 1 | 1 | 2 | | | Smith, James, 2d | 3 | 1 | 4 | | | Bowton, Avery | 1 | 1 | 2 | | |
| Sturgis, James | 2 | | 2 | | | Osborn, Aaron | 2 | 1 | 1 | | | Smith, Hezekiah | 3 | | 2 | | |
| Nash, Abraham | 2 | 1 | 2 | | | Stebbins, Samuel | 2 | 2 | 3 | | | Gray, Gilead | 1 | 4 | 4 | | |
| Nash, Abraham, 2d | 1 | 2 | 3 | | | Baker, Amos | 2 | 1 | 4 | | | Smith, Uriah | 1 | 1 | 4 | | |
| Omsted, Nathan | 2 | 1 | 3 | | | Stebbins, Benjamin | 1 | | 2 | | | Dean, Daniel, 2d | 1 | | 1 | | |
| Keeler, Timothy | 3 | | 2 | | | Smith, Jeremiah | 1 | 3 | 5 | | | Dean, Daniel, 2d | 2 | 1 | 4 | | |
| Northrup, Aaron | 3 | | 2 | | | How, Epenetus | 2 | | 6 | | | Burr, Samuel | 1 | 1 | 2 | | |
| Baldwin, John | 1 | | 2 | | | Olmsted, Ambros, 2d | 1 | 2 | 1 | | | Lobdell, Uriel | 2 | 1 | 4 | | |
| Goodrich, Revd Samuel | 1 | 1 | 4 | | | Waddy, Peter | 1 | 5 | 1 | | | Wheeler, Ichabod | 2 | 3 | 1 | | |
| Morris, John | 3 | | 3 | | | Olmsted, Ambros | 2 | 1 | 4 | | | Whittock, Robert | 2 | 2 | 3 | | |
| Olmsted, Jared | 2 | 2 | 7 | | | Stebbins, Ebenezer | 1 | 3 | 4 | | | Rundle, Shubael | 1 | 3 | 4 | | |
| Kellogg, Daniel | 2 | 2 | 3 | | | Smith, John | 3 | 2 | 2 | | | Warren, Michael | 1 | 3 | 4 | | |
| Kellogg, Nathan F | 1 | 3 | 4 | | | Hall, Josiah | 2 | 1 | 5 | | | Resiguie, Alexander | 1 | | 1 | | |
| Remerton, Stephen | 1 | 2 | 3 | | | Dowse, Mary | | 1 | 3 | | | Munro, William | 1 | 2 | 3 | | |
| Bennitt, Trowbridge | 1 | | 3 | | | Dauchey, Daniel | 1 | 2 | 3 | | | Rundle, Charles | 1 | 1 | 3 | | |
| Hine, Newton | 1 | 2 | 3 | | | Dauchey, John | 1 | 2 | 7 | | | Stebbins, Ann | 1 | 1 | 3 | | |
| Benedict, John, 2d | 1 | 1 | 4 | | | Dauchey, James | 1 | 2 | 2 | | | Dauchey, Vivus | 2 | 2 | 2 | | |
| Smith, Daniel, 4th | 1 | 2 | 1 | | | Jones, John | 2 | 2 | 5 | | | Bennitt, Isaac | 1 | | 3 | | |
| Chitterster, Daniel | 2 | | 2 | | | Folliot, Joseph | 1 | | 1 | | | Bennitt, Daniel | 1 | | 1 | | |
| Remington, Josiah | 1 | 1 | 1 | | | Folliot, Bartlit | 2 | | 1 | | | Resigue, William | 2 | 2 | 4 | | |
| Nash, Daniel | 1 | 1 | 2 | | | Smith, Job | 2 | | 4 | | | Bradley, Stephen | 1 | | 2 | | |
| Smith, Daniel, 2d | 1 | 1 | 5 | | | Smith, Daniel, 3d | 3 | 4 | 7 | | | Lobdell, Ebenezer | 1 | 2 | 2 | | |
| Northrup, Josiah | 1 | 3 | 4 | | | Smith, Sarah, 2d | | 2 | 6 | | | Bradley, Daniel | 1 | 1 | 1 | | |
| Keeler, Thaddeus | 1 | 3 | | | | Scott, Thomas | 1 | 1 | 1 | | | Livesay, James | 1 | 3 | 2 | | |
| Fairbanks, Samuel | 2 | | 2 | | | Scott, James, 2d | 1 | 3 | 2 | | | Olmsted, Justus | 2 | 1 | 2 | | |
| Northrup, Benjamin | 1 | 2 | 1 | | | Deforest, Hezekiah | 2 | | | | | Pulling, William | 1 | 2 | 2 | | |
| Mead, Jeremiah | 1 | 2 | 3 | | | Munson, Isaac | 1 | 1 | 2 | | | Sherwood, Jonathan | 2 | | 4 | | |
| Benedict, John | 1 | | 2 | | | Andros, Jonathan | 1 | 1 | 3 | | | Olmsted, Justus, 2d | 2 | 2 | 4 | | |
| Benedict, Abijah | 1 | 1 | 2 | | | Burt, Theophilus | 1 | 2 | 4 | | | Bryant, Samuel | 1 | 1 | 1 | | |
| Keeler, Martha | | | 2 | | | Partrick, James | 1 | 2 | 2 | | | Mead, William | 2 | 1 | 1 | | |
| Hoyt, Benjamin | 3 | 2 | 3 | | | Burt, Joshua | 1 | 3 | 1 | | | Gilbert, Abner | 1 | 4 | 4 | | |
| Olmsted, David | 2 | 3 | 3 | | | Read, Elias | 2 | 3 | 2 | | | Sherwood, Nehemiah | 3 | | 3 | | |
| Keeler, Timothy, Junr | 3 | 2 | 6 | | | Keeler, Levi | 1 | 3 | 3 | | | Bradley, Samuel | 4 | 2 | 3 | | |
| Olmsted, David, 3d | 1 | | 3 | | | Folliot, John | 1 | 4 | 1 | | | Mead, Joseph | 2 | 4 | 4 | | |
| Sturgis, Ward | 1 | 1 | 1 | | | Portman, Mary Ann | | | 1 | | | Mead, Hannah | | | 2 | | |
| Saintjohn, David | 1 | | 6 | | | Bennitt, Gabriel | 2 | 2 | 3 | | | Stewart, John | 1 | | 1 | | |
| Keeler, David | 1 | | 2 | | | Smith, Levi | 1 | 1 | 1 | | | Wilson, Thomas | 2 | 1 | 3 | | |
| Nash, Riah | 1 | 1 | 2 | | | Smith, Phinehas | 1 | 3 | 4 | | | Whittock, Justus | 1 | 2 | 3 | | |
| Benedict, Jesse | 3 | 1 | 3 | | | Folliot, Thankfull | 1 | 1 | 3 | | | Scribner, Uriah | 1 | | 2 | | |
| Seymour, Thomas | 3 | 1 | 3 | | | Deforest, Joseph | 1 | | 1 | | | Bryant, John | 1 | 1 | 1 | | |
| Olmsted, Ebenezer | 1 | 3 | 3 | | | Folliot, Jeremiah | 1 | | 1 | | | Wood, Jonathan | 1 | | 4 | | |
| Olmsted, Samuel, 2d | 2 | 3 | 5 | | | Sherman, John | 2 | 1 | 5 | | | Wood, Andrew | 1 | | 2 | | |
| Chambers, Nathan | 1 | | 6 | | | Mead, John | 2 | | 4 | | | Bennitt, Stephen | 2 | 2 | 3 | | |
| Northrup, John | 1 | | 3 | | | Scott, Gideon | 1 | 2 | 4 | | | Sturgis, Elnathan | 1 | | 2 | | |
| Olmsted, Mathew | 1 | 3 | 1 | | | Barnum, Abel | 1 | 2 | 7 | | | Sturgis, Nehemiah | 1 | 2 | 2 | | |
| Northrup, Elisabeth | 2 | 4 | 5 | | | Chapman, John | 1 | | 2 | | | Benedict, Gamaliel | 1 | 1 | 2 | | |
| Johnson, John | 1 | 2 | 1 | | | Barlow, John, 2d | 1 | | 2 | | | Starr, Sarah | | | 2 | | |
| Saintjohn, John | 1 | 1 | 2 | | | Hyatt, Thomas | 1 | 2 | 1 | | | Brush, Eliphelet | 2 | 3 | 6 | | |
| Benedict, Ezra | 1 | 2 | 2 | | | Scott, David | 2 | 2 | 2 | | | Smith, Elijah | 4 | 1 | 3 | | |
| Smith, Azor | 1 | | 1 | | | Smith, Gideon | 2 | 1 | 2 | | | Sherwood Nathan | 1 | | 3 | | |
| Berry, George | 1 | | 3 | | | Smith, David | 2 | 1 | 3 | | | Whitney, Capt Henry | 2 | | 3 | | |
| Barlow, John | 2 | 2 | 5 | | | Hyatt, Uzzell | 1 | 1 | 5 | | | Benedict, Comfort | 1 | 3 | 2 | | |
| Betts, Eunice | | | 2 | | | Depeere, John | 1 | 1 | 4 | | | Gates, Jonathan | 4 | 1 | 6 | | |
| Hawley, Elisha | 2 | 1 | 2 | | | Dann, Ezra | 1 | 1 | 6 | | | Foster, Jonah | 2 | 1 | 2 | | |
| Betts, Gideon | 1 | | 2 | | | Mead, Jaspar | 1 | | 4 | | | Pulling, Augustus | 1 | 3 | 7 | | |
| Smith, Nathan | 2 | 1 | 8 | | | Mills, Stephen | 1 | | 4 | | | Dolittle, Phinehas | 2 | 2 | 2 | | 1 |
| King, Joshua | 4 | | 4 | | | Dickens, Arnold | 1 | 2 | 6 | | | Northrup, Thomas | 1 | | 2 | | |
| Ingersol, Joseph | 1 | 1 | 3 | | | Keeler, Daniel | 2 | 1 | 6 | | | Sherwood, Reuben | 2 | 3 | 3 | | |
| Ingersol, Moss | 1 | | 3 | | | Whittock, Thaddeus | 1 | 2 | 3 | | | Pulling, Abigail | 2 | | 3 | | |
| Barns, Ambrose | 1 | 2 | 3 | | | Yabecomb, Gilbart | 1 | 2 | 1 | | | Northrup, Nathanl | 2 | | 6 | | |
| Olmsted, Daniel | 1 | | 2 | | | Morris, David | 1 | 1 | 2 | | | Keeler, John, 2d | 2 | 3 | 3 | | |
| Hawley, Thomas | 5 | 3 | 3 | | | Scott, James | 1 | | 1 | | | Finch, Peter | 1 | 5 | 9 | | |
| Olmsted, Daniel, 2d | 1 | 3 | 4 | | | Bowton, Timothy | 1 | 2 | 2 | | | Saintjohn, Thomas | 2 | | 5 | | |
| Hawley, Ebenezer | 2 | 1 | 2 | | | McFarden, Thomas | 1 | 1 | 1 | | | Weed, Jacob | 1 | 1 | 1 | | |
| Marvin, Uriah | 2 | | 3 | | | Hoyt, Samuel | 1 | 3 | 2 | | | Saintjohn, Samuel | 2 | 1 | 5 | | |
| Gilbart, David | 1 | 1 | 3 | | | Jones, Jacob, 2d | 1 | 2 | 2 | | | Barber, Benjamin | 2 | 2 | 2 | | |
| Hawley, Hezekiah | 1 | 1 | 3 | | | Whitney, Henry | 1 | 2 | 1 | | | Titus, John | 2 | 2 | 4 | | |
| Gilbart, Ebenezer | 1 | | 1 | | | Olmsted, Josiah | 1 | 1 | 1 | | | Wallace, William | 1 | 2 | 8 | 1 | 1 |
| Foster, Joseph | 1 | | | | | Jenkins, Calvin | 1 | | 3 | | | Smith, Jabez | 2 | | 5 | | |
| Smith, Jacob | 2 | 1 | 3 | | | Bears, Anthony | 1 | 2 | 4 | | | Smith, Matthew | 2 | | 3 | | |
| Seymour, Uriah | 1 | | 2 | | | Hoyt, David | 2 | 2 | 5 | | | Northrup, James | 1 | 5 | 4 | | |
| | | | | | | Jackson, Joseph | 1 | 4 | 2 | | | Sellick, Jesse | 1 | | 4 | | |

# HEADS OF FAMILIES—CONNECTICUT.

## FAIRFIELD COUNTY—Continued.

| NAME OF HEAD OF FAMILY. | Free white males of 16 years and upward, including heads of families. | Free white males under 16 years. | Free white females, including heads of families. | All other free persons. | Slaves. |
|---|---|---|---|---|---|
| **RIDGEFIELD TOWN—con.** | | | | | |
| Rockwell, William | 1 | | 3 | | |
| Northrup, Matthew | 1 | 1 | 3 | | |
| Birchard, Uriah | 1 | | 3 | | |
| Birchard, Isaiah | 2 | | 2 | | |
| Birchard, Jeremiah | 1 | 1 | 4 | | |
| Rockwell, Elisabeth | | | 1 | | |
| Leason, Prudence | | | 2 | | |
| Wilson, Abner | 2 | 2 | 5 | 1 | |
| Deforest, Uriah | 2 | 1 | 2 | | |
| Lynds, Benjamin | 2 | 1 | 1 | | |
| Sherwood, Ebenezer | 2 | | 1 | | |
| Coley, Daniel | 2 | 1 | 3 | | |
| Varnold, John | 1 | 1 | 3 | | |
| Rockwell, Abraham | 3 | 1 | 4 | | |
| Rockwell, Abijah | 1 | 2 | 3 | | |
| Rockwell, Daniel | 2 | 1 | 2 | | |
| Keeler, Samuel | 1 | 1 | 3 | | |
| Benedict, Timothy | 2 | 1 | 3 | | |
| Keeler, Timothy, 2d | 1 | 1 | 1 | | |
| Camp, Revd Samuel | 1 | 1 | 4 | | |
| Forrester, William | 3 | 2 | 5 | | |
| Keeler, Nehemiah | 1 | 3 | 4 | | |
| Grey, Joseph | 1 | 1 | 4 | | |
| Osborn, Gamaliel | 1 | | 4 | | |
| Abbott, James | 1 | 1 | 3 | | |
| Dykeman, Jonathan | 1 | | 3 | | |
| Abbott, Lemuel | 1 | 1 | 3 | | |
| Abbott, Lemuel, 2d | 1 | | 2 | | |
| Abbott, Stephen | 1 | 1 | 1 | | |
| Abbott, Silas | 1 | 2 | 1 | | |
| Arnold, Peleg | 1 | 1 | 2 | | |
| Leach, Christopher | 1 | 2 | 2 | | |
| Osborn, Jonah | 1 | 1 | 1 | | |
| Gates, Samuel | 1 | | 1 | | |
| Nickerson, Eliphaz | 1 | 2 | 1 | | |
| Rockwell, David | 2 | 1 | 5 | | |
| Crain, Zebulun | 4 | 4 | 3 | | |
| Rockwell, Joseph | 1 | | 1 | | |
| Thomas, Recompence, 2d | 2 | | 3 | | |
| Whitney, Ezekiel | 1 | 1 | 3 | | |
| Brush, Zophar | 1 | 2 | 2 | | |
| Fairchild, Ezekiel | 2 | 1 | 2 | | |
| Nickerson, William | 1 | 1 | 2 | | |
| Nickerson, James | 1 | | 1 | | |
| Nickerson, Barack | 1 | | 2 | | |
| Osborn, Abigail | 1 | 1 | 3 | | |
| Thomas, Recompence | 1 | 2 | 2 | | |
| Perry, John | 1 | | 1 | | |
| Norris, Stephen | 3 | 5 | 3 | | |
| Weed, Bartholomew | 2 | 3 | 5 | | |
| Starr, Peter | 1 | 2 | 2 | | |
| Scribner, John | 1 | 3 | 4 | | |
| Rockwell, Isaac | 1 | 1 | 1 | | |
| Stevens, Zachariah | 2 | 1 | 6 | | |
| Porter, James | 1 | | 1 | | |
| Platt, Samuel | 1 | 3 | 5 | | |
| Barber, Zachariah | 1 | 4 | 2 | | |
| Porter, Elisabeth | | 1 | 3 | | |
| Stevens, Nathan | 2 | 3 | 5 | | |
| Gorham, Lockwood | 1 | | 3 | | |
| Salmon, Stephen | 1 | 1 | 1 | | |
| Sears, Comfort | 1 | 1 | 6 | | |
| Sears, Knowles | 1 | 3 | 4 | | |
| Brush, Phillip | 1 | 2 | 2 | | |
| Sears, Daniel | 1 | 1 | 1 | | |
| Gage, Thomas | 1 | 1 | 1 | | |
| Gravy, Francis | 1 | | 2 | | |
| Keeler, Elijah | 2 | 2 | 7 | | |
| Rockwell, Henry | 1 | | 1 | | |
| Rockwell, Ebenezer | 1 | 2 | 2 | | |
| Pulling, Abraham | 1 | 3 | 2 | | |
| Foster, Jonah | 2 | 4 | 3 | | |
| Lee, William | 1 | 1 | 3 | | |
| **STRATFORD TOWN.** | | | | | |
| Judson, Pixly | 1 | 1 | 1 | | |
| Wells, Agar | 1 | 5 | 4 | | |
| Lewis, Isaac | 2 | 1 | 1 | | |
| Pixly, Peter | 1 | 2 | 3 | | |
| Hurd, Andrew | 1 | 1 | 3 | 1 | 2 |
| Benjamin, Elnathan | 1 | 5 | 2 | | |
| Benjamin, Samuel | 1 | | 1 | | |
| Judson, Abraham | 2 | 1 | 3 | | |
| Judson, Aaron | 2 | 1 | 2 | | 1 |
| Jones, Elnathan | 1 | 6 | 2 | | |
| Beardsly, Henery | 3 | | 1 | | |
| Beardsly, Matthew (Wid.) | | | 3 | | |
| Burritt, Silus | 1 | 1 | 2 | | |
| Beardsly, Ephraim | 2 | 2 | 3 | | |
| Benjamin, Philip | 1 | | 4 | | |
| Benjamin, John | 2 | 2 | 5 | | |
| Hawley, Abigail (Wid.) | 1 | | 4 | | |
| Brown, Isaac | 3 | 3 | 3 | | |

| NAME OF HEAD OF FAMILY. | Free white males of 16 years and upward, including heads of families. | Free white males under 16 years. | Free white females, including heads of families. | All other free persons. | Slaves. |
|---|---|---|---|---|---|
| **STRATFORD TOWN—con.** | | | | | |
| Benjamin, George | 3 | 3 | 7 | | 1 |
| Fairchild, John | 2 | 3 | 4 | | |
| Johnson, Samel W | 1 | | 1 | | 2 |
| Tomlinson, Phebe (Wid.) | | 1 | 3 | 2 | 1 |
| Walker, Robert | 1 | 1 | 7 | | 4 |
| Beers, Samel | 1 | | | | |
| Beers, Josiah | 1 | 1 | 4 | | |
| Collins, William B | 1 | 3 | 2 | | |
| Hawley, Ruth (Wid.) | | | 3 | | |
| Seirs, James | 1 | 3 | 4 | | 2 |
| Peck, John | 1 | 2 | 3 | | |
| Benjamin, John | 1 | 2 | 4 | | |
| Curtis, Jonas | 1 | | 1 | | |
| Wells, Benjamin | 3 | | 2 | | |
| Wells, William | 1 | 1 | 1 | | |
| Lilliston, James | 1 | | 3 | | |
| Hawley, Josiah | 1 | 1 | 4 | | |
| Whiting, Joseph | 1 | 3 | 3 | | 1 |
| Shelbey, Ebenezer | 2 | 3 | 5 | | |
| Wakman, Ephraim | 2 | 2 | 5 | | |
| Ufford, Samuel | 1 | 3 | 4 | | |
| Ufford, John | 1 | 2 | 4 | | |
| Ufford, Benjamin | 2 | 3 | 4 | | |
| Cow, James | 3 | 1 | 3 | | |
| Edward, Samuel | 3 | 4 | 6 | | |
| Curtis, Agar | 1 | 1 | 1 | | |
| Hurd, Jabez | 1 | | 1 | 3 | |
| Cannon, Lewis | 2 | | 1 | 3 | 2 |
| Gorham, Isaac | 2 | | 2 | | |
| Gorham, Nathan | 1 | 2 | 2 | | |
| Allen, Eben | 3 | 2 | 2 | | |
| Plum, Justis | 1 | 1 | 4 | | |
| Gorham, Nehemiah | 1 | 2 | 2 | 2 | |
| Southard, Samuel | 2 | | 4 | | |
| Silly, John | 3 | 1 | 6 | | |
| Warduher, Sarah | | | 2 | | |
| Osborn, Marah | | | 3 | | |
| Ward, Samuel | 1 | 1 | 5 | | |
| Curtis, Thomas | 2 | 5 | 2 | | |
| Paterson, Samuel | 1 | 1 | 6 | | |
| Clark, James | 3 | 1 | 7 | 2 | |
| Curtis, Henry | 1 | 1 | 6 | | |
| Wells, Joseph | 2 | 3 | 3 | | |
| Wells, Legrand | 2 | | 2 | | |
| Well, Benjamin | 1 | | 3 | | 1 |
| Woodhull, Stephen | 3 | 2 | 3 | | |
| Wheeler, Elnathan | 2 | 2 | 3 | | |
| Curtis, David | 1 | 1 | 5 | | |
| Curtis, Josiah | 3 | | 2 | | |
| Wheeler, Nathanel | 2 | 1 | 5 | | |
| Wheeler, Ephraim | 2 | 3 | 4 | | |
| Wheeler, Deborah | | | 3 | | |
| Wheeler, Elnathan, Jur | 1 | | 2 | | |
| Lewis, George | 1 | | 1 | 2 | 1 |
| Thompson, Stephen | 1 | 1 | 5 | 1 | |
| Judson, Stiles | 1 | 1 | 2 | | |
| Judson, Daniel | 2 | | 4 | 1 | 3 |
| Curtis, Stephen | 2 | | 2 | 1 | 2 |
| Gorham, George | 1 | 2 | 2 | | |
| Brothwell, Hezekiah | 1 | 4 | 1 | | |
| McCoy, Few | 1 | 2 | 1 | | |
| Curtis, Nehemiah | 3 | 3 | 5 | | |
| Wilcox, William | 2 | | 4 | | |
| Booth, Agar | 1 | 2 | 2 | | |
| Booth, Daniel | 4 | 1 | 2 | | |
| Well, Isaac | 1 | 2 | 3 | | 1 |
| Blackman, James | 1 | 2 | 3 | 1 | |
| Blackman, James | 1 | | 1 | | |
| Bindy, Nathan | 2 | | 1 | | 2 |
| Cartly, Ezra | 1 | | 2 | | 1 |
| Cartly, Ezra | 1 | 3 | 3 | | |
| Cartley, Zebelon | 1 | 3 | 4 | | |
| Sherwood, David | 1 | 2 | 4 | | |
| Clifford, Elizabeth | | | 2 | | |
| Warden, William | 2 | | 1 | | |
| Hubbill, Abijah | 1 | | 2 | | |
| Hubbill, Eunice (Wid.) | 1 | 2 | 2 | | |
| Wing, Charles | 1 | | 2 | | |
| Hoit, Eli | 1 | 2 | 2 | | |
| Hawley, Jabish | 2 | 1 | 4 | | |
| Hawley, Aaron | 5 | 2 | 2 | | 2 |
| Hoyt, Hanah (Wid.) | 1 | 1 | 1 | | 1 |
| Lymon, Robert | 2 | 2 | 4 | | |
| Phipeny, Ebenezer | 1 | 3 | 3 | | |
| Sturges, Lewis | 1 | 2 | 1 | | |
| Porter, Samuel | 1 | | 2 | | |
| Davis, Clark | 2 | | 4 | | |
| Willard, William | 1 | 4 | 2 | | |
| Hull, Stephen | 3 | 2 | 1 | | |
| Napp, Daniel | 1 | 1 | 3 | | |
| Shermon, Seth | 2 | | 2 | | 1 |
| Jennings, Eliphalet | 1 | 2 | 2 | | |
| Hawley, Woolcut | 2 | 2 | 2 | | |

| NAME OF HEAD OF FAMILY. | Free white males of 16 years and upward, including heads of families. | Free white males under 16 years. | Free white females, including heads of families. | All other free persons. | Slaves. |
|---|---|---|---|---|---|
| **STRATFORD TOWN—con.** | | | | | |
| Summers, Jabez | 1 | | 2 | | 2 |
| Starlin, Stephen | 1 | 2 | 1 | | |
| Starlin, Stephen, Jur | 1 | | 1 | | |
| Starlin, Abijah | 3 | 2 | 2 | | |
| Wakely, Jonathan | 2 | 1 | 4 | | |
| French, James B | 2 | 3 | 3 | | |
| Dudley, Asel | 1 | 2 | 2 | | |
| Hawley, Gregary | 1 | 3 | 2 | | |
| Summers, Stephen | 2 | 1 | 5 | | |
| Beach, Jabez | 1 | 1 | 1 | | |
| Summers, Abijah | 1 | 2 | 4 | | |
| Summers, Elnathan | 1 | 1 | 4 | | |
| Ciely, Denton | 1 | | 4 | | |
| Nichols, Reubin | 1 | | 3 | | |
| Gregory, James | 1 | | 2 | | |
| Summers, Aaron | 1 | 2 | 3 | | |
| Summers, Samuel | 4 | | 4 | | |
| Smith, John | 2 | | | | |
| Peterson, Isaac | 1 | 1 | 3 | | |
| Patchen, Salmon | 1 | | 3 | | |
| Seely, Elnathan | 2 | 2 | 2 | | |
| Gray, Reuel | 2 | 2 | 5 | | |
| Beardsley, Amos | 2 | 2 | 4 | | |
| Edward, Isaac | 1 | 4 | 4 | | |
| Seely, Agar | 1 | 1 | 3 | | |
| Seely, Benjamin | 2 | 2 | 5 | | |
| Burton, Joseph | 2 | 1 | 3 | | |
| Hach, Ebenezer | 1 | 1 | 1 | | |
| Beach, Isaac | 1 | 1 | 1 | | |
| Beardsley, David | 3 | | 2 | | |
| Beardsley, David, Junr | 2 | 3 | 1 | | |
| Beardsley, Aaron | 2 | 1 | 1 | | |
| Hayns, John | 1 | 2 | 3 | | |
| Edwards, Theophlus | 1 | | 1 | | |
| French, David | 3 | 1 | 4 | | |
| French, Samuel | 2 | 1 | 3 | | |
| French, John | 2 | | 1 | | |
| French, John | 1 | 1 | 1 | | |
| Curtis, Jones | 1 | | 1 | | |
| Curtis, Edmond | 3 | 1 | 4 | | |
| Wheeler, John | 4 | | 1 | | |
| Osborn, Nathanel | 1 | 1 | 5 | | |
| Beers, Elnathan | 1 | 2 | 2 | | |
| Beech, Jabez | 3 | 2 | 3 | | |
| Hogden (Widow) | | | 2 | | |
| Starling, Elijah | 3 | 2 | 2 | | |
| Beche, David | 2 | | 1 | | 1 |
| Wanright, William | 1 | | 3 | | |
| Curtis, Edmond | 3 | 5 | 2 | | |
| Booth, Silaman | 5 | 2 | 4 | | |
| Summers, David | 3 | 2 | 5 | | |
| Lane, Hanah | | | 1 | | |
| Curtis, John | 3 | | 5 | | |
| Turney, Samuel | 1 | | 1 | | |
| Turney, Ephraim | 1 | | 3 | | |
| Walker, Eliakim | 3 | | 3 | | |
| Midlebrook, Stephen | 2 | 1 | 2 | | |
| Midlebrook, Stephen, Jur | 1 | 2 | 1 | | |
| Beers, James | 1 | 1 | 5 | | |
| Tredwell, Sarah | | 1 | 5 | | |
| Turney, Robert | 1 | | | | |
| Turney, John | 1 | 2 | 4 | | |
| Midlebrook, Elizabeth | 1 | 1 | 2 | | |
| Midlebrook, John | 1 | | 1 | | |
| Fairchild, Daniel | 1 | | 2 | | |
| Turney, Daniel | 1 | | | | |
| Whiting, David | 1 | 2 | 1 | | |
| Midlebrook, Bine | 1 | | 2 | | |
| Fairweather, Zalmon | 1 | 1 | 2 | | |
| Turney, David | 2 | 2 | 8 | | |
| Turney, Elnathan | 1 | 1 | 2 | | |
| Turney, Gershom | 2 | 3 | 3 | | |
| Moyer, Nathaniel | 3 | 3 | 3 | | |
| Boor, David | 2 | 1 | 5 | | |
| Beebe, James | 1 | | 4 | | |
| Curtis, Joshua | 1 | 1 | 1 | | |
| Wakely, Thomas | 1 | 2 | 1 | | |
| Hawley, Elijah | 1 | | 2 | | |
| Jones, John | 1 | | 5 | | |
| Nichols, Jonathan | 2 | 3 | 4 | | 1 |
| Man, Richard | 1 | | 2 | | |
| Cable, William | 2 | | 2 | | |
| Curtis, Judson | 1 | 1 | 1 | | |
| Curtis, Judson, Junr | 1 | | 2 | | |
| French, Samuel, Junr | 1 | | 2 | | |
| Shermon, David | 1 | | 2 | | |
| Lewis, Samuel | 1 | 4 | 3 | | |
| Duncan, Charles | 2 | 2 | 2 | | |
| French, John | 1 | 1 | 1 | | |
| French, Samuel | 1 | 2 | 3 | | |
| Beech, Agar | 1 | 2 | 1 | | |
| Booth, Isaac | 2 | 2 | 2 | | |
| Ufford, John | 2 | | 5 | | |
| Ufford, Daniel | 1 | | 1 | | |

# FIRST CENSUS OF THE UNITED STATES.

## FAIRFIELD COUNTY—Continued.

| NAME OF HEAD OF FAMILY. | Free white males of 16 years and upward, including heads of families. | Free white males under 16 years. | Free white females, including heads of families. | All other free persons. | Slaves. | NAME OF HEAD OF FAMILY. | Free white males of 16 years and upward, including heads of families. | Free white males under 16 years. | Free white females, including heads of families. | All other free persons. | Slaves. | NAME OF HEAD OF FAMILY. | Free white males of 16 years and upward, including heads of families. | Free white males under 16 years. | Free white females, including heads of families. | All other free persons. | Slaves. |
|---|---|---|---|---|---|---|---|---|---|---|---|---|---|---|---|---|---|
| **STRATFORD TOWN**—con. | | | | | | **STRATFORD TOWN**—con. | | | | | | **STRATFORD TOWN**—con. | | | | | |
| Booth, David | 1 | | 2 | | 1 | Curtis, Samuel | 1 | 1 | 3 | | 1 | Beers, Abner | 2 | 1 | 2 | | 1 |
| Booth, David, Junr | 1 | | 4 | | 1 | Bennitt, Gidion | 1 | | 1 | | | Wells, James | 2 | | 4 | | |
| Ufford, Ebenezer | 2 | 2 | 3 | | | Bennitt, Benjamin | 1 | | 1 | | | Wells, Elias | 2 | 1 | 4 | | |
| Wetmore, Hezekiah | 1 | 2 | 3 | | 1 | Daton, Andrew | 1 | 2 | 4 | 1 | 2 | Thomson, David | 1 | | 2 | | |
| Seely, David | 2 | 2 | 6 | | | Brooks, William | 1 | 2 | 4 | | 1 | Beers, Jabez | 1 | | 3 | | |
| Hinman, Jonas | 1 | 2 | 3 | | | Fairchild, Robert | 2 | 3 | 3 | | | Curtis, Andrew | 1 | 1 | 2 | | |
| Booth, Filo | 1 | 3 | 3 | | | Walker, Joseph | 1 | 2 | | | | Clark, Samuel | 1 | 3 | 2 | | |
| Brinsley, Daniel | 1 | | 1 | 1 | | Brooks, Polly (Wid.) | | | 4 | 1 | | Peck, Judson | 1 | 1 | 5 | | |
| Coe, Zacheus | 2 | 2 | 4 | 1 | 1 | Tomlinson, Abraham | 1 | | 6 | | | Beers, Matthew | 2 | 1 | 1 | | |
| Coe, Aaron | 1 | 2 | 5 | | | Alent, Thomas | 1 | 2 | 2 | | 1 | Foot, Joseph | 2 | | 1 | | |
| Lamson, Nathanel | 1 | 1 | 4 | | | Witmon, Victory | 2 | | | | | Judson, William | 1 | 2 | 4 | | |
| French, Phebe | | | 2 | | | Lewis, Phinus | 1 | | 1 | | 1 | Curtis, David | 1 | 4 | 3 | | |
| Ufford, Samuel | 1 | 2 | 1 | | | Stebens, Stephen | 1 | 1 | 3 | | | Curtis, Judson | 1 | 1 | 3 | | |
| Wakely, Anna | | | 2 | 2 | | Curtis, Zelmon | 1 | 1 | 2 | | 1 | Curtis, Daniel | 1 | 1 | 6 | | |
| Beech, Eliakim | 1 | 3 | 2 | | | Deforest, Edward | 1 | 1 | 2 | | | Curtis, Agar | 1 | 3 | 1 | | |
| Hawley, Nero (Negro) | | | 4 | 4 | | McEuin, Abijah | 1 | 1 | 3 | | 1 | Peet, Stiles | 2 | | 5 | | |
| Beebe, Ruth | | | 3 | | | Judson, Abner | 1 | 1 | 4 | | | Curtis, Lewis | 2 | 1 | 6 | | |
| Edwards, Hezekiah | 1 | | 1 | | | Poor, Joshua | 1 | 2 | 5 | | | Walker, James | 1 | | 1 | | |
| Salmon, Richard | 1 | 1 | 5 | | | Hubill, Ebenezer | 3 | 4 | 3 | | | Walker, James, Junr | 1 | 3 | 2 | | |
| Beach, Elizabeth | | 3 | 1 | | | Deforist, Joseph | 1 | 2 | 6 | | 1 | Nichols, Sarah (Wid.) | 2 | | 3 | | |
| Beach, Agar, Junr | 2 | 1 | 2 | | | McEuin, Daniel | 1 | | 3 | | | Hurd, Gilead | 3 | | 3 | | |
| Beardsley, Lemuel | 1 | 2 | 3 | | | McEuin, John | 1 | 2 | 3 | | | Shermon, Nathan | 4 | 1 | 2 | | 1 |
| Hawley, Epharim | 2 | 1 | 2 | | 1 | McEuin, Matthew | 2 | 1 | 4 | | 1 | Pixley, William | 1 | 1 | 2 | | |
| Hawley, Andrew | 1 | | 2 | | | Coe, Ebenezer | 2 | 1 | 2 | | | Nichols, Nathaniel | 2 | 5 | 4 | | |
| Hawley, Mable | | | 1 | | | Birdsie, William | 1 | 1 | 1 | | | Taulsom, Elias | 2 | 1 | 3 | | |
| Diskom, Thomas | 1 | | 4 | | | Borough, Josiah | 1 | 1 | 2 | 7 | | Lewis, Stiles | 2 | 2 | 7 | | 2 |
| Siely, Betty (Wid.) | | | 2 | | | Porter, Stephen | 2 | 2 | 1 | | 2 | Crowel, Thomas | 3 | 1 | 6 | | |
| Peet, Daniel | 1 | 3 | 4 | | | Matcher, John | 2 | 1 | 3 | | | Toby (Negro) | | | | 3 | |
| Starlin, Ephraim | 3 | 2 | 5 | | | Robert, Wiliam | 1 | 1 | 2 | | | Hubbill, Samuel | 1 | 2 | 5 | | |
| Borough, Ciely | 1 | 2 | 3 | | | Beers, Joel | 1 | | 5 | | | Burrit, Stephen | 4 | | 2 | | |
| Summers, Daniel | 1 | 2 | 5 | | | Beers, Stephen | 2 | | 5 | | | Peet, Bersheba (Wid.) | 1 | 1 | 5 | | |
| Hayns, Lemuel | 1 | 4 | 3 | | | Plant, Solomon | 1 | 2 | | | | Patterson, Charity | | | 2 | | |
| Ives, Daniel | 1 | | 4 | | | Clark, Jerusha | 1 | 2 | 4 | | | Hubbill, Josiah | 2 | 2 | 2 | | |
| Wakely, Nehemiah | 1 | | 3 | | | Shermon, John | 1 | 1 | 3 | | | Lewis, Judson | 1 | 2 | 4 | | |
| Edwards, Elnathan | 1 | | 5 | | | Jones, Jasper | 1 | 2 | 2 | | | Hubbill, John | 2 | 2 | 3 | | |
| Hubbill, William | 1 | 2 | 6 | | | Nailer, John | 1 | 1 | 3 | | 1 | Lewis, Benjamin | 3 | 1 | 3 | | |
| Rose, William | 1 | 2 | 1 | | | Hows, Ebenezer | 1 | | 3 | | | Lewis, Joseph | 2 | | 2 | | 1 |
| Edwards, Nehemiah | 2 | | 2 | | | Cornwall, Thomas | 1 | 3 | 3 | | | Lamson (Widow) | | | 4 | | |
| Edwards, David | 1 | 1 | 3 | | | Lyons, David | 1 | 2 | 3 | | | Shermon, James | 2 | 1 | 4 | | |
| Edwards, Abel | 1 | 2 | 3 | | | Vos, Ebenezer | 1 | | 1 | | | Curtis, Fineus | 1 | 1 | 6 | | |
| Edwards, Couh | 1 | 1 | 3 | | | Fulsora, Mary | | | 2 | | | Curtis, Robert | 2 | 1 | 2 | | |
| Edwards, Reuben | 1 | 2 | 3 | | | Beardsly, John | 1 | 1 | 4 | | | Curtis, Joseph | 1 | 1 | 1 | | |
| Edwards, Thomas | 2 | | 3 | | 1 | Southard, William | 1 | | 1 | | | Bibbons, Timothy | 1 | | 3 | | |
| Edwards, John, 3d | 1 | 4 | 3 | | | Curtis, Abijah | 1 | 3 | 7 | | | Lampson, Nathanel | 2 | 3 | 3 | | |
| Edwards, David | 1 | | 2 | 2 | 2 | Curtis, Elihu | 1 | 2 | 3 | | | Philips, Thomas | 1 | | 1 | | |
| Edwards, John | 4 | 3 | 6 | | | Curtis, Daniel | 1 | 3 | 2 | | | Gorham (Widow) | | | 2 | | |
| Hubbill, Benjamin | 3 | | 6 | | | Frost, Stephen | 2 | 1 | 4 | | | Whiting, Samuel | 2 | 1 | 1 | | |
| Leman (Widow) | | | 3 | | | Wells, William | 1 | | 2 | | | Lewis, Filo | 1 | 4 | 2 | | |
| Wells, David | 2 | 1 | 3 | | | Thompson, David | 1 | 1 | 5 | | | Whiting, John | 1 | 1 | 3 | | |
| Wells, Gideon | 1 | 1 | 1 | | | Thomson, John | 1 | 1 | 5 | | | Walker, Phebe (Wid.) | | 1 | 2 | | |
| Hawly, Thomas | 4 | | 3 | | | Brooks, Abijah | 1 | 2 | 2 | | | Jones, Isaac | 1 | 2 | 1 | | |
| Bennitt, Samuel | 1 | | 3 | | | Walker, Joseph | 1 | 3 | 4 | 1 | 3 | Haris, Henery | 1 | | 2 | | |
| Hanes, William | 2 | 2 | 5 | | | Magraw, John | 1 | 1 | 3 | | | Barlow, David | 1 | 3 | 3 | | |
| Bulkley, Seth | 1 | 2 | 3 | | | Booth, John, Junr | 1 | 1 | | | | Osborn, Nathan | 3 | 2 | 2 | | |
| Sherwood, Stephen | 2 | 1 | 4 | | | Burritt, Hezekiah | 1 | | | | | Daton, Brewster | 2 | | 2 | | |
| Wakely, Molly (Wid.) | | | 1 | | | Burritt, Samuel | 2 | | 1 | | | Butler, Charles | 1 | 1 | 3 | | |
| Seely, Elijah | 1 | 1 | 1 | | | Burritt, Joseph | 2 | 2 | 4 | | | Lacy, Josiah | 2 | 1 | 5 | | 2 |
| Siely, Abel | 1 | | 1 | | | Gorham, Phebe | | | 2 | | | Peet, William | 1 | 3 | 4 | | |
| Peet, Elijah | 1 | 1 | 2 | | | Gorham, William | 1 | 2 | 3 | | | Allen, Nehemiah | 2 | | 2 | | |
| Wakely, David | 3 | 4 | 3 | | | Deforrest, Elihu | 3 | 1 | 5 | | | Allen, James | 2 | | 3 | | |
| Mitchel, Polly (Wid.) | 1 | 3 | 1 | | | Curtis, Samuel | 2 | | 4 | | | Baker, Jonathan | 1 | 2 | 3 | | |
| Beardsly, Benjamin | 2 | 3 | 4 | | | Cannon, James | 1 | | 3 | | 1 | Hawley, David | 1 | | 3 | | |
| Porter, Ephraim | 1 | 4 | 4 | | | Curtis, Jeremiah | 2 | | 3 | | | Young, Daniel | 3 | | 2 | | |
| Porter, Thomas | 3 | 1 | 4 | | | Burritt, Ephraim | 5 | | 3 | | | Clark, Ransom | 4 | 1 | 3 | | |
| Mallet, Philip | 1 | 4 | 3 | | | Russel, William | 1 | 5 | 3 | | | Smith, Justin | 1 | | 3 | | |
| Gregory, Gilman | 2 | 2 | 4 | | | Clifford, Elijah | 2 | 3 | 5 | | | Rose, Peter | 1 | 1 | 2 | | |
| Gregory, Enoch | 2 | 2 | 5 | | | Stretton, Anna | 2 | 3 | 4 | | | Hubbill, Amos | 3 | 3 | 2 | | 3 |
| Tredwell, Sarah | 1 | 1 | 6 | | | Nichols, Matthias | 2 | 3 | 6 | | 1 | Hinman, Isaac | 2 | 1 | 2 | | 1 |
| Beers, James | 1 | 1 | 2 | | | Osborn, Ephraim | 1 | 1 | 3 | | | Hubbill, Zalmon | 4 | 1 | 2 | | 2 |
| Coswell, Caleb | 2 | 1 | 3 | | | Elgar, Ezra | 2 | | 1 | | | Wilcox, Elisha | 1 | | 2 | | |
| Hubbard, Icabud | 2 | 2 | 4 | | | Curtis, Charles | 2 | 1 | 4 | | | Sherwood, Samuel | 1 | | 3 | | |
| Gregory, Samuel | 3 | 1 | 6 | | | Beardsley, Nathan | 2 | 3 | 3 | | | Brooks, Abijail (Wid.) | | 1 | 3 | | |
| Mallet, Joseph | 2 | 1 | 5 | | | Curtis, Esther (Wid.) | 1 | | 1 | | | Brooks, Benjamin | 1 | 3 | 4 | | |
| Gregory, Daniel | 1 | 1 | 5 | | | Siely, Mable | | | 3 | | | Benjamin, Aaron | 1 | 1 | 3 | | |
| Mallet, Seth | 1 | 2 | 2 | | | Beebe, Thomas | 1 | 1 | 2 | | | Brooks, John | 1 | | 2 | | |
| Jones, John | 1 | | 5 | | | Burrow, George | 4 | 1 | 2 | | | Benjamin, Asa | 1 | 1 | 1 | | |
| Midlebrook, Abiah | 1 | 2 | 4 | | | Blackman, Phineas | 2 | 1 | 3 | | | Beech, James | 1 | 2 | 3 | | |
| Mallet, Zacheriah | 1 | 3 | 5 | | | Wells, Hanah (Wid.) | 1 | 1 | 3 | | | Darrow, Nicholas | 1 | 1 | 6 | | |
| Whiting, David | 1 | 1 | 2 | | | Jones, Molly (Wid.) | | | 2 | | | Lake, Reubin | 2 | | 3 | | |
| Jerrald, Jame | 2 | 3 | 4 | | | Booth, John | 4 | 2 | 1 | | 2 | Wells, Jedediah F | 1 | 1 | 4 | | |
| Chambers, George | 1 | | 2 | | | Curtis, Joseph | 3 | 4 | 3 | | 2 | French, Gamaliel | 1 | 1 | 3 | | |
| Mallet, Samuel | 2 | 2 | 3 | | | Judson, Benjamin | 3 | | 3 | | | French, Benjamin | 1 | | 2 | | |
| Mallet, Zalmon | 1 | | 2 | | | Beardsly, Abraham | 3 | | 3 | | | Hall, Stephen | 1 | 2 | 8 | | |
| Mallet, David | 2 | 1 | 5 | | | Beardsly, Curtis | 1 | 4 | 2 | | | Beardsley (Widow) | | 2 | 3 | | |
| Mallet, Benjamin | 1 | | 1 | | | Booth, Hezekiah | 1 | 2 | 2 | | | Burrit, Charles | 2 | | 4 | | |
| Newreshic, Lewis | 1 | 1 | 3 | | | Booth, James | 1 | 2 | 4 | | | Parish, Joel | 1 | 1 | 4 | | |
| Mallet, Martha (Wid.) | 1 | 2 | 3 | | | Brooks, Isaac | 1 | 2 | 2 | | | Burriss, Stephen | 4 | 1 | 3 | | 2 |
| Mallet, John | 1 | 1 | 2 | | | Curtis, Stiles | 1 | 2 | 2 | | | Burrit, Elijah | 2 | | 7 | | |
| Siely, Phebe | | | 1 | | | Curtis, Edmond | 3 | 3 | 6 | | | Smith, Josiah | 1 | | 2 | | |
| Mallet, David, Junr | 2 | 3 | 3 | | | Curtis, Samuel | 1 | 1 | 1 | | | Smith, Jonathan | 1 | | 3 | | |
| Bennett, Nehemiah | | | 3 | | | Peck, Josiah | 1 | 3 | 3 | | | Borough, Griswell | 1 | 1 | 2 | | |
| Hall, Samuel | 1 | 3 | 3 | | | Curtis, Henery | 1 | | | | 1 | Booth, Samuel | 1 | 1 | 4 | | |
| Patterson, Hezekiah | 2 | 1 | 4 | | | Peck, Tabitha | | | 3 | | | Siely, Michael | 2 | | 5 | | |
| Osborn, William | 4 | 2 | 4 | | | Peck, Job | 2 | 4 | 2 | | | Siely, Seth | 2 | 1 | 3 | | |
| Curtis, Nehemiah | 1 | | 2 | | | Judson, Curtis | 1 | 1 | 2 | | | | | | | | |

# HEADS OF FAMILIES—CONNECTICUT.

## FAIRFIELD COUNTY—Continued.

| NAME OF HEAD OF FAMILY. | Free white males of 16 years and upward, including heads of families. | Free white males under 16 years. | Free white females, including heads of families. | All other free persons. | Slaves. | NAME OF HEAD OF FAMILY. | Free white males of 16 years and upward, including heads of families. | Free white males under 16 years. | Free white females, including heads of families. | All other free persons. | Slaves. | NAME OF HEAD OF FAMILY. | Free white males of 16 years and upward, including heads of families. | Free white males under 16 years. | Free white females, including heads of families. | All other free persons. | Slaves. |
|---|---|---|---|---|---|---|---|---|---|---|---|---|---|---|---|---|---|
| **STRATFORD TOWN—con.** | | | | | | **WESTON TOWN—con.** | | | | | | **WESTON TOWN—con.** | | | | | |
| Nichols, Philip | 3 | 1 | 4 | 1 | 3 | Wakeman, Daniel | 1 | 1 | 2 | | | Raymond, Ruth | 1 | | 1 | | |
| Barlow, Thomas | 1 | 3 | 4 | | | Sealy, Joseph | 2 | 1 | 4 | | | Jennings, Enoch | 1 | | 1 | | |
| Nichols, William | 1 | 1 | 7 | | | Oakly, Miles | 1 | 2 | 2 | | | Wadkins, William | 4 | 2 | 4 | | |
| Diseum, Robert | 3 | | 1 | | | Gilbert, Zalmon | 1 | 1 | 5 | | | Winton, John | 1 | | 1 | | |
| Siely, Michael | 1 | | 4 | | | Hubbill, Isaac | 1 | | 2 | | | Shermon, Andrew | 1 | 2 | 1 | | |
| Iarmgan, Jonathan | 1 | | 2 | | | Sealy, Nathaniel, Junr | 3 | 3 | 4 | | | Summers, Isaac | 1 | 1 | 4 | | |
| Bangs, Lemuel | 1 | | 2 | | | Dursy, Thomas, Junr | 1 | 1 | 3 | | | Summers, Elijah | 1 | 1 | 2 | | |
| Meeker, Isaac | 1 | 1 | 1 | | | Hubbill, Timothy | 2 | | 3 | | | Fairweather, Samuel | 1 | 1 | 1 | | |
| Hart, William | 1 | 1 | 4 | | | Siliman, David, 3d | 1 | 1 | 1 | | | Fairweather, Jonah | 1 | 1 | 2 | | |
| Taylor, William | 1 | | 2 | | | Jennings, Hezekiah | 2 | 1 | 2 | | | Winton, James | 1 | 3 | 2 | | |
| Diseum, James | 2 | | 2 | | | Crowfoot, James | 1 | 1 | 5 | | | Higgins, Isaac | 1 | | 2 | | |
| Beardsly, Silus | 1 | 4 | 1 | | | Sealy, Ephraim | 1 | 1 | 2 | | | Higgins, Abraham | 3 | 2 | 3 | | |
| Nichols, Thomas (Neg.) | | | | 5 | | Jennings, Nehimiah | 2 | 1 | 4 | | | Lacy, James | 1 | 1 | 2 | | |
| Frost, Joseph | 1 | 3 | 4 | | | Duncam, Edward | 1 | 1 | 2 | | | Gilbert, Thomas | 6 | 2 | 4 | | |
| Silemon, Hezekiah | 2 | 5 | 5 | | | Gilbert, John | 2 | | 2 | | | Curtis, Job | 1 | 3 | 4 | | |
| Lewis, Eli | 1 | 1 | 2 | | | Jennings, Hezekiah, Jr | 1 | 1 | 2 | | | Curtis, Benjamin | 2 | | 1 | | |
| Lewis, Nathaniel S | 2 | 1 | 3 | | | Wheeler, John | 2 | 1 | 3 | | | Curtis, John | 1 | 4 | 3 | | |
| Lewis, Nathan | 1 | 1 | 3 | | | Treadwell, David, Junr | 2 | 1 | 2 | | | Whealer, Eliphalet | 1 | 2 | 3 | | |
| Lewis, John | 1 | 1 | 7 | | | Oakly, Peter | 1 | 1 | 2 | | | Lyon, Ebenezer | 2 | | 5 | | |
| Lewis, Judson | 1 | 5 | 2 | | | Wheeler, Gideon | 1 | | 3 | | | Bennit, Thadeus | 2 | 2 | 4 | | |
| Thomson, Nehemiah | 1 | 2 | 3 | | | Mills, Ebenezer | 2 | | 3 | | | Murwin, John | 1 | 1 | 5 | | |
| Thomson, Abijah | 1 | 1 | 1 | | 1 | Foot, Nathan | 1 | 1 | 2 | | | Wheeler, Calvin | 1 | 1 | 6 | | |
| Burton, Samuel | 1 | 2 | 4 | | | Hill, Wakeman | 1 | 1 | 2 | | | Jones, John | 1 | 2 | 4 | | |
| Wilcox, Ephraim | 2 | 1 | 3 | | | Dimon, Benjamin | 3 | 1 | 3 | | | Homes, Daniel | 1 | | 7 | | |
| Wilcox, Elnathan | 1 | 2 | 2 | | | Burr, Moses | 2 | | 5 | | | Wheeler, Samuel | 1 | 1 | 2 | | |
| Wilcox, Nathan | 2 | | 3 | | | Adams, Abel | 1 | 2 | 3 | | | Darling, Samuel | 1 | 2 | 2 | | |
| Beardsly, Jeremiah | 2 | | 1 | 2 | | Lyon, Zacheriah | 2 | | 6 | | | Davis, Nathaniel | 1 | | 2 | | |
| Judson, Elihu | 1 | 1 | 3 | | | Odle, Daniel | 1 | 2 | 1 | | | Olmstead, Elijah | 3 | 4 | 5 | | |
| Judson, John | 1 | 3 | 2 | | | Judd, Reubin | 1 | 2 | 2 | | | Treadwell, Daniel | 2 | 2 | 3 | | |
| Wilcox, Gideon | 1 | 2 | 1 | | | Sealy, David | 1 | 1 | 4 | | | Gray, Daniel | 1 | | 3 | | |
| Wheeler, Samuel | 1 | 3 | 3 | | | Hall, Aaron | 1 | 3 | 5 | | | Lyon, Walter | 1 | 1 | 1 | | |
| Pendleton, William | 1 | 3 | 3 | | | Hall, Mary | | | 2 | | | Beardsly, Eliphalet | 1 | 3 | 2 | | |
| Lewis, Stephen | 1 | 2 | 3 | | 1 | Hall, Abel | 3 | 1 | 1 | | | Treadwell, Benjamin | 1 | 1 | 1 | | |
| Smith, John | 2 | 1 | 4 | | | Bennitt, James | 1 | 3 | 4 | | | Bennit, Samuel | 1 | 2 | 1 | | |
| Wells, Philip | 2 | 4 | 3 | | 1 | Bennitt, Aaron | 1 | | 1 | | | Jennings, Abraham | 1 | 4 | 5 | | |
| Thompson, Jonas | 2 | | 1 | | | Fairchild, Joel | 1 | | 2 | | | French, Ephraim | 2 | 2 | 4 | | |
| Booth, Abel | 1 | 2 | 8 | | | Wakelin, Samuel | 1 | | 1 | | | Lyon, Zacheriah, Junr | 1 | 2 | 3 | | |
| Hawly, Parson | 2 | 1 | 1 | | | Fairchild, Noami | | | 1 | | | Halis, John | 2 | 1 | 1 | | |
| Wells, Samuel | 1 | 2 | 2 | | 1 | Beardsly, Jabez | 2 | | 2 | | | Lacy, Joseph | 1 | | 5 | | |
| Wells, Stephen | 2 | | 2 | | 1 | Stratton, David | 2 | 2 | 3 | | | Wells, Samuel, Junr | 1 | 1 | 5 | | |
| Booth, Hilkiah | 2 | 1 | 2 | | | Nethersmith, Matthew | 2 | | 1 | | | Wells, Samuel | 3 | | 3 | | |
| Curtis, Isaac | 1 | | 2 | | | Summers, Henery | 2 | | 3 | | | Wells, Nathan | 1 | 1 | 2 | | |
| Clark, John | 1 | 2 | 2 | | | Bennitt, John | 3 | 1 | 2 | | | Lyon, Ezekiel | 1 | 4 | 2 | | |
| Juckets, Elijah | 1 | | 2 | | | Oakly, Jerad | 2 | 2 | 2 | | | Lyon, Sarah | | | 2 | | |
| Benson, Eben | 1 | 1 | 2 | | | Partlow, Abigail | | 2 | 2 | | | Fairchild, Gershom | 1 | 1 | 2 | | |
| Booth, Abijah | 3 | 2 | 3 | | | Shermon, Josiah | 4 | | 4 | | | Lyon, Gershom | 3 | 1 | 3 | | |
| Dayton, Brewster | 1 | 3 | 2 | | | Wadkins, Abel | 1 | 1 | 2 | | | Lyon, Daniel | 2 | 1 | 5 | | |
| Hawly, Edmond | 1 | 4 | 1 | | | Jennings, Hezekiah, 3d | 2 | 6 | 3 | | | Lyon, Thomas | 2 | 3 | 2 | | |
| Curtis, Silus | 1 | 5 | 6 | | 3 | Beach, Abel | 2 | 2 | 1 | 1 | | Lyon, Webb | 1 | 4 | 3 | | |
| Nodine, Lewis | 1 | 5 | 1 | | | Wheeler, Dimon | 1 | 1 | 2 | | | Lyon, Isaac | 1 | 3 | 4 | | |
| Russel, William | 1 | 5 | 2 | | | Lyon, Stephen | 1 | 4 | 2 | | | Edwards, Isaac | 1 | 1 | 1 | | |
| Cojah, Elizabeth | | 2 | 2 | | | Higby, Seth | 1 | 3 | 3 | | | Cardwell, John | 1 | 2 | 4 | | |
| Blackman, Zacheriah | 1 | 2 | 3 | | | Garit, David | 1 | 2 | 2 | | | Wakman, Samuel | 2 | 1 | 3 | 1 | 3 |
| Curtis, Elihu | 1 | 3 | 6 | | | Staples, Samuel | 1 | 4 | 1 | | | Wakman, Elijah | 1 | 3 | 3 | | |
| Curtis, John | 3 | 3 | 3 | | | Bennitt, Samuel | 1 | | 4 | | 1 | Wakeman, Samuel, Junr | 1 | | 4 | | |
| Birdsie, Thadeus | 1 | 1 | 2 | | | Siliman, David | 2 | 2 | 2 | | | Wheeler, Jabez | 1 | 1 | 2 | | |
| Tomlinson, Jabez N | 2 | 1 | 4 | | 1 | Jennings, William | 1 | 1 | 3 | | | Wheeler, Nathan | 2 | 2 | 4 | | |
| Birdsie, Ezra | 2 | 1 | 6 | | | Bennitt, Thomas | 1 | 2 | 3 | | | Olmstead, Daniel | 1 | | 2 | | |
| | | | | | | Silloman, Justus | 2 | 1 | 2 | | | Olmstead, Joseph | 1 | 1 | 3 | | |
| **WESTON TOWN.** | | | | | | Sherwood, Matthew | 1 | 2 | 2 | | | Thorp, Hezekiah | 1 | | 3 | | |
| Sherwood, John | 3 | 2 | 5 | | | Silliman, James | 1 | | 2 | | | Thorp, Samuel | 2 | 4 | 3 | | |
| Lyon, Andrew | 1 | | 1 | | 4 | Sanford, Sarah | | | 2 | | | Wakman, Lloyd | 1 | 3 | 3 | | |
| Treadwell, David | 2 | 3 | 2 | | | Bennitt, Content | | | 2 | | | Robertson, Jonathan | 2 | | 4 | | |
| Jacson, Francis | 1 | | 5 | | | Sherwood, Thomas | | | 2 | | | Gilbert, Joseph | 1 | 1 | 2 | | |
| Osbone, Jeremiah | 1 | 1 | 2 | | | Levitt, Josiah | 1 | 3 | 3 | | | Robertson, Jonathan, Jnr | 1 | | 3 | | |
| Stratton, Thomas | 1 | 2 | 2 | | | Sherwood, Daniel | 2 | 1 | 2 | | | Rockwell, Noah | 1 | 2 | 4 | | |
| Siely, Ebenezer | 1 | 1 | 3 | | | Hoyt, William | 1 | 2 | 1 | | | Bennitt, Nathan | 3 | 3 | 5 | | |
| Siely, Nathaniel | 3 | | 3 | | | Jackson, Daniel | 1 | 1 | 1 | | | Rockwell, John | 1 | 3 | 2 | | |
| Johnson, James | 2 | 1 | 4 | | | Jackson, John | 2 | | 1 | | | Cable, Nehemiah | 3 | 1 | 4 | | |
| Gilbert, Thadeus | 2 | 7 | 7 | | | Jackson, Nathan | 1 | | 1 | | | Hambleton, William | 1 | | 1 | | |
| Parrot, John | 3 | 1 | 3 | | | Jackson, Aden | 2 | | 2 | | | Gilbert, Reubin | 1 | 2 | 4 | | |
| Jewel, Hanah | | | 3 | | | Osborn, Jerad | 1 | 1 | 2 | | | Bradly, William | 2 | 1 | 2 | | |
| Cable, Ebenezer | 1 | | 2 | | | Sherwood, Thomas | 1 | | 2 | | | Fanton, Jonathan | 2 | 3 | 4 | | |
| Bradley, Joseph | 1 | | 3 | | | Hall, Byer | 1 | 1 | 2 | | | Godfry, Moses | 1 | 1 | 3 | | |
| Winton, Joseph | 1 | 2 | 5 | | | Odle, David | 1 | 2 | 2 | | 1 | Cable, Ruth | | | 2 | | |
| Cable, Joseph | 2 | | 3 | | | Beers, Ephraim | 3 | 1 | 3 | | | Morehouse, Daniel | 2 | 1 | 3 | 1 | 1 |
| Nichols, Daniel | 1 | 1 | 4 | | | Beers, David | 1 | 2 | 2 | | | Morehouse, Joseph | 1 | 1 | 3 | | |
| Redfield, Sarah | 2 | | 2 | | | Taylor, David | 2 | 2 | 6 | | | Morehouse, Banks | 1 | | 1 | | |
| Wheeler, Ezra | 1 | 4 | 3 | | | Taylor, Baroch | 2 | 2 | 2 | | | Dikeman, Hezekiah | 1 | 1 | 1 | | |
| Winton, Ezra | 2 | 3 | 1 | | | Whitehead, Nathaniel | 1 | 3 | 4 | | | Lockwood, John | 1 | 6 | 4 | | |
| Lyon, Joseph | 1 | | 2 | | | Wilson, Joseph | 2 | 4 | 1 | | | Abrahams, George H | 1 | 2 | 2 | | |
| Baldwin, Gabriel | 4 | 1 | 5 | | | Gold, Nathan | 1 | 1 | 2 | | | Cole, Jonathan | 1 | 2 | 4 | | |
| Sherwood, Amos | 2 | 5 | 5 | | | Baker, David | 1 | | 2 | | | Patchen, Jacob | 1 | 1 | 2 | | |
| Sherwod, Fanton | 1 | | 3 | | | Squire, Arel | 1 | 2 | 3 | | | Phinny, Jesse | 3 | 1 | 2 | | |
| Brindsmaid, Cyrus | 1 | | 2 | | | Barlow, Nehemiah | 1 | 1 | 2 | | | Duncan, Daniel | 4 | 2 | 4 | | |
| Brindsmde, Josiah | 1 | | 2 | | | Coble, Daniel | 3 | 2 | 2 | | | Rockwell, Jonah | 2 | 4 | 4 | | |
| Mills, Ebenezer | 1 | 2 | 2 | | | Goodsell, Samuel | 1 | | 2 | | | Sturges, Ezekiel | 1 | 1 | 3 | | |
| Bennitt, Daniel | 2 | 1 | 4 | | | Bradley, Isaac | 1 | 1 | 3 | 1 | | Sturges, Jabel | 4 | 1 | 2 | | |
| Sanford, Josiah | 2 | | 5 | | | Wakman, Nathan | 1 | 2 | 4 | | | Beers, Nathan | 1 | | 1 | | |
| Gregory, William | 2 | 1 | 2 | | | Turney, David | 1 | 4 | 2 | | | Beers, Pinkany | 1 | 3 | 2 | | |
| Wheeler, Elnathan | 1 | | 2 | | | Jennings, Philow | 1 | | 2 | | | Bigsbie, Ebenezer | 1 | 2 | 2 | | |
| Siliman, David, Junr | 3 | 2 | 8 | | | Sealy, Jesse | 2 | 3 | 2 | | | Squire, Seth | 1 | 1 | 3 | | |
| Bennitt, William | 1 | 1 | 2 | | | Beach, Nathaniel | 1 | 2 | 1 | | | Squire, Stephen | 1 | 1 | 2 | | |
| | | | | | | Levet, Josiah G | 1 | 3 | 2 | | | | | | | | |

# FIRST CENSUS OF THE UNITED STATES.

## FAIRFIELD COUNTY—Continued.

### WESTON TOWN—con.

| NAME OF HEAD OF FAMILY. | Free white males of 16 years and upward, including heads of families. | Free white males under 16 years. | Free white females, including heads of families. | All other free persons. | Slaves. |
|---|---|---|---|---|---|
| Gray, Anna | | | 2 | | |
| Andrews, Silliman | 3 | 2 | 5 | | |
| Rowland, Samuel | 2 | 2 | 4 | | |
| Burr, Moses | 1 | | 5 | | 1 |
| Higgens, Tommy | 1 | 3 | 1 | | 1 |
| Higgens, John | 1 | | 1 | | |
| Ogden, Joseph | 1 | 1 | 5 | | |
| Duncan, Jerard | 1 | 3 | 2 | | |
| Squire, Sealy | 2 | 4 | 4 | | |
| Sturges, James | 1 | 3 | 4 | | |
| Lockwood, Gideon | 1 | 4 | 3 | | |
| Squire, Thomas | 1 | 1 | 4 | | |
| Godfry, Jonathan | 1 | 2 | 3 | | |
| Godfry, David | 1 | | 1 | | |
| Godfry, Daniel | 1 | 2 | 1 | | |
| Godfry, Silliman | 2 | 2 | 4 | | |
| Osborn, William | 1 | | 3 | | |
| Osborn, Isaac | 1 | 4 | 3 | | |
| Osborn, Hezekiah | 3 | 1 | 3 | | |
| Patchen, George | 4 | 1 | 6 | | |
| Gilbert, Ebenezer | 1 | 2 | 4 | | |
| Morehouse, Michael | 1 | 2 | 2 | | |
| Brown, Elisha | 2 | 2 | 3 | | |
| Row, Daniel M | 1 | | 1 | | |
| Row, Beniah M | 2 | 1 | 5 | | |
| Thorp, Gershom | 1 | | 3 | | |
| Thorp, Jacob | 1 | | 3 | | |
| Gorham, Jacob (Negro) | | | | 3 | |
| Fanton, Gershom | 1 | | 1 | | |
| Wilkson, James | 1 | | 1 | | |
| Thorp, Nathan | 1 | 1 | 3 | | |
| Banks, Joseph | 1 | | 5 | | |
| Banks, Thomas | 1 | 3 | 3 | | |
| Nichols, Gold | 1 | | 3 | | |
| Treadwell, Joseph | 1 | 1 | 4 | | |
| Lyon, Ephraim | 3 | 1 | 4 | | |
| Davis, Joseph | 3 | 2 | 1 | | |
| Thorp, Jabez | 1 | 1 | 2 | | |
| Williams, Elnathan | 3 | 1 | 3 | | |
| Platt, Jesse | 2 | 2 | 5 | | |
| Gilbert, Andrew | 3 | 1 | 1 | | |
| Hull, Moses | 1 | 1 | 3 | | |
| Bradley, Ebenezer | 1 | 2 | 2 | | |
| Burr, Increase | 1 | 3 | 2 | | |
| Bennitt, Ezekiel | 1 | | 4 | | |
| Shermon, Sarah | | | | 2 | |
| Sturges, Moses | 1 | 2 | 3 | | |
| Nichols, John | 1 | 3 | 7 | 1 | |
| Burr, Eliphalet | 2 | | 2 | | |
| Nichols, Peter | 1 | 2 | 6 | | |
| Banks, Hezekiah | 2 | 1 | 5 | | |
| foot, Levi | 1 | 2 | 2 | | |
| Ryla, John | 1 | 2 | 3 | | |
| Baker, Samuel | 3 | 2 | 2 | | |
| Jennings, Benjamin | 3 | | 1 | | |
| Davis, Ebenezer | 2 | 1 | 2 | | |
| Canfield, Ezekiel | 1 | 2 | 5 | | |
| Davis, Ebenezer | 1 | | 2 | | |
| Cable, Isaac | 2 | 1 | 2 | | |
| Dimon, John | 1 | | 4 | | |
| Robertson, Seth | 1 | 2 | 3 | | |
| Fanton, Abel | 1 | | 3 | | |
| Murwin, David | 3 | | 2 | | |
| Bradley, Enos | 1 | 2 | 1 | | |
| Murwin, Seth | 1 | 1 | 1 | | |
| Murwin, Samuel | 2 | | 3 | | |
| Rowland, Jonathan | 2 | | 3 | | |
| Burr, John | 1 | 1 | 2 | | |
| Parrick, Molly | | 2 | 4 | | |
| Murwin, Eppepras | 1 | | 3 | | |
| Fanton, Nehemiah | 3 | 2 | 1 | | |
| Treadwell, Thomas | 3 | 1 | 2 | | |
| Treadwell, Nathan | 1 | 1 | 1 | | |
| Bradley, Francis | 1 | | 2 | | |
| Bradly, Gershom | 1 | 1 | 4 | | 2 |
| Bradley, Eliphalit | 1 | 2 | 2 | | 1 |
| Bradley, Gershom, Junr | 1 | | 2 | | |
| Perry, Job | 1 | 2 | 1 | | |
| Wakeman, Aaron | 2 | | 4 | | |
| Banks, Austin | 1 | 2 | 2 | | |
| Bradley, Levi | 1 | 1 | 2 | | |
| Gilbert, Lewis | 1 | 1 | 3 | | |
| Demon, Noah | 2 | 1 | 2 | | |
| Bradly, David | 1 | 1 | 3 | | 1 |
| Bradley, Lyman | 1 | 6 | 8 | | |
| Stocker, Mary | | | 3 | | |
| Davis, David | | | 2 | | |
| Davis, John | 1 | | 5 | | |
| Williams, Peter | 3 | 3 | 2 | | 1 |
| Fanton, Hezekiah | 1 | 3 | 4 | | |
| Murwin, Nathan | 1 | | 2 | | |
| Collyer, Thomas | 2 | 3 | 3 | | |
| Fanton, John, Junr | 1 | 1 | 2 | | |
| Sturges, Stephen | 1 | 2 | 9 | | |
| Fanton, John | 2 | | 1 | | 1 |
| Thorp, Ebenezer | 1 | | 5 | | |
| Thorp, Thadeus | 1 | 5 | 2 | | |
| Coley, Eliphalet | 2 | | 5 | | |
| Banks, Daniel | 1 | 2 | 1 | | |
| Thorp, Ebenezer, Junr | 1 | | 4 | | |
| Thorp, Peter | 1 | | 1 | | |
| Osborn, Ephraim | 1 | 3 | 3 | | |
| Dyars, Andrew | 2 | | 2 | | |
| Blackman, Nehemiah | 1 | 3 | 2 | | |
| Blackman, Daniel | 2 | 1 | 4 | | |
| Benton, Cyrus | 2 | 3 | 3 | | |
| Beleh, Josiah | 1 | | 4 | | |
| Sly, Thomas | 1 | 1 | 2 | | |
| Sawly, Thomas | 1 | 2 | 1 | | |
| Green, Solomon | 1 | | 2 | | |
| Smith, Seth | 1 | | 1 | | 1 |
| Hoyt, Seth | | 2 | 4 | | |
| French, Samuel | 1 | 2 | 4 | | |
| Hawley, David | 1 | | 1 | | |
| Hawley, Daniel | 1 | 1 | 3 | | |
| Harris, Robert | 1 | 3 | 2 | | |
| Sherwood, Joseph | 1 | 5 | 1 | | 1 |
| Hubbill, Nathaniel | 2 | 1 | 4 | | |
| Prince, William | 3 | 5 | 1 | 1 | |
| Bennit, Benjamin | 2 | 1 | 4 | | |
| Hall, Esbon | 1 | 3 | 4 | | |
| Beardsley, Benjamin | 2 | 3 | 5 | | |
| Steward, Charles | 1 | 3 | 3 | | |
| Porter, Joseph | 1 | 1 | 4 | | |
| Porter, David | 1 | 4 | 2 | | |
| Gregory, Samuel | 1 | | 4 | | |
| Daton, Sylus | 1 | | 3 | | |
| Booth, Thadeus | 2 | | 7 | | |
| Bennit, Isaac | 2 | 1 | 1 | | |
| Gilbert, Burr | 1 | | 3 | | |
| Bennit, Isaac | 1 | | | | |
| Baily, Henery | | | 2 | | |
| Hubbill, Stephen | 1 | 2 | 2 | | |
| Booth, John | 1 | | 1 | | |
| Broach, Mary | | 1 | 2 | | |
| Burton, Solomon | 2 | 4 | 3 | | |
| Simers, Hezekiah | 1 | 1 | 5 | | |
| Turril, Daniel | 1 | 4 | 2 | | |
| Gregory, Stephen | 2 | 1 | 3 | | |
| Hubbill, Seth | 1 | | 5 | | |
| Turril, Stephen | 2 | 3 | 3 | | |
| Hubbill, Ebenezer | 2 | | 3 | | |
| Summers, Nathan | 2 | 3 | 2 | | |
| Thorp, David | 1 | 3 | 5 | | |
| Sherwood, Levet | 1 | 1 | 2 | | |
| Fairchild, Ephraim | 3 | 1 | 3 | | |
| Hilton, Adkisson | 1 | | 3 | | |
| Gray, James | 2 | 1 | 2 | | |
| Coly, David, Junr | 1 | | 4 | | |
| Gray, Gideon | 1 | | 4 | | |
| Gray, Nathan | 1 | | 4 | | |
| Morehouse, Andrew | 1 | | 2 | | |
| Lyon, Hezekiah | 3 | 1 | 4 | | |
| Taylor, Jonathan | 1 | 1 | 1 | | |
| Dikman, John | 1 | 1 | 1 | | |
| Lockwood, Albert | 1 | 2 | 4 | | |
| Adams, Nathan | 3 | 2 | 6 | | |
| Bulkly, Talcot | 1 | 1 | 1 | | |
| Sherwood, Jabez | 2 | 2 | 3 | | |
| Sherwood, Seymour | 1 | | 2 | | |
| Smith, David | 2 | 3 | 2 | | |
| Gorham, Shubal | 2 | | 2 | | |
| Gray, Elijah | 2 | 5 | 2 | | |
| Coley, Morehouse | 1 | 1 | 2 | | 1 |
| Betterson, Joseph | 1 | 2 | 4 | | |
| Coley, Ebenezer | 5 | 1 | 4 | 3 | 5 |
| Crossman, Trowbridge | 1 | 2 | 1 | | |
| Thorp, John | 1 | 2 | 2 | | |
| Bennit, Elias | 1 | 3 | 4 | | |
| Adams, Squire | 2 | 1 | 2 | | |
| Adams, David | 1 | | 2 | | |
| Adams, Silaman | 1 | 3 | 2 | | |
| Coly, David | 2 | 1 | 2 | | |
| Morehouse, Nathan | 2 | 1 | 2 | | |
| Marvin, Brush | 1 | 1 | 2 | | |
| Osterbank, Moses | 2 | 1 | 4 | | |
| Dears, Benjamin | 2 | | 1 | | 1 |
| Noyes, John | 1 | 2 | 3 | | 1 |
| Rowland, Jeremiah | 2 | 3 | 2 | | |
| Persons, Peter | 3 | | 3 | | |
| Morehouse, Jesse | 1 | 3 | 2 | | |
| Godfry, Elias | 1 | 3 | 1 | | |
| Beers, Ezra | 1 | 1 | 2 | | |
| Godfry, Eleazer | 1 | | 1 | | |
| Godfry, David | 1 | 3 | 2 | | |
| Godfry, Cristopher | 1 | 3 | 2 | | |
| Beers, Isaac | 1 | 1 | 1 | | |
| Rowland, Daniel | 1 | 3 | 2 | | |
| Winkley, Henery | 1 | 1 | 3 | | |
| Bulkley, David | 1 | 2 | 3 | | |
| Godfry, Isaac | 1 | 1 | 2 | 1 | |
| Siely, Abel | 2 | | 2 | | |
| Beers, Nehemiah | 2 | 1 | 4 | | |
| Beers, Fanton | 1 | 2 | 3 | | |
| Beers, Ephraim | 2 | 1 | 2 | | |
| Beers, Jonathan | 1 | 1 | 6 | | |
| Brothington, Samuel | 1 | 3 | 3 | | |
| Coley, Jonathan | 2 | | 2 | | |
| Coley, Jonathan, Jur | 1 | 3 | 1 | | |
| Guire, Eben | 1 | 2 | 2 | | |
| Fanton, Zebulen | 1 | 1 | 3 | | |
| Gray, John | 2 | 2 | 3 | | |
| Morehouse, Jabez | 1 | | 2 | | |
| Lord, Sarah | 2 | 2 | 7 | | |
| Morehouse, David | 1 | 2 | 5 | | |
| Wood, Obadiah | 1 | 1 | 1 | | |
| Wood, Samuel | 2 | 1 | 2 | | 1 |
| Adams, Joshua | 1 | 2 | 3 | | |
| Sturges, Peter | 2 | 1 | 3 | | |
| Lockwood, John | 1 | 2 | 2 | | |
| Hutenack, Francis | 2 | 1 | 2 | | |
| Sherwood, Samuel B | 1 | 1 | 3 | | 2 |
| Dikeman, Eliphalet | 1 | 1 | 2 | | |
| Andrews, Daniel | 1 | 1 | 1 | 1 | 3 |
| Andrews, Daniel, Junr | 1 | 3 | 5 | | 1 |
| Fitch, Cuff (Negro) | | | | 9 | |
| Elwood, Joseph | 1 | 2 | 4 | | |

## HARTFORD COUNTY.

### BERLIN TOWN.

| NAME OF HEAD OF FAMILY. | Free white males of 16 years and upward, including heads of families. | Free white males under 16 years. | Free white females, including heads of families. | All other free persons. | Slaves. |
|---|---|---|---|---|---|
| Andrus, Moses | 3 | | 4 | | |
| Andrus, Nathaniel | 1 | | 2 | | |
| Atkins, Benjamin | 2 | | 3 | | |
| Andrus, Levi | 3 | 1 | 3 | | |
| Andrus, Hezekiah | 1 | 2 | 5 | | |
| Andrus, Hezekiah, Jr | 1 | 1 | 1 | | |
| Andrus, Josiah | 1 | | 3 | | |
| Andrus, Joseph | 2 | | 5 | | |
| Andrus, Elijah | 1 | 2 | 3 | | |
| Atkins, Hezekiah | 1 | 2 | 2 | | |
| Andrus, Moses, Jr | 1 | 2 | 6 | | |
| Booth, Nathan | 1 | 1 | 1 | | |
| Booth, Robert | 1 | 1 | 3 | | |
| Booth, Thomas | 1 | 1 | 2 | | |
| Belden, Leonard | 1 | 1 | 4 | | |
| Belden, Jonathan | 3 | 1 | 4 | | |
| Booth, Elisha | 1 | 1 | 5 | | |
| Booth, Elisha | 1 | 1 | 5 | | |
| Bass, Samuel | 1 | 3 | 4 | | |
| Bassett, Cornelius | 2 | | 6 | | |
| Booth, Joseph | 1 | 4 | 3 | | |
| Booth, James | 1 | 2 | 3 | | |
| Brunson, Elijah | 1 | | 2 | | |
| Brunson, Elijah, Jr | 1 | 4 | 2 | | |
| Brunson, Samuel | 1 | 3 | 3 | | |
| Booth, Nathan, Jr | 2 | 4 | 2 | | |
| Brunson, Noadiah | 1 | | 2 | | |
| Booth, Stephen | 1 | | 1 | | |
| Curtis, Ebenezer | 1 | 3 | 2 | | |
| Churchill, Nathaniel | 1 | 1 | 6 | | |
| Churchill, Nathaniel, Jr | 1 | 2 | 2 | | |
| Clark, Abel | 1 | 3 | 2 | | |
| Churchill, Stephen | 1 | 2 | 3 | | |
| Churchill, Sage | 1 | 1 | 2 | | |
| Cornwall, Robert | 3 | 1 | 3 | | |
| Cadwell, Roderic | | | | | |
| Clark, Solomon | 1 | 1 | 4 | | |
| Cone, Joshua | 1 | 3 | 5 | | |

# HEADS OF FAMILIES—CONNECTICUT.

## HARTFORD COUNTY—Continued.

### BERLIN TOWN—con.

| NAME OF HEAD OF FAMILY. | Free white males of 16 years and upward, including heads of families. | Free white males under 16 years. | Free white females, including heads of families. | All other free persons. | Slaves. |
|---|---|---|---|---|---|
| Couch, Ebenezer | 1 |  | 2 |  |  |
| Dewey, David | 3 |  | 2 |  |  |
| Dewey, Josiah | 1 | 2 | 2 |  |  |
| Dickenson, Samuel | 1 |  | 1 |  |  |
| Dickenson, Samuel, Jr. | 2 | 1 | 2 |  |  |
| Dickenson, Elijah | 1 | 1 | 3 |  |  |
| Doolittle, Ephraim | 2 | 2 | 4 |  |  |
| Daniels, David | 1 | 2 | 3 |  |  |
| Daley, Samuel | 1 | 1 | 2 |  |  |
| Dunham, David | 1 |  | 2 |  |  |
| Eddy, Charles | 2 | 4 | 5 |  |  |
| Frances, Elijah | 2 |  | 3 |  |  |
| Frances, James | 1 | 2 | 4 |  |  |
| Frances, Elijah, Jr | 1 | 1 | 1 |  |  |
| Frances, Justin | 1 | 1 | 3 |  |  |
| Gridley, Oliver | 1 | 1 | 5 |  |  |
| Griswold, Gideon | 1 |  | 3 |  |  |
| Griswold, Ashbel | 1 | 3 | 4 |  |  |
| Gladden, Samuel | 1 |  | 1 |  |  |
| Goodrich, David | 1 | 2 | 2 |  |  |
| Goodrich, Jediahah | 1 |  | 2 |  |  |
| Gridley, Thomas | 2 | 1 | 2 |  |  |
| Griswold, Experience |  |  | 1 |  |  |
| Goodrich, Isaac | 2 |  | 1 |  |  |
| Goodrich, Zenas | 1 | 2 | 2 |  |  |
| Halet, Mabel |  | 1 | 3 |  |  |
| Hart, Elijah | 3 | 1 | 3 |  |  |
| Hart, Thomas | 1 | 1 | 2 |  |  |
| Hart, Jehuda | 2 | 3 | 5 |  |  |
| Hart, Benjamin | 2 | 1 | 4 |  |  |
| Hart, Elizur | 4 | 2 | 4 |  |  |
| Hart, Elijah, Jr. | 2 | 4 | 2 |  |  |
| Hart, Judah | 1 | 3 | 5 |  |  |
| Hinsdale, John | 1 |  | 3 |  |  |
| Hinsdale, Elijah | 3 |  | 5 |  |  |
| Hollister, Rebecca |  | 1 | 5 |  |  |
| Hart, Bethel | 1 |  | 4 |  |  |
| Hart, Elisha | 1 | 2 | 5 |  |  |
| Hart, Asahel | 1 | 2 | 4 |  |  |
| Hotchkiss, Lemuel | 3 | 2 | 6 |  |  |
| Hart, Stephen | 2 |  | 3 |  |  |
| Hills, David | 2 | 1 | 1 |  |  |
| Hollister, Stephen | 1 | 1 | 2 |  |  |
| Hotchkiss, Ludwick | 1 | 3 | 4 |  |  |
| Hart, Aaron | 1 | 1 | 3 |  |  |
| Hollister, Thomas | 1 | 1 | 4 |  |  |
| Judd, Isaac | 1 |  | 2 |  |  |
| Judd, Anthony | 2 | 2 | 3 |  |  |
| Judd, Job | 2 | 2 | 2 |  |  |
| Judd, James | 1 | 3 | 4 |  |  |
| Judd, Daniel | 1 | 2 | 2 |  |  |
| Judd, Mary |  |  | 1 |  |  |
| Judd, John | 3 | 1 | 2 |  |  |
| North, Asher | 1 | 1 | 4 |  |  |
| Kilbourn, Timothy | 1 | 2 | 6 |  |  |
| Kilbourn, Seth | 1 | 2 | 2 |  |  |
| Kilbourn, Martha |  |  | 1 |  |  |
| Lee, Isaac | 1 |  | 1 | 2 |  |
| Lee, Isaac, Jr. | 2 | 2 | 4 |  |  |
| Langdon, John | 2 | 2 | 4 |  |  |
| Lewis, Adonijah | 2 | 1 | 2 |  |  |
| Lusk, John | 2 |  | 3 |  |  |
| Lusk, Elata |  |  | 3 |  |  |
| Lusk, David | 1 |  | 1 |  |  |
| Lusk, Seth | 1 | 2 | 3 |  |  |
| Lusk, David, Jr. | 1 | 2 | 3 |  |  |
| Lincoln, Simeon | 1 | 2 | 3 |  |  |
| Ludington, Daniel | 1 | 1 | 1 |  |  |
| Ludington, Collins | 1 |  | 2 | 1 |  |
| Lewis, James |  |  | 1 | 1 |  |
| Mather, David | 2 |  | 3 |  |  |
| Mather, Joseph, Jr. | 2 | 1 | 7 |  |  |
| Merrit, William | 1 |  | 1 |  |  |
| North, James | 3 | 4 | 5 |  |  |
| Ossgood, Jeremiah H. | 1 | 1 | 3 |  |  |
| Pratt, William | 1 | 3 | 4 |  |  |
| Pratt, Andrew | 1 |  | 3 |  |  |
| Penfield, Phinias | 1 | 2 | 5 |  |  |
| Penfield, Nathaniel | 2 | 2 | 3 |  |  |
| Roberts, Aaron | 1 |  | 1 |  |  |
| Roberts, Aaron, Jr. | 3 |  | 2 |  |  |
| Recor, Michael | 1 |  | 2 |  |  |
| Rugg, Solomon | 1 |  | 3 |  |  |
| Rice, Abigail |  |  | 4 |  |  |
| Smally, John | 3 |  | 5 |  |  |
| Smith, Joseph | 2 | 1 | 2 |  |  |
| Stanley, Timothy | 3 | 2 | 4 |  |  |
| Stanley, Gad | 3 | 2 | 6 |  |  |
| Smith, Samuel | 5 |  | 2 |  |  |
| Smith, Elnathan | 1 | 2 | 6 |  |  |
| Smith, Elijah | 1 | 3 | 2 |  |  |
| Stanley, Seth | 1 | 6 | 7 |  |  |
| Stanley, Lott | 2 | 2 | 8 |  |  |
| Stanley, Noah | 1 | 1 | 2 | 1 |  |
| Smith, Joel | 1 | 3 | 2 |  |  |
| Stanley, Ruth | 1 |  | 2 |  |  |
| Steele, Ebenezer | 1 |  | 3 |  |  |
| Steele, Ebenezer | 1 | 2 | 3 |  |  |
| Stedman, Charles, Jr. | 1 | 3 | 3 |  |  |
| Steele, Josiah | 1 | 2 | 4 |  |  |
| Steele, William | 1 | 2 | 2 |  |  |
| Steele, Selah | 1 | 1 | 2 |  |  |
| Shipman, Samuel | 2 | 3 | 4 |  |  |
| Stedman, John | 1 | 3 | 3 |  |  |
| Stedman, Thomas | 1 | 4 | 2 |  |  |
| Stiles, Robert | 1 | 2 | 2 |  |  |
| Seymour, Lewis | 1 | 1 | 1 |  |  |
| Sagden, Thomas | 1 | 3 | 4 |  |  |
| Smith, John | 1 |  | 3 |  |  |
| Woodruff, Seth | 1 |  | 2 |  |  |
| Woodruff, Amos | 1 | 2 | 5 |  |  |
| Woodford, Bissel | 2 | 2 | 3 |  |  |
| Webster, Joshua | 1 | 2 | 3 |  |  |
| Wright, Joseph | 1 | 5 | 1 |  |  |
| Wright, Reuben | 1 | 3 | 4 |  |  |
| White, Ezra | 1 | 1 | 2 |  |  |
| Whaples, Elezur | 1 | 1 | 2 |  |  |
| Woodruff, Gad | 1 | 1 | 1 |  |  |
| Wetherill, David | 2 | 2 | 1 |  |  |
| Wright, Ann |  |  | 4 |  |  |
| Warner, Thomas | 1 |  | 3 |  |  |
| Atwood, Josiah | 1 |  | 3 |  |  |
| Allyn, John B | 4 | 2 | 6 |  |  |
| Andrus, Amos | 2 |  | 1 |  |  |
| Brunson, Jesse | 1 | 2 | 5 |  |  |
| Brunson, Elnathan | 1 | 1 | 4 |  |  |
| Brunson, Asahel | 2 | 1 | 2 |  |  |
| Brunson, Luke | 2 | 2 | 6 |  |  |
| Barret, Robert | 2 |  | 2 |  |  |
| Belden, John | 1 |  | 2 |  |  |
| Belden, John, Jr. | 1 | 1 | 2 |  |  |
| Brown, Thomas | 1 |  | 1 |  |  |
| Brunson, Titus | 3 |  | 3 |  |  |
| Brunson, Nathaniel | 1 |  | 3 |  |  |
| Brunson, Ebenezer | 1 | 4 | 5 |  |  |
| Bailey, Jonathan | 1 | 1 | 1 |  |  |
| Brunson, John | 1 |  | 1 |  |  |
| Brunson, Roger | 2 | 1 | 1 |  |  |
| Barns, Jonathan | 2 | 3 | 3 | 1 | 1 |
| Ball, Oliver | 1 | 2 | 2 |  |  |
| Brunson, Abigail |  |  | 1 |  |  |
| Cowles, Asahel | 1 |  | 4 |  |  |
| Cowels, Samuel | 1 | 2 | 3 |  |  |
| Cowles, Jabez | 1 | 3 | 2 |  |  |
| Cole, Mathew | 2 | 1 | 3 |  |  |
| Cole, Selah | 1 | 1 | 4 |  |  |
| Cowles, Noah | 2 | 2 | 4 |  |  |
| Cole, Gideon | 1 | 2 | 7 |  |  |
| Cole, Stephen | 2 | 3 | 3 |  |  |
| Cole, Nathaniel | 2 | 1 | 1 |  |  |
| Crofoot, Epraim, Jr. | 1 | 2 | 1 |  |  |
| Cole, Rebecca | 1 |  | 4 |  |  |
| Cowles, Selah | 1 | 2 | 4 |  |  |
| Cole, John | 3 | 2 | 5 |  |  |
| Cole, Seth | 1 |  | 1 |  |  |
| Dickenson, Moses | 3 | 2 | 6 |  |  |
| Dunham, Barnabus | 3 |  | 5 |  |  |
| Gridley, Abel | 1 | 3 | 4 |  |  |
| Gridley, Clement | 1 | 1 | 3 |  |  |
| Bilbert, John | 1 |  | 1 |  |  |
| Gridley, Amos | 2 | 1 | 2 |  |  |
| Gridley, Selah | 1 | 2 | 3 |  |  |
| Gridley, Roger | 1 | 4 | 2 |  |  |
| Goodrich, Seth | 2 | 1 | 3 |  |  |
| Gridley, Judath | 1 |  | 2 |  |  |
| Howard, Edward | 2 |  | 1 |  |  |
| Hart, Gideon | 1 | 1 | 2 |  |  |
| Hart, Thomas, Jr. | 1 | 1 | 3 |  |  |
| Hooker, Elijah | 3 | 5 | 3 |  |  |
| Hooker, Samuel | 1 | 1 | 3 |  |  |
| Hart, Selah | 2 |  | 3 | 1 |  |
| Hart, Roger | 1 | 1 | 4 |  |  |
| Hooker, William | 1 | 2 | 3 |  |  |
| Hart, Hezekiah | 3 |  | 4 |  |  |
| Hurlbut, Calven | 2 | 3 | 5 |  |  |
| Hart, Oliver | 1 |  | 2 |  |  |
| Hart, Mathew | 2 |  | 3 |  |  |
| Hart, Mathew, Jr | 1 |  | 3 |  |  |
| Hurlbut, Isaac | 1 |  | 1 |  |  |
| Hills, Abraham | 1 |  | 3 |  |  |
| Hills, Gideon | 1 | 1 | 6 |  |  |
| Hill, Josiah | 1 |  | 2 |  |  |
| Hill, Jonathan | 2 |  | 1 |  |  |
| Hosington, John | 1 | 1 | 1 |  |  |
| Hosington, Salmon | 1 |  | 2 |  |  |
| Hart, Salmon | 2 | 1 | 4 |  |  |
| Hopkins, Caleb | 4 | 2 | 4 |  |  |
| Hopkins, Benjamin | 2 |  | 5 |  |  |
| Judd, Hezekiah | 1 | 1 | 5 |  |  |
| Jones, George | 1 | 2 | 1 |  |  |
| Judd, Gideon | 2 | 3 | 4 |  |  |
| Judd, Amos | 1 | 1 | 2 |  |  |
| Kelsey, William | 1 | 3 | 4 |  |  |
| Langton, Jonathan | 1 | 2 | 2 |  |  |
| Lee, Samuel | 1 | 1 | 1 |  |  |
| Lee, Oren | 3 | 1 | 2 |  |  |
| More, Roswell | 1 | 2 | 1 |  |  |
| Mather, Joseph | 1 | 1 | 2 |  |  |
| Mark, Miles | 1 |  | 2 |  |  |
| Measureall, Christopher | 1 |  | 1 |  |  |
| Norton, Stephen | 2 | 2 | 2 |  |  |
| Norton, Roger | 1 |  | 3 |  |  |
| Norton, Roger, Jr | 1 | 3 | 6 |  |  |
| Norton, Josiah | 2 | 4 | 4 |  |  |
| Parkerson, William | 2 | 1 | 3 |  |  |
| Peck, Isaac | 1 |  | 5 |  |  |
| Percival, James | 3 | 2 | 4 |  |  |
| Percival, James, Jr | 1 |  | 3 |  |  |
| Peck, Joseph | 1 | 2 | 6 |  |  |
| Peck, Oliver | 3 | 3 | 2 |  |  |
| Peck, Samuel | 2 | 1 | 2 |  |  |
| Peck, Eldad | 1 |  | 2 |  |  |
| Peck, Amos, Jr | 2 | 1 | 5 |  |  |
| Peck, Amos | 2 |  | 1 |  |  |
| Persons, John | 4 |  | 3 |  |  |
| Peck, Mathew | 1 |  | 2 |  |  |
| Prior, Mary |  | 2 | 3 |  |  |
| Root, Thomas | 2 |  | 2 |  |  |
| Root, Noah | 1 | 1 | 6 |  |  |
| Root, Job | 2 | 2 | 3 |  |  |
| Root, Daniel | 2 | 1 | 3 |  |  |
| Sexton, Simeon | 1 |  | 3 |  |  |
| Seymour, Jonathan | 2 |  | 4 |  |  |
| Stockin, John | 1 | 2 | 2 |  |  |
| Squire, Solomon | 1 |  | 2 |  |  |
| Stanley, Martha |  | 1 | 2 |  |  |
| Stanley, Elijah | 2 | 2 | 3 |  |  |
| Stanley, John | 1 | 3 | 2 |  |  |
| Stanley, Oliver | 1 | 1 | 3 |  |  |
| Scovill, Ezra | 1 | 1 | 4 |  |  |
| Stockin, Luther | 1 | 3 | 2 |  |  |
| Smith, Allyn | 2 | 3 | 6 |  |  |
| Smith, Asaph | 1 | 1 | 3 |  |  |
| Shepard, Isaiah | 1 |  | 2 |  |  |
| Smith, Solomon | 1 |  | 2 |  |  |
| Tryon, James | 2 | 1 | 4 |  |  |
| Upson, Benoni | 1 | 2 | 4 |  |  |
| Wells, Joseph | 2 |  | 3 |  |  |
| Wells, Joseph, Jr | 1 | 2 | 2 |  |  |
| Wells, Sylvester | 2 | 3 | 2 |  |  |
| Williams, Gideon | 2 | 1 | 3 |  |  |
| Wyard, Lemuel | 1 | 2 | 3 |  |  |
| Wilkinson, Amos | 1 | 1 | 4 |  |  |
| Winchell, Hezekiah | 1 | 1 | 2 |  |  |
| Winchell, Solomon | 1 | 1 | 2 |  |  |
| Winchell, Stephen | 1 |  | 3 |  |  |
| Warner, Daniel | 1 | 1 | 4 |  |  |
| Williams, Samuel | 2 | 2 | 4 |  |  |
| Winchell, William | 2 | 1 | 4 |  |  |
| Winchell, Salmon | 1 | 1 | 1 |  |  |
| Winchell, Roger | 1 | 1 | 1 |  |  |
| Andrus, George | 1 | 1 | 2 |  |  |
| Allis, Abel | 1 |  | 2 |  |  |
| Brandier, Elishama | 2 | 3 | 3 |  |  |
| Buckley, Selah | 1 | 1 | 2 |  |  |
| Barns, Eli | 4 |  | 2 |  |  |
| Buckley, Elias | 2 |  | 2 |  |  |
| Buckley, Elias, Jr. | 1 | 3 | 2 |  |  |
| Benton, Jonathan | 1 |  | 2 |  |  |
| Benton, Jonathan, Jr. | 1 | 4 | 3 |  |  |
| Buckley, Benjamin | 2 |  | 1 |  |  |
| Buckley, Jonathan | 1 | 1 | 4 |  |  |
| Buckley, Oliver | 1 | 2 | 2 |  |  |
| Belden, Ashbel | 1 |  | 2 |  |  |
| Buckley, David | 2 | 2 | 2 |  |  |
| Crutenden, Jonathan | 1 |  | 3 |  |  |
| Clark, Ezekiel | 1 |  | 4 |  |  |
| Cook, William | 2 | 1 | 3 |  |  |
| Cook, Lucius | 1 |  | 1 |  |  |
| Crofoot, Ephraim | 1 |  | 2 |  |  |
| Crofoot, Joseph | 1 |  | 1 |  |  |
| Cornwall, Nathaniel | 2 | 2 | 5 |  |  |
| Curtis, Giles | 1 |  | 2 |  |  |
| Clark, David | 2 | 4 | 3 |  |  |
| Danielson, Deborah |  |  | 2 |  |  |
| D. Wolf, Stephen | 1 | 1 | 5 |  |  |
| Deming, Moses | 1 | 1 | 2 | 1 |  |
| Deming, Moses, Jr. | 1 |  | 1 |  |  |
| Deming, Seth | 2 | 4 | 2 |  |  |
| Deming, Lardner | 1 | 2 | 1 |  |  |
| Deming, John | 1 |  | 2 |  |  |
| Deming, David | 1 | 1 | 2 |  |  |

## HARTFORD COUNTY—Continued.

| NAME OF HEAD OF FAMILY. | Free white males of 16 years and upward, including heads of families. | Free white males under 16 years. | Free white females, including heads of families. | All other free persons. | Slaves. | NAME OF HEAD OF FAMILY. | Free white males of 16 years and upward, including heads of families. | Free white males under 16 years. | Free white females, including heads of families. | All other free persons. | Slaves. | NAME OF HEAD OF FAMILY. | Free white males of 16 years and upward, including heads of families. | Free white males under 16 years. | Free white females, including heads of families. | All other free persons. | Slaves. |
|---|---|---|---|---|---|---|---|---|---|---|---|---|---|---|---|---|---|
| **BERLIN TOWN—con.** | | | | | | **BERLIN TOWN—con.** | | | | | | **BRISTOL TOWN—con.** | | | | | |
| Deming, Jacob | 1 | | 1 | | | Sage, Jedediah | 1 | 2 | 4 | | | Hall, Samuel | 2 | | 3 | | |
| Dunham, Solomon | 2 | 1 | 3 | 1 | | Sage, Solomon | 1 | 1 | 3 | | | Obverd, Thomas | 1 | 1 | 6 | | |
| Dunham, Warner | 2 | 1 | 2 | | | Sage, Zadock | 1 | 2 | 4 | | | Jones, Nathaniel | 1 | | 1 | | |
| Dunham, Elishama | 1 | 2 | 1 | | | Sage, Solomon, Jr | 1 | 2 | 5 | | | Conwell, Benjamin, Jr. | 1 | 2 | 3 | | |
| Deming, Israel | 1 | 1 | 5 | | | Squire, Elias | 1 | 2 | 4 | | | Johnson, Daniel, 2d | 1 | 2 | 1 | | |
| Dickenson, Nathaniel | 1 | | 1 | | | Sage, Jonathan | 1 | 1 | 2 | | | Brooks, Samuel | 2 | 1 | 1 | | |
| Dickenson, Nathaniel, Jr | 1 | | 2 | | | Sage, Abraham | 1 | 1 | 5 | | | Brooks, Samuel, Jr | 1 | | 1 | | |
| Dickinson, David | 1 | 2 | 3 | | | Savage, Selah | 1 | 1 | 3 | | | Benham, Joel | 2 | | 3 | | |
| Edwards, Josiah | 2 | 2 | 4 | | | Savage, Seth | 1 | 2 | 4 | | | Benham, James | 1 | 4 | 1 | | |
| Fuller, Ephraim | 1 | | 1 | | | Savage, Elisha | 1 | 1 | 4 | | | Tompkins, Phillip | 1 | | 4 | | |
| French, Daniel | 1 | | 5 | | | Savage, Elisha, Jr | 1 | 1 | 1 | | | Hotchkiss, Elijah | 1 | 3 | 2 | | |
| Flagg, Solomon | 2 | 3 | 4 | | | Smith, Wait | 2 | 2 | 3 | | | Spring, Timothy | 1 | 2 | 4 | | |
| Galpin, Peat | 2 | | 2 | | | Smith, Josiah | 2 | | 4 | | | Wheeler, William | 1 | 1 | 4 | | |
| Galpin, Benjamin | 2 | 1 | 1 | | | Stanley, Seth | 1 | 1 | 4 | | | Broock, Abraham | 3 | 2 | 2 | | |
| Galpin, Thomas | 2 | 1 | 5 | | | Sanford, Silas | 1 | 1 | 3 | | | Brooks, Isaac | 2 | 4 | 3 | | |
| Galpin, Joseph | 1 | 2 | 3 | | | Sage, Oliver | 1 | 1 | 1 | | | Linsley, Jacob | 3 | 3 | 2 | | |
| Goodrich, John | 1 | 1 | 2 | | | Sage, David | 1 | 1 | 1 | | | Leming, Judah | 1 | 1 | 3 | | |
| Gilbert, Seth | 1 | 1 | 7 | | | Wilcox, Israel | 1 | 1 | 5 | | | Johnson, Daniel | 2 | | 2 | | |
| Gilbert, Moses | 2 | 1 | 2 | | | Wilcox, Josiah | 3 | 2 | 5 | | | Rowe, Stephen | 1 | 3 | 2 | | |
| Gilbert, Hooker | 1 | 1 | 4 | | | Wilcox, Samuel | 1 | 4 | 1 | | | Peck, Lament | 2 | 2 | 3 | | |
| Gilbert, Jonathan | 2 | 1 | 2 | | | Wilcox, Sarah | | | 2 | | | Hungerford, Jacob | 1 | 4 | 2 | | |
| Gilbert, Jonathan, Jr | 1 | 1 | 2 | | | Wilcox, Jacob | 1 | 4 | 3 | | | Hungerford, Benjm | 1 | | 1 | | |
| Gilbert, Thomas | 1 | | | | | Webster, David | 2 | 1 | 2 | | | Gridley, Hezekiah | 2 | | 1 | | |
| Gilbert, Mary | | | 2 | | | Webster, David, Jr | 1 | 1 | 3 | | | Ives, Ammon | 1 | 1 | 2 | | |
| Goodrich, Elias | 1 | | 3 | | | Wright, Abraham | 1 | 4 | 3 | 1 | | Barns, Daniel | 1 | 4 | 2 | | |
| Goodrich, Salmon | 1 | 1 | 1 | | | Willcox, Stephen | 2 | 2 | 4 | | | Gridley, Asahel | 1 | 2 | 2 | | |
| Goodrich, Asahel | 1 | | 2 | | | Woodruff, Roswell | 1 | 2 | 1 | | | Cogswell, Robert | 1 | | 3 | | |
| Hart, Samuel | 1 | 2 | 4 | | | Woodruff, Selah | 1 | | | | | Peck, Zebulon | 2 | 3 | 7 | | |
| Hart, John | 2 | | 2 | | | Watson, John | 1 | 3 | 2 | | | Johnson, Daniel, Jr. | 1 | 1 | 4 | | |
| Hart, Levi | 2 | 1 | 3 | | | Wilton, Luther | 1 | 1 | 1 | | | Jearoms, Canuy | 1 | 2 | 2 | | |
| Hollister, Ephraim | 2 | 2 | 2 | | 1 | Tryall, William | 2 | 1 | 4 | | | Barns, Thomas | 2 | 3 | 4 | | |
| Hubbard, William, Jr | 1 | 1 | 1 | | | Porter, Eliphalet | 1 | 1 | 3 | | | Roberts, Seth | 1 | 2 | 2 | | |
| Hart, Asahel | 2 | | 1 | | | Buckley, Richard | 2 | | 3 | | | Thompson, Reuben | 2 | 1 | 4 | | |
| Hollister, Solomon | 1 | 2 | 4 | | | Bishop, Ebenezar | 1 | 1 | 1 | | | Roberts, Jabiz | 1 | | 3 | | |
| Hubbard, Samuel | 2 | 1 | 3 | | | Green, Perry | 1 | 1 | 1 | | | Stone, James | 1 | 3 | 3 | | |
| Hubbard, William | 2 | 1 | 2 | | | Fenn, Nathan | 2 | | 4 | | | Allyn, Samuel | 2 | 3 | 3 | | |
| Hubbard, Abijah | 1 | 2 | 3 | | | | | | | | | Allyn, Abel | 1 | 2 | 4 | | |
| Hubbard, Jonathan | 3 | 2 | 2 | | | **BRISTOL TOWN.** | | | | | | Johnson, Amos | 1 | 3 | 2 | | |
| Hubbard, George | 2 | 3 | 3 | | | Lewis, Roger | 2 | 3 | 4 | | | Bartholumew, Jacob | 3 | 2 | 5 | | |
| Hart, Zacheriah | 2 | 1 | 2 | | | Lewis, Eli | 3 | 1 | 8 | | | Upson, Friman | 2 | 2 | 5 | | |
| Hosford, Amos | 1 | | 5 | | | Lewis, Abel | 1 | 1 | 7 | | | Peck, Lyssim | 1 | | 4 | | |
| Hurlbut, Raphael | 2 | 3 | 3 | | | Buck, Deborah | | | 1 | | | Byington, Joseph | 1 | 4 | 3 | | |
| Hurlbut, James | 1 | 1 | 1 | | | Lewis, Josiah | 1 | | 2 | | | Mix, Timothy | 2 | 1 | 3 | | |
| Hurbut, Sarah | | | 2 | | | Lewis, Roger | 1 | 2 | 3 | | | Ives, Enos | 1 | 2 | 5 | | |
| Johnson, Samuel | 2 | 2 | 5 | | | Lewis, Josiah | 1 | 2 | 4 | | | Rogers, Nehemiah | 2 | | 1 | | |
| Kelsey, John | 2 | 2 | 2 | | | Lewis, Samuel | 3 | 3 | 4 | | | Rogers, Lent | 1 | 2 | 2 | | |
| King, Lois | 1 | 2 | 6 | | | Lewis, Mark | 1 | 2 | 2 | | | Lownsbury, Samuel | 1 | | 3 | | |
| Kelsey, Stephen | 1 | 2 | 2 | | | Thompson, Isaiah | 3 | 2 | 3 | | | Upson, Saul | 1 | | 4 | | |
| Kelsey, Charles | 2 | 2 | 4 | | | Roberts, Daniel | 1 | 2 | 1 | | | Byington, Noah | 1 | 1 | 3 | | |
| Kelsey, Ezekial | 1 | | 1 | | | Hart, Thomas | 1 | 1 | 3 | | | Lownsbury, David | 1 | | 3 | | |
| Kelsey, Ezekial, Jr | 1 | 1 | 5 | | | Gaylord, Elizur | 2 | | 2 | | | Jearoms, William, Jr | 1 | 1 | 4 | | |
| Kelsey, Asahel | 2 | 3 | 3 | | | Gaylord, Joseph | 1 | | 1 | | | Mix, Prime | | | | | 8 |
| Lee, John | 1 | | 2 | | | Gridley, Luke | 3 | | 6 | | | Jearoms, Benjamin | 1 | 1 | 2 | | |
| Lee, John, Jr | 1 | 1 | 2 | | | Newill, Samuel | 3 | 2 | 4 | | | Jearoms, Willm | 2 | | 2 | | 2 |
| Loveland, Elisha | 3 | 2 | 3 | | | Upson, Asa | 2 | | 2 | | | Freman, Peter | | | | 3 | |
| Mitchel, Joel | 1 | | 2 | | | Upson, Asa, Jr | 2 | 1 | 2 | | | Freeman, Cuff | | | | 3 | |
| Norton, Andrew | 2 | 1 | 3 | | | Newill, David | 3 | | 3 | | | Adams, Samuel | 1 | | 1 | | |
| Norton, Samuel | 1 | 1 | 3 | | | Root, Theodore | 2 | | 6 | | | Lee, John | 2 | 2 | 1 | | |
| Norton, Isaiah | 1 | 1 | 1 | | | Adams, Elisha | 1 | 2 | 1 | | | Lewis, David | 2 | 2 | 2 | | |
| Norton, Elnathan | 2 | 1 | 3 | | | Johnson, Chandler | 1 | 2 | 2 | | | Botchford, Theophilus | 1 | 3 | 4 | | |
| Norton, Elnathan, Jr | 1 | | 2 | | | Holt, Josiah | 1 | 1 | 2 | | | Haddfull, James | 5 | 2 | 4 | | |
| Norton, Solomon | 2 | 2 | 1 | | | Hungerford, Levi | 1 | 2 | 5 | | | Yate, Abel | 2 | 1 | 8 | | |
| North, Samuel | 1 | 2 | 4 | | | Linsley, Keturah | 1 | 3 | 4 | | | Yate, Thomas | 1 | | 1 | | |
| Norton, Jedidiah | 1 | | 1 | | | Hart, Gilbert | 1 | | 2 | | | Barns, Josiah | 1 | 2 | 1 | | |
| North, Isaac | 2 | | 2 | | | Rowe, Joseph | 3 | 1 | 2 | | | Peck, Susanna | | | 1 | | |
| North, Seth | 1 | 2 | 7 | | | Hendrick, Abel | 1 | 2 | 2 | | | Hendrick, John | 1 | 1 | 1 | | |
| North, Levi | 2 | 1 | 2 | | | Hitchcox, Nathaniel | 2 | | 2 | | | Hendrick, Daniel | 1 | | 2 | | |
| North, Abel | 1 | | 2 | | | Carrington, Lemuel | 2 | 3 | 4 | | | Hart, Benjamin | 1 | 1 | 5 | | |
| North, Jedediah | 1 | 1 | 4 | | | Mathews, Nathaniel | 2 | | 2 | | | Jeroams, Zerubbabel | 1 | 3 | 3 | | |
| North, Simeon | 2 | 2 | 2 | | | Mathews, Nathaniel, Jr. | 1 | | 2 | | | Bartholomew, Abram | 1 | | 3 | | |
| Nott, Charles | 1 | | 2 | | | Shelton, Isaac W | 1 | 1 | 5 | | | Wilcox, Benjamin | 1 | 3 | 2 | | |
| Nott, Charles, Jr | 1 | 3 | 1 | | | Arnold, Tennur | 1 | 4 | 2 | | | Wilcox, John | 1 | | 1 | | |
| North, Stephen | 1 | 1 | 1 | | | Ives, Amasa | 1 | 6 | 3 | | | Webster, Aaron | 1 | 1 | 5 | | |
| North, Joseph | 1 | 3 | 3 | | | Adams, Samuel, Jr | 1 | 3 | 3 | | | Richard, William | 1 | 2 | 8 | | |
| North, Samuel | 1 | | 2 | | | Mathews, John | 2 | 1 | 7 | | | Andrus, Ezekiel | 1 | 2 | 8 | | |
| Porter, Isaac | 1 | 3 | 4 | | | Andrus, Noah | 1 | 1 | 3 | | | Gladden, Jedidiah | 1 | 1 | 3 | | |
| Porter, Samuel | 2 | | 4 | | | French, Elisha | 1 | 2 | 1 | | | Palmer, Judah | 1 | | 2 | | |
| Porter, Samuel, 2d | 2 | 2 | 4 | | | Hart, Ithurel | 1 | 2 | 3 | | | Heron, Samuel | 1 | 7 | 5 | | |
| Porter, Samuel, 3d | 2 | | 2 | | | Hungerford, Thomas | 1 | 3 | 7 | | | Churchill, Benjm | 1 | 2 | 1 | | |
| Porter, Abel | 2 | | 6 | | | Mathews, Caleb | 4 | 2 | 3 | | | Churchill, Ira | 1 | | 1 | | |
| Porter, Aaron | 2 | 1 | 4 | | | Hill, Miles | 1 | | 1 | | | Churchill, Samuel | 1 | 1 | 2 | | |
| Porter, Abijah | 2 | 3 | 2 | | | Hill, Dan | 1 | 3 | 4 | | | Bradley, Abel | 1 | | 5 | | |
| Porter, Joseph, Jr | 1 | 1 | 2 | | | Ives, Lent | 1 | 3 | 5 | | | Marross, Elisha | 2 | 1 | 4 | | |
| Peck, Joseph | 3 | 1 | 4 | | | Gaylord, Joseph, 2d | 4 | 2 | 3 | | | Marross, Elijah | 1 | 1 | 3 | | |
| Peck, Jesse | 2 | | 3 | | | Gaylord, William | 1 | | 4 | | | Fox, Elisha | 2 | | 4 | | |
| Paterson, Edward | 2 | 2 | 1 | | | Hitchcock, Harvie | 1 | | 2 | | | Rich, Thaddeus | 1 | | 4 | | |
| Paterson, Sherbail | 3 | | 1 | | | Roberts, Joseph | 1 | 2 | 6 | | | Hall, Phebe | | 3 | 4 | | |
| Paterson, Elizabeth | | | 1 | | | Driggs, Daniel | 2 | | 2 | | | Root, Natha H | 1 | 2 | 6 | | |
| Presby, Charles | 3 | | 3 | | | Kate, Isaac | 1 | | 2 | | | Frisleer, Levi | 1 | | 2 | | |
| Riley, Roger | 1 | 4 | 4 | 1 | | Hill, Gaines | 1 | 2 | 2 | | | Barns, Amos | 2 | 1 | 2 | | |
| Root, John | 1 | | 3 | 1 | | Ledyard, Charles | 1 | 2 | 5 | | | Barns, Judah | 1 | 4 | 7 | | |
| Root, Asahel | 1 | | 2 | | | Fuller, Simeon | 2 | | 2 | | | Jearoms, Thomas | 3 | 1 | 15 | | |
| Richards, Joseph | 3 | 1 | 3 | | | Fuller, Edmund | 2 | | 1 | | | Johnson, Simeon | 1 | 7 | 5 | | |
| Richarson, Zebulon | 2 | | 5 | | | Scovil, Abijah | 1 | 1 | 4 | | | Johnson, Abigail | 1 | 5 | 1 | | |
| Steele, David | 2 | 1 | 2 | | | | | | | | | Ives, Reuben | 2 | 2 | 2 | | |

# HEADS OF FAMILIES—CONNECTICUT.

## HARTFORD COUNTY—Continued.

| NAME OF HEAD OF FAMILY. | Free white males of 16 years and upward, including heads of families. | Free white males under 16 years. | Free white females, including heads of families. | All other free persons. | Slaves. | NAME OF HEAD OF FAMILY. | Free white males of 16 years and upward, including heads of families. | Free white males under 16 years. | Free white females, including heads of families. | All other free persons. | Slaves. | NAME OF HEAD OF FAMILY. | Free white males of 16 years and upward, including heads of families. | Free white males under 16 years. | Free white females, including heads of families. | All other free persons. | Slaves. |
|---|---|---|---|---|---|---|---|---|---|---|---|---|---|---|---|---|---|
| **BRISTOL TOWN—con.** | | | | | | **BRISTOL TOWN—con.** | | | | | | **BRISTOL TOWN—con.** | | | | | |
| Lee, James | 2 | | 2 | | | Moses, Reuben | 1 | 1 | 3 | | | Covey, Jared | 1 | 2 | 4 | | |
| Andrus, Lament | 1 | 3 | 3 | | | Moses, Othaniel | 1 | 2 | 4 | | | Covey, Elisha | 1 | 1 | 3 | | |
| Woods, John | 1 | | 2 | | | Brown, Elisha | 1 | 3 | 2 | | | Covey, Silus | 1 | | 1 | | |
| Lee, W<sup>m</sup> | 2 | 2 | 4 | | | Page, Titus | 1 | 3 | 2 | | | Covey, Elijah | 1 | | 1 | | |
| Dannaly, John | 1 | | 1 | | | Barnes, Elijah | 1 | | 1 | | | Tubbs, Elijah | 1 | | 1 | | |
| Wilcox, Elijah | 4 | | 1 | | | Andruss, Sam<sup>u</sup> 1 | 1 | 2 | 3 | | | Hotchkiss, Samuel | 1 | 3 | 4 | | |
| Gaylord, David | 2 | 5 | 3 | | | Andruss, Sam<sup>u</sup> | 2 | 2 | 2 | | | Crandal, John | 1 | 1 | 5 | | |
| Gridley, Hezekiah, Jr | 1 | 2 | 2 | | | Andruss, Han | 1 | 1 | | | | Lewis, John | 1 | | 2 | | |
| Mitchel, W<sup>m</sup> | 1 | 4 | 4 | | | Moses, Othaniel | 1 | | 3 | | | Wilcox, John | 1 | 1 | 1 | | |
| Linsley, Jon<sup>th</sup> | 2 | 3 | 4 | | | Barnes, Lois | 1 | | 1 | | | Davis, Jon<sup>th</sup> | 2 | 3 | 4 | | |
| Rich, W<sup>m</sup> | 1 | 3 | 5 | | | Fuller, Ambros | 1 | 1 | 5 | | | Pettibone, Aexander | 1 | | 2 | | |
| Norton, Aaron | 1 | 5 | 2 | | | Woodruff, Seth | 2 | | 3 | | | Hemecage, Abraham | 1 | 4 | 5 | | |
| Rich, J<sup>no</sup> | 1 | 1 | 3 | | | Griswold, Jeremiah | 2 | 3 | 5 | | | Bacon, Joseph | 2 | | 5 | | |
| Roberts, W<sup>m</sup> | 1 | 3 | 3 | | | Humphrey, Jiles | 2 | 1 | 5 | | | Bacon, Roswell | 1 | 1 | 1 | | |
| Mitchel, Jotham | 1 | 1 | 3 | | | Smith, Phineas | 1 | 3 | 5 | | | Lewis, Benjamin | 1 | 1 | 8 | | |
| Robert, Gideon | 1 | 3 | 4 | | | Hill, Freeman | | | | 2 | | Bacon, Moses | 1 | 1 | 6 | | |
| Roberts, Amasa | 1 | 2 | 3 | | | Starks, Ichabod | 1 | | 1 | | | Rust, Alone | 1 | | 1 | | |
| Hungerford, Timothy | 1 | 3 | 4 | | | Starks, Ichabod, Jr | 1 | 3 | 4 | | | Doad, Ezra | 2 | 1 | 3 | | |
| Gaylord, J<sup>no</sup> | 1 | 4 | 3 | | | Woodford, Josiah | 1 | 2 | 2 | | | Cleveland, Ezra | 1 | 2 | 4 | | |
| Cowles, Mary | 1 | 1 | 1 | | | Cornwall, Benjamin | 1 | 2 | 1 | | | Rust, Amos | 1 | 2 | 2 | | |
| Gaylord, Jesse | 3 | | 2 | | | Nearing, John | 1 | 4 | 4 | | | Covil, Ebenezer | 1 | 2 | 2 | | |
| Gaylord, Elijah | 2 | | 3 | | | Pettibone, Chancey | 1 | 4 | 4 | | | Lewis, Stephen | 2 | | 4 | | |
| Gaylord, Elam | 1 | | 1 | | | Smith, Joseph | 1 | 1 | 2 | | | Doad, Amos | 1 | 1 | 4 | | |
| Gaylord, Samuel | 1 | | 2 | | | Petibone, Thodore | 1 | 4 | 4 | | | Doad, Stephen | 1 | 3 | 1 | | |
| Adams, Luke | 2 | 1 | 5 | | | Fuller, John | 2 | 1 | 3 | | | Willcox, Stephen | 1 | 3 | 1 | | |
| Trusdale, Joel | 1 | 1 | 2 | | | Hicox, Freeman | 1 | 1 | 3 | | | Doad, Jesse | 1 | 3 | 4 | | |
| Bowen, Bezahil | 1 | 1 | 4 | | | Mills, Job | 1 | 1 | 3 | | | Stephens, Joshua | 2 | 1 | 6 | | |
| Gridley, Moses | 1 | | 2 | | | Mills, J<sup>no</sup> | 2 | | 1 | | | Wiard, Seth | 2 | 1 | 6 | | |
| Murray, Thomas | 1 | | 1 | | | Mills, Noah | 1 | | 3 | | | Woodruff, Asa | 1 | | 3 | | |
| Norton, Isaac | 1 | | 1 | | | Foot, Samuel | 1 | | 3 | | | West, Hezekiah | 1 | 5 | 2 | | |
| Norton, Isaac, Jr | 1 | 2 | 4 | | | Higley, Ebenezer | 1 | | 2 | | | Yate, Ezra | 3 | 3 | 2 | | |
| Norton, Joel | 1 | 5 | 2 | | | Smith, Grove | 2 | | 4 | | | Lewis, Elisha | 1 | 1 | 1 | | |
| Gaylord, Jesse, Jr | 1 | 1 | 2 | | | Steele, Ebizur | 1 | | 2 | | | Lewis, Samuel | 1 | 1 | 1 | | |
| Beckwith, Samuel | 1 | 1 | 5 | | | Teil, Joseph | 1 | 1 | 2 | | | Main, Ezekiel | 1 | | 2 | | |
| Dutton, Oliver | 1 | 2 | 3 | | | Woodford, John | 3 | | 4 | | | Lewis, Eno | 1 | | 2 | | |
| Peck, Josiah | 1 | 1 | 4 | | | Gridley, Thomas | 1 | 2 | 3 | | | Burdock, Lewis | 2 | 3 | 2 | | |
| Woodruff, Ezekiel | 1 | | 3 | | | Way, Joseph | 3 | | 5 | | | Hotchkiss, Stephen, Jr | 2 | 1 | 5 | | |
| Hungerford, Jehiel | 1 | 3 | 3 | | | Boardman, Ephraim | 3 | 2 | 4 | | | Tubbs, Elisha | 1 | | 1 | | |
| Smith, Elihu | 1 | 2 | 3 | | | Brunson, Stephen | 2 | 2 | 5 | | | Bunnel, Nath<sup>a</sup> | 1 | 1 | 2 | | |
| Hodgekiss, James | 1 | | 3 | | | Farnsworth, Phillip H | 1 | 2 | 1 | | | Benham, Ebenezer | 2 | 1 | 1 | | |
| Newill, Abel | 3 | 2 | 4 | | | Hart, Ambrose | 1 | 3 | 2 | | | Webster, Justus | 2 | | 6 | | |
| Cowles, James | 2 | | 2 | | | Hart, Bliss | 1 | 3 | 2 | | | Webster, Justus, Jr | 1 | | 1 | | |
| Clark, Daniel | 1 | 1 | 3 | | | Beckwith, Thomas | 2 | 3 | 5 | | | Tharp, Linus | 1 | 2 | 3 | | |
| Hungerford, Stephen | 2 | | 3 | | | Stone, Nath<sup>a</sup> | 1 | 5 | 3 | | | Park, John | 2 | 2 | 4 | | |
| Norton, Isaac, 3<sup>d</sup> | 1 | 5 | 4 | | | Warner, Samuel | 1 | 3 | 4 | | | Robert, Freelove | 2 | 2 | 1 | | |
| Clark, Joel | 1 | 3 | 2 | | | Warner, Nathaniel | 1 | | 4 | | | Bird, John | 1 | | 4 | | |
| Hayford, Ira | 1 | | 4 | | | Warner, John | 1 | | 3 | | | Leming, David | 1 | 1 | 3 | | |
| Jearom, Asahel | 1 | | 2 | | | Parsons, Moses | 2 | | 2 | | | Bird, Ephraim | 2 | | 3 | | |
| Hayford, Joseph | 2 | 3 | 3 | | | Curtis, Ethan | 1 | 3 | | | | Bunel, Daniel, Jr | 1 | 1 | 2 | | |
| Carrington, Nath<sup>a</sup> | 1 | 1 | 2 | | | Curtis, Robert | 1 | 1 | 2 | | | Smith, Samuel, Jr | 1 | | 2 | | |
| Mathews, W<sup>m</sup> | 1 | | 1 | | | Perkins, Reuben | 2 | 1 | 4 | | | Smith, Samuel | 2 | | 8 | | |
| Smith, John | 1 | 1 | 1 | | | Perkins, Reuben, Jr | 1 | | 3 | | | Smith, Joseph | 2 | | 1 | | |
| Carrington, Jonathan | 1 | 3 | 7 | | | Peck, Caleb | 1 | 2 | 4 | | | Turner, Ephraim | 1 | 2 | 3 | | |
| Loury, Samuel | 1 | 4 | 5 | | | Marks, David | 1 | 2 | 3 | | | Smith, Joseph, J<sup>r</sup> | 1 | 2 | 2 | | |
| Barnes, Reuben | 1 | 6 | 1 | | | Wilmut, Thomas | 1 | 4 | 2 | | | Bellam, Lyman | 1 | 1 | 2 | | |
| Barnes, David | 1 | 1 | 1 | | | Cornwall, Cornilius | 1 | 2 | 6 | | | Smith, Amos | 1 | | 2 | | |
| Smith, John | 1 | 1 | 2 | | | Hamlin, Ebenezer | 1 | | 3 | | | Orsborn, Joseph | 2 | 1 | 1 | | |
| Garret, J<sup>no</sup> | 1 | 3 | 3 | | | Hamlin, Mark | 2 | 1 | 4 | | | Clark, Abel | 1 | | 2 | | |
| Warner, Nath<sup>n</sup> | 1 | | 2 | | | Miller, Jon<sup>th</sup> | 1 | 1 | 5 | | | Roberts, David | 1 | 1 | 6 | | |
| Scott, Ebenezer | 1 | 1 | 1 | | | Hart, Simeon, Jr | 1 | 1 | 3 | | | Robert, Martin | 1 | | 1 | | |
| Wolcott, Theodore | 2 | 2 | 1 | | | Hart, Simeon | 1 | | 2 | | | Roberts, Benjamin | 1 | 1 | 3 | | |
| Stone, Joseph | 2 | | 1 | | | Hart, Marcus | 1 | | 1 | | | Roberts, Jacob | 1 | | 2 | | |
| Spencer, Jared | 2 | | 3 | | | Friston, Zebulon | 2 | 1 | 4 | | | Little, Walter | 2 | 1 | 2 | | |
| Foot, Ichabod | 2 | 3 | 1 | | | Hotchkiss, Stephen | 1 | | 1 | | | Bacon, Andrew | 3 | 2 | 4 | | |
| Bartholomew, Jacob, Jr | 1 | | 1 | | | Taylor, Elezur | 2 | | 1 | | | Roberts, Jacob, Jr | 1 | 4 | 3 | | |
| Chapman, Sabethial | 1 | 2 | 4 | | | Driggs, Bartholomew | 3 | 4 | 2 | | | Clark, Dimon | 1 | | 3 | | |
| Peck, Seth | 2 | 1 | 2 | | | Elton, W<sup>m</sup> | 1 | 3 | | | | Bunnel, Bela | 2 | | 2 | | |
| Cone, Jere<sup>h</sup> | 1 | 2 | 5 | | | Spring, Ebenezer | 1 | 1 | | | | Curtis, Simeon | 1 | 1 | 4 | | |
| Griggs, Elliot | 1 | | 1 | | | Hotchkiss, Simeon | 1 | 2 | 2 | | | Frisbee, Hooker | 1 | 1 | 3 | | |
| Chapman, Josiah | 1 | | 1 | | | Brockway, Simeon | 1 | 1 | 1 | | | Brooks, Chancey | 1 | | 3 | | |
| Chapman, Josiah, Jr | 1 | | 2 | | | Frisbey, Daniel | 1 | | 2 | | | Lawry, John | 3 | 1 | 5 | | |
| Boardman, Moses | 1 | | 1 | | | Brockway, Samuel | 1 | | 2 | | | Stedman, Lemuel | 3 | 1 | 5 | | |
| Churchill, Asahel | 1 | 5 | 1 | | | Brockway, Samuel | 3 | 2 | 2 | | | Spencer, Joseph | 1 | | 2 | | |
| Linsley, Aaron | 2 | 4 | 3 | | | Gillett, Jeremiah | 1 | | 2 | | | Brooks, Thomas | 2 | 1 | 5 | | |
| Mix, Timothy | 1 | | 3 | | | Hart, Noadiah | 2 | | 2 | | | Bunnel, Titus | 1 | | 2 | | |
| Stone, Christopher | 1 | 3 | 1 | | | Bristo (Negro) | | | | 1 | | Lankton, Joseph | 2 | 5 | 3 | | |
| Stone, Solomon | 1 | | 3 | | | Hills, John | 1 | 1 | 2 | | | Johnson, Asahel | 2 | 3 | 6 | | |
| Hamlin, Dan | 1 | 1 | 3 | | | Humphreys, Solomon | 2 | 3 | 3 | | | Bailey, Nathan | 1 | 3 | 3 | | |
| Clark, Jude | 3 | 2 | 4 | | | Newton, Mathew | 3 | 5 | 4 | | | Marks, Edward | 1 | 2 | 1 | | |
| Clark, Marshal | 1 | | 4 | | | Burdock, Joshua | 1 | 1 | 1 | | | Marks, Zachariah | 1 | 1 | 1 | | |
| Grifiths, Dan<sup>el</sup> | 2 | | 1 | | | Burdock, Robert | 2 | 2 | 5 | | | Bunnel, Daniel | 2 | | 4 | | |
| Gillet, Ellick | 1 | | 2 | | | Willcox, Elias | 1 | 3 | 3 | | | Sedgwick, Samuel | 1 | 2 | 3 | | |
| Gillet, Reuben | 1 | 1 | 3 | | | Crumby, Samuel | 1 | 4 | 1 | | | Phelps, Joshua | 2 | 2 | 3 | | |
| Andrus, Ichabod | 1 | | 1 | | | Clark, Asa | 1 | 1 | 3 | | | Phelps, Joshua, Jr | 1 | | 2 | | |
| Beckwith, George | 3 | 3 | 6 | | | Davis, Roger | 1 | | 2 | | | Johnson, Enock | 1 | 2 | 6 | | |
| Hosmer, John | 1 | 1 | 2 | | | Covey, David | 1 | 3 | 2 | | | Whitmore, Jabez | 4 | 3 | 4 | | |
| Calver, Samuel | 2 | | 4 | | | Hitchcock, Joel | 1 | 2 | 2 | | | Warner, Samuel | 1 | 2 | 2 | | |
| Taylor, Wait | 1 | 4 | 6 | | | Hitchcock, Ashbel | 1 | 1 | 3 | | | Warner, Samuel, Jr | 1 | 3 | 2 | | |
| Woodruff, W<sup>m</sup> | 1 | 2 | 4 | | | Woodruff, Timothy | 1 | 2 | 1 | | | Brock, Phillis | | | 3 | | |
| Eaton, Daniel | 2 | 1 | 1 | | | Woodruff, Timothy, Jr | 1 | | 2 | | | Meacum, Jeremiah | 1 | | 3 | | |
| Belden, Benjamin | 2 | | 2 | | | Stilman, Amos | 1 | 3 | 4 | | | Gaylord, Joseph, J<sup>r</sup> | 1 | 5 | 2 | | |
| Fuller, Jesse | 1 | 2 | 5 | | | Neff, Arnold | 2 | 1 | 1 | | | Barnes, Wise | 1 | | 2 | | |
| Roberts, Lamberton | 1 | 2 | 3 | | | Palmeter, Jon<sup>th</sup> | 1 | 1 | 1 | | | Barnes, Joel | | | | | |
| Belden, Isaac | 2 | | 3 | | | Palmeter, Benjamin | 1 | | 2 | | | Ferry, Joshua | 1 | 1 | 6 | | |
| Dorman, Israel | 1 | 2 | 2 | | | | | | | | | Winston, John | 1 | 1 | 1 | | |

## HARTFORD COUNTY—Continued.

| NAME OF HEAD OF FAMILY. | Free white males of 16 years and upward, including heads of families. | Free white males under 16 years. | Free white females, including heads of families. | All other free persons. | Slaves. |
|---|---|---|---|---|---|
| BRISTOL TOWN—con. | | | | | |
| Hart, Ard | 1 | 1 | 2 | | |
| Hart, Lemuel | 1 | 1 | 3 | | |
| Hart, Jude | 1 | | 1 | | |
| Hart, Amos | 1 | 2 | 2 | | |
| Humphrey, Ozias | 1 | 3 | 6 | | |
| EAST HARTFORD TOWN. | | | | | |
| Williams, Eliphalet | 1 | 1 | 5 | | 1 |
| Pitkin, Daniel | 4 | 2 | 3 | | 1 |
| Burnham, Augustus | 2 | 2 | 2 | | |
| Wollcott, Roger | 3 | | 3 | 2 | |
| Burnham, George | 2 | 2 | 2 | | |
| Burnham, Eleazer | 1 | 3 | 1 | | |
| Burnham, Thomas | 1 | 1 | 1 | | |
| William, Joshua | 3 | | 5 | | |
| Williams, Jacob | 4 | 2 | 4 | | |
| Anderson, Asahel | 1 | | 2 | | |
| Gilman, George | 1 | 3 | 2 | | |
| Goodwin, Levi | 2 | 1 | 3 | | |
| Cowles, Timothy | 2 | 1 | 2 | | |
| Cowles, William | 2 | | 4 | | |
| Pitkin, Joshua | 5 | 1 | 2 | | 1 |
| Pitkin, Nathaniel | 1 | 2 | 3 | | |
| Pitkin, David | 1 | 1 | 2 | | |
| Pitkin, Joseph | 1 | | 2 | | |
| Olmsted, Nathaniel | 2 | 2 | 3 | | |
| Cowles, Eleazer | 4 | 1 | 2 | | |
| Cowles, Ashbel | 1 | 2 | 4 | | |
| Fowler, John | 1 | | 1 | | |
| Pitkin, William | 2 | | 4 | | |
| Pitkin, Ashbel | 1 | 1 | 4 | | |
| Pitkin, George, Senr | 2 | | 2 | | 5 |
| Pitkin, Epaphras | 4 | 1 | 3 | | 1 |
| Olmsted, William | 2 | 1 | 4 | | |
| Olmsted, Stephen | 1 | | 1 | | |
| Elmore, Aaron | 1 | 1 | 2 | | |
| Griswold, Shubael | 3 | 2 | 1 | | |
| Stanly, Theodore | 1 | | 3 | | |
| Olmsted, Ashbel | 2 | 2 | 5 | | |
| Olmstead, Ashbel, Jr | 1 | 2 | 1 | | |
| Olmsted, George | 3 | | 4 | | |
| Olmsted, Asahel | 2 | 2 | 5 | | |
| Olmsted, Thaddeus | 2 | | 2 | | |
| Olmsted, Samuel | 3 | | 5 | | |
| Olmsted, Samuel, Jr | 1 | | 1 | | |
| Cowles, Martha (Wid.) | 2 | 1 | 6 | | |
| Pitkin, Elisha, Jr | 1 | 3 | 2 | | 2 |
| Benjamin, James | 2 | 1 | 3 | | |
| Pitkin, John | 2 | 1 | 2 | | |
| Wyles, John | 1 | 1 | 2 | | |
| Woodbridge, Samuel | 5 | | 2 | | |
| Woodbridge, Russell | 1 | | 2 | | |
| Benjamin, Jonathan | 1 | 2 | 2 | | |
| Norton, Selah | 1 | 1 | 7 | | |
| Meackens, Joseph | 2 | | 4 | | 2 |
| Merrow, Nathan | 1 | 2 | 2 | | |
| Pitkin, Timothy | 1 | | 1 | | 2 |
| Flagg, Samuel | 4 | 1 | 2 | | 1 |
| Holmes, John | 1 | | 2 | | |
| Ford, Mathew | 1 | 2 | 3 | | |
| Woodbridge, Ward | 2 | 1 | 3 | | |
| Porter, John | 1 | 1 | 2 | | |
| Reynolds, John | 2 | 3 | 4 | | |
| Burnham, Stephen | 1 | 1 | 3 | | |
| Willcox, Jiles | 1 | 1 | 5 | | |
| Buckland, Mary | | 1 | 3 | | |
| White, Lemuel | 1 | 1 | | | |
| Burnham, Moses | 2 | | 2 | | |
| Pitkin, Roger | 2 | | 2 | | |
| Pitkin, Isaac | 1 | | 1 | | |
| Selby, David M | 1 | | 1 | | |
| Blancherd, Eunice | | 1 | 3 | | |
| Hill, Solomon | 2 | 2 | 6 | | |
| Pitkin, Jonathan | 3 | 2 | 5 | | |
| Goodwin, John | 2 | 3 | 4 | | |
| Goodwin, Joseph | 1 | 3 | 4 | | |
| Bement, Makens | 2 | 5 | 3 | | |
| Burnham, Theodore | 1 | 1 | 1 | | |
| Arnold, Mary | | | 2 | | |
| Williams, Elisha | 1 | 3 | 6 | | |
| Treat, Theodore | 1 | 2 | 2 | | |
| Burnham, Freeman | 1 | | 3 | | |
| Taylor, Giles | 1 | 1 | 2 | | |
| Cotton, David | 1 | | 3 | | |
| Cotton, Samuel | 4 | | 3 | | |
| Burnham, Rhoderic | 3 | 2 | 2 | | |
| Cheney, Benjamin | 1 | | 1 | | |
| Case, Thomas | 2 | 1 | 7 | | |
| Chapman, William | 1 | 2 | 7 | | |
| Gilman, Jonah | 4 | 4 | 4 | | |
| Gilman, Nathaniel | 2 | 1 | 3 | | |
| Kilbourn, Ashbel | 1 | 3 | 1 | | |
| Gilman, Elizabeth | 1 | | 1 | | |
| Gilman, David | 1 | | 3 | | |
| EAST HARTFORD TOWN—continued. | | | | | |
| Williams, Daniel | 1 | | 2 | | |
| Williams, Phineas | 1 | | 1 | | |
| Williams, John | 3 | 2 | 3 | | |
| Evens, Benoni | 1 | 4 | 4 | | |
| Burr, Jonathan | 2 | | 1 | | |
| Burnham, Timothy | 4 | | 3 | | |
| Burnham, Samuel | 1 | 2 | 1 | | |
| Burnham, Daniel | 5 | 1 | 2 | | |
| Anderson, Timothy | 1 | 1 | 3 | | |
| Burnham, Zenas | 1 | 3 | 4 | | |
| Belden, Nathan | 3 | 1 | 3 | | |
| Sage, John | 2 | 2 | 1 | | |
| Olmsted, Aaron | 1 | 2 | 5 | | |
| Olmsted, Jonathan | 2 | 3 | 3 | | |
| Rippenier, Christopher | 1 | | 5 | | |
| Brown, William | 1 | | 1 | | |
| Rippenier, Asahel | 1 | | 3 | | |
| Olmsted, Epaphras | 1 | | 3 | | |
| Olmsted, Benjamin | 1 | 2 | 3 | | |
| Williams, Edward | 2 | | 3 | | |
| Stanley, Jonathan | 2 | 2 | 2 | | |
| Firbbs, Ichabod | 2 | 1 | 4 | | |
| Kendall, John | 1 | 1 | 3 | | |
| Keeney, Benjamin | 1 | 2 | 4 | | |
| Norton, Samuel | 1 | 2 | 3 | | |
| Roberts, Nathaniel | 1 | 3 | 4 | | |
| Roberts, William | 1 | 2 | | | |
| Butler, Moses | 2 | 3 | 2 | | |
| Hills, Timothy | 2 | | 1 | | |
| Skinner, John | 1 | | 3 | | |
| Tinker, Jonathan | 2 | 2 | 2 | | |
| Pitkin, Elisha | 6 | 2 | 1 | | 5 |
| Roberts, George | 2 | | 5 | | |
| Hurlbut, Samuel | 1 | 1 | 3 | | |
| Pitkin, Thodore | 1 | 1 | 1 | | 2 |
| Hurlbut, John | 2 | 2 | 5 | | |
| Burnham, Aaron | 1 | 4 | 6 | | |
| Olmsted, Michael | 1 | | 3 | | |
| Burnham, Jerusha | | 1 | 5 | | |
| Hurlbut, Joseph | 3 | 2 | 4 | | |
| Reynolds, Charles | 2 | | 3 | | |
| Huntington, Silas | 2 | 1 | 5 | | |
| Crosby, David | 1 | 2 | 4 | | |
| Fowler, Samuel | 2 | | 3 | | |
| Bement, Edmund | 1 | | 2 | | |
| Jincks, Thankfull | | | 1 | | |
| Bidwell, Eodias | 1 | 2 | 3 | | |
| Bidwell, Ashbel | 1 | 1 | 2 | | |
| Bidwell, Joseph | 3 | 2 | 4 | | |
| Benton, Elisha | 1 | 1 | 1 | | |
| Bidwell, Asenath | | 1 | 3 | | |
| Bidwell, Mary | | 1 | 3 | | |
| Bellows, Isaac | 1 | | 1 | | |
| Bidwell, Elisha | 2 | 3 | 5 | | |
| Williams, Abraham | 4 | 1 | 5 | | |
| Hays, John | 3 | 3 | 3 | | |
| Gilman, Oliver | 2 | 1 | 4 | | |
| Case, Richard | 1 | 1 | 4 | | |
| Spencer, Gideon, Jr | 3 | 2 | 6 | | |
| Lyman, William | 1 | 4 | 3 | | |
| Kennedy, John | 1 | | 2 | | |
| Spencer, Gideon | 2 | | 2 | | |
| Spencer, John | 2 | 4 | 4 | | |
| Kennedy, Samuel | 2 | | 6 | | |
| Pratt, Moses | 2 | | 3 | | |
| Roberts, Elas | 2 | 1 | 9 | | |
| Roberts, Stephen | 1 | 3 | 1 | | |
| Dallaby, Samuel | 1 | 2 | 2 | | |
| Forbs, Thomas | 1 | 1 | 6 | | |
| Forbs, Aaron | 2 | 5 | 9 | | |
| Forbs, Timothy | 2 | 3 | 6 | | |
| Forbs, Elijah | 1 | 3 | 4 | | |
| Abby, Stephen | 5 | | 4 | | |
| Easton, Silas | 1 | 2 | 6 | | |
| Corning, William | 3 | 1 | 4 | | |
| Eaton, Justus | 3 | | 1 | | |
| Miller, Amaziah | 1 | 2 | 5 | | |
| Abbey, Stephen, Jr | 2 | | 2 | | |
| Chandler, Jonathan | 1 | 4 | 3 | | |
| Church, Samuel | 3 | 3 | 3 | | |
| Bidwell, John | 3 | 2 | 5 | | |
| Gulliver, Thomas | 1 | 1 | 1 | | |
| Taylor, John | 3 | 2 | 4 | | |
| Bidwell, Jonathan | 1 | 1 | 6 | | |
| Evens, Elisha | 1 | | 3 | | |
| Abbey, Jeduthan | 1 | 1 | 4 | | |
| Wallis, James | 2 | 1 | 1 | | |
| Little, David | 2 | 1 | 5 | | |
| Deming, Lemuel, Jr | 2 | 2 | 2 | | |
| Warren, William | 3 | | 3 | | |
| Warren, Daniel | 2 | | 5 | | |
| Warren, Edward | 1 | 3 | 3 | | |
| Wadsworth, Jerusha | | | 3 | | |
| Kilbourn, Russell | 3 | 2 | 6 | | |
| Easton, James | 2 | 2 | 6 | | |
| EAST HARTFORD TOWN—continued. | | | | | |
| Deming, David | 1 | 3 | 5 | | |
| Deming, Israel | 1 | 4 | 2 | | |
| Wyles, Thomas | 1 | 1 | 5 | | |
| Jutson, Roswell | 2 | | 6 | | |
| Risley, Benjamin | 4 | | 5 | | |
| Deming, Lemuel | 1 | | 5 | | |
| Williams, Timothy | 3 | 1 | 6 | | |
| Risley, John, Jr | 1 | 2 | 4 | | |
| Risley, John | 2 | 1 | 5 | | |
| Williams, Joseph | 4 | 4 | 3 | | |
| Roberts, Joseph | 5 | 1 | 3 | | |
| Firbbs, Edward | 2 | 1 | 2 | | |
| Bidwell, Samuel | 3 | | 7 | | |
| Treat, Mathias | 2 | 1 | 7 | | |
| Ensign, Moses | 1 | 1 | 1 | | |
| Hills, Epaphras | 1 | 2 | 4 | | |
| Williams, Solomon | 2 | | 2 | | |
| Wells, Jonathan | 3 | | 4 | | |
| Wells, Jonth, Jr | 1 | 4 | 2 | | |
| Fox, Joneal | 1 | 1 | 2 | | |
| Wells, John | 4 | | 4 | | |
| Butler, John | 1 | 4 | 3 | | |
| Humphreys, William | 1 | 2 | 2 | | |
| Smith, Eldad | 4 | 3 | 6 | | |
| Risley, Richard, Jr | 1 | 1 | 3 | | |
| Fox, Veniah | 1 | 1 | 3 | | |
| Warren, Elisha | 1 | | 2 | | |
| Risley, Richard | 2 | 1 | 3 | | |
| Risley, Eli | 1 | 1 | 4 | | |
| Wyles, David | 1 | | 6 | | |
| Treat, Jonathan | 1 | | 2 | | |
| Hills, Jonathan | 2 | | 2 | | |
| Hills, David | 4 | | 2 | | 2 |
| Hills, Elisha | 1 | 8 | 3 | | |
| Hills, Jonathan, 2d | 1 | | 2 | | |
| Hills, Caleb | 1 | 1 | 2 | | |
| Hills, Mabel | 1 | | 4 | | 3 |
| Hills, Joseph | 2 | | 2 | | |
| Allyn, Othnial | 1 | | 2 | | |
| Smith, Joseph | 1 | | 2 | | |
| Risley, Jeremiah | 1 | 1 | 2 | | |
| Wadsworth, Samuel | 1 | 1 | 5 | | |
| Little, Deodat | 3 | 3 | 2 | | |
| Warren, Ashbel | 1 | 1 | 1 | | |
| Buckley, Hannah | 1 | | 5 | | |
| Smith, Samuel | 2 | | 4 | | |
| Porter, Moses | 1 | | 3 | | |
| Buckland, Charles | 1 | 3 | 2 | | |
| Roberts, Jonathan | 2 | | 3 | | |
| Pratt, Russell | 2 | 1 | 4 | | |
| Abbey, Nehemiah | 1 | 2 | 5 | | |
| Chandler, Samuel | 3 | 2 | 4 | | |
| Buckland, Daniel | 1 | 4 | 3 | | |
| Spencer, John | 1 | | 4 | | |
| Roberts, David | 1 | | 1 | | |
| Smith, Nehemiah | 2 | 1 | 2 | | |
| Smith, Moses | 4 | 1 | 2 | | |
| Pratt, Eliab | 3 | | 2 | | |
| Risley, Joshua | 3 | 2 | 6 | | |
| Hills, William | 1 | 2 | 8 | | |
| Risley, Nehemiah | 1 | 3 | 1 | | |
| Risley, Levi | 1 | | 1 | | |
| Vibbert, Jesse | 1 | 2 | 3 | | |
| Vibbert, John | 1 | 1 | 1 | | |
| Vibbert, James | 2 | | 1 | | |
| Risley, Stephen | 1 | 3 | 6 | | |
| Wadsworth, William | 2 | 4 | 3 | | |
| Arnold, Joseph | 1 | 1 | 3 | | |
| Risley, George | 1 | 2 | 2 | | |
| Easton, Samuel | 1 | 2 | 6 | | |
| Firbs, Moses | 2 | 1 | 6 | | |
| Treat, Richard | 1 | | 5 | | |
| Kentfield, John | 1 | 3 | 2 | | |
| Phillips, John | 2 | | 5 | | |
| Porter, Nathan | 1 | 2 | 3 | | |
| Ocolow (Negro) | | | | 3 | |
| Kilbourn, Stephen | 1 | 2 | 5 | | |
| Porter, John | 2 | | 3 | | |
| Brewer, Daniel | 1 | 3 | 3 | | |
| Smith, John | 1 | 2 | 4 | | |
| Hall, Timothy | 1 | | 4 | | |
| Jones, David | 2 | | 5 | | |
| Brainard, Ezra | 1 | 1 | 3 | | |
| Porter, Job | 2 | 2 | 5 | | |
| Keeney, Joseph | 2 | 2 | 2 | | |
| Stebbin, Jonathan | 1 | 1 | 2 | | |
| Porter, Isaac | 1 | | 2 | | |
| Risley, George, 2d | 1 | | 2 | | |
| Porter, Roger | 3 | | 2 | | |
| Porter, Benjamin | 2 | 1 | 3 | | |
| Porter, William | 1 | 1 | 2 | | |
| Porter, Elijah | 1 | 2 | 2 | | |
| Fox, Ephraim | 3 | | 5 | | |
| Treat, Stephen | 1 | 1 | 2 | | |
| Roberts, John | 1 | 3 | 3 | | |

# HEADS OF FAMILIES—CONNECTICUT.

## HARTFORD COUNTY—Continued.

| NAME OF HEAD OF FAMILY. | Free white males of 16 years and upward, including heads of families. | Free white males under 16 years. | Free white females, including heads of families. | All other free persons. | Slaves. | NAME OF HEAD OF FAMILY. | Free white males of 16 years and upward, including heads of families. | Free white males under 16 years. | Free white females, including heads of families. | All other free persons. | Slaves. | NAME OF HEAD OF FAMILY. | Free white males of 16 years and upward, including heads of families. | Free white males under 16 years. | Free white females, including heads of families. | All other free persons. | Slaves. |
|---|---|---|---|---|---|---|---|---|---|---|---|---|---|---|---|---|---|
| EAST HARTFORD TOWN—continued. | | | | | | EAST HARTFORD TOWN—continued. | | | | | | EAST HARTFORD TOWN—continued. | | | | | |
| Roberts, Samuel | 1 | 2 | 2 | | | McKee, Nathaniel | 3 | 2 | 6 | | | Landpire, Abner | 1 | 2 | 5 | | |
| Roberts, Daniel | 1 | 2 | 2 | | | Buckland, Peter | 1 | 1 | 2 | | | Dart, Joseph | 1 | | 5 | 1 | |
| Roberts, Benjamin | 2 | 2 | 6 | | | Cheney, Timothy, Jr. | 1 | 2 | 1 | | | Dart, Sarah | | | 2 | | |
| Roberts, Ashbel | 1 | 2 | 2 | | | Bishop, Eleazer | 1 | 1 | 2 | | | Birdwell, Ozeas | 1 | 3 | 5 | | |
| Porter, Stephen | 1 | 3 | 4 | | | Deming, Benjamin | 1 | 1 | 2 | | | | | | | | |
| Fox, Ephraim, Jr | 1 | 2 | 1 | | | McKee, John | 1 | | 5 | | | EAST WINDSOR TOWN. | | | | | |
| Wadsworth, Thomas | 7 | 1 | 3 | | | Bryant, Timothy | 1 | | 6 | | | Burnham, Hannah | | 2 | 2 | | |
| Hills, Ashbell | 3 | 3 | 2 | | | Dewy, Nathaniel | 3 | | 4 | | | Wood, Robert | 2 | | 2 | | |
| Bills, John | 1 | 1 | 4 | | | Chase, Gidiliah | 1 | | 1 | | | Wood, John | 1 | | 1 | | |
| Risley, Moses | 1 | 1 | 6 | | | Brown, Benjamin | 2 | 2 | 5 | | | Moseley, Timothy | 1 | 3 | 2 | 1 | |
| Ritter, Daniel | 1 | 3 | 4 | | | Bartlet, Elizabeth | 1 | 1 | 2 | | | Bancroft, Abner | 2 | | 2 | | |
| Cowles, Samuel | 1 | 2 | 2 | | | Willson, Zilpah | 1 | 1 | 3 | | | Wolcott, Josiah | 1 | | 2 | | |
| Loomis, Israel | 1 | 1 | 3 | | | Wetherby, Seth | 2 | 1 | 8 | | | Anderson, George | 1 | | 2 | | |
| Risley, Jonathan | 2 | 3 | 2 | | | State, Thomas | 2 | | 2 | | | Gillet, Benjamin | 1 | 2 | 7 | | |
| Risley, Nathaniel | 1 | 2 | 3 | | | Hills, Joshua | 1 | 2 | 2 | | | Anderson, John | 1 | | 1 | | |
| Arnold, Samuel | 4 | 2 | 3 | | | Hills, Levi | 1 | 4 | 1 | | | Moreton, Abner | 1 | | 2 | | |
| Hills, Ebenezer | 1 | 4 | 4 | | | Hills, Nathan | 1 | 1 | 3 | | | Morton, Isaac | 1 | 2 | 1 | | |
| Hills, Eliphalet | 1 | 2 | 4 | | | Hills, Reuben | 1 | 2 | 2 | | | Morton, William | 1 | | 2 | | |
| Hills, Elijah | 1 | 4 | 1 | | | Hubbard, Jeremiah | 4 | 2 | 5 | | | Chase, Berrey | 1 | 2 | 3 | | |
| Hills, Russell, 1st | 1 | 2 | 1 | | | Treat, Henry | 2 | 3 | 2 | | | Rockwell, Joab | 1 | | 1 | | |
| Hills, Russell, 2d | 1 | 2 | 4 | | | Strickland, Benjamin | 1 | 2 | 4 | | | Elmore, Timothy | 1 | 1 | 4 | | |
| Deming, Elijah | 1 | 1 | 1 | | | Keeney, Thomas | 9 | 3 | 6 | | | Elmore, Eliphalet | 2 | 2 | 4 | | |
| Burnham, David | 2 | | 4 | | | Keeney, Eleazer | 3 | 1 | 4 | | | Elmore, Stephen | 1 | | 3 | | |
| Burnham, Oliver | 1 | 5 | 2 | | | Keeney, Benjamin | 2 | 1 | 5 | | | Elmore, Roswell | 1 | 4 | 4 | | |
| Tryon, Aaron | 1 | 1 | 5 | | | Keeney, Joseph | 3 | 1 | 4 | | | Mills, Roswell | 1 | 2 | 1 | | |
| Gilman, Solomon, Jr | 1 | 3 | 2 | | | Keeney, Simon | 1 | | 2 | | | Mills, Augustus | 1 | 1 | 3 | | |
| Roberts, Timothy | 3 | 2 | 5 | | | Keeney, Simon, Jr | 2 | 2 | 4 | | | Sutton, William | 1 | | 2 | | |
| Gilman, Solomon | 3 | 3 | 5 | | | Keeney, John | 3 | 5 | 2 | | | Wood, Obediah | 1 | 3 | 2 | | |
| Buckland, Aaron | 2 | | 5 | | | Keeney, Richard | 3 | 1 | 2 | | | Burr, Isaac | 1 | 1 | 2 | | |
| Chandler, Daniel | 3 | | 3 | | | Keeney, David, 2d | 1 | 2 | 4 | | | Wood, James | 1 | 3 | 2 | | |
| Cooley, Chancy | 1 | 1 | 1 | | | Hale, Isaac | 1 | 2 | 4 | | | Anderson, John, Jr | 1 | 3 | 4 | | |
| Buckland, Elisha | 2 | 2 | 2 | | | Webster, Jonathan | 1 | 1 | 2 | | | Kirkum, Philomon | 1 | | 2 | | |
| Simons, Samuel | 1 | 1 | 7 | | | Hollister, Josiah | 1 | 4 | 2 | | | Holman, Ebenezar | 2 | 2 | 4 | | |
| Loomis, Solomon | 1 | 1 | 3 | | | Bidwell, Stephen | 1 | | 2 | | | Elmore, Elizabeth | | 1 | 2 | | |
| Evens, Samuel | 1 | | 1 | | | Andrus, Ardon | 1 | | 2 | | | Bancroft, Samuel | 3 | 2 | 6 | | |
| Evens, Samuel, Jr | 1 | 2 | 2 | | | Woodruff, Gurdin | 1 | 2 | 4 | | | King, Theodore | 1 | 1 | 1 | | |
| Fletcher, William | 1 | 1 | 1 | | | Couch, Stephen | 1 | 1 | 6 | | | Filley, Silvanus | 1 | | 1 | | |
| Evens, David | 2 | 2 | 2 | | | Peck, Elijah | 2 | 2 | 3 | | | Diggins, Joseph | 2 | | 1 | | 1 |
| Skinner, Elias | 1 | 1 | 1 | | | Peck, Elijah, Jr | 1 | 5 | 2 | | | Wolcott, Permenis | 2 | 1 | 3 | | |
| Bissell, Ozias | 1 | 4 | 4 | | | Lucus, John | 1 | 3 | 4 | | | Fitch, Augustus | 2 | | 2 | | |
| Hammon, Jason | 2 | 1 | 2 | | | Couch, John | 3 | 4 | 2 | | | Fitch, John F | 1 | 1 | 2 | | |
| Keeney, George | 3 | 2 | 3 | | | Minor, Christopher | 2 | | 2 | | | Elmore, Joseph | 1 | 3 | 2 | | |
| Merryfield, Jonathan | 1 | 1 | 5 | | | Wyllys, John | 3 | | 1 | | | Bancroft, Thomas | 2 | 1 | 3 | | |
| Evans, Moses | 1 | 2 | 2 | | | Risley, Oliver | 1 | | 5 | | | Loomiss, Ezekiel | 2 | 1 | 2 | | |
| Anderson, William | 1 | | | | | Wallis, William | 2 | 2 | 5 | | | Wolcott, Roger | 2 | 1 | 2 | 1 | |
| Stibbins, Enos | 4 | 3 | 4 | | | Keeney, Isaac | 2 | 1 | 4 | | | Daniels, Stephen | 3 | | 2 | | |
| Dewy, Nathaniel | 1 | 1 | 2 | | | Dart, William | 2 | | 2 | | | Treat, Samuel | 1 | 2 | 5 | 1 | |
| Clark, Seth | 1 | | 1 | | | Fogarson, Elizabeth | | 4 | 5 | | | Wolcott, Samuel | 5 | 2 | 6 | | |
| Brewer, Daniel | 2 | | 2 | | | Keeney, Elijah | 1 | 1 | 6 | | | Gibbs, Stephen | 1 | 1 | 6 | | |
| Stedman, Nathan | 1 | 2 | 4 | | | Skinner, Augustus | 1 | 1 | 1 | | | Tudor, Samuel | 2 | | 3 | 1 | |
| Stedman, Timothy | 2 | 4 | 3 | | | Webster, Samuel | 1 | 2 | 5 | | | Stoughton, William | 1 | | 1 | | |
| Stedman, Comfort | | 4 | 3 | | | Hollister, John | 4 | 4 | 4 | | | Tudor, Elihu | 1 | 2 | 6 | | 1 |
| McKee, Elijah | 1 | 1 | 2 | | | Bidwell, Stephen | 1 | | 2 | | | Evans, Josiah | 1 | 3 | 3 | | |
| Corning, Malaca | 2 | 1 | 2 | | | Bidwell, Zebulon | 1 | 3 | 3 | | | Webb, Abigail | 2 | | 3 | | |
| Olcott, Samuel | 2 | 1 | 3 | | | Bidwell, David | 1 | | 4 | | | Avery, Samuel | 2 | 1 | 4 | | |
| Keeney, Alexander | 1 | 2 | 4 | | | Wallis, John | 2 | 1 | 4 | | | Walcott, William | 3 | | 2 | | |
| McKee, Joseph | 3 | 1 | 3 | | | Brown, Benjamin, Jr | 1 | 2 | 1 | | | Loomiss, Giles | 3 | 2 | 4 | | |
| McKee, Robert | 1 | 1 | 2 | | | Peck, Daniel | 1 | | 5 | | | Loomiss, Oliver | 2 | 1 | 5 | | |
| McKee, Andrew | 1 | 1 | 4 | | | Keeney, Alexander | 2 | | 2 | | | Porter, Nathaniel, Jr | 2 | 1 | 7 | | |
| McKee, Appleton | 1 | 2 | 1 | | | Pitkin, Richard, Jr | 3 | 2 | 5 | | | Porter, Hezekiah | 1 | | 4 | | |
| McKee, Robert, Jr | 1 | 2 | 4 | | | Pitkin, Richard | 3 | 1 | 3 | | | Porter, Wareham | 2 | | 1 | | |
| Webster, Eleazer | 1 | 1 | 3 | | | Cheeney, Timothy | 2 | | 5 | | | McClure, Revd David | 3 | 1 | 4 | | |
| McKee, Eleazer | 1 | | 2 | | | Cheeney, Silus | 2 | 1 | 2 | | | Rockwell, Jemima | | | 2 | | |
| Olcott, Nathaniel | 2 | | 4 | 1 | | Phelps, Benajah | 1 | 2 | 5 | | | Burnham, Abner | 2 | 4 | 2 | | |
| Webster, Ephraim | 2 | 6 | 1 | | | Pitkin, Eleazer | 1 | 1 | 2 | | | Heyden, Daniel | 4 | | 4 | | |
| Simons, Samuel | 2 | 2 | 6 | | | Man, Abeather | 2 | 1 | 3 | | | Stoughton, Russell | 1 | | 2 | | |
| Teal, John | 1 | 3 | 2 | | | Keeney, David | 1 | 1 | 5 | | | Stoughton, William | 1 | | 1 | 1 | |
| Spencer, Thomas, Jr | 3 | 1 | 1 | | | Porter, James | 1 | 2 | 5 | | | Wells, Esther | | | 2 | | |
| Brewer, Daniel | 1 | 1 | 3 | | | Skinner, Elias | 1 | 3 | 4 | | | King, Alexander | 3 | 4 | 2 | | |
| Spencer, Thomas | 4 | | 3 | | | Man, Benjamin | 1 | | 1 | | | Loomiss, John | 1 | | 3 | | |
| Marsh, Allyn | 1 | 2 | 6 | | | Cone, Russell | 2 | | 4 | | | Loomiss, Luke | 4 | | 2 | | |
| Marsh, Daniel | 2 | | 5 | | 2 | Bryant, Ebenezer | 2 | 1 | 4 | | | Chapin, Eliphalet | 3 | 1 | 5 | | |
| Cadwell, Reuben | 1 | | 2 | | | Evens, Ezekiel | 1 | 2 | 1 | | | Read, Ebenezer | 2 | 3 | | | |
| Olds, John | 1 | | 2 | | | Cheeney, Asahel | 2 | 2 | 2 | | | Read, Justus | 1 | | 4 | | |
| Olds, John, Jr | 2 | 2 | 3 | | | Smith, Ithemar | 1 | 2 | 3 | | | Bidwell, Ephraim | 1 | 2 | 3 | | |
| Wright, Aaron | 3 | 3 | 5 | | | Cone, Stephen | 3 | 1 | 4 | | | Wolcott, Benjamin | 2 | 3 | 5 | | |
| Case, David | 3 | 1 | 3 | | | Woodbridge, Deodat | 1 | 3 | 5 | 1 | | Newbury, Joseph | 3 | | 2 | | |
| Case, David, Jr | 1 | | 2 | | | Clark, Caty | 2 | | 4 | | | Newbury, John | 1 | 2 | 3 | | |
| Case, Joseph | 1 | | 9 | | | Buck, George | | 1 | 3 | | | Beamont, Jona | 1 | 1 | 2 | | |
| Case, Ashbel | 1 | 1 | 2 | | | Skinner, Jonathan | 1 | 1 | 3 | | | Hills, Anna | | | 3 | | |
| Simons, Israel | 2 | 3 | 5 | | | Swetland, Joseph | 2 | | 1 | | | Loomiss, Sarah | | | 2 | | |
| Simons, Israel | 1 | 2 | 3 | | | Swetland, Benjamin | 1 | | 2 | | | Porter, Naomi | | 1 | 2 | | |
| Benton, Joseph | 2 | 1 | 4 | | | Jones, John | 2 | 2 | 4 | | | Rockwell, Samuel | 1 | 3 | 4 | | |
| Simons, Joseph | 2 | 1 | 9 | | | Lyman, Joseph | 4 | 4 | 2 | | | Rockwell, David | 1 | | 2 | | |
| Cadwell, John | 1 | 3 | 5 | | | Flint, John | 1 | 4 | 2 | | | Newbury, Benjamin | 1 | | 3 | | |
| Cadwell, David | 1 | 1 | 2 | | | Flint, Joshua | 2 | 3 | 4 | | | Newbury, Amasa | 1 | 3 | 2 | | |
| Cadwell, Mathew | 1 | | 2 | | | Swetland, Daniel | 2 | 1 | 6 | | | Newbury, Chancey | 1 | 3 | 4 | | |
| Fox, Roswell | 1 | 2 | 6 | | | Dewy, Thomas | 1 | 4 | 3 | | | Skinner, Abijah | 1 | | 2 | | |
| Hills, Silus | 1 | 1 | 5 | | | Kilbourn, Benjamin | 2 | 1 | 3 | | | Hosmer, Joseph | 5 | 2 | 4 | | |
| Hills, Amos | 4 | 4 | 4 | | | Benjamin, Samuel | 2 | 2 | 3 | | | Skinner, Joseph | 2 | 3 | 2 | | |
| Vibbert, James | 3 | 3 | 4 | | | Millard, Andrew | 1 | 3 | 3 | | | Skinner, Azariah | 2 | | 2 | | |
| Loomis, Jonah | 1 | 2 | 6 | | | Deming, David | 3 | | 7 | | | Phelps, Jerejah | 3 | | 1 | | |
| Vibbert, David | 1 | 2 | 4 | | | Bissell, Russell | | 3 | 2 | | | Phelps, Daniel | 1 | | 2 | | |
| Glason, Moses | 1 | 2 | 4 | | | Bishop, Samuel | 1 | 4 | 1 | | | Baxter, Frances, Jr | 1 | 1 | 2 | | |
| Rich, Peter | 1 | 1 | 2 | | | Little, William | 1 | 3 | 3 | | | Olcott, Asahael | 1 | | 4 | | |
| Griswold, George | 1 | | 4 | | | Landpir, David | 1 | | 2 | | | Olcott, Benoni | | | 3 | | |

# FIRST CENSUS OF THE UNITED STATES.

## HARTFORD COUNTY—Continued.

| NAME OF HEAD OF FAMILY. | Free white males of 16 years and upward, including heads of families. | Free white males under 16 years. | Free white females, including heads of families. | All other free persons. | Slaves. |
|---|---|---|---|---|---|
| **EAST WINDSOR TOWN—continued.** | | | | | |
| Olcott, Eli | 1 | 1 | 2 | | |
| Wolcott, Erastus, Jr | 1 | 2 | 2 | | |
| Wolcott, Honererable Erastus | 3 | | 1 | | |
| Wolcott, Albertus | 1 | | 4 | | |
| Loomiss, Benajah | 1 | 1 | 4 | | |
| Wolcott, Ephraim | 3 | | 3 | | |
| Moore, Eli | 1 | | 3 | | |
| Moore, Wareham | 1 | 4 | 3 | | |
| Sherman, Nathaniel | 1 | 1 | 2 | | |
| Rockwell, William | 3 | 1 | 5 | | |
| Drake, Moses | 1 | | 1 | | |
| Stroughton, Alexander | 1 | 2 | 2 | | |
| Stoughton, Oliver | 2 | | 5 | | |
| Bliss, Stoughton | 1 | 2 | 4 | | |
| Rockwell, Charles | 1 | 1 | 4 | | |
| Flint, Archelaus | 2 | 3 | 1 | | |
| Rockwell, Nathaniel | 2 | 3 | 4 | | |
| Terry, Samuel | 3 | 2 | 4 | | |
| Gilman, Benjamin | 2 | | 3 | | |
| Higley, Nathan | 4 | 1 | 3 | | |
| Drake, Abiel | 1 | 1 | 3 | | |
| Stoughton, Augustus | 1 | 2 | 2 | | |
| Strong, Timothy | 2 | 2 | 2 | | |
| Strong, Nathaniel | 1 | | 2 | | |
| Strong, Nathaniel, Jr | 2 | 2 | 1 | | |
| Strong, John | 1 | | 1 | | |
| Strong, John | 1 | 2 | 2 | | |
| Drake, David | 1 | | 1 | | |
| Preston, Samuel | 1 | 1 | 2 | 1 | |
| Sadd, Mathew | 1 | | 4 | | |
| Drake, Amasa | 1 | 1 | 3 | | |
| Cook, Benjamin | 4 | | 2 | 1 | |
| Drake, Reuben | 3 | | 2 | | |
| Grant, Ebenezer | 1 | | 1 | | |
| Grant, Roswell | 3 | 1 | 2 | | |
| Grant, Aaron | 2 | 1 | 3 | | |
| Grant, Azariah | 1 | 1 | 6 | | |
| Virstile, William | | 1 | 3 | | 1 |
| Foster, Oliver | 1 | | 3 | | |
| Loomiss, Amasa, Jr | 1 | 1 | 3 | | |
| Bowers, Azel | 1 | | 1 | | |
| Mather, Charles | 3 | 1 | 4 | | 1 |
| Crosby, Simon | 1 | 3 | 2 | | |
| Bissell, Ebenezer | 2 | 1 | 3 | | |
| Smith, John | 1 | 1 | 4 | | |
| Dickerson, Obediah | 2 | 3 | 5 | | |
| Grant, Aaron, Jr | 1 | 1 | 3 | | |
| Grant, Reuben | 1 | 1 | 1 | | |
| Grant, Benjamin | 1 | | 2 | | |
| Wells, Noah | 3 | 1 | 3 | | |
| Wells, Mosses | 2 | | 1 | | |
| Day, Justus | 1 | | 2 | | |
| Day, Oliver | 1 | 1 | 2 | | |
| Bissell, Epaphras | 2 | 1 | 2 | 1 | |
| Bissell, Aaron | 3 | 1 | 3 | | |
| Bissell, Noah | 2 | 2 | 5 | | |
| Watson, John | 3 | 1 | 5 | 1 | 1 |
| Bissell, Elisha | 1 | 2 | 2 | | |
| May, Charles | 2 | | 2 | | |
| Burnap, Daniel | 4 | | 2 | | |
| Edwards, Rhodolfus | 1 | | 1 | | |
| Strickland, Richard | 3 | | 1 | | |
| Webster, Samuel | 3 | | 3 | | |
| Bissell, David | 5 | | 3 | | |
| Fenton, Francis | 1 | 2 | 4 | | |
| Wolcott, Elezur | 1 | | 1 | | |
| Bissell, Jonathan | 1 | 2 | 3 | | |
| Bissell, Justus | 1 | 1 | 3 | | |
| Loomis, Elihu | 1 | | 1 | | |
| Moore, Nathaniel | 1 | 1 | 3 | | |
| Morton, Elinor | 1 | 1 | 1 | | |
| Smith, Samuel | 1 | | 4 | | |
| Wood, Ruth | | | 1 | | |
| Bliss, Ellis | 2 | | 3 | | |
| Bliss, Anna | | | 1 | | 1 |
| Gaylord, Charles | 1 | 3 | 1 | | |
| Mitchell, Oliver | | | | 5 | |
| Chalke, William | 1 | | 3 | | |
| Stoughton, Elijah | 2 | 1 | 4 | | |
| Gaylord, Abiel | 1 | 6 | 5 | | |
| Bissell, William | 2 | | 3 | | |
| Bissell, Roswold | 1 | 2 | 3 | | |
| Bissell, Nathaniel | 1 | | 3 | | |
| Cram, John | 1 | 4 | 3 | | |
| Cahoon, Matha | | | 3 | | |
| Elsworth, Joel | 1 | | 4 | | |
| Pelton, Nathan | 2 | 2 | 3 | | |
| Pelton, Nathan, Jr | 1 | | 1 | | |
| Baxter, Levi | 1 | 2 | 1 | | |
| Elsworth, Frederic | 2 | 1 | 3 | | |
| Carpenter, Daniel | 1 | 2 | 2 | | |
| Watson, Ebenezer, Jr | 2 | 4 | 2 | | |
| French, John | 2 | | 2 | | |
| French, John, Jr | 1 | 2 | 3 | | |
| **EAST WINDSOR TOWN—continued.** | | | | | |
| Pinney, Jonª | 1 | 1 | 2 | | |
| Putnam, David | 3 | | 1 | | |
| Watson, Robert | 2 | 1 | 7 | | |
| Thompson, Alexander | 1 | 2 | 1 | | |
| Bullard, Josiah | 1 | 1 | 2 | | |
| Watson, Ebenezer | 1 | | 4 | | |
| Stoughton, Lemuel | 5 | | 6 | | |
| Watson, Sarah | | | 4 | | |
| Watson, Samuel | 2 | 3 | 1 | | |
| Wells, Lampson | 2 | 1 | 3 | | |
| Shaw, David | 1 | | 8 | | |
| Phelps, Daniel | 1 | | 3 | | |
| Phelps, Obadiah | 1 | | | | |
| Skinner, Samuel | 1 | 3 | 3 | | |
| Richardson, Edatha | | 1 | 3 | | |
| Munsell, Martin | 1 | 2 | 1 | | |
| Trumbull, David | 2 | 4 | 2 | | |
| Skinner, Mary | 1 | | 1 | | |
| Clark, Oliver | 1 | | 1 | | |
| Baxter, Francis | 2 | 1 | 3 | | |
| Stiles, Noah | 2 | | 1 | | |
| Prior, Joel | 2 | 4 | 4 | | |
| Orsborn, Thomas | 1 | 3 | 4 | | |
| McNight, Abigail | | | 1 | | |
| Orsborn, Ezra | 1 | 2 | 2 | | |
| Orsborn, Zebedee | 1 | 3 | 3 | | |
| Orsborn, Benjamin | 2 | | 3 | | |
| Prior, George | 1 | | 2 | | |
| Orsborn, Rebecka | | | 2 | | |
| Orsborn, Abel | 1 | 3 | 3 | | |
| Osborn, Martha | | | 3 | | |
| Orsborn, Ezekiel | 2 | 1 | 5 | | |
| Pasko, Jonathan | 1 | 2 | 2 | | |
| Morrison, John | 1 | | 2 | | |
| Parker, John | 1 | | 4 | | |
| Blodget, Elijah | 1 | 1 | 2 | | |
| Heath, Stephen | 3 | 2 | 6 | | |
| Bancraft, Isaac, Jr | 3 | 3 | 7 | | |
| Abbey, Obediah | 1 | 2 | 4 | | |
| Bancroft, John | 4 | | 3 | | |
| Fish, Levi | 2 | 3 | 4 | | |
| Eggleston, Joseph | 1 | | 1 | | |
| Fish, Benjamin | 1 | 2 | 2 | | |
| Booth, Aaron | 1 | | 3 | | |
| Pasko, Jonª | 3 | 1 | 1 | | |
| Pasko, James | 3 | 1 | 3 | | |
| Barber, Jonª | 2 | | 1 | | |
| Barber, Ashbel | 1 | | 1 | | |
| Barber, Oliver | 3 | 1 | 4 | | |
| Barber, Shadrack | 3 | 1 | 1 | | |
| Booth, Ephraim | 2 | 1 | 5 | | |
| Pease, James | 1 | 4 | 3 | | |
| Persons, William | 1 | 3 | 3 | | |
| Allyn, Zacheriah, Jr | 1 | 1 | 2 | | |
| Porter, Daniel | 1 | 1 | 2 | | |
| Pease, Joel | 2 | 2 | 3 | | |
| Fish, Jonª | 1 | | 1 | | |
| Utley, Joseph | 2 | | 2 | | |
| Kibbey, Phillip | 1 | | 2 | | |
| Elsworth, Daniel | 1 | | 5 | | |
| Phelps, Bethuel | 1 | 2 | 2 | 1 | |
| Benjamin, Allyn | 1 | 1 | 1 | | |
| Vorse, Samuel | 2 | 1 | 2 | | |
| Chamberlan, James | 2 | 1 | 1 | 1 | |
| Chamberlan, James, Jr | 1 | | 2 | | |
| Fox, Ashbel | 1 | 2 | 2 | | |
| Griswold, Roger | 1 | | 5 | | |
| Collins, Ebenezer | 2 | | 3 | | |
| Fish, Asa | 1 | 1 | 4 | | |
| Munsell, Jacob | 1 | | 2 | | |
| Lord, Joseph | 1 | 3 | 3 | | |
| Munsell, Silah | 1 | 3 | 2 | | |
| Lord, Jeremiah | 2 | | 1 | | |
| Lord, George | 1 | | 1 | | |
| Holt, Ebenezer | 2 | 1 | 3 | | |
| Booth, Calib | 1 | 4 | 5 | | |
| Blodget, Abner | 2 | 4 | 4 | | |
| Elmore, Joel | 1 | 1 | 3 | | |
| Markum, Abigail | | | 1 | | |
| Allyn, Samuel | 3 | 2 | 3 | | |
| Allyn, Hezekiah | 1 | 2 | 4 | | |
| Allyn, Samuel, Jr | 1 | 1 | 2 | | |
| Vining, Alexander | 1 | 4 | 2 | | |
| Bancroft, Edward | 1 | | 1 | | |
| Booth, Henry | 1 | 1 | 4 | | |
| Burnham, James | 1 | 1 | 3 | | |
| Fanning, Elisha | 1 | 1 | 3 | | |
| Potwine, Thomas, Jr | 1 | 4 | 2 | | |
| Wells, Hezekiah | 4 | 2 | 5 | | |
| Potwine, John | 1 | | 2 | | |
| Wells, Joshua | 1 | | 3 | | |
| Potwine, Revᵈ Thomas | 3 | 1 | 3 | | |
| Warrener, Aaron | 1 | | 2 | | |
| Orsborn, Samuel | 1 | | 5 | | |
| Whipple, Abraham | 1 | | 1 | | |
| **EAST WINDSOR TOWN—continued.** | | | | | |
| Watson, David | 1 | | 4 | | |
| Crane, Elishama | 1 | | 1 | | |
| Eli, Ephraim | 2 | 3 | 1 | | |
| Orsborn, Daniel | 6 | 2 | 3 | | |
| Allyn, Ebenezer | 1 | 5 | 4 | | |
| Munsell, Thomas | 1 | 1 | 2 | | |
| Elmore, Jacob | 2 | | 1 | | |
| Elmore, Noadiah | 1 | 1 | 1 | | |
| Bartlet, Jonathan | 1 | | 1 | | |
| Chapin, Daniel | 1 | 1 | 4 | | |
| Allyn, Peter | 2 | | 1 | | |
| Wolcott, Henery | 2 | 2 | 3 | | |
| Bissell, John | 1 | | 1 | | |
| Bartlet, Samuel | 3 | 1 | 1 | | |
| Stiles, Israel | 1 | | 1 | | |
| Stiles, Benoni | 1 | 2 | 1 | | |
| Wolcott, Gideon | 1 | | 1 | | |
| Stiles, Asahel | 2 | | 4 | | |
| Wade, Dredley | 1 | 2 | 2 | | |
| Brownley, Robert | 2 | | 1 | | |
| Clark, Jonathan | 1 | | 1 | | |
| Munsell, Corking | 1 | 1 | 2 | | |
| Clark, Ebenezer | 1 | | 1 | | |
| Munsell, Hannah | | | | | |
| Bartlet, John | 1 | 2 | 6 | | |
| Bissell, Moses | 2 | | 6 | | |
| Allyn, Benjamin | 1 | | 2 | | |
| Wolcott, Epaphras | 1 | | 5 | | |
| Wolcott, James | 1 | 2 | 1 | | |
| Allyn, Joseph | 3 | 1 | 2 | | |
| Cadwell, Levi | 2 | 2 | 4 | | |
| Allyn, Solomon | 2 | 1 | 3 | | |
| Allyn, Noah | 1 | 1 | 3 | | |
| Simons, Silas | 2 | 3 | 5 | | |
| Allyn, Luke | 1 | 1 | 4 | | 1 |
| Stiles, Samuel | 1 | 1 | 2 | | |
| Harper, James | 1 | 2 | 3 | | |
| Thompson, John | 1 | 2 | 1 | | |
| Thompson, James | 1 | | 1 | | |
| Thompson, William | 3 | 2 | 2 | | |
| Thompson, John, Jr | 2 | | 3 | | |
| Munsell, Elisha | 1 | | | | |
| Bullon, Jonª | 1 | 2 | 5 | | |
| Belknap, Job, Jr | 1 | 3 | 3 | | |
| Belknap, Job | 1 | 1 | 1 | | |
| Brayman, Daniel | 1 | | 5 | | |
| Pease, Stephen | 3 | | 1 | | |
| Belknap, Decsius | 1 | | 1 | | |
| Pease, Peter | 1 | 4 | 1 | | |
| Elsworth, Charles | 1 | | 1 | | |
| Elsworth, Josiah | 1 | 1 | | | |
| Persons, William | 1 | | 2 | | |
| Bancroft, Isaac | 3 | 2 | 5 | | |
| Ferry, Nathan | 1 | | 1 | | |
| Lord, Jeremʰ, Jr | 1 | 4 | 3 | | |
| Barber, Simon | 2 | | 5 | | |
| Loomiss, Roger | 1 | 2 | 6 | | |
| Loomiss, John, Jr | 3 | | 2 | | |
| Janes, Daniel | 4 | 3 | 3 | | |
| Chapin, Joseph | 1 | 1 | 4 | | |
| Bissell, Jerijah, Jr | 1 | 4 | 3 | | |
| Crane, Hezekiah | 1 | | 1 | | |
| Crane, David | 2 | 3 | 4 | | |
| Crane, Hezekiah, Jr | 3 | 1 | 5 | | |
| Crane, Rufus | 1 | 2 | 2 | | |
| Blodget, Phinias | 2 | 1 | 4 | | |
| Paine, Solomon | 1 | | 2 | | |
| Squires, Ezekiel | 2 | | 1 | | |
| Green, Jabez | 1 | 1 | 3 | | |
| Green, Roswold | 1 | 1 | 2 | | |
| Loomiss, Solomon | 1 | | 1 | | |
| Loomiss, Hezekiah | 1 | 1 | 2 | | |
| Abbey, Jeremiah | 3 | 1 | 3 | | |
| Gay, Levi | 1 | 2 | 5 | | |
| Paine, Rufus | 1 | 3 | 2 | | |
| Paine, Stephen, Jr | 1 | | 1 | | |
| Paine, Eliazer | 1 | 2 | 1 | | |
| Barber, George | 1 | | 1 | | |
| Crane, Aaron | 1 | 4 | 3 | | |
| Squire, Daniel | 1 | 3 | 3 | | |
| Chapin, Solomon | 1 | | 3 | | |
| Wolcott, Peter | 1 | 1 | 3 | | |
| Sadd, Elijah | 1 | 2 | | | |
| Sadd, Elisha | 1 | | 1 | | |
| Sadd, John | 2 | 2 | 2 | | |
| Bissell, Daniel | 2 | 4 | 5 | | |
| Grant, Isaac | 1 | | 2 | | |
| Bissell, Jerijah | 3 | 1 | 4 | | |
| Davis, Abel | 1 | | 5 | | |
| Freeman, Obed | | | | 8 | |
| Allyn, Israel | 2 | 2 | 4 | | |
| Armstrong, Rufus | 1 | | 3 | | |
| Bissell, Hezekiah | 2 | | 5 | | 1 |
| Webster, Daniel | 1 | | 1 | | |
| Elsworth, Benjamin | 2 | | 1 | | |

# HEADS OF FAMILIES—CONNECTICUT.

## HARTFORD COUNTY—Continued.

| NAME OF HEAD OF FAMILY. | Free white males of 16 years and upward, including heads of families. | Free white males under 16 years. | Free white females, including heads of families. | All other free persons. | Slaves. | NAME OF HEAD OF FAMILY. | Free white males of 16 years and upward, including heads of families. | Free white males under 16 years. | Free white females, including heads of families. | All other free persons. | Slaves. | NAME OF HEAD OF FAMILY. | Free white males of 16 years and upward, including heads of families. | Free white males under 16 years. | Free white females, including heads of families. | All other free persons. | Slaves. |
|---|---|---|---|---|---|---|---|---|---|---|---|---|---|---|---|---|---|
| **EAST WINDSOR TOWN—continued.** | | | | | | **EAST WINDSOR TOWN—continued.** | | | | | | **ENFIELD TOWN—con.** | | | | | |
| Elsworth, Job | 1 | 1 | 1 | | | Strong, Elijah | 2 | 2 | 4 | | | Reynolds, Samuel | 1 | 1 | 4 | | |
| Elsworth, Solomon | 5 | 3 | 4 | | | Grant, Oliver, 2d | 1 | | 1 | | | Prior, Azariah | 1 | | 2 | | |
| Morton, Alexander | 1 | 2 | 2 | | | Skinner, Daniel | 2 | | 3 | | | Churchill, Elijah | 1 | 2 | 2 | | |
| Drake, Gideon | 1 | 1 | 3 | | | Skinner, Oliver | 2 | 2 | 3 | | | McClester, John | 1 | | | | 1 |
| Starks, Ebenezar | 1 | | 1 | | | Filley, Mark | 1 | 2 | 9 | | | McClester, Elizabeth (Wid.) | | | 1 | | |
| Morton, John | 3 | 4 | 3 | | | Bissell, Timothy | 1 | 2 | 3 | | | McClester, James | 1 | 2 | 2 | | |
| Froet, Aaron | 1 | 3 | 3 | | | Bowers, John | 1 | 2 | 3 | | | Ware, Daniel | 1 | 1 | 2 | | |
| Sangor, Nathaniel | 2 | 2 | 2 | | | Bissell, Dan | 2 | 2 | 5 | | | Terry, Colo Nathaniel | 4 | 1 | 4 | | 1 |
| Charles (Negro) | | | 1 | 3 | | Bissell, Hannah | | | 3 | | | Feild, Doct Simeon | 3 | 1 | 4 | | |
| Wolcott, Simon | 2 | | 4 | | | Tuttle, Martha | | | 2 | | | Reynold, John, Esqr | 2 | 3 | 7 | | |
| Prior, Roswell | 1 | | 2 | | | Rockwell, Ebenezar | 3 | | 3 | | | Olmsted, Hannah (Wid.) | | | 1 | | |
| Dawner, Edmund | 2 | 1 | 2 | | | Rockwell, Ebenezar, Jr | 1 | 1 | 4 | | | Olmsted, Asa | 1 | 1 | 3 | | 1 |
| Orsborn, Jonathan | 1 | | 2 | | | Rockwell, James | 1 | 1 | 1 | | | King, Obadiah | 1 | | 3 | | |
| Starkweather, Benajah | 1 | | 1 | | | | | | | | | Kibbe, Margaret (Wid.) | 1 | 1 | 4 | | |
| Starkweather, Thomas | 1 | 3 | 5 | | | **ENFIELD TOWN.** | | | | | | Danna, Daniel | 2 | | 5 | | |
| Drake, Nathaniel | 1 | | | | | Fish, Eli | 1 | 3 | 2 | | | Geer, Elihu | 1 | 1 | 5 | | |
| Drake, Simeon | 2 | | 1 | | | Pease, William | 1 | 2 | 5 | | | Chandler, Nehemiah | 1 | | 1 | | |
| Drake, Nathaniel, Jr | 1 | 4 | 2 | | | Bullen, David | 2 | | 2 | | | Terry, Ephraim | 1 | 1 | 5 | | |
| Stedman, Stephen | 1 | | 1 | | | Bullen, Christopher | 1 | 1 | 3 | | | Diggins, Augustus | 1 | 1 | 4 | | 2 |
| Stedman, Stephen, Jr | 1 | 1 | 3 | | | Pratt, Thomas | 1 | 1 | 1 | | | Johnson, Jonathan | 2 | 1 | 3 | | |
| Drake, Shubel | 1 | | 1 | | | Pease, Moses | 1 | 1 | 5 | | | Prior, Ebenezer | 3 | | 5 | | |
| Drake, Ebenezer | 3 | | 4 | | | Pease, Moses, Jr | 1 | 2 | 1 | | | Kibbe, Isaac | 2 | 1 | 4 | | 1 |
| McCivers, Daniel | 1 | | 1 | | | Pease, Lemuel | 1 | 1 | 2 | | | Kibbe, Gains | 2 | 2 | 3 | | |
| House, Eliphalet | 1 | | 1 | | | Avery, John | 2 | 1 | 2 | | | Bush, Eli | 1 | 1 | 3 | | |
| Stoughton, Shem | 1 | 4 | 1 | | | Pease, Abiel | 1 | | 2 | | | Hale, Samuel | 1 | 3 | 6 | | |
| Rockwell, Silvanus | 1 | 3 | 3 | | | Webster, Joel | 1 | | 2 | | | Stockwell, Reuben | 2 | 4 | 4 | | |
| Rockwell, Joel | | 1 | 3 | | | Markum, Isaac | 1 | 1 | 1 | | | Terry, Samuel | 1 | 1 | 1 | | |
| Wolcott, Benjamin, 2d | 1 | | | | | Allyn, Moses | 4 | 1 | 5 | | | Terry, Benjamin, 2d | 1 | 1 | 2 | | |
| Rockwell, Amasa | 1 | | 1 | | | Allyn, Moses, Jr | 1 | 1 | 1 | | | Hale, Israel | 2 | | 2 | | |
| Grant, Justus | 1 | 4 | 1 | | | Allyn, Ebenezer | 2 | | 2 | | | Hillam, Eliphalet | 1 | 5 | 5 | | |
| Grant, Mathew | 1 | 2 | 1 | | | Allyn, Elijah | 1 | 1 | 1 | | | Hale, Thomas | 1 | | 2 | | |
| Grant, Oliver | 1 | | 3 | | | Warner, Eliphalet | 2 | 2 | 4 | | | Hale, Eli | 1 | 1 | 2 | | |
| Grant, Samuel R | 1 | 1 | 3 | | | Hall, Israel | 1 | | 2 | | | Meacham, Elizabeth (Widw) | | | 2 | | |
| Keeney, William | 1 | | 2 | | | Holkins, Joseph | 1 | | 3 | | | Meacham, Benjamin | 1 | 2 | 3 | | |
| Foster, Peletiah | 4 | | 5 | | | Holkins, Elijah | 2 | 1 | 3 | | | Griswold, Benajah | 1 | 2 | 2 | | |
| Grant, John | 1 | | 3 | | | Allyn, John | 4 | | 3 | | | Green, Obadiah | 1 | 1 | 4 | | |
| Grant, Edward C | 4 | 1 | 1 | | | Phelps, Noah | 1 | | 1 | | | Green, Mary (Wid.) | | | 3 | | |
| Johnson, Samuel | 1 | 1 | 1 | | | Markham, Nathan | 1 | | 3 | | | Anderson, Ashbel | 1 | 1 | 4 | | |
| Johnson, Feen | 1 | 2 | 3 | | | Parsons, Benjamin, 2d | 1 | 1 | 2 | | | Parsons, Christopher | 1 | | 2 | | |
| Elmore, Augustus | 1 | 1 | 2 | | | Butler, James | 1 | 2 | 7 | | | Parsons, Lemuel | 1 | 1 | 3 | | |
| Smith, Joseph | 2 | 3 | 3 | | | Holkins, Joel, Jr | 1 | | 1 | | | King, Naum | 3 | 4 | 3 | | |
| Kingsley, Salmon | 1 | 1 | 2 | | | Starns, Levi | 1 | 2 | 2 | | | Rush, Joshua, Jr | 1 | | 1 | | |
| Kingsley, Oren | 1 | 1 | 3 | | | Warner, John | 2 | | 1 | | | Pease, Noadiah | 1 | 4 | 5 | | |
| Kingsley, Stephen | 1 | | 1 | | | Warner, Hannah (Wd) | | | 3 | | | Kingsbury, Joseph | 2 | | 3 | | |
| Rockwell, Ephraim | 1 | 4 | 1 | | | Abbey, Richard | 1 | 1 | 2 | | | Monsen, Alexander | 1 | 2 | 5 | | |
| Corning, Nathan, Jr | 1 | | 3 | | | Abbey, Richard, Jr | 1 | 3 | 2 | | | Bucknel, Josiah | 4 | | 3 | | |
| Corney, Nathan | 3 | | 3 | | | Wilson, David | 1 | 1 | 2 | | | Metcalf, Thomas | 3 | | 3 | | |
| White, Freind | 3 | 1 | 4 | | | Booth, John | 1 | 2 | 2 | | | Fenton, Barry | 3 | | 3 | | |
| Goodale, Walter | 1 | 1 | 5 | | | Booth, Joel | 1 | | 2 | | | Terry, Selah | 3 | 1 | 4 | | |
| Goodale, Ebenezer | 3 | | 2 | | | Bement, Joseph | 1 | | 1 | | | Chaffer, William | 1 | | 7 | | |
| White, Henery | 2 | | 3 | | | Simons, Asahel | 5 | | 5 | | | Abbey, Thomas, 2d | 2 | 1 | 1 | | |
| Tryon, Aaron | 1 | 1 | 5 | | | Pease, Aaron, Jr | 1 | 4 | 7 | | | Brooks, Zerah | 3 | 3 | 5 | | |
| Evens, Allyn | 1 | 1 | 2 | | | Parsons, Ebenezer | 1 | | 5 | | | Alden, Amos | 2 | 1 | 3 | | |
| Fitch, White Roswold | 1 | 2 | 1 | | | Lord, William | 1 | | 2 | | | Terry, Shadrack | 3 | 2 | 2 | | |
| Fitch, Richard | 1 | | 2 | | | Ward, Thomas | 1 | | 1 | | | Brooks, William | 1 | | 3 | | |
| Elmore, Daniel | | 2 | 2 | | | Fenton, Truston | 1 | | 2 | | | Parsons, Hezekiah | 4 | | 2 | | |
| Benjamin, Elisha | 2 | 2 | 6 | | | Parsons, Joseph | 2 | 3 | 4 | | | Parsons, Hezekiah, Jr | 1 | 5 | 3 | | |
| Loomiss, Gideon | 3 | | 3 | | | Parsons, Thomas | 2 | 1 | 3 | | | Collins, John | 1 | 2 | 3 | | |
| Benjamin, Elisha, Jr | 1 | 1 | 2 | | | Bemont, Edmund | 1 | | 1 | | | Hale, John | 1 | 4 | 2 | | |
| Burkland, George | 1 | 3 | 4 | | | Bement, Dennis | 1 | 1 | 7 | | | Terry, Selah, Jr | 1 | | 3 | | |
| Brunson, Beriah | 1 | 2 | 2 | | | Holton, Elisha | 1 | | 4 | | | Meachum, Simeon | 1 | | 3 | | |
| Ludd, Ezekiel | 1 | | 1 | | | Parsons, Prudence (Wd) | | | 1 | | | Terry, Zeno | 1 | | 3 | | |
| Simons, Paul G | 2 | 1 | 1 | | | Parsons, Elijah | 3 | 3 | 5 | | | Handcock, William | 2 | 1 | 5 | | |
| Barber, Noah | 2 | 1 | 4 | | | Terry, Elijah | 4 | | 2 | | | Chandler, David | 1 | 3 | 5 | | |
| Munsell, Hezekiah | 1 | 5 | 2 | | | Booth, Levi | 2 | | 2 | | | Chandler, Joseph | 1 | 3 | 4 | | |
| Rockwell, Isaac | 2 | | 4 | | | Sabin, Thomas | 1 | | | | | Chandler, Joseph, Jr | 2 | 1 | 1 | | |
| Rockwell, Frances | 1 | 1 | 2 | | | Booth, Zacheriah | 1 | | 2 | | | Rumvil, John | 1 | | 3 | | |
| Fenton, William | 1 | 1 | 1 | | | Avery, Jonathan | 1 | 2 | 3 | | | Holkins, Joel | 2 | | 1 | | |
| Green, Barzilla | 2 | | 1 | | | Olmsted, Joseph | 2 | | 2 | | | Meacham, Asa | 1 | | 2 | | |
| Green, Azel | 1 | 3 | 5 | | | Booth, Joseph | 5 | | 6 | | | Bugbee, Jonathan | 1 | 1 | 2 | | |
| Cassee, Patrick | 1 | 2 | 2 | | | Pease, Ebenezer | 2 | 1 | 4 | | | Kingsbury, Lemuel | 3 | 4 | 4 | | |
| Watrous, Nathaniel | 1 | | 2 | | | Prior, Isaac | 1 | 3 | 5 | | | Bush, Jonathan | 2 | | 7 | | |
| Strong, Israel | 2 | 1 | 2 | | | Knight, Joseph | 3 | 1 | 2 | | | Bush, Joshua | 1 | 1 | 1 | | |
| Foster, Thomas | 2 | 2 | 5 | | | Knight, Thomas | 1 | | 1 | | | Terry, Daniel | 1 | 1 | 2 | | |
| Dorman, Stephen | 1 | 2 | 1 | | | Higley, Jeremiah | 1 | | 2 | | | Terry, Joseph | 1 | 3 | 5 | | |
| Stoughton, John | 1 | 2 | 4 | | | Pease, Sharon | 2 | | 4 | | | Terry, Ebenezer, 2d | 1 | | 5 | | |
| Webster, Cyrenus | 1 | 3 | 6 | | | Simons, Joel | 1 | 2 | 3 | | | Terry, Jacob | 3 | | 8 | | |
| Drake, Silas | 2 | 6 | 3 | | | Pease, Peter | 1 | 2 | 2 | | | Terry, Jacob, Jr | 1 | | 3 | | |
| Lathrop, Thatcher | 2 | | 3 | | | Griswold, Joseph | 2 | 1 | 3 | | | Terry, Julus | 1 | | 2 | | |
| Lathrop, David | 1 | 1 | 1 | | | Terry, Eliphalet, Esqr | 2 | 3 | 6 | | | Parsons, Jabez | 1 | | 3 | | |
| Morton, Deodat | 1 | 3 | 4 | | | Meacham, John | 6 | 3 | 2 | | | Hale, Jonn | 1 | | 1 | | |
| Gibbs, Ebenezer | 2 | 2 | 2 | | | Potter, Elam | 2 | 1 | 5 | | | Pease, James | 1 | 2 | 5 | | |
| Dart, Jabez | 2 | 2 | 6 | | | Pease, Ephm | 2 | | 2 | | 2 | Hale, David | 1 | | 3 | | |
| Stoughton, Jonathan | 1 | | 2 | | | Pridden, Revd Nehemiah | 1 | 1 | 3 | 1 | | Hale, David, Jr | 1 | 3 | 5 | | |
| Grant, Hezekiah | 1 | | 3 | | | Parsons, Benjn | 1 | | 2 | | | Hale, Ebenezer | 1 | 4 | 2 | | |
| Rockwell, Ezra | 1 | | 1 | | | Parsons, Simeon | 1 | 1 | | | | Pease, Joseph | 1 | | 2 | | |
| Rockwell, Daniel, 2d | 1 | 1 | 2 | | | Chapin, Azubah (Wid.) | 3 | | 5 | | | Pease, Gideon | 1 | | 2 | | |
| Smith, Samuel | 1 | 3 | 6 | | | Chapin, Nathaniel | 1 | | 3 | | | Stanley, Benjamin | 2 | 2 | 3 | | |
| Woodbridge, Ashbel | 1 | | 1 | | | Chapin, Nathaniel, Jr | 1 | 1 | 2 | | | Parsons, Wareham | 1 | 2 | 5 | | |
| Grant, Gideon | 2 | | 1 | | | Chapin, Simeon | 1 | 1 | 3 | | | Simons, Benjamin | 1 | | 3 | | |
| Grant, Gideon, Jr | 1 | | 3 | | | Pease, Zebulon | 2 | 5 | 3 | | | Simons, Benjamin, Jr | 1 | 5 | 4 | | |
| Grant, William | 1 | | 1 | | | Parsons, Peter | 2 | 3 | 4 | | | | | | | | |
| Rockebell, Daniel | 2 | 4 | 7 | | | Peirce, Joseph | 1 | 2 | 3 | | | | | | | | |
| Sadd, Thomas | 1 | | 1 | | | | | | | | | | | | | | |
| Sadd, Thomas, Jr | 2 | 2 | 4 | | | | | | | | | | | | | | |

## HARTFORD COUNTY—Continued.

| NAME OF HEAD OF FAMILY. | Free white males of 16 years and upward, including heads of families. | Free white males under 16 years. | Free white females, including heads of families. | All other free persons. | Slaves. | NAME OF HEAD OF FAMILY. | Free white males of 16 years and upward, including heads of families. | Free white males under 16 years. | Free white females, including heads of families. | All other free persons. | Slaves. | NAME OF HEAD OF FAMILY. | Free white males of 16 years and upward, including heads of families. | Free white males under 16 years. | Free white females, including heads of families. | All other free persons. | Slaves. |
|---|---|---|---|---|---|---|---|---|---|---|---|---|---|---|---|---|---|
| **ENFIELD TOWN—con.** | | | | | | **ENFIELD TOWN—con.** | | | | | | **FARMINGTON TOWN—continued.** | | | | | |
| Button, Elias | 1 | 3 | 2 | | | Billings, Thaddeus | 1 | 2 | 2 | | | Root, Hezekiah | 3 | 4 | 6 | | |
| Perkins, Daniel | 5 | | 2 | | | Billings, Eli | 1 | | 1 | | | Curtis, Solomon | 1 | 1 | 1 | | |
| Perkins, George | 1 | 1 | 1 | | | Eaton, Samuel | 1 | | 2 | | | Parsons, Thomas | 2 | 1 | 3 | | |
| Adams, Elijah | 1 | 3 | 3 | | | Eaton, Samuel, Jr | 1 | 1 | 6 | | | Monger, Levi | 1 | | 4 | | |
| Fairman, Ithemer | 1 | | 3 | | | Terry, Ebenezer | 2 | 1 | 4 | | | Parsons, Thomas, Jr | 1 | 1 | 1 | | |
| Pease, John, 3d | 2 | 3 | 4 | | | Terry, Hirum | 1 | | 2 | | | Kenada, Asa | 1 | 2 | 1 | | |
| Allyn, Jonathan | 1 | 2 | 2 | | | Pease, Commins | 1 | | 1 | | | Phinney, Oliver | 1 | | 1 | | |
| Gains, John | 2 | 1 | 3 | | | Pease, Heman | 1 | 2 | 3 | | | Phinney, Joshua | 1 | 2 | 2 | | |
| Chapin, Jeremiah | 1 | 1 | 2 | | | Pease, Commins, 2d | 1 | 3 | 5 | | | Gridley, Ebenezer | 2 | 2 | 3 | | |
| Pease, Gideon, 2d | 1 | 2 | 3 | | | Pease, David, 2d | 1 | 1 | 4 | | | Willcox, James | 1 | 2 | 2 | | |
| Pease, Isaac, 2nd | 1 | 6 | 1 | | | Billings, Nathaniel | 1 | 2 | 1 | | | Comes, Phineas | 2 | 2 | 8 | | |
| Sabin, David | 1 | 1 | 2 | | | Pease, Asa | 1 | 3 | 2 | | | Burrows, Barzilla | 1 | 1 | 2 | | |
| Pease, Ezekiel | 1 | | | | | Pease, Timothy | 1 | | 2 | | | Burrows, Joseph | 1 | 1 | 4 | | |
| Prior, Ezekiel | 1 | | 1 | | | Pease, Edward | 1 | 2 | 2 | | | Andruss, Ichabod | 1 | 1 | 3 | | |
| Prior, Zacheus | 3 | 1 | 5 | | | McGrigery, John | 1 | | 3 | | | Hamlin, Levi | 1 | 1 | 2 | | |
| Pease, Simon | 1 | 1 | 3 | | | Terry, Jonathan | 1 | | 2 | | | Shepard, Jesse | 1 | 1 | 2 | | |
| Pease, Israel | 3 | | 1 | | | Terry, David | 1 | 9 | 1 | | | Shepard, Amos | 2 | 2 | 3 | | |
| Comes, John | 2 | 1 | 6 | | | King, Benjamin | 5 | 2 | 3 | | | Smith, Lydia | | 2 | 4 | | |
| Collins, Edward, Esqr | 1 | | 1 | | | King, Joel | 1 | 3 | | | | Rowdan, James | 1 | 2 | 3 | | |
| Collins, Nathaniel | 1 | 1 | 3 | | | Hemingway, Samuel | 1 | | 2 | | | Hawley, Amos | 2 | 4 | 5 | | |
| Parsons, Eli | 1 | 3 | 3 | | | Marckum, Barzilla | 3 | | 2 | | | Churchill, Wm | 3 | | 1 | | |
| Kibbe, Elisha | 1 | | 3 | | 2 | Parsons, Eldad | 4 | 1 | 5 | | | Hawley, Abel | 1 | 2 | 6 | | |
| Bugbee, Nathaniel | 2 | 1 | 2 | | | Parsons, Asabel | 1 | 3 | 3 | | | Crampton, Miles | 2 | 1 | 4 | | |
| Pease, Samuel | 1 | 1 | 2 | | | Meachum, Abner | 1 | 2 | 2 | | | Hart, Thomas | 1 | 5 | 4 | | |
| Pease, Edward, 2d | 1 | 3 | 2 | | | Olmsted, Simeon | 2 | 5 | 3 | | | Hart, Ira | 2 | 3 | 4 | | |
| Parsons, Shubel | 1 | 3 | 4 | | | Chapin, Jabez | 2 | 2 | 3 | | | Hawley, Ebenezer | 1 | 6 | 3 | | |
| Pease, Hezekiah | 2 | | 6 | | | Cooley, Noah | 1 | 1 | 1 | | | Elsworth, William | 1 | | 2 | | |
| Eyers, Thomas | 1 | 1 | 5 | | | Shepard, Noah | 1 | | 2 | | | Curtis, Abner | 1 | 1 | 3 | | |
| Pease, Aaron | 2 | | 4 | | | Goold, John | 1 | 1 | 1 | | | Tubbs, Ammon | 1 | 1 | 2 | | |
| Terry, Solomon | 1 | 1 | 1 | | | Wood, Edward | 2 | | 6 | | | Lee, Amos | 2 | 2 | 3 | | |
| Chapin, Eliphalet | 1 | 1 | 2 | | | Bush, Aaron | 1 | | 1 | | | Bartholomew, Charles | 1 | | 4 | | |
| Pease, Jessee | 1 | 2 | 3 | | | Bush, Rufus | 1 | 2 | 4 | | | Rowe, Seth | 1 | 5 | 4 | | |
| Parsons, Nathaniel | 5 | 1 | 4 | | | Parker, Joseph | 1 | | 1 | | | Curtiss, Jesse | 1 | 2 | 5 | | |
| Pease, John, 2d | 2 | 3 | 2 | | | Baxter, William | 1 | 1 | 1 | | | Sweet, Palmer | 2 | 5 | 5 | | |
| Peirce, Abner | 1 | 2 | 1 | | | Talcott, Elizur | 3 | | 1 | | | Orvis, Zadock | 2 | 2 | 4 | | |
| Pease, Samuel, 2d | 2 | 2 | 5 | | | Parsons, Daniel | 1 | 1 | 3 | | | Barnes, Israel | 1 | 4 | 2 | | |
| Parsons, John | 2 | 5 | 3 | | | Parsons, Daniel, Jr | 1 | 1 | 1 | | | Alvord, Thomas G | 3 | 2 | 3 | | |
| Phelps, David | 1 | | 2 | | | Hills, Jacob | 1 | 1 | 4 | | | Wadsworth, Eliphalet | 2 | | 4 | | |
| Phelps, David, Jr | 1 | 4 | 2 | | | Emerson, Joseph | 2 | 1 | 4 | | | Mildren, Huldah | 1 | 1 | 2 | | |
| Phelps, Eldad | 2 | | 2 | | | Pease, Ruth (Wid.) | | 1 | 2 | | | Cowles, Elias | 3 | | 2 | | |
| Phelps, Eldad, Jr | 1 | | 2 | | | Booth, John, Jr | 1 | | 1 | | | Elsworth, Mary | | | 2 | | |
| Abbey, Thomas | 1 | 3 | 2 | | | Booth, Daniel | 1 | 2 | 4 | | | Hayden, David | 1 | 1 | 2 | | |
| Hubbard, Obediah | 3 | | 7 | | | Meachum, Joseph | 1 | | 1 | | | Langdon, Joseph | 2 | 4 | 5 | | |
| Pease, David | 2 | 1 | 5 | | | Pease, Benjamin | 8 | 4 | 16 | | | Sweet, Stephen | 1 | 2 | 1 | | |
| Hale, Daniel | 2 | | 4 | | | Pease, Elias | 1 | 2 | 2 | | | Grindley, Alexander | 2 | | 1 | | |
| Pease, Stone | 1 | 2 | 4 | | | Munsell, Zacheus | 1 | 1 | 6 | | | Byington, Jacob | 3 | | 3 | | |
| Chapin, Ebenezer | 4 | | 5 | | | Markham, Jehiel | 2 | 1 | 4 | | | Scott, Ezekiel | | 2 | 5 | | |
| Root, Benjamin | 1 | | 2 | | | Markham, Justus | 1 | 2 | 4 | | | Scott, Elisha | 2 | 1 | 6 | | |
| Root, Daniel | 1 | 4 | 6 | | | Parker, Samuel | 2 | 1 | 5 | | | Wadsworth, Eunice | | | 4 | | |
| Abbey, John | 1 | | 1 | | 1 | Pease, Isaac | 1 | 1 | 2 | | | Cowles, Ezekiel | 5 | 3 | 4 | | |
| Pease, Ephraim, 2d | 1 | 3 | 2 | | | Pease, Rufus | 1 | 3 | 2 | | | Welton, Joel | 1 | 2 | 2 | | |
| Abbey, Daniel | 2 | 3 | 4 | | | Pease, George | 1 | 2 | 1 | | | Tubbs, Amos | 1 | | 1 | | |
| Wright, Elezur | 2 | | 1 | | | | | | | | | Wadsworth, Luke | 2 | 3 | 7 | | |
| Abbey, John, 2d | 1 | 1 | 4 | | | **FARMINGTON TOWN.** | | | | | | Wadsworth, Wm | 2 | 3 | 2 | | |
| Abbey, John, 3d | 1 | | 4 | | | Warner, Demus | 1 | 2 | 3 | | | Hunt, James | 3 | | 2 | | |
| Pease, Nathan | 2 | 1 | 3 | | | Gridley, Isaac | 2 | 4 | 4 | | | Clark, Levi | 3 | | 2 | | |
| Allyn, David | 1 | | 3 | | | Gridley, Jonathan | 1 | | 1 | | | Root, Timothy | 4 | 1 | 3 | | |
| Ingram, Ebenezar | 2 | 2 | 3 | | | Jones, Samuel | 3 | | 1 | | | Root, Mark | 1 | | 1 | | |
| Thompson, Mathew | 3 | | 3 | | | Stedman, Elizabeth | | 1 | 2 | | | Cowles, Solomon, Jr | 5 | 3 | 8 | | |
| Markum, Darius | 2 | 3 | 4 | | | Gridley, Daniel | 1 | 2 | 2 | | | Cowles, Isaac | 4 | 3 | 5 | | |
| Meachum, Aaron | 1 | 2 | 5 | | | Porter, Prudince | | | | 5 | | Bidwell, Theodore | 3 | 1 | 4 | | |
| Parsons, Shubab | 1 | | 1 | | | Gridley, Rezin | 2 | | 4 | | | Kirkham, John | 1 | 1 | 3 | | |
| Collins, Eliphalet | 2 | 4 | 6 | | | Hamlin, John | 3 | 3 | 2 | | | Case, John | 2 | 1 | 1 | | |
| Thatcher, Thomas | 2 | 1 | 2 | | | Hamlin, Oliver | 1 | 1 | 1 | | | Case, Corvil | 1 | 2 | 1 | | |
| Terry, John | 1 | | 1 | | | Hamlin, Phinias | 1 | 1 | 1 | | | Curtis, Amos | 1 | 3 | 4 | | |
| Henry, John | 3 | 2 | 7 | | | Gridley, Noadiah | 3 | 1 | 4 | | | Cowles, Gideon | 1 | | 4 | | |
| Henery, Gager | 1 | 1 | | | | Cook, John | 2 | 2 | 3 | | | Cowles, Enos | 3 | 2 | 3 | | |
| Craw, Jonathan | 1 | | 1 | | | Hotchkiss, Ladwick | 1 | | 3 | | | Andruss, Timothy | 2 | 1 | 2 | | |
| Craw, David | 2 | 2 | 2 | | | Hotchkiss, Josiah | 2 | 1 | 3 | | | Kirham, Samuel | 1 | 2 | 1 | | |
| Griswold, Jonah | 1 | 4 | 4 | | | Root, Samuel | 2 | 2 | 3 | | | Porter, Elijah | 1 | 1 | 1 | | |
| Griswold, Shubel | 2 | 2 | 4 | | | Root, Elijah | 1 | 1 | 7 | | | Porter, Shubael | 1 | 1 | 1 | | |
| Griswold, Solomon | 1 | 1 | 6 | | | Root, Salmon | 1 | 2 | 6 | | | Bull, Jonathan | 1 | | 2 | | |
| Griswold, Jehiel | 1 | 4 | 3 | | | Hills, Joseph | 1 | 2 | 4 | | | Bull, Martin | 2 | | 2 | | |
| Shepard, Noah | 1 | | 2 | | | Hills, Chancey | 1 | 4 | 2 | | | Hawley, Isaac | 2 | 2 | 1 | | |
| Gowdy, Samuel | 2 | | 3 | | | Smally Jacob | 1 | 2 | 1 | | | Lee, Thomas, Jr | 1 | 1 | 1 | | |
| Gowdy, Robert | 1 | | 3 | | | Morse, Moses | 1 | 3 | 3 | | | Porter, George | 2 | | 4 | | |
| Gowdy, William | 1 | 2 | 2 | | | Wood, Eli | 2 | 1 | 2 | | | Buckley, Thomas | 2 | 1 | 2 | | |
| Jones, Caleb | 1 | | 2 | | | Deming, Samuel | 2 | | 1 | | 1 | Bidwell, Isaac | 2 | | 2 | | |
| Jones, Caleb, Jr | 1 | | 1 | | | Deming, Benjamin | 2 | | 2 | | | Wadsworth, Asahel | 4 | 1 | 4 | | |
| Jones, Ezra | 1 | 2 | 1 | | | Wilcox, Asa | 1 | 1 | 1 | | | Porter, Elijah, Jr | 1 | 1 | 1 | | |
| Gleason, Joseph | 1 | | 1 | | | Wilcox, Jesse | 1 | | 1 | | | Pitkin, Timothy | 3 | | 1 | | |
| Gleason, Jonah | 1 | 1 | 4 | | | Frisbee, Zebulon | 1 | | 1 | | | Cowles, Thomas | 2 | | 3 | | |
| Gleason, Isaac | 1 | 3 | 4 | | | Parsons, Isaac | 2 | 1 | 3 | | | Lewis, Thomas | 2 | 2 | 3 | | 1 |
| Gleason, Solomon | 1 | | 4 | | | Richards, Seth | 1 | 1 | 2 | | | Cowles, Amos | 2 | 1 | 3 | | |
| Gleason, Joseph, Jr | 1 | 2 | 4 | | | Richards, Samuel | 2 | | 2 | | | Deming, John | 2 | | 5 | | |
| Morrison, John | 2 | | 8 | | | Bishop, James | 2 | 1 | 2 | | | Deming, Chancey | 1 | | 2 | | |
| Parsons, Edward | 1 | | 5 | | | Hooper, Asahel | 4 | 1 | 3 | | | Mix, John | 1 | 2 | 5 | | |
| Sexton, Thomas | 3 | | 1 | | | Carrington, Elizabeth | | 1 | 5 | | | Shepard, Luther | 1 | | 2 | | |
| Fairman, Jared | 1 | 1 | 6 | | | Feney, Oziah | 1 | 1 | 2 | | | Lee, Seth | 2 | 5 | 6 | | |
| Sexton, Asabel | 1 | | 1 | | | Porter, Richard | 3 | | 2 | | | Whitman, Solomon, Jr | 2 | 3 | 5 | | |
| Pease, John | 1 | | 1 | | | Evans, Luther | 2 | 2 | 5 | | | Pond, Phineas | 1 | | 1 | | |
| Pease, Simeon, 2d | 1 | 2 | 1 | | | Lawry, Daniel | 1 | 4 | 3 | | | North, Reuben | 1 | 1 | 5 | | |
| Pease, Isaac, 3d | 2 | 3 | 3 | | | Hayford, John | 1 | | 2 | | | Woodruff, Oliver | 2 | 2 | 6 | | |
| Terry, Aseph | 1 | 2 | 4 | | | Gridley, Seth | 1 | 4 | 3 | | | Woodruff, Lois | 3 | 1 | 4 | | |
| Baxter, Frances | 1 | 1 | 1 | | | | | | | | | | | | | | |

# HEADS OF FAMILIES—CONNECTICUT.

## HARTFORD COUNTY—Continued.

| NAME OF HEAD OF FAMILY. | Free white males of 16 years and upward, including heads of families. | Free white males under 16 years. | Free white females, including heads of families. | All other free persons. | Slaves. | NAME OF HEAD OF FAMILY. | Free white males of 16 years and upward, including heads of families. | Free white males under 16 years. | Free white females, including heads of families. | All other free persons. | Slaves. | NAME OF HEAD OF FAMILY. | Free white males of 16 years and upward, including heads of families. | Free white males under 16 years. | Free white females, including heads of families. | All other free persons. | Slaves. |
|---|---|---|---|---|---|---|---|---|---|---|---|---|---|---|---|---|---|
| **FARMINGTON TOWN—continued.** | | | | | | **FARMINGTON TOWN—continued.** | | | | | | **FARMINGTON TOWN—continued.** | | | | | |
| Woodruff, Timothy | 1 | | 2 | | | Bird, Joseph | 1 | 3 | 3 | | | Thompson, Ruth | | | 4 | | |
| Woodruff, Abel | 1 | 1 | 3 | | | Wadsworth, Hezekiah | 3 | 5 | 4 | | | Thompson, Barnabas | 1 | 4 | 3 | | |
| Woodruff, Joshua | 2 | 2 | 2 | | | Barnes, Amos | 1 | 2 | 4 | | | Miller, Elisha | 2 | 4 | 5 | | |
| North, Samuel | 4 | 4 | 6 | | | Porter, John | 2 | 2 | 6 | 1 | | North, David | 1 | | 2 | | |
| North, Daniel | 3 | 1 | 5 | | | Porter, Lemuel | 1 | 1 | 1 | | | Lewis, Oliver | | 1 | 4 | | |
| Woodruff, Elijah, Jr | 2 | 1 | 3 | | | Hooker, Elnathan | 2 | 1 | 2 | | | Woodford, W<sup>m</sup> | 1 | 2 | 5 | | |
| Combs, Ebenezer | 1 | | 4 | | | Rowe, Isaiah | 2 | 1 | 5 | | | Woodford, Selah | 1 | 1 | 2 | | |
| Clark, Marvin | 1 | 2 | 5 | | | Youngs, Joshua | 1 | 3 | 1 | 2 | | Woodford, Samuel | 1 | 1 | 3 | | |
| Woodruff, Martin | 2 | 3 | 5 | | | Rowe, Samuel | 1 | | 2 | | | Everist, Solomon | 2 | | 2 | | |
| Hart, Joel | 1 | 1 | 4 | | | Barns, Moses | 1 | 2 | 4 | | | North, Isaiah | 2 | 1 | 5 | | |
| Woodruff, James | 1 | 2 | 4 | | | Barns, James | 3 | 3 | 7 | | | Woodford, Elijah | 1 | 4 | 4 | | |
| Hart, Lemuel | 1 | 1 | 1 | | | Brunson, Stephen | 5 | 4 | 4 | | | Woodford, Joseph | 4 | 2 | 6 | | |
| Hooker, Joseph | 2 | 4 | 2 | | | Woodruff, Reuben | 1 | 3 | 5 | | | Woodford, W<sup>m</sup>, Jr | 2 | 3 | 3 | | |
| Hooker, Noadiah | 2 | 3 | 7 | | | Woodruff, Noah | 4 | | 3 | | | Woodford, Dudley | 1 | 4 | 4 | | |
| Loomiss, Joseph | 2 | | 2 | | | Woodruff, Solomon | 1 | | 3 | | | Norton, Bethuel | 3 | 2 | 3 | | |
| Cowles, Elijah, Jr | 4 | 1 | 5 | | 1 | Clark, Dan | 3 | | 2 | | | Marshall, Eliakim | 3 | | 2 | | |
| Cowles, Elijah | 3 | | 4 | | | Whittlesey, Abner | 1 | 1 | 3 | | | Miller, Elijah | 1 | | 3 | | |
| Barker, Seth | 2 | 1 | 3 | | | Hinman, Amos | 1 | | 5 | | | Miller, Jonathan | 2 | | 1 | 1 | |
| Hart, Asa | 1 | 3 | 5 | | | Hayford, Elisha | 1 | 1 | 1 | | | Woodford, John | 1 | | 2 | | |
| Root, Samuel, Jr | 2 | 4 | 2 | | | Cook, Roswell | 2 | 2 | 2 | | | Woodford, Amos | 1 | 1 | 2 | | |
| Warren, Samuel | 2 | 2 | 4 | | | Winstone, John | 1 | 2 | 2 | | | Cummings, Samuel | 1 | | 1 | | |
| Porter, Joseph | 3 | 1 | 5 | | | Hayford, John | 1 | | 1 | | | Ingham, Jon<sup>th</sup> | 2 | 1 | 3 | | |
| Merrill, James | 1 | 4 | 1 | | | Potter, Philemon | 1 | 3 | 4 | | | Ingham, John | 1 | | 1 | | |
| Root, James | 1 | 2 | 3 | | | Peck, Abel | 1 | 1 | 3 | | | Ingham, Isaac | 1 | | 4 | | |
| Goodrich, Elijah | 1 | 4 | 4 | | | Tooley, Lemuel | 1 | 2 | 2 | | | Andrus, Mary | | 2 | 2 | | |
| Hart, William | 2 | 3 | 4 | | | Beckwith, Mabel | | | 2 | | | Hart, Elnathan | 2 | | 1 | | |
| Alvord, Thomas G., Jr | 1 | 2 | 2 | | | Woodruff, Elisha | 2 | 4 | 4 | | | Hart, Lineus | 1 | 2 | 1 | | |
| Judd, James | 2 | 2 | 5 | | | Beckwith, Jonah | 1 | 2 | 1 | | | Judd, Calvin | 1 | | 6 | | |
| Clark, Amos | 2 | 2 | 1 | | | Perry, Thomas | 1 | | 2 | | | Hinox, Salmon | 1 | 1 | 1 | | |
| Hart, Gad | 1 | 3 | 3 | | | Woodruff, Aaron | 2 | 1 | 4 | | | Hart, Ambrose | 2 | 1 | 3 | | |
| Strong, Elisha | 2 | 1 | 5 | | | North, Eli | 2 | 2 | 6 | | | Woodruff, Thomas | 2 | | 1 | | |
| Clark, Mathew | 1 | 2 | 2 | | | North, Asa | 1 | 2 | 4 | | | Woodruff, Medad | | 3 | 1 | | |
| Rice, Memusan | 1 | 4 | 2 | | | Parsons, Joshua | 2 | 2 | 1 | | | Woodruff, Gedar | 1 | 1 | 1 | | |
| Curtis, Gabriel | 2 | 2 | 2 | | | Cowles, Daniel, Jr | 1 | 2 | 1 | | | Woodford, Isaac | 2 | 4 | 3 | | |
| Curtis, Hannah | | | 3 | | | Porter, William | 1 | 2 | 6 | | | Thompson, Lott | 1 | 1 | 6 | | |
| Curtis, Silvanus | 2 | 1 | 3 | | | Hart, Reuben | 1 | 1 | 3 | | | Woodruff, Eldad | 2 | 4 | 3 | | |
| Curtis, Peter | 4 | 1 | 4 | | | Cowles, Daniel | 2 | 2 | 4 | | | Woodruff, Micah | 2 | 2 | 4 | | |
| Hart, John | 1 | 3 | 2 | 1 | | Woodford, Elijah | 1 | | 5 | | | Woodruff, Joseph | 2 | 5 | 4 | | |
| Hull, Eliakim | 2 | 2 | 7 | | | Lusk, James | 3 | 3 | 5 | | | Woodruff, Zebulon | 2 | | 1 | | |
| Andrus, Obadiah | 1 | | 5 | | | Cowles, Ziba | 2 | 2 | 4 | | | Foot, Jacob | 2 | 1 | 4 | | |
| Lewis, Phineas | 3 | | 4 | | | Hawley, Reuben | 1 | 6 | 3 | | | Hart, James | 1 | 1 | 2 | | |
| Thompson, Luke | 1 | 1 | 7 | | | Thomas, Zelpha | | | 2 | | | Durren, Stephen | 1 | 1 | 3 | | |
| Nott, Gershom | 1 | | | | | Brister, David | 1 | 3 | 5 | | | Potter, Nathaniel | 4 | | 1 | | |
| Curtis, Eleazer | 2 | | 3 | | | Fullar, John | 1 | 2 | 1 | | | Chidsuy, Joseph | 1 | 4 | 4 | | |
| Curtis, Daniel | 1 | | 2 | | | Fullar, Josiah | 1 | 1 | 1 | | | Hart, Hosea | 1 | | 3 | | |
| Richards, Samuel, Jr | 2 | 1 | 2 | | | Norton, Jedidiah | 2 | | 2 | | | Alderman, Timothy | 1 | 2 | 2 | | |
| Lee, Thomas | 2 | | 2 | | | Tillotson, Elias | 2 | 1 | 4 | | | Bunnel, Joseph | 1 | | 3 | | |
| Hooker, Roger | 3 | 1 | 3 | 1 | | Hart, Samuel | 1 | 1 | 2 | | | Tillotson, Daniel | 2 | 1 | 3 | | |
| Gleason, Isaac | 2 | | 2 | 1 | | Hart, Lent | 1 | 4 | 2 | | | Brockway, Joseph, Jr | 2 | | 4 | | |
| Hosmer, Timothy | 2 | 5 | 3 | | 1 | Hart, Munson | 1 | | 4 | | | Soper, Timothy | 3 | 3 | 2 | | |
| Hill, Amos | 1 | 3 | 5 | | | Peterson, Charles | 1 | 3 | 3 | | | Sturdivant, Azor | 2 | 1 | 2 | | |
| Andrus, Theodore | 1 | 2 | 3 | | | Tillotson, Ashbel | 1 | | 2 | | | Miller, Noah | 2 | 2 | 3 | | |
| Hicks, James | 1 | | 2 | | | Woodruff, Moses | 1 | 4 | 2 | | | Edson, Teracy | 2 | | 3 | | |
| Porter, Noah | 1 | 2 | 4 | | | Woodruff, Appleton | 1 | 2 | 2 | | | Brockway, Joseph | 1 | | 5 | | |
| Judd, W<sup>m</sup> | 3 | | 2 | | | Gridley, Obed | 1 | 1 | 3 | | | Frisbee, David | 1 | 1 | 5 | | |
| Judd, William S | 1 | 1 | 1 | | | North, Lott | 1 | 3 | 2 | | | Northway, Joseph | 2 | 3 | 2 | | |
| Street, Thankfull | | 2 | 3 | | | Hosford, Ezekiel | 4 | | 3 | | | Talcott, Job | 3 | 2 | 4 | | |
| Whitman, Solomon | 1 | 1 | 2 | | | Pratt, Elisha | 3 | | 2 | | | Sturdivant, James | 1 | 2 | 3 | | |
| Whitman, Elnathan | 1 | 1 | 3 | | | Langton, Solomon | 1 | 1 | 3 | | | Studivant, Ozar | 1 | 2 | 2 | | |
| Porter, Amos | 1 | 1 | 2 | | | Kelsey, Amos | 1 | 2 | 3 | | | Gleason, David | 1 | 5 | 1 | | |
| Welton, Benjamin | 1 | 2 | 2 | | | Gridley, Elijah | 3 | | 5 | | | Gleason, Samuel | 1 | 1 | 4 | | |
| Porter, Jesse | 1 | 1 | 3 | | | Thomson, Jonathan | 3 | | 2 | | 1 | Curtis, Gran | 1 | | 3 | | |
| Pratt, Mabel | | | 2 | | | Thompson, Daniel | 1 | 1 | 2 | 1 | | Norton, Samuel | 1 | 4 | 2 | | |
| Clark, Salmon | 1 | 1 | 1 | | | Andrus, Elijah | 3 | | 5 | | | Thompson, Abel | 1 | 2 | 2 | | |
| Norton, Reuben S | 1 | 2 | 3 | | | Thompson, Samuel | 3 | | 2 | | | Hawley, Elijah | 1 | 2 | 2 | | |
| Smith, Thomas | 2 | | 2 | | | Langdon, Ebenezer | 1 | 2 | 4 | | | Woodruff, Lott | 4 | 1 | 5 | | |
| Smith, Samuel | 2 | | 4 | | | Norton, Ichabod | 2 | 2 | 3 | | | Hawley, Joseph | 2 | 2 | 3 | 1 | |
| Thompson, John | 1 | 1 | 5 | | | Gillet, Noah | 1 | 4 | 2 | | | Hawley, Gad | 1 | 2 | 2 | | |
| Gillet, Abraham | 1 | 2 | 3 | | | Gillet, Isaac | 1 | 1 | 1 | | | Gridley, Timothy | 2 | 3 | 3 | | |
| Reynolds, John | 3 | | 3 | | | Gillett, Noadiah | 1 | 1 | 1 | | | Harrington, Elisha | 1 | 2 | 7 | | |
| Woodford, Roger | 1 | 5 | 3 | | | Gillett, Amos | 2 | | 1 | | | Selden, Joseph | 1 | 3 | 4 | | |
| Newill, Thomas | 3 | 3 | 3 | | | Willcox, Jesse | 1 | | 2 | | | Standley, Samuel | 1 | 1 | 2 | | |
| Roads, Joseph | 2 | 2 | 4 | | | Willcox, Eleazer | 1 | 2 | 2 | | | Standley, Samuel, Jr | 1 | 4 | 5 | | |
| Woodruff, John | 1 | 3 | 4 | | | Willcox, Ezra | 1 | 1 | 3 | | | Sedgwith, Stephen | 1 | 2 | 3 | | |
| Woodford, Charles | 1 | 3 | 3 | | | Willcox, Josiah | 1 | 2 | 2 | | | Sedgwith, Stephen, Jr | 1 | 2 | 1 | | |
| Humphry, Ralph | 1 | | 1 | | | Bishop, Benjamin | 1 | | 1 | | | Curtis, Josiah | 1 | 3 | 2 | | |
| Dyer, Joseph | 1 | 2 | 2 | | | Bishop, Samuel | 1 | 1 | 1 | | | Belden, John R | 2 | 1 | 5 | | |
| Woodruff, Aaron, Jr | 1 | 1 | 3 | | | Bishop, Thomas F | 2 | 2 | 4 | | | Olds, Ebenezer | 1 | | 2 | | |
| Lewis, Elijah | 1 | 2 | 2 | | | Hart, Gideon | 2 | 2 | 4 | | | More, Simeon | 1 | 2 | 4 | | |
| Woodruff, Judah | 3 | | 5 | | | Hart, Anthony | 1 | 1 | 3 | | | Goodwin, Morgan | 3 | 1 | 2 | | |
| Treadwell, John | 2 | 2 | 6 | | | Thomson, Timothy | 1 | | 2 | | | Farnsworth, Samuel | 1 | 1 | 1 | | |
| Woodruff, Joseph | 2 | 1 | 3 | | | Thompson, Thomas | 1 | 4 | 3 | | | Wells, Bayza | 2 | 4 | 2 | | |
| Thompson, Nathaniel | 1 | 2 | 3 | | | Woodford, Ezekiel | 1 | 4 | 3 | | | Wells, George | 1 | 1 | 1 | | |
| Welton, Solomon | 1 | | 2 | | | Miller, Anna | 1 | 1 | 3 | | | Wells, Elisha | 1 | 2 | 1 | | |
| Hayden, David, Jr | 1 | | 1 | | | Miller, Job | 1 | 2 | 2 | | | Wells, Elisha, Jr | 1 | 2 | 2 | | |
| M<sup>c</sup>Keinster, John | 1 | | 1 | | | Miller, Reuben | 1 | 2 | 2 | | | Grimes, John | 4 | 2 | 6 | | |
| Buck, Isaac | 3 | 3 | 6 | | | Miller, Solomon | 1 | 1 | 2 | | | Fisher, Timothy | 1 | 2 | 3 | | |
| Gridley, David | 1 | 3 | 5 | | | Miller, Ebenezer | 1 | | 2 | | | Shepard, Thomas | 1 | 1 | 4 | | |
| Peck, Samuel | 2 | 1 | 1 | | | Ford, W<sup>m</sup> | 2 | 2 | 2 | | | Rawley, Daniel | 1 | | 1 | | |
| North, John | 1 | 3 | 4 | | | Ford, Tho<sup>s</sup> | 2 | 4 | 6 | | | Cadwell, Peletiah | 1 | 5 | 2 | | |
| North, Seth | 1 | | 1 | | | Hawley, Rufus | 3 | 3 | 2 | | | Parsons, Hezekiak | 1 | 3 | 4 | | |
| Parks, Prudence | | 1 | 3 | | | Miller, Daniel | 1 | | 2 | | | Lord, Elisha | 1 | | 2 | | |
| Hull, Abraham | 1 | 2 | 4 | | | Thompson, Levi | | 2 | 6 | | | Cadwell, Mathew | 2 | 1 | 2 | | |
| Judd, Elizur | 1 | 2 | 3 | | | Thompson, Asa | 1 | 2 | 2 | | | | | | | | |

41

# FIRST CENSUS OF THE UNITED STATES.

## HARTFORD COUNTY—Continued.

| NAME OF HEAD OF FAMILY. | Free white males of 16 years and upward, including heads of families. | Free white males under 16 years. | Free white females, including heads of families. | All other free persons. | Slaves. | NAME OF HEAD OF FAMILY. | Free white males of 16 years and upward, including heads of families. | Free white males under 16 years. | Free white females, including heads of families. | All other free persons. | Slaves. | NAME OF HEAD OF FAMILY. | Free white males of 16 years and upward, including heads of families. | Free white males under 16 years. | Free white females, including heads of families. | All other free persons. | Slaves. |
|---|---|---|---|---|---|---|---|---|---|---|---|---|---|---|---|---|---|
| **FARMINGTON TOWN—continued.** | | | | | | **GLASTENBURY TOWN—continued.** | | | | | | **GLASTENBURY TOWN—continued.** | | | | | |
| Olcott, Jediah | 1 | | 3 | | | Hale, Elijah | 1 | 2 | 4 | | | Pulsifer, Huldah | | 2 | 2 | | |
| Cadwell, James | 2 | 4 | 3 | | | Hale, Asahel | 1 | | 2 | | | Pierce, Mary | | 1 | 2 | | |
| Burr, Noadiah, Jr | 1 | 3 | 2 | | | Hodge, Roswell | 1 | 1 | 1 | | | Pease, Peter | 1 | | 4 | | |
| Burr, Salmon | 1 | 1 | 1 | | | Hollister, Jonathan | 1 | | 3 | | | Rice, Eliphalet | 1 | 4 | 3 | | |
| Burr, Theodore | 1 | | 1 | | | Hodge, Eli | 1 | 3 | 3 | | | Rice, John | 1 | 2 | 1 | | |
| Burr, Samuel | 2 | | 3 | | | Hollister, Stephen | 2 | 1 | 5 | | | Rice, Samuel, Jr | 1 | 1 | 2 | | |
| Smith, John | 1 | 1 | 2 | | | Hale, Joseph, Jr | 1 | 3 | 3 | | 1 | Rice, Samuel | 2 | 2 | 2 | | |
| Burr, Titus | 2 | | 3 | | | Hale, Gideon | 4 | 3 | 5 | | | Risley, Benjamin | 2 | 1 | 2 | | |
| Burr, Noadiah | 3 | 3 | 6 | | | Hale, Elisha | 2 | 2 | 5 | 1 | | Risley, Job | 2 | 2 | 1 | | |
| Burr, Isaac | 1 | 2 | 4 | | | Hale, Theodore | 3 | 1 | 5 | | 9 | Robertson, David | 2 | 2 | 1 | | |
| Allyn, John | 1 | 2 | 4 | | | Hale, Timothy | 2 | | 2 | | | Risley, Joseph | 1 | 2 | 3 | | |
| Burr, Eunice | | 2 | 1 | | | Hale, David | 4 | | 5 | | | Risley, George | 1 | 3 | 2 | | |
| Kilbourn, Josiah | 1 | 1 | 2 | | | Hale, Ruth | 1 | | 4 | | 3 | Ranson, Harris | 1 | | 3 | | |
| Barnes, Simeon | 1 | 3 | 3 | | | Hollister, John | 1 | 5 | 5 | | | Smith, Jonathan | 1 | | | | |
| Barnes, Hartwell | 1 | 2 | 2 | | | Hale, John | 1 | 1 | 2 | | | Strickland, Stephen, Jr | 2 | 4 | 3 | | |
| North, Ashur | 1 | 3 | 4 | | | Hale, Mathew | 1 | | 2 | | | Stevens, George | 1 | 2 | 3 | | |
| Johnson, Prince | | | | 5 | | Hollister, Joseph | 1 | | 2 | | | Smith, Hannah | | | 2 | | |
| Auguster, Ceasar | | | | 4 | | Hubbard, Eleazer | 2 | | 3 | | | Sellew, John | 2 | 4 | 5 | | |
| Freman, Amos | | | | 3 | | Hale, David, Jr | 1 | 1 | 4 | | 1 | Stratton, Samuel, Jr | 1 | 2 | 6 | | |
| Buttler, Benjamin | | | | 7 | | Hale, Joseph | 2 | | 2 | | | Shipman, Stephen. Jr | 1 | | 1 | | |
| Kitt (Negro) | | | | 4 | | House, Samuel | 1 | 4 | 3 | | | Shipman, John | 2 | 1 | 5 | | |
| Nelson, Isaac | | | | 4 | | Hubbard, David | 1 | 3 | 1 | | | Smith, Jedediah | 1 | 2 | 1 | | |
| | | | | | | Hollister, Abraham | 1 | | 2 | | | Shipman, Stephen | 1 | | 1 | | |
| **GLASTENBURY TOWN.** | | | | | | Hollister, David | 1 | | 5 | | | Smith, Ebenezer | 1 | | 1 | | |
| | | | | | | Hale, Abagail | | | 2 | | | Smith, Benjamin | 1 | 1 | 4 | | |
| Alger, Ashbel | 2 | 5 | 4 | | | Hodge, Elijah | 2 | 2 | 3 | | | Stevens, Timothy | 1 | 2 | 4 | | |
| Andrus, Daniel | 1 | 2 | 3 | | | Hubbard, Prudence | | 1 | 3 | | | Strong, John | 2 | 1 | 3 | | |
| Avery, Abraham | 1 | 1 | 4 | | | House, Benjamin | 2 | 1 | 3 | | | Stocking, Ansel | 1 | | 3 | | |
| Andrews, Joseph | 1 | 2 | 2 | | | Hollister, Roswell | 3 | 2 | 2 | | | Stevens, Thomas | 3 | | 3 | | |
| Anderson, Sawney | | | | 4 | | Hale, George | 1 | | 3 | | 1 | Stevens, James | 2 | 2 | 3 | | |
| Alger, Roger | 1 | 1 | 3 | | | Hale, Josiah | 2 | 2 | 5 | 4 | | Stevens, Peter | 2 | 3 | 2 | | |
| Anthony (Negro) | | | | 3 | | House, Eleazer | 1 | 2 | 2 | | | Stevens, Josiah | 2 | | 2 | | |
| Bidwell, Isaac | 1 | 5 | 3 | | | House, John | 1 | 1 | 4 | | | Stratton, Samuel, 3d | 1 | 2 | 4 | | |
| Bidwell, Hezekiah | 1 | | 1 | | | Hollister, Amos | 2 | 2 | 3 | | | Stevens, Elijah | 2 | 3 | 5 | 1 | |
| Brooks, Joel | 1 | 5 | 4 | | | Hills, Joseph | 2 | 2 | 4 | | | Smith, William | 1 | | 2 | | |
| Brau, Jonathan, Esqr | 1 | 2 | 4 | | | Hollister, Joseph, Jr | 1 | 4 | 3 | | | Smith, Richard | 1 | | 1 | | |
| Benton, Ebenezer | 1 | 1 | 5 | | | Hodge, John | 2 | 1 | 2 | | | Smith, Elihu | 1 | 3 | 2 | | |
| Bidwell, Joseph | 2 | 3 | 3 | | | Hale, Charles | 4 | | 1 | | | Stratton, Samuel | 1 | 1 | 3 | | |
| Bidwell, Ephraim | 1 | 2 | 1 | | | Hollister, David, 3d | 1 | 1 | 3 | | | Smith, Abraham | 2 | | 4 | | |
| Bill, Aaron | 1 | 3 | 3 | | | Hodge, Jonathan | 1 | 4 | 2 | | | Smith, Bathoheba | | | 1 | | |
| Bidwell, David | 1 | | 2 | | | Hale, Benjamin | 2 | 2 | 4 | | | Stevens, William | 1 | 5 | 4 | | |
| Bill, Elizur | 2 | 3 | 2 | | | House, Elijah | 1 | 2 | 2 | | | Smith, Manoah | 1 | | 3 | | |
| Bill, Isaac | 1 | 1 | 7 | | | House, George | 1 | 2 | 2 | | | Smith, Samuel, 2d | 1 | 2 | 3 | | |
| Benton, Edward | 1 | 1 | 2 | | | House, Elizabeth | | | 2 | | | Sellers, Phillip | 3 | 5 | 7 | | |
| Benton, Josiah | 2 | 2 | 4 | | | Hunt, John | 1 | | 1 | | | Starr, John | 1 | 1 | 3 | | |
| Bidwell, Jonathan | 2 | 2 | 7 | | | Hunt, Samuel | 1 | 2 | 2 | | | Scott, Thomas | 1 | | 5 | | |
| Bidwell, Rebecca | 1 | | 2 | | | Jop, John | 1 | 1 | 2 | 1 | | Scott, Joseph | 1 | 2 | 2 | | |
| Bidwell, Allyn | 1 | 1 | 2 | | | Kilbourn, Mary | 1 | | 2 | 1 | | Stoddard, Ebenezar | 2 | | 2 | | |
| Bidwell, Samuel | 1 | 1 | 3 | | | Kilbourn, Abraham | 1 | | 1 | | | Stocking, Elisha | 1 | | 2 | | |
| Bumter, Shorum | | | | 2 | | Kibbard, Jonathan | 2 | | 3 | | | Strickland, Simeon | 1 | 2 | 4 | | |
| Coleman, Asaph | 2 | 2 | 3 | | | Lyman, Samuel | 2 | 1 | 3 | | | Talcott, John | 2 | 1 | 2 | | |
| Chapman, Jonah | 2 | 2 | 3 | | | Lewis, Abel | 1 | 1 | 2 | | | Talcott, George | 2 | 3 | 5 | | |
| Caswell, John | 2 | 1 | 5 | | | Loveland, Lazarus | 1 | 3 | 2 | | | Tryon, Thomas | 1 | 2 | 2 | | |
| Camp, Talcott | 1 | 4 | 3 | | | Loveland, Deborah | 1 | 1 | 3 | | | Talcott, Nathaniel | 2 | | 4 | | 2 |
| Covil, Ephraim | 3 | 1 | 2 | 1 | | Loveland, Eli | 1 | 1 | 5 | | | Tryon, Noah | 1 | 2 | 3 | | 1 |
| Case, Rachel (Wid.) | 2 | | 4 | | | Loveland, Solomon | 1 | 2 | 4 | | | Talcott, Elizur, Jr | 1 | 3 | 7 | | |
| Chapman, Tenant | 1 | 1 | 2 | | | Loveland, Thomas | 1 | | 1 | | | Treat, Peter | 2 | 1 | 5 | 1 | |
| Chapman, Jehiel | 1 | | 1 | | | Lannd, Hannah | | | 2 | | | Tryon, Elizuh | 3 | 5 | 5 | | |
| Chapel, Solomon | 1 | 1 | 3 | | | Moseley, William | 2 | 1 | 5 | | | Treat, Samuel | 2 | | 6 | | |
| Chapman, Amasa | 2 | 2 | 1 | | | Moseley, Syphax | | | | 5 | | Taylor, Samuel | 1 | 1 | 2 | | |
| Chapman, Asahel | 1 | | 3 | | | Miles, Daniel | 2 | | 2 | | | Treat, Dorotheus | 1 | 1 | 2 | | |
| Conley, John | 1 | 1 | 4 | | | Miller, Mathew | 2 | 1 | 6 | | | Treat, Charles | 2 | 3 | 2 | | |
| Densmore, Obadiah | 1 | 4 | 3 | | | Matson, Thomas, Jr | 1 | 3 | 4 | | | Talcott, Annar | | | 2 | | |
| Easton, Ephraim | 1 | | 1 | | | Miller, William, Jr | 2 | | 3 | | | Taylor, David | 1 | | 2 | | |
| Elles, Revd John | 2 | 1 | 6 | | | Matson, Joseph | 2 | 3 | 3 | | | Taylor, Azariah | 1 | 4 | 1 | | |
| Easton, Timothy | 1 | | 3 | | | Miller, Elizur | 1 | | 2 | | | Taylor, Joseph | 1 | 2 | 2 | | |
| Emons, Susanna | | | 1 | | | Matson, Thomas | 1 | | 1 | | | Talcott, Abraham | 1 | | 2 | | |
| Fox, Obadiah | 1 | 3 | 1 | | | Miller, William | 3 | 1 | 3 | | | Taylor, Jonathan | 1 | 2 | 5 | | |
| Flanckin, Banabas | 1 | 3 | 2 | | | Miller, Abijah | 2 | 1 | 5 | | 1 | Talcott, Elizur | 1 | 1 | 1 | | 1 |
| Fox, Samuel | 1 | | 3 | | | Moseley, Susanna | | | 1 | | | Tryon, William | 2 | 1 | 2 | | |
| Fox, Hosea | 1 | | | | | Moseley, Ebenezer | 1 | 3 | 2 | | | Taylor, George | 1 | 2 | 4 | | |
| Fox, Joseph | 1 | | 2 | | | Miller, John | 3 | 2 | 6 | | | Talcott, Nathaniel, Jr | 3 | 1 | 2 | | |
| Fox, Joseph, Jr | 1 | 2 | 4 | | | Moseley, Joseph | 5 | 1 | 3 | 1 | 2 | Tryon, William, Jr | 1 | 3 | 4 | | |
| Fox, Eleazer | 1 | 1 | 2 | | | Moseley, Demish | 1 | | 2 | 5 | | Treat, Elisha | 2 | 1 | 3 | | |
| Fox, David | 1 | | 2 | | | Moseley, Eunice | | | 2 | 3 | | Talcott, Ruth | | | 3 | | |
| Fuller, Barnabas | 1 | | 3 | | | Moseley, Richard | | | | 3 | | Talcott, Oliver | 2 | 1 | 3 | | |
| Fox, Asa | 1 | 1 | 3 | | | Nicholson, Frances | 1 | 2 | 4 | | | Treat, Gershom | 1 | 2 | 2 | | |
| Farris, Rhoda | | | 2 | | | Nichols, Nicholas | 1 | | 2 | | | Tenant, Caleb | 1 | 1 | 1 | | |
| Fruman, Samson | | | | 4 | | Nicholson, Joel | 2 | | 2 | | | Wheelar, Elnathan | 1 | | 1 | | |
| Goodrich, Isaac | 1 | | 3 | | | Nicholson, Ambrose, Jr | 2 | | 2 | | | Woodbridge, Howel | 2 | 5 | 5 | | |
| Goodrich, Wait, Jr | 1 | | 1 | | | Nicholson, Ambrose | 2 | | 3 | | | Whiting, Isaac | 1 | | 1 | | |
| Goodrich, David | 1 | | | | | Olive, Neptune | | | | 4 | | Willis, Eunice | 1 | 1 | 3 | 2 | 1 |
| Goodrich, David, Jr | 1 | 1 | 2 | | | Simbo, Prince | | | | 5 | | Wickham, David | 1 | | 1 | | |
| Goodrich, Noah | 2 | 3 | 1 | | | Plummer, Ebenezer | 1 | | 2 | | 2 | Ward, Daniel | 4 | | 3 | | |
| Goodrich, Wait | 2 | 1 | 3 | | | Plummer, Isaac | 2 | 2 | 2 | | | Wheelar, Lazarus | 1 | 2 | 2 | | |
| Goodrich, Jehiel | 1 | 5 | 2 | | | Pratt, David | 1 | 1 | 3 | | | Welles, Samuel | 1 | | 3 | | |
| Goodrich, Eliakim | 1 | 3 | 2 | | | Pratt, Daniel | 1 | | 4 | | | Welles, Joseph | 1 | 3 | 2 | | |
| Goodrich, Roswell | 1 | | 2 | | | Pratt, Mansah | 1 | 4 | 1 | | | Wright, Isaac | 2 | 2 | 4 | | |
| Goodrich, Elisha | 2 | 1 | 4 | | | Pease, David | 2 | 2 | 2 | | | Welles, John | 2 | 3 | 3 | | |
| Goodrich, Abigail | | | 3 | | | Pulsifer, Joseph | 3 | | 2 | | | Welles, Samuel, Jr | 2 | 2 | 3 | | |
| Glosender, John | 1 | 1 | 1 | | | Pulsifer, Sylvester | 1 | | 3 | | | Welles, Ephraim | 1 | | 1 | | |
| Goff, Elisha | 1 | | 2 | | | Price, Samuel | 1 | 4 | 2 | | | Welles, Jonathan | 4 | 1 | 5 | 1 | |
| Gains, Nathaniel | 2 | 1 | 2 | | | Polly, John | 1 | 3 | 2 | | | Wells, Isaac | 1 | | 1 | | |
| Gains, Dan | 1 | 1 | 1 | | | Peirce, Philip | 2 | 1 | 6 | | | Woodbridge, Theodore | 1 | 2 | 4 | | |
| Gains, John | 1 | 2 | 4 | | | Potter, Edward, Jr | 1 | 2 | 1 | | | Wright, Samuel | 3 | | 3 | | |

# HEADS OF FAMILIES—CONNECTICUT.

## HARTFORD COUNTY—Continued.

| NAME OF HEAD OF FAMILY. | Free white males of 16 years and upward, including heads of families. | Free white males under 16 years. | Free white females, including heads of families. | All other free persons. | Slaves. | NAME OF HEAD OF FAMILY. | Free white males of 16 years and upward, including heads of families. | Free white males under 16 years. | Free white females, including heads of families. | All other free persons. | Slaves. | NAME OF HEAD OF FAMILY. | Free white males of 16 years and upward, including heads of families. | Free white males under 16 years. | Free white females, including heads of families. | All other free persons. | Slaves. |
|---|---|---|---|---|---|---|---|---|---|---|---|---|---|---|---|---|---|
| **GLASTENBURY TOWN—continued.** | | | | | | **GLASTENBURY TOWN—continued.** | | | | | | **GLASTENBURY TOWN—continued.** | | | | | |
| Webster, Joshua | 1 | 2 | 2 | | | Hills, Elisha | 1 | 5 | 3 | | | Finley, David | 1 | 1 | 3 | | |
| Wares, Joseph | 1 | 2 | 4 | | | Homes, Appleton | 1 | 6 | 4 | | | Finley, John | 1 | 1 | 2 | | |
| Warren, John | 1 | 1 | 3 | | | House, Daniel | 2 | 2 | 4 | | | Finley, Solomon | 1 | 1 | 1 | | |
| Welles, Elijah | 1 | | 1 | | | House, Abner | 1 | 3 | 3 | | | Foot, Israel | 1 | 3 | 4 | | |
| Wells, Thaddeus | 1 | | 1 | | | Hunt, Thomas | 3 | 1 | 5 | | | Finley, Samuel | 2 | 1 | 2 | | |
| Williams, Jerusha | | | 3 | | | How, John, Jr | 1 | 2 | 3 | | | Loveland, Thomas | 3 | | 3 | | |
| Wright, Joseph | 1 | 3 | 1 | | | Hollister, Ichabod | 1 | 3 | 4 | | | Phelps, Timothy, Jr | 1 | | 1 | | |
| Wheelar, Silent | | | 2 | | | Hodge, Benjamin | 1 | 2 | 3 | | | Phelps, Timothy | 3 | 3 | 1 | | |
| Waterman, Asahel | 1 | 1 | 3 | | | Hodge, Benjamin, Jr | 2 | 3 | 1 | | | Phelps, John | 2 | 1 | 3 | 1 | |
| Andrews, Charles | 5 | 3 | 5 | | | Hollister, Nehemiah | 1 | 2 | 5 | | | Burden, Jerry | | | | 3 | |
| Andrews, Stephen | 1 | 1 | 1 | | | Hollister, Theodore | 2 | 1 | 3 | | | Skinner, Abraham, Jr | 1 | | 2 | 1 | |
| Andrews, Elisha | 1 | | 3 | | | Hollister, Nathaniel | 1 | 2 | 4 | | | Skinner, Deborah | 1 | 1 | 4 | | |
| Andrews, Elisha, Jr | 1 | 2 | 3 | | | Hollister, Elizur | 2 | 2 | 4 | 1 | | Strong, Amos | 2 | 2 | 4 | | |
| Andrews, John | 1 | 2 | 4 | | | Hollister, David, Jr | 1 | 2 | 3 | | | Skinner, Abraham | 2 | 1 | 3 | 1 | |
| Andrews, Benjamin, Jr | 1 | 1 | 5 | | | Hale, Thomathy, Jr | 1 | | 2 | | | Waters, Gideon | 1 | 1 | 2 | | |
| Andrews, David | 1 | 2 | 6 | | | Holden, Jonathan, Jr | 1 | | 1 | | | Warren, Henery | 1 | | 1 | | |
| Andrews, Benjamin | 3 | | 3 | | | Hills, John | 1 | 1 | 3 | | | Robberdore, August | | | | 4 | |
| Baker, Ephraim | 1 | 5 | 6 | | | Hubbard, Elizur, Jr | 2 | 2 | 3 | 1 | | Allyn, Peter | | | | 5 | |
| Buck, Libbeus | 1 | 4 | 3 | | | Hills, Libbeus | 1 | 1 | 2 | | | Janes, Frederic | | | | 8 | |
| Brooks, Josiah | 1 | 1 | 3 | | | Holmes, William | 1 | | 1 | | | | | | | | |
| Brooks, Samuel | 3 | | 2 | | | Hildrieth, William | 3 | 2 | 4 | | | **GRANBY TOWN.** | | | | | |
| Boles, Ezra | 1 | 4 | 3 | | | Huxford, William | 1 | | 1 | | | Holcomb, Hezekiah | 1 | 1 | 2 | | |
| Brewer, Dorothy | | | 4 | | | Jones, Parker | 1 | | 1 | | | Holcomb, Daniel | 3 | 1 | 2 | | |
| Blish, Thomas | 1 | 2 | 2 | | | Jones, Moses | 1 | | 1 | | | Holcomb, Hezekiah, Jr | 2 | 5 | 5 | | |
| Brooks, William | 1 | | 3 | | | Ingham, Joseph | 1 | 2 | 4 | | | Holcomb, Jesse | 2 | 3 | 3 | | |
| Brooks, Samuel, Jr | 3 | 1 | 4 | | | Jones, Lemuel | 2 | 2 | 6 | | | Holcomb, Noah | 2 | 1 | 6 | | |
| Covell, Eliphalet | 1 | 3 | 3 | | | Johnson, Levi | 1 | | 2 | | | Alford, Josiah | 3 | 1 | 3 | | |
| Covell, Jonathan | 1 | | 6 | | | Kuney, James | 1 | 1 | 4 | | | Alderman, Thankfull (Wid.) | 1 | 1 | 2 | | |
| Covell, Elijah | 2 | 4 | 2 | | | Kimberly, Mary | | | 3 | | | Barnes, Abraham | 1 | 2 | 2 | | |
| Covell, Philip | 1 | 4 | 3 | | | Loveland, John | 1 | 1 | 2 | | | Griffin, Benoni | 3 | | 1 | | |
| Covell, James | 1 | 1 | 1 | | | Loveland, Aaron | 1 | | 1 | | | Griffin, Abraham | 1 | 1 | 1 | | |
| Couch, Elisha | 1 | 3 | 2 | | | Loveland, Elizur | 2 | | 8 | | | Holcomb, Joshua | 1 | 3 | 4 | | |
| Covell, Samuel | 2 | 1 | 4 | | | Loveland, Levi | 2 | 3 | 4 | | | Holcomb, Caleb | 1 | 2 | 4 | | |
| Daniels, David | 1 | 2 | 2 | | | Loveland, Peletiah | 3 | 3 | 5 | | | Winchel, Jehiel | 1 | 1 | 4 | | |
| Dutton, William | 1 | 3 | 2 | | | Loveland, Nathan | 1 | 1 | 2 | | | Moore, Job | 3 | 1 | 1 | | |
| Dealing, Samuel | 2 | 1 | 1 | | | Moseley, Timothy | 3 | 1 | 3 | | | Crome, Samuel | 1 | 6 | 4 | | |
| Dickinson, Nathan, Jr | 1 | 1 | 1 | | | McLean, James | 3 | 2 | 5 | | | Adkins, Daniel | 1 | 1 | 1 | | |
| Dickinson, David, 3d | 1 | 3 | 8 | | | Nye, Solomon | 1 | 1 | 4 | | | Hayes, Daniel, Jr | 1 | 2 | 2 | | |
| Dickinson, David, Jr | 2 | 2 | 4 | | | Nye, Milatiah | 1 | | 1 | | | Toping, Josiah | 2 | 1 | 3 | | |
| Ellis, Revd James | 1 | 1 | 1 | | 1 | Nowland, Samuel | 2 | 2 | 7 | | | Toping, Josiah, Jr | 1 | 1 | 1 | | |
| Smith, Mabel | | | 3 | | | Newil, Sarah | | | 2 | | | Griffin, Stephen, 2d | 3 | 2 | 2 | | |
| Fox, David, Jr | 1 | 2 | 3 | | | Parsons, Samuel | 1 | | 4 | | | Higley, David | 3 | 1 | 2 | | |
| Fox, Lemuel | 1 | 1 | 4 | | | Risley, Thomas, Jr | 1 | | 3 | | | Edwards, Henery | 2 | | 3 | | |
| Fox, Levi | 1 | 1 | 2 | | | Risley, David | 1 | | 3 | | | Hayes, Daniel | 1 | | 2 | | |
| Fox, Richard | 1 | | 1 | | | Riley, Charles | 2 | | 1 | | | Heyes, Enock | 1 | 2 | 2 | | |
| Fox, Isaac | 2 | 2 | 3 | | | Risley, Reuben | 2 | 3 | 5 | | | Hayes, Honora (Wid.) | 1 | | 4 | | |
| Fox, Jonah | 2 | 1 | 5 | | | Risley, Thomas | 1 | 1 | 2 | | | Baker, Samuel | 2 | 1 | 3 | | |
| Fox, Thomas | 1 | | 4 | | | Smith, David | 1 | | 1 | | | Johnson, Asa | 3 | | 4 | | |
| Fox, Amasa | 1 | 1 | 1 | | | Smith, Asa | 1 | 3 | 2 | | | Pettibone, Chancey | 2 | 3 | 5 | 1 | |
| Fox, Amos | 1 | 4 | 3 | | | Smith, Samuel | 3 | 2 | 3 | | | Phelps, Isaac | 1 | 2 | 9 | | |
| Fox, Israel | 1 | 2 | 2 | | | Simons, Joseph | 2 | 4 | 4 | | | Pettibone, Ozias | 3 | | 4 | 5 | |
| Fox, Stephen | 1 | 2 | 4 | | | Sparks, Reuben | 1 | 2 | 5 | | | Jeut, Roger | 1 | 1 | 2 | | |
| Fox, Ebenezer | 1 | 2 | 6 | | | Shirtliff, Jonathan | 1 | | 5 | | | Rowe, Abijah | 2 | 1 | 3 | | |
| Fox, Martha | 1 | | 3 | | | Sparks, Thomas | 1 | 4 | 1 | | | Rice, Peter, Jr | 1 | 1 | 1 | | |
| Goff, Aaron | 2 | 1 | 3 | | | Strickland, Stephen | 1 | | 2 | | | Smith, Elijah | 1 | 2 | 3 | | |
| Goodale, Ebenezer | 2 | 2 | 3 | | | Skinner, Benjamin | 1 | 1 | 3 | | | Smith, James | 1 | 3 | 6 | | |
| Goodrich, Elijah H | 1 | 1 | 1 | | | Standish, Jeremiah | 2 | 2 | 6 | | | Hays, Joel | 3 | 1 | 2 | | |
| Goodale, Thomas | 1 | | 2 | | | Strickland, Howel | 1 | 1 | 1 | | | Hayes, Rufus | 1 | | 1 | | |
| Goodale, Joseph, Jr | 5 | 3 | 6 | | | Strickland, Nehemiah | 3 | 3 | 2 | | | Hayes, Amos | 1 | | 1 | | |
| Goodale, Joseph | 2 | | 5 | 1 | | Strickland, Stephen, 3d | 1 | 3 | 2 | | | Dibol, Benjamin | 1 | | 1 | | |
| Gosler, Timothy | 3 | 2 | 4 | | | Smith, Isaac | 2 | | 2 | | | Dibol, Heman | 1 | 1 | 1 | | |
| Gosler, Asa | 3 | 1 | 3 | | | Richardson, William | 1 | 3 | 2 | | | Hillyer, Pliny | 1 | 2 | 5 | 2 | |
| Gibson, Samuel | 3 | | 9 | | | Strickland, Nehemiah, Jr | 1 | 3 | 2 | | | Gold, Gurdon | 1 | | 1 | | |
| Goodale, Isaac | 1 | | 1 | | | Talcott, Jonathan | 1 | 3 | 1 | | | Dibol, Levi | 1 | 3 | 2 | | |
| Goodale, Avary | 1 | | 2 | | | Tubbs, Lemuel | 2 | 1 | 2 | | | Rice, Peter | 1 | | 2 | | |
| Goodale, Henery | 2 | | 3 | | | Treat, Jonathan, Jr | 1 | 2 | 1 | | | Rice, William | 1 | | 1 | | |
| Hills, Samuel | 1 | | 1 | | | Treat, Jonathan | 1 | | 1 | 1 | | Drownd, Nathaniel | 1 | 3 | 1 | | |
| Hills, Samuel, Jr | 1 | 3 | 2 | | | Treat, Charles | 1 | 4 | 2 | | | Ates, Abraham | 1 | 2 | 1 | | |
| Hills, Israel | 1 | 1 | 2 | | | Talcott, Isaac | 1 | 2 | 5 | | | Dibol, Benjamin, Jr | 2 | 2 | 3 | | |
| Hollister, Elisha | 4 | 1 | 4 | | | Tucker, Benjamin | 1 | 4 | 3 | | | Smith, Roger | 1 | 2 | 2 | | |
| Hollister, Aaron | 1 | 2 | 4 | | | Tryon, Joseph | 4 | | 4 | | | Brown, Justin | 1 | | 1 | | |
| Hollister, George | 1 | 2 | 5 | | | Tryon, George | 1 | 2 | 2 | | | Smith, Widow | | | 1 | | |
| House, Lazarus | 2 | 4 | 3 | | | Talcott, Jabez | 1 | 1 | 1 | | | Gillett, Elijah | 3 | 1 | 1 | | |
| Holmes, Charles | 1 | 5 | 5 | | | Tubbs, Ezekiel | 2 | 1 | 1 | | | Hayes, David | 1 | 3 | 3 | | |
| Hale, William | 2 | 1 | 4 | | | Tryon, Isaac | 1 | 5 | 4 | | | Hayes, Silus | 4 | | 2 | | |
| Huxford, William | 2 | | 2 | | | Williams, Isaac | 1 | 1 | 2 | | | Hayes, Samuel | 3 | | 2 | | |
| Hollister, Thomas | 1 | 1 | 6 | 1 | | Wilden, Peleg | 3 | 2 | 3 | | | Hayes, Pliny | 1 | 1 | 2 | | |
| Hubbard, Elizur | 2 | 3 | 2 | | | Wire, John | 2 | 3 | 4 | | | Hayes, Simeon | 1 | | 1 | | |
| Hollister, Gideon | 2 | 1 | 3 | | | Wire, Nehemiah | 1 | 2 | 4 | | | Hayes, Samuel, Jr | 1 | 1 | 4 | | |
| Hills, Daniel | 1 | 3 | 2 | | | Wickham, Hezekiah | 3 | 1 | 5 | | | Wright, Benjamin | 1 | | 4 | | |
| Hills, Josiah | 1 | 2 | 4 | | | Wickham, Hezekiah, Jr | 1 | 3 | 2 | | | Moore, Oliver | 1 | 1 | 1 | | |
| House, Frary | 1 | 2 | 5 | | | Waters, David | 1 | 3 | | | | Holcomb, Elihu | 1 | | 1 | | |
| Hollister, Israel | 1 | 3 | 6 | | | Wright, Daniel | 1 | | 3 | | | Barnard, David | 1 | 5 | 3 | | |
| Holden, Jonathan | 1 | 2 | 2 | | | Ackley, Stephen | 2 | | 3 | | | Hill, Elijah | 1 | 2 | 2 | | |
| House, Israel | 1 | 4 | 2 | | | Bigelow, David | 2 | 2 | 3 | | | Hurlbut, Jehiel | 1 | 2 | 2 | | |
| Hollister, Asahel | 1 | 1 | 2 | | | Blish, David | 3 | | 4 | | | Cook, Benjamin | 1 | 4 | 2 | | |
| Holden, John | 3 | | 1 | | | Chamberlain, William | 2 | | 3 | | | Salter, Rachel | | | 1 | | |
| Huxford, John | 1 | | 4 | | | Chamberlain, Elizabeth | | | 3 | | | Higley, Jonathan | 1 | 3 | 5 | | |
| House, Mathew | 1 | 2 | 4 | | | Chamberlain, Benjamin | 1 | 2 | 3 | | | Higley, Mary | | | 1 | | |
| Hale, Edward | 1 | 2 | 1 | | | Dunham, Levi | 1 | 5 | 2 | | | Alderman, Gad | 1 | 2 | 2 | | |
| How, Elisha | 4 | 1 | 6 | | | Dickinson, Thomas | 2 | 1 | 4 | | | Alderman, Lott | 1 | | 1 | | |
| House, Joel | 1 | 1 | 2 | | | Dickinson, Nathan | 1 | 4 | 4 | | | Swan, Joseph | 1 | 6 | 1 | | |
| Hale, Elizur | 2 | 3 | 2 | | | Dickinson, David | | | 4 | 3 | | | | | | | |
| Hale, Isaac | 2 | 1 | 1 | | 1 | Dewey, John | 1 | 3 | 4 | | | | | | | | |

43

## HARTFORD COUNTY—Continued.

| NAME OF HEAD OF FAMILY. | Free white males of 16 years and upward, including heads of families. | Free white males under 16 years. | Free white females, including heads of families. | All other free persons. | Slaves. | NAME OF HEAD OF FAMILY. | Free white males of 16 years and upward, including heads of families. | Free white males under 16 years. | Free white females, including heads of families. | All other free persons. | Slaves. | NAME OF HEAD OF FAMILY. | Free white males of 16 years and upward, including heads of families. | Free white males under 16 years. | Free white females, including heads of families. | All other free persons. | Slaves. |
|---|---|---|---|---|---|---|---|---|---|---|---|---|---|---|---|---|---|
| **GRANBY TOWN—con.** | | | | | | **GRANBY TOWN—con.** | | | | | | **GRANBY TOWN—con.** | | | | | |
| Eno, Elisha | 1 | 4 | 3 | | | Wright, Jeremiah | 1 | 1 | 4 | | | Case, Noah | 1 | | 1 | | |
| Griswold, Joseph | 1 | | 1 | | | Case, Micah | 1 | 2 | 4 | | | Case, Roger | 1 | | 4 | | |
| Griswold, Joseph, Jr | 1 | | 1 | | | Case, Rufus | 1 | 2 | 3 | | | Read, George | 1 | 1 | 1 | | |
| Alderman, Joseph | 1 | | 1 | | | Humphrey, Timothy | 1 | 2 | 4 | | | Read, David | 1 | 1 | 2 | | |
| Alderman, Joseph, Jr | 1 | 2 | 2 | | | Gillett, Adne | 1 | 1 | | | | Case, Noah, Jr | 1 | 2 | 4 | | |
| Alderman, Timothy | 1 | 2 | 2 | | | Case, William | 1 | | | | | Case, Simeon | 4 | 4 | 3 | | |
| Skinner, Hezekiah | 1 | | 1 | | | Wright, John | 1 | 1 | 2 | | | Case, Obed | 1 | 1 | 1 | | |
| Griffin, Thomas | 3 | | 4 | | | Holcomb, Dan | 2 | 3 | 5 | | | More, Damanes | 1 | | 1 | | |
| Griffin, Thomas, Jr | 1 | | 3 | | | Griffen, Nathaniel | 3 | | 1 | | | More, Jehiel | 1 | 1 | 2 | | |
| Alderman, Elnathan | 2 | 3 | 2 | | | Holcomb, Ozias | 4 | 2 | 2 | | | More, Benjamin | 1 | | 1 | | |
| Cook, Darius | 1 | 6 | 2 | | | Holcomb, Ozias, Jr | 1 | 1 | 1 | | | Case, Richard | 3 | 4 | 5 | | |
| Holcomb, Abel | 1 | 2 | 4 | | | Pratt, Timothy | 1 | | 3 | | | Case, Phineas | 1 | 1 | 5 | | |
| Alderman, Elijah | 1 | 3 | 5 | | | Reed, John, Jr | 2 | | 2 | | | Case, Richard, Jr | 1 | 3 | 4 | | |
| Holcomb, Simeon | 2 | 1 | 5 | | | Read, Rusell | 2 | 1 | 2 | | | Taylor, Russell | 1 | 4 | 1 | | |
| Messenger, Israel | 1 | 1 | 3 | | | Rice, John | 2 | 1 | 4 | | | Miller, Moses | 1 | 1 | 1 | | |
| Messenger, Amos | 1 | | 2 | | | Rice, Jessee | 1 | 1 | 2 | | | Miller, Ichabod | 1 | | 1 | | |
| Messenger, Nathaniel | 2 | | 4 | | | Phelps, Hezekiah | 1 | 1 | 1 | | | Case, George | 1 | 2 | 3 | | |
| Messenger, David | 1 | 2 | 3 | | | Phelps, Hez<sup>b</sup>, 2<sup>d</sup> | 1 | | 3 | | | Forward, Jesse | 1 | 4 | 3 | | |
| Messenger, Daniel | 1 | 1 | 2 | | | Vining, Richard | 2 | 3 | 3 | | | Holcomb, Ahas | 1 | | 1 | | |
| Couch, David | 2 | 1 | 7 | | | Grigny, Dan | 1 | | 1 | | | Veits, Benoni | 1 | | 1 | | |
| Hayes, Oliver | 1 | 3 | 4 | | | Wrathbun, Daniel | 1 | 2 | 1 | | | Veits, Luke | 1 | 3 | 5 | | |
| Gozzard, Moses | 2 | 3 | 3 | | | Higley, Joel | 2 | 1 | 5 | | | Stephens, Thomas | 1 | 2 | 3 | | |
| Perring, Elisha | 2 | 1 | 4 | | | Phelps, Abel | 3 | 2 | 4 | | | Hays, Zenas | 1 | 1 | 3 | | |
| Hugens, James | 4 | 1 | 2 | | | Banthore, W<sup>m</sup> | 2 | 2 | 2 | | | Holcomb, Ezekiel, Jr | 1 | 2 | 1 | | |
| Higley, Ozias | 2 | 3 | 4 | | | Frasure, Daniel | 3 | 1 | 4 | | | Gillett, Jabash | 1 | 2 | 3 | | |
| Higley, Asa | 2 | 1 | 3 | | | Griffen, Absalom | 1 | 2 | 2 | | | Gillett, Jacob | 1 | | | | |
| Holidy, Amos | 1 | 5 | 3 | | | Fletcher, Ephraim | 2 | 2 | 8 | | | Alderman, Epephras | 1 | 1 | 5 | | |
| Hayes, Benjamin | 3 | 2 | 5 | | | Holcomb, Benajah | 2 | 6 | 2 | | | Veits, Abner | 2 | 4 | 3 | | |
| Hayes, Jacob | 1 | 2 | 2 | | | Post, Aaron | 1 | | 2 | | | Rice, Joseph | 2 | 3 | 4 | | |
| Griffin, Joab | 1 | 4 | 3 | | | Holcomb, Roger, J<sup>r</sup> | | | 1 | | | Ormsby, Levi | 1 | 1 | 1 | | |
| Straten, Hannah | 3 | 3 | 1 | | | Coset, Reuben | 1 | | 2 | | | More, Rideout | 1 | 1 | 3 | | |
| Hicock, Jiles | 1 | | 1 | | | Compstock (Widow) | | | 1 | | | Veits, Seth | 2 | 4 | 5 | | |
| Hayes, Andrew | 3 | | 7 | | | Bulloph, Jonathan | 1 | 2 | 3 | | | Roe, Titus | 1 | 2 | 1 | | |
| Hayes, Andrew, Jr | 1 | 2 | 2 | | | Phelps, William | 1 | 2 | 3 | | | Gillet, Zacheus | 1 | 1 | 1 | | |
| Hays, Ezekiel | 2 | 2 | 2 | | | Phelps, Timothy | 1 | | 3 | | | Stephens, Edmond | 2 | 1 | 2 | | |
| Kilbourn, Lemuel | 1 | | 2 | | | Gains, Solomon | 2 | 1 | 2 | | | Griffin, Michael | 2 | 2 | 2 | | |
| Kilbourn, Filo | 1 | 1 | 1 | | | Cobler, Thos | 1 | 4 | 4 | | | Griffin, Elizabeth | | | 1 | | |
| Holidy, John | 1 | | 1 | | | Humphry, Ozias | 1 | | 2 | | | Veits, James | 1 | 2 | 3 | | |
| Strong, Elnathan | 2 | 3 | 4 | | | Rice, Pedi | | | 1 | | | Veits, Jonathan | 2 | | | | |
| Holcomb, Phineas | 2 | 1 | 3 | | | Rice, Jonah | 1 | 4 | 2 | | | Phelps, Elijah | 2 | 1 | 2 | | |
| Holcomb, Criss | 1 | | 1 | | | Butolph, Levi | 1 | 1 | 2 | | | Phelps, Shubel | 1 | 1 | 1 | | |
| Holcomb, Nahum | 1 | | 1 | | | Cap, Job | 2 | 2 | 2 | | | Miller, John | 1 | 1 | 4 | | |
| Holcomb, Reuben | 1 | | 1 | | | Holcomb, Silus | 1 | 1 | 1 | | | Stephens, Phinias | 1 | 3 | 4 | | |
| Holcomb, Noadiah | 1 | 3 | 3 | | | Clemens, Fardy | 1 | | 2 | | | Griffin, Elijah | 1 | 4 | 6 | | |
| Gozzard, Martin | 3 | 7 | 3 | | | Clemens, William | 1 | 2 | 2 | | | Griffin, Seth | 1 | 4 | 6 | | |
| Gozzard, Abel | 2 | | 1 | | | Colton, Elizabeth (Wid.) | | | 1 | | | Orsborn, David | 1 | 3 | 2 | | |
| Copt, Alexander | 3 | 1 | 3 | | | Copt, Frances | 2 | | 2 | | | Miller, Alexander | 1 | | 3 | | |
| Gozzard, John, Jr | 1 | 2 | 2 | | | Gaines, Luther | 1 | | 1 | | | Brown, Joseph | 1 | 3 | 2 | | |
| French, Asher | 1 | | 5 | | | Williams, W<sup>m</sup> | 1 | 3 | 5 | | | Holcomb, Obed | 1 | | 1 | | |
| Willcocks, David | 1 | 1 | 4 | | | Hayes, Dudley | 1 | 1 | 4 | | | Holcomb, Masa (Wid.) | 2 | 3 | 3 | | |
| Hays, Benajah | 1 | 3 | 1 | | | Hays, Dudley | 1 | 1 | 4 | | | Holcomb, David | 3 | | 1 | | |
| Hodgkiss, Ambrose | 1 | | 2 | | | Holcomb, Consider | 2 | 3 | 5 | | | Holcomb, David, Jr | 1 | | | | |
| Cosset, Timothy | 2 | | 3 | | | Gillett, Azariah | 1 | 5 | 2 | | | Bull, Abner | 2 | 1 | 3 | | |
| Bemon, Aaron | 2 | 3 | 4 | | | Gillett, Nathan | 3 | 4 | 2 | | | Griffin, Stephen | 2 | 2 | 4 | | |
| Pratt, Nathaniel | 1 | 3 | 3 | | | Holcomb, Roger | 2 | 1 | 8 | | | Roe, Daniel | 1 | 2 | 1 | | |
| Gillett, Joseph | 1 | 2 | 3 | | | Read, Benjamin | 2 | 3 | 3 | | | Pike, William | 1 | 1 | 1 | | |
| Gillett, Benoni | 1 | 3 | 2 | | | Gozzard, Fille | 2 | 2 | 5 | | | Holcomb, Ezekiel | 2 | 3 | 4 | | |
| Hays, Seth | 2 | 1 | 5 | | | Read, John | 1 | | | | | Granger, Israel | 2 | 2 | 2 | | |
| Gozzard, Isaac | 1 | 2 | 4 | | | Read, Abner | 1 | 3 | 2 | | | Halawa, Daniel | 1 | | 1 | | |
| Brewer, Benjamin | 2 | 1 | 3 | | | Hayes, William, Jr | 1 | 1 | 7 | | | Griffin, Stephen | 1 | | 2 | | |
| Gozzard, John | 1 | | 2 | | | Barber, Joseph | 1 | 2 | 1 | | | Hilyer, James | 1 | 1 | 1 | | |
| Gozzard, Nathan | 3 | 1 | 5 | | | Hoskins, John | 1 | | 1 | | | Hilyer, Asa | 2 | 2 | 2 | | |
| Gozzard, Ebenezer | 1 | 1 | 1 | | | Dibol, Moses, Jr | 1 | 2 | 2 | | | Hillyer, Theodorus | 1 | 2 | 3 | | |
| Gozzard, Ebenezer, Jr | 1 | 2 | 2 | | | Burr, Asa | 1 | 2 | 1 | | | Dunn, Samuel | 1 | 3 | 5 | | |
| Gozzard, Levi | 1 | 2 | 2 | | | Griffin, Mathew | 2 | | 3 | | | Spring, Thomas | 3 | 2 | 4 | | |
| Gozzard, Rufus | 1 | 2 | 2 | | | Dibol, Dan | 1 | 2 | 3 | | | Spring, Silvester | 1 | | 2 | | |
| Gozzard, Nicholus | 1 | 1 | 5 | | | Burr, Zebina | 1 | 2 | 3 | | | Burr, Adonijah | 2 | 2 | 3 | | |
| Griffin, John | 1 | 4 | 2 | | | Hilyer, Seth | 2 | 2 | 3 | | | Dibol, Moses | 1 | 1 | 3 | | |
| Messenger, Elijah | 2 | | 1 | | | Messenger, Nathaniel | 1 | | 1 | | | Dibol, Reuben | 1 | 1 | 3 | | |
| Holcomb, Peter | 2 | | 3 | | | Spring, Silvester | 1 | | 2 | | | More, Shadrack | 1 | | 3 | | |
| Holcomb, Asahel, 3<sup>d</sup> | 1 | 1 | 3 | | | Holcomb, Elijah | 4 | | 2 | | | More, Shadrack, Jr | 1 | 2 | 2 | | |
| Holcomb, Peter, Jr | 1 | 3 | 1 | | | Holcomb, Elijah, Jr | 1 | 2 | 2 | | | More, Roger | 1 | 1 | 2 | 1 | |
| Holcomb, Ebenezer | 1 | 1 | 1 | | | Read, Martin | 2 | 2 | 2 | | | Huse, Abraham | 1 | 3 | 2 | | |
| Holcomb, Abel, 2<sup>d</sup> | 1 | | 1 | | | Gains, Daniel | 2 | | 4 | | | Wadsworth, Timothy | 1 | 1 | 5 | | |
| Owen, Elijah | 1 | 1 | 1 | | | Slater, Benjamin | 2 | 2 | 3 | | | Moore, Eli | 1 | | 2 | | |
| Holcomb, John G | 1 | 2 | 1 | | | Moore, Ozias | 3 | 1 | 3 | | | More, Reuben | 1 | | | | |
| Gillett, Othenial | 1 | | | | | Holcomb, Asa | 2 | | 2 | | | Davis, William | 1 | | 5 | | |
| Gillett, Othenial, Jr | 1 | | 3 | | | Hays, William | 1 | | 1 | | | Bell, Elisha | 1 | 2 | 3 | | |
| Gillett, Buckler | 1 | 5 | 3 | | | Holcomb, Nathaniel | 1 | 1 | 1 | | | Willcox, John | 1 | | 4 | | |
| Gillett, Ephraim | 1 | 2 | 1 | | | Juett, Joseph | 2 | 2 | 2 | | | Williams, David | 1 | 1 | 3 | | |
| Holcomb, Adonijah | 1 | 2 | 6 | | | Phelps, Reuben | 1 | 1 | 7 | | | Gillett, Isaac | 1 | 1 | 6 | | |
| Gozzard, Ezra | 1 | 1 | 1 | | | Clark, Samuel | 1 | 1 | 2 | | | Holcomb, Nathan, Jr | 1 | 1 | 2 | | |
| Gozzard, Ezra | 1 | 2 | 2 | | | Bacon, Mary (Wid.) | 1 | | 2 | | | Clark, Eliphalet | 1 | 3 | 4 | | |
| Gozzard, Luther | 1 | | 1 | | | Holcomb, Eli | 1 | | 2 | | | Phelps, Noah | 1 | 3 | 4 | | |
| Case, Abel | 1 | | 1 | | | Pease, Naomi (Wid.) | | | 1 | | | Gillett, Levi | 1 | 2 | 3 | | |
| Swaine, Benjamin | 1 | 2 | 5 | | | Hawley, James | 1 | 1 | 2 | | | Jones, Hezekiah | 1 | 3 | 3 | | |
| Andrus, Ashael | 1 | 2 | 3 | | | Hawley, Thomas | 3 | 1 | 2 | | | Cushman, Solomon | 3 | 2 | 3 | | |
| Andrus, Abner | 1 | | 3 | | | Forward, Abel | 1 | | 2 | | | Phelps, Abijah | 2 | 1 | 4 | | |
| Weed, Aaron | 2 | 2 | 5 | | | Sage, Seth | 1 | 1 | 5 | | | Phelps, Levi | 1 | 3 | 4 | | |
| Bacon, Nathaniel | 2 | 1 | 4 | | | Spencer, Ebenezer | 1 | 3 | 2 | | | Cook, Jacob | 2 | 1 | 3 | | |
| Matson, Dorcas (Wid.) | 1 | 1 | 1 | | | Egeton, Ebenezer | 2 | 1 | 3 | | | Winchell, Mary | 2 | 1 | 1 | | |
| Weed, Deborah | | | | | | Egeton, Ebenezer, Jr | 1 | | 2 | | | Winchell, Simeon | 1 | | 1 | | |
| Weed, Moses | 1 | 3 | 3 | | | Segar, John | 1 | | 1 | | | Kellogg, Oliver | 1 | | 1 | | |
| Weld, Benjamin | 1 | 1 | 2 | | | Segar, Augustus | 1 | | 1 | | | Enos, David | 1 | 1 | 3 | | |
| Bacon, Celi | 1 | | 2 | | | | | | | | | More, Jonah | 2 | | 1 | | |

# HEADS OF FAMILIES—CONNECTICUT.

## HARTFORD COUNTY—Continued.

| NAME OF HEAD OF FAMILY. | Free white males of 16 years and upward, including heads of families. | Free white males under 16 years. | Free white females, including heads of families. | All other free persons. | Slaves. | NAME OF HEAD OF FAMILY. | Free white males of 16 years and upward, including heads of families. | Free white males under 16 years. | Free white females, including heads of families. | All other free persons. | Slaves. | NAME OF HEAD OF FAMILY. | Free white males of 16 years and upward, including heads of families. | Free white males under 16 years. | Free white females, including heads of families. | All other free persons. | Slaves. |
|---|---|---|---|---|---|---|---|---|---|---|---|---|---|---|---|---|---|
| **GRANBY TOWN—con.** | | | | | | **GRANBY TOWN—con.** | | | | | | **HARTFORD TOWN—con.** | | | | | |
| More, Joel | 3 | 4 | 3 | | | Barnes, Isaac | 2 | 3 | 3 | | | Bruster, Prince | 2 | 3 | 7 | | |
| More, Nathan | 2 | 2 | 5 | | | Huckins, James | 2 | | 1 | | | Boiles, Samuel | 1 | 1 | 2 | | |
| Griswold, Alexander | 2 | 3 | 3 | | | Huckins, Jonathan | 1 | 1 | 2 | | | Beebe, Adam | 1 | 2 | 1 | | |
| Clark, David, Jr | 1 | 3 | 3 | | | Day, Roswell | 1 | 1 | 3 | | | Caldwell, John | 2 | 2 | 6 | | |
| More, Joel, Jr | 1 | 1 | 1 | | | Day, Lues | 1 | 6 | 3 | | | Colton, Aaron | 3 | | 3 | | |
| Clark, David | 5 | 1 | 4 | | | Day, Timothy | 1 | 3 | 3 | | | Colt, Peter | 2 | 2 | 6 | | 1 |
| Clark, Cefus | 1 | 1 | 1 | | | Johnson, Daniel | 1 | 4 | 3 | | | Colt, Elisha | 2 | | 2 | | |
| Ross, William | 1 | | | | | Berwick, Elisha | 1 | | 1 | | | Calder, John | 3 | 1 | | | |
| Skinner, Roswell | 1 | 3 | 3 | | | Hoskins, Elijah | 1 | 2 | 3 | | | Caldwell, George | 1 | | 2 | | |
| Winchell, Oliver | 1 | | 4 | | | Gillett, Nathaniel, Jr | 2 | 4 | 6 | | | Caldwell, ——* | 1 | | | | |
| Thompson, Edward | 1 | 1 | 3 | | | Gillett, Nathaniel | 1 | | 1 | | | Cadwell, Elizabeth | | | 2 | | |
| Thompson, Edward, Jr | 1 | | 5 | | | Gillett, Timothy | 1 | 1 | 2 | | | Chenevard, John | 4 | | 5 | | |
| Thompson, Edmund | 1 | 1 | 2 | | | Holcomb, Ezra | 5 | 2 | 2 | | | Corning, Ezra | 2 | 3 | 3 | | |
| Lews, Simeon | 2 | 2 | 3 | | | Miller, Samuel | 1 | 1 | 5 | | | Cotton, Daniel | 2 | 1 | 3 | | |
| Winchell, Elisha | 3 | | 2 | | | Rowley, Roswell | 1 | 1 | 4 | | | Cadwell, Hezekiah | 2 | 2 | 4 | | |
| Winchell, Elisha, Jr | 1 | 4 | 2 | | | Strickland, Joseph | 1 | 1 | 1 | | | Corning, Asa | 6 | 1 | 7 | | |
| Winchell, Grove | 1 | 2 | 2 | | | Strickland, Joseph, Jr | 2 | 1 | 2 | | | Cadwell, Abram | 2 | | 2 | | |
| Thompson, Jemima | | | 1 | | | Forward, Joseph | 4 | 1 | 3 | | | Cables, John | 1 | 3 | 4 | | |
| Winchell, Jehiel | 1 | | | | | Forward, Reuben | 1 | 2 | 2 | | | Church, George | 1 | | 2 | | |
| Hoskins, Alson | 3 | 1 | 2 | | | Phelps, Ebenezer | 2 | 1 | 6 | | | Chapin, Aaron | 3 | 2 | 3 | | |
| Winchel, Nathaniel | 2 | 3 | 3 | | | Phelps, Nathaniel | 3 | | 2 | | | Cook, Aaron | 2 | 1 | 4 | | |
| Parker, Reuben | 4 | 1 | 1 | | | Phelps, Nathan | 1 | 1 | 2 | | | Church, Caleb | 4 | 2 | 2 | | |
| Clark, Joel | 2 | 2 | 3 | | | Phelps, Eliphalet | 1 | 1 | 4 | | | Caldwell, Charles | 1 | 1 | 6 | 1 | |
| Clark (Wid.) | | | 1 | | | Phelps, Nathaniel, Jr | 1 | | 1 | | | Cook, John | 1 | 1 | 9 | | |
| Phelps, Ruth (Wid.) | 1 | | 3 | | | Adams, Ephraim | 1 | 1 | 1 | | | Collins, Robert J | 1 | 3 | 4 | | |
| Clark, Jesse | 2 | | 4 | | | Wilkinson, Oliver | 1 | 1 | 3 | | | Cadwell, Nehemiah | 1 | | 4 | | |
| Rockwell, William | 1 | | 1 | | | Lyon, Aaron | 1 | | 4 | | | Cadwell, Nehemiah, Jr | 1 | 3 | 3 | | |
| Holcomb, Asahel, Jr | 3 | 1 | 2 | | | Leus, Hezekiah | 3 | 2 | 1 | | | Church, Asher | 1 | 2 | 3 | | |
| Goold, David | 1 | 3 | 2 | | | Kilbourn, James | 1 | | 1 | | | Cadwell, Jeduthan | 2 | 3 | 4 | | |
| Hillyer, Andrew | 1 | 2 | 4 | | | Bacon, James | 1 | | 4 | | | Cook, James | 2 | 1 | 1 | 1 | |
| Holcomb, Asahel, Jr | 3 | 1 | 1 | | | Strickland, Asahel | 1 | 4 | 4 | | | Church, James | 1 | | 1 | 1 | |
| Holcomb, Asahel, 4th | 1 | 1 | 2 | | | Colton (Wid.) | | 1 | 3 | | | Cook, William | 1 | 2 | 2 | | |
| Holcomb, Oliver | 1 | | 2 | | | Ross, Timothy | 1 | | 3 | | | Chapman, Alpheus | 1 | | 1 | | |
| Phelps, Basheba | 2 | 1 | 3 | | | Averett, Samuel | 3 | | 2 | | | Church, Joseph | 1 | 1 | 4 | | |
| Gillett, Joab | 1 | 2 | 2 | | | Clark, Aaron | 1 | 1 | 2 | | | Chapman, Andrew | 1 | 2 | 3 | | |
| Hill, John | 1 | | 2 | | | More, Isaac | 1 | | 1 | | | Chapman, Silas | 1 | 2 | 3 | | |
| Wright, Uring | 1 | | 2 | | | Jones, Daniel | 1 | | 1 | | | Cadwell, Ruth | | | 3 | | |
| Dewey, Isaac | 1 | | 1 | | | Hays, Levi | 1 | 3 | 2 | | | Curtis, Daniel | 1 | | 2 | | |
| Dewey, David | 1 | 4 | 3 | | | Holcomb, Martha (Wid.) | | | 1 | | | Clark, Ebenezer | 2 | | 5 | | |
| Dewey, Isaac | 1 | 1 | 5 | | | | | | | | | Clapp, Oliver | 2 | 2 | 5 | | |
| Dewey, Aaron | 1 | 1 | 3 | | | **HARTFORD TOWN.** | | | | | | Coop, David | 2 | | 2 | | |
| Copt, Alexander | 3 | 1 | 2 | | | Andrus, Silvanus | 1 | 1 | 5 | | | Center, John | 1 | 1 | 3 | | |
| Perring, Elisha | 2 | 1 | 4 | | | Ames, David | 1 | 1 | 1 | | | Church, Timothy | 1 | 1 | 2 | | |
| Kendall, Noadiah | 2 | 4 | 4 | | | Avery, John | 1 | 4 | 5 | 2 | 1 | Collier, William | 1 | 3 | 4 | | |
| Totten, Dorcas | | | 2 | | | Anderson, James | 3 | | 4 | | | Doolittle, Enos | 1 | 4 | 3 | | |
| Lampson, Joseph | 1 | | 2 | | | Adams, William | 1 | | 6 | 1 | | Denniss, Ebenezer | 1 | | 1 | | |
| Lampson, Ebenezer | 1 | 2 | 2 | | | Alford, Alpheus | | | 6 | | | Day, Samuel | 1 | 2 | 2 | | |
| Lampson, Benjamin | 1 | 1 | 3 | | | Alford, Lydia (widow) | | | 2 | | | Dickenson, Moses | 1 | | 1 | | |
| Lampson (Wid.) | | | 1 | | | Adams, Ebenezer | 2 | | 2 | | | Danforth, Edward | 3 | 1 | 4 | | |
| Haley, Israel | 1 | | 4 | | | Bull, Thomas | 2 | 2 | 4 | | | Day, Joseph | 2 | 2 | 1 | | |
| Lampson, Elnathan | 2 | | 2 | | | Bull, William | 1 | | 2 | | | Drake, Martha | | | 2 | | |
| Lampson, Samuel | 2 | 2 | 3 | | | Bull, George | 4 | | 2 | | | Davis, Philip | 1 | 2 | 6 | | |
| Hubbard, Elijah | 4 | 3 | 2 | | | Bull, Caleb | 3 | | 4 | | | Egleston, Elihu | 2 | 2 | 6 | | |
| More, Ruth | | | 4 | | | Bull, James | 3 | 1 | 2 | 1 | 1 | Ellery, William | 3 | | 4 | | |
| Holcomb, Judah, Jr | 2 | 2 | 3 | | | Bull, Hezekiah | 1 | | 4 | 1 | | Ensign, Thomas, Jr | 2 | | 1 | | |
| Holcomb, Judah, Esqr | 2 | | 2 | | | Bull, Frederic | 4 | 2 | 4 | 2 | | Ewing, William | 2 | | 2 | | |
| Gilbert, Ichabod | 2 | 3 | 2 | | | Bull, David | 2 | 2 | 6 | 2 | 1 | Fish, Miller | 5 | 1 | 3 | | |
| Hays, Obadiah | 1 | 3 | 3 | | | Bull, Isaac | 2 | 3 | 3 | | | Flagg, Joseph | 1 | | 3 | | |
| Ford, Adonijah | 1 | 3 | 4 | | | Brunson, Isaac | 2 | 1 | 1 | 2 | 2 | Fowler, Benjamin | 1 | 1 | 4 | | |
| Ford, Mathew | 1 | | 1 | | | Burr, Samuel | 3 | 2 | 6 | 1 | | Fish, Eliakim | 1 | | 3 | | |
| Holcomb, Joseph | 2 | 1 | 4 | | | Burr, Timothy | 3 | | 1 | | | Flagg, Jonathan | 2 | 2 | 3 | | |
| Holcomb, Joseph, Jr | 1 | 2 | 2 | | | Burr, Moses | 3 | | 4 | | | Fry, John | 1 | 1 | 2 | | |
| Cosset, Asa | 2 | 2 | 4 | | | Byington, Joel | 3 | 4 | 6 | | | Goodwin, John | 2 | 1 | 2 | | |
| Perring, Ruth | | | 3 | | | Bolles, John, 2d | 3 | 1 | 3 | | | Goodrich, Chancey | 3 | | 2 | | |
| Coley, Noah | 2 | 2 | 3 | | | Bunce, Isaac | | | | | | Goodman, Richard | 2 | 1 | 4 | | |
| Cosett, Rana | 1 | | 2 | | | Beebe, Adonijah | 2 | 2 | 2 | | | Gove, William | 2 | | 3 | | |
| Cosset, Silas | 1 | 4 | 1 | | | Burr, George | 1 | 5 | 4 | | | Goodwin, George | 3 | 4 | 5 | | |
| Hillyer, James, Jr | 1 | 3 | 3 | | | Beckwith, Samuel | 3 | 1 | 6 | | | Goodwin, William | 2 | 4 | 3 | | |
| Willcox, Sadoss | 2 | 2 | 3 | | | Burr, William | 3 | 2 | 4 | | | Goodwin, Theodore | 1 | | 1 | | |
| Robbins, Appleton | 1 | 1 | | | | Bigelow, Daniel | 1 | | 1 | | | Goodwin, Russell | 1 | | 1 | | |
| Trumble, Ephraim | 1 | | 1 | | | ——*, Nathan | 2 | 1 | 3 | | | Goodwin, Anna (Wid.) | 2 | 3 | 4 | | |
| Phelps, Roswell | 1 | 2 | 1 | | | Barnard, Joseph | 1 | | 2 | | | Goodwin, James | 3 | 2 | 2 | | |
| More, Micah | 1 | 1 | 1 | | | Belair, Thomas | 2 | 1 | 3 | | | Gray, Edward | 1 | 3 | 4 | | |
| Forward, Samuel | 1 | 3 | 5 | | | Burnham, George | 1 | 5 | 3 | | | Goodwin, Samuel | 2 | 1 | 2 | | |
| Bates, Zopha | 1 | | 2 | | | Barnard, Samuel | | | | | | Goodwin, David | 2 | 2 | 2 | | |
| Booth, Samuel | 1 | 1 | 2 | | | Beckwith, Josiah | 4 | | 2 | 1 | | Goodwin, Jonathan | 1 | 1 | 2 | | |
| Phelps, Roger | 1 | | 1 | | | Bunce, John, Jr | 1 | 3 | 1 | | | Goodwin, Allyn | 1 | | 2 | | |
| Attwet, Oliver | 1 | 2 | 3 | | | Barnard, Ebenezer | 2 | 1 | 4 | | | Goodwin, Mary | | | 3 | | |
| Owen, Alvin | 2 | 1 | 4 | | | Dwight, ——* | 4 | | 1 | | | Goodwin, Timothy | 1 | | | | |
| Bates, Lemuel | 3 | 1 | 1 | | | Bradley, Aaron | 2 | 3 | 3 | | | Grist, Joseph | 1 | | 2 | | |
| Gay, Richard, Jr | 1 | 4 | 3 | | | Buner, Timothy | 2 | 2 | 5 | | | Goodwin, Asher | 1 | 1 | 1 | | |
| Gay, Richard | 2 | 1 | 3 | | | Burkitt, Uriah | 3 | | 6 | | | Goodwin, Mary | | | 3 | | |
| Cornish, Joseph | 1 | 1 | 2 | | | Bolles, John | 4 | 2 | 5 | | | Hinsdale, Daniel | 4 | 2 | 6 | | |
| Cornish, Elizabeth | | | 1 | | | Burkitt, Thomas | 1 | 3 | 3 | | | Hart, Joseph | 2 | 1 | 2 | 4 | |
| Buck, Eliphalet | 2 | | 2 | | | Burkitt, John | 1 | 1 | 3 | | | Hosmer, James | 5 | 2 | 4 | | |
| Morse, Chester | 1 | 2 | 5 | | | Bryant, Benjamin | 1 | 1 | 2 | | | Hopkins, Asa | 3 | | 7 | | |
| Strong, Eli | 2 | 1 | 4 | | | Burt, Consider | 3 | 1 | 7 | | | Hopkins, Thomas | 1 | 2 | 4 | 1 | |
| Bartlet, Sylvanus | 1 | 3 | 5 | | | Burr, Joseph | 1 | 1 | 3 | | | Hall, John | 1 | 3 | 3 | | |
| Gillet, Oliver | 1 | 2 | 3 | | | Blanott, James | 2 | 2 | 2 | | | Hall, Asaph | 1 | | 2 | | |
| Burr, Adonijah, Jr | 1 | 3 | 2 | | | Benton, Asa | 2 | | 4 | | | Hall, William | 2 | | 3 | | |
| Jones, Levi | 1 | | 2 | | | Brainthwait, Robert | 4 | | 4 | | | Hequimburgh, Charles | 2 | 1 | 2 | | |
| Crittenton, Samuel | 1 | | 2 | | | Bunce, Jerusha | | | 3 | | | Henery, James | 1 | | 3 | | |
| More, Horace | 1 | | 3 | | | | | | | | | James, Webster | 3 | | 5 | | |
| More, Obed | 1 | 1 | 3 | | | Bolles, Stephen | 2 | 3 | 1 | | | Herrod, Jesse | 1 | | 2 | | |

* Illegible.

45

# FIRST CENSUS OF THE UNITED STATES.

## HARTFORD COUNTY—Continued.

| NAME OF HEAD OF FAMILY. | Free white males of 16 years and upward, including heads of families. | Free white males under 16 years. | Free white females, including heads of families. | All other free persons. | Slaves. | NAME OF HEAD OF FAMILY. | Free white males of 16 years and upward, including heads of families. | Free white males under 16 years. | Free white females, including heads of families. | All other free persons. | Slaves. | NAME OF HEAD OF FAMILY. | Free white males of 16 years and upward, including heads of families. | Free white males under 16 years. | Free white females, including heads of families. | All other free persons. | Slaves. |
|---|---|---|---|---|---|---|---|---|---|---|---|---|---|---|---|---|---|
| HARTFORD TOWN—con. | | | | | | HARTFORD TOWN—con. | | | | | | HARTFORD TOWN—con. | | | | | |
| Jones, Nathaniel | 1 | | 1 | | | Sloan, Robert | 1 | 2 | 2 | | | Brainard, Adonejah | 2 | 1 | 1 | | |
| Johnson, Shadrach | 1 | 1 | 2 | | | Suitar, John | 2 | 2 | 5 | | | Bigelow, Elisha | 2 | | 1 | | |
| Imley, William | 1 | 4 | 4 | 1 | | Stackhouse, Stacy | 3 | 4 | 3 | | | Bigelow, Elisha, Jr | 1 | 2 | 3 | | |
| Indicott, John | 1 | 4 | 3 | | | Steele, Thomas | 4 | 4 | 4 | | | Brau, John | 2 | | 1 | | |
| Jeffery, John | 2 | 3 | 6 | | | Spencer, Thomas | 1 | 2 | 1 | | | Bunce, Elizabeth (Wid.) | | 3 | 2 | | |
| Jepson, James | 1 | 1 | 4 | | | Skinner, Daniel | 1 | | 2 | | 2 | Butler, Daniel | 1 | 2 | 6 | | |
| Janes, Jonathan | 6 | 2 | 7 | 1 | 1 | Spencer, Theadore | 1 | 1 | 2 | | | Bigelow, Jonathan | 1 | 3 | 2 | | |
| Jones, John | 1 | 1 | 2 | | | Spencer, Epaphras | 1 | | 4 | | | Bunce, Roderic | 1 | 1 | 3 | | |
| Jones, Daniel | 4 | | 8 | | 1 | Spencer, Timothy | 2 | 3 | 5 | | | Barnard, Ashbel | 2 | 2 | 2 | | |
| Jones, Julius | 2 | 3 | 4 | | | Spencer, Ashbel | 2 | 3 | 5 | | | Benton, John | 1 | | 2 | 1 | |
| Jones, Samuel P | 1 | | 4 | | | Spencer, Michael | 1 | 2 | 2 | | | Bunce, James | 1 | 3 | 4 | | |
| Judd, Reuben | 2 | 4 | 4 | | | Sheldon, James | 2 | 2 | 3 | | | Butler, Jonathan | 2 | | 3 | | 3 |
| Judd, Simeon | 1 | 1 | 4 | | | Sheldon, John | 1 | | 2 | | | Barret, Elijah | 1 | 1 | 1 | | |
| Jones, Pantry | 1 | | 2 | | 1 | Sheldon, John, Jr | 1 | 5 | 5 | | | Bigelow, Jame | 2 | | 7 | | |
| Jones, Benjamin | 1 | | 1 | | | Skinner, Daniel, Jr | 1 | 2 | 2 | | | Bunce, Daniel | 1 | 1 | 4 | | |
| James, John | 2 | 3 | 5 | | | Spencer, Benjamin | 2 | 1 | 3 | | | Barrett, Jere | 1 | | 1 | | |
| Knox, James | 1 | 1 | 2 | | | Sanford, Thomas | 3 | 2 | 5 | | | Bunce, Asa | 1 | 3 | 2 | | |
| Kingsbury, Andrew | 1 | 1 | 5 | | | Spencer, John, Jr | 1 | 2 | 4 | | | Bigelow, John | 1 | 2 | 3 | | |
| Knox, William | 2 | 2 | 3 | 2 | | Smith, George | 2 | 2 | 2 | | | Barnard, Dorios | 2 | 3 | 1 | | |
| Knox, Jennet (Wid.) | 1 | 1 | 8 | 1 | | Seymour, Asa | 1 | 1 | 1 | | | Barnard, John | 4 | 1 | 4 | | |
| Kelsey, Levi | 1 | 3 | 4 | | | Sloan, Thomas | 3 | | 4 | | | Bigelow, Joseph | 2 | | | | |
| Kilbourn, Freeman | 2 | 2 | 5 | | | Seymour, Hezekiah | 1 | 3 | 2 | | | Bull, Jonathan | 2 | 2 | 6 | | |
| Kilbourn, Samuel | 1 | 2 | 3 | | | Shepard, Ashbel | 1 | 1 | 3 | | | Bigelow, Josiah | 1 | | 2 | | |
| Kellogg, Charles | 1 | | 1 | | | Skinner, Theodore | 1 | 2 | 3 | | | Bowen, Consider | 3 | 1 | 2 | | |
| Lyman, Timothy | 2 | 1 | 3 | | | Shepard, Richard | 2 | 3 | 5 | | | Benton, Nathaniel S | 1 | | 1 | | |
| Leffingwell, John | 4 | 1 | 5 | | | Skinner, Elisha | 1 | 5 | 1 | | | Boardman, William | 2 | 1 | 3 | | |
| Leidlie, Hugh | 3 | | 1 | | | Sanford, Isaac | 2 | 1 | 6 | | | Bliss, David | 1 | | 2 | | |
| Lawrence, John | 2 | 1 | 5 | | | Skinner, William | 1 | 1 | 1 | | | Bliss, Isaac | 3 | | 3 | | |
| Lawrence, William | 2 | 2 | 5 | | | Seymour, Thomas, Esqr | 8 | | 3 | 1 | | Bull, Aaron | 1 | 2 | 7 | | |
| Lowell, Willibe | 4 | 4 | 3 | | | Seymour, Robert | 1 | | 4 | | | Boardman, Revd Benjamin | 1 | | 1 | | 3 |
| Lord, John Haynes | 3 | 2 | 5 | | | Strong, Revd Nathan | 2 | 2 | 3 | 1 | | Benton, Samuel | 1 | 2 | 6 | | |
| Leffingwell, Joshua | 2 | 1 | 2 | | | Skinner, Jared | 1 | 1 | 3 | | | Babcock, Elisha | 2 | 5 | 4 | | |
| Lord, John H., Jr | 1 | | | | | Shepard, Charles | 1 | | 2 | | | Butler, Henry | 1 | 2 | 1 | | |
| Larkum, John | 1 | | 1 | | | Shepard, Uriah | 1 | | 4 | | | Barnard, Ebenezer, Jr | 2 | | 3 | | |
| Loud, Asa | 2 | 1 | 1 | | | Shepard, Elisha | 1 | 4 | | | | Beach, Miles | 3 | 2 | 4 | 1 | |
| Larkum, Rhoderic | 1 | 1 | 5 | | | Skinner, John | 1 | | 4 | | 1 | Butler, Richard | 2 | 1 | 5 | | |
| Lamb, James | 1 | 1 | 2 | | | Shepard, Timothy | 2 | 1 | | | | Butler, Moses | 1 | | 4 | | |
| Lee, George | 1 | | 3 | | | Sloan, Robert | 1 | 2 | 4 | | | Bull, Amos | 1 | 1 | 4 | 1 | 1 |
| Marsh, Mary | | | 5 | | | Sanford, Zach | 1 | | 2 | | | Benton, John, Jr | 2 | | 4 | | |
| Moseley, William | 1 | 2 | 2 | | | Savage, Luther | 1 | | 2 | | | Benton, Josiah | 1 | 2 | 2 | | |
| Morse, William | 1 | 2 | 2 | | | Stanley, Roswell | 1 | 1 | 3 | | | Bunce, Joseph | 1 | | 1 | | |
| Morgan, John | 2 | 1 | 3 | | | Stanley, Frederic | 1 | 2 | 5 | | | Buckland, Joshua | 1 | 3 | 2 | | |
| Merrill, George | 1 | | 3 | | 1 | Tiley, James | 1 | 2 | 4 | | | Bunce, John | 1 | | 4 | | |
| Marsh, Samuel | 4 | 1 | 4 | | | Talcott, Samuel | 2 | | 1 | | 1 | Benton, Ruth (Wid.) | | | 2 | | |
| Merrill, Hezekiah | 1 | 5 | 3 | | | Talcott, Samuel, Jr | 2 | 2 | 4 | | | Clapp, John | 1 | | 1 | | |
| Murray, Cotton | 1 | | 3 | | | Talcott, Joseph | 1 | 1 | 2 | | 1 | Carter, John | 1 | 4 | 4 | | |
| Marsh, Jesse | 2 | 1 | 2 | | | Thomas, John | 3 | 4 | 4 | | | Carter, Gidion | 2 | | 2 | | |
| Moore, Ebenezer | 3 | 1 | 4 | 1 | | Toocker, Joseph | 3 | 3 | 7 | | | Clapp, Roger | 1 | | 3 | | |
| McAlpine, John | 1 | 2 | 4 | | | Tisdale, Thomas | 5 | | 3 | | | Church, Timothy | 1 | 3 | 3 | | |
| Marsh, John | 1 | 3 | 2 | | 1 | Trumble, John | 1 | 2 | 5 | | | Chapman, Jonathan | 1 | 2 | 2 | | |
| Morgan, Devill | 1 | | 3 | | | Tiley, Samuel | 1 | | | | | Clerk, Josiah | 2 | 1 | 3 | | |
| Marsh, Samuel, 2d | 5 | | 6 | | | Turner, Samuel | 1 | 1 | 3 | | | Clapp, Thomas | 1 | 1 | 4 | | |
| Mire, William | 1 | 1 | 3 | | | Turner, Caleb | 2 | 2 | 2 | | | Carter, Joel | 1 | | 1 | | |
| Mason, Isaac | 1 | 1 | 2 | | | Taylor, Jonathan | 1 | | 1 | | | Clark, Samuel | 1 | 2 | 6 | | |
| Nichols, William | 1 | 1 | 3 | 1 | | Vibbert, Elisha | 1 | 3 | 5 | | | Clapp, Elijah | 1 | 2 | 3 | | |
| Nevins, John | 1 | 1 | 3 | | | Hatten, William | 1 | | 1 | | | Cole, Jacob | 1 | 2 | 4 | | |
| Newill, James | 1 | | | | | Weare, William | 3 | | 3 | | | Chester, Star | 3 | 1 | 4 | | |
| Olcott, Joseph | 1 | 2 | 5 | | | Woodward, Caleb | 1 | 1 | 1 | | | Dodd, John | 3 | | 2 | | |
| Ogden, Jacob | 1 | 1 | 8 | | | Wadsworth, Samuel | 2 | | 3 | | 3 | Dodd, Elisha | 2 | 4 | 2 | | |
| Olcott, Roderic | 1 | | 1 | | | Wadsworth, Thomas | 1 | | 3 | | | Dodd, Timothy | 1 | | 4 | | |
| Olcott, Samuel | 2 | | 5 | | 2 | Wadsworth, Rachel (Wid.) | | 2 | 4 | | | Dodd, Susan (Wid.) | | 1 | 3 | | |
| Olcott, Jonathan | 1 | | 2 | | | Wadsworth, David | 1 | 2 | 1 | | | Diggins, Luke | 1 | 1 | 1 | | |
| Oakes, David | 1 | 1 | 2 | | | Wadsworth, Joseph | 2 | 3 | 4 | | | Ensign, Moses | 1 | 1 | 1 | | |
| Olcott, Theodore | 2 | | 4 | | | Wadsworth, Roger | 2 | 3 | 8 | | | Ensign, Thomas | 1 | | 2 | | |
| Olcott, Hezekiah | 1 | 2 | 3 | | | Wadsworth, Elisha | 1 | | 1 | | | Ensign, James | 2 | 1 | 2 | | |
| Olcott, Timothy | 1 | | | | | Wadsworth, Jeremiah | 5 | 1 | 8 | | 4 | Ferry, Moses | 1 | 2 | 6 | | |
| Oakes, Isaac | 2 | 3 | 4 | | | Wadsworth, Gurdon | 1 | 1 | 5 | | | Frances, Asa | 7 | 4 | 3 | | |
| Olcott, Daniel | 2 | | 3 | 1 | | Wells, John | 3 | | 4 | | | Greenwood, Parson | 1 | 2 | 3 | | |
| Olcott, James | 1 | 2 | 4 | | | Wells, Ashbel, Jr | 5 | 2 | 6 | | | Grear, Mathew | 1 | 1 | 4 | | |
| Olcott, William, 2d | 1 | 1 | 3 | | | Wells, Thomas | 1 | | 2 | | | Camp, James | 1 | 1 | 1 | | |
| Pratt, James | 1 | | 3 | | | Winship, Samuel | 2 | 1 | 4 | | | Hender, Thomas | 1 | 3 | 4 | | |
| Porter, Solomon | 1 | 2 | 2 | | | Washbourn, Noah | 5 | 1 | 9 | | | Humphreys, Joseph | 2 | 2 | 4 | | |
| Phillips, Joseph | 2 | | 2 | | | Wells, James A | 1 | | 4 | | | Hide, Ezra | 1 | 1 | 1 | | |
| Pratt, William, Jr | 1 | | 2 | | | Watson, John | 5 | 1 | 4 | | | Hinsdale, James | 1 | | 1 | | |
| Pomeroy, Ralph | 4 | 1 | 3 | 1 | 2 | Waggoner, Henry | 1 | 1 | 2 | | | Hopkins, Moses | 1 | | 1 | | |
| Pratt, Zacheriah | 1 | 1 | 1 | | | Wadsworth, James | 1 | 3 | 2 | | | Hutchinson, Stephen | 2 | 4 | 3 | | |
| Pratt, George | 1 | | 1 | | | Wadsworth, Henry | 2 | 2 | 3 | | | Hempsted, Joshua | 1 | | 2 | | |
| Pratt, William | 5 | 2 | 2 | | | Wadsworth, Abigail | 1 | 1 | 4 | | | Hempsted, Josiah | 1 | | 4 | | |
| Phelps, Daniel, 2d | 2 | 1 | 3 | | | Webster, Noah, Jr | 2 | | 4 | | | Hosmer, William | 1 | 2 | 2 | | |
| Pratt, Joseph | 2 | 1 | 3 | | 1 | White, John | 1 | 1 | 8 | | | Hooker, William | 2 | 1 | 1 | | |
| Patten, Nathaniel | 3 | 1 | 4 | | | Waters, Thomas | 1 | | 1 | | | Hinsdale, Amos | 1 | | 1 | | |
| Perkins, Jabez | 3 | 4 | 1 | | | Wadsworth, George | 1 | | 3 | | | Hopkins, Lemuel | 1 | | 4 | 1 | |
| Perkins, Enoch | 1 | | 3 | 1 | | Wyllys, Samuel | 2 | 3 | 3 | | | Hildrup, Thomas | 1 | 5 | 3 | | |
| Patten Ruth (Wid.) | | | 6 | | | White, Consider | 1 | | 2 | | | Hudson, Barzilla | 7 | 2 | 7 | | |
| Root, Jesse | 3 | 1 | 2 | 1 | 1 | Winchell, John | 1 | | 1 | | | Howell, Ryal | 1 | 1 | 3 | | |
| Root, Jesse, Jr | 1 | | 2 | 1 | 1 | Andruss, John | 2 | 2 | 2 | | | Hunt, Alexander | 2 | | 3 | | 5 |
| Roberts, John | 1 | 2 | 6 | | | Andruss, William, Jr | 1 | | 3 | | | Hadlock, Reuben | 1 | 2 | 2 | | |
| Rowland, William | 1 | | 2 | | | Allyn, John | 3 | 2 | 4 | | | Hinsdale, William | 1 | 3 | 2 | | |
| Ramsey, Jonathan | 1 | 2 | 2 | | | Ashton, Joseph | 2 | | 4 | | | Holland, Benjamin | 1 | 5 | 1 | | |
| Roberts, Jonathan | 1 | 2 | 4 | | | Brunson, Mathew | 1 | 2 | 3 | | | Jones, Isaac | 1 | 1 | 2 | | |
| Roberts, Aaron | 1 | 1 | 2 | | | Bigelow, Alvin | 1 | 1 | 1 | | | Kneeland, Samuel | 2 | | 2 | | |
| Roberts, John, 2d | 1 | | 1 | | | Barnard, William | 1 | 1 | 4 | | | Kilbourn, James | 1 | 2 | 4 | | |
| Ritter, John | 1 | 1 | 1 | | | Butler, Norman | 2 | | 4 | 3 | | Kepple, John | 1 | | 2 | | |
| Spencer, Lina | | 1 | 3 | | | | | | | | | Kilbourn, John | 1 | | | | |
| Shortman, William | 1 | 2 | | | | | | | | | | | | | | | |

# HEADS OF FAMILIES—CONNECTICUT.

## HARTFORD COUNTY—Continued.

| NAME OF HEAD OF FAMILY. | Free white males of 16 years and upward, including heads of families. | Free white males under 16 years. | Free white females, including heads of families. | All other free persons. | Slaves. | NAME OF HEAD OF FAMILY. | Free white males of 16 years and upward, including heads of families. | Free white males under 16 years. | Free white females, including heads of families. | All other free persons. | Slaves. | NAME OF HEAD OF FAMILY. | Free white males of 16 years and upward, including heads of families. | Free white males under 16 years. | Free white females, including heads of families. | All other free persons. | Slaves. |
|---|---|---|---|---|---|---|---|---|---|---|---|---|---|---|---|---|---|
| **HARTFORD TOWN—con.** | | | | | | **HARTFORD TOWN—con.** | | | | | | **HARTFORD TOWN—con.** | | | | | |
| Loomis, George | 1 | | 2 | | | Cadwell, Thomas | 1 | 2 | 4 | | | Latimore, Wickham | 1 | | 3 | | |
| McLean, Niel | 2 | 6 | 3 | | | Cadwell, Hezekiah | 2 | 4 | 2 | | | Merrill, Jacob | 1 | 1 | 2 | | |
| Merrill, Charles | 2 | 3 | 3 | | | Cadwell, Aaron | 1 | 3 | 4 | | | Merrill, William | 1 | | 4 | | |
| Mygatt, Abigail | | | 2 | | | Cadwell, Joseph | 2 | 1 | 5 | | | Morgan, Charles | 2 | | 4 | | |
| Nichols, James | 1 | 3 | 2 | | | Cadwell, Rhoda | 1 | 2 | 2 | | | Mix, Elisha | 1 | 1 | 6 | | |
| Nichols, Eunice (Wid.) | | 1 | 1 | | | Con, Robert | 1 | | 2 | | | Merrill, Nathaniel | 1 | 1 | 5 | | |
| Olmsted, James | 1 | 5 | 5 | | | Dean, John | 1 | | 3 | | | Merrill, Abram | 2 | | 4 | | |
| Phillips, Richard | 1 | 2 | 1 | | | Frances, Elias | 1 | 2 | 6 | | | Mills, Jedediah | 3 | 3 | 6 | | |
| Rumbule, Phillip | 1 | 1 | 3 | | | Flagg, Abijah | 3 | 2 | 4 | | | Pelton, Jesse | 1 | | 3 | | |
| Seymour, Charles | 2 | 1 | 3 | | | Frances, Hezekiah | 1 | 2 | 2 | | | Olmsted, Timothy | 2 | 1 | 1 | | |
| Smith, Moses | 1 | 4 | 5 | | | Frances, Roswell | 1 | | 1 | | | Olmsted, Thomas | 2 | 1 | 4 | | |
| Steele, Jonathan | 1 | 1 | 4 | | | Gaylord, Moses | 1 | 3 | 4 | | | Olmsted, Frances F | 1 | 1 | 2 | | |
| Skinner, Jonathan | 1 | 4 | 1 | | | Goodwin, Titus | 1 | 1 | 2 | | | Rowe, David | 1 | 2 | 1 | | |
| Steele, Timothy | 2 | 1 | 4 | | | Goodman, Asa | 2 | 1 | 5 | | | Skinner, Joseph | 2 | 1 | 2 | | |
| Seymour, Aaron | 1 | 3 | 3 | | | Goodman, Richard | 3 | 1 | 7 | | | Seymour, Nathaniel | 2 | 1 | 2 | | |
| Seymour, Asa | 2 | | 3 | | | Goodman, Thomas | 1 | 1 | 2 | | | Seymour, Allyn | 1 | 3 | 4 | | |
| Seymour, Michael | 2 | 1 | 2 | | | Hooker, Daniel | 3 | 3 | 6 | | | Seymour, Charles | 2 | 2 | 5 | | |
| Seymour, Thomas Y | 2 | 1 | 3 | | | Heath, Peleg | 2 | 1 | 3 | | | Steele, Aaron | 2 | 1 | 3 | | |
| Skinner, Stephen | 1 | 2 | 3 | | | Henery, Aaron | 1 | 1 | 1 | | | Seymour, Norman | 1 | 4 | 2 | | |
| Seymour, Zebulon | 4 | | 4 | | | Hosmer, Elizabeth | | | 2 | | | Seymour, Moses | 1 | | 3 | | |
| Steele, John | 2 | 3 | 1 | | | Hurlbut, Amos | 1 | 1 | 5 | | | Seymour, Aaron | 1 | 5 | 4 | | |
| Skinner, Nathaniel | 1 | 5 | 3 | | 1 | Kelsey, Zacheus | 1 | 2 | 2 | | | Stanley, Hannah (Wid.) | 2 | 1 | 2 | | |
| Seymour, Daniel | 3 | 1 | 5 | | | Loomis, Zedekiah | 1 | 1 | 2 | | | Seymour, John | 2 | | 4 | | |
| Shepard, John | 1 | | 7 | 2 | | Lyman, Ichabod | 2 | 4 | 2 | | | Seymour, Eli | 1 | 1 | 3 | | |
| Skinner, Richard | 3 | 2 | 4 | | | Love, Charles | 1 | 1 | 2 | | | Stanley, Allyn | 1 | | 3 | | |
| Steele, Rachel (Wid.) | | | 4 | | | Lawrence, Amos | 1 | 1 | 3 | | | Stanley, Anna (Wid.) | 1 | 3 | 4 | | |
| Steele, Lemuel | 1 | 3 | 7 | | | Merry, John | 2 | 2 | 6 | | | Smith, Alvin | 2 | 1 | 2 | | |
| Seymour, Joseph Whiting | 1 | 1 | 2 | | | Merrill, Gideon | 1 | 3 | 3 | | | Smith, Frances | 1 | 3 | 1 | | |
| Seymour, Richard | 2 | 1 | 4 | | | Merrill, Samuel | 1 | 2 | 2 | | | Shepard, Sarah | | | 2 | | |
| Seymour, Freeman | 1 | 3 | 5 | | | Merrill, Thomas | 4 | | 3 | | | Stanley, Amaziah | 1 | 2 | 3 | | |
| Sheldon, Joseph | 1 | | 3 | | | Merrill, Thomas, Jr | 1 | 3 | 4 | | | Stanley, Noadiah | 1 | 2 | 3 | | |
| Sheldon, Roderic | 1 | 1 | 3 | | | Perkins, Revd Nathan | 1 | 3 | 4 | | | Stanley, James | 2 | 1 | 1 | | |
| Saunders, Abel | 1 | | 5 | | | Perkins, Caleb | 2 | 2 | 6 | | 1 | Tryon, Mary | | | 2 | | |
| Steele, James, Jr | 1 | 3 | 2 | | | Page, Levi | 1 | 2 | 2 | | | Tryon, William | 1 | | 5 | | |
| Seymour, George | 2 | 1 | 6 | | | Merrills, Anna | | | 4 | | | Wadsworth, Daniel | 1 | 3 | 3 | 1 | |
| Sheldon, Joseph, Jr | 1 | | 1 | 2 | | Steele, Ebenezer | 1 | 3 | 4 | | | Webster, Daniel | 1 | 1 | 4 | | |
| Steele, James | 3 | | 4 | | | Steele, Allyn | 3 | 2 | 2 | | | Wells, Elisha | 1 | 1 | 2 | | |
| Seymour, Calvin | 1 | 1 | 1 | | | Steele, Joel | 1 | 1 | 3 | | | Waters, Joseph | 1 | 1 | 2 | | |
| Shepard, Mary | 1 | | 3 | | | Steele, Frederic | 1 | 1 | 2 | | | Winter, Jonathan W | 1 | 1 | 1 | | |
| Tryon, Lydia (Wid.) | | | 2 | | | Steele, Moses | 1 | 4 | 3 | | | Webster, Noah | 2 | 3 | 3 | | |
| Taylor, Roswell | 1 | | 2 | | | Sedgwick, Abram | 1 | | 3 | | | Webster, Isaac, Jr | 1 | 3 | 2 | | |
| Taylor, Jesse | 1 | 1 | 3 | | | Shepard, Stephen | 2 | 1 | 5 | | | Webster, Stephen | 3 | 3 | 4 | | |
| Taylor, James | 2 | 3 | 3 | | | Shepard, Ashbel | 1 | 2 | 5 | | | King, Erastus | 1 | | 1 | | |
| Turner, Peletiah | 1 | 2 | 3 | | | Sedgwick, William | 4 | | 3 | | | Miller, Charles | 2 | 1 | 4 | | |
| Tucker, Isaac | 1 | | 2 | | | Seymour, Timothy | 1 | 4 | 5 | | | Sage, Calvin | 1 | 2 | 3 | | |
| Webster, Mathew | 2 | | 1 | | | Stillman, David | 2 | | 2 | | | Webster, Isaac | 2 | 1 | 2 | | |
| White, John, Jr | 1 | 1 | 5 | | | Wells, Ashbel | 1 | 1 | 5 | 2 | | | | | | | |
| White, John | 2 | | 4 | | | Whiting, Allyn | 3 | 1 | 4 | | | **SIMSBURY TOWN.** | | | | | |
| Webster, Samuel, 1st | 1 | | 2 | | | Whiting, Nathan H | 2 | 1 | 1 | | | Mosses, Michael | 2 | 4 | 3 | | |
| Webster, Medad | | 2 | 3 | | | Whitman, William | 2 | | 4 | | | Humphrey, Lott | 1 | | 4 | | |
| Warren, Elizur | 1 | 1 | 6 | | | Wadsworth, Elisha, Jr | 1 | 1 | 2 | | | Petibone, John | 2 | | 3 | | |
| Warner, Eli | 3 | | 2 | | | Whitman, John | 1 | 1 | 2 | | | Humphrey, Sylvanus | 2 | 2 | 1 | | |
| Wells, Elisha | 1 | | 1 | | | Whitman, Samuel | 2 | 1 | 2 | | | Harrington, Elisha | 1 | 2 | 3 | | |
| Waters, Benjamin | | | 3 | | | Whitman, John, Jr | 4 | | 5 | | | Phelps, David | 3 | 2 | 3 | | |
| Webster, Samuel, 2d | 1 | 3 | 5 | | | Wells, Ebenezer | 3 | 1 | 2 | | | Smith, Peter T | 1 | 1 | 2 | | |
| Wyllys, George | 3 | | 5 | 1 | 1 | Whiting, Joseph | 2 | 2 | 4 | | | Phelps, Noah A | 1 | 2 | 3 | | |
| Winship, Joseph | 4 | 1 | 5 | | | Whiting, Gurdin | 1 | | 1 | | | Humphrey, Jonathan | 2 | 1 | 4 | | |
| Wills, Jonathan | 3 | | 2 | | | Whiting, William | 1 | 1 | 3 | | | Cornish, James | 3 | 1 | 4 | | |
| Warren, Dorus | 1 | 1 | 2 | | | Bevins, Ebenezer | 3 | 1 | 3 | | | Cornish, Joel | 3 | 1 | 3 | | |
| Wood, Benjamin | 2 | | 1 | | | Butler, Joseph, Jr | 3 | 1 | 3 | | | Cornish, Elisha, Jr | 1 | 3 | 4 | | |
| Waters, William | 1 | | 2 | | | Butler, David | 3 | 3 | 5 | | | Humphrey, Amasa | 1 | 1 | 4 | | |
| Waters, Benjamin, Jr | 1 | 1 | 2 | | | Butler, Abel | 1 | 3 | 2 | | | Humphrey, Amaziah | 2 | 1 | 7 | | |
| Woodbridge, Joseph | 2 | 1 | 6 | | | Bidwell, Amos | 3 | | 4 | | | Cornish, George | 1 | 2 | 3 | | |
| Whitman, Abigail | 1 | | 3 | | | Belden, Rositer | | 1 | 2 | | | Humphrey, Elisha | 3 | 2 | 3 | | |
| Wheelar, Joseph | 2 | | 2 | | | Butler, Joseph | 1 | | 1 | | | Case, Giles | 1 | 2 | 2 | | |
| Wheeler, Samuel | | 1 | 3 | | | Croswell, Cabel | 1 | 3 | 4 | | | Humphrey, Martin | 1 | 2 | 3 | | |
| Willson, Stebbins | 1 | 2 | 4 | | | Crosby, Ebenezer | 1 | 2 | 5 | 1 | | Andruss, William | 1 | 1 | 2 | | |
| Waterman, Robert | 1 | 3 | 2 | | | Colton, Stephen | 2 | 1 | 6 | | | Penny, Abner | 1 | 5 | 4 | | |
| Wales, Horatio | 1 | | 1 | | | Colton, Abijah | 1 | 5 | 4 | | | Humphry, Asa | 1 | 2 | 1 | | |
| Wadsworth, Reubin | 1 | 2 | 3 | | | Collins, Seth | 2 | 1 | 4 | 1 | 1 | Humphry, Nathaniel | 2 | | 2 | | |
| Williamson, Dorotha | | 1 | 2 | | | Cadwell, Aaron | 1 | 1 | 2 | | | Andrus, Richard | 1 | 1 | 4 | | |
| Wyman, Solomon | 1 | | 1 | | | Deming, Gideon | 2 | 3 | 5 | | | Goodrich, Stephen | 1 | 2 | 3 | | |
| Wattles, Roswell | 1 | | 4 | | | Ensign, Elijah | 2 | | 3 | | | Humphrey, Campbell | 2 | | 4 | | |
| Hull, Prince | | | | 3 | | Ensign, Solomon | 2 | | 6 | | | Starter, James | 1 | 1 | 4 | | |
| Cutas, Aaron | | | | 2 | | Fox, Elisha | 1 | 1 | 1 | | | Ferry, John | 2 | 1 | 4 | | |
| Boston (Negro) | | | | 4 | | Faxton, Ebenezer | 3 | 3 | 7 | | | Case, Arial | 1 | 1 | 1 | | |
| Boston, Junior | | | | 3 | | Gray, Abial | 1 | | 1 | | | Case, Job | 2 | 3 | 2 | | |
| Rese, Willobe | | | | 6 | | Gilbert, Benjamin | 2 | 1 | 2 | | | Case, Charles, Jr | 2 | 1 | 2 | | |
| Sheldon, Prince | | | | 6 | | Gilbert, Charles | 2 | 1 | 2 | | | Case, Charles | 1 | 2 | 2 | | |
| Dege (Negro) | | | | 3 | | Gilbert, Jonathan | 2 | 1 | 4 | | | Terry, Samuel | 1 | 2 | 3 | | |
| Popp (Negro) | | | | 2 | | Goodman, Moses | 2 | 5 | 4 | | | Humphry, Daniel | 3 | 3 | 2 | | |
| Bear, Joseph | 2 | 1 | 1 | | | Gibbs, Clark | 1 | | 4 | | | Case, Amasa | 4 | 1 | 4 | | |
| Butler, Zacheus | 2 | 1 | 4 | | | Griswold, Josiah | 3 | 1 | 3 | | | Terry, John G | 2 | 3 | 5 | | |
| Brainard, Nathaniel | 1 | 1 | 3 | | | Hurlbut, Fitch | 1 | 1 | 3 | | | Eno, Jonathan | 2 | 2 | 6 | | |
| Balch, Jonathan B | 3 | 3 | 5 | | | Hurlbut, Joseph, Jr | 1 | 3 | 3 | | | Humphreys, Joseph | 1 | 3 | 4 | 1 | |
| Brau, Henry | 2 | 4 | 4 | | | Hurlbut, Christopher | 5 | 1 | 3 | | | Risley, Samuel | 1 | 1 | 2 | | |
| Brau, Moses | 1 | 1 | 3 | | | Hurlbut, Eli | 1 | 1 | 3 | | | Higley, Anna | | | 3 | | |
| Brau, Lenas | 4 | 1 | 1 | | | Hopkins, Stephen | 2 | | 2 | | | Case, Levi | 1 | | 2 | | |
| Butler, Gideon | 2 | 5 | 3 | | | Hopkins, William | 1 | 4 | 2 | | | Brown, Joseph | 1 | 1 | 2 | | |
| Brau, Thomas | 1 | 1 | 3 | | | Hurlbut, Lemuel | 3 | 1 | 2 | | | Viney, Elias | 3 | 5 | 3 | | |
| Belden, Simion | 1 | | 1 | | | Keyes, Amasa | 1 | 3 | 9 | 1 | 1 | Brunson, Oliver | 1 | 5 | 3 | | |
| Beardsly, Frances | | 3 | 2 | | | Kellogg, George | 2 | 1 | 2 | | | Owen, John C | 1 | | 2 | | |
| Combes, William | | | 3 | | | Kellogg, Ezekiel | 1 | 2 | 6 | | | Falmon, Benjamin | 1 | 2 | 6 | | |
| Center, Agnes | 1 | 1 | 4 | | | Love, William | 1 | | 2 | | | Birdwell, John | 1 | 1 | 2 | | |

35201—08——4

# FIRST CENSUS OF THE UNITED STATES.

## HARTFORD COUNTY—Continued.

| NAME OF HEAD OF FAMILY. | Free white males of 16 years and upward, including heads of families. | Free white males under 16 years. | Free white females, including heads of families. | All other free persons. | Slaves. | NAME OF HEAD OF FAMILY. | Free white males of 16 years and upward, including heads of families. | Free white males under 16 years. | Free white females, including heads of families. | All other free persons. | Slaves. | NAME OF HEAD OF FAMILY. | Free white males of 16 years and upward, including heads of families. | Free white males under 16 years. | Free white females, including heads of families. | All other free persons. | Slaves. |
|---|---|---|---|---|---|---|---|---|---|---|---|---|---|---|---|---|---|
| SIMSBURY TOWN—con. | | | | | | SIMSBURY TOWN—con. | | | | | | SIMSBURY TOWN—con. | | | | | |
| Mountain, Jonathain | 1 | | 5 | | | Hendrick, Philemon | 2 | | 4 | | | Barnard, Ebenezer | 1 | 2 | 3 | | |
| Phelps, Noah | 4 | 1 | 2 | | | Edgerton, Jonathan | 1 | 1 | 2 | | | Barnard, Samuel | 2 | 3 | 4 | | |
| Ensign, Isaac | 3 | 4 | 4 | | | Edgerton, Jedediah | 1 | 1 | 2 | | | Barnard, Frances | 2 | 4 | 3 | | |
| Weston, Noah | 1 | | 1 | | | Case, Seth | 2 | 2 | 5 | | | Adams, William | 1 | 2 | 6 | | |
| Pennyfur, Darius | 1 | 1 | 4 | | | Case, Amasa, Jr | 2 | 4 | 3 | | | Eno, Samuel | 1 | | 2 | | |
| Pettibone, Jacob | 2 | 1 | 3 | | | Tuller, Reuben | 1 | 1 | 6 | | | Gillitt, Joab | 1 | 1 | 5 | | |
| Payson, John | 1 | 1 | 8 | | | Willcocks, Roswold | 1 | | 2 | | | Piney, Abraham | 3 | 7 | 9 | | |
| Robe, Andrew | 1 | | 2 | | | Case, Moses | 1 | 1 | 7 | | | Tuller, James | 1 | | 2 | 1 | |
| Smith, Ebenezer | 1 | 3 | 4 | | | Buell, Solomon, Jr | 1 | 4 | 3 | | | Tuller, Eli | 2 | | 4 | | |
| Bidwell, James | 1 | 3 | 2 | | | Buell, Solomon | 2 | 2 | 3 | | | Eno, Joel | 3 | | 4 | | |
| Woodbridge, Theodore | 1 | 2 | 3 | | | Buell, William | 1 | 1 | 2 | | | Woodford, Solomon | 1 | 4 | 3 | | |
| Case, Reuben | 1 | 3 | 4 | | | Thomas, David | 1 | 2 | 5 | | | Kilbourn, Timothy | 2 | | 1 | | |
| Robbs, Phineas | 1 | 1 | 3 | | | Buell, William | 1 | 1 | 2 | | | Case, Caleb | 4 | 1 | 3 | | |
| Case, Jonathan | 2 | 1 | 1 | | | Case, Thomas | 1 | | 1 | | | Case, George | 1 | 3 | 3 | | |
| Stebins, Rev'd Samuel | 3 | 1 | 3 | | | Wells, Israel | 1 | | 2 | | | Case, Alexander | 1 | 3 | 4 | | |
| Case, Israel | 1 | 3 | 3 | | | More, Arcena | 1 | 2 | 1 | | | Barber, Thomas, 3d | 2 | 2 | 3 | | |
| Case, Isaac | 1 | 1 | 3 | | | Robe, Andrew, Jr | 1 | 1 | 4 | | | Case, Zenas | 4 | 2 | 3 | | |
| Phelps, Jonathan | 3 | 2 | 1 | | | Andrus, Jacob | 4 | 4 | 4 | | | Case, Benjamin | 2 | | 4 | | |
| Bird, Amy | 1 | 2 | 3 | | | Grimes, Joseph | 2 | | 3 | | | Brown, Eleazer | 1 | 2 | 3 | | |
| Andrus, William | 1 | | 3 | | | Fletcher, John | 2 | 3 | 5 | | | Foot, Elisha | 2 | 2 | 7 | | |
| Witch, Benjamin | 1 | | 2 | | | Case, Abel | 1 | 2 | 2 | | | Case, Ashbel | 1 | 4 | 2 | | |
| Pettibone, Dudley | 2 | 1 | 3 | | | Case, Asa | 1 | 2 | 5 | | | Goodwin, Joseph | 2 | 3 | 5 | | |
| Eddington, Isaac | 2 | | 4 | | | Jutson, Elisha | 1 | 2 | 1 | | | Foot, Grove | 1 | 3 | 1 | | |
| Humphrey, Jonathan | 2 | 1 | 5 | 1 | | Phelps, Daniel, Jr | 1 | 3 | 4 | | | Roberts, Lemuel | 2 | 2 | 6 | | |
| Pettibone, Jonathan | 2 | 6 | 4 | | 1 | Bacon, Daniel | 1 | 2 | 2 | | | Roberts, Nathaniel | 2 | 2 | 5 | | |
| Tuller, Joseph | 2 | 1 | 2 | | | Barber, Joel | 3 | 1 | 4 | | | Fitch, Selah | 1 | | 1 | | |
| Smith, James | 3 | 3 | 2 | | | Barber, Joel, Jr | 1 | | 3 | | | Case, Josiah | 1 | 4 | 3 | | |
| Case, Bartholomew | 3 | 5 | 2 | | | Tuller, Jacob | 3 | | 3 | | | Willcocks, Daniel | 3 | 3 | 4 | | |
| Tuller, Abel | 1 | | 4 | | | Bud, Abijah | 2 | 1 | 3 | | | Marshall, Alexander | 1 | 1 | 3 | | |
| Case, Roger | 3 | | 7 | | | Seward, Charles | 1 | 2 | 5 | | | Moses, Timothy | 2 | 1 | 3 | | |
| Petibone, Joseph | 3 | 2 | 6 | | | Priest, Asa | 1 | 1 | 3 | | | Adams, Hosea | 1 | 2 | 2 | | |
| Petibone, Abel | 2 | | 4 | | | Lilley, Moses | 2 | 2 | 4 | | | Nall, Mock | 1 | 1 | 4 | | |
| Tuller, Elisha | 4 | 1 | 3 | | | Higley, Isaac | 1 | 1 | 4 | | | Fox, John | 1 | | 1 | | |
| Latemore, Wait | 4 | 1 | 2 | | | Onsted, Daniel | 1 | 1 | 2 | | | Bliss, Ebenezer | 1 | 2 | 2 | | |
| Case, Benajah | 3 | 2 | 5 | | | Hill, Elijah | 1 | 1 | 4 | | | Case, Darius | 1 | 1 | 4 | | |
| Case, Jediah, Jr | 2 | 1 | 4 | | | Grant, Joshua | 1 | 2 | 5 | | | Adams, David, Jr | 1 | | 2 | | |
| Case, Jediah | 2 | 1 | 3 | | | Case, Isaac, Jr | 3 | 1 | 4 | | | Adams, David | 2 | | 2 | | |
| Pettibone, Abijah | 1 | | 3 | | | Case, Solomon | 2 | 1 | 5 | | | Adams, Ezra | 2 | 2 | 4 | | |
| Filer, Asa | 1 | 1 | 2 | | | Tuller, Elijah | 1 | 1 | 5 | | | Adams, George | 1 | 1 | 2 | | |
| Willcocks, Isaac | 1 | | 1 | | | Tullar, Joel | 1 | 1 | 3 | | | Willcocks, Jedediah | 1 | 2 | 2 | | |
| Hiccock, Daniel | 1 | | 1 | | | Tillotson, Zenas | 1 | | 1 | | | Priest, Darius | 1 | 2 | 3 | | |
| Wilcocks, Elijah | 3 | 2 | 7 | | | Tullar, Elijah, Jr | 1 | 1 | 3 | | | Grimes, Elisha | 4 | | 4 | | |
| Woodford, Levi | 1 | 1 | 2 | | | Wilcocks, Elijah, Jr | 1 | 1 | 2 | | | Grimes, Elisha, Jr | 2 | | 3 | | |
| Phelps, Samuel | 3 | 3 | 2 | | | Willcocks, Simeon | 1 | 1 | 2 | | | Adams, Sarah (Wid.) | 2 | | 6 | | |
| Phelps, Daniel | 1 | 2 | 3 | | | Willcocks, Elisha | 4 | 1 | 2 | | | Foot, John | 1 | 1 | 2 | | |
| Grant, Joshua | 1 | 3 | 4 | | | Higley, Simeon | 1 | 1 | 6 | | | Foot, John, Jr | 1 | 2 | 2 | | |
| Hill, Jediah | 1 | 1 | 2 | | | Higley, Bruster | 1 | | 1 | | | Brown, Hannah (Wid.) | 3 | 1 | 4 | | |
| Onsted, Daniel, Jr | 1 | 3 | 3 | | | Higley, Enoch | 1 | 1 | 3 | | | Case, Ephraim B | 1 | 1 | 2 | | |
| Hiccock, Helener (Wd) | | 3 | 2 | | | Terry, Solomon | 4 | 2 | 4 | | | Moses, Daniel | 1 | 3 | 2 | | |
| Barber, Jared | 1 | | 1 | | | Higley, Seth | 3 | 2 | 6 | | | Moses, Aaron | 2 | | 3 | | |
| Barber, Martha (Wid.) | | | 4 | | | Wilcock, Roger | 2 | 3 | 5 | | | Spencer, Caleb | 2 | 1 | 2 | | |
| Alford, Nathaniel, Jr | 1 | 1 | 1 | | | Case, Martin | 1 | 1 | 2 | | | Clarkland, James | 2 | | 2 | | |
| Humphrey, Margeret (Wid.) | 2 | 4 | 4 | | | Yates, John | 1 | | | | | Buttles, Joseph | 1 | 1 | 3 | | |
| Dealy, Jeremiah | 1 | 1 | 1 | | | Cotton, Eliakim | 1 | 2 | 1 | | | Latimore, Jiles | 3 | 3 | 3 | | |
| More, Jacob | 1 | | 2 | | | Adan, Oliver | 3 | 1 | 2 | | | Malson, Asa | 3 | 1 | 2 | | |
| Humphrey, Michael | 2 | 1 | 2 | | | Haskings, Shubael | 5 | | 3 | | | Willcox, Amos | 1 | 3 | 3 | | |
| Alderman, Eli | 1 | 2 | 3 | | | St. John, Elijah | 2 | 1 | 2 | | | Latimore, Jonathan | 3 | 1 | 7 | | |
| Hill, Eliazer | 2 | 1 | 2 | | | Russell, Jesse | 1 | 2 | 4 | | | Humphry, Ruggles | 1 | 1 | 2 | | |
| Alderman, Jonathan | 1 | 1 | 1 | | | Olmsted, Francis | 1 | 2 | 1 | | | Spencer, Roswell | 1 | 3 | 3 | | |
| Alderman, James | 1 | 2 | 3 | | | Case, Aaron, 2d | 1 | | 2 | | | Willcocks, Robert | 1 | | 3 | 1 | |
| Alderman, Jonathan, Jr | 1 | | 2 | | | Wilcox, Aaron | 4 | 1 | 2 | | | Mills, Ezekiel | 4 | 1 | 2 | | |
| Adans, Timothy | 1 | 1 | 5 | | | Case, Joseph | 3 | 1 | 2 | | | Grimes, Daniel, Jr | 1 | 3 | 2 | | |
| Alderman, Thomas | 3 | | 4 | | | Laurence, Samuel | 1 | | 2 | | | Grimes, Daniel | 4 | 1 | 2 | | |
| Thomas, Samuel | 1 | 3 | 4 | | | Andrus, Jonathan | 1 | 2 | 3 | | | Adans, William | 1 | | 3 | | |
| Andrews, Asahel | 1 | | | | | Tullar, Samuel | 3 | 4 | 3 | | | Willcox, Ira | 1 | | 2 | | |
| Humphrey, Levi | 1 | | 3 | | | Cornish, Daniel K | 1 | | 2 | | | Willcox, Charles | 1 | 2 | 5 | | |
| Reed, Silas | 2 | 5 | 2 | | | Higley, Sylvester | 1 | | 1 | | | Willcox, William | 1 | 5 | 2 | | |
| Adams, Roderic | 2 | 5 | 2 | | | Pinney, Aaron | 3 | 3 | 2 | | | Beach, Elihu | 1 | 2 | 4 | | |
| Case, George, 2d | 1 | 2 | 3 | | | Pinney, Jonathan | 4 | 2 | 3 | | | Moses, Elihu | 4 | 1 | 4 | | |
| Case, Roswell | 1 | 3 | 2 | | | Pinney, Levi | 1 | | 2 | | | Curtis, Eliphalet | 2 | 2 | 2 | | |
| Hoskins, Ashbel | 1 | 2 | 4 | | | Cook, Eleazer | 1 | 4 | 2 | | | Curtis, Eliphalet, Jr | 2 | 3 | 4 | | |
| Hoskins, Asa | *2 | 2 | 3 | | | Todd, Ambrose | 1 | | 2 | | | Humphry, James | 1 | 1 | 1 | | |
| Tiffery, Humphrey | 1 | 2 | 4 | | | Loomis, Frances | 1 | 3 | 7 | | | Cavelu, Thomas | 1 | 1 | 4 | | |
| Hoskins, Daniel | 1 | 1 | 3 | | | Foster, Zacheus | 1 | 2 | 7 | | | Grimes, Isaac | 2 | 1 | 9 | | |
| Hoskins, Asa | 1 | | 2 | | | Mitchelson, Eliphalet | 4 | 4 | 3 | | | Case, Abraham | 3 | 3 | 5 | | |
| Hase, Zedikiah | 1 | 1 | 4 | | | Eno, Isaac | 1 | | 2 | | | Case, Fithin | 2 | 3 | 2 | 1 | |
| Hase, Benjamin | 1 | 1 | 1 | | | Eno, Ive | 1 | 2 | 4 | | | Humphry, Charles | 3 | 2 | 4 | | |
| Andrus, William | 2 | | 1 | | | Trall, Ezekiel | 2 | 3 | 6 | | | Case, Daniel | 3 | | 2 | | |
| Slater, Shered | 1 | 2 | 2 | | | Adams, Abel | 1 | 3 | 5 | | | Case, Zacheus | 2 | 3 | 2 | | |
| Well, Abijah | 1 | 2 | 2 | | | Adams, Mathew | 4 | 1 | 3 | | | Leit, Samuel | 3 | | 2 | | |
| Bulloph, Daniel | 1 | | 3 | | | Griswold, Elisha | 4 | 1 | 3 | | | Leit, Daniel A | 1 | | 3 | | |
| Bulloph, Benoni | 1 | 2 | 2 | | | Griswold, Elisha, Jr | 2 | 7 | 4 | | | Tuller, Isaac | 2 | | 3 | | |
| Tuller, Joseph, Jr | 2 | 2 | 4 | | | Pratt, Ezra | 1 | 1 | 3 | | | Case, Hosea | 2 | | 6 | | |
| Phelps, Ozias | 2 | 2 | 5 | | | Comes, Ebenezer | 1 | | 3 | | | Case, Joseph A | 2 | | 2 | | |
| Bacom, Maskel | 3 | 2 | 5 | | | Kilbourn, Lemuel | 1 | 2 | 3 | | | Bidwell, Thomas | 1 | | 1 | | |
| Hoskins, John | 1 | | 4 | | | Griswold, Alexander | 1 | | 2 | | | Willcocks, Ezra | 3 | 3 | 5 | | |
| Hoskins, David | 1 | 3 | 2 | | | Clark, Daniel | 1 | | 4 | | | Willcox, Isaac | 1 | 3 | 6 | | |
| Andrus, Hezekiah | 1 | 2 | 7 | | | Seger, Michael | 3 | 3 | 5 | | | Case, Isaac | 1 | 3 | 6 | 1 | |
| Hoskins, Ezra | 3 | 1 | 2 | | | Seger, Joseph | 3 | 2 | 3 | | | Anderson, Daniel | 2 | | 8 | | |
| Tuller, Samuel | 2 | 4 | 4 | | | Wilson, John | 1 | 1 | 3 | | | Noble, William | 1 | 3 | 5 | | |
| Bacon, Masket, Jr | 3 | 1 | 3 | | | Griswold, Joel | 3 | 1 | 3 | | | Till, Joseph | 1 | | 4 | | |
| Moses, Zebne | 1 | 2 | 4 | | | Eno, Reuben | 1 | 3 | 2 | | | Case, Elias | 1 | 2 | 3 | 1 | |
| Holcomb, Benajah | 1 | | 6 | | | Griswold, Elijah | 1 | | 2 | | | Dill, Solomon | 2 | 1 | 3 | | |
| Holcomb, Benajah, Jr | 1 | 3 | 2 | | | Hoskins, Robert | 2 | 2 | 4 | | | Dycer, Thomas | 2 | 1 | 3 | | |
| | | | | | | Case, Aaron | 1 | 2 | 4 | | | Dycer, Thomas, Jr | 1 | 1 | 1 | | |

# HEADS OF FAMILIES—CONNECTICUT.

## HARTFORD COUNTY—Continued.

| NAME OF HEAD OF FAMILY. | Free white males of 16 years and upward, including heads of families. | Free white males under 16 years. | Free white females, including heads of families. | All other free persons. | Slaves. | NAME OF HEAD OF FAMILY. | Free white males of 16 years and upward, including heads of families. | Free white males under 16 years. | Free white females, including heads of families. | All other free persons. | Slaves. | NAME OF HEAD OF FAMILY. | Free white males of 16 years and upward, including heads of families. | Free white males under 16 years. | Free white females, including heads of families. | All other free persons. | Slaves. |
|---|---|---|---|---|---|---|---|---|---|---|---|---|---|---|---|---|---|
| **SIMSBURY TOWN—con.** | | | | | | **SOUTHINGTON TOWN.** | | | | | | **SOUTHINGTON TOWN— continued.** | | | | | |
| Dycer, Solomon | 1 | 1 | 3 | | | Smith, David | 1 | 1 | 4 | | | Lewis, Jabish | 1 | 1 | 4 | | |
| Humphrey, Frederic | 1 | 6 | 4 | | | Smith, Harvey | 1 | | 1 | | | Dunham, Cornelius | 2 | 3 | 7 | | |
| Adams, Benjamin | 2 | 1 | 5 | | | Smith, Simeon | 1 | 1 | 2 | | | Gridley, Asahel | 1 | 2 | 2 | | |
| Bacon, Frances | 2 | 3 | 2 | | | Potter, Paullinus | 1 | 1 | 3 | | | Smith, Ezariah | 1 | | 3 | | |
| Case, Ozias | 1 | 3 | 3 | | | Toot, Robert | 1 | 3 | 3 | | | Case, Jonathan | 1 | 1 | 5 | | |
| Case, Jerre | 2 | 2 | 2 | | | Smith, David, Jr | 3 | 5 | 5 | | | Carrington, Samuel | 1 | | 1 | | |
| Case, Daniel | 2 | 4 | 4 | | | Tyler, Jacob | 4 | 3 | 2 | | | Carrington, Samuel, Jr | 1 | 2 | 2 | | |
| Humphrey, Ezkiel, Jr | 1 | | 1 | | | Root, Joel | 1 | | 3 | | | Clark, Silas | 2 | 2 | 3 | | |
| Dyer, Daniel | 2 | 2 | 4 | | | Bunnel, Joseph | 2 | | 1 | | | Clark, Ezra | 1 | | 2 | | |
| Dycer, Benjamin | 1 | 2 | 1 | | | Woodruff, Lydia | 1 | | 3 | | | M<sup>c</sup>Kein, James | 1 | 1 | 3 | | |
| Dyer, Daniel | 2 | 2 | 4 | | | Woodruff, Samuel | 3 | | 4 | | | Hunt, Joel | 1 | 1 | 3 | | |
| Humphrey, Ezekiel | 2 | 3 | 6 | 1 | | Potter, Rhoda | | | 2 | | | Peck, Eliakim | 1 | | 1 | | |
| Garrett, Frances | 2 | 3 | 2 | | | Woodruff, Jonathan | 2 | 1 | 1 | | | Peck, Thomas | 1 | | 1 | | |
| Garrett, Rufus | 2 | 4 | 3 | | | Woodruff, Elisha | 2 | 4 | 5 | | | Peck, Eliakim, Jr | 1 | 3 | 2 | | |
| Humphrey, Samuel | 3 | 1 | 5 | | | Hash, David | 1 | | 2 | | | Peck, Isaac | 1 | 2 | 3 | | |
| Humphrey, Oliver | 3 | 5 | 2 | | | Rice, Mathew | 1 | | 5 | | | Peck, Selah | 1 | 1 | 1 | | |
| Humphrey, Samuel | 1 | 1 | 4 | | | Leavingston, John | 1 | | 2 | | | Beckwith, Mervin | 1 | 4 | 5 | | |
| Gleason, Chancey | 2 | 1 | 2 | 2 | | Tish, Solomon | 1 | 1 | 3 | | | Brunson, Benjamin | 1 | | 2 | | |
| Firbbs, Alisha | 2 | 2 | 2 | | | Tish, Isaac | 1 | 1 | 1 | | | Hart, Roswell | 2 | | 3 | | |
| Alford, Nathaniel | 2 | 2 | 4 | | | Curtiss, Samuel | 3 | 3 | 4 | 1 | | Hart, John | 1 | | 1 | | |
| Mills, Jared | 2 | 4 | 5 | | | Root, James | 1 | | 5 | | | Hart, John, Jr | 1 | 3 | 4 | | |
| Case, Daniel | 2 | 4 | 1 | | | Root, Stephen | 1 | 1 | 1 | | | Andrews, Jonathan | 1 | | 1 | | |
| Case, Dudley | 2 | | 2 | | | Day, Horatior | 1 | 3 | 2 | | | Andrews, Jonathan, Jr | 2 | 1 | 3 | | |
| Tuller, Amasa | 1 | 1 | 2 | | | Lewis, Hart | 2 | 3 | 4 | | | Barnes, John | 1 | | 3 | | |
| Higley, Obed | 1 | 1 | 3 | | | Tryon, John | 1 | 4 | 6 | | | Hart, Amos | 2 | 1 | 2 | | |
| Taylor, Noadiah | 2 | 1 | 3 | | | Norton, Charles | 3 | 3 | 3 | | | Hart, Chancey | 1 | 1 | 1 | | |
| Case, Elisha | 3 | 3 | 5 | | | Day, Stanley | 1 | 4 | 2 | | | Bradley, Nehemiah | 1 | 1 | 2 | | |
| Case, Truman | 1 | | 2 | | | Norton, Elnathan | 1 | 2 | 4 | | | Palmer, Judah | 1 | 2 | 2 | | |
| Harrington, Hezekiah | 1 | 1 | 6 | | | Ives, Samuel | 1 | 2 | 3 | | | Clark, Ephraim | 2 | 1 | 5 | | |
| Merring, Moam | 1 | 2 | 5 | | | Lyman, Noah | 1 | | 2 | | | Sloper, Hannah | 2 | | 2 | | |
| Seager, Joseph, Jr | 4 | | 4 | | | Wheador, Thomas | 1 | 1 | 7 | | | Sloper, Ursula (Wid.) | 1 | 1 | 3 | | |
| Seager, Elijah | 1 | 4 | 1 | | | Newill, John | 1 | 3 | 4 | | | Pardee, David | 1 | 1 | 3 | | |
| Crocker, John | 3 | 2 | 4 | | | Tisdale, William | 1 | 3 | 2 | | | Newill, Charles | 1 | 2 | 2 | | |
| Barber, Michael | 1 | 1 | 1 | | | Newill, Josiah | 1 | 1 | 1 | | | Larking, Scovill | 1 | 2 | 2 | | |
| Humphrey, Ichabod | 1 | 1 | 1 | | | Newill, Amos | 1 | 1 | 2 | | | Coles, Tho<sup>s</sup> | 2 | 1 | 5 | | |
| Petibone, David | 1 | | 3 | | | Johnson, Barnabas | 1 | | 1 | | | Barnes, Allyn | 1 | | 1 | | |
| Hoskins, Abel | 1 | 1 | 1 | | | Bradley, Dan | 2 | 4 | 2 | 1 | | Johnson, Stephen | 2 | 4 | 3 | | |
| Hubbard, Thaddeus | 1 | 2 | 1 | | | Durham, Silvanus | 4 | 2 | 3 | | | Hitchcock, Samuel | 1 | 1 | 4 | | |
| Barber, Thomas | 2 | 2 | 4 | | | Peck, Eleazer | 2 | | 2 | | | Hitchcock, Samuel, Jr | 1 | 3 | 2 | | |
| Barber, Elijah | 1 | 2 | 4 | | | Hungerford, John | 1 | 4 | 2 | | | Hitchcock, Caleb | 1 | 2 | 4 | | |
| Barber, Jesse | 1 | 2 | 2 | | | Bradley, Hemingway | 1 | | 2 | | | Lewis, William | 1 | | 1 | | |
| Barber, Samuel | 3 | 1 | 3 | | | More, Roswell | 1 | | 2 | | | Atwater, Herman | 1 | 1 | 3 | | |
| Barber, John | 1 | | 2 | | | Bradley, Ichabod | 1 | | 2 | | | Mathews, Moses, Jr | 1 | 5 | 4 | | |
| Barber, Jonathan | 1 | 1 | 2 | | | More, Roswell, Jr | 2 | 2 | 1 | | | Hitchcok, Amos | 1 | | 2 | | |
| Humphrey, Theophilus | 1 | 3 | 4 | | | Judd, Eunice | | | 2 | 1 | | Andrews, Thomas | 1 | | 1 | | |
| Taylor, William | 2 | 1 | 4 | | | Lewis, Isaac | 1 | | 3 | | | Andrews, Josiah | 2 | | 6 | 1 | |
| Taylor, Ozias | 1 | 1 | 5 | | | Winchell, Dan | 1 | 1 | 2 | | | Parsons, Amos | 1 | | 1 | | |
| Bacon, Joseph | 1 | 2 | 3 | | | Dunham, Solomon | 1 | 1 | 3 | | | Barrett, Benjamin | 3 | | 6 | | |
| Barber, John, Jr | 1 | 3 | 6 | | | Munson, Solomon | 1 | | 2 | | | Potter, Martin | 1 | | 1 | | |
| Case, Hosea, Jr | 1 | 1 | 2 | | | Munson, Jeros | 1 | | 1 | | | Munson, Esther | 1 | 1 | 2 | | |
| Messinger, Isaac | 3 | | 6 | | | Smith, Isaac | 2 | 1 | 4 | | | Barnes, Jon<sup>a</sup>, Sen<sup>r</sup> | 1 | | 2 | | |
| Barber, Michael | 1 | 2 | 3 | | | Bradley, Nathaniel | 1 | 3 | 3 | | | Royal, Jonathan | 1 | 1 | 2 | | |
| Humphrey, Abram | 1 | 1 | 1 | | | Bradley, James | 1 | | 3 | | | Deming, Selah | 1 | | 1 | | |
| Taylor, Ruth (Wid.) | | | 1 | | | Judd, Immer | 1 | | 1 | | | Lewis, Job | 3 | 2 | 3 | | |
| Barber, Reuben | 1 | 4 | 4 | | | Judd, Immer | 1 | 4 | 3 | | | Lewis, Seth | 1 | | 2 | | |
| Mills, Amasa | 2 | | 4 | | | Hazard, Stuart | 2 | 4 | 2 | | | Curtiss, Jeremiah | 1 | | 2 | | |
| Hillick, Jeremiah | 1 | 2 | 4 | | | Finch, Elam | 1 | 3 | 1 | | | Curtiss, Jonathan | 3 | 2 | 2 | | |
| Mills, Ephraim | 1 | 3 | 4 | | | Mass, Elihu | 1 | 2 | 1 | | | Robertson, William | 3 | 2 | 1 | 1 | 1 |
| Barber, Bildad | 3 | 3 | 4 | | | Dayton, Israel | 1 | 1 | 2 | | | Chapman, Levi | 1 | | 3 | | 1 |
| Taylor, John E | 1 | | 2 | | | James (Negro) | | | | 2 | | Lewis, Timothy | 2 | 4 | 4 | | |
| Adkins, Josiah | 1 | 2 | 5 | | | Clark, Enos | 2 | 2 | 4 | | | Atkins, Charles | 1 | 2 | 2 | | |
| Roberts, Anna (Wid.) | | | 2 | | | Pratt, Stephen | 1 | 2 | 3 | | | Atkins, Abigail | | | 3 | | |
| Eno, Abel | 1 | | 1 | | | Pratt, Christopher | 1 | 2 | 1 | | | Allyn, Daniel | 1 | 1 | 5 | | |
| Piney, Darius | 1 | 1 | 1 | | | Webster, Philologus | 1 | 2 | 2 | | | Root, Jonathan | 1 | | 2 | | |
| Kingson, Joseph | 3 | 2 | 4 | | | Wilcox, Justus | 1 | 1 | 2 | | | Root, Jonathan, Jr | 2 | 1 | 1 | 1 | 1 |
| Simons, Reuben | 3 | | 2 | | | Beckwith, Harey | 1 | | 2 | | | Andrus, Samuel | 1 | 1 | 6 | | |
| Fosbury, John | 1 | 4 | 2 | | | Andrews, Josiah, Jr | 1 | 3 | 2 | | | Hart, Levi | 2 | 3 | 6 | | |
| Enos, David | 2 | | 3 | | | Woodruff, Asa | 1 | 1 | 4 | | | Lee, Timothy | 1 | 5 | 6 | | |
| Willcox, George | 1 | 1 | 1 | | | Graniss, Aaron | 1 | 2 | 2 | | | Church, Samuel | 1 | 4 | 2 | | |
| Burdec, George | 1 | 4 | 2 | | | Frisbee, Ichabod | 2 | 2 | 1 | | | Andrus, Obadiah | 1 | | 1 | | |
| Bacon, James | 1 | 5 | 4 | | | Cogswell, David | 3 | | 2 | | | Andrus, Eleazer | 3 | 1 | 2 | | |
| Johnson, William | 1 | | | 3 | | Cogswell, David, Jr | 1 | | 3 | | | Peck, David | 2 | 3 | 5 | | |
| Richards, Sarah (Wid.) | 1 | 1 | 2 | | | Langton, Daniel, Jr | 2 | | 4 | | | Wadsworth, Theodore | 3 | 1 | 2 | | |
| Richards, Samuel | 1 | | 1 | | | Langton, Daniel | 3 | 1 | 4 | | | Howd, Whitehead | 4 | | 3 | | |
| Humphrey, Solomon | 2 | 1 | 2 | | | Langton, Job | 1 | | 2 | | | Clark, Elisha | 1 | 1 | 3 | | |
| Thomas, Solomon | 1 | | 2 | | | Langton, Asahel | 1 | 1 | 1 | | | White, Isaac | 2 | 5 | 2 | | |
| Case, Edward | 1 | 2 | 5 | | | Langton, Ruth | | | | 2 | | Crittenton, Nathaniel | 1 | 2 | 4 | | |
| Case, Solomon | 1 | 2 | 3 | | | Gridley, Joseph | 2 | 2 | 2 | | | Hitchcock, Josiah | 1 | 2 | 3 | | |
| Case, Timothy | 1 | 1 | 4 | | | Gridley, Ard | 1 | | 1 | | | Hitchcock, Ambrose | 1 | | 2 | | |
| Case, Jacob | 4 | 1 | 3 | | | Gridley, Ashbel | 1 | | 3 | | | Woodruff, Jason | 1 | 2 | 3 | | |
| Case, Jessee | 2 | 2 | 5 | | | Gridley, Noah | 1 | | 3 | | | Dawson, Timothy | 1 | 2 | 2 | | |
| Case, Elias | 4 | 3 | 4 | | | Mertin, Jethro | | | | 2 | | Curtiss, Ezekiel | 1 | 2 | 2 | | |
| Case, Abel | 1 | 3 | 3 | | | Newill, Simeon | 1 | 2 | 3 | | | Clark, Ithurill | 1 | | 4 | | |
| Case, Silas | 1 | 4 | 3 | | | Gridley, Elisha | 1 | 2 | 2 | | | Clark, Lewis | | 1 | 1 | | |
| Case, Simeon | 1 | | 1 | | | Munson, Stephen | 1 | 2 | 1 | | | Carter, Jacob | 1 | | 1 | | |
| Crocker, John | 2 | 2 | 3 | | | Deming, Mertain | 1 | | 1 | | | Carter, Levi | 1 | | 1 | | |
| Mills, Gideon | 2 | 2 | 7 | | | Newill, Mark | 1 | 6 | | | | Carter, Elihu | 2 | | 2 | | |
| Hill, John | 1 | | 4 | | | Deming, Lucy | 2 | | 2 | | | Crittenton, Amos | 1 | 1 | 1 | | |
| Hill, Jedediah | 1 | 3 | 1 | | | Whitcomb, Hiram | 2 | 2 | 3 | | | Woodruff, Levi | 1 | 3 | 3 | | |
| Moses, Abram | 2 | 2 | 3 | | | Newill, Pomeroy | 1 | 1 | 6 | | | Smith, James | 1 | | 2 | | |
| Hill, Darius | 1 | 3 | 4 | | | Newill, Isaac | 1 | | 5 | | | Jones, Nathaniel | 3 | 3 | 4 | | 1 |
| Humphrey, Jonathan | 2 | 1 | 6 | | | Newill, Isaac, Jr | 1 | 3 | 5 | | | Brunson, Silas | 1 | 3 | 3 | | |
| Case, Uriah | 2 | 3 | 8 | | | Langton, Seth | 2 | 1 | 3 | | | Barnes, Nathan, 3<sup>d</sup> | 1 | 3 | 3 | | |
| Cornish, Daniel King | 1 | | 2 | | | Curtiss, Solomon | 3 | 2 | 6 | | | Page, Ranor | 1 | 3 | 2 | | |

## HARTFORD COUNTY—Continued.

| NAME OF HEAD OF FAMILY. | Free white males of 16 years and upward, including heads of families. | Free white males under 16 years. | Free white females, including heads of families. | All other free persons. | Slaves. | NAME OF HEAD OF FAMILY. | Free white males of 16 years and upward, including heads of families. | Free white males under 16 years. | Free white females, including heads of families. | All other free persons. | Slaves. | NAME OF HEAD OF FAMILY. | Free white males of 16 years and upward, including heads of families. | Free white males under 16 years. | Free white females, including heads of families. | All other free persons. | Slaves. |
|---|---|---|---|---|---|---|---|---|---|---|---|---|---|---|---|---|---|
| **SOUTHINGTON TOWN— continued.** | | | | | | **SOUTHINGTON TOWN— continued.** | | | | | | **SOUTHINGTON TOWN— continued.** | | | | | |
| Beacher, Nathan | 1 | 1 | 2 | | | Thrash, Oliver | 2 | 2 | 1 | | | Coles, Calvin | 2 | | 6 | | |
| Graniss, Joel | 2 | 2 | 4 | | | Adkins, Samuel | 1 | 3 | 5 | | | Gillett, Nathan | 1 | 2 | 4 | | |
| Clark, John | 1 | | 1 | | | Neal, John | 1 | 2 | 2 | | | Gillett, Zachariah | 1 | 1 | 6 | | |
| Hart, Samuel | 1 | 1 | 2 | | | Merriman, Chancey | 1 | 3 | 4 | | | Hall, Heman | 1 | 2 | 7 | | |
| Carter, Daniel | 1 | 3 | 3 | 2 | | Whitman, Jonathan | 2 | | 3 | | | Harrison, David | 1 | 3 | 4 | | |
| Woodruff, John, Jr | 1 | 4 | 2 | | | Jude, Ellin | 2 | | 4 | | | Harrison, Mark | 1 | 3 | 5 | | |
| Woodruff, John | 1 | 2 | 2 | | | Neal, Timothy | 1 | | 1 | | | Mathews, Epaphras | 3 | | 1 | | |
| Squires, Samuel | 3 | 1 | 2 | | | Neal, Elijah | 1 | 2 | 2 | | | Hall, Curtiss | 2 | 1 | 6 | | |
| Blakely, Laban | 1 | 2 | 2 | | | Merriman (Wid.) | | | 5 | | | Barnes, Nathan | 1 | | 2 | | |
| Graniss, Stephen | 2 | 2 | 3 | | | Durin, Jonathan | 1 | | 1 | | | Tuttle, Zenas | 1 | | 2 | | |
| Mathews, Moses | 1 | | 1 | | | Durin, Noah | 1 | 2 | 1 | | | Johnson, Daniel, Jr | 1 | 1 | 1 | | |
| Cook, Martin | 1 | 1 | 2 | | | Plant, James | 1 | 3 | 4 | | | | | | | | |
| Carter, Abel | 1 | 1 | 3 | | | Rerry, Solomon | 1 | | 3 | | | **SUFFIELD TOWN.** | | | | | |
| Carter, John | 2 | 4 | 3 | | | Upson, Josiah | 2 | | 3 | | | | | | | | |
| Dutton, Benjamin | 1 | | 1 | | | Boardman, Catharine | | 1 | 2 | | | Phelps, Oliver | 3 | 2 | 3 | | 2 |
| Dutton, Timothy | 1 | 2 | 2 | | | Bradley, Benjamin | 1 | 3 | 3 | | | King, Alexander | 4 | 1 | 5 | | |
| Dutton, Benjamin, Jr | 1 | | 2 | | | Goodsell, Samuel | 1 | 3 | 3 | | | Leavitt, John | 1 | | 1 | | |
| Brunson, Phineas | 1 | | 2 | | | Porter, Joshua | 1 | 2 | 5 | 3 | | Granger, Gideon | 1 | 1 | 2 | 1 | |
| Thompson (Wid.) | | 1 | 1 | | | Pardee, Samuel | 1 | | 4 | | | Sheldon, Phineas | 3 | | 3 | | |
| Peck, Joel | 2 | 1 | 3 | | | Alcock, Jesse | 2 | 1 | 5 | | | Leavitt, Thaddeus | 2 | 1 | 3 | | |
| Norton, Ebenezer | 1 | 4 | 5 | | | Gerens, Russell | 1 | 3 | 2 | | | Granger, Amos | 1 | 3 | 2 | | |
| Durvin, Jonathan | 1 | 1 | 2 | | | Blakeley, Abner | 1 | 1 | 1 | | | Gay, Revd Ebenezer | 2 | | 2 | | 5 |
| Clark, Abraham | 1 | 2 | 2 | | | Churchill, David | 1 | 1 | 5 | | | Graham, Revd John | 1 | 2 | 1 | | |
| Bunnell, Amos | 1 | 1 | 3 | | | Baley, William | 1 | 4 | 2 | | | Hasting, Elder John | 4 | 1 | 4 | | |
| Clerk, Timothy | 2 | | 2 | | | Johnson, Ebenezer | 1 | | 2 | | | Granger, Zadoc | 2 | | 3 | | |
| Criessee, Gold | 2 | 1 | 3 | | | Baley, James | 1 | | 2 | | | Kent, Elihu | 2 | | 3 | | |
| Carter, Abel | 2 | 2 | 5 | | | Bruckot, Samuel | 2 | | 1 | | | Granger, John | 1 | | 2 | | |
| Dutton, Moses | 1 | 1 | 2 | | | Carter, Jacob, Jr | 3 | 2 | 4 | | | Hitchcock, Aaron | 1 | | 2 | | |
| Dutton, Joseph | 1 | 2 | 2 | | | Adkins, Chancey | 1 | 3 | 5 | | | Remington, Jona | 1 | | | | |
| Cook, Robert | 1 | | 2 | | | Sorith, Elkany | 1 | 2 | 5 | | | Granger, Abraham | 2 | 1 | 3 | | |
| Hall, Jacob | 1 | 2 | 2 | | | Wire, Daniel | 1 | 2 | 1 | | | Hanchett, Oliver | 5 | 1 | 5 | | |
| Bracket, Joel | 1 | | 2 | | | Duplax, Prince | | | | 5 | | King, Josiah | 3 | 1 | 3 | | |
| Dutton, Samuel | 1 | | 2 | | | Carter, Isaac | 1 | 3 | 2 | | | Sheldon, Simeon | 3 | 1 | 5 | | |
| Webster, Lucy | | | 3 | | | Powers, Barnabas | 1 | 1 | 3 | | | Pomeroy, Isaac | 2 | 3 | 3 | | |
| Brunson, Isaac | 1 | 2 | 2 | | | Neal, Noah | 2 | 1 | 2 | | | Lovijoy, Phineas | 2 | 1 | 5 | 1 | |
| Baldwin, Samuel | 1 | 2 | 3 | | | Clark, Israel | 1 | | 1 | | | Granger, Oliver | 2 | 4 | 5 | | |
| Hooker, Bryon | 2 | | 1 | | | Wire, Aaron | 3 | 2 | 3 | | | King, Ashbel | 4 | 3 | 2 | | |
| Hart, Varlines | 1 | | 3 | | | Rice, Elijah | 1 | 2 | 3 | | | Owen, Isaac | 3 | 1 | 6 | | |
| Coles, Ashbel | 2 | 2 | 3 | 1 | | Baley, James | 1 | 2 | 3 | | | Kent, John | 1 | 2 | 3 | | |
| Clark, Azenath | 1 | 2 | 2 | | | Smith, William | 1 | | 1 | | | Granger, Abner | 3 | | 7 | | |
| Dayton, Samuel | 1 | 3 | 4 | | | Beacher, Joseph | 2 | | 2 | | | Sheldon, Ebenezer | 2 | 2 | 4 | | |
| Woodruff, Phinas | 2 | 1 | 2 | | | Collins, Abel | 2 | | 2 | | | Loomis, Luther | 3 | 2 | 6 | | 2 |
| Fields, John | 1 | 2 | 2 | | | Pond, Moses | 2 | 3 | 3 | | | Phelps, Daniel | 1 | 2 | 3 | | |
| Pardee, Daniel | 1 | 1 | 2 | | | Johnson, Ebenezer | 1 | | 4 | | | Clark, Reuben | 1 | 3 | 3 | | |
| Ward, Rufus | 1 | 1 | 2 | | | Johnson, Levi | 1 | | 5 | | | Trumbul, Eli | 1 | 3 | 6 | | |
| Bray, Asa | 2 | 1 | 3 | | | Thornton, Samuel | 1 | 1 | 3 | | | King, Thaddeus | 2 | 3 | 2 | | |
| Bray, John | 1 | | 2 | | | Horton, Elisha | 1 | 2 | 4 | | | Williston, Consider | 3 | 2 | 2 | | |
| Woodruff, Robert | 1 | 1 | 5 | | | Beacher, Joseph, Jr | 1 | 2 | 2 | | | Hale, Samuel | 2 | 4 | 3 | | |
| Dickenson, George | 3 | 1 | 4 | | | Beacher, John | 2 | | | | | Notton, John | 2 | | 1 | | |
| Woodruff, Isaac | 2 | 1 | 5 | | | Beacher, Hezekiah | 1 | | 1 | | | Swan, Timothy | 1 | 1 | 3 | | |
| Woodruff, Obed | 1 | | 1 | | | Beacher, Erastus | 1 | | 1 | | | Austin, Seth | 1 | 1 | 4 | | 5 |
| Shepard, Samuel | 1 | | 2 | | | Scariott, Nathan | 1 | 2 | 3 | | | Granger, Gideon, 2d | 1 | 1 | 1 | | |
| Shepard, Samuel, Jr | 1 | | 3 | | | Scariott, James | 1 | 3 | 1 | | | Pease, Joseph | 5 | 1 | 5 | | 2 |
| Shepard, Nathaniel | 1 | 1 | 3 | | | Scariott, Jonathan | 1 | | 3 | | | Pease, Zeno | 1 | 1 | 4 | | |
| Hutson, Daniel | 2 | 2 | 2 | | | Bradley, Timothy | 3 | 2 | 5 | | | Pease, Seth | 2 | 2 | 2 | | |
| Sloper, Ambrose | 2 | | 2 | | | Bradley, Mise | 1 | 1 | 2 | | | Burbank, Seth | 1 | 2 | 1 | | |
| Lewis, Chancey | 1 | | 2 | | | Beacher, Amos | 2 | 2 | 3 | | | Granger, Charles | 4 | | 3 | | |
| Brunson, Joel | 1 | 2 | 1 | | | Robberts, Eli | 1 | | 2 | | | Hanchett, Ezra | 1 | 1 | 2 | | |
| Woodruff, Amos | 4 | | 5 | | | Plumb, Simeon | 3 | 1 | 3 | | | Leavitt, John, 2d | 1 | 2 | 3 | | |
| Newill, Samuel | 1 | 1 | 1 | | | Plum, Solomon | 1 | | 1 | | | Wilcocks, Ruth | | | 3 | | |
| Dickson, William | 2 | 1 | 5 | | | Beacher, Abel | 3 | | 5 | | | Wilcocks, Aaron | 1 | 3 | 2 | | |
| Hitchcock, Stephen | 2 | | 2 | | | Peck, Justus | 1 | 1 | 4 | | | Robbins, Ephraim | 2 | | 6 | | |
| Hart, Hawkins | 1 | | 2 | | | Peck, Elisha | 1 | 2 | 1 | | | Granger, Beldad, 2d | 1 | 1 | 1 | | |
| Woodruff, Mary | | | 2 | | | Beacher, Walter | 1 | 2 | 2 | | | Kent, Anna | 1 | | 2 | | |
| Barnes, Asa | 2 | 4 | 3 | 1 | | Finch, Gideon | 2 | 3 | 3 | | | Taylor, Gad | 4 | 2 | 6 | | |
| Barnes, William | 3 | | 4 | | | Minor, Joseph | 1 | 2 | 2 | | | Alden, Howard | 1 | | 3 | | |
| Barnes, Benjamin | 1 | 1 | 4 | | | Talmadge, Ichabod | 2 | | 4 | | | Field, Pardont | 1 | 1 | 2 | | |
| Barnes, Nathan, 2d | 1 | 1 | 1 | | | Linsley, Braniard | 1 | | 2 | | | Huntington, Hezekiah | 1 | 1 | 1 | | |
| Cowles, George | 1 | 2 | 2 | | | Upson, Thomas | 1 | 1 | | | | Kent, Elisha, 2d | 1 | 3 | 3 | | |
| Louse, Abram | 1 | 2 | 1 | | | Bracket, Zeure | 1 | 2 | 5 | | | Kent, Johnth Kellogg | 2 | 3 | 2 | | |
| Root, Josiah | 1 | 2 | 3 | | | Bracket, Amos | 1 | 3 | 2 | | | Kent, Hannah | | | 3 | | |
| Cowles, Josiah | 5 | 2 | 4 | | | Cleveland, Lemuel | 1 | 2 | 1 | | | Kent, Augustus | 1 | 3 | 5 | | |
| Upson, John | 3 | 4 | 5 | | | Smith, Joseph | 2 | 1 | 2 | | | Austin, Calvin | 2 | 2 | 4 | | |
| Smith, Samuel | 2 | 1 | 3 | | | Cleveland, Johnson | 1 | 1 | 4 | | | Thompson, Ardon | 2 | 3 | 4 | | |
| Hawley (Wid.) | | | 2 | | | Lane, Elijah | 1 | 2 | 4 | | | Sheldon, Martin | 2 | 2 | 3 | | |
| Persons, Abraham | 1 | | 1 | | | Lane, Joel | 1 | 2 | 2 | | | Sheldon, Jonathan | 2 | 1 | 4 | | |
| Upson, Amos | 5 | | 2 | | | Gillet, Ebenezer | 1 | 2 | 2 | | | Sheldon, Jonathan, Jr | 1 | 1 | 2 | | |
| Upson, Josiah | 2 | | 2 | | | Harrison, Jabez | 1 | 1 | 3 | | | Rice, Elezer | 2 | 1 | 6 | | |
| Upson, Timothy | 3 | 2 | 2 | | | Stephens, William | 1 | 2 | 2 | | | Phelps, Oliver | 1 | 1 | 3 | | |
| Moss, Theophilus | 1 | 2 | 2 | | | Hanson, Aaron | 2 | | 2 | | | Sheldon, Rachel | 2 | | 2 | | |
| Barnes, Nathaniel | 1 | | 3 | | | Potter, John | 1 | | 1 | | | Griswold, Collins | 2 | | 2 | | |
| Lewis, Nathan, Jr | 4 | 1 | 3 | | | Allcox, Daniel | 3 | | 6 | | | Sheldon, Benjamin | 1 | 1 | 3 | | |
| Lewis, Asahel | 3 | 1 | 2 | | | Stedman, Selah | 1 | 3 | 2 | | | Sheldon, Jacob | 2 | 3 | 4 | | |
| Merriman, Ebenezer | 3 | 5 | 3 | 1 | | Tuttle, Abraham | 1 | 2 | 2 | | | Sheldon, Daniel | 1 | | 2 | | |
| Lewis, Lemuel | 4 | 1 | 2 | | | Carter, Stephen | 1 | 1 | 2 | | | Sheldon, Gersham | 1 | 1 | 1 | | |
| Merriman, Pevis | 1 | 1 | 2 | | | Johnson, Daniel | 2 | 1 | 3 | | | King, Oliver | 2 | | 2 | | |
| Barnes, Nathaniel D | 1 | | 1 | | | Adkins, Luther | 2 | 1 | 5 | | | Harmon, Cephas | 2 | 1 | 1 | | |
| Hitchcock, David | 1 | | 8 | | | Brunson, John | 2 | 1 | 3 | | | Kent, Benajah | 1 | | 1 | | |
| Elwell, Isaac | 1 | 3 | 3 | | | Carter, Jonathan | 1 | 4 | 3 | | | Kent, Amos | 2 | | 2 | | |
| Noal, David | 2 | 2 | 2 | | | Barnes, Philimon | 1 | | 5 | | | Southwell, John | 1 | 2 | 5 | | |
| Finch, Joseph | 3 | 2 | 1 | | | Barnes, Mark | 1 | 1 | 2 | | | Austin, Caleb | 4 | 2 | 5 | | |
| Thrash, John | 1 | | 5 | | | Parker, Joseph | 2 | | 2 | | | Spencer, Eliphalet | 1 | | 5 | | |
| Thrash, Samuel | 2 | 3 | 3 | | | Upson, Isaac | 1 | 1 | 2 | | | Truesdall, Asa | 1 | 4 | 2 | | |
| Neal, Aaron | 1 | | 2 | | | Lewis, Nathaniel | 3 | 2 | 4 | | | Kent, Joseph | 2 | | 6 | | |
| Thrash, Reuben | 1 | 3 | 3 | | | Barnes, Farrington | 1 | | 2 | | | Hatheway, John | 1 | 1 | 2 | | |

# HEADS OF FAMILIES—CONNECTICUT.

## HARTFORD COUNTY—Continued.

### SUFFIELD TOWN—con.

| NAME OF HEAD OF FAMILY. | Free white males of 16 years and upward, including heads of families. | Free white males under 16 years. | Free white females, including heads of families. | All other free persons. | Slaves. |
|---|---|---|---|---|---|
| Lacey, Sizzardus | 1 | | | 4 | |
| Hathaway, Seth | 1 | 2 | 5 | | |
| Spencer, Rebeca | | 1 | 2 | | |
| Rising, Nathaniel, 2d | 1 | | 2 | | |
| Spencer, Hezekiah | 3 | 1 | 8 | | |
| Spencer, Daniel | 1 | | 4 | | |
| Palmer, Saul | | | | 4 | |
| Spencer, Augustus | 1 | 4 | 2 | | |
| Austin, Uriah | 1 | | 2 | | |
| Austin, Uriah, 2d | 2 | 1 | 2 | | |
| Remington, Benjamin | 2 | 2 | 4 | | |
| Remington, Isaac | 1 | 2 | 3 | | |
| Remington, Simeon | 1 | 2 | 3 | | |
| Pomeroy, Nathaniel | 1 | 2 | 2 | | |
| Remington, Asa | 3 | 1 | 4 | | 1 |
| Middleton, William | 1 | | 2 | | |
| Harmon, Phineas | 3 | | 3 | | |
| Sheldon, Oliver | 1 | 1 | 6 | | |
| Gillett, Daniel | 2 | 1 | 1 | | |
| Lacey, Jasper | 1 | 2 | 2 | | |
| Parsons, Oliver | 1 | 1 | 1 | | |
| Trumbull, Shadrack | 1 | 1 | 6 | | |
| Hale, Timothy | 1 | | 2 | | |
| Austins, Samuel | 3 | 1 | 2 | | |
| Rising, Jonathan | 4 | | 3 | | |
| Rising, Eli | 1 | 1 | 1 | | |
| Rising, Paul | 4 | 3 | 6 | | |
| Hathway, Ebenezer | 4 | | 2 | | |
| Todd, David | 2 | 3 | 5 | | 4 |
| Rowe, Moses | 1 | 4 | 4 | | |
| Rowe, John | 3 | 5 | 5 | | |
| Kirtland, John | 4 | | 5 | | |
| Bester, Daniel | 3 | 5 | 4 | | |
| Pierce, Luther | 1 | | 1 | | |
| Clevland, Frederic | 1 | | 8 | | |
| Hyde, Roger Eb'n | 1 | 3 | 2 | | |
| Hathaway, Asabel | 1 | 1 | 5 | | |
| Kellogg, Jonathan | 3 | | 2 | | |
| Pemberton, Thomas | 1 | 3 | 1 | | |
| Olds, Joseph | 1 | 1 | 1 | | |
| Lyman, Thaddeas | 1 | | 2 | | 1 |
| Olds, Josiah | 2 | | 2 | | |
| Olds, Josiah, 2nd | 2 | 4 | 2 | | |
| Phelps, Timothy | 5 | 2 | 2 | | |
| Phelps, Aaron | 3 | | 6 | | |
| Gunn, Elisha | 1 | 1 | 1 | | |
| King, David | 3 | 1 | 6 | | |
| Sheldon, John | 1 | | 1 | | |
| Sheldon, Josiah | 1 | 3 | 3 | | |
| Remington, Abijah | 1 | 2 | 4 | | |
| Peter (Negro) | | | | 3 | |
| Hastings, Benjamin | 2 | 3 | 5 | | |
| Remington, Elijah | 2 | 1 | 3 | | 1 |
| Allyn, Reuben, 2d | 1 | 1 | 2 | | |
| Allyn, Ebenezer | 1 | 1 | 5 | | |
| Allyn, Reuben | 1 | 3 | 5 | | |
| Leavitt, Enoch | 1 | 1 | 3 | | |
| Hastings, Abijah | 2 | 2 | 2 | | |
| Granger, Julius | 1 | 2 | 2 | | |
| Granger, Elijah | 2 | 2 | 7 | | |
| Remington, Amos | 1 | 3 | 4 | | |
| Hastings, Joseph | 2 | | 4 | | |
| Remington, Stephen | 1 | 2 | 9 | | |
| Remington, Hosea | 1 | 1 | 2 | | |
| Remington, Thomas | 1 | 2 | 5 | | |
| Barnard, Jacob | 1 | 1 | | | |
| Granger, Jacob | 1 | | 3 | | |
| Granger, Samuel | 2 | 1 | 4 | | |
| Hathway, Martin | 1 | 1 | 1 | | |
| Pomeroy, Amos | 1 | | 2 | | |
| Smith, Abisha | 1 | 2 | 2 | | |
| Pomeroy, John | 3 | 1 | 3 | | |
| Hathway, Samuel | 1 | | 2 | | |
| Hathway, Ebenezer | 1 | 2 | 2 | | |
| Hathway, John King | 1 | 6 | 3 | | |
| Hathway, Joel | 2 | 5 | 3 | | |
| Austin, Thomas | 3 | 3 | 3 | | |
| Smith, James | 1 | 3 | 4 | | |
| Smith, Ichabod | 1 | 2 | 5 | | |
| Smith, Seth | 3 | | 1 | | |
| Pomeroy, Asa | 1 | 3 | 4 | | |
| Pomeroy, Abigail | 1 | 1 | 3 | | |
| Palmer, Timothy | 2 | 1 | 8 | | |
| Mather, Increase | 4 | | 3 | | |
| Hoskins, Simeon | 1 | 1 | 2 | | |
| Spencer, Samuel | 3 | 2 | 3 | | |
| Street, James | 1 | 1 | 1 | | |
| Ives, John | 1 | | 2 | | |
| Rowes, Stephen | 1 | | 1 | | |
| Smith, Medad | 1 | 1 | 1 | | |
| Smith, Joseph | 2 | 1 | 9 | | |
| King, Joseph, 2d | 2 | 2 | 5 | | |
| Parsons, Ebenezer | 2 | 2 | 1 | | |
| Leavitt, Joshua | 2 | 2 | 3 | | |
| Monrow, Benjamin | 1 | | 3 | | |
| Hopkins, Jonathan | 3 | 1 | 2 | | |
| Barnard, Edmund | 3 | 2 | 6 | | |
| Addams, Zeb | 2 | | 1 | | |
| Addams, Zeb, 2d | 1 | 1 | 1 | | |
| Thompson, Mathew | 1 | 2 | 1 | | 1 |
| Sikes, Gideon | 1 | 1 | 3 | | |
| Woodcoalk, W'm | 3 | 1 | 1 | | |
| Grovener, Moses | 2 | 3 | 3 | | |
| Grovner, W'm | 1 | 1 | 1 | | |
| King, Jonathan | 1 | 1 | 3 | | |
| Perpoint, Joseph | 1 | 2 | 2 | | |
| French, John | 1 | 4 | 4 | | |
| Hall, Libeas | 1 | 1 | 1 | | |
| Adams, Zadock | 3 | 1 | 4 | | |
| Fowler, Bildad | 1 | 3 | 3 | | |
| Adams, Zadock, 2d | 1 | | 2 | | |
| Adams, Asabel | 1 | | 1 | | |
| Sykes, Victory | 1 | | 2 | | |
| Sykes, Samuel | 2 | 4 | 5 | | |
| Lane, Dan | 1 | | 1 | | |
| Allyn, Gidion | 1 | | 4 | | |
| Allyn, Gershom | 2 | 3 | 5 | | |
| Sykes, Paul | 1 | 2 | 3 | | |
| Sykes, David | 1 | 2 | 1 | | |
| Sykes, Victory, 2d | 1 | 4 | 1 | | |
| White, Nathan | 2 | 3 | 5 | | |
| Feany, William | 1 | | | | |
| Sykes, Lott | 2 | 2 | 4 | | |
| Sykes, Jonathan | 1 | 1 | 1 | | |
| Stiles, Chauncey | 1 | | 2 | | |
| Kent, Joel | 1 | 1 | 2 | | |
| Kent, Diana | 2 | 2 | 4 | | |
| Kent, Thomas | 1 | 4 | 2 | | |
| Adams, Samuel | 3 | 2 | 5 | | |
| Larnard, Amariah | 1 | 1 | 3 | | |
| Adams, Moses | 2 | 1 | 2 | | |
| Kindall, Simion | 1 | 3 | 2 | | 1 |
| Loomis, Nathaniel | 1 | 2 | 3 | | |
| Blunder, Samuel | 1 | 2 | 1 | | |
| Tobin, James | 2 | | 2 | | |
| Fuller, Joseph | 4 | | 3 | | |
| Granger, Benjamin | 2 | 1 | 2 | | |
| Lewis, John | 1 | 1 | 2 | | |
| Beebee, Ephraim | 1 | 3 | 1 | | |
| Lane, Gad | 1 | 5 | 3 | | |
| Kent, Seth, 2d | 1 | 3 | 1 | | |
| Gardner, Sherman | 1 | 2 | 3 | | |
| Kent, Zeno | 1 | 3 | 2 | | 1 |
| Kent, Seth | 1 | | 2 | | |
| Granger, Joseph | 1 | 1 | 2 | | |
| King, William | 2 | 1 | 4 | | |
| King, Seth | 1 | 2 | 3 | | |
| Beckwith, William | 1 | 4 | 4 | | |
| Norton, Seth | 1 | 6 | 3 | | |
| Dewy, John | 3 | | 3 | | |
| Tucker, Asa | 3 | | 3 | | |
| Norton, Daniel | 1 | | 2 | | |
| Rising, Nathaniel | 4 | | 5 | | |
| Rising, John | 1 | 4 | 3 | | |
| Smith, Eldad | 1 | | 1 | | |
| Parsely, Robert | 1 | | 1 | 1 | |
| Pero (Negro) | | | | 5 | |
| Howard, Joseph | 1 | | 3 | | |
| Parmeley, Elihu | 2 | 3 | 3 | | |
| Lewis, John, 2d | 1 | 1 | 2 | | |
| Lewis, John | 1 | 4 | 2 | | |
| Hathway, Charles | 3 | | 5 | | |
| Hathway, Thrall | 1 | 3 | 4 | | |
| Wootworth, Timothy | 1 | | 2 | | |
| Hathway, Charles, 2d | 1 | | 2 | | |
| M'cMorin, John | 2 | 2 | 4 | | |
| M'Moran, John, 2d | 1 | 1 | 5 | | |
| Hall, Nathaniel | 1 | 1 | 2 | | |
| Hall, John | 1 | | 2 | | |
| Spary, Elijah | 1 | 1 | 3 | | |
| Hough, Justin | 3 | 1 | 2 | | |
| Harmin, Benjamin, 2d | 2 | 3 | 4 | | |
| Spears, Moses | 2 | | 3 | | |
| Spears, Asabel | 1 | 1 | 3 | | |
| Pomeroy, Darkis | 1 | | 2 | | |
| Harmin, Benjamin | 1 | | 1 | | |
| Harmon, Abigail | 1 | 2 | 3 | | |
| King, Nathaniel | 2 | | 3 | | |
| King, Dan, 2d | 2 | 2 | 5 | | |
| Hitchcock, Chancey | 3 | 2 | 7 | | |
| Hanchett, Luke | 2 | | 7 | | |
| Hanchett, John | 1 | | 2 | | |
| Robbins, Elijah | 1 | 1 | 2 | | |
| Hanchett, David | 1 | 3 | 7 | | |
| Hanchett, John, 2d | 1 | 1 | 7 | | |
| Hubbard, Philip | 1 | | 1 | | |
| Austin, Joseph | 1 | | 4 | | |
| Austin, Joseph, 2d | 2 | 3 | 4 | | |
| Norton, John, 2d | 1 | 3 | 2 | | |
| Mark (Negro) | | | | 9 | |
| King, Joseph | 1 | | 2 | | |
| Wiggins, Josiah | 2 | 2 | 3 | | |
| Parsons, Reuben | 2 | | 4 | | |
| King, Isaac | 2 | 1 | 5 | | |
| Copty, Anna | 1 | | 2 | | |
| Graham, Daniel | 2 | | 1 | | |
| King, Gideon | 4 | | 3 | | |
| Harmon, Samuel | 2 | 3 | 6 | | |
| Sheldon, Elijah | 3 | | 3 | | |
| Wyman, Ebenezer | 2 | 1 | 5 | | |
| Gains, Samuel | 1 | 2 | 3 | | |
| Ingraham, Jeremiah, 2d | 1 | | 3 | | |
| Caton, Elizabeth | | | 2 | | |
| Harmon, Elias | 3 | 4 | 4 | | |
| Hale, Joseph | 1 | | 2 | | |
| Rowes, Gad | 1 | 4 | 3 | | |
| Spencer, Simeon | 1 | 2 | 3 | | |
| Spencer, John | 1 | 1 | 3 | | |
| Spencer, Reuben | 3 | 2 | 4 | | |
| Harmon, Ebenezer | 2 | 1 | 2 | | |
| Harmon, Israel | 1 | 3 | 3 | | |
| King, Theodore | 1 | 3 | 5 | | |
| Sheldon, Thomas | 1 | 2 | 2 | | |
| Gillett, Elihu | 1 | 1 | 1 | | |
| Pomeroy, Epephras | 1 | 1 | 1 | | |
| Pomeroy, Sarah | 1 | 1 | 6 | | |
| Pomeroy, Abagail | | | 2 | | |
| Warner, Thaddeus | 2 | 2 | 1 | | |
| Scott, William | 3 | 4 | 6 | | |
| Feland, Thomas | 2 | 3 | 3 | | |
| Nelson, Jereh | 2 | 1 | 7 | | |
| Nelson, Hosea | 1 | 2 | 2 | | |
| Nelson, Sarah | | | 4 | | |
| Denslow, Benjamin | 1 | 3 | 5 | | |
| Ingraham, Jeremiah | 3 | | 4 | | |
| Warner, Eli | 2 | 1 | 5 | | |
| Taylor, Thad | 3 | 2 | 5 | | |
| King, Ashur | 3 | 1 | 5 | | |
| Warner, Samuel | 2 | 3 | 5 | | |
| Gillet, Isaac | 1 | 1 | 3 | | |
| Dunam, Jabez | 2 | | 2 | | |
| Dunam, Jabez, 2d | 1 | 2 | 1 | | |
| Phelps, Ebenezer | 1 | 1 | 2 | | |
| Rising, James | 1 | | 3 | | |
| Lillie, Jonathan | 1 | 1 | 2 | | |
| Bush, Moses | 1 | 3 | 3 | | |
| Rising, Elijah | 1 | 2 | 2 | | |
| Rising, Abel | 2 | 3 | 3 | | |
| Rising, James, 2d | 1 | 1 | 1 | | |
| Rising, Jonah | 1 | 2 | 1 | | |
| Rising, Joel | 1 | | 2 | | |
| Spencer, Elisha | 3 | | 4 | | |
| Stiveson, Abner | 1 | 1 | 3 | | |
| Brown, John | 1 | 1 | 2 | | |
| Warner, Isaac | 1 | 1 | 2 | | |
| Warner, John | 1 | | 2 | | |
| Warner, John, 2d | 1 | 1 | 2 | | |
| Edwards, David | 2 | 2 | 4 | | |
| Trumbull, Levi | 2 | 2 | 3 | | |
| Olds, Stephen | 1 | 1 | 2 | | |
| Rocket, Josiah | 3 | | 2 | | |
| Parmatree, Joshua | 1 | 2 | 2 | | |
| Trumbull, Luther | 1 | 1 | 3 | | |
| Spencer, Elihu | 1 | 1 | 1 | | |
| Rising, Ebenezer | 1 | | 1 | | |
| Pease, Justin | 2 | 2 | 5 | | |
| Warner, Nathaniel | 1 | | 4 | | |
| Gillett, Calvin | 1 | | 3 | | |
| Warner, Silas | | 1 | 4 | | |
| Warner, Richard | 1 | 2 | 3 | | |
| Trumbull, Oliver | 1 | 2 | 2 | | |
| Remington, Elijah, 2d | 1 | 2 | 3 | | |
| Abbey, Justin | 1 | 1 | 2 | | |
| French, Amasa | 1 | | 2 | | |
| Stratton, John | 2 | 1 | 3 | | |
| Stratton, John, 2d | 1 | | 1 | | |
| Norton, Freegrace | 2 | 3 | 4 | | |
| Cannon, Joseph | 1 | | 2 | | |
| Blakely, Baley | 1 | 4 | 4 | | |
| Miller, Mike | 2 | 1 | 1 | | |
| More, Samuel | 1 | 1 | 1 | | |
| Moore, Daniel | 1 | | 2 | | |
| Phelps, Silas | 1 | 2 | 2 | | |
| Phelps, Elijah | 2 | 2 | 3 | | |
| Linsey, Robert | 1 | 6 | 3 | | |
| Edwards, Jonathan | 2 | | 3 | 1 | |
| Calver, Nathaniel | 1 | | 2 | | |
| Phelps, Judah | 2 | 4 | 3 | | |
| Warner, Moses | 2 | 6 | 6 | | |
| Granger, Elisha | 2 | 3 | 4 | | |
| Bellamy, Abner | 1 | 1 | 4 | | |
| Granger, Elisha, 2d | 1 | | 2 | | |
| Granger, Elihu | 1 | 5 | 1 | | |
| King, Eliphalet | 6 | 5 | 3 | | |
| King, William | 3 | | 3 | | |

# FIRST CENSUS OF THE UNITED STATES.

## HARTFORD COUNTY—Continued.

| NAME OF HEAD OF FAMILY. | Free white males of 16 years and upward, including heads of families. | Free white males under 16 years. | Free white females, including heads of families. | All other free persons. | Slaves. |
|---|---|---|---|---|---|
| **SUFFIELD TOWN—con.** | | | | | |
| King, Seth | 1 | 3 | 2 | | |
| Norton, Simeon | 2 | 4 | 3 | | |
| Leicester, Daniel | 1 | 2 | 3 | | |
| Bissell, Isaac | 1 | 4 | 3 | | |
| Granger, Bildad | 2 | 2 | 3 | | |
| Granger, Epaphras | 1 | | 2 | | |
| Remington, Nathaniel | 1 | 1 | 1 | | |
| King, Ebenezer, 2d | 1 | 1 | 2 | | |
| Hitchcock, Apollos | 1 | 5 | 1 | | |
| Towsley, Mike | 1 | | 3 | | |
| Dunlap, Brias | 1 | 1 | 3 | | |
| Remington, Nathaniel | 2 | 1 | 3 | | |
| Shaddock, Moses | 1 | 1 | 2 | | |
| Burbank, Ebenezer | 4 | 3 | 5 | | |
| Abbey, Peter | 1 | | 2 | | |
| Granger, Enock | 2 | 1 | 3 | | |
| Tuffie, Robert | 1 | 1 | 3 | | |
| King, Ebenezer | 3 | 2 | 6 | | |
| King, John | 1 | 1 | 1 | | |
| Leavitt, Stephen | | | | 2 | |
| Harmon, Joseph | 1 | 3 | 2 | | |
| Kindall, Amos | 1 | 1 | 2 | | |
| Kindall, Joshua | 1 | 1 | 4 | | |
| Kindall, Sarah | 1 | 2 | 4 | | 1 |
| Pease, Levi | 1 | 2 | 1 | | 1 |
| Lewis, Ezra | 1 | 2 | 1 | | |
| Hill, Stephen | 2 | 3 | 5 | | |
| King, Fidello | 1 | 1 | 3 | | |
| Granger, Rufus | 1 | | 1 | | |
| Cobbin, Josiah | 1 | | 2 | | |
| Granger, Eli | 1 | 2 | 3 | | |
| Williams, William | 2 | 2 | 1 | | |
| King, Dan | 4 | 2 | 9 | | |
| Archer, Thomas | 2 | 1 | 2 | | |
| Archer, Thomas, 2d | 1 | 3 | 2 | | |
| Holiday, William | 2 | 4 | 5 | | 1 |
| Holiday, Naoma | | 2 | 4 | | |
| Allyn, Chester | 2 | 2 | 3 | | |
| Tiley, Asa | 1 | 3 | 2 | | |
| Scott, Benjamin | 1 | | 1 | | |
| Nelson, Jeremiah, 2d | 1 | | 2 | | |
| **WETHERSFIELD TOWN.** | | | | | |
| Deming, Henry | 4 | 1 | 9 | | |
| Fosdick, William | 1 | 3 | 3 | | |
| Fosdick, Aanna | | | 3 | | |
| Bacon, Richard | 5 | 3 | 2 | | |
| Stevens, Isaac | 2 | | 1 | | |
| Webb, Joseph | 4 | 4 | 8 | 1 | 4 |
| Boardman, Elihu | 1 | 1 | 4 | | |
| Farnsworth, Joseph | 1 | 1 | 2 | | |
| Chester, Stephen | 2 | 1 | 4 | 3 | 1 |
| Dorr, Samuel | 2 | 4 | 4 | | |
| Stanley, George | 1 | | 3 | | |
| Hitchcock, Brenton | 1 | 1 | 2 | | |
| Woodward, —— | 1 | | 2 | | |
| May, Samuel, Jr | 1 | 6 | 3 | | |
| Gains, James | 1 | | 1 | | |
| Latimer, Bezᵘ | 2 | 3 | 1 | | |
| Willard, Josiah | 2 | | 1 | | |
| Draper, Aaron | 1 | 2 | 6 | 1 | |
| Balik, Ebenezar | 1 | 1 | 2 | | |
| Wright, Elijah | 2 | 3 | 2 | | 1 |
| Morrison, Hannah | | 2 | 1 | | |
| Barnard, Samuel | 2 | 1 | 2 | | |
| Beardsley, Hezekiah | 2 | 1 | 1 | | |
| Wright, Ashbel | 1 | | | | |
| Wright, David | 1 | 1 | 2 | | |
| Wright, Josiah | 4 | 1 | 2 | | |
| Fosdick, Ezekiel | 1 | 1 | 1 | | |
| Riley, Levi | 1 | 1 | 3 | | |
| Seymour, Elisha | 3 | | 1 | | |
| Deming, Richard | 1 | 2 | 5 | | |
| Loveland, John | 3 | 2 | 3 | | |
| Deming (Wid.) | 1 | 1 | 2 | | |
| Baxter, Elisha | 1 | | 5 | | |
| Griswold, Elisha | 1 | | 1 | | |
| Griswold, Margeret | 1 | 1 | 5 | | |
| Griswold, Frederic | 1 | 1 | 3 | | |
| Buckley, Sarah | 1 | | 2 | | |
| Dupu, Lims | 1 | | 4 | | |
| Combs, Andrew | 1 | | 3 | | |
| Wright, Josiah, Jr | 1 | | 3 | | |
| Hulbut, William | 3 | 1 | 3 | | |
| Hurlbut, Elijah | 1 | | 2 | | |
| Hurlbut, Stephen | 1 | 2 | 3 | | |
| Moses, Clerk | 1 | 1 | 3 | | |
| Hurlbut, Thomas | 4 | 1 | 2 | | |
| Tente, Ammon | 1 | | 2 | | |
| Goodrich, John | 1 | 4 | 3 | | |
| Bumbo, Harry | 1 | 2 | 1 | | |
| Stilman, Elisha | 2 | 1 | 3 | | |
| Russell, Timothy | 1 | 1 | 2 | | |
| Wells, Samuel, 2d | 1 | 1 | 2 | | |
| **WETHERSFIELD TOWN— continued.** | | | | | |
| Dix, Leonard | 1 | 4 | 2 | | |
| Dix, Jacob | 2 | 1 | 1 | | |
| Wright, Ebenezer | 1 | | 2 | | |
| Dix, Charles | 1 | 1 | 3 | | |
| Dix, Elisha | 1 | 3 | 2 | | |
| Boardman, Elisha | 1 | 1 | 3 | | |
| Johnson, James | | | 2 | | |
| Dillins (Wid.) | | | 2 | | |
| Churchill, Samuel | 2 | 1 | 1 | | |
| Montgue, Richard | 2 | 2 | 2 | | |
| Montague, George | 1 | | 2 | | |
| Churchill, Jesse | 3 | | 2 | | |
| Bunce, Richard | 1 | | 1 | | |
| Churchill, Levi | 1 | 2 | 3 | | |
| Combs, Joseph | 3 | 1 | 4 | | |
| Willard, Simon | 2 | 4 | 3 | | |
| Hatch, Moses | 1 | 1 | 3 | | |
| Blin, Hosea | 1 | 5 | 3 | | |
| Wells, Thomas, 2d | 2 | 2 | 3 | | |
| Kibby, John | 1 | 3 | 2 | | |
| Kibby, Dorothy | | 1 | 3 | | |
| Smith, Joseph | 1 | | 1 | | |
| Smith, Levi | 1 | 1 | 2 | | |
| Griswold, Ozias | 3 | 3 | 7 | | |
| Griswold, Jerusha | 1 | 2 | 2 | | |
| Rockwell, Samuel | 1 | 1 | 5 | | |
| North, Salmon | 2 | | 1 | | |
| Kibby, William | 1 | | 1 | | |
| Hatch, Zephaniah | 4 | | 2 | | |
| Hatch, James | 1 | 1 | 4 | | |
| Durham, David | 2 | | 1 | | |
| Waterbury, Joseph | 1 | 2 | 2 | | |
| Adams, Joseph | 1 | 2 | 2 | | |
| Warner, Robert | 1 | 3 | 2 | | |
| Montague, Moses | 1 | 2 | 1 | | |
| Montague, Anna | | | 3 | | |
| Montaigue, Seth | 1 | 2 | 3 | | |
| Adams, John | 1 | | 1 | | |
| Adams, Amasa | 1 | 3 | 4 | | |
| Blin, Solomon | 1 | 1 | 3 | | |
| Blin, William | 1 | 2 | 5 | | |
| Robbins, Joshua | 2 | 1 | 3 | | |
| Robbins, Joshua, 2d | 1 | | 2 | | |
| Robbins, Asa | 1 | 1 | 1 | | |
| Latimer, John | 1 | | 3 | | |
| Blin, Gershom | 2 | | 5 | | |
| Blin, Samuel | 2 | 2 | 4 | | |
| Warner, John | 2 | 1 | 2 | | |
| Ray, Flint | 1 | 2 | 6 | | |
| Adams, Benjamin | 4 | 1 | 7 | | |
| Havins, Thomas | 1 | 3 | 2 | | |
| Pembleton, —— | 1 | 2 | 3 | | |
| Adams, Camp | 2 | 1 | 7 | | |
| Warner, William | 1 | 2 | 3 | 1 | |
| Williams, Elisha | 1 | | 3 | | 2 |
| Crane, Abraham | 4 | | 4 | | |
| Crane, Joseph | 1 | 3 | 2 | | |
| Crane, Hezekiah | 1 | 4 | 5 | | |
| Loveland, William | 1 | 2 | 3 | | |
| Marks, William | 1 | | 3 | | |
| Harris, Hosea | 3 | 1 | 3 | | |
| Hart, Josiah | 1 | 1 | 6 | | |
| Dix, Moses | 3 | | 4 | | |
| Putman, John | 1 | 1 | 1 | | |
| Loveland, William | 1 | 2 | 3 | | |
| Barrett, Selah | 2 | 1 | 3 | | |
| Griffin, Simon | 2 | | 2 | | |
| Kibby, Richard | 1 | 1 | 2 | | |
| Crane, Ruth | | | 3 | | |
| Kibby, John | 2 | 1 | 1 | | |
| Crane, Curtis | 1 | 3 | 3 | | |
| Dix, Sarah | | | 4 | | |
| Crane, Ruth | 2 | | 2 | | |
| Dickenson, Hannah | | | 4 | | |
| Dickenson, Lucy | 3 | 1 | 3 | | |
| Coleman, Thomas | 1 | | 4 | | |
| Denniss, Allyn | 2 | | 1 | | |
| Brooks, Jonathan | 1 | | 3 | | |
| Hurlbut, Simon | 1 | 3 | 4 | | |
| Gooner, Quash | | | | 6 | |
| Robbins, Elisha | 1 | 2 | 3 | | |
| Robbins, Oliver | 4 | 2 | 4 | | |
| Robbins, Appleton | 2 | 2 | 6 | | |
| Wells, Jonathan | 1 | 1 | 1 | | |
| Hurlbut, Nathaniel | 1 | | 2 | | |
| Hurlbut, Nathaniel, 2d | 2 | 2 | 2 | | |
| Horner, Thomas | 1 | 2 | 1 | | |
| Benton, John | 2 | | 6 | | |
| Warner, Prudence | | | 2 | | |
| Warner, Aaron | 1 | | 2 | | |
| Warner, John, 3d | 1 | 1 | 3 | | |
| Belden, Rebecca | | 1 | 7 | | |
| Belden, John | 2 | | 1 | | |
| Warner, John, 2d | 1 | 2 | 6 | | |
| Robbins, David | 1 | | 3 | | |
| **WETHERSFIELD TOWN— continued.** | | | | | |
| Welles, Elisha | 1 | 3 | 2 | | |
| How, Elisha | 1 | 2 | 1 | | |
| Buckley, Charles | 1 | 2 | 3 | | |
| Buckley, John | 1 | | 3 | | |
| Treat, John | 1 | 3 | 2 | | |
| Treat, Charles | 2 | 1 | 3 | | |
| Treat, Damarus | | | 2 | | |
| Smith, Josiah | 3 | | 3 | | |
| Smith, James | 1 | 1 | 2 | | |
| Buckley, Benjamin | 1 | 3 | 3 | | |
| Clark, Roger | 1 | 1 | 3 | | |
| Palmer, Elizabeth | | | 1 | | |
| Hudson, John | 1 | 3 | 2 | | |
| Neff, John | 1 | | 3 | | |
| Dana, Thomas | 3 | 3 | 3 | | 1 |
| Smith, Israel | 3 | 1 | 4 | | |
| Smith, Jonathan | 4 | | 2 | | |
| Loomis, Silas | 1 | | 2 | | 2 |
| William, Ezekiel | 2 | 2 | 3 | 1 | 2 |
| Webb, Ebenezer | 1 | | 1 | | |
| Webb, Ezra | 1 | 1 | 2 | | |
| Fontaine, Luke | 1 | 1 | 2 | | 1 |
| Burnham, James | 1 | 5 | 3 | | |
| Kilbourn, Abigail | 1 | | 1 | | |
| Clark, Mary | | | 2 | | |
| Giles, Samuel | 1 | | 2 | | |
| Neuson, Thoˢ | | 3 | 6 | | 1 |
| Deming, Elezur | 1 | | 7 | | |
| Williams, Samuel W | 1 | | 6 | | 2 |
| Warner, Thomas | 1 | | 1 | | |
| Treat, Elisha | 1 | | 2 | | |
| Riley, Samuel | 2 | 2 | 2 | | |
| Boardman, Charles | 3 | | 4 | | |
| Riley, Christian | 1 | | 3 | | |
| Frances, James | 1 | 5 | 3 | | |
| Gladden, Josiah | 1 | 4 | 1 | | |
| Chester, John | 2 | 3 | 9 | 5 | 4 |
| Strong, William | 1 | | 2 | | |
| Willard, Stephen | 2 | 2 | 4 | | |
| Beadle, Jonathan | 3 | 2 | 6 | | |
| Storrs, Prince | 1 | 1 | 2 | | |
| Hurlbut, Elijah, Jr | 1 | 1 | 1 | | |
| Hurbut, Thomas, 2d | 1 | 1 | 4 | | |
| Boardman, Levi | 1 | 2 | 1 | | |
| Abbey, George | 1 | 1 | 3 | | |
| Fosdick, James | 1 | 1 | 1 | | |
| Mathews, Hugh | 1 | | 1 | | |
| Kibby, Christopher | 1 | 2 | 4 | | |
| Sampson, Will | | | | 7 | |
| Moreton, John | 2 | | 3 | | |
| Deming, Justus | 1 | 1 | 1 | | |
| Porter, Aaron | 1 | 1 | 4 | | |
| Buckley, Solomon | 1 | 3 | 5 | | |
| Palmer, Isaac | 1 | 3 | 2 | | |
| Welles, David | 1 | 2 | 3 | | |
| Riley, Levi | 2 | | 2 | | |
| Row, John | 1 | 3 | 2 | | |
| Burnham (Wid.) | | | 1 | 1 | |
| Burnham, Jeremiah | 1 | 2 | 4 | 1 | |
| Marsh, John | 1 | 3 | 6 | | |
| Riley, Ashbel | 2 | | 4 | | 2 |
| Aysault, Daniel | 1 | 1 | 3 | | 1 |
| Tryon, Moses | 1 | 4 | 4 | | |
| Williams, John | 1 | | 2 | | |
| Belden, Simeon | 4 | | 5 | | |
| Beldin, Ezekiel P | 1 | 1 | 5 | | 2 |
| Peirce, Samuel | 1 | 2 | 4 | | |
| Mitchel, James | 2 | 4 | 2 | | 3 |
| Mitchel, Stephen Mix | 3 | 5 | 5 | | 3 |
| Brigden, Michael | 2 | 2 | 3 | | |
| Riley, Justus | 4 | 2 | 5 | | |
| Deming, William | 2 | | 2 | | |
| Deming, James | 2 | 2 | 4 | | |
| Deming, Josiah | 4 | 3 | 3 | | |
| Stilman, Samuel | 1 | 1 | 3 | | |
| Chadwick, William | 3 | 1 | 3 | | |
| Stilman, Joseph | 4 | 2 | 6 | | |
| Stilman, Allyn | 1 | 1 | 2 | | |
| Robbins, Levi | 4 | | 4 | | |
| May, William | 2 | 1 | 4 | | |
| May, Hezekiah | 1 | | 1 | | |
| May, John | 1 | 4 | 3 | | |
| Buckley, Frances | 1 | 3 | 4 | | |
| Goodrich, Abigail | | | 5 | | 1 |
| Goodrich, John | 2 | 1 | 3 | | |
| Buner, Sarah | 1 | | 3 | | |
| Buner, Jonᵃ, Jr | 1 | 1 | 1 | | |
| Talcott, Moses | 1 | | 1 | | |
| Talcott, Mary | | | 1 | | |
| Talcott, Ebenezer | 4 | 1 | 3 | | |
| Talcott, Samuel | 1 | 1 | 2 | | 1 |
| Deming, William, Jr | 1 | 2 | 3 | | |
| Porter, Abigail | | | 2 | | |
| Butler, Frederic | 1 | 2 | 5 | 1 | |
| Wells, Bille | 4 | 1 | 3 | 1 | |

# HEADS OF FAMILIES—CONNECTICUT.

## HARTFORD COUNTY—Continued.

| NAME OF HEAD OF FAMILY. | Free white males of 16 years and upward, including heads of families. | Free white males under 16 years. | Free white females, including heads of families. | All other free persons. | Slaves. | NAME OF HEAD OF FAMILY. | Free white males of 16 years and upward, including heads of families. | Free white males under 16 years. | Free white females, including heads of families. | All other free persons. | Slaves. | NAME OF HEAD OF FAMILY. | Free white males of 16 years and upward, including heads of families. | Free white males under 16 years. | Free white females, including heads of families. | All other free persons. | Slaves. |
|---|---|---|---|---|---|---|---|---|---|---|---|---|---|---|---|---|---|
| WETHERSFIELD TOWN—continued. | | | | | | WETHERSFIELD TOWN—continued. | | | | | | WETHERSFIELD TOWN—continued. | | | | | |
| Noah, Will | | | | 4 | | Hale, James | 1 | 2 | 4 | | | Bradley, William | 1 | 2 | 3 | | |
| Woodhouse, Samuel | 1 | 1 | 4 | | | Hale, Elizabeth | 1 | | 4 | | | Hart, Seth | 3 | | 3 | | |
| Stilman, Nathaniel | 4 | | 2 | | | Hale, Benezer | 1 | 1 | 1 | | | Williams, Daniel | 2 | | 5 | | |
| Stillman, Allyn, Jr | 1 | | 2 | | | Curtis, Thomas | 2 | | 3 | | | Huntington, Josiah | 1 | 3 | 4 | | |
| Griswold, William | 1 | 2 | 1 | | | Goodrich, Joseph | 2 | 1 | 3 | | | Buckley, Justus | 1 | 2 | 2 | | |
| Griswold, Timothy | 3 | 2 | 2 | | | Brown, Edward | 2 | 1 | 2 | | | Foster, Samuel | 2 | | 6 | | 1 |
| Curtis, Samuel | 1 | 3 | 6 | | | Wolcott, Samuel | 1 | 1 | 2 | | | Benton, Esther | | 1 | 3 | | |
| Woodhouse, Anna | 2 | | 3 | | | Wolcott, Josiah | 1 | 2 | 1 | | | Nott, William | 1 | 2 | 2 | | 1 |
| Wolcott, Josiah | 1 | 1 | 1 | | | Wolcott, Solomon | 2 | 3 | 3 | | | Nott, John | 2 | | 1 | | 1 |
| Stilman, Nathᵃ, Jr | 1 | 2 | 4 | | | Wolcott, Elisha | 1 | | 1 | | 1 | Goodrich, Ichabod | 1 | | 3 | | |
| Hanmer, Samᵘ | 1 | 2 | 6 | | | Wolcott, Elisha, Jr | 1 | 2 | 4 | | | Ames, Benjamin | 1 | | 4 | | |
| Hanmer, Frances | 3 | | 4 | | | Robbins, Josiah | 1 | 2 | 3 | 1 | | Butler, Samuel | 2 | | 1 | | |
| Hanmer, John | 1 | | | | | Robbins, Josiah, 2ᵈ | 1 | 1 | 1 | | | Buckley, Paty | | 3 | 3 | | |
| Goodrich, Nathaniel, Jr | 3 | 3 | 2 | | | Robbins, Robert | 1 | | 1 | | | Williams, Elias | 1 | 1 | 1 | | 1 |
| Combs, Josiah | 1 | | 6 | | | Andrus, Elijah | 2 | | 4 | | | Williams, John | 2 | 3 | 3 | | |
| Weston, Benjamin | 1 | 1 | 7 | | | Willis, Seth | 1 | 1 | 4 | | | Collins, David | 3 | | 3 | | |
| Woodhouse, Samuel | 3 | | 4 | | | Wells, Joseph | 1 | 1 | 2 | | | Price, George | 1 | | 1 | | |
| Woodhouse, William | 1 | | 3 | | | Wells, Elijah | 1 | 3 | 8 | | | Williams, William | 2 | 2 | 4 | | |
| Boardman, Samuel | 1 | 2 | 5 | | | Wells, Christopher | 1 | | 2 | | | Robbins, Wait | 2 | 3 | 3 | | 1 |
| Buck, Samuel | 1 | | 3 | | | Wells, Joshua | 2 | | 3 | | | Robbins, Abijah, 2ᵈ | 2 | | 5 | | |
| Buck, John | 2 | | 5 | | | Wells, Joshua, Jr | 1 | 1 | 1 | | | Robbins, Frederic | | 4 | 4 | | |
| Woodhouse, John | 2 | 4 | 7 | | | Wells, Gideon | 1 | 1 | 1 | | | Robbins, Simeon | 1 | 3 | 5 | | |
| Woodhouse, Abijah | 1 | 2 | 3 | | | Wells, Levi | 1 | 1 | 1 | | | Goff, Josiah | 4 | 1 | 4 | | |
| Dabloughhai, Jonᵃ | 1 | | 3 | | | Morgan, Levi | 1 | | 2 | | | Riley, Ackley | 1 | 1 | 1 | | |
| Buck (Wid.) | | 1 | 3 | | | Roods, William | 2 | 2 | 4 | | | Dickenson, Elias | 4 | | 2 | | |
| Latimor, Solomon | 2 | | 5 | | | Roods, William, Jr | 1 | 1 | 2 | | | Buckley, Wetherby | 1 | 1 | 5 | | |
| Wells, Eli | 1 | 2 | 5 | | | Roods, Alexander | 3 | 3 | 5 | | | Riley, Jacob | 2 | 1 | 3 | | 3 |
| Wells, Chester | 5 | 1 | 5 | | | Roods, Mary | | | 1 | | | Calender, Elisha | 1 | 3 | 7 | | 1 |
| Wells, Theodore | 1 | | 4 | | | Combs, Joseph, Jr | 1 | | 2 | | | Buckley, Jehiel | 1 | 1 | 2 | | |
| Wells, Solomon | 4 | 1 | 3 | | | Blin, Unni | 1 | | 2 | | | Price, Jonathan | 1 | 2 | 4 | | |
| Goodrich, Josiah | 2 | 4 | 5 | | | Woolcut, Huldah | 1 | | 2 | | | Danforth, Thomas | 3 | | 5 | | 1 |
| Deming, Abel | 1 | 3 | 7 | | | Bunce, Jonᵃ | 1 | 4 | 3 | | | Robbins, Jacob | 2 | 3 | 3 | | |
| Deming, Daniel, Jr | 1 | 3 | 5 | | | Warner, Daniel | 4 | | 5 | | | Riley, Roger | 1 | 3 | 2 | | |
| Butler, Joseph | 2 | 2 | 3 | | | Warner, Levi | 1 | 1 | 2 | | | Gibbs, John | 2 | 1 | 6 | | |
| Wells, Prudence | | 1 | 3 | | 1 | Warner, Rhoda | | | 2 | | | Colver, Edward | 1 | 1 | 3 | | |
| Wells, John | 3 | 1 | 1 | | | Warner, Hannah | | | 2 | | | Holmes, Jonas | 1 | | 3 | | |
| Tryon, Abijah | 1 | 2 | 2 | | | Boardman, Elnathan | 1 | | 1 | | | Lewis, John | 1 | 2 | 3 | | 1 |
| Tryon, Josiah | 1 | | 3 | | | Boardman, Elijah | 2 | 2 | 2 | | | Williams, Jehiel | 2 | 4 | 5 | | |
| Standish, John | 1 | | 2 | | | Robbins, Zebulon | 1 | 2 | 2 | | | Goodrich, Israel | 1 | | 4 | | |
| Stoddard, Epephras | 1 | 1 | 6 | | | Robbins, Abigail | | | 2 | | | Demmonck, Joseph | 2 | | 3 | | |
| Deming, Simeon | 1 | 1 | 3 | | | Robbins, John | 2 | 2 | 3 | | | Belden, Mary | | | 2 | | |
| Will, Jephet | | | | 7 | | Boardman, Jonᵃ | 1 | | 1 | | | Samburn, Jedidiah | 1 | | 1 | | |
| Brendly, John | 1 | 2 | 3 | | | Boardman, Jonathan, Jr | 1 | 2 | 1 | | | Goodrich, Ebenezer | 4 | 1 | 3 | | |
| Beck, Josiah | 1 | | 1 | | | Boardman, Hannah | | | 3 | | | Goff, Gideon | 1 | | 3 | | |
| Buck, Josiah, Jr | 1 | 2 | 4 | | | Boardman, Jason | 1 | 1 | 3 | | | Goodrich, Thilcon | 2 | 2 | 4 | | |
| Buck, Daniel | 2 | 5 | 3 | | | Price, Richard | 2 | 1 | 5 | | | Selm, Patience | | | 1 | | |
| Deming, Peter | 1 | 2 | 4 | | | Adams, James | 1 | 2 | 3 | | | Deming, Frances | 1 | | 1 | | |
| Deming, Anora | | | 2 | | | Robbins, Elijah | 2 | 1 | 3 | | | Boardman, Return | 2 | | 1 | | |
| Standish, James | 1 | | 1 | | | Griswold, William | 2 | 1 | 5 | | 4 | Goodrich, Roger | 2 | 3 | 2 | | |
| Wright, Nathaniel | 3 | | 1 | | | Deming, Jonᵗʰ | 2 | | 6 | | | Cowing, Lois | | | 1 | | |
| Wright, Moses | 1 | 2 | 3 | | | Riley, Jabez | 2 | 1 | 5 | | | Churchill, Josiah | 1 | | 1 | | |
| Wright, Elizur | 2 | 1 | 3 | | | Morton, Benjamin | 1 | 3 | 3 | | | Goodrich, Elijah | 2 | | 3 | | |
| Butler, Roger | 1 | 2 | 2 | | | Morton, Abigail | | | 2 | | | Goodrich, Alpheus | 3 | 1 | 4 | | |
| Goodrich, Nathaniel | 2 | 1 | 2 | | | Buckley, Charles, 2ᵈ | 1 | 1 | 3 | | | Goodrich, Jerusha | 1 | | 3 | | |
| Goodrich, Israel | 1 | 1 | 3 | | | Robbins, Jason | 1 | | 1 | | | Wilson, Silus | 1 | | 3 | | |
| Butler, John | 1 | 1 | 6 | | | Smith, David | 1 | 1 | 2 | | | Smith, Susanna | | | 2 | | |
| Butler, John | 2 | 3 | 5 | | | Warner, Wait | 1 | 2 | 2 | | | Holmes, Levi | 1 | | 2 | | |
| Butler, Josiah | 2 | 3 | 1 | | | Edwards, John, 2ᵈ | 1 | 3 | 3 | | | Hands, Jonathan | 3 | | 3 | | |
| Butler, Hezekiah | 1 | | 2 | | | Edwards, John | 3 | 1 | 3 | | | Buckley, Joseph | | 4 | 4 | | |
| Butler, James | 2 | 2 | 3 | | | Demmack, Joseph, Jr | 1 | 1 | 2 | | | Buckley, Edward | 1 | 1 | 4 | | |
| Butler, William | 1 | 2 | 3 | | | Simons, William | 2 | 2 | 2 | | | Demmick, Samuel | 1 | 2 | 1 | | |
| Butler, Theodore | 1 | 2 | 2 | | | Church, Joseph | 2 | | 3 | | | Boardman, Frederic | 1 | | 1 | | |
| Willis, Ichabod | 3 | | 5 | | | Stebbins, Joseph | 1 | | 2 | | | Griswold, Mercy | | | 1 | | |
| Oconoland, Patrick | 1 | | | | | Buckley, Prescott | 2 | 1 | 7 | | | Holmes, Thomas | 1 | | 2 | | |
| Curtis, Josiah | 1 | | 1 | | | Bull, Aaron | 1 | 1 | 2 | | | Cleveland, Joseph | 1 | | 3 | | |
| Curtis, Levi | 1 | 2 | 5 | | | Hosford, Aaron | 2 | 2 | 4 | | | Williams, Ephraim | 4 | 3 | 2 | | |
| Frances, Josiah | 3 | 1 | 5 | | | McCombs, Andrew | 1 | 1 | 2 | | | Smith, Ezekiel | 1 | 2 | 4 | | |
| Curtis, James | 1 | | 1 | | | Riley, Stephen | 4 | 1 | 1 | | | Buckley, Christian | 1 | | 1 | | |
| Denniss, Dusen | 1 | | 1 | | | Stillman, William | 1 | 2 | 2 | | | Goodrich, Elihu | 1 | | 1 | | |
| Deming, Abigail | | | 1 | | | Stanley, James | 1 | | 2 | | 1 | Williams, Levi | 1 | | 2 | | |
| Deming, Hannah | 1 | 1 | 5 | | | Riley, John | 5 | 1 | 2 | | | Wilkinson, John | 1 | | 1 | | |
| Deming, Moses | | 2 | 2 | | 1 | Ames, Philemon | 1 | | 2 | | | Wright, Benjamin | 1 | | 2 | | |
| Wells, Samuel, 2ᵈ | 2 | | 3 | | 1 | Ames, William | 1 | | 1 | | | Hammond, James | 1 | 3 | 1 | | |
| Wells, Hezekiah | 1 | | 2 | | | Ames, Abagail | | | 3 | | | Wright, Daniel | 1 | 2 | 2 | | |
| Wells, Josiah | 1 | 1 | 2 | | | Robbins, John, Jr | 2 | 2 | 2 | | 1 | Griswold, Jehiel | 1 | 1 | 2 | | |
| Frances, John | 4 | 1 | 4 | | | Goodrich, Elizur | 1 | 2 | 2 | | | Goodrich, Gurdin, Jr | 1 | 3 | 5 | | |
| Deming, Josiah, Jr | 1 | 2 | 3 | | | Goodrich, Isaac | 1 | 1 | 2 | | | Mildram, Leydia | | | 3 | | |
| Goodrich, David | 4 | 3 | 4 | | | Grimes, Alexander | 2 | 6 | 4 | | | Miller, David | 1 | | 2 | | |
| Deming, Jessee | 1 | | 1 | | | Deming, Asa | 1 | 1 | 4 | | | Miller, Joseph | 1 | | 2 | | |
| Deming, John | 1 | 1 | 4 | 1 | | Pomeroy, Rachel | | | 4 | | | Riley, Sarah | | | 2 | | |
| Wells, Ruth | | 1 | 1 | | | Buckley, Prudence | 1 | 1 | 3 | | | Goodrich, Oliver | 2 | 3 | 3 | | |
| Franciss, Timothy | 2 | | 3 | | | Goodrich, William | 2 | 1 | 3 | | | Jager, Abraham | 1 | 2 | 2 | | |
| Hanmer, James | 1 | 1 | 9 | | | Belden, Bildad | 1 | 3 | 4 | | | Goodrich, Temperance | | | 1 | | |
| Flowers, Joseph | 3 | 1 | 3 | | | Stoddard, Ebenezer | 1 | | 4 | | | Mitchel, Calvin | 1 | 2 | 2 | | |
| Flowers, Simeon | 1 | | 2 | | | Chauncey, Eunice | | | 1 | | | Butler, Gideon | 1 | | 2 | | |
| Lewis, Joseph | 1 | 5 | 3 | | | Belden, Ezra | 2 | | 2 | | | Holmes, Daniel | 1 | | 2 | | |
| Clark, Ambrose | 1 | 1 | 2 | | | Whitmore, Hezekiah | 1 | 2 | 3 | | | Buckley, Hosea | 1 | 3 | 4 | | |
| Payne, Ambrose | 1 | 3 | 2 | | | Grimes, Josiah | 2 | | 4 | | | Buckley, Gersham | 1 | | 2 | | |
| Coleman, Peleg | 2 | 1 | 2 | | | Grimes, Abigail | 1 | | 3 | | | Butler, Benjamin | 1 | 4 | 2 | | |
| Porter, Israel | 2 | 2 | 2 | | | Webb, William | | | 2 | | | Curtis, Wait | 1 | | 2 | | |
| Clark, Theodore | 2 | | 2 | | | Ames, Daniel | 1 | 2 | 2 | | | Curtis, Josiah | 1 | | 4 | | |
| Harrison, Theodore | 1 | 3 | 3 | | | Williams, Jacob | 2 | | 6 | | | Butler, Joel | 1 | 1 | 2 | | |
| Clapp, Norman | 1 | 2 | 2 | | | Williams, Israel | 1 | | 3 | | | Griswold, Constant | 3 | 2 | 3 | | |
| Write, Lucy | | 1 | 2 | | | Higgins, Joseph | 1 | 2 | 3 | | | Miller, Nathaniel | 3 | 2 | 2 | | |
| Bunce, Josia | 2 | 4 | 4 | | | Bradley, David | 1 | | 2 | | | Rash, Jeremiah | 1 | 3 | 2 | | |
| Newbury, —— | 1 | | 2 | | | Williams, Moses | 1 | | 3 | | | Butler, Simeon | 1 | 1 | 3 | | |
| Deming, Ebenezer | 1 | 2 | 4 | | | | | | | | | | | | | | |

## HARTFORD COUNTY—Continued.

| NAME OF HEAD OF FAMILY. | Free white males of 16 years and upward, including heads of families. | Free white males under 16 years. | Free white females, including heads of families. | All other free persons. | Slaves. | NAME OF HEAD OF FAMILY. | Free white males of 16 years and upward, including heads of families. | Free white males under 16 years. | Free white females, including heads of families. | All other free persons. | Slaves. | NAME OF HEAD OF FAMILY. | Free white males of 16 years and upward, including heads of families. | Free white males under 16 years. | Free white females, including heads of families. | All other free persons. | Slaves. |
|---|---|---|---|---|---|---|---|---|---|---|---|---|---|---|---|---|---|
| **WETHERSFIELD TOWN—continued.** | | | | | | **WETHERSFIELD TOWN—continued.** | | | | | | **WINDSOR TOWN—con.** | | | | | |
| Butler, Richard | 1 | 1 | 1 | | | Lowry, David | 2 | | 3 | | | Hooker, Horrace | 2 | 2 | 6 | | |
| Butler, Zeebah | 1 | | 6 | | | Andrus, Eli | 1 | | 3 | | | Russell, Cornelius | 1 | 2 | 4 | | |
| Butler, David | 1 | 4 | 2 | | | Andrus, Abel | 3 | | 4 | | | Mather, Elijah | 3 | 1 | 1 | | |
| Collins, James | 2 | 2 | 4 | | | Kilbourn, Eunice | | | 2 | | | Elsworth, Eliz\* | | | 2 | | 1 |
| Collins, Robert | 2 | | 1 | | | Kilbourn, Simon | 1 | | 3 | | | Gillet, Alme | 1 | 2 | 1 | | |
| Collins, Abial | | | 3 | | | Wentworth, Sion | 1 | | 1 | | | Allen, Joseph | 1 | | 3 | | |
| Smith, Manus | 2 | | 1 | | | Lusk, James | 1 | 1 | 3 | | 1 | Drake, Dorson | 3 | 1 | 1 | | |
| Butler, Stephen | 1 | | 2 | | | Stoddard, Solomon | 1 | | 1 | | | Elsworth, Giles | 2 | | 2 | 1 | |
| Russell, Jonathan | 1 | 2 | 3 | | | Andrus, Elizur | 2 | 2 | 5 | | | Elsworth, Jonah | 3 | 3 | 3 | | |
| Russell, Thomas | 2 | 3 | 4 | | | Wells, Simon | 1 | 3 | 2 | | | Elsworth, Grove | 1 | 1 | 2 | | |
| Boardman, Levi | 1 | 1 | 1 | | | Andrus, Fitch | 1 | 1 | 3 | | | Barker, Ethan | 3 | | 1 | | |
| Collins, Levi | 1 | 1 | 4 | | | Buck, Amos | 2 | 2 | 4 | | | Russel, W\*m\* | 2 | 2 | 4 | | |
| Buckley, Jonathan | 1 | | 2 | | | Wells, Jamus | 4 | 3 | 6 | | | Mather, Elijah, Ju\*r\* | 1 | | 1 | | |
| Buckley, Stephen | 1 | 3 | 3 | | | Wells, Elijah | 2 | | 5 | | | Chapman, Taylor | 3 | 1 | 1 | | |
| Miller, Jerusha | | | 3 | | | Atwood, Asher | 2 | | 3 | | | Mather, Eliakim | 3 | 1 | 2 | | |
| Goodrich, Gurden | 2 | 1 | 3 | | | Wells, Roger | 1 | 2 | 3 | 1 | | Marshal, Amos | 1 | 1 | 3 | 1 | |
| Marsh, John | 1 | | 2 | | | Kellogg, Martin | 2 | 1 | 3 | | 2 | Stiles, Samuel | 2 | 1 | 5 | | |
| Marsh, John, Jr | 1 | 1 | 3 | | | Smith, Obadiah | 1 | 2 | 4 | | | Stoughton, Israel | 1 | | 5 | | |
| Marsh, Eli | 1 | 1 | 2 | | | Boardman, Israel | 2 | | 1 | | | Stoughton, Elisha | 1 | 2 | 3 | | |
| Bunce, Thomas | 1 | 3 | 4 | | | Williams, Elijah | 1 | 1 | 3 | | | Miller, Roswell | 1 | | 2 | | |
| Goodrich, Seth | 1 | 2 | 1 | | | Russell, David | 2 | | 4 | | | Allen, Sam\*l\* Ju | 1 | 1 | 3 | | 1 |
| Dickenson, Josiah | 1 | 2 | 3 | | | Andrus, Elias | 1 | 1 | 3 | | | Woolcott, Alex\*r\* | 1 | 3 | 2 | 2 | |
| Dickenson, Wait | 1 | 2 | 5 | | | Latimore, Luther | 2 | 1 | 3 | | | Rice, Aaron | 1 | 1 | 1 | | |
| Dickenson, Ozias | 1 | 5 | 5 | | | Landers, Samuel | 3 | | 3 | | | Hoskins, Ezekiel | 2 | 2 | 4 | | |
| Dickenson, Obadiah | 1 | 1 | 2 | | | Frances, Roger | 1 | 1 | 1 | | | Gaylord, John | 1 | 1 | 3 | | |
| Riley, Jasper | 1 | 2 | 2 | | | Wells, Absalom | 1 | 1 | 4 | | | Allen, Sam\*l\* W | 1 | 1 | 4 | | |
| Belden, David | 1 | 5 | 2 | | | Wells, Robert | 1 | 1 | 2 | | | Mather, Azariah, Ju | 1 | | 3 | | |
| Belden, Asa | 1 | | 3 | | | Wells, Robert, Jr | 1 | 2 | 2 | | | Holcomb, Elijah | 1 | 1 | 2 | | |
| Belden, Elisha | 1 | 1 | 2 | | | Whittlesey, Lemuel | 2 | 2 | 4 | 1 | | Pinney, Eliz\* | 2 | | 3 | | |
| Belden, John | 1 | | 3 | | | Hurlbut, Levi | 3 | 4 | 3 | | | Stiles, Ashbel | 2 | | 4 | | |
| Belden, Jeremiah | 1 | | 3 | | | Churchill, Joseph | 1 | 2 | 2 | | | Stiles, Job | 2 | | 2 | | |
| Deming, Jiles | 1 | | 4 | | | Coslet, Frances | 1 | | 1 | | | Elsworth, Hon\*bl\* Oliver, Esqr | 2 | 2 | 5 | 1 | |
| Deming, Leeman | 1 | 1 | 2 | | | Andrus, Sarah | | | 1 | | | Elsworth, David | 2 | 3 | 4 | | |
| Deming, Asahel | 1 | | 3 | | | Dickenson, Ebenezer | 2 | | 1 | | | Hindsdale, Theodore | 3 | 5 | 4 | | |
| Wright, Jiles | 1 | 2 | 2 | | | Dickenson, Wait S | 1 | 2 | 2 | | | Haydon, Thomas | 3 | 1 | 4 | | |
| Ceaser (Negro) | | | | 3 | | Frances, Josiah | 2 | 1 | 2 | | | Bissel, Eben\*r\* F | 2 | 1 | 1 | | |
| Collins, Simeon | 2 | 2 | 2 | | | Frances, Justus | 2 | 3 | 2 | | | Thrall, David | 1 | 2 | 3 | | |
| Belden, Abraham | 1 | 2 | 2 | | | Taylor, Benajah | 1 | 1 | 2 | | | Thrall, Jesse | 1 | 2 | 2 | | |
| Wright, Justus | 2 | | 3 | | | Merrill, Ebenezer | 1 | | 1 | | | Haydon, Isaac | 1 | 2 | 5 | | |
| Stow, Ebenezer | 2 | 1 | 4 | | | Wells, Levi | 1 | | 1 | | | Munsel, Alpheus | 2 | 2 | 2 | | |
| Holmes, John | 2 | 2 | 2 | | | Kellogg, Martin, Jr | 1 | 2 | 6 | | | Haydon, Nath\*l\* | 1 | | 2 | | |
| Belden, Oth\*o\* | 1 | 2 | 3 | | | Willard, Daniel | 2 | | 2 | | | Lamberton, Obed | 1 | | 1 | | |
| Belden, Richard | 2 | | 1 | | | Willard, Daniel, Jr | 2 | 1 | 1 | | | Lamberton, Moses | 1 | 1 | 3 | | |
| Belden, Richard, Jr | 1 | 2 | 2 | | | Deming, Frederic | 1 | 1 | 1 | | | Osburn, Jacob | 1 | | 2 | | |
| Blin, Hezekiah | 2 | 1 | 3 | | | Stoddard, Jonathan | 3 | | 3 | | | Bissel, Josiah | 2 | | 2 | | |
| Blin, David | 1 | | 1 | | | Guinea (Negro) | | | | 1 | | Bissel, Hezi\* (Wid.) | | 1 | 2 | | |
| Blin, Peter, Jr | 1 | 3 | 3 | | | Camp, Joseph | 1 | 3 | 5 | | | Welch, Lemuel | 1 | 1 | 5 | | |
| Blin, Peter | 1 | | 2 | | | Stoddard, Dorothy | | 2 | 2 | | | Haydon, Ezra | 2 | 2 | 6 | | 2 |
| Blin, Martha | 1 | 1 | 1 | | | Stodard, Joseph | 1 | 2 | 2 | | | Phelps, Bildad | 3 | | 5 | | 1 |
| Blin, Justus | 1 | 1 | 2 | | | Stoddard, David | 1 | 1 | 4 | | | Bissel, Ebin\*r\* F., Ju | 1 | | 1 | | 1 |
| Belden, Aaron | 4 | | 2 | | | Walcott, Abigail | | | 3 | | | Haydon, Nath\*l\* Ju | 4 | 2 | 4 | | |
| Belden, Moses | 1 | 1 | 4 | | | Kellogg, Stephen | 1 | 2 | 3 | | | Haydon, Levi | 4 | 4 | 4 | | 2 |
| Belden, Silas | 1 | 1 | 3 | | | Kellogg, Joseph | 1 | 1 | 1 | | | Haydon, Eben\*r\* | 1 | 1 | 1 | | |
| Wright, Charles | 1 | 1 | 6 | | | Hunn, Enos | 1 | 2 | 4 | | | Picket, Phinehas | 3 | 2 | 5 | | |
| Buckley, Theodore | 1 | 1 | 3 | | | Hinsdale, Zadock | 2 | 2 | 6 | | | Ensign, Amos | 2 | 1 | 2 | | |
| Sanford, Justus | 1 | 1 | 3 | | | Seymour, Elias | 2 | 1 | 6 | | | Haydon, John, Ju | 1 | 1 | 6 | | |
| Dix, Benjamin | 1 | 2 | 3 | | | Seymour, Ashbel | 1 | 4 | 2 | | | Haydon, Oliver | 1 | | 1 | | |
| Wolcott, Josiah | 2 | 2 | 4 | | | Seymour, Thankfull | 1 | | 2 | | | Haydon, John | 3 | 2 | 3 | | |
| Goodrich, John | 1 | 4 | 5 | | | Fox, Thomas | 1 | | 1 | | | Tucker, Gideon | 1 | | 2 | | |
| Goodrich, David | 2 | 3 | 2 | | | Pomp (Negro) | | | | 5 | | Sheldon, Remember | 1 | | 3 | | |
| Webster, Amos | 1 | 3 | 1 | | | Kellsey, Enock | 3 | 1 | 4 | | | Denslow, Joseph G | 1 | | 3 | | |
| Steele, Joseph | 1 | 3 | 3 | | | | | | | | | Russel, Jacob | 2 | 4 | 4 | | |
| Deming, Ephraim | 1 | | 2 | | | **WINDSOR TOWN.** | | | | | | Mather, Azariah | 1 | | 4 | | |
| Deming, Hannah | 1 | 1 | 4 | | | Alford, Jonathan | 2 | 4 | 1 | | | Gaylord, Eliakim | 2 | | 1 | | |
| Deming, Elias | 1 | 3 | 3 | | | Baldwin, Thomas | 1 | 3 | 5 | | | Gaylord, Eliakim, Ju | 1 | | 2 | | |
| Wolcott, Caleb | 1 | | 2 | | | Brown, Eph\*m\* | 3 | 1 | 3 | | | Denslow, Martin | 2 | 2 | 4 | | |
| Rockwell, Oziah | 1 | 2 | 3 | | | Denslow, Elijah | 3 | | 6 | | | Herskill, Jabez | 2 | 5 | 5 | | |
| Lark, Levi | 1 | 1 | 3 | | | Mather, Joseph | 3 | 1 | 2 | | | Denslow, Samuel | 1 | | 3 | | |
| Buterick, Edward | 1 | 1 | 1 | | | Brown, Elias | 1 | 3 | 1 | | | Fish, David | 1 | 3 | 3 | | |
| Churchill, Charles | 1 | 1 | 2 | | | Strong, Elisha | 1 | 3 | 7 | | | Eli, Daniel | 1 | 1 | 2 | | |
| Churchill, Solomon | 1 | | 1 | | | Benton, Elihu S | 2 | 1 | 5 | | | Gaylord, Eliazer | 1 | | 2 | | |
| Churchill, Samuel | 1 | 4 | 3 | | | Benton, Thomas | 2 | | 3 | | | Pinney, Martin | 3 | 1 | 4 | | |
| Churchill, Levi | 1 | 3 | 5 | | | Sill, Rich\*d\* L | 1 | 3 | 2 | | | Burge, Peletiah | 4 | 3 | 3 | | |
| Deming, Jara | 3 | | 4 | | | Sill, John | 1 | 3 | 1 | | | Dexter, Seth | 2 | 3 | 6 | | |
| Deming, Elizur | 2 | 2 | 3 | | | Allen, John, Ju | 1 | 2 | 2 | | | Clark, Oliver | 1 | 3 | 4 | | |
| Deming, Eliakim | 1 | | 3 | | | Wells, James | 2 | 1 | 2 | | | Sperry, Elijah | 1 | | 4 | | |
| Deming, Frances | 1 | 1 | 2 | | | Howard, Nath\*l\* | 1 | 4 | 1 | | | Wing, Lydia | 1 | 1 | 2 | | |
| Squire, John | 2 | 2 | 3 | | | Elsworth, Migail | | | 2 | | | Wing, Moses | 2 | | 4 | | |
| Richardson, Isael | 1 | 1 | 2 | | | Chaffee, Hez\*b\*, Jur | 3 | 1 | 2 | 2 | 1 | Allen, John | 2 | 4 | 6 | | |
| Blin, James | 2 | | 3 | | | Chaffee, Hezekiah | 3 | | 1 | | | Drake, Lora | 1 | | 2 | | |
| Wright, Abijah | 1 | | 4 | | | Hooker, James | 1 | | 7 | 1 | | Abby, Sam\*l\*, Ju | 1 | 2 | 1 | 1 | |
| Wright, Esther | 1 | 2 | 4 | | | Allen, Hannah | | | 4 | | | Barber, Elijah | 4 | 4 | 4 | | |
| Hurlbut, John | 1 | 2 | 4 | | | Gibbs, Charity | 3 | | 3 | | | Talcott, Dan\*l\* | 3 | 4 | 3 | | |
| Hurlbut, Mathew | 1 | | 2 | | | Elsworth, Eben\*r\* | 1 | 3 | 4 | | | Barber, Josiah | 1 | | 2 | | |
| Robbins, Unni | 3 | 1 | 5 | 1 | | Porter, Daniel | 1 | 3 | 2 | | | Barber, Josiah, Jur | 1 | 5 | 2 | | |
| Wolcott, George | 2 | 1 | 4 | | | Mack, Andrew | 1 | 4 | 1 | | | Allen, Sam\*l\* | 2 | | 2 | | |
| Hurlbut, Elias | 1 | 1 | 5 | | | Strong, Sarah | | | 3 | | | Barber, Thom\*a\* | 3 | | 1 | | |
| Gibbs, Lemuel | 1 | 1 | 1 | | | Filer, Samuel | 1 | | 2 | | | Barber, Eli | 1 | | 1 | | |
| Deming, Robert | 1 | 2 | 2 | | | Mather, Cotton | 1 | | 7 | | | Barber, Reuben | 1 | 1 | 3 | | |
| Blin, Jonathan | 2 | | 5 | | | Daboll, Jonathan | 2 | 3 | 3 | | | Mills, Elijah | 1 | | 3 | | |
| Belden, Joshua | 3 | 1 | 6 | | | Thrall, Eliz\* | 1 | | 2 | | | Drake, David | 3 | | 5 | | |
| Whaples, Eli | 1 | | 3 | | | Wilson, Moses | 2 | 3 | 4 | | | Drake, Phinehas | 2 | 1 | 3 | 1 | |
| Whaples, Reuben | 1 | 1 | 1 | | | Allen, John | 2 | 2 | 3 | | | Allen, Fitts | 2 | 1 | 3 | | |
| Holmes, Lemuel | 1 | | 4 | | | Allen, Charles | 1 | | 1 | | | Allen, Benj\*a\* | 1 | | | | |
| Phelps, Ephraim | 1 | | 4 | | | | | | | | | | | | | | |

# HEADS OF FAMILIES—CONNECTICUT.

## HARTFORD COUNTY—Continued.

| NAME OF HEAD OF FAMILY. | Free white males of 16 years and upward, including heads of families. | Free white males under 16 years. | Free white females, including heads of families. | All other free persons. | Slaves. | NAME OF HEAD OF FAMILY. | Free white males of 16 years and upward, including heads of families. | Free white males under 16 years. | Free white females, including heads of families. | All other free persons. | Slaves. | NAME OF HEAD OF FAMILY. | Free white males of 16 years and upward, including heads of families. | Free white males under 16 years. | Free white females, including heads of families. | All other free persons. | Slaves. |
|---|---|---|---|---|---|---|---|---|---|---|---|---|---|---|---|---|---|
| **WINDSOR TOWN—con.** | | | | | | **WINDSOR TOWN—con.** | | | | | | **WINDSOR TOWN—con.** | | | | | |
| Drake, Samuel | 2 | | | | | Griswold, Jonah | 2 | 1 | 1 | | | Steel, James | 1 | | 1 | | |
| Sheldon, Selah | 1 | 2 | 2 | | | Rigly, Richard | 2 | | 3 | | | Drake, Joseph | 2 | 3 | 2 | | |
| Wisland, Amos, Ju | 1 | 1 | 3 | | | Moore, Benj^a | 3 | 1 | 1 | | | Stoughton, Sam^l | 2 | 2 | 4 | | |
| Drake, Phinehas, J^ur | 1 | 2 | 4 | | | Denslow, Reuben | 1 | | 1 | | | Hubbard, Asa | 1 | 1 | 3 | | |
| Wesland, Joseph | 1 | | 4 | | | Pinney, Judah | 2 | 2 | 3 | | | Hubbard, Nath^l | 1 | 3 | 2 | | |
| Moore, Thom^s | 1 | | 3 | | | Pinney, Isaac | 1 | 1 | 2 | | | Bidwell, Jonathan | 1 | 3 | 6 | | |
| Barber, Moses | 3 | 1 | 3 | | | Griswold, George | 2 | | 5 | | | Hubbard, John | 1 | 3 | 1 | | |
| Barber, Aaron | 1 | 1 | 4 | | | Griswold, George, Ju | 1 | | 1 | | | Allen, Elisha | 1 | | 2 | | |
| Loomis, Joseph, Ju | 2 | 1 | 3 | | | Griswold, Francis | 1 | | 1 | | | Allen, Alex^r | 1 | 3 | 1 | | |
| Barber, Benoni | 1 | | 1 | | | Barns, Abel | 2 | 4 | 2 | | | Allen, Thomas | 1 | 2 | 5 | | |
| Loomis, Jerajah | 5 | | 3 | | | Griswold, Joab | 1 | 1 | 4 | | | Tiler, Roger | 1 | 3 | 4 | | |
| Loomis, Nijah | 1 | | 2 | | | Griswold, Joab, Ju | 1 | 1 | 2 | | | Burr, Amos | 1 | 1 | 2 | | |
| Warner, Loomis | 4 | | 3 | | | Griswold, Elihu | 1 | 1 | 7 | | | Wilson, Hez^h | 1 | 1 | 3 | | |
| Loomis, Benajah | 5 | 5 | 3 | | | Griswold, Elijah | 2 | 1 | 2 | | | Allen, George | 1 | | 3 | | |
| Strong, Abel | 1 | 3 | 4 | | | Griswold, Ziba | 3 | 3 | 7 | | | Wilson, Abiel | 1 | 1 | 3 | | |
| Elggleston, Thom^s | 3 | 4 | 1 | | | Marshall, Elisha | 2 | | 1 | | | Webster, James | 3 | 1 | 4 | | |
| Loomis, Watson | 1 | 1 | 1 | | | Marshall, Timothy | 1 | | 1 | | | Webster, Joseph | 3 | 2 | 2 | | |
| Loomis, Jedidiah | 1 | | 1 | | | Holcomb, Sam^l | 2 | | 2 | | | Webster, Hez^h | 2 | | 1 | | |
| Loomis, Jed, Jur | 1 | 4 | 1 | | | Owen, Aaron | 1 | | 1 | | | Grant, David | 2 | | | | |
| Loomis, Dan | 1 | | 2 | | | Phelps, W^m | 1 | | 3 | | | Allen, Solomon | 2 | 3 | 3 | | |
| Warner, John | 2 | | 2 | | | Phelps, Eli | 1 | | 2 | 1 | | Hubbard, Timothy | 2 | 2 | 5 | | |
| Cook, W^m | 1 | | 1 | | | Griswold, Abel | 2 | 5 | 3 | | | Risley, Zach | 1 | 2 | 5 | | |
| Alford, Jeremiah | 1 | | | | | Holcomb, Roderick | 1 | 1 | 2 | | | Hubbard, Abner | 1 | | 3 | | |
| Moore, Asa | 1 | | 3 | | | Griswold, Nath^l | 2 | 1 | 4 | | | Clark, George | 1 | 2 | 5 | | |
| Bestor, John | | | | 5 | | Griswold, Timothy | 1 | | 2 | | | Palmer, Jehiel | 3 | | 1 | | |
| Roberts, James | 2 | 1 | 5 | | | Holcomb, Martin | 4 | | 3 | | | Marshal, Sam^l | 1 | | 1 | | |
| Halsey, Phillip | 2 | 2 | 1 | | | Phelps, Enoch | 1 | | 1 | | | Barber, Hepzibah | | | 3 | | |
| Moore, Edw^d | 2 | 2 | 3 | | | Holcomb, Martin, Jur | 3 | 3 | 3 | | | Marshal, Sam, Jur | 1 | 2 | 1 | | |
| Chandler, Isaac | 3 | 1 | 2 | | | Holcomb, Joseph | 3 | 1 | 6 | | | Sanford, Rob^t | 1 | 3 | 3 | | |
| Moore, Roger | 1 | | | | | Griswold, Edw^d | 2 | 2 | 5 | | | Woodward, Oliver | 1 | 2 | 3 | | |
| Moore, Elisha | 3 | 2 | 3 | | | Blanchard, Jere | 5 | | 1 | | | Cadwell, Theodore | 1 | 2 | 3 | | |
| Phelps, Augustus | 2 | 1 | 4 | | | Mills, Naomi | | 2 | 3 | | | Palmer, Jonathan, Ju | 1 | 1 | 2 | | |
| Eggleston, Eph^m | 1 | 1 | 5 | | | Beebee, ——— | 1 | 1 | 2 | | | Filly, Jonathan | 3 | | 3 | | |
| Mather, Oliver | 3 | 4 | 2 | | | Griswold, Thomas | 1 | 1 | 1 | | | Ackley, Abner B | 3 | | 3 | | |
| Phelps, Eben^r | 1 | 1 | 3 | | | Porter, George | 1 | | 2 | 1 | | Hitchcock, Caleb | 2 | 1 | 4 | | |
| Moore, Hannah | 1 | | 2 | | | Wilson, Calvin | 1 | 1 | 4 | | | Bissell, Col. Hez^h | 1 | 2 | 6 | 1 | |
| Filley, John | 5 | 1 | 3 | | | Barnerd, Joseph | 3 | 2 | 6 | | | Gillit, Deborah | | | 3 | | |
| Allen, Jonah | 1 | | 1 | 1 | | Ross, John | 2 | 2 | 5 | | | Elmer, Eliakim | 1 | 1 | 1 | | |
| Newbury, Roger | 2 | 2 | 6 | 1 | 1 | Alford, Joseph | 2 | 3 | 4 | | | Butler, Nath^l | 2 | | 3 | | |
| Allen, Henry | 2 | 1 | 3 | | 1 | Griswold, Sylvanus | 5 | 2 | 2 | 2 | | Wait, W^m | 1 | 1 | 3 | | |
| Drake, Elihu | 2 | 1 | 3 | | | Phelps, Josias | 2 | | 2 | | | Andrus, Sam^l | 1 | 3 | 5 | | |
| Francis, W^m | 1 | 1 | 2 | | | Phelps, Josiah, 2^d | 1 | 1 | 3 | | | Barton, W^m | 1 | | 1 | | |
| Woolcott, Christopher | 3 | 2 | 5 | | | Owen, Nath^l | 2 | 2 | 3 | | | Elmer, Phinehas | 2 | 1 | 3 | | |
| Woolcott, George | 2 | 2 | 5 | | | Phelps, John | 3 | 1 | 4 | | | Fitch, Luther | 1 | | 1 | | |
| Utley, Joseph | 2 | 2 | 3 | | | Phelps, Isaac | 3 | 1 | 2 | | | Barber, James | 2 | 7 | 2 | | |
| Mather, Increase | 1 | | 2 | | | Phelps, Job | 1 | 2 | 3 | | | Drake, Noah | 1 | | 1 | | |
| Phelps, George | 1 | 2 | 2 | | | Barna, Joseph | 2 | 1 | 4 | | | Mills, Elijah | 1 | | 1 | | |
| Fitch, James | 2 | | 2 | | | Griswold, Isaac | 1 | 3 | 5 | | | Clark, Hosea | 1 | 2 | 3 | | |
| Loomis, Abiah | 2 | 2 | 4 | | | Case, Benoni | 2 | 2 | 5 | | | Drake, Moses | 1 | 1 | 4 | | |
| Loomis, George | 1 | 3 | 6 | | | Phelps, Shadrack | 2 | | 1 | | | Skinner, Isaac | 2 | | 2 | | |
| Loomis, Odiah | 1 | | 2 | | | Balcom, John | 2 | 2 | 2 | | | Skinner, Isaac, Ju | 1 | 1 | 4 | | |
| Holcomb, Elijah | 1 | | 3 | | | How, Edw^d | 1 | 2 | 2 | | | Delanna, W^m | 2 | | 1 | | |
| Roberts, Oliver | 2 | 1 | 1 | | | Day, Isaac | 1 | 2 | 2 | | | Hoskins, Increase | 4 | 1 | 4 | | |
| Fuller, Obadiah | 1 | 2 | 4 | | | May, John | 1 | | 4 | | | Higby, Job | 3 | | | | |
| Palmer, Benj^a | 1 | | 5 | | | Griswold, Hez^h | 1 | | 1 | | | Wills, Roger | 3 | 4 | 6 | | |
| Cook, Elisha | 1 | 1 | 4 | | | Miller, Abner | 1 | | 2 | | | Gillit, Abel, Ju | 2 | 4 | 4 | | |
| Brown, Stephen | 1 | 3 | 5 | | | Minor, John | 1 | 1 | 2 | | | Mills, Elihu | 1 | | 3 | | |
| Barber, Jerijah | 6 | | 4 | | | Thrall, John | 1 | 1 | 1 | | | Mills, Fred^k | 1 | 2 | 4 | | |
| Gillet, Dan^l | 2 | 1 | 5 | | | Latimer, Alex^r | 2 | | 2 | | | Latimer, Hez^h, Ju | 1 | 2 | 4 | | |
| Phelps, Roger | 2 | 1 | 3 | | | Phelps, Jacob | 1 | 1 | 5 | | | Newberry, Thomas | 2 | 1 | 4 | | |
| Phelps, Dan^l | 1 | 1 | 1 | | | Lawrence, Amos | 1 | 1 | 2 | | | Hoskins, Eli | 2 | 1 | 5 | | |
| Palmer, Jonathan | 3 | | 2 | | | Glazier, John | 1 | | 2 | | | Rowley, Sam^l | 1 | | 1 | | |
| Eno, Ashbel | 2 | | 4 | | | M^cLean, John | 1 | 3 | 4 | | | Filly, Luke | 2 | | 1 | | |
| Wilson, Phinehas | 3 | 3 | 2 | | | Waters, Bevil | 1 | | 2 | | | Filly, Jesse | 2 | | 1 | | |
| Phelps, Lanclot | 1 | 2 | 3 | | | Filley, Moses | 2 | 5 | 3 | | | Filly, Timothy | 1 | | 1 | | |
| Brown, Peter | 2 | 1 | 3 | | | M^cLean, Allen | 1 | 2 | 2 | | | Filly, David | 1 | 2 | 2 | | |
| Colt, Jabez | 2 | | 2 | | | Parsons, Doctor | 2 | 1 | 2 | | | Rowley, John | 1 | | 1 | | |
| Barber, Jonah | 2 | 2 | 3 | | | Loomis, Andrew | 1 | 4 | 3 | | | Rowley, Reuben | 1 | | 3 | | |
| Bolls, Ruth | | | 2 | | | Clark, Roger | 1 | 2 | 2 | | | Rowley, Philander | 1 | 2 | 2 | | |
| Barber, Gideon | 1 | 3 | 3 | | | Gillet, Jonah | 1 | 3 | 5 | | | Rowley, Roger | 1 | 2 | 3 | | |
| Marshall, Eliakim | 1 | | 2 | | | Gillet, Jonah, 2^d | 2 | 1 | 2 | | | Hempsted, Joshua | 1 | 1 | 2 | | |
| Marshal, Eliakim, Jur | 3 | 1 | 2 | | | Clark, Asahel | 1 | | 2 | | | Hall, Benajah | 1 | 2 | 3 | | |
| Palmer, Joel | 3 | 2 | 3 | | | Thrall, Isaac | 1 | 2 | 5 | | | Woolcott, Solomon | 1 | 3 | 3 | | |
| Barber, David, Ju | 1 | 3 | 3 | | | Loomis, Lydia | | | 2 | | | Cook, Eli | 2 | 3 | 1 | | |
| Dalton, Joseph | 1 | 1 | 1 | | | Clark, John | 2 | 2 | 4 | | | Latimer, Hez^h | 2 | 1 | 3 | | |
| Filley, Elisha | 2 | 3 | 3 | | | Latimer, George | 1 | 1 | 3 | | | Parsons, Hez^h | 1 | | 3 | | |
| Moore, Theophilus | 1 | | 1 | | | Loomis, Stephen | 1 | | 1 | | | Parsons, Pelitiah | 1 | | 4 | | |
| Allen, Moses | 1 | | 1 | | | Clark, Solomon | 1 | 2 | 4 | | | Fitch, Joseph | 3 | 1 | | | |
| Cook, Jonathan | 2 | | 1 | | | Eggleston, Sam^l | 2 | 3 | 6 | | | Cook, Job | 1 | 1 | 2 | | |
| Rowley, Thomas | 1 | 2 | 3 | | | Eggleston, Nath^l | 1 | | 1 | | | Mills, Diadema | | | 2 | | |
| Cook, Noah | 1 | 1 | 4 | | | Wilson, Joseph | 1 | 2 | 4 | | | Griswold, Simon | 2 | | 3 | | |
| Cook, Shubael | 1 | 3 | 2 | | | Gillit, Levi | 1 | 3 | 2 | | | Barns, Stephen | 2 | 2 | 5 | | |
| Wesland, Robert | 1 | 1 | 2 | | | Hoskins, Asa | 1 | 2 | 2 | | | Cook, Moses | 2 | | 6 | | |
| Cook, Josiah | 3 | | 2 | | | Gillit, Aaron | 1 | 1 | 2 | | | Riley, Nath^l | 1 | | 7 | | |
| Cook, Theophilus | 5 | | 3 | | | Hoskins, Zeb^a | 1 | | 2 | | | Fusbury, Anna | | | 2 | | |
| Filly, Amos | 2 | | 1 | | | Loomis, Elijah | 1 | 1 | 5 | | | Gray, W^m | 1 | 2 | 2 | | |
| White, Moses | 1 | 4 | 4 | | | Loomis, Reuben | 1 | | 2 | | | Cook, Abner | 2 | 1 | 2 | | |
| Drake, Dudley | 1 | 2 | 2 | | | Loomis, Abijah | 1 | 1 | 3 | | | Eggleston, Jonathan | 2 | 1 | 3 | | |
| Phelps, Cornelius | 1 | | 2 | | | Loomis, Jacob | 1 | 3 | 4 | | | Clark, Ira | 1 | 2 | 2 | | |
| Rowland, David S | 4 | 1 | 4 | | | Gillit, Amos | 2 | | 3 | | | Wilson, Joel | 1 | 3 | 4 | | |
| Phelps, Oliver | 2 | 2 | 4 | | | Allen, Jonth | 2 | 3 | 1 | | | Brown, Ezra | 2 | 1 | 8 | | |
| Phelps, James | 2 | 2 | 3 | 1 | | Allen, Solomon, Ju | 1 | | 4 | | | Wilson, Joel | 1 | | 2 | | |
| Phelps, Timothy | 2 | 1 | 3 | | | Gillit, Abel | 1 | | 2 | | | Gray, George | 1 | | 2 | | |
| Palmer, John | 1 | 5 | 2 | | | Grimes, Simeon | 1 | | 2 | | | Phelps, Charles | 1 | | 1 | | |
| Phelps, Job, J^nr | 1 | 3 | 5 | | | Lewis, Samuel | 2 | 1 | 2 | | | Phelps, Charles, Ju | 1 | | 2 | | |

# FIRST CENSUS OF THE UNITED STATES.

## HARTFORD COUNTY—Continued.

| NAME OF HEAD OF FAMILY. | Free white males of 16 years and upward, including heads of families. | Free white males under 16 years. | Free white females, including heads of families. | All other free persons. | Slaves. | NAME OF HEAD OF FAMILY. | Free white males of 16 years and upward, including heads of families. | Free white males under 16 years. | Free white females, including heads of families. | All other free persons. | Slaves. | NAME OF HEAD OF FAMILY. | Free white males of 16 years and upward, including heads of families. | Free white males under 16 years. | Free white females, including heads of families. | All other free persons. | Slaves. |
|---|---|---|---|---|---|---|---|---|---|---|---|---|---|---|---|---|---|
| **WINDSOR TOWN—con.** | | | | | | **WINDSOR TOWN—con.** | | | | | | **WINDSOR TOWN—con.** | | | | | |
| Phelps, Oliver | 1 | 1 | 1 | | | Cook, Joel | 1 | 2 | 2 | | | Owen, Elijah | 4 | 4 | 2 | | |
| Brown, Sam¹ | 2 | 1 | 3 | | | Cook, Pinny | 1 | 1 | 3 | | | Hollida, Daniel | 1 | | 3 | | |
| Griswold, Solomon | 3 | 1 | 8 | | | Kirk, Thomas | 1 | 2 | 2 | | | Phelps, Azariah | 3 | 2 | 4 | | |
| Phelps, Aaron, Ju | 1 | 1 | 2 | | | Thrall, John | 1 | | 1 | | | Winchel, Elihu | 1 | 1 | 1 | | |
| Phelps, Aron | 4 | 1 | 4 | 1 | | Hickoks, Ebenʳ | 1 | 5 | 1 | | | Pinney, John | 4 | | 3 | | |
| Enos, Sam¹ | 1 | 4 | 2 | | | Griswold, Matthew | 2 | 2 | 3 | 1 | | Hutchins, John | 1 | 1 | 1 | | |
| Manley, Allen | 3 | | 1 | | | Olden, Isaac | 3 | 3 | 3 | 1 | | Nungers, Israel | 3 | | 4 | | |
| Filly, Aaron | 1 | 1 | 4 | | | Thrall, John, 3ᵈ | 2 | 5 | 2 | | | Brown, John | 1 | | | | |
| Brown, Zadock | 1 | 2 | 3 | | | Thrall, ——* | 1 | 3 | 3 | | | Eno, James | 1 | 2 | 3 | | |
| Brown, Benjⁿ, Ju | 1 | 2 | 2 | | | Owen, ——* | 1 | 1 | 2 | | | Perkins, Joel | 1 | | 3 | | |
| Cotton, Sam¹ | 2 | 2 | 3 | | | Elsworth, ——* | 1 | 1 | 4 | | | Thrall, Benjⁿ | 1 | 2 | 3 | | |
| Brown, Benjⁿ | 1 | | 2 | | | Hubbard, A——* | 1 | 1 | 2 | | | Adams, Silas | 2 | 1 | 4 | | |
| Brown, Joseph | 1 | 2 | 2 | | | Phelps, Azariah, Ju | 1 | 1 | 3 | | | David, Sam¹ | 1 | | 2 | | |
| Filley, Jonathan | 3 | 1 | 2 | | | Mather, Nath¹ | 2 | | 3 | | | Hendrick, John | 1 | | | | 9 |
| Parsons, James | 1 | 4 | 4 | | | Marshal, Sam¹ | 1 | | | | | | | | | | |
| Brown, Alpheus | 1 | 2 | 4 | | | Owen, Stine | 1 | | | | | | | | | | |

## LITCHFIELD COUNTY.

| NAME OF HEAD OF FAMILY. | Free white males of 16 years and upward, including heads of families. | Free white males under 16 years. | Free white females, including heads of families. | All other free persons. | Slaves. | NAME OF HEAD OF FAMILY. | Free white males of 16 years and upward, including heads of families. | Free white males under 16 years. | Free white females, including heads of families. | All other free persons. | Slaves. | NAME OF HEAD OF FAMILY. | Free white males of 16 years and upward, including heads of families. | Free white males under 16 years. | Free white females, including heads of families. | All other free persons. | Slaves. |
|---|---|---|---|---|---|---|---|---|---|---|---|---|---|---|---|---|---|
| **BETHLEM TOWN.** | | | | | | **BETHLEM TOWN—con.** | | | | | | **BETHLEM TOWN—con.** | | | | | |
| Allen, Amos | 5 | | 2 | | | Green, Eleazer, 2ᵈ | 1 | 1 | 4 | | | Rose, Mabel | | | 1 | | |
| Allen, Samuel | 2 | 5 | 4 | | | Guernsey, Richard | 1 | 2 | 3 | | | Runney, Julius | 2 | | 3 | | |
| Ambler, David | 4 | | 5 | | | Gillet, Wheelor | 3 | 2 | 4 | | | Robartson, Solomon | 1 | 1 | 2 | | |
| Atwood, John | 2 | 3 | 4 | | | Goodrich, Waitstill | 2 | | 2 | | | Smith, Jonathan | 1 | | 2 | | |
| Atwood, Gideon | 1 | | | | | Green, Eleazer | 1 | 2 | 5 | | | Smith, Jonathan, Juʳ | 1 | 4 | 2 | | |
| Brace, Elisha | 3 | 1 | 5 | | | Hill, Jonathan | 2 | 1 | 3 | | | Stoddard, Curtis | 1 | 2 | 2 | | |
| Barnum, Tila | 1 | 2 | 6 | | | Hill, David | 1 | 1 | 5 | | | Stoddard, Elisha | 1 | | | | |
| Brownson, Abraham | 4 | 1 | 2 | | | Hand, Stephen | 1 | | 2 | | | Stoddard, John | 1 | 1 | 2 | | |
| Baldwin, Jacob | 3 | 1 | 9 | | | Hand, Elias | 1 | 3 | 4 | | | Sherwood, Amy | | | 1 | | |
| Baldwin, Eli | 1 | 2 | 2 | | | Hawley, Benjamin | 3 | | 3 | | | Skilton, Avery | 1 | 2 | 4 | | |
| Bellamy, David | 3 | 1 | 4 | 1 | | Hawley, Moses | 2 | 3 | 4 | | | Stilson, Joseph | 1 | 1 | 2 | | |
| Bellamy, Samuel | 1 | 3 | 3 | | | Hawley, Enos | 3 | | 7 | | | Stilson, Josiah | 1 | 4 | 3 | | |
| Butler, Darius | 1 | 2 | 1 | | | Hawley, Silas | 2 | 4 | 2 | | | Stilson, Abel | 1 | 3 | 3 | | |
| Bishop, Amos | 2 | 2 | 5 | | | Hawley, Azor | 1 | | | | | Steel, John | 3 | 1 | 5 | | |
| Bishop, Dan | 2 | 2 | 6 | | | Hannah, Robart | 1 | 3 | 5 | 1 | | Steel, Daniel | 1 | 1 | 2 | | |
| Bishop, Daniel | 1 | 2 | 2 | | | Hannah, James | 1 | 3 | 1 | | | Steel, Elisha | 2 | 3 | 6 | | |
| Bishop, Billy | 1 | 1 | 1 | | | Hannah, Alaxander | 3 | | 5 | | | Steel, John, 2ᵈ | 2 | 2 | 3 | | |
| Beach, Dan | 1 | | 4 | | | Hannah, Margaret | | | 1 | | | Strong, Daniel | 2 | 4 | 2 | | |
| Beacher, Hezekiah | 2 | 2 | 2 | | | Hannah, Daniel | 1 | 1 | 3 | | | Strong, Timothy | 4 | | 4 | | |
| Bird, Lucy | 1 | 4 | 2 | | | Hine, Dan | 3 | 1 | 5 | | | Strong, Samuel | 1 | | 4 | | |
| Bird, Atwood | 1 | 5 | 4 | | | Hine, Dan, Juʳ | 1 | 3 | 3 | | | Stevens, Dan | 1 | 1 | 1 | | |
| Burritt, William | 1 | 1 | 5 | | | Hinman, Enos | 2 | | 1 | | | Stiles, David | 1 | 3 | 1 | | |
| Blois, Francis | 1 | 3 | 5 | | | Hinman, James | 1 | | 1 | | | Smith, Daniel | 1 | 4 | 1 | | |
| Bacon, Josiah | 1 | | 3 | | | Hall, Ebenezer | 1 | 1 | 3 | | | Stoddard, Giddeon | 1 | | 1 | | |
| Bradley, Daniel | | | 1 | | | Hall, Bristor | 2 | | | | | Thomson, Henry | 1 | 3 | 4 | | |
| Burton, Nathan | 2 | 2 | 3 | | | Hitchcock, Abel | 1 | 3 | 3 | | | Twiss, John | 2 | 1 | 2 | | |
| Botsford, Daniel | 2 | | 2 | | | Hitchcock, Benjamin | 2 | 1 | 4 | | | Thomas, Enoch | 1 | 3 | 2 | | |
| Brown, David | 1 | 2 | 7 | | | Hitchcock, Jared | 2 | 3 | 2 | | | Thomson, Levi | 2 | 4 | 3 | | |
| Bishop, Deborah | | | 3 | | | Hitchcock, Lydia | | 3 | 3 | | | Thomson, Aaron | 2 | 2 | 2 | | |
| Baldwin, Joseph | 1 | 2 | 7 | | | Hull, Titus | 3 | 3 | 7 | 1 | | Thomson, Thomas | 1 | 1 | 3 | | |
| Clark, Amos | 2 | | 5 | | | Jackson, Theophilus | 1 | 3 | 4 | | | Thomson, Samuel | 1 | 1 | 2 | | |
| Clark, Friend | 1 | 2 | 4 | | | Jackson, Samuel | 1 | | 4 | | | Thomson, Zacheriah | 2 | 2 | 4 | | |
| Clark, Joshua | 2 | 2 | 3 | | | Jackson, Daniel | 1 | 3 | 3 | | | Wheelor, John | 3 | 2 | 5 | | |
| Churchel, Jonathan | 1 | | 1 | | | Judson, Abner | 3 | | 2 | | | Wheelor, Elizur | 1 | | 4 | | |
| Churchel, Oliver | 1 | | 2 | | | Kason, Alaxander | 2 | 1 | 4 | | | Way, Philemon | 1 | 1 | 4 | | |
| Crane, Robart | 3 | 1 | 4 | | | Kasson, Archibald | 1 | 1 | 1 | | | Way, Roswell | 1 | 2 | 2 | | |
| Cowles, Levi | 1 | 3 | 2 | | | Kasson, James | 5 | 2 | 4 | | | Tucker, Daniel | 1 | | 1 | | |
| Cowles, Asa | 1 | | 2 | | | Kason, James, Juʳ | 3 | 4 | 5 | | | Church, Joshua | 2 | | 4 | | |
| Curtis, Asa | 2 | 1 | 4 | | | Knap, Moses | 2 | 3 | 3 | | | Johnson, Truman | 1 | | 3 | | |
| Curtis, James | 1 | 1 | 2 | | | Linsley, Timothy | 1 | | 3 | | | | | | | | |
| Camp, David | 3 | 1 | 3 | | | Lewis, Oliver | 1 | | 5 | | | **CORNWALL TOWN.** | | | | | |
| Camp, David, 2ᵈ | 1 | 1 | 2 | | | Lewis, Ezekiel | 1 | 4 | 5 | | | Abbott, Daniel | 2 | 3 | 1 | | |
| Chapman, Nathaniel | 1 | | 5 | | | Lambert, Nehemiah | 1 | | 1 | | | Andrews, Andrew | 1 | 4 | 3 | | |
| Chapman, Michael | 1 | 1 | 2 | | | Leavitt, David | 1 | | 2 | | | Allen, Ebenezer | 1 | 3 | 1 | | |
| Chapman, Nathan | 1 | | 2 | | | Leavitt, David, Juʳ | 3 | 1 | 6 | | 1 | Angel, Henry | 1 | | 2 | | |
| Dunning, Elias | 3 | 1 | 2 | | | Meiggs, Phineas | 1 | 2 | 3 | | | Allen, Elijah | 2 | 4 | 3 | | |
| Davies, William | 2 | 1 | 7 | | | Meiggs, James | 1 | 1 | 4 | | | Andrews, Caleb | 2 | 1 | 2 | | |
| Doolittle, Thomas | 4 | | 2 | | | Martin, William | 4 | | 1 | | | Andrews, Lyman | 1 | 1 | 2 | | |
| Doolittle, Abner | 1 | 1 | 1 | | | Martin, Lucy | | 1 | 2 | | | Abbot, Samuel | 1 | | 3 | | |
| Doolittle, John | 1 | 2 | 3 | | | Martin, William, 2ᵈ | 1 | | 2 | | | Abbott, Gold | 1 | | 2 | | |
| D. Wolf, Levi | 1 | 1 | 1 | | | Martin, Simeon | 1 | | 2 | | | Beardsley, Jeames | 1 | | | | |
| Everit, Daniel | 2 | 1 | 4 | | | Martin, Andrew | 2 | | 1 | | | Bennham, Oliver | | | 3 | | |
| Everit, Eunice | 1 | | 3 | | | Martin, Seth | 2 | 1 | 4 | | | Bristol, Sarah | | 1 | 1 | | |
| Eagleston, James | 1 | 5 | 4 | | | Minor, Jonas | 1 | | 2 | | | Brownson, Jacob F | 1 | | 2 | | |
| Ford, Thomas | 2 | 2 | 6 | | | Munger, Merriman | 1 | 1 | 1 | | | Buel, Jesse | 3 | 1 | 7 | | |
| French, Gideon | 1 | 1 | 3 | | | Munger, Lewis | 2 | 1 | 2 | | | Bacon, Ebenezer | 1 | 4 | 4 | | |
| Frisbie, James | 2 | 1 | 3 | | | Munson, Ephraim | 1 | | 4 | | | Bierce, Austin | 4 | 1 | 3 | | |
| Frisbie, Amos | 2 | 2 | 3 | | | Parmely, Oliver | 3 | 1 | 4 | | | Bierce, Isaih | 1 | 3 | 5 | | |
| Frisbie, Jacob, 2ᵈ | 1 | 1 | 3 | | | Parmely, Oliver, Juʳ | 1 | | | | | Baldwin, Aaron | 1 | 2 | 2 | | |
| Frisbie, Jacob | 2 | 1 | 1 | | | Parmely, Samuel | 1 | | 2 | | | Bierce, Jeames | 1 | | 2 | | |
| Frost, Joseph | 1 | 1 | 2 | | | Parmely, Ebenezer | 1 | 2 | 1 | | | Beardsley, Nehemiah | 1 | 3 | 6 | | 1 |
| Foot, Robart | 1 | | 2 | | | Peet, Samuel | 3 | 1 | 5 | | | Burges, Samuel | 2 | 4 | 3 | | |
| Gordon, John | 2 | | 1 | | | Peet, Richard | 1 | 3 | 3 | | | Bonney, Titus | 2 | 1 | 2 | | |
| Gordon, George | 1 | | 2 | | | Prentice, John | 1 | 2 | 5 | | | Bierce, Joseph | 4 | 6 | 3 | | |
| Gaylord, Aaron | 2 | 1 | 5 | | | Prentice, Christopher | 3 | 4 | 5 | | | Bradford, John | 1 | | 3 | | |
| Galpen, Moses | 1 | | 2 | | | Parks, Anna | | 3 | 4 | | | Bradford, Jeames F | 1 | | 3 | | |
| Galpen, John | 2 | 3 | 4 | | | Parks, Elizur | 1 | | 4 | | | Bartholomew, Jesse | 1 | 2 | 4 | | |
| Guitteau, Joshua | 1 | | 2 | | | Purkins, Ebenezer | 1 | 2 | 3 | | | Bell, Benjamin | 1 | | 1 | | 1 |
| Guitteau, Simeon | 1 | | | | | Prichard, James | 1 | 1 | 2 | | | Brownson, Timothy | 1 | | 1 | | |
| Green, Eleazer | 1 | 3 | 4 | | | Robarts, Noah | 1 | 1 | 5 | | | | | | | | |

*Illegible.

# HEADS OF FAMILIES—CONNECTICUT.

## LITCHFIELD COUNTY—Continued.

| NAME OF HEAD OF FAMILY. | Free white males of 16 years and upward, including heads of families. | Free white males under 16 years. | Free white females, including heads of families. | All other free persons. | Slaves. | NAME OF HEAD OF FAMILY. | Free white males of 16 years and upward, including heads of families. | Free white males under 16 years. | Free white females, including heads of families. | All other free persons. | Slaves. | NAME OF HEAD OF FAMILY. | Free white males of 16 years and upward, including heads of families. | Free white males under 16 years. | Free white females, including heads of families. | All other free persons. | Slaves. |
|---|---|---|---|---|---|---|---|---|---|---|---|---|---|---|---|---|---|
| **CORNWALL TOWN—con.** | | | | | | **CORNWALL TOWN—con.** | | | | | | **CORNWALL TOWN—con.** | | | | | |
| Bordwin, Azeriah | | | | | | Hollister, Gershom | 1 | 1 | 6 | | | Stewart, Daniel | 2 | 1 | 4 | | |
| Birdsey, Ebenezer | 1 | 2 | 4 | | 1 | Heart, Silas | 1 | 2 | 3 | | | Swif, Rufus | 1 | | | | 4 |
| Bonney, Jarius | 1 | | 4 | | | Hyatt, Jesse | 1 | 1 | 6 | | | Scovil, Joseph | 1 | 1 | 3 | | |
| Bryan, Saviah | | | 2 | | | Harrisson, Daniel, 1st | 3 | | 2 | | | Sedgwik, John A | 1 | | | | |
| Bonney, Perez | 3 | 3 | 5 | | | Hall, Hezekiah | 1 | 1 | 3 | | | Stewart, Joseph | 1 | 1 | 4 | | |
| Bearce, Jeames, Junr | 3 | | 4 | | | How, Deliverance | 1 | 2 | 1 | | | Sedgwick, John | 6 | 3 | 6 | | |
| Bristol, John | 1 | | 1 | | | Hurlburt, Osias | 2 | 1 | 3 | | | Sleet, Eliphet | 1 | | | | |
| Bristol, Nathan | 1 | | 2 | | | Heart, Titus | 3 | 1 | 4 | | | Stertin, Jeames | 3 | 3 | 6 | | |
| Bristol, Amos | 2 | 3 | 6 | | | Harris, David | 1 | 3 | 1 | | | Stead, John | 3 | 2 | 3 | | |
| Baldwin, Henry | 1 | 2 | 4 | | | Hochkins, Joseph | 1 | 1 | 4 | | | Seward, Nathan | 1 | 3 | 2 | | |
| Benedict, Moses | 1 | 1 | 4 | | | Heart, Elias | 1 | 2 | 2 | | | Shephard, Ebemener | 1 | 1 | 3 | | |
| Brown, Daniel | 8 | 1 | 2 | | | Hartshorn, Joshua | 1 | 2 | 3 | | | Scott, Obediah | 1 | | 2 | | |
| Bates, Isaac | 2 | 1 | 6 | | | Hineman, John | 1 | | 1 | | | Smaley, Enoch | 1 | | 1 | | |
| Bailey, William | 2 | 1 | 7 | | | Jackson, Charles | 1 | | 1 | | | Squire, Abijah | | | 2 | | |
| Brownson, Jacob, 2d | 2 | 1 | 2 | | | Jackson, Ebenezer | 2 | 2 | 5 | | 1 | Stewart, Oliver | | 1 | 2 | | |
| Bierce, Hezekiah | 3 | 1 | 5 | | | Ives, Abel | 3 | 1 | 2 | | | Tanner, Consider | 1 | 4 | 4 | | |
| Bell, Ruth | 1 | | 4 | | | Johnson, Amos | 3 | 4 | 4 | | | Tanner, Trial | 1 | 3 | 4 | 8 | 1 |
| Bassot, Samuel | 1 | | 1 | | | Jackson, Isaih | 1 | 2 | 1 | | | Tanner, William | 2 | 1 | 4 | | |
| Bartholomew, Joseph | 1 | 4 | 2 | | | Jeffery, Ebenezer | 2 | | 1 | | | Thorn, Abel | 1 | 3 | 5 | | |
| Baldwin, Joseph | 1 | 1 | 2 | | | Johnson, Philemon | 2 | | 3 | | | Tuttle, Joel | 1 | 3 | 2 | | |
| Bishop, Ebenezer | 1 | | 4 | | | Jones, Zacheriah H | | 1 | | | | Tyler, Adonijah | 1 | | 1 | | |
| Baldwin, Joannah | 1 | | 1 | | | Johnson, William | 1 | 2 | 4 | | | Thomson, Martha | 1 | | 2 | | |
| Bliss, Simeon | 1 | 2 | 5 | | | Judson, Abel | 2 | 1 | 3 | | | Wilcox, Samuel | 3 | | 2 | | |
| Beach, Linus | 1 | 1 | 2 | | | Jackson, Ephm | 1 | 1 | 3 | | | Wilcox, Zadock | 1 | 1 | 4 | | |
| Clark, Silas, 2d | 1 | | 2 | | | Jennings, Lemuel | 3 | 1 | 4 | | | West, Josiah | 1 | 1 | 5 | | |
| Clark, David | 1 | 2 | 7 | | | Johnson, Amos | 1 | | 2 | | | Wickwin, Samuel | 4 | 1 | 2 | | |
| Cotter, Andrew | 1 | | | | | Luddington, Nathaniel | 1 | 2 | 1 | | | Wright, John | 2 | 1 | 3 | | |
| Clark, Hezzekiah | 1 | 1 | 7 | | | Lorain, Calvin | 1 | 1 | | | | Wadsworth, Samuel | 7 | | 3 | | |
| Clark, Benjamin | 1 | 1 | 1 | | | London, Charles | 1 | 1 | 1 | | | Wadsworth, Joseph | 2 | 3 | 4 | | |
| Carter, Hezekiah | 2 | | 6 | | | Linsley, Ephraim | 1 | 1 | 2 | | | Willougheby, Salmon | 1 | 2 | 3 | | |
| Cornwell, Eden B | 1 | 1 | 1 | | | Kellog, Judah | 2 | 2 | 3 | | 1 | Wadsworth, Jeams | 1 | 2 | 3 | | |
| Chiddester, William | 2 | 3 | 1 | | | Kutland, Jeames | 2 | 2 | 2 | | | Wickwin, Richard | 1 | | 2 | | |
| Clark, Nehemiah | 2 | 1 | 2 | | | Miner, Joseph | 3 | | 1 | | | Wickwin, Nathan | 1 | 1 | 2 | | |
| Catlin, Roger | 2 | 2 | 3 | | | Miles, Joseph | 1 | 1 | 1 | | | Wood, Samuel | 1 | | 2 | | |
| Cother, John | 1 | 1 | 2 | | | Miles, John | 1 | 3 | 2 | | | Wilson, Thomas | 1 | 1 | 1 | | |
| Carter, Philo | 1 | | 2 | | | Mallery, Eliakim | 3 | 3 | 4 | | | Wells, John | 1 | 3 | 4 | | |
| Carter, Salmon | 1 | | | | | Mead, Philip | 1 | 5 | 2 | | | Wood, Jonathan | 1 | 1 | 2 | | |
| Clather, Ambrose | 2 | 3 | 3 | | | Millard, John, 1st | 1 | 1 | 4 | | | Young, William | 1 | 3 | 3 | | |
| Carter, John | 3 | 2 | 2 | | | Millard, John, 2d | 5 | 2 | 5 | | | | | | | | |
| Camp, Amos | 2 | 2 | 2 | | | Morey, Asa | 2 | 3 | 1 | | | **HARWINTON TOWN.** | | | | | |
| Clark, Silas | 2 | 2 | 2 | | | Marvin, Nehemiah | 2 | | 6 | | | | | | | | |
| Crocker, Jonathan | 2 | 1 | 4 | | | Miles, Stephen | 1 | | 1 | | | Andrews, Silas | 3 | 1 | 5 | | |
| Crammer, William | 1 | 1 | 1 | | | Miles, Levi | 1 | | | | | Alford, Eli | 2 | 3 | 1 | | |
| Cole, Seth | 1 | 2 | 4 | | | Millard, Joel | 1 | 1 | 1 | | | Austin, Dan | 1 | 1 | 4 | | |
| Croner, Hannah | 2 | 1 | 4 | | | Millard, Nathan | 1 | 1 | 4 | | | Ames, Benjamin | 1 | 1 | 1 | | |
| Cadley, George | 1 | | 3 | | | May, Edward | 1 | | 1 | | | Abenatha, William | 2 | 2 | 5 | | |
| Dean, Benjamin | 3 | 2 | 3 | | | Marion, David | 1 | | 1 | | | Alford, Joab | 3 | | 3 | | |
| Dean, Samuel, 2d | 1 | | 1 | | | North, Stephen | 1 | 1 | 1 | | | Austin, Reuben | 1 | | 1 | | |
| Dibble, Silas | 1 | 1 | 3 | | | Olcott, John Easton | 1 | 2 | 2 | | | Alford, Alexander | 2 | 3 | 5 | | |
| Dibble, Jonathan | 1 | | 1 | | | Payne, Rufus | 1 | 5 | 3 | | | Andrews, David | 1 | | 1 | | |
| Dibbe, John | 1 | | 1 | | | Pratt, Abner | 1 | 1 | 6 | | | Alford, John | 1 | 3 | 4 | | |
| Dean, Samuel, 1st | 2 | | 2 | | | Pierce, Isaac | 1 | 1 | 4 | | | Bawaj, Thomas | 1 | 2 | 2 | | |
| Dean, John | 1 | 2 | 5 | | | Pierce, Joshua, 3d | 1 | | 2 | | | Bartholemew, Jacob | 3 | | 3 | | |
| Dibble, Isaac | 1 | | 2 | | | Proston, Stephen | 1 | 2 | 5 | | | Butt, Sabria | 1 | | 1 | | |
| Dibbe, Benjamin | 1 | | 2 | | | Pratt, David, 2d | 1 | 1 | 6 | | | Barber, Joshua | 2 | | 1 | | |
| Dibble, Israel | 3 | 2 | 2 | | | Pratt, David, 1st | 2 | | 2 | | | Barnes, Benjamin | 2 | 1 | 7 | | |
| Dibble, George | 2 | | 4 | | | Peck, Bennoni | 2 | 1 | 3 | | | Bill, Elijah, 1st | 1 | 1 | 4 | | |
| Dean, Reuben | 1 | 2 | 2 | | | Pratt, Jasper | 1 | 2 | 3 | | | Bill, Elijah, 2d | 1 | 2 | 1 | | |
| Dean, Reuben, 2d | 1 | | 1 | | | Paterson, Elkana | 2 | 1 | 4 | | | Bristol, Reuben, 2d | 1 | | 2 | | |
| Dickerson, Asahel | 1 | 2 | 3 | | | Pierce, Levi | 3 | | 4 | | | Barber, John, 2d | 1 | 2 | 2 | | |
| Dean, Thomas | 2 | 1 | 2 | | | Pierce, Joshua, 1st | 1 | | 1 | | 1 | Barnes, Zopar | 2 | 5 | 1 | | |
| Dextar, Sarah | | | 2 | | | Pierce, Joshua, 2d | 3 | | 2 | | | Butler, Josiah | 2 | | 2 | | 3 |
| Dickerson, Elijah | | | | | | Proston, David | 1 | | 2 | | | Barber, Reuben, 1st | 4 | | 2 | | |
| Dibbe, Clemens | 1 | 1 | 3 | | | Patterson, Mathew | 2 | 2 | 3 | | | Bull, John | 4 | 1 | 4 | | |
| Emons, Soloman | 1 | 3 | 5 | | | Pierce, John | 2 | 1 | 2 | | | Barber, Simeon | 1 | 3 | 2 | | |
| Everest, Daniel | 1 | 5 | 4 | | | Pierce, Seth | 3 | 2 | 8 | | | Bartholemew, Jeames | 1 | | 2 | | |
| Emons, Asaph | 2 | 3 | 2 | | | Rogers, Grace | | | 2 | | | Bartholemew, Reuben | 3 | 2 | 6 | | |
| Emons, Simeon | 1 | 2 | 2 | | | Rogers, Edward | 4 | 2 | 9 | | | Barber, Abner | 1 | 2 | 3 | | |
| Emons, Asa | 1 | 1 | 3 | | | Rogers, Timothy | 1 | 3 | 3 | | | Bull, Jesse | 2 | | 2 | | |
| Emons, Woodruff | 1 | | 1 | | | Rogers, Noah, 2d | 1 | | 2 | | | Brownson, Selah | 1 | 4 | 1 | | |
| Everston, Hannah | | 2 | 4 | | | Reed, John | 1 | 1 | | | | Bartholemew, John | 1 | | 1 | | |
| Freedom, Jack | | | | 4 | | Rexford, Samuel | | | 1 | | | Barber, Judah | 1 | | 1 | | |
| Foot, Jesse | 2 | 1 | 6 | | | Rogers, Noah | 6 | 3 | 5 | | 1 | Bartholemew, Andrew | 2 | 4 | 2 | | |
| Fox, Reuben | 1 | 2 | 5 | | | Reed, Holly | 1 | | | | | Bartholemew, Submit | 1 | | 3 | | |
| Ford, Oliver | 1 | 3 | 4 | | | Rouse, Elijah | 3 | | 1 | | | Baron, Aaron | 1 | 2 | 5 | | |
| Ford, Thaddeus | 1 | 2 | 4 | | | Rexford, David | 3 | 2 | 4 | | | Butler, Stephen | 1 | | 3 | | |
| Gold, Hezekiah | 1 | 1 | 2 | | | Russel, Ichabod | 1 | 2 | 4 | | | Brown, David | 1 | 2 | 3 | | |
| Gold, Benjamin | 2 | 2 | 3 | | | Saunders, Joshua | 1 | | 3 | | | Barber, Asahel | 1 | 1 | 3 | | |
| Gipson, Samuel | 2 | | 3 | | | Swift, Heman | 3 | 2 | 3 | | 3 | Bearce, Jeames, 1st | 1 | | 4 | | 2 |
| Gerrard, Jesse | 1 | 1 | 1 | | | Swift, Elisha | 1 | | 2 | | | Bristol, Reuben, 1st | 2 | 2 | 3 | | |
| Gold, Joseph Wakefield | 1 | 1 | | | 1 | Saunders, Ithamer | 3 | | 5 | | | Barber, Reuben, 2d | 2 | 1 | 4 | | |
| Graves, Asahel | 2 | 1 | 2 | | | Scovil, Jacob | 2 | | 2 | | | Bartholemew, Benjn | 1 | 3 | 4 | | |
| Green, Samuel, 1st | | | | 4 | | Saunders, Zelotes | 2 | 3 | 2 | | | Barber, Timothy | 1 | 1 | 4 | | |
| Green, Samuel, 2d | | | | 5 | | Stewart, John | 1 | 1 | 4 | | | Bradley, Joel | 1 | 2 | 3 | | |
| Green, Jacob | | | | 6 | | Shewood, Hannah | 2 | | 4 | | | Blakeley, Enos | 1 | 3 | 2 | | |
| Hallhet, John | 1 | 3 | 4 | | | Steel, Elijah, 1st | 1 | 1 | 4 | | | Barnes, Moses | 2 | 3 | 3 | | |
| Holcomb, John | 1 | 1 | 5 | | | Steel, Elijah, 2d | 1 | | 4 | | | Blakeley, Jonathan | 1 | | 2 | | |
| Hawkins, Abram | 4 | | 4 | | | Scovil, Timothy | 2 | | 4 | | | Basto, William | 3 | 1 | 3 | | |
| Harrisson, Daniel, 2d | 2 | 2 | 1 | | | Steel, Mathew M | 1 | 1 | 4 | | | Blakeley, Silas | 1 | 2 | 3 | | |
| Harrisson, Noah | 3 | | 4 | | | Stewart, Stephen | 1 | 2 | 4 | | | Baldwin, W. Samuel | 1 | 4 | 3 | | 1 |
| Hineman, Partrick | 1 | | 1 | 3 | | Scovil, Samuel, 1st | 4 | | 3 | | | Bartholemew, Margett | | | 1 | | |
| Hurlburt, Joab | 1 | 1 | 7 | | | Sawyer, Samuel | 2 | 1 | 6 | | | Bull, Michael | 1 | 2 | 1 | | |
| Heart, Soloman | 4 | 1 | 4 | | | Scovil, Stephen | 1 | 1 | 3 | | | Butler, Jesse | 2 | | 2 | | |
| Heart, Phineas | 2 | 1 | 2 | | | Stephen, Nathaniel | 4 | 1 | 5 | | | Curtis, David | 1 | 2 | 5 | | |
| Hopkins, Josiah | 1 | 5 | 2 | | | Scovil, Samuel, 2d | 1 | 1 | 2 | | | Castle, Joel | 2 | 4 | 2 | | |

# FIRST CENSUS OF THE UNITED STATES.

## LITCHFIELD COUNTY—Continued.

| NAME OF HEAD OF FAMILY. | Free white males of 16 years and upward, including heads of families. | Free white males under 16 years. | Free white females, including heads of families. | All other free persons. | Slaves. | NAME OF HEAD OF FAMILY. | Free white males of 16 years and upward, including heads of families. | Free white males under 16 years. | Free white females, including heads of families. | All other free persons. | Slaves. | NAME OF HEAD OF FAMILY. | Free white males of 16 years and upward, including heads of families. | Free white males under 16 years. | Free white females, including heads of families. | All other free persons. | Slaves. |
|---|---|---|---|---|---|---|---|---|---|---|---|---|---|---|---|---|---|
| HARWINTON TOWN—con. | | | | | | HARWINTON TOWN—con. | | | | | | KENT TOWN—continued. | | | | | |
| Crow, Damaras | | | 1 | | | Kellogg, Azeriah, 1st | 1 | 1 | 3 | | | Beardsley, Jabez | 3 | 3 | 5 | | |
| Catlin, Joel | 2 | 4 | 2 | | | Kellogg, Azeriah, 2d | 1 | 1 | 5 | | | Barnum, David | 3 | | 5 | | |
| Cook, Oliver | 2 | | 5 | | | King, David | 2 | 2 | 2 | | | Bates, Ichabod | 2 | 3 | 3 | | |
| Catlin, Jacob | 5 | | 6 | | | King, Lydia | | | 1 | | | Betts, Jesse | 1 | | 3 | | |
| Cooler, Isaac | 1 | 1 | 2 | | | Lee, Sarah | | | 1 | | | Botsford, David | 1 | | 4 | | |
| Catlin, Dan | 2 | 1 | 4 | | | Leach, Hezekiah | 1 | 3 | 4 | | | Barnes, Philip | 2 | 3 | 6 | | |
| Cook, Samuel | 2 | | 3 | | | Lanston, Jeames | 1 | 3 | 4 | | | Beebee, Daniel, 2d | 1 | 1 | 2 | | |
| Catlen, Daniel | 2 | 3 | 4 | | | Loomis, Isaih | 1 | | 4 | | | Beardsley, Philo | 3 | 2 | 2 | | |
| Catlen, Lewis | 1 | 1 | 3 | | | Lee, Theodore | 2 | 1 | 3 | | | Benedict, Jesse | 3 | 2 | 1 | | |
| Cleveland, Isaac | 2 | | 4 | | | Loomis, Ebenezer | 1 | 1 | 5 | | | Benedict, John | 1 | 2 | 2 | | |
| Conley, Wm Gaylord | 1 | 1 | | | | Loomis, Noah | 1 | 1 | 5 | | | Benedict, Elijah | 2 | 2 | 3 | | |
| Catlin, Abijah | 2 | 2 | 6 | | | Loomis, Giles | 1 | | 3 | | | Bull, Jacob | 3 | 1 | 6 | | |
| Catlin, Grover | 2 | | 1 | | | Moody, Thomas | 3 | 3 | 4 | | | Beach, Mary | | | 4 | | |
| Catlin, Hezekiah | 1 | 1 | 3 | | | Meachum, Jeremiah | 1 | | 3 | | | Brownson, Levi, 1st | 1 | | 5 | | |
| Cook, Joseph | 5 | 1 | 4 | | | Meriam, George | 1 | 4 | 4 | | | Brownson, Silas | 1 | 3 | 2 | | |
| Castle, Isaac | 1 | 4 | 2 | | | Morse, Amasa | 3 | 4 | 5 | | | Brownson, Wm | 1 | | 2 | | |
| Cook, Scad | 1 | | 4 | | | Merrill, Mead | 1 | 1 | 3 | | | Brownson, Levi, 2d | 1 | 3 | 2 | | |
| Cott, John | | 1 | 2 | | | Merwin, Stephen | 2 | 2 | 3 | | | Beamont, Tracy | 1 | 3 | 2 | | |
| Catlin, Jacob, 2d | 1 | 1 | 3 | | | Mechum, Nehemiah | 1 | | 3 | | | Barnum, John | 2 | 2 | 3 | | |
| Cook, Sylvanus | 1 | 1 | 3 | | | Mechum, Seth | 2 | 1 | 2 | | | Boardwell, Joel | 2 | 2 | 6 | | |
| Cook, Titus | 1 | 2 | 2 | | | Main, Ezekial | 1 | 3 | 3 | | | Bailey, John | 1 | 2 | 2 | | |
| Cott, Jonth Hanson | 3 | | 7 | | | Mansfield, David | 2 | 1 | 6 | | | Berry, Ebenezer | 2 | 3 | 6 | | |
| Catlin, Elisha | 2 | 2 | 4 | | | Meriam, William | 2 | 3 | 4 | | | Barley, Michael | 1 | 3 | 1 | | |
| Catlin, Isaac, 1st | 1 | 1 | 2 | | | Morse, Chauncy | 1 | 3 | 4 | | | Barlow, John | 3 | 2 | 6 | | |
| Cook, Daniel | 1 | 2 | 4 | | | Munson, Levi | 3 | 2 | 1 | | | Bently, Mary | | | 4 | | |
| Catlin, Isaac, 2d | 1 | 4 | 1 | | | Olcott, Jeames | 2 | | 2 | | | Bostwick, Ebenezer | 1 | 1 | 2 | | |
| Catlin, George, 2d | 1 | | 2 | | | Pierpont, Robert | 3 | | 5 | | | Chamberlain, Leander | 1 | | 1 | | |
| Catlin, Jonathan | 2 | | 3 | | | Pond, Josiah | 1 | | | | | Curtis, Hannah | | 1 | 1 | | |
| Cook, Joab | 1 | | 1 | | | Phelps, Oliver | 1 | | 2 | | | Chamberlain, Samuel | 2 | 2 | 4 | | |
| Catlin, Grover | 1 | 2 | 3 | | | Prindle, Mack | 5 | 2 | 5 | | | Caswell, Julius | 2 | | 4 | 2 | |
| Cook, Jonathan | 2 | 1 | 1 | | | Phelps, Josiah | 2 | 1 | 3 | | | Converse, Elijah | 3 | | 2 | | |
| Cook, Thomas | 2 | | 1 | | | Phelps, Samuel, 1st | 2 | | 2 | | | Chamberlain, Elizur | 2 | 1 | 1 | | |
| Catlin, Abram | 1 | | 3 | | | Perkins, Abner | 2 | 3 | 4 | | | Comstock, Abijah | 2 | 1 | 2 | | |
| Cook, William | 2 | | 4 | | | Peck, Gideon | 1 | 3 | 1 | | | Comstock, Gershom | 1 | | 3 | | |
| Curtis, Molly | | 1 | 2 | | | Peck, Solomon | 1 | 1 | 3 | | | Coleman, Aaron | 2 | 1 | 1 | 1 | |
| Carter, Stephen | 1 | | 2 | | | Phelps, Samuel, 2d | 1 | 1 | 2 | | | Comstock, David | 1 | | 2 | | |
| Deer, Eli | 2 | 3 | 4 | | | Potter, Jesse | 1 | | 1 | | | Campbell, Thomas | 1 | 1 | 2 | | |
| Davies, John | 2 | | 2 | | | Preston, John | 3 | 1 | 5 | | | Carter, Israel | 1 | 2 | 4 | | |
| Davies, Nathan | 3 | | 4 | | | Phelps, Uri | 1 | 1 | 3 | | | Comstock, Eliphlet | 1 | | 2 | | |
| Davies, Jeames | 1 | 1 | 4 | | | Royce, Nehemiah | 2 | 1 | 3 | | | Carter, Ithiel | 1 | | 1 | | |
| Elden, John | 1 | | 2 | | | Roseter, Jonathan | 1 | 1 | 6 | | | Chamberlain, Nathan | 1 | 4 | 3 | | |
| Ely, Jacob | 1 | 7 | 2 | | | Roseter, Amos | 1 | 2 | 6 | | | Chamberlain, Peleg | 1 | 1 | 5 | | |
| Evins, Asahel | 1 | 1 | 1 | | | Rogers, Hezekiah | 2 | 1 | 5 | | | Comstock, Peter | 1 | 2 | 3 | | 1 |
| Frisbie, Jabez | 2 | 2 | 4 | | | Smith, Amasa | 1 | 2 | 4 | | | Carter, Heman | 2 | | 2 | | |
| Foot, Darius | 1 | 1 | 2 | | | Smith, Jesse | 1 | 2 | 1 | | | Chamberlain, Jirah | 1 | 1 | 3 | | |
| Fitch, John | 1 | 3 | 4 | | | Smith, Asa, 1st | 1 | 1 | 3 | | | Case, Aaron | 1 | 4 | 3 | | |
| Frisbie, John, 1st | 2 | | 6 | | | Smith, Asa, 2d | 1 | 2 | 3 | | | Chamberlain, Bartlet | 1 | 3 | 3 | | |
| Frisbie, John, 2d | | | 4 | | | Smith, Jeremiah | 1 | 2 | 2 | | | Curtis, Martin | 1 | 1 | 5 | | |
| Filley, Jonah | 1 | 1 | 3 | | | Stone, Edmond | 1 | 2 | 1 | | | Clark, Cyrenus | 1 | 1 | 2 | | |
| Frisbier, Isaac | 2 | 1 | 2 | | | Stone, William | 2 | 2 | 4 | | | Calhoun, John | 1 | 4 | 4 | | |
| Frisbier, Enos | 1 | | 2 | | | Scovil, Ezekial | 5 | | 3 | | | Canfield, Andrew | 1 | 2 | 3 | | |
| Griswold, Janna | 1 | | 1 | | | Scovil, Joseph | 3 | 2 | 4 | | | Chase, Mary | 1 | | 1 | | |
| Gillott, Joel | 2 | 1 | 3 | | | Scovil, Daniel | 1 | 1 | 1 | | | Carter, Buel | 1 | | 1 | | |
| Gilbert, Jabez | 2 | 3 | 4 | | | Spencer, Silas | 1 | 3 | 5 | | | Chapman, Ben Thomas | 1 | | 3 | | |
| Griswold, Asa | 1 | 1 | 4 | | | Skinner, Ashbel | 4 | | 4 | | | Dailey, Jeames | 1 | 2 | 2 | | |
| Griswold, Benjamin | 1 | 1 | 4 | | | Skinner, Thomas | 1 | 2 | 6 | | | Dalton, John | 1 | 1 | 1 | | |
| Grannis, Enos | 2 | 3 | 2 | | | Skinner, Ira | 2 | | 2 | | | Dayton, Isaac | 3 | | 6 | | |
| Gridley, Abel | 3 | 2 | 3 | | | Stephens, Joshua | 2 | 3 | 5 | | | Delano, Sylvanus | 2 | 3 | 3 | | |
| Gridley, Silas | 2 | 3 | 2 | | | Sperry, Ebeneza | 1 | 1 | 2 | | | Dayton, Jonah | 1 | 2 | 6 | | |
| Graves, Stephen | 2 | 2 | 2 | | | Stoddard, Wells | 2 | 1 | 1 | | | Delano, Aaron | 2 | 2 | 2 | | |
| Gaylord, Chauny | 2 | 4 | 3 | | | Toles, Jacob | 1 | 3 | 2 | | | Dye, Daniel | 1 | | 2 | | |
| Gaylord, Elijah | 2 | | 2 | | | Tiler, Jonathan | 1 | 3 | 2 | | | Dodge, Stephen | 3 | 4 | 3 | | |
| Harvy, Thos | 1 | 4 | 1 | | | Tinsdale, Samuel | 2 | 1 | 2 | | | Dunham, Isaac | 1 | 1 | 6 | | |
| Hall, Elisha | 2 | | 3 | | | Williams, Thomas | 1 | | 2 | | | Dye, Elizabeth | | | 3 | | |
| Hale, Curtis | 2 | 3 | 5 | | | Wisson, Samuel | 1 | | 2 | | | Eliot, Nathan | 6 | 1 | 3 | | 3 |
| Hinsdale, Samuel | 2 | 2 | 2 | | | White, Nathaniel | 1 | 2 | 5 | | | Eliot, Abraham | 2 | 3 | 4 | | |
| Haydon, Elijah | 2 | 3 | 3 | | | Webster, Charles | 2 | 2 | 6 | | | Edward, Mary | | 3 | 2 | | |
| Hopkins, Hezekiah | 2 | 2 | 8 | | | Wooden, Calvin | 2 | 1 | 3 | | | Eaton, Moses | 1 | 2 | 3 | | |
| Haydon, Joseph | 2 | 3 | 4 | | | Webster, Cyprian | 2 | | 2 | | | Elton, Joseph | 1 | 3 | 3 | | |
| Hopkins, Uriah | 2 | 2 | 3 | | | Webster, Amos | 3 | 1 | 2 | | | Freeman, Call | | | | 4 | |
| Hopkins, Benjamin | 1 | | | | | Woodruf, Jesse | 1 | | 2 | | | Fairchild, Ezra | 1 | | 1 | | |
| Hungerford, Mathew | 1 | 3 | 6 | | | Wilson, John, 1st | 1 | | | | | Fairchild, Abel | 1 | 2 | 2 | | |
| Hungerford, Joseph | 1 | 1 | 3 | | | Wilson, Eli | 4 | 4 | 5 | | | Fairchild, Stephen | 2 | | 2 | | |
| Hough, Benoni | 1 | | 2 | | | Wilson, Abner | 1 | 4 | 5 | | | Fuller, Jeremiah | 2 | 1 | 3 | | |
| Homestone, Timothy | 2 | 2 | 4 | | | Wilson, John, 2d | 1 | 3 | 2 | | | Fuller, Ephraim | 2 | 1 | 5 | 1 | |
| Homestone, Joseph | 1 | | 5 | | | Wilson, Daniel | 2 | 2 | 4 | | | Fuller, Jacob | 4 | 1 | 7 | | |
| Homestone, Abram | 1 | 1 | 4 | | | Wilcox, Moses, 1st | 2 | | 2 | | | Fuller, Benajah | 1 | 2 | 4 | | |
| Hill, Asa | 2 | 2 | 1 | | | Wilcox, Moses, 2d | 1 | 1 | 1 | | | Fuller, Oliver | 2 | | 2 | | |
| Hungerford, Tertius | 1 | | | | | Watkins, John | 1 | 2 | 2 | | | Fuller, Abram | 3 | 2 | 5 | | 1 |
| Homestone, Abram, 2d | 1 | | 2 | | | Watkins, Henekiah | 1 | 1 | 2 | | | Felch, Ebenezer | 1 | 3 | 1 | | |
| Haydon, Samuel | 1 | 2 | 2 | | | Williams, Joshua | 1 | 1 | 4 | | | Fairchild, Samuel | 1 | | 1 | | |
| Haydon, William | 2 | | 4 | | | | | | | | | Freeland, Robert | 1 | 2 | 5 | | |
| Hinsdal, Ezra | 3 | 3 | 6 | | | KENT TOWN. | | | | | | Ghoram, Wakeman | 1 | | 2 | | |
| Harvy, William | 1 | 2 | 2 | | | | | | | | | Gibson, Isaih | | 2 | 4 | | |
| Johnson, Ebenezer | 2 | 2 | 4 | | | Berry, Joseph | 2 | 1 | 3 | | | Gregory, Fairweather | 1 | | 2 | | |
| Johnson, Benoni | 1 | 1 | 1 | | | Berry, Nathaniel | 5 | | 6 | 1 | | Ghoram, John | 3 | 1 | 5 | | |
| Johnson, Hamlen | 1 | 2 | 2 | | | Bates, Joseph | 1 | 2 | 6 | | | Geer, Ezra, 1st | 2 | | 2 | | |
| Johnson, Christopher | 4 | 5 | 3 | | | Beacher, Samuel | 2 | 1 | 3 | | | Geer, Ezra, 2d | 1 | 4 | 2 | | |
| Johnson, Ira | 1 | | 3 | | | Beacher, Abram | 3 | 5 | 3 | | | Gillet, Jonathan | 1 | 3 | 1 | | |
| Johnson, Samuel | 1 | 2 | 6 | | | Brown, Benjamin | 4 | | 6 | | | Geer, Elijah | 1 | | 1 | | |
| Johnson, Elisha | 1 | 4 | 2 | | | Benson, Noah | 1 | 1 | 1 | | | Gregory, Stephen | 1 | 1 | 5 | | |
| Johnson, Rufus | 1 | 2 | 6 | | | Beebee, Daniel | 3 | 2 | 4 | | | Geer, Nathaniel | 1 | 2 | 2 | | |
| Jones, George | 1 | 1 | 3 | | | Barnum, Amos | 1 | 1 | 4 | | | Greegory, Samuel | 1 | 2 | 3 | | |
| King, Joseph | 1 | | 6 | | | Beardsley, Ephraim | 3 | 2 | 4 | | | Greenill, Daniel | 1 | 1 | 3 | | |
| Kellogg, Allen | 1 | 1 | | | | Beardsley, David | 3 | | 3 | | | Gibbs, Robert | 1 | | 3 | | |

# HEADS OF FAMILIES—CONNECTICUT.

## LITCHFIELD COUNTY—Continued.

| NAME OF HEAD OF FAMILY. | Free white males of 16 years and upward, including heads of families. | Free white males under 16 years. | Free white females, including heads of families. | All other free persons. | Slaves. | NAME OF HEAD OF FAMILY. | Free white males of 16 years and upward, including heads of families. | Free white males under 16 years. | Free white females, including heads of families. | All other free persons. | Slaves. | NAME OF HEAD OF FAMILY. | Free white males of 16 years and upward, including heads of families. | Free white males under 16 years. | Free white females, including heads of families. | All other free persons. | Slaves. |
|---|---|---|---|---|---|---|---|---|---|---|---|---|---|---|---|---|---|
| **KENT TOWN—continued.** | | | | | | **KENT TOWN—continued.** | | | | | | **LITCHFIELD TOWN—con.** | | | | | |
| Hatch, Nathaniel | 4 | 2 | 5 | | 1 | Noble, Israel | 4 | 2 | 5 | | | Martin, Sam'l | 1 | 2 | 2 | | |
| Hubbel, Abijah | 1 | 4 | 5 | | | Phelps, Ebenezer | 1 | 3 | 1 | | | Collins, Charles | 2 | | 2 | | |
| Hall, Asa | 3 | 3 | 6 | | | Piet, John | 2 | 2 | 6 | | | Witton, Stephen | 3 | | 1 | | |
| Hath, Jethro | 3 | | 6 | | | Pratt, Peter | 2 | | 3 | | | Hubbard, Josiah | 1 | 1 | 7 | | |
| Hopkins, Noah | 1 | 2 | 2 | | | Payne, John | 3 | 3 | 6 | | | Noth, Seth | 1 | 1 | 2 | | |
| Hubbel, Jedediah | 1 | | 1 | | | Pratt, Joseph | 2 | 2 | 4 | | | Romain, Daniel | 2 | 3 | 2 | | |
| Hubbel, Samuel | 1 | 1 | 2 | | | Pratt, Noah | 2 | 1 | 4 | | | Smith, David | 1 | 3 | 2 | | |
| Hall, Mary | 1 | | 1 | | | Peck, Ebenezer | 1 | 3 | 1 | | | Bishshop, Samuel | 1 | 3 | 3 | | |
| Hopson, John | 1 | 1 | 1 | | | Percy, Ebenezer | 2 | 3 | 4 | | | Carter, Nathan | 1 | 3 | 4 | | |
| Hill, Daniel | 2 | 1 | 2 | | | Parish, Oliver | 1 | 1 | 2 | | | Butler, Abel | 3 | 2 | 2 | | |
| Hill, Jonathan | 1 | 3 | 2 | | | Read, Hezekiah | 4 | 2 | 3 | | | Mott, Samuel | 1 | 2 | 2 | | |
| Hubbel, David | 1 | 3 | 2 | | | Roots, Daniel | 1 | 4 | 2 | | | Ovatt, Samuel | 1 | 1 | 1 | | |
| How, Leavitt | 2 | | 2 | | | Ranson, John | 2 | | 2 | | | Ovatt, Samuel | 3 | 5 | 3 | | |
| Hoit, Ebenezer | 2 | | 3 | | | Roots, Gideon | 1 | | 3 | | | Murrin, Fowler | 2 | 3 | 4 | | |
| Rust, Abel | 2 | 1 | 5 | 1 | | Rust, Levi | 3 | 2 | 3 | | | Ovatt, Benjamin | 2 | 5 | 5 | | |
| Ross, Daniel | 2 | 2 | 3 | | | | | | | | | Norton, Aaron | 3 | 5 | 4 | | |
| Ross, Asher | 2 | 2 | 2 | | | **LITCHFIELD TOWN.** | | | | | | Catlin, Elisha | 1 | 1 | 1 | | |
| Sileman, John | 3 | | 5 | | | Smith, Jacob | 3 | 2 | 4 | | | Norval, Nathaniel | 1 | | 1 | | |
| Sturtevant, Samuel | 2 | 1 | 5 | | | Russell, William | 2 | 4 | | | | Atwood, Harvey | 1 | | 1 | | |
| Stewart, Silas | 1 | 1 | 4 | | | Granger, William | 2 | 3 | 1 | | | Buel, Timothy | 3 | 2 | 5 | | |
| Swift, Barzilla | 3 | 4 | 4 | | | B——*, Solomon | 1 | 1 | 2 | | | Norton, Nathaniel | 1 | 1 | 4 | | |
| Swetland, Joseph | 1 | 1 | 2 | | | Blake, Richard | 2 | 4 | 5 | | | Miles, Isaac | 1 | 3 | | | |
| Sturtevant, Zebedee | 3 | 2 | 2 | | | Crosbey, Simeon | 1 | 1 | 1 | | | Sheppard, Josiah | 1 | | 1 | | |
| Skiff, Nathan | 4 | 3 | 5 | | | Kilborn, Jeremiah | 1 | 2 | 2 | | | Driggs, Martin | 1 | 2 | 1 | | |
| Smith, Noah, 1st | 2 | 2 | 4 | | | Griswold, Median | 1 | | 5 | | | Merrill, Samuel | 1 | | 2 | | |
| Skiff, Joseph | 5 | | 2 | | | Smith, Charles | 1 | | 2 | | | Kilbron, John | 1 | 2 | 1 | | |
| Smith, Noah, 2d | 1 | 1 | 3 | | | Moodey, Mary | | | 2 | | | Lee, Rejoice | | | 1 | | |
| Segar, Joseph | 1 | 1 | 5 | | | Stone, Heman | 1 | 1 | 1 | | | Lee, Samuel | 2 | 2 | 2 | | |
| Smith, Elias | 1 | | 1 | | | Griswold, Jonathan | 1 | 1 | 6 | | | Ganes, Moses | 1 | 2 | 5 | | |
| Smith, Moses | 1 | 1 | 1 | | | Bartholomew, Noah | 2 | 2 | 4 | | | Paine, Abraham | 1 | 1 | 5 | | |
| Seeley, Elizabeth | | | 2 | | | Smith, Charles | 2 | | 1 | | | Paine, William | 1 | | 4 | | |
| Sloson, Nathan | 3 | 2 | 4 | | | Smith, David | 1 | 2 | 4 | | | Paine, William | 2 | | 3 | | |
| Skieff, Stephen | 4 | | 2 | | | Cluff, Isaac | 1 | | 2 | | | Paine, Ebenezer | 1 | | 2 | | |
| Spooner, Ebenezer | 3 | 3 | 4 | | | Waugh, John | 1 | 1 | 1 | | | Richard, Aaron | 3 | 2 | 4 | | |
| St. John, Timothy | 2 | 1 | 2 | | | Tthroop, Dan | 1 | 2 | 4 | | | Messenger, Reuben | 1 | 1 | 3 | | |
| Stuart, Jeames | 2 | 2 | 5 | | | Throop, Joseph | 1 | | 2 | | | Willey, Jonathan | 1 | | 3 | | |
| Swift, Asaph | 2 | 2 | 5 | | | Throop, Benjamin | 1 | 4 | 4 | | | Pike, Samuel | 3 | | 2 | | |
| Stevenson, Jeames | 1 | 1 | 3 | | | Bishop, Miles | 4 | 1 | 3 | | | Humpheys, Benonah | 3 | 1 | 3 | | |
| Smith, Noah Day | 2 | 1 | 3 | | | Hand, Timothy | 2 | 3 | 5 | | | Seymore, Elijah | 1 | 3 | 5 | 3 | |
| Stanton, Sarah | 1 | | 1 | | | Linley, Adam | 1 | | 2 | | 1 | Sheppard, Phinehas | 2 | 2 | 2 | | |
| Stewart, Robert | 1 | | 2 | | | Parmerly, Reuben | 1 | 2 | 3 | | | Dikerson, John | 1 | 2 | 4 | | |
| Townsend, Caleb | 1 | 2 | 3 | | | Potter, Joel | 1 | 3 | 1 | | | Ollcott, Thomas | 1 | | 2 | | |
| Thair, Ezekiel | 1 | 2 | 2 | | | Johns, Benjamin | 3 | | 2 | | | Olcott, James | 2 | 4 | 3 | | |
| Thomson, Elizur | 3 | | 3 | | | Stone, Stephen | 4 | | 6 | | | Roberts, Martin | 1 | 1 | 4 | | |
| Thomson, Daniel | 1 | 2 | 3 | | | Luddington, Eliphalet | 1 | 1 | 3 | | | Towner, Elijah | 2 | 1 | 2 | | |
| Terrill, Daniel | 2 | | 2 | | | Throop, William | 3 | 3 | 5 | | | Towner, Ephraim | 1 | 4 | 2 | | |
| Tuttle, Gideon | 2 | 1 | 3 | 1 | | Kannak, Hugh | 3 | 1 | 4 | | | Baldwin, Isaac | 2 | | 2 | | |
| Tayler, Hugh | 1 | 2 | 3 | | | Westover, Joseph | 2 | 2 | 2 | | | Burrel, Samuel | 2 | 1 | 1 | | 1 |
| Terrill, Abel | 1 | 5 | 4 | | | Moss, Asahel | 3 | | 3 | | | Higby, Patience | | 1 | 2 | | |
| Waller, Samuel | 1 | | 1 | | | Waugh, Robert | 2 | 2 | 6 | | | Lawrence, Jonas | 2 | 2 | 2 | | |
| Waller, Elijah | 2 | 2 | 4 | | | Waugh, Thomas | 1 | | 1 | | | Lawrence, Isaac | 1 | | 2 | | |
| Waller, Peter | 1 | 2 | 6 | | | Waugh, Samuel | 1 | 1 | 2 | | | Cobb, William | 1 | 1 | 1 | | |
| Worden, Joseph | 1 | 4 | 3 | | | Zitaw, Jehon | 2 | 3 | 4 | | | Tubbs, Simeon | 3 | | 3 | | |
| Whitney, Stephen | 2 | | 4 | | | Smedley, Nathan | 1 | 3 | 5 | | | Peet, William | 1 | | 1 | | |
| Winegar, Handriks | 1 | 3 | 2 | | | Comstock, Calvin | 1 | | 2 | 1 | | Kingsbury, Joshua | 1 | | 2 | | |
| Winegar, Mary | 2 | 1 | 2 | | | Foot, Timothy | 2 | 1 | 2 | | | Hide, Sam'l | 2 | 2 | 5 | | |
| Winegar, Samuel | 1 | 1 | 1 | | | Stoddard, Moses | 3 | 2 | 4 | | | Wadsworth, Ebene | 3 | | 2 | | |
| Wilson, William | 1 | 5 | 2 | | | Orton, Hezekiah | 1 | 1 | 1 | | | Woodard, David | 1 | 1 | 4 | | |
| Whitten, Thomas | 1 | 2 | 3 | | | Waugh, Alexander | 2 | 2 | 3 | | | White, Jedediah | 1 | 3 | 2 | 1 | |
| Hall, Timothy | 1 | 3 | 1 | | | Wickwire, James | 1 | 2 | 3 | | | Whitney, Joshua | 3 | 3 | 4 | | |
| Judd, Comfort | 1 | 3 | 3 | | | Keling, Asahel | 1 | 1 | 4 | | | Dutcher, Rulef | 3 | 1 | 3 | | 7 |
| Judd, Philip | 2 | | 3 | | | Churchel, Moses | 1 | | 3 | | | Hamlin, Reely | | | 2 | | |
| Judd, Matthew | 2 | 3 | 3 | | | Page, William | 1 | 1 | 2 | | | Buckenham, Isaac | 1 | | | | |
| Judd, Joseph | 3 | | 3 | | | Page, Daniel | 1 | 2 | 4 | | | Hantchet, Silvanus | 3 | 3 | 3 | | |
| Johnson, Daniel | 1 | | 1 | | | Stone, William | 1 | 1 | 2 | | | William, William | 1 | 2 | 5 | | |
| Keeney, Sylvester | 1 | 1 | 1 | | | Landon, James | 1 | 1 | 2 | | | Jule | | | | 5 | |
| Lee, Daniel | 1 | | 2 | | | Bissel, Benjamin | 1 | 3 | 4 | | | Hamlin, Thomas | 2 | 3 | 4 | | |
| Leonard, Silas | 2 | 2 | 3 | | | Dickenson, Molly | 1 | 1 | 2 | | | Gibbs, Silvanis | 1 | 1 | 4 | | |
| Lane, Richard | 1 | 3 | 4 | | | Dickenson, Reuben | 2 | 1 | 3 | | | Omsted, Hezekiah | 1 | 2 | 6 | | |
| Lane, Ephraim | 1 | 1 | 1 | | | Benton, Ebenezer | 4 | | 5 | | | Collins, Justice | 2 | | 3 | | |
| Lane, John | 1 | | 1 | | | Sanford, Joseph | 1 | 4 | 3 | | | Elmore, Sam'l | 3 | 1 | 5 | | |
| Lake, Samuel | 1 | 1 | 5 | | | Sanford, Joseph | 1 | 1 | 3 | | | Jewitt, Anney | | | 1 | | |
| Lynde, Reuben | 1 | 3 | 4 | | | Peck, Asa | 1 | 1 | 1 | | | Rockwell, Sam'l | 3 | 1 | 3 | | |
| Morgan, Caleb | 1 | 1 | 2 | | | Woodruff, Nathaniel | 1 | 1 | 4 | | | Canfield, Darius | 1 | | 1 | | |
| Martin, Manassat | 2 | | 4 | | | Woodruff, Philoe | 2 | 3 | 3 | | | Pardee, James | 2 | 1 | 2 | | |
| Main, John | 1 | 1 | 2 | | | Woodruff, Andrew | 1 | 3 | 6 | | | Pardee, Jonathan | 1 | | 2 | | |
| Main, Hannah | 1 | | 2 | | | Camp, Abel | 5 | 2 | 6 | | | Vandoore, Charles | 1 | | 2 | | |
| Morey, Thomas | 2 | 2 | 4 | | | Mansfield, Joseph | 3 | 2 | 4 | | | Grinnun, John | 1 | | 1 | | |
| Morris, Thomas, 1st | 1 | 1 | 2 | | | Harrisson, Thomas | 2 | 1 | 3 | | | Betts, Ezekiel | 1 | 2 | 3 | | |
| Morris, Thomas, 2nd | 1 | 2 | 2 | | | Ensign, Samuel | 4 | | 4 | | | King, George | 5 | 3 | 6 | | |
| Morgan, David | 2 | 3 | 5 | | | Harrison, Thomas | 1 | 1 | 1 | | | Evetts, James | 1 | | 2 | | |
| Morgan, Jonathan | 2 | 2 | 1 | | | Harrison, Levi | 2 | 1 | 4 | | | Smith, Asher | 2 | 2 | 3 | | |
| Mills, Hannah | 1 | 1 | 3 | | | Harrison, Elihue | 3 | | 2 | | | Beach, Jacob | 3 | | 2 | | |
| Morgan, Samuel | 1 | | 4 | | | Fraust, Samuel | 1 | | 2 | | | Beach, Francis | 1 | 1 | 1 | | |
| Mills, Peter | 1 | 3 | 3 | | | Rigs, Jeremiah | 1 | 3 | 4 | | | Rogers, Abeather | 1 | 4 | 3 | | |
| Miller, Samuel | 1 | 2 | 2 | | | Woodruff, Anna | | | 2 | | | Butler, Abel | 1 | 4 | 3 | | |
| Murray, Chloe | | | 3 | | | Woodruff, John | 1 | 1 | 2 | | | Dicingson, Thomas | 4 | 1 | 3 | | |
| Main, Caleb | 2 | 2 | 3 | | | Woodruff, Solomon | 1 | 1 | 1 | | | Dikingson, Thomas | 1 | 2 | 1 | | |
| Main, Jonathan | 1 | 4 | 5 | | | Woodruff, Charles | 1 | 1 | 1 | | | Sherman, Tesua | 1 | | 5 | | |
| Mills, Bradley | 1 | | 2 | | | Woodruff, Oliver | 1 | 1 | 2 | | | Wilson, Job | 2 | | 2 | | |
| Morgan, Jeames | 1 | 2 | 2 | | | Harrisson, Ephraim | | | 3 | 1 | | Roberts, Seth | 1 | 2 | 3 | | |
| Norecey, George | 1 | | 1 | | | Steel, Mary | 2 | | 2 | | | Squire, Justice | 1 | 3 | 1 | | |
| Norton, Silas | 2 | 1 | 4 | | | Mattoon Gorham | 1 | 4 | 3 | | | Beach, William | 1 | 3 | 1 | | |
| Nichols, Lewis | 2 | 2 | 2 | | | | | | | | | Baldwin, Bruin | 2 | 4 | 4 | | |

* Illegible.

## LITCHFIELD COUNTY—Continued.

### LITCHFIELD TOWN—con.

| NAME OF HEAD OF FAMILY. | Free white males of 16 years and upward, including heads of families. | Free white males under 16 years. | Free white females, including heads of families. | All other free persons. | Slaves. |
|---|---|---|---|---|---|
| Hills, Seth | 1 | 2 | 2 | | |
| Brown, William | 1 | 1 | 1 | | |
| Humphrey, Simion | 1 | 1 | 2 | | |
| Merrills, William | 2 | 1 | 3 | | |
| Merrills, Jonathan | 1 | 1 | 2 | | |
| Merrills, Jonathan | 1 | 1 | 3 | | |
| Case, Dudley | 4 | | 4 | 1 | |
| Slevell, James | 1 | 2 | 2 | | |
| Humphrey, Roswell | 2 | 1 | 1 | | |
| Bidwell, Thomas | 4 | | 4 | | |
| Bidwell, Riverious | 1 | 2 | 5 | 3 | |
| Garrot, John | 1 | 2 | 6 | | |
| Lenin, Justice | 3 | | 4 | | |
| Taylor, Obadiah | 1 | 1 | 3 | | |
| Nobles, William | 1 | 2 | 5 | | |
| Wallen, William | 1 | 1 | 2 | | |
| Ives, Nathan | 1 | 2 | 2 | | |
| Coles, Joseph | 2 | 3 | 3 | | |
| Ensign, Eliphalet | 2 | 1 | 2 | | |
| Pitkin, Stephen | 3 | 3 | 3 | | |
| Flowers, Gabrial | 1 | 3 | 2 | | |
| Henderson, John | 2 | 7 | 3 | | |
| Henderson, James | 3 | 6 | 3 | | |
| Tyler, Amos | 1 | 2 | 2 | | |
| Teplay, Ashbel | 2 | 3 | 4 | | |
| Ward, John | 2 | 3 | 4 | | |
| Duglis, Moses | 3 | 5 | 5 | | |
| Hurd, William | 1 | 2 | 3 | | |
| Tracy, Uriah | 1 | 1 | 5 | 1 | |
| Buell, Salmon | 2 | 3 | 4 | | |
| Barnes, Reuben | 2 | 1 | 6 | | |
| Collins, John | 3 | 2 | 5 | 1 | 1 |
| Addam, Joseph | 1 | | | | |
| Allen, John | 1 | | | | |
| Marvin, Raynold | 1 | | 1 | | |
| Kirbey, Ephraim | 1 | 1 | 4 | 3 | |
| Stanley, Rufus | 1 | | | | |
| Ruggles, Philoe | 1 | | | | |
| Dyre, Eliphalet | 1 | | | | |
| Martial, Deota | | | 1 | | |
| Morril, Robert | 1 | | | | |
| Bishshop, Seth | 1 | | 2 | | |
| Bishop, Seth, 2d | 1 | 2 | 3 | | |
| Spencer, Zacheus | 2 | 3 | 5 | | |
| Persons, Eliphas | 3 | 1 | 3 | | |
| Griswold, John | 1 | 3 | 3 | | |
| Landon, Thadeus | 1 | 3 | 1 | | |
| Parmeley, Mary | | | 3 | | |
| Fry, Rena | 1 | 1 | 1 | | |
| Dear, George | 1 | 3 | 3 | | |
| Motthop, Stephen | 1 | | 2 | | |
| Chase, Lot | 1 | 1 | 2 | | |
| Bristor, John | 1 | | | | |
| Burghes, Joseph | 1 | | 2 | | |
| Burges, Benjamin | 1 | | 1 | | |
| Griswold, Asahel | 2 | 3 | 7 | | |
| Smith, Eli | 2 | 3 | 3 | | |
| Whitmore, Clark | 1 | | 2 | | |
| Emmons, Williams | 1 | 2 | 4 | | |
| Dickemon, Ruth | | | 2 | | |
| Spencer, Samuel | 1 | | | | |
| Spencer, William | 1 | | | | |
| Wright, Jonathan | 2 | 4 | 7 | | |
| Perry, Israel | 1 | 4 | 3 | | |
| Catlin, Bradley | 1 | 3 | 3 | | |
| Whitmore, Timothy | 2 | 1 | 2 | | |
| Baker, Constant | 2 | 2 | 5 | | |
| Burges, James | 1 | 4 | 1 | | |
| Gibbs, Truman | 1 | 3 | 3 | | |
| Peck, George | 1 | | 3 | | |
| Coles, Stephen | 1 | | 4 | | |
| Pitkin, Timothy | 1 | | 1 | | |
| Baley, Joseph | 3 | | 4 | | |
| Standley, Timothy | 3 | | 1 | | |
| North, Ezekiel | 1 | 4 | 6 | | |
| Norton, Oliver | 1 | | 2 | | |
| Landon, Ozias | 1 | 1 | 3 | | |
| North, Joseph | 4 | 3 | 6 | | |
| Norton, Alexander | 3 | 2 | 4 | | |
| Waddoms, Solomon | 3 | 2 | 4 | | |
| Griswold, Jiles | 5 | 1 | 5 | | |
| Norton, Andrews | 4 | 2 | 1 | | |
| Kettell, Jonothan | 5 | 1 | 5 | | |
| Nash, Samuel | 1 | | | | |
| Goold, Thomas R | 1 | 1 | 3 | | |
| Sill, Elisha | 2 | 1 | 4 | | |
| Hale, Ebenezer | 1 | | 2 | | |
| Mayo, Elisha | 1 | 1 | 1 | | |
| Hale, Adino | 3 | | | | |
| Lockwood, Seth | 1 | 2 | 6 | | |
| Nash, Josiah | 2 | 3 | 3 | | |
| Nash, William | 1 | 2 | 9 | | |
| Brick, Moses | 2 | | 4 | | |
| Kellogg, Martin | 1 | 2 | 3 | | |
| Merrills, Joseph | 2 | 1 | 6 | | |

### LITCHFIELD TOWN—con.

| NAME OF HEAD OF FAMILY. | Free white males of 16 years and upward, including heads of families. | Free white males under 16 years. | Free white females, including heads of families. | All other free persons. | Slaves. |
|---|---|---|---|---|---|
| Mix, Isaac | 1 | | 1 | | |
| Stephens, Aaron | 1 | 1 | 1 | | |
| Sandiforth, Daniel | 1 | 3 | 9 | | |
| Seymore, Noah | 1 | 3 | 2 | | |
| Burnington, Ebenezer | 1 | 3 | 2 | | |
| Watson, Zachariah | 1 | 3 | 3 | | |
| Merrills, Marten | 1 | | 4 | | |
| Tryon, Ely | 1 | 2 | 3 | | |
| Merrills, Aaron | 1 | 4 | 5 | | |
| More, Josiah | 1 | 1 | 1 | | |
| Cotton, William | 1 | 2 | 2 | | |
| Bissel, Benjamin | 2 | 3 | 2 | | |
| Goodman, Thomas | 1 | 1 | 4 | | |
| Mather, Charles | 2 | 2 | 3 | | |
| Northawey, James | 1 | 4 | 5 | | |
| Watson, Levi | 4 | | 3 | | |
| Wells, Asahel | 1 | | 3 | 1 | |
| Grow, Ambroser | 1 | 1 | 5 | | |
| Averiss, Isaac | 2 | | 4 | | |
| Demmich, Solomon | 1 | 3 | 3 | | |
| Averiss, Ethan | 2 | 1 | 4 | | |
| Gibson, Roger | 1 | | 3 | | |
| Williams, John | 3 | 3 | 1 | | |
| Dickenson, Elisha | 2 | 1 | 2 | | |
| Dickenson, Ebin | 1 | | | | |
| Sawyer, Nathaniel | 3 | 1 | 6 | | |
| Gauslin, John | 1 | 3 | 4 | | |
| Ichabud, Seth | 1 | 1 | 2 | | |
| Camelon, John | 1 | 3 | 4 | | |
| Nilger, Sam | 1 | 2 | 5 | | |
| Minord, Frederick | 3 | 1 | 4 | | |
| Beebe, Amasa | 1 | 3 | 2 | | |
| Youngs, Soloman | 1 | | 3 | | |
| Chapman, Nehemiah | 1 | | 3 | | |
| Chapman, Caleb | 1 | | 2 | | |
| Bester, Seth | 3 | 4 | 5 | | |
| Coblium, Stephen | 3 | 1 | 3 | | |
| Bester, Job | 1 | 3 | 2 | | |
| Leanard, Benjaman | 1 | 3 | 3 | | |
| Benjamin, Phinehas | 1 | 1 | 3 | | |
| Smith, Theophelus | 1 | | 2 | | |
| Smith, Theophelus, 2d | 1 | 3 | 3 | | |
| Smith, Levi | 1 | 2 | 4 | | |
| Jackson, Amos | 1 | 3 | 3 | | |
| Hollister, Elisha | 3 | 1 | 4 | | |
| Chappel, Silas | 1 | 2 | 1 | | |
| Wilson, John | 1 | 2 | 3 | | |
| Miller, Joshua | 3 | 7 | 3 | | |
| Lovel, Joseph | 2 | | 6 | | |
| Denham, Jonathan | 2 | 1 | 3 | | |
| Studley, Joshua | 2 | 2 | 5 | | |
| Allen, Thomas | 1 | | 1 | | |
| Bailey, Joseph | 3 | 1 | 4 | | |
| Sturdephant, George | 2 | | | | |
| Swift, Philoe | 2 | | | | |
| Pangman, Adonijah | 1 | | 3 | | |
| Lenley, Joseph | 2 | | 4 | | |
| Monroe, Younglove | 1 | | 2 | | |
| Griswold, Adonijah | 3 | 1 | 3 | | |
| Monroe, Noah | 1 | 2 | 3 | | |
| Hamlin, Benjamin | 1 | 2 | 4 | | |
| Warren, Nathan¹ | 1 | 1 | 1 | | |
| Goold, Job | 3 | | 3 | | |
| Dicks, Charles | 1 | 2 | 2 | | |
| Noth, Juna | 1 | | 6 | | |
| Noth, Noah | 2 | | 3 | | |
| Rhiney, Daniel | 1 | 3 | 2 | | |
| Hurlburt, Levi | 1 | 1 | 3 | | |
| Leason, Noah | 1 | 2 | 4 | | |
| Aglestone, Joseph | 2 | 3 | 4 | | |
| Smith, Gidian | 2 | 2 | 5 | | |
| Philer, Stephen | 1 | 1 | 4 | | |
| Coe, Abner | 1 | | | | |
| Martial, Thomas | 5 | 1 | 3 | | |
| Philer, John | 1 | 1 | 3 | | |
| Hill, Benona | 2 | 1 | 4 | | |
| Philer, Silas | 2 | 3 | 3 | | |
| Drake, Noah | 1 | 2 | 1 | | |
| Sheppard, Stephen | 1 | | 3 | | |
| Agard, Solomon | 1 | 2 | 3 | | |
| Leach, Caleb | 1 | 5 | 1 | | |
| Loomise, Abraham | 1 | | 3 | | |
| Martial, Abner | 3 | | 2 | | |
| Drake, Joel | 2 | 4 | | | |
| Thrall, Noah | 2 | 1 | 3 | | |
| Whitmore, Samuel | 1 | | 3 | | |
| Burr, John | 2 | 3 | 4 | | |
| Stanley, Comfort | 1 | | 1 | | |
| Marther, Richard | 1 | 2 | 2 | | |
| Burr, Reuben | 2 | 2 | 4 | | |
| Burr, Russel | 3 | 3 | 3 | | |
| Hudson, Daniel | 2 | 1 | 5 | | |
| Stephens, Samuel | 3 | | 5 | | |
| Deming, Daniel | 3 | 4 | 6 | | |
| Haydon, Agustin | 3 | | | | |

### LITCHFIELD TOWN—con.

| NAME OF HEAD OF FAMILY. | Free white males of 16 years and upward, including heads of families. | Free white males under 16 years. | Free white females, including heads of families. | All other free persons. | Slaves. |
|---|---|---|---|---|---|
| Elmore, Abiath | 2 | 1 | 2 | | |
| Bierr, Hial | 1 | 3 | 3 | | |
| Austin, Thaniel | 1 | 3 | 3 | | |
| Frasier, George | 1 | | 4 | | |
| Loomise, Michael | 1 | 3 | 4 | | |
| Brown, Stepen | 1 | | 3 | | |
| Miller, Ebenezer | 1 | 1 | 2 | | |
| Doolittle, David | 2 | | 4 | | |
| Phernil, Benjamin | 1 | 2 | 4 | | |
| Loomise, Roswell | 1 | | 3 | | |
| Roberts, Henry | 1 | 3 | 2 | | |
| Philer, Ulissies | 1 | 2 | 5 | | |
| Tuttle, Clem | 1 | 2 | 2 | | |
| Tuttle, Isaac | 2 | 2 | 5 | | |
| Cook, Shubel | 1 | 1 | 3 | | |
| Shatdock, William | 1 | 2 | 3 | | |
| Babcok, Elias | 3 | 1 | 2 | | |
| Babcock, Rufiel | 1 | 2 | 1 | | |
| Martial, Joseph | 1 | 1 | 1 | | |
| Gibson, Ephraim | 2 | | 2 | | |
| Rowlenson, Asa | 2 | 4 | 1 | | |
| Rowlenson, John | 2 | | 2 | | |
| Rowlenson, William | 1 | 1 | 2 | | |
| Rowe, Samuel | 3 | 2 | 4 | | |
| Howe, Stephen | 1 | 4 | 3 | | |
| Barden, Seth | 2 | 2 | 5 | | |
| Southland, Beldwin | 2 | 1 | 1 | | |
| Deming, Daniel | 2 | 2 | 3 | | |
| White, John | 1 | 2 | 2 | | |
| Woodruff, Elias | 2 | 2 | 1 | | |
| Pates, Elisha | 1 | 2 | 1 | | |
| Landers, Joseph | 1 | | 1 | | |
| Hollister, David | 2 | 2 | 3 | | |
| Onton, Joseph | 1 | 1 | 5 | | |
| Croker, Oliver | 2 | | 4 | | |
| Goodrich, Ashbel | 1 | | 6 | | |
| Marsh, Isaiah | 1 | | 6 | | |
| Hamlin, Polley | | 1 | 1 | | |
| Gillet, Jonathan | 3 | 1 | 1 | | |
| Rennalds, Joel | 1 | 2 | 2 | | |
| Griffin, Thomas | 4 | 2 | 3 | | |
| Roland, David | 3 | 2 | 9 | | |
| Youngs, William | 1 | 2 | 2 | | |
| Chapman, William | 2 | 2 | 3 | | |
| Chapman, Pelatiah | 1 | 2 | 5 | | |
| Foster, John | 3 | 1 | 5 | | |
| Clark, William | 1 | 2 | 2 | | |
| McDonald, Jerrents | 1 | 1 | 3 | | |
| Hollester, Nathan | 1 | | 5 | | |
| Landen, Martha | | | 6 | | |
| Hollister, Joshua | 1 | | 3 | | |
| Lovell, Joshua | 2 | | 4 | | |
| Homer, David | 1 | 1 | 3 | | |
| Stanley, Comfort | 1 | 3 | 3 | | |
| Austin, David | 2 | 1 | 3 | | |
| Ward, David | 1 | 1 | 2 | | |
| Watter, Daniel | 1 | 3 | 1 | | |
| D Wolf, Benjamin | 1 | 1 | 2 | | |
| Swett, John | 2 | 5 | 5 | | |
| Watter, John | 1 | 5 | 3 | | |
| Cook, Arijah | 1 | 1 | 5 | | |
| Watter, Henry | 2 | 2 | 1 | | |
| Basten, John | 1 | | 2 | | |
| Munson, Caleb | 1 | | 1 | | |
| West, Judy | 1 | 1 | 2 | | |
| Crissey, David | 1 | 1 | 3 | | |
| Woodruff, Hezekiah | 2 | 2 | 5 | | |
| Woodruff, Isaac | 1 | | 3 | | |
| Hart, Luke | 3 | | 3 | | |
| Allen, John | 1 | 1 | 3 | | |
| Russel, David | 3 | 2 | 3 | | |
| Crissey, Israel | 1 | 1 | 2 | | |
| Aglestone, Daniel | 1 | 1 | 1 | | |
| Wolf, Daniel | 1 | | 1 | | |
| Right, John | 1 | 4 | 3 | | |
| Right, Charles | 2 | 4 | 3 | | |
| Right, Freedom | 1 | 2 | 6 | | |
| Smith, Zebina | 2 | 1 | 2 | | |
| Grenell, Michael | 1 | 2 | 5 | | |
| Smith, Jonaiah | 2 | 2 | 6 | | |
| Balcome, John | 2 | 3 | 6 | | |
| Palmer, Reuben | 1 | 3 | 2 | | |
| Palmer, Zazaries | 1 | 1 | 1 | | |
| Palmer, Solomon | 2 | 4 | 3 | | |
| Palmer, Benjamin | 1 | 4 | 3 | | |
| Morey, Abijah | 1 | 2 | 2 | | |
| Mills, Chancy | 2 | 3 | 3 | | |
| Mills, David | 2 | 2 | 3 | | |
| Mallery, Elisha | 2 | 6 | 6 | | |
| Dunnam, Jonathan | 2 | 4 | 4 | | |
| Mallery, Amos | 2 | | 1 | | |
| More, William | 1 | | 4 | | |
| White, Isaac | 2 | | 4 | | |
| Sawyer, Jesse | 2 | 1 | 4 | | |
| White, Samuel | 2 | 3 | 2 | | |

# HEADS OF FAMILIES—CONNECTICUT.

## LITCHFIELD COUNTY—Continued.

### LITCHFIELD TOWN—con.

| NAME OF HEAD OF FAMILY. | Free white males of 16 years and upward, including heads of families. | Free white males under 16 years. | Free white females, including heads of families. | All other free persons. | Slaves. |
|---|---|---|---|---|---|
| Smith, Jacob | 2 | 2 | 5 | | |
| Sheldon, George | 1 | | 2 | | |
| Peck, Frederick | 1 | 1 | 5 | | |
| Landon, George | 1 | | 2 | | |
| Knap, Jabez | 3 | 2 | 6 | | |
| Scordam, Henry | 1 | 2 | 1 | | |
| Curtiss, Aaron | 2 | | 3 | | |
| White, William | 1 | 3 | 1 | | |
| Mills, Aaron | 1 | 1 | 1 | 4 | |
| Churk, Nathan | 1 | 2 | 2 | | |
| Leanard, Fellows | 3 | | 1 | | |
| Blakesley, Samuel | 1 | 2 | 4 | | |
| Pierce, William | 2 | 2 | 3 | | |
| Cameron, Lauchland | 1 | | | | |
| Richeron, Thomas | 1 | 1 | 3 | | |
| Comering, Jacob | 1 | 2 | 5 | | |
| Horton, Elisha | 2 | | 2 | | |
| White, William | 2 | | 7 | | |
| Landon, Rufus | 1 | 3 | 2 | | |
| Landon, John | 1 | | 1 | | |
| Landon, David | 1 | | 4 | | |
| Landon, James | 2 | | 3 | | |
| Avery, Elisha | 2 | 1 | 5 | | |
| Commins, Jacom | 1 | | | | |
| Vaun, William | 1 | | | | |
| Towsby, Vistory S | 3 | 4 | 7 | | |
| Tousbey, Samuel | 2 | 1 | 1 | | |
| Loveland, Zile | 1 | 1 | 1 | | |
| Ensign, John | 2 | 5 | 6 | | |
| Smith, Seth | 4 | | 2 | | |
| Knickabocker, Isaac | 2 | 2 | 3 | | |
| Knickabocker, John | 1 | 1 | 2 | | |
| Rowlin, Luke | 1 | 3 | 2 | | |
| Knickerbocker, Solomon | 2 | 4 | 4 | | |
| Heath, David | 1 | 1 | 1 | | |
| Knickerbocker, Saml | 2 | 2 | 3 | | |
| Allen, Mathew | 1 | | 1 | | |
| Knickerbocker, Abraham | 3 | 3 | 6 | | |
| Parmerley, Theodore | 2 | 1 | 5 | | |
| Hill, Medad | 3 | 2 | 2 | | |
| Parmeley, Abraham | 1 | | 3 | 1 | |
| Lewis, Ebenezer | 1 | 1 | 4 | | |
| Barber, Sarah | | 2 | 2 | | |
| Holbrooks, Nathaniel | 1 | 1 | 3 | | |
| Hoopkins, Stephen | 1 | | 2 | | |
| Hopkins, Samuel | 2 | 1 | 3 | | |
| Thompson, John | 1 | | 1 | | |
| Thompson, John | 1 | | 2 | | |
| Baldwin, Stephen | 1 | 1 | 3 | | |
| Porter, Seth | 1 | 2 | 2 | | |
| Beach, Fisk | 2 | 1 | 5 | | |
| Rice, Josiah | 3 | 1 | 3 | | |
| Carrington, Mabel | 3 | 1 | 4 | | |
| Beach, Edmond | 2 | 2 | 4 | | |
| Beach, Edmond | 2 | 1 | 7 | | |
| Beach, Adney | 1 | 2 | 5 | | |
| Chapen, Samuel | 4 | | 2 | | |
| Merrills, Miah | 3 | 1 | 4 | | |
| Merrills, Jared | 3 | | 3 | | |
| Merrills, Elijah | 3 | | 4 | | |
| Adams, William | 1 | 3 | 6 | | |
| Merrills, Asher | 2 | 1 | 5 | | |
| Goodwin, Michael | 1 | 5 | 4 | | |
| Merrills, Benjamin | 2 | | 5 | | |
| Bardock, Amos | 2 | 3 | 5 | | |
| Goodwin, Moses | 1 | 2 | 3 | | |
| Goodwin, Elzer | 4 | | 6 | | |
| Goodwin, Tiras | 1 | 2 | 2 | | |
| Mills, Moses | 2 | 1 | 2 | | |
| Hale, Reuben | 1 | 1 | 3 | | |
| Barnes, Timothy | 1 | 1 | 3 | | |
| Barns, Israel | 1 | | 3 | | |
| Goodwin, Jonothan | 3 | | 4 | | |
| Cadwell, Phinehas | 1 | 1 | 4 | | |
| Bennams, Samuel | 1 | 1 | 1 | | |
| Merrills, Eliakim | 1 | | 4 | | |
| Bennom, Johial | 1 | 1 | 4 | | |
| Smith, Josiah | 1 | | 1 | | |
| Bennom, Samuel | 1 | 2 | 2 | | |
| Norton, Miles | 2 | 5 | 4 | | |
| Roberts, John | 1 | | 1 | | |
| Coleman, Josiah | 4 | | 5 | | |
| Newel, Nathan | 1 | | 1 | | |
| Newel, William | 1 | 1 | 4 | | |
| Spalden, Barbara | | | 3 | | |
| Sperry, Charles | 1 | | | | |
| Whitney, Stephen | 1 | | | | |
| Howe, Philop | 1 | 3 | 3 | | |
| Presson, David | 1 | 3 | 2 | | |
| Stephens, Daniel | 1 | 1 | 2 | 1 | |
| Brownwell, Aaron | 1 | 3 | 3 | | |
| Burt, Abraham | 3 | | 3 | | |
| Brownwell, Edward | 1 | 6 | 2 | | |
| Belknap, Jonathan | 1 | 1 | 4 | | |
| Johnson, Chancy | 1 | | 2 | | |
| Palmer, Simeon | 1 | 3 | 6 | | |
| Rickerson, Martha | | 1 | 3 | | |
| Green, John | 1 | 2 | 6 | | |
| Gleason, Ruful | 1 | | 2 | | |
| Tom | | | | 6 | |
| Watson, John | 3 | 2 | 4 | | |
| Thompson, Amos | 1 | | | | 4 |
| Sedgwick, Mary | | | 5 | | |
| Fanning, Sarah | | | | | |
| Pardy, Saml | 2 | 3 | 3 | | |
| Manning, David | 2 | | 3 | | |
| Dormond, Garsham | 1 | 2 | 2 | | |
| Bennet, Edmond | 3 | 3 | 4 | | |
| Persons, Enoch | 3 | 2 | 1 | | |
| Sanford, David | 1 | 1 | 2 | | |
| Summers, Asahel | 2 | 1 | 2 | | |
| Comp, Joel | 2 | 2 | 3 | | |
| Pettit, Solomon | 1 | | 1 | | |
| Hamlen, Nathen | 3 | 5 | 3 | | |
| Cheseton, Samuel | 1 | | 2 | | |
| Swift, Wilard | 1 | 2 | 3 | | |
| Furgason, Daniel | 1 | 1 | 3 | | |
| Dota, Timothy | 2 | | 1 | | |
| Fuller, Benjamin | 1 | | 4 | | |
| Commel, Daniel | 1 | | 3 | | |
| Ruxford, William | 1 | 3 | 3 | | |
| Minor, Joel | 2 | 3 | 3 | | |
| Gedion, John | 2 | 2 | 4 | | |
| Andrews, Nehemiah | 2 | 4 | | | |
| Hutchins, Anna | | | 2 | | |
| Hankok, Rachel | | | 2 | | |
| Lane, Enos | 3 | 3 | 2 | | |
| Hutchins, Benjamin | 1 | 1 | 2 | | |
| Wilcox, Jeremiah | 1 | | 3 | | |
| Church, Aaron | 1 | 2 | 3 | | |
| Smith, Martin | 2 | 2 | 3 | | |
| Spensor, Jessee | 1 | 1 | 2 | | |
| Smith, Havilah | 2 | 1 | 1 | | |
| Andrews, Nehemiah | 2 | 2 | 7 | | |
| Giddings, Benjamin | 1 | 3 | 3 | | |
| Akins, Acker | 1 | | 2 | | |
| Turner, Daniel | 1 | | 2 | | |
| Lawrence, John | 1 | 1 | 3 | | |
| Humphrey, Dudley | 1 | 1 | 3 | | |
| Mottbey, Johial | 1 | 1 | 1 | | |
| Watter, Joel | 2 | | 3 | | |
| Watter, Heman | 1 | | 1 | | |
| Watter, Elijah | 1 | 2 | 3 | | |
| Mack, Daniel | 2 | 3 | 3 | | |
| Mills, Edan | 1 | 3 | 1 | | |
| Nettleton, Joshua | 2 | 2 | 2 | | |
| Pomeroy, Simean | 1 | 2 | 4 | | |
| Mills, Laurance | 1 | 1 | 1 | | |
| Derby, John | 1 | | 1 | | |
| Lettleton, Roger | 1 | 1 | 3 | | |
| Austen, Saml | 1 | | 3 | | |
| Lewis, Edward | 2 | 1 | 3 | | |
| Mills, Michael | 4 | 1 | 4 | | |
| Phelps, Frind | 1 | 1 | 6 | | |
| Pardy, Ebenezer | 1 | 2 | 1 | | |
| Laurance, Grove | 1 | | 1 | | |
| Giddings, Joshua | 1 | 4 | 3 | | |
| Brockway, Edward | 4 | 2 | 9 | | |
| Spensor, Samuel | 1 | 1 | 2 | | |
| Gildersleaves, Obadiah | 1 | 1 | 1 | | |
| Brockway, Moses | 1 | 1 | 1 | | |
| Merrit, Sam | 1 | 1 | 3 | | |
| Beach, Sam | 1 | 1 | 2 | | |
| Jones, Benjamin | 1 | 2 | 2 | | |
| Tuttle, Isaah | 1 | 3 | 3 | | |
| Jones, Asahel | 1 | 2 | 4 | | |
| Hart, Hawkins | 3 | 2 | 3 | | |
| Munson, Ephraim | 2 | 2 | 3 | | |
| Munson, Wait | 1 | 1 | 3 | | |
| Gates, Theophelus L | 1 | 2 | 5 | | |
| Comore, Stephen | 1 | 2 | 3 | | |
| Betts, Bena Jah | 2 | | 5 | | |
| Bills, Benajah | 2 | | 5 | | |
| Rewick, Owen | 1 | 1 | 2 | | |
| Reed, Benin | 1 | | 1 | | |
| Fox, Ephraim | 1 | 1 | 2 | | |
| Clark, John | 1 | 1 | 2 | | |
| Bills, Joshua | 1 | | 2 | | |
| Danniels, Pelletiah | 1 | | 1 | | |
| Shovel, Michael | 2 | 3 | 5 | | |
| Phillip, William | 1 | | 1 | | |
| Church, Abisha | 1 | 1 | 2 | | |
| Cowdrey, Moses | 2 | | 5 | | |
| Mechum, Isaac | 1 | 4 | 5 | | |
| Church, Uriah | 2 | 1 | 2 | | |
| Perkins, Phinehas | 3 | 1 | 1 | | |
| Perkins, Eliphas | 1 | 5 | 4 | | |
| Mechur, Levi | 1 | | 2 | | |
| Dudley, Miles | 1 | 1 | 2 | | |
| Tibbots, Thomas | 3 | | 2 | | |
| Burr, Ebenr | 1 | | 6 | | |
| Rice, John | 1 | | 4 | | |
| Wilcox, Hesana | 2 | | 3 | | |
| Cotton, Michael | 1 | 3 | 2 | | |
| Galor, Timothy | 2 | 1 | 2 | | |
| Turner, Barts | 3 | | 1 | | |
| Goodwin, William | 1 | 1 | 2 | | |
| Thomson, Levi | 3 | 2 | 3 | | |
| Hall, Abraham | 1 | | 3 | | |
| Hall, Sam | 1 | 1 | 1 | | |
| Hall, Abraham, 2d | 1 | 1 | 3 | | |
| Goold, David | 4 | 3 | 6 | | |
| Bell, Jude | 1 | | 1 | | |
| Jinks, Eben | 1 | 1 | 3 | | |
| Humphey, Hoseah | 4 | | 2 | 1 | |
| Sheppard, Zebulon | 1 | 1 | 4 | | |
| Cadey, Lemuel | 2 | 3 | 6 | | |
| Johnson, Jacob | 2 | 4 | 5 | | |
| Tyler, Banijah | 1 | | 1 | | |
| Lowrey, Nathan | 2 | | 3 | | |
| Hammon, Dudley | 2 | 1 | 6 | | |
| Howe, Elisha | 1 | | 3 | | |
| Hale, Elihu | 1 | | 1 | | |
| Mott, Jonathan | 1 | | 2 | | |
| Bailey, Salmon | 1 | 2 | 1 | | |
| Yale, Elisha | 1 | 1 | 4 | | |
| Merrills, Joptha | 1 | 1 | 3 | | |
| Yale, Elisha, 2d | 1 | 1 | 3 | | |
| Howe, Jeremiah | 4 | 1 | 3 | | |
| Johnson, Timothy | 1 | | 2 | | |
| Johnson, Isaac | 1 | | 2 | | |
| Johnson, Levi | 2 | 1 | 2 | | |
| Howe, Joel | 1 | 3 | 1 | | |
| Harriss, Daniel | 1 | | 1 | | |
| Brown, Jerry | 3 | | 4 | | |
| Brown, John | 1 | 3 | 2 | | |
| Daming, Joel | 2 | 2 | 3 | | |
| Root, Caleb | 1 | | 1 | | |
| Barns, Gideon | 2 | | 3 | | |
| Clark, Reuben | 2 | | 1 | | |
| Smith, Asahel | 2 | 2 | 2 | | |
| Harger, Jabesh | 1 | 4 | 3 | | |
| Inenka, Charels | 1 | 1 | 4 | | |
| Cleavland, Aaron | 1 | | 3 | | |
| Perkins, Jason | 1 | 4 | 3 | | |
| Phelps, Samuel | 3 | 1 | 2 | | |
| Phelps, Samuel | 2 | 1 | 4 | | |
| Crosbey, Obed | 1 | | 4 | | |
| Crosbey, Samuel | 1 | 3 | 3 | | |
| Miller, Allen | 1 | 2 | 2 | | |
| Bates, Oliver | 2 | 3 | 4 | | |
| Hungerford, James | 1 | 1 | 5 | | |
| Bushnel, Daniel | 2 | | 5 | | |
| Hale, Reuben | 1 | 1 | 5 | | |
| Allen, Titus | 2 | | 5 | | |
| Treet, John | 1 | 2 | 5 | | |
| Fox, Jabes | 1 | 1 | 1 | | |
| Kilborn, Epephras | 1 | | 3 | | |
| Woodbridge, Samuel | 1 | 1 | 3 | | |
| Brau, Charles | 1 | | 5 | | |
| Dewey, Lenar | 1 | 3 | 3 | | |
| Smith, Reuben | 2 | 4 | 2 | | |
| Deming, Roswell | 1 | 2 | 1 | | |
| Clark, Rufus | 1 | 3 | 3 | | |
| Jakeway, Daniel | 1 | 1 | 3 | | |
| Root, Enoch | 3 | 1 | 7 | | |
| Lappedal, Peter | 1 | | | | |
| Goodrich, Isaac | 1 | 3 | 4 | | |
| Pettit, Saml | 4 | | 2 | | |
| Goold, Jonathan | 1 | 2 | 4 | | |
| Reed, Ethiel | 2 | 1 | 3 | | |
| Pettit, John | 2 | | 3 | | |
| Lilley, Hezekiah | 1 | 4 | 3 | | |
| Marchant, Elijah | 1 | | | | |
| Botsford, Ephream | 1 | | 1 | | |
| Williams, Eastes | | 2 | 1 | | |
| Botsford, Epriam, 2d | 1 | 3 | 6 | | |
| Marines, Ephraim | 2 | 1 | 4 | | |
| Pratt, Abreham | 1 | 1 | 3 | | |
| Sprague, Jonathan | 2 | | 1 | | |
| Chamberlain, Isaa | 2 | 3 | 7 | | |
| Guy, Dan | 3 | 2 | 4 | | |
| Pardee, Isaac | 2 | 1 | 3 | | 1 |
| Wanright, Thomas | 1 | | 1 | | |
| Heath, Obadiah | 1 | 1 | 2 | | |
| Heath, Hezekiah | 1 | 3 | 3 | | |
| Heath, Mehitabel | 1 | | 6 | | |
| Guy, Margaret | 3 | 1 | 6 | | |
| Guy, John | 1 | | | | |
| Marchant, Unice | 1 | | 2 | | |
| Marchant, Ashbel | 1 | 4 | 2 | | |
| Sprague, Simeon | 2 | 1 | 8 | | |
| Waldo, Syprean | 3 | 2 | 3 | | |

# LITCHFIELD COUNTY—Continued.

| NAME OF HEAD OF FAMILY. | Free white males of 16 years and upward, including heads of families. | Free white males under 16 years. | Free white females, including heads of families. | All other free persons. | Slaves. |
|---|---|---|---|---|---|
| **LITCHFIELD TOWN—con.** | | | | | |
| Kelsey, Noah | 1 | 1 | 2 | | |
| Bull, Jonathan | 2 | 1 | 2 | | |
| Parmer, William | 1 | 3 | 4 | | |
| Reed, Jonathan | 2 | 1 | 2 | | |
| Treet, Isaac | 1 | 1 | 2 | | |
| Barsley, John | 2 | | 1 | | |
| Foster, Polley | | | 1 | | |
| Jennins, Charles | 2 | 2 | 3 | | |
| Jewit, Caleb | 2 | | 3 | | |
| Cole, David | 4 | 2 | 5 | | |
| Chapman, Noah | 1 | | 1 | | |
| Averitt, John | 1 | 1 | 2 | | |
| Gregory, Joseph | 4 | 2 | 1 | | |
| S$^t$ John, Joel | 1 | | 1 | | |
| Harris, David | 3 | 2 | 5 | | |
| Seers, Stephen | 1 | 1 | 5 | | |
| Wolcott, Claudeus | 1 | 1 | 3 | | |
| Pardee, George | 2 | | 1 | | |
| Pardee, Moses | 1 | 2 | 3 | | |
| Sanford, Ezra | 1 | | 3 | | |
| Curtiss, Nathan$^l$ | 2 | 1 | 4 | | |
| Colkins, Elije | 2 | 1 | 4 | | |
| Colkins, Elija | 1 | 1 | 1 | | |
| Blake, Marana | 1 | 2 | 5 | | |
| Taylor, Joseph | 1 | 3 | 5 | | |
| Carr, William | 1 | 2 | 4 | | |
| Carr, Robert | 1 | | 3 | | |
| Cook, John | 1 | 3 | 2 | | |
| Miller, William | 1 | 2 | 2 | | |
| Phelps, Abraham | 1 | 1 | 3 | | |
| Ives, Abner | 3 | 3 | 7 | | |
| Ives, Jotheam | 2 | 3 | 3 | | |
| Phelps, Elijah | 1 | 4 | 3 | | |
| Carter, Ether | 1 | 4 | 3 | | |
| Dibble, Daniel | 1 | 2 | 4 | | |
| Eno, Eliphealet | 2 | | 1 | | |
| Furgeson, James | 2 | 3 | 7 | | |
| Brooker, John | 1 | 1 | 3 | | |
| Cruner, Peter | 1 | 5 | 2 | | |
| Luice, Ezekiel | 1 | 1 | 2 | | |
| Northaway, Ozias | 2 | 2 | 4 | | |
| Luice, Elisha | 1 | 1 | 1 | | |
| Woodruff, Marten | 2 | 4 | 4 | | |
| Wright, Jeremiah, No 1 | 1 | 3 | 4 | | |
| Shelden, Ephephsas | 3 | 4 | 3 | | 1 |
| Knap, Timothy | 1 | 1 | 1 | | |
| Kenton, Stephen | 2 | 3 | 4 | | |
| Fowlar, Noah | 1 | 5 | 7 | | |
| Avret, Israhel | 2 | 5 | 5 | | |
| Barber, Ely | 1 | 3 | 3 | | |
| Yale, James | 1 | 1 | 2 | | |
| Lyman, Ebenezer | 1 | 2 | 4 | | |
| Beach, Wait | 3 | 1 | 6 | | |
| Whitmore, Joel | 2 | | 3 | | |
| Leach, Nathan$^l$ | 1 | 1 | 4 | | |
| Lyman, Caleb | 3 | | 6 | | |
| Mastial, Raphel | 3 | | 3 | | |
| Bancroft, Noadiah | 2 | 2 | 3 | | |
| Phelps, Jonathan | 1 | 1 | 2 | | |
| Phelps, Benjamin | 4 | | 2 | | |
| Curtiss, Zebulon | 2 | 1 | 5 | | |
| Northerum, Eben$^r$ | 3 | 1 | 4 | | |
| Grant, Matthew | 3 | | 2 | | |
| Thrall, Pardon | 1 | 1 | 4 | | |
| Wilkinson, Jonathan | 1 | 1 | 6 | | |
| Fauster, Daniel | 1 | 1 | 3 | | |
| Sage, Daniel | 1 | 1 | 5 | | |
| Truscoat, Solon | 1 | 3 | 2 | | |
| Colking, John | 2 | 2 | 2 | | |
| Reed, Moses | 1 | 1 | 2 | | |
| Worden, Ebenezer | 1 | | 1 | | |
| Right, Jonathan | 1 | 1 | 1 | | |
| Wright, Elisha | 1 | 2 | 2 | | |
| Worthey, Benjamin | 1 | 2 | 4 | | |
| Corkings, Silas | 1 | | 1 | | |
| Fuller, Joseph | 1 | 1 | 2 | | |
| Fuller, Joshua | 1 | 3 | 5 | | |
| Lyman, Simeon | 1 | 2 | 5 | | |
| Dibble, Ebenezer | 1 | 5 | 5 | | |
| Hynes, George | 1 | | 4 | | |
| Boness, Amos | 1 | 4 | 5 | | |
| Hill, Michael, 2$^d$ | 1 | 2 | 4 | | |
| Hill, Michael | 1 | | 1 | | |
| Fuller, Johiel | 1 | 1 | 5 | | |
| Strong, Joel | 1 | 1 | 5 | | |
| Tickner, John | 2 | 5 | 2 | | |
| Deming, Hezekiah | 2 | | 3 | | |
| Rossiter, Benjamin | 2 | 1 | 5 | | |
| Cowls, Joseph | 3 | 4 | 4 | | |
| Barney, Thomas | 1 | 4 | 5 | | |
| Osmon, Thomas | 2 | 1 | 3 | | |
| Burrell, Charles | 2 | 3 | 3 | | |
| Bukley, Joseph | 2 | 2 | 4 | | |
| Hinsdale, Jacob | 2 | 1 | 4 | | |
| Holcomb, Elijah | 2 | 1 | 5 | | |
| Holcomb, Abraham | 2 | 2 | 4 | | |
| Buckley, Samuel | 3 | 3 | 3 | | |
| Holcomb, Noah | 3 | 3 | 5 | | |
| Rice, Chaney | 1 | | 1 | | |
| Buckley, Joseph | 2 | | 2 | | |
| Cowle, Jasen | 1 | | 3 | | |
| Hinman, Joseph | 2 | 3 | 2 | | |
| Right, John | 1 | 3 | 3 | | |
| Fellows, Abia | 4 | 3 | 2 | | |
| Marsh, Thankful | | | 2 | | |
| Lester, Andrew | 1 | | 4 | | |
| White, George | 1 | 1 | 2 | | |
| Bill, Jonathan | 1 | 1 | 2 | | |
| Bill, Jonathan, 2$^d$ | 1 | 1 | 6 | | |
| Wright, Ephraim | 2 | 2 | 1 | | |
| Spensor, Thomas | 2 | | 1 | | |
| Bushnal, Thomas | 1 | 1 | 4 | | |
| Rimington, Elihu | 1 | 2 | 2 | | |
| Banning, David | 2 | 1 | 1 | | |
| Banning, Dan$^l$ | 1 | | 1 | | |
| Adams, Daniel | 1 | | 2 | | |
| Bishnel, Alexander | 3 | | 6 | | |
| Selvey, Ephraim | 1 | 2 | 2 | | |
| Bush, Aaron | 1 | | 2 | | |
| Cole, Thankful | | | 3 | | |
| Brayne, Asahel | 2 | 2 | 4 | | |
| Selvey, William | 2 | | 2 | | |
| Hayner, Asahel | 1 | | 3 | | |
| Emmons, Lydia | 2 | 4 | 6 | | |
| Right, Ephraim | 1 | 1 | 5 | | |
| Mills, Timothy | 1 | | 2 | | |
| Case, Joseph | 1 | 3 | 4 | | |
| Mills, Samuel | 1 | 4 | 2 | | |
| Roberts, Nathaniel | 2 | 2 | 2 | | |
| Mason, Elijah | 2 | 3 | 5 | | |
| Mills, Constant | 1 | 1 | 2 | | |
| Wilson, Joseph | 2 | 1 | 6 | | |
| Gaylor, Adward | 1 | 2 | 3 | | |
| Gaylor, Ammon | 1 | 1 | 2 | | |
| Wilcox, Hosea | 1 | 2 | 3 | | |
| Lee, Miles | 1 | 4 | 3 | | |
| Humphrey, Michael | 1 | | 1 | | |
| Humphrey, Pelatiah | 1 | 2 | 1 | | |
| Foot, Asa | 2 | 4 | 4 | | |
| Corols, Ebenezer | 5 | 2 | 4 | | |
| Gaylor, Benjamin | 1 | | 2 | | |
| Bradley, John | 1 | 1 | 2 | | |
| Mills, Joseph | 4 | 1 | 3 | | |
| Case, Asahel | 4 | | 4 | | |
| Pettibone, Isaac | 1 | 3 | 3 | | |
| Norton, Stephen, 2$^d$ | 1 | 1 | 1 | | |
| Norton, Stephen | 4 | | 3 | | |
| Lawrence, Nehemiah | 2 | 1 | 2 | | |
| Lawrence, David | 1 | 3 | 5 | 6 | |
| Baccus, Silvenus | 2 | | 2 | | |
| Marsh, Rufus | 1 | | 3 | | |
| Pease, Calvin | 1 | 2 | 2 | | |
| Spaldwin, Edward | 4 | 1 | 4 | | |
| Plumb, Fredrerick | 1 | 2 | 1 | | |
| Peet, Anna | | | 3 | | |
| Brooks, John | 1 | 1 | 2 | | |
| Turner, Sam$^l$ | 2 | 1 | 1 | | |
| Howe, Nathan | 1 | | 2 | | |
| Baldwin, John | 3 | 1 | 4 | | |
| Waid, Josiah | 1 | | 5 | | |
| Gillet, Jonathan | 1 | 2 | 4 | | |
| Lane, Ashbel | 2 | 1 | 3 | | |
| Rathborn, Job | 3 | 1 | 4 | | |
| Ward, Abijah | 2 | | 1 | | |
| Kingsbury, William | 1 | 3 | 3 | | |
| Williams, James | 1 | | 1 | | |
| Smith, Nodeah | 2 | | 2 | | |
| Stephens, Abel | 2 | 2 | 8 | | |
| Hewit, Benjamin | 1 | 2 | 5 | | |
| Evans, John | 1 | 2 | 6 | | |
| Pardee, Thomas | 2 | 1 | 3 | | |
| Moxom, Adonijah | 2 | 3 | 3 | | |
| Randol, John | 2 | 1 | 3 | | |
| Randol, Solomon | 1 | | 2 | | |
| Ranal, Job | 1 | 1 | 2 | | |
| Jewit, Alpheus | 1 | 1 | 4 | | |
| Jones, Andrew | 2 | 2 | 5 | | |
| Pease, Allen | 2 | | 2 | | |
| Blakmore, Simeon | 1 | | 2 | | |
| Farling, Mechum | 1 | 3 | 4 | | |
| Lockwood, Unice | 1 | 3 | 3 | | |
| Slade, John | 1 | | 2 | | |
| Bard, Nathan | 1 | 1 | 2 | | |
| Bard, Nathan | 4 | 2 | 6 | | |
| Chapman, Elijah | 2 | | 1 | | |
| Downs, David | 2 | 3 | 4 | | |
| Osmon, Thomas | 2 | 1 | 3 | | |
| Karnes, Aaron | 1 | | 5 | | |
| Wilcox, Thomas | 1 | | 3 | | |
| Hunt, Russel | 4 | 1 | 4 | | |
| Hunt, Salmon | 1 | 3 | 1 | | |
| Hare, Silas | 1 | 1 | 3 | | |
| Gilbert, Rachel | 1 | 4 | 1 | | |
| Suttey, Sam$^l$ | 4 | | 3 | | |
| Seward, Daniel | 1 | | 1 | | |
| Crosbey, Sim | 2 | 1 | 3 | | |
| Wildar, Ephraim | 1 | 2 | 5 | | |
| Newton, Abraham | 2 | | 6 | | |
| Robinson, John | 1 | | 4 | | |
| Coe, Timothy | 1 | 1 | 4 | | |
| Camfield, Dan$^l$ | 1 | 3 | 4 | | |
| Cowdrey, Jacob | 3 | 3 | 3 | | |
| Sheppard, Olver | 1 | 2 | 2 | | |
| Galard, Nathan | 1 | | 2 | | |
| Williams, Israel | 1 | 3 | 1 | | |
| Newton, Abner | 1 | | 2 | | |
| Bushnel, Sam$^l$ | 1 | | 1 | | |
| Goodwin, Seth | 1 | 2 | 1 | | |
| Allyn, Jonathan | 1 | 1 | 2 | | |
| Senior, Dan$^l$ | 2 | 3 | 7 | 1 | |
| Hunt, Russel | 3 | | 1 | | |
| Goodrich, Benjamin | 2 | 1 | 2 | | |
| Curtiss, Josiah | 1 | 1 | 3 | | |
| Peck, Isaac | 1 | | 1 | | |
| Hubard, Edmond | 1 | 3 | 2 | | |
| Deen, Urah | 1 | | 1 | | |
| Carrier, Benjamin | 3 | 1 | 4 | | |
| Deen, John, 2$^d$ | 4 | 2 | 7 | | |
| Dean, Oliver | 3 | | 5 | | |
| Squire, Jessee | 2 | 3 | 5 | | |
| Deen, John | 2 | | 5 | | |
| Hug, Isaac | 1 | 3 | 2 | | |
| Barton, Andrew | 1 | 1 | 4 | | |
| Hosford, Anne | | | 3 | | |
| Hosford, Timothy | 1 | 1 | 6 | | |
| Huntington, James | 2 | 2 | 5 | | |
| Chamberlain, Joel | 1 | 4 | 2 | | |
| Hug, William | 1 | 1 | 2 | | |
| Curtiss, Samuel | 3 | | 6 | | |
| Rowley, David | 1 | 1 | 1 | | |
| Deen, Salmon | 1 | | 2 | | 2 |
| Holeburd, Timothy | 1 | | 3 | | |
| Holeburd, William | 2 | 1 | 1 | | |
| Holiburd, John | 1 | 1 | 1 | | |
| Hunt, Russel | 2 | 1 | 2 | | |
| Right, Elizer | 2 | 1 | 4 | | |
| Churchel, Benjamin | 1 | 3 | 3 | | |
| Smith, Elijah | 2 | 5 | 5 | | |
| Barns, Torhand | 1 | 1 | 4 | | |
| Grenold, Samuel | 1 | 1 | 1 | | |
| Spencer, Job | 3 | 1 | 5 | | |
| Spencer, Job, 2$^d$ | 2 | | 3 | | |
| Spencer, Eliphas | 2 | 2 | 2 | | |
| Owen Abner | 2 | | 2 | | |
| Miner, Asahel | 3 | 5 | 4 | | |
| Sharman, James | 1 | | 1 | | |
| Ballard, Jessee | 2 | 1 | 3 | | |
| Smith, Grove | 2 | | 4 | | |
| Seymore, David | 2 | | 3 | | |
| Shelden, Moses | 2 | 2 | 4 | | |
| Rolepau, Lettie | | | 1 | | |
| Sheldon, Ezra | 1 | 1 | 7 | | 2 |
| Norton, Lot | 3 | 3 | 1 | | |
| Kelsey, William | 1 | | 5 | | |
| Ely, Richard | 1 | 5 | 2 | | |
| Jennins, Timothy | 1 | 1 | 1 | | |
| Fitch, Elisha | 1 | 1 | 2 | | |
| Burress, Joseph | 3 | 2 | 3 | | |
| Conklin, Thomas | 2 | 3 | 7 | | |
| Tausly, Matthews | 3 | | 2 | | |
| Chapman, Tutus | 3 | 1 | 3 | | |
| Williams, Bennajah | 2 | 1 | 2 | | |
| Williams, Ephraim | 1 | | 3 | | |
| Chamberlain, Abner | 1 | 2 | 4 | | |
| Hubbard, Joseph | 3 | 1 | 4 | | |
| Owen, James | 2 | 1 | 7 | | |
| Goodsell, John | 1 | 1 | 1 | | |
| Eveth, Daniel | 1 | 3 | 2 | | |
| M$^c$Lin, John | 1 | 2 | 1 | | 1 |
| Strong, Adonijah | 2 | 4 | 3 | | |
| Marvin, Martin | 1 | | 3 | | |
| Benton, James | 1 | 1 | 1 | | |
| Chapman, Nathan | 1 | | 2 | | |
| Beebe, William | 1 | 1 | 2 | | |
| Jack | | | | | 1 |
| Bissel, John | 1 | 1 | 5 | | |
| Walton, William | 4 | | 4 | | |
| Reed, Joel | 2 | | 2 | | |
| Reed, Stephen | 3 | | 2 | | |
| Roberts, Elisha | 2 | 2 | 2 | | |
| Merills, Heck | 2 | 2 | 3 | | |
| Marsh, Anos | 1 | | 2 | | |
| Marsh, Job | 1 | | 3 | | |
| Merills, Soloman | 1 | 3 | 3 | | |
| Barnes, Charles | 3 | 2 | 4 | | |

# HEADS OF FAMILIES—CONNECTICUT.

## LITCHFIELD COUNTY—Continued.

| NAME OF HEAD OF FAMILY. | Free white males of 16 years and upward, including heads of families. | Free white males under 16 years. | Free white females, including heads of families. | All other free persons. | Slaves. | NAME OF HEAD OF FAMILY. | Free white males of 16 years and upward, including heads of families. | Free white males under 16 years. | Free white females, including heads of families. | All other free persons. | Slaves. | NAME OF HEAD OF FAMILY. | Free white males of 16 years and upward, including heads of families. | Free white males under 16 years. | Free white females, including heads of families. | All other free persons. | Slaves. |
|---|---|---|---|---|---|---|---|---|---|---|---|---|---|---|---|---|---|
| **LITCHFIELD TOWN—con.** | | | | | | **LITCHFIELD TOWN—con.** | | | | | | **LITCHFIELD TOWN—con.** | | | | | |
| Croe, Roger | 1 | 2 | 2 | | | Walter, Moses | 1 | 1 | 1 | | | Stephens, Roswell | 1 | 2 | 3 | | |
| Marsh, John | 1 | 1 | 3 | | | Walter, William | 2 | | 2 | | | Holt, Isaac | 5 | 1 | 3 | | |
| Marsh, Job | 3 | 2 | 3 | | | Walter, Clark | 1 | | | | 8 | Cravath, Sam¹ | 2 | 2 | 4 | | |
| Sheppard, Daniel | 2 | 2 | 3 | | | Orvis, Reuber | 1 | | 1 | | | Canfield, Dan¹ | 2 | 4 | 1 | | |
| Andruss, Eli | 2 | 4 | 6 | | | Stephens, Sam¹ | 1 | 2 | 2 | | | Morse, Andrew | 2 | | 1 | | |
| Neal, William | 1 | 2 | 2 | | | Jakins, George | 1 | | 2 | | | M°Cune, Garsham | 1 | | 1 | | |
| Neal, Aaron | 1 | 1 | 1 | | | Halley, Samu¹ | 2 | | 3 | | | M°Cune, Gersham | 1 | 2 | 2 | | |
| Neal, Enoch | 1 | 2 | 3 | | | Dimmick, David | 2 | 2 | 1 | | | M°Cune, Sam¹ | 1 | 3 | 4 | | |
| West, Aaron | 1 | 1 | 3 | | | Crevath, Samu¹ | 2 | | 2 | | | Smith, Eleazer | 1 | 3 | 4 | | |
| Thorp, Earle | 2 | 1 | 2 | | | Gillet, John | 1 | 2 | 4 | | | Alverd, Elihu | 2 | 1 | 5 | | |
| Dorson, Sibe | | 2 | 4 | | | Benedick, James | 1 | 2 | 3 | | | Wilcox, Elisha | 1 | 2 | 6 | | |
| Lone, Isaac | 1 | 3 | 4 | | | Benedick, Francis | 3 | | 4 | | | Blackman, Peter | 3 | 1 | 4 | | |
| Merrills, Siprean | 1 | 2 | 4 | | | Hawlley, Elisha | 1 | 3 | 3 | | | Smith, Samuel | 4 | 3 | 5 | | |
| Andrews, Nehemiah | 4 | 4 | 3 | | | Stephans, Simeon | 3 | 2 | 2 | | | Church, Silas | 2 | 2 | 4 | | |
| Tucker, Ephraim | 2 | 1 | 3 | | | Orvis, David | 1 | 3 | 4 | | | Bennet, John | 2 | 2 | 1 | | |
| Seymore, Uriah | 5 | 1 | | | | Grant, Roswell | 1 | | 3 | | | Keep, Jabez | 1 | 1 | 3 | | |
| Stephen, John | 1 | | 1 | | | Hungerford, Reuben | 3 | 2 | 4 | | | Jevel, Joseph | 2 | 4 | 6 | | |
| Wright, Ezekiel | 2 | 1 | 3 | | | Chamberlain, William | 1 | 2 | 3 | | | Camp, Jacob | 2 | 3 | 3 | | |
| Graves, Hubbard | 1 | 2 | 2 | | | Chamberlain, William | 2 | | 2 | | | Weeb, Isaac | 1 | 1 | 4 | | |
| Andrews, Ezra | 1 | 1 | 4 | | | Alverd, David | 1 | | 3 | | | Wholer, John | 2 | 2 | 2 | | |
| M'Canasy, Betty | | 3 | 5 | | | Bacon, John | 1 | 1 | 3 | | | Vosburgh, Jacob | 2 | 2 | 4 | | |
| Rust, Stephen | 1 | 2 | 1 | | | Holiburt, Martin | 1 | | 1 | | | Dacker, Jacob | 1 | | 1 | | |
| Seymore, Elias | 1 | 1 | 5 | | | Nash, John | 2 | | 3 | | | Hall, David | 1 | | 2 | | |
| Hursted, Roger | 1 | | 1 | | | Noth, Martin | 1 | | 2 | | | Camp, Luke | 2 | 2 | 3 | | |
| Gilbert, Jessee | 1 | | 2 | | | Elmore, Joseph | 1 | 1 | 2 | | | Weldon, Abraham | 1 | 2 | 2 | | |
| Atkins, James | 1 | | 1 | | | Knap, Joshua | 1 | 2 | 6 | | | Weldon, John | 3 | 1 | 4 | | |
| Russel, Elisha | 1 | | 2 | | | Everit, Josiah | 1 | 1 | 2 | | | Beemont, William | 2 | | 3 | | |
| Cadwell, Isaac | 1 | 2 | 4 | | | Holiburt, Sam¹ | 4 | 2 | 4 | | | Farnume, Philop | 1 | 1 | 2 | | |
| Goodwin, Eben' | 2 | 4 | 5 | | | Evaritt, Ebenezer | 2 | | 2 | | | Tuttle, Moses | 2 | | 3 | | |
| Goodwin, Eben' | 1 | | 3 | | | Avery, Daniel | 1 | 5 | 1 | | | Latten, John | 1 | 3 | 1 | | |
| Petton, John | 1 | | 1 | | | Everit, Ebenezer | 1 | 3 | 2 | | | Roach, William | 1 | 1 | 5 | | |
| Seymore, Hezekiah | 2 | 4 | 3 | | | Wood, Barney | 1 | 2 | 1 | | | Stanton, Joshua | 4 | 1 | 4 | | |
| Omsted, Roger | 2 | 1 | 3 | | | Smith, Samuel | 1 | 1 | 3 | | | Merchant, Joseph | 1 | | | | |
| Merrills, Benª | 3 | 7 | 7 | | | Chapman, Robert | 3 | 2 | 2 | | | Mason, Peter | 2 | 5 | 4 | | |
| Shelden, Roger | 2 | 4 | 5 | | | Wilson, Peter | 5 | 1 | 3 | | | Fletcher, Ebenezer | 2 | 3 | 6 | | |
| Marsh, Jonathan | 4 | | 5 | | | Tobins, John W | 1 | | 2 | | | James, Ethiel | 2 | 2 | 4 | | |
| Marsh, Daniel | 1 | 5 | 4 | | | Chapman, Robert | 1 | | 3 | | | Parx, James | 2 | 2 | 5 | | |
| Etton, Recompence | 1 | 4 | 2 | | | Tobins, James | 1 | 4 | 1 | | | Fitch, Joshua | 1 | 3 | 4 | | |
| Hinsdale, Elisha | 1 | 2 | 2 | | | Goodrich, Abner | 1 | 3 | 3 | | | Sirdam, Tunis | 4 | 1 | 6 | | |
| Goodwin, Jessee | 1 | 2 | 2 | | | Warner, Amasy | 1 | 1 | 4 | | | Dean, Joel | 1 | 2 | 2 | | |
| Johns, Joel | 1 | 3 | 3 | | | Wix, Rebacah | | | 1 | | | Lalintice, Jacob | 2 | | 4 | | |
| Kelsey, Enoch | 7 | 1 | 3 | | | Pomp | | | | | 7 | Corney, Andrew | 1 | 2 | 4 | | |
| Rowley, Levi | 2 | 3 | 6 | | | Fortier, Benjamin | 1 | 3 | 4 | | | Northorp, Samuel | 3 | 3 | 6 | | |
| Smith, John C | 1 | 2 | 1 | 2 | | Jones, James | 1 | 2 | 3 | | | Trowbridge, James | 2 | | 3 | | |
| Smith, Cotten M | 3 | 3 | 5 | 4 | | Gibson, Eliezer | 1 | 2 | 3 | | | Camp, Abial | 2 | 1 | 3 | | |
| Hunt, Isaac | 4 | 2 | 2 | | | Benjamin, Phinehas | 1 | 3 | 4 | | | Chapin, Phinehas | 3 | 3 | 3 | | |
| St. John, Silas | 2 | 2 | 4 | | | Morey, Nathaniel | 1 | | 1 | | | Chapin, Charles | 2 | 2 | 4 | | |
| Everitt, Isaah | 3 | 4 | 4 | | | Frisbie, Hezekiah | 3 | 4 | 4 | | | Ball, Erastus | 2 | | 2 | | |
| Hubbord, William A | 1 | 2 | 4 | | | Shaddock, Joseph | 1 | | 2 | | | Lotts, John H | 1 | 1 | 1 | | |
| Warner, Austin | 2 | 1 | 2 | | | Spensor, Alexander | 4 | | 2 | | | Camp, Joel | 3 | 2 | 5 | | |
| Smith, Paul | 1 | 1 | 1 | 2 | | Spensor, Hezekiah | 1 | 1 | 2 | | | Mix, Thomas | 3 | 1 | 1 | | |
| Canfield, Sam¹ | 3 | 1 | 5 | | | Hunt, Phinehas | 1 | 2 | 4 | | | Turner, Easter | | | 2 | | |
| Smith, Paul, 2d | 1 | 1 | 3 | | | Lawrence, John | 1 | 1 | 1 | | | Pollett, James | 1 | 1 | 3 | | |
| Tuller, John | 3 | | 7 | | | Hooker, Jessee | 1 | 2 | 5 | | | Eddy, Asa | 2 | 2 | 3 | | |
| Dota, Timothy, 2 | 2 | | 3 | | | Pratt, Joel | 1 | 2 | 3 | | | Coudry, Jonathan | 1 | 1 | 2 | | |
| Furgeson, Daniel | 1 | 1 | 3 | | | Stephens, Roswell | 1 | 2 | 3 | | | Whiting, Asa | 3 | 3 | 2 | | |
| Strong, Josiah | 2 | 1 | 2 | | | Knap, Luke | 3 | 1 | 5 | | | Bingham, Banajah | 1 | 1 | 2 | | |
| Backen, Daniel | 1 | 2 | 2 | | | Patrige, Stephen | 1 | 4 | 3 | | | Eddy, John | 1 | 1 | 1 | | |
| Goodrich, Elisha | 1 | 1 | 3 | | | Daniels, Jonathan | 1 | 2 | 4 | | | Scott, Etheel | 1 | 2 | 2 | | |
| Goodrich, Elizabeth | | | 2 | | | Stephens, Abel | 2 | | 8 | | | Curtis, Madad | 1 | | 1 | | |
| Goodrich, Joel | 2 | 3 | 2 | | | Tucker, Jedediah | 1 | 3 | 6 | | | Curtis, Sirus | 1 | | 2 | | |
| Pettit, Joel | 2 | | 2 | | | Darling, Abel | 1 | 4 | 5 | | | Hollister, Isaac | 2 | 3 | 2 | | |
| Burr, Walter | 1 | 3 | 6 | | | Stephens, James | 2 | 1 | 3 | | | Phelps, Elijah | 4 | 1 | 4 | | |
| Ashley, Abreham | 1 | 3 | 3 | | | Babcok, Elias | 3 | 1 | 2 | | | Monger, Reuben | 4 | 3 | 6 | 1 | |
| Holibert, Sam¹ | 1 | 2 | 2 | | | Babcok, Rufus | 1 | 2 | 1 | | | Lewis, Richard | 1 | | 2 | | |
| Basset, Joshua | 3 | | 3 | | | Martial, Joseph | 1 | 1 | 1 | | | Akins, Henry | 4 | 1 | 3 | | |
| Williams, Wait | 2 | 3 | 1 | | | Butler, Jererd | 3 | 3 | 4 | | | Curtis, Soloman | 1 | 2 | 2 | | |
| Holibert, Elisha | 2 | | 4 | | | Sturdaphant, James | 1 | 1 | 1 | | | Camp, Moses | 3 | 1 | 4 | | |
| Bartlet, Russel | 1 | 4 | 3 | | | Hils, Jessee | 1 | | 2 | | | Phelps, Darius | 2 | 1 | 3 | | |
| Taylor, Augustin | 1 | 1 | 2 | 3 | 2 | Whitmore, Abel | 2 | 3 | 2 | | | Coy, Ephraim | 1 | | 1 | 3 | |
| Smith, Phinehas | 2 | 4 | 2 | 1 | | Whitmore, Sam¹ | 1 | 1 | 2 | | | Rice, Nathan¹ | 5 | | 2 | | |
| Gallow, Joseph | 2 | | 4 | 1 | | Holibart, Martin | 1 | | 1 | | | Rice, Asa | 1 | 1 | 1 | | |
| Backen, Ebenses | 2 | 1 | 4 | | | Case, William | 1 | 3 | 4 | | | Cole, Dan¹ | 2 | | 2 | | |
| Goodwin, John | 1 | | 5 | | | Spensor, Thomas | 1 | 1 | 6 | | | Beach, Abner | 1 | 2 | 2 | | |
| Clark, Daniel | 1 | 2 | 1 | | | Braughton, Nathan | 1 | 2 | 2 | | | Johnson, Zebediah | 1 | 3 | 5 | | |
| Squre, Hulda | | | 2 | | | Murrin, David | 1 | | 1 | | | Burr, Ebenezer | 2 | 3 | 5 | | |
| Goodwin, John P | 3 | 4 | 4 | | | Blackman, Truman | 1 | | 1 | | | Jones, Joseph | 3 | 3 | 6 | | |
| Elmore, Elja | 3 | | 1 | | | Spalden, Isaac | 1 | 4 | 3 | | | Robons, Amenizsehana | 3 | 4 | 3 | | |
| Goodrich, William | 2 | 3 | 5 | | | Cammel, John | 1 | | 6 | | | Pettibone, Jiles | 2 | 1 | 7 | | |
| Freeman, John | 1 | 1 | 3 | | | Brister, John | 2 | 3 | 5 | | | More, William | 1 | 2 | 2 | | |
| Wadsworth, Josiah | 1 | 5 | 4 | | | Barden, Seth | 3 | 2 | 6 | | | Jailen, Isaac | 1 | 2 | 2 | | |
| Hawley, Samu¹ | 1 | 2 | 5 | | | Barden, Ebenezer | 1 | 1 | 1 | | | Phier, Horace | 1 | 2 | 4 | | |
| Bennedick, Benjamin | 1 | 1 | 4 | | | Barden, Timothy | 1 | | 1 | | | Moodey, Philop | 2 | 2 | 2 | | |
| Bennedick, Timothy | 3 | 1 | 5 | | | Merrills, Ephrm | 1 | 1 | 3 | | | Ranford, Joel | 1 | 3 | 1 | | |
| More, Simon | 1 | | 4 | | | Welch, Dan¹ | 1 | 3 | 2 | | | Case, Amos | 3 | 1 | 6 | | |
| Andrews, Dan¹ | 2 | 1 | 4 | | | Knap, Samu¹ | 2 | 1 | 3 | | | Allyn, Josiah | 1 | | 1 | | |
| Cook, Timothy | 1 | 3 | 2 | | | Gaylor, Joseph | 2 | 5 | 1 | 1 | | Sperry, Darius | 1 | 2 | 2 | | |
| Richard, Roswell | 1 | 2 | 3 | | | Gaylor, Ayer | 1 | 1 | 4 | | | Ranford, Daniel | 4 | 4 | 4 | | |
| Pardy, Charles | 2 | 2 | 2 | | | Gaylor, Marnory | | | 3 | | | Wilson, John | 1 | 2 | 3 | | |
| Richard, Elishu | 1 | 1 | 2 | | | Toby, Abraham | 2 | 2 | 2 | | | Crane, John | 3 | 2 | 2 | | |
| Richard, Jedediah, 2d | 1 | 5 | 2 | | | Gaylor, Sam¹ | 1 | | 2 | | | Johnson, Sherman | 1 | 3 | 5 | | |
| Richard, Jedediah | 1 | 1 | | | | Toby, Miles | 1 | | 1 | | | Johnson, Jonothan | 1 | 1 | 1 | | |
| Butler, Stephen | 1 | | 4 | | | Surdephant, Abijah | 1 | 1 | 1 | | | Allyn, Aaron | 2 | 1 | 2 | | |
| Butler, Hezekiah | 1 | | 2 | | | Toby, George | 2 | 1 | 5 | | | Wyldur, Jonathan | 2 | 2 | 3 | | |
| Bishop, Mimsa | | | 2 | 1 | | Murrey, Jasper | 4 | | 2 | 4 | | Austen, James | 2 | 2 | 5 | | |

35201—08——5

# FIRST CENSUS OF THE UNITED STATES.

## LITCHFIELD COUNTY—Continued.

| NAME OF HEAD OF FAMILY. | Free white males of 16 years and upward, including heads of families. | Free white males under 16 years. | Free white females, including heads of families. | All other free persons. | Slaves. | NAME OF HEAD OF FAMILY. | Free white males of 16 years and upward, including heads of families. | Free white males under 16 years. | Free white females, including heads of families. | All other free persons. | Slaves. | NAME OF HEAD OF FAMILY. | Free white males of 16 years and upward, including heads of families. | Free white males under 16 years. | Free white females, including heads of families. | All other free persons. | Slaves. |
|---|---|---|---|---|---|---|---|---|---|---|---|---|---|---|---|---|---|
| **LITCHFIELD TOWN—con.** | | | | | | **LITCHFIELD TOWN—con.** | | | | | | **LITCHFIELD TOWN—con.** | | | | | |
| Newill, Solomon | 2 | 5 | 4 | | | Bissel, Zebulon | 1 | 2 | 4 | | | Church, Ebenezer | 1 | 3 | 4 | | |
| King, Jonathan | 1 | 1 | 4 | | | Bissel, Benjamin | 1 | 3 | 3 | | | Cesar | | | | 3 | |
| Johnson, Reuben | 1 | | 3 | | | Thomas, Joseph | 1 | 1 | 1 | | | Griswold, Josiah | 1 | 3 | 2 | | |
| Sheppard, Moses | 2 | | 5 | | | Tryon, Joseph | 1 | 1 | 3 | | | Fairchild, David | 1 | 1 | 4 | | |
| Sheppard, Joseph | 2 | 1 | 3 | | | Tryon, John | 3 | | 3 | | | Roberts, Jude | 1 | 1 | 1 | | |
| Ward, James | 2 | 2 | 3 | | | Stone, John | 1 | 2 | 4 | | | Phelps, John | 2 | | 3 | | |
| Mason, Elisha | 2 | 1 | 4 | | | Taylor, Simeon | 1 | 1 | 2 | | | Pettiborn, Elijah | 1 | 6 | 2 | | |
| Mason, Harmon | 1 | | 1 | | | Kilborn, Jessee | 1 | 3 | 5 | | | Merrills, Noah | 1 | 4 | 2 | | |
| Mason, Joshua | 1 | | 2 | | | Kilborn, Jiles | 2 | | 3 | | | Porter, James | 4 | 4 | 5 | | |
| Moss, John | 1 | 3 | 5 | | | Howard, Ezekiel | 2 | | 2 | | | Phelps, Daniel | 1 | 2 | 3 | | |
| Gerret, Lydia | | 1 | 2 | | | Monger, Elisha S | 1 | 1 | 3 | | | Wakefield, Partrof | 1 | 4 | 3 | | |
| Wallace, Richard | 3 | 1 | 6 | | | Johnson, Lambard | 1 | 2 | 2 | | | Forson, Benjamin | 1 | | 2 | | |
| Goodwin, Joseph | 1 | 3 | 2 | | | Smith, Phinehas | 2 | 3 | 2 | | | Martin, Asahel | 1 | 2 | 3 | | |
| Seely, Justice | 2 | 1 | 2 | | | Carter, Thadeus | 1 | 1 | 2 | | | Cowls, Ira | 1 | 1 | 2 | | |
| Seeley, Ebenezer | 2 | 2 | 7 | | | Clemmons, Abijah | 1 | 1 | 2 | | | Allen, Justice | 1 | | | | |
| Seely, Benjamin | 1 | 1 | 3 | | | Orven, Phinehas | 1 | 2 | 1 | | | Walcott, John | 1 | | | | |
| Seeley, Nathaniel | 1 | | 1 | | | Smith, Nathaniel | 1 | | 1 | | | Andrews, Elijah | 2 | | 3 | | |
| Manning, Thomas | 1 | | 1 | | | Kilborn, Isaac | 1 | 1 | 4 | | | Pitkin, John | 1 | | 2 | | |
| McNiel, Isaac | 3 | 2 | 3 | | | Glass, James | 1 | 3 | 3 | | | Brown, John | 1 | | 1 | | |
| Loomis, Benjamin | 2 | 2 | 5 | | | Smith, Reuben | 2 | 1 | 2 | | | Pepper, John | 1 | | | | |
| Clark, Urial | 1 | 2 | 3 | | | Kilborn, John | 1 | | 1 | | | Morgan, Nathan | 1 | | 1 | | |
| Stacey, Samuel | 1 | 2 | 4 | | | Smith, Wait | 1 | | 1 | | | Simmons, Solomon | 2 | | 3 | | |
| Agard, Noah | 1 | 2 | 3 | | | Baldwin, Stephen | 2 | | 5 | | | Forbs, Elisha | 2 | 2 | 2 | | |
| Horford, John, 2d | 2 | 1 | 2 | | | Stodard, David | 2 | 1 | 2 | 1 | | Simmons, John | 1 | 1 | 3 | | |
| Horford, William, 2d | 2 | | 3 | | | Catlin, Rhoda | | 1 | 2 | | | Simmons, Rufus | 2 | | | | |
| Agard, Joseph | 1 | 4 | 2 | | | Kilborn, David | 4 | 3 | 4 | | | Grannis, William | 3 | | 4 | | |
| Andrews, William | 1 | | 1 | | | Stodard, Daniel | 1 | 1 | 2 | | | Motthrop, Isaac | 2 | 3 | 3 | | |
| Grant, Charles, 2d | 2 | 5 | 5 | | | Johnson, Benjamin | 1 | | 2 | | | Will | | | | 6 | |
| Agard, Mary | | | 2 | | | Odel, Daniel | 1 | 2 | 4 | | | Potler, Israel | 1 | 3 | 3 | | |
| Gerret, Joshua | 2 | | 3 | | | Hoskins, Daniel | 1 | 3 | 4 | | | Smith, Hezekiah | 1 | 1 | 1 | | |
| Gibbs, William | 2 | | 3 | | | Roe, Daniel | 1 | 3 | 5 | | | Page, Aaron | 1 | 1 | 1 | | |
| Gibbs, William | 1 | 1 | 3 | | | Hunt, Miloe | 1 | | 1 | | | Page, William | 1 | | 1 | | |
| Baldwin, Isaac, 2d | 2 | 4 | 3 | | 1 | Glover, Edward | 3 | 2 | 3 | | | Bessel, Isaac | 2 | 2 | 5 | | |
| Catlin, Thomas | 2 | 1 | 2 | | | Kilborn, Jessee | 1 | | 2 | | | Barnes, Samuel | 2 | | 4 | | |
| Skinner, Timothy | 5 | 3 | 4 | | | Bradley, Leming | 2 | | 2 | | | White, Ezra | 5 | 2 | 6 | | |
| Tallmadge, Benjamin | 1 | 3 | 4 | 1 | | Bradley, Aaron | 1 | 2 | 1 | | | Coldgrove, Joseph | 1 | | 2 | | |
| Sheldon, Daniel | 3 | 2 | 4 | | | Bradley, Comfort | 1 | 1 | 1 | | | Bogue, Daniel | 1 | 1 | 2 | | |
| Catlin, William | 2 | 1 | 5 | | | Smith, Nathaniel | 3 | 2 | 3 | | | Handy, Clemens | 4 | 1 | 8 | | |
| Parmerley, Amos | 2 | | 3 | | | Palmer, William | 1 | 1 | 4 | | | Norriss, Champfire | 2 | | 4 | | |
| Parmerly, Amos | 1 | 1 | 1 | | | Pierpoint, Eveland | 2 | 1 | 5 | | | Philley, Isaac | 2 | | 4 | | |
| Kilborn, Solomon, 2d | 2 | 1 | 2 | | | Pierpont, James | 3 | 3 | 3 | | | Beaman, Elisha | 14 | 2 | 4 | | |
| Kilborn, Solomon | 3 | | 3 | | | Johnson, Luther | 1 | | 5 | | | Wright, Jonathan | 1 | | 2 | | |
| Smith, Ruama | | 1 | 3 | | | Gibbs, Samuel | 3 | | 6 | | | Hewit, Joshua | 1 | 1 | 1 | | |
| Gates, Jehiel | 1 | 4 | 2 | | | Goodwin, Thomas | 3 | 1 | 3 | | | Prince | | | | 6 | |
| Bissel, Joseph | 1 | 2 | 1 | | | Farnham, Seth | 3 | 1 | 2 | | | Blakesley, Saml | 2 | 3 | 4 | | |
| Griswold, Zacheus | 3 | 1 | 3 | | | Goodwin, Nathaniel | 1 | | 3 | | | Rockwell, Elijah | 1 | 2 | 4 | | |
| Servant, James | 1 | | 2 | | | Goodwin, Elizabeth | 1 | | 2 | | | Blye, Paphroe | 1 | 1 | 3 | | |
| Merrills, Ephraim | 1 | 1 | 2 | | | Johnson, Jonathan | 1 | 4 | 4 | | | Rockwell, Elihue | 1 | | 3 | | |
| Wadhams, Moses | 1 | 2 | 3 | | | Harrison, David | 1 | 1 | 1 | | | Rockwell, Joseph | 1 | | | | |
| Ripner, Samuel | 1 | 2 | 2 | | | Johnson, Elizabeth | | | 1 | | | Rockwell, John | 1 | 2 | 2 | | |
| Wadhams, Seth | 3 | 2 | 3 | 1 | | Pero | | | | 3 | | Bidwell, Epiphras | 1 | 1 | 3 | | |
| Wadham, Jonathan | 2 | 2 | 3 | | | Deforrest, Isaac | 1 | 2 | 2 | | | Enos, Daniel | 2 | 1 | 2 | | |
| Leach, Phebe | 1 | 4 | 5 | | | Gibbs, Benjamin | 1 | | 1 | | | Bass, Anna | | 1 | 6 | | |
| Hoy, John | 1 | | 3 | | | Gibbs, Ethamon | 1 | 1 | 3 | | | Bass, Nathan | 1 | | 2 | | |
| Pratt, Isaac | 2 | | 3 | | | Linley, Joseph | 2 | | 4 | | | Wright, Moses | 3 | 1 | 8 | | |
| Pettibone, Judy | | | 2 | | | Peck, Elijah | 2 | 2 | 6 | | | Barber, Benjamin | 1 | 1 | 2 | | |
| Price, Paul | 1 | 2 | 3 | | | Huntington, Israel | 1 | | 2 | | | Hall, Daniel | 1 | 2 | 3 | | |
| Parmly, Standley | 1 | 1 | 1 | | | Peck, Levi | 1 | 3 | 8 | | | Rockwell, Saml | 17 | 4 | 3 | 1 | |
| Filley, Abraham | 3 | 1 | 2 | | | Woodruff, Benjamin | 1 | 1 | 6 | | | Seymore, Stephen | 1 | 4 | 2 | | |
| Pettus | | | | 4 | | Woodruff, Jacob | 1 | | 2 | | | Hopkins, Thomas | 2 | 2 | 1 | | |
| Jud, Benjamin | 1 | | 2 | | | Woodruff, W. Right | 1 | 1 | 2 | | | Taintor, Joseph | 1 | 3 | 2 | | |
| Kimberly, Jacob | 2 | 3 | 5 | | | Woodruff, Jacob | 2 | 2 | 3 | | | Buckingham, Andrew | 1 | | 4 | | |
| Preston, Samuel | 2 | 2 | 4 | | | Barnard, Saml | 1 | 1 | 1 | | | Pinney, David | 2 | | 3 | | |
| Stannard, Seth | 1 | 3 | 1 | | | Barnard, Saml | 1 | 4 | 2 | | | Pinney, Grove | 1 | | 3 | | |
| Hill, Huste | 2 | 2 | 6 | | | Gibbs, Justice | 2 | 2 | 6 | | | Pinney, Abraham | 1 | | 3 | | |
| Cook, Aaron | 1 | 3 | 2 | | | Gibbs, Remembrance | 3 | | 6 | | | Watter, Samuel | 1 | 2 | 3 | | |
| Philley, Remembrance | 2 | | 4 | | | Gibbs, Eldad | 1 | 1 | 1 | | | Aglestone, Daniel | 3 | | 3 | | |
| Smith, Heman | 1 | 3 | 2 | | | Morriss, James | 2 | 5 | 3 | | | Martial, Josiah | 1 | 3 | 4 | | |
| Beach, Joel | 2 | 2 | 3 | | | Woodruff, James | 1 | 2 | 3 | | | Howell, Edmond | 2 | 2 | 3 | | |
| Basset, Samuel | 2 | 2 | 5 | | | Moss, Joseph | 1 | | 1 | | | Chamberlain, Saml | 1 | | 2 | | |
| Ward, Danl | 1 | | 1 | | | Hall, Mary | 1 | 1 | 1 | | | Chamberlain, Saml | 2 | | 3 | | |
| Deer, Jonathan | 1 | 2 | 1 | | | Smith, Frien | 1 | | 1 | | | Sage, Enos | 1 | 5 | 1 | | |
| Deer, John | 1 | | 7 | | | Hall, Ephraim S | 1 | 1 | 2 | | | Stilman, Roger | 1 | 4 | 4 | | |
| Mott, Adam | 1 | 1 | 3 | | | Knap, Jerard | 2 | 1 | 1 | | | Stilman, Appleton | 2 | | 3 | | |
| Goit, Richard | 1 | 1 | 2 | | | Lyman, Ruth | | | 2 | | | Stilman, Robert | 1 | 2 | 2 | | |
| Grovier, Danl | 1 | 1 | 1 | | | Hyde, Enoch | 2 | | 3 | | | Hart, Josiah H | 2 | | 1 | | |
| Martial, John | 1 | 2 | 3 | | | Barns, Orange | 1 | | 3 | | | Preston, Charles | 1 | 3 | 3 | | |
| Leason, Noah | 1 | | 1 | | | Perkins, John | 1 | | 1 | | | Munson, Medad | 1 | 3 | 3 | | |
| Corbin, Danl | 3 | | 5 | | | Smith, Elnathan | 1 | | 2 | | | Gordon, Lewis | 1 | 2 | 1 | | |
| Corbin, Peter | 1 | | 1 | | | Woodward, John | 2 | | 3 | | | Scovel, Benjamin | 2 | | 2 | | |
| Vitelo, John | 1 | 2 | 2 | | | Boardman, Oliver | 1 | 3 | 3 | | | Reed, Josiah | 2 | 3 | 2 | | |
| Loomis, Mindwal | 2 | 1 | 4 | | | Colyer, Thomas | 3 | 4 | 3 | | | Little, Robert | 1 | 2 | 2 | | |
| Avarice, Hannah | 1 | 2 | 5 | | | Beach, Ebenezer | 1 | 1 | 2 | | | Crane, Martin | 1 | | 2 | | |
| Wilkinson, Jessee | 2 | 1 | 4 | | | Galpin, Amos | 2 | 1 | 3 | | | Adam, Thomas | 1 | 1 | | | |
| Andrews, Abraham | 1 | 3 | 2 | | | Trowbridge, Thomas | 2 | 3 | 1 | | | Kimball, Richard | 1 | 1 | 4 | | |
| Smith, Chancy | 1 | 1 | 3 | | | Bradley, Abraham | 1 | 1 | 3 | | | Stephens, Ebenezer | 3 | | 2 | | |
| Merrills, Aaron | 1 | | 3 | | | Wessells, Lawrence | 1 | | 2 | | | Stephens, Joel | 1 | | 1 | | |
| Stodard, Mary | 1 | 1 | 4 | | | Holley, Elnathan | 2 | 2 | 3 | | | Saunders, Thomas | 1 | | 2 | | |
| Kilborne, Lewis | 1 | 1 | 3 | | | Marsh, Ebenezer | 4 | | 3 | | | Smith, Nathen | 1 | | 2 | | |
| Kilborne, Benjamin | 1 | | 3 | | | Stone, Mary | 3 | | 2 | | | Evets, Stephen | 1 | 1 | 4 | | |
| Parmeley, Submit | | | 1 | | | Marsh, John | 3 | 1 | 2 | | | Beets, John | 1 | 1 | 4 | | |
| Bissel, Colvis | 1 | 2 | 3 | | | Beckwith, George | 1 | 1 | 4 | | | Moore, Amos | 1 | | 2 | | |
| Bissel, Archulus | 1 | 2 | 3 | | | Bull, Asa | 1 | 1 | 4 | | | Pinkerton, William | 1 | 1 | 1 | | |
| Joy, Submit | | | 1 | | | Catlin, Saml | 2 | | 6 | | | Thompson, Joel | 1 | | 1 | | |
| Bissel, Abagail | | | 2 | | | Crosbey, Jeremiah | 2 | | 1 | | | Thompson, James | 1 | | 1 | | |
| Stone, Deodama | 1 | | 3 | | | Wiling, John | 1 | 4 | 3 | | | Raynolds, John | 1 | 1 | 2 | | |

# HEADS OF FAMILIES—CONNECTICUT.

## LITCHFIELD COUNTY—Continued.

| NAME OF HEAD OF FAMILY. | Free white males of 16 years and upward, including heads of families. | Free white males under 16 years. | Free white females, including heads of families. | All other free persons. | Slaves. | NAME OF HEAD OF FAMILY. | Free white males of 16 years and upward, including heads of families. | Free white males under 16 years. | Free white females, including heads of families. | All other free persons. | Slaves. | NAME OF HEAD OF FAMILY. | Free white males of 16 years and upward, including heads of families. | Free white males under 16 years. | Free white females, including heads of families. | All other free persons. | Slaves. |
|---|---|---|---|---|---|---|---|---|---|---|---|---|---|---|---|---|---|
| **LITCHFIELD TOWN—con.** | | | | | | **LITCHFIELD TOWN—con.** | | | | | | **LITCHFIELD TOWN—con.** | | | | | |
| Whitmore, Saml | 3 | 1 | 4 | 1 | | Bartholmew, Saml | 2 | 4 | 5 | | | Phelps, Edward | 3 | | 2 | | |
| Woodward, Serenus | 3 | 4 | 2 | | | Bonney, Junis | 1 | 3 | 2 | | | Catlin, Abel | 1 | 2 | 5 | | |
| Johnson, Daniel | 2 | 3 | 2 | | | Bonney, Asahel | 1 | | 6 | | | Peck, Mary | 2 | 1 | | | |
| Johnson, Sarah | 2 | 1 | 2 | | | Tuttle, Noah | 3 | 2 | 5 | | | Horford, David | 1 | | 3 | | |
| Johnson, Polly | | 2 | 1 | | | Leach, Jonas | 1 | 3 | 5 | | | Gardenor, George | 1 | 2 | 3 | 1 | |
| Landon, Abagail | | | 2 | 1 | | Beach, Michael | 1 | 1 | 3 | | | Butler, David | 1 | | 2 | 1 | |
| Lott, Peter | 1 | | 3 | | | Squire, Clement | 2 | 3 | 4 | | | Phelps, John | 1 | 2 | 5 | | |
| Bushnel, Gideon | 2 | 1 | 3 | | | Kellog, Samuel | 3 | | 4 | | | Long, John | 1 | | | | |
| Fitch, Hezekiah | 3 | 5 | 4 | | | Merrils, Biezela | 1 | | 2 | | | Clark, Lyman | 2 | 3 | 4 | | |
| King, John | 1 | | 1 | | | Denison, William | 2 | 2 | 5 | | | Orsborn, John | 1 | | 1 | | |
| Cole, Saml | 1 | | 1 | | | Kellog, Helmont | 1 | 3 | 1 | | | Atwood, James | 1 | 1 | 4 | | |
| Piffer, Nathan C | 1 | | 1 | | | Thompson, Stephen | 3 | 1 | | 3 | | Addes, James | 2 | 2 | 1 | | |
| Murphey, James | 1 | 1 | 1 | | | Thomson, Edward | 1 | | 1 | | | Blin, Hosea | 2 | 2 | 6 | | |
| Palmer, Daniel | 1 | | 1 | | | Roberts, John | 1 | 1 | 5 | | | Baldwin, Phinehas | 2 | 2 | 3 | | |
| Montgomeroy, Hue | 1 | 1 | 2 | | | Lee, John | 1 | 3 | 3 | | | Taylor, Elisha | 1 | 1 | 3 | | |
| Whiting, William | 1 | | 4 | | | Barns, Abel | 1 | 3 | | | | Taylor, Joel | 1 | 1 | 2 | | |
| Bessel, John | 1 | 4 | 2 | | | Reed, Moses | 2 | | 2 | | | Hebard, Nathan | 1 | 2 | 6 | | |
| Wadhams, Abraham | 2 | 5 | 3 | | | Trumbull, Jonathan | 1 | | 5 | | | Whitmore, Caleb | 1 | | 1 | | |
| Landon, David | 1 | | 1 | | | Bates, Martin | 1 | 3 | 7 | | | Wallace, Anna | | 3 | 1 | | |
| Landon, David | 1 | 1 | 4 | | | Chapman, Reuben, 2d | 1 | | 1 | | | Phill | | | | 2 | |
| Wire, Thomas | 2 | 2 | 5 | | | Chapman, Reuben | 1 | 1 | 4 | | | Marsh, Ashbel | 1 | 1 | 1 | | |
| Mitcalf, John | 1 | 2 | 4 | | | Chapman, John C | 1 | 2 | 1 | | | Chapman, Caleb | 1 | | 2 | | |
| Brooks, Joseph | 1 | 3 | 2 | | | Landon, Ezekiel | 2 | 2 | 3 | | | Taylor, Benjamin | 1 | 1 | 4 | | |
| Collins, Ambrose | 2 | 5 | 3 | | | Bessel, George | 2 | | 2 | | | Smith, Henry | 1 | 1 | 4 | | |
| Loomice, Fitch | 1 | 2 | 2 | | | Grennold, Japer | 2 | | 1 | | | Dickenson, Friend | 1 | 4 | 2 | | |
| Drigs, Daniel | 2 | 1 | 4 | | | Landon, Ashbel | 1 | 1 | 3 | | | Taylor, Anna | | | 2 | | |
| Fleskey, Mary | | | 1 | | | Grennold, Seth | 1 | 1 | 1 | | | Pierce, Mary | | 2 | 7 | | |
| Loomis, Asahel | 1 | 1 | 5 | | | Landon, Nathan | 2 | 2 | 3 | | | Baldwin, Ashbel | 1 | 1 | 2 | | |
| Loomis, Joel | 1 | 4 | 5 | | | Kyes, William | 2 | 1 | 3 | | | Jones, Eliakim | 1 | | 4 | | |
| Loomis, Isaac | 1 | | | | 1 | Doud, Peleg | 2 | 1 | 3 | | | Matlocks, James | 3 | | 2 | | |
| Taylor, Stephen | 1 | 2 | 6 | | | Harrison, Jared | 2 | 2 | 5 | | | Starr, Daniel | 1 | 1 | 4 | | |
| Phelps, Juda | | | 4 | | | Lewis, Hendrick | 1 | 4 | 1 | | | Stanton, William | 2 | | 3 | | |
| Barber, Elihue | 1 | | 1 | | | Doud, Samuel | 3 | 1 | 3 | | | Seymore, Samuel | 2 | 1 | 3 | | |
| Austin, Andrew D | 3 | 5 | 3 | | | Bossworth, Nathan | 2 | 3 | 2 | | | Earl, Rafal | 1 | 1 | 2 | | |
| Austin, Aaron | 3 | 2 | 5 | | | Kelsey, Jonathan | 1 | | 2 | | | Seymore, Moses | 4 | 3 | 5 | | |
| Austin, Eliphalet | 3 | 3 | 6 | | | Colkins, Elisha | 2 | 1 | 2 | | | Barber, Ebenezer | 2 | | 1 | 1 | |
| Atwater, Aseph | 2 | 2 | 5 | | | Perrey, Benjamin | 1 | | 2 | | | Sanford, Oliver | 2 | | 2 | | |
| Wilson, Noah | 3 | 1 | 4 | | | Perrey, Amos | 1 | 2 | 1 | | | Sanford, Jonah | 2 | 1 | 3 | | |
| Wilson, Abijah | 3 | 1 | 4 | | | Rowley, Simeon | 2 | 1 | 3 | | | Cleavland, Benjamin | 1 | | | | |
| Wilson, Noah | 1 | 1 | 5 | | | Hamlin, David | 4 | 2 | 4 | | | Silkrigs, Jonathan G | 1 | | | | |
| Cook, Daniel | 1 | 1 | 1 | | | Fuller, Ebenezer | 1 | 5 | 3 | | | Emmons, Russel | 1 | 4 | 5 | | |
| Munson, John | 3 | 1 | 4 | | | Evarts, Saml | 1 | 4 | 5 | | | Emmons, Oliver | 1 | | 1 | | |
| Munson, Nathaniel | 2 | | 3 | | | Evarts, Ebenezer | 1 | 1 | 5 | | | Emmons, Abner | 1 | | 5 | | |
| Beach, Daniel | 2 | 1 | 4 | | | Anderson, John | 1 | 2 | 2 | | | Lampson, Daniel | 2 | 1 | 1 | | |
| Hinman, Samuel | 1 | 5 | 4 | | | Phelps, Ichabod | 3 | 3 | 4 | | | Woodruff, Levi | 3 | 1 | 3 | | |
| Hart, David | 1 | | 2 | | | Monger, William | 1 | | 1 | | | Agard, Hezekiah | 1 | 2 | 2 | | |
| Bartholemew, Isaac | 1 | 1 | 3 | | | Tubs, Luman | 2 | 1 | 1 | | | Knap, Abraham | 1 | 2 | 2 | | |
| Stephens, Abijah | 1 | 2 | 5 | | | Deen, Seth | 1 | | 1 | | | Hinsdale, Elias | 2 | 1 | 4 | | |
| Cook, Daniel | 1 | 2 | 2 | | | Reed, Elias | 1 | 4 | 7 | | | Farnham, Nathan | 1 | 1 | 1 | | |
| Webb, Jonathan | 1 | 2 | 5 | | | Holms, James | 2 | 2 | 2 | | | Trumbal, Ezekiel | 1 | | 3 | | |
| Webb, Jonathan | 1 | 1 | 1 | | | Eldredge, John | 2 | | 4 | | | Gibbs, David | 2 | 1 | 3 | | |
| Webb, David | 1 | 3 | 5 | | | Reed, John | 1 | | 1 | | | Gibbs, Reuben | 1 | 1 | 2 | | |
| Baldwin, David | 1 | 2 | 3 | | | Rowley, Johiel | 1 | 2 | 3 | | | Stodard, James | 2 | 1 | 2 | | |
| Cornwell, Samuel | 3 | | 4 | | | Cook, Joel | 1 | | 3 | | | Sanford, Moses | 2 | | 4 | | |
| Thomson, Jonathan | 2 | 1 | 3 | | | Hitchcock, Daniel | 1 | 2 | 2 | | | Chase, Amos | 3 | | 3 | | |
| Norton, Daniel | 6 | 2 | 6 | | | Parker, Benjamin | 3 | | 1 | | | Farnham, Gad | 2 | | 5 | | |
| Howe, Joseph | 2 | 1 | 4 | | | Holscombe, James | 1 | 1 | 4 | | | Emmons, Arther, 2d | 2 | 3 | 2 | | |
| Wright, Jabez | 3 | 1 | 2 | | | Goodhue, David | 1 | | 4 | | | Bartholemew, Luther | 1 | 1 | 3 | | |
| Gaylord, Joel | 2 | | 6 | | | Barber, Ephraim | 1 | 2 | 3 | | | Emmons, Arther | 1 | | 1 | | |
| Allyn, Joel | 4 | 2 | 3 | | | Case, Andrus | 1 | 2 | 6 | | | Emmons, Orrange | 1 | 3 | 2 | | |
| Wilson, Amos | 2 | 1 | 3 | | | Barber, David | 1 | 2 | 2 | | | Gallop, Benjamin | 1 | | 2 | | |
| Cook, Elihu | 1 | | 3 | | | Rice, Saml | 1 | 3 | 4 | | | Emmons, Phinehas | 1 | 2 | 4 | | |
| Wolcott, Gye | 2 | 2 | 3 | | | Hart, Seth | 3 | 3 | 3 | | | Brown, Joseph | 1 | | 2 | | |
| Loomiss, Richard | 2 | 3 | 3 | | | Messenger, Abner | 2 | 2 | 2 | | | Orton, Azariah | 2 | 4 | 6 | | |
| Higly, Sarah | | | 2 | | | Wilcox, Johiel | 1 | 3 | 2 | | | Barns, Timothy | 2 | | 5 | | |
| Loomis, Doritha | 2 | 1 | 2 | | | Barber, Abraham | 4 | 2 | 2 | | | Hall, John | 1 | 2 | 2 | | |
| Leach, Joshua | 1 | 2 | 5 | | | Barber, Jimsi | 1 | 2 | 2 | | | Farnham, John | 1 | 1 | 2 | | |
| Stoddard, Ebenezer | 1 | 1 | 3 | | | Barber, Jacob | 3 | 2 | 6 | | | Orton, Sedgwick | 2 | | 3 | | |
| Leach, Ebenezer | 1 | 2 | 3 | | | Basset, David | 2 | 2 | 4 | | | Dresser, Simeon | 1 | 1 | 4 | | |
| Baldwin, George | 2 | | 3 | | | Olcott, James | 2 | 4 | 3 | | | Kelley, Elizabeth | | 1 | 1 | | |
| Ray, Timothy | 1 | | 3 | | | Thompson, Samuel | 2 | | 2 | | | Barns, Enos | 2 | 3 | 3 | | |
| Leach, Richard | 2 | 3 | 4 | | | Graves, Alexander | 1 | 1 | 2 | | | Smedley, Ephraim | 2 | | 5 | | |
| Holebrook, Abijah | 2 | | 1 | | | Andrews, John | 2 | 4 | 5 | | | Barns, Gift | | | 3 | 5 | |
| Deming, Roswell | 1 | | 1 | | | Wilcox, Asahel | 2 | 6 | 2 | | | Ray, William | 1 | 3 | 1 | | |
| Perrey, Isaac | 1 | 1 | 1 | | | Sacket, Aaron | 2 | | 3 | | | Clark, Champion | 1 | 2 | 1 | | |
| Denison, Christopher | 1 | 4 | 4 | | | Buell, John | 2 | 2 | 2 | | | Moore, David | 1 | 1 | 2 | | |
| Apley, Ezekiel | 3 | 3 | 3 | | | Collens, Oliver | 2 | 1 | 5 | | | Shether, Saml | 1 | 1 | 1 | | |
| Grannis, Robart | 1 | 2 | | | | Kilborn, Appelton | 1 | 1 | 1 | | | Culver, Zebulon | 1 | 1 | 1 | | |
| McNire, James | 2 | | 5 | | | Graves, William | 1 | | 2 | | | Presson, Jermiah | 1 | 3 | 3 | | |
| Judd, Ebenezer | 2 | | 5 | | | Jones, Eaton | 1 | | 1 | | | Culver, Zebulon | 1 | | 4 | | |
| Bound, Joseph | 1 | 1 | 3 | | | Allen, Joseph | 1 | 1 | 2 | | | Culver, Stephen | 1 | 4 | 6 | | |
| Bradley, Azariah | 1 | 1 | 3 | | | McNeal, Roswell | 2 | 3 | 3 | | | Stone, Heber | 1 | 1 | 2 | | |
| Bacon, James | 1 | 1 | 1 | | | Buel, Norman | 1 | 2 | 3 | | | Woodruff, Samuel | 2 | 2 | 5 | | |
| Martial, Sarah | | | 2 | | | Buel, Archelus | 1 | 2 | 3 | | | Woodruff, Nathaniel | 2 | 1 | 1 | | |
| Whitmore, John | 2 | 2 | 4 | | | Cole, Joseph | 1 | 3 | | | | Poerpont, David | 2 | 1 | 1 | | |
| Miller, Asahel | 3 | 1 | 1 | | | McNiel, Archebald | 2 | | 6 | | | Buell, David | 1 | 2 | 4 | | 3 |
| Barber, Choxhebe | | | 1 | | | Bull, Eunuice | | | 5 | | | Lewis, Daniel W | 1 | | | | |
| Schovel, Ebenezer | 1 | | 4 | | | Bull, George | 2 | | 2 | 2 | | Raymond, William | | | 2 | | |
| Keyes, William | 1 | 2 | 2 | | | Peck, Rhoda | | 1 | 2 | | | Sheldorn, Saml | 3 | 2 | 2 | | |
| Horskins, Theodore | 1 | | 2 | | | Gillet, Amos | 2 | 2 | 3 | | | Baldwin, Isaac | 3 | | 3 | | |
| Hoanmen, Wait | 1 | 1 | 4 | | | Anderson, Joshua | 1 | 4 | 6 | | | Sprats, William | 2 | 2 | 4 | | |
| Ives, Lazarus | 2 | 1 | 5 | | | Catlin, Theodore | 3 | 2 | 5 | | | Demming, Julius | 3 | 3 | 3 | | 1 |
| Luther, Martin | 1 | 3 | 4 | | | Landon, David | 2 | 2 | 3 | | | Woolcott, Oliver | 3 | | 1 | | 6 |
| Orton, Darius | 1 | 1 | 4 | | | Parker, Ebenezer | 2 | | 3 | | | Reeve, Tapping | 1 | 2 | 3 | | |
| Maltbey, Jseph | 2 | 3 | 6 | | | McNiel, Alexander | 2 | | 1 | | 2 | | | | | | |

# FIRST CENSUS OF THE UNITED STATES.

## LITCHFIELD COUNTY—Continued.

### LITCHFIELD TOWN—con.

| NAME OF HEAD OF FAMILY. | Free white males of 16 years and upward, including heads of families. | Free white males under 16 years. | Free white females, including heads of families. | All other free persons. | Slaves. |
|---|---|---|---|---|---|
| Lewis, Osius | 5 | 1 | 3 | | |
| Barber, Stephen | 1 | 2 | 1 | | |
| Russel, Stephen | 1 | 1 | 5 | | |
| Marsh, Elisha | 2 | | 3 | | |
| Clemmons, John | 1 | 2 | 4 | | |
| Agard, Judah | 1 | 3 | 1 | | |
| McKinly, William | 1 | 3 | 4 | | |
| Marsh, Solomon | 2 | 3 | 5 | | 1 |
| Sanders, John | 1 | 2 | 5 | | |
| Smith, Benjamin | 3 | | 3 | | |
| Bishop, Silvanus | 2 | 1 | 2 | | |
| Stone, Reuben | 2 | 3 | 3 | | |
| Hughes, William | 1 | 2 | 3 | | |
| Hayson, Saml | 1 | | | | |
| Bates, Sarah | | 1 | 3 | | |
| Landon, John | 1 | 3 | 4 | | |
| Stone, Thomas | 2 | 2 | 2 | | |
| Bishop, Calvin | 1 | 2 | 2 | | |
| Woodcok, Saml | 2 | 1 | 6 | | |
| Woodcok, Jonathan | 1 | | | | |
| Griswold, Jacob | 2 | 1 | 1 | | |
| Stocker, Thadeus | 1 | 3 | 4 | | |
| Denison, Chaney | 2 | 1 | 2 | | |
| Stone, Silvanus | 1 | 2 | 1 | | |
| Stuard, Loas | | | 1 | | |
| Philips, Gideon | 2 | 1 | 3 | | |
| Benton, Nathaniel | 2 | 1 | 5 | | |
| Howard, Joseph | 1 | | 7 | | |
| Benton, Daniel | 1 | 1 | 1 | | |
| Swan, Nathan | 2 | | 4 | | |
| Benton, Abraham | 1 | | 1 | | |
| Hermom, Nicholas | 1 | | 2 | | |
| Gosling, Solomon | 1 | 1 | 2 | | |
| Stone, Jonah | 2 | 3 | 5 | | |
| Baldwin, William | 3 | 2 | 2 | | |
| Baldwin, James | 2 | | 4 | | |
| Worter, Benjamin | 1 | | 2 | | |
| Worter, Samuel | 2 | 2 | 3 | | |
| Wilmot, John | 1 | 3 | 2 | | |
| Taylor, John | 1 | | 3 | | |
| Merrills, Truman | 1 | | 3 | | |
| Humestone, Reuben | 3 | 1 | 3 | | |
| Catlin, Alexander | 3 | 1 | 6 | 1 | |
| Yale, Elsa | | | 2 | | |
| McNeil, Saml | 1 | 3 | 4 | | |
| Stone, Levi | 3 | 3 | 4 | | |
| Peck, Philoe | 1 | 1 | 4 | | |
| Phelps, Ariah | 1 | | | | |
| Kinney, Martha | 2 | 1 | 5 | | |
| Phillips, Samuel | 1 | 2 | 3 | | |
| Crissey, Presarved | 1 | 1 | 2 | | |
| Phillips, Samuel | 1 | 3 | 2 | | |
| Lymans, Aaron | 3 | | 5 | | |
| Lymans, Aaron | 1 | | 4 | | |
| Lymans, Hezikah | 1 | 4 | 5 | | |
| Lymans, William | 1 | 1 | 2 | | |
| Rockwell, David | 1 | 2 | 4 | | |
| Crissey, Solomon | 1 | | 5 | | |
| Russel, Stephen | 2 | 3 | 3 | | |
| Gowdy, Samuel | 1 | | 3 | | |
| Minor, Thomas | 2 | 7 | 3 | | |
| Wilcox, Mosas | 1 | 1 | 1 | | |
| Barbarer, James | 1 | 1 | 2 | | |
| Andrews, Samuel | 1 | 2 | 4 | | |
| Perkens, Gidian | 1 | 1 | 2 | | |
| Terry, Joseph | 1 | | 1 | | |
| Jones, William C | 1 | 1 | 1 | | |
| Jones, Isaac | 1 | 1 | 5 | | |
| Jones, Israel | 1 | | 1 | | |
| Jones, Saml | 1 | 3 | 6 | | |
| Jones, Thomas | 1 | 4 | 5 | | |
| Perkins, Phinehas | 1 | 4 | 4 | | |
| Chapman, William | 2 | 3 | 5 | | |
| Smith, Ephraim | 1 | 2 | 4 | | |
| Swat, Pelix | 1 | 4 | 5 | | |
| Barnes, Solomon | 1 | 1 | 1 | | |
| Palmer, Ambrose | 1 | 4 | 3 | | |
| Tucker, Reuben | 2 | 4 | 3 | | |
| Mott, Lemul | 1 | 2 | 1 | 2 | |
| Loomis, Daniel | 1 | 1 | 4 | | |
| Preston, Benjamin | 1 | 3 | 1 | | |
| Thompson, Elijah | 1 | 1 | 4 | | |
| Andrews, Abraham | 2 | 1 | 3 | | |
| Andrews, Theophilus | 1 | 4 | 4 | | |
| Kellogg, Seth | 1 | 4 | 3 | | |
| Thompson, Samuel | 1 | 1 | 2 | | |
| Benedick, Noah | 1 | 1 | 2 | | |
| Wilkeson, Levi | 1 | 3 | 2 | | |
| Benedick, Abijah | 1 | 1 | 1 | | |
| Turner, Titus | 2 | 3 | 3 | | |
| Sanford, Moses | 1 | 3 | 2 | | |
| Moss, Solomon | 2 | 3 | 2 | | |
| Washburn, William | 3 | | 3 | | |
| Graves, Benjamin | 1 | 1 | 3 | | |
| Little, Thomas | 1 | 1 | | | |
| Moss, Ives | 1 | | 3 | | |
| Sanford, Zacheus | 1 | 1 | 2 | | |
| Webster, John | 1 | 2 | 1 | | |
| Tharp, Asher | 1 | | 1 | | |
| Smith, Joshua | 1 | 1 | 6 | | |
| Smith, Elizabeth | 1 | | 2 | | |
| Crosby, Thomas | 2 | 1 | 5 | | |
| Webster, James | 1 | 4 | 2 | | |
| Grant, Jesse | 2 | 1 | 3 | | |
| Garnsey, Noah | 3 | 2 | 6 | | |
| Moss, Levi | 2 | 2 | 6 | | |
| Moss, Amos | 4 | 2 | 6 | | |
| Bidwell, Elijah | 1 | 3 | 3 | | |
| Webster, Charles, Jr | 1 | 2 | 1 | | |
| Catlin, Uriel | 3 | | 4 | | |
| Orsborn, Reuben | 1 | 3 | 2 | | |
| Murry, Philemon | 2 | 1 | 4 | | |
| Williams, Israel | 1 | 3 | 1 | | |
| Perkins, Saml | 1 | 4 | 2 | | |
| Johnson, Elias | 1 | 2 | 4 | | |
| Chamberlain, Moses | 2 | 5 | 2 | | |
| Bradley, Tina | 3 | 1 | 4 | | |
| Hotchkiss, Elihu | 2 | 1 | 5 | | |
| Mason, Luther | 1 | 2 | 2 | | |
| Webster, Stephen | 4 | 3 | 4 | | |
| Rowes, Winthrop | 1 | 2 | 6 | | |
| Roberts, John | 1 | 3 | 4 | | |
| Webster, Elijah | 1 | 3 | 2 | | |
| Webster, Benjamin | 2 | | 1 | | |
| Mason, Jonathan | 1 | | 2 | | |
| Mason, Rebacca | 2 | | 1 | | |
| Peck, Benjamin | 1 | 3 | 3 | | |
| Seeley, David | 3 | 3 | 1 | | |
| Ives, John | 2 | 2 | 5 | | |
| Shepperd, Joseph | 1 | 3 | 2 | | |
| Tuttle, Jery | 1 | 1 | 3 | | |
| Ford, Josephus | 1 | | 4 | | |
| Allyn, Jonathan | 1 | 1 | 2 | | |
| Ludington, Aaron | 1 | 1 | 2 | | |
| Thorn, William | 2 | | 4 | | |
| Barber, Reuben | 1 | 1 | 1 | | |
| Wilson, William | 1 | 2 | 2 | | |
| Hays, Asahel | 1 | 1 | 4 | | |
| Clinton, Samuel | 1 | | 4 | | |
| Menter, Daniel | 1 | 1 | 6 | | |
| Clinton, Henry | 1 | 1 | 3 | | |
| Keemann, Pelatiah | 1 | 4 | 2 | | |
| Hokim, Eli | 4 | 3 | 3 | | 9 |
| Weed, Ezra | 3 | 1 | 3 | | |
| Tiffany, Samuel | 1 | | 4 | | |
| Tayler, Abner | 1 | 2 | 2 | | |
| Tayler, Abner | 1 | | 2 | | |
| Zicke | | | | | 5 |
| Humphey, Ambrosi | 1 | 2 | 5 | | |
| Daniels, Pelatiah | 2 | | 2 | | |
| Daniels, Reuben | 1 | 4 | 2 | | |
| Gates, Jessie | 2 | 4 | 4 | | |
| Cowder, Ambrose | 1 | 3 | 1 | | |
| Cowder, Asa | 1 | 1 | 2 | | |
| Shipman, Jonathan | 3 | | 3 | | |
| Yates, Aaron | 1 | 3 | 3 | | |
| Phelps, Charles | 2 | 1 | 3 | | |
| Belden, Ebenezer | 1 | | 1 | | |
| Clark, Thomas | 3 | | 3 | | |
| Clark, Thaniel | 2 | 2 | 5 | | |
| Jones, Thomas | 1 | | 2 | | |
| Kirbey, Joseph | 1 | | 2 | | |
| Harkins, Nathan | 2 | | 2 | 1 | |
| Goodyer, Chancy | 1 | | 2 | | |
| Parker, Stephen | 1 | | 2 | | |
| Cole, Eleezer | 2 | 1 | 2 | | |
| Gideons, David | 4 | 5 | 7 | | |
| Borden, Asahel | 1 | 3 | 2 | | |
| Cone, Thomas | 2 | 2 | 4 | | |
| Borden, John | 4 | 1 | 4 | | |
| Ackley, Joel | 2 | | 4 | | |
| Remand, William, 2d | 6 | 1 | 3 | | |
| Bird, James | 6 | 3 | 7 | | |
| Bird, Thomas | 3 | 3 | 6 | | |
| Crane, Ezra | 2 | 3 | 1 | | |
| Bradley, Arial | 2 | | 3 | | |
| Averist, Jahiel | 2 | 1 | 3 | | |
| Spencer, Asahel | 1 | 2 | 6 | | |
| Slater, Francis | 4 | 3 | 8 | | 5 |
| Bushnal, Saml | 2 | | 2 | | |
| Brinsmade, John | 3 | | 2 | | |
| West, Amos | 1 | 1 | 1 | | |
| Landon, Elisha | 1 | 2 | 2 | | |
| Hinsdale, Moses | 1 | 2 | 4 | | |
| Brinsmade, Saml | 2 | 1 | 4 | | |
| Pempille, John | 1 | 2 | 3 | | |
| Averis, Elisha, 2d | 1 | 1 | 5 | | |
| Averis, Elisha | 1 | | | | |
| Carter, Moses | 3 | 1 | 5 | | |
| Dunbarr, David | 1 | 2 | 3 | | |
| Owen, Aaron | 1 | | 1 | 1 | |
| Chapin, Reuben | 2 | 2 | 4 | | |
| Sillick, Ezra | 3 | 1 | 6 | | |
| Sillick, Bethiel | 3 | 1 | 5 | | |
| Green, Nathaniel | 2 | 1 | 4 | | |
| Grinnol, Daniel | 1 | 2 | 3 | | |
| Lord, Elijah | 1 | | 3 | | |
| More, Samuel | 2 | 1 | 2 | | |
| More, Samuel, 2d | 3 | | 3 | | |
| Averis, Jared | 4 | 2 | 5 | | |
| Lyman, Simeon | 2 | 1 | 3 | | |
| Wright, James | 3 | 3 | 2 | | |
| Dickinson, Shirman | 1 | | 1 | | |
| Tryon, David | 1 | 1 | 4 | | |
| Reed, Thomas | 3 | 1 | 2 | | |
| Truman, Thaniel | 1 | 3 | 3 | | |
| Chapin, Charles | 1 | 2 | 6 | | |
| Jewell, Eliphalet | 3 | | 3 | 1 | |
| Beller, Saml | 1 | 2 | 3 | | |
| Camps, Hezekiah | 3 | 2 | 6 | | |
| Lee, Miles | 1 | | 3 | | |
| Howse, Bene | 2 | 2 | 3 | | |
| David, Daniel | 2 | 4 | 2 | | |
| Peck, James | 1 | 1 | 2 | | |
| La Clear, Francis | 1 | | 1 | | |
| Hall, Silas | 1 | 3 | 8 | | |
| White, Jacob | 2 | 3 | 4 | | |
| Scovel, Jonathan | 4 | 1 | 6 | | |
| Tyler, Solomon | 1 | | 3 | | |
| Pierce, Silas | 1 | 1 | 2 | | |
| Thornton, Ezra | 1 | 4 | 2 | | |
| Watter, Pierce | 1 | | 1 | | |
| Hawley, Samuel | 1 | 3 | 4 | | |
| Whiting, Christophar | 1 | 3 | 3 | | |
| Clark, Saml C | 1 | 1 | 3 | | |
| Miner, Reuben | 2 | | 3 | | |
| Miner, John | 1 | 3 | 3 | | |
| Roberts, Saml | 1 | 1 | 2 | | |
| Whealor, Isaac | 1 | 1 | 1 | | |
| Norton, Levi | 2 | 2 | 1 | | |
| Spensor, Stephen | 1 | 2 | 6 | | |
| Stanard, Abel | 1 | 2 | 6 | | |
| Church, John | 1 | 3 | 2 | | |
| Burton, Saml | 1 | 2 | 2 | | |
| Spensor, Elisha | 2 | 1 | 3 | | |
| Austen, David | 2 | 1 | 3 | | |
| Martial, Danl | 2 | 1 | 2 | | |
| Phelps, John | 3 | 3 | 3 | | |
| Phelps, Jedediah | 1 | 2 | 2 | | |
| Pease, Nathan | 1 | | 2 | | |
| Gillet, William | 1 | 1 | 3 | | |
| Walter, William | 4 | 6 | 8 | | |
| Smith, Joseph | 1 | 1 | 4 | | |
| Smith, Theodore | 1 | | 4 | | |
| Turner, John | 1 | | 2 | | |
| Turner, Hezekiah | 1 | 2 | 1 | | |
| Ives, Titus | 5 | 2 | 2 | | |
| Pease, Nathaniel | 2 | 1 | 4 | | 1 |
| Pease, Obadiah | 2 | | 2 | | |
| Stephen, Zebulon | 1 | 1 | 2 | | |
| Butler, Saml S | 1 | | 1 | | |
| Stephen, Nathaniel | 5 | 1 | 4 | | |
| Day, Thomas | 1 | 2 | 2 | | |
| Hatch, David | 1 | 3 | 2 | | |
| Baley, Hendrick | 1 | 3 | 1 | | |
| Pettiborn, Jiles | 4 | 5 | 1 | | |
| Gitteau, Ephraim | 3 | 1 | 1 | | |
| Welch, Elijah | 1 | | 1 | | |
| Stephen, Benjamin | 1 | 3 | 3 | | |
| Carter, Zebulon | 1 | 3 | 3 | | |
| Pinto, John | 1 | 2 | 2 | | |
| Stephens, Andrew | 1 | 3 | 2 | | |
| Whitmore, William | 2 | | 2 | | |
| Daniels, John | 2 | 3 | 5 | | |
| Clark, Joel | 1 | 5 | 3 | | |
| Church, Uriah | 1 | | 5 | | |
| Avery, William | 2 | 4 | 4 | | |
| Luce, Joshua | 1 | | 2 | | |
| Millerd, Joel | 1 | 1 | 2 | | |
| Tobins, Meriah | 1 | 1 | 2 | | |
| Spensor, Abel | 1 | | | | |
| Chafey, Joel | 2 | 2 | 7 | 1 | |
| Frink, Seth | 1 | | 2 | | |
| Church, Johiel | 3 | 1 | 3 | | |
| Church, Johiel, 2d | 1 | | 3 | | |
| Racksford, Joseph | 1 | 1 | 3 | | |
| Sciff, Samuel | 3 | 2 | 6 | | |
| Stjohn, Thomas | 3 | 1 | 4 | | |
| St. John, Uriah | 1 | | 2 | | |
| Youngslove, Saml | 1 | 2 | 2 | | |
| Younger, John | 1 | 3 | 5 | | |
| Cartwright, Betty | 1 | 1 | 2 | | |
| Sanford, Caleb | 1 | 2 | 2 | | |
| Pardy, Johiel | 1 | 3 | 4 | | |
| Miller, Jairs | 3 | | 4 | | |

# HEADS OF FAMILIES—CONNECTICUT.

## LITCHFIELD COUNTY—Continued.

### LITCHFIELD TOWN—con.

| NAME OF HEAD OF FAMILY. | Free white males of 16 years and upward, including heads of families. | Free white males under 16 years. | Free white females, including heads of families. | All other free persons. | Slaves. |
|---|---|---|---|---|---|
| Ackley, Thomas | 1 |  | 2 |  |  |
| Ackley, David | 2 |  | 2 |  |  |
| Muxum, Sam¹ | 1 |  | 2 |  |  |
| Howel, Edward | 1 |  | 1 |  |  |
| Abels, John | 1 | 1 | 2 |  |  |
| St. John, Timothy | 2 | 1 | 1 |  |  |
| Cube |  |  |  | 3 |  |
| St. John, Ezekiel | 1 |  | 2 |  |  |
| Harriss, George | 1 |  | 1 |  |  |
| Youngs, Benjamin | 3 | 1 | 3 | 1 |  |
| Ranford, Arther | 3 |  | 1 |  |  |
| Lord, John | 1 | 3 | 3 |  |  |
| Youngs, Samuel | 2 | 4 | 5 |  |  |
| Frink, Sam¹ | 1 | 2 | 5 |  |  |
| Everitt, Isaiah | 2 | 4 | 4 |  |  |
| Skift, Benjamin | 3 | 3 | 5 |  |  |
| Notts, Martin | 3 | 2 | 2 |  |  |
| M°Clure, Robert | 2 | 1 | 3 |  |  |
| Frisbey, Joseph | 2 | 2 | 2 |  |  |
| Stannard, Samuel | 2 | 2 | 5 |  |  |
| Griswold, Seth | 1 | 2 | 3 |  |  |
| Barber, William | 2 |  | 4 |  |  |
| Lucus, John | 2 | 1 | 3 |  |  |
| Breneson, Ozias | 4 | 1 | 3 |  |  |
| Ward, Amasa | 3 | 3 | 3 |  |  |
| Stannard, Ezra | 1 | 3 | 1 |  |  |
| Orvis, Roger | 2 | 1 | 7 |  |  |
| Stephen, Simeon | 1 | 1 | 3 |  |  |
| Buttler, Josiah | 1 |  | 4 |  |  |
| Walter, John | 1 | 3 | 2 |  |  |
| Hotchkins, Saml | 1 | 3 | 3 |  |  |
| Orvis Eleazer | 3 | 1 | 7 |  |  |
| Stuart, Sam¹ | 2 | 2 | 2 |  |  |
| Bull, James | 2 | 3 | 4 |  |  |
| Holt, Nicholas | 1 | 3 | 4 |  |  |
| Holt, Eliza | 1 | 1 | 2 |  |  |
| Kingsbury, Stephens | 1 | 1 | 2 |  |  |
| Holt, Isaac | 4 |  | 3 |  |  |
| Norton, Silvenus | 3 | 3 | 2 |  |  |
| Northaway, Sam¹ | 2 | 5 | 3 |  |  |
| Knap, Hezekiah | 1 | 4 | 3 |  |  |
| Spalding, Jacob | 3 | 1 | 3 |  |  |
| Knap, Samuel | 3 | 4 | 3 |  |  |
| Picket, Benjamin | 1 | 2 | 3 |  |  |
| Hoddy, Daniel | 1 | 1 | 4 |  |  |
| Green, Martin | 1 | 1 | 6 |  |  |
| Whipple, Joseph | 1 |  | 3 |  |  |
| Right, Justin | 1 | 1 | 4 |  |  |
| Nash, Polley |  |  | 2 |  |  |
| Wills, Seth | 2 | 2 | 3 |  |  |
| Hoskins, Joseph | 2 | 1 | 3 |  |  |
| Mills, Macy | 2 |  | 2 |  |  |
| Coe, Matthews | 4 | 5 | 4 |  |  |
| Brunson, Levi | 2 | 1 | 6 |  |  |
| Brunson, Binonah | 1 | 2 | 4 |  |  |
| Thompson, Elijah | 1 |  | 1 |  |  |
| Coe, Zedediah | 1 | 3 | 3 |  |  |
| Cane, Daniel | 1 | 4 | 3 |  |  |
| Griswoth, Phineas | 3 | 4 | 3 |  |  |
| Hamlin, Darling | 1 |  | 3 |  |  |
| Hamlin, Amasa | 2 | 2 | 3 | 1 |  |
| Hitchcocks, Sam¹ | 3 |  | 3 |  |  |
| Winages, Philip | 1 | 3 | 2 |  |  |
| Lamb, Johlel | 1 | 5 | 1 |  |  |
| Data, David | 2 | 3 | 2 |  |  |
| Data, Ezra | 1 | 3 | 1 |  |  |
| Kellogg, Olliver | 2 | 1 | 5 |  |  |
| Griswold, Ezeriah | 1 |  |  |  |  |
| Griswold, Ezeriah | 1 | 2 |  |  |  |
| Griswold, David | 1 |  | 2 |  |  |
| Strong, Joel | 1 | 2 | 1 |  |  |
| Hunter, Nathaniel | 1 | 2 | 5 |  |  |
| Whitford, John | 2 | 1 | 3 |  |  |
| Griswold, Daniel | 3 | 1 | 4 |  |  |
| Canfield, Judson | 1 | 2 | 2 | 3 | 1 |
| Lane, Jared | 1 | 1 | 2 |  |  |
| Conklin, Benjᵃ | 2 | 2 | 1 |  |  |
| Nott, Asa | 1 | 4 | 5 |  |  |
| Gay, David | 1 | 2 | 2 |  |  |
| Deming, Tom | 1 | 1 | 2 |  |  |
| Shuster, John | 1 | 2 | 4 |  |  |
| Riley, Sam¹ | 3 | 2 | 2 |  |  |
| Goodrich, Solomon | 3 |  | 2 |  |  |
| Elliot, Tom | 1 | 3 | 3 |  |  |
| Pellet, Enos | 2 |  | 3 | 3 |  |
| Marshnite, Zebalon | 1 |  |  |  |  |
| Pardee, Elijah | 1 | 3 | 3 |  |  |
| Jay, Elizabeth | 1 | 1 | 5 |  |  |
| Moses, Timothy | 2 | 1 | 2 |  |  |
| Fellows, Joseph | 3 | 2 | 4 |  |  |
| Demming, Bernard | 1 | 1 | 3 |  |  |
| Brown, James | 1 |  | 3 |  |  |
| Blakesley, Thomas | 2 | 1 | 3 |  |  |
| Benedict, Benjaman | 2 | 4 | 4 |  |  |
| Henshaw, James | 2 |  | 4 |  |  |

### LITCHFIELD TOWN—con.

| NAME OF HEAD OF FAMILY. | Free white males of 16 years and upward, including heads of families. | Free white males under 16 years. | Free white females, including heads of families. | All other free persons. | Slaves. |
|---|---|---|---|---|---|
| Elton, Ebenees | 2 | 1 | 5 |  |  |
| Curtess, Seth | 1 |  | 4 |  |  |
| Rockwell, William | 3 | 1 | 4 |  |  |
| Lawrence, Anson | 1 | 1 | 3 |  |  |
| Lawrence, Solomon | 1 | 3 | 3 |  |  |
| Stowe, Sam¹ | 2 | 1 | 4 |  |  |
| Rood, Marines | 4 | 3 | 3 |  |  |
| Clarke, Israel | 1 |  | 1 |  |  |
| Fellows, Ephraim | 2 | 2 | 3 |  |  |
| Fellows, Philemon | 3 | 1 |  |  |  |
| Mix, Chancey | 1 |  | 1 |  |  |
| Hopkins, Consider | 3 | 1 | 1 |  |  |
| Marsh, Jonathan | 2 | 2 | 4 |  |  |
| Merrills, John | 2 | 1 | 3 |  |  |
| Gilbert, Thodah | 2 | 1 | 5 |  |  |
| Smith, Martin | 1 |  | 1 |  |  |
| Moody, Eben | 2 | 3 | 6 |  |  |
| Bull, Asher | 1 | 6 | 3 |  |  |
| Smith, Elizer | 1 | 3 | 2 |  |  |
| Smith, Seth | 3 | 1 | 4 |  |  |
| Flowers, Elijah | 1 | 1 | 1 |  |  |
| Gilbert, Joseph | 1 | 3 | 6 |  |  |
| Gillet, Matthew | 2 | 2 | 6 |  |  |
| Hopkins, Roodrick | 1 |  | 1 |  |  |
| Pease, Violet |  |  | 1 | 1 |  |
| Gilbert, Theodosia |  |  | 3 | 2 |  |
| Gillet, Michael | 1 | 1 | 3 |  |  |
| Crittenton, James | 1 | 2 | 4 |  |  |
| Jones, Benjamin | 1 | 1 | 3 |  |  |
| Terrol, Lettie | 3 |  | 5 |  |  |
| Wells, Benjamin | 1 | 3 | 4 |  |  |
| Steel, William | 1 | 3 | 4 |  |  |
| Shephard, Eldad | 1 |  | 6 |  |  |
| Romnam, Meajah | 1 |  | 1 |  |  |
| Thompson, Elisha | 1 | 1 | 1 |  |  |
| Brace, William | 1 |  | 2 |  |  |
| Richards, Silas | 2 | 1 | 2 |  |  |
| Hutson, David | 2 | 3 | 2 |  |  |
| Childs, Timothy | 1 | 1 | 2 |  |  |
| Willoughby, Samuel | 1 |  | 3 |  |  |
| Richards, Charles | 3 | 1 | 3 |  |  |
| Hill, Samuel | 2 | 2 | 4 |  |  |
| Francis, Samuel | 1 |  | 1 |  |  |
| Hillhouse, Samuel | 1 | 1 | 4 |  |  |
| Collins, Philo | 2 |  | 3 |  |  |
| Willoughby, Josiah | 1 | 3 | 1 |  |  |
| Fargoe, James | 1 |  | 3 |  |  |
| Deming, Jonathan | 2 | 1 | 4 |  |  |
| Brooks, Asahel | 2 |  | 3 |  |  |
| Willoughby, Westil | 2 | 2 | 5 |  |  |
| Riley, John | 5 | 1 | 2 |  |  |
| Gilbert, Roda | 2 | 2 | 6 |  |  |
| Knickabocker, John | 1 | 2 | 2 |  |  |
| Hantchet, Joseph | 3 |  | 2 |  | 2 |
| Hantchet, Simeon | 1 | 4 | 2 |  |  |
| Tupper, Sam¹ | 2 | 1 | 2 |  |  |
| Hantchet, Luny |  |  | 1 |  |  |
| Hatchet, Jonah | 1 | 3 | 4 |  |  |
| Vandusen, Content | 2 |  | 2 |  |  |
| Barton, Roger | 4 | 1 | 5 |  |  |
| Barton, Joseph | 2 | 1 | 3 |  |  |
| Jackson, Jane |  | 2 | 3 |  |  |
| Jackaway, Simeon | 1 | 2 | 2 |  |  |
| Nickelson, Samuel | 1 | 4 | 2 |  |  |
| Nickelson, Ezra | 1 | 1 | 4 |  |  |
| Jackaway, Aaron | 3 | 1 | 3 |  |  |
| Wollner, Zebulon | 2 | 3 | 3 |  |  |
| Trupper, Thomas | 2 | 2 | 5 |  |  |
| Hantichet, John | 1 |  | 2 |  |  |
| Hantihet, Amos | 2 | 3 | 2 |  |  |
| Jacobs, Tuel | 1 | 4 | 3 |  |  |
| Hantchet, Ebenezer | 2 | 2 | 6 |  |  |
| Thomas, Benjamin | 1 | 1 | 3 |  |  |
| Knickabacker, John | 1 | 1 | 3 |  |  |
| Sweetland, Aaron | 1 | 1 | 1 |  |  |
| Nickerson, Uriah | 2 | 1 | 1 |  |  |
| Nicherson, Archelus | 1 | 1 | 2 |  |  |
| Tupper, William | 2 | 2 | 4 |  |  |
| Allen, Stephen | 2 | 1 | 3 |  |  |
| Baker, Martha | 2 | 2 | 3 |  |  |
| Benton, Isaac | 1 |  | 1 |  |  |
| Waters, John | 2 | 2 | 4 |  |  |
| Graves, Haynes | 2 | 2 | 3 |  |  |
| Graves, Ichabod | 1 | 1 | 3 |  |  |
| Mecantire, Stephen | 1 | 2 | 3 |  |  |
| Sellick, Noah | 1 | 2 | 3 |  |  |
| Graves, Anna | 1 | 1 | 5 |  |  |
| Johnson, James | 2 | 2 | 3 |  |  |
| Covel, Zenus | 1 | 2 | 3 |  |  |
| Griswold, George | 1 |  | 1 |  |  |
| Chipman, Thomas | 1 | 1 | 2 |  |  |
| Gane, Jude | 2 | 3 | 6 |  |  |
| Bradley, Daniel | 1 | 1 | 5 |  |  |
| Buell, Nathaniel | 4 | 1 | 5 |  |  |
| Canfield, Joseph, 2ᵈ | 1 | 1 | 1 |  |  |

### LITCHFIELD TOWN—con.

| NAME OF HEAD OF FAMILY. | Free white males of 16 years and upward, including heads of families. | Free white males under 16 years. | Free white females, including heads of families. | All other free persons. | Slaves. |
|---|---|---|---|---|---|
| Canfield, Joseph | 2 | 2 | 6 |  |  |
| Hoskins, Abel | 1 | 1 | 4 |  |  |
| Markem, James | 2 | 4 | 5 |  |  |
| Banning, Samuel | 3 | 2 | 5 |  |  |
| Philley, Jasper | 2 |  | 4 |  |  |
| Ormstid, Timothy | 4 | 2 | 5 |  |  |
| Trafford, William | 3 | 2 | 3 |  |  |
| Beebe, Elisha | 1 | 6 | 5 |  | 1 |
| Herford, Jeremiah | 1 | 1 | 3 |  |  |
| Crofford, William | 2 | 1 | 3 |  |  |
| Brown, Jacob | 3 |  | 2 |  |  |
| Deming, Daniel | 1 |  | 2 |  |  |
| Phelps, Simeon | 1 |  | 4 |  |  |
| Bebee, Daniel | 1 | 1 | 3 |  | 1 |
| Bebee, Solomon | 2 | 3 | 5 |  | 2 |
| Deen, Nathaniel | 2 |  | 3 |  |  |
| Deen, Roswell | 1 | 2 | 3 |  |  |
| Deen, Asa | 1 | 1 | 6 |  |  |
| Smith, Allen | 1 | 1 | 3 |  |  |
| Butler, Samuel | 2 | 3 | 3 |  |  |
| Wickwire, Ichabord | 2 | 4 | 1 |  |  |
| Bebee, Isaac | 2 | 3 | 4 |  |  |
| Towsley, Arial | 1 | 1 | 1 |  |  |
| Wolford, Jeremiah | 4 | 1 | 6 |  |  |
| Post, George | 1 | 2 | 6 |  |  |
| Villey, Cornelius | 7 | 2 | 2 |  |  |
| Burrill, Jonathan | 1 | 2 |  |  |  |
| Gleason, Arial | 2 |  | 4 |  |  |
| Hanmer, Benjamin | 1 | 2 | 3 |  |  |
| Barns, Job | 1 |  | 3 |  |  |
| Denmore, Patty |  |  | 3 |  |  |
| Hoogaboom, Jeremiah | 1 |  | 1 |  | 1 |
| Burd, Jonathan | 1 |  | 1 |  | 2 |
| Ensign, John | 2 |  | 1 |  |  |
| Loveman, Aaron | 1 | 1 | 1 |  |  |
| Hunt, Robert | 1 | 1 | 2 |  |  |
| Bowlis, George | 1 | 3 | 4 |  |  |
| Peek, John | 2 | 3 | 4 |  |  |
| Bushnal, Abraham | 2 | 4 | 6 |  |  |
| Bowman, Lydia | 1 | 3 | 1 |  |  |
| White, Elizer | 2 | 1 | 2 |  |  |
| Beach, Chancy | 1 | 6 | 4 |  |  |
| Robens, Easter |  |  | 1 | 1 |  |
| Sayer, Jesse | 1 |  | 1 |  |  |
| Elmon, John | 1 |  | 1 |  |  |
| Hale, Nathan | 1 | 2 | 6 | 1 | 1 |
| Johnson, Isaac | 2 |  | 3 |  |  |
| Barney, Samuel | 1 | 2 | 1 |  |  |
| Fuller, John | 2 |  | 4 |  |  |
| Peck, Calvin | 1 | 3 | 2 |  |  |
| Gray, Darias | 1 | 2 | 2 |  |  |
| Swift, Elisha | 1 |  |  |  |  |
| Corbey, Meriah |  |  | 2 |  |  |
| Bunson, William | 1 | 4 | 1 |  |  |
| Caldwell, James | 1 |  | 2 |  |  |
| Wells, Samuel | 1 | 2 | 3 |  |  |
| Wells, Noah | 1 |  | 2 |  |  |
| Monroe, Nathan | 1 | 2 | 4 |  |  |
| Fullerton, John | 1 |  | 2 |  |  |
| Johnson, James | 2 | 3 | 4 |  |  |
| Smith, Willard | 1 | 2 | 3 |  |  |
| Doolittle, Jonathan | 2 | 4 | 2 |  |  |
| Wallen, James | 1 | 2 | 3 |  |  |
| Hood, George | 2 | 1 | 3 |  |  |
| Fellows, Thomas | 2 |  | 3 |  |  |
| Harrison, Stephen | 2 | 3 | 5 |  |  |
| Mix, Martha |  |  | 1 | 3 |  |
| Ormsby, Amos | 1 | 2 | 1 |  |  |
| Franklin, John | 3 |  | 3 |  |  |
| Watson, Hezikah | 1 | 3 | 3 |  |  |
| Fellows, Lois |  |  | 2 |  |  |
| Stephens, Stafford | 3 | 1 | 4 |  |  |
| Watson, William | 2 | 3 | 5 |  |  |
| Wadsworth, John | 1 | 1 | 3 |  |  |
| Stanley, Robert | 3 | 1 | 4 |  |  |
| Bromwell, Ichabod | 2 |  | 5 |  |  |
| Williams, Jacob | 2 |  | 5 |  |  |
| Paxton, Allen | 6 |  | 2 |  |  |
| Lawrance, Gidian | 1 | 2 | 6 |  |  |
| Austin, Thadeus | 2 | 4 | 2 |  |  |
| Lawrance, Nehemiah | 1 | 2 | 2 |  |  |
| Burns, Simon | 1 | 2 | 4 |  |  |
| Jerrum, Lyman | 1 | 1 | 4 |  |  |
| Miller, Seth | 4 | 4 | 3 |  |  |
| Lawrance, Nathan | 2 |  | 2 |  |  |
| Stephens, Nathan | 2 | 1 | 5 |  |  |
| Stephens, Oliver | 1 | 2 | 2 |  |  |
| Lawrence, David | 2 |  | 4 |  |  |
| Lawrence, Jerry | 1 | 2 | 2 |  |  |
| Stephens, Zebulon | 2 | 1 | 4 |  |  |
| Stephens, Henry | 2 | 2 | 3 |  |  |
| Jackeway, Ebenezer | 2 | 2 | 4 |  |  |
| Foster, David | 1 |  | 2 |  |  |
| Atwood, William | 1 | 2 | 6 |  |  |
| Miller, Samuel | 2 | 3 | 4 |  |  |

# FIRST CENSUS OF THE UNITED STATES.

## LITCHFIELD COUNTY—Continued.

### LITCHFIELD TOWN—con.

| NAME OF HEAD OF FAMILY. | Free white males of 16 years and upward, including heads of families. | Free white males under 16 years. | Free white females, including heads of families. | All other free persons. | Slaves. |
|---|---|---|---|---|---|
| Mack, Benjamin | 1 | 1 | 1 | | |
| Coe, Elijah | 1 | 1 | 4 | | |
| Han, Titus | 2 | 3 | 5 | | |
| Benjamin, Samuel | 1 | 2 | 2 | | |
| Mack, Zebulon | 1 | 1 | 1 | | |
| Albertson, John P | 2 | 1 | 4 | | |
| Stiles, Saml | 1 | 3 | 3 | | |
| Evans, Benjamin | 1 | | 1 | | |
| Spelman, David | 1 | 1 | 6 | | |
| Mack, Gurdan | 1 | 2 | 2 | | |
| Money, Reuben | 1 | 3 | 4 | | |
| Coe, Phinehas | 1 | 3 | 2 | | |
| Ensignor, Daniel | 1 | 3 | 2 | | |
| Burnham, Reuben | 2 | 2 | 3 | | |
| Butler, Nathan | 3 | 2 | 4 | | |
| Gonyard, Spensor | 4 | 2 | 2 | | |
| Blakesley, Saml | 1 | 1 | 5 | | |
| Porter, Thomas | 1 | 1 | 3 | | |
| Miller, George T | 2 | 1 | 1 | | |
| Plumby, Ebenr | 1 | 2 | 2 | | |
| Olcott, Samuel | 1 | 1 | 4 | | |
| Brown, John | 2 | | 1 | | |
| Sweet, Joseph | 1 | 1 | 2 | | |
| Brown, Nathaniel | 1 | | 2 | | |
| Barber, William | 1 | | 1 | | |
| Norton, Levi | 1 | 1 | 2 | | |
| Norton, Thomas | 3 | 2 | 5 | | |
| Cady, Chester | 1 | 1 | 2 | | |
| Burr, Daniel | 1 | 1 | 7 | | |
| Beach, Lewis | 1 | 3 | 3 | | |
| Beach, John | 1 | 2 | 2 | | |
| Tibbots, Thomas | 1 | 2 | 3 | 1 | |
| Smith, Roda | 1 | 1 | 4 | | |
| Balcomb, Elias | 4 | 2 | 4 | | |
| Stanlif, Saml | 1 | 2 | 2 | | |
| Lee, Nathaniel | 1 | 2 | 5 | | |
| Brown, Edmond | 3 | | 2 | | |
| Cole, Noah | 1 | 3 | 2 | | |
| Tibbles, Samuel | 3 | 3 | 5 | | |
| Frank, Andrew | 1 | 3 | 3 | | |
| Nott, Abraham | 1 | 1 | 2 | | |
| Austin, Caleb | 1 | | 5 | | |
| Hinsdale, William | 1 | 2 | 1 | | |
| Fannig, Daniel | 4 | 1 | 5 | 2 | |
| Tooley, Nabby | | | 3 | | |
| Holmbeck, Abraham | 2 | 4 | 4 | 3 | |
| Belden, Charles | 2 | 1 | 4 | | |
| Belden, Charles | 3 | | 2 | | |
| Belden, Charles | 3 | 5 | 2 | | |
| Jupiter | | | | 1 | |
| Hide, Uriah | 2 | 1 | 8 | | |
| Beach, Zopher | 1 | 2 | 4 | | |
| Gannan, Edward | 2 | 2 | 5 | | |
| Bushnal, Abner | 1 | 2 | 3 | | |
| Porter, Elisha | 1 | | 2 | | |
| Spensor, Frederick | 1 | 1 | 7 | | |
| Stanley, Aaron | 1 | 3 | 6 | | |
| Wildeer, Gamaliall | 1 | 2 | 4 | | |
| Gilbert, David | 1 | | 2 | | |
| Ormsted, Isaac | 2 | 2 | 3 | | |
| Spensor, Jonah | 1 | 4 | 3 | | |
| Gun, Noble | 1 | 2 | 3 | | |
| Cady, Josiah | 1 | 3 | 3 | | |
| Wilard, Eunice | | | 1 | 2 | |
| Hall, Nathan | 1 | 1 | 2 | | |
| Beldon, Bartholomew | 1 | 2 | 4 | | |
| Haliburt, Elisha | 3 | 2 | 2 | | |
| Cuff | | | | 5 | |
| Andrews, Benajah | 2 | | 3 | | |
| Deming, Pelog | 1 | | | 1 | |
| Towrley, Levi | 1 | 1 | 1 | | |
| Hinsdale, Joseph | 3 | 1 | 2 | | |
| Kellogg, Elijah | 3 | | 2 | | |
| Kellogg, Joseph | 2 | 2 | 6 | | |
| Root, William | 2 | 1 | 6 | | |
| Philips, Benjamin | 1 | | 1 | | |
| Holcomb, Amasa | 3 | 1 | 4 | | |
| Fellows, John | 1 | | 2 | | |
| Parmely, Aaron | 1 | 5 | 3 | | |
| Whitney, John | 3 | 1 | 4 | | |
| Whitney, John, 2d | 2 | 1 | 3 | | |
| Austin, Levi | 1 | 3 | 4 | | |
| Perry, Elisha | 1 | 3 | 2 | | |
| Belcher, William | 2 | 1 | 2 | | |
| Throll, Aaron | 1 | 2 | 2 | | |
| Little, Otis | 1 | 2 | 2 | | |
| Witing, Benjamin | 2 | 2 | 3 | | |
| Bancroft, Eniam | 1 | 3 | 3 | | |
| Holmes, Seth | 4 | 1 | 3 | | |
| Sweet, Jonathan | 4 | 2 | 6 | | |
| Parmely, Standly | 1 | 1 | 1 | | |
| North, Ashbel | 2 | 1 | 2 | | |
| Whiting, John | 3 | | 3 | | |
| Coe, Ebenezer | 3 | | 3 | | |
| Comins, Samuel | 2 | 2 | 5 | | |

### LITCHFIELD TOWN—con.

| NAME OF HEAD OF FAMILY. | Free white males of 16 years and upward, including heads of families. | Free white males under 16 years. | Free white females, including heads of families. | All other free persons. | Slaves. |
|---|---|---|---|---|---|
| Loomis, Isanor | 2 | 2 | 5 | | |
| Thrall, Levi | 2 | 2 | 3 | | |
| Brau, Ariel | 2 | 5 | 2 | | |
| Spenscer, Aseph | 1 | 1 | 3 | | |
| Aglestone, James | 1 | | 2 | | |
| Benedick, Buchnel | 1 | 1 | 2 | | |
| Pratt, Adonijah | 1 | | 3 | | |
| Thrall, John | 1 | | 4 | | |
| Beach, John | 2 | 3 | 4 | | |
| Hodges, Ellane | 3 | 3 | 4 | | |
| West, David | 2 | 1 | 3 | | |
| Smith, Elisha | 2 | 1 | 4 | | |
| Loomis, Joel | 1 | | 2 | | |
| Williams, David | 1 | | 1 | | |
| Loomice, Moses | 2 | 1 | 4 | | |
| Loomice, Abner | 1 | 2 | 3 | | |
| Jagger, Phinihas | 1 | | 2 | | |
| Loomice, Shiphra | 4 | | 6 | | |
| Loomice, Mary | | | | | |
| Beach, Samuel | 2 | 1 | 4 | | |
| Loomice, Benona | 1 | 1 | 1 | | |
| Beach, Abel | 1 | 1 | 3 | | |
| Beach, Noah | 1 | 2 | 3 | | |
| Loomice, Ephraim | 4 | 1 | 3 | | |
| Grant, William | 3 | 1 | 3 | | |
| Loomice, Ephraim | 1 | 3 | 1 | | |
| Loomice, Aaron | 1 | 1 | 1 | | |
| Martial, Aaron | 1 | | 3 | | |
| Bowley, Samuel | 3 | 2 | 5 | | |
| Brunson, Ashbel | 1 | 3 | 4 | | |
| Aglestone, Benjamin | 3 | 3 | 4 | | |
| Wilson, Roger | 2 | 3 | 3 | | |
| North, Remembrance | 1 | 1 | 2 | | |
| Prichard, Eli | 1 | 1 | 3 | | |
| Prichard, Simain | 2 | 2 | 5 | | |
| Buell, Ashbel | 1 | 2 | 2 | | |
| Colver, Reuben | 1 | | 3 | | |
| Buell, Peter | 1 | 3 | 3 | | |
| Lord, Daniel | 4 | 3 | 6 | | |
| Ames, Chancey | 1 | 4 | 2 | | |
| Jones, Samul | 1 | 2 | 2 | | |
| Lee, Love | | | | | 1 |
| Lee, William | 1 | 4 | 4 | | |
| Colver, Azriah | 1 | 5 | 3 | | |
| Humerston, Joel | 1 | | 2 | | |
| Hart, Titus | 1 | 2 | 2 | | |
| Curtiss, Joseph | 2 | 1 | 5 | | |
| Moss, David | 2 | 3 | 3 | | |
| Hopson, Simeon | 1 | 2 | 5 | | |
| Moss, Simeon | 1 | | 3 | | |
| Barnes, Oliver | 1 | 4 | 3 | | |
| Bachelor, Reuben | 3 | | 3 | | |
| Preston, Noah | 2 | 3 | 1 | | |
| Spercy, Allen | 1 | 4 | 1 | | |
| Hall, Simes | 1 | | 1 | | |
| Hart, Ebenezer | 1 | 4 | 2 | | |
| Hopkins, Harriss | 2 | 1 | 4 | | |
| Hopkins, Harriss, 2d | 1 | | 1 | | |
| Bates, Henry | 2 | 1 | 2 | | |
| Humerston, Titus | 1 | 4 | 5 | | |
| Todd, Eli | 1 | 1 | 2 | | |
| Atwater, Richard | 1 | | 3 | | |
| Curtiss, Daniel | 1 | 1 | 4 | | |
| Way, Elijah | 1 | 1 | 2 | | |
| Todd, Ebenezer | 1 | 2 | 3 | | |
| Basset, Zopher | 1 | | | | |
| Todd, Ebenezer | 2 | | 3 | | |
| Homerston, John | 2 | 1 | 5 | | |
| Meriman, Amasa | 1 | | 1 | | |
| Sanford, Stephen | 1 | 3 | 2 | | |
| Lee, Saml | 1 | 2 | 1 | | |
| Hall, Nathaniel | 1 | 2 | 3 | | |
| Hall, Eleizer | 1 | | 2 | | |
| Ramond, William | 1 | 3 | 2 | | |
| Curtiss, Gideon | 1 | 1 | 3 | | |
| Evans, Isaac | 2 | 3 | 1 | | |
| Rice, Thadeus | 1 | | 2 | | |
| Cate | | | 6 | | |
| Jacobs, Heziran | 1 | 1 | 1 | | |
| Barns, Josiah | 1 | | 4 | | |
| Hammon, Dudley | 1 | 1 | 5 | | |
| Hammon, John | 2 | 3 | 1 | | |
| Barns, Samuel | 1 | | 3 | | |
| Root, Phinehas | 2 | 1 | 6 | | |
| Root, Asahel | 3 | | 3 | | |
| Thrall, Charles | 1 | 2 | 5 | | |
| Thrall, Friend | 1 | 5 | 3 | | |
| Harriss, Ebenezer | 2 | 2 | 3 | | |
| Norton, Sarah | 1 | 2 | 3 | | |
| Olcott, Harriet | 1 | 4 | 3 | | |
| Ensign, Elizer | 2 | 2 | 3 | | |
| Taylor, Prince | 2 | 3 | 4 | | |
| Ensign, Timothy | 1 | | 2 | | |
| Robertson, Noah | 1 | | 2 | | |
| Hatch, Nathan | 2 | 4 | 4 | | |

### LITCHFIELD TOWN—con.

| NAME OF HEAD OF FAMILY. | Free white males of 16 years and upward, including heads of families. | Free white males under 16 years. | Free white females, including heads of families. | All other free persons. | Slaves. |
|---|---|---|---|---|---|
| Sutley, David | 1 | 1 | 3 | | |
| Brau, Orange | 1 | 4 | 3 | | |
| Beach, Ezekiel | 2 | 2 | 2 | | |
| Goodrich, Giles | 1 | 3 | 2 | | |
| Birkshop, Abraham | 1 | | 4 | | |
| Cowdry, Jacob | 2 | 1 | 1 | | |
| Bushnel, Jedediah | 3 | | 3 | | |
| Crosbey, Timothy C | 1 | | 2 | | |
| Vreet, George | 1 | 2 | 2 | | |
| Bates, Aaron | 1 | 1 | 3 | | |
| Brau, Abel | 2 | 4 | 7 | | |
| Bushnel, Stephen | 2 | 5 | 4 | | |
| Barber, Samuel | 3 | 1 | 1 | | |
| Bushnel, Martin | 2 | 1 | 6 | | |
| Taylor, Chiles | 1 | 2 | 4 | | |
| Hokim, David | 2 | 2 | 1 | | |
| Root, Phinehas | 1 | 1 | 3 | | |
| Phelps, John | 2 | 3 | 3 | | |
| Judd, Alexr | 1 | 1 | 1 | | |
| Messenger, Nathaniel | 1 | | 1 | | |
| Root, Joel | 1 | | 2 | | |
| Whitaker, Samuel | 1 | 1 | 1 | | |
| Rowens, Richerson | 1 | 1 | 1 | | |
| Smith, Azariah | 1 | | 2 | | |
| Bishop, Jesse | 1 | 2 | 5 | | |
| Robens, Samuel | 1 | 2 | 2 | | |
| Osmon, Ashbel | 1 | 1 | 4 | | |
| Cowls, Timothy | 1 | 2 | 4 | | |
| Deen, Nathan | 1 | 2 | 3 | | |
| Dibble, Margret | | | 1 | | |
| Rudd, John | 2 | | 2 | | |
| Griswold, Saml | 2 | 1 | 5 | | |
| Deming, Andrew | 1 | 2 | 2 | 1 | |
| Bidwel, Eliezer | 1 | 6 | 1 | | |
| Hoskins, David | 1 | | 1 | | |
| Simons, William | 1 | | 1 | | |
| Veets, David | 4 | 2 | 4 | | |
| Kneeland, Isaac | 3 | 3 | 5 | | |
| Mills, Saml | 1 | 1 | 3 | | |
| Gowdey, James | 1 | 1 | 2 | | |
| Bidwel, Joseph | 2 | 1 | 1 | | |
| Seymour, Joseph, 2d | 1 | 3 | 2 | | |
| Seymour, Joseph | 2 | | 4 | | |
| Rockwell, John | 2 | 4 | 5 | | |
| Chub, Alexander | 1 | 2 | 2 | | |
| Whitmore, Increase | 1 | | 1 | | |
| Coe, Robert | 1 | 1 | 2 | | |
| Miller, Marcy | | 2 | 5 | | |
| Norton, Phinehas | 2 | 3 | 2 | | |
| Colver, Titus | 1 | | 1 | | |
| Ells, Ozias | 1 | | 1 | | |
| Collens, Nathaniel | 1 | 2 | 4 | | |
| Weldeer, Joseph | 2 | 5 | 3 | | |
| Merrills, John | 2 | 1 | 4 | | |
| Lewis, Nathaniel | 1 | | 2 | | |
| Hudson, John | 1 | 1 | 3 | | |
| Beach, David | 2 | 1 | 5 | | |
| Smith, Seth | 1 | 1 | 4 | | |
| Shepherd, Stephen | 1 | 2 | 3 | | |
| Francis, John | 2 | 3 | 5 | | |
| Bumps, Simeon | 3 | 1 | 2 | | |
| Gregory, Joseph | 1 | 3 | 2 | | |
| Jones, Benona | 1 | 2 | 3 | | |
| Cornwell, Isaac | 1 | 2 | 3 | | |
| Richerson, Stephen | 2 | 4 | 2 | | |
| Bampus, Nathanl | 2 | 1 | 2 | | |
| Nichelson, Sarah | 1 | | 2 | | |
| Allen, Pelletiah | 3 | 2 | 4 | | |
| Pike, James | 1 | | 3 | | |
| Addams, Richard | 3 | 3 | 5 | | |
| Andrews, Benjn | 2 | 1 | 3 | | |
| Case, Ozias | 2 | 1 | 3 | | |
| Case, Ezra | 1 | 2 | 5 | | |
| Jones, Isrehel | 3 | 4 | 6 | | |
| Huff, Caleb | 1 | 3 | 5 | | |
| Spencer, Thomas | 1 | 3 | 2 | | |
| Reed, Jacob | 1 | 2 | 3 | | |
| Taylor, Ebenezer | 1 | | 3 | | |
| Fuller, Thomas | 3 | 2 | 4 | | |
| Fuller, Eliphelet | 1 | 5 | 3 | | |
| Fuller, Samuel | 1 | | 3 | | |
| Beeman, Thomas | 2 | 2 | 4 | | |
| Beeman, Thomas, 2d | 1 | 2 | 2 | | |
| Moses, Martin | 2 | 4 | 2 | | |
| Tiffeny, Timothy | 1 | 2 | 2 | | |
| Burnham, Isaac | 1 | | 2 | | |
| Moses, Aaron | 1 | 1 | 4 | | |
| Moses, Ashbel | 2 | 2 | 1 | | |
| Holmes, Urial | 3 | 1 | 3 | | |
| Mechum, Joel | 3 | 1 | 5 | | |
| Sawyer, Jacob | 2 | 5 | 7 | | |
| Bushnell, William | 1 | 2 | 2 | | |
| Lawrance, Arial | 3 | 1 | 5 | 1 | |
| Lawrance, Arial | 4 | 2 | 2 | | |
| Pettibone, Samuel | 4 | | 4 | | |

# HEADS OF FAMILIES—CONNECTICUT.

## LITCHFIELD COUNTY—Continued.

| NAME OF HEAD OF FAMILY. | Free white males of 16 years and upward, including heads of families. | Free white males under 16 years. | Free white females, including heads of families. | All other free persons. | Slaves. | NAME OF HEAD OF FAMILY. | Free white males of 16 years and upward, including heads of families. | Free white males under 16 years. | Free white females, including heads of families. | All other free persons. | Slaves. | NAME OF HEAD OF FAMILY. | Free white males of 16 years and upward, including heads of families. | Free white males under 16 years. | Free white females, including heads of families. | All other free persons. | Slaves. |
|---|---|---|---|---|---|---|---|---|---|---|---|---|---|---|---|---|---|
| LITCHFIELD TOWN—con. | | | | | | LITCHFIELD TOWN—con. | | | | | | LITCHFIELD TOWN—con. | | | | | |
| Comstock, Secajah | 1 | | 1 | | | Cook, William | 2 | | 3 | | | Allyn, Cloe | | 2 | 4 | | |
| Thrall, Eli | 1 | | 2 | | | Henshaw, Benjamin | 5 | 1 | 2 | | | Weed, Jonas | 1 | 1 | 6 | | |
| Pettibone, Roswell | 1 | | 1 | | | Chub, Rachel | | | 3 | | | Phelps, Elkane | 3 | 2 | 6 | | |
| Cole, Amasa | 2 | 1 | 2 | | | Kellogg, Abraham | 1 | | 2 | | | Sweet, James | 2 | 3 | 5 | | |
| Gaylor, Roegs | 4 | 3 | 2 | | | Chub, Mindwell | | | 3 | | | Roberts, Poll | 1 | 3 | 3 | | |
| Phelps, Joel | 3 | 1 | 1 | | | Kellogg, Moses | 2 | 1 | 3 | | | Kellogg, Daniel | 1 | 1 | 4 | | |
| Humphrey, Asahel | 2 | 2 | 5 | | | Kellogg, Abraham | 1 | | 2 | | | Croe, Nathaniel | 1 | 1 | 2 | | |
| Malbey, Zacheus | 1 | 1 | 5 | | | Merrills, Joel | 1 | 1 | 2 | | | Croe, John | 1 | | 2 | | |
| Brown, Sam'l | 1 | 1 | 2 | | | Kellogg, Noah | 2 | 3 | 4 | | | Mills, David | 1 | | 1 | | |
| Malbey, Benjamin | 2 | 4 | 5 | | | Marsh, Moses | 1 | | 2 | | | More, King | 1 | | 3 | | |
| Cowls, Samuel | 4 | 1 | 2 | | | Sheldon, Ely | 1 | 3 | 3 | | | Barmer, James | 1 | | 3 | | |
| Blackesley, Mathew | 1 | | 3 | | | Ryder, Syvester | 2 | 2 | 1 | | | Messenger, Isaac | 3 | 1 | 5 | | |
| Grant, Joel | 2 | 2 | 4 | | | Merrills, Phinehas | 1 | 1 | 3 | | | Messenger, Elisha | 1 | 1 | 4 | | |
| Boardman, Joseph | 1 | 1 | 3 | | | Chapen, Phinehas | 1 | 1 | 1 | | | Messenger, Simeon | 3 | 3 | 4 | | |
| Grant, Elijah | 3 | | 3 | | | Russel, Josiah | 2 | 1 | 2 | | | Messenger, Moses | 1 | 2 | 2 | | |
| Clark, Daniel | 1 | 3 | 2 | | | Addams, Phinehas | 2 | 1 | 2 | | | Humphrey, Benona | 4 | 1 | 3 | | |
| Frisbey, Simeon | 1 | | 1 | | | Homer, James | 4 | | 3 | | | Merrit, John | 2 | 2 | 5 | | |
| Case, Asahel | 1 | 3 | 3 | | | Creny, John | 1 | 2 | 4 | | | Merrit, James | 2 | 2 | 5 | | |
| Foot, Luther | 1 | 2 | 3 | | | Jewel, Oliver | 3 | 5 | 6 | | | Case, Abner | 1 | 5 | 4 | | |
| Barber, Timothy | 1 | 1 | 2 | | | Jewell, Oliver, 2d | 1 | 2 | 2 | | | More, David | 1 | 4 | 3 | | |
| Mills, Samuel | 3 | 1 | 4 | | | Dorsey, Jeremiah | 2 | 2 | 2 | | | Bliss, Jad | 2 | | 5 | | |
| Bushnell, Daniel | 1 | 1 | 2 | | | Uri, John | 2 | | 1 | | | Rice, Wait | 1 | 3 | 2 | | |
| Banning, Abner | 1 | 5 | 3 | | | Parmerter, William | 1 | | 2 | | | Jones, Evan | 1 | 1 | 1 | | |
| Bill, Daniel | 1 | 2 | 3 | | | Herrick, Mary | | | 2 | | | Case, Simeon | 1 | 1 | 2 | | |
| Mechum, Johiel | 3 | | 2 | | | Moore, Daniel | 2 | | 1 | | | Parrey, John | 1 | 1 | 3 | | |
| Wildeer, John | 3 | | 3 | | | Moore, John | 4 | 3 | 3 | | | Copet, Marten | 2 | 3 | 4 | | |
| Gilman, Elihu | 2 | | 3 | | | Lee, Samuel | 3 | 1 | 2 | | | Copet, Timothy | 1 | 3 | 4 | | |
| Goodyer, Stephen | 1 | | 3 | | | Hutcheson, Asa | 1 | 2 | 4 | | | Miner | | | | 10 | |
| Allen, Chancy | 1 | 2 | 1 | | | Stanton, Elijah | 3 | 2 | 5 | | | Harris, William | 2 | | 4 | | |
| Wildeer, John | 1 | 1 | 3 | | | Mechum, Barnibus | 1 | | 2 | | | Miller, Sam | 1 | 1 | 4 | | |
| Beach, Sam'l | 2 | | 3 | | | Meigs, Janne | 2 | 1 | 3 | | | Case, Simeon | 1 | | 3 | | |
| Beach, Benonah | 2 | 1 | 5 | | | Weed, Belden | 1 | 1 | 2 | | | Emmons, Jonathan | 3 | | 1 | | |
| Atkins, Hezekiah | 2 | | 7 | | | Bruster, John | 2 | 2 | 2 | | | Muxum, Benjamin | 1 | | 2 | | |
| Atkens, Joseph | 1 | 2 | 4 | | | Edgarton, Nathan | 1 | 1 | 2 | | | Willer, William | 1 | | 1 | | |
| Ketchum, Stephen | 2 | | 4 | 1 | | Esmon, Nathan | 1 | | 3 | | | Geer, Charles | 1 | 1 | 1 | | |
| Obriont, Partrick | 1 | 3 | 3 | | | Avery, Sanford | 1 | | 2 | | | Dotee, Sarah | 1 | | 3 | | |
| Marsh, Nehenemiah | 1 | 2 | 3 | 1 | | Tush, Joseph | 1 | 1 | 4 | | | Knibloe, William | 2 | | 3 | | |
| Dugliss, Benajah | 3 | | 6 | | | Johnson, Elisha | 1 | 1 | 4 | | | Knibloe, Joseph | 2 | | 3 | | |
| Baker, Elisha | 2 | | 2 | | | Reed, Ebenezer | 1 | 2 | 2 | | | Hatch, Ebenezer | 2 | 1 | 4 | | |
| Cobb, Elijah W | 2 | 1 | 3 | | | Reed, Peter | 3 | | 3 | | | Stafford, John | 1 | 2 | 2 | | |
| Tausket, Mary | | | 1 | | | Bingham, Daniel | 2 | 1 | 5 | | | Tobey, Jonathan | 1 | 1 | 1 | | |
| Kingsbury, Sam'l | 5 | 1 | 3 | | | Bingham, Daniel, 2d | 2 | 3 | 4 | | | Nash, William | 1 | | 2 | | |
| Spalding, John | 1 | 3 | 2 | | | Russel, John | 2 | 3 | 3 | | | Tobey, Elisha | 5 | 4 | 5 | | |
| Adams, John | 1 | 4 | 4 | | | Smith, Gideon | 3 | 1 | 3 | | | Dillenor, Stephen | 2 | 1 | 7 | | |
| Fordes, Samuel | 4 | 1 | 2 | | | Sardam, Tunus | 1 | 2 | 4 | | | Dillenor, Thomas | 1 | 1 | 2 | | |
| Spalding, Asial | 1 | 2 | 1 | | | Sardam, Andrus | 4 | 1 | 3 | | | Dextor, Silas | 1 | 1 | 3 | | |
| Forbes, John | 1 | 2 | 2 | | | Harris, John | 2 | 4 | 5 | | | Cate | | | | 8 | |
| Mix, Daniel | 1 | 1 | 1 | | | Dutcher, Gabriel | 1 | 3 | 4 | | | Brockwey, Watston | 2 | 3 | 2 | | |
| Cook, Ephraim | 3 | 1 | 3 | | | Beeman, Samuel | 2 | 2 | 4 | | | Hunter, Ebenezer | 1 | | 2 | | |
| Curtiss, David | 1 | 1 | 2 | | | Wood, John | 1 | 2 | 4 | | | Norton, Gideon | 1 | | 1 | | |
| Jackson, John | 1 | 3 | 4 | | | Nichols, Philoe | 2 | | 4 | | | Willer, Daniel | 1 | 2 | 2 | | |
| Wright, Seth | 2 | 2 | 4 | | | Nichols, Caleb | 4 | 1 | 3 | | | Tober, Daniel | 1 | 2 | 6 | | |
| Linley, Sam'l | 3 | 1 | 2 | | | Dutcher, Ruluf, 3d | 1 | 3 | 2 | | | Muller, Samuel | 1 | 4 | 4 | | |
| Gleason, Ephraim | 2 | 1 | 5 | | | Hinsman, Benjamin | 1 | | 1 | | | Tewisdel, John | 3 | 4 | 3 | | |
| Cammel, John | 2 | 1 | 2 | | | Sheldon, Elisha, 2d | 1 | 2 | 3 | | | Winchel, Daniel | 2 | 4 | 4 | | |
| Hunt, Daniel | 2 | | 2 | | | Abanatha, Jiles | 1 | | 2 | | | Burgh, John | 1 | | 2 | | |
| Hunt, Daniel, 2d | 1 | 4 | 3 | | | Sheldon, Elisha | 1 | 1 | 1 | | 4 | Taylor, John | 2 | | 2 | | |
| Marsh, Jessie | 2 | 3 | 7 | | | Breant, Alexander | 1 | 2 | 2 | | | Burgher, David | 1 | 1 | 3 | | |
| Hucheson, Ezri | 1 | 1 | 2 | | | Jacobs, Salley | | 1 | 1 | | | Miller, Ebenezer | 3 | 3 | 5 | | |
| Hucheson, Ezri, 2d | 2 | 2 | 3 | | | Vandooser, Abraham | 3 | 1 | 1 | | | Burgher, Sim | 2 | 3 | 3 | | |
| Marvin, Joseph | 1 | 1 | 2 | | | Peck, Isaac | 2 | | 5 | | | Strong, John | 2 | 3 | 5 | | |
| Huchenson, Daniel | 1 | 3 | 5 | | | White, Herman | 1 | 4 | 3 | | | Griswell, Shubal | 3 | | 2 | | |
| Jackson, Elijah | 2 | 2 | 4 | | | Mallery, Samuel | 1 | | 2 | | | Bissel, Elijah | 1 | | 1 | | |
| Manfield, Ichabod | 1 | | 1 | | | Doolittle, Jessee | 1 | | 2 | | | Blake, Elijah | 2 | 4 | 3 | | |
| Curtiss, Josiah | 1 | 1 | 2 | | | Griffin, Ezri | 1 | | 2 | | | Bissel, Benjamin | 3 | 1 | 3 | | |
| Curtiss, Seth | 2 | | 2 | | | Rogers, Jonathan | 2 | 2 | 2 | | | Gaylor, Nehemiah | 2 | 1 | 4 | | |
| Cartright, Sam'l | 5 | 2 | 6 | | | Potter, Phinehas | 2 | 2 | 3 | | | Gaylor, Joseph | 1 | 2 | 2 | | |
| Abels, Slumon | 1 | 3 | 5 | | | Doolittle, Jessee | 2 | 1 | 2 | | | Gillet, Jabes | 4 | 1 | 7 | | |
| Abels, Elijah | 1 | | 1 | | | Potter, David | 1 | | 2 | | | Soper, David | 3 | 2 | 3 | | |
| Howe, Jeremiah | 1 | 2 | 1 | | | Potter, Ebenezer | 1 | 2 | 6 | | | Woodward, Samuel | 1 | 2 | 4 | | |
| Norton, Medad | 1 | 1 | 3 | | | Whealer, Nathan | 1 | 1 | 2 | | | Gillet, John | 1 | 4 | 3 | | |
| Collins, Cyprian | 3 | 2 | 2 | | | Potter, Daniel | 1 | 3 | 2 | | | Badelle, William | 3 | 4 | 6 | | |
| Smith, Chifleab | 2 | 1 | 3 | | | Potter, Elizar | 1 | 2 | 7 | | | White, Amy | | | 3 | | |
| Standley, William | 2 | | 4 | | | Whealer, Benjamin | 1 | 2 | 2 | | | Mills, Sam'l J | 2 | | 4 | 1 | |
| Lewis, Thomas | 3 | 4 | 4 | | | Miles, Lewis | 1 | 1 | 1 | | | Cook, Jessee | 3 | | 3 | | |
| Newel, Nathaniel | 1 | 1 | 2 | | | Rowley, Ebenezer | 1 | 3 | 4 | | | Gaylor, Elijah | 3 | 1 | 2 | | |
| Standley, Jessee | 2 | 2 | 4 | | | Bragnord, Othniah | 1 | 1 | 2 | | | Marther, Zachariah | 2 | 2 | 6 | | |
| Rice, Daniel | 2 | | 4 | | | Hatten, Stephen | 1 | 2 | 4 | | | Bissel, Hezekiah | 1 | 3 | 3 | | 2 |
| Norton, Bird Eye | 3 | 1 | 3 | | | Jop, John | 2 | 3 | 2 | | | Bissel, Ezekiel | 2 | 2 | 1 | | |
| Norton, Samuel | 2 | 1 | 6 | | | Shaw, John | 1 | 1 | 4 | | | Bissel, Eliphet | 1 | 2 | 1 | | |
| Dorod, John | 2 | | 3 | | | Thompson, Zebulon | 1 | 1 | 5 | | | Bissel, Ebenezer | 1 | 4 | 3 | | |
| Norton, Ebenezer | 2 | 2 | 4 | | | Rogers, Simeon | 1 | 1 | 4 | | | Loomis, Timothy | 1 | 4 | 5 | | |
| Davis, Abraham | 1 | | 1 | | | Wait, John | 1 | | 2 | | | Kelsey, Rachel | | | 2 | | |
| Goodwin, Abigal | 3 | 1 | 4 | | | Case, William | 1 | 4 | 6 | | | Kelsey, Nathan | 1 | | 2 | | |
| Lewis, Elihu | 1 | | 3 | 1 | | Kellogg, Elizer | 3 | 4 | 5 | | | Elsworth, Thomas | 2 | 2 | 4 | 1 | |
| Lewis, Nehemeah | 3 | 1 | 2 | | | Balcome, John | 1 | 1 | 2 | | | Rood, Moses | 1 | 3 | 2 | | |
| Orsborn, Samuel | 2 | 1 | 3 | | | Goodrich, Seth | 1 | 3 | 2 | | | Rood, Ebenezer | 3 | 4 | 5 | | |
| Markham, Ezekiel | 1 | 4 | 3 | | | More, Abijah | 2 | 3 | 6 | | | Buel, Jonothan | 4 | 1 | 2 | | |
| Cole, John | 2 | 1 | 7 | | | Whilford, Robert | 1 | 1 | 2 | | | Tharp, David | 3 | 3 | 2 | | |
| Gillet, Stephen | 1 | 1 | 1 | | | Cook, Richard | 1 | | 2 | | | Logan, Samuel | 2 | | 6 | | |
| Marsh, Jonothan | 1 | | 3 | | | Raydon, Samuel | 1 | 3 | 5 | | | Seeley, John | 1 | 1 | 5 | | |
| Loomis, Joseph | 1 | 2 | 3 | | | Catlin, Abraham | 1 | 3 | 4 | | | Wadhams, John | 3 | 1 | 3 | | |
| Steel, Isaac | 1 | 1 | 5 | | | Cleavland, Rufus | 1 | 5 | 3 | | | Norton, Ashbel | 1 | | 2 | | |
| Starling, John | 1 | 3 | 6 | | | Woodruff, Josiah | 2 | 2 | 6 | | | Buel, Jonothan | 1 | 1 | 2 | | |
| Merrills, Sarah | | 2 | 2 | | | Wead, Daniel | 1 | 2 | 3 | | | Cook, Amasa | 4 | | 2 | | |

## LITCHFIELD COUNTY—Continued.

### LITCHFIELD TOWN—con.

| NAME OF HEAD OF FAMILY. | Free white males of 16 years and upward, including heads of families. | Free white males under 16 years. | Free white females, including heads of families. | All other free persons. | Slaves. |
|---|---|---|---|---|---|
| Norvel, William | 1 | 1 | 2 | | |
| Lyman, Moses | 4 | 2 | 5 | | |
| Cook, Moses | 1 | 1 | 2 | | |
| Hagan, James | 1 | | 1 | | |
| Simmons, Perer | 1 | 3 | 4 | | |
| Farnham, Peter | 2 | | 1 | | |
| Wheeler, Josiah | 2 | | 1 | | |
| Waterman, David | 23 | 3 | 4 | | |
| Hawley, Luther | 1 | 5 | 3 | 1 | |
| Mingo, William | | | | 1 | |
| Porter, Joshua | 3 | | 5 | | 4 |
| Wheeler, Lemuel | 3 | | 2 | 1 | 2 |
| Coskins, Amos | 1 | 2 | 2 | | |
| Davis, Jacobus | 3 | 1 | 6 | 1 | |
| Lord, Joel | 2 | 1 | 3 | | |
| Lee, Robert W | 1 | 2 | 4 | | |
| Ball, Daniel | 4 | 2 | 4 | | |
| Griswold, John | 1 | | | | |
| Williams, Polley | | | 1 | | |
| Chittendon, Timothy | 2 | 1 | 4 | | |
| Chittendon, Timothy, 2d | 1 | 1 | 2 | | |
| Everts, Submit | | | 1 | | |
| Everts, Maryan | 2 | 1 | 3 | | |
| Eldridge, John | 3 | 3 | 3 | | |
| Everts, Nathan | 5 | 1 | 8 | | |
| Catoe | | | | 1 | |
| Marsh, George | 2 | 2 | 3 | | |
| Porter, Nicholas | 2 | 2 | 3 | 1 | |
| Atwood, Jedediah | 1 | 2 | 4 | 1 | |
| Miles, Stephen | 1 | 1 | 3 | | |
| Beyhal, Richard | 2 | 1 | 2 | | |
| Cook, Daniel | 1 | | 1 | | |
| Cook, Ezekiel | 1 | 1 | 2 | | |
| Cook, Simeon | 1 | | 1 | | |
| Tousley, Joseph | 2 | 1 | 4 | | |
| White, Israhel | 3 | | 4 | | |
| White, John | 1 | 3 | 3 | | |
| Wood, Elijah | 2 | 2 | 5 | | |
| Tousley, John | 1 | 2 | 3 | | |
| Colkins, Justice | 1 | 2 | 6 | | |
| Colkins, Silvanus | 1 | 1 | 1 | | |
| Ware, John | 1 | 1 | 3 | | |
| Willamson, John | 1 | 3 | 1 | | |
| Hill, John | 1 | | 1 | | |
| Barriss, David | 2 | | 1 | | |
| Martin, Eliphalet | 2 | 1 | 3 | | |
| Howe, John | 2 | 1 | 2 | | |
| Gilbert, John | 2 | 2 | 1 | | |
| Lyman, David | 1 | 6 | 3 | | |
| Curtis, Job | 3 | 1 | 4 | | |
| Lyman, Josiah | 1 | 1 | 2 | | |
| Morris, Daniel | 1 | 1 | 2 | | |
| Miller, David | 2 | | 2 | | |
| Cole, Samuel | 2 | 1 | 1 | | |
| Omsted, Roswell | 2 | 2 | 2 | | |
| More, Josiah | 2 | 2 | 4 | | |
| Dutton, John | 2 | 2 | 5 | | |
| Watson, Levi | 1 | 1 | 3 | | |
| Goodwin, Isaac | 2 | 3 | 5 | | |
| Coe, Seth | 1 | 1 | 4 | | |
| Foot, Roger | 2 | 1 | 1 | | |
| Loomis, Brigadeer | 1 | 1 | 4 | | |
| Austen, Isaac | 1 | | 4 | | |
| Soper, Joel | 2 | 1 | 1 | | |
| Elmon, Alexander | 1 | 5 | 3 | | |
| Dickenson, Susannah | | | 4 | | |
| Austen, Joel | 1 | 3 | 2 | | |
| Austen, Robert | 1 | 3 | 4 | | |
| Austen, Reuben | 1 | | 1 | | |
| Lyman, Francis | 1 | 2 | 4 | | |
| Tuttle, Elisha | 2 | 4 | 4 | | |
| Hills, Justice | 1 | 3 | 3 | | |
| Francis, Asahel | 3 | | 4 | | |
| Bunnel, Fradrick | 2 | 1 | 2 | | |
| Porter, Benjamin | 2 | 2 | 4 | | |
| Cuff | | | | 2 | |
| Tompson, Solomon | 1 | | 4 | | |
| Thompson, Elisha | 4 | 1 | 4 | | |
| Miles, Samuel | 2 | 2 | 3 | | |
| Munson, Thomas E | 2 | 1 | 6 | | |
| Thompson, James | 2 | 1 | 5 | | |
| Starr, Ephraim | 3 | 3 | 7 | | |
| Ives, Joseph | 4 | 2 | 3 | | |
| Thompson, David | 7 | | 4 | | |
| Pratt, Silas | 3 | 2 | 4 | | |
| Gordon, Samuel | 1 | 2 | 2 | | |
| Lewis, Judy | 1 | | 1 | | |
| Merrills, Nathaniel | 1 | 1 | 2 | | |
| Merriman, Ichabud | 1 | 3 | 4 | | |
| Peck, Zebulon | 1 | 2 | 1 | | |
| Hurlburt, Gidian | 2 | 2 | 3 | | |
| Parmerley, David | 1 | 1 | 3 | | |
| Veal, Joseph | 2 | | 3 | | |
| Landon, John | 1 | 3 | 5 | | |
| Crompton, Ebenezer | 3 | 4 | 4 | | |
| Clark, Lyman | 2 | 2 | 4 | | |
| Marsh, James | 2 | 2 | 2 | | |
| Webster, Charles | 1 | 3 | 2 | | |
| Orton, Saml | 3 | 1 | 5 | | |
| Stoddard, Briant | 1 | 3 | 5 | | |
| Marsh, Elijah | 3 | 2 | 3 | | |
| Marsh, Ambrose | 4 | | 2 | | |
| Marsh, Titus | 1 | 4 | 1 | | |
| Marsh, Thomas | 1 | | 2 | | |
| Peck, Cornelius | 1 | | 1 | | |
| Atwater, Abel | 1 | 2 | 4 | | |
| Birdwell, Stephen | 2 | 1 | 6 | | |
| Hart, Benjamin | 1 | 2 | 6 | | |
| Marsh, Roger | 5 | 3 | 3 | | |
| Humerston, Noah | 3 | 2 | 3 | | |
| Peck, Reeve | 2 | | 1 | | |
| Peck, Asahel | 1 | 2 | 1 | | |
| Hotchkiss, Eliphalet | 1 | 3 | 1 | | |
| Landon, Seth | 2 | 1 | 5 | | |
| Marsh, Rhoda | 1 | 1 | 6 | | |
| Stone, James | 2 | 1 | 4 | | |
| Lord, Leynde | 4 | 1 | 4 | | |
| Addams, Andrew | 2 | 1 | 5 | | |
| Punderson, Ahimea | 1 | | | | |
| Beach, Jessee | 1 | | | | |
| Cleaver, Tobias | 1 | | | | |
| Gatta, John I | | | | 1 | |
| Sterling, Elisha | 1 | | | | |
| Barnard, Hersey | 1 | | | | |
| Taylor, William | 1 | | | | |
| Addams, Andrew | 3 | 3 | 5 | 1 | 2 |
| Griffith, Edward | 1 | | 1 | | |
| Champion, Judas | 1 | | 4 | | 1 |
| Barnes, Amos | 1 | 2 | 3 | | |
| Smith, Reuben | 3 | | 6 | | |
| Peck, Reeve | 1 | 3 | 4 | | |
| Baldwin, Daniel | 1 | 2 | 6 | | |
| Baldwin, Nathaniel | 3 | 3 | 3 | | |
| Baldwin, Patience | | | | | |
| Smith, Matthew | 2 | | 4 | | |
| Baldwin, Samuel | 3 | | 3 | | |
| Smith, Israel | 1 | | 3 | | |
| Baldwin, Samuel | 1 | 2 | 3 | | |
| Bailey, Andrew | 1 | 4 | 2 | | |
| Hurd, David | 3 | 4 | 3 | | |
| Hall, Aseph | 2 | 1 | 2 | | |
| Henman, Phenehas | 3 | 2 | 5 | | |
| Humphry, Ashbel | 4 | 1 | 2 | | |
| Kimbal, Jacob | 2 | 3 | 5 | | |
| Standley, Timothy | 1 | 2 | 3 | | |
| Standley, Elisha | 1 | 2 | 4 | | |
| Filley, Jessee | 1 | | 3 | | |
| Fox, Stephen | 1 | 1 | 2 | | |
| Covel, David | 1 | 2 | 4 | | |
| Tyler, Abel | 1 | 2 | 3 | | |
| Branton, Michael | 2 | 2 | 1 | | |
| Willam, Isaac | 2 | 1 | 2 | | |
| Parsons, Benjamin | 1 | 5 | 2 | | |
| Pettibone, Abraham | 3 | | 4 | | 1 |
| Douglas, Samuel | 3 | 1 | 8 | | |
| Ensign, Eliphalet | 1 | 3 | 4 | | |
| Spensor, Nathaniel | 2 | 4 | 5 | | |
| Spensor, James | 1 | 2 | 4 | | |
| Basset, William | 1 | 1 | 4 | | |
| Spensor, Michael | 1 | 2 | 2 | | |
| Spenser, Ashbel | 1 | 2 | 5 | | |
| Spensor, John | 1 | 2 | 2 | | |
| Thompson, Eliphras | 1 | 2 | 3 | | |
| Coles, Asa | 2 | | 3 | | |
| Coles, Theodore | 2 | 3 | 2 | | |
| Tyler, Abial | 2 | 1 | 1 | | |
| Lomise, Isaac | 2 | 2 | 2 | | |
| Loomise, Israel | 2 | 2 | 5 | | |
| Jones, Benjamin | 1 | 1 | 3 | | |
| Wells, Timothy | 2 | 2 | 2 | | |
| Woodruff, Solomon | 3 | 4 | 6 | | |
| Merrells, Verijah | 3 | 1 | 2 | | |
| Austin, Aaron | 4 | 2 | 7 | | |
| Ives, Joseph | 1 | 2 | 4 | | |
| Goodrich, Isaac | 1 | 3 | 4 | | |
| Lord, Frederick | 1 | 2 | 2 | | |
| Tyler, Jedior | 2 | 5 | 3 | | |
| Gaylor, Wait | 1 | | 3 | | |
| Tyler, Amos | 1 | 1 | 2 | | |
| Warren, Mea | 1 | | | | |
| Wood, Elijah | 2 | 2 | 5 | | |
| Barnes, Reuben | 1 | 4 | 2 | | |
| Barnes, Timy | 3 | | 3 | | |
| Batterson, Hezekia | 2 | 2 | 3 | | |
| Harvey, Joel | 4 | 1 | 4 | | |
| Elvendolf, Tobias | 1 | 2 | 2 | 1 | 3 |
| Newel, Theodore | 1 | | 3 | | |
| Hensdale, Jacob | 1 | 2 | 2 | | |
| Rowe, Solomon | 1 | | 3 | | |
| Rood, David | 2 | 3 | 3 | | |
| Rood, Roger | 1 | 4 | 2 | | |
| Granger, Phinehas | 1 | 1 | 1 | | |
| Lawrence, Nathan | 2 | 1 | 3 | | |
| Detne, Benja | 1 | 1 | 3 | | |
| Benton, John | 1 | 1 | 1 | | |
| Hewit, Gershom | 1 | 2 | 7 | | |
| Pierce, Thomas | 3 | | 3 | | |
| Pierce, Amos | 2 | 4 | 5 | | |
| Pierce, Saml | 2 | 3 | 1 | 1 | 1 |
| Pierce, Pelahat | 3 | 1 | 3 | 1 | |
| Dunham, James | 2 | 1 | 2 | | |
| Dunham, Isaac | 1 | 2 | 1 | | |
| Pierce, Edward | 1 | 1 | 1 | | |
| Fenn, Theophelus | 2 | | 4 | | |
| Fellows, Stephen | 1 | 3 | 2 | | |
| Higbey, Isaac | 1 | 1 | 3 | | |
| Bacon, Andrew | 3 | 2 | 6 | | |
| Whitney, Cornelus | 1 | | 4 | | |
| Feeman, John | 3 | 2 | 4 | | |
| Capen, Timothy | 1 | 1 | 4 | | |
| Lawrence, Josiah | 1 | | 1 | | |
| Lawrence, Abel | 1 | 1 | 1 | | |
| Green, Willard | 2 | 1 | 3 | | |
| Burrel, Charles | 2 | 1 | 2 | | 2 |
| Burroll, Obed | 2 | 2 | 5 | | 1 |
| Green, Saml | 1 | 2 | 3 | | |
| Towner, Sarah | 1 | 1 | 3 | | |
| Bailey, Ithamon | 1 | 1 | 2 | | |
| Towner, Abi | | 2 | 1 | | |
| Beach, Linus | 3 | 1 | 4 | | |
| Beach, Mines | 1 | | 1 | | |
| Ives, Levi | 2 | 2 | | | |
| Benten, Josiah | 1 | | 2 | | |
| Balwin, Elisha | 1 | 1 | 3 | | |
| Newton, Isaac | 2 | 2 | 3 | | |
| Beach, Israel | 1 | 3 | 2 | | |
| Wetton, Elijah | 2 | 1 | 3 | | |
| Humphrey, David | 3 | 1 | 4 | | |
| Humphrey, Samuel | 3 | | 7 | | |
| Humphrey, Charles | 1 | 1 | 4 | | |
| Wallen, John | 1 | | 2 | | |
| Wallen, Thomas | 1 | 1 | 2 | | |
| Wallen, James | 1 | 3 | 4 | | |
| Hill, James | 1 | | 8 | | |
| Paine, Jessee | 1 | 1 | 4 | 3 | |
| Wilen, David | 1 | 1 | 4 | | |
| Coller, Olliver | 2 | 2 | 2 | | |
| Wallen, Daniel | 1 | 2 | 2 | | |
| Fox, Levi | 1 | 1 | 2 | | |
| Coller, John | 1 | | 3 | | |
| Coller, Isaac | 1 | 2 | 2 | | |
| Henman, Asher | 3 | 3 | 3 | | |
| Chaugorn, Mary | | | 2 | | |
| Merrills, Benajah | 2 | | 4 | | |
| Roberts, William | 2 | 1 | 3 | | |
| Willcox, Asa | 1 | 3 | 5 | | |
| Tayler, David | 1 | 2 | 2 | | |
| Willcox, Philander | 2 | | 6 | | |
| Clark, William | 1 | 1 | 2 | | |
| Hill, A Gift | 4 | 1 | 5 | | |
| Richard, Pelatiah | 1 | 2 | 4 | | |
| Mills, Benjamin | 3 | 1 | 4 | | |
| Mills, Dudley | 1 | | 4 | | |
| Merrills, Daniel | 1 | | 4 | | |
| Merrills, William | 1 | 1 | 4 | | |
| Barns, Roswell | 3 | | 4 | 1 | |
| Humphrey, Noah | 1 | 5 | 3 | | |
| Humphrey, Abraham | 2 | 1 | 7 | | |
| Pain, Ezri | 1 | | 2 | | |
| Gibbs, Gersham | 2 | 3 | 3 | | |
| Gibbs, Philoe | 1 | 1 | 1 | | |
| Plumb, Sarah | | 1 | 2 | | |
| Griswold, Timothy | 2 | | 3 | | |
| Frisbey, Noah | 2 | | 1 | | |
| Frisbey, Noah | 2 | | 3 | | |
| Welch, David | 5 | 1 | 2 | 2 | 2 |
| Page, Asa, 2d | 1 | 1 | 3 | | |
| Ackley, Saml | 1 | 1 | 3 | | |
| Landon, Daniel | 1 | 1 | 2 | | |
| Smith, Rebecca | | | 2 | | |
| Landon, Daniel | 1 | 1 | 4 | | |
| Bradley, Ellihue | 1 | 2 | 3 | | |
| Dickinson, Olliver | 1 | 5 | 3 | | |
| Stewart, Nathan | 2 | | 5 | | |
| Buel, Eunice | | | 3 | | |
| Welch, John | 1 | 1 | 2 | | 1 |
| Carter, Saml | 1 | | 2 | | |
| Clemmons, Abel | 1 | 1 | 3 | | |
| Robinson, Jerard | 1 | 1 | 3 | | |
| Dudley, William | 1 | | 2 | | |
| Landon, Abner | 3 | | 3 | | |
| Ludington, Stephen | 1 | 2 | 1 | | |
| Gibs, Nathan | 1 | | 2 | | |
| Gibs, Lydia | | | 3 | | |
| Brown, Stephen | 1 | 1 | 4 | | |
| Gibs, Zadock | 1 | 2 | 5 | | |
| Veal, Daniel | 1 | 1 | 2 | | |
| Catlin, Charles | 4 | 1 | 5 | | |

# HEADS OF FAMILIES—CONNECTICUT.

## LITCHFIELD COUNTY—Continued.

| NAME OF HEAD OF FAMILY. | Free white males of 16 years and upward, including heads of families. | Free white males under 16 years. | Free white females, including heads of families. | All other free persons. | Slaves. | NAME OF HEAD OF FAMILY. | Free white males of 16 years and upward, including heads of families. | Free white males under 16 years. | Free white females, including heads of families. | All other free persons. | Slaves. | NAME OF HEAD OF FAMILY. | Free white males of 16 years and upward, including heads of families. | Free white males under 16 years. | Free white females, including heads of families. | All other free persons. | Slaves. |
|---|---|---|---|---|---|---|---|---|---|---|---|---|---|---|---|---|---|
| **LITCHFIELD TOWN—con.** | | | | | | **NEW MILFORD TOWN—continued.** | | | | | | **NEW MILFORD TOWN—continued.** | | | | | |
| Graves, William | 1 | 3 | 2 | | | Baldwin, Abiel | 1 | 2 | 3 | | | Camp, Riverius | 1 | 3 | 1 | | |
| Day, John | 1 | | 2 | | | Baldwin, Israel | 1 | | 3 | | | Camp, Israel | 1 | | 2 | | |
| Morgan, Daniel | 1 | | 1 | | | Baldwin, John | 1 | 1 | 4 | | | Canfield, Ira | 1 | | 2 | | |
| Orsborn, Joseph | 1 | | 3 | | | Beacher, Elizur, 2d | 3 | | 3 | | | Cole, Jesse | 1 | 2 | 2 | | |
| Lyman, Moses | 1 | | | | | Beacher, Nathaniel | 2 | | 3 | | | Cole, Timothy | 1 | | 2 | | |
| Bissel, John | 2 | 1 | 4 | | | Bell, Jeams | 1 | 2 | 2 | | | Canfield, Oliver | 5 | 1 | 3 | | |
| Page, Asa | 1 | 3 | 3 | | | Buck, Enoch | 3 | 3 | 4 | | | Carpenter, John | 2 | 5 | 2 | | |
| Page, David | 1 | 3 | 3 | | | Bennett, Caleb | 1 | | 2 | | | Camp, Enos, 1st | 1 | | 1 | | |
| Smith, Benajah | 2 | 2 | 4 | | | Bennett, Gershom | 1 | 2 | 3 | | | Camp, Enos, 2d | 2 | 2 | 2 | | |
| Page, Abel | 1 | | 2 | | | Buckingham, Benjamin | 3 | 1 | 5 | | 1 | Canfield, Samuel | 4 | 2 | 3 | | 2 |
| Catlin, David | 1 | 4 | 3 | | | Botsford, Nathan | 2 | | 2 | | | Clark, Thomas, 1st | 2 | 1 | 3 | | |
| Can, Sarah | | 1 | 1 | | | Brownson, Noah | 3 | 3 | 3 | | | Cable, David | 1 | | 3 | | |
| Glass, John | 1 | 2 | 2 | | | Brownson, Mathew | 2 | 1 | 2 | | | Clark, Richard | 1 | 1 | 3 | | |
| Smedley, Gideon | 2 | 1 | 4 | | | Brownson, Benjamin | 1 | 3 | 3 | | | Camp, John | 1 | | | | |
| Spencer, Ephraim | 1 | 2 | 3 | | | Bennett, Abijah | 2 | 1 | 1 | | | Clark, Jeames | 1 | | | | |
| Cane, Edward | 2 | | 6 | | | Beard, David | 1 | | 1 | | | Canfield, Eunice | | | 3 | | |
| Doolittle, Benjamin | 3 | 3 | 7 | | | Buck, Sam Beebee | 1 | 1 | 6 | | | Couch, John, 2d | 1 | 1 | 2 | | |
| Doolittle, Fraderick | 1 | 2 | 3 | | | Buck, Jeames | 1 | 1 | 3 | | | Cole, John | 3 | 1 | 2 | | |
| Churchel, Jonathan | 1 | 2 | 5 | | | Benson, Benjamin, 1st | 2 | | 2 | | | Canfield, Elijah | 1 | 2 | 4 | | |
| Beach, Abner | 2 | 3 | 4 | | | Benson, Benjamin, 2d | 1 | 3 | 5 | | 1 | Clark, Joseph | 1 | 1 | 2 | | |
| Beach, Noah | 1 | 2 | 2 | | | Buck, Asaph | 1 | | 2 | | | Crane, Isaac C | 3 | | | | |
| Ward, William | 2 | 2 | 5 | | | Bradshaw, William | 2 | 3 | 5 | | | Crane, Ezra | 1 | | 1 | | |
| Plumb, Ebenezer | 3 | 4 | 6 | | | Bears, Ezra | 1 | 1 | 2 | | | Canfield, Azeriah | 1 | 1 | 3 | | |
| Colver, Joshua | 1 | 1 | 3 | | | Bears, Jeames, 1st | 2 | | 3 | | | Canfield, Levi | 1 | 1 | 3 | | |
| Strong, Anna | 2 | | 4 | | | Bears, Jeames, 2d | 1 | | 1 | | | Clark, John | 1 | 2 | 4 | | |
| Strong, Anna | 1 | | 1 | | | Buck, Ezekiel | 1 | | 1 | | | Camp, Nathan | 1 | 4 | 3 | | |
| Palms, Andrew | 1 | 1 | 3 | | | Buck, Benton | 1 | | 2 | | | Collar, Isaac | 1 | 2 | 6 | | |
| Buell, Solomon | 1 | 3 | 4 | | | Buck, Israel | 2 | 3 | 2 | | | Corbin, Philip | 1 | | 2 | | |
| Russel, John | 1 | 5 | 2 | | | Buck, Ephraim | 1 | | 1 | | | Canfield, Abel | 1 | 2 | 3 | | |
| Stone, Thomas W | 1 | | 2 | | | Bristol, Daniel | 1 | 1 | 4 | | | Canfield, David, 2d | 1 | 1 | 7 | | |
| Griswold, James | 1 | 1 | | | | Beach, Caleb | 1 | 1 | 2 | | | Canfield, David, 1st | 3 | | 1 | | |
| Ribborn, Jehiel | 1 | 2 | 6 | | | Bradley, Moses | 2 | | 7 | | | Deforest, Isaac | 2 | 1 | 4 | | |
| Plumb, Stephen | 1 | 3 | 5 | | | Benedict, Aaron | 3 | 2 | 4 | | | Dean, William | 1 | 2 | 1 | | |
| Webster, James | 1 | | 3 | | | Beardsley, Silas | 1 | | 1 | | | Dunning, Samuel | 2 | 2 | 5 | | |
| Hislop, Alford | 1 | 1 | 4 | | | Brownson, Asa | 1 | 1 | 2 | | | Downes, Jonathan | 3 | 1 | 2 | | |
| Stoddard, John | 3 | | 5 | | | Brownson, Ziba | 2 | 2 | 3 | | | Downes, Lemuel | 1 | 1 | 6 | | |
| Collins, William | 1 | 1 | 3 | | | Botts, Reuben | 5 | 3 | 5 | | 1 | Downes, Thomas | 1 | | 5 | | |
| Beach, Losior | 1 | 2 | 3 | | | Bristol, Richard | 6 | 1 | 4 | | | Downes, Elijah | 1 | 3 | 1 | | |
| Griswold, Syphrona | 1 | 2 | 2 | | | Baldwin, Asahel | 2 | 3 | 5 | | | Dayton, Eli | 2 | 2 | 3 | | |
| Tylford, Philathia | 1 | 2 | 2 | | | Bradley, Timothy | 2 | 4 | 5 | | | Dunning, Ezra | 1 | 2 | 2 | | |
| Palmer, Job | 1 | | 1 | | | Brownson, Isaac | 1 | | 4 | | | Deavenport, Benjamin | 1 | 2 | 3 | | |
| Gilbert, Calvin | 1 | | 1 | | | Burwell, Stephen | | 1 | 2 | | | Davies, Sarah | | | 2 | | |
| Beach, Sabin | 1 | 3 | 5 | | | Barnes, Sarah | | | 3 | | | Deavenport, David | 1 | 2 | 3 | | |
| Beach, David | 3 | | 3 | | | Beach, Abijah Hen? | 2 | | 2 | | | Deavenport, John | 2 | | 4 | | |
| Gilbert, Abner | 1 | 2 | 2 | | | Baldwin, Simeon | 1 | | 3 | | | Downes, Jonathan, 2d | 1 | 2 | 4 | | |
| Coe, Levi | 1 | 1 | 1 | | | Bull, David | 1 | | 4 | | | Everts, Stephen | 1 | 2 | 4 | | |
| Coe, Thomas | 2 | 1 | 2 | | | Bryan, Nathan | 1 | 2 | 5 | | | Earle, Benjamin | 1 | 2 | 2 | | |
| Pardey, Eli | 1 | 3 | 2 | | | Bulkley, John | 1 | | 1 | | | Everit, Daniel | 1 | 4 | 3 | | |
| Landon, Nathaniel | 1 | 1 | 1 | | | Bristol, Arial | 1 | 2 | 2 | | | Edward, Ebenezer | 1 | 1 | 3 | | |
| Landon, Martha | | 3 | 2 | | | Bass, Josiah | 1 | 1 | 4 | | | Edward, Edward | 1 | 1 | 5 | | |
| Orsborn, Jacob | 2 | | 1 | | | Buckingham, Abel | 2 | 5 | 2 | | | Ferris, David | 2 | 1 | 2 | | |
| Orsborn, John | 2 | 1 | 5 | | | Beardsley, John | 3 | | 1 | | | Ferris, Amasa | 1 | 2 | 3 | | |
| Orsborn, Jeremiah | 1 | 1 | 2 | | | Bushly, Ebenezer | 1 | 2 | 3 | | | Fenn, Joab | 2 | | 1 | | |
| Buel, Clive | 1 | 2 | 3 | | | Bass, Daniel | 1 | 1 | 1 | | | Feris, Zachariah | 3 | 3 | 4 | | |
| | | | | | | Burnham, Woolcott | 1 | | 5 | | | Fairchild, Abraham | 1 | 4 | 5 | | |
| **NEW MILFORD TOWN.** | | | | | | Booth, Elisha | 1 | 1 | 4 | | | Fairchild, Eleazer, 1st | 2 | 1 | 2 | | |
| Bostwick, Elisha | 1 | 2 | 2 | 6 | | Betts, William | 2 | | 3 | | | Fairchild, Eleazer, 2d | 1 | 2 | 1 | | |
| Bostwick, Oliver | 1 | 1 | 1 | | | Bobbett, Lemuel | 1 | 2 | 2 | | | Fairchild, Abel | 1 | 2 | 3 | | |
| Bostwick, Elizur | 1 | 2 | 1 | | | Bobbett, William | 1 | 2 | 1 | | | Farrand, Samuel | 2 | 2 | 4 | | |
| Bostwick, Joseph, 1st | 3 | 1 | 3 | | | Butler, Ezekiel | 1 | | 3 | | | Ferris, Joseph | 2 | 1 | 1 | | |
| Bostwick, Samuel | 1 | | 4 | | | Bush, Joel | 2 | 5 | 2 | | | Fenton, Solomon | 1 | 2 | 5 | | |
| Bostwick, Reuben, 1st | 2 | 1 | 3 | | | Benson, Bryan | 1 | 1 | 1 | | | Fits Jerald, Partrick | 1 | | | | |
| Bostwick, Ben Ruggles | 1 | 2 | 2 | | | Benson, Ambrose | 1 | | 2 | | | Ferris, Stephen | 2 | 1 | 3 | | |
| Bostwick, Benjamin | 3 | | 2 | | | Beacher, David | 2 | 1 | 2 | | | Firman, Richard | 3 | 3 | 4 | | |
| Bostwick, Jonathan | 8 | | 4 | | | Boardman, Homer | 1 | 2 | 2 | | | Fisher, N. Beacher | 1 | | 2 | | |
| Bostwick, Isaac | 4 | 1 | 2 | | | Baldwin, Nathaniel G | 1 | | 1 | | | Ford, Jonathan | 1 | 1 | 3 | | |
| Bostwick, Reuben, 2d | 2 | 1 | 4 | | | Beacher, John | 2 | 3 | 8 | | | Gillet, Abel | 1 | 1 | 3 | | |
| Bostwick, Salmon | 1 | | 2 | | | Bosworth, Joseph | 1 | 5 | 3 | | | Ghoram, Phineas | 1 | | 3 | | |
| Bostwick, David, 2d | 1 | | 1 | | | Camp, Job | 2 | 4 | 2 | | | Gunn, Gidion | 1 | 1 | 4 | | |
| Bostwick, Amos | 1 | 1 | 2 | | | Couch, Samuel | 3 | 2 | 3 | | | Gunn, Abner | 5 | | 3 | 1 | |
| Bostwick, Joseph, 2d | 3 | | 4 | | | Collins, Amos | 1 | | 2 | | | Gunn, Epenetus | 1 | 1 | 2 | | |
| Bostwick, Abel | 1 | | 2 | | | Canfield, Ithamar | 2 | 1 | 1 | 1 | | Garlick, Read | 2 | | 3 | | |
| Bostwick, Zackeriah | 1 | 2 | 2 | | | Camp, Heath | 2 | 1 | 3 | | | Garlick, Edmund | 1 | | 3 | | |
| Bostwick, Ichabod | 2 | 1 | 5 | | | Clark, William | 1 | 3 | 5 | | | Garlick, Samuel | 1 | 1 | 5 | | |
| Bostwick, Martin | 1 | 2 | 3 | | | Chatfield, Levi | 1 | 5 | 2 | | | Garlick, Heath | 1 | 1 | 1 | | |
| Bostwick, David, 1st | 2 | 2 | 3 | | | Clark, Daniel | 3 | | 5 | | | Gaylord, Benjamin | 3 | 3 | 3 | | |
| Bostwick, Nathan | 1 | 3 | 4 | | | Clark, Isaac | 1 | 1 | 4 | | | Gaylord, Aaron | 3 | 1 | 2 | | |
| Bostwick, John | 1 | | 1 | | | Comstack, Achilles | 1 | | 2 | | | Gaylord, Nathan | 1 | 3 | 3 | | |
| Bostwick, Medad | 1 | 2 | 1 | | | Chittenden, Stephen | 1 | 3 | 1 | | | Gaylord, Ebenezer | 1 | 2 | 4 | | |
| Boardman, Sherman | 3 | | 4 | 3 | | Comstack, John | 3 | | 2 | | | Gunn, Abel | 2 | | 2 | | |
| Bordman, Daniel | 4 | | 2 | 1 | | Canfield, Heath | 1 | 1 | 3 | | | Griswold, Stanley | 1 | | 2 | | |
| Baldwin, Ebenezer | 3 | 4 | 5 | | | Comstack, Samuel | 2 | | 1 | | | Ghorrum, David | 2 | | 3 | | |
| Baldwin, Theophilus | 2 | 2 | 5 | | | Camp, David | 2 | 1 | 2 | | | Garlick, Heath | 1 | | 3 | | |
| Bennett, Edward | 3 | 4 | 4 | | | Cole, Ichabod | 1 | | 3 | | | Gunn, Nathan | 1 | 2 | 2 | | |
| Brownson, Thomas | 1 | | 1 | | | Chittenden, Giles | 2 | 1 | 1 | | | Gaylord, William | 3 | 1 | 4 | | |
| Brownson, Reuben | 1 | 3 | 3 | | | Canfield, Philor | 2 | 2 | 3 | | | George, Sarah | | 3 | 2 | | |
| Botsford, Ena | 2 | 3 | 5 | | | Clark, Thomas, 2d | 2 | | 2 | | | Gratis, Nancy | | | | 1 | |
| Beach, Reuben | 1 | 2 | 3 | | | Clark, Edmond | 2 | 2 | 4 | | | Green, Jarus | 1 | 1 | 2 | 4 | |
| Bishop, Eler | 1 | 2 | 4 | | | Camp, Daniel | 2 | 2 | 2 | | | Gilbert, Hezekiah | 2 | 1 | 2 | | |
| Britterfield, Simeon | 1 | 1 | 1 | | | Canfield, Jeremiah | 2 | | 1 | | | Granger, George | 1 | 1 | 4 | | |
| Beach, Isaac | 2 | | 2 | | | Canfield, John | 1 | 2 | 4 | | | Hill, David | 1 | 2 | 2 | | |
| Baldwin, Jonah | 1 | | | | | Canfield, Lemuel | 1 | 4 | 3 | | | Hartwell, Samuel | 1 | 2 | 3 | | |
| Baker, Jesse | 1 | 1 | 3 | | | Cole, Nathaniel | 2 | | 2 | | | Holmes, Jeremiah | 1 | | 2 | | |
| Baldwin, Isaac | 1 | 2 | 6 | | | Couch, John, 1st | 3 | 3 | 4 | | | Holmes, Nathan | 1 | 2 | 3 | | |
| | | | | | | Cole, Solomon | 1 | | 2 | | | Hayes, Thomas | 3 | 3 | 5 | | |

# FIRST CENSUS OF THE UNITED STATES.

## LITCHFIELD COUNTY—Continued.

| NAME OF HEAD OF FAMILY. | Free white males of 16 years and upward, including heads of families. | Free white males under 16 years. | Free white females, including heads of families. | All other free persons. | Slaves. | NAME OF HEAD OF FAMILY. | Free white males of 16 years and upward, including heads of families. | Free white males under 16 years. | Free white females, including heads of families. | All other free persons. | Slaves. | NAME OF HEAD OF FAMILY. | Free white males of 16 years and upward, including heads of families. | Free white males under 16 years. | Free white females, including heads of families. | All other free persons. | Slaves. |
|---|---|---|---|---|---|---|---|---|---|---|---|---|---|---|---|---|---|
| **NEW MILFORD TOWN—continued.** | | | | | | **NEW MILFORD TOWN—continued.** | | | | | | **NEW MILFORD TOWN—continued.** | | | | | |
| Hendricks, Andrew | 1 | 3 | 2 | | | Mygatt, Jonathan | 3 | | 6 | | | Syllivan, Mott | | 1 | 2 | | |
| Hunt, Lewis | 1 | 2 | 4 | | | Masters, N. Shelton | 3 | 2 | 2 | | | Sperry, John | 2 | 2 | 2 | | |
| Hayt, Nathan | 1 | 1 | 5 | | | Marchant, Ezra | 3 | | 2 | | | Sherman, Ezra | 2 | | 1 | | |
| Hitchcock, William | 1 | 2 | 1 | | | Morehouse, Benjamin | 1 | 1 | 1 | | | Stilson, Revinus | 1 | 1 | 6 | | |
| Hustfield, Charles | 1 | | 2 | | | Morehouse, John, 2d | 1 | | 5 | | | Stilson, Nathan | 2 | 3 | 3 | | |
| Hotchkiss, Ebenezer | 1 | 1 | 2 | | | McEwen, William | 1 | | 2 | | | Stewart, Nathaniel | 2 | 1 | 5 | | |
| Hine, Noble | 3 | 2 | 9 | | | McEwen, John, 1st | 1 | | 2 | | | Sherman, Eli | 1 | 1 | 1 | | |
| Hitchcock, David | 2 | 2 | 3 | | | McEwen, John, 2d | 1 | 1 | 1 | | | Sherman, Daniel | 1 | 1 | 1 | | |
| Hull, John | 2 | 5 | | | | Mead, Daniel | 1 | 1 | 3 | | | Stilson, Truman | 1 | 3 | 4 | | |
| Hill, Silas | 4 | 2 | 3 | | | Murray, Nathan | 2 | 1 | 2 | | | Sanford, Benoni S | 1 | 2 | 2 | | |
| Hine, Daniel | 1 | 2 | 4 | | | Milligan, George | 1 | 1 | 1 | | | Stone, Reuben | 1 | 4 | 4 | | |
| Hill, Solomon, 1st | 1 | | 3 | | | Murray, Elisha | 2 | | 1 | | | Sherwood, Daniel | 1 | | 4 | | |
| Hallock, William | 1 | 4 | 2 | | | Morehouse, Squire | 1 | | 1 | | | Sherwood, Reuben | 1 | | | | |
| Hartwell, Joseph | 2 | 1 | 2 | | | Mead, Benjamin | 2 | | 4 | | | Smith, John, 2d | 2 | 1 | 2 | | |
| Hurd, William | 2 | 1 | 3 | | | Meker, Chauncy | 1 | 1 | 2 | | | Sanford, Samuel | 3 | 1 | 5 | | |
| Hurd, Abijah | 1 | | | | | McKentin, Duncan | 1 | 1 | 3 | | | Smith, Joel | 1 | 4 | 2 | | |
| Hurd, Hinman | 1 | | 1 | | | Northrop, Joel | 3 | | 4 | | | Sturtevant, John | 2 | 2 | 3 | | |
| Hine, Abel | 5 | 1 | 4 | | | Northrop, David | 3 | 4 | 5 | 2 | | Starr, Josiah | 3 | 2 | 4 | | |
| Hine, Stephen | 1 | 3 | 1 | | | Noble, David | 1 | 1 | 3 | | | Sanford, Liffe | 1 | 1 | 2 | | |
| Hollister, Abel | 5 | 1 | 4 | | | Noble, Daniel | 1 | 2 | 2 | | | Smith, Josiah | 1 | | 4 | | |
| Hatch, Isaac | 2 | 3 | 4 | | | Nichelson, Angus | 4 | 3 | 6 | 3 | | Stone, David | 1 | 1 | 2 | | |
| Hotech, John | 1 | 2 | 2 | | | Noble, Sylvanus | 2 | | 2 | | | Stone, Asahel | 3 | 3 | 2 | | |
| Hill, Samuel, 2d | 2 | 1 | 3 | | | Noble, Wakefield | 1 | | | | | Stone, Benjamin | 2 | 3 | 4 | | |
| Hill, Samuel | 1 | | 2 | | | Noble, Ezra | 3 | 2 | 4 | | | Summers, Samuel | 2 | | 1 | | |
| Hitchcock, Ira | 1 | 1 | 2 | | | Nichols, Isaac | 4 | 3 | 6 | | | Smith, George | 1 | | 1 | | |
| Hawley, Joseph | 1 | 2 | 4 | | | Nichols, Daniel | 1 | 1 | 6 | | | Summers, Andrew | 1 | 4 | 3 | | |
| Higgins, Joseph | 1 | | 3 | | | Norton, Robert | 3 | 1 | 3 | | | Sanford, Nehemiah | 2 | 2 | 4 | | |
| Hornet, John | 1 | 1 | 1 | | | Noble, Elisha | 1 | 3 | 2 | | | Squire, Joseph | 1 | 1 | 3 | | |
| Hendick, Eleazer | 1 | 1 | 3 | | | Noble, Asahel | 1 | | 1 | | | Smith, Eli | 2 | 2 | 4 | | 1 |
| Hurlbutt, David | 1 | | 3 | | | Noble, Sherman | 1 | 2 | 3 | | | Sanford, Nehemiah, 2d | 1 | 2 | 2 | | |
| Hurlbutt, Hezekiah | 1 | 1 | 1 | | | Norton, Rowland | 1 | 2 | 2 | | | Smith, Nathaniel | 1 | 1 | 3 | | |
| Hotchkiss, Solomon | 1 | 1 | 2 | | | Northrop, Caleb | 1 | 2 | 2 | | | Summers, Oliver | 1 | 3 | 1 | | |
| Hurlbutt, Gamaliel | 1 | | | | | Northrop, Solomon | 2 | 1 | 4 | | | Smith, George Clark | 1 | 3 | 4 | | |
| Hymes, Jeames | 1 | | 1 | | | Nichols, Samuel | 1 | | 1 | | | Sturtevant, John, 2d | 4 | 1 | 1 | | |
| Hitchcock, Nathan | 1 | 3 | 3 | | | Nichols, Robert | 1 | 1 | 3 | | | Stone, Benjamin | 1 | 1 | 5 | | |
| Hunt, Theophilus | 1 | 2 | 3 | | | Owen, Daniel | 1 | 1 | 6 | | | Sperry, Jared | 2 | 1 | 4 | | |
| Hitchcock, Aaron | 2 | | 4 | | | Osborn, Stephen | 1 | 4 | 7 | | | Stone, Julius | 2 | 2 | 5 | | |
| Hubbel, Watrous | 2 | | 2 | | | Ovaitt, Thomas | 1 | 2 | 2 | | | Stone, Canfield | 1 | | 2 | | |
| Hitchcock, Daniel | | 2 | 2 | | | Olmstead, Richard | 1 | 1 | 5 | | | Stone, Daniel | 2 | 1 | 2 | | |
| Hallock, Benjamin | 3 | 2 | 3 | | | Olmstead, David | 1 | 1 | 4 | | | Stone, Benajah | 1 | 3 | 3 | | |
| Hill, Solomon, 2d | 1 | 4 | 2 | | | Ovaitt, Samuel | 1 | 1 | 3 | | | Strict, Henry | 1 | | 5 | | |
| Jeasup, Jeames | 1 | 1 | 4 | | | Ovaitt, John | 1 | 1 | 3 | | | Stone, Ithiel | 1 | 2 | 3 | | |
| Jackson, Heny | 2 | 3 | 3 | | | Otis, Christopher | 2 | | 1 | | | Sealy, Benjamin | 1 | 1 | 1 | | 2 |
| Jackson, David | 1 | 2 | 5 | | | Pickett, Daniel | 2 | 1 | 2 | | | Smith, Thomas | 1 | | 3 | | |
| Jackson, Isaac | 1 | | 1 | | | Platt, Ephraim | 1 | 5 | 2 | | | Stilson, John | 2 | | 3 | | |
| Johnson, Isaac | 1 | | | | | Payne, William | 5 | 3 | 6 | | | Sturges, Augustus | 1 | 2 | 2 | | |
| Jacklin, Thaddeus | | | | 2 | | Picket, Abijah | 1 | 3 | 5 | | | Squire, Ebenezer | 1 | 1 | 2 | | |
| Johnson, Peter | 1 | | 5 | | | Platt, Jeremiah | 3 | 1 | 3 | | | Shelley, Abram | 1 | 2 | 2 | | |
| Ingersol, Buggs | 1 | 2 | 3 | | | Prince, Samuel | 1 | 3 | 3 | | | Sanford, Zacheriah, 1st | 3 | 2 | 3 | | |
| Knowles, William, 1st | 1 | | 1 | | | Prince, Edmond Howel | 2 | 2 | 5 | | | Seeley, Joseph | 1 | | 1 | | |
| Keeler, Ralph | 1 | 2 | 3 | | | Prince, Asa | 2 | 1 | 2 | | | Seeley, Abner | 3 | 1 | 2 | | |
| Knap, Joshua | 2 | 2 | 2 | | | Phippany, Jeames | 2 | 1 | 4 | | | Scamehorn, Cornelius | 1 | 1 | 2 | | |
| Knap, Francis | 1 | 3 | 4 | | | Phippany, Archibald | 2 | 2 | 3 | | | Smith, Abraham | 1 | | | | |
| Knowles, Arthur, 1st | 2 | 2 | 3 | | | Platt, Epinetus | 1 | 1 | 4 | | | Sperry, Alexander | 2 | 4 | 3 | | |
| Knowles, William, 2d | 1 | | 5 | | | Platt, Gideon | 1 | 2 | 2 | | | Sanford, Zacheriah, 2d | 1 | 2 | 3 | | |
| Keeney, Elias | 1 | 1 | 5 | | | Peck, Joseph | 2 | | 2 | | | Stone, Trueman | 1 | 1 | 1 | | |
| Keeler, Ebener | 1 | 1 | 2 | | | Platt, Nehemiah | 2 | 1 | 1 | | | Sears, John | 1 | | 2 | | |
| Ketchum, Aaron | 1 | 2 | 4 | | | Prout, Jesse | 1 | 2 | 4 | | | Stewart, Stephen | 1 | 4 | 2 | | |
| Knowles, Arthur, 2d | 1 | | 2 | | | Platt, Epinetus, 2d | 1 | 2 | 3 | | | Tomlinson Jabez | 1 | | 2 | | |
| Lake, Jeames | 1 | | 3 | | | Peet, Elnathan | 1 | | 2 | | | Thomas, Lemuel | 1 | 1 | 3 | | |
| Lyon, Lois | | | 3 | | | Peet, Daniel | 2 | 1 | 2 | | | Territt, John | 1 | 2 | 3 | | |
| Lory, Chauncy | 1 | 1 | 1 | | | Peet, Joseph | 1 | | 1 | | | Todd, Eli | 2 | 1 | 4 | | |
| Lynde, Daniel | 2 | | | | | Peet, Ithiel | 1 | 2 | 2 | | | Territt, Caleb | 3 | | 2 | | |
| Lamson, William, 1st | 1 | | 1 | | | Peet, Samuel | 3 | 1 | 2 | | | Territt, Isaac | 1 | 3 | 3 | | |
| Lamson, William, 2d | 3 | 2 | 4 | | | Peet, George | 1 | 3 | 2 | | | Treat, Gideon | 2 | 5 | 3 | | |
| Lamson, Silas | 1 | 3 | 1 | | | Phippeney, Nehemiah | 1 | 1 | 1 | | | Towner, Benjamin | 1 | | 2 | | |
| Lockwood, Josiah | 2 | 1 | 1 | | | Platt, Truman | 1 | 1 | 2 | | | Treat, John | 2 | 1 | 3 | | |
| Lockwood, Nathaniel | 2 | 2 | 5 | | | Platt, John | 1 | | 3 | | | Trobridge, Ebenezer | 1 | 3 | 3 | | |
| Lockwood, David | 1 | 2 | 2 | | | Phillips, Philip | | | | 2 | | Treat, Abijah | 1 | 2 | 2 | | |
| Lynde, Joseph | 1 | | 1 | | | Phillips, Reuben | | | | 7 | | Taylor, Nathaniel, 1st | 1 | | 2 | | 1 |
| Leach, Jeames | 1 | | 3 | | | Philips, Samuel | | | | 6 | | Taylor, Nathaniel, 2d | 1 | 1 | 2 | | |
| Lockwood, Jeames | 1 | 1 | 3 | | | Philips, Jeruel | | | | 4 | | Taylor, Nathaniel, 3d | 2 | 2 | 2 | 1 | 2 |
| Lockwood, Israel | 1 | 2 | 2 | | | Phenk, Daniel | 1 | 2 | 1 | | | Territt, Oliver | 2 | 2 | 3 | | |
| Lockwood, Nathan | 1 | | 1 | | | Peet, Lemuel | 2 | 2 | 5 | | | Tucker, Uriah | 3 | 1 | 4 | | |
| Lowly, Volentine | 2 | | | | | Porter, Nathaniel | 1 | | 4 | | | Taylor, William | 1 | 2 | 2 | | |
| Lamson, Sarah | | | 2 | | | Porter, Philo | 1 | 1 | 2 | | | Treadwell, Agur | 1 | | 4 | | |
| Morehouse, Stephen | 1 | 2 | 3 | | | Palmer, Polly | | | 1 | | | Territt, Joel | 1 | | 3 | | |
| Miles, Justus | 4 | | 1 | | | Peet, Nathan | 1 | 3 | 4 | | | Taylor, Daniel | 3 | 1 | 5 | | |
| Morehouse, John, 1st | 3 | 1 | 3 | | | Peet, Thaddeus | 3 | 2 | 5 | | | Taylor, Abram | 1 | | 2 | | |
| Miles, Stephen, 2d | 3 | 3 | 4 | | | Payne, Ezekiel | 2 | 1 | 1 | | | Territt, Jeames, 2d | 1 | 3 | 3 | | |
| Mygatt, Ben Star | 3 | 1 | 3 | | | Rundle, Jeremiah | 1 | | 4 | | | Territt, Jared | 1 | | 2 | | |
| McMehan, Cornelius | 1 | 3 | 4 | | | Richmond, Ephraim | 2 | 2 | 5 | | | Taylor, Eli | 2 | 1 | 6 | | |
| Marsh, John | 3 | 4 | 4 | | | Richmond, Jonathan | 1 | 3 | 5 | | | Territt, Jeames | 1 | 1 | 1 | | |
| Merwin, Abel | 2 | 2 | 2 | | | Richmond, Edmond | 1 | 3 | 1 | | | Territt, Joab | 2 | | 4 | | |
| Mead, Samuel | 1 | 3 | 4 | | | Read, Jacob | 1 | 2 | 5 | | | Thacher, Jacob | | | | 9 | |
| Morehouse, Lemuel | 1 | | | | | Ruggles, Joseph | 1 | 2 | 2 | | | Territt, Enoch | 1 | 1 | 2 | | |
| Morehouse, Stephen, 1st | 1 | 2 | 2 | | | Read, Jonathan Hanson | 1 | 1 | 4 | | | Treadwell, Hezekiah | 1 | 4 | 3 | | |
| Mygatt, Noah | 2 | 3 | 1 | | | Read, Asa | 1 | 1 | 3 | | | Territt, Nathan | 1 | 3 | 6 | | |
| Merwin, David, 2d | 2 | 2 | 2 | | | Robberts, Abraham | 2 | 2 | 2 | | | Territt, Caleb, 2d | 1 | 2 | 5 | | |
| Marsh, Samuel | 1 | 5 | 3 | | | Robberts, John | 3 | | 3 | | | Trobridge, Daniel | 1 | | 2 | | |
| Marsh, Joseph | 1 | 2 | 5 | | | Ruggles, Artemas | 1 | | 1 | | | Titus, Noah | 1 | 2 | 5 | | |
| Millan, Jeames | 1 | | 2 | | | Rowe, Thomas | 1 | 2 | 2 | | | Thair, Lemuel | 1 | 2 | 5 | | |
| Merwin, John | 2 | 2 | 5 | | | Ruggles, Isaac Mathew | 1 | 3 | 1 | | | Territt, Stephen | 2 | 5 | 4 | | |
| Merwin, David, 1st | 3 | 2 | 3 | | | Ruggles, Lad | 5 | 1 | 3 | | | Tillotson, Thomas | 1 | 1 | 2 | | |
| Merwin, Stephen | 1 | 2 | 4 | | | Smith, John, 1st | 2 | | 2 | | | Videto, Jeames | 4 | 1 | 2 | | |

# HEADS OF FAMILIES—CONNECTICUT.

## LITCHFIELD COUNTY—Continued.

| NAME OF HEAD OF FAMILY. | Free white males of 16 years and upward, including heads of families. | Free white males under 16 years. | Free white females, including heads of families. | All other free persons. | Slaves. |
|---|---|---|---|---|---|
| **NEW MILFORD TOWN—continued.** | | | | | |
| Vaughn, Philander | 1 | 1 | 2 | | |
| Whiteley, William | 1 | 4 | 2 | | |
| Wilkeson, Peter | 7 | | 3 | | |
| Wheeler, Dobson | 1 | | 1 | | |
| Wildman, Mathew, 2d | 1 | 1 | 6 | | |
| Wilkeson, Augustine | 1 | 1 | 1 | | |
| Woster, Peter | 1 | 1 | 1 | | |
| Wooster, Isaac | 1 | | 2 | | |
| Wilton, George | 2 | | 1 | | |
| Wooster, Jabez | 1 | | 1 | | |
| Warner, Reuben | 3 | 1 | 5 | | |
| Weller, Abel | 2 | 2 | 7 | | |
| Wilkerson, John | 2 | | 1 | | |
| Weeks, Samuel | 1 | 2 | 3 | | |
| Warner, Reuben, 2d | 1 | 4 | 4 | | |
| Warner, Lemuel | 1 | 1 | 1 | | |
| Warner, Asa | 2 | 1 | 7 | | |
| Wildman, Josiah | 2 | 1 | 4 | | |
| Warner, Elizuer | 3 | | 3 | | |
| Warner, John | 1 | 1 | 6 | | |
| Warner, John, 2d | 1 | 1 | 2 | | |
| Warner, Oliver | 2 | 1 | | | |
| Wildman, Matthew | 1 | | 3 | | |
| Winton, Abiel | 1 | 2 | 1 | | |
| Wells, Thomas | 3 | 2 | 5 | | |
| Wheaton, Esack | 1 | 4 | 3 | | |
| Wildman, Joseph | 2 | | 1 | | |
| Wadhams, Ingersol | 1 | 1 | 2 | | |
| Wadhams, Noah | 2 | | 1 | | |
| Wiggins, Arthur | 1 | 1 | 4 | | |
| West, Samuel | 1 | | 5 | | |
| Williams, Jabez | 1 | 3 | 3 | | |
| Welch, Paul, 1st | 4 | 1 | 2 | | |
| Welch, Paul, 2d | 1 | 3 | 4 | | |
| Williams, Ezra | 1 | | 3 | | |
| Wheeler, Jedediah | 1 | 1 | 1 | | |
| Wooster, Sylvester | 1 | 1 | 2 | | |
| Wilkeson, Abel | 1 | | 2 | | |
| Wilkeson, David | 2 | 1 | 6 | | |
| Warner, Elijah | 1 | 6 | 2 | | |
| Waller, Joseph | 3 | 1 | 1 | | |
| Warner, Orange | 5 | | 3 | | |
| **SOUTHBURY TOWN.** | | | | | |
| Allen, Edward | 1 | | 2 | | 3 |
| Allen, Gideon, 1st | 1 | 1 | 2 | | |
| Allen, Gideon, 2d | 1 | | 3 | | |
| Allen, David | 1 | | 3 | | |
| Allen, Jonah | 1 | 2 | 1 | | |
| Bateman, Stephen | 2 | | 6 | | |
| Brownson, Ebenezer | 1 | | 2 | | |
| Brownson, Ebenezer, 2d | 1 | 2 | 4 | | |
| Benham, Japhet | 2 | | 2 | | |
| Bulford, John | 1 | 2 | 3 | | |
| Brownson, Noah | 2 | 1 | 3 | | |
| Buritt, Anthony | 1 | 1 | 6 | | |
| Brownson, Elijah | 5 | 3 | 5 | | |
| Bates, Elias | 1 | | 2 | | |
| Bristol, Gad | 3 | 2 | 5 | | |
| Bristol, Gad, 2d | 1 | 1 | 1 | | |
| Bown, Park | 1 | 1 | 3 | | |
| Brownson, Abram | 4 | | 3 | | |
| Burr, William | 2 | 1 | 2 | | |
| Bristol, Thomas | 1 | | | | |
| Brises, Isaac | 2 | 2 | 3 | | |
| Bristol, P. Brigs | 1 | | | | |
| Bristol, Eliphlet | 1 | | 1 | | |
| Bristol, Justus | 3 | 2 | 5 | | |
| Bristol, Truman | 1 | | 1 | | |
| Burritt, Oliver | 2 | 2 | 3 | | |
| Barnes, Phineas | 2 | 1 | 4 | | |
| Booth, Smith | 1 | 2 | 5 | | |
| Baldwin, Joseph | 2 | 4 | 2 | | |
| Botsford, Samuel | 1 | | 4 | | |
| Blackman, Lemuel | 1 | 2 | 3 | | |
| Baldwin, Elijah | 1 | 2 | 3 | | |
| Bates, Eliakim | 1 | 2 | 1 | | |
| Birchard, Elijah | 1 | | 3 | | |
| Barlow, Dosin | | 2 | 2 | | |
| Brown, Thomas | 1 | | 2 | | |
| Bates, Josiah | 4 | 3 | 2 | | |
| Beebe, Asahel | 1 | | 1 | | |
| Bassett, Daniel | 2 | 3 | 6 | | |
| Bagley, Agnes | | 1 | 4 | | |
| Baldwin, Jerusha | 1 | | 3 | | |
| Brown, John | 2 | 2 | 2 | | |
| Booth, Elijah | 5 | 3 | 5 | | |
| Curtis, Israel, 1st | 1 | | 1 | | |
| Curtis, Israel, 2d | 2 | 1 | 6 | | |
| Curtis, Joseph | 2 | 1 | 3 | | |
| Curtis, Reuben | 2 | | 3 | | |
| Curtis, Benjamin | 1 | 3 | 2 | | |
| Curtis, Nathan | 3 | 1 | 4 | | |
| Curtis, Sarah | | | 1 | | |
| **SOUTHBURY TOWN—continued.** | | | | | |
| Curtis, Abijah | 1 | 3 | 4 | | |
| Curtis, Daniel | 1 | 1 | 1 | | |
| Curtis, Wait | 1 | 1 | 1 | | |
| Coe, Amos | 1 | 1 | 2 | | |
| Coe, Andrew, 2d | 1 | 2 | 3 | | |
| Cande, Samuel | 2 | 5 | 3 | | |
| Cande, Esther | 1 | | 2 | | |
| Cande, Timothy | 2 | 1 | 2 | | |
| Cande, David | 1 | 2 | 6 | | |
| Clark, Nathel C | 2 | 2 | 5 | | |
| Coggwell, Asa | 1 | 1 | 1 | | 5 |
| Curtis, Samuel | 2 | | 2 | 1 | |
| Coe, David | 1 | 3 | 5 | | |
| Chison, John | 1 | | 5 | | |
| Chatfield, Oliver | 3 | 1 | 4 | | |
| Coe, Andrew | 3 | 1 | 1 | | |
| Cumming, Simeon | | | | | |
| Drakeley, Samuel | 2 | 3 | 7 | | |
| Demmon, Isaac | 1 | | | | |
| Dudley, George | 2 | | 2 | | |
| Daniels, Samuel | 2 | 1 | 4 | | |
| Downes, Aaron | 2 | | 2 | | |
| Downes, Nathan | 2 | 1 | 2 | | |
| Downes, Benjamin | 3 | | 4 | | |
| Downes, Ebenezer | 1 | 1 | 4 | | |
| Downes, Moses | 2 | 1 | 2 | | |
| Downes, Truman | 1 | 2 | 4 | | |
| Downes, Wildman | 1 | 1 | 1 | | |
| Dawton, John | 1 | 2 | 5 | | |
| Edmond, John | 2 | 2 | 3 | | |
| Edmond, Jeames | 2 | 2 | 2 | | |
| Fairchild, Curtis | 2 | 3 | 2 | | |
| French, William | 4 | 1 | 2 | | |
| Fabrique, Bartemus | 4 | | 2 | | |
| Fabrique, David | 3 | 1 | 2 | | |
| Fairchild, Abijah | 1 | 1 | 3 | | |
| Glasier, Jacob | 1 | | 2 | | |
| Graham, Curtis | 2 | | 2 | | |
| Garrett, John | 1 | 2 | 4 | | |
| Garrett, Wait | 2 | 2 | 2 | | |
| Garrett, Frances | 1 | | 2 | | |
| Guthrie, Ebenezer | 4 | | 2 | | |
| Gibbs, Moor | 2 | 1 | 3 | | |
| Griswold, John | 1 | 1 | 3 | | |
| Galloway, Peter | | | | 2 | |
| Goss, Richard | 1 | 3 | 1 | | |
| Hinman, Truman | 4 | 1 | 4 | | 1 |
| Hinman, Eleazer | 1 | 3 | 2 | | |
| Hinman, Sherman | 4 | 1 | 6 | | |
| Hinman, John | 1 | 1 | 2 | | 1 |
| Hinman, Justus | 2 | | 2 | | |
| Hinman, Timothy | 1 | 2 | 2 | | 1 |
| Hinman, David | 2 | 2 | 1 | | |
| Hinman, Edward | 3 | | 3 | | 6 |
| Hinman, Lewis | 1 | | 1 | | |
| Hinman, Jonas | 1 | 1 | 4 | | |
| Hinman, Jonas, 2d | 1 | | 2 | | |
| Hinman, Silas | 1 | | 3 | | |
| Hinman, Abner | 1 | | | | |
| Hinman, Agus | 1 | 2 | 2 | | |
| Hinman, Joel | 1 | 3 | 5 | | |
| Hinman, Aaron | 1 | 3 | 4 | | |
| Hinman, Benjamin | 2 | | 1 | | |
| Hinman, Samuel | 1 | | 2 | | |
| Hinman, Francis | 1 | | 3 | | |
| Hinman, Titus | 1 | 1 | 2 | | |
| Hinman, Jonathan | 1 | 2 | 2 | | |
| Hinman, Wait | 2 | 1 | 2 | | |
| Hinman, Lemuel | 1 | 1 | 6 | | |
| Hinman, Daniel | 2 | 2 | 3 | | |
| Hinman, Adam | 2 | | 2 | | |
| Haun, Michael | 1 | | 3 | | |
| Hurd, Andrew | 1 | | 5 | | |
| Hurd, William | 3 | 2 | 3 | | |
| Hine, Elisha | 1 | 4 | 2 | | |
| Hicock, Amos | 3 | 1 | 2 | | 1 |
| Hicock, Benjamin | 3 | 4 | 5 | | |
| Hicock, Asa | 1 | 2 | 4 | | |
| Hicock, Justus | 1 | | 1 | | |
| Hawley, Richard | 3 | 1 | 3 | | |
| Hicock, Ithiel | 3 | | 2 | | |
| Hicock, Joseph | 1 | | 2 | | |
| Hicock, Joseph, 2d | 1 | 4 | 2 | | |
| Hymes, John | 1 | 1 | 2 | | |
| Hendrick, Zadock | 1 | 1 | 5 | | |
| Hendrick, Daniel | 1 | 1 | 2 | | |
| Hughs, William | 1 | | 2 | | |
| Heaton, Elizabeth | | | 1 | | |
| Hazen, Samuel | 1 | 4 | 3 | | |
| Holbrock, Joseph | 1 | 2 | 2 | | |
| Hicock, Silas | 2 | 4 | 3 | | |
| Jhonson, Asa | 3 | | 2 | | |
| Johnson, David | 3 | 1 | 2 | | |
| Johnson, Hyram | 1 | | 2 | | |
| Johnson, Solomon, 1st | 1 | 4 | 1 | | |
| **SOUTHBURY TOWN—continued.** | | | | | |
| Johnson, Solomon, 2d | 1 | 2 | 2 | | |
| Johnson, Timothy | 1 | 1 | 1 | | |
| Johnson, Gideon | 2 | | 3 | | |
| Johnson, Jeremiah | 1 | 2 | 5 | | |
| Johnson, Amos | 2 | 2 | 4 | | |
| Johnson, John, 1st | 1 | | 2 | | |
| Johnson, John, 2d | 1 | | 4 | | |
| Johnson, Justus | 1 | 3 | 4 | | |
| Johnson, Jehu | 1 | 3 | 4 | | |
| Jennings, Reuben | 2 | | | | |
| King, Elizabeth | | | 2 | | |
| Knap, Ebenr Kason | 2 | 1 | 1 | | |
| Kimberly, Adam | 1 | 2 | 6 | | |
| Kimberly, Thomas | 1 | | 1 | | |
| Lewis, Swignion | 1 | 1 | 3 | | |
| Lynes, Abram | 1 | 1 | 2 | | |
| Lewis, Nehemiah | 2 | 3 | 3 | | |
| Lewis, Beach | 1 | 3 | 1 | | |
| Lum, Henry | 2 | | 3 | | |
| Lumm, Adam | 3 | 4 | 5 | | |
| Leavenworth, Gideon | 5 | 1 | 2 | | |
| Leavenworth, John | 1 | 1 | 3 | | |
| Little, William | 2 | | 1 | | |
| Mitchel, Mathew | 2 | 3 | 1 | | |
| Mitchel, Simeon, 1st | 1 | | 3 | | 1 |
| Mitchel, David | 1 | 5 | 2 | | |
| Mitchel, Jonathan | 1 | 1 | 3 | | |
| Mitchel, Eleazer | 3 | 1 | 3 | | |
| Mitchel, Warren | 2 | 1 | 2 | | |
| Mitchel, Simeon, 2d | 2 | 1 | 5 | | |
| Moseley, Ineross | 2 | 1 | 3 | | |
| Munn, Jedediah, 2d | 1 | 1 | 3 | | |
| Munn, Jedediah 1st | 3 | | 5 | | |
| Mumn, Samuel | 1 | 2 | 5 | | |
| Mumm, David | 1 | 3 | 3 | | |
| Mallery, David | 1 | 2 | 4 | | |
| Mallett, Miles | 1 | 1 | 2 | | |
| Mallery, John | 3 | 1 | 6 | | |
| Mogg, Christian | 1 | 1 | 2 | | |
| Miner, Jehu | 1 | 1 | 5 | | |
| Munn, Asa | 1 | 1 | 3 | | |
| Osborn, Timothy | 2 | 1 | 2 | | |
| Osborn, Shadick | 1 | 2 | 5 | | |
| Osborn, Barnum | 1 | 1 | 2 | | |
| Osborn, Josiah | 1 | 2 | 5 | | |
| Penich, Samuel | 1 | 1 | 1 | | |
| Pierce, Joseph, 1st | 2 | 2 | 2 | | |
| Pierce, Joseph, 2d | 2 | 2 | 3 | | |
| Pierce, Abram | 2 | 2 | 4 | | |
| Pierce, Titus | 3 | 2 | 6 | | |
| Pierce, Nathan | 5 | 3 | 2 | | |
| Pierce, Justus | 3 | 3 | 4 | | |
| Pierce, Eunice | | | 2 | | |
| Pierce, Elijah | 2 | | 3 | | |
| Pierce, Joel | 3 | 3 | 3 | | |
| Peck, Elisha | 2 | | 1 | | |
| Peck, Zalmon | | 2 | 2 | | |
| Perkins, Elijah | 1 | 3 | 2 | | |
| Peck, Abijah | 1 | | | | |
| Page, Josiah | 1 | 3 | 2 | | |
| Post, Joseph | 1 | | 3 | | |
| Penich, David | 1 | 1 | 2 | | |
| Porter, Gideon | 1 | | 2 | | |
| Platt, William | 1 | | 2 | | |
| Platt, John | 1 | 2 | 2 | | |
| Platt, Stephen | 2 | 2 | 4 | | |
| Philips, Dolphin | | | | 4 | |
| Perry, Josiah | 1 | 5 | 6 | | |
| Perry, Lucana | | | 3 | | |
| Parks, John | 2 | | 2 | | |
| Peet, Stephen | 2 | 1 | 4 | | |
| Pardee, Eliphlet | 1 | 1 | 5 | | |
| Peet, Johiel | 1 | | | | |
| Russel, Benjamin | | | 2 | | |
| Raynold, Solomon | 1 | 1 | 3 | | |
| Richard, Truman | 2 | 3 | 2 | | |
| Rigbey, William | 1 | 2 | 4 | | |
| Starr, Robbin | | | | 2 | |
| Smith, Samuel | 1 | 1 | 2 | | |
| Smith, Elizabeth | | | 1 | | |
| Spring, Samuel | 1 | 1 | 1 | | |
| Stiles, Benjamin, 2d | 1 | | 2 | | |
| Stiles, Samuel | 2 | | | | |
| Stiles, Truman | 1 | | | | |
| Stiles, Benjamin | 3 | 1 | 3 | | |
| Stiles, David | 2 | 1 | 3 | | |
| Stiles, Nathan | 1 | 2 | 3 | | |
| Stiles, Ephraim | 3 | 1 | 5 | | |
| Stiles, Isaac | 1 | | 1 | | |
| Sanford, Joseph | 2 | 1 | 2 | | |
| Sanford, Nathaniel | 1 | 2 | 3 | | |
| Strong, Ebenezer | 3 | | 2 | | |
| Strong, Benjamin | 1 | 2 | 8 | | |
| Strong, Silah | 3 | 1 | 4 | | |
| Strong, Return | 1 | | 2 | | |

## LITCHFIELD COUNTY—Continued.

| NAME OF HEAD OF FAMILY. | Free white males of 16 years and upward, including heads of families. | Free white males under 16 years. | Free white females, including heads of families. | All other free persons. | Slaves. | NAME OF HEAD OF FAMILY. | Free white males of 16 years and upward, including heads of families. | Free white males under 16 years. | Free white females, including heads of families. | All other free persons. | Slaves. | NAME OF HEAD OF FAMILY. | Free white males of 16 years and upward, including heads of families. | Free white males under 16 years. | Free white females, including heads of families. | All other free persons. | Slaves. |
|---|---|---|---|---|---|---|---|---|---|---|---|---|---|---|---|---|---|
| **SOUTHBURY TOWN—continued.** | | | | | | **WARREN TOWN—con.** | | | | | | **WARREN TOWN—con.** | | | | | |
| Strong, Adino | 1 | 2 | 4 | | | Comstock, Martin Luther | 1 | 4 | 2 | | | Starr, Platt | 1 | 2 | 3 | | |
| Strong, Charles | 1 | | 4 | | | Carter, Joseph | 2 | 1 | 2 | | | Swift, Nathaniel, 2 | 2 | 1 | 8 | | |
| Strong, Elnathan | 4 | | 3 | | | Carter, Joseph, 2d | 1 | 3 | 3 | | | Spooner, John | 2 | 2 | 2 | | |
| Smith, Daniel | 1 | | 2 | | | Carter, Solomon | 1 | 2 | 2 | | | Spooner, William, 2d | 1 | 2 | 4 | | |
| Smith, Ebenezer | 4 | 1 | 3 | | | Carter, Samuel | 3 | 2 | 2 | | | Swan, Isaac | 3 | 2 | 5 | | |
| Smith, Elijah | 2 | 1 | 4 | | | Carter, Samuel, 2d | 1 | 2 | 2 | | | Swan, Amos | 3 | 2 | 3 | | |
| Stone, Mansfield | 2 | | 2 | | | Carter, Benjamin | 1 | 2 | 1 | | | Saunders, Benjamin | 2 | 1 | 4 | | |
| Stone, John | 2 | 2 | 2 | | | Carter, Adonijah | 1 | 3 | 3 | | | Spooner, Nathaniel | 1 | 1 | 1 | | |
| Summers, Jonah | 4 | | 6 | | | Carter, Bennoni | 1 | 5 | 2 | | 1 | Swift, Jabez | 1 | | 3 | | |
| Stoddard, Truman | 1 | 1 | 2 | | | Carter, Bradock | 1 | 3 | 1 | | | Stone, Willim | 1 | | 2 | | |
| Squire, Joseph | 1 | | 2 | | | Carter, Jirah | 1 | 2 | 2 | | | Spooner, William | 1 | | 2 | | |
| Squire, John, 2d | 1 | 2 | 1 | | | Carter, Berzilla | 1 | 1 | 1 | | | Starr, Peter | 2 | 4 | 4 | | |
| Squire, David | 4 | 2 | 7 | | | Cartis, Eleazer | 1 | 3 | 2 | | | Taylor, David | 1 | 5 | 4 | | |
| Squire, Stephen | 2 | 1 | 6 | | | Cartis, Augustine | 1 | 2 | 2 | | | Talmage, John | 2 | | 4 | | 1 |
| Sherman, Daniel | 1 | 2 | 4 | | | Curtis, Lysander | 1 | | | | | Tanner, Ephraim | 2 | 2 | 5 | | |
| Stanlif, Jeames | 1 | 2 | 3 | | | Curtis, Silas | 1 | | 7 | | | Taylor, Elias | 1 | 2 | 4 | | |
| Seward, Samuel | 2 | | 3 | | | Curtis, Milton | 1 | 1 | 1 | | | Taylor, Joseph, 2d | 2 | 2 | 4 | | |
| Seward, Solomon | 2 | 1 | 1 | | | Dunning, Benjamin | 3 | 1 | 8 | | | Tanner, Ebenezer | 2 | 1 | 2 | | |
| Skeels, John | 1 | 1 | | | | Eldred, Ward | 1 | | 1 | | 1 | Thomson, George | 1 | 1 | 3 | | |
| Stoddard, Cyreamus | 3 | | 2 | | | Eldred, Judah | 1 | 2 | 2 | | | Thomas, John | 1 | 1 | 5 | | |
| Skeels, Ephraim | 1 | | 3 | | | Eldred, Elisha | 1 | 2 | 2 | | | Webb, Josiah | 1 | 1 | 1 | | |
| Skeels, Ephraim, 2d | 1 | 5 | 3 | | | Eldred, Samuel | 1 | | 2 | | 1 | Whitlock, Samuel | 1 | | 5 | | |
| Squire, Daniel | 1 | 1 | 2 | | | Eldred, Jehoshaphet | 4 | | 2 | | | Whitlock, Joel | 1 | 1 | 5 | | |
| Smith, Zepheniah | 1 | 1 | 5 | | | Finny, John | 1 | 1 | 1 | | | Wedge, Isaac | 1 | 3 | 4 | | |
| Sperry, Ambrose | 1 | 4 | 3 | | | Finny, John, 2d | 1 | 2 | 2 | | | Wedge, Stephen | 1 | 1 | 2 | | |
| Stilson, George | 2 | | 2 | | | Finney, Jonah | 1 | 2 | 4 | | | Wedge, Asahel | 2 | 1 | 3 | | |
| Sperry, Alexander | 2 | 4 | 4 | | | Finney, Sylvester | 1 | | 6 | | | Woston, John | 1 | 1 | 1 | | |
| Sharp, Joab | | | | 5 | | Foster, Joseph | 2 | 1 | 3 | | | Wicks, Zadock | | | | 1 | |
| Tuttle, Nathaniel | 1 | 2 | 3 | | | Fuller, Amos | 1 | | 1 | | | Whitney, Joseph | 1 | 1 | 2 | | |
| Thomson, Esther | 3 | 1 | 6 | | 2 | Fuller, Abel, 1st | 1 | 2 | 2 | | | Weston, Samuel | 1 | 1 | 3 | | |
| Towner, Joseph | 1 | | 2 | | | Fuller, Abel, 2d | 1 | 2 | 1 | | | | | | | | |
| Towner, Joseph, 2d | 1 | 1 | 6 | | | Fuller, Adijah | 1 | | 2 | | | **WASHINGTON TOWN.** | | | | | |
| Towner, John | 2 | | 3 | | | Fuller, Asahel | 1 | 1 | 3 | | | Ackley, Hezekiah | 2 | 2 | 3 | | |
| Tuttle, Noah | 1 | 1 | 1 | | | Fuller, Daniel | 2 | 3 | 3 | | | Addams, Benjamin | 2 | 2 | 5 | | |
| Tuttle, Newton | 1 | 1 | 2 | | | Fuller, Howard | 3 | | 3 | | | Armstrong, Thomas | 3 | 3 | 4 | | |
| Treat, Bethuel | 4 | 1 | 8 | | | Gilbert, Ezra | 2 | 1 | 2 | | | Armstrong, Jeames | 2 | 2 | 1 | | |
| Ward, Macork | 3 | 4 | 2 | | | Gilbert, Truman | 1 | 4 | 2 | | | Averill, Samuel | 2 | | 1 | | |
| Ward, Bethuel | 2 | | 7 | | | Gilbert, Jabez | 1 | | | | | Averill, Percy | 2 | 4 | 5 | | |
| Wheeler, Obediah, 1st | 1 | 1 | 2 | | | Hitchcock, Jonathan | 1 | | 2 | | | Allen, Cornelius | 2 | | 1 | | |
| Wood, Joseph | 1 | | 3 | | | Hubbel, Ephiaim | 2 | 1 | 1 | | | Brown, John | 1 | 2 | 7 | | |
| Wheeler, John | 2 | 1 | 4 | | | Heart, Amasa | 1 | 5 | 4 | | | Baker, Ephraim | 2 | 5 | 7 | | |
| Wheeler, Zophas | 1 | | | | | Hawes, Samuel | 1 | 2 | 3 | | | Baker, Jesse | 2 | 1 | 4 | | |
| Wooster, Sylvester | 2 | 1 | 4 | | | Hopkins, Prince | 4 | 1 | 6 | | | Baker, Samuel | 1 | 4 | 1 | | |
| Wheeler, Amos | 1 | | | | | Hopkins, Nathan | 1 | | 1 | | | Baldwin, Enos | 2 | | 4 | | |
| Waggoner, Adam | 1 | | 2 | | | Holmes, Peleg | 1 | | 3 | | | Baldwin, Enos, 2d | 2 | 2 | 3 | | |
| Waggoner, David | 1 | 1 | 1 | | | Holmes, Israel | 1 | | 1 | | | Baldwin, Judah | 3 | 1 | 2 | | |
| White, Samuel | 1 | 1 | 4 | | | Holmes, Gershom | 1 | 1 | 3 | | | Baldwin, Asahel | 1 | 2 | 5 | | |
| Wheeler, Jesse | 2 | | 3 | | | Hopkins, Thomas | 1 | | | | | Baldwin, George | 2 | | 4 | | |
| Wheeler, Aden | 2 | 3 | 6 | | | Hopkins, Elijah | 2 | 1 | 8 | | | Baldwin, John | 1 | | 4 | | |
| Wheeler, Asa, 1st | 1 | 1 | 5 | | | Hopkins, Benjamin | 1 | 1 | 1 | | | Barnes, Elijah | 1 | 4 | 2 | | |
| Wheeler, Obediah, 2d | 2 | | 4 | | | Hoyt, Stephen | 2 | | 2 | | | Barnes, Asa | 2 | 2 | 3 | | |
| Wheeler, Joab | 1 | | 2 | | | Hawes, Isaac | 2 | 6 | 2 | | | Barnes, Eber | 1 | 1 | 2 | | |
| Wheeler, Ebenezer | 1 | 2 | 2 | | | Hurlburt, Solmon | 1 | | 4 | | | Barnes, Samuel | 1 | 2 | 1 | | |
| Wheeler, Agur | 1 | 4 | 4 | | | Hopkins, Joseph | 1 | 1 | 6 | | | Barnes, Daniel | 1 | 2 | 1 | | |
| Wheeler, Asa, 2d | 1 | 1 | 1 | | | Isles, Joshua | 1 | 1 | 5 | | | Beadsley, Wells | 1 | 3 | 3 | | |
| Wheeler, Johnson | 2 | 1 | 2 | | | Judd, Obediah | 1 | 2 | 2 | | | Brinsmade, Daniel | 3 | 1 | 6 | | |
| Wildman, David | 2 | 1 | 2 | | | Judd, Nathaniel | 1 | 1 | 2 | | | Brinsmade, Daniel N | 2 | | 1 | | |
| Wildman, Benjamin | 1 | 2 | 3 | | | Johnson, Nathaniel | 1 | 4 | 1 | | | Bosworth, Nathaniel | 1 | | 2 | | 1 |
| Ward, Zenas, 1st | 2 | 1 | 3 | | | Kent, Darius | 2 | | 4 | | | Bosworth, Nathaniel, 2d | 3 | 5 | 4 | | |
| Ward, Zenas, 2d | 1 | | 2 | | | London, William | 2 | | 2 | | | Burges, Jeames | 3 | 4 | 5 | | |
| Wilmot, Jonah | 2 | | 2 | | | Lord, John | 1 | 3 | 1 | | | Burges, Ebenezer | 1 | 3 | 3 | | |
| Warner, Noadiah | 2 | 2 | 3 | | | Lyon, Nathaniel | 1 | | 1 | | | Bears, Ebenezer | 1 | 1 | 1 | | |
| Wilmot, Alexander | 1 | 1 | 3 | | | Morris, Samuel | 1 | 2 | 3 | | | Bears, Philo | 1 | 2 | 3 | | |
| Wooden, Philo | 1 | 1 | 4 | | | Morris, Marget | | | 3 | | | Bears, Abel | 1 | | 3 | | |
| Wooden, Millow | 1 | | | | | Niel, Titus | 1 | 3 | 1 | | | Bears, Mathew | 1 | | 3 | | |
| Warner, Seth | | 2 | 2 | | | Newcomb, William | 1 | | 2 | | | Bryan, Richard | 3 | 3 | 4 | | |
| Williams | 1 | 2 | 1 | | | Palmer, Nathaniel | 2 | 2 | 3 | | | Byan, Samuel | 1 | 4 | 3 | | |
| Wolf, Christian | 1 | 2 | 3 | | | Palmer, Ezekiah | 3 | 2 | 2 | | | Byan, Zacheriah | 1 | 2 | 3 | | |
| | | | | | | Phelps, Truman | 1 | 1 | 2 | | | Bunce, Isaih | 1 | | 5 | | |
| **WARREN TOWN.** | | | | | | Phelps, David | 1 | 1 | 4 | | | Brown, Nathaniel | 1 | 4 | 5 | | |
| Andrews, Joseph | 2 | 3 | 2 | | | Palmer, Elijah | 2 | | 2 | | | Bosworth, Jeames Wood | 2 | 2 | 4 | | |
| Alger, Mathew | 1 | 1 | 2 | | | Patterson, John | 1 | | 2 | | | Beach, Benjamin | 3 | 2 | 2 | | |
| Alger, Nathan | 1 | | 2 | | | Peck, Phineas | 1 | 2 | 4 | | | Betts, Nehemiah | 1 | | 4 | | |
| Beamont, Timothy | 1 | 3 | 2 | | | Peters, Joseph | 2 | 1 | 5 | | | Blackman, N. Cady | 2 | | 7 | | |
| Beamont, Truman | 1 | 3 | 2 | | | Palmer, Ebenezer | 2 | | 1 | | | Brainard, Hen'y | 1 | 4 | 4 | | |
| Beamont, Park | 1 | 1 | 2 | | | Peet, Thaddeus | 1 | | 1 | | | Bulkley, Calvin | 1 | | 2 | | |
| Barnes, John, 1st | 1 | | 1 | | | Paush, Daniel | 1 | 2 | 3 | | | Camp, Jonah | 2 | 1 | 3 | | |
| Barnes, John, 2d | 1 | 3 | 1 | | | Pendal, Mary | | 2 | 3 | | | Camp, Isaac | 1 | 3 | 3 | | |
| Bliss, Sylvanus | 1 | | 1 | | | Roots, Isaac | 1 | 3 | 5 | | | Camp, Gideon | 1 | 6 | 5 | | |
| Bliss, Nezias | 1 | 1 | 2 | | | Sturtevant, Pelg | 1 | 3 | 5 | | | Camp, Chauncy | 2 | | 6 | | |
| Brownson, Asahel | 2 | | 3 | | | Strong, Eber | 1 | | 2 | | | Camp, Daniel | 2 | 1 | 1 | | |
| Brownson, John | 1 | 1 | 3 | | 2 | Strong, Philip | 1 | | 2 | | | Calhoun, Joseph | 1 | 1 | 2 | | |
| Beach, Reuben | 2 | 2 | 2 | | | Strong, Amasa | 3 | 3 | 1 | | | Calhoun, Jeames | 3 | 4 | 5 | | |
| Bery, Cyrus | 1 | 2 | 3 | | | Strong, Caverly | 1 | | | | | Calhoun, David | 1 | 2 | 2 | | |
| Bamont, Thomas | 3 | | 3 | | | Swetland, Lewis | 1 | 3 | 2 | | | Calhoun, Ebenezer | 1 | 2 | 5 | | |
| Beamont, Matthias | 1 | 1 | | | | Sacket, Alexander | 3 | 1 | 2 | | | Calhoun, George | 1 | 3 | 5 | | |
| Beamont, Daniel | 1 | | 5 | | | Sacket, Salmon | 1 | 1 | 1 | | | Calhoun, Tabitha | 1 | 3 | 2 | | |
| Beamont, Abel | 2 | 3 | 4 | | | Sacket, Reuben | 1 | 1 | 3 | | | Clark, Joseph | 3 | 2 | 5 | | |
| Beamont, Nathan | 1 | 1 | 2 | | | Sacket, Benjamin | 1 | 3 | 3 | | | Clark, Samuel | 2 | 4 | 5 | | |
| Barnes, Jasper | 1 | | 1 | | | Sackett, Justus | 3 | | 3 | | | Clark, Samuel, 2d | 1 | 1 | 2 | | |
| Beardsley, Jeames | 2 | | | | | Spooner, Ebenezer | 1 | 1 | 2 | | | Clark, William | 1 | 3 | 5 | | |
| Beamont, Ceasor | | | | 4 | | Smith, Peabody | 1 | 3 | 2 | | | | | | | | |
| Comstock, Abel | 2 | 2 | 2 | | | Stone, William, 2d | 1 | 1 | 1 | | | | | | | | |

## HEADS OF FAMILIES—CONNECTICUT.

### LITCHFIELD COUNTY—Continued.

| NAME OF HEAD OF FAMILY. | Free white males of 16 years and upward, including heads of families. | Free white males under 16 years. | Free white females, including heads of families. | All other free persons. | Slaves. | NAME OF HEAD OF FAMILY. | Free white males of 16 years and upward, including heads of families. | Free white males under 16 years. | Free white females, including heads of families. | All other free persons. | Slaves. | NAME OF HEAD OF FAMILY. | Free white males of 16 years and upward, including heads of families. | Free white males under 16 years. | Free white females, including heads of families. | All other free persons. | Slaves. |
|---|---|---|---|---|---|---|---|---|---|---|---|---|---|---|---|---|---|
| **WASHINGTON TOWN—continued.** | | | | | | **WASHINGTON TOWN—continued.** | | | | | | **WASHINGTON TOWN—continued.** | | | | | |
| Clark, Daniel | 1 | 1 | 2 | | | Keeney, John, 2d | 1 | | 1 | | | Tuttle, Eli | 4 | 3 | 5 | | |
| Clark, Marcy | 1 | | 1 | | | Keeney, Jacob | 1 | | 2 | | | Tuttle, Jonathan | 2 | | 6 | | |
| Canfield, Thomas | 2 | 1 | 3 | | | Keeney, Pearle | 2 | 5 | 3 | | | Titus, Joel | 3 | 5 | 6 | | |
| Canfield, Nathaniel | 2 | 2 | 3 | | | Keeney, Lyman | 1 | 1 | 1 | | | Titus, Onosimus | 3 | 1 | 3 | | |
| Coggwell, Roger | 5 | 1 | 5 | | | Knowles, Gid Benedict | 2 | 1 | 3 | | | Titus, Moses | 1 | 2 | 1 | | |
| Coggwell, Anna | | 2 | 3 | | | Keith, George | 2 | 3 | 3 | | | Treat, Bulah | | | 3 | | |
| Cary, Joseph | 1 | 2 | 2 | | | Keith | | | 3 | | | Woodruff, John | 3 | 2 | 4 | | |
| Curtis, Elizur | 1 | 2 | 3 | | | Kent, Eri | 1 | 1 | 3 | | | Whittlesey, Martin | 2 | 1 | 5 | | |
| Curtis, Joshua | 2 | 2 | 3 | | | Leavitt, Samuel | 2 | 2 | 4 | | | Whittlesey, John | 3 | 3 | 5 | | |
| Curtis, Abel | 1 | | 3 | | | Lacy, Ebenezer | 1 | 1 | 2 | | | Whittlesey, David | 2 | 1 | 2 | | |
| Cole, Thaddeus | 1 | 2 | 1 | | | Lemmon, Robert | 2 | 1 | 1 | | | Whittlesey, Joseph | 1 | 3 | 3 | | |
| Cooper, Timothy | 1 | | 3 | | | Lemmon, Robert, 2d | 1 | 2 | 4 | | | Wooden, Eri | 1 | 1 | 3 | | |
| Coggswell, Edward | 3 | 1 | 5 | | | Loggan, Mathew | 3 | 1 | 5 | | | Wooden, Elias | 1 | 1 | 3 | | |
| Coggswell, Edward, 2d | 1 | 1 | 2 | | | Loggan, Jeames | 2 | 2 | 4 | 1 | | Wheaton, Sylvester | 2 | | 3 | | |
| Cheritree, Reuben | 3 | 1 | 2 | | | Loggan, Johnson | 1 | 2 | 1 | | | Wheaton, Orange | 1 | 3 | 3 | | |
| Copley, Daniel | 1 | 2 | 1 | | | Lovejoy, Abner | 1 | | 4 | | | Warner, J. Ichabod | 1 | 2 | 6 | | |
| Dean, Elijah | 1 | 1 | 3 | | | Libberty, Jeff | | | | 4 | | Whitney, Hezekiah | 1 | 1 | 3 | | |
| Day, Jeremiah | 3 | 3 | 3 | | | Morse, Joseph | 1 | | 4 | | | Walker, David | 1 | | 4 | | |
| Davidson, John | 1 | 1 | 3 | | | Metcalf, Dan | 1 | 2 | 3 | | | | | | | | |
| Davies, John | 3 | 1 | 2 | | | Marchant, Sarah | | | 2 | | | **WATERTOWN TOWN.** | | | | | |
| Davies, John, 2d | 3 | 1 | 3 | | | Merwin, Noah | 2 | 1 | 6 | | | Allen, Ebenezer | 2 | 1 | 5 | | |
| Davies, Walter | 1 | 1 | 4 | | | Miers, Martin | 1 | 2 | 1 | | | Alling, Solomon | 1 | 1 | 1 | | |
| Davies, Jeams John | 1 | | | | | Mallerey, Elijah | 2 | | 3 | | | Allen, Jeames | 2 | 3 | 4 | | |
| Davies, David | 2 | 1 | 3 | | | Mallery, Ithamar | 1 | 2 | 3 | | | Avery, Ambrose | 1 | | 3 | | |
| Davies, Thomas | 1 | | 2 | | | Mitchel, Elnathan | 5 | | 3 | | | Atwater, Timothy | 1 | 1 | 2 | | |
| Durand, Samuel | 2 | 1 | | | | Mitchel, Simeon | 2 | 3 | 3 | | | Atkins, David | 1 | 2 | 3 | | |
| Davidson, Elizabeth | | | 1 | 1 | | Mitchel, David | 4 | 5 | | | 1 | Allen, Jeames, 2d | 1 | 3 | 3 | | |
| Dan, Abijah | 2 | 1 | 4 | | | Mitchel, Timothy | 2 | | 1 | | | Allen, David | 2 | 4 | 4 | | |
| Durker, Benjamin | 4 | 3 | 6 | | | Mitchel, William | 1 | | 6 | | | Atkins, Daniel | 1 | 1 | 5 | | |
| Durker, Jedediah | 1 | 1 | 2 | | | Mecher, David | 1 | 1 | 2 | | | Andrews, Justus | 1 | | 3 | | |
| Durkerson, Robert | 1 | 4 | 3 | | | Moger, Jeames | 1 | 1 | 1 | | | Avint, Amos | 1 | 2 | 3 | | |
| Easton, Joseph | 3 | 3 | 4 | | | Munson, John | 1 | 5 | 3 | | | Allen, John | 1 | 1 | 1 | | |
| Foot, David | 1 | 4 | 5 | | | Mayo, Elisha | 1 | 1 | 3 | | | Andrews, Reuben | 1 | 4 | 3 | | |
| Foot, Isaac | 1 | 5 | 2 | | | Mossley, Abner | 2 | 2 | 3 | | | Andrews, William | 1 | 2 | 2 | | |
| Foot, Aaron | 1 | 1 | 5 | | | Munger, Joel | 3 | | 3 | | | Avery, Benjamin | 1 | 2 | 2 | | |
| Farrand, Jonathan | 4 | 4 | 4 | 1 | | Munger, Joel, 2d | 1 | 1 | 2 | | | Atwood, Joseph | 1 | 2 | 2 | | |
| Farrand, John | 2 | 2 | 3 | | | Mead, Jeames | 2 | 3 | 2 | | | Andrews, Abram | 1 | | 2 | | |
| Frisbrie, Edward | 3 | | 6 | | | Newton, Ezekiel | 3 | | 2 | | | Atwood, Noble | 2 | 3 | 1 | | |
| Farmer, Thomas | 2 | 1 | 4 | | | Norton, Isachar | 2 | 2 | 3 | | | Atwood, Nathan | 1 | 1 | 2 | | |
| Ford, Samuel | 3 | 3 | 4 | | | Norton, Joel | 1 | 2 | 1 | | | Andrews, Ebenezer | 1 | | 1 | | |
| Ferry, Joseph | 1 | 2 | 7 | | | Northrop, Amos | 1 | 2 | 2 | | | Blakeley, Bela | 1 | | 3 | | |
| Ferry, Ebenezer | 1 | 4 | 3 | | | Northrop, Elijah | 1 | 2 | 2 | | | Beckwith, Jeames | 2 | | 2 | | |
| Ferry, Ezra | 1 | 1 | 2 | | | Nettleton, Daniel | 1 | 1 | 1 | 1 | | Beckwith, Zacheriah | 3 | | 6 | | |
| Fowler, Benjamin | 2 | | 2 | | | Oliver, Timothy | | | | 5 | | Brown, John | 1 | | | | |
| Fisher, Darius | 1 | | 1 | | | Older, Hannah | | 1 | 3 | | | Basset, Levi | 2 | 2 | 3 | | |
| Finn, Daniel | 1 | 2 | 3 | | | Patterson, Joseph | 1 | | 4 | | | Beach, Adna | 1 | | 3 | | |
| Galpin, Benjamin | 2 | 1 | 3 | | | Palmer, Zebulon | 1 | | 1 | | | Bearnes, Ebenezer | 1 | 1 | 2 | | |
| Gibson, Brinsmade | 2 | 2 | 6 | | | Parish, Isaac | 1 | 5 | 3 | | | Brown, Hezekiah | 1 | 1 | 1 | | |
| Gibson, William | 1 | 3 | 3 | | | Parish, Asa | 1 | | | | | Barnes, Eliphlet | 1 | 3 | 3 | | |
| Guthrie, Joseph | 5 | 1 | 6 | | | Parmely, Thomas | 4 | 2 | 4 | | | Blakeley, Moses | 2 | | 2 | | |
| Gunn, Phebe | 2 | | 1 | | | Parker, Amasa | 2 | 1 | 3 | | | Barnes, Joseph | 1 | | 1 | | |
| Goodsel, Isaac | 1 | 2 | 3 | | | Parker, Joseph | 2 | | 4 | | | Baldwin, Thaddeus | 2 | 2 | 5 | | |
| Goodsel, Thomas | 3 | 2 | 3 | | | Parker, Abner | 2 | 1 | 3 | | | Bunnet, Ambrose | 2 | | | | |
| Goodsel, Timothy | 3 | 1 | 2 | | | Parker, Abijail | 1 | 1 | 1 | | | Blakeley, Joel | 1 | 3 | 3 | | |
| Guthrie, Jeames | 1 | | 4 | | | Parker, Thomas | 2 | 3 | 5 | | | Blakeley, Judah | 3 | | 3 | | |
| Guthrie, Abraham | 1 | | 3 | | | Parks, William | 1 | 1 | 1 | | | Bartholemew, Daniel | 2 | 3 | 4 | | |
| Hurd, Levi | 1 | | 3 | | | Powel, John | 2 | 2 | 6 | | | Blakeley, Adna | 2 | | 2 | | |
| Handerson, William | 1 | 1 | 1 | | | Pratt, Abijah | 1 | 2 | 6 | 1 | | Blakeley, Eli | 1 | 4 | 5 | | |
| Holloway, John | 1 | 2 | 3 | | | Platt, John | 2 | 2 | 4 | | | Blakely, Sola | 1 | 1 | 1 | | |
| Hicock, Johnson | 3 | 2 | 2 | | | Platt, Zophar | 2 | 2 | 3 | | | Brownson, Amos | 3 | | 6 | | |
| Haslings, Seth | 3 | 3 | 4 | | | Peters, Eber | 2 | 1 | 2 | | | Blakeley, Annis | | | 2 | | |
| Hicock, Nathaniel | 2 | 1 | 3 | | | Palmer, John | 1 | 1 | 1 | | | Barker, Eliphlet | 2 | 4 | 2 | | |
| Hicock, Nathaniel | 4 | 2 | 2 | | | Parmeley, Truman | 1 | 2 | 3 | | | Bradley, Ebenezer, 2d | 2 | 2 | 2 | | |
| Hicock, Nathaniel, 2d | 1 | 1 | 3 | | | Pitcher, Truman | 1 | | 3 | | | Blakeley, Solomon | 1 | 1 | 2 | | |
| Hicock, Nathan, 2d | 2 | 1 | 3 | | | Pitcher, Susannah | | 1 | 4 | | | Barnes, Eli | 1 | 1 | 1 | | |
| Hicock, Elijah | 1 | 2 | 1 | | | Ranney, Nathan | 1 | | 3 | | | Bradley, Jared | 1 | | | | |
| Hicock, Joel | 1 | 1 | 3 | | | Royce, John | 1 | 1 | 4 | | | Blakeley, Samuel | 1 | 2 | 3 | | |
| Hicock, Thaddeus | 1 | | 1 | | | Royce, David | 3 | 1 | 4 | | | Barker, Miles | 1 | 1 | 1 | | |
| Hartwell, Joseph | 1 | 1 | 2 | | | Royce, Mark | 2 | 2 | 4 | | | Brownson, Noah Matt | 1 | 1 | | | |
| Harrison, Gideon | 1 | | 3 | | | Rude, Lester | 1 | 3 | 4 | | | Blakeley, Micajah | 1 | | | | |
| Herrick, Ephraim | 1 | 2 | 3 | | | Rude, Caleb | 2 | | 2 | | | Blakeley, Ashur | 3 | | 3 | | 2 |
| Hurd, Solomon | 3 | 1 | 3 | | | Rude, Caleb, 2d | 1 | 3 | 5 | | | Barnes, Nathaniel | 3 | 1 | 5 | | |
| Hurd, Sarah | | | 1 | | | Reynolds, John | 1 | | 3 | | | Blakeley, Amos | 1 | | 1 | | |
| Hollister, Gideon | 2 | 2 | 3 | | | Reynolds, David | 1 | 2 | 1 | | | Barnes, Daniel | 1 | 4 | 1 | | |
| Hollister, Gideon, 2d | 2 | 1 | 3 | | | Sharp, William | 1 | 2 | 6 | | | Barnes, Jonah | 1 | 1 | 3 | | |
| Hopson, William | 2 | 1 | 3 | | | Smith, John | 3 | 3 | 3 | | | Bradley, Philo | 1 | 2 | 1 | | |
| Howes, David | 4 | 1 | 1 | | | Smith, John, 2d | 2 | 2 | 4 | | | Bradley, Ebenezer | 1 | | 2 | | |
| Hinman, Michael | 1 | 1 | 4 | | | Smith, Moses | 1 | 2 | 3 | | | Brainard, Stephen | 1 | 1 | 2 | | |
| Hine, Jonathan | 3 | | 4 | | | Smith, Aaron | 1 | 1 | 4 | | | Barnes, Caleb | 1 | 5 | 1 | | |
| Hine, Andrew | 1 | 2 | 2 | | | Sherman, Peter | 5 | 2 | 5 | | | Baldwin, Israel | 1 | 3 | 1 | | |
| Hurlburt, Joseph | 2 | 1 | 2 | | | Stoddard, Jeames | 1 | 2 | 2 | | | Baldwin, Abel | 1 | | | | |
| Hurlburt, Samuel | 3 | 1 | 2 | | | Sherwood, Warren | 2 | | 3 | | | Bartholemew, Seth | 2 | 1 | 2 | | |
| Holdridge, Hezekiah | 1 | | | | | Swan, Samuel | 1 | 2 | 3 | | | Bradley, Anor | 1 | 3 | 4 | | |
| Hurd, Amos Asahel | 1 | 2 | 2 | | | Swan, Elizabeth | | | 3 | | | Beard, Azeriah | 2 | 1 | 7 | | |
| Hazen, Elijah | 2 | 1 | 3 | | | Smith, Samuel | 1 | | 5 | | | Brown, Elijah | 1 | 3 | | | |
| Hanford, William | 3 | 1 | 4 | | | Stilson, Eli | 1 | 1 | 1 | | | Brownson, Thomas | 2 | | 5 | | |
| Judson, David | 5 | 4 | 5 | | | Sharp, Eliakim | 1 | 1 | 2 | | | Brown, Zera | 1 | 3 | 3 | | |
| Judson, Abijail | | | 2 | | | Titus, Joseph | 1 | 2 | 2 | | | Bidwell, Jeremiah | 2 | 1 | 4 | | |
| Jordan, John | 1 | | 2 | | | Tuttle, Amos | 1 | 2 | 3 | | | Belding, Amos | 2 | | 2 | | |
| Johnes, Benjamin | 1 | 1 | 1 | | | Thorp, Peter | 1 | 1 | 3 | | | Buckingham, Epenetus | 2 | 1 | 4 | | |
| King, Oliver | 1 | | 2 | | | Treat, Sam Peat | 1 | | 2 | | | Buckingham, David | 1 | 2 | 2 | | |
| Keeney, Mark | 2 | 1 | 1 | | | Tracy, John | 3 | | 2 | | | Bidwell, Jacob | 2 | 2 | 5 | | |
| Krappen, Thomas | 1 | 2 | 5 | | | Tracy, Silas | 2 | 2 | 6 | | | Bradley, Nathaniel | 2 | 1 | 3 | | |
| Kimberly, David | 2 | 3 | 3 | | | Twiss, Samuel | 1 | | 3 | | | Baldwin, Alsop | 2 | 2 | 3 | | |
| Keeney, John | 1 | | 1 | | | Tibbals, Nathan | 1 | 2 | 2 | | | | | | | | |

# FIRST CENSUS OF THE UNITED STATES.

## LITCHFIELD COUNTY—Continued.

| NAME OF HEAD OF FAMILY. | Free white males of 16 years and upward, including heads of families. | Free white males under 16 years. | Free white females, including heads of families. | All other free persons. | Slaves. | NAME OF HEAD OF FAMILY. | Free white males of 16 years and upward, including heads of families. | Free white males under 16 years. | Free white females, including heads of families. | All other free persons. | Slaves. | NAME OF HEAD OF FAMILY. | Free white males of 16 years and upward, including heads of families. | Free white males under 16 years. | Free white females, including heads of families. | All other free persons. | Slaves. |
|---|---|---|---|---|---|---|---|---|---|---|---|---|---|---|---|---|---|
| WATERTOWN TOWN—continued. | | | | | | WATERTOWN TOWN—continued. | | | | | | WATERTOWN TOWN—continued. | | | | | |
| Brownson, Levi | 1 | 1 | 3 | | | Edward, Isaac | 1 | 1 | 2 | | | Hard, Anson | 1 | 3 | 1 | | |
| Blakeley, Jared | 1 | | | | | Edward, Nathaniel | 2 | | 6 | | | Hadeley, Gideon | 1 | 1 | 3 | | |
| Brown, Samuel | 1 | 1 | 3 | | | Egleston, John | 2 | 4 | 5 | | | Hammon, Thomas | 2 | 1 | 5 | | |
| Brigh, Elijah | 2 | 1 | 3 | | | Edward, Asahel | 1 | 4 | 2 | | | Hubbat, Hezekiah | 3 | | 3 | | |
| Byan, David | 2 | 2 | 6 | | | Frost, Samuel, 1st | 1 | | 2 | | | Hicocks, Ambrose, 2d | 2 | 1 | 5 | | |
| Baldwin, Theophilus | 1 | 6 | 2 | | | Frost, Samuel, 2nd | 1 | 1 | 1 | | | Hungeford, Jonas | 1 | 3 | 6 | | |
| Bryan, Benajah | 2 | 1 | 3 | | | Finn, Joseph | 2 | 3 | 5 | | | Hicocks, Caleb | 1 | | | | |
| Baldwin, David | 1 | 3 | 4 | | | Ferris, Nathan | 1 | 1 | 6 | | | Hicocks, Dick | | | | 3 | |
| Bassett, William | 1 | 2 | 6 | | | Frost, Solomon | 1 | 3 | 2 | | | Hicocks, Jonas | 2 | | 2 | | |
| Beard, Clark | 1 | 1 | 1 | | | Finn, Titus | 1 | 3 | 5 | | | Hotchkiss, Titus | 1 | 1 | 3 | | 1 |
| Barber, Samuel | 2 | 2 | 3 | | | Foot, Amos | 1 | 1 | 4 | | | Hicocks, Samuel | 1 | | 1 | | |
| Beard, George | 1 | | 1 | | | Fulson, David | 1 | 1 | 2 | | | Hicocks, Daniel | 2 | 3 | 6 | | |
| Bunnel, Hezekiah | 1 | | 2 | | | Foot, David | 1 | 4 | 4 | | | Hansson, Jared | 3 | 1 | 3 | | |
| Beckwith, Anna | | 2 | 2 | | | Finn, Thomas, 1st | 3 | 1 | 3 | | | Hungerford, Joel | 1 | 1 | 5 | | |
| Beardsley, Ebenezer | 2 | | 3 | | | Foot, Samuel | 1 | 1 | 3 | | | Hubbard, Joel, 1 | 1 | 2 | 4 | | |
| Baldwin, Samuel | 1 | | 2 | | | Foot, Thomas | 1 | | 2 | | | Hicocks, William | 4 | 2 | 5 | | |
| Blakeley, Thomas | 2 | 2 | 4 | | | Foot, John | 2 | 1 | 4 | | | Hicocks, Joseph | 1 | 2 | 2 | | |
| Brown, Daniel | 1 | 4 | 2 | | | Foot, Jacob | 3 | 1 | 7 | | | Hungerford, Jeames | 1 | 2 | 3 | | |
| Castle, Amasa | 1 | 2 | 6 | | | Finn, Samuel, 3d | 1 | | 2 | | | Hicocks, Phebe | | 1 | 2 | | |
| Castle, Abisha | 1 | 1 | 2 | | | Finn, Amos | 1 | 4 | 2 | | | Hicocks, Jeames | 1 | | 2 | | |
| Castle, Richard | 1 | 1 | 3 | | | Finn, Thomas, 2d | 1 | 1 | 4 | | | Hull, David, 1st | 2 | 1 | 2 | | |
| Camp, Isaac | 2 | 3 | 3 | | | Fulford, John | 2 | 1 | 8 | | | Hicocks, Mary | | 2 | 4 | | |
| Culver, Reuben | 1 | 2 | 3 | | | Foot, Thankful | 2 | 1 | 6 | | | How, Ephraim | 2 | 3 | 4 | | |
| Curtis, Jesse | 2 | 1 | 1 | | | Finn, Faar | 2 | 1 | 6 | | | Hicocks, Jared | 1 | 3 | 4 | | |
| Cook, Justus | 1 | | | | | Finn, Jason | 1 | 1 | 5 | | | Hull, David, 2d | 1 | | 2 | | |
| Curtis, Joseph | 2 | | 2 | | | Finn, Jacob | 2 | | 7 | | | Hubbard, Josiah | 1 | | 1 | | |
| Camp, Samuel | 2 | 2 | 4 | | | Finn, Jesse | 1 | 3 | 2 | | | Hitchcock, Samuel | 1 | | 4 | | |
| Camp, Ephraim | 2 | 1 | 2 | | | Finn, Ebenezer | 1 | | | | | Hubbart, David | 1 | 2 | 2 | | |
| Carrington, David | 1 | 5 | 2 | | | Finn, Samuel, 1st | 1 | 1 | 2 | | | Hicocks, Consider | 1 | 4 | 4 | | |
| Curtis, Samuel | 2 | | 3 | | | Finn, Aaron | 3 | 3 | 3 | | | Hicocks, Ambrose | 1 | 1 | 1 | | |
| Cook, Phebe | | | 2 | | | Finn, Samuel, 2d | 3 | | 5 | | | Hicocks, Hinman | 1 | 1 | 1 | | |
| Cook, Arba | 1 | 1 | 3 | | | Ford, Amos | 1 | 3 | 3 | | | Judd, Noah | 4 | 3 | 3 | | |
| Cook, Joel | 1 | 1 | 6 | | | Ford, Ebenezer | 1 | | 1 | | | Judd, Allen | 2 | 2 | 7 | | |
| Curtis, Isaac | 2 | | 2 | | | Ford, Daniel | 1 | 2 | 4 | | | Judd, Michael | 1 | 1 | 2 | | |
| Curtis, Jeames | 1 | 3 | 1 | | | Ford, Enos | 1 | | 4 | | | Judd, Levi | 1 | 2 | 3 | | |
| Camp, Benajah | 1 | 1 | 3 | | | Fost, Elisha | 1 | 1 | 2 | | | Judd, Dennis | 1 | 2 | 4 | | |
| Curtis, Elihu | 1 | 1 | 2 | | | Farnham, John | 2 | 1 | 1 | | | Judd, John, 1 | 2 | | 1 | | |
| Cooper, Jesse | 1 | 1 | 2 | | | Fancher, Ithiel | 1 | 1 | 3 | | | Judd, William | 1 | | 1 | | |
| Cusley, Jesse | 1 | | | | | Fenton, Benjamin | 2 | 2 | 1 | | | Judd, Asa | 2 | 3 | 4 | | |
| Curtis, Miles | 1 | | 1 | | | Foot, Simon | 1 | 1 | 3 | | | Judd, Merriam | 1 | | 2 | | |
| Cole, Timothy | 2 | 1 | 1 | | | Fancher, Sarah | | 1 | 3 | | | Judd, Samuel | 1 | 1 | 2 | | |
| Cowles, Ebenezer | 2 | 1 | 3 | | | Fancher, Jeames | 1 | | 3 | | | Jones, Sarah | | 1 | 1 | | |
| Curtis, Benjamin | 1 | 3 | 2 | | | Ford, Barnebas | 1 | 3 | 3 | | | Johnson, Isaac | 2 | | 1 | | |
| Curtis, Thomas | 1 | | 1 | | | Gilbert, Elisha | 1 | 2 | 4 | | | Johnson, Enos | 1 | 3 | 2 | | |
| Clark, Ichiel | 1 | 4 | 2 | | | Grannis, Hannah | | 2 | 1 | | | Jones, Timothy | 1 | 1 | 2 | | |
| Curtis, Zadock | 1 | 1 | 2 | | | Gridley, Hosea | 1 | 2 | 5 | | | Ives, Elnathan | 1 | 3 | 3 | | |
| Curtis, Oliver | 1 | 1 | 7 | | | Goodyer, David | 1 | 2 | 6 | | | Jerom, Robert | 1 | 1 | 4 | | |
| Cowles, Moses | 1 | 2 | 3 | | | Griggs, Solomon | 1 | 2 | 4 | | | Judd, Harvey | 1 | 1 | 2 | | |
| Cole, John | 1 | | | | | Griggs, Paul | 1 | 2 | 1 | | | Leavenworth, Asa | 2 | 1 | 3 | | |
| Cook, Jonah | 1 | 1 | 4 | | | Goss, Ebeneser | 3 | 1 | 2 | | | Luddington, David | 2 | | 4 | | |
| Curtis, Phineas | 1 | | 3 | | | Gaylord, Jotham | 1 | 3 | 2 | | | Lewis, Samuel | 1 | 1 | 2 | | |
| Culver, Daniel | 3 | 1 | 3 | | | Gaylord, Enos | 1 | 1 | 5 | | | Loomis, Faith | 1 | 1 | 2 | | |
| Cowles, Thomas | 3 | 1 | 3 | | | Guernsey, Joseph, 1st | 3 | 1 | 2 | | | Loomis, Oliver | 1 | 3 | 1 | | |
| Carrington, Eliphat | 1 | 2 | 4 | | | Guernsey, Joel | 1 | 2 | 2 | | | Lewis, Thankful | | | 1 | | |
| Coe, Denman | 1 | 2 | 5 | | | Guernsey, Ebenezer | 3 | 1 | 3 | | | Lockwood, Ezra | 5 | 3 | 4 | | |
| Clark, Oliver | 1 | | 2 | | | Guernsey, Daniel | 1 | 3 | 2 | | | Matthews, William | 1 | | 3 | | |
| Clark, Gamaliel | 3 | 3 | 5 | | | Guernsey, David | 2 | | 10 | | | Munson, Almond | 1 | 2 | 2 | | |
| Castle, John | 1 | 2 | 3 | | | Griggs, Noah, 1st | 2 | | 3 | | | Matthews, Lydia | | | 1 | | |
| Curtis, Eli | 1 | 1 | 1 | | | Griggs, Noah, 2 | 1 | | | | | Mozier, Zebulon | 1 | 4 | 3 | | |
| Cutler, Young Lorer | 4 | 1 | 3 | | | Givins, Shelden | 1 | | | | | Matthews, Samuel | 1 | 2 | 1 | | |
| Castle, Simeon | 1 | 2 | 5 | | | Guernsey, Eldad | 1 | 1 | 2 | | | Miller, Isaac | 1 | 3 | 2 | | |
| Dutton, Sarah | 1 | 1 | 3 | | | Guernsey, Southmayd | 1 | 1 | 3 | | | Marchant, Thomas, 1st | 2 | | 3 | | |
| Dunbar, David | 1 | | | | | Guernsey, Jonathan | 2 | | 2 | | | Morris, Isaac | 1 | | | | |
| Dunbar, Amos | 1 | 1 | 2 | | | Glasier, John | 1 | 1 | 1 | | | Morris, Amos | 1 | 1 | 2 | | |
| Dunbar, Joel | 1 | 2 | 3 | | | Guernsey, Joab | 2 | | 1 | | | Mead, Daniel | 1 | 1 | 3 | | |
| Dunbar, Aaron | 2 | 2 | 4 | | | Guernsey, Philo | 1 | | 3 | | | Mopley, John | 1 | | | | |
| Dunbar, Miles | 1 | 3 | 2 | | | Guernsey, Chauncy | 1 | 2 | | | | Mallery, Jacob | 1 | 2 | 2 | | |
| Darrow, Titus | 3 | 3 | 2 | | | Guernsey, Amos | 1 | | 7 | | | Munson, Obidiah | 3 | | 1 | | |
| Dodge, Ezra | 1 | 1 | 2 | | | Guernsey, Joseph, 2d | 1 | 1 | 3 | | | Matthews, Aaron | 1 | | 2 | | |
| Dunbar, Joseph | 1 | 2 | 2 | | | Guernsey, Abijah | 2 | 2 | 5 | | | Marp, Benoni | 1 | 2 | 2 | | |
| Doolittle, Eliasaph | 1 | 5 | 4 | | | Guernsey, Samuel | 2 | 1 | 4 | | | Merrills, Daniel | 2 | 1 | 2 | | |
| Darrow, Ebenezer, 2d | 1 | 2 | 1 | | | Guernsey, Thankfull | | | 3 | | | Matthews, Daniel | 1 | 2 | 2 | | |
| Darrow, Asa | 2 | 2 | 6 | | | Griggs, Jacob | 1 | 1 | 2 | | | Martin, Samuel | 1 | 2 | 3 | | |
| Dutton, P. Samuel | 2 | 1 | 2 | | | Gridley, Uriel | 1 | 1 | 2 | | | Merrills, John | 2 | | 2 | | |
| Dunbar, Jonathan | 1 | | | | | Heaton, Abram | 2 | 3 | 3 | | | Merriam, Isaac | 3 | 1 | 4 | | |
| Darrow, Ebenezer | 1 | | | | | Hornestone, Timothy | 1 | | 2 | | | Merriam, James | 2 | 1 | 2 | | |
| Dodg, Ira | 1 | 1 | 4 | | | Hall, Benjamin | 1 | 2 | 1 | | | Matthews, Thomas | 2 | 3 | 4 | | |
| Dayton, Michael | 1 | | 2 | | | Holt, Daniel | 1 | 2 | 2 | | | Matthews, Amos | 2 | 1 | 2 | | |
| Dutton, Thomas, 3d | 4 | 2 | 3 | | | Homestone, David | 1 | 1 | 3 | | | Merriam, Thomas, 2d | 1 | | 1 | | |
| Dayton, Justus | 2 | 3 | 4 | | | Hemmingway, Abram | 2 | | 4 | | | Mattoon, Amasa | 1 | 3 | 2 | | |
| Davies, Thomas | 1 | 1 | 1 | | | Hitchcock, Zachariah | 1 | 8 | 5 | | | Merriam, Joel | 2 | 2 | 2 | | |
| Dayton, Lyman | 1 | 1 | 2 | | | Homestone, Abel | 1 | 2 | 3 | | | Miles, Richard | 1 | 2 | 2 | | |
| Dayton, Abel | 1 | 1 | 1 | | | Heading, George | 1 | 1 | 2 | | | Merriam, Joseph | 1 | 2 | 2 | | |
| Doolittle, Uri | 3 | 2 | 2 | | | Hull, Ira | 1 | | | | | Merriam, Christopher | 3 | | 2 | | |
| Dutton, Thomas, 2d | 2 | 1 | 3 | | | Hawley, Samuel | 3 | | 2 | | | Merriam, Thomas, 1st | 2 | | 2 | | |
| Dayton, Charles | 2 | 3 | 3 | | | How, Zachariah | 2 | | 2 | | | Merriam, John | 2 | | 4 | | |
| Dayton, Alexander | 2 | | 2 | | | Homestone, Jose | 1 | 4 | 3 | | | Mattoon, John | 1 | | 2 | | |
| Dayton, Isaac | 1 | 2 | 1 | | | Homestone, Eliphet | 2 | 3 | 5 | | | Merriam, Charles | 3 | 1 | 2 | | |
| Dayton, David | 1 | 2 | 5 | | | Homestone, Thomas | 1 | 3 | 1 | | | Matthews, Stephen | 2 | | 2 | | |
| Dart, William | 1 | 2 | 3 | | | Hough, Benoni | 1 | 1 | 1 | | | Manoil, David | 2 | 2 | 3 | | |
| Davies, Jonathan | 1 | | 2 | | | Hill, James | 2 | 3 | 5 | | | Matthews, Phineas | 1 | | 2 | | |
| Dayton, Samuel | 1 | 1 | 2 | | | Hicocks, Joel | 1 | | 4 | | | Munson, William | 1 | 1 | 2 | | |
| Edward, Joseph | 1 | 2 | 2 | | | Hotchkiss, Truman | 1 | | 3 | | | Merriam, Marshal | 2 | 4 | 2 | | |
| Elton, Ebenezer | 3 | | 3 | | | How, Samuel | 1 | | 4 | | | Merrills, Mabel | 1 | | 2 | | |
| Edwards, Josiah | 1 | 1 | 1 | | | Hicocks, Samuel | 1 | | 1 | | | McDaniel, David | 3 | | 3 | | |
| Elton, John | 1 | 1 | 2 | | | Hicocks, Amos | 2 | 1 | 4 | | | McDaniel, James | 2 | 2 | 1 | | |

# HEADS OF FAMILIES—CONNECTICUT.

## LITCHFIELD COUNTY—Continued.

### WATERTOWN TOWN—continued.

| NAME OF HEAD OF FAMILY. | Free white males of 16 years and upward, including heads of families. | Free white males under 16 years. | Free white females, including heads of families. | All other free persons. | Slaves. |
|---|---|---|---|---|---|
| Marchant, Thomas, 2d | 1 | 1 | 3 | | |
| Munson, Heman | 1 | 4 | 1 | | |
| Northrop, Joseph | 1 | | | | |
| Northrop, Gideon | 1 | 3 | 5 | | |
| Northrop, Joseph | 1 | | | | |
| Northrop, Gideon, 2d | 1 | 3 | 5 | | |
| Northrop, Joel | 2 | 1 | 1 | | |
| Noble, Francis | 1 | 1 | 4 | | |
| Northrop, Jonathan | 2 | 1 | 4 | | |
| Nettleton, Joseph | 1 | 1 | 6 | | |
| Nettleton, Joseph, 2d | 1 | 1 | 2 | | |
| Nettleton, Susannah | | | 2 | | |
| Osborn, Zadock | 1 | 1 | 1 | | |
| Osborn, Amos | 1 | 1 | 2 | | |
| Osborn, Abijah | 1 | | 3 | | |
| Osborn, John | 1 | | 5 | | |
| Osborn, White | 1 | 1 | 3 | | |
| Peck, Samuel | 1 | | 1 | | |
| Preston, Caleb | 3 | 3 | 4 | | |
| Potter, Eliahson | 2 | 3 | 4 | | |
| Potter, Daniel | 1 | 2 | 3 | | |
| Potter, Lake | 2 | 1 | 3 | | |
| Potter, Jacob | 1 | 2 | 3 | | |
| Potter, Samuel | 3 | 2 | 4 | | |
| Potter, Demas | 1 | | | | |
| Potter, Zenas | 1 | | 1 | | |
| Potter, Thomas | 1 | | | | |
| Packer, Leut | 2 | 3 | 2 | | |
| Painter, Thomas W | 1 | 1 | 2 | | |
| Pond, Jonathan | 3 | 2 | 5 | | |
| Pond, Bartholemew, 1st | 2 | 3 | 3 | | |
| Pond, Ira | 1 | 1 | 1 | | |
| Painter, John | 2 | | 4 | | |
| Penfield, Jesse | 1 | 2 | 2 | | |
| Pond, Bartholemew, 2d | 1 | 1 | 3 | | |
| Parde, Stephen | 2 | 1 | 3 | | |
| Prindle, Chauncy | 1 | | 4 | | |
| Parker, John, 2d | 1 | | 1 | | |
| Painter, John, 2d | 1 | | 3 | | |
| Pulford, Dorcas | | | 3 | | |
| Prichard, Elijah | 1 | 2 | 2 | | |
| Prichard, Benjamin | 1 | 3 | 4 | | |
| Peck, Simeon | 2 | 2 | 2 | | |
| Prindle, David | 1 | 3 | 8 | | |
| Parker, John | 2 | 2 | 4 | | |
| Parker, Eli | 1 | 1 | 3 | | |
| Peck, Jeremiah | 1 | 1 | 4 | | |
| Prindle, Eleasor | 1 | 1 | 3 | | |
| Porter, Ebenezer | 2 | 2 | 4 | | |
| Pitcher, Jerusha | 1 | 1 | 4 | | |
| Peck, Elezier | 1 | | 2 | | |
| Preston, Amasa | 1 | 4 | 5 | | |
| Pond, Zera | 1 | 1 | 1 | | |
| Richard, Gideon | 1 | 1 | 3 | | |
| Ransom, Theophilus | 2 | 3 | 4 | 1 | |
| Richard, Ebenezer | 1 | | 3 | | |
| Raynold, Richard T | 2 | 1 | 2 | | |
| Raynold, Samuel, Junr | 1 | 2 | 6 | | |
| Richard, William | 1 | | | | |
| Richard, Benjamin, 1st | 1 | | 1 | | |
| Richard, Benjamin, 2d | 2 | 2 | 3 | | |
| Richard, Elizabeth | 1 | 1 | 3 | | |
| Robarts, Jonathan | 1 | 1 | 5 | | |
| Richard, Peter | 2 | | 2 | | |
| Roberts, Jesse | 1 | 2 | 2 | | |
| Rockwell, Jabez | 1 | | 2 | | |
| Rockwell, Benjamin | 1 | 3 | 2 | | |
| Royer, Samuel | 2 | 1 | 6 | | |
| Royer, Jacob | 1 | 4 | 4 | | |
| Rozer, David | 1 | | 6 | | |
| Sanford, David | 2 | | 1 | | |
| Scovill, William | 1 | 3 | 1 | | |
| Sutlif, Abel, 1st | 1 | | 2 | | |
| Sutliff, Abel, 2d | 3 | 1 | 6 | | |
| Sutliff, Lucas | 1 | | | | |
| Sutliff, Samuel | 1 | 2 | 1 | | |
| Sutliff, John | 2 | 3 | 5 | | |
| Sutliff, David | 1 | 3 | 2 | | |
| Sanford, Samuel | 3 | 2 | 1 | | |
| Sanford, Daniel, 2d | 2 | | 2 | | |
| Sanford, Joel | 1 | | 4 | | |
| Sanford, Jesse | 1 | 1 | 4 | | |
| Sanford, Ezekiel, 2d | 1 | 1 | 2 | | |
| Sanford, Stephen | 1 | | 2 | | |
| Scamon, Stephen, 1st | 1 | | 2 | | |
| Simons, Amos | 1 | 1 | 2 | | |
| Simon, Gideon | 2 | 3 | 3 | | |
| Simon, Abel | 3 | 2 | 4 | | |
| Skilton, David | 3 | 3 | 3 | 1 | |
| Stanley, Selah | 1 | 1 | 1 | | |
| Scovill, Samuel | 1 | | 2 | | |
| Scovill, Uri | 1 | 1 | 2 | | |
| Scovill, Eli | 1 | 2 | 1 | | |
| Scovill, Jesse | 1 | | 2 | | |
| Sperry, Lemuel | 1 | | 1 | | |
| Smith, David | 2 | 3 | 3 | | |
| Smith, Jeames | 1 | | 3 | | 1 |
| Soughton, Oliver | 1 | 3 | 4 | 1 | |
| Sanford, Ezekiel, 1st | 1 | 2 | 5 | | |
| Sanford, Amos | 1 | 3 | 1 | | |
| Smith, Isaac | 1 | | 1 | | |
| Smith, Stephen | 2 | 1 | 3 | | |
| Simons, Joseph | 2 | 4 | 3 | | |
| Southmayd, Samuel | 2 | | 4 | | |
| Scott, Hezekiah | 2 | | 3 | | |
| Scovill, Martha | | | 3 | | |
| Stoddard, John | 1 | 2 | 1 | | |
| Scott, Elicks | 1 | 2 | 5 | | |
| Stow, Ebenezer | 1 | 1 | 4 | | |
| Simons, Richard, 1st | 1 | 1 | 3 | | |
| Stoddard, Sampson | 1 | 4 | 4 | | |
| Scott, Jonathan | 3 | 4 | 1 | 1 | |
| Smith, Wart | 3 | 3 | 5 | | |
| Sitkuggs, Osi | 1 | | 2 | | |
| Scovill, Darius | 2 | 4 | 2 | | |
| Stoddard, Wills | 1 | | 1 | | |
| Scovill, William, 2d | 2 | 2 | 3 | | |
| Stilson, Amos | 1 | 2 | 3 | | |
| Steel, Elijah | 2 | 1 | 3 | | |
| Scott, Isaac | 2 | 1 | 1 | | |
| Steel, Ashbel | 2 | | 4 | | |
| Strickland, Samuel | 1 | 2 | 4 | | |
| Scott, Barnebes | 1 | | | | |
| Scott, Ebner | 1 | 2 | 3 | | |
| Sutton, Henr'y | 1 | 1 | 1 | | |
| Smith, Eliphlet | 1 | 2 | 4 | | |
| Smith, John | 3 | 2 | 4 | | |
| Simons, Samuel | 1 | 2 | 3 | | |
| Smith, Reuben | 1 | | 1 | | |
| Simons, Josiah | 1 | 3 | 3 | | |
| Scott, Uri | 1 | 1 | 1 | | |
| Singlehuff, John | 1 | | 3 | | |
| Scott, Eleazer, 1st | 1 | 1 | 5 | | |
| Simons, Richard, 2d | 1 | 1 | 1 | | |
| Scovill, Israel | 1 | 2 | 6 | | |
| Scott, Woolfy | 1 | 2 | 2 | | |
| Steel, Samuel | 1 | | 2 | | |
| Smith, Thomas | 1 | | 1 | | |
| Tuttle, John | 1 | | 2 | | |
| Truitt, Mattha | 2 | 1 | 4 | | |
| Tomkins, Feanes | 1 | 1 | 2 | | |
| Tomkins, Edmond | 1 | 2 | 2 | | |
| Titus, Amos | 1 | | 4 | | |
| Turner, David | 1 | 1 | 2 | | |
| Turner, Stephen | 2 | 1 | 3 | | |
| Treat, Richard | 2 | | 2 | | 1 |
| Tuttle, Obediah | 1 | 4 | 4 | | |
| Thomas, Samuel | 1 | | 1 | | |
| Tyler, Osias | 3 | 2 | 4 | | |
| Tomlinson, Victory | 2 | 2 | 2 | | |
| Tuttle, William | 1 | 3 | 3 | | |
| Todd, Samuel | 2 | | 2 | | |
| Todd, Edmond | 3 | | 3 | | |
| Todd, Elam | 1 | | | | |
| Tuttle, Noah | 2 | 4 | 3 | | |
| Turner, Bethuel | 1 | 2 | 1 | | |
| Todd, Lydia | | | 2 | | |
| Tuttle, Stephen | 1 | | 2 | | |
| Upson, Rusel | 1 | 1 | 2 | | |
| Upson, Joseph | 1 | 2 | 6 | | |
| Upson, Noah | 2 | 3 | 1 | | |
| Upson, Benjamin | 1 | | | | |
| Warner, Jeames | 2 | 2 | 5 | | |
| Warner, Noah | 1 | 1 | 2 | | |
| Warner, Elijah | 4 | 2 | 4 | | |
| Wright, Joseph Allen | 1 | 1 | 2 | 2 | |
| Warner, John | 1 | 5 | 3 | | |
| Warner, John, 3d | 1 | 1 | 5 | | |
| Welton, Eli, 1st | 2 | 2 | 2 | | |
| Welton, Eli, 2d | 1 | 1 | 1 | | |
| Woodruf, Gideon | 1 | | | | |
| Way, Thomas, 1st | 2 | 2 | 3 | | |
| Way, Thomas, 2d | 1 | | | | |
| Warner, David | 1 | 1 | 2 | | |
| Warner, Aaron | 1 | 2 | 2 | | |
| Warner, Osias | 1 | 5 | 4 | | |
| Wooden, Amos | 1 | 2 | 4 | | |
| Williams, John | 1 | | | | |
| Weed, Jesse | 3 | 2 | 6 | | |
| Way, Samuel | 1 | 3 | 3 | | |
| Wright, Amos | 1 | 1 | 2 | | |
| Worden, Thomas | 1 | 2 | 5 | | |
| Wheaton, Sarah | | | 2 | | |
| Williams, Thomas | 1 | 1 | 6 | | |
| Wetmore, Elizabeth | 3 | | 1 | | |
| Watson, William | 1 | 2 | 4 | | |
| Wade, Increse | 1 | 3 | 2 | | |
| Welton, Samuel | 1 | | 2 | | |
| Woodruff, Samuel | 1 | 1 | 2 | | |
| Warner, Elisha | 2 | | 1 | | |
| Wooden, Asa | 2 | 1 | 3 | | |
| Whitney, Ransford | 1 | 1 | 2 | | |
| Welton, Jesse | 1 | 2 | 4 | | |
| Woodruf, John | 2 | 5 | 2 | | |
| Woodruff, Sarah | 1 | 3 | 2 | | |
| Woodard, Elijah | 2 | 1 | 4 | | 1 |
| Williams, Daniel | 1 | | | | |
| Woodard, Antipas | 2 | 2 | 2 | | |
| Woodard, Edward | 1 | 3 | 2 | | |
| Wooard, John | 1 | 1 | 3 | | |
| Woodruff, Lambert | 1 | 4 | 1 | | |
| Welton, Stephen | 1 | | 1 | | |
| Welton, Dan | 2 | | 1 | | |
| Welton, Reuben | 2 | 2 | 5 | | |
| Welton, Josiah | 1 | 2 | 3 | | |
| Woodard, Israel | 3 | 2 | 4 | | |
| Williams, Timothy | 2 | | | | |
| Woodard, Nathan | 1 | 1 | 3 | | |
| Way, Abel | 1 | | 1 | | |
| Woodard, Abel | 4 | 2 | 4 | | |
| Williams, Jeames | 1 | 1 | 3 | | |
| Clark, Chauncy | 1 | 1 | 2 | | |

### WOODBURY TOWN.

| NAME OF HEAD OF FAMILY. | Free white males of 16 years and upward, including heads of families. | Free white males under 16 years. | Free white females, including heads of families. | All other free persons. | Slaves. |
|---|---|---|---|---|---|
| Atwood, Elijah | 2 | | 3 | | |
| Atwood, Nathan | 2 | 1 | 1 | | |
| Atwood, Jesse | 1 | 2 | 4 | | |
| Atwood, Elijah, 2d | 1 | 1 | 2 | | |
| Atwood, Oliver | 1 | 1 | 3 | | |
| Atwood, Elisha | 3 | 3 | 4 | | |
| Atwood, David | 1 | 2 | 2 | | 1 |
| Abenatha, John | 1 | 1 | 1 | | |
| Andrews, Benjamin | 2 | 1 | 2 | | |
| Aspenwall, Abel | 1 | 3 | 2 | | |
| Atwell, John | 3 | 1 | 5 | | |
| Armstrong, Isaac | 1 | 2 | 3 | | |
| Austin, Jesse | 1 | | 1 | | |
| Andrews, Thomas | 1 | 1 | 3 | | |
| Atwood, Skillars | 1 | | 2 | | |
| Baron, Jabez | 6 | 1 | 5 | | |
| Baron, Asahel | 1 | 1 | 2 | | |
| Baron, Jabez, 2d | 1 | 2 | 3 | | |
| Berham, Samuel | 4 | | 7 | | |
| Bradley, Searl | 2 | 1 | 1 | | |
| Bradley, Jehiel | 2 | 2 | 1 | | |
| Bears, Zacheriah | 2 | 1 | 6 | | |
| Bull, Thomas | 2 | 2 | 2 | | 2 |
| Bassett, Noah | 2 | 2 | 3 | | |
| Bears, Lewis | 1 | 1 | 1 | | |
| Bradley, Richard | 2 | 1 | 5 | | |
| Benham, Phineas | 3 | | 3 | | |
| Baldwin, Andrew | 3 | 1 | 4 | | |
| Brewster, David | 1 | 1 | 5 | | |
| Brothwell, F. Joseph | 2 | 1 | 4 | | |
| Benton, Jeremiah | 2 | 2 | 1 | | |
| Brougtron, Amos | 1 | 4 | 6 | | |
| Baldwin, Warner | 1 | 1 | 1 | | |
| Baldwin, Parmale | 1 | 3 | 4 | | |
| Benedict, Noah | 3 | 2 | 2 | | |
| Beach, Enos | 2 | | | | |
| Beach, John | 1 | 2 | 2 | | |
| Beach, Joel | 1 | | 1 | | |
| Baker, Jacob | 1 | 2 | 5 | | |
| Bates, Elias | 1 | 3 | 1 | | |
| Brownson, Abram | 2 | | 1 | | |
| Brownson, Abram, 2d | 1 | 1 | 1 | | |
| Brownson, Thomas | 1 | 2 | 3 | | |
| Brownson, Abel | 1 | 1 | 4 | | |
| Bassett, Samuel | 1 | 1 | 8 | | |
| Bassett, Isaac | 2 | 1 | 1 | | |
| Bailey, Charles | 2 | 1 | 5 | | |
| Bailey, Thomas | 1 | | 2 | | |
| Blakeley, Dan | 3 | 3 | 3 | | |
| Blakeley, Abram | 1 | 1 | 2 | | |
| Blakeley, Tilley | 2 | | | | |
| Bristol, Samuel | 1 | 2 | 2 | | |
| Bulford, John | 2 | 1 | 1 | | |
| Bostwick, Andrew | 3 | 2 | 4 | | |
| Booth, David | 2 | 4 | 2 | | |
| Booth, John | 1 | 1 | 4 | | |
| Baldwin, Lucy | | | 4 | | |
| Bears, Josiah | 1 | 2 | 3 | | |
| Black, Esther | | | | | |
| Blancher, Nathaniel | 1 | 2 | 4 | | |
| Blakeley, Jeames | 1 | | 3 | | |
| Barnes, John | 2 | | 2 | | |
| Brownson, Josiah | 1 | | 2 | | |
| Betts, Azor | | | | | |
| Beebe, Stephen | 1 | 1 | 2 | | |
| Benham, Smith | 1 | | 2 | | |
| Boyd, Francis | 2 | 2 | 2 | | |
| Bishop, William | 1 | 1 | 3 | | |
| Curtis, John | 3 | 2 | 2 | | |
| Curtis, David | 3 | 2 | 6 | | |

## LITCHFIELD COUNTY—Continued.

| NAME OF HEAD OF FAMILY. | Free white males of 16 years and upward, including heads of families. | Free white males under 16 years. | Free white females, including heads of families. | All other free persons. | Slaves. | NAME OF HEAD OF FAMILY. | Free white males of 16 years and upward, including heads of families. | Free white males under 16 years. | Free white females, including heads of families. | All other free persons. | Slaves. | NAME OF HEAD OF FAMILY. | Free white males of 16 years and upward, including heads of families. | Free white males under 16 years. | Free white females, including heads of families. | All other free persons. | Slaves. |
|---|---|---|---|---|---|---|---|---|---|---|---|---|---|---|---|---|---|
| **WOODBURY TOWN—continued.** | | | | | | **WOODBURY TOWN—continued.** | | | | | | **WOODBURY TOWN—continued.** | | | | | |
| Cunnigham, Garwood H. | 2 | 3 | 2 | | | Hall, William | 1 | 2 | 3 | | | Miner, John | 2 | | 5 | | |
| Crawfoot, Jeames | 3 | 2 | 2 | | | Hurd, Noah | 1 | 2 | 2 | | | Miner, Samuel | 1 | 2 | 2 | | |
| Cherway, Philmi | 1 | 6 | 3 | | | Hammon, David | 2 | | 1 | | | Miner, Thaddeus | 3 | 1 | 3 | | |
| Carr, Samuel | 1 | 2 | 5 | | | Hall, Mathew | 1 | 2 | 4 | | | Miner, Jeames | 1 | 3 | 3 | | |
| Clark, John | 1 | 3 | 5 | | | Hurlburt, Amos | 2 | 1 | 2 | | | Miner, Joseph | 1 | | 2 | | |
| Cussrey, Daniel | 2 | | 2 | | | Hurlburt, Damaras | 1 | | 2 | | | Miner, Adoniram | 1 | 2 | 1 | | |
| Coggshall, Daniel | 1 | | 3 | | | Hurd, Zadock | 2 | | 3 | | | Miner, Thomas | 1 | | 4 | | |
| Camp, Charity | 1 | | 1 | | | Heart, Jeames | 1 | | 3 | | | Miner, Israel | 4 | 1 | 5 | | |
| Crammer, Amos | 1 | 1 | 4 | | | Hyde, Ebenezer | 1 | 2 | 3 | | | Miner, Seth, 2d | 1 | | 1 | | |
| Castle, Israel | 2 | | 2 | | | Hurlburt, Gideon, 2d | 1 | 4 | 5 | | | Miner, Peace | 2 | 2 | 4 | | |
| Castle, Simeon | 1 | 2 | 5 | | | Hill, Aaron | 1 | | 4 | | | Miner, Peter | 2 | | 2 | | |
| Castle, Abram | 1 | 4 | 4 | | | Hull, Stephen | 1 | | 5 | | | Miner, Josiah | 1 | 1 | 4 | | |
| Castle, Samuel | 2 | 1 | 2 | | | Hull, Ebenezer | 3 | | 5 | | | Moramble, John | 1 | | 4 | | |
| Castle, Luke | 1 | | 1 | | | Hurlburt, Benjamin | 3 | | 4 | | | Morris, Mathew | 1 | 3 | 2 | | |
| Castle, Peter | 2 | 3 | 5 | | | Hurlburt, Comfort | | | 3 | | | Mitchel, Reuben | 1 | 1 | 5 | | |
| Castle, Reuben | 3 | 1 | 2 | | | Hunt, Ransom | 1 | | 2 | | | Mitchel, Nathaniel | 3 | 3 | 4 | | |
| Cap, C. John | 1 | 2 | 1 | | | Hurlburt, Nathaniel | 1 | | 1 | | | Mitchel, John, 2 | 1 | 1 | 6 | | |
| Clark, Benjamin | 1 | 3 | 3 | | | Hurlburt, Joel | 1 | 1 | 3 | | | Mitchel, Abijah | 1 | 1 | 3 | | |
| Canfield, Thomas | 2 | 2 | 3 | | 1 | Hine, Nathan | 1 | | 3 | | | Mitchel, John | 3 | 1 | 2 | | 1 |
| Canfield, Thomas, 2d | 2 | 2 | 4 | | | Hurd, Nathan, 2d | 1 | | 3 | | | Mitchel, Asahel | 1 | | 1 | | |
| Chatfield, Yarmouth | | | | 3 | | Ives, Asa | 1 | 2 | 2 | | | Mitchel, Daniel | 2 | | 1 | | |
| Crammr, Adam | 1 | | 1 | | | Ives, Anor, 1st | 1 | 2 | 4 | | | Mitchel, William | 2 | 1 | 2 | | |
| Castle, Booth | 1 | 2 | 2 | | | Ives, Anor, 2d | 1 | 1 | 1 | | | Marshal, Sarah | 1 | 4 | 3 | | |
| Demming, Phineas | 1 | 1 | 2 | | | Irwin, Andrew | 1 | | 1 | | | Maverill, John | 3 | 2 | 3 | | |
| Davidson, Jeames | 2 | 3 | 4 | | | Judson, Thomas | 1 | 2 | 4 | | | Munn, Daniel | 1 | 1 | 1 | | |
| Deforrest, John | 2 | 3 | 3 | | | Judson, Chapman | 1 | 2 | 3 | | | Munn, John | 1 | 2 | 2 | | |
| Dean, Samuel | 1 | | 3 | | | Judson, Joseph | 2 | 1 | 2 | | | Munn, Abel | 1 | 2 | 3 | | |
| Downes, Simeon | 1 | | 1 | | | Judson, Elisha | 2 | 3 | 4 | | | Munn, Gideon | 1 | 2 | 2 | | |
| Downes, Susannah | | 1 | 2 | | | Judson, Jonathan | 2 | 4 | 5 | | | Masters, John | 1 | | 1 | | |
| Dailey, Justus | 3 | 2 | 3 | | | Judson, Gideon | 2 | 1 | 4 | | | Masters, John, 2d | 2 | 3 | 3 | | |
| Easton, Eliphlet | 2 | | 1 | | | Judson, Isaih | 1 | | 1 | | | Mauray, David | 1 | | 3 | | |
| Edward, John | 2 | | 1 | | | Judson, Benjamin | 3 | 1 | 4 | | | Moody, Zimie | 2 | | 4 | | |
| Eastmon, Benjamin | 1 | 3 | 4 | | | Judson, John | 1 | 2 | 4 | | | Moody, Ebenezer | 1 | 1 | 1 | | |
| Eastman, Vespatian | 1 | | 3 | | | Judson, Noah | 4 | 1 | 4 | | | Munger, John | 1 | 2 | 5 | | |
| Titus (Eatheopian) | | | | 3 | | Judson, Joshua | 1 | | 3 | | | Mallery, John, 2d | 2 | 3 | 2 | | |
| Edgiton, Samuel | 1 | | 1 | | | Judson, Jeames | 2 | 2 | 4 | | | Mallery, David | 1 | 2 | 7 | | |
| Eastmon, Azeriah | 2 | 1 | 4 | | | Judson, Nehemiah | 2 | 4 | 4 | | | Mallery, Adna | 1 | | 1 | | |
| Eastman, Abner | 1 | | 3 | | | Judson, Hollister | 1 | | 4 | | | Mitchel, Beriah | 1 | | 1 | | |
| Easton, Norman | 1 | 2 | 5 | | | Judson, Emm | 1 | 2 | 2 | | | Mix, Abel | 2 | | 6 | | |
| Elderkin, Jedediah | 2 | 3 | 6 | | | Judson, David | 2 | 3 | 7 | | | Maltbie, Huldah | 1 | 3 | 4 | 1 | 1 |
| Eastman, Federich | 1 | 3 | 1 | | | Judson, Deborah | 2 | | 3 | | | Manvil, Simeon | 1 | 1 | 3 | | |
| Fairchild, Seth | 1 | | 5 | | | Judson, Seth | 1 | 1 | 1 | | | Marshal, Seth | 2 | | 2 | | |
| Flowers, Nathaniel | 1 | 1 | 3 | | | Judson, Daniel | 2 | 1 | 9 | | | Mitchel, Seth | 1 | 2 | 3 | | |
| French, Josiah | 1 | 1 | 3 | | | Judson, Nathan | 1 | 1 | 4 | | | Mallery, John | 1 | | 1 | | |
| Fusbrie, Ezekiel | 2 | | 3 | | | Jackson, David | 2 | 2 | 6 | | | Nihols, Gideon | 2 | 3 | 4 | | |
| Fusbrie, Noah | 1 | 2 | 3 | | | Jordan, Timothy | 2 | 1 | 2 | | | Nettleton, William | 1 | 2 | 4 | | |
| Galpin, Stephen | 1 | | 1 | | | Jackson, Comfort | 1 | 2 | 2 | | | Nettleton, Josiah | 1 | 1 | 3 | | |
| Galpin, Stephen Curtis | 1 | 2 | 4 | | | Judd, Daniel | 2 | 1 | 3 | | | Norton, George | 1 | | 2 | | |
| Galpin, Samuel | 3 | 1 | 2 | | | Jarvis, Thomas | 1 | | 4 | | | Norton, Austin | 1 | 3 | 3 | | |
| Galpin, Abram | 1 | | 3 | | | Keeler, Joseph | 1 | 1 | 4 | | | Northrop, Enoch | 1 | | 4 | | |
| Galpin, Curtis | 1 | | 3 | | | Kimberly, Jedediah | 1 | | 2 | | | Nichols, John | 1 | | | | |
| Glover, Budsery | 1 | 1 | 4 | | | Kimberly, Benjamin | 2 | 1 | 3 | | | Orton, Samuel | 1 | 5 | 4 | | |
| Gorden, Alexander | 2 | | 3 | | | Lyon, Bethuel | 1 | | 3 | | | Osborn, Nathan, 2d | 1 | 2 | 3 | | |
| Gibbs, Simeon | 1 | 2 | 3 | | | Lamson, Mitchel | 1 | 2 | 3 | | | Orton, John | 2 | 3 | 5 | | |
| Gilchrist, Damaras | | 1 | 4 | | | Leavenworth, Amos | 1 | 2 | 6 | | | Osborn, Nathan | 2 | | 1 | | |
| Gillet, David | 2 | 3 | 4 | | | Leavenworth, John | 2 | 1 | 3 | | | Odle, Walker | 1 | 1 | 1 | | |
| Galpin, Susannah | | | 3 | | | Linsley, Abiel | 2 | | 1 | | | Peet, Elnathan | 2 | | 2 | | |
| Griswold, Jonathan | 1 | 1 | 4 | | | Leavenworth, David | 2 | 1 | 3 | | | Pond, Dan | 1 | 1 | 5 | | |
| Hyde, Gideon | 2 | 1 | 3 | | | Leavenworth, Elihu | 1 | 3 | 2 | | 2 | Pond, Edward | 2 | | 5 | | |
| Hurd, Nathan | 1 | 2 | 4 | | 1 | Leavenworth, Gideon | 1 | 2 | 4 | | | Pollard, Isaac | 1 | | 6 | | |
| Hurd, Graham | 1 | 3 | 2 | | | Leavenworth, Moss | 1 | 3 | 2 | | | Prentice, Ameziah | 1 | 3 | 2 | | |
| Hurd, Andrew | 3 | | 2 | | | Lucas, Israel | 1 | 1 | | | | Percy, Nathaniel | 2 | | 1 | | |
| Hander, Shuball | 2 | | 2 | | | Leavenworth, Esther | | | 3 | | | Peck, Joseph | 2 | 2 | 4 | | |
| Huntington, Daniel | 2 | 2 | 6 | | | Lacy, Ezra | 1 | 1 | 3 | | | Percy, Joseph | 2 | | 4 | | |
| Hine, Joel | 1 | 2 | 1 | | | Martin, Solomon | 1 | | 2 | | | Prentice, Thomas | 1 | 1 | 3 | | |
| Hine, Jonah | 1 | | 2 | | | Martin, Amos | 2 | 1 | 4 | | | Prentice, Zackeriah | 1 | | 4 | | |
| Hull, Daniel | 2 | | 1 | | | Martin, John | 2 | | 4 | | | Price, Benjamin | 1 | 2 | 3 | | |
| Hotchkiss, Reuben | 1 | 3 | 1 | | | Martin, Elijah | 3 | 1 | 4 | | | Painter, Lamberton | 3 | 1 | 7 | | |
| Hurlbert, Turman | 2 | 5 | 1 | | | Martin, Nathan, 2d | 1 | 2 | 2 | | | Paterson, Andrew | 2 | 4 | 2 | | |
| Hurd, Wait | 1 | 2 | 5 | | | Martin, Abijah | 1 | | 2 | | | Peck, Hezekiah | 2 | 1 | 2 | | |
| Hall, John | 1 | | 2 | | | Martin, Jonas | 1 | 3 | 5 | | | Penery, Nathan | 1 | 1 | 1 | | |
| Hunt, Isaac | 2 | 2 | 2 | | | Martin, Samuel | 1 | 1 | 3 | | | Prentice, Ozias | 1 | 2 | 2 | | |
| Hunt, Isaac, 2d | 1 | 2 | 2 | | | Martin, Nathan | 2 | 3 | 2 | | | Prindle, John | 1 | | | (*) | |
| Hunt, Seth | 1 | 1 | 4 | | | Martin, Gold | 1 | | 1 | | | Pompey, London | | | | 1 | |
| Hunt, Gideon | 3 | | 1 | | | Martin, Thankful | | | 1 | | | Pompy (negro) | | | | 4 | |
| Hunt, William | 1 | | 2 | | | Martin, Isaac | 2 | 2 | 2 | | | Roots, Amos | 1 | 1 | 3 | | |
| Hunt, Lydia | 2 | | 3 | | | Mallery, Gideon | 1 | | 6 | | | Roots, John | 3 | 1 | 4 | | |
| Hand, Bendict | 1 | 2 | 4 | | | Mallery, Walker | 2 | 3 | 3 | | | Roots, Thomas | 1 | 1 | 4 | | |
| Hinman, Ephraim | 3 | 1 | 3 | | | Mallery, Thomas | 3 | | 4 | | | Roots, Jesse | 1 | 1 | 1 | | |
| Hurlburt, Amos | 1 | 2 | 4 | | | Mallery, David | 1 | 1 | 4 | | | Roots, Jesse, 2d | 1 | | 5 | | |
| Hurlburt, Thomas | 1 | 3 | 2 | | | Miner, Solomon | 1 | 4 | 3 | | | Roots, Amos, 2d | 1 | | 3 | | |
| Hurlburt, Ebenezer | 1 | | | | | Mallery, Aaron | 2 | | 4 | | | Russel, Benjamin | 1 | 6 | 3 | | |
| Hurlburt, Gideon | 1 | | 2 | | | Miner, Simeon | 1 | 2 | 4 | | | Roots, David | 1 | 1 | 5 | | |
| Hawley, Ann | | 2 | 4 | | | Miner, Gilbert | 1 | 1 | 3 | | | Ransom, Russel | 4 | 2 | 5 | | |
| Hurd, Simeon | 3 | 1 | 4 | | | Miner, Daniel | 4 | 2 | 3 | | | Rumsey, Nathan | 3 | | 1 | | |
| Hurd, Curtis | 2 | 2 | 6 | | | Miner, Seth | 2 | 1 | 4 | | | Rumsey, David | 2 | 3 | 2 | | |
| Hurd, Moses | 1 | 2 | 3 | | | Miner, David | 1 | 2 | 1 | | | Rogers, Jason | 1 | 6 | 4 | | |
| Hurd, Thaddeus | 3 | 3 | 5 | | | Miner, Preston | 1 | | 2 | | | Roots, Joseph | 1 | | 3 | | |
| Hurd, David | 1 | 1 | 3 | | | Miner, Mathew | 1 | 1 | 4 | | | Roots, Colonel | 2 | | | | |
| Hurd, David, 2d | 1 | 2 | 4 | | | Miner, Jonas | 1 | | 2 | | | Rogers, Phineas | 1 | 3 | 3 | | |
| Hough, Buel | 1 | 3 | 5 | | | Miner, Andrew | 4 | 1 | 2 | | | Rummery, Sarah | | 1 | 3 | | |
| Hodge, Philo | 2 | 1 | 4 | | | Miner, Benjamin | 1 | 1 | 1 | | | Rowel, Caleb | 1 | 2 | 3 | | |
| Hurd, Adam | 1 | 3 | 3 | | | Miner, Adam | 1 | 1 | 3 | | | Shelton, William | 1 | 1 | 1 | | |
| | | | | | | Miner, Nathan | 1 | | 3 | | | Strong, Solomon | 3 | 1 | 2 | | |

*Illegible.

# HEADS OF FAMILIES—CONNECTICUT.

## LITCHFIELD COUNTY—Continued.

| NAME OF HEAD OF FAMILY. | Free white males of 16 years and upward, including heads of families. | Free white males under 16 years. | Free white females, including heads of families. | All other free persons. | Slaves. | NAME OF HEAD OF FAMILY. | Free white males of 16 years and upward, including heads of families. | Free white males under 16 years. | Free white females, including heads of families. | All other free persons. | Slaves. | NAME OF HEAD OF FAMILY. | Free white males of 16 years and upward, including heads of families. | Free white males under 16 years. | Free white females, including heads of families. | All other free persons. | Slaves. |
|---|---|---|---|---|---|---|---|---|---|---|---|---|---|---|---|---|---|
| **WOODBURY TOWN— continued.** | | | | | | **WOODBURY TOWN— continued.** | | | | | | **WOODBURY TOWN— continued.** | | | | | |
| Strong, John | 2 | 2 | 2 | | | Stoddard, Ichabod | 1 | 2 | 3 | | | Thayer, Cornelius | 1 | 2 | 3 | | |
| Spalding, Jonas | 1 | 1 | 3 | | | Smith, Kinner | 1 | 2 | 1 | | | Taylor, Charles | 3 | | 2 | | |
| Stoddard, Seth | 1 | 3 | 2 | | | Smith, Asa | 1 | | 1 | | | Tuttle, Bostwick | 1 | | 2 | | |
| Stoddard, Israel | 2 | 3 | 3 | | | Smith, Bethel | 1 | 2 | 4 | | | Tuttle, Samuel | 1 | 3 | 4 | | |
| Stoddard, Gideon | 3 | | 4 | | | Smith, Sabra | | 1 | 2 | | | Terrill, Nathaniel | 1 | 4 | 1 | | |
| Spalding, Oliver | 1 | 1 | 2 | | | Smith, Robert | 1 | 2 | 2 | | | Terrill, Jonathan | 1 | 2 | 1 | | |
| Stoddard, Eunice | 2 | | 3 | | | Sherman, Mathew | 1 | 3 | 1 | | | Tyler, Ebenezer | 1 | 1 | 6 | | |
| Stoddard, Philo | 1 | 2 | 3 | | | Sherman, David | 5 | 1 | 2 | | | Thomas, Ira | 1 | | 2 | | |
| Stoddard, David | 2 | | 2 | | | Stoddard, Thaddeus | 1 | | 4 | | | Torrence, Samuel | 1 | 3 | 4 | | |
| Stoddard, David, 2d | 1 | 1 | 2 | | | Stoddard, Daniel | 1 | 1 | 4 | | | Woodman, Samuel | 1 | 3 | 4 | | |
| Stoddard, Elisha | 3 | 1 | 4 | | | Tuttle, Ezekiel | 2 | | 2 | | | Walker, Peter | 1 | 1 | 8 | | |
| Schuls, Samuel | 1 | 3 | 3 | | | Tuttle, Ayers | 1 | 2 | 2 | | | Walker, Samuel | 2 | 2 | 5 | | 1 |
| Shelton, Gershom | 1 | | | | | Tuttle, Aaron | 1 | | 1 | | | Way, Daniel | 1 | | 1 | | |
| Sanford, Nathan | 1 | 2 | 4 | | | Tuttle, Ephraim | 1 | | 2 | | | Warner, Nathan | 2 | 2 | 3 | | |
| Scott, Adoniram | 1 | | 2 | | | Tuttle, Andrew | 3 | 3 | 4 | | | Warner, Emm | | 1 | 5 | | |
| Smith, Amos | 1 | 2 | 1 | | | Tuttle, Daniel | 1 | 2 | 6 | | | Warner, Benjamin | 3 | 2 | 2 | | |
| Smith, Frederick | 1 | 1 | 2 | | | Tuttle, Abram | 1 | 1 | 2 | | | Warner, Ebenezer | 1 | | 2 | | |
| Smith, Nathaniel | 2 | 1 | 1 | | | Tuttle, David | 2 | 3 | 2 | | | Warner, Ebenezer, 2d | 2 | 3 | 6 | | |
| Smith, Samuel | 1 | | 2 | | | Tyler, Jeames | 2 | 2 | 2 | | | Warner, Thomas | 1 | 2 | 4 | | |
| Smith, Thomas | 1 | | 1 | | | Tyler, Jeames, 2d | 1 | | | | | Warner, Samuel | 1 | 3 | 3 | | |
| Shelton, Daniel | 2 | 3 | 4 | | | Tyler, Roswell | 1 | | 2 | | | Warner, Joseph | 2 | 1 | 3 | | |
| Sherwood, Jonathan | 1 | 3 | 4 | | | Tomlinson, Isaac | 3 | 1 | 3 | 1 | | Warner, Gideon | 1 | 1 | 4 | | |
| Sherman, Elijah | 6 | 4 | 4 | | | Tomlinson, Timothy | 1 | | | | | Warner, Saul | 1 | 3 | 3 | | |
| Sherman, Daniel | 1 | | 2 | | | Thomson, Hezekiah | 3 | 2 | 4 | | | Warner, Esther | 1 | | 2 | | |
| Sherman, Reuben | 2 | | 2 | | | Terrill, Lee | 1 | 2 | 3 | | | Warner, David | 1 | 1 | 3 | | |
| Sherman, Daniel, 2d | 1 | 1 | 4 | | | Terrill, Timothy | 1 | 1 | 3 | | | Warner, Rhoda | | 1 | 1 | | |
| Sherman, Solomon | 1 | | 2 | | | Towles, Nehemiah | 2 | 3 | 2 | | | Warner, Abijail | | | 2 | | |
| Stoters, Jonathan | 1 | | 3 | | | Towles, Ira | 1 | 3 | 2 | | | Walker, Joseph, 2d | 1 | 2 | 4 | | |
| Smith, Jonathan | 1 | 1 | 6 | | | Trobridge, John | 2 | 3 | 1 | | | Weller, Zacheriah | 3 | | 3 | | |
| Squire, Nathan | 1 | 1 | 1 | | | Taylor, Simeon | 1 | 3 | 4 | | | Weller, Samuel | 2 | 1 | 3 | | |
| Squire, Thomas | 1 | | | | | Townsend, Ezra | 1 | | | | | Weller, Daniel | 1 | 3 | 3 | | |
| Squire, Amos | 1 | 1 | 2 | | | Thomas, Charles | 2 | 1 | 4 | | | Wells, Thomas | 1 | 2 | 5 | | |
| Squire, Benjamin | 1 | 1 | 3 | | | Thomas, John | 1 | | | | | Wilcox, Stephen | 1 | 2 | 1 | | |
| Squire, Thomas, 2d | 1 | 2 | 5 | | | Thomas, Jeremiah | 1 | 4 | 6 | | | Way, Isaac | 1 | 2 | 4 | | |
| Smith, Phineas | 2 | 1 | 2 | | | Thomas, David | 1 | 3 | 4 | | | Wakeley, Henry | 1 | | 3 | | |
| Smith, Richard | 3 | | 2 | | | Thomas, Ebenezer | 2 | 3 | 4 | | | Wakeley, Platt | 1 | 1 | 2 | | |
| Sherman, John | 2 | | 5 | | | Thomas, Abram | 2 | 1 | 3 | | | Williams, David | 1 | 1 | 4 | | |
| Sherman, John, 2d | 1 | 1 | 3 | | | Thomas, Friend | 1 | 1 | 3 | | | Whitney, Samuel | 1 | 1 | 4 | | |
| Semour, John | 1 | | 1 | | | Talman, Ebenezer | 1 | 1 | 2 | | | Welles, Elijah | 1 | 1 | 4 | | |
| Semour, John, 2d | 1 | 1 | 1 | | | Talman, Josiah | 1 | 1 | 1 | | | Walker, Joseph | 1 | 1 | 1 | | |
| Semour, Joseph | 1 | 1 | 1 | | | Tomlinson, Samuel | 1 | 1 | 1 | | | Warner, Enos | 1 | 2 | 3 | | |
| Stoddard, Simeon | 1 | 1 | 1 | | | Tomkins, Joseph | 1 | 1 | 2 | | | | | | | | |

## MIDDLESEX COUNTY.

| NAME OF HEAD OF FAMILY. | Free white males of 16 years and upward, including heads of families. | Free white males under 16 years. | Free white females, including heads of families. | All other free persons. | Slaves. | NAME OF HEAD OF FAMILY. | Free white males of 16 years and upward, including heads of families. | Free white males under 16 years. | Free white females, including heads of families. | All other free persons. | Slaves. | NAME OF HEAD OF FAMILY. | Free white males of 16 years and upward, including heads of families. | Free white males under 16 years. | Free white females, including heads of families. | All other free persons. | Slaves. |
|---|---|---|---|---|---|---|---|---|---|---|---|---|---|---|---|---|---|
| **CHATHAM TOWN.** | | | | | | **CHATHAM TOWN—continued.** | | | | | | **CHATHAM TOWN—continued.** | | | | | |
| Akin, Reuben | 1 | | 3 | | | Goodrich, Richard | 1 | | 2 | | | Brown, Jonathan | 2 | 1 | 2 | | |
| Abby, Samuel | 3 | 1 | 3 | | | Goodrich, Jeremiah, Junr | 2 | 5 | 5 | | | Bidwell, Daniel | 2 | 3 | 6 | | |
| Abby, Benjamin | 1 | 6 | 1 | | | Goodrich, Joshua | 2 | 1 | 5 | | | Crittendon, Daniel | 1 | 2 | 4 | | |
| Andrews, Daniel | 1 | 3 | 1 | | | Goodrich, Solomon | 3 | 1 | 2 | | | Cornwell, Thomas | 1 | 1 | 5 | | |
| Akin, Samuel | 1 | 3 | 2 | | | Goodrich, Reuben | 1 | 3 | 3 | | | Cornwell, Nathaniel | 2 | 4 | 4 | | |
| Ames, Nicholas | 2 | 1 | 5 | | | Goodrich, Charles, Junr | 3 | | 4 | | | Cornwell, Samuel | 1 | 3 | 2 | | |
| Brown, Nathaniel | 4 | | 3 | | | Goodrich, Hezekiah | 6 | | 7 | | | Cornwell, Andrew | 1 | 3 | 2 | | |
| Brown, Richard | 1 | 2 | 4 | | | Gildersleeves, Obediah | 1 | | 2 | | | Chapman, David | 2 | 2 | 4 | | |
| Brown, Ebenezer | 1 | | 2 | | | Gildersleeves, Philip | 1 | 3 | 2 | | | Casheen, William | 1 | | 1 | | |
| Baley, Abraham | 2 | | 4 | | | Gleason, Joseph | 1 | 3 | 1 | | | Chapman, John | 1 | 4 | 3 | | |
| Baley, Recompence | 3 | | 2 | | | Gains, John | 2 | 1 | 3 | | | Chapman, Solomon | 1 | 2 | 3 | | |
| Bates, Job | 1 | | 2 | | | Goodrich, Jeremiah | 1 | | 1 | | | Churchell, Joseph | 3 | 1 | 2 | | 1 |
| Bates, David | 1 | 4 | 4 | | | Grimes, Joseph | 2 | | 1 | | | Cooper, George | 1 | | 2 | | |
| Bates, Abner | 1 | 1 | 2 | | | Hall, Samuel | 1 | | 1 | | | Cooper, John | 1 | | 2 | | |
| Bidwell, John | 1 | 6 | 3 | | | Hall, David | 1 | 2 | 3 | | | Chapman, Caleb | 1 | | 1 | | |
| Bartlett, John, Junr | 2 | 1 | 5 | | | Hall, Gideon | 1 | | 2 | | | Ellsworth, John | 1 | 1 | 5 | | |
| Bartlett, Moses | 1 | 1 | 2 | | | Hall, Abijah | 2 | 4 | 3 | | | Churchell, Daniel | 1 | 3 | 4 | | 1 |
| Buck, Samuel | 1 | 1 | 3 | | | Hall, Joel | 4 | 4 | 4 | | | Cheany, Daniel | 1 | 1 | 1 | | |
| Buck, Isaac | 1 | | 1 | | | Hale, Benjamin | 1 | | 6 | | | Crosby, John | 1 | | 2 | | |
| Bowers, Benajah | 1 | | 1 | | | Hale, Elisha | 1 | 1 | 2 | | | Chipman, Ebenezer | 1 | | 3 | | |
| Blague, Joseph | 2 | 1 | 2 | | | Hale, Daniel | 1 | | 2 | | | Chipman, Joseph | 1 | | | | |
| Brewer, Hezekiah | 3 | | 1 | | | Hale, Jonathan | 2 | 3 | 5 | | | Chipman, Barnabas | 1 | | | | |
| Belcher, Jonathan | 4 | 2 | 4 | | | Hall, Isaac | 1 | | 3 | | | Cooper, Thomas | 1 | 3 | 3 | | |
| Bacon, Beriah | 2 | | 3 | | | Hale, Elisha, Junr | 1 | 2 | 3 | | | Cooper, Deliverance | 1 | 1 | 3 | | |
| Bush, Moses | 1 | | 2 | | 3 | Hulbert, Gideon | 1 | 1 | 3 | | | Cooper, Timothy | 2 | 3 | 4 | | |
| Bush, Jonathan | 1 | 2 | 4 | | | Johnson, Jessey | 5 | 1 | 8 | | | Cooper, Harris S | 2 | 1 | 1 | | |
| Bush, George | 1 | 1 | 2 | 1 | | Kellogg, Joseph | 1 | 6 | 2 | | | Chappell, Jonathan | 1 | | 2 | | |
| Bliss, Thomas | 1 | | 3 | | | Knowles, Giles | 1 | 2 | 3 | | | McCleave, John | 1 | 1 | 2 | | |
| Bevins, Ezra | 1 | 1 | 1 | | | Knowles, Isaac | 1 | | 2 | | | McCorney, William, Junr | 1 | | 1 | | |
| Bush, Elisha | 1 | | | | | Knowles, Seth | 1 | 2 | 2 | | | McComb, John | 1 | | 1 | | |
| Brown, Samuel | 1 | 2 | 2 | | | Lewis, Moses | 1 | 1 | 4 | | | Norton, Jedediah | 1 | | 2 | | |
| Butler, John | 1 | 1 | 2 | | | Lewis, George, Junr | 2 | | 2 | | | Norcott, Abner | 1 | | | | |
| Boardman, Asa | 1 | | 3 | | | Lewis, George | 1 | | 3 | 1 | | Overton, Seth | 1 | 3 | 4 | | |
| Goodale, Henry | 2 | | 4 | | | Lee, Daniel | 1 | 2 | 11 | | | Pelton, John | 2 | | 3 | | |
| Crosby, William | 1 | | 1 | | | McCorney, William | 2 | | 1 | | | Pelton, Ithamar | 2 | 4 | 3 | | |
| Freeman, Cato | | | | 4 | | Maharr, James | 1 | 3 | 2 | | | Farmer, Aaron | 1 | 2 | 5 | | |
| Dixon, William | 4 | 3 | 7 | | | Butler, Samuel | 1 | 1 | 1 | | | Potter, Ezra | 1 | | 3 | | |
| Dean, Phinehas | 2 | 1 | 3 | | | Buck, Jeremiah | 2 | 2 | 1 | | | Phelps, Elisha | 1 | 1 | 2 | | |
| Davis, Charles | 1 | 2 | 3 | | | Bartlett, Thomas | 1 | 1 | 2 | | | Pelton, John, Junr | 1 | | 3 | | |
| Diggins, Welles | 1 | 1 | 4 | | | Bartlett, John | 1 | 1 | 1 | | | Pain, Reuben | 1 | 4 | 1 | | |
| Edy, Seth | 1 | 3 | 5 | | | Babbett, Jacob | 2 | 1 | 5 | | | Pane, Amasa | 1 | 1 | 1 | | |
| Edy, Thomas | 1 | 2 | 6 | | | Bebee, Richard | 1 | | 3 | | | Penfield, Simeon | 1 | | 2 | | |
| Fox, John | 2 | | 2 | | | Brewer, David | 1 | | 1 | | | Penfield, Jonathan | 1 | | 2 | | |
| Bagley, David | 1 | 4 | 2 | | | | | | | | | Penfield, John | 4 | 1 | 4 | | |
| Goodrich, Charles | 3 | | 4 | | | | | | | | | | | | | | |

# FIRST CENSUS OF THE UNITED STATES.

## MIDDLESEX COUNTY—Continued.

### CHATHAM TOWN—continued.

| NAME OF HEAD OF FAMILY. | Free white males of 16 years and upward, including heads of families. | Free white males under 16 years. | Free white females, including heads of families. | All other free persons. | Slaves. |
|---|---|---|---|---|---|
| Penfield, Jessey | 1 | 1 | 2 | | |
| Penfield, Samuel | 1 | 1 | 3 | | |
| Penfield, Amos | 1 | 2 | 4 | | |
| Penfield, Abel | 1 | 1 | 3 | | |
| Penfield, Simeon, Junr | 1 | 2 | 3 | | |
| Penfield, Abisha | 1 | 3 | 1 | | |
| Penfield, Stephen | 1 | 2 | 2 | | |
| Pelton, Johnson | 1 | | 1 | | |
| Pelton, Johnson, Junr | 2 | 1 | 6 | | |
| Pelton, Josiah | 3 | | 4 | | |
| Pelton, Joseph | 3 | | 3 | | |
| Pelton, Joseph, Junr | 1 | 3 | 2 | | |
| Pelton, Jonathan | 1 | 2 | 3 | | |
| Pelton, Abner | 1 | 3 | 4 | | |
| Pelton, Moses | 1 | | | | |
| Harrington, Jeremiah | 1 | 1 | 2 | | |
| Rensom, Peleg | 1 | | 1 | | |
| Pelton, Phinehas | 1 | | 1 | | |
| Robinson, David | 3 | | 2 | | |
| Reves, Samuel | 1 | | 1 | | |
| Ranny, Stephen | 1 | | 4 | | |
| Russell, Noadiah | 2 | | 2 | | |
| Russell, Timothy | 1 | | 3 | | |
| Ranny, George | 2 | 2 | 4 | | |
| Ranney, Thomas | 1 | 2 | 3 | | |
| Ranney, Stephen, Junr | 1 | | 2 | | |
| Reaves, John | 2 | 1 | 3 | | |
| Rass, Noah | 1 | | 3 | | |
| Randal, John | 1 | 3 | 5 | | |
| Rise, Benjamin | 2 | | 2 | | |
| Ranney, Jabez | 1 | 1 | 1 | | |
| Strong, Revd Cuprian | 1 | 4 | 5 | | |
| Sage, David, Esqr | 1 | | 4 | | |
| Sage, Joseph | 1 | 3 | 2 | | |
| Sage, Noah | 1 | 1 | 2 | | |
| Stocking, John | 1 | | 3 | | |
| Shields, James | 1 | | 1 | | |
| Schallenx, Abraham | 2 | 2 | 3 | | |
| Schallennex, Gideon | 1 | 4 | 3 | | |
| Savage, John | 1 | 2 | 4 | | |
| Savage, David | 1 | 2 | 1 | | |
| Savage, Luther | 1 | 1 | 4 | | |
| Stantliff, James, Junr | 1 | 1 | 3 | | |
| Smith, Noah | 1 | | 5 | | |
| Smith, Charles | 1 | 1 | 1 | | |
| Stow, Daniel, Junr | 1 | | 2 | | |
| Stewart, Robert | 1 | 1 | 2 | | |
| Sage, Enoch | 2 | 3 | 6 | | |
| Sage, Abner | 1 | 1 | 4 | 1 | |
| Strickland, Abel | 1 | 3 | 3 | | |
| Smith, Peter | 2 | | 3 | | |
| Stocking, David | 3 | 1 | 1 | | |
| Goodrich, John | 2 | 2 | 3 | | |
| Shepherd, John | 2 | | 2 | | |
| Strickland, Seth | 2 | | 4 | | |
| Shepherd, John, Junr | 1 | 1 | 1 | | |
| Shepherd, Amos | 1 | | 4 | | |
| Shepherd, Elisha | 4 | 3 | 2 | | |
| Shepherd, Daniel, Junr | 2 | 2 | 6 | | |
| Stewart, Daniel | 4 | 1 | 6 | 6 | 1 |
| Stewart, Michael | 2 | 1 | 5 | | |
| Stocking, Marshall | 3 | | 1 | | |
| Stocking, Moses | 1 | 1 | 2 | | |
| Shepherd, George | 1 | | 1 | | |
| Shepherd, Noah | 1 | | | | |
| Shepherd, Billy | 1 | | 1 | | |
| Shepherd, Elisha, Junr | 1 | | 2 | | |
| Gildersleeves, Phillip | 1 | 3 | 2 | | |
| Shepherd, Daniel | 3 | 2 | 6 | | |
| Stocking, Benjamin | 2 | | 2 | | |
| Tom, Stephen | | | | 6 | |
| Ufford, John | 1 | 1 | 4 | | |
| Ufford, Elakim | 2 | 1 | 2 | | |
| Ufford, John, Junr | 1 | | | | |
| Ufford, Jonathan | 2 | 4 | 5 | | |
| Vansant, Christopher | 1 | | 2 | | |
| White, Ebenezer, Esqr | 2 | 1 | 2 | | |
| White, David | 1 | | 3 | | |
| White, Noadiah, Junr | 1 | 3 | 4 | | |
| White, Noadiah | 3 | | 4 | | |
| White, Joseph | 1 | 4 | 3 | | |
| White, Josiah, Junr | 1 | 4 | 3 | | |
| White, George | 1 | | 1 | | |
| Willcox, Joseph | 1 | 1 | 4 | | |
| Willcox, Samuel | 1 | 1 | 4 | | |
| Wright, John | 1 | 3 | 3 | | |
| Woolcott, Joshua | 1 | | 1 | | |
| Waterman, Sylvenus | 1 | 1 | 1 | | |
| Waterman, Samuel | 1 | 1 | 3 | | |
| Willcox, Reuben | 1 | | 1 | | |
| Welles, Thomas | 2 | 3 | 6 | | |
| Willcox, Aaron | 3 | 2 | 3 | | |
| Witherell, Jonathan | 3 | 3 | 3 | | |
| Warner, Deliverance | 2 | 3 | 6 | | |
| Washbourn, John | 1 | | 2 | | |
| Wright, Jonas | 1 | 2 | 5 | | |
| Williams, William | 1 | 1 | 3 | | |
| Ackley, Oliver | 1 | 2 | 5 | | |
| Able, Ebel | 2 | 3 | 4 | | |
| Akins, Thomas | 1 | | 1 | | |
| Akins, Thomas, Junr | 1 | 2 | 6 | | |
| Akins, George | 1 | | 1 | | |
| Wood, Jason | 1 | 1 | 5 | | |
| Brainard, Daniel | 1 | 2 | 5 | | |
| Brainard, Seth | 2 | 1 | 4 | | |
| Bevins, Benjamin, Junr | 1 | | | | |
| Brown, Nathaniel | 1 | 2 | 2 | | |
| Buckley, Chauncey | 2 | | 2 | | |
| Bradford, Jeremiah | 2 | | 2 | | |
| Brainard, Jepthia | 1 | 3 | 2 | | |
| Bradford, Jeremiah, Junr | 1 | | 3 | | |
| Brainard, James | 2 | 4 | 6 | | |
| Bowers, Jonathan | 2 | 3 | 2 | | |
| Brainard, Simeon | 2 | 1 | 3 | | |
| Brainard, Simeon, Junr | 1 | 3 | 3 | | |
| Brainard, Ozias | 2 | 3 | 7 | | |
| Hollester, David B | 1 | | 4 | | |
| Brainard, Nathan | 2 | 4 | 6 | | |
| Hubbard, Royel | 1 | 1 | 1 | | |
| Brooks, Samuel | 1 | 3 | 5 | | |
| Crowell, Heman | 2 | 2 | 5 | | |
| Cary, Josiah | 1 | | 3 | | |
| Cary, Wait S | 1 | 2 | 2 | | |
| Cady, Ephraim | 1 | | 3 | | |
| Cook, Josiah | 1 | | 5 | | |
| Crittendon, Josiah | 1 | 3 | 2 | | |
| Clark, Jonathan | 1 | | 2 | 2 | |
| Clark, Elijah | 1 | | 2 | | |
| Cook, Mary | 1 | | 3 | | |
| Doan, Seth | 3 | | 1 | | 2 |
| Doan, Asaph | 1 | | 3 | | |
| Doan, Nathaniel, 2d | 2 | 1 | 3 | | |
| Doan, Nathaniel | 2 | 1 | 3 | | |
| Dart, Josiah | 2 | | 4 | | |
| Doan, Timothy | 1 | 2 | 3 | | |
| Daniels, Lemuel | 1 | | 1 | | |
| Daniels, Amasa | 2 | 5 | 3 | | |
| Exton, William | 1 | | 3 | | |
| Edy, John, Junr | 3 | | 2 | | |
| Edy, John, 3d | 1 | | | | |
| Freeman, Barnabas | 1 | 1 | 5 | | |
| Fuller, Amasa | 1 | 1 | 1 | | |
| Fuller, Abijah | 1 | | 2 | | |
| Fuller, Samuel | 2 | | 6 | | |
| Fuller, Thomas | 1 | | 2 | | |
| Freeman, Nathaniel | 2 | 1 | 2 | | |
| Griffen, Joshua | 1 | 1 | 4 | | |
| Goff, John | 2 | 2 | 4 | | |
| Goff, Ezekiel | 1 | 2 | 3 | | |
| Goff, Phillip | 2 | | 1 | | |
| Goff, Phillip, Junr | 1 | | 1 | | |
| Hubbard, Jedediah | 2 | 2 | 3 | | |
| Higgins, Israel | 2 | | 4 | | |
| Higgins, Israel, Junr | 1 | 1 | 2 | | |
| Hurd, Benjamin | 2 | 2 | 3 | | |
| Higgins, Thesiah | | | 2 | | |
| Wheat, Jonas | 2 | 4 | 4 | | |
| Hosmer, Zacheriah | 2 | 1 | 3 | | |
| Higgins, Lemuel | 1 | | 1 | | |
| Hosmer, Stephen, Junr | 1 | | 1 | | |
| Hosmer, Asa | 1 | | 3 | | |
| Holibard, Jehiel | 1 | 2 | 4 | | |
| Holibard, Elisha | 6 | 2 | 6 | | |
| Hurd, Joseph | 1 | 2 | 5 | | |
| Higgins, Lemuel, Junr | 1 | | 1 | | |
| Hubbard, Jedediah | 1 | | 2 | | |
| Hubbard, Calvin | 1 | | 1 | | |
| Hubbard, Timothy | 1 | | | | |
| Hurd, Jacob | 2 | | 2 | | |
| Hubbard, Abner | 1 | 2 | 1 | | |
| Hurd, Jessey | 1 | | 2 | | |
| Hubbard, Jessey | 2 | | 1 | | |
| Hubbard, George | 1 | 2 | 3 | | |
| Higgins, Timothy | 1 | | 1 | | |
| Holibard, David | 2 | 2 | 6 | | |
| Hosmer, Stephen | 1 | 2 | 2 | | |
| Hill, Daniel | 1 | | 2 | | |
| Hurd, Jacob, Junr | 1 | 2 | 2 | | |
| Holibard, William, Junr | 1 | 2 | 3 | | |
| Holibard, Reuben | 2 | 2 | 1 | | |
| Johnson, Joseph | 2 | 1 | 2 | | |
| Pelton, George | 1 | | 1 | | |
| Higgins, James | 1 | 2 | 3 | | |
| Hubbard, John, Junr | 4 | 3 | 5 | | |
| Higgins, Moses | 4 | 3 | 3 | | |
| Mayo, Richard | 2 | 2 | 4 | | |
| Polly, John | 1 | | | | |
| Purple, Josiah | 1 | 3 | 2 | | |
| Park, Joseph | 1 | | 7 | | |
| Park, John | 1 | 1 | 1 | | 1 |
| Rowley, Ebenezer | 1 | 2 | 3 | | |
| Ranney, Amos | 1 | 2 | 4 | | |
| Rowley, Gershom | 1 | | 2 | | |
| Rowley, Ithamar | 1 | 2 | 4 | | |
| Rider, John | 1 | 4 | 2 | | |
| Stocking, Reuben | 3 | 2 | 6 | | |
| Strong, Caleb | 1 | 4 | 6 | | |
| Shepherd, Elisha, Junr | 1 | | 2 | | |
| Strong, Benjamin | 1 | 3 | 2 | | |
| Shepherd, Abel | 1 | 3 | 6 | | |
| Smith, Enoch, Junr | 1 | 3 | 3 | | |
| Smith, Daniel | 2 | | 2 | | |
| Smith, Enoch | 1 | 1 | 3 | | 1 |
| Smith, Ralp | 3 | 2 | 3 | | |
| Smith, Heman | 1 | | 3 | | |
| Skeel, Asa | 2 | | 3 | | |
| Smith, Lemuel | 4 | | 3 | | |
| Swaddle, Sarah | | | | | |
| Smith, David | 4 | 2 | 5 | | |
| Smith, Timothy | 1 | 3 | 2 | | |
| Seldon, Thomas | 1 | 6 | 3 | | |
| Strong, John | 1 | 3 | 2 | | |
| Stocking, Abner | 1 | | 1 | | |
| Smith, Michael, Junr | 1 | 2 | 2 | | |
| Stocking, Amasa | 1 | 2 | 3 | | |
| Taylor, Noadiah | 3 | 2 | 5 | | |
| Smith, Benjamin | 4 | 4 | 5 | | |
| Strong, Josiah | 2 | 3 | 8 | | |
| Shepherd, Edward | 2 | 1 | 2 | | 2 |
| Shepherd, Edward, Junr | 1 | 1 | 2 | | |
| Sears Hezekiah | 3 | 2 | 7 | | |
| Seldon, Aaron | 1 | 2 | 4 | | |
| Smith, David | 1 | 1 | 2 | | |
| Taylor, Noadiah | 1 | | 1 | | |
| Taylor, Elisha | 1 | | 1 | | |
| Selden, David | 1 | 4 | 2 | | |
| Taylor, Samuel | 4 | 3 | 8 | | |
| Shepherd, Thomas | 1 | | 2 | | |
| Snow, Ebenezer | 1 | 1 | 2 | | |
| Wright, John | 1 | | 1 | | |
| Wright, William | 2 | 1 | 7 | | |
| Young, Samuel | 3 | 2 | 4 | | |
| Young, Elijah | 1 | 1 | 2 | | |
| Ackley, Thomas | 4 | | 1 | | |
| Ackley, Stephen | 3 | | 5 | | |
| Ackley, Levi | 1 | | | | |
| Alvord, Seth, Junr | 1 | 3 | 4 | | |
| Whitmore, Luther | 1 | 3 | 3 | | |
| Alvord, Orin | 1 | 1 | 5 | | |
| Alvord, Seth | 1 | 1 | 2 | | |
| Ackley, James, Junr | 1 | 1 | 1 | | |
| Ackley, Ezra | 1 | 1 | 8 | | |
| Alvord, Rend | 1 | 2 | 4 | | |
| Ackley, Elizabeth | | | | | |
| Ackley, Edward | 1 | 1 | 5 | | |
| Bailey, Ebenezer | 1 | 4 | 6 | | |
| Bailey, Robert | 1 | 4 | 4 | | |
| Brown, Samuel | 2 | | 1 | | |
| Brown, Samuel, Junr | 1 | 1 | 3 | | |
| Brainard, Othniel | 1 | 1 | 4 | | |
| Bailey, James | 2 | 1 | 2 | | |
| Bill, Erastus | 1 | | 2 | | |
| Bailey, Joshua, Junr | 1 | | 2 | | |
| Bailey, Joshua | 3 | | 4 | | |
| Bars, James | 2 | | 2 | | |
| Beebe, Comfort | 1 | | 1 | | |
| Babbett, Elijah | 1 | 1 | 5 | | |
| Bevin, William | 1 | | 2 | | |
| Bevin, Isaac | 1 | 3 | 5 | | |
| Bailey, Ichabod | 1 | 1 | 3 | | |
| Bailey, Solomon | 1 | | 3 | | |
| Arnold, Gideon | 1 | 1 | 3 | | |
| Arnold, Apollas | 1 | 1 | 3 | | |
| Bewell, Joseph | 3 | 2 | 3 | | |
| Colly, Stephen | 1 | | 1 | | |
| Carrier, Titus | 3 | 1 | 3 | | |
| Comstock, Jabez | 1 | | 3 | | |
| Cook, Richard | 1 | 1 | 3 | | |
| Chapham, Elezier | 1 | 3 | 7 | | |
| Carrier, Andrew | 2 | | 2 | | |
| Cole, Ebenezer | 1 | 2 | 1 | | |
| Cole, Ebenezer, Junr | 1 | 2 | 1 | | |
| Cole, Marcus | 1 | | 1 | | |
| Cole, Abner | 1 | 1 | 1 | | |
| Cone, Nathaniel | 1 | 2 | 5 | | |
| Clark, Nathaniel | | | | | |
| Bill, James | 2 | 2 | 4 | | |
| Clark, John, Esqr | 2 | | 1 | | |
| Caswell, John | 1 | | 3 | | |
| Caswell, Joseph | 1 | 1 | 5 | | |
| Cunning, George | 1 | | 4 | | |
| Clark, William | 1 | | 2 | | |
| Clark, David | 2 | 3 | 4 | | |
| Cowdry, Thomas | 2 | | 4 | | |

# HEADS OF FAMILIES—CONNECTICUT.

## MIDDLESEX COUNTY—Continued.

| NAME OF HEAD OF FAMILY. | Free white males of 16 years and upward, including heads of families. | Free white males under 16 years. | Free white females, including heads of families. | All other free persons. | Slaves. | NAME OF HEAD OF FAMILY. | Free white males of 16 years and upward, including heads of families. | Free white males under 16 years. | Free white females, including heads of families. | All other free persons. | Slaves. | NAME OF HEAD OF FAMILY. | Free white males of 16 years and upward, including heads of families. | Free white males under 16 years. | Free white females, including heads of families. | All other free persons. | Slaves. |
|---|---|---|---|---|---|---|---|---|---|---|---|---|---|---|---|---|---|
| **CHATHAM TOWN—continued.** | | | | | | **CHATHAM TOWN—continued.** | | | | | | **EAST HADDAM TOWN—continued.** | | | | | |
| Clark, Stephen | 1 | 1 | 2 | | | Smith, Isaac | 1 | | 1 | | | Brainerd, Bezaleel | 3 | | 4 | | |
| Cowdry, Nathaniel | 1 | | 1 | | | Smith, Isaac, Junr | 3 | 2 | 4 | | | Gates, Joseph | 2 | 4 | 4 | | |
| Cole, Moses | 2 | 2 | 8 | | | Smith, Ralph | 2 | 2 | 6 | | | Gates, Joshua | 2 | 1 | 4 | | |
| Cole, Hannah | 1 | 2 | 3 | | | Smith, Sparrow | 1 | 1 | 1 | | | Gates, Caleb | 1 | 3 | 2 | | |
| Caswell, Jonathan | 1 | 1 | 3 | | | Strong, Adonijah | 2 | 3 | 6 | | | Gates, Iona | 2 | 1 | 5 | | |
| Cook, Moses | 2 | 2 | 5 | | | Shepherd, Thomas | 2 | 1 | 3 | | | Olmstead, James | 2 | | 4 | 1 | |
| Clark, Amos | 1 | 1 | 3 | | | Shattuck, Randal | 2 | 2 | 3 | | | Moseley, Thos, Esqr | 1 | | 1 | | 2 |
| Clark, Jabez | 1 | 2 | 1 | | | Smith, Haziel | 1 | 2 | 3 | | | Moseley, Jona O | 1 | 1 | 2 | | 6 |
| Cowdry, Jonathan | 1 | | 1 | | | Sears, Elkanah | 2 | | 2 | | | Emmons, Joseph | 3 | 1 | 1 | | |
| Clark, Aaron | 1 | 1 | 1 | | | Sears, Isaac | 1 | 1 | 4 | | | Parsons, Revd Elijah | 2 | 1 | 3 | | |
| Dothick, Ananias | 1 | 2 | 5 | | | Sears, Willard | 1 | | 3 | | | Wadkins, Ephm | 1 | 1 | 5 | | |
| Davis, Comfort | 2 | 2 | 4 | | | Tennant, Moses | 1 | | 3 | | | Peck, Elisha | 2 | 1 | 2 | | |
| Daniels, Amos | 1 | 2 | 1 | | | Taylor, Stephen | 1 | 1 | 2 | | | Chapman, Polly | | 5 | 2 | | |
| Dailey, Joseph | 1 | 3 | 3 | | | Thomas, William | 1 | | 3 | | | Worthington, Elias | 1 | 1 | 2 | | 1 |
| Fuller, Timothy | 1 | | 2 | | | Tubbs, Lemuel | 1 | 1 | 2 | | | Gates, Bezaleel | 1 | 1 | 6 | | |
| Freeman, Sylvenus | 1 | 2 | 2 | | | Trowbridge, John, Junr | 1 | | 3 | | | Smith, Thos | 1 | 1 | | | |
| Freeman, Sylvenus, Junr | 1 | 1 | 2 | | | Trowbridge, Jonathan | 1 | 1 | 3 | | | Champion, Israel | 2 | | 2 | | |
| Fuller, Judge | 1 | | 1 | | | Welch, William | 1 | 2 | 4 | | | Champion, Reuben | 1 | | 1 | | 1 |
| Fuller, Ezra | 2 | | 2 | | | Welch, John | 1 | 4 | 3 | | | Brainerd, John | 2 | 3 | 6 | | |
| Goff, Samuel | 1 | 1 | 3 | | | Welch, Constant | 1 | 2 | 5 | | | Ackley, Elijah | 3 | 2 | 5 | | |
| Goff, James | 1 | 2 | 1 | | | White, Phillip | 1 | 1 | 4 | | | Brainerd, Amasa | 3 | 2 | 5 | | |
| Goff, Jonathan | 1 | 1 | 1 | | | White, Ephraim | 1 | | 3 | | | Brainerd, Joshua, 2d | 2 | | 3 | | |
| Goff, Josiah | 1 | 1 | 1 | | | Smith, Ezra | 2 | | 2 | | | Willey, David | 1 | 1 | 4 | | |
| Goff, Jacob | 1 | | 2 | | | Willey, John | 3 | 1 | 2 | | | Cone, Timo | 2 | 2 | 5 | | |
| Griffith, Stephen | 1 | 1 | 3 | | | White, William | 1 | 2 | 5 | | | Cone, Ebenezer | 2 | | 4 | | |
| Goff, Benjamin | 1 | | 3 | | | White, Moses | 1 | | 2 | | | Cone, Phinehas | 1 | 2 | 4 | | |
| Gates, Nehemiah | 1 | 1 | 1 | | | Waterhouse, Mary | | | 3 | | | Warner, Danl | 1 | 1 | 6 | | |
| Chappel, Caleb | 1 | 1 | 4 | | | West, Lemuel | 3 | 5 | 4 | | | Warner, Oliver | 3 | | 1 | | |
| Gates, George | 1 | 2 | 4 | | | Wood, Joel | 1 | 1 | 3 | | | Warner, Joseph | 3 | | 1 | | |
| Harding, Olive | 1 | | 1 | | | Witherel, Henry | 2 | | 1 | | | Ackley, Stephen | 2 | | 3 | | |
| Harding, Ebenezer | 1 | 2 | 6 | | | Webb, James | 2 | 2 | 5 | | | Arnold, John | 1 | | 2 | | |
| Hall, Calvin | 1 | | 1 | | | Ackley, James | 2 | 2 | 7 | | | Spencer, Jared W | 1 | 3 | 2 | | |
| Hinckley, John | 4 | 3 | 6 | | | Ackley, Samuel | 2 | 3 | 5 | | 1 | Ackley, Elijah | 1 | 1 | 3 | | |
| Hall, Dewy | 1 | 4 | 5 | | | Brainard, John | 4 | 4 | 7 | | | Ackley, Amasa | 2 | 3 | 3 | | |
| Harris, Ely | 1 | 7 | 2 | | | Brainard, Stephen | 4 | 2 | 6 | | | Warner, John | 2 | | 3 | | |
| Hall, Jabez | 2 | | 2 | | | Comstock, Christopher | 1 | | 1 | | | Beckwith, Francis | 1 | 1 | 1 | | |
| Hall, Abijah, Junr | 1 | | 2 | | | Mitchell, Zepheniah | 1 | 1 | 2 | 1 | | Church, Joseph | 3 | 1 | 3 | | |
| Hall, Ebenezer | 2 | | 2 | | | Mitchell, Zephaniah, Junr | 1 | 3 | 1 | | | Spencer, David | 1 | 2 | 4 | | |
| Hall, Seth | 1 | 1 | 2 | | | Mitchell, Asa | 1 | 1 | 2 | | | Willey, Jonathan | 1 | 1 | 5 | | |
| Hodge, Samuel | 1 | | 1 | | | Scovill, Lemuel | 1 | 3 | 3 | | | Gates, Brainerd | 1 | | 2 | | |
| Harding, Ephraim | 1 | 5 | 2 | | | Scovil, Abagail | | 1 | 5 | | | Fuller, Nathan | 1 | 1 | 5 | | |
| Harding, Nathaniel | 3 | 5 | 4 | | | Totten, Samuel | 1 | | 1 | 1 | | Brainerd, Joshua | 1 | | 1 | | |
| Hubbard, Seth | 1 | 3 | 6 | | | Trowbridge, Ebenezer | 2 | | 4 | | | Spencer, Gideon | 2 | | 2 | | |
| Jackson, Salah | 1 | 2 | 1 | | | Usher, Robert | 3 | 3 | 5 | | 1 | Andrews, John | 1 | 3 | 2 | | |
| Johnson, John | 1 | 2 | 5 | | | Williams, Thomas | 2 | 3 | 6 | | | Andrews, Joseph | 1 | 3 | 6 | | |
| Hallen, John, Junr | 1 | 1 | 3 | | | Miller, Daniel | 2 | | 2 | | | Andrews, Zephaniah | 2 | 3 | 3 | | |
| Hill, Samuel | 1 | 1 | 1 | | | Brooks, Mary | | 2 | 2 | | | Lyon, Josiah | 1 | 1 | 3 | | |
| Doolittle, Margaret | | | 3 | | | Cotton, James | 1 | | 1 | | | Fuller, Thankfull | | | 2 | | |
| Kilbourn, Samuel | 1 | 1 | 5 | | | Goff, Gideon | 1 | | 2 | | | Warner, Jabez | 2 | | 3 | | |
| Knolton, Stephen | 1 | | 2 | | | Hop, John | 2 | 4 | 4 | | | Warner, Seldon | 1 | 1 | 2 | | |
| Keys, Nathaniel | 1 | | 3 | | | Hosmer, Timothy | 1 | 2 | 2 | | | Gates, Timothy, Esqr | 2 | 2 | 5 | | 1 |
| Lucas, Samuel | 2 | | 3 | | | Hallen, John | 2 | 3 | 3 | | | Traicy, Nehh | 1 | 1 | 2 | | |
| Loveland, Daniel | 1 | 1 | 2 | | | | | | | | | Traicy, Gamaliel R | 1 | | 1 | | |
| Lewis, Nathan | 2 | 1 | 4 | | | **EAST HADDAM TOWN.** | | | | | | Selbe, Wm | 1 | | 1 | | |
| Lord, Eliphalet | 1 | | | | | | | | | | | Selbe, Jereh | 1 | 4 | 4 | | |
| Lucas, John | 1 | | 2 | | | Chapman, Jabez, Esqr | 11 | | 4 | 2 | | Mark, Hezh | 3 | 4 | 2 | | |
| Mott, Samuel | 2 | 1 | 3 | | | Gailston, Willm | 1 | 4 | 5 | | | Wright, Saml | 1 | 1 | 4 | | |
| Morgan, Amos | 2 | 3 | 7 | | | Percivall, Gordon | 1 | 4 | 3 | | | Gates, Thos | 1 | | 2 | | |
| Mott, Nathaniel | 2 | 1 | 3 | | | Palmes, Samel | 1 | 4 | 4 | | | Gates, Thos, Junr | 1 | 1 | 2 | | |
| Markham, Nathaniel | 1 | 2 | 4 | | | Johnson, Elijah | 1 | | 5 | | | Gates, Gideon | 1 | | 2 | | |
| Marklam, John | 1 | | 3 | | | Wenslow, Jesse | 1 | 3 | 4 | | | Tracy, Susanna | | 1 | 4 | | |
| Welch, William | 2 | 1 | 2 | | | Bunnel, Frank | | | 4 | | | Smith, Matthew | 1 | | 4 | | |
| Markham, James | 1 | 2 | 1 | | | Warner, Hannah | | | 2 | | | Smith, Jereh | 2 | 3 | 4 | | |
| Mathews, Asahel | 1 | 1 | 2 | | | Harvey, Willm | 1 | 3 | 2 | | | Spencer, Juda | 2 | | 4 | | |
| Newton, Asahel | 3 | 3 | 2 | | | Mitchell, Samel | 1 | 1 | 6 | | | Smith, Matthew, 2d | 1 | 3 | 4 | | |
| Nobles, Jonathan | 1 | | 1 | | | Sears, Matthew | 3 | | 1 | | 2 | Spencer, Mary | | | 4 | | |
| Norcott, Reuben | 1 | 2 | 3 | | | Anable, Abrm | 4 | 3 | 2 | | | Spencer, Jonathan | 1 | 2 | 2 | | |
| Norcott, William | 2 | | 5 | | | Spencer, Abigail | | | 1 | | | Spencer, Simeon | 1 | | 1 | | |
| Niles, David | 1 | 5 | 4 | | | Huntington, Jno | 2 | 2 | 5 | | | Fuller, Stephen | 1 | | 1 | | |
| Niles, Elisha | 1 | 1 | 3 | | | Belding, Stephen | 1 | 2 | 1 | | | Parmer, Levi | 3 | 2 | 5 | | |
| Norton, John | 1 | 2 | 7 | | | Atwood, Elijah | 3 | 2 | 8 | | | Ackley, Ephm | 3 | 4 | 1 | | 1 |
| Parmela, Bryan, Esqr | 2 | 1 | 2 | | | Atwood, Elijah, Junr | 1 | 1 | 3 | | | Andrews, Thos | 1 | 2 | 2 | | |
| Griffeth, Joshua, Junr | 1 | 1 | 2 | | | Brainerd, Eleazer | 3 | | 1 | | | Fox, Saml | 1 | 2 | 2 | | |
| Johnson, Isaac | 1 | 1 | 2 | | | Belding, David | 1 | 2 | 4 | | | Spencer, Solomon | 1 | 2 | 3 | | |
| Parsons, Revr Lemuel | 1 | 2 | 4 | | | Thomas, David | 1 | 3 | 2 | | | Spencer, Silas | 2 | 1 | 4 | | |
| Parmelee, John | 1 | 3 | 3 | | | Lord, Saml P | 5 | 3 | 6 | | 3 | Hall, Margaret | | | 4 | | |
| Rich, Samuel | 2 | 2 | 4 | | | Tinker, Silvanus | 3 | 1 | 5 | 1 | | Hall, Saml, Junr | 1 | 1 | 6 | | |
| Tupper, Mayo | 1 | 2 | 2 | | | Champion, Epaphras | 5 | 1 | 4 | 1 | | Hall, Thos | 1 | 1 | 5 | | |
| Purple, Edward | 2 | 2 | 6 | | | Metcalf, Elijah | 2 | 3 | 4 | | | Gates, Ephraim | 1 | | 6 | | |
| Park, Daniel | 2 | 4 | 5 | | | Tinker, Temperance | 1 | | 3 | | | Spencer, Sarah | | 1 | 1 | | |
| Parmela, Jonathan | 1 | | 1 | | | Marshal, Thos | 5 | 2 | 4 | | | Ely, Gabriel | 2 | 4 | 4 | | |
| Parmela, Jared | 1 | 2 | 5 | | | Green, James | 4 | 3 | 3 | | | Stocking, David | 1 | 1 | 3 | | |
| Rogers, Augustus | 2 | | 3 | | | Lyon, Humphrey | 3 | | 6 | | | Hall, Abner | 3 | 3 | 3 | | |
| Rowley, Asher | 1 | 1 | 2 | | | White, Amos | 3 | 3 | 7 | | | Olcott, Thos | 2 | | 2 | | |
| Remsen, Joseph | 1 | | 4 | | | Wacket (Freeman) | | | | 2 | | Cook, Gideon | 2 | 5 | 2 | | |
| Remsen, Joseph, Junr | 1 | | 4 | | | Daniels, Thos | 1 | 2 | 3 | | | Hurd, Robt | 1 | | 2 | | |
| Rich, Cornelius, Junr | 2 | 3 | 3 | | | Cone, Robs | 2 | 2 | 3 | | | Hurd, Crippin | 1 | 1 | 2 | | |
| Rogers, Timothy | 4 | | 3 | | | Harvey, Elisha | 2 | 1 | 3 | | | Bingham, Abel | 1 | 1 | 3 | | |
| Rich, Lemuel | 1 | | 2 | | | Bonfoy, Permit | 1 | | 4 | | | Spencer, Zachariah | 1 | 1 | 2 | | |
| Ranney, David | 1 | 1 | 2 | | | Goodspeed, Nathan | 1 | 2 | 5 | | | Rowley, Isaac | 1 | 1 | 1 | | |
| Sears, Ebenezer | 1 | | 4 | | | Crowell, Saml | 1 | 3 | 2 | | | Parmer, John | 1 | | 2 | | |
| Sears, David | 1 | | 1 | | | Spencer, David B | 4 | 1 | 4 | | | Fuller, Wm W | 1 | 2 | 3 | | |
| Sexton, Samuel | 2 | 3 | 5 | | | Ackley, Isaac C | 2 | 2 | 4 | | | Dick (negro) | | | | 4 | |
| Sexton, Jessey | 2 | 2 | 3 | | | Cone, George | 2 | 3 | 4 | | | Huntington, Saml, Junr | 2 | 1 | 3 | | |

## MIDDLESEX COUNTY—Continued.

### EAST HADDAM TOWN—continued.

| NAME OF HEAD OF FAMILY. | Free white males of 16 years and upward, including heads of families. | Free white males under 16 years. | Free white females, including heads of families. | All other free persons. | Slaves. |
|---|---|---|---|---|---|
| Huntington, Sam¹ | 1 | | 3 | | |
| Cillerman, Wᵐ | 2 | 2 | 4 | | |
| Kilbourn, Jonathan | 3 | | 5 | | |
| Chapman, Isaac | 2 | 3 | 6 | | |
| Chapman, Danˡˡ | 1 | 2 | 4 | | |
| Clark, Uriah | 1 | | 2 | | |
| Cone, Elisha | 2 | | 3 | | |
| Comstock, Jacob | 1 | 4 | 1 | | |
| Chappel, Joshua | 1 | 1 | 2 | | |
| Williams, Elijah | 1 | 1 | 2 | | |
| Chapinan, Timᵒ | 2 | 2 | 3 | | |
| Williams, Charles | 1 | 2 | 2 | | |
| Chapman, Francis | 2 | | 3 | | |
| Chapman, Ozias | 4 | 4 | 6 | | |
| Hurd, Crippin | 3 | 2 | 5 | | |
| Gates, Nathᵃ, 2ᵈ | 2 | 2 | 3 | | |
| Rowley, Eleazer | 3 | 2 | 6 | | |
| Ackley, Wᵐ | 3 | | 7 | | |
| Gates, Danˡ | 1 | 2 | 2 | | |
| Percival, John, Junʳ | 1 | 1 | 3 | | |
| Percival, John, Esqʳ | 2 | 1 | 5 | | |
| Fuller, David | 3 | | 2 | | |
| Fuller, Thoˢ | 1 | 1 | 3 | | |
| Fuller, Jehiel, 2ᵈ | 2 | 2 | 3 | | |
| Fuller, Jehiel | 2 | 1 | 5 | | |
| Fuller, Jrad | 1 | 1 | 2 | | |
| Taylor, Isaac | 2 | 1 | 3 | | |
| Gates, Noadiah | 2 | 4 | 3 | | |
| Gates, Phinehas | 1 | 4 | 4 | | |
| Chapman, Caleb | 1 | 4 | 5 | | |
| Chapman, Samˡ | 1 | 2 | 3 | | |
| Pike, Mary | | | 2 | | |
| Higgins, Elkina | 2 | 1 | 2 | | |
| Higgins, Dolle | | | 3 | | |
| Mobs, Samˡ | 1 | 1 | 1 | | |
| Gates, Oliver | 1 | 2 | 2 | | |
| Gates, Helen (Widᵉ) | | 1 | 2 | | |
| Cone, Joshua | 1 | | 1 | | |
| Cone, Hannah | 2 | 1 | 3 | | |
| Cone, Noadiah | 1 | 1 | 1 | | |
| Isham, John | 1 | 1 | 1 | | |
| Higgins, Jedʰ | 3 | 1 | 1 | 1 | |
| Higgins, Stephen | 1 | 2 | 4 | | |
| Hannibal, Joseph | 1 | 1 | 3 | | |
| Chapman, Zachʰ | 2 | 1 | 6 | | |
| Throop, Phebe | | 1 | 3 | | |
| Hurd, Thoˢ | 1 | 4 | 2 | | |
| Fowler, Joseph | 1 | 2 | 3 | | |
| Ransom, Amos | 4 | 2 | 3 | | |
| Brainerd, Jared | 1 | 1 | 3 | | |
| Starlin, Simon | 3 | 5 | 2 | | |
| Mason, Cooley | | | 1 | 7 | |
| Spencer, Amasah | 1 | 1 | 3 | | |
| Chapman, John | 1 | | | | |
| Rowley, Lydia | | | 2 | | |
| Clark, Samˡ | 1 | 1 | 6 | | |
| Randal, Amos | 1 | 1 | 3 | | |
| Usher, Hezʰ | 4 | 4 | 5 | | |
| Comstock, Phebe | | | 3 | | |
| Griffin, Geo | 4 | 2 | 5 | 1 | |
| Jewett, Nathan | 4 | 1 | 4 | | |
| Brown, Danˡ | 1 | 2 | 4 | | |
| Beckwith, Job | 1 | | 1 | 1 | |
| Chaddock, Silas | 1 | 2 | 2 | | |
| Baker, Mercy | 2 | 1 | 1 | | |
| Beckwith, Barzilla | 3 | 3 | 6 | | |
| Griffin, John | 1 | 3 | 2 | | |
| Griffin, Lemᵉˡ | 5 | 3 | 3 | | |
| Griffin, Nathan | 3 | | 2 | | |
| Jewitt, Nathan H | 2 | 2 | 3 | | |
| Jewitt, Sarah | 1 | 1 | 7 | | |
| Williams, Thoˢ | 1 | 2 | 2 | | |
| Bebee, Clark | 2 | 1 | 2 | | |
| Maynard, John | 2 | 2 | 5 | | |
| Dean, Samˡ | 1 | 3 | 3 | | |
| Pran, John | 1 | 1 | 2 | | |
| Rogers, Gordon | 1 | 3 | 3 | | |
| Rogers, John | 3 | 1 | 2 | | |
| Ackley, Simeon | 2 | | 2 | | |
| Hughs, John | 1 | 1 | 2 | | |
| Spencer, Israel, Esqʳ | 2 | | 2 | | |
| Spencer, Ebenezer | 1 | | 1 | | |
| Spencer, Seldon | 1 | 2 | 3 | | |
| Cone, Samˡ | 2 | | 3 | | |
| Cone, Roswell | 2 | 1 | 3 | | |
| Parmelee, Phinehas | 2 | | 2 | | |
| Post, Samˡ | 1 | 1 | 2 | | |
| Seldon, Joseph | 1 | 2 | 5 | | |
| Comstock, Israel | 1 | 1 | 2 | | |
| Willey, Samˡ | 2 | | 2 | | |
| Warner, Samˡ | 1 | 1 | 1 | | |
| Willey, Ezra | 1 | 1 | 2 | | |
| Warner, John, 2ᵈ | 2 | 1 | 6 | | |
| Hungerford, Joseph | 1 | 1 | 3 | | |
| Comstock, Jabez, 2ᵈ | 1 | 1 | 4 | | |
| Comstock, Jabez | 3 | 1 | 4 | | |
| Holmes, Christopher | 3 | 1 | 2 | | |
| Rawson, Erindol | 3 | 2 | 4 | | |
| Hungerford, Robᵗ | 2 | | 1 | | |
| Hungerford, Elijah | 1 | 2 | 4 | | |
| Marsh, Lemˡ | 1 | 2 | 6 | | |
| Marsh, Edmond | 2 | 2 | 3 | | |
| Usher, Oliver | 1 | | 2 | | |
| Warner, Joseph, 2ᵈ | 2 | 2 | 2 | | |
| Hungerford, Robᵗ, Juʳ | 1 | 3 | 2 | | |
| Beckwith, Nathˡ | 2 | 2 | 2 | | |
| Holmes, Elephalet, Esqʳ | 2 | 2 | 4 | | |
| Wilbee, Abᵐ | 1 | | 1 | | |
| Warner, Abᵐ | 1 | | 1 | | |
| Miner, Caziah | | | 1 | | |
| Cone, Juda | 1 | | 2 | | |
| Marsh, Samˡ | 1 | | 3 | | |
| Willey, Joseph | 1 | | 1 | | |
| Phelps, David | 1 | 1 | 3 | | |
| Willey, Ephᵐ, Junʳ | 1 | 2 | 3 | | |
| Beckwith, Joseph | 1 | | 1 | | |
| Beckwith, Chauncey | 1 | | 3 | | |
| Beckwith, Joseph, 2ᵈ | 1 | | 2 | | |
| Beckwith, Stephen | 1 | 1 | 3 | | |
| Harvey, Ithamar | 1 | 2 | 1 | | |
| Lyon, Elizabeth | | 1 | 2 | | |
| Hungerford, Zachʰ | 2 | 1 | 4 | | |
| Minor, Elihu | 1 | 2 | 1 | | |
| Hunn, Samˡ | 2 | 2 | 3 | | |
| Cone, Samˡ, 2ᵈ | 1 | 1 | 3 | | |
| Dutton, Joseph | 1 | | 2 | | |
| Crosby, Levi, 2ᵈ | 1 | 1 | 4 | | |
| Spencer, Reuben | 2 | 2 | 4 | | |
| Parker, John | 2 | 2 | 3 | | |
| Lord, Samˡ | 1 | 3 | 1 | | |
| Andrews, Asael | 1 | 4 | 3 | | |
| Vail, Revʳ Joseph | 1 | 3 | 3 | | |
| Willey, Noah | 1 | 4 | 3 | | |
| Freeman, Peter | | | 1 | 3 | |
| Willey, Seth | 1 | 2 | 4 | | |
| Willey, Cyrus | 1 | 1 | | | |
| Willey, Titus | 1 | | 3 | | |
| Hoel, Edwᵈ | 1 | 3 | 3 | | |
| Hunn, Mary | | | 2 | | |
| Little, John | 1 | 3 | 4 | | |
| Phelps, Samˡ | 1 | 1 | 3 | | |
| Hatch, Elnathan | 1 | 2 | 5 | | |
| Banning, Joseph | 1 | 5 | 3 | | |
| Crosby, Increase | 1 | | 3 | | |
| Crosby, Benjᵃ | 1 | 1 | 2 | | |
| Dixon, Edwᵈ | 1 | 1 | 1 | | |
| Crosby, Levi | 1 | | 4 | | |
| Crosby, Elijah | 1 | 1 | 2 | | |
| Bebee, John | 1 | 1 | 4 | | |
| Dewey, Israel | 1 | | 2 | | |
| Jewet, Gibbins | 2 | 1 | 4 | | |
| Willey, Aaron | 1 | 1 | 1 | | |
| Stewart, John | 1 | | 2 | | |
| Spencer, Joel | 2 | 1 | 3 | | |
| Hungerford, Nathˡ | 1 | 1 | 3 | | |
| Hungerford, Nathˡ, 2ᵈ | 2 | | 2 | | |
| Mather, Augustus | 1 | 2 | 4 | | |
| Spencer, Isaac, Juʳ Esqʳ | 2 | 4 | 2 | 1 | |
| Cone, Mary | 2 | 1 | 3 | | |
| Cone, Benjᵃ | 1 | | 3 | | |
| Gates, Zeprᵃ | 1 | | 2 | | |
| Cone, Jonᵃ | 2 | 1 | 2 | | |
| Stewart, Benjᵃ | 1 | 1 | 2 | | |
| Lyman, Revᵈ Wᵐ | 1 | | 2 | | |
| Southmayd, Danˡ | 1 | 2 | 4 | | |
| Spencer, Hannah | 2 | | 5 | | |
| Phillis (Freeman) | | | | 1 | |
| Buckley, Danˡ | 1 | 1 | 4 | | |
| Otis, Charles | 2 | 1 | 4 | | |
| Gates, Martha | 1 | | 4 | | |
| Estherbrooks, Hobert | 2 | 1 | 9 | | |
| Rose, Hannah | 1 | | 2 | | |
| Dutton, Russel | 1 | | 2 | | |
| Dutton, Samˡ | 2 | 2 | 1 | | |
| Minor, Turner | 1 | 2 | 3 | | |
| Bebee, Brockway | 3 | | 3 | | |
| Burnham, Nathˡ, 2ᵈ | 1 | 3 | 3 | | |
| Cone, Wᵐ | 3 | 1 | 4 | | |
| Gates, Joseph, 2ᵈ | 2 | 3 | 6 | | |
| Gates, Nathan | 3 | 1 | 4 | | |
| Warner, Jabez, 2ᵈ | 1 | 1 | 3 | 1 | |
| Clark, Sterlin | 1 | | 2 | | |
| Bebee, Abner | 4 | | 2 | | |
| Ingraham, Elkinah | 1 | 2 | 3 | | |
| Cone, George | 1 | 3 | 4 | | |
| Fuller, Benjᵃ | 1 | | 2 | | |
| Fox, Ebenezer | 2 | | 2 | | |
| Fox, Moses | 1 | | 2 | | |
| Willey, Susannah | | | 4 | | |
| Willey, Alford | 1 | | 2 | | |
| Chapman, Simeon | 2 | 1 | 4 | | |
| Ackley, Samˡ | 1 | 1 | 1 | | |
| Bebee, Caleb | 1 | 2 | 3 | | |
| Spencer, Timᵒ | 2 | 3 | 4 | | |
| Bebee, Avary | 1 | | 2 | | |
| Bebee, Phebee | 1 | | 1 | | |
| Fuller, Mary | 3 | | 2 | | |
| Wickwire, James | 2 | | 3 | | |
| Gilbert, Samˡ | 2 | 3 | 7 | | |
| Ransom, Joshua | 1 | 3 | 5 | | |
| Cone, Martin | 1 | | 2 | | |
| Marshe, Woodward | 2 | 2 | 2 | | |
| Arnold, Enoch | 2 | | 3 | | |
| Miller, Sarah | | | 2 | | |
| Lord, Elijah | 1 | | 3 | | |
| Dutton, Amasa | 4 | 5 | | | |
| Bebee, Nathan | 1 | | 3 | | |
| Fuller, Uriel | 1 | 2 | 5 | | |
| Willey, John | 1 | 1 | 2 | | |
| Willey, Jabez | 1 | 1 | 3 | | |
| Gates, Nathˡ | 1 | | 3 | | |
| Nolton, Thoˢ | 1 | | 2 | | |
| Clark, Asa | 1 | 2 | 4 | | |
| Burnham, David | 1 | | 3 | | |
| Burnham, Sylvester | 1 | | 3 | | |
| Arnold, Ephᵐ | 1 | 2 | 6 | | |
| Willey, Josiah | 2 | 1 | 1 | | |
| Wickham, David | 3 | 1 | 5 | | |
| Gates, Samˡ | 1 | 1 | 1 | | |
| Willey, Benaiah | 1 | | 3 | | |
| Arnold, Joseph | 2 | | 4 | | |
| Willey, G. Warren | 1 | | 3 | | |
| Ackley, Thoˢ | 1 | 1 | 1 | | |
| Niles, Daniel | 1 | | 1 | | |
| Cone, Joseph | 1 | | 2 | | |
| Spencer, Jared, Esqʳ | 1 | | 2 | | |
| Swan, Jabez | 2 | 2 | 6 | | 1 |
| Brainerd, Enoch | 2 | | 6 | | |
| Bebee, Ebenezer | 1 | 2 | 2 | | |
| Ackley, Nathˡ, 3ᵈ | 2 | | 5 | | |
| Olmstead, Daniel | 1 | 3 | 3 | | |
| Rich, Isaac | 1 | 4 | 5 | | |
| Brookes, Timothy | 1 | 2 | 2 | | |
| Bebee, Hannah | 1 | | 1 | | |
| Niles, John | 1 | 1 | 1 | | |
| Martin, Jonathan | 2 | 5 | 1 | | |
| Ackley, Gideon | 2 | | 1 | | |
| Dickinson, Simeon | 4 | 2 | 3 | | |
| Cone, Nehʰ | 1 | 2 | 6 | | |
| Andrews, Samˡ | 2 | 2 | 2 | | |
| Emmons, Noadʰ | 1 | 4 | 2 | | |
| Cone, Danˡ | 1 | 1 | 7 | | |
| Lee, Wᵐ | 1 | 2 | 1 | | |
| Davis, Joseph | 2 | | 6 | | |
| Cone, James | 3 | 4 | 3 | | |
| Cone, Silvanus | 2 | 1 | 3 | | |
| Cone, Solomon | 1 | 2 | 4 | | |
| Corkins, Aquilla | 1 | | 3 | | |
| Clark, Dan | 2 | | 4 | | |
| Cone, Israel | 1 | 2 | 3 | | |
| Marsh, John | 1 | | 3 | | |
| Stewart, Wᵐ | 1 | | 2 | | |
| Stewart, Wᵐ, 2ᵈ | 1 | 1 | 5 | | |
| Harvey, Robᵗ | 1 | | 6 | | |
| Harvey, Amasa | 2 | 5 | 2 | | |
| Fox, Joshua | 1 | 1 | 6 | | |
| Harvey, Russel | 2 | | 1 | | |
| Anderson, Robᵗ | 1 | 2 | 5 | | |
| Spencer, Isaac | 3 | 1 | 5 | | |
| Hungerford, Green | 1 | 2 | 6 | 1 | |
| Brockway, Enoch | 1 | | 4 | | |
| Harvey, Robᵗ, 2ᵈ | 2 | 4 | 2 | | |
| Hannibal, John | 2 | 2 | 2 | | |
| Harvey, Jonᵃ | 1 | | 2 | | |
| Willey, Ephᵐ | 1 | 2 | 4 | | |
| Graves, Benjᵃ | 1 | 1 | 1 | | |
| Harvey, Asa | 2 | 2 | 5 | | |
| Mack, Richᵈ | 1 | 2 | 2 | | |
| Graves, Elijah | 2 | 2 | 4 | | |
| Harvey, Ithamar, Jʳ | 1 | 1 | 3 | | |
| Harvey, Elisha | 2 | | 3 | | |
| Harvey, Zachra | 2 | 5 | 7 | | |
| Beckwith, Ezekiel B | 1 | 1 | 3 | | |
| Beckwith, Samˡ | 1 | 6 | 2 | | |
| Robins (Black) | | | | 3 | |
| Sparrow, Deborah | 2 | 1 | 6 | | |
| Stewart, Samˡ | 1 | 2 | 5 | | |
| Sparrow, Nathˡ | 2 | | 5 | | |
| Burnham, Nathan | 2 | 1 | 4 | | |
| Hinckley, Ebenʳ | 1 | | 2 | | |
| Bebee, Lydia | | | 3 | | |
| Stewart, Joseph | 1 | 1 | 3 | | |
| Fox, Ezekiel | 2 | 1 | 2 | | |
| Spencer, Matthias | 1 | | 2 | | |
| Spencer, Reuben | 1 | 2 | 5 | | |

# HEADS OF FAMILIES—CONNECTICUT.

## MIDDLESEX COUNTY—Continued.

| NAME OF HEAD OF FAMILY. | Free white males of 16 years and upward, including heads of families. | Free white males under 16 years. | Free white females, including heads of families. | All other free persons. | Slaves. | NAME OF HEAD OF FAMILY. | Free white males of 16 years and upward, including heads of families. | Free white males under 16 years. | Free white females, including heads of families. | All other free persons. | Slaves. | NAME OF HEAD OF FAMILY. | Free white males of 16 years and upward, including heads of families. | Free white males under 16 years. | Free white females, including heads of families. | All other free persons. | Slaves. |
|---|---|---|---|---|---|---|---|---|---|---|---|---|---|---|---|---|---|
| **EAST HADDAM TOWN—continued.** | | | | | | **HADDAM TOWN—continued.** | | | | | | **HADDAM TOWN—continued.** | | | | | |
| Smith, Thos, 2d | 3 | | 2 | | | Thomas, Ebenezer, Junr | 1 | 1 | 1 | | | Tyler, Joseph | 3 | 1 | 5 | | |
| Jones, Diad | 1 | 1 | 2 | | | Knowls, Elisha | 2 | | 3 | | | Tyler, Thomas | 1 | | 2 | | |
| Spencer, Wm | 1 | 1 | 3 | | | Knowls, William | 3 | | 3 | | | Tyler, Joseph, Junr | 1 | | 1 | | |
| Burnham, Joshua | 3 | 2 | 2 | | | Wakeley, Asa | 2 | 2 | 3 | | | Dickinson, Mehitible | 1 | | 3 | | |
| Bigelow, Joel | 1 | 1 | 2 | | | Knowls, Richard | 4 | | 3 | | | Dickinson, Obediah | 1 | 4 | 5 | | |
| Bigelow, Elisha | 2 | | 8 | | | Knowls, Richard, Junr | 1 | | | | | Dickinson, David | 1 | 2 | 5 | | |
| Fox, Gershom | 1 | 2 | 2 | | | Tibbels, Elizabeth | | | 1 | | | Dickerson, Esther | | | 1 | | |
| Fox, Wm | 1 | | 3 | | | Knowls, Walker | 1 | 2 | 3 | | | Dickinson, John | 1 | 1 | 4 | | |
| Ackley Simeon, Jr | 1 | 3 | 6 | | | Thomas, James | 2 | 1 | 5 | | | Arnold, Martha | | | 2 | | |
| Lord, Nathl | 2 | 1 | 5 | | | Doane, Phinehas | 3 | 1 | 7 | | | Arnold, David | 1 | 3 | 3 | | |
| Fuller, Levise | | | 2 | | | Hubbard, Joel | 5 | | 4 | | | Scovil, Josiah | 2 | | 5 | | |
| Rogers, Thos | 1 | 2 | 1 | | | Spencer, Elizur | 1 | 2 | 2 | | | Scovil, John, Junr | 1 | 3 | 3 | | |
| Fuller, Noadiah | 1 | | 1 | | | Spencer, Sarah | | | 3 | | | Tyler, Nathaniel, Junr | 1 | 2 | 2 | | |
| Fuller, Noadiah, Jr | 1 | | 3 | | | Hubbard, Benjamin | 1 | 1 | 3 | | | Shaler, Samuel | 1 | 3 | 2 | | |
| Fuller, Danl | 2 | 1 | 3 | | | Hubbard, Moses | 1 | 1 | 2 | | | Shaler, James | 1 | | 2 | | |
| Fuller, Elisha | 2 | | 2 | | | Hubbard, Samuel | 3 | | 2 | | | Smith, Charles | 1 | | 6 | | |
| Arnold, John, Jr | 3 | 2 | 4 | | | Hubbard, Samuel, Junr | 1 | 3 | 2 | | | Arnold, James | 1 | 2 | 5 | | |
| Morgan, Abijah | 2 | 3 | 5 | | | Thomas, Henry | 1 | 4 | 2 | | | Necho (Negro) | | | | 1 | |
| Williams, Abm | 1 | 1 | 4 | | | Knowles, James | 3 | 4 | 3 | | | Smith, Martha, 3d | | 3 | 2 | | |
| Church, Wm | 1 | | | | | Knowls, Joshua | 1 | | 1 | | | Dickinson, Stephen | 2 | | 2 | | |
| Church, Richd | 2 | 1 | 1 | | | Woodruff, D | 2 | 3 | 5 | | | Brainard, Eliakim, Junr | 1 | | 2 | | |
| Church, Oliver | 1 | | 2 | | | Sutliff, James | 1 | 2 | 2 | | | Brainard, Gideon, Junr | 1 | | 1 | | |
| Cone, Elihu | 1 | 2 | 5 | | | Hubbard, David | 1 | 1 | 7 | | | Lewis, Samuel | 2 | 2 | 7 | | |
| Bebee, Willm | 1 | | 3 | | | Hubbard, Jeremiah | 2 | | 3 | | | Venterhouse, John | 3 | | 3 | | |
| Plum Green | 1 | | 4 | | | Hubbard, Shalor | 1 | 3 | 7 | | | Dudley, Barzilla | 3 | 1 | 5 | | |
| Williams, Phillip | 2 | 1 | 2 | | | Hubbard, Jeremiah, Junr | 3 | 2 | 6 | | | Shaler, Reuben | 1 | 1 | 7 | | |
| Stocking, Ellis | | | 2 | | | Hubbard, Thomas, Junr | 1 | | 1 | | | Venterhouse, John, Junr | 1 | | 1 | | |
| Watson, John | 1 | 1 | 2 | | | Hubbard, Thomas | 2 | 2 | 8 | | | Shaler, Hezekiah, Junr | 1 | 1 | 1 | | |
| Watson, John, Junr | 1 | 2 | 3 | | | Spencer, David | 2 | | 1 | | | Sherman, Benjamin | 1 | 1 | 3 | | |
| Butler, Amos | 1 | 3 | 2 | | | Hubbard, Job | 3 | 1 | 4 | | | Shaler, Thomas | 1 | 3 | 4 | | |
| Lenneaux, Benja | 1 | | 2 | | | Spencer, Abner | 3 | | 4 | | | Shaler, Asa | 3 | 2 | 4 | | |
| Church, Ira | 1 | 1 | 5 | | | Hubbard, Timothy | 2 | | 2 | | | Smith, Joshua | 1 | 3 | 3 | | |
| Olmstead, Jehd | 3 | | 5 | | | Hubbard, Timothy, Junr | 1 | | 2 | | | Shaler Aaron | 1 | 2 | 1 | | |
| Olmstead, Roger | 1 | | | | | Hubbard, Calvin | 1 | 2 | 2 | | | Ely, William | 1 | 1 | 4 | | |
| Jones, Daniel | 1 | | 1 | | | Hubbard, Michael | 1 | | 1 | | | Ray, Peter | 3 | 2 | 4 | | |
| Smith, Ignatious | 3 | | 4 | | | Hubbard, Aaron | 2 | 2 | 7 | | | Ely, Moses | 1 | 1 | 2 | | |
| Smith, Jno H | 2 | 1 | 3 | | | Hubbard, James | 3 | | 3 | | | Ray, Levi | 1 | | 2 | | |
| Sheppardson, Jno | 1 | | 1 | | | Hubbard Jonathan | 1 | 1 | 3 | | | Ray, Joseph | 1 | | 1 | | |
| Sheppardson, Willm | 1 | 2 | 5 | | | Tibbells, Stephen | 1 | 1 | 3 | | | Russell, Stephen | 3 | 4 | 5 | | |
| Pecker, Nathl | 1 | | 2 | | | Clark, William | 2 | | 3 | | | Tyler, Nehemiah | 1 | 1 | 3 | | |
| Gates, Matthew | 1 | 2 | 2 | | | Clark, Adna | 1 | 1 | 2 | | | Ray, Isaac | 2 | | 2 | | |
| Olmstead, Bates | 2 | | 3 | | | Seward, John | 1 | | 1 | | | Rutty, Jonah | 2 | 1 | 5 | | |
| Beebee, Silas | | 2 | 2 | | | Burr, Joseph | 1 | 1 | 4 | | | Tyler, Simon | 3 | 3 | 3 | | |
| Beebee, Jehiel | 2 | 1 | 3 | | | Towner, Daniel | 1 | 1 | 1 | | | Rutty, Asa | 1 | | 2 | | |
| Gates, Timo, 2d | 1 | 2 | 2 | | | Brainard, Oliver | 1 | 2 | 3 | | | Tyler, Nathan | 4 | 1 | 3 | | |
| Lord, Willm | 1 | | 1 | | | Arnold, Christian | 1 | 2 | 2 | | | Smith, Wells | 1 | 2 | 2 | | |
| Emmons, Ithamar | 2 | 1 | 5 | | | Thomas, Evan | 1 | | 2 | | | Shaler, Simon | 2 | 1 | 4 | | |
| Emmons, Saml | 3 | 1 | 3 | | | Thomas, Roger | 1 | 4 | 4 | | | Shaler, Jeremiah | 1 | | 3 | | |
| Olmstead, Oliver | 2 | 2 | 2 | | | Smith, Jonathan | 4 | 4 | 4 | | | Ray, Nathaniel | 1 | 1 | 3 | | |
| Emmons, Daniel | 2 | | 2 | | | Wells Oliver | 1 | 1 | 6 | | | Shaler, Ezra | 3 | | 3 | | |
| Williams, Robinson | 1 | 1 | 2 | | | Brainard, Eliakim | 4 | 1 | 4 | | | Shaler, Hezekiah | 3 | 3 | 4 | | |
| Williams, Robinson, Jur | 1 | 2 | 2 | | | Brainard, Gideon | 5 | | 5 | | | Miller, Daniel | 4 | | 4 | | |
| Emmons, Ebenezer | 2 | | 1 | | | Smith, James | 1 | 1 | 3 | | | Finker, Samuel | 4 | | 4 | | |
| | | | | | | Smith, Hubbard | 1 | 1 | 3 | | | Ely, Jacob | 2 | | 6 | | |
| **HADDAM TOWN.** | | | | | | Brainard, Jessey | 1 | 4 | 3 | | | Ray, Jecaniah | 1 | | 3 | | |
| May, Revd Elerzer | 3 | 1 | 4 | 1 | | Smith, Frederick | 1 | 2 | 3 | | | Ray, Daniel | 1 | 1 | 4 | | |
| Brainard, Hezh, Esqr | 2 | | 3 | 1 | | Smith, Stephen, Junr | 1 | 4 | 4 | | | Ray, Constant | 1 | | 2 | | |
| Church, John | 1 | 2 | 3 | | | Porter, Ezra | 1 | | 2 | | | Bates, Daniel | 2 | 2 | 5 | | |
| Church, Thomas | 1 | 3 | 6 | | | Brainard, Phinehas, Junr | 2 | 2 | 4 | | | Bates, Jonathan | 1 | | 3 | | |
| Cone, Elisha | 1 | | 2 | | | Towner, Timothy | 3 | | 2 | | | Southward, Andrew | 1 | 1 | 3 | | |
| Smith, Sylvenus | 1 | 1 | 3 | | | Willcox, James | 1 | 1 | 1 | | | Brooks, Nathan | 2 | 2 | 3 | | |
| Brainard, William | 1 | 2 | 6 | | | Willcox, John | 3 | | 3 | | | Clark, Joseph | 2 | 3 | 6 | | |
| Brainard, Eber | 1 | 1 | 2 | | | Burr, Benjamin | 1 | 4 | 2 | | | Bates, Elihu | 3 | | 4 | | |
| Hazelton, Nathaniel | 2 | | 3 | | | Burr, Jonathan | 1 | 4 | 3 | | | Clark, Sarah | 1 | | 1 | | |
| Hazelton, Arnold | 1 | 2 | 2 | | | Burr, Nathaniel | 2 | | 1 | | | Bates, Joseph | 2 | | 1 | | |
| Haden, John | 1 | 1 | 2 | | | Porter, Edmund | 3 | | 3 | | | Bates Eleazer | 3 | 1 | 6 | | |
| Cone, Samuel | 1 | 3 | 2 | | | Smith, Aaron | 3 | 1 | 2 | | | Bates, Amos | 1 | 1 | 6 | | |
| Hazelton, Simeon | 1 | 1 | 3 | | | Smith, Jonathan | 1 | | 3 | | | Seldon, Seephas | 1 | | 5 | | |
| Hazelton, Hannah | | | 1 | | | Smith, John | 3 | 2 | 6 | | | Selden, Edward | 1 | | 5 | | |
| Fuller, Daniel | 2 | 2 | 3 | | | Smith, Stephen | 1 | | 1 | | | Selden, Joseph | 1 | | 5 | | |
| Welles, Joseph | 1 | | 1 | | | Tibbells, Eben | 1 | 3 | 4 | | | Brainard, Josiah, Junr | 5 | | 5 | | |
| Dart, Siras | 1 | 1 | 2 | | | Snow, Gideon | 1 | 4 | 4 | | | Clark, Robert | 2 | 4 | 4 | | |
| Arnold, Joseph | 2 | 1 | 1 | | | Gloding, Daniel | 1 | 1 | 5 | | | Arnold, Samuel B | 1 | 1 | 4 | | |
| Clark, James S | 1 | | 2 | | | Willcox, William | 1 | 1 | 3 | | | Arnold, Jabez | 6 | | 4 | | |
| Smith, Martha | | 1 | 1 | | | Spencer, Abigail | | | 2 | | | Arnold, Jacob | 1 | 3 | 5 | | |
| Smith, Hezekiah | 3 | 1 | 6 | | | Spencer, James | 1 | | 2 | | | Arnold, Benjamin | 1 | 1 | 5 | | |
| Merwin, Heman | 1 | 1 | 3 | | | Clark, Stephen | 2 | 4 | 4 | | | Brooks, Jabez | 2 | 3 | 5 | | |
| Kelsey, George | 1 | 4 | 1 | | | Johnson, Didemus | 1 | | 2 | | | Brooks, Amos | 3 | | 3 | | |
| Smith, William | 4 | 2 | 3 | | | Pelton, James | 2 | 3 | 5 | | | Brainard, Ezra, Esqr | 3 | 3 | 4 | | |
| Smith, Daniel, Junr | 5 | 4 | 3 | | | Taylor, Joseph | 2 | 3 | 1 | | | Brainard, Zadock | 2 | 2 | 1 | | |
| Chapman, Timothy | 1 | 1 | 2 | | | Burr, Nathaniel | 1 | 1 | 3 | | | Young, Asaph | 1 | | 2 | | |
| Arnold, Samuel | 4 | 2 | 5 | | | Clark, Aaron | 1 | | 3 | | | Brainard, Dudley | 1 | 1 | 6 | | |
| Clark, Samuel | 2 | 1 | 5 | | | Clark, Asher | 1 | | 1 | | | Brainard, Amos | 1 | 1 | 3 | | |
| Smith, Reuben | 2 | 2 | 3 | | | Auger, Isaac | 2 | | 1 | | | Tucker, Anner | | | 3 | | |
| Smith, Elias | 1 | 1 | 5 | | | Tyler Timothy | 1 | 1 | 1 | | | Brainard, Isaac | 1 | 3 | 2 | | |
| Brainard, Nehemiah, Esqr | 3 | 1 | 5 | | | Higgins, Hawse | 1 | | 1 | | | Brainard, Jona | 3 | 2 | 4 | | |
| Smith, Abisha | 1 | 1 | 3 | | | Higgins, Cornelius | 2 | 1 | 3 | | | Goff, Gideon | 2 | 1 | 4 | | |
| Shaler, Bezeleel | 2 | 2 | 7 | | | Auger, Joseph | 1 | | 2 | | | Brainard, Robert | 1 | | 2 | | |
| Brooks, Jonathan | 1 | 2 | 4 | | | Lewis, Thomas | 1 | 1 | 4 | | | Brainard, James | 1 | 1 | 2 | | |
| Brooks, Joseph, Esqr | 3 | | 5 | | | Lewis, Augustus | 1 | 4 | 2 | | | Tallbard, William | 2 | 2 | 4 | | |
| Brooks, Wakeman | 2 | 1 | 2 | | | Tyler, Abraham | 2 | 3 | 2 | | | Brainard, Jessey | 3 | 1 | 5 | | |
| Brooks, James | 1 | | 2 | | | Tyler, Samuel | 1 | 1 | 2 | | | Brainard, Cornelius | 2 | | 3 | | |
| Thomas, Ebenezer | 2 | | 6 | | | | | | | | | Higgins, James | 1 | 2 | 7 | | |
| | | | | | | | | | | | | Brainard, Jedediah | 2 | 2 | 3 | | |

# FIRST CENSUS OF THE UNITED STATES.

## MIDDLESEX COUNTY—Continued.

| Name of head of family. | Free white males of 16 years and upward, including heads of families. | Free white males under 16 years. | Free white females, including heads of families. | All other free persons. | Slaves. |
|---|---|---|---|---|---|
| **HADDAM TOWN—continued.** | | | | | |
| Brainard, Jedediah, Junr | 2 | 3 | 5 | | |
| Williams, Abraham | 4 | 3 | 9 | | |
| Chapman, Reuben | 3 | 2 | 3 | | |
| Brooks, Samuel, Junr | 2 | 2 | 4 | | |
| Day, Elisha | 3 | 1 | 4 | | |
| Selden, Elias | 2 | 4 | 3 | | |
| Northum, Samuel | 1 | 3 | 6 | | |
| Arnold, John | 4 | 1 | 5 | | |
| Arnold, Joshua | 1 | 4 | 5 | | |
| Cook, Amos | 2 | 1 | 6 | | |
| Willson, John | 1 | 1 | 8 | | |
| Bailey, Nehemiah | 2 | 1 | 5 | | |
| Childs, James R | 1 | 1 | 4 | | |
| Childs, Hannah | 1 | 2 | 2 | | |
| Childs, Thomas | 1 | 2 | 1 | | |
| Smith, Robert | 2 | | 2 | | |
| Childs, Sylvester | 1 | 1 | 2 | | |
| Kelly, Rebecca | | | 2 | | |
| Huntington, Jonathan | 2 | 1 | 5 | | |
| May, John | 1 | | 3 | | |
| Boardman, Luther | 3 | 1 | 2 | | |
| Sawyer, Ephraim | 2 | 1 | 3 | | |
| Eddy, Seveus | 3 | 3 | 3 | | |
| Brainard, David | 2 | | 6 | | 1 |
| Smith, Elihu | 2 | 1 | 3 | | |
| Scovel, William | 2 | 1 | 3 | | |
| Boardman, Chloe | | 1 | 2 | | |
| Brooks, Samuel | 3 | | 5 | | |
| Bailey, William | 3 | 3 | 5 | | |
| Wheeler, Job | 2 | 2 | 6 | | |
| Clark, Samuel, Junr | 2 | 4 | 3 | | |
| Bailey, John | 1 | | 1 | | |
| Bailey, Amos | 1 | 4 | 3 | | |
| Bailey, Elizabeth | | | 2 | | |
| Sutliff, Nathaniel | 1 | | 1 | | |
| Brainard, Martha | 1 | | 3 | | |
| Arnold, Joel | 1 | | 3 | 1 | |
| Brainard, Zachariah | 3 | 3 | 1 | | |
| Brainard, Elijah | 2 | 3 | 5 | | |
| Brainard, Samuel | 1 | 2 | 1 | | |
| Spencer, John | 1 | 1 | 2 | | |
| Skinner, Richard | 1 | 2 | 1 | | |
| Smith, David | 1 | 2 | 1 | | |
| Skinner, Ebenezer | 4 | | 2 | | |
| Chapman, Jonathan | 2 | 3 | 5 | | |
| Boardman, Jonathan | 1 | 3 | 3 | | |
| Bonfey, Bananuel | 1 | 3 | 4 | | |
| Higgins, Cornelius, Esqr | 2 | 1 | 2 | | |
| Spencer, Joseph | 2 | 1 | 4 | | |
| Spencer, Elihu | 1 | 1 | 3 | | |
| Brainard, Prosper | 3 | 2 | 3 | | |
| Spencer, Abigail | | 1 | 3 | | |
| Spencer, Stephen | 1 | 6 | 1 | | |
| Spencer, William | 1 | | 1 | | |
| Whitmore, Samuel B | 3 | | 4 | | |
| Bailey, Desire | 1 | 1 | 3 | | |
| Smith, Lewis | 1 | | 4 | | |
| Smith, John | 2 | | 4 | | |
| Smith, Israel | 1 | | 4 | | |
| Smith, John, Junr | 1 | 1 | 4 | | |
| Smith, Phinehas | 1 | 1 | 2 | | |
| Smith, Samuel | 1 | | 4 | | |
| Smith, Henry | 1 | | 4 | | |
| Clarke, Sylvenus | 1 | 1 | 4 | | |
| Clarke, James | 2 | 1 | 2 | | |
| Cone, Elisha, Junr | 2 | | 3 | | |
| Arnold, Ambross | 1 | 1 | 6 | | |
| Spencer, Daniel | 2 | 1 | 2 | | |
| Spencer, Elia | 1 | 3 | 2 | | |
| Brainard, William | 1 | 1 | 1 | | |
| Bailey, Oliver | 2 | 5 | 6 | | |
| Scovil, Samuel | 3 | 4 | 7 | | |
| Scovil, John | 1 | 2 | 5 | | |
| Scovil, Joseph | 1 | 3 | 2 | | |
| Harvey, Elisha | 2 | | 1 | | |
| Crook, Joseph | 2 | 5 | 2 | | |
| Crook, Whitmore | 1 | 2 | 2 | | |
| Bailey, Christopher | 1 | | 4 | | |
| Clark, William, Junr | 1 | 3 | 2 | | |
| Bailey, Eliakim | 1 | 1 | 1 | | |
| Brainard, Josiah, 3d | 2 | 1 | 2 | | |
| Bradford, Robert | 3 | | 2 | | |
| Spencer, Elisha | 2 | 5 | 5 | | |
| Crook, Thomas | 1 | 1 | 1 | | |
| Brainard, Jeremiah | 5 | | 2 | | |
| Sutliff, John | 2 | | 2 | | |
| Brainard, Nathaniel | 2 | 2 | 4 | | |
| McKnary, Martin | 1 | 3 | 2 | | |
| Brooks, Abigail | | | 2 | | |
| Crook, Shubell | 4 | | 4 | | |
| Johnson, John | 2 | | 4 | | |
| Bailey, Abijah | 2 | | 1 | | |
| Bailey, Timothy | 1 | 2 | 2 | | |
| Hubbard, Giles | 1 | 2 | 1 | | |
| Bailey, Jabez | 3 | 2 | 6 | | |
| **HADDAM TOWN—continued.** | | | | | |
| Bailey, Ephraim | 1 | | 2 | | |
| Bailey, Gideon, Junr | 4 | 5 | 5 | | |
| Bailey, Stephen | 3 | 1 | 8 | | |
| Walkley, Richard | 1 | 3 | 3 | | |
| Bailey, Caleb | 2 | 1 | 5 | | |
| Treadwell, Humphrey | 1 | | 2 | | |
| Brainard, Daniel | 2 | 1 | 4 | | |
| Sears, Charles | 3 | 5 | 3 | | |
| Brainard, John | 1 | 1 | 9 | | |
| Brainard, Heman | 1 | 2 | 4 | | |
| Brainard, Phinehas | 2 | | 2 | | |
| Bailey, Amy | | | 1 | | |
| Smith, James, 3d | 1 | 1 | 3 | | |
| Smith, William | 2 | 1 | 5 | | |
| Brainard, Bushnell | 2 | | 3 | | |
| Brainard, Aaron | 1 | 2 | 7 | | |
| Cone, Reuben | 1 | | 3 | | |
| Cone, Noadiah | 1 | 1 | 1 | | |
| Cone, James | 2 | | 6 | | |
| Thomas, Aaron | 2 | 1 | 5 | | |
| Clark, Joseph, Junr | 1 | 1 | 1 | | |
| Clark, Lydia | | 1 | 2 | | |
| Clark, Patience | | 2 | 2 | | |
| Clark, Hezekiah | 2 | | 2 | | |
| Clark, John | 2 | 3 | 2 | | |
| Brooks, Joshua | 2 | 3 | 3 | | |
| Wakeley, Solomon | 3 | 4 | 3 | | |
| Corn, Noah | 1 | 2 | 5 | | |
| Brooks, Abraham | 1 | | 7 | | |
| Dickinson, Joseph | 3 | 2 | 4 | | |
| Arnold, Joseph, Junr | 1 | 2 | 2 | | |
| Smith, Joseph | 1 | | 5 | | |
| Kelsey, Benjamin | 1 | 2 | 3 | | |
| Johnson, Isaac | 1 | 1 | 4 | | |
| Stannard, Samuel | 1 | 3 | 4 | | |
| Brooks, Porter | 1 | 2 | 6 | | |
| **KILLINGWORTH TOWN.** | | | | | |
| Towner, Daniel | 2 | | 3 | | |
| Towner, Reuben | 1 | 4 | 2 | | |
| Towner, Samuel | 1 | 1 | 1 | | |
| Rutty, Levi | 3 | | 2 | | |
| Stevens, Hubbell | 2 | 1 | 2 | | |
| Griswuld, Nathaniel | 1 | 2 | 3 | | |
| Parmela, Eliab | 1 | 1 | 2 | | |
| Griswould, Moses | 1 | 1 | 3 | | |
| Griswould, Ebenezer | 1 | 2 | 4 | | |
| Rutty, John | 1 | 2 | 2 | | |
| Clark, Abel | 1 | | 2 | | |
| Bowers, Zephaniah | 2 | 6 | 2 | | |
| Haden, Jacob | 1 | 4 | 3 | | |
| Parmalee, Nehemiah | 1 | 2 | 6 | | |
| Parmalee, Daniel | 1 | 2 | 3 | | |
| Parmalee, Rhoda | 2 | | 3 | | |
| Coan, Gaylor | 1 | | 1 | | |
| Willcox, Abel | 5 | | 2 | | |
| Willcox, Abel, Junr | 1 | 2 | 1 | | |
| Nettleton, Samuel, 2d | 2 | 3 | 5 | | |
| Pratt, Samuel | 2 | | 1 | | |
| Parmalee, Roswell | 4 | 2 | 3 | | |
| Parmalee, Amos | 1 | 3 | 4 | | |
| Stillman, George | 1 | 2 | 2 | | |
| Griffen, Samuel | 2 | 3 | 2 | | |
| Stone, Nehemiah | 1 | 2 | 5 | | |
| Turner, Elizabeth | | | 1 | | |
| Lord, Martin, Esqr | 3 | 2 | 6 | | |
| Lane, Hezekiah, Esqr | 3 | | 3 | | |
| Graves, Abner | 2 | 1 | 1 | | |
| Lane, Jabez | 1 | 5 | 2 | | |
| Parmalee, Ozias | 2 | 2 | 5 | | |
| Parmela, Constant | 2 | 1 | 2 | | |
| Lane, Elisha | 2 | 1 | 2 | | |
| Parmela, Cornelius | 3 | | 3 | | |
| Parmelee, Aaron | 1 | | 3 | | |
| Parmela, Josiah | 2 | 2 | 7 | | |
| Isbel, Israel | 1 | | 1 | | |
| Parmela, Braini | 1 | 3 | 1 | | |
| Parmela, David | 1 | | 1 | | |
| Parmela, Nathan | 1 | | 1 | | |
| Kelsey, Joseph | 1 | | 2 | | |
| Kelsey, Eber | 1 | 2 | 4 | | |
| Kelsey, Uriah | 2 | 1 | 4 | | |
| Parsons, Samuel, Junr | 1 | 2 | 1 | | |
| Willcox, Abraham | 1 | | 1 | | |
| Willcox, David | 2 | 1 | 4 | | |
| Graves, Sylvanus | 3 | | 5 | | |
| Lane, Joseph | 3 | | 3 | | |
| Lane, Joseph, Junr | 1 | | 2 | | |
| Hull, Nathan | 3 | 1 | 4 | | |
| Lane, John | 2 | | 3 | | |
| Lane, Arunah | 1 | | 1 | | |
| Stephens, Peter | 1 | 4 | 5 | | |
| Kelsey, David | 1 | | 1 | | |
| Kelsey, Jonathan | 2 | 1 | 2 | | |
| **KILLINGWORTH TOWN—continued.** | | | | | |
| Kelsey, David, Junr | 1 | 1 | 2 | | |
| Lane, John, Junr | 1 | 1 | 4 | | |
| Turner, Jacob | 1 | 1 | 2 | | |
| Blackslee, Daniel | 1 | 2 | 3 | | |
| Davis, Henry | 1 | 1 | 4 | | |
| Nettleton, James | 3 | 2 | 3 | | |
| Bishop, Thalmeno | 1 | 3 | 3 | | |
| Evarts, Joseph | 1 | | 2 | | |
| Norton, Moses | 2 | 4 | 2 | | |
| Norton, Eli | 1 | 2 | 1 | | |
| Norton, John | 2 | 1 | 3 | | |
| Norton, Joel | 1 | 2 | 3 | | |
| Nettleton, Daniel | 1 | 2 | 3 | | |
| Davis, Lemuel | 1 | 2 | 1 | | |
| Francis, James | 1 | 1 | 1 | | |
| Francis, Susannah | 1 | | 4 | | |
| Francis, Daniel | 1 | 2 | 6 | | |
| Linn, James | 3 | | 1 | | |
| Hull, Gurdon | 1 | 2 | 3 | | |
| Stephens, Lois | 1 | 4 | 4 | | |
| Griswould, Zenas | 1 | 2 | 1 | | |
| Davis, Solomon | 1 | 2 | 3 | | |
| Davis, Josiah | 1 | 2 | 4 | | |
| Kelsey, Stephen | 1 | 2 | 3 | | |
| Davis, James | 2 | 4 | 2 | | |
| Davis, Martha | 1 | 1 | 1 | | |
| Blakelee, David | 2 | | 2 | | |
| Brister, Bozaleel | 1 | 4 | 4 | | |
| Hill, James | 4 | 1 | 3 | | |
| Kelsey, Nathaniel | 2 | | 5 | | |
| Davis, Samuel | 2 | | 1 | | |
| Buell, Jeremiah, Junr | 2 | 1 | 7 | | |
| Higgins, Sarah | | | 1 | | |
| Kelsey, Bani | 1 | | 5 | | |
| Wheeler, Joseph | 2 | 1 | 2 | | |
| Parmela, Elias | 1 | 3 | 3 | | |
| Parmela, Ezra | 1 | | 2 | | |
| Parmelee, Jehiel | 1 | 4 | 4 | | |
| Parmelee, Samuel | 1 | | 6 | | |
| Kelsey, Joel | 1 | 4 | 2 | | |
| Isbel, Elias | 2 | 1 | 3 | | |
| Chappell, Jonathan | 1 | | 1 | | |
| Davis, Samuel, Junr | 2 | | 3 | | |
| Kelsey, Aaron | 1 | 1 | 1 | | |
| Stephens, Eliakim | 1 | | 3 | | |
| Nettleton, Josiah | 1 | 1 | 1 | | |
| Nettleton, Isaiah | 1 | | 6 | | |
| Bewell, Jeremiah | 1 | | 1 | | |
| Buell, Bela | 1 | 3 | 3 | | |
| Hull, Ezekiel | 2 | | 5 | | |
| Kelsey, Joseph, 2d | 1 | | 2 | | |
| Kelsey, Lemuel | 1 | | 2 | | |
| Franklin, Essi | 2 | 6 | 4 | | |
| Franlin, Jonathan | 1 | | 2 | | |
| Franlin, Samuel | 1 | 2 | 5 | | |
| Hull, Levi | 1 | 3 | 3 | | |
| Clark, Thomas | 1 | | 1 | | |
| Clark, Aaron | 1 | 1 | 2 | | |
| Nettleton, Samuel | 2 | | 4 | | |
| Jones, Daniel | 3 | 1 | 1 | | |
| Parmelee, Abner | 4 | | 2 | | |
| Phelps, Elexander | 1 | | 1 | | |
| Harris, Jedediah | 2 | 1 | 3 | | |
| Willcox, Nathan | 1 | | 2 | | |
| Willcox, Nathan, 3d | 1 | 5 | 2 | | |
| Stone, Benjamin | 1 | | 1 | | |
| Willcox, Joseph | 1 | 2 | 8 | | |
| Stone, Jedediah | 2 | | 5 | | |
| Stone, Jedediah, Junr | 1 | 1 | 1 | | |
| Williams, Jonathan | 1 | 1 | 4 | | |
| Jones, Phinehas | 1 | 2 | 2 | | |
| Willcox, Joel | 1 | 1 | 2 | | |
| Coan, Mulford | 1 | 1 | 2 | | |
| Smith, Samuel | 1 | 2 | 4 | | 1 |
| Stephens, Samuel, Junr | 1 | | 3 | | |
| Willcox, Adam | 3 | 1 | 3 | | |
| Brooker, Abraham | 1 | | 2 | | |
| Snow, John | 4 | | | | |
| Snow, William | 1 | | 2 | | |
| Lebarron, David | 3 | 2 | 5 | | |
| Isbel, Robert | 1 | | 1 | | |
| Nichols, Rebeca | | 3 | 1 | | |
| Hill, Noah | 1 | 4 | 2 | | |
| Turner, Abraham | 2 | 1 | 5 | | |
| Stevens, Samuel | 3 | | 5 | | |
| Stephens, Aaron | 1 | 1 | 4 | | |
| Brooker, Abraham | 1 | | 3 | | |
| Hull, Lucy | | | 4 | | |
| Willcox, Adam | 3 | 1 | 1 | | |
| Crane, Elisha | 2 | 1 | 1 | | |
| Crane, Elisha, Junr | 1 | 1 | 3 | | |
| Peirson, John, Esqr | 2 | | 4 | | |
| Willcox, Benjamin | 2 | | 2 | | |
| Buell, William | 1 | 2 | 3 | | |
| Butler, Houton | 2 | 1 | 2 | | |

# HEADS OF FAMILIES—CONNECTICUT.

## MIDDLESEX COUNTY—Continued.

| NAME OF HEAD OF FAMILY. | Free white males of 16 years and upward, including heads of families. | Free white males under 16 years. | Free white females, including heads of families. | All other free persons. | Slaves. |
|---|---|---|---|---|---|
| **KILLINGWORTH TOWN—continued.** | | | | | |
| Buell, Asa | 2 | 3 | 5 | | |
| Hull, Joel | 1 | | 6 | | |
| Hull, Roswell | 1 | 3 | 3 | | |
| Griswould, Nathaniel, 2d | 1 | 1 | 3 | | |
| Kelsey, Daniel | 1 | 3 | 3 | | |
| Parmelee, Daniel | 2 | 1 | 2 | | |
| Kelsey, Elisha | 1 | 1 | 3 | | |
| Kelsey, Martin | 2 | 5 | 4 | | |
| Kelsey, Oliver | 1 | | 3 | | |
| Ely, Revᵈ Henry | 3 | 1 | 5 | | |
| Pierson, Abraham, Esq. | 2 | 1 | 3 | | |
| Pierson, Dodo | 1 | 1 | 2 | | |
| Ward, Ichabod | 1 | 1 | 2 | | |
| Watrous, Josiah | 1 | | 1 | | |
| Redfield, Sylvenus | 1 | 2 | 6 | | |
| Porter, Ezra | 1 | 3 | 3 | | |
| Hull, James | 1 | 3 | 6 | | |
| Stevens, Thomas | 2 | | 1 | | |
| Stevans, Thomas, Junʳ | 4 | 3 | 4 | | |
| Hull, Lemuel | 1 | 1 | 2 | | |
| Pierson, Samuel | 3 | | 3 | | |
| Hull, Lemuel, Junʳ | 1 | 1 | 1 | | |
| Evits, Jehiel | 4 | | 3 | | |
| Evits, Jehiel, Junʳ | 2 | 1 | 3 | | |
| Houd, Edward | 3 | 1 | 4 | | |
| Chittendon, Daniel | 2 | 1 | 3 | | |
| Hull, Abner | 2 | 1 | 5 | | |
| Kelsey, Moses | 1 | | 3 | | |
| Hinkley, John | 1 | 1 | 7 | | |
| Davis, Ebenezer | 1 | 3 | 2 | | |
| Davis, Haydon | 1 | | 1 | | |
| Davis, Sibbell | | | 3 | | |
| Kelsey, Martha | 1 | | 1 | | |
| Stevens, Reuben | 5 | | 2 | | |
| Nettleton, John | 1 | 3 | 4 | | |
| Griswould, Samuel | 1 | 2 | 4 | | |
| Willson, Elijah, Junʳ | 1 | 3 | 3 | | |
| Walden, Nathaniel | 1 | | 3 | | |
| Willcox, Elijah | 1 | | 3 | | |
| Hull, Peter | 1 | | 1 | | |
| White, Dudley | 3 | 1 | 4 | | |
| Hull, Josiah | 2 | | 1 | | |
| Hull, Josiah, Junʳ | 1 | 1 | 3 | | |
| Kelsey, Augustus | 1 | | | | |
| Nettleton, Hannah | | | 1 | | |
| Nettleton, Damaras | 1 | 1 | 4 | | |
| Nettleton, Joseph | 1 | 1 | 1 | | |
| Nettleton, Abel | 2 | 1 | 3 | | |
| Butler, Stephen | 1 | | 1 | | |
| Redfield, Peleg | 1 | 1 | 1 | | |
| Pelton, Josiah | 3 | 4 | 3 | | |
| Redfield, Ambros | 1 | 3 | 3 | | |
| Dudley, Phinehas | 2 | 4 | 3 | | |
| Willcox, Simeon | 2 | 4 | 9 | | |
| Redfield, Constant | 1 | 2 | 5 | | |
| Willcox, Ebenezer | 2 | 1 | 3 | | |
| Dudley, Nathaniel | 3 | | 2 | | |
| Redfield, Seth | 1 | 5 | 1 | | |
| Redfield, George | 1 | | | | |
| Baldwin, Eliezer | 1 | 2 | 1 | | |
| Redfield, Josiah | 2 | 1 | 2 | | |
| Redfield, Tereny | 1 | 1 | 3 | | |
| Chittenden, Doseth | | | 1 | | |
| Farnham, Joseph, Junʳ | 2 | | 2 | | |
| Aldridge, Peter W | 3 | 1 | 2 | | |
| Farnham, Joseph | 2 | | 1 | | |
| Griswould, Joseph | 1 | | 4 | | |
| Stevens, Rebecca | | | 1 | | |
| Field, Daniel | 1 | 1 | 4 | | |
| Griswould, Abner | 1 | | 2 | | |
| Griswould, Giles | 2 | 1 | 2 | | |
| Griswould, Nathan | 3 | 1 | 2 | | |
| Williams, Mary | | | 2 | | |
| Crane, Rufas | 1 | 1 | 1 | | |
| Wilman, Jonathan | 1 | | 1 | | |
| Hull, Eliakim | 1 | | | | |
| Andrews, Silas | 1 | | 1 | | |
| Tooly, William | 1 | 1 | 4 | | |
| Tooly, Hannah | 2 | | 2 | | |
| Hull, George, 2d | 1 | 1 | 2 | | |
| Willcox, Nathan, 2d | 1 | | 7 | | |
| Hull, George | 1 | | 3 | | |
| Hull, Samuel | 1 | 5 | 1 | | |
| Farnham, Abner | 3 | 1 | 2 | | |
| Hull, Josiah | 1 | 1 | 3 | | |
| Hull, Joseph | 1 | | 2 | | |
| Stephens, Elias | 1 | 1 | 2 | | |
| Stevens, Jane | 2 | 3 | 3 | | |
| Trall, Oliver | 1 | | 2 | | |
| Hurd, Abraham | 3 | 2 | 1 | | |
| Hull, Abel | 1 | | 1 | | |
| Buell, David | 2 | 2 | 7 | | |
| Buell, Jedediah | 1 | 3 | 4 | | |
| Kelsey, Levi | 1 | 1 | 3 | | |
| Buell, David, 2d | 1 | | 2 | | |
| **KILLINGWORTH TOWN—continued.** | | | | | |
| Kelsey, Ezra | 1 | 1 | 2 | | |
| Buell, Nathaniel | 1 | | 2 | | |
| Spencer, John | 1 | 1 | 3 | 1 | |
| Willcox, Daniel | 1 | 1 | 2 | | |
| Willcox, John | 1 | | 1 | | |
| Griffen, Jared | 1 | | 2 | | |
| Hurd, Caleb L | 1 | 5 | 4 | | |
| Hurd, Seth | 1 | 1 | 4 | | |
| Hurd, Esther | 1 | | 2 | | |
| Ward, James | 4 | | 3 | | |
| Allen, Gideon | 3 | 1 | 3 | | |
| Kelsey, Ezra | 1 | 1 | 3 | | |
| Buell, John | 1 | 2 | 3 | | |
| Willcox, Stephen | 2 | | 5 | | |
| Hurd, Elnathan | 2 | | 1 | | |
| Hurd, Elnathan, 2d | 1 | 1 | 3 | | |
| Hurd, John | 1 | 1 | 4 | | |
| Griffen, Edward | 1 | 2 | 2 | | |
| Griswould, Daniel | 3 | 3 | 5 | | |
| Buell, Job, 2d | 1 | 1 | 4 | | |
| Carter, Jonas | 1 | | 1 | | |
| Buell, Job | 3 | | 4 | | |
| Buell, Josiah, 2d | 1 | 1 | 2 | | |
| Kelsey, Samuel | 1 | 3 | 6 | | |
| Bewell, Josiah | 3 | 1 | 3 | | |
| Buell, Benjamin | 1 | | 1 | | |
| Grace, Nicholass | 1 | | 2 | | |
| Stevens, Nathaniel | 1 | | 2 | | |
| Stevens, Phillip | 2 | 1 | 5 | | |
| Hilliard, Joseph | 3 | | 4 | | |
| Crane, Elias | 3 | | 1 | | |
| Redfield, Daniel | 1 | | 4 | | |
| Marble, Betsey | | | 2 | | |
| Young, Joseph | 2 | 6 | 2 | | |
| Redfield, Margarett | 1 | | 3 | | |
| Buell, Jonathan | 1 | 2 | 5 | | |
| Griffeth, Thomas | 1 | 2 | 2 | | |
| Morgan, Theophilus | 1 | 3 | 3 | | |
| Buell, Reuben | 2 | | 2 | | |
| Buell, James | 1 | 1 | 2 | | |
| Turner, Isaac | 1 | | 3 | | |
| Merrill, Benjamin | 2 | 1 | 4 | 1 | |
| Buell, Azariah | 2 | 1 | 3 | | |
| Kelsey, Amos | 3 | 2 | 3 | | |
| Kelsey, Dan | 4 | | 3 | | |
| Kelsey, Reuben | 1 | 2 | 2 | | |
| Carter, Josiah, Junʳ | 1 | 1 | 2 | | |
| Pierson, Phinehas | 2 | 2 | 3 | | |
| Willard, Peleg | 2 | | 2 | | |
| Willard, Elisha | 1 | 1 | 2 | | |
| Carter, Hubbell | 3 | 1 | 3 | | |
| Carter, Josiah | 2 | | 4 | | |
| Carter, Benjamin | 2 | 1 | 3 | | |
| Carter, Sarah | | | 3 | | |
| Grinnol, Barber | 2 | | 3 | | |
| Grinnol, William B | 1 | | 4 | | |
| Kelsey, Peter | 2 | | 5 | | |
| Redfield, Augustus | 1 | | 4 | | |
| Concklin, Esther | | | 1 | | |
| Dewolf, Elijah | 1 | | 3 | | |
| Dewolf, Elijah, 2d | 1 | 1 | 2 | | |
| Smith, Enoch | 1 | 2 | 4 | | |
| Peck, Daniel | 1 | 2 | 5 | | |
| Holmes, Cornelius | 2 | | 2 | | |
| Lane, Stephen | 2 | 1 | 7 | | |
| Pierson, Patience | | | 2 | 2 | |
| Pierson, Jedediah | 1 | 1 | 3 | | |
| Stevens, Jeremiah | 1 | 2 | 3 | | |
| Lane, Thatcher | 2 | 1 | 4 | | |
| Kelsey, Solomon | 1 | | 1 | | |
| Wright, James | 1 | 3 | 2 | | |
| Rositer, John, 2d | 1 | 1 | 2 | | |
| Kelsey, John | 2 | | 2 | | |
| Rositer, John | 1 | | 2 | | |
| Kelsey, Asa | 1 | 2 | 4 | | |
| Stevens, Jonas | 2 | | 2 | | |
| Elderkin, James | 2 | | 3 | | |
| Elderkin, Elisha | 1 | | 3 | | |
| Wright, Job, Esq. | 1 | 3 | 5 | | |
| Hilliard, Barzilla | 2 | | 3 | | |
| Eliott, Jerod, Junʳ | 1 | | 3 | | |
| Eliott, Jarod | 2 | 1 | 4 | 3 | |
| Dibble, David | 2 | 1 | 2 | | |
| Crane, Theophilus | 3 | 3 | 4 | | |
| Kelsey, Nathan | 2 | 2 | 1 | | |
| Griswould, Martin | 1 | | 1 | | |
| Willman, Zadock | 3 | 1 | 3 | | |
| Wright, Nathan | 1 | 2 | 4 | | |
| Chalker, Jessy | 2 | 1 | 2 | | |
| Kelsey, Samuel. 2d | 2 | 1 | 3 | | |
| Griswould, Josiah | 2 | | 2 | | |
| Chapman, Constant | 1 | 2 | 2 | | |
| Lane, Noah | 1 | 1 | 4 | 1 | |
| Wright, Grace | | | 1 | | |
| Merrill, Samuel | 2 | 2 | 4 | | |
| **KILLINGWORTH TOWN—continued.** | | | | | |
| Griffing, James N | 1 | 1 | 3 | | |
| Griffing, James | 1 | | 1 | | |
| Crane, Samuel | 3 | 1 | 7 | | |
| Stevens, Elnathan | 2 | 1 | 2 | | |
| Burrows, John | 1 | 1 | 2 | | |
| Buel, Hiel | 1 | 1 | 2 | | |
| Williams, Jonathan | 1 | 1 | 5 | | |
| Peck, Augustus | 2 | 1 | 2 | | |
| Buel, Hiel, 2d | 1 | | 1 | | |
| Redfield, Samuel | 1 | | 1 | | 1 |
| Redfield, Samuel, 3d | 1 | | 3 | | |
| Redfield, Eliphilalet | 3 | 1 | 3 | | |
| Kelsey, Josiah | 2 | 1 | 5 | | |
| Wright, Benjamin | 1 | 1 | 3 | | |
| Stevens, Jared | 1 | 3 | 5 | | |
| Merriam, George | 2 | 1 | 2 | | |
| Redfield, Samuel, 2d | 1 | 2 | 4 | | |
| Meryan, William, 2d | 1 | | 1 | 2 | |
| Redfield, Sylvester | 2 | 2 | 4 | | |
| Willcox, Joseph, 2d | 4 | 1 | 5 | 1 | 2 |
| Willcox, John | 1 | | 2 | | |
| Stanton, Adam | 4 | 1 | 7 | | |
| Triseth, William | 1 | 1 | 5 | | |
| Griffing, William | 2 | 1 | 4 | | |
| Eliott, George, Esqʳ | 5 | 1 | 4 | | 1 |
| Redfield, Simeon | 1 | | 2 | | |
| Belden, Samuel | 2 | 1 | 4 | | |
| Mansfield, Revᵈ Achileus | 2 | 2 | 5 | | |
| Eliott, William | 1 | 1 | 4 | | |
| Gale, Hannah | | | 4 | | |
| Hull, Oliver | 2 | 2 | 2 | | |
| Graves, John | 2 | 1 | 1 | | |
| L'Homedieu, William | 2 | | 2 | | |
| Eliott, Aaron | 1 | 3 | 4 | 1 | |
| Baldwin, Aaron | 1 | | 1 | | |
| Griffing, David | 1 | 1 | 1 | | |
| Hilliard, Walter | 1 | | 1 | | |
| Griffing, Benjamin | 1 | | 2 | | |
| Morgan, William, Esqʳ | 1 | 3 | 4 | | 4 |
| Farnum, Ozias | 1 | 3 | 4 | | |
| Kelsey, Silas | 2 | 1 | 3 | | |
| Willcox, John, 2d | 1 | 5 | 2 | | |
| Chatfield, Joseph | 2 | 3 | 2 | | |
| Griffing, Daniel | 2 | | 2 | | |
| Farnum, Hill | 1 | 2 | 3 | | |
| Wright, Reuben | 1 | | 1 | | |
| Elie (negro) | | | | 1 | |
| Evarts, David | 1 | 1 | 2 | | |
| Chatfield, Josiah | 3 | 2 | 3 | | |
| **MIDDLETOWN TOWN.** | | | | | |
| Hamlin, Hon. Jabez, Esqʳ | 2 | | 4 | | 5 |
| Miller, Asher, Esqʳ | 2 | 1 | 3 | | 1 |
| Hubbard, Elijah, Esqʳ | 3 | 1 | 4 | | 1 |
| Phillips, George, Esqʳ | 1 | 1 | 3 | | 1 |
| Starr, Elihu, Esqʳ | 1 | 2 | 6 | | 1 |
| Otis, Jonathan | 1 | | 1 | | 1 |
| Wetmore, Ichabod | 1 | | 9 | | |
| Bull, Samuel | 1 | 2 | 7 | | 2 |
| Fisk, Bozeʳ | 3 | 2 | 2 | | 1 |
| Whittlesey, Chauncey, Esqʳ | 2 | 1 | 5 | 1 | |
| Starr, George | 2 | 3 | 3 | | 2 |
| Woodruff, Ezekiel, Esqʳ | 1 | 2 | 4 | | |
| Storrs, Lemuel | 4 | 2 | 3 | 1 | |
| Cooper, Lamberton | 1 | 2 | 5 | | |
| Hobby, Winsley | 2 | | 2 | | 2 |
| Meigs, Giles | 3 | 3 | 9 | | |
| Warner, Robert | 4 | | 3 | | 1 |
| Canfield, Samuel | 4 | 1 | 5 | | |
| Sage, Ebenezer | 2 | | 1 | | 1 |
| Harrington, Abijah | 1 | 1 | 5 | | |
| Sebor, Jacob | 1 | 2 | 4 | | 1 |
| Richards, William | 1 | 1 | 4 | 1 | |
| Cornwell, James | 2 | 1 | 2 | | |
| Alsop, Richard | 1 | 2 | 4 | | |
| Hall, Anna | 1 | | 2 | | 2 |
| Parsons, William W., Esqʳ | 1 | | 3 | | |
| Brown, Nathaniel, Junʳ | 1 | 2 | 2 | | |
| Brewster, Jane | | | 1 | | |
| Goodrich, Samuel | 1 | 3 | 6 | | |
| Rawson, Elizabeth | | | 3 | | |
| Hall, John E | 1 | | 1 | | |
| Talcott, Mathew, Esqʳ | 3 | | 2 | | 1 |
| Starr, Timothy | 2 | | 3 | | |
| Cleaver, William | 1 | | | | |
| Bigelow, Elizabeth | 2 | 1 | 3 | | 3 |
| Bigelow, Timothy H | 1 | | 2 | | |
| Eglestom, Bennet | 1 | | 2 | | |
| Sage, Joseph | 1 | | 2 | | |
| Southmayd, William | 2 | 1 | 1 | | |

# FIRST CENSUS OF THE UNITED STATES.

## MIDDLESEX COUNTY—Continued.

### MIDDLETOWN TOWN—continued.

| NAME OF HEAD OF FAMILY. | Free white males of 16 years and upward, including heads of families. | Free white males under 16 years. | Free white females, including heads of families. | All other free persons. | Slaves. |
|---|---|---|---|---|---|
| Hubbard, Nehemiah, Jun r. | 4 | 1 | 3 | | |
| Tuch, Samuel | 1 | 2 | 4 | | |
| King, Joseph | 1 | | 1 | | |
| Pierce, Samuel | 1 | | 1 | | |
| Cleaver, William, Jun r. | 1 | | 2 | | |
| Campbell, Andrew | 2 | 3 | 6 | | |
| Nott, William | 1 | 2 | 1 | | |
| Dickinson, John | 1 | | 4 | 1 | |
| Alsop, Mary | | 1 | 8 | 5 | |
| Williams, Isaac | 1 | 1 | 2 | | |
| Nott, John | 1 | 3 | 1 | | |
| Banks, Hannah | | | 3 | | |
| Bailey, Hez. | 1 | 2 | 4 | | |
| Cotton, Samuel | 1 | 2 | 3 | | |
| Brigden, Thomas | 3 | 1 | 1 | | |
| Whitmore, Jacob, Jun r. | 1 | | 1 | | |
| Banks, John | 1 | 1 | 4 | | |
| Hall, Samuel | 1 | 1 | 3 | | |
| Redding, Edward | 1 | | 1 | | |
| Willis, Jamima | | | 2 | | |
| Babb, Sarah | | | 2 | | |
| Treadway, Amos, Jun r. | 1 | 1 | 3 | | |
| Banks, William | 1 | | 3 | | |
| Saxton, Knight | 1 | | 2 | | |
| Hall, Thomas | 3 | 2 | 4 | | |
| Pierce, Stephen | 1 | 2 | 3 | | |
| Starr, William | 2 | 1 | 4 | | |
| Rand, Robert | 2 | 4 | 2 | | |
| Ranney, Jonothan | 1 | 3 | 2 | | |
| Goodwin, Sukey | | 1 | 3 | | |
| Beamont, Mary | | 3 | 1 | | |
| Ingraham, Nathaniel G. | 4 | 3 | 3 | 1 | 2 |
| Hall, Jonathan A. | 1 | | 1 | | |
| Hinshaw, Joshua, Esq r. | 1 | 2 | 4 | | 1 |
| Tracy, Ebenezer | 1 | | 2 | 1 | |
| Washbourn, Ebenezer | 1 | 2 | 2 | | |
| Clark, Seth | 1 | | 1 | | |
| Pomeroy, Adino | 2 | 2 | 5 | | |
| Powers, Timothy | 1 | 3 | 3 | | |
| Whitmore, Jacob | 2 | 2 | 1 | | |
| Pickett, Thankfull | 1 | | 1 | | |
| Hulbert, Hezekiah | 4 | 3 | 8 | 2 | |
| Wallworth, Daniel | 1 | 4 | 1 | | |
| Douglass, William | 1 | | 3 | | |
| Starr, Thomas | 1 | | | | |
| Redfield, Frederick | 3 | 5 | 2 | | 2 |
| Goodwin, Thomas | 1 | | 2 | 3 | |
| Ginnason, Lucy | | | 1 | | |
| Southmayd, William, Jun r. | 1 | 1 | 1 | | |
| Fenno, Ephraim | 2 | 2 | 1 | | 1 |
| Boardman, Timothy | 3 | | 3 | | |
| Paddock, Zackeriah | 1 | | 1 | | |
| Winship, Samuel | 1 | 1 | 1 | | |
| Leverett, Mary | 2 | | 3 | | |
| Treat, Joseph | 1 | 1 | 2 | | |
| Meigs, John | 4 | 3 | 5 | | |
| Paddock, Seth | 2 | 2 | 3 | | |
| Parsons, Mehitable | 1 | 1 | 5 | 2 | 1 |
| Whitebread, Elizabeth | | | 2 | | |
| Treadway, Elijah, Esq r. | 1 | | 1 | | |
| Knap, Isaac | 1 | | 1 | | |
| Knap, Greenfield H. | 2 | | 3 | | |
| Cunningham, Samuel | 1 | 2 | 6 | | |
| Paddack, George | 2 | 1 | 2 | | |
| Starr, James | 2 | | 3 | | |
| Treadway, Amos | 2 | 1 | 2 | | |
| Treadway, Josiah | 1 | 1 | 3 | | |
| Sumner, Susannah | | | 2 | | 1 |
| Magill, Charles | 1 | 2 | 6 | | |
| Warner, William | 1 | 2 | 3 | | |
| Russell, John | 1 | 1 | 3 | | |
| Fairchild, Samuel | 1 | 1 | 3 | | |
| Clay, Stephen | 2 | 1 | 3 | 1 | |
| Daney, Jonathan | 3 | | 2 | 1 | |
| Gleason, Margarett | | | 2 | | |
| Sumner, William | 1 | 2 | 4 | | |
| Coy, Mary | | | 2 | | |
| Goodwin, Thomas, Jun r. | 1 | 1 | 3 | | |
| Henshaw, Mary | | | 1 | | |
| Willis, Joseph | 1 | 1 | 1 | | |
| Starr, Samuel, Jun r. | 1 | | 1 | | |
| Strong, Nathan | 2 | 3 | 5 | | |
| Winborne, Prince | 1 | | 3 | | |
| Phillips, Thompson | 3 | | 3 | | |
| Sage, Comfort, Esq r. | 4 | 1 | 3 | | 4 |
| Davis, John, Jun r. | 1 | 1 | 3 | | |
| Spooner, George | 1 | | 1 | | |
| Foster, John | 1 | 1 | 1 | | |
| Banks, Mary | | | 2 | | |
| Jarvis, Rev r. Abraham | 1 | 1 | 1 | | 2 |
| Whitmore, Ebenezer | 1 | 3 | 5 | | |
| Starr, Timothy, Jun r. | 1 | 5 | 3 | | |
| Strong, Elizabeth | 1 | | 1 | | |
| Cornwell, Elijah | 2 | 2 | 2 | | |
| Rockwell, Grove | 1 | | 2 | 1 | |
| Cadwell, John | 1 | 2 | 3 | | |
| Reardon, Simon | 1 | 1 | 1 | | |
| Johnson, Oliver | 1 | 1 | 2 | | |
| Tarbox, Benjamin | 1 | | 3 | | |
| Harris, John | 1 | 1 | 2 | | |
| Paddack, John | 1 | 3 | 6 | | |
| Frothingham, Samuel | 1 | 2 | 9 | | |
| Fletcher, Mary | | | 1 | | |
| Frothingham, Ebenezer | 1 | | 3 | | |
| Robbert, Elizabeth | | | 1 | | |
| Joyce, William | 1 | | 2 | | |
| Paddack, Samuel | 1 | 1 | 2 | | |
| Shaler, Nathaniel | 3 | 2 | 5 | | 1 |
| Johnson, Ashel | 2 | 2 | 3 | | |
| Starr, Josiah | 1 | 2 | 3 | | |
| Paddack, Robert | 1 | | 3 | | |
| Loveland, Darcus | | | 2 | 1 | |
| Redfield, Peleg | 1 | 1 | 1 | | |
| Parsons, Stephen | 2 | 5 | 5 | | |
| Sizer, Anthony | 1 | 1 | 2 | | |
| Willcox, Abell | 2 | 5 | 2 | | |
| Stow, John | 1 | 2 | 2 | | |
| Robert, Aaron | 1 | | 2 | | |
| Johnson, Jonathan | 2 | | 8 | | |
| Powers, Edward | 2 | 3 | 3 | | |
| Sizer, Daniel | 1 | 3 | 3 | | |
| Hull, Trustum | 1 | 1 | 2 | | |
| Buffham, Joshua | 1 | 1 | 1 | | |
| Bill, Martha | | | 1 | | |
| Nott, Mary | | | 5 | | |
| Bill, Solomon | 2 | | 2 | | |
| Fuller, Asa | 2 | 1 | 3 | | |
| Paddack, William | 1 | 2 | 6 | | |
| Gilbert, Joseph | 1 | 2 | 3 | | |
| Bill, Samuel | 1 | | 2 | | |
| Chamberlain, Samuel | 2 | 6 | 6 | | |
| Henry, James | 1 | 2 | 3 | | |
| Clark, Phebe | | | 1 | | |
| Goodwin, Samuel | 1 | | 2 | | |
| Starr, Thomas, Jun r. | 1 | | 1 | | |
| Ward, William | 1 | 3 | 2 | | |
| Darby, Partrick | 1 | 3 | 1 | | |
| Starr, Joseph | 1 | | 1 | | |
| Kelly, Hannah | | | 4 | | |
| Gaylord, Samuel | 1 | 3 | 3 | | |
| Sheers, Rebecca | | | 3 | | |
| Starr, Samuel | 1 | | 2 | | |
| Starr, Cloe | | | 1 | | |
| Starr, William, Jun r. | 1 | 3 | 2 | | |
| Redfield, William | 3 | | 3 | | |
| Stone, Ephraim | 2 | | 1 | | |
| Dickerson, Jacob | 1 | 2 | 2 | | |
| Huntington, Rev r Enoch | 1 | 3 | 7 | | |
| Hall, Joseph | 1 | 1 | 1 | | |
| Meigs, Return Jon a. | 1 | 1 | 2 | | |
| Hubbard, Jacob | 1 | 2 | 2 | | |
| Ingham, Joseph | 1 | | 3 | | |
| Vandeuerson, William | 1 | 2 | 3 | | |
| Starr, Anna | | | 4 | | |
| Nichols, Lois | 2 | | 5 | | |
| Russell, Samuel | 2 | 6 | 2 | | |
| Plum, Charles | 1 | 2 | 2 | | |
| Starr, Nathan | 5 | 2 | 6 | | |
| Cone, Joseph | 2 | 1 | 6 | | |
| Whittlesey, Bula | | | 3 | | |
| Nichols, Thadeus | 1 | 3 | 2 | | 1 |
| Sage, Esther | 1 | 1 | 3 | | |
| Starr, Vim. | 1 | | 1 | | |
| Tuch, Comfort | 2 | | 2 | | |
| Bow, Isaac | 1 | 4 | 3 | | |
| Tuch, Micajah | 1 | | 2 | | |
| Grace, John | 1 | 2 | 2 | | |
| Pousley, Samuel | 1 | | 2 | | |
| Stow, Solomon, Jun r. | 1 | | 2 | | |
| Tuch, Benjamin | 1 | 2 | 2 | | |
| Allen, Peter | 1 | 3 | 5 | | |
| Williams, Benjamin | 1 | 3 | 3 | | 2 |
| Magill, Arther | 3 | 2 | 6 | 1 | |
| Ranney, Stephen | 2 | | 2 | | 3 |
| Cotton, Elihu | 1 | 2 | 2 | | |
| Cotton, Elihu, Jun r. | 1 | 1 | 1 | | |
| Taylor, Jonathan | 1 | 2 | 2 | | |
| Cornwell, Timothy | 1 | 1 | 1 | | |
| Jepson, William | 1 | 1 | 2 | | |
| Giles, William | 1 | 2 | 2 | | |
| Bridgham, George | 1 | | 2 | | |
| Warner, Hope | | | 2 | 1 | 1 |
| Tuch, Enoch | 1 | 1 | 3 | | |
| Aird, David | 1 | 2 | 1 | | |
| Cotton, John | 1 | | 2 | | 2 |
| Cotton, Timothy | 1 | 1 | 2 | | |
| Gill, Abigail | | | 2 | | |
| Johnston, Samuel | 1 | 1 | 5 | | |
| Hosmer, Stephen T. | 2 | 1 | 3 | | 1 |
| Hosmer, Lydia | 1 | | 5 | | 1 |
| Foster, Edward | 1 | | 3 | | |
| Plum, Jacob | 1 | 2 | 3 | | |
| Doolittle, Abraham | 1 | 1 | 1 | | |
| Doolittle, Joshua | 1 | | 2 | | |
| Hamlin, Peter | | | | 2 | |
| Hollett, John | 1 | | 1 | | |
| Burnham, Ashbell | 2 | 2 | 8 | | |
| Smith, Joseph | 1 | 1 | 3 | | 2 |
| Lee, Josiah | 1 | | 3 | | |
| Keith, William | 1 | 5 | 4 | | |
| Scott, Lucreatia | | | 5 | | 2 |
| Powers, Gregory | 1 | 2 | 3 | | 1 |
| Osborn, Daniel | 1 | 1 | 3 | | |
| Mortimer, Phillip, Esq r. | 1 | | | | 11 |
| Munn, Olvir | 3 | | 3 | | |
| Fisher, Lydia | | 2 | 1 | | |
| Johonnot, Daniel | 1 | 3 | 2 | | |
| Starr, Jehosaphat, Jun r. | 2 | 4 | 2 | | |
| Wetmore, Hannah | 2 | 1 | 4 | | |
| Plum, Reuben | 3 | 3 | 5 | | |
| Rockwell, Edward, Jun r. | 1 | 4 | 3 | | |
| Wetmore, Jn e, Jun r. | 1 | 2 | 2 | | |
| Sage, Francis | 2 | 4 | 3 | | |
| Ranney, Stephen, Jun r. | 1 | 3 | 2 | | 3 |
| Woodward, Moses H. | 1 | 2 | 4 | | |
| Allen, Joel | 1 | 2 | 2 | | |
| Cotton, George | 1 | 1 | 3 | | |
| Osborn, John | 2 | 3 | 6 | | |
| Hawkins, Sarah | | | 2 | | |
| Sanford, Peleg | 2 | | 4 | | |
| Johnson, Samuel | 1 | | 1 | | |
| Johnson, Samuel, Jun r. | 1 | 1 | 2 | | |
| Ranney, Samuel W. | 1 | 2 | 3 | | |
| Plum, Walt | 2 | | 4 | | |
| Bacon, Joseph | 1 | 1 | 2 | | |
| Hulbert, Thomas | 2 | 2 | 8 | | |
| Peck, Timothy | 1 | 1 | 3 | | |
| Arnold, Asa Amasa | 1 | 1 | 4 | | |
| Richardson, Rowland | 1 | 3 | 4 | | |
| Spencer, Elizabeth | | 1 | 4 | | |
| Rockwell, Desiah | | 2 | 1 | | |
| Southern, Thomas | 1 | | 2 | | |
| Higbe, Noah | 1 | 2 | 4 | | |
| Mitchell, Mary | | | 3 | | |
| Rand, Thomas | 2 | 1 | 2 | | |
| Cuff (Negro) | | | | 4 | |
| Florah (Negro) | | | | 2 | |
| O'Daniel, Partrick | 2 | 3 | 3 | | |
| Griffin, Mary | 2 | 1 | 2 | | |
| Masterns, James | 1 | 1 | 1 | | |
| Thainer (Negro) | | | 3 | | |
| Sage, William, Jun r. | 2 | 1 | 4 | | |
| Canfield, Seba | 1 | 2 | 3 | | |
| Mackintire, Duncan | 3 | 1 | 3 | | |
| Bacon, William | 1 | 1 | 3 | | |
| Bacon, Rhoda (alias Hall) | | | 2 | | |
| Mahanna, John | 1 | | 2 | | |
| Wetmore, Esther | 1 | | 1 | | |
| Wetmore, John | 3 | | 2 | 1 | |
| Stow, David | 2 | 1 | 5 | | |
| Stow, Peter | 1 | 1 | 5 | | |
| Griffin, Ebenezer | 1 | 4 | 4 | | |
| Frasier, Mary | | | 2 | | |
| Winthrop, Mark | | | | 4 | |
| Starr, Joseph, 3 d. | 1 | 2 | 2 | | |
| Danforth, Martha | 2 | 1 | 2 | | |
| Plum, William, Esq r. | 1 | | 2 | | |
| Russell, Daniel | 2 | 3 | 2 | | |
| Cale, William | 1 | 1 | 1 | | |
| Doane, Nehemiah | | | | | |
| Williams, Peter | | | | 2 | |
| Ackraw (Negro) | | | | 2 | |
| Greenfield, Thomas | 1 | 1 | 3 | | |
| Redfield, Susannah | | 1 | 2 | | |
| Cornwell, William | 1 | 1 | 1 | | |
| Brown, Nathaniel | 1 | | 4 | | |
| Lucas, Pricilla | | | 1 | | |
| Gilbert, Asa | 1 | 1 | 1 | | |
| Goodwin, Jacob | 2 | 3 | 5 | | |
| Wright, Hannah | | | 1 | | |
| Creamore, George | 1 | | 1 | | |
| Henshaw, Sarah | | 2 | | | |
| Hill, Gershom | | | 1 | 1 | |
| Henshaw, Daniel | 1 | | 3 | | |
| Bacon, Isaac | 1 | 1 | 2 | | |
| Southmayd, Jonathan | 2 | 1 | 2 | | |
| Adkins, George | 3 | | 5 | | |
| Saxton, Jonathan | 1 | | 3 | | |
| Treadway, Phebe | | 1 | 3 | | |
| Driggs, Israel | 2 | | 5 | | |
| Barns, John | 2 | 1 | 2 | | |
| Hubbard, Hey | 2 | 3 | 2 | | |

# HEADS OF FAMILIES—CONNECTICUT.

## MIDDLESEX COUNTY—Continued.

| NAME OF HEAD OF FAMILY. | Free white males of 16 years and upward, including heads of families. | Free white males under 16 years. | Free white females, including heads of families. | All other free persons. | Slaves. | NAME OF HEAD OF FAMILY. | Free white males of 16 years and upward, including heads of families. | Free white males under 16 years. | Free white females, including heads of families. | All other free persons. | Slaves. | NAME OF HEAD OF FAMILY. | Free white males of 16 years and upward, including heads of families. | Free white males under 16 years. | Free white females, including heads of families. | All other free persons. | Slaves. |
|---|---|---|---|---|---|---|---|---|---|---|---|---|---|---|---|---|---|
| MIDDLETOWN TOWN—continued. | | | | | | MIDDLETOWN TOWN—continued. | | | | | | MIDDLETOWN TOWN—continued. | | | | | |
| Peck, Jessy S | 1 | | 1 | | | Augar, George | 1 | | 1 | | | Lucas, Samuel | 2 | 1 | 3 | | |
| Rogers, John | 2 | 1 | 5 | | | Croe, Asa | 1 | | 1 | | | Blake, Samuel | 1 | 2 | 2 | | |
| Doyle, John | 1 | | 6 | | | Robbards, Samuel C | 3 | 1 | 4 | | | Whitmore, Beriah | 1 | | 3 | | |
| Whitmore, Francis | 1 | | 2 | | | Tryon, Amos | 1 | 2 | 3 | | | Robbert, Fenno | 1 | | 2 | | |
| Miller, Caleb | 1 | 2 | 1 | | | Hubbard, Abijah | 1 | | 5 | | | Rockwell, Noadiah | 1 | 3 | 2 | | |
| Ames, Anthony | 1 | 1 | 2 | | | Hubbard, Oliver | 2 | 1 | 3 | | | Hedges, Henry, Junr | 2 | | 2 | | |
| Arnold, Ebenezer | 3 | 1 | 5 | | | Hubbard, Caleb | 1 | 4 | 4 | | | Prout, Oliver | 1 | 2 | 2 | | |
| Tryon, Elee | 1 | 6 | 2 | | | Bailey, Lowdon | 1 | 2 | 4 | | | Crowell, John | 2 | 1 | 2 | | |
| Trevana, Richard | 1 | | 2 | | | Hubbard, John | 1 | 3 | 1 | | | Crowell, John, Junr | 2 | | 3 | | |
| Markland, Jeremiah | 2 | 2 | 5 | | | Hubbard, Ephraim | 1 | 2 | 4 | | | Starr, David | 1 | 2 | 3 | | |
| Driggs, John | 1 | | 2 | | | Hubbard, Ama | | | 3 | | | Miles, Sarah | | 1 | 2 | | |
| Brown, William | 1 | | 4 | | | Butler, David | 1 | 1 | 2 | | | Hall, Calvin | 1 | | 3 | | |
| Frothingham, John | 1 | 2 | 2 | | | Clark, Daniel | 2 | 2 | 4 | | | Hall, Jacob | 1 | 3 | 3 | | |
| Robbard, Edward | 1 | 3 | 5 | | | Prior, Daniel | 1 | | 1 | | | Ward, Josiah | 2 | 3 | 6 | | |
| Ward, Samuel | 1 | 2 | 5 | | | Prior, Samuel | 1 | 1 | 3 | | | Ward, Josiah, Junr | 1 | 1 | 2 | | |
| Butler, John | 1 | | 3 | | | Prior, Elijah | 1 | 1 | 1 | | | Ward, John | 2 | 1 | 3 | | |
| Butler, Hannah | | | 2 | | | Hubbard, Solomon | 3 | 2 | 2 | | | Ward, John, 5th | 1 | 2 | 2 | | |
| Miller, Jonathan | 1 | 3 | 4 | | | Johnson, James | 1 | 3 | 2 | | | Crowell, Samuel | 1 | 2 | 3 | | |
| Miller, Edward | 1 | 2 | 2 | | | Johnson, Mehitable | | | 2 | | | Blake, John | 2 | | 5 | | |
| Markham, Samuel | 2 | 4 | 6 | | | Johnson, Caleb | 1 | 2 | 2 | | | Blake, Freelove | 1 | 3 | 2 | | |
| Ward, John, 4th | 2 | 1 | 3 | | | Tryon, Caleb | 1 | 1 | 5 | | | Crowell, Solomon | 1 | 2 | 3 | | |
| Bow, Samuel | 1 | 1 | 3 | | | Bailey, Ephraim | 1 | 2 | 1 | | | Crowell, Sarah | | | 1 | | |
| Sears, Nathan | 1 | 2 | 3 | | | Sears, Elisha | 2 | | 2 | | | Fairchild, Abigail | 1 | | 2 | | |
| Cotton, John, 2d | 1 | 1 | 2 | | | Hubbard, Jamansy | | | 2 | | | Fairchild, Joel | 1 | 3 | 3 | | |
| Miller, Jared | 1 | | 1 | | | Coe, Jessy | 2 | 2 | 4 | | | Crowell, Daniel | 1 | 4 | 4 | | |
| Daniels, John | 1 | | 1 | | | Rich, Eliakim | 1 | 3 | 1 | | | Prior, Oliver | 1 | 1 | 1 | | |
| Hubbard, Joseph | 1 | | 1 | | | Johnson, Partrick | 3 | | 5 | | | Hubbard, Micah | 1 | 3 | 5 | | |
| Hubbard, Manoah | 2 | 2 | 5 | | | Robbards, Nathaniel | 1 | 1 | 6 | | | Lucas, Moses | 1 | | 1 | | |
| Sumner, Elizabeth | 2 | 1 | 5 | | | Gilbert, John | 1 | 1 | 2 | | | Lucas, Moses. Junr | 1 | 2 | 7 | | |
| Hubbard, Eliphalet | 3 | | 2 | | | Hubbard, George | 4 | | 3 | | | Hubbard, Noadiah | 2 | 2 | 2 | | |
| Hubbard, Manoah, Junr | 1 | 1 | 3 | | | Clark, James | 1 | 3 | 3 | | | Hubbard, Noadiah, Junr | 3 | 1 | 1 | | |
| Weston, Darius | 1 | | 5 | | | Whitmore, Daniel | 1 | 1 | 2 | | | Barns, Daniel | 1 | | 3 | | |
| Bow, Peleg | 1 | 1 | 1 | | | Whitmore, Gordon | 2 | 1 | 5 | | | Barns, Martha | | 2 | 2 | | |
| Prior, Josiah | 1 | 2 | 5 | | | Lawrence, Roman | 1 | 3 | 2 | | | Adkins, Thomas | 2 | 2 | 2 | | |
| Tryon, David | 1 | 1 | 2 | | | Clark, Lamberton | 2 | 3 | 1 | | | Starr, Jehosaphat | 1 | | 1 | | |
| Tryon, David, Junr | 1 | | 2 | | | Clark, Ambros | 1 | 2 | 4 | | | Hubbard, Jabez | 2 | | 1 | | |
| Tryon, Elisha | 1 | 1 | 3 | | | Bidwell, Ashbell | 1 | 2 | 4 | | | Barns, Amos | 1 | | 3 | | |
| Tryon, Stephen | 1 | 2 | 3 | | | Davis, John | 2 | | 2 | | | Barns, Mary | 1 | | 3 | | |
| Nancarow, Edward | 1 | 1 | 2 | | | Miller, Joshua | 2 | 1 | 3 | | | Cornwell, Francis | 2 | | 3 | | |
| Bow, Amos | 2 | 3 | 4 | | | Powers, Henry | 1 | | 1 | | | Storms, James | | | | 3 | |
| Daniels, William | 3 | | 4 | | | Goff, David | 1 | 1 | 3 | | | Barns, Solomon | 1 | 1 | 2 | | |
| Griswold, Josiah | 1 | 1 | 3 | | | Starr, Daniel | 1 | 4 | 5 | | | Phillips, Peter | | | | 5 | |
| Robbard, Timothy | 1 | 3 | 5 | | | Braddock, Michael | 1 | | 5 | | | Barns, Thomas | 1 | 3 | 4 | | |
| Johnson, Elijah, Junr | 1 | 1 | 3 | | | Rogers, John, Junr | 1 | 1 | 3 | | | Johnson, Jonathan, Junr | 1 | | 2 | | |
| Johnson, Mary | | | 1 | | | Robbards, Nathaniel, Junr | 1 | 1 | 2 | | | Barnes, Ezekiel | 2 | | 1 | | |
| Brooks, David | 1 | | 3 | | | Lee, William | 1 | 5 | 5 | | | Barns, Giles | 1 | 1 | 5 | | |
| Hubbard, Abner | 1 | | 3 | | | Robbarts, Seth | 1 | 2 | 6 | | | Gilbert, Jonathan | 1 | 1 | 3 | | |
| Coe, Jessy, Junr | 1 | | 1 | | | Johnson, Stephen | 1 | 1 | 2 | | | Hubbard, Nehemiah | 3 | 1 | 2 | | |
| Hubbard, Elias | 1 | 1 | 1 | | | Johnson, William | 1 | 3 | 3 | | | Gilbert, Jonathan, Junr | 2 | 1 | 4 | | |
| Bates, Joseph | 1 | 1 | 2 | | | Johnson, Freelove | 1 | 1 | 5 | | | Doolittle, Mrs. Hannah | | | 4 | | |
| Clark, Giles | 1 | 2 | 6 | | | Johnson, Jedediah | 2 | | 2 | | | Adkins, Jessie | 1 | 1 | 2 | | |
| Griswold, Moses | 1 | 2 | 5 | | | Harris, William | 1 | 3 | 3 | | | Adkins, Samuel | 1 | | 3 | | |
| Butler, Samuel | 1 | 2 | 4 | | | Mitchell, Abner | 2 | 1 | 6 | | | Cornwell, Timothy | 3 | | 1 | | |
| Bow, Amos, Junr | 1 | 2 | 1 | | | Johnson, Martha | | | 3 | | | Adkins, Jabez | 1 | 2 | 1 | | |
| Bigelow, Frederick | 1 | 4 | 2 | | | Clark, Oliver | 3 | 2 | 5 | | | Adkins, Samuel, Junr | 2 | 1 | 3 | | |
| Johnson, Henry | 1 | 2 | 3 | | | Markham, Ebenezer | 1 | 4 | 3 | | | Lucas, Thomas | 2 | 1 | 1 | | |
| Lucas, Abner | 2 | 1 | 6 | | | Whitmore, Timothy | 1 | | 4 | | | Ward, Samuel, Junr | 2 | 2 | 4 | | |
| Brooks, Martha | | | 2 | | | Tryon, Thomas | 1 | | 1 | | | Hall, John | 3 | | 4 | | |
| Brooks, Joseph B | 1 | 1 | 2 | | | Tryon, Abel | 1 | 1 | 1 | | | Potter, John | 1 | 1 | 9 | | |
| Young, Sylvanus | 3 | 2 | 3 | | | Tryon, Josiah | 1 | 1 | 1 | | | Hubbard, Isaac | 1 | 4 | 3 | | |
| Carrier, Samuel | 1 | | 1 | | | Tryon, Jessy | 1 | | 2 | | | Adkins, Ephraim | 1 | | 2 | | |
| Bow, Abraham | 2 | 2 | 1 | | | Johnson, Timothy | 1 | 1 | 5 | | | Savage, Abijah | 1 | 4 | 7 | | |
| Whitmore, Stephen | 2 | 1 | 4 | | | Robbards, Rachel | | | 2 | | | Savage, Josiah | 2 | 1 | 2 | | |
| Cone, John | 3 | 2 | 3 | | | Crowell, Edward | 1 | 2 | 4 | | | Haskell, William | 1 | 3 | 5 | | |
| Carrier, Israel | 2 | 1 | 2 | | | Hubbard, Jeremiah | 1 | 2 | 3 | | | Savage, Josiah, Junr | 1 | 1 | 3 | | |
| Morgan, Simeon | 2 | 2 | 1 | | | Lord, James | 1 | 3 | 2 | | | Bishop, Leveritt | 1 | 2 | 3 | | |
| Morgan, Richard | 1 | | 1 | | | Roberts, Ebenezer | 1 | 1 | 3 | | | Sage, Timothy | 3 | 1 | 5 | | |
| Morgan, Richard, Junr | 1 | 1 | 3 | | | Robbert, Adonijah | 1 | 2 | 1 | | | Sage, Samuel | 1 | 1 | 3 | | |
| Morgan, Peter | 1 | 1 | 4 | | | Prout, John | 1 | 2 | 2 | | | Plum, Joshua | 1 | | 2 | | |
| Whitmore, Ebenezer | 2 | | 1 | | | Tryon, Charles | 4 | 4 | 5 | | | Edwards, Daniel | 2 | 2 | 5 | | |
| Whitmore, Jehiel | 1 | | 3 | | | Prout, Darcy | 1 | | 3 | | | Doxey, Henry | 1 | | 1 | | |
| Johnson, Seth | 1 | 3 | 4 | | | Brooks, Jabez | 2 | | 2 | | | Arnold, Daniel | 1 | 1 | 1 | | |
| Brooks, Noah | 1 | 3 | 3 | | | Johnson, Ebenezer | 3 | | 2 | | | Ranney, William | 2 | 1 | 1 | | |
| Clark, Francis | 2 | 1 | 3 | | | Prout, Harris | 1 | 2 | 3 | | | Eliott, John, Esqr | 1 | 1 | 3 | | 1 |
| Sears, Stephen | 3 | 2 | 3 | | | Brooks, Daniel | 1 | 2 | 2 | | | Williams, John | 2 | 2 | 4 | | |
| Swaddle, John | 2 | 1 | 5 | | | Robbards, Jonathan | 1 | 2 | 3 | | | Frairey, Samuel | 1 | 3 | 2 | | |
| Sears, John | 2 | 1 | 3 | | | Lee, Samuel | 1 | | 1 | | | Clark, James | 1 | 5 | 2 | | |
| Simmons, Samuel | 2 | | 2 | | | Shattuck, Robert | 1 | | 2 | | | Chauncey, Nathaniel, Esqr | 1 | | 1 | | |
| Butler, Davney | 2 | 1 | 4 | | | Harris, David | 1 | 1 | 2 | | | | | | | | |
| Thayer, Jonathan | 3 | | 4 | | | Sizer, Lemuel | 2 | 1 | 2 | | | Chauncey, Nathaniel, Junr | | | | | |
| Cook, William | 1 | | 4 | | | Lee, Samuel, Junr | 1 | | 2 | | | Smith, Edward | 1 | 1 | 4 | | |
| Miller, Stephen | 3 | 2 | 4 | | | Francis, Mary | | | 2 | | | Smith, James | 3 | 2 | 4 | | |
| Cunningham, Esther | | | 1 | | | Brewster, Elisha | 1 | 1 | 3 | | | Robinson, Robert | 1 | | 3 | | |
| Turpin, Henry | 1 | | 3 | | | Brooks, Jabez | 1 | | 3 | | | Sage, Nathan | 2 | 1 | 2 | | 2 |
| Driggs, Joseph | 1 | 1 | 2 | | | Brooks, Timothy | 1 | | 5 | | | Ranney, Ebenezer | 2 | 2 | 4 | | |
| Driggs, Joseph, Junr | 2 | 6 | 3 | | | Sizer, Eli | 1 | 1 | 3 | | | Stocking, Daniel | 1 | | 2 | | 1 |
| Pike, Charles | 1 | | 3 | | | Barrett, John | 1 | | 2 | | | Stocking William | 2 | 1 | 4 | | |
| Markham, Sarah | | | 1 | | | Woodward, Sibbel | | | 2 | | | Goodrich, Barsheba | | 1 | 3 | | |
| Robbards, Collins | 1 | 3 | 4 | | | Brooks, Jabez, Junr | 2 | | 2 | | | Stocking, Jozeb | 1 | 3 | 3 | | 1 |
| Ward, Abigail | 1 | | 3 | | | Brooks, Samuel | 2 | | 2 | | | White, Abagil | | 2 | 2 | | |
| Hubbard, Jonathan | 2 | 3 | 3 | | | Johnson, Jedediah, Junr | 2 | 3 | 5 | | | Gaylord, Jonathan | 1 | 2 | 4 | | |
| Prior, Jesse | 1 | 4 | 1 | | | Hedges, Isaac | 4 | | 6 | | | Gaylord, Wm C | 1 | 1 | 5 | | |
| Robbards, Hinkeman | 4 | | 3 | | | Robbards, Phinehas | 1 | 2 | 3 | | | White, Elias | 1 | 1 | 1 | | |
| Robbards, Noyes | 1 | 1 | 4 | | | Robbards, Simeon | 1 | | 2 | | | | | | | | |
| Butler, Samuel | 2 | 1 | 2 | | | | | | | | | | | | | | |

## MIDDLESEX COUNTY—Continued.

| NAME OF HEAD OF FAMILY. | Free white males of 16 years and upward, including heads of families. | Free white males under 16 years. | Free white females, including heads of families. | All other free persons. | Slaves. | NAME OF HEAD OF FAMILY. | Free white males of 16 years and upward, including heads of families. | Free white males under 16 years. | Free white females, including heads of families. | All other free persons. | Slaves. | NAME OF HEAD OF FAMILY. | Free white males of 16 years and upward, including heads of families. | Free white males under 16 years. | Free white females, including heads of families. | All other free persons. | Slaves. |
|---|---|---|---|---|---|---|---|---|---|---|---|---|---|---|---|---|---|
| MIDDLETOWN TOWN—continued. | | | | | | MIDDLETOWN TOWN—continued. | | | | | | MIDDLETOWN TOWN—continued. | | | | | |
| White, John | 3 | 4 | 8 | | | Gad, Marear | | | | 3 | | Willcox, John | 3 | | 4 | | |
| White, Timothy | 2 | 4 | 3 | | | Ward, Thomas | 3 | | 3 | | | Graves, Joseph | 1 | 2 | 7 | | |
| Stocking, Samuel | 1 | | 1 | | | Ward, Joshua | 1 | 1 | 2 | | | Boardman, Nathaniel | 2 | 2 | 4 | | |
| Savage, Giles | 1 | | 1 | | | Bacon, Jeremiah | 4 | 3 | 6 | | | Willcox, Jeremiah | 1 | 3 | 5 | | |
| Savage, Solomon | 1 | | 4 | | | Campbell, Andrew | 1 | | 1 | | | Dudley, Asahel | 3 | 1 | 4 | | |
| Ranney, Mary | | 2 | 1 | | | Lathrop, John | 1 | | 3 | | | Galpin, Samuel | 1 | 2 | 3 | | |
| Savage, Nathaniel | 1 | 2 | 3 | | | Doud, Cornwell | 1 | 4 | 3 | | | Willcox, Eli | 1 | 2 | 3 | | |
| Kirby, Hezekiah | 1 | 1 | 2 | | | Hough, Abigail | | | 2 | | | Robberts, Elijah | 1 | | 2 | | |
| Stow, Jonathan | 1 | | 2 | | | Adkins, Joel | 1 | 1 | 1 | | | Goodrich, Hosea | 1 | | 2 | | |
| Savage, Stephen | 1 | | 2 | | | Riley, Asher | 1 | 3 | 4 | | | Bailey, William | 1 | | 3 | | |
| Ellis, Nathaniel | 1 | 4 | 4 | | | Butler, Gershom | 4 | | 3 | | | Woods, Ruth | | 1 | 1 | | |
| Ellis, Daniel | 1 | 3 | 3 | | | Thrasher, Bezaleel | 2 | | | | | Boardman, Nathan | 1 | 2 | 4 | | |
| Robinson, James | 2 | 3 | 1 | | | Redding, Samuel | 1 | | 1 | | | Willcox, John, Junr | 2 | | 5 | | |
| Willcox, Eliphalett | 1 | 1 | 2 | | | Miller, Hoze | 1 | 1 | 6 | | | Willcox, Samuel | 1 | 3 | 1 | | |
| Butler, Benjamin | 1 | | 3 | | | Hubbard, Roswell | 1 | 2 | 1 | | | Willcox, Elijah | 2 | 3 | 4 | | |
| Butler, Comfort | 3 | | 2 | | | Thomas, Evan | 1 | 2 | 3 | | | Willcox, Joseph | 3 | 1 | 4 | | |
| Hamlin, Daniel | 1 | 2 | 3 | | | Plum, Abraham | 3 | | 3 | | | Bacon, Stephen | 1 | 2 | 4 | | |
| Riley, Joseph | 1 | 1 | 5 | | | Sears, Peter | | | | 5 | | Warner, John | 1 | 2 | 4 | | |
| Willcox, Elisha | 2 | 4 | 5 | | | Ranney, Abijah | 1 | 2 | 2 | | | Warner, Lois | 1 | | 2 | | |
| Willcox, Ozias | 3 | | 2 | | | Riley, Julius | 1 | 4 | 4 | | | Bacon, Joel | 2 | 2 | 6 | | |
| Savage, Sarah | | | 3 | | | Williams, Jehiel | 3 | 1 | 7 | | | Bacon, Noah | 3 | 1 | 3 | | |
| Savage, Amos | 1 | | 3 | | | Stocking, Seth | 1 | | 3 | | | Norton, Aaron | 2 | 2 | 7 | | |
| Clark, Sarah | 1 | | 2 | | | Kirby, Thomas | 4 | 1 | 4 | | | Norton, Isaiah | 1 | | 3 | | |
| McPherson, Joseph | 1 | | 2 | | | Smith, Abner | 3 | 2 | 3 | | | Higbe, Ephraim | 1 | 3 | 3 | | |
| Ranney, Hezekiah | 1 | 2 | 3 | | | Hamlin, John | 1 | 2 | 1 | | | Rexford, Benjamin | 1 | | 3 | | |
| Coy, Edy | 1 | 3 | 1 | | | Beldon, John | 1 | | 2 | | | Hall, David | 1 | 2 | 3 | | |
| Savage, Naomy | | | 2 | | | Beldon, Benjamin | 1 | | 1 | | | Higbe, Daniel | 4 | 6 | 2 | | |
| Willcox, James | 1 | | 2 | | | Chamberlain, Theodore | 1 | | | | | Joppen, William | 1 | | 2 | | |
| Gridley, Isaac, Esqr | 2 | 2 | 3 | | | Sage, John | 1 | | 1 | | | Higbe, Zacheus | 1 | | 2 | | |
| Spencer, Samuel | 2 | 1 | 8 | | | Sage, Simeon | 2 | 1 | 4 | | | Morgan, John | 1 | 4 | 7 | | |
| Gipson, John | 3 | 1 | 5 | | | Sage, Epaphras | 1 | 1 | 5 | | | Dudley, Joseph | 1 | | 3 | | |
| Willcox, Lois | | | 3 | | | Sage, Hezekiah | 3 | 3 | 5 | | | Higbe, Jeduthan | 1 | 1 | 2 | | |
| Johnson, Seth | 1 | 2 | 3 | | | Smith, Nathaniel | 1 | 2 | 2 | | | Higbe, Amos | 1 | | 2 | | |
| Hart, Seth | 2 | 2 | 1 | | | Sage, Lewis Samuel | 1 | | 2 | | | Higbe, David | 2 | 2 | 3 | | |
| Ranney, Nathaniel | 2 | | 5 | | | Sage, Lemuel | 1 | 1 | 1 | | | Crofoot, Elisha | 1 | 3 | 4 | | |
| Nichols, James | 1 | 1 | 2 | | | Sage, Joseph | 1 | 1 | 2 | | | Webster, Benjamin | 1 | | 1 | | |
| Ranny, Joseph | 1 | 3 | 3 | | | Perry, Christiany | | | 2 | | | Higbe Lemuel | 1 | | 1 | | |
| Sage, Amos | 2 | 3 | 3 | | | Robinson, Lydia | 1 | | 1 | | | Doolittle, Joel | 1 | 1 | 2 | | |
| Buckley, Revr Gershom | 1 | 1 | 3 | | | Savage, Daniel | 1 | 1 | 1 | | | Bacon, Phinehas | 2 | 1 | 5 | | |
| Stow, Joseph | 1 | 3 | 5 | | | Sage, Giles | 1 | 3 | 3 | | | Adkins, Benjamin | 1 | 2 | 3 | | |
| Stow, Zebulon | 1 | 5 | 2 | | 1 | Barnes, William | 1 | 2 | 2 | | | Allen, Ebenezer | 2 | 3 | 4 | | |
| Savage, Timothy | 1 | | 2 | | | Pryor, Amos | 1 | 2 | 3 | | | Bears, James | 1 | 2 | 2 | | |
| Savage, Jonathan | 3 | | | | | Lane, Letitia | | | 3 | | | Washbourn, Joseph | 5 | 2 | 5 | | |
| Bunnell, Joel | 1 | 2 | 4 | | | Robberts, Ruth | | 1 | 2 | | | Kentner, John P | 1 | 2 | 3 | | |
| Savage, William | 2 | 1 | 2 | | | Clark, Jonathan | 1 | | 2 | | | Kentner, Jeremiah | 1 | | 2 | | |
| Miller, James | 2 | 1 | 3 | | | Bivins, Ebenr | 1 | 1 | 2 | | | Roberts, David | 1 | 1 | 3 | | |
| Edwards, David, Junr | 2 | | 2 | | | Bacon, Ebenezer, Esqr | 3 | 2 | 4 | | | Wetmore, Seth | 4 | 4 | 6 | | 2 |
| Edwards, Churchel, Junr | 1 | 1 | 2 | | | Johnson, Asa | 1 | 3 | 1 | | | Whitmore, Jessey | 1 | 3 | 4 | | |
| Sage, Solomon | 1 | | 3 | | | Bacon, Sibbel | | 1 | 5 | | | Peter (Negro) | | | | 4 | |
| Sage, Elisha | 3 | 3 | 5 | | | Plum, Samuel, Junr | 2 | 1 | 3 | | | Hart, Ebenezer | 1 | 1 | | | |
| Sage, William | 4 | 4 | 4 | | | Plum, Samuel | 1 | | 3 | | | Jones, James | 1 | 1 | 1 | | |
| Gibson, Timothy | 2 | 1 | 3 | | | Plum, James | 1 | 2 | 3 | | | Merrow, John | 1 | | 4 | | |
| Kirby, Nehemiah | 2 | | 4 | | | Plum, Aaron | 1 | 2 | 3 | | | Merrow, Elisha | 1 | | 4 | | |
| Edwards, Churchell | 1 | | 1 | | | Plum, Jessey | 1 | 2 | 1 | | | Rockwell, Edward | 3 | 2 | 2 | | |
| Sage, Solomon, Junr | 1 | 2 | 2 | | | Robberts, Jessey | 1 | 1 | 6 | | | Kelly, Daniel | 1 | | 2 | | |
| White, Aaron | 2 | 1 | 4 | | | Gaylord, Elieazer | 1 | | 3 | | | Pratt, Jonathan | 1 | 1 | 2 | | |
| Robert, Recompence | 1 | 3 | 3 | | | Bacon, John | 1 | | 2 | | | Sizer, Abel | 1 | | 1 | | |
| Ray, Benjamin | 1 | 1 | 3 | | | Bacon, John, Junr | 1 | 5 | 4 | | | Southmayd, Partridge | 1 | 3 | 3 | | |
| Butler, Eli | 2 | 1 | 8 | | | Bonfy, Henry | 2 | 5 | 2 | | | Gears, Hezekiah | 2 | 1 | 1 | | |
| Kelsey, Israil | 4 | 2 | 4 | | | Hall, William | 2 | | 1 | | | Roper, Nathaniel | 1 | 1 | 2 | | |
| Shepherd, Joseph | 2 | 2 | 1 | | | Stow, Amos | 1 | 1 | 2 | | | Gilbert, Rhoda | | | 2 | | |
| Mildram, John | 1 | 3 | 3 | | | Clark, Benjamin | 1 | | 3 | | | Southmayd, Giles | 2 | 1 | 2 | | 1 |
| Treat, John | 1 | 2 | 1 | | | Clark, Daniel | 2 | 2 | 2 | | | Hall, Daniel | 2 | 4 | 4 | | 1 |
| Savage, Stephen | 1 | | 3 | | | Clark, Timothy | 2 | 1 | 7 | | | Wetmore, Oliver | 1 | 4 | 7 | 1 | 1 |
| Savage, Martha | | | 1 | | | Gouge, Nathaniel | 1 | 2 | 2 | | | Cotton, Ebenezer | 1 | | 3 | | 5 |
| Treat, Stephen, Junr | 1 | 3 | 3 | | | Johnson, Edward | 2 | 1 | 3 | | | Hall, Jabez | 1 | | 3 | | |
| Kirby, Daniel | 2 | | 1 | | | Willcox, Giles | 2 | 3 | 5 | | | Hamlin, Charles | 2 | 2 | 3 | | |
| Kirby, Sarah | 2 | | 2 | | | Doud, Benjamin | 2 | 1 | 3 | | | Marks, William | 1 | 1 | 1 | | |
| Shepherd, Jered | 1 | 2 | 3 | | | Cotton, James | 1 | | 3 | | | Miller, Giles | 1 | | 2 | | |
| Stow, Zachariah | 1 | | 3 | | | Cornwell, Ashbell | 1 | 4 | 4 | | | Miller, Giles, Junr | 1 | 1 | 2 | | |
| Hamlin, William, Junr | 3 | 3 | 6 | | | Doud, Richard | 1 | 2 | 4 | | | Coe, Nathan | 2 | | 6 | | |
| Hamlin, Abigail | 2 | | 4 | | | Doud, Phebe | | | 1 | | | Coe, Nathan, Junr | 1 | | 1 | | |
| Cornwell, Hart | 1 | | 2 | | | Hatch, Josiah | 1 | 2 | 3 | | | Griffin, Samuel | 1 | 3 | 3 | | |
| Cotton, Thomas | 1 | 1 | 1 | | | Elton, Bradley | 1 | 3 | 3 | | | Auger, Prosper | 1 | 2 | 4 | | |
| Cornwell, John | 2 | 1 | 3 | | | Hamlin, Patience | | | 3 | | | Roberts, John | 1 | | 1 | | |
| McKey, Phinehas | 2 | 1 | 2 | | | Treat, Stephen | 1 | 1 | 3 | | | Nichols, Silvenus | 1 | 1 | 3 | | |
| Ward, Joseph, Junr | 1 | 2 | 2 | 1 | | Ranney, Comfort | 1 | 1 | 1 | | | Richards, Sarah | | | 2 | | |
| Savage, Samuel | 1 | 3 | 5 | | | Bacon, William | 1 | 1 | 1 | | | Coe, John | | 1 | 3 | | |
| Clark, David | 1 | 2 | 2 | | | Clark, Joseph | 1 | 1 | 2 | | | Beebe, Zachariah | 1 | | 2 | | |
| Alvord, Daniel | 3 | 2 | 5 | | | Roberts, Reuben | 1 | 1 | 1 | | | Ward, Edward | 3 | 4 | 4 | | |
| Gilbert, Benjamin | 1 | | 4 | | | Lewis, Naboth | 1 | 1 | 1 | | | Jopping, Daniel | 2 | | 4 | | |
| Gilbert, Ebenezer | 1 | | 2 | 1 | | Minor, Revr Thomas | 1 | 3 | 2 | | | Guild, Jeremiah | 1 | 4 | 3 | | |
| Gilbert, Allen | 2 | 2 | 3 | | | Doolittle, Hannah | | | 3 | | | Ward, Abiel | | | 2 | | |
| Hamlin, William | 2 | | 3 | | | Doolittle, David | 1 | 1 | 2 | | | Guild, Samuel | 2 | 2 | 6 | | |
| Hamlin, Harris | 1 | | 3 | | | Doolittle, Joseph | 2 | 1 | 4 | | | Hale, Hezekiah | 1 | 1 | 1 | | |
| Cane, James | 1 | 1 | 1 | | | Doolittle, Alisha | 1 | 1 | 1 | | | Robberts, Asahel | 1 | | 1 | | |
| Ward, Michal | 1 | 2 | 4 | | | Clark, Michal | 1 | | 5 | | | Turner, John | 1 | | 2 | | |
| Cotton, Elisha | 1 | 3 | 3 | | | Treat, Rebecca | | | 2 | | | Clark, Daniel | 2 | 1 | 3 | | |
| Brown, Hugh | 1 | | 4 | | | Cornwell, Isaac | 2 | 5 | 3 | | | Clover, John | 1 | 4 | 4 | | |
| Cotton, Samuel | 1 | 2 | 3 | | | Cornwell, Nathaniel | 2 | 5 | 3 | | | Ward, James T | 2 | 4 | 4 | | |
| Cande, John | 1 | 4 | 3 | 1 | | Melona, Michael | 1 | 1 | 3 | | | Robberts, John | 1 | 1 | 1 | | |
| Cornwell, Caleb | 1 | | 4 | | | Robberts, Ebenezer | 1 | 2 | 3 | | | Robberts, E. Merril | 1 | | 2 | | |
| Johnson, Amos | 2 | | 1 | | | Geir, George | 1 | 2 | 3 | | | Coe, Joseph | 1 | 3 | 2 | | |
| Ward, Joseph | 1 | | 4 | 2 | | Robberts, Abel | 1 | 3 | 1 | | | Turner, Stephen | 2 | 2 | 4 | | |
| Ward, Bela | 1 | | 3 | | | Churchell, Amos, Esqr | 1 | 3 | 4 | | | Hoadley, Jehiel | 2 | | 3 | | |

# HEADS OF FAMILIES—CONNECTICUT.

## MIDDLESEX COUNTY—Continued.

| NAME OF HEAD OF FAMILY. | Free white males of 16 years and upward, including heads of families. | Free white males under 16 years. | Free white females, including heads of families. | All other free persons. | Slaves. | NAME OF HEAD OF FAMILY. | Free white males of 16 years and upward, including heads of families. | Free white males under 16 years. | Free white females, including heads of families. | All other free persons. | Slaves. | NAME OF HEAD OF FAMILY. | Free white males of 16 years and upward, including heads of families. | Free white males under 16 years. | Free white females, including heads of families. | All other free persons. | Slaves. |
|---|---|---|---|---|---|---|---|---|---|---|---|---|---|---|---|---|---|
| **MIDDLETOWN TOWN—continued.** | | | | | | **SAYBROOK TOWN—continued.** | | | | | | **SAYBROOK TOWN—continued.** | | | | | |
| Hand, Benjamin | 1 | | 4 | | | Morgan, Abraham | 3 | 2 | 5 | 1 | | Jones, Gideon | 3 | 1 | 2 | | |
| Freeman, David | 2 | | 2 | | | Clark, Saml | 2 | 1 | 4 | | | Chalker, Stephen | 2 | 2 | 3 | | |
| Ward, John | 2 | 3 | 5 | | 1 | Clark, Rufus | 1 | | 2 | | | Chalker, Abraham | 1 | 1 | 5 | | |
| Stow, Joshua | 1 | 1 | 4 | | | Hart, Saml | 2 | 1 | 5 | | 2 | Jones, Thomas | 2 | 1 | 3 | | |
| Wetmore, Asa | 2 | 2 | 7 | | | Hart, Jno | 2 | 3 | 4 | | | Jones, Israel | 1 | | 2 | | |
| Johnson, Hezekiah | 1 | | 2 | | | Shipman, Elias | 1 | 3 | 1 | | | Bushnell, Ira, 2d | 2 | 3 | 5 | | |
| Spencer, Ichabod | 1 | 4 | 4 | 1 | | Ingham, Thomas | 2 | | 2 | | | Babcock, Saml | 1 | 2 | 6 | | |
| Walker, James | 1 | 1 | 3 | | | Pratt, Timothy | 3 | 1 | 5 | | | Shipman, James | 1 | 1 | 4 | | |
| Roberts, David | 3 | 2 | 2 | | | Shipman, Samuel | 3 | | 2 | | | Sherman, Sarah | | | 2 | | |
| Hubbard, Robert | 1 | 4 | 3 | | | Shipman, Nathl | 2 | 3 | 2 | | | Mather, Hannah | | | 2 | | |
| Coe, David | 2 | 2 | 7 | | | Pratt, James | 1 | 1 | 3 | | | Whittlesey, Azariah | 2 | 1 | 5 | | |
| Birdsay, Hannah | | 2 | 5 | 2 | | Shipman, Jno | 1 | 1 | 2 | | | Sanford, Saml | 1 | | 2 | | |
| Miller, Elisha | 3 | 1 | 5 | | | Lord, Russel | 2 | 3 | 2 | | 1 | Sanford, Saml, 2d | 3 | | 2 | | |
| Kimball, Tyler | 1 | 1 | 2 | | | Lord, Andrew | 3 | 1 | 2 | | | Whittelsey, Ambrose | 2 | 1 | 3 | | |
| Camp, Edward | 1 | 1 | 5 | | | Lord, Martha | | | 2 | | | Whittelsey, Hezekiah | 3 | 1 | 2 | | |
| Camp, Lemuel | 1 | 3 | 3 | | | Hart, Elisha | 2 | 1 | 4 | | 1 | Whittelsey, Ambrose, 2d | 1 | 2 | 3 | | |
| Butler, Timothy | 1 | 2 | 4 | | | Hart, Mary | | | 2 | | 1 | Dudley, Saml | 2 | | 4 | | |
| Ward, William | 2 | | 4 | | | Ely, Elisha | 1 | 3 | 4 | | | Lord, Jeremiah | 2 | | 1 | | |
| Babbett, William | 1 | 1 | 5 | | | Willard, Joseph | 2 | 3 | 4 | | | Chapman, Esther | | | 3 | | |
| Ward, William, Junr | 1 | 1 | 1 | | | Newell, Benjamin | 1 | 1 | 2 | | | Harriss, Deliverance | | | 3 | | |
| Willey, Barzilla | 3 | 3 | 5 | | | Chalker, Abigail | | | 1 | | | Buckingham, Saml | 2 | 1 | 4 | | |
| Miller, Icabod | 2 | 2 | 3 | | | Willard, Nathl | 1 | 4 | 5 | | | Dudley, Jedediah | 1 | 1 | 7 | | |
| Wetmore, Joseph | 2 | 5 | 4 | | | Jones, Ezekiel | 1 | | 6 | 1 | | Whittelsey, David | 1 | 1 | 1 | | |
| Miller, Seth | 2 | 5 | 3 | | | Sandford, Rebekah | 1 | | 1 | | | Magney, Lucretia | | | 2 | 3 | |
| Miller, William | 1 | 2 | 6 | | | Jones, Isaac | 2 | 3 | 5 | | | Whittelsey, Saml W | 1 | | 2 | | |
| Stow, Elihu | 3 | | 4 | | | Chalker, Ezra | 1 | | 1 | | | Boles, Edgecombe | 1 | | 3 | | |
| Auger, Justice | 1 | 2 | 1 | | | Lord, Mary | | | 2 | 1 | 1 | Dudley, Anne | | | 4 | | |
| Camp, Asahel | 1 | | 3 | | | Jones, Parker | 1 | 1 | 3 | | | Dudley, Elisha | 1 | 1 | 1 | | |
| Coe, David | 1 | | 4 | 1 | | Jones, John | 1 | 1 | 1 | | | Kirtland, Asa | 1 | 5 | 3 | | |
| Coe, Eli | 1 | 3 | 3 | | | White, Oliver | 1 | | 1 | | | Shirtland, Wm E | 2 | 1 | 5 | | |
| Coe, Seth | 1 | 4 | 2 | | | Lilly (Negro) | | | | 2 | | Bates, Isaac | 2 | | 1 | | |
| Birdsey, David | 2 | 1 | 2 | | 1 | Pratt, Seth | 3 | 1 | 6 | | | Shipman, Jno | 1 | 1 | 2 | | |
| Birdsey, John, Junr | 1 | | 5 | 1 | | Lord, Wm | 1 | 1 | 3 | | | Glading, Wye | 1 | 1 | 1 | | |
| Lyman, David | 3 | 4 | 6 | | | Lord, Joel | 1 | | 1 | | | Glading, Rebekah | | | 2 | | |
| Birdsey, John | 1 | | 1 | 3 | | Lord, Abiel | 1 | | 3 | | | Glading, Ebenezer | 2 | | 1 | | |
| Birdsey, Abel | 1 | 2 | 1 | | | Reave, Pnyryer | 1 | 2 | 5 | | | Glading, Silas | 5 | | 4 | | |
| Miller, Isaac, Esqr | 2 | 2 | 7 | | 1 | Munn, Robert I | 1 | 1 | 3 | | | Pratt, Jno Clark | 1 | 2 | 3 | | |
| Hubbard, William | 1 | | 2 | | | Newell, Robert | 3 | | 3 | | | Pratt, Reuben | 2 | | 6 | | |
| Coe, Elisha | 1 | 2 | 5 | | | Newell, Robt, 2d | 1 | | 1 | | | Strakey, Stephen | 2 | 1 | 2 | | |
| Miller, Brainard | 2 | 3 | 3 | | | Tryon, Asa | 1 | 1 | 1 | | | Starkey, Charles | 1 | | 4 | | |
| Miller, Hezekiah | 1 | 2 | 3 | | | Waterhouse, Wm | 3 | | 3 | | | Pratt, Abraham | 3 | | 5 | | |
| Hambleton, Mary | | 1 | 2 | | | Buckingham, Elizabeth | 1 | | 1 | | | Pratt, Jeremiah | 1 | | 5 | | |
| Hawley, Stow | 4 | 3 | 5 | | | Waterhouse, Jno | 3 | | 5 | | | Pratt, Mary | | | 3 | | |
| Talcott, Hezekiah | 4 | 2 | 4 | | | Waterhouse, Ambrose | 1 | | 5 | | | Pratt, Charity | | 3 | 1 | | |
| Parsons, Aaron | 1 | | 2 | | | Parker, Wm | 3 | | 4 | | | Pratt, Jones | 1 | | 3 | | |
| Cone, Berial | 1 | 2 | 4 | | | Griffin, Jno | 1 | 1 | 5 | | | Pratt, Saml | 3 | 1 | 4 | | |
| Daniels, William | 1 | | 1 | | | Ayer, Travis | 1 | 1 | 3 | | | Tucker, Tabor | 1 | 1 | 1 | | |
| Miller, Jacob | 1 | 2 | 3 | | | Ayer, John | 1 | | 3 | | | Tucker, Richard | 1 | 1 | 3 | | |
| Birdsoy, Abigail | | 3 | 3 | | | Sill, Richard | 2 | 2 | 3 | | | Starkey, Noah | 3 | | 3 | | |
| Miller, William | 3 | 2 | 2 | | | Hill, Hiland | 1 | 1 | 3 | | | Starkey, Willm | 1 | | 3 | | |
| Miller, Ambros | 1 | 1 | 3 | | | Hill, Peleg | 1 | 2 | 2 | | | Trip, Willm | 1 | 3 | 5 | | |
| Rockwell, Joshua | 2 | 4 | 5 | | | Chapman, Elisha | 1 | 4 | 4 | | | Hill, James | 1 | 1 | 3 | | |
| Wetmore, John, 2d | 2 | 1 | 4 | | | Chapman, Pinehas | 3 | | 3 | | | Biggs, Willm | 1 | 2 | 1 | | |
| Wetmore, Daniel | 1 | 1 | 2 | | | Chapman, James | 1 | | 3 | | | Tiley, David | 1 | | 2 | | |
| Turner, Jonathan | 3 | | 2 | | | Chapman, Levi | 2 | 5 | 2 | | | Tucker, James | 1 | 2 | 2 | | |
| | | | | | | Bushnell, Pinehas | 1 | | 1 | | | Hill, Peleg | 1 | | 3 | | |
| **SAYBROOK TOWN.** | | | | | | Bushnell, Saml | 1 | | 2 | | | Haydon, Elias | 1 | 5 | 5 | | |
| Hotchkis, Revd Fredk W | 1 | 1 | 1 | | | Bushnell, Handly | 1 | 1 | 1 | | | Starkey, John | 1 | 1 | 4 | | |
| Hart, Willm, Esqr | 1 | 1 | 2 | 3 | 3 | Bushnell, Joshua | 1 | | 1 | | | Plumb, Joseph | 1 | | 2 | | |
| Pratt, Humphrey, Junr | 1 | 2 | 6 | | | Ely, Robert | 2 | 1 | 3 | | | Darrow, Jno | 3 | | 1 | | |
| Pratt, Humphrey | 1 | | 2 | | | Bushnell, Nathl | 1 | | 1 | | | Haydon, Jacob | 2 | 2 | 3 | | |
| Pratt, Elias | 1 | 2 | 2 | | | Bushnell, Elisha | 1 | | 1 | | | Pratt, Asa, 2d | 1 | 2 | 2 | | |
| Buckingham, Daniel | 1 | 1 | 3 | | | Bushnell, Nathl, 2d | 1 | | 1 | | | Pratt, Jno | 3 | 2 | 3 | | |
| Field, Saml | 1 | 2 | 4 | | | Bushnell, Daniel | 1 | | 2 | | | Pratt, Asa | 1 | | 5 | | |
| Pratt, Benjamin | 2 | 3 | 3 | | | Lee, George | 1 | | 2 | | | Pratt, Jno, 2d | 1 | 1 | 2 | | |
| Kirtland, Ambrose | 5 | | 2 | | | Lee, Saml | 1 | 2 | 3 | | | Williams, David | 2 | 1 | 6 | | |
| Williams, Charles | 3 | 1 | 2 | | | Bushnell, Elias | 2 | 3 | 3 | | | Williams, Ebenezer | 1 | | 5 | | |
| Blague, Giles | 1 | 2 | 3 | | | Chalker, Alexander | 1 | 1 | 3 | | | Pratt, Jane | 1 | | 5 | | |
| Tulley, Wm | 1 | 2 | 3 | | | Chalker, Gideon | 1 | | 1 | | | Scovell, Annah | | | 2 | | |
| Dickinson, Richard | 6 | 1 | 3 | | | Chalker, Moses | 1 | 1 | 2 | | | Williams, Jno | 2 | | 2 | | |
| Ingraham, Jno | 1 | 3 | 5 | | | Chalker, Oliver | 1 | | 1 | | | Scovell, Noah | 2 | 4 | 2 | | 1 |
| Ingraham, James | 1 | | 1 | | | Bushnell, Jonathan | 1 | | 2 | | | Lay, Saml | 2 | | 5 | | |
| Ingraham, Wm | 1 | 1 | 4 | | | Bushnell, Constant | 1 | 4 | 3 | | | Wilson, Nathl | 2 | | 3 | | |
| Ingraham, Daniel | 3 | | 3 | | | Dibble, John | 3 | 2 | 3 | | | Parker, Saml | 1 | 1 | 4 | | |
| Pierce, Thomas | 1 | 1 | 2 | | | Dibble, Josiah | 2 | 1 | 3 | | | Hayden, Eliakim | 3 | 2 | 2 | | |
| Cochran, Jno | 1 | 2 | 3 | | | Doty, Edward | 2 | | 2 | | | Haydon, Nehemiah | 1 | 3 | 3 | | |
| Cochran, Jno, 2d | 1 | | 2 | | | Doty, Benjamin | 1 | 2 | 5 | | | Haydon, Uriah | 3 | | 5 | | |
| Buckingham, Adonijah | 2 | | 5 | | | Bushnell, Handly, 2d | 1 | 1 | 2 | | | Lay, Robt | 2 | | 2 | | |
| Beaumont, Samuel | 1 | 2 | 4 | 1 | | Jones, Ezra | 1 | | 2 | | | Haydon, Ebenezer | 5 | | 3 | | |
| Kirtland, Martin | 1 | 1 | 4 | | | Doan, John | 1 | 3 | 3 | | | Pratt, Zephaniah | 4 | | 1 | | |
| Kirkland, Charles | 1 | | 4 | | | Chapman, Wm | 1 | 5 | 1 | | | Tucker, Joseph | 1 | 1 | 4 | | |
| Kirtland, Elizur | 1 | 1 | 2 | | | Chapman, Benja | 1 | | 4 | | | Pratt, Phinehas | 2 | 2 | 6 | | |
| Stilman, Saml | 1 | 1 | 4 | | | Tryon, Edward, 2d | 1 | | 3 | | | Pratt, Susannah | | | 4 | | |
| Ingham, Benjamin | 1 | 1 | 1 | | | Whittelsey, Hannah | | 1 | 1 | | | Phelps, Jno | 1 | | 2 | | |
| Tryon, Edward | 1 | 1 | 2 | | | Ingham, Ebenezer | 2 | 2 | 3 | | | Pratt, Jabez | 2 | | 1 | | |
| Newell, David | 1 | 2 | 5 | 2 | | Ingham, Wm | 1 | 3 | 4 | | | Pratt, Ezra | 2 | 4 | 2 | | |
| Clark, Ezra | 1 | 3 | 3 | | | Bushnell, Joseph | 2 | | 3 | | | Pratt, Robert | 2 | | 3 | 3 | |
| Tully, Saml, Esqr | 1 | 1 | 5 | | | Bushnell, Joseph, 2d | 2 | 1 | 2 | | | Denison, Mary | | | 3 | | |
| Tully, Elias | 1 | | 6 | | | Bushnell, Lemuel | 1 | | 2 | | | Denison, Ebenezer | 3 | | 3 | | |
| Shirtland, Saml | 2 | | 4 | | | Bushnell, Lemuel, 2d | 1 | 2 | 3 | | | Mather, Elisha | 1 | 3 | 3 | | |
| Shirtland, Saml, 2d | 1 | 2 | 4 | | | Chalker, Jacob | 3 | 3 | 4 | | | Holmes, Anne | 1 | | 3 | 1 | 1 |
| Lynde, Wm | 2 | 2 | 1 | | 2 | Ingham, Daniel | 3 | | 1 | | | Ely, Revd Richard | 2 | | 4 | | |
| | | | | | | Bushnell, Ira | 4 | 3 | 4 | | | Clark, Danforth | 3 | 1 | 6 | | |
| | | | | | | Bushnell, John | 3 | 1 | 5 | | | Williams, Richard | 1 | 2 | 5 | | |
| | | | | | | | | | | | | Knot, Josiah | 3 | 1 | 5 | | |

## MIDDLESEX COUNTY—Continued.

| NAME OF HEAD OF FAMILY. | Free white males of 16 years and upward, including heads of families. | Free white males under 16 years. | Free white females, including heads of families. | All other free persons. | Slaves. | NAME OF HEAD OF FAMILY. | Free white males of 16 years and upward, including heads of families. | Free white males under 16 years. | Free white females, including heads of families. | All other free persons. | Slaves. | NAME OF HEAD OF FAMILY. | Free white males of 16 years and upward, including heads of families. | Free white males under 16 years. | Free white females, including heads of families. | All other free persons. | Slaves. |
|---|---|---|---|---|---|---|---|---|---|---|---|---|---|---|---|---|---|
| SAYBROOK TOWN—con. | | | | | | SAYBROOK TOWN—con. | | | | | | SAYBROOK TOWN—con. | | | | | |
| Williams, Benjamin, 2d | 2 | 3 | 4 | | 1 | Southward, Nathan, 2d | 1 | | 4 | | | Stannard, Jno | 2 | 1 | 4 | | |
| Starkey, Timothy, Esqr | 2 | 4 | 4 | | 1 | Reed, Cornelius | 1 | 1 | 8 | | | Clark, Jno | 2 | 1 | 3 | | |
| Griswold, Selah | 1 | 3 | 2 | | | Callon, Ducan M | 2 | | 3 | | | Bushnell, Daniel | 1 | 2 | 3 | | |
| Pratt, Phebe | 1 | 1 | 4 | | | Shirland, Stephen | 2 | | 4 | | | Jones, Huldah | | 1 | 2 | | |
| Williams, Samuel | 1 | 7 | 3 | | | Lord, Doty | 2 | | 1 | | | Stokes, Richd | 1 | | 3 | | |
| Post, David | 5 | 3 | 4 | | | Kirtland, Abner | 1 | 4 | 5 | | | Post, Jedediah | 1 | | 3 | | |
| Post, David, Junr | 1 | 1 | 2 | | | Lord, Elijah | 3 | | 1 | | | Jones, Lewis | 1 | 6 | 3 | | |
| Lucass, Saml | 2 | 6 | 2 | | | Pratt, Benja | 1 | | 1 | | | Lay, James | 3 | 2 | 2 | | |
| Brockway, Elijah | 1 | 2 | 3 | | | Pratt, Jedh | 4 | 3 | 2 | | | Post, Isaac | 1 | | 5 | | |
| Denison, James | 2 | 4 | 3 | | | Pratt, Wm | 2 | 4 | 6 | | | Post, Joel | 1 | | 3 | | |
| Brockway, Ebenezer | 2 | 1 | 3 | | | Denison, Jno, 2d | 3 | 1 | 3 | | | Belding, Seymour | 2 | 1 | 3 | | |
| Jane, John | 1 | 4 | 4 | | | Dunnen, Jno | 1 | 2 | 3 | | | Post, Benjamin | 2 | 1 | 2 | | |
| Pelton, Wm | 3 | 1 | 6 | | | Scovell, Mathew | 2 | 5 | 4 | | | Dibble, Jonas | 2 | 2 | 3 | | |
| Ward, Smith | 3 | 2 | 4 | | | Beebe, Molly | 2 | 1 | 1 | | | Dibble, Jno P | 1 | 2 | 2 | | |
| Stilman, Charles | 1 | | 3 | | | Pratt, Mehitable | | | 3 | | | Post, Nathan | 1 | 1 | 3 | | |
| Pratt, Tabor | 1 | 4 | 3 | | | Widger, Jno | 1 | 2 | 1 | | | Post, Christopher | 3 | 2 | 5 | | |
| Pratt, Ozias | 1 | 3 | 3 | | | Havern, Edward | 1 | 2 | 2 | | | Post, Enoch | 2 | | 1 | | |
| Pratt, Gideon | 2 | 1 | 3 | | | Williams, Lydia | | | 1 | | | Post, Anne | | | 3 | | |
| Doan, Israel | 2 | 2 | 6 | | | Snow, Edmond | 3 | 1 | 4 | | | Spencer, Daniel | 1 | 2 | 2 | | |
| Buckingham, Reuben | 1 | 3 | 2 | | | Bull, Edward | 1 | 2 | 2 | | | Stannard, Jasper | 1 | 1 | 2 | | |
| Buckingham, Lucy | | 3 | | | | Bushnell, Daniel, 2d | 1 | | 1 | | | Jones, Norris | 1 | 3 | 3 | | |
| Pelton, Phinehas | 1 | | 5 | | | Bushnell, Francis | 1 | 2 | 5 | | | Spencer, Joseph, 2d | 1 | 5 | 4 | | |
| Denison, Robert | 2 | 1 | 6 | | | Bull, Jno | 1 | 2 | 4 | | | Spencer, Joseph | 2 | 1 | 2 | | |
| Butler, Saml | 1 | | 6 | | | Corbet, Joseph | 1 | 1 | 4 | | | Spencer, Peter | 3 | 2 | 3 | | |
| Champion, Stephen | 1 | 1 | 4 | | | Bushnell, Daniel | 2 | 2 | 4 | | | Wright, Saml | 2 | 1 | 2 | | |
| Grimes, Cyrus | 1 | | 4 | | | Graham, Jane | | | 1 | | | Hilliard, Bezaleel | 2 | | 7 | | |
| Buckingham, Saml | 3 | 4 | 3 | | | Devotion, Revr Jno | 1 | 1 | 3 | | | Stannard, Nathan | 1 | 3 | 2 | | |
| Andrews, Ichabod | 4 | 2 | 3 | | | Chapman, Martha | | 1 | 5 | | | Stannard, Ephraim | 1 | 2 | 4 | | |
| Tucker, Timothy | 4 | | 6 | | | Chapman, Caleb | 2 | 4 | 2 | | | Wright, Benja | 1 | 2 | 3 | | |
| Bebee, Mary | 1 | 1 | 3 | | | Keley, Rueben | 1 | 4 | 2 | | | Chapman, Jedediah | 1 | 1 | 2 | | 2 |
| Williams, Benja | 1 | | 3 | 2 | | Kebly, Jedediah | 2 | | 2 | | | Chapman, Jedediah, 2d | 1 | 4 | 2 | | |
| Scovell, Elijah | 2 | | 5 | | | Kelly, James | 1 | | 3 | | | Lay, John | 1 | 2 | 4 | | 2 |
| Hill, Willm | 4 | 2 | 3 | | | Bushnell, Jonathan | 2 | 2 | 4 | | | Wright, Josiah | 3 | | 4 | | |
| Dibble, George | 1 | | 4 | | | Chapman, Wm | 1 | 2 | 4 | | | Wright, Martin | 1 | | 1 | | |
| Dibble, Martin | 1 | 1 | 1 | | | Worthington, Wm | 1 | 2 | 2 | | | Kelly, Gemaliel | 1 | 1 | 1 | | |
| Post, Phinehas | 1 | 1 | 2 | | | Denison, Jedediah | 1 | 3 | 2 | | | Wright, Jeremh | 2 | 1 | 1 | | |
| Post, Nathan, 2d | 2 | 1 | 3 | | | Norriss, Oliver | 1 | 1 | 1 | | | L'Hommedieu, Henry | 2 | 1 | 3 | | 1 |
| Post, Josiah | 1 | 1 | 3 | | | Chapman, Labbeus | 1 | | 3 | | | Denison, Joseph | 2 | 3 | 4 | | |
| Dennison, Jno | 3 | 2 | 3 | | | Stannard, Abner | 2 | | 4 | | | Towner, Abraham | 3 | | 6 | | |
| Utter, Stephen | 4 | | 3 | | | Stannard, Joseph | | 1 | 4 | | | Carter, Joseph | 2 | | 2 | | |
| Buckley, Abraham | 1 | 4 | 2 | | | Redfield, James P | 1 | 1 | 4 | | | Lay, Asa | 2 | 2 | 6 | | |
| Platts, Jno | 1 | 2 | 5 | | | Stannard, Jno, 2d | 1 | | 3 | | | Hunter, Robert | 1 | | 1 | | |
| Buckley, Jemima | | 1 | 2 | | | Denison, Saml | 1 | | 3 | | | Wright, Ezekiel | 1 | 4 | 3 | | |
| Leister, Eliphalet | 1 | 1 | 1 | | | Denison, Asa | 1 | | 3 | | | Thompson, David | 1 | 2 | 2 | | |
| Platts, Dan | 1 | 1 | 4 | | | Post, Hezekh | 1 | 1 | 2 | | | Chittenden, John | 1 | 2 | 2 | | |
| Platts, Dan, 2d | 1 | 1 | 2 | | | Bartholomew, Wm | 1 | 2 | 3 | | | Post, Joshua | 2 | 2 | 5 | | |
| Jones, Saml, 2d | 1 | 4 | 2 | | | Kelly, Job | 1 | 2 | 4 | | | Stevens, Aaron | 2 | 2 | 4 | | |
| Stephens, Amos | 1 | 1 | 1 | | | Stannard, Job | 1 | 1 | 1 | | | Stannard, Josiah | 1 | 1 | 3 | | |
| Chalker, Daniel | 2 | 5 | 4 | | | Kelly, Ephm | 2 | 1 | 6 | | | Hull, Oliver | 1 | 3 | 2 | | |
| Stephens, Saml | 4 | 3 | 5 | | | Lay, Robert | 1 | 2 | 6 | | | Platts, Elisha | 2 | 2 | 7 | | |
| Tribble, James | 1 | 2 | 1 | | | Jones, Benjamin | 1 | | 1 | | | Stannard, Temperance | 1 | 1 | 2 | | |
| Bailey, Daniel | 1 | 1 | 1 | | | Jones, Benja, 2d | 1 | 1 | 2 | | | Benjamin, Richard | 3 | 2 | 2 | | |
| Pratt, Ether | 1 | | | | | Stannard, Peter | 1 | 3 | 2 | | | Baldwin, Josiah | 1 | | 2 | | |
| Bushnell, Phinehas | 1 | 2 | 7 | | | Stannard, Wm | 1 | 1 | 3 | | | Jones, Daniel | 1 | 1 | 6 | | |
| Bushnell, Jn. W | 4 | 3 | 4 | | | Ely, Jno | 1 | 2 | | | | Turner, John | 1 | 4 | 2 | | |
| Buckley, Conkling | 3 | 2 | 5 | | | Lay, Jona, Esqr | | | 4 | 1 | 1 | Mills, Revd Saml | 1 | 1 | 6 | | |
| Buckley, Wm | 2 | 2 | 9 | | | Lay, Ezra | 2 | 1 | 2 | | | Buckingham, John | 2 | 2 | 2 | | |
| Doan, Joel | 1 | 2 | 1 | | | Reed, Abigail | | | 1 | | | Silliman, Thomas, Esq | 1 | 2 | 2 | | |
| Post, James | 1 | 1 | 3 | | | Lay, Nathl | 1 | 1 | 1 | | | Canfield, Isaiah | 1 | 2 | 5 | | |
| Kelsey, Jeremiah | 1 | | 5 | | 1 | Bushnell, Benajah | 1 | | 1 | | | Southworth, Gideon | 1 | | 4 | | |
| Post, Isaac | 1 | 2 | 5 | | | Dee, Elijah | | 2 | 4 | | | Clark, Zelotes | 1 | 4 | 4 | | |
| Doan, Elkanah | 2 | 1 | 1 | | | Lay, Jeremh | 2 | 3 | 4 | | | Waterhouse, Abraham | 3 | | 8 | | |
| Platt, Noah | 1 | 1 | 3 | | | Dee, Danl | 1 | 2 | 4 | | | Southworth, Martin | 3 | 1 | 2 | | |
| Cone, David | 1 | 1 | 1 | | | Mordock, Wm | 2 | 1 | 6 | | 2 | Canfield, Joel | 3 | 1 | 2 | | |
| Sandford, Lois | | 1 | 4 | | | Dee, Wm | 1 | | 4 | | | Webb, Reynold | 2 | 2 | 2 | | |
| Post, Jonathan | 3 | | 2 | | | Doe, Mark | 1 | 1 | 4 | | | Waterhouse, Jno | 1 | 2 | 2 | | |
| Griffing, Abner | 1 | 2 | 5 | | | Mordock, Willm, 2d | 1 | | 3 | | | Waterhouse, Austin | 1 | 3 | 6 | | |
| Glading, Joseph | 1 | 2 | 2 | | | Wood, Mary | | 2 | 5 | | 1 | Waterhouse, Elijah | 1 | 1 | 1 | | |
| Clark, George, 2d | 1 | 2 | 2 | | | Lay, Simeon | 2 | 1 | 5 | | | Southworth, Isaac | 1 | | 3 | | |
| Clark, George | 3 | | 5 | | | Denison, Gideon | 2 | | 2 | | | Warner, Jona | 3 | 2 | 4 | | |
| Clark, Christopher | 3 | 2 | 3 | | | Belden, Mary | | | 2 | | | Leet, Edwd A | 3 | 1 | 2 | | |
| Clark, Paul | 1 | 3 | 2 | | | Hedges, Eleazer | 1 | 1 | 1 | | | Leet, Gideon | | | 2 | | |
| Buckingham, Hezekiah | 1 | | 2 | | 1 | Bushnell, Hezekiah | 1 | | 1 | | | Leet, Gideon, Junr | 2 | 1 | | | |
| Pratt, Thomas | 2 | 1 | 3 | | | Bushnell, Asa | 1 | 2 | 2 | | | Waterhouse, Abrm, Jr | 1 | | 3 | | |
| Comstock, Saml | 1 | | 1 | | | Bushnell, Reuben | 2 | 2 | 4 | | | Southworth, Nancy | | | 3 | | |
| Wardstark, Wm | 1 | 2 | 3 | | | Bushnell, Ebenezer | 1 | 2 | 2 | | | Church, Saml | 1 | 1 | 1 | | |
| Drone, Prince | 4 | | 3 | | | Champion, Thomas | 1 | | 1 | | | Church, Simeon | | | 1 | | |
| Pratt, Damaras | | | 3 | | | Champion, Nathan | 1 | 6 | 4 | | | Webb, Stephn | 2 | 1 | 3 | | |
| Bushnell, Ethen | 2 | | 2 | | | Denison, George | 1 | | 3 | | | Webb, Mary | | | 3 | | |
| Parker, Huldah | | | 1 | | | Denison, Stephen | 1 | 1 | 3 | | | Matery, John | 1 | 4 | 3 | | |
| Pratt, Simeon | 2 | 1 | 2 | | | Plant, Ethel | 1 | | 2 | | | Webb, Patience | | | 3 | | |
| Pratt, Jesse | 1 | 3 | 3 | | | Whittelsey, Joseph | 1 | 2 | 2 | | | Webb, Constant | 1 | 2 | 3 | | |
| Pratt, Benajah | 1 | | 1 | | | Hill, Henry | 1 | | 2 | | | Webb, Calvin | 1 | | 1 | | |
| Clark, Wm | 1 | 1 | 3 | | | Ingraham, Wm | 3 | 2 | 5 | | | Willard, Danl | 1 | 4 | 4 | | |
| Clark, Beamont, 2d | 1 | 1 | 3 | | | Spencer, Willm | 3 | 1 | 3 | | | Webb, James | 2 | 1 | 4 | | |
| Clark, Beamont | 3 | 2 | 5 | | | Jones, Zebulon | 2 | 1 | 3 | | | Parker, John | 1 | 1 | 2 | | |
| Waterhouse, Stephen | 1 | 1 | 2 | | | Spencer, Deborah | 2 | | 4 | | | Brooks, James | 1 | 1 | 3 | | |
| Birkingham, Hosmer | 1 | | 1 | | | Spencer, Caleb | 1 | 2 | 2 | | | Hough, Willm | 1 | 2 | 2 | | |
| Comstock, Saml, 2d | 4 | | 3 | | | Post, Jno | 2 | | 3 | | | Waterhouse, Josiah | 2 | | 3 | | |
| Bushnell, Reuben | 1 | | 3 | | | Hinkley, Ira | | | | 2 | 2 | Brooks, Simeon | 2 | 3 | 3 | | |
| Parker, Sarah | | | 1 | | | Spencer, Toby | | | | 2 | 2 | Bushnel, Doctr | | | | | |
| Parker, Jonathan | 1 | 3 | 2 | | | Jones, Augustus | 2 | 1 | 4 | | | Douglass, Danl | 4 | 2 | 5 | | |
| Clark, Peter | 4 | | 2 | | | Jones, Phinehas | 2 | | 3 | | | Douglass, Israel | 1 | 6 | 6 | | |
| Pratt, Deliverance | | | 3 | | | Jones, Ephraim | 1 | | 2 | | | Clark, Reuben | 2 | 2 | 4 | | |
| Southward, Nathan | 3 | 3 | 6 | | | Jones, Saml | 1 | 2 | 2 | | | Barker, John | 1 | 1 | 2 | | |

# HEADS OF FAMILIES—CONNECTICUT.

## MIDDLESEX COUNTY—Continued.

| NAME OF HEAD OF FAMILY. | Free white males of 16 years and upward, including heads of families. | Free white males under 16 years. | Free white females, including heads of families. | All other free persons. | Slaves. | NAME OF HEAD OF FAMILY. | Free white males of 16 years and upward, including heads of families. | Free white males under 16 years. | Free white females, including heads of families. | All other free persons. | Slaves. | NAME OF HEAD OF FAMILY. | Free white males of 16 years and upward, including heads of families. | Free white males under 16 years. | Free white females, including heads of families. | All other free persons. | Slaves. |
|---|---|---|---|---|---|---|---|---|---|---|---|---|---|---|---|---|---|
| **SAYBROOK TOWN—con.** | | | | | | **SAYBROOK TOWN—con.** | | | | | | **SAYBROOK TOWN—con.** | | | | | |
| Barker, Elisabeth | 1 | | 2 | | | Foster, Alpheus | 1 | 2 | 1 | | | Warner, Will<sup>m</sup> | 1 | 3 | 2 | | |
| Barker, Mary | 1 | | 3 | | | Waterhouse, Benj<sup>a</sup> | 3 | 5 | 3 | | | Parmelee, John | 1 | | 1 | | |
| Stebens, Benony | 1 | 2 | 5 | | | Grant, James | 1 | | 2 | | | Mitchell, W<sup>m</sup> | 3 | 1 | 2 | | 2 |
| Clark, Zach<sup>r</sup> | 1 | | 2 | | | Franklin, Caleb | 1 | 1 | 8 | | | Newbury, Nath<sup>l</sup> | 1 | | 1 | | |
| Clark, Jared | 3 | 2 | 4 | | | Warner, Phinehas | 2 | 3 | 2 | | | Warner, David | 1 | 1 | 2 | | 1 |
| Lewis, John | 3 | | 2 | | | Shipman, Michael | 1 | | | | | Dudley, Cyprian | 3 | | 1 | | |
| Lewis, Andrew | 1 | 1 | 2 | | | Ames, Sam<sup>el</sup> | 1 | | 2 | | | Webb, Will<sup>m</sup> | 2 | | 4 | | |
| Lewis, Joseph | 2 | 2 | 6 | | | Harriss, Nath<sup>l</sup> | 1 | | 3 | | | Baldwin, James | 2 | | 5 | | |
| Lyndes, Sam<sup>l</sup> | 3 | 1 | 5 | | | Shipman, Israel | 3 | 1 | 3 | | | M<sup>c</sup>Collum, Dan<sup>l</sup> | 1 | 1 | 1 | | |
| Stevens, Elijah | 2 | 3 | 6 | | | Southworth, Will<sup>m</sup> | 1 | | 5 | | | Parmelee, Mable | | | 2 | | |
| Hambleton, James | 1 | 3 | 2 | | | Waterhouse, Gideon | 2 | 3 | 5 | | | Deangelous, Lewis | 1 | 2 | 2 | | |
| Andrews (Wid<sup>o</sup>) | | | 6 | | | Mason, Elijah | 1 | 2 | 5 | | | Spencer, W<sup>o</sup> | | | 2 | | |
| Webb, Gid<sup>n</sup> | 1 | | 2 | | | Shipman, Joseph | 2 | 2 | 4 | | | Whittelsey (Wid<sup>o</sup>) | | | 2 | | |
| Spencer, Michael | 1 | 2 | 1 | | | Lyel, Robert | 1 | 1 | 2 | | | Clark, Joseph | 1 | | | | |
| Spencer, Dan | 1 | 1 | 2 | | | Clark, Gr<sup>st</sup> | 1 | 1 | 2 | | | Luke (Negro) | | | | 2 | |
| Church, Philemon | 1 | 2 | 5 | | | Shipman, Edw<sup>d</sup> | 3 | 2 | 5 | | | | | | | | |
| Cone, Aaron | 2 | 1 | 2 | | | Deangelous, Pascal | 1 | 1 | 2 | | 1 | | | | | | |

## NEW HAVEN COUNTY.

| NAME OF HEAD OF FAMILY. | Free white males of 16 years and upward, including heads of families. | Free white males under 16 years. | Free white females, including heads of families. | All other free persons. | Slaves. | NAME OF HEAD OF FAMILY. | Free white males of 16 years and upward, including heads of families. | Free white males under 16 years. | Free white females, including heads of families. | All other free persons. | Slaves. | NAME OF HEAD OF FAMILY. | Free white males of 16 years and upward, including heads of families. | Free white males under 16 years. | Free white females, including heads of families. | All other free persons. | Slaves. |
|---|---|---|---|---|---|---|---|---|---|---|---|---|---|---|---|---|---|
| **BRANFORD TOWN.** | | | | | | **BRANFORD TOWN—con.** | | | | | | **BRANFORD TOWN—con.** | | | | | |
| Page, Joel | 1 | | 3 | | | Maltby, Jonathan | 1 | 3 | 3 | | | Hoadly, Jonathan | 2 | 4 | 6 | | |
| Lent, Othimel | 1 | 1 | 3 | | | Baldwin, William | 1 | 2 | 4 | | | Rogers, Stephen | 2 | 1 | 2 | | |
| Linley, Isaac | 3 | | 3 | | | Butler, Benjamin | 1 | 1 | 4 | | | Hoadly, John | 1 | | 3 | | |
| Linley, John | 2 | 3 | 3 | | | Whiting, John | 1 | 1 | 3 | | | Hoadly, Abigail | | | 3 | | 3 |
| Linley, Rufus | 1 | 3 | 4 | | | Hubbard, John | 4 | | 1 | | | Jones, Jared | 1 | 1 | 2 | 1 | |
| Rose, Thomas | 2 | 2 | 4 | | | Tyler, Josiah | 1 | 1 | 2 | | | Rogers, Isaac | 1 | 3 | 4 | | |
| Page, Samuel | 2 | 1 | 3 | | | Millins, Charles | 2 | | 1 | | | Frisbie, Edward | 1 | 2 | 3 | | |
| Page, Amos | 1 | | 2 | | | Harrison, William | 2 | | | | | Jailor, Steward | 1 | 1 | 1 | | |
| Barker, Edward | 3 | 4 | 4 | | | Sheldon, Asher | 2 | | 1 | | | Palmer, Jerad | 1 | | 1 | | |
| Stint, Elizus | 1 | 4 | 4 | | 1 | Huggins, Hester | 1 | | 2 | | | Palmer, Barnabas | 1 | 2 | 1 | | |
| Russell, John | 1 | 3 | 4 | | | Gold, William | 3 | 1 | 5 | | 2 | Jones, Daniel | 1 | | 3 | | |
| Russell, Edward | 1 | | 2 | | | Tyler, Samuel | 1 | | 3 | | | Cooke, Demeb<sup>s</sup> | 1 | 1 | 5 | | |
| Plant, James | 1 | | 3 | | | Barker, Archelus | 1 | 2 | 4 | | | Rogers, John | 2 | 1 | 2 | | |
| Rose, Elizabeth | | | 4 | | | Blaxton, Sarah | | | 1 | 1 | | Houd, Hendrick | 2 | 2 | 5 | | |
| Smith, Allen | 1 | 2 | 4 | | | Hull, Ambrose | 1 | 2 | 1 | 1 | | Cooke, Isaiel | 3 | | 1 | | |
| Goodrich, Phineas | 3 | | 3 | | | Russel, John | 2 | 2 | 5 | | | Rogers, Abraham | 1 | 1 | 5 | | |
| Goodrich, Gidion | 1 | 2 | 4 | | | Welford, John | 1 | 2 | 4 | | | Barker, Timothy | 2 | 2 | 4 | | |
| Goodrich, Bethrolma | 2 | 5 | 4 | | | Palmer, Jonathan | 2 | 3 | 3 | | | Pond, Elias | 1 | 4 | 3 | | |
| Towner, Jonathan | 2 | 1 | 4 | | | Houd, Amie | 1 | | 2 | | | Frisbie, Ebenezur | 2 | 2 | 4 | | |
| Towner, Jacob | 1 | 1 | 5 | | | Ods, Martha | 1 | | 1 | | | Monro, George | 1 | | 1 | | |
| Bradley, Jerad | 1 | 5 | 4 | | 1 | Russell, Samuel | 1 | 2 | 1 | | 1 | Hotchkiss, Ira | 1 | 1 | 1 | | |
| Isaacs, Ralph | 1 | | 4 | 4 | | Stock, Moses | 1 | | | | | Frisbie, Rufus | 1 | | 2 | | |
| Plant, Benjamin | 2 | 1 | 3 | | | Russell, Samuel | 1 | 2 | 2 | | | Frisbie, Philomon | 1 | | 1 | | |
| D'Berrade, Charles | 2 | 1 | 1 | | 1 | Foot, Abraham | 1 | | 2 | | | Hoadly, Samuel | 2 | 4 | 5 | | |
| Spinks, Richard | 2 | 1 | 2 | | | Blackston, John | 4 | 3 | 3 | | | Fuller, Jemima | 1 | | 1 | | |
| Wheeton, Samuel | 1 | | 1 | | | Blakston, Stephen | 2 | | 2 | | 1 | Frisbie, Nathaniel | 3 | 2 | 3 | | |
| Wheeton, Mary | | | 1 | | | Willford, Elizabeth | | 1 | 2 | | | Palmer, Isaac | 1 | 5 | 2 | | |
| Grant, Margeret | | | 3 | | | Hubbard, Moses | 1 | 2 | 5 | | | Frisbie, Mary | 1 | | 3 | | |
| Tyler, Philomen | 1 | 2 | 3 | | | Foot, Ephraim | 2 | 2 | 2 | | | Gold, Thomas | 2 | 1 | 2 | | |
| Tyler, Joseph | 2 | | 2 | | | Tyler, Peter | 1 | 2 | 1 | | | Palmer, Nathaniel | 1 | 2 | 4 | | |
| Tyler, Samuel | 1 | 2 | 4 | | | Williams, Waram | 1 | 1 | 2 | | | Palmer, Benjamin | 3 | 3 | 4 | | |
| Cason, Thomas | 1 | 1 | 3 | | 1 | Russell, Penfield | 4 | | 5 | | | Fowler, Ely | 1 | | 4 | | |
| Waters, Temperance | | 1 | 5 | | | Blakston, Timothy | 1 | 1 | 6 | | | Hooper, James | 1 | 2 | 2 | | |
| Linly, Sarah | 1 | | 4 | | 2 | Hoadly, Samuel | 2 | 3 | 8 | | | Hoadly, James | 2 | 2 | 2 | | |
| Linly, Ebenezer | 1 | | 4 | | | Tyler, Obed | 1 | | 2 | | | Hoadly, Benjamin | 1 | 1 | 3 | | |
| Linly, Ebenezer, 2 | 1 | | 2 | 1 | | Barker, Joseph | 2 | | 5 | | | Frisbie, Joseph | 1 | 2 | 6 | | |
| Linly, Malik | 1 | | | 4 | | Hays, Ezekell | 2 | 3 | 5 | | | Frisbie, Mary | 1 | 1 | 3 | | |
| Chitsey, Roswell | 2 | 4 | 2 | | | Harrison, Farr | 1 | 4 | 4 | | | Griffin, Aron | 1 | 2 | 2 | | |
| Lamphin, Oliver | 1 | 1 | 3 | | | Baldwin, Samuel | 2 | | 2 | | | Palmer, Phebe | 1 | 1 | 3 | | |
| Cora, Rebecca | | 1 | 2 | | | Johnson, Timothy | 1 | 2 | 3 | | | Norton, Joel | 1 | | 6 | | |
| Trip, John | 2 | 3 | 3 | | | Beach, Elnathan | 4 | 2 | 4 | | | Chittenton, Levi | 1 | 1 | 3 | | |
| Linley, Obed | 1 | 3 | 3 | | | Goodrich, James | 1 | | 5 | | | Monro, William | 2 | 1 | 4 | | |
| Wheeton, Nathal | 1 | | 1 | | | Frisbie, Samuel | 2 | 1 | 4 | | | Monro, Fredrick | 1 | | 1 | | |
| Cooke, Elihu | 1 | 2 | 1 | | | Tyler, Patty | | 1 | 2 | | | Hoady, Silas | 1 | 2 | 3 | | |
| Gordon, Alexander | 1 | 2 | 3 | | | Tyler, Obed | 3 | | 2 | | | Gay, Amie | 1 | | 2 | 1 | |
| Whitney, John | 2 | | 1 | | | Beach, Ephrim | 3 | 1 | 2 | | 1 | Baldwin, Noah | 1 | 1 | 1 | | |
| Linly, Samuel | 2 | 2 | 3 | | | Beach, Ebenezer | 1 | 3 | 5 | | | Baldwin, Edward | 1 | 1 | 2 | | |
| Plant, Abraham | 1 | 1 | 5 | | | Norton, Thomas | 1 | 2 | 3 | | | Hoadly, Ralph | 1 | 3 | 4 | | |
| Ford, John | 1 | 2 | | | 2 | Bartholemew, Joseph | 1 | | 2 | | | Hoadly, Abigal | 1 | | 4 | | |
| Morris, Edmond | 1 | | 4 | | | Tyler, Soloman | 1 | 2 | 3 | | | Butler, John | 2 | | 1 | | |
| West, Agnes | | | 2 | | | Barker, Benjamin | 1 | 4 | 3 | | | Butler, Mathew | 3 | 2 | 2 | | |
| Parmalee, Joseph | 1 | 2 | 2 | | | Baldwin, James | 2 | | 3 | | | Baldwin, Moses | 1 | 2 | 3 | | |
| Foot, Stephen | 2 | 2 | 4 | | | Baldwin, Gamliel | 2 | | 1 | | | Page, Joseph | 1 | | 1 | | |
| Bradly, Timothy | 3 | 2 | 6 | | | Baldwin, John | 3 | 2 | 5 | | | Baldwin, Ephraim | 1 | 4 | 5 | | |
| Monro, Sarah | 2 | 1 | 4 | | | Harrison, Amie | 1 | 2 | 3 | | | Harrison, Timothy, 2<sup>d</sup> | 1 | 3 | 3 | | |
| Butler, Charles | 1 | 4 | 2 | | | Marchall, William | 2 | | 1 | | | Harrison, Timothy | 2 | 1 | 2 | | |
| Parrish, Ephraim | 2 | | 2 | | | Barker, Samuel | 1 | 1 | 5 | | | Houd, Joel | 1 | 3 | 3 | | |
| M<sup>c</sup>Queen, Trefina | | 3 | 3 | | | Harrison, Hester | 1 | 1 | 2 | 1 | | Baldwin, Samuel | 3 | 2 | 6 | | |
| Porter, Stephen | 1 | | 2 | | | Harrison, Peter | 1 | 3 | 6 | | | Baldwin, Aron | 2 | | 4 | | |
| Parmalie, Timothy | 1 | 1 | 1 | | | Beech, Harrison | 1 | 1 | 2 | | | Palmer, John | 4 | 2 | 4 | | |
| Baldwin, Nicodemus | 1 | 1 | 5 | | | Bartholomew, Benjamin | 1 | | 6 | 1 | | Potter, Joel | 2 | 2 | 3 | | |
| Barker, Russell | 1 | 2 | 2 | | | Garret, John | 1 | 2 | 6 | | 1 | Palmer, Stephan | 4 | 1 | 4 | | |
| Barker, James | 1 | | 1 | | | Rogers, Ephraim | 3 | 2 | 6 | | | Barker, Daniel | 1 | | 3 | | |
| Barker, Abigail | | | 1 | 1 | | Frisbie, Thomas | 1 | 2 | 6 | | | Barker, Job | 2 | | 2 | | |
| Gordon, Lidia | 1 | 1 | 3 | | | Ives, Joel | 2 | 1 | 4 | | | Harrison, Abraham | 2 | | 2 | | |
| Tyler, Benjamin | 1 | | 4 | | | Baldwin, Zacheus | 1 | 2 | 3 | | | Harrison, Nathan | 1 | 3 | 3 | | |
| Morris, Timothy | 5 | 1 | 4 | | | Rogers, Samuel | 2 | 2 | 4 | | | Byinton, Benjamin | 1 | 4 | | | |
| Rose, John | 1 | | 2 | | | Rogers, John | 3 | 2 | 3 | | | Woodward, Gaskin | 1 | | 1 | 1 | 1 |
| Attwater, Jason | 1 | | 4 | 1 | | Frisbie, William | 1 | 2 | 3 | | | Baldwin, Joel | 2 | 2 | 3 | | |
| Parish, Jonathan | 1 | 1 | 2 | | | | | | | | | Baldwin, Daniel | 3 | | 3 | | |

# FIRST CENSUS OF THE UNITED STATES.

## NEW HAVEN COUNTY—Continued.

| NAME OF HEAD OF FAMILY. | Free white males of 16 years and upward, including heads of families. | Free white males under 16 years. | Free white females, including heads of families. | All other free persons. | Slaves. |
|---|---|---|---|---|---|
| **BRANFORD TOWN—con.** | | | | | |
| Byington, Jonathan | 1 | 2 | 3 | | |
| Harrison, Daniel F | 1 | 2 | 3 | | |
| Pomp (Negroe) | | | | 7 | |
| Smith, Joseph | 2 | 1 | 3 | | |
| Harrison, Jerad | 1 | 1 | 5 | | |
| Rose, Justice | 1 | 1 | 5 | | 4 |
| Harrison, John | 1 | | 2 | | |
| Harrison, Samuel | 2 | | 3 | | |
| Ecels, Samuel | 2 | | 2 | 1 | |
| Russell, Timothy | 1 | | 3 | | |
| Rose, Daniel | 1 | 5 | 3 | | |
| Hoadly, Daniel | 3 | 3 | 4 | | |
| Russell, Ethal | 1 | 2 | 3 | | |
| Tyler, William | 2 | 2 | 5 | | |
| Russell, Ebenezer | 2 | 1 | 1 | | |
| Russell, Jonathan | 3 | 1 | 5 | | |
| Rose, Soloman | 3 | | 2 | | |
| Rose, Levi | 1 | 3 | 1 | | |
| Asher, Gad (Negroe) | | | | 8 | |
| Rose, Ruben | 2 | 1 | 5 | | |
| Page, Ruben | 1 | 1 | 2 | | |
| Ford, Lemuel | 2 | 2 | 4 | | 1 |
| Mulford, Nathan | 1 | 2 | 3 | | |
| Mulford, Barnabas | 2 | 1 | 2 | | |
| Wheeton, William | 3 | 3 | 2 | | |
| Page, Nathaniel | 4 | | 2 | | |
| Wheeton, Samuel | 1 | 2 | 5 | | |
| Barker, Justice | 1 | 1 | 3 | | |
| Wheeton, James | 3 | | 3 | | |
| Wheeton, Ruben | 2 | 1 | 4 | | |
| Smith, Jordan | 1 | | 2 | | |
| Wheeton, Roswell | 1 | 1 | 2 | | |
| Stone, Elihu | 2 | | 4 | | |
| Harrison, Jacob | 1 | | 4 | 1 | |
| Harrison, Asael | 2 | 1 | 3 | | |
| Page, Icabod | 1 | 3 | 3 | | |
| Renholds, Hezekiah | 2 | 4 | 3 | | |
| Bunnel, Josep | 1 | 1 | 6 | | |
| Harrison, James | 2 | 1 | 1 | | |
| Baldwin, Joseph | 1 | 1 | 4 | | |
| Page, Jacob | 1 | 2 | 1 | | |
| Hoffman, Samuel | 2 | | 2 | | |
| Cooke, Demetrus | 1 | | 1 | | |
| Harrison, Jeras | 2 | 1 | 2 | | |
| Johnson, Henry | 1 | | 4 | | |
| Merrick, Jonathan | 1 | 1 | 4 | | |
| Phillis (Negroe) | | | | 5 | |
| Otis, Joseph (Negroe) | | | | 6 | |
| Linly, Stephen | 1 | 2 | 4 | | |
| Rose, Samuel | 2 | 2 | 2 | | |
| Hale, Francis | 1 | 2 | 3 | | |
| Hale, Hannah | 1 | 1 | 2 | | |
| Linsley, Daniel | 2 | 2 | 3 | | |
| Foot, Jonathan | 3 | 1 | 3 | | |
| Rose, Nathan | 1 | 1 | 4 | | |
| Rose, Samuel | 3 | 1 | 3 | | |
| Boils, James | 2 | 1 | 5 | | |
| Palmer, Asael | 1 | 3 | 5 | | |
| Beers, John | 1 | | | | |
| Trusdale, Ebenezur | 1 | | 1 | | |
| Molthrop, Joseph | 1 | 1 | 4 | | |
| Linsley, Israel | 4 | 1 | 3 | | 1 |
| Harrison, Justice | 1 | 5 | 1 | | |
| Beers, Pitman | 1 | | 3 | | |
| Smith, Isaac | 2 | 2 | 3 | | |
| Palmer, Elijah | 1 | 1 | 2 | | |
| Bunnel, Jerus | 3 | 1 | 6 | | |
| Page, Benjamin | 1 | 1 | 3 | | 1 |
| Rogers, Josiah | 1 | | 5 | | |
| Rogers, David | 3 | | 4 | | |
| Rogers, Thomas | 4 | | 4 | | 4 |
| Pardie, Ebenezur | 1 | 3 | 2 | | |
| Rogers, Thomas, 2 | 2 | 2 | 5 | | |
| Butler, James | 1 | 1 | 1 | | |
| Robertson, John | 1 | | 3 | | |
| Smith, Dow | 1 | 3 | 6 | | |
| Harlow, Sarah | 1 | | 2 | | 2 |
| Baldwin, Israel | 1 | 4 | 3 | | |
| Monro, Andrew | 4 | 1 | 5 | | 2 |
| Linsley, Elizabeth | 1 | | 2 | | |
| Bunnel, Jacob | 4 | | 2 | | |
| Auger, Peter | 1 | 3 | 2 | | |
| Potter, John | 1 | | 1 | | |
| Potter, John, 2ᵈ | 1 | 4 | 1 | | |
| Plymouth, John | 2 | 2 | 3 | | |
| Bunnel, Jacob | 1 | 1 | 2 | | |
| Street, Louis | | 3 | 4 | | |
| Foot, Daniel | 2 | 1 | 3 | | |
| Auger, John | 1 | 3 | 4 | | |
| Foot, Daniel | 1 | 1 | 2 | | |
| Hotchkiss, Hannah | 1 | | 1 | | |
| Frisbie, Jonathan | 1 | 4 | 1 | | |
| Rogers, Ebenezur | 2 | 1 | 6 | | |
| Rogers, Elihu | 2 | 1 | 3 | | |
| Douglas, Hannah | 1 | 1 | 3 | | |
| **BRANFORD TOWN—con.** | | | | | |
| Frisbie, Jacob | 4 | 2 | 3 | | |
| Baldwin, Benjamin | 1 | 4 | 2 | | |
| Goodsall, Lidia | | | 2 | | |
| Johnson, Nathaniel | 1 | | 3 | | |
| Johnson, Rebecca | | | 1 | | |
| Baldwin, Phineas | 2 | | 2 | 1 | |
| Smith, James | 3 | | 1 | | |
| Finch, Jonathan | 1 | 1 | 2 | | |
| Williams, Stephen | 1 | 3 | 3 | | |
| Foot, Isaac | 3 | 2 | 6 | | |
| Harrison, Wooster | 1 | 1 | 1 | | 1 |
| Smith, Stephen | 1 | 1 | 1 | | |
| Bennet, Abigal | | | 1 | | |
| Barnell, John | 1 | 3 | 3 | | |
| Hawkins, Stephen | 1 | 2 | 2 | | |
| Tainter, Isaac | 1 | 1 | 1 | | |
| Auger, John | 1 | 1 | 1 | | |
| Auger, Joseph | 1 | 3 | 3 | | |
| Foot, Elisha | 2 | 1 | 1 | | |
| Foot, Ruben | 3 | 2 | 3 | | |
| Tainter, Michael | 1 | | | | |
| Tainter, Michael, 2ᵈ | 1 | 3 | 3 | | |
| Tainter, Medad | 1 | 1 | 4 | | |
| Rose, Samuel | 1 | 1 | 1 | 1 | |
| Tyler, Jonathan | 2 | 4 | 4 | | |
| Tyler, Isael | 2 | 4 | 3 | | |
| Seymore, Roger | 2 | 2 | 4 | | |
| Munson, Jonathan | 1 | 3 | 3 | | |
| Ingraham, Isaac | 1 | 1 | 7 | | |
| Bartholomew, Jonathan | 2 | 3 | 5 | | |
| Noyce, Mathew | 1 | | 1 | 1 | |
| Williams, Deavenport | 1 | 1 | 2 | | |
| Bartholomew, Samuel | 1 | | 1 | | |
| Bartholomew, Timothy | 2 | 2 | 2 | | |
| Rogers, Josep | 1 | 3 | 3 | | |
| Rogers, Joel | 1 | | 1 | | |
| Talmage, Soloman | 2 | 2 | 3 | | |
| Rose, Amajia | 1 | 2 | 2 | | |
| Tyler, Peter | 2 | 1 | 4 | | |
| Tyler, Paul | 1 | 1 | 1 | 1 | |
| Norton, Abraham | 1 | 1 | 2 | | |
| Farnum, Mary | | | 1 | | |
| Wheeton, William | 1 | 2 | 2 | | |
| Houde, Jude | 1 | | | | |
| Bartholomew, Benjamin, 2ᵈ | 1 | 1 | 3 | | |
| Clarke, Jonah | 1 | 1 | 3 | | |
| Pierson, Samuel | 1 | 1 | 2 | | |
| Pierson, Benjamin | 1 | | 4 | | |
| Meigs, Felix | 1 | | 1 | | |
| Houd, Thankfull | | | 1 | | |
| Baldwin, Elihu | 3 | | 6 | | |
| Baldwin, Sally | 1 | 1 | 5 | | |
| Kimberly, Isaac | 1 | 1 | 4 | | |
| Kimberly, Sherman | 1 | 1 | 1 | | |
| Maltby, Benjamin | 1 | | 2 | | |
| Maltby, Benjamin, 2 | 2 | 5 | 3 | | |
| Maltby, Stephen | 1 | 1 | 1 | | |
| Lindley, James | 1 | | 2 | | |
| Lindley, Josiah | 4 | 2 | 4 | | |
| Ward, Ambrose | 1 | 2 | 4 | | |
| Hoadly, Rufus | 3 | 3 | 6 | | |
| Maltby, John | 3 | 1 | 1 | | |
| Fowler, Josiah | 1 | 3 | 2 | | |
| Maltby, James | 1 | 1 | 3 | | |
| Lindley, Solman | 2 | | 2 | | |
| Foot, John | 2 | 1 | | | |
| Foot, Jerad | 2 | | 4 | | |
| Hoadley, Ebenezur | 1 | | 2 | | |
| Hoadley, Timothy | 1 | 2 | 1 | | |
| Harrison, Edward | 1 | 1 | 2 | | |
| Harrison, Amos | 3 | 2 | | | |
| Fowler, Josiah | 3 | | 2 | | 3 |
| Lindley, John | 1 | 2 | 3 | | |
| Page, John | 2 | 2 | 4 | | |
| Elwell, Samuel | 1 | 1 | 3 | | |
| Thomas, William | 1 | | 2 | | |
| Frisbie, Mary | | | 1 | | |
| Evens, William | 1 | | | | |
| Roser, Malachi | 1 | | 2 | | |
| Todd, Lidia | 1 | 1 | 2 | | |
| Bench, Phineas | 1 | | 1 | | |
| Finch, Ebenezer | 2 | 3 | 2 | | |
| **CHESHIRE TOWN.** | | | | | |
| Newton, Joseph | 1 | | 3 | | |
| Newton, Abner | 1 | | 2 | | |
| Newton, Jerad | 2 | 2 | 2 | | |
| Hull, Thelus | 1 | 2 | 3 | | |
| Newton, Cloe | 1 | 1 | 3 | | |
| Hull, Hannah | 1 | | 2 | | |
| Hull, Lidia | 1 | 1 | 1 | | |
| Root, Moses | 1 | 2 | 2 | | |
| Carrington, Daniel | 1 | 2 | 2 | | |
| **CHESHIRE TOWN—con.** | | | | | |
| Morse, Mary | | | 1 | | |
| Hull, Abeather | 1 | 1 | 1 | | |
| Attwater, Jesse | 1 | | 2 | | |
| Winchell, Ezeriah | 1 | | | | |
| Bishop, Jarad | 1 | 2 | 3 | | |
| Hill, Jonas | 2 | 3 | 5 | | |
| Hull, Abigal | 1 | | 1 | | |
| Parker, Job | 1 | 4 | 3 | | |
| Rice, Rebecca | | | 2 | | |
| Hull, Andrew, 2ᵈ | 1 | | 4 | 1 | |
| Brooks, Soloman | 1 | 1 | 3 | | |
| Reynolds, Squire | 1 | | 1 | | |
| Root, Judah | 2 | | 1 | | |
| Mathews, Amos | 1 | | 1 | | |
| Badger, Fredrick | 1 | | 4 | | |
| Hull, Luther | 1 | | 1 | | |
| Parker, Thankfull | 1 | 1 | 2 | | |
| Parker, Thomas | 1 | | 2 | | |
| Rice, Robert | 5 | | 3 | | |
| Parker, Levi | 1 | | 1 | | |
| Tuttle, Ebenezer | 1 | | | | |
| Merriman, Amos | 1 | | 3 | | |
| Parker, Edward | 1 | | 1 | | |
| Parker, Edward, 2ᵈ | 2 | 2 | 2 | | |
| Parker, William | 2 | 2 | 6 | | |
| Swift, Joseph | 2 | 2 | 3 | | |
| Hall, Timothy | 2 | 1 | 3 | | |
| Hall, Isaiah | 2 | 2 | 1 | | |
| Hall, Amassa | 1 | 3 | 5 | | |
| Hall, Timothy, 2ᵈ | 1 | 3 | 5 | | |
| Coles, Elisha | 1 | 2 | 5 | | |
| Yale, Job | 1 | 1 | 2 | | |
| Yale, Osiers | 1 | 1 | 1 | | |
| Thomas, Enoch | 1 | | 1 | | |
| Thomas, Enoch, 2ᵈ | 1 | 2 | 6 | | |
| Rice, John | 1 | | 4 | | |
| Curtis, Edward | 2 | 2 | 7 | | |
| Parker, Amos | 2 | 1 | 4 | | |
| Sanderson, William | 1 | 1 | 4 | | |
| Hough, Ambrose | 1 | 1 | 5 | | |
| Bradley, Peleg | 1 | | 1 | | |
| Miles, Joseph | 2 | 2 | 6 | | |
| Bristol, Benjamin | 1 | 1 | 1 | | |
| Liberty, Sharp (Negroe) | | | | 4 | |
| Clarke, Amassa | 1 | 4 | 2 | 1 | |
| Cooke, Samuel | 2 | | 4 | | |
| Andrews, Eneas | 1 | | 1 | | |
| Clarke, Stephen | 3 | | 3 | | |
| Andrews, Thomas | 1 | 3 | 2 | | |
| Ives, Abraham | 4 | 1 | 6 | | |
| Hull, Samuel | 1 | 1 | 1 | | |
| Hull, Epharus | 1 | | 1 | | |
| Hough, Ebenezer | 2 | 2 | 5 | | |
| Goodyear, Edward | 1 | 1 | 3 | | |
| Morse, Isaac | 1 | 5 | 3 | | 1 |
| Munson Amassa | 1 | 1 | 3 | | |
| Benham, John | 2 | | 3 | | |
| Benham, Warren | 1 | 1 | 2 | | |
| Lewis, Amassa | 3 | 1 | 5 | | |
| Bradley, Stephen | 2 | 5 | 5 | | |
| Attwater, Samuel | 1 | 1 | 5 | | |
| Lewis, Barnabas | 2 | 1 | 5 | | |
| Benham, Uriah | 2 | 3 | 4 | | |
| Ives, Zachariah | 3 | | 3 | | |
| Attwater, Timothy | 1 | 3 | 4 | | |
| Hull, Andrew | 1 | | 4 | | |
| Webb, Jonah | 1 | 2 | 2 | | |
| Hotchkiss, Daniel, 3ʳᵈ | 2 | 1 | 2 | | |
| Hudson, David | 1 | | 3 | | |
| Stevens, Willard | 1 | 2 | 1 | | |
| Tuttle, Edmond | 1 | | | | |
| Tuttle, Lazerus | 2 | 6 | 6 | | |
| Tuttle, Jecobed | 1 | 5 | 5 | | |
| Tuttle, Moses | 1 | | 1 | | |
| Tuttle, Samuel | 1 | 2 | 3 | | |
| Tuttle, Ephraim | 1 | | 6 | | |
| Attwater, Thomas | 1 | 1 | 3 | | |
| Persons, John | 3 | | 5 | | |
| Attwater, Ambrose | 5 | 3 | 6 | | |
| Attwater, Moses | 1 | 1 | 1 | | |
| Attwater, Lyman | 1 | | 1 | | |
| Conner, Elnathan | 2 | 1 | 3 | | |
| Attwater, Elihu | 1 | 1 | 3 | | |
| Bristol, Jonathan | 1 | | 2 | | |
| Andrews, Patience | | | 1 | | |
| Hall, Jonathan, 2 | 1 | 3 | 6 | | |
| Hotchkiss, Ruben | 1 | | 1 | | |
| Bristol, Zelus | 1 | 1 | 3 | | |
| Grannis, Eldad | 2 | 1 | 3 | | |
| Lewis, Thankfull | | | 3 | | |
| Andrews, Amos | 1 | 1 | 2 | | |
| Bristol, Austin | 2 | 2 | 2 | | |
| Winchel, Daniel | 1 | | 3 | | |
| Stedman, Sarah | | | 2 | | |
| Attwater, Hannah | 1 | 2 | 3 | | |

# HEADS OF FAMILIES—CONNECTICUT.

## NEW HAVEN COUNTY—Continued.

| NAME OF HEAD OF FAMILY. | Free white males of 16 years and upward, including heads of families. | Free white males under 16 years. | Free white females, including heads of families. | All other free persons. | Slaves. | NAME OF HEAD OF FAMILY. | Free white males of 16 years and upward, including heads of families. | Free white males under 16 years. | Free white females, including heads of families. | All other free persons. | Slaves. | NAME OF HEAD OF FAMILY. | Free white males of 16 years and upward, including heads of families. | Free white males under 16 years. | Free white females, including heads of families. | All other free persons. | Slaves. |
|---|---|---|---|---|---|---|---|---|---|---|---|---|---|---|---|---|---|
| **CHESHIRE TOWN—con.** | | | | | | **CHESHIRE TOWN—con.** | | | | | | **CHESHIRE TOWN—con.** | | | | | |
| Bristol, Thankfull | | | 3 | | | Bunnel, Israel | 2 | 5 | 3 | | | Peck Asa | 1 | | 1 | | |
| Stedman, Sarah | | | 2 | | | Smith, John | 1 | | 1 | | | Mathews, Hester | | | 1 | | |
| Bristol, Gideon | 1 | 2 | 5 | | | Ives, Ruben | 1 | | 1 | 1 | | Walton, Francis | 1 | 2 | 2 | | |
| Hill, Jonah | 1 | 2 | 5 | | | Hull, Hannah, 3rd | | 1 | 3 | | | Brunson, Ruben | 2 | 2 | 2 | | |
| Hotchkiss, Mineman | 2 | 2 | 1 | | | Hotchwick, Israel | 1 | 1 | 3 | | | Stone, Sarah | | | 2 | | |
| Page, Jared | 2 | 5 | 3 | | | Stanley, Whiting | 1 | 2 | 2 | | | Smith, Titus | 1 | 1 | 2 | | |
| Bristol, Thomas | 4 | | 4 | | | Smith, Elam | 2 | 1 | 3 | | | Cay, William | 1 | 3 | 2 | | |
| Bristol, Ezra | 1 | 2 | 2 | | | Thompson, Rockmary | | | 2 | | | Doolittle, Ephrahim | 1 | 1 | 1 | | |
| Gales, Nathaniel, 2 | 2 | | 6 | | | Johnson, Seth | 1 | 3 | 5 | | | Brooks, David | 2 | 2 | 7 | | |
| Gales, Nathaniel | 1 | 1 | 3 | | | Doolittle, Ebenezer | 3 | | 7 | | | Bradley, Roswell | 2 | 2 | 2 | | |
| Gales, Elias | 1 | | 1 | | | Doolittle, Benjamin H | 1 | 1 | 2 | | | Brooks. Jerry | 2 | 1 | 5 | | |
| Parker, Ebenezer | 2 | | 2 | | | Canfield, Timothy | 1 | 2 | 3 | | | Doolittle, Amos | 3 | 1 | 2 | | |
| Parker, Jabez | 1 | 1 | 2 | | | Bunnel, Louis | | | 1 | | | Lines, Rufus | 2 | 2 | 3 | | |
| Lines, Erastus | 1 | 2 | 4 | | | Hitchcock, Rufus | 2 | | 3 | | | Cooke, Mireman | 1 | 3 | 1 | | |
| Jones James | 1 | 4 | 1 | | | Hitchcock, Easter | 1 | | 3 | | | Cooke, Elizabeth | | | 3 | | |
| Bellamy, Arom | 1 | | 1 | 1 | | Doolittle, Silas | 1 | | 3 | | | Andrus, Phebe | | | 5 | | |
| Bellamy, Justus | 2 | 5 | 4 | | | Dorchester, Ruben | 1 | 2 | 7 | | | Peter (Negroe) | | | | 3 | |
| Cook, Cornelius | 2 | | 2 | | | Parker, Samuel | 1 | 1 | 5 | | | Brooks, Thomas | 2 | | 3 | | |
| Rice, Clarke | 2 | | 3 | | | Beach, Elnathan | 3 | 1 | 5 | | | Smith, Cooper | 1 | | 2 | | |
| Hull, Dick (Negroe) | | | | 2 | | Hall, Jonathan | 3 | 2 | 3 | | | Curtis, Gilbert | 1 | 1 | 3 | | |
| Bunnel, John | 1 | | 5 | | | Conner, Trisham | 1 | | 3 | | | Daly, Giles | 1 | 2 | 4 | | |
| Bunnel, Abner, 2nd | 2 | 2 | 4 | | | Bench, Samuel | 3 | 1 | 3 | | | Hitchwick, Jason | 2 | | 2 | | |
| Attwater, Ruben | 1 | 1 | 3 | | | Foot, John | 2 | 3 | 3 | | | Smith, Josiah, 2 | 1 | 1 | 2 | | |
| Barnes, David | 1 | | 1 | | | Andrews, Zinnus | 1 | 1 | 1 | | | Hall. Hannah | | | 3 | | |
| Doolittle, Isaac | 1 | 2 | 2 | | | Talmage, Samuel | 2 | | 3 | 1 | | Spencer, Seldon | 1 | 2 | 5 | | |
| Hotchkiss, Bela, 2nd | 1 | | 4 | | | Hotchkiss, Benjamin | 1 | | 1 | | | Plump, Benoni | 3 | 3 | 2 | | |
| Hall, Benjamin | 1 | | 2 | | | Hotchkiss, Bennan | 1 | 1 | 4 | 3 | | Smith, Ephrahim, 2nd | 2 | 6 | 2 | | |
| Arnold, Lidia | | 2 | 2 | | | Hotchkiss, Josiah | 1 | | 4 | | | Rice, Bennet | 1 | 4 | 4 | | |
| Bunnel, Abner | 1 | | 1 | | | Hotchkiss, Josiah, 2nd | 4 | | 4 | | | Hotchkiss, Adonijah | 1 | | 2 | | |
| Bunnel, Eneas | 1 | 2 | 4 | | | Meriam, Munson | 3 | | 4 | | | Doolittle, Benjamin | 4 | | 3 | | |
| Tyler, Ruth | 1 | | 3 | | | Meriam, Munson, 2 | 1 | | 2 | | | Cooke, Samuel, 2nd | 1 | 1 | 2 | | |
| Hall, Charles C | 1 | | | | | Meriam, Samuel | 1 | 1 | 3 | | | Hotchkis, Ephrim | 1 | 1 | 2 | | |
| Wainwright, Jonathan | 1 | 5 | 3 | | | Cooke, Aron | 1 | | | | | Preston, Ruben | 3 | 1 | 2 | | |
| Potter, Eldad | 1 | 3 | 2 | | | Jones, William | 1 | | 5 | | | Brooks, Amassa | 1 | 2 | 2 | | |
| Hitchcock, Amassa, 2nd | 1 | | 1 | | | Hotchkiss, Robert | 1 | | 4 | 2 | | Ren (Negroe) | | | | 3 | |
| Hitchcock, Valantine | 1 | 2 | 5 | | | Norton, Gold G | 1 | 2 | 4 | | | Ishmael (Negroe) | | | | 4 | |
| Hotchkiss, Elijah | 1 | | | | | Durrany, Samuel | 1 | 1 | 3 | | | Ives, Joel | 1 | | 2 | | |
| Hotchkiss, Henry | 1 | | 2 | | | Durany, Andrew, 2nd | 1 | | 1 | | | Ward, Timothy | 1 | | 4 | | |
| Hotchkiss, Jonah | 2 | 3 | 2 | | | Hitchcock, Amassa | 1 | 2 | 6 | | | Hummiston, Jesse | 1 | 1 | 3 | | |
| Bench, John | 2 | 2 | 3 | | | Hotchkiss, Willstell | 3 | 1 | 2 | | | Bunnel, David | 2 | | 6 | | |
| Ives, Nathaniel | 1 | | 1 | | | Hitchcock, David | 2 | 2 | 3 | | | Davis, Desire | | | 1 | | |
| Ives, Jotham | 1 | 1 | 4 | | | Hitchcock, Daniel | 3 | 1 | 2 | | | Bunnil, Ebenezer | 1 | 1 | 2 | | |
| Ives, Mathew | 2 | 1 | 2 | | | Hitchcock, Icobed | 1 | 1 | 3 | | | Thompson, Jesse | 1 | 1 | 1 | | |
| Bradley, Moses | 1 | | 1 | | | Brooks, David, 2 | 1 | | 3 | | | Badger, Edward | 1 | 2 | 6 | | |
| Bradley, Oliver | 2 | 3 | 3 | | | Hitchcock, Amos | 1 | 2 | 5 | | | Jones, Elisha | 1 | 3 | 3 | | |
| Bradley, Ruben | 1 | 1 | 7 | | | Hitchcock, Anna | | 1 | 3 | | | Morse, Titus | 2 | 2 | 2 | | |
| Gales, Thomas | 1 | 4 | 4 | | | Hitchcock, Harvey | 1 | | 1 | | | Bunnel, Joel | 1 | 1 | 2 | | |
| Bristol, Dick (Negroe) | | | | 3 | | Deering, Andrew | 3 | | 5 | | | Morse, Nathaniel | 4 | 1 | 3 | | |
| Hitchcock, John L | 1 | | 4 | | | Brooks, Cloe | 1 | 2 | 1 | | | Sutton, William | 1 | | 1 | | |
| Wilson, Benjamin | 1 | | 2 | | | Brooks, Gideon | 1 | | | | | Webb, Gideon | 1 | 1 | 1 | | |
| Parker, Stephen | 1 | 1 | 1 | | | Mathews, Elizabeth | | | 2 | | | Barnes, Elija | | | 2 | | |
| Smith, Anna | | | 1 | | | Mathews, Ephrim | 1 | 1 | 2 | | | Brooks, Henry | 1 | 1 | 2 | | |
| Twist, Benjamin | 1 | | 2 | | | Andrews, Samuel | 1 | 2 | 2 | | | Brooks, Henry 2nd | 1 | 4 | 4 | | |
| Miles, Burrage | 1 | | 1 | | | Andrews, Abel | 3 | 1 | 2 | | | Talmage, Josiah | 1 | 1 | 4 | | |
| Hull, Miles | 2 | | 2 | | | Andrews, Bela | 2 | 3 | 4 | | | Clarke, Samuel | 3 | 1 | 8 | | |
| Hotchkiss, Jason | 1 | 2 | 2 | | | Peck, Elijah | 1 | 3 | 2 | | | Gilkie, Peter | 1 | 5 | | | |
| Jolly, Martha | | | 2 | | | Upson, James | 1 | 1 | 2 | | | Doolittle, Obed | 1 | 4 | 3 | | |
| Hotchkiss, Ambrose | 1 | | | | | Doolittle, Ezra | 2 | 2 | 5 | | | Ives, Phineas | 1 | 5 | | | |
| Lawrence, Elihu | 1 | 3 | 2 | | | Merriman, Lent | 2 | 1 | 4 | | | Blakely, Moses | 2 | | 2 | | |
| Hitchcock, Bela | 2 | | 3 | | | Hall, John, 2nd | 1 | 3 | 3 | | | Morse, Moses | 3 | 3 | 4 | | |
| Beecher, Benjamin | 1 | 2 | 6 | | | Hall, John | | | 1 | 1 | | Doolittle, Abraham | 5 | | 2 | | |
| Wolcott, Abel | 2 | 1 | 2 | | | Hall, William | 1 | 4 | 4 | | | Morse, Josiah | 2 | | 1 | | |
| Attwater, Stephen | 1 | | 3 | | | Rice, Nathaniel | 1 | | 4 | 1 | | Benham, James | 1 | 1 | 4 | | |
| Attwater, Stephen, 2 | 2 | 1 | 4 | | | Rice, Ruben | 2 | 3 | 3 | 1 | | Collin, Joseph | 1 | 1 | 5 | | |
| Attwater, Titus | 1 | | 1 | | | Page, Ruben | 2 | 1 | 2 | | | Prindle, Sarah | | | 1 | | |
| Mallery, Daniel | 2 | 2 | 1 | | | Morse, Benjamin | | | 2 | 1 | | Todd, Caleb | 1 | 3 | 1 | | |
| Hitchcock, Asa | 1 | 1 | 2 | | | Rice, Levi | 2 | | 3 | | | Barnes, Ambrose | 2 | 1 | 2 | | |
| Attwater, John | 2 | 1 | 1 | | | Morse, Abigal | | | 3 | | | Hall, Jerad | 3 | 2 | 6 | | |
| Dalton, Daniel | 3 | 1 | 4 | | | Morse, Isaac Bower | 1 | | 1 | | | Andrews, Nathaniel | 1 | 1 | 2 | | |
| Attwater, Amos | 1 | | 4 | | | Morse, Jesse | 4 | 1 | 3 | | | Todd, Hezekiah | 1 | 1 | 3 | | |
| Sperry, Benjamin | 2 | | 5 | | | Morse, Samuel | 1 | | 4 | | | Hall, Jonah | 1 | 2 | 1 | | |
| Clarke, Stephen, 2nd | 1 | 1 | 2 | | | Morse, Thomas | 2 | 1 | 3 | | | Peirpoint, Ely | 1 | | 2 | | |
| Bunnil, Samuel | 1 | 1 | 1 | | | Flay, Diamond | 1 | 5 | 1 | | | Tyler, Joseph | 3 | 2 | 5 | | |
| Hitchcock, Mary | | | 1 | | | Brooks, Ebenezer, B | 1 | 3 | 2 | | | Blackley, Asa | 1 | 5 | 3 | | |
| Doolittle, Samuel | 1 | | 1 | | | Hotchkiss, Benjamin, 3 | 2 | | | | | Doolittle, Obed | 1 | 2 | 1 | | |
| Doolittle, Abner | 1 | 2 | 3 | | | Brunson, Martin | 2 | | 3 | | | Brooks, Joel | 1 | 2 | 2 | | |
| Doolittle, Ambrose | 2 | | 5 | | | Martin, John | 1 | 2 | | | | Tuttle, Moses, 2nd | 1 | 2 | 4 | | |
| Lewis, Ebenezer | 1 | 1 | 4 | | | Doolittle, Mosses | 1 | | | | | Bryant, John | 1 | 4 | 2 | | |
| Doolittle, Barney | 1 | | | | | Hotchkiss Benjamin | 1 | 1 | 1 | | | Beecher, Hezekiah | 1 | 2 | 6 | | |
| Smith, William | 1 | 1 | 2 | | | Hotchkiss, Ruth | | | 1 | | | Perkins, John | 1 | 1 | 1 | | |
| Hall, Ruben | 1 | | | | | Hoppen, Benjamin | 1 | | 1 | | | Hotchkiss, John, 3 | 1 | 1 | 2 | | |
| Andrews, Israel | 1 | 3 | 4 | | | Martin, Elizabeth | | | 2 | | | Hall, Ebenezer | 1 | 1 | 3 | | |
| Turrel, Ephraim, 2nd | 1 | 3 | 2 | | | Hitchcock, Aron | 2 | 1 | 2 | | | Hotchkiss, John, 2nd | 4 | 1 | 3 | | |
| Hall, Lidia | 1 | 1 | 4 | | | Attwater, Joseph | 2 | 2 | 2 | | | Williams, Aron | 3 | | 3 | | |
| Law, William | 4 | 3 | 5 | 1 | | Attwater, Benjamin | 4 | | 4 | 2 | | Hotchkiss, Henry, 2nd | 1 | 1 | 2 | | |
| Cornwell, Abijah | 2 | 1 | 3 | | | Benham, John, 2nd | 2 | | | | | Hotchkiss, Chauncy | 1 | | 2 | | |
| Atkins, Eber | 2 | 1 | 2 | | | Wright, Enos | 1 | | 3 | | | Hotchkiss, Lyman | 1 | | 2 | | |
| Clarke, William | 2 | | 4 | | | Munson, Peter | 2 | 3 | 1 | | | Turrel, Ephrim | 3 | 1 | 5 | | |
| Beecher, John | 2 | 2 | 6 | | | Ives, Phineas 2 | 2 | | 2 | | | Williams, John | 1 | 3 | 3 | | |
| Thompson, Samuel | 2 | | 1 | | | Naham, Peter (Negroe) | | | | 3 | | Hines, Hezekiah | 1 | 2 | 2 | | |
| Thompson, Asa | 1 | | 3 | | | Burr, Samuel | 1 | | 2 | | | Smith, Jarad | 1 | 3 | 2 | | |
| Parker, Caleb | 1 | 2 | 4 | | | Bunnel, Unice | | | 1 | 4 | | Hitchcock, Levi | 1 | 1 | 3 | | |
| Clarke, Andrew | 2 | | 6 | | | Andrews, Elizabeth | | | 2 | | | Smith, Ephrim | 1 | | 2 | | |
| McCurgen, Alexander | 1 | | 1 | | | Peck, John | 2 | 2 | 3 | | | Smith, Ephrm, 2 | 1 | 3 | 2 | | |
| Miriam, Icabod | 1 | 1 | 4 | | | Peck, John. 2nd | 1 | | 3 | | | Smith, Israel | 1 | 1 | 4 | | |

## NEW HAVEN COUNTY—Continued.

| NAME OF HEAD OF FAMILY. | Free white males of 16 years and upward, including heads of families. | Free white males under 16 years. | Free white females, including heads of families. | All other free persons. | Slaves. | NAME OF HEAD OF FAMILY. | Free white males of 16 years and upward, including heads of families. | Free white males under 16 years. | Free white females, including heads of families. | All other free persons. | Slaves. | NAME OF HEAD OF FAMILY. | Free white males of 16 years and upward, including heads of families. | Free white males under 16 years. | Free white females, including heads of families. | All other free persons. | Slaves. |
|---|---|---|---|---|---|---|---|---|---|---|---|---|---|---|---|---|---|
| **CHESHIRE TOWN—con.** | | | | | | **DERBY TOWN—con.** | | | | | | **DERBY TOWN—con.** | | | | | |
| Peck, Phineas | 1 | 3 | 3 | | | Clarke, William, 2nd | 1 | | 2 | | | Durand, Elizur | 3 | | 5 | | |
| Wilmot, Elijah | 2 | | 6 | | | Grany, Ebenezer | 2 | 4 | 4 | | 1 | Tomlinson, Auger | 2 | 1 | 5 | | |
| Tyler, Isaac | 2 | 1 | 1 | | | Wheeler, Joseph | 1 | 3 | 3 | 1 | | White, Daniel | 1 | 1 | 1 | | |
| Tyler, Amos | 1 | 1 | 1 | | | Davis, Nathan | 1 | 4 | 1 | | | Voce, Adam | 3 | 2 | 2 | | |
| Turrel, Enoch | 1 | | 1 | | | Judson, Isaac | 1 | | 2 | | | Lum, Ruben | 1 | 4 | 3 | | |
| Chatterton, Assael | 1 | | 3 | | | Hitchcock, David | 2 | 3 | 3 | | | Lum, Joseph | 1 | | 1 | | |
| Tyler, Enos | 1 | 1 | 3 | | | Smith, Abijah | 2 | 1 | 4 | | | Hull, Elizabeth | | | 2 | | |
| Hotchkiss, Jiles | 1 | 1 | 3 | | | Smith, Abraham | 1 | 3 | 1 | | | Bassett, Benjamin | 2 | 2 | 5 | | |
| Minick (Negroe) | | | | 3 | | Thompson, Abel | 1 | 3 | 1 | | | Bassett, Amos | 3 | 1 | 1 | 1 | 1 |
| Benham, Thomas | 1 | 3 | 2 | | | Wilcox, Abijah | 2 | | 2 | | | Tomlinson, Daniel | 2 | 4 | 3 | | |
| Andrew, Simeon | 1 | 1 | 3 | | | Putt, John (negroe) | | | | 3 | | Tomlinson, Nathaniel | 2 | 2 | 6 | | |
| Russell, Riverus | 1 | 2 | 4 | | | White, Joseph | 1 | 3 | 2 | | | Beardsley, Jonas | 2 | 3 | 6 | | |
| Burr, Jerad | 1 | | 3 | | | Gorham, George | 1 | 1 | 4 | | | Webster, Obed | 2 | 1 | 2 | | |
| Tyler, Isaac, 2nd | 2 | | 1 | 1 | | Johnson, Peter | 1 | | 3 | | | Pool, John | 2 | 1 | 3 | | |
| Sandford, John | 1 | 3 | 6 | | | Short, Joseph | 3 | 5 | 1 | | | Pool, Samuel | 1 | | 3 | | |
| Hines, Ambrose | 1 | | 1 | | | Holbrook, Daniel | 4 | 2 | 8 | | | Pool, Mary | | 1 | 3 | | |
| Hine, Silas | 1 | 2 | 2 | | | Parsons, Rena | 2 | 1 | 5 | | | Bassett, Joseph | 1 | 1 | 5 | | |
| Hotchkiss, Robert | 2 | | 2 | | | Lains, Henry | 2 | | 1 | | | Bassett, James | 2 | 4 | 3 | | |
| Russell, Nicholas | 1 | 1 | 1 | | | Hale, Samuel | 1 | 1 | 4 | | | Bassett, Samuel, 3d | 1 | | 1 | | |
| Ford, John | 1 | | 1 | | | Bradley, Eneas | 3 | | 2 | | | Tomlinson, Benjamin | 1 | | 2 | | |
| Ford, Nathaniel, 2 | 1 | | 2 | | | Bard, James | 2 | 1 | 2 | 1 | | Smith, Abner | 1 | | 2 | | |
| Ford, Nathaniel | 3 | | 1 | | | Tuller, Martin | 1 | | 5 | | | Bassett, Samuel | 1 | 1 | 2 | | |
| Hine, Ambrose, 2 | 1 | 2 | 4 | | | Coe, John | 1 | 2 | 4 | | | Tomlinson, David, 2nd | 2 | | 2 | | |
| Wilmot, Amos | 1 | | 3 | | | Hale, Abraham | 1 | | 2 | | | Durand, Noah | 1 | | 1 | | |
| Sperry, Joseph | 3 | | 2 | | | Phillip (Negroe) | | | | 6 | | Durand, Noah, 3rd | 1 | | 1 | | |
| Doolittle, Joseph | 2 | 3 | 3 | | | Johnson, Nathaniel | 3 | 1 | 2 | | | Botsford, Ebenezer | 1 | 1 | 2 | | |
| Sperry, Job | 1 | 1 | 1 | | | Johnson, Philo | 1 | 1 | 4 | | | Botsford, Samuel | 3 | | 3 | | |
| Sperry, Rhoda | | | 3 | | | Chatfield, Joseph | 2 | 1 | 4 | | | Botsford, Neamiah | 2 | 3 | 7 | | |
| McDonnal, Elves | 1 | | 2 | | | Hawkins, Abraham | 1 | | 4 | | | Botsford, Ezra | 1 | 2 | 3 | | |
| Brown, Nathan | 2 | | 2 | | | Johson, Amos | 1 | | 4 | | | Foot, Ezra | 1 | 2 | 3 | | |
| Brown, Isaac | 1 | 1 | 1 | | | Baldwin, Timothy | 2 | 1 | 1 | | 3 | Tomlinson, Benjamin, 2nd | 1 | 1 | 2 | | |
| Barns, Edmond | 1 | 1 | 4 | | | Baldwin, Thadeus | 1 | 3 | 6 | | | Hawkins, Samuel | 1 | 1 | 3 | | |
| Sandford, Gideon | 3 | | 4 | | | Baldwin, Timothy, 2nd | 1 | 1 | 2 | | 1 | Fairchild, Zachariah | 2 | | 2 | | |
| Williams, Ruben | 1 | 1 | 3 | | | Riggs, Joseph | 1 | 1 | 1 | | 1 | Hard, Wilson | 1 | | 4 | | |
| Nettleton, Ely | 1 | | 3 | | | Riggs, Joseph, 2nd | 3 | 2 | 4 | | | Canfield, Daniel | 1 | 1 | 2 | | |
| Wilmott, Joel | 1 | 1 | 4 | | | Waterhouse, Isaac | 1 | 1 | 3 | | | Bassett, Isaac | 1 | 1 | 4 | | |
| Wilmott, Elijah | 1 | | 3 | | | Pope, Joseph | 2 | 4 | 3 | | | Smith, Enoch | 1 | | 4 | | |
| Sandford, Henry | 1 | 2 | 2 | | | French, Samuel | 1 | | 2 | | | Bard, George | 1 | 2 | 2 | | |
| Sanford, Archibald | 1 | 2 | 2 | | | Pritchard, Philo | 1 | 1 | 2 | | | Tomlinson, Russell | 2 | 4 | 3 | | 2 |
| Wilmot, Asa | 1 | 1 | 4 | | | Hitchcock, Jonathan | 1 | 1 | 2 | | | Holbrook, Abel | 2 | | 2 | | |
| Hotchkiss, Noah | 2 | | 4 | | | Hitchcock, Jonathan, 2nd | 1 | 2 | 3 | | | Lewis, Ebenezer | 2 | 1 | 4 | | |
| Hotchkiss, John | 2 | | 4 | | | Loveman, Joseph | 1 | 2 | 2 | | | Fanton, Moses | 2 | 1 | | | |
| Hotchkiss, Ebenezer | 1 | 1 | 1 | | | French, Francis | 1 | 3 | 3 | | | Lewis, Philo | 1 | 3 | 2 | | |
| Hotchkiss, Daniel | 2 | | | | | Sherwood, Joseph | 1 | 2 | 2 | 1 | | Tucker, William | 1 | 2 | 2 | | |
| Hotchkiss, John C | 1 | 1 | 2 | | | Lovemond, Lewis | 1 | | 1 | | | Manville, James | 2 | 3 | 2 | | |
| Hitchcock, Lemuel | 1 | 3 | 4 | | | Blake, David | 1 | 2 | 3 | | | Tomlinson, Webb | 1 | 4 | 5 | | |
| Mathews, Joshua | 2 | | 2 | | | Prindle, Eneas | 1 | 1 | 5 | | | Mansfield, Nathan | 2 | 1 | 4 | | |
| Ives, William | 1 | | 4 | | | Pease, Elizabeth | | | 2 | | | Beeby, Martin | 2 | 1 | 4 | | |
| Merriman, Jehel | 1 | 1 | 3 | | | Keeney, Ethiel | 1 | | | | | Tomlinson, Henry | 3 | 5 | 3 | | |
| Merriman, Theophilus | 1 | | 2 | | | Davis, Nathan | 1 | 1 | | | | Smith, Andrew | 1 | 1 | 1 | | |
| Cooke, Clum | 2 | 2 | 3 | | | Wooden, Stephen | 1 | | | | | Graham, Andrew | 1 | 2 | 2 | | |
| Doolittle, Ruben | 1 | 2 | 1 | | | Whitney, William | 1 | 2 | 3 | | | Waterhouse, Andrew | 1 | 3 | 2 | | |
| Bristol, Ruben | 1 | | 4 | | | Whitney, Josiah | 1 | 1 | 3 | | | Holly, John | 1 | 5 | 3 | | |
| How, Joseph | 1 | 1 | 2 | | | Clarke, William | 2 | 4 | 4 | | 2 | Russell, Joseph | 1 | | 2 | | 1 |
| Lewis, Caleb | 1 | 1 | 4 | | | Hawkins, David | 2 | 3 | 2 | | | Russell, Samuel | 2 | 2 | 3 | | |
| Morse, Joel | 1 | 1 | 1 | | | Jackson, Jonathan | 3 | 1 | 3 | | | Lumn, Jonathan, 2nd | 3 | 2 | 4 | | |
| | | | | | | Prindle, John | 1 | 1 | 2 | | | Tomlinson, Elizabeth | | 1 | 2 | | |
| **DERBY TOWN.** | | | | | | Granis, David | 1 | 2 | 4 | | 4 | Wooster, Eprahim | 1 | 1 | 1 | | |
| Curtis, Oliver | 1 | | 2 | | | Hull, Abijah | 3 | 2 | 6 | | | Tomlinson, Isaac | 1 | 4 | 2 | | |
| Curtis, Sheldon | 1 | 2 | 3 | | | Hawkins, Moses | 1 | 2 | 2 | | | Lumn, Jonathan | 1 | | 2 | | |
| Craft, Edward | 2 | 4 | 4 | | | Hawkins, Isaac | 1 | 2 | 2 | | | Lumn, Samuel | 1 | 1 | 1 | | |
| Humphrey, Anna | | 2 | 4 | 3 | | Hawkins, Eli | 2 | | 4 | | | Lake, Elnathan | 1 | | 1 | | |
| Whitlesey, Joseph | 1 | | | | | Hawkins, Eli, 2nd | 2 | 2 | 4 | | | Bassett, John | 4 | 1 | 1 | | |
| Carter, Margerit | | 1 | 2 | | | Canfield, David | 1 | 1 | 4 | | | Smith, Christopher | 1 | 1 | 3 | | 6 |
| Hond, John | 2 | | 2 | 1 | 1 | Bassett, David | 1 | 3 | 2 | | | Holbrook, John | 2 | 2 | 2 | 1 | 1 |
| Kimberly, Liberty | 1 | 1 | 2 | | | Smith, Eneas | 1 | 4 | 5 | | | Holbrook, John, 2nd | 2 | | 3 | | |
| Humphreys, John | 3 | 3 | 5 | | 1 | Smith, Nathan | 4 | | 2 | | | English, Clement | 4 | | 3 | | |
| Burret, William, 2nd | 1 | | 2 | | | Smith, Andrew | 2 | | 3 | | | Nettleton, Jonah | 3 | 1 | 4 | | 4 |
| Smith, Abraham | 3 | 1 | 2 | | | Carpenter, Benjamin | 2 | | 1 | | | Jellet, Jeremiah | 2 | 2 | 3 | | |
| Smith, James | 1 | | 3 | | | Smith, Isaac | 1 | 3 | 3 | | | Holbrook, Nathan | 2 | 3 | | 1 | |
| Bartholemy, Claudius | 2 | 1 | 5 | | | Davis, Benjamin | 3 | | 3 | | | Johnson, Timothy | 1 | | 3 | | |
| Burret, William | 2 | 3 | 5 | | | Parson, Samuel | 1 | 1 | 2 | | | Johnson, Jeremiah | 2 | 1 | 3 | | |
| Hull, Samuel | 2 | 4 | 5 | 1 | 2 | Tomlinson, John | 1 | 2 | 4 | | | Durand, Ebenezer | 1 | 4 | 2 | | |
| Baldwin, Elizabeth | 1 | 1 | 5 | | | Alling, Samuel | 1 | 2 | 4 | | | Perkins, Ephraim | 4 | | 3 | | |
| Whitney, Stephen | 1 | | 3 | | | Smith, Josiah | 2 | 6 | 3 | | | Smith, John | 1 | 2 | | | |
| Tucker, Zephaniah | 2 | 2 | 3 | | | Nevis, Calver | 1 | | | | | Bunnel, Luke | 1 | | 2 | | |
| Mansfield, William | 1 | | 3 | | | Tomlinson, John | 2 | 1 | 3 | | | Wooster, Daniel | 1 | | 2 | | |
| Parson, Nathaniel | 1 | | 4 | | | Mucker, Ephraim | 1 | 2 | 2 | | | Durand, Nemiah | 1 | | 2 | | |
| Person, Abel | 2 | 3 | 1 | 1 | | Deforrest, Hannah | 4 | 1 | 5 | | | Durand, Joseph | 1 | 1 | 2 | | |
| Siverana, Nicholas | 2 | | 6 | | | D'Forrest, Gideon | 3 | | | | | Chatfield, Bennh | 1 | 3 | 2 | | |
| Hotchkiss, Leveret | 1 | 1 | 2 | | | Marshall, Bryan | 1 | 1 | 3 | | | Chatfield, Isaac | 1 | | 1 | | |
| Hawkins, Hannah | | | 2 | | | Marshall, Isaac E | 2 | | 3 | | | Bassett, Eben | 1 | | 1 | | |
| Horsey, Eunice | | 2 | 4 | | | Davis, Elias | 1 | | 2 | | | Chatfield, Dan | | | 4 | | |
| Starks, Daniel | 1 | 2 | 2 | | | Nicoll, Daniel | 1 | | 2 | | | Nicoll, Isaac | 3 | 2 | 3 | | |
| Todd, Daniel | 2 | 1 | 2 | | | Tomlinson, Sarah | | | 3 | | | Chatfield, John | 1 | 4 | 3 | | |
| Hotchkiss, Elizabeth | 1 | 1 | 6 | | | Lyman, Sarah | 1 | 2 | 2 | | | Chatfield, Gideon | 1 | 3 | 3 | | |
| Mansfield, Richard, 2nd | 2 | | 4 | | | Yale, Thomas | 2 | 1 | 4 | | | Durand, Elizabeth | 2 | | 3 | | |
| Gibb, Edward | 1 | 5 | 5 | | | Lister, Murry | 2 | | 3 | | | Bates, Elihu | 1 | 2 | 3 | | |
| Baldwin, Ruben | 1 | 5 | 3 | | | Morse, Joseph | 1 | 4 | 3 | | | Bales, Benjamin L | 1 | | 2 | | |
| Picket, Joseph | 1 | | 2 | | | Spencer, Joel | 2 | | 4 | | | Bunnel, Isaac | 1 | | 2 | | |
| Whitney, Henry | 1 | 2 | 1 | | | Durand, John | 1 | 2 | 2 | | | Pirkens, Daniel | 2 | 1 | 2 | | |
| Davis, Joseph | 2 | 4 | 1 | | | Morse, William | 4 | | 4 | | | Wooster, Nathaniel | 1 | | 2 | 1 | |
| Beers, John | 1 | 1 | 2 | | | Smith, Lucy | | 3 | 1 | | | Wooster, Aurther | 1 | | 1 | | |
| Clarke, Sheldon | 2 | 1 | 4 | | 1 | Smith, William | 1 | 2 | 3 | | | | | | | | |
| | | | | | | Durand, Noah, 2nd | 1 | | 4 | 3 | | | | | | | |

# HEADS OF FAMILIES—CONNECTICUT.

## NEW HAVEN COUNTY—Continued.

### DERBY TOWN—con.

| NAME OF HEAD OF FAMILY. | Free white males of 16 years and upward, including heads of families. | Free white males under 16 years. | Free white females, including heads of families. | All other free persons. | Slaves. |
|---|---|---|---|---|---|
| Hawkins, Silas | 1 | 1 | 5 | | |
| Hawkins, Zachariah | 2 | 1 | 2 | | 2 |
| Hawkins, Isaac | 1 | 3 | 1 | | |
| Hide, Daniel | 1 | | 1 | | |
| Parker, Soloman | 1 | 1 | 3 | | |
| Wooden, William | 2 | | 1 | | |
| Lewis, William, 2nd | 1 | 1 | 1 | | |
| Lewis, Charles | 1 | 1 | 1 | | |
| Lewis, William | 2 | 1 | 4 | | |
| Wooster, Joseph | 1 | 5 | 4 | | |
| Oatman, Samuel | 2 | 2 | 3 | | |
| Bryant, Isaac | 1 | | 2 | | |
| Wooster, Elizabeth | 1 | 1 | 2 | | |
| Warton, Abel | 1 | 1 | 1 | | |
| Hawkins, Dameras | 1 | | | | |
| Hide, Abijah | 2 | 2 | 5 | | |
| Hide, Nathaniel | 1 | | 1 | | |
| Hull, Abel | 1 | 3 | 4 | | |
| Hide, Asael | 1 | | 2 | | |
| Hide, Joseph | 1 | 1 | 1 | | |
| Jones, Joseph | 1 | 1 | 2 | | |
| Wentworth, James | 1 | 1 | 2 | | |
| Gibbons, John | 1 | | 1 | | |
| Hubbel, Joseph | 1 | 1 | 1 | | |
| Perry, Ezekiel | 1 | | 2 | | |
| Perry, John | 1 | | | | |
| Parsons, Eli | 2 | | 4 | | |
| Tomlinson, Noah | 1 | | 2 | | |
| Tomlinson, Noah, 2nd | 1 | 2 | 4 | | |
| Hubbell, Richard | 1 | 3 | 3 | | |
| Smith, Elizabeth | 1 | 2 | 3 | | |
| Lumn, Jonathan, 3rd | 1 | 4 | 4 | | |
| Hawkins, John | 1 | 4 | 1 | | |
| Sperry, Jonathan | 1 | 1 | 2 | | |
| Kimberly, Thomas | 1 | | 3 | | |
| Bassett, Edward | 1 | 1 | 2 | | |
| Bassett, John, 2nd | 2 | 2 | 2 | | |
| Griffin, Elizabeth | 3 | | 3 | | |
| Griffin, Jonathan | 1 | 2 | 1 | | |
| Beardsley, Eliakim | 2 | 2 | 4 | | |
| Bailey, Enock | 1 | 2 | 4 | | |
| Wooster, Ebenezer | 1 | | 1 | | |
| Perry, Caleb | 1 | 3 | 2 | | |
| Wooden, William, 2nd | 1 | | 5 | | |
| Clarke, Abel | 1 | 3 | 4 | | |
| Perry, Peter | 1 | | | | |
| Wooden, Charles | 1 | | 2 | | |
| Wright, Mosses | 2 | 1 | 7 | | |
| Hawkins, Elizabeth | 1 | 1 | 6 | | |
| Tomlinson, David | 2 | 2 | 3 | | |
| Perry, Joshua | 2 | 2 | 2 | | |
| Wooding, David | 1 | 1 | 2 | | |
| Perry, Gelverton | 1 | 3 | 3 | | |
| Pondman, Nathaniel | 1 | 1 | 2 | | |
| Perry, Gideon | 1 | 1 | 3 | | |
| Smith, Richard | 1 | | | | |
| Perry, Ezekel | 1 | | 2 | | |
| Wholf, Henry | 1 | | 3 | | |
| Bunnel, William | 1 | 2 | 3 | | |
| Twichel, David | 2 | 2 | 6 | | |
| Osborn, Joseph | 3 | 1 | 2 | | |
| Perry, James | 2 | 1 | 1 | | |
| Dutton, Ose | 1 | 2 | 4 | | |
| Sowers, Hannah | | | 3 | | |
| Strong, Josiah | 1 | 2 | 3 | | |
| Candie, Enos | 2 | 2 | 3 | | |
| Henman, Eben, 2nd | 2 | 2 | 3 | | |
| Henman, Eben | 1 | | 1 | | |
| Henman, Ephraim | 1 | 2 | 3 | | |
| Scott, Justis | 3 | 2 | 3 | | |
| Trumbel, Elizabeth | | | 1 | | |
| Brunson, David | 1 | 2 | 2 | | |
| Minott, Lewis | 2 | | | | |
| Hatch, Sherman | 1 | 4 | 1 | | |
| Tucker, Gideon | 1 | 3 | 2 | | |
| Hawkins, Peter | 1 | 2 | 4 | | |
| Bunnet, Hannah | | 1 | 2 | | |
| Burret, Benedict | 1 | | 3 | | |
| Candie, Gideon | 3 | 1 | 4 | | |
| Bunnels, Hannah | | | 1 | | |
| Candie, Moses | 1 | | 2 | | |
| Buckingham, Nathan | 3 | 1 | 4 | | |
| Osborn, Naboth | 1 | | | | |
| Osborn, Joseph | 1 | 5 | 1 | | |
| Townes, John | 1 | 5 | 2 | | |
| Bradley, Benjamin | 1 | 3 | 1 | | |
| Candie, Caleb | 3 | 5 | 5 | | |
| Buckingham, Ebenezer | 3 | | 3 | | |
| Smith, David | 1 | 2 | 1 | | |
| Candie, Justice | 1 | 4 | 2 | | |
| Wheeler, Samuel | 2 | 2 | 4 | | |
| Buckingham, Jerad | 1 | 1 | 1 | | |
| Turrel, Isaac | 1 | 3 | 3 | | |
| Twichet, David | 2 | 1 | 4 | | |
| Johnson, Phineas | 1 | 2 | 4 | | |
| Johnson, Timothy | 2 | | 4 | | |
| Candie, Neamiah | 2 | 4 | 3 | | |
| Wooster, Thomas | 2 | 2 | 4 | | |
| Riggs, John | 3 | 3 | 6 | | |
| Twichett, John | 2 | 1 | 4 | | |
| Twichet, Joseph | 2 | 2 | 1 | | |
| Twichet, Elizabeth | | | 3 | | |
| Botsford, John | 1 | 3 | 4 | | |
| Dean, Icabod | 1 | | 2 | | |
| Lyman, Russell | 1 | 1 | 6 | | |
| Osborn, Jerard | 1 | 3 | 3 | | |
| Twichet, Benjamin | 3 | 1 | 7 | | |
| Twichet, Enoch | 1 | | 4 | | |
| Wooster, Abel | 2 | 2 | 1 | | |
| Osborn, Thomas | 1 | | 1 | | |
| Wooster, Ebenezer | 1 | 2 | 3 | | |
| Tucker, Samuel | 1 | | 2 | | |
| Andrews, Ephrahim | 1 | 3 | 2 | | |
| Bunnel, Charles | 1 | 2 | 1 | | |
| Bunnel, Ruben | 1 | | 2 | | |
| Fairchild, Nathaniel | 2 | | 4 | | |
| Basset, Samuel, 2nd | 1 | 2 | 4 | | |
| Clarke, George | 1 | 4 | 1 | | |
| Tucker, Samuel | 1 | 1 | 1 | | |
| Tucker, Jonah | 1 | | | | |
| Twichet, Ebenezer | 1 | 2 | 2 | | |
| Wooster, Samuel | 1 | 1 | 3 | | |
| Clarke, Thomas | 2 | | 3 | | 1 |
| Basset, Abraham | 2 | 1 | 3 | | |
| Bassett, Miles | 1 | 1 | 1 | | |
| Davis, John | 2 | 3 | 2 | | |
| Church, John | 2 | | 2 | | |
| Churchill, John | 1 | 3 | 1 | | |
| Beecher, Hannah | 2 | 1 | 4 | | |
| Riggs, Ebenezer | 2 | 1 | 5 | | |
| Riggs, Edward | 2 | | 2 | | |
| Hitchcock, Samuel | 1 | 4 | 3 | | |
| Fairchild, Abiel | 1 | 1 | 1 | | |
| Kelly, Mathew | 1 | 1 | 3 | | |
| Riggs, James | 1 | 2 | 4 | | |
| Carpenter, Henry | 1 | | 4 | | |
| French, Nathaniel | 1 | 3 | 3 | | |
| Clarke, Thomas, 2nd | 2 | 2 | 3 | | |
| Johnson, Ebenezer | 1 | 2 | 1 | | |
| Johnson, Ebenezer | 2 | 2 | 2 | | |
| Judd, Sally | | | 2 | | |
| Riggs, Moses | 1 | 3 | 3 | | |
| Hine, Heil | 6 | | 3 | | |
| Smith, David | 1 | | 3 | | |
| Hine, Hezekiah | 2 | | 6 | | |
| Wilcox, John | 1 | 5 | 1 | | |
| Sandford, Zadock | 2 | 3 | 5 | | |
| Clark, Hezekiah | 2 | 2 | 2 | | |
| David, Riggs | 1 | 2 | 2 | | |
| Riggs, Joseph | 2 | 3 | 5 | | |
| Roger (Negroe) | | | | 3 | |
| Shubel (negroe) | | | | 4 | |
| Johnson, Alexander | 2 | 1 | 3 | | |
| Johnson, Timothy | 1 | | 3 | | |
| Johnson, Nathaniel | 1 | 2 | 3 | | |
| Johnson, Charles | 1 | 2 | 3 | | |
| Wheeler, Mosos | 2 | 3 | 6 | | |
| Cobin, Parish | 2 | 2 | 4 | | |
| Clarke, Moses | 1 | 1 | 3 | | |
| Washboun, Bowen | 1 | | 4 | | |
| Riggs, Thomas | 1 | | 2 | | |
| Fairchild, Joseph | 1 | 2 | 5 | | |
| Wheeler, Abel | 2 | 1 | 2 | | |
| Wheeler, Louis | | | 5 | | |
| Hicock, Ruben | 1 | 1 | 2 | | |
| Lines, Joseph | 1 | 2 | 2 | | |
| Andrews, Ebenezer | 1 | 2 | 4 | | |
| Mills, Asa | 1 | 1 | 1 | | |
| Andrews, Simeon | 1 | 3 | 3 | | |
| Potter, Joseph | 2 | 1 | 4 | | |
| Chatfield, Samuel | 2 | | 4 | | |
| Osborn, Joshua | 1 | 3 | 3 | | |
| Wheeler, Nathaniel | 2 | 1 | 2 | | |
| Wheeler, John | 1 | 3 | 3 | | |
| Edee, John | 1 | | 2 | | |
| Johnson, Hezekiah | 1 | 1 | 4 | | |
| Johnson, Asael | 1 | 2 | 3 | | |
| Johnson, Joseph | 1 | | 3 | | |
| Peck, Ebenezer | 1 | | 3 | | |
| Peck, Bezeliel | 1 | | 1 | | |
| Bristol (Negroe) | | | | 2 | |
| Holbrook, Daniel | 2 | 2 | 2 | | |
| Johnson, Isaac | 2 | 2 | 4 | | |
| French, Irael | 1 | 1 | 3 | | |
| French, Enoch | 1 | 2 | 3 | | |
| Chatfield, Joel | 1 | 3 | 2 | | |
| French, Charles | 1 | 2 | 3 | | |
| Smith, Samuel | 2 | 2 | 3 | | |
| Johson, Gideon | 1 | | | | |
| Gaston, Joseph | 1 | | 2 | | |
| Johnson, Eber B | 1 | | 4 | | |
| Johnson, Levi | 1 | | | | |
| Bosteck, Isaac | 1 | | 2 | | |
| Bosteck, Richard | 1 | | | | |
| White, John | 2 | 4 | 4 | | |
| Leek, James | 1 | | 4 | | |
| Page, Edmond | 2 | | 3 | | |
| Crawford, John | 1 | | 1 | | |
| Loveland, Trueman | 2 | 1 | 3 | | |
| Witmore, Turrel | 2 | 1 | 4 | | |
| Dayton, Phebe | 2 | 1 | 5 | 1 | |
| Beech, Benjamin | 1 | 1 | 2 | | |
| Loveland, Ashbel | 1 | 1 | 2 | | |
| Swift, John | 1 | 6 | 5 | | |
| Renny, Medad | 1 | 1 | 1 | | |
| Tomlinson, Levi | 1 | 1 | 8 | | |
| Wooster, Henry | 1 | | | | |
| Wooster, Henry, 2nd | 1 | | 2 | 1 | |
| Hawkins, Joseph | 1 | 1 | 5 | | |
| Roe, Daton | 1 | | 2 | | |
| Baldwin, James | 1 | 2 | 2 | | |
| Chatman, Ruben | 1 | 1 | 3 | | |
| Plant, Hester | 1 | 1 | 4 | | |
| Pritchard, James | 1 | 2 | 4 | | |
| Steel, Bradford, 2nd | 1 | 1 | 1 | | |
| Steel, Elisha | 2 | 1 | 1 | | |
| Sandford, Samuel | 1 | | | | |
| Pritchard, Leveret | 1 | | | | |
| Davis, Daniel | 2 | 3 | 2 | | |
| Steel, Bradford | 2 | | 2 | | 1 |
| Baldwin, Isaac | 2 | 3 | 3 | | |
| Hine, Amos | 1 | 1 | 2 | | |
| Smith, Jesse | 1 | 1 | 2 | | |
| Hitchcock, Ebenezer | 1 | 2 | 4 | | |
| Hargor, Edward | 1 | 1 | 6 | | |
| Cornish, John | 1 | | 2 | | |
| Bartis, Samuel | 1 | | 2 | | |
| Washborn, Josiah | 2 | | 2 | | |
| Wooster, James | 1 | | 2 | | |
| Wooster, John, 2nd | 1 | 1 | 2 | | |
| Stiles, Dan | 1 | | 1 | | |
| Wooden, Hezekiah | 2 | 2 | 2 | | |
| Canfield, Abiel | 2 | 2 | 3 | | |
| Wooster, Marchant | | 1 | 2 | | |
| Bassett, Abraham | 1 | 3 | 3 | | |
| Holbrook, Philo | 2 | 1 | 4 | | |
| Fowl, Lewis | 1 | 2 | 1 | | |
| Wooster, Abraham | 2 | | 1 | | |
| Miles, Jonathan | 2 | | 6 | | |
| Miles, Theophilus | 1 | 2 | 7 | | |
| Grinall, William | 1 | 1 | 4 | | |
| Keiny, William | 1 | 4 | 4 | | |
| Ronny, Ebenezer | 1 | 1 | 1 | | |
| Saben (Negroe) | | | | 7 | |
| Hine, Thomas | 2 | | 4 | | |
| Barty, John | 1 | | 4 | | |
| Deal, Charles | 1 | 2 | 1 | | |
| Harger, Philo | 3 | | 2 | | |
| Cambridge (Negroe) | | | | 5 | |
| Barnes, Icabod | 1 | 2 | 5 | | |
| Todd, Daniel, 2nd | 1 | 1 | 3 | | |
| Morris, David | 1 | | 3 | | |
| Plumb, Joshua | 1 | | | | |
| Plumb, Samuel | 2 | 2 | 5 | | |
| Hawkins, Daniel | 1 | | 3 | | |
| Putt, Christopher | 1 | | 1 | | |
| Prindle, Ebenezer | 2 | 1 | 2 | | |
| Hotchkiss, Eliphalet | 1 | | 1 | | |
| Mansfield, Richard | 2 | 1 | 4 | | 1 |
| Hotchkiss, Moses | 1 | | 2 | | |
| Merrel, Timothy | 1 | 3 | 1 | | |
| Smith, Abel | 1 | 1 | 1 | | |
| Baldwin, Silas | 1 | | 4 | | |
| Tucker, Reuben | 3 | 1 | 2 | | |
| Tucker, Daniel | 1 | | 2 | | |
| Frank (Negroe) | | | | 6 | |
| Thompson, Jabez | 2 | 4 | 4 | | |
| Burns, Titus | 1 | | | | |
| Hotchkiss, Thomas | 1 | | 1 | | |
| Burns, Titus, 2nd | 2 | 2 | 1 | | |
| Peter (Negroe) | | | | 2 | |
| Hawkins, Edward | 2 | 2 | 2 | | |
| Arger, Abraham | 1 | 1 | 1 | | |
| Arger, Mary | 1 | | 3 | | |
| Arger, Ephrahim | 1 | | 2 | | |
| Charles, William | 1 | | 2 | | |
| Wooster, Daniel | 1 | 2 | 4 | | 2 |
| Davis, Ruben | 1 | 1 | 2 | | |
| Delamore, Joseph | 2 | | 1 | | |
| Molthrop, Joseph | 2 | | 2 | | |
| Molthrop, Benjamin, 2nd | 1 | | 2 | | |
| Tuttle, Annie | | | 1 | | |

# FIRST CENSUS OF THE UNITED STATES.

## NEW HAVEN COUNTY—Continued.

| NAME OF HEAD OF FAMILY. | Free white males of 16 years and upward, including heads of families. | Free white males under 16 years. | Free white females, including heads of families. | All other free persons. | Slaves. | NAME OF HEAD OF FAMILY. | Free white males of 16 years and upward, including heads of families. | Free white males under 16 years. | Free white females, including heads of families. | All other free persons. | Slaves. | NAME OF HEAD OF FAMILY. | Free white males of 16 years and upward, including heads of families. | Free white males under 16 years. | Free white females, including heads of families. | All other free persons. | Slaves. |
|---|---|---|---|---|---|---|---|---|---|---|---|---|---|---|---|---|---|
| **DERBY TOWN—con.** | | | | | | **DURHAM TOWN—con.** | | | | | | **DURHAM TOWN—con.** | | | | | |
| Washbourn, John | 1 | | 1 | | | Wright, Asher | 1 | 1 | 5 | | | Parsons, Samuel | 2 | 1 | 2 | | |
| Row, Dan | 1 | 2 | 2 | | | Ades, Thomas | 1 | 1 | 2 | | | Lyman, Thomas | 2 | 2 | 3 | | 1 |
| Blake, Ruben | 1 | | 2 | | | Strong, Thomas | 3 | | 4 | | | Lyman, Abel | 1 | | 1 | | |
| Humphries, Isaac | 1 | 2 | 2 | | | Johnson, John | 4 | 1 | 5 | | | Parsons, Simeon | 2 | | 1 | | |
| Mark (negroe) | | | | 3 | | Scranton, Abraham | 6 | 3 | 4 | | | Coe, Charles | 2 | 1 | 2 | | |
| Clarke, Michael | 1 | 2 | 6 | | | Gillam, Benjamin | 1 | | 4 | | | Parsons, Sarah | | | 1 | | |
| Dorman, Samuel | 1 | 2 | 3 | | | Stow, Abraham | 2 | 1 | 1 | | | Parsons, Aaron | 1 | 3 | 2 | | |
| Mitchel, Whitney | 1 | | 1 | | | Seward, Samuel | 1 | | 2 | | | Butler, William | 1 | 3 | 3 | | |
| Harger, Ebenezer | 1 | 4 | 3 | | | Meeker, Daniel | 2 | | 1 | | | Coe, Abel | 1 | 1 | 2 | | 1 |
| Bartis, John, 2nd | 1 | 1 | 1 | | | Kelsey, Stephen | 2 | | 2 | | | Coe, Abel, 2nd | 2 | | 2 | | |
| Clinton, Ebenezer | 1 | 2 | 1 | | | Rositer, Mary | | | 2 | | | Coe, Josiah | 1 | 1 | 3 | | |
| Allen, David | 2 | 1 | 3 | | | Bishop, Jonas | 1 | | 2 | | | Coe, Asher | 2 | | 1 | | |
| Smith, Joseph | 1 | 2 | 2 | | | Dimick, Daniel | 1 | 2 | 5 | | | Spelman, Rohda | | 1 | 3 | | |
| Harrison, Levi | 1 | 1 | 1 | | | Burret, Israel | 1 | | 2 | | | Belknap, Ebenezur | 1 | | 2 | | |
| Hegleton, Abigal | | 2 | 2 | | | Coombs, John | 1 | 2 | 2 | | | Feild, Ambrose | 2 | 2 | 3 | | |
| Davis, Isaac | 1 | | 3 | | | Crocker, Jabez | 3 | | 3 | | | Chadock, Timothy | 2 | | 7 | | |
| Peirson, Joseph | 1 | 5 | 4 | | | Choker, Jabez, 2nd | 1 | 2 | 3 | | | Robinson, James | 1 | 3 | 2 | | |
| Waters, Richard | 1 | 1 | 4 | | | Crane, Lucretia | | | 1 | | | Brag, Benjamin | 1 | 1 | 2 | | |
| OCane, Jeremiah | 1 | | 4 | | | Crane, Mahitabel | | 2 | 4 | | | Squire, Phineas | 2 | 1 | 2 | | |
| OCane, Joseph | 1 | | | | | Crane, Fredrick | 1 | 3 | 3 | | | Squire, Thadeus | 3 | | 2 | | |
| Davis, Jabez | | | 2 | | | Loveland, Titus | 3 | 2 | 3 | | | Camp, Elnathan | 3 | 2 | 3 | | |
| Peirson, Amos | 2 | 1 | 1 | | | Crane, Henry | 1 | 3 | 5 | | | Butler, Jeremiah | 6 | 3 | 5 | | |
| Peirson, Isaac | 1 | 1 | 2 | | | Hull, Joseph | 1 | 1 | 3 | | | Lee, John | 1 | | 2 | | |
| Dyer, William | 1 | 2 | 2 | | | Hull, Josiah | 1 | | 3 | | | Strong, Seth | 1 | 1 | 2 | | |
| Homstead, Joseph | 1 | 5 | 1 | | | Hull, Cornelius | 3 | | 1 | | | Camp, John | 1 | | 1 | | |
| Hale, Beman | 2 | 3 | 1 | | | Hull, Sylvanus | 1 | 2 | 7 | | | Camp, Phineas | 3 | 3 | 5 | | |
| Tucker, Zapthali | 1 | 3 | 5 | | | Francis, Titus | 1 | 1 | 2 | | | Hall, John | 4 | 1 | 9 | | |
| Murry, Abraham | 1 | 1 | | | | Strong, Eliakim | 1 | 2 | 3 | | | Parsons, Sam F | 1 | 2 | 2 | | |
| Dove, Jack | 1 | | | | | Arnold, James | 1 | 2 | 2 | | | Chamberlane, Asa | 1 | 3 | 6 | | |
| Curtis, Samuel | 1 | | | | | Hinman, Elihu | 1 | | 4 | | | Bishop, James | 1 | | 2 | | |
| Blake, Isaac | 1 | 1 | 1 | | | Wells, Mary | | | 2 | | | Whiting, Samuel | 1 | 1 | 1 | | |
| Mansfield, Stephen | 1 | 1 | | | | Hinman, James | 2 | | 5 | | | Murrain, John | 1 | | 2 | | |
| Hotchkiss, Levi | 2 | 2 | 5 | | | Chrittenton, Hopestill | 1 | | 1 | | | Attwell, Mary | | 1 | 3 | | |
| Chatfield, Ebenezer | 1 | | | | | Loveman, John | 1 | 3 | 3 | | | Squire, Ambrose | 1 | | 1 | | |
| Gilbert, David | 1 | | | | | Strong, Medad | 1 | 3 | 3 | | | Parsons, Timothy | 3 | 1 | 3 | | |
| Miller, Elizabeth | | | 2 | | | Squire, Ebenezer | 1 | 2 | 2 | | | Baldwin, Ruben | 2 | 1 | 4 | | |
| Johnson, Mary | | | 1 | | | Chauncy, Elihu | 1 | | 1 | | | Baldwin, Noah | 3 | 1 | 3 | | |
| Hatch, Euson | 1 | 1 | 1 | | | Burrett, Charles | 1 | | 2 | | | Pasons, Samuel | 1 | 2 | | | |
| Loveland, Clarke | 1 | | 1 | | | Wadsworth, John M | 2 | 2 | 2 | | 2 | Parsons, David | 1 | | 1 | | |
| Loveland, Trent | 1 | | | | | Wadsworth, Hester | | | 1 | 1 | | Johnson, Thomas | 1 | | 1 | | |
| Northrop, Abigal | | | 2 | | | Squire, Abiather | 2 | 1 | 3 | | | Rice, Simeon | 1 | | 1 | | |
| Patchen, James | 1 | | 1 | | | Hicock, James | 2 | 2 | 2 | | | Weild, Samuel | 2 | 1 | 7 | | |
| Clarke, Ann | | 1 | 1 | | | Beamont, Jedutham | 1 | 1 | 1 | | | Brown, Ruben | 1 | 2 | 1 | | |
| Hinman, Philo | 1 | 1 | 5 | | | Camp, Samuel | 2 | 2 | 1 | | | Percy, Jane | | | 1 | | |
| Smith, Martha | | | 2 | | | Wilkinson, John | 1 | | 1 | | | Smith, Daniel | 1 | | 1 | | |
| Taylor, Henry | 1 | | | | | Goodrich, Elizur | 2 | 1 | 2 | 1 | | Austin, Jesse | 4 | | 3 | | 1 |
| Gillon, James | 1 | | | | | Camp, Ebenezur | 1 | 1 | 1 | | | Cooke, Thomas | 1 | | 4 | | |
| Turner, Henry | 1 | | | | | Chauncy, Elnathan | 3 | | 1 | | | Murrain, Miles | 2 | 2 | 7 | | |
| Jones, James | 1 | | | | | Spencer, Stephen | 1 | 3 | 1 | | | Baldwin, ABial | 4 | | 2 | | |
| Phillips, Elisha | 1 | | | | | Spencer, Roger | 2 | | 1 | | | Curtis, Abijah | 1 | 2 | 6 | | |
| Palson, Henry | 1 | | | | | Wheeton, Chapman | 1 | | 2 | | | Guernsey, Richmond | 1 | 1 | 1 | | |
| | | | | | | Meeker, John | 1 | | | | | Coe, Ann | | | 1 | | |
| **DURHAM TOWN.** | | | | | | Wells, Jonathan | 1 | | | | | Coe, John | 2 | 1 | 1 | | |
| | | | | | | Murry, Warren | 1 | | 1 | | | Fairchild, Edmond | 1 | 1 | 4 | | |
| Hart, Samuel | 4 | | 3 | | | King, John | 1 | 1 | 3 | | | Bates, Samuel | 2 | 1 | 5 | | |
| Coe, Morris | 1 | 5 | 2 | | | Chittenton, Gideon | 1 | 2 | 2 | | | Bates, Samuel, 2nd | 1 | 1 | 2 | | |
| Coe, Simeon | 1 | 5 | 3 | | | Parmalie, James | 1 | 1 | 2 | | | Bates, James | 1 | | 2 | | |
| Coe, Timothy | 1 | 2 | 4 | | | Wadsworth, James | 1 | | 2 | | | Bates, Daniel | 1 | | 2 | | |
| Parmalie, Eliphas | 4 | 2 | 3 | 2 | | Burret, Richard | 1 | 2 | 3 | | | Newton, Burrel | 4 | | 2 | | |
| Stow, Timothy | 1 | 2 | 3 | | | Camp, James | 3 | 1 | 2 | | | Bates, Curtis | 1 | 2 | 3 | | |
| Camp, Nathaniel | 2 | 3 | 1 | | | Hall, Timothy | 4 | 1 | 6 | | | Southmay'd, Daniel | 3 | | 4 | | |
| Spencer, John | 1 | 1 | 2 | | | Gillman, Asher | 1 | 2 | 1 | | | Picket, James | 1 | 1 | 1 | | |
| Norton, John | 1 | 2 | 4 | | | Hall, Sarah | | | 1 | | | Squire, Samuel | 1 | | 3 | | |
| Wright, Joseph | 1 | | 3 | | | Gurnsway, Lemuel | 1 | | 3 | | | Stevens, Thomas | 1 | 1 | 2 | | |
| Wright, Joseph, 2nd | 2 | 3 | 4 | | | Carr, Clement | 1 | 1 | 2 | | | Willcox, Ruben | 2 | | 3 | | |
| Bartlet, Abraham | 1 | 1 | 4 | | | Hull, Eliakim | 1 | 1 | 2 | | | Smith, Joseph | 1 | 4 | 4 | | |
| Seward, Moses | 4 | 2 | 2 | | | Picket, Benjamin | 2 | | 2 | | | Camp, Hezekiah | 1 | | 2 | | |
| Bartlet, Samuel | 2 | | 3 | | | Camp, Job | 8 | | 4 | | | Camp, Rejoice | 1 | 2 | 5 | | |
| Bartlet, Abraham | 1 | 1 | 3 | | | Spelman, Elizabeth | | 2 | 3 | | | Curtis, John | 2 | 1 | 2 | | |
| Meigs, Phineas | 1 | 1 | 1 | | | Smithson, Robert | 3 | | 3 | | | Curtis, Hannah | | | 1 | | 1 |
| Parmalie, Levi | 1 | 2 | 3 | | | White, Charles | 1 | 2 | 5 | | | Curtis, Anner | 2 | | 4 | | |
| Camp, Elias | 1 | 2 | 2 | | | Robinson, Ebenezur | 1 | 4 | 2 | | | Squire, Asher | 1 | 2 | 4 | | |
| Canfield, Asher | 1 | 2 | 3 | | | Gurnsey, Ebenezur | 2 | 1 | 2 | | | Johnson, John, 2nd | 2 | | 9 | | |
| Parmalie, Joel | 1 | 1 | 2 | | | Dunn, Timothy | 1 | | 1 | | | | | | | | |
| Parmalie, Camp | 1 | 1 | 2 | | | Norton, Hosias | 1 | | 2 | | | **EAST HAVEN TOWN.** | | | | | |
| Fowler, Caleb | 3 | 1 | 6 | | | Norton, Noah | 1 | | 2 | | | | | | | | |
| Camp, Ely | 1 | 1 | | | | Dunn, Timothy, 2nd | 1 | 2 | 2 | | | Hine, Henry F | 1 | | 1 | | |
| Camp, Phebe | | | 3 | | | Clarke, Nathaniel | 1 | 3 | 3 | | | Huse, John | 1 | 1 | 5 | | |
| Camp, Joseph | 1 | 1 | 3 | | | Tibbalds, Ebenezur | 4 | | 5 | | | Huse, Daniel | 1 | 1 | 2 | | |
| Camp, Elias | 2 | | 3 | | | Tibbalds, Joseph | 2 | 2 | 1 | | | Forbes, Johial | 5 | 1 | 7 | | 5 |
| Johnson, William | 1 | | 1 | | | Tibbalds, James | 2 | | 2 | | | Nails, Abraham | 1 | | 2 | | |
| Ceasar (Negroe) | | | | 6 | | Coles, Jesse | 2 | 1 | 6 | | | Pardie, Jerad | 1 | 2 | 2 | | 1 |
| Parmalie, Daniel | 1 | 2 | 4 | | | Robinson, James | 2 | 1 | 1 | | | Pardie, Molly | | | 2 | | 1 |
| Parmalie, Hezekiah | 1 | | 1 | | | Robinson, Nathaniel | 2 | | 1 | | | Smith, Job | 1 | 1 | 2 | | |
| Camp, Ezra | 1 | | 2 | | | Canfield, Gideon | 2 | | 1 | | | Wetmore, Charles | 1 | 1 | 2 | | |
| Larkins, Peter | 1 | 2 | 2 | | | Robinson, Asher | 2 | 1 | 4 | | | Day, Abigal | | | 4 | | |
| Norton, Stephen | 2 | | 2 | | | Robinson, Stephen | 1 | 1 | 2 | | | Atkins, Abigal | 1 | | 4 | | |
| Norton, Stephen, 2nd | 1 | 1 | 2 | | | Rose, Jiles | 1 | | 2 | | | Bradley, William | 1 | 1 | 4 | | |
| Hall, Luther | 1 | | 2 | | | Talcott, Noah | 1 | 2 | 5 | | | Smith, Ambrose | 1 | 2 | 4 | | |
| Strong, John | 1 | 1 | 4 | | | Davis, Amos | 2 | | 3 | | | Woodward, John, Junr | 4 | 3 | 3 | | 3 |
| Lose, John | 1 | 2 | 1 | | | Parsons, Ithamer | 2 | 2 | 6 | | | Tuttle, Joseph | 3 | 3 | 3 | | |
| Southward, Joseph | 1 | | 2 | | | Lyman, Noah | 2 | | 2 | | | Banns, Isaac | 1 | 2 | 4 | | |
| Crane, Jesse | 1 | | | | | Coe, Ann | | | 1 | | | Pardy, Jacob | 2 | | 4 | | |
| Crane, Zelock | 2 | 1 | 3 | | | Coe, Joel | 1 | 1 | 2 | | | Pardy, Abijah | 1 | 2 | 4 | | |
| Wright, Samuel | 1 | 3 | 1 | | | Parsons, Joseph | 1 | 2 | 4 | | | Pardy, Lidia | | | 4 | 1 | |

# HEADS OF FAMILIES—CONNECTICUT.

## NEW HAVEN COUNTY—Continued.

| NAME OF HEAD OF FAMILY. | Free white males of 16 years and upward, including heads of families. | Free white males under 16 years. | Free white females, including heads of families. | All other free persons. | Slaves. | NAME OF HEAD OF FAMILY. | Free white males of 16 years and upward, including heads of families. | Free white males under 16 years. | Free white females, including heads of families. | All other free persons. | Slaves. | NAME OF HEAD OF FAMILY. | Free white males of 16 years and upward, including heads of families. | Free white males under 16 years. | Free white females, including heads of families. | All other free persons. | Slaves. |
|---|---|---|---|---|---|---|---|---|---|---|---|---|---|---|---|---|---|
| **EAST HAVEN TOWN—con.** | | | | | | **EAST HAVEN TOWN—con.** | | | | | | **GUILFORD TOWN—con.** | | | | | |
| Pardy, Joseph | 1 | 2 | 2 | | | Burton, Ebenezer | 1 | 2 | 2 | | | Silas (Negroe) | | | | 2 | |
| Pardy, Leveret | 1 | 2 | 2 | | | Mallery, Asa | 1 | | 4 | | | Leet, Jerad | 1 | 1 | 3 | | |
| Pardy, Chandler | 1 | 1 | 2 | | | Granis, Isaac | 2 | | 4 | | | Fortner, Charles | 1 | | 3 | | |
| Morris, Amos, Junr | 1 | 2 | 8 | 1 | | Tuttle, Christopher | 1 | 1 | 4 | | | Morse, John | 1 | | 1 | | |
| Morris, Amos | 1 | 1 | 2 | | 1 | Tuttle, Stephan | 1 | 2 | 4 | | | Morse, David | 1 | 4 | 3 | | |
| Morris, John | 1 | 3 | 3 | | | Smith, Stephen | 2 | | 2 | | 3 | Leet, Daniel | 2 | 1 | 2 | | |
| Way, Timothy | 2 | 1 | 3 | | | Ludington, Jesse, Junr | 1 | | 3 | | | Leet, Ambrose | 1 | 3 | 3 | | |
| Smith, Samuel | 1 | 3 | 5 | | | Smith, Lydia | | | 3 | | | Leet, Palatine | 2 | 1 | 2 | | |
| Smith, Benjamin | 1 | 4 | 4 | | | Smith, Caleb | 1 | 1 | 2 | | | Leet, Amos | 1 | 3 | 6 | | |
| Thompson, Timothy | 3 | 3 | 4 | | | Tuttle, Daniel | 1 | 1 | 3 | | | Leet, Joel | 1 | | 1 | | |
| Bishop, Icabod | 1 | 2 | 3 | | | Landeraft, George | 1 | 3 | 1 | | | Leet, Soloman | 1 | | 2 | | |
| Bishop, Charles | 1 | | 3 | | 2 | Chitsey, Isaac | 3 | 1 | 3 | | | Leet, Elijah | 1 | 2 | 2 | | |
| Eveton, William | 2 | | 3 | | | Goodsell, Samuel | 1 | 3 | 4 | | | Leet, Pharos | 1 | 1 | 2 | | |
| Ford, Anna | | 1 | 1 | | | Hunt, John | 2 | 4 | 6 | | | Leet, Soloman, 2nd | 2 | 4 | 3 | | |
| Smith, Louis | | 2 | 3 | | | Chitsey, Ebenezur | 3 | | 5 | | | Leet, Thomas | 1 | 1 | 1 | | |
| Potter, Levi | 2 | | 4 | | | Granis, Elihu | 1 | | 5 | | | Leet, Victor | 1 | 2 | 1 | | |
| Mallery, Mabel | | | 2 | | | Chitsey, Levi | 1 | 6 | | | | Colvel, Nathaniel | 1 | 1 | 1 | 1 | 2 |
| Hemmingway, Enos | 1 | 2 | 4 | 1 | | Chitsey, James | 2 | | 1 | 2 | | Leet, Absolam | 2 | 1 | 2 | | |
| Street, Nicholas | 3 | 2 | 5 | 1 | | Thompson, Samuel | 2 | 2 | 3 | | | Elliott, John | 2 | 2 | 5 | 1 | 1 |
| Ferring, Zebelun | 2 | 4 | 4 | | | Cuff (Negroe) | | | | 5 | | Elliott, John, 2nd | 1 | | 1 | | 1 |
| Chitsey, Ephraim | 1 | | 2 | | | Dawson, Robert | 1 | 2 | 4 | | | Kirkham, William | | | | | |
| Hemmingway, John | 1 | 2 | 2 | | 1 | Smith, Samuel | 3 | 2 | 4 | | | Norton, Ebor | 1 | | 2 | | |
| Walker, Abigal | | | 5 | | | Smith, Mabel | 2 | | 3 | | | Norton, Timothy | 1 | | 1 | | |
| Smith, Laben | 1 | | 2 | | | Dayton, Nathaniel | 1 | 2 | 4 | | | Hill, Benjamin | 1 | | 2 | | |
| Hemmingway, Moses | 1 | 3 | 3 | | | Curtis, Phineas | 1 | | 4 | | | Bradley, Samuel | 1 | 4 | 2 | | |
| Smith, Nehamiah | 1 | 3 | 3 | | | Cooper, Levi | 1 | 1 | 4 | | | Bradley, Joseph | 1 | | 2 | | |
| Thompson, Moses | 1 | 2 | 5 | 1 | | Holt, Ebenezer | 1 | 2 | 2 | | | Bradley, James | 1 | 1 | 1 | | |
| Goodsell, John | 1 | 1 | 2 | | | Clarke, Daniel | 2 | | 1 | | 1 | Kirkham, Benjamin | 1 | 1 | 2 | | |
| Goodsell, John, Junr | 1 | 2 | 5 | | | Robinson, John | 3 | 1 | 3 | | | Fowler, Beldad | 1 | | 1 | | |
| Thompson, Amos | 2 | 1 | 6 | | | Robinson, Chandler | 1 | | 3 | | | Chrittenden, Timothy | 1 | 2 | 2 | | |
| Bradley, Josiah | 2 | | 4 | | | Thompson, Joel | 2 | 1 | 4 | | | Chrittenden, Nathaniel, 2nd | 1 | | 4 | | |
| Bradley, Daniel | 1 | 1 | 5 | | | Thompson, Jared | 1 | | 2 | | | Chittenden, Charles | 1 | | 1 | | |
| Chitsey, Deborah | | | 1 | | 1 | Molthrop, Joseph | 1 | 3 | 3 | | | Mercer, Absolam | 2 | 1 | 4 | | |
| Mallery, Levi | 1 | | 1 | | | Molthrop, Josiah | 2 | 1 | 3 | | | Vail, Jonathan | 1 | 1 | 1 | | |
| Bradley, Jacob | 3 | 1 | 2 | | | Fuller, John | 1 | | 4 | | | Hoadly, Samuel | 1 | 1 | 1 | | |
| Granis, Russell | 1 | 1 | 1 | | | Molthrop, Asher | 1 | 1 | 2 | | | Hotchkiss, Samuel | 1 | | 2 | | |
| Davidson, Andrew | 1 | 3 | 3 | | | Molthrop, Ely | 1 | | 2 | | | Hand, Joseph | 1 | | 1 | | |
| Row, Mathew | 1 | 2 | 4 | | | Molthrop, David | 1 | 2 | 2 | | | Ferral, George | 1 | 1 | 4 | | |
| Bradley, Stephen | 2 | | 1 | | 1 | Pardie, Mabel | | | 2 | | | Shally, Ebenezer | 1 | | 1 | | |
| Bradley, Stephen, Junr | 1 | 1 | 3 | | | Luddington, Jesse | 2 | 1 | 3 | | | Leet, James | 1 | 2 | 2 | | |
| Chitsey, John | 1 | 2 | 6 | | | Russell, Lidia | 1 | | 1 | | | Stevens, Samuel | 1 | 1 | 4 | | |
| Walker, William | 1 | 1 | 1 | | | Banns, Ebenezer | 2 | 2 | 3 | | | Fosdick, Abijah | 1 | | 4 | | |
| Mallery, Mary | 1 | 1 | 2 | | | Hemmingway, Samuel | 4 | 3 | 3 | | 4 | Stone, Levi | 1 | | 2 | | |
| Thompson, Stephen | 1 | 4 | 3 | | | Harrison, Philemon | 1 | 3 | 1 | | | Stone, Sibel | | | 2 | | |
| Austin, Joshua | 2 | 4 | 2 | 1 | | Smith, Ira | 1 | 1 | 2 | | | Hunt, John | 1 | 1 | 2 | | |
| Bradley, Simeon | 5 | 2 | 6 | | | Davenport, Samuel | 3 | 1 | 3 | | | Hall, John | 1 | | 1 | | |
| Bradley, Sarah | | | 2 | | | Brown, Hannah | 1 | 3 | 6 | | | Parmalie, David | 3 | 3 | 3 | | |
| Bradley, Gurdon | 1 | 3 | 5 | | | Rowe, Ezra | 1 | 5 | 4 | | | Miller, William | 2 | | 4 | | |
| Bradley, Elijah | 1 | 1 | 4 | | | Rowe, John | 2 | | 2 | | | Berry, Richard | 1 | 1 | 1 | | |
| Tyler, John | 3 | 1 | 1 | | | Mallery, Jesse | 1 | 2 | 2 | | | Parmalie, Joseph | 1 | | 3 | | |
| Thompson, Stephen | 1 | 1 | 2 | | | Ludington, Rachel | | | 1 | | | Raney, Ruben | 1 | | 3 | | |
| Luttenden, Samuel | 1 | 1 | 2 | | | Thompson, Elizabeth | | | 2 | | | Pendleton, Increase | 2 | | 3 | | |
| Mallery, Amos | 1 | | 2 | | | Woodward, John | 3 | 2 | 5 | | 2 | Pendleton, Joshua | 1 | | 3 | | |
| Hemmingway, Joseph | 2 | 6 | 3 | | 1 | Chitsey, Abraham | 2 | 2 | 5 | | | Barker, Ruth | 1 | 1 | 4 | | |
| Andrus, Jedediah | 1 | 1 | 4 | | | Pardy, Levi | 2 | 1 | 3 | | | Elliott, Abigal | 3 | | 5 | | |
| Forbes, Samuel | 1 | | 3 | | 1 | | | | | | | Elliott, William | 1 | 2 | 1 | | |
| Bradley, Ezeriah | 2 | 2 | 4 | | | **GUILFORD TOWN.** | | | | | | Bishop, Johson | 1 | | 4 | | |
| Bans, Abraham | 2 | 1 | 3 | | | Fowler, Noah, 2nd | 1 | 1 | 4 | | | Cadwell, Elias | 1 | 3 | 2 | | 1 |
| Forbes, Levi | 1 | 3 | 9 | | | Walstone, Thomas | 1 | 2 | 1 | | | Wells, Joseph | 2 | 1 | 4 | | |
| Augur, Daniel | 2 | | 2 | | | Fowler, Minor | 1 | 1 | 2 | | | Parmalie, Samuel | 1 | 1 | 2 | | |
| Augur, Philomen | 1 | 1 | 1 | | | Fowler, Noah | 1 | | 2 | 1 | | Elliott, Nathaniel | 1 | | 2 | | |
| Goodshell, Daniel | 1 | 1 | 2 | | | Norton, Felix | 2 | 4 | 5 | | | Parmalie, Andrew | 1 | | 1 | | |
| Eagleston, Elizabeth | | 1 | 2 | | | Norton, Elizabeth | | | 2 | | | Waters, Sarah | 1 | | 2 | | |
| Barnes, Levi | 1 | | | | | Norton, Rufus | 1 | 4 | 3 | | | Chrittenden, Joseph | 1 | | 3 | | |
| Barnes, Samuel | 2 | 2 | 3 | | | Norton, Molly | | | 3 | | | Chrittenden, Samuel | 1 | 1 | 3 | | |
| Huse, Rebecca | | 2 | 3 | | | Norton, Beriah | 2 | | 4 | | | Hunt, Thomas | 2 | | 4 | | |
| Tuttle, Samuel | 2 | 2 | 4 | | | Norton, John | 3 | 1 | 2 | | | Hunt, Thomas, 2nd | 1 | 1 | 2 | | |
| Goodsell, Daniel | 2 | | 3 | | | Leet, John | 2 | 1 | 5 | | | Parmalie, Linus | 1 | 2 | 3 | | |
| Forbes, Isaac | | 2 | 2 | 2 | | Goldsmith, John | 3 | | 5 | | | Parmalie, William | 3 | | 4 | | |
| Mallery, Benjamin | 2 | 2 | 4 | | | Goldsmith, John, 2nd | 1 | 1 | 2 | | | Bartlet, Hooker | 3 | 1 | 1 | | 1 |
| Sheppard, Samuel | 2 | 2 | 3 | | | Jones, Aron | 2 | 1 | 2 | | | Graves, Nathaniel | 2 | | 2 | | |
| Sheppard, Joseph | 1 | 1 | 2 | | | Stone, Jerad | 1 | | 2 | | | Griffin, Timothy | 1 | 6 | 3 | | |
| Barnes, Nathaniel | 1 | 2 | 3 | | | Stone, Mercy | | | 3 | | | Shelly, Timothy | 1 | | 5 | | |
| Sheppard, John | 1 | 2 | 4 | | | Burges, John | 1 | 1 | 1 | 1 | | Smith, John | 1 | 1 | 6 | | |
| Shepard, Stephen | 2 | | 3 | | | Norton, Ashbel | 1 | | 1 | | | Shelly, Joel | 1 | | | | |
| Granis, Mary | | | 2 | | | Norton, Jerad | 2 | | 2 | | | London (Negroe) | | | | 2 | |
| Bradley, Edmond | 1 | 1 | 3 | | | Benton, Jerad | 1 | 2 | 2 | | | Hill, Henry | 1 | 3 | 5 | | 1 |
| Sheppard, Thomas | 2 | 2 | 5 | | | Stone, James | 1 | 1 | 2 | | | Crittenton, Seth | 1 | 1 | 1 | | |
| Bradley, Ely | 2 | | 4 | | | Stone, Nathaniel | 4 | 1 | 5 | | | Colwell, Charles | 1 | | 1 | | |
| Banns, Ebenezer | 2 | 2 | 4 | | | Stone, Abner | 1 | 2 | 4 | | | Colwell, Ruth | | | 2 | | |
| Russell, Joseph | 3 | 2 | 2 | | | Benton, Samuel | 3 | | 1 | | | Redfield, John | 2 | | 2 | 2 | |
| Dennison, Jesse | 1 | 1 | | | | Hall, Isaac | 2 | | 3 | | | Redfield, John, 2nd | 1 | 1 | 3 | | |
| Townsend, Samuel | 1 | | 2 | | | Hall, Stephen | 1 | 2 | 2 | | | Fowler, Amos | 1 | | 2 | | |
| Hotchkiss, Joseph | 1 | 1 | 3 | | | Hall, Philomen | 3 | | 2 | | | Spencer, Mark | 1 | 5 | 3 | | |
| Andruss, Elisha | 3 | 1 | 4 | | | Johnson, John | 1 | 3 | 2 | | | Spencer, Miney | | 6 | 3 | | |
| Lucas, Richard | 1 | 1 | 2 | | | Saxton, Simion | 2 | 1 | 3 | | | Elliot, Joseph | 1 | 3 | 2 | | |
| Holt, Joseph | 2 | | 2 | | | Curren, James | 1 | | 4 | | | Fairchild, Mahitabel | | 4 | 2 | | |
| Luddenton, Mary | 2 | | 5 | | | Fowler, Andrew | 3 | 2 | 4 | | | Hallock, Israel | 1 | 1 | 2 | | |
| Granis, Joseph | 3 | | 1 | | | Hotchkiss, John | 2 | | 3 | | | Fairchild, Asher | 2 | 2 | 4 | | |
| Bradley, Isaac | 1 | 2 | 4 | | | Hotchkiss, Miles | 1 | | 2 | | | Foot, Eli | 1 | 5 | 2 | | |
| Holt, Samuel | 2 | 1 | 2 | | | Spencer, Uriah | 1 | | 4 | | | Powers, Thomas | 1 | 2 | 6 | | |
| Hotchkiss, Asa | 1 | | 2 | | | Stone, Miles | 1 | 1 | 5 | | | Hill, Thomas | 1 | | 6 | | |
| Russell, Edward | 1 | | 2 | | | Chittenden, Ambrose | 2 | | 5 | 1 | | Johnson, Nathaniel | 2 | | 3 | 6 | |
| Holt, Daniel | 2 | 2 | 6 | | | Prince (Negroe) | | | | 2 | | Benton, Caleb | 2 | 1 | 6 | | |
| Dinnison, John | 1 | 4 | 4 | | | | | | | | | | | | | | |

# FIRST CENSUS OF THE UNITED STATES.

## NEW HAVEN COUNTY—Continued.

### GUILFORD TOWN—con.

| NAME OF HEAD OF FAMILY. | Free white males of 16 years and upward, including heads of families. | Free white males under 16 years. | Free white females, including heads of families. | All other free persons. | Slaves. |
|---|---|---|---|---|---|
| Landon, Samuel | 1 |  | 3 |  |  |
| Handy, Anna |  |  | 1 |  |  |
| Landon, Jonathan | 1 | 1 | 2 |  |  |
| Landon, David | 1 | 3 | 1 |  |  |
| Tuttle, Joel | 4 |  | 8 |  |  |
| Stone, Medad | 1 |  | 4 |  | 1 |
| Collins, Pitman | 1 | 1 | 2 |  |  |
| Chalker, Isaac | 2 | 2 | 4 |  |  |
| Ward, Buley |  |  | 1 |  |  |
| Griffin, Joseph | 1 | 3 | 1 |  |  |
| Pyncheon, Joseph | 1 |  | 2 |  |  |
| Bosston, Nathaniel | 1 | 1 | 2 |  |  |
| Handy, Hetty |  | 1 | 2 |  |  |
| Murry, Thankfull |  | 2 | 1 |  |  |
| Johnson, Joel | 1 |  | 1 |  |  |
| Pyncheon, Thomas R | 2 | 1 | 4 | 1 |  |
| Woodward, Rosswell | 2 | 3 | 6 |  |  |
| Ruggles, Nathaniel | 1 | 1 | 1 |  |  |
| Griffin, Nathaniel | 1 |  | 2 | 1 |  |
| Ward, Thelas | 1 |  | 3 |  |  |
| Spencer, Christopher | 2 | 3 | 5 |  |  |
| Fowler, Elizabeth | 2 |  | 3 |  |  |
| Lines, Benjamin | 1 | 1 | 4 |  |  |
| Person, Submit |  | 1 | 3 |  |  |
| Griffin, Jasper | 1 | 1 | 1 | 1 |  |
| Hubbard, Deborah | 2 | 1 | 1 |  |  |
| Kimberley, George | 1 | 3 | 3 |  |  |
| Chittenton, Caleb | 1 | 1 | 1 |  |  |
| Stone, Bela | 1 |  | 3 |  |  |
| Stone, Ruben | 2 |  | 1 |  |  |
| Stone, Timothy | 1 | 1 | 1 |  |  |
| Collins, Joel | 2 | 2 | 4 |  |  |
| Crittenten, Nathaniel | 2 |  | 1 |  |  |
| Crittenton, Bela | 1 |  | 1 |  |  |
| Chrittenden, Nathaniel, 2nd | 1 |  | 1 |  |  |
| Roberson, Samuel | 1 |  | 1 |  |  |
| Stone, Abraham | 2 | 2 | 4 |  |  |
| Roberson, Samuel, 2 | 1 | 1 | 2 |  |  |
| Shelly, Shubal | 2 | 1 | 2 |  |  |
| Bishop, Seth | 1 |  | 2 |  |  |
| Stone, John | 1 | 1 | 2 |  |  |
| Veale, Joshua | 1 | 2 | 5 |  |  |
| Stone, Soloman | 1 | 1 | 2 |  | 1 |
| Griffin, Joel | 1 | 2 | 2 |  |  |
| Griffin, Peter | 1 |  | 1 |  |  |
| Green, Joseph | 1 | 1 | 1 |  |  |
| Stone, Benjamin | 2 | 1 | 4 |  |  |
| Woodward, Abraham | 1 | 3 | 2 |  |  |
| Stone, William | 1 |  | 2 |  |  |
| Chittenton, Joseph | 1 | 1 | 4 |  |  |
| Johnson, Samuel | 3 |  | 2 |  |  |
| Johnson, Nathaniel | 1 |  | 1 |  |  |
| Johnson, Samuel, 2nd | 1 | 2 | 2 |  |  |
| Ruggles, Nathaniel | 2 | 1 | 5 |  |  |
| Fowler, Joel | 1 |  | 1 |  |  |
| Hotchkiss, Hannah |  |  | 1 |  |  |
| Hemman, Aron | 3 | 1 | 1 |  |  |
| Veal, Jonathan | 2 |  | 6 |  |  |
| Norton, Elizabeth |  |  | 3 |  |  |
| Frisbie, Benjamin | 2 | 1 | 1 |  |  |
| Davis, John | 1 |  | 3 |  |  |
| Hill, Thomas | 3 | 1 | 2 |  |  |
| Redfield, Nathaniel | 1 | 1 | 1 |  |  |
| Evetts, Elyers | 1 |  | 2 |  |  |
| Evetts, Elyers, 2nd | 1 | 1 | 2 |  |  |
| Scot, James | 1 | 3 | 2 |  |  |
| Chittenton, Anna |  |  | 3 |  |  |
| Benton, Jabez | 3 | 2 | 2 |  |  |
| Scranton, Thomas, 2nd | 1 | 1 | 2 |  |  |
| Scranton, Samuel | 2 |  | 2 |  |  |
| Starr, William | 2 | 1 | 3 |  |  |
| Starr, John | 1 |  | 6 |  |  |
| Fowler, Abraham | 1 | 2 | 3 |  |  |
| Hall, Eliphalet | 2 | 1 | 2 |  |  |
| Evett, Lucy |  |  | 2 |  |  |
| Lee, Samuel | 1 |  | 2 |  |  |
| Lee, Levi | 1 | 3 | 2 |  |  |
| Lee, Timothy | 1 | 1 | 2 |  |  |
| Bishop, Jonathan | 1 |  | 2 |  |  |
| Bishop, David | 1 |  | 3 |  |  |
| Bishop, Jerad | 1 | 2 | 1 |  |  |
| Hall, Benjamin | 1 |  | 2 |  |  |
| Hall, Benjamin, 2nd | 1 | 1 | 3 |  |  |
| Chittenton, Joseph | 1 |  | 2 |  |  |
| Amos, James | 1 |  | 1 |  |  |
| Smith, Samuel | 1 | 1 | 3 |  |  |
| Downs, Griffin | 1 |  | 2 |  |  |
| Hotchkiss, Eber | 1 | 3 | 2 |  |  |
| Collins, Charles | 3 |  | 2 |  |  |
| Lee, William | 3 | 3 | 2 |  |  |
| Lee, Eton | 3 | 1 | 2 |  |  |
| Evetts, Abraham | 1 | 1 | 2 |  |  |
| Evetts, Samuel | 3 | 2 | 3 |  |  |
| Ward, Andrew | 2 | 1 | 3 |  |  |

### GUILFORD TOWN—con.

| NAME OF HEAD OF FAMILY. | Free white males of 16 years and upward, including heads of families. | Free white males under 16 years. | Free white females, including heads of families. | All other free persons. | Slaves. |
|---|---|---|---|---|---|
| Stone, Joseph | 2 |  | 2 |  |  |
| Dibble, Jane | 1 |  | 1 |  |  |
| Benton, James | 1 |  | 2 |  |  |
| Naughty, David | 2 | 2 | 3 | 1 |  |
| Naughty, David, 2nd | 1 | 2 | 1 |  |  |
| Johnson, Nathaniel | 1 |  | 2 |  |  |
| Parmalie, John | 1 |  | 2 |  |  |
| Parmalie, Joel | 1 | 2 | 2 |  |  |
| Parmalie, James | 1 | 2 | 2 |  |  |
| Parmalie, Eber | 1 |  | 3 |  |  |
| Parmalie, Ruben | 2 | 1 | 4 |  |  |
| Griswold, Joel | 1 | 1 | 2 |  |  |
| Griswold, Thomas | 1 | 1 | 2 |  |  |
| Griswold, Thomas, 2nd | 1 |  | 1 |  |  |
| Griswold, Miles | 1 |  | 3 |  |  |
| Davis, James | 1 |  | 1 |  |  |
| Hall, Miles | 1 | 1 | 1 |  |  |
| Stone, Luther | 1 | 1 | 1 |  |  |
| Benton, Silas | 4 | 3 | 1 |  |  |
| Hall, Mary |  |  | 3 |  |  |
| Johnson, Hill | 1 | 1 | 2 |  |  |
| Johnson, Miles | 1 | 2 | 3 |  |  |
| Bishop, David | 1 | 3 | 4 |  |  |
| Hotchkiss, Ebenezer | 2 | 1 | 2 |  |  |
| Hotchkiss, Ruben | 1 |  | 4 |  |  |
| Scranton, Thomas | 1 |  | 1 |  |  |
| Scranton, Nathaniel | 1 | 3 | 1 |  |  |
| Lee, Eber | 1 |  | 1 |  |  |
| Evetts, Samuel, 3rd | 1 | 1 | 2 |  |  |
| Bristol, Samuel | 1 | 1 | 3 |  |  |
| Parmalie, John, 2nd | 1 | 1 | 4 |  |  |
| Stanton, Daniel | 2 | 2 | 5 |  |  |
| Scovel, John | 2 |  | 3 |  | 1 |
| Wells, Joseph, 2nd | 1 |  | 3 |  |  |
| Fowler, Elizabeth |  |  | 1 |  | 1 |
| Hopson, Ebenezer | 1 | 2 | 4 |  |  |
| Parmalie, William | 1 | 2 | 2 |  |  |
| Graves, Ambrose | 1 |  | 2 |  |  |
| Burges, Thomas | 1 |  | 1 |  |  |
| Burges, Thomas, 2nd | 3 | 1 | 5 |  |  |
| Handy, Samuel | 1 | 2 | 3 |  |  |
| Hill, Nathaniel | 1 | 1 | 2 |  |  |
| Hill, Anna |  |  | 2 |  |  |
| Chittenden, Abraham | 1 |  | 1 |  |  |
| Chittenden, Abraham,2 | 2 | 2 | 3 |  |  |
| Colwell, Thomas | 2 |  | 6 |  |  |
| Bartlett, Samuel | 1 | 1 | 4 |  |  |
| Bartlett, Timothy | 1 | 1 | 1 |  |  |
| Griswold, Ezra | 1 | 1 | 5 |  |  |
| Griswold, John | 1 |  | 2 |  |  |
| Griswold, Molly |  |  | 2 |  |  |
| Parmalie, Nathaniel | 1 | 3 | 3 |  |  |
| Fowler, Ruben | 1 |  | 3 |  |  |
| Mann, Phillip | 2 |  | 1 |  |  |
| Chittenden, Noah | 1 |  | 5 |  |  |
| Collins, Darius | 2 |  | 5 |  |  |
| Griffin, Jasper | 1 | 4 | 2 |  |  |
| Crumbey, John | 1 | 2 | 5 |  |  |
| Ackley, Rebecca |  |  | 1 |  |  |
| Plum, Thankfull |  |  | 1 |  |  |
| Bishop, Elizabeth |  |  | 2 |  |  |
| Meigs, Nathaniel | 1 | 2 | 3 |  |  |
| Davis, James | 1 | 2 | 3 |  |  |
| Leet, John | 1 |  | 2 |  |  |
| Rossell, Mons | 1 |  | 2 | 2 | 1 |
| Shelly, Ruben | 1 |  | 1 |  |  |
| Fowler, Nathaniel | 1 | 2 | 2 |  |  |
| Shelly, Ruben, 2nd | 1 | 2 | 1 |  |  |
| Shelly, Medad | 1 |  | 1 |  |  |
| Murray, Daniel | 1 | 1 | 2 |  |  |
| Scovel, John | 1 | 1 | 3 |  |  |
| Happen, Gideon | 1 |  | 3 |  |  |
| Parmalie, Sarah |  |  | 2 |  |  |
| Leet, Ruben | 2 | 1 | 4 |  |  |
| Deming, Josiah J | 1 | 4 | 2 |  |  |
| Seward, David | 2 |  | 1 |  |  |
| Seward, David, 2nd | 1 |  | 4 |  |  |
| Seward, Timothy | 1 | 3 | 2 |  |  |
| Chittenton, Samuel | 1 |  | 2 |  |  |
| Evets, Aron | 2 |  | 3 |  |  |
| Evetts, Benjamin | 2 | 2 | 2 |  |  |
| Chittenton, Benjamin | 2 | 2 | 2 |  |  |
| Chittenton Abraham | 2 | 3 | 3 |  |  |
| Chittenton, David | 1 | 1 | 3 |  |  |
| Chittenton, Nathaniel | 1 |  | 3 |  |  |
| Evett, Timothy | 2 |  | 2 |  |  |
| Evett, Timothy, 2nd | 1 |  | 3 |  |  |
| Crittenton, Joseph | 1 |  | 3 |  |  |
| Crittenton, Huldy |  |  | 2 |  |  |
| Evett, Isaac | 2 | 4 | 3 |  |  |
| Evett, Daniel | 1 |  | 2 |  |  |
| Evett, Samuel | 2 | 2 | 5 |  |  |
| Norton, Hooker | 1 | 3 | 3 |  |  |
| Norton Ruben | 3 |  | 3 |  |  |
| Norton, Eber | 1 | 1 | 1 |  |  |

### GUILFORD TOWN—con.

| NAME OF HEAD OF FAMILY. | Free white males of 16 years and upward, including heads of families. | Free white males under 16 years. | Free white females, including heads of families. | All other free persons. | Slaves. |
|---|---|---|---|---|---|
| Norton, Aron | 2 | 1 | 5 |  |  |
| Evetts, Jonathan | 2 |  | 3 |  |  |
| Evetts, Ezra | 2 |  | 2 |  |  |
| Stanton, John | 1 |  | 1 |  |  |
| Evett, Moses | 1 |  | 1 |  |  |
| Crainton, John | 1 |  | 2 |  |  |
| Dudley, Thomas | 2 |  | 1 |  |  |
| Dudley, Eber | 1 |  |  |  |  |
| Bartlet, Joseph | 3 |  | 3 |  |  |
| Dudley, Samuel | 2 |  | 1 |  |  |
| Dudley, Jane |  | 1 | 2 |  |  |
| Ward, Elizabeth |  |  | 2 |  |  |
| Dudley, Amos | 2 | 3 | 2 |  |  |
| Hotchkiss, Isaac | 1 | 2 | 2 |  |  |
| Spinish, Nathaniel | 1 |  |  |  |  |
| Dudley, Caleb | 1 |  | 1 |  |  |
| Dudley, Nathaniel | 1 | 2 | 3 |  |  |
| Dudley Abraham | 1 | 2 | 2 |  |  |
| Dudley, Caleb 2 | 2 | 1 | 4 |  |  |
| Johnson, Benjamin | 1 |  | 2 |  |  |
| Johnson, Nathaniel | 1 |  | 1 |  |  |
| Benton, Seth | 1 |  | 2 |  |  |
| Shelly, Lucy |  |  | 1 |  |  |
| Hill, Thomas, 2nd | 3 | 1 | 2 |  |  |
| Powers, Thomas, 2nd | 1 |  |  |  |  |
| Norton, Ruben, 2 | 1 | 4 | 4 |  |  |
| Evett, David | 1 |  |  |  |  |
| Cleaveland, George | 1 |  |  |  |  |
| Hotchkiss, Amos | 2 |  | 2 |  |  |
| Wilson, Lucy |  |  | 1 |  |  |
| Shelly, Edmond | 1 | 3 | 2 |  |  |
| Hull, David | 1 |  | 1 |  |  |
| Hull, William | 1 |  | 2 |  |  |
| Collins, Freind | 1 | 2 | 3 |  |  |
| Ceasar (Negroe) |  |  |  |  | 3 |
| King, Charles | 1 | 1 | 3 |  |  |
| Lee, Deborah |  |  | 3 |  |  |
| Morse, John | 1 | 2 | 2 |  |  |
| Stone, Edmond | 1 |  |  |  |  |
| Ranney, George | 1 |  | 2 |  |  |
| Crampton, David | 1 | 2 | 5 |  |  |
| Manger, Ebenezer | 1 |  |  |  |  |
| Manger, Ebenezer, 2d | 1 | 2 | 2 |  |  |
| Manger, Jesse | 1 | 3 | 1 |  |  |
| Stone, Thomas | 1 |  | 2 |  |  |
| Cranton, Nathaniel | 1 |  | 2 |  |  |
| Cranton, Nathaniel, 2d | 1 | 2 | 2 |  |  |
| Stone, Seth | 1 | 1 | 1 |  |  |
| Stone, Mary |  |  | 3 |  |  |
| Bishop, Joiner | 1 |  | 3 |  |  |
| Bishop, James | 1 |  | 2 |  |  |
| Bishop, Hannah | 1 | 1 | 3 |  |  |
| Bishop, Lines | 1 |  | 3 |  |  |
| Bishop, Tabitha |  |  | 1 |  |  |
| Bassett, Elisha | 1 | 2 | 5 |  |  |
| Lee, Jonathan | 1 | 1 | 1 |  |  |
| Lee, Jonathan, 2nd | 1 |  | 2 |  |  |
| Smith, Jeffry | 1 | 3 | 1 |  |  |
| Bassett, William | 1 | 1 | 4 |  |  |
| Stone, Noah | 1 | 1 | 2 |  |  |
| Bishop, Russell | 1 |  | 2 |  |  |
| Wright, Benjamin | 3 | 1 | 3 |  |  |
| Crumton, Jonathan | 1 |  |  |  |  |
| Crumton, Jonathan, 2. | 2 |  | 1 |  |  |
| Shelly, John | 1 | 1 | 3 |  |  |
| Cramton, Asbel | 1 | 2 | 2 |  |  |
| Lee, Nathaniel | 3 |  | 4 |  |  |
| Dudley, Jonathan | 1 | 2 | 5 |  |  |
| Brown, Samuel | 2 |  | 2 |  |  |
| Wilcox, William | 2 | 2 | 2 |  |  |
| Willcox, Jonathan | 1 | 3 | 4 |  |  |
| Bradley, Simry | 4 | 1 | 5 |  |  |
| Veal, Nathaniel | 1 | 3 | 2 |  |  |
| Hand, Icabod | 1 | 4 | 3 |  |  |
| Judd, Jonathan | 1 | 2 | 3 |  |  |
| Blakely, Oliver | 1 | 4 | 3 |  |  |
| Conglin, Jacob | 1 |  |  |  |  |
| Stone, Rachel |  |  | 2 |  |  |
| Stone, William | 1 |  | 1 |  |  |
| Lee, Fredreck |  |  | 2 |  |  |
| Bradley, Timothy | 2 | 3 | 4 |  |  |
| Bradley, Anson | 1 |  |  |  |  |
| Feild, Joseph | 3 | 4 | 4 |  |  |
| Feild, Luke | 1 | 3 | 4 |  |  |
| Crittenton, Noah | 2 | 1 | 6 |  |  |
| Munger, Simeon | 2 |  | 2 |  |  |
| Munger, Josiah | 1 |  | 2 |  |  |
| Crumton, Hull | 1 | 1 | 1 |  |  |
| Crittenton, Edmond | 1 |  | 2 |  |  |
| Munger, Willis | 1 | 3 | 1 |  |  |
| Crumton, Darius | 1 |  | 2 |  |  |
| Evett, Stephen |  |  | 1 |  |  |
| Ripsey, Prinson | 1 | 1 | 3 |  |  |
| Graves, Temperance |  |  | 2 |  |  |
| Graves, Ezra | 1 |  | 2 |  |  |

# HEADS OF FAMILIES—CONNECTICUT.

## NEW HAVEN COUNTY—Continued.

| NAME OF HEAD OF FAMILY. | Free white males of 16 years and upward, including heads of families. | Free white males under 16 years. | Free white females, including heads of families. | All other free persons. | Slaves. | NAME OF HEAD OF FAMILY. | Free white males of 16 years and upward, including heads of families. | Free white males under 16 years. | Free white females, including heads of families. | All other free persons. | Slaves. | NAME OF HEAD OF FAMILY. | Free white males of 16 years and upward, including heads of families. | Free white males under 16 years. | Free white females, including heads of families. | All other free persons. | Slaves. |
|---|---|---|---|---|---|---|---|---|---|---|---|---|---|---|---|---|---|
| **GUILFORD TOWN—con.** | | | | | | **GUILFORD TOWN—con.** | | | | | | **GUILFORD TOWN—con.** | | | | | |
| Munger, Bela | 1 | 1 | 5 | | | Willcox, Edmond | 2 | 4 | 4 | | | Russell, Timothy | 2 | | 3 | | |
| Munger, James | 2 | 1 | 3 | | | Henderson, John | 3 | | 1 | | | Fowler, John | 1 | | 1 | | |
| Graves, Ebenezer | 3 | | 4 | | | Hand, Daniel | 1 | | 1 | 1 | | Fowler, Lucy | | 1 | 4 | | |
| Graves, Irael | 1 | | 3 | | | Hand, Daniel, 2nd | 1 | 2 | 1 | | | Fowler, Samuel | 1 | 1 | 1 | | |
| Bishop, Ebenezer | 1 | 2 | 4 | | | Dowd, Miles | 1 | 2 | 3 | | | Chitsey, Nathaniel | 1 | 1 | 1 | 1 | |
| Graves, Luman | 1 | 2 | 1 | | | Teal, Benjamin | 1 | 1 | 4 | | | Chitsey, Bathsheba | | | 6 | | |
| Thompson, David | 1 | 1 | 2 | | | Willard, Jerad | 1 | 1 | 5 | | | Baldwin, Timothy | 1 | 2 | 6 | | |
| Judd, Martha | | | 2 | | | Willard, James | 1 | | 1 | | | Cook, James | 1 | 1 | 1 | | |
| Bartlet, Ruben | | 2 | 2 | | | Dudley, Josiah | 1 | | 2 | | | Cook, Joshua | 1 | | 1 | | |
| Bartlet, Ruben, 2nd | 1 | | 1 | | | Dudley, Joseph | 2 | | 1 | | | Tom (Negroe) | | | 1 | | |
| Bartlet, Stephen | 2 | | 3 | | | Dowd, Abraham | 2 | | 1 | | | Dowd, Jeremiah | 1 | | | | |
| Bartlet, James | 1 | 2 | 4 | | | Dowd, Ruben | 1 | 3 | 3 | | | Roseter, Timothy | 1 | 1 | 2 | 1 | |
| Willcox, Ezra, 2 | 1 | 3 | 1 | | | Dudley, Simeon | 1 | 3 | 4 | | | Norton, Gideon | 1 | 1 | 3 | | |
| Scranton, John | 1 | 2 | 2 | | | Forster, Christopher | 1 | 2 | 3 | | | Norton, Abel | 1 | | 3 | | |
| Blakely, Abigal | | | 3 | | | Forster, Thomas | 1 | 3 | 2 | | | Rochester, Benjamin | 1 | | 3 | | 1 |
| Monger, Lidia | | | 2 | | | Dowd, Dedimos | 2 | | 3 | | | Kimberly, Abraham, 2nd | 3 | 2 | 4 | | |
| Monger, Johiel | 1 | | | | | Griffiths, Benjamin | 3 | 2 | 3 | | | Benton, Elihu | 2 | 4 | 4 | | |
| Evets, Ambrose | 3 | | 2 | | | Dowd, Asa | 1 | | 1 | | | Benton, Timothy | 3 | 1 | 3 | | |
| Dow'd, Zachariah | 1 | | 1 | | | Dowd, Asa, 2nd | 2 | 2 | 4 | | | Pond, Gad | 2 | 3 | 3 | | |
| Dow'd, Zachariah, 2nd | 1 | 2 | 3 | | | Meigs, Phineas | 2 | | 4 | | | Johnson, Isaac | 1 | 1 | 5 | | |
| Dowd, Soloman | 1 | 1 | 3 | | | Conglin, Isaac | 1 | | | | | Hall, Eber | 2 | 1 | 3 | | |
| Field, Timothy | 1 | 2 | 6 | | | Murry, Curtis | 1 | 2 | 1 | | | Benton, Lot | 1 | 1 | 3 | | |
| Graves, George | 1 | 1 | 1 | | | Bassett, Nathaniel | 1 | 1 | 3 | | | Bartlet, John | 3 | | 3 | | |
| Todd, Jonathan | 1 | | 1 | | | Hill, Icobad | 1 | 4 | 2 | | | Bartlet, Daniel | 2 | 1 | 1 | | |
| Scranton, Abraham | 1 | 3 | 3 | | | Maltby, Jane | | | 2 | | 2 | Philor, John | 1 | 2 | 2 | | |
| Jones, John | 1 | 4 | 3 | | | Forster, Sarah | | | 3 | 3 | | Bray, Thomas W | 1 | 6 | 5 | | |
| Dudley, Gilbert | 2 | 1 | 2 | | | Munger, Timothy | 1 | | 1 | | | Crittenton, Hull | 1 | | 2 | | |
| Lee, Silas | 1 | | 2 | | | Munger, Timothy, 2 | 1 | | 3 | | | Fowler, David | 2 | | 2 | | |
| Hill, Daniel | 1 | | 2 | | | Munger, Lines | 1 | 1 | 2 | | | Bishop, Samuel | 3 | | 2 | | |
| Hill, Timothy | 1 | | 5 | | | Munger, Josiah | 2 | | 1 | | | Fitch, Thomas | 1 | | 2 | | |
| Hart, Benjamin | 4 | | 3 | | | Blakley, Joshua | 2 | | 4 | | | Fitch, Samuel | 2 | 1 | 2 | | |
| Graves, Simeon | 1 | 1 | 3 | | | Dowd, John | 1 | | 7 | | | Dibble, Simus | 2 | | 1 | | |
| Graves, Timothy | 1 | 2 | 1 | | | Feild, Zacheriah | 1 | 1 | 6 | | | Bishop, Jesse | 1 | 1 | 3 | | |
| Graves, Elias | 1 | 1 | 3 | | | Leach, Oren | 1 | | 1 | | | Bishop, Hannah | | | 2 | | |
| Meigs, Timothy | 2 | 1 | 5 | 1 | | Field, Jedediah | 1 | 1 | 2 | | | Fowler, William | 1 | 3 | 4 | | |
| Bradley, Ashbel | 1 | 1 | 1 | | | Meigs, Abigal | 1 | | 4 | | | Dudley, Selah | 2 | 2 | | 1 | |
| Hill, Ruben, 2 | 1 | 1 | 4 | | | Field, Icobad | 1 | 1 | 2 | | | Fowler, Silas | 2 | 2 | 6 | | |
| Todd, John | 1 | | 1 | | | Cranton, Nathaniel | 1 | 1 | 4 | | | Hall, Ebenezer | 4 | | 3 | | |
| Todd, Jonathan | 2 | 2 | 2 | | | Leach, David | 1 | 2 | 2 | | | Rochester, Samuel | 1 | 1 | 1 | | |
| Willcox, Benjamin | 1 | 2 | 3 | | | Cranton, Josiah | 1 | 3 | 5 | | | Brooks, David S | 1 | | 2 | | |
| Scranton, Thomas | 1 | 5 | 4 | | | Hall, Zebulon | 1 | 3 | 4 | | | Wick, Edward | 3 | 1 | 3 | | |
| Mann, Elisha | 2 | | 2 | | | Cranton, Benjamin, 2 | 1 | 1 | 3 | | | Leet, Jarad | 1 | 1 | 3 | | |
| Scranton, Theobald | 1 | 1 | 1 | | | Fowler, Asher | 1 | | 4 | 1 | | Scranton, Torry | 1 | 1 | 3 | | |
| Graves, Eli | 2 | | 4 | | | Calhoun, Josiah | 1 | 1 | 1 | 1 | | Kimberly, Abraham | 1 | | 2 | | |
| Dudley, Bela | 1 | 3 | 3 | | | Pardie, James | 1 | | 4 | | | Chittenton, Daniel | 1 | 1 | 4 | | |
| Buckley, Aron | 2 | 3 | 5 | | | Field, Samuel | 3 | 3 | 3 | | | Stevens, Timothy | 1 | 2 | 3 | | |
| Buckley, Moses | 1 | | 1 | | | Johnson, Phineas | 3 | | 2 | | | Dudley, Luther | 1 | 5 | 1 | | |
| Murry, Amassa | 1 | | 2 | | | French, Didimus | 2 | 1 | 3 | | | Elwell, James | 1 | | 3 | | |
| Blakley, Moses | 1 | 1 | 1 | | | Johnson, Ruben | 1 | | 2 | | | Dudley, Medad | 4 | | 4 | | |
| Dowd, Joseph | 3 | 1 | 4 | | | Johnson, Isaac | 2 | | 1 | | | Dudley, Ambrose | 1 | 1 | 2 | | |
| Dowd, Timothy | 2 | 1 | 3 | | | Griswold, George | 1 | 1 | 2 | | | Tallman, Peter | 3 | | 6 | | |
| Dowd, Ebenezer | 4 | 3 | 1 | | | Bishop, Eneas | 4 | | 2 | | | Fowler, Stephen | 3 | 5 | 6 | | |
| Willard, Julius | 1 | 1 | 3 | | | Dowd, Thomas | 1 | | 4 | | | Fowler, Hannah | | | 2 | | |
| Meigs, Elias | 2 | | 6 | | | Doud, Moses | 2 | 1 | 4 | | | Hubbard, Ebor | 3 | 1 | 2 | | |
| Graves, Gilbert | 1 | | 3 | | | Doud, Job | 1 | 2 | 6 | | | Bishop, Elizabeth | | | 2 | | |
| Crane, Elisha | 1 | 1 | 6 | | | Crittenton, Soloman | 1 | | 2 | | | Hubbard, Abraham | 2 | 2 | 4 | | |
| Hand, Edmond | 2 | 2 | 1 | | | Cranton, Benjamin | 1 | | 1 | | | Parmalie, Ambrose | 1 | | 1 | | |
| Willard, Elias | 1 | 2 | 4 | | | Cranton, Edmond | 1 | | 3 | | | Stone, John | 1 | 2 | 2 | | |
| Willard, Stephen | 2 | | 1 | | | Cranton, Luther | 1 | 2 | 3 | | | Hubbard, Abraham, 2 | 1 | 1 | 1 | | |
| Willcox, Nathaniel | 2 | 2 | 5 | | | Stevens, Nathanirl | 1 | | | | | Wick, John | 1 | | 1 | | |
| Meigs, Daniel | 2 | 2 | 2 | | | Stevens, Nathaniel, 2nd | 2 | | 3 | | | Hubbard, John | 1 | 1 | 1 | | |
| Ward, Levi | 3 | | 3 | | | Scranton, Timothy | 2 | | 1 | | | Griswold, Nathaniel | 1 | 2 | 3 | | |
| Willard, Hiel | 1 | | | | | Scranton, Timothy, 2 | 1 | 3 | 1 | | | Griswold, Noah | 2 | | 2 | | |
| Hill, John | 2 | 1 | 6 | | | Dudley, David | 2 | | 1 | | | Stone, Eber | 1 | 1 | 2 | | |
| Bradley, Gillard | 2 | 1 | 3 | | | Dudley, Elizabeth | | | 4 | | | Stone, Ezra | 2 | | 2 | | |
| Bradley, Noah | 5 | 1 | 1 | | | Bishop, Sussannah | | | 2 | | | Dudley, Stephen | 3 | | | | |
| Meigs, Elish | 2 | 4 | 4 | | | Munger, Miles | 3 | 1 | 2 | | | Bishop, Nero | 1 | 2 | 2 | | |
| Hotchkiss, Thomas | 2 | | 4 | | | Munger, Cabe | 2 | 1 | 1 | | | Bishop, James | 1 | 4 | 2 | | |
| Murry, Abigal | | | 4 | | | Wheeler, Thomas | 1 | | 5 | | | Coan, John | 1 | 2 | 1 | | |
| Parmalie, Pheneas | 1 | | | | | Waikley, Ebenezer | 1 | 4 | 3 | | | Coan, John, 2nd | 1 | 1 | 2 | | |
| Meigs, Lucy | | | 2 | | | Bristol, Richard | 1 | | 2 | | | Fowler, Daniel | 1 | | 2 | | |
| Munger, Lyman | 1 | 2 | 2 | | | Chittenton, Daniel | 1 | | 1 | | | Dudley, Jerad | 1 | | 2 | | |
| Graves, Ambrose | 1 | | 3 | | | Hotchkiss, Noah | 3 | 2 | 2 | | | Dudley, Jerad, 2nd | 1 | 1 | 2 | | |
| Scranton, Josiah | 1 | 2 | 5 | | | Hopson, Amelia | | | 2 | | | Barnes, Lemuel | 1 | | 2 | | |
| Murry, Jesse | 1 | 2 | 2 | | | Hopson, John | 1 | 1 | 1 | | | Blakley, Joseph | 2 | | 5 | | |
| Murry, John | 2 | 1 | 4 | | | Norton, Noadiah | 2 | 2 | 4 | | | Roseter, William | 2 | 4 | 5 | | |
| Bishop, John | 2 | | 2 | | | Stone, Isaac | 1 | 2 | 5 | | | Fowler, Theophilus | 1 | 3 | 1 | | |
| Murry, Selah | 1 | | 1 | | | Stone, Aron, 2nd | 2 | | 1 | | | Bartlet, George | 1 | | 2 | | |
| Hill, Abraham | 1 | 1 | 2 | | | Dudley, David | 1 | | | | | Cain, Patrick | 1 | | 1 | | |
| Hill, Ruben | 1 | | 1 | | | French, Philomen | 3 | | 3 | | | Leet, Stephen | 1 | | 2 | | |
| Hill, James | 1 | 1 | 5 | | | Field, David | 1 | 2 | 2 | | | Chittenton, Simeon | 1 | 2 | 4 | | |
| Hill, Aron | 1 | 1 | 3 | | | Field, Benjamin | 1 | 3 | 1 | | | Rawlinson, Joseph | 2 | | 2 | | |
| Norton, Jesse | 1 | | 2 | | | Hill, James | 1 | 2 | 4 | | | Hill, Anna | | | 3 | | |
| Bishop, Elias | 1 | 1 | 2 | | | Cain, Latin | 1 | | 1 | | | Looper, Samuel F | 1 | | 2 | | |
| Bishop, John, 2 | 2 | | 3 | | | Richmond, Jacob | 4 | 1 | 3 | | | Looper, Samuel, 2nd | 3 | | 3 | | |
| Stannard, Elias | 1 | 5 | 4 | | | Richmond, Warner | 1 | | 2 | | | Brickwell, Zebulon | 1 | 1 | 5 | | |
| Coe, Thomas | 1 | 3 | 2 | | | Richmond, Hannah | 2 | 2 | 3 | | | Chittenten, Jerad | 1 | 3 | 3 | | |
| Willcox, Joseph | 1 | | 2 | | | Benton, Noah | 1 | | 1 | | | Chittenton, Amos | 1 | | 2 | | |
| Willcox, Joseph, 2nd | 1 | 1 | 3 | | | Dudley, Roswell | 1 | | 1 | | | Chittenton, Anson | 1 | 1 | 1 | | |
| Coe, Jedediah | 1 | | 3 | | | Johnson, Nathaniel | 1 | | 2 | | | Chittenton, Submit | | | 2 | | |
| Fenton, Israel | 1 | | 3 | | | Johnson, Benjamin | 1 | | 2 | | | Scranton, Jerad | 4 | 1 | 2 | 1 | 1 |
| Griswold, Jedidiah | 2 | | 3 | | | Spicer, Asher | 1 | 2 | 2 | | | Coan, Simeon | 1 | | | | |
| Griswold, Jedidiah, 2nd | 1 | | 3 | | | Fowler, Nathaniel | 2 | 2 | 4 | | | Philor, Joseph | 3 | | 3 | | |
| Willcox, Ezra | 3 | | 2 | | | Russell, Samuel R | 1 | | 2 | | | Fowler Ebenezer | 1 | | 1 | | |
| Wheaton, Rufus | 1 | | 3 | | | Fowler, Phineas | 2 | | 3 | | | Fowler, Caleb | | 1 | 2 | | |

99

## NEW HAVEN COUNTY—Continued.

| NAME OF HEAD OF FAMILY. | Free white males of 16 years and upward, including heads of families. | Free white males under 16 years. | Free white females, including heads of families. | All other free persons. | Slaves. | NAME OF HEAD OF FAMILY. | Free white males of 16 years and upward, including heads of families. | Free white males under 16 years. | Free white females, including heads of families. | All other free persons. | Slaves. | NAME OF HEAD OF FAMILY. | Free white males of 16 years and upward, including heads of families. | Free white males under 16 years. | Free white females, including heads of families. | All other free persons. | Slaves. |
|---|---|---|---|---|---|---|---|---|---|---|---|---|---|---|---|---|---|
| **GUILFORD TOWN—con.** | | | | | | **HAMDEN TOWN—con.** | | | | | | **HAMDEN TOWN—con.** | | | | | |
| Fowler, Oliver | 1 | | 1 | | | Martin, Samuel | 1 | 1 | 2 | | | Tuttle, Enos | 1 | | 1 | | |
| Collins, Daniel | 1 | 1 | 1 | | | Tuttle, Aron | 1 | 2 | 3 | | | Tuttle, Enos | 1 | 2 | 1 | | |
| Collins, Samuel | 1 | | | | | Cooke, Samuel | 1 | | 4 | | | Galend, Benjamin | 1 | | 1 | | |
| Collins, Ruth | | | 2 | 1 | 1 | Gilbert, Grigson | 1 | | 4 | | | Galend, Benjamin, 2nd | 1 | 2 | 4 | | |
| Collins, Augustus | 3 | 4 | 4 | | | Andrus, Samuel | 1 | 2 | 2 | | | Ives, Thomas | 1 | 1 | 2 | | |
| Stone, John | 3 | | 6 | | | Mix, Caleb | 2 | 1 | 3 | | | Tuttle, Hezekiah | 2 | | 4 | | |
| Grave, Benjamin | 3 | | 5 | | | Carrington, Elener | | | 1 | | | Perkins, Aron | 1 | | 1 | | |
| Grave, Abraham | 3 | | 4 | | | Brooks, Benjamin | 1 | 2 | 2 | | | Doolittle, Caleb | 3 | 1 | 3 | | |
| Griffin, Robert | 1 | | 2 | | | Munson, Joshua | 1 | | 2 | | | Perkins, John | 1 | 2 | 5 | | |
| Grave, Daniel | 1 | | 3 | | | Benham, Joseph | 2 | 2 | 3 | | | Sperry, John | 1 | 1 | 2 | | |
| Fowler, Ebenezer | 1 | 3 | 3 | | | Johnson, Noah | 1 | 1 | 1 | | | Bradley, Jason | 4 | 2 | 4 | | |
| Russell, Ebenezer | 1 | | 3 | | | Basett, James | 2 | 1 | 4 | | | Alling, Mabel | | | 3 | | |
| Rose, Joel | 1 | 2 | 4 | | | Wooden, Lidia | 1 | | 3 | | | Alling, Nathaniel | 3 | 1 | 1 | | |
| McCane, Barnabas | 1 | 4 | 6 | | | Hinton, Nathaniel | 3 | | 3 | | | Peck, Jesse | 1 | 1 | 1 | | |
| Atkins, Samuel | 1 | | 1 | | | Leek, Thomas | 1 | | 1 | | | Alling, Eli | 1 | | 1 | | |
| Dibble, Simus, 2nd | 1 | | 2 | | | Leek, Thomas, 2nd | 1 | 1 | 3 | | | Peck, Mosses | 1 | 1 | 4 | | |
| Bassett, Henry | 1 | | 2 | | | Alling, Joseph | 1 | | 1 | | | Alling, Nathaniel, 2nd | 1 | 1 | 3 | | |
| Fowler, Jonathan | 3 | | 3 | | | Chrittenton, Jerry | 3 | 1 | 2 | | | Spencer, Jabez | 2 | | 4 | | |
| Fowler, Joiner | 2 | 2 | 4 | | | Mansfield, J | 2 | 4 | 4 | | | Chatterton, Abraham | 1 | | 3 | | |
| Fowler, Josiah 2 | 1 | 2 | 6 | | | Cooper, Alling | 1 | 1 | 2 | | | Chatterton, Daniel | 1 | | 1 | | |
| Elliott, Timothy | 3 | 3 | 2 | | | Attwater, Samuel, 2nd | 1 | 2 | 6 | | | Chatterton, David | 1 | | 1 | | |
| Bishop, Ezra | 1 | | | | | Goodyear, Jesse | 2 | 1 | 4 | | | Hitchcock, Stephen | 2 | | 4 | | |
| Tyler, Molly | | | 1 | | | Goodyear, Theophilus | 3 | | 2 | | | Peck, Amos | 3 | | 4 | | |
| Dudley, Abigal | | | 1 | | | Goodyear, Titus | 1 | 2 | 3 | | | Roberts, Ebenezer | 1 | 1 | 1 | | |
| Bails, Deborah | | | 1 | | | Cooper, Beedy | 1 | | 1 | | | Munson, Ezra | 1 | | 4 | | |
| Stone, Osborne | 1 | 4 | 3 | | | Attwater, Samuel | 1 | | 3 | | | Peck, Joseph | 1 | | 3 | | |
| Bishop, Timothy | 3 | | 2 | | | Pardy, Joseph | 1 | | 2 | | | Hitchcock, Lidia | 1 | | 2 | | |
| Bishop, Ruben | 2 | 1 | 3 | | | Bradley, Eli | 2 | | 4 | | | Andrews, John | 1 | 1 | 5 | | |
| Fowler, Soloman | 1 | 2 | 3 | | | Pardie, Thomas | 1 | | 1 | | | Hitchcock, Samuel | 1 | 2 | 3 | | |
| Wright, Daniel | 1 | | 1 | | | Attwater, Caleb | 1 | 4 | 2 | | | Hitchcock, Jabez | 1 | 1 | 2 | | |
| | | | | | | Thompson, Henry | 1 | 3 | 4 | | | Attwater, Eneas | 1 | 2 | 4 | | |
| **HAMDEN TOWN.** | | | | | | Bassett, Hezekiah | 3 | 3 | 6 | | | Thomas, Isaac | 3 | 2 | 2 | | |
| Attwater, Medad | 1 | 2 | 4 | | | Seely, Isaac | 1 | 2 | 2 | | | Bradley, Elven | 2 | 2 | 3 | | |
| Attwater, Abigal | | 1 | 3 | | | Bassett, Mabel | | | 5 | | | Attwater, Jacob | 3 | | 1 | | |
| Attwater, Louis | | | 2 | | | Alling, Elisha | 1 | 1 | 5 | | | Ives, Ezra | 2 | 3 | 5 | | |
| Attwater, Joshua | 1 | 4 | 4 | | | Ives, Jonathan | 1 | | 1 | | | Warner, Abigal | | | 2 | | |
| Howell, Nicholas | 3 | | 3 | | | Ives, Jonathan, 2nd | 1 | 1 | 2 | | | Goodyear, Stephen | 2 | 1 | 4 | | |
| Attwater, David | 1 | 1 | 3 | | | Ives, Elam | 1 | | 1 | | | Leek, Timothy | 2 | | 1 | | |
| Attwater, Jerad | 1 | 2 | 1 | | | Ives, James | 3 | | 2 | | | Leek, Timothy, 2nd | 1 | 2 | 2 | | |
| Turner, Jabez | 2 | 4 | 2 | | | Pardie, Stephen | 2 | 2 | 3 | | | Dickerman, Jonathan, 2nd | 1 | 2 | 5 | | |
| Potter, Timothy, 2nd | 1 | 1 | 4 | | | Hotchkiss, Phebe | | | 2 | | | Andrus, Caleb | 1 | | 1 | | |
| Turner, Abraham | 1 | 1 | 1 | | | Dickerman, Hezekiah | 1 | 3 | 2 | | | Leek, Daniel | 1 | | 2 | | |
| Turner, Elisha | 1 | 1 | 1 | | | Bradley, Levi | 1 | 2 | 2 | | | Warner, David | 1 | 4 | 3 | | |
| Turner, Gurden | 2 | 4 | 5 | | | Gilbert, Joseph | 1 | 1 | 5 | | | Goodyear, Asa | 1 | | | | |
| Potter, Philomon | 3 | 3 | 2 | | | Goodyear, Timothy | 2 | 4 | 3 | | | Goodyear, Asa, 2nd | 1 | 1 | 5 | | |
| Cooper, Abraham, 2nd | 1 | 1 | 2 | | | Gilbert, Abraham | 1 | | 2 | | | Sugden, Lidia | 1 | | 3 | | |
| Potter, Joseph | 2 | 1 | 4 | | | Gilbert, Abraham, 2nd | 1 | 2 | 2 | | | Bassett, Timothy | 2 | 2 | 1 | | |
| Mansfield, Ebenezer | 2 | | 4 | | | Dickerman, Amos | 1 | | 2 | | | Wolcott, Noah | 4 | 1 | 5 | | |
| Potter, Timothy | 2 | 1 | 3 | | | Dickerman, Jonathan | 2 | | 2 | | | Alling, David | 1 | | 1 | | |
| Gilbert, Joseph | 2 | | 1 | | | Chapman, Elisha | 2 | 1 | 2 | | | Alling, Medad | 2 | | 1 | | |
| Potter, Chauncy | 1 | 1 | 1 | | | Bellamy, Samuel | 2 | | 2 | | 1 | Warner, Hezekiah | 3 | 3 | 2 | | |
| Marsen, Stephen | 1 | 1 | 3 | | | Dickerman, James | 2 | 1 | 3 | | | Warner, Benjamin | 1 | | 3 | | |
| Mencer, William | 1 | 1 | 1 | | | Kimberly, Ezra | 3 | 2 | 3 | | | Warner, Ebenezer | 2 | | 6 | | |
| Potter, Medad | 1 | | 2 | | | Hubbard, Joseph | 3 | 1 | 1 | | | Warner, Amos | 1 | | | | |
| Ball, Oliver | 1 | | 5 | | | Todd, Abner | 3 | 1 | 4 | | | Warner, Jesse | 1 | | 4 | | |
| Gill, John | 1 | 2 | 3 | | | Dickerman, Chauncy | 3 | 3 | 5 | | | Warner, Samuel | 1 | | | | |
| Gill, John, 2nd | 1 | | | | | Willis, Sarah | | | 2 | | | Warner, Ebenezer, 2nd | 1 | | | | |
| Hummiston, Samuel | 1 | 4 | 5 | | | Miles, Simeon | 1 | | 4 | | | Bradley, Gamaliel | 2 | 2 | 4 | | |
| Gill, Ebenezer M | 1 | 1 | 2 | | | Todd, Bethuel | 1 | | 1 | | | Crosby, Gad | 1 | | | | |
| Mansfield, Titus | 3 | | 2 | | | Munson, Justice | 1 | | 4 | | 1 | Pardie, Joel | 1 | | 1 | | |
| Tuttle, Daniel | 1 | | 2 | | | Munson, Bazael | 2 | | 3 | | | Goodyear, Gerad | 1 | | | | |
| Peckham, George | 1 | | 1 | | | Bishop, Nathaniel | 1 | 1 | 1 | | | Doolittle, Easter | | | 2 | | |
| Peckham, George, 2nd | 2 | | 2 | | | Gilbert, John | 2 | | 2 | | | Bracket, Hezekiah | 1 | 3 | 1 | | |
| Talmash, Daniel | 1 | | 3 | | | Beach, Asa | 1 | | 2 | | | Bristol (Negroe) | | | | 4 | |
| Tolmap, Daniel, 2nd | 1 | 3 | 5 | | | McDonald, Abigail | | 1 | 1 | | | Wolcott, H | | | 2 | | |
| Ford, Stephen | 1 | 3 | 5 | | | Dudley, Mercy | | | 1 | | | Andrus, Caleb | 1 | | 1 | | |
| Potter, Jesse | 1 | | 5 | | | Dickerman, Loley | 1 | 2 | 5 | | | Warner, Jonah | 1 | 1 | 2 | | |
| Potter, David | 1 | 1 | 3 | | | Dickerman, John | 1 | 2 | 3 | | | Potter, Amos | 1 | | 2 | | |
| Potter, David | 1 | | 1 | | | Doolittle, Titus | 1 | 1 | 6 | | | Hitchcock, Ebenezur | 2 | 1 | 3 | | |
| Potter, Abel | 1 | 1 | 2 | | | Johnson, Joseph | 2 | 3 | 8 | | | Hinton, Joseph | 1 | 1 | 1 | | |
| Ford, Joel | 2 | | 1 | | | Johnson, Joseph, 2nd | 1 | | 2 | | | Johnson, Timothy | 1 | 2 | 4 | | |
| Gilbert, Moses | 2 | 1 | 1 | | | Tuttle, Joatham | 1 | 2 | 2 | | | Alling, Joel | 1 | | | | |
| Cooper, Abraham | 1 | | 1 | | | Tuttle, Joel | 1 | 2 | 1 | | | Alling, Abraham | 1 | 1 | 5 | | |
| Basset, Theophilus | 1 | 1 | 2 | | | Tuttle, Abigal | | | 1 | | | Dorman, Benjamin | 1 | 2 | 3 | | |
| Basset, John | 1 | | 1 | | | Dickerman, Isaac | 2 | 3 | 3 | | | Dorman, Daniel | 1 | 3 | 2 | | |
| Basset, Amos | 1 | 2 | 3 | | | Frisbie, Luman | 2 | 3 | 3 | | | Gorham, Susanah | 1 | 1 | 4 | | |
| Ford, Moses | 2 | | 3 | | | Bennet, Ebenezer | | 3 | 1 | | | Smith, Abraham | 1 | 1 | 2 | | |
| Potter, Job | 1 | 3 | 7 | | | Munson, Job | 1 | 3 | 2 | | | Hitchcock, Ebenezur, 2nd | 1 | 1 | 4 | | |
| Humiston, Joseph | 2 | 2 | 3 | | | Mansfield, Hannah | | | 1 | | | Hummiston, David | 1 | 2 | 2 | | |
| Potter, Thomas | 1 | 3 | 3 | | | Bradley, Amassa | 1 | 4 | 1 | | | Munson, Isaac | 1 | 2 | 3 | | |
| Ford, Jonathan | 2 | 4 | 3 | | | Haush, Joseph | 1 | | 1 | | | Alling, Charles | 2 | 2 | 3 | | |
| Talmap, Hannah | | 3 | 2 | | | Bristol, Simeon | 1 | 2 | 3 | | 1 | Alling, Caleb | 1 | 3 | 8 | | |
| Howell, Nicholas | 1 | | | | | Bristol, George A | 1 | 2 | 2 | | | Hitchcock, Lidia | | | 3 | | |
| Carrington, Elizabeth | | 1 | 1 | | | Rice, Elisha | 1 | 2 | 1 | | | Munson, Jabez | 1 | 3 | 2 | | |
| Turner, Timothy | 1 | 1 | 1 | | | Attwater, Stephen | 2 | 1 | 5 | | | Munson, Eunice | 1 | | | | |
| Ford, Jonah | 1 | | 1 | | | Bradley, Aron | 2 | 1 | 1 | | | Munson, Levi | 1 | 1 | 3 | | |
| Potter, Moses | 3 | 2 | 4 | | | Bradley, Daniel | 1 | | 3 | | | Denshy, William | 2 | | 2 | | |
| Blakesley, Deborah | | | 3 | | | Bradley, Daniel, 2nd | 1 | 5 | 3 | | | Denshy, Eli | 2 | 1 | 2 | | |
| Tuttle, Jabez | 2 | 5 | 3 | | | Bradley, Joel | 2 | 2 | 2 | | 1 | Dorman, Joseph | 1 | | 1 | | |
| Tuttle, Aexander | 1 | 1 | 3 | | | Bradley, Jabez | 1 | | 2 | | | Dorman, Roger | 1 | 1 | 3 | | |
| Bassett, Abel | 2 | | 3 | | | Perkins, Elish | 2 | 1 | 6 | | | Dorman, Stephen | 1 | | | | |
| Todd, Job | 2 | 4 | 5 | | | Ives, Andrew | 1 | | 1 | | | Dorman, John | 1 | 2 | 2 | | |
| Todd, Joel | 3 | 1 | 5 | | | Bradley, Amos | 2 | 1 | 4 | | | Munson, David | 1 | 2 | 2 | | |
| Ives, Alling | 1 | 2 | 2 | | | Brooks, Abijah | 1 | | 2 | | | Boath, Jonathan | 1 | | 1 | | |
| | | | | | | Brooks, Louis | 1 | | 1 | | | | | | | | |

# HEADS OF FAMILIES—CONNECTICUT.

**NEW HAVEN COUNTY**—Continued.

| NAME OF HEAD OF FAMILY. | Free white males of 16 years and upward, including heads of families. | Free white males under 16 years. | Free white females, including heads of families. | All other free persons. | Slaves. | NAME OF HEAD OF FAMILY. | Free white males of 16 years and upward, including heads of families. | Free white males under 16 years. | Free white females, including heads of families. | All other free persons. | Slaves. | NAME OF HEAD OF FAMILY. | Free white males of 16 years and upward, including heads of families. | Free white males under 16 years. | Free white females, including heads of families. | All other free persons. | Slaves. |
|---|---|---|---|---|---|---|---|---|---|---|---|---|---|---|---|---|---|
| **HAMDEN TOWN**—con. | | | | | | **MILFORD TOWN**—con. | | | | | | **MILFORD TOWN**—con. | | | | | |
| Boath, Alexander | 1 | 1 | 1 | | | Fowler, Nathaniel | 2 | | 2 | | | Jillet, Eliphalet | 1 | | 1 | | |
| Boath, Elisha | 1 | | 1 | | | Fowler, Anna | 1 | 1 | 1 | | | Baldwin, Thadeus | 1 | 1 | 4 | 1 | |
| Maneer, John | 1 | 1 | 2 | | | Hoods, Catherine | | | 1 | | | Baldwin, Abraham | 2 | | 3 | | |
| Wooden, Isaac | 1 | 1 | 2 | | | Jones, Isaac | 3 | 3 | 4 | 1 | | Ceaser (Negroe) | | | | 3 | |
| Andrews, Timothy | 1 | | 2 | | | Lawrence, Katey | | 1 | 3 | | | Whitney, Isaac | 1 | | 3 | | |
| Gilbert, Asa | 1 | 1 | 3 | | | Miles, John | 4 | | 5 | | | Prime (Negroe) | | | | 2 | |
| Tuttle, Amos | 1 | | 2 | | | Green, Sarah | 1 | | 1 | | | Wetmore, Joseph | 1 | | | | |
| Gilbert, Daniel | 1 | 4 | 3 | | | Clarke, Mary | | | 2 | | | Beebie, Joel | 1 | | 2 | | |
| Gilbert, Mathew | 1 | | 1 | | | Jones, John | 1 | | 1 | | | Plumb, John | 2 | 3 | 4 | | |
| Wooden, Jaben | 1 | | 1 | | | Woods, Titus | 1 | 1 | 4 | | | Anderson, Atiny | 1 | 1 | 1 | | |
| Reed, Peter | 1 | 1 | 2 | | | Fowler, John | 1 | 1 | 2 | | | Prime (Negroe) | | | | 6 | |
| Alling, Icabod | 1 | 2 | 1 | | | Platt, Jiremiah | 4 | | 2 | | | Miles, Theophilus | 1 | 1 | 3 | | 1 |
| Alling, Desire | 1 | 1 | 3 | | | Buckingham, John | 2 | 2 | 3 | 2 | | Bull, Jeremiah | 1 | | 2 | | |
| Mix, Thomas | 1 | 2 | 3 | | | Buckingham, Gedion | 2 | 2 | 2 | 2 | | Baldwin, Isaac | 1 | 1 | 3 | | |
| Bassett, James | 1 | 1 | 1 | | | Bradley, Israel | 2 | 6 | 2 | | | Mallery, Daniel | 2 | 3 | 3 | | 1 |
| Jones, Pratt | 1 | 1 | 1 | | | Goldsmith, Joseph | 1 | | 2 | | | Baldwin, Jeremiah | 3 | | 4 | | |
| Dickerman, Louis | | | 2 | | | Donalds, Samuel | 1 | | 1 | | | Baldwin, David | 1 | | 1 | | |
| Dickerman, Hezekiah | 1 | | 2 | | | James (Negroe) | | | | 3 | | Attwater, William | 1 | 4 | 7 | | |
| Dickerman, Joseph | 1 | | 1 | | | Higby, Samuel | 2 | | 4 | | | Baldwin, Isaac, 2nd | 1 | | 2 | | |
| Wooden, Nathaniel | 2 | 1 | 2 | | | Plumb, Samuel | 1 | | 1 | | | Gowsley, William | 1 | | 1 | | |
| Wooden, Hannah | 1 | | 3 | | | Wise, Samuel | 1 | 1 | 3 | | | Gunn, Isaac | 1 | | 2 | | |
| Leforgess, Henry | 1 | 3 | 5 | | | Pry (Negroe) | | | | 6 | | Clarke, William | 3 | 2 | 6 | | |
| Wooden, Benjamin | 1 | 3 | 3 | | | Mallery, Mosses | 1 | 1 | 1 | | | Northrop, Lazerus | 1 | | | | |
| Hummiston, Nathaniel | 2 | | 1 | | | Clarke, Andrew | 2 | 1 | 4 | | | Camp, David | 1 | 2 | 3 | | |
| Attwater, Icabod | 1 | 2 | 2 | | | Britton, Newton | 1 | 1 | 3 | | 1 | Ford, Amos | 1 | 2 | 1 | | |
| Cooper, Samuel | 2 | 5 | 2 | | | Lockwood, William | 1 | | 3 | 1 | | Bisco, Ruth | | | 1 | | 1 |
| Cooper, Timothy | 3 | | 2 | | | Carrington, Edward | 2 | 2 | 5 | 1 | | Baldwin, Elnathan | 1 | 2 | 2 | | |
| Gilbert, Amos | 1 | 2 | 2 | | | Sheldon, Hannah | | | 2 | | | Tomlinson, William | 1 | | 3 | | |
| Gilbert, James | 1 | | 5 | | | Sears, Francis | 1 | | 3 | | | Nettleton, Caleb | 2 | 2 | 3 | | |
| Alling, Roger | 1 | 2 | 2 | | | Ingersall, Clement | 1 | | 2 | | | Stow, Jedediah | 1 | 3 | 2 | | |
| Hubbard, John | 2 | 4 | 3 | | | Green, Anna | | | 2 | 1 | | Baldwin, Advice | | | 2 | | |
| Dorman, Samuel | 1 | 2 | 1 | | | Glenny, William | 1 | | 3 | | | Baldwin, Elisha | 1 | | | | |
| Attwater, Zopher | 1 | 1 | 4 | | | Mallet, Lewis | 3 | 1 | 3 | | | Baldwin, Nathan | 3 | | 4 | | |
| Hotchkiss, Daniel | 1 | 2 | 2 | | | Miles, Tilla | 1 | 1 | 1 | | | Baldwin, Eliph | 1 | 1 | 3 | | 1 |
| Thomas, Caleb | 1 | 2 | 3 | | | Hepborn, Peter | 4 | 2 | 5 | | | Tibbalds, Arnold | 1 | | 2 | | |
| Whitty, John | 1 | | 1 | | | Perit, Peter | 1 | | 1 | | | Clarke, Jonathan | 1 | 1 | 2 | | |
| Demmons, Charles | 1 | | 1 | | | Davidson, James | 3 | | 2 | | | Tibbalds, Benedick | 1 | 2 | 3 | | |
| Ford, Daniel | 1 | | | | | Fowler, Nathaniel, 2nd | 1 | | 2 | | | Tibbalds, Samuel | 1 | 4 | 1 | | |
| Ford, Edward | 1 | | | | | Bristow, John | 1 | | 1 | | | Baldwin, Nathan, 2nd | 1 | 2 | 2 | | |
| Cooper, F | | | 1 | | | Bryant, Joseph | 1 | | | | | Bard, Abigel | | | 1 | 1 | |
| | | | | | | Galbin, Benjamin | 1 | | | | | Mills, David | 1 | 2 | 3 | | |
| **MILFORD TOWN.** | | | | | | Mallery, Moses | 2 | 1 | | | | Smith, Joel | 1 | 2 | 3 | | |
| Jellet, John | 3 | 1 | 1 | | | Bino, Watham | 1 | | 3 | | | Clarke, Joseph | 1 | 1 | 3 | | |
| Clarke, William | 1 | 3 | 3 | | | Sacket, Daniel | 1 | | 2 | | 1 | Camp, Ezra | 1 | 1 | 4 | 1 | 1 |
| Marren, John | 1 | 2 | 3 | | 3 | Stow, Samuel | 2 | | 1 | | | Ovet, Isaac | 1 | | 2 | | |
| Sadley, John | 1 | 1 | 1 | | | Dickenson, Sylvanus | 1 | 2 | 3 | 2 | | Clarke, Abraham | 1 | 1 | 4 | | 1 |
| Bens, Juno | 1 | | | | | Harpin, John | 1 | | 1 | | 1 | Collins, John | 2 | | 1 | | |
| Baldwin, Soloman | 1 | 1 | 1 | | | Baldwin, Phineas | 1 | 1 | 3 | | | Tibbalds, David | 1 | 3 | 2 | | |
| Baldwin, Daniel | 1 | | 1 | | | Stow, William | 1 | 1 | 2 | | | Camp, Mary | 1 | | 1 | | |
| Platt, Isaac | 1 | 3 | 3 | | | Barn, Andrew | 1 | 2 | 6 | | | Bard, Andrew | 1 | 2 | 2 | | |
| Purtree, John | 2 | 1 | 7 | | | Murren, David | 1 | 3 | 7 | | | Turrel, Samuel | 1 | | 3 | | |
| Plumb, Isaac | 1 | | 7 | | | Jellet, Zebulon | 2 | 1 | 3 | | | Turrel, David | 1 | | 1 | | |
| Bush, Lindie | 2 | | 2 | | | Davidson, Joseph | 1 | 1 | 1 | | | Clarke, Abel | 1 | | 3 | | |
| Beach, Thomas | 1 | 2 | 3 | | | De Witt, Garret | 1 | 2 | 3 | | 5 | Hine, Samuel | 2 | 4 | 2 | | |
| Burrel, Samuel | 2 | | | | | Coggeshall, William | 1 | 4 | 3 | | 2 | Tibbalds, Lemuel | 1 | 1 | 4 | | |
| Burrel, Samuel, 2nd | 1 | 2 | 2 | | | Bull, Henry | 1 | 2 | 3 | | | Baldwin, Josiah | 1 | 2 | 5 | | |
| Jellet, John, 2nd | 1 | 2 | 3 | | | Lartherbie, William | 2 | 1 | 1 | | | Northrop, Moses | 1 | | 3 | 1 | |
| Bunnel, John | 1 | 5 | 1 | | | Pond, Charles | 1 | 3 | 5 | | 2 | Smith, Hezekiah | 2 | 1 | 2 | | |
| Pritchard, Nathaniel | 1 | | 1 | | | Tomlinson, Abraham | 3 | | 3 | | | Smith, Caleb | 3 | 3 | 5 | | |
| Burrel, Jeremiah | 1 | 2 | 3 | | | Baldwin, Asbell | 3 | 1 | 4 | | | Bim, David | 2 | 4 | 3 | | 1 |
| Burrel, Daniel | 1 | 2 | 3 | | | Smith, Mary | 1 | | 4 | | | Camp, Elias | 2 | 3 | 3 | | |
| Beech, Thadeus | 1 | | 5 | | | Arnold, Abigal | | | 2 | | | Hine, George | 1 | | 1 | | |
| Beech, Samuel | 1 | 1 | 1 | | | Coggshall, Freegitt | 1 | | | | | Basset, Samuel | 1 | 3 | 3 | | |
| Parker, James | 1 | | 1 | | | De Wint, Garret N | 1 | | 1 | | | OCain, Antony | 1 | | 2 | | |
| Plump, Joseph | 1 | | | | | De Wint, Abraham N | 1 | | | | | Bassett, Samuel, 2nd | 2 | | 2 | | |
| Plump, Joseph, 2nd | 1 | 2 | 2 | 1 | | Tebbalds, James | 1 | | 1 | | | Bassett, David | 1 | 3 | 1 | | |
| Murrain, Miles | 1 | 5 | 3 | | 1 | Nettleton, Nathaniel | 1 | | 1 | | | Ovett, Ebenezer | 1 | | 6 | | |
| Ellis, Samuel | 1 | | 1 | | | Goldsmith, Gilbert | 1 | | 2 | | | Smith, Ebenezer | 1 | 2 | 3 | | |
| Ellis, Samuel, 2nd | 1 | | 2 | | | Baldwin, Heil | 3 | 2 | 4 | | | Peck, Abraham | 1 | 1 | 3 | | |
| Ellis, Hester | | | 1 | | | Perit, Peter | 2 | 1 | 1 | | | Northrop, Heth | 1 | 3 | 2 | | |
| Ellis, Sibel | | 1 | 2 | | | Mallet John | 1 | 1 | 1 | | | Nettleton, Thaddeus | 2 | 1 | 1 | | |
| Murdock, William | 1 | | | | | Vanduser, Thomas | 1 | 2 | 2 | | | Ovett, Nathan | 1 | | 1 | | |
| Pritchard, Nathaniel | 1 | | 3 | | | Hicock, Aron | 1 | | 1 | | | Mallery, Aron | 1 | 3 | 3 | | |
| Whiting, John | 2 | 1 | 1 | | | Gilbert, Katey | | | 1 | | | Basett, Isaac | 1 | 1 | 1 | | |
| Murren, Mary | 1 | | 2 | | 1 | Stow, Freelove | | | 1 | | | Bawley, John | 1 | | 2 | | |
| Clarke, Rebecca | | | 2 | | | Stow, Stephen | 1 | 3 | 4 | | | Clarke, Joseph | 1 | 2 | 3 | | 1 |
| Clarke, Amos | 1 | 1 | 3 | | | Stow, John | 1 | 3 | 1 | | | Peck, Benjamin | 2 | | 2 | | |
| Platt, Hannah | 2 | 2 | 3 | | | Thompson, James | 1 | | 1 | | | Hine, David | 1 | 3 | 3 | | |
| Clarke, Samuel | 2 | 3 | 2 | | 1 | Ball, Benedah | 3 | 1 | 3 | | | Beers, Benjamin | 1 | | | | |
| Smith, Isaac | 3 | 1 | 3 | | 2 | Bull, Temperance | | | 1 | | | Beers, John | 1 | 1 | 1 | | |
| Platt, Joseph | 1 | 1 | 2 | | | Miles, Daniel | 2 | 2 | 3 | | | Tuttle, Andrew | 1 | | 1 | | |
| Davinson, William | 1 | 3 | 3 | | | Goldsmith, William | 1 | | 4 | | | Tuttle, Andrew, 2nd | 1 | | 1 | | |
| Nott, William | 1 | | 3 | | | Goldsmith, James | 1 | | 1 | | | Ford, John | 1 | 1 | 5 | | |
| Jellet, Benjamin | 1 | 3 | 2 | | | Goldsmith, James, 2nd | 1 | 3 | 2 | | | Ford, John, 2nd | 1 | | 1 | | |
| Strong, John | 1 | | 2 | | | Beardsley, John | 1 | | 1 | | | Ford, Thomas | 1 | 1 | 4 | | |
| Trant, Philo | 2 | 2 | 3 | | | Gray, William | 1 | 2 | 1 | | | Ford, Thomas | 1 | | 2 | | |
| Bryan, Oliver | 1 | | 4 | | | Stevens, Eliphalet | 1 | 4 | 1 | | | Botchford, David | 2 | | 1 | | |
| Pond, Elizabeth | | | 3 | | | Tebbalds, Arnold | 1 | 3 | 3 | | | Botchford, Eli | 1 | 1 | 1 | | |
| Camp, Joab | 1 | 2 | 1 | | | Marchant, Ezra | 1 | | 2 | | | Peck, Samuel | 2 | | 2 | | |
| Woodruk, Barnabas | 2 | | 2 | | | Gibbs John | 1 | | 3 | | | Peck, Stephen | 2 | 1 | 1 | | |
| Sandford, John | 1 | | 1 | | | Smith, Joseph | 1 | 1 | 1 | | | Gunn, Stephen | 2 | | 2 | | |
| Sandford, Elisha | 1 | 1 | 6 | | | Camp, Samuel | 1 | 3 | 1 | | | Baldwin, Amos | 1 | | 1 | | |
| Wolcott, John | 1 | 2 | 4 | | | Camp, Hail | 1 | | 1 | | | Baldwin, Edward | 1 | | 3 | | |
| Sandford, Mother | 1 | 2 | 4 | | | Peck, John | 1 | 2 | 2 | | | Peck, Michael | 1 | 6 | 4 | | |
| | | | | | | Covert, Elerick | 3 | 1 | 2 | | | Smith, Jeremiah | 1 | 2 | 1 | | |

# FIRST CENSUS OF THE UNITED STATES.

## NEW HAVEN COUNTY—Continued.

| NAME OF HEAD OF FAMILY. | Free white males of 16 years and upward, including heads of families. | Free white males under 16 years. | Free white females, including heads of families. | All other free persons. | Slaves. | NAME OF HEAD OF FAMILY. | Free white males of 16 years and upward, including heads of families. | Free white males under 16 years. | Free white females, including heads of families. | All other free persons. | Slaves. | NAME OF HEAD OF FAMILY. | Free white males of 16 years and upward, including heads of families. | Free white males under 16 years. | Free white females, including heads of families. | All other free persons. | Slaves. |
|---|---|---|---|---|---|---|---|---|---|---|---|---|---|---|---|---|---|
| **MILFORD TOWN—con.** | | | | | | **MILFORD TOWN—con.** | | | | | | **MILFORD TOWN—con.** | | | | | |
| Carrington, Elias | 2 | 2 | 4 | | 1 | Treat, Jonathan | 1 | | 2 | | | Stevens, Thomas | 2 | | 3 | | |
| Higgins, Timothy | 3 | 1 | 5 | | | Fenn, Sarah | | 2 | 2 | | | Lambert, David | 3 | 2 | 4 | | |
| Hine, Joel | 3 | | 4 | | | Priden, Samuel | 1 | 3 | 3 | | | Trussell, Elizabeth | 1 | | 1 | | |
| Martin, Susannah | | | 1 | | | Woodruff, Joseph | 2 | 1 | 4 | | | Ben (Negroe) | | | | 6 | |
| Marchant, Mary | | | 2 | | | Platt, Joseph | 1 | 1 | 3 | | | Buckingham, Isaac | 1 | | 1 | | |
| Nettleton, Samuel | 1 | | 1 | | | Mallery, Samuel | 2 | | 5 | | | Pardy, Josiah | 1 | 2 | 7 | | |
| Fern, Mary | | 1 | 2 | | | Treat, Daniel | 3 | 1 | 3 | | | Woodruff, Mather | 2 | 1 | 5 | | |
| Clarke, Elizabeth | 2 | | 2 | | | Bukingham, Ephraim | 1 | 2 | 2 | | | Prindle, Josep | 1 | | 2 | | |
| Buckingham, Daniel | 1 | 2 | 3 | | 2 | Strong, Elnathan | 1 | | 1 | | | Lambeth, David, 2nd | 1 | 1 | 2 | | |
| Talmage, Ezra | 1 | | 1 | | | Stone, Samuel | 2 | 3 | 3 | | | Sacket, Jonathan | 1 | | | | |
| Strong, Ephrahim | 1 | | 1 | | | Clarke, Isaac | 1 | 1 | 5 | | 1 | Donnalds, Samuel, 2nd | 1 | | 1 | | |
| Strong, Ephrahim | 1 | 1 | 3 | | | Andrews, Charlotte | | 1 | 2 | | 1 | Isbel, Sarah | | | 2 | | |
| Marshal, Joseph | 2 | | 1 | | | Nettleton, Benijah | 1 | | 2 | | | Law, Jonathan | 1 | | 1 | | |
| Marshall, John | 1 | 1 | 3 | | | Fenn, Aron | 1 | | 2 | | | Ovet, Hannah | | | 2 | | |
| Northrop, Clement | 1 | 1 | 6 | | | Platt, Richard | 3 | 1 | 2 | | | | | | | | |
| Deering, Samuel | 2 | | 3 | | | Hine, Stephen | 1 | 1 | 2 | | 1 | **NEW HAVEN CITY.** | | | | | |
| Deering, Andrew | 1 | | | | | Woodruff, Phebe | | | 1 | 1 | | Plymate, William | 1 | 2 | 3 | | |
| Deering, John | 1 | 6 | 1 | | | Joe (Negroe) | | | | 4 | | Prinale, Charles | 2 | 1 | 5 | | |
| Deering, Ann | 2 | | 3 | | | Platt, Samuel | 2 | | 3 | | 1 | Cooke, David | 1 | | 2 | | |
| Clarke, Patty | 1 | | 1 | | | Platt, Sibel | 2 | | 1 | | | Hood, William | 1 | | 1 | | |
| Clarke, David | 2 | 4 | 4 | | | Clarke, Nathan | 2 | | 2 | | | Bonticon, Sussanah | | | 2 | | |
| Burk, John | 1 | | | | | Hine, Isaac | 1 | 1 | 3 | | | Sherman, Molly | | | 1 | | |
| Bristor, Elizabeth | | | 2 | | | Hine, Abraham | 1 | 1 | 5 | | | Jocelin, Simeon | 1 | | 2 | | |
| Sommers, Abel, 2 | 1 | 1 | 1 | | | Fenn, James | 3 | 1 | 1 | | | Bishop, Israel | 1 | 2 | 5 | | |
| Ashborn, Abigal | | | 1 | | | Bassett, Edward | 1 | 1 | 5 | | | Ells, Joseph | 1 | 1 | 2 | | |
| Bristol, Philco | 3 | 2 | 3 | | | Steward, John | 1 | 2 | 2 | | | Davis, Solomon, Junr | 1 | 1 | 1 | | |
| Hatch, Daniel | 1 | 4 | 3 | | | Pridden, John | 1 | 1 | 3 | | | Hitchcock, Samuel | 1 | 2 | 3 | | |
| Newton, John | 1 | 1 | 8 | | | Priden, Fletcher | 2 | | 5 | | | Bonticon, Susanah | 1 | 1 | 2 | | |
| Treat, Isaac | 2 | | 3 | | | Baldwin, Jerad | 2 | 3 | 3 | | | Bonticon, James | 1 | | | | |
| Clarke, Enoch | 1 | | 2 | | 1 | Pritchard, Isaac | 1 | 1 | 2 | | | Story, Nathaniel | 2 | 2 | 3 | | |
| Prudden, Jonathan | 1 | 1 | 2 | | | Pond, Peter | 1 | | 1 | | | Lyman, Mary | | | 3 | | |
| Clarke, Neahb | 1 | 1 | 2 | | | Tuller, David | 1 | | 2 | | | Covert, Samuel | 3 | 1 | 2 | | |
| Treat, Joseph | 2 | | 1 | | 2 | Colbrith, John | 2 | | 1 | | | Higby, Cheney | 1 | | 2 | | |
| Treat, Isaac | 1 | 1 | 2 | | | Downs, John, 2nd | 2 | 2 | 3 | | | Hopkins, Thomas | 3 | 1 | 2 | | |
| Treat, Robert | 1 | | 2 | | | Downs, John | 1 | | 1 | | | Hunt, Fredrick | 2 | 6 | 2 | | |
| Storer, Joseph | 1 | 2 | 3 | | | Bristol, David | 1 | | 1 | | | Stilman, Benjamin | 1 | 2 | 2 | | |
| Hine, John | 1 | 2 | 5 | | | Welsh, Martha | | | 1 | | | Gorham, Elias | 1 | | 2 | | |
| Hine, Joseph | 1 | 1 | 3 | | | Treat, Edmond | 1 | 1 | 1 | | | Gorham, Elizur | 1 | | 2 | | |
| Frost, Samuel | 2 | 1 | 1 | | | Malery, Benjamin | 1 | | 2 | | | Spencer, Nathaniel | 1 | 2 | 3 | | |
| Alling, Gidion | 1 | 2 | 4 | | | Bryant, Heil | 1 | | 1 | | 3 | Townsend, Soloman | 1 | | 2 | | |
| Woods, Samuell | 1 | 1 | 5 | | | Smith, William | 1 | 3 | | | | Brown, Elizur | 4 | | 4 | | |
| Clarke, Amos | 1 | | 2 | | | Clarke, Enock, 2nd | 1 | 3 | 2 | | 1 | White, Timothy | 1 | 4 | 5 | | |
| Evans, Evan | 1 | | 1 | | | Platt, Gideon | 2 | | 2 | | 1 | Alley, William | 1 | | 1 | | |
| Newton, Jonah | 2 | 1 | 5 | | 4 | Clarke, Elias | 1 | 3 | 2 | | 2 | Kindley, Joseph | 1 | 1 | | | |
| Summers, Henry | 2 | | 2 | | | Treat, Samuel | 1 | 1 | 3 | | | Wooster, Mary | | | 1 | | |
| Summers, Isaac | 1 | | 2 | | | Clarke, Benjamin | 1 | 2 | 2 | | | Wooster, Thomas | | | 6 | 3 | |
| Smith, John | 4 | | 3 | 1 | | Rogers, Jonathan | 1 | 2 | 3 | | | Hood, Samuel | 1 | 1 | 2 | | |
| Gillet, Eliphalet | 1 | | 1 | | | Bryant, John | 1 | 3 | 2 | | | Smith, Seymore | 1 | 1 | 3 | | |
| Gillet, Jonathan | 1 | | 1 | | | Fenn, Samuel | 2 | 2 | 6 | | | Wells, Gad | 1 | | 2 | | |
| Smith, Joseph | 1 | 1 | 3 | 1 | | Andrew, William | 2 | 1 | 2 | | 2 | Palmer, Elizabeth | 1 | | 1 | | |
| Smith, Samuel | 1 | 4 | 6 | 1 | | Bryant, Thomas | 1 | | 2 | | | Brown, Henry | 1 | | 3 | | |
| Jack (Negroe) | | | | 5 | | Woodruff, Mathew | 2 | 4 | 3 | | | Turner, Jesse | 1 | 3 | 3 | | |
| Peter (Negroe) | | | | 7 | | Nettleton, Isaac | 2 | 2 | 3 | | | Davis, Thomas | 1 | 1 | 1 | | |
| Munson, William | 1 | | 2 | | | Marks, Abraham | 1 | 2 | 1 | | | Parmalie, Jeremiah | 2 | | 3 | | |
| Rogers, Joseph | 1 | | 5 | | 1 | Buckingham, Joseph | 1 | | 2 | | | Dana, Revd James | 2 | 1 | 4 | | |
| Smith, David | 1 | 2 | 3 | | | Marks, Zacheriah | 2 | | 4 | | | Irwin, Sarah | | 3 | 1 | | |
| Summers, Abel | 3 | 1 | 5 | | | Treat, Francis | 1 | 1 | 2 | | | McKenzie, John | 1 | | 1 | | |
| Munson, Daniel | 1 | 4 | 6 | | | Treat, Richard | 1 | | 2 | | 1 | Humiston, Mary Ann | | 2 | 1 | | |
| Benjamin, Berzeler | 3 | 3 | 1 | | | Treat, John | 1 | | 1 | | | Warner, Jacob | 1 | 2 | 1 | | |
| Botsford, Aron | 1 | 1 | 1 | | | Treat, John, 2nd | 1 | | 2 | | | Peck, Thomas | 1 | | 1 | | |
| Bassett, Mary | | | 2 | | | Parker, Jeremiah | 1 | | 2 | | | Holmes, Joel | 1 | 3 | 3 | | |
| Turrel, Mary | | | 1 | | | Fenn, John | 1 | | 2 | | | Tinker, Amos | 1 | | 1 | | |
| Foot, John | 1 | | 2 | | | Fenn, Isaac | 1 | | 2 | | | Tucker, Noah | 1 | | 7 | | |
| Simeon (Negroe) | | | | 2 | | Welsh, Thomas | 2 | 1 | 5 | | | Hotchkiss, Eneas | 1 | | 2 | | |
| Joseph (Negroe) | | | | 3 | | Murrain, John, 3rd | 1 | 3 | 3 | | | Warner, Joseph | 1 | | 2 | | |
| Ovet, Ellick | 1 | | 2 | | | Pritchard, Martha | | | 3 | | | Leavenworth, Catherine | | 1 | 2 | | |
| Gunn, Anna | | | 2 | | | Bryant, Heil | 1 | | 2 | | | Denis, Samuel | 1 | | 2 | | |
| Roseter, Timothy W | 1 | | 1 | | | Molton, Joseph | 1 | 1 | 1 | | | Platt, Jerimiah | 2 | 1 | 4 | | 1 |
| Whiting, Joseph | 1 | 1 | 2 | | | Peck, Ephraim | 1 | | 1 | 1 | | Broome, Samuel | 3 | 2 | 6 | 2 | |
| Baldwin, Thankfull | | | 1 | | | Jeff (Negroe) | | | | 2 | | Hulse, Joseph | 1 | 3 | 5 | | |
| Morris, Richard | 1 | 2 | 2 | | | Gabriel, Peter | 1 | | 3 | | | Green, David | 1 | 1 | 1 | | |
| Merchant, Samuel | 2 | | 1 | | | Gabriel, Henry | 1 | | 3 | | | Wells, Mosses | 2 | | 4 | | |
| Burn, David | 1 | 2 | 4 | | | Bull, Benjamin | 2 | | 1 | 1 | | Thompson, Timothy | 2 | | 4 | | |
| Nando (Negroe) | | | | 1 | | Smith, Ebenezer | 1 | | 2 | | | Smith, Joshua | 1 | 4 | 5 | | |
| Camp, Nathaniel | 2 | 3 | 4 | | | Smith, Andrew | 1 | 1 | 2 | | | Hood, Richard | 3 | | 3 | | |
| Peck, John, 2nd | 1 | 1 | 2 | | | Bull, Anna | 1 | | 3 | | | English, Benjamin | 1 | 4 | 5 | | |
| Tomlinson, David | 2 | | | | | Peck, Hezekiah | 1 | | 2 | | | Tomlinson, Isaac | 4 | 2 | 4 | | |
| Bristow, Nathan | 1 | 6 | 2 | | | Baldwin, Justice | 1 | | 1 | 1 | | Cooke, George | 1 | 2 | 4 | | |
| Bristow, Richard | 1 | | | | | Isaacs, Isaac B | 1 | | 1 | | | Ray, Caleb | 1 | 1 | 2 | | |
| Clarke, Oliver | 1 | | 1 | | | Warren, Jonathan | 1 | | 2 | | | Catlin, Thomas | 1 | 3 | 2 | | |
| Northrop, Abel | 3 | 3 | 3 | | | Clarke, Thomas | 3 | | 3 | | | Tuttle, Abraham | 2 | | 1 | | |
| Smith, Benjamin | 1 | 1 | 3 | | | Mallery, Moses | 1 | 3 | 4 | | | Cuff (Negroe) | | | | 3 | |
| Lewis, Sarah | | | 2 | | | Treat, Stephen | 1 | 1 | 1 | | | Punderford, John | 1 | 3 | 3 | | |
| Baldwin, Sibel | | | 2 | | | Murrain, John | 1 | | 2 | | 1 | Montcalm, Mosses | 1 | 3 | 4 | | |
| Prindle, Charles | 2 | 1 | 2 | | | Platt, Benjamin | 1 | 2 | 3 | | | Brown, Jabez | 1 | 3 | 3 | | |
| Ovet, Isaac | 1 | 1 | 2 | | | Isbell, Israel | 1 | 1 | 4 | | | Storer, John | 2 | 3 | 3 | | |
| Summers, Agnes | | | 1 | | | Treat, Elisha | 1 | 2 | 2 | | 1 | Stilman, Ashbel | 2 | 4 | 1 | | |
| Botchford, Elnathan | 1 | | 1 | | | Hooker, John | 1 | | 2 | | | Bonticon, Thomas | 1 | 1 | 1 | | |
| Fowler, Timothy | 2 | 1 | 5 | | | Morris, Newton | 1 | 2 | 1 | | 1 | Storer, Sarah | 1 | | 4 | | |
| Fowler, William | 1 | 1 | 4 | | | Bradley, Jerad | 1 | | 2 | | | Bonticon, William | 1 | 1 | 2 | | |
| Treat, Joseph, 2nd | 1 | 1 | 5 | | | Hine, Titus | 1 | 2 | 2 | | | Sloan, Mary | | | 2 | | |
| Hine, Aron | 1 | | 2 | | | Congo (Negroe) | | | | 4 | | Mansfield, Ester | | | 2 | | |
| Pardie, Joseph | 1 | 1 | 1 | | | Pomp (Negroe) | | | | 3 | | Woodward, Richard | 4 | 1 | 2 | 1 | 2 |
| Clement, Isaac | 1 | 1 | 3 | | | Law, Benedick | 2 | 5 | 3 | | 1 | Russell, Samuel | 1 | | 3 | | |
| Treat, Robert | 2 | 1 | 2 | | | Lambert, Jesse | 2 | 1 | 2 | | | | | | | | |

# HEADS OF FAMILIES—CONNECTICUT.

## NEW HAVEN COUNTY—Continued.

| NAME OF HEAD OF FAMILY. | Free white males of 16 years and upward, including heads of families. | Free white males under 16 years. | Free white females, including heads of families. | All other free persons. | Slaves. | NAME OF HEAD OF FAMILY. | Free white males of 16 years and upward, including heads of families. | Free white males under 16 years. | Free white females, including heads of families. | All other free persons. | Slaves. | NAME OF HEAD OF FAMILY. | Free white males of 16 years and upward, including heads of families. | Free white males under 16 years. | Free white females, including heads of families. | All other free persons. | Slaves. |
|---|---|---|---|---|---|---|---|---|---|---|---|---|---|---|---|---|---|
| **NEW HAVEN CITY—con.** | | | | | | **NEW HAVEN CITY—con.** | | | | | | **NEW HAVEN CITY—con.** | | | | | |
| Sabins, Hezekiah | 1 | 1 | 2 | 4 | 1 | Lothrop, Unice | | | 5 | | | Gorham, Joseph | 1 | 3 | 1 | | |
| Graham, John | 1 | 2 | 3 | | | Mix, Joseph, 2nd | 2 | | 3 | | | Townsend, Elias | 1 | 1 | 5 | | |
| Tharp, Joel | 2 | 1 | 2 | | | Munson, Stephen | 1 | | 3 | | | Brown, Isaac | 1 | | 1 | | |
| Sherry, Joseph | 1 | | 3 | | | Noyse, Paul | 1 | 1 | 3 | | | Phipps, Daniel Goff | 1 | 3 | 3 | | |
| Lieke, John | 1 | 2 | 3 | | | Gardiner, David | | | | 6 | | Keif, Arthur | 1 | 1 | 4 | | |
| French, Edmond | 2 | 3 | 3 | | 1 | Adams, John | 1 | 1 | 2 | | | Austin, Elijah | 3 | 4 | 4 | | |
| Griffin, Rossiter | 1 | 1 | 2 | | | Bell, John | 1 | 1 | 1 | | | Trowbridge, Joseph E. | 1 | | 4 | | |
| Sandford, Benjamin | 1 | 1 | | | 5 | Dwight, Timothy | 1 | 4 | 3 | | | Trowbridge, Stephen | 1 | 1 | 1 | | |
| Perit, Job | 1 | | 2 | | | Nicoll, John | 2 | 1 | 4 | | 2 | Gobine, Nicholas | 1 | | 1 | | |
| Burke, Edmond | 1 | 1 | 2 | | | Bradley, Joseph | 2 | | 2 | | 2 | Trowbridge, Stephen, 3rd | 3 | | | | |
| Benedick, John | 1 | 2 | 1 | | | Mirriman, Silas | 3 | | 2 | | | Thomas, Samuel | 1 | | 1 | | |
| Downs, Nathaniel | 1 | | 2 | | | Mirriman, Marcus | 1 | 1 | 3 | | | Allen, Eneas | 1 | | 2 | | |
| Reiley, William | 1 | 1 | 1 | | | Turner, Enoch | | | 2 | | | Robinson, Catherine | | | 1 | | |
| Lewis, Sussanah | | | 1 | | | Drake, Joseph | 3 | 1 | 3 | | | Dinah (Negroe) | | | | 1 | |
| Molony, Downey | 1 | 2 | 1 | | | Mansfield, Henry | 1 | 1 | 2 | | | Hubbard, Leveret | 2 | 1 | 3 | 1 | 1 |
| Trickey, Jerard | 1 | 1 | 2 | | | Sabin, Hezekiah, 2nd | 1 | 4 | 2 | | | Brown, Robert | 5 | 3 | 4 | | |
| Jellet, Margret | | | 2 | | | Bradley, Abraham | 2 | 1 | 3 | | | Peck, Henry | 1 | 1 | 5 | | |
| Wilson, Sarah | | | 2 | | | Huggins, Heaton | 1 | | 1 | | | Trowbridge, William | 1 | 2 | 2 | | |
| Mulford, David | 2 | 1 | 1 | | | Mansfield, Jerad | 1 | | 1 | | | Larkin, Edward | 1 | 3 | 3 | | |
| Reed, David | 1 | | 1 | | | Bradley, Stephen | 1 | 1 | 3 | | | Oakes, Nathan | 6 | 1 | 7 | | |
| Mulford, Barnabas | 2 | 2 | 3 | | | Street, John | 2 | 1 | 1 | | | Ward, Ambros | 1 | | 3 | | |
| Thatcher, John | 1 | | 2 | | | Mix, Eldad | 1 | 2 | 4 | | | Peck, John | 1 | 1 | 1 | | |
| Buckly, William | 1 | | 2 | | | Morse, Abel | 4 | 3 | 2 | | 2 | Gold, Thomas | 1 | | 3 | | |
| Salls, James | 1 | 1 | 1 | | | Fitch, Jonathan | 5 | 5 | 3 | | 1 | Howell, Thomas | 1 | | 3 | | |
| Fenton, Nathaniel | 2 | | 4 | | | Stilwell, Elias | 1 | | 3 | | | Hubbard, Julia | | 1 | 2 | | |
| Peck, Gad | 1 | | 1 | | | Huggins, John | 1 | 1 | 3 | | | Bartholemew, Israel | 1 | 2 | 3 | | |
| Barber, Noah | 2 | 1 | 2 | | | Hotchkiss, Sussanah | | | 3 | | | Horcheild, William | 2 | | 1 | | |
| Walter, William | 3 | 3 | 4 | | | Spalding, John | 4 | | 1 | | | Howell, Thomas, Jr | 2 | 1 | 3 | | 1 |
| Miles, William | 1 | 2 | 5 | | | Horton, Samuel | 2 | | 2 | | | Sacket, Hannah | | | 1 | | |
| Townsend, Ebenezer | 3 | 3 | 4 | | | Townsend, Robert | 2 | 4 | 5 | | | Malone, Dansel | 1 | 3 | 2 | | |
| Smith, Edmond | 1 | 1 | 3 | | | Darling, Samuel | 1 | 3 | 3 | | | Hitchcock, Eliakim | 2 | 2 | 4 | | |
| Collis, Daniel | 3 | 1 | 5 | | | Trowbridge, Stephen | 2 | 2 | 4 | | | Holly, Josiah | 1 | 1 | 2 | | |
| Collony, Patrick | 1 | 1 | 3 | | | Howett, Joseph | 3 | 2 | 4 | | | Bailey, Elizabeth | | | 2 | | |
| Sabins, Jonathan | 1 | 1 | 6 | | | Tritten, Elizb | | 1 | 1 | | 3 | Little, Alexander | 1 | | 2 | | |
| Little, Alexander | 1 | | 2 | | | Attwater, Timothy | 1 | 3 | 6 | | | Osborn, Stephen | 5 | 5 | 4 | | |
| Throop, John R | 1 | 2 | 4 | | | Bishop, Sylvanus | 3 | 1 | 4 | | | Granis, Benjamin | 3 | 2 | 2 | | |
| Miles, John, 3rd | 1 | 3 | 2 | | | Miles, John | 2 | 1 | 1 | | | Miller, Caleb | 1 | | 1 | | |
| Trowbridge, John | 1 | 3 | 3 | | | Miles, Stephen | 1 | | 1 | | | Johnson, Thomas | 1 | | 1 | | |
| Bedford, Ad — | 1 | | 1 | | | Howell, Samuel | 1 | | 3 | | | Yorke, Henry | 2 | 2 | 6 | | |
| Collins, Luther | 1 | | 2 | | | Beecher, Mary | | | 3 | | | McNeil, William | 1 | 1 | 4 | | |
| Peck, Ebenezer | 4 | 2 | 2 | | | Munson, William | 1 | 3 | 4 | | | Hugins, Ebenezer | 1 | 4 | 4 | | |
| Peck, James | 1 | | 1 | | | Cleavland, Samuel | 1 | 2 | 3 | | | Prat, Samuel | 1 | | 3 | | |
| Powell, William | 2 | | 2 | | | Sisson, James | 1 | 1 | 4 | | | Alicocke, David | 3 | | 3 | | |
| Marsh, Robert | 1 | 2 | 1 | | | Hall, Abiel | | | 3 | | | Ward, Ambrose, Jr | 2 | 3 | 2 | | |
| Heyliger, John | 2 | 4 | 4 | | 1 | Whiting, Sarah | | 1 | 1 | | | Austin, Mahatibel | | | 1 | | |
| Wells, William | 1 | 1 | 3 | | | Whiting, Samuel | 1 | | 1 | | | Herrick, Stephen | 1 | | 5 | | |
| Meloy, Edward, 2nd | 1 | 1 | 2 | | | Whiting, Jonathan | | | 1 | | | Austin, Jonathan | 1 | 2 | 3 | | |
| Phipps, Solomon | 1 | | 4 | | | Whittlesey, Patty | 3 | | 3 | | | Hubbard, Revd Bela | 1 | 4 | 5 | | |
| Ward, John | 1 | | 1 | | | Hotchkiss, Lent | 2 | | 3 | | | Brigden, William | 1 | 2 | 3 | | |
| Davis, Thomas | 2 | 2 | 3 | | | Attwater, Thomas | 1 | 3 | 4 | 1 | | Alling, Bet (Negroe) | | | | 3 | |
| Brintnal, William | 2 | 2 | 6 | | | Northrop, Joel | 1 | 5 | 3 | 1 | | Denison, Martha | | 4 | 5 | | |
| Phipps, David | 1 | 2 | 4 | | | Chatterdon, Rodah | | | 3 | | | Chrittenton, Dolly | | 2 | 3 | | |
| Brown, Benjamin | 2 | 1 | 1 | | | Townsend, Jeremiah | 1 | 1 | 3 | | | Burnet, Jeremiah | 1 | 1 | 1 | | |
| Jocelin, Nathaniel | 1 | | 1 | | | Prout, Margeret | | | 2 | | | Johnson, Robert | 1 | | | | |
| Brown, Francis | 1 | 1 | 5 | | | Forbes, Elijah | 1 | 2 | 4 | | 2 | Stone, Cyrus | 1 | | | | |
| Helmes, William | 2 | 4 | 2 | | | Brown, Georgo | 1 | 2 | 2 | | | Peck, John | 1 | 2 | 2 | | |
| Prentice, Jonas | 2 | 1 | 5 | | | Tuttle, Abraham, 2d | 3 | 1 | 2 | 1 | | Ade, Aner | 1 | 1 | 2 | | |
| Fanning, David | 1 | 2 | 1 | | | Allen, Stephen | 1 | 1 | 5 | | | Mix, Jonathan | 2 | 4 | 3 | | |
| Forbes, Samuel | 1 | | 1 | | | Lymar, Elihu | 2 | | 1 | | 1 | Webber, John | 1 | 1 | 2 | | |
| Sherman, Samuel | 2 | 1 | 3 | | | Andrus, Phineas | 3 | 4 | 3 | | | Beecher, Isaac | 1 | | | | |
| Gilbert, Miriam | | | 2 | | | Smith, George | 1 | 3 | 2 | | 1 | Hoye, Nelly | | | 1 | | |
| Ward, Titus | 1 | | 1 | | | Gorham, Isaac | 1 | 1 | 2 | | | Howell, Cheney | 1 | 2 | 1 | | |
| Dorman, Amassa | 1 | 1 | 2 | | | Gurnsey, Isaac | | | 2 | | | McNeil, Archabald | 1 | 3 | 1 | | |
| Smith, Benjamin | 1 | 1 | 1 | 1 | | Thompson, William | 1 | | 1 | | | Mathews, Elizabeth | | | 1 | | |
| Crittenden, Lidia | | | 2 | | | Miles, Josep | 1 | | 1 | | | Sherman, William | 2 | 1 | 7 | | |
| Sherman, Lemuel | 1 | 3 | 1 | | | Townsen, Woodbridge | 1 | 1 | 1 | | | Bonticon, John | 1 | | 1 | | |
| Lane, James | 1 | | | | | Keeney, Michael | 1 | 1 | 2 | | | Bradley, Abraham | 1 | | 1 | | |
| Dougal, James | 3 | 1 | 3 | | | Forbes, Elias | 1 | 1 | 4 | | | Lyon, William | 2 | | 7 | | |
| Thomas, John | 1 | | 1 | | | Morgan, Jacob | 1 | 1 | 2 | | | Mix, Joseph | 2 | 3 | 5 | | |
| Dorman, David | 1 | 1 | 2 | | | Harrington, Benjamin | 1 | 1 | 3 | | | Lyon, Nathaniel | 2 | | 4 | | |
| Sharper (Negroe) | | | | 2 | | Davis, John | 1 | | 3 | | | Munson, Theophilus | 1 | | 2 | | |
| Hubbard, William G | 1 | | 3 | | | Hitchcock, John | 1 | | 1 | | | Hill, Hannah | | 1 | 2 | | |
| Hotchkiss, Stephen | 3 | 3 | 3 | | | Hatch, Zephaniah | | | 1 | | | Beardsley, Ebenezer | 3 | 2 | 2 | 1 | |
| Jack (Negroe) | | | | 1 | | Roberts, Josiah | 1 | 1 | 4 | | | Reed, Zackeriah | 2 | 2 | 5 | | |
| Gorham, Abigal | | | 2 | | | Snow, Samuel | 1 | | 2 | | | De Witt, Peter | 1 | | 2 | | |
| Smith, Joseph, 3rd | 2 | 2 | 3 | | | Bills, William | 3 | | 3 | | | Attwater, Jeremiah | 2 | 4 | 5 | | |
| Lines, Ezra | 1 | 1 | 4 | | | Wallace, William | 1 | 3 | 1 | | | McCraken, William | 1 | 4 | 4 | | 2 |
| Dummer, Nathaniel | | | 3 | | | Miller, John | 1 | | 2 | | 1 | Cutler, Richard | 1 | 4 | 7 | | |
| Dummer, Stephen | 2 | 4 | 3 | | | Davis, Enoch | 1 | 1 | 3 | | | Cooke, John | 3 | 3 | 2 | | |
| Munson, Samuel | 1 | 1 | 1 | | | Benham, Elisha | 1 | 1 | 5 | | | Kimberly, Nathaniel | 1 | 3 | 3 | | |
| Wilmot, Samuel | 1 | 2 | 3 | | | Rice, James | 2 | | 1 | | 1 | Beecher, Sussanah | 1 | 1 | 5 | | |
| Dennison, Rohda | | | 1 | | | Perit, Antony | 2 | | 1 | 1 | | Beecher, John | 1 | 1 | 1 | | |
| Pardee, Sarah | 1 | 2 | 3 | | | Brumham, John | 1 | | 2 | | | Cocker, James | 1 | | 1 | | |
| Bishop, Daniel | 4 | 5 | 3 | | | Trowbridge, Caleb | 2 | 4 | 3 | | | Davis, Isaac | 1 | | | | |
| Burret, Abel | 3 | 2 | 4 | | | Rice, Thomas | 1 | | 2 | | 2 | Miles, John, 3rd | 3 | | 4 | | |
| Mansfield, William | 1 | 2 | 4 | | | Trowbridge, Rutherford | 2 | 2 | 5 | | | Beecher, Thadius | 4 | 3 | 3 | | 1 |
| Ray, Martha | | | 2 | | | Morris, John | 2 | 1 | 3 | | | Wetmore, Hezekiah | 1 | 2 | 2 | 1 | |
| Dummer, Abraham | 1 | 1 | 3 | | | Clarke, John | 2 | 1 | 4 | | | Austin, Asa | 1 | 3 | 3 | | |
| Pinto, Polly | | 1 | 1 | | | Kirby, Abner | 1 | | 2 | | | Turner, Seth | 1 | 2 | 3 | | |
| Bishop, Samuel | 4 | | 4 | | | Trowbridge, Daniel | 1 | | 3 | | | Townsend, Isaac | 3 | 2 | 5 | | |
| Pinto, Jacob | 1 | | 2 | | | Trowbridge, Joseph | 1 | | 3 | | | Eld, Richard | 1 | 2 | 2 | | |
| Bishop, Isaac | 1 | 1 | 4 | | | Trowbridge, Mahbel | | | 3 | | | Townsend, Neeland | 4 | | 1 | | |
| Todd, Michael | 2 | | 4 | | 5 | Trowbridge, Newman | 3 | 3 | 3 | | | Adams, Polly | | | 2 | | |
| Chandler, John | 1 | 3 | 4 | | | Gorham, Timothy | 1 | | 1 | | | Bradley, Hannah | | | 3 | | |
| Jones, Timothy | 1 | 1 | 2 | | 1 | | | | | | | Smith, Joseph | 2 | | 3 | | |

## FIRST CENSUS OF THE UNITED STATES.

### NEW HAVEN COUNTY—Continued.

| NAME OF HEAD OF FAMILY. | Free white males of 16 years and upward, including heads of families. | Free white males under 16 years. | Free white females, including heads of families. | All other free persons. | Slaves. | NAME OF HEAD OF FAMILY. | Free white males of 16 years and upward, including heads of families. | Free white males under 16 years. | Free white females, including heads of families. | All other free persons. | Slaves. | NAME OF HEAD OF FAMILY. | Free white males of 16 years and upward, including heads of families. | Free white males under 16 years. | Free white females, including heads of families. | All other free persons. | Slaves. |
|---|---|---|---|---|---|---|---|---|---|---|---|---|---|---|---|---|---|
| NEW HAVEN CITY—con. | | | | | | NEW HAVEN CITY—con. | | | | | | NEW HAVEN CITY—con. | | | | | |
| Barney, Samuel | 1 | 2 | 5 | | | Williams, Hector (Negroe) | | | | 4 | | Dudley, Thomas | 1 | | 3 | | |
| Sabins, Sussanah | | | 2 | | | Potter, Noah | 1 | | 2 | | | Hatch, Amy | | | 1 | | |
| Hubbard, Levi | 2 | 1 | 2 | 1 | | Potter, Asa | 1 | 1 | 3 | | | Morrison (Widow) | | 1 | 1 | | |
| Cooladge, Henry | 3 | 1 | 2 | | | Geff (Negroe) | | | | 2 | | Rackerbrandt, John | 1 | | 3 | | |
| Bates, Mosses | 2 | 2 | 1 | | | Broughton, William | 1 | | 1 | | | Newall, Joshua | 2 | | 5 | | |
| Brigden, Jonathan | 1 | 2 | 2 | | | Dagget, Jacob | 1 | 1 | 5 | | | Dodd, John | 1 | 3 | 2 | | |
| White, John | 1 | | 1 | | | Hitchcock, Hannah | | | 1 | | | Gordon, Sarah | | | 2 | | |
| Carrington, Merrit | 2 | 1 | 2 | | | Jocelin, Pember | 2 | 2 | 4 | | | Pierpont, John | 2 | 3 | 3 | | |
| Cooke, William | 2 | 2 | 2 | | | Attwater, Mary | | | 1 | | | Miles, Elihu | | | 2 | | |
| Langmore, Alexander | 1 | | | | | Punderson, Daniel | 1 | | | | | Butler, Justas | 2 | 1 | 3 | | |
| Brown, Jacob | 3 | | 2 | 2 | | Prescot, Benjamin | 4 | 3 | 2 | | | Thatcher, Samuel | 1 | 1 | 5 | 1 | 2 |
| Gorham, Miles | 1 | 6 | 2 | | | Munson, Eneas | 3 | 3 | 2 | | 2 | Goodrich, Elijur | 2 | 1 | 4 | | 1 |
| Austin, David | 2 | | 2 | | | Beers, Nathan | 1 | 2 | 5 | | | Hillhouse, James | 1 | 2 | 7 | 2 | 1 |
| Wise, John | 1 | | 2 | | | Phelps, Timothy | 1 | | | | | Dodd, Guy | 1 | 2 | 5 | | |
| Wise, John, Jun^r | 1 | | 1 | | | Hotchkiss, Amos | 1 | 1 | 1 | | 1 | Smith, Joseph, 2^nd | 1 | 1 | 2 | | |
| Wise, Samuel | 1 | | 3 | | | Johnson, Abraham | 1 | 1 | 1 | | | Hillhouse, Mary | | 1 | 4 | | 3 |
| Austin, John | 3 | 2 | 3 | | | Ruben (Negroe) | | | | 2 | | Hillhouse, William | 1 | | | | |
| Crocker, Daniel | 1 | | 2 | | | Sperry, Eber | 1 | 1 | 2 | | | Higgins, Nemamiah | 1 | 3 | 3 | | |
| Gilbert, Caleb | 1 | | 2 | | | Gold, Peter | 1 | | 3 | | | Trowbridge, Joseph, 2^nd | 1 | 3 | 7 | | |
| Goodsell, Levi | 1 | | 1 | | | Henry, John | 1 | | | | | Parmalie, Hezekiah | 2 | 1 | 3 | | |
| Clarke, Tim | 2 | 2 | 2 | 1 | | Attwater, Stephen | 1 | 2 | 5 | | | Gibson, Hannah | | | 3 | | |
| Ord, John | 1 | | 2 | | | Gorham, Samuel | 1 | 3 | 3 | | | Tuttle, Richard | 1 | | 6 | | |
| Austin, William | 1 | 3 | 2 | | | Mix, Samuel | 1 | 2 | 4 | | | Belfast (Negroe) | | | | 5 | |
| Rice, Archabald | 1 | 1 | 1 | | | Mix, Elisha | 1 | 1 | 4 | | | Primus (Negroe) | | | | 3 | |
| Austin, Lidia | | | 1 | | | Mix, Hannah | | | 1 | | | Smith, Israel | 1 | | 1 | | |
| Bradley, Jonah | 2 | | 3 | | | Hotchkiss, Obadiah | 1 | | 2 | | | Dixon, James | 1 | | 3 | | |
| Mix, Sarah | | | 1 | | | Cooke, Miller | 2 | 1 | 2 | | | Luke (Negroe) | | | | 3 | |
| Mix, Thankfull | | 1 | 3 | | | Blakley, Tilley | 1 | 1 | 2 | | | Parmalie, Simion | 1 | 2 | 3 | | |
| Lines, James | 2 | | 1 | | | Burr, Josiah | 1 | 2 | 6 | | | Reed, Sussanah | | | 3 | | |
| Jack (Negro) | | | | 3 | | Page, Icabod | 1 | 1 | 2 | | | Mansfield, Richstead | 1 | 1 | 6 | | |
| Meloy, Edward | 3 | 2 | 1 | | | Dagget, Micajah | 1 | | | | | Mansfield, Moses | 1 | | 1 | | |
| Thompson, Joseph | 3 | | 6 | | | Chapman, Daniel | 2 | 2 | 1 | | | Edwards, Rev^d Jonathan | 3 | | 4 | | |
| Ford, Caleb | 2 | 2 | 4 | | | Hart, Rebeca | | 1 | 2 | | | Woodhull, Richard | 1 | | | | |
| Chappel, Patience | | 1 | 5 | | | Cooke, David | 1 | | 2 | | | Brainard, Joshua | 1 | | 1 | 2 | |
| Otty, William | 1 | | 3 | | | Macumber, Jeremiah | 2 | | | | | Lines, Major | 1 | 3 | 6 | | |
| Thompson, Jacob | 1 | 1 | 6 | 1 | 1 | Stevans, Leveret | 1 | 1 | 4 | | | Lines, Ebenezer | 1 | | 1 | | |
| Thompson, Jerad | 1 | 2 | 2 | | | Cambridge, Ruth | | | 2 | 2 | | Jones, Isaac | 1 | 4 | 4 | 1 | |
| Thompson, Isaac | 1 | 1 | 3 | | | Chatfield, Heil | 1 | | 2 | | | Ball, Hezekiah | 1 | | 3 | | |
| Clause, John | 1 | | 4 | | | Luke (Negroe) | | | | 4 | | Bird, Sarah | 1 | | 3 | | |
| Alley, Joseph | 1 | | 3 | | | Chittendon, Beriah | 1 | 2 | 2 | | | Breed, Newell | 2 | 2 | 1 | | |
| Gilbert, Elizabeth | | 2 | 3 | | | Griswold, Hannah | | | 2 | | | Stillwell, Mary | | | 2 | | |
| Gilbert, Isaac | 2 | 2 | 5 | | | Mansfield, Deborah | | | 1 | | | Dummer, Edward | 1 | | 1 | | |
| Bills, Thomas | 3 | | 2 | | | Hale, Hezekiah | 1 | 1 | 2 | | | Edwards, Perpont | 1 | 4 | 5 | | 2 |
| Bills, Thomas, 2^nd | 1 | | 1 | | | Munson, Israel | 5 | | 3 | | | Burrel, Thomas | 4 | 3 | 4 | | |
| Thompson, Jeremiah | 1 | | 1 | | | Munson, Joseph | 4 | 2 | 6 | | | Dwight, Samuel | 1 | | 2 | | |
| Dougal, David | 1 | 2 | 4 | | | Mix, John | 5 | 1 | 3 | | | Hubbard, Daniel | 1 | 2 | 1 | | |
| Gilbert, David | 1 | 2 | 2 | | | Townsend, Timothy | 1 | 1 | 2 | | | Wales, Rev^d Samuel | 2 | 3 | 2 | 1 | 1 |
| Gilbert, Amos | 1 | 2 | 4 | 1 | | Doolittle, Amos | 1 | 4 | 2 | | | Feilds, Thomas | 1 | 1 | 2 | | |
| Gilbert, Timothy | 1 | 2 | 2 | | | Ford, Ezra | 1 | | 7 | | | Punderson, Thomas | 3 | 3 | 3 | | |
| Hull, Samuel | 1 | 3 | 2 | | | Clarke, Parsons | 2 | | 2 | | | Punderson, Samuel | 1 | 2 | 5 | | |
| Dodd, Bishop | 1 | | 2 | | | Townsend, John | 2 | 1 | 3 | | | Alling Christopher | 1 | 1 | 5 | | |
| Barnes, Elizabeth | | 1 | 1 | | | Grenough, William | 1 | | 2 | | 2 | Hotchkiss, Ely | 2 | | 3 | | |
| Mix, Ester | | 3 | 1 | | | Molthrop, Enoch | 1 | | 3 | | | Reed, Daniel | 2 | 3 | 1 | | |
| Doolittle, Isaac | 1 | 1 | 4 | | | Barnes, Darcus | | | 1 | | | Gorham, Stephan | 1 | 4 | 4 | | |
| Noyce, William | 2 | 2 | 2 | | | Bradley, John | 1 | | 1 | | | Auger, Abraham | 1 | 1 | 2 | | |
| Beecher, David | 2 | 1 | 4 | | | Dagget, Ezra | 1 | | 3 | | | Fry, Christopher | 1 | | 2 | | |
| Hull, Joseph | 2 | | 2 | | | Barney, Hanover | 1 | 4 | 4 | | | Towers, Joshua | 1 | 3 | 2 | | |
| Fitch, Luther | 5 | 3 | 4 | | | Bradley, James | 2 | 2 | 5 | | | Attwater, Holbrook | 1 | 1 | 4 | | |
| Thompson, Phebe | | | 4 | | | Hotchkiss, Gabrael | 1 | 1 | 2 | | | Hill, Amos | 1 | | 1 | | |
| Fitch, Nathaniel | 2 | 5 | 3 | | | Wise, Rhoda | | | 1 | | | Hendrick, Coe | 1 | 2 | 1 | | |
| Green, Thomas | 3 | | 4 | | | Molthrop, Charles | 1 | | 3 | | | Tuttle, Hezekiah | 3 | | 2 | | |
| Attwater, Joel | 2 | 1 | 3 | | | Hotchkiss, Hezekiah | 2 | 2 | 5 | | 1 | Tuttle, Abner | 1 | 2 | 1 | | |
| Attwater, Ward | 1 | | 3 | | | Fisher, Hannah | | 2 | 2 | | | Alling, Hezekiah | 1 | | 1 | | |
| Potter, Statia | 1 | | 1 | | | Hanson, Christan | 1 | | 1 | | | Ives, Levi | 2 | 2 | 5 | | |
| Townsend, Jeremiah | 1 | 2 | 4 | | | Thompson, Abraham | 1 | | 1 | | | Scott, William | 1 | 1 | 4 | | |
| Potter, Livi | 1 | 1 | 1 | | | Marumberg, Abiel | 1 | 1 | | | | Benham, Lemuel | 1 | 2 | 5 | | |
| Green, Samuel | 2 | | 5 | | | Alling, Samuel | 1 | | 3 | | | Lenard, Tim (Negroe) | | | | 3 | |
| Attwater, Jeremiah | 3 | | 2 | 1 | | Parmalie, Sarah | | | 1 | | | Camp, Jesse | 2 | 1 | 3 | | |
| Stiles, Rev^d Ezra | 2 | 1 | 6 | 1 | | Dagget, Henry, 2^nd | 1 | 1 | 3 | | | Johnson, Peter | 2 | 3 | 6 | | |
| Beers, Elias | 1 | 2 | 4 | | | Hotchkiss, Asa | 1 | | 1 | | | Auger, Hezekiah | 2 | 1 | 6 | | |
| Beers, Isaac | 1 | 3 | 2 | | | Doolittle, Isaac | 3 | | 1 | | | Auger, Isaac | 1 | 3 | 2 | | |
| Goodrich, John | 2 | 3 | 4 | 1 | 1 | Hotchkiss, Josiah | 1 | 3 | 3 | | | Thompson, Abraham | 3 | 2 | 1 | | |
| Shipman, Elias | 2 | 4 | 6 | 1 | | Burr, Sturgis | 2 | 1 | 2 | | 1 | Mix, Anna | | | 1 | | |
| Hubbard, Mary | | | 2 | | | Prescot, James | 4 | 2 | 4 | | | Eli (Negroe) | | | | 6 | |
| Perit, Thadeus | 1 | 1 | 1 | | | Dagget, Henry | 1 | 3 | 4 | | | Tappen, John | 1 | 1 | 1 | | |
| Ingersal, Jonathan | 2 | 1 | 5 | | | Ball, Stephen | 2 | 1 | 1 | | | Nicolls, Christopher | 1 | 1 | 2 | | |
| Chittenden, Ebenezer | 1 | | 2 | | | Sherman, Roger | 3 | 1 | 8 | | | Hotchkiss, Hannah | | | 2 | | |
| Chittenden, Timothy | 1 | | 2 | | | Baldwin, Simion | 1 | 1 | 3 | 1 | | Attwater, Jonah | 1 | | 1 | | |
| Buel, Abel | 1 | 3 | 2 | | | Sherman, John | 2 | 2 | 4 | | | Smith, John | 1 | 1 | 3 | | |
| Dagget, David | 3 | 1 | 3 | 1 | | Parmalie, Ebenezer | 2 | | 2 | | 1 | Hotchkiss, Eneas | 1 | 1 | 4 | | |
| Scott, John | 1 | 2 | 4 | | | Peck, Joseph | 1 | | | | | Harry (Negroe) | | | | 2 | |
| Clarke, Samuel | 2 | 1 | 2 | | | Hays, Ezekiel | 4 | 2 | 6 | | | Hibbard, Samuel | 1 | 2 | 1 | | |
| Griswold, Samuel | 2 | 2 | 4 | | | Lucas, Amaziah | 1 | | | | | Mix, Timothy | 1 | | 1 | | |
| Gilbert, Margaret | | 1 | 3 | | | Leavenworth, Mark | 1 | 1 | 2 | 1 | | Dorchester, Abigel | | | 1 | | |
| Brown, Stephen | 1 | | 4 | | | Bradley, Phineas | 4 | | 5 | | | Murray, James | 1 | 2 | 4 | | |
| Baldwin, Theodore | 1 | 1 | 2 | | | Clarke, Russell | 2 | 1 | 5 | | | Robinson, Samuel | 1 | 1 | 3 | | |
| Mansfield, Daniel | 1 | | 2 | | | Smith, John | 1 | | 3 | 1 | | Oshall, John | 1 | | 2 | | |
| Graham (Widow) | | | 2 | | | Whiting, William J | 1 | | 3 | | | Warner, John | 2 | | 3 | 1 | |
| Osborn, Mahitabel | 1 | | 4 | | | Chauncy, Charles | 1 | 3 | 3 | 1 | 2 | Osborn, Hill | 1 | | | | |
| Beecher, Hiram | 1 | | 4 | | | Leavensworth, Ely | 1 | | 4 | | | Hotchkiss, Nemamiah | 1 | 3 | 4 | | |
| Gilbert, Elisha | 1 | 1 | 3 | | | Volumn, Lenard | 1 | | 3 | | | Peck, Nicholas | 1 | | 2 | | |
| Beecher, Sarah | | | 2 | | | Lamont, Mary Ann | | | 2 | | | Dagget, Sue (Negroe) | | | | 4 | |
| Thompson, Sarah | | 1 | 3 | | | Edwards, Cuff (Negroe) | | | | 4 | | Parrett, Martin | 1 | 2 | 4 | | |
| Gilbert, James | 2 | 1 | 5 | 1 | | | | | | | | | | | | | |

# HEADS OF FAMILIES—CONNECTICUT.

## NEW HAVEN COUNTY—Continued.

| NAME OF HEAD OF FAMILY. | Free white males of 16 years and upward, including heads of families. | Free white males under 16 years. | Free white females, including heads of families. | All other free persons. | Slaves. | NAME OF HEAD OF FAMILY. | Free white males of 16 years and upward, including heads of families. | Free white males under 16 years. | Free white females, including heads of families. | All other free persons. | Slaves. | NAME OF HEAD OF FAMILY. | Free white males of 16 years and upward, including heads of families. | Free white males under 16 years. | Free white females, including heads of families. | All other free persons. | Slaves. |
|---|---|---|---|---|---|---|---|---|---|---|---|---|---|---|---|---|---|
| **NEW HAVEN CITY—con.** | | | | | | **NEW HAVEN CITY—con.** | | | | | | **NEW HAVEN CITY—con.** | | | | | |
| Gain (Negroe) | | | | 1 | | Downey, James | 1 | | 3 | | | Murrain, Jonas | 1 | 2 | 2 | | |
| Amey (Negroe) | | | | 3 | | Thompson, Elisha | 4 | 3 | 5 | | | Murrain, Margaret | | | 3 | | |
| Lambert, George | 1 | 1 | 2 | | | Moore, Francis | 1 | | 5 | | | Clarke, Thadeus | 2 | 1 | 5 | | |
| Talmage, Timothy | 1 | | 2 | | | Baldwin, Silas | 1 | 1 | 2 | | | Clarke, Merrit | 1 | 7 | 1 | 1 | |
| Osborn, Mary | | | 3 | | | Bunce, David | 2 | 3 | 2 | | | Clarke, Abigal | 2 | | 2 | 1 | |
| Attwater, Eldad | 1 | 2 | 3 | | | Heppborn, Lewis | 1 | 1 | 4 | | | Murran, Joseph | 2 | | 2 | | 1 |
| Ball, Oliver | 1 | | 3 | | | Osborn, Medad | 2 | 2 | 5 | | | Platt, Josiah | 1 | | | | |
| Upsom, Jesse | 1 | 1 | 4 | | | Hotchkiss, Caleb | 1 | | 1 | | | Platt, Anna | 1 | 1 | 6 | | |
| Barnes, Ezra | 1 | 1 | 1 | | | Hotchkiss, Punderson | 2 | | 3 | | | Hoase, Sarah | | 2 | 5 | | |
| Place, Joe (Negroe) | | | | 2 | | Hotchkiss, Elisha | 1 | | 3 | | | Down, Job | 1 | 2 | 2 | | |
| Jane (Negroe) | | | | 10 | | Thompson, James | 1 | | 3 | | | Down, Benjamin | 3 | 3 | 8 | | |
| Granis, Nathaniel | 1 | 3 | 3 | | | Bradley, Soloman | 1 | | 4 | | | Down, Nathaniel | 2 | | 3 | | |
| Row, Stephan | 2 | 1 | 3 | | | Sperry, William | 4 | 3 | 3 | | | Plat, Mary | | | 1 | | |
| Osborn, Jeremiah | 1 | | 1 | | | Hotchkiss, John | 1 | 1 | 1 | | | Merrick, Josiah | 1 | | | | |
| Barnes, Soloman | 1 | 1 | 4 | | | Sperry, Levi | 1 | 2 | 3 | | | Hoy, Daniel | 1 | | | | |
| Alling, Roger | 1 | | 1 | | | Way, Job | 1 | | 2 | | | Thomas, Asael | 2 | | | | |
| Bracket, Mosses | 1 | | 3 | | | Sperry, Edon | 2 | 1 | 1 | | | Smith, Samuel B | 1 | 4 | 4 | | |
| Munson, David | 1 | 1 | 3 | | | Lines, Cornelius | 1 | 1 | 1 | | | Smith, Phlomon | 1 | 1 | 2 | | |
| Devenport, John | 1 | | 1 | | | Bradley, Griffin | 1 | | 2 | | | Candie, Isaac | 1 | 1 | 5 | | |
| Tuttle, Hoy | 1 | 2 | 3 | | | Warner, Abraham | 1 | | 3 | | | Bingley, Hannah | | | 1 | | |
| Osborn, Benjamin | 1 | 1 | 3 | | | Lines, Asbael | 1 | 3 | 5 | | | Kimberly, Asael | 1 | 3 | 3 | | |
| Attwater, David | 1 | 1 | 2 | | | Bradley, Erastus | 1 | 1 | 3 | | | Willington, Noah | 2 | | 3 | | |
| Ball, Joseph | 1 | | 1 | | | Bradley, Martha | | | 3 | | | Candie, Samuel | 1 | | 5 | | |
| Ball, David | 1 | 1 | 1 | | | Culver, John | 2 | 2 | 4 | | | Kimberly, Nathaniel | 1 | 2 | 3 | | |
| Brown, Bersheba | 1 | 1 | 3 | | | Dickerman, Isaac | 1 | 1 | 5 | | | Kimberly, Silas | 2 | 5 | 6 | | |
| Ceaser (Negroe) | | | | 3 | | Strong, Moses | 1 | | | | | Kimberly, Israel | 1 | 2 | | | |
| Humiston, Ebenezer | 1 | 3 | 3 | | | Dickerson, Benjamin | 2 | 1 | 1 | | | Kimberly, Mary | | | 2 | 1 | |
| Roles, James | | | 1 | | | Rexford, Phillip | 1 | | 1 | | | Kimberly, Gilead | 1 | 1 | 3 | | |
| Burke, Elizabeth | | | 1 | | | Baldwin, John | 2 | 1 | 4 | | | Reynolds, James | 1 | 1 | 1 | | 1 |
| Pendergrass, John | 1 | | 1 | | | Ball, Glover | 1 | 3 | 3 | | | Reynolds, James B | 1 | 1 | 2 | 1 | |
| Gowan, William | 1 | | | | | Ball, John | 2 | 2 | 5 | | | Reynolds, Fredrick | 1 | 1 | 2 | | |
| Hotchkiss, Leman | 1 | | | | | Ares, William | 1 | 3 | 4 | | | Catlin, John | 1 | | 2 | | |
| Carr, James | 1 | | | | | Harding, Fredrick | 1 | | 2 | | | Trowbridge, William | 1 | | 1 | | |
| Potter, Seate | 1 | | | | | Hull, David | 2 | 4 | 1 | | | Trowbridge, Samuel | 1 | 1 | 1 | | |
| McCoy, James | 1 | | | | | Johnson, Stephen | 1 | | 1 | | | Stevans, John | 1 | 1 | 1 | | |
| Isaacs, Brown | 1 | | | | | Johnson, Abraham | 1 | | 3 | | | Williams, Joatham | 1 | | 2 | | |
| Sperry, Joseph | 1 | | | | | Sabin, Charles | 1 | 1 | 3 | | | Bunham, Thomas | 1 | 1 | 3 | | |
| Smith, Jesse | 1 | | | | | Alling, Daniel | 4 | | 4 | | | Painter, Thomas | 1 | 1 | 2 | | |
| Pickets, William | 1 | | | | | Alling, Philo | 1 | 3 | 3 | | | Smith, Joseph | 1 | 1 | 4 | | |
| Law, Francis | 1 | | | | | Alling, Caleb | 1 | 1 | 4 | | | Smith, Samuel | 1 | | 5 | | |
| McHolland, Hugh | 1 | | | | | Alling, Silas | 2 | 3 | 3 | | | Smith, Darcus | 1 | 1 | 2 | | |
| Parral, David | 1 | | | | | Chaise, Isaac | 1 | | 1 | | | Smith, Wharam | 1 | | | | |
| Mathews, Thomas | 1 | | | | | Alling, Edward | 1 | 1 | 1 | 1 | | Beecher, Isaac | 1 | 1 | 4 | | |
| Lickleter, James | 1 | | | | | Russell, Samuel | 1 | 3 | 4 | | | Smith, Benjamin | 1 | 1 | 2 | | |
| Green, Daniel | 1 | | | | | Beecher, John | 1 | 2 | 3 | | | Smith, Thomas | 1 | | | | |
| Hicks, Samuel | 1 | | | | | Wolcot, Elisha | 1 | 3 | 1 | | | Smith, Nathan | 1 | 3 | 5 | | |
| Vanorden, John | 1 | | | | | Beecher, Medad | 1 | | 4 | | | Smith, George | 1 | | 1 | | |
| Clarke, Ebenezer | 1 | | | | | Beecher, Raphel | 1 | 1 | 6 | | | Smith, Jeremiah | 2 | | 6 | | |
| Bates, Elias | 1 | | | | | Beecher, Samuel | 1 | | 1 | | | Alling John | 1 | | 2 | | |
| Smith, Joseph | 1 | | | | | Beecher, Lowes | 1 | 1 | 3 | 1 | | Smith, Benjamin, 2nd | 1 | | 4 | | |
| Law, Francis | 1 | | | | | Alling, Amos | 1 | 1 | 3 | | | Steephens, Jesse | 1 | 3 | 3 | | |
| Tuft, Joshua | 1 | | | | | Humpherville, Ebenezer | 1 | | 2 | | | Bemmer, Mary | | | 3 | 2 | |
| Peet, Sherman | 1 | | | | | Humpherville, Joseph | 1 | 1 | 2 | | | Bemmer, Nathaniel | 1 | | 2 | | |
| McCurn, Malecton | 1 | | | | | Humpherville, Moses | 1 | | 2 | | | Ward, Thomas | 1 | 1 | 1 | | |
| Dummer, Jonathan | 1 | | | | | Humpherville, Lemuel | 2 | 1 | 6 | | | Trowbridge, David | 1 | | 1 | | |
| Little, Samuel | 1 | | | | | Pardie, Moses | 2 | | 5 | 1 | | Clarke, Mary | | | 4 | | |
| Raymond, John | 1 | | | | | Humpherville, Samuel | 1 | | 5 | | | Toles, Bethsheba | | | 1 | | |
| Jennings, William | 1 | | | | | Pardie, Sibel | 2 | | 3 | | | Clarke, Thompson | 1 | 1 | 7 | | |
| Miller, Stephen | 1 | | | | | Humpherville, Samuel | 1 | 1 | 2 | | | Beldin, Jerad | 1 | | 1 | | |
| Stephenson, Thomas | 1 | | | | | Smith, Nathan | 3 | | 4 | | | Belding, Rachel | | | 3 | | |
| Fenton, Jonathan | 1 | | | | | Smith, Gould | 1 | | 2 | | | Steephens, David | | 1 | 1 | | |
| Malery (Widow) | | | 1 | | | Meloy, John | 1 | 1 | 2 | | | Smith, Titus | 1 | 3 | 3 | | |
| Jutt, Joseph | 1 | | | | | Lancashire, Abigal | | | 1 | | | Smith, Huldy | 2 | | 1 | | |
| Dukerman, Elisha | 1 | | | | | Johnson, Eneas | 2 | | 3 | | | Thomas, Rhoda | | 1 | 1 | | |
| Smith, Thomas | 1 | | | | | Johnson, Ebenezer | 3 | 3 | 3 | | | Thomas, Aron | 1 | 3 | 5 | | |
| Bullard, Ely | 1 | | | | | Johnson, Lidla | | | 3 | | | Ward, Sibel | | 2 | 3 | | |
| Dickerman, Joseph | 1 | | | | | Alling, John | 1 | 1 | 4 | | | Thompson, Stephen | 1 | 1 | 2 | | |
| Mason, Peter | 1 | | | | | Loyd, Jabez | 1 | 1 | 1 | | | Smith, Eli | 1 | 1 | 1 | | |
| Wilmot, Thomas | 1 | | | 1 | | Thomas, Susanah | | | 1 | | | Smith, Andrew | 2 | 1 | 5 | | |
| Punderson, Lizey | | | 1 | | | Tuttle, Daniel | 2 | | 6 | | | James, Dolly | 1 | 1 | 2 | | |
| Wilmot, Ebenezer | 1 | | | | | Pool, Samuel | 1 | | 3 | | | Thomas, Edward | 3 | 1 | 5 | | |
| Beecher, Stephen | 1 | | | | | Alling, Susannah | | | 2 | | | Thomas, Daniel | 1 | | | 1 | |
| Gourd, Thomas | 1 | | | | | Johnson, John | 1 | 2 | 4 | | | Willoby, Christopher | 1 | 1 | 1 | | |
| Mix (Widow) | | | 1 | | | Beecher, Moses | 2 | | 4 | | | Thomas, Hester | | | 2 | | |
| Hendrick, Sarah | | 1 | 2 | | | Beecher, Moses, 2nd | 1 | 1 | 3 | | | Johnson, John | 2 | | 1 | | |
| Mallery, Elinor | | | 1 | | | Alling, Joseph | 3 | | 2 | | | Smith, Nehamiah | 1 | | | | |
| Warner, Elizabeth | | 1 | 1 | | | Alling, Stephen | 2 | 3 | 4 | | | Smith, Justice | 1 | 1 | 4 | | |
| Dennis, John | 1 | | | | | Thomas, Joseph | 1 | 5 | 3 | | | Thomas, Benjamin | 2 | | 5 | | |
| Mahan, Phillip | 1 | | | | | Prindle, Joseph | 2 | 1 | 3 | | | Beecher, Titus | 1 | | 5 | | |
| Clime, Pillip | 1 | 1 | 2 | | | Prindle, Elisha | 2 | 2 | 4 | | | Latherby, David | 1 | 1 | 4 | | |
| Atkins, Benoni | 2 | 1 | 5 | | | Prindle, John | 1 | 3 | 3 | | | Richard, John | 2 | 3 | 5 | | |
| Martin, John | 1 | 1 | 1 | | | Prindle, Elizabeth | | | 3 | | | Clarke, Daniel | 1 | | | | |
| Bradley, Lewis | 1 | 1 | 4 | | | Prindle, Dina | 1 | 2 | 3 | | | Ward, Henry | 1 | | | | |
| Bradley, Elizabeth | 1 | | 1 | | | Benham, David | 1 | | 4 | | | Thompson, Margeret | | | 1 | | |
| Bradley, Alexander | 1 | 1 | 3 | | | Stebbens, Uriah | 1 | 1 | 5 | | | Allen, Ebenezer | 1 | 2 | 5 | | |
| Drowney, Mary | | | 1 | | | Graham, Elenor | | | 1 | | | Allen, Elijah | 2 | | 3 | | |
| Bradley, Hezekiah | 1 | 1 | 5 | | | Smith, Oliver | 2 | 1 | 5 | | | Ward, John | 1 | | | | |
| Chatterton, Stephen | 1 | 1 | 1 | | | Bristol, David | 2 | 3 | 3 | | | | | | | | |
| Hotchkiss, Lemuel | 3 | 1 | 4 | 1 | | Bristol, David, 2nd | 2 | 1 | 1 | | | **NORTH HAVEN TOWN.** | | | | | |
| Hotchkiss, Lyman | 1 | | 3 | | | Jones, John | 2 | 1 | 4 | | | Tharp, Titus | 1 | 1 | 4 | | |
| Hotchkiss, Joshua | 2 | | 1 | | | Brown, Jonathan | 2 | | 3 | | | Tharp, Mosses | 1 | 1 | 2 | 1 | |
| New, John | 1 | | | | | Benham, John, 2nd | | 2 | 2 | | | Benham, Samuel | 1 | | | | |
| Hotchkiss, Silus | 3 | 3 | 2 | | | Benham, John | 3 | 1 | 3 | | | Thomas, Sarah | | | 1 | | |
| Hotchkiss, Elijur | 2 | 1 | 2 | | | Smith, Edward | 1 | 2 | 5 | | | Peter (Negroe) | | | | 3 | |
| Thompson, James | 2 | 4 | 2 | | | Benham, Gamaliel | 1 | 2 | 3 | | | | | | | | |

# FIRST CENSUS OF THE UNITED STATES.

## NEW HAVEN COUNTY—Continued.

### NORTH HAVEN TOWN—continued.

| Name of head of family. | Free white males of 16 years and upward, including heads of families. | Free white males under 16 years. | Free white females, including heads of families. | All other free persons. | Slaves. |
|---|---|---|---|---|---|
| White Sarah | | | 3 | | |
| Hull, Abner | 1 | | 2 | | |
| Blakesley, Enos | 1 | 1 | 3 | | |
| Barnes, Enoch | 1 | | 2 | | |
| Sandford, Jeremiah | 1 | | 1 | | |
| Tharp, Asa | 1 | 1 | 1 | | |
| Todd, Samuel | 1 | 4 | 1 | | |
| Barnes, Jonathan | 1 | | 1 | | |
| Smith, Abiel | 1 | | 2 | | |
| Bracket, Eneas | 1 | | 4 | | |
| Bracket, Eneas, 2nd | 1 | 3 | 3 | | |
| Spencer, John | 1 | | 1 | | |
| Holly, Miller | 1 | | 2 | | |
| Doolittle, Joseph | 1 | 3 | 3 | | |
| Tuttle, David | 1 | | 1 | | |
| Bradley, Diamond | 1 | 3 | 3 | | |
| Bradly, Joseph | 1 | | 2 | | |
| Bradley, Thomas | 1 | 2 | 2 | | |
| Day, William | 1 | 1 | 5 | 1 | |
| Ives, Noah | 3 | 2 | 3 | | |
| Ives, Daniel | 1 | 3 | 4 | | |
| Ives, Alling | 1 | | 1 | | |
| Ives, Sarah | 1 | | 5 | | |
| Walter, Mahitabel | | | 2 | | |
| Walter, Jacob | 2 | 2 | 2 | | |
| Todd, Seth | 2 | 1 | 5 | | |
| Bracket, Giles | 1 | 1 | 4 | | |
| Seeley, John | 2 | 2 | 1 | | |
| Tuttle, John | 1 | 1 | 4 | | |
| Ives, Sussanah | | | 1 | | |
| Mix, Samuel | 3 | | 5 | 1 | |
| Clarke, Caleb | 2 | 1 | 4 | | |
| Cooper, Joel | 1 | | | | |
| Cooper, Joel, 2nd | 2 | 1 | 1 | | |
| Cooper, Justice | 1 | | 4 | | |
| Cooper, Joseph | 1 | | 4 | | |
| Mix, Stephen | 1 | | 1 | | 1 |
| Eaton, Timothy | 1 | | 6 | | |
| Eaton, Titus | 2 | 1 | 1 | | |
| Brokes, Limeuel | 1 | 2 | 2 | | |
| Tharp, Samuel | 1 | | 6 | | |
| Fowler, Jeremiah | 1 | 4 | 5 | | |
| Mansfield, Richard | 2 | 2 | 1 | | |
| Dayton, John, 2nd | 1 | | 2 | | |
| Tomlinson, Robert | 1 | 1 | 4 | | |
| Starry, Nathan | 1 | 1 | 8 | | |
| Munson, Walter | 2 | | 3 | | |
| Munson, Mansfield | 1 | 1 | 3 | | |
| Passett, Joel | 2 | 2 | 3 | | |
| Simmons, Joshua | 1 | 3 | 4 | | |
| Cooper, Joseph, 2nd | 1 | 1 | 2 | | |
| Ives, James | 2 | 3 | 3 | | |
| Jacobs, Steven | 2 | 3 | 7 | | |
| Jacobs, Eli | 1 | | | | |
| Craine, William | 1 | 2 | 5 | | |
| Tuttle, Simeon | 1 | | 1 | | |
| Darling, Joseph | 1 | 1 | 3 | | |
| Arnold, John | 1 | 1 | 4 | | |
| Bishop, Joy | 1 | | 1 | | |
| Todd, Enos | 1 | 1 | 2 | 1 | |
| Dayton, Jonathan | 2 | 1 | 4 | | |
| Dayton, Cornelius | 1 | 1 | 2 | | |
| Todd, Isaac | 1 | 1 | 1 | | |
| Tharp, David, 2nd | 4 | | 1 | | |
| Tuttle, Deborah | 2 | | | | |
| Tuttle, Abigal | | | 2 | | |
| Tuttle, Joel | 1 | 2 | 4 | | |
| Tuttle, Jonathan | 2 | 1 | 3 | | |
| Eastman, Peter | 2 | 1 | 2 | 1 | |
| Bradley, Ebenezer | 1 | | 1 | | |
| Bradley, Ebenezer, 2nd | 1 | | | | |
| Tuttle, Soloman | 1 | 2 | 6 | | |
| Todd, Caleb | 1 | 1 | 2 | | |
| Todd, Lyman | 1 | | 2 | | |
| Tuttle, Hezekiah | 2 | 4 | 3 | | |
| Tuttle, Ethmah | 4 | 4 | 3 | | |
| Tuttle, Isaac | 1 | 1 | 1 | | |
| Buckley, Job | 2 | 1 | 4 | | |
| Todd, Ethmah | 1 | | | | |
| Tyler, Josep | 1 | 2 | 5 | | |
| Todd, Titus | 2 | 1 | 3 | | |
| Bracket, Samuel | 1 | | | | |
| Bassett, Joseph | 2 | 1 | 3 | | |
| Tuttle, Samuel | 1 | 1 | 2 | | |
| Bishop, Simion | 1 | 2 | 3 | | |
| Bishop, Benjamin | 4 | 1 | 3 | | |
| Bishop, Joy, 2nd | 3 | 2 | 5 | | |
| Blakeley, Seth | 1 | 2 | 6 | | |
| Blakeley, Zelus | 1 | | 4 | | |
| Hill, Stepen | 1 | 1 | 1 | | |
| Hill, John | 1 | | | | |
| Blakesley, Caleb | 1 | 3 | 2 | | |
| Tuttle, Ezra | 2 | 1 | 3 | | |
| Bishop, Abel | 3 | 3 | 2 | | |
| Bassett, Jehu | 1 | | 1 | | |
| Cooper, James | 1 | | 1 | | |
| Mansfield, Thomas | 2 | | 2 | | 2 |
| Humiston, Ephrahim | 3 | 1 | 4 | | |
| Bradley, Justus | 1 | 1 | 3 | | |
| Andrews, Mary | | 2 | 4 | | |
| Todd, Etham | 1 | | 4 | | |
| Tuttle, Limuel | 1 | | 2 | | |
| Turner, Edward | 1 | 1 | 2 | | |
| Ralph, Jonathan | 2 | 1 | 3 | | |
| Trumbull, Benjamin | 2 | 1 | 5 | | |
| Stiles, Clarke | 1 | 2 | 4 | | |
| Parker, John | 1 | 1 | 4 | | |
| Jacobs, Enoch | 1 | 2 | 3 | | |
| Todd, Daniel | 1 | 2 | 4 | | |
| Todd, Joel | 1 | | 1 | | |
| Todd, Soloman | 1 | | 2 | | |
| Todd, Hezekiah | 2 | 1 | 3 | | |
| Sacket, Joel | 1 | | | | |
| Peirpoint, Samuel | 2 | 1 | 4 | | |
| Todd, Bethuel | 1 | 1 | 3 | | |
| Thomas, Josiah | 1 | | 2 | | |
| Selby, Abraham | 1 | | 1 | | |
| Selby, Abraham, 2nd | 1 | 1 | 1 | | |
| Barnes, Benjamin | 1 | | | | |
| Parker, Edmond | 1 | 2 | 3 | | |
| Hull, Daniel | 2 | | 3 | | |
| Beach, Elasa | 2 | 4 | 6 | | |
| Sacket, Soloman | 1 | 2 | 4 | | |
| Ray, Enoch | 2 | | 3 | | |
| Sacket, Eli | 1 | 4 | 4 | | |
| Ray, Thomas | 1 | | | | |
| Beach, Giles | 2 | 1 | 1 | | |
| Beach, Nathaniel | 4 | 3 | 3 | | |
| Frost Titus | 2 | 3 | 3 | | |
| Frost, John | 1 | 1 | 2 | | |
| Frost, John, 2nd | 1 | 1 | 1 | | |
| Sandford, Thomas | 2 | | 1 | | |
| Heaton, John | 1 | 1 | 3 | | 2 |
| Heaton, John, 2nd | 2 | 2 | 3 | | |
| Burke, Ebenzer | 1 | | 2 | | |
| Stephens, Ashael | 1 | 1 | 1 | | |
| Bracket, Richard | 2 | | 3 | | |
| Barnes, Justice | 1 | 2 | 3 | | |
| Bracket, Levi | 2 | 2 | 3 | | |
| Bracket, Benjamin | 2 | 1 | 6 | | |
| Bracket, Abel | 1 | 2 | 3 | | |
| Bracket, Stephen | 1 | 2 | 2 | | |
| Button, Jedediah | 1 | 2 | 2 | | |
| Barnes, Seth | 2 | 2 | 3 | | |
| Barnes, David | 1 | 2 | 2 | | |
| Houghton, Giles | 2 | | 1 | | |
| Ray, Levi | 3 | 1 | 5 | | |
| Cooper, Caleb | 1 | | 3 | | |
| Barnes, John | | | 4 | | |
| Heaton, Calhoun | 3 | 2 | 3 | | |
| Sandford, Eliadia | 1 | | 3 | | |
| Humiston, Thomas | 1 | | 2 | | |
| Jacobs, David | 1 | | 1 | | |
| Jacobs, Soloman | 1 | 3 | 2 | | |
| Bracket, Ebenezer | 3 | | 3 | | |
| Sandford, John | 1 | | 5 | | |
| Sandford, William | 2 | 2 | 4 | | |
| Cooper, Thomas | 2 | 1 | | | |
| Bracket, John | 2 | | 1 | | |
| Bracket, Isaiah | 1 | 3 | 2 | | |
| Barnes, Noah | 1 | 2 | 3 | | |
| Cooper, Isaac | 2 | | 2 | | |
| Pardy, Eliphalet | 2 | 1 | 2 | | |
| Pardy, David | 1 | | 3 | | |
| Pardy, James | 1 | 1 | 4 | | |
| Pardie, John | 1 | | 3 | | |
| Cooper, Thomas | 1 | 4 | 3 | | |
| Cooper, John | 1 | 1 | 3 | | |
| Peirpoint, John | 1 | | 1 | | |
| Peirpoint, James | 2 | 1 | 4 | | |
| Peirpoint, Joseph | 2 | | 1 | | |
| Barnes, Joshua | 1 | | 2 | 3 | |
| Wolcutt, Thomas | 1 | | 3 | | |
| Peirpoint, Hezekiah | 1 | 1 | 3 | | |
| Barnes, Joel | 2 | 1 | 6 | | |
| Barnes, Jerry | 1 | 1 | 2 | | |
| Perth, Andrew | 1 | | 2 | | |
| Peirpoint, Thomas | 2 | 1 | 3 | | |
| Sacket, Samuel | 3 | | 3 | | |
| Bracket, Joseph | 2 | 3 | 3 | | |
| Jacobs, Joseph | 1 | 3 | 2 | | |
| Jacobs, Ezekiel | 1 | 1 | 2 | | |
| Robinson, Mosses | 1 | | 1 | | |
| Todd, Gideon | 2 | | 6 | | |
| Blakesley, Philomen | 1 | 1 | 2 | | |
| Blakesley, Amos | 1 | | 4 | | |
| Tharp, Abner | 1 | | 2 | | |
| Blakesley, Isaac | 1 | 2 | 3 | | |
| Hubbel, Lewis | 1 | 3 | 3 | | |
| Smith, John | 1 | 1 | 1 | | |
| Smith, Thankfull | | | 5 | 2 | |
| Smith, James | 1 | | 2 | | |
| Smith, Thomas | 1 | | 2 | | |
| Smith, Lidia | 1 | 1 | 2 | | |
| Peirpoint, Joseph | 1 | | 2 | | |
| Hull, Joseph | 1 | | 3 | | |
| Hull, Joseph, 2nd | 1 | 5 | 3 | | |
| Turner, Caleb | 1 | | 1 | | |
| Hull, John | 2 | 4 | 3 | | |
| Hull, Benjamin | 1 | 2 | 3 | | |
| Hull, Amie | 1 | | 3 | | |
| Peirpoint, Benjamin | 2 | 1 | 1 | | |
| Peirpoint, Giles | 1 | 2 | 4 | | |
| Peirpoint, Joel | 1 | | 2 | | |
| Todd, James | 1 | | 1 | | |
| Todd, Yale | 1 | 2 | 2 | | |
| Blakesley, Zopher | 3 | | 3 | | |
| Blakesley, Abraham | 1 | 2 | 1 | | |
| Blakesley, Joel | 2 | 2 | 5 | 1 | |
| Clarke, Phineas | 1 | 3 | 2 | | |
| Bassett, Jehu | 1 | | 4 | | |
| Clinton, Lawrence | 1 | 1 | 2 | | |
| Johnson, Stephen | 1 | | 2 | | |
| Bradley, Zewer | 1 | 1 | 4 | | |
| Bradley, Obed | 3 | 1 | 3 | | |
| Blakesley, Jonah | 1 | 2 | 2 | | |
| Tuttle, Ruben | 1 | | 2 | | |
| Jones, Samuel | 1 | 2 | 3 | | |
| Bradley, Joel | 1 | | 2 | | |
| Blakesley, John | 1 | | 2 | | |
| Bassett, Daniel | 2 | 1 | 2 | | |
| Bassett, Isaac | 1 | 1 | 1 | | |
| Bassett, Lidia | 1 | | 1 | | |
| Bassett, Samuel, 2nd | 1 | 4 | 3 | | |
| Bassett, Obed | 1 | | 2 | | |
| Bassett, Samuel | 1 | | 1 | | |
| Doolittle, Daniel | 3 | 3 | 5 | | |
| Alling, Joathem | 1 | 2 | 6 | | |
| Humiston, James | 1 | 3 | 4 | | |
| Hayes, John | 1 | | 2 | | |
| Tharp, Timothy | 1 | 1 | 3 | | |
| Bradley, Titus | 3 | 2 | 5 | | |
| Tharp, David | 3 | 2 | 1 | | |

### WALLINGFORD TOWN.

| Name of head of family. | Free white males of 16 years and upward, including heads of families. | Free white males under 16 years. | Free white females, including heads of families. | All other free persons. | Slaves. |
|---|---|---|---|---|---|
| Meeker, Nathaniel | 1 | | 1 | | |
| Gulbin, Oepas | | 1 | 1 | | |
| Butler, Comfort | 2 | 2 | 5 | | |
| Scovil, David | 1 | 3 | 3 | | |
| Yale, John | 2 | 2 | 4 | | |
| Hubbard, Watts | 2 | 2 | 4 | | |
| London, Charles | 1 | 1 | 2 | | |
| Lark, John | 2 | 1 | 2 | | |
| Lark, Solomon | 1 | | | | |
| Edwards, Jonathan | 1 | | | | |
| Farrington, Jeremiah | 2 | 1 | 4 | | |
| Crane, Daniel | 2 | | 5 | | |
| Austin, Noah | 2 | | 2 | | |
| Wholf, Seth D | 1 | 2 | 2 | | |
| Collins, Jonathan | 2 | 3 | 4 | | |
| Hall, Rufus | 2 | 1 | 4 | | |
| Collins, Edward | 1 | | 1 | | |
| Collins, Edward, 2nd | 1 | 1 | 2 | 1 | |
| Forster, Thomas | 6 | 1 | 3 | | |
| Stow, Thomas | 1 | 1 | 1 | | |
| Merriman, Jesse | 1 | 2 | 2 | | |
| Merriman, Josiah | 1 | 3 | 1 | | |
| Person, Joel | 1 | | 4 | | |
| Benham, Jerad | 1 | 3 | 3 | | |
| Robinson, John | 1 | | | | |
| Forster, Giles | 1 | 4 | 5 | | |
| Forster, Timothy | 2 | | 2 | | |
| Merriman, Caleb | 2 | | 2 | | |
| Merriman, Caleb, 2nd | 2 | 3 | 2 | | |
| Merriman, William | 2 | | 2 | | |
| Austin, John | 1 | | 1 | | |
| Merriman, Asaph | 2 | 4 | 3 | | |
| Meriman, Nathaniel | 2 | 1 | 2 | | |
| Merriman, Edmond | 1 | 2 | 3 | | |
| Merriman, Benjamin | 2 | 1 | 1 | | |
| Merriman, Jesse | 1 | | 1 | | |
| Miriman, John | 1 | 2 | 5 | 1 | |
| Mix, Joel | 1 | | 1 | | |
| Forster, Phebe | | | 2 | 1 | |
| Hough, Louis | 2 | | 2 | | |
| Hough, Samuel, 2nd | 1 | | 4 | | |
| Hough, Mathew | 1 | 2 | 2 | | |
| Hull, George | 1 | | | | |
| Barnes, Abel | 1 | 1 | 1 | | |
| Hough, Philip | 2 | | 2 | | |
| Hough, James | 2 | 4 | 3 | | |
| Scovel, Elizabeth | 2 | 1 | 4 | | |
| Scovel, Elisha | 1 | | 4 | | |
| Hollebut, Daniel | 1 | | | | |

# HEADS OF FAMILIES—CONNECTICUT.

## NEW HAVEN COUNTY—Continued.

### WALLINGFORD TOWN—continued.

| NAME OF HEAD OF FAMILY. | Free white males of 16 years and upward, including heads of families. | Free white males under 16 years. | Free white females, including heads of families. | All other free persons. | Slaves. |
|---|---|---|---|---|---|
| Forster, David | 1 | 2 | 3 | | |
| Shayler, Joseph | 2 | 1 | 5 | | |
| Piper, Jude | 1 | 2 | 4 | | |
| Ways, Abner | 1 | 1 | 1 | | |
| Hall, Elizabeth | 1 | 1 | 3 | | |
| Ways, John | 2 | 1 | 2 | | |
| Ives, Timothy | 1 | 2 | 5 | 1 | |
| Hall, Enos | 1 | 1 | 1 | | |
| Hall, Moses | 1 | 1 | 2 | | |
| Gale, Mathew | 1 | | 1 | | |
| Hall, Elisha | 1 | | 3 | | |
| Ives, Amos | 1 | 2 | 4 | | |
| Hull, Josiah, 2nd | 1 | 1 | 2 | | |
| Hall, Brenton | 3 | 5 | 4 | 1 | |
| Hall, Daniel | 2 | 1 | 4 | | |
| Yeoman, John | 1 | 2 | 5 | | |
| Bin, Isaac | 3 | | 5 | | |
| Ives, Elnathan | 2 | | 3 | | |
| Yale, Jonathan | 2 | 1 | 4 | | |
| Breford, Benjamin | 1 | 2 | 3 | | |
| Andrews, Thomas | 1 | 1 | 2 | | |
| Burres, John | 2 | 4 | 3 | | |
| Yale, Nathaniel | 2 | 3 | 3 | | |
| Yale, Daniel | 1 | 3 | 3 | | |
| Yale, Anna | | | 1 | | |
| Hough, Samuel | 1 | 2 | 3 | | |
| Darling, Samuel | 1 | 3 | 3 | | |
| Hall, Samuel | 2 | 3 | 4 | 2 | 1 |
| Collins, Daniel | 2 | 2 | 4 | 1 | |
| Lyman, Aron | 1 | | 1 | | |
| Willard, John | 1 | | 2 | | |
| Curtis, Levi | 1 | | 1 | | |
| Couch, John | 1 | | 1 | | |
| Couch, John, 2nd | 1 | 3 | 1 | | |
| Yale, Noah | 1 | | 1 | | |
| Yale, Amiton | 1 | | 2 | | |
| Perkins, Simeon | 2 | 3 | 5 | | |
| Coben, John | 1 | | 3 | | |
| Coben, James, 2nd | 1 | 2 | 2 | | |
| Merriman, Joseph | 3 | 1 | 4 | | |
| Andrews, Nicholas | 1 | | | | |
| Andrews, Lidia | | 1 | 4 | | |
| Andrews, Moses | 1 | 2 | 4 | | |
| Merriman, Ephrim | 1 | 2 | 4 | | |
| Merriman, Aron | 1 | 1 | 3 | | |
| Butler, Ezra | 1 | | 4 | | |
| Andrews, Sarah | | 1 | 1 | | |
| Bucket, Runnel | 1 | | | | |
| Merriman, Samuel | 1 | 1 | 2 | | |
| Todd, Caleb | 2 | | 3 | | |
| Merriman, Elisha | 1 | 2 | 2 | | |
| Yale, Nathaniel | 1 | | | | |
| Johnson, Israel | 1 | 2 | 3 | | |
| Livenston, Daniel | 1 | | 1 | | |
| Griswold, Giles | 1 | 2 | 6 | | |
| Lawrence, Elihu | 1 | 3 | 2 | | |
| Merriman, Titus | 2 | | 3 | | |
| Merriman, Joel | 1 | | | | |
| Carter, John | 1 | | 4 | | |
| Baldwin, Smith | 1 | | | | |
| Baldwin, Nathaniel | 1 | 1 | 1 | | |
| Collins, Giles | 2 | 1 | 6 | | |
| Duglass, Nathaniel | 1 | 1 | 4 | | |
| Douglass, Levi | 1 | | 3 | | |
| Holly, Abel | 1 | | 1 | | |
| Rice, Samuel | 2 | 2 | 5 | | |
| Rice, Ezekiel | 3 | 1 | 2 | | |
| Merriman, Amassa | 2 | 3 | 2 | | |
| Livenston, Eunice | | | 1 | | |
| Attwater, Isaac | 1 | 3 | 3 | | |
| Miles, John | 1 | | 1 | | |
| Hotchkiss, Samuel | 1 | | 1 | | |
| Attwater, Eunice | | 1 | 2 | | |
| Attwater, Stephen | 1 | | | | |
| Attwater, David | 1 | | | | |
| Holt, Nathaniel | 1 | 1 | 1 | | |
| Hall, Israel | 2 | 2 | 4 | | |
| Rice, Amassa | 1 | 2 | 5 | | |
| Hall, Aron | 2 | 1 | 5 | | |
| Johnson, Silder | 1 | | 2 | | |
| Rice, Ezra | 1 | 1 | 3 | | |
| Rice, Joel | 1 | 4 | 4 | | |
| Johnson, Samuel | 1 | 1 | 1 | | |
| Johnson, William B | 1 | 2 | 3 | | |
| Cole, Ebenezer | 2 | 1 | 2 | | |
| McKeys Daniel | 2 | | 2 | | |
| Robinson, Theophilus M | 1 | 2 | 3 | | |
| Robinson, Levi | 1 | 1 | 5 | | |
| Hough, Oliver | 1 | | | | |
| Holt, Aron | 2 | | 2 | | |
| Cowls, Timothy | 2 | 2 | 4 | | |
| Cowls, Joseph | 1 | | 1 | | |
| Johnson, William | 1 | 2 | 1 | | |
| Hall, Enos, 2nd | 1 | 1 | 3 | | |
| Yale, Ashal | 1 | 2 | | | |
| Holt, Daniel | 1 | 1 | 2 | | |
| Holt, Daniel, 2nd | 1 | | 1 | | |
| Holt, Benjamin | 1 | | 1 | | |
| Mitchell, Asaph | 1 | 1 | 2 | | |
| Austin, Abel | 4 | 1 | 5 | | |
| Andrews, Dana | 2 | 1 | 3 | | |
| Levit, Samuel | 1 | | 1 | | |
| Yale, Noah | 1 | | 2 | | 1 |
| Yale, Joel | 1 | 1 | 3 | | |
| Lyman, Phineas | 1 | 2 | 4 | | |
| Hubbard, Isaac | 2 | 2 | 4 | 1 | |
| Yale, Nathaniel | 1 | | 1 | | |
| Defforrest, David | 1 | | 1 | | |
| Clarke, Lamberton | 1 | | 4 | | |
| Hall, Joatham | 1 | | 3 | | |
| Aubony, Susannah | | 1 | 2 | | |
| Ives, John | 3 | 2 | 3 | | |
| Cooke, Benjamin | 1 | 3 | 4 | | |
| Merriman, Thomas | 1 | 1 | 4 | | |
| Brainard, David | 1 | | 1 | | |
| Francis, Joseph | 1 | | 5 | | |
| Merriman, Nathaniel | 1 | 1 | 4 | | |
| Hall, Street | 1 | | 2 | | |
| Morse, Joel | 1 | 3 | 1 | | |
| Metune, Ebenezer | 1 | | 2 | | |
| Molthrop, Timothy | 1 | | 1 | | |
| Matune, John | 1 | 1 | 1 | | |
| Matune, Caleb | 1 | | 5 | | |
| Tharp, Elnathan | 1 | 2 | 2 | | |
| Hall, Street T | 1 | | | | |
| Ackley, Dina | | | 4 | | |
| Alling, Archibald | 1 | 3 | 1 | | |
| Curtis, Philip | 1 | | 1 | | |
| Curtis, Phillip, 2nd | 1 | 1 | 1 | | |
| Curtis, Joseph | 1 | | 3 | | |
| Curtis, Joel | 1 | 2 | 2 | 1 | |
| Winston, John | 1 | | 2 | | |
| Durow, Daniel | 1 | 3 | 2 | | |
| Reed, John | 1 | 4 | 2 | | |
| Bertow, Benjamin | 1 | | 2 | | |
| Chipman, Joseph | 1 | 3 | 2 | | |
| Hart, Timothy | 1 | 3 | 2 | | |
| Ives, Amos | 1 | 5 | 3 | | |
| Wade, Ebenezer | 1 | 1 | 2 | | |
| Swift, James | 1 | 2 | 6 | | |
| Jones, Nathaniel | 1 | 1 | 2 | | |
| Jones, Ruben | 1 | 1 | 3 | | |
| Hall, Isaac | 4 | 3 | 1 | | 3 |
| Hall, Eliakim | 1 | | 3 | | |
| Hall, Hezekiah | 1 | 3 | 8 | | |
| Hall, Eliakim, 2nd | 1 | 2 | 8 | | 2 |
| Doolittle, Isaac | 1 | | 1 | | |
| Matune, Samuel | 1 | 1 | 3 | | |
| Booth, John | 1 | 2 | 5 | | |
| Hall, Asa | 1 | 2 | 2 | | |
| Hall, Ezekiel | 1 | | 1 | | |
| Blakely, Joseph | 1 | 1 | 3 | | |
| Fenn, Edward, 2nd | 2 | | 1 | | |
| Blakely, Joseph, 2 | 1 | 2 | 1 | | |
| Fenn, Austin | 2 | | 2 | | |
| Fenn, Edward | 1 | 1 | 3 | | |
| Hall, Thomas | 1 | | 1 | | 1 |
| Ives, Sarah | 2 | 1 | 5 | | |
| Hall, Amassa | 2 | 3 | 3 | | |
| Matune, Isaac | 2 | | 3 | | |
| Hall, David | 3 | 2 | 3 | | |
| Hall, David, 2nd | 1 | 1 | 1 | | |
| Francis, Amos | 1 | 3 | 4 | | |
| Francis, Jacob | 1 | | 2 | | |
| Francis, Joseph | 3 | | 2 | | |
| Ives, Abel | 1 | | 2 | | |
| Ives, John, 3rd | 1 | 3 | 2 | | |
| Ives, Icobod | 1 | 1 | 4 | | |
| London, Ambrose | 1 | 1 | 2 | | |
| Hall, Giles | 2 | 1 | 5 | | |
| Hall, Ephraim | 2 | 2 | 4 | | |
| Hall, Joshua | 1 | | 2 | | |
| Hall, Samuel, 2nd | 1 | | 3 | | |
| Hall, Luben | 1 | 1 | 3 | | |
| Hall, Benjamin | 3 | 2 | 2 | | |
| Douglass, John | 1 | 2 | 1 | | |
| Matune, Hester | | | 2 | | |
| Andrews, Marvel | 1 | | | | |
| Swift, Daniel | 1 | | 2 | | |
| Jolly, Martha | | | 2 | | |
| Hotchkiss, Ambrose | 1 | | | | |
| Baldwin, Elizabeth | | | 5 | | |
| Atkins, David | 2 | 1 | 2 | | |
| Graham, John | 1 | | 1 | | |
| Prout, John | 1 | | 1 | | |
| Miller, Constant | 1 | 4 | 4 | | |
| Baldwin, Samuel | 1 | 2 | 2 | | |
| Baldwin, Daniel | 1 | | 2 | | |
| Baldwin, Daniel, 2nd | 1 | | 2 | | |
| Yeamons, Elizabeth | | 4 | 3 | | |
| Hall, Phineas | 1 | | 2 | | |
| Hall, Phineas, 2nd | 1 | 2 | 2 | | |
| Hall, Levi | 1 | | | | |
| Hall, Benjamin | 1 | | 2 | | |
| Hall, Joash | 1 | 1 | 2 | | |
| Tharp, Jerad | 1 | | 1 | | |
| Wade, John, 2nd | 1 | 1 | 1 | | |
| Hall, John | 4 | 1 | 3 | | |
| Berry, Asael | 1 | 2 | 4 | | |
| Whiting, Samuel | 2 | 1 | 5 | | |
| Ives, Samuel | 2 | 2 | 4 | | |
| Ives, Bazelel | 1 | | 2 | | |
| Ives, John | 3 | 2 | 3 | | |
| Ives, Levi | 1 | 1 | 3 | | |
| Curtis, Abel | 4 | 2 | 4 | | |
| Hall, Isaac | 4 | 4 | 6 | | |
| Freeman (Negroe) | | | | 4 | |
| Perkins, Stephen | 1 | 1 | 2 | | |
| Hough, Ensign | 1 | 2 | 4 | | |
| Hall, Theophilus | 2 | 2 | 4 | | |
| Carter, Benjamin | 6 | 4 | 4 | | |
| Webb, John | 1 | | 1 | | |
| Baldwin, Ebenezer | 1 | | | | |
| Mitchel, Moses | 1 | | 2 | | |
| Mitchel, Zenus | 2 | 1 | 4 | | |
| Rinbal, Rachael | | | 1 | | |
| Smith, William | 1 | 1 | 1 | | |
| Curtis, Elisha | 1 | 1 | 4 | | |
| Avery, Edmond | 1 | 2 | 3 | | |
| Austin, John | 1 | 3 | 4 | | |
| Smith, Elizabeth | 1 | | 2 | | |
| Voce, Jesse | 1 | | 1 | | |
| Cooke, Jesse | 1 | 1 | 5 | | |
| Peck, Stephen | 2 | 1 | 4 | | |
| Ives, Abijah | 1 | 1 | 3 | | |
| Rice, Amos | 4 | | 3 | | |
| Clarke, Daniel | 2 | 1 | 2 | | |
| Curtis, Jacob | 1 | 1 | 2 | | |
| Hull, Eunice | | | 2 | | |
| Rice, James | 2 | 4 | 4 | | |
| Yale, Stephen | 2 | 2 | 3 | | |
| Peck, Nicholas | 1 | | 2 | | |
| Murren, Thomas | 4 | | 5 | | |
| Andrews, Anson | 2 | 4 | 2 | | |
| Clarke, Archibald | 2 | | 1 | | |
| Woodruf, Samuel | 1 | 2 | 2 | | |
| Mix, Josiah | 2 | 3 | 5 | | |
| Colly, George | 1 | 1 | 1 | | |
| Carter, John | 1 | | 4 | | |
| Pane, William | 1 | 1 | 1 | | |
| Day, Stephen | 1 | 3 | 6 | | |
| Day, Israel | 1 | | 1 | | |
| Tuttle, Chales | 2 | 1 | 4 | | |
| Beamont, Deoadah | 1 | 1 | 3 | | |
| Peck, Samuel | 2 | 1 | 6 | | |
| Chittenton, Benjamin | 1 | 4 | 2 | | |
| Andrews, Stephen | 3 | | 3 | | |
| Barnes, Samuel | 1 | 1 | 3 | | |
| Mansfield, John | 3 | 1 | 1 | | |
| Cooke, Amos | 1 | | 3 | | |
| Morse, Ebenezer | 3 | 1 | 4 | | |
| Johnson, Miles | 1 | 3 | 3 | | |
| Street, Caleb | 1 | 3 | 6 | | |
| Lewis, Samuel | 3 | 2 | 4 | | |
| Carrington, Jerem | 4 | 2 | 3 | | |
| Wettlesey, Elisha, 2 | 1 | 3 | 4 | | |
| Noyce, James | 1 | | 4 | | 1 |
| Bissinton, Robert | 1 | | 1 | | |
| Bissinton, Heil | 2 | 1 | 2 | | |
| Hall, Prudence | 1 | | 2 | | |
| Ackley, Aron | 2 | 3 | 6 | | |
| Bissenton, Asael | 2 | 1 | 6 | | |
| Rogers, Gideon | 2 | | 5 | | |
| McCleave, John | 1 | 1 | 2 | | |
| Merriman, Caleb | 1 | 3 | 2 | | 1 |
| Persons, Aron | 1 | 2 | 4 | | |
| Smith, Daniel | 1 | 3 | 1 | | |
| Gales, Moses | 2 | 1 | 2 | | |
| Street, Samuel | 1 | | 2 | | |
| Catlin, William | 1 | | 2 | | |
| Street, Elnathan | 1 | | 3 | | 2 |
| Potter, Jerad | 1 | | 3 | | |
| Hall, Charles | 1 | 3 | 3 | | |
| Carrington, Jerh, 2nd | 1 | 1 | 2 | | |
| Marks, James | 2 | | 3 | | |
| Marks, Levi | 1 | 2 | 1 | | |
| Doolittle, Daniel | 1 | | 1 | | |
| Vanette, James | 1 | 3 | 2 | | |
| Lovewell, Fredrick | 1 | | | | |
| Downs, Elizabeth | | | 1 | | |
| Downs, Sarah | | 1 | 2 | | |
| Ives, Fitch | 1 | | | | |
| Ives, Elnathan | 1 | | | | |
| Ives, Noel | 1 | | | | |

# FIRST CENSUS OF THE UNITED STATES.

## NEW HAVEN COUNTY—Continued.

### WALLINGFORD TOWN—continued.

| NAME OF HEAD OF FAMILY. | Free white males of 16 years and upward, including heads of families. | Free white males under 16 years. | Free white females, including heads of families. | All other free persons. | Slaves. |
|---|---|---|---|---|---|
| Camp, Amos | 1 | 1 | 1 | | |
| Hough, Joseph | 1 | 1 | 2 | | |
| Hough, Joseph, 2 | 2 | 1 | 5 | | |
| Hart, Benjamin | 1 | 1 | 5 | | |
| Yale, Samuel | 1 | 3 | 2 | | |
| Rice, Justice | 1 | 1 | 1 | | |
| Parker, Daniel | 2 | 1 | 4 | | |
| Rice, Abner | 1 | 4 | 3 | | |
| Rice, Moses | 1 | | 1 | | 5 |
| Rice, Amos | 1 | 1 | 2 | | |
| Hough, Ephrim | 2 | 3 | 5 | | |
| Hough, Andrew | 1 | 1 | 4 | | |
| Hough, Lidia | | | 1 | | |
| Baldwin, James | | 1 | 2 | | |
| Sanderson, William | 2 | | 3 | | |
| Davidson, John | 1 | 1 | 1 | | |
| Berry, Thomas | 1 | 1 | 2 | | |
| Cobin, Joseph | 1 | 1 | 1 | | |
| Alling, Amby | | | 1 | | |
| Rice, Joseph | 1 | 3 | 3 | | |
| Gale, Elihu | 1 | 3 | 5 | | |
| Andrews, Bartholomew | 2 | 1 | 3 | | |
| Hull, John | 1 | 2 | 3 | | |
| Wollcot, Samuel | 1 | 3 | 2 | | |
| Austin, Ezra | 1 | 1 | 4 | | |
| Hall, Andrew | 1 | | | | |
| Tyler, Samuel | 3 | 1 | 7 | | |
| Hough, Lent | 1 | 1 | 3 | | |
| Hull, Charles | 1 | 1 | 3 | | |
| Hull, Ebenezer | 1 | 2 | 4 | | |
| Stanley, Abraham | 1 | 1 | 1 | 2 | |
| Adwick, William | 1 | | | | |
| Bunker, James | 1 | | | | |
| Dudley, John | 2 | | 3 | | |
| Hall, Joel | 1 | 1 | 3 | | 1 |
| Newton, Aron | 1 | 1 | 1 | | |
| Cooke, Ephraim | 3 | 4 | 3 | | |
| Parker, Arnold | 1 | 1 | 2 | | |
| Ives, Abigal | | | 1 | | |
| Davison, Samuel | 1 | | | | |
| Davison, Anna | | | 3 | | |
| Tyler, John | 1 | | | | |
| Owing, Patience | | 1 | 2 | | |
| Tyler, Jerad | 3 | 1 | 3 | | |
| Persons, Samuel | 1 | | 3 | | |
| Clarke, James | 1 | 1 | 2 | | |
| Parker, Benjamin | 1 | 2 | 3 | | |
| Hill, Molly | | | 1 | | |
| Parker, Elliady | 2 | | 2 | | |
| Parker, Levi | 1 | 3 | 3 | | |
| Rice, Thadeus | 2 | | 6 | | |
| Hitchcock, Nathaniel | 1 | 1 | 5 | | |
| Beach, Mary | 1 | 1 | 3 | | |
| Gales, John | 1 | 1 | 2 | | |
| Preston, Samuel | 3 | 3 | 4 | | |
| Parker, Joshua | 2 | 3 | 7 | | |
| Distin, Josep | 2 | | 4 | | |
| Parker, Waitfull | 1 | | 1 | | |
| Parker, Charles | 2 | 1 | 2 | | |
| Hummiston, James | 2 | 1 | 2 | | |
| Hummiston, James, 2nd | 1 | | 1 | | |
| Ives, John | 2 | 2 | 7 | | |
| Beach, Moses | 1 | 2 | 2 | | |
| Beach, Titus | 1 | | | | |
| Rice, Samuel | | 1 | 2 | | |
| Cobert, James | 1 | 2 | 3 | | |
| Way, David | 1 | 1 | 3 | | |
| Yale, Joel | 1 | | 3 | | |
| Cobert, Hannah | | | 2 | | |
| Worthinton, Elizabeth | | 1 | 2 | | |
| Hitchcock, Hannah | | 1 | 4 | | |
| Parker, Gamaleel | 2 | 3 | 2 | | |
| Parker, Ephrim | 1 | 2 | 5 | | |
| Parker, Amos | 1 | | 3 | | |
| Hitchcock, Joash | 1 | 1 | 2 | | |
| Beach, William | 2 | | 3 | | |
| Johnson, Dan | 2 | 5 | 3 | | |
| Johnson, Soloman | 3 | 2 | 4 | | |
| Beach, Stephen | 1 | 4 | 5 | | |
| Conner, Elizabeth | 1 | | 5 | | |
| Bard, James | 3 | 1 | 1 | | |
| Parker, Isaac | 1 | 1 | 2 | | |
| Tyler, Jason | 1 | 1 | 3 | | |
| Johnson, Dayton | 3 | | 2 | | |
| Parker, Joseph | 2 | | 7 | | |
| Beech, John | 3 | 4 | 3 | | 1 |
| Cooke, Thaddeus | 2 | | 6 | | 5 |
| Preston, Benjamin | 1 | | 5 | | |
| Cooke, Samuel | 2 | 4 | 4 | | |
| Preston, Titus | 1 | 1 | 2 | | |
| Parker, Eliakim | 1 | 1 | 2 | | |
| Dudley, Zebulon | 2 | | 4 | | |
| Hitchcock, Dan | 1 | 4 | 5 | | |
| Johnson, John | 1 | 1 | 4 | | |
| How, Noah | 1 | 1 | 4 | | |
| Johnson, David | 1 | 4 | 2 | | |
| Frost, Amos | 1 | 1 | 2 | | |
| Tuttle, Benj | 1 | | 6 | | |
| Tuttle, Jonathan | 2 | 1 | 3 | | |
| Tuttle, Jetus | 1 | | | | |
| Johnson, Ephraim | 3 | | 3 | | |
| Johnson, Hezekiah | 2 | 1 | 5 | | |
| Fitch, Lidia | | | 3 | | |
| Dudley, Dyer | 1 | 5 | 5 | | |
| Jones, Theophilus | 1 | 1 | 2 | | 3 |
| Doolittle, Joseph | 2 | | 2 | | |
| Doolittle, Oliver | 1 | 1 | 3 | | |
| Merriman, George | 2 | 1 | 6 | | |
| Hall, Elihu | 1 | 4 | 3 | | 8 |
| Benham, Lettice | | | 3 | | |
| Hotchkiss, Anna | | | 1 | | |
| Stephensen, John | 1 | 4 | 2 | | |
| Munson, Eliphalet | 1 | 3 | 1 | | |
| Jones, Nicholas | 1 | | 4 | | |
| Doolittle, Ruben | 1 | 1 | 1 | | |
| Doolittle, Joel | 2 | 2 | 2 | | |
| Jack (Negroe) | | | | 1 | |
| Cooke, Molly | | 1 | 4 | | |
| Potter (Negroe) | | | | 2 | |
| Cooke, David | 1 | | | | |
| Kimberly, Thomas | 1 | | | | |
| Fenn, Benjamin | 1 | | | | |
| Hall, Benijah | 1 | 1 | 3 | | |
| Mix, John | 3 | 3 | 3 | | |
| Mix, Thomas | 1 | | | | |
| Andrews, Nathaniel | 1 | 3 | 2 | | |
| Andrews, Andrew | 1 | | 2 | | 1 |
| Williams, William | | | 2 | | |
| Ives, Charles | 1 | 1 | 3 | | |
| Winchester, Amajh | 1 | 2 | 3 | | |
| Ives, Joel | 1 | | | | 1 |
| Ives, Joel, 2nd | 1 | 2 | 3 | | |
| Morse, Jonathan | 2 | 3 | 6 | | |
| Morse, Jonathan | 1 | | | | |
| Morse, Levi | 2 | 1 | 2 | | |
| Morse, Bemijah | 1 | | 3 | | |
| Kemp, Charles | 1 | | 1 | | |
| Yale, Elihu | 1 | 1 | 2 | | |
| Jones, William | 1 | | 2 | | |
| Baldwin, David | 2 | 2 | 4 | | |
| Hull, Jeremiah | 1 | | 4 | | |
| Hart, Nathaniel | 3 | | 3 | | |
| Rice, Hannah | | 1 | 2 | | |
| Hough, James | 1 | 2 | 3 | | |
| Feild, Edmond | 7 | | 4 | | |
| Hull, John | 2 | 1 | 3 | | |
| Hough, Joseph | 1 | 1 | 2 | | |
| Hough, Joseph, 2nd | 2 | 1 | 5 | | |
| Hendrick, John | 1 | 3 | 3 | | |
| Ives, Ruben | 1 | 1 | 1 | | |
| Curtis, Nathaniel | 1 | 1 | 3 | | |
| Whittlesey, Elisha, 2nd | 1 | | | | |
| Attwater, Caleb | 1 | | | | |
| Yale Amassa | 1 | 2 | 2 | | |
| Hall, Titus | 2 | 2 | 4 | | |
| Smith, Elisha | 2 | 2 | 4 | | |
| Sheppard, Isaac | 2 | 1 | 4 | | |
| Honferd, Rubin | 2 | 1 | 3 | | |
| Merriman, Elisha | 1 | 2 | 4 | | |
| Hall, Sarah | | | 3 | | |
| Sheet, Hester | | | 2 | | |
| Parsons, Hester | | | 1 | | |
| Cole, Hannah | | 2 | 1 | | |
| Scarrot, James | 3 | 2 | 4 | | |
| Carter, Margeret | | | 1 | | |
| Samson (Negroe) | | | | 2 | |
| Attwater, Benjam | 1 | | 1 | | |
| Cooke, Peter | 2 | 3 | 2 | | |
| Stanley, Oliver | 3 | 2 | 2 | | |
| Cooke, Caleb | 2 | 1 | 4 | | |
| James, Rachael | 1 | | 1 | | |
| Rice, James | 1 | | | | |
| Baldwin, Benjn | 1 | | 1 | | |
| Voce, Charles | 1 | | 2 | | |
| Peck, Samuel, 3rd | 1 | | 2 | | |
| Cooke, Ambrose | 2 | 1 | 7 | | |
| Peck, Peter | 1 | 1 | 4 | | |
| Frisbee, Levi | 1 | 1 | 2 | | |
| Miles, Daniel | 1 | 2 | 4 | | |
| Austin, Elias | 1 | | 2 | | |
| Hull, Eldad | 1 | 1 | 2 | | |
| Cooke, Isaac | 1 | 1 | 5 | | |
| Ives, John, 4th | 2 | 3 | 5 | | |
| Carrington, Timothy | 1 | | 2 | | |
| Carrington, Lemuel | 1 | | 1 | | |
| Cooke, Attwater | 2 | 1 | 6 | | |
| Hull, Benjamin | 3 | | 3 | | |
| Tebbalds, Abner | 1 | | 1 | | |
| Lewis, Hester | | | 1 | | |
| Cooke, Meriman | 2 | 4 | 6 | | |
| Jepbell, Abel | 2 | 2 | 4 | | |
| Cooke, Hannah | | | 1 | | |
| Doolittle, Isaac | 1 | 1 | 1 | | |
| Peck, Abner | 1 | 4 | 4 | | |
| Culver, Charles | 1 | 1 | 2 | | |
| Culver, Benjamin | 1 | | 1 | | |
| Culver, Benjamin, 2nd | 1 | 3 | 3 | | |
| Bracket, Titus | 1 | 3 | 3 | | |
| Munson, Joshua | 1 | 3 | 4 | | |
| Williams, Willoby | 1 | 1 | 2 | | |
| Williams, Harmon | 1 | | 1 | | |
| Hall, Peter | 2 | 1 | | | 3 |
| Hall, Abell | 1 | 1 | 2 | | |
| Hall, Abell, 2nd | 1 | 1 | 3 | | |
| Hall, Daniel J | 1 | 2 | 3 | | |
| Hall, Arael | 1 | 1 | 1 | | |
| Hopson, Alvanus | 2 | 5 | 5 | | |
| Hopson, Rue | 1 | | 4 | | |
| Tharp, Abner | 1 | | 2 | | |
| Hopson, Ashbel | 1 | 4 | 5 | | |
| Hopson, Clement | 1 | 1 | 2 | | |
| Hall, Aron | 2 | 2 | 5 | | |
| Hall, Arael, 2nd | 1 | 2 | 2 | | |
| Ives, Joseph | 1 | | 1 | | |
| Hall, Andrew | 1 | 2 | 2 | | |
| Hall, Joel | 3 | 2 | 2 | | |
| Batholomew, Andw | 1 | 5 | 4 | | |
| Austin, Joshua | 2 | 2 | 3 | | |
| Bartholomew, Isaac | 1 | 5 | 4 | | |
| Bartholomew, Jona | 1 | 3 | 3 | | |
| Avery, Abner | 1 | 1 | | | |
| Avery, Abner, 2nd | 1 | 1 | 4 | | |
| Hopson, Samuel | 2 | 3 | 5 | | |
| Page, Isaac | 1 | | | | |
| Webber, Stephen | 1 | 2 | 3 | | |
| Page, Balthus | | | | | |
| Austin, Joel | 2 | 3 | 5 | | |
| Austin, Moses | 1 | 1 | 1 | | |
| Cooke, Titus | 1 | 2 | 2 | | |
| Dina (Negroe) | | | | 1 | |
| Cooke, Chancy | 1 | | 1 | | |
| Cooke, James | 1 | 1 | 2 | | |
| Culver, Hannah | | | 4 | | |
| Culver, Samuel | 1 | 2 | 3 | | |
| Culver, James | 1 | 1 | 4 | | |
| Luttinton, Oliver | 1 | 1 | 1 | | |
| Peck, Dan | 2 | | 1 | | |
| Culver, Ebenezer | 1 | 1 | 3 | | |
| Culver, John | 1 | 4 | 2 | | |
| Culver, Enoch | 1 | 1 | 3 | | |
| Culver, Enoch, 2nd | 1 | | 2 | | |
| Peck, Samuel | 2 | 3 | 5 | | |
| Todd, Heil | 1 | 5 | 1 | | |
| Hull, Heil | 1 | 6 | 2 | | |
| Hull, Peter, 2nd | 2 | 5 | 3 | | |
| Cooke, Aron | 3 | 3 | 4 | | 2 |
| Cooke, Abel | 2 | 7 | 1 | | |
| Cooke, Stephen | 1 | 3 | 3 | | |
| Cooke, Samuel | 1 | 1 | 4 | | |
| Collins, Uriah | 1 | | 3 | | |
| Todd, Asa | 1 | 2 | 6 | | |
| Munson, Joseph | 2 | 3 | 3 | | |
| Whitney, Enos | 1 | 1 | 2 | | |
| Munson, Samuel, 2nd | 1 | 1 | 2 | | |
| Munson, Isaac | 1 | 1 | 4 | | |
| Smith, Eli | 2 | | 2 | | |
| Munson, Samuel | 3 | | 1 | | |
| Lewis, Gerad | 2 | 3 | 3 | | |
| Todd, Stephen | 2 | | 6 | | |
| Katlin, Isaac | 1 | 1 | 6 | | |
| Munson, Ethel | 1 | 2 | 3 | | |
| Doolittle, Samuel | 2 | 2 | 2 | | |
| Alling, David | 1 | 1 | 3 | | |
| Street, Glover | 3 | 1 | 3 | | |
| Street, Samuel | 1 | | 2 | | |
| Rice, Thomas | 1 | 1 | 3 | | |
| Street, Samuel, 2nd | 1 | 2 | 2 | | |
| Alling, Daniel | 2 | 2 | 4 | | |
| Alling, Enos | 1 | 1 | 3 | | |
| Doolittle, Benjamin | 2 | 1 | 1 | | |
| Doolittle, Charles | 1 | 1 | 1 | | |
| Doolittle, Samuel, 2 | 1 | | 1 | | |
| Thompson, Elihu | 1 | | 1 | | |
| Bartholomew, Moses | 1 | 1 | 2 | | |
| Austin, Joseph | 1 | 1 | 2 | | |
| Wright, Samuel | 1 | | 1 | | |
| Houd, Daniel | 1 | | 3 | | |
| Ward, Amie | | | 5 | | |
| Johnson, Ward | 1 | 2 | 3 | | |
| Barker, John | 1 | | 2 | | |
| Barker, Edward | 2 | | 3 | | 3 |
| Barker, Abigail | | 4 | 2 | | |
| Clinton, Jesse | 1 | 1 | 2 | | |
| Catlin, Constant | 2 | | 4 | | |
| Ives, Caleb | 1 | | 2 | | |

# HEADS OF FAMILIES—CONNECTICUT.

## NEW HAVEN COUNTY—Continued.

| NAME OF HEAD OF FAMILY. | Free white males of 16 years and upward, including heads of families. | Free white males under 16 years. | Free white females, including heads of families. | All other free persons. | Slaves. | NAME OF HEAD OF FAMILY. | Free white males of 16 years and upward, including heads of families. | Free white males under 16 years. | Free white females, including heads of families. | All other free persons. | Slaves. | NAME OF HEAD OF FAMILY. | Free white males of 16 years and upward, including heads of families. | Free white males under 16 years. | Free white females, including heads of families. | All other free persons. | Slaves. |
|---|---|---|---|---|---|---|---|---|---|---|---|---|---|---|---|---|---|
| **WALLINGFORD TOWN—continued.** | | | | | | **WATERBURY TOWN—continued.** | | | | | | **WATERBURY TOWN—continued.** | | | | | |
| Bracket, Elisha | 1 | 2 | 4 | | | Cooke, Sarah | | | 1 | | | Welton, Oliver | 1 | | 1 | | |
| Thompson, Abel, 2nd | 1 | | 2 | | | Hopkins, Jesse | 1 | 1 | | | | Warner, Ruben | 1 | | 1 | | |
| Thompson, Abel | 1 | | 1 | | | Holmes, Israel | 1 | | | | | Welton, Richard | 2 | 3 | 4 | | |
| Doolittle, Ann | | | 1 | | | Nicol, Lidia | | | 1 | | | Scott, Edmond | 1 | 1 | 2 | | |
| Doolittle, John | 1 | | 3 | | | Bolt, Louis | | | 1 | | | Warner, Joseph, 2nd | 2 | 2 | 4 | | |
| Cornwell, Cornelius | 1 | | 2 | | | Nicol, Sussanah | | | 2 | | | Frost, Samuel | 1 | | 1 | | |
| Doolittle, Johnson | 1 | | | | | Nicoll, Polly | | | 1 | | | Taylor, Theodore | 1 | 3 | 1 | | |
| Bracket, Phebe | | | 3 | | | Welsh, Patrick | | | 1 | | | Frost, Timothy | 2 | | 7 | | |
| Bracket, Martha | | | 1 | | | Brunson, Joseph | 1 | | 4 | | | Leavenworth, Thomas | 1 | 1 | 1 | | |
| Rice, William | 1 | 1 | 1 | | | Porter, Daniel | 1 | | 1 | | | Turrel, Binjamin | 2 | 1 | 3 | | |
| Plump, Seth | 1 | | | | | Welton, Hy | 1 | | | | | Scott, Zebulon | 1 | | 1 | | |
| Bracket, Jerad | 1 | 1 | 1 | | | Cooke, Moses | 3 | 1 | 4 | | | Scott, Simeon | 1 | 5 | 4 | | |
| Spencer, Henry | 1 | 3 | 2 | | | McClaud, John | 1 | | 1 | | | Brown, Daniel | 2 | | 2 | | |
| Rice, Jesse | 1 | 3 | 3 | | | Knolton, John | 1 | | 1 | | | Brown, Daniel, 2nd | 1 | 3 | 5 | | |
| Abbot, Joseph | 2 | 2 | 6 | | | Nicol, Richard | 1 | | 1 | | | Brown, Asoph | 1 | 1 | 4 | | |
| Doolittle, Elizabeth | | 1 | 3 | | | Root, Eneas | 1 | 4 | 3 | | | Brown, Elias | 1 | 1 | 3 | | |
| Bradly, Isaac | 2 | | 1 | | | Nettleton, Elizh | 2 | | 5 | | | Brunson, Michael | 1 | 2 | 4 | | |
| Clarke, Job | 1 | 1 | 1 | | | Nicol, Simon | 1 | 2 | 5 | | | Brunson, Asher | 1 | | | | |
| Hall, Thankfull | 1 | 2 | 4 | | | Hoadly, Lemuel | 3 | 3 | 4 | | | Brown, Asa | 1 | 2 | 3 | | |
| Eran (Negroe) | | | | 2 | | Pritchett, Isaih | 1 | 1 | 2 | | | Merrill, Caleb | 2 | | 2 | | |
| Sharper (Negroe) | | | | 2 | | Brecket, Zenus | 2 | 2 | 3 | | | Richards, Elizabeth | 1 | 3 | 3 | | |
| Dutton, Eunice | 1 | 2 | 3 | | | Preshell, George, 2nd | 1 | 5 | 2 | | | Merrills, Nathanel | 1 | 3 | 2 | | |
| Dutton, Amos | 1 | | | | | Hotchkiss, Stephen | 1 | 1 | 5 | | | Brunson, Sibey | 4 | 5 | 6 | | |
| Hall, Stephen | 1 | 1 | 2 | | | Hotchkiss, Abraham | 3 | 2 | 3 | | | Munson, Hammon | 2 | 1 | 3 | | |
| Hall, Samuel, 2nd | 1 | 4 | 5 | | | Tyler, Ruben | 1 | | 4 | | | Clarke, John | 1 | 2 | 1 | | |
| Cooley, Arael | 3 | 1 | 3 | | | Ives, Steven | 2 | 1 | 3 | | | Brunson, Mary | | | 1 | | |
| Hall, Elisha | 3 | 1 | 5 | | | Paine, Joseph | 1 | 2 | 3 | | | Hicock, Jesse | | 1 | 2 | | |
| Attwater, Jeremh | 1 | | | | | Brunson, Samuel | 1 | 2 | 3 | | | Merrils, Icobad | 1 | 1 | 3 | | |
| Catlin, Jerham | 3 | 3 | 3 | | | Paine, Thomas | 1 | 3 | 3 | | | Tomkins, Elizabeth | 1 | 2 | 2 | | |
| Cooke, Augistin | 1 | | | | | Hill, Jarad | 2 | 2 | 3 | | | Buckingham, David | 2 | 1 | 2 | | |
| Beevel, Martin | 1 | 3 | 1 | | | Hill, Obadiah | 1 | 1 | 1 | | | Davis, Edward | 1 | 1 | 1 | | |
| Doolittle, Soloman | 2 | 2 | 5 | | | Peirpoint, Ezra | 1 | 2 | 3 | | | Tuttle, Jesse | 1 | 2 | 1 | | |
| Peck, Heil | | | 3 | | | Hotchkiss, Eldad | 1 | 1 | 2 | | | Warner, Elinor | | | 1 | | |
| Yale, Hannah | | | 3 | | | Blakley, Ebenezer | 2 | 3 | 5 | | | Welton, Amassa | 1 | 1 | 5 | | |
| Hull, Harvey | 1 | 1 | 3 | | | Benham, Thomas | 2 | 3 | 2 | | | Wetmore, John | 1 | | | | |
| Rice, Lucy | | | 1 | | | Dutton, Thomas | 1 | 1 | 2 | | | Osborn, Isaac | | 2 | 2 | | |
| Bunce, John | 1 | | | | | Hummiston, Joy | | | 2 | | | Hicock, Timothy | 1 | 2 | 6 | | |
| | | | | | | Munson, Elizabeth | 1 | 1 | 3 | | | Brown, James | 4 | 1 | 2 | | |
| **WATERBURY TOWN.** | | | | | | Root, Samuel | 1 | | 4 | | | Orton, Guy | 1 | | 1 | | |
| Hecock, John | 1 | 1 | 3 | | | Mix, Samuel | 1 | 3 | 1 | | | Miles, Simon | 1 | | 1 | | |
| Brunson, Ebenezur | 2 | 1 | 3 | | | Mix, Eldad | 2 | | 2 | | | Brown, Ebenezer | 1 | 2 | 3 | | |
| Brunson, Amassa | 1 | | 2 | | | Mix, Levi | 1 | | 1 | | | Leavenworth, Samuel | 2 | 1 | 4 | | |
| Baldwin, Benjamin | 1 | | 3 | | | Olds, Gersham | 1 | 3 | 1 | | | Tomkins, Philip | 2 | 1 | 4 | | |
| Hicock, Prosper | 1 | | | | | Hodley, Andrew | 1 | 1 | 2 | | | Warner, Abijah | 1 | 2 | 6 | | |
| Frost, Moses | 1 | | 3 | | | Callow, Miles | 1 | | 2 | | | Warner, Ephraim | 2 | | 2 | | |
| Tuttle, Hannah | | | 3 | | | Benham, Isaac | 1 | | 1 | | | Barnes, Jonathan | 1 | 2 | 3 | | |
| Taylor, David | 1 | | 2 | | | Boxton, John | 1 | | 2 | | | Conder, Daniel | 2 | 1 | 3 | | |
| Johnson, Abner | 1 | | 3 | | | Johnson, Cornelius | 1 | | 1 | | | Frost, Samuel, 2nd | 1 | 2 | 2 | | |
| Frost, Jason | 2 | | 4 | | | Johnson, Jesse | 1 | 1 | 5 | | | Frost, Isaac | 1 | 1 | 3 | | |
| Hopkins, Joseph | 2 | 1 | 3 | 1 | | Johnson, Lyman | 1 | 1 | 3 | | | Sortune, Mary | | | 3 | | |
| Judd, Samuel | 2 | 1 | 4 | | | Beech, Joseph | 1 | | | | | Bristow, Stephen | 1 | 2 | 3 | | |
| Brunson, Mark | 1 | 1 | 2 | | | Beach, Joseph, 2nd | 2 | 3 | 4 | | | Sanders, Nathaniel | 1 | 2 | 2 | | |
| Brunson, Ezra | 2 | 1 | 3 | | | Beach, Asa | 1 | 1 | 2 | | | Hine, David | 3 | | 1 | | |
| Fox, Ebenezer | 1 | 1 | 3 | | | Spony, Elizabeth | 1 | 2 | 2 | | | Kellock, Morton | 2 | 3 | 4 | | |
| Harrison, Lemuel | 1 | | 1 | | | Hoadly, Nathl | 1 | | 2 | | | Kellock, Joseph | 1 | | 2 | | |
| Leavenworth, Mark | 1 | 1 | 2 | | 1 | Hoadley, Asa | 2 | | 3 | | | Merril, Elizabeth | 1 | 1 | 4 | | |
| Leavenworth, William | 1 | 1 | 3 | | | Munson, William | 1 | 1 | 2 | | | Benedick, Aron | 2 | 2 | 5 | | |
| Brunson, Stephen | 1 | 2 | 4 | | | Hummiston, Bennet | 1 | 2 | 1 | | | Thompson, John | 3 | 2 | 7 | | |
| Scovel, Samuel | 2 | 1 | 2 | | | Betram, Benjamin | 2 | 1 | 1 | | | Morris, William | 1 | 6 | 2 | | |
| Upson, Benjamin | 3 | 1 | 3 | | | Benham, Shadreck | 1 | 2 | 3 | | | Brunson, Rosswell | 1 | 1 | 4 | | |
| Beardsley, Levi | 1 | 1 | 3 | | | Hitchcock, Benjamin | 1 | 6 | 3 | | | Atwell, Thomas | 1 | 2 | 3 | | |
| Porter, Phineas | 1 | 2 | 5 | | | Merriman, Joel | 1 | 2 | 3 | | | Munson, Caleb | 1 | 5 | 1 | | |
| Pritchet, David | 1 | 2 | 4 | | | Austin, Edmond | 2 | 3 | 4 | | | Clarke, John | 2 | 1 | 2 | | |
| Baldwin, Isaac | 3 | | 4 | | 1 | Cartie, Phineas | 1 | 3 | 7 | | | Hine, Benjamin | 2 | 1 | 2 | | |
| Warner, Ephraim | 2 | 2 | 3 | | | Johnson, Cornilus, 2nd | 1 | 3 | 1 | | | Abbot, Daniel | 1 | | 1 | | |
| Baldwin, Jonathan | 1 | | 4 | | | Upson, Samuel | 3 | 1 | 3 | | | Abbot, David | 1 | 1 | 2 | | |
| Baldwin, Noah | 1 | 4 | 4 | | | Munson, Soloman | 1 | 2 | 1 | | | Nicoll, Samuel | 1 | 2 | 2 | | |
| Young, Happy | | | 3 | | | Frost, David | 2 | | 3 | | | Morris, Major | 1 | 4 | 4 | | |
| Porter, Preserve | 1 | 2 | 2 | | 5 | Frost, Jesse | 1 | 1 | 3 | | | Scovel, Asa | 1 | | 2 | | |
| Porter, Timothy | 2 | 2 | 4 | | | Bartholomew, Abial | 1 | 2 | | | | Scovel, Desire | 1 | | 1 | | |
| Nicoll, John | 3 | 1 | 8 | | 3 | Bartholomew, Seth | 1 | | 4 | | | Nicoll, Benjamin | 1 | | 3 | | |
| Welton, David | 1 | 3 | 3 | | | Bartholomew, Osi | 1 | 3 | 2 | | | Scovell, Seldon | 1 | | 3 | | |
| Welton, Martha | | | 1 | | | Frisbie, Ruben | 1 | 3 | 5 | | | Scovel, Selah | 2 | 2 | 2 | | |
| Pomp (Negroe) | | | | 4 | | Warner, Ebenezer | 1 | | 1 | | | Fenn, Samuel | 1 | 2 | 3 | | |
| Judd, Stephen | 1 | 1 | 3 | | | Warner, Justice | 1 | 2 | 4 | | | Richardson, Nathaniel | 1 | 1 | 3 | | |
| Cossett, John | 2 | | 2 | | | Warner, Mark | 1 | 2 | 4 | | | Richardson, Eber | 1 | | 1 | | |
| Brown, Daniel | 3 | | 1 | | | Austin, James | 1 | | 2 | | | Bartholomew, Joseph | 1 | | 3 | | |
| Silkrogs, Nicholas | 1 | | 2 | | | Turrel, Amos | 2 | | 3 | | | Brunson, Levi | 1 | | 2 | | |
| Richards, Huldy | | | 2 | | | Grillery, Daniel | 1 | | 2 | | | Barnes, Thomas | 1 | 1 | 2 | | |
| Whitney, James | 3 | | 2 | | | Wooster, Miles | 1 | 2 | 6 | | | Richardson, Thomas | 1 | 1 | 2 | | |
| Brunson, Daniel | 2 | 1 | 5 | | | Pritchet, Roger | 1 | | 2 | | | Pritchard, Archibald | 1 | 1 | 1 | | |
| Cooke, Charles | 1 | | 2 | | | Warner, Josiah | 2 | 2 | 4 | | | Merril, David | 1 | 1 | 5 | | |
| Cooke, James | 1 | 1 | 2 | | | Pritchet, Abraham | 2 | 2 | 2 | | | Judson, Eber | 1 | 4 | 2 | | |
| Adams, Arael | 1 | | 1 | | | Pritchet, Amos | 2 | 3 | 4 | | | Berman, Josiah | 2 | 1 | 5 | | |
| Adams, William | 2 | | 2 | | | Welton, Levi | 2 | 3 | 7 | | | Wilmot, Abijah | 2 | 2 | 2 | | |
| Adams, Sebinus | 1 | 1 | 3 | | | Warner, Andrew | 1 | 4 | 5 | | | Wilmot, Silas | 1 | | 1 | | |
| Scott, Samuel | 1 | | 3 | | | Worthington, John | 2 | 1 | 3 | | | Crilley, Henry | 1 | 1 | 2 | | |
| Scott, Ashley | 1 | | 3 | | | Munson, Samuel | 2 | 2 | 4 | | | Brunson, Isaac | 1 | 1 | 3 | | |
| Adams, William, 2nd | 2 | 2 | 2 | | | Warner, James H | 1 | 2 | 3 | | | Brunson, Ethal | 1 | | 1 | | |
| Scovel, Timothy | 1 | 1 | 1 | | | Welton, Andrew | 1 | 2 | 3 | | | Brunson, Isaac, 2nd | 2 | 1 | 2 | | |
| Nicoll, Elizabeth | | | 1 | | | Harrit, Stephen | 1 | | 2 | | | Brunson, Eli | 3 | 1 | 6 | | |
| Harrison, James | 1 | | | | | Welton, Stephen | 1 | 3 | 4 | | | Brunson, Arael | 2 | 1 | 3 | | |
| Durand, Samuel | 1 | | | | | Barnes, Ezekeal | 1 | 3 | 2 | | | Brunson, Elizabeth | 1 | 3 | 3 | | |
| Beardsley, Jabez | 1 | | | | | Smith, Ephraim | 2 | 4 | 1 | | | Brunson, Josiah | | | 3 | | |
| | | | | | | Welton, John | 2 | 3 | 5 | | | Brunson, Abel | 2 | 1 | 4 | | |

# FIRST CENSUS OF THE UNITED STATES.

## NEW HAVEN COUNTY—Continued.

### WATERBURY TOWN—continued.

| NAME OF HEAD OF FAMILY. | Free white males of 16 years and upward, including heads of families. | Free white males under 16 years. | Free white females, including heads of families. | All other free persons. | Slaves. |
|---|---|---|---|---|---|
| Brunson, Theo | 1 | 2 | 5 | | |
| Brunson, Seth | 1 | 3 | 3 | | |
| Brunson, Titus | 2 | 3 | 3 | | |
| Brunson, Jesse | 1 | 2 | 2 | | |
| Scovel, John | 1 | | 3 | | |
| Tyler, Daniel | 1 | | 3 | | |
| Tyler, Daniel, 2nd | 1 | 3 | 2 | | |
| Tomkins, David | 1 | 1 | 4 | | |
| Munson, Abner | 2 | 3 | 4 | | |
| Munson, Caleb | 1 | | 1 | | |
| Munson, Benjamin | 4 | | | | |
| Sackett, Siam D | 1 | | 2 | | |
| Brunson, Josiah, 2nd | 2 | 4 | 2 | | |
| Brunson, David | 1 | 1 | 3 | | |
| Newton, Miles | 1 | 3 | 2 | | |
| Porter, Mark | 1 | 3 | 3 | | |
| Hinman, Amos | 1 | | 3 | | |
| Porter, David | 2 | 3 | 3 | | |
| Peck, Ward | 1 | | 4 | | |
| Porter, James | 2 | 1 | 4 | | |
| Fenn, Benjamin | 1 | | 4 | | |
| Peck, Augustus | 1 | 1 | 2 | | |
| Osborn, Abner | 1 | 1 | 2 | | |
| Scovel, Amos | 1 | 1 | 1 | | |
| Beman, Benjamin | 1 | 3 | 3 | | |
| Porter, Timothy, 2nd | 1 | 1 | 3 | | |
| Buckingham, Samuel | 1 | 2 | 2 | | |
| Ratford, James | 1 | 1 | 3 | | |
| Fenn, Gamaliel | 1 | 2 | 3 | | |
| Bates, Benjamin | 1 | 5 | 4 | | |
| Smith, Levi | 1 | 3 | 2 | | |
| Scott, Ruben | 1 | 1 | 1 | | |
| Scott, Abel | 1 | 2 | 6 | | |
| Scovel, Noah | 1 | 2 | 1 | | |
| Welton, Lemuel | 1 | | 2 | | |
| Areston, Gad | 1 | | | | |
| Lewis, Silas | 1 | 3 | 2 | | |
| Saxton, Ebenezer | 1 | 1 | 2 | | |
| Scott, Amos, 2nd | 1 | 1 | 1 | | |
| Wooster, David | 2 | 1 | 8 | | |
| Scott, Ebenezer | 1 | 1 | 4 | | |
| Harrison, Samuel | 1 | 1 | 5 | | |
| Gunn, Samuel | 3 | 3 | 2 | | |
| Scovel, Timothy, 2. | 1 | 1 | 2 | | |
| Hotchkiss, Thelus | 1 | | 2 | | |
| Brunson, Andrew | 2 | | 4 | | |
| Bates, Gamaliel | 1 | 2 | 3 | | |
| Adams, John | 1 | 2 | 5 | | |
| Pritchett, John | 2 | | 3 | | |
| Pritchett, James | 1 | | 1 | | |
| Hall, Ezra | 2 | 2 | 4 | | |
| Nicoll, Samuel | 1 | | 1 | | |
| Clarke, David | 2 | | 2 | | |
| Pritchet, George | 1 | 1 | 3 | | |
| Clarke, Samuel | 2 | 1 | 2 | 1 | |
| Pritchett, John | 1 | 1 | 4 | | |
| Wooster, Wait | 1 | | 2 | | |
| Sperry, Jacob | 1 | 2 | 4 | | |
| Blakely, Ruben | 3 | 2 | 3 | | |
| Porter, Elizabeth | 2 | | 3 | | |
| Chatfield, Daniel | 3 | 1 | 2 | | |
| Sperry, Jesse | 2 | 1 | 5 | | |
| Roberts, Joel | 1 | 1 | 5 | | |
| Clarke, William | 1 | 2 | 4 | | |
| Platt, Gideon | 2 | 3 | 3 | | |
| Pardie, Phyphe | | | 5 | | |
| Scovell, Amaziah | 2 | 4 | 2 | | |
| Bradley, Enos | 1 | 3 | 3 | | |
| Wooster, Elizabeth | 1 | 1 | 3 | | |
| Pope, Jacob | 1 | | 2 | | |
| Scott, Enoch | 2 | 1 | 2 | | |
| Cowell, James | 1 | 4 | 2 | | |
| Thayer, Hester | | | 2 | | |
| Upson, Daniel | 2 | | 2 | | |
| Hotchkiss, Arael | 2 | 2 | 3 | | |
| Warner, Eneas | 3 | 3 | 4 | | |
| Cambie, Noah | 2 | 1 | 2 | | |
| Fulford, Titus | 1 | | 2 | | |
| Beebe, Elizabeth | 1 | 1 | 1 | | |
| Frisby, Elizabeth | 1 | | 2 | | |
| Frisbee, John | 1 | 1 | 1 | | |
| Anderson, Asa | 1 | 2 | 1 | | |
| Wakely, David | 2 | 1 | 2 | | |
| Wakley, Ebenezer | 1 | | 1 | | |
| Frisby, Charles | 1 | 3 | 2 | | |
| Grilly, Sirus | 1 | 2 | 3 | | |
| Grilley, Teuly | 1 | | 3 | | |
| Norton, Hseas | 2 | 2 | 3 | | |
| Norton, Zebel | 1 | 3 | 1 | | |
| Talmage, John | 1 | 3 | 2 | | |
| Thrasher, Elnathan | 1 | 2 | 3 | | |
| Frisby, Judas | 1 | 2 | 4 | | |
| Upson, Ashbel | 1 | 1 | 1 | | |
| Seward, Amos | 1 | 1 | 4 | | |
| Wilcox, Philomen | 1 | 1 | 2 | | |
| Scott, Timothy | 1 | | 3 | | |
| Dana, Daniel | 1 | 2 | 2 | | |
| Stalief, Joseph | 1 | | 2 | | |
| Stalief, Joseph, 2nd | 2 | 3 | 4 | | |
| Hopkins, Simeon | 2 | 2 | 5 | | |
| Hopkins, Isaac | 1 | | 4 | | |
| Silkrags, Trunans | | 1 | 2 | | |
| Hotchkiss, Wait | 2 | 3 | 2 | | |
| Obed (Negroe) | | | | 5 | |
| Hotchkiss, Joel | 1 | | 3 | | |
| Norton, Noah W | 1 | 1 | 2 | | |
| Tuttle, Daniel | 3 | 3 | 5 | | |
| Byington, Benjamin | 3 | 3 | 5 | | |
| Atkins, Joseph | 3 | 2 | 5 | | |
| Talmage, Jacob | 1 | 2 | 2 | | |
| Upson, Charles | 1 | 5 | 2 | | |
| Mallery, Joseph | 1 | 2 | 3 | | |
| Weston, Abraham | 2 | 2 | 10 | | |
| Upson, Ezekiel | 2 | | 7 | | |
| Byington, Daniel | 3 | 2 | 5 | | |
| Curtis, Abel | 2 | 4 | 4 | | |
| Beecher, Amos | 1 | 1 | 3 | | |
| Williams, Obed | 1 | 5 | 7 | | |
| Thomas, James | 1 | 3 | 4 | | |
| Alcock, James | 1 | 1 | 8 | | |
| Rinny, John | 1 | | 2 | | |
| Barnes, Josiah | 1 | 3 | 4 | | |
| Welton, Eliakim | 1 | | 1 | | |
| Welton, Eliakim, 2nd | 2 | 2 | 2 | | |
| Alcocke, David | 2 | 3 | 5 | | |
| Alcock, John | 3 | | 1 | | |
| Alcock, John, 2nd | 1 | 2 | 1 | | |
| Alcock, Samuel | 2 | 1 | 2 | | |
| Alcock, Soloman | 1 | | 3 | | |
| Wilton, Benjamin | 1 | 2 | 2 | | |
| Richards, Street | 2 | 2 | 3 | | |
| Wilson, Thomas | 2 | 3 | 7 | | |
| Shatlief, Nathaniel | 3 | 1 | 5 | | |
| Mills, John | 1 | | | | |
| Rowley, Eli | 1 | 1 | 3 | | |
| Rowley, William | 1 | | 2 | | |
| Rowley, William, 2nd | 1 | | 1 | | |
| Scott, Nathan | 1 | 1 | 2 | | |
| Hicock, Abraham | 1 | | 3 | | |
| Nicoll, Samuel | 1 | 2 | 3 | | |
| Nicol, Joseph | 1 | 2 | 3 | | |
| Scott, Samuel, 2nd | 1 | 2 | 1 | | |
| Frisbie, Israel | 1 | 2 | 2 | | |
| Scott, John | 1 | | 2 | | |
| How, Daniel | 1 | | | | |
| Gunn, Abigal | 2 | 1 | 3 | | |
| Scott, Amos, 2nd | 1 | 3 | 2 | | |
| Palmer, Samuel | 1 | 2 | 3 | | |
| Scott, Joseph | 1 | | 1 | | |
| Smith, Ephrim | 1 | | 1 | | |
| Gunn, Jabamah | 4 | 3 | 4 | | |
| Osborn, Thomas | 2 | 3 | 3 | | |
| Osborn, Daniel | 2 | | 1 | | |
| Gunn, Nathaniel | 2 | | 6 | | |
| Gunn, Abel | 1 | 2 | 1 | | |
| Peck, Joseph | 1 | 1 | 1 | | |
| Webb, Nancy | | | 1 | | |
| Osborn, Abraham | 2 | | 3 | | |
| Osborn, Abraham, 2nd | 1 | | 3 | | |
| Osborn, Andrew | 1 | 1 | 2 | | |
| Osborn, Peter | 1 | | | | |
| Osborn, Ezra | 1 | 2 | 3 | | |
| Osborn, John | 1 | | 1 | | |
| Osborn, Daniel, 2nd | 2 | | 1 | | |
| Pits, Richard | 1 | 2 | 3 | | |
| Bruster, Stephen | 1 | 2 | 3 | | |
| Lownsby, John | 1 | 1 | 2 | | |
| Cupper, Cornelius | 1 | | 1 | | |
| Judd, Roswell | 1 | 2 | 6 | | |
| Porter, Samuel, 2nd | 1 | 4 | 4 | | |
| Condy, Timothy | 2 | | 3 | | |
| Scott, Isaac | 1 | 1 | 3 | | |
| Scott, Thadeus | 1 | 2 | 1 | | |
| Scott, Abner | 1 | | 3 | | |
| Todd, Walter | 1 | 1 | 3 | | |
| Judd, Chauncy | 1 | 1 | 2 | | |
| Morgan, Isaac | 1 | 1 | 3 | | |
| Porter, Samuel | 1 | | 1 | | |
| Porter, Ebenezer | 1 | 3 | 3 | | |
| Judd, Isaac | 2 | 3 | 1 | | |
| Williams, Ruben | 1 | 2 | 2 | | |
| Williams, Mary | | | 1 | | |
| Smith, Elizabeth | | | 1 | | |
| Osborn, Elijah | 1 | 3 | 3 | | |
| Smith, John | 1 | 1 | 7 | | |
| Woodruff, Jonah | 1 | 4 | 3 | | |
| Adams, Abraham | 1 | | 2 | | |
| Judd, Isaac, 2 | 1 | 3 | 4 | | |
| Adams, Ely | 2 | 2 | 2 | | |
| Scott, Enoch, 2nd | 1 | 4 | 1 | | |
| Lewis, David | 1 | 2 | 4 | | |
| Warner, Stephen | 3 | | 2 | | |
| Scott, Gideon | 1 | | 1 | | |
| Scott, Caleb | 1 | 1 | 3 | | |
| Scott, Samuel, 2nd | 1 | 1 | 1 | | |
| Lewis, Eunice | 1 | | 3 | | |
| Porter, Nathaniel | 1 | 2 | 4 | | |
| Spencer, Culver | 2 | 1 | 1 | | |
| Hoadley, Culpeper | 1 | 1 | 2 | | |
| Culver, Amos | 2 | 2 | 4 | | |
| Buckly, Daniel | 1 | 1 | 1 | | |
| Lewis, John | 1 | | 1 | | |
| Lewis, Samuel S | 1 | 2 | 2 | | |
| Hoadley, Ebenezer | 1 | 2 | 2 | | |
| Hoadley, Philo | 1 | 1 | 1 | | |
| Chatfield, Samuel | 1 | | 4 | | |
| Chatfield, Samuel, 2nd | 1 | | 3 | | |
| Beebe, Ruben | 1 | 4 | 6 | | |
| Camp, Samuel | 1 | | 4 | | |
| Beecher, Daniel | 2 | 2 | 6 | | |
| Warner, Joseph | 2 | 2 | 2 | | |
| Porter, Francis | 1 | 3 | 2 | | |
| Caukins, Roswell | 2 | 2 | 3 | | |
| Rush, Phebe | | | 1 | | |
| Clarke, Chauncy | 1 | 1 | 2 | | |
| Scott, Josiah | 1 | | 1 | | |
| Alcock, Isaac | 1 | | 1 | | |
| Lane, Daniel | 1 | 1 | 1 | | |
| Minor, Caleb | 1 | 1 | 2 | | |
| Stevens, Nathan | 2 | 3 | 5 | | |
| Twicket, Joseph | 1 | | 1 | | |
| Bicket, David | 1 | 1 | 2 | | |
| Byington, Jerad | 1 | | | | |
| Minor, Jud | 1 | | 4 | | |
| Hine, Ebenezer | 1 | | 4 | | |
| Potter, Lemuel | 2 | 3 | 3 | | |
| Turrel, Icobald | 1 | 3 | 2 | | |
| Porter, Freeman | 1 | 1 | 4 | | |
| Porter, Thomas, 2nd | 2 | 1 | 3 | | |
| Hoadley, William | 1 | 2 | 3 | | |
| Porter, Ashbel | 2 | 1 | 2 | | |
| Porter, Asbell, 2nd | 1 | 1 | 1 | | |
| Hoadly, Jude | 2 | 1 | 2 | | |
| Stevens, Elijah | 6 | 3 | | | |
| Fowler, Abraham | 2 | 2 | 3 | | |
| Turrel, Jerad | 1 | 1 | 2 | | |
| Turrel, Isaiah | 4 | 2 | 5 | | |
| Hicox, Samuel | 2 | 1 | 5 | | |
| Hicox, Gideon | 2 | | 4 | | |
| Scott, Uriah | 1 | | 2 | | |
| Turrel, Oliver | 1 | | 2 | 1 | |
| Osborn, Arael | 1 | | 2 | | |
| Osborn, Amos | 2 | 2 | 2 | | |
| Norton, David | 1 | | 2 | | |
| Norton, Cyrus | 1 | 4 | 4 | | |
| Smith, Anthony | 1 | 4 | 4 | | |
| Beebe, Israel | 2 | 1 | 1 | | |
| Porter, Ezekol | 1 | | 2 | | |
| Morris, David | 1 | 2 | 3 | | |
| Hine, Hezekiah | 1 | 1 | 3 | | |
| Turrel, Israel | 1 | 1 | 4 | | |
| Byington, Jerad | 4 | 4 | 2 | | |
| Webb, Daniel | 1 | 2 | 2 | | |
| Smith, Austin | 2 | 1 | 2 | | |
| Beebe, David | 1 | 3 | 7 | | |
| Osborn, Thaddeus | 1 | | 1 | | |
| Hichson, Eneas | 1 | 1 | 2 | | |
| Ells, Linthell | 1 | 1 | 5 | | |
| Wooster, Walter | 2 | 3 | 2 | | |
| Beebe, Borden | 1 | | 2 | | |
| Hall, Prindle | 2 | 2 | 3 | | |
| Ames, Samuel | 1 | 1 | 3 | | |
| Hopkins, John | 3 | | 3 | | |
| Hopkins, David | 1 | | | | |
| Gibbord, Timothy | 3 | 3 | 2 | | |
| Horton, John | 3 | | 1 | | |
| Horton, Calvin | 1 | 3 | 1 | | |
| Hotchkiss, Amos | 2 | 2 | 3 | | |
| Turrel, Isaac | 1 | | 1 | | |
| Hopkins, Joseph, 2nd | 2 | 1 | 4 | | |
| Philis (Negroe) | | | | 2 | |
| Payne, David | 1 | | 5 | | |
| Hotchkiss, Gideon | 4 | | 2 | | |
| Hotchkiss, Eber | 1 | 1 | 2 | | |
| Todd, Samuel | 1 | 3 | 3 | | |
| Riggs, John | 2 | | 2 | | |
| Riggs, Abner | 1 | 4 | 2 | | |
| Tinker, Absolum | 1 | 3 | 4 | | |
| Hotchkiss, Fredrick | 1 | | 1 | | |
| Tyler, Abraham | 1 | 3 | 4 | | |
| Turrel, Josiah | 3 | 1 | 1 | | |
| Hine, Isaac | 2 | 1 | 3 | | |

# HEADS OF FAMILIES—CONNECTICUT.

## NEW HAVEN COUNTY—Continued.

| NAME OF HEAD OF FAMILY. | Free white males of 16 years and upward, including heads of families. | Free white males under 16 years. | Free white females, including heads of families. | All other free persons. | Slaves. | NAME OF HEAD OF FAMILY. | Free white males of 16 years and upward, including heads of families. | Free white males under 16 years. | Free white females, including heads of families. | All other free persons. | Slaves. | NAME OF HEAD OF FAMILY. | Free white males of 16 years and upward, including heads of families. | Free white males under 16 years. | Free white females, including heads of families. | All other free persons. | Slaves. |
|---|---|---|---|---|---|---|---|---|---|---|---|---|---|---|---|---|---|
| **WATERBURY TOWN—continued.** | | | | | | **WOODBRIDGE TOWN—continued.** | | | | | | **WOODBRIDGE TOWN—continued.** | | | | | |
| Root, Joseph | 1 | 5 | 2 | | | Baldwin, Jerad | 1 | | 4 | | | Sperry, Ebenezer | 2 | 1 | 3 | | |
| Spencer, Ansel | 1 | | 2 | | | Booth, Hester | 1 | | 2 | | 1 | Sperry, Eliakim | 1 | 3 | 3 | | |
| Hickson, Gideon, 2nd | 2 | | 2 | | | Lines, James | 1 | 1 | 2 | | | Sperry, Amos | 1 | 2 | 2 | | |
| Hickson, James | 2 | 1 | 2 | | | Dibble, John | 4 | 1 | 3 | 1 | | Sperry, Lidia | | | 3 | | |
| Turrel, Enoch | 1 | 3 | 2 | | | Lines, Samuel | 2 | 1 | 2 | | | Bradley, Abner | 4 | 2 | 4 | | |
| Beebe, Zina | 2 | 4 | 2 | | | Lumsdale, Hatham | 1 | 3 | 4 | 1 | | Ford, Jesse | 3 | 1 | 6 | | |
| Morgan, Arael | 1 | 2 | 1 | | | Lines, Daniel | 1 | 1 | 1 | | | Perkins, Unice | | | 3 | 4 | |
| Paine, Philemon | 1 | 1 | 1 | | | Lines, Darus | | 1 | 2 | | | Clarke, Elioney | 2 | 1 | 2 | | |
| Burret, Benjamin | 1 | 1 | 2 | | | Jim (Negroe) | | | | 2 | | Darling, Thomas | 2 | 2 | 1 | | |
| Peck, David | 1 | | 3 | | | Lines, Alvin | 1 | 1 | 3 | | | Darling, Abigal | | | 3 | | 4 |
| Farrel, Joel | 1 | 1 | 4 | | | Lines, Linus | 1 | | 3 | | | Clarke, David | 1 | | 1 | | |
| Lane, Asael | 1 | | | | | Beecher, Linus | 1 | | 1 | | | Sperry, Asa | 1 | 3 | 4 | | |
| Lane, Nathaniel | 1 | | | | | Adams, Rebecca | | | 1 | | | Jim (Negroe) | | | | 5 | |
| Welton, Eliakim, 2nd | 1 | | 3 | | | Alling, Marahel | 2 | 3 | 5 | | | Clarke, Martin | 1 | | 3 | | |
| Welton, Ebenezer | 1 | | 3 | | | Thomas, Amos | 2 | 2 | 1 | | | Sperry, David | 2 | | 3 | | |
| Turrel, Elihu | 1 | 2 | 2 | | | Beecher, Ephraim | 1 | 2 | 6 | | | Sperry, Joel | 1 | 3 | 3 | | |
| Smith, Austin | 1 | | 1 | | | Sherman, Amos | 2 | | 3 | | | Marten, Francis | 1 | 2 | 4 | | |
| Lewis, John, 2nd | 3 | 2 | 2 | | | Sherman, Jese | 1 | 1 | 1 | | | Hotchkiss, Jonas | 2 | | 1 | | |
| Grant, John | 1 | 3 | 2 | | | Johnson, Job | 1 | 5 | 2 | | | Hitchcock, Eneas | | | 1 | | |
| Thomas, Elisha | 1 | 4 | 4 | | | Johnson, Isaac | 1 | | 2 | | | Carrington, Samuel | 1 | 2 | 4 | | |
| Higgs, John | 1 | | 2 | | | Johnson, Mary | | 2 | 2 | | | Carrington, Noadiah | 1 | | 2 | | |
| Lewis, Abraham | 2 | | 5 | | | Sperry, Asa | 1 | | 2 | | | Peck, Silas | 1 | 1 | 2 | | |
| Judd, Ebenezer | 1 | 3 | 4 | | | Howell, Henry | 1 | | | | | Carrington, Peter | 1 | | 2 | | |
| Beebe, Joseph | 1 | 3 | 3 | | | Downs, Joseph | 1 | 1 | 5 | | | Syrus (Negroe) | | | | 2 | |
| Frisbie, Josiah | 1 | 1 | 1 | | | Alling, Daniel | 1 | | 1 | | | Dorman, Samuel | 1 | 2 | 4 | | |
| | | | | | | Buckingham, John | 1 | | | | | Hull, Joel | 1 | | | | |
| **WOODBRIDGE TOWN.** | | | | | | Smith, Israel | 1 | | 1 | | | Pond, Phineas | 1 | | | | |
| Brown, Jonathan | 1 | | 2 | | | Hine, David | 1 | 1 | 2 | | | Clarke, Nathan | 2 | 1 | 3 | | |
| Bristol, Eunice | 1 | 3 | 3 | | | Clinton, Anson | 1 | | 1 | | | Curtis, Nathan | 1 | | 1 | | |
| Smith, Heil | 1 | 2 | 1 | | | Platt, Nathaniel | 1 | 1 | 4 | 1 | | Allen, Elenor | | | 1 | | |
| Baldwin, Richard | 2 | 5 | 4 | | | Smith, David | 1 | 1 | 3 | | | Andrews, Anna | | 1 | 3 | | |
| Northrop, Isaac | 1 | 2 | 4 | | | Beach, Benjamin | 1 | 5 | 3 | | | Hitchcock, Daniel | 1 | | | | |
| Baldwin, Enoch | 1 | 5 | 4 | | | Smith, Nathan | 1 | | 4 | | | Hitchcock, Phineas | 1 | | | | |
| Baldwin, Charles | 4 | 2 | 5 | | 1 | Smith, Nathan, 2nd | 1 | | | | | Hitchcock, Eneas | 1 | | | | |
| Pardie, Samuel | 1 | 3 | 4 | | | Peck, Phineas | 2 | | 2 | | | Alling, Noah | 1 | 2 | 2 | | |
| Sandford, Moses | 2 | | 1 | | | Peck, Samuel | 1 | 2 | 3 | | | Alling, Lemuel | 1 | 3 | 4 | | |
| Baldwin, Henry | 1 | 1 | 3 | | | Clarke, Lar | 2 | 3 | 4 | 1 | | Andrews, Caleb | 1 | 1 | 6 | | |
| Baldwin, Henry, 2nd | 1 | | 1 | | | Gun, George | 2 | 1 | 2 | | | Humpherville, John | 1 | 4 | 2 | | |
| Osborn, Elisha | 1 | 1 | 3 | 1 | | Smith, Abel | 1 | 3 | 3 | | | Downs, Samuel, 2nd | 1 | 1 | 2 | | |
| Smith, Jesse | 1 | 4 | 1 | | | Clarke, David | 1 | | 1 | | | Brooks, Asshael | 1 | 3 | 3 | | |
| Ford, Illard | 1 | 2 | 3 | | | Peck, Hannah | | 2 | 3 | | | Gilbert, Linus | 2 | 3 | 4 | | |
| Andrus, Timothy | 1 | | | | | Clarke, George | 2 | 1 | 2 | | | Downs, Samuel | 2 | | 1 | | |
| Baldwin, Andrew | 2 | | 3 | | | Bradly, Alling | 1 | 2 | 3 | | | Downs, Ebenezur | 2 | 1 | 5 | | |
| Trent, Abijah | 2 | 2 | 4 | | | Newton, Samuel | 3 | 2 | 4 | | | Downs, Felix | 1 | | 2 | | |
| Baldwin, Josiah | 3 | 1 | 2 | | | Gilbert, Soloman | 1 | 1 | 4 | | | Gilbert, Samuel | 1 | 2 | 6 | | |
| Sandford, Isaac | 2 | | 1 | | | Gilbert, Ely | 1 | 2 | 4 | | | Johnson, Jesse | 2 | 2 | 3 | | |
| Sandford, Abel | 1 | | 3 | | | Ford, David | 2 | 1 | 3 | | | Goodyear, Joel | 2 | 1 | 4 | | |
| Tinker, Oliver | 2 | | 2 | | | Hemmingway, Isaac | 1 | | 2 | | | Hotchkiss, Benjamin | 2 | 1 | 4 | | |
| Northrop, Job | 2 | 2 | 2 | | | Murring, Joseph | 1 | 1 | 2 | | | Beecher, Weeler | 1 | | 2 | | |
| Hine, Charles | 3 | 1 | 3 | | | Murring, Fletcher | 1 | 1 | 3 | | | Sandford, David | 3 | 3 | 6 | | |
| Hine, Stephen | 1 | 2 | 6 | | | Murring, Joseph, 2nd | 1 | | 4 | | | Sperry, Isaac | 1 | | 5 | | |
| Hine, David | 1 | | 1 | | | Newton, Enoch | 2 | 1 | 3 | 1 | | Morris, Asa | 1 | 3 | 1 | | |
| Newton, Samuel, 2nd | 1 | | 1 | | | Andrus, Judah | 1 | 1 | 7 | | | Toles, Abraham | 1 | 1 | 2 | | |
| Dibble, Philo | 1 | 2 | 1 | | | Newton, Roger | 1 | 1 | 3 | | | Humpherville, Ebenezer | 1 | 3 | 2 | | |
| Hotchkiss, Soloman | 1 | 2 | 3 | | | Russell, William | 1 | 1 | 5 | | | Sandford, Stephen | 1 | 2 | 5 | | |
| Clinton, Laurence | 1 | | 2 | | | Russell, Richard, 2nd | 1 | 2 | 3 | | | Dickerman, Timothy | 1 | | 1 | | |
| Clinton, Samuel | 1 | 4 | 2 | | | Russell, Richard | 1 | | | | | Toles, Lazurus | 1 | 4 | 4 | | |
| Smith, Daniel | 1 | 2 | 5 | | | Perkins, Jonathan | 2 | 1 | 2 | | | Ceasar (Negroe) | | | | 5 | |
| Northrop, Job, 2nd | 1 | 3 | 5 | | | Perkins, David | 1 | 2 | 4 | | | Beecher, Isaac | 2 | 1 | 2 | | |
| Hine, Moses | 1 | 1 | 3 | | | Main, Russel | 1 | | | | | Beecher, Hezekiah | 1 | 3 | 4 | | |
| Booth, Walter | 1 | 2 | 4 | | | Perkins, Rachel | | | 1 | | | Peck, Hiram | 1 | 2 | 2 | | |
| Sperry, Richard | 2 | | 6 | | | Beecher, Burr | 3 | 1 | 4 | | | Hotchkiss, Elias | 2 | 2 | 1 | | |
| Northrup, Philo | 1 | 1 | 3 | | | Huntington Asa | 3 | 1 | 3 | | | Hotchkiss, Joel | 1 | 2 | 6 | | |
| Baldwin, Thomas | 3 | 3 | 5 | | | Russel, Stephen | 1 | 2 | 2 | | | Peck, Sarah | | | 3 | | |
| Baldwin, Barnabas | 3 | | 2 | | 2 | Hull, Amassa | 1 | | | | | Peck, Elizabeth | 1 | 2 | 4 | | |
| Andrus, Elijah | 1 | 1 | 4 | | | Walker, Webber | 1 | | | | | Wooden, Elizabeth | 1 | 2 | 2 | | |
| Baldwin, Barnabas, 2nd | 1 | 4 | 1 | | | Ford, Isaac | 2 | | 2 | 1 | | Perkins, Archibald | 1 | 3 | 3 | | |
| Downs, Seth | 2 | 1 | 3 | | | Ford, Vincen | 1 | | 2 | | | Wooden, John | 3 | 3 | 3 | | |
| Beecher, Ebenezur | 2 | 2 | 3 | | | Carrington, Allen | 2 | | 2 | | | Tuttle, Nathaniel | 2 | 2 | 4 | | |
| Beecher, Nicholas | 1 | | 1 | | | Perkins, Amos | 2 | 1 | 2 | | | Wooden, Edmond | 1 | 2 | 3 | | |
| Beecher, Sarah | | | 3 | | | Perkins, Elizabeth | 1 | 4 | 2 | | | Todd, Josiah | 3 | 1 | 5 | | |
| Beecher, Enoch | 1 | 2 | 2 | | | Perkins, Amos, 2nd | 1 | | 2 | | | Hotchkiss, Daniel | 2 | 3 | 2 | | |
| Beecher, Joseph | 1 | 4 | 2 | | | Peck, Dan | 1 | 1 | 4 | | | Hotchkiss, Soloman | 1 | 2 | 2 | | |
| Whiting, Sarah | 1 | | 4 | | | Peck, Henry | 1 | 1 | 2 | | | Tuttle, Uriah | 3 | 5 | 2 | | |
| Andrews, David | 1 | | 1 | | | Peck, Amie | | | 1 | | | Hammiston, Joel | 1 | 2 | 3 | | |
| Andrews, Barnes | 1 | | 3 | | | Parmer, Bethseba | | | 2 | | | Wheeler, Joel | 1 | 1 | 3 | | |
| Bradley, Andrew | 1 | | 1 | | | Hotchkiss, David | 1 | 2 | 6 | | | Bradley, Ruben | 3 | 1 | 2 | | |
| Bradley, Silas | 1 | | 2 | | | Cooke, David | 1 | | 1 | | | Ives, Abel | 2 | | 2 | | |
| Peck, Molly | | | 3 | | | Osborn, Samuel | 3 | 2 | 4 | | 2 | Perkins, Adonijah | 2 | 1 | 2 | | |
| Peck, Benjamin | 1 | | 4 | | | Perkins, Ellas | 1 | 3 | 2 | | | Beecher, Hannah | 2 | 1 | 4 | | |
| Osborn, Elijah | 1 | 1 | 3 | | | Thompson, Thadeus | 1 | 2 | 3 | | | Bishop, Ebenezer | 1 | 4 | 3 | | |
| Thomas, Ephrahim | 1 | 2 | 4 | | | Alling, Roger | 1 | 3 | 4 | | | Bishop, Joseph | 1 | | | | |
| Bradley, Timothy | 2 | | 3 | | | Smith, David | 1 | 2 | 5 | | | Hotchkiss, Joel, 2nd | 1 | 1 | 7 | | |
| Bradley, Wilmot | 1 | 2 | 3 | | | Smith, Titus | 1 | 1 | 1 | | | Talmage, Alsop | 1 | 2 | 5 | | |
| Beecher, Jonathan | 1 | | 1 | | | Smith Adney | 1 | 4 | 2 | | | Beecher, Jesse | 2 | 1 | 5 | | |
| Bradley, Timothy, 2nd | 1 | 1 | 1 | | | Johnson, Niamiah | 1 | | 2 | | | Russell John | 3 | 1 | 3 | | |
| Bradly, Charles | 2 | 3 | 7 | | | Russell, Daniel | 1 | 1 | 8 | | | Sperry, Simeon | 3 | 1 | 5 | | |
| Bradley, Benjamin | 1 | | 4 | | | Sperry, Thomas | 1 | 2 | 3 | | | Thompson, Daniel | 1 | | 3 | | |
| Geers, Caleb | 1 | 1 | 2 | | | Sperry, James | 1 | 2 | 3 | | | Osborn, James | 1 | | 2 | | |
| Sperry, Nathaniel | 1 | 2 | 4 | | | Sperry, Caleb | 1 | | 2 | | | Downs, Jacob | 1 | 2 | 4 | | |
| Thomas, Ruben | 1 | | 2 | | | Sperry, Samuel | 1 | 3 | 3 | | | Sperry, Job | 1 | | 4 | | |
| Johnson, Samuel | 1 | 3 | 3 | | | Peck, Stephen | 2 | 2 | 4 | | | Carry, Margaret | 1 | | | | |
| Peas, Mary | | | 2 | | | Sperry, Lent | 2 | 2 | 4 | | | Sperry, Lois | 1 | | | | |
| | | | | | | Sperry, Amie | | | 2 | | | Merriman, Moses | 1 | 1 | 2 | | |
| Smith, Hezekiah | 2 | 1 | 3 | | | Sperry, Samuel | 1 | 3 | 5 | | | Toles, Hannah | | | 2 | | |
| | | | | | | Salton, George | 2 | 1 | 1 | | | Wooden, Cyrus | 1 | | | | |

35201—08——8

111

# FIRST CENSUS OF THE UNITED STATES.

## NEW HAVEN COUNTY—Continued.

| NAME OF HEAD OF FAMILY. | Free white males of 16 years and upward, including heads of families. | Free white males under 16 years. | Free white females, including heads of families. | All other free persons. | Slaves. | NAME OF HEAD OF FAMILY. | Free white males of 16 years and upward, including heads of families. | Free white males under 16 years. | Free white females, including heads of families. | All other free persons. | Slaves. | NAME OF HEAD OF FAMILY. | Free white males of 16 years and upward, including heads of families. | Free white males under 16 years. | Free white females, including heads of families. | All other free persons. | Slaves. |
|---|---|---|---|---|---|---|---|---|---|---|---|---|---|---|---|---|---|
| **WOODBRIDGE TOWN—continued.** | | | | | | **WOODBRIDGE TOWN—continued.** | | | | | | **WOODBRIDGE TOWN—continued.** | | | | | |
| Todd, Rachael | 1 | | 5 | | | Wilmot, Walter | 1 | 4 | 1 | | | Hine, Joel | 1 | 2 | 3 | | |
| Hummiston, Abel | 1 | 3 | 4 | | | Tuttle, Jeremiah | 1 | 1 | 3 | | | Pardie, William | 1 | | 2 | | |
| Hummiston, Daniel | 1 | | 1 | | | Tolles, Jerad | 1 | 5 | 2 | | | Attwater, Moses | 1 | 1 | 3 | | |
| Warren, Nathen | 1 | 3 | 2 | | | John (Negroe) | | | | 1 | | Newton, Christopher | 1 | 3 | 3 | | |
| Perkins, Ruben | 2 | 3 | 4 | | | Sperry, Demas | 1 | 2 | 1 | | | Buckhingham, Oliver | 1 | 1 | 1 | | |
| Sperry, Amie | 1 | | 1 | | | Downs, Joseph | 2 | 1 | 2 | | | Buckhingham, Abijah | 1 | | 1 | | |
| Sandford, Jonathan | 1 | 2 | 2 | | | Rinsley, Sarah | | | 4 | | | Sandford, Raymond | 1 | 3 | 5 | | |
| Barnes, Jacob | 1 | 2 | 6 | | | Sperry, Elizabeth | 2 | 3 | 6 | | | Tim (Negroe) | | | | 5 | |
| Johnson, Hezekiah | 1 | 2 | 4 | | | Tolles, Lamberton | 3 | | 8 | | | Underwood, John | 1 | | 1 | | |
| Johnson, Eliphalet | 1 | 4 | 4 | | | Thomas, Garthom | 3 | | 1 | | | Nettleton, John | 1 | 1 | 2 | | |
| Foot, Isaac | 1 | 1 | 2 | | | Thomas, Noah | 1 | 2 | 3 | 1 | | Tyrell, John | 1 | 2 | 2 | | |
| Beecher, Isaac, 2nd | 1 | | 1 | | | Sperry, Hezekiah | 1 | 3 | 8 | | | Andrew, Sarah | | 2 | 1 | | |
| Baldwin, Mathew | 2 | | 1 | | | Peck, Timothy | 1 | | 1 | | | Downs, Sarah | | | 1 | | |
| Benham, Elihu | 1 | 3 | 4 | | | Attwater, Amos | 1 | 1 | 3 | | | Hotchkiss, Elisha | 1 | 1 | 2 | | |
| Smith, Lamberton | 2 | 1 | 2 | | | Hitchcock, Amos | 2 | | 1 | | | Prince, Nathaniel | 1 | 2 | 3 | | |
| Thomas, Moses | 1 | | 1 | | | Martin, Israel | 1 | | 2 | | | Tyrell, Eliakin | 1 | 5 | 2 | | |
| Smith, Ezekiel | 1 | 4 | 3 | | | Nelson, Silus | 1 | 2 | 3 | | | Tyrell, Philomin | 1 | | 2 | | |
| Wheeler, Simion | 1 | 1 | 3 | | | Wolcot, Joseph | 1 | | 2 | | | Warren, Edward | 2 | 2 | 3 | | |
| Collins, Joel | 1 | 2 | 6 | | | Goodyer, Theophilus | 1 | | | | | Bino, Samuel | 1 | | 2 | | |
| Turrel, Jesse | 1 | 2 | 1 | | | Goodyer, Simeon | 1 | | | | | Bino, Ruth | | | 1 | | |
| Perkins, Israel | 2 | | 2 | | | Beers, Nathan | 1 | 2 | 3 | | | Hotchkiss, Isaac | 1 | 2 | 3 | | |
| Perkins, Rossannah | | | 3 | | | Alling, John | 1 | | | | | Wheeler, James | 1 | 2 | 6 | | |
| Kimbal, Thomas | 1 | 2 | 1 | | | Smith, Niamiah (Negroe) | | | | 2 | | Northrop, Gideon | 1 | 1 | 1 | | |
| Sperry, Ezra, 2nd | 1 | | 1 | | | Rowland, Jesse | 1 | 3 | 4 | | | Clarke, Aron | 3 | 1 | 2 | | |
| Bencher, Justus | 1 | 1 | 3 | | | Hoadley, Amasia | 1 | 3 | 2 | | | Ward, Abel | 1 | | | | |
| Peck, Samuel | 1 | 5 | 3 | | | Attwater, David | 1 | 1 | 3 | | | Smith, Poly Carp | | | 1 | | |
| Thomas, John | 3 | 1 | 3 | | | Driver, Lidia | | 2 | 2 | | | Beach, Samuel | 1 | 1 | 2 | | |
| Smith, Jonathan | 1 | 3 | 4 | | | Hummiston, Asa | 1 | | 2 | | | Clarke, Elizabeth | 2 | 2 | 2 | | |
| Sperry, Ezra | 2 | | 5 | | | Russell, Robert | 2 | | 1 | | | Chatfield, Hannah | 1 | | | | |
| Beecher, Daniel | 3 | | 2 | | 1 | Lownbury, Stephen | 1 | 1 | 3 | | | Thomas, John, 2 | 1 | 1 | 2 | | |
| Hitchcock, William | 1 | | 3 | | | Lownbury, Elias | 1 | 2 | 1 | | | Tolles, Daniel | 1 | 2 | 6 | | |
| Ball, Timothy | 1 | 1 | 6 | | | Peck, Chester | 1 | | | | | Hotchkiss, Jacob | 2 | 1 | 4 | | |
| Ball, Mary | | | 2 | | | Lownbury, Timothy | 2 | | 2 | | | Sacket, Jonathan | 1 | | 1 | | |
| Hitchcock, Medad | 2 | | 1 | | | Lownbury, Timothy, 2nd | 1 | | 2 | | | Hitchcock, Joseph | 1 | 1 | 3 | | |
| Lines, Abel | 1 | 1 | 4 | | | Hotchkiss, James | 1 | 1 | 2 | | | Hitchcock, Ebenezer | 1 | 1 | 4 | | |
| Hotchkiss, Joseph | 3 | 1 | 2 | | | Collins, Joseph | 1 | | | | | Russell, James | 2 | 1 | 7 | | |
| Hotchkiss, Abraham | 1 | 4 | 2 | | | Collins, Joseph, 2d | 1 | 1 | 1 | | | Tuttle, Caleb | 1 | 1 | 3 | | |
| Attwater, Jonathan | 3 | | 2 | | | Collins, Benjamin | 1 | | | | | Johnson, Joseph | 1 | 4 | 3 | | |
| Hooker, Hezekiah | 1 | 2 | 1 | | | Morris, Benjamin | 1 | | 3 | | | Carrington, Abraham | 1 | 2 | 3 | | |
| Sandford, Elihu, 2nd | 1 | 3 | | | | Turrel, Phineas | 2 | 6 | 5 | | | Carrington, David | 1 | | 1 | | |
| Holly, Stephen | 1 | 1 | | | | Wilmot, David | 1 | 1 | 4 | | | Hitchcock, Joseph | 2 | 3 | 5 | | |
| Holley, Stephen, 2nd | 1 | | 1 | | | Wilmot, Volantine | 1 | | 1 | | | Thomas, David | 2 | 1 | 5 | | |
| Pane, Abraham | 1 | 1 | 2 | | | Wilmot, Volantine, 2nd | 1 | 1 | 2 | | | Lines, Eber | 1 | | 3 | | |
| Thomas, James | 1 | | | | | Brown, Timothy | 2 | 1 | 3 | | | Lines, John | 1 | | 2 | | |
| Warren, Abigal | | | 1 | | | Hotchkiss, Stephen | 1 | | 1 | | | Lines, Ebenezer | 1 | | 2 | | |
| Johnson, Eden | 1 | 2 | 3 | | | Hotchkiss, Jabez | 1 | | 2 | | | Lines, Luke | 1 | 1 | 3 | | |
| Sperry, Elam | 1 | | 2 | | | Beacher, Jerad | 2 | 1 | 3 | 1 | | Sandford, Hitabel | | | 1 | | |
| Sperry, Ruben | 2 | 2 | 3 | | | French, David | 3 | 2 | 6 | | | Baldin, Mathew, 2 | 1 | 1 | 1 | | |
| Sperry, N | 3 | 2 | 5 | | | Thomas, Hezekiah | 1 | | 3 | | | Clarke, Joseph | | | | | |
| Sandford, Elihu | 1 | | 2 | | | Hotchkiss, Eziekel | 1 | 2 | 2 | | | Lownsbury, Lyles | 1 | 3 | 1 | | |
| Hotchkiss, Samuel | 1 | 1 | 2 | | | Thomas, Amos | 1 | 1 | 2 | | | Beers, David | 1 | | 1 | | |
| Perkins, Peter | 4 | 1 | 4 | | | | | | | | | Hotchkiss, Hetty | | | 1 | | |

## NEW LONDON COUNTY.

| NAME OF HEAD OF FAMILY. | Free white males of 16 and upward | Under 16 | Free white females | All other free | Slaves | NAME OF HEAD OF FAMILY. | M16+ | M<16 | F | Other | Slaves | NAME OF HEAD OF FAMILY. | M16+ | M<16 | F | Other | Slaves |
|---|---|---|---|---|---|---|---|---|---|---|---|---|---|---|---|---|---|
| Coburn, Samuel | 1 | | 2 | | | Grunstel, John | 1 | 1 | 2 | | | Avory, Jonathan | 2 | 4 | 3 | | |
| Able, Alpheus | 3 | 1 | 3 | | | Grunstel, James | 1 | | 2 | | | Palmer, Asa | 1 | 1 | 3 | | |
| Perrigo, Ezekiel | 1 | 2 | 3 | | | James, John | 1 | | 1 | | | Palmer, John | 2 | 1 | 2 | | |
| Bushnal, John | 1 | 1 | 2 | | | Knight, Asa | 2 | 1 | 2 | | | Lothrop, Jedediah | 1 | 1 | 4 | | |
| Hartshorn, Oliver | 1 | 1 | 2 | | | Cumstock, Daniel | 1 | 1 | 2 | | | Burnham, Benjamin | 3 | 1 | 3 | | |
| Dodge, Joshua | 1 | 1 | 4 | | | Webb, Jonathan | 1 | 2 | 5 | | | Bishop, Caleb | 4 | 2 | 3 | | 2 |
| Perkins, John | 9 | 4 | 4 | | | Knight, Issabel | | | 2 | | | Potter, William | 1 | 1 | 6 | | |
| Perkins, Levi | 2 | 2 | 4 | | | Perrigo, Ebenezer | 1 | 2 | 4 | | | Smith, Thomas | 1 | 2 | 2 | | |
| Overton, Aaron | 1 | | 2 | | | Knight, David, Junr | 1 | 2 | 4 | | | Capron, William | 1 | | 1 | | |
| Fuller, John | 1 | 4 | 3 | | | Knight, Phineas | 2 | 1 | 3 | | | Williams, Ezra | 1 | 1 | 3 | | |
| Fuller, Jacob | 1 | 1 | 1 | | | Knight, David | 2 | 1 | 2 | | | Burnham, Jedediah | 1 | 2 | 3 | | 1 |
| Fuller, Ebenezer | 1 | 2 | 3 | | | French, Joseph | 1 | 2 | 1 | | | Lapum, David | 1 | | | | |
| Guy (Negro) | | | | | 2 | Clark, David | 1 | 1 | 1 | | | Kinsman, Jeremiah, Junr | 3 | 1 | 6 | | |
| Perkins, Frederick | 4 | 2 | 4 | | | Hide, Asa | 4 | 5 | 4 | | | Stephens, Moses | 3 | 1 | 3 | | |
| Perkins, Joshua | 5 | 2 | 5 | | | Bishop, Joshua | 1 | 2 | | | | Stephens, Levi | 1 | | 2 | | |
| Coburn, Cornelius | 1 | 1 | 2 | | | Bishop, Nathl | 1 | | 2 | | | Kinsman, Jeremiah | 3 | | 3 | 8 | |
| Bishop, Mary | 1 | 2 | 4 | | | Roathburn, William | 1 | 2 | 3 | | | Wintworth, William | 2 | 5 | 4 | | |
| Cutler, Daniel | 2 | | 6 | | | Mingham, John | 3 | | 4 | | | Crosby, Ezra | 1 | | 2 | | |
| Cutler, Eleazer | 1 | 1 | 3 | | | Smith, Elkanah | 1 | 1 | 4 | | | Cleaveland, John | 1 | 4 | 1 | | |
| James, Saml | 1 | | 3 | | | Kingsley, Hezekiah | 1 | 1 | 3 | | | Craps (Negro) | | | | 6 | |
| Perrigo, John | 1 | | 1 | | | Clark, Perry | 4 | | 5 | | | Safford, Solomon | 1 | 1 | 3 | | |
| Manning, Luther | 2 | 1 | 2 | | | Petingall, Lemuel | 2 | | 2 | | | Safford, Jedediah | 2 | 1 | 5 | | |
| Perrigo, William | 2 | 1 | 6 | | | Simons, Thomas | 1 | 1 | 1 | | | Hide, Barnabas | 1 | | 3 | | |
| Tubs, Daniel | 1 | 2 | 5 | | | Bingham, John, Junr | 1 | | | | | Calkins, Able, Junr | 2 | 1 | 5 | | |
| Perrigo, William, Junr | 1 | 2 | 4 | | | Bottom, James | 1 | 2 | 4 | | | Braman, Daniel | 1 | | 3 | | |
| Cutler, Samuel | 3 | 3 | 3 | | | James (Negro) | | | | 7 | | Thillam, Samuel | 1 | | 2 | | |
| Farnum, Elijah | 1 | 4 | 2 | | | Peter (Negro) | | | | 4 | | Whaley, Theophilus | 1 | | 3 | | |
| Kingsley, Diah | 1 | 2 | 2 | | | Davis, John | 1 | 1 | 1 | | | Perkins, Olive | 2 | 1 | 4 | | |
| Able, Zacheus | 1 | | 1 | | | Smith, Nathl | 1 | 3 | 3 | | | Perkins, Joseph | 1 | | 1 | | |
| French, Pheba | 1 | | 2 | | | Huntington, Barnabas | 3 | 1 | 3 | | | Perkins, Solomon | 2 | 3 | 5 | | |
| Lee, Andrew | 4 | 4 | 5 | | | Stephens, John | 3 | 1 | 5 | | | Perkins, Jacob | 4 | 2 | 4 | | |
| Farnum, Henry | 3 | 2 | 2 | | | Roathburn, Thomas | 3 | 4 | 3 | | | Fitch, John | 1 | 2 | 3 | | |
| Bushnul, Nathan | 2 | 2 | 7 | | | Morse, Rufus | 1 | 1 | 3 | | | Bundy, Joshua | 1 | | 3 | | |
| Bushnul, Joseph | 2 | 1 | 3 | | | Roathburn, Asa | 1 | 2 | 4 | | | Bottom, Daniel | 1 | | 4 | | |
| Bushnul, Ezekiel | 2 | | 4 | | | Bishop, Samuel | 1 | 3 | 5 | | | Bottom, Daniel, Junr | 1 | | 2 | | |
| Bushnul, Aaron | 2 | 4 | 4 | | | Isaac (Negro) | | | | 5 | | Morrow, Thomas | 1 | 1 | 2 | | |
| Lovett, Saml | 4 | 2 | 6 | | | Adams, William | 7 | 2 | 7 | | | Whipple, Rebecka | | | 1 | | |
| Williams, John | 1 | | 2 | | | Lewis (Negro) | | | | 8 | | | | | | | |

# HEADS OF FAMILIES—CONNECTICUT.

## NEW LONDON COUNTY—Continued.

| NAME OF HEAD OF FAMILY. | Free white males of 16 years and upward, including heads of families. | Free white males under 16 years. | Free white females, including heads of families. | All other free persons. | Slaves. |
|---|---|---|---|---|---|
| Bottom, Amaziah | 1 | | 2 | | |
| Kimball, Jedediah | 1 | 4 | 3 | | |
| Sheldon, William | 1 | 3 | 3 | | |
| Smith, Joseph | 1 | | 1 | | |
| Smith, Daniel | 1 | 2 | 2 | | |
| Caulkins, William | 1 | 1 | 3 | | |
| Pharough (Negro) | | | | 6 | |
| Jackson, John | 1 | 3 | 3 | | |
| Denison, James | 3 | 1 | 6 | | |
| Jackson, Jonathan | 1 | | 1 | | |
| Clark, Ezra | 2 | 4 | 6 | | 1 |
| Bishop, Ezra | 3 | 3 | 4 | | |
| Bishop, Ebenezer | 3 | 1 | 5 | 1 | |
| Lothrop, Septemius | 3 | 2 | 6 | 2 | |
| Willoughby, Elijah | 4 | 1 | 4 | | |
| Baldwin, Joseph | 2 | | 3 | | |
| Baldwin, Rufus | 1 | 2 | 4 | | |
| Burnham, James | 3 | 1 | 3 | | |
| Herrington, Andw | 1 | | 3 | | |
| Herrington, Stephen | 1 | 1 | 1 | | |
| Lothrop, Simeon | 3 | 2 | 4 | | |
| Clark, Andw | 4 | 1 | 3 | 1 | |
| Craft, Rhoda | | | 2 | | |
| Clark, Samuel | 1 | 2 | 2 | | |
| King, Joseph | 2 | 1 | 3 | | |
| Goodel, Ruben | 1 | 2 | 1 | | |
| Sly, Thomas | 2 | | 1 | | |
| Jehu (Negro) | | | | 6 | |
| Larrance, Jonathan | 2 | | 3 | | |
| Gorton, Joseph | 1 | 4 | 2 | | |
| Larrance, Samuel | 2 | | 1 | | |
| Read, Samuel | 1 | 1 | 3 | | |
| Kuzer, Nathl | 1 | 3 | 4 | | |
| Kuzer, Samuel | 1 | | 1 | | |
| Kirtland, Hannah | 1 | | 1 | | |
| Yerrington, Ruben | 2 | 3 | 2 | | |
| Bishop, John | 2 | | 2 | | |
| Autherton, Isaac | 1 | | 3 | | |
| Branch, Stephen | 3 | 4 | 4 | | |
| Read, Asa | 1 | 2 | 5 | | |
| Read, Joseph | 1 | | 1 | | |
| Read, Amos | 1 | 4 | 4 | | |
| Herrington, Joseph | 2 | 1 | 2 | | |
| Eames, John | 2 | 1 | 4 | | |
| Tracy, Jesse | 3 | 5 | 5 | | |
| Tracy, Andw | 1 | 2 | 4 | | |
| Tracy, Ebenezer | 4 | 1 | 6 | | |
| Tracy, Elijah | 2 | 1 | 2 | | |
| Smith, James | 1 | | 1 | | |
| Read, Jabez | 2 | 1 | 3 | | |
| Read, John | 1 | 3 | 5 | 1 | |
| Baker, Enoch | 3 | 1 | 3 | | |
| Gordon, Elexander | 1 | 2 | 2 | 1 | |
| Preston, Daniel | 1 | 3 | 2 | | |
| Caulkins, Jonathan | 1 | 1 | 3 | | |
| Button, Joshua | 1 | | 3 | | |
| Morgan, Elisha | 2 | 3 | 8 | | |
| John (Negro) | | | | 3 | |
| Cato (Negro) | | | | 3 | |
| Eames, Cumfort | 1 | | 1 | | |
| Fanning, Charles | 1 | 3 | 5 | | 1 |
| Jewet, Joseph | 2 | | 3 | | |
| Kimball, Levi | 2 | 2 | 9 | | |
| Draper, Fisher | | 2 | 2 | | |
| Jewet, Eleazer | 1 | | 2 | | |
| Taylor, Nathan | 1 | 3 | 3 | | |
| Brown, John | 1 | 2 | 2 | | |
| Whealer, Parley | 1 | 1 | 1 | | |
| Wilson, John | 3 | 2 | 4 | | |
| Clark, Daniel | 1 | | 5 | | |
| Morgan, Dudley | 2 | 2 | 4 | | |
| Smith, Samuel | 1 | 2 | 4 | | |
| Norman, John | 2 | 1 | 3 | | |
| Woodard, Ruben | 1 | 1 | 4 | | |
| Smith, Jonathan | 1 | | 3 | | |
| Rose, Thomas | 1 | 2 | 4 | 1 | |
| Rose, Asa | 1 | | 5 | | |
| Rose, Sarah | | | 3 | | |
| Moore, James | 2 | | 2 | | |
| Adams, Asael | 2 | 2 | 4 | | |
| Sipeo (Negro) | | | | 6 | |
| Geers, Roger | 1 | 3 | 4 | | |
| Geers, Christopher | 1 | | 1 | | |
| Quive, Elijah | 1 | | 1 | 1 | |
| Coit, Oliver | 2 | 3 | 4 | | |
| Phillups, Genworence | | 1 | 2 | 1 | |
| Tracy, Samuel | 1 | | 3 | | |
| Keeney, Benjamin | 1 | 1 | 3 | | |
| Belshaw, William | 3 | 3 | 3 | | |
| Phillups, Levi | 1 | | 1 | | |
| Phillups, Squire | 1 | 3 | 3 | | |
| Phillups, Jonathan | 1 | 3 | 2 | | |
| Keigwin, James | 1 | 1 | 3 | | |
| Mulkins, John | 1 | | 2 | | |
| Lothrop, Azariah | 1 | 3 | 2 | | |
| Pope, Ansil | 1 | 2 | 5 | | |
| Kuzer, Elisha | 1 | | 1 | | |
| Davis, Samuel | 1 | 3 | 5 | | |
| Moody (Negro) | | | | 6 | |
| Rich, Solomon | 1 | 1 | 2 | 2 | |
| John (Negro) | | | | 1 | |
| Harris, Lydia | 1 | | 2 | | |
| Peter (Negro) | | | | 3 | |
| Avory, James | 2 | 2 | 5 | | |
| Geer, Robert | 1 | | 3 | | |
| Absolum (Negro) | | | | 6 | |
| Avory, Gideon | 2 | 3 | 5 | | |
| Avory, William | 2 | 2 | 3 | | |
| Hatch, Elisabeth | | | | 1 | |
| Jackson, Thomas | 2 | | 1 | | |
| Coit, Benjamin | 3 | 4 | 4 | 1 | |
| Quive, Lemuel | 2 | 2 | 5 | | |
| Greene, David | 2 | 2 | 7 | | |
| Greene, Winter | 7 | 2 | 5 | | |
| Greene, John | 1 | | 3 | | |
| Belshaw, Joseph | 1 | 3 | 6 | | |
| Gates, John | 1 | 2 | 2 | | |
| Tucker, William | 2 | 1 | 5 | | |
| Coit, Samuel | 1 | | 1 | | 1 |
| Quive, Henry | 1 | 1 | 2 | | |
| Coit, Samuel, Junr | 3 | 1 | 4 | | |
| Partridge, Asa, Junr | 1 | | 3 | | |
| Fanning, Frederick | 1 | | 2 | | |
| Smith, David | 4 | 5 | 4 | | |
| Blunt, Ambrus | 2 | 1 | 3 | | |
| Blunt, Walter | 1 | 1 | 1 | | |
| Johnson, Stephen | 4 | 1 | 4 | | |
| Waters, Lydia | | 1 | 1 | | |
| Walton, Daniel | 2 | | 8 | | |
| Austin, Thomas | 3 | | 2 | | |
| Walton, Oliver | 2 | 4 | 5 | | |
| Clarke, Lydia | | | 3 | | |
| Olin, Philup | 3 | 5 | 5 | | |
| Blunt, Elisha | 1 | 1 | 3 | | |
| Bennett, Daniel | 2 | 5 | 3 | | |
| Fry, Peleg | 1 | 2 | 4 | | |
| Gorton, Stephen | 1 | | 2 | | |
| Tylar, John | 2 | 3 | 2 | 2 | |
| Tylar, John, Junr | 1 | 3 | 3 | | |
| Geer, Nathan | 1 | 1 | 5 | | |
| Phillups, Jeramiah | 2 | 3 | 4 | | |
| Coit, John | 3 | 2 | 6 | | |
| Geers, Daniel | 1 | | 3 | | |
| Avery, John, Junr | 1 | 2 | 4 | | |
| Lord, Nathl | 2 | 2 | 5 | | |
| Yerrington, Abraham | 1 | | 2 | | |
| Tucker, Ephraim | 2 | 2 | 3 | | |
| Adams, Daniel | 1 | 2 | 2 | | |
| Gates, Mary | | | 4 | | |
| Bennett, Jacob | 2 | | 2 | | |
| Parks, Ruben | 1 | 1 | 1 | | |
| Cleft, Amos | 3 | 1 | 3 | | |
| Pero (Negro) | | | | 5 | |
| Pike (Negro) | | | | 6 | |
| Tylar, Elisha | 3 | 1 | 5 | | |
| Tracy, Lucy | | | 3 | | |
| Tylar, Joseph | 1 | | 3 | | |
| Tylar, James | 2 | 2 | 3 | | |
| Covey, Kinyon | 1 | | 3 | | |
| Cogswell, Nathl | 4 | 1 | 3 | | |
| Kenney Asa | 2 | | 3 | | |
| Brown, Jacob | 1 | 1 | 2 | | |
| Bliss, Jona | 2 | 1 | 1 | | |
| Potter, Gideon | 2 | 4 | 6 | | |
| Baxter, Jesse | 1 | | 6 | | |
| Freman, Abigail | 1 | | 3 | | |
| Kenney, Jacob | 4 | 3 | 2 | | |
| Bassett, James | 1 | 2 | 4 | | |
| Cook, Thadeus | 2 | 3 | 6 | | |
| Wade, William | 1 | 1 | 1 | | |
| Cheesborough, Thomas | 1 | 2 | 4 | | |
| Hatch, Jeremi | 1 | | 2 | | |
| Hatch, Elisha | 1 | 1 | 3 | | |
| Gates, James | 3 | 3 | 3 | | |
| Absolum (Negro) | | | | 2 | |
| Stanton, Jabez | 1 | 1 | 4 | | |
| Stanton, William | 1 | | 3 | | |
| Geer, Able | 2 | 2 | 4 | | |
| Prentice, Manassa | 2 | 2 | 2 | | |
| Morgan, James | 2 | 1 | 5 | | |
| Geer, Lebeus | 1 | 4 | 3 | | |
| Lester, Moses | 3 | 2 | 6 | | |
| Geer, Stephen | 1 | 1 | 2 | | |
| Geer, Elisha | 2 | 1 | 6 | | |
| Bliss, Saml | 1 | 1 | 2 | | |
| Bliss, Silas | 2 | 1 | 2 | | |
| Whealer, Edward | 1 | | 1 | | |
| Smith, Darius | 1 | | 2 | | |
| Clark, Perry | 2 | 1 | 3 | | |
| Parks, David | 1 | | 2 | | |
| Stanton, Jabez | 2 | 2 | 6 | | |
| Bruster, Simon | 4 | 1 | 7 | | 2 |
| Freman, Caleb | 1 | | 2 | | |
| Freman, Saml | 3 | | 4 | | |
| Freman, Peleg | 1 | 1 | 5 | | |
| Freman, Mary | 2 | | 1 | | |
| Rude, Lydia | 1 | | 2 | | |
| Morse, William | 1 | 1 | 5 | | |
| Morse, Daniel | 2 | | 2 | | |
| Morgan, Benjamin | 1 | | 2 | | |
| Geer, Silsbey | 1 | | 2 | | |
| Johnson, William | 1 | | 1 | | |
| Benjamin, John | 1 | 1 | 3 | | |
| Palmer, Darius | 1 | 2 | 3 | | |
| Nickols, William | 1 | 2 | 1 | | |
| Prentice, Eleazer | 3 | 1 | 2 | | |
| Lester, Elisha | 2 | 2 | 5 | | |
| Leonard, Saml | 2 | 2 | 3 | | |
| Stanton, Nathan | 1 | 1 | 2 | | |
| Stanton, Robart, Junr | 2 | | 1 | | |
| Stanton, Robart | 1 | | 1 | | |
| Leonard, Saml, Junr | 1 | 1 | 2 | 1 | |
| Denison, Elijah | 2 | | 1 | | |
| Stanton, David | 2 | 1 | 4 | | |
| Stanton, Saml | 1 | 1 | 2 | | |
| Maine, Peres | 1 | | 2 | | |
| Burton, Israel | 1 | | 6 | | |
| Palmer, Gershom | 1 | | 2 | | |
| Ray, Daniel | 2 | | 4 | | |
| Bramin, Prudence | 2 | 2 | 3 | | |
| Herrick, Israel | 2 | 1 | 5 | | |
| Randal, Nathan | 1 | 4 | 5 | | |
| Ray, Amos | 1 | 3 | 3 | 1 | 1 |
| Dorrance, Gershom | 3 | | 1 | | |
| Herrick, Isaac | 1 | | 2 | | |
| Herrick, Ephraim | 1 | 2 | 5 | | |
| Wilbur, Joseph | 1 | 5 | 2 | | |
| Kimball, Nathan | 3 | 1 | 4 | | |
| Frink, James | 1 | 2 | 2 | | |
| Stanton, David, Junr | 1 | 1 | 5 | | |
| Brown, Parley | 2 | 4 | 6 | | |
| Tylar, Samuel | 3 | 1 | 4 | | |
| Bordman, Hezekiah | 3 | 2 | 5 | | |
| Branch, Thomas | 3 | 1 | 5 | | |
| Guile, Abraham | 2 | 1 | 3 | | |
| Cook, Barton | 4 | | 6 | | |
| Cook, John | 4 | 3 | 5 | | |
| Samson, William | 1 | 1 | 1 | | |
| Sherman, Elisabeth | | | 1 | | |
| Holly, Manchester | 1 | 1 | 3 | | |
| Stuart, Elexander | 1 | 3 | 8 | | 1 |
| Keeney, Ezra | 2 | 1 | 1 | | 1 |
| Boardman, David | 2 | 1 | 7 | | |
| Yemmons, Saml | 1 | 2 | 2 | | |
| Rouse, Simeon | 4 | | 2 | | |
| Starkweather, Joseph | 2 | 3 | 2 | | |
| Reynolds, Ebenr | 2 | 2 | 3 | 3 | |
| Lewis, Mary | | | 3 | | |
| Maine, Peckham | 1 | 1 | 2 | | |
| Killam, Nathan | 1 | | 2 | | |
| Barns, Elijah | 2 | 3 | 6 | | |
| Bromley, Preserved | 2 | | 1 | | |
| Starkweather, Ephraim | 1 | 1 | 3 | | |
| Chapman, William | 2 | | 4 | | |
| Holt, Nathl | 1 | 1 | 2 | | |
| Capron, Giles | 2 | 1 | 6 | | |
| Pollard, Joseph | 1 | | 2 | | |
| Johnson, Benjamin | 1 | | 2 | | |
| Keeney, Gideon | 3 | | 4 | | |
| Herrick, Elijah | 1 | | 4 | | |
| Rose, Daniel | 3 | 3 | 3 | 1 | |
| Huntington, Andw | 2 | 1 | 2 | | |
| Avery, Solomon | 1 | | 1 | | |
| Partridge, Elijah | 2 | 3 | 1 | | |
| Partridge, Asa | 1 | 2 | 3 | | |
| Love, Robart | 1 | | 1 | | |
| Weeden, Elijah | 2 | 2 | 6 | | |
| Davis, Joseph | 1 | | 2 | | |
| Herrick, Nathan | 1 | 1 | 3 | | |
| Herrick, Amos | 1 | | 2 | | |
| Partridge, James | 3 | 3 | 6 | | |
| Belshaw, Nathan | 1 | 1 | 2 | | |
| Bottom, Joseph | | | | | |
| Whealer, John | 1 | 5 | 1 | | |
| Guile, Joseph | 1 | 3 | 2 | | |
| Partridge, John | 1 | | 1 | | |
| Gates, Joseph | 1 | 3 | 4 | | |
| Gates, Elijah | 1 | | 1 | 1 | |
| Wanton (Negro) | | | | 3 | |
| Whitman, John | 1 | 1 | 2 | | |
| Partridge, Ruben | 2 | 3 | 4 | | |
| Bennett, Elias | 1 | 1 | 3 | | |
| Daniels, Oliver | 3 | | 3 | | |
| Woodard, Moses | 1 | 2 | 7 | | |
| Geer, James | 2 | 1 | 2 | | |
| Rose, Anna | 2 | | 8 | | |
| Coit, Daniel | 1 | 1 | 4 | | |
| Prentice, Elisha | 1 | 1 | 4 | | |

113

# FIRST CENSUS OF THE UNITED STATES.

## NEW LONDON COUNTY—Continued.

| NAME OF HEAD OF FAMILY. | Free white males of 16 years and upward, including heads of families. | Free white males under 16 years. | Free white females, including heads of families. | All other free persons. | Slaves. |
|---|---|---|---|---|---|
| Cogswell, John | 1 | 1 | 2 | | |
| Hartshorn, Jonathan | 1 | 2 | 2 | | |
| Guile, Samuel | 2 | 1 | 4 | | |
| Keeney, Henry | 1 | 1 | 2 | | |
| Ray, Stephen | 1 | 2 | 2 | | |
| Ray, John | 2 | 1 | 5 | | |
| Ray, Gideon | 1 | | 3 | | |
| Burton, Nathan | 1 | | 1 | | |
| Burton, Israel | 1 | | 3 | | |
| Hutcherson, Amos | 2 | 2 | 5 | | |
| Bromley, Israel | 1 | 3 | 2 | | |
| Parrish, Roswell | 1 | 2 | 2 | | |
| Benjamins, Jedediah | 1 | | 1 | | |
| Brown, John | 4 | 2 | 3 | | |
| Rix, Hannah | 2 | | 4 | | |
| Billings, Joseph | 1 | | 1 | | |
| Maine, Rufus | 1 | 4 | 4 | | |
| Rix, Thomas | 2 | 2 | 4 | | |
| Small, William | 1 | | 1 | | |
| Rix, Theophilus | 1 | 2 | 3 | | |
| Woodburn, Pruda | 1 | | 3 | | |
| Amos, Elisabeth | | | | | |
| Lambert, Thomas | 1 | 2 | 3 | | |
| Herrick, Eleazer | 2 | 1 | 3 | | |
| Kimball, John | 1 | | 1 | | |
| Benjamin, Abiel | 1 | | 1 | | |
| Benjamin, Abiel Jun^r | 1 | 6 | 3 | | |
| Benjamins, Ezra | 2 | 2 | 3 | | |
| Badcock, Benjamin | 2 | 3 | 4 | | |
| Geer, Jonathan | 1 | | 1 | | |
| Blodgett, William | 1 | | | | |
| Frink, Diah | 1 | 1 | 2 | | |
| Brown, Amos, Jun^r | 1 | 2 | 3 | | |
| Grant, W^m | 1 | 2 | 2 | | |
| Brown, Walter | 2 | 2 | 3 | | |
| Brown, Amos | 2 | 5 | 3 | | |
| Robins, Moses | 2 | | 4 | 1 | |
| Crasy, Robert | 1 | 1 | 2 | | |
| Keeney, David | 1 | 2 | 4 | | |
| Davis, Thara | 2 | 2 | 4 | | |
| Halsey, W^m | 2 | | 3 | | |
| Safford, Thomas | 2 | 1 | 5 | | |
| Guile, Elisha | 1 | 1 | 2 | | |
| Frink, And^w | 4 | | 2 | | |
| Brumley, Christopher | 1 | 4 | 5 | | |
| Safford, John | 3 | 2 | 2 | | |
| Safford, Johnson | 1 | 1 | 2 | | |
| Starkweather, Jesse | 1 | 2 | 6 | | |
| James, John | 2 | 2 | 6 | 1 | |
| Tylar, Caleb | 2 | | 3 | 1 | 1 |
| Tylar, Joseph | 2 | 2 | 3 | | |
| Spicer, Oliver | 1 | | 1 | | |
| Crasy, John | 3 | 2 | 4 | | 1 |
| Palmer, George | 1 | 4 | 3 | | |
| Tylar, Lemuel | 2 | | 5 | | |
| Peters, Nathan | 2 | 2 | 5 | | |
| Morgan, John | 3 | 4 | 5 | | |
| Forthsides, Charles | 1 | 4 | 3 | | |
| Jones, Simeon | 1 | | 4 | | |
| Billings, Randall | 3 | 5 | 1 | | |
| Palmer, Jesse | 1 | 1 | 4 | | |
| Downing, John | 1 | 2 | 3 | | |
| Parks, Hannah | | | 1 | | |
| Edwards, William | 1 | | 1 | | |
| Smith, Jon^a | 1 | 2 | 3 | | |
| Crasy, Robart, Jun^r | 1 | | 4 | | |
| Tracy, Isael | 2 | 1 | 7 | | |
| Forbs, Nathan | 3 | 1 | 2 | | |
| Andrus, Solomon | 1 | | 1 | | |
| Rude, Zachariah | 3 | 2 | 2 | | |
| York, Elisha | 2 | 3 | 5 | | |
| Cook, Cyprian | 1 | 1 | 3 | | |
| Leonard, Nicholas | 1 | | 2 | | |
| Morse, David | 2 | 4 | 3 | | |
| Brown, Walter, Jun^r | 1 | | 2 | | |
| Meach, Lucy | | | 2 | | |
| Rude, Ezekiel | 2 | 1 | 3 | | |
| Meach, Moses | 2 | 2 | 5 | | |
| Smith, Asa | 2 | 4 | 9 | | |
| Meach, Jacob | 4 | 2 | 4 | | |
| Clark, Timothy, Jun^r | 1 | 3 | 3 | | |
| Mott, Samuel | 4 | 2 | 5 | 1 | |
| Bestow, Calvin | 3 | | 3 | | |
| Bruster, Eunice | | 1 | 1 | | |
| Mott, Edward | 3 | | 7 | | |
| Downer, Joshua | 4 | 4 | 3 | | 1 |
| Treat, Samuel | 1 | | 2 | | |
| Brown, William | 1 | 3 | 4 | | |
| Rix, Nathan | 1 | 1 | 2 | | |
| Gavett, John | 1 | | 2 | | |
| Morgan, James, Jun^r | 1 | 1 | 2 | 1 | |
| Button, Roswell | 5 | 5 | 6 | | |
| Downer, Avory | 1 | 3 | 1 | | |
| Tracy, Edward | 1 | 2 | 3 | | |
| Brown, Amos, Jun^r | 1 | | 2 | | |
| Grant, William | 1 | 1 | 3 | | |
| Winter, Frederick | 3 | 1 | 8 | | |
| Plummer, Mary | | | 2 | | |
| Gates, Ebenezer | 1 | 1 | 2 | | |
| Chapman, Cumfort, Jun^r | 1 | 2 | 2 | | |
| Avory, Richerson | 1 | | 3 | | |
| Dunwell, Stephen | 1 | 1 | 3 | | |
| Winter, Amos | 1 | 1 | 3 | | |
| Crandall, Benjamin | 1 | 3 | 1 | | |
| Button, Mathias | 1 | 3 | 4 | | |
| Parks, Elisha | 2 | 2 | 2 | | |
| Stanton, Nathan | 1 | 1 | 2 | | |
| Parks, Silas | 1 | 1 | 2 | | |
| Parks, Elijah | 2 | 2 | 4 | | |
| Geer, John W | 1 | 4 | 2 | | |
| Parks, Paul | 2 | 1 | 4 | | |
| Baley, Jeremiah | 2 | | 4 | | |
| Baley, Samuel | 1 | | 3 | | |
| Freman, Ebenezer | 1 | | 2 | | |
| Thomas, Abigail | | | 3 | | |
| Avory, Ebenezer | 2 | 3 | 5 | | |
| Story, Solomon | 2 | 1 | 3 | | |
| Kimball, Elisha | 1 | 4 | 4 | | |
| Winter, Ebenezer | 1 | | 4 | | |
| Halsey, Jeremiah | 4 | 4 | 8 | 1 | 2 |
| Parks, Roswell | 1 | 3 | 2 | | |
| Parks, Abijah | 1 | | 3 | | |
| Parks, Abijah, Jun^r | 1 | | 3 | | |
| Parks, Asa | 2 | 1 | 3 | | |
| Cook, Isaiah | 2 | 4 | 3 | | |
| Woodard, Thomas | 2 | 2 | 4 | | |
| Avory, Samuel | 2 | | 3 | | |
| Avory, David | 1 | 2 | 2 | | |
| Avory, John | 3 | 2 | 2 | | |
| Avory, Isaac | 3 | 2 | 6 | | |
| Avory, Amos | 2 | 1 | 3 | 2 | |
| Winter, Jonah | 1 | 2 | 3 | 1 | |
| Swan, Timothy | 1 | 5 | 3 | | |
| Thomas, Daniel | 1 | 2 | 6 | | |
| Killam, Samuel | 1 | 2 | 6 | | |
| Whipple, Luther | 1 | 3 | 7 | | |
| Bruster, Jacob | 1 | 2 | 4 | | |
| Gates, Thomas | 2 | 1 | 2 | | |
| Gates, Cyrus | 1 | 4 | 4 | | |
| Beard, William | 3 | | 2 | | |
| Chapman, Cumfort | 3 | | 1 | | |
| Gates, Daniel | 3 | 2 | 6 | | |
| Prentice, Elisha | 1 | 1 | 4 | | |
| Harris, Andrew | 1 | 1 | 2 | | |
| Crasy, Oliver | 3 | 1 | 5 | 1 | |
| Bruster, Dorothy | 1 | | 2 | | |
| Bruster, Daniel | 3 | 3 | 4 | | |
| Standish, Israel | 1 | 4 | 4 | | |
| Standish, Amasa | 1 | 4 | 4 | | |
| Gion, Luke | 1 | 2 | 3 | | |
| Newton, Jacob | 1 | 3 | 2 | | |
| Comb, Thomos | 2 | | 3 | | |
| Smith, Jonathan | 1 | | 4 | | |
| Holt, Jesse | 1 | | 5 | | |
| Jones, Stephen | 1 | 1 | 1 | | |
| Smith, Silas | 1 | 5 | 1 | | |
| Ruel, Elijah | 1 | | 1 | | |
| Roath, Daniel | 1 | | 1 | | |
| Roath, Rufus | 1 | 2 | 3 | | |
| Randall, Joseph | 2 | | 2 | | |
| Roath, Betsy | | 1 | 2 | | |
| Wintworth, Amos | 1 | | 2 | | |
| Roath, Benjamin | 2 | 1 | 5 | | |
| Peter (Negro) | | | | 3 | |
| Roath, Sam^l | 2 | 1 | 2 | | |
| Roath, John | 2 | 2 | 3 | | |
| Roath, Silas | 1 | 2 | 4 | | |
| Cook, William | 1 | 2 | 3 | | |
| Williams, Moses | 1 | 1 | 1 | | |
| Roath, Joseph | 1 | 2 | 3 | | |
| Downs, Sarah | | | 2 | | |
| Rose, Peleg | 1 | 3 | 2 | | |
| Bromley, Dewey | 1 | 1 | 4 | | |
| Spicer, Daniel | 1 | 1 | 2 | | |
| Spicer, Asa | 1 | | 2 | | |
| Mortimer, Benjamin | 1 | | 4 | | |
| Corning, Elisha | 2 | 4 | 3 | | |
| Corning, Loami | 2 | 3 | 5 | | |
| Corning, Samuel | 1 | 1 | 1 | | |
| Coy, Nathan | 1 | 3 | 2 | | |
| Wilcox, Elisha | 1 | | 1 | | |
| Wilcox, Joseph | 1 | | 1 | | |
| Cato (Negro) | | | | 5 | |
| Brown, George | 1 | | 1 | | |
| Longwood, Mathew | 1 | | 1 | | |
| Tracy, Elisha | 1 | | 1 | | |
| Gideons, Joseph | 1 | 1 | 7 | | |
| Tracy, John | 1 | 1 | 2 | | |
| Smith, Ephraim | 1 | 1 | 5 | | |
| Avory, James | 3 | 4 | 3 | | |
| Badcock, Ichabod, Jun^r | 2 | 4 | 4 | | |
| Morgan, Simeon | 1 | 1 | 3 | | |
| Buttors, William | | | | | |
| Williams, Moses, Jun^r | 1 | 1 | 3 | | |
| Stilman, Zeporah | 1 | | 3 | | |
| Bruster, Jon^a, Jun^r | 2 | 1 | 2 | | |
| Pride, Absolum | 2 | | 2 | | |
| Story, Jonathan | 1 | 2 | 7 | | |
| Story, Eben^r | 1 | 3 | 2 | | |
| Williams, Jesse | 3 | | 2 | | |
| Penninian, William | 1 | | 2 | | |
| Story, Mehitable | | 1 | 1 | | |
| Holdrige, William | 2 | 1 | 1 | | |
| Winslow, William | 1 | 2 | 1 | | |
| Craige, Robart | 1 | | 1 | | |
| Aderton, Samuel | 1 | 3 | 3 | | |
| Ford, John | 1 | 1 | 2 | | |
| Bruster, Jabez | 3 | 5 | 3 | | |
| Bruster, Nathan | 2 | 1 | 4 | | |
| Bruster, Elijah | 3 | 2 | 3 | | |
| Harkness, John | 2 | 2 | 6 | | |
| Capron, Simeon | 1 | 2 | 3 | | |
| Bruster, Jonathan | 3 | 3 | 3 | | |
| Allen, Ebenezer | 1 | | 1 | | |
| Clark, Roger | 1 | 1 | 2 | | |
| Pollard, Barsheba | | | 2 | | |
| Pollard, Nabby | | | 3 | | |
| Wight, John | 1 | | 4 | | |
| Worthington, Dan | 1 | 5 | 4 | | |
| Rust, Prudence | | 1 | 4 | | |
| Punderson, Ebenezer, Jun^r | 1 | 1 | 4 | | 2 |
| Page, Philemon | 1 | 1 | 2 | | |
| Punderson, Ebenezer | 1 | | 2 | | |
| Billings, Benjamin | 1 | | 2 | | |
| Billings, William | 1 | | 1 | | |
| Whipple, Jonathan | 1 | 3 | 2 | | |
| Holerige, Elisha | 1 | 1 | 2 | | |
| Capron, Samuel | 3 | 3 | 5 | | |
| Rose, Joseph | 2 | | 4 | | |
| Thurber, Luther | 1 | | 1 | | |
| Whipple, Elijah | 1 | 2 | 2 | | |
| Pollard, John | 1 | 1 | 4 | | |
| Chapman, Obadiah | 2 | 1 | 4 | | |
| Whipple, Joseph | 1 | | 2 | | |
| Brown, Elias | 3 | 3 | 3 | | 1 |
| Badcock, Ichabod | 3 | 1 | 5 | | |
| Brown, Eunice | | | 2 | | |
| Kimball, Moses | 3 | | 2 | | |
| Kimball, Asa | 3 | 2 | 3 | | |
| Stodard, Mortimer | 2 | 2 | 4 | | |
| Standish, Levi | 1 | | 4 | | |
| Starkweather, Richard | 1 | | 3 | | |
| Badcock, Christopher | 1 | 1 | 5 | | |
| Read, Christopher | 1 | | 3 | | |
| Badcock, Joseph S | 1 | 1 | 5 | | |
| Prince (Negro) | | | | 1 | 4 |
| Huntley, Thomas | 1 | 2 | 2 | | |
| Brown, David | 1 | 1 | 3 | | |
| Button, William | 1 | | 1 | | |
| Button, Shubael | 1 | 1 | 1 | | |
| Teel, Joseph | 5 | 4 | 3 | | |
| Bruster, Silas | 1 | 1 | 2 | | |
| Williams, Samuel | 2 | | 5 | | |
| Williams, Simeon | 2 | | 1 | | |
| Crandall, Christopher | 1 | 3 | 2 | | |
| Gideons, Solomon | 2 | 5 | 5 | | |
| Pembleton, Joshua | 2 | 3 | 6 | | |
| Standish, Nathan | 2 | 4 | 4 | | |
| Baldwin, Joseph | 1 | 3 | 3 | | |
| Davis, William | 1 | | 3 | | |
| Guile, Nathan | 1 | | 3 | | |
| Bramin, John | 2 | 2 | 5 | | |
| Read, Samuel | 1 | 2 | 5 | | |
| Corning, Nehemiah | 2 | | 2 | | |
| Corning, Uriah | 1 | 3 | 3 | | |
| Truman, Jonathan | 2 | 2 | 3 | 1 | |
| Pride, Asa | 2 | | 2 | | |
| Adams, Abraham | 1 | 1 | 2 | | |
| Wight, Joseph | 1 | | | | |
| Champlin, Silas | 2 | 1 | 2 | | |
| Story, Jabez | 2 | 1 | 2 | | |
| Pride, William | 4 | 1 | 7 | | |
| Smith, John | 1 | | 3 | | |
| Benjamins, Asa | 2 | 1 | 2 | | |
| Harvey, Ruth | | | 2 | | |
| Weever, Elijah | 1 | | 2 | | |
| Vale, William | 1 | 4 | 1 | | |
| Patterson, James | 1 | | 2 | | |
| Ellis, Samuel | 1 | | 3 | | |
| Harvey, Phillup | 2 | 4 | 3 | | |
| Andrus, Jude | 1 | | 2 | | |
| Andrus, Joseph | 1 | | 3 | | |
| Saunders, Wait | 2 | | 3 | | |
| Badcock, Elihu | 1 | 1 | 3 | | |
| Ginnings, Jonathan | 1 | | 3 | | |
| Saunders, Elisha | 3 | 2 | 7 | | |
| Andrus, John | 1 | | 3 | | |
| Hasskall, Roger | 2 | | 3 | | |
| Fitch, Cordelia | 1 | | 3 | | |
| Hilyard, Benjamin | 1 | 4 | 3 | | |

# HEADS OF FAMILIES—CONNECTICUT.

## NEW LONDON COUNTY—Continued.

| NAME OF HEAD OF FAMILY. | Free white males of 16 years and upward, including heads of families. | Free white males under 16 years. | Free white females, including heads of families. | All other free persons. | Slaves. | NAME OF HEAD OF FAMILY. | Free white males of 16 years and upward, including heads of families. | Free white males under 16 years. | Free white females, including heads of families. | All other free persons. | Slaves. | NAME OF HEAD OF FAMILY. | Free white males of 16 years and upward, including heads of families. | Free white males under 16 years. | Free white females, including heads of families. | All other free persons. | Slaves. |
|---|---|---|---|---|---|---|---|---|---|---|---|---|---|---|---|---|---|
| Wilcox, Isaiah | 1 | 2 | 2 | | | Eglestone, David | 1 | 2 | 3 | | | Palmer, George | 1 | 1 | 1 | | |
| Fitch, Benaijah | 2 | | 2 | 1 | | Bentley, Ezekiel | 1 | 4 | 2 | | | Coats, Rufus | 1 | 3 | 2 | | |
| Fitch, Elijah | 3 | | 3 | 1 | | Woodard, Content | 1 | | 2 | | | Coats, William | 2 | | 2 | 1 | |
| Fitch, Thomas | 1 | 1 | 2 | | | Morgan, Jonathan | 2 | 1 | 5 | | | Brown, Stephen | 2 | 2 | 5 | | |
| Fitch, Nathaniel | 1 | 3 | 2 | | | Searls, William | 1 | 3 | 4 | | | Plumb, Samuel | 1 | 2 | 4 | | |
| Downs, Joshua | 1 | | 1 | | | Swan, Patience | 1 | 1 | 4 | | | Palmer, Joseph | 2 | | 4 | | |
| Bushnell, Joseph | 1 | 2 | 3 | | | Swan, David | 1 | | 1 | | | Palmer, Gershon | 1 | 3 | 3 | | |
| Mix, Rufus | 1 | 2 | 2 | | | Swan, Charles | 1 | 4 | 2 | | | Palmer, Ethel | 3 | 1 | 3 | | |
| Tracy, Moses | 1 | | 3 | | | Swan, Robart | 2 | 2 | 4 | | | Palmer, Elias Sanford | 2 | 4 | 6 | | |
| Standish, Sam¹ | 1 | | 2 | | | Brown, Silvanus | 1 | 5 | 2 | | | Palmer, Ichabod | 2 | | 3 | | |
| Morse, Mary | 1 | | 2 | | | Brown, Humphrey | 1 | 1 | 2 | | | Palmer, Peleg | 1 | 1 | 1 | | |
| Bruster, Joseph | 1 | 4 | 2 | | | Swan, Nathan | 1 | 4 | 3 | | | Lamphear, John | 1 | 3 | 1 | | |
| Parks, Moses | 3 | 4 | 5 | | | Smith, Thomas | 1 | 1 | 6 | | | Palmer, Gilbert | 1 | 1 | 2 | | |
| Demming, Jabez | 1 | 2 | 5 | | | Swan, Timothy | 1 | | 2 | | | Palmer, Sanford | 1 | | 2 | | |
| Pride, Elijah | 2 | 3 | 3 | | | Ayrs, Joseph | 2 | 1 | 5 | | | Crandall, Amos | 1 | | 2 | | |
| Chote, Abigail | | | 2 | | | Browning, Jeremi | 1 | 3 | 2 | | | Bromley, Jesse | 1 | | 2 | | |
| Chote, John | 1 | 1 | 4 | | | Palmer, Michael | 1 | 2 | 1 | | | Frink, Amos | 3 | 2 | 3 | | |
| Harvey, George | 1 | | 2 | | | Meach, Moses | 5 | 3 | 5 | 1 | | Darrow, Lemuel | 1 | 1 | 3 | | |
| Cook, Asael | 3 | 3 | 5 | | | Barns, Nehemiah | 1 | 3 | 1 | | | Thompson, Robart | 1 | 2 | 4 | | |
| Cook, James | 1 | 2 | 3 | | | Moore, David | 1 | 1 | 3 | | 1 | Thompson, James | 4 | | 3 | | |
| Grinell, Mathew | 1 | 1 | 2 | | | Harvey, Peter | 1 | 1 | 3 | | | Thompson, James, Junr | 1 | 3 | 2 | | |
| Tracy, Joseph | 1 | 2 | 1 | | | York, Collins | 2 | 1 | 3 | | | Roggers, Jonathan | 2 | | 2 | | |
| Rockwell, Samuel | 1 | 3 | 3 | | | Frink, Hannah | 1 | | 2 | | | Thompson, Elexander | 1 | | 1 | | |
| Bruster, Judah | 1 | 3 | 5 | | | Hewet, Jonas | 3 | 1 | 7 | | | Thompson, Moses | 1 | | 2 | | |
| Larreby, James | 1 | | 2 | | | Billings, Sanford | 4 | 2 | 4 | | | Wilcox, Collins | 1 | 2 | 5 | | |
| Davis, Samuel | 2 | 2 | 3 | | | Greene, Caleb | 3 | | 3 | | | Young, Nicholas | 1 | 1 | 7 | | |
| Cook, Elisha | 2 | 2 | 4 | | | Hewet, Henry | 3 | | 3 | | | Worden, Nath¹ | 2 | | 3 | | |
| Cook, Daniel | 2 | 1 | 4 | 1 | | Hewet, Simeon | 1 | | 2 | | | Taylor, Sanford | 3 | 1 | 6 | | |
| Spicer, Able | 1 | 1 | 2 | | | Hewet, Sam¹ | 1 | | 4 | | | Nun, Samuel | 2 | | 2 | | |
| Palmer, Jedediah | 2 | 2 | 7 | | | Hakes, George | 1 | | 1 | | | Wilcox, Francis | 2 | 3 | 1 | | |
| Tracy, Miner | 2 | 2 | 5 | 1 | | Hilyard William | 1 | 2 | 3 | | | Wilcox, Daniel | 4 | 5 | 4 | | |
| Clark, John | 3 | 2 | 2 | | | Baldwin, Theophilus | 1 | | 2 | | | Northrop, Sam¹ | 1 | 1 | 2 | | |
| Aldrige, Jane | 1 | | 2 | | | Billings, Daniel | 1 | 1 | 8 | | | Weever, Jonathan | 1 | 1 | 2 | | |
| Clark, Ebenezer | 3 | 1 | 5 | | | Billings, Elisha | 1 | 3 | 2 | | | Eglestone, Joseph | 2 | | 5 | | |
| Bruster, Simeon, Junr | 3 | 1 | 6 | | | Billings, Benaijah, Junr | 1 | 1 | 3 | | | Palmeter, Joseph | 1 | 5 | 1 | | |
| Ayrs, Nathan | 6 | 2 | 6 | | | Billings, Benaijah | 1 | | 2 | | | Palmeter, Silas | 1 | | 5 | | |
| Storsy, Abigail | 1 | | 2 | | | Baldwin, Zeba | 1 | 6 | 1 | | | Palmeter, Paul | 1 | 4 | 2 | | |
| Stersy, Consider | 1 | 1 | 5 | | | Baldwin, David | 3 | 1 | 4 | | | Homes, Thomas | 6 | | 4 | | |
| Meach, David | 4 | 1 | 6 | | | Baldwin, John | 3 | 4 | 5 | | | Worden, Daniel | 1 | | | | |
| Will (Negro) | | | | 3 | | Brown, Asa | 2 | 4 | 4 | | | Roggers, Jonathan | 1 | | 2 | | |
| Morgan, Simeon | 3 | 1 | 7 | | | Swan, Jesse | 2 | 3 | 6 | | | Brown, Nehemiah | 2 | 2 | 6 | | 1 |
| Morgan, Daniel | 2 | 3 | 5 | | | Lamb, Lemuel | 3 | 4 | 3 | | | Brown, Christopher | 2 | | 7 | | |
| Herrick, Rufus | 1 | | 2 | | | Herrick, Ebenr | 1 | 1 | 1 | | | Popple, George | 1 | 1 | 3 | | |
| Lester, Timothy | 1 | 5 | 2 | | | Woodard, Park | 1 | | 3 | | | Galley, James | 1 | | 1 | | |
| Lester, Elijah | 1 | 4 | 7 | 1 | | Frink, Stephen | 1 | 1 | 3 | | | Dye, Easter | | | 1 | | |
| Back, Elisabeth | | | 1 | | | Woodard, Asa | 1 | | 3 | | | Weever, Lodowick | 1 | 2 | 3 | | |
| Graves, Jonathan | 1 | 2 | 2 | | | Brown, Jesse | 2 | 2 | 6 | | | Chapman, Nathan | 3 | | 3 | | |
| Coit, Whealer | 4 | 1 | 8 | | | Church, Nath¹ | 1 | 4 | 1 | | | Chapman, Amos | 2 | 2 | 4 | | |
| Hart, Levi | 1 | 2 | 2 | | | Searls, John | 1 | 3 | 2 | | | Chapman, Joseph | 3 | 3 | 5 | | |
| Herrick, Ephraim | 1 | 1 | 3 | | | Jones, Sam¹ | 1 | 1 | 2 | | | Chapman, Andrew, Junr | 2 | 3 | 4 | | |
| Austin, Edward | 1 | | 4 | | | Jones, William | 1 | | 4 | | | Chapman, Nahum | 1 | 3 | 2 | | |
| Button, Joseph | 2 | 1 | 4 | | | Wilcox, Oliver | 2 | 2 | 5 | | | Crandall, Charles | 2 | 1 | 4 | | |
| Morgan, Daniel, Junr | 1 | 3 | 7 | | 1 | Geer, Thomas | 1 | 4 | 2 | | | Parks, Malvin | 2 | 3 | 4 | | |
| Swan, Elisha | 3 | | 7 | | | Hodge, Benjamin | 1 | 2 | 2 | | | Brown, William | 3 | | 2 | | |
| Sharp (Negro) | | | | 2 | | Eglestone, Ichabod, Junr | 2 | | 1 | 1 | | York, Bel | 3 | 1 | 3 | | |
| Meach, Aaron | 2 | 2 | 2 | | | Briston & Philup (Negro) | | | | | 2 | York, James | 1 | 1 | 6 | | |
| Andrus, Eli | 1 | 2 | 3 | | | Edwards, Peleg | 3 | 2 | 4 | | | York, Bel, Junr | 2 | 1 | 8 | | |
| Waldo, Cornelius | 1 | | 1 | | | Eglestone, Ichabod | 1 | 2 | 2 | | | Lamphear, Shubael | 1 | 1 | 2 | | |
| Meach, Daniel | 3 | 2 | 5 | | | Palmer, Jemima | 1 | | 2 | | | Lamphear, Roswell | 1 | | | | |
| Smith, Seth | 1 | | 1 | | | Eglestone, Ichabod, 3d | 1 | | 2 | | | Maine, Lyman | | | 2 | | |
| Smith, Chester | 1 | 1 | 2 | | | Eglestone, Dennis | 1 | 1 | 2 | | | Maine, Jonas | 1 | 2 | 2 | | |
| Bromley, John | 1 | 1 | 4 | | | Maine, Nath¹ | 1 | 3 | 3 | | | Yemmons, Thomas | 1 | 1 | 1 | 1 | |
| Culver, Jeremiah | 2 | 2 | 3 | | | Eglestone, Winlock | 1 | 4 | 3 | | | Brud, Jabez | 1 | 1 | 4 | | |
| Yerrington, Joseph | 3 | | 5 | | | Edward, Christopher | 1 | | 2 | | | Brud, Joseph, Junr | 1 | 1 | 5 | | |
| Chapman, Adinah | 1 | | 3 | | | Billings, Nathan | 1 | 3 | 4 | | | Brud, Allen | 1 | | 1 | | 1 |
| Button, Zebulun | 1 | 2 | 1 | | | Eglestone, Joseph | 4 | 2 | 7 | | | Bromley, Jabez | 1 | 4 | 4 | | |
| Starkweather, Arthur | 2 | 4 | 2 | | | Beba, Stephen | 1 | | 2 | | | Geer, Joseph | 2 | | 1 | | |
| Starkweather, Robert | 1 | 1 | 3 | | | Baker, William | 1 | 1 | 4 | | | Geer, George | 1 | 4 | 1 | | |
| Starkweather, Charles | 1 | 3 | 2 | | | Crandall, Baley | 1 | 3 | 2 | | | Northrop, Samuel | 1 | 1 | 1 | | |
| Starkweather, John | 1 | 5 | 3 | | | Crandall, Isaiah | 1 | | 4 | | | Brown, Dan¹ | 3 | 1 | 5 | | |
| Kimball, John | 2 | 1 | 4 | | | Eglestone, Benedick | 2 | | 6 | | | Coats, Wm, Junr | 2 | 6 | 3 | | |
| Prentice, John | 3 | | 4 | | | Hadsall, Stephen | | 1 | 2 | | | Parks, Peter | 2 | | 2 | | |
| Prentice, John, Junr | 1 | 1 | 1 | | | Burdick, Ira | 2 | | 1 | | | Burdick, Samuel | 3 | 1 | 1 | | |
| Prentice, Thomas | 2 | | 2 | 1 | | Tiff, Joseph | 2 | 2 | 1 | | | Burdick, Abraham | 3 | 3 | 4 | | |
| Bruster, Elisabeth | | | 2 | | | Tiff, John | 1 | 1 | 3 | | | Coon, Lebues | 1 | 1 | 1 | | |
| Prentice, Samuel | 2 | 1 | 4 | | | Mott, Jonathan | 1 | | 2 | | | Parmeter, Joshua | 1 | | 2 | | |
| Utley, Peleg | 1 | 2 | 2 | | | Stafford, Andrew | 1 | 2 | 6 | | | Burdick, Daniel | 1 | | 3 | | |
| Prentice, Joshua | 2 | 3 | 3 | | | Crandall, Amos, Junr | 2 | 3 | 4 | | | Tanner, Joseph | 1 | 1 | 2 | | |
| Smith, Joseph | 5 | 3 | 3 | | | Austin, Edward | 1 | 1 | 6 | | | Palmer, Stephen | 1 | 2 | 3 | | |
| Denison, Avory | 2 | 1 | 3 | | | Austin, Jedediah | 1 | | 2 | | | Maine, Asa | 3 | 1 | 5 | | |
| Denison, Daniel | 2 | 3 | 7 | | | Austin, William | 1 | 2 | 1 | | | Maine, Asa, Junr | 1 | | 1 | | |
| Denison, Elisha | 2 | 2 | 5 | | | Palmer, Stutely | 1 | 2 | 4 | | | Maine, Peter | 1 | | 1 | | |
| Prentice, Lucy | 1 | | 3 | | | Whealer, David | 1 | | 2 | | | Maine, Peter, Junr | 2 | 4 | 4 | | |
| Eames, Joseph | 2 | 3 | 3 | | | Tiff, Oliver | 1 | 3 | 4 | | | Maine, Peter, 3d | 1 | | 1 | | |
| Crasey, George | 2 | 3 | 2 | | | Roads, Anthony | 3 | 1 | 3 | | | Heby, Christopher | 3 | 2 | 2 | | |
| Sears, Remington | 3 | 1 | 3 | | | Palmer, Wait | 1 | | 2 | | | Cole, Sands | 1 | | 1 | | |
| Whealer, Ephraim | 2 | 1 | 5 | | | Palmer, Mody | 1 | | 2 | | | Collins, Stephen | 1 | 1 | 2 | | |
| Billings, Samuel | 1 | | 4 | | | Brown, Jabez | 1 | 1 | 3 | | | Collins, Mehitable | | | 2 | | |
| Billings, Otis | 1 | | 1 | | | Badcock, Timothy | 2 | 1 | 3 | | | Brown, Nathan | 1 | 2 | 4 | | |
| Billings, Samuel, Junr | 2 | | 3 | | | Palmer, Vorce | 1 | 3 | 5 | | | Langothy, Thomas | 1 | | 1 | | |
| Swan, Edward | 2 | 3 | 2 | 1 | | Badcock, Joshua | 4 | 5 | 4 | | | Langothy, John | 1 | 3 | 3 | | |
| Swan, Thomas | 3 | 2 | 5 | 2 | | Lewis, Jonathan | 1 | | 3 | | | Davis, William | 2 | 1 | 1 | | |
| Fanning, Richard | 2 | 1 | 2 | | | Cleaveland, Pheba | | | 3 | | | Maine, David, Junr | 1 | 1 | 2 | | |
| Wilkinson, George | 2 | 2 | 2 | | | Burdet, Thomson | 1 | 3 | 4 | | | Langothy, Benjamin | 2 | 4 | 6 | | |
| Woodard, Caleb | 2 | 3 | 5 | | | Downs, Joseph | 2 | 4 | 5 | | | Burdick, Elijah | 1 | 2 | 3 | | |
| Worden, Sitorster | 1 | 4 | 2 | | | Palmer, William | 1 | 1 | 6 | | | Allen, Ichabod | 1 | | 4 | | |
| Jones, Charles | 1 | 1 | 2 | | | | | | | | | Crandall, Peter | 1 | | 1 | | |

## NEW LONDON COUNTY—Continued.

| NAME OF HEAD OF FAMILY. | Free white males of 16 years and upward, including heads of families. | Free white males under 16 years. | Free white females, including heads of families. | All other free persons. | Slaves. | NAME OF HEAD OF FAMILY. | Free white males of 16 years and upward, including heads of families. | Free white males under 16 years. | Free white females, including heads of families. | All other free persons. | Slaves. | NAME OF HEAD OF FAMILY. | Free white males of 16 years and upward, including heads of families. | Free white males under 16 years. | Free white females, including heads of families. | All other free persons. | Slaves. |
|---|---|---|---|---|---|---|---|---|---|---|---|---|---|---|---|---|---|
| Allen, John | 1 | | 1 | | | Williams, Benadam | 1 | 4 | 4 | | 4 | Grant, John | 1 | 6 | 2 | | |
| Spalding, Asa | 1 | 3 | 5 | | | Coats, John | 3 | | 4 | | | Whealer, Paul | 1 | 1 | 6 | | |
| Roberson, John | 3 | 1 | 6 | | | Coats, David | 1 | 2 | 1 | | | Noyce, Joseph | 3 | 2 | 5 | | |
| Wills, Thomas | 2 | 4 | 5 | | | Coats, Amos | 1 | 2 | 2 | | | Frink, Isaac | 3 | 1 | 4 | | |
| Greene, John | 1 | 3 | 3 | | | Grey, Robart | 2 | 2 | 6 | | | Champlin, Joseph | 3 | | 3 | | 1 |
| Vors, Edward | 1 | 1 | 1 | | | Brown, David | 1 | 2 | 2 | | | Palmer, John | 1 | | | | |
| Reynolds, Thomas | 1 | 2 | 3 | | | Thomson, Joseph | 1 | 1 | 2 | | | Hull, Latham | 2 | 4 | 5 | | 2 |
| Welles, David | 1 | 2 | 5 | | | Tiff, Oliver | 1 | 4 | 3 | | | Utley, John | 1 | 2 | 2 | | |
| Bentley, George | 2 | | 3 | | | Coats, Bartholemu | 2 | 3 | 6 | | | Hull, Stephen | 1 | 1 | 1 | | |
| Stanton, Joshua | 4 | 4 | 6 | | | Stuart, Nathan | 2 | 3 | 6 | | | Whealer, Joseph | 1 | 7 | 1 | | |
| Wilcox, Nathan | 2 | | 3 | | | Coats, Edward | 2 | 1 | 4 | | | Whealer, Joshua | 1 | | 4 | | |
| Wilcox, David | 1 | | 2 | | | Coats, Betsy | 2 | 2 | 4 | | | Brown, Asher | 1 | 4 | 3 | | |
| Collins, Daniel | 2 | 1 | 3 | | | Williams, Isaac, Junr | 1 | 2 | 6 | | 2 | Geary, Thomas | 1 | 3 | 5 | | 1 |
| Hall, Stephen | 2 | 4 | 6 | | | Hilyard, William, Junr | 2 | 1 | 3 | | | Williams, Ephraim | 1 | 1 | 2 | | 2 |
| Burdick, Ezekiel | 1 | | 3 | | | Hilyard, John | 1 | 2 | 4 | | | Gibeons, John | 1 | 2 | 6 | | |
| Miner, Asa | 2 | | 4 | | | Browning, Jeremiah | 3 | 2 | 4 | 1 | | Otis, Jonathan | 1 | 2 | 4 | | |
| Crum, Arnold | 1 | 3 | 1 | | | York, Oliver | 1 | 2 | 5 | | | Tosbery, John | | | | 5 | |
| Badcock, Paul | 3 | 1 | 5 | | | Brown, Jared | 1 | 2 | 3 | | | Fish, Jason | 3 | 1 | 3 | | |
| Stanton, William | 1 | | 4 | | | Harvey, Paul | 1 | 2 | 4 | | | Fish, Titus | 2 | | 2 | | |
| Worden, Walter | 1 | 1 | 2 | | | Ayrs, Joseph, Junr | 2 | 5 | 4 | | | Fish, David | 1 | 2 | 5 | | |
| Palmer, Wm, Junr | 1 | 2 | 2 | | | Hilyard, Azariah | 1 | 3 | 1 | | | Schoolcraft, Samuel | 1 | | 1 | | |
| Palmer, William | 1 | | 3 | | | Newton, Ebenezer | 1 | 1 | 5 | | | Baley, David | 1 | 2 | 6 | | |
| Loomis, Timothy | 1 | 1 | 2 | | | Miner, Simeon | 2 | | 3 | | | Baley, Able | 1 | 3 | 3 | | |
| Nugen, John | 1 | | 3 | | | Avory, Elias | 1 | | 1 | | | Bennett, Aaron | 3 | 2 | 6 | | |
| Lewis, Beriah | 1 | 4 | 5 | | | Plumb, Nathl | 1 | | 4 | | | Bennett, David | 1 | | 2 | | |
| Richerson, John | 1 | 1 | 3 | | | Plumb, James | 2 | 4 | 4 | | | Bennett, Elisha | 1 | 3 | 5 | | |
| Pemberton, Stephen | 2 | | 3 | | | Brown, Jonas | 2 | 1 | 6 | | | Hemstead, Robart | 3 | 2 | 4 | | |
| Dewey, Christopher | 2 | 1 | 4 | | | Miner, James | 1 | 1 | 3 | | | Hemstead, Robart, Junr | 1 | | 2 | | |
| Hall, Simeon | 1 | 2 | 2 | | | Miner, Nathan | 2 | | 1 | | | Hemstead, Samuel | 1 | 5 | 3 | | |
| Brown, Zebulun | 1 | 1 | 4 | | | Miner, Nathan, Junr | 1 | | 1 | | | Lewis, Volentine | 1 | 5 | 3 | | |
| Church, David | 1 | 1 | 3 | | | Avory, Luther | 1 | 4 | 3 | | | Mulkey, Timothy | 1 | 4 | 7 | | |
| Allen, Jonathan | 1 | | 1 | | | Stow, Samuel | 1 | 2 | 3 | | | Gallup, John | 1 | 3 | 3 | | |
| Allen, Jonathan, Junr | 1 | 1 | 2 | | | Burdick, John | 1 | 3 | 2 | | | Brumley, Simion | 1 | 3 | 3 | | |
| Collins, Amos | 3 | 2 | 6 | | | Sisson, William | 3 | 2 | 7 | | | Miner, Samuel | 2 | 1 | 4 | | |
| Brown, Simeon | 1 | 4 | 6 | | | Avory, Stephen, Junr | 5 | 2 | 6 | | | Miner, Peres | 1 | | 2 | | |
| Hall, Ruben | 2 | 1 | 5 | 1 | | Peckham, Thomas | 1 | 2 | 2 | | | Whittles, Isaac | | 1 | 3 | | |
| Bentley, George, Junr | 1 | 3 | 4 | | | Swan, John | 5 | 1 | 4 | | | Satille, Elisha | 2 | 4 | 4 | | |
| Button, John | 3 | 5 | 8 | | | Elliot, John | 1 | 1 | 1 | | | Cheesborough, Christopher | 1 | 4 | 1 | | |
| Partlow, Thomas | 1 | | 2 | | | Hewet, Rufus | 2 | | 2 | | | Williams, Ebenezer, Junr | 1 | 1 | 2 | | |
| Partlow, Azariah | 2 | 2 | 5 | | | Avory, John | 1 | | 3 | | | Williams, Nathl | 1 | 3 | 2 | | |
| Miner, Daniel | 2 | | 2 | | 1 | Leeds, Jedediah | 1 | 1 | 3 | | | Williams, Thomas | 1 | | 2 | | |
| Crum, Joseph | 3 | 2 | 6 | | | Hewet, Elias | 1 | | | | | Miner, Richerson | 1 | 1 | 6 | | |
| Whealer, Hannah | | | 3 | | | Hewet, Rufus, Junr | | | 2 | | | Avory, Stephen | 2 | | 2 | | |
| Brown, Nathan, 3d | 1 | 2 | 2 | | | Peckham, John | 2 | 1 | 4 | | | Denison, John | 2 | | 3 | | |
| Brown, Mathew | 1 | | 2 | | | Peckham, Benjamin | 1 | 3 | 4 | | | Eldridge, Christopher | 3 | | 3 | | |
| Brown, Simeon | 1 | | 1 | | | Whealer, Hosea | 2 | 3 | 5 | | | Denison, And{w} | 3 | 3 | 4 | | |
| Brown, Joshua, Junr | 1 | | 3 | 1 | | Whealer, John, Junr | 1 | 2 | 3 | | | Miner, Daniel, Junr | 1 | 4 | 4 | | |
| Brown, Jeptha | 1 | 1 | 2 | | | Grant, Josiah | 1 | 2 | 5 | | | Wilcox, Robart | 1 | 3 | 3 | | |
| Brown, Josiah | 1 | | 3 | | | Palmer, Nehemiah | 2 | 1 | 7 | | | Wilcox, Jeremi | 1 | | 2 | | 1 |
| Larkin, Moses | 1 | 1 | 2 | | | Elexander, James | 1 | | 5 | | | Smith (Negro) | | | | 7 | |
| Frink, Samuel | 1 | | 2 | | | Brown, Robart | 2 | 1 | 3 | | | Wilcox, Arnold | 3 | | 3 | | |
| Dye, William | 2 | 3 | 6 | | | Whealer, Thomas, 2d | 1 | 2 | 3 | | | York (Negro) | | | | 4 | |
| Randall, Robart | 2 | 6 | 2 | | | Roberson, William | 1 | | 1 | | | Williams, Ebenezer | 1 | 2 | 2 | | |
| Brown, Nathan, Junr | 3 | 2 | 5 | | | Grant, Amos | 1 | 2 | 2 | | | Fish, Sirus | 1 | | 2 | | |
| Bromley, David | 2 | | 4 | | | Brud, Stephen | 1 | 1 | 2 | | | Daverson, Christopher | 2 | 3 | 2 | | |
| Palmer, Jonathan, Junr | 1 | 1 | 7 | | | Grant, Oliver | 1 | | 3 | | | Daverson, Daniel | 1 | 3 | 1 | | |
| Welch, Charles | 3 | 3 | 4 | | | Grant, Oliver, Junr | 1 | 5 | 3 | | | Williams, Nehemiah | 3 | | 1 | | |
| Stanton, Robart | 1 | 5 | 4 | | | Hewet, Dudley | 1 | 1 | 3 | | | Williams, Park | 1 | 4 | 3 | | |
| Grant, Noah | 1 | 3 | 3 | | | Avory, Christopher | 1 | 1 | 2 | | | Williams, Eleazer | 1 | | 6 | 1 | |
| Brown, Jeremi | 2 | 4 | 7 | | | Avory, Christopher, Junr | 1 | 1 | 1 | | | Hudson, John | 3 | | 3 | | |
| Brown, James | 1 | 2 | 4 | | | Hewet, Charles | 4 | | 4 | | | Williams, Gilbert | 1 | | | | |
| Brown, Eleazer | 2 | 1 | 4 | | | Brud, Joseph | 1 | 3 | 3 | | | Denison, Daniel, Junr | 2 | 1 | 6 | | 1 |
| Maine, Daniel | 1 | 3 | 5 | | | Whealer, Amos | 1 | 3 | 3 | | 4 | Williams, Uriah | 1 | 2 | 3 | | |
| Crandall, Ebor | 2 | 4 | 4 | | | Whealer, Jeremi | 1 | | | | | Williams, Isaac | 1 | | 1 | | |
| Thurston, Edward | 2 | 4 | 5 | | | Greene, John | 2 | 4 | 3 | | | Denison, Joseph | 1 | | 1 | | 1 |
| Maine, Amos | 3 | 1 | 8 | | | Brumley, Joshua | 1 | 1 | 5 | | | Copp, Saml | 1 | 3 | 9 | | |
| York, John | 3 | 1 | 6 | | | Badcock, Nathl | 2 | | 4 | | | Denison, John, 3d | 1 | 3 | 2 | 4 | 1 |
| Homes, Joshua | 1 | 3 | 4 | 1 | | Brumley, David | 1 | 2 | 4 | | | Denison, Amos | 1 | 3 | 4 | 1 | 1 |
| Homes, Edward | 1 | | 2 | | | Denison, George | 5 | 3 | 6 | | | Denison, Peleg | 1 | 3 | 4 | 1 | |
| Maine, David | 2 | 4 | 4 | | | Davis, Joseph | 1 | 1 | 3 | | | Whipple, Amos | 1 | 1 | 6 | | |
| Maine, Timothy | 3 | 1 | 3 | | | Denison, Nathaniel | 1 | | 4 | | | Whipple, William | 1 | | 2 | | |
| Maine, Timothy, Junr | 1 | 1 | 3 | | | Meach, Elkanah | 3 | 2 | 3 | | | Shaw, Amos | 1 | 1 | 2 | | |
| Maine, Benaijah | 3 | 3 | 6 | | | Gardiner, Abiel | 4 | 2 | 3 | | | Whealer, Lester | 1 | 3 | 6 | | |
| Williams, William | 1 | | 1 | 3 | | Vincent, William | 1 | 2 | 3 | | | Williams, Elisha | 1 | | 2 | | 4 |
| Williams, William, Junr | 1 | 2 | 1 | | | Burington, Eliphelet | 2 | 3 | 3 | | | Denison, Joseph, Junr | 1 | 5 | 6 | | |
| Williams, John, 2d | 3 | 3 | 3 | | | Noyce, James | 1 | 1 | 4 | | | Amon (Negro) | | | | 7 | |
| Laws, John | 1 | 1 | 2 | | | Hinckley, Thomas | 1 | 2 | 4 | | | Lewis, Ichabod | 1 | | 1 | | |
| Utley, Elijah | 3 | | 1 | | | Helme, Oliver | 2 | 2 | 4 | | | White, Mary | 1 | | 2 | | |
| Badcock, John | 2 | | 2 | | | Richerson, Salmon | 3 | | 3 | | | Prince (Negro) | | | | 3 | |
| Homes, James | 1 | 3 | 4 | | | Brand, Thomas | 1 | 3 | 3 | | | Holdridge, Nathl | 1 | 1 | 1 | | |
| Brigs, Ithamer | 2 | 1 | 2 | | | Whealer, Sheppard | 1 | 2 | 3 | 1 | | Whittles, Isaac, Junr | 1 | 2 | 2 | | |
| Maine, Luther | 1 | 1 | 2 | | | Clark, Arnold | 1 | 1 | 3 | | | Denison, Oliver | 1 | | 2 | | |
| Bill, Joseph | 1 | | 6 | | | Badcock, Elias | 1 | | 2 | | | Stanton, Danl | 3 | | 5 | | |
| Hakes, Richard | 5 | 6 | 7 | | | Button, George | 2 | | 2 | | | Witter, William | 1 | 1 | 2 | | |
| York, Allen | 1 | | 3 | | | Greene, Mathew | 3 | | 2 | | | Stanton, Saml, 3d | 1 | 1 | 3 | | |
| Swan, Mary | | | 4 | | | Grant, Joshua | 1 | 4 | 3 | | | Whealer, Richard | 4 | 1 | 3 | | |
| York, Jesse | 3 | 2 | 2 | | | Grant, Gilbert | 1 | 2 | 4 | | | Whealer, Jonathan | 1 | | 1 | | |
| Peabody, Saml | 2 | | 2 | | | Grant, Noah, Junr | 1 | 1 | 2 | | | Whealer, Jonathan, Junr | 3 | | 3 | | |
| Peabody, Thomas | 3 | 3 | 5 | | | Munsill, Phineas | 2 | 2 | 2 | | | Page, Joseph | 3 | 1 | 5 | 1 | 3 |
| Brown, Jedediah, Junr | 1 | 5 | 2 | | 1 | Whealer, John | 2 | 1 | 3 | | | Ingraham, Nathl | 2 | 2 | 3 | | |
| Hammon, Thomas | 1 | 3 | 6 | | | Whealer, John, 3d | 1 | | 3 | | | Champlin, Charles | 2 | 3 | 5 | | |
| Fellows, Ephraim | 2 | | 6 | | | Niles, Surviah | | | 2 | | 3 | Collins, Daniel | 1 | 5 | 4 | | |
| Homes, Jared | 1 | | 2 | | | Whealer, Thomas | 2 | 1 | 5 | 1 | | Hubbard, Peter | 1 | 2 | 3 | | |
| Homes, Jeremi | 1 | 4 | 6 | 1 | | Williams, Washam | | | 3 | 1 | | Gallup, Amos | 2 | 2 | 2 | | |
| Homes, John | 1 | 2 | 7 | | 3 | Williams, Washam, Junr | 1 | | 2 | | | Stanton, Wait | 2 | 1 | 1 | | |
| Smith, Lemuel | 1 | 2 | 3 | | | McDaniel, James | 1 | 2 | 2 | | | | | | | | |
| Hewet, Isaac | 1 | | 4 | | | | | | | | | | | | | | |

# HEADS OF FAMILIES—CONNECTICUT.

## NEW LONDON COUNTY—Continued.

| NAME OF HEAD OF FAMILY. | Free white males of 16 years and upward, including heads of families. | Free white males under 16 years. | Free white females, including heads of families. | All other free persons. | Slaves. | NAME OF HEAD OF FAMILY. | Free white males of 16 years and upward, including heads of families. | Free white males under 16 years. | Free white females, including heads of families. | All other free persons. | Slaves. | NAME OF HEAD OF FAMILY. | Free white males of 16 years and upward, including heads of families. | Free white males under 16 years. | Free white females, including heads of families. | All other free persons. | Slaves. |
|---|---|---|---|---|---|---|---|---|---|---|---|---|---|---|---|---|---|
| Dewey, Joseph | 1 | | 1 | | | Billings, Amos | 2 | 4 | 5 | 1 | | Shaw, Peleg | 1 | | 3 | | |
| Hallans, Amos | 3 | 2 | 4 | 1 | | Frink, Isaac | 2 | | 6 | | | Slack, Able | 1 | 1 | 2 | | |
| Vincent, Joseph | 1 | 4 | 10 | | | Whealer, Rufus | 1 | 1 | 1 | | 2 | Slack, William | 1 | 1 | 7 | | |
| Hubbard, Eliphelet | 2 | 4 | 1 | | | Randall, Jedediah | 1 | 1 | 1 | 1 | 2 | Cheesborough, Asa | 1 | 1 | 4 | | |
| Cheesborough, Robart | 1 | 3 | 6 | 1 | | Dickerson, Ichabod | 1 | | 1 | | | Noyce, Gershom | 1 | | 1 | | |
| Palmer, Thomas | 2 | 1 | 2 | | | Leeds, Thomas | 1 | 2 | 3 | | | Burdick, Lodowick | 1 | 1 | 2 | | |
| Whealer, Elisha | 1 | 1 | 1 | | | Miner, Peleg | 2 | 2 | 2 | | | Cheesborough, William | 2 | 1 | 3 | | |
| Randall, Thomas | 2 | 4 | 8 | 1 | 2 | Denison, Elisha | 4 | 1 | 4 | 1 | 2 | Tenny, Jeremiah | 1 | 2 | 1 | | |
| Hancock, Elihu | 1 | | 1 | | | Smith, Roswell | 1 | 1 | 2 | | | Cheesborough, Saml | 5 | 2 | 8 | | |
| Grey, Jonathan | 1 | | 2 | 2 | | Brown, Roswell | 2 | 2 | 1 | | | Burch, Henry | 2 | 2 | 6 | | |
| Dewey, Deborah | 3 | 2 | 3 | | | Brown, Jedediah | 3 | 1 | 4 | | | Loper, Abraham | 1 | 1 | 3 | | |
| Haley, Edmund | 1 | 1 | 2 | | | Randall, Roswell | 1 | | 2 | | | Cheesborough, Jedediah | 5 | | 4 | | |
| Belshaw, John | 3 | 1 | 1 | | | Randall, William | 1 | 1 | 2 | | 1 | Cheesborough, Rebecka 3d | | 2 | 3 | | |
| Fellows, Nathl, 3d | 1 | 1 | 1 | | | Baldwin, Asa | 1 | 1 | 4 | | | Yemmons, Daniel | 2 | 3 | 3 | | |
| Fellows, Nathl, 2d | 4 | 1 | 4 | | | Badcock, Joseph | 1 | 1 | 2 | | | Yemmons, Moses | 3 | | 4 | | |
| Fellows, Nathl | 1 | | 2 | | | Frink, Asa | 2 | 2 | 6 | | | Palmer, Abijah | 1 | | | | |
| Cheesborough, Nathl, 2d | 3 | 4 | 4 | | 1 | Burdick, Christopher | 3 | 2 | 2 | | | Palmer, Simeon | 1 | 1 | 4 | | |
| Haley, John | 3 | 1 | 4 | | | Brown, Samuel | 3 | | 4 | | | Palmer, Jesse | 2 | | 2 | | |
| Hinckley, Able | 4 | 1 | 4 | | | Randall, John, Junr | 1 | 7 | 3 | | | Cheesborough, Amos | 1 | | 1 | | |
| Noyce, Peleg | 4 | 2 | 5 | 1 | 1 | Weever, Joshua | 1 | 1 | 3 | | | Cheesborough, Saml, 2d | 2 | 1 | 6 | | |
| Welden, Jonathan | 1 | 2 | 5 | | | Miner, Christopher | 2 | 5 | 3 | | | Cheesborough, John | 1 | | 1 | | |
| Burdick, Nathl | 1 | 1 | 3 | | | Miner, Thomas | 3 | 2 | 4 | | | Dennis, Betsy | | 1 | 2 | | 1 |
| Williams, Robart | 1 | 1 | 4 | | | Miner, James, Junr | | | 2 | | 2 | Lewis, Asa | 1 | 1 | 5 | | |
| Harvey, James | 1 | | 1 | | | Miner, Daniel | 1 | | | | | Solomon (Negro) | | | | 3 | |
| Cheesborough, Zebulun, Junr | 1 | 2 | 3 | | | Brud, Lucy | 2 | 3 | 2 | 1 | | Miner, Hemstead | 2 | | 3 | | |
| Graves, Saml | 2 | 5 | 4 | | | Brud, Nathan | 2 | | 3 | | | Baldwin, Silvester | 2 | 1 | 4 | | |
| Buttles, George | 2 | 1 | 4 | | | Brud, Nathan, Junr | 1 | 1 | 1 | | | Palmer, Noyce | 4 | 1 | 5 | 2 | |
| Hubbard, Eliphelet | 2 | 1 | 3 | | | Brud, Oliver | 1 | 5 | 2 | | | Thomson, Jedediah | 1 | | | | |
| Eliot, James | 1 | 1 | 2 | | | Brud, Samuel | 1 | 2 | 2 | | | Thomson, David | 1 | 2 | 5 | | |
| Patterson, Amasa | 1 | 1 | 3 | | | Whealer, Peres | 1 | 1 | 2 | | | Cheesborough, Peleg | 1 | 4 | 6 | 1 | 1 |
| Spargo, Edward | 1 | 1 | | | | Miner, Peres, Junr | 1 | | 2 | | | Cheesborough, Zebulum | 3 | 1 | 5 | | |
| Whipples, Joseph | 2 | | 3 | | | Randall, John | 4 | 1 | 4 | | 4 | Phelps, Charles | 1 | | 3 | | |
| Whipples, Robart | 1 | 2 | 3 | | | Weever, Jonathan, Junr | 1 | 3 | 6 | | 1 | Phelps, Charles, Junr | 1 | | 3 | | |
| Hancock, James | 1 | | 3 | | | Allen, Thomas | 2 | 3 | 4 | | | Lewis, Elisha | 2 | | 2 | | |
| Hancock, Nathan | 1 | 2 | 3 | | | Swan, George | 1 | 3 | 3 | | 1 | Lewis, Elisha, Junr | 1 | 2 | 3 | | |
| Burdick, Elisha | 2 | 3 | 4 | | | Roads, Simon | 2 | | 1 | | 2 | Hancock, John | 1 | | 3 | | |
| Jaquis, Robart | 1 | 1 | 2 | | | Stales, Adam | 3 | 2 | 3 | | | Cheesborough, Pheba | 1 | 2 | 4 | | |
| Cheesborough, Nathl | 2 | 2 | 5 | | | Hinkley, Elijah | 1 | 3 | 6 | | | Burdick, Oliver | 1 | 1 | 5 | | |
| Irish, John | 4 | 2 | 6 | | | Frink, Prentice | 4 | 4 | 3 | | | Johnson, Nathan | 1 | 4 | 5 | | |
| Lewis, William | 2 | 3 | 6 | | | Miner, Charles | 1 | 2 | 8 | | 1 | Miner, Humstead, Junr | 1 | | 2 | | |
| Lewis, William, Junr | 1 | 1 | 1 | | | Barber, Henry | 2 | 3 | 3 | | | Stanton, William, 3d | 1 | | 3 | | |
| Hancock, Joseph | 1 | | 2 | | | Ingraham, Hezekiah | 1 | 2 | 3 | | | Palmer, Henry | 1 | | 1 | | |
| Dean, James | 5 | 2 | 3 | 1 | | Miner, Ephraim | 1 | 1 | 2 | | | Brown, Elias | 1 | 1 | 2 | | |
| Denison, Robart | 1 | 2 | 4 | | | Will (Negro) | | | | 3 | | Burdick, Thomson | 2 | 1 | 3 | | |
| Cheesborough, William, 3d | | | | | | Dewey, David | 1 | 1 | 2 | | | Cheesborough, William, 4th | 1 | | 2 | | |
| Baldwin, Silvester, Junr | 1 | 1 | 3 | | | Otis, James | 1 | 2 | 2 | | | Worden, Mary | | | 2 | | |
| Denison, Beba | 1 | 3 | 5 | | | Laten, Joseph | 3 | 2 | 4 | | | Stephens, Sarah | | | 1 | | |
| Denison, Darius | 1 | 3 | 6 | | | Babcock, Henry | 4 | | 4 | | | Pero (Negro) | | | | 1 | |
| Miner, David | 1 | 1 | 6 | | | Bradford, Elexander | 1 | 1 | 2 | 1 | | Palmer, Asa | 1 | 1 | 2 | | 1 |
| Miner, David, Junr | 1 | 1 | 2 | | | Stanton, John | 3 | 1 | 2 | | | Pendleton, Andrew | 1 | 1 | 3 | | |
| Slight, Joseph | 1 | | 2 | | | Blivin, John | 1 | | 2 | | | Palmer, Elijah | 2 | 3 | 6 | | |
| Miner, Rufus | 3 | | 2 | | | Sheffield, George | 1 | 2 | 5 | | | Cheesborough, Bridgett | 1 | | 5 | | |
| Miner, William | 2 | 3 | 5 | | | Davis, John | 1 | 3 | 2 | | | Norden, Benjamin | 4 | | 3 | | |
| Miner, Thomas | 1 | 3 | 5 | | | Davis, Thomas | 2 | 2 | 2 | | | Homes, Silas | 1 | 2 | 4 | | |
| Miner, Manassa | 1 | 2 | 4 | | | Hinckley, John | 2 | 1 | 3 | | | Roathburn, Joshua | 1 | | 1 | | |
| Wilcox, Edward | 1 | | 2 | | | Harvey, James | 1 | 1 | 4 | | | Rothburn, Achors | 1 | 2 | 1 | | |
| Wilcox, John | 1 | 1 | 1 | | | Burdick, Peter | 1 | 1 | 3 | | | Sheffield, Achors | 2 | | 8 | | |
| Mason, Samuel | 2 | | 2 | | 1 | Stanton, Thomas | 3 | | 3 | | 4 | Palmer, Amos | 1 | 2 | 5 | | |
| Mason, Elnathan | 1 | 2 | 3 | | | Will (Negro) | | | | 1 | | Brand, Lucy | | | 2 | | |
| Mason, Andw | 1 | | 1 | 3 | | Stanton, Eli | 1 | | 5 | | | Eales, Joseph | 4 | | 2 | | |
| Denison, Pheba | | | 2 | | | Stanton, Jesse | 1 | | | | | Cutler, Benjamin | 1 | 1 | 2 | | |
| Wilcox, Ebenr | 2 | | 2 | | | Peters (Negro) | | | | 2 | | Spencer, John | 1 | 3 | 1 | | |
| Mason, Nehemiah | 1 | 2 | 5 | | | Baldwin, Jonathan | 2 | | 3 | | | Cables, Michael | 2 | 2 | 4 | | |
| Cuff (Negro) | | | | 5 | | | | | | | | Billingham, John | 2 | | 2 | | |
| Denison, George | 2 | 2 | 4 | 4 | | Stanton, Thomas, Junr | 1 | 3 | 5 | | | Elliot, Mary | | | 3 | | |
| Denison, Nathan | 2 | 1 | | | | Stanton, Thomas | 1 | 3 | 4 | | | Palmer, Nathan | 2 | | 2 | | |
| Brown, Joshua | 3 | 2 | 6 | | | Slack, Amos | 2 | 1 | 2 | | | Palmer, Eliakim | 1 | 1 | 3 | | |
| Williams, Joshua | 2 | 1 | 2 | | | Palmer, Moses | 1 | 1 | 4 | | | Cobb, Ebenezer | 3 | 3 | 3 | | |
| Williams, Mercy | | 1 | 4 | | 2 | Badcock, Simon | 1 | 3 | 4 | | | Pendleton, Eunice | | | 2 | 6 | |
| Brown, Peter | 1 | 2 | 3 | | | Hinkley, Nathan | 1 | 2 | 6 | | | Tripp, James | 3 | 2 | 6 | | |
| Thomson, Nathl | 1 | 2 | 2 | | | Brown, Joshua, Junr | 3 | 3 | 1 | | | Tripp, Nathl | 1 | 2 | 1 | | |
| Palmer, Nathl | 3 | 2 | 5 | | 3 | Dorrel, Thomas | 2 | 3 | 4 | | | Rhoads, James | 2 | | 3 | | 2 |
| Bell, Joseph | 1 | 4 | | | | Hinkley, Mary | | | 1 | | | Brown, Stephen | 1 | | 2 | | |
| Woodbrige, Dudley | 4 | | 2 | | 3 | Noyce, James | 1 | | 4 | | 2 | Niles, Paul | 1 | | 2 | | |
| Denison, George, Junr | 1 | 4 | 4 | | 3 | Noyce, John | 3 | | 2 | 2 | | Niles, Paul, Junr | 1 | | 1 | | |
| Denison, William | 1 | 2 | 4 | | | Noyce, James, Junr | 2 | 6 | 2 | 1 | | Stanton, William | 1 | 1 | 5 | | |
| Stanton, William | 1 | | 3 | | 3 | Cheesborough, William, 2d | 1 | 4 | 5 | 1 | 1 | Tribe, John | 1 | 1 | 1 | | |
| Stanton, Nathan | 2 | 2 | 3 | | | Palmer, William | 1 | 1 | 2 | | | Sattille, Samuel | 1 | 5 | 3 | | |
| Denison, Isaac | 1 | 4 | 5 | 2 | | Palmer, James, Junr | 2 | 2 | 3 | | | Waldren, Lowis | 2 | 4 | 3 | | |
| Denison, Beeba, 2d | 1 | 1 | 3 | | | Palmer, Roswell | 1 | | 2 | | | Cobb, Elkanah | 1 | 3 | 2 | 1 | |
| Denison, Frederick | 1 | | 2 | | | Palmer, Hannah | | | 2 | | | Miner, Clemment | 2 | | 1 | | |
| Denison, Henry | 1 | 1 | 2 | | | Stanton, Peleg | 1 | 1 | 5 | 1 | | Miner, William | 1 | | 1 | | |
| Adams, Simeon | 1 | 4 | 6 | | | Palmer, Samuel | 1 | 5 | 2 | 2 | | Sheffield, Burdick, Junr | 1 | 3 | 3 | | |
| Williams, John | 2 | | 2 | 4 | | Badcock, Robart | 2 | 1 | 4 | | | Bottom, Saml H | 1 | | 2 | | |
| Williams, John, 3d | 3 | 3 | 6 | 3 | | Palmer, James | 2 | | 3 | | | Sheffield, William, 2d | 1 | 1 | 1 | | |
| Gardiner, Abigail | | | 1 | 2 | | Crandall, Nathl | 1 | 1 | 2 | | | Denison, Mary | | | 2 | 4 | |
| Adams, Simeon | | | | | | Crandall, Paul | 1 | 2 | 5 | | | Denison, John, 2d | | | 1 | 1 | 2 |
| Niles, Nathan | 6 | 1 | 3 | | | Brown, William | 1 | | 2 | | | Denison, John, 4th | 1 | | 3 | | 1 |
| Parks, John | 1 | 2 | 3 | | | Lamphear, Benjamin | 1 | | 2 | | | Smith, Oliver | 3 | 1 | 4 | | |
| Pero (Negro) | | | | 5 | | Lamphear, John | 1 | 1 | 1 | | | Sheffield, William | 1 | 4 | 2 | | |
| Hallam, Abigail | | 2 | 2 | | | Lamphear, Elisha | 1 | 1 | 1 | | | Terrett, William | 2 | 2 | 3 | | |
| Quash (Negro) | | | | 3 | | Palmer, Ruben | 1 | | 2 | | | Hilyard, Oliver | 1 | | 2 | | |
| Gallup, Levi | 1 | 2 | 2 | | | Palmer, Daniel | 1 | 3 | 2 | | | Ash, Michael | 3 | 1 | 5 | | |
| Gallup, Ezra | 1 | 2 | 3 | | | Palmer, Denison | 3 | 2 | 6 | | | Fanning, Gilbert | 2 | 2 | 5 | | |
| Gallup, Silas | 1 | 2 | 5 | | | | | | | | | Woodruff, Hezekiah | 2 | 1 | 5 | | |
| Cheesborough, James | 1 | | 2 | | | | | | | | | | | | | | |

# FIRST CENSUS OF THE UNITED STATES.

## NEW LONDON COUNTY—Continued.

| NAME OF HEAD OF FAMILY. | Free white males of 16 years and upward, including heads of families. | Free white males under 16 years. | Free white females, including heads of families. | All other free persons. | Slaves. |
|---|---|---|---|---|---|
| Sanford, Elisha | 3 | 1 | 3 | | |
| Rothburn, Volentine | 1 | | 1 | | |
| Niles, Sands | 1 | | 2 | | 1 |
| Cheesborough, Naboth | 1 | 3 | 3 | | |
| Stanton, Samuel | 2 | | 2 | | |
| Stanton, Zebulun | 2 | 3 | 2 | | |
| Burch, Billings | 1 | 1 | 4 | | |
| Crary, Jonathan | 1 | 1 | 4 | | |
| Larrey, John | 2 | | 3 | | |
| Smith, Nathan | 2 | | 1 | | |
| Palmer, Nathan, Jun<sup>r</sup> | 2 | 2 | 2 | | 1 |
| Smith, Edward | 1 | 3 | 3 | | |
| Roberson, Thomas | 2 | 2 | 2 | | |
| Wilcox, Joshua | 1 | 3 | 3 | | |
| Sloane, William | 1 | | 2 | | |
| Durfee, James | 1 | 3 | 2 | | |
| Fellows, Elnathan | 2 | 2 | 4 | | |
| Brud, Prentice | 1 | | 5 | | |
| Burch, Samuel | 1 | 2 | 4 | | |
| Palmer, Robart | 1 | 2 | 2 | | |
| Palmer, Peleg | 1 | 1 | 3 | | |
| Worden, Henry | 1 | 3 | 2 | | |
| Swan, Joshua | 4 | | 3 | | |
| Potter, Hannah | | | 2 | | |
| How, Mary | 2 | | 1 | | |
| Avory, Patience | | 1 | 2 | | |
| Hall, Joshua | 2 | | 3 | | |
| Ellis, Edward | 1 | 2 | 4 | | |
| Wood, Gophar | 1 | 3 | 2 | | |
| Gardiner, Thomas | 1 | 1 | 1 | | |
| Hickcox, Thomas | 2 | | 2 | | |
| Fowler, Gideon | 1 | | 2 | | |
| Palmer, Amos, 2<sup>d</sup> | 1 | 4 | 1 | | |
| Lewis, Sarah | | | 2 | | |
| Bliss, Mary | | | 3 | | |
| Hart, Lewis | 1 | 1 | 2 | | |
| Stanton Azariah | 1 | | 3 | | |
| Lewis, Robartson | 1 | 1 | 1 | | |
| Ammy, Emanuel | 1 | | 2 | | |
| Robbins, Ezekiel | 1 | | 1 | | |
| Bebe, John | 1 | 1 | 3 | | |
| Crary, Humphery | 1 | | 2 | | |
| Copp, Joseph | 1 | 1 | 3 | | |
| Stanton, Eben<sup>r</sup> | 1 | 1 | 2 | | |
| Hancock, Edward | 1 | | 2 | | |
| Hancock, Nathan | 1 | 1 | 3 | | |
| Spencer, Caleb | 1 | | 3 | | |
| Mitchel, Moses | 1 | | 1 | | |
| Hancock, Zebulun | 1 | 2 | 3 | | |
| Brown, Peleg | 1 | 3 | 5 | | 4 |
| Brown, Mary | 3 | | 1 | 1 | |
| Homes, Jabez | 1 | | 3 | | |
| Hancock, Edward, 2<sup>d</sup> | 2 | 1 | 7 | | |
| Rothburn, John | 2 | 3 | 6 | | |
| Miner, Nath<sup>l</sup> | 1 | | 1 | 1 | |
| Sheffield, Isaac | 2 | | 3 | | |
| Sheffield, Amos | 1 | 1 | 2 | | |
| Sheffield, Isaac, Jun<sup>r</sup> | 1 | 4 | 2 | | |
| Dewey, Lemuel | 2 | 1 | 2 | | |
| Cotterall, Thomas P | 1 | | 1 | | |
| Hancock, James | 1 | 1 | 2 | | |
| Hancock, Nath<sup>l</sup> | 1 | 1 | 3 | | |
| Rosseter, Elnathan | 1 | | 1 | | |
| Kinyon, Augustus | 1 | | 3 | | |
| Nugen, John | 2 | 1 | 2 | | |
| Crary, Peter | 6 | 2 | 3 | | |
| Smith, Benjamin | 2 | 2 | 1 | | |
| Elles, Benjamin | 1 | | 2 | | 2 |
| McCurdy, John | 1 | 4 | 3 | | |
| Sheppard, James | 1 | | | | |
| Woodbridge, James | 2 | | 4 | | |
| Noyce, Thomas | 3 | 3 | 3 | | |
| Lord, Dan<sup>l</sup> | 2 | 1 | 1 | | |
| Packer, Frelove | | | 4 | | |
| Crandall, Jonathan | 3 | 2 | 3 | | |
| Crary, Nathan | 1 | 1 | 2 | | 3 |
| Crary, Isaac | 1 | 5 | 3 | | |
| Dinah (Negro) | | | | 2 | |
| Eldridge, Charles | 2 | | 1 | | |
| Eldridge, Charles, Jun<sup>r</sup> | 1 | | 2 | | 1 |
| Eldridge, Sam<sup>l</sup> | 3 | 1 | 7 | | |
| Frink, Jabez | 6 | | 2 | | |
| Frink, Jabez, Jun<sup>r</sup> | 1 | | 3 | | |
| Gallup, Jesse | 1 | 2 | 5 | | 1 |
| Gallup, Samuel | 3 | 2 | 7 | | |
| Gallup, Joshua | 1 | 1 | 1 | | |
| Gallup, Josiah | 1 | | 2 | | 1 |
| Gallup, Jacob | 2 | 1 | 3 | | |
| Gallup, Nathan | 4 | | 4 | 1 | |
| Gallup, Ebenezer | 1 | 4 | 2 | | |
| Gallup, Henry | 4 | | 2 | | 1 |
| Williams, Seth | 1 | 1 | 3 | 1 | |
| Williams, Henry | 2 | 1 | 1 | | |
| Holdrige, Benajiah | 2 | 5 | 5 | | |
| Freman, Hannah | | | 3 | | |
| Morgan, Christopher | 2 | 1 | 6 | | 2 |
| Stanton, Prudence | 1 | 1 | 4 | | |
| Williams, Peleg | 2 | 2 | 3 | | |
| Brown, Cumfort | 1 | 2 | 3 | | 2 |
| Morgan, John | 1 | 1 | 2 | | |
| Morgan, Stephen | 2 | | 4 | | |
| Billings, Stephen | 1 | 1 | 3 | | 3 |
| Brown, Ezekiel | 1 | 4 | 3 | | |
| Morgan, Rebecka | | | 2 | | |
| Hilyard, Jonathan | 2 | 4 | 4 | | |
| Morgan, Shapley | 1 | 1 | 4 | | |
| Morgan, Shapley, Jun<sup>r</sup> | 1 | 1 | 1 | | |
| Morgan, William A | 1 | 5 | 4 | | |
| Gray, Benjamin | 2 | 1 | 5 | | |
| Allins, Ephraim | 2 | 5 | 5 | | |
| Stanton, Thankfull | 1 | | 3 | | |
| Smith, Nehemiah | 2 | | 2 | | |
| Parks, Jacob | 1 | 1 | 1 | | |
| Brown, Elkanah | 1 | 1 | 2 | | |
| Billings, John | 1 | 1 | 2 | | |
| Spicer, Sarah | | | 2 | | |
| Giles, Thomas | 3 | 2 | 4 | | |
| Bellows, Nath<sup>l</sup> | 1 | | 1 | | |
| Bellows, John | 2 | | 5 | | |
| Allen, James | 2 | 3 | 5 | 1 | |
| Brown, Nath<sup>l</sup> | 1 | 1 | 2 | | |
| Brown, Ann | | | 2 | | |
| Mallerson, Thomas | 1 | 2 | 3 | | |
| Williams, Richard | 3 | | 2 | | |
| Williams, Isaac | 1 | 3 | 4 | | |
| Allen, David | 2 | | 1 | | |
| Hewet, Elkanah | 1 | 2 | 3 | | |
| Brown, Hannah | | 1 | 2 | | |
| Halsey (Negro) | | | | 3 | |
| Geer, Amos | 2 | | 7 | | |
| Geer, Ebenezer | 1 | 2 | 1 | | |
| Geer, James | 1 | 1 | 1 | | 1 |
| Green, Joseph | 1 | 1 | 2 | | |
| Brown, Ebenezer | 2 | | 7 | | |
| Geer, Robart | 1 | | 3 | | 5 |
| Stodard, Margarett | | | 2 | | |
| Geer, Mary | | | 2 | | |
| Geer, Richard | 4 | 1 | 5 | | |
| Geer, Benjamin | 2 | 4 | 4 | | 1 |
| Forthsides, Robert | 1 | 1 | 3 | | |
| Chapman, Joseph, 2<sup>d</sup> | 2 | 3 | 4 | | |
| Williams, Aaron | 2 | | 1 | | |
| Maynard, John | 3 | | 1 | | |
| Pettis, Benj<sup>a</sup> | 1 | | 3 | | |
| Ethridge, Sarah | 2 | 1 | 2 | | |
| Miner, John O | 1 | 1 | 2 | | |
| Holdrige, Rufus | 1 | 1 | 2 | | |
| Bayler, Noah | 2 | 1 | 4 | | |
| Allen, Hannah | 2 | | 3 | | |
| Palmeter, Phineas | 1 | 1 | 3 | | |
| Morgan, Eben<sup>r</sup> | 3 | | 3 | | |
| Newton, Mark | 2 | 2 | 5 | | |
| Newton, Agrippa | 1 | | 2 | | |
| Chapman, Joseph | 2 | 1 | 4 | | |
| Spicer, Edward | 2 | | 3 | | |
| Allen, Tryall | 2 | 1 | 4 | | |
| Perkins, John | 1 | 3 | 5 | | |
| Lamb, Silas | 1 | 1 | 1 | | |
| Lamb, Asa | 1 | | 3 | | |
| Lamb, Silas, Jun<sup>r</sup> | 1 | 2 | 1 | | |
| Steadman, Sarah | | | 4 | | |
| Lamb, William | 1 | 1 | 1 | | |
| Morgan, Nathan | 1 | 2 | 2 | | |
| Avory, Simeon | 2 | 6 | 3 | | |
| Morgan, Solomon | 2 | | 2 | | |
| Morgan, William | 3 | 1 | 5 | | |
| Keeney, Aaron | 2 | 4 | 3 | | |
| Dabol, Benjamin | 1 | | 4 | | |
| Belton, Jonas | 1 | | 6 | | 3 |
| Brown, W<sup>m</sup> | 1 | 4 | 3 | | |
| Brown, Geshom | 4 | | 3 | | |
| Gray, Phillup | 5 | 1 | 5 | | |
| Perkins, Jacob | 3 | 1 | 2 | | |
| Perkins, Mary | | | 4 | | |
| Stanton, Sam<sup>l</sup> | 1 | 3 | 2 | | |
| Hallet, Thomas | 1 | 1 | 5 | | |
| Parks, Hezekiah | 1 | 6 | 6 | | |
| Fanning, Elisabeth | 1 | | 2 | | |
| Derby, Jedediah | 2 | | 1 | | 1 |
| Latham, Carey | 1 | 2 | 5 | | |
| Latham, Joseph | 4 | 6 | 3 | | |
| Williams, John | 1 | | 3 | | 1 |
| Williams, Carey | 1 | 1 | 3 | | |
| Williams, Peter | 1 | 2 | 3 | | |
| Stanton, Isaac | 1 | | 4 | | |
| Spicer, Oliver | 2 | | 4 | | |
| Spicer, Amos | 1 | | 2 | | |
| Avory, Benaijah | 1 | | 6 | | |
| Williams, Amos | 1 | | 3 | | |
| Williams, John, Jun<sup>r</sup> | 1 | | 4 | | |
| Avory, Daniel | 2 | 4 | 4 | | |
| Avory, David | 1 | 2 | 3 | | |
| Chapman, Joshua | 1 | | 4 | | |
| Chapman, Amos | 1 | 1 | 2 | | |
| Smith, Joshua | 1 | | 2 | | |
| Newton, Christopher | 1 | | 1 | | 1 |
| Lamb, John | 1 | 2 | 1 | | |
| Morgan, Israel | 1 | | 9 | | 1 |
| Powers, John | 1 | 2 | 5 | | |
| Hide, Phineas | 1 | 1 | 5 | | |
| Parks, Mary | 1 | | 3 | | |
| Meach, Aaron | 1 | 1 | 1 | | |
| Fanning, Elkanah | 2 | 1 | 1 | | |
| Avory, Jacob | 2 | | 2 | | |
| Avory, Theophilus | 1 | 1 | 3 | | |
| Spicer, John | 2 | 1 | 5 | | |
| Avory, Constant | 2 | | 2 | | |
| Avory, Theophilus, Jun<sup>r</sup> | 1 | 3 | 2 | | |
| Avory, James, Jun<sup>r</sup> | 4 | 2 | 3 | | |
| Standish, Israel | 1 | 3 | 4 | | |
| Morgan, Jacob | 1 | | 2 | | |
| Spicer, Edward, Jun<sup>r</sup> | 1 | 6 | 1 | | |
| Avory, Isaac | 2 | 3 | 6 | | |
| Smith, Sam<sup>l</sup> | 2 | | 3 | | |
| Adams, Joseph | 1 | 3 | 7 | | |
| Gates, John | 1 | 1 | 1 | | |
| Pelton, Eben<sup>r</sup> | 1 | | 1 | | |
| Andrus, Sam<sup>l</sup> | 1 | | 1 | | |
| Newton, Sam<sup>l</sup> | 1 | | 1 | | |
| Williams, Robart | 1 | | 5 | | |
| Avory, Jacob, Jun<sup>r</sup> | 1 | | 3 | | |
| Chapman, David | 1 | | 1 | | |
| Chapman, Asa | 1 | | 2 | | |
| Andrus, Elisha | 1 | 2 | 1 | | |
| Shoals, John | 3 | | 5 | | |
| Chapman, Levi | 2 | 2 | 10 | | |
| Stodard, Robart | 1 | | | | |
| Stodard, Robart, Jun<sup>r</sup> | 1 | 3 | 3 | | |
| Stodard, Dan<sup>l</sup> | 1 | 2 | 2 | | |
| Geers, Gurden | 1 | 2 | 2 | | |
| Holdrige, William | 1 | 2 | 4 | | |
| Bill, Benajiah | 1 | 1 | 1 | | |
| Stodard, James | 1 | | 2 | | |
| Stodard, James, Jun<sup>r</sup> | 2 | 4 | 2 | | |
| Spicer, Silas | 2 | 2 | 7 | | |
| Stodard, Deborah | | | 3 | | |
| Allen, Thomas | 1 | 5 | 4 | | |
| Allen, Mary | 1 | 1 | 4 | | |
| Mallerson, Elisha | 1 | 1 | 2 | | |
| Avory, John | 2 | | 2 | | |
| Avory, John, Jun<sup>r</sup> | 1 | 2 | 4 | | |
| Avory, Amos | 1 | 1 | 2 | | |
| Smith, Job. I | 1 | | 3 | 1 | |
| Starry, Oliver | 2 | 2 | 2 | | |
| Bill, Joshua | 1 | 2 | 3 | | |
| Newton, Able | 2 | 3 | 7 | | |
| Shoals, Mary | 2 | 2 | 4 | | |
| Marks, Aholiab | 1 | 1 | 2 | | |
| Waldren, Isaac | 1 | | 2 | | |
| Stodard, Jonathan | 1 | 1 | 1 | | |
| Stodard, Ichabod | 4 | 3 | 4 | | |
| Williams, Christopher | 1 | 2 | 2 | | |
| Newbury, Nathan | 1 | 1 | 3 | | |
| Stodard, Mark | 2 | 3 | 5 | | |
| Smith, William | 1 | 5 | 3 | | |
| Hewet, Henry | 1 | 1 | 3 | | |
| Pelton, Thomas | 1 | | 3 | | |
| Allen, Park | 2 | | 3 | 1 | |
| Allen, Park, Jun<sup>r</sup> | 1 | | 3 | | |
| Newton, Elijah | 1 | 1 | 3 | | |
| Mallerson, Joseph | 3 | 1 | 6 | | |
| Allen, Robart | 1 | | 2 | | |
| Allen, Thomas, Jun<sup>r</sup> | 1 | 2 | 2 | | |
| Elderkin, Elisabeth | | | 3 | | |
| Morgan, Thomas | 2 | 2 | 3 | | |
| Morgan, Thomas, Jun<sup>r</sup> | 1 | | 2 | | |
| Chester, Charles | 1 | | 1 | | |
| Allen, Edna | 1 | | 2 | | |
| Elderkin, Roxa | | 1 | | | |
| Allen, Joseph | 1 | | 3 | 1 | |
| Stodard, Raiph, Jun<sup>r</sup> | 3 | 3 | 2 | | |
| Havens, Jonathan | 1 | 4 | 2 | | |
| Avory, Nathan | 1 | | 2 | | |
| Mallerson, Ezra | 1 | 2 | 3 | | |
| Mallerson, Roswell | 1 | 2 | 4 | | |
| Lester, Amos | 1 | | 1 | | |
| Bill, Phineas | 2 | 2 | 6 | | |
| Lester, Peter, Jun<sup>r</sup> | 1 | | 2 | | |
| Baker, Sam<sup>l</sup> | 1 | 1 | 4 | | |
| Daton, Richard | 2 | | 2 | | |
| Rought, Daniel | 1 | 1 | 2 | | |
| Badcock, Sarah | | | 2 | | |
| Davis, Jasper | 1 | 6 | 1 | | |
| Williams, Mary | 3 | 1 | 2 | | |
| Jones, John | 1 | | 2 | | |
| Hallabutt, Raiph | 2 | 1 | 5 | | |
| Widger, And<sup>w</sup> | 1 | | 2 | | |
| Culver, Peter | 2 | | 3 | | |
| Auther, Elisha | 1 | | 1 | | |
| James (Negro) | | | | 4 | |
| Allen, John | 2 | | 3 | | |

# HEADS OF FAMILIES—CONNECTICUT.

## NEW LONDON COUNTY—Continued.

| NAME OF HEAD OF FAMILY. | Free white males of 16 years and upward, including heads of families. | Free white males under 16 years. | Free white females, including heads of families. | All other free persons. | Slaves. | NAME OF HEAD OF FAMILY. | Free white males of 16 years and upward, including heads of families. | Free white males under 16 years. | Free white females, including heads of families. | All other free persons. | Slaves. | NAME OF HEAD OF FAMILY. | Free white males of 16 years and upward, including heads of families. | Free white males under 16 years. | Free white females, including heads of families. | All other free persons. | Slaves. |
|---|---|---|---|---|---|---|---|---|---|---|---|---|---|---|---|---|---|
| Geer, Israel | 1 | | 5 | | | Starr, Vine | 3 | 1 | 1 | | | Heath, William | 1 | 4 | 4 | | |
| Geer, Jacob | 4 | | 1 | | | Latham, Robart | 1 | 1 | 1 | | 2 | Roads, William | 1 | 1 | 2 | | |
| Clark, Ruben | 1 | | 1 | | | Street, James | 1 | | 2 | | | Mitchel, Francis | 2 | 4 | 3 | | |
| Allen, Nathan | 2 | 1 | 2 | | | Baley, Jonᵃ, Junʳ | 2 | 4 | 1 | | | White, Christopher | 2 | 3 | 3 | | |
| Allen, Elisabeth | 1 | 1 | 3 | | | Ingraham, Flexander | 1 | 3 | 2 | | | Avory, Peter, 2ᵈ | 1 | 1 | 1 | 1 | 1 |
| Latham, Thomas | 2 | 2 | 3 | | | Lester, Samˡ, Junʳ | 1 | 2 | 3 | | | Ledgyard, Ebenʳ, 2ᵈ | 1 | | 3 | | |
| Smith, Samˡ, Junʳ | 2 | 1 | 6 | 1 | | Lester, Samˡ | 1 | | 1 | | | Burdick, Walter | 3 | 2 | 5 | | |
| Dirskall, Asa | 1 | 1 | 3 | | | Knowls, Danˡ & Son | 4 | | 2 | | | Read, Elexander | 1 | | | | |
| Widger, Eli | 1 | 1 | 2 | | | Forthsides, Nathan | 1 | | 4 | | | Warren, Thomas | 1 | 1 | 2 | | |
| Widger, John | 1 | | 2 | | | Forthsides, William | 1 | 3 | 2 | | | Williams, Peter | 1 | 2 | 4 | | |
| Ruff, Sarah | | 2 | 1 | | | Woodmansee, John | 1 | 3 | 6 | | | Chester, Giles | 1 | 1 | 4 | | |
| Plumb, George | 1 | 2 | 2 | | | Wood, William, Junʳ | 1 | 2 | 3 | | | Darrow, Nathan | 1 | 3 | 2 | | |
| Geer, Easter | 1 | | 3 | | 1 | Woodbridge, Micha | 1 | 1 | 2 | | | Chester, Simeon | 1 | 1 | 1 | | |
| Widger, Samˡ | 4 | 2 | 5 | | | Fanning, Thomas | 1 | 2 | 4 | | | Mason, Henry | 1 | 3 | 2 | | |
| Smith, James, Junʳ | 3 | 2 | 5 | | | Culver, Thomas | 1 | 2 | 4 | | | Lester, Lucretia | | 1 | 4 | | |
| Smith, Richard | 1 | | 2 | | | Latham, Christopher, Junʳ | 1 | 2 | 2 | | | Prentice, Amos | 3 | 1 | 5 | | |
| Smith, Richard, Junʳ | 1 | 3 | 2 | | | Lester, Christopher | | | | | | Latham, Edward | 3 | 1 | 2 | | 1 |
| Boles, Roberson | 1 | | 2 | | | Lewis, Peleg | 1 | 1 | 4 | | | Whealer, Ephraim | 1 | | 1 | | |
| Perkins, Solomon | 3 | | 4 | | | Woodard, Lucretia | 1 | 1 | 3 | | | Jeffers, Edward | 2 | | 1 | | |
| Perkins, Ebenʳ | 2 | 1 | 2 | | | Culver, Daniel | 1 | 1 | 1 | | | Baley, Ezekiel | 1 | 2 | 1 | | |
| Perkins, Jacob, 2ᵈ | 1 | | 1 | | | Lester, Elisabeth | | | 2 | | | Baley, Elisabeth | 1 | | 3 | | |
| Perkins, Elisabeth | | 2 | 3 | | | Newton, Ama | 1 | 1 | 5 | | | Latham, Elisabeth | | 1 | 3 | | |
| Swift, William | 1 | 2 | 4 | | | Starr, Thomas | 1 | 1 | 5 | | | Avory, Rufus | 3 | 4 | 2 | | |
| Bill, Benjamin | 3 | 1 | 3 | | | Starr, William | 1 | 5 | 3 | | | Ledgyard, Ann | | 1 | 3 | 1 | 1 |
| Avory, Amos | 3 | 1 | 4 | | | Mills, James | 2 | | 3 | | | Harvey, John | 1 | | 1 | | |
| Roberson, Elias | 1 | | 2 | | | Lester, Mary | 3 | | 2 | | | Leeds, Wᵐ | 2 | 3 | 4 | | |
| Morgan, Temperance | | | 1 | 1 | | Lester, Thomas | 1 | 1 | 4 | | | Ledyard, Ebenʳ | 4 | 3 | 2 | | 1 |
| David, David | 1 | 1 | 3 | | | Lester, Danˡ | 1 | 1 | 2 | | | Avory, Ebenʳ | 2 | | 2 | | 1 |
| Stodard, Tabitha | 1 | | 1 | | | Lester, Sarah | 1 | 1 | 3 | | 2 | Griffen, John | 1 | | 2 | | |
| Sheffield, Paul | 1 | | 1 | | | Taylor, Job | 1 | 2 | 6 | | | Gore, Able | 1 | 1 | 3 | | |
| Stodard, Silas | 1 | 3 | 4 | | | Shoals, Whealer | 1 | 1 | 3 | | | Latham, Betsy | | 1 | 3 | | |
| Stodard, Wait | 2 | | 1 | | | Budington, Walter, Junʳ | 1 | 4 | 6 | | | Thomson, Elisabeth | 1 | | 4 | | |
| Kennedy, John | 1 | | 2 | | | Badcock, Isaac | 1 | 3 | 4 | | | Yerrington, Ezekiel | 1 | | 5 | | |
| Williams, Thomas | 1 | 1 | 3 | | | Muxley, Jonᵃ | 1 | | 2 | | | Chipman, Samˡ, Junʳ | 1 | | 2 | | |
| Lester, Asa | 1 | 1 | 3 | | | Latham, Jasper | 2 | 1 | 5 | | 1 | Lankford, Joseph | 1 | 1 | 2 | | |
| Lester, Nathan | 2 | 1 | 3 | | | Latham, Mary | | 1 | 5 | | | Leeds, Ann | 1 | | 2 | | |
| Lester, Peter | 2 | 1 | 2 | | | Barber, John | 1 | 4 | 5 | | | Latham, Jonᵃ | 1 | | 2 | | |
| Allen, Amos | 2 | 2 | 3 | | | Smith, Charles | 2 | 2 | 4 | | | Latham, William, Junʳ | 2 | 4 | 6 | | 2 |
| Read, James | 1 | 1 | 1 | | | Andrus, James | 1 | | 4 | | | Avory, Ebenʳ, 2ᵈ | 1 | 3 | 4 | | |
| Latham, Lucy | 1 | 1 | 2 | | | Gallup, Gardiner | 1 | 1 | 1 | | | Avory, Pheba | | 2 | 3 | | |
| Stodard, Ralph | 1 | | 1 | 1 | | Brown, Peter | 1 | 1 | 3 | | | Avory, Caleb, 2ᵈ | 1 | | 2 | | |
| Stodard, Vine | 1 | 5 | 3 | | | Hill, Easter | 1 | 2 | 2 | | | Chester, Isaac | 2 | | 3 | | |
| Shoals, John | 3 | | 2 | | | Fanning, Jonᵃ, Junʳ | 1 | | 2 | | | Chester, Thomas | 3 | | 5 | | |
| Tammage, Elisha | 1 | 1 | 1 | | | Muxley, Elisabeth | 1 | | 2 | | | Avory, Latham | 2 | 2 | 3 | 1 | |
| Avory, Hannah | | | 2 | | 1 | Waterhouse, Amos | 1 | 2 | 2 | | | Starr, Jesse | 1 | 3 | 3 | | |
| Giles, Thomas, Junʳ | 1 | 3 | 5 | | | Devenport, William | 1 | 1 | 1 | | | Hawlet, Josiah | 2 | | 3 | | |
| Baley, Simeon | 1 | 2 | 1 | | | Deball, Mary | | | 3 | | | Widger, John | 1 | 1 | 2 | | |
| Bundy, Robart | 1 | 2 | 2 | | | Deball, Samˡ | 1 | 1 | 2 | | | Primes (Negro) | | | | 5 | |
| Smith, James | 3 | 5 | 5 | | | Davis, Daniel | 1 | | 5 | | | Chester, Ann | | 1 | 1 | | |
| Smith, Samˡ, 3ᵈ | 1 | | 2 | | | Morgan, John | 4 | 1 | 3 | | | Latham, Ann | | 2 | 4 | | |
| Lamb, Hannah | | 1 | 2 | | | Deball, John | 2 | 4 | 3 | | | Latham, Sigleton | 1 | | 3 | | |
| Starr, Joseph | 1 | | 1 | | 6 | Turner, Amos | 2 | 3 | 3 | | | Dodge, Mary | | 1 | 5 | | |
| Perkins, Rufus | 2 | 7 | 2 | | | Turner, Amos, Junʳ | 1 | 1 | 1 | | | Brown, John | 1 | 1 | 3 | | |
| Perkins, Jabez | 1 | 3 | 2 | | | Turner, Ezekiel | 2 | 1 | 3 | | | Daniels, Frank | 1 | 1 | 3 | | |
| Lewis, Joseph | 1 | 1 | 2 | | | Avory, Peter | | | | | 3 | Moore, Frederick | 1 | 1 | 2 | | |
| Lewis, Deborah | | 1 | 4 | | | Daniels, John | 1 | 3 | 2 | | | Chipman, Christopher | 1 | 5 | 2 | | |
| Muxley, Joseph | 1 | | 4 | | | Shoals, Susanna | | 1 | 1 | | | Thays, Thomas | 1 | | 1 | | |
| Dexter, Elisha | 1 | 3 | 2 | | | Daniels, John, Junʳ | 1 | 1 | 1 | | | Williams, Theoda | | 1 | 7 | | |
| Perkins, Youngs | 1 | 3 | 2 | | | Elexander, William | 2 | | 4 | | | Williams, John, 3ᵈ | 1 | | 1 | | |
| Hemmingar, John | 1 | 1 | 2 | | | Start, Daniel | 1 | 1 | 3 | | | Hall, Mary | | | 2 | | |
| Smith, Jeremiah | 2 | 2 | 1 | | | Allen, Miner | 1 | 1 | 3 | | | Avory, Youngs | 1 | 1 | 3 | | |
| Woodworth, Assel | 1 | | 3 | | | Chalsea, Wᵐ | 1 | 1 | 2 | | | Avory, Park, Junʳ | 1 | 2 | 3 | | 2 |
| Baley, Elijah | 1 | 1 | 2 | | | William (Negro) | | | | 8 | | Burch, Isaac | 1 | 2 | 2 | | |
| Baley, Dudley | 1 | 1 | 2 | | | Pharough (Negro) | | | | 3 | | Avory, Park | 2 | | 3 | | 2 |
| Tayler, John | 2 | 1 | 3 | | | Edgcomb, David | 1 | 2 | 3 | | | Ayrs, Daniel | 1 | 2 | 1 | | |
| Perkins, Mary | | | 2 | | | Edgcomb, Jabez | 1 | | 2 | | | Brown, Jesse | 2 | 1 | 4 | | 2 |
| Adams, David | 1 | 1 | 2 | | | Avory, Thomas | 3 | 2 | 7 | | | Gallup, Joseph | 3 | 1 | 4 | | |
| Fish, Thomas | 1 | 1 | 5 | | | Smith, Rufus | 3 | 1 | 2 | | | Morgan, Youngs | 2 | 2 | 4 | | |
| Fish, Jonathan | 1 | | 3 | | | Edgcomb, Samˡ | 3 | | 2 | | | Avory, William | 3 | | 3 | | 1 |
| Fish, George | 1 | 2 | 2 | | | Edgcomb, Samˡ, Junʳ | 1 | 1 | 1 | | | Morgan, James | 2 | | 7 | | |
| Niles, Nathˡ | 3 | | 3 | | 3 | Smith, Jabez | 1 | 1 | 3 | | 1 | Morgan, James, Junʳ | 1 | 1 | 3 | | |
| Niles, Elisha | 1 | 2 | 2 | | 1 | Smith, Gilbert & Son | 2 | 1 | 2 | | 1 | Ceaser (Negro) | | | | 3 | |
| Baley, Obadiah | 1 | 4 | 5 | | | Smith, Denison | 1 | | 2 | | | Clark, Josiah | 3 | 6 | 3 | 1 | |
| Baley, Azubah | | | 5 | | | Walworth, Joshua | 1 | 1 | 1 | | | Latham, William, 3ᵈ | 1 | 2 | 2 | | |
| Starr, John | 2 | 1 | 5 | | | Chipman, Samˡ | 2 | | 4 | | | Hoskins, Ebenʳ | 1 | 3 | 2 | | |
| Culver, Amos | 2 | | 3 | | | Niles, Thomas | 4 | 2 | 2 | | | Avory, Benjamin | 3 | 3 | 5 | | |
| Woodworth, Oliver | 1 | | 3 | | | Daball, Nathan | 1 | 2 | 3 | | | Champlin, John | 1 | 1 | 4 | | |
| Andrus, Benjᵃ | 1 | 4 | 4 | | | Lewis, William | 1 | 2 | 2 | | | Davis, Robart | 1 | | 3 | | |
| Saunders, Gideon | 2 | | 2 | | | Chaple, Edward | 1 | 2 | 4 | | | Roggers, Amos | 1 | 4 | 2 | | |
| Woodworth, Joseph | 1 | 1 | 3 | | | Stark, Solomon | 1 | 1 | 4 | | | Guard, Daniel | 2 | | 1 | | |
| Adams, Samˡ | 2 | | 2 | | | Stark, Daniel, Junʳ | 1 | 1 | 2 | | | Roggers, Ebenʳ | 1 | 5 | 3 | | |
| Perkins, Obadiah | 4 | 4 | 4 | | | Whitman, Isaac | 2 | 3 | 3 | | | Avory, Caleb | 1 | 1 | 3 | | |
| Woodmansee, Joseph | 1 | 1 | 2 | | | Baley, John, Junʳ | 1 | | 1 | | | Havens, Silvester | 1 | 1 | 3 | | |
| Baley, John | 2 | 1 | 2 | 1 | | Whitman, Timothy, Junʳ | 1 | 2 | 2 | | | Latham, Joseph | 1 | 1 | 1 | | |
| Baley, Joseph | 2 | 3 | 5 | | | Whitman, Timothy | 2 | 1 | 3 | | | Chipman, William | 1 | 7 | 2 | | |
| Pembleton, Jabez | 1 | 1 | 3 | | | Culver, Moses | 1 | 2 | 3 | | | Avory, Deborah | 3 | 3 | 3 | | |
| Baley, Jonathan | 3 | 1 | 2 | | | Culver, Joseph | 1 | | 4 | | | Brand, Benjamin | 1 | 5 | 3 | | |
| Daball, John | 1 | | 4 | | | Culver, Eunice | 1 | 1 | 5 | | | Burrows, Silas | 2 | 1 | 5 | 1 | |
| Avory, James | 2 | 2 | 2 | | | Hart, Jemima | 2 | | 4 | | | Crum, Charles | 1 | | 3 | | |
| Avory, John | 2 | | 3 | | 1 | Baley, Joseph, Junʳ | 1 | 3 | 3 | | | Burrows, John | 1 | 1 | 3 | | |
| Avory, Pruda | 1 | | 2 | 4 | | Baley, Pethust | 1 | 3 | 1 | | | Burrows, James | 1 | 1 | 3 | | |
| Budington, Walter | 2 | 2 | 4 | 1 | | Lamb, Timothy | 3 | 3 | 6 | | | Gaurd, Nathan | 1 | | 1 | | |
| Latham, Christopher | 3 | | 3 | | | Lamb, Samuel | 1 | 5 | 6 | | | Burrows, Joseph | 1 | 1 | 4 | | |
| Wood, John | 1 | | 3 | | | Clark, Obed | 1 | 3 | 2 | | | Tylar, Solomon | 1 | | 1 | | |
| Wood, William | 1 | | 3 | | | | | | | | | Latham, Jasper | 1 | 5 | 1 | | |
| Wood, Samˡ | 1 | | 1 | | | | | | | | | Latham, John | 1 | | 1 | | |
| Wood, John, Junʳ | 1 | 1 | 2 | | | | | | | | | Latham, Joseph | 1 | 2 | 3 | | |

# FIRST CENSUS OF THE UNITED STATES.

## NEW LONDON COUNTY—Continued.

| NAME OF HEAD OF FAMILY. | Free white males of 16 years and upward, including heads of families. | Free white males under 16 years. | Free white females, including heads of families. | All other free persons. | Slaves. |
|---|---|---|---|---|---|
| Morgan, Timothy | 3 | 1 | 4 | | |
| Morgan, Saml | 1 | 1 | 1 | | |
| Palmer, George | 2 | 2 | 2 | | |
| Ashley, James | 1 | | 2 | | |
| Palmer, Elihu | 1 | 1 | 3 | | |
| Morgan, Joshua | 1 | 1 | 4 | | |
| Sawer, James | 1 | | 2 | | |
| Fitch, Hannah | 3 | | 1 | | |
| Potter, Thomas | 1 | 1 | 2 | | |
| Burrows, Lemuel | 1 | 1 | 2 | | |
| Burrows, William | 1 | 1 | 3 | | |
| Ashby, Edward | 5 | | 2 | | |
| Williams, Solomon | 1 | 4 | 3 | | |
| Rothburn, Elijah | 1 | 1 | 5 | | |
| Burrows, Nathan, Junr | 1 | 4 | 1 | | |
| Fish, John | 1 | | 1 | | |
| Fish, John, Junr | 1 | | 2 | | |
| Fish, Saml | 1 | 3 | 1 | | |
| Tiff, Solomon | 1 | 3 | 4 | | |
| Brice, Robart | 1 | 3 | 2 | | |
| Burrows, Elisha | 1 | | 6 | | |
| Fish, Ebenr | 1 | 2 | 4 | | |
| Gaurd, Elisha | 1 | | 3 | | |
| Gaurd, Saml | 1 | | 3 | | |
| Middleton, George | 3 | | 4 | | |
| Lewis, David | 1 | 2 | 3 | | |
| Baker, Joshua | 1 | 5 | 2 | | |
| Gates, Zebadiah | 1 | 1 | 3 | | |
| Gates, Sarah | 1 | | 2 | | |
| Wilcox, Mary | | | 1 | | |
| Taylor, Joseph | 3 | 3 | 4 | | |
| Williams, Saml | 1 | | 2 | | |
| Brightman, Henry | 2 | | 3 | | |
| Brightman, Henry, Junr | 1 | | 2 | | |
| Latham, William | 1 | 2 | 5 | | |
| Billings, Mary | | | 1 | | |
| Smith, Simeon | 1 | 2 | 7 | 1 | |
| Walworth, Sarah | 3 | | 3 | | |
| Burrows, Saml | 1 | 4 | 2 | | |
| Sabins, Saml | 1 | | 1 | | |
| Packer, Joseph | 2 | | 4 | | |
| Packer, Benjamin | 1 | | 1 | | |
| Packer, John | 2 | 1 | 3 | | |
| Packer, John, Junr | 1 | 1 | 4 | | |
| Packer, Surviah | | | 1 | | |
| Ashby, John | 1 | 2 | 3 | | |
| Packer, Elisha | 2 | 4 | 6 | | |
| Packer, Abigail | | | 2 | | |
| Packer, Joseph | 1 | 2 | 8 | 1 | |
| Parks, Joseph | 2 | 3 | 4 | | |
| Volph, Anthony | 1 | 1 | 3 | | |
| Burrows, Lemuel, Junr | 2 | 1 | 5 | | |
| Packer, Danl | 3 | 1 | 1 | | 1 |
| Packer, Elam | 1 | | 4 | | |
| Packer, Eldrige | 1 | 1 | 2 | | |
| Packer, Edward | 1 | | 2 | | 1 |
| Packer, James | 1 | 1 | 3 | | |
| Niles, Saml | 1 | 1 | 2 | | |
| Burrows, Nathan | 2 | 2 | 9 | | |
| Eldrige, Thomas, 2d | 1 | 2 | 1 | | |
| Niles, Nathan | 1 | 1 | 2 | | |
| Burrows, Danl | 2 | 1 | 4 | | |
| Enos, John | 1 | | 1 | | |
| Fish, Nathan | 4 | | 5 | | |
| Fish, Sands | 1 | 1 | 3 | | |
| Parks, Joseph | 3 | | 2 | | |
| Parks, Thomas | 2 | | 1 | | |
| Smith, William, 2d | 1 | 1 | 4 | | |
| Clark, Aaron | 1 | | 3 | | |
| Haley, Jeremiah | 3 | 2 | 2 | | |
| Holdrige, Saml | 1 | 2 | 4 | | |
| Stodard, Elisha | 1 | 2 | 3 | | |
| Holdrige, Saml, Junr | 1 | 2 | 2 | | |
| Parks, Nathl | 3 | | 4 | | |
| Denison, Jona | 2 | | 2 | | |
| Burnett, Rachel | | | 3 | | |
| Prince (Negro) | | | | 2 | |
| Welles, Thomas | 1 | 3 | 2 | | |
| Welles, Wait | 2 | | 4 | | |
| Sisson, James | 1 | 1 | 4 | | |
| Hix, John | 2 | 2 | 3 | | |
| Haley, Caleb | 2 | 1 | 2 | | |
| Morgan, Jesse | 1 | | 4 | | |
| Eldrige, James | 1 | 1 | 2 | 5 | |
| Clark, Francis | 1 | 1 | 3 | | |
| Williams, Caleb | 2 | 4 | 2 | | 1 |
| Hix, John, Junr | 1 | | 3 | | |
| Fish, Aaron | 2 | 1 | 4 | | |
| Fish, Sprage | 1 | 1 | 1 | | |
| Langothy, John | 1 | | 2 | | |
| Crary, Nathan, Junr | 1 | 3 | 6 | 1 | |
| Burrows, Hubbard | 1 | | 1 | | |
| Burrows, Jona | 2 | 1 | 6 | | |
| Ingraham, William | 1 | | 3 | | |
| Eldrige, Daniel | 1 | | 5 | | |
| Spicer, William | 1 | 2 | | | |
| Burrows, John | 1 | | 2 | | |
| Lydia (Negro) | | | | 2 | |
| Baley, Thadeus | 3 | 2 | 6 | | |
| Baley, Jedediah | 1 | | 1 | | |
| Burrows, Paul | 1 | 4 | 5 | | |
| Williams, Saml, 3d | 1 | 4 | 8 | | |
| Start, Ebenr | 1 | | 2 | | |
| Waterhouse, Jabez | 3 | | 3 | | |
| Waterhouse, Timothy | 3 | 2 | 4 | | |
| Waterhouse, Timothy, 2d | 1 | 3 | 1 | | |
| Enos, Joshua | 2 | | 9 | | |
| Gallup, Benadam, 2d | 3 | 2 | 3 | | |
| Gallup, Benadam | 1 | | 3 | | 4 |
| Gallup, Isaac | 1 | 1 | 2 | | |
| Morgan, Jedediah | 2 | 1 | 5 | | |
| Lee, Joseph | 1 | 1 | 2 | | |
| Geer, Robart | 1 | 3 | 8 | | |
| Geer, David | 2 | 3 | 4 | | |
| Rose, Robart | 2 | | 2 | | |
| Rose, Robart, Junr | 2 | 1 | 4 | | |
| Swan, Elias | 1 | 2 | 3 | | |
| Shadrack (Negro) | | | | 7 | |
| Gallup, Nehemiah | 1 | 3 | 3 | | |
| Williams, Saml, Junr | 3 | 4 | 3 | | |
| Barns, Ezra | 2 | 3 | 5 | | |
| Fish, Ambrus | 2 | 1 | 3 | | |
| Fanning, Jona | 1 | 1 | 1 | | |
| Fanning, Phineas | 1 | 3 | 3 | | |
| Brown, William, Junr | 1 | 2 | 3 | | |
| Fanning, David | 1 | 1 | 4 | | |
| Steadman, John | 1 | | 1 | | |
| Steadman, Benjamin | 2 | 3 | 5 | | |
| Jones, Samuel | 3 | 2 | 6 | | |
| Miner, Joshua | 1 | | 3 | | |
| Dixon, John | 1 | | 1 | | |
| Dixon, Robart | 1 | 2 | 3 | 2 | |
| Williams, Wm | 1 | | 2 | | |
| Williams, William, 2d | 1 | 3 | 3 | 2 | |
| Williams, Elisha | 1 | | 2 | 1 | |
| Williams, Joseph, Junr | 1 | 1 | 4 | | |
| Williams, Joseph | 1 | | 2 | | |
| Wood, Elisabeth | | 1 | 5 | | |
| Stanton, Joseph | 3 | 2 | 5 | | |
| Stanton, John | 1 | 1 | 1 | | |
| Lucas, Park | 1 | | 1 | | |
| Holley, Joseph | 1 | 3 | 3 | | |
| Fish, Elias | 1 | 1 | 2 | | |
| Stodard, Increase | 1 | | 2 | | |
| Williams, Roger | 1 | 1 | 5 | | |
| Brown, Nathl, Junr | 1 | 2 | 6 | | |
| Brown, James | 2 | 2 | 4 | | |
| Barns, Simeon | 1 | | 4 | | |
| Barns, Easter | | | 1 | | |
| Packer, John, 3d | 1 | 3 | 2 | | |
| Holdrige, Phineas | 3 | 2 | 5 | | |
| Barns, Jesse, 2d | 1 | | 1 | | |
| Barns, Jesse | 1 | 1 | 3 | | |
| Hewet, Stanton | 2 | 2 | 1 | | |
| Lester, Ebenr | 2 | 3 | 6 | | |
| Lester, Guy | 1 | | 3 | | |
| Smith, Moses | 1 | 2 | 4 | | |
| Lee, Squire | 2 | 2 | 4 | | |
| Eyrs, Elisha | 2 | 1 | 5 | | |
| Brown, Gershom, Junr | 1 | | 2 | | |
| Brown, Ruben | 1 | 2 | 1 | | |
| Parks, Mathew, Junr | 1 | 2 | 3 | 1 | |
| Hewet, Israel | 1 | | 4 | | |
| Bellows, Darius | 1 | | 1 | | |
| Bellows, Asa | 1 | 1 | 1 | | |
| Noyce, Charles | 1 | 2 | 2 | | |
| Worden, James | 1 | | 2 | | |
| Worden, Joseph | 2 | 3 | 2 | | |
| Cumstock, Simeon | 1 | 4 | 1 | | |
| Baker, Daniel | 2 | 1 | 3 | | |
| Williams, Margaret | 1 | 1 | 3 | | |
| Park, Stephen | 1 | | | | |
| Lucas, William | 2 | | 1 | | |
| Grant, Beriah | 1 | 2 | 4 | | |
| Brown, Amos | 1 | 2 | 2 | | |
| Brown, Cumfort, 2d | 1 | 2 | 3 | | |
| Morgan, Joseph | 1 | 3 | 3 | | 1 |
| Roach, Thomas | 1 | 1 | | | |
| Thomas, Abigail | | | 3 | | |
| Hubbard, William | 1 | 1 | 4 | 1 | |
| Isham, Joseph, 2d | 1 | | 1 | | 4 |
| Worthington, Asa | 1 | 3 | 4 | | |
| Cook, John | 1 | | 3 | | |
| Wright, Dudley | 2 | | 3 | | 3 |
| Watrus, John R | 1 | 1 | 2 | | 1 |
| Buckley, Charles, Junr | 1 | 1 | 1 | | |
| Townsend, William | 1 | 1 | 3 | | |
| Tainter, John | 3 | 4 | 1 | 1 | |
| Tainter, Roger | 1 | | 1 | | |
| Wack, Lydea | | 1 | 3 | 1 | |
| Hall, William | 1 | | 3 | | |
| Clark, Darius | 1 | 1 | | | |
| Buckley, William | 2 | | 1 | | 1 |
| Foot, Daniel | 2 | 3 | 2 | | |
| Whitney, Daniel | 1 | | 1 | | |
| Foot, Charles | 2 | | 5 | | |
| Clark, John | 1 | 2 | 5 | | |
| Clark, Ezra, Junr | 2 | 1 | 3 | | |
| Welles, John | 2 | 4 | 4 | | |
| Buckley, Joseph | 4 | 2 | 4 | | |
| Chamberlain, John | 3 | 2 | 2 | | |
| Huntley, Harris | 4 | 3 | 4 | | |
| Hall, Ephraim | 1 | | | | |
| Bill, Annis | | | 1 | 1 | |
| Johnson, Joseph | 1 | 2 | 4 | | |
| Burnham, Catharine | | | 3 | | |
| Hazard, Samuel | 2 | 5 | 6 | | 2 |
| Clark, Lucy | | | 2 | 1 | |
| Watrus, Theodore | 1 | 2 | 3 | | |
| Clark, Elihu | 3 | | 2 | | 1 |
| Clark, Ezra | 3 | | 1 | | |
| Freman, Timothy | 1 | | | | |
| Freman, Calvin | 1 | 1 | 2 | | |
| Foot, Joseph | 2 | 2 | 6 | | |
| Bridges, Edmund | 2 | 3 | 4 | | |
| Foot, Hosea | 3 | | 3 | 1 | 1 |
| Peter (Negro) | | | | 10 | |
| Kellog, Russell | 1 | 1 | 2 | | |
| Foot, Ruhamah | 4 | | 4 | | |
| Judd, Daniel | 4 | | 2 | | |
| Judd, Timothy | 1 | 2 | 3 | | |
| Beckwith, Francis | 1 | 1 | 1 | | |
| Pratt, John | 1 | 3 | 5 | | |
| Albert, Obed | 3 | 4 | 7 | | |
| Pratt, Daniel, Junr | 3 | | 2 | | |
| Pratt, Daniel | 1 | | 2 | | |
| Gillet, Ela | 3 | 1 | 4 | | |
| Taylor, Joseph | 3 | | 3 | 1 | 3 |
| Northam, Asa | 1 | | | | |
| Northam, Jonathan, Junr | 1 | 2 | 1 | | |
| Alvord, Rachel | | | 1 | | |
| Kellog, Elisha | 1 | 1 | 4 | | |
| Hatch, Benjamin | 2 | | 2 | | |
| Jones, Isaac | 1 | 1 | 2 | | |
| McCrackin, James | 1 | 3 | 1 | | |
| Kellog, Israel | 1 | 2 | 4 | | |
| Chamberlain, Roswell | 2 | | 5 | | |
| Adams, Saml | 3 | | 4 | | |
| Carrier, Isaac | 1 | 4 | 2 | | |
| Staples, John | 1 | 2 | 2 | | |
| Skinner, John | 1 | 2 | 4 | | |
| Bass, Jonathan | 1 | 1 | 2 | | |
| Pratt, Daniel, 3d | 1 | 3 | 3 | | |
| Mitchel, John | 1 | 1 | 2 | | |
| Mitchel, Amasa | 1 | 1 | 1 | | |
| Mitchel, Joseph | 1 | | 1 | | |
| Mitchel, Asa | 1 | | 1 | | |
| Ransom, Joseph | 1 | 3 | 1 | | |
| Reede, Rufus | 1 | 4 | 4 | | |
| Woodworth, John | 1 | 1 | 2 | | |
| Skinner, Stephen | 1 | 4 | 4 | | |
| Strong, Amos | 3 | 1 | 1 | | |
| Carrier, Samuel | 3 | | 4 | | |
| Carrier, John | 2 | 3 | 2 | | |
| Bigalow, Ira | 1 | 2 | 2 | | |
| Niles, Ambrus | 2 | 3 | 5 | | |
| Niles, Darkas | 1 | 1 | 2 | | |
| Drinkwater, Ebenezer B | 1 | 2 | 3 | | |
| Carrier, Thomas, Junr | 1 | 1 | 7 | | |
| Carrier, Joseph | 3 | | 1 | | |
| Skinner, Noah, Junr | 1 | 1 | 1 | | |
| Foot, Charles | 3 | 2 | 2 | | |
| Skinner, David | 4 | 4 | 4 | | 1 |
| Eales, John | 1 | 2 | 8 | | 1 |
| Buel, Elisha | 2 | | 3 | | |
| Foot, Roger | 1 | | 2 | | |
| Lord, Ebenezer | 2 | 3 | 5 | | 1 |
| Fox, Appleton | 1 | 3 | 2 | | |
| Lord, Epafras | 1 | | 1 | | 3 |
| Lord, John | 1 | 1 | 1 | | 1 |
| Lord, Ichabod | 1 | 3 | 5 | | |
| Lord, Elisha | 2 | 4 | 3 | | |
| Bowers, Ephraim | 1 | 3 | 1 | | |
| Kneeland, Morey | | | | | |
| McCall, Daniel | 1 | 3 | 6 | | |
| Carter, Eleazer | 2 | | 2 | | |
| Deane, Abner | 2 | | 2 | | 1 |
| Strong, David | 1 | 3 | 3 | 1 | |
| Huntington, David | 1 | | 1 | | |
| Isham, Samuel | 2 | 2 | 6 | | |
| Buel, Elijah | 1 | | 3 | | |
| Buel, Elijah, Junr | 2 | 1 | 2 | | |
| Root, Benjamin | 2 | 2 | 2 | | |
| Boles, Joshua | 1 | 1 | 3 | | |
| Curtis, Benjamin | 3 | 1 | 1 | | |
| Dayton, Henry | 5 | | 5 | | |
| Finley, Samuel | 1 | 3 | 2 | | |
| Judd, Daniel, Junr | 4 | 2 | 5 | | |
| Blush, Asa | 1 | 1 | 2 | | |

# HEADS OF FAMILIES—CONNECTICUT.

## NEW LONDON COUNTY—Continued.

| Name of head of family. | Free white males of 16 years and upward, including heads of families. | Free white males under 16 years. | Free white females, including heads of families. | All other free persons. | Slaves. |
|---|---|---|---|---|---|
| Caton, James | 1 | | | | |
| Carrier, Thomas | 4 | 1 | 4 | | |
| Lord, Theodore | 3 | 1 | 7 | | |
| Carter, Ezra | 1 | 4 | 3 | | |
| Kneeland, David | 2 | 3 | 5 | | |
| Adams, John | 1 | | 2 | | |
| Miller, David | 2 | 2 | 3 | | |
| Strong, Ebenezer | 1 | 2 | 4 | | |
| Ingraham, Jacob | 1 | 2 | 5 | | |
| Berry, Joseph | 1 | 2 | 4 | | |
| Curtis, Isaac | 1 | | 1 | | |
| Willis, Jeduthan | 1 | 2 | 4 | | |
| Taylor, Stephen | 1 | 1 | 4 | | |
| Blush, Ezra | 1 | 1 | 2 | | |
| Blush, Easter | | | 2 | | |
| Stodard, William | 1 | 1 | 1 | | |
| Ingraham, Jonathan | 2 | 3 | 4 | | |
| Coleman, Ebenezer | 2 | 2 | 8 | | |
| McCall, Jacob | 2 | 2 | 5 | | |
| Goff, Joshua | 1 | | 1 | | |
| Watrus, Lazarus | 1 | 4 | 3 | | |
| Bigalow, Azariah | 4 | 2 | 4 | | |
| Bigalow, Daniel | 3 | 1 | 4 | | |
| Goff, Sam¹ | 1 | | 3 | | |
| Goff, Cumfort | 2 | 1 | 2 | | |
| Goff, Charles | 1 | 1 | 5 | | |
| Goff, Cumfort, Junr | 1 | 2 | 3 | | |
| Goff, Squire | 1 | 2 | 3 | | |
| Goff, Gansey | 1 | | 1 | | |
| Isham, John | 2 | 1 | 1 | | |
| Isham, Noah | 1 | 1 | | | |
| Watrus, Joseph | 2 | | 2 | | |
| Watrus, Henry | 1 | | 3 | | |
| Adams, David | 1 | | 1 | | |
| Staples, Elijah | 1 | | 2 | | |
| Staples, Benjamin | 1 | 1 | 1 | | |
| Staples, Elijah, Junr | 1 | 1 | 4 | | |
| Adams, Benjamin | 1 | | 2 | | |
| Adams, Benjamin, 2d | 1 | | 2 | | |
| Warner, Nath¹ | 1 | | 1 | | |
| Foot, Nath¹ | 1 | | 1 | | |
| Foot, Aaron | 2 | 3 | 5 | | |
| Day, Abraham | 1 | | 2 | | |
| Day, Elijah | 1 | 2 | 2 | | |
| Babbit, Jacob | 1 | 1 | 1 | | |
| Hill, Thomas | 2 | | 3 | | |
| Williams, Weeks | 1 | | 1 | | |
| Williams, Daniel | 1 | 4 | 2 | | |
| Williams, Elijah | 1 | 5 | 4 | | |
| Watrus, Timothy | 2 | 4 | 1 | | |
| Bigalow, Ezra | 2 | 1 | 2 | | |
| Brown, Sam¹ | 1 | 4 | 1 | | |
| Gifford, Caleb | 1 | 1 | 3 | | |
| Scovil, Judah | 3 | | 7 | | |
| Crocker, Joseph | 1 | 1 | 2 | | |
| Dunham, Eleazer | 1 | 1 | 1 | | |
| Dunham, Eleazer, 2d | 1 | | 3 | | |
| Miner, David | 2 | 1 | 1 | | |
| Worthington, Gad | 1 | 1 | 5 | | 1 |
| Day, Joseph | 2 | | 3 | | |
| Skinner, Noah | 1 | | 2 | | |
| Skinner, Sam¹ | 1 | 1 | 2 | | |
| Taylor, Ezra | 1 | 2 | 2 | | |
| Sexton, George | 1 | 2 | 3 | 1 | |
| Sexton, Betsy | 1 | | 3 | | |
| Day, Amasa | 2 | 1 | 5 | | |
| Day, Jesse | 1 | 2 | 2 | | |
| Day, Asa | 1 | | 1 | | |
| Prince (Negro) | | | | 2 | |
| Foot, Adonijah | 1 | 1 | 3 | | |
| Foot, Ruben | 1 | | 1 | | |
| Northum, Jonathan | 3 | | 5 | | |
| Lothrop, Oliver | 1 | 1 | 5 | 1 | |
| Watrus, Samuel | 2 | 2 | 3 | | |
| Tracy, Daniel | 2 | 2 | 1 | | |
| Young, Robart | 1 | 1 | 2 | | |
| Ramsdale, Ezra | 1 | 3 | 2 | | |
| Brown, Amasa | 1 | 1 | 3 | | |
| Peter (Negro) | | | | 2 | |
| Pomp (Negro) | | | | 3 | |
| Susanna (Negro) | | | | 2 | |
| Jack (Negro) | | | | 5 | |
| Yemmons, David | 1 | 5 | 5 | | |
| Yemmons, Sarah | | | 2 | | |
| Isham, John, Junr | 2 | 2 | 5 | | 7 |
| Blish, John | 2 | 2 | 5 | | 1 |
| Woodbridge, Timothy | 1 | 1 | 2 | 5 | |
| Williams, Charles | 2 | 1 | 1 | | |
| Robins, Robart | 3 | 3 | 5 | | |
| Sabins, Phenias | 2 | 3 | 3 | | |
| Isham, Joseph | 1 | 1 | 1 | | |
| Jones, John | 1 | 2 | 1 | | |
| Bigalow, John | 3 | | 5 | | |
| Bigalow, Sarah | | | 4 | | |
| McCan, Francis | 1 | | 2 | | |
| Crocker, Simeon | 1 | 3 | 3 | | |
| Herrick, Isaac | 1 | 1 | | | |
| Crocker, Timothy | 1 | 4 | 1 | | |
| Saxton, James | 1 | 2 | 4 | | |
| Doras (Negro) | | | | 2 | |
| Shattuck, Robart | 1 | 3 | 2 | | |
| Shattuck, David | 1 | | 2 | | |
| Loomis, Solomon | 2 | 2 | 3 | | |
| Loomis, Samuel | 1 | 2 | 3 | | |
| Dunham, William | 1 | 1 | 1 | | |
| Lewis, Sarah | 2 | | 2 | | |
| Lord, Ezekiel | 1 | 2 | 4 | | |
| Umstead, John | 4 | | 3 | | |
| Champion, Henry | 3 | 1 | 2 | | 2 |
| Champion, Henry, Junr | 2 | 2 | 4 | | |
| Worthington, Erastus | 1 | 1 | 2 | | |
| Carrier, Lovina | | | 2 | | |
| Isham, Joshua | 1 | | 1 | | |
| Foot, Nath¹, Junr | 1 | 2 | 4 | | |
| Carrier, Uriah | 3 | 2 | 3 | | |
| Smith, Elijah | 1 | 3 | 2 | | |
| Wetmore, Joseph | 1 | 4 | 2 | | |
| Isham, Isaac | 2 | 1 | 3 | | |
| Isham, Isaac, Junr | 1 | 2 | 6 | | |
| Bigsby, Green | 1 | | 1 | | |
| Brainard, William | 2 | 4 | 4 | | |
| Cone, Cephas | 1 | 2 | 5 | | |
| Fuller, Joseph | 1 | 3 | 1 | | |
| Gates, John | 1 | | 2 | | |
| Devenport, Eliphalet | 1 | 1 | 1 | | |
| Williams, Nathan | 1 | 2 | 5 | | |
| Buckley, Joshua | 2 | 1 | 3 | 4 | 5 |
| Bigalow, Jonathan | 1 | 1 | 4 | | |
| Bigalow, James | 1 | | 3 | | |
| Swan, Asa | 1 | 2 | 6 | | |
| Roggers, Sam¹ | 1 | 3 | 2 | | |
| Buckley, Abigail | | | 1 | | 4 |
| Buckley, Daniel | 2 | 3 | 3 | | 1 |
| Welles, Chaunsey | 1 | 4 | 3 | | |
| Brown, Stephen | 1 | 3 | 2 | | |
| Buckley, David | 2 | 1 | 5 | | |
| Dodge, Thomas | 3 | | 6 | | |
| Johnson, John | 1 | | 1 | | |
| Quash (Negro) | | | | 2 | |
| Vira (Negro) | | | | 3 | |
| Webster, Stephen | 1 | | 2 | | |
| Webster, Elisabeth | | | 3 | | |
| Webster, Levi | 3 | | 1 | | |
| Hopson, John | 1 | | 1 | | |
| Buckley, Roger | 5 | 4 | 3 | 2 | 3 |
| Kellog, Abigail | 1 | | 2 | | |
| Kellog, Ebenr | 1 | 2 | 4 | | |
| Kellog, Butler | 1 | | 1 | | |
| Tainter, Charles | 2 | 1 | 9 | 2 | |
| Buckley, Elijah | 1 | 2 | 5 | | |
| Gillet, Nehemiah | 2 | 1 | 5 | | |
| Burnham, David | 1 | 1 | 4 | | |
| Gillet, Joseph | 3 | 3 | 6 | | |
| Fuller, Elijah | 1 | 2 | 3 | | |
| Fuller, Hannah | 1 | | 5 | | |
| Fox, Jacob | 1 | 3 | 4 | | |
| Roberson, Samuel | 1 | | 2 | | |
| Worthington, Abigail | 1 | 3 | 2 | 2 | 2 |
| Buckley, John | 2 | 3 | 7 | | |
| Boham (Negro) | | | | 5 | |
| Clark, Nath¹ | 2 | | 2 | | |
| Clark, Gurdon | 1 | | 2 | | |
| Gillet, Joseph, Junr | 1 | 1 | 3 | | |
| Mun, Isaiah | 2 | | 2 | | |
| Strong, Ambrus | 3 | 2 | 2 | 1 | |
| Roggers, Josiah | 1 | 1 | 6 | | |
| Bettis, Thomas | 1 | | 1 | | |
| Chamberlain, Nath¹, Junr | 1 | 2 | 1 | | |
| Gillet, Lydia | 3 | 1 | 6 | | |
| Archer, Crispass | 1 | | 4 | | |
| Puffer Sarah | | | 3 | | |
| Strong, Zebulun | 4 | 1 | 4 | | |
| Coleman, Daniel | 1 | 2 | 3 | | |
| Watrus, William | 1 | | 1 | | |
| Welles, Israel W | 2 | 1 | 2 | | |
| Little, Ephraim | 1 | 3 | 3 | | |
| Wright, Mehitable | 1 | | 2 | | |
| Chamberlain, Nath¹ | 2 | | 2 | | |
| Chamberlain, Erastus | 1 | 2 | 3 | | |
| Wright, John | 2 | 3 | 5 | 1 | |
| Jacob (Negro) | | | | 4 | |
| Carter (Negro) | | | | 10 | |
| Bennett, Daniel | 2 | | 1 | | |
| Coleman, Ambrus | 1 | 2 | 2 | | |
| Dale, Sam¹ | 1 | | 1 | | |
| Mariner, Mary | | 1 | 3 | | |
| Kellog, Abner | 1 | 3 | 5 | | |
| Chamberlain, Job | 2 | | 1 | | |
| Welles, Ann | | | 1 | | |
| Welles, Martin | 2 | 4 | 3 | | |
| Isham, Daniel | 4 | | 2 | | |
| Otis, John | 3 | 1 | 4 | | |
| Otis, John I | 1 | 2 | 3 | | |
| Otis, James | 3 | | | | |
| Brown, Ephraim | 1 | 3 | 3 | | |
| Welch, Daniel, Junr | 1 | 1 | 1 | | |
| Welles, Amos | 5 | 3 | 2 | | |
| Morgan, Joshua | 1 | 3 | 4 | | |
| Welles, Ephraim | 2 | 1 | 4 | | |
| Scovil, Solomon | 2 | | 3 | | |
| McCarter, John, Junr | 1 | 1 | 4 | | |
| Welch, Daniel | 1 | | | | |
| Mason, Peter | 2 | 1 | 3 | | |
| Ways, John | 1 | 1 | 3 | | |
| Brown, Ezra | 1 | 1 | 7 | | |
| Prince (Negro) | | | | 3 | |
| Rosseter, Stephen | 3 | 1 | 4 | | |
| Randall, Arunah | 1 | 4 | 3 | | |
| Rothburn, Able | 1 | 3 | 5 | | |
| Holms, George | 1 | 3 | 6 | | |
| Holms, Sam¹ | 2 | 4 | 4 | | |
| Ransom, William | 1 | 1 | 3 | | |
| Chamberlain, Fredom | 2 | 1 | 2 | | 1 |
| Cremor, I | 1 | | 2 | | |
| Otis, Nath¹, 3d | 1 | 1 | 3 | | |
| Treadway, Asa | 2 | 1 | 5 | | |
| Beebe, Joab | 1 | | 2 | | |
| Jones, Mary | | | 1 | | |
| Lothrop, Ebenezer | 3 | 1 | 4 | | |
| Gates, Josiah | 4 | | 2 | | |
| Gates, Thomas | 1 | 3 | 3 | | |
| Gates, Able | 1 | 1 | 2 | | |
| Gates, Sam¹ | 2 | 1 | 5 | | |
| Rothburn, Moses | 1 | | 2 | | |
| Rothburn, Moses | 1 | 4 | 2 | | |
| Rothburn, Joshua | 1 | | 1 | | |
| Rothburn, Joshua, Junr | 1 | 3 | 5 | | |
| Harris, Joseph | 1 | 1 | 4 | | |
| Harris, Nath¹ | 3 | 3 | 7 | | |
| Homes, John | 1 | 3 | 4 | | |
| Buckley, Peter | 4 | 1 | 5 | | 1 |
| Chapman, Abner, Junr | 2 | 1 | 1 | 1 | |
| Newton, Asael | 1 | 1 | 4 | | |
| Way, Barsheba | 4 | | 2 | | |
| Buckley, Peter, Junr | 3 | | 5 | | |
| Randall, Asa | 3 | 2 | 4 | | |
| Randall, Silvester | 2 | 2 | 2 | | |
| Randall, Rufus | 1 | 2 | 5 | | |
| Brown (Negro) | | | | 3 | |
| Randall, Abraham | 1 | 3 | 2 | | |
| Tennant, John | 1 | 2 | 2 | | |
| Stark, Silas | 2 | | 4 | | |
| Welles, Oliver | 4 | 5 | 4 | | |
| Randall, Elias | 2 | 1 | 2 | | |
| Palmer, George | 2 | | 4 | | |
| Palmer, Humphrey | 1 | 1 | 3 | | |
| Palmer, Christopher, 2d | 1 | | 1 | | |
| Allen, Ichabod | 1 | | 1 | | |
| Randall, Joseph | 2 | | 3 | | |
| Vibber, Thomas | 3 | 2 | 3 | | |
| Wightman, Allen | 2 | | 3 | | |
| Palmer, Christopher | 3 | 1 | 5 | | |
| Bouge, Jeremiah | 1 | 1 | 5 | | |
| Randall, Amos | 1 | 2 | 3 | | |
| Palmer, Elias, Junr | 1 | 2 | 3 | | |
| Morgan, Jonathan, 2d | 1 | 1 | 4 | | |
| Palmer, Elias | 5 | 2 | 2 | | |
| Juba (Negro) | | | | 3 | |
| Cavarly, John, Junr | 1 | 1 | 1 | | |
| Beeba, Peter | 1 | | 3 | | |
| Cavarly, John | 1 | 1 | 2 | | |
| Cavarly, Phillup | 3 | 1 | 2 | | |
| Hall, Joshua | 1 | 4 | 5 | | |
| Otis, Nath¹ | 2 | 2 | 6 | | |
| Wright, Azariah | 5 | 1 | 7 | 1 | |
| Clark, Daniel | 3 | | 5 | | |
| Kellog, Samuel | 2 | | 2 | | 1 |
| Hill, Abner | 2 | 1 | 4 | | |
| Morgan, Jona | 1 | 3 | 2 | | |
| Edward (Negro) | | | | 6 | |
| Kellog, Daniel | 2 | 3 | 3 | | |
| Kellog, Amos | 2 | 3 | 2 | | |
| Chamberlain, Jarus | 1 | 1 | 1 | | |
| Rowley, Jesse | 1 | 2 | 4 | | |
| Boston (Negro) | | | | 5 | |
| Jefferson, Joseph | 2 | | 2 | | |
| Skinner, Thomas | 4 | 3 | 2 | 1 | 1 |
| Watrus, John | 4 | | 2 | 1 | |
| Buckley, Charles | 2 | 6 | 4 | | |
| Little, Justin | 2 | | 2 | | 1 |
| Mather, Gibeons | 2 | 1 | 1 | | |
| Brud, John | 2 | | 2 | 1 | |
| Buckley, Eliphelet | 1 | 2 | 7 | | |
| Pomroy, Noah | 2 | 1 | 4 | | |
| Foot, Abigail | 2 | | 2 | 1 | |
| Hall, William | 1 | 1 | 3 | | |
| Cone, Simon | 3 | 2 | 6 | 1 | 1 |
| Kitterfield, Elisabeth | | | 2 | | |
| Kilburn, David | 4 | 2 | 6 | | |
| Baker Asa | 2 | | 2 | | |

# FIRST CENSUS OF THE UNITED STATES.

## NEW LONDON COUNTY—Continued.

| NAME OF HEAD OF FAMILY. | Free white males of 16 years and upward, including heads of families. | Free white males under 16 years. | Free white females, including heads of families. | All other free persons. | Slaves. | NAME OF HEAD OF FAMILY. | Free white males of 16 years and upward, including heads of families. | Free white males under 16 years. | Free white females, including heads of families. | All other free persons. | Slaves. | NAME OF HEAD OF FAMILY. | Free white males of 16 years and upward, including heads of families. | Free white males under 16 years. | Free white females, including heads of families. | All other free persons. | Slaves. |
|---|---|---|---|---|---|---|---|---|---|---|---|---|---|---|---|---|---|
| Graves, Asa | 1 | 1 | 2 | | | Lothrop, Daniel | 1 | 1 | 3 | | | Higgins, David | 1 | 2 | 3 | | |
| Ceaser (Negro) | | | | 2 | | Loverige, Noah | 1 | | 2 | | | Marvin, Timothy | 4 | 4 | 4 | | |
| Wyles, David | 1 | 3 | 5 | | | Loverige, John | 1 | | 1 | | | Gould, James, Jun<sup>r</sup> | 3 | 1 | 5 | | |
| Kilburn, Elijah | 2 | 3 | 5 | | | Carter, John | 3 | | 2 | | | Mervin, Elisha | 2 | | 2 | | |
| Beadle, Benjamin | 2 | 6 | 5 | | | Carter, Clark | 2 | 3 | 1 | | | Mervin, Joseph | 1 | 2 | 2 | | |
| Keeney, Jonathan | 2 | 1 | 2 | | | Treadway, Alpheus | 1 | 1 | 2 | | | Anderson, Thomas | 3 | 1 | 4 | | |
| Beckwith, Jasper | 1 | 2 | 3 | | | Harris, Elias | 1 | | 3 | | | Harvey, Joseph | 2 | | 4 | | |
| Wolcott, Solomon | 2 | 2 | 4 | | | Sheridan, Mary | | | 3 | | | Prince (Negro) | | | | 5 | |
| Chapman, Gideon | 2 | 3 | 3 | | | Hambleton, James | 1 | | 3 | | | Lee, Abner | 1 | 1 | 3 | | |
| Chapman, Abner | 1 | | 1 | | | Hambleton, James, 2<sup>d</sup> | 1 | 2 | 2 | | | Lee, Dan | 1 | 1 | 2 | | |
| Bigalow, Asa | 3 | 3 | 3 | 3 | | Loverige, Abner | 1 | 3 | 4 | 1 | | Lord, Abner | 1 | | 2 | | |
| Graves, Peter, Jun<sup>r</sup> | 2 | | 4 | | | Loverige, William | 1 | 4 | 2 | | | Lord, Abner, Jun<sup>r</sup> | 1 | 1 | 5 | 1 | 1 |
| Ransom, Amy | 1 | 1 | 2 | | | Waterman, Zebulun | 2 | 3 | 3 | | | M<sup>c</sup>Cary, Sam<sup>l</sup>, Jun<sup>r</sup> | 2 | | 2 | | |
| Newton, Israel, Jun<sup>r</sup> | 1 | 1 | 4 | | | Treadway, David | 1 | 1 | 6 | | | M<sup>c</sup>Cary, Elisabeth | 3 | 3 | 4 | | |
| Newton, Israel, 3<sup>d</sup> | 1 | | 3 | | | Hambleton, Gurdon | 1 | | 2 | | | Otis, Robart | 2 | | 1 | | |
| Beeba, Robart | 2 | | 3 | | | Henry, Robart | 1 | 4 | 4 | | | Otis, Robart, Jun<sup>r</sup> | 1 | | 1 | | |
| Newton, Israel | 1 | 1 | 1 | | | Treadway, Abigail | 1 | 1 | 4 | | | M<sup>c</sup>Intosh, Rachel | | | 2 | | |
| Newton, Asa | 1 | 2 | 3 | 2 | | Williams, John | 4 | | 4 | | | Ely, Seth | 3 | 1 | 5 | | |
| Ransom, Asael | 1 | 2 | 6 | 1 | | Henry, John | 3 | 4 | 6 | 2 | | Mingo (Negro) | | | | 3 | |
| Newton, Able | 1 | 1 | 1 | | | Towser, Richard | 2 | 2 | 3 | | | Rothburn, Ebenezer | 2 | | 2 | | |
| Newton, John | 1 | | 1 | | | Towser, Julias | 2 | 1 | 5 | | | Ransom, Stephen | 1 | 2 | 3 | | |
| Ransom, Amasa | 1 | 3 | 4 | 1 | | Fassion (Negro) | | | | 3 | | Cumstock, Joab | 2 | | 4 | | |
| Morgan, Sam<sup>l</sup> | 2 | 4 | 4 | | | Beba, Timothy | 2 | 2 | 2 | | | Bouge, Richard | 1 | | 1 | | |
| Jones, Amos | 3 | 1 | 4 | | | Duglass, John | 1 | 2 | | | | Cumstock, Abner | 2 | 1 | 4 | | |
| Jones, Amos, 3<sup>d</sup> | 1 | | 2 | | | Duglass, Robart | 1 | | | | | Cumstock, Abner, 2<sup>d</sup> | 1 | 4 | 1 | | |
| Rothburn, Job | 1 | 5 | 4 | | | Seabury, John | 2 | | 3 | 1 | | Cumstock, Asa | 3 | 1 | 5 | | |
| Purple, David | 1 | 1 | 2 | | | Mumford, John | 5 | 3 | 7 | 1 | 3 | Cumstock, Easter | 2 | 1 | 3 | | |
| Newton, James | 1 | 2 | 1 | | | Beba, Clark | 3 | 1 | 3 | | | Cumstock, Hezekiah | 1 | 1 | 2 | | |
| Bigalow, Bond | 1 | 3 | 3 | | | Pomp (Negro) | | | | 7 | | Matson, William | 2 | 2 | 3 | | 2 |
| Chapman, Elisha | 2 | 1 | 2 | | | Miner, Jonathan | 1 | 1 | | | | Peck, Daniel | 4 | | 4 | | |
| Chapman, Ichabod, Jun<sup>r</sup> | 2 | 2 | 4 | | | Ransom, Israel | 1 | 3 | 1 | | | Church, Josiah | 1 | | 5 | | |
| Chapman, Gidion, Jun<sup>r</sup> | 1 | 2 | 3 | | | Ransom, James | 1 | 2 | 2 | | | Church, John | 1 | | 2 | | |
| Loverige, Edward | 3 | 1 | 5 | | | Tiffany, Eben<sup>r</sup>, Jun<sup>r</sup> | 1 | 2 | 3 | | | Hains, Charles | 3 | | 2 | | |
| Ransom, Bliss | 4 | 4 | 4 | | | Tiffany, Eben<sup>r</sup> | 5 | 1 | 5 | | | Seldon, Elijah | 1 | 3 | 2 | | |
| Lester, Jonathan | 1 | | 1 | | | Baker, Matthias W | 1 | 1 | 1 | | | Warner, Chapman | 1 | 1 | 4 | | |
| Kilborn, Elisabeth | | | 2 | | | Chapman, Abraham | 1 | 2 | 3 | | | Brooks, Sam<sup>l</sup> | 1 | 2 | 2 | | |
| Eads, Eleazer | 1 | | 2 | | | Story, Sam<sup>l</sup> | 1 | 1 | 4 | | | Fox, Joshua | 1 | 1 | 3 | | |
| Graves, Arvil | 1 | | 1 | | | Wood, David | 1 | | 2 | | | Alwood, Mariam | | | 3 | | |
| Chapman, Noah | 1 | 1 | 4 | | | Wood, David, Jun<sup>r</sup> | 1 | | 1 | | | Warner, Jonathan | 2 | | 2 | | 1 |
| Jones, Amos, Jun<sup>r</sup> | 2 | 4 | 4 | | | Perkins, Jon<sup>a</sup> | 3 | | 6 | | | Warner, Selden | 1 | 2 | 1 | | |
| Tiffany, Philomon | 1 | | 4 | | | Perkins, Joshua | 2 | 3 | 2 | | | Selden, Elisabeth | 1 | | 1 | | |
| Loverige, David | 1 | | 2 | 2 | | Eames, Lucy | | | 2 | | | Selden, Dudley | 1 | | | | |
| Sipro (Negro) | | | | 6 | | Beckwith, Ephraim | 1 | 1 | 4 | | | Selden, Ely | 2 | | 5 | | 1 |
| Craw, Jesse | | | | | | Huntley, Hoel | 1 | 2 | 2 | | | Lorther, Levi | 1 | 2 | 2 | | |
| Church, Sam<sup>l</sup> | 2 | | | | | Mackintosh, Lothlin | 1 | 2 | 2 | | | Selden, Samuel | 1 | 2 | 2 | | 2 |
| Warner, Elihu | 1 | 3 | 5 | | | Huntley, Benaijah | 1 | | 1 | | | Church, Ezra | 1 | 1 | 1 | | |
| Loomis, Samuel | 4 | 1 | 3 | | | Bouge, James | 3 | 3 | 3 | | | Saunders, Sam<sup>l</sup> | 1 | 4 | 3 | | |
| Williams, Enos | 1 | 2 | 3 | | | Huntley, Nehemiah | 1 | | 1 | | | Saunders, John | 2 | | 2 | | |
| Gustin, Walter | 1 | 2 | 3 | | | Clark, Dan<sup>l</sup> | 2 | 4 | 6 | | | Saunders, John, Jun<sup>r</sup> | 1 | 2 | 3 | | |
| Treadway, John | 1 | 1 | 7 | | | Tillotson, Simeon | 1 | | 2 | | | Greene, John | 1 | | 3 | | |
| Tarball, William | 2 | 2 | 5 | | | Wood, Margarett | | 2 | 5 | | | Miller, William | 1 | 1 | 1 | | |
| Denison, Gilbert | 1 | 1 | 2 | 2 | | Bouge, James, Jun<sup>r</sup> | 1 | | 1 | | | Saunders, Simeon | 1 | | 3 | | |
| Worthington, Elijah | 5 | 1 | 2 | | | Beckwith, Daniel | 1 | 3 | 1 | | | Pratt, David B | 1 | 3 | 5 | | |
| Way, John | 1 | 1 | 1 | | | Daniel (Negro) | | | | 4 | | Banning, John | 1 | | 1 | | |
| Worthington, William | 1 | 2 | 5 | 1 | | Lee, Benjamin | 1 | 2 | 4 | | | Brockway, Ezra | 1 | | | | |
| Dean, Christopher | 1 | 3 | 3 | 1 | | Eames, John | 1 | 2 | 2 | | | Phelps, Mary | | 1 | 3 | 1 | |
| Worthington, Joel | 2 | 3 | 3 | | 1 | Armstead, Joseph | 1 | 5 | 2 | | | Niles, Ambrus, 2<sup>d</sup> | 1 | | 2 | | |
| Miller, Thomas | 3 | 2 | 3 | | | Park, Lee | 2 | | 2 | | | Niles, Ambrus | 1 | 1 | 2 | | |
| Chapman, William | 2 | 1 | 4 | | | Lee, Seth | 1 | 2 | 5 | | | Mentor, John | 1 | | | | |
| Kilburn, Hezekiah | 2 | | 1 | | | Pratt, Edward | 1 | 3 | 2 | | | Wood, John | 1 | 1 | 4 | | |
| Ferman, John | 1 | 2 | 6 | | | Leach, Manassa | 2 | 3 | 6 | | | Beba, Abner | 1 | 3 | 4 | | |
| Marshall, Jeremiah | 3 | 3 | 5 | | | Mather, Frederick | 1 | 3 | 4 | | | Butler, William | 1 | | 2 | | |
| Bergen, Mercy | | | | 2 | 2 | Mather, Eleazer, Jun<sup>r</sup> | 1 | 5 | 2 | | | Cumstock, Jesse | 2 | 1 | | | |
| Treadway, Charles | 1 | | 2 | | | Tillotson, Mary | 1 | | 1 | | | Phelps, Jonathan | 1 | 3 | 1 | | |
| Treadway, Elijah | 1 | 2 | 4 | | | Mather, Eleazer | 1 | 1 | 1 | | | Smith, Phineas | 1 | 1 | 1 | | |
| Chapman, Jonathan | 1 | 3 | 4 | | | Emerson, Stephen | 1 | | 2 | | | Cumstock, Noah | 1 | 4 | 4 | | |
| Ferman, David | 1 | | 1 | | | Minor, Eben<sup>r</sup> | | 2 | 2 | | | Beba, David | 2 | | 3 | | |
| Welles, Joshua | 1 | | | | | Rise, Ruel | 3 | 1 | 3 | | | Emerson, Abraham | 1 | 2 | 3 | | |
| Daniels, Asa | 3 | 3 | 4 | | | Beba, Azariah | 1 | 3 | 2 | | | Emerson, Abraham, 2<sup>d</sup> | 1 | 2 | 3 | | |
| Domine (Negro) | | | | 3 | | Cuff (Negro) | | | | 4 | | Harron, John | 1 | 2 | 4 | | |
| Dodge, Benjamin | 1 | 3 | 2 | | | Phillups, Michael | 1 | 1 | 4 | | | Reynolds, John | 1 | 2 | 3 | | |
| Otis, Nath<sup>l</sup>, Jun<sup>r</sup> | 1 | 1 | 2 | | | Way, Peter | 1 | 1 | 4 | | | Phelps, Samuel | 1 | 3 | 2 | | |
| Rothburn, Jon<sup>a</sup> | 1 | | 2 | | | Mitchel, George | 1 | 2 | 1 | | | Peter (Negro) | | | | 5 | |
| Waters, Sam<sup>l</sup> | 2 | 1 | 2 | | | Colt, Samuel | 2 | 5 | 2 | | | Mitchel, John | 2 | 1 | 5 | | |
| Beckwith, Caleb | 1 | 1 | 1 | | | Spencer, Ichabod | 2 | 4 | 3 | | | Brockway, Ebenezer | 5 | 1 | 4 | | |
| Beba, Easter | | | 4 | | | Wright (Negro) | | | | 5 | | Brockway, Zebulun | 1 | 1 | 1 | | |
| Warner, Nathan | 1 | | 1 | | | Pumham (Negro) | | | | 4 | | Harrison, Elihu | 2 | 3 | 2 | | |
| Warner, Oliver | 1 | 3 | 2 | | | Sam<sup>l</sup> (Negro) | | | | 6 | | Curwin, Theophilus | 1 | | | | |
| Bacon, Pierpoint | 2 | | 1 | 1 | 6 | Sipro (Negro) | | | | 5 | | Brockway, Gamaliel | 4 | 1 | 4 | | |
| Gardiner, William | 2 | 3 | 3 | | | Beba, Lemuel | 1 | | 5 | | | Brockway, William | 2 | | 3 | | |
| Loomis, Israel | 3 | 2 | 4 | 1 | | Roggers, Gedion | 1 | 1 | 1 | | | Brockway, Richard | 1 | | 3 | | |
| Dodge, Jonathan, Jun<sup>r</sup> | 1 | 2 | 7 | | | Griffin, Joshua | 1 | 1 | 2 | | | Brockway, Richard, 2<sup>d</sup> | 1 | | 1 | | |
| Dodge, Jonathan | 1 | | 1 | | | Griffin, Nathan | 1 | | 2 | | | Brockway, Clark | 1 | | 1 | | |
| Dodge, Daniel | 1 | 1 | 3 | | | Griffin, Jasper | 2 | 1 | 3 | | | Brockway, Eliphelet | 2 | 2 | 5 | | |
| Morgan, Abigail | 1 | 2 | 4 | | | Griffin, John | 1 | 2 | 2 | | | Brockway, Ezra | 1 | | 1 | | |
| Buel, Jacob | 3 | | 2 | | | Griffin, Sarah | 3 | 2 | 4 | | | Banning, Ebenezer | 3 | 2 | 4 | | |
| Loomis, John | 4 | 4 | 2 | | | Lord, John | 6 | 2 | 6 | | 4 | Ely, Abner | 4 | | 3 | | |
| Morgan, Benjamin | 1 | | 3 | | | Tinker, Joshua | 2 | 2 | 4 | | | Ely, Elijah | 4 | | | | |
| Graves, Peter | 1 | 1 | 1 | | | Huntley, Lydia | | | 4 | | | Wade, Hannah | | | 3 | | |
| Morgan, William | 1 | 1 | 2 | | | Colt, Harris | 2 | | 4 | 1 | | Miller, Elisha | 1 | 1 | 2 | | |
| Gardiner, Abraham | 1 | | 2 | | | Phelps, Thadeus | 1 | 4 | 6 | | | Brockway, Abner | 1 | 5 | 2 | | |
| Ransom, James | 4 | | 4 | 1 | | Gould, James | 2 | | 4 | | | Laplass, Jonathan | 1 | | 2 | | |
| Peck, Elias | 2 | 2 | 5 | | | Gould, John | 1 | 1 | 4 | | | Brockway, John | 2 | 1 | 2 | | |
| Treadway, James | 1 | | 2 | | | Gould, Walter | 1 | | 4 | | | Brockway, Lowis | 1 | | 2 | | |
| Jones, Jabez | 3 | 2 | 3 | | | Colt, Desire | 2 | 1 | 3 | | 2 | Smith, Nath<sup>l</sup> | 1 | 1 | 4 | | |
| Jones, Jabez, Jun<sup>r</sup> | 1 | 2 | 2 | | | Bingham, Elijah | 3 | 1 | 1 | | | Ransom, Ruben | 3 | 2 | 2 | | |
| Hambleton, Abial | 1 | 1 | 1 | | | Lee, Stephen | 1 | 1 | 3 | | | Rothburn, Sam<sup>l</sup> | 1 | | 2 | | |

# HEADS OF FAMILIES—CONNECTICUT.

## NEW LONDON COUNTY—Continued.

| NAME OF HEAD OF FAMILY. | Free white males of 16 years and upward, including heads of families. | Free white males under 16 years. | Free white females, including heads of families. | All other free persons. | Slaves. |
|---|---|---|---|---|---|
| Perkins, John | 3 | 2 | 6 | | |
| Sawyer, Ephraim | 1 | 2 | 4 | | |
| Harrison, Hipsebah | | 1 | 2 | | |
| Ely, James | 3 | 2 | 3 | | |
| Tiffany, Nathan | 2 | 1 | 3 | | |
| Lord, Sam¹ | 2 | 1 | 4 | | |
| Marvin, Elisha, 2d | 3 | 2 | 8 | | |
| Miller, Volentine | 2 | 2 | 4 | | |
| Wade, John | 1 | 1 | 4 | | |
| Wade, Abraham | 1 | 1 | 3 | | |
| Boon, Henry | 2 | | 5 | | |
| Harvey, Joshua | 1 | | 1 | | |
| Brockway, Benjamin | 1 | 4 | 2 | | |
| Butler, John | 1 | | 5 | | |
| Sterling, William | 3 | 5 | 3 | | |
| Sill, William | 1 | | 3 | | |
| Hide, Elisabeth | | 1 | 1 | | |
| Mark, Ezra | 2 | 1 | 8 | | |
| Reaves, Israel | 1 | | 5 | | |
| Howard, David | 1 | 1 | 5 | | |
| Ely, Amy | 2 | 1 | 4 | | |
| Ely, Gurden | 1 | 1 | 2 | | |
| Tucker, Phillup | 1 | 2 | 3 | | |
| Ely, Ann | | 2 | 4 | | |
| Huntley, Mary | | | 2 | | |
| Sterling, Jacob | 1 | | 5 | | |
| Sill, Giles | 2 | 4 | 7 | | |
| Sterling, Samuel | 4 | 1 | 4 | | |
| Sterling, John | 2 | 2 | 3 | | |
| Brown, Henry | 3 | 3 | 5 | | |
| Sterling, Betsy | | | 2 | | |
| Huntley, Elihu | 1 | 2 | 5 | | |
| Hays, Abigail | 1 | | 3 | | |
| Ely, Denison | 1 | | 1 | | |
| Stark, Samuel | 1 | 1 | 3 | | |
| Wade, George | 2 | | 2 | | |
| Tiffany, Mary | | | 2 | | |
| Tiffany, Mary, Junr | | 2 | 3 | | |
| Bump, John | 2 | 4 | 2 | | |
| Brooks, Silas | 1 | 1 | 3 | | |
| Ely, Elihu | 2 | 4 | 5 | | |
| Selden, Ezra | 3 | 1 | 5 | | |
| Perkins, William | 3 | 3 | 3 | | |
| Ely, Ezra | 2 | | 1 | | |
| Miner, Wm | 1 | 1 | 4 | | |
| Ely, Adriel | 2 | 2 | 5 | | |
| Ceaser (Negro) | | | | 7 | |
| Ely, Welles | 3 | | 2 | | |
| Ely, Daniel | 1 | | 5 | | |
| Ely, Christopher | 3 | 1 | 1 | | |
| Ely, Marsh | 1 | 1 | 6 | | |
| Ely, Cullick | 3 | 1 | 3 | | |
| Ely, David | 1 | 1 | 2 | 1 | |
| Ely, Cullick, Junr | 1 | | 1 | | |
| Mack, Josiah | 3 | 3 | 5 | | |
| Ely, Josiah | 4 | 1 | 4 | | |
| Beckwith, George | 1 | | 2 | | |
| Beckwith, George, Junr | 1 | 2 | 4 | | |
| Perkins, Samuel | 1 | 1 | 2 | 1 | |
| Perkins, Abraham | 1 | 2 | 3 | | |
| Lord, Amos | 1 | | 2 | | |
| Peck, Sarah | 1 | | 5 | | |
| Munsill, John | 2 | | 3 | | |
| Munsill, John | 1 | | 3 | | |
| Munsill, Thomas | 1 | 2 | 1 | | |
| Ely, Gabriel | 1 | 1 | 5 | | |
| Mack, Samuel, Junr | 1 | 1 | 2 | | |
| Miller, Thomson | 1 | 1 | 1 | | |
| Ransom, David | 1 | 3 | 2 | | |
| Mather, Samuel | 2 | 1 | 4 | 1 | |
| Lord, Daniel | 4 | | 4 | 1 | |
| Pierson, Peter | 1 | 2 | 3 | | |
| Lord, Marvin | 1 | 2 | 4 | | |
| Lord, Benjamin | 6 | 1 | 3 | | |
| Lord, Ruben | 2 | 2 | 6 | | |
| Lord, Sarah | 1 | 2 | 6 | | |
| Lord, Josiah | 1 | 2 | 1 | | |
| Ransom, Edward | 1 | 2 | 5 | | |
| Giles, John | 1 | 2 | 2 | | |
| Colt, Benjamin | 1 | 1 | 2 | | |
| Mather, Nath¹ | 2 | 1 | 2 | | |
| Tinker, Stephen | 1 | 2 | 1 | | |
| Lord, Enoch | 4 | | 3 | 1 | 5 |
| Lord, Richard | 3 | | 2 | | |
| Glover, Jeremiah | 1 | 1 | 4 | | |
| Burnham, Joseph | 1 | | 3 | | |
| Burnham, James | 1 | 1 | 3 | | |
| Burnham, Josiah | 1 | | 3 | | |
| Denison, Samuel | 1 | 3 | 5 | | |
| Clark, Roswell | 3 | 1 | 6 | | |
| Smith, Latham | 1 | 4 | 3 | | |
| Dowsack, Gospur | 3 | 3 | 2 | | |
| Higgins, Cristian | 2 | | 4 | | |
| Higgins, Silvanus | 2 | | 4 | | |
| Burnham, Josiah | 1 | | 3 | | |
| Roggers, Ebenezer | 1 | | 3 | | |
| Roggers, Able | 1 | 1 | 3 | | |
| Roggers, Richard | 1 | 3 | 1 | | |
| Miner, Daniel | 3 | 1 | 5 | | |
| Peck, Samuel | 1 | 1 | 6 | | |
| Peck, Darius | 2 | 2 | 3 | | |
| Burt, Joseph | 2 | 3 | 4 | | |
| Beckett, Josiah | 2 | 1 | 2 | | |
| Roggers, Pheba | | 2 | 2 | | |
| Roland, Benjamin | 1 | 2 | 2 | | |
| Hide, Elisabeth | 2 | 1 | 4 | | |
| Lord, Joseph | 1 | 1 | 5 | | |
| Bennett, John | 1 | | 1 | | |
| Robins, Silas | 1 | 2 | 3 | | |
| Huntley, Zephaniah | 1 | | 1 | | |
| Sill, Silas | 1 | 2 | 3 | | |
| Sill, David F | 3 | 1 | 4 | | |
| Matson, Israel | 2 | | 3 | | |
| Hall, Able | 2 | 4 | 7 | | |
| Jerom, Elisabeth | | | 1 | | |
| Brockway, Elisha | 1 | 3 | 2 | | |
| Woolf, Samuel | 1 | 2 | 3 | | |
| Sill, Samuel | 1 | | 4 | | |
| Wade, Elihu | 4 | 1 | 5 | | |
| Wade, Elisha | 2 | | 4 | | |
| Read, Joseph | 1 | | 4 | | |
| Sill, John | 2 | | 3 | 1 | |
| Beckwith, Watrus | 3 | 1 | 2 | | |
| Peck, John | 2 | 3 | 5 | | |
| Noyce, Calvin | 1 | 1 | 3 | | |
| Noyce, Joseph | 1 | 2 | 1 | 2 | |
| Noyce, William | 2 | | 1 | 5 | |
| Noyce, William, Junr | 1 | | 3 | 1 | |
| Clark, Silvanus | 1 | 3 | 2 | | |
| Huntley, Asher | 1 | | 2 | | |
| Wicks, Joseph | 1 | | 3 | | |
| Miller, Weltha | | | 2 | | |
| Miller, Silas | 1 | 2 | 6 | | |
| Hill, Samuel | 3 | | 3 | | |
| Marvin, Joseph | 2 | 1 | 2 | | |
| Griswould, Mathew | 4 | 2 | 3 | | 1 |
| Griswould, Mathew, 2d | 3 | | 1 | | |
| Griswould, John | 3 | 2 | 6 | | |
| Noyce, John | 1 | | 1 | | |
| Lay, Lee | 1 | 4 | 4 | 1 | |
| Denison, Easter | | 3 | 4 | | |
| Champion, Ezra | 1 | 2 | 3 | | |
| Watrus, Easter | 1 | | 1 | | |
| Woolf, William D | 2 | 1 | 4 | | |
| York (Negro) | | | | 2 | |
| Eldrige, Jonathan | 2 | 5 | 6 | | |
| Huntley, Phineas | 2 | 2 | 4 | | |
| Smith, Richard, 2d | 2 | 4 | 4 | | |
| Gardiner, Thomas | 1 | | 4 | | |
| Beckwith, Phineas | 1 | | 4 | | |
| Miller, Ezra | 1 | 1 | 5 | | |
| Smith, Amos | 1 | 2 | 1 | | |
| Wait, Loen | 1 | 3 | 6 | | |
| Griffen, Sam¹ | 3 | | 3 | | |
| Chadwick, Ruben | 2 | 2 | 5 | | |
| Comb, Henry | 1 | 2 | 2 | | |
| Chadwick, Guy | 2 | | 3 | | |
| Chadwick, Hannah | 1 | | 4 | | |
| Wait, Richard | 2 | | 1 | | |
| Wait, Remick | 1 | 2 | 2 | | |
| Wait, John | 2 | 2 | 4 | | |
| Miller, Joseph | 1 | | 1 | | |
| Havens, John | 1 | | 3 | | |
| Chadwick, Richard | 1 | | 3 | | |
| Chadwick, George | 1 | | 6 | | |
| Nevee, Peter | 1 | 3 | 2 | | |
| DeWoolf, Stephen | 1 | 2 | 2 | | |
| Wait, Richard, Junr | 3 | 2 | 5 | | |
| Lay, Robart | 3 | | 2 | | |
| Ingraham, Parnall | | | 1 | | |
| Wait, Joseph | 2 | | 1 | | |
| Anderson, John | 1 | | 1 | | |
| Anderson, John, 2d | 1 | 2 | 3 | | |
| Clark, John | 2 | | 1 | | |
| Beckwith, Sam¹ | 1 | 1 | 3 | | |
| Walker, Joseph | 1 | 2 | 1 | | |
| Smith, Silvanus | 2 | 1 | 5 | | |
| Tinker, Amos | 1 | | 3 | | |
| Tinker, Joseph | 2 | 3 | 3 | | |
| Smith, Stephen | 1 | | 4 | | |
| Watrus, Gideon | 1 | 3 | 2 | | |
| Miner, Jesse | 1 | 2 | 2 | | |
| Gilbert, John | 1 | | 2 | | |
| Brockway, Elias | 1 | 2 | 2 | | |
| Champion, Elisabeth | | | 1 | | |
| Chadwick, Ezra | 1 | | 3 | | |
| Champion, Stephen | 1 | 1 | 3 | | |
| Champion, Ruben | 1 | 1 | 4 | | |
| Baker, John | 1 | 2 | 3 | | |
| Chadwick, Stephen | 1 | 2 | 2 | | |
| Clark, Lemuel | 2 | 1 | 4 | | |
| Scovil, Martin | 1 | | 1 | | |
| Roland, Nath¹ | 1 | | 4 | | |
| Roland, Ezra | 1 | | 2 | | |
| Hudson, Stephen | 2 | | 4 | | |
| Loveman, Susanna | | | 1 | | |
| Auger, Roger G | 1 | 2 | 4 | | |
| Champion, Elisha | 1 | | 8 | | |
| Champion, Lynds | 1 | 2 | 1 | | |
| Champion, Roswell | 1 | 2 | 2 | | |
| Havens, Edward | 1 | 2 | 4 | | |
| Chadwick, Allen | 1 | 3 | 3 | | |
| Roland, Asael | 1 | 1 | 2 | | |
| Roland, Levi | 3 | 3 | 2 | | |
| Salem (Negro) | | | | 2 | |
| Champlin, Nathan | 3 | | 3 | | |
| Champion, Henry | 2 | | 1 | | |
| Peck, Joseph | 1 | 2 | 1 | | |
| Auger, Lucy | | | 1 | | |
| Suaney, John | 2 | 2 | 4 | | |
| Miner, Elias | 2 | 3 | 2 | | |
| Ray, Daniel | 1 | | 3 | | |
| Robins, Nathan | 2 | | 1 | | |
| Peck, Lebeus | 1 | 1 | 3 | | |
| Marvin, Mathew | 2 | 2 | 6 | | |
| Champlin, William | 1 | 1 | 3 | | |
| Minor, Seth | 1 | 2 | 4 | | |
| Brown, Jeremiah | 1 | | 2 | | |
| Lay, Joseph | 2 | | 1 | | |
| Daniels, Daniel, 2d | 1 | 3 | 1 | | |
| Welch, John | 1 | | 4 | | |
| Johnson, Stephen | 1 | | 6 | | 1 |
| Mather, Lucinda | | 2 | 2 | | |
| Lay, John, 3d | 1 | 1 | 1 | | |
| Watrus, Gershom | 2 | 2 | 3 | | |
| Watrus, Phineas | 3 | | 1 | | |
| Daniels, Daniel | 1 | | 2 | | |
| Champlin, Silas | 1 | 2 | 1 | | |
| Robins, Ezra | 2 | 1 | 2 | | |
| Robins, Elisha | 2 | | 4 | | |
| Lay, Elisha | 3 | 2 | 3 | | 1 |
| Lay, William | 4 | | 5 | | 1 |
| Ingraham, Samuel | 2 | | 1 | | |
| Lee, Ezra | 1 | | 4 | | |
| Greenfield, James | 1 | 2 | 3 | | |
| Hobart, Sam¹ | 1 | 3 | 4 | | |
| Smith, William | 2 | 1 | 3 | | |
| Greenfield, Archibauld S | 1 | | 2 | | |
| Lay, John | 2 | 2 | 4 | | |
| Lay, John, 2d | 2 | 1 | 3 | | |
| Johnson, Abigail | 1 | | 4 | | |
| Marvin, Benjamin | 2 | 1 | 4 | | |
| Porter, Edward | 1 | | 2 | | |
| Hall, Samuel | 1 | | 1 | | |
| Parsons, Marshfield | 1 | | 4 | | 4 |
| McCurdy, Ann | 2 | 1 | 3 | | |
| Mather, Sam¹, Junr | 3 | 3 | 9 | 1 | 4 |
| Kent, Mehitable | 1 | | 2 | | |
| King, Paul | 1 | | 1 | | |
| Mather, Sarah | | | 2 | | |
| Tinker, Nathan | 2 | 2 | 4 | | |
| Mather, Joseph | 1 | | 2 | | |
| Persons, John | 1 | | 5 | | |
| Mather, Silvester | 2 | | 2 | | |
| Smith, Joseph | 2 | 1 | 4 | | |
| Tinker, Amos, Junr | 1 | | 3 | | |
| Higgins, Benjamin | 1 | 1 | 4 | | |
| Smith, Joseph, 4th | 1 | 2 | 5 | 1 | |
| Hollester, Lucretia | 1 | | 5 | | |
| Morgan, Elijah | 3 | | 3 | | |
| Smith, Ichabod | 2 | | 2 | | |
| Mather, Jehalada | 3 | 1 | 5 | | |
| Beckwith, Roswell | 1 | 2 | 2 | | |
| Minor, Martin | 2 | | 4 | | |
| Marvin, Zachariah | 2 | 2 | 3 | | |
| More, Able | 1 | 1 | 3 | | |
| Tinker, Peter | 1 | 1 | 2 | | |
| Wilkerson, Malachi | 1 | | 3 | | |
| Mather, Timothy | 1 | 2 | 4 | | |
| Mather, Timothy, 2d | 3 | 2 | 5 | | |
| Kellog, Martin | 3 | 2 | 5 | | |
| Marvin, Moses | 1 | 1 | 4 | | |
| Read, George | 2 | | 4 | | |
| Lamphear, Ruth | 1 | | 3 | | |
| Peck, Mathew | 1 | 1 | 3 | | |
| Lay, Peter | 1 | | 3 | | |
| Peck, Jasper | 3 | 1 | 5 | | |
| Marvin, Zachariah, 2d | 2 | 3 | 1 | | |
| Tucker, Stephen | 3 | 1 | 3 | | |
| Wood, David | 2 | | 8 | | |
| Clark, Gurdon | 2 | 1 | 6 | | |
| Rogers, Able | 1 | | 1 | | |
| Marvin, Sam¹ | 2 | 3 | 4 | | |
| Bartholick, Martin | 2 | | 1 | | |
| Bartholick, Thomas | 2 | | 2 | | |
| Fitch, Elijah | 1 | | 1 | | |
| Peck, Reynold | 3 | 2 | 3 | | |
| Wilson, George | 1 | 2 | 1 | | |
| Peck, Martha | | | 5 | | |
| Peck, Hannah | | 1 | 4 | | |
| Peck, Latt | 1 | | 2 | | |

# FIRST CENSUS OF THE UNITED STATES.

## NEW LONDON COUNTY—Continued.

| Name of head of family. | Free white males of 16 years and upward, including heads of families. | Free white males under 16 years. | Free white females, including heads of families. | All other free persons. | Slaves. |
|---|---|---|---|---|---|
| Royce, Elisha | 2 | 2 | 4 | | |
| Chadwick, James | 1 | 1 | 2 | | |
| Bramble, John | 1 | 1 | 4 | | |
| Wade, Martin | 2 | 1 | 5 | | |
| Gillet, Joseph | 1 | 3 | 4 | | |
| Tucker, Job | 1 | 1 | 2 | | |
| Lester, Jeremiah | 1 | 2 | 2 | | |
| Dorr, George | 1 | 1 | 5 | | |
| Smith, Richard | 2 | | 3 | | |
| Lee, Thomas | 2 | 2 | 4 | | |
| Griswould, Andrus | 1 | 2 | 4 | | |
| Lee, Elisha | 5 | 2 | 2 | | 1 |
| Lee, Elisha, Junr | 1 | 1 | 4 | | |
| Griswould, George | 2 | 2 | 5 | | |
| Beckwith, Martin | 1 | | 3 | | 1 |
| Keeney, Samuel | 2 | 1 | 3 | | |
| Lester, Noah | 1 | 3 | 6 | | |
| Lester, Joshua | 1 | | 2 | | |
| Lee, John M | 2 | | 1 | | |
| Gould, Francis | 2 | | | | |
| Read, Enoch | 1 | 2 | 5 | | |
| Mather, John | 1 | | 1 | | |
| Mather, John, 2d | 2 | 2 | 3 | | |
| Hall, Ezra | 3 | 3 | 5 | | |
| Gillet, Daniel | 1 | 2 | 1 | | |
| Gillet, Ezra | 1 | 1 | 2 | | |
| Gillet, Reynold | 1 | 1 | 2 | | |
| Sill, Samuel | 1 | | 2 | | |
| Sill, Isaac | 1 | 2 | 5 | | |
| Huntley, Martin | 1 | 4 | 1 | | |
| Huntley, Jasper | 1 | 1 | 2 | | |
| Roggers, Daniel | 1 | 1 | 1 | | |
| Huntley, Amos | 1 | 1 | 3 | | |
| Huntley, Rice | 1 | | 2 | | |
| Huntley, Marvin | 1 | | 2 | | |
| Munsill, Timothy | 1 | 3 | 2 | | |
| Huntley, Ruben | 1 | 3 | 2 | | |
| Huntley, James | 3 | 3 | 2 | | |
| Pierson, Eli | 1 | 3 | 2 | | |
| Roggers, Saml | 3 | 1 | 2 | | |
| Roggers, Isaiah | 2 | 2 | 2 | | |
| Minor, Jesse | 3 | 3 | 4 | | |
| Peck, Dan | 1 | 2 | 1 | | |
| Belot, John | 1 | 2 | 1 | | |
| Beckwith, Lebeus | 1 | | 2 | | |
| Mack, William | 1 | 1 | 3 | | |
| Mack, Ebenezer | 1 | 1 | 2 | | |
| Smith, Ithamer | 2 | | 3 | | |
| Miner, Ebenr | 1 | | 1 | | |
| Miner, Whitfield | 1 | 1 | 1 | | |
| Brockway, Edward | 3 | | 5 | | |
| Bouge, Elisha | 1 | | 2 | | |
| Bouge, John | 1 | | 3 | | |
| Gee, William | 1 | | 2 | | |
| Gee, Zophar | 1 | 1 | 1 | | |
| Gee, William, Junr | 1 | | 2 | | |
| Peck, Silas | 1 | | 1 | | |
| Lewis, James | 2 | 1 | 3 | | |
| Huntley, William | 1 | | 2 | | |
| Beckwith, Buel | 1 | 4 | 3 | | |
| Smith, Samuel | 4 | | 2 | | |
| Tubs, John M | 2 | | 2 | | |
| Howard, David | 1 | | 2 | | |
| Read, Robart | 1 | 1 | 2 | | |
| Huntley, Reynold | 3 | 3 | 3 | | |
| Mack, Zophar | 2 | 1 | 3 | | |
| Roggers, Jonathan | 1 | 2 | 2 | | |
| Tubs, Ahimus | 1 | 3 | 4 | | |
| Beckwith, Ezra | 1 | 1 | 4 | | |
| Beckwith, Nathan | 1 | 1 | 4 | | |
| Smith, Russell | 2 | | 2 | | |
| Peck, David | 5 | | 3 | | |
| Smith, Nehemiah | 3 | 1 | 1 | | |
| Lewis, John | 2 | 1 | 3 | | |
| Belshaw, Joseph | 1 | | 2 | | |
| Maxson, Tony | 1 | 3 | 1 | | |
| Lewis, George | 4 | 1 | 4 | | |
| Smith, Joseph | 1 | | 2 | | |
| Lee, Jason | 2 | 2 | 5 | | |
| Beckwith, Jedediah | 1 | | 1 | | |
| Beba, Jedediah | 1 | | 1 | | |
| Ryon, James | 3 | 1 | 2 | | |
| Smith, David | 1 | | 2 | | |
| Smith, Edward | 1 | | 1 | | |
| Kettles, Benjamin | 1 | | 2 | | |
| Smith, Seth | 2 | 3 | 3 | | |
| Beckwith, Stephen | 2 | | 2 | | |
| Cumstock, Saml | 2 | 3 | 4 | | |
| Tubs, Peter | 1 | 2 | 2 | | |
| Smith, Elisha | 2 | 1 | 2 | | |
| Johnson, John | 3 | 1 | 2 | | |
| Johnson, Reynold | 1 | 1 | 2 | | |
| Winslow, Job | 3 | 2 | 5 | | |
| Roggers, Rowland | 1 | | 2 | | |
| Brown, David | 3 | 1 | 2 | | |
| Lewis, Daniel | 1 | 1 | 1 | | |
| Smith, Zadock | 1 | 1 | 5 | | |
| Miller, George | 3 | 6 | 3 | | |
| Bush, Amaziah | 2 | 1 | 1 | | |
| George (Negro) | | | | 7 | |
| Powers, Joshua | 1 | 3 | 4 | | |
| Gorton, Benjamin | 2 | 4 | 4 | | |
| Manwaring, Josiah | 2 | | 6 | | |
| Manwaring, Latham | 1 | | 1 | | |
| Manwaring, Adam | 1 | 1 | 1 | | |
| Manwaring, Nathl | 1 | 2 | 4 | | |
| Denison, William | 2 | | 2 | | |
| Denison, Ashbael | 1 | 1 | 2 | | |
| Church, Fairbanks | 1 | | 7 | | |
| Lester, Andw | 1 | 2 | 5 | | |
| Manwaring, Peter | 1 | | 3 | | |
| Beckwith, Perigreen | 1 | 3 | 1 | | |
| Beckwith, Elijah | 1 | 1 | 2 | | |
| Latham, Joseph | 1 | 2 | 3 | | |
| Latham, David | 1 | | 1 | | |
| Latham, John | 1 | 4 | 1 | | |
| Champlin, Edward | 1 | 1 | 3 | | |
| Champlin, Caleb | 1 | 2 | 1 | | |
| Champlin, Edward, 2d | 1 | 1 | 1 | | |
| Dowsett, Amos | 1 | 2 | 2 | | |
| Griswould, Saml | 3 | | 1 | | |
| Lewis, Sirus | 3 | 1 | 2 | | |
| Smith, Joseph | 1 | | 4 | | |
| Roggers, Saml, 2d | 2 | 3 | 3 | | |
| Way, Thomas | 2 | 2 | 1 | | |
| Way, Elisha | 1 | | 6 | | |
| Way, Thomas, 2d | 2 | | 2 | | |
| Smith, Thomas | 1 | | 3 | | |
| Smith, Dudley | 1 | 1 | 2 | | |
| Smith, Stephen | 1 | | 3 | | |
| Tillotson, Bela | 1 | | 4 | | |
| Tillotson, Isaac | 1 | 1 | 2 | | |
| Tinker, Nathan | 1 | 2 | 2 | | |
| Beckwith, Absolum | 2 | 1 | 4 | | |
| Beckwith, Nathl | 1 | | 1 | | |
| Tillerson, John | 3 | 2 | 4 | | |
| Huntley, Dan | 1 | | 1 | | |
| Watrus, Gordon, 2d | 1 | 1 | 1 | | |
| Shipman, William | 1 | | 3 | | |
| Shipman, Abner | 1 | 6 | 2 | | |
| Read, William | 1 | 2 | 3 | | |
| Read, Pheba | | | 4 | | |
| Tillotson, George | 1 | 2 | 2 | | |
| Moore, John | 2 | 4 | 4 | | |
| Tillotson, William | 1 | | 1 | | |
| Chapman, Ezekiel | 1 | 1 | 2 | | |
| Avory, Silvanus | 1 | 1 | 2 | | |
| Luther, Benjamin | 1 | 1 | 1 | | |
| Tillotson, Daniel | 1 | | 1 | | |
| Avory, Pheba | 1 | 2 | 5 | | |
| Tillotson, Jacob | 2 | 2 | 4 | | |
| Avory, Martha | 2 | | 2 | | |
| Chapman, Amy | 1 | 2 | 3 | | |
| Smith, Josiah | 1 | | 3 | | |
| Smith, Josiah, 2d | 1 | 1 | 3 | | |
| Roland, Henry | 1 | | 2 | | |
| Tillotson, Simeon | 1 | | | | |
| Chapman, Edward, 2d | 1 | 2 | 1 | | |
| Chapman, Elisabeth | | 2 | 3 | | |
| Avory, Jona | 1 | | 1 | | |
| Avory, Abraham | 1 | | 1 | | |
| Way, George, Junr | 2 | 1 | 5 | | |
| Tubs, John B | 1 | | 3 | | |
| Beckwith, Zenos | 3 | 2 | 4 | | |
| Beckwith, Thomas | 1 | 1 | 1 | | |
| Beckwith, Abner | 1 | 2 | 2 | | |
| Brooks, Noah | 1 | | 4 | | |
| Moore, Eunice | | | 1 | | |
| Tinker, Saml | 1 | 3 | 3 | | |
| Lee, Lemuel | 1 | 3 | 4 | | |
| Lee, Sabra | | | 3 | | |
| Way, Daniel | 2 | 2 | 4 | | |
| Spencer, Calvin | 2 | | 1 | | |
| Miner, Elisha, 2d | 1 | | 4 | | |
| Peckwith, Joseph | 1 | | 2 | | |
| Caulkins, Elisabeth | | 4 | 7 | | 1 |
| Wait, Thomas G | 1 | | 1 | | |
| Brockway, Woolston | 1 | 3 | 4 | | |
| Miner, Elisha | 1 | 1 | 1 | | |
| Miner, William | 1 | 1 | 3 | | |
| Warren, Moses | 1 | | 2 | | |
| Warren, Moses, 2d | 2 | 2 | 3 | | |
| Beckwith, Mary | 1 | 1 | 2 | | |
| Way, Durin | 1 | 1 | 1 | | |
| Moore, Joshua | 1 | | 5 | | |
| Moore, Deborah | | | 2 | | |
| Ayres, Daniel | 2 | 1 | 1 | | |
| Ayres, Easter | | | 2 | | |
| Huntley, Daniel, 2d | 1 | 1 | 2 | | |
| Morgan, Jona | 1 | 3 | 3 | | |
| Austin, Edward | 1 | 4 | 5 | | |
| Hains, Elisabeth | | | 4 | | |
| Sullard, Jacob | 1 | | 3 | | |
| Sullard, James | 1 | 1 | 3 | | |
| Chapman, Peter | 2 | | 3 | | |
| Chapman, Edward | 4 | 1 | 3 | | |
| Buckley, John | 1 | | 3 | | 1 |
| Miner, Easter | 1 | | 5 | | |
| Roggers, Peleg | 1 | | 1 | | |
| Way, Joseph | 3 | 2 | 2 | | |
| Tinker, Durin | 4 | 2 | 2 | | |
| Tinker, William | 3 | 1 | 3 | | |
| Mack, Ebenr | 2 | 1 | 4 | | |
| Dodge, Jeremiah | 1 | 1 | 4 | | |
| Demay, Samuel | 1 | | 3 | | |
| Beckwith, Jesse, 2d | 1 | 6 | 2 | | |
| Beckwith, Jesse | 1 | 1 | 2 | | |
| Strickland, Peter | 2 | 3 | 5 | | |
| Watrus, Gusdon | 2 | 2 | 4 | | |
| Watrus, Pheba | | | 2 | | |
| Moore, Joseph | 1 | 1 | 2 | | |
| Tinker, William, 2d | 1 | 2 | 1 | | |
| Moore, William | 1 | | 1 | | |
| Beckwith, Jonathan | 1 | 1 | 4 | | |
| Miner, Champlin | 1 | | 1 | | |
| Roggers, Samuel, 3d | 1 | 3 | 2 | | |
| Tinker, Silvanus | 1 | | 1 | | |
| Way, Reynold | 1 | 2 | 4 | | |
| Miner, Stephen | 1 | 2 | 4 | | |
| Bishop, Joseph | 2 | 2 | 4 | | |
| Miner, Volentine | | | | | |
| Fox, Ezekiel | 1 | | 2 | | 3 |
| Fox, Brinton | 1 | 4 | 3 | | |
| Austin, Joseph B | 1 | | 2 | | |
| Allen, Saml | 1 | | 2 | | |
| Fergo, Joshua, 2d | 1 | 2 | 2 | | |
| Fergo, Joshua | 1 | | 1 | | |
| Scarot, Thomas | 1 | 1 | 3 | | |
| Chaple, Danl | 1 | 3 | 4 | | |
| Cobb, Benjamin | 1 | | 2 | | |
| Allen, Jason | 3 | 2 | 3 | | 2 |
| Fox, Saml | 2 | 4 | 4 | | 1 |
| Fox, Elisha | 2 | 1 | 6 | | |
| Comstock, Zebulun | 1 | 3 | 7 | | |
| Robarts, George | 1 | | 1 | | |
| Foresides, Timothy | 1 | | 2 | | |
| Foresides, Latham | 1 | 1 | 2 | | |
| Lyons, John | 2 | 1 | 3 | | |
| Condall, James | 2 | 1 | 2 | | |
| Chaple, John | 4 | 1 | 5 | | |
| Condall, Jonathan | 1 | 2 | 3 | | |
| Roles, Daniel | 2 | 1 | 3 | | |
| Cumstock, Jared | 2 | 2 | 6 | | |
| Turner, Isaac | 1 | 4 | 3 | | |
| Fergo, Robart | 3 | | 3 | | |
| Fergo, Stanton | 2 | 1 | 4 | | |
| Scribner, Ann | | | 1 | 4 | |
| Chaple, Andrew | 1 | 2 | 2 | | |
| Lester, Isaac | 1 | | 3 | | |
| Turner, Thomas | 1 | | 1 | | |
| Lester, Norman | 1 | 1 | 2 | | |
| Stebbins, Edward | 1 | 4 | 5 | | |
| Stebbins, Jabez | 2 | 1 | 2 | | |
| Cumstock, Thomas | 1 | | 2 | | |
| Wickwise, Lucretia | 1 | | 2 | | |
| Cumstock, Ransford | 2 | 3 | 4 | | |
| Cumstock, Peter | 2 | 4 | 6 | | |
| Cumstock, Oliver | 2 | 1 | 2 | | |
| Clayton, Peter | 1 | 1 | 2 | | |
| Dolebear, John | 2 | 3 | 4 | 1 | 3 |
| Smith, Nathan | 3 | | 2 | | |
| Raymond, Joshua | 2 | 1 | 5 | 1 | 2 |
| Vallet, Jeremiah, 3d | 4 | 2 | 6 | | |
| Baker, Joshua | 1 | 2 | 2 | | |
| Cook, Roswell | 2 | 2 | 3 | | 1 |
| Miner, George | 1 | | 1 | | |
| Atwell, Lucretia | | 1 | 2 | | |
| Atwell, Benjamin | 3 | | 3 | | |
| Atwell, George | 1 | | 2 | | |
| Lester, Elihu | 1 | 1 | 2 | | |
| Capple, Nathl | 1 | 2 | 2 | | |
| Dart, David | 1 | 2 | 4 | | |
| Bishop, Thomas | 1 | 3 | 5 | | |
| Dart, Solomon | 3 | 3 | 4 | | |
| Chaple, Easter | | 1 | 7 | | |
| York (Negro) | | | | 2 | |
| McFall, William | 1 | 2 | 2 | | |
| Chaple, Richard | 3 | | 3 | | |
| Turner, Thomas, 2d | 3 | 3 | 5 | | |
| Foresides, John | 2 | 3 | 2 | | |
| Bishop, Sarah | 1 | 3 | 2 | | |
| Thompson, John | 1 | 2 | 2 | | |
| Bishop, John | 1 | 2 | 3 | | |
| Bishop, Clemment | 3 | 1 | 2 | | |
| Wix, James | 1 | 2 | 3 | | |
| Miner, Ananias | 1 | | 2 | | |
| Prentice, Saml | 1 | | 2 | | |
| Bishop, Daniel | 2 | | 3 | | |
| Davis, Joseph | 2 | | 2 | | |
| Davis, Benaijah | 1 | 2 | 2 | | |
| Cobb, Simeon, 2d | 1 | 1 | 2 | | |

# HEADS OF FAMILIES—CONNECTICUT.

## NEW LONDON COUNTY—Continued.

| NAME OF HEAD OF FAMILY. | Free white males of 16 years and upward, including heads of families. | Free white males under 16 years. | Free white females, including heads of families. | All other free persons. | Slaves. | NAME OF HEAD OF FAMILY. | Free white males of 16 years and upward, including heads of families. | Free white males under 16 years. | Free white females, including heads of families. | All other free persons. | Slaves. | NAME OF HEAD OF FAMILY. | Free white males of 16 years and upward, including heads of families. | Free white males under 16 years. | Free white females, including heads of families. | All other free persons. | Slaves. |
|---|---|---|---|---|---|---|---|---|---|---|---|---|---|---|---|---|---|
| Davis, Micaijah | 1 | 1 | 2 | | | Allen, Stephen, 2d | 1 | 2 | 4 | | | Roggers, Jaheil | 1 | 1 | 6 | | |
| Matimer, George | 1 | 1 | 7 | | | Miner, Roswell | 1 | 2 | 1 | | | Roggers, Thomas, 2d | 1 | 3 | 2 | | |
| Latimer, Jonathan | 1 | 2 | 4 | | | Miner, Jonathan | 3 | 2 | 2 | | | Roggers, Andrew | 1 | 2 | 2 | | |
| Latimer, Henry | 3 | | 5 | 1 | | Thompson, William | 3 | | 1 | | | Chapple, James, 2d | 1 | | 2 | | |
| Baker, Josiah | 2 | | 5 | | | Thompson, Samuel | 1 | | 2 | | | Dirskall, Daniel | 1 | | 2 | | |
| Colt, John | 2 | 1 | 2 | | | Denison, George | 1 | 2 | 4 | | | Mosier, Elijah | 1 | | 3 | | |
| Chapple, Lebeus | 2 | 3 | 3 | | | Miner, Joshua | 1 | | 1 | | | Smith, Joseph | 1 | 3 | 3 | | |
| Latimer, Amos | 3 | 1 | 3 | | | Miner, Lemuel | 1 | 1 | 4 | | | Brown, Amy | | | 3 | | |
| Latimer, Nathan, 2d | 1 | 3 | 2 | | | Miner, Richard | 1 | | 2 | | | Lester, Silas | 1 | | 1 | | |
| Latimer, Nathan | 2 | | 5 | | | Chapman, Alpheus | 2 | | 4 | | | Brown, Thomas | 2 | 2 | 3 | | |
| Latimer, Hallam | 1 | 1 | 3 | | | Miner, Abiather | 2 | 1 | 3 | | | Forthsides, Timothy, 2d | 1 | 3 | 2 | | |
| Martenus, Goodard | 1 | 1 | 3 | | | Fergo, William | 1 | | 1 | | | Wickwire, Jonas | 1 | 2 | 3 | | |
| Johnson, Larrance | 1 | 4 | 1 | | | Chapel, Atwell | 3 | 2 | 2 | | | Boles, Stephen | 1 | 1 | 2 | | |
| Boan (Negro) | | | | 7 | | Thompson, Nathl | 1 | 2 | 4 | | | Cumstock, James | 2 | 3 | 2 | | |
| Miner, Samuel | 2 | | 1 | | | Chapman, Betsy | | | 1 | | | Church, Amos | 1 | | 2 | | |
| Beckwith, Saml | 2 | 3 | 2 | | | Manwaring, Asa | 1 | 1 | 1 | | | Church, Mary | 1 | | 2 | | |
| Johnson, Lucy | 1 | | 1 | | | Atwell, Richard | 1 | 1 | 5 | | | Falley, James | 1 | | 2 | | |
| Mosier, Noman | 2 | | 3 | | | Dolbear, George | 2 | 1 | 3 | | | Sheffield, Saml | 1 | 1 | 6 | | |
| Manwaring, George | 1 | 2 | 6 | | | Avory, Elihu | 1 | 1 | 4 | | | Cumstock, Mary | 1 | | 3 | | |
| Manwaring, George, 2d | 1 | | 1 | | | Otis, Nathl | 2 | 2 | 6 | | | Waterhouse, Thomas | 1 | 3 | 3 | 2 | |
| White, Ezekiel | 1 | 1 | 4 | | | Gardiner, David, 2d | 1 | 6 | 4 | | | Cumstock, Nathan | 1 | 2 | 5 | | |
| White, Ezekiel, 2d | 1 | 1 | 2 | | | Beba, Amos | 2 | 3 | 3 | | | Cumstock, Jason | 1 | 3 | 2 | | |
| Cobb, Joseph | 1 | | 2 | | | Fish, Joseph | 1 | 7 | 3 | | | Baker, Hepsibah | | 1 | 3 | | |
| Boles, Joseph | 1 | 1 | 4 | | | Daniels, Asa | 1 | 2 | 1 | | | Roggers, Martha | 1 | | 4 | | |
| Homes, Jabez | 1 | 2 | 5 | | | Williams, Nathl | 1 | 2 | 1 | | | Roggers, Joseph | 1 | | 2 | | |
| Brown, Sarah | 1 | 1 | 3 | | | Hopkins, Benjamin | 1 | | 4 | | | Shoals, Jabez | 1 | 2 | 5 | | |
| Gurley, John | 1 | 1 | 4 | | | Avory, Isaac | 1 | 2 | 3 | | | Church, Mary, 2d | | 1 | 1 | | |
| Waley, James | 4 | 1 | 4 | | | Roggers, Nathan | 1 | | 3 | | | Palmer, Ruben | 1 | 2 | 5 | | |
| Johnson, Caleb | 1 | | 4 | | | Denison, Margarett | 2 | | 3 | | | Condall, David | 1 | 2 | 3 | | |
| Chaple, John | 1 | 2 | 5 | | | Manwaring, Christopher | 1 | | 4 | | | Roggers, Jeremiah | 1 | 1 | 5 | | |
| Cobb, Simeon | 3 | 1 | 6 | | | Cumstock, Peres | 1 | | 2 | | | Condall, John | 1 | | 2 | | 1 |
| Chaple, Jedediah | 1 | 2 | 3 | | | Avory, Amy | | | 3 | | | Cumstock, Elisha | 1 | 2 | 3 | | |
| Swaddle, Saml | 2 | 1 | 4 | | | Manwaring, John | 1 | 1 | 1 | | | Cumstock, Daniel | 1 | 1 | 4 | | |
| Chaple, Ezekiel, 2d | 3 | | 5 | | | West, Joshua | 1 | 2 | 2 | | | Amy (Negro) | | | | 1 | |
| Chaple, William, 2d | 3 | | 2 | | | Cumstock, Nathl | 2 | | 7 | 1 | | Whealer, William | 1 | 3 | 6 | | |
| Austin, Jonathan | 3 | 4 | 4 | | | Apley, Roswell | 1 | 1 | 3 | | | Church, Jonathan | 1 | 3 | 4 | | |
| Chaple, John, 2d | 1 | 1 | 3 | | | Willoughby, Bridget | | | 1 | | | Vallet, Jeremiah, 2d | 2 | | 5 | | |
| Austin, Zebadiah | 1 | | 2 | | | Willoughby, Bliss | 1 | | 1 | | | Goff, William | 2 | | 1 | | |
| Mosier, Stephen | 1 | 2 | 2 | | | Cato (Negro) | | | | 6 | | Roggers, James | 1 | 2 | 1 | | |
| Miner, Volentine | 1 | 2 | 1 | | | Ceaser (Negro) | | | | 5 | | Roggers, Jonathan | 1 | 1 | 1 | | |
| Brown, Cumstock | 1 | | 2 | | | Hammon, Isaac | 1 | 1 | 5 | | | Cumstock, George | 2 | | 2 | | |
| Page, Joseph | 1 | 1 | 1 | | | Hammon, Joseph | 1 | | 4 | | | Chapple, James | 1 | | 2 | | |
| Chaple, William, 3d | 1 | 2 | 3 | | | Cumstock, Joshua | 1 | 1 | 1 | | | Horton, James | 4 | 1 | 2 | | 1 |
| Chaple, Ezekiel | 1 | 1 | 1 | | | Crocker, John | 1 | | 2 | | | Raymond, Nathl | 2 | 2 | 2 | | 1 |
| Latimer, Samuel | 1 | | 1 | | | Hilhouse, John | 2 | 1 | 4 | 2 | | Raymond, George | 2 | | 2 | | |
| Fitch, Thomas | 1 | 1 | 5 | | | Camp, Elither | 1 | 2 | 2 | | | Leach, John | 2 | | 4 | | |
| Chaple, Saml | 1 | 1 | 1 | | | Raymond, Christopher | 2 | 1 | 3 | 2 | | Wickwire, Jeremiah | 4 | | 2 | | |
| Gilbert, Jona | 3 | 1 | 3 | 2 | | Hilhouse, Thomas | 3 | 2 | 1 | 1 | | Bradford, Saml | 2 | | 4 | | |
| Atwell, Benjamin | 2 | | 5 | | | Bradford, Joseph | 4 | 1 | 5 | | | Roggers, Thomas | 1 | | 1 | | |
| Allen, Nathan | 3 | 2 | 4 | | | Waley, David | 1 | 2 | 3 | | | Bradford, Nathl | 1 | | 1 | | |
| Avory, George | 1 | | 2 | | | Leffingwell, Benjamin | 2 | 3 | 5 | | | Hill, Jonathan | 1 | 3 | 6 | | |
| Turner, Mathew | 4 | 2 | 4 | | | Payton, George | 1 | | 1 | | | Allen, Joseph | 2 | | 4 | | |
| Turner, Perigreen | 1 | 1 | 2 | | | Chapman, Jonathan | 3 | | 2 | | | Baker, James | 1 | | 1 | | |
| Duglass, Joshua | 2 | 2 | 4 | | | Leffingwell, Caleb | 1 | | 1 | | | Baker, Jared | 3 | | 1 | | |
| Loomis, Jacob | 1 | 2 | 4 | | | Nobles, James | 1 | | 2 | | | Horton, Lebeus | 1 | | 2 | | |
| Ransom, Elijah | 2 | 1 | 8 | 3 | | Nobles, James, 2d | 1 | 2 | 4 | | | Chapman, Joseph | 1 | 1 | 3 | | |
| Latimer, Stephen | 1 | 1 | 4 | | | Nobles, William | 1 | 3 | 3 | | | Beckwith, Isaac | 1 | 1 | 4 | | |
| Condall, Daniel | 1 | 1 | 4 | | | Hammon, Josiah | 1 | 2 | 2 | | | Wood, Miss | | | 2 | | |
| Dashon, Joseph | 3 | 1 | 2 | | | Tracy, Moses | 1 | 2 | 3 | | | Boles, Thomas | 2 | 1 | 6 | | |
| Gallup, Thomas P | 3 | | 4 | | | Billings, Mathew | 1 | 3 | 1 | | | Perkins, Mary | | | 3 | | |
| Miner, Lebeus | 1 | | 2 | | | Maples, Stephen | 2 | 3 | 5 | | | Baker, Gideon | 2 | | 3 | | |
| Miner, Zebadiah | 1 | 1 | 3 | | | Williams, Elisabeth | | | 2 | | | Tuttle, Pelatiah | 1 | 3 | 1 | | |
| Eames, John | 1 | | 3 | | | Raymond, Josiah | 2 | 2 | 1 | | | Church, Peleg | 3 | 1 | 1 | | |
| Dolebear, Saml | 2 | 1 | 2 | 2 | | Partin, John | 1 | 1 | 3 | | | Whealer, Ephraim | 1 | | 1 | | |
| Bliss, Pelatiah | 1 | 2 | 2 | | | Homes, Samuel | 1 | 1 | 2 | | | Nickerson, Daniel | 1 | 3 | 2 | | |
| Bradford, Benjamin | 1 | 1 | 1 | | | Davis, John | 2 | 4 | 2 | | | Miner, Abiather | 2 | | 2 | | |
| Roggers, Asa | 1 | 2 | 5 | | | Hosmer, Graves | 1 | | | | | Williams, Easter | 1 | 1 | 1 | | |
| Homes, Elisha | 1 | 1 | 4 | | | Hilhouse, William | 1 | | 3 | 1 | 2 | Horton, John | 3 | 3 | 6 | | |
| Roggers, Nathl | 2 | | 1 | | | Raymond, Mulford | 1 | 1 | 4 | | 1 | Chapman, Nathl | 2 | 2 | 2 | | |
| Roggers, Nathl, 2d | 1 | 2 | 3 | | | Gardiner, John | 1 | | | | | Adgate, John | 1 | | 4 | | |
| Roggers, Jabez | 2 | | 2 | | | Raymond, Lemuel | 1 | 2 | 1 | | 1 | Adgate, Thomas | 1 | 3 | 2 | | |
| Roggers, Ebenezer | 2 | 2 | 3 | | | Raymond, Lucy | 1 | | 1 | | 1 | Boles, Amos | 3 | | 4 | | |
| Harris, Ephraim | 1 | 4 | 6 | | | Bill, Charles | 1 | 2 | 6 | | | Rose, Rufus | 1 | 2 | 2 | | |
| Roggers, Gurdon | 1 | 1 | 1 | | | Hatch, Zephaniah | 1 | 2 | 3 | | | Smith, Ebenr | 3 | | 2 | | |
| Williams, John | 3 | | 4 | | | Maples, William, 2d | 1 | 2 | 4 | | | Smith, Ebenr, 2d | 1 | 2 | 5 | | |
| Beckwith, Jasper | 2 | 1 | 3 | | | Bland, James | 1 | 1 | 5 | | | Whealer, Ephraim, 2d | 1 | 6 | 6 | | |
| Burk, William | 1 | 2 | 3 | | | Raymond, John | 2 | 2 | 2 | | 1 | Williams, Oliver | 1 | | 2 | | |
| Roggers, Alpheus | 1 | 1 | 5 | | | Waley, Elexander | 2 | | 3 | | | Cumstock, Joseph | 1 | 4 | 6 | | |
| Worthington, Sarah | | 1 | 2 | | | Waley, Jonathan | 2 | 2 | 3 | | | Atwell, Samuel | 2 | | 2 | | |
| Worthington, Dan | 1 | | 1 | | | Robbins, Mary | | | 1 | | | Woodworth, Joshua | 1 | 3 | 6 | | |
| Derttrick, John | 1 | 4 | 3 | | | Maples, Stephen, Junr | 1 | 1 | 4 | | | Eames, Danl | 1 | | 6 | | |
| Rothburn, Simeon | 2 | 4 | 4 | | | Story, Samuel | 1 | 1 | 3 | | | Adgate, Asa | 1 | | 1 | | |
| Palmer, Able | 2 | 4 | 2 | 1 | | Munson, Henry | 1 | 2 | 2 | | | Church, Joseph | 1 | 1 | 3 | | |
| Whipple, Frederick | 1 | 1 | 3 | | | Fitch, Joseph | 3 | 1 | 3 | | 1 | Atwell, John | 1 | | 2 | | |
| Chester, Joseph | 4 | 1 | 10 | | | Fitch, Sherwood | 1 | | 2 | 1 | | Dersy (Negro) | | | | 4 | |
| Chester, Joseph, 2d | 1 | 3 | 1 | | | Avory, Thomas | 1 | 1 | 2 | | | Eames, Ebenezer | 1 | | 1 | | |
| Billings, Stephen | 1 | 3 | 3 | | | Vibber, Nathl | 1 | 2 | 5 | | | Brown, John | 1 | 1 | 1 | | |
| Stanton, John | 1 | 1 | 1 | | | Vibber, William | 1 | 5 | 3 | | | Brown, Daniel, 2d | 1 | | 2 | | |
| Rothburn, Saml | 1 | 2 | 2 | | | Fitch, Andrus | 2 | 3 | 4 | | | Spink, Asa | 1 | 1 | 4 | | |
| Roggers, James | 1 | 1 | 2 | | | Maples, John | 1 | 1 | 2 | | | Roggers, Frederick | 1 | | 1 | | |
| Waley, Samuel | 1 | 4 | 3 | | | Maples, Joseph | 2 | 3 | 5 | | | Roggers, Asa | 1 | 2 | 2 | | |
| Whipple, Silas | 3 | | 2 | | | Munroe, Joshua | 1 | 2 | 1 | | | Ceaser (Negro) | | | | 2 | |
| Turner, Joshua | 1 | 2 | 2 | | | Chapple, William | 1 | 2 | 2 | | | Rebecka (Negro) | | | | 4 | |
| Allen, Stephen | 1 | | 1 | | | Maples, Josiah | 1 | 3 | 4 | | | Jewet, David H | 2 | 2 | 5 | | 1 |
| Moore, Miles | 1 | | 3 | | | Morris, James | 1 | | 2 | | | Whealer, James | 1 | 5 | 4 | | |
| Fergo, Nehemiah | 1 | 2 | 1 | | | Bradford, Peres | 3 | 2 | 3 | | | Palmer, Saml | 1 | | 1 | | |
| Darrow, Christopher | 2 | 3 | 2 | | | Homes, Seth W | 2 | 2 | 3 | | | Swaddle, Jemima | | 1 | 3 | | |

## NEW LONDON COUNTY—Continued.

| Name of head of family. | Free white males of 16 years and upward, including heads of families. | Free white males under 16 years. | Free white females, including heads of families. | All other free persons. | Slaves. | Name of head of family. | Free white males of 16 years and upward, including heads of families. | Free white males under 16 years. | Free white females, including heads of families. | All other free persons. | Slaves. | Name of head of family. | Free white males of 16 years and upward, including heads of families. | Free white males under 16 years. | Free white females, including heads of families. | All other free persons. | Slaves. |
|---|---|---|---|---|---|---|---|---|---|---|---|---|---|---|---|---|---|
| Bishop, Betsy | | 1 | 1 | | | Eames, Josiah | 1 | | 2 | | | Boles, John & Son | 3 | 1 | 5 | | |
| Waterman, Nehemiah | 1 | | 1 | | | Woodworth, Jabez | 2 | | 3 | | | Hinman, Elisha | 2 | 1 | 4 | | 2 |
| Waterman, Nehemiah, 2d | 4 | 1 | 2 | | | Huntington, Christopher | 2 | | 2 | | | Hallam, George | 1 | | 1 | 2 | 2 |
| Gifford, Stephen | 2 | | 3 | | | Ford, Joseph | 1 | 1 | 7 | | | Smith, David | 3 | 1 | 5 | | 4 |
| Gifford, Susanna | | 2 | 1 | | | Ford, Roswell | 1 | | 1 | | | Newbury, Davis | 1 | 1 | 3 | | |
| Birchird, Jesse | 4 | 1 | 3 | | | Osgood, Josiah | 1 | 1 | 2 | | | Smith, Sarah | | | 2 | | |
| Hilyard, Dennis | 1 | 1 | 3 | | | Lothrop, Zebadiah | 3 | 1 | 2 | | | Roggers, Elexander | 3 | 2 | 6 | | |
| Baldwin, Ebenr | 1 | | 1 | | 1 | Woodworth, Ziba | 1 | | 1 | | | Roggers, Nathl | 1 | | 3 | | |
| Backuss, Oliver | 1 | 1 | 3 | | | Gardiner, Gurdon | 1 | 1 | 1 | | | Hambleton, John | 2 | 1 | 2 | | |
| Waterman, John | 3 | 1 | 4 | | | Smith, Wm | 2 | 2 | 3 | | | Hambleton, Gurdon | 1 | 1 | 3 | | |
| McCall, John | 2 | 1 | 2 | | | Fish, Nathl | 2 | 2 | 6 | | | Lester, Levi | 1 | 3 | 3 | | |
| Story, William | 1 | 1 | 5 | | | Fish, William | 5 | 3 | 5 | | | Boles, Deborah | 1 | 1 | 1 | | |
| Brown, Wm | 1 | | 4 | | | Cardwell, William | 1 | 4 | 4 | | | Roggers, John | 1 | 3 | 4 | | |
| Johnson, Ebenr | 4 | 1 | 3 | | | Bingham, David | 2 | 1 | 2 | | | Walden, John | 1 | 3 | 3 | | |
| Edgcomb, John | 1 | | 3 | | | Walworth, Benjamin | 2 | 4 | 3 | | | Roggers, Mary | | | 2 | | |
| Lothrop, Simeon | 2 | 1 | 2 | | | Lothrop, Jedediah | 2 | | 2 | | | Shaw, Thomas, 2d | 1 | | 1 | | |
| Lathrop, Andrew, Junr | 1 | | 2 | | | Whiting, Caleb | 3 | | 2 | | | Whealer, Guy | 1 | 2 | 3 | | |
| Avory, Nathl | 1 | 1 | 1 | | | Avory, Ezekiel | 1 | | 2 | | | Avory, Frederick | 1 | 2 | 3 | | |
| Tillotson, Saml | 1 | 1 | 2 | | | Gardiner, Stephen | 1 | | 4 | | | Whealer, Zachius | 1 | | 3 | 1 | |
| Baulding, Eliphelet | 2 | 2 | 7 | | | Gardiner, Daniel | 2 | 3 | 3 | | | Roggers, John, 3d | 2 | 3 | 4 | | |
| Bingham, Nathan | 2 | 3 | 5 | | | Gardiner, William | 2 | 2 | 4 | | | Roggers, Saml | 1 | | 2 | | |
| Lothrop, Saml | 2 | 1 | 3 | | | Gardiner, John | 1 | 2 | 3 | | | Burns, Daniel | 1 | 1 | 1 | | |
| Persons, Joseph | 2 | 1 | 4 | | | Gardiner, Jona | 1 | | 2 | | | Waterhouse, John | 2 | 3 | 4 | | |
| Deane, David | 1 | 2 | 3 | | | Gardiner, Jonathan, 2d | 1 | 1 | 3 | | | Roggers, Saml, 2d | 2 | 3 | 2 | | |
| Able, Jesse | 2 | 2 | 3 | | | Gardiner, Lemuel | 1 | | 2 | | | Roggers, Lite | 2 | | 5 | | |
| Able, Saml | 1 | 1 | 2 | | | Frink, Christopher | 2 | 2 | 2 | | | Roggers, James, 2d | 1 | 1 | 3 | | |
| Squire, Josiah | 1 | | 1 | | | Gardiner, Simeon | 1 | 2 | 4 | | | Prentice, Easter | 1 | 2 | 2 | | |
| Backuss, Ozias | 1 | 1 | 2 | | | Condon, Timothy | 2 | | 5 | | | Robart (Negro) | | | | 3 | |
| Fitch, Asa | 5 | 3 | 3 | 1 | | Gardiner, David | 1 | 1 | 3 | | | Boles, Joshua | 2 | 1 | 3 | | |
| Lothrop, Uriah | 1 | 1 | 4 | 1 | | Avory, Samuel | 2 | | 5 | | | Simons, Ann | 1 | | 3 | | |
| Able, Theophilus | 1 | 1 | 2 | | | Gardiner, Isaac | 1 | 2 | 2 | | | Frink, David | 2 | 3 | 4 | | |
| Able, Simeon | 3 | 1 | 5 | | | Gustin, Amos | 1 | 3 | 4 | | | Boles, Enoch | 1 | 1 | 5 | | |
| Birchird, Ezra | 4 | | 3 | | | Fox, Jedediah | 2 | 1 | 6 | | | Learned, Amasa | 1 | 4 | 5 | 1 | 1 |
| Moredock, Jona | 1 | 1 | 4 | | | Gardiner, David, Junr | 1 | 2 | 5 | | | Richards, William | 1 | 1 | 6 | | |
| Caulkins, Durkee | 1 | | 1 | | | Minor, Daniel | 1 | 1 | 4 | | | Richards, Saml | 2 | 1 | 5 | | |
| Caulkins, Thomas | 1 | | 5 | | | Vergoson, John | 1 | 1 | 4 | | | Bliss, Abraham | 2 | 1 | 2 | | |
| Baker, Asa | 2 | | 3 | | | Vergoson, Diah | 1 | 1 | 2 | | | Hallam, Robart | 1 | 2 | 2 | | |
| Throop, Wm | 2 | 4 | 4 | | | Loomer, Ebenr | 1 | 1 | 3 | | | Richards, Jabez | 1 | 3 | 5 | | |
| Throop, Benja | 3 | 1 | 4 | | | Leffingwell, Clark | 1 | 1 | 2 | | | Smith, Paul | 1 | 1 | 3 | | |
| Edgerton, Lucy | | | 4 | | | Roggers, Peter | 1 | 2 | 2 | | | Smith, King | 1 | 2 | 2 | | |
| Roberson, Saml | 1 | 3 | 3 | | | Nobles, Diah | 1 | 2 | 5 | | | Smith, Hezekiah | 1 | 1 | 1 | | |
| Downer, Richard | 3 | 1 | 5 | | | Lothrop, Sarah | | 1 | 2 | | | Smith, Elijah | 1 | | 3 | | |
| Marshall, Abiel | 1 | | 2 | | | Leffingwell, Saml | 1 | | 1 | | | Roggers, Jona | 1 | | 1 | | |
| Allen, Jason | 1 | 1 | 2 | | | Leffingwell, Saml, 2d | 1 | 1 | 5 | | | Beba, Abijah | 1 | 2 | 2 | | |
| West, Nathan | 1 | | 2 | | | Leffingwell, Roswell | 3 | | 4 | | | Smith, John | 1 | 3 | 2 | | |
| West, Elias | 2 | 1 | 5 | | | Leffingwell, Presilla | 1 | 1 | 5 | | | Smith, Hugh | 1 | 4 | 3 | | |
| Lathrop, Asa | 2 | 2 | 4 | | | Leffingwell, Andrew | 2 | 1 | 2 | | | Smith, Simon | 2 | 4 | 4 | | |
| Fox, Jemima | | | 1 | | | Nobles, Mary | | 1 | 3 | | | Smith, Ezekiel | 1 | 2 | 2 | | |
| Downer, Uriah | 1 | 1 | 2 | | | Post, Stephen | 1 | 2 | 1 | | | Fergo, Thomas | 1 | 3 | 3 | | 1 |
| West, Asael | 3 | | 1 | | | Beckwith, Lemuel | 1 | | 5 | | | Smith, Mercy | | | 2 | | |
| Whitman, Abraham | 1 | | 2 | | | Post, John | 2 | 1 | 4 | | | Smith, Samuel | 1 | | 1 | | |
| Whitman, John | 2 | 4 | 3 | | | Post, Nathl | 1 | | 2 | | | Smith, Saml, 2d | 1 | 3 | 5 | | |
| Whitman, Volentine | 2 | 2 | 3 | | | Gemima (Negro) | | | | 2 | | Smith, Daniel, 2d | 1 | 1 | 3 | | |
| Smith, Elisha | 1 | | 1 | | | Reynolds, Hezekiah | 1 | | 1 | | | Smith, Thomas | 4 | | 4 | | |
| Woodworth, Asa | 3 | 2 | 4 | | | Johnson, Eliphalet | 1 | 1 | 3 | | | Luther, Levi | 1 | 1 | 5 | | |
| Lamphear, George | 1 | 2 | 4 | | | Loomer, Arnold | 1 | | 1 | | | Lee, Levi | 2 | 1 | 5 | | |
| Houghf, David | 2 | 1 | 4 | | | Sangor, Asael | 1 | | 1 | | | Dart, Roger | 1 | | 6 | | |
| Houghf, Jabez | 5 | | 4 | | | Loomer, Lovina | | 1 | 2 | | | Daniels, Peter | 1 | 1 | 1 | | |
| Crocker, William | 1 | 1 | 2 | | | Ford, John | 1 | | 2 | | | Latimer, Lemuel | 1 | | 3 | | |
| Spicer, Elderkin | 1 | | 1 | | | Whitman, Daniel | 1 | | 1 | | | Mago, Thomas | 1 | 2 | 4 | | |
| Lothrop, Andw | 2 | 1 | 6 | | | Senot, Thomas | 1 | | 4 | | | Daniels, Nathan, 2d | 2 | | 6 | | |
| Woodworth, Benjamin | 2 | | 1 | | | Gazer, Simon, & Dan. | 3 | 2 | 4 | | | Chapple, Peter | 1 | | 1 | | |
| Collins, Nathl | 1 | 2 | 2 | | | Gardiner, Caleb | 1 | 2 | 2 | | | Dart, Saml | 1 | | 3 | | |
| Able, Hezekiah | 2 | | 6 | | | Whitman, Amos | 1 | 2 | 1 | | | Avory, Wait | 1 | | 3 | | |
| Woodworth, Benja, 2d | 1 | 1 | 2 | | | Fagins (Negro) | | | | 5 | | Walden, Elisabeth | | 1 | 2 | | |
| Ford, Charles | 1 | | 3 | | | Harris, William | 1 | 1 | 2 | | | Thomson, Benjamin | 1 | 3 | 2 | | |
| Fish, John | 1 | 2 | 2 | | | Durkee, William | 1 | 1 | 2 | | | Chapman, Lemuel | 1 | | 7 | | |
| Rudd, Daniel | 1 | 2 | 5 | | | Huntington, Thomas | 1 | 1 | 3 | | | Lee, Edgcomb | 1 | | 5 | | |
| Balding, Oliver | 1 | 2 | 2 | | | Lothrop, Jedediah, 2d | 2 | 2 | 3 | | | Strickland, Amos | 1 | 1 | 3 | | |
| Whitman, Zorobable | 3 | 1 | 5 | | | Vergoson, Jeremiah | 1 | | 3 | | | Strickland, William | 1 | | 3 | | |
| Harris, Benjamin | 2 | 2 | 3 | | | Whitman, Israel | 2 | | 3 | | | Strickland, Sarah | 1 | | 2 | | |
| Scott, John | 2 | 1 | 4 | | | Harris, Peter | 2 | 1 | 3 | | | Boles, James | 1 | | 4 | | |
| Houghf, Ebenr | 2 | 1 | 3 | | | Harris, Peter | 1 | 2 | 3 | | | Boles, Joseph | 3 | | 1 | | |
| Waterman, Benjamin | 2 | 1 | 5 | | | Metcalf, Jabez | 1 | 1 | 1 | | | Dart, William | 4 | 2 | 2 | | |
| Johnson, John | 1 | 2 | 3 | | | Wait, Marvin | 1 | 2 | 4 | 1 | 2 | Dart, William, Junr | 1 | 1 | 1 | | |
| Hinson, William | 1 | | 4 | | | Deshon, John | 2 | 2 | 4 | | 4 | Sharp, Joseph | 1 | | 2 | | |
| Hinson, William, Junr | 1 | 1 | 3 | | | Wright, David | 1 | 2 | 4 | | | Quinley, Jeremiah | 1 | 1 | 1 | | |
| Sangor, Trijah | 1 | | 2 | | | Roberson, Archibauld | 1 | | 5 | | | Quinley, Thomas | 1 | 2 | 5 | | |
| Plumb, Peter | 1 | | 1 | | | Chapman, Elisabeth | 5 | | 2 | | | Freman (Negro) | | | | 4 | |
| Step (Negro) | | | | 1 | | Caulkins, Pember | 4 | | 3 | 1 | 3 | Strickland, Peter | 2 | | 2 | | |
| Samson (Negro) | | | | 4 | | Melally, Michael | 1 | 1 | 3 | | 5 | Strickland, Peter, 3d | 1 | | 1 | | |
| Tuley, Amos | 1 | | 6 | | | Latimer, Saml | 3 | | 3 | | | Thomson, Charles | 2 | | 3 | | |
| Fergo, Daniel | 1 | 2 | 2 | | | Latimer, Richard | 1 | | 3 | | | Eames, Daniel | 2 | | 3 | | |
| Ammon (Negro) | | | | 6 | | Pool, Thomas | 2 | 1 | 3 | | | Whippie, Titus | 2 | 3 | 2 | | 1 |
| Ceaser (Negro) | | | | 3 | | Deshon, Richard | 4 | 2 | 4 | | 1 | Duglass, Joseph | 2 | 2 | 7 | | |
| Fox, Roswell | 3 | 1 | 4 | | | Brainard, Jeremiah | 1 | 2 | 4 | | 1 | Douglas, David | 3 | | 2 | | |
| Read, Christopher | 1 | 1 | 1 | | | Coit, Joshua | 1 | | 4 | | | Douglass, Stephen | 1 | 3 | 1 | | |
| Eames, Joseph | 1 | 2 | 2 | | | Shaw, Thomas | 2 | | 5 | 1 | | Eames, Saml | 2 | 5 | 2 | | |
| Houghf, John | 4 | 2 | 6 | | | Ceaser (Negro) | | | | 5 | | Brooks, Daniel | 1 | 1 | 1 | | |
| Crocker, Thomas | 1 | 1 | 3 | | | Williams, George | 2 | | 10 | 3 | | Dodge, James | 1 | | 1 | | |
| Crocker, Asa | 1 | | | | | Smith, Joshua | 1 | 2 | 3 | | | Gitchel, Joseph | 1 | | 1 | | |
| Durkee, Sabin | 1 | | 2 | | | Boles, Thomas | 2 | 1 | 6 | | | Dart, Ebenr | 3 | | 7 | | |
| Backuss, Ebenr | 1 | 4 | 2 | | | Powers, Saml | 3 | 4 | 4 | | 3 | Dart, Ebenr, Junr | 1 | 1 | 1 | | |
| Huntington, Isaac | 2 | 1 | 3 | | | Greene, Benja | 2 | 1 | 5 | | | Waterhouse, Nathl | 3 | 1 | 6 | | |
| Huntington, Elijah | 1 | 3 | 4 | | | Strickland, Peter, Junr | 2 | 2 | 3 | | | Caulkins, Thomas | 1 | | 2 | | |
| Caulkins, Christopher | 3 | | 2 | | | Greene, Christopher | 2 | 2 | 5 | | | Butler, John, Junr | 3 | 1 | 6 | | |
| Culver, Lemuel | 1 | 1 | 2 | 5 | | | | | | | | Prentice, Joseph | | | | | |

# HEADS OF FAMILIES—CONNECTICUT.

## NEW LONDON COUNTY—Continued.

| NAME OF HEAD OF FAMILY. | Free white males of 16 years and upward, including heads of families. | Free white males under 16 years. | Free white females, including heads of families. | All other free persons. | Slaves. |
|---|---|---|---|---|---|
| Duglass, Thomas | 3 | | 8 | | |
| Douglass, Daniel | 2 | 5 | 2 | | |
| Duglass, James | 1 | | 1 | | |
| Duglass, Silvanus | 1 | | 2 | | |
| Duglass, James, 2d | 1 | | 3 | | |
| Watrus, Elijah | 3 | 2 | 4 | | |
| Caulkins, Saml | 2 | 1 | 3 | | |
| Richards, Nehemiah | 3 | 3 | 4 | | |
| Powers, Michael | 1 | | 3 | | |
| Powers, Joseph | 1 | | 3 | | |
| Eames, Joseph | 1 | 1 | 1 | | |
| Powers, Michael, 2d | 1 | 1 | 4 | | |
| Holt, Wm | 1 | | 2 | | |
| Holt, Asa | 1 | 3 | 1 | | |
| Chapple, Walter | 2 | | 2 | | |
| Chapple, William | 1 | 1 | 3 | | |
| Way, Azariah | 3 | | 1 | | |
| Duglass, Saml | 1 | 2 | 2 | | |
| Beba, Thadeus | 2 | 1 | 3 | | |
| Caulkins, Lemuel | 1 | 5 | 1 | | |
| Hall, Aaron | 1 | 1 | 3 | | |
| Chapple, Barsheba | 1 | | 2 | | |
| Knight, John | 1 | 1 | 3 | | |
| Daniels, James | 2 | | 3 | | |
| Daniels, Thomas | 1 | 1 | 1 | | |
| Fox, Jesse | 1 | | 3 | | |
| Fergo, William | 1 | 1 | 2 | | |
| Champlin, Isaac | 1 | 3 | 3 | | |
| Watrus, Sarah | | | 2 | | |
| Gibson, Roger | 2 | | 1 | | |
| Phillups, John | 2 | 2 | 3 | | |
| Daniels, Nehemiah | 1 | | 3 | | |
| Daniels, Joseph | 1 | 1 | 2 | | |
| Butler, James | 1 | | 4 | | |
| Butler, John | 1 | 1 | 5 | | |
| Bishop, Jona | 1 | 4 | 5 | | |
| Daniels, Saml | 3 | | 1 | | |
| Fergo, Moses | 3 | | 2 | | |
| Moore, Hannah | | | 1 | | |
| Daniels, Jasper | 1 | 1 | 1 | | |
| Crocker, Amos | 1 | 1 | 4 | | |
| Daniels, Job | 1 | 4 | 2 | | |
| Daniels, Nehemiah, 2d | 1 | | 3 | | |
| Morgan, William | 1 | | 1 | | |
| Beckwith, Isaac | 1 | 1 | 3 | | |
| Brown, Eleazer | 1 | 2 | 4 | | |
| Beba, James | 3 | 1 | 6 | | |
| Hall, Joshua | 3 | | 2 | | |
| Dart, Daniel | 1 | 1 | 3 | | |
| Strickland, John | 3 | 8 | 2 | | |
| Bartholemy, Saml | 1 | 1 | 2 | | |
| Dart, James | 1 | 2 | 2 | | |
| Miner, Jabez | 1 | | 3 | | |
| Gorton, Collins | 1 | 2 | 4 | | |
| Avory, Elisha | 2 | | 1 | | |
| Manwaring, Isaac | 1 | | 4 | | |
| Kenyon, Pain | 1 | 3 | 2 | | |
| Tabor, Saml | 3 | 1 | 2 | | |
| Tabor, Saml, Junr | 1 | 2 | 5 | | |
| Page, Jeremiah | 2 | 4 | 3 | | |
| Fosdike, Clemment | 1 | 3 | 2 | | |
| Beckwith, Ezekiel, 2d | 1 | | 2 | | |
| Crocker, Daniel | 1 | 4 | 2 | | |
| Wordon, Wait | 1 | 3 | 2 | | |
| Lane, William | 1 | 2 | 4 | | |
| Darrow, James | 2 | 1 | 1 | | |
| Brown, Zachariah | 1 | | 2 | | |
| Crocker, Constant | 2 | 1 | 2 | | |
| Ayres, Elisha | 1 | | 4 | | |
| Beba, Eliphelet | 1 | 3 | 2 | | |
| Keeney, William | 1 | 4 | 2 | | |
| Horton, Benjamin | 1 | | 5 | | |
| Daniels, Isaac | 1 | | 1 | | |
| Manwaring, Thomas | 1 | 1 | 6 | | |
| Raymond, Caleb | 2 | | 3 | 1 | |
| Moore, Joshua | 2 | | 1 | | |
| Crocker, Lydia | | 1 | 2 | | |
| Chaple, Jonathan | 1 | 1 | 2 | | |
| Bishop, Susanna | | | 2 | | |
| Beba, Joseph | 1 | | 5 | | |
| Clark, Nathl | 1 | 2 | 5 | 2 | |
| Bramin, Paul | 1 | | 1 | | |
| Daniels, Nathan | 1 | | 6 | | |
| Dart, Richard | 1 | | 1 | | |
| Stuart, Elisha | 2 | | 4 | | |
| Morgan, Samuel | 1 | | 6 | | |
| Duglass, George | 1 | | 10 | 1 | |
| Duglass, William | 3 | | 3 | | |
| Morgan, Grace | | | 1 | | |
| Morgan, John | 1 | | 2 | | |
| Whipple, Anthony | 2 | | 3 | | |
| Morgan, George | 2 | 2 | 3 | | |
| Bill, Timothy | 1 | 1 | 1 | | |
| Baker, Sarah | | | 1 | | |
| Baker, John | 1 | | 4 | | |
| Morgan, Edward | 2 | | 4 | | |
| Morgan, Phillip | 2 | 1 | 2 | | |
| Leach, Stephen | 1 | 3 | 3 | | |
| Leach, Ephraim | 1 | | 2 | | |
| Culver, Joseph | 1 | 2 | 1 | | |
| Tinker, Joseph | 1 | 1 | 4 | | |
| Whipples, John | 3 | 1 | 4 | | |
| Beba, Azariah | 3 | | 2 | | |
| Beba, Richard | 1 | 1 | 2 | | |
| Leach, Daniel | 1 | | 2 | | |
| Beckwith, Elisha | 1 | 1 | 3 | | |
| Howard, John | 1 | | 1 | | |
| Chaple, Isaac | 1 | 1 | 4 | | |
| Thomson, James | 2 | | 3 | | |
| Latimer, Daniel | 1 | 1 | 1 | | 1 |
| Latimer, Pickett | 1 | | | | |
| Chaple, Isaac, Junr | 1 | 1 | 3 | | |
| Harding, Jeremiah | 1 | 2 | 2 | | |
| Atwell, Thomas | 1 | | 2 | | |
| Hemstead, Jonathan | 1 | 2 | 5 | | 1 |
| Maynard, Stephen | 4 | 1 | 7 | | |
| Ryan, Rebecka | 1 | | 2 | | |
| Staplin, Edward | 1 | | 1 | | |
| Richards, Edward | 1 | | 4 | | |
| Doyle, Peter | 1 | 1 | 2 | | |
| Chapman, Nathl | 1 | | 1 | | |
| Harden, Thomas | 3 | | 4 | | |
| Williams, Daniel | 1 | 1 | 2 | | |
| Chapman, Eliphelet | 1 | 3 | 1 | | |
| Clifford, Silvester | 2 | | 1 | 1 | |
| Clifford, Joseph | 1 | 3 | 2 | | |
| Read, Charles | 1 | 2 | 5 | | |
| Cannon, Robart | 1 | 2 | 1 | | |
| Chapman, Jason | 1 | | 4 | | |
| Marshall, Joseph | 1 | 1 | 5 | | |
| Boles, Saml | 1 | 3 | 5 | | |
| Avory, Charles | 1 | 1 | 2 | | |
| Richards, John | 1 | | 1 | | 2 |
| Hatch, Deborah | | 1 | 2 | | |
| Roggers, Ichabod | 1 | 2 | 5 | | |
| Richards, Nathl | 2 | 1 | 4 | | 2 |
| Huntington, Jedediah | 1 | 2 | 7 | | |
| Sistarre, Gabriel | 2 | 3 | 4 | | 3 |
| Green, Timothy | 5 | 4 | 5 | | 3 |
| Burns, John | 1 | 1 | 4 | | |
| Edgcomb, Jesse | 2 | | 4 | | |
| Chapman, Easter | | | 2 | | |
| Hemstead, Nathl, 3d | 1 | 1 | 2 | | |
| Manwaring, Robart | 3 | 2 | 5 | | |
| Hemstead, Nathl, Junr | 2 | 2 | 3 | | |
| Richards, David | 1 | | 1 | | |
| Chapman, Hannah | | | 2 | | |
| Hemstead, Benjamin | 1 | 3 | 4 | | |
| Ashcraft, William | 1 | 2 | 2 | | |
| Froud, Robart | 1 | | 2 | | 1 |
| Ashcraft, Edward | 1 | 3 | 1 | | |
| Dart, Caleb | 1 | 3 | 2 | | |
| Mosier, Saml | 1 | | 2 | | |
| Dart, Benja | 1 | 1 | 3 | | |
| Dart, Ruth | | | 4 | | |
| Beba, Saml, Junr | 2 | 2 | 4 | | |
| Chaple, Jesse | 1 | 1 | 2 | | |
| Chaple, Eunice | | | 3 | | |
| Manwaring, Jabez | 1 | 1 | 3 | | |
| Leach, Mary | | | 1 | | |
| Stebbins, Joseph | 1 | | 1 | | |
| Brown, Sarah | | | 2 | | |
| Chaple, Richard | 1 | | 2 | | |
| Stebbins, John | 1 | 2 | 2 | | |
| Armstrong, Peter | 1 | 1 | 3 | | |
| Miner, Stephen | 1 | | 1 | | |
| Miner, Lydia | | | 2 | | |
| Tinker, Benja | 3 | | 2 | | |
| King, Charles | 1 | | 2 | | |
| Tinker, Benjamin, 2d | 1 | 1 | 2 | | |
| Beba, Ephraim | 1 | 2 | 5 | | |
| Manwaring, Oliver | 1 | 2 | 2 | | |
| Crocker, Thomas | 2 | 1 | 2 | | |
| Crocker, Isaac | 1 | | 1 | | |
| Crocker, Stephen | 2 | 1 | 5 | | |
| Beckwith, Jason | 1 | 2 | 1 | | |
| Newbury, Stedman | 1 | 3 | 4 | | |
| Crocker, Joshua | 1 | | 1 | | |
| Beba, Saml | 1 | | 1 | | |
| Beckwith, Seth | 1 | 2 | 2 | | |
| Hicks, Saml | 1 | 1 | 2 | | |
| Crocker, Nehemiah | 1 | 2 | 2 | | |
| Smith, George | 3 | 1 | 2 | | |
| Mossett, Thomas | 1 | | 2 | | |
| Caulkins, Lydia | | | 4 | | |
| Morrison, Joseph | 1 | | 3 | | |
| Cumstock, Martha | | | 2 | | |
| Howard, Sarah | 1 | 2 | 2 | | |
| Lovett, Joseph | 1 | 2 | 4 | | |
| Miner, Jonathan | 1 | | 6 | | |
| Darrow, Zadock | 2 | | 2 | | |
| Darrow, Lemuel | 1 | 3 | 4 | | |
| Howard, Daniel | 1 | 4 | 5 | | |
| Stuart, William | 3 | 1 | 2 | | |
| Caulkins, Jedediah | 1 | 2 | 1 | | |
| Caulkins, Ezra | 1 | 1 | 1 | | |
| Beckwith, John | 1 | | 3 | | |
| Beckwith, Caleb | 1 | 1 | 1 | | |
| Miner, Silvester | 1 | 1 | 1 | | |
| Beckwith, John, Junr | 1 | 2 | 6 | | |
| Pember, Ezekiel | 1 | | 1 | | |
| Darrow, Ebenr | 1 | 2 | 2 | | |
| Gardiner, Benaijah | 3 | 3 | 1 | | 3 |
| Durfee, Sarah | 1 | | 3 | | 6 |
| Taylor, Simon | 1 | 3 | 4 | | |
| Miner, Amos | 1 | 1 | 3 | | |
| Prentice, Stephen | 1 | 1 | 2 | | |
| Manchester, Thomas | 1 | | 2 | | |
| Prentice, Stephen, Junr | 1 | 2 | 3 | | |
| Beckwith, Frederick | 3 | 1 | 5 | | |
| Brown, Charles | 2 | 3 | 5 | | |
| Beckwith, Noah | 1 | 5 | 2 | | |
| Soper, John | 1 | | 2 | | |
| Chapple, Wm | 1 | 2 | 4 | | |
| Newbury, Richard | 1 | 1 | 3 | | |
| Newbury, Samuel | 1 | 1 | 2 | | |
| Maynard, Naomi | | | 1 | | |
| Darrow, William | 1 | 2 | 3 | | |
| Lester, Timothy | 1 | | 1 | | |
| Crocker, Jonathan | 2 | 2 | 2 | | |
| Mallery, David | 1 | 2 | 4 | | |
| Beba, Rufus | 2 | 1 | 1 | | |
| Tabor, Jeremiah | 1 | | 3 | | |
| Moore, William | 2 | 1 | 4 | | |
| Daniels, Noah | 1 | | 1 | | |
| Leach, David | 1 | 2 | 2 | | |
| Tinker, John | 1 | | 3 | | |
| Tinker, John, Junr | 1 | 1 | 2 | | |
| Durfee, Thomas | 1 | | 2 | | |
| Shaw, Daniel | 2 | 1 | 3 | | 1 |
| Chapple, Elisabeth | | | 1 | | |
| Chapple, Lydia | | 1 | 2 | | |
| Munro, Joshua | 1 | 1 | 2 | | |
| Tinker, Saml | 1 | 4 | 1 | | |
| Stebbins, John, 2d | 1 | 1 | 2 | | |
| Fergo, Zacheus | 1 | | 2 | | |
| White, Hannah | | | 2 | | |
| Miner, Hugh | 2 | | 5 | | |
| Roggers, David | 1 | 6 | 4 | | |
| Davis, William | 1 | 1 | 2 | | |
| Beba, Theophilus | 2 | 1 | 3 | | |
| Beba, Othiniel | 1 | 4 | 1 | | |
| Darrow, Ebenr | 1 | | 3 | | |
| Chapple, George | 2 | 1 | 2 | | |
| Badcock, Daniel | 1 | 1 | 2 | | |
| Beba, Jared | 1 | | 1 | | |
| Miner, Samuel | 1 | 3 | 3 | | |
| Tinker, Perry | 1 | 1 | 1 | | |
| Beba, Ruben | 1 | | 3 | | |
| Finger, William | 1 | 1 | 3 | | |
| Crocker, Amos | 1 | 3 | 1 | | |
| Chapman, James | 1 | 1 | 2 | | |
| Holt, Daniel | 2 | 3 | 4 | | |
| Truman, Daniel | 2 | | 3 | | 1 |
| Fox, Edward | 1 | | 1 | | |
| Carter, John | 1 | 1 | 3 | | |
| Henry, Daniel | 1 | | 1 | | |
| Harris, Joseph | 2 | 2 | 2 | | 1 |
| Miller, Jeremiah | 3 | 1 | 4 | | 2 |
| Way, Jerusha | 1 | | 2 | | |
| Smith, John | 1 | | 2 | | |
| Gardiner, Rufus | 1 | | 3 | | |
| Hemstead, William | 2 | 2 | 5 | | |
| Norris, Henry | 1 | | 1 | | |
| Keeney, Amos | 1 | 2 | 3 | | |
| Watrus, Benjamin | 1 | 1 | 2 | | |
| Lewis, Joseph | 1 | | 1 | | |
| Smith, Joseph | 1 | | 2 | | |
| Teague, Jerusha | | | 2 | 1 | |
| Cato (Negro) | | | | 3 | |
| Fowler, John | 1 | 4 | 2 | | |
| Maynard, Ebenr | 1 | 2 | 2 | | |
| Maynard, Christopher | 1 | 2 | 4 | | |
| Roggers, Ebenr | 1 | | 2 | 1 | |
| Roggers, Thomas | 1 | | 1 | | |
| Roggers, David | 2 | | 1 | | |
| Rogers, Zebulun | 1 | 2 | 3 | | |
| Rogers, Clark | 1 | 1 | 4 | | |
| Rogers, Ephraim | 1 | 1 | 2 | | |
| Rogers, Nathan | 1 | | 2 | | |
| Rogers, Jona | 1 | 3 | 1 | | |
| Rogers, Phineas | 1 | | 2 | | |
| Westcott, William | 2 | 4 | 3 | | |
| Pacston, Shubael | 1 | | 1 | | |
| Chub, Joseph | | 1 | 4 | | |
| Darrow, Jedediah | 2 | 1 | 2 | | |
| Crandall, Phinias | 2 | 1 | 4 | | |
| Fox, Benja | 2 | | 2 | | |
| Fox, Samuel | 1 | | 2 | | |
| Jerom, Richard | 1 | 1 | 5 | | |
| Rogers, James | 1 | | 1 | | 4 |

## NEW LONDON COUNTY—Continued.

| NAME OF HEAD OF FAMILY. | Free white males of 16 years and upward, including heads of families. | Free white males under 16 years. | Free white females, including heads of families. | All other free persons. | Slaves. | NAME OF HEAD OF FAMILY. | Free white males of 16 years and upward, including heads of families. | Free white males under 16 years. | Free white females, including heads of families. | All other free persons. | Slaves. | NAME OF HEAD OF FAMILY. | Free white males of 16 years and upward, including heads of families. | Free white males under 16 years. | Free white females, including heads of families. | All other free persons. | Slaves. |
|---|---|---|---|---|---|---|---|---|---|---|---|---|---|---|---|---|---|
| Dayton, Joseph | 1 | | 1 | | | Perkin, Richard W | 2 | 1 | 4 | 1 | 2 | Coit, Thomas, Jun<sup>r</sup> | 1 | 1 | 3 | | |
| Daton, Ephraim | 1 | 1 | 1 | | | Winthrop, Frank | 3 | 2 | 4 | | 1 | Goddard, Ebenezer | 1 | 3 | 2 | | |
| Tabor, Pardon | 2 | | 1 | | 1 | Howard, W<sup>m</sup> | 1 | 1 | 2 | | | Hurlburt, Daniel | 1 | | 2 | | |
| Allen, Thomas, Jun<sup>r</sup> | 2 | 4 | 4 | | 1 | Strowd, Richard | 1 | | 2 | | | Warner, —— | 1 | | 2 | | |
| Beba, Jethro | 1 | 2 | 3 | | | Slater, Zerobabel | 2 | | 3 | | | Payne, Phoebe | 2 | | 1 | | |
| Brooks, Ezekiel | 1 | | 1 | | | Fellows, Joseph | 1 | 2 | 2 | | | Norcute, John | 1 | 1 | 3 | | |
| Brooks, Ezekiel, 2<sup>d</sup> | 1 | 3 | 1 | | | Melona, William | 1 | 1 | 2 | | | Buckley, Charles | 1 | 3 | 4 | | |
| Rothburn, W<sup>m</sup> | 1 | 4 | 5 | | | Tinker, Daniel | 1 | 3 | 3 | | | Fosdick, Nicoll | 2 | 2 | 3 | | 1 |
| Beba, Jon<sup>a</sup> | 1 | 1 | 2 | | | Fellows, Isaac | 1 | | 4 | | | Mumford, Giles | 2 | 1 | 4 | | 1 |
| Beba, William | 1 | 1 | 2 | | | Packwood, Joseph | 1 | 1 | 6 | | | Hempstead, Stephen | 3 | 4 | 3 | | |
| Beba, Guy | 1 | 3 | 6 | | | Rogers, John | 1 | 1 | 5 | | | Smith, Joseph | | 2 | 2 | | |
| Beba, Jabez | | | 2 | | | Hancock, Thomas | 1 | 1 | 3 | | | Tabor, Job | 2 | 4 | 6 | | 1 |
| Beba, Paul | 1 | 1 | 3 | | | Potter, Ann | | | 2 | 3 | | Stimel, John | 1 | 1 | 2 | | |
| Beba, Jabez, 2<sup>d</sup> | 1 | 2 | 2 | | | Sampson (Negro) | | | | 6 | | Fergo, Hannah | | | 1 | | |
| Rogers, Daniel | 1 | | 2 | | | Harry (Negro) | | | | 4 | | Tilley, John | 1 | | 1 | | |
| Chapple, Sam<sup>l</sup> | 1 | 3 | 5 | | | Sarah (Negro) | | | | 3 | | Dart, Job | 1 | | 3 | | |
| Tinker, Ezekiel | 1 | 1 | 2 | | | Gordon, John | 1 | 2 | 3 | | | Proctor, Abel | 1 | 2 | 4 | | |
| Welles, Lucy | | | 3 | | | Bloyd, Margaret | | | | 1 | | Douglass, Richard, 1<sup>st</sup> | 1 | 3 | 4 | | |
| Beba, Jeduthan | 2 | 1 | 3 | | | Whipple, John | 1 | 1 | 1 | | | Rathbun, Job | 1 | | 2 | | 1 |
| Daton, Zophar | 2 | | 2 | | | Phink, Adam | 1 | | 3 | | | Wescott, Elizabeth | | | 2 | | |
| Beckwith, Timothy, 2<sup>d</sup> | 1 | 1 | 2 | | | Fernando, Frances | 1 | 1 | 2 | | | Stockman, Jacob | 1 | 3 | 1 | | |
| Beckwith, Timothy | 2 | 2 | 5 | | | Gesting, John | 1 | | 1 | | | Spence, Deborah | | 1 | 5 | | |
| Edwards, Roger | 1 | | 1 | | | Mason, Patience | | 2 | 4 | | | Jones, Thomas | 1 | | 3 | | |
| Bur, Purcy | 1 | 3 | 2 | | | Smith, Henry | 1 | 1 | 1 | | | Manwaring, David | 2 | | 5 | | |
| Moore, William, 2<sup>d</sup> | 3 | 2 | 5 | | | Beebee, Burgess | 1 | | 1 | | | Miner, Ephraim | 2 | 1 | 5 | 2 | |
| Rogers, Solomon | 1 | 3 | 4 | | | Culver, Christopher | 1 | 2 | 2 | | | Douglass, Jonathan | 2 | 4 | 2 | | |
| Rogers, Stephen | 1 | 2 | 2 | | | Beebee, Grace | 3 | | 6 | | | Starr, Joshua | 4 | 4 | 4 | | 1 |
| Rogers, Isaac | 1 | 2 | 2 | | | Ryon, William | 1 | | 5 | | | Penniman, James | 5 | 1 | 3 | | |
| Fowler, Morris | 2 | 1 | 1 | | | Holt, Jonathan | 1 | 2 | 1 | | | Wheat, Samuel | 2 | 4 | 3 | | 3 |
| Wix, Joseph | 1 | 3 | 1 | | | Gristing, James | 1 | 1 | 4 | | | Durivage, Nicholas | 4 | 3 | 3 | | 1 |
| Avory, Griswould | 4 | | 4 | | | Jones, Aaron | 1 | 2 | 1 | | | Stewart, William | 2 | | 4 | | 2 |
| Brown, Benj<sup>a</sup> | 3 | 3 | 3 | | | Harris, James | 1 | | 2 | | | Saltonstall, Gurdon | 1 | 1 | 2 | | |
| Maynard, James | 1 | 2 | 3 | | | Harvey, —— | | 1 | 2 | 2 | | Elliott, Clark | 2 | | 1 | | |
| Brown, Jeremiah | 2 | 4 | 5 | | | Holt, William | 1 | 1 | 2 | | | Rogers, George | 4 | 1 | 8 | | |
| Jerom, Benjamin | 1 | 5 | 4 | | | Squier, John | 1 | | 1 | | | Hill, James | 1 | 5 | 2 | 1 | |
| Brown, James | 2 | 2 | 1 | | | Culver, James | 1 | | | | | Luke, John | 1 | 2 | 1 | | 1 |
| Harris, Eliphelet, 2<sup>d</sup> | 1 | | 1 | | | Crowly, William | | | 1 | | | Law, Richard | 2 | 2 | 3 | 2 | 1 |
| Sprage, Lucy | | | 2 | | | Dart, John | 1 | 2 | 1 | | | Wild, John | 2 | 1 | 3 | | |
| Wyllis, William | 1 | | 4 | | | Holt, Elizabeth | 1 | 1 | 3 | | | Matters, James | 1 | | 2 | | |
| Brown, John | 1 | 1 | 4 | | | Codner, Cata | | | 1 | | | Leech, James | 1 | 1 | 1 | | |
| Harris, Eliphelet | 2 | 2 | 4 | | | Coit, Patty | | 2 | 1 | | | Young, Joseph | 1 | | 1 | | |
| Harris, Daniel | 1 | 1 | 4 | | 1 | Harris, Jasper | 1 | | 2 | | | Beckwith, David | 1 | 1 | 3 | | |
| Chapple, Alpheus | 1 | | 2 | | | Penveer, John | 1 | | 1 | | | Clark, Isaac | 1 | | 2 | | |
| Harris, Ezra | 1 | | 2 | | | Holt, Ebenezer | 1 | | 3 | | | Dennis, John | 1 | | 2 | | |
| West, Daniel | 1 | | 1 | 1 | | Smith, James | 2 | 1 | 2 | | | Craw, Sarah | | | 2 | | |
| Harris, Thomas | 1 | 1 | 5 | | | Watrous, Stephen | 1 | 1 | 1 | | | Richards, Daniel W | 2 | 1 | 2 | | |
| Lester, John | 2 | | 4 | | | Wheat, William | 1 | | 2 | | | Percival, Monsieur | 1 | | 3 | 1 | 1 |
| Harris, John | 1 | | 3 | | | Manning, Latham | 1 | | 1 | | | Skinner, William | 1 | 1 | 1 | | |
| Harris, Sarah | 1 | | 3 | | | Hempstead, Nath<sup>l</sup> | 1 | 1 | 2 | | | Skinner, William, 2<sup>d</sup> | 1 | 2 | 2 | | |
| Harris, Noah | 1 | 1 | 2 | | | Hempstead, Samuel | 1 | 1 | 1 | | | Dickinson, Nath<sup>l</sup> | 1 | 3 | 4 | | |
| Harris, John, 3<sup>d</sup> | 1 | 1 | 2 | | | Proud, Robert | 1 | | | | | Holt, Stephen | 3 | 2 | 3 | | |
| Lester, Amos | 1 | | 2 | | | Hempstead, Joshua | 1 | 2 | 2 | | | Way, Ebenezer | 1 | 2 | 1 | | |
| Harris, Walter | 2 | 1 | 3 | | | Hamilton, Rebecca | 1 | 2 | 1 | | | Harris, Peter B | 1 | 1 | 6 | | |
| Newbury, Mary | | | 2 | | | Miner, Turner | 2 | 2 | 4 | | | Burrows, Roswell | 5 | | 2 | | |
| Harris, Daniel, 2<sup>d</sup> | 1 | 1 | 2 | | | Christophers, Peter | 6 | 1 | 3 | 2 | 2 | Latimer, William | 1 | 2 | 1 | | |
| Way, Nath<sup>l</sup> | 1 | | 2 | | | Coit, William | 1 | | 4 | | 2 | Palmer, Hannah | | | 1 | | |
| Kenney, John | 2 | 4 | 3 | | | Wolcott, Simon | 2 | 1 | 8 | | | Edmunds, —— | | | 2 | | |
| Keney, Dan<sup>l</sup> | 1 | 3 | 2 | | | Douglass, Richard | 1 | | 1 | | | La Roche, John | 1 | 1 | 2 | | |
| Tinker, Edward | 1 | | 1 | | | Shields, Hannah | | | 1 | | | Chapman, Oliver | 4 | | 3 | | |
| Tinker, Josiah | 1 | | 1 | | | Weaver, William | 1 | 4 | 2 | | | Pero, Barsheba | | 1 | 3 | | |
| Tinker, Jeremiah | 1 | | 1 | | | Miner, Hugh | 1 | | 2 | | | Emerson, Joseph | 1 | 2 | 3 | | |
| Lewis, Mary | | 1 | 3 | | | Starr, Jonathan | 1 | | 2 | | | Weeden, Isaac | 1 | 1 | 3 | | |
| Prentice, John | 1 | 1 | 1 | | | Freeman, Henry | 1 | | 3 | 1 | | Angell, James | 1 | 4 | 2 | | |
| Barber, Benjamin | 1 | | 2 | | | Crawford, John | 1 | 1 | 2 | | | Potter, Joshua | 2 | 4 | 7 | | |
| Harris, Nath<sup>l</sup> | 1 | 4 | 2 | | | Carroll, Nancy | | | 2 | | | Powers, Sylvester | 1 | 2 | 2 | | |
| Rogers, Israel | 1 | | 3 | | | Silvia (Negro) | | | | 2 | | Rice, Thomas | 1 | | 2 | | |
| Harris, John, 2<sup>d</sup> | 3 | 1 | 6 | | | Chapman, John | 1 | 2 | 3 | | | Wignall, William | 1 | 1 | 2 | | |
| Fox, Daniel | 1 | | 3 | | | Sherman, James | 1 | 1 | 2 | | | Miller, James | 1 | 2 | 4 | | |
| Carrol, John | 1 | 1 | 1 | | | Holt, Eben | 3 | 2 | 4 | | | Fish, Seabury | 3 | | 2 | | |
| West, Jabez | 1 | 1 | 1 | | | Rogers, Hannah | | 2 | 4 | | | Lathrop, John | 1 | | 2 | | |
| Cumstock, John | 1 | 2 | 4 | | | Brown, Wheeler | 3 | 5 | 3 | | | Douglass, Sperry | 1 | 2 | 3 | | |
| Harris, Roswell | 1 | 1 | 3 | | | Turner, Sarah | | | 2 | | | Brooks, Jonathan | 2 | 1 | 2 | | |
| Darrow, Nicholas | 1 | 3 | 5 | | | Coit, Joseph | 2 | 3 | 4 | | 3 | Cottril, James | 1 | | 3 | | |
| Harris, Henry | 1 | 1 | 1 | | | Starr, Lucy | | | 4 | | | Bloyd, John | 1 | 1 | 2 | | |
| Lewis, Edward | 1 | | 1 | | | Champlin, Elizabeth | 2 | 2 | 4 | | | Smith, Asa | 1 | | 4 | | |
| Daniels, Jeremiah | 1 | 1 | 2 | | | Bradley, Joshua | 1 | 1 | 4 | | | Manning, Gamaliel | 2 | | | | |
| Paterson, James | 1 | 1 | 4 | | | Crocker, John | 1 | 2 | 3 | | | Smith, Dayton | 1 | 1 | 3 | | |
| Fink, Adam | 1 | | 2 | | | Buddington, Walter | 1 | | 1 | | | Douglass, Ebenezer | 1 | 3 | 6 | 3 | |
| Coit, Sam<sup>l</sup> | 1 | 1 | 2 | | | Clark, John | 1 | | 2 | | | Brown, Joseph | 1 | | 1 | | |
| Coit, John | 1 | | 1 | | | Watson, John | 1 | 1 | 2 | | | Richards, Mary | | | 2 | | |
| Coit, Sam<sup>l</sup>, 2<sup>d</sup> | 1 | 4 | 2 | | | Rockwell, Merit | 1 | 1 | 2 | | | Potter, John | 3 | 4 | 2 | | |
| Mason, Sam<sup>l</sup> | 1 | 2 | 3 | | | Harris, William | 4 | 2 | 2 | | | Potter, William | 1 | 1 | 1 | | |
| Devenport, Welthy | | | 4 | 2 | | Dodge, Ezra | 1 | | 1 | | | Harvey, Thomas | 1 | | 1 | | |
| Mason, Japhet | 1 | | 1 | | | Ryon, Irena | | | 1 | 2 | | Harvey, William | 1 | | 2 | | |
| Thorp, Nath<sup>l</sup> | 1 | 2 | 3 | | | Short, Hannah | | | 2 | | | Hart, James | 1 | 2 | 2 | | |
| Thorp, Nath<sup>l</sup>, 2<sup>d</sup> | 1 | 1 | 1 | | | Lampheer, James | 1 | 1 | 7 | | | Jack (Negro) | | | | 3 | |
| Stone, John | 1 | 3 | 4 | | | Gardiner, Mary | 1 | | 2 | | | Malay, Aliff | | | 2 | | |
| Thorp, Ezekiel | 1 | | 3 | | | Shepherd, John | 1 | 3 | 4 | | 1 | Hempstead, Hallam | 1 | 1 | 2 | | |
| Thorp, Amos | 1 | 1 | 4 | | | Tilley James | 9 | 6 | 4 | | 2 | Jeffery, Thomas | 1 | | 3 | | |
| Davis, Ruben | 1 | | 3 | | | Miller, John | 2 | 3 | 4 | | 2 | Jeffery, James | 1 | | 1 | | |
| Holt, Thomas | 2 | 2 | 2 | | | Winthrop, Ann | | | 2 | | | Nicholl, Owen | 1 | | 1 | | |
| Miller, Frelove | | 1 | 1 | | | Starr, Jonathan, Jun<sup>r</sup> | 1 | 3 | 7 | 1 | | Brooks, James | 1 | | 1 | | |
| Wicks, Rebecka | | | 1 | | | Starr, Jared | 2 | 3 | 3 | 1 | 1 | Jeffery, Charles, 2<sup>d</sup> | 2 | | 6 | | |
| Ceaser (Negro) | | | | 2 | | Way, John | 1 | 1 | 2 | | | Hewitt, Nathaniel | 3 | | 1 | | |
| Jones, Henry | 1 | 1 | 3 | | | Avery, George D | 2 | 3 | 6 | | | Bayley, Nathan, Jun<sup>r</sup> | 1 | 4 | 5 | | |
| Dart, Prudence | | | 4 | | | Fink, Jacob | 1 | | 3 | | | Craw, Amasa | 1 | | 1 | | |
| Harding, Thomas, 2<sup>d</sup> | 1 | 1 | 6 | | | Saltonstall, Winthrop | 1 | | 2 | | 3 | Springer, John | 1 | 2 | 3 | | |

# HEADS OF FAMILIES—CONNECTICUT.

## NEW LONDON COUNTY—Continued.

| NAME OF HEAD OF FAMILY. | Free white males of 16 years and upward, including heads of families. | Free white males under 16 years. | Free white females, including heads of families. | All other free persons. | Slaves. | NAME OF HEAD OF FAMILY. | Free white males of 16 years and upward, including heads of families. | Free white males under 16 years. | Free white females, including heads of families. | All other free persons. | Slaves. | NAME OF HEAD OF FAMILY. | Free white males of 16 years and upward, including heads of families. | Free white males under 16 years. | Free white females, including heads of families. | All other free persons. | Slaves. |
|---|---|---|---|---|---|---|---|---|---|---|---|---|---|---|---|---|---|
| Woodard, John | 2 | | 1 | | | Deepu, John | 1 | | 3 | | | Taylor, John | 1 | | 2 | | |
| Jeffery, Moses | 2 | 2 | 3 | | | Blackley, Margaret | | | 3 | | | Ayers, Joseph | 3 | | 3 | | |
| Bayley, Nathan | 2 | | 2 | | | Piner, Lydia | | | 4 | | | Ayers, John | 1 | | 3 | 1 | |
| Manierre, Lewis | 2 | 3 | 4 | | | Prentice, Ebenr | 1 | 1 | 2 | | | Ayers, Squire | 1 | 2 | 5 | | |
| Jeffery, Charles | 1 | | 1 | | | Richards, Guy | 3 | 4 | 7 | | | Ayers, Timothy | 1 | 5 | 3 | | |
| Whipple, Thomas | 1 | 4 | 4 | | | House, George | 1 | 1 | 2 | | | Abell, Martin | 1 | 1 | 2 | | |
| Taylor, John | 1 | | 1 | | | Coats, Frederick | 1 | | 2 | | | Abell, Parnell | 1 | | 2 | | |
| Chapell, Edward | 2 | 2 | 5 | | 3 | Hallam, Edward | 2 | | 2 | 1 | | Peck, Phinehas | 3 | 3 | 3 | | |
| Colbert, Temperance | | 1 | 2 | | | Higgins, William | 1 | 2 | 2 | | | Samson, Jonathan | 1 | 2 | 2 | | |
| Harris, Francis | 1 | 1 | 3 | | | Goodfaith, David | 1 | 1 | 1 | | | Ladd, Joseph | 2 | 2 | 2 | | |
| Holt, James | 1 | 1 | 3 | | | Carrol, James | 1 | 2 | 4 | | | Hyde, Joseph | 2 | 2 | 2 | | |
| Perry, Eliahim | 1 | | 2 | 1 | | Hurlbut, Elisabeth | 3 | | 5 | | 3 | Stoddard, Solomon | 2 | | 2 | | |
| Dunton, Ebenezer | 1 | 2 | 11 | | | Whittemore, Saml | 1 | 3 | 3 | | | Edgerton, Ariel | 1 | 3 | 3 | | |
| Foster, Benjamin | 1 | 1 | 2 | 1 | | Gordon, John | 2 | 3 | 3 | | | Scott, Joseph | 3 | 3 | 4 | | |
| Waldo, John | 1 | | 1 | | | Winthrop, Elisabeth | 1 | | 3 | | 1 | Munsell, John | 1 | 2 | 2 | | |
| Simmonds, John | 1 | 1 | 3 | | | Sebor, Jacob | 1 | 1 | 7 | 2 | | Edgerton, Elizabeth | | | 2 | | |
| Holmes, James | 2 | 3 | 4 | | 2 | Saltonstall, Roswell | 4 | 3 | 7 | | 1 | Edgerton, Samuel | 2 | | 4 | | |
| Treby, John | 2 | 1 | 4 | | | Hallam, John | 1 | 3 | 3 | | 1 | Edgerton, Zebulon | 1 | | 3 | | |
| Young, James | 1 | | 3 | | | Seabury, Saml, 2d | 1 | 1 | 2 | | | Gazer, John | 4 | | 4 | | |
| Dyian, Philip | 1 | | 3 | | | Tabor, Wardon T | 2 | | 4 | | | Abell, Cherub | 1 | 2 | 1 | | |
| Billings, Lament | | 1 | 7 | | | Elliot, Daniel | 1 | 4 | | | | Barstow, Yetonce | 2 | | 4 | | |
| Rice, Mary | | | 1 | | | Young, James | 1 | 1 | 4 | | | Currin, Phinehas | 1 | 4 | 1 | | |
| Treby, Isaac | 2 | | 4 | | | Jackson, John | 1 | 2 | 3 | | | Bourne, Amos | 1 | | 2 | | |
| Stacy, Rebecca | | | 3 | | | Wilson, Thomas | 1 | | 1 | | | Hyde, Mary | | | 2 | | |
| Douglass, Mary | | | 1 | | | Kimball, Chester | 1 | 2 | 1 | | | Hyde, Isaac | 2 | 1 | 2 | | |
| Trott, Jonathan | 3 | 1 | 4 | | | Ward, John | 2 | | 1 | | | Hyde, Elihu | 2 | | 2 | | |
| Mumford, David | 3 | 1 | 4 | 1 | 1 | Stark, William | 1 | | 2 | | | Armstrong, Lee | 1 | 2 | 3 | | |
| Saltonstall, Nathaniel | 1 | 2 | 4 | | | Beba, James | 1 | 2 | 2 | | | Perry, Seth | 1 | 1 | 8 | | |
| Robinsone, Patrick | 2 | 3 | 3 | | | Miller, Henry | 2 | | 2 | | | Gazer, Levi | 2 | 1 | 3 | | |
| Bolles, Isaiah | 1 | 5 | 4 | | | Collins, Thomas | 1 | 1 | 2 | | | Denison, Eleazar | 4 | 3 | 5 | | |
| Gale, Luther | 2 | | 2 | | | Owen, John | 2 | 5 | 7 | | | Rogers, John | 1 | 1 | 1 | | |
| Hewit, Gurdon | 4 | 2 | 2 | | | Stark, Benjamin | 1 | 2 | 1 | | | Manning, Josiah | 1 | | 2 | | |
| Plumb, Samuel | 1 | 2 | 2 | | | Swain, Peter | 1 | 2 | 2 | | | Edgerton, Nathan | 1 | 1 | 2 | | |
| Lyman, Elisha | 1 | 1 | 1 | | | Colvin, Gabriel | 1 | 1 | 1 | | | Edgerton, Hannah | | | 3 | | |
| Lee, Elizabeth | | | 2 | | | McDonald, Mathew | 1 | | | | | Belshaw, Thomas | 3 | 2 | 4 | 1 | |
| Pool, David | 1 | 2 | 4 | | | Hall, Jenny | | | | | | Gazer, Daniel | 2 | 1 | 4 | | |
| Cornhill, Job | 3 | 2 | 5 | | | Culver, Samuel | 1 | 3 | 4 | | | Gazer, Aaron | 2 | | 1 | | |
| Powers, Sylvester | 1 | 2 | 2 | | | Wally, John | 1 | 1 | 1 | | | Hyde, Vaniah | 1 | 2 | 3 | | |
| Zants, Monsieur | 1 | | 4 | | | Simons, Chapman | 1 | 1 | 4 | | | Barker, Mary | 1 | | 1 | | 1 |
| Manwaring, John | 1 | | 2 | | | Williams, Visalamos | 1 | 1 | 2 | | | Ladd, Daniel | 2 | 3 | 7 | | |
| Cheney, Samuel | 1 | 1 | 1 | | | Bush, Henry | 2 | 1 | 2 | | | Tracy, Josiah | 1 | | 2 | | |
| Newport, Sarah | | | 1 | | | Simmons, Sarah | | | 1 | | | Tracy, Calvin | 1 | 2 | 3 | | |
| Clay, Patience | | | 3 | | | Simmons, Sally | | 1 | 1 | | | Tracy, Eliphalet | 1 | | 2 | | |
| Seabury, Samuel | 2 | 2 | 4 | | 2 | Brooks, Thadeus | 2 | 3 | 3 | | | Smith, Asahel | 1 | | 4 | | |
| Freeman, Mary | | | 7 | | | Rogers, Benjamin | 2 | 4 | 4 | | | Tracy, Elisha | 2 | | 3 | | |
| Richards, Guy | 1 | | | | | Briggs, William | 2 | 2 | 4 | | | Throop, Cary | 3 | | 3 | | |
| Allen, Thomas | 1 | 1 | 2 | | 1 | Peters, James | 1 | | 2 | | | Ellis, Benjamin | 1 | 1 | 3 | | |
| Badet, Peter | 1 | 1 | 2 | | | Gardiner, Henry | 1 | | 1 | | | Hyde, Daniel, Junr | 2 | 3 | 1 | | |
| Coit, Boradel | | 1 | 5 | | | Shapley, Mary | 2 | | 1 | | | Rogers, Uriah | | | | | |
| Belden, Samuel | 3 | | 5 | | 1 | Colefax, Abigail | | | 4 | | | Hartshorn, Zebadiah | 1 | 1 | 1 | | |
| Smith, Simeon | 4 | 2 | 5 | | | Hinman, Cate | | | 4 | | | Kingsbury, Daniel | 1 | | 1 | | |
| Burrows, Daniel | 6 | 2 | 3 | | | Hichcox, Ebenr | 1 | | 2 | | | Pepper, Michael | 1 | 1 | 1 | | |
| Stebbins, Lucy | 1 | | 1 | | | Chapman, Danl | 1 | | 2 | | | Sholes, Miner | 1 | 1 | 2 | | |
| Walker, John | 1 | 1 | 2 | | | Griswould, Elisha | 1 | | 2 | | | French, Joshua | 2 | 1 | 3 | | |
| Packwood, Nabby | | 1 | 2 | | 2 | Griswould, Saml | 3 | 2 | 6 | | | Edgerton, Jos. Kingsbury | 1 | 1 | 4 | | |
| Rogers, Fanny | | 3 | 1 | | | Lord, Nathan | 2 | 7 | 5 | | | Hartshorn, Nathan | 1 | 2 | 3 | | |
| Owen, Joseph | | | 2 | | | Mills, Mehitable | | | 2 | | | Hartshorn, Sarah | | | 2 | | |
| Champlin, John | 3 | 3 | 2 | | | Roberson, Nathan | 3 | 1 | 3 | | | Hartshorn, Sarah | | | 1 | | |
| Lee, Thomas | 1 | 3 | 1 | | | Gideons, Nathl | 2 | 2 | 5 | | | Edgerton, Zebulon, Junr | 1 | 3 | 2 | | |
| Prince, Kimball | 1 | 2 | 2 | | | Fillemore, Cumfort | 2 | 3 | 6 | | | Woodworth, Amasa | 1 | 1 | 2 | | |
| Adams, Bela | 1 | | 1 | | 1 | Fillemore, Amaziah | 1 | 1 | 3 | | | Nott, Abigail | | | 3 | | |
| Brooks, William | 1 | 1 | 2 | | | Kingsley, Eliphelet | 2 | | 3 | | | Smith, Abner | 1 | 3 | 3 | | |
| Adams, David | 1 | 1 | 3 | | | Armstrong, Isaiah | 1 | 4 | 1 | | | Peck, Darius | 2 | 1 | 1 | | |
| Newcomb, Sarah | | | 2 | | | Griswould, Ebenr | 4 | | 5 | | | Munsell, Henry | 4 | | 5 | | |
| Sistarre, Gabriel, 2d | 1 | 1 | 3 | 1 | | Armstrong, Bela | 1 | 4 | 3 | | | Bugby, Samuel | 1 | 3 | 2 | | |
| Pitman, William | 3 | 2 | 3 | | | Barker, John | 4 | 2 | 6 | | | Hyde, Asa | 2 | 2 | 3 | | |
| Woodard, Abisha | 5 | 3 | 7 | 1 | | Barker, John, 2d | 1 | | 2 | | | Pember, Jacob | 1 | 2 | 2 | | |
| Plumb, John | 1 | | 3 | | | Backeus, Ezekiel | 1 | 1 | 2 | | | Hyde, Mehitabel | | | 3 | | |
| Goodard, Mary | 1 | 2 | 3 | | | Armstrong, John | 3 | | 3 | | | Hyde, Matthew | 1 | 3 | 1 | | |
| Merrils, Mary | 1 | | 4 | | | Armstrong, Amos | 3 | 3 | 3 | | | Ingraham, Joseph | 1 | | 1 | | |
| Saltonstall, Dudley | 3 | | 3 | | 1 | Armstrong, Asa | 2 | | 2 | | | Ingraham, Rachel | | | 2 | | |
| Hall, Sarah | | | 3 | | | Kingsley, Alpheus | 1 | 2 | 5 | | | Grunslit, Benjamin | 1 | 1 | 3 | | |
| Dixon, Thomas | 1 | 1 | 1 | | | Fox, Martha | | | 2 | | | Hyde, Eli | 3 | 1 | 7 | | |
| Rudge, Sampson | 1 | 2 | 3 | | | Kingsley, William | 2 | 2 | 3 | | | Hyde, Thomas | 2 | 1 | 4 | | |
| Wix, Deborah | | 1 | 2 | | | Ellis, John | 2 | 1 | 5 | | | Rudd, Jonathan | 2 | 1 | 2 | | |
| Thomas, John | 1 | 1 | 2 | | | Ladd, Samuel | 3 | 1 | 6 | | | Rudd, Samuel | 1 | 1 | 2 | | |
| Smith, Ephraim | 1 | 1 | 3 | | | Ladd, Ezekiel | 2 | 1 | 6 | | | Huntington, Elisha | 1 | 2 | 4 | | |
| Daniel (Negro) | | | | 2 | | Samson, Joseph | 2 | 1 | 4 | | | Rudd, Prosper | 1 | | 3 | | |
| Bolton, James | 1 | | 2 | | | Bruster, Stephen | 2 | 2 | 2 | | | Woodworth, Amos | 2 | 1 | 3 | | |
| Crawson, Asa | 1 | 1 | 2 | | | Ladd, Jeremiah | 3 | 1 | 2 | | | Abell, Oliver | 1 | 4 | 1 | | |
| Thomson, Robart | 1 | | 3 | | | Hazen, Moses | 2 | | 2 | | | Hyde, Solomon | 1 | 2 | 3 | | |
| Markaniff, Charles | 1 | | 2 | | | Hazen, Joseph | 1 | 1 | 1 | | | Camp, James M | 2 | 3 | 4 | | |
| Rogers, James | 4 | 3 | 4 | | 2 | Ladd, David, 2d | 1 | | 1 | | | Rogers, Uriah, Junr | 2 | 1 | 3 | | |
| Burn, James | 1 | | 1 | | | Ladd, Jedediah | 1 | | 4 | | | Hyde, Abel | 1 | 1 | 3 | | |
| Rogers, Jason | 2 | 2 | 3 | | 1 | Ladd, Andw | 1 | | 4 | | | Tracy, Peter | 2 | | 5 | | |
| Deshon, Daniel | 1 | 2 | 2 | | | Story, Ephraim | 1 | | 2 | | | Hyde, Joshua | 1 | | 6 | | |
| Deshon, Henry | 2 | 1 | 2 | 1 | | Smith, Joshua | 2 | | 2 | | | Fessenden, Samuel | 1 | 1 | 2 | | |
| Susant, James | 1 | | 1 | 1 | | Smith, Joshua, 2d | 1 | | 1 | | | Fox, Edmund | 1 | | 2 | | |
| Fitsgerald, John | 1 | | 2 | | | Cook, John | 1 | 2 | 2 | | | Lebbeus (Negro) | | | | 9 | |
| Ward, Crittendon | 1 | 1 | 1 | | | Ladd, Abner | 3 | 2 | 6 | | | Wood, Phinehas | 1 | 1 | 1 | | |
| Channing, Henry | 1 | 2 | 2 | 1 | | Armstrong, James | 1 | 1 | 3 | | | Crocker, Ezekiel | 2 | 1 | 2 | | |
| Richards, Elisabeth | | | 1 | 1 | | Huntley, Calvin | 1 | 1 | 3 | | | Crocker, Diah | 2 | | 2 | | |
| Manwaring, Lydia | | | 1 | | | Smith, John | 3 | | 3 | | | Backus, Hugh | 2 | | 2 | | |
| Colefax, George | 2 | 2 | 5 | | | Smith, Saml | 1 | | 3 | | | Calkins, Hugh | 2 | | 1 | | |
| Copp, Joseph | 1 | 1 | 1 | | | Armstrong, Hope | 2 | | 2 | | | Hartshorn, Andrew | 1 | 1 | 4 | | |
| Edgerton, James | 1 | 1 | 2 | | | Armstrong, Pelatiah | 1 | | 1 | | | Griswold, Diah | 1 | | 2 | | |
| Blackley, John | 1 | 1 | 3 | | | Sabin, Benajah | 2 | 1 | 3 | | | | | | | | |

# FIRST CENSUS OF THE UNITED STATES.

## NEW LONDON COUNTY—Continued.

| NAME OF HEAD OF FAMILY. | Free white males of 16 years and upward, including heads of families. | Free white males under 16 years. | Free white females, including heads of families. | All other free persons. | Slaves. | NAME OF HEAD OF FAMILY. | Free white males of 16 years and upward, including heads of families. | Free white males under 16 years. | Free white females, including heads of families. | All other free persons. | Slaves. | NAME OF HEAD OF FAMILY. | Free white males of 16 years and upward, including heads of families. | Free white males under 16 years. | Free white females, including heads of families. | All other free persons. | Slaves. |
|---|---|---|---|---|---|---|---|---|---|---|---|---|---|---|---|---|---|
| Penhally, Richard | 1 | 4 | 2 | | | Lathrop, Darius | 1 | | 2 | | | Lehomidieu, Grover | 3 | 4 | 7 | | |
| Hazen, Jacob | 2 | 1 | 4 | | | Griswold, Abell | 2 | 1 | 2 | | | King, Walter | 2 | | 5 | | |
| Armstrong, Ezra | 2 | | 5 | | | Morse, John | 1 | 5 | 5 | | | Bruster, Seabury | 2 | 2 | 2 | | |
| Hartshorn, Ebenezer | 1 | | 1 | | | Lathrop, Jonathan | 4 | 1 | 3 | | | Carew, Simeon | 2 | 1 | 3 | | |
| Hartshorn, Eben, Junr | 2 | 2 | 5 | | | Lathrop, Zachariah | 2 | 4 | 6 | | | Lester, Jona | 3 | 3 | 3 | | |
| Ladd, David | 2 | 2 | 3 | | | Chappell, Nathan | 1 | | 1 | | | Niles, Robart | 2 | 1 | 2 | | |
| Deans, Levi | 1 | 1 | 3 | | | Lathrop, Jeremiah | 2 | 3 | 5 | | | Geers, Squire | 2 | | 5 | | |
| Willes, Henry | 2 | | 2 | | | Caulkins, Daniel | 1 | | 2 | | | Ewen, Edward | 1 | 2 | 2 | | |
| Willes, Joshua | 1 | 1 | 1 | | | Abell, Caleb | 1 | 1 | 2 | | | Story, Henry | 1 | 1 | 2 | | |
| Nott, Samuel | 2 | 2 | 4 | | | Allen, Hezekiah | 1 | 1 | 2 | | | Story, Henry, 2d | 1 | 1 | 2 | | |
| Waterman, Ezekiel | 2 | 2 | 2 | | | Lord, Lucy | | | 3 | | | Story, James | 1 | 1 | 1 | | |
| Packer, John | 2 | 1 | 3 | | | Woodworth, Asa | 1 | 1 | 2 | | | Herrick, Elijah | 2 | 3 | 4 | | |
| Sanford, Kingsbury | 1 | 4 | 3 | | | French, Samuel | | | 2 | | | Deolph, Prissillah | | | 3 | | |
| Sanford, Bethiah | 1 | | 4 | | | French, Daniel | 1 | 2 | 2 | | | Story, Ephraim | 2 | | 3 | | |
| Starr, Abigail | | | 3 | | | Smith, Roger | 1 | | 2 | | | Lester, William | 1 | 2 | 2 | | |
| Lathrop, John | 2 | | 1 | | | Wentworth, Elizabeth | | | 1 | | | Wattles, Elijah | 2 | | 4 | | |
| Hyde, Joseph, Junr | 1 | 2 | 3 | | | Kirtland, Jabez | 1 | 3 | 2 | | | Wade, James | 2 | 2 | 4 | | |
| Willes, Jabez | 1 | | 1 | | | Bushnell, Jason | 1 | 2 | 2 | | | Hall, Daniel | 1 | 2 | 4 | | |
| Ellis, William | 1 | 1 | 4 | | | Kirtland, Joshua | 1 | 4 | 2 | | | Parker, Timothy | 2 | 2 | 3 | | |
| Ellis, Daniel | 2 | 1 | 2 | | | Downing, Christopher | 1 | | 1 | | | Tracy, David | 1 | | 1 | | |
| Peck, Joseph | 1 | 1 | 3 | | | Perkins, Robert | 1 | 4 | 5 | | | Leffingwell, Mathew. 2d | 1 | 1 | 2 | | |
| Peck, Syril | 1 | 2 | 7 | | | Woodworth, Asa, Junr | 3 | | 3 | | | Bryan, Timothy | 1 | 1 | 1 | | |
| Hyde, Ezekiel | 2 | | 2 | | | Burnham, James | | | 3 | | | Beckwith, William | 1 | | 1 | | |
| Chapman, Stephen | 1 | 2 | 4 | | | Burnham, Roger | 1 | 2 | 2 | | | Gilbert, George | 1 | 1 | 4 | | |
| Smith, Obadiah | 1 | 1 | 3 | | | Abell, Thomas | 2 | 1 | 7 | | | Beckwith, Nathan | 1 | | 1 | | |
| Backus, Eunice | | 3 | 2 | | | Burnham, Samuel | 1 | | 1 | | | Jeffers, Peter | 1 | 1 | 2 | | |
| Hartshorn, Elijah | 1 | 1 | 2 | | | Tracy, Jabez, Junr | 1 | 1 | 2 | | | Waterman, John | 2 | 1 | 4 | | |
| Smith, Joshua, 3d | 2 | | 1 | | | Tracy, Daniel | 1 | | 3 | | | Waterman, Peter | 1 | | 3 | | |
| Smith, Andrew | 2 | 2 | 5 | | | Tracy, Esanius | 1 | 2 | 1 | | | Elderkin, John | 1 | 2 | 2 | | |
| Smith, Sarah | 1 | | 2 | | | Quy (Negro) | | | | 2 | 1 | Wade, Jona | 1 | | 1 | | |
| Fox, David | 3 | 1 | 2 | | | Lathrop, Jabez | 1 | | 1 | | | Webb, John | 3 | | 3 | | |
| Hyde, Taber | 2 | | 1 | | | Lathrop, Lucy | 2 | 1 | 2 | | | Willet, John, Junr | 1 | 1 | 2 | | |
| Hyde, Andrew | 1 | 3 | 4 | | | Hughes, John | 2 | 1 | 1 | | | Murry, Semore | 1 | 2 | 2 | | |
| Hyde, Benjamin | 1 | 1 | 3 | | | Allen, John | 2 | 3 | 4 | | | Billings, Alpheus | 2 | 3 | 6 | | |
| Hastings, Roswell | 1 | 3 | 3 | | | Jack (Negro) | | | | 1 | | Vorce, Wm | 1 | | 3 | | |
| Hastings, Dan | 1 | 1 | 1 | | | Leech, Elijah | 1 | 4 | 3 | | | Sutliff, Jannah | | | 2 | | |
| James (Negro) | | | | | 2 | Jones, Rufus | 1 | 2 | 3 | | | Geer, Uziel | 2 | | 2 | | |
| Champion, John | 1 | | 2 | | | Johnson, Nathan | 2 | 1 | 3 | | | Williams, Elijah | 1 | | 4 | | |
| Champion, Henry V | 3 | 2 | 5 | | | Kingsley, Josiah | 2 | | 3 | | | Chapman, Nancy | | | 1 | | |
| Forry, Micajah | 1 | | 4 | | | Kingsley, Eleazar | 1 | 1 | 8 | | | Fitch, Hannah | | | 4 | | |
| Metcalf, Eliphalet | 2 | 1 | 1 | | | Bushnell, David | 1 | 4 | 3 | | | Baker, John | 1 | 2 | 2 | | |
| Ellis, Stephen | 2 | | 3 | | | Bushnell, John | | | | | | Peirce, John | 3 | | 2 | | |
| Tracy, Joshua | 1 | 1 | 2 | | | Bushnell, Mary | 1 | 1 | 4 | | | Day, John | 1 | 3 | 2 | | |
| Huntington, Azariah | 3 | 1 | 3 | | | Meeker, Josiah | 1 | 1 | 1 | | | Willet, John | 1 | | 2 | | |
| Sabin, Elijah | 1 | | 1 | | | Jones, Amos | 1 | 1 | 2 | | | Willet, Jedediah | 1 | 2 | 1 | | |
| Sabin, Jedediah | 1 | 1 | 1 | | | Bushnell, Jonathan | 1 | | 1 | | | Ewen, Edward, Junr | 1 | | 1 | | |
| Tracy, Josiah, Junr | 2 | | 7 | 1 | | Bushnell, Jonathan, Junr | 1 | 2 | 2 | | | Hewet, Solomon | 3 | 2 | 2 | | |
| Tracy, Hezekiah | 1 | 1 | 3 | 1 | | Lord, Hezekiah | 1 | | 3 | | | Larrance, Jona | 1 | 2 | 2 | | |
| Tracy, Dudley | 1 | 2 | 3 | | | Williams, Solomon | 1 | 4 | 4 | | | Calkins, Hugh | 1 | | 1 | | |
| Tracy, John | 3 | 1 | 5 | | | Walbridge, Gustavus | 1 | | 1 | | | Whiting, Ebenr | 3 | 4 | 6 | | 2 |
| Bentley, Eleazar | 1 | | 2 | | | Walbridge, Ebenezer | 1 | | 1 | | | Destouch, Sirace | 1 | 1 | 3 | | 7 |
| Edgerton, Elisha | 2 | 5 | 5 | | | Wall, James | 1 | 2 | 4 | | | Whipple, Joshua | 1 | | 3 | | |
| Edgerton, Abel | 1 | 1 | 4 | | | Brown, Samuel | 1 | | 2 | | | Baker, Pemberton | 1 | 3 | 3 | | |
| Tracy, Naomi | 1 | 1 | 3 | | | Yeomans, Joshua | 1 | 3 | 3 | | | Ceaser (Negro) | | | | 4 | |
| Edgerton, Hezekiah | 2 | 2 | 6 | | | Reeves, Ebenezer | 2 | 1 | 3 | | | Craige, Mary | 1 | | 4 | | |
| Edgerton, Hezekiah, Junr | 1 | | 2 | | | Barker, William | 1 | 3 | 2 | | | Kelley, John | 2 | | 4 | | |
| Tracy, Daniel | 4 | | 4 | | | Bushnell, Elisabeth | 1 | | 3 | | | Cheney, Abiel, 2d | 1 | 1 | 5 | | |
| Hyde, Taber, Junr | 1 | 2 | 2 | | | Hazen, Jacob | 1 | 1 | 1 | | | Brooks, Gurdon | 1 | | 2 | | |
| Tracy, John, Junr | 1 | 2 | 3 | | | Wayres, Archibald | 1 | | 4 | | | Barker, Stephen, 2d | 1 | | 2 | | |
| Lathrop, Ephraim | 1 | 2 | 2 | | | Derly, Blanchard | 1 | 2 | 4 | | | Day, James | 3 | 2 | 2 | | |
| Fitch, Benjamin B | 2 | | 1 | | | Derly, Blanchard, Junr | 1 | | 2 | | | Williams, Joseph | 5 | 3 | 6 | | 2 |
| Hyde, Daniel | 4 | 1 | 5 | | | Belshaw, Samuel | 1 | 4 | 1 | | | Fitch, Ebenr | 1 | 1 | 3 | | |
| Mason, David | 2 | | 5 | | | Lunt, Sarah | | | 2 | | | Cowdre, Isaac | 1 | 1 | 4 | | |
| Johnson, Isaac | 1 | 2 | 2 | | | Leffingwell, Matthew | 6 | 1 | 3 | | | Woodworth, Darius | 1 | 1 | 2 | | |
| Johnson, Oliver | 1 | | 2 | | | Bushnell, Caleb | 2 | | 3 | | | Brud, John | 2 | | 5 | | 1 |
| Lathrop, James | 1 | | 2 | | | Bushnell, Richard | 1 | 2 | 2 | | | Huntington, Jona | 3 | 3 | 3 | | |
| Lathrop, Ezekiel | 1 | 1 | 3 | | | Parish, Nathaniel | 2 | | 2 | | | Huntington, Daniel | 1 | | 3 | | |
| Lathrop, Abigail | | | 1 | | | Leffingwell, Phinehas | 1 | 6 | 3 | | | Clemment, Jeremiah | 1 | | 2 | | |
| Lathrop, Arunah | 2 | 1 | 3 | | | Fitch, Gideon | 1 | | 4 | | | Braddock, John | 1 | | 2 | | |
| Maynard, James | 1 | 1 | 3 | | | Fitch, Gideon, Junr | 1 | | 1 | | | Smith, Jona | 1 | 2 | 4 | | |
| Pettis, Ichiel | 1 | 2 | 3 | 1 | | Huntington, Jared | 1 | 4 | 4 | | | Osburn, David | 1 | 2 | 3 | | |
| Lathrop, Walter | 1 | 3 | 3 | | | Goodell, Benjamin | 2 | 1 | 4 | | | Christee, James | 2 | 3 | 4 | | |
| Lord, Sylvanus | 1 | | 3 | | | Ormsby, Samuel | 2 | 1 | 4 | | | Leffingwell, Hart | 2 | | 2 | | |
| Tinney, Asa | 1 | 5 | 4 | | | Senter, John | 1 | | 5 | | | Lord, Jabez | 1 | 3 | 4 | | |
| Tinney, Reuben | 1 | 1 | 3 | | | Giffords, Jeremiah | 2 | 1 | 7 | | | Dennis, Benjamin | 1 | | 2 | | 1 |
| Tinney, Mary | | | 2 | | | Morgan, Darius | 1 | 2 | 2 | | | Coit, Farewell | 1 | 1 | 2 | | |
| Lathrop, Priscilla | 2 | | 2 | | | Giffords, John | 2 | 2 | 2 | | | Holden, Phineas | 1 | | 2 | | |
| Bret, William | 1 | | 1 | | | Starr, Jona | 6 | 2 | 6 | | 1 | Tracy, Isaac | 2 | 2 | 3 | | |
| Hewitt, Jedidiah | 4 | 1 | 2 | | | Carew, Elpheleb | 2 | 4 | 6 | 2 | | Backeus, Betsy | 1 | 2 | 9 | 1 | |
| Cary, Diah | 1 | | 1 | | | Leach, Thomas | 1 | | 2 | | | Denison, Benadam | 1 | 3 | 6 | | 1 |
| Hyde, Sarah | 2 | 1 | 2 | | | Hazen, Darius | 1 | 4 | 4 | | | Backeus, Ezra | 2 | | 3 | | |
| Backus, Joshua | 1 | 1 | 2 | | | Williams, Ashur | 2 | 1 | 4 | | | Kelley, Daniel | 1 | 1 | 2 | | |
| Abell, Ira | 1 | 2 | 3 | | | Lathrop, Jedidiah | 2 | 1 | 4 | | | Loring, Surviah | | | 2 | | |
| Lilly, Amariah | 1 | 2 | 5 | | | Pitcher, Elijah | 3 | 6 | 2 | | | Brud, Shubael | 1 | | 4 | | |
| Giffords, Samuel | 2 | 1 | 4 | | | Burnham, Elias | 2 | 3 | 4 | | | Swaddle, John | 1 | 1 | 2 | | |
| Rogers, James | 3 | | 5 | | | Burnham, Zaccheus | 1 | | 1 | | | Burdett, Edward | 1 | 1 | 1 | | |
| Rogers, Eleazar | 1 | | 2 | | | Willet, Joshua | 1 | | 3 | | | Fillemore, Timothy | 1 | | 1 | | |
| Edgerton, Simon | 2 | 1 | 2 | | | Lathrop, Zephaniah | 3 | 1 | 5 | | | Read, Mary | | | 2 | | |
| Edgerton, Stephen | 1 | 1 | 3 | | | Roath, Frederick | 1 | | 1 | | | Stephens, William | 1 | | 2 | | |
| Tracy, Jabez | 1 | 1 | 5 | | | Carpenter, Alfred | 1 | 2 | 2 | | | Barker, Stephen | 2 | 4 | 2 | | |
| Ellis, Joseph | 2 | 1 | 4 | | | Palmeter, Jesse | 1 | | 1 | | | Culver, Stephen | 1 | | 1 | | |
| Birchard, John | 1 | 2 | 6 | | | Maples, Jona | 1 | | 5 | | | Lanman, Peter | 4 | 1 | 5 | | |
| Armstrong, Joseph | 1 | | 1 | | | Woodworth, Jasper | 3 | 1 | 2 | | | Daverson, Brazilla | 4 | 1 | 4 | | |
| Armstrong, Phinehas | 1 | 1 | 6 | | | Adams, Solomon | 1 | 2 | 3 | | | Perkins, Erastus | 1 | 4 | 3 | | |
| Armstrong, Elijah | 2 | 1 | 2 | | | Woodworth, Simeon | 1 | | 2 | | | Daverson, William | 1 | | 3 | | |
| Armstrong, Jabez | 1 | 3 | 2 | | | Mumford, Thomas | 3 | 2 | 5 | | 1 | Marvin, Elihu | | 1 | 4 | | |
| | | | | | | Colt, Thomas | 3 | | 2 | | 3 | Colt, William | 6 | 1 | 5 | | 1 |

# HEADS OF FAMILIES—CONNECTICUT.

## NEW LONDON COUNTY—Continued.

| NAME OF HEAD OF FAMILY. | Free white males of 16 years and upward, including heads of families. | Free white males under 16 years. | Free white females, including heads of families. | All other free persons. | Slaves. | NAME OF HEAD OF FAMILY. | Free white males of 16 years and upward, including heads of families. | Free white males under 16 years. | Free white females, including heads of families. | All other free persons. | Slaves. | NAME OF HEAD OF FAMILY. | Free white males of 16 years and upward, including heads of families. | Free white males under 16 years. | Free white females, including heads of families. | All other free persons. | Slaves. |
|---|---|---|---|---|---|---|---|---|---|---|---|---|---|---|---|---|---|
| Whipple, Zephaniah | 1 | 4 | 1 | | | Bliss, Elijah | 1 | | 2 | | | Burchird, Elisha | 3 | 3 | 2 | | |
| Peabody, Asa | 1 | 1 | 3 | | 1 | Bliss, Thomas | 2 | | 2 | | 1 | Avory, Samuel | 2 | 3 | 4 | | |
| Peabody, Prentice | 1 | 3 | 5 | | | Silsby, Jonª | 1 | 1 | 2 | | | Huntington, John | 2 | | 1 | | |
| Young, Nabby | | | 2 | | | Smith, John, 2d | 1 | 4 | 2 | | | Huntington, Felix | 5 | 2 | 7 | | |
| Huxley, Eunice | | | 2 | | | Roath, David | 2 | | 4 | | | Huntington, Ezra | 1 | 3 | 5 | | |
| Kelley, Hezekiah | 4 | | 2 | | | Roath, Joseph | 1 | 1 | 6 | | | Huntington, Benjamin | 2 | 1 | 3 | | |
| Tylar, John | 2 | 1 | 6 | | | Roath, Jonª | 1 | | | | | Tracy, Daniel | 3 | | 6 | | |
| Buswell, Lemuel | 2 | 2 | 3 | | | Roath, Stephen | | | 1 | | | Darrow, Michael | 1 | | 1 | | |
| Bingham, Simeon | 1 | | 1 | | | Roath, Eleazer | 1 | 2 | 3 | | | Post, John | 1 | 1 | 1 | | |
| Story, Solomon | 1 | 2 | 3 | | | Roath, Samˡ | 2 | 3 | 2 | | | Lothrop, Darcas | | | 2 | | |
| Choat, Eunice | | | 2 | | | Roggers, Presilla | | | 3 | | | Danforth, John | 3 | | 5 | | |
| Vale, Christopher | 2 | 1 | 3 | | | Lamb, John | 1 | 1 | 1 | | | Danforth, Hannah | | | 2 | | |
| Welcop, John | 1 | 1 | 2 | | | Culver, Benjamin | 1 | 1 | 1 | | | Spicer, Joshua | 1 | | 2 | | |
| Brown, William | 1 | | 1 | | | Headen, Noah | 2 | | 4 | | | Larthly, Mary | | 1 | 2 | | |
| Young, John | 1 | 1 | 4 | | | Winchester, Joel | 1 | | 3 | | | Hall, Nathan | 2 | | 1 | | |
| Wilber, Jeremiah | 1 | 2 | 1 | | | Dennis, Samˡ | 1 | 2 | 3 | | | Grist, Ann | | | 2 | | |
| Thomas, James | 1 | | 1 | | | Sutliff, John | 1 | 2 | 2 | | | Huntington, Elisha | 1 | 3 | 3 | | |
| Freman, Hezekiah | 2 | 1 | 5 | | | Mehagan, Dennis | 1 | | | | | Lancaster, John | 3 | | 2 | | |
| Warren, Lemuel | 1 | 1 | 4 | | | Elderkin, James | 1 | | 1 | | | Strong, Joseph | 2 | 2 | 3 | | 1 |
| Corning, John | 2 | 1 | 1 | | | Sherman, John | 1 | 2 | 2 | | | Huntington, Zachariah | 2 | 2 | 4 | 1 | 1 |
| Whipple, Wᵐ | 1 | 1 | 4 | | | Smith, Patience | | 1 | 1 | | | Huntington, Joshua | 2 | 1 | 4 | | |
| Dennis, Russel | 2 | 1 | 3 | | | Hill, John | 1 | | 2 | | | Tracy, Mundator | 2 | 3 | 4 | | |
| Howland, Joseph | 4 | 2 | 9 | | | Hendricks, Benjamin | 1 | 1 | 2 | | | Able, Hannah | | 1 | 1 | | |
| Moore, David | 2 | 4 | 3 | | | Billings, Henry | 1 | 1 | 1 | | | Huntington, Andʷ | 2 | 3 | 5 | | |
| Lamb, Jesse | 1 | | 1 | | | Keeney, Newcomb | 2 | 2 | 1 | | | Tracy, Samˡ | 3 | 1 | 3 | | |
| Harris, Jeremiah | 2 | 5 | 5 | | | Carew, Daniel | 1 | 1 | 3 | | | Jones, Parmenus | 1 | | 3 | | |
| Perkins, Andʷ | 2 | | 5 | | | Fanning, Thomas | 3 | 1 | 5 | | | Huntington, Samˡ | 2 | | 4 | 2 | 1 |
| Perkins, Hezekiah | 2 | 3 | 3 | | | Huntington, Frederick | 2 | 1 | 4 | | | Gale, Joseph | 1 | 2 | 2 | | |
| Lothrop, Lydia | 2 | 4 | 5 | | | Corning, Bliss | 2 | 2 | 2 | | | Abbot, Danˡ | 1 | 3 | 5 | | |
| Perkins, Jabez | 3 | | 2 | | | Shipman, Nathˡ | 5 | 1 | 2 | | | Leach, Jeremiah | 2 | 1 | 2 | | |
| Hambleton, Jonas | 4 | | 4 | | | Dennis, George | 1 | | 3 | | 2 | Townshend, Nathˡ | 1 | 2 | 3 | | |
| Hambleton, Solomon | 2 | | 3 | | | Moore, John | 2 | 3 | 5 | | | Huntington, Simeon | 2 | 2 | 6 | | |
| Kingsley, Eunice | | | 2 | | | Derby, Erastus | 1 | | 1 | | | Nevins, David | 5 | 7 | 5 | | |
| Leffingwell, Hart, 2d | 1 | | 1 | | | Lothrop, Elijah | 2 | 1 | 3 | | 4 | Charlton, Charles | 2 | | 5 | | |
| Smith, Zebadiah | 1 | 2 | 5 | | | Lothrop, Simon | 1 | 2 | 2 | | 1 | Lothrop, Asa | 3 | | 6 | | |
| How, Abner | 3 | 2 | 4 | | | Weston, Amaziah | 2 | 1 | 3 | | | Young, Thomas | 1 | 2 | 3 | | |
| Bruster, Phillup | 1 | 1 | 1 | | | Leffingwell, Elisha | 1 | 2 | 5 | | | Carew, Joseph | 2 | | 3 | | |
| Backeus, Erastus | 1 | 2 | 1 | | 2 | Goodel, Silas | 1 | 1 | 5 | | | Turner, John | 1 | | 3 | | |
| Ginnings, Zephaniah | 2 | 2 | 2 | | | Cato (Negro) | | | | 5 | | Sam (Negro) | | | | 4 | |
| Perkins, Jabez, Junʳ | 3 | 1 | 3 | | | Bena (Negro) | | | | 6 | 1 | Mix, John | 1 | 2 | 5 | | |
| Dᵉ Witt, Jacob | 1 | 2 | 3 | | | Kingsley, Joseph | 3 | | 4 | | | Roggers, David | 2 | | 1 | | |
| Lothrop, Elijah, Junʳ | 3 | 3 | 4 | | | Leffingwell, Hezekiah | 2 | 1 | 5 | | | Gilden, Issabell | | | 2 | | |
| McCurdy, Lynds | 2 | 2 | 4 | | | Savage, Cornelius | 1 | 3 | 1 | | | McDonald, Elexander | 1 | 1 | 2 | | |
| Huntington, Levi | 2 | 3 | 6 | | | Hendricks, Daniel | 1 | | 1 | | | Miner, Seth | 2 | 2 | 3 | 1 | |
| Norman, Joshua | 2 | 1 | 4 | | | Nicols, John | 1 | 1 | 2 | | | Sloakum, Edward | 1 | | 2 | | |
| Wetmore, Izrahiah | 1 | 1 | 3 | | 1 | Castle, Anthony | 1 | 2 | 4 | | | Dean, Samˡ | 1 | 1 | 2 | | |
| Demming, Elizer | 1 | | 1 | | | Reynolds, Joseph | 3 | 2 | 5 | | | Carpenter, Joseph | 4 | 2 | 6 | | |
| Bill, Ephraim | 3 | 1 | 2 | | 2 | Barral, Lewis | 1 | 2 | 2 | | | Brown, Jesse | 1 | 3 | 4 | | 1 |
| King, Thomas | 5 | 3 | 4 | 1 | | Bliss, John | 5 | | 2 | | | Griswould, Roger | 2 | 3 | 2 | | |
| Cheney, Abiel | 1 | | 1 | | | Williams, Hezekiah | 1 | 1 | 3 | | | Carpenter, Gardiner | 1 | | 2 | | |
| Lathrop, Samuel | 1 | | 3 | | | Fanning, Ann | | | 1 | | | Peck, Bela | 2 | 2 | 2 | | 1 |
| Silsby, Polly | | | 1 | | | London (Negro) | | | | 2 | | Jones, Ebenʳ | 3 | | 3 | | |
| Smith, Daniel | 1 | 1 | 4 | | | Pettis, Abigail | | | 1 | | | Spalding, Asa | 1 | 1 | 3 | | |
| Smith, Jonª | 1 | 2 | 2 | | | Leffingwell, Thomas | 2 | | 3 | | | Stockwell, Elisabeth | | 1 | 1 | | |
| Barrett, William | 3 | | 2 | | | Coit, Joseph | 2 | | 2 | | | Manning, Diah | 1 | 1 | 5 | | |
| Coit, Benjamin | 1 | 2 | 3 | | | Leffingwell, Samˡ | 1 | | 6 | | | Cole, Mary | | | 2 | | |
| Demming, Wᵐ | 1 | | 4 | | | Linkhorn, James | 1 | | 1 | | | Lord, Eleazer | 3 | 1 | 3 | 1 | |
| Wattles, Henry | 2 | | 3 | | | Winter, Abner | 1 | | 4 | | | Lord, Abigail | | | 2 | | |
| Brooks, Benjamin | 1 | 1 | 3 | | | Winship, Philemon | 1 | 1 | 1 | | | Lord, Daniel | 1 | 1 | 1 | | |
| Roath, Ebenezer | 1 | 1 | 3 | | | Richards, John | 1 | 2 | 3 | | | Lothrop, Azariah | 5 | 3 | 6 | 1 | 3 |
| Badcock, Thomas | 1 | 3 | 1 | | | Norman, Caleb | 1 | | 1 | | | Leffingwell, Bela | 1 | | 1 | | |
| Champlin, Rowland | 3 | 4 | 4 | | | Marsh, Jonathan | 1 | 1 | 4 | | | Wedge, David | 1 | | 1 | | |
| Jones, Benjamin | 2 | | 4 | | | Leffingwell, William | 1 | 2 | 3 | | | Otis, Joseph | 1 | 1 | 2 | | |
| Easter (Negro) | | | | 3 | | Leffingwell, Christopher | 5 | 2 | 10 | | | Backeus, Elisabeth | | | 2 | | |
| Frisby, Jonathan | 1 | 1 | 3 | | | Firgo, Elisha | 1 | | 1 | | | Backeus, Rufus | 7 | 3 | 3 | | |
| Corning, Deborah | | | 2 | | | Cox, William | 1 | 7 | 4 | | | Backeus, John | 2 | | 3 | | |
| Waterman, Ignatius | 1 | | 3 | | | Harland, Thomas | 6 | 7 | 7 | | | Jack (Negro) | | | | 1 | |
| Winchester, Amaziah | 2 | | 2 | | | Williams, Thomas | 4 | 1 | 2 | | | Backeus, Elijah | 6 | 2 | 3 | 1 | 1 |
| Disskoll, Adam | 1 | 3 | 2 | | | Primus (Negro) | | | | 2 | | Noyce, Dolly | | | 1 | | |
| Elderkin, Frederick | 1 | | 4 | | | Huntington John, 2d | 3 | 3 | 5 | | | Woodbridge, Samuel | 2 | 2 | 6 | 1 | |
| Buswell, Lemuel, Junʳ | 2 | 1 | 1 | | | Billings, Mary | | | 3 | | | Prince (Negro) | | | | 3 | |
| Rockwell, Elisabeth | 2 | | 2 | | | Hubbard, Thomas | 2 | 6 | 2 | | | Roggers, Theophilus | 1 | 1 | 3 | | |
| Clemment, Peabody | 2 | | 1 | | | Bushneel, Ebenʳ | 1 | 1 | 2 | | | Pomp (Negro) | | | | 1 | 1 |
| Kelley, Joseph | 1 | | 3 | | | Cleaveland, Irena | | | 1 | | | Sutton (Negro) | | | | 2 | |
| Gordon, George | 1 | 1 | 2 | | | Carew, Ebenʳ | 7 | 3 | 5 | | | Caulkins, Andʷ | 1 | | 2 | | |
| Daverson, — | | | 1 | | | Lothrop, Zebadiah | 1 | | 3 | | | Waterman, Arunah | 1 | 5 | 5 | | |
| Trapp, Caleb | 1 | | 4 | | | Avory, Richard | 3 | | 2 | | | Waterman, Lucy | | | 2 | | |
| Moore, Jonª | 1 | | 1 | | | Maynord, Asael | 1 | | 2 | | | Yale, Joseph | 1 | 2 | 4 | | |
| Edwards, David | 1 | | 3 | | | Rockwell, Amy | | | 2 | | | Waterman, Eunice | 1 | | 2 | | |
| Farnum, John | 2 | 2 | 1 | | | Manning, Rockwell | 1 | 1 | 2 | | | Tracy, Andʷ | 4 | 2 | 6 | 1 | |
| Trapp, Samˡ | 1 | | 1 | | | Lothrop, Rufus | 2 | 1 | 2 | 2 | 1 | Roggers, Zabdiel | 2 | 4 | 10 | | |
| Joy, Richard | 1 | | 2 | | | Lothrop, Joshua | 2 | 1 | 3 | 1 | 2 | Ornsby, Ephraim | 1 | | 4 | | |
| Crandall, Samuel | 2 | | 3 | | | Case, Simeon | 2 | | 2 | | | Winter, Jacob | 2 | 2 | 3 | | |
| Brooks, Guy | 1 | | 4 | | | Lothrop, Jerusha | | 1 | 3 | | | Tracy, Fridirick | 2 | 3 | 6 | | |
| Rogers, Nehemiah | 1 | 1 | 4 | | | Lothrop, Thomas | 2 | 3 | 5 | | 1 | Marshall, Thomas | 1 | 1 | 2 | | |
| Cullis, James | 1 | | 1 | | | Coit, Daniel | 2 | 1 | 6 | 1 | 1 | Hide, James, 2d | 3 | 4 | 4 | | |
| Bates, Henry | 1 | 1 | 2 | | | Adgate, Eunice | 3 | | 2 | | | Hide, Abiel | 3 | 3 | 5 | | |
| S (Negro) | | | | 7 | | Case, Samˡ | 2 | 1 | 2 | | | Waterman, William | 2 | | 4 | | |
| Leffingwell, Benajah | 3 | 1 | 2 | | | Cobb, Nathan | 3 | 1 | 5 | | | Griswould, Isaac | 1 | 1 | 5 | 1 | |
| Joy, William | 1 | 1 | 5 | | | Brown, Surviah | | | 2 | | | Clark, Elisha | 1 | | 1 | | |
| Joy, William, Junʳ | 1 | | 3 | | | Coney, Edward | 1 | 1 | 3 | | | Silva (Negro) | | | | 2 | |
| Trapp, Ephraim | 1 | 1 | 3 | | | Mix, James | 1 | 2 | 2 | | | Lord, Simon | 1 | 1 | 4 | | |
| Hinckley, Vorce | 1 | 1 | 5 | | | Case, Ebenʳ | 2 | | 2 | | | Wintworth, Lemuel | 1 | 3 | 4 | | |
| Elderkin, Martha | | | 1 | | | Beba, David | 1 | | 1 | | | Culver, Jonathan | 5 | 2 | 6 | | |
| Coy, David | 1 | 2 | 1 | | | Case, Asael | 1 | | 1 | | | Hide, Ebenʳ | 3 | 2 | 5 | | |
| Arnold, Caleb | 1 | 1 | 2 | | | Pots, Christopher | 2 | 2 | 2 | | | Hide, James | 1 | | 3 | | |
| Strange, Hannah | | | 1 | | | Burchird, Gideon | 2 | 1 | 3 | | | Gibeons, Gerard | 1 | 1 | 3 | | |

## NEW LONDON COUNTY—Continued.

| NAME OF HEAD OF FAMILY. | Free white males of 16 years and upward, including heads of families. | Free white males under 16 years. | Free white females, including heads of families. | All other free persons. | Slaves. | NAME OF HEAD OF FAMILY. | Free white males of 16 years and upward, including heads of families. | Free white males under 16 years. | Free white females, including heads of families. | All other free persons. | Slaves. | NAME OF HEAD OF FAMILY. | Free white males of 16 years and upward, including heads of families. | Free white males under 16 years. | Free white females, including heads of families. | All other free persons. | Slaves. |
|---|---|---|---|---|---|---|---|---|---|---|---|---|---|---|---|---|---|
| Waller, Silas | 1 | 2 | 2 | | | Barret, Ezekiel | 1 | 3 | 2 | | | Tracy, Philemon | 1 | 1 | 2 | | |
| Collier, John | 2 | | 3 | | | Sabins, Sarah | 1 | 1 | 2 | | | Tainter, Joseph | 1 | | 3 | | |
| Waller, Hannah | | | 1 | | | Wintworth, Abigail | | | 1 | | | Hide, Elisha | 1 | 1 | 4 | | |
| Avory, Elisha | 1 | 1 | 4 | | | Belshaw, Jonᵃ | 1 | | 2 | | | Mansfield, William | 1 | 1 | 7 | | |
| Thatcher, John | 1 | 4 | 1 | | | Lord, Ebenʳ | 1 | | 4 | | | Chapman, Joseph | 1 | 2 | 5 | | |
| Clark, Watrus | 2 | 4 | 3 | | | Chapple, Nathan, 2ᵈ | 3 | | 3 | | | Doyle, Richard | 1 | | 1 | | |
| Thomas (Negro) | | | | 5 | | Morgan, William | 3 | 1 | 3 | | | Johnson, Eliphelet | 1 | 2 | 3 | | |
| Poor house | 2 | 2 | 3 | | | Frost, Ebenʳ | 1 | 4 | 4 | | | Wade, Sarah | | | 1 | | |
| Huntington, Simon | 4 | 1 | 2 | 1 | | Tracy, Nathan | 1 | 1 | 3 | | | Reynolds, Gamaliel | 2 | | 3 | | |
| Huntington, Samˡ, Junʳ | 1 | 1 | 4 | | | Duglass, Daniel | 1 | | 4 | | | Nutter, John | 2 | | 4 | | |
| Huntington, Daniel | 1 | | 1 | | | Giffords, Samˡ, Junʳ | 1 | 1 | 2 | | | Post, Samˡ | 2 | | 3 | | |
| Richerson, Asa | 2 | 2 | 5 | | | Thomas, Thomas L | 4 | 3 | 5 | | | Latham, Peter | 1 | 2 | 6 | | |
| Roath, Robart | 1 | | | | | Bryan, John | 2 | 1 | 4 | | | Arnold, Prudence | 1 | | 4 | | |
| Griswould, Joseph | 2 | 1 | 3 | | | Brigden, Timothy | 1 | 2 | 1 | | | Will (Negro) | | | | 6 | |
| Lamb, Richard | 2 | 2 | 3 | | | Thomas, Simeon | 1 | | 5 | | | Ark (Negro) | | | | 5 | |
| Carew, Palmer | 2 | 1 | 4 | | | Dulongpre, Ann | 1 | | 3 | | | Avory, Ann | | | 2 | | |
| Gilson, Jonᵃ | 1 | | 2 | | | Tracy, Peres | 2 | | 2 | | | Waterman, Timothy | 2 | | 3 | | 2 |
| Thatcher, Samˡ | 1 | 2 | 2 | | | Able, Joshua | 1 | 1 | 2 | | | Turner, Phillup | 2 | 1 | 6 | | |
| Huntington, Eliphelet | 2 | 2 | 5 | | | Waterman, Uriah | 2 | | 2 | | | Trumbull, John | 2 | 6 | 4 | | |
| Dennis, George, 2ᵈ | 1 | 1 | 5 | | | Huntington, Benjamin | 7 | 1 | 6 | | | Tracy, Uriah | 1 | | 3 | | |
| Caulkins, Simon | 1 | 1 | 1 | | | Grover, Ebenʳ | 1 | | 3 | | | Collier, Benjᵃ | 2 | | 2 | | |
| Thomas, Ebenʳ | 2 | 5 | 6 | | | Hartshorn, Rufus | 1 | | | | | Baker, Ephraim | 3 | 1 | 2 | | |
| Tracy, Jared | 2 | 2 | 6 | | | Bride, Ann | | | 1 | | | Tracy, Elisha | 1 | | 3 | | |
| Cleaveland, Aaron | 3 | 3 | 5 | | | Bristo (Negro) | | | | 4 | | | | | | | |
| Armstrong, Worth | 1 | 2 | 3 | | | Hide, Zebadiah | 2 | 2 | 3 | | | | | | | | |

## TOLLAND COUNTY.

### BOLTON TOWN.

| NAME OF HEAD OF FAMILY. | Free white males of 16 years and upward, including heads of families. | Free white males under 16 years. | Free white females, including heads of families. | All other free persons. | Slaves. | NAME OF HEAD OF FAMILY. | Free white males of 16 years and upward, including heads of families. | Free white males under 16 years. | Free white females, including heads of families. | All other free persons. | Slaves. | NAME OF HEAD OF FAMILY. | Free white males of 16 years and upward, including heads of families. | Free white males under 16 years. | Free white females, including heads of families. | All other free persons. | Slaves. |
|---|---|---|---|---|---|---|---|---|---|---|---|---|---|---|---|---|---|
| Coleman, Jnᵒ, Jr | 1 | 1 | 2 | | | Lyman, Jacob | 2 | 1 | 3 | | | Evans, Thoˢ | 1 | | 1 | | |
| Coleman, Jnᵒ | 1 | 3 | 2 | | | Isam, Timᵒ | 6 | 2 | 4 | | | Hyde, Josˢ | 2 | 2 | 4 | | |
| Waterman, Ezra | 3 | 1 | 4 | | | Tolcot, Jonᵃ | 1 | 2 | 3 | | | Tolcot, Seth | 3 | | 3 | | |
| Talcot, Josᵘ | 2 | 3 | 5 | | | Atherton, Jnᵒ | 1 | 4 | 4 | | | Tolcot, Justus | 1 | | 3 | | |
| Phillips, Elijah | 4 | 1 | 4 | | | Swetland, Luke | 1 | 1 | 4 | | | Rude (Widow) | | | 3 | | |
| Fowler, James | 2 | 1 | 2 | | | Bishop, Thoˢ | 2 | | 2 | | | Tolcot, Caleb | 2 | 1 | 2 | | |
| Chapman, James | 1 | 4 | 2 | | | Dart, Jonᵃ | 2 | 1 | 3 | | | Simons, James | 2 | 5 | 2 | | |
| Herkin, Aaron | 1 | 1 | 5 | | | Lomis, Elijah | 2 | 1 | 7 | | | Ellis (Widow) | | | 2 | | |
| Hollister, Appleton | 1 | 2 | | | | Dart, Jonᵃ | 1 | 1 | 2 | | | Dart, Jnᵒ | 2 | 1 | 4 | | |
| Bartletts, Chaˢ | | | 2 | | | Lomis, Amasa | 1 | 2 | 2 | | | King, Elijah | 3 | 1 | 4 | | |
| Post, Josˢ | 2 | | 3 | | | Lomis, Abner | 1 | 3 | 2 | | | King, Samˡ | 2 | 1 | 3 | | |
| Griswould, George | 1 | 1 | 3 | | | Lomis, Jacob | 2 | | 3 | | | Fields, Thoˢ | 1 | | 3 | | |
| Ringe, Isaac | 1 | 2 | 1 | | | Lomis, Charles | 1 | 2 | 6 | | | Chapman, Thoˢ | 1 | 4 | 5 | | |
| Cone, Jared | 2 | | 2 | | | Webster, Thoˢ | 1 | | 2 | | | Webster, Asahel | 2 | 1 | 4 | | |
| White, Joel | 1 | | 3 | | | Webster, David | 3 | 1 | 4 | | | Root, Daniel | 1 | | 2 | | |
| Alvert, Saul | 3 | | 3 | | | Bishop, Jnᵒ | 2 | 4 | 4 | | | Byers, Leonard | 1 | | 5 | | |
| White, Jabez | 1 | | 5 | | | Bishop, Samˡ | 1 | 2 | 2 | | | Skinner, Ruben | 2 | 2 | 6 | | |
| White, Elijah | 5 | 2 | 4 | | 1 | Raynolds, Ruben | 1 | | 2 | | | Chapman, Lemˡ | 2 | 2 | 5 | | |
| Bliss, Mrˢ | 1 | 1 | 2 | | | Lomis, Levy | 1 | 4 | 5 | | | Ladd, Elijah | 3 | 3 | 4 | | |
| Clark, Emˢ | 1 | 1 | 1 | | | Lomis, Andrew | 1 | 1 | 1 | | | Mᶜᶜlen, Alexander | 3 | 2 | 5 | | |
| Strong, Aaron | 2 | 4 | 3 | | | Huckins, Joshuᵃ | 1 | 1 | 1 | | | Mᶜᶜlen, Lethman | 1 | | 3 | | |
| Spencer, Timᵒ | 1 | 5 | 3 | | | Huckins, Jnᵒ C | 1 | 1 | 1 | | | Brownson, Allin | 1 | 1 | 1 | | |
| Taylor, Jnᵒ | 1 | 1 | 3 | | | Bowing, Jnᵒ | 1 | 1 | 1 | | | Taylor, Nathˡ | 1 | 3 | 2 | | |
| Webster, Josˢ | 1 | | 3 | | | Dart, Alvin | 1 | 1 | 1 | | | Ryder, Cornelius | 1 | 2 | 4 | | |
| Andrews, Elisha | 1 | 1 | 2 | | | Lomis, Thoˢ | 1 | 4 | 2 | | | Hunt, Abner | 2 | 1 | 2 | | |
| Skinner, Richard | 1 | | 2 | | | Trumbull, Benjᵃ | 1 | | 1 | | | Dorchester, David | 2 | 3 | 2 | | |
| Skinner, Uriah | 1 | 1 | 2 | | | Colton, Jonᵃ | 2 | 2 | 5 | | | Dorchester, Danˡ | 1 | 1 | 5 | | |
| Skinner, Samˡ | 1 | 1 | 2 | | | Lomis, Mathew | 2 | | 2 | | | Lomis, Elijah, Jr | 1 | 1 | 2 | | |
| Clark, Jnᵒ | 4 | 1 | 2 | | | Ringe, Thos | 2 | 2 | 1 | | | Fowler, Gordan | 2 | 2 | 5 | | |
| Fox, Jacob | 1 | 3 | 5 | | | Skinner, Israel | 2 | 1 | 4 | | | Lomis, Roger | 2 | | 2 | | |
| Skinner, Richard | 2 | | 1 | | | Robinson, Benjᵃ | 1 | 2 | 4 | | | Dorchester, David, Jr | 1 | 2 | 6 | | |
| Skinner, Daniel | 1 | 6 | 3 | | | Skinner, Jonᵃ | 3 | | 3 | | | Lomis, Roswel | 1 | | 5 | | |
| Farmer, Aaron | 1 | 1 | 2 | | | Carver, Samˡ, Jr | 2 | 2 | 5 | | | Pain, Jnᵒ | 1 | 2 | 5 | | |
| Gay, Icabod | 1 | | 2 | | | Hamman, Elijah | 2 | 1 | 2 | | | Lomis, Hezekiah | 1 | 2 | 2 | | |
| Phelps, Israel | 1 | | 5 | | | Hamman, Nathˡ | 4 | 6 | 7 | | | Grant, Elnathan | 1 | | 4 | | |
| Littel, Wᵐ | 1 | | 2 | | | Carver, Samˡ | 2 | | 2 | | | Hall, George | 1 | | 2 | | |
| Hubbard, Nathˡ | 1 | 4 | 1 | | | Bruce (Widow) | | | 1 | | | West, Ira | 1 | 4 | 5 | | |
| Taylor, David | 4 | | 3 | | | Welles, Benjᵃ | 2 | 1 | 4 | | | Grant, Cyras | 4 | 2 | 6 | | |
| Strong, David | 2 | | 1 | | | Smith, Victore | 1 | 1 | 3 | | | Mᶜᵛay, Jnᵒ | 3 | | 3 | | |
| MᶜColton, Revᵈ | 2 | 1 | 3 | | | Wilson, Wᵐ | 1 | 4 | 5 | | | Walden, Emˢ | 1 | 2 | 1 | | |
| Wanner, Davᵈ | 4 | | 4 | | | Howard, Samˡ | 1 | 1 | 2 | | | Mᶜkinna, Alexander | 2 | 4 | 2 | | |
| Carver, Ebenʳ | 2 | 3 | 3 | | | Hoskins, Wᵐ | 3 | 1 | 3 | | | Brown, Eber | 2 | 1 | 3 | | |
| White, Thoˢ | 2 | 3 | 4 | | | Risley, Richard | 2 | | 3 | | | Mᶜkinna, Alexander, Jr | 1 | 1 | 1 | | |
| Cone, Jared, Jr | 1 | 1 | 3 | | | Tolcot, Elijah | 1 | 3 | 3 | | | Cheesbrooks, Jabez | 2 | 3 | 5 | | |
| Alvert, Saul, Jr | 4 | 3 | 3 | | | Tucker, Josˢ | 2 | 1 | 1 | | | Chapman, Nathᵃ | 1 | 4 | 1 | | |
| Griswould, Danᵉˡ | 2 | | 2 | | | Tucker, Emˢ | 2 | 1 | 1 | | | Hunt, Wᵐ | 1 | | 1 | | |
| Woodworth, Samˡ | 1 | | 1 | | | Welles, Elezer | 1 | | 1 | | | Driggs, Jnᵒ | 3 | 2 | 6 | | |
| Dart, Wᵐ | 1 | 2 | 1 | | | Welles, Jarreᵈ | 1 | | 2 | | | Hawkins, Eliakim | 3 | 1 | 6 | | |
| Strong, Ebʳ | 1 | | 2 | | | Tolcot, Elijah | 1 | 1 | 5 | | | Smith, David | 4 | 1 | 4 | | |
| Brownson, Jabez | 1 | 1 | 2 | | | Marchall, Icabod | 3 | | 3 | | | Simons (Widow) | | | 4 | | |
| Dart, Jnᵒ | 1 | 2 | 3 | | | Carver, Jonᵃ | 2 | 4 | 3 | | | Lord, Danˡ | 2 | 2 | 1 | | |
| Goodrich, Moses | 1 | 3 | 8 | | | Carver, Josˢ | 5 | 2 | 4 | | | Ladd, Ezekˡ | 1 | | 2 | | |
| Howard, Benjᵃ | 2 | 1 | 2 | | | Dewey, Solᵒ | 1 | 3 | 3 | | | Chapman, Jonᵃ | 2 | 1 | 3 | | |
| Mᶜkee, Nathˡ | 1 | 3 | 3 | | | Tucker, Elijah | 3 | 1 | 7 | | | Chapman, Eleze | 1 | 1 | 3 | | |
| Gay, Pearce | 1 | 1 | 1 | | | Tolcot, Benjᵃ | 5 | | 4 | | | Ladd, David | 1 | 1 | 4 | | |
| Howard, Jnᵒ | 1 | 2 | 4 | | | Olcutt, Ezekˡ | 3 | 1 | 3 | | | Chapman, James | 1 | 1 | 1 | | |
| Strickland, Jonas | 2 | 3 | 4 | | | Daniels, Jnᵒ | 3 | | 5 | | | Pain, Roswel | 4 | 2 | 6 | | |
| Howard, Benjᵃ, Jr | 1 | | 2 | | | Walker, Jnᵒ | 3 | | 3 | | | Sparks, Jnᵒ | 4 | | 1 | | |
| Goodrich, Crafts | 1 | | 1 | | | Johns, Abijah | 2 | 2 | 3 | | | Tolcot, Samˡ | 1 | | 4 | | |
| Strong, Leroy | 1 | 2 | 2 | | | Daniels, Jnᵒ, Jr | 2 | 2 | 1 | | | Lomis, Elijah | 3 | 1 | 4 | | |
| Strong, Nathᵃ | 2 | | 1 | | | Walker, Jnᵒ, 2ᵈ | 2 | 2 | 1 | | | Brown, Wᵐ | 1 | 5 | 2 | | |
| Bingham, Asa | 2 | 1 | 3 | | | Pain, Wᵐ | 1 | | 2 | | | Lord, Benjᵃ | 3 | | 3 | | |
| Strong, Judas | 1 | 1 | 1 | | 1 | Pain, Benajah | 1 | | 3 | | | Carpenter, Noah | 3 | 3 | 3 | | |
| Strong, Charles | 1 | 1 | 1 | | | Lomis, Josˢ | 1 | 1 | 3 | | | West, Abel | 1 | 1 | 4 | | |

# HEADS OF FAMILIES—CONNECTICUT.

## TOLLAND COUNTY—Continued.

| NAME OF HEAD OF FAMILY. | Free white males of 16 years and upward, including heads of families. | Free white males under 16 years. | Free white females, including heads of families. | All other free persons. | Slaves. | NAME OF HEAD OF FAMILY. | Free white males of 16 years and upward, including heads of families. | Free white males under 16 years. | Free white females, including heads of families. | All other free persons. | Slaves. | NAME OF HEAD OF FAMILY. | Free white males of 16 years and upward, including heads of families. | Free white males under 16 years. | Free white females, including heads of families. | All other free persons. | Slaves. |
|---|---|---|---|---|---|---|---|---|---|---|---|---|---|---|---|---|---|
| **BOLTON TOWN—con.** | | | | | | **COVENTRY TOWN—con.** | | | | | | **COVENTRY TOWN—con.** | | | | | |
| Brownson, Isaac | 2 | 2 | 2 | | | Edwards, Warham | 1 | 2 | 1 | | | Lyman, Asa | 1 | 3 | 4 | | |
| Perry, Jos | 1 | 4 | 4 | | | Richardson, Amos | 2 | 1 | 5 | | | Dorman, Dudley | 2 | 1 | 4 | | |
| Tonkum, Peter | 1 | 2 | 2 | | | Swetland, Levi | 2 | | 4 | | | Parker, Canda | 3 | | 2 | | |
| Fich, Jm | 3 | | 3 | | | Robinson, Saml | 3 | 1 | 2 | | | Howard, Nthel | 2 | 2 | 2 | | |
| Webster, Elijah | 1 | 5 | 2 | | | Brown, Thos | 2 | 1 | 3 | | | Dow, Levy | 1 | 4 | 2 | | |
| Smith, Jona | 2 | 2 | 2 | | | Pomeroy, Elenr | 2 | 3 | 5 | | 1 | Dow, Calvin | 1 | | | | |
| Thrawl, Leml | 1 | 1 | 1 | | | Tolcot, Jos | 2 | 3 | 4 | | | Porter, Uriah | 1 | | 2 | | |
| Shrinner, Elijah | 1 | 3 | 3 | | | Parker, Jos | 1 | 1 | 3 | | | Taylor, Jno | 2 | 1 | 3 | | |
| Millard, Levit | 1 | 1 | 2 | | | Page, Gad | 1 | | 2 | | | Rose, Timo | 3 | 6 | 3 | | |
| Flint, Tolcot | 2 | 1 | 2 | | | Chapple, Noah | 1 | 2 | 2 | | | Huntington, Rev. J | 1 | 3 | 5 | | |
| Tucker, Jona | 1 | 2 | 2 | | | Crocker (Widow) | | | 3 | | | Fich, Jno | 1 | 3 | 4 | | |
| Bissel, Luthry | 1 | 1 | 2 | | | Devenport, Thos | 2 | 1 | 8 | | | Devensport, Richard | 1 | | 1 | | |
| Johnsin (Widow) | | 1 | 1 | | | Parker, Josiah | 1 | | 1 | | | Parmerly, Jno | 1 | | 2 | | |
| Foot, Noah | 1 | 3 | 5 | | | Parker, Nathan | 1 | 3 | 2 | | | Brigham, Tiphet | 1 | | 3 | | |
| Wiles, Jonas | 2 | | 1 | | | Case, Tuball | 1 | 2 | 1 | | | Robinson, Danl | 2 | 1 | 7 | | |
| Tolcot, Benja, 2d | 1 | 2 | 3 | | | Edwards, Jams | 1 | | 2 | | | Dow, Em, 2d | 1 | 3 | 3 | | |
| Kellogg, Rev. Em | 2 | 1 | 2 | | | Richardson, Justus | 1 | 4 | 3 | | | Robinson, Saml | 2 | 2 | 3 | | |
| Strong, Jacob | 1 | 1 | 1 | | | Wright, Elijah | 2 | 1 | 5 | | | Cushman, Minerva | 1 | | 6 | | |
| Chapman, Phineas | 1 | 1 | 7 | | | Wright, Elijah, 2d | 2 | 1 | 1 | | | Manning, Calvin | 1 | 3 | 6 | | |
| Kellogg, Eber | 1 | 2 | 3 | | | Turner, Robt | 1 | | 2 | | | Curtis, Bilvad | 1 | 2 | 1 | | |
| Emerson, Jabez | 2 | | 3 | | | Richardson, Stephen | 2 | 1 | 3 | 2 | | Meade, Jno | 1 | 2 | 2 | | |
| King (Widow) | | | 2 | | | Case, Benjm | 2 | 3 | 2 | | | Allin, Sam | 2 | | 1 | | |
| King, Lelah | 1 | | 2 | | | Avery, Amos | 1 | 1 | 3 | | | Coleman, Eber, 2d | 1 | 1 | 4 | | |
| King, Dawn | 1 | 5 | 4 | | | Walbridge, Jno | 1 | 1 | 2 | | | Warin, Martin | 1 | 2 | 4 | | |
| King, Ruben | 1 | 2 | 5 | | | Walbridge, Leml | 1 | 2 | 3 | | | Coleman, Em | 2 | 4 | 3 | | |
| King, Gidn | 3 | | 3 | | | Reddington, Jno | 2 | | 3 | | | Boinington, Oliver | 2 | 5 | 3 | | |
| King, Stephen | 2 | 1 | 3 | | | Kingsbury, Saml | 3 | 1 | 3 | | | Cook, Jesse | 1 | 2 | 4 | | |
| King, Oliver | 2 | 3 | 1 | | | Richardson, Jona | 3 | | 2 | | | Coleman, Nathl | 1 | 1 | 4 | | |
| King, Daniel | 1 | 1 | 2 | | | Hendy (Widow) | | | 3 | | | Coleman, Timo | 1 | | 4 | | |
| Sage, Ruben | 1 | 3 | 2 | | | Fowler, Israel | 3 | | 7 | | | Robinson, Jno | 2 | 2 | 6 | | |
| Pearl, Joshua | 2 | 3 | 4 | | | Ellis, Nathl | 1 | 4 | 3 | | | Robinson, Ralph | 1 | | 6 | | |
| Skinner, Jno | 2 | 1 | 3 | 1 | | Babcock, David | 1 | 3 | 3 | | | Standley, Moses | 2 | 1 | 2 | | |
| Richardson, Ezekiel | 1 | 3 | 2 | | | Lomis, Daniel | 4 | 2 | 6 | | | Fields, Benn | 2 | 3 | 6 | | |
| Webster, Ransford | 1 | | 2 | | | Lomis, Dan | 1 | 4 | 5 | | | Robinson, Danl | 1 | 4 | 6 | | |
| Johns, Thos | 1 | 1 | 5 | | | Lomis, Elisha | 2 | 2 | 2 | | | Carpenter, Timo | 2 | 1 | 5 | | |
| King, Leml | 2 | | 3 | 3 | | Andrews, Em | 4 | 1 | 3 | | | Stanly, Caleb | 1 | 3 | 3 | | |
| | | | | | | Waldo, Nathan | 1 | | 3 | | | Rose, Frederick | 1 | 1 | 4 | | |
| **COVENTRY TOWN.** | | | | | | Brewster, Jacob | 2 | 1 | 5 | | | Turner, Jos | 1 | | 1 | | |
| Porter, Noah | 1 | 3 | 8 | | | Wheldon, Jona | 2 | | 3 | | | Turner, Saml | 1 | | 1 | | |
| Cook, Jesse | 2 | 1 | 8 | | | Manley, Joseph | 2 | 2 | 3 | | | Denty, Mathew | 1 | 2 | 4 | | |
| Porter, Isaiah | 1 | 1 | 1 | | | Lomis, Jno | 3 | 2 | 6 | | | Grover, Benja | 1 | 1 | 3 | | |
| Porter, Jona | 2 | 1 | 4 | | | Hibbard, David | 2 | | 2 | | | Porter (Widow) | 1 | | 3 | | |
| Bruster, Benjn | 1 | 3 | 1 | | | Parmer, Nathl | 2 | 4 | 1 | | | Carpenter, Jos | 2 | 3 | 5 | | |
| Buel, Benjn | 2 | 1 | 7 | | | Lomis, Danl, Jr | 1 | 1 | 2 | | | Brigham, Thos | 1 | | 2 | | |
| Brewster, Israel | 1 | 1 | 3 | | | Wheeler (Widow) | | 2 | 4 | | | Strong, Benajah | 3 | 1 | 6 | | |
| Little, Saml | 2 | 2 | 4 | | | Brewster, Peter | 2 | 1 | 4 | | | Root, Medad | 1 | 1 | 5 | | |
| Brown, Abm | 1 | | 1 | | | Hunt, Elipht | 3 | 1 | 4 | | | Root, Jona | 3 | | 3 | | |
| Chamberlain (Widow) | | | 2 | | | Page, Elias | 1 | 2 | 3 | | | House, Jona | 1 | | 5 | | |
| Kingsbury, Wm | 1 | 2 | 1 | | | Hibbert, Silas | 2 | | 1 | | | Greenleaf, David | 1 | 1 | 3 | | |
| Badcock, Jno | 1 | 3 | 4 | | | Strong, Reve N | 2 | 1 | 3 | | | Cristee, Jno | 1 | 2 | 1 | | |
| Baxter, Wm | 1 | 1 | 5 | | | Carpenter, Noah | 3 | 3 | 4 | | | Hawkins (Widow) | | | 2 | | |
| Carpenter, Wm | 3 | 1 | 4 | | | King, Silas | 4 | | 7 | | | Hawkins, Rodolphus | 1 | 4 | 1 | | |
| Chapple, Stephen | 2 | 2 | 4 | | | Fuller, Jona | 2 | 2 | 3 | | | Langdon, Chancey | 1 | | 2 | | |
| Lamb, Benjn | 2 | | 3 | | | Badger, Danl | 1 | | 2 | | | Root, En | 3 | 1 | 6 | | |
| Allin, Saml | 2 | 1 | 1 | | | Badger, Danl | 1 | | 2 | | | Root, Jesse | 4 | 1 | 3 | 1 | 3 |
| Grover, Isaac | 1 | 1 | 4 | | | Badger, Moses | 1 | 4 | 4 | | | Ripley, Jm | 1 | 1 | 1 | | |
| Barnard, Jos | 2 | 1 | 2 | | | Pearce, Oliver | 1 | | 3 | | | Fitch, Henry | 1 | | 1 | | |
| Carpenter, Elipt | 3 | 1 | 8 | | | Carpenter, Levi | 3 | | 3 | | | White, Adno | 1 | 5 | 1 | | |
| Bissel, Mathew | 1 | 1 | 5 | | | Carpenter, Elijah | 2 | 2 | 2 | | | Root, Wm | 1 | 3 | 3 | | |
| Miner, Isaac | 1 | 2 | 4 | | | Wilson, Rust | 2 | 1 | 2 | | | Ripley, Jabez | 1 | 3 | 4 | 1 | |
| Woodward, Moses | 1 | 4 | 3 | | | Johns, Elihu | 1 | 4 | 4 | | | Parme, Gersham | 2 | 2 | 10 | | |
| Woodward, Nathl | 4 | 2 | 5 | | | Cooly, Saml | 2 | 2 | 3 | | | Brigham, Don | 1 | 3 | 6 | | |
| Hawkins, Jos | 2 | 3 | 4 | | | Bourns, Wm | 1 | 3 | 2 | | | Sherman, Jabez | 2 | | 5 | | |
| Hatch, Dan | 1 | 4 | 2 | | | Waldo (Widow) | 1 | 1 | 3 | | | Richarson, Hezekiah | 1 | 2 | 7 | | |
| Hunt, Gad | 2 | 3 | 4 | | | Willson, Wm | 1 | | 2 | | | Sanford, Elisha | 1 | 2 | 4 | | |
| Root, Ezra | 1 | 2 | 4 | | | Field, Saml | 1 | | 2 | | | Ringe, Danl | 1 | | 1 | | |
| Jewet, Icaood | 3 | 1 | 3 | | | Wilson, Jno | 1 | 3 | 2 | | | Carpenter, Silas | 2 | 2 | 2 | | |
| Jewet, Icabod, 2d | 1 | 1 | 3 | | | Long, Lemuel | 2 | 1 | 1 | 1 | | Rose, Jehiel | 3 | 2 | 2 | | |
| Edgerton, Jabez | 1 | 1 | 2 | | | Long, Lemuel, 2d | 2 | 1 | 5 | | | Ringe, Wm | 2 | 2 | 4 | | |
| Edwards, Adonijah | 1 | 1 | 4 | | | Porter, Abel | 2 | 1 | 5 | | | Edwards, Josu | 1 | 2 | 2 | | |
| Ladd, Saml | 2 | | 2 | | | Kingsbury, Eber | 3 | 2 | 6 | | | Dorman, Amos | 3 | 1 | 4 | | |
| Molbourn, Godfry | 1 | | 4 | | | Avery, Jabez | 1 | 1 | 3 | | | Edward, Warham | 1 | | 2 | | |
| Tiffany, Ol | 1 | | 4 | | | Hilyard, Jos | 1 | 1 | 1 | | | Brown, Richard | 1 | 4 | 3 | | |
| Malbone, Charles | 1 | 1 | 3 | | | Lyman, Elijah | 1 | | 4 | | | Brigham, Gersham | 1 | 1 | 1 | | |
| Manning, Andrew | 2 | 2 | 3 | | | Avery, Amos | 2 | 2 | 3 | | | Dunham, Stephen | 1 | | 2 | | |
| Scripter, Sime | 1 | | 1 | 2 | | Bockwell, Amorialo | 2 | | 4 | | | Brown, Eleph | 2 | 1 | 2 | | |
| Dorman, Danl | 1 | | 4 | | | Kingsbury, Em | 2 | 2 | 4 | | | Devensport, Richard | 1 | | 4 | | |
| Cogswell, Benjn | 2 | 1 | 3 | | | Vislon, Elijah | 1 | | 6 | 6 | | Dunham, Elezer | 1 | 2 | 5 | | |
| French, Abner | 1 | 6 | 3 | | | Ladd, Jno | 2 | 2 | 2 | 1 | | Dimock, Timo, Jr | 1 | | 1 | | |
| Dean, Wm | 1 | 4 | 3 | | | Crosman, Eber | 1 | 2 | 4 | | | Rose, Saml | 2 | 3 | 4 | | |
| Cogswell, Amos | 1 | 3 | 7 | | | Dow, Em | 1 | 4 | 1 | | | Dimock, Timo | 3 | 1 | 3 | | |
| Hunt, Sime | 3 | | 1 | | | Jud, Thos | 3 | | 2 | | | Dimock, Jno | 1 | | 4 | | |
| Wintworth, Ezekiel | 1 | | 2 | | | Parker (Widow) | | | 1 | | | Carpenter, Jno | 1 | | 1 | | |
| Gurley, Phineas | 1 | 2 | 5 | | | Hale, David | 5 | 1 | 8 | | | Sprague, Perez | 2 | 1 | 1 | | |
| Chamberlain, Edmn | 1 | 3 | 1 | | | Porter, Thos | 2 | 2 | 1 | | | Coleman, Levy | 1 | | 2 | | |
| Wintworth, Ebenr | 2 | 1 | 4 | | | Wright, Nathel | 2 | 1 | 4 | | | Robinson (Widow) | | 1 | 3 | | |
| Herrick Jos | 2 | | 1 | | | Grant (Widow) | | | 2 | | | Fuller, Jos | 1 | 1 | 3 | | |
| White, Saml | 1 | 2 | 3 | | | Parker, Soln | 2 | 2 | 5 | | | Fich, Pen | 1 | 1 | 2 | | |
| White, Jona | 1 | 1 | 1 | | | Gears, Jedediah | 1 | 3 | 3 | | | Robinson, Hezekiah | 1 | | 2 | | |
| Lyman, David | 1 | 1 | 1 | | | Huchinson, Em | 1 | 5 | 4 | | | Robinson, Isaac | 1 | 2 | 2 | | |
| Brown, Ebenr | 2 | | 2 | | | Doubleday, Jos | 3 | | 3 | | | Robinson, Jno | 1 | | 2 | | |
| Thompson, Jona | 1 | 1 | 2 | | | Devenport, Umphry | 2 | 2 | 3 | | | Robinson, Wm | 3 | 3 | 3 | | |
| Root, Nathl | 1 | 3 | 4 | | | Ellis, Jno | 2 | 3 | 5 | | | Woodworth, Josi | 1 | | 3 | | |
| Brown, Jos | 1 | 4 | 3 | | | Hale, Richard | 1 | 2 | 4 | | | Fitch, Jos | 1 | | 2 | | |
| | | | | | | Devenport, Benjn | 2 | 2 | 1 | | | Fitch, Abner | 1 | | 3 | | |

133

# FIRST CENSUS OF THE UNITED STATES.

## TOLLAND COUNTY—Continued.

| NAME OF HEAD OF FAMILY. | Free white males of 16 years and upward, including heads of families. | Free white males under 16 years. | Free white females, including heads of families. | All other free persons. | Slaves. | NAME OF HEAD OF FAMILY. | Free white males of 16 years and upward, including heads of families. | Free white males under 16 years. | Free white females, including heads of families. | All other free persons. | Slaves. | NAME OF HEAD OF FAMILY. | Free white males of 16 years and upward, including heads of families. | Free white males under 16 years. | Free white females, including heads of families. | All other free persons. | Slaves. |
|---|---|---|---|---|---|---|---|---|---|---|---|---|---|---|---|---|---|
| **COVENTRY TOWN—con.** | | | | | | **ELLINGTON TOWN—con.** | | | | | | **ELLINGTON TOWN—con.** | | | | | |
| Turner (Widow) | 2 | | 2 | | | Kingsbury, Dur | 1 | | 3 | | | Fitch, Medin | 2 | | 2 | | |
| Fitch, Abner, Jr | 3 | 4 | 4 | | | Pomler, Elija | 3 | 1 | 3 | | | Wells, Levi | 3 | | 4 | 1 | |
| Cook, Nathl | 1 | 2 | 3 | | | Bingham, Ithm | 1 | 1 | 2 | | | Isam, Benjn | 2 | | 1 | | |
| Hamman, Zephn | 2 | | 4 | | | Hyde, Mathew | 4 | | 3 | | | Carpenter, Ruggles | 1 | | 2 | | |
| Babcock, Zebulon | 2 | 4 | 4 | | | Maher, Dan | 1 | 2 | 1 | | | Allen, Jos | 1 | 1 | 2 | | |
| Babcock, Robd | 1 | | 2 | | | McCray, Jno | 1 | 1 | 3 | | | Hall, Jno | 3 | 2 | 4 | | |
| Edwards, Benajah | 2 | | 5 | | | Bartlet, Elepht | 1 | | 1 | | | Gifford, Siba | 2 | 2 | 5 | | |
| Cook, Shubal | 2 | 1 | 1 | | | Warner, Daniel | 3 | 2 | 3 | | | Bartlett, Edm | 3 | 1 | 1 | | |
| Babcock, Wm | 1 | | 2 | | | Denison, Jona | 1 | 1 | 3 | | | Nucrum, Saml | 1 | 3 | 5 | | |
| Babcock, Roger | 1 | 2 | 3 | | | Stephens, Heny | 2 | 1 | 5 | | | Waldo, Bethuel | 3 | | 3 | | |
| Cushman, Atherton | 3 | | 3 | | | Hombbord, Isaac | 3 | | 3 | | | Johnson, Convus | 1 | | 1 | | |
| Babcock, Robd | 3 | 1 | 3 | | | Reed (Widow) | 1 | 4 | 4 | | | Foster, Charles | 1 | 1 | 2 | | |
| Turner, Amos | 1 | | 2 | | | Parker, Jno | 1 | 1 | 4 | | | Chapman, Hoseah | 1 | 2 | 4 | | |
| Turner, Jethro | 2 | 5 | 5 | | | Barber, Jona | 2 | | 6 | | | Chapman, Jabez | 2 | 3 | 6 | | |
| Brown, Nathl | 1 | 2 | 2 | | | Porter, Jno | 1 | 1 | 2 | | | Grant, Jona | 1 | | 2 | | |
| Cushman, Em | 1 | 4 | 4 | | | Wise, Ruben | 1 | 1 | 3 | | | Pomber, Andrew | 2 | 1 | 2 | | |
| Coleman, Saml | 3 | 3 | 5 | | | Kingsbury, Somo | 1 | | 2 | | | Sessions, Saml | 2 | 2 | 5 | | |
| Coleman, Asa | 2 | 1 | 7 | | | Cushman, Alverton | 1 | | 3 | | | Purple, Ezra | 1 | 4 | 4 | | |
| Rust, Nath. W | 1 | 2 | 2 | | | Smith, Jno | 1 | | 1 | | | Mills, Peter | 1 | 2 | 2 | | |
| Larriby (Widow) | | | 2 | | | Smith, Isaac | 1 | | 2 | | | Graton, Nathl | 1 | 1 | 2 | | |
| Turner, Caleb | 1 | 1 | 4 | | | Wadsworth, Icabod | 2 | 2 | 4 | | | Clark, Warham | 1 | 2 | 5 | | |
| Curtis, Heny | 3 | | 3 | | | Goodale, Eler | 1 | 2 | 2 | | | Smith, Grace | 1 | | 4 | | |
| Meads, Jno | 1 | 1 | 3 | | | Clark, Danl | 1 | 4 | 4 | | | Hare, Stephen | 1 | 1 | 3 | | |
| Manley, George | 2 | 2 | 3 | | | Emerson, Jabez | 1 | | 2 | | | Jones, Danl | 1 | | 2 | | |
| Badcock, Timo | 1 | | 2 | | | Wallis, Wm | 1 | | 6 | | | Uttley, Timo | 1 | | 1 | | |
| Ladd, Elisha | 1 | 2 | 2 | | | Wallis, Abm | 1 | 1 | 2 | | 1 | Uttley, Stephen | 1 | | 1 | | |
| Badcock, Elihu | 3 | 2 | 2 | | | Goodrich, Thos | 3 | | 2 | | | Hills, Elijah | 3 | | 1 | | |
| Baker, Timo | 2 | 5 | 3 | | | Kenada, Thos | 1 | 2 | 4 | | | Charles, Jno | 2 | | 2 | | |
| Baker, Blund | 1 | 1 | 5 | | | Smith, Moses | 1 | 2 | 5 | | | Grover, Edm | 1 | | 3 | | |
| Baker, Asa | 1 | | 4 | | | Spears, Wm | 4 | 1 | 5 | | | Pease, Thos | 1 | 3 | 3 | | |
| Timons, Elijah | 1 | 1 | 2 | | | Bakon, Jno | 1 | 4 | 2 | | | Woodworth, Jesse | 1 | | 4 | | |
| Dow, Umphus | 2 | 2 | 5 | | | Fuller, Jacob | 3 | 1 | 4 | | | Andrews, Saml | 2 | 5 | 4 | | |
| Johnes, Saml | 1 | 3 | 3 | | | Belnap, Simn | 2 | | 4 | | | Shurtliff, Jno | 1 | | 5 | | |
| Jones, Elias | 1 | 3 | 3 | | | Peas, Jona | 3 | 3 | 4 | | | King, Saml | 3 | 2 | 7 | | |
| Jones (Widow) | 2 | | 2 | | | Daman, Natha | 1 | 2 | 1 | | | Torry, Elijah | 1 | 2 | 4 | | |
| Peters (Widow) | | | 1 | | | Stiles, Jno | 1 | 2 | 2 | | | Newton, Jno | 1 | | 2 | | |
| Fieldon, Jno | 1 | 2 | 6 | | | Warner, Saml | 1 | 1 | 1 | | | Jinks, Jno | 3 | | 3 | | |
| Hows, Asa | 1 | 3 | 2 | | | Bingham, Ithm | 2 | 1 | 5 | | | Braman, Jos | 1 | 2 | 2 | | |
| Lomis, Israel | 1 | 5 | 2 | | | McCray, Wm | 3 | 1 | 3 | | | Newton, Moses | 1 | 2 | 2 | | |
| Sprague, Saml | 2 | 1 | 5 | | | McCray, Calvin | 1 | 1 | 1 | | | Warner, Phillip | 2 | 2 | 4 | | |
| Sprague, Saml, Jr | 1 | | 5 | | | Pearse (Widow) | 1 | | 1 | | | Durfy, Eber | 1 | | 3 | | |
| Lomis, Zadock | 3 | 1 | 7 | | | Pearse, Em | 2 | 3 | 5 | | | Russel, Eben | 3 | 1 | 5 | | |
| Sprague, Elisha | 1 | 2 | 5 | | | Stone, Stephen | 1 | | 1 | | | Lomis, Justus | 1 | 1 | 5 | | |
| Lockwood, Rev. S | 2 | | 2 | | 1 | Stone, Dane | 1 | 1 | 2 | | | Dewey, Josu | 1 | 1 | 2 | | |
| Walbridge, Saml | 1 | 1 | 3 | | | Strong, Phineas | 2 | 1 | 2 | | | Porter, Ruben | 1 | 2 | 4 | | |
| Mordoch, Jona | 2 | | 7 | | | Holton, Timo | 4 | 4 | 7 | | 1 | Russell, Hezekiah | 3 | 2 | 9 | | |
| Walbridge, Jona | 2 | 3 | 3 | | | McKnite, Jno | 2 | 1 | 3 | | | Brag, Edwd | 1 | | 1 | | |
| Thompson, Thos | 1 | 1 | 1 | | | Jennings, Em | 2 | 2 | 3 | | | Sabine, Thos | 2 | 1 | 2 | | |
| Skinner, Daniel | 1 | 1 | 1 | | | Thompson, Saml | 2 | 2 | 2 | | | Newel, Nathl | 5 | | 6 | | |
| Jones, Benjn | 2 | | 1 | | | Thompson, Israel | 1 | | 2 | | | Porter, Jos | 1 | 1 | 2 | | |
| Jones, Silas | 2 | 2 | 1 | | | Thompson, Luther | 1 | | 1 | | | Carver, Ralph | 1 | 1 | 1 | | |
| Jones, Noah | 3 | 2 | 7 | | | Thompson, Wm | 2 | 5 | 3 | | | Woodworth, Peleg | 2 | | 2 | | |
| Lyman, Silas | 1 | | 1 | | | Elsworth, Charles | 1 | 3 | 3 | | | Banister, Levi | 1 | 1 | 7 | | |
| Blackman, Aaron | 1 | 3 | 2 | | | Hamblengton, Paul | 1 | | 5 | | | Durfey, Jno | 1 | 2 | 2 | | |
| Blackman, Benjn | 2 | 2 | 2 | | | Hamblengton (Widow) | 3 | 1 | 3 | | | Buck, Eben | 1 | | 1 | | |
| Blackman, Benjn, Jr | 2 | 1 | 2 | | | Scovel, Isaac | 2 | 3 | 3 | | | Bradley, Ruben | 3 | | 4 | | |
| House, Benjn | 1 | 6 | 2 | | | Parsons, Saml | 2 | | 2 | | | Chubbuck, Eben | 2 | | 3 | | |
| Lyman, Joab | 3 | 2 | 6 | | | Sanger, Danl | 1 | 1 | 3 | | | Chubbuck, Nathl | 1 | 1 | 1 | | |
| House, Sam | 2 | 1 | 5 | | | Belnap, Frances | 1 | 1 | 1 | | | Charter, Allen | 1 | 4 | 3 | | |
| Smith, Experience | 1 | | 1 | | | Green, Danl | 1 | 1 | 5 | | | Charter, Jno, Jr | 1 | | 3 | | |
| Badger, Enoch | 2 | 4 | 8 | | | McKinstry, Elezer | 3 | 3 | 7 | | | Ray, Adonijah | 5 | 1 | 3 | | |
| Blakeman, Elijah | 1 | | 1 | | | Whitney, Jos | 1 | 2 | 3 | | | Aldridge, Nathan | 4 | | 3 | | |
| Wheldon, Jno | 2 | 1 | 4 | | | Barkley, Jona | 2 | | 4 | | | Keath, James | 2 | 1 | 7 | | |
| Dow, Pelitiah | 1 | | 7 | | | Snow, Sylvanus | 1 | 2 | 3 | | | Slawter, Anthony | 1 | 3 | 5 | | |
| Simon (Widow) | | 1 | 2 | | | Davis, Daniel | 1 | | 1 | | | Frost, Josu | 1 | 3 | 2 | | |
| Daggett, Isaiah | 1 | 5 | 2 | | | Parker, Em | 1 | | 2 | | | Fentons, Old | | | 2 | | |
| Dagget, Saml | 1 | | 1 | | | Levit, Jame | 1 | 2 | 4 | | | Slawter, Moses | 1 | 3 | 4 | | |
| Lawrence, Heny | 1 | 2 | 3 | | | Abbot, Moses | 1 | 1 | 2 | | | Briant, Danl D | 1 | 1 | 1 | | |
| Hendy, Elipt | 2 | 5 | 3 | | | Buckley, Alexander | 1 | 1 | 2 | | | Edson, Benjn | 1 | 1 | 3 | | |
| Lomis, Nathl | 2 | 4 | 2 | | | Charter, George | 1 | 5 | 4 | | | Bigsbee, Jno | 1 | | 2 | | |
| Aynsworth, Jno | 1 | 1 | 3 | | | Penna, Elezear | 2 | 1 | 7 | | | Demming, Aaron | 1 | 2 | 2 | | |
| Babcock, Jno | 1 | | 3 | 1 | | Blodget, Josiah | 2 | 3 | 3 | | | Negros (Free) | | | | 15 | 2 |
| Aynsworth, Ebenr | 3 | | 2 | | | Penna, Jos | 5 | 2 | 1 | | | | | | | | |
| Robinson, Em | 1 | | 3 | | | Cotton, Isaac | 1 | 2 | 1 | | | **HEBRON TOWN.** | | | | | |
| Burnap, Christopher | 1 | 2 | 5 | | | Abbot, Joseph | 4 | 3 | 6 | | | Button, Jos | 1 | | 3 | | |
| Patten, David | 3 | | 2 | | | McKinna, James | 2 | | 2 | | | Button (Widow) | | | 3 | | |
| Lomis, Heny | 1 | | 5 | | | McKinna, James, 3d | 1 | 4 | 4 | | | Isam, Jos | 1 | 2 | 1 | | |
| Barnaby, James | 1 | 1 | 1 | | | McKinna, Andrew | 2 | | 6 | | | Hutchinson, Jona | 2 | 1 | 3 | | |
| Dart, Levi | 1 | | 1 | | | McKinna, James | 1 | | 6 | | | Culver, David | 6 | | 4 | | |
| White, Danl | 2 | 2 | 6 | | | McKinna, Wm | 3 | 2 | 6 | | | Sumner, Ruben | 3 | | 3 | | |
| Burnap, Abm | 3 | | 4 | | | Chapman, Saml | 2 | 2 | 3 | | | Webster, Elijah | 1 | 2 | 3 | | |
| Badcock, Danl | 1 | 3 | 2 | | | Elsworth, Daniel | 3 | | 6 | | | Skinner, Danl | 5 | 1 | 2 | | |
| Crocker, James | 1 | 1 | 2 | | | Elsworth, Gordon | 3 | | 2 | | | Wells, Bateman | 1 | | 7 | | |
| Richardson, Em | 1 | 1 | 4 | | | Nash, Eben | 3 | 4 | 5 | | | Wells, Rufus | 1 | 3 | 5 | | |
| Kingsbury, Nathl | 1 | 2 | 3 | | | Kimball, Adm | 1 | 1 | 3 | | | Ingram, Danl | 2 | | 1 | | |
| Kingsbury, Jos | 1 | 2 | 7 | | | Baker, Let | 1 | 3 | 5 | | | Wells, Shipman | 2 | 1 | 1 | | |
| Atherton, Elijah | 2 | 3 | 6 | 3 | | Craw, Jno | 4 | 1 | 3 | | | Sawyer, Jno | 1 | | 4 | | 1 |
| McCoy, Jno | 1 | 1 | 2 | | | Varnum, Wm | 1 | 3 | 3 | | | Phelps, Elezer | 1 | 1 | 5 | | |
| Fitch, Jm | 1 | 1 | 3 | | | Little, Rufus | 1 | | 4 | | | Wells, Thos | 3 | 1 | 4 | | |
| Fitch, Jeptha | 1 | 2 | 2 | | | Fuller, Frederick | 1 | 2 | 2 | | | Horton, Eli, Jr | 1 | 1 | 2 | | |
| | | | | | | Snow, Natha | 3 | | 2 | | | Hutchinson, Jos | 1 | | 4 | | |
| **ELLINGTON TOWN.** | | | | | | Buckley, Alexander | 3 | 1 | 4 | | | Hutchinson, Jabez | 1 | | 3 | | |
| | | | | | | Parker, Jno | 1 | 2 | 2 | | | Post, Jedediah | 2 | | 4 | | |
| Steel, James | 4 | 1 | 6 | | | Mug, Icabod | 2 | | 1 | | | Post, David | 3 | 4 | 3 | | |
| Mills, Stone | 3 | 1 | 2 | | | Tayler, Jno | 1 | 3 | 3 | | | Merrils Jno | 4 | | 3 | | |
| Chapman, Jabez | 1 | 1 | 2 | | | Cross, Jno | 1 | 1 | 2 | | | | | | | | |

# HEADS OF FAMILIES—CONNECTICUT.

## TOLLAND COUNTY—Continued.

| NAME OF HEAD OF FAMILY. | Free white males of 16 years and upward, including heads of families. | Free white males under 16 years. | Free white females, including heads of families. | All other free persons. | Slaves. | NAME OF HEAD OF FAMILY. | Free white males of 16 years and upward, including heads of families. | Free white males under 16 years. | Free white females, including heads of families. | All other free persons. | Slaves. | NAME OF HEAD OF FAMILY. | Free white males of 16 years and upward, including heads of families. | Free white males under 16 years. | Free white females, including heads of families. | All other free persons. | Slaves. |
|---|---|---|---|---|---|---|---|---|---|---|---|---|---|---|---|---|---|
| **HEBRON TOWN—con.** | | | | | | **HEBRON TOWN—con.** | | | | | | **HEBRON TOWN—con.** | | | | | |
| Post, Jos | 2 | 5 | 4 | | | Smith, Nathl | 1 | 1 | 2 | | | White, Jos | 4 | 1 | 6 | | |
| Fieldon, Saml | 1 | 1 | 4 | | | Hosford, Dudley | 2 | 1 | 9 | | | Beach, Elijha | 3 | 1 | 5 | | |
| Brown, James | 1 | 2 | 1 | | | Bowls, Wm | 2 | 6 | 3 | | | Mann, Abijah | 3 | 2 | 5 | | |
| Ellis, Jabez | 4 | | 3 | | | Darbey, Danl | 1 | | 1 | | | Skinner, Benja | 3 | | 2 | | |
| Tolcot, Wm | 1 | 1 | 4 | 1 | | Gillet, Aaron | 1 | 2 | 2 | | | Skinner, David | 1 | 1 | 2 | | |
| Post, James | 2 | | 3 | | | Rayman (Wid.) | | 1 | 2 | | | Beach, Elijha | 1 | | 2 | | |
| Brown, James | 1 | 5 | 1 | | | Jones, Gid | 2 | 1 | 2 | | | Somers, Sylvester | 5 | 5 | 7 | | |
| Curtis (Wid.) | 1 | 1 | 2 | | | Jones, Benajah | 3 | 1 | 5 | | | Dunnum, Jona | 2 | 1 | 2 | | |
| Calver, David | 1 | 3 | 1 | | | Smith, Benjn | 2 | 1 | 3 | | | Felcher, Michael | 1 | 1 | 2 | | |
| Curtis, Jno | 1 | | 2 | | | Kellogg, Moses | 2 | 1 | 5 | | | Porter, Nehemiah | 2 | 3 | 5 | | |
| Wright, Jude | 1 | | 1 | | | Fuller, Nathel | 2 | 3 | 6 | | | Carver, David | 4 | | 2 | | |
| Horton, Saml | 1 | 1 | 4 | | | Darbey, Nthel | 1 | | 2 | | | Carver, David, Jr | 1 | 4 | 1 | | |
| Davis, Zepha | 1 | 3 | 4 | | | Kellogg, Moses, Jr | 1 | | 2 | | | Root, Dan | 1 | 1 | 2 | | |
| Tolcot, Gad | 3 | 2 | 3 | | 1 | Kellog, Martin | 1 | 1 | 1 | | | Phelps, Horner | 1 | 2 | 4 | | |
| Daniels, Ezekl | 3 | 2 | 2 | | | Fuller, Nathl | 2 | 3 | 5 | | | Porter, Joel | 3 | 3 | 4 | | |
| Gears, Saml | 2 | 2 | 3 | | | Darbey, Nathl | 1 | | 2 | | | Porter, Increas | 1 | 3 | 5 | | |
| Dunham, Timo | 5 | 1 | 5 | | | Phelps, Ruben | 1 | 3 | 3 | | | Webster, Martin | 1 | 1 | 5 | | |
| Dunham, Isacc | 1 | | 2 | | | Smith, Benjn | 2 | 1 | 4 | | | Anabal, Anson | 1 | 3 | 3 | | |
| Perrin, Soln | 1 | 3 | 3 | | | Kellogg, Martin, Jr | 1 | 1 | 1 | | | Badger, Neha | 2 | | 1 | | |
| Root, Josa | 1 | 1 | 6 | | | Root, Jonah | 2 | 4 | 3 | | | Gillit, Ezekl | 4 | | 2 | | |
| Sumner, Wm | 1 | | 4 | | | Horton, Ezekiel | 3 | 2 | 5 | | | Pomeroy, Elihu | 1 | 4 | 2 | | |
| Finley, Jno | 2 | 1 | 3 | | | Norton, David | 1 | 1 | 3 | | | Gillit, Charles | 1 | 1 | 1 | | |
| Roswell, Nehm | 1 | 1 | 3 | | | Brown, Jona | 3 | 2 | 6 | | | Gillit, Amasa | 1 | | 3 | | |
| Hall, Amos | 2 | 2 | 5 | | | Chapple, Jno | 3 | 1 | 3 | | | Barber, Bela | 3 | 2 | 3 | | |
| Ford, Luther | 1 | 2 | 2 | | | Chapple, David | 1 | 1 | 1 | | | Corkins, Jedediah | 1 | 1 | 2 | | |
| Rollow, Zachary | 3 | 1 | 2 | | | Cone, Zachy | 3 | 4 | 2 | | | Bliss (Wid.) | 1 | 1 | 10 | | |
| Mc——, Jos | 3 | | 3 | | | Sutton, Jno | 2 | | 3 | | | Fuller, Roger | 3 | 5 | 9 | | |
| Bucks, David | 2 | 2 | 4 | | | White, James | 3 | 2 | 8 | | | Phelps, Aaron | 2 | 2 | 4 | | |
| Allin, Wm | 2 | 2 | 3 | | | Swetland, Joel | 2 | 2 | 1 | | | Townsend, Jona | 1 | 2 | 1 | | |
| Root (Widow) | | | 1 | | | Sanger, Sola | 1 | 1 | 3 | | | Kellogg, Revd Mr | 2 | 1 | 3 | | |
| Rollow, Wm | 4 | 2 | 4 | | | Jones, Jona | 3 | 1 | 4 | | | Gilbert, Sylvester | 2 | 4 | 5 | | 2 |
| Post, Jacob | 2 | 1 | 3 | | | Jones, Saml | 1 | 4 | 1 | | | Dutton, Timo | 6 | | 5 | | 1 |
| Post, Thos | 4 | 2 | 3 | | | Bingham, Stephen | 4 | 4 | 3 | | | Jones, Joel | 3 | | 2 | | |
| Norton, Sola | 2 | 1 | 4 | | | Bewel, Jno | 7 | 4 | 6 | 1 | | Phelps, Eber | 2 | | 5 | | |
| Gilbert, Saml | 4 | 3 | 4 | 3 | | Parker, Jos | 1 | 3 | 5 | | | Gilbert, Jno | 1 | 4 | 9 | | 1 |
| Cass, Jos W | 2 | 1 | 3 | | | Townsend, David | 1 | 1 | 3 | | | Strong, Elezer | 2 | | 2 | | |
| Brown, Thos | 2 | 2 | 4 | | | Blackman, Wm | 1 | 3 | 5 | | | Strong, David | 1 | 3 | 5 | | |
| Graves, Elijah | 1 | 3 | 4 | | | Powel, Aaron | 1 | 2 | 2 | | | Stiles, Stephen | 4 | 2 | 7 | | |
| Sutton, David | 1 | | 2 | | | Clark, Benia | 3 | 1 | 2 | | | Bessel, Levi | 1 | 5 | 4 | | |
| Pratt, James | 1 | | 1 | | | Kingsbury, Denson | 2 | 1 | 4 | | | Filer, Saml | 3 | | 3 | | |
| Peters, Jno | 2 | | 3 | 1 | | Swetland, Azariah | 2 | | 3 | | | Coleman (Wid.) | 1 | | 3 | | |
| Peters, Jona | 1 | 1 | 4 | | | Swetland, Peter | 3 | 3 | 3 | | | Phelps, Amos | 7 | 2 | 3 | | |
| Peters, Wm | 1 | 2 | 2 | | | Swetland, Aaron | 2 | 3 | 3 | | | Man, Joel | 3 | 3 | 2 | | |
| Willes, Thos, Jr | 2 | 2 | 5 | | | Wells, Timo | 2 | 1 | 3 | | | Huntington, Sola | 3 | 3 | 6 | | |
| West, Ruben | 2 | 3 | 2 | | | White, Adonjah | 1 | 4 | 4 | | | Barber, Stephen | 1 | | 3 | | |
| Brown, Ezekiel | 1 | 2 | 1 | | | Townsend, David, Jr | 2 | 1 | 4 | | | Barber, Stephen, Jr | 3 | | 3 | | |
| Bliss, Abel | 1 | 1 | 3 | | | White, James | 1 | 1 | 4 | | | Phelps, Abner | 1 | 1 | 3 | | |
| Lothrop, Revd J | 3 | | 2 | | | Hows, Luke | 1 | | 1 | | | Tillotson, Abm, Jr | 2 | 2 | 1 | | |
| Wells, Jno | 2 | 4 | 2 | | | Lomis, Ahiel | 2 | | 2 | | | Root (Wid.) | 1 | | 2 | | |
| Post, Gordan | 4 | 2 | 4 | | | Lomis, Jos | 2 | | 2 | | | Root, Abel | 2 | 2 | 2 | | |
| Huchinson, Jno | 1 | 1 | 1 | | | Buel, Benja | 3 | | 2 | 3 | | Rude, Jno | 2 | 3 | 5 | | |
| Huchinson, Jona | 2 | | 3 | | | Cone, Zachy | 3 | 4 | 2 | | | Wintr, Niolas | 1 | 1 | 3 | | |
| Huchinson, Israel | 1 | 2 | 1 | | | Jones, Gid, Jr | 1 | 1 | 2 | | | Mann, Jos | 3 | 1 | 2 | | |
| Gilbert, Jno | 1 | | 1 | | | Jones, Abner | 3 | 2 | 4 | | | Barber, Obd | 1 | 1 | 1 | | |
| Phelps, Icabod | 1 | | 2 | | | Jones, Oliver | 2 | | 2 | | | Norton, Francis | 2 | 3 | 7 | | |
| Phelps, Icabod, Jr | 1 | 1 | 4 | | | Mervin, Elihu | 2 | 1 | 4 | | | Stewart, Jno | 2 | 3 | 3 | | |
| Tillotson, Elezr | 2 | 1 | 2 | | | Barker, Aaron | 1 | 2 | 4 | | | Tillotson, Abm | 2 | 1 | 1 | | |
| Bushnoll, Danl | 2 | | 1 | | | Airs, Jno | 2 | 2 | 2 | | | Phelps, Syvanus | 2 | 1 | 4 | | |
| Brown, Danl | 1 | 4 | 2 | | | Kelleg, Jno | 2 | 1 | 3 | | | Root, Caleb | 4 | 1 | 3 | | |
| Trumbel, Asa | 3 | 2 | 8 | 1 | 1 | Pepone, Silas | 3 | 5 | 1 | | | Bliss, Elis | 1 | 3 | 6 | | |
| Hall, Seth | 1 | | 2 | | | Jones, Ezekiel | 4 | 3 | 9 | | | Marble, Thos | 2 | | 2 | | |
| Hall, Jona | 1 | 2 | 3 | | | Danish, Jona | 1 | 1 | 3 | | | Owen, David | 2 | 1 | 5 | | |
| Mc——, Ralph | 1 | 3 | 7 | | | Tuch, Richard | 1 | 1 | 1 | | | Root, Dan | 1 | | 2 | | |
| Wilcocks, Jehiel | 2 | 4 | 5 | | | Danish, Ezkl | 1 | 2 | 2 | | | Beach, Azariah | 3 | 1 | 4 | | |
| Horton, Stephen | 2 | 2 | 4 | | | Danish, Neham | 3 | 1 | 6 | | | Backus, Ezra | 2 | 1 | 3 | | |
| Horton, Sampson | 1 | 1 | 4 | | | Jones, Samuel | 2 | 4 | 5 | | | Phelps, Jos | 2 | 1 | 1 | | |
| Ingram, Jos | 1 | 2 | 4 | | | Jones, Joel | 4 | 1 | 2 | 1 | | Phelps, Jos, Jr | 1 | 1 | 6 | | |
| Darbay, Wm | 3 | 4 | 2 | | | Beach, Jno | 1 | | 1 | | | Buel, Icabod | 2 | 1 | 3 | | |
| Root, Danl | 3 | 1 | 4 | | | Archer, Amasa | 1 | 1 | 2 | | | Strong, Phenias | 1 | 1 | 4 | | |
| Case, Roger | 3 | 2 | 3 | | | Jones, Jedediah | 1 | 1 | 2 | | | Phelps, Roswel | 1 | 1 | 3 | | |
| Loveman, Alpheas | 2 | 3 | 4 | | | Archer, Jnn | 1 | | 2 | | | Phelps, Saml | 1 | 1 | 3 | | |
| Wartis (Wid.) | 3 | | 2 | | | Dean, Amos | 2 | 2 | 5 | | | Mann, Jno | 1 | 1 | 3 | | |
| Buck, Wm, Jr | 2 | 3 | 2 | | | Risley, Saml | 2 | 4 | 4 | | | Mann, Andrew | 3 | 3 | 3 | | |
| Fox, Abm | 1 | | 2 | | | Washborn, Levi | 1 | 2 | 6 | | | Man, Elijah | 3 | 3 | 7 | | |
| Fox, Jael | 1 | 3 | 1 | | | Archer, Benja | 1 | 2 | 3 | | | Burge, Jona | 1 | 1 | 4 | | |
| Root, Ebenr | 2 | 2 | 4 | | | Peas, Nhel | 1 | 1 | 2 | | | Porter, Gaylan | 2 | 2 | 1 | | |
| Acheley, Jno | 1 | 2 | 4 | | | Chapman, Em | 2 | 2 | 2 | | | Tarbox, Jona | 1 | 4 | 5 | | |
| Root, Jona | 3 | 3 | 3 | | | Wright, Enos | 1 | 2 | 3 | | | Townsend, Jona | 2 | 2 | 4 | | |
| Phelps, Soln | 1 | 1 | 1 | 4 | | Northam, Jno | 2 | 2 | 1 | | | Phelps, Cornelus | 2 | 1 | 2 | | |
| Phelps, Soln, Jr | 1 | 2 | 3 | | | Mc——, Orlander | 1 | 1 | 2 | | | Phelps, Roger | 3 | 1 | 8 | | |
| Phelps, Ashbel | 2 | 1 | 2 | 1 | | Hamblin, Eben | 1 | 2 | 5 | | | Basset, Abel | 1 | 1 | 3 | 1 | |
| Nothenn, Elijah | 3 | 1 | 3 | | | Wright, Saml | 1 | 3 | 5 | | | Phelps, Sylvanus | 2 | 1 | 4 | | |
| Tillotson, Elezer | 3 | 1 | 7 | | | Darbey, Jno | 1 | 1 | 4 | | | Bissel, Hezekiah | 3 | 1 | 5 | | |
| Bewel, Wm | 2 | | 1 | | | Niles, Nathl | 1 | 3 | 3 | | | Phelps, Frederick | 2 | 2 | 6 | | |
| Curtis, Ruben | 2 | 4 | 5 | | | Cullom, George | 1 | 1 | 1 | | | Gillet, Jno | 1 | 1 | 3 | | |
| Owen, Aziel | 1 | | 3 | | | Felcher, Miael | 1 | 1 | 1 | | | Barber, David | 2 | 3 | 4 | | |
| Owen (Wid.) | 2 | | 4 | | | Dunnum, Jona | 1 | | 2 | | | Wass, Jno | 2 | 2 | 6 | | |
| Carrver, Amos | 1 | 1 | 1 | | | Jillitt, Israel | 1 | | 3 | | | Baxter, Aaron | 1 | 2 | 4 | | |
| Phelps, Ruben | 1 | 4 | 1 | | | White, Deah | 4 | | 3 | | | Carver, Alderich | 1 | 2 | 3 | | |
| Smith, Nathn | 3 | 1 | 1 | | | Ford, Isaa | 3 | 3 | 5 | | | Leanarvas, Jno | 1 | | 1 | | |
| Hosford, Danl | 3 | 5 | 6 | | | Brown, Amasa | 1 | 2 | 4 | | | Barber, David | 3 | 1 | 2 | | |
| Collings, Luis | 1 | 1 | 1 | | 1 | Gay, Joel | 1 | 2 | 3 | | | White, Daniel | 1 | 1 | 1 | | |
| Hosford, Enos | 2 | | 5 | | | Parker, Peletiah | 3 | | 6 | | | Parmer, Stephen | 2 | 2 | 3 | | |
| Nelomd, Jona | 3 | 3 | 6 | | | Porter, Danl | 1 | 3 | 2 | | | Got, Danl | 1 | | 2 | | |
| Kellogg, Danl | 3 | | 6 | | | Parker, Wimans | 1 | | 3 | | | Burge, Jno | 1 | 3 | 3 | | |
| Kellegg, Elijah | 3 | 1 | 1 | | | Stiles, Aaron | 2 | 1 | 4 | | | Tayler, Benja | 1 | 2 | 4 | | |

## TOLLAND COUNTY—Continued.

| NAME OF HEAD OF FAMILY. | Free white males of 16 years and upward, including heads of families. | Free white males under 16 years. | Free white females, including heads of families. | All other free persons. | Slaves. | NAME OF HEAD OF FAMILY. | Free white males of 16 years and upward, including heads of families. | Free white males under 16 years. | Free white females, including heads of families. | All other free persons. | Slaves. | NAME OF HEAD OF FAMILY. | Free white males of 16 years and upward, including heads of families. | Free white males under 16 years. | Free white females, including heads of families. | All other free persons. | Slaves. |
|---|---|---|---|---|---|---|---|---|---|---|---|---|---|---|---|---|---|
| HEBRON TOWN—con. | | | | | | SOMERS TOWN—con. | | | | | | SOMERS TOWN—con. | | | | | |
| Parmer, Jos<sup>u</sup> | 1 | | 3 | | | Pease, David | 3 | 3 | 7 | | | Pease, Levi, Jr | 1 | | 3 | | |
| Tayler, Jn<sup>o</sup> | 1 | 1 | 4 | | | Parsons, Seth | 1 | | 2 | | | Kibbee, Tim<sup>o</sup> | 1 | | 4 | | |
| Dewey, Aaron | 1 | 2 | 7 | | | Pease, Sam<sup>l</sup> | 1 | | 3 | | | Felt, David | 1 | 2 | 2 | | |
| Jones, Sam<sup>l</sup>, Jr | 2 | 3 | 2 | | | Ward, Jacob | 1 | | 3 | | | Hamblenton, Asa | 2 | 3 | 2 | | |
| Wartis, Jos | 3 | 2 | 4 | | | Wood, Dan<sup>l</sup> | 3 | 3 | 1 | | | Sexton, Stephen | 2 | 2 | 3 | | |
| Wartis (Wid.) | | | 1 | 1 | | Jones, Dan<sup>l</sup> | 1 | | 2 | | | Prentice, Jn<sup>o</sup> | 2 | 1 | 2 | | |
| Phelps, Elihu | 1 | 1 | 1 | | | Jones, Silas | 1 | 2 | 7 | | | Jones, Benj<sup>a</sup> | 1 | 3 | 2 | | |
| Wartis, Enos | 1 | 1 | 1 | | | Spencer, Obed<sup>h</sup> | 1 | 2 | 6 | | | Orcutt, Jacob | 2 | 2 | 3 | | |
| Cutting, Zadock | 1 | 1 | 1 | | | Shephard, Isaac | 2 | 1 | 2 | | | Morehouse, David | 1 | 1 | 2 | | |
| Wartis, Phel<sup>a</sup> | 1 | | | | | Spencer, Jon<sup>a</sup> | 2 | 1 | 3 | | | M<sup>c</sup>Llewer, David | 1 | 1 | 5 | | |
| Foot, Ambros | 1 | 3 | 1 | | | Spencer, Eber | 2 | 1 | 2 | | | Luce, Luke | 2 | 2 | | | |
| Ingram, Nath<sup>l</sup> | 2 | 1 | 2 | | | Spencer, Hezekiah | 3 | 2 | 4 | | | Parsons, Seth | 2 | | 3 | | |
| Foot, Stephen | 1 | 2 | 2 | | | Spencer, Hez., Jr | 1 | 1 | 4 | | | Kibbe, Elisha | 3 | 1 | 3 | | |
| Crouch, Tho<sup>s</sup> | 3 | 7 | 3 | | | Goudy, Alexander | 1 | 1 | 3 | | | Kibbe, Zerah | 2 | 2 | 1 | | |
| Crouch, Ruben | 1 | | 1 | | | Shepherd, Jacob | 1 | 1 | 5 | | | Pease, Noah | 1 | 1 | 1 | | |
| Clark, Noah | 1 | 1 | 2 | | | Billing, Jn<sup>o</sup> | 2 | 2 | 4 | | | Pease, Giles | 2 | 1 | 1 | | |
| Got, Jn<sup>o</sup> | 1 | 1 | 2 | | | Billings, Sol<sup>o</sup> | 2 | | 2 | | | Pease, Richard | 2 | 2 | 3 | | |
| Crouch, Christopher | 2 | 2 | 4 | | | Collings, Jn<sup>o</sup> | 1 | 2 | 4 | | | Pease, Rob<sup>t</sup> | 1 | 2 | 5 | | |
| Tarbox, David | 3 | 5 | 3 | | | Fords, Jn<sup>o</sup> | 1 | 1 | 3 | | | Sexton, Joseph | 4 | 2 | 2 | | |
| Porter, Tim<sup>o</sup> | 3 | | 3 | | | Fords, Jn<sup>o</sup>, Jr | 1 | 3 | 1 | | | Sexton, Joseph, 2<sup>d</sup> | 2 | 4 | 4 | | |
| Tarbox, Zenas | 1 | 3 | 4 | | | Billings, Elijah | 2 | 3 | 3 | | | Saxton, Daniel | 1 | 2 | 5 | | |
| Tarbox, Sol<sup>o</sup> | 2 | 1 | 4 | | | Jones, Isahar | 2 | 3 | 2 | | | Collins, Jos | 1 | 5 | 2 | | |
| Tarbox, Godfry | 1 | | 4 | | | Halbert, Jabes | 1 | 4 | 3 | | | Jones, Jiles | 1 | 1 | 2 | | |
| Parmer, Sam<sup>l</sup> | 2 | | 1 | | | Jones, Stephen | 2 | 2 | 3 | | | Brace, Lt | 1 | 2 | 4 | | |
| Rus, Jn<sup>o</sup> | 3 | | 3 | | | Jones, Benj<sup>a</sup> | 2 | 2 | 4 | | | Brown, Jn<sup>o</sup> | 3 | 1 | 3 | | |
| Bridge, Asa | 1 | 2 | 3 | | | Ward, James | 1 | 2 | 5 | | | Cooley, Tho<sup>s</sup> | 5 | 3 | 5 | | |
| Cutting, Isaac | 1 | | 4 | | | Chaffee, Serrel | 1 | 2 | 4 | | | Fuller, W<sup>m</sup> | 1 | 1 | 2 | | |
| Porter, Jonah | 1 | 5 | 4 | | | Collins, Jabez | 2 | 3 | 4 | | | Pease, Alphe | 1 | 1 | 2 | | |
| Wright, Sam<sup>l</sup> | 2 | 1 | 3 | | | Parsons, Nath<sup>l</sup> | 2 | | 1 | | | Tiffany, Nath<sup>l</sup> | 2 | | 4 | | |
| Barber, Oliver | 3 | 3 | 5 | | | Parsons, Stephen | 1 | | 3 | | | Painter, Jn<sup>o</sup> | 1 | 1 | 6 | | |
| Barber, Obedi | 1 | 3 | 4 | | | Kibbe, Joel | 1 | 2 | 1 | | | Purna, Peter | 1 | | | | |
| Tillotson, Jn<sup>o</sup> | 1 | | 2 | | | Parsons, Ezra | 2 | 1 | 3 | | | Inman, Edward | 3 | 1 | 5 | | |
| Wartis, Jn<sup>o</sup> | 1 | | 2 | | | Kibbe, Gordon | 1 | | 1 | | | Prat, Ashbel | 1 | 2 | 4 | | |
| Fuller, Eber | 1 | | 3 | 9 | | Kibbe, Elijah | 1 | 1 | 3 | | | Pollet, Rob<sup>t</sup> | 2 | 3 | 4 | | |
| Housie, Elijah | 5 | | 5 | 1 | 1 | Pease, Noah | 3 | 2 | 2 | | | Ford, Jos | 1 | 1 | 1 | | |
| Yonguer, Ebn<sup>r</sup> | 1 | 2 | 3 | 7 | | Raynolds, Sam<sup>l</sup> | 1 | 1 | 3 | | | Coy, David | 3 | 2 | 5 | | |
| | | | | | | Davis, Corn<sup>s</sup> | 1 | | 1 | | | Phillips, Jon<sup>a</sup> | 2 | | 6 | | |
| SOMERS TOWN. | | | | | | Backus, Revd. C. | 1 | 1 | 3 | | | Horton, Aaron | 1 | 3 | 3 | | |
| Chapin (Wid.) | 2 | 1 | 7 | | | Pitkin, Tho<sup>s</sup> | 1 | 1 | 3 | | | Winchester, Benj<sup>n</sup> | 2 | 3 | 5 | | |
| Thompson, George | 1 | 1 | 4 | | | Pitkin, Calvin | 1 | 1 | 2 | | | Dwight, Jos | 1 | 2 | 2 | | |
| Chapin, Moses | 3 | 1 | 5 | | | Dwight, Alpheus | 1 | 2 | 3 | | | Fords, Tim<sup>o</sup> | 3 | 3 | 5 | | |
| Wood, Harber | 3 | 1 | 2 | | | Fowler, David | 2 | | 3 | | | Meacham, Jos | 4 | 2 | 4 | | |
| Newcrum, Du<sup>r</sup> | 4 | 2 | 2 | | 3 | Meachem, Sam<sup>l</sup> | 2 | | 5 | | | Scott, W<sup>m</sup> | 1 | 3 | 1 | | |
| Pease, Joel | 1 | 1 | 3 | | | Allen, Nath<sup>l</sup> | 2 | 3 | 5 | | | Utley, Asahel | 1 | 1 | 2 | | |
| Kibbe, Bildad | 1 | 1 | 4 | | | Davis, Aaron | 1 | | 2 | | | Kibbe, Tim<sup>o</sup>, 2<sup>d</sup> | 2 | 3 | 2 | | |
| Cooly, Luke | 1 | 3 | 1 | 1 | | Morehouse, Tho<sup>s</sup> | 1 | | 2 | | | Fuller, Lukus | 3 | 2 | 3 | | |
| Dickinson, Noah | 3 | 4 | 6 | | | Root, Tim<sup>o</sup> | 1 | | 6 | | | Kibbe, Elijah | 1 | 2 | 2 | | |
| Cooly, Nath<sup>l</sup> | 2 | 2 | 4 | | | Root, Jos | 1 | 3 | 3 | | | Kibbe, Edward | 1 | | 1 | | |
| Prentice, James | 2 | | 6 | | | Chapin, Seth | 1 | | 1 | | | Kibbe, Noah | 1 | 1 | 1 | | |
| Howard, Jos | 2 | | 3 | | | Jones, Benj<sup>a</sup> | 1 | | 2 | | | Cook, W<sup>m</sup> | 1 | 3 | 4 | | |
| Howard, Charles | 1 | 1 | 1 | | | Pitkin, Paul | 1 | 3 | 2 | | | Prentice, Stephen | 1 | | 1 | | |
| Dunbar, Jabe | 1 | | 2 | | | Chapin, Sam<sup>l</sup> | 1 | 4 | 4 | | | | | | | | |
| Kibbe, Lemuel | 1 | 5 | 2 | | | Chapin, Elias | 2 | 1 | 1 | | | STAFFORD TOWN. | | | | | |
| Kibbe, Israel, Jr | 2 | 1 | 2 | | | Chapin, Aaron | 2 | 1 | 3 | | | Agar, Jos<sup>u</sup> | 1 | 2 | 3 | | |
| Fuller, Stephen | 1 | 3 | 3 | | | Davis, Jobe | 2 | 2 | 1 | | | Alden, Jos<sup>u</sup> | 3 | 1 | 4 | | |
| Kibbe, Dan<sup>l</sup> | 2 | | 1 | | | Davis, James | 1 | 2 | 4 | | | Alden, Elisha | 4 | 3 | 4 | | |
| Kibbe, Frederick | 1 | 1 | 2 | | | Root, Jacob | 3 | | 1 | | | Amadown, Jn<sup>o</sup> | 1 | | 4 | | |
| Elmer, W<sup>m</sup> | 1 | 2 | 3 | | | Root, Eben<sup>r</sup> | 1 | 1 | 2 | | | Addams, Sol<sup>a</sup> | 1 | 1 | 1 | | |
| Phelps, Benj<sup>n</sup> | 2 | 2 | 3 | | | Kibbe, Moses | 1 | 2 | 3 | | | Avery, Jabez | 3 | | 4 | | |
| Kibbe, Jed<sup>h</sup> | 1 | 3 | 4 | | | Ladd, Jn<sup>o</sup> | 1 | 1 | 3 | | | Abbot, Stephen | 1 | | 1 | | |
| Kibbe, Israel | 1 | | 4 | | | Buck, Tho<sup>s</sup> | 2 | 1 | 2 | | | Blodget, Josa | 4 | 1 | 3 | | |
| Kibbe, Ed<sup>d</sup> | 1 | 3 | 5 | | | Elis, Oliver | 1 | | 6 | | | Bass, Codsida | 1 | 1 | 1 | | |
| Burge, Jon<sup>a</sup> | 1 | 4 | 3 | | | Hunt, Jos | 1 | | 1 | | | Babcock, Hozeah | 1 | | 1 | | |
| Fuller, Ja<sup>s</sup> | 1 | 1 | 6 | | | Hunt, Peter | 1 | 3 | 2 | | | Bolton, Dan<sup>l</sup> | 2 | 2 | 5 | | |
| Russel, Jn<sup>o</sup> | 2 | 1 | 7 | | | Richardson, Stephen | 1 | 3 | 4 | | | Butler, Zeb<sup>di</sup> | 1 | 2 | 4 | | |
| Russel, W<sup>m</sup> | 1 | | 3 | | | Wood, Dan<sup>l</sup> | 1 | | 4 | | | Blodget, Ab<sup>m</sup> | 2 | 2 | 2 | | |
| Cooly, James | 3 | | 2 | | | Buel, Joseph | 3 | 2 | 4 | | | Bloget, Tim<sup>o</sup> | 1 | 1 | 5 | | |
| Sheldon, Charles | 2 | 3 | 6 | | | Wardwel, David | 3 | | 2 | | | Blodget, Sylvanus | 2 | 1 | 3 | | |
| Hall, Sam<sup>l</sup> | 4 | 2 | 3 | | | Kibbe, Peter, Jr | 1 | 2 | 2 | | | Blodget, Dan<sup>l</sup> | 2 | | 2 | | |
| Davis, Isaac | 1 | 1 | 3 | | | Parsons, Stephen | 1 | | 1 | | | Blodget, Paul, 2<sup>d</sup> | 1 | | 3 | | |
| Spencer, Isr<sup>l</sup> | 2 | | 3 | | | Richardson, David | 1 | | 2 | | | Blodget, Paul | 1 | 1 | 4 | | |
| White, Sam | 1 | 2 | 4 | | | Pease, Stephen | 2 | 1 | 2 | | | Bass, Zeph<sup>h</sup> | 1 | 2 | 1 | | |
| Purchase, Tho<sup>s</sup> | 1 | 1 | 1 | | | Richardson, David, Jr. | 2 | 1 | 2 | | | Bascom, Dan<sup>l</sup> | 2 | | 1 | | |
| Wardwell, Nath<sup>el</sup> | 1 | | 3 | | | Horton, Moses | 1 | 3 | 1 | | | Bartlett, E<sup>m</sup> | 2 | 2 | 4 | | |
| Hall, Jos<sup>a</sup> | 1 | 2 | 3 | | | Cosly, George | 2 | 1 | 5 | | | Bartlett, Sam<sup>l</sup> | 2 | 3 | 3 | | |
| Hall, Alpheus | 1 | | 1 | | | Wood, Jn<sup>o</sup> | 6 | 1 | 3 | | | Bigsbee, Sol<sup>m</sup> | 1 | | 1 | | |
| Hall, Veasny | 3 | 3 | 3 | | | Burton, Christopher | 1 | 1 | 2 | | | Bradley, Mercy | | | 3 | | |
| Kimball, Sam<sup>l</sup> | 2 | 2 | 4 | | | Pratt, Eliakim | 1 | | 2 | | | Bradley, Jonah | 1 | 1 | 2 | | |
| M<sup>c</sup>Gregory, Eben<sup>r</sup> | 1 | 1 | 4 | | | Pomeroy, Jos<sup>a</sup> | 3 | 1 | 2 | | | Carpenter, Jn<sup>o</sup> | 1 | 2 | 4 | | |
| Hall, Zadock | 1 | 1 | 4 | | | Pomeroy, Jn<sup>o</sup> | 5 | 1 | 5 | | | Carpenter, W<sup>m</sup> | 1 | 2 | 1 | | |
| Hall, Libny | 1 | 1 | 4 | | | Felt, Sam<sup>l</sup> | 2 | 5 | 5 | | | Chaffee, Darius | 1 | | 2 | | |
| Swetland, Tho<sup>s</sup> | 1 | 1 | 3 | | | Buck, Isaac | 1 | 1 | 1 | | | Clark, Neh<sup>m</sup> | 1 | | 1 | | |
| Pease, James | 1 | | 2 | | | Wood, Josiah | 1 | 1 | 3 | | | Carue*, Revd Mr | | | 3 | | |
| Clark, Amo<sup>s</sup> T. | 2 | 1 | 3 | | | Jenning, Benj<sup>n</sup> | 1 | | 4 | | | Cross, Sam | 1 | 5 | 3 | | |
| Allen, Asa | 2 | 4 | 4 | | | Adams, Sol<sup>o</sup> | 1 | 1 | 4 | | | Convus, Jesse | 2 | | 4 | | |
| Hall, Luke | 1 | 1 | 4 | | | Parsons, W<sup>m</sup> | 1 | 2 | 4 | | | Convus, Jos | 1 | 2 | 6 | | |
| Jones, David | 1 | 3 | 3 | | | Buckley, Dan<sup>l</sup> | 1 | | 2 | | | Convus, Darius | 1 | | 2 | | |
| Brace, David | 1 | 2 | 2 | | | M<sup>c</sup>Gound (Wid.) | | | 1 | | | Convus, James | 1 | 6 | 2 | | |
| Wallice, Ab<sup>m</sup> | 1 | 2 | 5 | | | Cooly, Ruben | 1 | | 1 | | | Convus, Asa | 1 | 3 | 2 | | |
| Slate, Ezek<sup>l</sup> | 3 | 3 | 4 | | | M<sup>c</sup>Gee (Wid.) | | 2 | 4 | | | Cross, Stephen | 2 | | 3 | | |
| Billings, Sam<sup>l</sup> | 2 | 3 | 4 | | | Burbanks, Dan<sup>l</sup> | 1 | 4 | 5 | | | Crandal, Urich | 1 | 1 | 1 | | |
| Lomis, Phillip | 1 | 1 | 5 | | | Kibbe, Peter | 4 | | 2 | | 1 | Crandal, Abijah | 1 | | 2 | | |
| Pease, Col<sup>n</sup> | 2 | 2 | 3 | 1 | | Sykes, Ruben | 3 | 1 | 4 | | 1 | Cushman, W<sup>m</sup> | 3 | 3 | 6 | | |

*Nonresident.

# HEADS OF FAMILIES—CONNECTICUT.

## TOLLAND COUNTY—Continued.

| NAME OF HEAD OF FAMILY. | Free white males of 16 years and upward, including heads of families. | Free white males under 16 years. | Free white females, including heads of families. | All other free persons. | Slaves. | NAME OF HEAD OF FAMILY. | Free white males of 16 years and upward, including heads of families. | Free white males under 16 years. | Free white females, including heads of families. | All other free persons. | Slaves. | NAME OF HEAD OF FAMILY. | Free white males of 16 years and upward, including heads of families. | Free white males under 16 years. | Free white females, including heads of families. | All other free persons. | Slaves. |
|---|---|---|---|---|---|---|---|---|---|---|---|---|---|---|---|---|---|
| **STAFFORD TOWN—con.** | | | | | | **STAFFORD TOWN—con.** | | | | | | **STAFFORD TOWN—con.** | | | | | |
| Carpenter, Jno | 3 | 1 | 3 | | | Harwood, Jno | 2 | 2 | 5 | | | Stoel, Robt | 1 | 2 | 4 | | |
| Carpenter, Nathan | 1 | | 3 | | | Hall, Wm | 3 | | 2 | | | Scott, Philip | 1 | 1 | 3 | | |
| Convus (Wid.) | | 1 | 3 | | | Holmes, Josi | 2 | 1 | 3 | | | Saxton, George | 1 | 2 | 2 | | |
| Convus, Josi | 2 | 1 | 6 | | | Holmes, Jona | 1 | | 2 | | | Stone, James | 1 | 1 | 4 | | |
| Cushman, Solm | 3 | 1 | 2 | | | Hows, Israel | 2 | 2 | 4 | | | Sanger, Jno | 2 | 1 | 3 | | |
| Convus, Sola | 1 | 2 | 5 | | | Hyde, Nathl | 1 | | 3 | | | Townsend, Benja | 1 | | 2 | | |
| Coy, Aaron | 1 | 1 | 1 | | | Hitchcock, Jona | 1 | 2 | 2 | | | Torry, James | 2 | 5 | 3 | | |
| Colebourn, Eben | 4 | 2 | 4 | | | Johnson, Seth | 2 | | 2 | | | Townsend, Jno | 1 | | 1 | | |
| Colebourn, Saml | 2 | 1 | 2 | | | Hunt, Jesse | 4 | | 5 | | | Townsend, Gibs | 1 | | 3 | | |
| Colebourn, Jos | 1 | 4 | 5 | | | Holloway, Danl | 1 | 1 | 4 | | | Thrasher, Eben | 2 | 2 | 3 | | |
| Colebourn (Wid.) | 1 | 1 | 1 | | | Johnson, Nathl | 3 | 1 | 3 | | | Thrasher, Christopher | 3 | 1 | 3 | | |
| Colebourn, Danl | 1 | 3 | 4 | | | Jones, Elijah | 1 | 3 | 4 | | | Thrasher, Sampson | 1 | 1 | 3 | | |
| Colebourn, Ruben | 1 | 3 | 5 | | | Johnson, Sampson | 1 | | 1 | | | Thrasher, Noah | 1 | 3 | 3 | | |
| Convus, Joseph | 1 | 2 | 3 | | | Jennings, Robt | 1 | | 4 | | | Tupper, Solm | 1 | | 1 | | |
| Convus, Stephen | 2 | 1 | 4 | | | Johnson, Ebenr | 1 | 1 | 3 | | | Torry, Jame, Jr | 2 | 2 | 2 | | |
| Canvil (Wid.) | | 1 | 2 | | | Johnson, Em | 1 | 4 | 2 | | | Torry, Amos | 1 | 1 | 3 | | |
| Cross, Noah | 2 | 4 | 4 | | | Johnson, Abner | 1 | 1 | 6 | | | Torry, Ezra | 1 | 2 | 4 | | |
| Cushman, Nathl | 1 | 2 | 2 | | | Johnson, Jona | 3 | 3 | 6 | | | Thompson, Asa | 1 | | 2 | | |
| Chapman, Jno | 2 | 3 | 4 | | | Igard, Benjn | 1 | 3 | 6 | | | Thompson, Heny | 2 | 1 | 1 | | |
| Cushman, Isaac | 1 | 2 | 2 | | | Johnson, Charles | 1 | | 3 | | | Thrasher, Josu | 1 | 1 | 1 | | |
| Chaffee, Amos | 2 | 2 | 3 | | | Johnson, Abel | 1 | 1 | 2 | | | Willard, Rev. I | 1 | 1 | 4 | | |
| Cady, Ruben | 1 | 4 | 2 | | | Johnson, Nathan | 2 | 3 | 4 | | | Wardwell, Eber | 1 | 5 | 3 | | |
| Cady, Asa | 1 | 1 | 4 | | | Johnson, David | 2 | 1 | 4 | | | Whisler, Zadock | 1 | 2 | 2 | | |
| Cady, Jesse | 1 | 1 | 7 | | | Jinks, Wm | 2 | 4 | 2 | | | West, Abbe | 1 | 2 | 2 | | |
| Cady, Abner | 1 | 2 | 2 | | | Kendal, Eben | 1 | 3 | 2 | | | Wakefield, Levy | 1 | | 4 | | |
| Cady, Jedediah | 1 | | 5 | | | Kent, Josi | 2 | | 3 | | | Wakefield, Elijah | 1 | | 3 | | |
| Cady, Hez | 1 | 3 | 3 | | | Kent, Jabez | 3 | 1 | 4 | | | Wakefield, Jno | 1 | | 2 | | |
| Chapin, Elias | 1 | 1 | 3 | | | Kent, Benja | 2 | 2 | 6 | | | Walbridge, Amos | 4 | 2 | 5 | | |
| Chapin, Aaron | 1 | 3 | 4 | | | Lyon, Lymon | 1 | 3 | 5 | | | Walbridge, Wm | 1 | 3 | 4 | | |
| Carpenter, Danl | 1 | | 3 | | | Lard, Wm | 3 | 1 | 2 | | | Wallis, James | 1 | 1 | 2 | | |
| Carpenter, Moses | 1 | 2 | 1 | | | Leach, Calvin | 1 | 2 | 2 | | | Washbourn, Ezra | 2 | 5 | 3 | | |
| Carpenter, David | 1 | 1 | 2 | | | Lull, James | 2 | | 2 | | | Whore, Edw | 1 | | 2 | | |
| Cushman, Urich | 1 | 1 | 2 | | | Lee, Saml | 1 | 1 | 2 | | | Washbourn, Ezra, Jr | 2 | | 1 | | |
| Kimbal, Daniel | 1 | 4 | 2 | | | Little, Robt | 1 | | 1 | | | Web, Elipht | 1 | 2 | 5 | | |
| Dunoty, Francis | 1 | | 2 | | | Molton, Salmon | 1 | 4 | 1 | | | Wakefield, Ziel | 1 | 2 | 2 | | |
| Dunbar, Benja | 1 | 3 | 3 | | | Molton, Jona | 3 | 1 | 2 | | | Washbourn, Wm | 1 | 1 | 3 | | |
| Drake, Levy | 2 | 5 | 2 | | | Molton, Barnard | 1 | 2 | 3 | | | Washburn, Sola | 1 | | 1 | | |
| Davis, Jo | 1 | | 1 | | | Molton, Eben | 2 | 1 | 1 | | | Washbourn, Natha | 1 | 1 | 3 | | |
| Davis, Danl | 1 | 1 | 1 | | | Miller, Cornelius | 1 | | 1 | | | Washbourn, Sola | 2 | | 5 | | |
| Davis, Noah | 3 | 3 | 5 | | | Maker, Danl | 3 | | 4 | | | Washbourn, Moses | 1 | 2 | 6 | | |
| Davis, Moses | 3 | | 1 | | | Molton, Stephen | 3 | 1 | 2 | | | Whittikar, Abm | 1 | 1 | 2 | | |
| Davis, Jesse | 1 | | 4 | | | Molton, Stephen, Jr | 1 | 2 | 2 | | | Washburn, Wm | 2 | 1 | 5 | | |
| Dimock, Sylvanus | 2 | 1 | 2 | | | Morse, James | 4 | 2 | 6 | | | Wood, Nathn | 1 | 2 | 3 | | |
| Davis, Benja | 2 | | 2 | | | Mercy, Jno | 1 | | 1 | | | Wood, Abner | 3 | 2 | 7 | | |
| Davis, Benjn, Jr | 1 | 1 | 2 | | | Moulton, Howard | 3 | 2 | 6 | | | Warner, Moses | 1 | 2 | 5 | | |
| Davis, Noah, Jr | 1 | 3 | 3 | | | Moulton, Jos | 1 | | 1 | | | Whittikar, Jona, 2d | 1 | | 5 | | |
| Davis, Jno | 1 | 1 | 6 | | | Miller, Cornelius | 1 | 1 | 2 | | | Wood, Natha | 1 | 2 | 4 | | |
| Davis, Aaron | 3 | 3 | 3 | | | Marchal, Ruben | 1 | 2 | 6 | | | Whittikar, Stephen | 1 | | 3 | | |
| Davis, Leml | 1 | 4 | 3 | | | Newton, Jona | 1 | 1 | 2 | | | Welch, Jude | | 1 | 1 | | |
| Edson, Eliab | 2 | 2 | 3 | | | Nedom, Dan | 1 | | 2 | | | Whittikar, Jona | 3 | 1 | 3 | | |
| Eaton, Jno | 2 | 4 | 3 | | | Nedom, Nehm | 2 | 1 | 3 | | | Winter, Jos | 1 | 5 | 4 | | |
| Edson, Calvin | 2 | | 4 | | | Nelson, Wm | 1 | 2 | 1 | | | Woodworth, Charles | 1 | 4 | 3 | | |
| Edson, Jacob | 3 | 1 | 6 | | | Nelson, George | 1 | | 5 | | | Washburn, Nehm | 1 | 2 | 2 | | |
| Edson, Peter | 1 | 2 | 3 | | | Knox, Adam | 1 | 2 | 2 | | | Wesley, Wm | 1 | | 1 | | |
| Edson, Levi | 2 | 1 | 4 | | | Nash, Phneas | 1 | 3 | 4 | | | Webster, Jos | 2 | 3 | 2 | | |
| Estes, Stephen | 1 | 5 | 3 | | | Orcutt, Timo | 1 | 1 | 2 | | 1 | Burrows, Amos | 1 | 2 | 1 | | |
| Eaton, Aaron | 4 | 1 | 3 | | | Orcutt, Nathl | 2 | | 2 | | | Phillips, Jno | 1 | | 4 | | |
| Elethrop, Saml | 1 | 2 | 1 | | | Orcutt, Jabez | 1 | 3 | 5 | | | Burge, Edwd | 1 | 4 | 3 | | |
| Elethrop, Jno | 1 | | 3 | | | Orcutt, Stephens | 1 | 4 | 1 | | | Bester, Jno | 2 | | 4 | | |
| Ellis, Timo | 1 | 1 | 2 | | | Orcutt, David | 1 | | 2 | | | Foot, Jesse | 1 | 5 | 3 | | |
| Ellis, Cyrus | 2 | 1 | 1 | | | Orcutt, Icabod | 2 | | 4 | | | Barret, Benjn | 1 | 2 | 4 | | |
| Ellis, Benja | 4 | | 4 | | | Orcutt, Solm | 2 | | 2 | | 1 | Barret, James | 1 | 3 | 4 | | |
| Ellis, Jos | 1 | 2 | 3 | | | Orcutt, Natha | 2 | | 2 | | | Barret, Jno | 1 | 1 | 1 | | |
| Eaton, Wm | 1 | 1 | 2 | | | Orcutt, Danl | 2 | | 2 | | | Russel, Rider | 1 | | 2 | | |
| Eaton, Saml | 1 | 1 | 4 | | | Pinna, Isaac | 2 | 1 | 3 | | | Allden, Zepha | 1 | | 2 | | |
| Foster, Revd Mr | 1 | | 3 | | | Phelps, Jno | 3 | 1 | 4 | | | Pasco, Jos | 1 | | 3 | | |
| Fuller, David | 2 | 1 | 4 | | | Phelps, Jose | 2 | | 2 | | | Pasco, Jona | 2 | 3 | 2 | | |
| Fuller (Wid.) | | | 1 | | | Pooler, Jno | 1 | | 2 | | | Fuller, Jose | 2 | | 5 | | |
| Forget, Jno | 2 | 1 | 5 | | | Pool, James | 2 | 3 | 4 | | | Skinner, Jo | 2 | | 3 | | |
| Forget, Elijah | 1 | 4 | 2 | | | Pool, Jona | 3 | 1 | 2 | | | Avay, Danl | 1 | 3 | 2 | | |
| Fish, Elijah | 2 | 1 | 2 | | | Perry, Ruben | 1 | 3 | 4 | | | Gager, Saml | 1 | | 3 | | |
| Fuller, Wm | 1 | 1 | 6 | | | Parsons, David | 7 | | 6 | | | Bester, Abel | 1 | 1 | 5 | | |
| Fuller, Hez | 1 | 2 | 3 | | | Pattin, Nathl | 3 | 4 | 4 | | | Dimock, Amasa | 2 | 1 | 4 | | |
| Farmer, Timo | 1 | 1 | 1 | | | Pattin, Wm | 3 | 1 | 4 | | | Dimock, Timo | 1 | 1 | 1 | | |
| Fuller, Saml | 3 | 1 | 4 | | | Pulnam, Cornelius | 1 | 2 | 4 | | | Dimock, Timo, Jr | 1 | 2 | 2 | | |
| Foot, Isaac | 1 | 4 | 3 | | | Pattin, Jno | 2 | 3 | 4 | | | Clust, Jona | 3 | 1 | 3 | | |
| Fays, David | 2 | 2 | 3 | | | Parker, Or | 1 | 2 | 2 | | | Carton, Caleb | 1 | 3 | 2 | | |
| Guthery, Saml | 3 | | 3 | | | Pease, Jno | 1 | 2 | 2 | | | Eaton, Saml | 3 | 2 | 1 | | |
| Gibs, Josi | 1 | 1 | 4 | | | Richardson, Isaac | 1 | 3 | 3 | | | Dimock, Jno | 3 | | 1 | | |
| Gay, Eben | 2 | 2 | 4 | | | Richardson, Natha | 1 | | 4 | | | Burows, Jona | 1 | 2 | 5 | | |
| Gilman, Wm | 2 | | 2 | | | Richardson, Gershom | 1 | 1 | 4 | | | Bourns, Moses | 1 | 3 | 2 | | |
| Green, Jno | 1 | 1 | 3 | | | Richardson, Jno | 1 | | 2 | | | Clust, Timo | 2 | 1 | 2 | | |
| Gordon (Widow) | | | 3 | | | Ross, Wm | 1 | 1 | 4 | | | Rice, David | 1 | 1 | 5 | | |
| Gordon, Gardner | 1 | | 3 | | | Russel, Saml | 2 | | 3 | | | Allin, Saml | 1 | 2 | 5 | | |
| Hall, Moses | 1 | 3 | 2 | | | Ryder, Benjn | 1 | 3 | 3 | | | Sawyer, Jno | 2 | 1 | 3 | | |
| Hyde, Em | 3 | | 4 | | | Rockwell, Saml | 4 | 1 | 7 | | | | | | | | |
| Hyde, Em, Jr | 1 | 2 | 3 | | | Smith, David | 1 | 2 | 4 | | | **TOLLAND TOWN.** | | | | | |
| Hickson, Jos | 1 | | 1 | | | Sessons, Benj | 1 | 2 | 2 | | | Holmes, Nathel | 2 | 2 | 3 | | |
| Hickson, Nathl, Jr | 1 | 2 | 6 | | | String, David | 3 | 2 | 6 | | | Nye, Jno | 2 | | 2 | | |
| Hall, Em | 3 | 1 | 3 | | | Smith, Abijah | 1 | | 1 | | | Hinkley, Icabod | 4 | 3 | 10 | | |
| Hodg, Jno | 1 | 1 | 3 | | | Strickland, Saml | 1 | 3 | 2 | | | Holmes, Jazaniah | 1 | 3 | 3 | | |
| Hornes, David | 1 | 1 | 4 | | | Stanton, Robt | 1 | 2 | 1 | | | Tyler (Widow) | | | 4 | | |
| Harris (Wid.) | | 1 | 3 | | | Sawyer, Cornelius | 2 | 3 | 3 | | | Eaton, Jno | 4 | 1 | 2 | | |
| Harris, Robt | | 2 | 3 | | | Searls, Jno | 1 | 2 | 3 | | | Eldridge, Solomon | 1 | | 4 | | |
| Harris, Eben | 1 | 3 | 2 | | | Scott, Stephen | 1 | 1 | 5 | | | | | | | | |

## TOLLAND COUNTY—Continued.

### TOLLAND TOWN—con.

| NAME OF HEAD OF FAMILY. | Free white males of 16 years and upward, including heads of families. | Free white males under 16 years. | Free white females, including heads of families. | All other free persons. | Slaves. |
|---|---|---|---|---|---|
| Fellows, Isaac | 2 | 3 | 4 | | |
| Nye, Samuel | 2 | | 4 | | |
| Nye, Hezekiah | 1 | 4 | 1 | | |
| Hows, Ebenr | 2 | 4 | 2 | | |
| Scott (Widow) | | | 2 | | |
| Lothrop, Jno | 3 | | 4 | | |
| Bradley, Jabez | 2 | 3 | 5 | | |
| Lothrop (Widow) | 1 | | 2 | | |
| Davis, Jos | 1 | | 2 | | |
| Robinson, Joshua | 3 | 1 | 4 | | |
| Harvey, Nathan | 2 | | 4 | | |
| Rawdin, Thos | 2 | 1 | 3 | | |
| Crandal, Samuel | 2 | 1 | 4 | | |
| Bester, Jno | 2 | 1 | 3 | | |
| Barnard, Moses | 1 | 1 | 3 | | |
| Barnard, Wm | 1 | 1 | 1 | | |
| Robinson, Ruben | 1 | 1 | 2 | | |
| Cook, Stephen | 1 | 1 | 3 | | |
| Holbrook, Elias | 3 | 3 | 4 | | |
| Avery, Asael | 4 | | 2 | | |
| Steel, Elezer | 3 | | 3 | | |
| Steel, Ashbel | 1 | | 1 | | |
| Stearns (Widow) | | 1 | 3 | | |
| Barns, Jona | 2 | 1 | 1 | | |
| Chapman, Isham | 1 | | 4 | | |
| Grant, Em, Jr | 1 | | 3 | | |
| Shepherd, Benoni | 2 | 1 | 5 | 1 | |
| Williams, Wilks | 1 | 1 | 3 | | |
| Grosvenor, Wm | 2 | | 2 | 1 | |
| Spencer, Ebenr | 1 | 3 | 3 | | |
| Bond, Thadeus | 4 | 1 | 3 | | |
| Williams, Rev. N | 4 | | 2 | | |
| Howard, Asa | 1 | 1 | 1 | | |
| Howard, Thos | 3 | 6 | 3 | | |
| Steel, Stephen | 2 | | 2 | | |
| Steel, Perez | 1 | 3 | 4 | | |
| Woodward, Elisha | 2 | | 2 | | |
| Parker, Phineas | 1 | 1 | 4 | | |
| Parker, James | 1 | | 3 | | |
| Luce, Jos | 1 | 1 | 4 | | |
| Cobb, David | 2 | 3 | 2 | | |
| Steel, Elezr, Jr | 1 | 4 | 1 | | |
| Norris, Jno | 2 | 2 | 5 | | |
| Thomas, Jno | 2 | 1 | 1 | | |
| Hammon, Elezr | 1 | 3 | 6 | | |
| Lomis, Simon | 1 | 2 | 1 | | |
| Tupper, Jos | 2 | 5 | 2 | | |
| Hawkins, Jno | 1 | | 1 | | |
| Hawkins, George | 1 | 4 | 4 | | |
| Tonkum, Gidn | 1 | | 1 | | |
| Grover, Jabez | 1 | 1 | 2 | | |
| Edwards, Jabez | 2 | 3 | 2 | | |
| Caswell, Lemuel | 1 | 4 | 4 | | |
| Carpenter, Timo | 1 | 1 | 1 | | |
| Carpenter, Comfort | 2 | 1 | 3 | | |
| Grover, Ebenr | 4 | 4 | 6 | | |
| Rawding, Ezra | 1 | 2 | 1 | | |
| Whipple, Saml | 4 | 2 | 1 | | |
| Lomis, Soln | 2 | 5 | 3 | | |
| Winslow, Jno | 1 | 1 | 1 | | |
| Griggs, Jno | 1 | 2 | 6 | | |
| Yongue, Moses | 1 | 2 | 3 | | |
| Norris, Benjn | 4 | 1 | 2 | | |
| Hammon, James | 1 | 4 | 7 | | |
| Ryder, Jno | 3 | | 3 | | |
| Humphries, Saml | 1 | 1 | 5 | | |
| Grover, Jno | 5 | 2 | 4 | | |
| Clap, Increas | 1 | 5 | 4 | | |
| Barrows, Wills | 2 | 2 | 3 | | |
| Baker, Thephilus | 2 | 2 | 5 | | |
| Webster, Timo | 1 | 1 | 4 | | |
| Cobb, Jeduthron | 4 | 3 | 6 | 1 | 1 |
| Hilyard, Miner | 2 | 2 | 3 | | |
| Jennes, Amos | 3 | 1 | 2 | | |
| Stearns, Jos | 1 | 4 | 4 | | |
| West, Soln | 1 | 2 | 5 | | |
| Cobb, Daniel | 2 | 1 | 2 | | |
| Baxter, Simn | 1 | 2 | 3 | | |
| Studley, Jos | 2 | 4 | 5 | | |
| Griggs, Saml | 1 | 1 | 3 | | |
| Barrows, Jno | 2 | 2 | 1 | | |
| Edgerton, Oliver | 1 | 2 | 1 | 1 | 1 |
| Hews, Danl | 1 | 2 | 2 | | |
| Edgerton, Danl | 3 | 4 | 6 | | |
| Haskel, Elijah | 1 | 3 | 3 | | |
| Hart, Jno | 1 | 1 | 3 | 1 | 1 |
| Long (Widow) | | | 2 | | |
| Griggs (Widow) | | 1 | 3 | | |
| Squire, Danl | 3 | 1 | 2 | | |
| Goodspead, Nathl | 1 | 1 | 1 | | |
| Steel, Jno | 2 | 2 | 7 | | |
| Wheeler (Widow) | | 1 | 2 | | |
| Crow, Simon | 1 | | 3 | | |
| Warren, Jno | 2 | 3 | 5 | | |
| Cheedle, Rufus | 1 | | 2 | | |

### TOLLAND TOWN—con.

| NAME OF HEAD OF FAMILY. | Free white males of 16 years and upward, including heads of families. | Free white males under 16 years. | Free white females, including heads of families. | All other free persons. | Slaves. |
|---|---|---|---|---|---|
| Lothrop, Icabod | 1 | 1 | 1 | | |
| Whiton, Elijah | 1 | 1 | 3 | | |
| Lothrop, Hope | 2 | 5 | 6 | | |
| Carpenter, Simo | 1 | 1 | 3 | | |
| Luce, Jona | 2 | | 4 | | |
| Mumford, Irad | 1 | 4 | 4 | | |
| Alford, Jno | 1 | 2 | 3 | | |
| Richardson, Lemul | 3 | 3 | 4 | | |
| Benton, Jacob | 1 | 2 | 4 | | |
| Benton, Danl | 1 | 1 | 4 | | |
| Scott, Zebediah | 2 | | 1 | | |
| Luce, Mark | 2 | 1 | 3 | | |
| Kenndy, David | 2 | | 4 | | |
| Abbot, Jno | 1 | 1 | 4 | | |
| Willes, Soln | 3 | 2 | 3 | | |
| Burge (Widow) | | | 2 | | |
| Stimpson, Stephen | 3 | 2 | 6 | | |
| Davis, Benjn | 1 | | 3 | | |
| Paulk, Ammi | 1 | 2 | 4 | | |
| Polk, David | 1 | 1 | 1 | | |
| Griggs, Josu | 2 | 1 | 4 | | |
| Robinson, Eber | 3 | 2 | 3 | | |
| Whittlesey, Saml | 1 | | 2 | | |
| Stimpson, Thos | 2 | | 1 | | |
| Hatch, Elezer | 3 | 1 | 6 | | |
| Lothrop, S. (Widow of) | | | 1 | | |
| Baker, Titus | 2 | | 1 | | |
| Baker, Titus, Jr | 1 | 1 | 2 | | |
| Weston (Widow) | 1 | | 3 | | |
| Baker, Danl | 2 | 2 | 6 | | |
| Baker, Ebenr | 2 | 1 | | | |
| Welles, Thos | 1 | 4 | 1 | | |
| Baker, Jos | 3 | 2 | 2 | | |
| Cady, Amos | 2 | 3 | 4 | | |
| Cady, Nahum | 2 | 1 | 6 | | |
| Field, Danl | 3 | 1 | 4 | | |
| Reed, Shubal | 4 | | 3 | | |
| Reed, Saml | 1 | 2 | 3 | | |
| Kaggan, Saml | 2 | 1 | 4 | | |
| Hull, Stephen | 3 | 4 | 5 | | |
| Delano, Sylvanus | 1 | | 2 | | |
| Polk, Em | 1 | 2 | 3 | | |
| Strong, Elnathan | 3 | | 3 | | |
| Tobey, Saml | 1 | 4 | 3 | | |
| Eaton, Soln | 1 | 3 | 2 | | |
| Shurtliff, Jno | 1 | | 1 | | |
| Chapman, Eliakim | 1 | 2 | 3 | 7 | |
| Chapman, Elijah | 3 | 1 | 1 | | |
| Chapman, Elijah, Jr | 2 | 2 | 4 | | |
| Chapman, Ashbel | 1 | | 3 | 2 | 1 |
| Chapman, Simo | 3 | 5 | 2 | | |
| Chapman, Samuel | 1 | | 2 | | |
| Stanley, Jno | 2 | 2 | 4 | | |
| Baker, Jno | 1 | | 1 | | |
| Baker, Haman | 2 | | 3 | | |
| Kingsbury, Nathel | 3 | 1 | 5 | | 1 |
| Aychinson, Bazzallet | 4 | 2 | 4 | | |
| Aychinson, Baza, Jr | 1 | 2 | 2 | | |
| Johnson, Elihu | 2 | 2 | 6 | | |
| Kingsbury, Nathl, Jr | 2 | 1 | 4 | | |
| Kingsbury, Rust | 1 | 2 | 5 | | |
| Cartson, Jno | 1 | 3 | 3 | | |
| Cartson, Darius | 2 | 2 | 3 | | |
| Blodget, Silas | 2 | | 1 | | |
| Benton, Timo | 3 | 2 | 4 | | |
| Peck, Jos | 1 | 1 | 2 | | |
| Aberns, Saml | 3 | | 2 | | |
| Aberns, Saml, Jr | 1 | 2 | 2 | | |
| Smith, Danl | 4 | 4 | 3 | | |
| King, Saml | 1 | 1 | 5 | | |
| Ladd, Elial | 2 | 2 | 2 | | |
| Post, Jazaniah | 1 | 1 | 4 | | |
| Sessions, Amasa | 1 | 2 | 5 | | |
| Ladd, Akijah | 1 | 1 | 1 | | |
| Newel, Danl | 1 | 1 | 1 | | |
| Betts, Timo | 1 | 1 | 4 | | |
| Huntington, Jno | 1 | 2 | 2 | | |
| Huntington, Elisha | 1 | 2 | 2 | | |
| Huntington (Widow) | | | 2 | | |
| Baxter, Alexander | 1 | 2 | 3 | | |
| Benton, Jona | 1 | 4 | 3 | | |
| White, Ebenr | 1 | 1 | 2 | | |
| Benton, Cyrus | 1 | 6 | 3 | | |
| Ladd, Jona | 2 | | 2 | | |
| Wheelerson, Jos | 1 | | 1 | | |
| Smith, Allan | 1 | | 3 | | |
| Isham, Asher | 1 | | 3 | | |
| Boothe, Peter | 1 | | 5 | | |
| Russel, Jona | 2 | 1 | 6 | | |
| Ryder, Enos | 1 | 3 | 2 | | |
| West, David | 1 | 3 | 2 | | |
| Baker, Jna, Jr | 2 | 1 | 5 | | |
| Preston, Enos | 1 | | 2 | | |
| Ward, Obediah | 1 | 5 | 2 | | |
| Heath, Simo | 1 | | 2 | | |

### TOLLAND TOWN—con.

| NAME OF HEAD OF FAMILY. | Free white males of 16 years and upward, including heads of families. | Free white males under 16 years. | Free white females, including heads of families. | All other free persons. | Slaves. |
|---|---|---|---|---|---|
| Heath, Isaac | 1 | 1 | 2 | | |
| Able, Asa | 1 | | 1 | | |
| Burchard, Walter | 1 | 1 | 3 | | |
| Carpenter, Ruben | 2 | 2 | 5 | | |
| Ingersol, Richard | 1 | 1 | 1 | | |
| West, Jabez | 1 | 1 | 2 | | |
| West, Ruful | 2 | | 4 | | |
| West, Job | 3 | 1 | 3 | | |
| Hows, James | 1 | 1 | 2 | | |
| Delano, Barna | 1 | 1 | 4 | | |
| Wilson, Jacob | 1 | 2 | 3 | | |
| Jewet, David | 2 | 3 | 5 | | |
| Baker, Seth | 1 | 2 | 1 | | |
| Ryder, Saml | 1 | | 3 | | |
| Wood, Jno | 2 | 1 | 7 | | |
| Ladd, Saml | 3 | 2 | 3 | | |
| Bates, Jos | 1 | | 2 | | |
| Baxter, Jedediah | 1 | 2 | 1 | | |
| Hare (Widow) | | | 2 | | |
| Borac, Jared | 1 | | | | |
| Rogers, Benjn | 1 | | 2 | | |
| Heney, Asa | 1 | 2 | 4 | | |
| Barton, Elkane | 1 | | 3 | | |
| Lillibridge, Thos | 2 | 2 | 3 | | |
| Lillibridge, Jon | 1 | 3 | 3 | | |
| Hartch, Jos | 2 | 4 | 7 | | |
| Cogswell, Wm | 1 | 1 | 2 | | |
| West, Jn | 2 | 2 | 5 | | |
| Baker, Elezer | 2 | 1 | 2 | | |
| Morgan, Joshua | 2 | 3 | 4 | | |
| Carlton, Richard | 1 | 3 | 2 | | |
| Baldwin, Asa | 1 | 1 | 4 | | |
| Woodward, Amos | 1 | 1 | 6 | | |
| Harth, Alma | 2 | 2 | 6 | | |
| Grant, Em | 4 | 2 | 2 | | |
| Grant, Eber | 1 | 2 | 4 | | |
| Dornah, Edward | 2 | 2 | 4 | | |
| Marnard, Zachariah | 1 | 1 | 3 | | |
| Howard, Stephen | 1 | 3 | 2 | | |

### UNION TOWN.

| NAME OF HEAD OF FAMILY. | Free white males of 16 years and upward, including heads of families. | Free white males under 16 years. | Free white females, including heads of families. | All other free persons. | Slaves. |
|---|---|---|---|---|---|
| Williams, Wm | 3 | | 3 | | |
| Foster, Edward | 2 | 4 | 4 | | |
| McKnawt, James | 1 | 1 | 1 | | |
| Gay, Amasa | 1 | | 3 | | |
| Walker, Benjn | 1 | | 1 | | |
| Walker, Timo | 2 | 2 | 5 | | |
| Lewes, Jona | 2 | 3 | 6 | | |
| Newel, Nathl | 2 | 2 | 5 | | |
| Walker, Benjn, 2d | 1 | 2 | 3 | | |
| Sprague, Thos | 2 | 1 | 5 | | |
| Write, Saml | 1 | 2 | 4 | | |
| Sessions, Ebenr | 2 | 1 | 2 | | |
| Merriman, Edw | 3 | 1 | 2 | | |
| Taylor, Thos | 2 | 2 | 4 | | |
| Horton, Benjn | 1 | 3 | 4 | | 1 |
| Bowls, Lemuel | 1 | 2 | 4 | | |
| Trimklin, Ic | 1 | 1 | 3 | | |
| Childs, Penuel | 1 | 4 | 2 | | |
| Armer, Jno | 2 | | 1 | | |
| Moses, Jno | 1 | | 2 | | |
| Moses (Wid.) | 1 | | 2 | | |
| Armer, James | 1 | 5 | 2 | | |
| Badger, Jm | 4 | 2 | 5 | | |
| Armstrong, Elias | 1 | | 1 | | |
| Munger, Jno | 2 | 3 | 1 | | |
| Armer, James | 1 | | 2 | | |
| Stone, Jos | 2 | | 5 | | |
| Merrifield, Ithm | 1 | | 1 | | |
| Coy, Levy | 1 | 2 | 2 | | |
| Clark, Jno | 2 | | 3 | | |
| Convus, Josi | 1 | | 1 | | |
| Sessons, Abijah | 3 | 1 | 7 | | |
| Bates, Davd | 2 | 1 | 3 | | |
| Pearce, Francis | 1 | 2 | 2 | | |
| Olney, Ezekl | 1 | 3 | 5 | | |
| Crawford, Saml | 3 | 4 | 5 | | |
| Burley, Soln | 2 | 2 | 6 | | |
| Convus, Benjn | 1 | 3 | 4 | | |
| Howard, Manassa | 1 | 1 | 2 | | |
| Lally, Jno | 1 | 1 | 1 | | |
| Lawson, Thos | 2 | | 3 | | |
| Coy, Archabal | 3 | 1 | 5 | | |
| Lawson, Robt | 1 | 1 | 3 | | |
| Farebanks, Jos | 2 | 3 | 4 | | |
| Paul (Wid.) | | | 2 | | |
| Lawson, David | 1 | | 3 | | |
| Mattason, Wm | 2 | 2 | 3 | | |
| Hows, David | 2 | | 3 | | |
| Lawson, Jno | 3 | 1 | 3 | | |
| Paul, Robt, 2d | 1 | | 2 | | |
| Convus, Noah | 1 | 2 | 3 | | |
| Eneas, Jos | 2 | 3 | 2 | | |
| Hunt, Jno | 1 | 3 | 3 | | |

# HEADS OF FAMILIES—CONNECTICUT.

## TOLLAND COUNTY—Continued.

| NAME OF HEAD OF FAMILY. | Free white males of 16 years and upward, including heads of families. | Free white males under 16 years. | Free white females, including heads of families. | All other free persons. | Slaves. | NAME OF HEAD OF FAMILY. | Free white males of 16 years and upward, including heads of families. | Free white males under 16 years. | Free white females, including heads of families. | All other free persons. | Slaves. | NAME OF HEAD OF FAMILY. | Free white males of 16 years and upward, including heads of families. | Free white males under 16 years. | Free white females, including heads of families. | All other free persons. | Slaves. |
|---|---|---|---|---|---|---|---|---|---|---|---|---|---|---|---|---|---|
| **UNION TOWN—con.** | | | | | | **WILLINGTON TOWN—con.** | | | | | | **WILLINGTON TOWN—con.** | | | | | |
| Utley, Jonᵃ | 1 | 3 | 7 | | | Church, Asa | 2 | 3 | 4 | | | Crocker, Jos | 3 | 1 | 5 | | |
| Backus, Jos | 1 | 2 | 1 | | | Sanger, Azariah | 3 | | 2 | | | Sawing, George | 1 | 4 | 4 | | |
| Rube, Jnᵒ | 1 | 3 | 4 | | | Vintin, Seth | 1 | 3 | 1 | | | Brown, Jas | 2 | | 3 | | |
| Gasby, Caleb | 2 | 2 | 5 | | | Thare, Shadrick | 1 | 1 | 5 | | | Eldridge, Jesse | 2 | | 1 | | |
| Shaw, Gid | 1 | 3 | 3 | | | Peery (Wid.) | | 1 | 1 | | | Eldridge (Wid.) | | 1 | 2 | | |
| Abbot, Wᵐ | 2 | 3 | 5 | | | Niles, James | 2 | 2 | 4 | | | Eldridge, Jos | 1 | 1 | 5 | | |
| Sessions, Jnᵒ | 2 | 3 | 4 | | | Perry, Samˡ | 1 | 1 | 1 | | | Eldridge, Zooth | 2 | 3 | 2 | | |
| Sessions, Waller | 1 | | 3 | | | Thompson, Jnᵒ | 2 | 2 | 3 | | | Crocker, Zebⁿ | 2 | 1 | 2 | | |
| Leach, Robᵗ | 1 | 1 | 1 | | | Works, Henʳʸ | 2 | 4 | 2 | | | Crocker, Stephen | 1 | | 2 | | |
| Martin, Samˡ | 1 | | 2 | | | Pool, Timᵒ | 1 | 2 | 1 | | | Dumnum, Samˡ | 1 | | 1 | | |
| Newel, Jacob | 2 | 2 | 4 | | | Whitmore, Jacob | 1 | 4 | 3 | | | Vintin, Samˡ | 1 | 2 | 4 | | |
| Burley, Jacob | 1 | | 4 | | | Jacobs, Jos | 1 | | 1 | | | Crocker, Samˡ | 1 | | 5 | | |
| More, David | 1 | 3 | 3 | | | Lillibridge, Benjᵃ | 2 | 1 | 2 | | 1 | Root, Nathˡ | 1 | | 3 | | |
| Godman, Jnᵒ | 3 | 1 | 3 | | | Jinnings, Thoˢ | 1 | | 1 | | | Scott, Jos | 1 | | 1 | | |
| Paul, Robᵗ | 1 | | 2 | | | Tyler, Broadstreat | 1 | 1 | 3 | | | Rice, Jnᵒ | 1 | | 2 | | |
| Sessions, Nathˡ | 1 | 2 | 5 | | | Tyler, James | 1 | | 2 | | | Holt, Nathˡ | 2 | | 1 | | |
| Kenna, Nathᵃⁿ | 2 | 4 | 3 | | | Jennings, David | 2 | | 2 | | | Holt, Nathˡ, 2ᵈ | 1 | 1 | 3 | | |
| Sprague, Jameˢ | 1 | 1 | 3 | | | Cummings, Simᵉ | 1 | | 4 | | | Preston, Darius | 2 | 1 | 4 | | |
| Thompson, Jameˢ | 1 | | 2 | | | Tyler, Broadᵗ, 2ᵈ | 1 | | 2 | | | Weston, Abᵐ | 1 | 2 | 3 | | |
| Hiscock, Stephen | 1 | 2 | 3 | | | Sibley, Jnᵒ | 2 | 1 | 2 | | | Weston, Samˡ | 3 | | 4 | | |
| Griggs, Jos | 3 | 3 | 5 | | | Sanger, Noadᵗ | 2 | 2 | 6 | | | Grant, Minor | 1 | 4 | 2 | | |
| Morris, Henʳʸ | 1 | 1 | 1 | | | Mackintosh, Andrew | 2 | 2 | 3 | | | Holt, Andrew | 1 | | 2 | | |
| Wales, Solᵃ | 2 | 2 | 4 | | | Dorman, Micajah | 3 | | 1 | | | Holt, James | 3 | 2 | 3 | | |
| May, Rufus | 1 | 2 | 4 | | | Davis, Jnᵒ | 1 | 1 | 2 | | | Holt, Timᵒ | 2 | | 2 | | |
| String, Samˡ | 2 | | 8 | | | Davis, Avery | 1 | 2 | 3 | | | Wheeler, Asa | 1 | 3 | 4 | | |
| Dodge, Nathˡ | 1 | 1 | 5 | | | Amedown, Jedediah | 1 | 3 | 3 | | | Buknall (Wid.) | | 1 | 3 | | |
| Twist, David | 2 | | 5 | | | Hewit, Danˡ | 1 | 3 | 4 | | | Johnson, Elisha | 2 | 1 | 3 | | |
| Fisk, Jnᵒ | 1 | 3 | 3 | | | Lillibridge, David | 2 | 1 | 4 | | | Eldridge, Wᵐ | 1 | 3 | 1 | | |
| Bass, Jos | 1 | 1 | 1 | | | Lillibridge, Clark | 1 | | 3 | | | Scott, Jn | 3 | 1 | 2 | | |
| Whiton, Caleb | 1 | 2 | 3 | | | Sawying, Jnᵒ | 2 | 1 | 3 | | | Hull, Hazard | 1 | 4 | 2 | | |
| Munger, Edʷ | 1 | 5 | 3 | | | Pomeroy, Noah | 1 | 1 | 1 | | | Topliff, Clement | 3 | | 3 | | |
| Sessions, Nathˡ | 1 | 2 | 5 | | | Pearl (Wid.) | | | 1 | | | Utley, Jnᵒ | 2 | 1 | 5 | | |
| Wales, Elijah | 1 | 4 | 4 | | | Hastings, James | 3 | | 2 | | | Richardson, Jnᵒ | 1 | 3 | 4 | | |
| Rothbone, David | 1 | 1 | 1 | | | Amadown, Moses | 1 | 1 | 4 | | | Fenton, Elezʳ | 1 | 3 | 2 | | |
| Strong, Alexander | 1 | 2 | 5 | | | Flint, Jonᵃ | 1 | 3 | 1 | | | Holt, Philᵃ | 1 | 1 | 1 | | |
| More, Wᵐ | 2 | 3 | 2 | | | Amadown, Henry | 4 | | 2 | | | Fuller, Danˡ | 2 | | 3 | | |
| More, James | 4 | 4 | 2 | | | Andrews, George | 3 | 1 | 3 | | | Root, Nathˡ | 2 | | 2 | | |
| More, James | 1 | 1 | 1 | | | Smith, Jnᵒ | 3 | 2 | 5 | | | Vintin, David | 1 | | 2 | | |
| More (Wid.) | 1 | 1 | 3 | | | Wever, Benjᵃ | 1 | 2 | 3 | | | Stoel, Samuel | 1 | 2 | 2 | | |
| More, Icabod | 1 | 1 | 3 | | | Johnson, Jnᵒ | 3 | 1 | 6 | | | Stoel, Asa | 1 | 1 | 2 | | |
| Lomis, Abner | 2 | 1 | 3 | | | Johnson, Danˡ | 1 | 1 | 3 | | | Hancks, Elijah | 1 | 4 | 2 | | |
| Burley, Jos | 2 | 3 | 5 | | | Chapman, Jason | 1 | 2 | 4 | | | Eldridge, Micajah H | 1 | 1 | 2 | | |
| Booth, Isaac | 1 | | 3 | | | Albray, Peter | 1 | 1 | 2 | | | Fuller, Danel | 2 | | 3 | | |
| Thompson, David | 2 | 3 | 1 | | | Jennings, Nathan | 2 | 1 | 3 | | | Jennings, Nathˡ | 1 | 3 | 2 | | |
| Holt, Seth | 1 | 1 | 4 | | | Goodale, Jnᵒ | 1 | 2 | 3 | | | Hatch, Justus | 1 | 1 | 3 | | |
| Semans, Abel | 2 | 1 | 3 | | | Hewit, Asa | 1 | 1 | 1 | | | Pearl, Timᵒ | 2 | 1 | 3 | | |
| Paul, Mathew | 2 | | 4 | | | Johnson, David | 1 | 1 | 2 | | | Fenton, Samˡ | 1 | | 5 | | |
| | | | | | | Mane, Josᵃ | 1 | 1 | 3 | | | Fenton, Asa | 2 | 4 | 6 | | |
| **WILLINGTON TOWN.** | | | | | | Mane, Ruben | 1 | 2 | 1 | | | Fenton, Adonijah | 1 | 4 | 2 | | |
| Nye, Benjⁿ | 3 | 4 | 4 | | | Mane, Elias | 2 | | 2 | | | Fenton, Solᵃ | 1 | 1 | 2 | | |
| James, Amos | 2 | 1 | 2 | | | Mane, Andrew | 1 | | 1 | | | Fenton, Luke | 1 | | 2 | | |
| Merrick, Stephen | 2 | 1 | 5 | | | Robinson (Wid.) | | | 3 | | | Fenton, Jos | 1 | | 7 | | |
| Farley, Jnᵒ | 3 | | 8 | | | Robinson, Bethul | 1 | 2 | 6 | | | Rice, Thoˢ | 2 | 1 | 2 | | |
| Farley, Samˡ | 1 | 2 | 1 | | | Robinson, Sabin | 1 | 1 | 3 | | | Pearle, Oliver | 1 | 2 | 3 | | |
| Parsons, Jos | 2 | 1 | 2 | | | Mane, Andrew, Jr | 1 | 1 | 5 | | | Glayer, Silas | 3 | 2 | 5 | | |
| Merrick, Thoˢ | 1 | | 1 | | | Fuller, Jnᵒ | 2 | 2 | 2 | | | Antissel, Silas | 1 | 4 | 7 | | |
| Merrick, Timᵒ | 3 | 1 | 2 | | | Weber, Thoˢ | 1 | 3 | 6 | | | Antissel, Pheneas | 1 | 4 | 2 | | |
| Merrick, Jnᵒ | 2 | | 1 | | | Wheeler, Jos | 1 | | 3 | | | Smith, Jos | 3 | | 4 | | |
| Merrick, Jnᵒ, Jr | 1 | 3 | 2 | | | Nelson, James | 1 | | 1 | | | Preston, Darius | 1 | 1 | 1 | | |
| Johnson, Wᵐ | 1 | 1 | 3 | | | Fisk, Rufus | 1 | 2 | 5 | | | Britt, Eᵐ | 2 | 1 | 4 | | |
| Hinkley, Jnᵒ | 1 | 2 | 3 | | | Weber, Jnᵒ | 1 | | 5 | | | Parks, Jonᵃ | 2 | 2 | 3 | | |
| Hinkley, David | 1 | 1 | 2 | | | Culver, James | 1 | 2 | 4 | | | Cushman, Elezer | 1 | | 2 | | |
| Abby, Samˡ | 2 | | 1 | | | Wever (Wid.) | | 1 | 5 | | | Cushman, Elezer, 2ᵈ | 1 | 3 | 6 | | |
| Bates, Danᵉˡ | 1 | | 1 | | | Wever, David | 2 | | 2 | | | Cushman, Eliphᵗ | 1 | 2 | 2 | | |
| Hatch, David | 3 | | 6 | | | Sibley, Ezra | 1 | 1 | 2 | | | Cushman, Thoˢ | 1 | 1 | 1 | | |
| Fellows, Varny | 2 | | 4 | | | Scripter, Elezer | 3 | 3 | 6 | | | Johnson, Abel | 1 | 2 | 3 | | |
| Nobles, Revᵈ. G | 2 | 2 | 3 | | | Stanton, Samˡ | 1 | 3 | 5 | | | Holt, Elijah | 2 | | 4 | | |
| Nobles, Solⁿ | 1 | 1 | 1 | | | Damock, Geduthon | 1 | 3 | 2 | | | Dunton, Samˡ | 2 | 3 | 3 | | |
| Holmes, Abel | 1 | 3 | 4 | | | Peck, Thoˢ | 3 | 1 | 1 | | | Rice (Wid.) | | | 2 | | |
| Kenada, Jonᵃ | 1 | | 4 | | | Newcum, Joˢ | 1 | 4 | 3 | | | Heath, Ebenʳ | 2 | 1 | 2 | | |
| Rice, Jnᵒ, Jr | 1 | | 1 | | | Carie, Nathˡ | 2 | 2 | 4 | | | Lee, Danˡ | 1 | 4 | 5 | | |
| Olcut, Caleb | 1 | 1 | 4 | | | Scripter, Jnᵒ | 2 | 1 | 3 | | | Marcy, Zebʰ | 2 | | 5 | | |
| Sparkes, Jos | 1 | | 1 | | | Gleason, Elezer | 1 | 3 | 4 | | | Stiles, Galo | 2 | 2 | 11 | | |
| Jennings, Nathˡ, 2ᵈ | 1 | 2 | 2 | | | Fenton, Elijah | 2 | | 2 | | | Holt, Isaac | 2 | | 6 | | |
| Jennings (Wid.) | | 1 | 2 | | | Fenton, Jnᵒ | 2 | 1 | 2 | | | Case, Jonⁿ | 1 | | 1 | | |
| Hows, Haman | 2 | 1 | 4 | | | Fenton, Nathˡ | 1 | 3 | 2 | | | Woodward, Abner | 1 | | 1 | | |
| Weston, Jonᵃ | 1 | 2 | 2 | | | Thompson, Justus | 1 | 1 | 2 | | | Teel, Isaac | 1 | 2 | 3 | | |
| Curtis, Ramson | 2 | 4 | 3 | | | Thompson, Jonᵃ | 1 | 2 | 6 | | | Root, Timᵒ | 3 | | 5 | | |
| Marcy, Zebediah, 2ᵈ | 1 | | 4 | | | Dimack, Jos | 1 | 1 | 5 | | | Becknal, Elezer | 1 | 1 | 1 | | |
| Davis, George | 1 | 1 | 2 | | | Root (Widow) | | 1 | 2 | | | Demock, Jos | 1 | 1 | 2 | | |
| Clyder, Jos | 2 | 5 | 4 | | | Taylor, Elisha | 1 | 3 | 4 | | | Belnap, Jonⁿ | 1 | 3 | 1 | | |
| Fuller, Elisha | 3 | 1 | 2 | | | Pearl, Timᵒ | 2 | 1 | 3 | | | Brown, Shubal | 1 | | 2 | | |
| Pearl, Richard | 1 | 4 | 3 | | | Johnson, Samˡ | 1 | 4 | 3 | | | Jenning (Wid.) | | 1 | 2 | | |
| Pearl, Frederick | 1 | | 2 | | | Fenton, Elezer | 3 | 1 | 3 | | | Fenton, Jnᵒ | 1 | | 1 | | |
| Flint, Asher | 2 | 1 | 1 | | | Taylor, Thoˢ | 1 | 3 | 5 | | | Sibley, Moses | 1 | 2 | 2 | | |
| | | | | | | Holt, Caleb | 1 | 3 | 1 | | | Johnson, Isaac | 2 | | 2 | 17 | |

# FIRST CENSUS OF THE UNITED STATES.

## WINDHAM COUNTY.

| NAME OF HEAD OF FAMILY. | Free white males of 16 years and upward, including heads of families. | Free white males under 16 years. | Free white females, including heads of families. | All other free persons. | Slaves. | NAME OF HEAD OF FAMILY. | Free white males of 16 years and upward, including heads of families. | Free white males under 16 years. | Free white females, including heads of families. | All other free persons. | Slaves. | NAME OF HEAD OF FAMILY. | Free white males of 16 years and upward, including heads of families. | Free white males under 16 years. | Free white females, including heads of families. | All other free persons. | Slaves. |
|---|---|---|---|---|---|---|---|---|---|---|---|---|---|---|---|---|---|
| **ASHFORD TOWN.** | | | | | | **ASHFORD TOWN—con.** | | | | | | **ASHFORD TOWN—con.** | | | | | |
| Wright, Nathan | 4 | 1 | 4 | | | Gasper, Joseph | 1 | | 2 | | | Kendall, Isaac | 1 | 1 | 3 | | |
| Knolton, Thomas | 2 | 4 | 3 | | | Hall, Job | 2 | 2 | 2 | | | Clark, John | 1 | 3 | 3 | | |
| Knolton, Ezra | 1 | | 3 | | | Stanley, Jerem^h | 2 | | 2 | | | Clark, Israel | 2 | 1 | 2 | | |
| Reed, Mathew | 2 | 3 | 2 | | | Whiton, Whitfield | 1 | 2 | 3 | | | Leonard, Benj^a | 2 | 1 | 1 | | |
| Phillips, Augustus | 1 | 1 | 2 | | | Buffington, William | 1 | 1 | 2 | | | Triscot, Joseph | 2 | 2 | 6 | | |
| Squire, Ephraim | 1 | 3 | 5 | | | Chapman, Benj^a | 2 | 2 | 5 | | | Howe, James | 1 | 3 | 4 | | |
| Johnson, Sam^l | 3 | | 2 | 1 | | Hill, Thomas | 1 | 5 | 2 | | | Boutle, Ezra | 3 | | 3 | | |
| Johnson, Sam^l | 2 | 1 | 2 | | | Haws, Eli | 2 | | 5 | | | Snow, Sam^l, Jn^r | 2 | 2 | 4 | | |
| Preston, Abraham | 1 | 3 | 5 | | | Pratt, Benj^n | 1 | 1 | 1 | | | Abbot, Stephen | 2 | | 1 | | |
| Bugbe, James | 2 | 2 | 5 | | | Knox, Sam^l | 1 | 5 | 2 | | | Snow, William | 2 | 5 | 7 | | |
| Russ, Azariah | 3 | 1 | 4 | | | Snow, Stephen, Jn^r | 1 | 1 | 3 | | | Mercy, Reubin | 5 | 1 | 6 | | |
| Tappin, Richard | 1 | | 2 | | | Potter, Silas | 2 | 5 | 5 | | | Macy, Mathew | 1 | | 4 | | |
| Snow, Oliver | 2 | 1 | 1 | | | Hillyard, Isaac | 1 | | 1 | | | Chandler, Stephen | 1 | 1 | 1 | | |
| Southward, John | 1 | | 5 | | | Dimmock, Timothy | 1 | 1 | 5 | | | Howe, Neh^h | 2 | | 5 | | |
| Snow, Stephen | 4 | | 3 | 3 | | Knox, William | 1 | 2 | 4 | | | Perkins, Isaac | 3 | 4 | 4 | | |
| Bugbe, Sam^l | 1 | 2 | 4 | | | Freemans, John | | | | 2 | | Cook, Aaron | 2 | 1 | 2 | | |
| Woodward, John | 2 | 1 | 3 | | | Hall, Uriah | 1 | 3 | 3 | | | Simmons, Abel | 4 | 4 | 5 | | |
| Clark, Benj^a | 3 | | 3 | | 2 | Grosvenor, Ezra | 1 | 3 | 3 | | | Davis, Willard | 2 | 1 | 3 | | |
| Snow, Jona^th | 1 | 1 | 3 | | | Wilcox, Thomas | 5 | 3 | 3 | | | Preston, Zera | 1 | 3 | 4 | | |
| Stebbins, Thomas | 2 | 3 | 5 | | | Robins, Thomas | 1 | 1 | 4 | | | Dow, Abel | 2 | 1 | 2 | | |
| Webb, Jabez | 1 | 2 | 3 | | | Robins, Clark | 1 | 3 | 3 | | | Woodward, Jason | 3 | 2 | 2 | | |
| Smith, Sarah | | | 2 | | | Robins, Benj^a | 1 | 3 | 3 | | | Gould, Jonathan | 2 | 1 | 2 | | |
| Bicknall, Zacha^h | 3 | | 4 | | | Curtiss, Henry | 1 | 1 | 2 | | | Wilson, Jacob | 1 | | 2 | | |
| Bicknall, John | 3 | 1 | 4 | | | Young, Thomas | 1 | 3 | 3 | | | Pond, Enoch | 2 | 3 | 6 | | |
| Welch, Solomon | 1 | | 4 | | | Kingsbury, Sam^l | 3 | | 2 | | | Mason, Eben^r | 2 | | 2 | | |
| Fletcher, Benj^a | 1 | 3 | 2 | | | Bass, Sam^l | 2 | 4 | 6 | | | Russell, Benj^n | 1 | | 2 | | |
| Cross, Nathan | 1 | | 3 | | | Snell, William | 1 | | 2 | | | Leamphere, Sam^l | 2 | 2 | 3 | | |
| Fletcher, Richard | 3 | | 4 | | | Snell, William, Jn^r | 1 | 2 | 1 | | | Burnam, Isaac | 3 | 2 | 5 | | |
| Snow, Simon | 1 | 2 | 1 | | | Preston, Hovey | 1 | 2 | 5 | | | Richards, Thaddeus | 2 | 2 | 4 | | |
| Yeomans, John | 1 | | 1 | | | Eldridge, Hezekiah | 1 | 3 | 3 | | | Bullard, Calvin | 1 | 2 | 3 | | |
| Aspenweil, Peter | 4 | | 3 | | | Eaton, Josiah | 1 | 3 | 2 | | | Chubb, William | 1 | 1 | 1 | | |
| Wright, Benj^a | 1 | 2 | 4 | | | Henfield, William | 1 | 1 | 1 | | | Chapman, David | 1 | 4 | 6 | | |
| Chaffee, Josiah, Jn^r | 1 | 1 | 1 | | | Eastman, Peter | 3 | 2 | 4 | | | Smith, John | 1 | 1 | 3 | | |
| Eldridge, Steph^n | 1 | 1 | 1 | | | Brook, Abijah | 2 | 1 | 2 | | | Loomis, Abner | 3 | | 5 | | |
| Eaton, Elisabeth | | 2 | 2 | | | Preston, John | 2 | 1 | 4 | | | Snow, Sam^l, Sen^r | 1 | 1 | 2 | | |
| Parker, Reuben | 1 | 1 | 1 | | | Preston, Medinah | 3 | 4 | 4 | | | Mason, John | 1 | 2 | 2 | | |
| Abbe, Isaac | 3 | | 1 | | | Amadown, Joseph | 2 | 4 | 6 | | | Eaton, Eben^r | 2 | 2 | 5 | | |
| Owen, Eben^r | 1 | 1 | 6 | | | Ward, Ichabod | 2 | 2 | 5 | | | Dowe, Abel | 1 | 1 | 2 | | |
| Owen, Eleaz^r | 2 | 3 | 3 | | | Whiton, Joseph | 1 | 6 | 7 | | | Dowe, Cyrus | 4 | 1 | 2 | | |
| Fay, Jedediah | 4 | 1 | 5 | | | Whiton, Hannah | 2 | | 5 | | | Watkins, Jedediah | 1 | 3 | 3 | | |
| Donset, Jonathan | 1 | | 4 | | | Smith, Simeon | 4 | 2 | 7 | | | Sumner, Edward | 4 | 2 | 3 | | |
| Cummins, David | 2 | 1 | 8 | | | Smith, Ezra | 1 | | 1 | | | Payne, Noah | 1 | 5 | 8 | | |
| Sibley, Ezekel | 2 | 1 | 1 | | | Huntington, Thomas | 2 | 2 | 4 | | | Abbot, John | 5 | 4 | 7 | | |
| Fay, Jed^h, Jn^r | 1 | 2 | 3 | | | Dudley, Nicholas | 1 | 1 | 2 | | | Tucker, Rufus | 1 | 4 | 2 | | |
| Hale, John | 3 | 5 | 5 | | | Howard, Lucy | | 1 | 2 | | | Brown, John | 1 | 2 | 4 | | |
| Warner, Thomas | 1 | 1 | 1 | | | Brooks, Nath^l | 1 | 3 | 1 | | | Broughton, John | 1 | 1 | 4 | | |
| Dunham, John | 2 | 1 | 3 | | | Craine, Roger | 1 | 1 | 5 | | | Owen, Benj^a | 2 | 2 | 4 | | |
| Connel, Jere^h | 1 | 1 | 6 | | | Sanders, Duty | 1 | | 3 | | | Burlingham, Nathan | 1 | 2 | 2 | | |
| Sharp, Solomon | 1 | 2 | 6 | | | Bozworth, John | 2 | 3 | 5 | | | Watkins, Amasa | 3 | | 4 | | |
| Maine, Tho^s | 2 | 3 | 4 | | | Grant, Hamlinton | 2 | 1 | 1 | | | Scarborough, Stephen | 1 | 2 | 3 | | |
| Smith, Eben^e | 1 | 1 | 4 | | | Sanders, Isachar | 1 | 2 | 2 | | | Brown, Obediah | 1 | | 2 | | |
| Knowlton, Abraham | 5 | 3 | 3 | | | Sanders, Stephen A | 1 | 1 | 1 | | | Humphrey, Lucy | | 2 | 1 | | |
| Farnam, Manassa | 2 | 1 | 3 | | | Keyes, Sampson | 2 | 1 | 5 | 1 | | Russell, James | 1 | 2 | 2 | | |
| Wickwire, Solomon | 1 | | 1 | 2 | | Knolton, Fredrick | 1 | 1 | 4 | | | Hynes, James | 2 | 2 | 2 | | |
| Spearks, Isaiah | 1 | 4 | 4 | | | Utley, Sam^l | 2 | 3 | 2 | | | Wales, Nathan | 1 | 4 | 3 | | |
| Hanks, Benj^a | 1 | 2 | 3 | | | Moseley, Luther | 1 | | 3 | | | Kyes, Solomon | 3 | | 5 | | |
| Dyer, James | 2 | | 9 | | | Barker, Joshua | 3 | 4 | 3 | | | Brown, Ambrose | 1 | 1 | 2 | | |
| Bragg, Thomas | 1 | 2 | 4 | | | James, Benj^a | 2 | 3 | 5 | | | Dean, Simeon | 1 | | 2 | | |
| Farnam, Stephen | 1 | | 2 | | | Palmer, Benj^a | 2 | 3 | 2 | | | Bartlet, Dan^l | 3 | 6 | 6 | | |
| Farnam, Benj^a | 1 | 3 | 2 | | | Chaffee, Jonathan | 2 | 2 | 4 | | | Rogers, Moses | 1 | 1 | 4 | | |
| Poor House | 3 | | 3 | | | Smith, Asa | 2 | 1 | 4 | | | Works, Joseph | 2 | 2 | 9 | | |
| Chaffee, Jona^th | 1 | | 3 | | | Utley, Abigal | 1 | 1 | 3 | | | Bozworth, Allen | 3 | | 6 | | 1 |
| Slater, Benj^a | 1 | 5 | 3 | | | Royce, William | 1 | | 4 | | | Frinck, Mary | 1 | 3 | 2 | | |
| Smith, George | | | | 11 | | Bishop, Jere^h | 2 | 1 | 2 | | | Watkins, Sarah | | | 4 | | |
| Walker, Sam^l | 1 | 2 | 4 | | | Phillips, Elijah | 2 | 2 | 6 | | | Cheedle, Increase | 2 | | 5 | | |
| Walker, Eben^r | 1 | 2 | 3 | | | Palmer, Joseph | 3 | 5 | 6 | | | Bozward, Eben^r | 5 | | 5 | | |
| Walker, James | 1 | | 3 | | | Lewis, Dan^l | 1 | 2 | 6 | | | Works, John | 3 | | 2 | | |
| Waker, Mary | 3 | | 2 | | | Chapman, Jacob | 2 | | 4 | | | Spalding, Josiah | 5 | 1 | 5 | | |
| Chaffe, Josiah, Sen^r | 3 | 1 | 5 | | | Chapman, Penelope | | | 2 | | | Watkins, Thaddeus | 1 | 2 | 2 | | |
| Robinson, Timothy | 2 | | 3 | | | Marcy, Thomas | 2 | 1 | 2 | | | Fitz, Daniel | 1 | 2 | 1 | | |
| Bugbe, Amos | 1 | 1 | 7 | | | Byles, Eben^r | 3 | 3 | 8 | | | Wright, Eben^r | 3 | 2 | 10 | | |
| Bugbe, Josiah | 2 | 1 | 2 | | | Knolton, Mehitabel | 1 | | 3 | | | Allen, David | 2 | 4 | 2 | | |
| Porter, Abigal | | | 4 | | | Johnson, Marver | 1 | 1 | 5 | | | Howard, Ephraim | 4 | | 7 | | |
| Warren, John | 4 | 1 | 7 | | | Preston, Jareb | 2 | 3 | 7 | | | Watkins, William | 1 | 1 | 1 | | |
| Knolton, Dan^l | 2 | 1 | 3 | | | Ellis, John | 3 | 2 | 5 | | | Scarborough John | 2 | | 2 | | |
| Butler, Stephen | 1 | | 2 | | | Brown, Mary | | | 2 | | | Scarborough, Joseph | 1 | 1 | 2 | | |
| Hall, Robert | 1 | 3 | 2 | | | Heath, Eben^r | 1 | | 2 | | | Briggs, John | 1 | 3 | 1 | | |
| Tiffany, Ezek^l | 1 | 1 | 1 | | | Torrey, David | 1 | 2 | 2 | 1 | | Hiscock, David | 1 | 4 | 1 | | |
| Woodward, Joseph | 4 | 1 | 3 | | | Dana, Jacob | 2 | | 3 | | | Allen, Timothy | 4 | 1 | 4 | | |
| Walker, Benj^a | 3 | | 5 | | | Messinger, Elisabeth | 1 | 1 | 4 | | | Bugbee, Isaiah | 3 | 3 | 4 | | |
| Watkins, Pheneas | 1 | 1 | 1 | | | Preston, Zeph^h | 1 | 1 | 2 | | | Carpenter, Hez^a | 3 | 3 | 5 | | |
| Lamb, Nathan | 1 | 3 | 5 | | | Dana, Jedediah | 1 | 3 | 3 | | | Bugbee, Jesse | 1 | 5 | 2 | | |
| Hanks, John | 2 | 3 | 3 | | | Burnam, Joseph | 3 | 3 | 4 | | | Parkhurst, — | 1 | 1 | 2 | | |
| Hannam, Justus | 1 | | 3 | | | Clark, Eleph^t | 1 | 2 | 2 | | | Carpenter, Dan | 1 | | 1 | | |
| Whiton, James | 2 | 3 | 8 | | | Badcock, Timothy | 2 | 2 | 4 | | | Fisher, Olcott | 1 | 3 | 2 | | |
| Huges, Jona^th | 1 | 2 | 2 | | | Smith, John | 2 | 2 | 3 | | | Howard, Sam^l | 1 | 1 | 3 | | |
| Chaffee, Dareus | | | 3 | | | Snow, Joseph | 2 | 2 | 4 | | | Carpenter, Joel | 2 | | 2 | | |
| Birchard, Prince | 3 | | 6 | | | Snow, Benj^n | 1 | 1 | 6 | | | Howard, Jona^th | 2 | 3 | 5 | | |
| Dimmock, Elias | 3 | 1 | 4 | | | Snow, Bela | 1 | 1 | 2 | | | Coats, Benj^n | 1 | | 1 | | |
| Waker, Sam^l, Jn^r | 1 | 1 | 4 | | | Hende, Joseph | 1 | 4 | 1 | | | Judson, Andrew | 1 | 5 | 3 | | |
| Marcy, Sam^l | 2 | 2 | 3 | | | Hende, Caleb | 2 | | 2 | | | Pettis, John | 4 | 2 | 8 | | |
| Person, Benj^a | 4 | | 1 | | | Ewings, Thomas | 1 | | 4 | | | Bowen, Joseph | 3 | 2 | 2 | | |
| Dimmock, Dan^l | 1 | 3 | 2 | | | Brown, David | 2 | 3 | 5 | | | Bowen, John | 1 | 3 | 3 | | |
| Farnam, Solomon | 1 | | 3 | | | Snow, James | 1 | 3 | 2 | | | Bowen, Barre | 1 | 1 | 1 | | |
| Russell, John | 2 | 2 | 3 | | | Kendal, Eli | 2 | 1 | 3 | | | Burnam, John | 1 | 1 | 3 | | |

# HEADS OF FAMILIES—CONNECTICUT.

## WINDHAM COUNTY—Continued.

| NAME OF HEAD OF FAMILY. | Free white males of 16 years and upward, including heads of families. | Free white males under 16 years. | Free white females, including heads of families. | All other free persons. | Slaves. |
|---|---|---|---|---|---|
| **ASHFORD TOWN—con.** | | | | | |
| Snow, Robert | 3 | | 2 | | |
| Parrish, Eliphaz | 1 | 3 | 4 | | |
| Badger, John | 1 | 3 | 3 | | |
| Cheney, Benjⁿ | 2 | 2 | 4 | | |
| Sumner, Robert | 1 | 1 | 3 | | |
| Horton, Moses | 1 | | 2 | | |
| Badger, Ezekel | 2 | 1 | 2 | | |
| Russell, John | 1 | 5 | 3 | | |
| Case, Elipht | 1 | | 3 | | |
| Strickland, Nathl | 1 | | 1 | | |
| Tufts, Peter | 1 | 3 | 2 | | |
| Sumner, John | 2 | 2 | 5 | | |
| Foster, Stephen | 1 | | 2 | | |
| Tufts, Aaron | 3 | 3 | 6 | | |
| Beamus, Jonathan | 1 | 3 | 6 | | |
| Mumford, Jeremiah | 1 | 2 | 2 | | |
| Bowls, David, Jnr | 1 | 1 | 3 | | |
| Nichalls, Jonathⁿ | 2 | 2 | 4 | | |
| Kendal, Joseph, Jnr | 1 | 2 | 1 | | |
| Averil, John | 1 | 2 | 1 | | |
| Kendall, Joseph | 4 | 3 | 4 | | |
| Bowls, David | 2 | 2 | 4 | 2 | 1 |
| Chamberlin, Edmond | 2 | 2 | 6 | | |
| Bozworth, Aaron | 1 | 4 | 7 | | |
| Badger, Ezra | 1 | 2 | 1 | | |
| Havens, Jeriah | 1 | 1 | 2 | | |
| Sumner, Benjⁿ | 4 | | 4 | | |
| Kendal, Smith | 1 | 2 | 1 | | |
| Carperter, Comfort | 1 | 2 | 2 | | |
| Work, Josiah, Senr | 2 | 1 | 3 | | |
| Sumner, James F | 2 | 2 | 5 | | |
| Sumner, Samuel | 2 | 3 | 5 | | |
| Works, Ingolsby | 2 | 1 | 3 | | |
| Sumner, Ebenr | 3 | 1 | 6 | | |
| Clap, Seth | 1 | 4 | 1 | | |
| Simmon, Abel, Senr | 1 | 3 | 4 | | |
| Havens, Simons | 2 | 2 | 5 | | |
| Burnam, Nathan | 1 | 3 | 2 | | |
| Lyon, Nathan | 1 | 2 | 1 | | |
| Beamous, Ephraim | 3 | | 1 | | |
| Wilson, Elias | 1 | | 2 | | |
| Lyon, Ephraim | 3 | 1 | 5 | | |
| Eastmaⁿ, Ebenr | 4 | | 3 | | |
| Chapman, Jonathan | 1 | | 3 | | |
| Chapman, Jonaⁿ, Jnr | 1 | 6 | 3 | | |
| Chapman, Jonah | 3 | 3 | 2 | | |
| Mason, Ebenr | 1 | 6 | 3 | | |
| Peck, Joseph | 1 | 3 | 2 | | |
| Peck, Lyda | | | 3 | | |
| Peck, John | 2 | 1 | 2 | | |
| Clark, Leml | 2 | 4 | 2 | | |
| Snow, Arunnah | 1 | 2 | 4 | | |
| Spring, Saml | 3 | | 1 | | |
| Spalding, Ephraim | 2 | 2 | 4 | | |
| Wilson, Jacob, Jnr | 1 | 4 | 2 | | |
| Snow, Billarky | 1 | 3 | 3 | | |
| Dodge, Ephraim | 1 | 1 | 3 | | |
| Bullard, Luther | 1 | 1 | 2 | | |
| Bullard, William | 3 | | 2 | | |
| Harton, Moses, Jnr | 1 | 2 | 3 | | |
| Sanders, Eseck | 2 | 6 | 7 | 1 | |
| Angell, Stephⁿ | 1 | 1 | 3 | | |
| Craine, Roger | 1 | 2 | 4 | | |
| Smith, Hubard | 1 | 3 | 3 | | |
| Dimmock, Isaac | 2 | 2 | 4 | | |
| Lewis, Enock, Senr | 1 | | 1 | | |
| Lewis, Israel | 1 | 5 | 1 | | |
| Kyes, Edward | 2 | 4 | 2 | | |
| Brown, Roswell | 1 | 1 | 1 | | |
| Walker, Stephen | 1 | 4 | 4 | | |
| Chaffee, Joseph | 2 | 4 | 5 | | |
| Holt, Ezekiel | 1 | | 1 | | |
| Lawson, Ebenr | 1 | 3 | 4 | | |
| Fanam, Asa | 3 | | 4 | | |
| Sheppard, James | 1 | | 1 | | |
| Ward, Phebe | | | 1 | | |
| Kasson, Saml | 1 | | 1 | | |
| Kasson, Saml, Jnr | 1 | 2 | 1 | | |
| Walker, Ephm | 2 | 1 | 2 | | |
| Chapman, Joseph | 2 | | 3 | | |
| Chapman, Elias | 2 | 2 | 3 | | |
| Chapman, Thomas | 1 | | 1 | | |
| Chaffee, David | 3 | 2 | 4 | | |
| Abbe, Jonathan | 2 | 3 | 5 | | |
| Robins, David | 1 | | 1 | | |
| Loomis, Danl | 2 | 2 | 3 | | |
| Miller, Solomon | 1 | 1 | 3 | | |
| Henfield, Benjⁿ | 1 | 2 | 3 | | |
| Loomis, John | 1 | 2 | 2 | | |
| Walker, Ebenr, Jnr | 1 | | 3 | | |
| Walker, William | 3 | 1 | 3 | | |
| Walker, Ebenr, Senr | 2 | | 3 | | |
| Backus, Adonijah | 2 | 1 | 3 | | |
| Smith, Abijah | 1 | | 3 | | |
| Suitleif, Sylvester | 2 | 1 | 3 | | |
| Tyler, Saml | 1 | 2 | 1 | | |
| **ASHFORD TOWN—con.** | | | | | |
| Tyler, Job | 2 | 1 | 3 | | |
| Chapman, Christopher | 1 | 1 | 4 | | |
| Johnson, Reubin | 1 | 3 | 3 | | |
| Rathbon, John | 2 | 1 | 3 | | |
| Barney, Mary | | | 3 | | |
| Coy, Luke | 1 | 1 | 2 | | |
| Chapman, Thomas | 3 | | 2 | | |
| Chapman, Oliver | 1 | 1 | 1 | | |
| Brown, Danl | 1 | 4 | 1 | | |
| Brown, John, Senr | 3 | | 3 | | |
| Burnam, Freeman | 1 | 1 | 3 | | |
| Kyes, Edward | 1 | 5 | 1 | | |
| **BROOKLYNE TOWN.** | | | | | |
| Harras, Reuben | 1 | 4 | 7 | | |
| Rogers, Josiah | 1 | | 3 | | |
| Harris, Paul | 1 | 1 | 6 | | |
| Brown, John | 1 | | 4 | | |
| Allen, Parker | 1 | 1 | 3 | | |
| Harriss, Ebenr | 1 | 1 | 1 | | |
| Harris, Saml | 1 | 6 | 3 | | |
| Perrit, Joseph | 2 | 1 | 4 | | |
| Staples, Abel | 1 | 4 | 3 | | |
| Cady, Ebenr | 1 | 3 | 2 | | |
| Withy, Eunice | | | 1 | | |
| Stanton, Thomas | 2 | 1 | 5 | | |
| Benjamin, Barzl | 1 | | 2 | | |
| Dean, Saml | 3 | 1 | 4 | | |
| Merrit, Thomas | 3 | 1 | 5 | | |
| Davison, Peter | 3 | 3 | 2 | | |
| Litchfield, Eleazr | 1 | 2 | 2 | | |
| Hewit, Stephen | 1 | 2 | 4 | | |
| Tyler, Asa | 2 | 3 | 4 | | |
| Winter, Nathan | 2 | 1 | 4 | 1 | |
| Alworth, James | 2 | 2 | 4 | | |
| Winter, Josiah | 2 | 2 | 1 | | |
| Pooles, Amasa | 1 | 3 | 2 | | |
| Copeland, James | 3 | 2 | 3 | | |
| Cady, Gideon | 2 | 1 | 5 | | |
| Cady, Asail | 1 | 1 | 3 | | |
| Fasset, John | 1 | | 3 | | |
| Roe, Isaac | 2 | 1 | 3 | | |
| Downing, Jededh | 3 | 2 | 5 | | |
| Frazier, John | 1 | 1 | 2 | | |
| Randal, Jobe | 1 | | 3 | | |
| Davison, Joseph | 3 | 2 | 4 | | |
| Davison, Joseph, Jnr | 1 | 1 | 4 | 1 | |
| Bacon, Nehemiah | 2 | | 3 | | |
| Cady, Benjⁿ | 3 | 1 | 5 | | |
| Cady, Jonathⁿ | 1 | 1 | 3 | | |
| Bowman, Walter | 1 | 4 | 6 | | |
| Cady, John | 3 | 2 | 3 | | |
| Searls, Salter | 3 | 4 | 3 | | |
| Clark, Caleb | 2 | 1 | 3 | | |
| Bowman, Elisha | 3 | 3 | 4 | | |
| Geers, John | 3 | 3 | 3 | | |
| Morgan, Roswell | 1 | 2 | 3 | | |
| Brown, Alpheus | 2 | 3 | 5 | | |
| Carder, — | 2 | 1 | 3 | | |
| Shepard, Benjⁿ | 2 | | 2 | | |
| Shepard, Whitmore | 2 | 1 | 3 | | |
| Litchfield, Israel | 3 | | 3 | | |
| Litchfield, John | 3 | 2 | 4 | | |
| Baker, John | 4 | 1 | 5 | | |
| Quivy, Amasa | 1 | 1 | 2 | | |
| Baker, Joseph, Jnr | 2 | 1 | 4 | | |
| Fuller, Josiah | 1 | | 3 | | |
| Adam, William, Senr | 7 | 1 | 7 | | |
| Cady, Naham | 1 | 1 | 3 | | |
| Clark, Moses | 1 | | 2 | | |
| Clark, Danl | 1 | 1 | 5 | | |
| Palmer, Thaddeus | 1 | 3 | 2 | | |
| Cady, Uriah | 1 | | 4 | | |
| Cady, Danl | 2 | 2 | 6 | | |
| Hastings, Dyeer | 4 | | 7 | | |
| Baker, Stephen | 2 | | 5 | | |
| Putnam, Reubin | 1 | 5 | 1 | | |
| Goodale, Abijah | 1 | 1 | 3 | | |
| Litchfield, Uriah | 1 | | 2 | | |
| Cook, Danl | 1 | 1 | 1 | 1 | |
| Sterns, Daniel | 3 | 1 | 3 | | |
| Baker, Erastus | 4 | 2 | 3 | | |
| Spalding, Ebenr | 4 | 3 | 3 | | |
| Payne, Seth, Jnr | 2 | 2 | 5 | | |
| Baker, William | 2 | 2 | 4 | | |
| Gilbert, Eleazr | 2 | 3 | 6 | | |
| Whitney, Josiah | 2 | | 6 | | |
| Tyler, Danl, Jnr | 4 | 6 | 4 | | |
| Jefford, John | 2 | | 4 | | |
| Herrick, Benjⁿ | 1 | 4 | 4 | | |
| Herrick, Rufus | 2 | | 5 | | |
| Finch, Stephen | | | | 6 | |
| Tyler, Danl | 3 | | 3 | 1 | |
| Miles, Joshua | 5 | 2 | 4 | | |
| **BROOKLYNE TOWN—con.** | | | | | |
| William, Benjⁿ, Jr | 1 | 2 | 6 | | |
| Pike, John, Jr | 4 | | 3 | | |
| Stephens, John | 1 | 2 | 3 | | |
| Allen, Joseph | 1 | 1 | 7 | | |
| Pike, Jonⁿ | 2 | 2 | 2 | | |
| Kindal, David | 1 | | 2 | | |
| Kindal, John | 1 | | 5 | | |
| Eaton, Ezekl, Jr | 3 | 1 | 7 | | |
| Pellet, Jonaⁿ | 2 | 1 | 6 | | |
| Butts, Saml | 4 | 1 | 6 | | |
| Copeland, Jonaⁿ | 1 | 3 | 3 | | |
| Peirce, Timaus | 2 | 3 | 5 | | |
| Peirce, Dillano | 2 | 4 | 4 | | |
| Dorrance, James | 2 | 2 | 4 | | |
| Smith, William | 4 | 2 | 4 | | |
| Murdock, Andrus | 6 | 1 | 3 | | |
| Woodward, Ward | 2 | 5 | 5 | | 1 |
| Cogshall, Nathl | 3 | 2 | 3 | | |
| Allen, Jabez | 2 | 2 | 6 | | |
| Darke, William, Jr | 2 | 6 | 5 | | 1 |
| Weaver, John | 1 | | 1 | | |
| Weaver, Rimington | 1 | 3 | 4 | | |
| Whittiker, Saml | 1 | 1 | 1 | | |
| Adams, Peter | 4 | | 5 | | |
| Adams, Philemon | 3 | 3 | 3 | | |
| Miles, Thomas | 1 | 3 | 4 | | |
| Wilson, Ignatus | 1 | | 3 | | |
| Hubard, William | 3 | 1 | 2 | | |
| Prince, Abel | 2 | 1 | 1 | | |
| Adams, Shubael | 1 | 2 | 2 | | |
| Weaver, Anna | | | 4 | | |
| Hubard, Ebⁿ | 1 | 2 | 3 | | |
| Denison, David | 2 | | 2 | | |
| Adams, Noah | 3 | 1 | 3 | | |
| Hulet, Nehemh | 1 | 1 | 4 | | |
| Kelly, William | 3 | 5 | 5 | | |
| Ashcraft, Jedediah | 2 | 3 | 6 | | |
| Ashcraft, John | 3 | 1 | 4 | | |
| Howard, Charles | 2 | | 2 | | |
| Adams, Ephraim | 1 | | 3 | | |
| Adams, Abner | 2 | | 2 | | |
| Tyler, Joseph | 2 | 2 | 4 | | |
| Frost, Jonas | 3 | 1 | 4 | | |
| Darke, James | 1 | 1 | 2 | | |
| Fogg, Danl | 1 | | 2 | 7 | 4 |
| Badcock, Jerah | 2 | 1 | 4 | | |
| Brown, Shubael | 2 | 3 | 3 | | |
| Cady, Eliakim | 1 | 3 | 4 | | |
| Eldridge, James | 4 | 6 | 6 | 3 | 2 |
| Withy, James | 4 | 2 | 5 | | |
| Hide, Jakey & Co | 2 | 3 | 5 | | |
| Scarborough, Ebenr | 1 | 2 | 3 | | |
| Scarborough, Saml | 2 | 4 | 6 | | |
| Barret, William | 3 | 1 | 5 | | |
| Gilbert, Wilks | 1 | 4 | 6 | | |
| Williams, Saml, Jnr | 2 | 5 | 2 | | |
| Pike, Ebenr | 4 | | 6 | | |
| Deaolph, Charles | 2 | 6 | 2 | | |
| Pike, Willard | 1 | 1 | 2 | | |
| Smith, Thomas | 3 | 1 | 3 | | |
| Spalding, Caleb | 4 | | 2 | | |
| Spalding, Abel | 2 | | 2 | | |
| Prince, Timothy, Jnr | 2 | 1 | 4 | | |
| Cushman, Isaac | 3 | 2 | 7 | | |
| Peirce, Benjⁿ | 2 | 1 | 3 | | |
| Payne, Seth | 2 | 1 | 3 | | |
| Prince, Timoty | 1 | | 2 | | |
| Miles, Jesse | 1 | 3 | 1 | 5 | |
| Baker, Joseph | 1 | 3 | 4 | | |
| Putnam, Danl | 3 | 1 | 5 | | |
| Winchester, Jabez | 1 | 1 | 5 | | |
| Cushman, William | 1 | 4 | 2 | | |
| Phillemore, Willm | 1 | | 2 | | |
| Williams, Roger | 1 | 1 | 4 | | |
| Fling, Lemuel | 1 | 1 | 3 | | |
| Frazier, Elijah | 1 | 3 | 4 | | |
| Gilbert, Joseph | 3 | 1 | 4 | | |
| Fasset, Adonijah | 6 | 1 | 4 | | |
| Chapman, Amazh | 3 | | 2 | | |
| Collar, Jonathan | 2 | 2 | 5 | | |
| Davis, Danl | 1 | 3 | 4 | | |
| Malborne, Peter | | | | 3 | |
| Williams, Stephen | 2 | 4 | 4 | | |
| Williams, Martha | | 2 | 2 | | |
| Williams, Roger | 3 | 1 | 3 | | |
| Weeks, Ebenr | 3 | 7 | 5 | | |
| Ingolls, Saml | 3 | 1 | 5 | | |
| Williams, Saml | 3 | | 6 | | |
| Ward, Saml | 2 | | 1 | | |
| Putnam, Israel | 3 | 2 | 5 | | 1 |
| Scarborough, Joseph | 4 | 5 | 7 | | |
| Holmes, Nathl | 1 | 1 | 1 | | |
| Cleavland, Pheneas | 1 | | 1 | | |
| Johnson, Stephen | 1 | 2 | 2 | | |
| Cleavland, Joseph | 2 | 2 | 3 | | |
| Dayley, Benjⁿ | | | | 3 | |

## WINDHAM COUNTY—Continued.

| NAME OF HEAD OF FAMILY. | Free white males of 16 years and upward, including heads of families. | Free white males under 16 years. | Free white females, including heads of families. | All other free persons. | Slaves. |
|---|---|---|---|---|---|
| **CANTERBURY TOWN.** | | | | | |
| Wills, Gideon | 2 | 1 | 3 | | |
| Cleavland, Eliphaz | 2 | 2 | 2 | | |
| Amy, Christopher | | | 2 | 2 | |
| Amirell, Job | | | | 7 | |
| Lyons, John | 2 | 2 | 3 | | |
| Safford, Joseph | 1 | 2 | 5 | | |
| Pellet, Hez\a, Jn | 2 | 2 | 3 | | |
| Kendal, Phineas | 2 | 3 | 4 | | |
| Backus, Elisha | 3 | 1 | 3 | | |
| Backus, Stephen | 3 | | 3 | | |
| Payne, Luther | 2 | | 4 | | |
| Bingham, Gurdon | 1 | 4 | 1 | | |
| Bingham, Luther | 5 | | 5 | | |
| Ward, Ichabod | 2 | 2 | 4 | | |
| Fitch, Jabez | 3 | 2 | 8 | 1 | |
| Fitch, John | 7 | 1 | 4 | | |
| Hough, Walter | 3 | 3 | 3 | | |
| Lord, William | 1 | 3 | 3 | | |
| Obrian, William | 1 | 2 | 2 | | |
| Brewster, Walter | 1 | 1 | 1 | | |
| Bacon, Abner | 2 | 1 | 4 | | |
| Felch, Sam\l | 2 | 1 | 4 | | |
| Andross, Fredrick | 3 | 4 | 1 | | |
| Bacon, Jacob | 2 | 2 | 2 | 1 | |
| Spalding, Jacob | 1 | 1 | 4 | | |
| Hough, Erastus | 1 | | 1 | | |
| Fisk, Darius | 2 | 1 | 8 | | |
| Washburn, Eli | 1 | 1 | 3 | | |
| Backus, Timothy | 1 | 1 | 5 | | |
| Spalding, Ezekiel | 2 | 1 | 3 | | |
| Aspinwall, William | 1 | 3 | 5 | | |
| Tracy, Zurriah | 1 | | 3 | | |
| Cob, James | 2 | | 3 | | |
| Ainsworth, Anne | | 1 | 4 | | |
| Adams, Nathan, Jn | 4 | 1 | 6 | | |
| Brown, Jede\h | 1 | 1 | 3 | | |
| Johnson, Obediah | 2 | 1 | 3 | | |
| Ainsworth, Nathan\l | 1 | 2 | 5 | | |
| Hyde, Jonathan | 4 | | 3 | | |
| Finny, Joshua, Jr | 2 | 2 | 4 | | |
| Fitch, Rebeca, Jr | 1 | 1 | 4 | | |
| Dyer, James | 4 | 1 | 8 | | |
| Adams, Roger, Jr | 2 | | 4 | | |
| Bawldin, Jacob | 2 | 1 | 2 | | |
| Devenport, Paul | 5 | 3 | 6 | | |
| Adams, Elihu, Jr | 3 | 2 | 4 | | |
| Webb, Christopher | 1 | 4 | 1 | | |
| Baldwin, David | 2 | 2 | 3 | | |
| Justin, George | 2 | 1 | 6 | | |
| Stearkweather, Bilchar | 1 | 1 | 4 | | |
| Carter, Sam\l | 3 | 1 | 4 | | |
| Ainsworth, Joseph | 4 | | 5 | | |
| Adams, Phineas | 2 | 1 | 1 | | |
| Cobb, Ephnah | 2 | 1 | 3 | | |
| Payne, Solomon | 4 | 1 | 5 | | |
| Edwards, Dan\l, Jr | 3 | 2 | 4 | | |
| Dyer, Jareh, Sr | 4 | 2 | 6 | | |
| Dyer, Elijah | 5 | 1 | 4 | | |
| Finney, Asa | 1 | | 1 | | |
| Ainsworth, William | 2 | 1 | 4 | | |
| Ainsworth, Will\m, Jr | 2 | 1 | 2 | | |
| Bennet, Eben\r | 2 | 2 | 5 | | |
| Farnam, Joseph | 2 | 4 | 3 | | |
| Justin, Nicholas | 2 | | 2 | | |
| Mott, Gershom | 1 | | 1 | | |
| Larrabe, Silas | 1 | 1 | 3 | | |
| Dyer, Eben\r | 1 | 3 | 3 | | |
| Whitford, David | 1 | 1 | 4 | | |
| King, Elisha | 1 | 2 | 2 | | |
| Gould, Edmond | 1 | 2 | 2 | | |
| Morse, Charles | 3 | 2 | 4 | | |
| Adams, Levi | 1 | 1 | 2 | | |
| Stevens, Adams | 2 | 3 | 6 | | |
| Adams, Parker | 2 | 2 | 3 | | |
| Dulop, James | 3 | 3 | 4 | | |
| Muth, Abiah | 1 | 2 | 3 | | |
| Smith, Asa | 1 | 6 | 4 | | |
| Leach, Mary | | | 1 | | |
| Rude, Nathan | 1 | 2 | 5 | | |
| Justin, William | 1 | | 2 | | |
| Green, Eunice | | 2 | 2 | | |
| Williams, Elijah | 2 | 2 | 5 | | |
| Mott, Jere\h, Sr | 3 | | 4 | | |
| Lyon, Eben\r | 2 | 3 | 2 | | |
| Kingsley, Jabez | 1 | 1 | 1 | | |
| Rathbon, Joseph | 1 | 3 | 2 | | |
| Rathbon, Sybil | | 2 | 2 | | |
| Justin, Walcott | 1 | 1 | 1 | | |
| Lyon, Ephraim | 1 | 2 | 4 | | |
| Smith, Benj\a | 1 | | 3 | | |
| Apley, James | 2 | 4 | 2 | | |
| Wentworth, John | 2 | 5 | 4 | | |
| Dimmock (Wid.) | | | 5 | | |
| Wentworth, William | 1 | | 4 | | |
| Allen, Pratt | 1 | 1 | 1 | | |
| **CANTERBURY TOWN— continued.** | | | | | |
| Cotton, Tho\s | 1 | 1 | 3 | | |
| Morse, James | 1 | 1 | 5 | | |
| Francis, John | 1 | | 1 | | |
| Winter, Asa | 1 | 2 | 3 | | |
| Winchester, Andrew | 1 | | 2 | | |
| Brewster, Peleg | 1 | | 1 | | |
| Brewster, Jededi\h | 1 | 3 | 4 | | |
| William, Isaiah | 3 | 3 | 4 | | |
| Bennet, Elijah | 1 | | 2 | | |
| Payne, Esther | | | 2 | | |
| Carver, David, Sr | 3 | 2 | 7 | | |
| Park, Nathan | 2 | 1 | 2 | | |
| Smith, Benj\a | 1 | | 3 | | |
| Smith, John | 2 | 1 | 7 | | |
| Butts, Josiah | 1 | 3 | 3 | | |
| Adams, Bradford | 1 | 2 | 4 | | |
| Herrick, John | 4 | | 3 | | |
| Fuller, Benj\n | 1 | 1 | 3 | | |
| Perkins, William | 1 | | 3 | | |
| Perkins, Leonard | 1 | 2 | 1 | | |
| Adams, Tho\s, Sr | 2 | 1 | 3 | | |
| Peck, Reubin | 1 | 3 | 4 | | |
| Wood, Augustus | 1 | 1 | 2 | | |
| Allen, Barnabas | 1 | | 5 | 1 | |
| Allen, Jared | 1 | 3 | 2 | | |
| Waldo, Edward | 2 | 1 | 3 | | |
| Jewit, Tho\s | 1 | 1 | 5 | | |
| Smith, Jacob | 2 | | 5 | | |
| Park, Reubin | 2 | 1 | 3 | | |
| Parks, Simeon | 2 | | 5 | | |
| Butts, Sherekiah | 4 | | 2 | | |
| Butts, Gideon | 1 | 2 | 2 | | |
| Butts, Eben\r | 1 | | 7 | | |
| Adams, Joseph | 1 | 3 | 4 | | |
| Silsby, John | 1 | | 4 | | |
| Safford, Joseph | 4 | 1 | 5 | | |
| Safford, Rufus | 1 | 1 | 2 | | |
| Meach, Esther | 1 | 2 | 2 | | |
| Parks, Eben\r | 1 | 1 | 2 | | |
| Carter, Joseph | 2 | | 2 | | |
| Butts, Stephen | 3 | 1 | 6 | | |
| Justin, Charles | 1 | 2 | 1 | | |
| Parks, John | 2 | 3 | 2 | | |
| Rose, David | 2 | 3 | 7 | | |
| Rose, John | 1 | 1 | 3 | | |
| Beston, John | 2 | 2 | 7 | | |
| Bond, Jonas | 1 | 1 | 3 | | |
| Beston, Sam\l | 4 | 3 | 4 | | |
| Bond, William | 1 | | 6 | | |
| Wright, Sam\l | 1 | 3 | 7 | | |
| Brown, Waldo | 1 | | 1 | | |
| Woodward, Peter | 1 | 2 | 5 | | |
| Beston, John | 1 | | 2 | | |
| Winchester, Andrew | 1 | | 2 | | |
| Herrick, John | 2 | | 2 | | |
| Herrick, John | 3 | 2 | 5 | | |
| Frost, Henry | 2 | 2 | 3 | | |
| Adams, James | 2 | 2 | 4 | | |
| Frost, Dan\l | 1 | 2 | 2 | | |
| Leach, Joel | 1 | 2 | 2 | | |
| Austin, Sarah | 1 | | 4 | | |
| Adams, Timothy | 2 | 1 | 5 | | |
| Herrick, Asael | 1 | 1 | 1 | | |
| Fish, Nathan | 1 | 1 | 4 | | |
| Bingham, Gidion | 1 | 1 | 2 | | |
| Adams, Sam\l | 1 | | 2 | | |
| Payne, Luther | 2 | | 4 | | |
| Kendal, Peter | 2 | 2 | 2 | | |
| Smith, Jarus | 1 | 4 | 2 | | |
| Johnson, Joel | 1 | | 2 | | |
| More, Joseph | 4 | 2 | 3 | | |
| Pellet, Sarah | 1 | 1 | 5 | | |
| Hough, John | 1 | | 3 | | |
| Buswell, Tho\s | 2 | 2 | 3 | 1 | |
| Cleavland, Timothy | 4 | | 4 | 1 | |
| Payne, Sam\l | 1 | 2 | 3 | | |
| Adams, Elishah | 2 | 1 | 3 | | |
| Bacon, Joseph | 1 | | 1 | | |
| Cleavland, Perez | 2 | 1 | 4 | | |
| Spalding, Pearl | 1 | 1 | 2 | | |
| Pellet, Rufus | 2 | 3 | 5 | | |
| Pellet, Joseph | 2 | 3 | 2 | | |
| Adams, John | 3 | 3 | 7 | | |
| Tyler, John | 1 | | 2 | | |
| Tyler, Zebulon | 4 | | 1 | | |
| Obrion, John | 1 | 2 | 6 | | |
| Button, John | 2 | 2 | 3 | | |
| Wheeler, John | 3 | 1 | 4 | | |
| Bradford, John, Jur | 1 | 2 | 2 | | |
| Bradford, Sam\l | 2 | 1 | 5 | | |
| Bradford, Tho\s | 3 | | 4 | | |
| Adams, Sam\l | 2 | 2 | 2 | | |
| Adams, Eben\r | 1 | 3 | 4 | | 1 |
| Cady, Abijah | 3 | | 4 | | |
| Adams, Cornelius | 1 | 5 | 6 | | |
| **CANTERBURY TOWN— continued.** | | | | | |
| Stanton, Amon, sr | 2 | 2 | 4 | | |
| Clark, Seth | 1 | 1 | 2 | | |
| Simons, Francis | 1 | | 1 | | |
| Wheeler, Jonath\a | 2 | 5 | 5 | | |
| Geer, Jacob | 2 | | 2 | | 1 |
| Warren, Moses | 2 | 3 | 1 | | |
| Tyler, Oliver | 1 | 3 | 4 | | |
| Smith, Mary | | | 4 | | |
| Brown, Benj\a | 3 | 1 | 5 | | |
| Knowling, Asa | 1 | 2 | 3 | | |
| Morse, Benj\a | 2 | 2 | 6 | | |
| Foster, Dan\l | 1 | | 2 | | |
| Litchfeld, David | 2 | 2 | 4 | | |
| Constable, William | 1 | | 2 | | |
| Parrish, Lem\l | 2 | 2 | 4 | | |
| Parrish, Roswell | 1 | 2 | 3 | | |
| Falkner, Caleb | 1 | 1 | 4 | | |
| Masi, Anthony | 4 | | 5 | | |
| Bradford, John | 1 | 3 | 3 | | |
| Bradford, Josiah, sr | 3 | 2 | 5 | | |
| Olney, Hez\a | 2 | 3 | 9 | | |
| Hibard, Rufus | 1 | 3 | 4 | | |
| Ransford, Joseph | 1 | | 3 | | |
| Ransford, David | 1 | 1 | 6 | | |
| Ransford, Joseph | 1 | 1 | 2 | | |
| Ransford, Richard | 2 | 2 | 3 | | |
| Adams, William | 1 | 1 | 3 | | |
| Carew, William | 1 | | 4 | | |
| Hyde, Josiah, Ju\r | 1 | 1 | 1 | | |
| Hyde, Josiah | 2 | | 5 | | |
| Hyde, Neh\h | 2 | | 2 | | |
| thayer, Ezekiel | 1 | 6 | 6 | | |
| Staples, John | 3 | 4 | 2 | | |
| Johnson, Rufus | 2 | 2 | 2 | 1 | |
| Glass, Silas | 1 | 1 | 4 | | |
| Davis, Mary | | | 4 | | |
| Burgess, Asa | 1 | 3 | 5 | | |
| Downing, Henry | 1 | 3 | 7 | | |
| Downing, Stephen | 2 | 2 | 2 | | |
| Downing, Phineas | 2 | 1 | 2 | | |
| Downing, Phineas, Ju | 1 | 1 | 3 | | |
| Dowing, Dan\l | 1 | 3 | 1 | | |
| Hebard, Eben\r | 1 | 1 | 3 | | |
| Dowing, Jona\a | 4 | | 3 | | |
| Hebard, William | 4 | 1 | 3 | | |
| Hebard, Will\m, Jr | 1 | 4 | 5 | | |
| Darbe, Eleaz\r | 1 | | 2 | | |
| Darbe, Rufus | 1 | 2 | 4 | | |
| Douset, Joseph | 1 | 1 | 4 | | |
| Williamson, Joseph | 2 | 1 | 2 | | |
| Burge, Joseph | 1 | 2 | 4 | | |
| Spiner, Elijah | 1 | 3 | 2 | | |
| Henry, Sam\l | 1 | 1 | 4 | | |
| Gordon, Alexander | 3 | 5 | 5 | | |
| Parks, Peter, sr | 2 | 2 | 2 | | |
| Parks, Jesse | 1 | | 2 | | |
| Backus, Isaac | 2 | 1 | 3 | | |
| Backus, Nathan | 1 | | 4 | | |
| Shaw, William | 1 | | 2 | | |
| Waldo, Zach\h | 2 | 1 | 2 | | |
| Sanders, Peter | 1 | | 3 | | |
| Williamson, Cornelious | 1 | 1 | 3 | | |
| Williamson, Caleb | 3 | | 3 | | |
| Williamson, George | 2 | 2 | 4 | | |
| Williamson, Caleb, Sen\r | 1 | | 2 | | |
| Raymond, Joshua | 3 | 1 | 3 | | |
| Shaw, Benj\a | 1 | | 1 | | |
| Avery, David | 3 | 1 | 3 | | |
| Davis, Jonathan | 1 | | 3 | | |
| Hyde, Elasa | 1 | 3 | 5 | | |
| Sheppard, Asa | 2 | 1 | 2 | | |
| Bacon, Benj\a, Ju\r | 2 | 1 | 4 | | |
| Bacon, Benj\a | 4 | 1 | 3 | | |
| Johnson, William | 4 | 1 | 6 | 1 | |
| Hyde, Benj\a | 1 | 2 | 2 | | |
| Johnson, John | 3 | 2 | 8 | | |
| Payne, David | 1 | | 3 | | |
| Cleavland, Moses, sr | 4 | 2 | 5 | | |
| Stevens, Robert | 1 | 1 | 5 | | |
| Hyde, Nathan | 1 | 1 | 3 | | |
| Cleavland, Shubail | 1 | 2 | 5 | | |
| Justin, Miner | 1 | 1 | 1 | | |
| Hyde, Isaac | 2 | 1 | 4 | | |
| Clark, Theoph\u | 2 | 1 | 3 | | |
| Cleavland, Josiah | 2 | 1 | 3 | | |
| Brown, Eben\r | 3 | | 4 | | |
| Hyde, Comfort | 2 | 2 | 5 | | |
| Spalding, Tho\s | 1 | 2 | 2 | | |
| Ransom, Sam\l | 1 | | 3 | | |
| Bacon, Asa | 2 | 1 | 5 | | |
| Palmer, Elihu | 3 | | 3 | | |
| Chaffee, Eben\r | 2 | 2 | 5 | | |
| Pike, Joseph | 1 | | 2 | | |
| Pike, James | 1 | | 2 | | |
| Pike, Amos | 3 | 1 | 3 | | |

# HEADS OF FAMILIES—CONNECTICUT.

## WINDHAM COUNTY—Continued.

| NAME OF HEAD OF FAMILY. | Free white males of 16 years and upward, including heads of families. | Free white males under 16 years. | Free white females, including heads of families. | All other free persons. | Slaves. | NAME OF HEAD OF FAMILY. | Free white males of 16 years and upward, including heads of families. | Free white males under 16 years. | Free white females, including heads of families. | All other free persons. | Slaves. | NAME OF HEAD OF FAMILY. | Free white males of 16 years and upward, including heads of families. | Free white males under 16 years. | Free white females, including heads of families. | All other free persons. | Slaves. |
|---|---|---|---|---|---|---|---|---|---|---|---|---|---|---|---|---|---|
| **CANTERBURY TOWN—continued.** | | | | | | **HAMPTON TOWN—continued.** | | | | | | **HAMPTON TOWN—continued.** | | | | | |
| Harris, John | 1 | 2 | 4 | | | Griffin, Ebenr | 2 | 2 | 5 | | | Farnam, Hannah | | 1 | 1 | | |
| Hyde, David | 1 | 1 | 2 | | | Fuller, John, Jnr | 1 | 1 | 2 | | | Farnam, Jereh | 1 | 3 | 3 | | |
| Cleavland, Asa | 2 | | 2 | | | Fuller, John | 4 | 2 | 2 | | | Greenslit, Elijah | 1 | 3 | 2 | | |
| **HAMPTON TOWN.** | | | | | | Fuller, Benja | 2 | 5 | 2 | | | Durkee, William | 3 | 1 | 3 | | |
| Moseley, Flavel | 2 | | 2 | | | Hammond, Hezekiah | 3 | 3 | 2 | | | Martin, Benja | 2 | | 9 | | |
| Utley, Saml | 2 | 1 | 3 | | | Moseley, Saml | 2 | 1 | 4 | 1 | | Molton, Tabatha | | | 3 | | |
| Hammond, Josiah | 3 | 1 | 7 | | | Moseley, Ebenr | 2 | 2 | 5 | | | Martin, Joseph | 1 | 2 | 3 | | |
| Goodale, Aaron | 2 | 1 | 3 | | | Simons, Elijah | 2 | | 4 | | | Flint, Nathl | 2 | 1 | 2 | | |
| Moseley, Joseph | 2 | 3 | 5 | | | Sessions, John | 5 | 2 | 3 | | | Flint, Phens | 1 | 3 | 2 | | |
| Moseley, Ebenezer, Junr | 1 | 1 | 2 | | | Martin, George | 2 | | 3 | | | Martin, William | 3 | 4 | 6 | | |
| Hovey, Ebenr | 2 | 1 | 3 | | | Ringe, Martha | 1 | 1 | 4 | | | Jennings, Seth | 1 | 3 | 1 | | |
| Clark, Timothy | 1 | 1 | 3 | | | Orms, Hannah | | | 1 | | | Meachum, Seth | 1 | | 1 | | |
| Holt, Nehemiah | 1 | 1 | 3 | | | Hovey, John | 4 | 1 | 4 | | | Rogers, Jeduthon | 2 | | 1 | | |
| Holt, Nehemh, Jnr | 1 | | 5 | | | Brewster, John | 3 | 1 | 3 | | | Park, Jacob | 1 | 5 | 3 | | |
| Lamphear, Jedeh | 2 | 2 | 4 | | | Stedman, Thos | 4 | 3 | 4 | | | Burnam, Josiah | 2 | 2 | 1 | | |
| Lyon, Robert | 1 | 1 | 7 | | | Greenslit, Joel | 2 | 1 | 7 | | | Upton, Lucy | 1 | | 3 | | |
| Moseley, Uriel | 1 | 1 | 1 | | | Stedman, Thos, Jnr | 2 | 1 | 4 | | | Fisk, Jonathan | 1 | | 1 | | |
| Robins, Nathl | 1 | | 2 | | | Fuller, Della | | | 1 | | | | | | | | |
| Huntington, William | 2 | 2 | 5 | | | Wheat, Benja | 1 | | 3 | | | **KILLINGLEY TOWN.** | | | | | |
| Spearks, Lemuel | 2 | 2 | 3 | | | Collins, Josiah | 1 | 1 | 4 | | | Hutchins, Silas | 1 | 2 | 2 | | |
| Clark, Pheneas | 2 | 4 | 5 | | | Jackson, Thos | 2 | | 1 | | | Hutchins, John | 1 | 4 | 2 | | |
| Ringe, John | 1 | | 1 | | | Crocker, Elizabeth | | | 1 | | | Hutchins, Amasa | 1 | 1 | 1 | | |
| Ringe, Richd | 1 | 1 | 4 | | | Hovey, Chloe | | 1 | 2 | | | Hutchins, Shubal | 1 | | 6 | | |
| Martin, Richd | 2 | 1 | 2 | | | Brown, Henry | 3 | 1 | 5 | | | Hutchins, Ezra | 2 | 5 | 3 | | |
| Clark, Jonathn | 1 | 1 | 2 | | | Farnam, William | 3 | | 6 | | | Sprague, John | 2 | 1 | 4 | | |
| Robins, John | 2 | | 4 | | | Ormsby, Jereh | 2 | 2 | 4 | | | Key, John | 1 | 6 | 2 | | |
| Durke, Wm, Jnr | 1 | 1 | 2 | | | Abbot, Asa | 1 | 1 | 4 | | | Barret, Amos | 2 | 4 | 2 | | |
| Loomiss, Jonathan | 2 | 2 | 6 | | | Burnap, James | 1 | 1 | 6 | | | Spalding, Benja | 2 | 1 | 6 | | |
| Robins, Mary | | | 1 | | | Martin, Amasa | 1 | 2 | 2 | | | Kingsbury, Asa | 2 | 2 | 3 | | |
| Fuller, Daniel | 3 | 1 | 4 | 1 | | Blanchard, John | 1 | | 1 | | | Cleavland, Jesse | 2 | 1 | 3 | | |
| Hewit, Robert | 1 | 2 | 2 | | | Cheedle, Benjamin | 2 | | 4 | | | Wilson, Andrew | 2 | 3 | 5 | | |
| Utley, Amos | 2 | 2 | 2 | | | Abbot, Benja | 1 | 2 | 4 | | | Barret, Jonathan | 2 | 3 | 4 | | |
| Fuller, William | 3 | 1 | 1 | | | Abbot, Benja, Jnr | 1 | | 3 | | | Farnam, James | 2 | 3 | 4 | | |
| Fuller, Joseph | 2 | 5 | 4 | | | Parker, John | 3 | | 2 | | | Farnam, Daniel | 1 | 1 | 3 | | |
| Stedman, Hannah | 2 | 1 | 4 | | | Smith, Solomon, Jnr | 2 | 1 | 2 | | | Farnam, Eleazr | 1 | | 5 | | |
| Ford, Abraham | 3 | 1 | 8 | | | Fisk, Jona, Jnr | 1 | 3 | 2 | | | Sprague, Danl | 3 | 1 | 5 | | |
| Martin, Nathl | 1 | 1 | 3 | | | Burnam, Josiah | 1 | 2 | 3 | | | Spalding, Davis | 3 | 1 | 9 | | |
| Durke, Elipht | 2 | 2 | 3 | | | Neff, William | 1 | 3 | 2 | | | Spalding, Nathl | 2 | 1 | 3 | | |
| Hodgkins, Thomas | 2 | | 4 | | | Randall, Elijah | 1 | 2 | 5 | | | Wright, Saml | 2 | | 4 | | |
| Holt, Paul, Senr | 2 | | 3 | | | Porrage, Jabez | | | | | 5 | Grover, Jonathan | 3 | 1 | 5 | | |
| Durke, Henry | 3 | 2 | 4 | | | Burnam, Joseph | 1 | 1 | 3 | | | Reynolds, Alexander | 2 | 2 | 2 | | |
| Holt, Abiel | 2 | | 2 | | | Flint, Nathl, Jnr | 1 | 1 | 4 | | | Leavens, Isaac | 2 | 1 | 4 | | |
| Burnam, Joseph | 1 | 1 | 3 | | | Upton, John | 2 | 2 | 3 | | | Reynolds, Elisha | 1 | 2 | 5 | | |
| Robinson, Clifford | 1 | 4 | 1 | | | Burnam, Danl | 2 | 3 | 2 | | | Spalding, Simon | 3 | 5 | 4 | | |
| Clark, Ebenr | 1 | 2 | 3 | | | Smith, Solomon | 2 | 1 | 3 | | | Hutchins, Isaac | 1 | 3 | 6 | | |
| Simons, Elijah | 1 | 3 | 2 | | | Fuller, Abijah | 2 | 4 | 5 | | | Spalding, Zadock | 1 | 4 | 4 | 2 | |
| Kennedy, David | 2 | | 3 | | | Elliot, William | 3 | 2 | 4 | | | Danielson, James | 2 | 2 | 2 | | |
| Bill, Roswell | 2 | 1 | 4 | | | Fisk, David | 2 | 3 | 6 | | | Fasset, Ruben | 1 | 2 | 2 | | |
| Flint, Danl | 1 | 2 | 2 | | | Spence, Silas | 1 | 3 | 8 | | | Hutchins, Zadock | 2 | 1 | 5 | | |
| Clark, Titus | 1 | | 1 | | | Alsworth, William | 2 | | 6 | | | Hutchins, Penuel | 2 | 2 | 1 | 1 | 1 |
| Clark, Danl | 1 | 2 | 3 | | | Dodge, David | 2 | 2 | 2 | | | Stephens, Cypian | 1 | | 1 | | |
| Richardson, John | 2 | 3 | 6 | | | Rude, Jason | 1 | 1 | 3 | | | Stearns, Elias | 1 | 3 | 3 | | |
| Buck, Judah | 2 | 2 | 7 | | | Fenton, David | 1 | | 1 | | | Stearns, Boaz | 1 | 4 | 5 | | |
| Walcott, Moses | 2 | 3 | 3 | | | Hebard, Warner | 1 | | 1 | | | Stearns, Joseph | 2 | 1 | 4 | | |
| Martin, William, Jnr | 2 | 2 | 4 | | | Howard, Stephen | 2 | | 2 | | | Davis, Barnabas | 1 | 2 | 6 | | |
| Butlar, William | 1 | | 2 | | | Spencer, David | 1 | 1 | 3 | | | Key, Wilson | 1 | 1 | 2 | | |
| Butlar, Hannah | | | 4 | | | Ashley, Abner | 2 | 4 | 3 | | | Key, Nathl | 2 | 2 | 3 | | |
| Holt, Paul, Jnr | 1 | 3 | 5 | | | Ashley, Joseph | 1 | 3 | 4 | | | Reynolds, John | 1 | | 1 | | |
| Kingsbury, Jonath | 3 | 5 | 7 | | | Jewit, Ebenr | 2 | 1 | 5 | | | Reynolds, David | 1 | 1 | 4 | | |
| Utley, Amos, Jnr | 1 | | 1 | | | Smith, James | 1 | 4 | 3 | | | Dixon, James | 2 | 4 | 6 | | |
| Flint, Benjn | 1 | 2 | 4 | | | Fuller, Jonatha | 3 | 2 | 3 | | | Danielson, William | 1 | | 3 | | 1 |
| Clark, Jeremiah, Jnr | 1 | 4 | 5 | | | Fuller, Aaron | 3 | 2 | 4 | | | Dixon, Thomas | 1 | 4 | 4 | | |
| Clark, Amos | 1 | 1 | 1 | | | Kimball, Danl | 2 | 1 | 2 | | | Cundal, William | 2 | 3 | 4 | | |
| Clark, Jeremiah | 1 | | 1 | | | Durkee, Benja | 2 | 3 | 3 | | | Cheamberlin, Benjamin | 2 | 2 | 1 | | |
| Martin, Joseph, Jnr | 1 | 4 | 3 | | | Farnam, Zebudh | 2 | 1 | 2 | | | Hall, Thomas | 2 | | 3 | | |
| Clark, Stephen | 1 | 4 | 3 | | | Fullar, Thos | 4 | 1 | 2 | 1 | | Busbee, Jona | 1 | | 1 | | |
| Clark, Hannah | | | 3 | | | Durke, Andrew | 2 | 3 | 5 | | | Young, Caleb | 1 | 4 | 2 | | |
| Ford, Benjamin | 1 | 2 | 4 | | | Dorrance, Alexr | 1 | | 1 | | | Danielson, Samuel | 3 | 1 | 5 | 5 | 3 |
| Ford, Amos | 1 | 1 | 4 | | | Dorrance, Saml | 2 | 3 | 4 | | | Robinson, Isaiah | 1 | 4 | 5 | | |
| Clark, Amos, Jnr | 1 | 1 | 2 | | | Durke, Jereh | 2 | 3 | 3 | | | Day, Thomas | 1 | 3 | 2 | 1 | |
| Molton, Benja | 1 | 4 | 5 | | | Holt, Zebeh | 3 | 2 | 6 | | | Colier, Joseph | 1 | | 2 | | |
| Holt, William, Jnr | 3 | 2 | 4 | | | Simons, Shubael | 1 | 1 | 5 | | | William, Eleazr | 2 | | 1 | | |
| Holt, Joshua | 3 | 1 | 2 | | | Holt, Jonah | 2 | 4 | 3 | | | Fisher, John | 2 | 4 | 3 | | |
| Denison, Daniel | 2 | 1 | 6 | | | Preston, Jacob | 3 | 1 | 6 | | | Green, Henry | 2 | | 3 | | |
| Clark, John | 1 | 4 | 3 | | | Butts, John | 1 | 1 | 2 | | | Fuller, Peter | | | | 4 | |
| Allen, Saml | 1 | | 2 | | | Martin, David | 3 | 2 | 5 | | | Biggs, Adam | 1 | | 3 | | |
| Hovey, Jonath | 3 | 4 | 6 | | | Fuller, Saml | 2 | 3 | 4 | | | Wheaton, Simon | 1 | 1 | 5 | | |
| Joslin, David | 3 | 1 | 5 | | | Geer, Ebenr S. | 2 | 2 | 1 | | | Fuller, John | 3 | | 3 | | 1 |
| Avery, Abel | 3 | 1 | 3 | | | Downing, Jonath | 1 | 1 | 5 | | | Whiting, Cornelius | 1 | 2 | 3 | | |
| Ford, Amos, Jnr | 1 | 1 | 2 | | | Cleavland, Silas, Jnr | 1 | 3 | 3 | | | Hulet, Allim | 3 | 1 | 4 | | |
| Blanchard, Elias | 2 | 1 | 5 | | | Waldo, John E. | 1 | 3 | 3 | | | Hulet, David | 2 | 2 | 6 | | |
| Jennings, Nathan | 1 | 2 | 3 | | | Jewit, Benja, Jnr | 2 | 3 | 5 | | | Youngs, Othoniel | 2 | 4 | 3 | | |
| Utley, Thos | 2 | 2 | 7 | | | Curtiss, John | 4 | | 4 | | | Hulet, Mehitable | 2 | | 5 | | |
| Kimball, Asa | 1 | | 1 | | | Curtis, John, Jnr | 2 | 1 | 3 | | | Baker, Jonathan | 1 | 2 | 2 | | |
| Abbot, Nathan | 1 | 1 | 1 | | | Williams, Nathan | 1 | | 5 | | | Davis, Gyas | 1 | 3 | 1 | | |
| Grow, Thomas | 2 | | 7 | | | Dorset, Joseph | 2 | 1 | 2 | | | Petingall, Nathl | 1 | | 3 | | |
| Grow, Thomas, Jnr | 3 | 3 | 9 | | | Snow, Abraham | 2 | 2 | 2 | | | Mitchell, Jotha | 1 | | 3 | | |
| Pearl, Phillip | 3 | 3 | 4 | | | Bennet, Francis | 1 | | 2 | | | Bassett, Isaac | 2 | 3 | 3 | | |
| Abbot, Henry | 1 | 2 | 2 | | | Keys, James | 1 | | 2 | | | Warren, Ephraim | 3 | 1 | 4 | | |
| Ford, Nathanel | 2 | 2 | 1 | | | Colborn, Edward | 2 | | 2 | | | Brewster, Nathl | 1 | 2 | 5 | | |
| Martin, Benja | 1 | | 9 | | | Avery, Uriah | 1 | | 4 | | | Clavland, Jacob | 1 | 1 | 2 | | |
| Cummins, Stephen | 1 | 2 | 4 | | | Spalding, Amos | 2 | | 2 | | | Slater, Jeremiah | 2 | | 2 | | |
| Roger, Benjn | | | | 2 | | Howard, William | 5 | 4 | 6 | | | Simmons, Benja | 3 | 3 | 3 | | |
| | | | | | | Howard, James | 5 | 3 | 6 | 1 | | Young, Ezekel | 1 | 2 | 3 | | |
| | | | | | | Bennet, Isaac | 2 | 1 | 7 | | | | | | | | |

## WINDHAM COUNTY—Continued.

| NAME OF HEAD OF FAMILY. | Free white males of 16 years and upward, including heads of families. | Free white males under 16 years. | Free white females, including heads of families. | All other free persons. | Slaves. | NAME OF HEAD OF FAMILY. | Free white males of 16 years and upward, including heads of families. | Free white males under 16 years. | Free white females, including heads of families. | All other free persons. | Slaves. | NAME OF HEAD OF FAMILY. | Free white males of 16 years and upward, including heads of families. | Free white males under 16 years. | Free white females, including heads of families. | All other free persons. | Slaves. |
|---|---|---|---|---|---|---|---|---|---|---|---|---|---|---|---|---|---|
| KILLINGLEY TOWN—con. | | | | | | KILLINGLEY TOWN—con. | | | | | | KILLINGLEY TOWN—con. | | | | | |
| Graves, Whitney | 1 | | 7 | | | Whittemore, Joshua | 2 | 2 | 5 | | | Grow, Nath¹ | 1 | 2 | 4 | | |
| Hicks, David | 1 | 1 | 2 | | | Weaver, Timothy | 2 | 3 | 6 | | | Learned, James, Jnʳ | 1 | 1 | 1 | | |
| Hopkins, Jenks | 1 | 1 | 2 | | | Bordon, John | 1 | | 1 | | | Perry, Sylvanus | 2 | 2 | 5 | | |
| Adams, Abel | 3 | 3 | 9 | | | Buck, Aaron | 1 | 3 | 3 | | | Brooks, John | 1 | | 2 | | |
| Slater, Abraham, Senʳ | 2 | | 3 | | | Day, David | 3 | 1 | 3 | | | Carpenter, Oliver | 1 | 3 | 3 | | |
| Slater, Abraham, Jnʳ | 1 | 1 | 3 | | | Carder, John | 2 | 3 | 5 | | | Torrey, Anne | | 3 | 1 | | |
| Mattison, Royall | 1 | 1 | 2 | | | Mays, Ephraim | 1 | 2 | 2 | | | Hawkins, Uriah | 1 | 4 | 1 | | |
| Young, Joel | 1 | 2 | 4 | | | Bassitt, John | 4 | 1 | 3 | | | Adams, Edward | 1 | 2 | 2 | | |
| Page, James | 2 | | 3 | | | Whittemore, Danˡ | 1 | 2 | 4 | | | Learned, Theophilus | 1 | 2 | 3 | | |
| Baker, Jonas | 1 | 4 | 4 | | | Kinsbury, Jeduthan | 3 | | 5 | | | Leavins, Rowland | 2 | 3 | 5 | | |
| Baker, Nathan | 1 | 3 | 3 | | | Russell, David | 3 | | 3 | | | Key, Daniel | 1 | 3 | 3 | | |
| Baker, Thomas | 1 | | 2 | | | Starkweather, Elijah | 3 | | 3 | | | Levins, Elisabeth | 1 | 1 | 4 | | |
| Russell, John | 3 | 3 | 3 | | | Whitmore, Pearley | 1 | 1 | 4 | | | Levins, Benjᵃ | 1 | | 3 | | |
| Baker, Joel | 1 | 2 | 2 | | | Cady, Isaiah | 3 | 1 | 5 | | | Buck, Samuel, Jnʳ | 1 | 2 | 2 | | |
| Moffat, Mathew | 1 | 6 | 2 | | | Mitchell, Zebudiah | 1 | 1 | 1 | | | Howe, Isaac Cady | 1 | 4 | 4 | | |
| Spearks, Samˡ | 2 | 2 | 3 | | | Warren, Eleazʳ, Jnʳ | 2 | 5 | 3 | | | Brown, David | 1 | 2 | 2 | | |
| Moffat, Andrew | 1 | 1 | 5 | | | Coman, Stephen | 1 | 1 | 4 | | | Wheaton, Resolved | 2 | | 5 | | |
| Spearks, John | 1 | 3 | 4 | | | Hopkins, Charles | 2 | 1 | 4 | | | Whipple, Jesse | 3 | 4 | 3 | | |
| Martin, John, Jnʳ | 1 | 2 | 2 | | | Warren, Eleazʳ | 4 | 1 | 3 | | | Buck, Jonathan | 1 | | 1 | | |
| Graves, Isachar | 1 | 5 | 2 | | | Warren, Ephraim | 3 | 1 | 4 | | | Buck, David | 1 | | 1 | | |
| Martin, John | 1 | 1 | 2 | | | Jurdon, Martin | 1 | 1 | 1 | | | Brown, Othniel | 1 | 2 | 3 | | 1 |
| Tarbox, Caleb | 1 | | 1 | | | Cook, Stephen | 1 | 2 | 1 | | | Waterman, Gideon | 2 | | | | |
| Woodcock, Israel | 1 | | 5 | | | Fisher, Barzillia | 3 | 1 | 4 | | | Adams, Joseph | 1 | 3 | 1 | | |
| Hulet, Oliver | 3 | 1 | 4 | | | Dexter, Joseph | 2 | 1 | 4 | | | Falshaw, John | 6 | | 6 | | |
| Carey, Benjᵃ | 1 | 4 | 2 | | | Stevens, Oliver | 2 | 1 | 2 | | | Deane, Ezra | 3 | 2 | 4 | | |
| Baker, Samˡ | 1 | | 2 | | | Aldridge, Abner | 1 | 1 | 2 | | | Peirce, William | 2 | 3 | 2 | | |
| Kingsbury, Samˡ | 1 | 3 | 2 | | | Eames, Mack | 2 | | 3 | | | Cutlar, Ephraim | 2 | | 7 | | |
| Jowls, John | 1 | 2 | 2 | | | Lawrence, Elihu | 2 | 1 | 4 | | | Coop, David | 2 | 2 | 3 | | 1 |
| Short, Siloam | 3 | 1 | 7 | | | Lawrence, John | 1 | 2 | 2 | | | Howe, Sampson | 2 | 5 | 5 | | |
| Eaton, John & co | 2 | 1 | 6 | | | Leach, Ebenʳ | 2 | 1 | 4 | | | Atkins, Elisha | 1 | 2 | 5 | | |
| Foster, Weaver | 1 | 1 | 2 | | | Bigford, Thomas | 1 | 1 | 5 | | | Buck, David | 3 | 1 | 5 | | |
| Cady, David | 1 | 3 | 3 | | | Tucker, Richard | 3 | 1 | 3 | | | Learned, James | 1 | 2 | 2 | | |
| Day, Noah | 1 | 3 | 5 | | | Burges, William | 1 | | 2 | | | Buck, Daniel | 1 | | 1 | | |
| Eaton, Timothy | 3 | | 3 | | | Burges, Thomas | 2 | 2 | 5 | | | Cady, Joseph | 4 | 1 | 2 | | |
| Weaver, Constant | 1 | 4 | 3 | | | Bullock, Danˡ | 1 | 1 | 3 | | | Cady, Jonathan | 3 | | 4 | | |
| Day, Jonathan | 2 | 1 | 5 | | | Chase, Edward | 1 | 5 | 2 | | | Kent, George | 1 | 1 | 4 | | |
| Knight, David | 1 | 1 | 2 | | | Chase, David | 2 | | 2 | | | Buck, Reuben | 1 | 1 | 3 | | |
| Cady, Joseph | 2 | | 1 | | | Chase, Oliver &c | 3 | 3 | 8 | | | Miles, Eleazer | 1 | 1 | 1 | | |
| Dalley, Field | 2 | | 4 | | | Campbell, Sylvanus | 1 | 3 | 3 | | | Buck, Samuel | 3 | | 2 | | |
| Burlington, Benjⁿ | 1 | 1 | 2 | | | Brown, Andrew | 2 | 2 | 2 | | | Spalding, Obedʰ | 2 | 3 | 5 | | |
| Day, Jonathan | 1 | | 2 | | | Bartlet, Richard | 4 | 1 | 4 | | | Converse, Jesse | 1 | 1 | 1 | | |
| Whitney, Asa | 1 | 1 | 2 | | | Mason, Pellatiah | 3 | 3 | 7 | | | Bishop, Parker | 1 | 1 | 3 | | |
| Day, Abner | 1 | 3 | 2 | | | Whitney, Samˡ | 2 | 2 | 4 | | | Cutlar, Benjamin | 2 | 3 | 7 | | |
| Bush, John | 2 | 1 | 4 | | | Mitchell, Ezekiel | 1 | 1 | 2 | | | Johnson, Resolved | 1 | 1 | 2 | | 1 |
| Parks, Isaac | 1 | 3 | 2 | | | Campbell, William | 1 | | 1 | | | Torrey, Oliver | 3 | 1 | 3 | | |
| Day, David | 1 | 2 | 2 | | | Cape, Demas | | | | 6 | | Torrey, Hubard | 3 | | 2 | | |
| Burlingham, Edmond | 1 | 1 | 2 | | | Tucker, Timothy | 2 | 1 | 2 | | | Torrey, Joseph | 2 | | 3 | | |
| Moffat, John | 1 | 3 | 3 | | | Talbert, Benjamin | 1 | 1 | 6 | | | Warner, Benjamin | 4 | 1 | 6 | | |
| Moffat, John, Jnʳ | 1 | 3 | 3 | | | Prague, Joseph | 1 | 3 | 3 | | | Converse, Jonathan | 1 | 2 | 2 | | |
| Day, Levi | 1 | 3 | 2 | | | Brown, Isaiah | 1 | 4 | 2 | | | Graves, John | 2 | 4 | 4 | | |
| Smith, Elisha | 2 | 6 | 4 | | | Horton, Jotham | 2 | 4 | 2 | | | Wallin, Cornelious | 3 | 1 | 5 | | |
| Day, Jonathan, Jnʳ | 2 | 3 | 2 | | | Brown, Stephen | 2 | 4 | 4 | | | Cutlar, Peter | 3 | 3 | 4 | | |
| Burlington, Hopkins | 1 | 3 | 2 | | | Wheelock, Samˡ | 1 | | 1 | | | Reynolds, David | 1 | 1 | 3 | | |
| Barrows, William | 1 | 4 | 3 | | | Durfee, William | 5 | | 6 | | | Brown, Nebudiah | 4 | 3 | 8 | | |
| Barrows, Thomas | 1 | 2 | 4 | | | Hopkins, Richard | 1 | 1 | 3 | | | Babbet, Edward, Jnʳ | 1 | | 1 | | |
| Bennet, Joseph | 2 | | 1 | | | Turtels, Benjamin | 2 | 1 | 4 | | | Green, Edward | 1 | 2 | 5 | | |
| Harridon, Benjamin | 1 | 2 | 5 | | | Bateman, Benjamin | 2 | 3 | 5 | | | Bowen, Eleazʳ | 2 | | 2 | | |
| Preston, Danˡ | 1 | 2 | 4 | | | Aldridge, Levi | 2 | 4 | 3 | | | Cutlar, Azariah | 3 | 3 | 6 | | |
| Twogood, Samˡ | 1 | 1 | 2 | | | Carpenter, Lou | 3 | 3 | 3 | | | Cutlar, David | 1 | 2 | 2 | | |
| Pooler, Allen | 2 | | 2 | | | Smith, Joseph | 1 | | 1 | | | Leonard, Enoch | | | 2 | | |
| Adams, Abijah | 3 | 1 | 3 | | | Laws, David | 2 | 2 | 3 | | | Johnson, Aholiab | 1 | 1 | 4 | | |
| Whitney, Matthias | 1 | 3 | 4 | | | Brown, Nathˡ | 1 | | 1 | | | | | | | | |
| Randall, James | 1 | 2 | 3 | | | Brown, Zachⁿ | 2 | 4 | 2 | | | LEBANON TOWN. | | | | | |
| Sharp, Reubin & co | 2 | | 5 | | | Brown, Josiah &c | 2 | 1 | 2 | | | | | | | | |
| Warker, Comfort | 1 | 1 | 4 | | | Ferrows, Benjamin | 1 | 3 | 5 | | | Kennie, Nathan | 2 | 2 | 6 | | |
| Pidge, John | 2 | 1 | 4 | | | Covill, Ebenʳ | 2 | 3 | 3 | | | Kasson, Joseph | 1 | 4 | 3 | | |
| Alswerth, John | 1 | 2 | 3 | | | Smith, John, Senʳ | 1 | | 3 | | | Brooks, Isaac | 2 | | 5 | | |
| Owens, Josiah | 4 | | 7 | | | Herrington, Jonathan | 3 | 1 | 3 | | | Ford, Abraham | 1 | | 3 | | |
| Cooper, Peter | 2 | | 2 | | | Herrington, Jonᵃ, Jnʳ | 1 | | 1 | | | Badcock, Nathan | 2 | 3 | 1 | | |
| Durfee, John | 1 | 1 | 4 | | | Cutlar, Isaac | 1 | 2 | 2 | | | Seabury, Samˡ | 2 | 1 | 2 | | |
| Anderson, Samˡ | 1 | 3 | 2 | | | Herrington, John | 1 | 1 | 2 | | | Manning, John | 1 | 3 | 2 | | |
| Eames, Samˡ | 1 | 5 | 4 | | | Herrington, Othniel | 1 | | 1 | | | House, John | 3 | 5 | 7 | | |
| Bates, Oliver | 2 | | 2 | | | Smith, John | 1 | 1 | 1 | | | Avery, Joseph | 2 | 2 | 6 | | |
| Bowen, James | 1 | 1 | 2 | | | Smith, Hezᵃ | 1 | 1 | 5 | | | Payne, Joseph | 2 | 1 | 1 | | |
| Spalding, Silas | 1 | 3 | 3 | | | Cutlar, Roberd | 1 | 2 | 5 | | | Payne, Joel | 1 | 1 | 2 | | |
| Dexter, Andrew | 2 | 1 | 4 | | | Corban, Elipht | 1 | 2 | 3 | | | Badger, Abner | 1 | 4 | 2 | | |
| Day, Israel | 1 | 4 | 3 | | | Babbet, Edward | 3 | | 2 | | | Clark, James | | | | 2 | |
| Day, Comfort | 1 | 1 | 4 | | | Beston, William | 1 | 5 | 4 | | | Sprague, Benjⁿ | 1 | 2 | 4 | 1 | |
| Whitney, Jonᵃ | 1 | 2 | 3 | | | Cady, Joseph | 4 | 3 | 5 | | | Perkins, John | 1 | 1 | 4 | | |
| Short, Seth | 1 | | 3 | | | Covil, Daniel &c | 5 | | 7 | | | Perkins, Thoˢ | 2 | 1 | 2 | | |
| Rude, Isaac | 1 | 2 | 1 | | | Fisk, Ephraim | 3 | 4 | 6 | | | Cook, John | 2 | 1 | 2 | | |
| Rude, Jacob | 1 | 1 | 4 | | | Herrington, Jeremiah | 2 | 1 | 2 | | | Wheeler, William | 1 | 2 | 3 | | |
| Slack, Joseph | 1 | 1 | 4 | | | Bowen, Oliver | 1 | 3 | 4 | | | Perkins, Samˡ | 1 | 3 | 3 | | |
| Slack, William | 2 | | 2 | | | Bartlet, Edward | 1 | 1 | 5 | | | Fitch, Jabez | 3 | | 3 | | |
| Winter, Nathan | 2 | | 3 | | | Collins, Richard | 4 | | 2 | | | Dagget, John | | 1 | 2 | | |
| Day, Elias | 1 | 4 | 2 | | | Whitmore, Benjⁿ | 1 | 2 | 3 | | | Hutchinson, Eleazʳ, Jnʳ | 1 | 2 | 1 | | |
| Dexter, Phillip | 1 | 1 | 2 | | | Moffet, Eleazʳ | 3 | | 2 | | | Simms, William | 4 | 1 | 4 | | |
| Howard, Joseph | 2 | | 5 | | | Converse, Eleazʳ | | 2 | 5 | | | Hutchinson, Eleazʳ | 3 | 1 | 6 | | |
| Day, John | 1 | 2 | 6 | | | Leach, John | 2 | 2 | 7 | | | Hutchinson, Eleazʳ, 3ᵈ | 2 | 3 | 5 | | |
| Warren, Isaac | 2 | 3 | 2 | | | Hull, Thomas | 1 | 1 | 1 | | | Reed, Danˡ | 3 | 3 | 5 | | |
| Sanders, Prudence A | | | 1 | 1 | | Wilson, Ebenʳ | 4 | | 3 | | | Bill, Elisha | 3 | 3 | 6 | | |
| Boyden, Elham | 3 | 2 | 2 | | | Hartwell, Nathaniel | 1 | | 2 | | | Hutchinson, Samˡ | 3 | 1 | 4 | | |
| Selden, Caleb | 2 | 4 | 4 | | | Talbert, Jared | 2 | 2 | 5 | | | White, Aaron | 1 | | 1 | | |
| Allen, Caleb | 3 | 3 | 5 | | | Salsbury, Gilbert | 2 | 5 | 4 | | | Hebard, Lindon | 1 | | 2 | | |
| Allen, Thaddeus | 1 | | 2 | | | Covill, Samˡ | 2 | 2 | 5 | | | Deman, John | | | | | |

# HEADS OF FAMILIES—CONNECTICUT.

## WINDHAM COUNTY—Continued.

| NAME OF HEAD OF FAMILY. | Free white males of 16 years and upward, including heads of families. | Free white males under 16 years. | Free white females, including heads of families. | All other free persons. | Slaves. | NAME OF HEAD OF FAMILY. | Free white males of 16 years and upward, including heads of families. | Free white males under 16 years. | Free white females, including heads of families. | All other free persons. | Slaves. | NAME OF HEAD OF FAMILY. | Free white males of 16 years and upward, including heads of families. | Free white males under 16 years. | Free white females, including heads of families. | All other free persons. | Slaves. |
|---|---|---|---|---|---|---|---|---|---|---|---|---|---|---|---|---|---|
| **LEBANON TOWN—con.** | | | | | | **LEBANON TOWN—con.** | | | | | | **LEBANON TOWN—con.** | | | | | |
| Loomis, Asa | 1 | 1 | 1 | | | Lee, Solomon | 1 | 3 | 3 | | | Howard, Caleb | 2 | | | | |
| Dunham, Daniel | 2 | 3 | 8 | | | Waterman, Andrew | 3 | 1 | 3 | | | Loomis, Eleazr | 1 | 2 | 4 | | |
| Little, Gamaliel | 1 | 3 | 7 | | | Yeomans, Daniel | 2 | 4 | 4 | | | Waterman, Joseph | 2 | 3 | 1 | | |
| Linkon, Abijah | 4 | | 1 | | | Polly, Joshua | 1 | | 2 | | | Hyde, Zebediah | 1 | 4 | 2 | 1 | |
| Barker, Priscilla | 2 | 2 | 4 | | | Wattles, Joshua | 1 | 4 | 1 | | | Barber, Jeremiah | 1 | 4 | 3 | | |
| Mason, Elijah, Senr | 1 | 1 | 1 | | 28 | Badger, Abigal | | | 3 | | | Stearkweather, Nathl | 1 | 1 | 6 | | |
| Throope, Dan | 1 | 2 | 4 | | | Jones, Daniel | 1 | | 4 | | | Dutton, Ebenr | 2 | 1 | 3 | | |
| Throope, Joseph | 1 | 4 | 2 | | | Ingraham, Daniel | 3 | 1 | 5 | | | Abel, Joseph | 1 | 2 | 7 | | |
| Throope, Benjamin | 1 | 3 | 4 | | | Bolls, Asa | 3 | | 7 | | | Southward, Beriah | 3 | | 5 | | |
| Payne, Seth | 2 | 4 | 6 | | | McCaul, Archs | 3 | 2 | 2 | | 1 | Leach, Joseph | 4 | 1 | 4 | | |
| Payne, Stephen | 2 | 2 | 3 | | | Thomas, Elihu | 1 | 1 | 7 | | | Lyman, Jonath | 3 | 1 | 3 | | |
| Tisdale, Elijah | 7 | 4 | 7 | | | Hill, Phillip | 2 | | 1 | | | Thomas, James | 2 | 2 | 3 | | |
| Hutchinson, Daniel | 1 | 1 | 1 | | | Wattles, Thos | 1 | 2 | 4 | | | Lyman, William | 3 | 2 | 5 | | |
| Hatch, Samuel | 3 | 2 | 4 | | | Fitch, Nathan | 2 | | 1 | | | Porter, Nathl | 2 | | 3 | 1 | |
| Hunt, Walter | 1 | 1 | 4 | | | Hunt, Jonath | 1 | 3 | 6 | | | Bushnell, Ebenezr | 3 | 4 | 3 | | |
| Champion, Salmon | 3 | 3 | 5 | | | Wattles, Mason | 2 | | 1 | | | Trumbull, Jonathan | 1 | 1 | 5 | 2 | |
| Phelps, Elijah | 2 | 1 | 3 | | | Wattles, Charles | 1 | 2 | 5 | | | Robinson, Ichabod | 2 | 1 | 3 | | 3 |
| Payne, Stephen, Jur | 3 | 3 | 7 | | | Thomas, Amos, Jnr | 1 | 2 | 2 | | | Wood, Josiah | 1 | 1 | 6 | | |
| Badcock, Elijah | 2 | 3 | 4 | | | Wattles, Belcher | 1 | 2 | 3 | | | Wattles, Denison | 1 | 2 | 2 | 1 | |
| Lathrop, Zebulon | 3 | 2 | 4 | | | Wattles, Ichabod | 3 | 3 | 3 | | | Fitch, Isaac | 1 | | 3 | | |
| Johnson, John, Jur | 2 | 1 | 6 | | | Alden, Andrew | 1 | 3 | 2 | | | Taintor, John | 1 | 1 | 4 | 1 | |
| Johnson, John | 1 | | 1 | | 1 | Rogers, Nathanl, Senr | 1 | 2 | 4 | | | White, Enoch | 2 | 3 | 3 | | 1 |
| Snow, Abraham | 1 | | 1 | | | Frink, William | 5 | | 8 | | | Lisk, Ebenezr | 1 | | 5 | | |
| Payne, Benjn | 2 | 2 | 4 | | | Medcalf, Ebenezr | 3 | 2 | 4 | | | Gay, Asael | 2 | 1 | 4 | | |
| Badcock, Abijah | 2 | 2 | 7 | | | Capills, Thomas, & Josiah Rogers | 2 | 1 | 4 | | | Crowel, Ebenr | 2 | 1 | 3 | | |
| Seabury, Abigal | | | 4 | | | | | | | | | Clark, John | 2 | | 3 | | 1 |
| Stearkweather, Nathan | 4 | | 2 | | | Lamphear, Elijah | 2 | 2 | 2 | | | Rockwill, Jonah | 4 | 3 | 6 | | |
| Williams, George | 5 | 5 | 5 | | | Coleman, John | | | 3 | | | Young, David | 4 | 2 | 4 | | |
| Payne, Benjamin, Jnr | 1 | 1 | 2 | | | Harrison, Silas | 1 | 3 | 4 | | | Green, Robert | 1 | | 2 | | |
| Bliss, Amos | 3 | 1 | 8 | | | Coleman, John, Jnr | 1 | 2 | 1 | | | Lyman, Jabez | 1 | | 3 | | |
| Tisdale, Eliphalet | 1 | | 2 | | | Coleman, Jason | 1 | 2 | 4 | | | Strong, Oliver | 2 | 1 | 2 | | |
| Turner, Mary | 1 | 1 | 4 | | | Carter, James | 2 | | 2 | | | Payne, Dan | 1 | 1 | 7 | | |
| Gross, Saml | 1 | 2 | 3 | | | Dilla, Riva | 1 | 3 | 8 | | | Chappel, Caleb | 1 | 1 | 6 | | |
| Tisdale, Ebenezr | 1 | | 3 | | | Waters, Aaron | 3 | 3 | 3 | 1 | | Strong, Daniel, Jnr | 4 | 2 | 7 | | |
| Hyde, Moses | 3 | 1 | 4 | | | Miners, David | 1 | 4 | 4 | | | Bozworth, Ichabod | 1 | 2 | 4 | | |
| Williams, Honr William | 2 | 2 | 4 | 2 | | Lee, Israel, Jnr | 1 | 3 | 5 | | | Strong, Daniel | 3 | 1 | 3 | | |
| Trumbull, David | 4 | 3 | 7 | | | Lee, Israel, Senr | 2 | 3 | 3 | | | Loomiss, Thomas | 2 | 2 | 6 | | |
| Williams, Thomas | 3 | 3 | 4 | | | Mason, Jeremiah | 4 | | 4 | 1 | 2 | William, William, Jnr | 2 | 2 | 3 | | |
| Ely, Zebulon | 1 | 2 | 4 | 1 | | Learned, Joseph | 1 | | 3 | | | Clark, Jacob | 1 | 1 | 1 | | |
| Huntington, William | 2 | 1 | 3 | | 1 | Kingsley, Timoy | 2 | | 3 | | | Clark, Jerom | 3 | 1 | 3 | | |
| Hyde, Elijah | 3 | 2 | 6 | | | Kingsley, Nathanl | 1 | 2 | 6 | | | Loomiss, Thomas, Jnr | 2 | 3 | 3 | | |
| Abell, Caleb | 2 | 1 | 6 | | | Payne, John | 1 | 1 | 4 | | | Bartlet, John | 3 | 3 | 4 | | |
| Medcalf, Eliphalet | 1 | 3 | 5 | | | Stark, Abiel | 1 | 2 | 5 | | | Brewster, Benjamin | 3 | | 2 | 2 | 1 |
| Medcalf, David | 2 | 2 | 7 | | | Steark, Nathan | 2 | 3 | 4 | | | Hall, Christopher | 1 | 2 | 1 | | |
| Fitch, Andrew | 1 | 3 | 2 | | | Rogers, Jeremiah | 1 | 2 | 3 | | | Clark, Jonathan | 1 | | 4 | | |
| Huntington, William | 5 | | 2 | 1 | | Lathrop, James | 1 | 1 | 2 | | | Williams, Jehiel | 3 | 4 | 3 | | |
| Brewster, Comfort | 3 | 1 | 5 | | | McKensey, George | 1 | 2 | 4 | | | Wilcox, Ephraim | 1 | 1 | 4 | | |
| Lovegrove, Edward | 1 | 1 | 3 | | | Lathrop, Charles | 2 | 3 | 4 | | | Clark, Andrew | 1 | 1 | 2 | | |
| Huntington, Oliver | 3 | 3 | 5 | | | Lathrop, Abiel | 1 | 1 | 6 | | | Clark, Nathan | 1 | 1 | 2 | | |
| Beamon, Samuel | 1 | 2 | 6 | | | Thomas, Amos | 2 | 4 | 8 | 1 | 1 | Clark, Silas | 5 | | 3 | | |
| Hyde, Elijah, Senior | 1 | 2 | 3 | | | Thomas, Abijah | 4 | 2 | 4 | | 1 | Chappel, Amaziah | 1 | 3 | 4 | | |
| Russ, Jehiel | 1 | 2 | 6 | | | Hyde, William | 2 | 5 | 4 | | | Bliss, Ezra | 4 | | 1 | | |
| Fitch, Ichabod | 2 | 3 | 8 | 2 | | Bigelow, Otis | 2 | 5 | 3 | | | Hyde, Oliver | 1 | | 6 | | |
| Hyde, Benjamin | 3 | 3 | 5 | | | Abel, Simon | 2 | 2 | 5 | | | Bill, Jonath | 1 | 1 | 3 | | |
| Mason, James F | 2 | 1 | 3 | | | Bartlet, Chandler | 1 | 3 | 5 | | | Clark, Jared | 3 | 1 | 4 | | |
| Waterman, Simeon | 2 | 3 | 6 | | | Bartlet, Judah | 1 | 4 | 5 | | | Clark, Daniel | 3 | | 5 | | |
| Hyde, Samuel | 4 | 2 | 7 | 1 | | Capells, John | 2 | 3 | 5 | | | Abell, Solomon | 2 | 2 | 6 | | |
| Little, William | 4 | 1 | 7 | | | Thorp, Aaron | 3 | 4 | 7 | | | Abell, Eliphl | 1 | 2 | 1 | | |
| Pettiss, James | 2 | 3 | | 6 | | Bartlet, Ichabod | 3 | 3 | 3 | | 1 | Abel, Danl | 2 | 1 | 2 | | |
| Medcalf, Jabez | 4 | 3 | 6 | 12 | | Jordon, Asa | 3 | | 3 | | | Abel, Elijah | 2 | 3 | 3 | | |
| Medcalf, Abigal | | | 6 | 1 | 2 | Steark, Joshua | 3 | 2 | 4 | | | Gurley, John | 2 | | 2 | | |
| Medcalf, Zebulon | 3 | | 4 | | | Hobbs, Edmond | 1 | | 3 | | | Green, Robert | 1 | | 2 | | |
| Medcalf, Peter | 1 | 1 | 2 | | | Whitman, William | 1 | 2 | 3 | | | Woodworth, Walter | 1 | | 2 | | |
| Alden, William | 1 | 1 | 2 | | | Gay, Elisha | 1 | 1 | 1 | | | White, Sylvanus | 2 | 1 | 4 | | |
| Huntington, Andrew | 1 | 4 | 4 | | | Hill, Abner | 1 | | 1 | | | Dewey, Barzeliel | 1 | 2 | 1 | | |
| Lisk, Andrew | 2 | 1 | 4 | | | Mantle, Jacob | 1 | 1 | 2 | | | Doubleday, Elisha | 1 | 2 | 5 | | |
| Chappel, Oliver | 1 | 3 | 5 | | | Roger, Nathel, Jnr | 2 | 1 | 5 | | | Doubleday, Jesse | 1 | 1 | 5 | | |
| Flint, Martha | | 1 | 3 | | | Stone, Timothy | 4 | | 3 | 1 | | Marsh, Anne | 1 | | 4 | | |
| McCawl, John | 2 | 2 | 2 | | | Hinkley, Dyer I | 3 | | 6 | 2 | | Payne, Dan | 1 | | 2 | | |
| Fitch, Abraham | 3 | | 4 | | | Hinkley, Jared | 4 | 1 | 3 | | | Williams, John | 1 | 1 | 2 | | |
| Loomis, Joseph | 4 | 3 | 3 | | | Dutton, Ambrose | 1 | 2 | 2 | | | McCaul, Roger | 2 | 1 | 2 | | |
| Palmer, Nehemiah | 2 | | 2 | | | Shapley, John | 1 | 3 | 2 | | | Williams, William, 3d | 2 | 3 | 4 | | |
| Bissell, Daniel | 3 | 3 | 7 | | | Bewel, Oliver | 4 | | 6 | | | Williams, Charles | 4 | 2 | 4 | | |
| Bewel, Abel | 1 | | 2 | | | Hinkley, Ebenr | 3 | 1 | 3 | | | Bascomb, William | 2 | | 2 | | |
| Bewel, Josiah | 1 | 2 | 5 | | | Thomas, Peleg | 2 | 1 | 4 | 1 | | Cole, Jonathn | 1 | 1 | 2 | | |
| Bewel, William | 1 | 1 | 6 | | | Butler, Patk | 2 | 1 | 3 | | | Richardson, Humphrey | 1 | | 2 | | |
| Palmer, Jabez | 1 | 2 | 6 | | | West, Ebenezr | 4 | 1 | 5 | | | Fuller, David | 1 | 1 | 1 | | |
| Hyde, Daniel | 1 | 2 | 5 | | | Sumner, Jonath | 1 | 1 | 4 | | | Porter, Reuben | 2 | 2 | 6 | | |
| Brown, Sarah | | | | | 1 | Tillotson, Danl | 2 | | 4 | | | Hunt, Saml | 2 | 3 | 5 | | |
| Clark, James | 4 | 2 | 7 | | | Clark, Dan | 2 | 1 | 5 | | | Allen, Jared | 1 | | 4 | | |
| Williams, Isaac | 2 | 4 | 4 | | | Alden, Walter | 1 | | 5 | | | Spencer, Peter | 3 | 5 | 3 | | |
| Williams, Vitch | 2 | 1 | 4 | | | Martin, Anderson | 1 | 2 | 6 | | | Williams, Isaiah | 1 | 2 | 5 | | |
| Bissell, Joseph W | 4 | 2 | 4 | | 1 | Smith, Frederick | 2 | 1 | 2 | | | Williams, Simon | 4 | 1 | 7 | | |
| Wattles, Oliver | 2 | | 9 | | | Hutchinson, Eleazer | 2 | 1 | 1 | | | Stiles, Benjamin | 2 | 2 | 4 | | |
| McCawl, Green | 1 | 1 | 2 | | | Hutchinson, Elisha | 3 | 1 | 9 | | | Palmer, Amos | 1 | 2 | 4 | | |
| Brown, John | 2 | 2 | 4 | | 2 | Mason, Elijah, Jnr | 2 | 2 | 4 | | | Cuningham, Peleg | 1 | | 2 | | |
| Williams, Fredrick | 1 | 2 | 2 | | | Terry, Ephraim | 4 | 3 | 5 | | | McCaul, Holbart | 2 | 3 | 3 | 1 | 1 |
| McCawl, Ozias | 1 | 4 | 3 | | | Terry, Saml | 2 | | 2 | | | Bristol (Negro) | | | | 3 | |
| Williams, Jonath | 4 | | 3 | | | Coye, Joseph | 2 | 2 | 4 | | | Jeffords, Robin | | | | 5 | |
| Fowler, Adonijah | 2 | 3 | 6 | | 1 | Webster, Josiah | 3 | 1 | 4 | | | Bewel, Daniel | 1 | 2 | 3 | | |
| Medcalf, Andrew | 1 | | 3 | 1 | | Smith, Jacob | 1 | | 3 | | | Clark, Moses | 3 | 1 | 2 | | |
| Harris, Phillip | 2 | 3 | 3 | | | Smith, Elijah | 1 | 1 | 4 | | | West, David | 1 | 2 | 2 | | |
| Whitely, John | 1 | 2 | 3 | | | Bemount, Isaiah | | 1 | 4 | | | Haynes, Daniel | 1 | 3 | 4 | | |
| Fowler, John | 2 | | 4 | | | Smith, Abijah | 3 | 1 | 2 | | | Haynes, Sylvester | 1 | | 1 | | |
| | | | | | | Bacon, Ebenezr | 1 | 1 | 3 | | | Bliss, Peltiah | 1 | 1 | 3 | | |

145

# WINDHAM COUNTY—Continued.

| NAME OF HEAD OF FAMILY. | Free white males of 16 years and upward, including heads of families. | Free white males under 16 years. | Free white females, including heads of families. | All other free persons. | Slaves. | NAME OF HEAD OF FAMILY. | Free white males of 16 years and upward, including heads of families. | Free white males under 16 years. | Free white females, including heads of families. | All other free persons. | Slaves. | NAME OF HEAD OF FAMILY. | Free white males of 16 years and upward, including heads of families. | Free white males under 16 years. | Free white females, including heads of families. | All other free persons. | Slaves. |
|---|---|---|---|---|---|---|---|---|---|---|---|---|---|---|---|---|---|
| **LEBANON TOWN—con.** | | | | | | **LEBANON TOWN—con.** | | | | | | **LEBANON TOWN—con.** | | | | | |
| Tyler, Danl | 4 | 1 | 4 | | | Hill, Joseph | 2 | 3 | 3 | | | Beston, Joseph | 1 | 1 | 2 | | |
| Clark, Roswell | 1 | 2 | 4 | | | Newcomb, Joseph | 1 | 2 | 4 | | | Cole, David | 3 | 1 | 4 | | |
| Wright, Mehitable | 1 | 1 | 4 | | | Clark, David | 3 | 3 | 7 | | | Bliss, Elias | 1 | | 1 | | |
| Clark, Ambrose | 1 | 2 | 1 | | | Allen, Joshua | 3 | 2 | 6 | | | Chappel, Elijah | 1 | | 5 | | |
| Coleman, Noah | 2 | 4 | 3 | | | Hunt, Elijah | 2 | 2 | 7 | | | Sulard, Joseph | 2 | 1 | 5 | | |
| Williams, Ambrose | 1 | 1 | 2 | | | Allen, Saml | 2 | | 4 | | | Beston, Saml | 1 | 1 | 4 | | |
| Watrous, Jonath | 1 | 1 | 3 | | | Hartshorne, Ezekel | 2 | 2 | 5 | | | Pinney, James | 4 | 2 | 6 | | |
| William, Israel | 2 | 1 | 3 | | | Woodworth, Ebenezr | 1 | | 3 | | | Loomis, Ezra | 1 | | 1 | | |
| Medcalf, Levi | 1 | 4 | 3 | | | Woodworth, Elipht | 4 | 4 | 8 | | | Porter, Abraham | 1 | 1 | 4 | | |
| Bell, Oliver | 6 | 2 | 9 | | | Fitch, Nathl | 2 | 4 | 4 | | | Porter, Elikm | 1 | 4 | 3 | | |
| Medcalf, Reuben | 2 | 1 | 3 | | | Hunt, Eldad | 2 | 5 | 2 | | | Hoolbrook, John | 1 | 4 | 4 | | |
| Brewster, Ichabod | 3 | 3 | 6 | | | Brewster, Wadsworth | 3 | 3 | 6 | | | Brewster, Experience | | | 4 | | |
| Wilcox, Abraham | 1 | 3 | 3 | | | Lyman, William | 2 | 3 | 3 | | | Bissell, Elisha | 3 | 1 | 4 | | |
| Bill, Abial | 1 | 3 | 2 | | | Kingsbury, Asa | 1 | 2 | 1 | | | Hunt, Joseph | 3 | 2 | 7 | | |
| Porter, Laton | 1 | 1 | 4 | | | Badcock, Amos | 1 | 3 | 4 | | | Thomas, Elipht | 1 | 1 | 3 | | |
| West, Levi | 1 | 1 | 1 | | | Thomson, Saml | 1 | 4 | 5 | | | Hoolbrook, Abel | 2 | | 3 | | |
| Bascomb, Abial | 1 | 1 | 5 | | | Loomis, Nathan | 1 | 2 | 5 | | | Brewster, Saml | 1 | 2 | 1 | | |
| Spafford, Nathan | 2 | 3 | 5 | | | Manley, Sylvester | 1 | 3 | 2 | | | Porter, John | 2 | 2 | 3 | | |
| West, Amos | 1 | | 1 | | | Baxter, William | 2 | 1 | 4 | | | Bennet, Robert | 3 | | 1 | | |
| Webster, Zurvey | 1 | 1 | 3 | | | Woodward, Israel | 1 | 1 | 1 | | | Bliss, Zenas | 1 | 1 | 1 | | |
| Lamb, Rufus | 2 | 1 | 5 | | | Woodward, Eleazr | 2 | 4 | 3 | | | Loomiss, Joseph | 2 | 1 | 2 | | |
| Harriss, Phillip | 1 | 1 | 3 | | | Woodward, Israel, Jnr | 3 | 2 | 4 | | | Wright, Joel | 1 | 2 | 3 | | |
| Marsh, Dan | 2 | 3 | 9 | | | Gary, Thadeus | 1 | | 4 | | | Williams, John, Jnr | 1 | 4 | 2 | | |
| Webster, Ruth | 3 | 3 | 9 | | | Woodworth, Swift | 1 | 3 | 4 | | | Loomiss, Benoni | 1 | 3 | 5 | | |
| Cuff (Wido.) | | | | 4 | | Lyman, Benja | 1 | 3 | 5 | | | Buckingham, William | 1 | | 2 | | |
| Webster, James | 2 | 4 | 9 | | | Gary, Seth | 1 | | 1 | | | Williams, John | 2 | 4 | 4 | | |
| Bissell, Benjamin | 1 | 3 | 2 | | | Garey, Elijah | 1 | | 2 | | | Little, Consider | 2 | 3 | 2 | | |
| Bissell, Partridge | 1 | 1 | 2 | | | Tickner, Isaac | 3 | 4 | 2 | | | Abel, Jonath | 2 | 2 | 4 | | |
| Bissell, Joseph F | 1 | | 2 | | | Bliss, Henry | 2 | 1 | 6 | | | Backus, Whiting | 2 | 3 | 7 | | |
| Finney, Joseph | 1 | 2 | 2 | | | Little, John | 1 | 4 | 3 | | | Bailey, Isaac, Jnr | 5 | 1 | 6 | | |
| Hill, Consider, Senr | 3 | 1 | 4 | | | Little, Gamaliel | 2 | 2 | 7 | | | Bailey, Isaac | 2 | 2 | 4 | | |
| Hill, Darious | 2 | 1 | 2 | | | Wright, Jabez | 1 | 1 | 2 | | | Medcalf, Saml | 2 | 2 | 4 | | |
| Pryor, Azarior | 3 | | 6 | 1 | | Wright, Jeriah | 1 | 4 | 3 | | | Dewey, Elipht | 1 | 2 | 2 | | |
| Case, Levi | 2 | 1 | 6 | | | Chapman, James | 1 | | 2 | | | Gross, Simon | 2 | 2 | 4 | | |
| Antrim, Francis | 1 | 4 | 5 | | | Little, John | 2 | 4 | 3 | | | Gillet, Isaac | 2 | 5 | 3 | | |
| Ward, William | 1 | | 4 | | | Wood, Benja | 2 | | 2 | | | Gillet, Mary (Wido.) | | 1 | 4 | | |
| Calkins, Solomon | 3 | | 2 | | | Bliss, Saml | 2 | 1 | 5 | | | Gay, Saml | 2 | 3 | 5 | | |
| Crocker, Simon | 3 | | 3 | | | Loomis, Simon | 4 | 2 | 4 | 1 | | Loomiss, Ezekiel | 2 | 3 | 3 | | |
| Crocker, Adonijah | 2 | 1 | 4 | | | Clark, Simon | 1 | 1 | 3 | | | Bliss, Samuel | 3 | 1 | 6 | | |
| Woodworth, Jeremiah | 1 | 1 | 2 | | | Clark, Asael | 2 | 4 | 5 | | | Loomiss, Abraham | 2 | 2 | 4 | | |
| Wills, Eleazr | 1 | 3 | 1 | | | Clark, Flavel | 1 | 2 | 2 | | | Bliss, Joseph | 3 | | 4 | | |
| Clarck, Saml | 1 | 2 | 5 | | | Brockway, Thomas | 2 | 2 | 9 | 2 | | Hyde, Nathl | 2 | 1 | 4 | | |
| Smith, Elijah | 1 | | 2 | | | Leamphear, Jabez | 1 | 1 | 4 | | | Lee, Nathan | 1 | | 4 | | |
| Tilden, Daniel | 5 | 1 | 8 | | | Barker, Saml | 1 | | 2 | | | Loomiss, Jacob | 1 | | 4 | | |
| Mason, James | 1 | 3 | 8 | | | Bill, Thomas | 2 | | 3 | | | Goodwin, Saml | 1 | 1 | 2 | | |
| Snow, Francis | 3 | 4 | 4 | | | Loomis, Joel | 1 | 3 | 2 | | | Tilden, Ebenr | 1 | 2 | 2 | | |
| Fitch, Ammi | 3 | 2 | 3 | | | Woodworth, James | 3 | 1 | 5 | | | Bailey, Saml, Jnr | 2 | | 3 | | |
| Seabury, Saml, Jnr | 1 | 1 | 2 | | | Guild, Saml | 1 | 2 | 5 | | | Brown, Thomas | 1 | 1 | 2 | | |
| Murdock, William | 2 | 2 | 7 | | | Huntington, David | 1 | 2 | 4 | | | Bailey, Saml, Senr | 2 | 2 | 3 | | |
| Hovey, Nathan | 1 | 2 | 2 | | | Hunt, Eldad | 2 | 5 | 4 | | | Clark, John | 1 | | 3 | | |
| Swift, Rowland, Jnr | 1 | 1 | 4 | | | Dunham, Hannah | | | 3 | | | Bettis, James | 2 | | 2 | | |
| Cheevers, Nathan | 2 | 3 | 4 | | | Lyman, Jesse | 4 | | 3 | | | Torrey, Asa | 6 | 1 | 2 | | |
| Swift, Rowland | 4 | 2 | 6 | | | Bounce, Aaron | 1 | 2 | 2 | | | Groscup, John | 1 | | 2 | | |
| Goodin, William | 1 | 1 | 4 | | | Abbot, James | 2 | 3 | 5 | | | Hoolbrook, Timoy | 2 | 2 | 4 | | |
| Goodwin, Johnath | 2 | 1 | 2 | | | Strong, David, Jnr | 1 | | 2 | | | Bailey, James | 4 | 4 | 6 | | |
| Clark, Abigal | 2 | 1 | 4 | | | Fish, Saml | 2 | 1 | 4 | | | Vaughn, Martha | | | 2 | | |
| Bailey, Elisha | 2 | 1 | 2 | | | Helms, Christopher | 1 | 1 | 4 | | | Dewey, John | 1 | 1 | 4 | | |
| Ford, Jacob | 1 | | 2 | | | Newcomb, Paul | 2 | 6 | 2 | | | Loomis, Israel, Jnr | 3 | 2 | 5 | | |
| Davis, Lathrop | 2 | 3 | 4 | | | Strong, David | 2 | | 4 | | | Dewey, Danl | 2 | 3 | 4 | | |
| Swift, William | 2 | | 1 | | | Sprague, Dan | 2 | 1 | 3 | | | Loomis, Simon | 2 | 2 | 1 | | |
| Thatcher, Abigal | | | 2 | | | Crocker, James | 1 | | 2 | | | Dewey, Woodward | 2 | | 3 | | |
| Bayley, Sexton | 4 | 1 | 3 | | | Gary, Eneas | 1 | 2 | 2 | | | Hill, Ephraim | | | 2 | | |
| Swift, Charles | 3 | 4 | 6 | | | Nye, Silas | 1 | | 1 | | | Loomiss, Israel | 2 | 1 | 7 | | |
| Kingsley, Oliver | 3 | 1 | 2 | | | Hyde, Nathl, Jnr | 1 | 1 | 7 | | | Loomiss, John | 1 | 4 | 5 | | |
| Kingsley, Asael | 1 | 2 | 1 | | | Richardson, James | 1 | 1 | 5 | | | Arnold, John | 2 | 3 | 5 | | |
| Brooks, Thomas | 1 | 1 | 3 | | | Bennet, Hinchman | 3 | | 7 | | | Lyman, Fredrick | 1 | | 2 | | |
| Newcomb, Jesse | 1 | 5 | 3 | | | Richardson, Eleazr | 2 | 2 | 4 | | | Tiffeny, Recompense | 1 | | 2 | | |
| Newcomb, John | 2 | 3 | 3 | | | Wright, Charles | 1 | 2 | 5 | | | Syms, George | 2 | 1 | 2 | | |
| Clark, Jonath | 2 | 1 | 5 | | | Hyde, Nathl, Senr | 2 | | 1 | | | Manning, Eleazr | 1 | 1 | 3 | | |
| Collins, Rufus | 3 | 1 | 4 | | | Bennet, Simon | 1 | 1 | 4 | | | | | | | | |
| Dewey, Abraham, Senr | 2 | 1 | 4 | | | Payne, James | 1 | 3 | 2 | | | **MANSFIELD TOWN.** | | | | | |
| Dewey, Abraham, Jnr | 1 | | 2 | | | Marble, John | 1 | 4 | 4 | | | | | | | | |
| Collins, Eleazr | 1 | 3 | 5 | | | Gary, Gilbert | 2 | 3 | 4 | | | Chaplin, Benja | 6 | 2 | 3 | | 3 |
| Collins, Rufus, Jnr | 1 | 4 | 4 | | | Garey, Ebenezr | 2 | | 6 | | | Storrs, John | 2 | 1 | 2 | | |
| Kingsley, Timo | 1 | | 3 | | | Woodworth, Jehiel | 1 | 1 | 5 | | | Lyon, Chester | 1 | 1 | 2 | | |
| Gillet, Isaac | 2 | 4 | 3 | | | Stearns, Roswill | 2 | | 4 | | | Mopley, Nathl | 2 | | 4 | | |
| Beamont, William | 1 | | 2 | | | English, Abiel | 1 | 2 | 3 | | | Robins, Solomon | 2 | 3 | 3 | | |
| Beamont, Dan | 1 | 2 | 2 | | | Woodworth, Lebens | 3 | | 3 | | | Preston, Danl | 2 | 2 | 3 | | |
| Scovil, Elizebith | 2 | 1 | 4 | | | Treadaway, David | 1 | 1 | 3 | | | Edgerton, Abel | 1 | | 2 | | |
| Hebard, Luther | 1 | | 1 | | | Little, Gamaliel, Jnr | 2 | 2 | 1 | | | Butler, Danl | 2 | 2 | 3 | | |
| Hill, James | 1 | | 5 | | | Finney, David | 3 | 2 | 4 | | | Williams, Lucretia | | | 2 | | |
| Thatcher, Benja | 5 | | 5 | | | Prince, Abijah | | | | 3 | | Edgerton, David | 1 | | 3 | | |
| Dingley, John | 1 | | 5 | | | Yeomans, Giles | 3 | | 5 | 1 | | Edgerton, John | 2 | 1 | 3 | | |
| Carpenter, Dan | 1 | | 3 | | | Sweatland, Jonah | 1 | 4 | 5 | | | Hartshorne, Andrew | 2 | 1 | 2 | | |
| Carpenter, Paul | 1 | 1 | 3 | | | Treadaway, William | 2 | 3 | 4 | | | Phelps, Moses | 2 | 3 | 4 | | |
| Dewey, Solomon | 1 | 2 | 3 | | | Rude, Jeremiah | 3 | 2 | 5 | | | Storrs, Judah | 3 | 2 | 5 | 1 | |
| Fuller, Saml | 1 | | 2 | | | Brown, Azariah | 1 | | 7 | | | Carey, Ebenr | 3 | 2 | 5 | | |
| Fuller, Bezl | 5 | 2 | 3 | | | White, Nathl | 2 | 2 | 5 | | | Clark, James | 1 | 1 | 6 | | |
| Fuller, Abiaal | 3 | 3 | 3 | | | West, Saml | 2 | 1 | 8 | | | Clark, Oliver | 4 | 1 | 2 | | |
| Tickner, James | 1 | | 2 | | | Phelps, John | 3 | 4 | 4 | | | Clark, Israel | 2 | 4 | 4 | | |
| Dewey, Israel | 2 | 1 | 3 | | | Newcomb, Bethewel | 3 | 4 | 10 | | | Clark, Lemuel | 5 | | 6 | | |
| Maxwill, John | 2 | 2 | 3 | | | Post, Pheneas | 1 | 5 | 5 | | | Rust, Eunice | 2 | 1 | 7 | | |
| Dewey, Eliphalet | 1 | | 2 | | | Thomas, Daniel | 1 | 4 | 3 | | | Huntington, Whitman | 3 | | 2 | | |
| Buckingham, Jedediah | 5 | | 2 | | | Gates, Zebulon | 1 | 4 | 2 | | | Clark, Nathan | 2 | 2 | 1 | | |
| Buckingham, Thomas | 1 | 1 | 5 | | | Chapman, Joshua | 1 | 1 | 1 | | | Gates, Susanna | | 1 | 4 | | |

# HEADS OF FAMILIES—CONNECTICUT.

## WINDHAM COUNTY—Continued.

| NAME OF HEAD OF FAMILY. | Free white males of 16 years and upward, including heads of families. | Free white males under 16 years. | Free white females, including heads of families. | All other free persons. | Slaves. | NAME OF HEAD OF FAMILY. | Free white males of 16 years and upward, including heads of families. | Free white males under 16 years. | Free white females, including heads of families. | All other free persons. | Slaves. | NAME OF HEAD OF FAMILY. | Free white males of 16 years and upward, including heads of families. | Free white males under 16 years. | Free white females, including heads of families. | All other free persons. | Slaves. |
|---|---|---|---|---|---|---|---|---|---|---|---|---|---|---|---|---|---|
| MANSFIELD TOWN—con. | | | | | | MANSFIELD TOWN—con. | | | | | | MANSFIELD TOWN—con. | | | | | |
| Owen, Timothy | 3 | | 1 | | | Fenton, Rusba | | 3 | 2 | | | Crain, Danl | 1 | 3 | 4 | | |
| Tracy, Israel | 1 | 4 | 4 | | | Fenton, Joseph | 2 | | 3 | | | Johnson, William | 1 | | 2 | | |
| Stoel, Josiel | 2 | 3 | 5 | | | Fenton, Ebenezr, Senr | 1 | | 1 | | | Pierce, Enoch | 1 | 2 | 3 | | |
| Southward, Nathl | 1 | 3 | 4 | | | Fenton, Jonathan | 1 | | 2 | | | Royce, David | 2 | 3 | 2 | | |
| Abbe, Solomon | 2 | 1 | 2 | | | Dexter, Nathan | 1 | 2 | 1 | | | Royce, James, Jnr | 1 | 4 | 3 | | |
| Curtiss, Mary | | | 3 | | | Birchard, Joseph | 2 | | 4 | | | Royce, Solomon | 1 | 4 | 3 | | |
| Smith, Uriah | 2 | 1 | 2 | | | Conant, Seth | 1 | 5 | 1 | | | Royce, Phillip | 2 | 2 | 4 | | |
| Booth, Henry | 1 | | 3 | | | Wheaton, Jacob | 2 | 1 | 8 | | | Bundy, John | 2 | 2 | 3 | | |
| Balch, Vivian | 1 | | 3 | | | Whitmore, Aaron | 3 | 1 | 4 | | | Dimmik, Joseph | 1 | 2 | 3 | | |
| Balch, Israel | 2 | 3 | 3 | | | Parker, James | 1 | 3 | 4 | | | Kidder, Nathl, Senr | 1 | 1 | 4 | | |
| Church, Abner | 2 | 1 | 1 | | | Harriss, Daniel | 2 | 1 | 9 | | | Storrs, Royal | 1 | | 4 | | |
| Linkon, Lemuel | 1 | 2 | 2 | | | Warner, Eleazr | 2 | | 5 | | | Waldo, Jesse | 1 | | 3 | 1 | |
| Thompson, Jared | 5 | | 2 | | | Bozworth, Nathl | 1 | 2 | 3 | | | Waldo, Roger | 2 | | 1 | | |
| Swift, Barzillia | 3 | 4 | 4 | | | Barrows, Thomas | 2 | 4 | 5 | | | Molton, Asa | 2 | | 2 | | |
| Bingham, Oliver | 1 | 2 | 3 | | | Olcott, John | 1 | 4 | 2 | 1 | | Royce, David | 1 | | 1 | | |
| Cushman, Joab | 1 | | 2 | | | Swift, John | 4 | 2 | 4 | | | Molton, Mary | | 1 | 3 | | |
| Abbe, Nathan | 1 | | 2 | | | Upham, Noah | 2 | 2 | 3 | | | Hovey, Aaron | 3 | 1 | 3 | | |
| Hovey, Jonath | 2 | 2 | 2 | | | Upham, Joseph | 1 | | 3 | | | Bicknal, Moses | 3 | 3 | 7 | | |
| Tilden, Ithamar | 3 | 2 | 2 | | | Swift, Thomas | 3 | 5 | 5 | | | Fairwell, Thomas | 1 | 4 | 3 | 1 | 1 |
| Parker, Ephraim | 3 | 1 | 4 | | | Southward, Joseph | 2 | 1 | 2 | | | Finney, Joseph | 1 | | | | |
| King, John | 3 | | 3 | | | Wood, Saml | 2 | 2 | 7 | | | Thompson, Saml | 3 | 2 | 4 | | |
| Badger, Jonathn | 1 | 4 | 3 | | | Bugbee, Hannah | 1 | | 2 | | | Freeman, Fredrick | 2 | 3 | 5 | | |
| Porter, Saml | 1 | 1 | 2 | | | Jones Jacob | 2 | 1 | 3 | | | Johnson, William, Jnr | 1 | | 2 | | |
| Ainy, Ambrose | 1 | | 2 | | | Russill, Thomas | 1 | 1 | 1 | | | Topliff, Calvan | 4 | 2 | 5 | | |
| Hartshorne, Joseph | 1 | 2 | 6 | | | Balch, Henry | 1 | 3 | 3 | | | Peirce, Saml | 1 | | 4 | | |
| Stutson, Anne | 1 | | 4 | | | Nichols, Jonathn | 4 | | 4 | | | Peirce, Enoch | 2 | | 3 | | |
| Bingham, Eleazr | 3 | 2 | 5 | | | Allen, Heza | 3 | 1 | 4 | | | Perin, Seth | 3 | 5 | 2 | | |
| Stearkweather, Joel | 2 | | 3 | 1 | | Huntington, Abner | 4 | 3 | 7 | | | Beardly, Gershom | 2 | 2 | 5 | | |
| Keaton, — | 1 | | 3 | | | Plumb, Daniel | 2 | 2 | 3 | | | Storrs, Cordial | 1 | 2 | 2 | | |
| Allen, Heza | 3 | | 4 | | | Crain, Hezekiah | 2 | 3 | 3 | | | Calkins, James | 2 | 1 | 3 | | |
| Ross, Ebenezr | 2 | 3 | 3 | | | Conant, Benajh | 1 | | 3 | | | Dexter, Jonath | 5 | 2 | 8 | | |
| Trumbull, Walter | 2 | 1 | 2 | | | Conant, Shubael | 2 | 1 | 4 | | | Taylor, Joseph | 3 | 1 | 1 | | |
| Bawldin, Ebenezr | 3 | 3 | 3 | | | Salter, Mary | 1 | 1 | 4 | | 2 | Russ, Stephen | 1 | 2 | 3 | | |
| Sessions, Leonard | 1 | 1 | 2 | | | Salter, John | 3 | 1 | 3 | | | Turner, Prince | 1 | 1 | 5 | | |
| Hunt, John | 2 | | 2 | | | Southward, Constant | 2 | | 3 | | | Badcock, John | 2 | 1 | 3 | | |
| Hunt, Joseph | 1 | 1 | 2 | | | Trumbull, William | 1 | 1 | 6 | | | Williams, Jesse | 3 | 2 | 6 | | |
| Raies, Moses | 1 | | 1 | | | Campbell, Peter | 1 | 1 | 2 | | | Dunham, Jacob | 1 | 2 | 2 | | |
| Hutchins, Benjn | 2 | 1 | 2 | | | Hall, Theophilus | 1 | 4 | 3 | | | Peirce, Fred'k, & Jarum Topliff | 2 | 1 | 2 | | |
| Adams, Lucy | 2 | 1 | 3 | 1 | | Nicholls, Lemuel | 2 | 1 | 2 | | | Parrish, Abigal | 1 | 1 | 3 | | |
| Southward, Saml | 4 | 2 | 9 | | | Triscatt, Dorathy | | | 2 | | | Dunham, James | 1 | 2 | 2 | | |
| Martin, Ebenezr | 1 | 5 | 2 | | | Hovey, Jonathn | 2 | 1 | 7 | | | Fuller, Jonathn | 1 | 2 | 5 | | |
| Stowel, Amasa | 1 | 1 | 1 | | | Balch, William | 1 | 2 | 2 | | | Slater, Eleazr | 1 | 5 | 5 | | |
| Arnold, John | 1 | | 1 | | | Hodges, Ephram | 1 | 3 | 4 | | | Johnson, Joseph | 1 | | 3 | | |
| Martin, John | 1 | | 2 | | | Kennedy, Daniel | 2 | 1 | 4 | | | Johnson, William, Jnr | 1 | 2 | 2 | | |
| Whittemore, Joseph, Jr | 1 | 2 | 1 | | | Kennedy, Daniel, Jnr | 1 | | 1 | | | Reed, Nathan | 1 | 1 | 1 | | |
| Sergeants, Saml | 4 | 1 | 6 | | | Fletcher, Seth | 1 | 3 | 1 | | | Evens, Arad | 1 | 1 | 2 | | |
| Storrs, Mary | | 1 | 1 | | | Turner, Elijah | 1 | 2 | 3 | | | Welch, Moses Cook | 2 | 3 | 8 | | |
| Hearsay, James | 1 | 2 | 2 | | | Hanks, Benjn | 2 | 3 | 4 | | | Allen, Simeon | 1 | 1 | 3 | | |
| Southward, Josiah | 1 | 1 | 6 | | | Fuller, Timothy | 1 | 1 | 3 | | | Conant, Joseph | 2 | | 2 | | |
| Storrs, Experience | 3 | 1 | 4 | | | Hanks, Uriah | 3 | 2 | 3 | | | Conant, Josiah, Jnr | 1 | 3 | 3 | 1 | |
| Conant, Eleazr | 2 | 3 | 4 | | | Newcomb, Thos | 1 | | 3 | | | Wood, Timothy | 1 | | 1 | | |
| Storrs, Dan | 3 | 5 | 5 | | | Webster, Moses | 1 | 2 | 5 | | | Ames, Amos | 1 | 1 | 3 | | |
| Collins, Benjn | 1 | | 3 | | | Royce, Asa | 1 | 1 | 4 | | | Dexter, Silas | 1 | 2 | 1 | | |
| Cushman, Isaac | 1 | 1 | 2 | | | Cross, Peter | 4 | 2 | 4 | | | Whitehouse, Thomas | 1 | 1 | 3 | | |
| Aspenwell, Prince | 2 | | 4 | | | Nicholls, Thomas | 1 | 1 | 2 | | | Cheamberlin, Oliver | 2 | 4 | 2 | | |
| Hull, Elias | 1 | 4 | 2 | | | Thompson, Isaac | 4 | 1 | 4 | | | Turner, Saml | 2 | 5 | 2 | | |
| Bibbens, Timothy | 1 | 1 | 1 | | | Freeman, John | 1 | 3 | 4 | | | Dimmick, Shubael | 8 | 1 | 4 | | |
| Dodge, Edward | 2 | 1 | 5 | | | Gurley, Zebulon | 3 | 3 | 7 | | | Turner, Stephen | 1 | | 3 | | |
| Storrs, Amariah | 4 | 1 | 4 | | | Royce, Byram | 1 | 1 | 3 | | | Turner, Timothy | | 4 | 3 | | |
| Whittemore, Saml | 2 | | | | | Parker, Zachariah, Jr | 1 | | 2 | | | Turner, Pheneas | 1 | 3 | 4 | | |
| Hartshore, Danl | 2 | 2 | 4 | | | Parker, Zach | 3 | | 4 | | | Dimmick, Edward | 2 | 1 | 3 | | |
| Barrows, David | 1 | 4 | 3 | | | Barrows, Ethan | 1 | 2 | 3 | | | Cheamberlain, Seth | 1 | | 1 | | |
| Abbe, Elijah | 1 | 1 | 1 | | | Baldwin, Danl | 4 | | 3 | | | Reed, Amasa | 3 | 2 | 3 | | |
| Abbe, Solomon, Jnr | 3 | 2 | 5 | | | Simons, Darious | 2 | 3 | 3 | | | Barrows, Isaac, 2d | 1 | 2 | 4 | | |
| Abbe, Bathsheba | 1 | | 1 | | | Shumway, Joseph | 2 | 3 | 8 | | | Stewart, Thomas | 1 | 1 | 2 | | |
| Hall, Josiah | 3 | 1 | 3 | | | Newcomb, Bradford | 1 | 3 | 2 | | | Waldo, Jesse, Senr | 2 | | 2 | 1 | |
| Campbell, Zuril | 3 | 5 | 5 | | | Royce, Zurel | 1 | 3 | 2 | | | Stewart, Saml | 1 | 4 | 5 | | |
| McCaul, Eleazr | 2 | 1 | 5 | | | Kidder, Nathl | 1 | 1 | | | | Slater, Saml | 1 | | 2 | | |
| Kidder, James | 2 | 2 | 2 | | | Eaton, Jacob | 2 | | 4 | | | Badcock, Josiah | 3 | 1 | 2 | | |
| Hopkins, Elisha | 1 | 2 | 1 | | | Eldridge, Elisha | 1 | 1 | 2 | | | Spafford, Jesse | 3 | 1 | 3 | | |
| Dodge, William | 1 | 4 | 3 | | | Gilbert, John | 1 | | 2 | | | Dunham, Danl | 3 | 1 | 2 | | |
| McCaul, Mary | | | 2 | | | Cross, Ruebin | 2 | | 1 | | | Dimmock, Eliph | 1 | | 2 | | |
| Kitch, Benjn | 1 | 3 | 1 | | | Fuller, Timothy | 1 | 1 | 4 | | | Dimmock, Oliver | 2 | 4 | 4 | | |
| Storrs, Josiah | 5 | 4 | 8 | | | Parker, Joshua | 2 | 2 | 4 | | | Nicholls, John | 1 | | 4 | | |
| Simons, Jonathan | 2 | 1 | | | | Anderson, Lemuel | 1 | | 3 | | | Dunham, Danl | 3 | 1 | 2 | | |
| Calkins, James | 1 | | 4 | | | Barrows, Robert | 2 | 3 | 5 | | | Turner, Isaac | 1 | 5 | 4 | | |
| Conant, Sylvanus | 1 | 3 | 7 | | | Sergeants, Isaac, Jnr | 1 | | 4 | | | Dunham, Phebe | | | 4 | | |
| Freeman, Azariah | 2 | 2 | 2 | | | Howe, Danl | 4 | 1 | 2 | | | Dunham, Jonath | 1 | 2 | 3 | | |
| Barrows, Phillip | 1 | | 3 | | | Storrs, Benjn | 2 | 3 | 4 | | | Tilden, Joshua | 2 | 2 | 7 | | |
| McCaul, Elijah | 1 | 1 | 1 | | | Sergeants, Isaac | 2 | 1 | 4 | | | Dunham, Seth | 2 | | 5 | | |
| Atwood, Heman | 2 | 3 | 3 | | | Freeman, Skiff | 2 | 4 | 5 | | | Medcalf, Ebenezr | 5 | 1 | 7 | | |
| Dunham, Elisha | 1 | | 3 | | | Davis, Joseph | 2 | 1 | 4 | | | Wood, Timothy | 1 | | 2 | | |
| Fenton, Ebenr | 2 | | 1 | | | Davis, Elizabeth | 1 | 1 | 2 | | | Brigham, Stephen | 4 | 2 | 6 | | |
| Atwood, Thomas | 1 | 3 | 1 | | | Freeman, Rebecca | 1 | | 3 | | | Williams, Amariah | 2 | 3 | 7 | | |
| Atwood, Hannah | 1 | 1 | 8 | | | Baldwin, Joseph | 3 | | 4 | | | Hovey, Joseph | 3 | 3 | 5 | | |
| Atwood, Nathl | 4 | 1 | 5 | | | Dimmick, Lot | 3 | 2 | 4 | | | Utley, Oliver | 1 | 1 | 4 | 1 | |
| Dunham, Bangs | 2 | 3 | 2 | | | Hovey, Jacob | 1 | 4 | 3 | | | Wright, Chloe | | | 4 | | |
| Philps, Nathl | 2 | 1 | 4 | | | Dimmik, Hezah | 1 | 3 | 8 | | | Willis, Willm | | | 4 | | |
| Phelps, Joseph | 1 | | 2 | | | Marcy, Benjamin | 1 | 1 | 3 | | | Spafford, Abraham | 1 | 1 | 2 | | |
| Thomson, Joseph | 1 | 1 | 6 | | | Royce, James | 2 | 1 | 2 | | | King, James | 1 | 3 | 3 | | |
| Fenton, Nathl | 1 | 1 | 2 | | | Hovey, Enoch | 2 | 1 | 2 | | | King, Saml | 2 | | 6 | | |
| Eaton, Nathl | 1 | 1 | 4 | | | Hebard, Eliphaz | 1 | 3 | 3 | | | Simons, Elipht | 1 | | 2 | | |
| Russell, Benjamin | 1 | 4 | 2 | | | Freeman, Edmond | 1 | | 2 | | | Barrows, Thomas | 4 | 1 | 4 | | |
| Newcomb, Submit | | | 5 | | | Hosmer, Eunice | | | 3 | | | Barrows, Eleazr | 1 | 2 | 4 | | |
| Brown, Jonathan | 3 | 2 | 2 | | | Thompson, Saml, Jr | 1 | 1 | 1 | 1 | | | | | | | |

# WINDHAM COUNTY—Continued.

| NAME OF HEAD OF FAMILY. | Free white males of 16 years and upward, including heads of families. | Free white males under 16 years. | Free white females, including heads of families. | All other free persons. | Slaves. | NAME OF HEAD OF FAMILY. | Free white males of 16 years and upward, including heads of families. | Free white males under 16 years. | Free white females, including heads of families. | All other free persons. | Slaves. | NAME OF HEAD OF FAMILY. | Free white males of 16 years and upward, including heads of families. | Free white males under 16 years. | Free white females, including heads of families. | All other free persons. | Slaves. |
|---|---|---|---|---|---|---|---|---|---|---|---|---|---|---|---|---|---|
| **MANSFIELD TOWN—con.** | | | | | | **PLAINFIELD TOWN—con.** | | | | | | **PLAINFIELD TOWN—con.** | | | | | |
| Wright, Ebenez<sup>r</sup> | 2 | 1 | 4 | | | Phillips, William | 2 | 1 | 3 | | | Wheeler, Aaron | 3 | | 4 | | |
| Barrows, Jabez | 3 | 2 | 4 | | | Dowe, John | 4 | 1 | 6 | | | Kingsbury, James | 2 | 2 | 3 | | |
| Abbot, David | 1 | 2 | 3 | | | Spalding, Stephen | 2 | 2 | 3 | | | Pierce, Samuel | 2 | 1 | 3 | | |
| Hanks, Silas | 2 | 1 | 6 | | | Sharkweather, Anne | | 1 | 2 | | | Fuller, Benj<sup>n</sup> | 2 | 1 | 4 | | |
| Beemus, Levi | 1 | 2 | 1 | | | Dunworth, Charles | 1 | 3 | 2 | | | French, Stuman | 2 | 2 | 3 | | |
| Huntington, Jonas | 5 | 2 | 6 | | | Parks, Neh<sup>eh</sup> | 4 | 3 | 11 | | | Hall, John | 2 | 1 | 1 | | 2 |
| Bennet, Jesse | 1 | 1 | 2 | | | Robinson, Josiah | 2 | 3 | 6 | | | Thurstone, Sam<sup>l</sup> | 1 | 3 | 3 | | |
| Bennet, Joshua | 1 | | 3 | | | Collins, Peter | 1 | | 1 | | | Wilson, Abraham | 2 | 2 | 4 | | |
| Gurley, Jacob B | 5 | 1 | 5 | | | Sharkweather, Richard | 1 | 1 | 1 | | | Hall, John, Jn<sup>r</sup> | 1 | 1 | 2 | | |
| Gurley, Daniel | 2 | 6 | 2 | | | Benjamin, Simeon | 1 | 1 | 2 | | | Stranaham, James | 3 | 2 | 4 | | |
| Gurley, Sam<sup>l</sup> | 3 | 1 | 5 | | | Sweet, Benj<sup>n</sup> | 1 | 4 | 2 | | | Hinsbury, Eben | 2 | | 2 | | |
| Gurley, Ephraim | 2 | 1 | 1 | | | Cole, Spencer | 1 | 1 | 2 | | | Walling, Ezekiel | 2 | 2 | 5 | | |
| Gurley, Jonathan | 2 | 1 | 6 | | | Dean, Josiah | 1 | 1 | 5 | | | Wilch, David | 1 | | 2 | | |
| Willis, James | 2 | 2 | 3 | | | Spalding, Dan<sup>l</sup> | 1 | 1 | 2 | | | Kennedy, Mary | 1 | | 2 | | |
| Willis, Micajah | 1 | 3 | 2 | | | Whipple, Zebulon | 4 | 1 | 5 | 1 | | Hill, Dan<sup>l</sup> | 3 | | 5 | | |
| Willis, James, Jn<sup>r</sup> | 1 | 3 | 5 | | | Dean, Christopher | 1 | 1 | 4 | | | Wheeler, Moses | 1 | 4 | 3 | | |
| Dimmock, Peter | 3 | 1 | 7 | | | Phillips, Asa | 2 | 2 | 4 | | | Lane, Hez<sup>a</sup> | 1 | 2 | 5 | | |
| Turner, Eleaz<sup>r</sup> | 1 | | 3 | | | Glover, Nathan | 2 | | 4 | | | Ashbury, Tho<sup>s</sup> | 1 | | 1 | | |
| Dexter, Isaac | 2 | 1 | 3 | | | Badcock, Silas | 1 | 2 | 1 | | 1 | Parkhurst, David | 2 | | 5 | | |
| Dexter, Dan<sup>l</sup> | 1 | 1 | 2 | | | Clark, Stephen | 3 | 6 | 4 | 1 | | Hutit, Nath<sup>l</sup> | 2 | | 4 | | |
| Craine, Hez<sup>a</sup> | 1 | 1 | 2 | | | Clark, Silas, Jr | 2 | 6 | 2 | | | Parkhurst, Job | 1 | 3 | 4 | | |
| Craine, Elisha | 1 | 2 | 4 | | | Crary, Benj<sup>n</sup> | 2 | 1 | 3 | 2 | | Parkhurst, Lem<sup>l</sup> | 3 | | 2 | | |
| Gurley, William | 3 | 3 | 3 | | | Harris, Sears | 3 | 1 | 3 | | | Millar, James | 1 | 2 | 2 | | |
| Dexter, David | 1 | 3 | 6 | | | Gallop, John | 2 | 1 | 4 | | | Millar, Sanders | 3 | 2 | 3 | | |
| Dunham, John | 1 | 2 | 7 | | | Kinsman, Newport | | | | 2 | | Whipple, Jonathan | | | | 3 | |
| Russ, John | 1 | | 3 | | | Starkweather, Jekey | 3 | 1 | 6 | | | Gallop, Jonath<sup>n</sup> | 1 | 2 | 1 | | |
| Wright, Amaziah | 1 | 3 | 7 | | | Heard, Josiah | 1 | 1 | 5 | | | Maine, Nath<sup>l</sup> | 2 | 2 | 1 | | |
| Davis, Jonath<sup>n</sup> | 2 | 1 | 3 | | | Tanner, William | 1 | 1 | 1 | | | Wall, William | 2 | 1 | 2 | | |
| Davis, Thomas | 3 | 1 | 5 | | | Williams, Tho<sup>s</sup> | 2 | 2 | 1 | | | Spalding, Azariah | 1 | 1 | 3 | | |
| Wright, Eleaz<sup>r</sup> | 1 | 1 | 6 | | | Bailey, Caleb | 1 | 1 | 1 | | | Care, Eben<sup>r</sup> | 1 | 3 | 3 | | |
| Nichall, Sam<sup>l</sup> | 1 | 3 | 4 | | | Gallop, Eben<sup>r</sup> | 2 | 1 | 2 | | 2 | Pope, Rich<sup>d</sup> | 5 | 2 | 5 | | |
| Nichalls, Nath<sup>l</sup> | 1 | 2 | 3 | | | Welch, John | 2 | | 2 | | | Parkhurst, Pierce | 1 | 1 | 2 | | |
| Waters, Jacob | 1 | | 2 | | | Woodward, Elias | 7 | 1 | 8 | | | Carey, Joseph | 1 | 3 | 4 | | |
| Barrows, Solomon | 1 | 3 | 3 | | | Satterlee, Nath<sup>l</sup> | 5 | 2 | 5 | | | Backus, Stephen | 1 | 1 | 4 | | |
| Bennet, Nath<sup>l</sup> | 2 | | 5 | | | Dixon, William | 2 | 3 | 3 | 1 | | Backus, Andrew | 3 | 1 | 4 | | 1 |
| Storrs, Tho<sup>s</sup> | 4 | 3 | 6 | | | Harris, Nathan | 5 | 3 | 5 | | | Spalding, Jonath<sup>n</sup> | 1 | 2 | 4 | | |
| Waters, Jacob, Jn<sup>r</sup> | 2 | 4 | 4 | | | Rude, William | 1 | 3 | 2 | | | Wheeler, Ephraim | 5 | 2 | 7 | | |
| Bennet, Nath<sup>l</sup>, Jn<sup>r</sup> | 1 | 3 | 5 | | | Pearks, Robert | 1 | 1 | 3 | | | Cutlar, William | 7 | 2 | 4 | | |
| Turner, Phillip | 1 | 3 | 1 | | | Sheldon, Eunice | 1 | 1 | 2 | | | Hall, Joseph, Jn | 2 | 3 | 2 | | |
| Cumins, William | 1 | 3 | 2 | | | Spaldin, Jesse | 1 | 1 | 3 | | | Champton, Paul | 2 | 3 | 5 | | |
| Snow, Eben<sup>r</sup> | 1 | | 3 | | | Hopkins, George | 2 | 4 | 5 | | | Ansell, Nath<sup>l</sup> | 3 | 1 | 2 | 1 | 1 |
| Barrows, Lemuel | 3 | 1 | 4 | | | Johnson, Sylvester | 2 | | 2 | | | Dunlop, Joshua | 3 | 1 | 6 | | |
| Conant, John | 2 | 1 | 3 | | | Herrick, Andrew | 3 | | 3 | | | Howe, Robert | 1 | 4 | | | |
| Eldridge, Lemuel | 2 | 4 | 3 | | | Colegrove, Jonath<sup>n</sup> | 1 | 3 | 5 | | | Burton, Uriah | 2 | | 2 | | |
| Barrows, Elisha, Jn<sup>r</sup> | 1 | 2 | 3 | | | Hall, Sam<sup>l</sup> | 3 | 1 | 6 | | | Spalding, Philip | 3 | 2 | 5 | | |
| Hall, Nath<sup>l</sup> | 1 | 2 | 5 | | | Bradford, James | 2 | 2 | 4 | | | Hall, Caleb, Jr | 2 | 3 | 5 | | |
| Hall, Gershom | 2 | 1 | 3 | | | Palmer, Vose | 1 | 2 | 2 | | | Herd, Jacob | 1 | 1 | 3 | | |
| Barrows, Gershom | 2 | 3 | 5 | | | Andrus, Akel | 2 | 2 | 4 | | | Stern, Nath<sup>l</sup> | 4 | 1 | 4 | | |
| Slate, Ezekel | 2 | 1 | 6 | | | Pastelot, Aseal | 2 | | 1 | | | Corey, Josiah | 1 | 1 | 1 | | |
| Barrows, Jabez | 3 | 1 | 3 | | | Pryor, Benj<sup>n</sup> | 2 | 1 | 5 | | | Sheppard, Simon | 3 | 1 | 2 | | |
| Hall, James | 2 | 3 | 5 | | | Garey, John | 1 | 2 | 5 | | | Pryor, Joseph | 1 | 5 | 3 | | |
| Hall, Susanna | | | 2 | | | Hall, Stephen | 2 | 1 | 4 | | | Warren, Ezra | 1 | 5 | 6 | | |
| Whittemore, Joseph | | | 2 | | | Gray, Jenney | 2 | | 4 | | | Branch, Moses | 5 | 1 | 4 | | |
| Bennet, Asa | 1 | 3 | 3 | | | Sabin, Nath<sup>l</sup> | 1 | 2 | 3 | | | Dow, Sam<sup>l</sup> | 2 | 1 | 1 | | |
| Barrows, Tho<sup>s</sup>, 3<sup>d</sup> | 1 | 4 | 3 | | | Taylor, George | 3 | 1 | 3 | | | Gallop, Benj<sup>n</sup> | 1 | 2 | 4 | | |
| Barrows, Jesse | 1 | 3 | 1 | | | Wilbar, William | 1 | | 2 | | | Douglass, John | 3 | | 5 | 7 | |
| Hall, Andrew | 3 | 3 | 6 | | | Nicholls, Joseph | 1 | 1 | 2 | | | Stevens, Hepsibah, Sr | | | 5 | | |
| Palmer, Nathan | 4 | 1 | 5 | | | Phillips, John | 4 | 2 | 4 | | | Perkins, Elisha | 6 | 9 | 7 | 1 | |
| Nesbit, Nathan | 1 | 1 | 3 | | | Webb, Joshua | 2 | 2 | 4 | | | Hun, Jonathan | 2 | 1 | 3 | | |
| Barrows, Joshua | 1 | 3 | 3 | | | Potter, Nehemiah | 1 | 1 | 2 | | | Smith, Luther | 1 | 1 | 7 | 1 | |
| Storrs, Sam<sup>l</sup> | 2 | 2 | 5 | | | Clark, William | 2 | | 4 | | | Herd, Thomas | 1 | | 1 | | |
| Storrs, Jehiel | 2 | 2 | 4 | | | Phillips, Joseph | 1 | | 2 | | | Perce, William | 3 | | 2 | | |
| Barrows, Isaac | 2 | | 5 | | | Shinger, Sarah | 1 | | 2 | | | Tuckerman, Jacob | 2 | | 1 | | |
| Bennet, James | 1 | 2 | 6 | | | Crandal, Christopher | 1 | 2 | 5 | | | Bottom, Joshua | 2 | 1 | 4 | | |
| Barrows, Elisha | 2 | 2 | 4 | | | French, John | 2 | 4 | 5 | | | Jones, Ephraim & co | 3 | 4 | 6 | | |
| Turner, Thomas | 1 | 1 | 2 | | | Dexter, Sam<sup>l</sup> | 2 | 4 | 3 | | | Badcock, Jack | | | | 8 | |
| Turner, Stephen | 1 | 3 | 3 | | | Kenney, Manuel | 4 | 2 | 4 | | | Eaton, Eben<sup>r</sup> | 5 | 3 | 6 | 1 | |
| Turner, Elijah | 1 | | 4 | | | Sheppard, Reubin | 3 | 1 | 5 | | | Robinson, William | 1 | 2 | 1 | | |
| Fitch, Josiah | 2 | 4 | 6 | | | Douglass, James | 2 | 2 | 4 | | | Bennedict, Joel | 1 | 3 | 6 | | |
| Hall, Nath<sup>l</sup> | 4 | 2 | 5 | | | Simmons, Tho<sup>s</sup> | 1 | 2 | 5 | | | Bottom, Abel | 1 | | 2 | | |
| Davisson, Dan<sup>l</sup> | 1 | | 2 | | | Hall, Stephen | 1 | 2 | 1 | | | Gordon, James | 4 | 1 | | | |
| Harriss, John | 1 | 2 | 4 | | | Miller, Alexander, Jn<sup>r</sup> | 2 | 1 | 2 | | | Stevens, Jeduthan | 1 | 1 | 6 | | |
| Stearn, Boaz | 2 | 2 | 7 | | | Murdock, George, Jn | 2 | 4 | 7 | | | Lightfoot, Robert | 2 | | 2 | | |
| Balcom, Joseph | 2 | 2 | 5 | | | Dunham, Dan<sup>l</sup> | 2 | | 5 | | | Farlin, Hitchcock | 1 | 1 | 2 | | |
| Hunt, Nath<sup>l</sup> | 1 | 1 | 5 | | | Burges, John | 3 | | 2 | | | Avery, John | 2 | 1 | 2 | | |
| Jacobs, Benj<sup>n</sup> | 4 | 2 | 4 | | | Warren, Nath<sup>l</sup> | 1 | 2 | 1 | | | Fox, Sam<sup>l</sup> | 5 | 1 | 3 | 1 | |
| Simons, Nathan | 2 | 2 | 2 | | | M<sup>c</sup>Cinster, Hugh | 1 | 2 | 1 | 4 | | Pierce, John | 1 | 1 | 2 | | |
| Pryor, Joshua | 3 | 2 | 2 | | | Parks, Sam<sup>l</sup> | 1 | 3 | 2 | | | Coops, Eben<sup>r</sup> | 1 | 1 | 2 | | |
| Perkins, Phillip | 2 | 4 | 7 | | | Corey, Josiah, Sen<sup>r</sup> | 1 | 1 | 3 | | | Pierce, Timothy | 2 | | 3 | | |
| Jacobs, Joseph | 3 | 3 | 7 | | | Marsh, Nath<sup>l</sup> | 3 | 4 | 3 | | | Spalding, Andrew | 3 | | 4 | 1 | |
| Fuller, Ezra | 1 | | 2 | | | Warren, Jotham | 2 | 3 | 4 | | | Spalding, Hez<sup>a</sup> | 1 | 2 | 4 | | |
| Smith, Solomon | 1 | | 1 | | | Robinson, Eben<sup>r</sup> & co | 2 | 4 | 6 | 1 | | Spalding, Ezra | 1 | 2 | 4 | 2 | |
| Arnold, Nathan | 1 | 2 | 2 | | | Chase, Benj<sup>n</sup> | 4 | 3 | 2 | | | Dorrance, George | 2 | 1 | 2 | | |
| Huntington, Eleaz<sup>r</sup> | 3 | 2 | 8 | | | Wood, Noah | 4 | 1 | 3 | | | Ingraham, Reubin | 1 | 2 | 4 | | |
| Lane, James | 4 | 1 | 4 | | | Boyd, Abraham | 1 | 3 | 2 | | | Dunlop, Ledly, Jn | 2 | 4 | 3 | | |
| Huntington, Eleaz<sup>r</sup>, Jn<sup>r</sup> | 1 | | 2 | | | Richardson, William | 1 | 5 | 3 | | | Peire, Tho<sup>s</sup> | 1 | 2 | 3 | | 1 |
| | | | | | | Bordon, Joseph | 1 | 1 | 2 | | | Pierce, Josiah | 1 | 4 | 4 | | |
| **PLAINFIELD TOWN.** | | | | | | Bush, Stephen | 1 | 1 | 4 | | | Spalding, Joseph | 1 | | 2 | | |
| | | | | | | Levins, William | 3 | | 2 | | | Herrick, Andrew | 1 | 2 | 4 | | |
| Maxwell, James | 2 | 3 | 4 | | | Hall, Joshua | 1 | | 3 | 5 | | Sheppard, Joseph | 2 | 1 | 4 | | |
| Aply, John | 2 | | 2 | | | Hall, Jon<sup>a</sup> | 1 | 2 | 6 | | | Spalding, Reubin | 2 | 1 | 5 | | |
| Spalding, Sam<sup>l</sup> | 2 | 2 | 5 | | | Dean, Abijah | 2 | 1 | 6 | | | Knight, Isaac | 1 | 1 | 6 | 1 | |
| Palmer, Walter | 1 | 1 | 4 | 1 | | Hall, David | 1 | | 2 | | | Wheeler, Jonas | 2 | | 1 | | |
| Clark, Benj<sup>n</sup> | 1 | 1 | 2 | | | Witbert, Abner, Sr | 2 | | 4 | | | Herrick, Elisabeth | | | 3 | | |
| Phillips, Aaron | 3 | | 1 | | | Nicholls, Joseph | 2 | | 3 | | | Parrish, Elijah | 1 | 1 | 3 | | |

# HEADS OF FAMILIES—CONNECTICUT.

## WINDHAM COUNTY—Continued.

| NAME OF HEAD OF FAMILY. | Free white males of 16 years and upward, including heads of families. | Free white males under 16 years. | Free white females, including heads of families. | All other free persons. | Slaves. |
|---|---|---|---|---|---|
| **PLAINFIELD TOWN—con.** | | | | | |
| Wheeler, Saml | 2 | 4 | 5 | | |
| Howe, Noah | 1 | 1 | 2 | | |
| Cullar, William, Jr | 6 | | 3 | | |
| Cullar, Jonathan | 1 | 2 | 1 | | |
| Lester, Timothy | 5 | 2 | 6 | 4 | |
| Sheppard, Abraham | 4 | 2 | 5 | 1 | |
| Sheppard, John | 2 | 2 | 6 | 3 | 1 |
| Thurston, David | 2 | 1 | 2 | 4 | |
| Compton, William | 1 | 2 | 2 | | |
| Healey, Resolved | 2 | 1 | 3 | | |
| Key, Uriah | 2 | 1 | 3 | | |
| Key, Nathl | 2 | 1 | 5 | | |
| Davis, David | 1 | 1 | 6 | | |
| Howe, Jonathn | 1 | 1 | 2 | | |
| Picket, John | 1 | | 2 | | |
| Knight, Saml | 2 | 3 | 5 | 1 | |
| Parkhurst, Saml | 2 | 1 | 4 | 1 | |
| Sheppard, Stephen | 2 | 2 | 4 | | |
| Parkhurst, Isaac | 3 | 2 | 6 | | |
| Parkis, James | 3 | | 6 | | |
| Parkis, William | 2 | | 1 | | |
| Hammot, Jonathn | 3 | 2 | 6 | | |
| Cleavland, Truman | 2 | | 1 | | |
| Cleavland, Jesse | 2 | 1 | 4 | | |
| Russell, Josiah | 2 | 2 | 4 | | |
| Morse, Solomon | 1 | 1 | 1 | | |
| Morgan, Isaac | 4 | 1 | 6 | 1 | |
| Smith, Saml | 3 | 2 | 7 | | |
| Kenney, Cogshall | 2 | 2 | 3 | | |
| Sheppard, Lyda | | 1 | 3 | | |
| Sheppard, John | 2 | 1 | 9 | | |
| Kenny, David | 3 | 3 | 6 | | |
| Austin, Caleb | 1 | | 2 | | |
| Johnson, Jacob | 3 | 3 | 3 | 1 | |
| Spalding, Miner | 1 | 2 | 3 | | |
| Peise, Willard | 1 | | 2 | | |
| Cornet, Gideon | 2 | | 4 | | |
| Cornett, Gideon, 2d | 1 | 1 | 4 | | |
| Bennet, Stephen | 1 | | 3 | | |
| Russell, Jonah | 1 | 4 | 2 | | |
| Barber, John | 1 | | 2 | | |
| Morgan, Solomon | 3 | 3 | 6 | | |
| **POMFRET TOWN.** | | | | | |
| Grosvenor, Seth | 4 | 4 | 9 | | 1 |
| Dyer, John | 2 | 1 | 1 | | |
| Grosvenor, Ebenr | 5 | 2 | 5 | | |
| Grosvenor, Leml | 3 | 4 | 3 | 1 | |
| Gorton, John | 2 | 3 | 2 | | |
| Sabin, Josiah | 2 | 1 | 2 | | 1 |
| Sabin, Willm | 1 | 2 | 5 | | |
| Ainsworth, Jededh | 2 | 2 | 5 | | |
| Lee, Cyril | 2 | 3 | 3 | | |
| Chandler, Henry | 2 | 2 | 3 | | |
| Denison, Jabez | 2 | 1 | 2 | | |
| Sabin, Joseph | 1 | 3 | 4 | 1 | |
| Whitwell, An | 1 | 1 | 2 | | |
| Payson, John | 3 | 2 | 7 | | |
| Chandler, Joseph | 1 | 4 | 6 | 1 | |
| Chandler, Peter | 5 | 3 | 6 | 1 | |
| Underwood, Josiah | 2 | 3 | 3 | | |
| Greggs, Sarah | 1 | 2 | 5 | | |
| Shumway, Elijah | 1 | 2 | 1 | | |
| Aplin, James | 1 | 1 | 2 | | |
| Dresser, John | 1 | 2 | 3 | | |
| Chub, Prentiece | 3 | 1 | 7 | | 1 |
| Stephens, Nathanl | 1 | 2 | 3 | | |
| Goodale, David | 4 | 3 | 3 | | |
| Fuller, Caleb | 1 | | 3 | | |
| Grosvenor, Oliver | 2 | 3 | 3 | | |
| Laurence (Wido) | 1 | | 2 | | |
| Webster, Stephen | 1 | 4 | 4 | | |
| Gary, William | 5 | | 3 | | |
| Gary, Josiah | 1 | 2 | 2 | | |
| Cook, Eleazr | 1 | | 3 | | |
| Cook, Lot | 2 | 1 | 3 | | |
| White, Danl | 4 | 3 | 7 | | |
| Vose, Leml | 2 | | 4 | | |
| Bugbe, Thos | 1 | 1 | 3 | | |
| Smith, John R | 1 | 4 | 4 | | |
| Sabin, Elihu | 1 | 2 | 2 | | |
| Sawyer, James | 2 | 1 | 1 | | |
| Perrin, Saml | 3 | 1 | 1 | | |
| Lamb, John | 1 | 3 | 5 | | |
| Clark, Saml | 1 | 3 | 2 | | |
| Below, Peter | 2 | 2 | 4 | | |
| Flying, Abijah | 5 | 2 | 4 | | |
| Carpenter, Saml | 1 | | 1 | | |
| Dresser, Nathan | 2 | 2 | 3 | | |
| Herrington, Elisha | 1 | 1 | 3 | | |
| Leffingwell, Jereh | 3 | 1 | 1 | | |
| Gleason, Elisha | 2 | 2 | 5 | 1 | |
| Adams, Elihu | 3 | | 3 | | |
| Williams, James | 1 | 1 | 4 | | |
| **POMFRET TOWN—con.** | | | | | |
| Foster, Joseph | 1 | 1 | 3 | | |
| Holmes, Ebenr | 4 | 1 | 3 | | |
| Williams, Joshua | 1 | 3 | 3 | | |
| Durkee, Benjn | 2 | 2 | 7 | | |
| Cotton, John | 3 | | 3 | | |
| Cotton, Simon | 2 | 3 | 6 | | 1 |
| Smith, Benjn | 3 | 1 | 3 | | |
| Cheamberlin, Harvey | 2 | 1 | 2 | | |
| Westcoat, Hukely | 1 | 1 | 2 | 1 | |
| William, Stephen | 2 | 2 | 5 | | |
| Knight, Edward | 3 | 2 | 5 | | |
| Inman, Thos | 5 | 3 | 4 | | |
| White, Adam | 1 | 2 | 5 | 1 | 1 |
| Dana, Elijah | 2 | 2 | 3 | | |
| Ellis, Benjn | 3 | 2 | 5 | | |
| Hubard, Willard | 1 | 2 | 4 | | |
| McIntire, Benjn | 1 | 1 | 5 | | |
| Holmes, Benjn | 1 | 2 | | | |
| Richmond, John | 2 | | 3 | | |
| Grosvenor, Asa | 1 | 3 | 6 | | |
| May, Ithamar | 2 | 3 | 5 | | |
| Sabin, Jonathan | 3 | 1 | 3 | | |
| Bartholomew, Leonard | 1 | | 2 | | |
| Allen, Jonathan | 2 | | 3 | | |
| Allen, Nathl | 2 | 1 | 2 | | |
| Smith, Henry | 1 | 1 | 2 | | |
| Underwood, Lott | 2 | 1 | 2 | | |
| Sabin, Peter | 2 | 3 | 6 | | |
| Carpenter, Simon | 3 | | 5 | | |
| James, Freeman | 1 | 1 | 2 | | |
| Angel (Wid.) | 1 | 2 | 3 | | |
| Cady, Penuel | 2 | 1 | 4 | 1 | |
| Kingsley, Pardon | 4 | 1 | 4 | | |
| Sole, Jonathn | 1 | 2 | 1 | | |
| Phillips, Barnard | 1 | 2 | 4 | | |
| Detray, Peter | 1 | 1 | 2 | | |
| Child, Payson | 2 | 1 | 1 | 2 | |
| Cleavland, Aaron | 2 | 3 | 7 | | |
| White, James | 2 | | 2 | | |
| Quithy, Philip | 1 | 1 | 3 | | |
| Waters, John, sr | 3 | 2 | 5 | | |
| Liscomb, Thos | 1 | 1 | 6 | | |
| Collar, Isaac | 1 | 2 | 2 | | |
| Brown, David | 1 | 1 | 2 | | |
| Brown, Joseph | 1 | | 3 | | |
| Field, Jeremiah | 3 | 2 | 4 | | |
| Putnam, Peter S | 2 | 3 | 9 | | |
| Barry, John | 2 | 3 | 9 | | |
| Williams, Nehemiah | 1 | 2 | 5 | | 1 |
| White, Antipass | 1 | 3 | 4 | | |
| Kinsbury, Ebenr | 5 | 1 | 5 | | |
| Molhone, Evan | 1 | 2 | 6 | | 1 |
| Newel, Danl | 3 | | 3 | | |
| Chandler, Josiah | 3 | 2 | 4 | | |
| Waldo, Joanna | | | 3 | | |
| Averill, Stephen | 4 | 3 | 3 | | |
| Chandler, Philemon | 1 | 2 | 2 | | |
| Fay, John | 1 | | 2 | | |
| Cornel, Ezekiel | 4 | | 2 | | 1 |
| Holmes, David | 1 | | 2 | | |
| Spalding, Reubin | 4 | 1 | 2 | | |
| Stone, William | 2 | 1 | 1 | | |
| Perry, John | 1 | | 1 | | |
| Jenkinbottom, Obediah | 2 | | 2 | | |
| Randal, Jonathan | 2 | 2 | 2 | | 3 |
| Franklin, —— | 3 | 2 | 4 | | |
| sharp, Caleb | 2 | | 2 | | |
| Goodale, Richard | 1 | 4 | 7 | | |
| White, Jacob | 1 | 2 | 4 | | |
| Griggs, Heza | 1 | 2 | 4 | | |
| Chandler, Silas | 3 | 3 | 6 | | |
| Grosvenor, Chester | 1 | 1 | 3 | | |
| Wharton, James | 1 | 2 | 4 | | |
| Dana, Saml | 1 | 1 | 4 | | |
| Sharp, Gershom | 2 | | 1 | | |
| Cheedle, Elisabeth | | 1 | 2 | | |
| Sharp, Gershom, Secnd | 2 | 1 | 8 | | |
| Langworthy, Timothy | 1 | 1 | 4 | | |
| Tucker, Ephraim | 4 | 3 | 4 | | |
| Underwood, Timothy | 1 | 1 | 1 | | |
| Capron, John | 5 | | 6 | | |
| Cargell, Benjn | 4 | 3 | 5 | 1 | |
| Hosmer (Widow) | 1 | 2 | 3 | | |
| Gregg, Joseph | 1 | 2 | 5 | | |
| Sharp, Asa | 2 | 4 | 4 | | |
| Sabin, Isaac | 2 | 1 | 4 | | |
| Grosvenor, Thos | 4 | 2 | 4 | 1 | 2 |
| Waldo, Saml | 1 | 2 | 5 | | |
| Hall, Jonathn | 2 | 2 | 3 | 1 | 1 |
| Hubard, Benjn, Jnr | 5 | 3 | 5 | | |
| Putnam, Aaron | 2 | 1 | 5 | | 2 |
| Waldo, Abigene | 2 | 1 | 3 | | |
| William, John | 2 | 1 | 3 | | |
| Sabin, Joshua | 2 | 1 | 4 | | |
| Howard, Caleb | 1 | 1 | 8 | | |
| **POMFRET TOWN—con.** | | | | | |
| Brayton, David | 1 | 1 | 2 | | |
| Cleavland, Solomon | 2 | 1 | 4 | | |
| Dresser, Ebenr | 1 | | 3 | | |
| Brayton, Thos | 2 | 2 | 4 | | |
| Sessions, Amasa | 2 | 1 | 2 | | |
| Grosvenor, Amos | 4 | 1 | 1 | | |
| Ingalls, Zebulon, sr | 4 | 2 | | | |
| Dresser, Saml | 2 | | 5 | | |
| Baxter, Robert | 2 | 2 | 3 | | |
| Sessions, Squire | 4 | | 1 | | |
| Whipple, Saml | 2 | 3 | 3 | | |
| Trowbridge, Danl | 3 | 3 | 7 | | |
| Sawyer, Prescot | 2 | | 2 | | |
| Sawyer, William | 2 | 2 | 2 | | |
| Cuningham, Peter | 1 | 3 | 4 | | |
| Work, Alexander | 1 | 1 | 2 | | |
| Trowbridge, John | 2 | 1 | 4 | | |
| Grosvenor, Joshua, Jr | 1 | 1 | 4 | | |
| Grosvenor, Joshua | 1 | 4 | 4 | | |
| Wheeler, John | 3 | 1 | 4 | | |
| Ruggles, Edward | 2 | 1 | 4 | | |
| Stoddord, Ebenr | 2 | 1 | 2 | | |
| Lyon, Zurviah | 1 | 1 | 4 | | |
| Hoel, Ephraim | 3 | 2 | 4 | | |
| Chace, Seth | 4 | 3 | 4 | | |
| Slade, Jonathan | 1 | 3 | 4 | | |
| Trowbridge, James | 2 | 4 | 5 | | |
| Wheaton, James | 1 | 4 | 3 | | |
| Mathson, Nathn | 1 | 1 | 3 | | |
| Osgood, Zachh | 3 | 1 | 5 | | |
| Davison, Pheneas | 1 | 1 | 5 | | |
| Osgood, Appleton | 1 | 2 | 1 | | |
| Osgood, William, Jnr | 2 | 5 | 2 | | |
| Hartshorne, Saml | 2 | 1 | 3 | | |
| Stowel, Lemuel | 4 | 2 | 7 | | |
| Coats, Elisabeth | 1 | | 2 | | |
| Utley (Wido) | | 1 | 2 | | |
| Craft, Saml | 3 | 2 | 6 | | 1 |
| Gould, Jonathn | 1 | | 4 | | |
| Sumnar, Saml | 4 | | 6 | | |
| Ashley, Rachel | 1 | 2 | 4 | | |
| Adams, Noah | 2 | 2 | 2 | | |
| Greggs, Saml | 2 | 1 | 6 | | |
| Utley, Stephen | 2 | 2 | 5 | | |
| Ruggles, Benjn | 2 | 2 | | | |
| Greggs, Nathan | 1 | | 3 | 2 | |
| Greggs, David | 2 | 2 | 3 | | |
| Dodge, Neheh | 2 | 2 | 5 | | |
| Lyon, Thos | 1 | 1 | 4 | | |
| Abbot, William | 2 | | 3 | | |
| Trobridge, Mary | | | 4 | | |
| Lyon, Walter | 1 | 2 | 2 | | |
| Goodale, Zachh | 4 | 1 | 6 | | |
| Williams, Freelove | 1 | | 5 | | |
| Trusdell, Jeduthem | 1 | 3 | 1 | | |
| Goodale, Caleb | 1 | 2 | 2 | | |
| Goodale, Meachum | 1 | 2 | 3 | | |
| Sharp, David | 2 | 2 | 4 | | |
| Ingalls, Benjn | 2 | 1 | 3 | | |
| Kenny, Amos | 3 | 1 | 5 | | |
| Sharp, John | 3 | | 2 | | |
| Stevens, Leml | 1 | 3 | 2 | | |
| Raymond, Amazh | 1 | 1 | 2 | | |
| Winter, Ephraim | 2 | | 4 | | |
| Plank, William | 1 | 1 | 3 | | |
| Plank, Zebudiah | 1 | 4 | 2 | 2 | |
| Record, Silas | 2 | | 1 | | |
| Holmes, Jonathan | 1 | 2 | 3 | | |
| Ingalls, Joseph | 1 | 1 | 2 | | |
| Ingalls, Peter | 1 | 2 | 5 | | |
| Sharp, Robert | 2 | 1 | 1 | | |
| Bennet, John | 2 | | 2 | | |
| Dean, Nathan | 2 | | 1 | | |
| Sharp, Ruth | | 1 | 3 | | |
| Ingalls, Saml | 1 | | 5 | | |
| Webber, Benjn | 1 | 2 | 3 | | |
| Ingalls, John | 2 | | 4 | | |
| Sharp, Abigail | 2 | | 2 | | |
| Ingall, Thos | 1 | | 3 | | |
| Goodale, Danl | 1 | 3 | 3 | | |
| Allen, Benjn | 1 | | 3 | | |
| Fish, Danl | 2 | | 1 | | |
| Pratt, Danl | 2 | | 3 | | |
| Copeland, William | 1 | | 3 | | |
| Warner, Jared | 2 | 3 | 6 | 1 | 1 |
| Stoel, Elisha | 2 | 1 | 5 | | |
| Lord, Elisha | 3 | 2 | 9 | 2 | |
| Ingalls, Leml | 3 | 3 | 7 | | |
| Goodale, Amasa | 1 | 3 | 6 | | |
| Ruggles, Edward | 1 | | 4 | | |
| Ingalls, Ephraim | 2 | 2 | 4 | | |
| Boutwell, —— | 1 | | 2 | | |
| Field, William | 1 | 3 | 2 | | |
| Stephens, Aaron | 1 | | 1 | | |
| Childs, Charles | 1 | 1 | 6 | | |

149

## WINDHAM COUNTY—Continued.

| NAME OF HEAD OF FAMILY. | Free white males of 16 years and upward, including heads of families. | Free white males under 16 years. | Free white females, including heads of families. | All other free persons. | Slaves. | NAME OF HEAD OF FAMILY. | Free white males of 16 years and upward, including heads of families. | Free white males under 16 years. | Free white females, including heads of families. | All other free persons. | Slaves. | NAME OF HEAD OF FAMILY. | Free white males of 16 years and upward, including heads of families. | Free white males under 16 years. | Free white females, including heads of families. | All other free persons. | Slaves. |
|---|---|---|---|---|---|---|---|---|---|---|---|---|---|---|---|---|---|
| POMFRET TOWN—con. | | | | | | THOMPSON TOWN—con. | | | | | | THOMPSON TOWN—con. | | | | | |
| Force, Eben<sup>r</sup> | 1 | 1 | 2 | | | Green, Eben<sup>r</sup> | 1 | | 1 | | | Gleason, Nath<sup>l</sup> | 1 | 2 | 4 | | |
| Sharp, William | 3 | 2 | 4 | | | Moffat, Micajah | 3 | 1 | 2 | | | Turtolot, Erick | 1 | | 1 | | |
| Cresey, Eben<sup>r</sup> | 2 | | 2 | | | Burrall, John | 2 | 3 | 5 | | | Turtolot, Joshua | 2 | 1 | 5 | | |
| Payne, Nathan | 1 | 3 | 6 | 1 | | Wakefield, John | 2 | 1 | 4 | | | Turtolot, Barnabas | 2 | 2 | 5 | | |
| THOMPSON TOWN. | | | | | | Green, Dexter | 1 | 2 | 2 | | | Turtolot, Mich<sup>l</sup> | 2 | 1 | 3 | | |
| | | | | | | Whitmon, John | 1 | | 1 | | | Turtolot, Isaac | 1 | 2 | 4 | | |
| | | | | | | Cutlar, Sam<sup>l</sup> | 1 | | 1 | | | Newall, Sam<sup>l</sup> | 2 | 2 | 4 | | |
| Johnson, Smith | 3 | 2 | 5 | | | Blackman, Jacob | 1 | 2 | 5 | | | Jacobs, John, Jn<sup>r</sup> | 1 | 4 | 3 | | |
| Halsey, Samuel | 1 | 1 | 2 | | | Moffat, Eli | 1 | 1 | 2 | | | Russell, William | 2 | 2 | 2 | | |
| Plank, Robert | 1 | 2 | 6 | | | Wilson, James | 2 | 2 | 4 | | | Smith, Israel | 1 | 2 | 5 | | |
| Brown, Jesse | 1 | 4 | 5 | | | Marrion, Joseph, Jn<sup>r</sup> | 4 | 3 | 6 | | | Cummins, Josiah, Jr | 1 | 1 | 5 | | |
| Underwood, William | 1 | 1 | 4 | | | Marrion, Israel | 1 | 2 | 4 | | | Haskall, Jon<sup>h</sup> | 1 | 4 | 8 | | |
| Gay, Elisha | 4 | 1 | 4 | | | Marrion, Joseph | 1 | | 1 | | | Soams, Consider | 2 | 1 | 3 | | |
| Sessions, Darious | 1 | 1 | 3 | | | Marrion, Benj<sup>n</sup> | 1 | 1 | 1 | | | Jammes, Solomon | 1 | 6 | 4 | | |
| Parks, Isaac | 1 | 2 | 5 | | | Harriss, Joseph | 2 | 1 | 3 | | | Fay, Sam<sup>l</sup> | 2 | 2 | 5 | | |
| Lee, Joel | 1 | 5 | 7 | | | Carrol, Amos | 4 | | 2 | | | Freeman, Joseph | 3 | 2 | 2 | | |
| Gay, Richard | 2 | | 3 | | | Richard, Dan<sup>l</sup> | 1 | | 2 | | | Haskall, David | 1 | 2 | 1 | | |
| Learned, Dan<sup>l</sup> | 3 | 5 | 4 | | | Russell, Joseph | 2 | 3 | 4 | | | Alton, David | 1 | 2 | 7 | | |
| Gimman, George | 1 | 1 | 7 | | | Richards, Israel | 1 | 4 | 6 | | | Davis, Thomas | 1 | 3 | 1 | | |
| Brown, Joseph | 2 | 3 | 4 | | | Smith, Abraham | 2 | 1 | 2 | | | Trumbull, John | 1 | 2 | 3 | | |
| Larned, Simon | 2 | 3 | 4 | | | Burral, Benjamin | 1 | | 4 | | | Town, Joseph | 3 | 1 | 6 | | |
| Gay, Eben<sup>e</sup> | 2 | 2 | 5 | | | Wood, Ephraim A | 1 | | 3 | | | Town, Joseph, Jn<sup>r</sup> | 1 | 2 | 2 | | |
| Willis, Joab | 1 | 6 | 2 | | | Morse, Joshua | 3 | | 3 | | | Grant, Tho<sup>s</sup> & co | 2 | | 5 | | |
| Lee, Allen | | 1 | 4 | | | Dike, Thomas | 1 | 3 | 5 | | | Prince, Sam<sup>l</sup> | 1 | 3 | 3 | | |
| Lee, Joseph | 1 | 3 | 2 | | | Dike, James | 1 | 1 | 4 | | | Elliot, Sam<sup>l</sup> | 1 | 1 | 2 | | |
| Woodward, John | 1 | 2 | 3 | | | Bigsby, Sam<sup>l</sup> | 1 | | 2 | | | Elliot, Tho<sup>s</sup>, Jn<sup>r</sup> | 1 | 3 | 2 | | |
| Record, Joseph | 1 | | | | | Bigsby, Jacob | 1 | 3 | 1 | | | Stone, Jon<sup>a</sup> | 1 | 1 | 4 | | |
| Thayer, Reubin | 1 | 1 | 3 | | | Bigsby, Moses | 1 | 1 | 1 | | | Town, William | 1 | 2 | 1 | | |
| Lee, Jona<sup>th</sup> | 3 | 1 | 3 | | | Pratt, John | 1 | | 4 | | | Stone, Levi | 1 | 2 | 5 | | |
| Thayer, Nath<sup>l</sup> | 1 | 3 | 3 | | | Rodes, James | 2 | | 1 | | | Beston, Asa | 1 | | 2 | | |
| Ruggles, Sam<sup>l</sup> | 1 | 1 | 1 | | | Burlingham, Ezekiel | 1 | 6 | 6 | | | Whittemore, Caleb | 1 | 2 | 1 | | |
| Demon, Joseph | 1 | 2 | 2 | | | Turtolot, Israel | 1 | 3 | 3 | | | Fay, Neh<sup>h</sup>, Sen<sup>r</sup> | 1 | | 2 | | |
| Converse, Payne | 3 | 4 | 4 | | | Kimball, Sam<sup>l</sup> | 2 | 2 | 4 | | | Belcher, David | 2 | 2 | 3 | | |
| Davis, Simon | 3 | 2 | 8 | | | Jacob, John | 4 | 1 | 1 | | | Prince, Robert | 1 | 4 | 3 | | |
| Paul, David | 1 | 2 | 6 | | | Atwell, John | 2 | 2 | 2 | | | Prince, Joseph | 2 | 1 | 3 | | |
| Griggsby, Nath<sup>l</sup> | 1 | 2 | 2 | | | Bales, Elijah | 3 | 5 | 3 | | | Prince, Eben<sup>r</sup> | 2 | | 2 | | |
| Merriam, Benj<sup>a</sup> | 3 | 1 | 4 | | | Martin, John | 3 | 1 | 4 | | | Whitmore, William | 1 | | 2 | | |
| Wilson, John | 1 | 2 | 5 | | | Mason, Hale | 1 | 2 | 1 | | | Whitmore, William, Jn<sup>r</sup> | 2 | 4 | 4 | | |
| Learned, Henry | 1 | 2 | 5 | | | Cummins, Josiah | 2 | | 4 | | | Ormsbe, Tho<sup>s</sup> | 2 | | 2 | | |
| Whitmore, Jabez | 1 | 3 | 4 | | | Bigsby, Nathan | 3 | 2 | 5 | | | Crosby, Elijah | 1 | 2 | 2 | | |
| Wilson, Sam<sup>l</sup> | 3 | 3 | 6 | | | Watson, Mathew | 2 | | 2 | | | Elliot, Roger | 1 | 2 | 3 | | |
| Paul, Jonathan | 1 | 3 | 2 | | | Town, Archelous | 2 | 2 | 3 | | | Stone, Barsom | 3 | 3 | 4 | | |
| Cleft, Obed<sup>h</sup> | 5 | 2 | 8 | | | Duncan, William | 1 | 1 | 6 | | | Upham, Ivory | 2 | | 5 | | |
| Learned, Benj<sup>n</sup> | 2 | 3 | 5 | | | Wilson, Sharp | | | | | 2 | Upham, Luther | 3 | | 7 | | |
| Russell, Jon<sup>a</sup>, Jn<sup>r</sup> | 3 | 2 | 4 | | | Watson, Abigal | 6 | 4 | 5 | | | Curtiss, Japhet | 1 | 3 | 6 | | |
| Briggs, Jon<sup>a</sup> | 1 | 1 | 4 | | | Luther, Isaac | 1 | | 1 | | | Upham, Jonath<sup>a</sup> | 1 | | 2 | | |
| Russell, Dan<sup>l</sup> | 2 | 1 | 6 | | | Bailey, John | 2 | 1 | 3 | | | Upham, Isaac | 1 | 3 | 1 | | |
| Russell, Jon<sup>a</sup> | 1 | 3 | 2 | | | Keith, John | 4 | 3 | 6 | | | Alby, Joseph | 2 | 2 | 2 | | |
| Hicks, Chase | 1 | 1 | 5 | | | Russell, Noadiah | 3 | 1 | 2 | | 1 | Childs, Nath<sup>l</sup> | 2 | | 3 | | |
| Hopkins, Jere<sup>h</sup> | 1 | 4 | 2 | | | Dresser, Asa | 1 | | 2 | | | Shiffields, Nath<sup>l</sup> | 2 | | 3 | | |
| Cutlar, Solomon | 1 | 2 | 4 | | | Dresser, Jacob | 3 | 2 | 7 | | 6 | Child, Elijah | 1 | 3 | 2 | | |
| Blackmore, Ezekel | 1 | 2 | 3 | | | Cooper, John | 1 | 2 | 2 | | | Converse, Elijah | 1 | 2 | 3 | | |
| Reynolds, Jacob | 1 | 1 | 1 | | | Flint, Joseph | 2 | | 4 | | | Curtiss, Charles | 1 | 2 | 3 | | |
| Green, Seth | 1 | 2 | 4 | | | Flint, Davis | 1 | 2 | 7 | | | Haughton, Edward | 1 | 3 | 4 | | |
| Green, Pheneas | 1 | | 3 | | | Wilson, Jonathan | 2 | | 6 | | | Payne, Joseph | 1 | | 1 | | |
| Leonard, Giliver | 1 | 2 | 3 | | | Keith, Stephen | 3 | 3 | 4 | | | Hendrick, Dan<sup>l</sup> | 1 | | 1 | | |
| Plank, John | 1 | | 1 | | | Bartholomew, Benjamin | 1 | 2 | 4 | | | Copeland, William | 1 | 1 | 2 | | |
| Richmond, Michael | 2 | | 4 | | | Nichols, Elijah | 3 | 1 | 2 | | | Stone, Simon | 2 | 1 | 6 | | |
| Richmond, Oliver | 1 | 2 | 5 | | | Elliot, Thomas | 2 | 2 | 2 | | | Corban, Moses | 2 | 1 | 1 | | |
| Westcoat, Amos | 2 | 1 | 4 | | | Elliot, John | 1 | 2 | 2 | | | Atwood, Francis | 1 | | 2 | | |
| Converse, Jacob | 3 | 3 | 6 | | | Elliot, Joel | 2 | 1 | 3 | | | Bowen, Asa | 1 | 2 | 4 | | |
| Comstock, Israel | 3 | 2 | 3 | | | Green, John | 2 | 2 | 3 | | | Ormsby, Jesse | 1 | 1 | 1 | | |
| Benson, Barack | 1 | 2 | 3 | | | Bates, Isackas | 2 | 2 | 3 | | | Jewit, Joseph | 2 | 2 | 7 | | |
| Coats, Benj<sup>n</sup> | 1 | 1 | 6 | | | White, David | 1 | 3 | 1 | | | Blackmar, Jona<sup>th</sup> | 1 | | 2 | | |
| Robins, Seth | 1 | 1 | 1 | | | White, Jona<sup>th</sup> | 1 | | 2 | | | Carpenter, Elijah | 1 | 2 | 2 | | |
| Robins, John | 2 | 1 | 2 | | | Johnson, Jotham | 1 | 2 | 2 | | | Potter, Edmond | 1 | 1 | 1 | | |
| Knap, Lemuel | 2 | 1 | 6 | 2 | | Starr, Eben<sup>r</sup> | 2 | 6 | 3 | | | Barret, John | 1 | 1 | 2 | | |
| Gleason, John | 1 | 1 | 4 | | | Woodward, Comfort | 1 | 2 | 3 | | | Elliot, Francis | 2 | | 2 | | |
| Robins, David | 1 | 2 | 2 | | | Stockwell, Peter | 2 | 2 | 5 | | | Elithorp, Nath<sup>l</sup> | 3 | | 3 | | |
| Mason, Abraham | 2 | | 6 | | | Plummer, Israel | 1 | | 3 | | | Elithorp, Henry | 2 | 3 | 3 | | |
| Jocelin, Edward | 1 | 2 | 5 | | | Stockwell, Israel | 2 | | 5 | | | Barrows, Printrise | 3 | 1 | 3 | | |
| Jocelin, Israel | 1 | 1 | 7 | | | Beston, Jeremiah | 2 | 3 | 5 | | | White, Jacob | 3 | 1 | 1 | | |
| Porter, Jona<sup>n</sup> | 2 | 1 | 6 | | | Walker, Andrew | 1 | 4 | 2 | | | Elliot, John | 3 | 1 | 2 | | |
| Cole, Isaac | 1 | 1 | 3 | | | Robinson, Aaron | 2 | 1 | 4 | | | Nichols, Elijah | 2 | 1 | 2 | | |
| Porter, Flint | 1 | 1 | 4 | | | Robinson, Moses | 2 | 1 | 10 | | | Gay, Richard | 2 | | 2 | | |
| Jinkham, Abel | 1 | 3 | 3 | | | Cole, Isaac | 2 | 2 | 3 | | | Luther | 3 | 1 | 5 | | |
| Coats, James | 1 | | 1 | | | Plumber, John | 1 | 3 | 6 | | | Lee, Joel | 2 | 3 | 5 | | |
| Cutlar, Amos | 3 | 2 | 4 | | | Porter, Jonathan | 3 | 1 | 9 | | | Parks, Isaac | 2 | 1 | 6 | | |
| Polluck, Charles | 2 | | 4 | | | Carrol, Nath<sup>l</sup> | 1 | 2 | 4 | | | Cady, John | 2 | 2 | 3 | | |
| Coats, Hez<sup>h</sup> | 1 | | 1 | | | Bigsby, Aaron | 1 | 1 | 3 | | | Bundy, Eben<sup>r</sup> | 5 | | 7 | | |
| Jocelin, Joseph | 3 | 2 | 3 | | | Bigsby, Jesse | 1 | 3 | 1 | | | Ellis, Jona<sup>th</sup> | 4 | | 3 | | |
| Wheeler, Jeremiah | 1 | 3 | 2 | | | Billows, Hez<sup>a</sup> | 1 | 3 | 3 | | | Keith, Peter | 3 | 1 | 5 | | |
| Jacobs, Asa | 1 | | | | | Bigsby, Amos | 2 | | 2 | | | Keith, Barack | 1 | 3 | 3 | | |
| Joslin, Jesse | 1 | | 3 | | | May, Sam<sup>l</sup> | 2 | 4 | 2 | | | Dwight, William | 2 | 5 | 3 | | |
| Emerson, Simeon | 2 | 3 | 3 | | | Rich, Israel | 3 | | 5 | | | Nichalls, Jon<sup>a</sup>, Jn<sup>r</sup> | 3 | 1 | 4 | | |
| Leggs, Thomas | 1 | 1 | 1 | | | Brown, Rufus | 1 | 2 | 3 | | | Prince, Abel | 1 | 2 | 2 | | |
| Hoyle, Richard | 1 | 2 | 4 | | | Howard, Simon | 1 | 2 | 4 | | | Barret, Joseph | 2 | | 3 | | |
| Hoyle, W<sup>m</sup> | 1 | | 2 | | | Howard, Eben<sup>r</sup> | 1 | | 7 | | | Everden, Walter | 1 | 1 | 2 | | |
| Covil, Eben<sup>r</sup> | 2 | 3 | 5 | | | Bates, John | 2 | 2 | 3 | | | Perrin, Dan<sup>l</sup> | 2 | 5 | 4 | | |
| Allen, Abraham | 2 | 7 | 8 | | | Cummins, Amos | 1 | 1 | 2 | | | Elliot, Asael | 2 | 2 | 3 | | |
| Green, Benj<sup>n</sup> | 1 | 2 | 4 | | | Brown, Stephen | 2 | 1 | 3 | | | Thayer, Phillip | 2 | 2 | 2 | | |
| Fitz, Eben<sup>r</sup> | 2 | 1 | 2 | | | Ballard, Zach<sup>us</sup> | 2 | 1 | 3 | | | Alger, Nath<sup>l</sup> | 2 | 3 | 4 | | |
| Green, Amos | 4 | 2 | 4 | | | Stone, Henry & Co | 3 | 4 | 3 | | | Alger, Abraham | 1 | 2 | 1 | | |
| Barret, John | 2 | 2 | 2 | | | Carrol, John | 1 | 3 | 3 | | | Chaffee, Abiel | 2 | 3 | 8 | | |
| Burrall, Jacob | 1 | 1 | 1 | | | | | | | | | | | | | | |

# HEADS OF FAMILIES—CONNECTICUT.

## WINDHAM COUNTY—Continued.

| NAME OF HEAD OF FAMILY. | Free white males of 16 years and upward, including heads of families. | Free white males under 16 years. | Free white females, including heads of families. | All other free persons. | Slaves. | NAME OF HEAD OF FAMILY. | Free white males of 16 years and upward, including heads of families. | Free white males under 16 years. | Free white females, including heads of families. | All other free persons. | Slaves. | NAME OF HEAD OF FAMILY. | Free white males of 16 years and upward, including heads of families. | Free white males under 16 years. | Free white females, including heads of families. | All other free persons. | Slaves. |
|---|---|---|---|---|---|---|---|---|---|---|---|---|---|---|---|---|---|
| **THOMPSON TOWN—continued.** | | | | | | **VOLUNTOWN TOWN—continued.** | | | | | | **VOLUNTOWN TOWN—continued.** | | | | | |
| Hosmer, David | 1 | 1 | 3 | | | Stiles, Amos | 1 | | 3 | 1 | | Griffin, George | 2 | 3 | 4 | | |
| Bennet, James | 2 | 2 | 4 | | | Gordon, John | 1 | | 3 | | | Stephens, Simon | 2 | 2 | 4 | | |
| Barret, Moses | 1 | 4 | 5 | | | Cambell, Joseph | 3 | | 4 | | | Green, Jonathan | 1 | 3 | 2 | | |
| Spalding, Saml | 1 | 1 | 1 | | | Gordon, John, Jnr | 2 | 2 | 3 | | | Green, Benja | 1 | | 1 | | |
| Barret, Lemul | 3 | 4 | 7 | | | Douglass, John, Senr | 2 | 3 | 3 | | | Peirce, Preserved | 1 | 1 | 1 | | |
| Alton, William | 3 | 2 | 5 | | | Kegwin, William | 2 | | 6 | | | Randall, Isaac | 1 | | 1 | | |
| Carpenter, Saml | 3 | 3 | 6 | | | Kegwin, Nicholas | 2 | | 6 | | | Crandal, Ezra | 1 | 1 | 1 | | |
| Alton, John | 3 | 3 | 4 | | | Frink, Usual | 2 | 1 | 3 | | | Bligh, Benja | 4 | 3 | 2 | | |
| Barret, Oliver | 3 | 3 | 4 | | | Frink, Zachh | 2 | | 2 | | | Campbell, Allen | 2 | 4 | 7 | | |
| Hosmer, James | 3 | 1 | 2 | | | Dixon, John, Senr | 1 | | 1 | | | Larkham, John | 2 | 1 | 5 | | |
| Corban, Moses | 4 | 2 | 7 | | | Kennedy, David | 3 | 3 | 4 | | | Shepard, Nathl | 2 | 1 | 4 | | |
| Corban, Clement | 2 | 5 | 3 | | | Stuart, Saml | 2 | 3 | 8 | | 1 | Larkham, Lott | 2 | 1 | 3 | | |
| Houghton, Ephraim | 3 | | 4 | | | Frink, Saml | 1 | 1 | 4 | | | Colegrove, Benja | 3 | | 3 | | |
| Palmer, Saml | 3 | 2 | 4 | | | Campbell, Noble | 1 | 2 | 6 | | | Green, Saml | 1 | 2 | 5 | | |
| Corban, Jonath | 1 | 3 | 4 | | | Wyley, Joseph | 4 | | 6 | | | Douglass, William | 2 | 1 | 4 | | |
| Corban, Peleg | 2 | 3 | 5 | | | Pulman, John | 1 | 4 | 3 | | | Lewis, Saml | 2 | 2 | 5 | | |
| Chaffee, Thomas | 1 | 2 | 4 | | | Budlong, Joseph | 2 | 2 | 4 | | | Wintor, Weedon | 1 | 2 | 1 | | |
| Childs, Nathl | 2 | 1 | 3 | | | Budlong, David | 1 | 1 | 3 | | | Poplestone, Gideon | 1 | | 1 | | |
| Childs, Elijah | 1 | 3 | 2 | | | Rode, William | 1 | | 1 | | | Weaver, Thos | 3 | 5 | 3 | | |
| Converse, Elijah | 1 | 1 | 3 | | | Lewis, Caleb | 1 | 1 | 1 | | | Douglass, William, Jnr | 1 | 1 | 2 | | |
| Hebard, Jona | 1 | | 1 | | | Adams, Stephen | 3 | 2 | 2 | | | Peirce, Edward | 1 | 2 | 2 | | |
| Winter, Asa | 1 | 1 | 4 | | | Adams, William | 1 | 1 | 1 | | | Martin, Stephen | 2 | 2 | 5 | | |
| Humes, Saml | 2 | 1 | 3 | | | Adams, Reubin | 1 | | 4 | | | Campbell, James | 3 | | 6 | | |
| Chaffee, Chester | 2 | 2 | 3 | | | Wilkinson, William, Jnr | 2 | 1 | 4 | | | Palmer, Roswill | 1 | | 1 | | |
| Chaffee, James | 1 | 1 | 6 | | | Campbell, John | 1 | 3 | 3 | | | Campbell, William | 1 | 3 | 5 | | |
| Chaffee, Calvan | 1 | 1 | 2 | | | Kennedy, Daniel | 2 | 2 | 6 | | | Campbell, Partrick | 1 | 1 | 1 | | |
| Chaffee, Saml | 1 | 2 | 3 | | | Partelow, Jonas | 1 | 1 | 3 | | | Blyth, Joseph | 1 | 2 | 2 | | |
| Winter, Amasa | 1 | 2 | 1 | | | Partelow, Thomas | 2 | | 6 | | | Jackson, Elias | 1 | 3 | 4 | | |
| Webster, John | 3 | | 5 | | | Wedge, Amos | 2 | 1 | 6 | | | Hoxey, Joseph | 3 | 1 | 4 | | |
| Perry, Josiah | 2 | 1 | 4 | | | Kennedy, Joseph | 1 | 2 | 3 | | | Gallop, Saml | 1 | 3 | 8 | | |
| Brown, Joseph | 1 | | 1 | | | Gates, Phineas | 1 | 3 | 2 | | | Campbell. Archibald | 2 | 2 | 5 | | |
| Brown, Joseph, Jnr | 1 | 1 | 2 | | | Alexander, Joseph | 3 | | 4 | | | Wilkinson, James Y | 1 | | 2 | | |
| Brown, Henry | 1 | 1 | 4 | | | Campbell, Amos | 4 | 1 | 7 | | | Lewis, Caleb | 1 | 1 | 1 | | |
| Thayer, Oliver | 3 | 1 | 3 | | | Alexander, James, Jnr | 2 | 1 | 1 | | | Layton, Noyes | 1 | 1 | 3 | | |
| Rawson, Nathl | 1 | 1 | 1 | | | Campbell, James, Jnr | 1 | | 2 | | | Lewis, Asa | 1 | 1 | 1 | | |
| Fairbanks, Benja | 2 | | 3 | | | Hunter, John | 1 | | 3 | | | Mathewson, Joshua | 1 | 2 | 2 | | |
| Bowers, John, Jnr | 1 | 3 | 4 | | | Stanton, Joseph | 1 | 4 | 4 | | | Gorton, William | 2 | 1 | 3 | | |
| Palmer, Saml | 1 | | 1 | | | Sweet, Ezekiel | 2 | 2 | 4 | | | Stewart, John | 2 | 1 | 6 | | |
| Phips, Jason | 4 | 2 | 5 | | | Alexander, John | 1 | 2 | 7 | | | Briggs, James | 2 | 1 | 4 | 1 | |
| Whitmore, John | 2 | 2 | 2 | | | Wyley, Moses | 1 | 4 | 5 | | | Campbell, John | 3 | | 4 | | |
| Brown, Nathan | 2 | 1 | 2 | | | Swift, James | 1 | | 1 | | | Jackson, Robert | 1 | | 2 | | |
| Brown, Rufus | 1 | 4 | 2 | | | Lewis, Eleazr | 1 | 3 | 5 | | | Gallop, John | 1 | 3 | 4 | | |
| Brown, Charles | 2 | 2 | 3 | | | Bowdist, Joseph | 1 | 1 | 1 | | | Briggs, William | 1 | 4 | 2 | | 1 |
| Bowers, John | 1 | 2 | 5 | | | Colegrove, Benjn, Jnr | 1 | 1 | 1 | | | Montgomery, John | 1 | 1 | 2 | | |
| Bowers, Alpheus | 1 | | 1 | | | Rhodes, John | 4 | 4 | 3 | | | Porter, Micaiah | 2 | 4 | 2 | | |
| Houghton, Ephraim | 2 | | 3 | | | Rodes, John, Jnr | 1 | | 2 | | | Gordon, Maryam | 4 | | 2 | | |
| Holbrook, Thos | 1 | | 2 | | | Coats, Heza | 1 | 1 | 1 | | | Gallop, Wheeler | 2 | 1 | 4 | 1 | |
| Corban, Ezra | 1 | 2 | 3 | 1 | | Brown, John | 3 | | 3 | | | Hutchinson, Elisha | 1 | 4 | 3 | | |
| Brown, Aaron | 1 | | 6 | | | Robins, Saml | 3 | 2 | 6 | | | Gallop, Bennadam | 1 | 2 | 2 | 1 | |
| Holbrook, John | 5 | 1 | 6 | | | Morgan, Peter | 2 | 1 | 3 | | | Prince (Negro) | | | | 3 | |
| Green, Ira | 1 | 2 | 2 | | | Lewis, Nathan | 2 | | 3 | | | Button, Newberry | 1 | 4 | 3 | | |
| Blackmore, Levi | 3 | | 2 | | | Robins, Saml, Jnr | 1 | 2 | 3 | | | McGollsgal, James | 2 | 1 | 4 | | |
| Bugbee, Cathare | 1 | | 2 | | | Cady, Martha | 4 | 2 | 4 | | | Busey, Titus | 2 | 3 | 1 | | 3 |
| Sumner, Danl | 1 | 2 | 4 | | | Kenney, Saml | 2 | 2 | 5 | | | Matthewson, George | 1 | 1 | 7 | | |
| Gleason, William | 2 | 1 | 5 | | | Kenney, James | 3 | 3 | 3 | | | Mathewson, Dutifull | 1 | 1 | 2 | | |
| Chandler, Theophilus | 2 | 2 | 3 | | | Morgan, Eleanor | 1 | | 3 | | | Mathewson, Reuben | 1 | 1 | 1 | | |
| Sabin, Peter | 1 | 1 | 3 | | | Fish, Saml | 2 | 1 | 4 | | | Sweet, Ebenr | 1 | 1 | 1 | | |
| | | | | | | Robins, Lorin | 4 | 2 | 4 | | | Smith, John | | | | 3 | |
| **VOLUNTOWN TOWN.** | | | | | | Kenney, Abel | 1 | 3 | 6 | | | Bailey, Adonijah | 2 | | 1 | | |
| Dorrance, Archibald | 3 | 1 | 3 | 1 | | Kenney, Ira | 3 | 3 | 5 | | | Congdoll, Benjn | 2 | 2 | 2 | | |
| Hard, Josiah | 3 | 1 | 3 | | | Robins, Moses | 2 | 2 | 3 | | | Wilson, Robert | 3 | 1 | 3 | | |
| Spener, George | 1 | 3 | 4 | | | Fisk, Elias, &c | 3 | 4 | 7 | | | Vaughn, Danl | 2 | 3 | 4 | | |
| Henry, John | 3 | 1 | 4 | 1 | | Peirce, William | 1 | 1 | 2 | | | Vaughn, Jesse | 5 | 3 | 6 | | |
| Kenyon, John | 2 | 3 | 7 | | | Fisk, Moses, Senr | 1 | | 2 | | | Mathson, Thomas | 1 | 2 | 3 | | |
| Kenyon, Saml | 1 | 3 | 3 | | | Fisk, Moses, Jnr | 1 | 3 | 3 | | | Mathewson, Caleb | 1 | 1 | 3 | | |
| Smith, Ebenr | 3 | 3 | 3 | | | Wilkinson, William | 2 | | 2 | | | Whitford, Asa | 1 | 2 | 3 | | |
| Burlingham, Nathan | 4 | 1 | 3 | | | Houston, John | 1 | 1 | 3 | 1 | 1 | Wilbar, Oliver | 2 | 3 | 3 | | |
| Potter, Phillip | 3 | 2 | 5 | | | Gallop, Benja | 3 | 1 | 11 | | | Marcy, Jereh | 2 | | 2 | | |
| Tuckerman, Benjamin | 1 | 2 | 1 | | | Davis, Bill | 2 | 3 | 3 | | | Wyley, John | 1 | 1 | 4 | | |
| Dixon, Robert | 5 | 2 | 7 | | 11 | Palmer, Benjn | 3 | | 3 | 1 | | Mathewson, Jesse | 2 | 1 | 2 | | |
| Amy, Elisha | 2 | 1 | 8 | | | Palmer, Elihu | 2 | 2 | 5 | | | Harris, Jonathn | 2 | 3 | 3 | | |
| Smith, Francis | 3 | 2 | 6 | | | Hillyard, Jonathan | 1 | 1 | 5 | | | Green, Jonathan | 1 | 1 | 1 | | |
| Avery, Joseph | 2 | 1 | 4 | | | Ray, Gershom | 1 | 2 | 3 | | | Stone, William | 1 | 1 | 1 | | |
| Green, John | 2 | 2 | 2 | | | Palmer, Jonath | 1 | 3 | 6 | | | Douglass, Saml | 3 | 2 | 5 | | |
| Dorrance, Lemuel | 2 | 3 | 5 | | 2 | Palmer, Joseph | 2 | 2 | 3 | | | Thompson, Thomas | 2 | 1 | 4 | | |
| Smith, Phebe | 2 | | 2 | | | Gilman, Robert | 2 | 1 | 4 | | | Pentnodle, George | 1 | 1 | 1 | | |
| Pearks, Robert | 1 | 1 | 3 | | | Randall, Amos | 2 | 4 | 5 | | | Peavey, Ichabd | 2 | 3 | 3 | | |
| Dixon, Thomas | 2 | 1 | 2 | | | Randall, Peleg | 1 | 3 | 3 | | | Bennet, William | 1 | 1 | 3 | | |
| Gallop, David | 2 | | 1 | | | Randall, Nicholas | 2 | 4 | 3 | | | Bennet, Benjn | 1 | 2 | 2 | | |
| Dixon, John | 3 | 4 | 7 | | | Gallop, William | 2 | 2 | 3 | | | Knox, James | 1 | 2 | 3 | | |
| Gordon, Thomas | 2 | | 1 | | 2 | Gallop, Jabez | 1 | 1 | 2 | | | Knox, Andrew | 1 | 2 | 3 | | |
| Edmonds, Andrew | 3 | 4 | 4 | | | Gallop, Lyda | 1 | 2 | 4 | | | Montgomery, Robert | 2 | 1 | 4 | | |
| Gordon, Archibald | 1 | 1 | 4 | | | Newton, Mathew | 3 | 2 | 3 | | | Montgomery, Asa | 2 | 4 | 6 | | |
| Gallop, Isaac | 3 | | 3 | | | Corning, Benja | 1 | 1 | 2 | | | Riser, Thos | 1 | 1 | 1 | | |
| Gallop, Nathl | 2 | | 2 | | | Newton, Jabez | 1 | 2 | 3 | | | Gibson, James | 1 | 1 | 1 | | |
| Gallop, William | 2 | 1 | 3 | | | Brown, John, Jnr | 1 | 2 | 2 | | | Angell, Thos | 1 | 1 | 1 | | |
| Cole, Thomas | 2 | 1 | 3 | | | Palmer, Elyh | 1 | 3 | 5 | | | Kinyon, Sylvester | 3 | 1 | 2 | | |
| Douglass, John | 3 | 4 | 5 | | | Stanbury, John | 1 | 2 | 3 | | | Burges, Thos | 1 | 1 | 4 | | |
| Gallop, Nathl | 2 | 1 | 3 | | | Safford, Mary | | | 3 | | | Burges, Benyh | 2 | 4 | 4 | | |
| Gallop, Saml | 1 | 1 | 2 | | | Palmer, Ziba | 1 | 4 | 1 | | | Montgomery, Josiah | 1 | 1 | 1 | | |
| Dow, Benjn | 2 | 1 | 3 | | | Randall, Joseph | 2 | 1 | 3 | | | Spence, Joshua | 2 | 3 | 8 | | |
| Frink, Matthias | 2 | 2 | 3 | | | Palmer, Uriel | 1 | 3 | 1 | | | Green, Thos | 1 | | 1 | | |
| Dow, Ebenr | 3 | 1 | 3 | | | Palmer, Pheneas | 1 | | 2 | | | Frink, Joshua | 3 | 4 | 5 | | |
| Dow, Nathan | 2 | | 2 | | | Newton, Desire | | | 2 | | | Montgomery, Sarah | 2 | 1 | 4 | | |
| | | | | | | Coon, Joseph | 1 | | 2 | | | Phillips, John | 1 | | 3 | | |

# FIRST CENSUS OF THE UNITED STATES.

## WINDHAM COUNTY—Continued.

| NAME OF HEAD OF FAMILY. | Free white males of 16 years and upward, including heads of families. | Free white males under 16 years. | Free white females, including heads of families. | All other free persons. | Slaves. | NAME OF HEAD OF FAMILY. | Free white males of 16 years and upward, including heads of families. | Free white males under 16 years. | Free white females, including heads of families. | All other free persons. | Slaves. | NAME OF HEAD OF FAMILY. | Free white males of 16 years and upward, including heads of families. | Free white males under 16 years. | Free white females, including heads of families. | All other free persons. | Slaves. |
|---|---|---|---|---|---|---|---|---|---|---|---|---|---|---|---|---|---|
| **VOLUNTOWN TOWN—continued.** | | | | | | **WINDHAM TOWN—continued.** | | | | | | **WINDHAM TOWN—continued.** | | | | | |
| Stedman, Harry | 2 | 1 | 2 | | | Jennings, Eunice | 1 | | 3 | | | Swift, Zeph | 1 | 1 | 2 | | |
| Perkins, Amos | 2 | 4 | 3 | | | Abbe, Elisha | 3 | 2 | 6 | | | Robinson, Daniel | 2 | 2 | 7 | | |
| Perkins, Newman | 1 | 1 | 2 | | | Hebard, Paul | 2 | | 1 | | 1 | Bingham, Ebenr | 2 | 2 | 3 | | |
| Perkins, Elisha | 1 | 1 | 2 | | | Ripley, John | 1 | 3 | 3 | | | White, Elisha | 1 | 3 | 1 | | |
| Perkins, Oliver | 3 | 1 | 3 | | | Frink, Andrew | 2 | 2 | 4 | | | Spafford, Asa | 3 | | 1 | | |
| Franklin, Abel | 1 | | 1 | | | Huntington, Solomon | 2 | 1 | 4 | | | Spafford, Pheneas | 1 | 2 | 2 | | |
| Franklin, Uriah | 2 | 2 | 3 | | | Webb, Samuel | 3 | 2 | 7 | | | Spafford, Eliphalet | 2 | 1 | 4 | | |
| William, William | 3 | 1 | 3 | | | Ripley, Hezekiah | 1 | 3 | 5 | | | Sawyer, Joshua | 4 | 2 | 4 | | |
| Williams, Benja | 1 | | 5 | | | Elderkin, Joshua | 1 | | 2 | | | Downing, Benja | 1 | 2 | 4 | | |
| Williams, William, Ju | 1 | | 2 | | | Brewster, Asa | 1 | 1 | 2 | | | Fitch, Eleazr, Senior | 1 | | 2 | | |
| Denison, Nathl | 1 | | 3 | | | Robinson, Deborah | | | 2 | | | Cuningham, Robert | 1 | 3 | 1 | | |
| Boyd, Joseph | 1 | 2 | 2 | | | Lee, Samuel | 4 | 2 | 6 | | | Fitch, Shubael | 1 | 2 | 4 | | |
| Wood, Elisha | 1 | 1 | 1 | | | Skinner, Jonath | 2 | 1 | 4 | | | Backus, Demetrious | 1 | | 6 | | |
| Dixon, John | 1 | 1 | 1 | | | Follet, Abner | 1 | 2 | 8 | | | Calkins, Nathl S | 1 | 3 | 3 | | |
| Geary, Ezekiel | 2 | 3 | 5 | | | Crane, Eunice | 1 | | 5 | | | Sawyer, Mathius | 2 | | 1 | | |
| Dixon, Thos | 5 | 1 | 5 | | | Buck, Daniel | 3 | 2 | 3 | | | Balcam, Azariah | 1 | 4 | 3 | | |
| Bennet, Ezra | 1 | 2 | 3 | | | Robinson, Eleazer | 1 | 1 | 1 | | | Millard, Benja | 2 | 3 | 3 | | |
| Coloil, Saml | 3 | 1 | 3 | | | Flint, John | 1 | 3 | 3 | | | Sawyer, Asael | 1 | 1 | 4 | | |
| Knight, John | 1 | | 2 | | | Ormsby, Eliphalet | 1 | 2 | 4 | | | Skiffe, Joseph | 2 | | 2 | | |
| Mansfield, John | 1 | 2 | 2 | | | Badger, Saml | 1 | | 1 | | | Molton, James | 2 | | 2 | | |
| Mansfield, Calvin | 1 | 2 | 2 | | | Young, William | 1 | | 4 | | | Robinson, Isaac | 2 | 1 | 8 | | |
| Dorrance, James | 2 | 1 | 4 | | | Perkins, Daniel | 1 | 1 | 6 | | 1 | Abbe, Saml | 1 | 1 | 3 | | |
| Gastin, John | 2 | | 2 | | | Elderkin, Joshua B | 2 | 2 | 6 | | | Carey, Zurveyh | 2 | | 2 | | |
| Cole, John | 1 | | 1 | | | Badger, Joseph | 2 | 1 | 2 | | | Elderkin, Bela | 2 | 6 | 4 | | |
| Cole, Heza | 2 | | 3 | | | Francis, David | 1 | | 2 | | | Bingham, John | 1 | 1 | 3 | | |
| Hitt, John | 1 | 1 | 2 | | | Lord, Solomon | 2 | | 2 | | | Bingham, Elias | 1 | 1 | 2 | | |
| French, Isaac | 1 | 3 | 4 | | | Hovey, Jacob | 4 | 3 | 4 | | | Howes, Zenas | 3 | 1 | 3 | | |
| Young, Jonah | 1 | 3 | 7 | | | Wales, Nathaniel | 4 | 3 | 8 | | | Fitch, Roswell | 1 | 1 | 3 | | |
| Titus, Simon | 1 | 2 | 2 | | | Wales, Jonathan | 2 | 2 | 6 | | | Hewit, Lewis | 1 | 1 | 6 | | |
| Titus, Ebenr | 1 | | 1 | | | Wales, William | 1 | 1 | 4 | | | Simons, Nathan | 1 | | 6 | | |
| Titus, Comfort | 3 | 2 | 2 | | | Spafford, John | 2 | 1 | 7 | | | Fitch, Jesse | 2 | 4 | 3 | | |
| Kenyon, Giles | 1 | 2 | 4 | | | Palmer, Enos | 2 | 2 | 5 | | | Fitch, Stephen | 1 | 2 | 4 | | |
| Kenyon, Freeman | 1 | | 2 | | | Palmer, Seth | 2 | 1 | 3 | | | Howes, Zachh | 1 | | 2 | | |
| Kenyon, Azariah | 1 | | 2 | | | Palmer, Joseph | 3 | 1 | 5 | | | Crowel, John | 2 | 1 | 3 | | |
| Kenyon, Gardiner | 1 | 1 | 3 | | | Palmer, Eliphalet | 1 | 2 | 5 | | | Molton, William | 3 | | 3 | | |
| Gore, Saml | 2 | | 2 | | | Palmer, Eleazer | 1 | 2 | 3 | | | Shaw, Thomas | 2 | 1 | 3 | | |
| Adams, Silas | 1 | | 4 | | | Kingsley, Ezra | 1 | 5 | 3 | | | Tracy, Prince | 3 | | 3 | | |
| Mason, Jinks | 1 | 1 | 3 | | | Burnet, James | 5 | 3 | 6 | | | Allen, Daniel | 4 | 1 | 2 | | |
| King, Jonatha | 1 | 1 | 2 | | | Manning, Josiah | 2 | | 5 | | 1 | Howes, Zachh | 1 | 2 | 5 | | |
| James, Anthony | 1 | | 1 | | | Church, Lemuel | 1 | 2 | 2 | | | Wills, Jacob | 2 | | 2 | | |
| Seldon, Charles | 1 | 4 | 4 | | | Manning, Joel | 1 | 1 | 4 | | | Clark, Abel | 1 | 1 | 5 | | |
| Bennet, John | 1 | 1 | 3 | | | Kingley, Eliphaz | 2 | 2 | 5 | | | Hebard, Joseph | 2 | | 3 | | |
| Rhodes, John | 1 | 1 | 2 | | | Palmer, Josiah | 2 | 4 | 3 | | | Young, Saml | 4 | 3 | 5 | | |
| Cole, Noah | 4 | 5 | 2 | | | Hebard, Jared | 1 | 4 | 4 | | | Brown, Stephen | 3 | 2 | 4 | | |
| Hill, Robert | 2 | 2 | 2 | | | Spencer, David | 1 | | 4 | | | Brown, John | 5 | 1 | 6 | | |
| Hill, Aves | 1 | | 2 | | | Spencer, Jeduthan | 1 | 4 | 2 | | | Murdock, Eliphalet | 3 | | 8 | | 1 |
| Hill, Danl | 1 | | 6 | | | Carey, Nathl | 2 | 1 | 1 | | | Tracy, Prince | 3 | | 2 | | |
| Hill, Parker | 1 | 1 | 4 | | | Hebard, Zebulon | 3 | 2 | 4 | | | Murdock, Anne | 1 | 1 | 3 | | |
| Hill, Jonathn | 1 | 2 | 6 | | | Hebard, Samuel | 2 | 1 | 4 | | | Young, William | 3 | 3 | 3 | | |
| James, Zephh | 1 | 4 | 1 | | | Huntington, Nathan | 4 | | 7 | | | Woodward, Cathrine | | | 2 | | |
| Eaton, Joshua | 1 | 1 | 2 | | | Cleft, Waterman | 3 | 1 | 8 | | | Dunham, George | 1 | | 2 | | |
| Henry, James | 1 | | 3 | | | Carey, Hezekiah | 1 | 1 | 3 | | | Spafford, Moses | 3 | 1 | 8 | | |
| Whiton, Amos | 3 | 1 | 2 | | | Tracy, Percy | 2 | | 2 | | | Warner, Nathl | 2 | 2 | 7 | | |
| Covill, Abraham | 1 | | 2 | | | Reed, David | 2 | 3 | 4 | | | Howes, Zachh, Jnr | 1 | 2 | 5 | | |
| Colvil, Ephriam | 1 | 1 | 1 | | | Reed, Beriah | 2 | | 4 | | | Hovey, David | 4 | 3 | 4 | | |
| Winston, Azariah | 1 | 2 | 2 | | | Spencer, Samuel | 1 | | 3 | | | Maxwell, Joshua | 2 | 1 | 3 | | |
| Hammond, Saml | 1 | 1 | 3 | | | Fitch, Christopher | 1 | 2 | 3 | | | Bingham, Joseph | 2 | | 1 | | |
| Jocelin, Thos | 1 | 3 | 4 | | | Fitch, Eleazr, 3d | 1 | | 1 | | | Bingham, Ralph | 1 | 1 | 3 | | |
| Howard, Jesse | 1 | 2 | 3 | | | Bingham, Alfred | 1 | 1 | 1 | | | Bingham, Gideon | 2 | | 6 | | |
| Brown, Anthony | 1 | 2 | 2 | | | Flint, James | 1 | 1 | 2 | | | Button, Joshua | 1 | 3 | 3 | | |
| Bennet, Joseph | 1 | 3 | 4 | | | Backus, Calvin | 1 | | 3 | | | Jennings, Zephh | | | 2 | 5 | |
| Hill, Cromwell | 1 | 1 | 2 | | | Ormsby, John | 3 | | 2 | | | Spafford, Oliver | 1 | | 2 | | |
| Newton, Isaac | 1 | 1 | 1 | | | Smith, Miner | 1 | | 4 | | | Dewey, Alpheus | 2 | 1 | 4 | | |
| Hyde, Squire | 1 | | 3 | | | Backus, Abner | 1 | 1 | 1 | | | Mingo, Primus | | | | 4 | |
| Millar, John | 1 | | 2 | | | Manning, Fredrick | 1 | 2 | 3 | | | Phlps, Paul | 2 | 6 | 2 | | |
| | | | | | | Miner, Rufus | 2 | | 5 | | | Gaser, Jason | 2 | 4 | 4 | | |
| **WINDHAM TOWN.** | | | | | | Taylor, Nathan | 2 | | 1 | | | Smith, Oliver | 2 | | 2 | | |
| | | | | | | Gray, Thomas | 1 | | 5 | | | Robinson, William | 2 | 1 | 3 | | |
| Dyer, Hone Eliphalet | 1 | | 1 | 1 | 8 | Gilbert, Jabez | 2 | | 2 | | | Huntington, Nathl | 2 | 1 | 5 | | |
| Staniford, John | 3 | 2 | 4 | | | Huntington, John | 2 | 3 | 3 | | | Bass, Ebenr | 5 | 4 | 8 | | |
| Backus, Bela | 3 | 2 | 4 | | | Denison, Susanna | | | 3 | | | Manning, Hezekiah | 2 | 2 | 4 | | |
| Elderkin, Jedediah | 1 | 2 | 3 | | | Sawyer, Elijah | 2 | 1 | 8 | | | Carey, Oliver | 1 | | 3 | | |
| Carey, Marey | 1 | | 2 | | | Ripley, Eleazr | 3 | | 1 | | | Perrit, John | 3 | 2 | 3 | 2 | |
| Abbe, Pheneas | 1 | 7 | 4 | | | Ripley, Ebenezer | 2 | 3 | 1 | | | Smith, Eleazer | 1 | | 1 | | |
| Fitch, Eleazr, Jr | 2 | 2 | 3 | | | Barrows, Sylvanus | 1 | 1 | 1 | | | Tracy, Zebh | 2 | 1 | 2 | 1 | |
| Kennedy, Isaac | 2 | 2 | 4 | | | Frink, Lathrop | 1 | | 3 | | | Lillie, Jared | 2 | | 2 | | |
| Tileston, Thomas | 2 | 1 | 3 | | | Elderkin, Lyda | | | 4 | | | Parsons, Jesse | | | 7 | 2 | |
| Brewster, Benjamin | 4 | | 2 | | 1 | Larrabe, Timothy | 4 | 2 | 5 | | 5 | Abbe, Sampson | | | | | |
| Gray, Saml | 1 | | 4 | | 2 | Page, John | 3 | 2 | 3 | | | Smith, Ephraim | 1 | 3 | 5 | | |
| Clark, Jabez | 1 | | 2 | | | Johnson, Joseph | 1 | 1 | 3 | | | Persons, Theodotious | 1 | 1 | 4 | | |
| Backus, Nathl | 3 | 1 | 5 | | | Duvit, Henry | 2 | 2 | 6 | | | Cogshall, James | 1 | 1 | 2 | | 1 |
| Fitch, John | 1 | 3 | 4 | | | Warren, Nathl | 2 | 1 | 1 | | | Devotion, Ebenezr | 5 | 3 | 4 | | |
| Webb, Peter | 1 | 1 | 3 | | | Flint, Jemima | | | 4 | | | Manning, Seabury | 1 | | 2 | | |
| Barker, John | 1 | | 2 | | | Jennings, Jonath | 1 | 2 | 3 | | | Kingsley, Elisha | 2 | | 2 | | |
| Hebard, Jonathan | 1 | 1 | 1 | | | White, Stephen | 4 | | 6 | | 2 | Webb, John | 2 | 3 | 3 | | |
| Stanley, Fredrick | 1 | 1 | 1 | | | Clark, John | 1 | | 6 | | | Cheney, Pemul | 3 | | 2 | | |
| Clark, John | 1 | | 2 | | | Fitch, Olive | | 1 | 6 | | | Palmer, Marshal | 2 | 1 | 2 | | |
| Badger, Edmond | 4 | 2 | 3 | | | Huntington, Heza | 1 | | 2 | | | Dorrance, David | 2 | 4 | 2 | | 1 |
| Brown, Edward | 1 | | 2 | | | Jones, John | 1 | | 4 | | | Kyes, John | 2 | 1 | 5 | | 1 |
| Abbe, Shubael | 2 | 2 | 7 | | 2 | Dyer, Thomas | 2 | 1 | 4 | | | Webb, John | 2 | 2 | 4 | | |
| Miner, Stephen | 2 | 1 | 3 | | | Lathrop, Benjamin | 2 | 3 | 3 | | | Lillie, Chester | 2 | 4 | 2 | | |
| Webb, Nathl | 1 | 2 | 2 | | | Ormsby, Stephen | 2 | 1 | 5 | | | Ripley, Gamaliel | 2 | 4 | 4 | | 1 |
| Ripley, Ralph | 1 | 4 | 3 | | | Elderkin, Alfred | 1 | | 5 | | | Hovey, Saml | 1 | | 2 | | |
| Backus, Ebene | 3 | 2 | 3 | | | Hebard, Nathl | 4 | 2 | 1 | | | Giles, William | 1 | | 3 | | |
| Huntington, Roger | 2 | 1 | 3 | | | Tozier, Charles | 1 | | 4 | | | Webb, Lebeus | 1 | 2 | 2 | | |
| Reed, Thomas | 1 | 3 | 3 | | | Barrows Sylvanus Jnr | 1 | | 3 | | | Webb Jared | 2 | | 4 | | |

# HEADS OF FAMILIES—CONNECTICUT.

## WINDHAM COUNTY—Continued.

| NAME OF HEAD OF FAMILY. | Free white males of 16 years and upward, including heads of families. | Free white males under 16 years. | Free white females, including heads of families. | All other free persons. | Slaves. |
|---|---|---|---|---|---|
| **WINDHAM TOWN—con.** | | | | | |
| Mudge, Charles | 1 | 3 | 3 | | |
| Hurlbert, Alfred | 1 | 1 | 3 | | |
| Palmer, John | 2 | 1 | 3 | | |
| Waldon, John | 1 | 1 | 2 | | |
| Waldon, John, Jnr | 1 | | 6 | | |
| Bingham, Jereh | 1 | 2 | 2 | | |
| Kimball, Deliverance | | | 3 | | |
| White, Asa | 3 | 4 | 5 | | |
| Bingham, Uriah | 1 | 3 | 2 | | |
| Bingham, Jereh | 1 | 2 | 3 | | |
| Pettingall, Solomon | 1 | | 4 | | |
| Allen, Joseph | 1 | 2 | 4 | | |
| Allen, Asael | 3 | 2 | 3 | | |
| Adams, Asa | 1 | | 1 | | |
| Smith, Nathl | 1 | | 1 | | |
| Lasell, Josiah | 2 | 3 | 4 | | |
| Kingsley, John | 1 | 2 | 4 | | |
| Kingsley, Asael | 1 | | 1 | | |
| Lillie, Elisha | 2 | 1 | 5 | | |
| Carey, William | 1 | 5 | 5 | | |
| Rudd, Nathl | 2 | | 3 | | |
| Walton, Joseph | 1 | 2 | 3 | | |
| Lillie, Nathan | 1 | | 5 | | |
| Webb, Ebenezr | 1 | | 2 | | |
| Baker, Walter | 1 | 1 | 7 | | |
| Rudd, William | 2 | 2 | 5 | | |
| Rudd, Jonathan | 3 | 2 | 5 | | |
| Waldo, Zachus | 4 | 1 | 2 | | |
| Waldo, Zachus, Jnr | 1 | 2 | 2 | | |
| Bingham, Jedediah | 1 | 2 | 7 | | |
| Bingham, Saml | 2 | 2 | 5 | | |
| Baker, Aaron | 3 | 5 | 7 | | |
| Baker, John | 2 | 4 | 6 | | |
| Hebard, Nathan | 3 | 2 | 7 | | |
| Bingham, Nathl | 2 | 1 | 3 | | |
| Bingham, Isaac | 1 | | 4 | | |
| Smith, Benjn | 1 | 3 | 5 | | |
| Wood, Isaih | 2 | 1 | 2 | | |
| Wood, Mary | | | 6 | | |
| Smith, Jonah | 2 | | 7 | | |
| Jackson, Andrew | | | | 2 | |
| White, Prince | | | | 5 | |
| Geer, Saml | 2 | 3 | 7 | | |
| Linkon, Thomas | 4 | 4 | 7 | | |
| Rouse, Jabez | 1 | | 1 | | |
| Cuningham, Anne | | | 3 | | |
| Hanson, Edward | | | | 8 | |
| Phillips, Saml | | | | 2 | |
| Lynes, John | | | | 6 | |
| Robinson, Asa, Jnr | 2 | 4 | 3 | | |
| Linkon, Nathan | 2 | 2 | 4 | | |
| Linkon, Jonah | 1 | | 4 | | |
| Bebbons, Benjn | 1 | | 1 | | |
| Martin, Jonathan | 2 | 2 | 6 | | |
| Welch, John | 2 | | 3 | | |
| Spafford, Jehiel | 1 | 3 | 3 | | |
| Rathborne, Ezra | | | | 6 | |
| Phillips, John | | | | 4 | |
| Hebard, Gideon | 2 | 2 | 5 | | |
| Welch, John, Jnr | 1 | 2 | 5 | | |
| Snow, Thomas | 1 | 1 | 6 | | |
| Wheeler, David | 1 | 2 | 1 | | |
| Carey, Roger | 1 | 2 | 5 | 2 | |
| Littlefield, Ebenezr | 1 | 1 | 4 | | |
| Francis, Manning | 1 | 1 | 7 | | |
| Gennings, McHanah | 1 | | 3 | | |
| Robinson, Asa | 2 | | 5 | | |
| Robinson, Levi | 1 | | 2 | | |
| Robinson, James | 2 | 3 | 5 | | |
| Robinson, Reubin | 2 | 1 | 2 | | |
| Robinson, Rubin, Jnr | 1 | 1 | 4 | | |
| Baker, Elijah | 1 | 3 | 3 | | |
| Robinson, Jacob | 3 | 1 | 3 | | |
| Morgan, Saml | 2 | 1 | 4 | | |
| Morgan, Nathan | 1 | 1 | 4 | | |
| Bingham, Thomas | 2 | 1 | 2 | | |
| Luce, Ebenezer | 2 | 1 | 7 | | |
| Smith, Josiah | 1 | 2 | 6 | | |
| Bottom, Asa | 2 | 5 | 3 | | |
| Palmer, Veniah | 1 | 1 | 3 | | |
| Palmer, Jonah | 3 | 1 | 5 | | |
| Robinson, Saml | 1 | | 2 | | |
| Ringe, Amy | | | 2 | | |
| Morgan, Asher | 1 | 1 | 3 | | |
| Carey, Jonath | 1 | 4 | 2 | | |
| Lathrop, Ebenezer | 3 | 2 | 4 | 1 | |
| Southward, William | 1 | 4 | 2 | | |
| Burnam, Andrew | 3 | 1 | 4 | | |
| Badcock, Beriah | 1 | 1 | 2 | | |
| Burnam, James | 1 | 1 | 2 | | |
| Johnson, Levi | 3 | | 6 | | |
| Lease, John | 1 | 1 | 1 | | |
| Carey, James | 1 | 3 | 4 | 1 | |
| Holt, Benjamin | 2 | | 2 | | |
| **WINDHAM TOWN—con.** | | | | | |
| Kimball, Peltiah | 3 | 1 | 4 | | |
| Huntington, Elipht | 1 | | 3 | | |
| Robinson, Abner | 4 | 1 | 7 | 1 | |
| Burnam, John | 2 | 3 | 2 | | |
| Robinson, Experience | 2 | 1 | 3 | | |
| Robinson, Elias | 1 | 1 | 3 | | |
| Webb, Stephen | 5 | 3 | 8 | | |
| Luce, Mehitable | 1 | 2 | 5 | | |
| Meachum, Joseph | 3 | 1 | 8 | | |
| Kingsley, Jonath | 2 | 3 | 5 | | |
| Ripley, William | 2 | 2 | 3 | | |
| Fox, Jabez | 1 | 2 | 5 | | |
| Walker, Asael | 1 | 1 | | 2 | |
| Lathrop, Roswell | 2 | 5 | 2 | | |
| Jennings, John | 1 | 1 | 5 | | |
| Hutchins, Elizabeth | | | 1 | | |
| Cross, John | 1 | 1 | 2 | | |
| Bingham, Jonath | 3 | 1 | 5 | | |
| Cross, William | 2 | 1 | 2 | | |
| Johnson, David | 2 | 1 | 3 | | |
| Cross, Joseph | 1 | 2 | 1 | | |
| Linkon, Nathl | 3 | | 3 | | |
| Flint, John, Senr | 1 | 4 | 4 | | |
| Stowel, Jonath | 2 | 2 | 6 | | |
| Tilden, Littice | | | 4 | | |
| Kingsbury, Thomas | 1 | 1 | 6 | | |
| Linkon, John | 3 | 4 | 2 | | |
| Dains, Ephm | 2 | 3 | 4 | | |
| Abbe, Joshua | 2 | 4 | 3 | | |
| Abbe, Joshua, Jnr | 2 | 3 | 8 | | |
| Sessions, Joseph | 1 | | 3 | | |
| Geer, Aaron | 2 | 2 | 2 | | |
| Geer, Saml | 2 | 3 | 6 | | |
| Perkins, Cudge | | | | 6 | |
| Welch, Peter | | | | | 2 |
| Geer, Amos | 1 | 1 | 2 | | |
| Orcutt, John | 2 | | 1 | | |
| Walcott, Nathl | 1 | 1 | 3 | | |
| Kennedy, David | 1 | 1 | 1 | | |
| Kennedy, John | 1 | | 1 | | |
| Gennings, Zebulon | 2 | 1 | 1 | | |
| Dains, Axenbridge | 1 | | 1 | | |
| Dains, Thomas | 1 | | 3 | | |
| Neff, Benjn | 2 | 2 | 1 | | |
| Neff, Oliver | 1 | | 3 | | |
| Spalding, James | 1 | 5 | 8 | | |
| Dain, Lemuel | 1 | 3 | 3 | | |
| Colburn, Robert | 1 | | 1 | | |
| Colburn, Sylvanus | 1 | | 4 | | |
| Rogers, Oliver | 2 | 1 | 6 | | |
| Colburn, Ithamar | 1 | 1 | 3 | | |
| Robinson, Simeon, Jnr | 1 | 2 | 5 | | |
| Jinnings, Menoah | | | 1 | | |
| Chester, Jonathan | 1 | 1 | 2 | | |
| Jennings, Ebenezr | 1 | 2 | 3 | | |
| Smith, Mathew | 1 | 1 | 3 | | |
| Huntley, Elijah | 1 | | 6 | | |
| Robinson, Simeon | 1 | | 1 | | |
| Walcott, Jabez | 1 | | 3 | | |
| Aims, William | 1 | 1 | 2 | | |
| Aims, Asa | 1 | 3 | 6 | | |
| Abbe, Nathl | 1 | | 1 | | |
| Neff, John | 1 | 5 | 1 | | |
| Kinsbury, Saml | 1 | 1 | 4 | | |
| Parrish, John | 1 | 2 | 1 | | |
| Jennings, John | 2 | 1 | 1 | | |
| Linkon, Danl | 1 | 1 | 3 | | |
| Fisk, John | 1 | 2 | 3 | | |
| Larrabe, Sith | 1 | 2 | 3 | | |
| Preston, William | 1 | | 7 | | |
| Badcock, Joseph, Jnr | 2 | 2 | 5 | | |
| Badcock, Joseph | 1 | | 2 | | |
| Badcock, Nathan | 2 | 3 | 2 | | |
| Badcock, Danl | 3 | 2 | 2 | | |
| Warner, William | 3 | 3 | 4 | | |
| Cartright, Cyrus | 1 | 3 | 3 | | |
| Fox, Jesse | 3 | 1 | 7 | | |
| Kidder, Luther | 3 | | 2 | | |
| Allen, William | 1 | 2 | 6 | | |
| Allen, Abner | 1 | 2 | 4 | | |
| Fuller, Nathl | 1 | 2 | 3 | | |
| Robinson, Andrew | 1 | 2 | 1 | | |
| Ashley, Jonathan | 1 | 2 | 5 | | |
| Ashley, David | 1 | 3 | 2 | | |
| Parrish, John, Jnr | 2 | 2 | 8 | | |
| Blackman, Jonath | 1 | 1 | 1 | | |
| Flint, Saml | 1 | 1 | 2 | | |
| Jennings, Stephen | 1 | 4 | 3 | | |
| Martin, George | 1 | 3 | 1 | | |
| Bibbens, Elijah | 3 | 1 | 8 | | |
| Bibbens, Benjn | 1 | | 1 | | |
| Spafford, Oliver | | | 2 | 1 | |
| Thatcher, Asa | 2 | 1 | 3 | | |
| Snow, Thomas | 1 | 1 | 6 | | |
| **WINDHAM TOWN—con.** | | | | | |
| Wheeler, David | 1 | 2 | 1 | | |
| Bibbens, William | 2 | 3 | 4 | | |
| Welch, Reuben | 1 | 1 | 7 | | |
| Welch, Jeremiah | 2 | 3 | 4 | | |
| Dyer, Benjamin | 1 | 2 | 5 | | |
| Gray, Ebenezr | 1 | 1 | 3 | | |
| **WOODSTOCK TOWN.** | | | | | |
| Chandler, Anne | 1 | 1 | 6 | | |
| Brock, David | 2 | | 3 | | |
| Morse, Abiel | 2 | 5 | 7 | | |
| Tucker, Stephen | 6 | 4 | 5 | | |
| May, Caleb | 3 | 1 | 4 | | |
| May, Thos | 3 | 1 | 4 | | |
| Russell, William | 2 | 2 | 5 | 2 | |
| Tucker, Zephh | 2 | 1 | 4 | | |
| May, Stephen | 3 | 3 | 8 | | |
| Childs, Elisha | 3 | 3 | 8 | | |
| May, Silas | 1 | 2 | 4 | | |
| Taylor, Micah | 1 | 2 | 2 | | |
| Johnson, Joshua | 2 | 2 | 5 | | |
| Torrey, Elisha | 3 | 3 | 2 | | |
| Allard, Uriah | 2 | | 3 | | |
| Comstock, John | 3 | | 6 | | |
| Carpenter, Ephraim | 1 | 2 | 3 | | |
| Rawney, William | 1 | 3 | 3 | | |
| Childs, Abiel | 2 | 2 | 5 | | |
| Blackmar, Adonijah | 3 | | 5 | | |
| Haven, Abraham | 2 | 1 | 4 | | |
| Chanler, Seth | 3 | 3 | 6 | | |
| Sumner, Moses | 1 | 1 | 3 | | |
| Dayley, Jacob | 3 | 1 | 5 | | |
| Sumner, Sarah | | | 3 | | |
| Bullard, Asa | 2 | 1 | 1 | | |
| Child, Obediah | 2 | 2 | 2 | | |
| Williams, David | 2 | 1 | 4 | | |
| Allard, Danl | 1 | 2 | 4 | | |
| May, Joshua | 3 | 3 | 4 | | |
| May, Joseph | 1 | 1 | 2 | | |
| Allard, William | 2 | 1 | 2 | | |
| Dawson, Ebenr | 3 | 3 | 5 | | |
| Buckman, Stephen | 2 | 3 | 5 | | |
| Murry, James | 1 | 1 | 4 | | |
| Cheamberlin, Abiel | 1 | 3 | 3 | | |
| Child, Elias | 2 | | 2 | | |
| Long, Josiah | 2 | | 2 | | |
| Fox, Joseph | 1 | | 3 | | |
| Bacon, Benjn | 2 | 2 | 5 | | 2 |
| Childs, Nathl | 5 | 1 | 5 | | |
| Childs, Alpha | 2 | 3 | 3 | | |
| Walker, Leonard | 2 | | 1 | | |
| Jones, Samuel | 1 | 2 | 3 | | |
| Bacon, Parker | 3 | 1 | 4 | | |
| White, Peregrine | 5 | 2 | 4 | | |
| Lyon, Danl | 3 | 2 | 8 | | |
| Lyon, Stephen | 1 | 1 | 1 | | 1 |
| Child, Timothy | 3 | | 5 | | |
| Stone, Isaac | 3 | | 1 | | |
| Morris, William | 1 | 5 | 3 | | |
| Bradford, Samuel | 1 | 3 | 4 | | |
| May, Eleakin | 2 | 3 | 4 | | |
| Rawson, David | 2 | 2 | 2 | | |
| Brown, Andrew | 2 | 2 | 5 | | |
| Carpenter, Davis | 2 | 3 | 7 | | |
| Marcy, Uriah | 1 | | 2 | | |
| Marcy, Elisha | 1 | 2 | 3 | | |
| Phillips, William | 3 | 4 | 4 | | |
| Perrin, John | 3 | | 1 | | |
| Tucker, Stephen, Senr | 3 | | 3 | | |
| Goodale, Lemuel | 2 | | 6 | | |
| Foster, Jacob | 1 | 1 | 2 | | |
| Child, Amasa | 1 | 1 | 6 | | |
| Plummer, Ebenr | 1 | 1 | 1 | | |
| Vinton, Timothy | 1 | | | | |
| Eddy, Benjn | 2 | | 4 | | |
| Eddy, Lew | 1 | 2 | 4 | | |
| Child, Henry | 6 | 2 | 8 | | |
| Child, Peter | 4 | 1 | 4 | | |
| Gould, Besaliel | 1 | 2 | 4 | | |
| Lyon, Nehemiah | 4 | 3 | 4 | | |
| Richmond, Edward | 2 | 5 | 5 | | |
| Walker, Pheneas | 6 | 3 | 4 | | |
| Child, Asa | 3 | | 2 | 1 | |
| Allard, Peter | 3 | 1 | 3 | | |
| Jackson, Benjn | 1 | 1 | 2 | | |
| Corban, Abijah | 1 | 1 | 5 | | |
| Carpenter, Ezekiel | 2 | | 2 | | |
| Bacon, Saml | 2 | 2 | 4 | | |
| Sibley, Asa | 2 | 1 | 1 | | |
| White, Cornelious | 1 | 3 | 4 | | |
| Barret, Ephraim | 2 | 1 | 2 | | |
| Barret, John | 2 | 2 | 2 | | |
| Barret, Danl | 2 | 4 | 5 | | |

## WINDHAM COUNTY—Continued.

| NAME OF HEAD OF FAMILY. | Free white males of 16 years and upward, including heads of families. | Free white males under 16 years. | Free white females, including heads of families. | All other free persons. | Slaves. | NAME OF HEAD OF FAMILY. | Free white males of 16 years and upward, including heads of families. | Free white males under 16 years. | Free white females, including heads of families. | All other free persons. | Slaves. | NAME OF HEAD OF FAMILY. | Free white males of 16 years and upward, including heads of families. | Free white males under 16 years. | Free white females, including heads of families. | All other free persons. | Slaves. |
|---|---|---|---|---|---|---|---|---|---|---|---|---|---|---|---|---|---|
| WOODSTOCK TOWN—continued. | | | | | | WOODSTOCK TOWN—continued. | | | | | | WOODSTOCK TOWN—continued. | | | | | |
| Holmes, Eben<sup>r</sup> | 1 | 1 | 1 | 1 | | Mercy, Ichabod | 2 | 3 | 3 | | | Grosvener, Caleb | 1 | 3 | 3 | | |
| Holmes, Eben<sup>r</sup>, Jn<sup>r</sup> | 1 | 4 | 3 | | | Clark, Nath<sup>l</sup> | 1 | | 2 | | | Perry, Elijah | 1 | | 5 | | |
| Chapman, W<sup>m</sup> | 1 | 1 | 2 | | | Flyn, John | 2 | 2 | 6 | | | Clark, Joseph | 2 | 1 | 3 | | |
| Chapman, William, Jn<sup>r</sup> | 2 | 3 | 4 | | | Child, Rufus | 2 | 1 | 1 | | | Perrin, Dan<sup>l</sup> | 2 | 3 | 4 | | |
| Bowen, William | 2 | 1 | 3 | | | Williams, Elijah | 3 | 2 | 1 | | | Camp, Simeon | 1 | | 4 | | |
| Nigas, Silas | 1 | | 3 | 1 | | Horton, Jonas | 2 | 1 | 6 | | | Bugbe, Caleb | 3 | 2 | 6 | | |
| Sanger, Pearley | 2 | 2 | 2 | | | Richardson, John | 2 | 2 | 4 | | | Stoddard, Eben<sup>e</sup> | 1 | 2 | 3 | | |
| Woodbury, David | 2 | 1 | 3 | | | Lyon, Isaiah | 2 | 2 | 2 | | | Dean, Abiel | 3 | | 4 | | |
| Torrey, Sam<sup>l</sup> | 2 | 1 | 6 | | | Lyon, Jona<sup>th</sup> | 5 | 2 | 8 | | | Carpenter, Dan | 1 | 1 | 1 | | |
| Kimball, Jed<sup>d</sup> | 3 | | 2 | | | Lyon, W<sup>m</sup> | 1 | 3 | 4 | | | Austin, Jacob | 4 | | 5 | | |
| Howlet, Sam<sup>l</sup> | 2 | | 1 | | | Lyon, Elijah | 2 | 3 | 1 | | | Dean, Zeph<sup>h</sup> | 3 | 2 | 3 | | |
| Bugbee, James | 3 | 3 | 8 | | | Lyon, Benjamin | 5 | | 2 | | | Howard, Benj<sup>n</sup> | 6 | 2 | 5 | | |
| Chaffee, Stephen | 2 | | 1 | | | Mason, Elias | 3 | 2 | 5 | | | Howard, Amasa | 1 | | 7 | | |
| Chaffee, Josiah | 2 | 2 | 5 | | | Kingsley, Uriah | 1 | | 2 | | | Howard, David | 2 | 1 | 7 | | |
| Tucker, Eph<sup>m</sup> | 3 | 1 | 2 | | | Martin, David | 1 | 3 | 1 | | | Wally, John | | | | 4 | |
| Cummins, Perker | 2 | 1 | 4 | | | Mascroft, Jacob | 4 | 3 | 11 | | | Green, Charles | 2 | 1 | 3 | | |
| Hosmer, Abel | 1 | 2 | 7 | | | Morse, Jedediah | 3 | 4 | 8 | | | Mason, Noah | 4 | 2 | 6 | | |
| Perrin, W<sup>m</sup> | 2 | | 4 | | | Lyon, William, Jn<sup>r</sup> | 1 | 4 | 5 | | | Wheeler, James | 2 | 2 | 3 | | |
| Perrin, Amos | 3 | 3 | 4 | | | Lyon, Tho<sup>s</sup> | 1 | 1 | 1 | | | Hosmer, Menassah, Sen<sup>r</sup> | 2 | 4 | 6 | | |
| Child, Nath<sup>l</sup> | 5 | | 4 | | | Johnson, Willard | 1 | | 3 | | | Hosmer, Menassah | 2 | 1 | 2 | | |
| Hosmer (Wido.) | 1 | 2 | 2 | | | Skinner, William, Jn<sup>r</sup> | 1 | 2 | 5 | | | Macy, Asael | 2 | 4 | 7 | | |
| Allen, Jonathan | 2 | | 3 | | | Nicholls, Ezekiel | 2 | 3 | 5 | | | Wilbar, William | 2 | 1 | 4 | | 1 |
| Bartholomew, Leonard | 1 | 1 | 2 | | | Ainsworth, Darious | 2 | 4 | 3 | | | Corbin, William | 3 | 3 | 5 | | |
| Peak, Joseph, &c | 3 | 2 | 5 | | | Coburn, Eben<sup>r</sup> | 2 | 5 | 5 | | | Corban, Asael | 3 | | 3 | | |
| Bartholomew, Benj<sup>n</sup> | 1 | | 4 | | | Coburn, David | 1 | | 3 | | | Corban, John | 2 | 1 | 3 | | |
| Frisell, Joseph | 4 | 2 | 2 | | | Dewing, Hez<sup>a</sup> | 1 | 1 | 2 | | | Morse, David | 1 | 2 | 2 | | |
| Payne, Dan<sup>l</sup> | 3 | 2 | 8 | 1 | | Dewing, Michael | 1 | | 1 | | | Cutlar, Jesse | 1 | 2 | 2 | | |
| Johnson, Uriah | 1 | | 9 | | | Lyon, Wareham | 2 | 1 | 6 | | 1 | Bartholomew, Sam<sup>l</sup> | 1 | 1 | 3 | | |
| Griggs, Abijah | 2 | | 1 | | | Paul, Daniel | 1 | 1 | 4 | | | Lyon, Amos | 3 | 1 | 4 | | |
| Sanger, John | 2 | 1 | 7 | | | Coats, Sam<sup>l</sup> | 2 | 1 | 4 | | | Underwood, Lemuel | 1 | 2 | 3 | | |
| Holmes, David | 3 | 2 | 5 | | | Doyt, Abiel | 2 | 1 | 6 | | | Bartholomew, Sam<sup>l</sup> | 3 | 2 | 6 | | |
| Riley, Sam<sup>l</sup> | 1 | | 3 | | | Morris, Sam<sup>l</sup> | 3 | | 2 | | | Leonard, Jacob | 3 | 3 | 4 | | |
| Lindley, Dan<sup>l</sup> | 3 | 2 | 3 | | | Peabody, Richard | 2 | | 5 | | | Mercy, Israel | 1 | 2 | 6 | | |
| McClallen, Sam<sup>l</sup> | 6 | 2 | 4 | 1 | 2 | Abbot, Nathan | 5 | 3 | 3 | | | Macy, Jona<sup>th</sup> | 2 | 1 | 6 | | |
| Newell, Tho<sup>s</sup> | 2 | 1 | 3 | | | William, Stephen | 3 | | 3 | | 1 | Thayer, Mebisheth | 1 | 1 | 4 | | |
| Bowen, Mathew | 2 | 2 | 3 | | | Bugbee, Elijah | 2 | 4 | 5 | | | Morse, John | 3 | | 3 | | |
| Carryl, Ephraim | 4 | 4 | 4 | | | Johnson, William | 1 | 1 | 2 | | | Cheamberlin, Elisha | 3 | 2 | 4 | | |
| William, David | 3 | 2 | 3 | | | Linkon, Zeph<sup>h</sup> | 3 | | 4 | | | Easterbrooks, Oliver | 3 | 1 | 5 | | |
| Hammond, Josiah | 2 | 1 | 2 | | | Blanchard, John | 2 | 1 | 5 | | | Cheamberlin, Rubin | 1 | 1 | 4 | | |
| Lyman, Eliphalet | 2 | 2 | 5 | | | Lyon, Eben<sup>r</sup> | 2 | 6 | 3 | | | Mercy, Abraham | 1 | 2 | 6 | | |
| Bartholomew, John | 2 | 1 | 5 | | | Barton, Michael | 1 | 2 | 3 | | | Smith, Dan<sup>l</sup> | 1 | 2 | 6 | | |
| Chandler, Meriam | 3 | 1 | 7 | | 2 | Bugbee, Jonath<sup>a</sup> | 2 | 1 | 7 | | | Dodge, Eunice | 1 | | 3 | | |
| Fox, Tho<sup>s</sup> | 2 | 1 | 6 | | | Richmond, Abner | 1 | 2 | 1 | | | Broughton, Amos | 2 | 2 | 5 | | |
| Kingsley, Rufus | 1 | | 2 | | | Richmond, Joseph | 2 | 1 | 4 | | | Gage, Joel | 2 | 2 | 4 | | |
| Merey, John | 3 | 3 | 2 | | | Bowen, Henry | 2 | 4 | 2 | | | Gage, Thaddeus | 1 | 1 | 2 | | |
| Holmes, William | 1 | 2 | 3 | | | Morse, Lyda | | | 3 | | | Gage, Elisha | 1 | 3 | 4 | | |
| Easterbrooks, Peleg | 2 | 2 | 2 | | | Bartholomew, Sarah | | | 3 | | | Underwood, Josiah | 1 | 3 | 2 | | |
| Fairfield, David | 2 | | 3 | | | Ferker, Eleaz<sup>r</sup> | 5 | 4 | 5 | | | Goodale, Asa | 3 | | 5 | | |
| Bolls, Jesse | 3 | 5 | 4 | | | Perrin, Moses | 2 | | 2 | | | Clark, David | 2 | 2 | 3 | | |
| Sprague, John | 1 | 1 | 6 | | | Lillie, Eben<sup>r</sup> | 3 | 1 | 6 | | | Clark, Seth | 2 | | 3 | | |
| Leonard, Mary | 1 | 2 | 4 | | | Chandler, Moses | 3 | | 7 | | | Gage, Aaron | 1 | 2 | 1 | | |
| Badcock, Nathan<sup>l</sup> | 2 | 3 | 3 | | | Johnson, Peter | 1 | | 2 | | | Mercy, Israel, Jn<sup>r</sup> | 1 | 1 | 6 | | |
| Easterbrook, Moses | 3 | 3 | 4 | | | Johnson, Stephen | 1 | 3 | 2 | | | Craft, David | 1 | 1 | 2 | | |
| Barret, Smith | 1 | 1 | 2 | | | Skinner, Abraham | 2 | | 4 | | 1 | Clark, Asael | 3 | | 3 | | |
| Holebrook, Jobe | 2 | 4 | 6 | | | Payne, Stephen | 1 | | 1 | | | Cady, Luther | 1 | 1 | 2 | | |
| Lathrop, Benj<sup>n</sup> | 1 | 3 | 3 | | | Mercy, Nath<sup>l</sup> | 2 | 2 | 3 | | | Ainsworth, Joseph | 2 | 3 | 3 | | |
| Lyon, Nath<sup>l</sup> | 1 | 1 | 3 | | | Wilkinson, Rhodes | 2 | 2 | 4 | | | Key, Joseph | 1 | 2 | 2 | | |
| Trisdal, Darias | 1 | 3 | 2 | | | Bradford, George | 3 | 1 | 4 | | | Cole, Nathan | 2 | 2 | 5 | | |
| Holbrook, Calvan | 1 | 2 | 3 | | | Bradford, Essick | 1 | | 2 | | | Thompson, Ichabod | 1 | 2 | 2 | | |
| Judge (Negro) | | | | 4 | | Coltney, George | 4 | | 7 | | | Lyon, Dan<sup>l</sup> | 2 | 2 | 2 | | |
| Simons, Asael | 1 | 1 | 2 | | | Perrin, Elijah | 2 | 1 | 3 | | | Jackson, Nehemiah | 2 | 2 | 3 | | |
| Chaffee, Noah | 1 | 2 | 6 | | | Howlet, John | 2 | 4 | 3 | | | Eddy, Levy | 1 | 2 | 3 | | |
| Bugbee, Jed<sup>h</sup> | 1 | 3 | 5 | | | Fuller, Nath<sup>l</sup> | 1 | 1 | 3 | | | Mashcraft, John | 2 | 1 | 3 | | |
| Bugbee, Thomas | 2 | 1 | 3 | | | Greggs, Ichabod | 2 | 3 | 5 | | | Goodale, John | 3 | 1 | 4 | | |
| Bugbe, Thomas, Jn<sup>r</sup> | 2 | 1 | 1 | | | Smith, Eben<sup>r</sup> | 3 | 2 | 9 | | 1 | Doyt, James | 3 | 3 | 3 | | |
| Manning, Bela | 2 | 1 | 4 | | | Morris, Lemuel | 5 | 4 | 5 | | | Fox, John | 1 | | 4 | | |
| Howlet, Sam<sup>l</sup>, Jun<sup>r</sup> | 1 | 4 | 3 | | | Bugbe, Rufus | 4 | 2 | 3 | | | Child, Tho<sup>s</sup> | 1 | 1 | 4 | | |
| Gay, Calvin | 1 | 3 | 4 | | | Mathewson, Israil | 1 | 3 | 7 | | | Child, Lem<sup>l</sup> | 2 | 2 | 5 | | |
| Spears, Mary | 1 | 1 | 3 | | | Skinner, Stephen | 2 | 3 | 3 | | | Underwood, Neh<sup>h</sup> | 3 | 4 | 4 | | |
| Cheamberlin, John | 2 | 1 | 3 | | | Payne, Luter | 2 | 1 | 6 | | | Bugbee, Dan<sup>l</sup> | 5 | 2 | 4 | | |
| Skinner, William | 2 | 2 | 5 | | | Salisbury, Richard | 1 | 1 | 6 | | | Lyon, Sabry | 3 | | 3 | | |
| Chaffee, Sam<sup>l</sup> | 3 | 1 | 6 | | | Martin, Henry | 1 | 5 | 3 | | | Perrin, John | 3 | | 1 | | |
| Chaffee, Benj<sup>n</sup> | 2 | | 5 | | | Barber, William | 3 | | 4 | | | Broadway, Eleaz<sup>r</sup> | 2 | 1 | 3 | | |
| Bradford, George | 1 | | 2 | | | Howard, Peter | 3 | 3 | 2 | | | Ainsworth, William | 1 | 1 | | | 1 |
| Skinner, Priscilla | | | 4 | | | Carpenter, Joseph | 1 | 1 | 4 | | | Perrin, Isaiah | | | 2 | | |
| Darke, Alpheus | 2 | 1 | 3 | | | Perrin, David | 5 | 1 | 6 | | | Corban, Silas | 4 | 2 | 7 | | |
| Martin, William | 4 | 1 | 4 | | | Perrin, Stephen | 2 | 1 | 3 | | | Childs, Shubael | 1 | | | | |
| Lyon, George | 2 | | 5 | | | Childs, Elias | 3 | | 1 | | | Hull, Amos | | | | 3 | |
| Willowbe, Isaac | 1 | | 3 | | | Sheppard, William | 2 | 3 | 3 | | | Fairfield, Eleanor | 1 | 1 | 3 | | |
| Hurlburt, Elijah | 1 | | 5 | | | Perrin, Timothy | 2 | 2 | 4 | | | Barret, Joseph | 3 | 4 | 2 | | |
| Payson, Asa | 1 | 3 | 1 | | | Bugbee, William | 2 | 1 | 3 | | | Barret, Hannah | | 1 | 2 | | |
| Manning, William | 1 | 1 | | | | Childs, Jacob | 2 | 3 | 4 | | | | | | | | |

# INDEX.[1]

Abanatha, Jiles, 69.
Abbe, Bathsheba, 147.
Abbe, Elijah, 147.
Abbe, Elisha, 152.
Abbe, Isaac, 140.
Abbe, Jonathan, 141.
Abbe, Joshua, 153.
Abbe, Joshua, Jn$^r$, 153.
Abbe, Nathan, 147.
Abbe, Nath$^l$, 153.
Abbe, Pheneas, 152.
Abbe, Sampson, 152.
Abbe, Sam$^l$, 152.
Abbe, Shubael, 152.
Abbe, Solomon, 147.
Abbe, Solomon, Ju$^r$, 147.
Abbet, Thadeus, 27.
Abbey, Daniel, 40.
Abbey, George, 52.
Abbey, Jeduthan, 36.
Abbey, Jeremiah, 38.
Abbey, John, 40.
Abbey, John, 2$^d$, 40.
Abbey, John, 3$^d$, 40.
Abbey, Justin, 51.
Abbey, Levi, 80.
Abbey, Nehemiah, 36.
Abbey, Obediah, 38.
Abbey, Peter, 52.
Abbey, Richard, 39.
Abbey, Richard, Jr., 39.
Abbey, Stephen, Jr, 36.
Abbey, Thomas, 40.
Abbey, Thomas, 2$^d$, 39.
Abbot, Asa, 143.
Abbot, Benj$^n$, 143.
Abbot, Benj$^n$, Jn$^r$, 143.
Abbot, Daniel, 109.
Abbot, Dan$^l$, 131.
Abbot, David, 109.
Abbot, David, 148.
Abbot, Gold, 56.
Abbot, Henry, 143.
Abbot, James, 146.
Abbot, Jn$^o$, 138.
Abbot, John, 140.
Abbot, Joseph, 109.
Abbot, Joseph, 134.
Abbot, Moses, 134.
Abbot, Nathan, 143.
Abbot, Nathan, 154.
Abbot, Samuel, 56.
Abbot, Stephen, 136.
Abbot, Stephen, 140.
Abbot, W$^m$, 139.
Abbot, William, 149.
Abbott, Aaron, 22.
Abbott, Daniel, 56.
Abbott, Ebenezer, 21.
Abbott, Enoch, 23.
Abbott, Eunice, 22.
Abbott, James, 22.
Abbott, James, 29.
Abbott, Jedediah, 21.
Abbott, John, 22.
Abbott, Jonathan, 23.
Abbott, Lemuel, 29.
Abbott, Lemuel, 2$^d$, 29.
Abbott, Seth, 21.
Abbott, Silas, 29.
Abbott, Stephen, 23.
Abbott, Stephen, 29.
Abby, Benjamin, 79.
Abby, Samuel, 79.
Abby, Sam$^l$, 139.
Abby, Sam$^l$, Ju., 54.
Abby, Stephen, 36.
Abel, Butler, 59.
Abel, Dan$^l$, 145.
Abel, Elijah, 14.
Abel, Elijah, 145.
Abel, Jona$^{th}$, 146.
Abel, Joseph, 145.
Abel, Simon, 145.
Abell, Caleb, 130.
Abell, Caleb, 145.
Abell, Cherub, 129.
Abell, Eliph$^t$, 145.
Abell, Ira, 130.
Abell, Martin, 129.
Abell, Oliver, 129.
Abell, Parnell, 129.
Abell, Solomon, 145.
Abell, Thomas, 130.

Abels, Elijah, 69.
Abels, John, 67.
Abels, Slumon, 69.
Abenatha, John, 77.
Abenatha, William, 57.
Aberns, Sam$^l$, 138.
Aberns, Sam$^l$, Jr., 138.
Able, Alpheus, 112.
Able, Asa, 138.
Able, Ebel, 80.
Able, Hannah, 131.
Able, Hezekiah, 126.
Able, Jesse, 126.
Able, Joshua, 132.
Able, Sam$^l$, 126.
Able, Simeon, 126.
Able, Theophilus, 126.
Able, Zacheus, 112.
Abrahams, George H., 31.
Absolum (Negro), 113.
Absolum (Negro), 113.
Acheley, Jn$^o$, 135.
Ackley, Abner B., 55.
Ackley, Amasa, 81.
Ackley, Aron, 107.
Ackley, David, 19.
Ackley, David, 67.
Ackley, Dina, 107.
Ackley, Edward, 80.
Ackley, Elijah, 81.
Ackley, Elijah, 81.
Ackley, Elizabeth, 80.
Ackley, Eph$^m$, 81.
Ackley, Ezra, 81.
Ackley, Gideon, 82.
Ackley, Hezekiah, 74.
Ackley, Isaac C., 81.
Ackley, James, 81.
Ackley, James, Jun$^r$, 80.
Ackley, Joel, 66.
Ackley, Levi, 80.
Ackley, Nath$^l$, 3$^d$, 82.
Ackley, Oliver, 80.
Ackley, Rebecca, 98.
Ackley, Sam$^l$, 70.
Ackley, Samuel, 81.
Ackley, Sam$^l$, 82.
Ackley, Simeon, 82.
Ackley, Simeon, Jr, 83.
Ackley, Stephen, 43.
Ackley, Stephen, 80.
Ackley, Stephen, 81.
Ackley, Thomas, 67.
Ackley, Thomas, 80.
Ackley, Tho$^s$, 82.
Ackley, W$^m$, 82.
Ackraw (Negro), 86.
Acorn, Thomas, 22.
Acorns, Daniel, 19.
Adam, Thomas, 64.
Adam, William, Sen., 141.
Adams, Aaron, 23.
Adams, Abel, 81.
Adams, Abel, 48.
Adams, Abel, 144.
Adams, Abijah, 144.
Adams, Abner, 141.
Adams, Abraham, 27.
Adams, Abraham, 110.
Adams, Abraham, 114.
Adams, Amasa, 5.
Adams, Arael, 109.
Adams, Asa, 153.
Adams, Asabel, 51.
Adams, Asael, 113.
Adams, Bela, 129.
Adams, Benjamin, 49.
Adams, Benjamin, 52.
Adams, Benjamin, 121.
Adams, Benjamin, 2$^d$, 121
Adams, Bradford, 142.
Adams, Camp, 52.
Adams, Cornelius, 142.
Adams, Daniel, 62.
Adams, Daniel, 113.
Adams, David, 32.
Adams, David, 48.
Adams, David, 119.
Adams, David, 121.
Adams, David, 129.
Adams, David, J$^r$, 48.
Adams, Ebenezer, 45.
Adams, Eben$^r$, 142.

Adams, Edward, 144.
Adams, Elihu, 149.
Adams, Elihu, Jr., 142.
Adams, Elijah, 40.
Adams, Elisha, 34.
Adams, Elishah, 142.
Adams, Ely, 110.
Adams, Ephraim, 13.
Adams, Ephraim, 45.
Adams, Ephraim, 141.
Adams, Ezra, 48.
Adams, George, 48.
Adams, Hosea, 48.
Adams, James, 53.
Adams, James, 142.
Adams, John, 15.
Adams, John, 52.
Adams, John, 69.
Adams, John, 103.
Adams, John, 110.
Adams, John, 121.
Adams, John, 142.
Adams, Joseph, 15.
Adams, Joseph, 27.
Adams, Joseph, 52.
Adams, Joseph, 118.
Adams, Joseph, 142.
Adams, Joseph, 144.
Adams, Joshua, 32.
Adams, Levi, 142.
Adams, Lucy, 147.
Adams, Luke, 35.
Adams, Mary (W$^d$), 23.
Adams, Mathew, 48.
Adams, Moses, 51.
Adams, Nathan, 15.
Adams, Nathan, 32.
Adams, Nathan, Jn., 142.
Adams, Nathaniel, 12.
Adams, Noah, 141.
Adams, Noah, 149.
Adams, Parker, 142.
Adams, Peter, 24.
Adams, Peter, 141.
Adams, Pheneas, 142.
Adams, Philemon, 141.
Adams, Polly, 103.
Adams, Rebecca, 111.
Adams, Roderic, 48.
Adams, Roger, Jr., 142.
Adams, Samuel, 34.
Adams, Samuel, 51.
Adams, Sam$^l$, 119.
Adams, Sam$^l$, 120.
Adams, Sam$^l$, 142.
Adams, Sam$^l$, 142.
Adams, Samuel, Jr., 34.
Adams, Sarah (Wid.), 48.
Adams, Sebinus, 109.
Adams, Silaman, 32.
Adams, Silas, 56.
Adams, Silas, 152.
Adams, Simeon, 117.
Adams, Solomon, 130.
Adams, Sol$^n$, 136.
Adams, Squire, 32.
Adams, Stephen, 12.
Adams, Stephen, 14.
Adams, Stephen, 15.
Adams, Stephen, 151.
Adams, Tho$^s$, Sr., 142.
Adams, Timothy, 142.
Adams, William, 45.
Adams, William, 45.
Adams, William, 61.
Adams, William, 109.
Adams, William, 112.
Adams, William, 142.
Adams, William, 151.
Adams, William, 2$^{nd}$, 109.
Adams, Zadock, 51.
Adams, Zadock, 2$^d$, 51.
Adan, Oliver, 48.
Adans, Timothy, 48.
Adans, William, 48.
Addam, Joseph, 60.
Addams, Andrew, 70.
Addams, Andrew, 70.
Addams, Benjamin, 74.
Addams, Phinehas, 69.
Addams, Richard, 68.

Addams, Sol$^n$, 136.
Addams, Zeb, 51.
Addams, Zeb, 2$^d$, 51.
Addes, James, 65.
Addington, John, 15.
Ade, Aner, 103.
Aderton, Samuel, 114.
Ades, Thomas, 96.
Adgate, Asa, 125.
Adgate, Eunice, 131.
Adgate, John, 125.
Adgate, Thomas, 125.
Adkins, Benjamin, 88.
Adkins, Chancey, 50.
Adkins, Daniel, 43.
Adkins, Ephraim, 87.
Adkins, George, 86.
Adkins, Jabez, 87.
Adkins, Jessie, 87.
Adkins, Joel, 88.
Adkins, Josiah, 49.
Adkins, Luther, 50.
Adkins, Samuel, 50.
Adkins, Samuel, 87.
Adkins, Samuel, Jun$^r$, 87.
Adkins, Thomas, 87.
Adwick, William, 108.
Agar, Jos$^u$, 136.
Agard, Hezekiah, 65.
Agard, Joseph, 64.
Agard, Judah, 66.
Agard, Mary, 64.
Agard, Noah, 64.
Agard, Solomon, 60.
Aglestone, Benjamin, 68.
Aglestone, Daniel, 60.
Aglestone, Daniel, 64.
Aglestone, James, 68.
Aglestone, Joseph, 60.
Aims, Asa, 153.
Aims, William, 153.
Ainsworth, Anne, 142.
Ainsworth, Darious, 154.
Ainsworth, Jeded$^h$, 149.
Ainsworth, Joseph, 142.
Ainsworth, Joseph, 154.
Ainsworth, Nathan$^l$, 142.
Ainsworth, William, 142.
Ainsworth, William, 154.
Ainsworth, Will$^m$, Jr., 142.
Ainy, Ambrose, 147.
Aird, David, 86.
Airs, Jn$^o$, 135.
Akin, Reuben, 79.
Akin, Samuel, 79.
Akins, Acker, 61.
Akins, George, 80.
Akins, Henry, 63.
Akins, Thomas, 80.
Akins, Thomas, Jun$^r$, 80.
Albert, Obed, 120.
Albertson, John P., 68.
Albin, John, 17.
Albray, Peter, 139.
Alby, Joseph, 150.
Alcock, Isaac, 110.
Alcock, James, 110.
Alcock, Jesse, 50.
Alcock, John, 110.
Alcock, John, 2$^{nd}$, 110.
Alcock, Samuel, 110.
Alcock, Soloman, 110.
Alcocke, David, 110.
Alden, Amos, 39.
Alden, Andrew, 145.
Alden, Elisha, 136.
Alden, Howard, 50.
Alden, Jos$^u$, 136.
Alden, Walter, 145.
Alden, William, 145.
Alderman, Eli, 48.
Alderman, Elijah, 44.
Alderman, Elnathan, 44.
Alderman, Epephras, 44.
Alderman, Gad, 43.
Alderman, James, 48.
Alderman, Jonathan, 48.
Alderman, Jonathan, Jr., 48.
Alderman, Joseph, 44.
Alderman, Joseph, Jr., 44.
Alderman, Lott, 43.
Alderman, Thankfull (Wid.), 43.

Alderman, Thomas, 48.
Alderman, Timothy, 41.
Alderman, Timothy, 44.
Aldridge, Abner, 144.
Aldridge, Levi, 144.
Aldridge, Nathan, 134.
Aldridge, Peter W., 85.
Aldrige, Jane, 115.
Alent, Thomas, 30.
Alexander, James, Ju$^r$, 151.
Alexander, John, 151.
Alexander, Joseph, 151.
Alford, Alexander, 57.
Alford, Alpheus, 45.
Alford, Eli, 57.
Alford, Jeremiah, 55.
Alford, Joab, 57.
Alford, John, 57.
Alford, Jn$^o$, 138.
Alford, Jonathan, 54.
Alford, Joseph, 55.
Alford, Josiah, 43.
Alford, Lydia (widow), 45.
Alford, Nathaniel, 49.
Alford, Nathaniel, Jr., 48.
Alger, Abraham, 150.
Alger, Ashbel, 42.
Alger, Mathew, 74.
Alger, Nathan, 74.
Alger, Nath$^l$, 150.
Alger, Roger, 42.
Alicocke, David, 103.
Allan, Moses, 12.
Allard, Dan$^l$, 153.
Allard, Peter, 153.
Allard, Uriah, 153.
Allard, William, 153.
Allcox, Daniel, 50.
Allden, Zeph$^a$, 137.
Allen, Abner, 153.
Allen, Abraham, 150.
Allen, Alex$^r$, 55.
Allen, Amos, 56.
Allen, Amos, 119.
Allen, Asa, 136.
Allen, Asael, 153.
Allen, Barnabas, 142.
Allen, Benjamin, 13.
Allen, Benj$^n$, 54.
Allen, Benj$^n$, 149.
Allen, Caleb, 144.
Allen, Chancy, 69.
Allen, Charles, 54.
Allen, Cornelius, 74.
Allen, Daniel, 152.
Allen, David, 14.
Allen, David, 73.
Allen, David, 75.
Allen, David, 96.
Allen, David, 118.
Allen, David, 140.
Allen, Eben, 29.
Allen, Ebenezer, 13.
Allen, Ebenezer, 56.
Allen, Ebenezer, 75.
Allen, Ebenezer, 88.
Allen, Ebenezer, 105.
Allen, Ebenezer, 114.
Allen, Edna, 118.
Allen, Edward, 73.
Allen, Elenor, 111.
Allen, Elethan, 13.
Allen, Elijah, 56.
Allen, Elijah, 105.
Allen, Eliphilet, 13.
Allen, Elisabeth, 119.
Allen, Elisha, 55.
Allen, Eneas, 103.
Allen, Fitts, 54.
Allen, Gabriel, 12.
Allen, George, 14.
Allen, George, 55.
Allen, Gershom, 12.
Allen, Giddeon, 19.
Allen, Gideon, 85.
Allen, Gideon, 1$^{st}$, 73.
Allen, Gideon, 2$^d$, 73.
Allen, Hannah, 54.
Allen, Hannah, 118.
Allen, Henry, 55.
Allen, Hezekiah, 130.
Allen, Hez$^a$, 147.
Allen, Hez$^a$, 147.

[1] No attempt has been made in this publication to correct mistakes in spelling made by the deputy marshals, but the names have been reproduced as they appear upon the census schedules.

# INDEX.

Allen, Ichabod, 115.
Allen, Ichabod, 121.
Allen, Jabez, 141.
Allen, James, 30.
Allen, James, 118.
Allen, Jared, 142.
Allen, Jared, 145.
Allen Jason, 124.
Allen Jason, 126.
Allen, Jeames, 75.
Allen Jeames, 2d, 75.
Allen, Joel, 86.
Allen, John, 13.
Allen, John, 18.
Allen, John, 26.
Allen, John, 54.
Aller, John, 54.
Allen, John, 54.
Allen, John, 60.
Allen, John, 60.
Allen, John, 75.
Allen, John, 116.
Allen, John, 118.
Allen, John, 130.
Allen, John, Jur, 54.
Allen, Jonah, 55.
Allen, Jonah, 73.
Allen, Jonth., 55.
Allen, Jonathan, 116.
Allen, Jonathan, 149.
Allen, Jonathan, 154.
Allen, Jonathan, Junr, 116.
Allen, Joseph, 54.
Allen, Joseph, 65.
Allen, Joseph, 118.
Allen, Joseph, 125.
Allen, Jos., 134.
Allen, Joseph, 141.
Allen, Joseph, 153.
Allen, Joshua, 146.
Allen, Justice, 64.
Allen, Mary, 118.
Allen, Mathew, 61.
Allen, Miner, 119.
Allen, Moses, 55.
Allen, Nathan, 119.
Allen, Nathan, 125.
Allen, Nathl, 136.
Allen, Nathl, 149.
Allen, Nehemiah, 30.
Allen, Park, 118.
Allen, Park, Junr, 118.
Allen, Parker, 141.
Allen, Pelletiah, 68.
Allen, Peter, 86.
Allen, Pratt, 142.
Allen, Robart, 118.
Allen, Saml, 54.
Allen, Samuel, 56.
Allen, Saml, 124.
Allen, Saml, 143.
Allen, Saml, 146.
Allen, Saml, Ju., 54.
Allen, Saml W., 54.
Allen, Simeon, 147.
Allen, Solomon, 55.
Allen, Solomon, Ju., 55.
Allen, Stephen, 13.
Allen, Stephen, 67.
Allen, Stephen, 103.
Allen, Stephen, 125.
Allen, Stephen, 2d, 125.
Allen, Thaddeus, 144.
Allen, Thomas, 55.
Allen, Thomas, 60.
Allen, Thomas, 117.
Allen, Thomas, 118.
Allen, Thomas, 129.
Allen, Thomas, Junr, 118.
Allen, Thomas, Junr, 128.
Allen, Timothy, 140.
Allen, Titus, 61.
Allen, Tryall, 118.
Allen, William, 13.
Allen, William, 19.
Allen, William, 153.
Alley, Joseph, 104.
Alley, William, 102.
Allin, Saml, 133.
Allin, Sam., 133.
Allin, Saml, 137.
Allin, Wm, 135.
Alling, Abraham, 100.
Alling, Amby, 108.
Alling, Amos, 105.
Alling, Archibald, 107.
Alling, Bet (Negroe), 103.
Alling, Caleb, 100.
Alling, Caleb, 105.
Alling, Charles, 100.
Alling, Christopher, 104.
Alling, Daniel, 105.
Alling, Daniel, 108.
Alling, Daniel, 111.
Alling, David, 100.
Alling, David, 108.
Alling, Desire, 101.
Alling, Edward, 105.
Alling, Eli, 100.
Alling, Elisha, 100.
Alling, Enos, 108.
Alling, Gidion, 102.
Alling, Hezekiah, 104.
Alling, Icabod, 101.

Alling, Joathem, 106.
Alling, Joel, 100.
Alling, John, 105.
Alling, John, 105.
Alling, John, 112.
Alling, Joseph, 100.
Alling, Joseph, 105.
Alling, Lemuel, 111.
Alling, Emanuel, 118.
Alling, Mabel, 100.
Alling, Marahel, 111.
Alling, Medad, 100.
Alling, Nathaniel, 100.
Alling, Nathaniel, 2nd, 100.
Alling, Noah, 111.
Alling, Philo, 105.
Alling, Roger, 101.
Alling, Roger, 105.
Alling, Roger, 111.
Alling, Samuel, 94.
Alling, Samuel, 104.
Alling, Silas, 105.
Alling, Solomon, 75.
Alling, Stephen, 105.
Alling, Susannah, 105.
Allins, Ephraim, 118.
Allis, Abel, 33.
Allomas, Amos, 111.
Allyn, Aaron, 63.
Allyn, Abel, 34.
Allyn, Benjamin, 38.
Allyn, Chester, 52.
Allyn, Cloe, 69.
Allyn, Daniel, 49.
Allyn, David, 40.
Allyn, Ebenezar, 51.
Allyn, Ebenezer, 38.
Allyn, Ebenezer, 39.
Allyn, Elijah, 39.
Allyn, Gershom, 51.
Allyn, Gidion, 51.
Allyn, Hezekiah, 38.
Allyn, Israel, 38.
Allyn, Joel, 65.
Allyn, John, 39.
Allyn, John, 42.
Allyn, John, 46.
Allyn, John B., 33.
Allyn, Jonathan, 40.
Allyn, Jonathan, 62.
Allyn, Jonathan, 66.
Allyn, Joseph, 38.
Allyn, Josiah, 63.
Allyn, Luke, 38.
Allyn, Moses, 39.
Allyn, Moses, Jr., 39.
Allyn, Noah, 38.
Allyn, Othnial, 36.
Allyn, Peter, 28.
Allyn, Peter, 43.
Allyn, Reuben, 51.
Allyn, Reuben, 2d, 51.
Allyn, Samuel, 34.
Allyn, Samuel, 38.
Allyn, Samuel, Jr., 38.
Allyn, Solomon, 38.
Allyn, Zacheriah, Jr., 38.
Alsop, Mary, 86.
Alsop, Richard, 85.
Alswerth, John, 144.
Alsworth, William, 143.
Alton, David, 150.
Alton, John, 151.
Alton, William, 151.
Alverd, David, 63.
Alverd, Elihu, 63.
Alvert, Saul, 132.
Alvert, Saul, Jr, 132.
Alvord, Daniel, 88.
Alvord, John, 13.
Alvord, Orin, 80.
Alvord, Rachel, 120.
Alvord, Rend, 80.
Alvord, Seth, 80.
Alvord, Seth, Junr, 80.
Alvord, Thomas G., 40.
Alvord, Thomas G., Jr., 41.
Alwood, Mariam, 122.
Alworth, James, 141.
Amadown, Henry, 139.
Amadown, Jno, 136.
Amadown, Joseph, 140.
Amadown, Moses, 139.
Ambler, David, 56.
Ambler, Isaac, 26.
Ambler, Jacob, 25.
Ambler, John, 11.
Ambler, Joseph, 25.
Ambler, Joshua, 25.
Ambler, Mercy, 22.
Ambler, Peter, 11.
Ambler, Squire, 11.
Ambler, Stephen, 11.
Amedown, Jedediah, 139.
Ames, Abagail, 53.
Ames, Amos, 147.
Ames, Anthony, 87.
Ames, Benjamin, 53.
Ames, Benjamin, 57.
Ames, Chancey, 68.
Ames, Daniel, 53.
Ames, David, 45.
Ames, Everit, 10.
Ames, Nicholas, 79.

Ames, Philemon, 53.
Ames, Samel, 91.
Ames, Samuel, 110.
Ames, William, 53.
Amey (Negroe), 105.
Amirell, Job, 142.
Ammon (Negro), 126.
Ammy, Emanuel, 118.
Amon (Negro), 116.
Amos, Elisabeth, 114.
Amos, James, 98.
Amy, Christopher, 142.
Amy, Elisha, 151.
Amy (Negro), 125.
Anabal, Anson, 135.
Anable, Abrm, 81.
Anderson, Asa, 110.
Anderson, Asahel, 36.
Anderson, Ashbel, 39.
Anderson, Atiny, 101.
Anderson, Daniel, 10.
Anderson, Daniel, 48.
Anderson, George, 37.
Anderson, Isaac, 16.
Anderson, James, 45.
Anderson, Jeremiah, 16.
Anderson, John, 37.
Anderson, John, 65.
Anderson, John, 123.
Anderson, John, Jr., 37.
Anderson, John, 2d, 123.
Anderson, Joseph, 16.
Anderson, Joshua, 65.
Anderson, Lemuel, 147.
Anderson, Robt, 82.
Anderson, Saml, 144.
Anderson, Sawney, 42.
Anderson, Stephen, 16.
Anderson, Thomas, 122.
Anderson, Timothy, 36.
Anderson, Zinnus, 16.
Anderson, William, 37.
Andres, Jeremiah, 26.
Andres, John, 26.
Andress, Eden, 12.
Andress, Eliakam, 12.
Andress, John, 12.
Andress, John, Jur, 12.
Andress, Robert, 12.
Andress, Robert, Jur, 12.
Andrew, Sarah, 112.
Andrew, Simeon, 94.
Andrew, William, 102.
Andrews, Abel, 93.
Andrews, Abraham, 64.
Andrews, Abraham, 66.
Andrews, Abram, 75.
Andrews, Amos, 92.
Andrews, Andrew, 56.
Andrews, Andrew, 108.
Andrews, Anna, 111.
Andrews, Anson, 107.
Andrews, Asael, 82.
Andrews, Asahel, 48.
Andrews, Barnes, 111.
Andrews, Bartholomew, 108.
Andrews, Bela, 93.
Andrews, Benajah, 68.
Andrews, Benjamin, 43.
Andrews, Benjn, 68.
Andrews, Benjamin, 77.
Andrews, Benjamin, Jr., 43.
Andrews, Caleb, 56.
Andrews, Caleb, 111.
Andrews, Charles, 43.
Andrews, Charlotte, 102.
Andrews, Dana, 107.
Andrews, Daniel, 63.
Andrews, Danl, 63.
Andrews, Daniel, 79.
Andrews, Daniel, Junr, 32.
Andrews, David, 43.
Andrews, David, 57.
Andrews, David, 111.
Andrews, Ebenezer, 27.
Andrews, Ebenezer, 75.
Andrews, Ebenezer, 95.
Andrews, Elijah, 64.
Andrews, Elisha, 43.
Andrews, Elisha, 132.
Andrews, Elisha, Jr., 43.
Andrews, Elizabeth, 93.
Andrews, Em, 133.
Andrews, Eneas, 92.
Andrews, Ephraim, 95.
Andrews, Ezra, 63.
Andrews, Francis, 27.
Andrews, George, 139.
Andrews, Hannah, 10.
Andrews, Ichabod, 90.
Andrews, Israel, 95.
Andrews, John, 13.
Andrews, John, 43.
Andrews, John, 65.
Andrews, John, 81.
Andrews, John, 100.
Andrews, Jonathan, 49.
Andrews, Jonathan, Jr., 49.
Andrews, Joseph, 42.
Andrews, Joseph, 74.
Andrews, Joseph, 81.
Andrews, Josiah, 49.
Andrews, Josiah, Jr., 49.

Andrews, Justus, 75.
Andrews, Lidia, 107.
Andrews, Lyman, 56.
Andrews, Marvel, 107.
Andrews, Mary, 106.
Andrews, Moses, 107.
Andrews, Nathaniel, 93.
Andrews, Nathaniel, 108.
Andrews, Nehemiah, 61.
Andrews, Nehemiah, 61.
Andrews, Nehemiah, 63.
Andrews, Nicholas, 107.
Andrews, Patience, 92.
Andrews, Reuben, 75.
Andrews, Samuel, 10.
Andrews, Samuel, 66.
Andrews, Samuel, 93.
Andrews, Saml, 82.
Andrews, Saml, 134.
Andrews, Sarah, 27.
Andrews, Sarah, 107.
Andrews, Seth, 27.
Andrews, Silas, 57.
Andrews, Silas, 85.
Andrews, Silliman, 32.
Andrews, Simeon, 95.
Andrews, Stephen, 43.
Andrews, Stephen, 107.
Andrews, Theophilus, 66.
Andrews, Thomas, 13.
Andrews, Thomas, 49.
Andrews, Thomas, 77.
Andrews, Thos, 81.
Andrews, Thomas, 92.
Andrews, Thomas, 107.
Andrews, Timothy, 101.
Andrews (Wido), 91.
Andrews, William, 64.
Andrews, William, 75.
Andrews, Zephaniah, 81.
Andrews, Zinnus, 93.
Andros, Jonathan, 28.
Andross, Fredrick, 142.
Andrus, Abel, 54.
Andrus, Abner, 44.
Andrus, Akel, 148.
Andrus, Amos, 33.
Andrus, Ardon, Jur, 12.
Andrus, Ashael, 44.
Andrus, Benja, 119.
Andrus, Caleb, 100.
Andrus, Caleb, 100.
Andrus, Daniel, 42.
Andrus, Eleazer, 49.
Andrus, Eli, 54.
Andrus, Eli, 115.
Andrus, Elias, 54.
Andrus, Elijah, 32.
Andrus, Elijah, 41.
Andrus, Elijah, 53.
Andrus, Elijah, 111.
Andrus, Elisha, 118.
Andrus, Elizur, 54.
Andrus, Ezekiel, 34.
Andrus, Fitch, 54.
Andrus, George, 33.
Andrus, Hezekiah, 32.
Andrus, Hezekiah, 48.
Andrus, Hezekiah, Jr., 32.
Andrus, Ichabod, 35.
Andrus, Jacob, 33.
Andrus, James, 119.
Andrus, Jedediah, 97.
Andrus, John, 114.
Andrus, Jonathan, 48.
Andrus, Joseph, 114.
Andrus, Josiah, 32.
Andrus, Judah, 111.
Andrus, Jude, 114.
Andrus, Lament, 35.
Andrus, Levi, 32.
Andrus, Mary, 41.
Andrus, Moses, 32.
Andrus, Moses, Jr., 32.
Andrus, Nathaniel, 32.
Andrus, Noah, 34.
Andrus, Obadiah, 41.
Andrus, Obadiah, 49.
Andrus, Phebe, 93.
Andrus, Phineas, 103.
Andrus, Richard, 47.
Andrus, Samuel, 49.
Andrus, Saml, 55.
Andrus, Samuel, 100.
Andrus, Saml, 118.
Andrus, Sarah, 54.
Andrus, Silvanus, 45.
Andrus, Solomon, 114.
Andrus, Theodore, 41.
Andrus, Timothy, 111.
Andrus, William, 48.
Andrus, William, 48.
Andruss, Eli, 63.
Andruss, Han, 35.
Andruss, Elisha, 97.
Andruss, Ichabod, 40.
Andruss, Samu, 135.
Andruss, Samu I., 35.
Andruss, Timothy, 40.
Andruss, William, 47.
Andruss, William, Jr., 46.

Anebal, Antoni, 14.
Anebal, Ebenezer, 18.
Angel, Henry, 56.
Angel (Wid.), 149.
Angell, James, 128.
Angell, Stephn, 141.
Angell, Thos, 151.
Ann (Negro), 21.
Anne (Negro), 21.
Ansell, Nathl, 148.
Anthony (Negro), 42.
Antissel, Pheneas, 139.
Antissel, Silas, 139.
Antrim, Francis, 146.
Apley, Ezekiel, 65.
Apley, James, 142.
Apley, Roswell, 125.
Aplin, James, 149.
Aply, John, 148.
Archer, Amasa, 135.
Archer, Benja, 135.
Archer, Benja, 135.
Archer, Crispass, 121.
Archer, John, 24.
Archer, Thomas, 52.
Archer, Thomas, 2d, 52.
Ares, William, 105.
Areston, Gad, 110.
Arger, Abraham, 95.
Arger, Ephraim, 95.
Arger, Mary, 95.
Ark (Negro), 132.
Armer, Abigail (Wd), 16.
Armer, James, 138.
Armer, James, 138.
Armer, Jno, 138.
Armstead, Joseph, 122.
Armstrong, Amos, 129.
Armstrong, Asa, 129.
Armstrong, Bela, 129.
Armstrong, Elias, 139.
Armstrong, Elijah, 130.
Armstrong, Ezra, 130.
Armstrong, Hope, 129.
Armstrong, Isaac, 77.
Armstrong, Isaiah, 129.
Armstrong, Jabez, 130.
Armstrong, James, 129.
Armstrong, Jeames, 74.
Armstrong, John, 129.
Armstrong, Joseph, 130.
Armstrong, Lee, 129.
Armstrong, Pelatiah, 129.
Armstrong, Peter, 127.
Armstrong, Phinehas, 130.
Armstrong, Rufus, 38.
Armstrong, Thomas, 74.
Armstrong, Worth, 132.
Arnold, Abigal, 101.
Arnold, Ambross, 84.
Arnold, Apollas, 80.
Arnold, Asa Amasa, 86.
Arnold, Benjamin, 83.
Arnold, Caleb, 131.
Arnold, Christian, 83.
Arnold, Daniel, 87.
Arnold, David, 83.
Arnold, Ebenezer, 87.
Arnold, Enoch, 82.
Arnold, Ephm, 82.
Arnold, Gideon, 80.
Arnold, Isaac, Junr, 23.
Arnold, Jabez, 83.
Arnold, Jacob, 22.
Arnold, Jacob, 83.
Arnold, James, 83.
Arnold, James, 96.
Arnold, Joel, 84.
Arnold, John, 81.
Arnold, John, 84.
Arnold, John, 106.
Arnold, John, 146.
Arnold, John, 147.
Arnold, John. Jr., 83.
Arnold, Joseph, 36.
Arnold, Joseph, 82.
Arnold, Joseph, 83.
Arnold, Joseph, Junr, 84.
Arnold, Joshua, 84.
Arnold, Lidia, 93.
Arnold, Martha, 83.
Arnold, Mary, 36.
Arnold, Mary (Wd), 24.
Arnold, Nathan, 148.
Arnold, Peleg, 29.
Arnold, Prudence, 132.
Arnold, Samuel, 87.
Arnold, Samuel, 83.
Arnold, Samuel B., 83.
Arnold, Tennur, 34.
Arnolds, Isaac, 23.
Ash, Michael, 117.
Ash, Samuel, 15.
Ashborn, Abigal, 102.
Ashbury, Thos, 148.
Ashby, Edward, 120.
Ashby, John, 120.
Ashcraft, Edward, 127.
Ashcraft, Jedediah, 141.
Ashcraft, John, 141.
Ashcraft, William, 127.
Asher, Gad (Negroe), 92.
Ashley, Abner, 143.

# INDEX.

Ashley, Abreham, 63.
Ashley, David, 153.
Ashley, James, 120.
Ashley, Jonathan, 153.
Ashley, Joseph, 143.
Ashley, Rachel, 149.
Ashton, Joseph, 46.
Aspenvall, Abel, 77.
Aspenwell, Peter, 140.
Aspenwell, Prince, 147.
Aspinwall, William, 142.
Ates, Abraham, 43.
Atherton, Elijah, 134.
Atherton, Simo, 132.
Atkens, Joseph, 69.
Atkins, Abigail, 49.
Atkins, Abigal, 96.
Atkins, Benjamin, 32.
Atkins, Benoni, 105.
Atkins, Charles, 49.
Atkins, Daniel, 75.
Atkins, David, 75.
Atkins, David, 107.
Atkins, Eber, 93.
Atkins, Elisha, 144.
Atkins, Hezekiah, 32.
Atkins, Hezekiah, 69.
Atkins, James, 63.
Atkins, Joseph, 110.
Atkins, Samuel, 100.
Attwater, Abigal, 100.
Attwater, Ambrose, 92.
Attwater, Amos, 93.
Attwater, Amos, 112.
Attwater, Benjamin, 93.
Attwater, Benjamn, 108.
Attwater, Caleb, 100.
Attwater, Caleb, 108.
Attwater, David, 100.
Attwater, David, 105.
Attwater, David, 107.
Attwater, David, 112.
Attwater, Eldad, 105.
Attwater, Elihu, 92.
Attwater, Eneas, 100.
Attwater, Eunice, 107.
Attwater, Hannah, 92.
Attwater, Holbrook, 104.
Attwater, Icabod, 101.
Attwater, Isaac, 107.
Attwater, Jacob, 100.
Attwater, Jason, 91.
Attwater, Jerad, 100.
Attwater, Jeremiah, 103.
Attwater, Jeremiah, 104.
Attwater, Jeremh, 109.
Attwater, Jesse, 92.
Attwater, Joel, 104.
Attwater, John, 93.
Attwater, Jonah, 104.
Attwater, Jonathan, 112.
Attwater, Joseph, 93.
Attwater, Joshua, 100.
Attwater, Louis, 100.
Attwater, Lyman, 92.
Attwater, Mary, 104.
Attwater, Medad, 100.
Attwater, Moses, 92.
Attwater, Moses, 112.
Attwater, Ruben, 93.
Attwater, Samuel, 92.
Attwater, Samuel, 100.
Attwater, Samuel, 2nd, 100.
Attwater, Stephen, 93.
Attwater, Stephen, 100.
Attwater, Stephen, 104.
Attwater, Stephen, 107.
Attwater, Stephen, 2d, 93.
Attwater, Thomas, 92.
Attwater, Thomas, 103.
Attwater, Timothy, 92.
Attwater, Timothy, 103.
Attwater, Titus, 93.
Attwater, Ward, 104.
Attwater, William, 101.
Attwater, Zopher, 101.
Attwell, Mary, 96.
Attwet, Oliver, 45.
Atwater, Abel, 70.
Atwater, Aseph, 65.
Atwater, Herman, 49.
Atwater, Richard, 68.
Atwater, Timothy, 75.
Atwell, Benjamin, 124.
Atwell, Benjamin, 125.
Atwell, George, 124.
Atwell, John, 77.
Atwell, John, 125.
Atwell, John, 150.
Atwell, Lucretia, 124.
Atwell, Richard, 125.
Atwell, Samuel, 125.
Atwell, Thomas, 109.
Atwell, Thomas, 127.
Atwood, Asher, 54.
Atwood, David, 77.
Atwood, Elijah, 77.
Atwood, Elijah, 81.
Atwood, Elijah, Junr, 81.
Atwood, Elijah, 2d, 77.
Atwood, Elisha, 77.
Atwood, Francis, 150.
Atwood, Gideon, 56.

Atwood, Hannah, 147.
Atwood, Harvey, 59.
Atwood, Heman, 147.
Atwood, James, 65.
Atwood, Jedediah, 70.
Atwood, Jesse, 77.
Atwood, John, 50.
Atwood, Joseph, 75.
Atwood, Josiah, 33.
Atwood, Nathan, 75.
Atwood, Nathan, 77.
Atwood, Nathl, 147.
Atwood, Noble, 75.
Atwood, Oliver, 77.
Atwood, Skillars, 77.
Atwood, Thomas, 147.
Atwood, William, 67.
Aubony, Susannah, 107.
Auction, Thomas, 23.
Augar, George, 87.
Auger, Abraham, 104.
Auger, Hezekiah, 104.
Auger, Isaac, 83.
Auger, Isaac, 104.
Auger, John, 92.
Auger, John, 92.
Auger, Joseph, 83.
Auger, Joseph, 92.
Auger, Justice, 89.
Auger, Lucy, 123.
Auger, Peter, 92.
Auger, Prosper, 88.
Auger, Roger G., 123.
Angur, Daniel, 97.
Augur, Philomen, 97.
Auguster, Ceasar, 42.
Austen, David, 66.
Austen, Isaac, 70.
Austen, James, 63.
Austen, Joel, 70.
Austen, Reuben, 70.
Austen, Robert, 70.
Austen, Samel, 61.
Austin, Aaron, 65.
Austin, Aaron, 70.
Austin, Abel, 107.
Austin, Amos, 107.
Austin, Andrew D., 65.
Austin, Asa, 103.
Austin, Caleb, 50.
Austin, Caleb, 68.
Austin, Caleb, 149.
Austin, Calvin, 50.
Austin, Charles, 25.
Austin, Dan., 57.
Austin, David, 60.
Austin, David, 104.
Austin, Edmond, 109.
Austin, Edward, 115.
Austin, Edward, 115..
Austin, Edward, 124.
Austin, Elias, 108.
Austin, Elijah, 103.
Austin, Eliphalet, 65.
Austin, Ezra, 108.
Austin, Isaiah, 5.
Austin, Jacob, 154.
Austin, James, 109.
Austin, Jedediah, 115.
Austin, Jesse, 77.
Austin, Jesse, 96.
Austin, Joel, 108.
Austin, John, 104.
Austin, John, 106.
Austin, Jonathan, 103.
Austin, Jonathan, 125.
Austin, Joseph, 51.
Austin, Joseph, 108.
Austin, Joseph, 2d, 51.
Austin, Joseph B., 124.
Austin, Joshua, 97.
Austin, Joshua, 108.
Austin, Levi, 68.
Austin, Lidia, 104.
Austin, Mahatibel, 103.
Austin, Moses, 108.
Austin, Noah, 106.
Austin, Reuben, 57.
Austin, Samuel, 25.
Austin, Sarah, 142.
Austin, Seth, 50.
Austin, Thadeus, 67.
Austin, Thaniel, 60.
Austin, Thomas, 51.
Austin, Thomas, 113.
Austin, Uriah, 51.
Austin, Uriah, 2d, 51.
Austin, William, 104.
Austin, William, 115.
Austin, Zebadiah, 125.
Austins, Samuel, 51.
Auther, Elisha, 118.
Autherton, Isaac, 113.
Avarice, Hannah, 64.
Avay, Dan., 137.
Averett, Samuel, 45.
Averil, John, 141.
Averill, Percy, 74.
Averill, Samuel, 74.
Averill, Stephen, 149.
Averis, Elisha, 66.
Averis, Elisha, 2d, 66.
Averis, Jared, 66.

Averiss, Ethan, 60.
Averiss, Isaac, 60.
Averist, Jahiel, 66.
Averitt, John, 62.
Avery, Abel, 143.
Avery, Abner, 108.
Avery, Abner, 2nd, 108.
Avery, Abraham, 42.
Avery, Ambrose, 75.
Avery, Amos, 133.
Avery, Amos, 133.
Avery, Asael, 138.
Avery, Benjamin, 75.
Avery, Daniel 63.
Avery, David, 142.
Avery, Edmond, 107.
Avery, Elisha, 61.
Avery, George D., 128.
Avery, Jabez, 133.
Avery, Jabez, 136.
Avery, John, 15.
Avery, John, 39.
Avery, John, 45.
Avery, John, 148.
Avery, John, Junr, 113.
Avery, Revd John, 24.
Avery, Jonathan, 39.
Avery, Joseph, 144.
Avery, Joseph, 151.
Avery, Peter, 16.
Avery, Samuel, 37.
Avery, Sanford, 69.
Avery, Solomon, 113.
Avery, Uriah, 143.
Avery, William, 66.
Avint, Amos, 75.
Avory, Abraham, 124.
Avory, Amos, 114.
Avory, Amos, 118.
Avory, Amos, 119.
Avory, Amy, 125.
Avory, Ann, 132.
Avory, Benaijah, 118.
Avory, Benjamin, 119.
Avory, Caleb, 119.
Avory, Caleb, 2d, 119.
Avory, Charles, 127.
Avory, Christopher, 116.
Avory, Christopher, Junr, 116.
Avory, Constant, 118.
Avory, Daniel, 118.
Avory, David, 114.
Avory, David, 118.
Avory, Deborah, 119.
Avory, Ebenezer, 114.
Avory, Ebenr, 119.
Avory, Ebenr, 2d, 119.
Avory, Elias, 116.
Avory, Elihu, 125.
Avory, Elisha, 127.
Avory, Elisha, 132.
Avory, Ezekiel, 126.
Avory, Frederick, 126.
Avory, George, 125.
Avory, Gideon, 113.
Avory, Griswould, 128.
Avory, Hannah, 119.
Avory, Isaac, 114.
Avory, Isaac, 118.
Avory, Isaac, 125.
Avory, Jacob, Junr, 118.
Avory, James, 113.
Avory, James, 114.
Avory, James, 119.
Avory, James, Junr, 118.
Avory, John, 114.
Avory, John, 116.
Avory, John, 118.
Avory, John, 119.
Avory, John, Junr, 118.
Avory, Jonathan, 112.
Avory, Jona, 124.
Avory, Latham, 119.
Avory, Luther, 116.
Avory, Martha, 124.
Avory, Nathan, 118.
Avory, Nathl, 126.
Avory, Park, 119.
Avory, Park, Junr, 119.
Avory, Patience, 118.
Avory, Peter, 119.
Avory, Peter, 2d, 119.
Avory, Pheba, 119.
Avory, Pheba, 124.
Avory, Pruda, 119.
Avory, Richard, 131.
Avory, Richerson, 114.
Avory, Rufus, 119.
Avory, Samuel, 114.
Avory, Samuel, 126.
Avory, Samuel, 131.
Avory, Silvanus, 124.
Avory, Simeon, 118.
Avory, Stephen, 116.
Avory, Stephen, Junr, 116.
Avory, Theophilus, 118.
Avory, Theophilus, Junr, 118.
Avory, Thomas, 119.
Avory, Thomas, 125.
Avory, Wait, 126.
Avory, William, 113.
Avory, William, 119.

Avory, Youngs, 119.
Avret, Israhel, 62.
Aychinson, Bazzallet, 138.
Aychinson, Baza., Jr, 138.
Ayer, Jno, 89.
Ayer, Travis, 89.
Ayers, John, 129.
Ayers, Squire, 129.
Ayers, Timothy, 129.
Aynsworth, Ebenr, 134.
Aynsworth, Jno, 134.
Ayres, Benjamin, 22.
Ayres, Bradley, 25.
Ayres, Easter, 124.
Ayres, Elisha, 127.
Ayres, Daniel, 124.
Ayres, John, 25.
Ayres, Jonathan, 26.
Ayres, Joseph, 129.
Ayrs, Daniel, 119.
Ayrs, Joseph, 11b.
Ayrs, Joseph, Junr, 116.
Ayrs, Nathan, 115.
Aysault, Daniel, 52.

B——, Solomon, 59.
Babb, Sarah, 86.
Babbet, Edward, 144.
Babbet, Edward, Jnr, 144.
Babbet, Stephen, 17.
Babbett, Elijah, 80.
Babbett, Jacob, 79.
Babbett, William, 89.
Babbit, Jacob, 121.
Babcock, David, 133.
Babcock, Elisha, 46.
Babcock, Henry, 117.
Babcock, Hozeah, 136.
Babcock, Isaiah, 19.
Babcock, Jno, 134.
Babcock, Robd, 134.
Babcock, Robd, 134.
Babcock, Roger, 134.
Babcock, Rufiel, 60.
Babcock, Saml, 89.
Babcock, Wm, 134.
Babcock, Zebulon, 134.
Babck, Elias, 60.
Babcok, Elias, 63.
Babcok, Rufus, 63.
Baccus, Silvenus, 62.
Bachelor, Reuben, 68.
Back, Elisabeth, 115.
Backen, Daniel, 63.
Backen, Ebenses, 63.
Backeus, Betsy, 130.
Backeus, Elijah, 131.
Backeus, Elisabeth, 131.
Backeus, Erastus, 131.
Backeus, Ezekiel, 129.
Backeus, Ezra, 130.
Backeus, John, 131.
Backeus, Rufus, 131.
Backsster, Arline, 27.
Backus, Abner, 152.
Backus, Adonijah, 141.
Backus, Andrew, 148.
Backus, Asa, 129.
Backus, Bela, 152.
Backus, Revd. C., 136.
Backus, Calvin, 152.
Backus, Demetrious, 152.
Backus, Ebene, 113.
Backus, Elisha, 142.
Backus, Eunice, 130.
Backus, Ezra, 135.
Backus, Isaac, 142.
Backus, Jos., 139.
Backus, Joshua, 130.
Backus, Nathan, 142.
Backus, Nathl, 152.
Backus, Stephen, 148.
Backus, Stephen, 142.
Backus, Timothy, 142.
Backus, Whiting, 146.
Backuss, Ebenr, 126.
Backuss, Oliver, 126.
Backuss, Ozias, 126.
Bacom, Maskel, 48.
Bacon, Abner, 142.
Bacon, Andrew, 35.
Bacon, Andrew, 70.
Bacon, Asa, 142.
Bacon, Benjn, 142.
Bacon, Benjn, 153.
Bacon, Benjn, Junr, 142.
Bacon, Beriah, 79.
Bacon, Celi, 44.
Bacon, Daniel, 48.
Bacon, Ebenezer, 56.
Bacon, Ebenezr, 88.
Bacon, Ebenezer, Esqr, 88.
Bacon, Ephraim, 15.
Bacon, Frances, 49.
Bacon, Isaac, 86.
Bacon, Jacob, 142.
Bacon, James, 45.
Bacon, James, 49.
Bacon, James, 65.
Bacon, Jeremiah, 88.
Bacon, Joel, 88.
Bacon, John, 63.
Bacon, John, 88.

Bacon, John, Junr, 88.
Bacon, Joseph, 35.
Bacon, Joseph, 49.
Bacon, Joseph, 86.
Bacon, Joseph, 142.
Bacon, Josiah, 56.
Bacon, Mary (Wid.), 44.
Bacon, Masket, Jr, 48.
Bacon, Moses, 35.
Bacon, Nathaniel, 44.
Bacon, Nehemiah, 141.
Bacon, Noah, 88.
Bacon, Parker, 153.
Bacon, Phinehas, 88.
Bacon, Pierpoint, 122.
Bacon, Rhoda (alias Hall), 86.
Bacon, Richard, 52.
Bacon, Roswell, 35.
Bacon, Saml, 153.
Bacon, Sibbel, 88.
Bacon, Stephen, 88.
Bacon, William, 86.
Bacon, William, 88.
Badcock, Abijah, 145.
Badcock, Amos, 146.
Badcock, Benjamin, 114.
Badcock, Beriah, 153.
Badcock, Christopher, 114.
Badcock, Daniel, 127.
Badcock, Danl, 134.
Badcock, Danl, 153.
Badcock, Elias, 116.
Badcock, Elihu, 114.
Badcock, Elihu, 117.
Badcock, Elihu, 134.
Badcock, Elijah, 145.
Badcock, Ichabod, 114.
Badcock, Ichabod, Junr, 114.
Badcock, Isaac, 119.
Badcock, Jack, 148.
Badcock, Jereh, 141.
Badcock, John, 116.
Badcock, Jno, 133.
Badcock, John, 147.
Badcock, Joseph, 117.
Badcock, Joseph, 153.
Badcock, Joseph, Junr, 153.
Badcock, Joseph S., 114.
Badcock, Joshua, 115.
Badcock, Josiah, 147.
Badcock, Nathan, 144.
Badcock, Nathan, 153.
Badcock, Nathl, 116.
Badcock, Nathanl, 154.
Badcock, Paul, 116.
Badcock, Robart, 117.
Badcock, Sarah, 118.
Badcock, Silas, 148.
Badcock, Simon, 117.
Badcock, Thomas, 131.
Badcock, Timothy, 115.
Badcock, Timo, 134.
Badcock, Timothy, 140.
Badelle, William, 69.
Badet, Peter, 129.
Badger, Abigal, 145.
Badger, Abner, 144.
Badger, Danl, 133.
Badger, Danl, 133.
Badger, Edmond, 152.
Badger, Edward, 93.
Badger, Enoch, 134.
Badger, Ezekel, 141.
Badger, Ezra, 141.
Badger, Fredrick, 92.
Badger, Jm, 138.
Badger, John, 141.
Badger, Jonathn, 147.
Badger, Joseph, 152.
Badger, Moses, 133.
Badger, Neh., 135.
Badger, Saml, 152.
Bagger, John, 20.
Bagley, Agnes, 73.
Bagley, David, 79.
Bailey, Abijah, 84.
Bailey, Adonijah, 151.
Bailey, Amos, 84.
Bailey, Amy, 84.
Bailey, Andrew, 70.
Bailey, Caleb, 84.
Bailey, Caleb, 148.
Bailey, Charles, 77.
Bailey, Christopher, 84.
Bailey, Daniel, 90.
Bailey, Desire, 84.
Bailey, Ebenezer, 80.
Bailey, Eliakim, 84.
Bailey, Elisha, 146.
Bailey, Elizabeth, 84.
Bailey, Elizabeth, 103.
Bailey, Enock, 95.
Bailey, Ephraim, 84.
Bailey, Ephraim, 87.
Bailey, Gideon, Junr, 84.
Bailey, Hezekiah, 18.
Bailey, Hez., 86.
Bailey, Ichabod, 80.
Bailey, Isaac, 146.
Bailey, Isaac, Jnr, 146.
Bailey, Ithamon, 70.
Bailey, Jabez, 84.
Bailey, James, 80.

158 INDEX.

Bailey, James, 146.
Bailey, John, 58.
Bailey, John, 84.
Bailey, John, 150.
Bailey, Jonathan, 33.
Bailey, Joseph, 60.
Bailey, Joshua, 80.
Bailey, Joshua, Jun$^{r}$, 80.
Bailey, Lowdon, 87.
Bailey, Nathan, 35.
Bailey, Nehemiah, 34.
Bailey, Oliver, 84.
Bailey, Robert, 80.
Bailey, Salmon, 61.
Bailey, Sam$^{l}$, Ju$^{r}$, 146.
Bailey, Sam$^{l}$, Sen$^{r}$, 146.
Bailey, Solomon, 80.
Bailey, Stephen, 84.
Bailey, Thomas, 77.
Bailey, Timothy, 84.
Bailey, William, 57.
Bailey, William, 84.
Bailey, William, 88.
Bails, Deborah, 100.
Baily, Henery, 32.
Baker, Amos, 28.
Baker, Asa, 121.
Baker, Asa, 126.
Baker, Asa, 134.
Baker, Blun$^{d}$, 134.
Baker, Constant, 60.
Baker, Daniel, 120.
Baker, Dan$^{l}$, 138.
Baker, David, 31.
Baker, Ebenezer, 12.
Baker, Eben$^{r}$, 138.
Baker, Elezer, 138.
Baker, Elijah, 153.
Baker, Elisha, 69.
Baker, Enoch, 113.
Baker, Ephraim, 43.
Baker, Ephraim, 74.
Baker, Ephraim, 132.
Baker, Erastus, 141.
Baker, Gideon, 125.
Baker, Haman, 138.
Baker, Hepsibah, 125.
Baker, Jacob, 77.
Baker, James, 22.
Baker, James, 125.
Baker, Jared, 125.
Baker, Jesse, 71.
Baker, Jesse, 74.
Baker, Joel, 144.
Baker, John, 123.
Baker, John, 127.
Baker, John, 130.
Baker, Jn$^{o}$, 138.
Baker, John, 141.
Baker, John, 153.
Baker, Jn$^{o}$, J$^{r}$, 138.
Baker, Jonas, 144.
Baker, Jonathan, 30.
Baker, Jonathan, 143.
Baker, Jos., 138.
Baker, Joseph, 141.
Baker, Joseph, Jn$^{r}$, 141.
Baker, Joshua, 120.
Baker, Joshua, 124.
Baker, Josiah, 125.
Baker, Let, 134.
Baker, Martha, 67.
Baker, Matthias W., 122.
Baker, Mercy, 82.
Baker, Nathan, 144.
Baker, Pemberton, 130.
Baker, Samuel, 32.
Baker, Samuel, 43.
Baker, Samuel, 74.
Baker, Sam$^{l}$, 118.
Baker, Sam$^{l}$, 144.
Baker, Sam$^{l}$, 153.
Baker, Sarah, 127.
Baker, Seth, 138.
Baker, Stephen, 141.
Baker, Thephilus, 138.
Baker, Thomas, 144.
Baker, Tim$^{o}$, 134.
Baker, Titus, 138.
Baker, Titus, Jr., 138.
Baker, Walter, 153.
Baker, William, 115.
Baker, William, 141.
Bakon, Jn$^{o}$, 134.
Balcam, Azariah, 152.
Balch, Henry, 147.
Balch, Israel, 147.
Balch, Jonathan B., 47.
Balch, Vivian, 147.
Balch, William, 147.
Balcom, John, 55.
Balcom, Joseph, 148.
Balcomb, Elias, 68.
Balcome, John, 60.
Balcome, John, 69.
Baldin, Mathew, 2$^{d}$, 112.
Balding, Oliver, 126.
Baldwin, Aaron, 56.
Baldwin, Aaron, 85.
Baldwin, Abel, 75.
Baldwin, ABial, 96.
Baldwin, Abiel, 71.
Baldwin, Abigail, 21.
Baldwin, Abraham, 20.
Baldwin, Abraham, 101.
Baldwin, Advice, 101.
Baldwin, Alsop, 75.
Baldwin, Amos, 20.
Baldwin, Amos, 101.
Baldwin, Andrew, 77.
Baldwin, Andrew, 111.
Baldwin, Aron, 91.
Baldwin, Asa, 117.
Baldwin, Asa, 138.
Baldwin, Asahel, 71.
Baldwin, Asahel, 74.
Baldwin, Asbeil, 101.
Baldwin, Ashbel, 65.
Baldwin, Barnabas, 111.
Baldwin, Barnabas, 2$^{nd}$, 111
Baldwin, Benjamin, 92.
Baldwin, Benj$^{n}$, 108.
Baldwin, Benjamin, 109.
Baldwin, Bruin, 59.
Baldwin, Caleb, 20.
Baldwin, Charles, 111.
Baldwin, Clark, 20.
Baldwin, Daniel, 70.
Baldwin, Daniel, 91.
Baldwin, Daniel, 101.
Baldwin, Daniel, 107.
Baldwin, Dan$^{l}$, 147.
Baldwin, Daniel, 2$^{nd}$, 107
Baldwin, David, 20.
Baldwin, David, 65.
Baldwin, David, 76.
Baldwin, David, 101.
Baldwin, David, 108.
Baldwin, David, 115.
Baldwin, David, 142.
Baldwin, Ebenezer, 71.
Baldwin, Ebenezer, 107.
Baldwin, Eben$^{r}$, 126.
Baldwin, Edward, 91.
Baldwin, Edward, 101.
Baldwin, Eli, 56.
Baldwin, Eliezer, 85.
Baldwin, Elihu, 92.
Baldwin, Elijah, 73.
Baldwin, Eliph., 101.
Baldwin, Elisha, 101.
Baldwin, Elizabeth, 94.
Baldwin, Elizabeth, 107.
Baldwin, Elnathan, 101.
Baldwin, Enoch, 111.
Baldwin, Enos, 74.
Baldwin, Enos, 2$^{d}$, 74.
Baldwin, Ephraim, 91.
Baldwin, Gabriel, 31.
Baldwin, Gamliel, 91.
Baldwin, George, 65.
Baldwin, George, 74.
Baldwin, Heil, 101.
Baldwin, Henry, 57.
Baldwin, Henry, 111.
Baldwin, Henry, 2$^{d}$, 111.
Baldwin, Isaac, 19.
Baldwin, Isaac, 59.
Baldwin, Isaac, 65.
Baldwin, Isaac, 71.
Baldwin, Isaac, 95.
Baldwin, Isaac, 101.
Baldwin, Isaac, 109.
Baldwin, Isaac, 2$^{d}$, 64.
Baldwin, Isaac, 2$^{nd}$, 101.
Baldwin, Israel, 71.
Baldwin, Israel, 75.
Baldwin, Israel, 92.
Baldwin, Jacob, 56.
Baldwin, James, 66.
Baldwin, James, 91.
Baldwin, James, 91.
Baldwin, James, 95.
Baldwin, James, 108.
Baldwin, Jerad, 102.
Baldwin, Jerad, 111.
Baldwin, Jeremiah, 101.
Baldwin, Jerusha, 73.
Baldwin, Joannah, 57.
Baldwin, Joel, 91.
Baldwin, John, 19.
Baldwin, John, 28.
Baldwin, John, 62.
Baldwin, John, 71.
Baldwin, John, 74.
Baldwin, John, 91.
Baldwin, John, 105.
Baldwin, John, 115.
Baldwin, Jonah, 71.
Baldwin, Jonathan, 109.
Baldwin, Jonathan, 117.
Baldwin, Joseph, 56.
Baldwin, Joseph, 57.
Baldwin, Joseph, 73.
Baldwin, Joseph, 92.
Baldwin, Joseph, 113.
Baldwin, Joseph, 114.
Baldwin, Joseph, 147.
Baldwin, Josiah, 90.
Baldwin, Josiah, 101.
Baldwin, Josiah 111.
Baldwin, Judah, 74.
Baldwin, Justice, 102.
Baldwin, Lucy, 77.
Baldwin, Mathew, 21.
Baldwin, Mathew, 112.
Baldwin, Moses, 91.
Baldwin, Nathan, 101.
Baldwin. Nathan, 2$^{nd}$, 101.
Baldwin, Nathaniel, 70.
Baldwin, Nathaniel, 107.
Baldwin, Nathaniel G., 71.
Baldwin, Nicodemus, 91.
Baldwin, Noah, 91.
Baldwin, Noah, 96.
Baldwin, Noah, 109.
Baldwin, Parmale, 77.
Baldwin, Patience, 70.
Baldwin, Phineas, 92.
Baldwin, Phineas, 101.
Baldwin, Phinehas, 65.
Baldwin, Richard, 111.
Baldwin, Ruben, 94.
Baldwin, Ruben, 96.
Baldwin, Rufus, 113.
Baldwin, Sally, 92.
Baldwin, Samuel, 50.
Baldwin, Samuel, 70.
Baldwin, Samuel, 70.
Baldwin, Samuel, 76.
Baldwin, Samuel, 91.
Baldwin, Samuel, 91.
Baldwin, Samuel, 107.
Baldwin, Sibel, 102.
Baldwin, Silas, 95.
Baldwin, Silas, 105.
Baldwin, Silvester, 117.
Baldwin, Silvester, Jun$^{r}$, 117.
Baldwin, Simeon, 71.
Baldwin, Simion, 104.
Baldwin, Smith, 107.
Baldwin, Soloman, 101.
Baldwin, Stephen, 61.
Baldwin, Stephen, 64.
Baldwin, Sweeten, 20.
Baldwin, Thaddeus, 75.
Baldwin, Thadeus, 94.
Baldwin, Thadeus, 101.
Baldwin, Thankfull, 102.
Baldwin, Theodore, 104.
Baldwin, Theophilus, 71.
Baldwin, Theophilus, 76.
Baldwin, Theophilus, 115.
Baldwin, Thomas, 54.
Baldwin, Thomas, 111.
Baldwin, Timothy, 94.
Baldwin, Timothy, 99.
Baldwin, Timothy, 2$^{nd}$, 94.
Baldwin, W. Samuel, 57
Baldwin, Warner, 77.
Baldwin, William, 66.
Baldwin, William, 91.
Baldwin, Zacheus, 91.
Baldwin, Zeba, 115.
Bales, Benjamin L., 94.
Bales, Elijah, 150.
Baley, Able, 116.
Baley, Abraham, 79.
Baley, Azubah, 119.
Baley, Benjamin, 12.
Baley, Benona, 12.
Baley, David, 116.
Baley, Dudley, 119.
Baley, Ebenezer, 12.
Baley, Elijah, 119.
Baley, Elisabeth, 119.
Baley, Ezekiel, 119.
Baley, Hendrick, 66.
Baley, James, 50.
Baley, James, 50.
Baley, Jedediah, 120.
Baley, Jeremiah, 114.
Baley, John, 119.
Baley, John, Jun$^{r}$, 119.
Baley, Jonathan, 119.
Baley, Jon$^{a}$, Jun$^{r}$, 119.
Baley, Joseph, 60.
Baley, Joseph, 119.
Baley, Joseph, Jun$^{r}$, 119.
Baley, Obadiah, 119.
Baley, Pethust, 119.
Baley, Recompence, 79.
Baley, Samuel, 12.
Baley, Samuel, 114.
Baley, Simeon, 119.
Baley, Thadeus, 120.
Baley, William, 50.
Balik, Ebenezar, 52.
Ball, Benedah, 101.
Ball, Daniel, 70.
Ball, David, 105.
Ball, Eliphlet, 19.
Ball, Erastus, 63.
Ball, Glover, 105.
Ball, Hezekiah, 104.
Ball, John, 105.
Ball, Joseph, 105.
Ball, Mary, 112.
Ball, Oliver, 33.
Ball, Oliver, 100.
Ball, Oliver, 105.
Ball, Stephen, 104.
Ball, Timothy, 112.
Ball, Wait, 19.
Ballard, Jessee, 62.
Ballard, Zach$^{us}$, 150.
Balwin, Elisha, 70.
Bamont, Thomas, 74.
Bampus, Nathan$^{l}$, 68.
Bancraft, Isaac, Jr., 38.
Bancraft, Oliver, 20.
Bancroft, Abner, 37.
Bancroft, Edward, 38.
Bancroft, Emiam, 68.
Bancroft, Isaac, 38.
Bancroft, John, 38.
Bancroft, Noadiah, 62.
Bancroft, Samuel, 37.
Bancroft, Thomas, 37.
Bangs, Lemuel, 31.
Bangs, Lemwell, 15.
Banister, Levi, 134.
Banks, Austin, 32.
Banks, Benjamin, 16.
Banks, Benjamin, Jn$^{r}$, 13.
Banks, Daniel, 13.
Banks, Daniel, 16.
Banks, Daniel, 32.
Banks, David, 13.
Banks, David, 17.
Banks, David, 28.
Banks, Ebenezer, 15.
Banks, Elijah, 13.
Banks, Elizabeth, 13.
Banks, Elizabeth (W$^{d}$), 16.
Banks, Gershom, 13.
Banks, Gershom, Jn$^{r}$, 13.
Banks, Hannah, 86.
Banks, Hezekiah, 32.
Banks, Hyat, 27.
Banks, Isaac, 13.
Banks, James, 15.
Banks, Jesse, 27.
Banks, Jesse, Jun$^{r}$, 27.
Banks, John, 13.
Banks, John, 86.
Banks, Jonathan, 13.
Banks, Joseph, 13.
Banks, Joseph, 15.
Banks, Joseph, 27.
Banks, Joseph, 32.
Banks, Joshua, 16.
Banks, Mary, 86.
Banks, Moses, 13.
Banks, Nathan, 13.
Banks, Nehemiah, 13.
Banks, Nehemiah, Jn$^{r}$, 13.
Banks, Samuel, 13.
Banks, Samuel, 24.
Banks, Sarah, 13.
Banks, Seth, 27.
Banks, Talcott, 13.
Banks, Thadeus, 27.
Banks, Thomas, 32.
Banks, William, 86.
Banning, Abner, 69.
Banning, David, 62.
Banning, Ebenezer, 122.
Banning, John, 122.
Banning, Joseph, 82.
Banning, Sam$^{l}$, 62.
Banning, Samuel, 67.
Banns, Ebenezer, 97.
Banns, Ebenezer, 97.
Banns, Isaac, 96.
Bans, Abraham, 97.
Banthore, W$^{m}$, 44.
Barbarer, James, 66.
Barber, Aaron, 55.
Barber, Abner, 57.
Barber, Abraham, 65.
Barber, Asahel, 57.
Barber, Ashbel, 38.
Barber, Bela, 135.
Barber, Benjamin, 11.
Barber, Benjamin, 28.
Barber, Benjamin, 64.
Barber, Benjamin, 128.
Barber, Benoni, 55.
Barber, Bildad, 49.
Barber, Choxhebe, 65.
Barber, David, 65.
Barber, David, 135.
Barber, David, 135.
Barber, David, Ju., 55.
Barber, Ebenezer, 65.
Barber, Eli, 54.
Barber, Elihue, 65.
Barber, Elijah, 49.
Barber, Elijah, 54.
Barber, Ely, 62.
Barber, Ephraim, 65
Barber, George, 38.
Barber, Gideon, 55.
Barber, Henry, 117.
Barber, Hepzibah, 55.
Barber, Jacob, 65.
Barber, James, 55.
Barber, Jared, 48.
Barber, Jeremiah, 145.
Barber, Jerijah, 55.
Barber, Jesse, 49.
Barber, Jimsi, 65.
Barber, Joel, 48.
Barber, Joel, Jr., 48.
Barber, John, 49.
Barber, John, 119.
Barber, John, 149.
Barber, John, Jr., 49.
Barber, John, 1$^{st}$, 57.
Barber, John, 2$^{d}$, 57.
Barber, Jonah, 55.
Barber, Jon$^{a}$, 38.
Barber, Jonathan, 49.
Barber, Jn$^{o}$, 134.
Barber, Joseph, 44.
Barber, Josiah, 54.
Barber, Josiah, Jur., 54.
Barber, Judah, 57.
Barber, Martha (Wid.), 48.
Barber, Michael, 49.
Barber, Michael, 49.
Barber, Moses, 55.
Barber, Noah, 39.
Barber, Noah, 103.
Barber, Ob$^{d}$, 135.
Barber, Obedi., 136.
Barber, Oliver, 38.
Barber, Oliver, 136.
Barber, Reuben, 49.
Barber, Reuben, 54.
Barber, Reuben, 66.
Barber, Reuben, 1$^{st}$, 57.
Barber, Reuben, 2$^{d}$, 57.
Barber, Samuel, 49.
Barber, Samuel, 68.
Barber, Samuel, 76.
Barber, Sarah, 61.
Barber, Shadrack, 38.
Barber, Simeon, 57.
Barber, Simon, 38.
Barber, Stephen, 66.
Barber, Stephen, 135.
Barber, Stephen, Jr., 135.
Barber, Thomas, 49.
Barber, Thom$^{s}$, 54.
Barber, Thomas, 3$^{d}$, 48
Barber, Timothy, 57.
Barber, Timothy, 69.
Barber, William, 67.
Barber, William, 68.
Barber, William, 154.
Barber, Zachariah, 29.
Bard, Abigel, 101.
Bard, Alexander, 16.
Bard, Andrew, 101.
Bard, George, 94.
Bard, James, 94.
Bard, James, 108.
Bard, Nathan, 62.
Bard, Nathan, 62.
Barden, Ebenezer, 63.
Barden, Seth, 60.
Barden, Seth, 63.
Barden, Timothy, 63.
Bardock, Amos, 61.
Barker, Aaron, 135.
Barker, Abigal, 91.
Barker, Abigal, 108.
Barker, Archelus, 91.
Barker, Benjamin, 91.
Barker, Daniel, 91.
Barker, Edward, 91.
Barker, Edward, 108.
Barker, Eliphlet, 75.
Barker, Elisabeth, 91.
Barker, Ethan, 54.
Barker, James, 91.
Barker, Job, 91.
Barker, John, 90.
Barker, John, 108.
Barker, John, 129.
Barker, John, 152.
Barker, John, 2$^{d}$, 129.
Barker, Joseph, 91.
Barker, Joshua, 140.
Barker, Justice, 92.
Barker, Mary, 91.
Barker, Mary, 129.
Barker, Miles, 75.
Barker, Priscilla, 145.
Barker, Russell, 91.
Barker, Ruth, 97.
Barker, Samuel, 91.
Barker, Sam$^{l}$, 146.
Barker, Seth, 41.
Barker, Stephen, 130.
Barker, Stephen, 2$^{d}$, 130.
Barker, Timothy, 91.
Barker, William, 130.
Barkley, Jon$^{a}$, 134.
Barley, Michael, 58.
Barlow, Aaron, 27.
Barlow, Daniel, 14.
Barlow, David, 14.
Barlow, David, 18.
Barlow, David, 30.
Barlow, Dosin, 73.
Barlow, Edmon, 14.
Barlow, Gershom, 27.
Barlow, John, 28.
Barlow, John, 58.
Barlow, John, 2$^{d}$, 28.
Barlow, Nehemiah, 10.
Barlow, Nehemiah, 31.
Barlow, Samuel, 17.
Barlow, Samuel, 17.
Barlow, Thomas, 31.
Barmer, James, 69.
Barn, Daniel, 101.
Barna, Joseph, 55.
Barnaby, James, 134.
Barnard, Ashbel, 46.
Barnard, David, 43.
Barnard, Dorios, 46.

# INDEX.

Barnard, Ebenezer, 45.
Barnard, Ebenezer, 48.
Barnard, Ebenezer, Jr., 46.
Barnard, Edmund, 51.
Barnard, Frances, 48.
Barnard, Hersey, 70.
Barnard, Jacob, 51.
Barnard, John, 46.
Barnard, Joseph, 45.
Barnard, Jos., 133.
Barnard, Moses, 138.
Barnard, Samuel, 45.
Barnard, Samuel, 48.
Barnard, Samuel, 52.
Barnard, Sam'l, 64.
Barnard, Sam¹, 64.
Barnard, William, 46.
Barnard, W^m, 138.
Barnell, John, 92.
Barnerd, Joseph, 55.
Barnes, Abel, 106.
Barnes, Abraham, 43.
Barnes, Allyn, 49.
Barnes, Ambrose, 93.
Barnes, Amos, 41.
Barnes, Amos, 70.
Barnes, Asa, 50.
Barnes, Asa, 74.
Barnes, Benjamin, 50.
Barnes, Benjamin, 57.
Barnes, Benjamin, 106.
Barnes, Caleb, 75.
Barnes, Charles, 62.
Barnes, Daniel, 74.
Barnes, Daniel, 75.
Barnes, Darcus, 104.
Barnes, David, 35.
Barnes, David, 93.
Barnes, David, 106.
Barnes, Eber, 74.
Barnes, Eli, 75.
Barnes, Elija, 93.
Barnes, Elijah, 35.
Barnes, Elijah, 74.
Barnes, Eliphlet, 75.
Barnes, Elizabeth, 104.
Barnes, Enoch, 106.
Barnes, Ezekael, 109.
Barnes, Ezekiel, 87.
Barnes, Ezra, 105.
Barnes, Farrington, 50.
Barnes, Hartwell, 42.
Barnes, Icabod, 95.
Barnes, Isaac, 45.
Barnes, Israel, 40.
Barnes, Jacob, 112.
Barnes, Jasper, 74.
Barnes, Jerry, 106.
Barnes, Joel, 35.
Barnes, Joel, 106.
Barnes, John, 24.
Barnes, John, 49.
Barnes, John, 77.
Barnes, John, 106.
Barnes, John, Jun^r, 24.
Barnes, John, 1^st, 74.
Barnes, John, 2^d, 74.
Barnes, Jonah, 75.
Barnes, Jonathan, 106.
Barnes, Jonathan, 109.
Barnes, Jon^a, Sen^r, 49.
Barnes, Joseph, 75.
Barnes, Joshua, 106.
Barnes, Josiah, 110.
Barnes, Justice, 106.
Barnes, Lemuel, 99.
Barnes, Levi, 97.
Barnes, Lois, 35.
Barnes, Mark, 50.
Barnes, Moses, 57.
Barnes, Nathan, 50.
Barnes, Nathan, 2^d, 50.
Barnes, Nathan, 3^d, 49.
Barnes, Nathaniel, 50.
Barnes, Nathaniel, 75.
Barnes, Nathaniel, 97.
Barnes, Nathaniel D., 50.
Barnes, Noah, 106.
Barnes, Oliver, 68.
Barnes, Philmon, 50.
Barnes, Philip, 58.
Barnes, Phineas, 73.
Barnes, Reuben, 35.
Barnes, Reuben, 60.
Barnes, Reuben, 70.
Barnes, Samuel, 64.
Barnes, Samuel, 74.
Barnes, Samuel, 97.
Barnes, Samuel, 107.
Barnes, Sarah, 71.
Barnes, Seth, 106.
Barnes, Simeon, 42.
Barnes, Soloman, 105.
Barnes, Solomon, 66.
Barnes, Thomas, 109.
Barnes, Timothy, 61.
Barnes, Tim^ty, 70.
Barnes, William, 50.
Barnes, William, 88.
Barnes, Wise, 35.
Barnes, Zopar, 57.
Barney, Hanover, 104.
Barney, Mary, 141.

Barney, Samuel, 67.
Barney, Samuel, 104.
Barney, Thomas, 62.
Barns, Abel, 55.
Barns, Abel, 65.
Barns, Ambrose, 28.
Barns, Amos, 34.
Barns, Amos, 87.
Barns, Daniel, 34.
Barns, Daniel, 87.
Barns, Easter, 120.
Barns, Edmond, 94.
Barns, Eli, 33.
Barns, Elijah, 113.
Barns, Enos, 65.
Barns, Ezra, 120.
Barns, Gideon, 61.
Barns, Gift, 65.
Barns, Giles, 87.
Barns, Israel, 61.
Barns, James, 19.
Barns, James, 41.
Barns, Jesse, 120.
Barns, Jesse, 2^d, 120.
Barns, Job, 67.
Barns, John, 86.
Barns, Jonathan, 33.
Barns, Jona., 138.
Barns, Josiah, 34.
Barns, Josiah, 68.
Barns, Judah, 34.
Barns, Martha, 87.
Barns, Mary, 87.
Barns, Moses, 41.
Barns, Nehemiah, 115.
Barns, Orange, 64.
Barns, Roswell, 70.
Barns, Samuel, 68.
Barns, Simeon, 120.
Barns, Solomon, 87.
Barns, Stephen, 19.
Barns, Stephen, 55.
Barns, Thomas, 34.
Barns, Thomas, 87.
Barns, Timothy, 65.
Barns, Torhand, 62.
Barns, William, 19.
Barnum, Abel, 12.
Barnum, Abel, 18.
Barnum, Abel, 28.
Barnum, Abijah, 11.
Barnum, Abijah, Jn^r, 11.
Barnum, Amos, 18.
Barnum, Benjamin, 1^st, 11.
Barnum, Benjamin, 2^d, 11.
Barnum, Daniel, 12.
Barnum, David, 12.
Barnum, David, 19.
Barnum, David, 19.
Barnum, David, 58.
Barnum, Ebenezer, 10.
Barnum, Eleazer, 11.
Barnum, Elijah, 12.
Barnum, Eliphilet, 10.
Barnum, Ephraim, 12.
Barnum, Ephraim, 12.
Barnum, Eunice, 12.
Barnum, Eunice, 17.
Barnum, Ezbon, 10.
Barnum, Ezra, 11.
Barnum, Gabriel, 11.
Barnum, Isaac, 10.
Barnum, Jesby, 11.
Barnum, John, 10.
Barnum, John, 12.
Barnum, John, 58.
Barnum, John, Jn^r, 11.
Barnum, Joseph, 11.
Barnum, Joseph, 12.
Barnum, Joseph, Jn^r, 11.
Barnum, Josiah, 10.
Barnum, Judah, 11.
Barnum, Justus, 11.
Barnum, Lazerus, 12.
Barnum, Levi, 12.
Barnum, Mathew, 12.
Barnum, Mathew, Jn^r, 12.
Barnum, Nathanel, 11.
Barnum, Noah, 10.
Barnum, Olive, 11.
Barnum, Olive, 11.
Barnum, Samuel, 11.
Barnum, Samuel, 19.
Barnum, Seth, 11.
Barnum, Stephen, 11.
Barnum, Stephen, 19.
Barnum, Tila, 18.
Barnum, Timothy, 19.
Barnum, Timothy, J^r, 19.
Barnum, Zadock, 18.
Baron, Aaron, 57.
Baron, Asahel, 77.
Baron, Jabez, 77.
Baron, Jabez, 2^d, 77.
Barral, Lewis, 131.
Barret, Amos, 143.
Barret, Benj^n, 137.
Barret, Dan¹, 153.
Barret, Elijah, 46.
Barret, Ephraim, 153.
Barret, Ezekiel, 132.
Barret, Hannah, 154.
Barret, James, 137.

Barret, Jn°, 137.
Barret, John, 150.
Barret, John, 150.
Barret, John, 153.
Barret, Jonathan, 143.
Barret, Joseph, 150.
Barret, Joseph, 154.
Barret, Lemu¹, 151.
Barret, Moses, 151.
Barret, Oliver, 151.
Barret, Robert, 33.
Barret, Smith, 154.
Barret, William, 141.
Barrett, Jere, 46.
Barrett, John, 87.
Barrett, Selah, 52.
Barrett, William, 49.
Barrett, William, 131.
Barriss, David, 70.
Barrows, David, 147.
Barrows, Eleaz^r, 147.
Barrows, Elisha, 148.
Barrows, Elisha, Ju^r, 148.
Barrows, Ethan, 147.
Barrows, Gershom, 148.
Barrows, Isaac, 148.
Barrows, Isaac, 2^d, 147.
Barrows, Jabez, 148.
Barrows, Jabez, 148.
Barrows, Jesse, 148.
Barrows, Jn°, 138.
Barrows, Joshua, 148.
Barrows, Job, 21.
Barrows, Lemuel, 148.
Barrows, Phillip, 147.
Barrows, Printrise, 150.
Barrows, Robert, 147.
Barrows, Solomon, 148.
Barrows, Sylvanus, 152.
Barrows, Sylvanus, Ju^r, 152.
Barrows, Thomas, 144.
Barrows, Thomas, 147.
Barrows, Thomas, 147.
Barrows, Tho^s, 3^d, 148.
Barrows, William, 144.
Barrows, Wills, 138.
Barry, John, 149.
Bars, James, 80.
Barsley, John, 62.
Barstow, Yetonce, 129.
Bartholemew, Andrew, 57.
Bartholemew, Benj^n, 57.
Bartholemew, Daniel, 75.
Bartholemew, Isaac, 65.
Bartholemew, Israel, 103.
Bartholemew, Jacob, 57.
Bartholemew, Jeames, 57.
Bartholemew, John, 57.
Bartholemew, Joseph, 91.
Bartholemew, Margett, 57.
Bartholemew, Reuben, 57.
Bartholemew, Seth, 75.
Bartholemew, Submit, 57.
Bartholemy, Claudius, 94.
Bartholemy, Sam¹, 127.
Bartholick, Martin, 123.
Bartholick, Thomas, 123.
Bartholmew, Moses, 108.
Bartholmew, Sam¹¹, 65.
Bartholomew, Abra^m, 34.
Bartholomew, Benjamin, 91.
Bartholomew, Benjamin, 150.
Bartholomew, Benj^n, 154.
Bartholomew, Benjamin, 2^nd, 92.
Bartholomew, Charles, 40.
Bartholomew, Isaac, 108.
Bartholomew, Jacob, Jr., 35.
Bartholomew, Jesse, 56.
Bartholomew, John, 154.
Bartholomew, Jonathan, 92.
Bartholomew, Jon^a, 108.
Bartholomew, Joseph, 57.
Bartholomew, Joseph, 109.
Bartholomew, Leonard, 149.
Bartholomew, Leonard, 154.
Bartholomew, Luther, 65.
Bartholomew, Noah, 59.
Bartholomew, Osi, 109.
Bartholomew, Samuel, 92.
Bartholomew, Sam¹, 154.
Bartholomew, Sam¹, 154.
Bartholomew, Sarah, 154.
Bartholomew, Seth, 109.
Bartholomew, Timothy, 92.
Bartholomew, W^m, 90.
Bartholumew, Jacob, 34.
Bartis, John, 2^d, 96.
Bartis, Samuel, 95.
Bartlet, Abraham, 96.
Bartlet, Abraham, 96.
Bartlet, Chandler, 145.
Bartlet, Daniel, 99.
Bartlet, Dan¹, 140.
Bartlet, Edward, 144.
Bartlet, Eliph^t, 134.
Bartlet, Elizabeth, 37.
Bartlet, George, 99.
Bartlet, Hooker, 97.
Bartlet, Ichabod, 145.
Bartlet, James, 99.
Bartlet, John, 38.
Bartlet, John, 99.

Bartlet, John, 145.
Bartlet, Jonathan, 38.
Bartlet, Joseph, 98.
Bartlet, Judah, 145.
Bartlet, Richard, 144.
Bartlet, Ruben, 99.
Bartlet, Ruben, 2^nd, 99.
Bartlet, Russel, 63.
Bartlet, Samuel, 38.
Bartlet, Samuel, 96.
Bartlet, Stephen, 99.
Bartlet, Sylvanus, 45.
Bartlett, Daniel, 27.
Bartlett, Ed^m, 134.
Bartlett, E^m, 136.
Bartlett, John, 79.
Bartlett, John, Jun^r, 79.
Bartlett, Moses, 79.
Bartlett, Nathaniel, 27.
Bartlett, Samuel, 98.
Bartlett, Samuel, 136.
Bartlett, Thomas, 79.
Bartlett, Timothy, 98.
Bartletts, Cha^r, 132.
Barton, Andrew, 62.
Barton, Elkane, 138.
Barton, Joseph, 67.
Barton, Michael, 154.
Barton, Roger, 67.
Barton, W^m, 55.
Bartram, James, 12.
Bartram, Job, 21.
Bartram, John, 11.
Bartram, Mary, 14.
Bartrum, Daniel, 27.
Bartrum, David, 27.
Bartrum, Jabez, 18.
Bartrum, Noah, 18.
Bartrum, Paul, 27.
Barty, John, 95.
Bascom, Dan¹, 136.
Bascomb, Abial, 146.
Bascomb, William, 145.
Basett, Isaac, 101.
Basett, James, 100.
Bass, Anna, 64.
Bass, Benjamin, 19.
Bass, Codsida, 136.
Bass, Daniel, 71.
Bass, Eben^r, 152.
Bass, Elijah, 19.
Bass, John, 18.
Bass, Jonathan, 120.
Bass, Joseph, 18.
Bass, Joseph, 19.
Bass, Jos., 139.
Bass, Josiah, 71.
Bass, Nathan, 64.
Bass, Newcomb, 10.
Bass, Samuel, 32.
Bass, Sam¹, 140.
Bass, Thomas, 18.
Bass, Zeph^b, 136.
Basset, Abel, 135.
Basset, Abraham, 95.
Basset, Amos, 100.
Basset, David, 65.
Basset, Hennery, 18.
Basset, Joel, 20.
Basset, John, 18.
Basset, John, 20.
Basset, John, 100.
Basset, Joshua, 63.
Basset, Levi, 75.
Basset, Samuel, 64.
Basset, Samuel, 101.
Basset, Samuel, 2^d, 95.
Basset, Theophilus, 100.
Basset, William, 70.
Basset, Zopher, 68.
Bassett, Abel, 100.
Bassett, Abraham, 95.
Bassett, Amos, 94.
Bassett, Benjamin, 94.
Bassett, Cornelius, 32.
Bassett, Daniel, 73.
Bassett, Daniel, 106.
Bassett, David, 94.
Bassett, David, 101.
Bassett, Eben, 94.
Bassett, Edward, 95.
Bassett, Edward, 102.
Bassett, Elisha, 98.
Bassett, Henry, 100.
Bassett, Hezekiah, 100.
Bassett, Isaac, 77.
Bassett, Isaac, 94.
Bassett, Isaac, 106.
Bassett, Isaac, 143.
Bassett, James, 94.
Bassett, James, 101.
Bassett, James, 113.
Bassett, Jehu, 106.
Bassett, Jehu, 113.
Bassett, John, 94.
Bassett, John, 2^nd, 95.
Bassett, Joseph, 94.
Bassett, Joseph, 106.
Bassett, Lidia, 106.
Bassett, Mabel, 100.
Bassett, Mary, 102.
Bassett, Miles, 95.
Bassett, Nathaniel, 99.

Bassett, Noah, 77.
Bassett, Obed, 106.
Bassett, Samuel, 77.
Bassett, Samuel, 94.
Bassett, Samuel, 106.
Bassett, Samuel, 2^nd, 101.
Bassett, Samuel, 2^nd, 106.
Bassett, Samuel, 3^d, 94.
Bassett, Timothy, 100.
Bassett, William, 76.
Bassett, William, 98.
Bassitt, John, 144.
Bassot, Samuel, 57.
Basten, John, 60.
Basto, William, 57.
Bateman, Benjamin, 144.
Bateman, Stephen, 73.
Bates, Aaron, 68.
Bates, Abner, 79.
Bates, Amos, 83.
Bates, Benjamin, 110.
Bates, Charles, 26.
Bates, Curtis, 96.
Bates, Daniel, 83.
Bates, Daniel, 96.
Bates, Dan^el, 139.
Bates, David, 26.
Bates, David, 79.
Bates, David, 138.
Bates, Eleazer, 83.
Bates, Eliakim, 73.
Bates, Elias, 73.
Bates, Elias, 77.
Bates, Elias, 105.
Bates, Elihu, 83.
Bates, Elihu, 94.
Bates, Gamaliel, 110.
Bates, Gershom, 26.
Bates, Henry, 68.
Bates, Henry, 131.
Bates, Ichabod, 58.
Bates, Isaac, 19.
Bates, Isaac, 57.
Bates, Isaac, 89.
Bates, Isackas, 150.
Bates, James, 27.
Bates, James, 96.
Bates, Jerom, 26.
Bates, Job, 79.
Bates, John, 27.
Bates, John, 150.
Bates, John, Jun^r, 26.
Bates, Jonathan, 27.
Bates, Jonathan, 83.
Bates, Joseph, 58.
Bates, Joseph, 83.
Bates, Joseph, 87.
Bates, Jos., 138.
Bates, Josiah, 73.
Bates, Justus, 27.
Bates, Lemuel, 45.
Bates, Martin, 65.
Bates, Mary (W^d), 26.
Bates, Mosses, 104.
Bates, Nehemiah, 24.
Bates, Oliver, 61.
Bates, Oliver, 144.
Bates, Samuel, 96.
Bates, Samuel, 2^nd, 96.
Bates, Sarah, 66.
Bates, William, 26.
Bates, Zopha, 45.
Batholomew, And^w, 108.
Batterson, George, 13.
Batterson, Hezekiah, 70.
Batterson, James, 12.
Batterson, James, 22.
Batterson, James, Jn^r, 12.
Batterson, John, 12.
Batterson, John, Jn^r, 12.
Batterson, Jorge, Jn^r, 12.
Batterson, Pawel, 22.
Batterson, Stephen, 24.
Batterson, William, 13.
Baul, Doct^r J., 24.
Baulding, Eliphelet, 126.
Bawaj, Thomas, 57.
Bawlden, Calep, 11.
Bawlden, Dudley, 13.
Bawlden, Elias, 17.
Bawlden, Samuel, 11.
Bawlden, Thaddeus, 10.
Bawlden, Tibbals, 10.
Bawldin, Ebenez^r, 147.
Bawldin, Jacob, 142.
Bawley, John, 101.
Baxter, Aaron, 135.
Baxter, Alexander, 138.
Baxter, Elisha, 52.
Baxter, Frances, 40.
Baxter, Frances, Jr., 37.
Baxter, Francis, 83.
Baxter, Jedediah, 138.
Baxter, Jesse, 113.
Baxter, Levi, 38.
Baxter, Robert, 149.
Baxter, Sim^n, 138.
Baxter, William, 40.
Baxter, W^m, 133.
Baxter, William, 146.
Baxto, Reuben, 23.
Bay, Thomas, 15.
Bayler, Noah, 118.

# INDEX.

Bayley, Nathan, 129.
Bayley, Nathan, Jun$^r$, 128.
Bayley, Sexton, 146.
Beach, Abel, 31.
Beach, Abel, 68.
Beach, Abijah Hen$^y$, 71.
Beach, Abner, 63.
Beach, Abner, 71.
Beach, Adna, 75.
Beach, Adney, 61.
Beach, Agar, Jun$^r$, 30.
Beach, Asa, 100.
Beach, Asa, 109.
Beach, Azariah, 135.
Beach, Benjamin, 74.
Beach, Benjamin, 111.
Beach, Benonah, 69.
Beach, Caleb, 71.
Beach, Chancy, 67.
Beach, Dan., 56.
Beach, Daniel, 65.
Beach, David, 68.
Beach, David, 71.
Beach, Ebenezer, 17.
Beach, Ebenezer, 64.
Beach, Ebenezer, 71.
Beach, Ebenezer, 91.
Beach, Edmond, 61.
Beach, Edmond, 61.
Beach, Elasa, 106.
Beach, Elihu, 48.
Beach, Elijha, 135.
Beach, Elijha, 135.
Beach, Elizabeth, 30.
Beach, Elnathan, 91.
Beach, Elnathan, 93.
Beach, Enos, 77.
Beach, Ephrim, 91.
Beach, Ezekiel, 68.
Beach, Fisk, 61.
Beach, Francis, 59.
Beach, Giles, 106.
Beach, Hezekiah, 17.
Beach, Isaac, 29.
Beach, Isaac, 71.
Beach, Israel, 70.
Beach, Jabez, 29.
Beach, Jacob, 59.
Beach, Jessee, 70.
Beach, Joel, 64.
Beach, Joel, 77.
Beach, John, 17.
Beach, John, 20.
Beach, John, 68.
Beach, John, 68.
Beach, John, 77.
Beach, Jn$^o$, 135.
Beach, John, Jun$^r$, 19.
Beach, Joseph, 2$^{nd}$, 109.
Beach, Lazarus, 20.
Beach, Lewis, 68.
Beach, Linus, 57.
Beach, Linus, 70.
Beach, Losior, 71.
Beach, Mary, 58.
Beach, Mary, 108.
Beach, Michael, 65.
Beach, Miles, 46.
Beach, Mines, 70.
Beach, Moses, 108.
Beach, Nathaniel, 31.
Beach, Nathaniel, 106.
Beach, Noah, 68.
Beach, Noah, 71.
Beach, Reuben, 74.
Beach, Sabin, 71.
Beach, Sam., 61.
Beach, Samuel, 68.
Beach, Sam'l, 69.
Beach, Samuel, 112.
Beach, Stephen, 108.
Beach, Thomas, 101.
Beach, Titus, 108.
Beach, Wait, 62.
Beach, William, 59.
Beach, William, 108.
Beach, Zopher, 68.
Beacher, Abel, 50.
Beacher, Abram, 58.
Beacher, Amos, 50.
Beacher, David, 71.
Beacher, Elizur, 2$^d$, 71.
Beacher, Erastus, 50.
Beacher, Hezekiah, 50.
Beacher, Hezekiah, 56.
Beacher, Jerad, 112.
Beacher, John, 50.
Beacher, John, 71.
Beacher, Joseph, 50.
Beacher, Joseph, Jr., 50.
Beacher, Nathan, 50.
Beacher, Nathaniel, 71.
Beacher, Samuel, 58.
Beacher, Walter, 50.
Beachgood, John, 24.
Beadle, Benjamin, 122.
Beadle, Jonathan, 52.
Beadsley, Wells, 74.
Beaman, Elisha, 64.
Beamon, Samuel, 145.
Beamont, Abel, 74.
Beamont, Ceasor, 74.
Beamont, Daniel, 74.

Beamont, Dan., 146.
Beamont, Deoadah, 107.
Beamont, Jedutham, 96.
Beamont, Jon$^a$, 37.
Beamont, Mary, 86.
Beamont, Matthias, 74.
Beamont, Nathan, 74.
Beamont, Park, 74.
Beamont, Timothy, 74.
Beamont, Tracy, 58.
Beamont, Truman, 74.
Beamont, William, 146.
Beamous, Ephraim, 141.
Beamus, Jonathan, 141.
Bear, Joseph, 47.
Bearce, Jeames, 57.
Bearce, Jeames, Jun$^r$, 57.
Beard, Azeriah, 75.
Beard, Charles, 17.
Beard, Clark, 76.
Beard, David, 17.
Beard, David, 71.
Beard, David, Ju$^r$, 17.
Beard, George, 76.
Beard, Joel, 18.
Beard, Robert, 16.
Beard, Samuel, 18.
Beard, William, 114.
Beardly, Gershom, 147.
Beardslee, Aaron, 17.
Beardslee, Abijah, 18.
Beardslee, Benjamin, 17.
Beardslee, Benjamin, Jun$^r$, 17.
Beardslee, Calep, 18.
Beardslee, Daniel, 12.
Beardslee, Daniel, 17.
Beardslee, David, 18.
Beardslee, David, 18.
Beardslee, David, 19.
Beardslee, Eli, 17.
Beardslee, Elijah, 18.
Beardslee, Eliot, 18.
Beardslee, Elisha, 17.
Beardslee, Elizabeth, 17.
Beardslee, George, 17.
Beardslee, Giddeon, 18.
Beardslee, Giddeon, Ju$^r$, 18.
Beardslee, Hall, 18.
Beardslee, Hennery, 17.
Beardslee, Isaac, 17.
Beardslee, Israel, 17.
Beardslee, Jered, 17.
Beardslee, John, 18.
Beardslee, John, 18.
Beardslee, Joseph, 18.
Beardslee, Joseph, 18.
Beardslee, Joshua, 17.
Beardslee, Josiah, 17.
Beardslee, Josiah, 18.
Beardslee, Lemwell, 17.
Beardslee, Lewis, 17.
Beardslee, Luke, 17.
Beardslee, Moses, 18.
Beardslee, Nathan S., 18.
Beardslee, Nehemiah, 19.
Beardslee, Obediah, 18.
Beardslee, Philo, 17.
Beardslee, Phineus, 18.
Beardslee, Samuel, 18.
Beardslee, Samuel, 18.
Beardslee, Stephen, 17.
Beardslee, Thaddeus, 17.
Beardslee, Thomas, 17.
Beardslee, William, 17.
Beardslee, Zalmon, 18.
Beardslee, Zeph., 18.
Beardslee, Zepheniah, 18.
Beardsley, Aaron, 29.
Beardsley, Abigail, 20.
Beardsley, Abigail (Wid.), 19.
Beardsley, Amos, 29.
Beardsley, Benjamin, 32.
Beardsley, David, 29.
Beardsley, David, 58.
Beardsley, Ebenezer, 76.
Beardsley, Ebenezer, 103.
Beardsley, Eliakim, 95.
Beardsley, Elias, 19.
Beardsley, Ephraim, 58.
Beardsley, Hezekiah, 52.
Beardsley, Jabez, 58.
Beardsley, Jabez, 109.
Beardsley, Jeames, 56.
Beardsley, Jeames, 74.
Beardsley, Jesse, 29.
Beardsley, John, 71.
Beardsley, John, 81.
Beardsley, Jonas, 94.
Beardsley, Jonathan, 19.
Beardsley, Josiah, 19.
Beardsley, Lemuel, 30.
Beardsley, Levi, 109.
Beardsley, Nathan, 30.
Beardsley, Nehemiah, 56.
Beardsley, Philo, 58.
Beardsley, Samuel, 19.
Beardsley, Silas, 71.
Beardsley (Widow), 30.
Beardsly, Abraham, 30.
Beardsly, Benjamin, 30.
Beardsly, Curtis, 30.
Beardsly, David, Jun$^r$, 29.
Beardsly, Eliphalet, 31.

Beardsly, Ephraim, 29.
Beardsly, Frances, 47.
Beardsly, Henery, 29.
Beardsly, Jabez, 31.
Beardsly, Jeremiah, 31.
Beardsly, John, 30.
Beardsly, Matthew (Wid.), 29.
Beardsly, Silus, 31.
Bearmore, Nathan$^{el}$, 15.
Bearnes, Ebenezer, 75.
Bears, Abel, 74.
Bears, Anthony, 28.
Bears, Ebenezer, 74.
Bears, Ezra, 71.
Bears, James, 88.
Bears, Jeames, 1$^{st}$, 71.
Bears, Jeames, 2$^d$, 71.
Bears, Josiah, 77.
Bears, Lewis, 77.
Bears, Mathew, 74.
Bears, Nathan, 28.
Bears, Philo, 74.
Bears, Zacheriah, 77.
Beaumont, Samuel, 89.
Beba, Abijah, 126.
Beba, Abner, 122.
Beba, Amos, 125.
Beba, Azariah, 122.
Beba, Azariah, 127.
Beba, Clark, 122.
Beba, David, 122.
Beba, David, 131.
Beba, Easter, 122.
Beba, Eliphelet, 127.
Beba, Ephraim, 127.
Beba, Guy, 128.
Beba, Jabez, 128.
Beba, Jabez, 2$^d$, 128.
Beba, James, 127.
Beba, James, 129.
Beba, Jared, 127.
Beba, Jedediah, 124.
Beba, Jeduthan, 128.
Beba, Jethro, 128.
Beba, Jon$^a$, 128.
Beba, Joseph, 127.
Beba, Lemuel, 122.
Beba, Othiniel, 127.
Beba, Paul, 128.
Beba, Richard, 127.
Beba, Robart, 122.
Beba, Ruben, 127.
Beba, Rufus, 127.
Beba, Sam$^l$, 127.
Beba, Sam$^l$, Jun$^r$, 127.
Beba, Stephen, 115.
Beba, Thadeus, 127.
Beba, Theophilus, 127.
Beba, Timothy, 122.
Beba, William, 128.
Bebbons, Benj$^n$, 153.
Bebe, John, 118.
Bebee, Abner, 82.
Bebee, Avary, 82.
Bebee, Brockway, 82.
Bebee, Caleb, 82.
Bebee, Clark, 82.
Bebee, Daniel, 67.
Bebee, Ebenezer, 82.
Bebee, Hannah, 82.
Bebee, Isaac, 67.
Bebee, John, 82.
Bebee, Lydia, 82.
Bebee, Lydia (W$^d$), 26.
Bebee, Mary, 90.
Bebee, Nathan, 82.
Bebee, Phebee, 82.
Bebee, Richard, 79.
Bebee, Solomon, 67.
Bebee, Will$^m$, 83.
Beche, David, 29.
Beck, Josiah, 53.
Becknal, Elezer, 139.
Beckett, Josiah, 123.
Beckwith, Abner, 124.
Beckwith, Absolum, 124.
Beckwith, Anna, 76.
Beckwith, Barzilla, 82.
Beckwith, Buel, 124.
Beckwith, Caleb, 122.
Beckwith, Caleb, 127.
Beckwith, Chauncey, 82.
Beckwith, David, 128.
Beckwith, Daniel, 122.
Beckwith, Elijah, 124.
Beckwith, Elisha, 127.
Beckwith, Ephraim, 122.
Beckwith, Ezekiel, 2$^d$, 127.
Beckwith, Ezekiel B., 82.
Beckwith, Ezra, 124.
Beckwith, Francis, 81.
Beckwith, Francis, 120.
Beckwith, Frederick, 127.
Beckwith, George, 35.
Beckwith, George, 64.
Beckwith, George, 123.
Beckwith, George, Jun$^r$, 123.
Beckwith, Harey, 49.
Beckwith, Isaac, 125.
Beckwith, Isaac, 128.
Beckwith, Jason, 127.
Beckwith, Jasper, 122.
Beckwith, Jasper, 125.
Beckwith, Jeames, 75.

Beckwith, Jedediah, 124.
Beckwith, Jesse, 124.
Beckwith, Jesse, 2$^d$, 124.
Beckwith, Job, 82.
Beckwith, John, 127.
Beckwith, John, Jun$^r$, 127.
Beckwith, Jonah, 41.
Beckwith, Jonathan, 124.
Beckwith, Joseph, 124.
Beckwith, Joseph, 2$^d$, 82.
Beckwith, Josiah, 45.
Beckwith, Lebeus, 124.
Beckwith, Lemuel, 126.
Beckwith, Mabel, 41.
Beckwith, Martin, 124.
Beckwith, Mary, 124.
Beckwith, Mervin, 49.
Beckwith, Nathan, 124.
Beckwith, Nathan, 130.
Beckwith, Nath$^l$, 82.
Beckwith, Nath$^l$, 124.
Beckwith, Noah, 127.
Beckwith, Perigreen, 124.
Beckwith, Phineas, 123.
Beckwith, Roswell, 123.
Beckwith, Samuel, 35.
Beckwith, Samuel, 45.
Beckwith, Sam$^l$, 82.
Beckwith, Sam$^l$, 123.
Beckwith, Sam$^l$, 125.
Beckwith, Seth, 127.
Beckwith, Stephen, 82.
Beckwith, Stephen, 124.
Beckwith, Thomas, 35.
Beckwith, Thomas, 124.
Beckwith, Timothy, 128.
Beckwith, Timothy, 2$^d$, 128.
Beckwith, Watrus, 123.
Beckwith, William, 51.
Beckwith, William, 130.
Beckwith, Zacheriah, 75.
Beckwith, Zenos, 124.
Bedford, Ad, 103.
Bedient, Gilead, 24.
Bedient, Jesse, 24.
Bedient, John, 24.
Bedient, Mordecai, 24.
Beeba, Peter, 121.
Beeba, Robert, 122.
Beebe, Adam, 45.
Beebe, Adonijah, 45.
Beebe, Amasa, 60.
Beebe, Asahel, 73.
Beebe, Borden, 110.
Beebe, Comfort, 80.
Beebe, David, 12.
Beebe, David, 110.
Beebe, Edmond, 12.
Beebe, Elisha, 67.
Beebe, Elizabeth, 110.
Beebe, Israel, 110.
Beebe, James, 29.
Beebe, Joab, 121.
Beebe, Joseph, 12.
Beebe, Joseph, 111.
Beebe, Joseph, Jur, 12.
Beebe, Lemuel, 12.
Beebe, Lemuel, Jur, 12.
Beebe, Molly, 90.
Beebe, Ruben, 110.
Beebe, Ruth, 90.
Beebe, Stephen, 77.
Beebe, Thomas, 30.
Beebe, William, 62.
Beebe, Zachariah, 88.
Beebe, Zina, 111.
Beebee, ——, 55.
Beebee, Burgess, 128.
Beebee, Daniel, 58.
Beebee, Daniel, 2$^d$, 58.
Beebee, Ephraim, 51.
Beebee, Ethel, 12.
Beebee, Grace, 110.
Beebee, Jehiel, 83.
Beebee, Silas, 83.
Beebie, Joel, 101.
Beeby, Martin, 94.
Beech, Agar, 29.
Beech, Benjamin, 95.
Beech, Eliakim, 30.
Beech, Harrison, 91.
Beech, Jabez, 29.
Beech, James, 30.
Beech, John, 108.
Beech, Joseph, 109.
Beech, Lazarus, 27.
Beech, Samuel, 101.
Beech, Thadeus, 101.
Beecher, Amos, 110.
Beecher, Benjamin, 93.
Beecher, Burr, 111.
Beecher, Daniel, 110.
Beecher, Daniel, 112.
Beecher, David, 104.
Beecher, Ebenezur, 111.
Beecher, Enoch, 111.
Beecher, Ephrahim, 111.
Beecher, Hannah, 95.
Beecher, Hannah, 111.
Beecher, Hezekiah, 93.
Beecher, Hezekiah, 111.
Beecher, Hiram, 104.
Beecher, Isaac, 103.

Beecher, Isaac, 105.
Beecher, Isaac, 111.
Beecher, Isaac, 2$^{nd}$, 112.
Beecher, Jesse, 111.
Beecher, John, 93.
Beecher, John, 103.
Beecher, John, 105.
Beecher, Jonathan, 111.
Beecher, Joseph, 111.
Beecher, Linus, 111.
Beecher, Lowes, 105.
Beecher, Mary, 103.
Beecher, Medad, 105.
Beecher, Moses, 105.
Beecher, Moses, 2$^{nd}$, 105.
Beecher, Nicholas, 111.
Beecher, Raphel, 105.
Beecher, Samuel, 105.
Beecher, Sarah, 104.
Beecher, Sarah, 111.
Beecher, Stephen, 105.
Beecher, Sussanah, 103.
Beecher, Thadius, 103.
Beecher, Titus, 105.
Beecher, Weeler, 111.
Beeman, Josiah, 10.
Beeman, Samuel, 69.
Beeman, Thomas, 68.
Beeman, Thomas, 2$^d$, 68.
Beemont, William, 63.
Beemus, Levi, 148.
Beerdslee, John, 14.
Beers, Abner, 30.
Beers, Andrew, 20.
Beers, Archebus, 17.
Beers, Barnabus, 17.
Beers, Benjamin, 101.
Beers, Daniel, 21.
Beers, David, 14.
Beers, David, 20.
Beers, David, 31.
Beers, David, 112.
Beers, David, Jn$^r$, 12.
Beers, David, Jun$^r$, 14.
Beers, Eben, 20.
Beers, Elias, 20.
Beers, Elias, 104.
Beers, Elnathan, 29.
Beers, Elnathan, 32.
Beers, Ephraim, 31.
Beers, Ephraim, 32.
Beers, Ezekiel, 23.
Beers, Ezra, 32.
Beers, Fanton, 32.
Beers, Finious, 20.
Beers, Gershom, 27.
Beers, Isaac, 32.
Beers, Isaac, 104.
Beers, Jabez, 30.
Beers, James, 24.
Beers, James, 29.
Beers, James, 30.
Beers, Joel, 30.
Beers, John, 20.
Beers, John, 92.
Beers, John, 94.
Beers, John, 101.
Beers, Jonathan, 32.
Beers, Joseph, 14.
Beers, Joseph, 18.
Beers, Joseph, Jn$^r$, 14.
Beers, Josiah, 29.
Beers, Lewis, 17.
Beers, Matthew, 30.
Beers, Moses, 22.
Beers, Moses, Jun$^r$, 22.
Beers, Nathan, 14.
Beers, Nathan, 23.
Beers, Nathan, 31.
Beers, Nathan, 104.
Beers, Nathan, 112.
Beers, Nathan, Jn$^r$, 14.
Beers, Nathaniel, 17.
Beers, Nathaniel, 21.
Beers, Nehemiah, 32.
Beers, Noah, 18.
Beers, Oliver, 20.
Beers, Pinkany, 31.
Beers, Pitman, 92.
Beers, Reubin, 14.
Beers, Samuel, 14.
Beers, Samuel, 21.
Beers, Samuel, 21.
Beers, Sam$^l$, 29.
Beers, Samuel, Jn$^r$, 14.
Beers, Sarah (Wid.), 20.
Beers, Simeon, 21.
Beers, Sirus, 20.
Beers, Stephen, 30.
Beers, Tine, 18.
Beers, Truman, 20.
Beets, John, 64.
Beevel, Martin, 109.
Belair, Thomas, 45.
Belcher, David, 150.
Belcher, Elisha, 16.
Belcher, Jonathan, 79.
Belcher, William, 68.
Belden, Aaron, 54.
Belden, Abraham, 54.
Belden, Asa, 54.
Belden, Ashbel, 33.
Belden, Benjamin, 35.

INDEX. 161


Belden, Bildad, 53.
Belden, Charles, 68.
Belden, Charles, 68.
Belden, Charles, 68.
Belden, David, 54.
Belden, Ebenezer, 66.
Belden, Elisha, 54.
Belden, Ezra, 53.
Belden, Isaac, 35.
Belden, Jeremiah, 54.
Belden, John, 33.
Belden, John, 52.
Belden, John, 54.
Belden, John, Jr., 33.
Belden, John R., 41.
Belden, Jonathan, 32.
Belden, Joshua, 54.
Belden, Leonard, 32.
Belden, Mary, 53.
Belden, Mary, 90.
Belden, Moses, 54.
Belden, Nathan, 36.
Belden, Oth$^o$. 54.
Belden, Rebecca, 52.
Belden, Richard, 54.
Belden, Richard, Jr., 54.
Belden, Rositer, 47.
Belden, Samuel, 85.
Belden, Samuel, 129.
Belden, Silas, 54.
Belden, Simeon, 52.
Belden, Simion, 47.
Beldin, Ezekiel P., 52.
Beldin, Jerad, 105.
Belding, Amos, 75.
Belding, Asa, 21.
Belding, Benjamin, 27.
Belding, David, 21.
Belding, David, 81.
Belding, John, 22.
Belding, Rachel, 105.
Belding, Samuel, 21.
Belding, Seymour, 90.
Belding, Stephen, 81.
Belding, Thomas, 21.
Beldon, Bartholomew, 68.
Beldon, Benjamin, 83.
Beldon, John, 88.
Beleh, Josiah, 32.
Belfast (Negroe), 104.
Belknap, Deceius, 38.
Belknap, Ebenezur, 96.
Belknap, Job, 38.
Belknap, Job, Jr., 38.
Belknap, Jonathan, 61.
Bell, Abraham, 24.
Bell, Benjamin, 56.
Bell, Elisha, 44.
Bell Jeams, 71.
Bell, Joannah (W$^d$), 25.
Bell, John, 26.
Bell, John, 103.
Bell, John, Jun$^r$, 26.
Bell, Jonathan, 26.
Bell, Joseph, 117.
Bell, Jude, 61.
Bell, Noah, 25.
Bell, Oliver, 146.
Bell, Ruth, 57.
Bell, Stephen, 25.
Bell, Thaddeus, 26.
Bell, Thaddeus, J$^r$, 26.
Bellam, Lyman, 35.
Bellamy, Abner, 51.
Bellamy, Arom, 93.
Bellamy, David, 56.
Bellamy, Justus, 93.
Bellamy, Samuel, 56.
Bellamy, Samuel, 100.
Beller, Sam$^l$, 66.
Bellknapp, Abel, 23.
Bellows, Asa, 120.
Bellows, Darius, 120.
Bellows, Isaac, 36.
Bellows, John, 118.
Bellows, Nath$^l$, 118.
Belnap, Frances, 134.
Belnap, Jo$^n$, 139.
Belnap, Sim$^n$, 134.
Belot, John, 124.
Below, Peter, 149.
Belshaw, John, 117.
Belshaw, Jon$^a$, 132.
Belshaw, Joseph, 113.
Belshaw, Joseph, 124.
Belshaw, Nathan, 113.
Belshaw, Samuel, 130.
Belshaw, Thomas, 129.
Belshaw, William, 113.
Belton, Jonas, 118.
Beman, Benjamin, 110.
Bement, Dennis, 39.
Bement, Edmund, 36.
Bement, Joseph, 39.
Bement, Makens, 36.
Bemmer, Mary, 105.
Bemmer, Nathaniel, 105.
Bemon, Aaron, 44.
Bemont, Edmund, 39.
Bemount, Isaiah, 145.
Ben (Negroe), 102.
Bena (Negro), 131.
Bench, John, 93.
Bench, Phineas, 92.
Bench, Samuel, 93.
Bencher, Justus, 112.
Benedick, Abijah, 66.
Benedick, Aron, 109.
Benedick, Buchnel, 68.
Benedick, Francis, 63.
Benedick, James, 63.
Benedick, John, 103.
Benedick, Noah, 66.
Benedict, Aaron, 71.
Benedict, Abigail, 11.
Benedict, Abijah, 28.
Benedict, Abraham, 10.
Benedict, Abraham, Jn$^r$, 10.
Benedict, Asa, 11.
Benedict, Asor, 11.
Benedict, Benjaman, 67.
Benedict, Calep, 11.
Benedict, Comfort, 28.
Benedict, Daniel, 11.
Benedict, David, 11.
Benedict, Ebenezer, 11.
Benedict, Ebenezer, 11.
Benedict, Eliakam, 10.
Benedict, Eliakam, 12.
Benedict, Elijah, 11.
Benedict, Elijah, 58.
Benedict, Ezra, 11.
Benedict, Ezra, 28.
Benedict, Gamaliel, 28.
Benedict, Hezekiah, 12.
Benedict, Jesse, 28.
Benedict, Jesse, 58.
Benedict, John, 28.
Benedict, John, 58.
Benedict, John, 2$^d$, 28.
Benedict, Jonas, 11.
Benedict, Joseph, 11.
Benedict, Joshua, 10.
Benedict, Lemwell, 11.
Benedict, Michael, 10.
Benedict, Moses, 57.
Benedict, Nathan, 11.
Benedict, Noah, 77.
Benedict, Noble 11.
Benedict, Peter, 10.
Benedict, Samuel, 1$^{st}$, 11.
Benedict, Samuel, 2$^d$, 11.
Benedict, Stephen B., 11.
Benedict, Thadeus, 27.
Benedict, Theofelus, 11.
Benedict, Thomas 11.
Benedict, Timothy, 11.
Benedict, Timothy, 29.
Benedict, Zadock, 11.
Benham, David, 105.
Benham, Ebenezer, 35.
Benham, Elihu, 112.
Benham, Elisha, 103.
Benham, Gamaliel, 105.
Benham, Isaac, 109.
Benham, James, 34.
Benham, James, 93.
Benham, Japhet, 73.
Benham, Jerad, 106.
Benham, Joel, 34.
Benham, John, 92.
Benham, John, 105.
Benham, John, 2$^{nd}$, 93.
Benham, John, 2$^{nd}$, 105.
Benham, Joseph, 100.
Benham, Lemuel, 104.
Benham, Lettice, 108.
Benham, Phineas, 77.
Benham, Samuel, 105.
Benham, Shadreck, 109.
Benham, Smith, 77.
Benham, Thomas, 94.
Benham, Thomas, 109.
Benham, Uriah, 92.
Benham, Warren, 92.
Benjamin, Aaron, 30.
Benjamin, Abiel, 114.
Benjamin, Abiel, Jun$^r$, 114.
Benjamin, Allyn, 38.
Benjamin, Asa, 30.
Benjamin, Barz$^l$, 141.
Benjamin, Berzeler, 102.
Benjamin, Elisha, 39.
Benjamin, Elisha, Jr., 39.
Benjamin, Elnathan, 29.
Benjamin, George, 29.
Benjamin, James, 36.
Benjamin, John, 29.
Benjamin, John, 29.
Benjamin, John, 113.
Benjamin, Jonathan, 36.
Benjamin, Philip, 29.
Benjamin, Phinehas, 60.
Benjamin, Phinehas, 63.
Benjamin, Richard, 90.
Benjamin, Samuel, 29.
Benjamin, Samuel, 37.
Benjamin, Samuel, 68.
Benjamin, Simeon, 148.
Benjamins, Asa, 114.
Benjamins, Ezra, 114.
Benjamins, Jedediah, 114.
Bennams, Samuel, 61.
Bennedick, Benjamin, 63.
Bennedick, Timothy, 63.
Bennedict, Asel, 12.
Bennedict, Ashel, 11.
Bennedict, Benajah, 12.
Bennedict, Benjamin, 12.
Bennedict, Caleb, 22.
Bennedict, Caleb, 26.
Bennedict, Calep, Ju$^r$, 11.
Bennedict, Comfort, 12.
Bennedict, David, Ju$^r$, 12.
Bennedict, Ebenezer, Ju$^r$, 11.
Bennedict, Eleazer, 12.
Bennedict, Elezer, 11.
Bennedict, Elezer, 18.
Bennedict, Eli, 24.
Bennedict, Elizabeth (W$^d$), 21.
Bennedict, Ephraim, 11.
Bennedict, Ezra, 23.
Bennedict, Hezekiah, 23.
Bennedict, Hezekiah, Ju$^r$, 12.
Bennedict, Ira, 12.
Bennedict, Isaac, 12.
Bennedict, Isaac, 22.
Bennedict, James, 12.
Bennedict, James, 23.
Bennedict, James, J$^r$, 23.
Bennedict, Jesse, 14.
Bennedict, Jesse, 23.
Bennedict, Joel, 148.
Bennedict, John, 12.
Bennedict, John, 18.
Bennedict, John, 23.
Bennedict, John, Ju$^r$, 12.
Bennedict, Jonah, 12.
Bennedict, Jonathan, 12.
Bennedict, Joseph, 12.
Bennedict, Lemuel, 12.
Bennedict, Levi, 12.
Bennedict, Mary, 10.
Bennedict, Mary (W$^d$), 23.
Bennedict, Nathanel, 12.
Bennedict, Nathaniel, 12.
Bennedict, Nathaniel, 22.
Bennedict, Nathaniel, J$^r$, 22.
Bennedict, Nehemiah, 23.
Bennedict, Nehemiah, J$^r$, 23.
Bennedict, Oliver, 12.
Bennedict, Samuel, 12.
Bennedict, Samuel, 23.
Bennedict, Seth, 12.
Bennedict, Stephen, 23.
Bennedict, Thaddeus, 12.
Bennedict, Thaddeus, 22.
Bennedict, Thomas, 12.
Bennedict, Thomas, 12.
Bennedict, Thomas, 22.
Bennedict, Thomas, 2$^{nd}$, 23.
Bennedict, William, 12.
Bennedict, William, 21.
Bennet, Abigal, 92.
Bennet, Andrew, 24.
Bennet, Asa, 148.
Bennet, Benjamin, 19.
Bennet, Benj$^n$, 151.
Bennet, Benjamin, Ju$^r$, 19.
Bennet, Daniel, 13.
Bennet, Daniel, 17.
Bennet, Daniel, 18.
Bennet, Daniel N., 19.
Bennet, David, 10.
Bennet, Deliverance, 12.
Bennet, Ebenezer, 24.
Bennet, Ebenezer, 100.
Bennet, Eben$^r$, 142.
Bennet, Edmond, 61.
Bennet, Elijah, 142.
Bennet, Ezra, 152.
Bennet, Francis, 143.
Bennet, Hayns, 12.
Bennet, Hinchman, 146.
Bennet, Isaac, 143.
Bennet, Jabez, 13.
Bennet, James, 13.
Bennet, James, 148.
Bennet, James, 151.
Bennet, Jesse, 13.
Bennet, Jesse, 148.
Bennet, John, 10.
Bennet, John, 63.
Bennet, John, 149.
Bennet, John, 152.
Bennet, Joseph, 13.
Bennet, Joseph, 144.
Bennet, Joseph, 152.
Bennet, Joseph W., 14.
Bennet, Joshua, 148.
Bennet, Moses, 13.
Bennet, Moses, 23.
Bennet, Nathan, 13.
Bennet, Nathan, 18.
Bennet, Nath$^l$, 148.
Bennet, Nath$^l$, Jn$^r$, 148.
Bennet, Robert, 146.
Bennet, Silas, 17.
Bennet, Silas, 24.
Bennet, Simon, 146.
Bennet, Stephen, 14.
Bennet, Stephen, 149.
Bennet, Thaddeus, 14.
Bennet, Thomas, 12.
Bennet, William, 13.
Bennet, William, 151.
Bennett, Aaron, 116.
Bennett, Abijah, 71.
Bennett, Abraham, 20.
Bennett, Caleb, 19.
Bennett, Caleb, 71.
Bennett, Daniel, 113.
Bennett, Daniel, 121.
Bennett, David, 116.
Bennett, Edward, 71.
Bennett, Elias, 113.
Bennett, Elisha, 116.
Bennett, Gershom, 71.
Bennett, Jacob, 113.
Bennett, James, 19.
Bennett, John, 123.
Bennett, Nathan, 22.
Bennett, Nehemiah, 30.
Bennett, Thomas, 19.
Bennham, Oliver, 56.
Bennit, Benjamin, 32.
Bennit, Daniel, 27.
Bennit, David, 22.
Bennit, Elias, 32.
Bennit, Isaac, 32.
Bennit, Isaac, 32.
Bennit, Josiah, 28.
Bennit, Samuel, 31.
Bennit, Thadeus, 31.
Bennitt, Aaron, 31.
Bennitt, Abel, 19.
Bennitt, Amos, 19.
Bennitt, Benjamin, 30.
Bennitt, Content, 31.
Bennitt, Daniel, 28.
Bennitt, Daniel, 31.
Bennitt, Ezekiel, 32.
Bennitt, Gabriel, 28.
Bennitt, Gidion, 30.
Bennitt, Isaac, 28.
Bennitt, James, 31.
Bennitt, John, 31.
Bennitt, Miles, 27.
Bennitt, Nathan, 31.
Bennitt, Richard, 19.
Bennitt, Samuel, 30.
Bennitt, Samuel, 31.
Bennitt, Shubel, 27.
Bennitt, Stephen, 28.
Bennitt, Thomas, 31.
Bennitt, Trowbridge, 28.
Bennitt, William, 31.
Bennom, Johial, 61.
Bennom, Samuel, 61.
Bens, Juno, 101.
Benson, Ambrose, 71.
Benson, Barack, 150.
Benson, Benjamin, 1$^{st}$, 71.
Benson, Benjamin, 2$^d$, 71.
Benson, Bryan, 71.
Benson, Eben, 31.
Benson, Noah, 58.
Benten, Josiah, 70.
Bentley, Eleazar, 130.
Bentley, Ezekiel, 115.
Bentley, George, 116.
Bentley, George, Jun$^r$, 116.
Bently, Mary, 58.
Bento, Silus, 27.
Benton, Abraham, 66.
Benton, Asa, 45.
Benton, Caleb, 97.
Benton, Cyrus, 32.
Benton, Cyrus, 138.
Benton, Daniel, 66.
Benton, Dan$^{el}$, 138.
Benton, Ebenezer, 42.
Benton, Ebenezer, 59.
Benton, Edward, 42.
Benton, Elihu, 99.
Benton, Elihu S., 54.
Benton, Elisha, 36.
Benton, Esther, 53.
Benton, Isaac, 67.
Benton, Jabez, 98.
Benton, Jacob, 138.
Benton, James, 62.
Benton, James, 98.
Benton, Jerad, 97.
Benton, Jeremiah, 77.
Benton, John, 46.
Benton, John, 52.
Benton, John, 70.
Benton, John, Jr., 46.
Benton, Jonathan, 33.
Benton, Jon$^a$, 138.
Benton, Jonathan, Jr., 33.
Benton, Joseph, 37.
Benton, Josiah, 42.
Benton, Josiah, 46.
Benton, Lot, 99.
Benton, Nathaniel, 66.
Benton, Nathaniel S., 46.
Benton, Noah, 99.
Benton, Ruth (Wid.), 46.
Benton, Samuel, 46.
Benton, Samuel, 97.
Benton, Sealey, 17.
Benton, Seth, 98.
Benton, Silas, 98.
Benton, Thomas, 54.
Benton, Timothy, 99.
Benton, Tim$^o$, 138.
Bergen, Mercy, 122.
Berham, Samuel, 77.
Berman, Josiah, 109.
Berry, Asael, 107.
Berry, Ebenezer, 58.
Berry, George, 28.
Berry, Joseph, 58.
Berry, Joseph, 121.
Berry, Nathaniel, 58.
Berry, Richard, 97.
Berry, Thomas, 108.
Bertow, Benjamin, 107.
Berwick, Elisha, 45.
Bery, Cyrus, 74.
Bescoro, Nathan, 20.
Bessel, George, 65.
Bessel, Isaac, 64.
Bessel, John, 65.
Bessel, Levi, 135.
Bessy, Bridget (W$^d$), 21.
Bessy, Peleg, 22.
Bester, Abel, 137.
Bester, Daniel, 51.
Bester, Job, 60.
Bester, Jn$^o$, 137.
Bester, Jn$^o$, 138.
Bester, Seth, 60.
Beston, Asa, 150.
Beston, Jeremiah, 150.
Beston, John, 142.
Beston, John, 142.
Beston, Joseph, 146.
Beston, Sam$^l$, 142.
Beston, Sam$^l$, 146.
Beston, William, 144.
Bestor, John, 55.
Bestow, Calvin, 114.
Betram, Benjamin, 109.
Betterson, Joseph, 32.
Bettes, James, 11.
Bettey, Daniel, 11.
Bettis, James, 146.
Bettis, Thomas, 121.
Betts, Abigail (W$^d$), 21.
Betts, Abijah, 21.
Betts, Abner, 20.
Betts, Azor, 77.
Betts, Bena Jah, 61.
Betts, Benjamin, 21.
Betts, Benjamin, 26.
Betts, Burrell, 22.
Betts, Daniel, 21.
Betts, Daniel, 23.
Betts, Elijah, 21.
Betts, Elijah, 21.
Betts, Enoch, 24.
Betts, Eunice, 28.
Betts, Ezekiel, 59.
Betts, Gideon, 28.
Betts, Hezekiah, 21.
Betts, Isaac, 21.
Betts, Isaac, Jun., 21.
Betts, Jeremiah, 23.
Betts, Jesse, 21.
Betts, Jesse, 58.
Betts, John, 21.
Betts, Mary (W$^d$), 21.
Betts, Matthew, 22.
Betts, Moses, 13.
Betts, Moses, 21.
Betts, Nehemiah, 74.
Betts, Peter, 23.
Betts, Peter, 24.
Betts, Peter, Jun$^r$, 23.
Betts, Reuben, 21.
Betts, Ruth (W$^d$), 23.
Betts, Samuel, 23.
Betts, Samuel, 23.
Betts, Sarah (W$^d$), 16.
Betts, Seth, 23.
Betts, Silas, 23.
Betts, Stephen, 21.
Betts, Stephen, 22.
Betts, Stephen, 27.
Betts, Stephen, 3$^d$, 23.
Betts, Thaddeus, 21.
Betts, Thomas, 21.
Betts, Tim$^o$, 138.
Betts, William, 71.
Betts, William M., 23.
Betty, James, 21.
Bevin, Isaac, 80.
Bevin, William, 80.
Bevins, Benjamin, Jun$^r$, 80.
Bevins, Ebenezer, 47.
Bevins, Ezra, 79.
Bewel, Abel, 145.
Bewel, Isaac, 145.
Bewel, Jn$^o$, 135.
Bewel, Josiah, 145.
Bewel, Oliver, 145.
Bewel, W$^m$, 135.
Bewel, William, 145.
Bewell, Jeremiah, 84.
Bewell, Joseph, 80.
Bewell, Josiah, 85.
Beyhal, Richard, 70.
Bibbens, Benj$^n$, 153.
Bibbens, Elijah, 153.
Bibbens, Timothy, 147.
Bibbens, William, 153.
Bibbins, Israel, 14.

# INDEX.

Bibbons, Timothy, 30.
Bicket, David, 110.
Bicknal, Moses, 147.
Bicknall, John, 140.
Bicknall, Zacha.h, 140.
Bidwel, Eliezer, 68.
Bidwel, Joseph, 68.
Bidwell, Allyn, 42.
Bidwell, Amos, 47.
Bidwell, Asenath, 36.
Bidwell, Ashbel, 36.
Bidwell, Ashbell, 87.
Bidwell, Daniel, 79.
Bidwell, David, 37.
Bidwell, David, 42.
Bidwell, Elijah, 66.
Bidwell, Elisha, 36.
Bidwell, Eodias, 36.
Bidwell, Ephraim, 37.
Bidwell, Ephraim, 42.
Bidwell, Epiphras, 64.
Bidwell, Hezekiah, 42.
Bidwell, Isaac, 40.
Bidwell, Isaac, 42.
Bidwell, Jacob, 75.
Bidwell, James, 48.
Bidwell, Jeremiah, 75.
Bidwell, John, 36.
Bidwell, John, 79.
Bidwell, Jonathan, 36.
Bidwell, Jonathan, 42.
Bidwell, Jonathan, 55.
Bidwell, Joseph, 36.
Bidwell, Joseph, 42.
Bidwell, Mary, 36.
Bidwell, Rebecca, 42.
Bidwell, Riverious, 60.
Bidwell, Samuel, 36.
Bidwell, Samuel, 42.
Bidwell, Stephen, 37.
Bidwell, Stephen, 37.
Bidwell, Theodore, 40.
Bidwell, Thomas, 48.
Bidwell, Thomas, 60.
Bidwell, Zebulon, 37.
Bierce, Austin, 56.
Bierce, Hezekiah, 57.
Bierce, Isaih, 56.
Bierce, Jeames, 56.
Bierce, Joseph, 56.
Bierr, Hial, 60.
Bigalow, Asa, 122.
Bigalow, Azariah, 121.
Bigalow, Bond, 122.
Bigalow, Daniel, 121.
Bigalow, Ezra, 121.
Bigalow, Ira, 120.
Bigalow, James, 121.
Bigalow, John, 121.
Bigalow, Jonathan, 121.
Bigalow, Sarah, 121.
Bigelow, Alvin, 46.
Bigelow, Daniel, 45.
Bigelow, David, 43.
Bigelow, Elisha, 46.
Bigelow, Elisha, 83.
Bigelow, Elisha, Jr., 46.
Bigelow, Elizabeth, 85.
Bigelow, Frederick, 87.
Bigelow, Jame, 46.
Bigelow, Joel, 83.
Bigelow, John, 46.
Bigelow, Jonathan, 46.
Bigelow, Joseph, 46.
Bigelow, Josiah, 46.
Bigelow, Otis, 145.
Bigelow, Timothy H., 85.
Bigford, Thomas, 144.
Biggs, Adam, 143.
Biggs, Will.m, 89.
Bigsbee, J.no, 134.
Bigsbee, Sol.m, 136.
Bigsbie, Ebenezer, 31.
Bigsby, Aaron, 150.
Bigsby, Amos, 150.
Bigsby, Gracy (W.d), 22.
Bigsby, Green, 121.
Bigsby, Jacob, 150.
Bigsby, Jesse, 150.
Bigsby, Moses, 150.
Bigsby, Nathan, 150.
Bigsby, Sam.l, 150.
Bilbert, John, 33.
Bill, Aaron, 42.
Bill, Abial, 146.
Bill, Annis, 120.
Bill, Benajah, 118.
Bill, Benjamin, 119.
Bill, Charles, 125.
Bill, Daniel, 69.
Bill, Elijah, 1st, 57.
Bill, Elijah, 2d, 57.
Bill, Elisha, 144.
Bill, Elizur, 42.
Bill, Ephraim, 131.
Bill, Erastus, 80.
Bill, Isaac, 42.
Bill, James, 80.
Bill, Jonathan, 62.
Bill, Jona.th, 145.
Bill, Jonathan, 2d, 62.
Bill, Joseph, 116.
Bill, Joshua, 118.

Bill, Martha, 86.
Bill, Phineas, 118.
Bill, Roswell, 143.
Bill, Samuel, 86.
Bill, Solomon, 86.
Bill, Thomas, 146.
Bill, Timothy, 127.
Billing, J.no, 136.
Billinghast, John, 117.
Billings, Alpheus, 130.
Billings, Amos, 117.
Billings, Benaijah, 115.
Billings, Benaijah, Jun.r, 115.
Billings, Benjamin, 114.
Billings, Daniel, 115.
Billings, Eli, 40.
Billings, Elijah, 136.
Billings, Elisha, 115.
Billings, Henry, 131.
Billings, John, 118.
Billings, Joseph, 114.
Billings, Lament, 129.
Billings, Mary, 120.
Billings, Mary, 131.
Billings, Mathew, 125.
Billings, Nathan, 115.
Billings, Nathaniel, 40.
Billings, Otis, 115.
Billings, Randall, 114.
Billings, Samuel, 115.
Billings, Sam.l, 136.
Billings, Samuel, Jun.r, 115.
Billings, Sanford, 115.
Billings, Sol.n, 136.
Billings, Stephen, 118.
Billings, Stephen, 125.
Billings, Thaddeus, 40.
Billings, William, 114.
Billows, Hez.a, 150.
Bills, Benajah, 61.
Bills, John, 37.
Bills, Joshua, 61.
Bills, Thomas, 104.
Bills, Thomas, 2nd, 104.
Bills, William, 103.
Bim, David, 101.
Bin, Isaac, 107.
Bindy, Nathan, 29.
Bingham, Abel, 81.
Bingham, Alfred, 152.
Bingham, Asa, 132.
Bingham, Banajah, 63.
Bingham, Daniel, 69.
Bingham, Daniel, 2d, 69.
Bingham, David, 126.
Bingham, Ebenz.r, 152.
Bingham, Eleaz.r, 147.
Bingham, Elias, 152.
Bingham, Elijah, 122.
Bingham, Gideon, 152.
Bingham, Gidion, 142.
Bingham, Gurdon, 142.
Bingham, Isaac, 153.
Bingham, Ith.m, 134.
Bingham, Ith.m, 134.
Bingham, Jedediah, 153.
Bingham, Jere.h, 153.
Bingham, Jere.h, 153.
Bingham, John, 152.
Bingham, John, Jun.r, 112.
Bingham, Jona.th, 153.
Bingham, Joseph, 152.
Bingham, Luther, 142.
Bingham, Nathan, 126.
Bingham, Nath.l, 153.
Bingham, Oliver, 147.
Bingham, Ralph, 152.
Bingham, Sam.l, 153.
Bingham, Simeon, 131.
Bingham, Stephen, 135.
Bingham, Thomas, 153.
Bingham, Uriah, 153.
Bingley, Hannah, 105.
Bino, Ruth, 112.
Bino, Samuel, 112.
Bino, Watham, 101.
Birchard, Elijah, 73.
Birchard, Isaiah, 29.
Birchard, James, 23.
Birchard, Jemima (W.d), 23.
Birchard, Jeremiah, 29.
Birchard, Jesse, 22.
Birchard, John, 130.
Birchard, Joseph, 147.
Birchard, Prince, 140.
Birchard, Uriah, 29.
Birchird, Ezra, 126.
Birchird, Jesse, 126.
Bird, Amy, 48.
Bird, Atwood, 56.
Bird, Ephraim, 35.
Bird, James, 66.
Bird, John, 35.
Bird, Joseph, 41.
Bird, Lucy, 56.
Bird, Sarah, 104.
Bird, Thomas, 66.
Birdsay, Hannah, 89.
Birdsey, Abel, 89.
Birdsey, Abigail, 89.
Birdsey, David, 89.
Birdsey, Ebenezer, 57.
Birdsey, John, 18.

Birdsey, John, 89.
Birdsey, John, Jun.r, 89.
Birdsie, Ezra, 31.
Birdsie, Thadeus, 31.
Birdsie, William, 30.
Birdslee, Joseph, 18.
Birdwell, John, 47.
Birdwell, Ozeas, 37.
Birdwell, Stephen, 70.
Birkingham, Hosmer, 90.
Birkshop, Abraham, 68.
Birrchard, Daniel, 21.
Bisco, Ruth, 101.
Biscow, John, 21.
Biscow, Sarah (Wid.), 20.
Bishnel, Alexander, 62.
Bishop, Abel, 106.
Bishop, Abijah, 24.
Bishop, Alexander, 24.
Bishop, Amos, 56.
Bishop, Benjamin, 41.
Bishop, Benjamin, 106.
Bishop, Betsy, 126.
Bishop, Billy, 56.
Bishop, Caleb, 112.
Bishop, Calvin, 66.
Bishop, Caty (W.d), 26.
Bishop, Charles, 97.
Bishop, Clemment, 124.
Bishop, Dan., 56.
Bishop, Daniel, 56.
Bishop, Daniel, 103.
Bishop, Daniel, 124.
Bishop, David, 98.
Bishop, David, 98.
Bishop, Deborah, 56.
Bishop, Ebenezar, 34.
Bishop, Ebenezer, 57.
Bishop, Ebenezer, 99.
Bishop, Ebenezer, 111.
Bishop, Ebenezer, 113.
Bishop, Eleazer, 37.
Bishop, Eler, 71.
Bishop, Elias, 99.
Bishop, Elizabeth, 98.
Bishop, Elizabeth, 99.
Bishop, Eneas, 99.
Bishop, Ezra, 100.
Bishop, Ezra, 113.
Bishop, Hannah, 98.
Bishop, Hannah, 99.
Bishop, Icabod, 97.
Bishop, Isaac, 103.
Bishop, Israel, 102.
Bishop, Jacob, 22.
Bishop, James, 40.
Bishop, James, 96.
Bishop, James, 98.
Bishop, James, 99.
Bishop, Jarad, 92.
Bishop, Jerad, 98.
Bishop, Jere.h, 140.
Bishop, Jesse, 68.
Bishop, Jesse, 99.
Bishop, John, 99.
Bishop, John, 113.
Bishop, J.no, 132.
Bishop, John, 2d, 99.
Bishop, Johson, 97.
Bishop, Joiner, 98.
Bishop, Jonas, 96.
Bishop, Jonathan, 24.
Bishop, Jonathan, 96.
Bishop, Jon.a, 127.
Bishop, Jonathan A., 11.
Bishop, Joseph, 111.
Bishop, Joseph, 124.
Bishop, Joshua, 112.
Bishop, Joy, 106.
Bishop, Joy, 2nd, 106.
Bishop, Leveritt, 87.
Bishop, Lines, 98.
Bishop, Mary, 112.
Bishop, Miles, 59.
Bishop, Mimsa, 63.
Bishop, Nathan, 11.
Bishop, Nathaniel, 100.
Bishop, Nath.l, 112.
Bishop, Nero, 99.
Bishop, Parker, 144.
Bishop, Parsons, 26.
Bishop, Peter, 26.
Bishop, Ruben, 100.
Bishop, Russell, 98.
Bishop, Samuel, 24.
Bishop, Samuel, 37.
Bishop, Samuel, 41.
Bishop, Samuel, 99.
Bishop, Samuel, 103.
Bishop, Samuel, 112.
Bishop, Sam.l, 132.
Bishop, Sarah, 124.
Bishop, Seth, 98.
Bishop, Seth, 2d, 60.
Bishop, Silas, 24.
Bishop, Silvanus, 66.
Bishop, Simion, 106.
Bishop, Stephen, 25.
Bishop, Stephen, Jun.r, 25.
Bishop, Susanna, 127.
Bishop, Sussannah, 99.
Bishop, Sylvanus, 103.

Bishop, Tabitha, 98.
Bishop, Thalmeno, 84.
Bishop, Thomas, 124.
Bishop, Tho.s, 132.
Bishop, Thomas F., 41.
Bishop, Timothy, 100.
Bishop, William, 77.
Bishshop, Samuel, 59.
Bishshop, Seth, 60.
Bissel, Abagail, 64.
Bissel, Archulus, 64.
Bissel, Benjamin, 59.
Bissel, Benjamin, 60.
Bissel, Benjamin, 64.
Bissel, Benjamin, 69.
Bissel, Colvis, 64.
Bissel, Ebenezer, 69.
Bissel, Eben.r F., 54.
Bissel, Eben.r F., Ju., 54.
Bissel, Elijah, 69.
Bissel, Eliphet, 69.
Bissel, Ezekiel, 69.
Bissel, Hezekiah, 69.
Bissel, Hezekiah, 135.
Bissel, Hezi.h (Wid.), 54.
Bissel, John, 62.
Bissel, John, 71.
Bissel, Joseph, 64.
Bissel, Josiah, 54.
Bissel, Luthry, 133.
Bissel, Mathew, 133.
Bissel, Zebulon, 64.
Bissell, Aaron, 38.
Bissell, Benjamin, 146.
Bissell, Daniel, 38.
Bissell, Dan., 39.
Bissell, Daniel, 145.
Bissell, David, 38.
Bissell, Ebenezer, 38.
Bissell, Elisha, 38.
Bissell, Elisha, 146.
Bissell, Epaphras, 38.
Bissell, Hannah, 39.
Bissell, Col. Hez.h, 55.
Bissell, Isaac, 52.
Bissell, Jerijah, 38.
Bissell, Jerijah, Jr., 38.
Bissell, John, 38.
Bissell, Jonathan, 38.
Bissell, Joseph F., 146.
Bissell, Joseph W., 145.
Bissell, Justus, 38.
Bissell, Moses, 38.
Bissell, Nathaniel, 38.
Bissell, Noah, 38.
Bissell, Ozias, 37.
Bissell, Partridge, 146.
Bissell, Roswold, 38.
Bissell, Russell, 37.
Bissell, Timothy, 39.
Bissell, William, 38.
Bissenton, Asael, 107.
Bissinton, Heil, 107.
Bissinton, Robert, 107.
Bivins, Eben.r, 88.
Black, Esther, 77.
Black, Step (negro), 22.
Blackesley, Mathew, 69.
Blackley, Admer, 22.
Blackley, Asa, 93.
Blackley, John, 129.
Blackley, Margaret, 129.
Blacklidge, George, 18.
Blacklidge, Pamey, 18.
Blackman, Aaron, 134.
Blackman, Ager, 18.
Blackman, Asahel, 17.
Blackman, Benj.n, 134.
Blackman, Benj.n, Jr., 134.
Blackman, Daniel, 32.
Blackman, David, 18.
Blackman, David, 18.
Blackman, Ebenezer, 10.
Blackman, Edward, 19.
Blackman, Eli, 17.
Blackman, Ephraim, 18.
Blackman, Jacob, 150.
Blackman, James, 21.
Blackman, James, 29.
Blackman, James, 29.
Blackman, Joel, 18.
Blackman, John, 13.
Blackman, John, 20.
Blackman, John, Jun.r, 21.
Blackman, Jonas, 18.
Blackman, Jona.th, 153.
Blackman, Joseph, 20.
Blackman, Josiah, 20.
Blackman, Lemuel, 73.
Blackman, N. Cady, 74.
Blackman, Nehemiah, 32.
Blackman, Niram, 10.
Blackman, Peter, 63.
Blackman, Philo, 10.
Blackman, Phineas, 30.
Blackman, Reuben, 20.
Blackman, Ruth, 17.
Blackman, Samuel, 18.
Blackman, Samuel, 18.
Blackman, Timothy, 17.
Blackman, Treuman, 21.
Blackman, Truman, 63.

Blackman, William, 18.
Blackman, W.m, 135.
Blackman, Zacheriah, 31.
Blackmar, Adonijah, 153.
Blackmar, Jona.th, 150.
Blackmon, Ezekel, 150.
Blackmore, Levi, 151.
Blackslee, Daniel, 84.
Blacksly, Benjamin, 23.
Blackston, John, 91.
Blague, Giles, 89.
Blague, Joseph, 79.
Blake, David, 94.
Blake, Elijah, 69.
Blake, Freelove, 87.
Blake, Isaac, 96.
Blake, John, 87.
Blake, Marana, 62.
Blake, Richard, 59.
Blake, Ruben, 96.
Blake, Samuel, 87.
Blakelee, David, 84.
Blakeley, Abner, 50.
Blakeley, Abram, 77.
Blakeley, Adna, 75.
Blakeley, Amos, 75.
Blakeley, Annis, 75.
Blakeley, Ashur, 75.
Blakeley, Bela, 75.
Blakeley, Dan, 77.
Blakeley, Eli, 75.
Blakeley, Enos, 57.
Blakeley, Jared, 76.
Blakeley, Jeames, 77.
Blakeley, Joel, 75.
Blakeley, Jonathan, 57.
Blakeley, Judah, 75.
Blakeley, Micajah, 75.
Blakeley, Moses, 75.
Blakeley, Samuel, 75.
Blakeley, Silas, 57.
Blakeley, Solomon, 75.
Blakeley, Thomas, 76.
Blakeley, Tilley, 77.
Blakeley, Zelus, 106.
Blakely, Abigail, 99.
Blakely, Baley, 51.
Blakely, Joseph, 107.
Blakely, Laban, 50.
Blakely, Moses, 93.
Blakely, Obidiah, 16.
Blakely, Oliver, 98.
Blakely, Ruben, 110.
Blakely, Sola, 75.
Blakeman, Elijah, 134.
Blakesley, Abraham, 106.
Blakesley, Amos, 106.
Blakesley, Caleb, 106.
Blakesley, Deborah, 100.
Blakesley, Enos, 106.
Blakesley, Isaac, 106.
Blakesley, Joel, 106.
Blakesley, John, 106.
Blakesley, Jonah, 106.
Blakesley, Philomen, 106.
Blakesley, Samuel, 61.
Blakesley, Sam.l, 64.
Blakesley, Sam.l, 68.
Blakesley, Seth, 106.
Blakesley, Thomas, 67.
Blakesley, Zopher, 106.
Blakley, Ebenezer, 109.
Blakley, Joseph, 99.
Blakley, Joseph, 2d, 107.
Blakley, Joshua, 99.
Blakley, Moses, 99.
Blakley, Tilley, 104.
Blakmore, Simeon, 62.
Blakston, Stephen, 91.
Blakston, Timothy, 91.
Blanchard, Elias, 143.
Blanchard, Jacob, 25.
Blanchard, Jere, 55.
Blanchard, John, 143.
Blanchard, John, 154.
Blanchard, William, 25.
Blancher, Nathaniel, 77.
Blancherd, Eunice, 36.
Bland, James, 125.
Blanott, James, 45.
Blaxton, Sarah, 91.
Bligh, Benj.n, 151.
Blin, David, 54.
Blin, Gershom, 52.
Blin, Hezekiah, 54.
Blin, Hosea, 52.
Blin, Hosea, 65.
Blin, James, 54.
Blin, Jonathan, 54.
Blin, Justus, 54.
Blin, Martha, 54.
Blin, Peter, 54.
Blin, Peter, Jr., 54.
Blin, Samuel, 54.
Blin, Solomon, 52.
Blin, Unni, 53.
Blin, William, 52.
Blish, David, 43.
Blish, John, 121.
Blish, Thomas, 43.
Bliss, Abel, 135.
Bliss, Abraham, 126.
Bliss, Amos, 145.

# INDEX.

Bliss, Anna, 38.
Bliss, David, 46.
Bliss, Ebenezer, 48.
Bliss, Elias, 146.
Bliss, Elijah, 131.
Bliss, Elis, 125.
Bliss, Ellis, 38.
Bliss, Ezra, 145.
Bliss, Henry, 146.
Bliss, Isaac, 46.
Bliss, Jad, 69.
Bliss, John, 131.
Bliss, Jon$^a$, 113.
Bliss, Joseph, 146.
Bliss, Mary, 118.
Bliss, M$^{rs}$, 132.
Bliss, Nezias, 74.
Bliss, Pelatiah, 125.
Bliss, Peltiah, 145.
Bliss, Sam$^l$, 113.
Bliss, Sam$^l$, 146.
Bliss, Samuel, 146.
Bliss, Silas, 113.
Bliss, Simeon, 57.
Bliss, Stoughton, 38.
Bliss, Sylvanus, 74.
Bliss, Thomas, 79.
Bliss, Thomas, 131.
Bliss (Wid.), 135.
Bliss, Zenas, 146.
Blivin, John, 117.
Blodget, Abner, 38.
Blodget, Ab$^m$, 136.
Blodget, Dan$^l$, 136.
Blodget, Elijah, 38.
Blodget, Josa, 136.
Blodget, Josiah, 134.
Blodget, Paul, 136.
Blodget, Paul, 2$^d$, 136.
Blodget, Phinias, 38.
Blodget, Silas, 138.
Blodget, Sylvanus, 136.
Blodgett, William, 114.
Bloget, Tim$^o$, 136.
Bloidell, Thomas, 27.
Blois, Francis, 56.
Bloomer, William, 22.
Bloyd, John, 128.
Bloyd, Margaret, 128.
Blunder, Samuel, 51.
Blunt, Ambrus, 113.
Blunt, Elisha, 113.
Blunt, Walter, 113.
Blush, Asa, 120.
Blush, Easter, 121.
Blush, Ezra, 121.
Blye, Paphroe, 64.
Blyth, Joseph, 151.
Boan (Negro), 125.
Boardman, Asa, 79.
Boardman, Rev$^d$ Benjamin, 46.
Boardman, Catharine, 50.
Boardman, Charles, 52.
Boardman, Chloe, 84.
Boardman, David, 113.
Boardman, Elihu, 52.
Boardman, Elijah, 53.
Boardman, Elisha, 52.
Boardman, Elnathan, 53.
Boardman, Ephraim, 35.
Boardman, Frederic, 53.
Boardman, Hannah, 53.
Boardman, Homer, 71.
Boardman, Israel, 54.
Boardman, Jason, 53.
Boardman, Jon$^a$, 53.
Boardman, Jonathan, 84.
Boardman, Jonathan, Jr., 53.
Boardman, Joseph, 69.
Boardman, Levi, 52.
Boardman, Levi, 54.
Boardman, Luther, 84.
Boardman, Moses, 35.
Boardman, Nathan, 88.
Boardman, Nathaniel, 88.
Boardman, Oliver, 64.
Boardman, Return, 53.
Boardman, Samuel, 53.
Boardman, Sherman, 71.
Boardman, Timothy, 86.
Boardman, William, 46.
Boardwell, Joel, 58.
Boath, Alexander, 101.
Boath, Elisha, 101.
Boath, Jonathan, 100.
Bobbett, Lemuel, 71.
Bobbett, William, 71.
Bobbit, Samuel, 20.
Bochford, Abel, 19.
Bochford, Abraham, 19.
Bochford, Clemon, 20.
Bochford, Elijah, 19.
Bochford, Gideon, 20.
Bochford, Gideon, 20.
Bochford, Jabez, 19.
Bochford, Jerid, 20.
Bochford, Joel, 20.
Bochford, John, 19.
Bochford, Moses, 20.
Bochford, Theopholus, 20.
Bockwell, Amoriah, 133.
Bogue, Daniel, 64.
Boham (Negro), 121.

Boils, James, 92.
Boinington, Oliver, 133.
Boles, Amos, 125.
Boles, Deborah, 126.
Boles, Edgecombe, 89.
Boles, Enoch, 126.
Boles, Ezra, 43.
Boles, James, 126.
Boles, John & Son, 126.
Boles, Joseph, 125.
Boles, Joseph, 125.
Boles, Joshua, 120.
Boles, Joshua, 126.
Boles, Roberson, 119.
Boles, Sam$^l$, 127.
Boles, Stephen, 125.
Boles, Thomas, 125.
Boles, Thomas, 126.
Bolles, Isaiah, 129.
Bolles, John, 45.
Bolles, John, 2$^d$, 45.
Bolles, Samuel, 45.
Bolles, Stephen, 45.
Bolls, Asa, 145.
Bolls, Jesse, 154.
Bolls, Ruth, 55.
Bolt, David, 23.
Bolt, Louis, 109.
Bolt, William, 22.
Bolton, Dan$^l$, 136.
Bolton, James, 129.
Bond, Jonas, 142.
Bond, Thadeus, 138.
Bond, William, 142.
Boness, Amos, 62.
Bonfey, Bananuel, 84.
Bonfoy, Permit, 81.
Bonfy, Henry, 88.
Bonney, Asahel, 65.
Bonney, Jarius, 57.
Bonney, Junis, 65.
Bonney, Perez, 57.
Bonney, Titus, 56.
Bonticon, James, 102.
Bonticon, John, 103.
Bonticon, Susanah, 102.
Bonticon, Sussanah, 102.
Bonticon, Thomas, 102.
Bonticon, William, 102.
Boon, Henry, 123.
Boor, Jonathan, 29.
Booth, Aaron, 38.
Booth, Abel, 10.
Booth, Abel, 31.
Booth, Abiel, 19.
Booth, Abijah, 31.
Booth, Abraham, 21.
Booth, Agar, 29.
Booth, Asael, 19.
Booth, Ashbell, 17.
Booth, Calib, 38.
Booth, Daniel, 19.
Booth, Daniel, 29.
Booth, Daniel, 40.
Booth, David, 19.
Booth, David, 30.
Booth, David, 77.
Booth, David, Jun$^r$, 30.
Booth, Elijah, 73.
Booth, Elisha, 32.
Booth, Elisha, 32.
Booth, Elisha, 71.
Booth, Ephraim, 38.
Booth, Ezra, 19.
Booth, Filo, 30.
Booth, Henry, 38.
Booth, Henry, 147.
Booth, Hester, 111.
Booth, Hezekiah, 20.
Booth, Hezekiah, 30.
Booth, Hilkiah, 31.
Booth, Isaac, 18.
Booth, Isaac, 29.
Booth, Isaac, 139.
Booth, James, 20.
Booth, James, 30.
Booth, James, 32.
Booth, Joel, 39.
Booth, John, 30.
Booth, John, 32.
Booth, John, 39.
Booth, John, 107.
Booth, John, Jun$^r$, 30.
Booth, John, Jr., 40.
Booth, Jonathan, 19.
Booth, Joseph, 32.
Booth, Joseph, 39.
Booth, Levi, 29.
Booth, Lewis, 17.
Booth, Nathan, 17.
Booth, Nathan, 32.
Booth, Nathan, Jr, 17.
Booth, Nathan, Jr., 32.
Booth, Nathanel, 17.
Booth, Olive (Wid.), 19.
Booth, Phebe (Wid.), 19.
Booth, Philo, 10.
Booth, Reuben, 20.
Booth, Robert, 82.
Booth, Samuel, 17.
Booth, Samuel, 30.
Booth, Samuel, 45.

Booth, Silaman, 29.
Booth, Silas, 17.
Booth, Smith, 73.
Booth, Stephen, 32.
Booth, Thadeus, 32.
Booth, Thomas, 31.
Booth, Walter, 111.
Booth, Zacheriah, 39.
Boothe, Peter, 138.
Borac, Jared, 138.
Borden, Asahel, 66.
Borden, John, 66.
Bordman, Daniel, 71.
Bordman, Hezekiah, 113.
Bordon, John, 144.
Bordon, Joseph, 148.
Bordwin, Azariah, 57.
Borough, Ciely, 30.
Borough, Griswell, 30.
Borough, Josiah, 30.
Boscon, Patience, 20.
Bosston, Nathaniel, 98.
Bossworth, Nathan, 66.
Bosteck, Isaac, 95.
Bosteck, Richard, 95.
Boston, Junior, 47.
Boston (Negro), 47.
Boston (Negro), 121.
Bostwick, Abel, 71.
Bostwick, Amos, 71.
Bostwick, Andrew, 77.
Bostwick, Ben Ruggles, 71.
Bostwick, Benjamin, 10.
Bostwick, Benjamin, 71.
Bostwick, David, 1$^{st}$, 71.
Bostwick, David, 2$^d$, 71.
Bostwick, Ebenezer, 58.
Bostwick, Elethan H., 18.
Bostwick, Elisha, 71.
Bostwick, Elizur, 71.
Bostwick, Ichabod, 71.
Bostwick, Isaac, 71.
Bostwick, John, 71.
Bostwick, Jonathan, 71.
Bostwick, Joseph, 1$^{st}$, 71.
Bostwick, Joseph, 2$^d$, 71.
Bostwick, Levi, 10.
Bostwick, Martin, 71.
Bostwick, Medad, 71.
Bostwick, Nathan, 71.
Bostwick, Oliver, 71.
Bostwick, Reuben, 1$^{st}$, 71.
Bostwick, Reuben, 2$^d$, 71.
Bostwick, Salmon, 71.
Bostwick, Samuel, 71.
Bostwick, William, 19.
Bostwick, Zackeriah, 71.
Bosworth, Jeames Wood, 74.
Bosworth, Joseph, 71.
Bosworth, Nathaniel, 74.
Bosworth, Nathaniel, 2$^d$, 74.
Botchford, David, 101.
Botchford, Eli, 101.
Botchford, Elnathan, 102.
Botchford, James, 10.
Botchford, Joseph, 19.
Botchford, Theophilus, 34.
Botsford, Aron, 102.
Botsford, Daniel, 56.
Botsford, David, 58.
Botsford, Ebenezer, 94.
Botsford, Ena, 71.
Botsford, Ephream, 61.
Botsford, Epriam, 2$^d$, 61.
Botsford, Ezra, 94.
Botsford, John, 95.
Botsford, Nathan, 71.
Botsford, Neamiah, 94.
Botsford, Samuel, 73.
Botsford, Samuel, 94.
Bottom, Abel, 148.
Bottom, Amaziah, 113.
Bottom, Asa, 153.
Bottom, Daniel, 112.
Bottom, Daniel, Jun$^r$, 112.
Bottom, James, 112.
Bottom, Joseph, 113.
Bottom, Joshua, 148.
Bottom, Sam$^l$ H., 117.
Botts, Reuben, 71.
Bouge, Elisha, 124.
Bouge, James, 122.
Bouge, James, Jun$^r$, 122.
Bouge, Jeremiah, 121.
Bouge, John, 124.
Bouge, Richard, 122.
Boughton, Abijah, 11.
Boughton, David, Jn$^r$, 11.
Boughton, Joseph, 11.
Boughton, Thomas, 11.
Bounce, Aaron, 146.
Bound, Joseph, 65.
Bourne, Amos, 129.
Bourns, Moses, 137.
Bourns, W$^m$, 133.
Boutain, Daniel, 26.
Boutain, David, 22.
Boutain, Eleazer, 22.
Boutain, Eleazer, Jun$^r$, 22.
Boutain, Joshua, 22.
Boutain, Nathan, 27.
Boutain, Samuel, 22.
Boutain, Sarah (W$^d$), 22.

Boutain, Seth, 22.
Boutain, William, 22.
Boutain, Zarius, 22.
Boutle, Ezra, 140.
Bouton, David, 27.
Bouton, Mathew, 11.
Boutwell, ——, 149.
Bow, Abraham, 87.
Bow, Amos, 87.
Bow, Amos, Jun$^r$, 87.
Bow, Isaac, 86.
Bow, Peleg, 87.
Bow, Samuel, 87.
Bowdish, William, 19.
Bowdist, Joseph, 151.
Bowen, Asa, 150.
Bowen, Barre, 140.
Bowen, Bezahil, 35.
Bowen, Consider, 46.
Bowen, Eleaz$^r$, 144.
Bowen, Henry, 154.
Bowen, James, 144.
Bowen, John, 140.
Bowen, Joseph, 140.
Bowen, Mathew, 154.
Bowen, Oliver, 144.
Bowen, William, 154.
Bowers, Alpheus, 151.
Bowers, Azel, 38.
Bowers, Benajah, 79.
Bowers, Ephraim, 120.
Bowers, John, 39.
Bowers, John, 151.
Bowers, John, Jn$^r$, 151.
Bowers, Jonathan, 80.
Bowers, Zephaniah, 84.
Bowing, Jn$^o$, 132.
Bowley, Samuel, 68.
Bowlis, George, 67.
Bowls, David, 141.
Bowls, David, Jn$^r$, 141.
Bowls, Lemuel, 138.
Bowls, W$^m$, 135.
Bowman, Elisha, 141.
Bowman, Lydia, 67.
Bowman, Walter, 141.
Bown, Park, 73.
Bowton, Avery, 28.
Bowton, Daniel, 11.
Bowton, David, 11.
Bowton, Eli, 11.
Bowton, Roger, 28.
Bowton, Timothy, 28.
Boxton, John, 109.
Boyd, Abraham, 148.
Boyd, Francis, 77.
Boyd, Joseph, 152.
Boyden, Elnam, 144.
Bozward, Eben$^r$, 140.
Bozworth, Aaron, 141.
Bozworth, Allen, 140.
Bozworth, Ichabod, 145.
Bozworth, John, 140.
Bozworth, Nath$^l$, 147.
Brace, David, 136.
Brace, Elisha, 56.
Brace, Lt., 136.
Brace, William, 67.
Bracket, Abel, 106.
Bracket, Amos, 50.
Bracket, Benjamin, 106.
Bracket, Ebenezer, 106.
Bracket, Elisha, 109.
Bracket, Eneas, 106.
Bracket, Eneas, 2$^{nd}$, 106.
Bracket, Giles, 106.
Bracket, Hezekiah, 100.
Bracket, Isaiah, 106.
Bracket, Jerad, 109.
Bracket, Joel, 50.
Bracket, John, 106.
Bracket, Joseph, 106.
Bracket, Levi, 106.
Bracket, Martha, 109.
Bracket, Mosses, 105.
Bracket, Phebe, 109.
Bracket, Richard, 106.
Bracket, Samuel, 106.
Bracket, Stephen, 106.
Bracket, Titus, 108.
Bracket, Zeure, 50.
Braddock, John, 130.
Braddock, Michael, 87.
Bradford, Benjamin, 125.
Bradford, Eloxander, 117.
Bradford, Essick, 154.
Bradford, George, 154.
Bradford, George, 154.
Bradford, Hennery, 17.
Bradford, James, 148.
Bradford, Jeames F., 56.
Bradford, Jeremiah, 80.
Bradford, Jeremiah, Jun$^r$, 80.
Bradford, John, 56.
Bradford, John, 142.
Bradford, John, Jr, 142.
Bradford, Joseph, 125.
Bradford, Josiah, sr., 142.
Bradford, Nath$^l$, 125.
Bradford, Peres, 125.
Bradford, Robert, 84.
Bradford, Samuel, 153.
Bradford, Sam$^l$, 125.

Bradford, Sam$^l$, 142.
Bradford, Tho$^s$, 142.
Bradley, Aaron, 45.
Bradley, Aaron, 64.
Bradley, Abel, 13.
Bradley, Abel, 34.
Bradley, Abner, 111.
Bradley, Abraham, 64.
Bradley, Abraham, 103.
Bradley, Abraham, 103.
Bradley, Adad, 13.
Bradley, Albin, 13.
Bradley, Alexander, 105.
Bradley, Amassa, 100.
Bradley, Amos, 100.
Bradley, Andrew, 111.
Bradley, Anor, 75.
Bradley, Anson, 98.
Bradley, Arial, 66.
Bradley, Aron, 100.
Bradley, Ashbel, 99.
Bradley, Azariah, 65.
Bradley, Benjamin, 50.
Bradley, Benjamin, 95.
Bradley, Benjamin, 111.
Bradley, Comfort, 64.
Bradley, Daniel, 13.
Bradley, Daniel, 28.
Bradley, Dan., 49.
Bradley, Daniel, 56.
Bradley, Daniel, 67.
Bradley, Daniel, 97.
Bradley, Daniel, 100.
Bradley, Daniel, 2$^d$, 100.
Bradley, David, 13.
Bradley, David, 53.
Bradley, Diamond, 106.
Bradley, Ebenezer, 32.
Bradley, Ebenezer, 75.
Bradley, Ebenezer, 106.
Bradley, Ebenezer, 2$^d$, 75.
Bradley, Ebenezer, 2$^{nd}$, 106.
Bradley, Edmond, 97.
Bradley, Elethan, 13.
Bradley, Eli, 100.
Bradley, Elijah, 27.
Bradley, Elijah, 97.
Bradley, Elisha, 13.
Bradley, Eliphalit, 32.
Bradley, Elizebeth, 105.
Bradley, Ellihue, 70.
Bradley, Elven, 100.
Bradley, Ely, 97.
Bradley, Eneas, 94.
Bradley, Enos, 32.
Bradley, Enos, 110.
Bradley, Ephraim, 19.
Bradley, Erastus, 105.
Bradley, Ezeriah, 97.
Bradley, Frances, 13.
Bradley, Francis, 32.
Bradley, Gamaleil, 100.
Bradley, Gershom, Jun$^r$, 32.
Bradley, Gillard, 99.
Bradley, Griffin, 105.
Bradley, Gurdon, 97.
Bradley, Hannah, 103.
Bradley, Hemingway, 49.
Bradley, Hezekiah, 13.
Bradley, Hezekiah, 105.
Bradley, Ichabod, 49.
Bradley, Isaac, 31.
Bradley, Isaac, 97.
Bradley, Israel, 101.
Bradley, Jabez, 100.
Bradley, James, 138.
Bradley, Jacob, 97.
Bradley, James, 49.
Bradley, James, 97.
Bradley, James, 104.
Bradley, Jared, 75.
Bradley, Jason, 100.
Bradley, Jehiel, 77.
Bradley, Jerad, 91.
Bradley, Jerad, 102.
Bradley, Joel, 57.
Bradley, Joel, 99.
Bradley, Joel, 106.
Bradley, John, 13.
Bradley, John, 62.
Bradley, John, 104.
Bradley, Jonah, 104.
Bradley, Jonah, 136.
Bradley, Jonathan, 19.
Bradley, Joseph, 13.
Bradley, Joseph, 31.
Bradley, Joseph, 97.
Bradley, Joseph, 103.
Bradley, Joshua, 128.
Bradley, Josiah, 97.
Bradley, Justus, 106.
Bradley, Leming, 64.
Bradley, Levi, 32.
Bradley, Levi, 100.
Bradley, Lewis, 105.
Bradley, Lyman, 32.
Bradley, Mable, 13.
Bradley, Martha, 105.
Bradley, Mercy, 136.
Bradley, Mise, 50.
Bradley, Moses, 71.
Bradley, Moses, 93.
Bradley, Nathan, 13.

164 INDEX.

Bradley, Nathan, 13.
Bradley, Nathaniel, 49.
Bradley, Nathaniel, 75.
Bradley, Nehemiah, 49.
Bradley, Noah, 99.
Bradley, Obed, 106.
Bradley, Oliver, 93.
Bradley, Peleg, 92.
Bradley, Peter, 13.
Bradley, Phillip B., Esqr, 28.
Bradley, Philo, 75.
Bradley, Phineas, 104.
Bradley, Richard, 77.
Bradley, Roswell, 93.
Bradley, Ruben, 93.
Bradley, Ruben, 111.
Bradley, Ruben, 134.
Bradley, Samuel, 13.
Bradley, Samuel, 28.
Bradley, Samuel, 97.
Bradley, Sarah, 97.
Bradley, Searl, 77.
Bradley, Seth, 13.
Bradley, Silas, 111.
Bradley, Simeon, 97.
Bradley, Simry, 98.
Bradley, Soloman, 105.
Bradley, Stephen, 28.
Bradley, Stephen, 92.
Bradley, Stephen, 97.
Bradley, Stephen, 103.
Bradley, Stephen, Junr, 97.
Bradley, Thomas, 106.
Bradley Timothy, 50.
Bradley, Timothy, 71.
Bradley, Timothy, 98.
Bradley, Timothy, 111.
Bradley, Timothy, 2nd, 111.
Bradley, Tina, 66.
Bradley, Titus, 106.
Bradley, Walter, 13.
Bradley, William, 53.
Bradley, William, 96.
Bradley, Wilmot, 111.
Bradley, Zalmon, 13.
Bradley, Zewer, 106.
Bradly, Alling, 111.
Bradly, Charles, 111.
Bradly, David, 32.
Bradly, Gershom, 32.
Bradly, Isaac, 109.
Bradly, Joseph, 106.
Bradly, Timothy, 91.
Bradly, William, 31.
Bradshaw, William, 71.
Brag, Benjamin, 96.
Brag, Edwd, 134.
Bragg, Thomas, 140.
Bragnord, Othniah, 69.
Brainard, Aaron, 84.
Brainard, Adonejah, 46.
Brainard, Amos, 83.
Brainard, Bushnell, 84.
Brainard, Cornelius, 83.
Brainard, Daniel, 80.
Brainard, Daniel, 84.
Brainard, David, 84.
Brainard, David, 107.
Brainard, Dudley, 83.
Brainard, Eber, 83.
Brainard, Eliakim, 83.
Brainard, Eliakim, Junr, 83.
Brainard, Elijah, 84.
Brainard, Ezra, 36.
Brainard, Ezra, Esqr, 83.
Brainard, Gideon, 83.
Brainard, Gideon, Junr, 83.
Brainard, Heman, 84.
Brainard, Hen'y, 74.
Brainard, Hezh, Esqr, 83.
Brainard, Isaac, 83.
Brainard, James, 80.
Brainard, James, 83.
Brainard, Jedediah, 83.
Brainard, Jedediah, Junr, 84.
Brainard, Jepthia, 80.
Brainard, Jeremiah, 84.
Brainard, Jeremiah, 126.
Brainard, Jessey, 83.
Brainard, Jessey, 83.
Brainard, John, 81.
Brainard, John, 84.
Brainard, Jona, 83.
Brainard, Joshua, 104.
Brainard, Josiah, 83.
Brainard, Josiah, Junr, 83.
Brainard, Josiah, 3d, 84.
Brainard, Martha, 84.
Brainard, Nathan, 80.
Brainard, Nathaniel, 47.
Brainard, Nathaniel, 84.
Brainard, Nehemiah, Esqr, 83.
Brainard, Oliver, 83.
Brainard, Othniel, 80.
Brainard, Ozias, 80.
Brainard, Phinehas, 84.
Brainard, Phinehas, Junr, 83.
Brainard, Prosper, 84.
Brainard, Robert, 83.
Brainard, Samuel, 84.
Brainard, Seth, 80.
Brainard, Simeon, 80.
Brainard, Simeon, Junr, 80.
Brainard, Stephen, 75.
Brainard, Stephen, 81.
Brainard, William, 83.
Brainard, William, 84.
Brainard, William, 121.
Brainard, Zachariah, 84.
Brainard, Zadock, 83.
Brainerd, Amasa, 81.
Brainerd, Bezaleel, 81.
Brainerd, Eleazer, 81.
Brainerd, Enoch, 82.
Brainerd, Jared, 82.
Brainerd, John, 81.
Brainerd, Joshua, 81.
Brainerd, Joshua, 2d, 81.
Brainthwait, Robert, 45.
Braman, Daniel, 112.
Braman, Jos., 134.
Bramble, John, 124.
Bramin, John, 114.
Bramin, Paul, 127.
Bramin, Prudence, 113.
Branch, Moses, 148.
Branch, Stephen, 113.
Branch, Thomas, 113.
Brand, Benjamin, 119.
Brand, Lucy, 117.
Brand, Thomas, 116.
Brandier, Elishama, 33.
Branton, Michael, 70.
Brau, Abel, 68.
Brau, Ariel, 68.
Brau, Charles, 61.
Brau, Hanah (Wid.), 19.
Brau, Henry, 47.
Brau, John, 46.
Brau, Jonathan, Esqr, 42.
Brau, Lenas, 47.
Brau, Moses, 47.
Brau, Orange, 68.
Brau, Thomas, 47.
Braughton, Nathan, 63.
Bray, Asa, 50.
Bray, John, 50.
Bray, Thomas W., 99.
Brayman, Daniel, 38.
Brayne, Asahel, 62.
Brayton, David, 149.
Brayton, Thos, 149.
Breant, Alexander, 69.
Brecket, Zenus, 109.
Breed, Newell, 104.
Breford, Benjamin, 107.
Brendly, John, 53.
Breneson, Ozias, 67.
Bret, William, 130.
Breto, Isaac, 23.
Brewer, Benjamin, 44.
Brewer, Daniel, 36.
Brewer, Daniel, 37.
Brewer, Daniel, 37.
Brewer, David, 79.
Brewer, Dorothy, 43.
Brewer, Hezekiah, 79.
Brewer, John, 12.
Brewster, Asa, 152.
Brewster, Benjamin, 145.
Brewster, Benjamin, 152.
Brewster, Comfort, 145.
Brewster, David, 77.
Brewster, Elisha, 87.
Brewster, Experience, 146.
Brewster, Ichabod, 146.
Brewster, Israel, 133.
Brewster, Jacob, 133.
Brewster, Jane, 85.
Brewster, Jededh, 142.
Brewster, John, 143.
Brewster, Nathl, 143.
Brewster, Peleg, 142.
Brewster, Peter, 133.
Brewster, Saml, 146.
Brewster, Wadsworth, 146.
Brewster, Walter, 142.
Briant, Danl D., 134.
Brice, Robart, 120.
Brick, Moses, 60.
Brickwell, Zebulon, 99.
Bride, Ann, 132.
Bridge, Asa, 136.
Bridges, Edmund, 120.
Bridgham, George, 86.
Brigden, Jonathan, 104.
Brigden, Michael, 52.
Brigden, Thomas, 86.
Brigden, Timothy, 132.
Brigden, William, 103.
Briggs, Caleb, 25.
Briggs, Ezra, 25.
Briggs, Hannah (Wd), 25.
Briggs, Hannah, Jr (Wd), 25.
Briggs, James, 151.
Briggs, John, 140.
Briggs, Jona, 150.
Briggs, Stephen, 25.
Briggs, William, 129.
Briggs, William, 151.
Briggs, Zepheniah, 19.
Briggsby, Hopkins, 22.
Briggsby, John, 22.
Briggsby, John, 22.
Briggsby, Joseph, 22.
Briggsby, Moses, 22.
Brigh, Elijah, 76.
Brigham, Don, 133.
Brigham, Gersham, 133.
Brigham, Stephen, 147.
Brigham, Thos, 133.
Brigham, Tiphet, 133.
Brightman, Henry, 120.
Brightman, Henry, Junr, 120.
Brigs, Ithamer, 116.
Brindsmaid, Cyrus, 31.
Brindsmde, Josiah, 31.
Brinsley, Daniel, 30.
Brinsmade, Daniel, 74.
Brinsmade, Daniel N., 74.
Brinsmade, John, 66.
Brinsmade, Saml, 66.
Brintnal, William, 103.
Brises, Isaac, 73.
Brister, Bozaleel, 84.
Brister, David, 41.
Brister, Isarel, 10.
Brister, John, 63.
Brister, Joseph, 20.
Brister, Soloman, 26.
Bristo (Negro), 35.
Bristo (Negro), 132.
Bristol, Amos, 57.
Bristol, Arial, 71.
Bristol, Austin, 92.
Bristol, Benjamin, 92.
Bristol, Daniel, 71.
Bristol, David, 102.
Bristol, David, 105.
Bristol, David, 2nd, 105.
Bristol, Dick (Negroe), 93.
Bristol, Eliphlet, 73.
Bristol, Eunice, 111.
Bristol, Ezra, 93.
Bristol, Gad, 73.
Bristol, Gad, 2d, 73.
Bristol, George A., 100.
Bristol, Gideon, 93.
Bristol, John, 57.
Bristol, Jonathan, 92.
Bristol, Justus, 73.
Bristol, Nathan, 57.
Bristol (Negro), 145.
Bristol (Negroe), 95.
Bristol (Negroe), 100.
Bristol, P. Brigs, 73.
Bristol, Phico, 102.
Bristol, Reuben, 1st, 57.
Bristol, Reuben, 2d, 57.
Bristol, Richard, 71.
Bristol, Richard, 99.
Bristol, Ruben, 94.
Bristol, Samuel, 77.
Bristol, Samuel, 98.
Bristol, Sarah, 56.
Bristol, Simeon, 100.
Bristol, Thankfull, 93.
Bristol, Thomas, 73.
Bristol, Thomas, 93.
Bristol, Truman, 73.
Bristol, Zelus, 92.
Briston & Philup (Negro), 115.
Bristor, Elizabeth, 102.
Bristor, John, 60.
Bristow, John, 101.
Bristow, Nathan, 102.
Bristow, Richard, 102.
Bristow, Stephen, 109.
Britt, Em, 139.
Britterfield, Simeon, 71.
Britton, Newton, 101.
Broach, Mary, 32.
Broadway, Eleazr, 154.
Brock, David, 153.
Brock, Phillis, 35.
Brockway, Abner, 122.
Brockway, Benjamin, 123.
Brockway, Clark, 122.
Brockway, Ebenezer, 90.
Brockway, Ebenezer, 122.
Brockway, Edward, 61.
Brockway, Edward, 124.
Brockway, Elias, 123.
Brockway, Elijah, 90.
Brockway, Elipheiet, 122.
Brockway, Elisha, 123.
Brockway, Enoch, 82.
Brockway, Ezra, 122.
Brockway, Ezra, 122.
Brockway, Gamaliel, 122.
Brockway, John, 122.
Brockway, Joseph, 41.
Brockway, Joseph, Jr., 41.
Brockway, Lowis, 122.
Brockway, Moses, 61.
Brockway, Richard, 122.
Brockway, Richard, 2d, 122.
Brockway, Samuel, 35.
Brockway, Samuel, 35.
Brockway, Simeon, 35.
Brockway, Thomas, 146.
Brockway, William, 122.
Brockway, Woolston, 124.
Brockway, Zebulun, 122.
Brockwey, Watston, 69.
Brokes, Limeuel, 106.
Bromley, David, 116.
Bromley, Dewey, 114.
Bromley, Israel, 114.
Bromley, Jabez, 115.
Bromley, Jesse, 115.
Bromley, John, 115.
Bromley, Preserved, 113.
Bromwell, Ichabod, 67.
Bronson, Alford, 19.
Broock, Abraham, 34.
Brook, Abijah, 140.
Brooker, Abraham, 84.
Brooker, Abraham, 84.
Brooker, John, 62.
Brookes, Anna (Wd), 24.
Brookes, Timothy, 82.
Brooks, Abigail, 84.
Brooks, Abijah, 30.
Brooks, Abijah, 100.
Brooks, Abijail (Wid.), 30.
Brooks, Abraham, 84.
Brooks, Amassa, 93.
Brooks, Amos, 83.
Brooks, Asahel, 67.
Brooks, Asshael, 111.
Brooks, Benjamin, 30.
Brooks, Benjamin, 100.
Brooks, Benjamin, 131.
Brooks, Chancey, 35.
Brooks, Cloe, 93.
Brooks, Daniel, 87.
Brooks, Daniel, 126.
Brooks, David, 87.
Brooks, David, 93.
Brooks, David, 2d, 93.
Brooks, David S., 99.
Brooks, Ebenezer B., 93.
Brooks, Ezekiel, 128.
Brooks, Ezekiel, 2d, 128.
Brooks, Gideon, 93.
Brooks, Gurdon, 130.
Brooks, Guy, 131.
Brooks, Henry, 93.
Brooks, Henry, 2nd, 93.
Brooks, Isaac, 30.
Brooks, Isaac, 34.
Brooks, Isaac, 144.
Brooks, Jabez, 83.
Brooks, Jabez, 87.
Brooks, Jabez, 87.
Brooks, Jabez, Junr, 87.
Brooks, James, 83.
Brooks, James, 90.
Brooks, James, 128.
Brooks, Jerry, 93.
Brooks, Joel, 42.
Brooks, Joel, 93.
Brooks, John, 30.
Brooks, John, 62.
Brooks, John, 144.
Brooks, Jonathan, 52.
Brooks, Jonathan, 83.
Brooks, Jonathan, 128.
Brooks, Joseph, 65.
Brooks, Joseph, Esqr, 83.
Brooks, Joseph B., 87.
Brooks, Joshua, 84.
Brooks, Josiah, 43.
Brooks, Lemuel, 22.
Brooks, Lemuel, Junr, 22.
Brooks, Louis, 100.
Brooks, Martha, 87.
Brooks, Mary, 81.
Brooks, Nathan, 83.
Brooks, Nathl, 140.
Brooks, Noah, 87.
Brooks, Noah, 124.
Brooks, Polly (Wid.), 30.
Brooks, Porter, 84.
Brooks, Samuel, 34.
Brooks, Samuel, 43.
Brooks, Samuel, 80.
Brooks, Samuel, 84.
Brooks, Samuel, 87.
Brooks, Saml, 122.
Brooks, Samuel, Jr., 34.
Brooks, Samuel, Jr., 43.
Brooks, Samuel, Junr, 84.
Brooks, Silas, 123.
Brooks, Simeon, 90.
Brooks, Soloman, 92.
Brooks, Thadeus, 129.
Brooks, Thomas, 10.
Brooks, Thomas, 35.
Brooks, Thomas, 93.
Brooks, Thomas, 146.
Brooks, Thomas, Jur, 10.
Brooks, Timothy, 87.
Brooks, Wakeman, 83.
Brooks, William, 11.
Brooks, William, 30.
Brooks, William, 39.
Brooks, William, 43.
Brooks, William, 129.
Brooks, Zerah, 39.
Broome, Samuel, 102.
Brothington, Daniel, 12.
Brothington, Samuel, 32.
Brothwell, Benjamin, 15.
Brothwell, F. Joseph, 77.
Brothwell, Hezekiah, 29.
Brothwell, Joseph, 15.
Brothwell, Thomas, 14.
Broughton, Amos, 154.
Broughton, John, 140.
Broughton, William, 104.
Brougtron, Amos, 77.
Brown, Aaron, 151.
Brown, Abigail (Wd), 26.
Brown, Abm, 133.
Brown, Alpheus, 56.
Brown, Alpheus, 141.
Brown, Amasa, 121.
Brown, Amasa, 135.
Brown, Ambrose, 140.
Brown, Amos, 114.
Brown, Amos, 120.
Brown, Amos, Junr, 114.
Brown, Amos, Junr, 114.
Brown, Amy, 125.
Brown, Andrew, 144.
Brown, Andrew, 153.
Brown, Ann, 118.
Brown, Anthony, 152.
Brown, Asa, 109.
Brown, Asa, 115.
Brown, Asher, 116.
Brown, Asoph, 109.
Brown, Azariah, 146.
Brown, Bazaleel, 15.
Brown, Benjamin, 37.
Brown, Benjn, 56.
Brown, Benjamin, 58.
Brown, Benjamin, 103.
Brown, Benja, 128.
Brown, Benjn, 142.
Brown, Benjamin, Jr., 37.
Brown, Benjn, Ju., 56.
Brown, Bersheba, 105.
Brown, Charles, 19.
Brown, Charles, 127.
Brown, Charles, 151.
Brown, Christopher, 115.
Brown, Cumfort, 118.
Brown, Cumfort, 2d, 120.
Brown, Cumstock, 125.
Brown, Daniel, 57.
Brown, Daniel, 76.
Brown, Danl, 82.
Brown, Daniel, 109.
Brown, Daniel, 109.
Brown, Danl, 115.
Brown, Danl, 135.
Brown, Danl, 141.
Brown, Daniel, 2nd, 109.
Brown, Daniel, 2d, 125.
Brown, David, 16.
Brown, David, 56.
Brown, David, 57.
Brown, David, 114.
Brown, David, 116.
Brown, David, 124.
Brown, David, 140.
Brown, David, 144.
Brown, David, 149.
Brown, Ebenezer, 79.
Brown, Ebenezer, 109.
Brown, Ebenezer, 118.
Brown, Ebenr, 133.
Brown, Ebenr, 142.
Brown, Eber, 132.
Brown, Edmond, 68.
Brown, Edward, 53.
Brown, Edward, 152.
Brown, Eleazer, 48.
Brown, Eleazer, 116.
Brown, Eleazer, 127.
Brown, Elepht, 133.
Brown, Elias, 54.
Brown, Elias, 109.
Brown, Elias, 114.
Brown, Elias, 117.
Brown, Elijah, 75.
Brown, Elisha, 18.
Brown, Elisha, 32.
Brown, Elisha, 35.
Brown, Elizur, 102.
Brown, Elkanah, 118.
Brown, Enos, 24.
Brown, Ephm, 54.
Brown, Ephraim, 121.
Brown, Eunice, 114.
Brown, Ezekiel, 118.
Brown, Ezekiel, 135.
Brown, Ezra, 55.
Brown, Ezra, 121.
Brown, Francis, 26.
Brown, Francis, 103.
Brown, George, 103.
Brown, George, 114.
Brown, Gershom, Junr, 120.
Brown, Geshom, 118.
Brown, Hannah, 97.
Brown, Hannah, 118.
Brown, Hannah (Wid.), 48.
Brown, Henry, 102.
Brown, Henry, 123.
Brown, Henry, 143.
Brown, Henry, 151.
Brown, Hezekiah, 75.
Brown, Hugh, 88.
Brown, Humphrey, 115.
Brown, Isaac, 26.
Brown, Isaac, 29.
Brown, Isaac, 94.
Brown, Isaac, 103.
Brown, Isaiah, 144.
Brown, Jabez, 102.
Brown, Jabez, 115.

# INDEX.

Brown, Jacob, 67.
Brown, Jacob, 104.
Brown, Jacob, 113.
Brown, James, 10.
Brown, James, 11.
Brown, James, 16.
Brown, James, 24.
Brown, James, 67.
Brown, James, 109.
Brown, James, 116.
Brown, James, 120.
Brown, James, 128.
Brown, James, 135.
Brown, James, 135.
Brown, Jas., 139.
Brown, Jared, 116.
Brown, Jedediah, 22.
Brown, Jedediah, 117.
Brown, Jedeh, 142.
Brown, Jedediah, Junr, 116.
Brown, Jeremi, 116.
Brown, Jeptha, 116.
Brown, Jeremiah, 123.
Brown, Jeremiah, 128.
Brown, Jerry, 61.
Brown, Jesse, 22.
Brown, Jesse, 115.
Brown, Jesse, 119.
Brown, Jesse, 131.
Brown, Jesse, 150.
Brown, John, 51.
Brown, John, 56.
Brown, John, 61.
Brown, John, 64.
Brown, John, 68.
Brown, John, 73.
Brown, John, 74.
Brown, John, 75.
Brown, John, 113.
Brown, John, 114.
Brown, John, 119.
Brown, John, 125.
Brown, John, 128.
Brown, Jno, 136.
Brown, John, 140.
Brown, John, 141.
Brown, John, 145.
Brown, John, 151.
Brown, John, 152.
Brown, John, Jnr, 151.
Brown, John, Senr, 141.
Brown, Jonas, 116.
Brown, Jonathan, 23.
Brown, Jonathan, 26.
Brown, Jonathan, 79.
Brown, Jonathan, 105.
Brown, Jonathan, 111.
Brown, Jona, 135.
Brown, Jonathan, 147.
Brown, Joseph, 24.
Brown, Joseph, 44.
Brown, Joseph, 47.
Brown, Joseph, 56.
Brown, Joseph, 65.
Brown, Joseph, 128.
Brown, Jos., 133.
Brown, Joseph, 149.
Brown, Joseph, 150.
Brown, Joseph, 151.
Brown, Joseph, Jnr, 151.
Brown, Joshua, 117.
Brown, Joshua, Junr, 116.
Brown, Joshua, Junr, 117.
Brown, Josiah, 15.
Brown, Josiah, 116.
Brown, Josiah, &c., 144.
Brown, Justin, 43.
Brown, Laurence, 16.
Brown, Levi, 15.
Brown, Major, 16.
Brown, Mary, 118.
Brown, Mary, 140.
Brown, Mathew, 116.
Brown, Mercy, 25.
Brown, Nathan, 22.
Brown, Nathan, 94.
Brown, Nathan, 115.
Brown, Nathan, 151.
Brown, Nathan, Junr, 116.
Brown, Nathan, 3d, 116.
Brown, Nathel, 25.
Brown, Nathaniel, 68.
Brown, Nathaniel, 74.
Brown, Nathaniel, 79.
Brown, Nathaniel, 80.
Brown, Nathaniel, 86.
Brown, Nathl, 118.
Brown, Nathl, 134.
Brown, Nathl, 144.
Brown, Nathaniel, Junr, 85.
Brown, Nathl, Junr, 120.
Brown, Nebudiah, 144.
Brown (Negro), 121.
Brown, Nehemiah, 16.
Brown, Nehemiah, 115.
Brown, Obediah, 140.
Brown, Othniel, 144.
Brown, Parley, 113.
Brown, Peleg, 118.
Brown, Peter, 16.
Brown, Peter, 55.
Brown, Peter, 117.
Brown, Peter, 119.

Brown, Rebecca (Wd), 26.
Brown, Rebecca, 2d (Wd), 24.
Brown, Richard, 79.
Brown, Richard, 133.
Brown, Robart, 116.
Brown, Robert, 103.
Brown, Roger, 16.
Brown, Roswell, 117.
Brown, Roswell, 141.
Brown, Ruben, 96.
Brown, Ruben, 120.
Brown, Rufus, 150.
Brown, Rufus, 151.
Brown, Ruth, 18.
Brown, Samuel, 10.
Brown, Samuel, 13.
Brown, Saml, 56.
Brown, Saml, 69.
Brown, Samuel, 76.
Brown, Samuel, 79.
Brown, Samuel, 80.
Brown, Samuel, 98.
Brown, Samuel, 117.
Brown, Saml, 121.
Brown, Samuel, 130.
Brown, Samuel, Junr, 80.
Brown, Sarah, 125.
Brown, Sarah, 127.
Brown, Sarah, 145.
Brown, Sherman, 15.
Brown, Shubael, 141.
Brown, Shubal, 139.
Brown, Silvanus, 115.
Brown, Simeon, 116.
Brown, Simeon, 116.
Brown, Stepen, 60.
Brown, Stephen, 55.
Brown, Stephen, 70.
Brown, Stephen, 104.
Brown, Stephen, 115.
Brown, Stephen, 117.
Brown, Stephen, 121.
Brown, Stephen, 144.
Brown, Stephen, 150.
Brown, Stephen, 152.
Brown, Surviah, 131.
Brown, Thomas, 33.
Brown, Thomas, 73.
Brown, Thomas, 125.
Brown, Thos, 133.
Brown, Thos, 135.
Brown, Thomas, 146.
Brown, Timothy, 112.
Brown, Waldo, 142.
Brown, Walter, 114.
Brown, Walter, Junr, 114.
Brown, Wheeler, 128.
Brown, William, 36.
Brown, William, 60.
Brown, William, 87.
Brown, William, 114.
Brown, William, 115.
Brown, William, 117.
Brown, Wm, 118.
Brown, Wm, 126.
Brown, William, 131.
Brown, Wm, 132.
Brown, William, Junr, 120.
Brown, Zachariah, 127.
Brown, Zachu, 144.
Brown, Zadock, 56.
Brown, Zobulun, 116.
Brown, Zera, 75.
Browning, Jeremi, 115.
Browning, Jeremiah, 116.
Brownley, Robert, 38.
Brownson, Abel, 77.
Brownson, Abraham, 56.
Brownson, Abram, 73.
Brownson, Abram, 77.
Brownson, Abram, 2d, 77.
Brownson, Allin, 132.
Brownson, Amos, 75.
Brownson, Asa, 71.
Brownson, Asahel, 74.
Brownson, Benjamin, 71.
Brownson, Ebenezer, 73.
Brownson, Ebenezer, 2d, 73.
Brownson, Elijah, 73.
Brownson, Isaac, 71.
Brownson, Isaac, 133.
Brownson, Jabez, 132.
Brownson, Jacob, 2d, 57.
Brownson, Jacob F., 56.
Brownson, John, 74.
Brownson, Josiah, 77.
Brownson, Levi, 76.
Brownson, Levi, 1st, 58.
Brownson, Levi, 2d, 58.
Brownson, Mathew, 71.
Brownson, Noah, 71.
Brownson, Noah Matt, 75.
Brownson, Reuben, 71.
Brownson, Selah, 57.
Brownson, Silas, 58.
Brownson, Thomas, 71.
Brownson, Thomas, 75.
Brownson, Thomas, 77.
Brownson, Timothy, 56.
Brownson, Wm, 58.
Brownson, Ziba, 71.
Brownwell, Aaron, 61.

Brownwell, Edward, 61.
Bruce (Widow), 132.
Bruckot, Samuel, 50.
Brud, Allen, 115.
Brud, Jabez, 115.
Brud, John, 121.
Brud, John, 130.
Brud, Joseph, 116.
Brud, Joseph, Junr, 115.
Brud, Lucy, 117.
Brud, Nathan, 117.
Brud, Nathan, Junr, 117.
Brud, Oliver, 117.
Brud, Prentice, 118.
Brud, Samuel, 117.
Brud, Shubael, 130.
Brud, Stephen, 116.
Brumham, John, 103.
Brumley, Christopher, 114.
Brumley, David, 116.
Brumley, Joshua, 116.
Brumley, Simion, 116.
Brundage, Gabriel, 16.
Brundage, Joseph, 15.
Brundage, Sarah, 16.
Brunson, Abel, 109.
Brunson, Abigail, 33.
Brunson, Amassa, 109.
Brunson, Amos, 11.
Brunson, Andrew, 110.
Brunson, Arael, 109.
Brunson, Asahel, 33.
Brunson, Ashbel, 68.
Brunson, Asher, 109.
Brunson, Benjamin, 49.
Brunson, Beriah, 39.
Brunson, Binonah, 67.
Brunson, Daniel, 109.
Brunson, David, 95.
Brunson, David, 110.
Brunson, Ebenezer, 33.
Brunson, Ebenezur, 109.
Brunson, Eli, 109.
Brunson, Elijah, 32.
Brunson, Elijah, Jr., 32.
Brunson, Elizabeth, 109.
Brunson, Elnathan, 33.
Brunson, Ethal, 109.
Brunson, Ezra, 11.
Brunson, Ezra, 109.
Brunson, Isaac, 45.
Brunson, Isaac, 50.
Brunson, Isaac, 109.
Brunson, Isaac, 2nd, 109.
Brunson, Jesse, 33.
Brunson, Jesse, 110.
Brunson, Joel, 50.
Brunson, John, 33.
Brunson, John, 50.
Brunson, Joseph, 109.
Brunson, Josiah, 109.
Brunson, Josiah, 2nd, 110.
Brunson, Levi, 67.
Brunson, Levi, 109.
Brunson, Luke, 33.
Brunson, Mark, 109.
Brunson, Martin, 93.
Brunson, Mary, 109.
Brunson, Mathew, 46.
Brunson, Michael, 109.
Brunson, Nathaniel, 33.
Brunson, Noadiah, 32.
Brunson, Oliver, 47.
Brunson, Phineas, 50.
Brunson, Roger, 33.
Brunson, Rosswell, 109.
Brunson, Ruben, 93.
Brunson, Samuel, 32.
Brunson, Samuel, 109.
Brunson, Seth, 110.
Brunson, Sibey, 109.
Brunson, Silas, 49.
Brunson, Stephen, 35.
Brunson, Stephen, 41.
Brunson, Stephen, 109.
Brunson, Thaddeus, 11.
Brunson, Theo., 110.
Brunson, Titus, 33.
Brunson, Titus, 110.
Brush, Amos, 19.
Brush, Benjamin, 16.
Brush, Benjamin, 24.
Brush, Eliphelet, 28.
Brush, James, 16.
Brush, Jonas, 19.
Brush, Joseph, 10.
Brush, Phillip, 29.
Brush, Shubeal, 16.
Brush, Stephen, 19.
Brush, Thomas, 19.
Brush, Thomas, 2d, 19.
Brush, Zacheus, 19.
Brush, Zophar, 29.
Bruster, Benjn, 133.
Bruster, Calep, 14.
Bruster, Daniel, 114.
Bruster, Dorothy, 114.
Bruster, Elijah, 114.
Bruster, Elisabeth, 115.
Bruster, Eunice, 114.
Bruster, Jabez, 114.
Bruster, Jacob, 114.

Bruster, John, 69.
Bruster, Jonathan, 114.
Bruster, Jona, Junr, 114.
Bruster, Joseph, 115.
Bruster, Judah, 115.
Bruster, Nathan, 114.
Bruster, Phillup, 131.
Bruster, Prince, 45.
Bruster, Seabury, 130.
Bruster, Silas, 114.
Bruster, Simon, 113.
Bruster, Simon, Junr, 115.
Bruster, Stephen, 110.
Bruster, Stephen, 129.
Bryan, Benajah, 76.
Bryan, John, 132.
Bryan, Nathan, 71.
Bryan, Oliver, 101.
Bryan, Richard, 74.
Bryan, Saviah, 57.
Bryan, Timothy, 130.
Bryant, Benjamin, 45.
Bryant, Ebenezer, 37.
Bryant, Heil, 102.
Bryant, Heil, 102.
Bryant, Isaac, 95.
Bryant, John, 28.
Bryant, John, 93.
Bryant, John, 102.
Bryant, Joseph, 101.
Bryant, Samuel, 28.
Bryant, Thomas, 102.
Bryant, Timothy, 37.
Buck, Aaron, 144.
Buck, Abner, 19.
Buck, Amos, 54.
Buck, Asaph, 71.
Buck, Benton, 71.
Buck, Daniel, 19.
Buck, Daniel, 53.
Buck, Daniel, 144.
Buck, Daniel, 152.
Buck, David, 144.
Buck, David, 144.
Buck, Deborah, 34.
Buck, Eben, 134.
Buck, Eliphalet, 45.
Buck, Enoch, 71.
Buck, Ephraim, 71.
Buck, Ezekiel, 71.
Buck, George, 37.
Buck, Isaac, 41.
Buck, Isaac, 79.
Buck, Isaac, 136.
Buck, Israel, 71.
Buck, Jeames, 71.
Buck, Jeremiah, 79.
Buck, John, 53.
Buck, Jonathan, 144.
Buck, Josiah, 19.
Buck, Josiah, Jr., 53.
Buck, Judah, 143.
Buck, Reuben, 144.
Buck, Samuel, 53.
Buck, Samuel, 79.
Buck, Samuel, 144.
Buck, Samuel, Jnr, 144.
Buck, Sam. Beebee, 71.
Buck, Thos, 136.
Buck (Wid.), 53.
Buck, William, 43.
Buck, Wm, Jr., 135.
Buckenham, Isaac, 59.
Bucket, Runnel, 107.
Buckhingham, Abijah, 112.
Buckhingham, Oliver, 112.
Buckingham, Abel, 71.
Buckingham, Adonijah, 89.
Buckingham, Andrew, 64.
Buckingham, Benjamin, 71.
Buckingham, Curtis, 10.
Buckingham, Daniel, 89.
Buckingham, Daniel, 102.
Buckingham, David, 75.
Buckingham, David, 109.
Buckingham, Ebenezer, 95.
Buckingham, Elizabeth, 89.
Buckingham, Enoch, 17.
Buckingham, Epenetus, 75.
Buckingham, Gedion, 101.
Buckingham, Hezekiah, 90.
Buckingham, Isaac, 102.
Buckingham, Jedediah, 146.
Buckingham, Jerad, 85.
Buckingham, John, 90.
Buckingham, John, 101.
Buckingham, John, 111.
Buckingham, Joseph, 102.
Buckingham, Lucy, 90.
Buckingham, Nathan, 95.
Buckingham, Reuben, 90.
Buckingham, Samel, 89.
Buckingham, Saml, 90.
Buckingham, Samuel, 110.
Buckingham, Thomas, 146.
Buckingham, William, 146.
Buckland, Aaron, 37.
Buckland, Charles, 36.
Buckland, Daniel, 36.
Buckland, Elisha, 37.
Buckland, Joshua, 46.
Buckland, Mary, 36.
Buckland, Peter, 37.

Buckley, Abigail, 121.
Buckley, Abraham, 90.
Buckley, Alexander, 134.
Buckley, Alexander, 134.
Buckley, Aron, 99.
Buckley, Benjamin, 33.
Buckley, Benjamin, 52.
Buckley, Charles, 52.
Buckley, Charles, 121.
Buckley, Charles, 128.
Buckley, Charles, Junr, 120.
Buckley, Charles, 2d, 53.
Buckley, Chauncey, 80.
Buckley, Christian, 53.
Buckley, Conkling, 90.
Buckley, Dan1, 82.
Buckley, Daniel, 121.
Buckley, Dan1, 136.
Buckley, David, 33.
Buckley, David, 121.
Buckley, Edward, 53.
Buckley, Elias, 33.
Buckley, Elias, Jr., 33.
Buckley, Elijah, 121.
Buckley, Eliphelet, 121.
Buckley, Frances, 52.
Buckley, Gersham, 53.
Buckley, Revr Gershom, 88.
Buckley, Hannah, 36.
Buckley, Hosea, 53.
Buckley, Jehiel, 53.
Buckley, Jemima, 90.
Buckley, Job, 106.
Buckley, John, 52.
Buckley, John, 121.
Buckley, John, 124.
Buckley, Jonathan, 33.
Buckley, Jonathan, 54.
Buckley, Joseph, 53.
Buckley, Joseph, 62.
Buckley, Joseph, 120.
Buckley, Joshua, 121.
Buckley, Justus, 51.
Buckley, Moses, 99.
Buckley, Oliver, 33.
Buckley, Paty, 53.
Buckley, Peter, 121.
Buckley, Peter, Junr, 121.
Buckley, Prescott, 53.
Buckley, Prudence, 53.
Buckley, Richard, 34.
Buckley, Roger, 121.
Buckley, Samuel, 62.
Buckley, Sarah, 52.
Buckley, Selah, 33.
Buckley, Solomon, 52.
Buckley, Stephen, 54.
Buckley, Theodore, 54.
Buckley, Thomas, 40.
Buckley, Wetherby, 53.
Buckley, Wm, 90.
Buckley, William, 120.
Buckly, Daniel, 110.
Buckly, William, 103.
Buckman, Stephen, 153.
Bucknel, Josiah, 39.
Bucks, David, 135.
Bud, Abijah, 48.
Buddington, Walter, 128.
Budington, Walter, 119.
Budington, Walter, Junr, 119.
Budlong, David, 151.
Budlong, Joseph, 151.
Buel, Abel, 104.
Buel, Archelus, 65.
Buel, Benjn, 133.
Buel, Benjn, 135.
Buel, Clive, 71.
Buel, Elijah, 120.
Buel, Elijah, Junr, 120.
Buel, Elisha, 120.
Buel, Eunice, 70.
Buel, Hiel, 85.
Buel, Hiel, 2d, 85.
Buel, Icabod, 135.
Buel, Jacob, 122.
Buel, Jesse, 65.
Buel, Jonothan, 69.
Buel, Jonothan, 69.
Buel, Joseph, 136.
Buel, Norman, 65.
Buel, Timothy, 59.
Buell, Asa, 85.
Buell, Ashbel, 68.
Buell, Azariah, 85.
Buell, Bela, 84.
Buell, Benjamin, 85.
Buell, David, 65.
Buell, David, 85.
Buell, David, 2d, 85.
Buell, James, 85.
Buell, Jedediah, 85.
Buell, Jeremiah, Junr, 84.
Buell, Job, 85.
Buell, Job, 2d, 85.
Buell, John, 65.
Buell, John, 85.
Buell, Jonathan, 85.
Buell, Josiah, 2d, 85.
Buell, Nathaniel, 67.
Buell, Nathaniel, 85.
Buell, Peter, 68.
Buell, Reuben, 85.

# INDEX.

Buell, Salmon, 60.
Buell, Solomon, 48.
Buell, Solomon, 71.
Buell, Solomon, Jr., 48.
Buell, William, 48.
Buell, William, 48.
Buell, William, 84.
Buffham, Joshua, 86.
Buffington, William, 140.
Bugbe, Amos, 140.
Bugbe, Caleb, 154.
Bugbe, James, 140.
Bugbe, Josiah, 140.
Bugbe, Rufus, 154.
Bugbe, Sam$^l$, 140.
Bugbe, Tho$^s$, 149.
Bugbe, Thomas, Ju$^r$, 154.
Bugbee, Cathar$^e$, 151.
Bugbee, Dan$^l$, 154.
Bugbee, Elijah, 154.
Bugbee, Hannah, 147.
Bugbee, Isaiah, 140.
Bugbee, James, 154.
Bugbee, Jed$^h$, 154.
Bugbee, Jesse, 140.
Bugbee, Jonathan, 39.
Bugbee, Jonath$^n$, 154.
Bugbee, Nathaniel, 40.
Bugbee, Thomas, 154.
Bugbee, William, 154.
Bugby, Samuel, 129.
Bukingham, Ephraim, 102.
Bukley, Joseph, 62.
Buknall (Wid.), 139.
Bulford, John, 73.
Bulford, John, 77.
Bulkley, Aaron, 27.
Bulkley, Abigail, 12.
Bulkley, Abraham, 13.
Bulkley, Andrew, 14.
Bulkley, Calvin, 74.
Bulkley, Daniel, 13.
Bulkley, David, 32.
Bulkley, Deborah, 14.
Bulkley, Ebenezer, 14.
Bulkley, Elihue, 14.
Bulkley, Gershom, 14.
Bulkley, Gershom, 2$^d$, 14.
Bulkley, Hannah, 14.
Bulkley, James, 15.
Bulkley, James, Jn$^r$, 14.
Bulkley, John, 71.
Bulkley, Jonathan, 19.
Bulkley, Joseph, 13.
Bulkley, Joseph, 14.
Bulkley, Joseph, 2$^d$, 14.
Bulkley, Josiah, 14.
Bulkley, Luther, 10.
Bulkley, Nathan, 13.
Bulkley, Nathan, 14.
Bulkley, Peter, 13.
Bulkley, Peter, 13.
Bulkley, Peter, 27.
Bulkley, Seth, 30.
Bulkley, Turney, 13.
Bulkley, William, 15.
Bulkly, Peter, Jun$^r$, 27.
Bulkly, Talcot, 32.
Bull, Aaron, 46.
Bull, Aaron, 53.
Bull, Abner, 44.
Bull, Amos, 46.
Bull, Anna, 102.
Bull, Asa, 64.
Bull, Asher, 67.
Bull, Benjamin, 102.
Bull, Caleb, 45.
Bull, David, 45.
Bull, David, 71.
Bull, Edward, 90.
Bull, Enunice, 65.
Bull, Frederic, 45.
Bull, George, 45.
Bull, George, 65.
Bull, Henry, 101.
Bull, Hezekiah, 45.
Bull, Isaac, 45.
Bull, Jacob, 58.
Bull, James, 45.
Bull, James, 67.
Bull, Jeremiah, 101.
Bull, Jesse, 57.
Bull, John, 57.
Bull, Jno., 90.
Bull, Jonathan, 40.
Bull, Jonathan, 46.
Bull, Jonathan, 62.
Bull, Martin, 40.
Bull, Michael, 57.
Bull, Samuel, 85.
Bull, Temperance, 101.
Bull, Thomas, 45.
Bull, Thomas, 77.
Bull, William, 45.
Bullard, Asa, 153.
Bullard, Calvin, 140.
Bullard, Ely, 105.
Bullard, Josiah, 38.
Bullard, Luther, 141.
Bullard, William, 141.
Bullen, Christopher, 39.
Bullen, David, 39.
Bullock, Dan$^l$, 144.

Bullon, Jon$^a$, 38.
Bulloph, Benoni, 48.
Bulloph, Daniel, 48.
Bulloph, Jonathan, 44.
Bumbo, Harry, 52.
Bump, John, 123.
Bumps, Simeon, 68.
Bumter, Shorum, 42.
Bunce, Asa, 46.
Bunce, Daniel, 46.
Bunce, David, 105.
Bunce, Elizabeth (Wid.), 46.
Bunce, Isaac, 45.
Bunce, Isaih, 74.
Bunce, James, 46.
Bunce, Jerusha, 45.
Bunce, John, 46.
Bunce, John, 109.
Bunce, John, Jr., 45.
Bunce, Jon$^a$, 53.
Bunce, Joseph, 46.
Bunce, Josia, 53.
Bunce, Richard, 52.
Bunce, Roderic, 46.
Bunce, Thomas, 54.
Bundy, Ebenezer, 17.
Bundy, Eben$^r$, 150.
Bundy, John, 147.
Bundy, Joshua, 112.
Bundy, Robart, 119.
Bunel, Daniel, Jr., 35.
Buner, Jon$^a$, Jr., 52.
Buner, Sarah, 52.
Buner, Timothy, 45.
Bunham, Thomas, 105.
Bunker, James, 108.
Bunnel, Abner, 93.
Bunnel, Abner, 2$^d$, 93.
Bunnel, Bela, 35.
Bunnel, Charles, 95.
Bunnel, Daniel, 35.
Bunnel, David, 93.
Bunnel, Eneas, 93.
Bunnel, Fradrick, 70.
Bunnel, Frank, 81.
Bunnel, Gershom, 12.
Bunnel, Hannah, 24.
Bunnel, Hezekiah, 76.
Bunnel, Isaac, 94.
Bunnel, Israel, 93.
Bunnel, Jacob, 92.
Bunnel, Jacob, 92.
Bunnel, Jerus, 92.
Bunnel, Job, 10.
Bunnel, Joel, 93.
Bunnel, John, 93.
Bunnel, John, 101.
Bunnel, Josep, 92.
Bunnel, Joseph, 41.
Bunnel, Joseph, 49.
Bunnel, Louis, 93.
Bunnel, Luke, 94.
Bunnel, Nath$^a$, 95.
Bunnel, Ruben, 95.
Bunnel, Titus, 85.
Bunnal, Unice, 93.
Bunnel, William, 95.
Bunnell, Amos, 50.
Bunnell, Joal, 88.
Bunnels, Hannah, 95.
Bunnet, Ambrose, 75.
Bunnet, Hannah, 95.
Bunnil, Ebenezer, 93.
Bunnil, Samuel, 93.
Bunson, William, 67.
Bur, Purcy, 128.
Burbank, Ebenezer, 52.
Burbank, Seth, 50.
Burbanks, Dan$^l$, 136.
Burch, Billings, 118.
Burch, Henry, 117.
Burch, Isaac, 119.
Burch, Samuel, 118.
Burch, William, 20.
Burch, William, 20.
Burchard, Elijah, 12.
Burchard, Walter, 138.
Burchin, William, 20.
Burchird, Elisha, 131.
Burchird, Gideon, 131.
Burd, Jonathan, 67.
Burdec, George, 49.
Burden, Jerry, 43.
Burdet, Thomson, 115.
Burdett, Edward, 130.
Burdick, Abraham, 115.
Burdick, Christopher, 117.
Burdick, Daniel, 115.
Burdick, Elijah, 115.
Burdick, Elisha, 117.
Burdick, Ezekiel, 116.
Burdick, Lodowick, 117.
Burdick, Nath$^l$, 117.
Burdick, Oliver, 117.
Burdick, Peter, 117.
Burdick, Samuel, 115.
Burdick, Thomson, 117.
Burdick, Walter, 119.
Burdock, Joshua, 35.
Burdock, Lewis, 35.
Burdock, Robert, 35.
Burdrick, Ira, 115.
Burdrick, John, 116.

Burge, Edw$^d$, 137.
Burge, Jn$^o$, 135.
Burge, Jon$^a$, 135.
Burge, Jon$^a$, 136.
Burge, Joseph, 142.
Burge, Peletiah, 54.
Burge (Widow), 138.
Burges, Beney$^h$, 151.
Burges, Benjamin, 60.
Burges, Ebenezer, 74.
Burges, James, 60.
Burges, Jeames, 74.
Burges, John, 97.
Burges, John, 148.
Burges, Samuel, 56.
Burges, Thomas, 98.
Burges, Thomas, 144.
Burges, Tho$^s$, 151.
Burges, Thomas, 2$^d$, 98.
Burges, William, 144.
Burgess, Asa, 142.
Burgh, Charles, 69.
Burgher, David, 69.
Burgher, Sim., 69.
Burghes, Joseph, 60.
Burington, Eliphelet, 116.
Buritt, Anthony, 73.
Burk, John, 102.
Burk, William, 125.
Burke, Ebenzer, 106.
Burke, Edmond, 103.
Burke, Elizabeth, 105.
Burkitt, John, 45.
Burkitt, Thomas, 45.
Burkitt, Uriah, 45.
Burkland, George, 39.
Burkout, Peter, 22.
Burley, Ebenezer, 19.
Burley, Jacob, 139.
Burley, Jos., 139.
Burley, Sarah (W$^d$), 16.
Burley, Silas, 16.
Burley, Sol$^n$, 138.
Burlingham, Edmond, 144.
Burlingham, Ezekiel, 150.
Burlingham, Nathan, 140.
Burlingham, Nathan, 151.
Burlington, Benj$^a$, 144.
Burlington, Hopkins, 144.
Burn, David, 102.
Burn, James, 129.
Burnam, Andrew, 153.
Burnam, Dan$^l$, 143.
Burnam, Freeman, 141.
Burnam, Isaac, 140.
Burnam, James, 153.
Burnam, John, 140.
Burnam, John, 153.
Burnam, Joseph, 140.
Burnam, Joseph, 143.
Burnam, Joseph, 143.
Burnam, Josiah, 143.
Burnam, Josiah, 143.
Burnam, Nathan, 141.
Burnap, Ab$^m$, 134.
Burnap, Christopher, 134.
Burnap, Daniel, 38.
Burnap, James, 143.
Burnet, James, 152.
Burnet, Jeremiah, 95.
Burnet, Rev$^d$ Matthias, 21.
Burnett, Rachel, 120.
Burnham, Aaron, 36.
Burnham, Abner, 37.
Burnham, Ashbell, 86.
Burnham, Augustus, 36.
Burnham, Benjamin, 112.
Burnham, Catharine, 120.
Burnham, Daniel, 36.
Burnham, David, 37.
Burnham, David, 82.
Burnham, David, 121.
Burnham, Eleazer, 36.
Burnham, Elias, 130.
Burnham, Freeman, 36.
Burnham, George, 36.
Burnham, George, 45.
Burnham, Hannah, 37.
Burnham, Isaac, 68.
Burnham, James, 38.
Burnham, James, 52.
Burnham, James, 113.
Burnham, James, 123.
Burnham, James, 130.
Burnham, Jedediah, 112.
Burnham, Jeremiah, 52.
Burnham, Jerusha, 36.
Burnham, Joseph, 123.
Burnham, Joshua, 83.
Burnham, Josiah, 123.
Burnham, Moses, 36.
Burnham, Nathan, 82.
Burnham, Nath$^l$, 2$^d$, 82.
Burnham, Oliver, 37.
Burnham, Reuben, 68.
Burnham, Rhoderic, 36.
Burnham, Roger, 130.
Burnham, Samuel, 36.
Burnham, Samuel, 130.
Burnham, Stephen, 36.
Burnham, Sylvester, 82.
Burnham, Theodore, 36.
Burnham, Thomas, 36.

Burnham, Timothy, 36.
Burnham (Wid.), 52.
Burnham, Woolcott, 71.
Burnham, Zaccheus, 130.
Burnham, Zenas, 36.
Burnington, Ebenezer, 60.
Burns, Daniel, 126.
Burns, John, 127.
Burns, Simon, 67.
Burns, Titus, 95.
Burns, Titus, 2$^{nd}$, 95.
Burows, Jon$^a$, 137.
Burr, Aaron, 14.
Burr, Abel, 27.
Burr, Adonijah, 44.
Burr, Adonijah, Jr, 45.
Burr, Amos, 45.
Burr, Asa, 44.
Burr, Benjamin, 83.
Burr, Bud, 13.
Burr, Charles, 14.
Burr, Charles, 27.
Burr, Daniel, 12.
Burr, Daniel, 68.
Burr, David, 12.
Burr, David, Jn$^r$, 12.
Burr, David, 3$^d$, 14.
Burr, Ebenezer, 13.
Burr, Ebenezer, 61.
Burr, Ebenezer, 63.
Burr, Ebenezer, 2$^d$, 14.
Burr, Ebenezer, 3$^d$, 13.
Burr, Edmon, 13.
Burr, Elijah, 15.
Burr, Elijah, 27.
Burr, Eliphalet, 32.
Burr, Eunice, 12.
Burr, Eunice, 42.
Burr, Ezekiel, 27.
Burr, George, 13.
Burr, George, 45.
Burr, Gershom, 14.
Burr, Hezekiah, 14.
Burr, Hosea, 17.
Burr, Increase, 13.
Burr, Increase, 32.
Burr, Isaac, 14.
Burr, Isaac, 37.
Burr, Isaac, 42.
Burr, James, 17.
Burr, Jehue, 17.
Burr, Jerad, 94.
Burr, Jesse, 13.
Burr, Jesse, 2$^d$, 15.
Burr, Joel, 27.
Burr, John, 13.
Burr, John, 32.
Burr, John, 60.
Burr, John, Jn$^r$, 14.
Burr, Jonathan, 36.
Burr, Jonathan, 83.
Burr, Joseph, 13.
Burr, Joseph, 27.
Burr, Joseph, 45.
Burr, Joseph, 83.
Burr, Josiah, 104.
Burr, Moses, 31.
Burr, Moses, 32.
Burr, Moses, 45.
Burr, Nathan, 14.
Burr, Nathan, 27.
Burr, Nathaniel, 83.
Burr, Nathaniel, 83.
Burr, Nehemiah, 14.
Burr, Noadiah, 42.
Burr, Noadiah, Jr., 42.
Burr, Noah, 21.
Burr, Oliver, 11.
Burr, Osias, 14.
Burr, Peter, 14.
Burr, Reuben, 60.
Burr, Russel, 60.
Burr, Salmon, 42.
Burr, Samuel, 13.
Burr, Samuel, 28.
Burr, Samuel, 42.
Burr, Samuel, 45.
Burr, Samuel, 93.
Burr, Samuel, 1$^{st}$, 14.
Burr, Samuel, 3$^d$, 14.
Burr, Seth, 27.
Burr, Stephen, 27.
Burr, Sturgis, 104.
Burr, Talcott, 13.
Burr, Thaddeus, 14.
Burr, Theodore, 42.
Burr, Timothy, 13.
Burr, Timothy, 45.
Burr, Titus, 42.
Burr, Wakeman, 14.
Burr, Walter, 63.
Burr, William, 14.
Burr, William, 45.
Burr, William, 73.
Burr, Zalmon, 13.
Burr, Zebina, 44.
Burral, Benjamin, 150.
Burral, Samuel, 22.
Burrall, Jacob, 150.
Burrall, John, 150.
Burrel, Charles, 70.
Burrel, Daniel, 101.
Burrel, Jeremiah, 101.

Burrel, Samuel, 101.
Burrel, Samuel, Jr, 23.
Burrel, Samuel, 2$^d$, 101.
Burrel, Thomas, 104.
Burrel, William, 59.
Burrell, Charles, 62.
Burrell, Sarah, 24.
Burres, John, 107.
Burress, Joseph, 62.
Burret, Abel, 103.
Burret, Benedict, 95.
Burret, Benjamin, 111.
Burret, Israel, 96.
Burret, Richard, 96.
Burret, William, 94.
Burret, William, 2$^d$, 94.
Burrett, Charles, 96.
Burrill, Jonathan, 67.
Burrill, Stephen, 19.
Burriss, Stephen, 25.
Burrit, Charles, 30.
Burrit, Elijah, 30.
Burrit, Franses, 10.
Burrit, John, 17.
Burrit, Philip, 11.
Burrit, Stephen, 30.
Burrit, Wakeman, 13.
Burritt, Amos, 20.
Burritt, Ephraim, 30.
Burritt, Hezekiah, 30.
Burritt, Joseph, 30.
Burritt, Oliver, 73.
Burritt, Rebeckah (Wid.), 20.
Burritt, Samuel, 30.
Burritt, Silus, 29.
Burritt, William, 30.
Burritt, William, 56.
Burroll, Obed, 70.
Burrow, George, 30.
Burrows, Amos, 137.
Burrows, Barzilla, 40.
Burrows, Dan$^l$, 120.
Burrows, Daniel, 129.
Burrows, Elisha, 120.
Burrows, Hubbard, 120.
Burrows, James, 119.
Burrows, John, 85.
Burrows, John, 119.
Burrows, John, 120.
Burrows, Jon$^a$, 120.
Burrows, Joseph, 40.
Burrows, Joseph, 119.
Burrows, Lemuel, 120.
Burrows, Lemuel, Jun$^r$, 120.
Burrows, Nathan, 120.
Burrows, Nathan, Jun$^r$, 120.
Burrows, Paul, 120.
Burrows, Roswell, 128.
Burrows, Sam$^l$, 120.
Burrows, Silas, 119.
Burrows, William, 120.
Burt, Abraham, 61.
Burt, Consider, 45.
Burt, Joseph, 123.
Burt, Joshua, 28.
Burt, Richard, 14.
Burt, Theophilus, 28.
Burton, Christopher, 136.
Burton, Ebenezer, 97.
Burton, Israel, 113.
Burton, Israel, 114.
Burton, Joseph, 29.
Burton, Nathan, 56.
Burton, Nathan, 114.
Burton, Samuel, 31.
Burton, Sam$^l$, 66.
Burton, Solomon, 32.
Burton, Uriah, 148.
Burwell, Stephen, 71.
Busbee, Jon$^a$, 143.
Busey, Titus, 151.
Bush, Aaron, 40.
Bush, Aaron, 62.
Bush, Amaziah, 124.
Bush, David, 16.
Bush, Eli, 39.
Bush, Elisha, 79.
Bush, George, 79.
Bush, Henry, 129.
Bush, Joel, 71.
Bush, John, 144.
Bush, Jonathan, 39.
Bush, Jonathan, 79.
Bush, Joseph, 15.
Bush, Joshua, 39.
Bush, Lindie, 101.
Bush, Moses, 51.
Bush, Moses, 79.
Bush, Rufus, 40.
Bush, Samuel, 16.
Bush, Samuel, 25.
Bush, Stephen, 148.
Bush, William, 15.
Bushly, Ebenezer, 71.
Bushnal, Abner, 68.
Bushnal, Abraham, 67.
Bushnal, John, 112.
Bushnal, Sam$^l$, 66.
Bushnal, Thomas, 62.
Bushneel, Eben$^r$, 131.
Bushnel, Daniel, 61.
Bushnel, Doct$^r$, 90.
Bushnel, Gideon, 65.

# INDEX.

Bushnel, Jedediah, 68.
Bushnel, Martin, 68.
Bushnel, Sam¹, 62.
Bushnel, Stephen, 68.
Bushnell, Asa, 90.
Bushnell, Benajah, 90.
Bushnell, Caleb, 130.
Bushnell, Constant, 89.
Bushnell, Daniel, 69.
Bushnell, Daniel, 89.
Bushnell, Daniel, 90.
Bushnell, Daniel, 90.
Bushnell, Daniel, 2ᵈ, 90.
Bushnell, David, 130.
Bushnell, Ebenezer, 90.
Bushnell, Ebenezʳ, 145.
Bushnell, Elias, 89.
Bushnell, Elisabeth, 130.
Bushnell, Elisha, 89.
Bushnell, Ethen, 90.
Bushnell, Francis, 90.
Bushnell, Handly, 89.
Bushnell, Handly, 2ᵈ, 89.
Bushnell, Hezekiah, 90.
Bushnell, Ira, 89.
Bushnell, Ira, 2ᵈ, 89.
Bushnell, Jason, 130.
Bushnell, John, 89.
Bushnell, John, 130.
Bushnell, Jnᵒ. W., 90.
Bushnell, Jonathan, 89.
Bushnell, Jonathan, 90.
Bushnell, Jonathan, 130.
Bushnell, Jonathan, Junʳ, 130.
Bushnell, Joseph, 89.
Bushnell, Joseph, 115.
Bushnell, Joseph, 2ᵈ, 89.
Bushnell, Joshua, 89.
Bushnell, Lemuel, 89.
Bushnell, Lemuel, 2ᵈ, 89.
Bushnell, Mary, 130.
Bushnell, Nathan, 89.
Bushnell, Nath¹, 89.
Bushnell, Nath¹, 2ᵈ, 89.
Bushnell, Phinehas, 90.
Bushnell, Pinehas, 89.
Bushnell, Reuben, 90.
Bushnell, Reuben, 90.
Bushnell, Richard, 130.
Bushnell, Sam¹, 89.
Bushnell, William, 68.
Bushnoll, Dan¹, 185.
Bushnul, Aaron, 112.
Bushnul, Ezekiel, 112.
Bushnul, Joseph, 112.
Bushnul, Nathan, 112.
Buswell, Lemuel, 131.
Buswell, Lemuel, Junʳ, 131.
Buswell, Thoˢ, 142.
Buterick, Edward, 54.
Butlar, Hannah, 143.
Butlar, William, 143.
Butler, Abel, 47.
Butler, Abel, 59.
Butler, Amos, 83.
Butler, Benjamin, 53.
Butler, Benjamin, 88.
Butler, Benjamin, 91.
Butler, Charles, 30.
Butler, Charles, 91.
Butler, Comfort, 88.
Butler, Comfort, 106.
Butler, Daniel, 46.
Butler, Dan¹, 146.
Butler, Darius, 56.
Butler, David, 47.
Butler, David, 54.
Butler, David, 65.
Butler, David, 87.
Butler, Davney, 87.
Butler, Eli, 88.
Butler, Ezekiel, 71.
Butler, Ezra, 107.
Butler, Frederic, 52.
Butler, Gershom, 88.
Butler, Gideon, 47.
Butler, Gideon, 53.
Butler, Hannah, 87.
Butler, Henry, 46.
Butler, Hezekiah, 53.
Butler, Hezekiah, 63.
Butler, Houton, 84.
Butler, James, 39.
Butler, James, 53.
Butler, James, 92.
Butler, James, 127.
Butler, Jeremiah, 96.
Butler, Jererd, 63.
Butler, Jesse, 57.
Butler, Joel, 53.
Butler, John, 36.
Butler, John, 53.
Butler, John, 79.
Butler, John, 87.
Butler, John, 91.
Butler, John, 123.
Butler, John, 127.
Butler, John, Junʳ, 126.
Butler, Jonathan, 46.
Butler, Joseph, 47.
Butler, Joseph, 53.
Butler, Joseph, Jr., 47.
Butler, Josiah, 53.

Butler, Josiah, 57.
Butler, Justas, 104.
Butler, Mathew, 91.
Butler, Moses, 36.
Butler, Moses, 46.
Butler, Nathan, 68.
Butler, Nath¹, 55.
Butler, Norman, 46.
Butler, Patᵏ, 145.
Butler, Richard, 46.
Butler, Richard, 54.
Butler, Roger, 53.
Butler, Samuel, 53.
Butler, Samuel, 67.
Butler, Samuel, 79.
Butler, Samuel, 87.
Butler, Samuel, 87.
Butler, Sam¹, 90.
Butler, Sam¹ S., 66.
Butler, Simeon, 53.
Butler, Stephen, 54.
Butler, Stephen, 57.
Butler, Stephen, 63.
Butler, Stephen, 85.
Butler, Stephen, 140.
Butler, Theodore, 53.
Butler, Timothy, 89.
Butler, William, 53.
Butler, William, 96.
Butler, William, 122.
Butler, Zacheus, 47.
Butler, Zebᵈⁱ, 136.
Butler, Zeebah, 54.
Butolph, Levi, 44.
Butt, Sabria, 57.
Buttersby, Wᵐ, 23.
Buttersworth, John, 22.
Buttler, Benjamin, 42.
Buttler, Josiah, 67.
Buttles, George, 117.
Buttles, Joseph, 48.
Button, Elias, 40.
Button, George, 116.
Button, Jedediah, 106.
Button, John, 116.
Button, John, 142.
Button, Joseph, 115.
Button, Jos., 134.
Button, Joshua, 113.
Button, Joshua, 152.
Button, Mathias, 114.
Button, Newberry, 151.
Button, Roswell, 114.
Button, Shubael, 114.
Button (Widow), 134.
Button, William, 114.
Button, Zebulun, 115.
Buttonton, Nehemiah, 14.
Buttonton, Walter, 14.
Buttonton, William, 14.
Buttors, William, 114.
Butts, Ebenʳ, 142.
Butts, Gideon, 142.
Butts, Isaac, 19.
Butts, John, 143.
Butts, Josiah, 142.
Butts, Sam¹, 141.
Butts, Sherekiah, 142.
Butts, Stephen, 142.
Buxton, Dorras (Wᵈ), 17.
Buxton, James, 25.
Buxton, John, 25.
Buxton, Mercy (Wᵈ), 25.
Buxton, Peter, 25.
Buxton, Samuel, 25.
Byan, David, 76.
Byan, Samuel, 74.
Byan, Zacheriah, 74.
Byers, Leonard, 132.
Byington, Benjamin, 110.
Byington, Daniel, 110.
Byington, Jacob, 40.
Byington, Jerad, 110.
Byington, Jerad, 110.
Byington, Joel, 45.
Byington, John, 27.
Byington, John, 27.
Byington, Jonathan, 92.
Byington, Joseph, 34.
Byington, Noah, 34.
Byinton, Benjamin, 91.
Byles, Ebenʳ, 140.

Cable, Abner, 18.
Cable, Benjamin, 23.
Cable, David, 71.
Cable, Ebenezer, 24.
Cable, Ebenezer, 31.
Cable, George, 13.
Cable, Gershom, 23.
Cable, Isaac, 32.
Cable, Joseph, 31.
Cable, Martha (Wᵈ), 23.
Cable, Nehemiah, 31.
Cable, Rebekah, 15.
Cable, Ruth, 31.
Cable, Samuel, 14.
Cable, Thomas, 12.
Cable, William, 29.
Cables, John, 45.
Cables, Michael, 117.
Cadey, Lemuel, 61.
Cadley, George, 57.

Cadwell, Aaron, 47.
Cadwell, Aaron, 47.
Cadwell, Abram, 45.
Cadwell, David, 37.
Cadwell, Elias, 97.
Cadwell, Elizabeth, 45.
Cadwell, Hezekiah, 45.
Cadwell, Hezekiah, 47.
Cadwell, Isaac, 63.
Cadwell, James, 42.
Cadwell, Jeduthan, 45.
Cadwell, John, 37.
Cadwell, John, 86.
Cadwell, Joseph, 47.
Cadwell, Levi, 38.
Cadwell, Mathew, 37.
Cadwell, Mathew, 41.
Cadwell, Nehemiah, 45.
Cadwell, Nehemiah, Jr., 45.
Cadwell, Peletiah, 41.
Cadwell, Phinehas, 61.
Cadwell, Reuben, 37.
Cadwell, Rhoda, 47.
Cadwell, Roderic, 32.
Cadwell, Ruth, 45.
Cadwell, Theodore, 55.
Cadwell, Thomas, 47.
Cady, Abijah, 142.
Cady, Abner, 137.
Cady, Amos, 138.
Cady, Asa, 137.
Cady, Asail, 141.
Cady, Benjⁿ, 141.
Cady, Chester, 68.
Cady, Dan¹, 141.
Cady, David, 144.
Cady, Eben¹, 141.
Cady, Eliakim, 141.
Cady, Ephraim, 80.
Cady, Gideon, 141.
Cady, Hez., 137.
Cady, Isaiah, 144.
Cady, Jedediah, 137.
Cady, Jesse, 137.
Cady, John, 141.
Cady, John, 150.
Cady, Jonathⁿ, 141.
Cady, Jonathan, 144.
Cady, Joseph, 144.
Cady, Joseph, 144.
Cady, Joseph, 144.
Cady, Josiah, 68.
Cady, Luther, 154.
Cady, Martha, 151.
Cady, Naham, 141.
Cady, Nahum, 138.
Cady, Penuel, 149.
Cady, Ruben, 137.
Cady, Uriah, 141.
Cahoon, Matha, 38.
Cain, Hugh, 28.
Cain, Latin, 99.
Cain, Patrick, 99.
Calder, John, 45.
Caldvin, David, 47.
Caldwell, ——, 45.
Caldwell, Charles, 45.
Caldwell, George, 45.
Caldwell, James, 67.
Caldwell, John, 45.
Cale, William, 86.
Calender, Elisha, 53.
Calhoun, David, 74.
Calhoun, Ebenezer, 74.
Calhoun, George, 74.
Calhoun, Jeames, 74.
Calhoun, John, 58.
Calhoun, Joseph, 74.
Calhoun, Josiah, 99.
Calhoun, Tabitha, 74.
Calkin, Israel, 18.
Calkins, Able, Junʳ, 112.
Calkins, Hugh, 129.
Calkins, Hugh, 130.
Calkins, James, 147.
Calkins, James, 147.
Calkins, Nath¹ S., 152.
Calkins, Solomon, 146.
Callon, Ducan M., 90.
Callow, Miles, 109.
Calver, David, 135.
Calver, Nathaniel, 51.
Calver, Samuel, 35.
Cambell, Joseph, 151.
Camble, Noah, 110.
Cambridge (Negroe), 95.
Cambridge, Ruth, 104.
Camelon, John, 60.
Cameron, Lauchland, 61.
Camfield, Dan¹, 62.
Cammel, John, 63.
Cammel, John, 69.
Camp, Abel, 59.
Camp, Abial, 63.
Camp, Abraham, 10.
Camp, Amos, 57.
Camp, Amos, 108.
Camp, Asahel, 89.
Camp, Benajah, 76.
Camp, Charity, 78.
Camp, Chauncy, 74.
Camp, Daniel, 71.
Camp, Daniel, 74.

Camp, David, 56.
Camp, David, 71.
Camp, David, 101.
Camp, David, 2ᵈ, 56.
Camp, Ebenezur, 96.
Camp, Edward, 89.
Camp, Elias, 96.
Camp, Elias, 96.
Camp, Elias, 101.
Camp, Elither, 125.
Camp, Elnathan, 96.
Camp, Ely, 96.
Camp, Enos, 1ˢᵗ, 71.
Camp, Enos, 2ᵈ, 71.
Camp, Ephraim, 76.
Camp, Ezra, 96.
Camp, Ezra, 101.
Camp, Gideon, 74.
Camp, Hail, 101.
Camp, Heath, 71.
Camp, Hezekiah, 20.
Camp, Hezekiah, 96.
Camp, Isaac, 21.
Camp, Isaac, 74.
Camp, Isaac, 76.
Camp, Isaac, Junʳ, 21.
Camp, Israel, 71.
Camp, Israel, 96.
Camp, Jacob, 63.
Camp, James, 46.
Camp, James M., 129.
Camp, Jesse, 104.
Camp, Joab, 101.
Camp, Job, 71.
Camp, Job, 96.
Camp, Joel, 21.
Camp, Joel, 63.
Camp, John, 71.
Camp, John, 96.
Camp, Jonah, 74.
Camp, Jonathan, 21.
Camp, Joseph, 54.
Camp, Joseph, 96.
Camp, Julius, 20.
Camp, Lemuel, 89.
Camp, Levi, 10.
Camp, Luke, 63.
Camp, Mary, 101.
Camp, Moses, 63.
Camp, Nathan, 10.
Camp, Nathan, 71.
Camp, Nathaniel, 96.
Camp, Nathaniel, 102.
Camp, Phebe, 96.
Camp, Phineas, 96.
Camp, Rejoice, 96.
Camp, Richard, 21.
Camp, Riverius, 71.
Camp, Samuel, 76.
Camp, Samuel, 96.
Camp, Samuel, 101.
Camp, Samuel, 110.
Camp, Revᵈ Samuel, 29.
Camp, Simeon, 154.
Camp, Talcott, 42.
Campbell, Allen, 151.
Campbell, Amos, 151.
Campbell, Andrew, 86.
Campbell, Andrew, 88.
Campbell, Archibald, 151.
Campbell, James, 151.
Campbell, James, Jnʳ, 151.
Campbell, John, 151.
Campbell, John, 151.
Campbell, Noble, 151.
Campbell, Partrick, 151.
Campbell, Peter, 147.
Campbell, Sylvanus, 144.
Campbell, Thomas, 58.
Campbell, William, 144.
Campbell, William, 151.
Campbell, Zuril, 147.
Camps, Hezekiah, 66.
Can. Sarah, 71.
Cande, David, 73.
Cande, Esther, 73.
Cande, John, 88.
Cande, Samuel, 73.
Cande, Timothy, 73.
Candie, Caleb, 95.
Candie, Enos, 95.
Candie, Gideon, 95.
Candie, Isaac, 105.
Candie, Justice, 95.
Candie, Moses, 95.
Candie, Neamiah, 95.
Candie, Samuel, 105.
Cane, Daniel, 67.
Cane, Edward, 71.
Cane, James, 88.
Canfield, Abel, 71.
Canfield, Abiel, 95.
Canfield, Andrew, 58.
Canfield, Asher, 96.
Canfield, Azeriah, 71.
Canfield, Daniel, 94.
Canfield, Darius, 59.
Canfield, David, 94.
Canfield, David, 1ˢᵗ, 71.
Canfield, David, 2ᵈ, 71.
Canfield, Elijah, 71.
Canfield, Eunice, 71.

Canfield, Ezekiel, 32.
Canfield, Gideon, 96.
Canfield, Heath, 71.
Canfield, Ira, 71.
Canfield, Isaiah, 90.
Canfield, Ithamar, 71.
Canfield, Jeremiah, 71.
Canfield, Joel, 90.
Canfield, John, 71.
Canfield, Joseph, 67.
Canfield, Joseph, 2ᵈ, 67.
Canfield, Judson, 67.
Canfield, Lemuel, 71.
Canfield, Levi, 71.
Canfield, Nathaniel, 75.
Canfield, Oliver, 71.
Canfield, Philor, 71.
Canfield, Samuel, 12.
Canfield, Sam¹, 63.
Canfield, Samuel, 71.
Canfield, Samuel, 85.
Canfield, Seba, 86.
Canfield, Thomas, 75.
Canfield, Thomas, 78.
Canfield, Thomas, 2ᵈ, 78.
Canfield, Timothy, 93.
Cannon, James, 30.
Cannon, John, 23.
Cannon, John, Junʳ, 21.
Cannon, Joseph, 51.
Cannon, Lewis, 29.
Cannon, Robart, 127.
Cannon, Samuel, 14.
Canon, James, 21.
Canvil (Wid.), 137.
Cap, C. John, 78.
Cap, Job, 44.
Cape, Demas, 144.
Capells, John, 145.
Capen, Timothy, 70.
Capills, Thomas, & Josiah Rogers, 145.
Capple, Nath¹, 124.
Capron, Giles, 113.
Capron, John, 149.
Capron, Samuel, 114.
Capron, Simeon, 114.
Capron, William, 112.
Carder, ——, 141.
Carder, John, 144.
Cardwell, John, 31.
Cardwell, William, 126.
Caro, Ebenʳ, 148.
Carew, Daniel, 131.
Carew, Ebenʳ, 131.
Carew, Eliphelet, 130.
Carew, Joseph, 131.
Carew, Palmer, 132.
Carew, Simeon, 130.
Carew, William, 142.
Carey, Benjⁿ, 144.
Carey, Ebenʳ, 146.
Carey, Hezekiah, 152.
Carey, James, 153.
Carey, Jonaᵗʰ, 153.
Carey, Joseph, 148.
Carey, Marey, 152.
Carey, Nath¹, 152.
Carey, Oliver, 152.
Carey, Roger, 153.
Carey, William, 153.
Carey, Zurveyⁿ, 152.
Cargell, Benjⁿ, 149.
Carie, Nath¹, 139.
Carington, Daniel N., 11.
Carlee, John, 19.
Carlton, Richard, 138.
Carman, John, 10.
Carpenter, Alfred, 130.
Carpenter, Barnard, 19.
Carpenter, Barnee, 19.
Carpenter, Benedict, 18.
Carpenter, Benjamin, 94.
Carpenter, Comfort, 138.
Carpenter, Comfort, 141.
Carpenter, Daniel, 38.
Carpenter, Dan¹, 137.
Carpenter, Dan., 140.
Carpenter, Dan., 146.
Carpenter, Dan., 154.
Carpenter, David, 137.
Carpenter, Davis, 153.
Carpenter, Elijah, 133.
Carpenter, Elijah, 150.
Carpenter, Elipt., 133.
Carpenter, Ephraim, 153.
Carpenter, Ezekiel, 153.
Carpenter, Gardiner, 131.
Carpenter, Henry, 95.
Carpenter, Hezᵃ, 140.
Carpenter, Isaiah, 19.
Carpenter, Joel, 140.
Carpenter, John, 71.
Carpenter, Jnᵒ, 133.
Carpenter, Jnᵒ, 136.
Carpenter, Jnᵒ, 137.
Carpenter, Joseph, 131.
Carpenter, Jos., 133.
Carpenter, Joseph, 154.
Carpenter, Levi, 133.
Carpenter, Lou, 144.
Carpenter, Moses, 137.
Carpenter, Nathan, 137.

168 INDEX.


Carpenter, Noah, 132.
Carpenter, Noah, 133.
Carpenter, Oliver, 144.
Carpenter, Paul, 146.
Carpenter, Ruben, 138.
Carpenter, Ruggles, 134.
Carpenter, Sam$^{l}$, 149.
Carpenter, Sam$^{l}$, 151.
Carpenter, Silas, 133.
Carpenter, Sim$^{o}$, 138.
Carpenter, Simon, 149.
Carpenter, Tim$^{o}$, 133.
Carpenter, Tim$^{o}$, 138.
Carpenter, William, 17.
Carpenter, W$^{m}$, 133.
Carpenter, W$^{m}$, 136.
Carr, Clement, 96.
Carr, James, 105.
Carr, Robert, 62.
Carr, Samuel, 78.
Carr, William, 62.
Carrier, Andrew, 80.
Carrier, Benjamin, 62.
Carrier, Isaac, 120.
Carrier, Israel, 87.
Carrier, John, 120.
Carrier, Joseph, 120.
Carrier, Lovina, 121.
Carrier, Samuel, 87.
Carrier, Samuel, 120.
Carrier, Thomas, 121.
Carrier, Thomas, Jun$^{r}$, 120.
Carrier, Titus, 80.
Carrier, Uriah, 121.
Carrigal, Henry, 25.
Carrihart, Hacaliah, 16.
Carrington, Abraham, 112.
Carrington, Allen, 111.
Carrington, Daniel, 92.
Carrington, David, 76.
Carrington, David, 112.
Carrington, Edward, 101.
Carrington, Elener, 100.
Carrington, Elias, 102.
Carrington, Eliphat, 76.
Carrington, Elizabeth, 40.
Carrington, Elizabeth, 100.
Carrington, Jerem., 107.
Carrington, Jer$^{h}$, 2$^{nd}$, 107.
Carrington, Jonathan, 35.
Carrington, Lemuel, 35.
Carrington, Lemuel, 108.
Carrington, Mabel, 61.
Carrington, Merrit, 104.
Carrington, Nath$^{a}$, 35.
Carrington, Noadiah, 111.
Carrington, Peter, 111.
Carrington, Samuel, 49.
Carrington, Samuel, 111.
Carrington, Samuel, Jr., 49.
Carrington, Timothy, 108.
Carrol, Amos, 150.
Carrol, James, 129.
Carrol, John, 128.
Carrol, John, 150.
Carrol, Nath$^{l}$, 150.
Carroll, Nancy, 128.
Carrver, Amos, 135.
Carry, Margaret, 111.
Carryl, Ephraim, 154.
Carsey, Devonshier, 18.
Carson, Walter, 14.
Carter, Abel, 50.
Carter, Abel, 50.
Carter, Adonijah, 74.
Carter, Benjamin, 74.
Carter, Benjamin, 85.
Carter, Benjamin, 107.
Carter, Bennoni, 74.
Carter, Berzilla, 74.
Carter, Bradock, 74.
Carter, Buel, 58.
Carter, Clark, 122.
Carter, Daniel, 50.
Carter, Ebenezer, 23.
Carter, Eleazer, 120.
Carter, Elihu, 49.
Carter, Ether, 62.
Carter, Ezra, 121.
Carter, Gidion, 46.
Carter, Heman, 58.
Carter, Hezekiah, 57.
Carter, Hubbell, 85.
Carter, Isaac, 50.
Carter, Israel, 58.
Carter, Ithiel, 58.
Carter, Jacob, 49.
Carter, Jacob, Jr., 50.
Carter, James, 145.
Carter, Jirah, 74.
Carter, Joel, 46.
Carter, John, 23.
Carter, John, 46.
Carter, John, 50.
Carter, John, 57.
Carter, John, 107.
Carter, John, 107.
Carter, John, 122.
Carter, John, 127.
Carter, Jonas, 85.
Carter, Jonathan, 50.
Carter, Joseph, 74.
Carter, Joseph, 90.
Carter, Joseph, 142.
Carter, Joseph, 2$^{d}$, 74.
Carter, Josiah, 85.
Carter, Josiah, Jun$^{r}$, 85.
Carter, Levi, 49.
Carter, Margeret, 108.
Carter, Margerit, 94.
Carter, Moses, 66.
Carter, Nathan, 59.
Carter, (Negro), 121.
Carter, Philo, 57.
Carter, Salmon, 57.
Carter, Samuel, 23.
Carter, Sam$^{l}$, 70.
Carter, Samuel, 74.
Carter, Sam$^{l}$, 142.
Carter, Samuel, 2$^{d}$, 74.
Carter, Sarah, 85.
Carter, Solomon, 74.
Carter, Stephen, 50.
Carter, Stephen, 58.
Carter, Thadeus, 64.
Carter, Zebulon, 66.
Cartie, Phineas, 109.
Cartis, Augustine, 74.
Cartis, Eleazer, 74.
Cartley, Zebelon, 29.
Cartly, Ezra, 29.
Cartly, Ezra, 29.
Carton, Caleb, 137.
Cartright, Cyrus, 153.
Cartright, Sam$^{l}$, 69.
Cartson, Darius, 138.
Cartson, Jn$^{o}$, 138.
Cartwright, Betty, 66.
Carue, Rev$^{d}$ M$^{r}$, 136.
Carver, Alderich, 135.
Carver, David, 135.
Carver, David, Jr., 135.
Carver, David, Sr., 142.
Carver, Eben$^{r}$, 132.
Carver, Jn$^{o}$, 132.
Carver, Jos., 132.
Carver, Melzer, 24.
Carver, Ralph, 134.
Carver, Sam$^{l}$, 132.
Carver, Sam$^{l}$, Jr., 132.
Cary, Diah, 130.
Cary, Joseph, 75.
Cary, Josiah, 80.
Cary, Wait S., 80.
Cary, William, 14.
Case, Aaron, 48.
Case, Aaron, 58.
Case, Aaron, 2$^{d}$, 48.
Case, Abel, 44.
Case, Abel, 48.
Case, Abel, 49.
Case, Abner, 69.
Case, Abraham, 48.
Case, Alexander, 48.
Case, Amasa, 47.
Case, Amasa, Jr., 48.
Case, Amos, 63.
Case, Andrus, 65.
Case, Arial, 47.
Case, Asa, 48.
Case, Asael, 131.
Case, Asahel, 62.
Case, Asahel, 69.
Case, Ashbel, 37.
Case, Ashbel, 48.
Case, Bartholomew, 48.
Case, Benajah, 48.
Case, Benjamin, 48.
Case, Benj$^{m}$, 133.
Case, Benoni, 55.
Case, Caleb, 48.
Case, Charles, 47.
Case, Charles, J$^{r}$, 47.
Case, Corvil, 40.
Case, Daniel, 48.
Case, Daniel, 49.
Case, Daniel, 49.
Case, Darius, 48.
Case, David, 37.
Case, David, Jr., 37.
Case, Dudley, 49.
Case, Dudley, 60.
Case, Eben$^{r}$, 131.
Case, Edward, 49.
Case, Elias, 48.
Case, Elias, 49.
Case, Eliph$^{t}$, 141.
Case, Elisha, 49.
Case, Ephraim B., 48.
Case, Ezra, 68.
Case, Fithin, 48.
Case, George, 44.
Case, George, 48.
Case, George, 2$^{d}$, 48.
Case, Giles, 47.
Case, Hosea, 48.
Case, Hosea, Jr., 49.
Case, Isaac, 48.
Case, Isaac, 48.
Case, Isaac, Jr., 48.
Case, Israel, 48.
Case, Jacob, 49.
Case, Jediah, 48.
Case, Jediah, Jr., 48.
Case, Jerre, 49.
Case, Jessee, 49.
Case, Job, 47.
Case, John, 40.
Case, Jonathan, 48.
Case, Jonathan, 49.
Case, Jon$^{a}$, 139.
Case, Joseph, 37.
Case, Joseph, 48.
Case, Joseph, 62.
Case, Joseph A., 48.
Case, Josiah, 48.
Case, Levi, 47.
Case, Levi, 146.
Case, Martin, 48.
Case, Micah, 44.
Case, Moses, 48.
Case, Noah, 44.
Case, Noah, J$^{r}$, 44.
Case, Obed, 44.
Case, Ozias, 49.
Case, Ozias, 68.
Case, Phineas, 44.
Case, Rachel (Wid.), 42.
Case, Reuben, 48.
Case, Richard, 36.
Case, Richard, 44.
Case, Richard, Jr., 44.
Case, Roger, 44.
Case, Roger, 48.
Case, Roger, 135.
Case, Roswell, 48.
Case, Rufus, 44.
Case, Sam$^{l}$, 131.
Case, Seth, 48.
Case, Silas, 49.
Case, Simeon, 44.
Case, Simeon, 49.
Case, Simeon, 69.
Case, Simeon, 69.
Case, Simcon, 131.
Case, Solomon, 48.
Case, Solomon, 49.
Case, Thomas, 36.
Case, Thomas, 48.
Case, Timothy, 49.
Case, Truman, 49.
Case, Tuball, 133.
Case, Uriah, 49.
Case, William, 44.
Case, William, 63.
Case, William, 69.
Case, Zacheus, 48.
Case, Zenas, 48.
Casheen, William, 79.
Cason, Thomas, 91.
Cass, Jo$^{s}$ W., 135.
Cassee, Patrick, 39.
Castle, Abisha, 76.
Castle, Abram, 78.
Castle, Amasa, 76.
Castle, Anthony, 131.
Castle Booth, 78.
Castle, Isaac, 58.
Castle, Israel, 78.
Castle, Joel, 57.
Castle, John, 76.
Castle, Luke, 78.
Castle, Peter, 11.
Castle, Peter, 78.
Castle, Reuben, 78.
Castle, Richard, 76.
Castle, Samuel, 78.
Castle, Simeon, 76.
Castle, Simeon, 78.
Caswell, John, 42.
Caswell, John, 80.
Caswell, Jonathan, 81.
Caswell, Joseph, 80.
Caswell, Julius, 58.
Caswell, Lemuel, 138.
Cate, 68.
Cate, 69.
Catlin, Abel, 65.
Catlin, Abijah, 58.
Catlin, Abraham, 69.
Catlin, Abram, 58.
Catlin, Alexander, 66.
Catlin, Bradley, 60.
Catlin, Charles, 70.
Catlin, Constant, 108.
Catlin, Dan., 58.
Catlin, Daniel, 58.
Catlin, David, 71.
Catlin, Elisha, 58.
Catlin, Elisha, 59.
Catlin, George, 2$^{d}$, 58.
Catlin, Grover, 58.
Catlin, Grover, 58.
Catlin, Hezekiah, 58.
Catlin, Isaac, 1$^{st}$, 58.
Catlin, Isaac, 2$^{d}$, 58.
Catlin, Jacob, 58.
Catlin, Jacob, 2$^{d}$, 58.
Catlin, Jerham, 109.
Catlin, Joel, 58.
Catlin, John, 105.
Catlin, Jonathan, 58.
Catlin, Lewis, 58.
Catlin, Rhoda, 64.
Catlin, Roger, 57.
Catlin, Sam$^{l}$, 64.
Catlin, Theodore, 65.
Catlin, Thomas, 64.
Catlin, Thomas, 102.
Catlin, Uriel, 66.
Catlin, William, 64.
Catlin, William, 107.
Cato, (Negro), 11.
Cato, (Negro), 12.
Cato (Negro), 20.
Cato (Negro), 113.
Cato (Negro), 114.
Cato (Negro), 125.
Cato (Negro), 127.
Cato (Negro), 131.
Catoe, 70.
Caton, Elizabeth, 51.
Caton, James, 121.
Caukins, Roswell, 110.
Caulkins, And$^{w}$, 131.
Caulkins, Christopher, 126.
Caulkins, Daniel, 130.
Caulkins, Durkee, 126.
Caulkins, Elisabeth, 124.
Caulkins, Ezra, 127.
Caulkins, Jedediah, 127.
Caulkins, Jonathan, 113.
Caulkins, Lemuel, 127.
Caulkins, Lydia, 127.
Caulkins, Pember, 126.
Caulkins, Sam$^{l}$, 127.
Caulkins, Simon, 132.
Caulkins, Thomas, 126.
Caulkins, Thomas, 126.
Caulkins, William, 113.
Cavarly, John, 121.
Cavarly, John, Jun$^{r}$, 121.
Cavarly, Phillup, 121.
Cavelu, Thomas, 48.
Cay, William, 93.
Ceasar (Negroe), 96.
Ceasar (Negroe), 98.
Ceasar (Negroe), 111.
Ceaser (Negro), 54.
Ceaser (Negro), 119.
Ceaser (Negro), 122.
Ceaser (Negro), 123.
Ceaser (Negro), 125.
Ceaser (Negro), 125.
Ceaser (Negro), 126.
Ceaser (Negro), 126.
Ceaser (Negro), 128.
Ceaser (Negro), 130.
Ceaser (Negroe), 101.
Ceaser (Negroe), 105.
Celogg, Eliphilet, 11.
Center, Agnes, 47.
Center, John, 45.
Cesar, 64.
Chace, Seth, 149.
Chaddock, Silas, 82.
Chadock, Timothy, 96.
Chadwick, Allen, 123.
Chadwick, Ezra, 123.
Chadwick, George, 123.
Chadwick, George, 2$^{d}$, 123.
Chadwick, Guy, 123.
Chadwick, Hannah, 123.
Chadwick, James, 124.
Chadwick, Richard, 123.
Chadwick, Ruben, 123.
Chadwick Stephen, 123.
Chadwick, William, 52.
Chafey, Joel, 66.
Chaffe, Josiah, Sen$^{r}$, 140.
Chaffee, Abiel, 150.
Chaffee, Amos, 137.
Chaffee, Benj$^{n}$, 154.
Chaffee, Calvan, 151.
Chaffee, Chester, 151.
Chaffee, Dareus, 140.
Chaffee, Darius, 136.
Chaffee, David, 141.
Chaffee, Eben$^{r}$, 142.
Chaffee, Hezekiah, 54.
Chaffee, Hez$^{h}$, J$^{ur}$, 54.
Chaffee, James, 151.
Chaffee, Jona$^{th}$, 140.
Chaffee, Jonathan, 140.
Chaffee, Joseph, 141.
Chaffee, Josiah, 154.
Chaffee, Josiah, J$^{nr}$, 140.
Chaffee, Noah, 154.
Chaffee, Sam$^{l}$, 151.
Chaffee, Sam$^{l}$, 154.
Chaffee, Serrel, 136.
Chaffee, Stephen, 154.
Chaffee, Thomas, 151.
Chaffer, William, 39.
Chaise, Isaac, 105.
Chalke, William, 38.
Chalker, Abigail, 89.
Chalker, Abraham, 89.
Chalker, Alexander, 89.
Chalker, Daniel, 90.
Chalker, Ezra, 89.
Chalker, Gideon, 89.
Chalker, Isaac, 98.
Chalker, Jacob, 89.
Chalker, Jessy, 85.
Chalker, Moses, 89.
Chalker, Oliver, 89.
Chalker, Stephen, 89.
Chalsea, W$^{m}$, 119.
Chamberlain, Abner, 62.
Chamberlain, Bartlet, 58.
Chamberlain, Benjamin, 43.
Chamberlain, Edman, 133.
Chamberlain, Elizabeth, 43.
Chamberlain, Elizur, 58.
Chamberlain, Erastus, 121.
Chamberlain, Fredom, 121.
Chamberlain, Isaa, 61.
Chamberlain, Jarus, 121.
Chamberlain, Jirah, 58.
Chamberlain, Job, 121.
Chamberlain, Joel, 62.
Chamberlain, John, 120.
Chamberlain, Leander, 58.
Chamberlain, Moses, 66.
Chamberlain, Nathan, 58.
Chamberlain, Nath$^{l}$, 121.
Chamberlain, Nath$^{l}$, Jun$^{r}$, 121.
Chamberlain, Peleg, 58.
Chamberlain, Roswell, 120.
Chamberlain, Samuel, 58.
Chamberlain, Sam$^{l}$, 64.
Chamberlain, Sam$^{l}$, 64.
Chamberlain, Samuel, 86.
Chamberlain, Theodore, 88.
Chamberlain (Widow), 133.
Chamberlain, William, 43.
Chamberlain, William, 63.
Chamberlain, William, 63.
Chamberlain, James, 38.
Chamberlan, James, Jr., 38.
Chamberlane, Asa, 96.
Chamberlin, Edmond, 141.
Chambers, Asa, 19.
Chambers, George, 30.
Chambers, Nathan, 28.
Chambers, Thomas, 20.
Champion, Elisabeth, 123.
Champion, Elisha, 123.
Champion, Epaphras, 81.
Champion, Ezra, 123.
Champion, Henry, 121.
Champion, Henry, 123.
Champion, Henry, Jun$^{r}$, 121.
Champion, Henry V., 130.
Champion, Israel, 81.
Champion, John, 130.
Champion, Judas, 70.
Champion, Lynds, 123.
Champion, Nathan, 90.
Champion, Reuben, 81.
Champion, Roswell, 123.
Champion, Ruben, 123.
Champion, Salmon, 145.
Champion, Stephen, 90.
Champion, Stephen, 123.
Champion, Thomas, 90.
Champlin, Caleb, 124.
Champlin, Charles, 116.
Champlin, Edward, 124.
Champlin, Edward, 2$^{d}$, 124.
Champlin, Elizabeth, 128.
Champlin, Isaac, 127.
Champlin, John, 119.
Champlin, John, 129.
Champlin, Joseph, 116.
Champlin, Nathan, 123.
Champlin, Rowland, 131.
Champlin, Silas, 114.
Champlin, Silas, 123.
Champlin, William, 123.
Champton, Paul, 148.
Chancy, Woolcott, 14.
Chandler, Anne, 153.
Chandler, Daniel, 37.
Chandler, David, 39.
Chandler, Henry, 149.
Chandler, Isaac, 55.
Chandler, John, 19.
Chandler, John, 103.
Chandler, Jonathan, 36.
Chandler, Joseph, 39.
Chandler, Joseph, 149.
Chandler, Joseph, Jr., 39.
Chandler, Josiah, 149.
Chandler, Meriam, 154.
Chandler, Moses, 154.
Chandler, Nehemiah, 39.
Chandler, Peter, 149.
Chandler, Philemon, 149.
Chandler, Samuel, 36.
Chandler, Silas, 149.
Chandler, Stephen, 140.
Chandler, Theophilus, 151.
Chanler, Seth, 153.
Channing, Henry, 120.
Chapel, Atwell, 125.
Chapel, Solomon, 42.
Chapell, Edward, 129.
Chapen, Phinehas, 69.
Chapen, Samuel, 61.
Chapham, Elezier, 80.
Chapin, Aaron, 45.
Chapin, Aaron, 136.
Chapin, Aaron, 137.
Chapin, Azubah (Wid.), 39.
Chapin, Charles, 63.
Chapin, Charles, 66.
Chapin, Daniel, 38.
Chapin, Ebenezer, 40.
Chapin, Elias, 136.
Chapin, Elias, 137.
Chapin, Eliphalet, 37.
Chapin, Eliphalet, 40.
Chapin, Jabez, 40.

INDEX. 169


Chapin, Jeremiah, 40.
Chapin, Joseph, 38.
Chapin, Moses, 136.
Chapin, Nathaniel, 39.
Chapin, Nathaniel, Jr., 39.
Chapin, Phinehas, 63.
Chapin, Reuben, 66.
Chapin, Sam$^{l}$, 136.
Chapin, Seth, 136.
Chapin, Simeon, 39.
Chapin, Solomon, 38.
Chapin (Wid.), 136.
Chaple, Andrew, 124.
Chaple, Dan$^{l}$, 124.
Chaple, Easter, 124.
Chaple, Edward, 119.
Chaple, Eunice, 127.
Chaple, Ezekiel, 125.
Chaple, Ezekiel, 2$^{d}$, 125.
Chaple, Isaac, 127.
Chaple, Isaac, Jun$^{r}$, 127.
Chaple, Jedediah, 125.
Chaple, Jesse, 127.
Chaple, John, 124.
Chaple, John, 125.
Chaple, John, 2$^{d}$, 125.
Chaple, Jonathan, 127.
Chaple, Richard, 124.
Chaple, Richard, 127.
Chaple, Sam$^{l}$, 125.
Chaple, William, 2$^{d}$, 125.
Chaple, William, 3$^{d}$, 125.
Chaplin, Benj$^{n}$, 146.
Chapman, Abner, 122.
Chapman, Abner, Jun$^{r}$, 121.
Chapman, Abraham, 122.
Chapman, Adinah, 115.
Chapman, Albert, 12.
Chapman, Alpheus, 45.
Chapman, Alpheus, 125.
Chapman, Amasa, 42.
Chapman, Amaz$^{h}$, 141.
Chapman, Amos, 115.
Chapman, Amos, 118.
Chapman, Amy, 124.
Chapman, Andrew, 45.
Chapman, Andrew, Jun$^{r}$, 115.
Chapman, Asa, 118.
Chapman, Asahel, 42.
Chapman, Ashbel, 138.
Chapman, Benj$^{n}$, 89.
Chapman, Benj$^{n}$, 140.
Chapman, Ben Thomas, 58.
Chapman, Betsy, 125.
Chapman, Caleb, 60.
Chapman, Caleb, 65.
Chapman, Caleb, 79.
Chapman, Caleb, 82.
Chapman, Caleb, 90.
Chapman, Christopher, 141.
Chapman, Collins, 20.
Chapman, Constant, 85.
Chapman, Cumfort, 114.
Chapman, Cumfort, Jun$^{r}$, 114.
Chapman, Daniel, 13.
Chapman, Dan$^{ll}$, 82.
Chapman, Daniel, 104.
Chapman, Dan$^{l}$, 129.
Chapman, David, 79.
Chapman, David, 118.
Chapman, David, 140.
Chapman, Denne, 13.
Chapman, Easter, 127.
Chapman, Edward, 124.
Chapman, Edward, 2$^{d}$, 124.
Chapman, Eleze, 132.
Chapman, Eliakim, 138.
Chapman, Elias, 141.
Chapman, Elijah, 62.
Chapman, Elijah, 138.
Chapman, Elijah, Jr., 138.
Chapman, Eliphelet, 127.
Chapman, Elisabeth, 124.
Chapman, Elisabeth, 126.
Chapman, Elisha, 89.
Chapman, Elisha, 100.
Chapman, Elisha, 122.
Chapman, E$^{m}$, 135.
Chapman, Esther, 89.
Chapman, Ezekiel, 124.
Chapman, Francis, 82.
Chapman, Gideon, 122.
Chapman, Gidion, Jun$^{r}$, 122.
Chapman, Hannah, 127.
Chapman, Hoseah, 134.
Chapman, Ichabod, Jun$^{r}$, 122.
Chapman, Isaac, 82.
Chapman, Isham, 138.
Chapman, Jabez, 134.
Chapman, Jabez, 134.
Chapman, Jabez, Esq$^{r}$, 81.
Chapman, Jacob, 140.
Chapman, James, 12.
Chapman, James, 89.
Chapman, James, 127.
Chapman, James, 132.
Chapman, James, 132.
Chapman, James, 146.
Chapman, Jason, 127.
Chapman, Jason, 139.
Chapman, Jedediah, 90.
Chapman, Jedediah, 2$^{d}$, 90.
Chapman, Jehiel, 42.
Chapman, John, 12.
Chapman, John, 28.
Chapman, John, 79.
Chapman, John, 82.
Chapman, John, 128.
Chapman, Jn$^{o}$, 137.
Chapman, John C., 65.
Chapman, Jonah, 42.
Chapman, Jonah, 141.
Chapman, Jonathan, 46.
Chapman, Jonathan, 84.
Chapman, Jonathan, 122.
Chapman, Jonathan, 125.
Chapman, Jon$^{a}$, 132.
Chapman, Jonathan, 141.
Chapman, Jona$^{n}$, Jn$^{r}$, 141.
Chapman, Joseph, 115.
Chapman, Joseph, 118.
Chapman, Joseph, 125.
Chapman, Joseph, 132.
Chapman, Joseph, 141.
Chapman, Doct$^{r}$ Joseph, 24.
Chapman, Joseph, 2$^{d}$, 118.
Chapman, Joshua, 10.
Chapman, Joshua, 118.
Chapman, Joshua, 146.
Chapman, Josiah, 35.
Chapman, Josiah, Jr., 35.
Chapman, Labbeus, 90.
Chapman, Lemuel, 126.
Chapman, Lem$^{l}$, 132.
Chapman, Levi, 49.
Chapman, Levi, 89.
Chapman, Levi, 118.
Chapman, Lovel, 13.
Chapman, Martha, 90.
Chapman, Michael, 56.
Chapman, Nahum, 115.
Chapman, Nancy, 130.
Chapman, Nathan, 56.
Chapman, Nathan, 62.
Chapman, Nathan, 115.
Chapman, Nath$^{n}$, 132.
Chapman, Nathaniel, 56.
Chapman, Nath$^{l}$, 125.
Chapman, Nath$^{l}$, 127.
Chapman, Nehemiah, 60.
Chapman, Noah, 62.
Chapman, Noah, 122.
Chapman, Obadiah, 114.
Chapman, Oliver, 128.
Chapman, Oliver, 141.
Chapman, Ozias, 82.
Chapman, Pelatiah, 60.
Chapman, Penelope, 140.
Chapman, Peter, 124.
Chapman, Phineas, 133.
Chapman, Pinehas, 89.
Chapman, Polly, 81.
Chapman, Reuben, 65.
Chapman, Reuben, 84.
Chapman, Reuben, 2$^{d}$, 65.
Chapman, Robert, 22.
Chapman, Robert, 63.
Chapman, Robert, 63.
Chapman, Sabethial, 35.
Chapman, Sam$^{l}$, 82.
Chapman, Sam$^{l}$, 134.
Chapman, Samuel, 138.
Chapman, Sarah, 12.
Chapman, Silas, 45.
Chapman, Simeon, 82.
Chapman, Sim$^{o}$, 138.
Chapman, Solomon, 79.
Chapman, Stephen, 130.
Chapman, Taylor, 54.
Chapman, Tenant, 42.
Chapman, Tho$^{s}$, 132.
Chapman, Thomas, 141.
Chapman, Thomas, 141.
Chapman, Tim$^{o}$, 82.
Chapman, Timothy, 83.
Chapman, Tutus, 62.
Chapman, William, 36.
Chapman, William, 60.
Chapman, William, 66.
Chapman, W$^{m}$, 89.
Chapman, W$^{m}$, 90.
Chapman, William, 113.
Chapman, William, 122.
Chapman, W$^{m}$, 154.
Chapman, William, Jn$^{r}$, 154.
Chapman, William E., 25.
Chapman, Zach$^{h}$, 82.
Chappel, Amaziah, 145.
Chappel, Caleb, 81.
Chappel, Caleb, 145.
Chappel, Elijah, 146.
Chappel, Joshua, 82.
Chappel, Oliver, 145.
Chappel, Patience, 104.
Chappel, Silas, 60.
Chappell, Jonathan, 79.
Chappell, Jonathan, 84.
Chappell Nathan, 130.
Chapple, Alpheus, 128.
Chapple, Barsheba, 127.
Chapple, David, 135.
Chapple, Elisabeth, 127.
Chapple, George, 127.
Chapple, James, 125.
Chapple, James, 2$^{d}$, 125.
Chapple, Jn$^{o}$, 135.
Chapple, Lebeus, 125.
Chapple, Lydia, 127.
Chapple, Nathan, 2$^{d}$, 132.
Chapple, Noah, 133.
Chapple, Peter, 126.
Chapple, Sam$^{l}$, 128.
Chapple, Stephen, 133.
Chapple, Walter, 127.
Chapple, William, 125.
Chapple, W$^{m}$, 127.
Chapple, William, 127.
Charles, Jn$^{o}$, 134.
Charles (Negro), 39.
Charles, William, 95.
Charlton, Charles, 131.
Charter, Allen, 134.
Charter, George, 134.
Charter, Jn$^{o}$, Jr., 134.
Chase, Amos, 65.
Chase, Benj$^{n}$, 148.
Chase, Berrey, 37.
Chase, David, 144.
Chase, Edward, 144.
Chase, Giddeon, 19.
Chase, Gidiliah, 37.
Chase, Isaac, 10.
Chase, Lot, 60.
Chase, Mary, 58.
Chase, Oliver, &c., 144.
Chatfield, Benn$^{h}$, 94.
Chatfield, Dan., 94.
Chatfield, Daniel, 110.
Chatfield, Ebenezer, 96.
Chatfield, Gideon, 94.
Chatfield, Hannah, 112.
Chatfield, Heil, 104.
Chatfield, Isaac, 94.
Chatfield, Joel, 95.
Chatfield, John, 94.
Chatfield, Joseph, 85.
Chatfield, Joseph, 94.
Chatfield, Josiah, 85.
Chatfield, Lemuel, 18.
Chatfield, Levi, 71.
Chatfield, Oliver, 73.
Chatfield, Samuel, 95.
Chatfield, Samuel, 110.
Chatfield, Samuel, 2$^{nd}$, 110.
Chatfield, Yarmouth, 78.
Chatman, Ruben, 95.
Chatterdon, Rodah, 103.
Chatterton, Abraham, 100.
Chatterton, Assael, 94.
Chatterton, Daniel, 100.
Chatterton, David, 100.
Chatterton, Stephen, 105.
Chaugorn, Mary, 70.
Chauncey, Eunice, 53.
Chauncey, Nathaniel, Esq$^{r}$, 87.
Chauncey, Nathaniel, Jun$^{r}$, 87.
Chauncy, Charles, 104.
Chauncy, Elihu, 96.
Chauncy, Elnathan, 96.
Cheamberlain, Seth, 147.
Cheamberlin, Abiel, 153.
Cheamberlin, Benjamin, 143.
Cheamberlin, Elisha, 154.
Cheamberlin, Harvey, 149.
Cheamberlin, John, 154.
Cheamberlin, Oliver, 147.
Cheamberlin, Rubin, 154.
Cheany, Daniel, 79.
Cheedle, Benjamin, 143.
Cheedle, Elisabeth, 149.
Cheedle, Increase, 140.
Cheedle, Rufus, 138.
Cheehan, Nathanel, 11.
Cheeney, Asahel, 37.
Cheeney, Silus, 37.
Cheeney, Thomas, 37.
Cheesborough, Amos, 117.
Cheesborough, Asa, 117.
Cheesborough, Bridgett, 117.
Cheesborough, Christopher, 116.
Cheesborough, James, 117.
Cheesborough, Jedediah, 117.
Cheesborough, John, 117.
Cheesborough, Naboth, 118.
Cheesborough, Nath$^{l}$, 117.
Cheesborough, Nath$^{l}$, 2$^{d}$, 117.
Cheesborough, Peleg, 117.
Cheesborough, Pheba, 117.
Cheesborough, Rebecka, 3$^{d}$, 117.
Cheesborough, Robart, 117.
Cheesborough, Sam$^{l}$, 117.
Cheesborough, Sam$^{l}$ 2$^{d}$, 117.
Cheesborough, Thomas, 113.
Cheesborough, William, 117.
Cheesborough, William, 2$^{d}$, 117.
Cheesborough, William, 3$^{d}$, 117.
Cheesborough, William, 4$^{th}$, 117.
Cheesborough, Zebulum, 117.
Cheesborough, Zebulun, Jun$^{r}$, 117.
Cheesbrooks, Jabez, 132.
Cheevers, Nathan, 146.
Chenevard, John, 45.
Cheney, Abiel, 131.
Cheney, Abiel, 2$^{d}$, 130.
Cheney, Benjamin, 36.
Cheney, Benj$^{n}$, 141.
Cheney, Pemui, 152.
Cheney, Samuel, 129.
Cheney, Timothy, Jr., 37.
Cheritree, Reuben, 75.
Cherry, Poll, 16.
Cherway, Philmi, 78.
Cheseton, Samuel, 61.
Chester, Ann, 119.
Chester, Charles, 118.
Chester, Giles, 119.
Chester, Isaac, 119.
Chester, John, 52.
Chester, Jonathan, 153.
Chester, Joseph, 125.
Chester, Joseph, 2$^{d}$, 125.
Chester, Simeon, 119.
Chester, Star, 46.
Chester, Stephen, 52.
Chester, Thomas, 119.
Chiddester, William, 57.
Chidsuy, Joseph, 41.
Child, Amasa, 153.
Child, Asa, 153.
Child, Elias, 153.
Child, Elijah, 150.
Child, Henry, 153.
Child, Lem$^{l}$, 154.
Child, Nath$^{l}$, 154.
Child, Obediah, 153.
Child, Payson, 149.
Child, Peter, 153.
Child, Rufus, 154.
Child, Tho$^{s}$, 154.
Child, Timothy, 153.
Childs, Abiel, 153.
Childs, Alpha, 153.
Childs, Charles, 149.
Childs, Elias, 154.
Childs, Elijah, 151.
Childs, Elisha, 153.
Childs, Hannah, 84.
Childs, Jacob, 154.
Childs, James R., 84.
Childs, Nath$^{l}$, 150.
Childs, Nath$^{l}$, 151.
Childs, Nath$^{l}$, 153.
Childs, Pennel, 138.
Childs, Shuball, 154.
Childs, Sylvester, 84.
Childs, Thomas, 84.
Childs, Timothy, 67.
Chipman, Barnabas, 79.
Chipman, Christopher, 119.
Chipman, Ebenezer, 79.
Chipman, Joseph, 79.
Chipman, Joseph, 107.
Chipman, Sam$^{l}$, 119.
Chipman, Sam$^{l}$, Jun$^{r}$, 119.
Chipman, Thomas, 67.
Chipman, William, 119.
Chison, John, 73.
Chistester, Sarah (W$^{d}$), 23.
Chitester, Abraham, 21.
Chitester, Henry, 23.
Chitester, Moses, 17.
Chitsey, Abraham, 97.
Chitsey, Bathsheba, 99.
Chitsey, Deborah, 97.
Chitsey, Ebenezur, 97.
Chitsey, Ephrahim, 97.
Chitsey, Isaac, 97.
Chitsey, James, 97.
Chitsey, John, 97.
Chitsey, Levi, 97.
Chitsey, Nathaniel, 99.
Chitsey, Roswell, 91.
Chittenden, Abraham, 98.
Chittenden, Abraham, 2$^{d}$, 98.
Chittenden, Ambrose, 97.
Chittenden, Charles, 97.
Chittenden, Doseth, 85.
Chittenden, Ebenezer, 104.
Chittenden, Giles, 71.
Chittenden, John, 90.
Chittenden, Noah, 98.
Chittenden, Stephen, 71.
Chittenden, Timothy, 104.
Chittendon, Beriah, 104.
Chittendon, Daniel, 85.
Chittendon, Timothy, 70.
Chittendon, Timothy, 2$^{d}$, 70.
Chittenten, Jerad, 99.
Chittenton, Abraham, 98.
Chittenton, Amos, 99.
Chittenton, Anna, 98.
Chittenton, Anson, 99.
Chittenton, Benjamin, 98.
Chittenton, Benjamin, 107.
Chittenton, Caleb, 98.
Chittenton, Daniel, 99.
Chittenton, Daniel, 99.
Chittenton, David, 98.
Chittenton, Gideon, 96.
Chittenton, Joseph, 98.
Chittenton, Joseph, 98.
Chittenton, Levi, 91.
Chittenton, Nathaniel, 98.
Chittenton, Samuel, 98.
Chittenton, Simeon, 99.
Chittenton, Submit, 99.
Chitterster, Daniel, 28.
Chittester, Abraham, 26.
Chittester, David, 26.
Chittester, Nathan, 26.
Choat, Eunice, 131.
Choker, Jabez, 2$^{nd}$, 96.
Chote, Abigail, 115.
Chote, John, 115.
Christee, James, 130.
Christophers, Peter, 128.
Chrittenden, Joseph, 97.
Chrittenden, Nathaniel, 2$^{nd}$, 97.
Chrittenden, Nathaniel, 2$^{nd}$, 98.
Chrittenden, Samuel, 97.
Chrittenden, Timothy, 97.
Chrittenton, Dolly, 103.
Chrittenton, Hopestill, 96.
Chrittenton, Jerry, 100.
Chub, Alexander, 68.
Chub, Joseph, 127.
Chub, Mindwell, 69.
Chub, Prentiece, 149.
Chub, Rachel, 69.
Chubb, William, 140.
Chubbuck, Eben, 134.
Chubbuck, Nath$^{l}$, 134.
Church, Aaron, 61.
Church, Abisha, 61.
Church, Abner, 147.
Church, Amos, 125.
Church, Asa, 139.
Church, Asher, 45.
Church, Caleb, 45.
Church, Daniel, 10.
Church, Daniel, 21.
Church, David, 116.
Church, Ebenezer, 21.
Church, Ebenezer, 64.
Church, Elizabeth, 11.
Church, Ezra, 122.
Church, Fairbanks, 124.
Church, George, 45.
Church, Ira, 83.
Church, James, 45.
Church, Johiel, 66.
Church, Johiel, 2$^{nd}$, 66.
Church, John, 66.
Church, John, 83.
Church, John, 95.
Church, John, 122.
Church, Jonathan, 125.
Church, Joseph, 45.
Church, Joseph, 53.
Church, Joseph, 81.
Church, Joseph, 125.
Church, Joshua, 56.
Church, Josiah, 122.
Church, Lemuel, 152.
Church, Mary, 125.
Church, Mary, 2$^{d}$, 125.
Church, Nath$^{l}$, 115.
Church, Oliver, 83.
Church, Peleg, 125.
Church, Philemon, 91.
Church, Rich$^{d}$, 83.
Church, Samuel, 36.
Church, Samuel, 49.
Church, Sam$^{l}$, 90.
Church, Sam$^{l}$, 122.
Church, Silas, 63.
Church, Simeon, 90.
Church, Thomas, 83.
Church, Timothy, 45.
Church, Timothy, 46.
Church, Uriah, 61.
Church, Uriah, 66.
Church, W$^{m}$, 83.
Church, Winter, 11.
Churchel, Benjamin, 62.
Churchel, Jonathan, 56.
Churchel, Jonathan, 71.
Churchel, Moses, 59.
Churchel, Oliver, 56.
Churchell, Amos, Esq$^{r}$, 88.
Churchell, Daniel, 79.
Churchell, Joseph, 79.
Churchill, Asahel, 35.
Churchill, Benj$^{m}$, 34.
Churchill, Charles, 54.
Churchill, David, 50.
Churchill, Elijah, 39.
Churchill, Ira, 34.
Churchill, Jesse, 52.
Churchill, John, 95.
Churchill, Joseph, 54.
Churchill, Josiah, 53.
Churchill, Levi, 52.
Churchill, Levi, 54.
Churchill, Nathaniel, 32.
Churchill, Nathaniel, Jr., 32.
Churchill, Sage, 32.
Churchill, Samuel, 34.
Churchill, Samuel, 52.
Churchill, Samuel, 54.
Churchill, Solomon, 54.
Churchill, Stephen, 32.
Churchill, W$^{m}$, 40.
Churk, Nathan, 61.
Ciely, Denton, 29.
Cillerman, W$^{m}$, 82.
Clap, Increas, 138.
Clap, Seth, 141.
Clapp, Benjamin, 16.
Clapp, Elijah, 46.
Clapp, James, 16.
Clapp, John, 46.
Clapp, Joseph, 16.
Clapp, Norman, 53.

# INDEX.

Clapp, Oliver, 45.
Clapp, Phebe (W^d), 16.
Clapp, Roger, 46.
Clapp, Thomas, 16.
Clapp, Thomas, 46.
Clarck, Sam^l, 146.
Clark, Aaron, 45.
Clark, Aaron, 81.
Clark, Aaron, 83.
Clark, Aaron, 84.
Clark, Aaron, 120.
Clark, Abel, 32.
Clark, Abel, 35.
Clark, Abel, 84.
Clark, Abel, 152.
Clark Abigal, 146.
Clark, Abraham, 50.
Clark, Abraham E., 17.
Clark, Adna, 83.
Clark, Ambros, 87.
Clark, Ambrose, 53.
Clark, Ambrose, 146.
Clark, Amos, 41.
Clark, Amos, 56.
Clark, Amos, 81.
Clark, Amos, 143.
Clark, Amos, Jn^r, 143.
Clark, Amos T., 136.
Clark, And^w, 113.
Clark, Andrew, 145.
Clark, Arnold, 116.
Clark, Asa, 35.
Clark, Asa, 82.
Clark, Asael, 146.
Clark, Asael, 154.
Clark, Asahel, 55.
Clark, Asher, 83.
Clark, Azenath, 50.
Clark, Beamont, 90.
Clark, Beamont, 2^d, 90.
Clark, Benj, 148.
Clark, Benja, 135.
Clark, Benjamin, 57.
Clark, Benjamin, 78.
Clark, Benjamin, 88.
Clark, Benj^n, 140.
Clark, Blagg, 17.
Clark, Caleb, 141.
Clark, Caty, 37.
Clark, Cefus, 45.
Clark, Champion, 65.
Clark, Chauncy, 77.
Clark, Christopher, 90.
Clark, Cyrenus, 58.
Clark, Danforth, 89.
Clark, Daniel, 35.
Clark, Dan., 41.
Clark, Daniel, 48.
Clark, Daniel, 63.
Clark, Daniel, 69.
Clark, Daniel, 71.
Clark, Daniel, 75.
Clark, Dan., 82.
Clark, Daniel, 87.
Clark, Daniel, 88.
Clark, Daniel, 88.
Clark, Daniel, 113.
Clark, Daniel, 121.
Clark, Dan^l, 122.
Clark, Dan^l, 134.
Clark, Dan^l, 141.
Clark, Dan^l, 143.
Clark, Dan., 145.
Clark, Daniel, 145.
Clark, Darius, 120.
Clark, David, 33.
Clark, David, 45.
Clark, David, 57.
Clark, David, 80.
Clark, David, 88.
Clark, David, 112.
Clark, David, 146.
Clark, David, 154.
Clark, David, Jr., 45.
Clark, Dimon, 35.
Clark, Ebenezer, 38.
Clark, Ebenezer, 45.
Clark, Ebenezer, 74.
Clark, Ebenezer, 115.
Clark, Eben^r, 143.
Clark, Edmond, 71.
Clark, Elihu, 120.
Clark, Elijah, 80.
Clark, Eliphalet, 44.
Clark, Eleph^t, 140.
Clark, Elisha, 17.
Clark, Elisha, 49.
Clark, Elisha, 131.
Clark, Enos, 49.
Clark, Ephraim, 49.
Clark, E^m, 132.
Clark, Ezekiel, 33.
Clark, Ezra, 49.
Clark, Ezra, 89.
Clark, Ezra, 113.
Clark, Ezra, 120.
Clark, Ezra, Jun^r, 120.
Clark, Flavel, 146.
Clark, Francis, 87.
Clark, Francis, 120.
Clark, Friend, 56.
Clark, Gamaliel, 76.
Clark, George, 17.

Clark, George, 18.
Clark, George, 55.
Clark, George, 90.
Clark, George, 2^d, 90.
Clark, Giles, 87.
Clark, Gr^nt, 91.
Clark, Gurdon, 121.
Clark, Gurdon, 123.
Clark, Hannah, 143.
Clark, Hezekiah, 17.
Clark, Hezekiah, 18.
Clark, Hezekiah, 84.
Clark, Hezekiah, 95.
Clark, Hezzekiah, 57.
Clark, Hosea, 55.
Clark, Ichiel, 76.
Clark, Ira, 55.
Clark, Isaac, 71.
Clark, Isaac, 128.
Clark, Israel, 50.
Clark, Israel, 140.
Clark, Israel, 146.
Clark, Ithurill, 49.
Clark, Jabez, 81.
Clark, Jabez, 152.
Clark, Jacob, 145.
Clark, James, 10.
Clark, James, 18.
Clark, James, 29.
Clark, James, 87.
Clark, James, 87.
Clark, James, 144.
Clark, James, 145.
Clark, James, 145.
Clark, James S., 83.
Clark, Jared, 91.
Clark, Jared, 145.
Clark, Jeames, 71.
Clark, Jeremiah, 143.
Clark, Jeremiah, Jn^r, 143.
Clark, Jerom, 145.
Clark, Jerusha, 30.
Clark, Jesse, 45.
Clark, Joel, 35.
Clark, Joel, 45.
Clark, Joel, 66.
Clark, John, 17.
Clark, John, 50.
Clark, John, 55.
Clark, John, 61.
Clark, John, 71.
Clark, John, 78.
Clark, John, 84.
Clark, Jn^o, 90.
Clark, John, 115.
Clark, John, 120.
Clark, John, 123.
Clark, John, 128.
Clark, Jn^o, 132.
Clark, Jn^o, 138.
Clark, John, 140.
Clark, John, 143.
Clark, John, 145.
Clark, John, 146.
Clark, John, 152.
Clark, John, 152.
Clark, John, Esq^r, 80.
Clark, Jonathan, 38.
Clark, Jonathan, 80.
Clark, Jonathan, 88.
Clark, Jonath^n, 143.
Clark, Jonathan, 145.
Clark, Jona^th, 146.
Clark, Joseph, 10.
Clark, Joseph, 71.
Clark, Joseph, 74.
Clark, Joseph, 83.
Clark, Joseph, 88.
Clark, Joseph, 91.
Clark, Joseph, 154.
Clark, Joseph, Jun^r, 84.
Clark, Joshua, 56.
Clark, Josiah, 119.
Clark, Jude, 145.
Clark, Lamberton, 87.
Clark, Lemuel, 123.
Clark, Lem^l, 141.
Clark, Lemuel, 146.
Clark, Levi, 40.
Clark, Lewis, 49.
Clark, Lucy, 120.
Clark, Lydia, 84.
Clark, Lyman, 65.
Clark, Lyman, 70.
Clark, Marcy, 75.
Clark, Marshal, 35.
Clark, Marvin, 41.
Clark, Mary, 10.
Clark, Mary, 52.
Clark, Mathew, 41.
Clark, Michal, 88.
Clark, Moses, 141.
Clark, Moses, 145.
Clark, Nathan, 17.
Clark, Nathan, 145.
Clark, Nathan, 146.
Clark, Nathan, 2^d, 18.
Clark, Nathan, 3^d, 18.
Clark, Nathaniel 80.
Clark, Nath^l, 121.
Clark, Nath^l, 127.
Clark, Nath^l, 154.

Clark, Nath^el C., 73.
Clark, Nehemiah, 57.
Clark, Neh^m, 136.
Clark, Noah, 136.
Clark, Obed, 119.
Clark, Oliver, 10.
Clark, Oliver, 38.
Clark, Oliver, 54.
Clark, Oliver, 76.
Clark, Oliver, 87.
Clark, Oliver, 146.
Clark, Patience, 84.
Clark, Paul, 90.
Clark, Perry, 112.
Clark, Perry, 113.
Clark, Peter, 90.
Clark, Phebe, 86.
Clark, Pheneas, 143.
Clark, Ransom, 30.
Clark, Reuben, 50.
Clark, Reuben, 61.
Clark, Reuben, 90.
Clark, Richard, 71.
Clark, Robert, 83.
Clark, Roger, 52.
Clark, Roger, 55.
Clark, Roger, 114.
Clark, Roswell, 123.
Clark, Roswell, 146.
Clark, Ruben, 119.
Clark, Rufus, 61.
Clark, Rufus, 89.
Clark, Salmon, 41.
Clark, Samuel, 17.
Clark, Samuel, 30.
Clark, Samuel, 44.
Clark, Samuel, 46.
Clark, Samuel, 74.
Clark, Sam^l, 82.
Clark, Samuel, 83.
Clark, Sam^l, 89.
Clark, Samuel, 113.
Clark, Sam^l, 149.
Clark, Samuel, Jun^r, 84.
Clark, Samuel, 2^d, 74.
Clark, Sam^l C., 66.
Clark, Sarah, 17.
Clark, Sarah, 83.
Clark, Sarah, 88.
Clark, Seth, 37.
Clark, Seth, 86.
Clark, Seth, 142.
Clark, Seth, 154.
Clark, Silas, 49.
Clark, Silas, 57.
Clark, Silas, 145.
Clark, Silas, Jr., 148.
Clark, Silas, 2^d, 57.
Clark, Silvanus, 123.
Clark, Simon, 146.
Clark, Solomon, 32.
Clark, Solomon, 55.
Clark, Stephen, 81.
Clark, Stephen, 83.
Clark, Stephen, 143.
Clark, Stephen, 148.
Clark, Sterlin, 82.
Clark, Thaniel, 66.
Clark, Theodore, 53.
Clark, Theoph^u, 142.
Clark, Thomas, 66.
Clark, Thomas, 84.
Clark, Thomas, 1^st, 71.
Clark, Thomas, 2^d, 71.
Clark, Timothy, 88.
Clark, Timothy, 143.
Clark, Timothy, Jun^r, 114.
Clark, Titus, 143.
Clark, Uriah, 82.
Clark, Urial, 64.
Clark, Warham, 134.
Clark, Watrus, 132.
Clark, (Wid.), 45.
Clark, William, 60.
Clark, William, 70.
Clark, William, 71.
Clark, William, 74.
Clark, William, 80.
Clark, William, 83.
Clark, W^m, 90.
Clark, William, 148.
Clark, William, Jun^r, 84.
Clark, Zachariah, 19.
Clark, Zach^r, 91.
Clark, Zelotes, 90.
Clarke, Abel, 95.
Clarke, Abel, 101.
Clarke, Abigal, 105.
Clarke, Abraham, 101.
Clarke, Amassa, 92.
Clarke, Amos, 101.
Clarke, Amos, 102.
Clarke, Andrew, 93.
Clarke, Andrew, 101.
Clarke, Ann, 96.
Clarke, Archibald, 107.
Clarke, Aron, 112.
Clarke, Benjamin, 102.
Clarke, Caleb, 106.
Clarke, Chauncy, 110.
Clarke, Daniel, 97.
Clarke, Daniel, 105.
Clarke, Daniel, 107.

Clarke, David, 102.
Clarke, David, 110.
Clarke, David, 111.
Clarke, David, 111.
Clarke, Ebenezer, 105.
Clarke, Elias, 102.
Clarke, Elioney, 111.
Clarke, Elizabeth, 102.
Clarke, Elizabeth, 112.
Clarke, Enoch, 102.
Clarke, Enock, 2^nd, 102.
Clarke, George, 95.
Clarke, George, 111.
Clarke, Isaac, 102.
Clarke, Israel, 67.
Clarke, James, 84.
Clarke, James, 108.
Clarke, Job, 109.
Clarke, John, 103.
Clarke, John, 109.
Clarke, John, 109.
Clarke, Jonah, 92.
Clarke, Jonathan, 101.
Clarke, Joseph, 101.
Clarke, Joseph, 101.
Clarke, Joseph, 112.
Clarke, Lamberton, 107.
Clarke, Lar, 111.
Clarke, Lydia, 113.
Clarke, Martin, 111.
Clarke, Mary, 101.
Clarke, Mary, 105.
Clarke, Merrit, 105.
Clarke, Michael, 96.
Clarke, Moses, 95.
Clarke, Nathan, 102.
Clarke, Nathan, 111.
Clarke, Nathaniel, 96.
Clarke, Neah^h, 102.
Clarke, Oliver, 102.
Clarke, Parsons, 104.
Clarke, Patty, 102.
Clarke, Phineas, 106.
Clarke, Rebecca, 101.
Clarke, Russell, 104.
Clarke, Samuel, 93.
Clarke, Samuel, 101.
Clarke, Samuel, 104.
Clarke, Samuel, 110.
Clarke, Sheldon, 94.
Clarke, Stephen, 92.
Clarke, Stephen, 2^nd, 93.
Clarke, Sylvenus, 84.
Clarke, Thadeus, 105.
Clarke, Thomas, 95.
Clarke, Thomas, 102.
Clarke, Thomas, 2^nd, 95.
Clarke, Thompson, 105.
Clarke, Tim, 104.
Clarke, William, 93.
Clarke, William, 94.
Clarke, William, 101.
Clarke, William, 101.
Clarke, William, 110.
Clarke, William, 2^nd, 94.
Clarkland, James, 48.
Clason, Enoch, 24.
Clason, Isaac, 16.
Clason, Samuel, 24.
Clason, Seth, 25.
Clason, Solomon, 24.
Clason, Stephen, 24.
Clather, Ambrose, 57.
Clause, John, 104.
Clavland, Jacob, 143.
Clay, Patience, 129.
Clay, Stephen, 86.
Clayton, Peter, 124.
Cleaveland, Aaron, 132.
Cleaveland, George, 98.
Cleaveland, Irena, 131.
Cleaveland, John, 19.
Cleaveland, John, 112.
Cleaveland, Pheba, 115.
Cleaver, Tobias, 70.
Cleaver, William, 85.
Cleaver, William, Jun^r, 86.
Cleavland, Aaron, 61.
Cleavland, Aaron, 149.
Cleavland, Asa, 143.
Cleavland, Benjamin, 65.
Cleavland, Eliphaz, 142.
Cleavland, Jesse, 143.
Cleavland, Jesse, 149.
Cleavland, Joseph, 141.
Cleavland, Josiah, 143.
Cleavland, Moses, sr., 142.
Cleavland, Perez, 142.
Cleavland, Pheneas, 141.
Cleavland, Rufus, 69.
Cleavland, Samuel, 103.
Cleavland, Shubail, 142.
Cleavland, Silas, Jn^r, 143.
Cleavland, Solomon, 149.
Cleavland, Timothy, 142.
Cleavland, Truman, 149.
Cleft, Amos, 113.
Cleft, Obed^h, 150.
Cleft, Waterman, 152.
Clemens, Fardy, 44.
Clemens, William, 44.
Clement, Isaac, 102.
Clemment, Jeremiah, 130.

Clemment, Peabody, 131.
Clemmons, Abel, 70.
Clemmons, Abijah, 64.
Clemmons, John, 66.
Clenton, Antine, 18.
Clerk, Josiah, 46.
Clerk, Timothy, 50.
Cleveland, Ezra, 35.
Cleveland, Isaac, 58.
Cleveland, Johnson, 50.
Cleveland, Joseph, 53.
Cleveland, Lemuel, 50.
Clevland, Frederic, 51.
Clifford, Elijah, 30.
Clifford, Elizabeth, 29.
Clifford, Joseph, 127.
Clifford, Silvester, 127.
Clift, William, 12.
Clime, Pillip, 105.
Clinton, Allen, 23.
Clinton, Anson, 111.
Clinton, Ebenezer, 96.
Clinton, Henry, 66.
Clinton, Jesse, 108.
Clinton, Joseph, 23.
Clinton, Laurence, 111.
Clinton, Lawrence, 106.
Clinton, Samuel, 66.
Clinton, Samuel, 111.
Clock, Abraham, 26.
Clock, Comfort (W^d), 26.
Clock, John, 26.
Clock, Jonas, 24.
Clock, Martin, 24.
Clock, Martin, J^r, 24.
Clock, Nathaniel, 26.
Clock, Sarah (W^d), 26.
Close, Abraham, 16.
Close, Benjamin, 16.
Close, Ellihu, 16.
Close, Gilbert, 15.
Close, Hannah (W^d), 16.
Close, Jonathan, 15.
Close, Joseph, 16.
Close, Odel, 16.
Close, Odel, Jun^r, 16.
Clover, John, 88.
Cluff, Isaac, 59.
Clust, Jon^a, 137.
Clust, Tim^o, 137.
Clyder, Jos. 139.
Coan, Gaylor, 84.
Coan, John, 99.
Coan, John, 2^nd, 99.
Coan, Mulford, 84.
Coan, Simeon, 99.
Coats, Amos, 116.
Coats, Bartholemu, 116.
Coats, Benj^n, 140.
Coats, Benj^n, 150.
Coats, Betsy, 116.
Coats, David, 116.
Coats, Edward, 116.
Coats, Elisabeth, 149.
Coats, Frederick, 129.
Coats, Hez^h, 150.
Coats, Hez^a, 151.
Coats, James, 150.
Coats, John, 116.
Coats, Rufus, 115.
Coats, Sam^l, 154.
Coats, William, 115.
Coats, W^m, Jun^r, 115.
Cob, James, 142.
Coban, Daniel, 17.
Cobb, Benjamin, 124.
Cobb, Daniel, 138.
Cobb, David, 138.
Cobb, Ebenezer, 117.
Cobb, Elijah W., 69.
Cobb, Elkanah, 117.
Cobb, Ephnah, 142.
Cobb, Jeduthron, 138.
Cobb, Joseph, 125.
Cobb, Nathan, 131.
Cobb, Simeon, 125.
Cobb, Simeon, 2^d, 124.
Cobb, William, 59.
Cobbin, Josiah, 52.
Coben, James, 2^nd, 107.
Coben, John, 107.
Cobert, Hannah, 108.
Cobert, James, 108.
Cobin, Joseph, 108.
Cobin, Parish, 95.
Coble, Daniel, 31.
Cobler, Tho^s, 44.
Coblium, Stephen, 60.
Coburn, Cornelius, 112.
Coburn, David, 154.
Coburn, Eben^r, 154.
Coburn, Samuel, 112.
Cochran, Jn^o, 89.
Cochran, Jn^o, 2^d, 89.
Cocker, James, 103.
Codner, Cata, 128.
Coe, Aaron, 30.
Coe, Abel, 96.
Coe, Abel, 2^nd, 96.
Coe, Abner, 60.
Coe, Amos, 73.
Coe, Andrew, 73.

# INDEX.

Coe, Andrew, 2ᵈ, 73.
Coe, Ann, 96.
Coe, Ann, 96.
Coe, Asher, 96.
Coe, Charles, 96.
Coe, David, 73.
Coe, David, 89.
Coe, David, 89.
Coe, Denman, 76.
Coe, Ebenezer, 30.
Coe, Ebenezer, 68.
Coe, Eli, 89.
Coe, Elijah, 68.
Coe, Elisha, 89.
Coe, Jedediah, 99.
Coe, Jessy, 87.
Coe, Jessy, Junʳ, 87.
Coe, Joel, 96.
Coe, John, 88.
Coe, John, 94.
Coe, John, 96.
Coe, Jonathan, 16.
Coe, Joseph, 88.
Coe, Josiah, 96.
Coe, Levi, 71.
Coe, Matthews, 67.
Coe, Morris, 96.
Coe, Nathan, 88.
Coe, Nathan, Junʳ, 88.
Coe, Phinehas, 68.
Coe, Reuben, 16.
Coe, Robert, 68.
Coe, Seth, 70.
Coe, Seth, 89.
Coe, Simeon, 96.
Coe, Thomas, 71.
Coe, Thomas, 99.
Coe, Timothy, 62.
Coe, Timothy, 96.
Coe, Zacheus, 30.
Coe, Zedediah, 67.
Coggeshall, William, 101.
Coggshall, Daniel, 78.
Coggshall, Freegift, 101.
Coggswell, Dunlap, 26.
Coggswell, Edward, 75.
Coggswell, Edward, 2ᵈ, 75.
Coggwell, Anna, 75.
Coggwell, Asa, 73.
Coggwell, Roger, 75.
Cogshall, James, 152.
Cogshall, Nathˡ, 141.
Cogswell, Amos, 133.
Cogswell, Asael, 19.
Cogswell, Benjⁿ, 133.
Cogswell, David, 49.
Cogswell, David, Jr., 49.
Cogswell, John, 114.
Cogswell, Nathˡ, 113.
Cogswell, Robert, 34.
Cogswell, Wᵐ, 138.
Coit, Benjamin, 113.
Coit, Benjamin, 131.
Coit, Boradel, 129.
Coit, Daniel, 113.
Coit, Daniel, 131.
Coit, Farewell, 130.
Coit, John, 113.
Coit, John, 128.
Coit, Joseph, 128.
Coit, Joseph, 131.
Coit, Joshua, 126.
Coit, Oliver, 113.
Coit, Patty, 128.
Coit, Samuel, 113.
Coit, Samuel, Junʳ, 113.
Coit, Samˡ, 128.
Coit, Samˡ, 2ᵈ, 128.
Coit, Thomas, 130.
Coit, Thomas, Junʳ, 128.
Coit, Whealer, 115.
Coit, William, 128.
Coit, William, 130.
Cojah, Elizabeth, 31.
Colbert, Temperance, 129.
Colborn, Edward, 143.
Colbrith, John, 102.
Colburn, Ithamar, 153.
Colburn, Robert, 153.
Colburn, Sylvanus, 153.
Coldgrove, Joseph, 64.
Cole, Abner, 80.
Cole, Amasa, 69.
Cole, Asa, 21.
Cole, Danˡ, 63.
Cole, David, 62.
Cole, David, 146.
Cole, Ebenezer, 80.
Cole, Ebenezer, 107.
Cole, Ebenezer, Junʳ, 80.
Cole, Eleezer, 66.
Cole, Elezer, 10.
Cole, Gideon, 33.
Cole, Hannah, 81.
Cole, Hannah, 108.
Cole, Hezekiah, 17.
Cole, Hezᵃ, 152.
Cole, Hyman, 19.
Cole, Ichabod, 71.
Cole, Isaac, 150.
Cole, Isaac, 150.
Cole, Jacob, 46.
Cole, Jesse, 71.

Cole, John, 33.
Cole, John, 69.
Cole, John, 71.
Cole, John, 76.
Cole, John, 152.
Cole, Jonathan, 21.
Cole, Jonathan, 31.
Cole, Jonathan, 145.
Cole, Joseph, 65.
Cole, Marcus, 80.
Cole, Mary, 131.
Cole, Mathew, 33.
Cole, Moses, 81.
Cole, Nathan, 154.
Cole, Nathaniel, 33.
Cole, Nathaniel, 71.
Cole, Noah, 68.
Cole, Noah, 152.
Cole, Rebecca, 33.
Cole, Samˡ, 65.
Cole, Samuel, 70.
Cole, Sands, 115.
Cole, Selah, 33.
Cole, Seth, 33.
Cole, Seth, 57.
Cole, Solomon, 71.
Cole, Spencer, 148.
Cole, Stephen, 33.
Cole, Thaddeus, 75.
Cole, Thankful, 62.
Cole, Thomas, 21.
Cole, Thomas, 151.
Cole, Timothy, 71.
Cole, Timothy, 76.
Colebourn, Danˡ, 137.
Colebourn, Eben, 137.
Colebourn, Joˢ, 137.
Colebourn, Ruben, 137.
Colebourn, Samˡ, 137.
Colebourn (Wid.), 137.
Colefax, Abigail, 129.
Colefax, George, 129.
Colegrove, Benjⁿ, 151.
Colegrove, Benjⁿ, Jnʳ, 151.
Colegrove, Jonathⁿ, 148.
Coleman, Aaron, 58.
Coleman, Ambrus, 121.
Coleman, Asa, 134.
Coleman, Asaph, 42.
Coleman, Danˡ, 121.
Coleman, Ebenezer, 121.
Coleman, Ebeʳ, 2ᵈ, 133.
Coleman, Eᵐ, 133.
Coleman, Jason, 145.
Coleman, Jnᵒ, 132.
Coleman, John, 145.
Coleman, Jnᵒ, Jrˡ, 132.
Coleman, John, Jnʳ, 145.
Coleman, Josiah, 61.
Coleman, Levy, 133.
Coleman, Nathˡ, 133.
Coleman, Noah, 146.
Coleman, Pelig, 53.
Coleman, Samˡ, 134.
Coleman, Thomas, 52.
Coleman, Timᵒ, 133.
Coleman (Wid.), 135.
Coles, Asa, 70.
Coles, Ashbel, 50.
Coles, Calvin, 50.
Coles, Elisha, 92.
Coles, Jesse, 96.
Coles, Joseph, 60.
Coles, Levi, 11.
Coles, Stephen, 60.
Coles, Theodore, 70.
Coles, Thoˢ, 49.
Coley, Daniel, 29.
Coley, Ebenezer, 32.
Coley, Eliphalet, 32.
Coley, Gershom, 27.
Coley, Jesse, 27.
Coley, Jonathan, 32.
Coley, Jonathan, Jr, 32.
Coley, Morehouse, 32.
Coley, Noah, 45.
Coley, Onisimus, 27.
Coley, Samuel, 27.
Colking, John, 62.
Colkins, Elija, 2ᵈ, 62.
Colkins, Elije, 62.
Colkins, Elisha, 65.
Colkins, Justice, 70.
Colkins, Silvanus, 70.
Collar, Isaac, 71.
Collar, Isaac, 149.
Collar, Jonathan, 141.
Collens, Nathaniel, 68.
Collens, Oliver, 65.
Coller, Isaac, 70.
Coller, John, 70.
Coller, Joseph, 143.
Coller, Olliver, 70.
Collier, Benjⁿ, 132.
Collier, John, 132.
Collier, William, 45.
Collin, Joseph, 93.
Collings, Jnᵒ, 136.
Collings, Luis, 135.
Collins, Abel, 50.
Collins, Abial, 54.
Collins, Ambrose, 65.
Collins, Amos, 71.

Collins, Amos, 116.
Collins, Augustus, 100.
Collins, Benjamin, 112.
Collins, Benjⁿ, 147.
Collins, Charles, 59.
Collins, Charles, 98.
Collins, Cyprian, 69.
Collins, Daniel, 100.
Collins, Daniel, 107.
Collins, Daniel, 116.
Collins, Daniel, 116.
Collins, Darius, 98.
Collins, David, 53.
Collins, Ebenezer, 38.
Collins, Edward, 106.
Collins, Edward, Esqʳ, 40.
Collins, Edward, 2ᵈ, 106.
Collins, Eleazʳ, 146.
Collins, Eliphalet, 40.
Collins, Freind, 98.
Collins, Giles, 107.
Collins, Jabez, 136.
Collins, James, 54.
Collins, Joel, 98.
Collins, Joel, 112.
Collins, John, 39.
Collins, John, 60.
Collins, John, 101.
Collins, Jonathan, 106.
Collins, Joseph, 112.
Collins, Joseph, 2ⁿᵈ, 112.
Collins, Josiah, 143.
Collins, Justice, 59.
Collins, Levi, 54.
Collins, Luther, 103.
Collins, Mehitable, 115.
Collins, Nathaniel, 40.
Collins, Nathˡ, 126.
Collins, Peter, 148.
Collins, Philo, 67.
Collins, Pitman, 98.
Collins, Richard, 144.
Collins, Robert, 54.
Collins, Robert J., 45.
Collins, Rufus, 146.
Collins, Rufus, Jnʳ, 146.
Collins, Ruth, 100.
Collins, Samuel, 100.
Collins, Seth, 47.
Collins, Simeon, 54.
Collins, Stephen, 115.
Collins, Thomas, 129.
Collins, Uriah, 108.
Collins, William, 71.
Collins, William B., 29.
Collis, Daniel, 125.
Collony, Patrick, 103.
Colly, George, 107.
Colly, Stephen, 80.
Collyer, Thomas, 32.
Coloil, Samˡ, 152.
Colson, Joseph, 21.
Colt, Benjamin, 123.
Colt, Desire, 122.
Colt, Elisha, 45.
Colt, Harris, 122.
Colt, Jabez, 55.
Colt, John, 125.
Colt, Peter, 45.
Colt, Samuel, 122.
Coltney, George, 154.
Colton, Abijah, 47.
Colton, Elizabeth (Wid.), 44.
Colton, Jonᵃ, 132.
Colton, Joseph, 47.
Colton (Wid.), 45.
Colvel, Nathaniel, 97.
Colver, Azriah, 68.
Colver, Edward, 53.
Colver, Joshua, 71.
Colver, Reuben, 68.
Colver, Titus, 68.
Colvil, Ephraim, 152.
Colvin, Gabriel, 129.
Colwell, Charles, 97.
Colwell, Ruth, 97.
Colwell, Thomas, 98.
Coly, David, 32.
Coly, David, Junʳ, 32.
Colyer, Thomas, 64.
Coman, Stephen, 144.
Comb, Henry, 123.
Comb, Thomos, 114.
Combes, William, 47.
Combs, Andrew, 52.
Combs, Ebenezer, 41.
Combs, John, 11.
Combs, Joseph, 52.
Combs, Joseph, Jr., 53.
Combs, Josiah, 53.
Combs, William, 11.
Comering, Jacob, 61.
Comes, Ebenezer, 48.
Comes, John, 40.
Comes, Phineas, 40.
Comestock, Aaron, 22.
Comestock, David, Jr, 21.
Comestock, Elizabeth (Wᵈ), 25.
Comestock, Enoch, 22.
Comestock, Enoch, 26.
Comestock, Moses, 22.

Comestock, Nathan, 23.
Comestock, Samuel, 22.
Comins, Samuel, 68.
Commel, Daniel, 61.
Commins, Jacom, 61.
Comore, Stephen, 61.
Comp, Joel, 61.
Compstock (Widow), 44.
Comstalk, Daniel, 11.
Comstalk, Mercy, 12.
Comstalk, Stephen, 10.
Comstock, Abel, 74.
Comstock, Abijah, 23.
Comstock, Abijah, 58.
Comstock, Abijah, Jʳ, 23.
Comstock, Achilles, 71.
Comstock, Caleb, 25.
Comstock, Calvin, 59.
Comstock, Christopher, 81.
Comstock, David, 25.
Comstock, David, 58.
Comstock, Eliphlet, 58.
Comstock, Gershom, 58.
Comstock, Israel, 82.
Comstock, Israel, 150.
Comstock, Jabez, 80.
Comstock, Jabez, 82.
Comstock, Jabez, 2ᵈ, 82.
Comstock, Jacob, 82.
Comstock, John, 71.
Comstock, John, 153.
Comstock, Martin Luther, 74.
Comstock, Peter, 58.
Comstock, Phebe, 25.
Comstock, Samuel, 71.
Comstock, Samˡ, 90.
Comstock, Sarah, 23.
Comstock, Samˡ, 2ᵈ, 90.
Comstock, Secajah, 69.
Comstock, Strong, 23.
Comstock, Thomas, 23.
Comstock, Zebulun, 124.
Compton, William, 149.
Con, Robert, 47.
Conant, Benajʰ, 147.
Conant, Eleazʳ, 147.
Conant, John, 148.
Conant, Joseph, 147.
Conant, Josiah, Jnʳ, 147.
Conant, Seth, 147.
Conant, Shubael, 147.
Conant, Sylvanus, 147.
Concklin, Esther, 85.
Condall, Daniel, 125.
Condall, David, 125.
Condall, James, 124.
Condall, John, 125.
Condall, Jonathan, 124.
Conder, Daniel, 109.
Condon, Timothy, 126.
Condy, Timothy, 110.
Cone, Aaron, 91.
Cone, Benjⁿ, 82.
Cone, Berial, 89.
Cone, Cephas, 121.
Cone, Danˡ, 82.
Cone, David, 90.
Cone, Ebenezer, 81.
Cone, Elihu, 83.
Cone, Elisha, 82.
Cone, Elisha, 83.
Cone, Elisha, Junʳ, 84.
Cone, George, 81.
Cone, George, 82.
Cone, Hannah, 82.
Cone, Israel, 82.
Cone, James, 82.
Cone, James, 84.
Cone, Jared, 132.
Cone, Jared, Jr, 132.
Cone, Jerᵇ, 35.
Cone, John, 87.
Cone, Jonᵃ, 82.
Cone, Joseph, 86.
Cone, Joshua, 32.
Cone, Joshua, 82.
Cone, Martin, 82.
Cone, Mary, 82.
Cone, Nathaniel, 80.
Cone, Nehᵇ, 82.
Cone, Noadiah, 82.
Cone, Noadiah, 84.
Cone, Phinehas, 81.
Cone, Reuben, 84.
Cone, Robᵗ, 81.
Cone, Roswell, 82.
Cone, Russell, 37.
Cone, Samˡ, 82.
Cone, Samuel, 83.
Cone, Samˡ, 2ᵈ, 82.
Cone, Silvanus, 82.
Cone, Simon, 121.
Cone, Solomon, 82.
Cone, Stephen, 37.
Cone, Thomas, 66.
Cone, Timᵒ, 81.
Cone, Wᵐ, 82.
Cone, Zachʸ, 135.
Cone, Zachʸ, 135.
Coneklin, John, 23.
Coney, Edward, 131.

Congdoll, Benjⁿ, 151.
Conger, Ephraim, 18.
Conger, Joel, 19.
Conglin, Isaac, 99.
Conglin, Jacob, 98.
Congo (Negroe), 102.
Conklin, Benjⁿ, 67.
Conklin, Mary (Wᵈ), 16.
Conklin, Thomas, 62.
Conley, John, 42.
Conley, Wᵐ Gaylord, 58.
Connel, Jereʰ, 140.
Conner, Elizabeth, 108.
Conner, Elnathan, 92.
Conner, Trisham, 93.
Constable, William, 142.
Convass, Demor, 11.
Converse, Eleazʳ, 144.
Converse, Elijah, 58.
Converse, Elijah, 150.
Converse, Elijah, 151.
Converse, Jacob, 150.
Converse, Jesse, 144.
Converse, Jonathan, 144.
Converse, Payne, 150.
Convus, Asa, 136.
Convus, Benjⁿ, 138.
Convus, Darius, 136.
Convus, James, 136.
Convus, Jesse, 136.
Convus, Jos., 136.
Convus, Joseph, 137.
Convus, Josⁱ, 137.
Convus, Josⁱ, 138.
Convus, Noah, 138.
Convus, Sola, 137.
Convus, Stephen, 137.
Convus (Wid.), 137.
Conwell, Benjamin, Jr., 34.
Cook, Aaron, 45.
Cook, Aaron, 64.
Cook, Aaron, 140.
Cook, Abner, 55.
Cook, Amasa, 69.
Cook, Amos, 84.
Cook, Arba, 76.
Cook, Arijah, 60.
Cook, Asael, 115.
Cook, Barton, 113.
Cook, Benjamin, 38.
Cook, Benjamin, 43.
Cook, Cornelius, 93.
Cook, Cyprian, 114.
Cook, Daniel, 58.
Cook, Daniel, 65.
Cook, Daniel, 65.
Cook, Daniel, 70.
Cook, Daniel, 115.
Cook, Danˡ, 141.
Cook, Darius, 44.
Cook, Eleazer, 48.
Cook, Eleazʳ, 149.
Cook, Eli, 55.
Cook, Elihu, 65.
Cook, Elisha, 55.
Cook, Elisha, 115.
Cook, Ephraim, 69.
Cook, Ezekiel, 70.
Cook, Gideon, 81.
Cook, Isaiah, 114.
Cook, Jacob, 44.
Cook, James, 45.
Cook, James, 99.
Cook, James, 115.
Cook, Jesse, 133.
Cook, Jesse, 133.
Cook, Jessee, 69.
Cook, Joab, 58.
Cook, Job, 55.
Cook, Joel, 56.
Cook, Joel, 65.
Cook, Joel, 76.
Cook, John, 40.
Cook, John, 45.
Cook, John, 62.
Cook, John, 113.
Cook, John, 120.
Cook, John, 129.
Cook, John, 144.
Cook, Jonah, 76.
Cook, Jonathan, 55.
Cook, Jonathan, 58.
Cook, Joseph, 58.
Cook, Joseph P., 11.
Cook, Joseph P., Jr., 11.
Cook, Joshua, 99.
Cook, Josiah, 55.
Cook, Josiah, 80.
Cook, Justus, 76.
Cook, Lot, 149.
Cook, Lucius, 33.
Cook, Martin, 50.
Cook, Mary, 80.
Cook, Moses, 55.
Cook, Moses, 70.
Cook, Moses, 81.
Cook, Nathˡ, 134.
Cook, Noah, 55.
Cook, Oliver, 58.
Cook, Phebe, 76.
Cook, Pinny, 56.
Cook, Richard, 69.
Cook, Richard, 80.

# INDEX.

Cook, Robert, 50.
Cook, Roswell, 41.
Cook, Roswell, 124.
Cook, Samuel, 11.
Cook, Samuel, 58.
Cook, Scad, 58.
Cook, Shubael, 55.
Cook, Shubal, 134.
Cook, Shubel, 60.
Cook, Simeon, 70.
Cook, Stephen, 138.
Cook, Stephen, 144.
Cook, Sylvanus, 58.
Cook, Thadeus, 113.
Cook, Theophilus, 55.
Cook, Thomas, 11.
Cook, Thomas, 58.
Cook, Timothy, 63.
Cook, Titus, 58.
Cook, William, 33.
Cook, William, 45.
Cook, W$^m$, 55.
Cook, William, 58.
Cook, William, 69.
Cook, William, 87.
Cook, William, 114.
Cook, W$^m$, 136.
Cooke, Abel, 108.
Cooke, Ambrose, 108.
Cooke, Amos, 107.
Cooke, Aron, 93.
Cooke, Aron, 108.
Cooke, Attwater, 108.
Cooke, Augistin, 109.
Cooke, Benjamin, 107.
Cooke, Caleb, 108.
Cooke, Chancy, 108.
Cooke, Charles, 109.
Cooke, Clum, 94.
Cooke, David, 102.
Cooke, David, 104.
Cooke, David, 108.
Cooke, David, 111.
Cooke, Demeb$^s$, 91.
Cooke, Demetrus, 92.
Cooke, Elihu, 91.
Cooke, Elizabeth, 93.
Cooke, Ephrahim, 108.
Cooke, George, 102.
Cooke, Hannah, 108.
Cooke, Isaac, 108.
Cooke, Isaiel, 91.
Cooke, James, 108.
Cooke, James, 109.
Cooke, Jesse, 107.
Cooke, John, 103.
Cooke, Merliam, 108.
Cooke, Miller, 104.
Cooke, Mireman, 93.
Cooke, Molly, 108.
Cooke, Moses, 109.
Cooke, Peter, 108.
Cooke, Samuel, 92.
Cooke, Samuel, 100.
Cooke, Samuel, 108.
Cooke, Samuel, 108.
Cooke, Samuel, 108.
Cooke, Samuel, 2$^{nd}$, 93.
Cooke, Sarah, 109.
Cooke, Stephen, 108.
Cooke, Thaddeus, 108.
Cooke, Thomas, 96.
Cooke, Titus, 108.
Cooke, William, 104.
Cooladge, Henry, 104.
Cooler, Isaac, 58.
Cooley, Arael, 109.
Cooley, Chancy, 37.
Cooley, Hezekiah, 12.
Cooley, John, 13.
Cooley, Noah, 40.
Cooley, Tho$^s$, 136.
Coolly, Sam$^l$, 133.
Cooly, James, 136.
Cooly, Luke, 136.
Cooly, Nath$^l$, 136.
Cooly, Ruben, 136.
Coombs, John, 96.
Coon, Joseph, 151.
Coon, Lebues, 115.
Coop, David, 45.
Coop, David, 144.
Cooper, Abraham, 100.
Cooper, Abraham, 2$^{nd}$, 100.
Cooper, Alling, 100.
Cooper, Beedy, 100.
Cooper, Caleb, 106.
Cooper, Deliverance, 79.
Cooper, F., 101.
Cooper, George, 79.
Cooper, Harris S., 79.
Cooper, Isaac, 106.
Cooper, James, 106.
Cooper, Jesse, 76.
Cooper, Joel, 106.
Cooper, Joel, 2$^{nd}$, 106.
Cooper, John, 79.
Cooper, John, 106.
Cooper, John, 150.
Cooper, Joseph, 106.
Cooper, Joseph, 2$^{nd}$, 106.
Cooper, Justice, 106.
Cooper, Lamberton, 85.
Cooper, Levi, 97.

Cooper, Peter, 144.
Cooper, Samuel, 101.
Cooper, Thomas, 79.
Cooper, Thomas, 106.
Cooper, Thomas, 106.
Cooper, Timothy, 75.
Cooper, Timothy, 79.
Cooper, Timothy, 101.
Coops, Eben$^r$, 148.
Copeland, James, 141.
Copeland, Jona$^s$, 141.
Copeland, William, 149.
Copeland, William, 150.
Copet, Marten, 69.
Copet, Timothy, 69.
Copley, Daniel, 75.
Copp, Sam$^l$, 116.
Copp, Joseph, 118.
Copp, Joseph, 129.
Copt, Alexander, 44.
Copt, Alexander, 45.
Copt, Frances, 44.
Copty, Anna, 51.
Cora, Rebecca, 91.
Corban, Abijah, 153.
Corban, Asael, 154.
Corban, Clement, 151.
Corban, Elipht., 144.
Corban, Ezra, 151.
Corban, John, 154.
Corban, Jona$^{th}$, 151.
Corban, Moses, 150.
Corban, Moses, 151.
Corban, Peleg, 151.
Corban, Silas, 154.
Corbet, Joseph, 90.
Corbey, Meriah, 67.
Corbin, Dan$^l$, 64.
Corbin, Peter, 64.
Corbin, Philip, 71.
Corbin, William, 154.
Corey, Josiah, 148.
Corey, Josiah, Sen$^r$, 148.
Corkings, Silas, 62.
Corkins, Aquilla, 82.
Corkins, Jedediah, 135.
Corn, Noah, 84.
Cornel, Ezekiel, 149.
Cornet, Gideon, 149.
Cornett, Gideon, 2$^d$, 149.
Corney, Allen, 17.
Corney, Andrew, 63.
Corney, Nathan, 39.
Cornhill, Job, 129.
Corning, Asa, 45.
Corning, Benj$^a$, 151.
Corning, Bliss, 131.
Corning, Deborah, 131.
Corning, Elisha, 114.
Corning, Ezra, 45.
Corning, John, 131.
Corning, Loami, 114.
Corning, Malaca, 37.
Corning, Nathan Jr., 39.
Corning, Nehemiah, 114.
Corning, Samuel, 114.
Corning, Uriah, 114.
Corning, William, 36.
Cornish, Daniel K., 48.
Cornish, Daniel King, 49.
Cornish, Elisha, J$^r$, 47.
Cornish, Elizabeth, 45.
Cornish, George, 47.
Cornish, James, 47.
Cornish, Joel, 47.
Cornish, John, 95.
Cornish, Joseph, 45.
Cornwall, Benjamin, 35.
Cornwall, Cornilius, 35.
Cornwall, John, 16.
Cornwall, Nathaniel, 33.
Cornwall, Robert, 32.
Cornwall, Thomas, 30.
Cornwell, Abijah, 93.
Cornwell, Andrew, 79.
Cornwell, Ashbell, 88.
Cornwell, Caleb, 88.
Cornwell, Cornelius, 109.
Cornwell, Eden B., 57.
Cornwell, Elijah, 86.
Cornwell, Francis, 87.
Cornwell, Hart, 85.
Cornwell, Isaac, 68.
Cornwell, Isaac, 88.
Cornwell, James, 85.
Cornwell, John, 10.
Cornwell, John, 88.
Cornwell, Nathan, 10.
Cornwell, Nathaniel, 79.
Cornwell, Nathaniel, 88.
Cornwell, Samuel, 65.
Cornwell, Samuel, 79.
Cornwell, Thomas, 79.
Cornwell, Timothy, 86.
Cornwell, Timothy, 87.
Cornwell, William, 86.
Corols, Ebenezer, 62.
Coset, Reuben, 44.
Cosett, Rana, 45.
Cosher, Abel, 19.
Cosher, Benjamin, 11.
Cosher, Enoch, 18.
Coskins, Amos, 70.

Coslet, Frances, 54.
Cosly, George, 136.
Cosset, Asa, 45.
Cosset, Silas, 45.
Cosset, Timothy, 44.
Cossett, John, 109.
Coswell, Caleb, 30.
Cother, John, 57.
Cott, John, 58.
Cott, Jon$^{th}$ Hanson, 58.
Cotter, Andrew, 57.
Cotterall, Thomas P., 118.
Cotton, Daniel, 45.
Cotton, David, 36.
Cotton, Ebenezer, 88.
Cotton, Eliakim, 48.
Cotton, Elihu, 86.
Cotton, Elihu, Jun$^r$, 86.
Cotton, Elisha, 88.
Cotton, George, 86.
Cotton, Isaac, 134.
Cotton, James, 81.
Cotton, James, 88.
Cotton, John, 86.
Cotton, John, 149.
Cotton, John, 2$^d$, 87.
Cotton, Michael, 61.
Cotton, Samuel, 36.
Cotton, Sam$^l$, 56.
Cotton, Samuel, 86.
Cotton, Samuel, 88.
Cotton, Samuel, 149.
Cotton, Thomas, 88.
Cotton, Tho$^s$, 142.
Cotton, Timothy, 86.
Cotton, William, 60.
Cottril, James, 128.
Couch, Abraham, 13.
Couch, David, 23.
Couch, David, 44.
Couch, Ebenezer, 33.
Couch, Elijah, 27.
Couch, Elisha, 43.
Couch, Giddeon, 13.
Couch, John, 27.
Couch, John, 37.
Couch, John, 107.
Couch, John, 1$^{st}$, 71.
Couch, John, 2$^d$, 71.
Couch, John, 2$^{nd}$, 107.
Couch, Joshua, 13.
Couch, Josiah, 27.
Couch, Nehemiah, 12.
Couch, Rachel (W$^d$), 24.
Couch, Samuel, 71.
Couch, Simon, 13.
Couch, Simon, 27.
Couch, Simon, 28.
Couch, Stephen, 27.
Couch, Stephen, 37.
Couch, Thomas, 27.
Coudry, Jonathan, 63.
Covel, David, 70.
Covel, Zenus, 67.
Covell, Elijah, 43.
Covell, Eliphalet, 43.
Covell, James, 43.
Covell, Jonathan, 43.
Covell, Philip, 43.
Covell, Samuel, 43.
Covert, Elerick, 101.
Covert, Samuel, 102.
Covey, David, 35.
Covey, Elijah, 35.
Covey, Elisha, 35.
Covey, Jared, 35.
Covey, Kinyon, 113.
Covey, Silus, 35.
Covil, Daniel, &c., 144.
Covil, Ebenezer, 35.
Covil, Eben$^r$, 150.
Covil, Ephraim, 42.
Covill, Abraham, 152.
Covill, Eben$^r$, 144.
Covill, Sam$^l$, 144.
Cow, James, 29.
Cowder, Ambrose, 66.
Cowder, Asa, 66.
Cowdre, Isaac, 130.
Cowdrey, Jacob, 62.
Cowdrey, Moses, 61.
Cowdry, Jacob, 68.
Cowdry, John, 18.
Cowdry, Jonathan, 81.
Cowdry, Nathaniel, 81.
Cowdry, Thomas, 80.
Cowell, James, 110.
Cowels, Samuel, 33.
Cowing, Lois, 53.
Cowle, Jasen, 62.
Cowles, Amos, 40.
Cowles, Asa, 56.
Cowles, Asahel, 33.
Cowles, Ashbel, 36.
Cowles, Daniel, 41.
Cowles, Daniel, Jr., 41.
Cowles, Ebenezer, 76.
Cowles, Eleazer, 40.
Cowles, Elias, 40.
Cowles, Elijah, 41.
Cowles, Elijah, Jr., 41.
Cowles, Enos, 40.

Cowles, Ezekiel, 40.
Cowles, George, 50.
Cowles, Gideon, 40.
Cowles, Isaac, 40.
Cowles, Jabez, 33.
Cowles, James, 35.
Cowles, Josiah, 50.
Cowles, Levi, 56.
Cowles, Martha (Wid.), 36.
Cowles, Mary, 35.
Cowles, Moses, 76.
Cowles, Noah, 33.
Cowles, Samuel, 37.
Cowles, Selah, 33.
Cowles, Solomon, Jr, 40.
Cowles, Thomas, 40.
Cowles, Thomas, 76.
Cowles, Timothy, 36.
Cowles, William, 36.
Cowles, Ziba, 41.
Cowley, James, 21.
Cowls, Ira, 64.
Cowls, Joseph, 62.
Cowls, Joseph, 107.
Cowls, Samuel, 69.
Cowls, Timothy, 68.
Cowls, Timothy, 107.
Cox, William, 10.
Cox, William, 131.
Coy, Aaron, 137.
Coy, Archabal, 138.
Coy, David, 131.
Coy, David, 136.
Coy, Edy, 88.
Coy, Ephraim, 63.
Coy, Jesse, 122.
Coy, Levy, 138.
Coy, Luke, 141.
Coy, Mary, 86.
Coy, Nathan, 114.
Coye, Joseph, 145.
Coza (Negro), 21.
Craft, David, 12.
Craft, David, 154.
Craft, Edward, 94.
Craft, Rhoda, 113.
Craft, Sam$^l$, 149.
Craft, Stephen, 23.
Craige, Mary, 130.
Craige, Robart, 114.
Crain, Dan$^l$, 147.
Crain, Hezekiah, 147.
Crain, Zebulun, 29.
Craine, Elisha, 148.
Craine, Hez$^a$, 148.
Craine, Roger, 140.
Craine, Roger, 141.
Craine, William, 106.
Crainton, John, 98.
Cram, John, 38.
Crammer, Amos, 78.
Crammer, William, 57.
Crammr, Adam, 78.
Crampton, David, 98.
Crampton, Miles, 40.
Cramton, Asbel, 98.
Crandal, Abijah, 136.
Crandal, Christopher, 148.
Crandal, Ezra, 151.
Crandal, John, 35.
Crandal, Samuel, 138.
Crandal, Urich, 136.
Crandall, Amos, 115.
Crandall, Amos, Jun$^r$, 115.
Crandall, Baley, 116.
Crandall, Benjamin, 114.
Crandall, Charles, 115.
Crandall, Christopher, 114.
Crandall, Ebor, 116.
Crandall, Isaiah, 115.
Crandall, Jonathan, 118.
Crandall, Nath$^l$, 117.
Crandall, Paul, 117.
Crandall, Peter, 115.
Crandall, Phinias, 127.
Crandall, Samuel, 131.
Crane, Aaron, 38.
Crane, Abraham, 52.
Crane, Curtis, 52.
Crane, Daniel, 106.
Crane, David, 38.
Crane, Elias, 85.
Crane, Elisha, 84.
Crane, Elisha, 99.
Crane, Elisha, Jun$^r$, 84.
Crane, Elishama, 38.
Crane, Eunice, 152.
Crane, Ezra, 66.
Crane, Ezra, 71.
Crane, Fredrick, 96.
Crane, Henry, 96.
Crane, Hezekiah, 38.
Crane, Hezekiah, 52.
Crane, Hezekiah, Jr., 38.
Crane, Isaac C., 71.
Crane, Jesse, 96.
Crane, John, 63.
Crane, Joseph, 52.
Crane, Lucretia, 96.
Crane, Mahitabel, 96.
Crane, Martin, 64.
Crane, Robart, 56.
Crane, Rufas, 85.
Crane, Rufus, 38.

Crane, Ruth, 52.
Crane, Ruth, 52.
Crane, Samuel, 85.
Crane, Theophilus, 85.
Crane, Zelock, 96.
Cranton, Benjamin, 99.
Cranton, Benjamin, 2$^d$, 99.
Cranton, Edmond, 99.
Cranton, Josiah, 99.
Cranton, Luther, 99.
Cranton, Nathaniel, 98.
Cranton, Nathaniel, 99.
Cranton, Nathaniel, 2$^d$, 98.
Craps (Negro), 112.
Crary, Benj$^n$, 148.
Crary, Humphery, 118.
Crary, Isaac, 118.
Crary, James, 11.
Crary, Jonathan, 118.
Crary, Nathan, 118.
Crary, Nathan, Jun$^r$, 120.
Crary, Peter, 118.
Crasey, George, 115.
Crasy, John, 114.
Crasy, Oliver, 114.
Crasy, Robart, Jun$^r$, 114.
Crasy, Robert, 114.
Cravath, Sam$^l$, 63.
Craufford, Thomas, 24.
Craw, Amasa, 128.
Craw, David, 40.
Craw, Jesse, 122.
Craw, Jn$^o$, 134.
Craw, Jonathan, 40.
Craw, Reubin, 19.
Craw, Sarah, 128.
Crawfoot, Daniel, 12.
Crawfoot, Jeames, 78.
Crawfoot, Josiah, 12.
Crawfoot, Mathew, 12.
Crawfoot, Samuel, 12.
Crawfoot, Samuel, Ju$^r$, 12.
Crawford, John, 95.
Crawford, John, 128.
Crawford, Sam$^l$, 138.
Crawson, Asa, 129.
Creamore, George, 86.
Cremor, I., 121.
Creny, John, 69.
Cresey, Eben$^r$, 150.
Crevath, Sam$^{nl}$, 63.
Criessee, Gold, 50.
Crilley, Henry, 109.
Crissey, David, 60.
Crissey, Israel, 60.
Crissey, Presarved, 66.
Crissey, Solomon, 66.
Crissy, Abraham, 26.
Crissy, Jesse, 26.
Crissy, Mary (W$^d$), 26.
Crissy, Nathaniel, 26.
Crissy, Nath$^{el}$, Jr, 26.
Crissy, Samuel, 26.
Crissy, William, 26.
Cristee, Jn$^o$, 133.
Crittenden, Lidia, 103.
Crittendon, Daniel, 79.
Crittendon, Josiah, 80.
Crittenten, Nathaniel, 98.
Crittenton, Amos, 49.
Crittenton, Bela, 98.
Crittenton, Edmond, 98.
Crittenton, Huldy, 98.
Crittenton, Hull, 99.
Crittenton, James, 67.
Crittenton, Joseph, 98.
Crittenton, Nathaniel, 49.
Crittenton, Noah, 98.
Crittenton, Samuel, 45.
Crittenton, Seth, 97.
Crittenton, Soloman, 99.
Crocker, Adonijah, 146.
Crocker, Amos, 127.
Crocker, Amos, 127.
Crocker, Asa, 126.
Crocker, Constant, 127.
Crocker, Daniel, 104.
Crocker, Daniel, 127.
Crocker, Diah, 129.
Crocker, Elizabeth, 143.
Crocker, Ezekiel, 129.
Crocker, Isaac, 127.
Crocker, Jabez, 96.
Crocker, James, 134.
Crocker, James, 146.
Crocker, John, 49.
Crocker, John, 49.
Crocker, John, 125.
Crocker, John, 128.
Crocker, Jonathan, 57.
Crocker, Jonathan, 127.
Crocker, Joseph, 121.
Crocker, Jos., 139.
Crocker, Joshua, 127.
Crocker, Lydia, 127.
Crocker, Nehemiah, 127.
Crocker, Sam$^l$, 139.
Crocker, Simeon, 121.
Crocker, Simon, 146.
Crocker, Stephen, 127.
Crocker, Stephen, 139.
Crocker, Thomas, 126.
Crocker, Thomas, 127.

# INDEX.

Crocker, Timothy, 121.
Crocker (Widow), 133.
Crocker, William, 126.
Crocker, Zeb$^n$, 139.
Croe, Asa, 87.
Croe, John, 69.
Croe, Nathaniel, 69.
Croe, Roger, 63.
Crofford, William, 67.
Crofoot, David, 27.
Crofoot, Elisha, 88.
Crofoot, Joseph, 33.
Crofoot, Ephraim, 33.
Crofoot, Ephraim, Jr., 33.
Croford, Ebenezer, 23.
Croford, Joseph, 23.
Croford, Samuel, 23.
Croker, Oliver, 60.
Crome, Samuel, 43.
Crompton, Ebenezer, 70.
Croner, Hannah, 57.
Croney, Elizabeth, 16.
Crook, Joseph, 84.
Crook, Shubell, 84.
Crook, Thomas, 84.
Crook, Whitmore, 84.
Crosbey, Jeremiah, 64.
Crosbey, Obed, 61.
Crosbey, Samuel, 61.
Crosbey, Simeon, 59.
Crosbey, Sim., 62.
Crosbey, Timothy C., 68.
Crosby, Benj$^a$, 82.
Crosby, David, 36.
Crosby, Ebenezer, 47.
Crosby, Elijah, 82.
Crosby, Elijah, 150.
Crosby, Ezra, 112.
Crosby, Gad, 100.
Crosby, Increase, 82.
Crosby, John, 79.
Crosby, Levi, 82.
Crosby, Levi, 2$^d$, 82.
Crosby, Simon, 38.
Crosby, Thomas, 66.
Crosby, William, 79.
Crosman, Eber, 133.
Cross, Jn$^o$, 134.
Cross, John, 153.
Cross, Joseph, 153.
Cross, Nathan, 140.
Cross, Noah, 137.
Cross, Peter, 147.
Cross, Ruebin, 147.
Cross, Sam., 136.
Cross, Stephen, 136.
Cross, William, 153.
Crossman, Trowbridge, 32.
Croswell, Cabel, 47.
Crouch, Christopher, 136.
Crouch, Ruben, 136.
Crouch, Tho$^s$, 136.
Crow, Damaras, 58.
Crow, Simon, 138.
Crowel, Eben$^r$, 145.
Crowel, John, 152.
Crowel, Thomas, 30.
Crowell, Daniel, 87.
Crowell, Edward, 87.
Crowell, Heman, 80.
Crowell, John, 87.
Crowell, John, Jun$^r$, 87.
Crowell, Sam$^l$, 81.
Crowell, Samuel, 87.
Crowell, Sarah, 87.
Crowell, Solomon, 87.
Crowfoot, Daniel, 20.
Crowfoot, Elihu, 20.
Crowfoot, Ezra, 11.
Crowfoot, Isaac, 20.
Crowfoot, Israel, 27.
Crowfoot, James, 27.
Crowfoot, James, 31.
Crowfoot, John, 20.
Crowfoot, John, 20.
Crowfoot, Joseph, 11.
Crowfoot, Levi, 6.
Crowfoot, Molly (Wid.), 20.
Crowfoot, Sealee, 12.
Crowfoot, Seth, 11.
Crowfoot, Stephen, 19.
Crowfoot, Uriah, 27.
Crowly, William, 128.
Crum, Arnold, 116.
Crum, Charles, 119.
Crum, Joseph, 116.
Crumbey, John, 98.
Crumby, Samuel, 35.
Crumton, Darius, 98.
Crumton, Hull, 98.
Crumton, Jonathan, 98.
Crumton, Jonathan, 2$^d$, 98.
Cruner, Peter, 62.
Crutenden, Jonathan, 33.
Cube, 67.
Cuff, 68.
Cuff, 70.
Cuff (Negro), 86.
Cuff (Negro), 117.
Cuff (Negro), 122.
Cuff (Negroe), 97.
Cuff (Negroe), 102.

Cuff (Wido.), 146.
Cullar, Jonathan, 149.
Cullar, William, Jr., 149.
Cullis, James, 131.
Cullom, George, 135.
Culver, Amos, 110.
Culver, Amos, 119.
Culver, Benjamin, 108.
Culver, Benjamin, 131.
Culver, Benjamin, 2$^{nd}$, 108.
Culver, Charles, 108.
Culver, Christopher, 128.
Culver, Daniel, 76.
Culver, Daniel, 119.
Culver, David, 134.
Culver, Ebenezer, 108.
Culver, Enoch, 108.
Culver, Enoch, 2$^{nd}$, 108.
Culver, Eunice, 119.
Culver, Hannah, 108.
Culver, James, 108.
Culver, James, 128.
Culver, James, 139.
Culver, Jeremiah, 115.
Culver, John, 105.
Culver, John, 108.
Culver, Jonathan, 131.
Culver, Joseph, 119.
Culver, Joseph, 127.
Culver, Lemuel, 126.
Culver, Moses, 119.
Culver, Peter, 118.
Culver, Reuben 76.
Culver, Samuel, 108.
Culver, Samuel, 129.
Culver, Stephen, 65.
Culver, Stephen, 130.
Culver, Thomas, 119.
Culver, Zebulon, 65.
Culver, Zebulon, 65.
Cumins, William, 148.
Cumming, Simeon, 73.
Cummings, Samuel, 41.
Cummings, Sim$^e$, 139.
Cummins, Amos, 150.
Cummins, Asa, 11.
Cummins, David, 140.
Cummins, Josiah, 150.
Cummins, Josiah, Jr, 150.
Cummins, Perker, 154.
Cummins, Stephen, 143.
Cumstock, Abner, 122.
Cumstock, Abner, 2$^d$, 122.
Cumstock, Asa, 122.
Cumstock, Daniel, 112.
Cumstock, Daniel, 125.
Cumstock, Easter, 122.
Cumstock, Elisha, 125.
Cumstock, George, 125.
Cumstock, Hezekiah, 122
Cumstock, James, 125.
Cumstock, Jared, 124.
Cumstock, Jason, 125.
Cumstock, Jesse, 122.
Cumstock, Joab, 122.
Cumstock, John, 128.
Cumstock, Joseph, 125.
Cumstock, Joshua, 125.
Cumstock, Martha, 127.
Cumstock, Mary, 125.
Cumstock, Nathan, 125.
Cumstock, Nath$^l$, 125.
Cumstock, Noah, 122.
Cumstock, Oliver, 124.
Cumstock, Peres, 125.
Cumstock, Peter, 124.
Cumstock, Ransford, 124.
Cumstock, Sam$^l$, 125.
Cumstock, Simeon, 120.
Cumstock, Thomas, 124.
Cundal, William, 143.
Cuningham, Anne, 153.
Cuningham, Peleg, 145.
Cuningham, Peter, 149.
Cuningham, Robert, 152.
Cunning, George, 80.
Cunningham, Abigail, 16.
Cunningham, Esther, 87.
Cunningham, Garwood H., 78.
Cunningham, Samuel, 86.
Cupper, Cornelius, 110.
Curren, James, 97.
Currin, Phinehas, 129.
Curtess, Seth, 67.
Curtis, Abel, 17.
Curtis, Abel, 75.
Curtis, Abel, 107.
Curtis, Abel, 110.
Curtis, Abijah, 19.
Curtis, Abijah, 30.
Curtis, Abijah, 73.
Curtis, Abijah, 96.
Curtis, Abner, 40.
Curtis, Agar, 29.
Curtis, Agar, 30.
Curtis, Amos, 40.
Curtis, Andrew, 17.
Curtis, Andrew, 30.
Curtis, Anner, 96.
Curtis, Asa, 12.
Curtis, Asa, 56.
Curtis, Benjamin, 19.

Curtis, Benjamin, 31.
Curtis, Benjamin, 73.
Curtis, Benjamin, 76.
Curtis, Benjamin, 120.
Curtis, Bilvad, 133.
Curtis, Charles, 30.
Curtis, Daniel, 30.
Curtis, Daniel, 41.
Curtis, Daniel, 45.
Curtis, Daniel, 73.
Curtis, David, 29.
Curtis, David, 30.
Curtis, David, 57.
Curtis, David, 77.
Curtis, Ebenezer, 32.
Curtis, Edmond, 29.
Curtis, Edmond, 29.
Curtis, Edmond, 30.
Curtis, Edward, 92.
Curtis, Eleazer, 41.
Curtis, Elethan, 18.
Curtis, Eli, 76.
Curtis, Elihu, 30.
Curtis, Elihu, 31.
Curtis, Elihu, 76.
Curtis, Elihue, 18.
Curtis, Elijah, 17.
Curtis, Elijah, 18.
Curtis, Eliphalet, 48.
Curtis, Eliphalet, Jr, 48.
Curtis, Elisha, 107.
Curtis, Elizur, 75.
Curtis, Ephraim, 18.
Curtis, Esther (Wid.), 30.
Curtis, Ethan, 35.
Curtis, Ezra, 17.
Curtis, Fineus, 30.
Curtis, Filo, 19.
Curtis, Gabriel, 41.
Curtis, Gilbert, 93.
Curtis, Giles, 33.
Curtis, Gold, 20.
Curtis, Gran., 41.
Curtis, Hannah, 41.
Curtis, Hannah, 58.
Curtis, Hannah, 96.
Curtis, Henery, 29.
Curtis, Henery, 30.
Curtis, Hennery, 18.
Curtis, Heny, 134.
Curtis, Isaac, 17.
Curtis, Isaac, 31.
Curtis, Isaac, 76.
Curtis, Isaac, 121.
Curtis, Israel, 1$^{st}$, 73.
Curtis, Israel, 2$^d$, 73.
Curtis, Jacob, 107.
Curtis, James, 17.
Curtis, James, 17.
Curtis, James, 53.
Curtis, James, 56.
Curtis, Jeames, 76.
Curtis, Jeremiah, 25.
Curtis, Jeremiah, 30.
Curtis, Jesse, 76.
Curtis, Job, 31.
Curtis, Job, 70.
Curtis, Joel, 107.
Curtis, John, 29.
Curtis, John, 31.
Curtis, John, 31.
Curtis, John, 77.
Curtis, John, 96.
Curtis, Jn$^o$, 135.
Curtis, John, Jn$^r$, 143.
Curtis, Jonas, 29.
Curtis, Jonathan, 17.
Curtis, Jonathan, 25.
Curtis, Jones, 29.
Curtis, Joseph, 30.
Curtis, Joseph, 30.
Curtis, Joseph, 73.
Curtis, Joseph, 76.
Curtis, Joseph, 107.
Curtis, Joshua, 29.
Curtis, Joshua, 75.
Curtis, Josiah, 19.
Curtis, Josiah, 29.
Curtis, Josiah, 41.
Curtis, Josiah, 53.
Curtis, Josiah, 53.
Curtis, Judson, 30.
Curtis, Judson, Jun$^r$, 29.
Curtis, Levi, 18.
Curtis, Levi, 53.
Curtis, Levi, 107.
Curtis, Lewis, 30.
Curtis, Lysander, 74.
Curtis, Madad, 63.
Curtis, Martin, 58.
Curtis, Matthew, 19.
Curtis, Miles, 76.
Curtis, Milton, 74.
Curtis, Molly, 58.
Curtis, Nathan, 73.
Curtis, Nathan, 111.
Curtis, Nathaniel, 108.
Curtis, Nehemiah, 19.
Curtis, Nehemiah, 29.
Curtis, Nehemiah, 30.

Curtis, Nirum, 20.
Curtis, Oliver, 76.
Curtis, Oliver, 94.
Curtis, Peter, 41.
Curtis, Philip, 107.
Curtis, Phillip, 2$^{nd}$, 107.
Curtis, Phineas, 76.
Curtis, Phineas, 97.
Curtis, Ramson, 139.
Curtis, Rebecca (W$^d$), 25.
Curtis, Reuben, 73.
Curtis, Reubin, 11.
Curtis, Robert, 17.
Curtis, Robert, 30.
Curtis, Robert, 35.
Curtis, Ruben, 135.
Curtis, Samuel, 11.
Curtis, Samuel, 30.
Curtis, Samuel, 30.
Curtis, Samuel, 30.
Curtis, Samuel, 53.
Curtis, Samuel, 73.
Curtis, Samuel, 96.
Curtis, Sarah, 73.
Curtis, Sheldon, 94.
Curtis, Silas, 18.
Curtis, Silas, 74.
Curtis, Silus, 31.
Curtis, Silvanus, 41.
Curtis, Simeon, 35.
Curtis, Sirus, 63.
Curtis, Soloman, 63.
Curtis, Solomon, 40.
Curtis, Stephen, 11.
Curtis, Stephen, 11.
Curtis, Stephen, 29.
Curtis, Stiles, 18.
Curtis, Stiles, 20.
Curtis, Stiles, 30.
Curtis, Temperence, 18.
Curtis, Thomas, 29.
Curtis, Thomas, 53.
Curtis, Thomas, 76.
Curtis, Timothy, 17.
Curtis, Timothy, 25.
Curtis, Wait, 53.
Curtis, Wait, 73.
Curtis (Wid.), 135.
Curtis, William, 18.
Curtis, Zadock, 76.
Curtis, Zalmon, 20.
Curtis, Zelmon, 31.
Curtiss, Aaron, 61.
Curtiss, Charles, 150.
Curtiss, Daniel, 68.
Curtiss, David, 69.
Curtiss, Ezekiel, 49.
Curtiss, Gideon, 68.
Curtiss, Henry, 140.
Curtiss, Japhet, 150.
Curtiss, Jeremiah, 49.
Curtiss, Jesse, 40.
Curtiss, John, 143.
Curtiss, Jonathan, 49.
Curtiss, Joseph, 68.
Curtiss, Josiah, 62.
Curtiss, Josiah, 69.
Curtiss, Mary, 147.
Curtiss, Nathan$^l$, 62.
Curtiss, Samuel, 49.
Curtiss, Samuel, 62.
Curtiss, Seth, 69.
Curtiss, Solomon, 49.
Curtiss, Zebulon, 62.
Curwin, Theophilus, 122.
Cushman, Alverton, 134.
Cushman, Atherton, 134.
Cushman, Elezer, 139.
Cushman, Elezer, 2$^d$ 139.
Cushman, Elipht., 139.
Cushman, E$^m$, 134.
Cushman, Isaac, 137.
Cushman, Isaac, 141.
Cushman, Isaac, 147.
Cushman, Joab, 147.
Cushman, Minerva, 133.
Cushman, Nath$^l$, 137.
Cushman, Sol$^m$, 137.
Cushman, Solomon, 44.
Cushman, Tho$^s$, 139.
Cushman, Urich, 137.
Cushman, W$^m$, 136.
Cushman, William, 141.
Cusley, Jesse, 76.
Cussrey, Daniel, 78.
Cutas, Aaron, 47.
Cutlar, Amos, 150.
Cutlar, Azariah, 144.
Cutlar, Benjamin, 144.
Cutlar, David, 144.
Cutlar, Ephraim, 144.
Cutlar, Isaac, 144.
Cutlar, Jesse, 154.
Cutlar, Peter, 144.
Cutlar, Roberd, 144.
Cutlar, Sam$^l$, 150.
Cutlar, Solomon, 150.
Cutlar, William, 148.
Cutler, Benjamin, 117.
Cutler, Daniel, 112.
Cutler, Eleazer, 112.

Cutler, Richard, 103.
Cutler, Samuel, 112.
Cutler, Young Lorer, 76.
Cutting, Isaac, 136.
Cutting, Zadock, 136.

Daball, John, 119.
Daball, Nathan, 119.
Dabloughhai, Jon$^a$, 53.
Dabol, Benjamin, 118.
Daboll, Jonathan, 54.
Dacker, Jacob, 63.
Dagget, David, 104.
Dagget, Ezra, 104.
Dagget, Henry, 104.
Dagget, Henry, 2$^{nd}$, 104.
Daggot, Jacob, 104.
Dagget, John, 144.
Dagget, Micajah, 104.
Dagget, Sam$^l$, 134.
Dagget, Sue (Negroe), 104.
Daggett, Isaiah, 134.
Dailey, Field, 144.
Dailey, Jeames, 58.
Dailey, Joseph, 81.
Dailey, Justus, 78.
Dain, Lemuel, 153.
Dains, Axenbridge, 153.
Dains, Eph$^m$, 153.
Dains, Thomas, 153.
Dale, Sam$^l$, 121.
Daley, Benjamin, 15.
Daley, Samuel, 33.
Dallaby, Samuel, 36.
Dalton, Daniel, 93.
Dalton, John, 58.
Dalton, Joseph, 55.
Daly, Giles, 93.
Daman, Nath$^a$, 134.
Daming, Joel, 61.
Damock, Geduthon, 139.
Dan, Abijah, 75.
Dan, Nathan, 26.
Dan, Nathaniel, 26.
Dan, Squire, 25.
Dana, Daniel, 110.
Dana, Elijah, 149.
Dana, Jacob, 140.
Dana, Rev$^d$ James, 102.
Dana, Jedediah, 140.
Dana, Sam$^l$, 149.
Dana, Thomas, 52.
Daney, Jonathan, 86.
Danforth, Edward, 45.
Danforth, Hannah, 131.
Danforth, John, 131.
Danforth, Martha, 86.
Danforth, Thomas, 53.
Daniel (Negro), 122.
Daniel (Negro), 129.
Daniels, Amasa, 80.
Daniels, Amos, 81.
Daniels, Asa, 122.
Daniels, Asa, 125.
Daniels, Daniel, 123.
Daniels, Daniel, 2$^d$, 123.
Daniels, David, 33.
Daniels, David, 43.
Daniels, Ezek$^l$, 135.
Daniels, Frank, 119.
Daniels, Isaac, 127.
Daniels, James, 127.
Daniels, Jasper, 127.
Daniels, Jeremiah, 128.
Daniels, Job, 127.
Daniels, John, 66.
Daniels, John, 87.
Daniels, John, 119.
Daniels, Jn$^o$, 132.
Daniels, John, Jun$^r$, 119.
Daniels, Jn$^o$, Jr, 132.
Daniels, Jonathan, 63.
Daniels, Joseph, 127.
Daniels, Lemuel, 80.
Daniels, Nathan, 127.
Daniels, Nathan, 2$^d$, 126.
Daniels, Nehemiah, 127.
Daniels, Nehemiah, 2$^d$, 127
Daniels, Noah, 127.
Daniels, Oliver, 15.
Daniels, Pelatiah, 66.
Daniels, Peter, 126.
Daniels, Reuben, 66.
Daniels, Samuel, 73.
Daniels, Sam$^l$, 127.
Daniels, Stephen, 37.
Daniels, Tho$^s$, 81.
Daniels, Thomas, 127.
Daniels, William, 87.
Daniels, William, 89.
Danielson, Deborah, 33.
Danielson, James, 143.
Danielson, Samuel, 143.
Danielson, William, 143.
Danish, Ezk$^l$, 135.
Danish, Jon$^a$, 135.
Danish, Neham., 135.
Dann, Ezra, 28.
Danna, Daniel, 39.
Dannaly, John, 35.
Danniels, Pelletiah, 61.
Darbay, W$^m$, 135.

# INDEX.

Darbe, Eleazr, 142.
Darbe, Rufus, 142.
Darbey, Danl, 135.
Darbey, Jos, 135.
Darbey, Nthel, 135.
Darbey, Nathl, 135.
Darby, Partrick, 86.
Darke, Alpheus, 154.
Darke, James, 141.
Darke, William, Jr., 141.
Darling, Abel, 63.
Darling, Abigal, 111.
Darling, Benjamin, 27.
Darling, Joseph, 106.
Darling, Samuel, 31.
Darling, Samuel, 103.
Darling, Samuel, 107.
Darling, Thomas, 111.
Darrow, Asa, 76.
Darrow, Benjamin, 14.
Darrow, Christopher, 125.
Darrow, Daniel, 12.
Darrow, Ebenezer, 76.
Darrow, Ebenr, 127.
Darrow, Ebenr, 127.
Darrow, Ebenezer, 2d, 76.
Darrow, James, 16.
Darrow, James, 127.
Darrow, Jedediah, 127.
Darrow, Jno, 89.
Darrow, Lemuel, 115.
Darrow, Lemuel, 127.
Darrow, Michael, 131.
Darrow, Nathan, 119.
Darrow, Nicholas, 30.
Darrow, Nicholas, 128.
Darrow, Sarah (Wd), 16.
Darrow, Titus, 76.
Darrow, William, 127.
Darrow, Zadock, 127.
Dart, Alvin, 132.
Dart, Benja, 127.
Dart, Caleb, 127.
Dart, Daniel, 127.
Dart, David, 124.
Dart, Ebenr, 126.
Dart, Ebenr, Junr, 126.
Dart, Jabez, 39.
Dart, James, 127.
Dart, Job, 18.
Dart, Job, 128.
Dart, John, 128.
Dart, Jno, 132.
Dart, Jno, 132.
Dart, Jona, 132.
Dart, Jona, 132.
Dart, Joseph, 37.
Dart, Josiah, 80.
Dart, Levi, 134.
Dart, Prudence, 128.
Dart, Richard, 127.
Dart, Roger, 126.
Dart, Ruth, 127.
Dart, Saml, 126.
Dart, Sarah, 37.
Dart, Siras, 83.
Dart, Solomon, 124.
Dart, William, 37.
Dart, William, 76.
Dart, William, 126.
Dart, Wm, 132.
Dart, William, Junr, 126.
Dascomb, John, 17.
Dascomb, Wm, 24.
Dashon, Joseph, 125.
Data, David, 67.
Data, Ezra, 67.
Daton, Andrew, 30.
Daton, Benjamin, 17.
Daton, Brewster, 30.
Daton, Ephraim, 128.
Daton, Hezekiah, 20.
Daton, Richard, 118.
Daton, Sylus, 32.
Daton, Zophar, 128.
Dauchey, Daniel, 28.
Dauchey, James, 28.
Dauchey, John, 28.
Dauchey, Nathan, 28.
Dauchey, Phillip, 28.
Dauchey, Vivus, 28.
Davenport, Deodate, 26.
Davenport, Deodate, 26.
Davenport, James, Esqr, 24.
Davenport, John, 25.
Davenport, John, Junr, 24.
Davenport, Samuel, 97.
Davenport, Silas, 24.
Daverson, ——, 131.
Daverson, Brazilla, 130.
Daverson, Christopher, 116.
Daverson, Daniel, 116.
Daverson, William, 130.
David, Daniel, 66.
David, David, 119.
David, Riggs, 95.
David, Saml, 56.
Davidson, Andrew, 97.
Davidson, Elizabeth, 75.
Davidson, James, 101.
Davidson, Jeames, 78.
Davidson, John, 75.
Davidson, John, 108.

Davidson, Joseph, 101.
Davies, David, 75.
Davies, Jeames, 58.
Davies, Jeams John, 75.
Davies, John, 58.
Davies, John, 75.
Davies, John, 2d, 75.
Davies, Jonathan, 76.
Davies, Nathan, 58.
Davies, Sarah, 71.
Davies, Thomas, 75.
Davies, Thomas, 76.
Davies, Walter, 75.
Davies, William, 56.
Davinson, William, 101.
Davis, Aaron, 136.
Davis, Aaron, 137.
Davis, Abel, 38.
Davis, Abraham, 25.
Davis, Abraham, 69.
Davis, Amos, 96.
Davis, Avery, 139.
Davis, Barnabas, 143.
Davis, Benaijah, 124.
Davis, Benjamin, 17.
Davis, Benjamin, 94.
Davis, Benja, 137.
Davis, Benja, 138.
Davis, Benja, Jr, 137.
Davis, Bill, 151.
Davis, Charles, 79.
Davis, Clark, 29.
Davis, Comfort, 81.
Davis, Corna, 136.
Davis, Daniel, 95.
Davis, Daniel, 119.
Davis, Daniel, 134.
Davis, Danl, 137.
Davis, Danl, 141.
Davis, David, 32.
Davis, David, 149.
Davis, Desire, 93.
Davis, Ebenezer, 32.
Davis, Ebenezer, 32.
Davis, Ebenezer, 85.
Davis, Edward, 109.
Davis, Elias, 94.
Davis, Elias, 16.
Davis, Elizabeth, 147.
Davis, Enoch, 103.
Davis, George, 10.
Davis, George, 139.
Davis, Gyas, 143.
Davis, Haydon, 85.
Davis, Henry, 84.
Davis, Isaac, 15.
Davis, Isaac, 96.
Davis, Isaac, 103.
Davis, Isaac, 136.
Davis, Jabez, 13.
Davis, Jabez, 96.
Davis, Jacobus, 70.
Davis, James, 21.
Davis, James, 84.
Davis, James, 98.
Davis, James, 98.
Davis, James, 136.
Davis, Jasper, 118.
Davis, Jesse, 137.
Davis, Jobe, 136.
Davis, John, 13.
Davis, John, 27.
Davis, John, 32.
Davis, John, 87.
Davis, John, 95.
Davis, John, 98.
Davis, John, 103.
Davis, John, 112.
Davis, John, 114.
Davis, John, 117.
Davis, John, 125.
Davis, Jno, 127.
Davis, Jno, 139.
Davis, John, Junr, 86.
Davis, Jonth, 35.
Davis, Jonathan, 142.
Davis, Jonathn, 148.
Davis, Joseph, 32.
Davis, Joseph, 82.
Davis, Joseph, 94.
Davis, Joseph, 113.
Davis, Joseph, 116.
Davis, Joseph, 124.
Davis, Jo., 137.
Davis, Jos, 138.
Davis, Joseph, 147.
Davis, Joshua, 14.
Davis, Josiah, 84.
Davis, Lathrop, 146.
Davis, Lemuel, 84.
Davis, Leml, 137.
Davis, Martha, 84.
Davis, Mary, 142.
Davis, Micaijah, 125.
Davis, Moses, 137.
Davis, Nathan, 94.
Davis, Nathan, 94.
Davis, Nathaniel, 31.
Davis, Noah, 137.
Davis, Noah, Jr, 137.
Davis, Philip, 45.
Davis, Robart, 119.
Davis, Roger, 35.

Davis, Ruben, 95.
Davis, Ruben, 128.
Davis, Samuel, 84.
Davis, Samuel, 113.
Davis, Samuel, 115.
Davis, Samuel, Junr, 84.
Davis, Sibbell, 85.
Davis, Simon, 150.
Davis, Solomon, 84.
Davis, Solomon, Junr, 102.
Davis, Stephen, 15.
Davis, Stephen, Jr., 16.
Davis, Thara, 114.
Davis, Thomas, 12.
Davis, Thomas, 102.
Davis, Thomas, 103.
Davis, Thomas, 117.
Davis, Thomas, 148.
Davis, Thomas, 150.
Davis, Willard, 140.
Davis, William, 18.
Davis, William, 44.
Davis, William, 115.
Davis, William, 127.
Davis, Zephn, 135.
Davison, Anna, 108.
Davison, Joseph, 141.
Davison, Joseph, Jnr, 141.
Davison, Peter, 141.
Davison, Pheneas, 149.
Davison, Samuel, 108.
Davison, Zacherius, 17.
Davisson, Danl, 148.
Daw, Isaac, 12.
Dawner, Edmund, 39.
Dawson, Ebenr, 153.
Dawson, Robert, 97.
Dawson, Timothy, 49.
Dawton, John, 73.
Day, Abigal, 96.
Day, Abner, 144.
Day, Abraham, 121.
Day, Amasa, 121.
Day, Asa, 121.
Day, Comfort, 144.
Day, David, 144.
Day, David, 144.
Day, Elias, 144.
Day, Elijah, 121.
Day, Elisha, 84.
Day, Horatior, 49.
Day, Isaac, 55.
Day, Israel, 107.
Day, Israel, 144.
Day, James, 130.
Day, Jeremiah, 75.
Day, Jesse, 121.
Day, John, 71.
Day, John, 130.
Day, John, 144.
Day, Jonathan, 19.
Day, Jonathan, 144.
Day, Jonathan, 144.
Day, Jonathan, Jnr, 144.
Day, Joseph, 45.
Day, Joseph, 121.
Day, John, 102.
Day, Justus, 38.
Day, Levi, 144.
Day, Lues, 45.
Day, Noah, 144.
Day, Oliver, 38.
Day, Roswell, 45.
Day, Samuel, 43.
Day, Stanley, 49.
Day, Stephen, 107.
Day, Thomas, 66.
Day, Thomas, 143.
Day, Timothy, 45.
Day, William, 106.
Dayley, Benja, 141.
Dayley, Jacob, 153.
Dayton, Abel, 76.
Dayton, Abraham, 15.
Dayton, Alexander, 76.
Dayton, Amos, 106.
Dayton, Brewster, 31.
Dayton, Charles, 76.
Dayton, Cornelius, 106.
Dayton, David, 76.
Dayton, Eli, 71.
Dayton, Henry, 120.
Dayton, Isaac, 58.
Dayton, Isaac, 76.
Dayton, Israel, 49.
Dayton, John, 2nd, 106.
Dayton, Jonah, 58.
Dayton, Jonathan, 106.
Dayton, Joseph, 128.
Dayton, Justus, 76.
Dayton, Lyman, 76.
Dayton, Michael, 76.
Dayton, Nathaniel, 97.
Dayton, Phebe, 95.
Dayton, Samuel, 50.
Dayton, Samuel, 76.
D'Berrade, Charles, 91.
Deal, Charles, 95.
Deal, George, 25.
Dealing, Samuel, 43.
Dealy, Jeremiah, 48.
Dean, Abiel, 154.
Dean, Abijah, 148.
Dean, Amos, 135.

Dean, Benjamin, 57.
Dean, Christopher, 122.
Dean, Christopher, 148.
Dean, Daniel, 2d, 28.
Dean, Daniel, 2d, 28.
Dean, Ebenezer, 25.
Dean, Elijah, 75.
Dean, Icabod, 95.
Dean, James, 117.
Dean, Joel, 63.
Dean, John, 11.
Dean, John, 47.
Dean, John, 57.
Dean, Josiah, 148.
Dean, Nathan, 149.
Dean, Phinehas, 79.
Dean, Reuben, 57.
Dean, Reuben, 2d, 57.
Dean, Samuel, 78.
Dean, Saml, 82.
Dean, Saml, 131.
Dean, Saml, 141.
Dean, Samuel, 1st, 57.
Dean, Samuel, 2d, 57.
Dean, Simeon, 140.
Dean, Thomas, 57.
Dean, William, 71.
Dean, Wm, 133.
Dean, Zephh, 154.
Deane, Abner, 120.
Deane, David, 126.
Deane, Ezra, 144.
Deangelous, Lewis, 91.
Deangelous, Pascal, 91.
Deans Levi, 130.
Deaolph, Charles, 141.
Dear, George, 60.
Dears, Benjamin, 22.
Deavenport, Benjamin, 71.
Deavenport, David, 71.
Deavenport, John, 71.
Deball, John, 119.
Deball, Mary, 119.
Deball, Saml, 119.
Dee, Danl, 90.
Dee, Elijah, 90.
Dee, Mark, 90.
Dee, Wm, 90.
Deen, Asa, 67.
Deen, John, 62.
Deen, John, 2d, 62.
Deen, Nathan, 68.
Deen, Nathaniel, 67.
Deen, Oliver, 62.
Deen, Roswell, 67.
Deen, Salmon, 62.
Deen, Seth, 65.
Deen, Urah, 62.
Deepu, John, 129.
Doer, Eli, 58.
Deer, John, 64.
Deer, Jonathan, 64.
Deering, Andrew, 93.
Deering, Andrew, 102.
Deering, Ann, 102.
Deering, John, 102.
Deering, Samuel, 102.
Defforrest, David, 107.
Deforest, Alexander, 20.
Deforest, Ebenezer, 23.
Deforest, Edward, 30.
De Forest, Elihue 11.
De Forest, Hezekiah, 17.
Deforest, Hezekiah, 28.
Deforest, Isaac, 23.
Deforest, Isaac, 71.
Deforest, Joseph, 28.
Deforest, Lemuel, 21.
De Forest, Nehemiah, 17.
De Forest, Nehemiah, 18.
De Forest, Othenial, 17.
Deforest, Samuel, 15.
De Forest, Samuel, 17.
Deforest, Sarah (Wd), 23.
Deforest, Uriah, 29.
Deforist, Joseph, 30.
Deforrest, Elihu, 30.
D'Forrest, Gideon, 94.
Deforrest, Hannah, 94.
Deforrest, Isaac, 64.
Deforrest, John, 78.
Defres, Reuben, 25.
Dege (Negro), 47.
Delamore, Joseph, 95.
Delanna, Wm, 55.
Delano, Aaron, 58.
Delano, Barno, 138.
Delano, Sylvanus, 58.
Delano, Sylvanus, 138.
Deman, John, 144.
Demay, Samuel, 124.
DMill, Anthony, 24.
DMill, Joseph, 24.
Deming, Abel, 53.
Deming, Abigail, 53.
Deming, Andrew, 68.
Deming, Anora, 53.
Deming, Asa, 53.
Deming, Asahel, 54.
Deming, Benjamin, 37.
Deming, Benjamin, 40.
Deming, Chancey, 40.
Deming, Daniel, 60.

Deming, Daniel, 60.
Deming, Daniel, 67.
Deming, Daniel, Jr., 53.
Deming, David, 33.
Deming, David, 36.
Deming, David, 37.
Deming, Ebenezer, 53.
Deming, Elezur, 52.
Deming, Eliakim, 54.
Deming, Elias, 54.
Deming, Elijah, 37.
Deming, Elizur, 54.
Deming, Ephraim, 54.
Deming, Frances, 53.
Deming, Frances, 54.
Deming, Frederic, 54.
Deming, Gideon, 47.
Deming, Hannah, 53.
Deming, Hannah, 54.
Deming, Henry, 52.
Deming, Hezekiah, 62.
Deming, Israel, 34.
Deming, Israel, 36.
Deming, Jacob, 34.
Deming, James, 52.
Deming, Jara, 54.
Deming, Jessee, 53.
Deming, Jiles, 54.
Deming, John, 33.
Deming, John, 40.
Deming, John, 53.
Deming, Jonathan, 67.
Deming, Jonth, 53.
Deming, Josiah, 52.
Deming, Josiah J., 98.
Deming, Josiah, Jr., 53.
Deming, Justus, 52.
Deming, Lardner, 33.
Deming, Leeman, 54.
Deming, Lemuel, 36.
Deming, Lemuel, Jr., 36.
Deming, Lucy, 49.
Deming, Mertain, 49.
Deming, Moses, 33.
Deming, Moses, 53.
Deming, Moses, Jr., 33.
Deming, Pelog, 68.
Deming, Peter, 53.
Deming, Richard, 52.
Deming, Robert, 54.
Deming, Roswell, 61.
Deming, Roswell, 65.
Deming, Samuel, 40.
Deming, Selah, 49.
Deming, Seth, 33.
Deming, Simeon, 53.
Deming, Tom, 67.
Deming (Wid.), 52.
Deming, William, 52.
Deming, William, Jr., 52.
Demmack, Joseph, Jr., 53.
Demmich, Solomon, 60.
Demmick, Samuel, 53.
Demming, Aaron, 134.
Demming, Bernard, 67.
Demming, Elizer, 131.
Demming, Jabez, 115.
Demming, Julius, 65.
Demming, Phineas, 78.
Demming, Wm, 131.
Demmon, Isaac, 73.
Demmon, Nathaniel, 21.
Demmonck, Joseph, 53.
Demmons, Charles, 101.
Demock, Jos., 139.
Demon, Joseph, 150.
Demon, Noah, 32.
Denham, Jonathan, 60.
Denis, Samuel, 102.
Denison, Amos, 116.
Denison, Andw, 116.
Denison, Asa, 90.
Denison, Ashbael, 124.
Denison, Avory, 115.
Denison, Beba, 117.
Denison, Beeba, 2d, 117.
Denison, Benadam, 130.
Denison, Chaney, 66.
Denison, Christopher, 65.
Denison, Daniel, 115.
Denison, Daniel, 143.
Denison, Daniel, Junr, 116.
Denison, Darius, 117.
Denison, David, 141.
Denison, Easter, 123.
Denison, Ebenezer, 89.
Denison, Eleazar, 129.
Denison, Elijah, 113.
Denison, Elisha, 115.
Denison, Elisha, 117.
Denison, Frederick, 117.
Denison, George, 90.
Denison, George, 116.
Denison, George, 117.
Denison, George, 125.
Denison, George, Junr, 117.
Denison, Gideon, 90.
Denison, Gilbert, 122.
Denison, Henry, 117.
Denison, Isaac, 117.
Denison, Jabez, 149.
Denison, James, 90.
Denison, James, 113.

INDEX. 175

Denison, Jedediah, 90.
Denison, John, 116.
Denison, Jn$^{o}$, 90.
Denison, John, 2$^{d}$, 117.
Denison, John, 3$^{d}$, 116.
Denison, John, 4$^{th}$, 117.
Denison, Jon$^{a}$, 120.
Denison, Jon$^{a}$, 134.
Denison, Joseph, 90.
Denison, Joseph, 116.
Denison, Joseph, Jun$^{r}$, 116.
Denison, Margarett, 125.
Denison, Martha, 103.
Denison, Mary, 89.
Denison, Mary, 117.
Denison, Nathan, 117.
Denison, Nathaniel, 116.
Denison, Nath$^{l}$, 152.
Denison, Oliver, 116.
Denison, Peleg, 116.
Denison, Pheba, 117.
Denison, Robart, 117.
Denison, Robert, 90.
Denison, Sam$^{l}$, 90.
Denison, Samuel, 123.
Denison, Stephen, 90.
Denison, Susanna, 152.
Denison, William, 65.
Denison, William, 117.
Denison, William, 124.
Denmore, Patty, 67.
Dennis, Benjamin, 130.
Dennis, Betsy, 117.
Dennis, George, 131.
Dennis, George, 2$^{d}$, 132.
Dennis, John, 105.
Dennis, John, 128.
Dennis, Russel, 131.
Dennis, Sam$^{l}$, 131.
Dennison, Jesse, 97.
Dennison, Jn$^{o}$, 90.
Dennison, Rohda, 103.
Denniss, Allyn, 52.
Denniss, Dusen, 53.
Denniss, Ebenezer, 45.
Denshy, Eli, 100.
Denshy, William, 100.
Denslow, Benjamin, 51.
Denslow, Elijah, 54.
Denslow, Joseph G., 54.
Denslow, Martin, 54.
Denslow, Reuben, 55.
Denslow, Samuel, 54.
Densmore, Obadiah, 42.
Denton, Benjamin, 22.
Denton, Humphry, 15.
Denty, Mathew, 133.
Deolph, Prissillah, 130.
Depeere, John, 28.
Derby, Erastus, 131.
Derby, Jedediah, 118.
Derby, John, 61.
Derly, Blanchard, 130.
Derly, Blanchard, Junr., 130.
Dersy (Negro), 125.
Derttrick, John, 125.
Deshon, Daniel, 129.
Deshon, Henry, 129.
Deshon, John, 126.
Deshon, Richard, 126.
Destouch, Sirace, 130.
Detne, Benj$^{a}$, 70.
Detray, Peter, 149.
Devenport, Benj$^{a}$, 133.
Devenport, Eliphalet, 121.
Devenport, John, 105.
Devenport, Paul, 142.
Devenport, Tho$^{s}$, 133.
Devenport, Umphry, 133.
Devenport, Welthy, 128.
Devenport, William, 119.
Devensport, Richard, 133.
Devensport, Richard, 133.
Devern, John, 27.
Devotion, Ebenez$^{r}$, 152.
Devotion, Rev$^{r}$ Jn$^{o}$, 90.
Dewey, Aaron, 45.
Dewey, Aaron, 136.
Dewey, Abraham, Jn$^{r}$, 146.
Dewey, Abraham, Sen$^{r}$, 146.
Dewey, Alpheus, 152.
Dewey, Barzeliel, 145.
Dewey, Christopher, 116.
Dewey, Dan$^{l}$, 146.
Dewey, David, 33.
Dewey, David, 45.
Dewey, David, 117.
Dewey, Deborah, 117.
Dewey, Eliphalet, 146.
Dewey, Eliph$^{t}$, 146.
Dewey, Isaac, 45.
Dewey, Israel, 82.
Dewey, Israel, 146.
Dewey, John, 43.
Dewey, John, 146.
Dewey, Joseph, 117.
Dewey, Jos$^{u}$, 134.
Dewey, Josiah, 33.
Dewey, Lemuel, 118.
Dewey, Lenar, 61.
Dewey, Sol$^{n}$, 132.
Dewey, Solomon, 146.
Dewey, Woodward, 146.
Dewing, Hez$^{a}$, 154.
Dewing, Michael, 154.
De Wint, Abraham N., 101.
De Wint, Garret N., 101.
De Witt, Garret, 101.
D$^{e}$ Witt, Jacob, 131.
De Witt, Peter, 103.
D Wolf, Benjamin, 60.
Dewolf, Elijah, 85.
Dewolf, Elijah, 2$^{d}$, 85.
D Wolf, Levi, 56.
D. Wolf, Stephen, 33.
D$^{e}$ Woolf, Stephen, 123.
Dewy, Isaac, 45.
Dewy, John, 51.
Dewy, Nathaniel, 37.
Dewy, Nathaniel, 37.
Dewy, Thomas, 37.
Dextar, Sarah, 57.
Dexter, Andrew, 144.
Dexter, Dan$^{l}$, 148.
Dexter, David, 148.
Dexter, Elisha, 119.
Dexter, Isaac, 148.
Dexter, Jona$^{th}$, 147.
Dexter Joseph, 144.
Dexter, Nathan, 147.
Dexter, Phillip, 144.
Dexter, Sam$^{l}$, 148.
Dexter, Seth, 54.
Dexte$^{r}$, Silas, 69.
Dexter, Silas, 147.
Dibbe, Benjamin, 57.
Dibbe, Clemens, 57.
Dibbe, John, 57.
Dibble, Anne (W$^{d}$), 26.
Dibble, Daniel, 12.
Dibble, Daniel, 62.
Dibble, David, 85.
Dibble, Ebenezer, 62.
Dibble, Rev$^{d}$ Ebenezer, 24.
Dibble, Eli, 12.
Dibble, Elisha, 11.
Dibble, Ezra, 10.
Dibble, Ezra, 12.
Dibble, Ezra, Ju$^{r}$, 10.
Dibble, George, 24.
Dibble, George, 57.
Dibble, George, 90.
Dibble, Isaac, 57.
Dibble, Israel, 57.
Dibble, Jane, 98.
Dibble, Jeddediah H., 12.
Dibble, John, 26.
Dibble, John, 89.
Dibble, John, 111.
Dibble, Jn$^{o}$ P., 90.
Dibble, Jonas, 90.
Dibble, Jonathan, 57.
Dibble, Josiah, 89.
Dibble, Levi, 10.
Dibble, Margret, 68.
Dibble, Martin, 90.
Dibble, Nathan, 12.
Dibble, Nehemiah, 12.
Dibble, Philo, 111.
Dibble, Samuel, 12.
Dibble, Silas, 57.
Dibble, Simus, 99.
Dibble, Simus, 2$^{nd}$, 100.
Dibble, Solomon, 25.
Dibble, Tar, 11.
Dibble, Thomas, 12.
Dibol, Benjamin, 43.
Dibol, Benjamin, Jr., 43.
Dibol, Dan., 44.
Dibol, Heman, 43.
Dibol, Levi, 43.
Dibol, Moses, 44.
Dibol, Moses, Jr., 44.
Dibol, Reuben, 44.
Dicingson, Thomas, 59.
Dick, Betty, 18.
Dick (negro), 81.
Dickemon, Ruth, 60.
Dickens, Arnold, 28.
Dickenson, Deborah (W$^{d}$), 23.
Dickenson, Ebenezer, 54.
Dickenson, Ebin, 60.
Dickenson, Elias, 53.
Dickenson, Elijah, 33.
Dickenson, Elisha, 60.
Dickenson, Friend, 65.
Dickenson, George, 50.
Dickenson, Hannah, 52.
Dickenson, Josiah, 54.
Dickenson Lucy, 52.
Dickenson, Molly, 59.
Dickenson, Moses, 33.
Dickenson, Moses, 45.
Dickenson, Nathaniel, 34.
Dickenson, Nathaniel, Jr., 34.
Dickenson, Obadiah, 54.
Dickenson, Ozias, 54.
Dickenson, Reuben, 59.
Dickenson, Samuel, 33.
Dickenson, Samuel, Jr., 33.
Dickenson, Susannah, 70.
Dickenson, Sylvanus, 101.
Dickenson, Wait, 54.
Dickenson, Wait S., 54.
Dickerman, Amos, 100.
Dickerman, Chauncy 100.
Dickerman, Hezekiah, 100.
Dickerman, Hezekiah, 101.
Dickerman, Isaac, 100.
Dickerman, Isaac, 105.
Dickerman, James, 100.
Dickerman, John, 100.
Dickerman, Jonathan, 100.
Dickerman, Jonathan, 2$^{nd}$, 100.
Dickerman, Joseph, 101.
Dickerman, Joseph, 105.
Dickerman, Loley, 100.
Dickerman, Louis, 101.
Dickerman, Timothy, 111.
Dickerson, Asahel, 57.
Dickerson, Benjamin, 105.
Dickerson, Elijah, 57.
Dickerson, Esther, 83.
Dickerson, Ichabod, 117.
Dickerson, Jacob, 86.
Dickerson, Obediah, 38.
Dickerson, Zadoc, 27.
Dickinson, David, 34.
Dickinson, David, 43.
Dickinson, David, 83.
Dickinson, David, Jr., 43.
Dickinson, David, 3$^{d}$, 43.
Dickinson, John, 83.
Dickinson, John, 86.
Dickinson, Joseph, 84.
Dickinson, Mehitible, 83.
Dickinson, Nathan, 43.
Dickinson, Nathan, Jr., 43.
Dickinson, Nath$^{l}$, 128.
Dickinson, Noah, 136.
Dickinson, Obediah, 83.
Dickinson, Olliver, 70.
Dickinson, Richard, 89.
Dickinson, Shirman, 66.
Dickinson, Simeon, 82.
Dickinson, Stephen, 83.
Dickinson, Thomas, 43.
Dicks, Charles, 60.
Dickson, William, 50.
Diggins, Augustus, 39.
Diggins, Joseph, 37.
Diggins, Luke, 46.
Diggins, Welles, 79.
Dightman, Daniel, 11.
Dightman, Thaddeus, 10.
Dightman, Thomas, 10.
Dike, James, 150.
Dike, Thomas, 150.
Dikeman, Daniel, 24.
Dikeman, Eliphalet, 32.
Dikeman, Frederick, 27.
Dikeman, Hezekiah, 31.
Dikeman, John, J$^{r}$, 24.
Dikeman, Levi, 21.
Dikerson, John, 59.
Dikingson, Thomas, 59.
Dikman, John, 32.
Dill, Solomon, 48.
Dilla, Riva, 145.
Dillabrose, Martin, 24.
Dillenor, Stephen, 69.
Dillenor, Thomas, 69.
Dillins (Wid.), 52.
Dimack, Jos., 139.
Dimick, Daniel, 96.
Dimmick, David, 63.
Dimmick, Edward, 147.
Dimmick, Lot, 147.
Dimmick, Shubael, 147.
Dimmik, Hez$^{ah}$, 147.
Dimmik, Joseph, 147.
Dimmock, Dan$^{l}$, 140.
Dimmock, Elias, 140.
Dimmock, Eliph$^{t}$, 147.
Dimmock, Isaac, 141.
Dimmock, Oliver, 147.
Dimmock, Peter, 148.
Dimmock, Timothy, 140.
Dimmock (Wid.), 142.
Dimock, Amasa, 137.
Dimock, Dan$^{l}$, 133.
Dimock, Jn$^{o}$, 137.
Dimock, Jn$^{o}$, Jr., 137.
Dimock, Sylvanus, 137.
Dimock, Tim$^{o}$, 133.
Dimock, Tim$^{o}$, 137.
Dimock, Tim$^{o}$, J$^{r}$, 133.
Dimon, Benjamin, 31.
Dimon, Daniel, 14.
Dimon, Gold, 20.
Dimon, Gold, 21.
Dimon, John, 32.
Dimon, Nimrod, 17.
Dimon, Samuel, 13.
Dimon, Thomas, 27.
Dimon, William, 14.
Dina (Negroe), 108.
Dinah (Negro), 118.
Dinah (Negroe), 103.
Dingley, John, 146.
Dinnison, John, 97.
Dirskall, Asa, 119.
Dirskall, Daniel, 125.
Disbrow, Asahel, 13.
Disbrow, Asahel, 19.
Disbrow, Elias, 13.
Disbrow, Hennery, 19.
Disbrow, Isaac, 13.
Disbrow, Jabez, 13.
Disbrow, Jason, 13.
Disbrow, John, 13.
Disbrow, Joseph, 19.
Disbrow, Joshua, 13.
Disbrow, Justis, 12.
Disbrow, Levi, 13.
Disbrow, Thaddeus, 13.
Diseum, James, 31.
Diseum, Robert, 31.
Diskom, Thomas, 30.
Disskoll, Adam, 131.
Distin, Josep, 108.
Dix, Benjamin, 54.
Dix, Charles, 52.
Dix, Elisha, 52.
Dix, Jacob, 52.
Dix, Leonard, 52.
Dix, Moses, 52.
Dix, Sarah, 52.
Dixon, Edw$^{d}$, 82.
Dixon, George, 19.
Dixon, James, 104.
Dixon, James, 143.
Dixon, John, 120.
Dixon, John, 151.
Dixon, John, 152.
Dixon, John, Sen$^{r}$, 151.
Dixon, Robart, 120.
Dixon, Robert, 151.
Dixon, Thomas, 129.
Dixon, Thomas, 143.
Dixon, Thomas, 151.
Dixon, Tho$^{s}$, 152.
Dixon, William, 79.
Dixon, William, 148.
Dixson, John, 24.
Doad, Amos, 35.
Doad, Ezra, 35.
Doad, Jesse, 35.
Doad, Stephen, 35.
Doan, Asaph, 80.
Doan, Elkanah, 90.
Doan, Israel, 90.
Doan, Joel, 90.
Doan, John, 89.
Doan, Nathaniel, 80.
Doan, Nathaniel, 2$^{d}$, 80.
Doan, Seth, 80.
Doan, Timothy, 80.
Doane, Nehemiah, 86.
Doane, Phinehas, 83.
Dodd, Bishop, 104.
Dodd, Elisha, 46.
Dodd, Guy, 104.
Dodd, John, 46.
Dodd, John, 104.
Dodd, Susan (Wid.), 46.
Dodd, Timothy, 46.
Dodg, Ira, 76.
Dodge, Benjamin, 122.
Dodge, Daniel, 122.
Dodge, David, 143.
Dodge, Edward, 147.
Dodge, Ephraim, 141.
Dodge, Eunice, 154.
Dodge, Ezra, 76.
Dodge, Ezra, 128.
Dodge, James, 126.
Dodge, Jeremiah, 124.
Dodge, Jonathan, 122.
Dodge, Jonathan, Jun$^{r}$, 122.
Dodge, Joshua, 112.
Dodge, Mary, 119.
Dodge, Nath$^{l}$, 139.
Dodge, Nehe$^{h}$, 149.
Dodge, Stephen, 58.
Dodge, Thomas, 121.
Dodge, William, 147.
Dogharty, Andrew, 25.
Dolbear, George, 125.
Dolebear, John, 124.
Dolebear, Sam$^{l}$, 125.
Dolittle, Phinehas, 28.
Domine (Negro), 122.
Donald, Lewis M., 25.
Donalds, Samuel, 101.
Donnalds, Samuel, 2$^{nd}$, 102.
Doolittle, Abner, 56.
Doolittle, Abner, 93.
Doolittle, Abraham, 86.
Doolittle, Abraham, 93.
Doolittle, Alisha, 88.
Doolittle, Ambrose, 93.
Doolittle, Amos, 93.
Doolittle, Amos, 104.
Doolittle, Ann, 109.
Doolittle, Barney, 93.
Doolittle, Benjamin, 71.
Doolittle, Benjamin, 93.
Doolittle, Benjamin, 108.
Doolittle, Benjamin H., 93.
Doolittle, Caleb, 100.
Doolittle, Charles, 108.
Doolittle, Daniel, 106.
Doolittle, Daniel, 107.
Doolittle, David, 60.
Doolittle, David, 88.
Doolittle, Easter, 100.
Doolittle, Ebenezer, 93.
Doolittle, Eliasaph, 76.
Doolittle, Elizabeth, 109.
Doolittle, Enos, 45.
Doolittle, Ephrahim, 93.
Doolittle, Ephraim, 33.
Doolittle, Ezra, 93.
Doolittle, Frederick, 71.
Doolittle, Hannah, 88.
Doolittle, Mrs. Hannah, 87.
Doolittle, Isaac, 93.
Doolittle, Isaac, 104.
Doolittle, Isaac, 104.
Doolittle, Isaac, 107.
Doolittle, Isaac, 108.
Doolittle, Jessee, 69.
Doolittle, Jessee, 69.
Doolittle, Joel, 88.
Doolittle, Joel, 108.
Doolittle, John, 56.
Doolittle, John, 109.
Doolittle, Johnson, 109.
Doolittle, Jonathan, 67.
Doolittle, Joseph, 88.
Doolittle, Joseph, 94.
Doolittle, Joseph, 106.
Doolittle, Joseph, 108.
Doolittle, Joshua, 86.
Doolittle, Margaret, 81.
Doolittle, Mosses, 93.
Doolittle, Obed, 93.
Doolittle, Obed, 93.
Doolittle, Oliver, 108.
Doolittle, Ruben, 94.
Doolittle, Ruben, 108.
Doolittle, Samuel, 93.
Doolittle, Samuel, 108.
Doolittle, Samuel, 2$^{d}$, 108.
Doolittle, Silas, 93.
Doolittle, Soloman, 109.
Doolittle, Thomas, 56.
Doolittle, Titus, 100.
Doolittle, Uri, 76.
Doras (Negro), 121.
Dorchester, Abigel, 104.
Dorchester, Dan$^{l}$, 132.
Dorchester, David, 132.
Dorchester, David, J$^{r}$, 132.
Dorchester, Ruben, 93.
Doreset, Jonathan, 140.
Doreset, Joseph, 142.
Dorman, Amassa, 103.
Dorman, Amos, 133.
Dorman, Benjamin, 100.
Dorman, Daniel, 100.
Dorman, Dan$^{l}$, 133.
Dorman, David, 103.
Dorman, Dudley, 133.
Dorman, Israel, 35.
Dorman, Joseph, 100.
Dorman, John, 100.
Dorman, Micajah, 139.
Dorman, Roger, 100.
Dorman, Samuel, 96.
Dorman, Samuel, 101.
Dorman, Samuel, 111.
Dorman, Stephen, 39.
Dorman, Stephen, 100.
Dormond, Garsham, 61.
Dornah, Edward, 138.
Dorod, John, 69.
Dorr, George, 124.
Dorr, Samuel, 52.
Dorrance, Alex$^{r}$, 143.
Dorrance, Archibald, 151.
Dorrance, David, 152.
Dorrance, George, 148.
Dorrance, Gershom, 113.
Dorrance, James, 141.
Dorrance, James, 152.
Dorrance, Lemuel, 151.
Dorrance, Sam$^{l}$, 143.
Dorrel, Thomas, 117.
Dorset, Joseph, 143.
Dorsey, Jeremiah, 69.
Dorson, Sibe, 63.
Dota, Timothy, 61.
Dota, Timothy, 2$^{d}$, 63.
Dota, William, 16.
Dotee, Sarah, 69.
Dothick, Ananias, 81.
Doty, Benjamin, 89.
Doty, Edward, 89.
Doubleday, Elisha, 145.
Doubleday, Jesse, 145.
Doubleday, Jos., 133.
Doud, Benjamin, 88.
Doud, Cornwell, 88.
Doud, Job, 99.
Doud, Moses, 99.
Doud, Peleg, 65.
Doud, Phebe, 88.
Doud, Richard, 88.
Doud, Samuel, 65.
Dougal, David, 104.
Dougal, James, 103.
Douglas, David, 126.
Douglas, Hannah, 92.
Douglas, Samuel, 70.
Douglass, Dan$^{l}$, 90.
Douglass, Daniel, 127.
Douglass, Ebenezer, 128.
Douglass, Israel, 90.
Douglass, James, 148.
Douglass, John, 107.
Douglass, John, 148.
Douglass, John, 151.
Douglass, John, Sen$^{r}$, 151.

35201—08——12

# INDEX.

Douglass, Jonathan, 128.
Douglass, Levi, 107.
Douglass, Mary, 129.
Douglass, Nathan, 10.
Douglass, Richard, 128.
Douglass, Richard, 1st, 128.
Douglass, Sam¹, 151.
Douglass, Sperry, 128.
Douglass, Stephen, 126.
Douglass, William, 86.
Douglass, William, 151.
Douglass, William, Jnr, 151.
Dove, Jack, 96.
Dow, Abel, 140.
Dow, Benjn, 151.
Dow, Calvin, 133.
Dow, Ebenr, 151.
Dow, Em, 133.
Dow, Em, 2d, 133.
Dow, Levy, 133.
Dow, Nathan, 151.
Dow, Pelitiah, 134.
Dow, Sam¹, 148.
Dow, Umphus, 134.
Dowd, Abraham, 99.
Dowd, Asa, 99.
Dowd, Asa, 2nd, 99.
Dowd, Dedimos, 99.
Dowd, Ebenezer, 99.
Dowd, Jeremiah, 99.
Dowd, John, 99.
Dowd, Joseph, 99.
Dowd, Miles, 99.
Dowd, Ruben, 99.
Dowd, Soloman, 99.
Dowd, Thomas, 99.
Dowd, Timothy, 99.
Dow'd, Zachariah, 99.
Dow'd, Zachariah, 2nd, 99.
Dowe, Abel, 140.
Dowe, Cyrus, 140.
Dowe, John, 148.
Dowing, Dan¹, 142.
Dowing, Jonan, 142.
Down, Benjamin, 105.
Down, Job, 105.
Down, Nathaniel, 105.
Downer, Avory, 114.
Downer, Joshua, 114.
Downer, Richard, 126.
Downer, Uriah, 126.
Downes, Aaron, 73.
Downes, Benjamin, 73.
Downes, Ebenezer, 73.
Downes, Elijah, 71.
Downes, Jonathan, 71.
Downes, Jonathan, 2d, 71.
Downes, Lemuel, 71.
Downes, Moses, 73.
Downes, Nathan, 73.
Downes, Simeon, 78.
Downes, Susannah, 78.
Downes, Thomas, 71.
Downes, Truman, 73.
Downes, Wildman, 73.
Downey, James, 105.
Downing, Benjan, 152.
Downing, Christopher, 130.
Downing, Henry, 142.
Downing, Jededh, 141.
Downing, John, 114.
Downing, Jonath, 143.
Downing, Phineas, 142.
Downing, Phineas, Ju., 142.
Downing, Stephen, 142.
Downs, Abel, 13.
Downs, Chauncy, 13.
Downs, David, 62.
Downs, Ebenezur, 111.
Downs, Elizabeth, 107.
Downs, Felix, 111.
Downs, Griffin, 98.
Downs, Jacob, 111.
Downs, John, 13.
Downs, John, 17.
Downs, John, 102.
Downs, John, 2nd, 102.
Downs, Joseph, 13.
Downs, Joseph, 18.
Downs, Joseph, 111.
Downs, Joseph, 112.
Downs, Joseph, 115.
Downs, Joshua, 115.
Downs, Mary, 13.
Downs, Nathaniel, 103.
Downs, Samuel, 111.
Downs, Samuel, 2nd, 111.
Downs, Sarah, 107.
Downs, Sarah, 112.
Downs, Sarah, 114.
Downs, Seth, 111.
Downs, William, 24.
Downs, Woolcot, 23.
Dowsack, Gospur, 123.
Dowse, Mary, 28.
Dowsett, Amos, 124.
Doxey, Henry, 87.
Doyle, John, 87.
Doyle, Peter, 127.
Doyle, Richard, 132.
Doyt, Abiel, 154.
Doyt, James, 154.
Drake, Abiel, 38.

Drake, Amasa, 38.
Drake, David, 38.
Drake, David, 54.
Drake, Dorson, 54.
Drake, Dudley, 55.
Drake, Ebenezer, 39.
Drake, Elihu, 55.
Drake, Gideon, 39.
Drake, Joel, 55.
Drake, Joseph, 55.
Drake, Joseph, 103.
Drake, Levy, 137.
Drake, Lora, 54.
Drake, Martha, 45.
Drake, Moses, 38.
Drake, Moses, 55.
Drake, Nathaniel, 39.
Drake, Nathaniel, Jr., 39.
Drake, Noah, 55.
Drake, Noah, 60.
Drake, Phinehas, 54.
Drake, Phinehas, Jnr, 55.
Drake, Reuben, 38.
Drake, Samuel, 55.
Drake, Shubel, 39.
Drake, Silas, 39.
Drake, Simeon, 39.
Drakeley, Samuel, 73.
Draper, Aaron, 52.
Draper, Fisher, 113.
Draper, Giddeon, 19.
Dresser, Asa, 150.
Dresser, Ebenr, 149.
Dresser, Jacob, 150.
Dresser, John, 149.
Dresser, Nathan, 149.
Dresser, Sam¹, 149.
Dresser, Simeon, 65.
Drew, Isaac, 27.
Drew, John, 27.
Drew, John, 27.
Drew, Peter, 27.
Driggs, Bartholomew, 35.
Driggs, Daniel, 34.
Driggs, Israel, 86.
Driggs, Martin, 59.
Driggs, John, 87.
Driggs, Jno, 132.
Driggs, Joseph, 87.
Driggs, Joseph, Junr, 87.
Drigs, Daniel, 65.
Drinkwater, Ebenezer B., 120.
Driskill, Timothy, 19.
Driver, Lidia, 112.
Drone, Prince, 90.
Drownd, Nathaniel, 43.
Drowney, Mary, 105.
Dudley, Abigal, 100.
Dudley, Abraham, 98.
Dudley, Ambrose, 99.
Dudley, Amos, 98.
Dudley, Anne, 89.
Dudley, Asahel, 88.
Dudley, Asel, 29.
Dudley, Barzilla, 83.
Dudley, Bela, 99.
Dudley, Caleb, 98.
Dudley, Caleb, 2d, 98.
Dudley, Cyprian, 91.
Dudley, David, 99.
Dudley, David, 99.
Dudley, Dyer, 108.
Dudley, Eber, 98.
Dudley, Elizabeth, 99.
Dudley, Elisha, 89.
Dudley, George, 73.
Dudley, Gilbert, 99.
Dudley, Isaac, 88.
Dudley, Jane, 98.
Dudley, Jedediah, 89.
Dudley, Jerad, 99.
Dudley, Jerad, 2d, 99.
Dudley, John, 108.
Dudley, Jonathan, 98.
Dudley, Joseph, 99.
Dudley, Josiah, 99.
Dudley, Luther, 99.
Dudley, Medad, 99.
Dudley, Mercy, 100.
Dudley, Miles, 61.
Dudley, Nathaniel, 85.
Dudley, Nathaniel, 98.
Dudley, Nicholas, 140.
Dudley, Phinehas, 85.
Dudley, Roswell, 99.
Dudley, Sam¹, 89.
Dudley, Samuel, 99.
Dudley, Selah, 99.
Dudley, Simeon, 99.
Dudley, Stephen, 99.
Dudley, Thomas, 98.
Dudley, Thomas, 104.
Dudley, William, 70.
Dudley, Zebulon, 108.
Duglass, Daniel, 132.
Duglass, George, 127.
Duglass, James, 127.
Duglass, James, 2d, 127.
Duglass, John, 122.
Duglass, Joseph, 126.
Duglass, Joshua, 125.
Duglass, Nathaniel, 107.
Duglass, Robart, 122.

Duglass, Sam¹, 127.
Duglass, Silvanus, 127.
Duglass, Thomas, 127.
Duglass, William, 127.
Duglis, Moses, 60.
Dugliss, Benajah, 69.
Dukerman, Elisha, 105.
Dulongpre, Ann, 132.
Dulop, James, 142.
Dummer, Abraham, 103.
Dummer, Edward, 104.
Dummer, Jonathan, 105.
Dummer, Nathaniel, 103.
Dummer, Stephen, 103.
Dumnum, Sam¹, 139.
Dun, Michael, 16.
Dunam, Jabez, 51.
Dunam, Jabez, 2d, 51.
Dunbar, Aaron, 76.
Dunbar, Amos, 76.
Dunbar, Benjn, 137.
Dunbar, David, 76.
Dunbar, Jabe, 136.
Dunbar, Joel, 76.
Dunbar, Jonathan, 76.
Dunbar, Joseph, 76.
Dunbar, Miles, 76.
Dunbarr, David, 66.
Duncam, Edward, 31.
Duncan, Charls, 29.
Duncan, Daniel, 31.
Duncan, Jerard, 32.
Duncan, William, 150.
Duncomb, John, 14.
Dunham, Bangs, 147.
Dunham, Barnabus, 33.
Dunham, Cornelius, 49.
Dunham, Daniel, 145.
Dunham, Dan¹, 147.
Dunham, Dan¹, 147.
Dunham, Dan¹, 148.
Dunham, David, 33.
Dunham, Eleazer, 121.
Dunham, Eleazer, 2d, 121.
Dunham, Elezer, 133.
Dunham, Elisha, 147.
Dunham, Elishama, 34.
Dunham, George, 152.
Dunham, Hannah, 146.
Dunham, Isaac, 58.
Dunham, Isaac, 70.
Dunham, Isacc, 135.
Dunham, Jacob, 147.
Dunham, James, 70.
Dunham, James, 147.
Dunham, John, 140.
Dunham, John, 148.
Dunham, Jonath, 147.
Dunham, Levi, 43.
Dunham, Phebe, 147.
Dunham, Seth, 147.
Dunham, Solomon, 34.
Dunham, Solomon, 49.
Dunham, Stephen, 133.
Dunham, Timo, 135.
Dunham, Warner, 34.
Dunham, William, 121.
Dunlap, Brias, 52.
Dunlop, Joshua, 148.
Dunlop, Ledly, Jn., 148.
Dunn, Reuben, 25.
Dunn, Samuel, 44.
Dunn, Timothy, 96.
Dunn, Timothy, 2d, 96.
Dunnam, Jonathan, 60.
Dunnen, Benjamin, 17.
Dunnen, Eli, 10.
Dunnen, Giddeon, 10.
Dunnen, Isaac, 17.
Dunnen, Jered, 10.
Dunnen, Jeremiah, 10.
Dunnen, John, 10.
Dunnen, Jno, 90.
Dunnen, John, Jur, 10.
Dunnen, Joseph, 10.
Dunnen, Liverius, 10.
Dunnen, Luther, 10.
Dunnen, Nathan, 10.
Dunnen, Reubin, 10.
Dunnen, Woolcott, 10.
Dunnin, David, 23.
Dunning, Aaron, 23.
Dunning, Benjamin, 74.
Dunning, Daniel, 23.
Dunning, Elias, 56.
Dunning, Ezra, 71.
Dunning, Moses, 23.
Dunning, Richard, 21.
Dunning, Samuel, 71.
Dunnum, Jona, 135.
Dunnum, Jona, 135.
Dunoty, Francis, 137.
Dunton, Ebenezer, 129.
Dunton, John, 120.
Dunwell, Stephen, 114.
Dunworth, Charles, 148.
Duplax, Prince, 50.
Dupu, Lims, 52.
Duran, Joseph, 22.
Durand, Ebenezer, 94.
Durand, Elizabeth, 94.
Durand, Elizur, 94.
Durand, John, 94.

Durand, Joseph, 94.
Durand, Nemiah, 94.
Durand, Noah, 94.
Durand, Noah, 2nd, 94.
Durand, Noah, 3rd, 94.
Durand, Samuel, 75.
Durand, Samuel, 109.
Durany, Andrew, 2nd, 93.
Durfee, James, 118.
Durfee, John, 144.
Durfee, Sarah, 127.
Durfee, Thomas, 127.
Durfee, William, 144.
Durfey, Jos., 134.
Durfy, Eber, 134.
Durham, David, 52.
Durham, Silvanus, 49.
Durin, Jonathan, 50.
Durin, Noah, 50.
Durivage, Nicholas, 128.
Durke, Andrew, 143.
Durke, Eliphr, 143.
Durke, Henry, 143.
Durke, Jereh, 143.
Durke, Wm, Jnr, 143.
Durkee, Benjn, 143.
Durkee, Benjn, 149.
Durkee, Sabin, 126.
Durkee, William, 126.
Durkee, William, 143.
Durker, Benjamin, 75.
Durker, Jedediah, 75.
Durkerson, Robert, 75.
Durow, Daniel, 107.
Durrany, Samuel, 93.
Durren, Stephen, 41.
Dursy, Thomas, Junr, 31.
Durvin, Jonathan, 50.
Dutcher, Gabriel, 69.
Dutcher, Rulef, 59.
Dutcher, Ruluf, 3d, 69.
Dutton, Amasa, 82.
Dutton, Ambrose, 145.
Dutton, Amos, 109.
Dutton, Benjamin, 50.
Dutton, Benjamin, Jr., 50.
Dutton, Ebenr, 145.
Dutton, Eunice, 109.
Dutton, Joel, 19.
Dutton, John, 70.
Dutton, Joseph, 50.
Dutton, Joseph, 82.
Dutton, Moses, 50.
Dutton, Oliver, 35.
Dutton, Ose, 95.
Dutton, P. Samuel, 76.
Dutton, Russel, 82.
Dutton, Samuel, 50.
Dutton, Sarah, 76.
Dutton, Sam¹, 82.
Dutton, Thomas, 109.
Dutton, Thomas, 2d, 76.
Dutton, Thomas, 3d, 76.
Dutton, Timothy, 50.
Dutton, Timo, 135.
Dutton, William, 43.
Duvit, Henry, 152.
Dwight, ——, 45.
Dwight, Alpheus, 136.
Dwight, Jos., 136.
Dwight, Samuel, 104.
Dwight, Timothy, 13.
Dwight, Timothy, 103.
Dwight, William, 150.
Dyars, Andrew, 32.
Dycer, Benjamin, 49.
Dycer, Solomon, 49.
Dycer, Thomas, 48.
Dycer, Thomas, Jr, 48.
Dye, Daniel, 58.
Dye, Easter, 115.
Dye, Elizabeth, 58.
Dye, William, 116.
Dyer, Benjamin, 153.
Dyer, Daniel, 49.
Dyer, Daniel, 49.
Dyer, Ebenr, 142.
Dyer, Elijah, 142.
Dyer, Hone Eliphalet, 152.
Dyer, James, 140.
Dyer, James, 142.
Dyer, Jareh, Sr., 142.
Dyer, John, 149.
Dyer, Joseph, 41.
Dyer, Thomas, 152.
Dyer, William, 96.
Dyian, Philip, 129.
Dykeman, Jonathan, 29.
Dyre, Eliphalet, 60.

Eads, Eleazer, 122.
Eagleston, Elizabeth, 97.
Eagleston, James, 56.
Eales, John, 120.
Eales, Joseph, 117.
Eames, Cumfort, 113.
Eames, Dan¹, 125.
Eames, Daniel, 126.
Eames, Ebenezer, 125.
Eames, John, 113.
Eames, John, 122.
Eames, John, 125.
Eames, Joseph, 115.

Eames, Joseph, 126.
Eames, Joseph, 127.
Eames, Josiah, 126.
Eames, Lucy, 122.
Eames, Mack, 144.
Eames, Sam¹, 126.
Eames, Sam¹, 144.
Earl, Rafal, 65.
Earle, Benjamin, 71.
Easter (Negro), 131.
Easterbrook, Moses, 154.
Easterbrooks, Oliver, 154.
Easterbrooks, Peleg, 154.
Eastman, Abner, 78.
Eastman, Ebenr, 141.
Eastman, Federich, 78.
Eastman, Joseph, 18.
Eastman, Peter, 106.
Eastman, Peter, 140.
Eastman, Vespatian, 78.
Eastmon, Azeriah, 78.
Eastmon, Benjamin, 78.
Easton, Eliphlet, 78.
Easton, Ephraim, 42.
Easton, James, 36.
Easton, Joseph, 75.
Easton, Norman, 78.
Easton, Samuel, 36.
Easton, Silas, 36.
Easton, Timothy, 42.
Eaton, Aaron, 137.
Eaton, Daniel, 35.
Eaton, Ebenr, 140.
Eaton, Ebenr, 148.
Eaton, Elisabeth, 140.
Eaton, Ezek¹, Jr., 141.
Eaton, Jacob, 147.
Eaton, Jno, 137.
Eaton, Jno, 137.
Eaton, John & co., 144.
Eaton, Joshua, 152.
Eaton, Josiah, 140.
Eaton, Justus, 91.
Eaton, Moses, 58.
Eaton, Nath¹, 147.
Eaton, Samuel, 40.
Eaton, Sam¹, 137.
Eaton, Sam¹, 137.
Eaton, Samuel, Jr., 40.
Eaton, Solm, 138.
Eaton, Timothy, 106.
Eaton, Timothy, 144.
Eaton, Titus, 106.
Eaton, Wm, 137.
Ecels, Samuel, 92.
Eddington, Isaac, 48.
Eddy, Asa, 63.
Eddy, Benjn, 153.
Eddy, Charles, 33.
Eddy, John, 63.
Eddy, Levy, 154.
Eddy, Lew, 153.
Eddy, Seveus, 84.
Edee, John, 95.
Eden, David, 16.
Edgarton, Nathan, 69.
Edgcomb, David, 119.
Edgcomb, Jabez, 119.
Edgcomb, Jesse, 127.
Edgcomb, John, 126.
Edgcomb, Sam¹, 119.
Edgcomb, Sam¹, Junr, 119.
Edgerly, John, 15.
Edgerton, Abel, 130.
Edgerton, Abel, 146.
Edgerton, Ariel, 129.
Edgerton, Dan¹, 138.
Edgerton, David, 146.
Edgerton, Elisha, 130.
Edgerton, Elizabeth, 129.
Edgerton, Hannah, 129.
Edgerton, Hezekiah, 130.
Edgerton, Hezekiah, Junr, 130.
Edgerton, Jabez, 133.
Edgerton, James, 129.
Edgerton, Jedediah, 48.
Edgerton, John, 146.
Edgerton, Jonathan, 48.
Edgerton, Jos. Kingsbury, 129.
Edgerton, Lucy, 129.
Edgerton, Nathan, 129.
Edgerton, Oliver, 138.
Edgerton, Samuel, 129.
Edgerton, Simon, 129.
Edgerton, Stephen, 130.
Edgerton, Zebulon, 129.
Edgerton, Zebulon, Junr, 120.
Edgiton, Samuel, 78.
Edmond, Jeames, 73.
Edmond, John, 73.
Edmond, Robert, 28.
Edmonds, Andrew, 151.
Edmonds, William, 19.
Edmunds, ——, 128.
Edson, Benjn, 134.
Edson, Calvin, 137.
Edson, Eliab, 137.
Edson, Jacob, 137.
Edson, Levi, 137.
Edson, Peter, 137.
Edson, Teracy, 41.
Edward, Asahel, 76.
Edward, Christopher, 115.

# INDEX.

Edward, Ebenezer, 71.
Edward, Edward, 71.
Edward, Isaac, 29.
Edward, Isaac, 76.
Edward, John, 78.
Edward, Joseph, 76.
Edward, Mary, 58.
Edward, Nathaniel, 76.
Edward (Negro), 121.
Edward, Samuel, 29.
Edward, Warham, 133.
Edwards, Abel, 30.
Edwards, Adonijah, 133.
Edwards, Ager, 17.
Edwards, Benajah, 134.
Edwards, Churchel, Junr, 88.
Edwards, Churchell, 88.
Edwards, Couh, 30.
Edwards, Cuff (Negroe), 104.
Edwards, Daniel, 87.
Edwards, Danl, Jr., 142.
Edwards, David, 30.
Edwards, David, 30.
Edwards, David, 30.
Edwards, David, 51.
Edwards, David, 131.
Edwards, David, Junr, 88.
Edwards, Elnathan, 30.
Edwards, Henery, 43.
Edwards, Hezekiah, 30.
Edwards, Isaac, 31.
Edwards, Jabez, 138.
Edwards, Jame, 133.
Edwards, John, 30.
Edwards, John, 53.
Edwards, John, 2d, 53.
Edwards, John, 3d, 30.
Edwards, Jonathan, 51.
Edwards, Jonathan, 106.
Edwards, Revd Jonathan, 104.
Edwards, Josiah, 34.
Edwards, Josiah, 76.
Edwards, Josu, 133.
Edwards, Nehemiah, 30
Edwards, Peleg, 115.
Edwards, Perpont, 104.
Edwards, Reuben, 30.
Edwards, Rhodolfus, 38.
Edwards, Roger, 128.
Edwards, Theophlus, 29.
Edwards, Thomas, 30.
Edwards, Warham, 133.
Edwards, William, 17.
Edwards, William, 114.
Edy, John, Junr, 80.
Edy, John, 3d, 80.
Edy, Seth, 79.
Edy, Thomas, 79.
Egeton, Ebenezer, 44.
Egeton, Ebenezer Jr., 44.
Eggleston, Ephm, 55.
Eggleston, Jonathan, 55.
Eggleston, Joseph, 38.
Eggleston, Nathl, 55.
Eggleston, Saml, 55.
Eglestom, Bennet, 85.
Egleston, Elihu, 45.
Egleston, John, 76.
Eglestone, Benedick, 115.
Eglestone, David, 115.
Eglestone, Dennis, 115.
Eglestone, Ichabod, 115.
Eglestone, Ichabod, Junr, 115.
Eglestone, Ichabod, 3d, 115.
Eglestone, Joseph, 115.
Eglestone, Joseph, 115.
Eglestone, Winlock, 115.
Eld, Richard, 103.
Elden, John, 58.
Elderkin, Alfred, 152.
Elderkin, Bela, 152.
Elderkin, Elisabeth, 118.
Elderkin, Elisha, 85.
Elderkin, Frederick, 131.
Elderkin, James, 85.
Elderkin, James, 131.
Elderkin, Jedediah, 78.
Elderkin, Jedediah, 152.
Elderkin, John, 130.
Elderkin, Joshua, 152.
Elderkin, Joshua B., 152.
Elderkin, Lyda, 152.
Elderkin, Martha, 131.
Elderkin, Roxa, 118.
Eldred, Elisha, 74.
Eldred, Jehoshaphet, 74.
Eldred, Judah, 74.
Eldred, Samuel, 74.
Eldred, Ward, 74.
Eldredge, John, 65.
Eldridge, Charles, 118.
Eldridge, Charles, Junr, 118.
Eldridge, Christopher, 116.
Eldridge, Elisha, 147.
Eldridge, Hezekiah, 140.
Eldridge, James, 141.
Eldridge, Jesse, 139.
Eldridge, John, 70.
Eldridge, Jos., 139.
Eldridge, Lemuel, 148.
Eldridge, Micajah H., 139.
Eldridge, Saml, 118.
Eldridge, Solomon, 137.

Eldridge, Stepha, 140.
Eldridge (Wid.), 139.
Eldridge, Wm, 139.
Eldridge, Zooth, 139.
Eldrige, Daniel, 120.
Eldrige, James, 120.
Eldrige, Jonathan, 123.
Eldrige, Thomas, 2d, 120.
Elethrop, Jno, 137.
Elethrop, Saml, 137.
Elexander, James, 116.
Elexander, William, 119.
Elgar, Ezra, 30.
Elggleston, Thoms, 55.
Eli, Daniel, 54.
Eli, David, 17.
Eli, Ephraim, 38.
Eli (Negroe), 104.
Elie (Negro), 85.
Eliot, Abraham, 58.
Eliot, Andrew, 14.
Eliot, James, 117.
Eliot, Nathan, 58.
Eliott, Aaron, 85.
Eliott, George, Esqr, 85.
Eliott, Jarod, 85.
Eliott, Jerod, Junr, 85.
Eliott, John, Esqr, 87.
Eliott, William, 85.
Elis, Oliver, 136.
Elithorp, Henry, 150.
Elithorp, Nathl, 150.
Ellery, William, 45.
Elles, Benjamin, 118.
Elles, Jeremiah, 22.
Elles, Jeremiah B., 23.
Elles, John, 22.
Elles, Revd John, 42.
Elles, Moses C., 23.
Elliot, Asael, 150.
Elliot, Daniel, 129.
Elliot, Francis, 150.
Elliot, Joel, 150.
Elliot, John, 116.
Elliot, John, 150.
Elliot, John, 150.
Elliot, Joseph, 97.
Elliot, Mary, 117.
Elliot, Roger, 150.
Elliot, Saml, 150.
Elliot, Thomas, 150.
Elliot, Thos, Jnr, 150.
Elliot, Tom, 67.
Elliot, William, 143.
Elliott, Abigal, 97.
Elliott, Clark, 128.
Elliott, Elijah, 97.
Elliott, John, 2nd, 97.
Elliott, Nathaniel, 97.
Elliott, Ezra, 150.
Elliott, Timothy, 100.
Elliott, William, 97.
Ellis, Benjamin, 129.
Ellis, Benja, 137.
Ellis, Jacob, 149.
Ellis, Cyrus, 137.
Ellis, Daniel, 88.
Ellis, Daniel, 130.
Ellis, Edward, 118.
Ellis, Hester, 101.
Ellis, Jabez, 135.
Ellis, Revd James, 43.
Ellis, John, 129.
Ellis, Jno, 133.
Ellis, John, 140.
Ellis, Jonath, 150.
Ellis, Joseph, 130.
Ellis, Jos., 137.
Ellis, Nathaniel, 88.
Ellis, Nathl, 133.
Ellis, Samuel, 101.
Ellis, Samuel, 114.
Ellis, Samuel, 2nd, 101.
Ellis, Sibel, 101.
Ellis, Stephen, 130.
Ellis, Timothy, 18.
Ellis, Timo, 137.
Ellis (Widow), 132.
Ellis, William, 130.
Ells, Joseph, 102.
Ells, Linthell, 110.
Ells, Ozias, 68.
Ellsworth, John, 79.
Elmer, Eliakim, 55.
Elmer, Elijah, 55.
Elmer, Hezekiah, 12.
Elmer, Phinehas, 55.
Elmer, Wm, 136.
Elmon, Alexander, 70.
Elmon, John, 67.
Elmore, Aaron, 36.
Elmore, Abiath, 60.
Elmore, Augustus, 39.
Elmore, Daniel, 39.
Elmore, Eliphalet, 37.
Elmore, Elizabeth, 37
Elmore, Elja, 63.
Elmore, Jacob, 38.
Elmore, Joel, 38.
Elmore, Joseph, 37.
Elmore, Joseph, 63.
Elmore, Noadiah, 38.
Elmore, Roswell, 37.

Elmore, Saml, 59.
Elmore, Stephen, 37.
Elmore, Timothy, 37.
Elsworth, ——, 56.
Elsworth, Benjamin, 38.
Elsworth, Charles, 38.
Elsworth, Charles, 134.
Elsworth, Daniel, 38.
Elsworth, Daniel, 134.
Elsworth, David, 54.
Elsworth, Ebenr, 54.
Elsworth, Eliza, 54.
Elsworth, Frederic, 38.
Elsworth, Giles, 54.
Elsworth, Gordon, 134.
Elsworth, Grove, 54.
Elsworth, Job, 39.
Elsworth, Joel, 38.
Elsworth, Jonah, 54.
Elsworth, Josiah, 38.
Elsworth, Mary, 40.
Elsworth, Migail, 54.
Elsworth, Honbl Oliver, Esqr., 54.
Elsworth, Solomon, 39.
Elsworth, Thomas, 69.
Elsworth, William 40.
Elton, Bradley, 88.
Elton, Ebenees, 47.
Elton, Ebenezer, 76.
Elton, John, 76.
Elton, Joseph, 58.
Elton, Wm, 35.
Elvendolf, Tobias, 70.
Elwell, Isaac, 50.
Elwell, James, 99.
Elwell, Samuel, 92.
Elwood, Abijah, 13.
Elwood, Abraham, 13.
Elwood, Hezekiah, 12.
Elwood, Joseph, 32.
Elwood, Nathan, 12.
Elwood, Richard, 12.
Elwood, Rion, 20.
Elwood, Thomas, 14.
Ely, Abner, 122.
Ely, Adriel, 123.
Ely, Amy, 123.
Ely, Ann, 123.
Ely, Christopher, 123.
Ely, Cullick, 123.
Ely, Cullick, Junr, 123.
Ely, Daniel, 123.
Ely, David, 123.
Ely, Denison, 123.
Ely, Elihu, 123.
Ely, Elijah, 122.
Ely, Elisha, 89.
Ely, Ezra, 123.
Ely, Gabriel, 81.
Ely, Gabriel, 123.
Ely, Gurden, 123.
Ely, Revr Henry, 85.
Ely, Jacob, 58.
Ely, Jacob, 83.
Ely, James, 123.
Ely, Jno, 90.
Ely, Josiah, 123.
Ely, Marsh, 123.
Ely, Moses, 83.
Ely, Richard, 62.
Ely, Revr Richard, 89.
Ely, Robert, 89.
Ely, Seth, 122.
Ely, Welles, 123.
Ely, William, 83.
Ely, Zebulon, 145.
Emerson, Abraham, 122.
Emerson, Abraham, 2d, 122.
Emerson, Jabez, 133.
Emerson, Jabez 134.
Emerson, Joseph, 40.
Emerson, Joseph, 128.
Emerson, Simeon, 150.
Emerson, Stephen, 122.
Emmons, Abner, 65.
Emmons, Arther, 65.
Emmons, Arther, 2d, 65.
Emmons, Daniel, 83.
Emmons, Ebenezer, 83.
Emmons, Ithamar, 83.
Emmons, Jonathan, 69.
Emmons, Joseph, 81.
Emmons, Lydia, 65.
Emmons, Noadh, 82.
Emmons, Oliver, 65.
Emmons, Orrange, 65.
Emmons, Phinehas, 65.
Emmons, Russel, 65.
Emmons, Saml, 83.
Emmons, Williams, 60.
Emons, Asa, 57.
Emons, Asaph, 57.
Emons, Simeon, 57.
Emons, Soloman, 57.
Emons, Susanna, 42.
Emons, Woodruff, 57.
Eneas, Jos., 138.
English, Abiel, 146.
English, Benjamin, 102.
English, Clement, 94.
Eno, Abel, 49.

Eno, Ashbel, 55.
Eno, Eliphealet, 62.
Eno, Elisha, 44.
Eno, Isaac, 48.
Eno, Ive, 48.
Eno, James, 56.
Eno, Joel, 48.
Eno, Jonathan, 47.
Eno, Reuben, 48.
Eno, Samuel, 48.
Enos, Daniel, 64.
Enos, David, 44.
Enos, David, 49.
Enos, John, 120.
Enos, Joshua, 120.
Enos Saml, 56.
Ensign, Amos, 54.
Ensign, Elijah, 47.
Ensign, Eliphalet, 60.
Ensign, Eliphalet, 70.
Ensign, Elizer, 68.
Ensign, Isaac, 48.
Ensign, James, 46.
Ensign, John, 61.
Ensign, John, 67.
Ensign, Moses, 36.
Ensign, Moses, 46.
Ensign, Samuel, 59.
Ensign, Solomon, 47.
Ensign, Thomas, 46.
Ensign, Thomas, Jr., 45.
Ensign, Timothy, 68.
Ensignor, Daniel, 68.
Eran (Negroee), 109.
Esmon, Nathan, 69.
Estes, Stephen, 137.
Estherbrooks, Hobert, 82.
Ethridge, Sarah, 118.
Etton, Recompence, 63.
Evans, Benjamin, 68.
Evans, Daniel, 27.
Evans, Evan, 102.
Evans, Isaac, 68.
Evans, John, 62.
Evans, Joseph, 23.
Evans, Josiah, 37.
Evans, Luther, 49.
Evans, Moses, 37.
Evans, Thos, 132.
Evaritt, Ebenezer, 63.
Evarts, David, 85.
Evarts, Ebenezer, 65.
Evarts, Joseph, 84.
Evarts, Saml, 65.
Evens, Allyn, 39.
Evens, Arad, 147.
Evens, Benoni, 36.
Evens, David, 37.
Evens, Elisha, 36.
Evens, Ezekiel, 37.
Evens, Samuel, 37.
Evens, Samuel, Jr., 37.
Evens, William, 92.
Everden, Walter, 150.
Everest, Daniel, 57.
Everct, Richard, 21.
Everist, Solomon, 41.
Everit, Daniel, 56.
Everit, Daniel, 71.
Everit, Ebenezer, 63.
Everit, Eunice, 56.
Everit, Josiah, 63.
Everitt, Isaah, 63.
Everitt, Isaiah, 67.
Eversley, John, 21.
Everston, Hannah, 57.
Everts, Maryan, 70.
Everts, Nathan, 70.
Everts, Stephen, 71.
Everts, Submit, 70.
Evertson, Evert, 22.
Eveth, Daniel, 62.
Eveton, William, 97.
Evets, Ambrose, 99.
Evets, Aron, 98.
Evets, Stephen, 64.
Evett, Daniel, 98.
Evett, David, 98.
Evett, Isaac, 98.
Evett, Lucy, 98.
Evett, Moses, 98.
Evett, Samuel, 98.
Evett, Stephen, 98.
Evett, Timothy, 98.
Evett, Timothy, 2nd, 98.
Evetts, Abraham, 98.
Evetts, Benjamin, 98.
Evetts, Elyers, 98.
Evetts, Elyers, 2nd, 98.
Evetts, Ezra, 98.
Evetts, James, 59.
Evetts, Jonathan, 98.
Evetts, Samuel, 98.
Evetts, Samuel, 3rd, 98.
Evins, Asahel, 58.
Evits, Jehiel, 85.
Evits, Jehiel, Junr, 85.
Ewen, Edward, 130.
Ewen, Edward, Junr, 130.
Ewing, William, 45.
Ewings, Thomas, 140.
Exton, William, 80.

Eyers, Thomas, 40.
Eyrs, Elisha, 120.

Fabrique, Bartemus, 73.
Fabrique, David, 73.
Fagins (Negro), 126.
Fairbanks, Benjn, 151.
Fairbanks, Samuel, 28.
Fairchild, Abel, 58.
Fairchild, Abel, 71.
Fairchild, Abiel, 95.
Fairchild, Abigail, 87.
Fairchild, Abijah, 73.
Fairchild, Abraham, 27.
Fairchild, Abraham, 71.
Fairchild, Ager, 20.
Fairchild, Alexander, 18.
Fairchild, Andrew, 19.
Fairchild, Apheus, 20.
Fairchild, Asher, 97.
Fairchild, Clemon, 20.
Fairchild, Curtis, 73.
Fairchild, Daniel, 29.
Fairchild, David, 64.
Fairchild, Ebenr, 66.
Fairchild, Edmond, 96.
Fairchild, Eleazer, 1st, 71.
Fairchild, Eleazer, 2d, 71.
Fairchild, Enoch, 8.
Fairchild, Ephraim, 32.
Fairchild, Ezekiel, 16.
Fairchild, Ezekiel, 29.
Fairchild, Ezra, 58.
Fairchild, Filo, 20.
Fairchild, Gershom, 31.
Fairchild, James, 20.
Fairchild, James, 20.
Fairchild, Joel, 31.
Fairchild, Joel, 87.
Fairchild, John, 17.
Fairchild, John, 20.
Fairchild, John, 27.
Fairchild, John, 29.
Fairchild, Jonathan, 20.
Fairchild, Joseph, 18.
Fairchild, Joseph, 95.
Fairchild, Joseph, Jur, 17.
Fairchild, Josiah, 20.
Fairchild, Mahitabel, 97.
Fairchild, Nathaniel, 95.
Fairchild, Noami, 31.
Fairchild, Oliver, 16.
Fairchild, Peter, 20.
Fairchild, Ranson, 21.
Fairchild, Robert, 30.
Fairchild, Samuel, 21.
Fairchild, Samuel, 27.
Fairchild, Samuel, 58.
Fairchild, Samuel, 86.
Fairchild, Seth, 20.
Fairchild, Seth, 78.
Fairchild, Silus, 20.
Fairchild, Stephen, 27.
Fairchild, Stephen, 58.
Fairchild, William A., 19.
Fairchild, Zachariah, 94.
Fairchild, Zadoc, 20.
Fairfield, David, 154.
Fairfield, Eleanor, 154.
Fairman, Ithemer, 40.
Fairman, Jared, 40.
Fairweather, Benjamin, 14.
Fairweather, Hanford, 22.
Fairweather, Jonah, 31.
Fairweather, Samuel, 31.
Fairweather, Thomas, 23.
Fairweather, Zalmon, 29.
Fairwell, Thomas, 147.
Falkner, Caleb, 142.
Falley, James, 125.
Falmon, Benjamin, 47.
Falshaw, John, 144.
Fanam, Asa, 141.
Fancher, David, 26.
Fancher, David, Junr, 26.
Fancher, Ithiel, 76.
Fancher, Jeames, 76.
Fancher, Sarah, 76.
Fancher, Silvanus, 26.
Fancher, Silvanus, Jr, 26.
Fannig, Daniel, 68.
Fanning, Ann, 131.
Fanning, Charles, 113
Fanning, David, 103.
Fanning, David, 120.
Fanning, Elisabeth, 118.
Fanning, Elisha, 38.
Fanning, Elkanah, 118.
Fanning, Frederick, 113.
Fanning, Gilbert, 117.
Fanning, Jona, 120.
Fanning, Jona, Junr, 119.
Fanning, Phineas, 120.
Fanning, Richard, 115.
Fanning, Sarah, 61.
Fanning, Thomas, 119.
Fanning, Thomas, 131.
Fanton, Abel, 32.
Fanton, Gershom, 32.
Fanton, Hezekiah, 32.
Fanton, John, 32.
Fanton, John, Junr, 32.

# INDEX.

Fanton, Jonathan, 18.
Fanton, Jonathan, 31.
Fanton, Moses, 94.
Fanton, Nehemiah, 32.
Fanton, Zebulen, 32.
Farebanks, Jos., 138.
Fargoe, James, 67.
Farley, Jn$^o$, 139.
Farley, Sam$^l$, 139.
Farlin, Hitchcock, 148.
Farling, Mechum, 62.
Farmer, Aaron, 132.
Farmer, Filo, 20.
Farmer, Thomas, 75.
Farmer, Tim$^o$, 137.
Farmon, Henery, 19.
Farmon, Jeabud, 19.
Farnam, Benj$^a$, 140.
Farnam, Daniel, 143.
Farnam, Eleaz$^r$, 143.
Farnam, Hannah, 143.
Farnam, James, 143.
Farnam, Jere$^h$, 143.
Farnam, Joseph, 142.
Farnam, Manassa, 140.
Farnam, Solomon, 140.
Farnam, Stephen, 140.
Farnam, William, 143.
Farnam, Zebud$^a$, 143.
Farnham, Abner, 85.
Farnham, Gad, 65.
Farnham, John, 65.
Farnham, John, 76.
Farnham, Joseph, 85.
Farnham, Joseph, Jun$^r$, 85.
Farnham, Nathan, 65.
Farnham, Peter, 70.
Farnham, Seth, 64.
Farnsworth, Joseph, 52.
Farnsworth, Phillip H., 35.
Farnsworth, Samuel, 41.
Farnum, Elijah, 112.
Farnum, Henry, 112.
Farnum, Hill, 85.
Farnum, John, 131.
Farnum, Mary, 92.
Farnum, Ozias, 85.
Farnum, Peter, 17.
Farnume, Philop, 63.
Farrand, John, 75.
Farrand, Jonathan, 75.
Farrand, Samuel, 71.
Farrel, Joel, 111.
Farrington, Jeremiah, 106.
Farris, Rhoda, 42.
Fasset, Adonijah, 141.
Fasset, John, 141.
Fasset, Ruben, 143.
Fassion (Negro), 122.
Fauster, Daniel, 62.
Faxton, Ebenezer, 47.
Fay, Jedediah, 140.
Fay, Jed$^h$, Jn$^r$, 140.
Fay, John, 149.
Fay, Neh$^h$, Sen$^r$, 150.
Fay, Sam$^l$, 150.
Fays, David, 137.
Fealds, William, 19.
Feany, William, 51.
Feeman, John, 70.
Feild, Ambrose, 96.
Feild, Edmond, 108.
Feild, Joseph, 98.
Feild, Luke, 98.
Feild, Doc$^t$ Simeon, 39.
Feild, Zacheriah, 99.
Feilds, Thomas, 104.
Feland, Thomas, 51.
Felch, Ebenezer, 58.
Felch, Sam$^l$, 142.
Felcher, Miael, 135.
Felcher, Michael, 135.
Fellows, Abia, 62.
Fellows, Elnathan, 118.
Fellows, Ephraim, 67.
Fellows, Ephraim, 116.
Fellows, Isaac, 128.
Fellows, Isaac, 138.
Fellows, John, 68.
Fellows, Joseph, 67.
Fellows, Joseph, 128.
Fellows, Lois, 67.
Fellows, Nath$^l$, 117.
Fellows, Nath$^l$, 2$^d$, 117.
Fellows, Nath$^l$, 3$^d$, 117.
Fellows, Philemon, 67.
Fellows, Stephen, 70.
Fellows, Thomas, 67.
Fellows, Varny, 139.
Felt, David, 136.
Felt, Sam$^l$, 136.
Feney, Oziah, 40.
Fenn, Aron, 102.
Fenn, Austin, 107.
Fenn, Benjamin, 108.
Fenn, Benjamin, 110.
Fenn, Edward, 107.
Fenn, Edward, 2$^d$, 107.
Fenn, Gamaliel, 110.
Fenn, Isaac, 102.
Fenn, James, 102.
Fenn, Joab, 71.
Fenn, John, 102.

Fenn, Nathan, 34.
Fenn, Samuel, 102.
Fenn, Samuel, 109.
Fenn, Sarah, 102.
Fenn, Theophelus, 70.
Fenno, Ephraim, 86.
Fenton, Adonijah, 139.
Fenton, Asa, 139.
Fenton, Barry, 39.
Fenton, Benjamin, 76.
Fenton, David, 143.
Fenton, Eben$^r$, 147.
Fenton, Ebenez$^r$, Sen$^r$, 147.
Fenton, Elezer, 139.
Fenton, Elez$^r$, 139.
Fenton, Elijah, 139.
Fenton, Francis, 38.
Fenton, Israel, 99.
Fenton, Jn$^o$, 139.
Fenton, Jn$^o$, 139.
Fenton, Jonathan, 105.
Fenton, Jonathan, 147.
Fenton, Jos., 139.
Fenton, Joseph, 147.
Fenton, Luke, 139.
Fenton, Nathaniel, 103.
Fenton, Nath$^l$, 139.
Fenton, Nath$^l$, 147.
Fenton, Rusba, 147.
Fenton, Sam$^l$, 139.
Fenton, Solomon, 71.
Fenton, Sol$^a$, 139
Fenton, Truston, 39.
Fenton, William, 39.
Fentons, Old, 134.
Fergo, Daniel, 126.
Fergo, Hannah, 128.
Fergo, Joshua, 24.
Fergo, Joshua, 2$^d$, 124.
Fergo, Moses, 127.
Fergo, Nehemiah, 125.
Fergo, Robart, 124.
Fergo, Stanton, 124.
Fergo, Thomas, 126.
Fergo, William, 125.
Fergo, William, 127.
Fergo, Zacheus, 127.
Feris, Zachariah, 71.
Ferman, David, 122.
Ferman, John, 122.
Fern, Mary, 102.
Fernando, Frances, 128.
Ferral, George, 97.
Ferring, Zebelun, 97.
Ferris, Abel, 20.
Ferris, Amasa, 71.
Ferris, Ashford, 15.
Ferris, David, 15.
Ferris, David, 71.
Ferris, David, Jr., 15.
Ferris, Rev$^d$ Ebenezer, 24.
Ferris, Jabez, 16.
Ferris, James, 25.
Ferris, Jeduthan, 15.
Ferris, Jeremiah, 15.
Ferris, Jonah, 25.
Ferris, Joseph, 16.
Ferris, Joseph, 17.
Ferris, Joseph, 20.
Ferris, Joseph, 71.
Ferris, Joseph, Jun$^r$, 16.
Ferris, Josiah, 16.
Ferris, Mary (W$^d$), 17.
Ferris, Moses, 15.
Ferris, Nathan, 21.
Ferris, Nathan, 76.
Ferris, Nathaniel, 15.
Ferris, Nath$^el$, Jun$^r$, 15.
Ferris, Oliver, 15.
Ferris, Park, 15.
Ferris, Peter, 20.
Ferris, Ransford A., 25.
Ferris, Samuel, 15.
Ferris, Samuel, 15.
Ferris, Samuel, 20.
Ferris, Shubeal, 15.
Ferris, Solomon, 16.
Ferris, Solomon, Jun$^r$, 16.
Ferris, Stephen, 15.
Ferris, Stephen, 71.
Ferris, Thomas, 16.
Ferris, Timothy, 16.
Ferris, Zacheriah, 20.
Ferrows, Benjamin, 144.
Ferry, Benjamin, 12.
Ferry, Ebenezer, 12.
Ferry, Eliphilet, 12.
Ferry, Ezra, 75.
Ferry, John, 47.
Ferry, Joseph, 75.
Ferry, Joshua, 35.
Ferry, Moses, 46.
Ferry, Nathan, 38.
Ferrys, Joshua, 12.
Ferrys, Sarah, 12.
Fesher, Eleaz$^r$, 154.
Fessenden, Samuel, 129.
Fiarchild, Andrew, 27.
Fich, J$^m$, 133.
Fich, Jn$^o$, 133.
Fich, P$^en$, 133.
Field, Aaron, 16.
Field, Benjamin, 99.

Field, Daniel, 85.
Field, Dan$^l$, 138.
Field, David, 99.
Field, Icobad, 99.
Field, Jedediah, 99.
Field, Jeremiah, 149.
Field, Pardont, 50.
Field, Sam$^l$, 89.
Field, Samuel, 99.
Field, Sam$^l$, 133.
Field, Timothy, 99.
Field, Uriah, 16.
Field, William, 149.
Fieldin, James, 11.
Fieldon, Jn$^o$, 134.
Fieldon, Sam$^l$, 135.
Fields, Ben$^a$, 133.
Fields, John, 50.
Fields, Tho$^s$, 132.
Fifer, Simon, 24.
Filer, Asa, 48.
Filer, Samuel, 54.
Filer, Sam$^l$, 135.
Fillemore, Amaziah, 129.
Fillemore, Cumfort, 129.
Fillemore, Timothy, 130.
Filley, Abraham, 64.
Filley, Elisha, 55.
Filley, Jessee, 70.
Filley, John, 55.
Filley, Jonah, 58.
Filley, Jonathan, 56.
Filley, Mark, 39.
Filley, Moses, 55.
Filley, Silvanus, 37.
Filly, Aaron, 56.
Filly, Amos, 55.
Filly, David, 55.
Filly, Jesse, 55.
Filly, Jonathan, 55.
Filly, Luke, 55.
Filly, Timothy, 55.
Finch, Dan, 22.
Finch, Ebenezer, 92.
Finch, Elam, 49.
Finch, Ezekiel, 16.
Finch, Ezekiel, 16.
Finch, Gideon, 50.
Finch, Hannah (W$^d$), 25.
Finch, Ichabod, 24.
Finch, Isaac, 16.
Finch, Jacob, 11.
Finch, John, 23.
Finch, John, Jun$^r$, 24.
Finch, Jonathan, 16.
Finch, Jonathan, 92.
Finch, Jonathan, Jr, 16.
Finch, Joseph, 50.
Finch, Nathanel, 11.
Finch, Nathaniel, 16.
Finch, Nathaniel, 25.
Finch, Peluk, 11.
Finch, Peter, 28.
Finch, Ruth, 21.
Finch, Seth, 25.
Finch, Stephen, 141.
Finch, Timothy, 16.
Finch, Timothy, Jr, 16.
Finch, Titus, 26.
Finch, William, 16.
Finch, William, 23.
Finch, William N., 16.
Finchly, George, 24.
Finger, William, 127.
Fink, Adam, 128.
Fink, Jacob, 128.
Finker, Samuel, 83.
Finley, David, 43.
Finley, John, 43.
Finley, Jn$^o$, 135.
Finley, Samuel, 43.
Finley, Samuel, 120.
Finley, Solomon, 43.
Finn, Aaron, 76.
Finn, Amos, 76.
Finn, Daniel, 75.
Finn, Ebenezer, 76.
Finn, Faar, 76.
Finn, Jacob, 76.
Finn, Jason, 76.
Finn, Jesse, 76.
Finn, Joseph, 76.
Finn, Samuel, 1$^{st}$, 76.
Finn, Samuel, 2$^d$, 76.
Finn, Samuel, 3$^d$, 76.
Finn, Thomas, 1$^{st}$, 76.
Finn, Thomas, 2$^d$, 76.
Finn, Titus, 76.
Finne, Jesse, 27.
Finney, Asa, 142.
Finney, David, 146.
Finney, Elded, 19.
Finney, Jonah, 74.
Finney, Joseph, 146.
Finney, Joseph, 147.
Finney, Sylvester, 74.
Finny, Elisha, 23.
Finny, John, 74.
Finny, John, 2$^d$, 74.
Finny, Joshua, Jr., 142.
Finny, Solomon, 16.
Firbbs, Alisha, 49.
Firbbs, Edward, 36.

Firbbs, Ichabod, 36.
Firbs, Moses, 36.
Firgo, Elisha, 131.
Firman, Richard, 71.
Fish, Aaron, 120.
Fish, Ambrus, 120.
Fish, Asa, 38.
Fish, Benjamin, 38.
Fish, Dan$^l$, 149.
Fish, David, 54.
Fish, David, 116.
Fish, Eben$^r$, 120.
Fish, Eli, 39.
Fish, Eliakim, 45.
Fish, Elias, 120.
Fish, Elijah, 137.
Fish, George, 119.
Fish, Jason, 116.
Fish, John, 120.
Fish, John, 126.
Fish, John, Jun$^r$, 120.
Fish, Jon$^a$, 38.
Fish, Jonathan, 119.
Fish, Joseph, 125.
Fish, Levi, 38.
Fish, Miller, 45.
Fish, Nathan, 120.
Fish, Nathan, 142.
Fish, Nath$^l$, 126.
Fish, Sam$^l$, 120.
Fish, Sam$^l$, 146.
Fish, Sam$^l$, 151.
Fish, Sands, 120.
Fish, Seabury, 128.
Fish, Sirus, 116.
Fish, Sprage, 120.
Fish, Thomas, 119.
Fish, Titus, 116.
Fish, William, 126.
Fisher, Barzillia, 144.
Fisher, Darius, 75.
Fisher, Hannah, 104.
Fisher, John, 143.
Fisher, Lydia, 86.
Fisher, N. Beacher, 71.
Fisher, Olcott, 140.
Fisher, Timothy, 41.
Fisk, Boze, 85.
Fisk, Darius, 142.
Fisk, David, 143.
Fisk, Elias & c., 151.
Fisk, Ephraim, 144.
Fisk, Jn$^o$, 139.
Fisk, John, 153.
Fisk, Jonathan, 143.
Fisk, Jon$^a$, Jn$^r$, 143.
Fisk, Moses, Jn$^r$, 151.
Fisk, Moses, Sen$^r$, 151.
Fisk, Rufus, 139.
Fisk, William, 16.
Fitch, Abijah, 23.
Fitch, Abner, 133.
Fitch, Abner, Jr., 134.
Fitch, Abraham, 145.
Fitch, Ammi, 146.
Fitch, Andrew, 145.
Fitch, Andrus, 125.
Fitch, Arael, 27.
Fitch, Asa, 126.
Fitch, Augustus, 37.
Fitch, Benaijah, 115.
Fitch, Benjamin B., 130.
Fitch, Bushnel, 23.
Fitch, Christopher, 152.
Fitch, Cordelia, 104.
Fitch, Cuff (Negro), 32.
Fitch, Eben$^r$, 130.
Fitch, Eleaz$^r$, Jr, 152.
Fitch, Eleaz$^r$, Senior, 152.
Fitch, Eleaz$^r$, 3$^d$, 152.
Fitch, Elijah, 24.
Fitch, Elijah, 115.
Fitch, Elijah, 123.
Fitch, Elisha, 62.
Fitch, Gideon, 130.
Fitch, Gideon, Jun$^r$, 130.
Fitch, Hannah, 120.
Fitch, Hannah, 130.
Fitch, Haynes, 21.
Fitch, Hen$^y$, 133.
Fitch, Hezekiah, 65.
Fitch, Ichabod, 145.
Fitch, Isaac, 145.
Fitch, Jabez, 142.
Fitch, Jabez, 144.
Fitch, Col. Jabez, 16.
Fitch, James, 21.
Fitch, James, 55.
Fitch, J$^m$, 134.
Fitch, James, Jun$^r$, 21.
Fitch, Jeptha, 134.
Fitch, Jesse, 152.
Fitch, John, 23.
Fitch, John, 58.
Fitch, John, 112.
Fitch, John, 142.
Fitch, John, 152.
Fitch, John F., 37.
Fitch, Jonathan, 103.
Fitch, Joseph, 23.
Fitch, Joseph, 55.
Fitch, Joseph, 125.
Fitch, Jos., 133.

Fitch, Joseph P., 24.
Fitch, Joshua, 63.
Fitch, Josiah, 148.
Fitch, Lidia, 108.
Fitch, Luther, 55.
Fitch, Luther, 104.
Fitch, Medi$^n$, 134.
Fitch, Nathan, 145.
Fitch, Nathaniel, 104.
Fitch, Nathaniel, 115.
Fitch, Nath$^l$, 146.
Fitch, Olive, 152.
Fitch, Rebeca, Jr., 142.
Fitch, Rebecca (W$^d$), 21.
Fitch, Richard, 39.
Fitch, Roswell, 152.
Fitch, Samuel, 24.
Fitch, Samuel, 99.
Fitch, Samuel, Jun$^r$, 24.
Fitch, Selah, 48.
Fitch, Seymore, 23.
Fitch, Sherwood, 125.
Fitch, Shubael, 152.
Fitch, Stephen, 23.
Fitch, Stephen, 152.
Fitch, Theophilus, 23.
Fitch, Thomas, 99.
Fitch, Thomas, 115.
Fitch, Thomas, 125.
Fitch, Thomas, Esq$^r$, 21.
Fitch, Timothy, 21.
Fitch, White Roswold, 39.
Fitch, William, 24.
Fitch, William, 24.
Fitsgerald, John, 129.
Fits Jerald, Partrick, 71.
Fitz, Daniel, 140.
Fitz, Eben$^r$, 150.
Flagg, Abijah, 47.
Flagg, Jonathan, 45.
Flagg, Joseph, 45.
Flagg, Samuel, 45.
Flagg, Solomon, 34.
Flanckin, Banabas, 42.
Flay, Diamond, 93.
Fleskey, Mary, 65.
Fletcher, Benj$^a$, 140.
Fletcher, Ebenezer, 63.
Fletcher, Ephraim, 44.
Fletcher, John, 48.
Fletcher, M. (W$^d$), 15.
Fletcher, Mary, 86.
Fletcher, Richard, 140.
Fletcher, Seth, 147.
Fletcher, William, 37.
Flin, Thomas, 12.
Fling, Lemuel, 141.
Flint, Archelaus, 38.
Flint, Asher, 139.
Flint, Benj$^a$, 143.
Flint, Dan$^l$, 143.
Flint, Davis, 150.
Flint, James, 152.
Flint, Jemima, 152.
Flint, John 37.
Flint, John, 152.
Flint, John, Sen$^r$, 153.
Flint, Jon$^a$, 139.
Flint, Joseph, 150.
Flint, Joshua, 37.
Flint, Martha, 145.
Flint, Nath$^l$, 143.
Flint, Nath$^l$, Jur$^r$, 143.
Flint, Phen$^s$, 143.
Flint, Sam$^l$, 153.
Flint, Tolcot, 133.
Florah (Negro), 86.
Flowers, Elijah, 67.
Flowers, Gabrial, 60.
Flowers, Joseph, 53.
Flowers, Nathaniel, 78.
Flowers, Simeon, 53.
Flying, Abijah, 149.
Flyn, John, 154.
Fogarson, Elizabeth, 37.
Fogg, Dan$^l$, 141.
Follet, Abner, 152.
Folliot, Bartlit, 28.
Folliot, Jeremiah, 28.
Folliot, John, 28.
Folliot, Joseph, 28.
Folliot, Thankfull, 28.
Fontaine, Luke, 52.
Foot, Aaron, 75.
Foot, Aaron, 121.
Foot, Abel, 10.
Foot, Abigail, 121.
Foot, Abraham, 91.
Foot, Adonijah, 121.
Foot, Ambros, 136.
Foot, Amos, 76.
Foot, Asa, 62.
Foot, Asa, 91.
Foot, Charles, 120.
Foot, Daniel, 20.
Foot, Daniel, 21.
Foot, Daniel, 92.
Foot, Daniel, 120.
Foot, Darius, 75.
Foot, David, 75.
Foot, David, 76.
Foot, Edward, 20.

# INDEX.

Foot, Eli, 97.
Foot, Elisha, 21.
Foot, Elisha, 48.
Foot, Elisha, 92.
Foot, Ephraim, 91.
Foot, Ezra, 94.
Foot, Filo, 20.
Foot, George, 20.
Foot, George, 20.
Foot, Grove, 48.
Foot, Hosea, 120.
Foot, Ichabod, 35.
Foot, Isaac, 75.
Foot, Isaac, 92.
Foot, Isaac, 112.
Foot, Isaac, 137.
Foot, Israel, 43.
Foot, Jacob, 41.
Foot, Jacob, 76.
Foot, Jehiel, 20.
Foot, Jerad, 92.
Foot, Jesse, 57.
Foot, Jesse 137
Foot, John, 11.
Foot, John, 48.
Foot, John, 76.
Foot, John, 92.
Foot, John, 93.
Foot, John, 102.
Foot, John, Jr, 48.
Foot, Jonathan, 92.
Foot, Joseph, 20.
Foot, Joseph, 30.
Foot, Joseph, 120.
foot, Levi, 32.
Foot, Luther, 69.
Foot, Nathan, 31.
Foot, Nath¹, 121.
Foot, Nath¹, Junr, 121.
Foot, Noah, 133.
Foot, Patience, 10.
Foot, Peter, 20.
Foot, Petcr, 20.
Foot, Robart, 56.
Foot, Roger, 70.
Foot, Roger, 120.
Foot, Ruben, 121.
Foot, Ruhamah, 120.
Foot, Samuel, 35.
Foot, Samuel, 76.
Foot, Samuel, 92.
Foot, Simon, 76.
Foot, Stephen, 91.
Foot, Stephen, 136.
Foot, Thankful, 76.
Foot, Thomas, 76.
Foot, Timothy, 59.
Forbes, Elias, 103.
Forbes, Elijah, 103.
Forbes, Isaac, 97.
Forbes, Johial, 96.
Forbes, John, 69.
Forbes, Levi, 97.
Forbes, Samuel, 97.
Forbes, Samuel, 103.
Forbs, Aaron, 36.
Forbs, Elijah, 36.
Forbs, Elisha, 36.
Forbs, Nathan, 114.
Forbs, Thomas, 36.
Forbs, Timothy, 36.
Force, Ebenr, 150.
Ford, Abraham, 143.
Ford, Abraham, 144.
Ford, Adonijah, 45.
Ford, Amos, 76.
Ford, Amos, 101.
Ford, Amos, 143.
Ford, Amos, Jur, 143.
Ford, Anna, 97.
Ford, Barnebas, 76.
Ford, Benjamin, 143.
Ford, Caleb, 104.
Ford, Charles, 126.
Ford, Daniel, 76.
Ford, Daniel, 101.
Ford, David, 111.
Ford, Ebenezer, 76.
Ford, Edward, 101.
Ford, Enos, 76.
Ford, Ezra, 104.
Ford, Illard, 111.
Ford, Isaa, 135.
Ford, Isaac, 111.
Ford, Jacob, 146.
Ford, Jesse, 111.
Ford, Joel, 100.
Ford, John, 91.
Ford, John, 94.
Ford, John, 101.
Ford, John, 114.
Ford, John, 126.
Ford, John, 2nd, 101.
Ford, Jonah, 100.
Ford, Jonathan, 71.
Ford, Jonathan, 100.
Ford, Joseph, 126.
Ford, Jos, 136.
Ford, Josephus, 66.
Ford, Lemuel, 92.
Ford, Luther, 135.
Ford, Mathew, 36.
Ford, Mathew, 45.

Ford, Moses, 100.
Ford, Nathaniel, 94.
Ford, Nathanel, 143.
Ford, Nathaniel, 2d, 94.
Ford, Oliver, 57.
Ford. Roswell, 126.
Ford, Samuel, 75.
Ford, Stephen, 100.
Ford, Thaddeus, 57.
Ford, Thos, 41.
Ford, Thomas, 56.
Ford, Thomas, 101.
Ford, Thomas, 101.
Ford, Vincen, 111.
Ford, Wm, 41.
Fordes, Samuel, 69.
Fords, Jno, 136.
Fords, Jno, Jr., 136.
Fords, Timo, 136.
Foresides, John, 124.
Foresides, Latham, 124.
Foresides, Timothy, 124.
Forgerson, John, 11.
Forget, Elijah, 137.
Forget, Jno, 137.
Forrester, William, 29.
Forry, Micajah, 130.
Forson, Benjamin, 64.
Forster, Christopher, 99.
Forster, David, 107.
Forster, Giles, 106.
Forster, Phebe, 106.
Forster, Sarah, 99.
Forster, Thomas, 99.
Forster, Thomas, 106.
Forster, Timothy, 106.
Forthsides, Charles, 114.
Forthsides, Nathan, 119.
Forthsides, Robert, 118.
Forthsides, Timothy, 2d, 125.
Forthsides, William, 119.
Fortier, Benjamin, 63.
Fortner, Charles, 97.
Forward, Abel, 44.
Forward, Jesse, 44.
Forward, Joseph, 45.
Forward, Reuben, 45.
Forward, Samuel, 45.
Fosbury, John, 49.
Fosdick, Aanna, 52.
Fosdick, Abijah, 97.
Fosdick, Ezekiel, 52.
Fosdick, James, 52.
Fosdick, Nicoll, 128.
Fosdick, William, 52.
Fosdike, Clemment, 127.
Fost, Elisha, 76.
Foster, Alpheus, 91.
Foster, Asa, 19.
Foster, Benjamin, 129.
Foster, Charles, 134.
Foster, Danl, 142.
Foster, David, 67.
Foster, Edward, 86.
Foster, Edward, 138.
Foster, Jacob, 153.
Foster, Jesse, 11.
Foster, John, 60.
Foster, John, 86.
Foster, Jonah, 28.
Foster, Jonah, 29.
Foster, Joseph, 28.
Foster, Joseph, 74.
Foster, Joseph, 149.
Foster, Oliver, 38.
Foster, Peletiah, 39.
Foster, Polley, 62.
Foster, Revd Mr, 137.
Foster, Samuel, 53.
Foster, Stephen, 141.
Foster, Thomas, 39.
Foster, Weaver, 144.
Foster, Zacheus, 48.
Fountain, Moses, 24.
Fourge, Sarah, 14.
Fowl, Lewis, 95.
Fowlar, Noah, 62.
Fowler, Abraham, 98.
Fowler, Abraham, 110.
Fowler, Adonijah, 145.
Fowler, Amos, 97.
Fowler, Andrew, 97.
Fowler, Anna. 101.
Fowler, Asher, 99.
Fowler, Beldad, 97.
Fowler, Benjamin, 45.
Fowler, Benjamin, 75.
Fowler, Bildad, 51.
Fowler, Caleb, 96.
Fowler, Caleb, 100.
Fowler, Daniel, 99.
Fowler, David, 99.
Fowler, David, 136.
Fowler, Ebenezer, 99.
Fowler, Ebenezer, 100.
Fowler, Elizabeth, 98.
Fowler, Elizabeth, 98.
Fowler, Ely, 91.
Fowler, Gideon, 118.
Fowler, Gordan, 132.
Fowler, Hannah, 99.
Fowler, Israel, 133.
Fowler. James, 132.

Fowler, Jeremiah, 106.
Fowler, Joel, 98.
Fowler, John, 36.
Fowler, John, 99.
Fowler, John, 101.
Fowler, John, 127.
Fowler, John, 145.
Fowler, Joiner, 100.
Fowler, Jonathan, 100.
Fowler, Joseph, 82.
Fowler, Josiah, 92.
Fowler, Josiah, 92.
Fowler, Josiah, 2d, 100.
Fowler, Lucy, 99.
Fowler, Minor, 97.
Fowler, Morris, 128.
Fowler, Nathaniel, 98.
Fowler, Nathaniel, 99.
Fowler, Nathaniel, 101.
Fowler, Nathaniel, 2nd, 101.
Fowler, Nehemiah, 15.
Fowler, Noah, 97.
Fowler, Noah, 2nd, 97.
Fowler, Oliver, 100.
Fowler, Phineas, 99.
Fowler, Ruben, 98.
Fowler, Samuel, 36.
Fowler, Samuel, 99.
Fowler, Silas, 99.
Fowler, Soloman, 100.
Fowler, Stephen, 14.
Fowler, Stephen, 99.
Fowler, Theophilus, 99.
Fowler, Timothy, 102.
Fowler, William, 99.
Fowler, William, 102.
Fox, Abm, 135.
Fox, Amasa, 43.
Fox, Amos, 43.
Fox, Appleton, 120.
Fox, Asa, 42.
Fox, Ashbel, 38.
Fox, Benja, 127.
Fox, Brinton, 124.
Fox, Daniel, 128.
Fox, David, 42.
Fox, David, 130.
Fox, David, Jr., 43.
Fox, Ebenezer, 43.
Fox, Ebenezer, 82.
Fox, Ebenezer, 109.
Fox, Edmund, 129.
Fox, Edward, 127.
Fox, Eleazer, 34.
Fox, Elisha, 34.
Fox, Elisha, 47.
Fox, Elisha, 124.
Fox, Ephraim, 36.
Fox, Ephraim, 61.
Fox, Ephraim, Jr, 37.
Fox, Ezekiel, 82.
Fox, Ezekiel, 124.
Fox, Gershom, 83.
Fox, Hosea, 42.
Fox, Isaac, 43.
Fox, Israel, 43.
Fox, Jabes, 61.
Fox, Jabez, 153.
Fox, Jacob, 121.
Fox, Jacob, 132.
Fox, Jael, 135.
Fox, Jedediah, 126.
Fox, Jemima, 126.
Fox, Jesse, 127.
Fox, Jesse, 153.
Fox, John, 48.
Fox, John, 79.
Fox, John, 154.
Fox, Jonah, 43.
Fox, Jonathan, 21.
Fox, Joneal, 36.
Fox, Joseph, 42.
Fox, Joseph, 153.
Fox, Joseph, Jr., 42.
Fox, Joshua, 82.
Fox, Joshua, 122.
Fox, Lemuel, 43.
Fox, Levi, 43.
Fox, Levi, 70.
Fox, Martha, 43.
Fox, Martha, 129.
Fox, Moses, 82.
Fox, Obadiah, 42.
Fox, Reuben 57.
Fox, Richard, 43.
Fox, Roswell, 37.
Fox, Roswell, 126.
Fox, Samuel, 42.
Fox, Saml, 81.
Fox, Saml, 124.
Fox, Samuel, 127.
Fox, Saml, 148.
Fox, Stephen, 43.
Fox, Stephen, 70.
Fox, Thomas, 43.
Fox, Thomas, 54.
Fox, Thos, 154.
Fox, Veniah, 36.
Fox, Wm, 83.
Frairey, Samuel, 87.
Frances, Asa, 46.
Frances, Elias, 47.
Frances, Elijah, 33.

Frances, Elijah, Jr., 33.
Frances, Hezekiah, 47.
Frances, James, 33.
Frances, James, 52.
Frances, John, 53.
Frances, Josiah, 53.
Frances, Josiah, 54.
Frances, Justin, 33.
Frances, Justus, 54.
Frances, Roger, 54.
Frances, Roswell, 47.
Francis, Amos, 107.
Francis, Asahel, 70.
Francis, Daniel, 84.
Francis, David, 152.
Francis, Jacob, 107.
Francis, James, 84.
Francis, John, 68.
Francis, John, 142.
Francis, Joseph, 107.
Francis, Joseph, 107.
Francis, Manning, 153.
Francis, Mary, 87.
Francis, Samuel, 67.
Francis, Susannah, 84.
Francis, Titus, 96.
Francis, Wm, 55.
Franciss, Timothy, 53.
Frank, Andrew, 68.
Frank (Negroe), 95.
Frank, Robin, 10.
Frank, Andw, 114.
Franklin, ——, 149.
Franklin, Abel, 152.
Franklin, Caleb, 91.
Franklin, Essi, 84.
Franklin, John, 67.
Franklin, Samuel, 84.
Franklin, Uriah, 152.
Franlin, Jonathan, 84.
Frasier, Daniel, 12.
Frasier, George, 60.
Frasier, Mary, 86.
Frasier, William, 17.
Frasure, Daniel, 44.
Fraust, Samuel, 59.
Frazier, Elijah, 141.
Frazier, John, 141.
Freedom, Jack, 57.
Freeland, Robert, 58.
Freeman, Azariah, 147.
Freeman, Barnabas, 80.
Freeman, Call, 58.
Freeman, Cato, 79.
Freeman, Cuff, 34.
Freeman, David, 89.
Freeman, Edmond, 147.
Freeman, Fredrick, 147.
Freeman, Henry, 128.
Freeman, John, 63.
Freeman, John, 147.
Freeman, Joseph, 150.
Freeman, Mary, 129.
Freeman, Nathaniel, 80.
Freeman (Negroe), 107.
Freeman, Obed, 38.
Freeman, Peter, 82.
Freeman, Rebecca, 147.
Freeman, Skiff, 147.
Freeman, Sylvenus, 81.
Freeman, Sylvenus, Junr, 81.
Freeman, Thomas, 27.
Freemans, John, 140.
Freman, Abigail, 113.
Freman, Amos, 42.
Freman, Caleb, 120.
Freman, Calvin, 120.
Freman, Ebenezer, 114.
Freman, Hannah, 118.
Freman, Hezekiah, 131.
Freman, Mary, 113.
Freman (Negro), 126.
Freman, Peleg, 113.
Freman, Peter, 34.
Freman, Saml, 113.
Freman, Timothy, 120.
French, Abner, 17.
French, Abner, 133.
French, Amasa, 51.
French, Asher, 44.
French, Benjamin, 30.
French, Charles, 95.
French, Daniel, 34.
French, Daniel, 130.
French, David, 29.
French, David, 112.
French, Didimus, 99.
French, Ebenezer, 17.
French, Edmond, 103.
French, Elisha, 34.
French, Enoch, 95.
French, Ephraim, 31.
French, Francis, 94.
French. Gamaliel, 20.
French, Gamaliel, 30.
French, Gideon, 56.
French, Irael, 95.
French, Isaac, 152.
French, James, 17.
French, James B., 29.
French, Jeheil, 17.
French, Jeriel, 17.
French, John, 18.
French, John, 29.

French, John, 29.
French, John, 29.
French, John, 38.
French, John, 51.
French, John, 148.
French, John, Jr., 38.
French, Jonas, 18.
French, Jonathan, 18.
French, Joseph, 18.
French, Joseph, 112.
French, Joshua, 129.
French, Josiah, 78.
French, Nathaniel, 95.
French, Othenial, 17.
French, Pheba, 112.
French, Phebe, 30.
French, Philomen, 99.
French, Samuel, 10.
French, Samuel, 29.
French, Samuel, 29.
French, Samuel, 32.
French, Samuel, 94.
French, Samuel, 130.
French, Samuel, Junr, 29.
French, Stuman, 148.
French, Wells, 10.
French, William, 18.
French, William, 73.
Frinck, Mary, 140.
Frink, Amos, 115.
Frink, Andw, 114.
Frink, Andrew, 152.
Frink, Asa, 117.
Frink, Christopher, 126.
Frink, Danl, 151.
Frink, David, 126.
Frink, Diah, 114.
Frink, Hannah, 115.
Frink, Isaac, 116.
Frink, Isaac, 117.
Frink, Jabez, 118.
Frink, Jabez, Junr, 118.
Frink, James, 113.
Frink, Joshua, 151.
Frink, Lathrop, 151.
Frink, Matthias, 151.
Frink, Prentice, 117.
Frink Saml, 67.
Frink, Samuel, 116.
Frink, Seth, 66.
Frink, Stephen, 115.
Frink, Usual, 151.
Frink, William, 145.
Frink, Zachh, 151.
Frisbee, David, 41.
Frisbee, Hooker, 35.
Frisbee, Ichabod, 49.
Frisbee, John, 110.
Frisbee, Levi, 108.
Frisbee, Zebulon, 40.
Frisbey, Daniel, 35.
Frisbey, Joseph, 67.
Frisbey, Noah, 70.
Frisbey, Noah, 70.
Frisbey, Simeon, 69.
Frisbie, Amos, 56.
Frisbie, Benjamin, 98.
Frisbie, Ebenezur, 91.
Frisbie, Edward, 91.
Frisbie, Hezekiah, 63.
Frisbie, Israel, 110.
Frisbie, Jabez, 58.
Frisbie, Jacob, 56.
Frisbie, Jacob, 2d, 56.
Frisbie, Jacob, 92.
Frisbie, James, 56.
Frisbie, John, 1st, 58.
Frisbie, John, 2d, 58.
Frisbie, Jonathan, 92.
Frisbie, Joseph, 91.
Frisbie, Josiah, 111.
Frisbie, Luman, 100.
Frisbie, Mary, 91.
Frisbie, Mary, 91.
Frisbie, Mary, 92.
Frisbie, Nathaniel, 91.
Frisbie, Philomon, 91.
Frisbie, Ruben, 109.
Frisbie, Rufus, 91.
Frisbie, Samuel, 91.
Frisbie, Thomas, 91.
Frisbie, William, 91.
Frisbier, Enos, 58.
Frisbier, Isaac, 58.
Frisbrie, Edward, 75.
Frisby, Charles, 110.
Frisby, Elizabeth, 110.
Frisby, Jonathan, 131.
Frisby, Judas, 110.
Frisell, Joseph, 154.
Frisleer, Levi, 34.
Friston, Zebulon, 35.
Froet, Aaron, 39.
Frost, Amos, 108.
Frost, Danl, 142.
Frost, David, 109.
Frost, Ebenr, 132.
Frost, Henry, 142.
Frost, Isaac, 109.
Frost, Jason, 109.
Frost, Jesse, 109.
Frost, John, 106.
Frost, John, 2nd, 106.

180 INDEX.


Frost, Jonas, 141.
Frost, Joseph, 27.
Frost, Joseph, 31.
Frost, Joseph, 56.
Frost, Josu, 134.
Frost, Moses, 109.
Frost, Samuel, 102.
Frost, Samuel, 109.
Frost, Samuel, 1st, 76.
Frost, Samuel, 2nd, 76.
Frost, Samuel, 2nd, 109.
Frost, Solomon, 76.
Frost, Stephen, 30.
Frost, Timothy, 109.
Frost, Titus, 106.
Frothingham, Ebenezer, 86.
Frothingham, John, 87.
Frothingham, Samuel, 86.
Froud, Robart, 127.
Fruman, Samson, 42.
Fry, Christopher, 104.
Fry, John, 45.
Fry, Peleg, 113.
Fry, Rena, 60.
Fry, Thomas, 13.
Fulford, Edmon, 18.
Fulford, John, 76.
Fulford, Oliver, 20.
Fulford, Titus, 110.
Fullar, John, 41.
Fullar, Josiah, 41.
Fullar, Thos, 143.
Fuller, Aaron, 143.
Fuller, Abel, 1st, 74.
Fuller, Abel, 2d, 74.
Fuller, Abiaal, 146.
Fuller, Abijah, 80.
Fuller, Abijah, 143.
Fuller, Abram, 58.
Fuller, Adijah, 74.
Fuller, Amasa, 80.
Fuller, Ambros, 35.
Fuller, Amos, 74.
Fuller, Asa, 86.
Fuller, Asahel, 74.
Fuller, Barnabas, 42.
Fuller, Benajah, 58.
Fuller, Benjamin, 61.
Fuller, Benja, 82.
Fuller, Benjn, 142.
Fuller, Benjn, 143.
Fuller, Benjn, 148.
Fuller, Bezl, 146.
Fuller, Caleb, 149.
Fuller, Danel, 139.
Fuller, Daniel, 74.
Fuller, Danl, 83.
Fuller, Daniel, 83.
Fuller, Danl, 139.
Fuller, Daniel, 143.
Fuller, David, 82.
Fuller, David, 137.
Fuller, David, 139.
Fuller, David, 145.
Fuller, Della, 143.
Fuller, Ebenezer, 65.
Fuller, Ebenezer, 112.
Fuller, Eber, 136.
Fuller, Edmund, 34.
Fuller, Elijah, 121.
Fuller, Eliphelet, 68.
Fuller, Elisha, 83.
Fuller, Elisha, 139.
Fuller, Ephraim, 34.
Fuller, Ephraim, 58.
Fuller, Ezra, 81.
Fuller, Ezra, 148.
Fuller, Frederick, 134.
Fuller, Hannah, 121.
Fuller, Hez., 137.
Fuller, Howard, 74.
Fuller, Jacob, 58.
Fuller, Jacob, 112.
Fuller, Jacob, 134.
Fuller, Jas, 136.
Fuller, Jehiel, 82.
Fuller, Jehiel, 2d, 82.
Fuller, Jemima, 91.
Fuller, Jeremiah, 58.
Fuller, Jesse, 35.
Fuller, Johiel, 62.
Fuller, John, 35.
Fuller, John, 67.
Fuller, John, 97.
Fuller, John, 112.
Fuller, John, 143.
Fuller, John, 143.
Fuller, John, Jnr, 143.
Fuller, Jona, 133.
Fuller, Jonathn, 143.
Fuller, Jonathn, 147.
Fuller, Joseph, 19.
Fuller, Joseph, 51.
Fuller, Joseph, 62.
Fuller, Joseph, 121.
Fuller, Jos., 133.
Fuller, Jose, 137.
Fuller, Joseph, 143.
Fuller, Joshua, 62.
Fuller, Josiah, 141.
Fuller, Jrad, 82.
Fuller, Judge, 81.
Fuller, Levise, 83.
Fuller, Lukus, 136.
Fuller, Mary, 82.
Fuller, Nathan, 81.
Fuller, Nathel, 135.
Fuller, Nathl, 135.
Fuller, Nathl, 153.
Fuller, Nathl, 154.
Fuller, Noadiah, 83.
Fuller, Noadiah, Jr, 83.
Fuller, Obadiah, 55.
Fuller, Oliver, 58.
Fuller, Peter, 143.
Fuller, Roger, 135.
Fuller, Samuel, 68.
Fuller, Samuel, 80.
Fuller, Saml, 137.
Fuller, Saml, 143.
Fuller, Saml, 146.
Fuller, Simeon, 34.
Fuller, Stephen, 81.
Fuller, Stephen, 136.
Fuller, Thankfull, 81.
Fuller, Thomas, 68.
Fuller, Thomas, 80.
Fuller, Thos, 82.
Fuller, Timothy, 81.
Fuller, Timothy, 147.
Fuller, Timothy, 147.
Fuller, Uriel, 82.
Fuller (Wid.), 137.
Fuller, Wm, 136.
Fuller, Wm, 137.
Fuller, William, 143.
Fuller, Wm W., 81.
Fullerton, John, 67.
Fulson, David, 76.
Fulsora, Mary, 30.
Furgason, Daniel, 61.
Furgeson, Daniel, 63.
Furgeson, James, 62.
Fusbrie, Ezekiel, 78.
Fusbrie, Noah, 78.
Fusbury, Anna, 55.

Gabriel, Henry, 102.
Gabriel, Peter, 102.
Gad, Marear, 88.
Gage, Aaron, 154.
Gage, Elisha, 154.
Gage, Joel, 154.
Gage, Thaddeus, 154.
Gage, Thomas, 29.
Gager, Saml, 137.
Gailston, Willm, 81.
Gain (Negroe), 105.
Gaines, Luther, 44.
Gains, Dan., 42.
Gains, Daniel, 44.
Gains, James, 52.
Gains, John, 40.
Gains, John, 42.
Gains, John, 79.
Gains, Nathaniel, 42.
Gains, Samuel, 51.
Gains, Solomon, 44.
Galard, Nathan, 62.
Galbin, Benjamin, 101.
Gale, Elihu, 108.
Gale, Hannah, 85.
Gale, Isaac, 25.
Gale, Joseph, 131.
Gale, Luther, 129.
Gale, Mathew, 107.
Gale, Wm, 25.
Galend, Benjamin, 100.
Galend, Benjamin, 2nd, 100.
Galer, Reuben, 25.
Gales, Elias, 93.
Gales, John, 108.
Gales, Moses, 107.
Gales, Nathaniel, 93.
Gales, Nathaniel, 2d, 93.
Gales, Thomas, 93.
Galley, James, 115.
Gallop, Benjamin, 65.
Gallop, Benjn, 148.
Gallop, Benja, 151.
Gallop, Bennadam, 151.
Gallop, David, 151.
Gallop, Ebenr, 148.
Gallop, Isaac, 151.
Gallop, Jabez, 151.
Gallop, John, 148.
Gallop, John, 151.
Gallop, Jonathn, 148.
Gallop, Lyda, 151.
Gallop, Nathl, 151.
Gallop, Nathl, 151.
Gallop, Saml, 151.
Gallop, Saml, 151.
Gallop, Wheeler, 151.
Gallop, William, 151.
Gallop, William, 151.
Gallow, Joseph, 63.
Galloway, Peter, 73.
Gallup, Amos, 116.
Gallup, Benadam, 120.
Gallup, Benadam, 2d, 120.
Gallup, Ebenezer, 118.
Gallup, Ezra, 117.
Gallup, Gardiner, 119.
Gallup, Henry, 118.
Gallup, Isaac, 120.
Gallup, Jacob, 118.
Gallup, Jesse, 118.
Gallup, John, 116.
Gallup, Joseph, 119.
Gallup, Joshua, 118.
Gallup, Josiah, 118.
Gallup, Levi, 117.
Gallup, Nathan, 118.
Gallup, Nehemiah, 120.
Gallup, Samuel, 118.
Gallup, Silas, 117.
Gallup, Thomas P., 125.
Galor, Timothy, 61.
Galpen, John, 56.
Galpen, Moses, 56.
Galpin, Abram, 78.
Galpin, Amos, 64.
Galpin, Benjamin, 34.
Galpin, Benjamin, 75.
Galpin, Curtis, 78.
Galpin, Joseph, 34.
Galpin, Peat, 34.
Galpin, Samuel, 78.
Galpin, Samuel, 88.
Galpin, Stephen, 78.
Galpin, Stephen Curtis, 78.
Galpin, Susannah, 78.
Galpin, Thomas, 34.
Gane, Jude, 67.
Ganes, Moses, 59.
Gannan, Edward, 68.
Gardenor, George, 65.
Gardiner, Abiel, 116.
Gardiner, Abigail, 117.
Gardiner, Benaijah, 127.
Gardiner, Caleb, 126.
Gardiner, Daniel, 126.
Gardiner, David, 103.
Gardiner, David, 126.
Gardiner, David, Junr, 126.
Gardiner, David, 2d, 125.
Gardiner, Gurdon, 126.
Gardiner, Henry, 129.
Gardiner, Isaac, 126.
Gardiner, John, 125.
Gardiner, John, 126.
Gardiner, Jona, 126.
Gardiner, Jonathan, 2d, 126.
Gardiner, Lemuel, 126.
Gardiner, Mary, 128.
Gardiner, Rufus, 127.
Gardiner, Simeon, 126.
Gardiner, Stephen, 126.
Gardiner, Thomas, 118.
Gardiner, Thomas, 123.
Gardiner, William, 122.
Gardiner, William, 122.
Gardiner, William, 126.
Gardner, Sherman, 51.
Garey, Ebenezr, 146.
Garey, Elijah, 146.
Garey, John, 148.
Garit, David, 31.
Garlic, Hennery, 18.
Garlick, David, 71.
Garlick, Edmund, 71.
Garlick, Heath, 71.
Garlick, Read, 71.
Garlick, Samuel, 71.
Garner, William, 22.
Garnsey, Noah, 66.
Garret, Jno, 35.
Garret, John, 91.
Garrett, Frances, 49.
Garrett, Frances, 73.
Garrett, John, 73.
Garrett, Rufus, 49.
Garrett, Wait, 73.
Garrot, John, 60.
Gary, Eneas, 146.
Gary, Gilbert, 146.
Gary, Josiah, 149.
Gary, Seth, 146.
Gary, Thadeus, 146.
Gary, William, 149.
Gasby, Caleb, 139.
Gaser, Jason, 152.
Gasper, Joseph, 140.
Gastin, John, 152.
Gaston, Joseph, 95.
Gates, Able, 121.
Gates, Bezaleel, 81.
Gates, Brainerd, 81.
Gates, Caleb, 81.
Gates, Cyrus, 114.
Gates, Danl, 82.
Gates, Daniel, 113.
Gates, Daniel, 114.
Gates, Ebenezer, 114.
Gates, Elijah, 113.
Gates, Ephraim, 81.
Gates, George, 81.
Gates, Gideon, 81.
Gates, Helen (Wido), 82.
Gates, Iona, 81.
Gates, Jehiel, 64.
Gates, Jessie, 66.
Gates, John, 113.
Gates, John, 118.
Gates, John, 121.
Gates, Jonathan, 28.
Gates, Joseph, 81.
Gates, Joseph, 113.
Gates, Joseph, 2d, 82.
Gates, Joshua, 81.
Gates, Josiah, 121.
Gates, Martha, 82.
Gates, Mary, 113.
Gates, Matthew, 83.
Gates, Moses, 22.
Gates, Nathan, 82.
Gates, Nathn, 2d, 82.
Gates, Nathl, 82.
Gates, Nehemiah, 81.
Gates, Noadiah, 82.
Gates, Noah, 28.
Gates, Oliver, 82.
Gates, Phineas, 151.
Gates, Phinehas, 82.
Gates, Samuel, 22.
Gates, Samuel, 29.
Gates, Saml, 82.
Gates, Saml, 121.
Gates, Samuel, Jr, 22.
Gates, Sarah, 120.
Gates, Susanna, 146.
Gates, Theophelus L., 61.
Gates, Thos, 81.
Gates, Thomas, 114.
Gates, Thomas, 121.
Gates, Thos, Junr, 81.
Gates, Timothy, Esqr, 81.
Gates, Timo, 2d, 83.
Gates, Zebadiah, 120.
Gates, Zebulon, 146.
Gates, Zepra, 82.
Gatta, John I., 70.
Gaurd, Elisha, 120.
Gaurd, Nathan, 119.
Gaurd, Saml, 120.
Gauslin, John, 60.
Gavett, John, 114.
Gay, Amasa, 138.
Gay, Amie, 91.
Gay, Asael, 145.
Gay, Calvin, 154.
Gay, David, 67.
Gay, Eben, 137.
Gay, Ebene, 150.
Gay, Revd Ebenezer, 50.
Gay, Elisha, 145.
Gay, Elisha, 150.
Gay, Icabod, 132.
Gay, Joel, 135.
Gay, Levi, 38.
Gay, Pearce, 132.
Gay, Richard, 45.
Gay, Richard, 150.
Gay, Richard, 150.
Gay, Richard, Jr., 45.
Gay, Saml, 146.
Gayler, Elizabeth (Wd), 21.
Gaylor, Adward, 62.
Gaylor, Ammon, 62.
Gaylor, Ayer, 63.
Gaylor, Benjamin, 62.
Gaylor, Elijah, 69.
Gaylor, Joseph, 63.
Gaylor, Joseph, 69.
Gaylor, Marnory, 63.
Gaylor, Nehemiah, 69.
Gaylor, Roegs, 69.
Gaylor, Saml, 63.
Gaylor, Wait, 70.
Gaylord, Aaron, 56.
Gaylord, Aaron, 71.
Gaylord, Abiel, 38.
Gaylord, Benjamin, 71.
Gaylord, Charles, 38.
Gaylord, Chauny, 58.
Gaylord, David, 35.
Gaylord, Ebenezer, 71.
Gaylord, Elam, 35.
Gaylord, Eliakim, 54.
Gaylord, Eliakim, Jn, 54.
Gaylord, Eliazer, 54.
Gaylord, Elieazer, 88.
Gaylord, Elijah, 35.
Gaylord, Elijah, 58.
Gaylord, Elizur, 34.
Gaylord, Enos, 76.
Gaylord, Jesse, 35.
Gaylord, Jesse, Jr., 35.
Gaylord, Joel, 65.
Gaylord, Jno, 35.
Gaylord, John, 54.
Gaylord, Jonathan, 87.
Gaylord, Joseph, 34.
Gaylord, Joseph, Jr, 35.
Gaylord, Joseph, 2d, 34.
Gaylord, Jotham, 76.
Gaylord, Moses, 47.
Gaylord, Nathan, 71.
Gaylord, Samuel, 35.
Gaylord, Samuel, 86.
Gaylord, William, 34.
Gaylord, William, 71.
Gaylord, Wm C., 87.
Gazer, Aaron, 129.
Gazer, Dan. *See* Simon & Dan. Gazer, 126.
Gazer, Daniel, 129.
Gazer, John, 129.
Gazer, Levi, 129.
Gazer, Simon & Dan., 126.
Gears, Hezekiah, 88.
Gears, Jedediah, 133.
Gears, Saml, 135.
Geary, Ezekiel, 152.
Geary, Thomas, 116.
Gedion, John, 61.
Gee, William, 124.
Gee, William, Junr, 124.
Gee, Zophar, 124.
Geer, Aaron, 153.
Geer, Able, 113.
Geer, Amos, 118.
Geer, Amos, 153.
Geer, Benjamin, 118.
Geer, Charles, 69.
Geer, David, 120.
Geer, Easter, 119.
Geer, Ebenezer, 118.
Geer, Ebenr S., 143.
Geer, Elihu, 39.
Geer, Elijah, 58.
Geer, Elisha, 113.
Geer, Ezra, 1st, 58.
Geer, Ezra, 2d, 58.
Geer, George, 115.
Geer, Israel, 119.
Geer, Jacob, 119.
Geer, Jacob, 142.
Geer, James, 113.
Geer, James, 118.
Geer, John W., 114.
Geer, Jonathan, 114.
Geer, Joseph, 115.
Geer, Lebeus, 113.
Geer, Mary, 118.
Geer, Nathan, 113.
Geer, Nathaniel, 58.
Geer, Richard, 118.
Geer, Robart, 118.
Geer, Robart, 120.
Geer, Robert, 113.
Geer, Saml, 153.
Geer, Saml, 153.
Geer, Silsbey, 113.
Geer, Stephen, 113.
Geer, Thomas, 115.
Geer, Uziel, 130.
Geers, Caleb, 111.
Geers, Christopher, 113.
Geers, Daniel, 113.
Geers, Gurden, 118.
Geers, John, 141.
Geers, Roger, 113.
Geers, Squire, 130.
Geff (Negroe), 104.
Geir, George, 88.
Gemima (Negro), 126.
Gennings, McHanah, 153.
Gennings, Zebulon, 153.
George, Amos, 18.
George (Negro), 124.
George, Sarah, 71.
Gerens, Russell, 50.
Gerrard, Jesse, 57.
Gerret, Joshua, 64.
Gerret, Lydia, 64.
Gerrineau, Peter, 16.
Gesting, John, 128.
Ghoram, John, 58.
Ghoram, Phineas, 71.
Ghoram, Wakeman, 58.
Ghorrum, David, 71.
Gibb, Edward, 94.
Gibbons, John, 95.
Gibbord, Timothy, 110.
Gibbs, Benjamin, 64.
Gibbs, Charity, 54.
Gibbs, Clark, 47.
Gibbs, David, 65.
Gibbs, Ebenezer, 39.
Gibbs, Eldad, 64.
Gibbs, Ethamon, 64.
Gibbs, Gersham, 70.
Gibbs, Hannah, 17.
Gibbs, John, 53.
Gibbs, John, 101.
Gibbs, Justice, 64.
Gibbs, Lemuel, 54.
Gibbs, Moor, 73.
Gibbs, Philoe, 70.
Gibbs, Remembrance, 64.
Gibbs, Reuben, 65.
Gibbs, Robert, 58.
Gibbs, Samuel, 22.
Gibbs, Samuel, 64.
Gibbs, Silvanis, 59.
Gibbs, Simeon, 78.
Gibbs, Stephen, 37.
Gibbs, Truman, 60.
Gibbs, William, 64.
Gibbs, William, 64.
Gibeons, Gerard, 131.
Gibeons, John, 116.
Gibs, Josi, 137.
Gibs, Lydia, 70.
Gibs, Nathan, 70.
Gibs, Zadock, 70.
Gibson, Brinsmade, 75.
Gibson, Eliezer, 63.
Gibson, Ephraim, 60.
Gibson, Hannah, 104.
Gibson, Isaih, 58.
Gibson, James, 151.
Gibson, Roger, 60.

# INDEX.

Gibson, Roger, 127.
Gibson, Samuel, 43.
Gibson, Timothy, 88.
Gibson, William, 75.
Giddeons, Jonathan, 19.
Giddeons, Joseph, 19.
Giddeons, William, 19.
Giddeons, Zebulon, 19.
Giddings, Benjamin, 61.
Giddings, Joshua, 61.
Gideons, David, 66.
Gideons, Joseph, 114.
Gideons, Nath¹, 129.
Gideons, Solomon, 114.
Gifford, Caleb, 121.
Gifford, Siba, 134.
Gifford, Stephen, 126.
Gifford, Susanna, 126.
Giffords, Jeremiah, 130.
Giffords, John, 130.
Giffords, Samuel, 130.
Giffords, Sam¹, Junʳ, 132.
Gilbart, Abner, 28.
Gilbart, David, 28.
Gilbart, Ebenezer, 28.
Gilbert, Abner, 71.
Gilbert, Abraham, 18.
Gilbert, Abraham, 100.
Gilbert, Abraham, 2ⁿᵈ, 100.
Gilbert, Ager, 18.
Gilbert, Allen, 88.
Gilbert, Amos, 101.
Gilbert, Amos, 104.
Gilbert, Andrew, 32.
Gilbert, Asa, 86.
Gilbert, Asa, 101.
Gilbert, Benjamin, 24.
Gilbert, Benjamin, 47.
Gilbert, Benjamin, 88.
Gilbert, Burr, 32.
Gilbert, Caleb, 104.
Gilbert, Calvin, 71.
Gilbert, Charles, 47.
Gilbert, Daniel, 101.
Gilbert, David, 68.
Gilbert, David, 96.
Gilbert, David, 104.
Gilbert, Ebenezer, 32.
Gilbert, Ebenezer, 88.
Gilbert, Eleazʳ, 141.
Gilbert, Elihue, 17.
Gilbert, Elisha, 76.
Gilbert, Elisha, 104.
Gilbert, Elizabeth, 104.
Gilbert, Ely, 111.
Gilbert, Ezra, 74.
Gilbert, George, 130.
Gilbert, Grigson, 100.
Gilbert, Hezekiah, 71.
Gilbert, Hooker, 34.
Gilbert, Ichabod, 45.
Gilbert, Isaac, 104.
Gilbert, Jabez, 58.
Gilbert, Jabez, 74.
Gilbert, Jabez, 152.
Gilbert, James, 101.
Gilbert, James, 104.
Gilbert, Jessee, 63.
Gilbert, Joel, 18.
Gilbert, John, 17.
Gilbert, John, 20.
Gilbert, John, 31.
Gilbert, John, 70.
Gilbert, John, 87.
Gilbert, John, 100.
Gilbert, John, 123.
Gilbert, Jnᵒ, 135.
Gilbert, Jnᵒ, 135.
Gilbert, John, 147.
Gilbert, Jonathan, 34.
Gilbert, Jonathan, 47.
Gilbert, Jonathan, 87.
Gilbert, Jonᵃ, 125.
Gilbert, Jonathan, Jr., 34.
Gilbert, Jonathan, Junʳ, 87.
Gilbert, Joseph, 31.
Gilbert, Joseph, 67.
Gilbert, Joseph, 86.
Gilbert, Joseph, 100.
Gilbert, Joseph, 100.
Gilbert, Joseph, 141.
Gilbert, Katey, 101.
Gilbert, Lemwell, 18.
Gilbert, Lewis, 32.
Gilbert, Linus, 111.
Gilbert, Margaret, 104.
Gilbert, Mary, 34.
Gilbert, Mathew, 101.
Gilbert, Miriam, 103.
Gilbert, Moses, 34.
Gilbert, Moses, 100.
Gilbert, Nathan, 25.
Gilbert, Obediah, 17.
Gilbert, Rachel, 62.
Gilbert, Reubin, 31.
Gilbert, Rhoda, 88.
Gilbert, Roda, 67.
Gilbert, Sam¹, 82.
Gilbert, Samuel, 111.
Gilbert, Sam¹, 135.
Gilbert, Seth, 20.
Gilbert, Seth, 34.
Gilbert, Soloman, 111.
Gilbert, Stephen, 20.
Gilbert, Sylvester, 135.
Gilbert, Thadeus, 31.
Gilbert, Theodosia, 67.
Gilbert, Thodah, 67.
Gilbert, Thomas, 18.
Gilbert, Thomas, 31.
Gilbert, Thomas, 34.
Gilbert, Timothy, 104.
Gilbert, Truman, 74.
Gilbert, Wilks, 141.
Gilbert, Zalmon, 31.
Gilchrist, Damaras, 78.
Gilden, Issabell, 131.
Gildersleeves, Obadiah, 61.
Gildersleeves, Obediah, 79.
Gildersleeves, Phillip, 79.
Gildersleeves, Phillip, 80.
Gildersleve, Finch, 23.
Giles, John, 123.
Giles, Samuel, 52.
Giles, Thomas, 118.
Giles, Thomas, Junʳ, 119.
Giles, William, 86.
Giles, William, 152.
Gilkie, Peter, 93.
Gill, Abigail, 86.
Gill, Ebenezer M., 100.
Gill, John, 100.
Gill, John, 2ⁿᵈ, 100.
Gillam, Benjamin, 96.
Gillet, Aaron, 135.
Gillet, Abel, 71.
Gillet, Abraham, 41.
Gillet, Alme, 54.
Gillet, Amos, 65.
Gillet, Benjamin, 37.
Gillet, Dan¹, 55.
Gillet, Daniel, 124.
Gillet, David, 78.
Gillet, Ebenezer, 50.
Gillet, Ela, 120.
Gillet, Eliphalet, 102.
Gillet, Elick, 35.
Gillet, Ezra, 124.
Gillet, Isaac, 41.
Gillet, Isaac, 51.
Gillet, Isaac, 146.
Gillet, Isaac, 146.
Gillet, Jabes, 69.
Gillet, John, 63.
Gillet, John, 69.
Gillet, Jnᵒ, 135.
Gillet, Jonah, 55.
Gillet, Jonah, 2ᵈ, 55.
Gillet, Jonathan, 58.
Gillet, Jonathan, 60.
Gillet, Jonathan, 62.
Gillet, Jonathan, 102.
Gillet, Joseph, 121.
Gillet, Joseph, 124.
Gillet, Joseph, Junʳ, 121.
Gillet, Lydia, 121.
Gillet, Mary (Wido.), 146.
Gillet, Matthew, 67.
Gillet, Michael, 67.
Gillet, Nehemiah, 121.
Gillet, Noah, 41.
Gillet, Oliver, 45.
Gillet, Reuben, 35.
Gillet, Reynold, 124.
Gillet, Stephen, 69.
Gillet, Wheelor, 56.
Gillet, William, 24.
Gillet, William, 66.
Gillet, Zacheus, 44.
Gillett, Adne, 44.
Gillett, Amos, 41.
Gillett, Azariah, 44.
Gillett, Benoni, 44.
Gillett, Buckler, 44.
Gillett, Calvin, 51.
Gillett, Daniel, 51.
Gillett, Elihu, 51.
Gillett, Elijah, 43.
Gillett, Ephraim, 44.
Gillett, Isaac, 44.
Gillett, Jabash, 44.
Gillett, Jacob, 44.
Gillett, Jeremiah, 35.
Gillett, Joab, 45.
Gillett, Joseph, 44.
Gillett, Levi, 44.
Gillett, Nathan, 44.
Gillett, Nathan, 50.
Gillett, Nathaniel, 45.
Gillett, Nathaniel, Jʳ, 45.
Gillett, Noadiah, 41.
Gillett, Othenial, 44.
Gillett, Othenial, Jʳ, 44.
Gillett, Timothy, 45.
Gillett, Zachariah, 50.
Gillit, Aaron, 55.
Gillit, Abel, 55.
Gillit, Abel, Ju., 55.
Gillit, Amasa, 135.
Gillit, Amos, 55.
Gillit, Charles, 135.
Gillit, Deborah, 55.
Gillit, Ezek¹, 135.
Gillit, Levi, 55.
Gillitt, Joab, 48.
Gillman, Asher, 96.
Gillon, James, 96.
Gillott, Joel, 58.
Gilman, Benjamin, 38.
Gilman, David, 36.
Gilman, Elihu, 69.
Gilman, Elizabeth, 36.
Gilman, Evans, 24.
Gilman, George, 36.
Gilman, Jonah, 36.
Gilman, Nathaniel, 36.
Gilman, Oliver, 36.
Gilman, Robert, 151.
Gilman, Solomon, 37.
Gilman, Solomon, Jʳ, 37.
Gilman, Wᵐ, 137.
Gilson, Jonᵃ, 132.
Gimman, George, 150.
Ginnason, Lucy, 86.
Ginnings, Jonathan, 114.
Ginnings, Zephaniah, 131.
Gion, Luke, 114.
Gipson, John, 88.
Gipson, Samuel, 57.
Gitchel, Joseph, 126.
Gitteau, Ephraim, 66.
Givins, Shelden, 76.
Gladden, Jedidiah, 34.
Gladden, Josiah, 52.
Gladden, Samuel, 33.
Glading, Ebenezer, 89.
Glading, Joseph, 90.
Glading, Rebekah, 89.
Glading, Silas, 89.
Glading, Wye, 89.
Glasier, Jacob, 73.
Glasier, John, 76.
Glason, Moses, 37.
Glass, James, 64.
Glass, John, 71.
Glass, Silas, 142.
Glayer, Silas, 139.
Glazier, John, 55.
Gleason, Arial, 67.
Gleason, Chancey, 49.
Gleason, David, 41.
Gleason, Elezer, 139.
Gleason, Elisha, 149.
Gleason, Ephraim, 69.
Gleason, Isaac, 40.
Gleason, Isaac, 41.
Gleason, John, 150.
Gleason, Jonah, 40.
Gleason, Joseph, 40.
Gleason, Joseph, 79.
Gleason, Joseph, Jr., 40.
Gleason, Margarett, 86.
Gleason, Nath¹, 150.
Gleason, Ruful, 61.
Gleason, Samuel, 41.
Gleason, Solomon, 40.
Gleason, William, 151.
Glenny, William, 101.
Gloding, Daniel, 83.
Glosender, John, 42.
Glover, Benjamin, 20.
Glover, Budsery, 78.
Glover, Christopher, 12.
Glover, Daniel, 20.
Glover, Edward, 64.
Glover, Elias, 20.
Glover, Henary, 20.
Glover, James, 20.
Glover, Jeremiah, 123.
Glover, John, 20.
Glover, Lemuel, 27.
Glover, Nathan, 148.
Glover, Solimon, 20.
Glover, Zalmon, 20.
Gobine, Nicholas, 103.
Goddard, Ebenezer, 128.
Godfry, Cristopher, 32.
Godfry, Daniel, 32.
Godfry, David, 32.
Godfry, Ebenezer, 13.
Godfry, Eleazer, 32.
Godfry, Elias, 32.
Godfry, Hannah, 14.
Godfry, Isaac, 32.
Godfry, John, 14.
Godfry, Jonathan, 13.
Godfry, Jonathan, 32.
Godfry, Mary, 12.
Godfry, Moses, 31.
Godfry, Nathan, 13.
Godfry, Samuel, 27.
Godfry, Silliman, 32.
Godfry, Stephen, 13.
Godman, Jnᵒ, 139.
Goff, Aaron, 43.
Goff, Benjamin, 81.
Goff, Charles, 121.
Goff, Cumfort, 121.
Goff, Cumfort, Junʳ, 121.
Goff, David, 87.
Goff, Elisha, 42.
Goff, Ezekiel, 80.
Goff, Gansey, 121.
Goff, Gideon, 53.
Goff, Gideon, 81.
Goff, Gideon, 83.
Goff, Jacob, 81.
Goff, James, 81.
Goff, John, 80.
Goff, Jonathan, 81.
Goff, Joshua, 121.
Goff, Josiah, 53.
Goff, Josiah, 81.
Goff, Peter, 15.
Goff, Phillip, 80.
Goff, Phillip, Junʳ, 80.
Goff, Samuel, 81.
Goff, Sam¹, 121.
Goff, Squire, 121.
Goff, William, 125.
Goit, Richard, 64.
Gold, Benjamin, 57.
Gold, Gurdon, 43.
Gold, Hezekiah, 57.
Gold, Joseph Wakefield, 57.
Gold, Nathan, 31.
Gold, Peter, 104.
Gold, Samuel, 27.
Gold, Thomas, 91.
Gold, Thomas, 103.
Gold, William, 91.
Goldsmith, Gilbert, 101.
Goldsmith, James, 101.
Goldsmith, James, 2ⁿᵈ, 101.
Goldsmith, John, 97.
Goldsmith, John, 2ⁿᵈ, 97.
Goldsmith, Joseph, 101.
Goldsmith, William, 101.
Gonyard, Spensor, 68.
Goodale, Aaron, 143.
Goodale, Abijah, 141.
Goodale, Amasa, 149.
Goodale, Asa, 154.
Goodale, Avary, 43.
Goodale, Caleb, 149.
Goodale, Dan¹, 149.
Goodale, David, 149.
Goodale, Ebenezer, 39.
Goodale, Eler, 134.
Goodale, Henery, 43.
Goodale, Henry, 79.
Goodale, Isaac, 43.
Goodale, Jnᵒ, 139.
Goodale, John, 154.
Goodale, Joseph, 43.
Goodale, Joseph, Jr., 43.
Goodale, Lemuel, 153.
Goodale, Meachum, 149.
Goodale, Richard, 149.
Goodale, Thomas, 43.
Goodale, Walter, 39.
Goodale, Zachʰ, 149.
Goodard, Mary, 129.
Goodel, Ruben, 113.
Goodel, Silas, 131.
Goodell, Benjamin, 130.
Goodfaith, David, 129.
Goodhue, David, 65.
Goodin, William, 146.
Goodluck, London, 18.
Goodman, Asa, 47.
Goodman, Moses, 47.
Goodman, Richard, 45.
Goodman, Richard, 47.
Goodman, Thomas, 47.
Goodman, Thomas, 60.
Goodrich, Abigail, 42.
Goodrich, Abigail, 52.
Goodrich, Abner, 63.
Goodrich, Alpheus, 53.
Goodrich, Asahel, 34.
Goodrich, Ashbel, 60.
Goodrich, Barsheba, 87.
Goodrich, Benjamin, 62.
Goodrich, Bethrolma, 91.
Goodrich, Chancey, 45.
Goodrich, Charles, 79.
Goodrich, Charles, Junʳ, 79.
Goodrich, Crafts, 132.
Goodrich, David, 35.
Goodrich, David, 42.
Goodrich, David, 42.
Goodrich, David, 54.
Goodrich, David, Jr., 42.
Goodrich, Ebenezer, 53.
Goodrich, Eliakim, 42.
Goodrich, Elias, 34.
Goodrich, Elihu, 53.
Goodrich, Elijah, 41.
Goodrich, Elijah, 53.
Goodrich, Elijah H., 43.
Goodrich, Elijur, 104.
Goodrich, Elisha, 42.
Goodrich, Elisha, 53.
Goodrich, Elizabeth, 63.
Goodrich, Elizur, 53.
Goodrich, Elizur, 96.
Goodrich, Gidion, 53.
Goodrich, Giles, 68.
Goodrich, Gurden, 54.
Goodrich, Gurdin, Jr., 53.
Goodrich, Hezekiah, 79.
Goodrich, Hosea, 88.
Goodrich, Ichabod, 53.
Goodrich, Isaac, 42.
Goodrich, Isaac, 53.
Goodrich, Isaac, 61.
Goodrich, Isaac, 70.
Goodrich, Israel, 53.
Goodrich, Israel, 53.
Goodrich, James, 91.
Goodrich, Jediahah, 33.
Goodrich, Jehiel, 42.
Goodrich, Jeremiah, 79.
Goodrich, Jeremiah, Junʳ, 79.
Goodrich, Jerusha, 53.
Goodrich, Joel, 63.
Goodrich, John, 34.
Goodrich, John, 52.
Goodrich, John, 52.
Goodrich, John, 54.
Goodrich, John, 80.
Goodrich, John, 104.
Goodrich, Joseph, 53.
Goodrich, Joshua, 79.
Goodrich, Josiah, 53.
Goodrich, Moses, 132.
Goodrich, Nathaniel, 53.
Goodrich, Nathaniel, Jr., 53.
Goodrich, Noah, 42.
Goodrich, Oliver, 53.
Goodrich, Phineas, 91.
Goodrich, Reuben, 79.
Goodrich, Richard, 79.
Goodrich, Roger, 53.
Goodrich, Roswell, 42.
Goodrich, Salmon, 34.
Goodrich, Samuel, 85.
Goodrich, Revᵈ Samuel, 28.
Goodrich, Seth, 33.
Goodrich, Seth, 54.
Goodrich, Seth, 69.
Goodrich, Solomon, 67.
Goodrich, Solomon, 79.
Goodrich, Stephen, 47.
Goodrich, Temperance, 53.
Goodrich, Thilcon, 53.
Goodrich, Thoˢ, 134.
Goodrich, Wait, 42.
Goodrich, Wait, Jr., 42.
Goodrich, Waitstill, 56.
Goodrich, William, 53.
Goodrich, William, 63.
Goodrich, Zenas, 33.
Goodsall, Lidia, 92.
Goodsel, Isaac, 75.
Goodsel, Thomas, 75.
Goodsel, Timothy, 75.
Goodsell, Daniel, 97.
Goodsell, David, 13.
Goodsell, Epaphras, 13.
Goodsell, James, 13.
Goodsell, John, 12.
Goodsell, John, 62.
Goodsell, John, 97.
Goodsell, John Junʳ, 97.
Goodsell, Levi, 104.
Goodsell, Lewis, 13.
Goodsell, Samuel, 31.
Goodsell, Samuel, 50.
Goodsell, Samuel, 97.
Goodsell, Thomas, 13.
Goodshell, Daniel, 97.
Goodspead, Nath¹, 138.
Goodspeed, Nathan, 81.
Goodwin, Abigal, 69.
Goodwin, Allyn, 45.
Goodwin, Anna (Wid.), 45.
Goodwin, Asher, 45.
Goodwin, David, 45.
Goodwin, Ebenʳ, 63.
Goodwin, Ebenʳ, 63.
Goodwin, Elizabeth, 64.
Goodwin, Elzer, 61.
Goodwin, George, 45.
Goodwin, Isaac, 70.
Goodwin, Jacob, 86.
Goodwin, James, 45.
Goodwin, Jessee, 63.
Goodwin, John, 36.
Goodwin, John, 45.
Goodwin, John, 63.
Goodwin, John P., 63.
Goodwin, Johnᵗʰ, 146.
Goodwin, Jonathan, 45.
Goodwin, Jonothan, 61.
Goodwin, Joseph, 36.
Goodwin, Joseph, 48.
Goodwin, Joseph, 64.
Goodwin, Levi, 36.
Goodwin, Mary, 45.
Goodwin, Mary, 45.
Goodwin, Michael, 61.
Goodwin, Morgan, 41.
Goodwin, Moses, 61.
Goodwin, Nathaniel, 64.
Goodwin, Russell, 45.
Goodwin, Samuel, 45.
Goodwin, Samuel, 86.
Goodwin, Sam¹, 146.
Goodwin, Seth, 62.
Goodwin, Sukey, 86.
Goodwin, Theodore, 45.
Goodwin, Thomas, 64.
Goodwin, Thomas, 86.
Goodwin, Thomas, Junʳ, 86.
Goodwin, Timothy, 45.
Goodwin, Tiras, 61.
Goodwin, Titus, 47.
Goodwin, William, 45.
Goodwin, William, 61.
Goodyear, Asa, 100.

# INDEX.

Goodyear, Asa, 2nd, 100.
Goodyear, Edward, 92.
Goodyear, Gerad, 100.
Goodyear, Jesse, 100.
Goodyear, Joel, 111.
Goodyear, Stephen, 100.
Goodyear, Theophilus, 100.
Goodyear, Timothy, 100.
Goodyear, Titus, 100.
Goodyer, Chancy, 66.
Goodyer, David, 76.
Goodyer, Simeon, 112.
Goodyer, Stephen, 69.
Goodyer, Theophilus, 112.
Goold, David, 45.
Goold, David, 61.
Goold, Job, 60.
Goold, John, 40.
Goold, Jonathan, 61.
Goold, Thomas R., 60.
Gooner, Quash, 52.
Gorden, Alexander, 78.
Gordon, Alexander, 91.
Gordon, Alexander, 142.
Gordon, Archibald, 151.
Gordon, Elexander, 113.
Gordon, Gardner, 137.
Gordon, George, 56.
Gordon, George, 131.
Gordon, James, 148.
Gordon, John, 56.
Gordon, John, 128.
Gordon, John, 129.
Gordon, John, 151.
Gordon, John, Jnr, 151.
Gordon, Lewis, 64.
Gordon, Lidia, 91.
Gordon, Maryam, 151.
Gordon, Samuel, 70.
Gordon, Sarah, 104.
Gordon, Thomas, 151.
Gordon (Widow), 137.
Gore, Able, 119.
Gore, Saml., 152.
Gorham, Abigal, 103.
Gorham, Benjamin, 11.
Gorham, Ebenezer, 12.
Gorham, Echabod, 19.
Gorham, Elias, 102.
Gorham, Elizur, 102.
Gorham, George, 29.
Gorham, George, 94.
Gorham, Hannah (Wd), 26.
Gorham, Isaac, 27.
Gorham, Isaac, 29.
Gorham, Isaac, 103.
Gorham, Isaac, Junr, 27.
Gorham, Jaber, 27.
Gorham, Jacob (Negro), 32.
Gorham, Joseph, 103.
Gorham, Joseph, Jnr, 12.
Gorham, Lockwood, 29.
Gorham, Meeker, 19.
Gorham, Miles, 104.
Gorham, Nathan, 29.
Gorham, Nehemiah, 29.
Gorham, Phebe, 30.
Gorham, Samuel, 23.
Gorham, Samuel, 104.
Gorham, Shubal, 32.
Gorham, Stephan, 104.
Gorham, Susanah, 100.
Gorham, Timothy, 103.
Gorham (Widow), 30.
Gorham, William, 30.
Gorton, Benjamin, 124.
Gorton, Collins, 127.
Gorton, John, 149.
Gorton, Joseph, 113.
Gorton, Stephen, 113.
Gorton, William, 151.
Gosler, Asa, 43.
Gosler, Timothy, 43.
Gosling, Solomon, 66.
Goss, Ebeneser, 76.
Goss, Richard, 73.
Got, Danl, 135.
Got, Jno, 136.
Gotham, Daniel, 26.
Goudy, Alexander, 136.
Gouge, Nathaniel, 88.
Gould, Aaron, 13.
Gould, Besaliel, 153.
Gould, David, 13.
Gould, Dimon, 13.
Gould, Echobod, 13.
Gould, Edmond, 142.
Gould, Elizabeth, 14.
Gould, Francis, 124.
Gould, Isaac, 14.
Gould, James, 122.
Gould, James, Junr, 122.
Gould, Jesse, 13.
Gould, John, 122.
Gould, Jonathan, 140.
Gould, Jonathn, 149.
Gould, Luther, 14.
Gould, Nathan, 13.
Gould, Samuel, 13.
Gould, Stephen, 13.
Gould, Talcott, 14.
Gould, Walter, 122.
Gould, William, 19.

Gourd, Thomas, 105.
Gove, William, 45.
Gowan, William, 105.
Gowdey, James, 68.
Gowdy, Robert, 40.
Gowdy, Samuel, 40.
Gowdy, Samuel, 66.
Gowdy, William, 40.
Gowsley, William, 101.
Gozzard, Abel, 44.
Gozzard, Ebenezer, 44.
Gozzard, Ebenezer, Jr., 44.
Gozzard, Ezra, 44.
Gozzard, Ezra, 44.
Gozzard, Fille, 44.
Gozzard, Isaac, 44.
Gozzard, John, 44.
Gozzard, John, Jr., 44.
Gozzard, Levi, 44.
Gozzard, Luther, 44.
Gozzard, Martin, 44.
Gozzard, Moses, 44.
Gozzard, Nathan, 44.
Gozzard, Nicholus, 44.
Gozzard, Rufus, 44.
Grace, John, 86.
Grace, Nicholass, 85.
Graham, Andrew, 94.
Graham, Curtis, 73.
Graham, Daniel, 51.
Graham, Elenor, 105.
Graham, Jane, 90.
Graham, John, 103.
Graham, John, 107.
Graham, Revd John, 50.
Graham (Widow), 104.
Granger, Abner, 50.
Granger, Abraham, 50.
Granger, Amos, 50.
Granger, Benjamin, 51.
Granger, Bildad, 52.
Granger, Bildad, 2d, 50.
Granger, Charles, 50.
Granger, Eli, 52.
Granger, Elihu, 51.
Granger, Elijah, 51.
Granger, Elisha, 51.
Granger, Elisha, 2d, 51.
Granger, Enock, 52.
Granger, Epaphras, 52.
Granger, George, 71.
Granger, Gideon, 51.
Granger, Gideon, 2d, 50.
Granger, Israel, 44.
Granger, Jacob, 51.
Granger, John, 50.
Granger, Joseph, 51.
Granger, Julius, 51.
Granger, Oliver, 50.
Granger, Phinehas, 70.
Granger, Rufus, 52.
Granger, Samuel, 51.
Granger, William, 59.
Granger, Zadoc, 50.
Granis, Benjamin, 103.
Granie, David, 94.
Granis, Elihu, 97.
Granis, Isaac, 97.
Granis, Joseph, 97.
Granis, Mary, 97.
Granis, Nathaniel, 105.
Granis, Russell, 97.
Graniss, Aaron, 49.
Graniss, Joel, 50.
Graniss, Stephen, 50.
Grannis, Eldad, 92.
Grannis, Enos, 58.
Grannis, Hannah, 76.
Grannis, Robart, 65.
Grannis, William, 64.
Grant, Aaron, 38.
Grant, Aaron, Jr., 38.
Grant, Amos, 116.
Grant, Azariah, 38.
Grant, Benjamin, 38.
Grant, Beriah, 120.
Grant, Charles, 2d, 64.
Grant, Cyrus, 132.
Grant, Darius, 13.
Grant, David, 55.
Grant, Ebenezer, 38.
Grant, Eber, 138.
Grant, Edward C., 39.
Grant, Elijah, 69.
Grant, Elnathan, 132.
Grant, Em, 138.
Grant, Em, Jr, 138.
Grant, Gideon, 39.
Grant, Gideon, Jr., 39.
Grant, Gilbert, 116.
Grant, Hamlinton, 140.
Grant, Hezekiah, 39.
Grant, Isaac, 38.
Grant, James, 91.
Grant, Jesse, 66.
Grant, Joel, 69.
Grant, John, 39.
Grant, John, 111.
Grant, John, 116.
Grant, Jona, 134.
Grant, Joshua, 48.
Grant, Joshua, 48.
Grant, Joshua, 116.

Grant, Josiah, 116.
Grant, Justus, 39.
Grant, Margeret, 91.
Grant, Mathew, 39.
Grant, Matthew, 62.
Grant, Minor, 150.
Grant, Noah, 116.
Grant, Noah, Junr, 116.
Grant, Oliver, 39.
Grant, Oliver, 116.
Grant, Oliver, Junr, 116.
Grant, Oliver, 2nd, 39.
Grant, Reuben, 38.
Grant, Roswell, 38.
Grant, Roswell, 63.
Grant, Samuel R., 39.
Grant, Thos & co., 150.
Grant (Widow), 133.
Grant, William, 39.
Grant, William, 68.
Grant, Wm, 114.
Grant, William, 114.
Grany, Ebenezer, 94.
Gratis, Nancy, 71.
Graton, Nathl, 134.
Grave, Abraham, 100.
Grave, Benjamin, 100.
Grave, Daniel, 100.
Graves, Abner, 84.
Graves, Alexander, 65.
Graves, Ambrose, 98.
Graves, Ambrose, 99.
Graves, Anna, 67.
Graves, Arvil, 122.
Graves, Asa, 122.
Graves, Asahel, 57.
Graves, Benjamin, 66.
Graves, Benja, 82.
Graves, Ebenezer, 99.
Graves, Eli, 99.
Graves, Elias, 99.
Graves, Elijah, 82.
Graves, Elijah, 135.
Graves, Ezra, 19.
Graves, Ezra, 98.
Graves, George, 99.
Graves, Gilbert, 99.
Graves, Haynes, 99.
Graves, Hubbard, 63.
Graves, Ichabod, 67.
Graves, Irael, 99.
Graves, Isachar, 144.
Graves, Jedediah, 19.
Graves, John, 85.
Graves, John, 144.
Graves, Jonathan, 115.
Graves, Joseph, 88.
Graves, Luman, 99.
Graves, Nathaniel, 97.
Graves, Peter, 122.
Graves, Peter, Junr, 122.
Graves, Saml, 117.
Graves, Simeon, 99.
Graves, Stephen, 99.
Graves, Sylvanus, 84.
Graves, Temperance, 98.
Graves, Timothy, 99.
Graves, Whitney, 144.
Graves, William, 65.
Graves, William, 71.
Gravy, Francis, 29.
Gray, Abial, 47.
Gray, Anna, 94.
Gray, Benjamin, 118.
Gray, Daniel, 31.
Gray, Darias, 67.
Gray, Ebenezr, 153.
Gray, Edward, 45.
Gray, Elias, 19.
Gray, Elijah, 32.
Gray, George, 55.
Gray, Giddeon, 12.
Gray, Gideon, 32.
Gray, Gilead, 27.
Gray, Gilead, 28.
Gray, Hannah (Wd), 22.
Gray, Hezekiah, 10.
Gray, Isaac, 27.
Gray, James, 27.
Gray, James, 32.
Gray, Jenney, 148.
Gray, Joel, 28.
Gray, John, 27.
Gray, John, 32.
Gray, Joseph, 23.
Gray, Joseph, 19.
Gray, Justus, 12.
Gray, Justus, 28.
Gray, Moses, 19.
Gray, Nathan, 23.
Gray, Nehemiah, 13.
Gray, Phillup, 118.
Gray, Reuel, 29.
Gray, Saml, 152.
Gray, Seth, 20.
Gray, Siliman, 13.
Gray, Solomon, 12.
Gray, Stephen, 27.
Gray, Thomas, 152.
Gray, William, 13.
Gray, William, 21.
Gray, Wm, 55.

Gray, William, 101.
Grear, Mathew, 46.
Greegory, Samuel, 58.
Green, Abraham, 24.
Green, Amos, 24.
Green, Amos, 150.
Green, Anna, 101.
Green, Azel, 39.
Green, Barzilla, 39.
Green, Benja, 150.
Green, Benja, 151.
Green, Caleb, 16.
Green, Caleb, 22.
Green, Charles, 16.
Green, Charles, 154.
Green, Daniel, 22.
Green, Daniel, 105.
Green, Danl, 134.
Green, David, 102.
Green, Dexter, 150.
Green, Ebenr, 150.
Green, Edward, 144.
Green, Eleazer, 56.
Green, Eleazer, 56.
Green, Eleazer, 2d, 56.
Green, Eunice, 142.
Green, Henry, 143.
Green, Ira, 151.
Green, Jabez, 31.
Green, Jacob, 57.
Green, James, 16.
Green, James, 81.
Green, Jarus, 71.
Green, John, 16.
Green, John, 61.
Green, Jno, 137.
Green, John, 150.
Green, John, 151.
Green, Jonathan, 151.
Green, Jonathan, 151.
Green, Joseph, 9.
Green, Joseph, 98.
Green, Joseph, 118.
Green, Martin, 67.
Green, Mary (Wid.), 39.
Green, Mercy (Wd), 24.
Green, Nathaniel, 66.
Green, Obadiah, 39.
Green, Orastus, 11.
Green, Perry, 34.
Green, Pheneas, 150.
Green, Robert, 145.
Green, Robert, 145.
Green, Roswold, 38.
Green, Samuel, 12.
Green, Sam, 70.
Green, Samuel, 104.
Green, Saml, 151.
Green, Samuel, 1st, 57.
Green, Samuel, 2d, 57.
Green, Sarah, 101.
Green, Seth, 150.
Green, Solomon, 32.
Green, Thomas, 104.
Green, Thos, 151.
Green, Timothy, 127.
Green, Willard, 70.
Greene, Benja, 126.
Greene, Caleb, 115.
Greene, Christopher, 126.
Greene, David, 113.
Greene, John, 113.
Greene, John, 116.
Greene, John, 116.
Greene, John, 122.
Greene, Mathew, 116.
Greene, Winter, 113.
Greenfield, Archibauld S., 123.
Greenfield, James, 123.
Greenfield, Thomas, 86.
Greenill, Daniel, 58.
Greenleaf, David, 133.
Greenslit, Elijah, 143.
Greenslit, Joel, 143.
Greenslit, Titus, 22.
Greenwood, Parson, 46.
Gregg, Joseph, 149.
Greggs, David, 149.
Greggs, Ichabod, 154.
Greggs, Nathan, 149.
Greggs, Saml, 149.
Greggs, Sarah, 149.
Gregory, Aaron, 23.
Gregory, Aaron M., 19.
Gregory, Abijah, 23.
Gregory, Abraham, 21.
Gregory, Daniel, 23.
Gregory, Daniel, 30.
Gregory, Deborah, 11.
Gregory, Denton, 21.
Gregory, Dolly (Wd), 23.
Gregory, Ebenezer, 11.
Gregory, Ebenezer, 21.
Gregory, Ebenezer 23.
Gregory, Ebenezer, Junr, 23.
Gregory, Enoch, 30.
Gregory, Ezra, 11.
Gregory, Ezra, 23.
Gregory, Fairweather, 58.
Gregory, Gilman, 30.
Gregory, Isaac, 22.
Gregory, Isaac, Jr, 22.

Gregory, Isaiah, 23.
Gregory, Jabez, 23.
Gregory, James, 18.
Gregory, James, 29.
Gregory, Jeheel, 23.
Gregory, John, 10.
Gregory, John, 11.
Gregory, John, 21.
Gregory, John, Jur, 10.
Gregory, Joseph, 62.
Gregory, Joseph, 68.
Gregory, Josiah, 24.
Gregory, Mathew, 11.
Gregory, Monson, 11.
Gregory, Moses, 23.
Gregory, Moses, 23.
Gregory, Nathan, 11.
Gregory, Nathan, 11.
Gregory, Nathan, 23.
Gregory, Nathaniel, 11.
Gregory, Ralph, 19.
Gregory, Rebecca (Wd), 23.
Gregory, Samuel, 11.
Gregory, Samuel, 21.
Gregory, Samuel, 21.
Gregory, Samuel, 30.
Gregory, Samuel, 31.
Gregory, Seely, 21.
Gregory, Silas, 21.
Gregory, Silas, 23.
Gregory, Stephen, 21.
Gregory, Stephen, 32.
Gregory, Stephen, 58.
Gregory, Thomas, 10.
Gregory, Thomas, 23.
Gregory, William, 31.
Gregory, Zaccheus, 28.
Grenell, Michael, 60.
Grennold, Japer, 65.
Grennold, Seth, 65.
Grenold, Samuel, 62.
Grenough, William, 104.
Grey, Jonathan, 117.
Grey, Joseph, 26.
Grey, Joseph, 29.
Grey, Robart, 116.
Gridley, Abel, 33.
Gridley, Abel, 58.
Gridley, Amos, 33.
Gridley, Ard, 49.
Gridley, Asahel, 34.
Gridley, Asahel, 49.
Gridley, Ashbel, 49.
Gridley, Clement, 33.
Gridley, Daniel, 40.
Gridley, David, 41.
Gridley, Ebenezer, 40.
Gridley, Elijah, 41.
Gridley, Elisha, 49.
Gridley, Hezekiah, 34.
Gridley, Hezekiah, Jr., 35.
Gridley, Hosea, 76.
Gridley, Isaac, 40.
Gridley, Isaac, Esqr, 88.
Gridley, Jonathan, 40.
Gridley, Joseph, 49.
Gridley, Judath, 33.
Gridley, Luke, 33.
Gridley, Moses, 35.
Gridley, Noadiah, 40.
Gridley, Noah, 49.
Gridley, Obed, 41.
Gridley, Oliver, 33.
Gridley, Rezin, 40.
Gridley, Roger, 33.
Gridley, Selah, 33.
Gridley, Seth, 40.
Gridley, Silas, 58.
Gridley, Thomas, 33.
Gridley, Thomas, 35.
Gridley, Timothy, 41.
Gridley, Uriel, 76.
Griffen, Absalom, 44.
Griffen, Edward, 85.
Griffen, Jared, 85.
Griffen, John, 119.
Griffen, Joshua, 80.
Griffen, Nathaniel, 44.
Griffen, Samuel, 84.
Griffen, Saml, 123.
Griffeth, Thomas, 85.
Griffin, Abner, 20.
Griffin, Abraham, 43.
Griffin, Amos, 20.
Griffin, Aron, 91.
Griffin, Benoni, 43.
Griffin, Catherine, 10.
Griffin, Ebenezer, 86.
Griffin, Ebenr, 143.
Griffin, Elijah, 44.
Griffin, Elizabeth, 44.
Griffin, Elizabeth, 95.
Griffin, Ezri, 69.
Griffin, Geo., 82.
Griffin, George, 151.
Griffin, Jasper, 98.
Griffin, Jasper, 122.
Griffin, Joab, 44.
Griffin, Joel, 98.
Griffin, John, 44.
Griffin, John, 82.
Griffin, Jno., 89.

# INDEX.

Griffin, John, 122.
Griffin, Jonathan, 12.
Griffin, Jonathan, 95.
Griffin, Joseph, 20.
Griffin, Joseph, 27.
Griffin, Joseph, 98.
Griffin, Joshua, 122.
Griffin, Lem¹, 82.
Griffin, Mary, 86.
Griffin, Mathew, 44.
Griffin, Michael, 44.
Griffin, Nathan, 82.
Griffin, Nathan, 122.
Griffin, Nathaniel, 98.
Griffin, Peter, 98.
Griffin, Reubin, 20.
Griffin, Robert, 99.
Griffin, Rossiter, 103.
Griffin, Samuel, 88.
Griffin, Sarah, 122.
Griffin, Seth, 44.
Griffin, Simon, 52.
Griffin, Stephen, 44.
Griffin, Stephen, 44.
Griffin, Stephen, 2ᵈ, 43.
Griffin, Thomas, 44.
Griffin, Thomas, 60.
Griffin, Thomas, Jr, 44.
Griffin, Timothy, 97.
Griffin, William, 12.
Griffing, Abner, 90.
Griffing, Benjamin, 85.
Griffing, Daniel, 85.
Griffing, David, 85.
Griffing, James, 85.
Griffing, James N., 85.
Griffing, William, 85.
Griffith, Edward, 70.
Griffith, Joshua, Junr, 81.
Griffith, Stephen, 81.
Griffith, Wm, 23.
Griffiths, Benjamin, 99.
Grifiths, Danˡ, 35.
Grigg, Alexander, 16.
Grigg, Henry, 16.
Griggs, Abijah, 154.
Griggs, Elliot, 35.
Griggs, Hezª, 149.
Griggs, Jacob, 76.
Griggs, Jno, 138.
Griggs, Jos., 139.
Griggs, Josu, 138.
Griggs, Noah, 1st, 76.
Griggs, Noah, 2ᵈ, 76.
Griggs, Paul, 76.
Griggs, Samˡ, 138.
Griggs, Solomon, 76.
Griggs (Widow), 138.
Griggsby, Nathˡ, 150.
Grigny, Dan., 44.
Grillery, Daniel, 109.
Grilley, Teuly, 110.
Grilly, Sirus, 110.
Grimes, Abigail, 53.
Grimes, Alexander, 53.
Grimes, Cyrus, 90.
Grimes, Daniel, 48.
Grimes, Daniel, Jr, 48.
Grimes, Elisha, 48.
Grimes, Elisha, Jr., 48.
Grimes, Isaac, 48.
Grimes, John, 41.
Grimes, Joseph, 48.
Grimes, Joseph, 79.
Grimes, Josiah, 53.
Grimes, Simeon, 55.
Grinall, William, 95.
Grindley, Alexander, 40.
Grinnell, Mathew, 115.
Grinnol, Barber, 85.
Grinnol, Daniel, 66.
Grinnol, William B., 85.
Grinnun, John, 59.
Grist, Ann, 131.
Grist, Joseph, 45.
Gristing, James, 128.
Griswell, Shubal, 69.
Griswold, Abel, 55.
Griswold, Abell, 130.
Griswold, Adonijah, 60.
Griswold, Alexander, 45.
Griswold, Alexander, 48.
Griswold, Asa, 58.
Griswold, Ashebel, 60.
Griswold, Ashbel, 33.
Griswold, Benajah, 39.
Griswold, Benjamin, 58.
Griswold, Collins, 50.
Griswold, Constant, 53.
Griswold, Daniel, 67.
Griswold, David, 67.
Griswold, Diah, 129.
Griswold, Edwd, 55.
Griswold, Elihu, 55.
Griswold, Elijah, 48.
Griswold, Elijah, 55.
Griswold, Elisha, 48.
Griswold, Elisha, 52.
Griswold, Elisha, Jr., 48.
Griswold, Experience, 33.
Griswold, Ezeriah, 67.
Griswold, Ezeriah, 67.
Griswold, Ezra, 98.

Griswold, Francis, 55.
Griswold, Frederic, 52.
Griswold, George, 37.
Griswold, George, 55.
Griswold, George, 67.
Griswold, George, 99.
Griswold, George, Juˢ., 55.
Griswold, Gideon, 33.
Griswold, Giles, 107.
Griswold, Hannah, 104.
Griswold, Hezh, 55.
Griswold, Isaac, 55.
Griswold, Jacob, 66.
Griswold, James, 71.
Griswold, Janna, 58.
Griswold, Jedidiah, 99.
Griswold, Jedidiah, 2nd, 99.
Griswold, Jehiel, 40.
Griswold, Jehiel, 53.
Griswold, Jeremiah, 35.
Griswold, Jerusha, 52.
Griswold, Jiles, 60.
Griswold, Joab, 55.
Griswold, Joab, Ju., 55.
Griswold, Joel, 48.
Griswold, Joel, 98.
Griswold, John, 60.
Griswold, John, 70.
Griswold, John, 73.
Griswold, John, 98.
Griswold, Jonah, 40.
Griswold, Jonah, 55.
Griswold, Jonathan, 59.
Griswold, Jonathan, 78.
Griswold, Joseph, 39.
Griswold, Joseph, 44.
Griswold, Joseph, Jr., 44.
Griswold, Josiah, 47.
Griswold, Josiah, 64.
Griswold, Josiah, 98.
Griswold, Margeret, 52.
Griswold, Matthew, 56.
Griswold, Median, 59.
Griswold, Mercy, 53.
Griswold, Miles, 98.
Griswold, Molly, 98.
Griswold, Moses, 87.
Griswold, Nathˡ, 55.
Griswold, Nathaniel, 99.
Griswold, Noah, 99.
Griswold, Ozias, 52.
Griswold, Roger, 38.
Griswold, Samˡ, 68.
Griswold, Samuel, 104.
Griswold, Selah, 90.
Griswold, Seth, 67.
Griswold, Shubael, 36.
Griswold, Shubel, 40.
Griswold, Simon, 55.
Griswold, Solomon, 40.
Griswold, Solomon, 56.
Griswold, Stanley, 71.
Griswold, Sylvanus, 55.
Griswold, Syphrona, 71.
Griswold, Thomas, 55.
Griswold, Thomas, 98.
Griswold, Thomas, 2nd, 98.
Griswold, Timothy, 53.
Griswold, Timothy, 55.
Griswold, Timothy, 70.
Griswold, William, 53.
Griswold, William, 53.
Griswold, Zacheus, 64.
Griswold, Ziba, 55.
Grisworth, Phineas, 67.
Griswould, Abner, 85.
Griswould, Andrus, 124.
Griswould, Daniel, 85.
Griswould, Danˡ, 132.
Griswould, Ebenezer, 84.
Griswould, Ebenr, 129.
Griswould, Elisha, 129.
Griswould, George, 124.
Griswould, George, 132.
Griswould, Giles, 85.
Griswould, Isaac, 131.
Griswould, John, 123.
Griswould, Joseph, 85.
Griswould, Joseph, 132.
Griswould, Josiah, 85.
Griswould, Martin, 85.
Griswould, Mathew, 123.
Griswould, Mathew, 2ᵈ, 123.
Griswould, Moses, 84.
Griswould, Nathan, 85.
Griswould, Nathaniel, 84.
Griswould, Nathaniel, 2ᵈ, 85.
Griswould, Roger, 131.
Griswould, Samuel, 85.
Griswould, Samˡ, 124.
Griswould, Samˡ, 129.
Griswould, Zenas, 84.
Groscup, John, 146.
Gross, Samˡ, 145.
Gross, Simon, 146.
Grosvener, Caleb, 154.
Grosvenor, Amos, 149.
Grosvenor, Asa, 149.
Grosvenor, Chester, 149.
Grosvenor, Ebenr, 149.
Grosvenor, Ezra, 140.
Grosvenor, Joshua, 149.
Grosvenor, Joshua, Jr., 149.

Grosvenor, Lemˡ, 149.
Grosvenor, Oliver, 149.
Grosvenor, Seth, 149.
Grosvenor, Thoˢ, 149.
Grosvenor, Wm, 138.
Grovener, Moses, 51.
Grover, Benjª, 133.
Grover, Ebenr, 132.
Grover, Ebenr, 138.
Grover, Edm, 134.
Grover, Hannah, 104.
Grover, Isaac, 133.
Grover, Jabez, 138.
Grover, Jno, 138.
Grover, Jonathan, 143.
Grovier, Danˡ, 64.
Grovner, Wm, 51.
Grow, Ambroser, 60.
Grow Nathˡ, 144.
Grow, Thomas, 143.
Grow, Thomas, Jnr, 143.
Grumman, Ezra, 21.
Grumman, Isaac, 21.
Grumman, Jeremiah, 21.
Grumman, John, 21.
Grumman, Nehemiah, 21.
Grumman, Thomas, 21.
Grummon, Samuel, Jr, 22.
Grunslit, Benjamin, 129.
Grunstel, James, 112.
Grunstel, John, 112.
Guard, Daniel, 119.
Gucnsey, Ezra, 24.
Guernsey, Abijah, 76.
Guernsey, Amos, 76.
Guernsey, Chauncy, 76.
Guernsey, Daniel, 76.
Guernsey, David, 76.
Guernsey, Ebeneser, 76.
Guernsey, Eldad, 76.
Guernsey, Joab, 76.
Guernsey, Joel, 76.
Guernsey, Jonathan, 76.
Guernsey, Joseph, 1st, 76.
Guernsey, Joseph, 2ᵈ, 76.
Guernsey, Philo, 76.
Guernsey, Richard, 56.
Guernsey, Richmond, 96.
Guernsey, Samuel, 15.
Guernsey, Samuel, 76.
Guernsey, Southmayd, 76.
Guernsey, Thankfull, 76.
Guernsey, Zacheus, 24.
Guild, Jeremiah, 88.
Guild, Samuel, 88.
Guild, Jr., 88.
Guild, Samˡ, 146.
Guile, Abraham, 113.
Guile, Elisha, 114.
Guile, Joseph, 113.
Guile, Nathan, 114.
Guile, Samuel, 114.
Guinea (Negro), 54.
Guire, Eben, 32.
Guire, John, 27.
Guire, Mathew, 28.
Guire, Samuel, 27.
Guire, Stephen, 13.
Guire, Thadius, 27.
Guitteau, Joshua, 56.
Guitteau, Simeon, 56.
Gulbin, Oepas, 106.
Gulliver, Thomas, 36.
Gun, Abel, 10.
Gun, George, 111.
Gun, Joseph, 10.
Gun, Noble, 58.
Gunn, Aaron, 22.
Gunn, Abel, 71.
Gunn, Abel, 110.
Gunn, Abigal, 110.
Gunn, Abner, 71.
Gunn, Anna, 102.
Gunn, Elisha, 51.
Gunn, Epenetus, 71.
Gunn, Gideon, 71.
Gunn, Isaac, 101.
Gunn, Jabamah, 110.
Gunn, Nathan, 71.
Gunn, Nathaniel, 110.
Gunn, Phebe, 75.
Gunn, Samuel, 110.
Gunn, Stephen, 101.
Gunn, William, 16.
Gurley, Daniel, 148.
Gurley, Ephraim, 148.
Gurley, Jacob B., 148.
Gurley, John, 125.
Gurley, John, 145.
Gurley, Jonathan, 148.
Gurley, Phineas, 133.
Gurley, Samˡ, 148.
Gurley, William, 148.
Gurley, Zebulon, 147.
Gurnsey, Ebenezur, 96.
Gurnsey, Isaac, 103.
Gurnsway, Lemuel, 96.
Gustin, Amos, 126.
Gustin, Walter, 122.
Guthery, Samˡ, 137.
Guthrie, Abraham, 75.
Guthrie, Ebenezer, 73.
Guthrie, Jeames, 75.
Guthrie, Joseph, 75.
Guy, Danˡ, 61.

Guy, John, 61.
Guy, Margaret, 61.
Guy (Negro), 112.
Guyer, Luke, 24.

Hach, Ebenezer, 29.
Haddfull, James, 34.
Hadeley, Gideon, 76.
Haden, Jacob, 84.
Haden, John, 83.
Hadlock, Reuben, 46.
Hadsall, Stephen, 115.
Hagan, James, 70.
Hains, Charles, 122.
Hains, Elisabeth, 124.
Hait, David, 26.
Hait, Elijah, 26.
Hait, Elijah, Junr, 23.
Hait, Elizabeth (Wd), 26.
Hait, Frederick, Junr, 26.
Hait, Isaac, 25.
Hait, Jesse, 25.
Hait, Jonas, 25.
Hait, Jonathan, Jr, 25.
Hait, Jonathan, 3ᵈ, 25.
Hait, Joseph, Junr, 24.
Hait, Josiah, 24.
Hait, Nathan, 26.
Hait, Nathaniel, 3ᵈ, 26.
Hait, Peter, 26.
Hait, Samuel, Junr, 26.
Hait, Samuel, 3ᵈ, 24.
Hait, Seth, 25.
Hait, Uriah, 26.
Hakes, George, 115.
Hakes, Richard, 116.
Halawa, Daniel, 44.
Halbert, Jabes, 136.
Hale, Abagail, 42.
Hale, Abraham, 94.
Hale, Adino, 60.
Hale, Asahel, 42.
Hale, Beman, 96.
Hale, Benezer, 53.
Hale, Benjamin, 42.
Hale, Benjamin, 79.
Hale, Charles, 42.
Hale, Curtis, 58.
Hale, Daniel, 40.
Hale, Daniel, 79.
Hale, David, 39.
Hale, David, 42.
Hale, David, 133.
Hale, David, Jr., 39.
Hale, David, Jr., 42.
Hale, Ebenezer, 39.
Hale, Ebenezer, 60.
Hale, Edward, 43.
Hale, Eli, 39.
Hale, Elihu, 61.
Hale, Elijah, 42.
Hale, Elisha, 42.
Hale, Elisha, 79.
Hale, Elisha, Junr, 79.
Hale, Elizabeth, 53.
Hale, Elizur, 43.
Hale, Francis, 92.
Hale, Frary, 43.
Hale, George, 42.
Hale, Gideon, 42.
Hale, Hannah, 92.
Hale, Hezekiah, 88.
Hale, Hezekiah, 104.
Hale, Isaac, 37.
Hale, Isaac, 43.
Hale, Israel, 39.
Hale, James, 53.
Hale, John, 39.
Hale, John, 42.
Hale, John, 140.
Hale, Jonˢ, 39.
Hale, Jonathan, 79.
Hale, Joseph, 42.
Hale, Joseph, 51.
Hale, Joseph, Jr., 42.
Hale, Josiah, 42.
Hale, Mathew, 42.
Hale, Nathan, 67.
Hale, Reuben, 61.
Hale, Richard, 133.
Hale, Ruth, 42.
Hale, Samuel, 39.
Hale, Samuel, 50.
Hale, Samuel, 94.
Hale, Theodore, 42.
Hale, Thomas, 39.
Hale, Timothy, Jr., 43.
Hale, Timothy, 42.
Hale, Timothy, 51.
Hale, William, 43.
Haleburd, Hosea, 14.
Halet, Mabel, 33.
Haley, Caleb, 120.
Haley, Edmund, 117.
Haley, Jeremiah, 120.
Haley, John, 117.
Haliburt, Elisha, 68.
Halis, John, 31.
Hall, Aaron, 31.
Hall, Aaron, 127.
Hall, Abel, 31.

Hall, Abell, 108.
Hall, Abell, 2nd, 108.
Hall, Abiel, 103.
Hall, Abijah, 79.
Hall, Abijah, Junr, 81.
Hall, Able, 123.
Hall, Abner, 81.
Hall, Abraham, 61.
Hall, Abraham, 2ᵈ, 61.
Hall, Alpheus, 136.
Hall, Amassa, 92.
Hall, Amassa, 107.
Hall, Amos, 135.
Hall, Andrew, 108.
Hall, Andrew, 108.
Hall, Andrew, 148.
Hall, Anna, 85.
Hall, Arael, 108.
Hall, Arael, 2nd, 108.
Hall, Aron, 107.
Hall, Aron, 108.
Hall, Asa, 59.
Hall, Asa, 107.
Hall, Asaph, 45.
Hall, Aseph, 70.
Hall, Benajah, 55.
Hall, Benijah, 108.
Hall, Benjamin, 15.
Hall, Benjamin, 76.
Hall, Benjamin, 93.
Hall, Benjamin, 98.
Hall, Benjamin, 107.
Hall, Benjamin, 107.
Hall, Benjamin, 2nd, 98.
Hall, Brenton, 107.
Hall, Bristor, 56.
Hall, Byer, 31.
Hall, Caleb, Jr., 148.
Hall, Calvin, 81.
Hall, Calvin, 87.
Hall, Charles, 107.
Hall, Charles C., 93.
Hall, Christopher, 145.
Hall, Curtiss, 50.
Hall, Daniel, 64.
Hall, Daniel, 88.
Hall, Daniel, 107.
Hall, Daniel, 123.
Hall, Daniel, 130.
Hall, Daniel J., 108.
Hall, David, 12.
Hall, David, 63.
Hall, David, 79.
Hall, David, 88.
Hall, David, 107.
Hall, David, 148.
Hall, David, 2nd, 107.
Hall, Dewy, 81.
Hall, Ebenezer, 14.
Hall, Ebenezer, 27.
Hall, Ebenezer, 56.
Hall, Ebenezer, 81.
Hall, Ebenezer, 93.
Hall, Ebenezer, 99.
Hall, Eber, 99.
Hall, Eleizer, 68.
Hall, Elephalet, 98.
Hall, Eliakim, 107.
Hall, Eliakim, 2nd, 107.
Hall, Elihu, 108.
Hall, Elisha, 58.
Hall, Elisha, 107.
Hall, Elisha, 109.
Hall, Elizabeth, 107.
Hall, Em, 137.
Hall, Enos, 107.
Hall, Enos, 2nd, 107.
Hall, Ephraim, 107.
Hall, Ephraim, 120.
Hall, Ephraim S., 64.
Hall, Esbon, 32.
Hall, Ezekiel, 107.
Hall, Ezra, 110.
Hall, Ezra, 124.
Hall, George, 18.
Hall, George, 132.
Hall, Gershom, 148.
Hall, Gideon, 79.
Hall, Giles, 107.
Hall, Hannah, 21.
Hall, Hannah, 93.
Hall, Heman, 50.
Hall, Hezekiah, 57.
Hall, Hezekiah, 107.
Hall, Ichobud, 14.
Hall, Isaac, 79.
Hall, Isaac, 97.
Hall, Isaac, 107.
Hall, Isaac, 107.
Hall, Isaiah, 92.
Hall, Israel, 39.
Hall, Irsael, 107.
Hall, Israel, 107.
Hall, Jabez, 79.
Hall, Jabez, 81.
Hall, Jabez, 88.
Hall, Jacob, 50.
Hall, Jacob, 87.
Hall, James, 14.
Hall, James, 148.
Hall, Jenny, 129.
Hall, Jerad, 93.
Hall, Joash, 107.

# INDEX.

Hall, Joatham, 107.
Hall, Job, 140.
Hall, Joel, 79.
Hall, Joel, 108.
Hall, Joel, 108.
Hall, John, 14.
Hall, John, 19.
Hall, John, 45.
Hall, John, 51.
Hall, John, 65.
Hall, John, 78.
Hall, John, 87.
Hall, John, 93.
Hall, John, 96.
Hall, John, 97.
Hall, John, 107.
Hall, Jn°, 134.
Hall, John, 148.
Hall, John, Jn\*, 148.
Hall, John, 2nd, 93.
Hall, John E., 85.
Hall, Jonah, 93.
Hall, Jonathan, 93.
Hall, Jon\*, 135.
Hall, Jon\*, 148.
Hall, Jonath\*, 149.
Hall, Jonathan, 2d, 92.
Hall, Jonathan A., 86.
Hall, Joseph, 14.
Hall, Joseph, 86.
Hall, Joseph, Jn., 148.
Hall, Joshua, 107.
Hall, Joshua, 118.
Hall, Joshua, 121.
Hall, Joshua, 127.
Hall, Jos\*, 136.
Hall, Joshua, 148.
Hall, Josiah, 28.
Hall, Josiah, 147.
Hall, Levi, 107.
Hall, Libeas, 51.
Hall, Libny, 136.
Hall, Lidia, 93.
Hall, Liman, 14.
Hall, Luben, 107.
Hall, Luke, 136.
Hall, Luther, 96.
Hall, Margaret, 81.
Hall, Mary, 31.
Hall, Mary, 59.
Hall, Mary, 64.
Hall, Mary, 98.
Hall, Mary, 119.
Hall, Mathew, 78.
Hall, Miles, 98.
Hall, Moses, 107.
Hall, Moses, 137.
Hall, Nathan, 68.
Hall, Nathan, 131.
Hall, Nathaniel, 51.
Hall, Nathaniel, 68.
Hall, Nath¹, 148.
Hall, Nath¹, 148.
Hall, Peter, 108.
Hall, Phebe, 34.
Hall, Philomen, 97.
Hall, Phineas, 107.
Hall, Phineas, 2nd, 107.
Hall, Prindle, 110.
Hall, Prudence, 107.
Hall, Rhoda, 86.
Hall, Robert, 140.
Hall, Ruben, 93.
Hall, Ruben, 116.
Hall, Rufus, 106.
Hall, Samuel, 30.
Hall, Samuel, 34.
Hall, Sam., 61.
Hall, Samuel, 79.
Hall, Sam¹, 81.
Hall, Samuel, 86.
Hall, Samuel, 107.
Hall, Sam¹, 136.
Hall, Sam¹, 148.
Hall, Sam¹, Jun\*, 81.
Hall, Samuel, 2nd, 107.
Hall, Samuel, 2nd, 109.
Hall, Sarah, 96.
Hall, Sarah, 108.
Hall, Sarah, 129.
Hall, Seth, 19.
Hall, Seth, 81.
Hall, Seth, 135.
Hall, Silas, 66.
Hall, Simeon, 116.
Hall, Simes, 68.
Hall, Stephen, 30.
Hall, Stephen, 97.
Hall, Stephen, 109.
Hall, Stephen, 116.
Hall, Stephen, 148.
Hall, Stephen, 148.
Hall, Street, 107.
Hall, Street T., 107.
Hall, Susanna, 148.
Hall, Thankfull, 109.
Hall, Theophilus, 107.
Hall, Theophilus, 147.
Hall, Tho\*, 81.
Hall, Thomas, 86.
Hall, Thomas, 107.
Hall, Thomas, 143.
Hall, Timothy, 36.

Hall, Timothy, 59.
Hall, Timothy, 92.
Hall, Timothy, 96.
Hall, Timothy, 2nd, 92.
Hall, Titus, 108.
Hall, Uriah, 140.
Hall, Veasny, 136.
Hall, William, 14.
Hall, William, 20.
Hall, William, 45.
Hall, William, 78.
Hall, William, 88.
Hall, William, 93.
Hall, William, 120.
Hall, William, 121.
Hall, Wm, 137.
Hall, Zadock, 136.
Hall, Zebulon, 99.
Hallabutt, Ralph, 118.
Hallam, Abigail, 117.
Hallam, Edward, 129.
Hallam, George, 126.
Hallam, John, 129.
Hallam, Robart, 126.
Hallans, Amos, 117.
Hallebert, David, 10.
Hallebert, Job, 19.
Hallebert, John, 18.
Hallen, John, 81.
Hallen, John, Jun\*, 81.
Hallester, Giddeon, 18.
Hallester, Jonathan, 19.
Hallet, Thomas, 118.
Halley, Samu¹, 63.
Hallhet, John, 57.
Hallins, Abigail, 15.
Hallock, Benjamin, 72.
Hallock, Israel, 97.
Hallock, William, 72.
Halsey, Jeremiah, 114.
Halsey (Negro), 118.
Halsey, Phillip, 55.
Halsey, Samuel, 150.
Halsey, Wm, 114.
Hamblen, David, 10.
Hamblen, Elisha, 10.
Hamblen, William, 10.
Hamblengton, Paul, 134.
Hamblengton (Widow), 134.
Hamblenton, Asa, 136.
Hambleton, Abial, 122.
Hambleton, Alexander, 17.
Hambleton, Eliakam, 11.
Hambleton, Gurdon, 122.
Hambleton, Gurdon, 126.
Hambleton, James, 91.
Hambleton, James, 128.
Hambleton, James, 2d, 122.
Hambleton, John, 10.
Hambleton, John, 19.
Hambleton, John, 126.
Hambleton, Jonas, 131.
Hambleton, Joseph, 11.
Hambleton, Joseph, 11.
Hambleton, Mary, 89.
Hambleton, Paul, 10.
Hambleton, Silas, 11.
Hambleton, Solomon, 131.
Hambleton, William, 31.
Hamblin, Cornelius, 18.
Hamblin, Eben, 135.
Hamilton, Rebecca, 128.
Hamlen, Nathen, 61.
Hamlin, Abigail, 88.
Hamlin, Amasa, 67.
Hamlin, Benjamin, 60.
Hamlin, Charles, 88.
Hamlin, Dan., 35.
Hamlin, Daniel, 88.
Hamlin, Darling, 67.
Hamlin, David, 65.
Hamlin, Ebenezer, 35.
Hamlin, Harris, 88.
Hamlin, Hon. Jabez, Esq\*, 85.
Hamlin, John, 40.
Hamlin, John, 88.
Hamlin, Levi, 40.
Hamlin, Mark, 35.
Hamlin, Oliver, 40.
Hamlin, Patience, 88.
Hamlin, Peter, 86.
Hamlin, Phinias, 40.
Hamlin, Polley, 60.
Hamlin, Reely, 59.
Hamlin, Thomas, 59.
Hamlin, William, 88.
Hamlin, William, Jun\*, 88.
Hamlinton, Benjamin, 27.
Hamman, Elijah, 132.
Hamman, Nath¹, 132.
Hamman, Zeph\*, 134.
Hammiston, Joel, 111.
Hammon, David, 78.
Hammon, Dudley, 61.
Hammon, Dudley, 68.
Hammon, Elez\*, 138.
Hammon, Isaac, 125.
Hammon, James, 138.
Hammon, Jason, 37.
Hammon, John, 68.
Hammon, Joseph, 125.
Hammon, Josiah, 125.
Hammon, Thomas, 76.

Hammon, Thomas, 116.
Hammond, Hezekiah, 143.
Hammond, James, 53.
Hammond, Josiah, 143.
Hammond, Josiah, 154.
Hammond, Sam¹, 152.
Hammot, Jonath\*, 149.
Han, Titus, 68.
Hanchett, David, 51.
Hanchett, Ezra, 50.
Hanchett, John, 51.
Hanchett, John, 2d, 51.
Hanchett, Luke, 51.
Hanchett, Oliver, 50.
Hancks, Elijah, 139.
Hancock, Edward, 118.
Hancock, Edward, 2d, 118.
Hancock, Elihu, 117.
Hancock, James, 117.
Hancock, James, 118.
Hancock, John, 117.
Hancock, Joseph, 117.
Hancock, Nathan, 117.
Hancock, Nathan, 118.
Hancock, Nath¹, 118.
Hancock, Thomas, 128.
Hancock, Zebulon, 118.
Hand, Bendict, 78.
Hand, Benjamin, 89.
Hand, Daniel, 99.
Hand, Daniel, 2d, 99.
Hand, Edmond, 99.
Hand, Elias, 56.
Hand, Icabod, 98.
Hand, Joseph, 97.
Hand, Stephen, 56.
Hand, Timothy, 59.
Handcock, William, 39.
Hander, Shuball, 78.
Handerson, William, 75.
Hands, Jonathan, 53.
Handy, Anna, 98.
Handy, Clemens, 64.
Handy, Hetty, 98.
Handy, Samuel, 98.
Hanes, William, 30.
Hanford, Abraham, 22.
Hanford, Alexander, 22.
Hanford, Betty, 12.
Hanford, Daniel, 21.
Hanford, Ebenezer, 22.
Hanford, Ebenezer, Jun\*, 22.
Hanford, Eleazer, 24.
Hanford, Eleazer, Jun\*, 23.
Hanford, Eliphalet, 22.
Hanford, Hannah (Wd), 23.
Hanford, Hayns, 13.
Hanford, Hezekiah, 21.
Hanford, Hezekiah, Jun\*, 21.
Hanford, Jedediah, 21.
Hanford, John, 12.
Hanford, John, 23.
Hanford, Jorge, 12.
Hanford, Levi, 22.
Hanford, Levi, 24.
Hanford, Mary (Wd), 22.
Hanford, Mary (Wd), 22.
Hanford, Moses, 22.
Hanford, Nehemiah, 23.
Hanford, Ozias, 23.
Hanford, Phineas, Jun\*, 24.
Hanford, Samuel, 22.
Hanford, Samuel, Jun\*, 22.
Hanford, Stephen, 24.
Hanford, Theophilus, 22.
Hanford, Timothy, 22.
Hanford, Uriah, 23.
Hanford, William, 75.
Hankok, Rachel, 61.
Hanks, Benj\*, 140.
Hanks, Benj\*, 147.
Hanks, John, 140.
Hanks, Silas, 148.
Hanks, Uriah, 147.
Hanmer, Benjamin, 67.
Hanmer, Frances, 53.
Hanmer, James, 53.
Hanmer, John, 53.
Hanmer, Samu, 53.
Hannah, Alexander, 56.
Hannah, Daniel, 56.
Hannah, James, 56.
Hannah, Margaret, 56.
Hannah, Robart, 56.
Hannah, Justus, 140.
Hannibal, John, 82.
Hannibal, Joseph, 82.
Hanson, Aaron, 50.
Hanson, Christian, 104.
Hanson, Edward, 153.
Hansson, Jared, 76.
Hantchet, Ebenezer, 67.
Hantchet, Joseph, 67.
Hantchet, Luny, 67.
Hantchet, Silvanus, 59.
Hantchet, Simeon, 67.
Hantichet, John, 67.
Hantihet, Amos, 67.
Happen, Gideon, 98.
Hard, Anson, 76.
Hard, Josiah, 151.

Hard, Wilson, 94.
Harden, Thomas, 127.
Harding, Ebenezer, 81.
Harding, Ephraim, 81.
Harding, Fredrick, 105.
Harding, Jeremiah, 127.
Harding, Nathaniel, 81.
Harding, Olive, 81.
Harding, Thomas, 2d, 128.
Hare, Silas, 62.
Hare, Stephen, 134.
Hare (Widow), 138.
Harger, Ebenezer, 96.
Harger, Jabesh, 61.
Harger, Philo, 95.
Hargor, Edward, 95.
Haris, Henery, 30.
Harkins, Nathan, 66.
Harkness, John, 114.
Harland, Thomas, 131.
Harlow, Sarah, 92.
Harmin, Benjamin, 51.
Harmin, Benjamin, 2d, 51.
Harmon, Cephas, 50.
Harmon, Ebenezer, 51.
Harmon, Elias, 51.
Harmon, Iaguish, 51.
Harmon, Israel, 51.
Harmon, Joseph, 52.
Harmon, Phineas, 51.
Harmon, Samuel, 51.
Harmony, Nicholas, 16.
Harper, James, 38.
Harpin, John, 101.
Harras, Reuben, 141.
Harridon, Benjamin, 144.
Harrington, Abijah, 85.
Harrington, Benjamin, 103.
Harrington, Elisha, 41.
Harrington, Elisha, 47.
Harrington, Hezekiah, 49.
Harrington, Jeremiah, 80.
Harris, Andrew, 114.
Harris, Benjamin, 126.
Harris, Daniel, 113.
Harris, Daniel, 126.
Harris, Daniel, 128.
Harris, Daniel, 2d, 128.
Harris, David, 57.
Harris, David, 62.
Harris, David, 87.
Harris, Eben, 137.
Harris, Elias, 122.
Harris, Eliphelet, 128.
Harris, Eliphelet, 2d, 128.
Harris, Ely, 81.
Harris, Ephraim, 125.
Harris, Ezra, 128.
Harris, Francis, 129.
Harris, Henry, 128.
Harris, Hosea, 52.
Harris, James, 128.
Harris, Jasper, 128.
Harris, Jedediah, 84.
Harris, Jeremiah, 131.
Harris, John, 69.
Harris, John, 86.
Harris, John, 128.
Harris, John, 143.
Harris, John, 2d, 128.
Harris, John, 3d, 128.
Harris, Jonath\*, 151.
Harris, Joseph, 121.
Harris, Joseph, 127.
Harris, Nathan, 148.
Harris, Nath¹, 121.
Harris, Nath¹, 128.
Harris, Noah, 128.
Harris, Paul, 141.
Harris, Peter, 126.
Harris, Peter B., 128.
Harris, Phillip, 145.
Harris, Rob\*, 137.
Harris, Robert, 32.
Harris, Roswell, 128.
Harris, Sam¹, 141.
Harris, Sarah, 128.
Harris, Sears, 148.
Harris, Thomas, 128.
Harris, Walter, 128.
Harris (Wid.), 137.
Harris, William, 21.
Harris, William, 69.
Harris, William, 87.
Harris, William, 126.
Harris, William, 128.
Harrison, Abraham, 91.
Harrison, Amie, 91.
Harrison, Amos, 92.
Harrison, Asael, 92.
Harrison, Daniel F., 92.
Harrison, David, 50.
Harrison, David, 64.
Harrison, Edward, 92.
Harrison, Elihu, 122.
Harrison, Elihue, 59.
Harrison, Farr, 91.
Harrison, Gideon, 75.
Harrison, Hester, 91.
Harrison, Hipsebah, 123.
Harrison, Jabez, 50.
Harrison, Jacob, 92.
Harrison, James, 92.

Harrison, James, 109.
Harrison, Jared, 65.
Harrison, Jerad, 92.
Harrison, Jeras, 92.
Harrison, John, 92.
Harrison, Justice, 92.
Harrison, Lemuel, 109.
Harrison, Levi, 91.
Harrison, Levi, 96.
Harrison, Mark, 50.
Harrison, Nathan, 91.
Harrison, Peter, 91.
Harrison, Philemon, 97.
Harrison, Samuel, 92.
Harrison, Samuel, 110.
Harrison, Silas, 145.
Harrison, Stephen, 67.
Harrison, Theodore, 53.
Harrison, Thomas, 59.
Harrison, Timothy, 91.
Harrison, Timothy, 2nd, 91.
Harrison, William, 91.
Harrison, Wooster, 92.
Harriss, Daniel, 61.
Harriss, Daniel, 147.
Harriss, Deliverance, 89.
Harriss, Ebenezer, 68.
Harriss, Eben\*, 141.
Harriss, George, 67.
Harriss, John, 148.
Harriss, Joseph, 150.
Harriss, Nath¹, 91.
Harriss, Phillip, 146.
Harrisson, Daniel, 1st, 57.
Harrisson, Daniel, 2d, 57.
Harrisson, Ephraim, 59.
Harrisson, Noah, 57.
Harrisson, Thomas, 59.
Harrit, Stephen, 109.
Harron, John, 122.
Harrop, Joseph, 18.
Harry (Negro), 21.
Harry (Negro), 128.
Harry (Negroe), 104.
Hart, Aaron, 33.
Hart, Ambrose, 35.
Hart, Ambrose, 41.
Hart, Amos, 36.
Hart, Amos, 49.
Hart, Anthony, 41.
Hart, Ard, 36.
Hart, Asa, 41.
Hart, Asahel, 33.
Hart, Asahel, 34.
Hart, Benjamin, 33.
Hart, Benjamin, 34.
Hart, Benjamin, 70.
Hart, Benjamin, 99.
Hart, Benjamin, 108.
Hart, Bethel, 33.
Hart, Bliss, 35.
Hart, Chancey, 49.
Hart, David, 65.
Hart, Ebenezer, 68.
Hart, Ebenezer, 88.
Hart, Elijah, 33.
Hart, Elijah, Jr., 33.
Hart, Elisha, 33.
Hart, Elisha, 89.
Hart, Elizur, 33.
Hart, Elnathan, 41.
Hart, Gad, 41.
Hart, Gideon, 33.
Hart, Gideon, 41.
Hart, Gilbert, 34.
Hart, Hawkins, 50.
Hart, Hawkins, 61.
Hart, Hezekiah, 33.
Hart, Hosea, 41.
Hart, Ira, 40.
Hart, Ithurel, 34.
Hart, James, 41.
Hart, James, 128.
Hart, Jehuda, 33.
Hart, Jemima, 119.
Hart, Joel, 24.
Hart, Joel, 41.
Hart, John, 34.
Hart, John, 41.
Hart, John, 49.
Hart, Jn°, 89.
Hart, Jn°, 138.
Hart, John, Jr., 49.
Hart, Joseph, 45.
Hart, Josiah, 52.
Hart, Josiah H., 64.
Hart, Judah, 33.
Hart, Jude, 36.
Hart, Lemuel, 36.
Hart, Lemuel, 41.
Hart, Lent, 41.
Hart, Levi, 34.
Hart, Levi, 49.
Hart, Levi, 115.
Hart, Lewis, 118.
Hart, Lineus, 41.
Hart, Luke, 60.
Hart, Marcus, 35.
Hart, Mary, 89.
Hart, Mathew, 33.
Hart, Mathew, Jr., 33.
Hart, Munson, 41.
Hart, Nathaniel, 108.

# INDEX.

Hart, Noadiah, 35.
Hart, Oliver, 33.
Hart, Rebeca, 104.
Hart, Reuben, 41.
Hart, Roger, 33.
Hart, Roswell, 49.
Hart, Salmon, 33.
Hart, Samuel, 34.
Hart, Samuel, 41.
Hart, Samuel, 50.
Hart, Sam$^l$, 89.
Hart, Samuel, 96.
Hart, Selah, 33.
Hart, Seth, 53.
Hart, Seth, 65.
Hart, Seth, 88.
Hart, Simeon, 35.
Hart, Simeon, Jr., 35.
Hart, Stephen, 33.
Hart, Thomas, 33.
Hart, Thomas, 34.
Hart, Thomas, 40.
Hart, Thomas, Jr., 33.
Hart, Timothy, 107.
Hart, Titus, 68.
Hart, Varlines, 50.
Hart, William, 31.
Hart, William, 41.
Hart, Will$^m$, Esq$^r$, 89.
Hart, Zacheriah, 34.
Hartch, Jo$^n$, 138.
Harth, Alma, 138.
Harton, Moses, Jn$^r$, 141.
Hartshore, Dan$^l$, 147.
Hartshorn, Andrew, 129.
Hartshorn, Eben, Jun$^r$, 130.
Hartshorn, Ebenezer, 130.
Hartshorn, Elijah, 130.
Hartshorn, John, 129.
Hartshorn, Jonathan, 114.
Hartshorn, Joshua, 57.
Hartshorn, Nathan, 129.
Hartshorn, Oliver, 112.
Hartshorn, Rufus, 132.
Hartshorn, Sarah, 129.
Hartshorn, Zebadiah, 129.
Hartshorne, Andrew, 146.
Hartshorne, Ezekel, 146.
Hartshorne, Joseph, 147.
Hartshorne, Sam$^l$, 149.
Hartwell, Joseph, 72.
Hartwell, Joseph, 75.
Hartwell, Nathaniel, 144.
Hartwell, Samuel, 71.
Harvey, ——, 128.
Harvey, Amasa, 82.
Harvey, Asa, 82.
Harvey, Elisha, 81.
Harvey, Elisha, 82.
Harvey, Elisha, 84.
Harvey, George, 115.
Harvey, Ithamar, 82.
Harvey, Ithamar, Jr, 82.
Harvey, James, 117.
Harvey, James, 117.
Harvey, Joel, 70.
Harvey, John, 119.
Harvey, Jon$^a$, 82.
Harvey, Joseph, 122.
Harvey, Joshua, 123.
Harvey, Nathan, 138.
Harvey, Paul, 116.
Harvey, Peter, 115.
Harvey, Phillup, 114.
Harvey, Rob$^t$, 82.
Harvey, Rob$^t$, 2$^d$, 82.
Harvey, Russel, 82.
Harvey, Ruth, 114.
Harvey, Thomas, 128.
Harvey, Will$^m$, 81.
Harvey, William, 128.
Harvey, Zachra, 82.
Harvy, Tho$^s$, 58.
Harvy, William, 58.
Harwood, Jn$^o$, 137.
Hase, Benjamin, 48.
Hase, Zedikiah, 48.
Hash, David, 49.
Haskall, David, 150.
Haskall, Jon$^h$, 150.
Haskel, Elijah, 138.
Haskell, William, 87.
Haskings, Shubael, 48.
Haslings, Seth, 75.
Hasskall, Roger, 114.
Hasting, Elder John, 50.
Hastings, Abijah, 51.
Hastings, Benjamin, 51.
Hastings, Dan, 130.
Hastings, Dyeer, 141.
Hastings, James, 139.
Hastings, Joseph, 51.
Hastings, Roswell, 130.
Hatch, Amy, 104.
Hatch, Benjamin, 120.
Hatch, Daniel, 102.
Hatch, Dan., 133.
Hatch, David, 66.
Hatch, David, 139.
Hatch, Deborah, 127.
Hatch, Ebezer, 69.
Hatch, Elezer, 138.
Hatch, Elisabeth, 113.

Hatch, Elisha, 113.
Hatch, Elnathan, 82.
Hatch, Euson, 96.
Hatch, Hennery, 18.
Hatch, Isaac, 72.
Hatch, James, 52.
Hatch, Jeremi, 113.
Hatca, John, 18.
Hatch, Josepn, 21.
Hatch, Josiah, 88.
Hatch, Justus, 139.
Hatch, Moses, 52.
Hatch, Nathan, 68.
Hatch, Nathaniel, 59.
Hatch, Samuel, 145.
Hatch, Sherman, 95.
Hatch, Zephaniah, 52.
Hatch, Zephaniah, 103.
Hatch, Zephaniah, 125.
Hatcher, Joshua, 21.
Hatchet, Jonah, 67.
Hath, Jethro, 59.
Hathaway, Asabel, 51.
Hathaway, Seth, 51.
Hatheway, John, 50.
Hathway, Charles, 51.
Hathway, Charles, 2$^d$, 51.
Hathway, Ebenezer, 51.
Hathway, Ebenezer, 51.
Hathway, Joel, 51.
Hathway, John King, 51.
Hathway, Martin, 51.
Hathway, Samuel, 51.
Hathway, Thrall, 51.
Hatten, Stephen, 69.
Hatten, William, 46.
Haughton, Edward, 150.
Haun, Michael, 73.
Haush, Joseph, 100.
Haven, Abraham, 153.
Havens, Edward, 123.
Havens, Jeriah, 141.
Havens, John, 123.
Havens, Jonathan, 118.
Havens, Silvester, 119.
Havens, Simons, 141.
Havern, Edward, 90.
Havins, Thomas, 52.
Hawes, Isaac, 74.
Hawes, Samuel, 74.
Hawkins, Abraham, 94.
Hawkins, Abram, 57.
Hawkins, Dameras, 95.
Hawkins, Daniel, 95.
Hawkins, David, 94.
Hawkins, Edward, 95.
Hawkins, Eleakim, 132.
Hawkins, Eli, 94.
Hawkins, Eli, 2$^d$, 94.
Hawkins, Elizabeth, 95.
Hawkins, George, 138.
Hawkins, Hannah, 94.
Hawkins, Isaac, 94.
Hawkins, Isaac, 95.
Hawkins, John, 95.
Hawkins, Jn$^o$, 138.
Hawkins, Joseph, 95.
Hawkins, Jo$^s$, 133.
Hawkins, Moses, 94.
Hawkins, Peter, 95.
Hawkins, Rodolphus, 133.
Hawkins, Samuel, 94.
Hawkins, Sarah, 86.
Hawkins, Silas, 95.
Hawkins, Stephen, 92.
Hawkins, Uriah, 144.
Hawkins (Widow), 133.
Hawkins, William, 11.
Hawkins, Zachariah, 95.
Hawlet, Josiah, 119.
Hawley, Aaron, 29.
Hawley, Abel, 17.
Hawley, Abel, 21.
Hawley, Abel, 43.
Hawley, Abigail (Wid.), 29.
Hawley, Amos, 40.
Hawley, Andrew, 30.
Hawley, Ann, 78.
Hawley, Anne, 18.
Hawley, Anne, 18.
Hawley, Azor, 56.
Hawley, Benjamin, 21.
Hawley, Benjamin, 56.
Hawley, Catherin, 13.
Hawley, Charrity, 17.
Hawley, Closen, 10.
Hawley, Daniel, 32.
Hawley, David, 18.
Hawley, David, 30.
Hawley, David, 32.
Hawley, Ebenezer, 28.
Hawley, Ebenezer, 40.
Hawley, Elias, 17.
Hawley, Elijah, 17.
Hawley, Elijah, 17.
Hawley, Elijah, 25.
Hawley, Elijah, 29.
Hawley, Elijah, 41.
Hawley, Elisha, 28.
Hawley, Enos, 55.
Hawley, Ephraim, 30.
Hawley, Ephraim, 17.
Hawley, Ga$^d$, 41.

Hawley, Giddeon, 17.
Hawley, Gregary, 29.
Hawley, Hezekiah, 28.
Hawley, Isaac, 10.
Hawley, Isaac, 19.
Hawley, Isaac, 40.
Hawley, Israel, 17.
Hawley, James, 44.
Hawley, Jedidah, 10.
Hawley, Job, 17.
Hawley, John, 11.
Hawley, John, 18.
Hawley, Jonathan, 17.
Hawley, Joseph, 17.
Hawley, Joseph, 21.
Hawley, Joseph, 27.
Hawley, Joseph, 41.
Hawley, Joseph, 72.
Hawley, Josiah, 29.
Hawley, Jotham, 21.
Hawley, Liverius, 10.
Hawley, Luther, 70.
Hawley, Mable, 30.
Hawley, Milton, 18.
Hawley, Moses, 56.
Hawley, Nehemiah, 10.
Hawley, Nero (Negro), 30.
Hawley, Reuben, 41.
Hawley, Richard, 73.
Hawley, Rufus, 41.
Hawley, Ruth, 17.
Hawley, Ruth (Wid.), 29.
Hawley, Samu$^l$, 63.
Hawley, Samuel, 66.
Hawley, Samuel, 76.
Hawley, Sarah, 10.
Hawley, Silas, 14.
Hawley, Silas, 56.
Hawley, Stow, 89.
Hawley, Thomas, 17.
Hawley, Thomas, 28.
Hawley, Thomas, 44.
Hawley, Walleson, 17.
Hawley (Wid.), 50.
Hawley, William, 21.
Hawley, William, 27.
Hawley, Woolcut, 29.
Hawlley, Elisha, 63.
Hawly, Edmond, 31.
Hawly, Elijah, 29.
Hawly, Parson, 31.
Hawly, Thomas, 30.
Haws, Eli, 140.
Hawse, Jabes, 10.
Hayden, David, 40.
Hayden, David, Jr., 41.
Hayden, Eliakim, 89.
Haydon, Agustin, 60.
Haydon, Ebenezer, 89.
Haydon, Eben$^r$, 54.
Haydon, Elias, 89.
Haydon, Elijah, 58.
Haydon, Ezra, 54.
Haydon, Isaac, 54.
Haydon, Jacob, 89.
Haydon, John, 54.
Haydon, John, Ju., 54.
Haydon, Joseph, 58.
Haydon, Levi, 54.
Haydon, Nath$^l$, 54.
Haydon, Nath$^l$, Ju., 54.
Haydon, Nehemiah, 89.
Haydon, Oliver, 54.
Haydon, Samuel, 58.
Haydon, Thomas, 54.
Haydon, Uriah, 89.
Haydon, William, 58.
Hayes, Abraham, 15.
Hayes, Abraham, J$^r$, 16.
Hayes, Amos, 43.
Hayes, Andrew, 44.
Hayes, Andrew, Jr., 44.
Hayes, Benjamin, 44.
Hayes, Daniel, 43.
Hayes, Daniel, Jr., 43.
Hayes, David, 43.
Hayes, Dudley, 44.
Hayes, Eunice (W$^d$), 23.
Hayes, Honora (Wid.), 43.
Hayes, Jacob, 44.
Hayes, John, 22.
Hayes, John, 106.
Hayes, Oliver, 44.
Hayes, Pliny, 43.
Hayes, Rufus, 43.
Hayes, Samuel, 43.
Hayes, Samuel, Jr., 43.
Hayes, Silus, 43.
Hayes, Simeon, 43.
Hayes, Thomas, 71.
Hayes, William, Jr., 44.
Hayford, Elisha, 41.
Hayford, Ira, 35.
Hayford, John, 40.
Hayford, John, 41.
Hayford, Joseph, 35.
Hayner, Asahel, 62.
Haynes, Daniel, 145.
Haynes, Sylvester, 145.
Hayns, John, 29.
Hayns, Lemuel, 30.
Hays, Abigail, 123.
Hays, Asahel, 66.

Hays, Benajah, 44.
Hays, Dudley, 44.
Hays, Elizabeth, 18.
Hays, Ezekeil, 91.
Hays, Ezekiel, 44.
Hays, Ezekiel, 104.
Hays, James, 11.
Hays, Jesse, 18.
Hays, Joel, 43.
Hays, John, 36.
Hays, Joseph, 15.
Hays, Levi, 45.
Hays, Nathan, 14.
Hays, Nehemiah, 14.
Hays, Obadiah, 45.
Hays, Peter, 12.
Hays, Seth, 44.
Hays, Stephen, 17.
Hays, William, 15.
Hays, William, 44.
Hays, Zenas 44.
Hayson, Sam$^l$, 66.
Hayt, Ezra, 26.
Hayt, Nathan, 72.
Hazard, Samuel, 120.
Hazard, Stuart, 49.
Hazelton, Arnold, 83.
Hazelton, Hannah, 83.
Hazelton, Nathaniel, 83.
Hazelton, Simeon, 83.
Hazen, Darius, 130.
Hazen, Elijah, 75.
Hazen, Jacob, 130.
Hazen, Jacob, 130.
Hazen, Joseph, 129.
Hazen, Moses, 129.
Hazen, Samuel, 73.
Heacock, Benjamin, 12.
Heacock, Daniel, 12.
Heacock, Ebenezer, 12.
Heacock, Samuel, 11.
Headen, Noah, 131.
Heading, George, 76.
Healey, George, 17.
Healey, Resolved, 149.
Heard, Josiah, 148.
Heard, Oliver C., 20.
Hearsay, James, 147.
Heart, Amasa, 74.
Heart, Elias, 57.
Heart, Jeames, 78.
Heart, Phineas, 57.
Heart, Silas, 57.
Heart, Soloman, 57.
Heart, Titus, 57.
Heath, David 61.
Heath, Eben$^r$, 139.
Heath, Eben$^r$, 140.
Heath, Hezekiah, 61.
Heath, Isaac, 138.
Heath, Mehitabel, 61.
Heath, Obadiah, 61.
Heath, Peleg, 47.
Heath, Sim$^o$, 138.
Heath, Stephen, 38.
Heath, William, 119.
Heaton, Abram, 76.
Heaton, Calhoun, 106.
Heaton, Elizabeth, 73.
Heaton, John, 106.
Heaton, John, 106.
Hebard, Eben$^r$, 142.
Hebard, Eliphaz, 147.
Hebard, Gideon, 153.
Hebard, Jared, 152.
Hebard, Jon$^a$, 151.
Hebard, Jonathan. 152.
Hebard, Joseph, 152.
Hebard, Lindon, 144.
Hebard, Luther, 146.
Hebard, Nathan, 65.
Hebard, Nathan, 153.
Hebard, Nath$^l$, 152.
Hebard, Paul, 152.
Hebard, Samuel, 152.
Hebard, Warner, 143.
Hebard, William, 142.
Hebard, Will$^m$, Jr., 142.
Hebard, Zebulon, 152.
Heby, Christopher, 115.
Hecock, Beth$^l$, 21.
Hecock, Ebenezer, 23.
Hecock, John, 109.
Hecock, Nathan$^e$$^l$, 21.
Hecock, Noah, 21.
Hecock, Samuel, 24.
Hecock, Thomas, 24.
Hedges, Eleazer, 90.
Hedges, Henry, Jun$^r$, 87.
Hedges, Isaac, 87.
Hegleton, Abigal, 96.
Helme, Oliver, 116.
Helmes, William, 103.
Helms, Christopher, 146.
Hemecage, Abraham, 35.
Hemman, Aron, 98.
Hemingway, Samuel, 40.
Hemmingar, John, 119.
Hemmingway, Abram, 76.
Hemmingway, Enos, 97.
Hemmingway, Isaac, 111.
Hemmingway, John, 97.
Hemmingway Joseph, 97.

Hemmingway, Moses, 97.
Hemmingway, Samuel, 97.
Hempstead, Hallam, 128.
Hempstead, Joshua, 128.
Hempstead, Nath$^l$, 128.
Hempstead, Samuel, 128.
Hempstead, Stephen, 128.
Hempsted, Joshua, 46.
Hempsted, Joshua, 55.
Hempsted, Josiah, 46.
Hemstead, Benjamin, 127.
Hemstead, Jonathan, 127.
Hemstead, Nath$^l$, Jun$^r$, 127.
Hemstead, Nath$^l$, 3$^d$, 127.
Hemstead, Robart, 116.
Hemstead, Robart, Jun$^r$, 116.
Hemstead, Samuel, 116.
Hemstead, William, 127.
Hende, Caleb, 140.
Hende, Joseph, 140.
Hender, Thomas, 46.
Henderson, James, 60.
Henderson, John, 60.
Henderson, John, 99.
Hendick, Eleazer, 72.
Hendric, William, 15.
Hendrick, Abel, 34.
Hendrick, Benjamin, 19.
Hendrick, Coe, 104.
Hendrick, Daniel, 34.
Hendrick, Daniel, 73.
Hendrick, Dan$^l$, 150.
Hendrick, Deodate, 21.
Hendrick, James, 19.
Hendrick, John, 19.
Hendrick, John, 34.
Hendrick, John, 56.
Hendrick, John, 108.
Hendrick, Nathan, 21.
Hendrick, Nathaniel, 24.
Hendrick, Peter, 21.
Hendrick, Philemon, 48.
Hendrick, Samuel, 19.
Hendrick, Samuel, 19.
Hendrick, Sarah, 105.
Hendrick, Zadock, 73.
Hendricks, Andrew, 72.
Hendricks, Benjamin, 131.
Hendricks, Daniel, 131.
Hendy, Elipt, 134.
Hendy (Widow), 133.
Heneries, Elizabeth, 11.
Henery, Aaron, 47.
Henery, Gager, 40.
Henery, James, 45.
Henery, Obediah, 12.
Heney, Asa, 138.
Henfield, Benj$^n$, 141.
Henfield, William, 140.
Henman, Asher, 70.
Henman, Eben, 95.
Henman, Eben, 2$^{nd}$, 95.
Henman, Ephrahim, 95.
Henman, Nathan, 17.
Henman, Phenehas, 70.
Henman, Samuel, 17.
Hennerics, Ellis, 21.
Henneries, Abner, 13.
Henneries, Samuel, 13.
Henry, Daniel, 127.
Henry, James, 86.
Henry, James, 152.
Henry, John, 40.
Henry, John, 104.
Henry, John, 122.
Henry, John, 151.
Henry, Robart, 122.
Henry, Sam$^l$, 142.
Hensdale, Jacob, 70.
Henshaw, Benjamin, 69.
Henshaw, Daniel, 86.
Henshaw, James, 67.
Henshaw, Mary, 86.
Henshaw, Samuel, 86.
Hepborn, Peter, 101.
Heppborn, Lewis, 105.
Hequimburgh, Charles, 45.
Herd, Jacob, 148.
Herd, Thomas, 148.
Herford, Jeremiah, 67.
Herkin, Aaron, 132.
Hermom, Nicholas, 66.
Heron, Samuel, 34.
Heron, William, 27.
Herrick, Amos, 113.
Herrick, Andrew, 148.
Herrick, Andrew, 148.
Herrick, Asael, 142.
Herrick, Benj$^n$, 141.
Herrick, Eben$^r$, 115.
Herrick, Eleazer, 114.
Herrick, Elijah, 113.
Herrick, Elijah, 130.
Herrick, Elisabeth, 148.
Herrick, Ephraim, 75.
Herrick, Ephraim, 113.
Herrick, Ephraim, 115.
Herrick, Isaac, 113.
Herrick, Isaac, 121.
Herrick, Israel, 113.
Herrick, John, 142.
Herrick, John, 142.
Herrick, John, 142.

# INDEX.

Herrick, Jos., 133.
Herrick, Mary, 69.
Herrick, Nathan, 113.
Herrick, Rufus, 115.
Herrick, Rufus, 141.
Herrick, Stephen, 103.
Herrington, Andw, 113.
Herrington, Elisha, 149.
Herrington, Jeremiah, 144.
Herrington, John, 144.
Herrington, Jonathan, 144.
Herrington, Jona, Jnr, 144.
Herrington, Joseph, 113.
Herrington, Othniel, 144.
Herrington, Stephen, 113.
Herrod, Jesse, 45.
Herskill, Jabez, 54.
Hevelan, Nathanel, 19.
Hevelan, Thomas, 18.
Heveland, Isaac, 19.
Heveland, Roger, 19.
Hewet, Charles, 116.
Howet, Dudley, 116.
Hewet, Elias, 116.
Hewet, Elkanah, 118.
Hewet, Henry, 115.
Hewet, Henry, 118.
Hewet, Isaac, 116.
Hewet, Israel, 120.
Hewet, Jonas, 115.
Hewet, Rufus, 116.
Hewet, Rufus, Junr, 116.
Hewet, Saml, 115.
Hewet, Simeon, 115.
Hewet, Solomon, 130.
Hewet, Stanton, 120.
Hewit, Asa, 139.
Hewit, Benjamin, 62.
Hewit, Danl, 139.
Hewit, Gershom, 70.
Hewit, Gurdon, 129.
Hewit, Joshua, 64.
Hewit, Lewis, 152.
Hewit, Robert, 143.
Hewit, Stephen, 141.
Hewitt, Jedidiah, 130.
Hewitt, Nathaniel, 128.
Hews, Danl, 138.
Heyden, Daniel, 37.
Heyes, Enock, 43.
Heyliger, John, 103.
Hibard, Rufus, 142.
Hibbard, David, 133.
Hibbard, Elisha, 19.
Hibbard, Jonathan, 16.
Hibbard, Nathanel, 19.
Hibbard, Nathaniel, 16.
Hibbard, Peter, 18.
Hibbard, Samuel, 104.
Hibbert, Silas, 133.
Hiccock, Daniel, 48.
Hiccock, Helener (Wd), 48.
Hichcox, Ebenr, 129.
Hichson, Eneas, 110.
Hick, John, 18.
Hickcox, Thomas, 118.
Hickoks, Ebenr, 56.
Hicks, Chase, 150.
Hicks, David, 144.
Hicks, James, 41.
Hicks, Samuel, 105.
Hicks, Saml, 127.
Hickson, Gideon, 2nd, 111.
Hickson, James, 111.
Hickson, Jos, 137.
Hickson, Nathl, Jr., 137.
Hicock, Abraham, 110.
Hicock, Ambrose, 2d, 76.
Hicock, Amos, 73.
Hicock, Aron, 101.
Hicock, Asa, 73.
Hicock, Benjamin, 73.
Hicock, Elijah, 75.
Hicock, Ithiel, 73.
Hicock, James, 96.
Hicock, Jesse, 109.
Hicock, Jiles, 44.
Hicock, Joel, 75.
Hicock, Johnson, 75.
Hicock, Joseph, 73.
Hicock, Joseph, 2d, 73.
Hicock, Justus, 73.
Hicock, Nathan, 75.
Hicock, Nathan, 2d, 75.
Hicock, Nathaniel, 75.
Hicock, Nathaniel, 2d, 75.
Hicock, Prosper, 109.
Hicock, Ruben, 95.
Hicock, Silas, 73.
Hicock, Thaddeus, 75.
Hicock, Timothy, 109.
Hicocks, Ambrose, 76.
Hicocks, Amos, 76.
Hicocks, Caleb, 76.
Hicocks, Consider, 76.
Hicocks, Daniel, 76.
Hicocks, Dick, 76.
Hicocks, Hinman, 76.
Hicocks, Jared, 76.
Hicocks, Jeames, 76.
Hicocks, Joel, 76.
Hicocks, Jonas, 76.
Hicocks, Joseph, 76.

Hiscock, Mary, 76.
Hicocks, Phebe, 76.
Hicocks, Samuel, 76.
Hicocks, Samuel, 76.
Hicocks, William, 76.
Hicox, Freeman, 35.
Hicox, Gideon, 110.
Hicox, Samuel, 110.
Hide, Abiel, 131.
Hide, Abijah, 95.
Hide, Asa, 112.
Hide, Asael, 95.
Hide, Barnabas, 112.
Hide, Daniel, 95.
Hide, Ebenr, 131.
Hide, Eliakam, 17.
Hide, Elisabeth, 123.
Hide, Elisabeth, 123.
Hide, Elisha, 17.
Hide, Elisha, 132.
Hide, Ezra, 46.
Hide, Jakey & Co., 141.
Hide, James, 131.
Hide, James, 2d, 131.
Hide, John, 12.
Hide, John, Jnr, 12.
Hide, Joseph, 12.
Hide, Joseph, 95.
Hide, Nathaniel, 95.
Hide, Phineas, 118.
Hide, Samuel, 17.
Hide, Saml, 59.
Hide, Uriah, 68.
Hide, Zebadiah, 132.
Higbe, Amos, 88.
Higbe, Daniel, 88.
Higbe, David, 88.
Higbe, Ephraim, 88.
Higbe, Jeduthan, 88.
Higbe, Lemuel, 88.
Higbe, Noah, 86.
Higbe, Zacheus, 88.
Higbey, Isaac, 70.
Higby, Cheney, 102.
Higby, Job, 55.
Higby, Patience, 59.
Higby, Samuel, 101.
Higby, Seth, 31.
Higgens, John, 32.
Higgens, Tommy, 32.
Higgins, Abraham, 31.
Higgins, Benjamin, 123.
Higgins, Cornelius, 83.
Higgins, Cornelius, Esqr, 84.
Higgins, Cristian, 123.
Higgins, David, 122.
Higgins, Dolle, 82.
Higgins, Elkina, 82.
Higgins, George, 19.
Higgins, Hawse, 83.
Higgins, Isaac, 31.
Higgins, Israel, 80.
Higgins, Israel, Junr, 80.
Higgins, James, 80.
Higgins, James, 83.
Higgins, Jedh, 82.
Higgins, Joseph, 53.
Higgins, Joseph, 72.
Higgins, Lemuel, 80.
Higgins, Lemuel, Junr, 80.
Higgins, Moses, 80.
Higgins, Nemamiah, 104.
Higgins, Sarah, 84.
Higgins, Silvanus, 123.
Higgins, Stephen, 82.
Higgins, Thesiah, 80.
Higgins, Timothy, 80.
Higgins, Timothy, 102.
Higgins, William, 129.
Higgs, John, 111.
Higley, Anna, 47.
Higley, Asa, 44.
Higley, Bruster, 48.
Higley, David, 43.
Higley, Ebenezer, 35.
Higley, Enoch, 48.
Higley, Isaac, 48.
Higley, Jeremiah, 39.
Higley, Joel, 44.
Higley, Jonathan, 43.
Higley, Mary, 43.
Higley, Nathan, 38.
Higley, Obed, 49.
Higley, Ozias, 44.
Higley, Seth, 48.
Higley, Simeon, 48.
Higley, Sylvester, 48.
Higly, Sarah, 65.
Hildrieth, William, 43.
Hildrup, Thomas, 46.
Hilhouse, John, 125.
Hilhouse, Thomas, 125.
Hilhouse, William, 125.
Hill, Aaron, 78.
Hill, Abner, 121.
Hill, Abner, 145.
Hill, Abraham, 99.
Hill, AGift, 70.
Hill, Allel, 27.
Hill, Amos, 41.
Hill, Amos, 104.
Hill, Andrew, 27.
Hill, Anna, 98.

Hill, Anna, 99.
Hill, Aron, 99.
Hill, Asa, 58.
Hill, Aves, 152.
Hill, Benjamin, 97.
Hill, Benona, 60.
Hill, Consider, Senr, 146.
Hill, Cromwell, 152.
Hill, Daniel, 27.
Hill, Daniel, 27.
Hill, Dan., 34.
Hill, Daniel, 59.
Hill, Daniel, 80.
Hill, Daniel, 99.
Hill, Danl, 148.
Hill, Danl, 152.
Hill, Darious, 146.
Hill, Darius, 49.
Hill, David, 27.
Hill, David, 56.
Hill, David, 71.
Hill, Easter, 119.
Hill, Ebenezer, 18.
Hill, Eliazer, 48.
Hill, Elijah, 43.
Hill, Elijah, 48.
Hill, Eliphilet, 13.
Hill, Ephraim, 146.
Hill, Esther (Wd), 23.
Hill, Ezekiel, 27.
Hill, Freeman, 35.
Hill, Gaines, 34.
Hill, Gershom, 86.
Hill, Hannah, 103.
Hill, Henry, 90.
Hill, Henry, 97.
Hill, Hiland, 89.
Hill, Huste, 64.
Hill, Icobad, 99.
Hill, Isaac, 18.
Hill, James, 70.
Hill, James, 76.
Hill, James, 84.
Hill, James, 89.
Hill, James, 99.
Hill, James, 128.
Hill, James, 146.
Hill, Jarad, 109.
Hill, Jedediah, 49.
Hill, Jediah, 48.
Hill, John, 45.
Hill, John, 49.
Hill, John, 70.
Hill, John, 99.
Hill, John, 106.
Hill, John, 131.
Hill, Jonah, 93.
Hill, Jonas, 92.
Hill, Jonathan, 19.
Hill, Jonathan, 33.
Hill, Jonathan, 56.
Hill, Jonathan, 59.
Hill, Jonathan, 125.
Hill, Jonathn, 152.
Hill, Joseph, 13.
Hill, Joseph, 14.
Hill, Joseph, 146.
Hill, Josiah, 33.
Hill, Mary, 18.
Hill, Medad, 61.
Hill, Michael, 62.
Hill, Michael, 2d, 62.
Hill, Miles, 34.
Hill, Molly, 108.
Hill, Nathaniel, 98.
Hill, Noah, 84.
Hill, Obadiah, 109.
Hill, Parker, 152.
Hill, Peleg, 89.
Hill, Peleg, 89.
Hill, Phillip, 145.
Hill, Robert, 152.
Hill, Ruben, 99.
Hill, Ruben, 2d, 99.
Hill, Samuel, 67.
Hill, Samuel, 72.
Hill, Samuel, 81.
Hill, Samuel, 123.
Hill, Samuel, 2d, 72.
Hill, Silas, 72.
Hill, Solomon, 36.
Hill, Solomon, 1st, 72.
Hill, Solomon, 2d, 72.
Hill, Stepen, 106.
Hill, Stephen, 52.
Hill, Thomas, 13.
Hill, Thomas, 97.
Hill, Thomas, 98.
Hill, Thomas, 121.
Hill, Thomas, 140.
Hill, Thomas, 2nd, 98.
Hill, Timothy, 99.
Hill, Wakeman, 31.
Hill, William, 13.
Hill, Willm, 90.
Hillam, Eliphalet, 39.
Hillard, Jacy, 27.
Hillhouse, James, 104.
Hillhouse, Mary, 104.
Hillhouse, Samuel, 67.
Hillhouse, William, 104.
Hilliard, Barzilla, 85.

Hilliard, Bezaleel, 90.
Hilliard, Joseph, 85.
Hilliard, Thurstain, 27.
Hilliard, Walter, 85.
Hillick, Jeremiah, 49.
Hills, Abraham, 33.
Hills, Amos, 37.
Hills, Anna, 37.
Hills, Ashbell, 37.
Hills, Caleb, 36.
Hills, Chancey, 40.
Hills, Daniel, 43.
Hills, David, 33.
Hills, David, 36.
Hills, Ebenezer, 37.
Hills, Elijah, 37.
Hills, Elijah, 134.
Hills, Eliphalet, 37.
Hills, Elisha, 36.
Hills, Elisha, 43.
Hills, Epaphras, 36.
Hills, Gideon, 33.
Hills, Israel, 43.
Hills, Jacob, 40.
Hills, Jessee, 63.
Hills, John, 35.
Hills, John, 43.
Hills, Jonathan, 36.
Hills, Jonathan, 2d, 36.
Hills, Joseph, 36.
Hills, Joseph, 40.
Hills, Joseph, 42.
Hills, Joshua, 37.
Hills, Josiah, 43.
Hills, Justice, 70.
Hills, Levi, 37.
Hills, Libbeus, 43.
Hills, Mabel, 36.
Hills, Nathan, 37.
Hills, Reuben, 37.
Hills, Russell, 1st, 37.
Hills, Russell, 2d, 37.
Hills, Samuel, 43.
Hills, Samuel, Jr., 43.
Hills, Seth, 60.
Hills, Silus, 37.
Hills, Timothy, 36.
Hills, William, 36.
Hillyard, Isaac, 140.
Hillyard, Jonathan, 151.
Hillyer, Andrew, 45.
Hillyer, Asa, 44.
Hillyer, James, Jr, 45.
Hillyer, Pliny, 43.
Hillyer, Theodorus, 44.
Hilton, Adkisson, 32.
Hilyard, Azariah, 116.
Hilyard, Benjamin, 114.
Hilyard, Dennis, 126.
Hilyard, John, 116.
Hilyard, Jonathan, 118.
Hilyard, Jos., 133.
Hilyard, Miner, 138.
Hilyard, Oliver, 117.
Hilyard, William, 115.
Hilyard, William, Junr, 116.
Hilyer, James, 44.
Hilyer, Seth, 44.
Hinckley, Able, 117.
Hinckley, Ebenr, 82.
Hinckley, John, 81.
Hinckley, John, 117.
Hinckley, Thomas, 116.
Hinckley, Vorce, 131.
Hindsdale, Theodore, 54.
Hine, Abel, 72.
Hine, Abraham, 102.
Hine, Ambrose, 2d, 94.
Hine, Amos, 95.
Hine, Andrew, 75.
Hine, Aron, 102.
Hine, Benjamin, 109.
Hine, Charles, 111.
Hine, Dan., 56.
Hine, Daniel, 72.
Hine, Dan., Jur, 56.
Hine, David, 101.
Hine, David, 109.
Hine, David, 111.
Hine, Ebenezer, 110.
Hine, Elisha, 73.
Hine, George, 101.
Hine, Heil, 95.
Hine, Henry F., 96.
Hine, Hezekiah, 95.
Hine, Hezekiah, 110.
Hine, Isaac, 102.
Hine, Isaac, 110.
Hine, Joel, 78.
Hine, Joel, 102.
Hine, Joel, 112.
Hine, John, 102.
Hine, Jonah, 78.
Hine, Jonathan, 75.
Hine, Joseph, 102.
Hine, Moses, 111.
Hine, Nathan, 78.
Hine, Newton, 28.
Hine, Noble, 72.
Hine, Samuel, 101.
Hine, Silas, 94.
Hine, Stephen, 72.

Hine, Stephen, 102.
Hine, Stephen, 111.
Hine, Thomas, 95.
Hine, Titus, 102.
Hineman, John, 57.
Hineman, Partrick, 57.
Hines, Ambrose, 94.
Hines, Hezekiah, 93.
Hinkley, David, 139.
Hinkley, Dyer I., 145.
Hinkley, Ebenr, 145.
Hinkley, Elijah, 117.
Hinkley, Icabod, 137.
Hinkley, Ira, 90.
Hinkley, Jared, 145.
Hinkley, John, 85.
Hinkley, Jno, 139.
Hinkley, Mary, 117.
Hinkley, Nathan, 117.
Hinman, Aaron, 73.
Hinman, Abner, 73.
Hinman, Adam, 73.
Hinman, Agus, 73.
Hinman, Amos, 41.
Hinman, Amos, 110.
Hinman, Benjamin, 73.
Hinman, Cate, 129.
Hinman, Daniel, 73.
Hinman, David, 20.
Hinman, David, 73.
Hinman, Edward, 73.
Hinman, Eleazer, 73.
Hinman, Elihu, 96.
Hinman, Elisha, 126.
Hinman, Enos, 56.
Hinman, Ephraim, 78.
Hinman, Francis, 73.
Hinman, Isaac, 30.
Hinman, James, 56.
Hinman, James, 96.
Hinman, Joel, 73.
Hinman, John, 73.
Hinman, Jonas, 30.
Hinman, Jonas, 73.
Hinman, Jonas, 2d, 73.
Hinman, Jonathan, 73.
Hinman, Joseph, 62.
Hinman, Justus, 73.
Hinman, Lemuel, 73.
Hinman, Lewis, 73.
Hinman, Mary, 20.
Hinman, Michael, 75.
Hinman, Philo, 96.
Hinman, Samuel, 65.
Hinman, Samuel, 73.
Hinman, Sherman, 73.
Hinman, Silas, 73.
Hinman, Timothy, 73.
Hinman, Titus 73.
Hinman, Truman, 73.
Hinman, Wait, 73.
Hinox, Salmon, 41.
Hinsbury, Eben, 148.
Hinsdal, Ezra, 58.
Hinsdale, Amos, 46.
Hinsdale, Daniel, 45.
Hinsdale, Elias, 65.
Hinsdale, Elijah, 33.
Hinsdale, Elisha, 63.
Hinsdale, Jacob, 62.
Hinsdale, James, 46.
Hinsdale, John, 33.
Hinsdale, Joseph, 68.
Hinsdale, Moses, 66.
Hinsdale, Samuel, 58.
Hinsdale, William, 46.
Hinsdale, William, 68.
Hinsdale, Zadock, 54.
Hinshaw, Joshua, Esqr, 86.
Hinsman, Benjamin, 69.
Hinson, William, 126.
Hinson, William, Junr, 126.
Hinton, Joseph, 100.
Hinton, Nathaniel, 100.
Hiscock, David, 140.
Hiscock, Stephen, 139.
Hislop, Alford, 71.
Hitchcock, Aaron, 50.
Hitchcock, Aaron, 72.
Hitchcock, Abel, 56.
Hitchcock, Amassa, 93.
Hitchcock, Amassa, 2nd, 93.
Hitchcock, Ambrose, 49.
Hitchcock, Amos, 93.
Hitchcock, Amos, 112.
Hitchcock, Anna, 93.
Hitchcock, Apollos, 52.
Hitchcock, Aron, 93.
Hitchcock, Asa, 93.
Hitchcock, Ashbel, 35.
Hitchcock, Bela, 93.
Hitchcock, Benjamin, 56.
Hitchcock, Benjamin, 109.
Hitchcock, Brenton, 52.
Hitchcock, Caleb, 49.
Hitchcock, Caleb, 55.
Hitchcock, Chancey, 51.
Hitchcock, Daniel, 65.
Hitchcock, Daniel, 72.
Hitchcock, Daniel, 93.
Hitchcock, Dan., 108.
Hitchcock, Daniel, 111.
Hitchcock, David, 50.

INDEX. 187


Hitchcock, David, 72.
Hitchcock, David, 93.
Hitchcock, David, 94.
Hitchcock, Easter, 93.
Hitchcock, Ebenezer, 95.
Hitchcock, Ebenezer, 112.
Hitchcock, Ebenezur, 100.
Hitchcock, Ebenezur, 2$^{nd}$, 100.
Hitchcock, Eliakim, 103.
Hitchcock, Eneas, 111.
Hitchcock, Eneas, 111.
Hitchcock, Hannah, 104.
Hitchcock, Hannah, 108.
Hitchcock, Harvey, 93.
Hitchcock, Harvie, 34.
Hitchcock, Icobed, 93.
Hitchcock, Ira, 72.
Hitchcock, Jabez, 100.
Hitchcock, Jared, 56.
Hitchcock, Joash, 108.
Hitchcock, Joel, 35.
Hitchcock, John L., 93.
Hitchcock, Jonathan, 74.
Hitchcock, Jonathan, 94.
Hitchcock, Jon$^{a}$, 137.
Hitchcock, Jonathan, 2$^{nd}$, 94.
Hitchcock, Joseph, 15.
Hitchcock, Joseph, 112.
Hitchcock, Joseph, 112.
Hitchcock, Josiah, 49.
Hitchcock, Jotham, 103.
Hitchcock, Lemuel, 94.
Hitchcock, Levi, 93.
Hitchcock, Lidia, 100.
Hitchcock, Lidia, 100.
Hitchcock, Lydia, 56.
Hitchcock, Mary, 93.
Hitchcock, Medad, 112.
Hitchcock, Nathan, 72.
Hitchcock, Nathaniel, 108.
Hitchcock, Phineas, 111.
Hitchcock, Rufus, 93.
Hitchcock, Samuel, 49.
Hitchcock, Samuel, 76.
Hitchcock, Samuel, 95.
Hitchcock, Samuel, 100.
Hitchcock, Samuel, 102.
Hitchcock, Samuel, Jr., 49.
Hitchcock, Stephen, 50.
Hitchcock, Stephen, 100.
Hitchcock, Thomas, 15.
Hitchcock, Valantine, 93.
Hitchcock, William, 72.
Hitchcock, William, 112.
Hitchcock, Zachariah, 76.
Hitchcocks. Sam$^{l}$, 67.
Hitchcok, Amos, 49.
Hitchcox, Nathaniel, 34.
Hitchwick, Jason, 93.
Hitt, John, 152.
Hix, John, 120.
Hix, John, Jun$^{r}$, 120.
Hoadley, Amasia, 112.
Hoadley, Asa, 109.
Hoadley, Culpeper, 110.
Hoadley, Ebenezer, 110.
Hoadley, Ebenezur, 92.
Hoadley, Jehiel, 88.
Hoadley, Philo, 110.
Hoadley, Timothy, 92.
Hoadley, William, 110.
Hoadly, Abigal, 91.
Hoadly, Abigal, 91.
Hoadly, Benjamin, 91.
Hoadly, Daniel, 92.
Hoadly, Isaac, 91.
Hoadly, James, 91.
Hoadly, John, 91.
Hoadly, Jonathan, 91.
Hoadly, Jude, 110.
Hoadly, Lemuel, 109.
Hoadly, Nath$^{l}$, 109.
Hoadly, Ralph, 91.
Hoadly, Rufus, 92.
Hoadly, Samuel, 91.
Hoadly, Samuel, 91.
Hoadly, Samuel, 97.
Hoady, Silas, 91.
Hoanmen, Wait, 65.
Hoase, Sarah, 105.
Hobart, Sam$^{l}$, 123.
Hobbs, Edmond, 145.
Hobby, Abraham, 15.
Hobby, Benjamin, 15.
Hobby, Charles, 15.
Hobby, David, 16.
Hobby, Ebenezer, 15.
Hobby, Henry, 24.
Hobby, Hezekiah, 15.
Hobby, Jabez Mead, 15.
Hobby, John, 15.
Hobby, Jonathan, 16.
Hobby, Joseph, 15.
Hobby, Joseph, Jun$^{r}$, 15.
Hobby, Mills, 15.
Hobby, Seymore, 16.
Hobby, Thomas, 15.
Hobby, Thomas, Jun$^{r}$, 15.
Hobby, Winsley, 85.
Hochkins, Joseph, 57.
Hoddy, Daniel, 67.
Hodg, Jn$^{o}$, 137.
Hodgden, David, 14.
Hodge, Abel, 19.
Hodge, Benjamin, 43.
Hodge, Benjamin, 115.
Hodge, Benjamin, Jr., 43.
Hodge, Eli, 42.
Hodge, Elijah, 42.
Hodge, Job, 23.
Hodge, John, 42.
Hodge, Jonathan, 42.
Hodge, Philo, 78.
Hodge, Roswell, 42.
Hodge, Samuel, 81.
Hodge, Thomas, 19.
Hodgekiss, James, 35.
Hodges, Ellane, 68.
Hodges, Ephram, 147.
Hodges, Ezra, 10.
Hodges, Thaddeus, 19.
Hodgkins, Thomas, 143.
Hodgkiss, Ambrose, 44.
Hodley, Andrew, 109.
Hoel, Edw$^{d}$, 82.
Hoel, Ephraim, 149.
Hoffman, Samuel, 92.
Hogden (Widow), 29.
Hoit, Deodate, 25.
Hoit, Ebenezer, 59.
Hoit, Eli, 29.
Hoit, Mary, 24.
Hoit, Nezer, 25.
Hokim, David, 68.
Hokim, Eli, 66.
Holbrock, Joseph, 73.
Holbrook, Abel, 94.
Holbrook, Calvan, 154.
Holbrook, Daniel, 94.
Holbrook, Daniel, 95.
Holbrook, Elias, 138.
Holbrook, John, 94.
Holbrook, John, 151.
Holbrook, John, 2$^{nd}$, 94.
Holbrook, Nathan, 94.
Holbrook, Philo, 95.
Holbrook, Tho$^{s}$, 151.
Holbrooks, Nathaniel, 61.
Holcomb, Abel, 44.
Holcomb, Abel, 2$^{d}$, 44.
Holcomb, Abraham, 62.
Holcomb, Adonijah, 44.
Holcomb, Ahas, 44.
Holcomb, Amasa, 68.
Holcomb, Asa, 44.
Holcomb, Asahel, Jr., 45.
Holcomb, Asahel, Jr., 45.
Holcomb, Asahel, 3$^{d}$, 44.
Holcomb, Asahel, 4$^{th}$, 45.
Holcomb, Benajah, 44.
Holcomb, Benajah, 48.
Holcomb, Benajah, Jr., 48.
Holcomb, Caleb, 43.
Holcomb, Consider, 44.
Holcomb, Criss, 44.
Holcomb, Daniel, 43.
Holcomb, Dan., 44.
Holcomb, David, 44.
Holcomb, David, Jr., 44.
Holcomb, Ebenezer, 44.
Holcomb, Eli, 44.
Holcomb, Elihu, 43.
Holcomb, Elijah, 44.
Holcomb, Elijah, 54.
Holcomb, Elijah, 55.
Holcomb, Elijah, 62.
Holcomb, Elijah, Jr., 44.
Holcomb, Ezekiel, 44.
Holcomb, Ezekiel, Jr., 44.
Holcomb, Ezra, 45.
Holcomb, Hezekiah, 43.
Holcomb, Hezekiah, J$^{r}$, 43.
Holcomb, Jesse, 43.
Holcomb, John, 57.
Holcomb, John G., 44.
Holcomb, Joseph, 45.
Holcomb, Joseph, 55.
Holcomb, Joseph, J$^{r}$, 45.
Holcomb, Joshua, 43.
Holcomb, Judah, Esq$^{r}$, 45.
Holcomb, Judah, J$^{r}$, 45.
Holcomb, Luther, 12.
Holcomb, Martha (Wid.), 45.
Holcomb, Martin, 55.
Holcomb, Martin, J$^{ur}$, 55.
Holcomb, Masa (Wid.), 44.
Holcomb, Nahum, 44.
Holcomb, Nathan, J$^{r}$, 44.
Holcomb, Nathaniel, 44.
Holcomb, Noadiah, 44.
Holcomb, Noah, 43.
Holcomb, Noah, 62.
Holcomb, Obed, 44.
Holcomb, Oliver, 45.
Holcomb, Ozias, 44.
Holcomb, Ozias, Jr., 44.
Holcomb, Peter, 44.
Holcomb, Peter, J$^{r}$, 44.
Holcomb, Phineas, 44.
Holcomb, Reuben, 44.
Holcomb, Roderick, 55.
Holcomb, Roger, 44.
Holcomb, Roger, J$^{r}$, 44.
Holcomb, Sam$^{l}$, 55.
Holcomb, Silus, 44.
Holcomb, Simeon, 44.
Holden, John, 43.
Holden, Jonathan, 43.
Holden, Jonathan, Jr., 43.
Holden, Phineas, 130.
Holdridge, Hezekiah, 75.
Holdridge, Nath$^{l}$, 116.
Holdrige, Benaijah, 118.
Holdrige, Phineas, 120.
Holdrige, Rufus, 118.
Holdrige, Sam$^{l}$, 120.
Holdrige, Sam$^{l}$, Jun$^{r}$, 120.
Holdrige, William, 114.
Holdrige, William, 118.
Holebrook, Abijah, 65.
Holebrook, Jobe, 154.
Holeburd, Timothy, 62.
Holeburd, William, 62.
Holeburton, Thomas, 14.
Holeburton, William, 14.
Holerige, Elisha, 114.
Holibard, David, 80.
Holibard, Elisha, 80.
Holibard, Jehiel, 80.
Holibard, Reuben, 80.
Holibard, William, Jun$^{r}$, 80.
Holibart, Martin, 63.
Holibert, Elisha, 63.
Holibert, Sam$^{l}$, 63.
Holiburd, John, 62.
Holiburt, Martin, 63.
Holiburt, Sam$^{l}$, 63.
Holiday, Naoma, 52.
Holiday, William, 52.
Holidy, Amos, 44.
Holidy, John, 44.
Holkins, Elijah, 39.
Holkins, Joel, 39.
Holkins, Joel, Jr., 39.
Holkins, Joseph, 39.
Holland, Benjamin, 46.
Hollebut, Daniel, 106.
Hollester, David B., 80.
Hollester, Lucretia, 123.
Hollester, Nathan, 60.
Hollett, John, 86.
Holley, Elnathan, 64.
Holley, Joseph, 120.
Holley, Stephen, 2$^{nd}$, 112.
Hollibert, Daniel, 24.
Hollibert, James, 23.
Hollibert, John, 24.
Hollibert, Joseph, 21.
Hollibert, Stephen, 24.
Hollida, Daniel, 56.
Hollister, Aaron, 43.
Hollister, Abel, 72.
Hollister, Abraham, 42.
Hollister, Amos, 42.
Hollister, Appleton, 132.
Hollister, Asahel, 43.
Hollister, David, 42.
Hollister, David, 60.
Hollister, David, Jr., 43.
Hollister, David, 3$^{d}$, 42.
Hollister, Elisha, 43.
Hollister, Elisha, 60.
Hollister, Elizur, 43.
Hollister, Ephraim, 34.
Hollister, George, 43.
Hollister, Gershom, 57.
Hollister, Gideon, 43.
Hollister, Gideon, 75.
Hollister, Gideon, 2$^{d}$, 75.
Hollister, Ichabod, 43.
Hollister, Isaac, 63.
Hollister, Israel, 43.
Hollister, John, 37.
Hollister, John, 42.
Hollister, Jonathan, 42.
Hollister, Joseph, 42.
Hollister, Joseph, Jr., 42.
Hollister, Joshua, 60.
Hollister, Josiah, 37.
Hollister, Nathaniel, 43.
Hollister, Nehemiah, 43.
Hollister, Rebecca, 33.
Hollister, Roswell, 42.
Hollister, Solomon, 34.
Hollister, Stephen, 33.
Hollister, Stephen, 42.
Hollister, Theodore, 43.
Hollister, Thomas, 33.
Hollister, Thomas, 43.
Holloway, Dan$^{l}$, 137.
Holloway, John, 75.
Holly, Abel, 107.
Holly, Abraham, 25.
Holly, Abraham, Jun$^{r}$, 26.
Holly, David, 24.
Holly, Enoch, 26.
Holly, Francis, 25.
Holly, Increas, 26.
Holly, John, 23.
Holly, John, 26.
Holly, John, 94.
Holly, John, Jun$^{r}$, 26.
Holly, John W., 24.
Holly, Josiah, 103.
Holly, Lois (W$^{d}$), 15.
Holly, Manchester, 113.
Holly, Martha (W$^{d}$), 24.
Holly, Miller, 106.
Holly, Nathan, 24.
Holly, Numan, 24.
Holly, Stephen, 25.
Holly, Stephen, 112.
Holly, Stephen, J$^{r}$, 25.
Holman, Ebenezar, 37.
Holmbeck, Abraham, 68.
Holmes, Abel, 139.
Holmes, Anne, 89.
Holmes, Benjamin, 15.
Holmes, Benj$^{n}$, 149.
Holmes, Charles, 43.
Holmes, Christopher, 82.
Holmes, Cornelius, 85.
Holmes, Daniel, 53.
Holmes, David, 149.
Holmes, David, 154.
Holmes, Ebenezer, 16.
Holmes, Eben$^{r}$, 149.
Holmes, Eben$^{r}$, 154.
Holmes, Eben$^{r}$, Jn$^{r}$, 154.
Holmes, Elephalet, Esq$^{r}$, 82.
Holmes, Gershom, 74.
Holmes, Isaac, 15.
Holmes, Isaac, 23.
Holmes, Israel, 74.
Holmes, Israel, 109.
Holmes, Jabez, 16.
Holmes, James, 129.
Holmes, Jazaniah, 137.
Holmes, Jeremiah, 71.
Holmes, Joel, 102.
Holmes, John, 26.
Holmes, John, 36.
Holmes, John, 54.
Holmes, Jonas, 53.
Holmes, Jon$^{n}$, 137.
Holmes, Jonathan, 149.
Holmes, Jos$^{i}$, 137.
Holmes, Lemuel, 54.
Holmes, Levi, 53.
Holmes, Nathan, 71.
Holmes, Nath$^{l}$, 141.
Holmes, Nathel, 137.
Holmes, Peleg, 74.
Holmes, Reuben, 16.
Holmes, Seth, 68.
Holmes, Stephen, 15.
Holmes, Thatford, 19.
Holmes, Thomas, 53.
Holmes, Urial, 68.
Holmes, William, 43.
Holmes, William, 154.
Holms, George, 121.
Holms, James, 65.
Holms, Sam$^{l}$, 121.
Holscombe, James, 65.
Holt, Abiel, 143.
Holt, Andrew, 139.
Holt, Aron, 107.
Holt, Asa, 127.
Holt, Benjamin, 107.
Holt, Benjamin, 153.
Holt, Caleb, 139.
Holt, Daniel, 13.
Holt, Daniel, 76.
Holt, Daniel, 97.
Holt, Daniel, 107.
Holt, Daniel, 127.
Holt, Daniel, 2$^{nd}$, 107.
Holt, Eben, 128.
Holt, Ebenezer, 38.
Holt, Ebenezer, 97.
Holt, Ebenezer, 128.
Holt, Elijah, 139.
Holt, Eliza, 67.
Holt, Elizabeth, 128.
Holt, Ezekiel, 141.
Holt, Isaac, 63.
Holt, Isaac, 67.
Holt, Isaac, 139.
Holt, James, 129.
Holt, James, 139.
Holt, Jesse, 114.
Holt, Jonathan, 128.
Holt, Jona$^{th}$, 143.
Holt, Joseph, 97.
Holt, Joshua, 143.
Holt, Josiah, 34.
Holt, Nathaniel, 107.
Holt, Nath$^{l}$, 113.
Holt, Nath$^{l}$, 139.
Holt, Nath$^{l}$, 2$^{d}$, 139.
Holt, Nehemiah, 143.
Holt, Nehem$^{h}$, Jn$^{r}$, 143.
Holt, Nicholas, 67.
Holt, Paul, Jn$^{r}$, 143.
Holt, Paul, Sen$^{r}$, 143.
Holt, Phil$^{n}$, 139.
Holt, Samuel, 97.
Holt, Seth, 139.
Holt, Stephen, 128.
Holt, Thomas, 128.
Holt, Tim$^{o}$, 139.
Holt, W$^{m}$, 127.
Holt, William, 128.
Holt, William, Jn$^{r}$, 143.
Holt, Zebe$^{h}$, 143.
Holton, Elisha, 39.
Holton, Tim$^{o}$, 134.
Hombbord, Isaac, 134.
Homer, David, 60.
Homer, James, 69.
Homerston, John, 68.
Homes, Appleton, 43.
Homes, Daniel, 31.
Homes, Edward, 116.
Homes, Elisha, 125.
Homes, Jabez, 118.
Homes, Jabez, 125.
Homes, James, 116.
Homes, Jared, 116.
Homes, Jeremi, 116.
Homes, John, 116.
Homes, John, 121.
Homes, Joshua, 116.
Homes, Samuel, 125.
Homes, Seth W., 125.
Homes, Silas, 117.
Homes, Thomas, 115.
Homestead, Joseph, 96.
Homestone, Abel, 76.
Homestone, Abram, 58.
Homestone, Abram, 2$^{d}$, 58.
Homestone, David, 76.
Homestone, Eliphet, 76.
Homestone, Jose, 76.
Homestone, Joseph, 58.
Homestone, Thomas, 76.
Homestone, Timothy, 58.
Hond, John, 94.
Honferd, Rubin, 108.
Hood, George, 67.
Hood, Richard, 102.
Hood, Samuel, 102.
Hood, William, 102.
Hoods, Catherine, 101.
Hoogaboom, Jeremiah, 67.
Hooker, Bryon, 50.
Hooker, Daniel, 47.
Hooker, Elijah, 33.
Hooker, Elnathan, 41.
Hooker, Hezekiah, 112.
Hooker, Horrace, 54.
Hooker, James, 54.
Hooker, Jessee, 63.
Hooker, John, 102.
Hooker, Joseph, 41.
Hooker, Noadiah, 41.
Hooker, Roger, 41.
Hooker, Samuel, 33.
Hooker, William, 33.
Hooker, William, 46.
Hoolbrook, Abel, 146.
Hoolbrook, John, 146.
Hoolbrook, Timo$^{y}$, 146.
Hooper, Asahel, 40.
Hooper, James, 91.
Hoopkins, Stephen, 61.
Hop, John, 81.
Hopkins, Asa, 45.
Hopkins, Benjamin, 33.
Hopkins, Benjamin, 58.
Hopkins, Benjamin, 74.
Hopkins, Benjamin, 125.
Hopkins, Caleb, 33.
Hopkins, Charles, 144.
Hopkins, Consider, 67.
Hopkins, David, 110.
Hopkins, Elijah, 74.
Hopkins, Elisha, 147.
Hopkins, George, 148.
Hopkins, Harriss, 68.
Hopkins, Harriss, 2$^{d}$, 68.
Hopkins, Hezekiah, 58.
Hopkins, Isaac, 110.
Hopkins, Jenks, 144.
Hopkins, Jere$^{h}$, 150.
Hopkins, Jesse, 109.
Hopkins, John, 110.
Hopkins, Jonathan, 51.
Hopkins, Joseph, 74.
Hopkins, Joseph, 109.
Hopkins, Joseph, 2$^{nd}$, 110.
Hopkins, Josiah, 57.
Hopkins, Lemuel, 46.
Hopkins, Moses, 46.
Hopkins, Nathan, 74.
Hopkins, Noah, 59.
Hopkins, Prince, 74.
Hopkins, Richard, 144.
Hopkins, Roodrick, 67.
Hopkins, Samuel, 61.
Hopkins, Simeon, 110.
Hopkins, Stephen, 47.
Hopkins, Thomas, 45.
Hopkins, Thomas, 64.
Hopkins, Thomas, 74.
Hopkins, Thomas, 102.
Hopkins, Uriah, 58.
Hopkins, William, 47.
Hoppen, Benjamin, 93.
Hopson, Alvanus, 108.
Hopson, Amelia, 99.
Hopson, Ashbel, 108.
Hopson, Clement, 108.
Hopson, Ebenezer, 98.
Hopson, John, 59.
Hopson, John, 99.
Hopson, John, 121.
Hopson, Rue, 108.
Hopson, Samuel, 108.
Hopson, Simeon, 68.
Hopson, William, 75.
Horcheild, William, 103.
Horford, David, 65.

# INDEX.

Horford, John, 2d, 64.
Horford, William, 2d, 64.
Horner, Thomas, 52.
Hornes, David, 137.
Hornestone, Timothy, 76.
Hornet, John, 72.
Horsey, Eunice, 94.
Horskins, Theodore, 65.
Horton, Aaron, 136.
Horton, Benjamin, 127.
Horton, Calvin, 110.
Horton, Eli, Jr., 134.
Horton, Elisha, 50.
Horton, Elisha, 61.
Horton, Ezekiel, 135.
Horton, Ezra, 138.
Horton, James, 125.
Horton, John, 110.
Horton, John, 125.
Horton, Jonas, 154.
Horton, Jotham, 144.
Horton, Lebues, 125.
Horton, Moses, 136.
Horton, Moses, 141.
Horton, Sampson, 135.
Horton, Samuel, 103.
Horton, Sam$^l$, 135.
Horton, Stephen, 135.
Horton, Timothy, 16.
Hosford, Aaron, 53.
Hosford, Amos, 34.
Hosford, Anne, 62.
Hosford, Dan$^l$, 135.
Hosford, Dudley, 135.
Hosford, Enos, 135.
Hosford, Ezekiel, 41.
Hosford, Timothy, 62.
Hosington, John, 33.
Hosington, Salmon, 33.
Hoskins, Abel, 49.
Hoskins, Abel, 67.
Hoskins, Alson, 45.
Hoskins, Asa, 48.
Hoskins, Asa, 48.
Hoskins, Asa, 55.
Hoskins, Ashbel, 48.
Hoskins, Daniel, 48.
Hoskins, Daniel, 64.
Hoskins, David, 48.
Hoskins, David, 68.
Hoskins, Eben$^r$, 119.
Hoskins, Eli, 55.
Hoskins, Elijah, 45.
Hoskins, Ezekiel, 54.
Hoskins, Ezra, 48.
Hoskins, Increase, 55.
Hoskins, John, 44.
Hoskins, John, 48.
Hoskins, Joseph, 67.
Hoskins, Robert, 48.
Hoskins, Simeon, 51.
Hoskins, W$^m$, 132.
Hoskins, Zeb$^a$, 55.
Hosmer, Abel, 154.
Hosmer, Asa, 80.
Hosmer, David, 151.
Hosmer, Elizabeth, 47.
Hosmer, Eunice, 147.
Hosmer, Graves, 125.
Hosmer, James, 45.
Hosmer, James, 151.
Hosmer, John, 35.
Hosmer, Joseph, 37.
Hosmer, Lydia, 86.
Hosmer, Menassah, 154.
Hosmer, Menassah, Sen$^r$, 154.
Hosmer, Stephen, 80.
Hosmer, Stephen, Jun$^r$, 80.
Hosmer, Stephen T., 86.
Hosmer, Timothy, 41.
Hosmer, Timothy, 81.
Hosmer, William, 46.
Hosmer (Widow), 149.
Hosmer (Wido.), 154.
Hosmer, Zachariah, 80.
Hotchkins, Sam$^l$, 67.
Hotchkis, Ephrim, 93.
Hotchkis, Rev$^d$ Fred$^k$ W., 89.
Hotchkiss, Abraham, 109.
Hotchkiss, Abraham, 112.
Hotchkiss, Adonijah, 93.
Hotchkiss, Ambrose, 93.
Hotchkiss, Ambrose, 107.
Hotchkiss, Amos, 98.
Hotchkiss, Amos, 104.
Hotchkiss, Amos, 110.
Hotchkiss, Anna, 108.
Hotchkiss, Arael, 110.
Hotchkiss, Asa, 97.
Hotchkiss, Asa, 104.
Hotchkiss, Bela, 2$^d$, 93.
Hotchkiss, Benjamin, 93.
Hotchkiss, Benjamin, 93.
Hotchkiss, Benjamin, 111.
Hotchkiss, Benjamin, 3$^d$, 93
Hotchkiss, Bennan, 93.
Hotchkiss, Caleb, 105.
Hotchkiss, Chauncy, 93.
Hotchkiss, Daniel, 94.
Hotchkiss, Daniel, 101.
Hotchkiss, Daniel, 111.
Hotchkiss, Daniel, 3$^d$, 92.
Hotchkiss, David, 111.

Hotchkiss, Ebenezer, 72.
Hotchkiss, Ebenezer, 94.
Hotchkiss, Ebenezer, 98.
Hotchkiss, Eber, 98.
Hotchkiss, Eber, 110.
Hotchkiss, Eldad, 109.
Hotchkiss, Elias, 111.
Hotchkiss, Elihu, 66.
Hotchkiss, Elijah, 34.
Hotchkiss, Elijah, 93.
Hotchkiss, Elijur, 105.
Hotchkiss, Eliphalet, 70.
Hotchkiss, Eliphalet, 95.
Hotchkiss, Elisha, 105.
Hotchkiss, Elisha, 112.
Hotchkiss, Elizabeth, 94.
Hotchkiss, Ely, 104.
Hotchkiss, Eneas, 102.
Hotchkiss, Eneas, 104.
Hotchkiss, Eziekel, 112.
Hotchkiss, Fredrick, 110.
Hotchkiss, Gabrael, 104.
Hotchkiss, Gideon, 110.
Hotchkiss, Hannah, 92.
Hotchkiss, Hannah, 98.
Hotchkiss, Hannah, 104.
Hotchkiss, Henry, 93.
Hotchkiss, Henry, 2$^{nd}$, 93.
Hotchkiss, Hetty, 112.
Hotchkiss, Hezekiah, 104.
Hotchkiss, Ira, 98.
Hotchkiss, Isaac, 98.
Hotchkiss, Isaac, 112.
Hotchkiss, Jabez, 112.
Hotchkiss, Jacob, 112.
Hotchkiss, James, 112.
Hotchkiss, Jason, 93.
Hotchkiss, Jiles, 94.
Hotchkiss, Joel, 110.
Hotchkiss, Joel, 111.
Hotchkiss, Joel, 2$^{nd}$, 111.
Hotchkiss, John, 94.
Hotchkiss, John, 97.
Hotchkiss, John, 105.
Hotchkiss, John, 2$^d$, 93.
Hotchkiss, John, 3$^d$, 93.
Hotchkiss, John C., 94.
Hotchkiss, Jonah, 93.
Hotchkiss, Jonas, 111.
Hotchkiss, Joseph, 97.
Hotchkiss, Joseph, 112.
Hotchkiss, Joshua, 105.
Hotchkiss, Josiah, 40.
Hotchkiss, Josiah, 93.
Hotchkiss, Josiah, 104.
Hotchkiss, Josiah, 2$^d$, 93.
Hotchkiss, Ladwick, 40.
Hotchkiss, Leman, 105.
Hotchkiss, Lemuel, 33.
Hotchkiss, Lemuel, 105.
Hotchkiss, Lent, 103.
Hotchkiss, Leverbet, 94.
Hotchkiss, Levi, 96.
Hotchkiss, Ludwick, 33.
Hotchkiss, Lyman, 93.
Hotchkiss, Lyman, 105.
Hotchkiss, Miles, 97.
Hotchkiss, Mineman, 93.
Hotchkiss, Moses, 95.
Hotchkiss, Nemamiah, 104.
Hotchkiss, Noah, 94.
Hotchkiss, Noah, 99.
Hotchkiss, Obadiah, 104.
Hotchkiss, Phebe, 100.
Hotchkiss, Punderson, 105.
Hotchkiss, Reuben, 78.
Hotchkiss, Robert, 93.
Hotchkiss, Robert, 94.
Hotchkiss, Ruben, 92.
Hotchkiss, Ruben, 98.
Hotchkiss, Ruth, 93.
Hotchkiss, Samuel, 35.
Hotchkiss, Samuel, 97.
Hotchkiss, Samuel, 107.
Hotchkiss, Samuel, 112.
Hotchkiss, Silus, 105.
Hotchkiss, Simeon, 35.
Hotchkiss, Soloman, 111.
Hotchkiss, Soloman, 111.
Hotchkiss, Solomon, 72.
Hotchkiss, Stephen, 35.
Hotchkiss, Stephen, 103.
Hotchkiss, Stephen, 109.
Hotchkiss, Stephen, 111.
Hotchkiss, Stephen, Jr., 35.
Hotchkiss, Sussanah, 103.
Hotchkiss, Thelus, 110.
Hotchkiss, Thomas, 95.
Hotchkiss, Thomas, 99.
Hotchkiss, Titus, 76.
Hotchkiss, Truman, 76.
Hotchkiss, Wait, 110.
Hotchkiss, Willstell, 93.
Hotchwick, Israel, 93.
Hotech, John, 72.
Houd, Amie, 91.
Houd, Daniel, 108.
Houd, Edward, 85.
Houd, Hendrick, 91.
Houd, Joel, 91.
Houd, Thankfull, 92.
Houde, Jude, 92.
Hough, Abigail, 88.

Hough, Ambrose, 92.
Hough, Andrew, 108.
Hough, Benoni, 58.
Hough, Benoni, 76.
Hough, Buel, 78.
Hough, Ebenezer, 92.
Hough, Ensign, 107.
Hough, Ephrim, 108.
Hough, Erastus, 142.
Hough, James, 106.
Hough, James, 108.
Hough, John, 142.
Hough, Joseph, 108.
Hough, Joseph, 108.
Hough, Joseph, 2$^d$, 108.
Hough, Joseph, 2$^{nd}$, 108.
Hough, Justin, 51.
Hough, Lent, 108.
Hough, Lidia, 108.
Hough, Louis, 106.
Hough, Mathew, 106.
Hough, Oliver, 107.
Hough, Philip, 106.
Hough, Samuel, 107.
Hough, Samuel, 2$^{nd}$, 106.
Hough, Walter, 142.
Hough, Will$^m$, 90.
Houghf, David, 126.
Houghf, Eben$^r$, 126.
Houghf, Jabez, 126.
Houghf, John, 126.
Houghton, Ephraim, 151.
Houghton, Ephraim, 151.
Houghton, Giles, 106.
House, Abner, 43.
House, Benjamin, 42.
House, Benj$^n$, 134.
House, Daniel, 43.
House, Eleazer, 42.
House, Elijah, 42.
House, Eliphalet, 39.
House, Elizabeth, 42.
House, George, 42.
House, George, 129.
House, Israel, 43.
House, Joel, 43.
House, John, 42.
House, John, 144.
House, Jon$^a$, 133.
House, Lazarus, 43.
House, Mathew, 43.
House, Samuel, 42.
House, Sam. 134.
House, William, 43.
Housie, Elijah, 136.
Houston, John, 151.
Hovey, Aaron, 147.
Hovey, Chloe, 143.
Hovey, David, 152.
Hovey, Eben$^r$, 143.
Hovey, Enoch, 147.
Hovey, Jacob, 147.
Hovey, Jacob, 152.
Hovey, John, 143.
Hovey, Jona$^{th}$, 143.
Hovey, Jona$^{th}$, 147.
Hovey, Jonath$^n$, 147.
Hovey, Joseph, 147.
Hovey, Nathan, 146.
Hovey, Sam$^l$, 152.
How, Abner, 131.
How, Daniel, 110.
How, Deliverance, 57.
How, Edw$^d$, 55.
How, Elisha, 43.
How, Elisha, 52.
How, Epenetus, 28.
How, Ephraim, 76.
How, John, Jr., 94.
How, Joseph, 94.
How, Leavitt, 59.
How, Mary, 118.
How, Noah, 108.
How, Samuel, 76.
How, Zachariah, 76.
Howard, Amasa, 154.
Howard, Asa, 138.
Howard, Benj$^n$, 132.
Howard, Benjamin, 154.
Howard, Benj$^n$, Jr, 132.
Howard, Caleb, 145.
Howard, Caleb, 149.
Howard, Charles, 136.
Howard, Charles, 141.
Howard, Daniel, 16.
Howard, Daniel, 127.
Howard, David, 123.
Howard, David, 124.
Howard, David, 154.
Howard, Eben$^r$, 150.
Howard, Edward, 33.
Howard, Ephraim, 140.
Howard, Ezekiel, 64.
Howard, James, 143.
Howard, Jesse, 152.
Howard, John, 127.
Howard, Jn$^o$, 132.
Howard, Joseph, 51.
Howard, Joseph, 66.
Howard, Jos., 136.
Howard, Joseph, 144.
Howard, Lucy, 140.

Howard, Manassa, 138.
Howard, Nath$^l$, 54.
Howard, Nth$^{el}$, 133.
Howard, Peter, 154.
Howard, Sam$^l$, 132.
Howard, Sam$^l$, 140.
Howard, Sarah, 26.
Howard, Sarah, 127.
Howard, Simon, 150.
Howard, Stephen, 138.
Howard, Stephen, 143.
Howard, Tho$^s$, 138.
Howard, W$^m$, 128.
Howard, William, 143.
Howd, Whitehead, 49.
Howe, Bowers, 26.
Howe, Dan$^l$, 147.
Howe, David, 26.
Howe, Ebenezer, 16.
Howe, Ebenezer, 26.
Howe, Elisha, 61.
Howe, Isaac, 16.
Howe, Isaac Cady, 144.
Howe, Jacob, 26.
Howe, Jeremiah, 61.
Howe, Jeremiah, 69.
Howe, Joel, 61.
Howe, John, 70.
Howe, Jonathan, 15.
Howe, Jonath$^n$, 149.
Howe, Joseph, 65.
Howe, Nathan, 26.
Howe, Nathan, 62.
Howe, Neh$^{eh}$, 140.
Howe, Noah, 149.
Howe, Philop, 61.
Howe, Robert, 148.
Howe, Sampson, 144.
Howe, Sarah (W$^d$), 26.
Howe, Silvanus, 16.
Howe, Stephen, 60.
Howel, Edward, 67.
Howel, Ben$^n$, 66.
Howell, Cheney, 103.
Howell, Edmond, 64.
Howell, Henry, 111.
Howell, Nicholas, 100.
Howell, Nicholas, 100.
Howell, Ryal, 46.
Howell, Samuel, 103.
Howell, Thomas, 103.
Howell, Thomas, Jr, 103.
Howes, David, 75.
Howes, Noah, 26.
Howes, Prince, 26.
Howes, Prince, Jun$^r$, 26.
Howes, Zach$^h$, 152.
Howes, Zach$^h$, 152.
Howes, Zach$^h$, Jn$^r$, 152.
Howes, Zenas, 152.
Howett, Joseph, 103.
Howland, Joseph, 131.
Howlet, John, 154.
Howlet, Sam$^l$, 154.
Howlet, Sam$^l$, Jun$^r$, 154.
Hows, Asa, 134.
Hows, David, 138.
Hows, Ebenezer, 30.
Hows, Eben$^r$, 138.
Hows, Hamam, 139.
Hows, Israel, 137.
Hows, James, 138.
Hows, Luke, 135.
Howse, Ben$^n$, 66.
Howse, Edmon, 19.
Howse, Zacheriah, 18.
Hoxey, Joseph, 151.
Hoy, Daniel, 105.
Hoy, John, 64.
Hoye, Nelly, 103.
Hoyle, Richard, 150.
Hoyle, W$^m$, 150.
Hoyt, Ager, 10.
Hoyt, Amos, 12.
Hoyt, Asa, 12.
Hoyt, Asa, 22.
Hoyt, Benjamin, 12.
Hoyt, Benjamin, 28.
Hoyt, Comfort, 10.
Hoyt, Comfort, 12.
Hoyt, Daniel, 11.
Hoyt, Daniel, 11.
Hoyt, Daniel, 23.
Hoyt, Daniel D., 11.
Hoyt, David, 10.
Hoyt, David, 23.
Hoyt, David, 25.
Hoyt, David, 28.
Hoyt, Drake, Jn$^r$, 11.
Hoyt, Eleazer, 11.
Hoyt, Eleazer, 12.
Hoyt, Eli, 10.
Hoyt, Elijah, 11.
Hoyt, Elizabeth (W$^d$), 25.
Hoyt, Enos, 11.
Hoyt, Epenetus, 25.
Hoyt, Frederick, 25.
Hoyt, Gould, 23.
Hoyt, Hanah (Wid.), 29.
Hoyt, Hanford, 26.
Hoyt, Hannah (W$^d$), 24.

Hoyt, Henry, 22.
Hoyt, Isaac, 22.
Hoyt, Jacob, 26.
Hoyt, James, 12.
Hoyt, James, 25.
Hoyt, Jesse, 12.
Hoyt, Jesse, 23.
Hoyt, Jesse, Jun$^r$, 25.
Hoyt, Job, 22.
Hoyt, John, 11.
Hoyt, John, 22.
Hoyt, John, 23.
Hoyt, John, 26.
Hoyt, John, Jun$^r$, 23.
Hoyt, John, Jun$^r$, 24.
Hoyt, John, 3$^d$, 26.
Hoyt, Jonathan, 11.
Hoyt, Jonathan, 22.
Hoyt, Jonathan, 26.
Hoyt, Josep, 3$^d$, 25.
Hoyt, Joseph, 26.
Hoyt, Joseph, 4$^{th}$, 25.
Hoyt, Joshua, 12.
Hoyt, Josiah, 25.
Hoyt, Justice, 22.
Hoyt, Justus, 11.
Hoyt, Mary (W$^d$), 22.
Hoyt, Matthew, 23.
Hoyt, Moses, 19.
Hoyt, Moses, 22.
Hoyt, Nathan, 11.
Hoyt, Nathan, 22.
Hoyt, Nathanel, 12.
Hoyt, Nathaniel, 24.
Hoyt, Nathaniel, Jun$^r$, 26.
Hoyt, Nehemiah, 23.
Hoyt, Noah, 11.
Hoyt, Ruth (W$^d$), 25.
Hoyt, Samuel, 12.
Hoyt, Samuel, 12.
Hoyt, Samuel, 26.
Hoyt, Samuel, 28.
Hoyt, Samuel, 4$^{th}$, 24.
Hoyt, Samuel, 5$^{th}$, 24.
Hoyt, Sarah (W$^d$), 22.
Hoyt, Sarah (W$^d$), 22.
Hoyt, Seth, 32.
Hoyt, Silas, 25.
Hoyt, Stephen, 23.
Hoyt, Stephen, 74.
Hoyt, Thaddeus, 10.
Hoyt, Thaddeus, 23.
Hoyt, Thaddeus, 25.
Hoyt, Thomas, 12.
Hoyt, Thomas, 22.
Hoyt, Timothy, 21.
Hoyt, Timothy, 23.
Hoyt, Walter, 18.
Hoyt, Warren, 26.
Hoyt, Water, 23.
Hoyt, Waterbury, 26.
Hoyt, William, 23.
Hoyt, William, 24.
Hoyt, William, 31.
Hubard, Benj$^n$, Jur, 149.
Hubard, Eb$^n$, 141.
Hubard, Edmond, 62.
Hubard, Willard, 149.
Hubard, William, 141.
Hubbard, A——, 56.
Hubbard, Aaron, 83.
Hubbard, Abijah, 34.
Hubbard, Abijah, 87.
Hubbard, Abner, 55.
Hubbard, Abner, 83.
Hubbard, Abner, 87.
Hubbard, Abraham, 99.
Hubbard, Abraham, 2$^d$, 99.
Hubbard, Ama, 55.
Hubbard, Asa, 55.
Hubbard, Rev$^d$ Bela, 103.
Hubbard, Benjamin, 83.
Hubbard, Caleb, 87.
Hubbard, Calvin, 80.
Hubbard, Calvin, 83.
Hubbard, Daniel, 104.
Hubbard, David, 42.
Hubbard, David, 83.
Hubbard, Deborah, 98.
Hubbard, Ebor, 99.
Hubbard, Eleazer, 42.
Hubbard, Elias, 87.
Hubbard, Elijah, 45.
Hubbard, Elijah, Esq$^r$, 85.
Hubbard, Eliphalet, 87.
Hubbard, Eliphelet, 117.
Hubbard, Eliphelet, 117.
Hubbard, Elizur, 43.
Hubbard, Elizur, Jr., 43.
Hubbard, Ephraim, 87.
Hubbard, George, 34.
Hubbard, George, 80.
Hubbard, George, 87.
Hubbard, Giles, 84.
Hubbard, Hez., 86.
Hubbard, Icabud, 30.
Hubbard, Isaac, 87.
Hubbard, Isaac, 107.
Hubbard, Jabez, 87.
Hubbard, Jacob, 86.
Hubbard, Jamansy, 87.
Hubbard, James, 83.

INDEX. 189

Hubbard, Jedediah, 80.
Hubbard, Jedediah, 80.
Hubbard, Jeremiah, 37.
Hubbard, Jeremiah, 83.
Hubbard, Jeremiah, 87.
Hubbard, Jeremiah, Jun$^{r}$, 83.
Hubbard, Jessey, 80.
Hubbard, Job, 83.
Hubbard, Joel, 83.
Hubbard, Joel, 1$^{st}$, 76.
Hubbard, John, 55.
Hubbard, John, 87.
Hubbard, John, 91.
Hubbard, John, 99.
Hubbard, John, 101.
Hubbard, John, Jun$^{r}$, 80.
Hubbard, Jonathan, 34.
Hubbard, Jonathan, 83.
Hubbard, Jonathan, 87.
Hubbard, Joseph, 62.
Hubbard, Joseph, 87.
Hubbard, Joseph, 100.
Hubbard, Josiah, 59.
Hubbard, Josiah, 76.
Hubbard, Julia, 103.
Hubbard, Justin, 14.
Hubbard, Leveret, 103.
Hubbard, Levi, 104.
Hubbard, Manoah, 87.
Hubbard, Manoah, Jun$^{r}$, 87.
Hubbard, Mary (W$^{d}$), 24.
Hubbard, Mary, 104.
Hubbard, Micah, 87.
Hubbard, Michael, 83.
Hubbard, Moses, 83.
Hubbard, Moses, 91.
Hubbard, Nath$^{l}$, 55.
Hubbard, Nath$^{l}$, 132.
Hubbard, Nehemiah, 87.
Hubbard, Nehemiah, Jun$^{r}$, 86.
Hubbard, Noadiah, 87.
Hubbard, Noadiah, Jun$^{r}$, 87.
Hubbard, Obediah, 40.
Hubbard, Oliver, 87.
Hubbard, Peter, 116.
Hubbard, Philip, 51.
Hubbard, Prudence, 42.
Hubbard, Robert, 89.
Hubbard, Roswell, 88.
Hubbard, Royel, 80.
Hubbard, Samuel, 34.
Hubbard, Samuel, 83.
Hubbard, Samuel, Jun$^{r}$, 83.
Hubbard, Sarah, 13.
Hubbard, Seth, 81.
Hubbard, Shalor, 83.
Hubbard, Solomon, 87.
Hubbard, Thaddeus, 49.
Hubbard, Thomas, 83.
Hubbard, Thomas, 131.
Hubbard, Thomas, Jun$^{r}$, 83.
Hubbard, Timothy, 55.
Hubbard, Timothy, 80.
Hubbard, Timothy, 83.
Hubbard, Timothy, Jun$^{r}$, 83.
Hubbard, Watts, 106.
Hubbard, William, 17.
Hubbard, William, 34.
Hubbard, William, 89.
Hubbard, William, 120.
Hubbard, William, Jr., 34.
Hubbard, William G., 103.
Hubbart, David, 76.
Hubbat, Hesekiah, 76.
Hubbel, Abijah, 59.
Hubbel, David, 59.
Hubbel, Ephiaim, 74.
Hubbel, Jedediah, 59.
Hubbel, Joseph, 95.
Hubbel, Lewis, 106.
Hubbel, Samuel, 59.
Hubbel, Watrous, 72.
Hubbell, Aaron, 14.
Hubbell, Abel, 14.
Hubbell, Amos, 18.
Hubbell, Barrack, 19.
Hubbell, Coleman, 10.
Hubbell, Daniel, 15.
Hubbell, David, 17.
Hubbell, David, 2$^{d}$, 18.
Hubbell, Eleazer, 19.
Hubbell, Elisha, 18.
Hubbell, Ephraim, 18.
Hubbell, Ezra, 10.
Hubbell, Gershom, 13.
Hubbell, Giddeon, 15.
Hubbell, Giddeon, 17.
Hubbell, Giddeon, 18.
Hubbell, Giddeon, 19.
Hubbell, Giddeon, 19.
Hubbell, Isaac, 14.
Hubbell, Jabez, 14.
Hubbell, Jeremiah, 17.
Hubbell, Joel, 14.
Hubbell, John, 13.
Hubbell, John, 18.
Hubbell, John, 18.
Hubbell, Lidea, 14.
Hubbell, Mathew, 17.
Hubbell, Mathew, 18.
Hubbell, Noah, 11.
Hubbell, Richard, 14.
Hubbell, Richard, 95.
Hubbell, Silevant, 12.
Hubbell, Timothy, 18.
Hubbell, William, 17.
Hubbell, Zadoch, 21.
Hubbill, Abijah, 29.
Hubbill, Amos, 30.
Hubbill, Benjamin, 30.
Hubbill, Comfort, 19.
Hubbill Ebenezer 32.
Hubbill, Enoch, 19.
Hubbill, Eunice (Wid.), 29.
Hubbill, Isaac, 31.
Hubbill, Jepthan, 20.
Hubbill, John, 19.
Hubbill, John, 30.
Hubbill, Josiah, 30.
Hubbill, Lewis, 19.
Hubbill, Nathaniel, 32.
Hubbill, Samuel, 30.
Hubbill, Seth, 32.
Hubbill, Stephen, 32.
Hubbill, Timothy, 31.
Hubbill, Wiliam, 30.
Hubbill, Zalmon, 30.
Hubble, David, 13.
Hubble, Jehiel, 15.
Hubble, Nathan, 21.
Hubble, Thaddeus, 21.
Hubbord, Daniel, 17.
Hubbord, Henry, 17.
Hubbord, William A., 63.
Hubby, Benjamin, 15.
Hubill, Ebenezer, 30.
Huchenson, Daniel, 69.
Hucheson, Ezri, 69.
Hucheson, Ezri, 2$^{d}$, 69.
Huchinson, E$^{m}$, 133.
Huchinson, Israel, 135.
Huchinson, Jn$^{o}$, 135.
Huchinson, Jon$^{a}$, 135.
Huckins, James, 45.
Huckins, Jn$^{o}$ C., 132.
Huckins, Jonathan, 45.
Huckins, Joshu$^{a}$, 132.
Hudson, Barzilla, 46.
Hudson, Daniel, 60.
Hudson, David, 92.
Hudson, John, 52.
Hudson, John, 68.
Hudson, John, 116.
Hudson, Stephen, 123.
Huff, Caleb, 68.
Hug, Isaac, 62.
Hug, William, 62.
Hugens, James, 44.
Huges, Jona$^{th}$, 140.
Huggins, Heaton, 103.
Huggins, Hester, 91.
Huggins, John, 103.
Hughes, John, 130.
Hughes, William, 66.
Hughs, John, 82.
Hughs, William, 73.
Hugins, Ebenezer, 103.
Hulbert, Gideon, 79.
Hulbert, Hezekiah, 86.
Hulbert, Thomas, 86.
Hulbut, William, 52.
Hulet, Allim, 143.
Hulet, David, 143.
Hulet, Mehitable, 143.
Hulet, Nehem$^{h}$, 141.
Hulet, Oliver, 144.
Hull, Abeather, 92.
Hull, Abel, 85.
Hull, Abel, 95.
Hull, Abigal, 92.
Hull, Abijah, 94.
Hull, Abner, 85.
Hull, Abner, 106.
Hull, Abraham, 10.
Hull, Abraham, 41.
Hull, Amassa, 111.
Hull, Ambrose, 91.
Hull, Amie, 106.
Hull, Amos, 154.
Hull, Andrew, 92.
Hull, Andrew, 2$^{nd}$, 92.
Hull, Benjamin, 106.
Hull, Benjamin, 108.
Hull, Chapman, 27.
Hull, Charles, 108.
Hull, Cornelius, 96.
Hull, Daniel, 13.
Hull, Daniel, 78.
Hull, Daniel, 106.
Hull, David, 14.
Hull, David, 27.
Hull, David, 98.
Hull, David, 105.
Hull, David, 1$^{st}$, 76.
Hull, David, 2$^{d}$, 76.
Hull, Dick (Negroe), 93.
Hull, Ebenezer, 78.
Hull, Ebenezer, 108.
Hull, Eldad, 108.
Hull, Eliakim, 41.
Hull, Eliakim, 85.
Hull, Eliakim, 96.
Hull, Elias, 147.
Hull, Elijah, 20.
Hull, Eliphalit, 20.
Hull, Eliphilet, 13.
Hull, Elizabeth, 94.
Hull, Epharus, 92.
Hull, Esther (W$^{d}$), 26.
Hull, Eunice, 107.
Hull, Ezekiel, 13.
Hull Ezekiel, 84.
Hull, George, 85.
Hull, George, 106.
Hull, George, 2$^{d}$, 85.
Hull, Gurdon, 84.
Hull, Hannah, 92.
Hull, Hannah, 3$^{rd}$, 93.
Hull, Harvey, 109.
Hull, Hazard, 139.
Hull, Heil, 108.
Hull, Ira, 76.
Hull, James, 85.
Hull, Jeddediah, 15.
Hull, Jeremiah, 108.
Hull, Joel, 85.
Hull, Joel, 111.
Hull, John, 13.
Hull, John, 20.
Hull, John 27.
Hull, John, 27.
Hull, John, 72.
Hull, John, 106.
Hull, John, 108.
Hull, John, 108.
Hull, Joseph, 18.
Hull, Joseph, 85.
Hull, Joseph, 96.
Hull, Joseph, 104.
Hull, Joseph, 106.
Hull, Joseph, 2$^{nd}$, 106.
Hull, Josiah, 85.
Hull, Josiah, 85.
Hull, Josiah, 96.
Hull, Josiah, Jun$^{r}$, 85.
Hull, Josiah, 2$^{nd}$, 107.
Hull, Latham, 116.
Hull, Lemuel, 85.
Hull, Lemuel, Jun$^{r}$, 85.
Hull, Levi, 84.
Hull, Lidia, 92.
Hull, Lucy, 84.
Hull, Luther, 92.
Hull, Miles, 93.
Hull, Moses, 32.
Hull, Nathan, 84.
Hull, Nehemiah, 27.
Hull, Oliver, 85.
Hull, Oliver, 90.
Hull, Peter, 27.
Hull, Peter, 85.
Hull, Peter, 2$^{nd}$, 108.
Hull, Prince, 47.
Hull, Roswell, 85.
Hull, Samuel, 18.
Hull, Samuel, 85.
Hull, Samuel, 92.
Hull, Samuel, 94.
Hull, Samuel, 104.
Hull, Seth, 27.
Hull, Silas, 28.
Hull, Sirenus, 27.
Hull, Stephen, 13.
Hull, Stephen, 29.
Hull, Stephen, 78.
Hull, Stephen, 116.
Hull, Stephen, 138.
Hull, Sylvanus, 96.
Hull, Thelus, 92.
Hull, Thomas, 144.
Hull, Titus, 56.
Hull, Trustum, 86.
Hull, William, 14.
Hull, William, 98.
Hull, Zalmon, 27.
Hulse, Joseph, 102.
Humerston, Joel, 68.
Humerston, Noah, 70.
Humerston, Titus, 68.
Humes, Sam$^{l}$, 151.
Humestone, Reuben, 66.
Humiston, Ebenezer, 105.
Humiston, Ephrahim, 106.
Humiston, James, 106.
Humiston, Joseph, 100.
Humiston, Mary Ann, 102.
Humiston, Thomas, 106.
Hummiston, Abel, 112.
Hummiston, Asa, 112.
Hummiston, Bennet, 109.
Hummiston, Daniel, 112.
Hummiston, David, 100.
Hummiston, James, 108.
Hummiston, James, 2$^{nd}$, 108.
Hummiston, Jesse, 93.
Hummiston, Joy, 109.
Hummiston, Nathaniel, 101.
Hummiston, Samuel, 100.
Humpherville, Ebenezer, 105.
Humpherville, Ebenezer, 111.
Humpherville, John, 111.
Humpherville, Joseph, 105.
Humpherville, Lemuel, 105.
Humpherville, Moses, 105.
Humpherville, Samuel, 105.
Humpherville, Samuel, 105.
Humphey, Ambrosi, 66.
Humphey, Hoseah, 61.
Humpheys, Benonah, 59.
Humphrey, Abraham, 70.
Humphrey, Abram, 49.
Humphrey, Amasa, 47.
Humphrey, Amaziah, 47.
Humphrey, Anna, 94.
Humphrey, Asahel, 69.
Humphrey, Benona, 69.
Humphrey, Campbell, 47.
Humphrey, Charles, 70.
Humphrey, David, 70.
Humphrey, Dudley, 61.
Humphrey, Elisha, 47.
Humphrey, Ezekiel, 49.
Humphrey, Ezekiel, Jr., 49.
Humphrey, Frederic, 49.
Humphrey, Ichabod, 49.
Humphrey, Jiles, 35.
Humphrey, Jonathan, 47.
Humphrey, Jonathan, 48.
Humphrey, Jonathan, 49.
Humphrey, Levi, 48.
Humphrey, Lott, 47.
Humphrey, Lucy, 140.
Humphrey,Margeret (Wid.), 48.
Humphrey, Martin, 47.
Humphrey, Michael, 48.
Humphrey, Michael, 62.
Humphrey, Noah, 70.
Humphrey, Oliver, 49.
Humphrey, Ozias, 36.
Humphrey, Pelatiah, 62.
Humphrey, Roswell, 60.
Humphrey, Samuel, 49.
Humphrey, Samuel, 49.
Humphrey, Samuel, 70.
Humphrey, Simion, 60.
Humphrey, Solomon, 49.
Humphrey, Sylvanus, 47.
Humphrey, Theophilus, 49.
Humphrey, Timothy, 44.
Humphreys, John, 94.
Humphreys, Joseph, 46.
Humphreys, Joseph, 47.
Humphreys, Solomon, 35.
Humphreys, William, 36.
Humphries, Isaac, 96.
Humphries, Sam$^{l}$, 138.
Humphry, Asa, 47.
Humphry, Ashbel, 70.
Humphry, Charles, 48.
Humphry, Daniel, 47.
Humphry, James, 48.
Humphry, Nathaniel, 47.
Humphry, Ozias, 44.
Humphry, Ralph, 41.
Humphry, Ruggles, 48.
Hun, Jonathan, 148.
Hungeford, Jonas, 76.
Hungerford, Benj$^{m}$, 34.
Hungerford, Elijah, 82.
Hungerford, Ezra, 19.
Hungerford, Green, 82.
Hungerford, Isaiah, 19.
Hungerford, Jacob, 34.
Hungerford, James, 61.
Hungerford, Jeames, 76.
Hungerford, Jehiel, 35.
Hungerford, Joel, 76.
Hungerford, John, 49.
Hungerford, Joseph, 58.
Hungerford, Joseph, 82.
Hungerford, Josiah, 19.
Hungerford, Levi, 34.
Hungerford, Mary, 19.
Hungerford, Mathew, 58.
Hungerford, Nath$^{l}$, 82.
Hungerford, Nath$^{l}$, 2$^{d}$, 82.
Hungerford, Reuben, 63.
Hungerford, Rob$^{t}$, 82.
Hungerford, Rob$^{t}$, Ju$^{r}$, 82.
Hungerford, Stephen, 35.
Hungerford, Tertius, 58.
Hungerford, Thomas, 34.
Hungerford, Timothy, 35.
Hungerford, Uriah, 19.
Hungerford, Zach$^{h}$, 82.
Hunn, Enos, 54.
Hunn, Mary, 82.
Hunn, Saml., 82.
Hunt, Abner, 132.
Hunt, Alexander, 46.
Hunt, Daniel, 69.
Hunt, Daniel, 2$^{d}$, 69.
Hunt, Eldad, 146.
Hunt, Eldad, 146.
Hunt, Elijah, 146.
Hunt, Eliph$^{t}$, 133.
Hunt, Fredrick, 102.
Hunt, Gad, 133.
Hunt, Gideon, 78.
Hunt, Isaac, 63.
Hunt, Isaac, 78.
Hunt, Isaac, 2$^{d}$, 78.
Hunt, James, 40.
Hunt, Jesse, 137.
Hunt, Joel, 49.
Hunt, John, 26.
Hunt, John, 42.
Hunt, John, 97.
Hunt, John, 97.
Hunt, Jn$^{o}$, 138.
Hunt, John, 147.
Hunt, Jona$^{th}$, 145.
Hunt, Jos., 136.
Hunt, Joseph, 146.
Hunt, Joseph, 147.
Hunt, Lewis, 72.
Hunt, Lydia, 78.
Hunt, Miloe, 64.
Hunt, Nath$^{l}$, 148.
Hunt, Peter, 136.
Hunt, Phinehas, 63.
Hunt, Ransom, 78.
Hunt, Robert, 67.
Hunt, Russel, 62.
Hunt, Russel, 62.
Hunt, Russel, 62.
Hunt, Salmon, 62.
Hunt, Samuel, 42.
Hunt, Sam$^{l}$, 145.
Hunt, Seth, 78.
Hunt, Sim$^{e}$, 133.
Hunt, Theophilus, 72.
Hunt, Thomas, 43.
Hunt, Thomas, 97.
Hunt, Thomas, 2$^{nd}$, 97.
Hunt, Walter, 145.
Hunt, William, 78.
Hunt, W$^{m}$, 132.
Hunte, William, 23.
Hunter, Ebenezer, 69.
Hunter, John, 151.
Hunter, Nathaniel, 67.
Hunter, Robert, 90.
Huntington, Abner, 147.
Huntington, And$^{w}$, 113.
Huntington, And$^{w}$, 131.
Huntington, Andrew, 145.
Huntington, Asa, 111.
Huntington, Azariah, 130.
Huntington, Barnabas, 112.
Huntington, Benjamin, 131.
Huntington, Benjamin, 132.
Huntington, Christopher, 126.
Huntington, Daniel, 78.
Huntington, Daniel, 130.
Huntington, Daniel, 132.
Huntington, David, 120.
Huntington, David, 146.
Huntington, Eleaz$^{r}$, 148.
Huntington, Eleaz$^{r}$, Jn$^{r}$, 148.
Huntington. Elijah, 126.
Huntington, Eliphelet, 132.
Huntington, Eliph$^{t}$, 153.
Huntington, Elisha, 129.
Huntington, Elisha, 131.
Huntington, Elisha, 138.
Huntington, Rev$^{r}$ Enoch. 86.
Huntington, Ezra, 131.
Huntington, Felix, 131.
Huntington, Frederick, 131.
Huntington, Hezekiah, 50.
Huntington, Hez$^{a}$, 152.
Huntington, Isaac, 126.
Huntington, Israel, 64.
Huntington, Rev. J., 133.
Huntington, James, 62.
Huntington, Jared, 130.
Huntington, Jedediah, 127.
Huntington, Jn$^{o}$, 81.
Huntington, John, 131.
Huntington, Jn$^{o}$, 138.
Huntington, John, 152.
Huntington, John, 2$^{d}$, 131.
Huntington, Jonas, 148.
Huntington, Jonathan, 84.
Huntington, Jon$^{a}$, 130.
Huntington, Joshua, 131.
Huntington, Josiah, 53.
Huntington, Levi, 131.
Huntington, Nathan, 152.
Huntington, Nath$^{l}$, 152.
Huntington, Oliver, 145.
Huntington, Roger, 152.
Huntington, Sam$^{l}$, 82.
Huntington, Sam$^{l}$, 131.
Huntington, Sam$^{l}$, Jun$^{r}$, 81.
Huntington, Sam$^{l}$, Jun$^{r}$, 132.
Huntington, Silas, 36.
Huntington, Simeon, 131.
Huntington, Simon, 132.
Huntington, Sol$^{n}$, 135.
Huntington, Solomon, 152.
Huntington, Thomas, 126.
Huntington, Thomas, 140.
Huntington, Whitman, 146.
Huntington (Widow), 138.
Huntington, William, 143.
Huntington, William, 145.
Huntington, William, 145.
Huntington, Zachariah, 131.
Huntley, Amos. 124.
Huntley, Asher, 123.
Huntley, Benaijah, 122.
Huntley, Calvin, 129.
Huntley, Dan., 124.
Huntley, Daniel, 2$^{d}$, 124.
Huntley, Elihu, 123.
Huntley, Elijah, 153.
Huntley, Harris, 120.
Huntley, Hoel, 122.
Huntley, James, 124.
Huntley, Jasper, 124.
Huntley, Lydia, 122.
Huntley, Martin, 124.
Huntley, Marvin, 124.

# INDEX.

Huntley, Mary, 123.
Huntley, Nehemiah, 122.
Huntley, Phineas, 123.
Huntley, Reynold, 124.
Huntley, Rice, 124.
Huntley, Ruben, 124.
Huntley, Thomas, 114.
Huntley, William, 124.
Huntley, Zephaniah, 123.
Hurbut, Sarah, 34.
Hurbut, Thomas, 2d, 52.
Hurd, Abel, 10.
Hurd, Abijah, 72.
Hurd, Abraham, 17.
Hurd, Abraham, 85.
Hurd, Adam, 78.
Hurd, Ammon, 21.
Hurd, Amos 20.
Hurd, Amos Asahel, 75.
Hurd, Andrew, 29.
Hurd, Andrew, 73.
Hurd, Andrew, 78.
Hurd, Benjamin, 80.
Hurd, Caleb L., 85.
Hurd, Crippin, 81.
Hurd, Crippin, 82.
Hurd, Curtis, 20.
Hurd, Curtis, 78.
Hurd, David, 18.
Hurd, David, 70.
Hurd, David, 78.
Hurd, David, 2d, 78.
Hurd, Ebenezer, 17.
Hurd, Elethan, 18.
Hurd, Elnathan, 85.
Hurd, Elnathan, 2d, 85.
Hurd, Esther, 85.
Hurd, Finious, 20.
Hurd, Gilead, 30.
Hurd, Graham, 78.
Hurd, Hinman, 72.
Hurd, Jabesh, 10.
Hurd, Jabez, 29.
Hurd, Jacob, 80.
Hurd, Jacob, Junr, 80.
Hurd, Jessey, 80.
Hurd, John, 19.
Hurd, John, 85.
Hurd, Jonathan, 21.
Hurd, Joseph, 80.
Hurd, Levi, 75.
Hurd, Mead, 17.
Hurd, Moses, 78.
Hurd, Nathan, 78.
Hurd, Nathan, 2d, 78.
Hurd, Nehemiah, 17.
Hurd, Nirum, 19.
Hurd, Noah, 78.
Hurd, Philo, 17.
Hurd, Robt, 81.
Hurd, Samuel, 18.
Hurd, Sarah, 75.
Hurd, Seth, 85.
Hurd, Simeon, 78.
Hurd, Solomon, 75.
Hurd, Thaddeus, 78.
Hurd, Thos, 82.
Hurd, Wait, 78.
Hurd, William, 60.
Hurd, William, 72.
Hurd, William, 73.
Hurd, Zadock, 78.
Hurlbert, Alfred, 153.
Hurlbert, Turman, 78.
Hurlburt, Amos, 78.
Hurlburt, Amos, 78.
Hurlburt, Benjamin, 78.
Hurlburt, Comfort, 78.
Hurlburt, Damaras, 78.
Hurlburt, Daniel, 128.
Hurlburt, Ebenezer, 78.
Hurlburt, Elijah, 154.
Hurlburt, Gideon, 78.
Hurlburt, Gideon, 2d, 78.
Hurlburt, Gidian, 70.
Hurlburt, Joab, 57.
Hurlburt, Joel, 78.
Hurlburt, Joseph, 75.
Hurlburt, Levi, 60.
Hurlburt, Nathaniel, 78.
Hurlburt, Osias, 57.
Hurlburt, Samuel, 75.
Hurlburt, Solmon, 74.
Hurlburt, Thomas, 78.
Hurlbut, Amos, 47.
Hurlbut, Calven, 33.
Hurlbut, Christopher, 47.
Hurlbut, Eli, 47.
Hurlbut, Elias, 54.
Hurlbut, Elijah, 52.
Hurlbut, Elijah, Jr., 52.
Hurlbut, Elisabeth, 129.
Hurlbut, Fitch, 47.
Hurlbut, Isaac, 33.
Hurlbut, James, 34.
Hurlbut, Jehiel, 43.
Hurlbut, John, 36.
Hurlbut, John, 54.
Hurlbut, Joseph, 36.
Hurlbut, Joseph, Jr., 47
Hurlbut, Lemuel, 47.
Hurlbut, Levi, 54.
Hurlbut, Mathew, 54.

Hurlbut, Nathaniel, 52.
Hurlbut, Nathaniel, 2d, 52.
Hurlbut, Raphael, 34.
Hurlbut, Samuel, 36.
Hurlbut, Simion, 52.
Hurlbut, Stephen, 52.
Hurlbut, Thomas, 52.
Hurlbutt, David, 72.
Hurlbutt, Gamaliel, 72.
Hurlbutt, Giddeon, 12.
Hurlbutt, Hezekiah, 72.
Hursted, Roger, 63.
Huse, Abraham, 44.
Huse, Daniel, 96.
Huse, John, 96.
Huse, Rebecca, 97.
Husted, Abraham, 16.
Husted, Andrew, 11.
Husted, Benjamin, 16.
Husted, Jared, 16.
Husted, Jonathan, 26.
Husted, Joseph, 15.
Husted, Moses, 16.
Husted, Moses, Jr, 16.
Husted, Nathan, 16.
Husted, Peter, 16.
Husted, Thaddeus, 22.
Husted, Thaddeus, 25.
Husted, Zebulon, 25.
Hustfield, Charles, 72.
Hutcherson, Amos, 114.
Hutcheson, Asa, 69.
Hutchins, Amasa, 143.
Hutchins, Anna, 61.
Hutchins, Benjamin, 61.
Hutchins, Benjn, 147.
Hutchins, Elizabeth, 153.
Hutchins, Ezra, 143.
Hutchins, Isaac, 143.
Hutchins, John, 58.
Hutchins, John, 143.
Hutchins, Penuel, 143.
Hutchins, Shubal, 143.
Hutchins, Silas, 143.
Hutchins, Zadock, 143.
Hutchinson, Daniel, 145.
Hutchinson, Eleazr, 144.
Hutchinson, Eleazer, 145.
Hutchinson, Eleazr, Jnr, 144.
Hutchinson, Eleazr, 3d, 144.
Hutchinson, Elisha, 145.
Hutchinson, Elisha, 151.
Hutchinson, Jabez, 134.
Hutchinson, Jonn, 134.
Hutchinson, Jos., 134.
Hutchinson, Saml, 144.
Hutchinson, Stephen, 46.
Hutenack, Francis, 32.
Hutit, Nathl, 148.
Hutson, Daniel, 50.
Hutson, David, 67.
Hutton, Samuel, 24.
Huxford, John, 43.
Huxford, William, 43.
Huxford, William, 43.
Huxley, Eunice, 131.
Hyat, Samuel, 23.
Hyatt, Abraham, 23.
Hyatt, Daniel, 21.
Hyatt, Elvin, 21.
Hyatt, Isaac, 21.
Hyatt, Jesse, 57.
Hyatt, John, 23.
Hyatt, Mary (Wd), 21.
Hyatt, Stephen, 24.
Hyatt, Nathl, 116.
Hyatt, Thomas, 23.
Hyatt, Thomas, 28.
Hyatt, Uzzeil, 28.
Hyde, Abel, 129.
Hyde, Andrew, 130.
Hyde, Asa, 129.
Hyde, Benjamin, 130.
Hyde, Benjn, 142.
Hyde, Benjamin, 145.
Hyde, Comfort, 142.
Hyde, Daniel, 130.
Hyde, Daniel, 145.
Hyde, Daniel, Junr, 129.
Hyde, David, 143.
Hyde, Ebenezer, 78.
Hyde, Elasa, 142.
Hyde, Eli, 129.
Hyde, Elihu, 129.
Hyde, Elijah, 145.
Hyde, Elijah, Senior, 145.
Hyde, Em, 137.
Hyde, Em, Jr, 137.
Hyde, Enoch, 64.
Hyde, Ezekiel, 130.
Hyde, Gideon, 78.
Hyde, Isaac, 142.
Hyde, Jonathan, 142.
Hyde, Joseph, 129.
Hyde, Jos., 132.
Hyde, Joseph, Junr, 130.
Hyde, Joshua, 129.
Hyde, Josiah, 142.
Hyde, Josiah, Jur, 142.
Hyde, Mary, 129.
Hyde, Mathew, 134.
Hyde, Matthew, 129.
Hyde, Mehitabel, 129.

Hyde, Moses, 145.
Hyde, Nathan, 142.
Hyde, Nathl, 137.
Hyde, Nathl, 146.
Hyde, Nathl, Jnr, 146.
Hyde, Nathl, Senr, 146.
Hyde, Nehh, 142.
Hyde, Oliver, 145.
Hyde, Roger Ebn, 51.
Hyde, Samuel, 145.
Hyde, Sarah, 130.
Hyde, Solomon, 129.
Hyde, Squire, 152.
Hyde, Taber, 130.
Hyde, Taber, Junr, 130.
Hyde, Thomas, 129.
Hyde, Vaniah, 129.
Hyde, William, 106.
Hyde, William, 145.
Hyde, Zebediah, 145.
Hymes, Jeames, 72.
Hymes, John, 73.
Hynes, George, 62.
Hynes, James, 140.

Iarmgan, Jonathan, 31.
Ichabud, Seth, 60.
Igard, Benjn, 137.
Imley, William, 46.
Indicott, John, 46.
Inenka, Charels, 61.
Ingall, Thos, 149.
Ingalls, Benjl, 149.
Ingalls, David, 149.
Ingalls, Ephraim, 149.
Ingalls, John, 149.
Ingalls, Joseph, 149.
Ingalls, Leml, 149.
Ingalls, Peter, 149.
Ingalls, Zebulon, sr., 149.
Ingersal, Jonathan, 104.
Ingersail, Clement, 101.
Ingersol, Buggs, 72.
Ingersol, Elizabeth (Wd), 25.
Ingersol, Joseph, 28.
Ingersol, Mary (Wd), 25.
Ingersol, Moss, 28.
Ingersol, Nathaniel, 15.
Ingersol, Richard, 138.
Ingersoll, Elizabeth (Wd), 16.
Ingersoll, Simon, 16.
Ingham, Daniel, 89.
Ingham, Ebenezer, 89.
Ingham, Isaac, 41.
Ingham, John, 41.
Ingham, Jonth, 41.
Ingham, Joseph, 43.
Ingham, Joseph, 86.
Ingham, Thomas, 89.
Ingham, Wm, 89.
Ingolls, Saml, 141.
Ingraham, Benjamin, 89.
Ingraham, Daniel, 89.
Ingraham, Daniel, 145.
Ingraham, Elexander, 119.
Ingraham, Elkinah, 82.
Ingraham, Hezekiah, 117.
Ingraham, Isaac, 92.
Ingraham, Jacob, 121.
Ingraham, James, 89.
Ingraham, Jeremiah, 51.
Ingraham, Jeremiah, 2d, 51.
Ingraham, Jno, 89.
Ingraham, Jonathan, 121.
Ingraham, Joseph, 129.
Ingraham, Nathl, 116.
Ingraham, Nathaniel G., 86.
Ingraham, Parnall, 123.
Ingraham, Rachel, 129.
Ingraham, Reubin, 145.
Ingraham, Samuel, 123.
Ingraham, Wm, 89.
Ingraham, Wm, 90.
Ingraham, William, 120.
Ingram, Danl, 134.
Ingram, Ebenezar, 40.
Ingram, Jos., 135.
Ingram, Nathl, 136.
Inman, Edward, 136.
Inman, Thos, 149.
Ireland, Abraham, 16.
Ireland, Job, 16.
Irish, John, 117.
Irwin, Andrew, 78.
Irwin, Sarah, 102.
Isaac (Negro), 112.
Isaacs, Brown, 105.
Isaacs, Isaac, 23.
Isaacs, Isaac B., 102.
Isaacs, Ralph, 91.
Isam, Benjn, 134.
Isam, Jos., 134.
Isam, Timo, 132.
Isbel, Elias, 84.
Isbel, Israel, 84.
Isbel, Robert, 84.
Isbel, Sarah, 102.
Isbell, Israel, 84.
Isham, Asher, 138.
Isham, Daniel, 121.
Isham, Isaac, Junr, 121.
Isham, John, 82.
Isham, John, 121.

Isham, John, Junr, 121.
Isham, Joseph, 121.
Isham, Joseph, 2d, 120.
Isham, Joshua, 121.
Isham, Noah, 121.
Isham, Samuel, 120.
Ishmael (Negroe), 93.
Isles, Joshua, 74.
Ives, Abel, 57.
Ives, Abel, 107.
Ives, Abel, 111.
Ives, Abigal, 108.
Ives, Abijah, 107.
Ives, Abner, 62.
Ives, Abraham, 92.
Ives, Alling, 100.
Ives, Alling, 106.
Ives, Amasa, 34.
Ives, Ammon, 34.
Ives, Amos, 107.
Ives, Amos, 107.
Ives, Andrew, 100.
Ives, Anor, 1st, 78.
Ives, Anor, 2d, 78.
Ives, Asa, 78.
Ives, Bazelel, 107.
Ives, Caleb, 108.
Ives, Charles, 108.
Ives, Daniel, 30.
Ives, Daniel, 106.
Ives, Elam, 100.
Ives, Elnathan, 76.
Ives, Elnathan, 107.
Ives, Elnathan, 107.
Ives, Enos, 34.
Ives, Ezra, 100.
Ives, Fitch, 107.
Ives, Icobod, 107.
Ives, James, 100.
Ives, James, 106.
Ives, Joel, 91.
Ives, Joel, 93.
Ives, Joel, 108.
Ives, Joel, 2nd, 108.
Ives, John, 51.
Ives, John, 66.
Ives, John, 107.
Ives, John, 107.
Ives, John, 108.
Ives, John, 3d, 107.
Ives, John, 4th, 108.
Ives, Jonathan, 100.
Ives, Jonathan, 2nd, 100.
Ives, Joseph, 70.
Ives, Joseph, 70.
Ives, Joseph, 108.
Ives, Jotham, 93.
Ives, Jotheam, 62.
Ives, Lazarus, 65.
Ives, Lent, 34.
Ives, Levi, 70.
Ives, Levi, 104.
Ives, Levi, 107.
Ives, Mathew, 93.
Ives, Nathan, 60.
Ives, Nathaniel, 93.
Ives, Noah, 106.
Ives, Noel, 107.
Ives, Phineas, 93.
Ives, Phineas, 2d, 93.
Ives, Reuben, 34.
Ives, Ruben, 93.
Ives, Ruben, 108.
Ives, Samuel, 49.
Ives, Samuel, 107.
Ives, Sarah, 106.
Ives, Sarah, 107.
Ives, Steven, 109.
Ives, Sussanah, 106.
Ives, Thomas, 100.
Ives, Timothy, 107.
Ives, Titus, 66.
Ives, William, 94.
Ives, Zachariah, 92.

Jack, 62.
Jack (negro), 26.
Jack (Negro), 104.
Jack (Negro), 121.
Jack (Negro), 128.
Jack (Negro), 130.
Jack (Negro), 131.
Jack (Negroe), 102.
Jack (Negroe), 103.
Jack (Negroe), 108.
Jackaway, Aaron, 67.
Jackaway, Simeon, 67.
Jackeway, Ebenezer, 67.
Jacklin, Thaddeus, 72.
Jackson, Aden, 131.
Jackson, Amos, 60.
Jackson, Andrew, 153.
Jackson, Benjn, 153.
Jackson, Charles, 57.
Jackson, Comfort, 78.
Jackson, Daniel, 10.
Jackson, Daniel, 21.
Jackson, Daniel, 28.
Jackson, Daniel, 31.
Jackson, Daniel, 56.
Jackson, David, 10.
Jackson, David, 27.
Jackson, David, 72.

Jackson, David, 78.
Jackson, Ebenezer, 57.
Jackson, Elias, 151.
Jackson, Elijah, 69.
Jackson, Ephraim, 10.
Jackson, Ephm, 57.
Jackson, Ezekiel, 27.
Jackson, Gershom, 10.
Jackson, Hannah, 23.
Jackson, Henry, 72.
Jackson, Isaac, 72.
Jackson, Isaih, 57.
Jackson, Jane, 67.
Jackson, John, 28.
Jackson, John, 31.
Jackson, John, 69.
Jackson, John, 113.
Jackson, John, 129.
Jackson, Jonathan, 94.
Jackson, Jonathan, 113.
Jackson, Joseph, 28.
Jackson, Mary (Wd), 22.
Jackson, Nathan, 15.
Jackson, Nathan, 22.
Jackson, Nathan, 31.
Jackson, Nehemiah, 154.
Jackson, Rachel (Wd), 21.
Jackson, Robert, 12.
Jackson, Robert, 151.
Jackson, Salah, 81.
Jackson, Samuel, 56.
Jackson, Stephen, 27.
Jackson, Theophilus, 56.
Jackson, Thomas, 113.
Jackson, Thos, 143.
Jackson, William, 17.
Jacob, John, 150.
Jacob (Negro), 121.
Jacobs, Asa, 150.
Jacobs, Benjn, 148.
Jacobs, David, 106.
Jacobs, Eli, 106.
Jacobs, Enoch, 106.
Jacobs, Ezekiel, 106.
Jacobs, Heziran, 68.
Jacobs, John, Jnr, 150.
Jacobs, Joseph, 106.
Jacobs, Joseph, 148.
Jacobs, Jos., 139.
Jacobs, Salley, 69.
Jacobs, Soloman, 106.
Jacobs, Steven, 106.
Jacobs, Tuel, 67.
Jacson, Aaron, 27.
Jacson, Francis, 31.
Jager, Abraham, 53.
Jagger, Joannah, 24.
Jagger, Phinihas, 68.
Jailen, Isaac, 63.
Jailor, Steward, 91.
Jakeway, Daniel, 61.
Jakins, George, 63.
James, Amos, 139.
James, Anthony, 152.
James, Benjn, 140.
James, Dolly, 105.
James, Ethiel, 63.
James, Freeman, 149.
James, Hezekiah, 21.
James, John, 46.
James, John, 112.
James, John, 114.
James (Negro), 23.
James (Negro), 49.
James (Negro), 112.
James (Negro), 118.
James (Negro), 130.
James (Negroe), 101.
James, Peter, 23.
James, Rachael, 108.
James, Saml, 112.
James, Webster, 45.
James, Zephh, 152.
Jammes, Solomon, 150.
Jane, John, 90.
Jane (Negroe), 105.
Janes, Daniel, 38.
Janes, Frederic, 43.
Janes, Jonathan, 46.
Jaquis, Robart, 117.
Jarvis, Revr Abraham, 86.
Jarvis, Catharine, 26.
Jarvis, Henry, 21.
Jarvis, Jesse, 21.
Jarvis, John, 22.
Jarvis, Martha (Wd), 24.
Jarvis, Samuel, 24.
Jarvis, Samuel, 27.
Jarvis, Samuel (Comp), 23.
Jarvis, Stephen, 10.
Jarvis, Stephen, 21.
Jarvis, Thomas, 78.
Jarvis, William, 23.
Jay, Elizabeth, 67.
Jearom, Asahel, 35.
Jearoms, Benjamin, 34.
Jearoms, Canuy, 34.
Jearoms, Thomas, 34.
Jearoms, Willm, 34.
Jearoms, William, Jr., 34.
Jeasup, Jeames, 72.
Jeff (Negroe), 102.
Jeffers, Edward, 119.

# INDEX.

Jeffers, Peter, 130.
Jefferson, Joseph, 121.
Jeffery (Black), 16.
Jeffery, Charles, 129.
Jeffery, Charles, 2ᵈ, 128.
Jeffery, Ebenezer, 57.
Jeffery, James, 128.
Jeffery, John, 46.
Jeffery, Moses, 128.
Jeffery, Samuel, 25.
Jeffery, Thomas, 128.
Jefford, John, 141.
Jeffords, Robin, 145.
Jehu (Negro), 113.
Jellet, Abraham, 20.
Jellet, Benjamin, 101.
Jellet, Canfield, 18.
Jellet, Jeremiah, 94.
Jellet, John, 20.
Jellet, John, 101.
Jellet, John, 2ⁿᵈ, 101.
Jellet, Margret, 103.
Jellet, Moses, 20.
Jellet, Zebulon, 101.
Jenkinbottom, Obediah, 149.
Jenkins, Calvin, 28.
Jennes, Amos, 138.
Jenning, Benjⁿ, 136.
Jenning (Wid.), 139.
Jennings, Aaron, 13.
Jennings, Abel, 15.
Jennings, Abraham, 31.
Jennings, Benjamin, 32.
Jennings, Burrit, 12.
Jennings, David, 13.
Jennings, David, 14.
Jennings, David, 14.
Jennings, David, 139.
Jennings, Ebenezʳ, 153.
Jennings, Edmond, 13.
Jennings, Eliphalet, 29.
Jennings, Eᵐ, 134.
Jennings, Enoch, 13.
Jennings, Enoch, 31.
Jennings, Eunice, 152.
Jennings, Ezra, 15.
Jennings, Gershom, 13.
Jennings, Hezekiah, 31.
Jennings, Hezekiah, Jr., 31.
Jennings, Hezekiah, 3ᵈ, 31.
Jennings, Isaac, 14.
Jennings, Jacob, 23.
Jennings, Jeremiah, 14.
Jennings, Joel, 13.
Jennings, John, 13.
Jennings, John, 153.
Jennings, John, 153.
Jennings, Jonatʰ, 152.
Jennings, Joshua, 13.
Jennings, Lemuel, 57.
Jennings, Liman, 14.
Jennings, Mathew, 15.
Jennings, Moses, 14.
Jennings, Nathan, 14.
Jennings, Nathan, 139.
Jennings, Nathan, 143.
Jennings, Nathanel, 14.
Jennings, Nathˡ, 139.
Jennings, Nathˡ, 2ᵈ, 139.
Jennings, Nehimiah, 31.
Jennings, Noah, 14.
Jennings, Peter, 14.
Jennings, Peter, 14.
Jennings, Philow, 31.
Jennings, Reuben, 73.
Jennings, Robert, 15.
Jennings, Robᵗ, 137.
Jennings, Seth, 23.
Jennings, Seth, 143.
Jennings, Stephen, 153.
Jennings, Thaddeus, 13.
Jennings (Wid.), 139.
Jennings, William, 13.
Jennings, William, 31.
Jennings, William, 105.
Jennings, Zacherius, 14.
Jennings, Zephʰ, 152.
Jennins, Charles, 17.
Jennins, Timothy, 62.
Jepbell, Abel, 108.
Jepson, James, 46.
Jepson, William, 86.
Jermain, Elizabeth, 16.
Jeroams, Zerubbabel, 34.
Jerod, John, 13.
Jerom, Benjamin, 128.
Jerom, Elisabeth, 123.
Jerom, Richard, 127.
Jerom, Robert, 76.
Jerrald, Jame, 30.
Jerrold, Jabez, 19.
Jerrum, Lyman, 67.
Jesop, Ebenezer, 13.
Jesop, Ebenezer, Jnʳ, 12.
Jeut, Roger, 43.
Jevel, Joseph, 63.
Jewel, Hanah, 31.
Jewel, Oliver, 69.
Jewell, Eliphalet, 66.
Jewell, Oliver, 2ᵈ, 69.
Jewet, David, 138.
Jewet, David H., 125.
Jewet, Eleazer, 113.

Jewet, Gibbins, 82.
Jewet, Icabod, 133.
Jewet, Icabod, 2ᵈ, 133.
Jewet, Joseph, 137.
Jewett, Nathan, 82.
Jewit, Alpheus, 62.
Jewit, Benjⁿ, Jnʳ, 143.
Jewit, Caleb, 62.
Jewit, Ebenʳ, 143.
Jewit, Joseph, 150.
Jewit, Thoˢ, 142.
Jewitt, Anney, 59.
Jewitt, Nathan H., 82.
Jewitt, Sarah, 82.
Jezup, Blackledge, 24.
Jezup, Blacklege, Junʳ, 24.
Jezup, Ebenezer, 15.
Jezup, Elizabeth, 26.
Jezup, Elizabeth (Wᵈ), 15.
Jezup, Jonathan, 15.
Jezup, Joseph, 24.
Jezup, Samuel, 25.
Jezup, Silvanus, 15.
Jhonson, Asa, 73.
Jillet, Eliphalet, 101.
Jillitt, Israel, 135.
Jim (Negroe), 111.
Jim (Negroe), 111.
Jincks, Thankfull, 36.
Jinkham, Abel, 150.
Jinks, Eben, 61.
Jinks, Jnᵒ, 134.
Jinks, Wᵐ, 134.
Jinnings, Menoah, 153.
Jinnings, Thoˢ, 139.
Jocelin, Edward, 150.
Jocelin, Israel, 150.
Jocelin, Joseph, 150.
Jocelin, Nathaniel, 103.
Jocelin, Pember, 104.
Jocelin, Simeon, 102.
Jocelin, Thoˢ, 152.
Joe (Negroe), 102.
John (Negro), 113.
John (Negro), 113.
John (Negroe), 112.
Johnes, Benjamin, 75.
Johnes, Samˡ, 134.
Johns, Abijah, 132.
Johns, Benjamin, 59.
Johns, Elihu, 133.
Johns, Joel, 63.
Johns, Thoˢ, 133.
Johnsin (Widow), 133.
Johnson, Abel, 20.
Johnson, Abel, 137.
Johnson, Abel, 139.
Johnson, Abigail, 34.
Johnson, Abigail, 123.
Johnson, Abner, 109.
Johnson, Abner, 137.
Johnson, Abraham, 104.
Johnson, Abraham, 105.
Johnson, Aholiab, 144.
Johnson, Alexander, 95.
Johnson, Amos, 34.
Johnson, Amos, 57.
Johnson, Amos, 57.
Johnson, Amos, 73.
Johnson, Amos, 88.
Johnson, Asa, 43.
Johnson, Asa, 88.
Johnson, Asael, 95.
Johnson, Asahel, 35.
Johnson, Ashel, 86.
Johnson, Barnabas, 49.
Johnson, Benjamin, 64.
Johnson, Benjamin, 98.
Johnson, Benjamin, 99.
Johnson, Benjamin, 113.
Johnson, Benoni, 58.
Johnson, Caleb, 87.
Johnson, Caleb, 125.
Johnson, Chancy, 61.
Johnson, Chandler, 34.
Johnson, Charles, 95.
Johnson, Charles, 137.
Johnson, Christopher, 58.
Johnson, Convus, 134.
Johnson, Cornelius, 109.
Johnson, Cornilus, 2ⁿᵈ, 109.
Johnson, Daniel, 34.
Johnson, Daniel, 45.
Johnson, Daniel, 50.
Johnson, Daniel, 59.
Johnson, Daniel, 65.
Johnson, Dan., 108.
Johnson, Danˡ, 139.
Johnson, Daniel, Jr., 34.
Johnson, Daniel, Jr., 50.
Johnson, Daniel, 2ᵈ, 34.
Johnson, David, 73.
Johnson, David, 108.
Johnson, David, 137.
Johnson, David, 139.
Johnson, David, 153.
Johnson, Dayton, 108.
Johnson, Didemus, 83.
Johnson, Ebenezer, 17.
Johnson, Ebenezer, 50.
Johnson, Ebenezer, 50.
Johnson, Ebenezer, 58.
Johnson, Ebenezer, 87.
Johnson, Ebenezer, 95.

Johnson, Ebenezer, 95.
Johnson, Ebenezer, 105.
Johnson, Ebenʳ, 126.
Johnson, Eben, 137.
Johnson, Eber B., 95.
Johnson, Eden, 112.
Johnson, Edward, 88.
Johnson, Elias, 66.
Johnson, Elihu, 138.
Johnson, Elijah, 81.
Johnson, Elijah, Junʳ, 87.
Johnson, Eliphalet, 112.
Johnson, Eliphalet, 126.
Johnson, Eliphelet, 132.
Johnson, Elisha, 58.
Johnson, Elisha, 69.
Johnson, Elisha, 139.
Johnson, Elizabeth, 26.
Johnson, Elizabeth, 64.
Johnson, Eᵐ, 137.
Johnson, Eneas, 105.
Johnson, Enoch, 20.
Johnson, Enock, 35.
Johnson, Enos, 76.
Johnson, Ephraim, 17.
Johnson, Ephraim, 108.
Johnson, Feen, 39.
Johnson, Freelove, 87.
Johnson, Gideon, 73.
Johnson, Hamlen, 58.
Johnson, Henry, 15.
Johnson, Henry, 87.
Johnson, Henry, 92.
Johnson, Hezekiah, 89.
Johnson, Hezekiah, 95.
Johnson, Hezekiah, 108.
Johnson, Hezekiah, 112.
Johnson, Hill, 98.
Johnson, Hyram, 73.
Johnson, Ira, 58.
Johnson, Isaac, 61.
Johnson, Isaac, 67.
Johnson, Isaac, 72.
Johnson, Isaac, 76.
Johnson, Isaac, 81.
Johnson, Isaac, 84.
Johnson, Isaac, 95.
Johnson, Isaac, 99.
Johnson, Isaac, 99.
Johnson, Isaac, 111.
Johnson, Isaac, 130.
Johnson, Isaac, 139.
Johnson, Israel, 107.
Johnson, Jacob, 61.
Johnson, James, 16.
Johnson, James, 31.
Johnson, James, 52.
Johnson, James, 67.
Johnson, James, 67.
Johnson, James, 87.
Johnson, Jedediah, 87.
Johnson, Jedediah, Junʳ, 87.
Johnson, Jehu, 73.
Johnson, Jeremiah, 73.
Johnson, Jeremiah, 94.
Johnson, Jesse, 109.
Johnson, Jesse, 111.
Johnson, Jessey, 79.
Johnson, Job, 111.
Johnson, Joel, 20.
Johnson, Joel, 98.
Johnson, Joel, 142.
Johnson, John, 20.
Johnson, John, 28.
Johnson, John, 81.
Johnson, John, 84.
Johnson, John, 96.
Johnson, John, 97.
Johnson, John, 105.
Johnson, John, 105.
Johnson, John, 108.
Johnson, John, 121.
Johnson, John, 124.
Johnson, John, 126.
Johnson, John, 142.
Johnson, John, 145.
Johnson, Jnᵒ, 139.
Johnson, John, Jnʳ, 145.
Johnson, John, 1ˢᵗ, 73.
Johnson, John, 2ᵈ, 73.
Johnson, John, 2ⁿᵈ, 96.
Johnson, Jonathan, 39.
Johnson, Jonathan, 63.
Johnson, Jonathan, 64.
Johnson, Jonathan, 86.
Johnson, Jonathan, Junʳ, 87.
Johnson, Joseph, 80.
Johnson, Joseph, 95.
Johnson, Joseph, 100.
Johnson, Joseph, 112.
Johnson, Joseph, 120.
Johnson, Joseph, 147.
Johnson, Joseph, 152.
Johnson, Joseph, 2ⁿᵈ, 100.
Johnson, Joshua, 153.
Johnson, Jotham, 150.
Johnson, Justus, 73.
Johnson, Lambard, 64.
Johnson, Larrance, 125.
Johnson, Levi, 43.
Johnson, Levi, 50.

Johnson, Levi, 61.
Johnson, Levi, 95.
Johnson, Levi, 153.
Johnson, Lidia, 105.
Johnson, Lucy, 125.
Johnson, Luther, 64.
Johnson, Lyman, 109.
Johnson, Martha, 87.
Johnson, Marver, 140.
Johnson, Mary, 87.
Johnson, Mary, 96.
Johnson, Mary, 111.
Johnson, Mehitable, 87.
Johnson, Miles, 98.
Johnson, Miles, 107.
Johnson, Moses, 22.
Johnson, Nathan, 117.
Johnson, Nathan, 130.
Johnson, Nathan, 137.
Johnson, Nathanel, 12.
Jonhson, Nathaniel, 74.
Johnson, Nathaniel, 92.
Johnson, Nathaniel, 94.
Johnson, Nathaniel, 95.
Johnson, Nathaniel, 97.
Johnson, Nathaniel, 98.
Johnson, Nathaniel, 98.
Johnson, Nathaniel, 98.
Johnson, Nathaniel, 99.
Johnson, Nathˡ, 137.
Johnson, Niamiah, 111.
Johnson, Noah, 100.
Johnson, Obediah, 142.
Johnson, Oliver, 86.
Johnson, Oliver, 130.
Johnson, Partrick, 87.
Johnson, Peter, 72.
Johnson, Peter, 94.
Johnson, Peter, 104.
Johnson, Peter, 154.
Johnson, Philemon, 57.
Johnson, Philo, 94.
Johnson, Phineas, 95.
Johnson, Phineas, 99.
Johnson, Polly, 65.
Johnson, Prince, 42.
Johnson, Rebecca, 92.
Johnson, Resolved, 144.
Johnson, Reuben, 64.
Johnson, Reubin, 141.
Johnson, Reynold, 124.
Johnson, Robert, 103.
Johnson, Ruben, 99.
Johnson, Rufus, 58.
Johnson, Rufus, 142.
Johnson, Sampson, 137.
Johnson, Samuel, 16.
Johnson, Samuel, 34.
Johnson, Samuel, 39.
Johnson, Samuel, 58.
Johnson, Samuel, 86.
Johnson, Samuel, 98.
Johnson, Samuel, 107.
Johnson, Samuel, 111.
Johnson, Samˡ, 139.
Johnson, Samˡ, 140.
Johnson, Samˡ, 140.
Johnson, Samuel, Junʳ, 86.
Johnson, Samuel, 2ⁿᵈ, 98.
Johnson, Samˡ W., 29.
Johnson, Sarah, 65.
Johnson, Seth, 87.
Johnson, Seth, 88.
Johnson, Seth, 93.
Johnson, Seth, 137.
Johnson, Shadrach, 46.
Johnson, Sherman, 63.
Johnson, Silder, 107.
Johnson, Simeon, 34.
Johnson, Smith, 150.
Johnson, Soloman, 108.
Johnson, Solomon, 1ˢᵗ, 73.
Johnson, Solomon, 2ᵈ, 73.
Johnson, Stephen, 49.
Johnson, Stephen, 87.
Johnson, Stephen, 105.
Johnson, Stephen, 106.
Johnson, Stephen, 113.
Johnson, Stephen, 123.
Johnson, Stephen, 141.
Johnson, Stephen, 154.
Johnson, Sylvester, 148.
Johnson, Thomas, 15.
Johnson, Thomas, 96.
Johnson, Thomas, 103.
Johnson, Timothy, 61.
Johnson, Timothy, 73.
Johnson, Timothy, 87.
Johnson, Timothy, 91.
Johnson, Timothy, 94.
Johnson, Timothy, 95.
Johnson, Timothy, 95.
Johnson, Timothy, 100.
Johnson, Truman, 56.
Johnson, Uriah, 154.
Johnson, Ward, 63.
Johnson, Willard, 154.
Johnson, William, 15.
Johnson, William, 49.
Johnson, William, 57.
Johnson, William, 87.
Johnson, William, 96.
Johnson, William, 107.

Johnson, William, 113.
Johnson, Wᵐ, 139.
Johnson, William, 142.
Johnson, William, 147.
Johnson, William, 154.
Johnson, William, Jnʳ, 147.
Johnson, William, Jnʳ, 147.
Johnson, William B., 107.
Johnson, Zebediah, 63.
Johnston, Samuel, 86.
Johonnot, Daniel, 86.
Johson, Amos, 94.
Johson, Gideon, 95.
Jolly, Martha, 93.
Jolly, Martha, 107.
Jones, Aaron, 128.
Jones, Abner, 135.
Jones, Amos, 122.
Jones, Amos, 130.
Jones, Amos, Junʳ, 122.
Jones, Amos, 3ᵈ, 122.
Jones, Andrew, 62.
Jones, Arou, 97.
Jones, Asa, 26.
Jones, Asahel, 61.
Jones, Augustus, 90.
Jones, Benajah, 135.
Jones, Benjaman, 61.
Jones, Benjamin, 24.
Jones, Benjamin, 46.
Jones, Benjamin, 67.
Jones, Benjamin, 70.
Jones, Benjamin, 90.
Jones, Benjamin, 131.
Jones, Benjⁿ, 134.
Jones, Benjⁿ, 136.
Jones, Benjⁿ, 136.
Jones, Benjⁿ, 136.
Jones, Benjⁿ, 2ᵈ, 90.
Jones, Benona, 68.
Jones, Caleb, 40.
Jones, Caleb, Jr., 40.
Jones, Charles, 115.
Jones, Daniel, 45.
Jones, Daniel, 46.
Jones, Daniel, 83.
Jones, Daniel, 84.
Jones, Daniel, 90.
Jones, Daniel, 91.
Jones, Danˡ, 134.
Jones, Danˡ, 136.
Jones, Daniel, 145.
Jones, David, 36.
Jones, David, 136.
Jones, Diad, 83.
Jones, Eaton, 65.
Jones, Ebenezer, 28.
Jones, Ebenʳ, 131.
Jones, Ebenezer, Junʳ, 25.
Jones, Ebenezer, 2ᵈ, 28.
Jones, Captᵗ Ebenezer, 24.
Jones, Eliakim, 65.
Jones, Elias, 134.
Jones, Elijah, 22.
Jones, Elijah, 137.
Jones, Elisha, 93.
Jones, Elnathan, 29.
Jones, Enos, 25.
Jones, Ephraim, 25.
Jones, Ephraim, 90.
Jones, Ephraim & co., 148.
Jones, Evan, 69.
Jones, Ezekiel, 89.
Jones, Ezekiel, 135.
Jones, Ezra, 40.
Jones, Ezra, 89.
Jones, George, 33.
Jones, George, 86.
Jones, Gideon, 89.
Jones, Gid., 135.
Jones, Gid., Jr., 135.
Jones, Henry, 128.
Jones, Hezekiah, 44.
Jones, Huldah, 90.
Jones, Isaac, 30.
Jones, Isaac, 46.
Jones, Isaac, 66.
Jones, Isaac, 89.
Jones, Isaac, 101.
Jones, Isaac, 104.
Jones, Isaac, 120.
Jones, Isahar, 136.
Jones, Israel, 66.
Jones, Israel, 89.
Jones, Isrehel, 68.
Jones, Jabez, 122.
Jones, Jabez, Jnʳ, 122.
Jones, Jacob, 147.
Jones, Jacob, 2ᵈ, 28.
Jones, James, 63.
Jones, James, 88.
Jones, James, 93.
Jones, James, 96.
Jones, Jared, 91.
Jones, Jasper, 30.
Jones, Jedediah, 135.
Jones, Jiles, 136.
Jones, Joel, 135.
Jones, John, 28.
Jones, John, 29.
Jones, John, 30.
Jones, John, 31.

# INDEX.

Jones, John, 37.
Jones, John, 46.
Jones, John, 89.
Jones, John, 99.
Jones, John, 101.
Jones, John, 105.
Jones, John, 118.
Jones, John, 121.
Jones, John, 152.
Jones, Jon\<sup>a</sup>, 135.
Jones, Joseph, 63.
Jones, Joseph, 95.
Jones, Josiah, 25.
Jones, Julius, 46.
Jones, Lemuel, 43.
Jones, Levi, 45.
Jones, Lewis, 24.
Jones, Lewis, 90.
Jones, Mary, 121.
Jones, Molly (Wid.), 30.
Jones, Moses, 43.
Jones, Nathaniel, 34.
Jones, Nathaniel, 46.
Jones, Nathaniel, 49.
Jones, Nathaniel, 107.
Jones, Nicholas, 108.
Jones, Noah, 134.
Jones, Norris, 90.
Jones, Oliver, 135.
Jones, Pantry, 46.
Jones, Parker, 43.
Jones, Parker, 89.
Jones, Parmenus, 131.
Jones, Phinehas, 84.
Jones, Phinehas, 90.
Jones, Pratt, 101.
Jones, Reuben, 26.
Jones, Ruben, 107.
Jones, Rufus, 130.
Jones, Samuel, 26.
Jones, Samuel, 40.
Jones, Sam\<sup>l</sup>, 66.
Jones, Samu\<sup>l</sup>, 68.
Jones, Sam\<sup>l</sup>, 90.
Jones, Samuel, 106.
Jones, Sam\<sup>l</sup>, 115.
Jones, Samuel, 120.
Jones, Sam\<sup>l</sup>, 135.
Jones, Samuel, 135.
Jones, Samuel, 153.
Jones, Samuel, Jun\<sup>r</sup>, 26.
Jones, Sam\<sup>l</sup>, Jr., 136.
Jones, Sam\<sup>l</sup>, 2\<sup>d</sup>, 90.
Jones, Samuel P., 46.
Jones, Sarah, 76.
Jones, Silas, 134.
Jones, Silas, 136.
Jones, Simeon, 114.
Jones, Stephen, 114.
Jones, Stephen, 136.
Jones, Theophilus, 108.
Jones, Thomas, 26.
Jones, Thomas, 66.
Jones, Thomas, 66.
Jones, Thomas, 89.
Jones, Thomas, 128.
Jones, Timithy, 103.
Jones, Timothy, 76.
Jones (Widow), 134.
Jones, William, 93.
Jones, William, 108.
Jones, William, 115.
Jones, William C., 66.
Jones, Zacheriah H., 57.
Jones, Zebulon, 90.
Jop, John, 42.
Jop, John, 69.
Joppen, William, 88.
Jopping, Daniel, 88.
Jordan, John, 75.
Jordan, Timothy, 78.
Jordon, Asa, 145.
Jordon, W\<sup>m</sup>, 16.
Joseph, 23.
Joseph (Negroe), 102.
Joslin, David, 143.
Joslin, Jesse, 150.
Jowls, John, 144.
Joy, Richard, 131.
Joy, Submit, 64.
Joy, William, 131.
Joy, William, Jun\<sup>r</sup>, 131.
Joyce, John, 11.
Joyce, Sarah (W\<sup>d</sup>), 15.
Joyce, William, 86.
Juba (Negro), 121.
Jube (Negro), 11.
Juckets, Elijah, 31.
Jud, Benjamin, 64.
Jud, Tho\<sup>s</sup>, 133.
Judah, David, 12.
Judd, Abigail, 12.
Judd, Abner, 11.
Judd, Alex\<sup>r</sup>, 68.
Judd, Allen, 76.
Judd, Amos, 33.
Judd, Anthony, 33.
Judd, Asa, 76.
Judd, Balmerim, 17.
Judd, Benjamin, 12.
Judd, Calvin, 41.
Judd, Chauncy, 110.
Judd, Comfort, 59.

Judd, Daniel, 12.
Judd, Daniel, 33.
Judd, Daniel, 78.
Judd, Daniel, 120.
Judd, Daniel, Jun\<sup>r</sup>, 120.
Judd, David, 12.
Judd, Dennis, 76.
Judd, Ebenezer, 12.
Judd, Ebenezer, 65.
Judd, Ebenezer, 111.
Judd, Elihue, 12.
Judd, Elijah, 27.
Judd, Elizur, 41.
Judd, Eunice, 49.
Judd, Gideon, 33.
Judd, Harvey, 76.
Judd, Hezekiah, 33.
Judd, Immer, 49.
Judd, Immer, 49.
Judd, Isaac, 33.
Judd, Isaac, 110.
Judd, Isaac, 2\<sup>d</sup>, 110.
Judd, Jacob, 11.
Judd, James, 33.
Judd, James, 41.
Judd, Job, 33.
Judd, John, 33.
Judd, John, 1\<sup>st</sup>, 76.
Judd, Jonathan, 98.
Judd, Joseph, 59.
Judd, Levi, 76.
Judd, Martha, 99.
Judd, Marthew, 59.
Judd, Mary, 33.
Judd, Merriam, 76.
Judd, Michael, 76.
Judd, Nathaniel, 74.
Judd, Noah, 76.
Judd, Obediah, 74.
Judd, Philip, 59.
Judd, Reuben, 46.
Judd, Reubin, 31.
Judd, Roswell, 110.
Judd, Sally, 95.
Judd, Samuel, 12.
Judd, Samuel, 76.
Judd, Samuel, 109.
Judd, Simeon, 46.
Judd, Stephen, 109.
Judd, Thomas, 1\<sup>st</sup>, 11.
Judd, Thomas, 2\<sup>d</sup>, 11.
Judd, Timothy, 120.
Judd, W\<sup>m</sup>, 41.
Judd, William, 76.
Judd, William S., 41.
Jude, Ellin, 50.
Judge (Negro), 154.
Judson, Aaron, 29.
Judson, Abel, 20.
Judson, Abel, 57.
Judson, Abijail, 75.
Judson, Abner, 30.
Judson, Abner, 56.
Judson, Abraham, 29.
Judson, Ager, 18.
Judson, Ager, Ju\<sup>r</sup>, 18.
Judson, Andrew, 140.
Judson, Benjamin, 30.
Judson, Benjamin, 78.
Judson, Chapman, 78.
Judson, Curtis, 30.
Judson, Daniel, 29.
Judson, Daniel, 78.
Judson, David, 75.
Judson, David, 78.
Judson, Deborah, 78.
Judson, Eber, 109.
Judson, Elihu, 31.
Judson, Elijah, 20.
Judson, Elisha, 78.
Judson, Emm, 78.
Judson, Ephraim, 17.
Judson, Ezekiel, 17.
Judson, Gideon, 78.
Judson, Hollister, 78.
Judson, Isaac, 18.
Judson, Isaac, 94.
Judson, Isaih, 78.
Judson, James, 17.
Judson, Jeames, 78.
Judson, Joel, 10.
Judson, John, 17.
Judson, John, 18.
Judson, John, 21.
Judson, John, 24.
Judson, John, 31.
Judson, John, 78.
Judson, John, 3\<sup>d</sup>, 17.
Judson, Jonathan, 17.
Judson, Jonathan, 78.
Judson, Joseph, 24.
Judson, Joseph, 78.
Judson, Joshua, 8.
Judson, Lemwell, 17.
Judson, Lewis, 17.
Judson, Nathan, 78.
Judson, Nathanel, 17.
Judson, Nathan\<sup>el</sup>, 20.
Judson, Nehemiah, 78.
Judson, Noah, 78.
Judson, Phineus, 17.
Judson, Pixly, 29.
Judson, Samuel, 18.

Judson, Sarah, 20.
Judson, Seth, 78.
Judson, Silas, 18.
Judson, Stiles, 29.
Judson, Thomas, 78.
Judson, William, 78.
Juett, Joseph, 44.
Jule, 59.
June, Abisha, 25.
June, Abner, 25.
June, Ezra, 25.
June, Israel, 25.
June, Israel, J\<sup>r</sup>, 25.
June, Jabez, 22.
June, Joel, 25.
June, Joshua, 25.
June, Nathaniel, 25.
June, Silas, 25.
June, Thomas, 25.
June, William, 25.
Jupiter, 68.
Jurden, David, 18.
Jurden, Edmon, 18.
Jurdon, Martin, 144.
Justin, Charles, 142.
Justin, George, 142.
Justin, Miner, 142.
Justin, Nicholas, 142.
Justin, Thomas, 142.
Justin, William, 142.
Jutson, Elisha, 48.
Jutson, Peter, 40.
Jutson, Roswell, 36.
Jutt, Joseph, 105.

Kaggan, Sam\<sup>l</sup>, 138.
Kannak, Hugh, 59.
Karnes, Aaron, 62.
Kason, Alaxander 56.
Kason, James, Ju\<sup>r</sup>, 56.
Kasson, Archibald, 56.
Kasson, James, 56.
Kasson, Joseph, 144.
Kasson, Sam\<sup>l</sup>, 141.
Kasson, Sam\<sup>l</sup>, Jn\<sup>r</sup>, 141.
Kate, Isaac, 34.
Katlin, Isaac, 108.
Keath, James, 134.
Keaton, ——, 147.
Kebly, Jedediah, 90.
Keeler, Aaron, 23.
Keeler, Aaron, 23.
Keeler, Anne (W\<sup>d</sup>), 21.
Keeler, Daniel, 28.
Keeler, David, 10.
Keeler, David, 23.
Keeler, David, 28.
Keeler, Ebener, 72.
Keeler, Elijah, 22.
Keeler, Elijah, 29.
Keeler, Elisha, 10.
Keeler, Elizabeth, 22.
Keeler, Isaac, 22.
Keeler, Isaac, 22.
Keeler, Isaac, 23.
Keeler, Jabez, 28.
Keeler, James, 23.
Keeler, Jeremiah, 23.
Keeler, Jeremiah, 28.
Keeler, John, 10.
Keeler, John, 28.
Keeler, John, Ju\<sup>r</sup>, 10.
Keeler, John, 2\<sup>d</sup>, 28.
Keeler, Joseph, 78.
Keeler, Justice, 23.
Keeler, Levi, 28.
Keeler, Luke, 23.
Keeler, Martha, 28.
Keeler, Mathew, 28.
Keeler, Matthew, Jun\<sup>r</sup>, 28.
Keeler, Nathan, 10.
Keeler, Nathan, 22.
Keeler, Nathaniel, 21.
Keeler, Nehemiah, 29.
Keeler, Paul, 28.
Keeler, Philip, 21.
Keeler, Phinehas, 23.
Keeler, Ralph, 72.
Keeler, Samuel, 22.
Keeler, Samuel, 23.
Keeler, Samuel, 29.
Keeler, Sarah, 10.
Keeler, Seth, 23.
Keeler, Stephen, 22.
Keeler, Stephen, 23.
Keeler, Thaddeus, 23.
Keeler, Thaddeus, 28.
Keeler, Thomas, 23.
Keeler, Timothy, 22.
Keeler, Timothy, 28.
Keeler, Timothy, Jun\<sup>r</sup>, 28.
Keeler, Timothy, 2\<sup>d</sup>, 29.
Keelogg, Martin, 19.
Keemann, Pelatiah, 66.
Keeney, Aaron, 118.
Keeney, Alexander, 37.
Keeney, Alexander, 37.
Keeney, Amos, 127.
Keeney, Benjamin, 36.
Keeney, Benjamin, 37.
Keeney, Benjamin, 113.
Keeney, David, 37.

Keeney, David, 114.
Keeney, David, 2\<sup>d</sup>, 37.
Keeney, Eleazer, 37.
Keeney, Elias, 72.
Keeney, Elijah, 37.
Keeney, Ethiel, 94.
Keeney, Ezra, 113.
Keeney, George, 37.
Keeney, Gideon, 113.
Keeney, Henry, 114.
Keeney, Isaac, 37.
Keeney, Jacob, 75.
Keeney, John, 37.
Keeney, John, 75.
Keeney, John, 2\<sup>d</sup>, 75.
Keeney, Jonathan, 122.
Keeney, Joseph, 36.
Keeney, Joseph, 37.
Keeney, Lyman, 75.
Keeney, Mark, 75.
Keeney, Michael, 103.
Keeney, Newcomb, 131.
Keeney, Pearle, 75.
Keeney, Richard, 37.
Keeney, Samuel, 124.
Keeney, Simon, 37.
Keeney, Simon, Jr., 37.
Keeney, Sylvester, 59.
Keeney, Thomas, 37.
Keeney, William, 39.
Keeney, William, 127.
Keep, Jabez, 63.
Kegwin, Nicholas, 151.
Kegwin, William, 151.
Keif, Arthur, 103.
Keigwin, James, 113.
Keiny, William, 95.
Keith, 75.
Keith, Barack, 150.
Keith, George, 75.
Keith, John, 150.
Keith, Peter, 150.
Keith, Stephen, 150.
Keith, William, 86.
Keley, Rueben, 90.
Keling, Asahel, 59.
Kellagg, Enos, 23.
Kellagg, Epenetus, 23.
Kellagg, Isaac, 22.
Kellagg, James, 23.
Kellagg, Jarvis, 23.
Kellagg, John, 22.
Kellagg, Jonathan, 22.
Kellagg, Nathan, 22.
Kellagg, Samuel, 22.
Kellagg, Stephen, 23.
Kelleg, Jn\<sup>o</sup>, 135.
Kellegg, Elijah, 135.
Kellegg, Moses, 135.
Kelley, Daniel, 130.
Kelley, Elizabeth, 65.
Kelley, Hezekiah, 131.
Kelley, John, 130.
Kelley, Joseph, 131.
Kellock, Joseph, 109.
Kellock, Morton, 109.
Kellog, Abigail, 121.
Kellog, Abner, 121.
Kellog, Amos, 121.
Kellog, Butler, 121.
Kellog, Daniel, 121.
Kellog, Eben\<sup>r</sup>, 121.
Kellog, Elisha, 120.
Kellog, Helmont, 65.
Kellog, Israel, 120.
Kellog, Judah, 57.
Kellog, Martin, 123.
Kellog, Martin, 135.
Kellog, Russell, 120.
Kellog, Samuel, 65.
Kellog, Samuel, 121.
Kellogg, Abraham, 69.
Kellogg, Abraham, 69.
Kellogg, Allen, 58.
Kellogg, Azeriah, 1\<sup>st</sup>, 58.
Kellogg, Azeriah, 2\<sup>d</sup>, 58.
Kellogg, Charles, 46.
Kellogg, Daniel, 28.
Kellogg, Daniel, 69.
Kellogg, Dan\<sup>l</sup>, 135.
Kellogg, Eber, 133.
Kellogg, Elijah, 68.
Kellogg, Elizer, 69.
Kellogg, Rev. E\<sup>m</sup>, 133.
Kellogg, Ezekiel, 47.
Kellogg, George, 47.
Kellogg, Jonathan, 51.
Kellogg, Joseph, 54.
Kellogg, Joseph, 68.
Kellogg, Joseph, 79.
Kellogg, Martin, 54.
Kellogg, Martin, 60.
Kellogg, Martin, Jr., 54.
Kellogg, Martin, Jr., 135.
Kellogg, Moses, 69.
Kellogg, Moses, Jr, 135.
Kellogg, Nathan F., 28.
Kellogg, Noah, 69.
Kellogg, Oliver, 44.
Kellogg, Oliiver, 67.
Kellogg, Rev'd Mr., 135.
Kellogg, Seth, 66.
Kellogg, Stephen, 54.

Kellsey, Enock, 54.
Kellsey, Levi, 85.
Kelly, Daniel, 88.
Kelly, Eph\<sup>m</sup>, 90.
Kelly, Gemaliel, 90.
Kelly, Hannah, 86.
Kelly, James, 90.
Kelly, Job, 90.
Kelly, Mathew, 95.
Kelly, Rebecca, 84.
Kelly, William, 141.
Kelogg, Martin, 17.
Kelogg, Martin, Ju\<sup>r</sup>, 19.
Kelsey, Aaron, 84.
Kelsey, Amos, 41.
Kelsey, Amos, 85.
Kelsey, Asa, 85.
Kelsey, Asahel, 34.
Kelsey, Augustus, 85.
Kelsey, Bani, 84.
Kelsey, Benjamin, 84.
Kelsey, Charles, 34.
Kelsey, Daniel, 85.
Kelsey, Dan, 85.
Kelsey, David, 84.
Kelsey, David, Jun\<sup>r</sup>, 84.
Kelsey, Eber, 84.
Kelsey, Elisha, 85.
Kelsey, Enoch, 63.
Kelsey, Ezekial, 84.
Kelsey, Ezekial, Jr., 34.
Kelsey, Ezra, 85.
Kelsey, Ezra, 85.
Kelsey, George, 83.
Kelsey, Israil, 88.
Kelsey, Jeremiah, 90.
Kelsey, Joel, 84.
Kelsey, John, 34.
Kelsey, John, 85.
Kelsey, Jonathan, 65.
Kelsey, Jonathan, 84.
Kelsey, Joseph, 84.
Kelsey, Joseph, 2\<sup>d</sup>, 84.
Kelsey, Josiah, 85.
Kelsey, Lemuel, 84.
Kelsey, Levi, 46.
Kelsey, Martha, 85.
Kelsey, Martin, 85.
Kelsey, Moses, 85.
Kelsey, Nathan, 69.
Kelsey, Nathan, 85.
Kelsey, Nathaniel, 84.
Kelsey, Noah, 62.
Kelsey, Oliver, 85.
Kelsey, Peter, 85.
Kelsey, Rachel, 69.
Kelsey, Reuben, 85.
Kelsey, Samuel, 85.
Kelsey, Samuel, 2\<sup>d</sup>, 85.
Kelsey, Silas, 85.
Kelsey, Solomon, 85.
Kelsey, Stephen, 34.
Kelsey, Stephen, 84.
Kelsey, Stephen, 96.
Kelsey, Uriah, 84.
Kelsey, William, 33.
Kelsey, William, 62.
Kelsey, Zacheus, 47.
Kemp, Charles, 108.
Kenada, Asa, 40.
Kenada, Jon\<sup>a</sup>, 139.
Kenada, Tho\<sup>s</sup>, 134.
Kendal, Eben, 137.
Kendal, Eli, 140.
Kendal, Joseph, Jn\<sup>r</sup>, 141.
Kendal, Peter, 142.
Kendal, Phineas, 142.
Kendal, Smith, 141.
Kendall, Isaac, 140.
Kendall, John, 36.
Kendall, Joseph, 141.
Kendall, Noadiah, 45.
Keney, Dan\<sup>l</sup>, 128.
Kenna, Nath\<sup>an</sup>, 139.
Kenndy, David, 138.
Kennedy, Daniel, 147.
Kennedy, Daniel, 151.
Kennedy, Daniel, Jn\<sup>r</sup>, 147.
Kennedy, David, 143.
Kennedy, David, 151.
Kennedy, David, 153.
Kennedy, Isaac, 152.
Kennedy, John, 36.
Kennedy, John, 119.
Kennedy, John, 153.
Kennedy, Joseph, 151.
Kennedy, Mary, 148.
Kennedy, Samuel, 36.
Kenney, Abel, 151.
Kenney, Asa, 113.
Kenney, Cogshall, 149.
Kenney, Ira, 151.
Kenney, Jacob, 113.
Kenney, James, 151.
Kenney, John, 128.
Kenney, Manuel, 148.
Kenney, Sam\<sup>l</sup>, 151.
Kennie, Nathan, 144.
Kenny, Amos, 149.
Kenny, David, 149.
Kent, Amos, 50.
Kent, Anna, 50.
Kent, Augustus, 50.

INDEX. 193


Kent, Benajah, 50.
Kent, Benj$^{n}$, 137.
Kent, Darius, 74.
Kent, Diana, 51.
Kent, Elihu, 50.
Kent, Elisha, 2$^{d}$, 50.
Kent, Eri, 75.
Kent, George, 144.
Kent, Hannah, 50.
Kent, Jabez, 137.
Kent, Joel, 51.
Kent, John, 50.
Kent, John$^{th}$ Kellogg, 50.
Kent, Joseph, 50.
Kent, Jos$^{i}$, 137.
Kent, Mehitable, 123.
Kent, Seth, 51.
Kent, Seth, 2$^{d}$, 51.
Kent, Thomas, 51.
Kent, Zeno, 51.
Kentfield, John, 36.
Kentner, Jeremiah, 88.
Kentner, John P., 88.
Kenton, Stephen, 62.
Kenworthy, Thomas, 24.
Kenyon, Azariah, 152.
Kenyon, Freeman, 152.
Kenyon, Gardiner, 152.
Kenyon, Giles, 152.
Kenyon, John, 151.
Kenyon, Pain, 127.
Kenyon, Sam$^{l}$, 151.
Kepple, John, 46.
Kerbey, Robert, 19.
Ketchum, Aaron, 72.
Ketchum, Isaac, 23.
Ketchum, Peter, 23.
Ketchum, Stephen, 69.
Kettell, Jonothan, 60.
Kettles, Benjamin, 124.
Key, Daniel, 144.
Key, John, 143.
Key, Joseph, 154.
Key, Nath$^{l}$, 143.
Key, Nath$^{l}$, 149.
Key, Uriah, 149.
Key, Wilson, 143.
Keyes, Amasa, 47.
Keyes, Sampson, 140.
Keyes, William, 65.
Keys, James, 143.
Keys, Nathaniel, 81.
Kibbard, Jonathan, 42.
Kibbe, Amoriah, 136.
Kibbe, Bildad, 136.
Kibbe, Dan$^{l}$, 136.
Kibbe, Ed$^{d}$, 136.
Kibbe, Edward, 136.
Kibbe, Elijah, 136.
Kibbe, Elijah, 136.
Kibbe, Elisha, 40.
Kibbe, Elisha, 136.
Kibbe, Frederick, 136.
Kibbe, Gains, 39.
Kibbe, Gordon, 136.
Kibbe, Isaac, 39.
Kibbe, Israel, 136.
Kibbe, Israel, Jr., 136.
Kibbe, Jed$^{h}$, 136.
Kibbe, Joel, 136.
Kibbe, Lemuel, 136.
Kibbe, Margaret (Wid.), 39.
Kibbe, Moses, 136.
Kibbe, Noah, 136.
Kibbe, Peter, 136.
Kibbe, Peter, Jr., 136.
Kibbe, Tim$^{o}$, 2$^{d}$, 136.
Kibbe, Zerah, 136.
Kibbee, Tim$^{o}$, 136.
Kibbey, Phillip, 38.
Kibby, Christopher, 52.
Kibby, Dorothy, 52.
Kibby, John, 52.
Kibby, Richard, 52.
Kibby, Thomas, 52.
Kibby, William, 52.
Kidder, James, 147.
Kidder, Luther, 153.
Kidder, Nath$^{l}$, 147.
Kidder, Nath$^{l}$, Sen$^{r}$, 147.
Kilborn, Appelton, 65.
Kilborn, David, 64.
Kilborn, Elisabeth, 122.
Kilborn, Epephras, 61.
Kilborn, Isaac, 64.
Kilborn, Jeremiah, 59.
Kilborn, Jessee, 64.
Kilborn, Jessee, 64.
Kilborn, Jiles, 64.
Kilborn, John, 64.
Kilborn, Solomon, 64.
Kilborn, Solomon, 2$^{d}$, 64.
Kilborne, Benjamin, 64.
Kilborne, Lewis, 64.
Kilbourn, Abigail, 52.
Kilbourn, Abraham, 42.
Kilbourn Ashbel, 36.
Kilbourn, Benjamin, 37.
Kilbourn, Eunice, 54.
Kilbourn, Filo, 44.
Kilbourn, Freeman, 46.
Kilbourn, James, 45.
Kilbourn, James, 46.
Kilbourn, John, 46.
Kilbourn, Jonathan, 82.
Kilbourn, Josiah, 42.
Kilbourn, Lemuel, 44.
Kilbourn, Lemuel, 48.
Kilbourn, Martha, 33.
Kilbourn, Mary, 42.
Kilbourn, Russell, 36.
Kilbourn, Samuel, 46.
Kilbourn, Samuel, 81.
Kilbourn, Seth, 33.
Kilbourn, Simon, 54.
Kilbourn, Stephen, 36.
Kilbourn, Timothy, 33.
Kilbourn, Timothy, 48.
Kilbron, John, 59.
Kilburn, David, 121.
Kilburn, Elijah, 122.
Kilburn, Hezekiah, 122.
Killam, Nathan, 113.
Killam, Samuel, 114.
Kimbal, Daniel, 137.
Kimbal, Jacob, 70.
Kimbal, Thomas, 112.
Kimbald, Richard, 64.
Kimball, Ad$^{m}$, 134.
Kimball, Asa, 114.
Kimball, Asa, 143.
Kimball, Chester, 129.
Kimball, Dan$^{l}$, 143.
Kimball, Deliverance, 153.
Kimball Elisha, 114.
Kimball, Jedediah, 113.
Kimball, Jed$^{d}$, 154.
Kimball, John, 114.
Kimball, John, 115.
Kimball, Levi, 113.
Kimball, Moses, 114.
Kimball, Nathan, 113.
Kimball, Peltiah, 153.
Kimball, Sam$^{l}$, 136.
Kimball, Sam$^{l}$, 150.
Kimball, Tyler, 89.
Kimberley, George, 98.
Kimberly, Abraham, 99.
Kimberly, Abraham, 2$^{nd}$, 99.
Kimberly, Adam, 73.
Kimberly, Asael, 105.
Kimberly, Benjamin, 78.
Kimberly, David, 75.
Kimberly, Ezra, 100.
Kimberly, Gilead, 105.
Kimberly, Isaac, 92.
Kimberly, Israel, 105.
Kimberly, Jacob, 64.
Kimberly, Jedediah, 78.
Kimberly, Liberty, 94.
Kimberly, Mary, 43.
Kimberly, Mary, 105.
Kimberly, Nathaniel, 103.
Kimberly, Nathaniel, 105.
Kimberly, Sherman, 92.
Kimberly, Silas, 105.
Kimberly, Thomas, 73.
Kimberly, Thomas, 95.
Kimberly, Thomas, 108.
Kimble, Fitch, 20.
Kindal, David, 141.
Kindal, John, 141.
Kindall, Amos, 52.
Kindall, Joshua, 52.
Kindall, Sarah, 52.
Kindall, Simion, 51.
Kindley, Joseph, 102.
King, Alexander, 37.
King, Alexander, 50.
King, Ashbel, 50.
King, Ashur, 51.
King, Benjamin, 40.
King, Charles, 98.
King, Charles, 127.
King, Dan., 52.
King, Daniel, 133.
King, Dan., 2$^{d}$, 51.
King, David, 20.
King, David, 51.
King, David, 58.
King, Dawn, 133.
King, Ebenezer, 52.
King, Ebenezer, 2$^{d}$, 52.
King, Elijah, 132.
King, Eliphalet, 51.
King, Elisha, 142.
King, Elizabeth, 73.
King, Erastus, 47.
King, Fidello, 52.
King, George, 59.
King, Gideon, 51.
King, Gid$^{n}$, 133.
King, Isaac, 51.
King, James, 147.
King, Joel, 40.
King, John, 52.
King, John, 65.
King, John, 96.
King, John, 147.
King, Jonathan, 51.
King, Jonathan, 64.
King, Jonath$^{n}$, 152.
King, Joseph, 51.
King, Joseph, 58.
King, Joseph, 86.
King, Joseph, 113.
King, Joseph, 2$^{d}$, 51.
King, Joshua, 28.
King, Josiah, 50.
King, Lelah, 133.
King, Lem$^{l}$, 133.
King, Lois, 34.
King, Lydia, 58.
King, Nathaniel, 51.
King, Naum, 39.
King, Obadiah, 39.
King, Oliver, 50.
King, Oliver, 75.
King, Oliver, 133.
King, Paul, 123.
King, Richard, 13.
King, Ruben, 133.
King, Sam$^{l}$, 132.
King, Sam$^{l}$, 134.
King, Sam$^{l}$, 138.
King, Sam$^{l}$, 147.
King, Seth, 51.
King, Seth, 52.
King, Silas, 133.
King, Stephen, 133.
King, Thaddeus, 50.
King, Theodore, 37.
King, Theodore, 51.
King, Thomas, 131.
King, Walter, 130.
King (Widow), 133.
King, William, 51.
King, William, 51.
Kingley, Eliphaz, 152.
Kingsbury, Andrew, 46.
Kingsbury, Asa, 143.
Kingsbury, Asa, 146.
Kingsbury, Daniel, 129.
Kingsbury, Denson, 135.
Kingsbury, Dur, 134.
Kingsbury, Eber, 133.
Kingsbury, E$^{m}$, 133.
Kingsbury, James, 148.
Kingsbury, Jona$^{th}$, 143.
Kingsbury, Joseph, 39.
Kingsbury, Jos., 134.
Kingsbury, Joshua, 59.
Kingsbury, Lemuel, 39.
Kingsbury, Nath$^{l}$, 134.
Kingsbury, Nath$^{l}$, 138.
Kingsbury, Nath$^{l}$, J$^{r}$, 138.
Kingsbury, Rust, 138.
Kingsbury, Sam'l, 69.
Kingsbury, Sam$^{l}$, 133.
Kingsbury, Sam$^{l}$, 140.
Kingsbury, Sam$^{l}$, 144.
Kingsbury, Som$^{o}$, 134.
Kingsbury, Stephens, 67.
Kingsbury, Thomas, 153.
Kingsbury, William, 62.
Kingsbury, W$^{m}$, 133.
Kingsley, Alpheus, 129.
Kingsley, Asael, 146.
Kingsley, Asael, 153.
Kingsley, Diah, 112.
Kingsley, Eleazar, 130.
Kingsley, Eliphelet, 129.
Kingsley, Elisha, 152.
Kingsley, Eunice, 131.
Kingsley, Ezra, 152.
Kingsley, Hezekiah, 112.
Kingsley, Jabez, 142.
Kingsley, John, 153.
Kingsley, Jona$^{th}$, 153.
Kingsley, Joseph, 131.
Kingsley, Josiah, 130.
Kingsley, Nathan$^{l}$, 145.
Kingsley, Oliver, 146.
Kingsley, Oren, 39.
Kingsley, Pardon, 149.
Kingsley, Rufus, 154.
Kingsley, Salmon, 39.
Kingsley, Stephen, 39.
Kingsley, Timo$^{y}$, 145.
Kingsley, Tim$^{o}$, 146.
Kingsley, Uriah, 154.
Kingsley, William, 129.
Kingson, Joseph, 49.
Kinney, Martha, 66.
Kinsbury, Eben$^{r}$, 149.
Kinsbury, Jeduthan, 144.
Kinsbury, Sam$^{l}$, 153.
Kinsman, Jeremiah, 112.
Kinsman, Jeremiah, Jun$^{r}$, 112.
Kinsman, Newport, 148.
Kinyon, Augustus, 118.
Kinyon, Sylvester, 151.
Kirbey, Ephraim, 60.
Kirbey, Joseph, 66.
Kirby, Abner, 103.
Kirby, Daniel, 88.
Kirby, Hezekiah, 88.
Kirby, Nehemiah, 88.
Kirby, Sarah, 88.
Kirby, Thomas, 88.
Kirham, Samuel, 40.
Kirk, Thomas, 56.
Kirkham, Benjamin, 97.
Kirkham, John, 40.
Kirkham, William, 97.
Kirkland, Charles, 89.
Kirkum, Philomon, 37.
Kirtland, Abner, 90.
Kirtland, Ambrose, 89.
Kirtland, Asa, 89.
Kirtland, Elizur, 89.
Kirtland, Hannah, 113.
Kirtland, Jabez, 130.
Kirtland, John, 51.
Kirtland, Joshua, 130.
Kirtland, Martin, 89.
Kitch, Benj$^{n}$, 147.
Kitt (Negro), 42.
Kitterfield, Elisabeth, 121.
Knap, Abraham, 65.
Knap, Eben$^{r}$ Kason, 73.
Knap, Francis, 72.
Knap, Greenfield H., 86.
Knap, Hezekiah, 67.
Knap, Isaac, 86.
Knap, Jabez, 61.
Knap, Jerard, 64.
Knap, Joshua, 63.
Knap, Joshua, 72.
Knap, Lemuel, 150.
Knap, Luke, 63.
Knap, Moses, 56.
Knap, Samu$^{l}$, 63.
Knap, Samuel, 67.
Knap, Timothy, 62.
Knapp, Amy (W$^{d}$), 15.
Knapp, Anne (W$^{d}$), 16.
Knapp, Benjamin, 11.
Knapp, Benjamin, 14.
Knapp, Bracy, 11.
Knapp, Caleb, 22.
Knapp, Charles, 15.
Knapp, Charles, 24.
Knapp, Daniel, 11.
Knapp, Daniel, 15.
Knapp, Daniel, 24.
Knapp, David, 11.
Knapp, David, 15.
Knapp, Eben, 15.
Knapp, Ebenezer, 15.
Knapp, Elnathan, 11.
Knapp, Elnathan, J$^{nr}$, 11.
Knapp, Enos, 15.
Knapp, Epenetus, 24.
Knapp, Fransis, 10.
Knapp, Gilbert, 15.
Knapp, Hannah (W$^{d}$), 16.
Knapp, Henery, 11.
Knapp, Hezekiah, 26.
Knapp, Israel, 16.
Knapp, Jacob, 25.
Knapp, James, 11.
Knapp, James, 14.
Knapp, James, 18.
Knapp, James, 24.
Knapp, James, J$^{r}$, 24.
Knapp, Jeremiah, 15.
Knapp, John, 10.
Knapp, John, 10.
Knapp, John, 14.
Knapp, John, 16.
Knapp, John, 25.
Knapp, John, J$^{nr}$, 14.
Knapp, Jonah, 16.
Knapp, Jonathan, 16.
Knapp, Joseph, 16.
Knapp, Joshua, 11.
Knapp, Joshua, 16.
Knapp, Joshua, J$^{r}$, 15.
Knapp, Joshua, 3$^{d}$, 16.
Knapp, Moses, 18.
Knapp, Nathan, 24.
Knapp, Nathan, Jun$^{r}$, 27.
Knapp, Nathaniel, 25.
Knapp, Noah, 11.
Knapp, Oliver, 18.
Knapp, Peter, 25.
Knapp, Phebe (W$^{d}$), 15.
Knapp, Rachel (W$^{d}$), 15.
Knapp, Samuel, 15.
Knapp, Samuel, 25.
Knapp, Shubeal, 16.
Knapp, Silvanus, 24.
Knapp, Timothy, 15.
Knapp, Uriah, 16.
Knapp, Usial, 25.
Knapp, William, 15.
Knapp, William, 25.
Kneeland, David, 121.
Kneeland, Isaac, 68.
Kneeland, Morey, 120.
Kneeland, Samuel, 46.
Knibloe, Joseph, 69.
Knibloe, William, 69.
Knickabacker, John, 67.
Knickabocker, John, 67.
Knickabocker, Isaac, 61.
Knickabocker, John, 61.
Knickerbocker, Abraham, 61.
Knickerbocker, Sam$^{l}$, 61.
Knickerbocker, Solomon, 61.
Knight, Asa, 112.
Knight, David, 112.
Knight, David, 144.
Knight, David, Jun$^{r}$, 112.
Knight, Edward, 149.
Knight, Isaac, 148.
Knight, Issabel, 112.
Knight, John, 127.
Knight, John, 152.
Knight, Doct$^{r}$ Jonath$^{n}$, 21.
Knight, Joseph, 39.
Knight, Phineas, 112.
Knight, Sam$^{l}$, 149.
Knight, Thomas, 39.
Knolton, Dani$^{l}$, 140.
Knolton, Ezra, 140.
Knolton, Fredrick, 140.
Knolton, John, 109.
Knolton, Mehitabel, 140.
Knolton, Stephen, 81.
Knolton, Thomas, 140.
Knot, Josiah, 89.
Knowles, Arthur, 1$^{st}$, 72.
Knowles, Arthur, 2$^{d}$, 72.
Knowles, Gid Benedict, 75.
Knowles, Giles, 79.
Knowles, Isaac, 79.
Knowles, James, 83.
Knowles, Seth, 79.
Knowles, William, 1$^{st}$, 72.
Knowles, William, 2$^{d}$, 72.
Knowling, Asa, 142.
Knowls, Dan$^{l}$ & Son, 119.
Knowls, Elezer, 10.
Knowls, Elisha, 83.
Knowls, Joshua, 83.
Knowls, Richard, 83.
Knowls, Richard, Jun$^{r}$, 83.
Knowls, Walker, 83.
Knowls, William, 83.
Knowlton, Abraham, 140.
Knox, Adam, 137.
Knox, Andrew, 151.
Knox, James, 46.
Knox, James, 151.
Knox, Jennet (Wid.), 46.
Knox, Sam$^{l}$, 140.
Knox, William, 46.
Knox, William, 140.
Krappen, Thomas, 75.
Kuney, James, 43.
Kutland, Jeames, 57.
Kuzer, Elisha, 113.
Kuzer, Nath$^{l}$, 113.
Kuzer, Samuel, 113.
Kyes, Edward, 141.
Kyes, Edward, 141.
Kyes, John, 152.
Kyes, Solomon, 140.
Kyes, William, 65.

Laberee, Bennedict, 18.
Laberee, James, 18.
Lacey, Jasper, 51.
Lacey, Sizzardus, 51.
La Clear, Francis, 66.
Lacy, Aaron, 12.
Lacy, Abel, 12.
Lacy, Anne, 18.
Lacy, Chancy, 18.
Lacy, Daniel, 15.
Lacy, David, 15.
Lacy, Ebenezer, 75.
Lacy, Ezra, 78.
Lacy, James, 31.
Lacy, John, 15.
Lacy, Joseph, 31.
Lacy, Josiah, 30.
Lacy, Margeret, 15.
Lacy, Richard, 20.
Lacy, Sarah (Wid.), 20.
Ladd, Abner, 129.
Ladd, Akijah, 138.
Ladd, And$^{w}$, 129.
Ladd, Daniel, 129
Ladd, David, 130.
Ladd, David, 132.
Ladd, David, 2$^{d}$, 129.
Ladd, Elial, 138.
Ladd, Elijah, 132.
Ladd, Elisha, 134.
Ladd, Ezekiel, 129.
Ladd, Ezek$^{l}$, 132.
Ladd, Jedediah, 129.
Ladd, Jeremiah, 129.
Ladd, Jn$^{o}$, 133.
Ladd, Jn$^{o}$, 136.
Ladd, Jon$^{a}$, 138.
Ladd, Joseph, 129.
Ladd, Samuel, 129.
Ladd, Sam$^{l}$, 133.
Ladd, Sam$^{l}$, 138.
Lains, Henry, 94.
Lake, David, 21.
Lake, Elnathan, 94.
Lake, Jabes, 18.
Lake, Jeames, 72.
Lake, John, 21.
Lake, Peter, 21.
Lake, Reubin, 30.
Lake, Samuel, 59.
Lalintice, Jacob, 63.
Lally, Jos., 138.
Lamb, Asa, 118.
Lamb, Benj$^{n}$, 133.
Lamb, Hannah, 119.
Lamb, James, 46.
Lamb, Jesse, 131.
Lamb, Johiel, 67.

# INDEX.

Lamb, John, 118.
Lamb, John, 131.
Lamb, John, 149.
Lamb, Lemuel, 115.
Lamb, Nathan, 140.
Lamb, Richard, 132.
Lamb, Rufus, 146.
Lamb, Samuel, 119.
Lamb, Silas, 118.
Lamb, Silas, Jun[r], 118.
Lamb, Timothy, 119.
Lamb, William, 118.
Lambart, David, 21.
Lambert, David, 102.
Lambert, George, 105.
Lambert, Jesse, 102.
Lambert, Nehemiah, 56.
Lambert, Thomas, 114.
Lamberton, Moses, 54.
Lamberton, Obed, 54.
Lambeth, David, 2[nd], 102.
Lamont, Mary Ann, 104.
Lamphear, Benjamin, 117.
Lamphear, Elijah, 145.
Lamphear, Elisha, 117.
Lamphear, George, 126.
Lamphear, Jede[h], 143.
Lamphear, John, 115.
Lamphear, John, 117.
Lamphear, Roswell, 115.
Lamphear, Ruth, 123.
Lamphear, Shubael, 115.
Lampheer, James, 128.
Lamphin, Oliver, 91.
Lampson, Benjamin, 45.
Lampson, Daniel, 65.
Lampson, Ebenezer, 45.
Lampson, Elnathan, 45.
Lampson, Joseph, 45.
Lampson, Nathan[el], 30.
Lampson, Samuel, 45.
Lampson (Wid.), 45.
Lamson, Mitchel, 78.
Lamson, Nathan[el], 30.
Lamson, Sarah, 72.
Lamson, Silas, 72.
Lamson (Widow), 30.
Lamson, William, 1[st], 72.
Lamson, William, 2[d], 72.
Lancashire, Abigail, 105.
Lancaster, John, 131.
Landen, Martha, 60.
Landeraft, George, 97.
Landers, Joseph, 60.
Landers, Samuel, 54.
Landon, Abagail, 65.
Landon, Abner, 70.
Landon, Ashbel, 65.
Landon, Daniel, 70.
Landon, Daniel, 70.
Landon, David, 61.
Landon, David, 65.
Landon, David, 65.
Landon, David, 65.
Landon, David, 98.
Landon, Elisha, 66.
Landon, Ezekiel, 65.
Landon, George, 61.
Landon, James, 59.
Landon, James, 61.
Landon, John, 61.
Landon, John, 66.
Landon, John, 70.
Landon, Jonathan, 98.
Landon, Martha, 71.
Landon, Nathan, 65.
Landon, Nathaniel, 71.
Landon, Ozias, 60.
Landon, Rufus, 61.
Landon, Samuel, 98.
Landon, Seth, 70.
Landon, Thadeus, 60.
Landpir, David, 37.
Landpire, Abner, 37.
Lane, Arunah, 84.
Lane, Assel, 111.
Lane, Ashbel, 62.
Lane, Dan., 51.
Lane, Daniel, 110.
Lane, Elijah, 50.
Lane, Elisha, 84.
Lane, Enos, 61.
Lane, Ephraim, 59.
Lane, Gad, 51.
Lane, Hanah, 29.
Lane, Hez[a], 148.
Lane, Hezekiah, Esq[r], 84.
Lane, Jabez, 84.
Lane, James, 103.
Lane, James, 148.
Lane, Jared, 67.
Lane, Joel, 50.
Lane, John, 15.
Lane, John, 59.
Lane, John, 84.
Lane, John, Jun[r], 84.
Lane, Joseph, 84.
Lane, Joseph, Jun[r], 84.
Lane, Letitia, 88.
Lane, Nathaniel, 111.
Lane, Noah, 85.
Lane, Richard, 59.
Lane, Stephen, 85.

Lane, Thatcher, 85.
Lane, William, 127.
Langdon, Chancey, 133.
Langdon, Ebenezer, 41.
Langdon, John, 33.
Langdon, Joseph, 40.
Langin, Timothy, 11.
Langmore, Alexander, 104.
Langothy, Benjamin, 115.
Langothy, John, 115.
Langothy, John, 120.
Langothy, Thomas, 115.
Langton, Asahel, 49.
Langton, Daniel, 49.
Langton, Daniel, Jr., 49.
Langton, Job, 49.
Langton, Jonathan, 33.
Langton, Ruth, 49.
Langton, Seth, 49.
Langton, Solomon, 41.
Langworthy, Timothy, 149.
Lankford, Joseph, 119.
Lankton, Joseph, 35.
Lanman, Peter, 130.
Lannd, Hannah, 42.
Lanston, Jeames, 58.
Lapener, Antony, 17.
Laplass, Jonathan, 122.
Lappedal, Peter, 61.
Lapum, David, 112.
Lard, W[m], 137.
Lark, John, 106.
Lark, Levi, 54.
Lark, Solomon, 106.
Larkham, John, 151.
Larkham, Lott, 151.
Larkin, Edward, 103.
Larkin, Joshua, 17.
Larkin, Moses, 116.
Larking, Scovill, 49.
Larkins, Peter, 96.
Larkum, John, 46.
Larkum, Rhoderic, 54.
Larnard, Amariah, 51.
Larned, Simon, 150.
La Roche, John, 128.
Larrabe, Silas, 142.
Larrabe, Sith, 153.
Larrabe, Timothy, 152.
Larrance, Jonathan, 113.
Larrance, Jon[a], 130.
Larrance, Samuel, 113.
Larreby, James, 115.
Larrey, John, 118.
Larriby (Widow), 134.
Lartherbie, William, 101.
Larthly, Mary, 131.
Lasell, Josiah, 153.
Latemore, Wait, 48.
Laten, Joseph, 117.
Latham, Ann, 119.
Latham, Betsy, 119.
Latham, Carey, 118.
Latham, Christopher, 119.
Latham, Christopher, Jun[r], 119.
Latham, David, 124.
Latham, Edward, 119.
Latham, Elisabeth, 119.
Latham, Jasper, 119.
Latham, Jasper, 119.
Latham, John, 119.
Latham, John, 124.
Latham, Jon[a], 119.
Latham, Joseph, 118.
Latham, Joseph, 119.
Latham, Joseph, 119.
Latham, Joseph, 124.
Latham, Lucy, 119.
Latham, Mary, 119.
Latham, Peter, 132.
Latham, Robart, 119.
Latham, Sigleton, 119.
Latham, Thomas, 119.
Latham, William, 120.
Latham, William, Jun[r], 119.
Latham, William, 3[d], 119.
Latherby, David, 105.
Lathrop, Abiel, 145.
Lathrop, Abigail, 130.
Lathrop, Andrew, Jun[r], 126.
Lathrop, Arunah, 130.
Lathrop, Asa, 126.
Lathrop, Benjamin, 152.
Lathrop, Benj[a], 154.
Lathrop, Charles, 145.
Lathrop, Darius, 130.
Lathrop, David, 39.
Lathrop, Ebenezer, 153.
Lathrop, Ephraim, 130.
Lathrop, Ezekiel, 130.
Lathrop, Jabez, 130.
Lathrop, James, 130.
Lathrop, James, 145.
Lathrop, Jedidiah, 130.
Lathrop, Jeremiah, 130.
Lathrop, John, 88.
Lathrop, John, 128.
Lathrop, John, 130.
Lathrop, Jonathan, 130.
Lathrop, Lucy, 130.
Lathrop, Priscilla, 130.
Lathrop, Roswell, 153.
Lathrop, Samuel, 131.

Lathrop, Thatcher, 39.
Lathrop, Walter, 130.
Lathrop, Zachariah, 130.
Lathrop, Zebulon, 145.
Lathrop, Zephaniah, 130.
Latimer, Alex[r], 55.
Latimer, Amos, 125.
Latimer, Bez[u], 52.
Latimer, Daniel, 127.
Latimer, George, 55.
Latimer, Hallam, 125.
Latimer, Henry, 125.
Latimer, Hez[h], 55.
Latimer, Hez[h], Ju., 55.
Latimer, John, 52.
Latimer, Jonathan, 125.
Latimer, Lemuel, 126.
Latimer, Nathan, 125.
Latimer, Nathan, 2[d], 125.
Latimer, Pickett, 127.
Latimer, Richard, 126.
Latimer, Samuel, 125.
Latimer, Sam[l], 125.
Latimer, Stephen, 125.
Latimer, William, 128.
Latimor, Solomon, 53.
Latimore, Jiles, 48.
Latimore, Jonathan, 48.
Latimore, Luther, 54.
Latimore, Wickham, 47.
Laton, Abraham, 27.
Lator, Preserv'd, 27.
Lattain, Benjamin, 20.
Lattain, Jacob, 20.
Lattain, Joseph, 20.
Lattain, Luke, 20.
Latten, John, 63.
Lattin, David, 18.
Lattin, Thomas, 18.
Laurance, Grove, 61.
Laurence, Samuel, 48.
Laurence, Timothy, 25.
Laurence (Wido.), 149.
Law, Benedick, 102.
Law, Francis, 105.
Law, Francis, 105.
Law, Jonathan, 102.
Law, Richard, 128.
Law, William, 93.
Lawrance, Arial, 68.
Lawrance, Gidian, 67.
Lawrance, Nathan, 67.
Lawrance, Nehemiah, 67.
Lawrence, Abel, 70.
Lawrence, Amos, 47.
Lawrence, Amos, 55.
Lawrence, Anson, 67.
Lawrence, Arial, 68.
Lawrence, David, 62.
Lawrence, David, 67.
Lawrence, Elihu, 93.
Lawrence, Elihu, 107.
Lawrence, Elihu, 144.
Lawrence, Hen[y], 134.
Lawrence, Isaac, 59.
Lawrence, Jerry, 67.
Lawrence, John, 46.
Lawrence, John, 61.
Lawrence, John, 63.
Lawrence, John, 144.
Lawrence, Jonas, 59.
Lawrence, Josiah, 70.
Lawrence, Katey, 101.
Lawrence, Nathan, 70.
Lawrence, Nehemiah, 62.
Lawrence, Roman, 87.
Lawrence, Solomon, 67.
Lawrence, William, 46.
Lawry, Daniel, 40.
Lawry, John, 35.
Laws, David, 144.
Laws, John, 116.
Lawson, David, 138.
Lawson, Ebcn[r], 141.
Lawson, Jn[o], 138.
Lawson, Rob[t], 138.
Lawson, Tho[s], 138.
Lay, Asa, 90.
Lay, Elisha, 123.
Lay, Ezra, 90.
Lay, James, 90.
Lay, Jerem[h], 90.
Lay, John, 90.
Lay, John, 123.
Lay, John, 2[d], 123.
Lay, John, 3[d], 123.
Lay, Jon[a], Esq[r], 90.
Lay, Joseph, 123.
Lay, Lee, 123.
Lay, Nath[l], 90.
Lay, Peter, 123.
Lay, Robart, 123.
Lay, Rob[t], 89.
Lay, Robert, 90.
Lay, Sam[l], 89.
Lay, Simeon, 90.
Lay, William, 123.
Layton, Noyes, 151.
Leach, Amos, 19.
Leach, Caleb, 60.
Leach, Calvin, 137.
Leach Christopher, 29.
Leach, Daniel, 18.

Leach, Daniel, 127.
Leach, David, 99.
Leach, David, 127.
Leach, Ebenezer, 65.
Leach, Eben[r], 144.
Leach, Echabod, 18.
Leach, Ephraim, 127.
Leach, Hezekiah, 58.
Leach, Jeames, 72.
Leach, Jeremiah, 131.
Leach, Joel, 142.
Leach, John, 27.
Leach, John, 125.
Leach, Jonas, 65.
Leach, Joseph, 145.
Leach, Joshua, 65.
Leach, Manassa, 122.
Leach, Mary, 18.
Leach, Mary, 127.
Leach, Mary, 142.
Leach, Nathan[l], 62.
Leach, Oren, 99.
Leach, Phebe, 64.
Leach, Richard, 65.
Leach, Rob[t], 139.
Leach, Stephen, 127.
Leach, Thomas, 130.
Leach, William, 144.
Leamphear, Jabez, 146.
Leamphere, Sam[l], 140.
Leanard, Benjaman, 60.
Leanard, Fellows, 61.
Leanarvas, Jn[o], 135.
Learned, Amasa, 126.
Learned, Benj[s], 150.
Learned, Dan[l], 150.
Learned, Henry, 150.
Learned, James, 144.
Learned, James, Jn[r], 144.
Learned, Joseph, 145.
Learned, Theophilus, 144.
Lease, John, 153.
Leason, Noah, 60.
Leason, Noah, 64.
Leason, Prudence, 29.
Leavens, Isaac, 104.
Leavensworth, Ely, 104.
Leavenworth, Amos, 78.
Leavenworth, Asa, 76.
Leavenworth, Catherine, 102.
Leavenworth, David, 78.
Leavenworth, Elihu, 78.
Leavenworth, Esther, 78.
Leavenworth, Gideon, 73.
Leavenworth, Gideon, 78.
Leavenworth, John, 73.
Leavenworth, John, 78.
Leavenworth, Mark, 104.
Leavenworth, Mark, 109.
Leavenworth, Moss, 78.
Leavenworth, Samuel, 109.
Leavenworth, Thomas, 109.
Leavenworth, William, 109.
Leavingston, John, 49.
Leavins, Rowland, 144.
Leavitt, David, 56.
Leavitt, David, Ju[r], 56.
Leavitt, Enoch, 51.
Leavitt, John, 50.
Leavitt, John, 2[d], 50.
Leavitt, Joshua, 51.
Leavitt, Samuel, 75.
Leavitt, Stephen, 52.
Leavitt, Thaddeus, 50.
Lebarron, David, 84.
Lebbeus (Negro), 129.
Ledgyard, Eben[r], 2[d], 119.
Ledyard, Ann, 119.
Ledyard, Charles, 34.
Ledyard, Eben[r], 119.
Lee, Abner, 122.
Lee, Allen, 150.
Lee, Amos, 40.
Lee, Andrew, 112.
Lee, Benjamin, 122.
Lee, Cyril, 149.
Lee, Daniel, 28.
Lee, Daniel, 59.
Lee, Daniel, 79.
Lee. Dan., 122.
Lee, Dan[l], 139.
Lee, Deborah, 98.
Lee, Eber, 98.
Lee, Edgcomb, 126.
Lee, Elias, 28.
Lee, Elijah, 28.
Lee, Elisha, 124.
Lee, Elisha, Jun[r], 124.
Lee, Elizabeth, 129.
Lee, Enos, 27.
Lee, Enos, 33.
Lee, Eton, 98.
Lee, Ezra, 123.
Lee, Fredreck, 98.
Lee, George, 46.
Lee, George, 89.
Lee, Isaac, 33.
Lee, Israel, Jr., 33.
Lee, Israel, Jn[r], 145.
Lee, Israel, Sen[r], 145.
Lee, James, 35.
Lee, Jason, 124.
Lee, Joel, 150.

Lee, Joel, 150.
Lee, John, 28.
Lee, John, 34.
Lee, John, 34.
Lee, John, 65.
Lee, John, 96.
Lee, John, Jr., 34.
Lee, John M., 124.
Lee, Jonathan, 98.
Lee, Jonat[h], 150.
Lee, Jonathan, 2[nd], 98.
Lee, Joseph, 120.
Lee, Joseph, 150.
Lee, Josiah, 86.
Lee, Lemuel, 124.
Lee, Levi, 98.
Lee, Levi, 126.
Lee, Love, 68.
Lee, Miles, 62.
Lee, Miles, 66.
Lee, Nathan, 146.
Lee, Nathaniel, 68.
Lee, Nathaniel, 98.
Lee, Oren, 33.
Lee, Rejoice, 59.
Lee, Robert W., 70.
Lee, Sabra, 124.
Lee, Samuel, 33.
Lee, Samuel, 59.
Lee, Sam[l], 68.
Lee, Samuel, 69.
Lee, Samuel, 87.
Lee, Sam[l], 89.
Lee, Samuel, 98.
Lee, Sam[l], 137.
Lee, Samuel, 152.
Lee, Samuel, Jun[r], 87.
Lee, Sarah, 58.
Lee, Seth, 28.
Lee, Seth, 40.
Lee, Seth, 52.
Lee, Silas, 99.
Lee, Silus, 27.
Lee, Solomon, 145.
Lee, Squire, 120.
Lee, Stephen, 21.
Lee, Stephen, 122.
Lee, Theodore, 58.
Lee, Thomas, 41.
Lee, Thomas, 124.
Lee, Thomas, 129.
Lee, Thomas, Jr., 40.
Lee, Timothy, 49.
Lee, Timothy, 98.
Lee, William, 29.
Lee, W[m], 35.
Lee, William, 68.
Lee, W[m], 82.
Lee, William, 87.
Lee, William, 98.
Leech, Elijah, 130.
Leech, James, 128.
Leeds, Abraham, 26.
Leeds, Ann, 119.
Leeds, Carey, 26.
Leeds, Elisha, 26.
Leeds, Elizabeth (W[d]), 26.
Leeds, Gideon, 26.
Leeds, Jedediah, 116.
Leeds, Mary (W[d]), 26.
Leeds, Thomas, 117.
Leeds, W[m], 119.
Leek, Daniel, 100.
Leek, James, 95.
Leek, Thomas, 100.
Leek, Thomas, 2[nd], 100.
Leek, Timothy, 100.
Leek, Timothy, 2[nd], 100.
Leemnis, George, 24.
Leet, Absolam, 97.
Leet, Ambrose, 97.
Leet, Amos, 97.
Leet, Daniel, 97.
Leet, Edw[d] A., 90.
Leet, Elijah, 97.
Leet, Gideon, 90.
Leet, Gideon, Jun[r], 90.
Leet, James, 97.
Leet, Jarad, 99.
Leet, Jerad, 97.
Leet, Joel, 97.
Leet, John, 97.
Leet, John, 98.
Leet, Palatine, 97.
Leet, Pharos, 97.
Leet, Ruben, 98.
Leet, Soloman, 97.
Leet, Soloman, 2[nd], 97.
Leet, Stephen, 99.
Leet, Thomas, 97.
Leet, Victor, 97.
Leffingwell, Andrew, 126.
Leffingwell, Bela, 131.
Leffingwell, Benaijah, 131.
Leffingwell, Benjamin, 125.
Leffingwell, Caleb, 125.
Leffingwell, Christopher, 131.
Leffingwell, Clark, 125.
Leffingwell, Elisha, 131.
Leffingwell, Hart, 130.
Leffingwell, Hart, 2[d], 131.
Leffingwell, Hezekiah, 131.
Leffingwell, Jere[h], 149.

# INDEX.

Leffingwell, John, 46.
Leffingwell, Joshua, 46.
Leffingwell, Mathew, 2d, 130.
Leffingwell, Matthew, 130.
Leffingwell, Phinehas, 130.
Leffingwell, Presila, 126.
Leffingwell, Roswell, 126.
Leffingwell, Saml, 126.
Leffingwell, Saml, 131.
Leffingwell, Saml, 2d, 126.
Leffingwell, Thomas, 131.
Leffingwell, William, 131.
Leforgess, Henry, 101.
Leggs, Thomas, 150.
Lehomidieu, Grover, 130.
L'Homedieu, William, 85.
L'Hommedieu, Henry, 90.
Leicester, Daniel, 52.
Leidlie, Hugh, 46.
Leister, Eliphalet, 90.
Leit, Daniel A., 48.
Leit, Samuel, 48.
Lekes, Ephraim, 20.
Leman (Widow), 30.
Leming, David, 35.
Leming, Judah, 34.
Lemmon, Robert, 75.
Lemmon, Robert, 2d, 75.
Lenard, Tim (Negroe), 104.
Lenenworth, Daniel, 17.
Lenin, Justice, 60.
Lenley, Joseph, 60.
Lenneaux, Benja, 83.
Lenslee, James, 11.
Lenslee, Lemuel, 11.
Lent, Othimel, 91.
Leonard, Benja, 140.
Leonard, Enoch, 144.
Leonard, Giliver, 150.
Leonard, Jacob, 154.
Leonard, Mary, 154.
Leonard, Nicholas, 114.
Leonard, Saml, 113.
Leonard, Saml, Junr, 113.
Leonard, Silas, 59.
Leonard, Timothy, 23.
Lester, Amos, 118.
Lester, Amos, 128.
Lester, Andrew, 62.
Lester, Andw, 124.
Lester, Asa, 119.
Lester, Christopher, 119.
Lester, Danl, 119.
Lester, Ebenr, 120.
Lester, Elihu, 124.
Lester, Elijah, 115.
Lester, Elisabeth, 119.
Lester, Elisha, 113.
Lester, Guy, 120.
Lester, Isaac, 124.
Lester, Jeremiah, 124.
Lester, John, 17.
Lester, John, 128.
Lester, Jonathan, 122.
Lester, Jona, 130.
Lester, Joshua, 124.
Lester, Levi, 126.
Lester, Lucretia, 119.
Lester, Mary, 119.
Lester, Moses, 113.
Lester, Nathan, 119.
Lester, Noah, 124.
Lester, Norman, 124.
Lester, Peter, 119.
Lester, Peter, Junr, 118.
Lester, Saml, 119.
Lester, Saml, Junr, 119.
Lester, Sarah, 119.
Lester, Silas, 125.
Lester, Thomas, 119.
Lester, Timothy, 115.
Lester, Timothy, 127.
Lester, Timothy, 149.
Lester, William, 130.
Lettleton, Roger, 61.
Leus, Hezekiah, 45.
Levensworth, Edmon, 18.
Levensworth, Giddeon, 18.
Leverett, Mary, 86.
Levet, Josiah G., 31.
Levins, Benja, 144.
Levins, Elisabeth, 144.
Levins, William, 148.
Levit, Jame, 134.
Levit, Samuel, 107.
Levitt, Josiah, 31.
Lewes, Jona, 138.
Lewis, Abel, 17.
Lewis, Abel, 34.
Lewis, Abel, 42.
Lewis, Abraham, 19.
Lewis, Abraham, 111.
Lewis, Adonijah, 33.
Lewis, Amassa, 92.
Lewis, Andrew, 91.
Lewis, Asa, 117.
Lewis, Asa, 151.
Lewis, Asahel, 50.
Lewis, Augustus, 83.
Lewis, Barnabas, 92.
Lewis, Beach, 18.
Lewis, Beach, 73.
Lewis, Benjamin, 30.
Lewis, Benjamin, 35.
Lewis, Beriah, 116.
Lewis, Birdsley, 17.
Lewis, Caleb, 94.
Lewis, Caleb, 151.
Lewis, Caleb, 151.
Lewis, Chancey, 50.
Lewis, Charles, 95.
Lewis, Daniel, 16.
Lewis, Daniel, 121.
Lewis, Danl, 140.
Lewis, Daniel W., 65.
Lewis, David, 34.
Lewis, David, 110.
Lewis, David, 120.
Lewis, Deborah, 119.
Lewis, Ebenezer, 17.
Lewis, Ebenezer, 17.
Lewis, Ebenezer, 61.
Lewis, Ebenezer, 93.
Lewis, Ebenezer, 94.
Lewis, Edward, 61.
Lewis, Edward, 128.
Lewis, Eleazr, 151.
Lewis, Eli, 31.
Lewis, Eli, 34.
Lewis, Elihu, 69.
Lewis, Elijah, 18.
Lewis, Elijah, 41.
Lewis, Elisha, 35.
Lewis, Elisha, 117.
Lewis, Elisha, Junr, 117.
Lewis, Eno, 35.
Lewis, Enock, Senr, 141.
Lewis, Eunice, 110.
Lewis, Everit, 17.
Lewis, Ezekiel, 56.
Lewis, Ezra, 52.
Lewis, Filo, 30.
Lewis, Floria, 18.
Lewis, Fredrick, 17.
Lewis, George, 29.
Lewis, George, 79.
Lewis, George, 124.
Lewis, George, Junr, 79.
Lewis, Gerad, 108.
Lewis, Hart, 49.
Lewis, Hendrick, 65.
Lewis, Hester, 108.
Lewis, Ichabod, 116.
Lewis, Isaac, 16.
Lewis, Isaac, 29.
Lewis, Isaac, 49.
Lewis, Revd Isaac, 15.
Lewis, Israel, 141.
Lewis, Jabish, 49.
Lewis, James, 33.
Lewis, James, 124.
Lewis, Job, 49.
Lewis, John, 31.
Lewis, John, 35.
Lewis, John, 51.
Lewis, John, 51.
Lewis, John, 53.
Lewis, John, 91.
Lewis, John, 110.
Lewis, John, 124.
Lewis, John, 2d, 51.
Lewis, John, 2nd, 111.
Lewis, Jonathan, 14.
Lewis, Jonathan, 25.
Lewis, Jonathan, 115.
Lewis, Joseph, 30.
Lewis, Joseph, 53.
Lewis, Joseph, 91.
Lewis, Joseph, 119.
Lewis, Joseph, 127.
Lewis, Josiah, 34.
Lewis, Josiah, 34.
Lewis, Judson, 30.
Lewis, Judson, 31.
Lewis, Judy, 70.
Lewis, Lemuel, 50.
Lewis, Lothrop, 14.
Lewis, Mark, 34.
Lewis, Mary, 113.
Lewis, Mary, 128.
Lewis, Moses, 79.
Lewis, Naboth, 88.
Lewis, Nathan, 31.
Lewis, Nathan, 81.
Lewis, Nathan, 151.
Lewis, Nathan, Jr, 50.
Lewis, Nathaneel, 17.
Lewis, Nathaniel, 50.
Lewis, Nathaniel, 68.
Lewis, Nathaniel S., 31.
Lewis (Negro), 112.
Lewis, Nehemeah, 69.
Lewis, Nehemiah, 73.
Lewis, Oliver, 31.
Lewis, Oliver, 56.
Lewis, Osius, 66.
Lewis, Peleg, 119.
Lewis, Philo, 94.
Lewis, Phineas, 41.
Lewis, Phinus, 30.
Lewis, Richard, 63.
Lewis, Robartson, 118.
Lewis, Roger, 34.
Lewis, Roger, 34.
Lewis, Samuel, 17.
Lewis, Samuel, 29.
Lewis, Samuel, 34.
Lewis, Samuel, 35.
Lewis, Samuel, 55.
Lewis, Samuel, 76.
Lewis, Samuel, 83.
Lewis, Samuel, 107.
Lewis, Saml, 151.
Lewis, Samuel S., 110.
Lewis, Sarah, 17.
Lewis, Sarah, 102.
Lewis, Sarah, 118.
Lewis, Sarah, 121.
Lewis, Seth, 49.
Lewis, Silas, 110.
Lewis, Sirus, 124.
Lewis, Stephen, 31.
Lewis, Stephen, 35.
Lewis, Stiles, 30.
Lewis, Sussanah, 103.
Lewis, Swignion, 73.
Lewis, Thankful, 76.
Lewis, Thankfull, 99.
Lewis, Thomas, 17.
Lewis, Thomas, 40.
Lewis, Thomas, t9.
Lewis, Thomas, 83.
Lewis, Timothy, 49.
Lewis, Volentine, 116.
Lewis, Walker, 17.
Lewis, Wells, 17.
Lewis, William, 49.
Lewis, William, 95.
Lewis, William, 117.
Lewis, William, 119.
Lewis, William, Junr, 117.
Lewis, William, 2nd, 95.
Lewis, Zacheriah, 17.
Lews, Simeon, 45.
Libberty, Jeff, 75.
Liberty, Sharp (Negroe), 92.
Lickleter, James, 105.
Lieke, John, 103.
Lightfoot, Robert, 148.
Like, Andrew, 10.
Lilley, David, 61.
Lilley, Moses, 48.
Lillibridge, Benja, 139.
Lillibridge, Clark, 139.
Lillibridge, David, 139.
Lillie, Chester, 152.
Lillie, Ebenr, 154.
Lillie, Elisha, 153.
Lillie, Jared, 152.
Lillie, Jonathan, 51.
Lillie, Nathan, 145.
Lilliston, James, 29.
Lilly Amariah, 130.
Lilly (Negro), 89.
Lincoln, Simeon, 33.
Lindley, Danl, 154.
Lindley, James, 92.
Lindley, John, 92.
Lindley, Josiah, 28.
Lindley, Josiah, 92.
Lindley, Solman, 92.
Lindslee, Mathew, 11.
Lines, Abel, 112.
Lines, Alvin, 111.
Lines, Asbael, 105.
Lines, Benjamin, 98.
Lines, Cornelius, 105.
Lines, Darus, 111.
Lines, Daniel, 111.
Lines, Ebenezer, 112.
Lines, Eber, 112.
Lines, Erastus, 93.
Lines, Ezra, 103.
Lines, James, 104.
Lines, James, 111.
Lines, John, 112.
Lines, Joseph, 95.
Lines, Linus, 111.
Lines, Luke, 112.
Lines, Major, 104.
Lines, Rufus, 98.
Lines, Samuel, 111.
Linkhorn, James, 131.
Linkon, Abijah, 145.
Linkon, Danl, 153.
Linkon, John, 153.
Linkon, Jonah, 153.
Linkon, Lemuel, 147.
Linkon, Nathan, 153.
Linkon, Nathl, 153.
Linkon, Thomas, 153.
Linkon, Zephh, 154.
Linley, Adam, 59.
Linley, Isaac, 91.
Linley, John, 91.
Linley, Joseph, 64.
Linley, Obed, 91.
Linley, Rufus, 91.
Linley, Saml, 69.
Linly, Ebenezer, 91.
Linly, Ebenezer, 2d, 91.
Linly, Malik, 91.
Linly, Samuel, 91.
Linly, Sarah, 91.
Linly, Stephen, 92.
Linn, James, 84.
Linsey, Robert, 51.
Linsley, Aaron, 35.
Linsley, Abiel, 78.
Linsley, Braniard, 50.
Linsley, Daniel, 92.
Linsley, Elizabeth, 92.
Linsley, Ephraim, 57.
Linsley, Israel, 92.
Linsley, Jacob, 34.
Linsley, Jonth, 35.
Linsley, Keturah, 34.
Linsley, Timothy, 56.
Lion, Calep, 14.
Lion, Eliphilet, 13.
Lion, Jese, 13.
Lion, Jesse, 13.
Lion, Joseph, 13.
Lion, Joseph, Jnr, 13.
Lion, Seth, 13.
Lion, Wakeman, 13.
Liscomb, Thos, 149.
Lisk, Andrew, 145.
Lisk, Ebenezr, 145.
Lister, Murry, 94.
Litchfield, David, 142.
Litchfield, Eleazr, 141.
Litchfield, Israel, 141.
Litchfield, John, 141.
Litchfield, Uriah, 141.
Lithbridge, Jon, 138.
Lithbridge, Thos, 138.
Littel, Wm, 132.
Little, Alexander, 103.
Little, Consider, 146.
Little, David, 36.
Little, Deodat, 36.
Little, Ebenezer, 26.
Little, Ephraim, 121.
Little, Gamaliel, 145.
Little, Gamaliel, 146.
Little, Gamaliel, Jnr, 146.
Little, James, 27.
Little, John, 26.
Little, John, 82.
Little, John, 146.
Little, John, 146.
Little, Justin, 121.
Little, Otis, 68.
Little, Robert, 64.
Little, Robt, 137.
Little, Rufus, 134.
Little, Samuel, 105.
Little, Saml, 133.
Little, Thomas, 66.
Little, Walter, 35.
Little, William, 37.
Little, William, 73.
Little, William, 145.
Littlefield, Ebenezr, 153.
Livenston, Daniel, 107.
Livenston, Eunice, 107.
Livesay, James, 28.
Lobdell, Caleb, 28.
Lobdell, Ebenezer, 28.
Lobdell, Josiah, 28.
Lobdell, Phillip, 28.
Lobdell, Uriel, 28.
Lobden, Daniel, 10.
Lobden, John, 10.
Lobden, Lewis, 10.
Lockwood, Abigail (Wd), 25.
Lockwood, Abraham, 15.
Lockwood, Albert, 32.
Lockwood, Amos, 16.
Lockwood, Andrew, 15.
Lockwood, Anny (Wd), 15.
Lockwood, Caleb, 15.
Lockwood, Charles, 24.
Lockwood, Daniel, 24.
Lockwood, Daniel, 24.
Lockwood, Daniel, Jr, 26.
Lockwood, David, 26.
Lockwood, David, 72.
Lockwood, David, Junr, 25.
Lockwood, Ebenezer, 21.
Lockwood, Edmond, 24.
Lockwood, Edward, 15.
Lockwood, Eliphalet, 21.
Lockwood, Eliphalet, 24.
Lockwood, Elizabeth (Wd), 25.
Lockwood, Elnathan, 26.
Lockwood, Enos, 15.
Lockwood, Ephraim, 22.
Lockwood, Ezra, 76.
Lockwood, Frederick, 15.
Lockwood, Freelove (Wd), 25.
Lockwood, George, 15.
Lockwood, Gershom, 16.
Lockwood, Gershom, 23.
Lockwood, Gershom, 25.
Lockwood, Gideon, 32.
Lockwood, Gilbert, 15.
Lockwood, Hannah (Wd), 25.
Lockwood, Hezekiah, 21.
Lockwood, Isaac, 10.
Lockwood, Isaac, 24.
Lockwood, Israel, 16.
Lockwood, Israel, 72.
Lockwood, Jacob, 22.
Lockwood, Jacob, 24.
Lockwood, James, 23.
Lockwood, Jared, 24.
Lockwood, Jeames, 72.
Lockwood, John, 15.
Lockwood, John, 21.
Lockwood, John, 22.
Lockwood, John, 31.
Lockwood, John, 32.
Lockwood, Jonathan, 15.
Lockwood, Jonathan, 25.
Lockwood, Jonathan, Jr., 17.
Lockwood, Jonathan, 3d, 15.
Lockwood, Joseph, 15.
Lockwood, Joseph, 23.
Lockwood, Josiah, 25.
Lockwood, Josiah, 72.
Lockwood, Martha (Wd), 23.
Lockwood, Mary (Wd), 15.
Lockwood, Matthew, 21.
Lockwood, Nathan, 72.
Lockwood, Nathan, 15.
Lockwood, Nathaniel, 16.
Lockwood, Nathaniel, 25.
Lockwood, Nathaniel, 72.
Lockwood, Noah, 15.
Lockwood, Philip, 15.
Lockwood, Reuben, 25.
Lockwood, Rev. S., 134.
Lockwood, Samuel, 15.
Lockwood, Samuel, 22.
Lockwood, Samuel, Jr., 16.
Lockwood, Sarah, 16.
Lockwood, Sarah (Wd), 23.
Lockwood, Seth, 60.
Lockwood, Shubeal, 16.
Lockwood, Stephen, 12.
Lockwood, Stephen, 15.
Lockwood, Stephen, 16.
Lockwood, Stephen, 23.
Lockwood, Thaddeus, 15.
Lockwood, Thaddeus, 25.
Lockwood, Thomas, 21.
Lockwood, Titus, 25.
Lockwood, Unice, 62.
Lockwood, William, 101.
Logan, Samuel, 69.
Loggan, Jeames, 75.
Loggan, Johnson, 75.
Loggan, Mathew, 75.
Lomis, Abner, 132.
Lomis, Abner, 139.
Lomis, Ahiel, 135.
Lomis, Amasa, 132.
Lomis, Andrew, 132.
Lomis, Charles, 132.
Lomis, Daniel, 133.
Lomis, Dan. 133.
Lomis, Danl, Jr, 133.
Lomis, Elijah, 132.
Lomis, Elijah, 132.
Lomis, Elijah, Jr, 132.
Lomis, Elisha, 133.
Lomis, Henry, 134.
Lomis, Hezekiah, 132.
Lomis, Israel, 134.
Lomis, Jacob, 132.
Lomis, Jne, 133.
Lomis, Jos., 132.
Lomis, Jos, 135.
Lomis, Justus, 134.
Lomis, Levy, 132.
Lomis, Mathew, 132.
Lomis, Nathl, 134.
Lomis, Phillip, 136.
Lomis, Roger, 132.
Lomis, Roswel, 132.
Lomis, Simon, 138.
Lomis, Soln, 138.
Lomis, Thos, 132.
Lomis, Zadock, 134.
Lomise, Isaac, 70.
Londen, John, 16.
London, Ambrose, 107.
London, Charles, 57.
London, Charles, 106.
London (Negro), 131.
London (Negroe), 97.
London, William, 74.
Lone, Isaac, 63.
Long, John, 65.
Long, Josiah, 153.
Long, Lemuel, 133.
Long, Lemuel, 2d, 133.
Long (Widow), 138.
Longwell, Stephen, 25.
Longwood, Mathew, 114.
Loomer, Arnold, 126.
Loomer, Ebenr, 126.
Loomer, Lovina, 126.
Loomice, Aaron, 68.
Loomice, Abner, 68.
Loomice, Benona, 68.
Loomice, Ephraim, 68.
Loomice, Ephraim, 68.
Loomice, Fitch, 65.
Loomice, Mary, 68.
Loomice, Moses, 68.
Loomice, Shiphra, 68.
Loomis, Abiah, 55.
Loomis, Abijah, 55.
Loomis, Abner, 140.
Loomis, Andrew, 55.
Loomis, Asa, 145.
Loomis, Asahel, 65.
Loomis, Benajah, 55.
Loomis, Benjamin, 55.
Loomis, Brigadeer, 70.
Loomis, Dan., 55.

# INDEX.

Loomis, Daniel, 66.
Loomis, Dan¹, 141.
Loomis, Doritha, 65.
Loomis, Ebenezer, 58.
Loomis, Eleaz$^r$, 145.
Loomis, Elihu, 38.
Loomis, Elijah, 55.
Loomis, Ezra, 146.
Loomis, Faith, 76.
Loomis, Frances, 48.
Loomis, George, 47.
Loomis, George, 55.
Loomis, Giles, 58.
Loomis, Hezekiah, 38.
Loomis, Isaac, 65.
Loomis, Isaih, 58.
Loomis, Isanor, 68.
Loomis, Israel, 37.
Loomis, Israel, 122.
Loomis, Israel, Jn$^r$, 146.
Loomis, Jacob, 55.
Loomis, Jacob, 125.
Loomis, Jedidiah, 55.
Loomis, Jed, Jur., 55.
Loomis, Jerajah, 55.
Loomis, Joel, 65.
Loomis, Joel, 68.
Loomis, Joel, 146.
Loomis, John, 122.
Loomis, John, 141.
Loomis, Jonah, 37.
Loomis, Joseph, 69.
Loomis, Joseph, 145.
Loomis, Joseph, Ju., 55.
Loomis, Luther, 50.
Loomis, Lydia, 55.
Loomis, Mindwal, 64.
Loomis, Nathan, 146.
Loomis, Nathaniel, 51.
Loomis, Nijah, 55.
Loomis, Noah, 58.
Loomis, Odiah, 55.
Loomis, Oliver, 76.
Loomis, Reuben, 55.
Loomis, Samuel, 121.
Loomis, Samuel, 122.
Loomis, Silas, 52.
Loomis, Simon, 146.
Loomis, Simon, 146.
Loomis, Solomon, 37.
Loomis, Solomon, 121.
Loomis, Stephen, 55.
Loomis, Timothy, 69.
Loomis, Timothy, 116.
Loomis, Watson, 55.
Loomis, Zedekiah, 47.
Loomise, Abraham, 60.
Loomise, Israel, 70.
Loomise, Michael, 60.
Loomise, Roswell, 60.
Loomiss, Abraham, 146.
Loomiss, Amasa, Jr., 38.
Loomiss, Benajah, 38.
Loomiss, Benoni, 146.
Loomiss, Ezekiel, 37.
Loomiss, Ezekiel, 146.
Loomiss, Gideon, 39.
Loomiss, Giles, 37.
Loomiss, Israel, 146.
Loomiss, Jacob, 146.
Loomiss, John, 37.
Loomiss, John, 146.
Loomiss, John, Jr., 38.
Loomiss, Jonathan, 143.
Loomiss, Joseph, 41.
Loomiss, Joseph, 146.
Loomiss, Luke, 37.
Loomiss, Oliver, 37.
Loomiss, Richard, 65.
Loomiss, Roger, 38.
Loomiss, Sarah, 37.
Loomiss, Solomon 38.
Loomiss, Thomas, 145.
Loomiss, Thomas, Jn$^r$, 145.
Looper, Samuel, 2$^d$, 99.
Looper, Samuel F., 99.
Loper, Abraham, 117.
Lorain, Calvin, 57.
Lorain, David, 23.
Lord, Abiel, 89.
Lord, Abigail, 131.
Lord, Abner, 122.
Lord, Abner, Jun$^r$, 122.
Lord, Amos, 123.
Lord, Andrew, 89.
Lord, Benjamin, 123.
Lord, Benj$^n$, 132.
Lord, Daniel, 68.
Lord, Dan¹, 118.
Lord, Daniel, 123.
Lord, Daniel, 131.
Lord, Dan¹, 132.
Lord, Doty, 90.
Lord, Ebenezer, 120.
Lord, Eben$^r$, 132.
Lord, Eleazer, 131.
Lord, Elijah, 66.
Lord, Elijah, 82.
Lord, Elijah, 90.
Lord, Eliphalet, 81.
Lord, Elisha, 41.
Lord, Elisha, 120.
Lord, Elisha, 149.

Lord, Enoch, 123.
Lord, Epafras, 120.
Lord, Ezekiel, 121.
Lord, Frederick, 70.
Lord, George, 38.
Lord, Gold, 27.
Lord, Hezekiah, 130.
Lord, Ichabod, 120.
Lord, Jabez, 130.
Lord, James, 87.
Lord, Jeremiah, 38.
Lord, Jeremiah, 89.
Lord, Jerem$^h$, Jr., 38.
Lord, Joel, 70.
Lord, Joel, 89.
Lord, John, 67.
Lord, John, 74.
Lord, John, 120.
Lord, John, 122.
Lord, John Haynes, 46.
Lord, John H., Jr., 46.
Lord, Joseph, 38.
Lord, Joseph, 123.
Lord, Josiah, 123.
Lord, Leynde, 70.
Lord, Lucy, 130.
Lord, Martha, 89.
Lord, Martin, Esq$^r$, 84.
Lord, Marvin, 123.
Lord, Mary, 89.
Lord, Nathan, 129.
Lord, Nath¹, 83.
Lord, Nath¹, 113.
Lord, Richard, 123.
Lord, Ruben, 123.
Lord, Russel, 89.
Lord, Sam¹, 82.
Lord, Sam¹, 112.
Lord, Sam¹ P., 81.
Lord, Sarah, 32.
Lord, Sarah, 123.
Lord, Simon, 131.
Lord, Solomon, 152.
Lord, Sylvanus, 130.
Lord, Theodore, 121.
Lord, William, 39.
Lord, Will$^m$, 83.
Lord, W$^m$, 89.
Lord, William, 142.
Loreing, Joseph, 17.
Loring, Surviah, 130.
Lorther, Levi, 122.
Lory, Chauncy, 72.
Lose, John, 96.
Lothrop, And$^w$, 126.
Lothrop, Asa, 131.
Lothrop, Azariah, 113.
Lothrop, Azariah, 131.
Lothrop, Daniel, 122.
Lothrop, Darcas, 131.
Lothrop, Ebenezer, 121.
Lothrop, Elijah, 131.
Lothrop, Elijah, Jun$^r$, 131.
Lothrop, Hope, 138.
Lothrop, Icabod, 138.
Lothrop, Rev$^d$ J., 135.
Lothrop, Jedidiah, 112.
Lothrop, Jedidiah, 126.
Lothrop, Jedidiah, 2$^d$, 126.
Lothrop, Jerusha, 131.
Lothrop, Jn$^o$, 138.
Lothrop, Joshua, 131.
Lothrop, Lydia, 131.
Lothrop, Oliver, 121.
Lothrop, Rufus, 131.
Lothrop, S. (Widow of), 138.
Lothrop, Sam¹, 126.
Lothrop, Sarah, 126.
Lothrop, Septemius, 113.
Lothrop, Simeon, 113.
Lothrop, Simeon, 126.
Lothrop, Simon, 131.
Lothrop, Thomas, 131.
Lothrop, Unice, 103.
Lothrop, Uriah, 126.
Lothrop (Widow), 138.
Lothrop, Zebadiah, 126.
Lothrop, Zebadiah, 131.
Lott, Peter, 65.
Lotts, John H., 63.
Loud, Asa, 46.
Lounsbury, David, 25.
Lounsbury, Elijah, 25.
Lounsbury, Enos, 25.
Lounsbury, Gideon, 25.
Lounsbury, Jacob, 25.
Lounsbury, James, 25.
Lounsbury, John, 25.
Lounsbury, Michael, 25.
Lounsbury, Monmouth, 25.
Lounsbury, Nathan, 25.
Lounsbury, Nath$^{el}$, 25.
Lounsbury, Nath$^{el}$, Jr, 25.
Loury, Samuel, 35.
Louse, Abram, 50.
Love, Charles, 47.
Love, Robart, 113.
Love, William, 47.
Lovegrove, Edward, 145.
Lovejoy, Abner, 75.
Lovel, Joseph, 60.
Loveland, Aaron, 43.
Loveland, Ashbel, 95.

Loveland, Clarke, 96.
Loveland, Daniel, 81.
Loveland, Darcus, 86.
Loveland, Deborah, 42.
Loveland, Eli, 42.
Loveland, Elisha, 34.
Loveland, Elizur, 43.
Loveland, John, 43.
Loveland, John, 52.
Loveland, Lazarus, 42.
Loveland, Levi, 43.
Loveland, Nathan, 43.
Loveland, Peletiah, 43.
Loveland, Solomon, 42.
Loveland, Thomas, 42.
Loveland, Thomas, 43.
Loveland, Titus, 96.
Loveland, Trent, 96.
Loveland, Trueman, 95.
Loveland, William, 52.
Loveland, William, 52.
Loveland, Zile, 61.
Loveless, Richard, 11.
Lovell, Joshua, 60.
Loveman, Aaron, 67.
Loveman, Alpheas, 135.
Loveman, John, 96.
Loveman, Joseph, 94.
Loveman, Susanna, 123.
Lovemond, Lewis, 94.
Loverige, Abner, 122.
Loverige, David, 122.
Loverige, Edward, 122.
Loverige, John, 122.
Loverige, Noah, 122.
Loverige, William, 122.
Lovett, Joseph, 127.
Lovewell, Fredrick, 107.
Lovijoy, Phineas, 50.
Lowell, Willibe, 64.
Lowly, Volentine, 72.
Lownbury, Elias, 112.
Lownbury, Stephen, 112.
Lownbury, Timothy, 112.
Lownbury, Timothy, 2$^{nd}$, 112.
Lownsbury, David, 34.
Lownsbury, Lyles, 112.
Lownsbury, Samuel, 34.
Lownsby, John, 110.
Lowrey, Nathan, 61.
Lowry, David, 54.
Loyd, Jabez, 105.
Lucas, Abner, 87.
Lucas, Amaziah, 104.
Lucas, Israel, 78.
Lucas, John, 81.
Lucas, Moses, 87.
Lucas, Moses, Jun$^r$, 87.
Lucas, Park, 120.
Lucas, Pricilla, 86.
Lucas, Richard, 97.
Lucas, Samuel, 81.
Lucas, Samuel, 87.
Lucas, Thomas, 87.
Lucas, William, 120.
Lucass, Sam¹, 90.
Luce, Ebenezer, 153.
Luce, Jon$^a$, 138.
Luce, Jos., 138.
Luce, Joshua, 66.
Luce, Luke, 136.
Luce, Mark, 61.
Luce, Mehitable, 153.
Lucus, John, 37.
Lucus, John, 67.
Ludd, Ezekiel, 39.
Luddenton, Mary, 97.
Luddington, David, 76.
Luddington, Eliphalet, 59.
Luddington, Jesse, 97.
Luddington, Nathaniel, 57.
Ludeman, John, 11.
Ludington, Aaron, 66.
Ludington, Collins, 33.
Ludington, Daniel, 33.
Ludington, Jesse, Jun$^r$, 97.
Ludington, Rachel, 97.
Ludington, Stephen, 70.
Luice, Elisha, 62.
Luice, Ezekiel, 62.
Luke, John, 128.
Luke (Negro), 91.
Luke (Negroe), 104.
Luke (Negroe), 104.
Lull, James, 137.
Lum, Henry, 73.
Lum, Joseph, 94.
Lum, Ruben, 94.
Lumm, Adam, 73.
Lumn, Jonathan, 94.
Lumn, Jonathan, 2$^{nd}$, 94.
Lumn, Jonathan, 3$^{rd}$, 95.
Lumn, Samuel, 94.
Lumsdale, Hatham, 111.
Lunt, Sarah, 130.
Lusk, David, 33.
Lusk, David, Jr., 33.
Lusk, Elata, 33.
Lusk, James, 41.
Lusk, James, 54.
Lusk, John, 33.
Lusk, Seth, 33.

Luther, 150.
Luther, Benjamin, 124.
Luther, Isaac, 150.
Luther, Levi, 126.
Luther, Martin, 65.
Luttenden, Samuel, 97.
Luttinton, Oliver, 108.
Lydia (Negro), 120.
Lyel, Robert, 91.
Lyman, Abel, 96.
Lyman, Aron, 107.
Lyman, Asa, 133.
Lyman, Benj$^n$, 146.
Lyman, Caleb, 62.
Lyman, David, 70.
Lyman, David, 89.
Lyman, David, 133.
Lyman, Ebenezer, 62.
Lyman, Elijah, 133.
Lyman, Eliphalet, 154.
Lyman, Elisha, 129.
Lyman, Francis, 70.
Lyman, Fredrick, 146.
Lyman, Ichabod, 47.
Lyman, Jabez, 145.
Lyman, Jacob, 132.
Lyman, Jesse, 146.
Lyman, Joab, 134.
Lyman, Jona$^{th}$, 145.
Lyman, Joseph, 37.
Lyman, Josiah, 70.
Lyman, Mary, 102.
Lyman, Moses, 70.
Lyman, Moses, 71.
Lyman, Noah, 49.
Lyman, Noah, 96.
Lyman, Phineas, 107.
Lyman, Russell, 95.
Lyman, Ruth, 64.
Lyman, Samuel, 42.
Lyman, Sarah, 94.
Lyman, Silas, 134.
Lyman, Simeon, 62.
Lyman, Simeon, 66.
Lyman, Thaddeas, 51.
Lyman, Thomas, 96.
Lyman, Timothy, 46.
Lyman, William, 36.
Lyman, William, 145.
Lyman, William, 146.
Lyman, Rev$^d$ W$^m$., 82.
Lymans, Aaron, 66.
Lymans, Aaron, 66.
Lymans, Hezikah, 66.
Lymans, William, 66.
Lymar, Elihu, 103.
Lymon, Robert, 29.
Lynde, Daniel, 72.
Lynde, Joseph, 72.
Lynde, Reuben, 59.
Lynde, W$^m$, 89.
Lyndes, Sam¹, 91.
Lynds, Benjamin, 29.
Lynes, Abram, 73.
Lynes, John, 27.
Lynes, John, 153.
Lyon, Aaron, 45.
Lyon, Amos, 16.
Lyon, Amos, 154.
Lyon, Andrew, 27.
Lyon, Andrew, 31.
Lyon, Arel, 27.
Lyon, Benjamin, 15.
Lyon, Benjamin, 154.
Lyon, Bethuel, 78.
Lyon, Betty, 19.
Lyon, Caleb, 15.
Lyon, Caleb, Jun$^r$, 16.
Lyon, Chester, 146.
Lyon, Daniel, 15.
Lyon, Daniel, 16.
Lyon, Daniel, 27.
Lyon, Daniel, 31.
Lyon, Dan¹, 153.
Lyon, Daniel, 3$^d$, 15.
Lyon, David, 15.
Lyon, Ebenezer, 31.
Lyon, Eben$^r$, 142.
Lyon, Eben$^r$, 154.
Lyon, Elijah, 154.
Lyon, Elizabeth, 82.
Lyon, Ephraim, 32.
Lyon, Ephraim, 141.
Lyon,Ephraim, 142.
Lyon, Ezekiel, 31.
Lyon, Ezra, 27.
Lyon, Filo, 27.
Lyon, George, 154.
Lyon, Gershom, 31.
Lyon, Gilbert, 15.
Lyon, Gilbert, Jun$^r$, 15.
Lyon, Grace, 27.
Lyon, Hezekiah, 32.
Lyon, Humphrey, 81.
Lyon, Isaac, 31.
Lyon, Isaiah, 154.
Lyon, James, 15.
Lyon, James, Jun$^r$., 15.
Lyon, James, 3$^d$, 15.
Lyon, Job, 15.
Lyon, Jona$^{th}$, 154.

Lyon, Joseph, 31.
Lyon, Joshua, 15.
Lyon, Josiah, 81.
Lyon, Lemuel, 27.
Lyon, Lois, 72.
Lyon, Lymon, 137.
Lyon, Nathan, 27.
Lyon, Nathan, 141.
Lyon, Nathaniel, 27.
Lyon, Nathaniel, 103.
Lyon, Nath¹, 154.
Lyon, Nehemiah, 153.
Lyon, Noah, 16.
Lyon, Palatia, 22.
Lyon, Robert, 143.
Lyon Sabry, 154.
Lyon, Sarah, 31.
Lyon, Shubeal, 15.
Lyon, Stephen, 15.
Lyon, Stephen, 31.
Lyon, Stephen, 153.
Lyon, Thomas, 31.
Lyon, Tho$^s$, 149.
Lyon, Tho$^s$, 154.
Lyon, Walter, 31.
Lyon, Walter, 149.
Lyon, Wareham, 154.
Lyon, Webb, 31.
Lyon, William, 103.
Lyon, W$^m$, 154.
Lyon, William, Jn$^r$ 154.
Lyon, Zacheriah, 31.
Lyon, Zacheriah, Jun$^r$, 31.
Lyon, Zurviah, 149.
Lyons, David, 30.
Lyons, John, 124.
Lyons, John, 142.

M$^c$——, Jos., 135.
M$^c$——, Orlander, 135.
M$^c$——, Ralph, 135.
M$^c$Alpine, John, 46.
M$^c$Call, Daniel, 120.
M$^c$Call, Jacob, 121.
M$^c$Call, John, 126.
M$^c$Can, Francis, 121.
M'Canasy, Betty, 63.
M$^c$Cane, Barnabas, 100.
M$^c$Carter, John, Jun$^r$, 121.
M$^c$Cary, Elisabeth, 122.
M$^c$Cary, Sam¹, Jun$^r$, 122.
MCaul Angus, 16.
M$^c$Caul, Arch$^a$, 145.
M$^c$Caul, Eleaz$^r$, 147.
M$^c$Caul, Elijah, 147.
M$^c$Caul, Holbart, 145.
M$^c$Caul, Mary, 147.
M$^c$Caul, Roger, 145.
M$^c$Cawl, Green, 145.
M$^c$Cawl, John, 145.
M$^c$Cawl, Ozias, 145.
M$^c$Cimter, Hugh, 148.
M$^c$Civers, Daniel, 39.
M$^c$Clallen, Sam¹, 154.
M$^c$Clane, John, 10.
M$^c$Claud, John, 109.
M$^c$Cleave, John, 79.
M$^c$Cleave, John, 107.
M$^c$Clen, Alexander, 132.
M$^c$Clen, Lethman, 132.
M$^c$Clester, Eliza$^{th}$ (Wid.), 39.
M$^c$Clester, James, 39.
M$^c$Clester, John, 39.
M$^c$Clure, Rev$^d$ David, 37.
M$^c$Clure, Robert, 67.
M$^c$Collum, Dan¹, 91.
M$^c$Colton, Rev, 132.
M$^c$Comb, John, 79.
M$^c$Combs, Andrew, 53.
M$^c$Corney, William, 79.
M$^c$Corney, William, Jun$^r$, 79.
M$^c$Coy, Few, 29.
M$^c$Coy, James, 105.
M$^c$Coy, Jn$^o$, 134.
M$^c$Crackin, James, 120.
M$^c$Craken, William, 103.
M$^c$Cray, Calvin, 134.
M$^c$Cray, Jn$^o$, 134.
M$^c$Cray, W$^m$, 134.
M$^c$Cune, Garsham, 63.
M$^c$Cune, Gersham, 63.
M$^c$Cune, Sam¹, 63.
M$^c$Curdy, Ann, 123.
M$^c$Curdy, John, 118.
M$^c$Curdy, Lynds, 131.
M$^c$Curgen, Alexander, 93.
M$^c$Curn, Malecton, 105.
M$^c$Daniel, David, 76.
M$^c$Daniel, James, 76.
M$^c$Daniel, James, 116.
M$^c$Donald, Abigal, 100.
M$^c$Donald, Elexander, 131.
M$^c$Donald, Jerrents, 60.
M$^c$Donald, Mathew, 129.
M$^c$Donnal, Elves, 94.
M$^c$Euin, Abijah, 30.
M$^c$Euin, Daniel, 30.
M$^c$Euin, John, 30.
M$^c$Euin, Matthew, 30.
M$^c$Ewen, John, 1$^{st}$, 72.
M$^c$Ewen, John, 2$^d$, 72.
M$^c$Ewen, William, 72.
M$^c$Fall, William, 124.

# INDEX. 197

McFarden, Thomas, 28.
McGee (Wid.), 136.
McGollsgal, James, 151.
McGound (Wid.), 136.
McGregory, Ebenr, 136.
McGrigery, John, 40.
McHolland, Hugh, 105.
McIntire, Benjn, 149.
McIntosh, Rachel, 122.
Mack, Andrew, 54.
Mack, Benjamin, 68.
Mack, Daniel, 61.
Mack, Ebenezer, 124.
Mack, Ebenr, 124.
Mack, Gurdan, 68.
Mack, Josiah, 123.
Mack, Richd, 82.
Mack, Samuel, Junr, 123.
Mack, William, 124.
Mack, Zebulon, 68.
Mack, Zophar, 124.
McKay, John, 16.
McKee, Andrew, 37.
McKee, Appleton, 37.
McKee, Eleazer, 37.
McKee, Elijah, 37.
McKee, John, 37.
McKee, Joseph, 37.
McKee, Nathaniel, 37.
McKee, Nathl, 132.
McKee, Robert, 37.
McKee, Robert, Jr., 37.
McKein, James, 49.
McKeinster, John, 41.
McKensey, George, 145.
McKentin, Duncan, 72.
McKenzie, John, 102.
McKey, Phinehas, 88.
McKeys, Daniel, 107.
McKinly, William, 66.
McKinna, Alexander, 132.
McKinna, Alexander, Jr., 132.
McKinna, Andrew, 134.
McKinna, James, 134.
McKinna, James, 134.
McKinna, James, 3d, 134.
McKinna, Wm, 134.
McKinstry, Elezer, 134.
Mackintire, Duncan, 86.
Mackintosh, Andrew, 139.
Mackintosh, Lothlin, 122.
McKnary, Martin, 84.
McKnawt, James, 138.
McKnite, Jno, 134.
McKune, James, 18.
McLean, Allen, 55.
McLean, James, 43.
McLean, John, 55.
McLean, Niel, 47.
McLin, John, 62.
McLlewer, David, 136.
McMehan, Cornelius, 72.
McMoran, John, 2d, 51.
McMorin, John, 51.
McNab, Alexander, 23.
McNeal, Roswell, 65.
McNeil, Archabald, 103.
McNeil, Saml, 66.
McNeil, William, 103.
McNiel, Alexander, 65.
McNiel, Archebald, 65.
McNiel, Isaac, 64.
McNight, Abigail, 38.
McNire, James, 65.
McPherson, Joseph, 88.
McQueen, Trefina, 91.
McRay, James, 14.
Macumber, Jeremiah, 104.
McVay, Jno, 132.
Macy, Asael, 154.
Macy, Jonath, 154.
Macy, Mathew, 140.
Magill, Arther, 86.
Magill, Charles, 86.
Magney, Lucretia, 89.
Mago, Thomas, 126.
Magraw, John, 30.
Mahan, Phillip, 105.
Mahanna, John, 86.
Maharr, James, 79.
Maher, Dan, 134.
Main, Caleb, 59.
Main, Ezekial, 58.
Main, Ezekiel, 35.
Main, Hannah, 59.
Main, John, 59.
Main, Jonathan, 59.
Main, Russel, 111.
Maine, Amos, 116.
Maine, Asa, 115.
Maine, Asa, Junr, 115.
Maine, Benaijah, 116.
Maine, Daniel, 116.
Maine, David, 116.
Maine, David, Junr, 115.
Maine, Jonas, 115.
Maine, Luther, 116.
Maine, Lyman, 115.
Maine, Nathl, 115.
Maine, Nathl, 148.
Maine, Peckham, 113.
Maine, Peres, 113.
Maine, Peter, 115.

Maine, Peter, Junr, 115.
Maine, Peter, 3d, 115.
Maine, Rufus, 114.
Maine, Thos, 140.
Maine, Timothy, 116.
Maine, Timothy, Junr, 116.
Maker, Danl, 137.
Malay, Aliff, 128.
Malbey, Benjamin, 39.
Malbey, Jonathan, 14.
Malbey, Zacheus, 69.
Malbone, Charles, 133.
Malborne, Peter, 141.
Malery, Benjamin, 102.
Malery, Calep, 17.
Malery, Daniel, 27.
Malery, Daniel, 27.
Malery, Ebenezer, 20.
Malery, John, 27.
Malery, Jonathan, 27.
Malery, Mary (Wid.), 20.
Malery, Nathan, 27.
Malery, Samuel, 27.
Malery, Thomas, 20.
Malery (Widow), 105.
Mallerey, Elijah, 75.
Mallerson, Elisha, 118.
Mallerson, Ezra, 118.
Mallerson, Joseph, 118.
Mallerson, Roswell, 118.
Mallerson, Thomas, 118.
Mallery, Aaron, 78.
Mallery, Adna, 78.
Mallery, Amos, 60.
Mallery, Amos, 97.
Mallery, Aron, 101.
Mallery, Asa, 97.
Mallery, Benajah, 18.
Mallery, Benjamin, 97.
Mallery, Daniel, 93.
Mallery, Daniel, 101.
Mallery, David, 73.
Mallery, David, 78.
Mallery, David, 78.
Mallery, David, 127.
Mallery, Eliakim, 57.
Mallery, Elinor, 105.
Mallery, Elisha, 60.
Mallery, Gideon, 17.
Mallery, Gideon, 78.
Mallery, Ithamar, 75.
Mallery, Jacob, 76.
Mallery, Jesse, 97.
Mallery, John, 73.
Mallery, John, 78.
Mallery, John, 2d, 78.
Mallery, Joseph, 110.
Mallery, Levi, 14.
Mallery, Levi, 97.
Mallery, Mabel, 97.
Mallery, Mary, 97.
Mallery, Moses, 101.
Mallery, Moses, 102.
Mallery, Mosses, 101.
Mallery, Samuel, 69.
Mallery, Samuel, 102.
Mallery, Thomas, 78.
Mallery, Walker, 78.
Mallet, Benjamin, 30.
Mallet, David, 80.
Mallet, David, Junr, 30.
Mallet, Edmon, 10.
Mallet, John, 30.
Mallet, John, 101.
Mallet, Joseph, 30.
Mallet, Lewis, 14.
Mallet, Lewis, 101.
Mallet, Martha (Wid.), 30.
Mallet, Philip, 30.
Mallet, Philo, 17.
Mallet, Samuel, 30.
Mallet, Seth, 30.
Mallet, Zacheriah, 30.
Mallet, Zalmon, 30.
Mallett, Miles, 73.
Mallory, Capt Nathan, 21.
Mallory, Polly (Wd), 21.
Malone, Danael, 103.
Malson, Asa, 48.
Maltbey, Jseph, 65.
Maltbie, David, 24.
Maltbie, Huldah, 78.
Maltby, Benjamin, 92.
Maltby, Benjamin, 2d, 92.
Maltby, James, 92.
Maltby, Jane, 99.
Maltby, John, 92.
Maltby, Jonathan, 91.
Maltby, Stephen, 92.
Man, Abeather, 37.
Man, Benjamin, 37.
Man, Elijah, 135.
Man, Jabez, 18.
Man, Joel, 135.
Man, Richard, 17.
Man, Richard, 29.
Manchant, Enoch, 27.
Manchester, Thomas, 127.
Mand, Dependence, 17.
Mane, Andrew, 139.
Mane, Andrew, Jr., 139.
Mane, Elias, 139.
Mane, Josa, 139.

Mane, Ruben, 139.
Maneer, John, 101.
Manfield, Ichabod, 69.
Manger, Ebenezer, 98.
Manger, Ebenezer, 2d, 98.
Manger, Jesse, 98.
Manierre, Lewis, 129.
Manley, Allen, 56.
Manley, George, 134.
Manley, Joseph, 133.
Manley, Sylvester, 146.
Mann, Abijah, 135.
Mann, Andrew, 135.
Mann, Elisha, 99.
Mann, Jno, 135.
Mann, Jos, 135.
Mann, Phillip, 98.
Manning, Andrew, 133.
Manning, Bela, 154.
Manning, Calvin, 133.
Manning, David, 61.
Manning, Diah, 131.
Manning, Eleazr, 146.
Manning, Fredrick, 152.
Manning, Gamaliel, 128.
Manning, Hezekiah, 152.
Manning, Joel, 152.
Manning, John, 144.
Manning, Josiah, 129.
Manning, Josiah, 152.
Manning, Latham, 128.
Manning, Luther, 112.
Manning, Rockwell, 131.
Manning, Seabury, 152.
Manning, Thomas, 64.
Manning, William, 154.
Mannon, Samuel, 17.
Manoil, David, 76.
Mansfield, Revd Achileus, 85.
Mansfield, Calvin, 152.
Mansfield, David, 104.
Mansfield, David, 58.
Mansfield, Deborah, 104.
Mansfield, Ebenezer, 100.
Mansfield, Ester, 102.
Mansfield, Hannah, 100.
Mansfield, Henry, 103.
Mansfield, J., 100.
Mansfield, Jerad, 103.
Mansfield, John, 107.
Mansfield, John, 152.
Mansfield, Joseph, 59.
Mansfield, Moses, 104.
Mansfield, Nathan, 94.
Mansfield, Richard, 95.
Mansfield, Richard, 106.
Mansfield, Richard, 2nd, 94.
Mansfield, Richstead, 104.
Mansfield, Stephen, 96.
Mansfield, Thomas, 106.
Mansfield, Titus, 100.
Mansfield, William, 94.
Mansfield, William, 103.
Mansfield, William, 132.
Manson, Ebenezer, 11.
Mantle, Jacob, 145.
Manvil, Simeon, 78.
Manville, James, 94.
Manwaring, Adam, 124.
Manwaring, Asa, 125.
Manwaring, Christopher, 125.
Manwaring, David, 128.
Manwaring, George, 125.
Manwaring, George, 2d, 125.
Manwaring, Isaac, 127.
Manwaring, Jabez, 127.
Manwaring, John, 125.
Manwaring, John, 129.
Manwaring, Josiah, 124.
Manwaring, Latham, 124.
Manwaring, Lydia, 129.
Manwaring, Nathl, 124.
Manwaring, Oliver, 127.
Manwaring, Peter, 124.
Manwaring, Robart, 127.
Manwaring, Thomas, 127.
Maples, John, 125.
Maples, Jona, 130.
Maples, Josiah, 125.
Maples, Stephen, 125.
Maples, Stephen, Junr, 125.
Maples, William, 125.
Maples, William, 2d, 125.
Marble, Betsey, 85.
Marble, John, 146.
Marble, Thos, 135.
Marchal, Ruben, 137.
Marchall, Icabod, 132.
Marchall, William, 91.
Marchant, Ashbel, 61.
Marchant, Chaney, 27.
Marchant, Elenar, 27.
Marchant, Elijah, 61.
Marchant, Ezra, 72.
Marchant, Ezra, 101.
Marchant, Mary, 102.
Marchant, Sarah, 75.
Marchant, Thomas, 1st, 76.
Marchant, Thomas, 2d, 77.
Marchant, Unice, 61.
Marckum, Barzilla, 40.
Marcy, Benjamin, 147.
Marcy, Elisha, 153.

Marcy, Jereh, 151.
Marcy, Saml, 140.
Marcy, Thomas, 140.
Marcy, Uriah, 153.
Marcy, Zebh, 139.
Marcy, Zebediah, 2d, 139.
Mariner, Mary, 121.
Marines, Ephraim, 61.
Marion, David, 57.
Mark, Ezra, 123.
Mark, Hezh, 81.
Mark, Miles, 33.
Mark (Negro), 51.
Mark (negroe), 96.
Markaniff, Charles, 129.
Markem, James, 67.
Markham, Ebenezer, 87.
Markham, Ezekiel, 69.
Markham, James, 81.
Markham, Jehiel, 40.
Markham, Justus, 40.
Markham, Nathan, 39.
Markham, Nathaniel, 81.
Markham, Samuel, 87.
Markham, Sarah, 87.
Marklam, John, 81.
Markland, Jeremiah, 87.
Marks, Abraham, 102.
Marks, Aholiab, 118.
Marks, David, 35.
Marks, Edward, 35.
Marks, James, 107.
Marks, Levi, 107.
Marks, Mordica, 17.
Marks, William, 52.
Marks, William, 88.
Marks, Zachariah, 35.
Marks, Zacheriah, 102.
Markum, Abigail, 38.
Markum, Darius, 40.
Markum, Isaac, 39.
Marnard, Zachariah, 138.
Marp, Benoni, 76.
Marren, John, 101.
Marrion, Benja, 150.
Marrion, Israel, 150.
Marrion, Joseph, 150.
Marrion, Joseph, Junr, 150.
Marross, Elijah, 34.
Marross, Elisha, 34.
Marsen, Stephen, 100.
Marsh, Allyn, 37.
Marsh, Ambrose, 70.
Marsh, Anne, 145.
Marsh, Anos, 62.
Marsh, Ashbel, 65.
Marsh, Daniel, 37.
Marsh, Daniel, 63.
Marsh, Dan., 146.
Marsh, Ebenezer, 64.
Marsh, Edmond, 82.
Marsh, Eli, 54.
Marsh, Elijah, 70.
Marsh, Elisha, 66.
Marsh, George, 70.
Marsh, Isaiah, 60.
Marsh, James, 70.
Marsh, Jesse, 46.
Marsh, Jessie, 69.
Marsh, Job, 62.
Marsh, Job, 63.
Marsh, John, 46.
Marsh, John, 52.
Marsh, John, 54.
Marsh, John, 63.
Marsh, John, 64.
Marsh, John, 72.
Marsh, John, 82.
Marsh, John, Jr., 54.
Marsh, Jonathan, 63.
Marsh, Jonathan, 67.
Marsh, Jonathan, 69.
Marsh, Jonathan, 131.
Marsh, Joseph, 72.
Marsh, Leml, 82.
Marsh, Mary, 46.
Marsh, Moses, 69.
Marsh, Nathl, 148.
Marsh, Nehenemiah, 69.
Marsh, Rhoda, 70.
Marsh, Robert, 103.
Marsh, Roger, 70.
Marsh, Rufus, 62.
Marsh, Samuel, 46.
Marsh, Samuel, 72.
Marsh, Saml, 82.
Marsh, Samuel, 2d, 46.
Marsh, Solomon, 66.
Marsh, Thankful, 62.
Marsh, Thomas, 70.
Marsh, Titus, 70.
Marshal, Amos, 54.
Marshal, Eliakim, Jur, 55.
Marshal, Joseph, 102.
Marshal, Saml, 55.
Marshal, Saml, 55.
Marshal, Sam., Jur., 55.
Marshal, Sarah, 78.
Marshal, Seth, 78.
Marshal, Thos, 81.
Marshall, Abiel, 126.
Marshall, Alexander, 48.
Marshall, Andrew, 15.

Marshall, Bryan, 94.
Marshall, Eliakim, 41.
Marshall, Eliakim, 55.
Marshall, Elisha, 55.
Marshall, Ezra, 15.
Marshall, Gilbert, 16.
Marshall, Henry, 16.
Marshall, Isaac, 15.
Marshall, Isaac E., 94.
Marshall, Jeremiah, 122.
Marshall, John, 102.
Marshall, Joseph, 127.
Marshall, Polly, 24.
Marshall, Thomas, 15.
Marshall, Thomas, 131.
Marshall, Timothy, 55.
Marshe, Woodward, 82.
Marshnite, Zebalon, 67.
Marten, Francis, 111.
Martenus, Goodard, 125.
Marther, Richard, 60.
Marther, Zachariah, 69.
Martial, Aaron, 68.
Martial, Abner, 60.
Martial, Danl, 66.
Martial, Deota, 60.
Martial, John, 64.
Martial, Joseph, 60.
Martial, Joseph, 63.
Martial, Josiah, 64.
Martial, Sarah, 65.
Martial, Thomas, 60.
Martin, Abijah, 78.
Martin, Amasa, 143.
Martin, Amos, 78.
Martin, Anderson, 145.
Martin, Andrew, 56.
Martin, Asahel, 64.
Martin, Benjn, 143.
Martin, Benjn, 143.
Martin, David, 143.
Martin, David, 154.
Martin, Ebenezr, 147.
Martin, Elijah, 78.
Martin, Eliphalet, 70.
Martin, Elizabeth, 93.
Martin, George, 143.
Martin, George, 153.
Martin, Gold, 78.
Martin, Henry, 154.
Martin, Israel, 112.
Martin, Isaac, 78.
Martin, John, 78.
Martin, John, 93.
Martin, John, 105.
Martin, John, 144.
Martin, John, 147.
Martin, John, 150.
Martin, John, Jnr, 144.
Martin, Jonas, 78.
Martin, Jonathan, 82.
Martin, Jonathan, 153.
Martin, Joseph, 143.
Martin, Joseph, Jnr, 143.
Martin, Lucy, 56.
Martin, Manassat, 59.
Martin, Nathan, 78.
Martin, Nathan, 2d, 78.
Martin, Nathl, 143.
Martin, Richd, 143.
Martin, Saml, 59.
Martin, Samuel, 76.
Martin, Samuel, 78.
Martin, Samuel, 144.
Martin, Saml, 139.
Martin, Seth, 56.
Martin, Simeon, 56.
Martin, Solomon, 78.
Martin, Stephen, 151.
Martin, Susannah, 102.
Martin, Thankful, 78.
Martin, William, 56.
Martin, William, 143.
Martin, William, 154.
Martin, William, Jnr, 143.
Martin, William, 2d, 56.
Marumberg, Abiel, 104.
Marvin, Barna, 23.
Marvin, Benjamin, 22.
Marvin, Benjamin, 123.
Marvin, Brush, 32.
Marvin, David, 23.
Marvin, Elihu, 130.
Marvin, Elisha, 2d, 123.
Marvin, Hercules, 22.
Marvin, Martin, 62.
Marvin, Joseph, 69.
Marvin, Joseph, 123.
Marvin, Matthew, 21.
Marvin, Mathew, 123.
Marvin, Moses, 123.
Marvin, Nehemiah, 57.
Marvin, Ozias, Junr, 23.
Marvin, Majr Ozias, 23.
Marvin, Raynold, 60.
Marvin, Saml, 21.
Marvin, Samuel, 3d, 21.
Marvin, Seth, 21.
Marvin, Stephen, 23.
Marvin, Timothy, 122.
Marvin, Uriah, 28.
Marvin, Zachariah, 123.

# INDEX.

Marvin, Zachariah, 2d, 123.
Marwell, Edward, 27.
Mascroft, Jacob, 154.
Mashcraft, John, 154.
Masi, Anthony, 142.
Mason, Abraham, 150.
Mason, Andw, 117.
Mason, Cooley, 82.
Mason, David, 130.
Mason, Ebenr, 140.
Mason, Ebenr, 141.
Mason, Elias, 154.
Mason, Elijah, 62.
Mason, Elijah, 91.
Mason, Elijah, Jnr, 145.
Mason, Elijah, Senr, 145.
Mason, Elisha, 64.
Mason, Elnathan, 117.
Mason, Hale, 150.
Mason, Harmon, 64.
Mason, Henry, 119.
Mason, Isaac, 46.
Mason, James, 146.
Mason, James F., 145.
Mason, Japhet, 128.
Mason, Jeremiah, 145.
Mason, Jinks, 152.
Mason, John, 140.
Mason, Jonathan, 66.
Mason, Joshua, 64.
Mason, Luther, 66.
Mason, Nehemiah, 117.
Mason, Noah, 154.
Mason, Patience, 128.
Mason, Pellatiah, 144.
Mason, Peter, 63.
Mason, Peter, 105.
Mason, Peter, 121.
Mason, Rebacca, 66.
Mason, Samuel, 117.
Mason, Saml, 128.
Mass, Elihu, 49.
Masterns, James, 86.
Masters, James, 19.
Masters, John, 78.
Masters, John, 2d, 78.
Masters, N. Shelton, 72.
Mastial, Raphel, 62.
Matcher, John, 30.
Matery, John, 90.
Mather, Augustus, 82
Mather, Azariah, 54.
Mather, Azariah, Ju., 54.
Mather, Charles, 38.
Mather, Charles, 60.
Mather, Cotton, 54.
Mather, David, 33.
Mather, Eleazer, 122.
Mather, Eleazer, Junr, 122.
Mather, Eliakim, 54.
Mather, Elijah, 54.
Mather, Elijah, Jur, 54.
Mather, Elisha, 89.
Mather, Frederick, 122.
Mather, Gibeons, 121.
Mather, Hannah, 89.
Mather, Increase, 51.
Mather, Increase, 55.
Mather, Jehaiada, 123.
Mather, John, 124.
Mather, John, 2d, 124.
Mather, Joseph, 24.
Mather, Joseph, 33.
Mather, Joseph, 54.
Mather, Joseph, 123.
Mather, Joseph, Jr., 33.
Mather, Lucinda, 123.
Mather, Revd Moses, 26.
Mather, Nathl, 56.
Mather, Nathl, 123.
Mather, Noyes, 24.
Mather, Oliver, 55.
Mather, Samuel, 27.
Mather, Samuel, 123.
Mather, Saml, Junr, 123.
Mather, Sarah, 123.
Mather, Silvester, 123.
Mather, Timothy, 123.
Mather, Timothy, 2d, 123.
Mathews, Amos, 92.
Mathews, Asahel, 81.
Mathews, Caleb, 34.
Mathews, Elizabeth, 93.
Mathews, Elizabeth, 103.
Mathews, Epaphras, 50.
Mathews, Ephrim, 93.
Mathews, Giddeon, 18.
Mathews, Hester, 93.
Mathews, Hugh, 52.
Mathews, John, 12.
Mathews, John, 34.
Mathews, Joshua, 94.
Mathews, Moses, 50.
Mathews, Moses, Jr., 49.
Mathews, Nathaniel, 25.
Mathews, Nathaniel, Jr., 34.
Mathews, Thomas, 105.
Mathews, Wm, 35.
Mathewson, Caleb, 151.
Mathewson, Dutifull, 151.
Mathewson, Israil, 154.
Mathewson, Jesse, 151.
Mathewson, Joshua, 151.

Mathewson, Reuben, 151.
Mathson, Nathn, 149.
Mathson, Thomas, 151.
Matimer, George, 125.
Matlocks, James, 65.
Matson, Dorcas (Wid.), 44.
Matson, Israel, 123.
Matson, Joseph, 42.
Matson, Thomas, 42.
Matson, Thomas, Jr., 42.
Matson, William, 122.
Mattason, Wm, 138.
Matters, James, 128.
Matthews, Aaron, 76.
Matthews, Amos, 76.
Matthews, Daniel, 76.
Matthews, Lydia, 76.
Matthews, Phineas, 76.
Matthews, Samuel, 76.
Matthews, Stephen, 76.
Matthews, Thomas, 76.
Matthews, William, 76.
Matthewson, George, 151.
Matthias, Bethial (Wd), 26.
Mattison, Royall, 144.
Mattoon, Amasa, 76.
Mattoon, Gorham, 59.
Mattoon, John, 76.
Matune, Caleb, 107.
Matune, Hester, 107.
Matune, Isaac, 107.
Matune, John, 107.
Matune, Samuel, 107.
Mauray, David, 78.
Maverill, John, 78.
Maxfield, Eber, 22.
Maxfield, Joseph, 10.
Maxson, Tony, 124.
Maxwell, James, 148.
Maxwell, Joshua, 152.
Maxwill, John, 146.
May, Caleb, 153.
May, Charles, 38.
May, Edward, 57.
May, Eleakin, 153.
May, Revd Elerzer, 83.
May, Hezekiah, 52.
May, Ithamar, 149.
May, John, 52.
May, John, 55.
May, John, 84.
May, Joseph, 153.
May, Joshua, 153.
May, Rufus, 139.
May, Saml, 150.
May, Samuel, Jr., 52.
May, Silas, 153.
May, Stephen, 153.
May, Thos, 153.
May, William, 52.
Maynard, Christopher, 127.
Maynard, Ebenr, 127.
Maynard, James, 128.
Maynard, James, 130.
Maynard, John, 82.
Maynard, John, 118.
Maynard, Naomi, 127.
Maynard, Stephen, 127.
Maynerd, Elisha, 16.
Maynord, Asael, 131.
Mayo, Elisha, 60.
Mayo, Elisha, 75.
Mayo, Richard, 80.
Mays, Ephraim, 144.
Meach, Aaron, 115.
Meach, Aaron, 118.
Meach, Daniel, 115.
Meach, David, 115.
Meach, Elkanah, 116.
Meach, Esther, 64.
Meach, Jacob, 114.
Meach, Lucy, 114.
Meach, Moses, 114.
Meach, Moses, 115.
Meacham, Asa, 39.
Meacham, Benjamin, 39.
Meacham, Elizabeth(Widw),39.
Meacham, John, 39.
Meacham, Jos, 136.
Meachem, Saml, 136.
Meachum, Aaron, 40.
Meachum, Abner, 40.
Meachum, Jeremiah, 58.
Meachum, Joseph, 40.
Meachum, Joseph, 153.
Meachum, Seth, 143.
Meachum, Simeon, 39.
Meackens, Joseph, 36.
Meacum, Jeremiah, 35.
Mead, Abel, 15.
Mead, Abigail (Wd), 16.
Mead, Abigail (Wd), 16.
Mead, Abijah, 22.
Mead, Abraham, 16.
Mead, Amos, 15.
Mead, Andrew, 15.
Mead, Azor, 22.
Mead, Benjamin, 16.
Mead, Benjamin, 72.
Mead, Calvin, 16.
Mead, Daniel, 16.
Mead, Daniel, 72.
Mead, Daniel, 76.

Mead, David, 16.
Mead, David, 22.
Mead, Ebenezer, 16.
Mead, Eber, 25.
Mead, Edmond, 17.
Mead, Edward, 15.
Mead, Elias, 27.
Mead, Eliphalet, Junr, 16.
Mead, Elkanah, 15.
Mead, Enos, 16.
Mead, Ezra, 24.
Mead, Ezra, 28.
Mead, Hannah, 28.
Mead, Henry, 15.
Mead, Henry, Junr, 16.
Mead, Israel, 15.
Mead, Jabez, 15.
Mead, Jared, 15.
Mead, Jaspar, 15.
Mead, Jasper, 16.
Mead, Jeames, 75.
Mead, Jehiel, 16.
Mead, Jeremiah, 17.
Mead, Jeremiah, 22.
Mead, Jeremiah, 27.
Mead, Jeremiah, 28.
Mead, Jeremiah, Junr., 15.
Mead, Jesse, 16.
Mead, John, 15.
Mead, John, 28.
Mead, John, Junr, 16.
Mead, John Betts, 21.
Mead, Jonah, 15.
Mead, Jonathan, 16.
Mead, Joseph, 15.
Mead, Joseph, 22.
Mead, Joseph, 28.
Mead, Joshua, 15.
Mead, Jotham, 16.
Mead, Matthew, 15.
Mead, Matthew, 22.
Mead, Mehitable (Wd), 22.
Mead, Nathaniel, 16.
Mead, Nathaniel, Junr, 15.
Mead, Nathel, 3d, 15.
Mead, Nehemiah, 15.
Mead, Nehemiah, Jr, 15.
Mead, Peter, 16.
Mead, Philip, 57.
Mead, Prudence (Wd), 17.
Mead, Reuben, 25.
Mead, Reuben, Junr, 24.
Mead, Ruth (Wd), 16.
Mead, Samuel, 72.
Mead, Sarah (Wd), 25.
Mead, Shadrach, 16.
Mead, Sibela (Wd), 16.
Mead, Silas, 16.
Mead, Smith, 15.
Mead, Stephen, 15.
Mead, Thaddeus, 22.
Mead, Titus, 15.
Mead, Titus, Junr, 15.
Mead, Uriah, 27.
Mead, Whitman, 16.
Mead, William, 28.
Mead, Zacheus, 16.
Mead, Zebediah, 16.
Meade, Jno, 133.
Meads, Jno, 134.
Meaker, David, 26.
Measureall, Christopher, 33.
Mecantire, Stephen, 67.
Mecher, David, 75.
Mechum, Barnibus, 69.
Mechum, Isaac, 61.
Mechum, Joel, 68.
Mechum, Johiel, 69.
Mechum, Nehemiah, 58.
Mechum, Seth, 58.
Mechur, Levi, 61.
Medcalf, Abigal, 145.
Medcalf, Andrew, 145.
Medcalf, David, 145.
Medcalf, Ebenezr, 145.
Medcalf, Ebenezr, 147.
Medcalf, Eliphalet, 145.
Medcalf, Jabez, 145.
Medcalf, Levi, 146.
Medcalf, Peter, 145.
Medcalf, Reuben, 146.
Medcalf, Saml, 146.
Medcalf, Zebulon, 145.
Meecker, Josiah, 130.
Meeker, Abigail, 14.
Meeker, Benjamin, 13.
Meeker, Daniel, 13.
Meeker, Daniel, 96.
Meeker, David, 15.
Meeker, David, 20.
Meeker, Elonyer, 27.
Meeker, Ephraim, 27.
Meeker, Hezekiah, 15.
Meeker, Ichobud, 14.
Meeker, Igaci, 27.
Meeker, Isaac, 27.
Meeker, Isaac, 31.
Meeker, John, 96.
Meeker, Jonathan, 27.
Meeker, Joseph, 13.
Meeker, Justus, 14.
Meeker, Liman, 14.

Meeker, Nathaniel, 106.
Meeker, Ogden, 27.
Meeker, Peter, 14.
Meeker, Seth, 13.
Meeker, Seth, 27.
Meeker, Seth, Jnr, 12.
Meeker, Stephen, 13.
Meeker, Thankfull, 14.
Mehagan, Dennis, 131.
Meiggs, Jesso, 56.
Meiggs, Phineas, 56.
Meigs, Abigal, 99.
Meigs, Daniel, 99.
Meigs, Elish, 99.
Meigs, Elias, 99.
Meigs, Felix, 92.
Meigs, Giles, 85.
Meigs, Janne, 69.
Meigs, John, 86.
Meigs, Lucy, 99.
Meigs, Nathaniel, 98.
Meigs, Phineas, 96.
Meigs, Phineas, 99.
Meigs, Return Jona, 86.
Meigs, Timothy, 99.
Meker, Chauncy, 72.
Melally, Michael, 126.
Melona, Michael, 88.
Melona, William, 128.
Meloy, Edward, 104.
Meloy, Edward, 2d, 103.
Meloy, John, 105.
Mencer, William, 100.
Menter, Daniel, 66.
Mentor, 21.
Mentor, John, 122.
Mentor, Thomas, 24.
Mercer, Absolam, 97.
Merchant, John, 19.
Merchant, Joseph, 63.
Merchant, Samuel, 102.
Mercy, Abraham, 154.
Mercy, Ichabod, 154.
Mercy, Israel, 154.
Mercy, Israel, Jnr, 154.
Mercy, Jno, 137.
Mercy, Nathl, 154.
Mercy, Reubin, 140.
Merey, John, 154.
Meriam, George, 58.
Meriam, Munson, 93.
Meriam, Munson, 2d, 93.
Meriam, Samuel, 93.
Meriam, William, 58.
Merills, Heck, 62.
Merills, Soloman, 62.
Meriman, Amasa, 68.
Meriman, Nathaniel, 106.
Merit, Ebenezer, 27.
Merrel, Timothy, 95.
Merrells, Verijah, 70.
Merriam, Benja, 150.
Merriam, Charles, 76.
Merriam, Christopher, 76.
Merriam, George, 85.
Merriam, Isaac, 76.
Merriam, James, 76.
Merriam, Joel, 76.
Merriam, John, 76.
Merriam, Joseph, 76.
Merriam, Marshal, 76.
Merriam, Thomas, 1st, 76.
Merriam, Thomas, 2d, 76.
Merrick, Jno, 139.
Merrick, Jno, Jr., 139.
Merrick, Jonathan, 92.
Merrick, Josiah, 105.
Merrick, Stephen, 139.
Merrick, Thos, 139.
Merrick, Timo, 139.
Merrifield, Ithm, 138.
Merril, David, 109.
Merril, Abram, 47.
Merril, Benjamin, 85.
Merril, Caleb, 109.
Merril, Charles, 47.
Merril, Ebenezer, 54.
Merril, George, 46.
Merril, Gideon, 47.
Merril, Hezekiah, 46.
Merril, Jacob, 47.
Merril, James, 41.
Merril, Mead, 58.
Merril, Moses, 41.
Merril, Nathaniel, 47.
Merril, Samuel, 47.
Merril, Samuel, 59.
Merril, Samuel, 85.
Merril, Thomas, 47.
Merril, Thomas, Jr., 47.
Merril, William, 47.
Merrills, Aaron, 60.
Merrills, Aaron, 64.
Merrills, Aaron, 47.
Merrills, Asher, 61.
Merrills, Benajah, 70.
Merrills, Benjamin, 61.
Merrills, Bena, 63.
Merrills, Daniel, 76.
Merrills, Daniel, 70.
Merrills, Eliakim, 61.
Merrills, Elijah, 61.

Merrills Ephm, 63.
Merrills, Ephraim, 64.
Merrills, Jared, 61.
Merrills, Jeptha, 61.
Merrills, Joel, 69.
Merrills, John, 67.
Merrills, John, 68.
Merrills, John, 76.
Merrills, Jonathan, 60.
Merrills, Jonathan, 60.
Merrills, Joseph, 60.
Merrills, Mabel, 76.
Merrills, Marten, 60.
Merrills, Miah, 61.
Merrills, Nathaniel, 70.
Merrills, Noah, 64.
Merrills, Phinehas, 69.
Merrills, Sarah, 69.
Merrills, Siprean, 63.
Merrills, Truman, 66.
Merrills, William, 60.
Merrills, William, 70.
Merrils, Biezela, 65.
Merrils, Icobad, 109.
Merrils, Jno, 134.
Merrils, Mary, 129.
Merrils, Nathanel, 109.
Merriman, Amassa, 107.
Merriman, Amos, 92.
Merriman, Aron, 107.
Merriman, Asaph, 106.
Merriman, Benjamin, 106.
Merriman, Caleb, 106.
Merriman, Caleb, 107.
Merriman, Caleb. 2nd, 106.
Merriman, Chancey, 50.
Merriman, Ebenezer, 50.
Merriman, Edmond, 106.
Merriman, Edw, 138.
Merriman, Elisha, 107.
Merriman, Elisha, 108.
Merriman, Ephrim, 107.
Merriman, George, 108.
Merriman, Ichabud, 70.
Merriman, Jehel, 94.
Merriman, Jesse, 106.
Merriman, Jesse, 106.
Merriman, Joel, 107.
Merriman, Joel, 109.
Merriman, Joseph, 107.
Merriman, Josiah, 106.
Merriman, Lent, 93.
Merriman, Moses, 111.
Merriman, Nathaniel, 107.
Merriman, Pevis, 50.
Merriman, Samuel, 107.
Merriman, Theophilus, 94.
Merriman, Thomas, 107.
Merriman, Titus, 107.
Merriman (Wid.), 50.
Merriman, William, 106.
Merring, Moam, 49.
Merrit, Abraham, 15.
Merrit, Abraham, 15.
Merrit, Adam, 16.
Merrit, James, 69.
Merrit, Jesse, 15.
Merrit, John, 69.
Merrit, Jonathan, 16.
Merrit, Nathan, 16.
Merrit, Nathan, Junr, 16.
Merrit, Nathaniel, 16.
Merrit, Nehemiah, 16.
Merrit, Sam., 61.
Merrit, Solomon, 15.
Merrit, Thomas, 141.
Merrit, William, 33.
Merritt, Eben, 16.
Merrow, Elisha, 88.
Merrow, John, 88.
Merrow, Nathan, 36.
Merry, John, 47.
Merryfield, Jonathan, 37.
Mertin, Jethro, 49.
Mervin, Elihu, 135.
Mervin, Elisha, 122.
Mervin, Joseph, 122.
Merwin, Abel, 72.
Merwin, David, 1st, 72.
Merwin, David, 2d, 72.
Merwin, Heman, 83.
Merwin, John, 72.
Merwin, Noah, 75.
Merwin, Stephen, 58.
Merwin, Stephen, 72.
Meryan, William, 2d, 85.
Mesnard, John, 16.
Messenger, Abner, 65.
Messenger, Amos, 44.
Messenger, Daniel, 44.
Messenger, David, 44.
Messenger, Elijah, 44.
Messenger, Elisha, 69.
Messenger, Isaac, 69.
Messenger, Israel, 44.
Messenger, Moses, 69.
Messenger, Nathaniel, 44.
Messenger, Nathaniel, 44.
Messenger, Nathaniel, 68.
Messenger, Reuben, 59.
Messenger, Simeon, 69.
Messinger, Elisabeth, 140.
Messinger, Isaac, 49.

# INDEX.

Metcalf, Dan., 75.
Metcalf, Elijah, 81.
Metcalf, Eliphalet, 130.
Metcalf, Jabez, 126.
Metcalf, Thomas, 39.
Metune, Ebenezer, 107.
Middlebrook, Jonathan, 13.
Middlebrook, Jonathan, 23.
Middlebrook, Oliver, 13.
Middlebrook, Samuel, 23.
Middlebrook, Somers, 23.
Middlebrook, Sylvanus, 13.
Middleton, George, 120.
Middleton, Peter, 17.
Middleton, William, 51.
Midlebrook, Abiah, 30.
Midlebrook, Bine, 29.
Midlebrook, Elizabeth, 29.
Midlebrook, John, 29.
Midlebrook, Stephen, 29.
Midlebrook, Stephen, Jur, 29.
Miers, Martin, 75.
Mildram, John, 88.
Mildram, Leydia, 53.
Mildren, Huldah, 40.
Miles, Burrage, 93.
Miles, Daniel, 42.
Miles, Daniel, 101.
Miles, Daniel, 108.
Miles, Eleazer, 144.
Miles, Elihu, 104.
Miles, Isaac, 59.
Miles, Jesse, 141.
Miles, John, 57.
Miles, John, 92.
Miles, John, 101.
Miles, John, 103.
Miles, John, 107.
Miles, John, 3rd, 103.
Miles, John, 3rd, 103.
Miles, Jonathan, 95.
Miles, Josep, 103.
Miles, Joseph, 57.
Miles, Joshua, 141.
Miles, Justus, 72.
Miles, Levi, 57.
Miles, Lewis, 69.
Miles, Richard, 76.
Miles, Samuel, 70.
Miles, Sarah, 87.
Miles, Simeon, 100.
Miles, Simon, 109.
Miles, Stephen, 57.
Miles, Stephen, 70.
Miles, Stephen, 103.
Miles, Stephen, 2d, 72.
Miles, Theophilus, 95.
Miles, Theophilus, 101.
Miles, Thomas, 141.
Miles, Tilla, 101.
Miles, William, 103.
Millan, Jeames, 72.
Millar, James, 148.
Millar, John, 152.
Millar, Sanders, 148.
Millard, Andrew, 37.
Millard, Benja, 152.
Millard, Joel, 57.
Millard, John, 1st, 57.
Millard, John, 2d, 57.
Millard, Levit, 133.
Millard, Nathan, 57.
Miller, Abijah, 42.
Miller, Abner, 55.
Miller, Alexander, 44.
Miller, Alexander, Jnr, 148.
Miller, Allen, 61.
Miller, Amaziah, 36.
Miller, Ambros, 89.
Miller, Andrew, 16.
Miller, Anna, 41.
Miller, Asahel, 65.
Miller, Asher, Esqr, 85.
Miller, Brainard, 89.
Miller, Caleb, 87.
Miller, Caleb, 103.
Miller, Charles, 47.
Miller, Constant, 107.
Miller, Cornelius, 137.
Miller, Cornelus, 137.
Miller, Daniel, 41.
Miller, Daniel, 81.
Miller, Daniel, 83.
Miller, David, 53.
Miller, David, 70.
Miller, David, 121.
Miller, Ebenezer, 41.
Miller, Ebenezer, 60.
Miller, Ebenezer, 69.
Miller, Edward, 87.
Miller, Elijah, 41.
Miller, Elisha, 41.
Miller, Elisha, 89.
Miller, Elisha, 122.
Miller, Elizabeth, 96.
Miller, Elizur, 42.
Miller, Ezra, 123.
Miller, Frelove, 128.
Miller, George, 124.
Miller, George T., 68.
Miller, Giles, 88.
Miller, Giles, Junr, 88.
Miller, Henry, 129.
Miller, Hezekiah, 89.
Miller, Hoze, 88.
Miller, Icabod, 89.
Miller, Ichabod, 44.
Miller, Isaac, 76.
Miller, Isaac, Esqr, 89.
Miller, Jacob, 89.
Miller, Jairs, 66.
Miller, James, 88.
Miller, James, 128.
Miller, Jared, 87.
Miller, Jeremiah, 127.
Miller, Jerusha, 54.
Miller, Job, 41.
Miller, John, 15.
Miller, John, 42.
Miller, John, 44.
Miller, John, 103.
Miller, John, 128.
Miller, Jonth, 35.
Miller, Jonathan, 41.
Miller, Jonathan, 87.
Miller, Joseph, 53.
Miller, Joseph, 123.
Miller, Joshua, 60.
Miller, Joshua, 87.
Miller, Marcy, 68.
Miller, Mathew, 42.
Miller, Mike, 51.
Miller, Moses, 44.
Miller, Nathaniel, 53.
Miller, Noah, 41.
Miller, Reuben, 41.
Miller, Roswell, 54.
Miller, Samuel, 45.
Miller, Samuel, 59.
Miller, Samuel, 67.
Miller, Sam., 69.
Miller, Sarah, 82.
Miller, Seth, 67.
Miller, Seth, 89.
Miller, Silas, 123.
Miller, Solomon, 41.
Miller, Solomon, 141.
Miller, Stephen, 87.
Miller, Stephen, 105.
Miller, Thomas, 122.
Miller, Thomson, 123.
Miller, Volentine, 123.
Miller, Weltha, 123.
Miller, William, 42.
Miller, William, 62.
Miller, William, 89.
Miller, William, 89.
Miller, William, 97.
Miller, William, 122.
Miller, William, Jr., 42.
Millerd, Joel, 66.
Milligan, George, 72.
Millins, Charles, 91.
Mills, Aaron, 61.
Mills, Alexander, 24.
Mills, Amasa, 49.
Mills, Amos, 16.
Mills, Andrew, 20.
Mills, Asa, 95.
Mills, Augustus, 37.
Mills, Benjamin, 70.
Mills, Bradley, 59.
Mills, Chancy, 60.
Mills, Constant, 62.
Mills, Daniel, 12.
Mills, Daniel, 20.
Mills, David, 60.
Mills, David, 69.
Mills, David, 101.
Mills, Denton, 28.
Mills, Diadema, 55.
Mills, Dudley, 70.
Mills, Ebenezer, 31.
Mills, Ebenezer, 31.
Mills, Edan, 61.
Mills, Elihu, 55.
Mills, Elijah, 54.
Mills, Elijah, 55.
Mills, Elisha, 17.
Mills, Ephraim, 49.
Mills, Ezekiel, 48.
Mills, Ezra, 26.
Mills, Fredk, 55.
Mills, George, 24.
Mills, Gideon, 49.
Mills, Hannah, 59.
Mills, Isaac, 17.
Mills, James, 18.
Mills, James, 119.
Mills, Jared, 49.
Mills, Jedediah, 17.
Mills, Jedediah, 47.
Mills, Job, 35.
Mills, John, 11.
Mills, John, 24.
Mills, Jno, 35.
Mills, John, 110.
Mills, Joseph, 12.
Mills, Joseph, 62.
Mills, Laurance, 61.
Mills, Macy, 67.
Mills, Mehitable, 129.
Mills, Michael, 61.
Mills, Moses, 61.
Mills, Naomi, 55.
Mills, Nathel, 25.
Mills, Noah, 35.
Mills, Peter, 59.
Mills, Peter, 134.
Mills, Roswell, 37.
Mills, Samuel, 16.
Mills, Samuel, 18.
Mills, Samuel, 62.
Mills, Samuel, 69.
Mills, Saml, 68.
Mills, Revd Saml, 90.
Mills, Saml J., 69.
Mills, Stephen, 20.
Mills, Stephen, 28.
Mills, Stone, 134.
Mills, Timothy, 62.
Millson, Daniel, 12.
Miner, 67.
Miner, Abiather, 125.
Miner, Abiather, 125.
Miner, Adam, 78.
Miner, Adoniram, 78.
Miner, Amos, 127.
Miner, Ananias, 124.
Miner, Andrew, 78.
Miner, Asa, 116.
Miner, Asahel, 62.
Miner, Benjamin, 78.
Miner, Caziah, 82.
Miner, Champlin, 124.
Miner, Charles, 117.
Miner, Christopher, 117.
Miner, Clemment, 117.
Miner, Daniel, 78.
Miner, Daniel, 116.
Miner, Daniel, 117.
Miner, Daniel, 123.
Miner, Daniel, Junr, 116.
Miner, David, 78.
Miner, David, 117.
Miner, David, 121.
Miner, David, Junr, 117.
Miner, Easter, 124.
Miner, Ebenr, 124.
Miner, Elias, 123.
Miner, Elisha, 124.
Miner, Elisha, 2d, 124.
Miner, Ephraim, 117.
Miner, Ephraim, 128.
Miner, George, 124.
Miner, Gilbert, 78.
Miner, Hemstead, 117.
Miner, Hugh, 127.
Miner, Hugh, 128.
Miner, Humstead, Junr, 117.
Miner, Isaac, 133.
Miner, Israel, 78.
Miner, Jabez, 127.
Miner, James, 116.
Miner, James, Junr, 117.
Miner, Jeames, 78.
Miner, Jehu, 73.
Miner, Jesse, 123.
Miner, John, 66.
Miner, John, 78.
Miner, John O., 118.
Miner, Jonas, 78.
Miner, Jonathan, 122.
Miner, Jonathan, 125.
Miner, Jonathan, 127.
Miner, Joseph, 57.
Miner, Joseph, 78.
Miner, Joshua, 120.
Miner, Joshua, 125.
Miner, Josiah, 78.
Miner, Lebeus, 125.
Miner, Lemuel, 125.
Miner, Lydia, 127.
Miner, Manassa, 117.
Miner, Mathew, 78.
Miner, Nathan, 78.
Miner, Nathan, 116.
Miner, Nathan, Junr, 116.
Miner, Nathl, 118.
Miner, Peace, 78.
Miner, Peleg, 117.
Miner, Peres, 116.
Miner, Peres, Junr, 117.
Miner, Peter, 78.
Miner, Preston, 78.
Miner, Reuben, 66.
Miner, Richard, 125.
Miner, Richerson, 116.
Miner, Roswell, 125.
Miner, Rufus, 117.
Miner, Rufus, 152.
Miner, Samuel, 78.
Miner, Samuel, 116.
Miner, Samuel, 125.
Miner, Samuel, 127.
Miner, Seth, 78.
Miner, Seth, 131.
Miner, Seth, 2d, 78.
Miner, Silvester, 127.
Miner, Simeon, 78.
Miner, Simeon, 116.
Miner, Solomon, 78.
Miner, Stephen, 124.
Miner, Stephen, 127.
Miner, Stephen, 152.
Miner, Thaddeus, 78.
Miner, Thomas, 78.
Miner, Thomas, 117.
Miner, Thomas, 117.
Miner, Turner, 128.
Miner, Volentine, 124.
Miner, Volentine, 125.
Miner, Whitfield, 124.
Miner, William, 117.
Miner, William, 117.
Miner, Wm, 123.
Miner, William, 124.
Miner, Zebadiah, 125.
Miners, David, 145.
Mingham, John, 112.
Mingo (Negro), 122.
Mingo, Primus, 152.
Mingo, William, 70.
Minick (Negroe), 94.
Minor, Caleb, 110.
Minor, Christopher, 37.
Minor, Daniel, 126.
Minor, Ebenr, 122.
Minor, Elihu, 82.
Minor, Jesse, 124.
Minor, Joel, 61.
Minor, John, 16.
Minor, John, 55.
Minor, Jonas, 56.
Minor, Joseph, 50.
Minor, Jud, 110.
Minor, Martin, 123.
Minor, Seth, 123.
Minor, Thomas, 66.
Minor, Revd Thomas, 88.
Minor, Turner, 82.
Minord, Frederick, 60.
Minott, Lewis, 95.
Mire, William, 46.
Miriam, Icabod, 93.
Miriman, John, 106.
Mirriman, Marcus, 103.
Mirriman, Silas, 103.
Mitcalf, John, 65.
Mitchel, Abijah, 78.
Mitchel, Amasa, 120.
Mitchel, Asa, 120.
Mitchel, Asahel, 78.
Mitchel, Beriah, 78.
Mitchel, Calvin, 53.
Mitchel, Daniel, 78.
Mitchel, David, 25.
Mitchel, David, 73.
Mitchel, David, 75.
Mitchel, Eleazer, 73.
Mitchel, Elnathan, 75.
Mitchel, Francis, 119.
Mitchel, George, 122.
Mitchel, James, 52.
Mitchel, Joel, 34.
Mitchel, John, 13.
Mitchel, John, 18.
Mitchel, John, 78.
Mitchel, John, 120.
Mitchel, John, 122.
Mitchel, John, 2d, 78.
Mitchel, Jonathan, 73.
Mitchel, Joseph, 120.
Mitchel, Jotham, 35.
Mitchel, Revd Justice, 22.
Mitchel, Mathew, 73.
Mitchel, Moses, 107.
Mitchel, Moses, 118.
Mitchel, Nathaniel, 78.
Mitchel, Polly (Wid.), 30.
Mitchel, Reuben, 78.
Mitchel, Seth, 78.
Mitchel, Simeon, 75.
Mitchel, Simeon, 1st, 73.
Mitchel, Simeon, 2d, 73.
Mitchel, Stephen Mix, 52.
Mitchel, Timothy, 75.
Mitchel, Warren, 73.
Mitchel, Whitney, 96.
Mitchel, Wm, 35.
Mitchel, William, 75.
Mitchel, William, 78.
Mitchel, Zacheriah, 17.
Mitchel, Zenus, 107.
Mitchell, Abner, 87.
Mitchell, Asa, 81.
Mitchell, Asaph, 107.
Mitchell, Ezekiel, 144.
Mitchell, Jothn, 143.
Mitchell, Mary, 86.
Mitchell, Oliver, 38.
Mitchell, Saml, 81.
Mitchell, Wm, 91.
Mitchell, Zebudiah, 144.
Mitchell, Zephaniah, Junr, 81.
Mitchell, Zepheniah, 81.
Mitchelson, Eliphalet, 48.
Mix, Abel, 78.
Mix, Anna, 104.
Mix, Caleb, 100.
Mix, Chancey, 67.
Mix, Daniel, 69.
Mix, Eldad, 103.
Mix, Eldad, 109.
Mix, Elisha, 47.
Mix, Elisha, 104.
Mix, Ester, 104.
Mix, Hannah, 104.
Mix, Isaac, 60.
Mix, James, 131.
Mix, Joel, 106.
Mix, John, 40.
Mix, John, 104.
Mix, John, 108.
Mix, John, 131.
Mix, Jonathan, 103.
Mix, Joseph, 103.
Mix, Joseph, 2nd, 103.
Mix, Josiah, 107.
Mix, Levi, 109.
Mix, Martha, 67.
Mix, Prime, 34.
Mix, Rufus, 115.
Mix, Samuel, 104.
Mix, Samuel, 106.
Mix, Samuel, 109.
Mix, Sarah, 104.
Mix, Stephen, 106.
Mix, Thankfull, 104.
Mix, Thomas, 63.
Mix, Thomas, 101.
Mix, Thomas, 108.
Mix, Timothy, 34.
Mix, Timothy, 35.
Mix, Timothy, 104.
Mix (Widow), 105.
Mobs, Saml, 82.
Moffat, Andrew, 144.
Moffat, Eli, 150.
Moffat, John, 144.
Moffat, John, Jnr, 144.
Moffat, Mathew, 144.
Moffat, Micajah, 150.
Moffet, Eleazr, 144.
Mogenot, John, 20.
Moger, Jeames, 75.
Mogg, Christian, 73.
Molbourn, Godfry, 133.
Molhone, Evan, 149.
Molony, Downey, 103.
Molthrop, Asher, 97.
Molthrop, Benjamin, 95.
Molthrop, Benjamin, 2nd, 95.
Molthrop, Charles, 104.
Molthrop, David 97.
Molthrop, Ely, 97.
Molthrop, Enoch, 104.
Molthrop, Joseph, 92.
Molthrop, Joseph, 97.
Molthrop, Josiah. 97.
Molthrop, Timothy, 107.
Molton, Asa, 147.
Molton, Barnard, 137.
Molton, Benja, 143.
Molton, Eben, 137.
Molton, James, 152.
Molton, Jona, 137.
Molton, Joseph, 102.
Molton, Mary, 147.
Molton, Salmon, 137.
Molton, Stephen, 137.
Molton, Stephen, Jr., 137.
Molton, Tabatha, 143.
Molton, William, 152.
Money, Reuben, 68.
Monger Elisha S., 64.
Monger Johiel, 99.
Monger, Lidia, 99.
Monger, Levi, 40.
Monger, Reuben, 63.
Monger, William, 65.
Monro, Andrew, 92.
Monro, Fredrick, 91.
Monro, George, 91.
Monro, Sarah, 91.
Monro, William, 91.
Monroe, Nathan, 67.
Monroe, Noah, 60.
Monroe, Younglove, 60.
Monrow, Benjamin, 51.
McRow, David, 27.
Monsen, Alexander, 39.
Monson, Levi, 11.
Montague, Anna, 52.
Montague, George, 52.
Montague, Moses, 52.
Montaigue, Seth, 52.
Montcalm, Mosses, 102.
Montgomeroy, Hue, 65.
Montgomery, Asa, 151.
Montgomery, John, 151.
Montgomery, Josiah, 151.
Montgomery, Robert, 151.
Montgomery, Sarah, 151.
Montgue, Richard, 52.
Moodey, Mary, 59.
Moodey, Philop, 63.
Moody, Eben, 67.
Moody, Ebenezer, 78.
Moody (Negro), 113.
Moody, Thomas, 58.
Moody, Zimie, 78.
Moor, Robert, 18.
Moore, Amos, 64.
Moore, Asa, 55.
Moore, Benja, 55.
Moore, Daniel, 51.
Moore, Daniel, 69.
Moore, David, 65.
Moore, David, 115.
Moore, David, 131.
Moore, Deborah, 124.
Moore, Ebenezer, 46.
Moore, Edwd, 55.
Moore, Eli, 38.

# INDEX.

Moore, Eli, 44.
Moore, Elisha, 55.
Moore, Eunice, 124.
Moore, Francis, 105.
Moore, Frederick, 119.
Moore, Hannah, 55.
Moore, Hannah, 127.
Moore, James, 113.
Moore, Job, 43.
Moore, John, 69.
Moore, John, 124.
Moore, John, 131.
Moore, Jonª, 131.
Moore, Joseph, 124.
Moore, Joshua, 124.
Moore, Joshua, 127.
Moore, Miles, 125.
Moore, Nathaniel, 38.
Moore, Oliver, 43.
Moore, Ozias, 44.
Moore, Roger, 55.
Moore, Theophilus, 55.
Moore, Thomˢ, 55.
Moore, Wareham, 38.
Moore, William, 124.
Moore, William, 127.
Moore, William, 2ᵈ, 128.
Mopley, John, 76.
Mopley, Nathˡ, 146.
Moramble, John, 78.
Mordock, Jonª, 134.
Mordock, Wᵐ, 90.
Mordock, Willᵐ, 2ᵈ, 90.
More, Abijah, 69.
More, Able, 123.
More, Arcena, 48.
More, Benjamin, 44.
More, Damanes, 44.
More, David, 69.
More, David, 139.
More, Horace, 45.
More, Icabod, 139.
More, Isaac, 45.
More, Jacob, 48.
More, James, 139.
More, James, 139.
More, Jehiel, 44.
More, Joel, 45.
More, Joel, Jr., 45.
More, Jonah, 44.
More, Joseph, 142.
More, Josiah, 60.
More, Josiah, 70.
More, King, 69.
More, Micah, 45.
More, Nathan, 45.
More, Obed, 45.
More, Reuben, 44.
More, Rideout, 44.
More, Roger, 44.
More, Roswell, 33.
More, Roswell, 49.
More, Roswell, Jr., 49.
More, Ruth, 45.
More, Samuel, 51.
More, Samuel, 66.
More, Samuel, 2ᵈ, 66.
More, Shadrack, 44.
More, Shadrack, Jr., 44.
More, Simeon, 41.
More, Simon, 63.
More (Wid.), 139.
More, William, 60.
More, William, 63.
More, Wᵐ, 139.
Moredock, Jonª, 126.
Morehouse, Aaron, 27.
Morehouse, Abijah, 14.
Morehouse, Abraham, 13.
Morehouse, Abraham, 14.
Morehouse, Andrew, 32.
Morehouse, Banks, 31.
Morehouse, Beebe, 27.
Morehouse, Benjamin, 72.
Morehouse, Daniel, 27.
Morehouse, Daniel, 31.
Morehouse, David, 14.
Morehouse, David, 24.
Morehouse, David, 27.
Morehouse, David, 32.
Morehouse, David, 136.
Morehouse, Ebenezer, 13.
Morehouse, Elijah, 14.
Morehouse, Elijah, 27.
Morehouse, Eunice, 13.
Morehouse, Gershom, 27.
Morehouse, Gershom, 27.
Morehouse, Groman, 13.
Morehouse, Hezekiah, 19.
Morehouse, Isaac, 14.
Morehouse, Jabez, 32.
Morehouse, Jared, 23.
Morehouse, Jesse, 32.
Morehouse, John, 10.
Morehouse, John, 13.
Morehouse, John, 19.
Morehouse, John, 27.
Morehouse, John, 1ˢᵗ, 72.
Morehouse, John, 2ᵈ, 72.
Morehouse, Joseph, 31.
Morehouse, Joshua, 26.
Morehouse, Lemuel, 72.
Morehouse, Michael, 24.

Morehouse, Michael, 32.
Morehouse, Nathan, 32.
Morehouse, Peter, 14.
Morehouse, Samuel, 13.
Morehouse, Samuel, 24.
Morehouse, Sarah (Wᵈ), 22.
Morehouse, Seth, 14.
Morehouse, Solomon, 23.
Morehouse, Squire, 72.
Morehouse, Stephen, 24.
Morehouse, Stephen, 72.
Morehouse, Stephen, 1ˢᵗ, 72.
Morehouse, Thaddeus, 10.
Morehouse, Thosˢ, 136.
Morehouse, Uriah, 14.
Morehouse, William, 14.
Moreton, Abner, 37.
Moreton, John, 52.
Morey, Abijah, 60.
Morey, Asa, 57.
Morey, Nathaniel, 63.
Morey, Thomas, 59.
Morgan, Abigail, 122.
Morgan, Abijah, 83.
Morgan, Abraham, 89.
Morgan, Amos, 81.
Morgan, Arael, 111.
Morgan, Asher, 153.
Morgan, Benjamin, 113.
Morgan, Benjamin, 122.
Morgan, Caleb, 59.
Morgan, Charles, 47.
Morgan, Christopher, 118.
Morgan, Daniel, 71.
Morgan, Daniel, 115.
Morgan, Daniel, Junʳ, 115.
Morgan, Darius, 130.
Morgan, David, 59.
Morgan, Devill, 46.
Morgan, Dudley, 113.
Morgan, Ebenʳ, 118.
Morgan, Edward, 127.
Morgan, Eleanor, 151.
Morgan, Elijah, 123.
Morgan, Elisha, 113.
Morgan, George, 127.
Morgan, Grace, 127.
Morgan, Isaac, 110.
Morgan, Isaac, 149.
Morgan, Israel, 118.
Morgan, Jacob, 103.
Morgan, Jacob, 118.
Morgan, James, 22.
Morgan, James, 113.
Morgan, James, 119.
Morgan, James, Junʳ, 114.
Morgan, James, Junʳ, 119.
Morgan, Jeames, 59.
Morgan, Jedediah, 120.
Morgan, Jesse, 113.
Morgan, John, 21.
Morgan, John, 46.
Morgan, John, 88.
Morgan, John, 114.
Morgan, John, 118.
Morgan, John, 119.
Morgan, John, 127.
Morgan, Jonathan, 59.
Morgan, Jonathan, 115.
Morgan, Jonª, 121.
Morgan, Jonª, 124.
Morgan, Jonathan, 2ᵈ, 121.
Morgan, Joseph, 27.
Morgan, Joseph, 98.
Morgan, Joshua, 120.
Morgan, Joshua, 121.
Morgan, Joshua, 138.
Morgan, Levi, 53.
Morgan, Nathan, 64.
Morgan, Nathan, 118.
Morgan, Nathan, 153.
Morgan, Nathanel, 27.
Morgan, Peter, 87.
Morgan, Peter, 151.
Morgan, Phillup, 127.
Morgan, Rebecka, 118.
Morgan, Richard, 87.
Morgan, Richard, Junʳ, 87.
Morgan, Roswell, 141.
Morgan, Samuel, 59.
Morgan, Samˡ, 120.
Morgan, Samˡ, 122.
Morgan, Samuel, 127.
Morgan, Samˡ, 153.
Morgan, Shapley, 118.
Morgan, Shapley, Junʳ, 118.
Morgan, Simeon, 87.
Morgan, Simeon, 114.
Morgan, Simeon, 115.
Morgan, Soloman, 149.
Morgan, Solomon, 118.
Morgan, Stephen, 115.
Morgan, Temperance, 119.
Morgan, Theophilus, 85.
Morgan, Thomas, 118.
Morgan, Thomas, Junʳ, 118.
Morgan, Timothy, 120.
Morgan, William, 118.
Morgan, William, 122.
Morgan, William, 127.
Morgan, William, 132.
Morgan, William, Esqʳ, 85.
Morgan, William A., 118.

Morgan, Youngs, 119.
Morgen, Joseph, 27.
Morgin, Abijah, 27.
Morgin, Hezekiah, 20.
Moris, Shadrack, 11.
Morrel, Jacob, 15.
Morril, Robert, 60.
Morris, Amos, 20.
Morris, Amos, 97.
Morris, Amos, Junʳ, 97.
Morris, Asa, 111.
Morris, Benjamin, 112.
Morris, Daniel, 20.
Morris, Daniel, 70.
Morris, David, 28.
Morris, David, 95.
Morris, David, 110.
Morris, Edmond, 91.
Morris, Ephraim, 11.
Morris, Henry, 139.
Morris, Isaac, 76.
Morris, James, 125.
Morris, John, 28.
Morris, John, 97.
Morris, John, 103.
Morris, Lemuel, 154.
Morris, Major, 109.
Morris, Marget, 74.
Morris, Mathew, 78.
Morris, Newton, 102.
Morris, Richard, 102.
Morris, Revᵈ Robert, 15.
Morris, Samuel, 11.
Morris, Samuel, 74.
Morris, Samˡ, 154.
Morris, Thomas, 1ˢᵗ, 59.
Morris, Thomas, 2ⁿᵈ, 59.
Morris, Timothy, 91.
Morris, William, 109.
Morris, William, 153.
Morrison, Hannah, 52.
Morrison, John, 38.
Morrison, John, 40.
Morrison, Joseph, 127.
Morrison (Widow), 104.
Morriss, James, 64.
Morrow, Thomas, 112.
Morse, Abel, 103.
Morse, Abiel, 153.
Morse, Abigal, 93.
Morse, Amasa, 58.
Morse, Andrew, 63.
Morse, Bemijah, 108.
Morse, Benjamin, 93.
Morse, Benjª, 142.
Morse, Charles, 142.
Morse, Chauncy, 58.
Morse, Chester, 45.
Morse, Daniel, 113.
Morse, David, 97.
Morse, David, 114.
Morse, David, 154.
Morse, Ebenezer, 107.
Morse, Isaac, 92.
Morse, Isaac Bower, 93.
Morse, James, 137.
Morse, James, 142.
Morse, Jedediah, 154.
Morse, Jesse, 93.
Morse, Joel, 94.
Morse, Joel, 107.
Morse, John, 97.
Morse, John, 98.
Morse, John, 130.
Morse, John, 154.
Morse, Jonathan, 108.
Morse, Jonathan, 108.
Morse, Joseph, 75.
Morse, Joseph, 94.
Morse, Joshua, 150.
Morse, Josiah, 93.
Morse, Levi, 108.
Morse, Lyda, 154.
Morse, Mary, 92.
Morse, Mary, 115.
Morse, Moses, 40.
Morse, Moses, 93.
Morse, Nathaniel, 93.
Morse, Rufus, 93.
Morse, Samuel, 93.
Morse, Solomon, 149.
Morse, Thomas, 93.
Morse, Titus, 93.
Morse, William, 46.
Morse, William, 94.
Morse, William, 150.
Mortimer, Benjamin, 114.
Mortimer, Phillip, Esqʳ, 86.
Morton, Abigail, 53.
Morton, Alexander, 39.
Morton, Benjamin, 53.
Morton, Deadat, 39.
Morton, Elinor, 38.
Morton, Isaac, 37.
Morton, John, 39.
Morton, William, 37.
Moseley, Demish, 42.
Moseley, Ebenezer, 42.
Moseley, Ebenʳ, 143.
Moseley, Eunice, Junʳ, 143.
Moseley, Eunice, 42.
Moseley, Flavel, 143.

Moseley, Ineross, 73.
Moseley, Jonª O., 81.
Moseley, Joseph, 42.
Moseley, Joseph, 143.
Moseley, Luther, 140.
Moseley, Richard, 42.
Moseley, Samˡ, 143.
Moseley, Susanna, 42.
Moseley, Syphax, 42.
Moseley, Thosˢ, Esqʳ, 81.
Moseley, Timothy, 37.
Moseley, Timothy, 43.
Moseley, Uriel, 143.
Moseley, William, 42.
Moseley, William, 46.
Moses, Aaron, 48.
Moses, Abner, 68.
Moses, Abram, 49.
Moses, Ashbel, 68.
Moses, Clerk, 52.
Moses, Daniel, 48.
Moses, Elihu, 48.
Moses, Jnº, 138.
Moses, Martin, 68.
Moses, Othaniel, 35.
Moses, Othaniel, 35.
Moses, Reuben, 35.
Moses, Timothy, 48.
Moses, Timothy, 67.
Moses (Wid.), 138.
Moses, Zebne, 48.
Mosher, George, 13.
Mosher, James, 19.
Mosier, Daniel, 15.
Mosier, Elijah, 125.
Mosier, Henry, 16.
Mosier, James, 15.
Mosier, Noman, 125.
Mosier, Rachel (Wᵈ), 27.
Mosier, Samˡ, 127.
Mosier, Stephen, 125.
Moss, Amasa, 11.
Moss, Amos, 66.
Moss, Asahel, 59.
Moss, Daniel, 17.
Moss, David, 68.
Moss, Elihue, 18.
Moss, Elizabeth, 18.
Moss, Isaac, 17.
Moss, Ives, 66.
Moss, John, 18.
Moss, John, 64.
Moss, Joseph, 17.
Moss, Joseph, 64.
Moss, Levi, 66.
Moss, Simeon, 68.
Moss, Solomon, 66.
Moss, Theophilus, 50.
Moss, William, 18.
Mosses, Michael, 47.
Mossett, Thomas, 127.
Mossley, Abner, 75.
Mott, Adam, 64.
Mott, Edward, 114.
Mott, Gershom, 142.
Mott, Jerehᵇ, Sr., 142.
Mott, Jonathan, 61.
Mott, Jonathan, 115.
Mott, Lemuˡ, 66.
Mott, Nathaniel, 81.
Mott Reuben, 21.
Mott, Samuel, 59.
Mott, Samuel, 81.
Mott, Samuel, 114.
Mott, William, 21.
Mottbey, Johial, 61.
Motthop, Stephen, 60.
Motthrop, Isaac, 64.
Moulton, Howard, 137.
Moulton, Josˢ, 137.
Mountain, Jonathain, 48.
Moxom, Adonijoh, 62.
Moyer, Nathaniel, 29.
Mozier, Zebulon, 76.
Mucker, Ephrahim, 94.
Mudge, Charles, 153.
Mug, Icabod, 134.
Mulford, Barnabas, 92.
Mulford, Barnabas, 103.
Mulford, David, 103.
Mulford, Nathan, 92.
Mulkey, Timothy, 116.
Mulkins, John, 113.
Muller, Samuel, 69.
Mumford, David, 129.
Mumford, Giles, 128.
Mumford, Irad, 138.
Mumford, Jeremiah, 141.
Mumford, John, 122.
Mumford, Thomas, 130.
Mumm, David, 73.
Mumn, Samuel, 73.
Mun, Isaiah, 121.
Munday, Sarah, 24.
Munger, Bela, 99.
Munger, Cabe, 99.
Munger, Edwʳ, 139.
Munger, James, 99.
Munger, Joel, 75.
Munger, Joel, 2ᵈ, 75.
Munger, John, 78.
Munger, Jnº, 138.
Munger, Josiah, 98.

Munger, Josiah, 99.
Munger, Lewis, 56.
Munger, Lines, 99.
Munger, Lyman, 99.
Munger, Merriman, 56.
Munger, Miles, 99.
Munger, Simeon, 98.
Munger, Timothy, 99.
Munger, Timothy, 2ᵈ, 99.
Munger, Willis, 98.
Mungo, Simeon, 27.
Munn, Abel, 78.
Munn, Asa, 73.
Munn, Daniel, 78.
Munn, Gideon, 78.
Munn, Jedediah, 1ˢᵗ, 73.
Munn, Jedediah, 2ᵈ, 73.
Munn, John, 78.
Munn, Olvir, 86.
Munn, Robert I., 89.
Munro, Joseph, 28.
Munro, Joshua, 127.
Munro, William, 28.
Munroe, Joshua, 125.
Munrow, John, 17.
Munsel, Alpheus, 54.
Munsell, Corking, 38.
Munsell, Elisha, 38.
Munsell, Hannah, 38.
Munsell, Henry, 129.
Munsell, Hezekiah, 39.
Munsell, Jacob, 38.
Munsell, John, 129.
Munsell, Martin, 38.
Munsell, Silah, 38.
Munsell, Thomas, 38.
Munsell, Zacheus, 40.
Munsill, John, 123.
Munsill, John, 123.
Munsill, Phineas, 116.
Munsill, Thomas, 123.
Munsill, Timothy, 124.
Munson, Abner, 110.
Munson, Almond, 76.
Munson, Amassa, 92.
Munson, Bazael, 16.
Munson, Benjamin, 110.
Munson, Caleb, 60.
Munson, Caleb, 109.
Munson, Caleb, 110.
Munson, Daniel, 102.
Munson, David, 100.
Munson, David, 105.
Munson, Eliphalet, 108.
Munson, Elizabeth, 109.
Munson, Eneas, 104.
Munson, Ephraim, 56.
Munson, Ephraim, 61.
Munson, Esther, 49.
Munson, Ethel, 108.
Munson, Eunice, 100.
Munson, Ezra, 100.
Munson, Hammon, 109.
Munson, Heman, 77.
Munson, Henry, 125.
Munson, Isaac, 28.
Munson, Isaac, 100.
Munson, Isaac, 108.
Munson, Israel, 104.
Munson, Jabez, 100.
Munson Jeros, 49.
Munson, Job, 100.
Munson, John, 65.
Munson, John, 75.
Munson, Jonathan, 92.
Munson, Joseph, 104.
Munson, Joseph, 108.
Munson, Joshua, 100.
Munson, Joshua, 108.
Munson, Justice, 100.
Munson, Levi, 58.
Munson, Levi, 100.
Munson, Mansfield, 106.
Munson, Medad, 64.
Munson, Nathaniel, 65.
Munson, Obidiah, 76.
Munson, Peter, 93.
Munson, Samuel, 103.
Munson, Samuel, 108.
Munson, Samuel, 109.
Munson, Samuel, 2ⁿᵈ, 108.
Munson, Soloman, 109.
Munson, Solomon, 49.
Munson, Stephen, 49.
Munson, Stephen, 103.
Munson, Theophelus, 27.
Munson, Theophilus, 103.
Munson, Thomas E., 70.
Munson, Wait, 61.
Munson, Walter, 106.
Munson, William, 76.
Munson, William, 102.
Munson, William, 103.
Munson, William, 105.
Murdock, Andrus, 141.
Murdock, Anne, 152.
Murdock, Eliphalet, 152.
Murdock, George, Jn., 148.
Murdock, William, 101.
Murdock, William, 146.
Murphey, James, 65.
Murrain, Job, 96.
Murrain, John, 102.

# INDEX.

Murrain, John, 3rd, 102.
Murrain, Jonas, 105.
Murrain, Margeret, 105.
Murrain, Miles, 96.
Murrain, Miles, 101.
Murran, Joseph, 105.
Murray, Chloe, 59.
Murray, Cotton, 46.
Murray, Daniel, 24.
Murray, Daniel, 98.
Murray, Elisha, 72.
Murray, James, 104.
Murray, Nathan, 72.
Murray, Thomas, 35.
Murren, David, 101.
Murren, Mary, 101.
Murren, Thomas, 107.
Murrey, Jasper, 63.
Murrey, Pattern, 19.
Murrin, Abijah, 13.
Murrin, Andrew, 10.
Murrin, David, 63.
Murrin, Ebenezer, 13.
Murrin, Fowler, 59.
Murrin, Isaac, 10.
Murrin, Levi, 10.
Murrin, Meeker, 13.
Murrin, Nathan, 10.
Murrin, Samuel, 10.
Murrin, Samuel, Jur, 10.
Murring, Fletcher, 111.
Murring, Joseph, 111.
Murring, Joseph, 2nd, 111.
Murry, Abigal, 99.
Murry, Abraham, 96.
Murry, Amassa, 99.
Murry, Benjamin, 10.
Murry, Curtis, 99.
Murry, James, 153.
Murry, Jesse, 99.
Murry, John, 99.
Murry, Philemon, 66.
Murry, Selah, 99.
Murry, Semore, 130.
Murry, Thankfull, 98.
Murry, Warren, 96.
Murwin, David, 32.
Murwin, Eppepras, 32.
Murwin, John, 31.
Murwin, Nathan, 32.
Murwin, Samuel, 32.
Murwin, Seth, 32.
Muth, Abiah, 142.
Muxley, Elisabeth, 119.
Muxley, Jona, 119.
Muxley, Joseph, 119.
Muxum, Benjamin, 69.
Muxum, Saml, 67.
Mygatt, Abigail, 47.
Mygatt, Ben Star, 72.
Mygatt, Comfort, 12.
Mygatt, Eli, 10.
Mygatt, Jonathan, 72.
Mygatt, Noah, 72.
Mygatt, Philo, 11.

Nahan, Peter, (Negroe), 93.
Nailer, John, 30.
Nails, Abraham, 96.
Nall, Mock, 48.
Nancarow, Edward, 87.
Nando (Negroe), 102.
Nanneistran, Charles, 18.
Napp, Daniel, 29.
Napp, David, 27.
Napp, David, 27.
Napp, Jonathan, 27.
Napp, Rebecka, 27.
Nash, Aaron, 23.
Nash, Abraham, 28.
Nash, Abraham, 2d, 28
Nash, Daniel, 23.
Nash, Daniel, 28.
Nash, David, 22.
Nash, Eben, 134.
Nash, Ebenezer, 21.
Nash, Edward, 22.
Nash, Eliakam, 19.
Nash, Francis, 16.
Nash, John, 24.
Nash, John, 63.
Nash, Josiah, 60.
Nash, Micajah, 23.
Nash, Nathan, 22.
Nash, Nathanel, 11.
Nash, Phneas, 137.
Nash, Polley, 67.
Nash, Riah, 28.
Nash, Samuel, 24.
Nash, Samuel, 60.
Nash, Thomas, 13.
Nash, Thomas, Jnr, 13.
Nash, William, 22.
Nash, William, 60.
Nash, William, 69.
Naughty, David, 98.
Naughty, David, 2nd, 98.
Neal, Aaron, 50.
Neal, Aaron, 63.
Neal, Elijah, 50.
Neal, Enoch, 63.
Neal, John, 50.
Neal, Noah, 50.

Neal, Timothy, 50.
Neal, William, 63.
Nearing, Henery, 10.
Nearing, John, 35.
Nearnin, John H., 10.
Nearnin, Joseph, 10.
Necho (Negro), 83.
Nedom, Dan., 137.
Nedom, Nehm, 137.
Neff, Arnold, 35.
Neff, Benjn, 153.
Neff, John, 52.
Neff, John, 153.
Neff, Oliver, 153.
Neff, William, 143.
Negros (Free), 134.
Nelomd, Jona, 135.
Nelson, George, 137.
Nelson, Hosea, 51.
Nelson, Isaac, 42.
Nelson, James, 139.
Nelson, Jereh, 51.
Nelson, Jeremiah, 2d, 52.
Nelson, Sarah, 51.
Nelson, Silus, 112.
Nelson, Wm, 137.
Neptune, 22.
Nesbit, Nathan, 148.
Nethersmith, Matthew, 31.
Nettleton, Abel, 85.
Nettleton, Benijah, 102.
Nettleton, Caleb, 101.
Nettleton, Damaras, 85.
Nettleton, Daniel, 75.
Nettleton, Daniel, 84.
Nettleton, Elizh, 109.
Nettleton, Ely, 94.
Nettleton, Hannah, 85.
Nettleton, Isaac, 102.
Nettleton, Isaiah, 84.
Nettleton, James, 84.
Nettleton, John, 85.
Nettleton, John, 112.
Nettleton, Jonah, 94.
Nettleton, Joseph, 77.
Nettleton, Joseph, 85.
Nettleton, Joseph, 2d, 77.
Nettleton, Joshua, 61.
Nettleton, Josiah, 78.
Nettleton, Josiah, 84.
Nettleton, Nathaniel, 101.
Nettleton, Samuel, 84.
Nettleton, Samuel, 102.
Nettleton, Samuel, 2d, 84.
Nettleton, Susannah, 77.
Nettleton, Thaddeus, 101.
Nettleton, William, 78.
Neuson, Thos, 52.
Nevee, Peter, 123.
Nevins, David, 131.
Nevins, John, 46.
Nevis, Calver, 94.
New, John, 105.
Newall, Joshua, 104.
Newall, Saml, 150.
Newberry, Thomas, 55.
Newbury, ——, 53.
Newbury, Amasa, 37.
Newbury, Benjamin, 37.
Newbury, Chancey, 37.
Newbury, Davis, 126.
Newbury, John, 37.
Newbury, Joseph, 37.
Newbury, Mary, 128.
Newbury, Nathan, 118.
Newbury, Nathl, 91.
Newbury, Richard, 127.
Newbury, Roger, 55.
Newbury, Samuel, 127.
Newbury, Stedman, 127.
Newcomb, Bethewel, 146.
Newcomb, Bradford, 147.
Newcomb, Jesse, 146.
Newcomb, John, 146.
Newcomb, Joseph, 146.
Newcomb, Paul, 146.
Newcomb, Sarah, 129.
Newcomb, Submit, 147.
Newcomb, Thos, 147.
Newcomb, William, 74.
Newcrum, Dur, 136.
Newcum, Jos, 139.
Newel, Danl, 138.
Newel, Danl, 149.
Newel, Frances, 23.
Newel, Jacob, 139.
Newel, Nathan, 61.
Newel, Nathaniel, 69.
Newel, Nathl, 134.
Newel, Nathl, 138.
Newel, Theodore, 70.
Newel, William, 61.
Newell, Benjamin, 89.
Newell, David, 89.
Newell, Robert, 89.
Newell, Robt, 2d, 89.
Newell, Thos, 154.
Newill, Sarah, 43.
Newill, Abel, 35.
Newill, Amos, 49.
Newill, Charles, 49.
Newill, David, 34.
Newill, Isaac, 49.

Newill, Isaac, Jr., 49.
Newill, James, 46.
Newill, John, 49.
Newill, Josiah, 49.
Newill, Mark, 49.
Newill, Pomeroy, 49.
Newill, Samuel, 34.
Newill, Samuel, 50.
Newill, Simeon, 49.
Newill, Solomon, 64.
Newill, Thomas, 41.
Newport, Sarah, 129.
Newreshic, Lewis, 30.
Newton, Able, 118.
Newton, Able, 122.
Newton, Abner, 62.
Newton, Abner, 92.
Newton, Abraham, 62.
Newton, Agrippa, 118.
Newton, Ama, 119.
Newton, Aron, 108.
Newton, Asa, 122.
Newton, Asael, 121.
Newton, Asahel, 81.
Newton, Burrel, 96.
Newton, Christopher, 112.
Newton, Christopher, 118.
Newton, Cloe, 92.
Newton, David, 17.
Newton, Desire, 151.
Newton, Ebenezer, 116.
Newton, Elijah, 118.
Newton, Enoch, 111.
Newton, Ezekiel, 75.
Newton, Isaac, 70.
Newton, Isaac, 152.
Newton, Israel, 122.
Newton, Israel, Junr, 122.
Newton, Israel, 3d, 122.
Newton, Jabez, 151.
Newton, Jacob, 114.
Newton, James, 122.
Newton, Jerad, 92.
Newton, John, 102.
Newton, John, 122.
Newton, Jno, 134.
Newton, Jonah, 102.
Newton, Jona, 137.
Newton, Joseph, 92.
Newton, Mark, 118.
Newton, Mathew, 35.
Newton, Mathew, 151.
Newton, Miles, 110.
Newton, Moses, 134.
Newton, Roger, 111.
Newton, Samuel, 111.
Newton, Saml, 118.
Newton, Samuel, 2nd, 111.
Nich (Negro), 26.
Nichall, Saml, 148.
Nichalls, Jonathl, 141.
Nichalls, Jona, Jnr, 150.
Nichalls, Nathl, 148.
Nichelson, Angus, 72.
Nichelson, Sarah, 68.
Nicholl, Owen, 128.
Nicholls, Ezekiel, 154.
Nicholls, John, 147.
Nicholls, Joseph, 148.
Nicholls, Joseph, 148.
Nicholls, Lemuel, 147.
Nicholls, Thomas, 147.
Nichols, Benjamin, 17.
Nichols, Caleb, 69.
Nichols, Daniel, 26.
Nichols, Daniel, 31.
Nichols, Daniel, 72.
Nichols, Daniel, Junr, 25.
Nichols, David, 13.
Nichols, David, 17.
Nichols, Ebenezer, 10.
Nichols, Ebenezer, 13.
Nichols, Elethan, 17.
Nichols, Elijah, 20.
Nichols, Elijah, 150.
Nichols, Elijah, 150.
Nichols, Enoch, 22.
Nichols, Enos, 22.
Nichols, Ephraim, 13.
Nichols, Eunice (Wid.), 47.
Nichols, Gold., 32.
Nichols, Hezekiah, 14.
Nichols, Isaac, 72.
Nichols, James, 17.
Nichols, James, 21.
Nichols, James, 24.
Nichols, James, 88.
Nichols, James, 47.
Nichols, James, Jr, 24.
Nichols, Jeremiah, 22.
Nichols, Jesse, 13.
Nichols, John, 14.
Nichols, John, 32.
Nichols, John, 78.
Nichols, Jonathan, 22.
Nichols, Jonathan, 23.
Nichols, Jonathan, 29.
Nichols, Jonathn, 147.
Nichols, Joseph, 125.
Nichols, Lemuel, 21.
Nichols, Lewis, 59.
Nichols, Lois, 86.
Nichols, Mansfield, 17.

Nichols, Matthias, 30.
Nichols, Moses, 12.
Nichols, Moses, 24.
Nichols, Nathan, 31.
Nichols, Nathaniel, 30.
Nichols, Nehemiah, 22.
Nichols, Nicholas, 42.
Nichols, Paul, 14.
Nichols, Peter, 21.
Nichols, Peter, 32.
Nichols, Philip, 17.
Nichols, Philip, 31.
Nichols, Philo, 21.
Nichols, Philoe, 69.
Nichols, Rebeca, 84.
Nichols, Reubin, 29.
Nichols, Richard, 20.
Nichols, Robert, 19.
Nichols, Robert, 25.
Nichols, Robert, 72.
Nichols, Samuel, 11.
Nichols, Samuel, 72.
Nichols, Samuel, 20.
Nichols, Sarah (Wid.), 30.
Nichols, Silvenus, 88.
Nichols, Squire, 14.
Nichols, Thaddeus, 23.
Nichols, Thadeus, 86.
Nichols, Thomas (Neg.), 31.
Nichols, Tiles, 17.
Nichols, William, 10.
Nichols, William, 31.
Nichols, William, 46.
Nicholson, Ambrose, 42.
Nicholson, Ambrose, Jr., 42.
Nicholson, Frances, 42.
Nicholson, Joel, 42.
Nickelson, Ezra, 67.
Nickerson, Archelus, 67.
Nickerson, Barack, 29.
Nickerson, Daniel, 125.
Nickerson, Eliphaz, 29.
Nickerson, James, 29.
Nickerson, Samuel, 67.
Nickerson, Uriah, 67.
Nickerson, William, 29.
Nickols, William, 113.
Nicol, Joseph, 110.
Nicol, Lidia, 109.
Nicol, Richard, 109.
Nicol, Simon, 109.
Nicol, Sussanah, 109.
Nicoll, Benjamin, 109.
Nicoll, Daniel, 94.
Nicoll, Elizabeth, 109.
Nicoll, Isaac, 94.
Nicoll, John, 103.
Nicoll, John, 109.
Nicoll, Polly, 109.
Nicoll, Samuel, 109.
Nicoll, Samuel, 110.
Nicoll, Samuel, 110.
Nicolls, Christopher, 104.
Nicols, John, 131.
Niel, Titus, 74.
Nigas, Silas, 154.
Niholls, Gideon, 78.
Nikerson, Hannah, 12.
Niles, Ambrus, 120.
Niles, Ambrus, 122.
Niles, Ambrus, 2d, 122.
Niles, Daniel, 82.
Niles, Darkas, 120.
Niles, David, 81.
Niles, Elisha, 81.
Niles, Elisha, 119.
Niles, James, 139.
Niles, John, 82.
Niles, Nathan, 117.
Niles, Nathan, 120.
Niles, Nathl, 119.
Niles, Nathl, 135.
Niles, Paul, 117.
Niles, Paul, Junr, 117.
Niles, Robart, 130.
Niles, Saml, 120.
Niles, Sands, 118.
Niles, Surviah, 116.
Niles, Thomas, 119.
Niles, William, 17.
Nilger, Sam, 60.
Noah, Will, 53.
Noal, David, 50.
Noble, Asahel, 72.
Noble, Daniel, 72.
Noble, David, 72.
Noble, Elethan, 10.
Noble, Elisha, 72.
Noble, Ezra, 72.
Noble, Francis, 77.
Noble, Israel, 59.
Noble, Jesse, 10.
Noble, Sherman, 72.
Noble, Sylvanus, 72.
Noble, Wakefield, 72.
Noble, William, 48.
Nobles, Diah, 126.
Nobles, Revd. G., 139.
Nobles, James, 125.
Nobles, James, 2d, 125.
Nobles, Jonathan, 81.
Nobles, Mary, 126.
Nobles, Soln, 139.

Nobles, William, 60.
Nobles, William, 125.
Nodine, Fredrick, 18.
Nodine, Lewis, 31.
Nolton, Thos, 82.
Norcott, Abner, 79.
Norcott, Dennis, 16.
Norcott, Reuben, 81.
Norcott, William, 81.
Norcute, John, 128.
Norden, Benjamin, 117.
Norecey, George, 59.
Norman, Caleb, 131.
Norman, John, 113.
Norman, Joshua, 131.
Norris, Benjn, 138.
Norris, Henry, 127.
Norris, Jno, 138.
Norris, Stephen, 29.
Norriss, Champfire, 64.
Norriss, Oliver, 90.
North, Abel, 34.
North, Asa, 41.
North, Ashbel, 68.
North, Asher, 33.
North, Ashur, 42.
North, Daniel, 41.
North, David, 41.
North, Eli, 41.
North, Ezekiel, 60.
North, Isaac, 34.
North, Isaiah, 41.
North, James, 33.
North, Jedediah, 34.
North, John, 41.
North, Joseph, 34.
North, Joseph, 60.
North, Levi, 34.
North, Lott, 41.
North, Remembrance, 68.
North, Reuben, 40.
North, Salmon, 52.
North, Samuel, 34.
North, Samuel, 41.
North, Seth, 34.
North, Seth, 41.
North, Simeon, 34.
North, Stephen, 34.
North, Stephen, 57.
Northam, Asa, 120.
Northam, Jno, 135.
Northam, Jonathan, Junr, 120.
Northaway, Ozias, 62.
Northaway, Saml, 67.
Northawey, James, 60.
Northerum, Ebenr, 62.
Northop, Lawrence, 20.
Northorp, Abraham, 19.
Northorp, Joseph, 63.
Northrop, Abel, 20.
Northrop, Abel, 102.
Northrop, Abigal, 96.
Northrop, Amos, 19.
Northrop, Amos, 75.
Northrop, Andrew, 10.
Northrop, Anne, 10.
Northrop, Asa, 10.
Northrop, Caleb, 72.
Northrop, Clement, 102.
Northrop, David, 10.
Northrop, David, 19.
Northrop, David, 72.
Northrop, Drake, 10.
Northrop, Elijah, 75.
Northrop, Enoch, 78.
Northrop, Enos, 10.
Northrop, Ezra, 10.
Northrop, George, 20.
Northrop, Gideon, 20.
Northrop, Gideon, 77.
Northrop, Gideon, 112.
Northrop, Gideon, 2d, 77.
Northrop, Heth, 101.
Northrop, Isaac, 10.
Northrop, Isaac, 19.
Northrop, Isaac, 111.
Northrop, Isaiah, 19.
Northrop, Job, 111.
Northrop, Job, 2nd, 111.
Northrop, Joel, 72.
Northrop, Joel, 77.
Northrop, Joel, 103.
Northrop, John, 20.
Northrop, Jonathan, 77.
Northrop, Joseph, 77.
Northrop, Joseph, 10.
Northrop, Joshua, 10.
Northrop, Joshua, Jur, 10.
Northrop, Lazerus, 101.
Northrop, Mary, 10.
Northrop, Moses, 101.
Northrop, Nathanel, 20.
Northrop, Nehemiah, 20.
Northrop, Peter, 20.
Northrop, Ruth (Wid.), 20.
Northrop, Saml, 115.
Northrop, Samuel, 115.
Northrop, Solomon, 72.
Northrop, Wait, 10.
Northrop, William, 20.
Northrup, Aaron, 28.
Northrup, Benjamin, 28.

# INDEX.

Northrup, Elisabeth, 28.
Northrup, James, 28.
Northrup, John, 28.
Northrup, Josiah, 28.
Northrup, Matthew, 29.
Northrup, Nathan[el], 28.
Northrup, Philo, 111.
Northrup, Thomas, 28.
Northum, Jonathan, 121.
Northum, Samuel, 84.
Northway, Joseph, 41.
Norton, Aaron, 35.
Norton, Aaron, 59.
Norton, Aaron, 88.
Norton, Abel, 99.
Norton, Abraham, 92.
Norton, Alexander, 60.
Norton, Andrew, 34.
Norton, Andrews, 60.
Norton, Aron, 98.
Norton, Ashbel, 69.
Norton, Ashbel, 97.
Norton, Austin, 78.
Norton, Beriah, 97.
Norton, Bethuel, 41.
Norton, Bird Eye, 69.
Norton, Charles, 49.
Norton, Cyrus, 110.
Norton, Daniel, 51.
Norton, Daniel, 65.
Norton, David, 110.
Norton, David, 135.
Norton, Ebenezer, 50.
Norton, Ebenezer, 69.
Norton, Eber, 98.
Norton, Ebor, 97.
Norton, Eli, 84.
Norton, Elizabeth, 97.
Norton, Elizabeth, 98.
Norton, Elnathan, 34.
Norton, Elnathan, 49.
Norton, Elnathan, Jr., 34.
Norton, Felix, 97.
Norton, Filo, 20.
Norton, Francis, 135.
Norton, Freegrace, 51.
Norton, George, 78.
Norton, Gideon, 69.
Norton, Gideon, 99.
Norton, Gold G., 93.
Norton, Hooker, 98.
Norton, Hosias, 96.
Norton, Hseas, 110.
Norton, Ichabod, 41.
Norton, Isaac, 35.
Norton, Isaac, Jr., 35.
Norton, Isaac, 3[d], 35.
Norton, Isachar, 75.
Norton, Isaiah, 34.
Norton, Isaiah, 88.
Norton, Jedediah, 79.
Norton, Jedidiah, 34.
Norton, Jedidiah, 41.
Norton, Jerad, 97.
Norton, Jesse, 99.
Norton, Joel, 35.
Norton, Joel, 75.
Norton, Joel, 84.
Norton, Joel, 91.
Norton, John, 81.
Norton, John, 84.
Norton, John, 96.
Norton, John, 97.
Norton, John, 2[d], 51.
Norton, Josiah, 83.
Norton, Levi, 66.
Norton, Levi, 68.
Norton, Lot, 62.
Norton, Medad, 69.
Norton, Miles, 61.
Norton, Molly, 97.
Norton, Moses, 84.
Norton, Nathan, 20.
Norton, Nathaniel, 59.
Norton, Noadiah, 99.
Norton, Noah, 96.
Norton, Noah W., 110.
Norton, Oliver, 60.
Norton, Phinehas, 68.
Norton, Reuben S., 41.
Norton, Robert, 72.
Norton, Roger, 33.
Norton, Roger, Jr., 33.
Norton, Rowland, 72.
Norton, Ruben, 98.
Norton, Ruben, 2[d], 98.
Norton, Rufus, 97.
Norton, Samuel, 34.
Norton, Samuel, 36.
Norton, Samuel, 41.
Norton, Samuel, 69.
Norton, Sarah, 68.
Norton, Selah, 36.
Norton, Seth, 51.
Norton, Silas, 59.
Norton, Silvenus, 67.
Norton, Simeon, 52.
Norton, Solomon, 34.
Norton, Sol[a], 135.
Norton, Stephen, 33.
Norton, Stephen, 62.
Norton, Stephen, 96.
Norton, Stephen, 2[d], 62.

Norton, Stephen, 2[nd], 96.
Norton, Thomas, 68.
Norton, Thomas, 91.
Norton, Timothy, 97.
Norton, Zebel, 110.
Norval, Nathaniel, 59.
Norvel, William, 70.
Noth, Juna, 60.
Noth, Martin, 63.
Noth, Noah, 60.
Noth, Seth, 59.
Nothenn, Elijah, 135.
Nott, Abigail, 129.
Nott, Abraham, 68.
Nott, Asa, 67.
Nott, Charles, 34.
Nott, Charles, Jr., 34.
Nott, Gershom, 41.
Nott, John, 53.
Nott, John, 86.
Nott, Joseph, 86.
Nott, Mary, 86.
Nott, Samuel, 130.
Nott, William, 53.
Nott, William, 86.
Nott, William, 101.
Notton, John, 50.
Notts, Martin, 67.
Nowland, Samuel, 43.
Noyce, Calvin, 123.
Noyce, Charles, 120.
Noyce, Dolly, 131.
Noyce, Gershom, 117.
Noyce, James, 107.
Noyce, James, 116.
Noyce, James, 117.
Noyce, James, Jun[r], 117.
Noyce, John, 117.
Noyce, John, 123.
Noyce, Joseph, 116.
Noyce, Joseph, 123.
Noyce, Mathew, 92.
Noyce, Peleg, 117.
Noyce, Thomas, 118.
Noyce, William, 104.
Noyce, William, 123.
Noyce, William, Jun[r], 123.
Noyes, John, 32.
Noyse, Joseph, 14.
Noyse, Paul, 103.
Nucrum, Sam[l], 134.
Nugen, John, 116.
Nugen, John, 118.
Numan, Benjamin, 25.
Numan, Clark, 25.
Numan David, 25.
Numan, Ezra, 25.
Numan, Israel, 25.
Numan, Nathaniel, 25.
Numan, Nehemiah, 25.
Numan, Platt, 25.
Numan, Samuel, 25.
Numan, Stephen, 24.
Nun, Samuel, 115.
Nungers, Israel, 56.
Nutt, Robert, 16.
Nutter, John, 132.
Nye, Benj[a], 139.
Nye, Hezekiah, 138.
Nye, Jn[o], 137.
Nye, Milatiah, 43.
Nye, Samuel, 138.
Nye, Silas, 146.
Nye, Solomon, 43.

Oakes, David, 46.
Oakes, Isaac, 46.
Oakes, Nathan, 103.
Oakley, Gilbert, 19.
Oakley, Jeremiah, 19.
Oakly, Jerad, 31.
Oakly, Miles, 31.
Oakly, Peter, 31.
Oatman, Samuel, 95.
Obed (Negroe), 110.
Obrian, William, 142.
Obrion, John, 142.
Obriont, Partrick, 69.
Obverd, Thomas, 34.
OCain, Antony, 101.
OCane, Jeremiah, 96.
OCane, Joseph, 96.
Ocolow (Negro), 30.
Oconoland, Patrick, 53.
O'Daniel, Partrick, 86.
Odel, Daniel, 64.
Odel, Nathaniel, 22.
Odle, Aaron, 17.
Odle, Daniel, 31.
Odle, David, 31.
Odle, Isaac, 14.
Odle, John, 17.
Odle, Nehemiah S., 14.
Odle, Sarah, 14.
Odle, Walker, 78.
Ods, Martha, 91.
Ogden, Bethuel, 14.
Ogden, David, 14.
Ogden, Ebenezer, 12.
Ogden, Hezekiah, 13.
Ogden, Jacob, 46.
Ogden, Jean, 14.
Ogden, Jesse, 21.
Ogden, John, 12.

Ogden, Joseph, 32.
Ogden, Moses, 13.
Ogden, Samuel, 13.
Ogden, Sturges, 14.
Oglesby, Rev[d] Geo., 21.
Olcott, Asahael, 37.
Olcott, Benoni, 37.
Olcott, Daniel, 46.
Olcott, Eli, 38.
Olcott, Harriet, 68.
Olcott, Hezekiah, 46.
Olcott, James, 46.
Olcott, James, 59.
Olcott, James, 65.
Olcott, Jeames, 58.
Olcott, Jediah, 42.
Olcott, John, 147.
Olcott, John Easton, 57.
Olcott, Jonathan, 46.
Olcott, Joseph, 46.
Olcott, Nathaniel, 37.
Olcott, Roderic, 46.
Olcott, Samuel, 37.
Olcott, Samuel, 46.
Olcott, Samuel, 68.
Olcott, Theodore, 46.
Olcott, Tho[s], 81.
Olcott, Timothy, 46.
Olcott, William, 2[d], 46.
Olcut, Caleb, 139.
Olcutt, Ezek[l], 132.
Olden, Isaac, 56.
Older, Hannah, 75.
Olds, Ebenezer, 41.
Olds, Gersham, 109.
Olds, John, 37.
Olds, John, Jr., 37.
Olds, Joseph, 51.
Olds, Josiah, 51.
Olds, Josiah, 2[nd], 51.
Olds, Stephen, 51.
Olin, Philup, 113.
Olive, Neptune, 42.
Oliver, Timothy, 75.
Ollcott, Thomas, 59.
Olmsted, Ashbel, Jr, 36.
Olmstead, Bates, 83.
Olmstead, Daniel, 31.
Olmstead, Daniel, 82.
Olmstead, David, 72.
Olmstead, Elijah, 31.
Olmstead, James, 81.
Olmstead, Jeh[d], 83.
Olmstead, John, 31.
Olmstead, Oliver, 83.
Olmstead, Richard, 72.
Olmstead, Roger, 83.
Olmsted, Aaron, 36.
Olmsted, Ambros, 28.
Olmsted, Ambros, 2[d], 28.
Olmsted, Asa, 39.
Olmsted, Asahel, 36.
Olmsted, Ashbel, 36.
Olmsted, Benjamin, 36.
Olmsted, Catharine (W[d]), 24.
Olmsted, Daniel, 10.
Olmsted, Daniel, 2[d], 28.
Olmsted, Darius, 24.
Olmsted, David, 22.
Olmsted, David, 28.
Olmsted, David, 2[d], 28.
Olmsted, David, 3[d], 28.
Olmsted, Ebenezer, 28.
Olmsted, Epaphras, 36.
Olmsted, Frances F., 47.
Olmsted, Francis, 48.
Olmsted, George, 36.
Olmsted, Hannah (Wid.), 39.
Olmsted, James, 22.
Olmsted, James, 24.
Olmsted, James, 28.
Olmsted, James, 47.
Olmsted, James, 2[d], 24.
Olmsted, Jared, 28.
Olmsted, Jesse, 23.
Olmsted, Jonathan, 36.
Olmsted, Joseph, 22.
Olmsted, Joseph, 39.
Olmsted, Josiah, 28.
Olmsted, Justus, 36.
Olmsted, Justus, 2[d], 28.
Olmsted, Lydia (W[d]), 22.
Olmsted, Mathew, 28.
Olmsted, Michael, 36.
Olmsted, Nathan, 22.
Olmsted, Nathaniel, 24.
Olmsted, Nathaniel, 36.
Olmsted, Phebe (W[d]), 24.
Olmsted, Reuben, 21.
Olmsted, Reuben, 24.
Olmsted, Samuel, 22.
Olmsted, Samuel, 24.
Olmsted, Samuel, 24.
Olmsted, Samuel, 28.
Olmsted, Samuel, 36.
Olmsted, Samuel, Jr, 36.
Olmsted, Samuel, 2[d], 28.
Olmsted, Silvanus, 21.
Olmsted, Simeon, 40.
Olmsted, Stephen, 36.
Olmsted, Thaddeus, 36.

Olmsted, Thomas, 47.
Olmsted, Timothy, 47.
Olmsted, William, 36.
Olmstord, Grace, 27.
Olney, Ezek[l], 138.
Olney, Hez[a], 142.
Omsted, Hezekiah, 59.
Omsted, Nathan, 28.
Omsted, Roger, 63.
Omsted, Roswell, 70.
Onsted, Daniel, 48.
Onsted, Daniel, Jr., 48.
Onton, Joseph, 60.
Orcutt, Dan[l], 137.
Orcutt, David, 137.
Orcutt, Icabod, 137.
Orcutt, Jabez, 137.
Orcutt, Jacob, 136.
Orcutt, John, 153.
Orcutt, Nath[a], 137.
Orcutt, Nath[l], 137.
Orcutt, Sol[m], 137.
Orcutt, Stephens, 137.
Orcutt, Tim[o], 137.
Ord, John, 104.
Orms, Hannah, 143.
Ormsbe, Tho[s], 81.
Ormsby, Amos, 67.
Ormsby, Eliphalet, 152.
Ormsby, Jere[h], 143.
Ormsby, Jesse, 150.
Ormsby, John, 152.
Ormsby, Samuel, 130.
Ormsby, Stephen, 152.
Ormsted, Isaac, 68.
Ormstid, Timothy, 67.
Ornsby, Ephraim, 131.
Orsborn, Abel, 38.
Orsborn, Benjamin, 38.
Orsborn, Daniel, 38.
Orsborn, David, 44.
Orsborn, Ezekiel, 38.
Orsborn, Ezra, 38.
Orsborn, Jacob, 71.
Orsborn, Jeremiah, 71.
Orsborn, John, 65.
Orsborn, John, 71.
Orsborn, Jonathan, 39.
Orsborn, Joseph, 35.
Orsborn, Joseph, 71.
Orsborn, Rebecka, 38.
Orsborn, Reuben, 66.
Orsborn, Samuel, 38.
Orsborn, Samuel, 69.
Orsborn, Thomas, 38.
Orsborn, Zebedee, 38.
Orton, Azariah, 65.
Orton, Darius, 65.
Orton, Guy, 109.
Orton, Hezekiah, 59.
Orton, John, 78.
Orton, Sam[l], 70.
Orton, Samuel, 78.
Orton, Sedgwick, 65.
Orven, Phinehas, 64.
Orvis, David, 63.
Orvis, Eleazer, 67.
Orvis, Reuber, 63.
Orvis, Roger, 67.
Orvis, Zadock, 40.
Osbone, Jeremiah, 31.
Osborn, Aaron, 19.
Osborn, Aaron, 28.
Osborn, Abel, 14.
Osborn, Abigail, 13.
Osborn, Abigail, 29.
Osborn, Abijah, 77.
Osborn, Abner, 110.
Osborn, Abraham, 110.
Osborn, Abraham, 2[nd], 110.
Osborn, Amos, 77.
Osborn, Amos, 110.
Osborn, Andrew, 110.
Osborn, Arael, 110.
Osborn, Barnum, 73.
Osborn, Benjamin, 105.
Osborn, Daniel, 12.
Osborn, Daniel, 14.
Osborn, Daniel, 14.
Osborn, Daniel, 86.
Osborn, Daniel, 110.
Osborn, Daniel, 2[nd], 110.
Osborn, David, 10.
Osborn, David, 11.
Osborn, David, 14.
Osborn, Ebenezer, 13.
Osborn, Ebenezer, Jn[r], 14.
Osborn, Edward, 20.
Osborn, Elezer, 19.
Osborn, Elijah, 110.
Osborn, Elijah, 111.
Osborn, Elisha, 111.
Osborn, Ephraim, 30.
Osborn, Ephraim, 32.
Osborn, Ezra, 110.
Osborn, Gamaliel, 29.
Osborn, Gershom, 14.
Osborn, Hezekiah, 32.
Osborn, Hill, 104.
Osborn, Howes, 14.
Osborn, Isaac, 32.
Osborn, Isaac, 109.

Osborn, Israel, 10.
Osborn, Jacob, 21.
Osborn, James, 10.
Osborn, Jerad, 31.
Osborn, Jerard, 95.
Osborn, Jeremiah, 105.
Osborn, John, 14.
Osborn, John, 18.
Osborn, John, 77.
Osborn, John, 86.
Osborn, John, 110.
Osborn, John, 111.
Osborn, Jonah, 29.
Osborn, Jonathan, 19.
Osborn, Joseph, 11.
Osborn, Joseph, 95.
Osborn, Joseph, 95.
Osborn, Joshua, 95.
Osborn, Josiah, 73.
Osborn, Levi, 11.
Osborn, Levi, 13.
Osborn, Mable, 14.
Osborn, Mahitabel, 104.
Osborn, Marah, 29.
Osborn, Martha, 38.
Osborn, Mary, 105.
Osborn, Medad, 95.
Osborn, Moses, 12.
Osborn, Naboth, 95.
Osborn, Nathan, 30.
Osborn, Nathan, 78.
Osborn, Nathan, 2[d], 78.
Osborn, Nathan[el], 29.
Osborn, Peter, 110.
Osborn, Reubin, 19.
Osborn, Samuel, 17.
Osborn, Samuel, 111.
Osborn, Shadick, 73.
Osborn, Stephen, 14.
Osborn, Stephen, 72.
Osborn, Stephen, 103.
Osborn, Thaddeus, 110.
Osborn, Thomas, 95.
Osborn, Thomas, 110.
Osborn, Timothy, 73.
Osborn, White, 77.
Osborn, William, 30.
Osborn, William, 32.
Osborn, Zadock, 77.
Osburn, David, 130.
Osburn, Jacob, 54.
Osgood, Appleton, 149.
Osgood, Josiah, 126.
Osgood, William, Jn[r], 149.
Osgood, Zach[h], 149.
Oshall, John, 104.
Osmon, Ashbel, 68.
Osmon, Thomas, 62.
Osmon, Thomas, 62.
Ossgood, Jeremiah H., 33.
Osterbank, Moses, 32.
Otis, Charles, 82.
Otis, Christopher, 72.
Otis, James, 117.
Otis, James, 121.
Otis, John, 121.
Otis, John I., 121.
Otis, Jonathan, 85.
Otis, Jonathan, 116.
Otis, Joseph, 131.
Otis, Joseph (Negroe), 92.
Otis, Nath[l], 121.
Otis, Nath[l], 125.
Otis, Nath[l], Jun[r], 122.
Otis, Nath[l], 3[d], 121.
Otis, Robart, 122.
Otis, Robart, Jun[r], 122.
Otty, William, 104.
Ovaitt, John, 72.
Ovaitt, Samuel, 72.
Ovaitt, Thomas, 72.
Ovatt, Benjamin, 59.
Ovatt, Samuel, 59.
Ovatt, Samuel, 59.
Overton, Aaron, 112.
Overton, Seth, 79.
Ovet, Ellick, 102.
Ovet, Hannah, 102.
Ovet, Isaac, 101.
Ovet, Isaac, 102.
Ovett, Ebenezer, 101.
Ovett, Nathan, 101.
Owen, ——, 56.
Owen, Aaron, 55.
Owen, Aaron, 66.
Owen, Abner, 62.
Owen, Alvin, 45.
Owen, Aziel, 135.
Owen, Benj[a], 140.
Owen, Daniel, 72.
Owen, David, 135.
Owen, Eben[e], 140.
Owen, Eleaz[r], 140.
Owen, Elijah, 44.
Owen, Elijah, 56.
Owen, Isaac, 50.
Owen, James, 62.
Owen, John, 129.
Owen, John C., 47.
Owen, Joseph, 129.
Owen, Nath[l], 55.
Owen, Stine, 56.
Owen, Timothy, 147.

# INDEX.

Owen (Wid.), 135.
Owens, Josiah, 144.
Owing, Patience, 108.
Oysterbanks, David, 12.
Oysterbanks, David, Jnr, 13.
Oysterbanks, Isaac, 12.
Oysterbanks, Joshua, 12.

Paching, Ebenezer, 21.
Packer, Abigail, 120.
Packer, Benjamin, 120.
Packer, Danl, 120.
Packer, Edward, 120.
Packer, Eldrige, 120.
Packer, Elam, 120.
Packer, Elisha, 120.
Packer, Frelove, 118.
Packer, James, 120.
Packer, John, 120.
Packer, John, 130.
Packer, John, Junr, 120.
Packer, John, 3d, 120.
Packer, Joseph, 120.
Packer, Joseph, 120.
Packer, Leut, 77.
Packer, Surviah, 120.
Packeton, Dennis, 26.
Packwood, Joseph, 128.
Packwood, Nabby, 129.
Pacston, Shubael, 127.
Paddack, George, 86.
Paddack, John, 86.
Paddack, Robert, 86.
Paddack, Samuel, 86.
Paddack, Seth, 86.
Paddack, William, 86.
Paddock, Zackeriah, 86.
Page, Aaron, 64.
Page, Abel, 18.
Page, Abel, 71.
Page, Amos, 91.
Page, Asa, 71.
Page, Asa, 2d, 70.
Page, Balthus, 108.
Page, Benjamin, 92.
Page, Daniel, 59.
Page, David, 71.
Page, Edmond, 95.
Page, Elias, 133.
Page, Gad, 133.
Page, Icabod, 92.
Page, Icabod, 104.
Page, Isaac, 108.
Page, Jacob, 92.
Page, James, 144.
Page, Jared, 93.
Page, Jeremiah, 127.
Page, Joel, 91.
Page, John, 92.
Page, John, 152.
Page, Jonathan, 19.
Page, Joseph, 91.
Page, Joseph, 116.
Page, Joseph, 125.
Page, Josiah, 73.
Page, Levi, 47.
Page, Nathaniel, 92.
Page, Philemon, 114.
Page, Ranor, 49.
Page, Ruben, 92.
Page, Ruben, 93.
Page, Samuel, 19.
Page, Samuel, 91.
Page, Titus, 35.
Page, William, 59.
Page, William, 64.
Pain, Benajah, 132.
Pain, Ezrl, 70.
Pain, Jno, 134.
Pain, Reuben, 79.
Pain, Roswel, 132.
Pain, Wm, 132.
Paine, Abraham, 59.
Paine, Ebenezer, 59.
Paine, Eliazer, 38.
Paine, Jessee, 70.
Paine, Joseph, 109.
Paine, Philemon, 111.
Paine, Rufus, 38.
Paine, Solomon, 38.
Paine, Stephen, Jr., 38.
Paine, Thomas, 109.
Paine, William, 59.
Paine, William, 59.
Painter, John, 77.
Painter, Jno, 136.
Painter, John, 2d, 77.
Painter, Lamberton, 78.
Painter, Thomas, 105.
Painter, Thomas W., 77.
Palmer, Abijah, 117.
Palmer, Able, 125.
Palmer, Ambrose, 66.
Palmer, Amme, 10.
Palmer, Amos, 117.
Palmer, Amos, 145.
Palmer, Amos, 2d, 118.
Palmer, Asa, 112.
Palmer, Asa, 117.
Palmer, Asael, 92.
Palmer, B. (Wd), 15.
Palmer, Barnabas, 91.
Palmer, Benjn, 55.

Palmer, Benjamin, 60.
Palmer, Benjamin, 91.
Palmer, Benjn, 140.
Palmer, Benjn, 151.
Palmer, Christopher, 121.
Palmer, Christopher, 2d, 121.
Palmer, Daniel, 65.
Palmer, Daniel, 117.
Palmer, Darius, 113.
Palmer, Denham, 15.
Palmer, Denison, 117.
Palmer, Ebenezer, 74.
Palmer, Eleazer, 152.
Palmer, Eliakim, 117.
Palmer, Elihu, 120.
Palmer, Elias, 121.
Palmer, Elias, Junr, 121.
Palmer, Elias Sanford, 115.
Palmer, Elihu, 142.
Palmer, Elihu, 151.
Palmer, Elijah, 74.
Palmer, Elijah, 92.
Palmer, Elijah, 117.
Palmer, Eliphalet, 152.
Palmer, Elizabeth, 52.
Palmer, Elizabeth, 102.
Palmer, Elliot, 115.
Palmer, Elyh, 151.
Palmer, Enos, 16.
Palmer, Enos, 152.
Palmer, Ethel, 115.
Palmer, Ezekial, 74.
Palmer, George, 114.
Palmer, George, 115.
Palmer, George, 120.
Palmer, George, 121.
Palmer, Gershom, 113.
Palmer, Gershon, 115.
Palmer, Gideon, 16.
Palmer, Gilbert, 115.
Palmer, Hannah, 117.
Palmer, Hannah, 128.
Palmer, Henry, 117.
Palmer, Humphrey, 121.
Palmer, Ichabod, 115.
Palmer, Isaac, 52.
Palmer, Isaac, 91.
Palmer, Israel, 16.
Palmer, Jabez, 145.
Palmer, James, 117.
Palmer, James, Junr, 117.
Palmer, Jedediah, 115.
Palmer, Jehiel, 55.
Palmer, Jemima, 115.
Palmer, Jerad, 91.
Palmer, Jeremiah, 24.
Palmer, Jesse, 114.
Palmer, Jesse, 117.
Palmer, Job, 71.
Palmer, Joel, 55.
Palmer, John, 15.
Palmer, John, 55.
Palmer, John, 75.
Palmer, John, 91.
Palmer, John, 112.
Palmer, John, 116.
Palmer, John, 153.
Palmer, John W., 16.
Palmer, Jonah, 153.
Palmer, Jonathan, 16.
Palmer, Jonathan, 55.
Palmer, Jonathan, 91.
Palmer, Jonath, 151.
Palmer, Jonathan, Ju., 55.
Palmer, Jonathan, Junr, 116.
Palmer, Joseph, 115.
Palmer, Joseph, 140.
Palmer, Joseph, 151.
Palmer, Joseph, 152.
Palmer, Josiah, 152.
Palmer, Judah, 34.
Palmer, Judah, 49.
Palmer, L. (Wd), 15.
Palmer, Levi, 16.
Palmer, Marshal, 152.
Palmer, Messenger, 16.
Palmer, Michael, 115.
Palmer, Mody, 115.
Palmer, Moses, 117.
Palmer, Nathan, 117.
Palmer, Nathan, 148.
Palmer, Nathan, Junr, 118.
Palmer, Nathaniel, 74.
Palmer, Nathaniel, 91.
Palmer, Nathl, 117.
Palmer, Nehemiah, 116.
Palmer, Nehemiah, 145.
Palmer, Noyce, 117.
Palmer, Peleg, 115.
Palmer, Peleg, 118.
Palmer, Phebe, 91.
Palmer, Pheneas, 151.
Palmer, Polly, 15.
Palmer, Reuben, 60.
Palmer, Robart, 118.
Palmer, Roswell, 117.
Palmer, Roswill, 151.
Palmer, Ruben, 117.
Palmer, Ruben, 125.
Palmer, Samuel, 16.
Palmer, Samuel, 110.
Palmer, Samuel, 117.
Palmer, Saml, 125.

Palmer, Saml, 151.
Palmer, Saml, 151.
Palmer, Samuel, Jr., 16.
Palmer, Sanford, 115.
Palmer, Saul, 51.
Palmer, Seth, 16.
Palmer, Seth, 152.
Palmer, Simeon, 61.
Palmer, Simeon, 117.
Palmer, Smith, 15.
Palmer, Solomon, 60.
Palmer, Stephan, 91.
Palmer, Stephen, 15.
Palmer, Stephen, 115.
Palmer, Stutely, 115.
Palmer, Thaddeus, 141.
Palmer, Thomas, 117.
Palmer, Timothy, 51.
Palmer, Titus, 16.
Palmer, Uriel, 151.
Palmer, Veniah, 153.
Palmer, Vorce, 115.
Palmer, Vose, 148.
Palmer, Wait, 115.
Palmer, Walter, 148.
Palmer, William, 64.
Palmer, William, 115.
Palmer, William, 116.
Palmer, William, 117.
Palmer, Wm, Junr, 116.
Palmer, Winas, 16.
Palmer, Zazaries, 60.
Palmer, Zebulon, 75.
Palmer, Ziba, 151.
Palmes, Samel, 81.
Palmeter, Benjamin, 35.
Palmeter, Jesse, 130.
Palmeter, Jonth, 35.
Palmeter, Joseph, 115.
Palmeter, Paul, 115.
Palmeter, Phineas, 118.
Palmeter, Silas, 115.
Palmitter, Geaner, 14.
Palms, Andrew, 71.
Palson, Henry, 96.
Pane, Aaron, 19.
Pane, Abraham, 112.
Pane, Amasa, 79.
Pane, David, 17.
Pane, Samuel, 17.
Pane, William, 107.
Pangman, Adonijah, 60.
Parcks, Michael, 20.
Parde, Stephen, 77.
Pardee, Daniel, 50.
Pardee, David, 49.
Pardee, Elijah, 67.
Pardee, Eliphlet, 73.
Pardee, George, 62.
Pardee, Isaac, 61.
Pardee, James, 59.
Pardee, Jonathan, 59.
Pardee, Moses, 62.
Pardee, Sarah, 103.
Pardee, Thomas, 62.
Pardey, Eli, 71.
Pardie, Ebenezur, 92.
Pardie, James, 99.
Pardie, Jerad, 96.
Pardie, Joel, 100.
Pardie, John, 106.
Pardie, Joseph, 102.
Pardie, Mabel, 97.
Pardie, Molly, 96.
Pardie, Phyphe, 110.
Pardie, Sibel, 105.
Pardie, Stephen, 100.
Pardie, Thomas, 100.
Pardie, William, 112.
Pardy, Abijah, 96.
Pardy, Asher, 19.
Pardy, Chandler, 97.
Pardy, Charles, 63.
Pardy, David, 106.
Pardy, Ebenezer, 61.
Pardy, Eliphalet, 106.
Pardy, Jacob, 96.
Pardy, James, 106.
Pardy, Johiel, 66.
Pardy, John, 25.
Pardy, Joseph, 100.
Pardy, Josiah, 102.
Pardy, Leveret, 97.
Pardy, Levi, 97.
Pardy, Lidia, 96.
Pardy, Saml, 61.
Pardy, Stephen, 19.
Parish, Asa, 75.
Parish, Isaac, 144.
Parish, Joel, 30.
Parish, Jonathan, 91.
Parish, Nathaniel, 130.
Parish, Oliver, 59.
Park, Daniel, 81.
Park, Jacob, 143.
Park, John, 35.
Park, John, 80.
Park, Joseph, 80.
Park, Lee, 122.

Park, Nathan, 142.
Park, Reubin, 142.
Park, Stephen, 120.
Parker, Abijail, 75.
Parker, Abner, 75.
Parker, Amasa, 75.
Parker, Amos, 92.
Parker, Amos, 108.
Parker, Arnold, 108.
Parker, Benjamin, 65.
Parker, Benjamin, 108.
Parker, Caleb, 93.
Parker, Canda, 133.
Parker, Charles, 108.
Parker, Daniel, 108.
Parker, Ebenezer, 65.
Parker, Ebenezer, 93.
Parker, Edmond, 106.
Parker, Edward, 92.
Parker, Edward, 2nd, 92.
Parker, Eli, 77.
Parker, Eliakim, 108.
Parker, Elliady, 108.
Parker, Ephraim, 147.
Parker, Ephrim, 108.
Parker, Em, 134.
Parker, Gamaleel, 108.
Parker, Huldah, 90.
Parker, Isaac, 108.
Parker, Jabez, 93.
Parker, James, 101.
Parker, James, 138.
Parker, James, 147.
Parker, Jeremiah, 102.
Parker, Job, 92.
Parker, John, 38.
Parker, John, 77.
Parker, John, 82.
Parker, John, 90.
Parker, John, 106.
Parker, Jno., 134.
Parker, John, 143.
Parker, Jno, 134.
Parker, John, 2d, 77.
Parker, Jonathan, 90.
Parker, Joseph, 40.
Parker, Joseph, 50.
Parker, Joseph, 75.
Parker, Joseph, 108.
Parker, Jos., 133.
Parker, Jos., 135.
Parker, Joshua, 108.
Parker, Joshua, 147.
Parker, Josiah, 133.
Parker, Levi, 92.
Parker, Levi, 108.
Parker, Nathan, 133.
Parker, Or, 137.
Parker, Peletiah, 135.
Parker, Phineas, 138.
Parker, Reuben, 45.
Parker, Reuben, 140.
Parker, Samuel, 40.
Parker, Saml, 89.
Parker, Samuel, 93.
Parker, Sarah, 90.
Parker, Soloman, 95.
Parker, Soln, 133.
Parker, Stephen, 66.
Parker, Stephen, 93.
Parker, Thankfull, 92.
Parker, Thomas, 75.
Parker, Thomas, 92.
Parker, Timothy, 130.
Parker, Waitful, 108.
Parker, Wimans, 135.
Parker, Wm, 89.
Parker, William, 92.
Parker, Zachh, 147.
Parker, Zachariah, Jr, 147.
Parkerson, William, 33.
Parkhurst, ——, 140.
Parkhurst, David, 148.
Parkhurst, Isaac, 149.
Parkhurst, Job, 148.
Parkhurst, Leml, 148.
Parkhurst, Pierce, 148.
Parkhurst, Saml, 149.
Parkis, James, 149.
Parkis, William, 149.
Parks, Abijah, Junr, 114.
Parks, Anna, 56.
Parks, Asa, 114.
Parks, David, 113.
Parks, Ebenr, 142.
Parks, Elijah, 114.
Parks, Elisha, 114.
Parks, Elizur, 56.
Parks, Hannah, 114.
Parks, Hezekiah, 118.
Parks, Isaac, 144.
Parks, Isaac, 150.
Parks, Isaac, 150.
Parks, Jacob, 118.
Parks, James, 23.
Parks, Jesse, 142.
Parks, John, 73.
Parks, John, 117.
Parks, John, 142.
Parks, Jona, 139.
Parks, Joseph, 120.

Parks, Joseph, 120.
Parks, Malvin, 115.
Parks, Mary, 118.
Parks, Mathew, Junr, 120.
Parks, Moses, 115.
Parks, Nathl, 120.
Parks, Neheh, 148.
Parks, Paul, 114.
Parks, Peter, 115.
Parks, Peter, Sr., 142.
Parks, Prudence, 41.
Parks, Roswell, 114.
Parks, Ruben, 113.
Parks, Saml, 148.
Parks, Silas, 114.
Parks, Simeon, 142.
Parks, Thomas, 120.
Parks, William, 75.
Parmalee, Amos, 84.
Parmalee, Daniel, 84.
Parmalee, Joseph, 91.
Parmalee, Nehemiah, 84.
Parmalee, Ozias, 84.
Parmalee, Rhoda, 84.
Parmalee, Roswell, 84.
Parmalie, Ambrose, 99.
Parmalie, Andrew, 97.
Parmalie, Camp, 96.
Parmalie, Daniel, 98.
Parmalie, David, 97.
Parmalie, Ebenezer, 104.
Parmalie, Eber, 98.
Parmalie, Eliphas, 96.
Parmalie, Hezekiah, 96.
Parmalie, Hezekiah, 104.
Parmalie, James, 96.
Parmalie, James, 98.
Parmalie, Jeremiah, 102.
Parmalie, Joel, 96.
Parmalie, Joel, 98.
Parmalie, John, 98.
Parmalie, John, 2nd, 98.
Parmalie, Joseph, 97.
Parmalie, Levi, 96.
Parmalie, Linus, 97.
Parmalie, Nathaniel, 38.
Parmalie, Pheneas, 99.
Parmalie, Ruben, 98.
Parmalie, Samuel, 97.
Parmalie, Sarah, 98.
Parmalie, Sarah, 104.
Parmalie, Simion, 104.
Parmalie, Timothy, 91.
Parmalie, William, 97.
Parmalie, William, 98.
Parmatree, Joshua, 51.
Parme, Gersham, 133.
Parmela, Braini, 84.
Parmela, Bryan, Esqr, 81.
Parmela, Constant, 84.
Parmela, Cornelius, 84.
Parmela, David, 84.
Parmela, Eliab, 84.
Parmela, Elias, 84.
Parmela, Ezra, 84.
Parmela, Jared, 81.
Parmela, Jonathan, 81.
Parmela, Josiah, 84.
Parmela, Nathan, 84.
Parmelee, Aaron, 84.
Parmelee, Abner, 84.
Parmelee, Daniel, 85.
Parmelee, Jehiel, 84.
Parmelee, John, 81.
Parmelee, John, 91.
Parmelee, Mable, 91.
Parmelee, Phinehas, 82.
Parmelee, Samuel, 84.
Parmeley, Abraham, 61.
Parmeley, Elihu, 51.
Parmeley, Mary, 60.
Parmeley, Submit, 64.
Parmeley, Truman, 75.
Parmely, Aaron, 68.
Parmely, Ebenezer, 56.
Parmely, Noah, 20.
Parmely, Oliver, 56.
Parmely, Oliver, Jur, 56.
Parmely, Samuel, 56.
Parmely, Standly, 61.
Parmely, Thomas, 75.
Parmer, Aaron, 79.
Parmer, Bethseba, 111.
Parmer, John, 81.
Parmer, Josu, 136.
Parmer, Levi, 81.
Parmer, Nathl, 133.
Parmer, Saml, 136.
Parmer, Stephen, 135.
Parmer, William, 62.
Parmerley, Amos, 64.
Parmerley, David, 70.
Parmerley, Theodore, 61.
Parmerly, Amos, 64.
Parmerly, Jno, 133.
Parmerly, Reuben, 59.
Parmerter, William, 69.
Parmeter, Joshua, 115.
Parmly, Standley, 64.
Parral, David, 105.
Parret, Abraham, 14.
Parret, John, 13.
Parrett, Martin, 104.

# INDEX.

Parrey, John, 69.
Parrick, Molly, 32.
Parrish, Abigal, 147.
Parrish, Elijah, 148.
Parrish, Eliphaz, 141.
Parrish, Ephraim, 91.
Parrish, John, 153.
Parrish, John, Jn$^r$, 153.
Parrish, Lem$^l$, 142.
Parrish, Roswell, 114.
Parrish, Roswell, 142.
Parrit, David, 13.
Parrot, John, 15.
Parrot, John, 31.
Parsely, Robert, 51.
Parson, Nathaniel, 94.
Parson, Samuel, 94.
Parsons, Aaron, 89.
Parsons, Aaron, 96.
Parsons, Abijah, 27.
Parsons, Amos, 49.
Parsons, Asabel, 40.
Parsons, Benj$^a$, 39.
Parsons, Benjamin, 70.
Parsons, Benjamin, 2$^d$, 39.
Parsons, Christopher, 39.
Parsons, Daniel, 40.
Parsons, Daniel, Jr., 40.
Parsons, David, 96.
Parsons, David, 137.
Parsons, Doctor, 55.
Parsons, Ebenezer, 39.
Parsons, Ebenezer, 51.
Parsons, Edward, 40.
Parsons, Eldad, 40.
Parsons, Eli, 40.
Parsons, Eli, 95.
Parsons, Elijah, 27.
Parsons, Elijah, 39.
Parsons, Rev$^d$ Elijah, 81.
Parsons, Ezra, 136.
Parsons, Hester, 108.
Parsons, Hezekiah, 39.
Parsons, Hoz$^h$, 55.
Parsons, Hezekiah, Jr., 39.
Parsons, Hezekiak, 41.
Parsons, Isaac, 40.
Parsons, Ithamer, 96.
Parsons, Jabez, 39.
Parsons, James, 56.
Parsons, Jesse, 152.
Parsons, John, 40.
Parsons, Jonathan, 27.
Parsons, Jonathan, 39.
Parsons, Joseph, 39.
Parsons, Joseph, 96.
Parsons, Jos., 139.
Parsons, Joshua, 41.
Parsons, Lemuel, 39.
Parsons, Rev$^r$ Lemuel, 81.
Parsons, Marshfield, 123.
Parsons, Mehitable, 86.
Parsons, Moses, 35.
Parsons, Nathan, 14.
Parsons, Nathaniel, 40.
Parsons, Nath$^l$, 136.
Parsons, Oliver, 51.
Parsons, Pelitiah, 55.
Parsons, Peter, 39.
Parsons, Prudence (W$^d$), 39.
Parsons, Rena, 94.
Parsons, Reuben, 51.
Parsons, Samuel, 43.
Parsons, Samuel, 96.
Parsons, Sam$^l$, 136.
Parsons, Samuel, Jun$^r$, 84.
Parsons, Sam F., 96.
Parsons, Sarah, 96.
Parsons, Sarah (W$^d$), 17.
Parsons, Seth, 136.
Parsons, Seth, 136.
Parsons, Shubab, 40.
Parsons, Shubel, 40.
Parsons, Simeon, 39.
Parsons, Simeon 96.
Parsons, Stephen, 86.
Parsons, Stephen, 126.
Parsons, Stephen, 136.
Parsons, Thomas, 39.
Parsons, Thomas, 40.
Parsons, Thomas, J$^r$, 40.
Parsons, Timothy, 96.
Parsons, Wareham, 39.
Parsons, W$^m$, 136.
Parsons, William W., Esq$^r$, 85.
Partelow, Jonas, 151.
Partelow, Thomas, 151.
Partin, John, 125.
Partlow, Abigail, 31.
Partlow, Azariah, 116.
Partlow, Thomas, 116.
Partrick, James, 28.
Partridge, Asa, 113.
Partridge, Asa, Jun$^r$, 113.
Partridge, Elijah, 113.
Partridge, James, 113.
Partridge, John, 113.
Partridge, Ruben, 113.
Parx, James, 63.
Pasco, John, 125.
Pasco, Jon$^a$, 137.
Pasco, Jos., 137.
Pasko, James, 38.
Pasko, Jonathan, 38.
Pasko, Sarah, 38.
Pasons, Samuel, 96.
Passett, Joel, 106.
Pastelot, Aseal, 148.
Patch, Ezra, 10.
Patch, Quint, 10.
Patch, Thompson, 10.
Patch William, 11.
Patchen, David, 14.
Patchen, Elijah, 15.
Patchen, George, 32.
Patchen, Jacob, 31.
Patchen, James, 14.
Patchen, James, 96.
Patchen, Josiah, 14.
Patchen, Salmon, 29.
Patchen, Woolcott, 14.
Patching, Abigail (W$^d$), 24.
Patching, Daniel, 24.
Patchon, Arael, 27.
Paterson, Andrew, 78.
Paterson, Edward, 34.
Paterson, Elizabeth, 34.
Paterson, Elkana, 57.
Paterson, James, 128.
Paterson, Samuel, 29.
Paterson, Sherbail, 34.
Pates, Elisha, 60.
Patrick, Abraham, 21.
Patrick, Asa, 24.
Patrick, Ellen (W$^d$), 21.
Patrick, Ellen (W$^d$), 24.
Patrick, John, 24.
Patrick, Noah, 24.
Patrick, Samuel, 23.
Patrige, Stephen, 63.
Patten, David, 134.
Patten, Nathaniel, 46.
Patten, Ruth (Wid.), 46.
Patterson, Amasa, 117.
Patterson, Charity, 30.
Patterson, Hezekiah, 30.
Patterson, James, 18.
Patterson, James, 114.
Patterson, John, 13.
Patterson, John, 74.
Patterson, Joseph, 75.
Patterson, Mark, 18.
Patterson, Mathew, 57.
Patterson, Samuel, 18.
Pattin, Jn$^o$, 137.
Pattin, Nath$^l$, 137.
Pattin, W$^m$, 137.
Paul, Daniel, 154.
Paul, David, 150.
Paul, Jonathan, 150.
Paul, Mathew, 139.
Paul, Rob$^t$, 139.
Paul, Rob$^t$, 2$^d$, 138.
Paul (Wid.), 138.
Paulk, Ammi, 138.
Paush, Daniel, 74.
Paxton, Allen, 67.
Payn, Urana, 17.
Payne, Ambrose, 53.
Payne, Benj$^a$, 145.
Payne, Benjamin, Jn$^r$, 145.
Payne, Dan., 145.
Payne, Dan., 145.
Payne, Dan$^l$, 154.
Payne, David, 110.
Payne, David, 142.
Payne, Esther, 142.
Payne, Ezekiel, 72.
Payne, James, 146.
Payne, Joel, 144.
Payne, John, 59.
Payne, John, 145.
Payne, John, Sam$^l$, 136.
Payne, Joseph, 144.
Payne, Joseph, 150.
Payne, Luter, 154.
Payne, Luther, 142.
Payne, Luther, 142.
Payne, Nathan, 150.
Payne, Noah, 140.
Payne, Phoebe, 128.
Payne, Rufus, 57.
Payne, Sam$^l$, 142.
Payne, Seth, 141.
Payne, Seth, 145.
Payne, Seth, Jn$^r$, 141.
Payne, Solomon, 142.
Payne, Stephen, 145.
Payne, Stephen, 154.
Payne, Stephen, Jn$^r$, 145.
Payne, William, 72.
Payson, Asa, 154.
Payson, John, 48.
Payson, John, 149.
Payton, George, 125.
Peabody, Asa, 131.
Peabody, Prentice, 131.
Peabody, Richard, 154.
Peabody, Sam$^l$, 116.
Peabody, Thomas, 116.
Peak, Joseph &c., 154.
Pearce, Francis, 138.
Pearce, Oliver, 133.
Pearks, Robert, 148.
Pearks, Robert, 151.
Pearl, Frederick, 139.
Pearl, Joshua, 133.
Pearl, Phillip, 143.
Pearl, Richard, 139.
Pearl, Tim$^o$, 139.
Pearl, Tim$^o$, 139.
Pearl (Wid.), 139.
Pearle, Oliver, 139.
Pearse, E$^m$, 134.
Pearse (Widow), 134.
Peas, Jon$^a$, 134.
Peas, Mary, 111.
Peas, Nhe$^l$, 135.
Pease, Aaron, 40.
Pease, Aaron, Jr., 39.
Pease, Abiel, 39.
Pease, Allen, 62.
Pease, Alphe, 136.
Pease, Asa, 40.
Pease, Benjamin, 40.
Pease, Calvin, 62.
Pease, Col$^n$, 136.
Pease, Commins, 40.
Pease, Commins, 2$^d$, 40.
Pease, David, 40.
Pease, David, 42.
Pease, David, 136.
Pease, David, 2$^d$, 40.
Pease, David, 111.
Pease, Ebenezer, 39.
Pease, Edward, 40.
Pease, Edward, 2$^d$, 40.
Pease, Elias, 40.
Pease, Elizabeth, 94.
Pease, Eph$^m$, 39.
Pease, Ephraim, 2$^d$, 40.
Pease, Ezekiel, 40.
Pease, George, 40.
Pease, Gideon, 39.
Pease, Gideon, 2$^d$, 40.
Pease, Giles, 136.
Pease, Heman, 40.
Pease, Hezekiah, 40.
Pease, Isaac, 2$^{nd}$, 40.
Pease, Isaac, 3$^d$, 40.
Pease, Israel, 40.
Pease, James, 38.
Pease, James, 39.
Pease, James, 136.
Pease, Jessee, 40.
Pease, Joel, 38.
Pease, Joel, 136.
Pease, John, 40.
Pease, Jn$^o$, 137.
Pease, John, 2$^d$, 40.
Pease, John, 3$^d$, 40.
Pease, Joseph, 39.
Pease, Joseph, 50.
Pease, Justin, 51.
Pease, Lemuel, 39.
Pease, Levi, 52.
Pease, Levi, J$^r$, 136.
Pease, Moses, 39.
Pease, Moses, Jr., 39.
Pease, Naomi (Wid.), 44.
Pease, Nathan, 40.
Pease, Nathan, 66.
Pease, Nathaniel, 66.
Pease, Noadiah, 39.
Pease, Noah, 136.
Pease, Noah, 136.
Pease, Obadiah, 66.
Pease, Peter, 38.
Pease, Peter, 39.
Pease, Peter, 42.
Pease, Richard, 136.
Pease, Rob$^t$, 136.
Pease, Rufus, 40.
Pease, Ruth (Wid.), 40.
Pease, Samuel, 40.
Pease, Sam$^l$, 136.
Pease, Samuel, 2$^d$, 40.
Pease, Seth, 50.
Pease, Sharon, 39.
Pease, Simeon, 2$^d$, 40.
Pease, Simon, 40.
Pease, Stephen, 38.
Pease, Stephen, 136.
Pease, Stone, 40.
Pease, Tho$^s$, 134.
Pease, Timothy, 40.
Pease, Violet, 67.
Pease, William, 39.
Pease, Zebulon, 39.
Pease, Zeno, 50.
Peavey, Ichab$^d$, 151.
Peck, Aaron, 16.
Peck, Abel, 41.
Peck, Abijah, 10.
Peck, Abijah, 11.
Peck, Abijah, 73.
Peck, Abner, 108.
Peck, Abraham, 16.
Peck, Abraham, 101.
Peck, Amie, 111.
Peck, Amos, 33.
Peck, Amos, 100.
Peck, Amos, Jr., 33.
Peck, Asa, 59.
Peck, Asa, 93.
Peck, Asahel, 70.
Peck, Asher, 21.
Peck, Augustus, 85.
Peck, Augustus, 110.
Peck, Bela, 131.
Peck, Benjamin, 12.
Peck, Benjamin, 16.
Peck, Benjamin, 66.
Peck, Benjamin, 101.
Peck, Benjamin, 111.
Peck, Bennoni, 57.
Peck, Bezeliel, 95.
Peck, Caleb, 35.
Peck, Calvin, 12.
Peck, Calvin, 67.
Peck, Chester, 112.
Peck, Cornelius, 70.
Peck, Daniel, 37.
Peck, Daniel, 85.
Peck, Dan., 108.
Peck, Dan., 111.
Peck, Daniel, 122.
Peck, Dan., 124.
Peck, Darius, 24.
Peck, Darius, 123.
Peck, Darius, 129.
Peck, David, 10.
Peck, David, 16.
Peck, David, 21.
Peck, David, 49.
Peck, David, 2$^d$, 40.
Peck, David, 111.
Peck, David, 124.
Peck, Ebenezer, 15.
Peck, Ebenezer, 21.
Peck, Ebenezer, 59.
Peck, Ebenezer, 95.
Peck, Ebenezer, 103.
Peck, Eldad, 33.
Peck, Eleazer, 49.
Peck, Elezier, 77.
Peck, Eli, 20.
Peck, Eliakam, 10.
Peck, Eliakim, 49.
Peck, Eliakim, Jr., 49.
Peck, Elias, 122.
Peck, Elijah, 37.
Peck, Elijah, 64.
Peck, Elijah, 93.
Peck, Elijah, Jr., 37.
Peck, Eliphilet, 11.
Peck, Eliphilet, 12.
Peck, Elisha, 50.
Peck, Elisha, 73.
Peck, Elisha, 81.
Peck, Elizabeth, 111.
Peck, Elizabeth (Wid.), 20.
Peck, Enoch, 21.
Peck, Enos, 21.
Peck, Ephraim, 102.
Peck, Ephraim, 16.
Peck, Ephraim, 19.
Peck, Ezra, 11.
Peck, Ezra, 20.
Peck, Fredrerick, 61.
Peck, Gad, 103.
Peck, George, 15.
Peck, George, 60.
Peck, Gideon, 16.
Peck, Gideon, 58.
Peck, Gilbert, 16.
Peck, Hannah, 111.
Peck, Hannah, 123.
Peck, Heil, 109.
Peck, Henery, 20.
Peck, Hennery, 10.
Peck, Henry, 103.
Peck, Henry, 111.
Peck, Heth, 20.
Peck, Heth, Jun$^r$, 20.
Peck, Hezekiah, 78.
Peck, Hezekiah, 102.
Peck, Hiram, 111.
Peck, Isaac, 15.
Peck, Isaac, 16.
Peck, Isaac, 20.
Peck, Isaac, 33.
Peck, Isaac, 49.
Peck, Isaac, 62.
Peck, Isaac, 69.
Peck, Isaac, 3$^d$, 15.
Peck, Isarel, 21.
Peck, Israel, 16.
Peck, Jabez, 21.
Peck, James, 66.
Peck, James, 103.
Peck, Jasper, 123.
Peck, Jeremiah, 15.
Peck, Jeremiah, 77.
Peck, Jesse, 12.
Peck, Jesse, 34.
Peck, Jesse, 100.
Peck, Jessy S., 87.
Peck, Job, 30.
Peck, Joel, 50.
Peck, John, 10.
Peck, John, 11.
Peck, John, 21.
Peck, John, 29.
Peck, John, 93.
Peck, John, 101.
Peck, John, 103.
Peck, John, 103.
Peck, John, 141.
Peck, John, 2$^d$, 93.
Peck, John, 2$^d$, 102.
Peck, Joseph, 12.
Peck, Joseph, 15.
Peck, Joseph, 21.
Peck, Joseph, 33.
Peck, Joseph, 34.
Peck, Joseph, 72.
Peck, Joseph, 78.
Peck, Joseph, 100.
Peck, Joseph, 104.
Peck, Joseph, 110.
Peck, Joseph, 123.
Peck, Joseph, 130.
Peck, Jos., 138.
Peck, Joseph, 141.
Peck, Joshua, 20.
Peck, Josiah, 30.
Peck, Josiah, 35.
Peck, Judson, 30.
Peck, Justus, 50.
Peck, Lament, 34.
Peck, Latt, 123.
Peck, Lebens, 123.
Peck, Levi, 11.
Peck, Levi, 20.
Peck, Levi, 64.
Peck, Livenus, 21.
Peck, Lyda, 141.
Peck, Lyssim, 34.
Peck, Martha, 123.
Peck, Mary, 65.
Peck, Mathew, 33.
Peck, Mathew, 123.
Peck, Matthew, 20.
Peck, Michael, 101.
Peck, Miel, 10.
Peck, Molly, 111.
Peck, Moses, 15.
Peck, Moses, 20.
Peck, Mosses, 100.
Peck, Nathan, 21.
Peck, Nathaniel, 15.
Peck, Nathaniel, 20.
Peck, Nicholas, 104.
Peck, Nicholas, 107.
Peck, Oliver, 33.
Peck, Peter, 108.
Peck, Philoe, 66.
Peck, Phineas, 74.
Peck, Phineas, 94.
Peck, Phineas, 111.
Peck, Phinehas, 129.
Peck, Reeve, 70.
Peck, Reeve, 70.
Peck, Reubin, 142.
Peck, Reynold, 123.
Peck, Rhoda, 65.
Peck, Roberts, 15.
Peck, Samuel, 15.
Peck, Samuel, 20.
Peck, Samuel, 33.
Peck, Samuel, 41.
Peck, Samuel, 77.
Peck, Samuel, 101.
Peck, Samuel, 107.
Peck, Samuel, 108.
Peck, Samuel, 112.
Peck, Samuel, 123.
Peck, Samuel, Jr, 16.
Peck, Samuel, 3$^d$, 16.
Peck, Samuel, 3$^d$, 108.
Peck, Samuel F., 111.
Peck, Sarah, 111.
Peck, Sarah, 123.
Peck, Sarah (Wid.), 20.
Peck, Selah, 49.
Peck, Seth, 35.
Peck, Shadrack, 20.
Peck, Silas, 111.
Peck, Silas, 124.
Peck, Simeon, 77.
Peck, Solomon, 16.
Peck, Solomon, 58.
Peck, Stephen, 11.
Peck, Stephen, 101.
Peck, Stephen, 107.
Peck, Stephen, 111.
Peck, Susanna, 34.
Peck, Syril, 130.
Peck, Tabitha, 30.
Peck, Theophilus, 16.
Peck, Thomas, 49.
Peck, Thomas, 102.
Peck, Tho$^s$, 139.
Peck, Timothy, 86.
Peck, Timothy, 112.
Peck, Ward, 110.
Peck, Zalmon, 73.
Peck, Zebulon, 34.
Peck, Zebulon, 70.
Pecker, Nath$^l$, 83.
Peckham, Benjamin, 116.
Peckham, George, 100.
Peckham, George, 2$^{nd}$, 100.
Peckham, John, 116.
Peckham, Thomas, 116.
Peckwith, Joseph, 124.
Peek, John, 67.
Peery (Wid.), 139.
Peet, Anna, 62.
Peet, Bersheba (Wid.), 30.
Peet, Daniel, 30.
Peet, Daniel, 72.
Peet, Elijah, 30.
Peet, Elnathan, 72.
Peet, Elnathan, 78.
Peet, George, 72.

# INDEX.

Peet, Ithiel, 72.
Peet, Johiel, 73.
Peet, John, 27.
Peet, Joseph, 72.
Peet, Lemuel, 72.
Peet, Nathan, 72.
Peet, Richard, 56.
Peet, Samuel, 56.
Peet, Samuel, 72.
Peet, Sherman, 105.
Peet, Stephen, 73.
Peet, Stiles, 30.
Peet, Thaddeus, 72.
Peet, Thaddeus, 74.
Peet, William, 30.
Peet, William, 59.
Peirce, Abner, 40.
Peirce, Benj$^n$, 141.
Peirce, Dillano, 141.
Peirce, Edward, 151.
Peirce, Enoch, 147.
Peirce, Fred'k, and Jarum Topliff, 147.
Peirce, John, 130.
Peirce, Joseph, 39.
Peirce, Philip, 42.
Peirce, Preserved, 151.
Peirce, Samuel, 52.
Peirce, Sam$^l$, 147.
Peirce, Timaus, 141.
Peirce, William, 144.
Peirce, William, 151.
Peirce, Tho$^s$, 148.
Peirpoint, Benjamin, 106.
Peirpoint, Ely, 93.
Peirpoint, Ezra, 109.
Peirpoint, Giles, 106.
Peirpoint, Hezekiah, 106.
Peirpoint, James, 106.
Peirpoint, Joel, 106.
Peirpoint, John, 106.
Peirpoint, Joseph, 106.
Peirpoint, Joseph, 106.
Peirpoint, Samuel, 106.
Peirpoint, Thomas, 106.
Peirson, Amos, 96.
Peirson, Isaac, 96.
Peirson, John, Esq$^r$, 84.
Peirson, Joseph, 96.
Peise, Willard, 149.
Pellet, Enos, 67.
Pellet, Hez$^a$, Jn$^r$, 142.
Pellet, Jona$^n$, 141.
Pellet, Joseph, 142.
Pellet, Rufus, 142.
Pellet, Sarah, 142.
Pelton, Abner, 80.
Pelton, Eben$^r$, 118.
Pelton, George, 80.
Pelton, Ithamar, 79.
Pelton, James, 83.
Pelton, Jesse, 47.
Pelton, John, 79.
Pelton, John, Jun$^r$, 79.
Pelton, Johnson, 80.
Pelton, Johnson, Jun$^r$, 80.
Pelton, Jonathan, 80.
Pelton, Joseph, 80.
Pelton, Joseph, Jun$^r$, 80.
Pelton, Josiah, 80.
Pelton, Josiah, 85.
Pelton, Moses, 80.
Pelton, Nathan, 28.
Pelton, Nathan, Jr., 38.
Pelton, Phinehas, 80.
Pelton, Phinehas, 90.
Pelton, Thomas, 118.
Pelton, W$^m$, 90.
Pember, Ezekiel, 127.
Pember, Jacob, 129.
Pemberton, Stephen, 116.
Pemberton, Thomas, 51.
Pembleton, ——, 52.
Pembleton, Jabez, 119.
Pembleton, Joshua, 114.
Pempille, John, 66.
Penayre, Amos, 26.
Pendal, Mary, 74.
Pendergrass, John, 105.
Pendleton, Andrew, 117.
Pendleton, Eunice, 117.
Pendleton, Increase, 97.
Pendleton, Joshua, 97.
Pendleton, William, 31.
Penery, Nathan, 78.
Penfield, Abel, 80.
Penfield, Abisha, 80.
Penfield, Amos, 80.
Penfield, James, 14.
Penfield, James, Jn$^r$, 14.
Penfield, Jesse, 77.
Penfield, Jessey, 80.
Penfield, John, 19.
Penfield, John, 79.
Penfield, Jonathan, 79.
Penfield, Lewis, 18.
Penfield, Nathaniel, 33.
Penfield, Peter, 18.
Penfield, Phinias, 33.
Penfield, Samuel, 14.
Penfield, Samuel, 80.
Penfield, Simeon, 79.
Penfield, Simeon, Jun$^r$, 80.

Penfield, Stephen, 80.
Penhally, Richard, 130.
Penich, David, 73.
Penich, Samuel, 73.
Penna, Elezer, 134.
Penna, Jos., 134.
Penniman, James, 128.
Penniman, William, 114.
Penny, Abner, 47.
Penny, Jane, 10.
Pennyfur, Darius, 48.
Penoyre, Gould S., 26.
Penoyre, Isaac, 26.
Penoyre, Martha (W$^d$), 26.
Penoyre, Samuel, 26.
Pentnodle, George, 151.
Penveer, John, 128.
Pepone, Silas, 135.
Pepper, Dan$^l$, 19.
Pepper, John, 64.
Pepper, Michael, 129.
Pepper, Seth, 19.
Pepper, Stephen, 19.
Pepper, Stephen, Jr., 19.
Perce, William, 148.
Percival, James, 33.
Percival, James, Jr., 33.
Percival, John, Esq$^r$, 82.
Percival, John, Jun$^r$, 82.
Percival, Monsieur, 128.
Porcivall, Gordon, 81.
Percy, Ebenezer, 59.
Percy, Jane, 96.
Percy, Joseph, 78.
Percy, Nathaniel, 78.
Perin, Seth, 147.
Perit, Antony, 103.
Perit, Job, 103.
Perit, Peter, 101.
Perit, Peter, 101.
Perit, Thadeus, 104.
Perkens, Gidian, 66.
Perkin, Richard W., 128.
Perkins, Abner, 58.
Perkins, Abraham, 123.
Perkins, Adonijah, 111.
Perkins, Amos, 111.
Perkins, Amos, 152.
Perkins, Amos, 2$^{nd}$, 111.
Perkins, And$^w$, 131.
Perkins, Archibald, 111.
Perkins, Aron, 100.
Perkins, Caleb, 47.
Perkins, Cudge, 153.
Perkins, Daniel, 40.
Perkins, Daniel, 152.
Perkins, David, 111.
Perkins, Eben$^r$, 119.
Perkins, Elias, 111.
Perkins, Elijah, 73.
Perkins, Eliphas, 61.
Perkins, Elisabeth, 119.
Perkins, Elish, 100.
Perkins, Elisha, 148.
Perkins, Elisha, 152.
Perkins, Elizabeth, 111.
Perkins, Enoch, 46.
Perkins, Ephraim, 94.
Perkins, Erastus, 130.
Perkins, Frederick, 112.
Perkins, George, 40.
Perkins, Gideon, 95.
Perkins, Hezekiah, 131.
Perkins, Isaac, 140.
Perkins, Israel, 112.
Perkins, Jabez, 46.
Perkins, Jabez, 119.
Perkins, Jabez, 131.
Perkins, Jabez, Jun$^r$, 131.
Perkins, Jacob, 112.
Perkins, Jacob, 118.
Perkins, Jacob, 2$^d$, 119.
Perkins, Jason, 61.
Perkins, Joel, 56.
Perkins, John, 64.
Perkins, John, 93.
Perkins, John, 100.
Perkins, John, 112.
Perkins, John, 118.
Perkins, John, 123.
Perkins, John, 144.
Perkins, Jonathan, 111.
Perkins, Jon$^a$, 122.
Perkins, Joseph, 112.
Perkins, Joshua, 112.
Perkins, Joshua, 122.
Perkins, Leonard, 142.
Perkins, Levi, 112.
Perkins, Mary, 118.
Perkins, Mary, 119.
Perkins, Mary, 125.
Perkins, Rev$^d$ Nathan, 47.
Perkins, Newman, 152.
Perkins, Obadiah, 119.
Perkins, Olive, 112.
Perkins, Oliver, 152.
Perkins, Peter, 112.
Perkins, Phillip, 148.
Perkins, Phinehas, 61.
Perkins, Phinehas, 66.
Perkins, Rachel, 111.
Perkins, Reuben, 35.
Perkins, Reuben, Jr., 35.
Perkins, Robert, 130.

Perkins, Rossannah, 112.
Perkins, Ruben, 112.
Perkins, Rufus, 119.
Perkins, Sam$^l$, 66.
Perkins, Samuel, 123.
Perkins, Samuel, 144.
Perkins, Simeon, 107.
Perkins, Solomon, 112.
Perkins, Solomon, 119.
Perkins, Stephen, 107.
Perkins, Tho$^s$, 144.
Perkins, Unice, 111.
Perkins, William, 123.
Perkins, William, 142.
Perkins, Youngs, 119.
Pero, 64.
Pero, Barsheba, 128.
Pero (Negro), 51.
Pero (Negro), 113.
Pero (Negro), 117.
Pero (Negro), 117.
Perpoint, Joseph, 51.
Perrey, Amos, 65.
Perrey, Benjamin, 65.
Perrey, Isaac, 65.
Perrigo, Ebenezer, 112.
Perrigo, Ezekiel, 112.
Perrigo, John, 112.
Perrigo, William, 112.
Perrigo, William, Jun$^r$, 112.
Perrin, Amos, 154.
Perrin, Dan$^l$, 150.
Perrin, Dan$^l$, 154.
Perrin, David, 154.
Perrin, Elijah, 154.
Perrin, Isaiah, 154.
Perrin, John, 153.
Perrin, John, 154.
Perrin, Moses, 154.
Perrin, Sam$^l$, 149.
Perrin, Sol$^n$, 135.
Perrin, Stephen, 154.
Perrin, Timothy, 154.
Perrin, W$^m$, 154.
Perring, Elisha, 44.
Perring, Elisha, 45.
Perring, Ruth, 45.
Perritt, John, 152.
Perrit, Joseph, 141.
Perry, Abijah, 18.
Perry, Abner, 18.
Perry, Abner, Jr, 18.
Perry, Bennitt, 20.
Perry, Caleb, 95.
Perry, Christiany, 88.
Perry, Daniel, 27.
Perry, David, 17.
Perry, David, 28.
Perry, Ebenezer, 14.
Perry, Eliahim, 129.
Perry, Elihu, 27.
Perry, Elijah, 18.
Perry, Elijah, 154.
Perry, Elisha, 19.
Perry, Elisha, 68.
Perry, Ezekiel, 95.
Perry, Ezra, 21.
Perry, Rev$^d$ Filo, 20.
Perry, Gelverton, 95.
Perry, Israel, 60.
Perry, Jabez, 14.
Perry, James, 18.
Perry, James, 95.
Perry, Job, 32.
Perry, John, 14.
Perry, John, 27.
Perry, John, 29.
Perry, John, 95.
Perry, John, 149.
Perry, Jonathan, 14.
Perry, Joseph, 13.
Perry, Joseph, 18.
Perry, Jo$^s$, 133.
Perry, Joshua, 95.
Perry, Josiah, 73.
Perry, Josiah, 151.
Perry, Lucana, 73.
Perry, Miah, 14.
Perry, Nathan, 13.
Perry, Nathanel, Jn$^r$, 14.
Perry, Peter, 14.
Perry, Peter, 95.
Perry, Ruben, 137.
Perry, Sam$^l$, 139.
Perry, Seth, 129.
Perry, Sylvanus, 144.
Perry, Thadeus, 27.
Perry, Thomas, 13.
Perry, Thomas, 41.
Persall, John, 12.
Persall, Samuel, 12.
Persall, Samuel, Jn$^r$, 12.
Person, Abel, 94.
Person, Benj$^n$, 140.
Person, Joel, 106.
Person, Submit, 98.
Persons, Abraham, 50.
Persons, Aron, 107.
Persons, Darius, 63.
Persons, Eliphas, 60.
Persons, Enoch, 61.

Persons, John, 33.
Persons, John, 92.
Persons, John, 123.
Persons, Joseph, 126.
Persons, Peter, 32.
Persons, Samuel, 108.
Persons, Theodotious, 152.
Persons, Timothy, 27.
Persons, William, 38.
Persons, William, 38.
Perth, Andrew, 106.
Peter (Negro), 21.
Peter (Negro), 26.
Peter (Negro), 51.
Peter (Negro), 88.
Peter (Negro), 112.
Peter (Negro), 113.
Peter (Negro), 114.
Peter (Negro), 120.
Peter (Negro), 121.
Peter (Negro), 122.
Peter (Negroe), 93.
Peter (Negroe), 95.
Peter (Negroe), 102.
Peter (Negroe), 105.
Peters, Eber, 75.
Peters, James, 129.
Peters, Jn$^o$, 135.
Peters, Jon$^a$, 135.
Peters, Joseph, 74.
Peters, Nathan, 114.
Peters (Negro), 117.
Peters (Widow), 134.
Peters, W$^m$, 135.
Peterson, Charles, 41.
Peterson, Isaac, 29.
Petibone, Abel, 48.
Petibone, David, 49.
Petibone, John, 47.
Petibone, Joseph, 48.
Petibone, Thodore, 35.
Petingall, Lemuel, 112.
Petingall, Nath$^l$, 143.
Petten, Samuel, 26.
Pettibone, Abijah, 48.
Pettibone, Abraham, 70.
Pettibone, Aexander, 35.
Pettibone, Chancey, 35.
Pettibone, Chancey, 43.
Pettibone, Dudley, 48.
Pettibone, Isaac, 62.
Pettibone Jacob, 48.
Pettibone, Jiles, 63.
Pettibone, Jonathan, 48.
Pettibone, Judy, 64.
Pettibone, Ozias, 43.
Pettibone, Roswell, 69.
Pettibone, Samuel, 68.
Pettiborn, Elijah, 64.
Pettiborn, Jiles, 66.
Pettingall, Solomon, 153.
Pettis, Abigail, 131.
Pettis, Benj$^a$, 118.
Pettis, Ichiel, 130.
Pettis, John, 140.
Pettiss, James, 145.
Pettit, Joel, 63.
Pettit, John, 61.
Pettit, Sam$^l$, 61.
Pettit, Solomon, 61.
Petton, John, 63.
Pettus, 64.
Pharough (Negro), 113.
Pharough (Negro), 119.
Phelmer, John, 11.
Phelps, Aaron, 135.
Phelps, Aaron, Ju., 56.
Phelps, Abel, 44.
Phelps, Abijah, 44.
Phelps, Abner, 135.
Phelps, Abraham, 62.
Phelps, Amos, 135.
Phelps, Ariah, 66.
Phelps, Aron, 56.
Phelps, Ashbel, 135.
Phelps, Augustus, 55.
Phelps, Azariah, 56.
Phelps, Azariah, Ju., 56.
Phelps, Basheba, 45.
Phelps, Benajah, 37.
Phelps, Benjamin, 62.
Phelps, Benj$^a$, 136.
Phelps, Bethuel, 38.
Phelps, Bildad, 54.
Phelps, Charles, 55.
Phelps, Charles, 66.
Phelps, Charles, 117.
Phelps, Charles, Ju., 55.
Phelps, Charles, Jun$^r$, 117.
Phelps, Cornelius, 55.
Phelps, Cornelus, 135.
Phelps, Daniel, 37.
Phelps, Daniel, 38.
Phelps, Daniel, 48.
Phelps, Daniel, 50.
Phelps, Dan$^l$, 55.
Phelps, Daniel, Jr., 48.
Phelps, Daniel, 2$^d$, 46.
Phelps, David, 40.
Phelps, David, 47.

Phelps, David, 74.
Phelps, David, 82.
Phelps, David, Jr., 40.
Phelps, Ebenezer, 45.
Phelps, Ebenezer, 51.
Phelps, Eben$^r$, 55.
Phelps, Ebenezer, 59.
Phelps, Eber, 135.
Phelps, Edward, 65.
Phelps, Eldad, 40.
Phelps, Eldad, Jr., 40.
Phelps, Elexander, 84.
Phelps, Elezer, 134.
Phelps, Eli, 55.
Phelps, Elihu, 136.
Phelps, Elijah, 44.
Phelps, Elijah, 51.
Phelps, Elijah, 62.
Phelps, Elijah, 63.
Phelps, Elijah, 145.
Phelps, Eliphalet, 45.
Phelps, Elisha, 79.
Phelps, Elkane, 69.
Phelps, Enoch, 55.
Phelps, Ephraim, 54.
Phelps, Frederick, 135.
Phelps, Frind, 65.
Phelps, George, 55.
Phelps, Hezekiah, 55.
Phelps, Hez$^h$, 2$^d$, 44.
Phelps, Horner, 135.
Phelps, Icabod, 135.
Phelps, Icabod, Jr, 135.
Phelps, Ichabod, 65.
Phelps, Isaac, 43.
Phelps, Isaac, 55.
Phelps, Israel, 132.
Phelps, Jacob, 55.
Phelps, James, 55.
Phelps, Jedediah, 66.
Phelps, Jerejah, 37.
Phelps, Job, 55.
Phelps, Job, Jn$^r$, 55.
Phelps, Joel, 69.
Phelps, John, 43.
Phelps, John, 55.
Phelps, John, 64.
Phelps, John, 65.
Phelps, John, 66.
Phelps, John, 68.
Phelps, Jno., 89.
Phelps, Jn$^o$, 137.
Phelps, Jonathan, 48.
Phelps, Jonathan, 62.
Phelps, Jonathan, 122.
Phelps, Joseph, 18.
Phelps, Jo$^s$, 135.
Phelps, Jos$^e$, 137.
Phelps, Joseph, 146.
Phelps, Joseph, 147.
Phelps, Jo$^s$, Jr., 135.
Phelps, Joshua, 35.
Phelps, Joshua, Jr., 35.
Phelps, Josiah, 58.
Phelps, Josiah, 2$^d$, 55.
Phelps, Josias, 55.
Phelps, Juda, 65.
Phelps, Judah, 51.
Phelps, Lanclot, 55.
Phelps, Levi, 44.
Phelps, Mary, 122.
Phelps, Moses, 146.
Phelps, Nathan, 45.
Phelps, Nathaniel, 45.
Phelps, Nathaniel, Jr., 45.
Phelps, Noah, 39.
Phelps, Noah, 44.
Phelps, Noah, 48.
Phelps, Noah A., 47.
Phelps, Obadiah, 38.
Phelps, Oliver, 50.
Phelps, Oliver, 50.
Phelps, Oliver, 55.
Phelps, Oliver, 56.
Phelps, Oliver, 58.
Phelps, Ozias, 48.
Phelps, Reuben, 45.
Phelps, Roger, 45.
Phelps, Roger, 55.
Phelps, Roger, 135.
Phelps, Roswel, 135.
Phelps, Roswell, 45.
Phelps, Ruben, 135.
Phelps, Ruben, 135.
Phelps, Ruth (Wid.), 45.
Phelps, Samuel, 48.
Phelps, Samuel, 61.
Phelps, Samuel, 61.
Phelps, Sam$^l$, 82.
Phelps, Samuel, 122.
Phelps, Sam$^l$, 135.
Phelps, Samuel, 1$^{st}$, 58.
Phelps, Samuel, 2$^d$, 58.
Phelps, Shadrack, 55.
Phelps, Shubel, 44.
Phelps, Silas, 51.
Phelps, Simeon, 67.
Phelps, Sol$^n$, 135.
Phelps, Sol$^n$, Jr, 135.
Phelps, Sylvanus, 135.
Phelps, Syvanus, 135.
Phelps, Thadeus, 122.
Phelps, Timothy, 43.

# INDEX.

Phelps, Timothy, 44.
Phelps, Timothy, 51.
Phelps, Timothy, 55.
Phelps, Timothy, 104.
Phelps, Timothy, Jr., 43.
Phelps, Truman, 74.
Phelps, Uri, 58.
Phelps, William, 19.
Phelps, William, 44.
Phelps, W$^m$, 55.
Phenk, Daniel, 72.
Phernil, Benjamin, 60.
Phier, Horace, 63.
Philer, John, 60.
Philer, Silas, 60.
Philer, Stephen, 60.
Philer, Ulissies, 60.
Philips, Benjamin, 68.
Philips, Dolphin, 73.
Philips, Gideon, 66.
Philips, Jeruel, 72.
Philips, John, 13.
Philips, Samuel, 72.
Philips, Thomas, 13.
Philips, Thomas, 30.
Philis (Negroe), 110.
Phill, 65.
Phillemore, Will$^m$, 141.
Philley, Isaac, 64.
Philley, Jasper, 67.
Philley, Remembrance, 64.
Phillip (Negroe), 94.
Phillip, William, 61.
Phillips, Aaron, 148.
Phillips, Abiel, 11.
Phillips, Asa, 148.
Phillips, Augustus, 140.
Phillips, Barnard, 149.
Phillips, Ebenezer, 22.
Phillips, Elijah, 132.
Phillips, Elijah, 140.
Phillips, Elisha, 96.
Phillips, George, Esq$^r$, 85.
Phillips, John, 36.
Phillips, Jn$^o$, 137.
Phillips, John, 148.
Phillips, John, 151.
Phillips, John, 153.
Phillips, Jon$^a$, 136.
Phillips, Joseph, 46.
Phillips, Joseph, 148.
Phillips, Peter, 87.
Phillips, Philip, 72.
Phillips, Reuben, 72.
Phillips, Richard, 47.
Phillips, Samuel, 66.
Phillips, Samuel, 66.
Phillips, Sam$^l$, 153.
Phillips, Samuel H., 11.
Phillips, Thompson, 86.
Phillips, William, 148.
Phillips, William, 153.
Phillis (Freeman), 82.
Phillis (Negroe), 92.
Phillo, Benjamin, 24.
Phillo, Isaac, 21.
Phillo, James, 24.
Phillo, John, 21.
Phillups, Genworence, 113.
Phillups, Jeramiah, 113.
Phillups, John, 127.
Phillups, Jonathan, 113.
Phillups, Levi, 113.
Phillups, Michael, 122.
Phillups, Squire, 113.
Philor, John, 100.
Philor, Joseph, 99.
Philps, Nath$^l$, 147.
Phlps, Paul, 152.
Philup (Negro). See Briston & Philup (Negro), 115.
Phink, Adam, 128.
Phinney, Joshua, 40.
Phinney, Oliver, 40.
Phinny, Jesse, 31.
Phipeny, Ebenezer, 29.
Phipeny, Nehemiah, 14.
Phippany, Archibald, 72.
Phippany, Jeames, 72.
Phippeney, Nehemiah, 72.
Phipps, Daniel Goff, 103.
Phipps, David, 103.
Phipps, Solomon, 103.
Phips, Jason, 151.
Picket, Abijah, 72.
Picket, Benjamin, 19.
Picket, Benjamin, 67.
Picket, Benjamin, 96.
Picket, David, 10.
Picket, Ebenezer, 11.
Picket, Ebenezer, Jn$^r$, 11.
Picket, Hannah, 12.
Picket, James, 96.
Picket, John, 149.
Picket, Joseph, 94.
Picket, Phinehas, 54.
Picket, Polly I., 19.
Picket, Thomas, 10.
Pickets, William, 105.
Pickett, Daniel, 72.
Pickett, Ezra, 22.
Pickett, Thankfull, 86.
Picksley, David, 17.

Pidge, John, 144.
Pierce, Abram, 73.
Pierce, Amos, 70.
Pierce, David, 11.
Pierce, Edward, 70.
Pierce, Elijah, 73.
Pierce, Enoch, 147.
Pierce, Eunice, 73.
Pierce, Isaac, 57.
Pierce, Joel, 73.
Pierce, John, 57.
Pierce, John, 148.
Pierce, Joseph, 1$^{st}$, 73.
Pierce, Joseph, 2$^d$, 73.
Pierce, Joshua, 104.
Pierce, Joshua, 1$^{st}$, 57.
Pierce, Joshua, 2$^d$, 57.
Pierce, Joshua, 3$^d$, 57.
Pierce, Josiah, 148.
Pierce, Justus, 73.
Pierce, Levi, 57.
Pierce, Luther, 51.
Pierce, Mary, 42.
Pierce, Mary, 65.
Pierce, Nathan, 73.
Pierce, Pelahat, 70.
Pierce, Sam$^l$, 70.
Pierce, Samuel, 86.
Pierce, Samuel, 148.
Pierce, Seth, 57.
Pierce, Silas, 66.
Pierce, Stephen, 86.
Pierce, Thomas, 70.
Pierce, Thomas, 89.
Pierce, Timothy, 148.
Pierce, Titus, 73.
Pierce, William, 61.
Piercy, Nathanel, 18.
Pierpoint, Eveland, 64.
Pierpont, James, 64.
Pierpont, John, 104.
Pierpont, Robert, 58.
Pierson, Abraham, Esq$^r$, 85.
Pierson, Benjamin, 92.
Pierson, Dodo, 85.
Pierson, Eli, 124.
Pierson, Jedediah, 85.
Pierson, John, 14.
Pierson, Patience, 85.
Pierson, Peter, 123.
Pierson, Phinehas, 85.
Pierson, Samuel, 85.
Pierson, Samuel, 92.
Piet, John, 59.
Piffer, Nathan C., 65.
Pike, Amos, 142.
Pike, Charles, 87.
Pike, Eben$^r$, 141.
Pike, James, 68.
Pike, James, 142.
Pike, John, Jr., 141.
Pike, Jon$^a$, 19.
Pike, Joseph, 142.
Pike, Mary, 82.
Pike (Negro), 113.
Pike, Samuel, 69.
Pike, Willard, 141.
Pike, William, 14.
Pike, William, 44.
Pine, Samuel, 16.
Piner, Lydia, 129.
Piney, Abraham, 48.
Piney, Darius, 49.
Pinkerton, William, 64.
Pinna, Isaac, 137.
Pinney, Aaron, 48.
Pinney, Abraham, 64.
Pinney, David, 64.
Pinney, Eliz$^a$, 54.
Pinney, Grove, 64.
Pinney, Isaac, 55.
Pinney, James, 146.
Pinney, John, 56.
Pinney, Jon$^a$, 38.
Pinney, Jonathan, 48.
Pinney, Judah, 55.
Pinney, Levi, 48.
Pinney, Martin, 54.
Pinto, Jacob, 103.
Pinto, John, 66.
Pinto, Polly, 103.
Piper, Jude, 107.
Pirkens, Daniel, 94.
Pitcher, Elijah, 130.
Pitcher, Jerusha, 77.
Pitcher, Susannah, 75.
Pitcher, Truman, 87.
Pitkin, Ashbel, 36.
Pitkin, Calvin, 136.
Pitkin, Daniel, 36.
Pitkin, David, 36.
Pitkin, Eleazer, 37.
Pitkin, Elisha, 36.
Pitkin, Elisha, Jr., 36.
Pitkin, Epaphras, 36.
Pitkin, George, Sen$^r$, 36.
Pitkin, Isaac, 36.
Pitkin, John, 36.
Pitkin, John, 64.
Pitkin, Jonathan, 36.
Pitkin, Joseph, 36.
Pitkin, Joshua, 36.
Pitkin, Nathaniel, 36.

Pitkin, Paul, 136.
Pitkin, Richard, 37.
Pitkin, Richard, Jr., 37.
Pitkin, Roger, 36.
Pitkin, Stephen, 60.
Pitkin, Theodore, 36.
Pitkin, Tho$^s$, 136.
Pitkin, Timothy, 36.
Pitkin, Timothy, 40.
Pitkin, Timothy, 60.
Pitkin, William, 36.
Pitman, William, 129.
Pits, Richard, 110.
Pixley, William, 30.
Pixly, Peter, 29.
Place, Joe (Negroe), 105.
Plank, John, 150.
Plank, Robert, 150.
Plank, William, 149.
Plank, Zebudiah, 149.
Plant, Abraham. 91.
Plant, Benjamin, 91.
Plant, Ethel, 90.
Plant, Hester, 95.
Plant, James, 50.
Plant, James, 91.
Plant, Solomon, 30.
Plat, Mary, 105.
Platt, Anna, 105.
Platt, Benjamin, 102.
Platt, David, 18.
Platt, Ebenezer, 12.
Platt, Ephraim, 72.
Platt, Epinetus, 72.
Platt, Epinetus, 2$^d$, 72.
Platt, Gideon, 72.
Platt, Gideon, 102.
Platt, Gideon, 110.
Platt, Hannah, 101.
Platt, Hezekiah, 27.
Platt, Isaac, 27.
Platt, Isaac, 27.
Platt, Isaac, 101.
Platt, Jabez, 23.
Platt, Jarvis, 20.
Platt, Jeremiah, 72.
Platt, Jerimiah, 102.
Platt, Jesse, 20.
Platt, Jesse, 32.
Platt, Jiremiah, 101.
Platt, John, 23.
Platt, John, 72.
Platt, John, 73.
Platt, John, 75.
Platt, Jonas, 27.
Platt, Jonas, Jun$^r$, 27.
Platt, Joseph, 11.
Platt, Joseph, 23.
Platt, Joseph, 101.
Platt, Joseph, 102.
Platt, Joseph Y., 26.
Platt, Josiah, 19.
Platt, Josiah, 105.
Platt, Justin, 20.
Platt, Mary, 27.
Platt, Moses, 18.
Platt, Nathan, 10.
Platt, Nathaniel, 111.
Platt, Nehemiah, 72.
Platt, Noah, 90.
Platt, Philip, 27.
Platt, Richard, 102.
Platt, Samuel, 23.
Platt, Samuel, 29.
Platt, Samuel, 102.
Platt, Sibel, 102.
Platt, Stephen, 73.
Platt, Timothy, 20.
Platt, Truman, 72.
Platt, William. 73.
Platt, Zebulon, 27.
Platt, Zophar. 75.
Platts, Dan., 90.
Platts, Dan., 2$^d$, 90.
Platts, Elisha, 90.
Platts, Jn$^o$ , 90.
Plum, Aaron, 88.
Plum, Abraham. 88.
Plum, Charles, 86.
Plum, Green, 83.
Plum, Jacob, 86.
Plum, James, 88.
Plum, Jessey, 88.
Plum, Joseph, 87.
Plum, Justis, 29.
Plum, Reuben, 86.
Plum, Samuel, 88.
Plum, Samuel, Jun$^r$, 88.
Plum, Solomon, 50.
Plum, Thankfull, 98.
Plum, Wait, 86.
Plum, William, Esq$^r$, 86.
Plumb, Daniel, 147.
Plumb, Ebenezer, Jr., 126.
Plumb, Fredrerick, 62.
Plumb, George, 119.
Plumb, Isaac, 101.
Plumb, James, 116.
Plumb, John, 101.
Plumb, John, 129.
Plumb, Joseph, 89.
Plumb, Joshua, 95.
Plumb, Nath$^l$, 116.

Plumb, Peter, 126.
Plumb, Samuel, 95.
Plumb, Samuel, 101.
Plumb, Samuel, 115.
Plumb, Samuel, 129.
Plumb, Sarah. 70.
Plumb, Simeon, 50.
Plumb, Stephen, 71.
Plumber, John, 150.
Plumby, Eben$^r$, 68.
Plummer, Ebenezer, 42.
Plummer, Eben$^r$, 153.
Plummer, Isaac 42.
Plummer, Israel, 150.
Plummer, Mary, 114.
Plump, Benoni, 93.
Plump, Joseph, 101.
Plump, Joseph, 2$^d$, 101.
Plump, Seth, 109.
Plymate, William, 102.
Plymouth, John. 92.
Poerpont, David, 65.
Polk, David, 138.
Polk, E$^m$, 138.
Pollard, Barsheba 114.
Pollard, Isaac, 78.
Pollard, John, 114.
Pollard, Joseph, 113.
Pollard, Nabby, 114.
Pollet, James, 63.
Pollet, Rob$^t$, 136.
Polley, John, 13.
Polluck, Charles, 150.
Polly, John, 42.
Polly, John, 80.
Polly, Joshua, 145.
Pomber, Andrew, 134.
Pomeroy, Abagail, 51.
Pomeroy, Abigail, 51.
Pomeroy, Adino, 86.
Pomeroy, Amos, 51.
Pomeroy, Asa, 51.
Pomeroy, Darkis, 51.
Pomeroy, Elen$^r$, 133.
Pomeroy, Elihu, 135.
Pomeroy, Epephras, 51.
Pomeroy, Isaac, 50.
Pomeroy, John, 51.
Pomeroy, Jn$^o$, 136.
Pomeroy, Jos$^a$, 51.
Pomeroy, Nathaniel, 51.
Pomeroy, Noah, 139.
Pomeroy, Rachel, 53.
Pomeroy, Ralph, 46.
Pomeroy, Sarah, 51.
Pomeroy, Simean, 61.
Pomler, Elij$^a$, 134.
Pomp, 63.
Pomp (Negro), 21.
Pomp (Negro), 54.
Pomp (Negro), 121.
Pomp (Negro), 122.
Pomp (Negro), 131.
Pomp (Negroe), 92.
Pomp (Negroe), 102.
Pomp (Negroe), 109.
Pompey, London, 78.
Pompy (negro), 78.
Pomroy, Joel, 15.
Pomroy, Noah, 121.
Pond, Bartholemew, 1$^{st}$, 77.
Pond, Bartholemew, 2$^d$, 77.
Pond, Charles, 101.
Pond, Dan., 78.
Pond, Edward, 78.
Pond, Elias, 91.
Pond, Elizabeth, 101.
Pond, Enoch, 140.
Pond, Gad, 99.
Pond, Ira, 77.
Pond, Jonathan, 77.
Pond, Josiah, 58.
Pond, Moses, 50.
Pond, Peter, 102.
Pond, Phineas, 40.
Pond, Phineas, 111.
Pond, Zera, 77.
Pondman, Nathaniel, 95.
Pool, David, 129.
Pool, James, 137.
Pool, John, 17.
Pool, John, 94.
Pool, Jon$^a$, 137.
Pool, Mary, 94.
Pool, Samuel, 94.
Pool, Samuel, 105.
Pool, Thomas, 126.
Pool, Tim$^o$, 139.
Pooler, Allen, 144.
Pooler, Jn$^o$, 137.
Pooles, Amasa, 141.
Poor house, 132.
Poor House, 140.
Poor, Jonathan, 13.
Poor, Joshua, 30.
Pope, Ansil, 113.
Pope, Charles, 21.
Pope, Jacob, 110.
Pope, Joseph, 94.
Pope, Rich$^d$, 148.
Poplestone, Gideon, 151.
Popp (Negro), 47.
Popple, George, 115.

Porrage, Jabez, 143.
Porter, Aaron, 34.
Porter, Aaron, 52.
Porter, Abel, 34.
Porter, Abel, 133.
Porter, Abigail, 52.
Porter, Abigal, 140.
Porter, Abijah, 34.
Porter, Abraham, 146.
Porter, Amos, 41.
Porter, Asbell, 2$^{nd}$, 110.
Porter, Ashbel, 110.
Porter, Benjamin, 36.
Porter, Benjamin, 70.
Porter, Daniel, 38.
Porter, Daniel, 54.
Porter, Daniel, 109.
Porter, Dan$^l$, 135.
Porter, David, 32.
Porter, David, 110.
Porter, Ebenezer, 77.
Porter, Ebenezer, 110.
Porter, Edmund, 83.
Porter, Edward, 123.
Porter, Elijah, 36.
Porter, Elijah, 40.
Porter, Elijah, Jr., 40.
Porter, Elik$^m$, 146.
Porter, Eliphalet, 34.
Porter, Elisabeth, 29.
Porter, Elisha, 68.
Porter, Elizabeth, 110.
Porter, Ephraim, 30.
Porter, Ezekel, 110.
Porter, Ezra, 83.
Porter, Ezra, 85.
Porter, Flint, 150.
Porter, Francis, 110.
Porter, Freeman, 110.
Porter, Gaylan, 135.
Porter, George, 40.
Porter, George, 55.
Porter, Gideon, 73.
Porter, Hezekiah, 37.
Porter, Increas, 135.
Porter, Isaac, 34.
Porter, Isaac, 36.
Porter, Isaiah, 133.
Porter, Israel, 53.
Porter, James, 29.
Porter, James, 64.
Porter, James, 110.
Porter, Jesse, 41.
Porter, Job, 36.
Porter, Joel, 135.
Porter, John, 11.
Porter, John, 11.
Porter, John, 14.
Porter, John, 36.
Porter, John, 36.
Porter, John, 41.
Porter, Jn$^o$, 134.
Porter, John, 146.
Porter, Jonah, 136.
Porter, Jon$^a$, 133.
Porter, Jona$^n$, 150.
Porter, Jonathan, 150.
Porter, Joseph, 32.
Porter, Joseph, 41.
Porter, Jos., 134.
Porter, Joseph, Jr., 34.
Porter, Joshua, 10.
Porter, Joshua, 50.
Porter, Joshua, 70.
Porter, Laton, 146.
Porter, Lemuel, 41.
Porter, Manoah, 11.
Porter, Mark, 110.
Porter, Micaiah, 151.
Porter, Moses, 36.
Porter, Naomi, 37.
Porter, Nathan, 36.
Porter, Nathaniel, 17.
Porter, Nathaniel, 72.
Porter, Nathaniel, 110.
Porter, Nath$^l$, 145.
Porter, Nathaniel, Jr., 37.
Porter, Nehemiah, 135.
Porter, Nicholas, 70.
Porter, Noah, 41.
Porter, Noah, 133.
Porter, Philo, 72.
Porter, Phineas, 109.
Porter, Preserve, 109.
Porter, Prudince, 40.
Porter, Reuben, 145.
Porter, Richard, 40.
Porter, Roger, 36.
Porter, Ruben, 134.
Porter, Samuel, 29.
Porter, Samuel, 34.
Porter, Samuel, 110.
Porter, Sam$^l$, 147.
Porter, Samuel, 2$^d$, 34.
Porter, Samuel, 2$^d$, 110.
Porter, Samuel, 3$^d$, 34.
Porter, Seth, 61.
Porter, Shubael, 34.
Porter, Solomon, 46.
Porter, Stephen, 30.
Porter, Stephen, 37.
Porter, Stephen, 91.

# INDEX.

Porter Thomas, 30.
Porter, Thomas, 68.
Porter, Thoˢ, 133.
Porter, Thomas, 2ⁿᵈ, 110.
Porter, Timothy, 109.
Porter, Timᵒ, 136.
Porter, Timothy, 2ⁿᵈ, 110.
Porter, Uriah, 133.
Porter, Wareham, 37.
Porter (Widow), 133.
Porter, William, 36.
Porter, William, 41.
Portman, Mary Ann, 28.
Post, Aaron, 44.
Post, Anne, 90.
Post, Benjamin, 90.
Post, Christopher, 90.
Post, David, 90.
Post, David, 134.
Post, David, Junʳ, 90.
Post, Enoch, 90.
Post, George, 67.
Post, Gordan, 135.
Post, Hezekʰ, 90.
Post, Isaac, 90.
Post, Isaac, 90.
Post, Jacob, 135.
Post, James, 90.
Post, James, 135.
Post, Jazaniah, 138.
Post, Jedediah, 90.
Post, Jedediah, 134.
Post, Joel, 90.
Post, Jnᵒ, 90.
Post, John, 126.
Post, John, 131.
Post, Jonathan, 90.
Post, Joseph, 73.
Post, Joˢ, 132.
Post, Jos., 135.
Post, Joshua, 90.
Post, Josiah, 90.
Post, Nathan, 90.
Post, Nathan, 2ᵈ, 90.
Post, Nathˡ, 126.
Post, Pheneas, 146.
Post, Phinehas, 90.
Post, Samˡ, 82.
Post, Samˡ, 132.
Post, Stephen, 126.
Post, Thoˢ, 135.
Potleett, James, 63.
Potler, Israel, 64.
Pots, Christopher, 131.
Potter, Abel, 100.
Potter, Amos, 100.
Potter, Ann, 128.
Potter, Asa, 104.
Potter, Chauncy, 100.
Potter, Daniel, 69.
Potter, Daniel, 77.
Potter, David, 69.
Potter, David, 100.
Potter, David, 100.
Potter, Demas, 77.
Potter, Ebenezer, 69.
Potter, Edmond, 150.
Potter, Edward, Jr., 42.
Potter, Elam, 39.
Potter, Eldad, 93.
Potter, Eliahson, 77.
Potter, Elizer, 69.
Potter, Ezra, 79.
Potter, Gideon, 113.
Potter, Hannah, 118.
Potter, Jacob, 77.
Potter, James, 19.
Potter, Jerad, 107.
Potter, Jesse, 58.
Potter, Jesse, 100.
Potter, Job, 100.
Potter, Joel, 59.
Potter, Joel, 91.
Potter, John, 50.
Potter, John, 87.
Potter, John, 92.
Potter, John, 128.
Potter, John, 2ⁿᵈ, 92.
Potter, Joseph, 95.
Potter, Joseph, 100.
Potter, Joshua, 128.
Potter, Lake, 77.
Potter, Lemuel, 110.
Potter, Levi, 97.
Potter, Livi, 104.
Potter, Martin, 49.
Potter, Medad, 100.
Potter, Milton, 19.
Potter, Moses, 100.
Potter, Nathaniel, 41.
Potter (Negroe), 108.
Potter, Nehemiah, 148.
Potter, Noah, 104.
Potter, Paullinus, 49.
Potter, Philemon, 41.
Potter, Phillip, 151.
Potter, Philomon, 100.
Potter, Phinehas, 69.
Potter, Rhoda, 49.
Potter, Samuel, 77.
Potter, Seate, 105.
Potter, Silas, 140.
Potter, Statia, 104.

Potter, Thomas, 77.
Potter, Thomas, 100.
Potter, Thomas, 120.
Potter, Timothy, 100.
Potter, Timothy, 2ⁿᵈ, 100.
Potter, William, 112.
Potter, William, 128.
Potter, Zenas, 77.
Potwine, John, 38.
Potwine, Thomas, Jr., 38.
Potwine, Revᵈ Thomas, 38.
Pousley, Samuel, 86.
Powel, Aaron, 135.
Powel, John, 75.
Powell, William, 103.
Powers, Barnabas, 50.
Powers, Edward, 86.
Powers, Gregory, 86.
Powers, Henry, 87.
Powers, John, 118.
Powers, Joseph, 127.
Powers, Joshua, 124.
Powers, Michael, 127.
Powers, Michael, 2ᵈ, 127.
Powers, Samˡ, 126.
Powers, Sylvester, 128.
Powers, Sylvester, 129.
Powers, Thomas, 97.
Powers, Thomas, 2ⁿᵈ, 98.
Powers, Timothy, 86.
Poyson, John, 48.
Prague, Joseph, 144.
Pran, John, 82.
Prat, Ashbel, 136.
Prat, Samuel, 103.
Pratt, Abijah, 75.
Pratt, Abner, 57.
Pratt, Abraham, 89.
Pratt, Abreham, 61.
Pratt, Adonijah, 68.
Pratt, Andrew, 33.
Pratt, Asa, 89.
Pratt, Asa, 2ᵈ, 89.
Pratt, Benajah, 89.
Pratt, Benjamin, 89.
Pratt, Benjᵃ, 90.
Pratt, Benjᵃ, 140.
Pratt, Charity, 89.
Pratt, Christopher, 49.
Pratt, Damaras, 90.
Pratt, Daniel, 42.
Pratt, Daniel, 120.
Pratt, Danˡ, 149.
Pratt, Daniel, Junʳ, 120.
Pratt, Daniel, 3ᵈ, 120.
Pratt, David, 89.
Pratt, David, 1ˢᵗ, 57.
Pratt, David, 2ᵈ, 57.
Pratt, David B., 122.
Pratt, Deliverance, 90.
Pratt, Edward, 122.
Pratt, Eliab, 36.
Pratt, Eliakim, 136.
Pratt, Elias, 89.
Pratt, Elisha, 41.
Pratt, Ether, 90.
Pratt, Ezra, 48.
Pratt, Ezra, 89.
Pratt, George, 46.
Pratt, Gideon, 89.
Pratt, Humphrey, 89.
Pratt, Humphrey, Junʳ, 89.
Pratt, Isaac, 64.
Pratt, Jabez, 89.
Pratt, James, 46.
Pratt, James, 89.
Pratt, James, 135.
Pratt, Jane, 89.
Pratt, Jasper, 57.
Pratt, Jedʰ, 90.
Pratt, Jeremiah, 89.
Pratt, Jesse, 90.
Pratt, Joel, 63.
Pratt, Jnᵒ, 89.
Pratt, John, 120.
Pratt, John, 150.
Pratt, Jnᵒ, 2ᵈ, 89.
Pratt, Jnᵒ Clark, 89.
Pratt, Jonathan, 88.
Pratt, Jones, 89.
Pratt, Joseph, 46.
Pratt, Joseph, 59.
Pratt, Mabel, 41.
Pratt, Mansah, 42.
Pratt, Mary, 89.
Pratt, Mehitable, 90.
Pratt, Moses, 36.
Pratt, Nathaniel, 44.
Pratt, Noah, 59.
Pratt, Ozias, 90.
Pratt, Peter, 59.
Pratt, Phebe, 90.
Pratt, Phinehas, 89.
Pratt, Reuben, 89.
Pratt, Robert, 89.
Pratt, Russell, 36.
Pratt, Samuel, 84.
Pratt, Samˡ, 89.
Pratt, Seth, 89.
Pratt, Silas, 70.
Pratt, Simeon, 90.
Pratt, Stephen, 49.
Pratt, Susannah, 89.

Pratt, Tabor, 90.
Pratt, Thomas, 39.
Pratt, Thomas, 90.
Pratt, Timothy, 44.
Pratt, Timothy, 89.
Pratt, William, 33.
Pratt, William, 46.
Pratt, Wᵐ, 90.
Pratt, William, Jr., 46
Pratt, Zacheriah, 46.
Pratt, Zephaniah, 89.
Prentice, Ameziah, 78.
Prentice, Amos, 119.
Prentice, Christopher, 56.
Prentice, Easter, 126.
Prentice, Ebenʳ, 129.
Prentice, Eleazer, 113.
Prentice, Elisha, 113.
Prentice, Elisha, 114.
Prentice, James, 136.
Prentice, John, 56.
Prentice, John, 115.
Prentice, John, 128.
Prentice, Jnᵒ, 136.
Prentice, John, Junʳ, 115.
Prentice, Jonas, 103.
Prentice, Joseph, 126.
Prentice, Joshua, 115.
Prentice, Lucy, 115.
Prentice, Manassa, 113.
Prentice, Ozias, 78.
Prentice, Samuel, 115.
Prentice, Samˡ, 124.
Prentice, Stephen, 127.
Prentice, Stephen, 136.
Prentice, Stephen, Junʳ, 127.
Prentice, Thomas, 78.
Prentice, Thomas, 115.
Prentice, Zackeriah, 78.
Presbrey, Joseph, 11.
Presby, Charles, 34.
Prescot, Benjamin, 104.
Prescot, James, 104.
Preshell, George, 2ⁿᵈ, 109.
Presson, David, 61.
Presson, Jermiah, 65.
Preston, Abraham, 140.
Preston, Amasa, 77.
Preston, Benjamin, 66.
Preston, Benjamin, 108.
Preston, Caleb, 77.
Preston, Charles, 64.
Preston, Daniel, 113.
Preston, Daniel, 144.
Preston, Danˡ, 146.
Preston, Darius, 139.
Preston, Darius, 139.
Preston, Enos, 138.
Preston, Hovey, 140.
Preston, Jacob, 143.
Preston, Jareb, 140.
Preston, John, 58.
Preston, John, 140.
Preston, Medinah, 140.
Preston, Noah, 68.
Preston, Ruben, 93.
Preston, Samuel, 38.
Preston, Samuel, 64.
Preston, Samuel, 108.
Preston, Titus, 108.
Preston, William, 153.
Preston, Zephʰ, 140.
Preston, Zera, 140.
Price, Benjamin, 78.
Price, David, 13.
Price, David, 22.
Price, Ebenezer, 28.
Price, George, 53.
Price, Hezekiah, 13.
Price, Hurd, 28.
Price, Jonathan, 53.
Price, Paul, 64.
Price, Richard, 53.
Price, Samuel, 42.
Price, Zalmon, 13.
Prichard, Benjamin, 77.
Prichard, Eli, 68.
Prichard, Elijah, 77.
Prichard, James, 56.
Prichard, Simain, 68.
Pridden, John, 102.
Pridden, Revᵈ Nehemiah, 39.
Pride, Absolum, 114.
Pride, Asa, 114.
Pride, Elijah, 115.
Pride, William, 114.
Priden, Fletcher, 102.
Priden, Samuel, 102.
Priest, Asa, 48.
Priest, Darius, 48.
Prime (Negroe), 101.
Prime (Negroe), 101.
Primes (Negro), 119.
Primus (Negro), 131.
Primus (Negroe), 104.
Prinale, Charles, 102.
Prince, 64.
Prince, Abel, 141.
Prince, Abel, 150.
Prince, Abijah, 146.
Prince, Asa, 72.
Prince, Ebenʳ, 150.
Prince, Edmond Howel, 72.

Prince, Joseph, 150.
Prince, Kimball, 129.
Prince, Nathaniel, 112.
Prince (Negro), 114.
Prince (Negro), 116.
Prince (Negro), 120.
Prince (Negro), 121.
Prince (Negro), 121.
Prince (Negro), 122.
Prince (Negro), 131.
Prince (Negro), 151.
Prince (Negro), 97.
Prince, Robert, 150.
Prince, Samuel, 72.
Prince, Samˡ, 150.
Prince, Timᵒˡʸ, 141.
Prince, Timothy, Juʳ, 141.
Prince, William, 32.
Prindle, Aaron, 19.
Prindle, Abiel, 20.
Prindle, Abijah, 20.
Prindle, Amos, 18.
Prindle, Charles, 102.
Prindle, Chauncy, 77.
Prindle, Danˡ, 20.
Prindle, David, 77.
Prindle, Dina, 105.
Prindle, Ebenezer, 95.
Prindle, Eleasor, 77.
Prindle, Elisha, 105.
Prindle, Elizabeth, 105.
Prindle, Eneas, 94.
Prindle, Isaac, 17.
Prindle, John, 78.
Prindle, John, 94.
Prindle, John, 105.
Prindle, Jonas, 20.
Prindle, Jonathan, 20.
Prindle, Josep, 102.
Prindle, Joseph, 20.
Prindle, Joseph, 105.
Prindle, Lazarus, 20.
Prindle, Mack, 58.
Prindle, Philimon, 20.
Prindle, Samuel, 20.
Prindle, Sarah, 93.
Prindle, Sirus, 20.
Pringle, Ephraim, 20.
Prior, Azariah, 39.
Prior, Daniel, 87.
Prior, Ebenezer, 39.
Prior, Elijah, 87.
Prior, Ezekiel, 40.
Prior, George, 38.
Prior, Isaac, 39.
Prior, Jesse, 87.
Prior, Joel, 38.
Prior, Josiah, 87.
Prior, Mary, 33.
Prior, Oliver, 87.
Prior, Roswell, 39.
Prior, Samuel, 87.
Prior, Zacheus, 40.
Pritchard, Archibald, 109.
Pritchard, Isaac, 102.
Pritchard, James, 95.
Pritchard, Leveret, 95.
Pritchard, Martha, 102.
Pritchard, Nathaniel, 101.
Pritchard, Nathaniel, 101.
Pritchard, Philo, 94.
Pritchet, Abraham, 109.
Pritchet, Amos, 109.
Pritchet, David, 109.
Pritchet, George, 110.
Pritchet, Roger, 109.
Pritchett, Isaih, 109.
Pritchett, James, 110.
Pritchett, John, 110.
Pritchett, John, 110.
Proctor, Abel, 128.
Proston, David, 57.
Proston, Stephen, 57.
Proud, Robert, 128.
Prout, Darcy, 87.
Prout, Harris, 87.
Prout, Jesse, 72.
Prout, John, 87.
Prout, John, 107.
Prout, Margeret, 103.
Prout, Oliver, 87.
Provost, Samuel, 25.
Provost, Thomas, 26.
Prudden, Jonathan, 102.
Pry (Negroe), 101.
Pryor, Azarior, 146.
Pryor, Benjᵃ, 148.
Pryor, John, 88.
Pryor, Joseph, 148.
Pryor, Joshua, 148.
Puffer, Sarah, 121.
Pughby, Samuel, 16.
Pulford, Dorcas, 77.
Pulford, Lewis, 18.
Pulling, Abigail, 28.
Pulling, Abraham, 29.
Pulling, Augustus, 28.
Pulling, William, 28.
Pulman, John, 151.
Pulnam, Cornelius, 137.
Pulsifer, Huldah, 42.
Pulsifer, Joseph, 42.
Pulsifer, Sylvester, 42.

Pumham (Negro), 122.
Punderford, John, 102.
Punderson, Ahimea, 70.
Punderson, Daniel, 104.
Punderson, Ebenezer, 114.
Punderson, Ebenezer, Junʳ, 114.
Punderson, Lizey, 105.
Punderson, Samuel, 104.
Punderson, Thomas, 104.
Purchase, Thoˢ, 136.
Purdy, Daniel, 16.
Purdy, Elizabeth (Wᵈ), 16.
Purdy, Nathan, 16.
Purdy, Ruth (Wᵈ), 16.
Purkins, Ebenezer, 56.
Purna, Peter, 136.
Purple, David, 122.
Purple, Edward, 81.
Purple, Ezra, 134.
Purple, Josiah, 80.
Purtree, John, 101.
Putman, John, 52.
Putnam, Aaron, 13.
Putnam, Aaron, 149.
Putnam, Danˡ, 141.
Putnam, David, 38.
Putnam, Israel, 141.
Putnam, Peter S., 149.
Putnam, Reubin, 141.
Putt, Christopher, 95.
Putt, John (negroe), 94.
Pyncheon, Joseph, 98.
Pyncheon, Thomas R., 98.

Quash (Negro), 117.
Quash (Negro), 121.
Quinley, Jeremiah, 126.
Quinley, Thomas, 126.
Quintard, Isaac, 16.
Quintard, Isaac, 24.
Quintard, James, 22.
Quintard, Peter, 22.
Quintard, Peter, 24.
Quithy, Phillip, 149.
Quive, Elijah, 113.
Quive, Henry, 113.
Quive, Lemuel, 113.
Quivy, Amasa, 141.
Quy (Negro), 130.

Rackerbrandt, John, 104.
Racksford, Joseph, 66.
Raies, Moses, 147.
Ralph, Jonathan, 106.
Ramond, William, 68.
Rample, George, 20.
Ramsdale, Ezra, 121.
Ramsey, Jonathan, 46.
Ranal, Job, 62.
Rand, Robert, 86.
Rand, Thomas, 86.
Randal, Amos, 82.
Randal, Jobe, 141.
Randal, John, 80.
Randal, Jonathan, 149.
Randal, Nathan, 113.
Randall, Abraham, 121.
Randall, Amos, 121.
Randall, Amos, 151.
Randall, Arunah, 121.
Randall, Asa, 121.
Randall, Elias, 121.
Randall, Elijah, 143.
Randall, Isaac, 151.
Randall, James, 144.
Randall, Jedediah, 117.
Randall, John, 117.
Randall, John, Junʳ, 117.
Randall, Joseph, 114.
Randall, Joseph, 121.
Randall, Joseph, 151.
Randall, Nicholas, 151.
Randall, Peleg, 151.
Randall, Robart, 116.
Randall, Roswell, 117.
Randall, Rufus, 117.
Randall, Silvester, 121.
Randall, Thomas, 117.
Randall, William, 117.
Randol, John, 62.
Randol, Solomon, 62.
Raney, Ruben, 97.
Ranford, Arther, 67.
Ranford, Daniel, 63.
Ranford, Joel, 63.
Ranney, Abijah, 88.
Ranney, Amos, 80.
Ranney, Comfort, 88.
Ranney, David, 81.
Ranney, Ebenezer, 87.
Ranney, George, 98.
Ranney, Hezekiah, 88.
Ranney, Jabez, 80.
Ranney, Jonothan, 86.
Ranney, Mary, 88.
Ranney, Nathan, 75.
Ranney, Nathaniel, 88.
Ranney, Samuel W., 86.
Ranney, Stephen, 86.
Ranney, Stephen, Junʳ, 80.
Ranney, Stephen, Junʳ, 86.
Ranney, Thomas, 80.
Ranney, William, 87.

# INDEX.

Ranny, George, 80.
Ranny, Joseph, 88.
Ranny, Stephen, 80.
Ransford, David, 142.
Ransford, Joseph, 142.
Ransford, Joseph, 142.
Ransford, Richard, 142.
Ransley, William, 18.
Ransom, Amasa, 122.
Ransom, Amos, 82.
Ransom, Amy, 122.
Ransom, Asael, 122.
Ransom, Bliss, 122.
Ransom, David, 123.
Ransom, Edward, 123.
Ransom, Elijah, 125.
Ransom, Israel, 122.
Ransom, James, 122.
Ransom, Joseph, 120.
Ransom, Joshua, 82.
Ransom, Ruben, 122.
Ransom, Russel, 78.
Ransom, Sam¹, 142.
Ransom, Stephen, 122.
Ransom, Theophilus, 77.
Ransom, William, 121.
Ranson, Harris, 42.
Ranson, John, 59.
Rash, Jeremiah, 53.
Rass, Noah, 80.
Ratford, James, 110.
Rathbon, John, 141.
Rathbon, Joseph, 142.
Rathbon, Sybil, 142.
Rathborn, Job, 62.
Rathborne, Ezra, 153.
Rathbun, Job, 128.
Rathburn, Susannah, 16.
Rawdin, Thoˢ, 138.
Rawding, Ezra, 138.
Rawley, Daniel, 41.
Rawlinson, Joseph, 99.
Rawney, William, 153.
Rawson, David, 153.
Rawson, Elizabeth, 85.
Rawson, Erindol, 82.
Rawson, Nath¹, 151.
Ray, Adonijah, 134.
Ray, Amos, 113.
Ray, Benjamin, 88.
Ray, Caleb, 102.
Ray, Constant, 83.
Ray, Daniel, 83.
Ray, Daniel, 113.
Ray, Daniel, 123.
Ray, Enoch, 106.
Ray, Flint, 52.
Ray, Gershom, 151.
Ray, Gideon, 114.
Ray, Isaac, 83.
Ray, Jecaniah, 83.
Ray, John, 114.
Ray, Joseph, 83.
Ray, Levi, 83.
Ray, Levi, 106.
Ray, Martha, 103.
Ray, Nathaniel, 83.
Ray, Peter, 83.
Ray, Stephen, 114.
Ray, Thomas, 106.
Ray, Timothy, 65.
Ray, William, 65.
Raydon, Samuel, 69.
Rayman (Wid.), 135.
Rayment, Daniel, 14.
Rayment, Isaac, 11.
Raymond, Aaron, 22.
Raymond, Abigail (Wᵈ), 21.
Raymond, Abraham, 23.
Raymond, Amazʰ, 149.
Raymond, Asahel, 21.
Raymond, Benjamin, 21.
Raymond, Caleb, 127.
Raymond, Christopher, 125.
Raymond, Clapp, 21.
Raymond, Clapp, Jʳ, 21.
Raymond, Comfort, 23.
Raymond, David, 22.
Raymond, Ebenezer, 22.
Raymond, Edward, 22.
Raymond, Eliakim, 22.
Raymond, Esther (Wᵈ), 23.
Raymond, George, 22.
Raymond, George, 125.
Raymond, Gershom, 22.
Raymond, Gershom, Jʳ, 22.
Raymond, Hezekiah, 22.
Raymond, Jesse, 23.
Raymond, John, 22.
Raymond, John, 105.
Raymond, John, 125.
Raymond, Joshua, 124.
Raymond, Joshua, 142.
Raymond, Josiah, 21.
Raymond, Josiah, 125.
Raymond, Justin, 20.
Raymond, Lemuel, 26.
Raymond, Lemuel, 125.
Raymond, Lucy, 125.
Raymond, Luke, 26.
Raymond, Moses, 22.
Raymond, Mulford, 125.

Raymond, Naphtha, 22.
Raymond, Nathaniel, 22.
Raymond, Nath¹, 125.
Raymond, Nathᵉˡ, Jr, 22.
Raymond, Paul, 22.
Raymond, Ruth, 31.
Raymond, Samuel, 22.
Raymond, Seth, 21.
Raymond, Seth, 21.
Raymond, Simon, 22.
Raymond, Stephen, 26.
Raymond, Uriah, 22.
Raymond, Wᵐ, 23.
Raymond, Wᵐ, 23.
Raymond, William, 65.
Raymong, David, 12.
Raymong, David, 18.
Raymong, Elijah, 12.
Raymong, Jesse, 18.
Raymong, William, 13.
Raymong, William, Jnʳ, 13.
Raynold, Richard T., 77.
Raynold, Samuel, Junʳ, 77.
Raynold, Solomon, 73.
Raynolds, John, 64.
Raynolds, Ruben, 132.
Raynolds, Sam¹, 136.
Read, Abner, 44.
Read, Amos, 113.
Read, Asa, 72.
Read, Asa, 113.
Read, Benjamin, 44.
Read, Charles, 127.
Read, Christopher, 114.
Read, Christopher, 126.
Read, David, 44.
Read, Ebenezer, 37.
Read, Elexander, 119.
Read, Eli, 27.
Read, Elias, 28.
Read, Enoch, 124.
Read, George, 44.
Read, George, 123.
Read, Hezekiah, 27.
Read, Hezekiah, 59.
Read, Jabez, 113.
Read, Jacob, 72.
Read, James, 119.
Read, John, 27.
Read, John, 44.
Read, John, 113.
Read, Jonathan Hanson, 72.
Read, Joseph, 113.
Read, Joseph, 123.
Read, Justus, 37.
Read, Martin, 44.
Read, Mary, 130.
Read, Pheba, 124.
Read, Robart, 124.
Read, Rusell, 44.
Read, Samuel, 113.
Read, Samuel, 114.
Read, William, 124.
Read, Zalmon, 27.
Reardon, Simon, 86.
Reave, Pnyryer, 89.
Reaves, Israel, 123.
Reaves, John, 80.
Rebecka (Negro), 125.
Recor, Michael, 83.
Record, Joseph, 150.
Record, Silas, 149.
Redding, Edward, 86.
Redding, Samuel, 88.
Reddington, Jnᵒ, 133.
Redfield, Ambros, 85.
Redfield, Augustus, 85.
Redfield, Constant, 85.
Redfield, Daniel, 85.
Redfield, Ebenezer, 12.
Redfield, Eliphilalet, 85.
Redfield, Frederick, 86.
Redfield, George, 85.
Redfield, James, 13.
Redfield, James, Jnʳ, 12.
Redfield, James P., 90.
Redfield, John, 97.
Redfield, John, 2ⁿᵈ, 97.
Redfield, Josiah, 85.
Redfield, Lucretia, 14.
Redfield, Margarett, 85.
Redfield, Nathaniel, 98.
Redfield, Peleg, 85.
Redfield, Peleg, 85.
Redfield, Samuel, 85.
Redfield, Samuel, 2ᵈ, 85.
Redfield, Samuel, 3ᵈ, 85.
Redfield, Sarah, 85.
Redfield, Seth, 85.
Redfield, Simeon, 85.
Redfield, Susannah, 86.
Redfield, Sylvenus, 85.
Redfield, Sylvester, 85.
Redfield, Tereny, 85.
Redfield, William, 86.
Reed, Abigail, 22.
Reed, Abigail, 90.
Reed, Amasa, 147.
Reed, Benjamin, 22.
Reed, Benjᵃ, 61.
Reed, Beriah, 152.
Reed, Cornelius, 90.
Reed, Daniel, 104.

Reed, Danˡ, 144.
Reed, David, 103.
Reed, David, 152.
Reed, Ebenezer, 69.
Reed, Captᵗ Eli, 22.
Reed, Elias, 65.
Reed, Ethiel, 61.
Reed, Holly, 57.
Reed, Jacob, 68.
Reed, Jesse, 22.
Reed, Joel, 62.
Reed, John, 22.
Reed, John, 57.
Reed, John, 65.
Reed, John, 107.
Reed, John, Jr., 44.
Reed, Jonathan, 27.
Reed, Jonathan, 62.
Reed, Josiah, 64.
Reed, Mathew, 140.
Reed, Matthew, 23.
Reed, Moses, 62.
Reed, Moses, 65.
Reed, Nathan, 27.
Reed, Nathan, 147.
Reed, Peter, 69.
Reed, Peter, 101.
Reed, Samˡ, 138.
Reed, Shubal, 138.
Reed, Silas, 48.
Reed, Stephen, 62.
Reed, Sussanah, 104.
Reed, Thaddeus, 22.
Reed, Thomas, 66.
Reed, Thomas, 152.
Reed, Timothy, 26.
Reed (Widow), 134.
Reed, William, 22.
Reed, William, Junʳ, 22.
Reed, Zackeriah, 103.
Reede, Rufus, 120.
Reels, John, 17.
Reeve, Tapping, 65.
Reeves, Ebenezer, 130.
Relley, William, 18.
Remand, William, 2ᵈ, 66.
Remerton, Stephen, 28.
Remington, Abijah, 51.
Remington, Amos, 51.
Remington, Asa, 51.
Remington, Benjamin, 51.
Remington, Elijah, 51.
Remington, Elijah, 2ᵈ, 51.
Remington, Hosea, 51.
Remington, Isaac, 51.
Remington, Jonᵃ, 50.
Remington, Josiah, 28.
Remington, Nathaniel, 52.
Remington, Nathaniel, 52.
Remington, Simeon, 51.
Remington, Stephen, 51.
Remington, Thomas, 51.
Remsen, Joseph, 81.
Remsen, Joseph, Junʳ, 81.
Ren (Negroe), 93.
Renholds, Hezekiah, 92.
Rennalds, Joel, 60.
Renny, Ebenezer, 95.
Renny, Medad, 95.
Rensom, Peleg, 80.
Renton, James, 22.
Reryy, Solomon, 50.
Rese, Willobe, 47.
Resigue, William, 28.
Resigue, Alexander, 28.
Resiguie, Jacob, 28.
Resiguie, Jacob, 2ᵈ, 28.
Resiguie, James, 28.
Ressique, James, 23.
Reves, Samuel, 80.
Rewick, Owen, 61.
Rexford, Benjamin, 88.
Rexford, David, 57.
Rexford, Elisha, 17.
Rexford, Phillip, 105.
Rexford, Samuel, 57.
Reynold, John, Esqʳ, 39.
Reynolds, Alexander, 143.
Reynolds, Ambrose, 16.
Reynolds, Benjamin, 16.
Reynolds, Briggs, 15.
Reynolds, Charles, 36.
Reynolds, Daniel, 15.
Reynolds, David, 75.
Reynolds, David, 143.
Reynolds, David, 144.
Reynolds, Ebenʳ, 113.
Reynolds, Elisha, 15.
Reynolds, Elizabeth (Wᵈ), 16.
Reynolds, Elihu, 15.
Reynolds, Ezekiel, 15.
Reynolds, Ezra, 16.
Reynolds, Fredrick, 105.
Reynolds, Gamaliel, 132.
Reynolds, Hezekiah, 126.
Reynolds, Horton, 15.
Reynolds, Isaac, 22.
Reynolds, Jacob, 150.
Reynolds, James, 105.
Reynolds, James B., 105.
Reynolds, Joannah (Wᵈ), 16.
Reynolds, John, 36.

Reynolds, John, 41.
Reynolds, John, 75.
Reynolds, John, 122.
Reynolds, John, 143.
Reynolds, Jonathan, 16.
Reynolds, Joseph, 15.
Reynolds, Joseph, 16.
Reynolds, Joseph, 131.
Reynolds, Nathan, 16.
Reynolds, Nathaniel, 15.
Reynolds, Nathᵉˡ, Jr, 15.
Reynolds, Peroz, 25.
Reynolds, Philo, 15.
Reynolds, Richardson, 25.
Reynolds, Samuel, 15.
Reynolds, Samuel, 39.
Reynolds, Squire, 92.
Reynolds, Thomas, 116.
Rhiney, Daniel, 60.
Rhoads, James, 117.
Rhodes, John, 151.
Rhodes, John, 152.
Ribborn, Jehiel, 71.
Rice, Aaron, 54.
Rice, Abigail, 33.
Rice, Abner, 108.
Rice, Amassa, 107.
Rice, Amos, 107.
Rice, Amos, 108.
Rice, Archabald, 104.
Rice, Asa, 63.
Rice, Bennet, 93.
Rice, Chaney, 62.
Rice, Clarke, 93.
Rice, Daniel, 69.
Rice, David, 137.
Rice, Elezer, 50.
Rice, Elijah, 63.
Rice, Eliphalet, 42.
Rice, Elisha, 100.
Rice, Ezekiel, 107.
Rice, Ezra, 107.
Rice, Hannah, 108.
Rice, James, 103.
Rice, James, 107.
Rice, James, 108.
Rice, Jesse, 109.
Rice, Jessee, 44.
Rice, Joel, 43.
Rice, Joel, 107.
Rice, John, 42.
Rice, John, 44.
Rice, John, 61.
Rice, John, 92.
Rice, Jnᵒ, 139.
Rice, Jnᵒ, Jʳ, 139.
Rice, Jonah, 44.
Rice, Joseph, 44.
Rice, Joseph, 108.
Rice, Josiah, 61.
Rice, Justice, 108.
Rice, Levi, 93.
Rice, Lucy, 109.
Rice, Mary, 129.
Rice, Mathew, 49.
Rice, Memusan, 41.
Rice, Moses, 108.
Rice, Nathanˡ, 63.
Rice, Nathaniel, 93.
Rice, Pedi, 44.
Rice, Peter, 43.
Rice, Peter, Jr., 43.
Rice, Rebecca, 92.
Rice, Robert, 92.
Rice, Ruben, 93.
Rice, Samuel, 42.
Rice, Samˡ, 65.
Rice, Samuel, 107.
Rice, Samuel, 108.
Rice, Samuel, Jr., 42.
Rice, Simeon, 96.
Rice, Thadeus, 68.
Rice, Thadeus, 108.
Rice, Thomas, 103.
Rice, Thomas, 108.
Rice, Thomas, 128.
Rice, Thoˢ, 139.
Rice, Wait, 69.
Rice (Wid.), 139.
Rice, William, 43.
Rice, William, 109.
Rich, Cornelius, Junʳ, 81.
Rich, Eliakim, 87.
Rich, Isaac, 82.
Rich, Israel, 150.
Rich, Jnᵒ, 35.
Rich, Lemuel, 81.
Rich, Peter, 37.
Rich, Samuel, 81.
Rich, Solomon, 113.
Rich, Thaddeus, 34.
Rich, Wᵐ, 35.
Richard, Aaron, 59.
Richard, Abigail (Wᵈ), 22.
Richard, Benjamin, 1ˢᵗ, 77.
Richard, Benjamin, 2ᵈ, 77.
Richard, Danˡ, 150.
Richard, Ebenezer, 77.
Richard, Elishu, 63.
Richard, Elizabeth, 77.
Richard, Gershom, 22.
Richard, Gideon, 77.
Richard, Jedediah, 63.

Richard, Jedediah, 2ᵈ, 63.
Richard, John, 23.
Richard, John, 105.
Richard, Pelatiah, 70.
Richard, Peter, 77.
Richard, Roswell, 63.
Richard, Stephen, 21.
Richard, Truman, 73.
Richard, William, 34.
Richard, William, 77.
Richards, Charles, 67.
Richards, Daniel W., 128.
Richards, David, 127.
Richards, Edmond, 23.
Richards, Edward, 127.
Richards, Elisabeth, 129.
Richards, Elizabeth, 109.
Richards, Guy, 129.
Richards, Guy, 129.
Richards, Huldy, 109.
Richards, Israel, 150.
Richards, Jabez, 126.
Richards, James, 23.
Richards, James, Junʳ, 23.
Richards, Jesse, 23.
Richards, John, 127.
Richards, John, 131.
Richards, Joseph, 34.
Richards, Mary, 128.
Richards, Nathan, 22.
Richards, Nathˡ, 127.
Richards, Nehemiah, 127.
Richards, Rebecca (Wᵈ), 22.
Richards, Samuel, 40.
Richards, Samuel, 49.
Richards, Samˡ, 126.
Richards, Samuel, Jr., 41.
Richards, Sarah, 88.
Richards, Sarah (Wid.), 49.
Richards, Seth, 40.
Richards, Silas, 67.
Richards, Street, 110.
Richards, Thaddeus, 140.
Richards, William, 85.
Richards, William, 126.
Richardson, Amos, 133.
Richardson, David, 136.
Richardson, David, Jr., 136.
Richardson, Eber, 109.
Richardson, Edatha, 38.
Richardson, Eleazʳ, 146.
Richardson, Eᵐ, 134.
Richardson, Ezekiel, 133.
Richardson, Gershom, 137.
Richardson, Humphrey, 145.
Richardson, Isaac, 137.
Richardson, Isael, 54.
Richardson, James, 146.
Richardson, Jnᵒ, 137.
Richardson, Jnᵒ, 139.
Richardson, John, 143.
Richardson, John, 154.
Richardson, Jonᵃ, 133.
Richardson, Justus, 133.
Richardson, Lemˡ, 138.
Richardson, Natha., 137.
Richardson, Nathaniel, 109.
Richardson, Rowland, 86.
Richardson, Stephen, 133.
Richardson, Stephen, 136.
Richardson, Thomas, 136.
Richardson, William, 43.
Richardson, William, 148.
Richarson, Hezekiah, 133.
Richarson, Zebulon, 34.
Richeron, Thomas, 61.
Richerson, Asa, 132.
Richerson, John, 116.
Richerson, Salmon, 116.
Richerson, Samuel, 18.
Richerson, Stephen, 68.
Richmond, Abner, 154.
Richmond, Edmond, 72.
Richmond, Edward, 153.
Richmond, Ephraim, 72.
Richmond, Hannah, 99.
Richmond, Jacob, 99.
Richmond, John, 149.
Richmond, Jonathan, 72.
Richmond, Joseph, 154.
Richmond, Michael, 150.
Richmond, Oliver, 150.
Richmond, Warner, 99.
Rickerson, Martha, 61.
Rider, John, 10.
Rider, John, 80.
Rigbey, William, 73.
Riggs, Abner, 110.
Riggs, Ebenezer, 95.
Riggs, Edward, 95.
Riggs, James, 95.
Riggs, John, 95.
Riggs, John, 110.
Riggs, Joseph, 28.
Riggs, Joseph, 94.
Riggs, Joseph, 95.
Riggs, Joseph, 2ⁿᵈ, 94.
Riggs, Moses, 95.
Riggs, Thomas, 95.
Right, Charles, 60.
Right, Elizer, 62.
Right, Ephraim, 62.
Right, Freedom, 60.

INDEX. 209

Right, John, 60.
Right, John, 62.
Right, Jonathan, 62.
Right, Justin, 67.
Rigly, Richard, 55.
Rigs, Jeremiah, 59.
Riley, Ackley, 53.
Riley, Ashbel, 52.
Riley, Asher, 88.
Riley, Charles, 43.
Riley, Christian, 52.
Riley, Jabez, 53.
Riley, Jacob, 53.
Riley, Jasper, 54.
Riley, John, 53.
Riley, John, 67.
Riley, Joseph, 88.
Riley, Julius, 88.
Riley, Justus, 52.
Riley, Levi, 52.
Riley, Levi, 52.
Riley, Nathl, 55.
Riley, Roger, 34.
Riley, Roger, 53.
Riley, Samuel, 52.
Riley, Saml, 67.
Riley, Saml, 154.
Riley, Sarah, 53.
Riley, Stephen, 53.
Rimington, Elihu, 62.
Rinbal, Rachael, 107.
Rines, Daniel, 17.
Rinevault, William, 19.
Ringe, Amy, 153.
Ringe, Danl, 133.
Ringe, Isaac, 132.
Ringe, John, 143.
Ringe, Martha, 143.
Ringe, Richd, 143.
Ringe, Thos., 132.
Ringe, Wm, 133.
Rinny, John, 110.
Rinsley, Sarah, 112.
Rion, Jeremiah, 19.
Ripley, Ebenezer, 152.
Ripley, Eleazr, 152.
Ripley, Gamaliel, 152.
Ripley, Hezekiel, 13.
Ripley, Hezekiah, 152.
Ripley, Jabez, 133.
Ripley, Jm, 133.
Ripley, John, 152.
Ripley, Ralph, 152.
Ripley, William, 153.
Ripner, Samuel, 64.
Rippenier, Asahel, 36.
Rippenier, Christopher, 36.
Ripsey, Prinson, 98.
Rise, Benjamin, 80.
Rise, Ruel, 122.
Riser, Thos, 151.
Rising, Abel, 51.
Rising, Ebenezer, 51.
Rising, Eli, 51.
Rising, Elijah, 51.
Rising, James, 51.
Rising, James, 2d, 51.
Rising, Joel, 51.
Rising, John, 51.
Rising, Jonah, 51.
Rising, Jonathan, 51.
Rising, Nathaniel, 51.
Rising, Nathaniel, 2d, 51.
Rising, Paul, 51.
Risley, Benjamin, 36.
Risley, Benjamin, 42.
Risley, David, 43.
Risley, Eli, 36.
Risley, George, 36.
Risley, George, 42.
Risley, George, 2d, 36.
Risley, Jeremiah, 36.
Risley, Job, 42.
Risley, John, 36.
Risley, John, Jr., 36.
Risley, Jonathan, 37.
Risley, Joseph, 42.
Risley, Joshua, 36.
Risley, Levi, 36.
Risley, Moses, 37.
Risley, Nathaniel, 37.
Risley, Nehemiah, 36.
Risley, Oliver, 37.
Risley, Reuben, 43.
Risley, Richard, 36.
Risley, Richard, 132.
Risley, Richard, Jr, 36.
Risley, Samuel, 47.
Risley, Saml, 135.
Risley, Stephen, 36.
Risley, Thomas, 43.
Risley, Thomas, Jr, 43.
Risley, Zach., 55.
Ritch, James, 15.
Ritch, John, 15.
Ritch, John, 23.
Ritch, Lemuel, 15.
Ritch, Mary (Wd), 15.
Ritch, Thomas, 15.
Ritter, Daniel, 37.
Ritter, John, 46.
Rix, Hannah, 114.
Rix, Nathan, 114.
Rix, Theophilus, 114.
Rix, Thomas, 114.
Roach, Thomas, 120.
Roach, William, 63.
Roads, Anthony, 115.
Roads, Joseph, 41.
Roads, Simon, 117.
Roads, William, 119.
Roath, Benjamin, 114.
Roath, Betsy, 114.
Roath, Daniel, 114.
Roath, David, 131.
Roath, Ebenezer, 131.
Roath, Eleazer, 131.
Roath, Frederick, 130.
Roath, John, 114.
Roath, Jona, 131.
Roath, Joseph, 114.
Roath, Joseph, 131.
Roath, Robart, 132.
Roath, Rufus, 114.
Roath, Saml, 114.
Roath, Saml, 131.
Roath, Silas, 114.
Roath, Stephen, 131.
Roathburn, Asa, 112.
Roathburn, Joshua, 117.
Roathburn, Thomas, 112.
Roathburn, William, 112.
Robart (Negro), 126.
Robarts, George, 124.
Robards, Jonathan, 77.
Robarts, Noah, 56.
Robartson, Solomon, 56.
Robbard, Edward, 87.
Robbard, Timothy, 87.
Robbards, Collins, 87.
Robbards, Hinkeman, 87.
Robbarts, Jonathan, 87.
Robbards, Nathaniel, 87.
Robbards, Nathaniel, Junr, 87.
Robbards, Noyes, 87.
Robbards, Phinehas, 87.
Robbards, Rachel, 87.
Robbards, Samuel C., 87.
Robbards, Simeon, 87.
Robbarts, Seth, 87.
Robberdore, August 43.
Robbert, Adonijah, 87.
Robbert, Elizabeth, 86.
Robbert, Fenno, 87.
Robberts, Abel, 88.
Robberts, Abraham, 72.
Robberts, Asahel, 88.
Robberts, E. Merril, 88.
Robberts, Ebenezer, 88.
Robberts, Eli, 50.
Robberts, Elijah, 88.
Robberts, Jessey, 88.
Robberts, John, 72.
Robberts, John, 88.
Robberts, Ruth, 88.
Robbins, Abigail, 53.
Robbins, Abijah, 2d, 53.
Robbins, Appleton, 45.
Robbins, Appleton, 52.
Robbins, Asa, 52.
Robbins, David, 52.
Robbins, Elijah, 51.
Robbins, Elijah, 53.
Robbins, Elisha, 52.
Robbins, Ephraim, 50.
Robbins, Ezekiel, 118.
Robbins, Frederic, 53.
Robbins, Jacob, 53.
Robbins, Jason, 53.
Robbins, John, 53.
Robbins, John, Jr., 53.
Robbins, Joshua, 52.
Robbins, Joshua, 2d, 52.
Robbins, Josiah, 53.
Robbins, Josiah, 2d, 53.
Robbins, Levi, 52.
Robbins, Mary, 125.
Robbins, Oliver, 52.
Robbins, Robert, 53.
Robbins, Simeon, 53.
Robbins, Unni, 54.
Robbins, Wait, 53.
Robbins, Zebulon, 53.
Robbs, Phineas, 48.
Robe, Andrew, 48.
Robe, Andrew, Jr., 48.
Robens, Easter, 67.
Robens, Samuel, 68.
Roberson, Archibauld, 126.
Roberson, Elias, 119.
Roberson, John, 14.
Roberson, John, 116.
Roberson, John, Jnr, 14.
Roberson, Nathan, 129.
Roberson, Samuel, 98.
Roberson, Samuel, 121.
Roberson, Saml, 126.
Roberson, Samuel, 2d, 98.
Roberson, Thomas, 118.
Roberson, William, 14.
Roberson, William, 116.
Robert, Aaron, 86.
Robert, Freelove, 35.
Robert, Gideon, 35.
Robert, Martin, 35.
Robert, Recompence, 88.
Robert, William, 30.
Roberts, Aaron, 33.
Roberts, Aaron, 46.
Roberts, Aaron, Jr., 33.
Roberts, Amasa, 35.
Roberts, Amos, 26.
Roberts, Anna (Wid.), 49.
Roberts, Ashbel, 37.
Roberts, Benjamin, 35.
Roberts, Benjamin, 37.
Roberts, Daniel, 34.
Roberts, Daniel, 37.
Roberts, David, 35.
Roberts, David, 36.
Roberts, David, 88.
Roberts, David, 89.
Roberts, Ebenezer, 87.
Roberts, Ebenezer, 100.
Roberts, Elas, 36.
Roberts, Elisha, 62.
Roberts, George, 36.
Roberts, Henry, 60.
Roberts, Jabiz, 34.
Roberts, Jacob, 35.
Roberts, Jacob, Jr., 35.
Roberts, James, 55.
Roberts, Jesse, 77.
Roberts, Joel, 110.
Roberts, John, 36.
Roberts, John, 46.
Roberts, John, 61.
Roberts, John, 65.
Roberts, John, 66.
Roberts, John, 88.
Roberts, John, 2d, 46.
Roberts, Jonathan, 36.
Roberts, Jonathan, 46.
Roberts, Joseph, 34.
Roberts, Joseph, 36.
Roberts, Josiah, 103.
Roberts, Jude, 64.
Roberts, Lamberton, 35.
Roberts, Lemuel, 48.
Roberts, Luke, 12.
Roberts, Martin, 59.
Roberts, Nathaniel, 36.
Roberts, Nathaniel, 48.
Roberts, Nathaniel, 62.
Roberts, Oliver, 55.
Roberts, Philip, 27.
Roberts, Poll, 69.
Roberts, Reuben, 88.
Roberts, Samuel, 37.
Roberts, Saml, 66.
Roberts, Seth, 34.
Roberts, Seth, 59.
Roberts, Stephen, 36.
Roberts, Thomas, 20.
Roberts, Timothy, 37.
Roberts, William, 11.
Roberts, Wm, 35.
Roberts, William, 36.
Roberts, William, 70.
Roberts, Zelotus, 11.
Robertson, David, 42.
Robertson, John, 92.
Robertson, Jonathan, 31.
Robertson, Jonathan, Jnr, 31.
Robertson, Mercy, 23.
Robertson, Noah, 68.
Robertson, Seth, 32.
Robertson, William, 49.
Robins, Benjn, 140.
Robins (Black), 82.
Robins, Clark, 140.
Robins, David, 141.
Robins, David, 150.
Robins, Elisha, 123.
Robins, Ephraim, 15.
Robins, Ezra, 123.
Robins, John, 143.
Robins, John, 150.
Robins, Lorin, 151.
Robins, Mary, 143.
Robins, Moses, 114.
Robins, Moses, 151.
Robins, Nathan, 123.
Robins, Nathl, 143.
Robins, Robart, 121.
Robins, Saml, 151.
Robins, Saml, Jur, 151.
Robins, Seth, 150.
Robins, Silas, 123.
Robins, Solomon, 146.
Robins, Thomas, 140.
Robinson, Aaron, 150.
Robinson, Abner, 153.
Robinson, Andrew, 153.
Robinson, Asa, 153.
Robinson, Asa, Jur, 153.
Robinson, Asher, 96.
Robinson, Benjn, 132.
Robinson, Bethul, 139.
Robinson, Catherine, 103.
Robinson, Chandler, 97.
Robinson, Clifford, 143.
Robinson, Danl, 133.
Robinson, Danl, 133.
Robinson, Daniel, 152.
Robinson, David, 80.
Robinson, Deborah, 152.
Robinson, Ebenezur, 96.
Robinson, Ebenr, & co., 148.
Robinson, Eber, 138.
Robinson, Eleazer, 152.
Robinson, Elias, 153.
Robinson, Em, 134.
Robinson, Experience, 153.
Robinson, Hezekiah, 133.
Robinson, Ichabod, 145.
Robinson, Isaac, 133.
Robinson, Isaac, 152.
Robinson, Isaiah, 143.
Robinson, Jacob, 153.
Robinson, James, 88.
Robinson, James, 96.
Robinson, James, 96.
Robinson, James, 153.
Robinson, Jerard, 70.
Robinson, John, 62.
Robinson, John, 97.
Robinson, John, 106.
Robinson, Jno, 133.
Robinson, Jno, 133.
Robinson, Joshua, 138.
Robinson, Josiah, 148.
Robinson, Levi, 107.
Robinson, Levi, 153.
Robinson, Lydia, 88.
Robinson, Moses, 150.
Robinson, Mosses, 106.
Robinson, Nathaniel, 96.
Robinson, Ralph, 133.
Robinson, Reubin, 153.
Robinson, Robert, 87.
Robinson, Ruben, 138.
Robinson, Rubin, Jnr, 153.
Robinson, Sabin, 139.
Robinson, Samuel, 104.
Robinson, Saml, 133.
Robinson, Saml, 133.
Robinson, Saml, 153.
Robinson, Simeon, 153.
Robinson, Simeon, Jnr, 153.
Robinson, Stephen, 96.
Robinson, Theophilus M., 107.
Robinson, Timothy, 140.
Robinson (Widow), 133.
Robinson (Wid.), 139.
Robinson, Wm, 133.
Robinson, William, 148.
Robinson, William, 152.
Robinsone, Patrick, 129.
Robons, Amenizsehana, 63.
Rochester, Benjamin, 99.
Rochester, Samuel, 99.
Rockebell, Daniel, 39.
Rocket, Josiah, 51.
Rockwell, Abijah, 29.
Rockwell, Abraham, 29.
Rockwell, Amasa, 39.
Rockwell, Amy, 131.
Rockwell, Benjamin, 77.
Rockwell, Charles, 38.
Rockwell, Clapp, 23.
Rockwell, Daniel, 29.
Rockwell, Daniel, 2d, 39.
Rockwell, David, 29.
Rockwell, David, 37.
Rockwell, David, 66.
Rockwell, Desiah, 86.
Rockwell, Ebenezar, 39.
Rockwell, Ebenezar, Jr., 39.
Rockwell, Ebenezer, 29.
Rockwell, Edward, 88.
Rockwell, Edward, Junr, 86.
Rockwell, Elihue, 64.
Rockwell, Elijah, 64.
Rockwell, Elisabeth, 29.
Rockwell, Elisabeth, 131.
Rockwell, Ephraim, 39.
Rockwell, Ezra, 39.
Rockwell, Frances, 39.
Rockwell, Grove, 86.
Rockwell, Henry, 29.
Rockwell, Isaac, 29.
Rockwell, Isaac, 39.
Rockwell, Jabez, 77.
Rockwell, James, 28.
Rockwell, James, 39.
Rockwell, Jemima, 37.
Rockwell, Joab, 37.
Rockwell, Joel, 39.
Rockwell, John, 23.
Rockwell, John, 31.
Rockwell, John, 64.
Rockwell, John, 68.
Rockwell, Jonah, 31.
Rockwell, Joseph, 21.
Rockwell, Joseph, 29.
Rockwell, Joseph, 64.
Rockwell, Joseph, Jr, 21.
Rockwell, Joshua, 89.
Rockwell, Mercy, 12.
Rockwell, Merit, 128.
Rockwell, Nathaniel, 38.
Rockwell, Noadiah, 87.
Rockwell, Noah, 31.
Rockwell, Oziah, 54.
Rockwell, Samuel, 37.
Rockwell, Samuel, 52.
Rockwell, Saml, 59.
Rockwell, Saml, 64.
Rockwell, Samuel, 115.
Rockwell, Saml, 137.
Rockwell, Silvanus, 39.
Rockwell, Stephen, 25.
Rockwell, Thaddeus, 28.
Rockwell, William, 29.
Rockwell, William, 38.
Rockwell, William, 45.
Rockwell, William, 67.
Rockwill, Jonah, 145.
Rode, William, 151.
Rodes, James, 150.
Rodes, John, Jnr, 151.
Roe, Daniel, 44.
Roe, Daniel, 64.
Roe, Daton, 95.
Roe, Isaac, 141.
Roe, Titus, 44.
Roger, Benjn, 143.
Roger, Nathel, Jnr, 145.
Roger (Negroe), 95.
Rogers, Abeather, 59.
Rogers, Able, 123.
Rogers, Abraham, 91.
Rogers, Augustus, 81.
Rogers, Benjamin, 129.
Rogers, Benjn, 138.
Rogers, Clark, 127.
Rogers, Daniel, 128.
Rogers, David, 13.
Rogers, David, 92.
Rogers, Ebenezur, 92.
Rogers, Edward, 57.
Rogers, Eleazar, 130.
Rogers, Elihu, 92.
Rogers, Ephraim, 91.
Rogers, Ephraim, 127.
Rogers, Fanny, 129.
Rogers, George, 128.
Rogers, Gideon, 107.
Rogers, Gordon, 82.
Rogers, Grace, 57.
Rogers, Hannah, 128.
Rogers, Hezekiah, 23.
Rogers, Hezekiah, 58.
Rogers, Isaac, 91.
Rogers, Isaac, 128.
Rogers, Israel, 128.
Rogers, James, 27.
Rogers, James, 127.
Rogers, James, 129.
Rogers, James, 130.
Rogers, Jason, 78.
Rogers, Jason, 129.
Rogers, Jeduthon, 143.
Rogers, Jeremiah, 145.
Rogers, Joel, 92.
Rogers, John, 22.
Rogers, John, 82.
Rogers, John, 87.
Rogers, John, 91.
Rogers, John, 91.
Rogers, John, 128.
Rogers, John, 129.
Rogers, John, Junr, 87.
Rogers, Jonathan, 69.
Rogers, Jonathan, 102.
Rogers, Jona, 127.
Rogers, Josep, 92.
Rogers, Joseph, 23.
Rogers, Joseph, 102.
Rogers, Josiah, 92.
Rogers, Josiah, 141.
Rogers, Josiah. *See* Capills, Thomas, 145.
Rogers, Lemuel, 21.
Rogers, Lent, 34.
Rogers, Mary (Wd), 21.
Rogers, Medad, 18.
Rogers, Moses, 140.
Rogers, Nathan, 127.
Rogers, Nathanl, Senr, 145.
Rogers, Nehemiah, 34.
Rogers, Nehemiah, 131.
Rogers, Noah, 57.
Rogers, Noah, 2d, 57.
Rogers, Oliver, 153.
Rogers, Phineas, 78.
Rogers, Phineas, 127.
Rogers, Samuel, 91.
Rogers, Simeon, 69.
Rogers, Solomon, 128.
Rogers, Stephen, 91.
Rogers, Stephen, 128.
Rogers, Thos, 83.
Rogers, Thomas, 92.
Rogers, Thomas, 2d, 92.
Rogers, Timothy, 57.
Rogers, Timothy, 81.
Rogers, Uriah, 21.
Rogers, Uriah. *See* Hyde, Daniel, Junr, 129.
Rogers, Uriah, Junr, 129.
Rogers, Zebulun, 127.
Roggers, Able, 123.
Roggers, Alpheus, 125.
Roggers, Amos, 119.
Roggers, Andrew, 125.
Roggers, Asa, 125.
Roggers, Asa, 125.
Roggers, Daniel, 124.

# INDEX.

Roggers, David, 127.
Roggers, David, 127.
Roggers, David, 131.
Roggers, Eben'r, 119.
Roggers, Ebenezer, 123.
Roggers, Ebenezer, 125.
Roggers, Eben'r, 127.
Roggers, Elexander, 126.
Roggers, Frederick, 125.
Roggers, Gedion, 122.
Roggers, Gurdon, 125.
Roggers, Ichabod, 127.
Roggers, Isaiah, 124.
Roggers, Jabez, 125.
Roggers, Jaheil, 125.
Roggers, James, 125.
Roggers, James, 125.
Roggers, James, 2d, 126.
Roggers, Jeremiah, 125.
Roggers, John, 126.
Roggers, John, 3d, 126.
Roggers, Jonathan, 115.
Roggers, Jonathan, 115.
Roggers, Jonathan, 124.
Roggers, Jonathan, 125.
Roggers, Jona, 126.
Roggers, Joseph, 125.
Roggers, Josiah, 121.
Roggers, Lite, 126.
Roggers, Martha, 125.
Roggers, Mary, 126.
Roggers, Nathan, 125.
Roggers, Nathl, 125.
Roggers, Nathl, 126.
Roggers, Nathl, 2d, 125.
Roggers, Peleg, 124.
Roggers, Peter, 126.
Roggers, Pheba, 123.
Roggers, Presilla, 131.
Roggers, Richard, 123.
Roggers, Rowland, 124.
Roggers, Saml, 121.
Roggers, Saml, 124.
Roggers, Saml, 126.
Roggers, Saml, 2d, 124.
Roggers, Saml, 2d, 126.
Roggers, Samuel, 3d, 124.
Roggers, Theophilus, 131.
Roggers, Thomas, 125.
Roggers, Thomas, 127.
Roggers, Thomas, 2d, 125.
Roggers, Zabdiel, 131.
Roland, Asael, 123.
Roland, Benjamin, 123.
Roland, David, 60.
Roland, Ezra, 123.
Roland, Henry, 124.
Roland, Levi, 123.
Roland, Nathl, 123.
Rolepau, Lettie, 62.
Roles, Daniel, 124.
Roles, James, 105.
Rollins, Aaron, 14.
Rollow, Wm, 135.
Rollow, Zachary, 135.
Romain, Daniel, 59.
Romnam, Meajah, 67.
Rood, David, 70.
Rood, Ebenezer, 69.
Rood, John, 10.
Rood, Marines, 67.
Rood, Moses, 69.
Rood, Roger, 70.
Roods, Alexander, 53.
Roods, Mary, 53.
Roods, William, 53.
Roods, William, Jr., 53.
Root, Abel, 135.
Root, Asahel, 34.
Root, Asahel, 68.
Root, Benjamin, 40.
Root, Benjamin, 120.
Root, Caleb, 61.
Root, Caleb, 135.
Root, Daniel, 33.
Root, Daniel, 40.
Root, Daniel, 132.
Root, Danl, 135.
Root, Dan., 135.
Root, En, 133.
Root, Ebenr, 135.
Root, Ebenr, 136.
Root, Elijah, 40.
Root, Eneas, 109.
Root, Enoch, 61.
Root, Ezra, 133.
Root, Hezekiah, 40.
Root, Jacob, 136.
Root, James, 41.
Root, James, 49.
Root, Jesse, 46.
Root, Jesse, 133.
Root, Jesse, Jr., 46.
Root, Job, 33.
Root, Joel, 49.
Root, Joel, 68.
Root, John, 34.
Root, Jonah, 135.
Root, Jonathan, 49.
Root, Jona, 133.
Root, Jona, 135.
Root, Jonathan, Jr., 49.

Root, Joseph, 111.
Root, Jos., 136.
Root, Josa, 135.
Root, Josiah, 50.
Root, Judah, 92.
Root, Mark, 40.
Root, Medad, 133.
Root, Moses, 92.
Root, Nathl, 133.
Root, Nathl, 139.
Root, Nathl, 139.
Root, Naths H., 34.
Root, Noah, 33.
Root, Phinehas, 68.
Root, Phinehas, 68.
Root, Salmon, 40.
Root, Samuel, 40.
Root, Samuel, 109.
Root, Samuel, Jr., 41.
Root, Stephen, 49.
Root, Theodore, 34.
Root, Thomas, 33.
Root, Timothy, 40.
Root, Timo, 136.
Root, Timo, 139.
Root (Widow), 135.
Root (Wid.), 135.
Root (Widow), 139.
Root, William, 68.
Root, Wm, 133.
Roots, Amos, 78.
Roots, Amos, 2d, 78.
Roots, Colonel, 78.
Roots, Daniel, 59.
Roots, David, 78.
Roots, Gideon, 59.
Roots, Isaac, 74.
Roots, Jesse, 78.
Roots, Jesse, 2d, 78.
Roots, John, 78.
Roots, Joseph, 78.
Roots, Thomas, 78.
Roper, Nathaniel, 88.
Rose, Amajia, 92.
Rose, Asa, 113.
Rose, Daniel, 92.
Rose, Daniel, 113.
Rose, David, 142.
Rose, Elisha, 113.
Rose, Elizabeth, 91.
Rose, Frederick, 133.
Rose, Hannah, 82.
Rose, Jehiel, 133.
Rose, Jiles, 96.
Rose, Joel, 100.
Rose, John, 91.
Rose, John, 142.
Rose, Joseph, 114.
Rose, Justice, 92.
Rose, Levi, 92.
Rose, Mabel, 56.
Rose, Nathan, 92.
Rose (Negro), 21.
Rose, Peleg, 114.
Rose, Peter, 30.
Rose, Robart, 120.
Rose, Robart, Junr, 120.
Rose, Ruben, 92.
Rose, Rufus, 125.
Rose, Samuel, 92.
Rose, Samuel, 92.
Rose, Samuel, 92.
Rose, Saml, 133.
Rose, Sarah, 113.
Rose, Soloman, 92.
Rose, Thomas, 91.
Rose, Thomas, 113.
Rose, Timo, 133.
Rose, William, 30.
Roser, Malachi, 92.
Roseter, Asa, 58.
Roseter, Jonathan, 58.
Roseter, Timothy, 99.
Roseter, Timothy W., 102.
Roseter, William, 99.
Rositer, John, 85.
Rositer, John, 2d, 85.
Rositer, Mary, 96.
Ross, Asher, 59.
Ross, Daniel, 59.
Ross, Ebenezr, 147.
Ross, John, 55.
Ross, Robert, 14.
Ross, Timothy, 45.
Ross, William, 45.
Ross, Wm, 137.
Rossell, Mons, 98.
Rosseter, Elnathan, 118.
Rosseter, Stephen, 121.
Rossiter, Benjamin, 62.
Roswell, Nehm, 135.
Rothbone, David, 139.
Rothburn, Able, 121.
Rothburn, Achors, 117.
Rothburn, Ebenezer, 122.
Rothburn, Elijah, 120.
Rothburn, Job, 122.
Rothburn, John, 118.
Rothburn, Jonathan, 121.
Rothburn, Jona, 122.
Rothburn, Joshua, 121.
Rothburn, Joshua, Junr, 121.
Rothburn, Moses, 121.

Rothburn, Saml, 122.
Rothburn, Saml, 125.
Rothburn, Simeon, 125.
Rothburn, Volentine, 118.
Rothburn, Wm, 128.
Rought, Daniel, 118.
Rouse, Elijah, 57.
Rouse, Jabez, 153.
Rouse, Simeon, 113.
Row, Beniah M., 32.
Row, Dan., 96.
Row, Daniel M., 32.
Row, Ebenezer, 13.
Row, Ebenezer, Jnr, 13.
Row, John, 52.
Row, Mathew, 97.
Row, Stephan, 105.
Rowdan, James, 40.
Rowe, Abijan, 43.
Rowe, David, 47.
Rowe, Ezra, 97.
Rowe, Isaiah, 41.
Rowe, John, 51.
Rowe, John, 97.
Rowe, Joseph, 34.
Rowe, Moses, 51.
Rowe, Samuel, 41.
Rowe, Samuel, 60.
Rowe, Seth, 40.
Rowe, Solomon, 70.
Rowe, Stephen, 34.
Rowe, Thomas, 72.
Rowel, Caleb, 78.
Rowel, Jacob, 17.
Rowel, Valentine, 16.
Rowel, Wm, 16.
Rowens, Richerson, 68.
Rowes, Gad, 51.
Rowes, Stephen, 51.
Rowes, Winthrop, 66.
Rowland, Abigail, 14.
Rowland, Andrew, 14.
Rowland, Daniel, 32.
Rowland, David S., 55.
Rowland, Israel, 27.
Rowland, Jabez, 20.
Rowland, Jeremiah, 32.
Rowland, Jesse, 112.
Rowland, Jonathan, 32.
Rowland, Samuel, 32.
Rowland, Thomas, 27.
Rowland, William, 46.
Rowlenson, Asa, 60.
Rowlenson, John, 60.
Rowlenson, William, 60.
Rowley, Asher, 81.
Rowley, David, 62.
Rowley, Ebenezer, 69.
Rowley, Ebenezer, 80.
Rowley, Eleazer, 82.
Rowley, Eli, 110.
Rowley, Gershom, 80.
Rowley, Isaac, 81.
Rowley, Ithamar, 80.
Rowley, Jesse, 121.
Rowley, Johiel, 65.
Rowley, John, 55.
Rowley, Levi, 63.
Rowley, Philander, 55.
Rowley, Reuben, 55.
Rowley, Roger, 55.
Rowley, Roswell, 45.
Rowley, Saml, 55.
Rowley, Simeon, 65.
Rowley, Thomas, 55.
Rowley, William, 110.
Rowley, William, 2nd, 110.
Rowlin, Luke, 61.
Royal, Jonathan, 49.
Royce, Asa, 147.
Royce, Byram, 147.
Royce, David, 75.
Royce, David, 147.
Royce, David, 147.
Royce, James, 147.
Royce, James, Jnr, 147.
Royce, John, 75.
Royce, Mark, 75.
Royce, Nehemiah, 58.
Royce, Phillip, 147.
Royce, Solomon, 147.
Royce, William, 140.
Royce, Zurel, 147.
Royer, Jacob, 77.
Royer, Samuel, 77.
Rozer, David, 77.
Rube, Jno, 139.
Ruben (Negroe), 104.
Rudd, Daniel, 126.
Rudd, John, 68.
Rudd, Jonathan, 129.
Rudd, Jonathan, 153.
Rudd, Nathl, 153.
Rudd, Prosper, 129.
Rudd, Samuel, 129.
Rudd, William, 153.
Rude, Caleb, 75.
Rude, Caleb, 2d, 75.
Rude, Ezekiel, 114.
Rude, Isaac, 144.
Rude, Jacob, 144.

Rude, Jason, 143.
Rude, Jeremiah, 146.
Rude, Jno, 135.
Rude, Joseph, 148.
Rude, Lester, 75.
Rude, Lydia, 113.
Rude, Nathan, 142.
Rude (Widow), 132.
Rude, Zachariah, 114.
Rudge, Sampson, 129.
Rudles, Timothy, 10.
Ruel, Elijah, 114.
Ruff, Sarah, 119.
Rugg, Solomon, 33.
Ruggles, Artemas, 72.
Ruggles, Benjn, 149.
Ruggles, Edward, 149.
Ruggles, Edward, 149.
Ruggles, Isaac Mathew, 72.
Ruggles, Joseph, 72.
Ruggles, Lad, 72.
Ruggles, Nathaniel, 98.
Ruggles, Nathaniel, 98.
Ruggles, Philoe, 60.
Ruggles, Saml, 150.
Rugles, Abijah, 10.
Rugles, Ashbell, 10.
Rugles, Benjamin, 10.
Rugles, Bostwick, 10.
Rugles, Eden, 10.
Rugles, Joseph, 10.
Rugles, Samuel, 10.
Rumbule, Phillip, 47.
Rummery, Sarah, 78.
Rumsey, David, 78.
Rumsey, Ephraim, 27.
Rumsey, Nathan, 78.
Rumvil, John, 39.
Rundle, Amy (Wd), 15.
Rundle, Amy (Wd), 16.
Rundle, Charles, 16.
Rundle, Charles, 28.
Rundle, Elizabeth (Wd), 15.
Rundle, Experience, 19.
Rundle, Jeremiah, 15.
Rundle, Jeremiah, 72.
Rundle, Nathaniel, 15.
Rundle, Phinehas, 16.
Rundle, Rachel (Wd), 16.
Rundle, Reuben, 15.
Rundle, Samuel, 15.
Rundle, Samuel, 16.
Rundle, Shubael, 28.
Rundle, Solomon, 15.
Rundle, Timothy, 15.
Rundle, William, 19.
Runnels, Anne, 14.
Runney, Julius, 56.
Rus, Jno, 136.
Rush, Joshua, Jr., 39.
Rush, Phebe, 110.
Russ, Azariah, 140.
Russ, Jehiel, 145.
Russ, John, 148.
Russ, Stephen, 147.
Russel, Benjamin, 73.
Russel, Benjamin, 78.
Russel, David, 60.
Russel, Eben, 134.
Russel, Elisha, 63.
Russel, Ichabod, 57.
Russel, Isaac, 137.
Russel, Jacob, 54.
Russel, John, 69.
Russel, John, 71.
Russel, John, 91.
Russel, Jno, 136.
Russel, Jona, 138.
Russel, Josiah, 69.
Russel, Rider, 137.
Russel, Stephen, 66.
Russel, Stephen, 66.
Russel, Stephen, 111.
Russel, William, 30.
Russel, William, 31.
Russel, Wm, 54.
Russel, Wm, 136.
Russell, Benjn, 140.
Russell, Benjamin, 147.
Russell, Cornelius, 54.
Russell, Daniel, 86.
Russell, Daniel, 111.
Russell, Danl, 150.
Russell, David, 54.
Russell, David, 144.
Russell, Ebenezer, 92.
Russell, Ebenezer, 100.
Russell, Edward, 91.
Russell, Edward, 97.
Russell, Ethal, 92.
Russell, Hezekiah, 134.
Russell, James, 140.
Russell, Jesse, 48.
Russell, John, 86.
Russell, John, 91.
Russell, John, 111.
Russell, John, 112.
Russell, John, 140.
Russell, John, 141.
Russell, John, 144.
Russell, Jonah, 149.
Russell, Jonathan, 54.
Russell, Jonathan, 92.

Russell, Jona, 150.
Russell, Jona, Jnr, 150.
Russell, Joseph, 94.
Russell, Joseph, 97.
Russell, Joseph, 125.
Russell, Josiah, 149.
Russell, Lidia, 97.
Russell, Nicholas, 94.
Russell, Noadiah, 55.
Russell, Noadiah, 150.
Russell, Penfield, 91.
Russell, Richard, 111.
Russell, Richard, 2nd, 111.
Russell, Riverus, 94.
Russell, Robert, 112.
Russell, Samuel, 86.
Russell, Samuel, 91.
Russell, Samuel, 91.
Russell, Samuel, 94.
Russell, Samuel, 102.
Russell, Samuel, 105.
Russell, Samuel R., 99.
Russell, Stephen, 83.
Russell, Thomas, 54.
Russell, Timothy, 52.
Russell, Timothy, 80.
Russell, Timothy, 92.
Russell, Timothy, 99.
Russell, William, 59.
Russell, William, 111.
Russell, William, 150.
Russell, William, 153.
Russill, Thomas, 147.
Russique, Mary, 22.
Russique, Nathan, 22.
Rust, Abel, 59.
Rust, Alom, 35.
Rust, Amos, 35.
Rust, Eunice, 146.
Rust, Levi, 59.
Rust, Nath. W., 134.
Rust, Prudence, 114.
Rust, Stephen, 63.
Rutty, Asa, 83.
Rutty, John, 84.
Rutty, Jonah, 83.
Rutty, Levi, 84.
Ruxford, William, 61.
Ryan, Rebecka, 127.
Ryder, Benja, 137.
Ryder, Cornelius, 132.
Ryder, Enos, 138.
Ryder, Jno, 138.
Ryder, Saml, 138.
Ryder, Syvester, 69.
Ryla, John, 32.
Ryon, Irena, 128.
Ryon, James, 124.
Ryon, William, 128.

S —— (Negro), 131.
Saben (Negroe), 95.
Sabin, Benajah, 129.
Sabin, Charles, 105.
Sabin, David, 40.
Sabin, Elihu, 149.
Sabin, Elijah, 130.
Sabin, Hezekiah, 2nd, 103.
Sabin, Isaac, 149.
Sabin, Jedediah, 130.
Sabin, Jonathan, 149.
Sabin, Joseph, 149.
Sabin, Joshua, 149.
Sabin, Josiah, 149.
Sabin, Nathl, 148.
Sabin, Peter, 149.
Sabin, Peter, 151.
Sabin, Thomas, 39.
Sabin, Willm, 149.
Sabine, Thos, 134.
Sabins, Hezekiah, 103.
Sabins, Jonathan, 103.
Sabins, Phenias, 121.
Sabins, Saml, 120.
Sabins, Sarah, 132.
Sabins, Sussanah, 104.
Sacket, Aaron, 65.
Sacket, Alexander, 74.
Sacket, Benjamin, 74.
Sacket, Cornelius, 101.
Sacket, Eli, 106.
Sacket, Hannah, 103.
Sacket, Joel, 106.
Sacket, Jonathan, 102.
Sacket, Jonathan, 112.
Sacket, Joseph, 15.
Sacket, Justice, 15.
Sacket, Reuben, 74.
Sacket, Salmon, 74.
Sacket, Samuel, 106.
Sacket, Soloman, 106.
Sackett, Justus, 74.
Sackett, Nathel, 15.
Sackett, Peter, 16.
Sackett, Siam D., 110.
Sadd, Elijah, 38.
Sadd, Elisha, 38.
Sadd, John, 38.
Sadd, Mathew, 38.
Sadd, Thomas, 39.
Sadd, Thomas, Jr., 39.
Sadley, John, 101.
Safford, Jedediah, 112.

INDEX. 211


Safford, John, 114.
Safford, Johnson, 114.
Safford, Joseph, 142.
Safford, Joseph, 142.
Safford, Mary, 151.
Safford, Rufus, 142.
Safford, Solomon, 112.
Safford, Thomas, 114.
Sagden, Thomas, 33.
Sage, Abner, 80.
Sage, Abraham, 34.
Sage, Amos, 88.
Sage, Calvin, 47.
Sage, Comfort, Esqr, 86.
Sage, Daniel, 62.
Sage, David, 34.
Sage, David, Esqr, 80.
Sage, Ebenezer, 85.
Sage, Elisha, 88.
Sage, Enoch, 80.
Sage, Enos, 64.
Sage, Epaphras, 88.
Sage, Esther, 86.
Sage, Francis, 86.
Sage, Giles, 88.
Sage, Hezekiah, 88.
Sage, Jedediah, 34.
Sage, John, 36.
Sage, John, 88.
Sage, Jonathan, 34.
Sage, Joseph, 80.
Sage, Joseph, 85.
Sage, Joseph, 88.
Sage, Lemuel, 88.
Sage, Lewis Samuel, 88.
Sage, Nathan, 87.
Sage, Noah, 80.
Sage, Oliver, 34.
Sage, Ruben, 133.
Sage, Samuel, 87.
Sage, Seth, 44.
Sage, Simeon, 88.
Sage, Solomon, 88.
Sage, Solomon, 34.
Sage, Solomon, Jr., 34.
Sage, Solomon, Junr, 88.
Sage, Timothy, 87.
Sage, William, 88.
Sage, William, Junr, 80.
Sage, Zadock, 34.
Sails, James, 103.
St John, Amy (Wd), 21.
St John, Anna, 23.
St John, Anna (Wd), 23.
St John, Benona, 23.
St John, Caleb, 23.
St John, Daniel, 23.
St. John, David, 22.
Saintjohn, David, 28.
St. John, Elijah, 48.
St. John, Ezekiel, 67.
St. John, Ezra, 22.
St John, Hannah (Wd), 25.
St John, Hezekiah, 23.
St John, Isaac, 22.
St John, Jesse, 23.
St John, Joel, 62.
St John, John, 21.
St John, John, 22.
Saintjohn, John, 28.
St John, Capt John, 24.
St John, Jonathan, 22.
St John, Josiah, 21.
St John, Justice, 22.
St John, Matthew, Junr, 23.
St John, Matthias, 23.
St John, Nathan, 23.
St John, Nehemiah, 23.
St John, Nehemiah, Jr, 23.
St John, Peter, 23.
St John, Phinehas, 23.
Saintjohn, Samuel, 28.
St. John, Selleck, 22.
St John, Silas, 22.
St. John, Silas, 63.
St John, Stephen, 21.
St John, Stephen, Junr, 23.
Saintjohn, Thomas, 28.
Stjohn, Thomas, 66.
St. John, Timothy, 59.
St. John, Timothy, 67.
St. John, Uriah, 66.
St John, William, 21.
St John, Wm, Junr, 21.
Salem (Negro), 123.
Salisbury, Richard, 154.
Salmon, Asael, 27.
Salmon, Richard, 30.
Salmon, Stephen, 29.
Salsbury, Gilbert, 144.
Salter, John, 147.
Salter, Mary, 147.
Salter, Rachel, 43.
Salton, George, 111.
Saltonstall, Dudley, 129.
Saltonstall, Gurdon, 128.
Saltonstall, Nathaniel, 129.
Saltonstall, Roswell, 129.
Saltonstall, Winthrop, 128.
Sam (Negro), 131.
Samburn, Jedidiah, 53.
Sampson (Negro), 128.
Sampson, Will, 52.
Samson, Jonathan, 129.
Samson, Joseph, 129.
Samson (Negro), 126.
Samson (Negroe), 108.
Samson, William, 113.
Saml (Negro), 122.
Sander, John M., 18.
Sanders, Aaron, 17.
Sanders, Duty, 140.
Sanders, Eseck, 141.
Sanders, Isachar, 140.
Sanders, John, 66.
Sanders, Nathaniel, 109.
Sanders, Peter, 142.
Sanders, Prudence A., 144.
Sanders, Stephen A., 140.
Sanders, William, 19.
Sanderson, William, 92.
Sanderson, William, 108.
Sandford, Abel, 111.
Sandford, Benjamin, 103.
Sandford, David, 111.
Sandford, Eliadia, 106.
Sandford, Elihu, 112.
Sandford, Elihu, 2nd, 112.
Sandford, Elisha, 101.
Sandford, Gideon, 94.
Sandford, Henry, 94.
Sandford, Hitabel, 112.
Sandford, Isaac, 111.
Sandford, Jeremiah, 106.
Sandford, John, 94.
Sandford, John, 101.
Sandford, John, 106.
Sandford, Jonathan, 112.
Sandford, Lois, 90.
Sandford, Moses, 111.
Sandford, Mother, 101.
Sandford, Raymond, 112.
Sandford, Rebekah, 89.
Sandford, Samuel, 95.
Sandford, Stephen, 111.
Sandford, Thomas, 106.
Sandford, William, 106.
Sandford, Zadock, 95.
Sandiforth, Daniel, 60.
Sanford, Aaron, 27.
Sanford, Amos, 77.
Sanford, Archibald, 94.
Sanford, Benoni S., 72.
Sanford, Bethiah, 130.
Sanford, Biah, 27.
Sanford, Caleb, 66.
Sanford, Daniel, 2d, 77.
Sanford, David, 61.
Sanford, David, 77.
Sanford, Ebenezer, 27.
Sanford, Eli, 27.
Sanford, Elias, 27.
Sanford, Elisha, 118.
Sanford, Elisha, 133.
Sanford, Elnathan, 27.
Sanford, Ezekiel, 27.
Sanford, Ezekiel, 1st, 77.
Sanford, Ezekiel, 2d, 77.
Sanford, Ezra, 27.
Sanford, Ezra, 62.
Sanford, Hezekiah, 19.
Sanford, Hezekiah, 27.
Sanford, Hezekiah, 27.
Sanford, Isaac, 46.
Sanford, James, 19.
Sanford, James, 27.
Sanford, Jesse, 77.
Sanford, Joel, 10.
Sanford, Joel, 77.
Sanford, John, 27.
Sanford, John, Junr, 19.
Sanford, Jonah, 65.
Sanford, Jonas, 20.
Sanford, Jonathan, 20.
Sanford, Joseph, 59.
Sanford, Joseph, 59.
Sanford, Joseph, 73.
Sanford, Josiah, 31.
Sanford, Justus, 54.
Sanford, Kingsbury, 130.
Sanford, Lemuel, 27.
Sanford, Liffe, 72.
Sanford, Moses, 65.
Sanford, Moses, 66.
Sanford, Nathan, 22.
Sanford, Nathan, 79.
Sanford, Nathanel, 20.
Sanford, Nathaniel, 73.
Sanford, Nehemiah, 72.
Sanford, Nehemiah, 2d, 72.
Sanford, Oliver, 27.
Sanford, Oliver, 65.
Sanford, Peleg, 86.
Sanford, Peter, 27.
Sanford, Robt., 55.
Sanford, Samuel, 19.
Sanford, Samuel, 72.
Sanford, Samuel, 77.
Sanford, Samel, 89.
Sanford, Samel, 2d, 89.
Sanford, Sarah, 27.
Sanford, Sarah, 31.
Sanford, Seth, 27.
Sanford, Silas, 34.
Sanford, Soloman, 20.
Sanford, Stephen, 68.
Sanford, Stephen, 77.
Sanford, Thomas, 19.
Sanford, Thomas, 46.
Sanford, William, 19.
Sanford, Zach., 46.
Sanford, Zacheriah, 1st, 72.
Sanford, Zacheriah, 2d, 72.
Sanford, Zacheus, 66.
Sanger, Azariah, 139.
Sanger, Danl, 134.
Sanger, Jno, 137.
Sanger, John, 154.
Sanger, Noadt, 139.
Sanger, Pearley, 154.
Sanger, Soln, 135.
Sangor, Asael, 126.
Sangor, Nathaniel, 39.
Sangor, Trijah, 126.
Sarah (Negro), 128.
Sardam, Andrus, 69.
Sardam, Tunus, 69.
Satille, Elisha, 116.
Satterlee, Nathl, 148.
Sattille, Samuel, 117.
Saunders, Abel, 47.
Saunders, Benjamin, 74.
Saunders, Elisha, 114.
Saunders, Gideon, 119.
Saunders, Holmes, 22.
Saunders, Ithamer, 57.
Saunders, Jabez, 21.
Saunders, John, 23.
Saunders, John, 122.
Saunders, John, Junr, 122.
Saunders, John, Senr, 22.
Saunders, Joshua, 57.
Saunders, Saml, 122.
Saunders, Simeon, 122.
Saunders, Thomas, 23.
Saunders, Thomas, 64.
Saunders, Wait, 114.
Saunders, Zelotes, 57.
Savage, Abijah, 87.
Savage, Amos, 88.
Savage, Cornelius, 131.
Savage, Daniel, 88.
Savage, David, 80.
Savage, Elisha, 34.
Savage, Elisha, Jr., 34.
Savage, Giles, 88.
Savage, John, 80.
Savage, Jonathan, 88.
Savage, Josiah, 87.
Savage, Josiah, Junr, 87.
Savage, Luther, 46.
Savage, Luther, 80.
Savage, Martha, 88.
Savage, Naomy, 88.
Savage, Nathaniel, 88.
Savage, Samuel, 88.
Savage, Sarah, 88.
Savage, Selah, 34.
Savage, Seth, 34.
Savage, Solomon, 88.
Savage, Stephen, 88.
Savage, Stephen, 88.
Savage, Timothy, 88.
Savage, William, 88.
Sawer, James, 120.
Sawing, George, 139.
Sawly, Thomas, 32.
Sawyer, Asael, 152.
Sawyer, Cornelius, 137.
Sawyer, Elijah, 152.
Sawyer, Ephraim, 84.
Sawyer, Ephraim, 123.
Sawyer, Jacob, 68.
Sawyer, James, 149.
Sawyer, Jesse, 60.
Sawyer, Jno, 134.
Sawyer, Jno, 137.
Sawyer, Joshua, 152.
Sawyer, Mathius, 152.
Sawyer, Nathaniel, 60.
Sawyer, Prescot, 149.
Sawyer, Samuel, 57.
Sawyer, William, 149.
Sawying, Jno, 139.
Saxton, Daniel, 136.
Saxton, Ebenezer, 110.
Saxton, George, 137.
Saxton, James, 121.
Saxton, Jonathan, 86.
Saxton, Knight, 86.
Saxton, Simion, 97.
Sayer, Jesse, 67.
Scamehorn, Cornelius, 72.
Scamon, Stephen, 1st, 77.
Scarborough, Ebenr, 141.
Scarborough, John, 140.
Scarborough, Joseph, 140.
Scarborough, Joseph, 141.
Scarborough, Saml, 141.
Scarborough, Stephen, 140.
Scariott, James, 50.
Scariott, Jonathan, 50.
Scariott, Nathan, 50.
Scarot, Thomas, 124.
Scarrot, James, 108.
Schallen, Abraham, 80.
Schallennex, Gideon, 80.
Schoolcraft, Samuel, 116.
Schovel, Ebenezer, 65.
Schuls, Samuel, 79.
Sciff, Samuel, 66.
Scofield, Abraham, 25.
Scofield, Abraham, Jr, 25.
Scofield, Benjamin, 25.
Scofield, Billy, 25.
Scofield, Daniel, 25.
Scofield, David, 25.
Scofield, Edward, 25.
Scofield, Elias, 25.
Scofield, Elisha, 24.
Scofield, Enos, 11.
Scofield, Epenetus, 25.
Scofield, Gershom, 26.
Scofield, Gideon, 25.
Scofield, Gilbert, 26.
Scofield, Hait, 26.
Scofield, Henry, 26.
Scofield, Israel, 25.
Scofield, Jacob, 25.
Scofield, Jacob, Jr, 25.
Scofield, Jacob, 3d, 26.
Scofield, James, 18.
Scofield, James, 24.
Scofield, James, Junr, 25.
Scofield, James, 3d, 25.
Scofield, John, 25.
Scofield, John, 5th, 26.
Scofield, Jonas, 25.
Scofield, Jonathan H., 25.
Scofield, Joseph, 26.
Scofield, Joseph, Junr, 25.
Scofield, Josiah, 25.
Scofield, Josiah, 25.
Scofield, Josiah, Junr, 26.
Scofield, Josiah W., 25.
Scofield, Nathan, 25.
Scofield, Nathaniel, 24.
Scofield, Nathel, Junr, 25.
Scofield, Nezer, 25.
Scofield, Peter, 22.
Scofield, Peter, 25.
Scofield, Reuben, 25.
Scofield, Samuel, 25.
Scofield, Samuel, Jr, 25.
Scofield, Samuel, 3d, 25.
Scofield, Sarah (Wd), 25.
Scofield, Seeley, 25.
Scofield, Selleck, 26.
Scofield, Seth, 25.
Scofield, Silvanus, 25.
Scofield, Silvanus, 26.
Scofield, Silvanus, Junr, 25.
Scofield, Stephen, 11.
Scofield, Stephen, 25.
Scofield, Thaddeus, 25.
Scofield, Uriah, 25.
Scofield, Warren, 25.
Scofield, Weed, 25.
Scogel, James, 12.
Soordam, Henry, 61.
Scot, James, 98.
Scott, Aaron, 22.
Scott, Abel, 110.
Scott, Abner, 110.
Scott, Adoniram, 79.
Scott, Amos, 2nd, 110.
Scott, Amos, 2nd, 110.
Scott, Ashley, 109.
Scott, Barnebes, 77.
Scott, Benjamin, 52.
Scott, Caleb, 110.
Scott, David, 28.
Scott, Ebenezer, 35.
Scott, Ebner., 77.
Scott, Ebenezer, 110.
Scott, Edmond, 109.
Scott, Eleazer, 22.
Scott, Eleazer, 2d, 77.
Scott, Elicks, 77.
Scott, Elisha, 40.
Scott, Enoch, 110.
Scott, Enoch, 2nd, 110.
Scott, Etheel, 63.
Scott, Ezekiel, 40.
Scott, Gideon, 28.
Scott, Gideon, 110.
Scott, Hezekiah, 77.
Scott, Isaac, 77.
Scott, Isaac, 110.
Scott, James, 28.
Scott, James, 2d, 28.
Scott, John, 22.
Scott, John, 104.
Scott, John, 110.
Scott, John, 126.
Scott, Jn., 139.
Scott, Jonathan, 77.
Scott, Joseph, 42.
Scott, Joseph, 110.
Scott, Joseph, 129.
Scott, Jos., 139.
Scott, Josiah, 110.
Scott, Justis, 95.
Scott, Lucreatia, 86.
Scott, Nathan, 110.
Scott, Obediah, 57.
Scott, Philip, 137.
Scott, Ruben, 110.
Scott, Samuel 109.
Scott, Samuel, 2nd, 110.
Scott, Samuel, 2nd, 110.
Scott, Simeon, 109.
Scott, Stephen, 137.
Scott, Thadeus, 110.
Scott, Thomas, 28.
Scott, Thomas, 42.
Scott, Timothy, 110.
Scott, Uri, 77.
Scott, Uriah, 110.
Scott (Widow), 138.
Scott, William, 18.
Scott, William, 22.
Scott, William, 51.
Scott, William, 104.
Scott, Wm, 136.
Scott, William, 141.
Scott, Wm, Junr, 22.
Scott, Woolfy, 77.
Scott, Zebediah, 138.
Scott, Zebulon, 109.
Scovel, Amos, 110.
Scovel, Asa, 109.
Scovel, Benjamin, 64.
Scovel, Desire, 109.
Scovel, Elisha, 106.
Scovel, Elizabeth, 106.
Scovel, Isaac, 134.
Scovel, John, 98.
Scovel, John, 98.
Scovel, John, 110.
Scovel, Jonathan, 66.
Scovel, Noah, 110.
Scovel, Samuel, 109.
Scovel, Selah, 109.
Scovel, Timothy, 109.
Scovel, Timothy, 2d, 110.
Scovel, William, 84.
Scovell, Amaziah, 110.
Scovell, Annah, 89.
Scovell, Elijah, 90.
Scovell, Mathew, 90.
Scovell, Noah, 89.
Scovell, Seldon, 109.
Scovil, Abagail, 81.
Scovil, Abijah, 34.
Scovil, Daniel, 58.
Scovil, David, 106.
Scovil, Elizebith, 146.
Scovil, Ezekial, 58.
Scovil, Jacob, 57.
Scovil, John, 84.
Scovil, John, Junr, 83.
Scovil, Joseph, 57.
Scovil, Joseph, 58.
Scovil, Joseph, 84.
Scovil, Josiah, 83.
Scovil, Judah, 121.
Scovil, Martin, 123.
Scovil, Samuel, 84.
Scovil, Samuel, 1st, 57.
Scovil, Samuel, 2d, 57.
Scovil, Solomon, 121.
Scovil, Stephen, 57.
Scovil, Timothy, 57.
Scovill, Darius, 77.
Scovill, Eli, 77.
Scovill, Ezra, 33.
Scovill, Israel, 77.
Scovill, Jesse, 77.
Scovill, Lemuel, 81.
Scovill, Martha, 77.
Scovill, Samuel, 77.
Scovill, Uri, 77.
Scovill, William, 77.
Scovill, William, 2d, 77.
Scranton, Abraham, 96.
Scranton, Abraham, 99.
Scranton, Jerad, 99.
Scranton, John, 99.
Scranton, Josiah, 99.
Scranton, Nathaniel, 98.
Scranton, Samuel, 98.
Scranton, Theobald, 99.
Scranton, Thomas, 98.
Scranton, Thomas, 99.
Scranton, Thomas, 2nd, 98.
Scranton, Timothy, 99.
Scranton, Timothy, 2d, 99.
Scranton, Torry, 99.
Scribner, Abraham, 23.
Scribner, Ann, 124.
Scribner, Enoch, 23.
Scribner, Ezra, 24.
Scribner, John, 29.
Scribner, Levi, 23.
Scribner, Matthew, 23.
Scribner, Osias, 19.
Scribner, Rachel, 28.
Scribner, Stephen, 21.
Scribner, Thomas, 23.
Scribner, Uriah, 22.
Scribner, Uriah, 28.
Scripter, Elezer, 139.
Scripter, Jno, 139.
Scripter, Sime, 133.
Scudder, Elizabeth (Wd), 21.
Scudder, Roberd, 13.
Seabury, Abigal, 145.
Seabury, John, 122.
Seabury, Samuel, 129.
Seabury, Saml, 144.
Seabury, Saml, Jnr, 146.
Seabury, Saml, 2d, 129.
Seager, Elijah, 49.
Seager, Joseph, Jr., 49.

212 INDEX.


Sealee, Abel, 19.
Sealee, Bradley, 19.
Sealee, Deborah, 15.
Sealee, Ezra, 14.
Sealee Giddeon, 17.
Sealee, James, 12.
Sealee, Liman, 18.
Sealee, Seth, 15.
Sealy, Benjamin, 72.
Sealy, David, 31.
Sealy, Ephraim, 31.
Sealy, Jesse, 31.
Sealy, Joseph, 31.
Sealy, Nathaniel, Jun$^{r}$, 31.
Searls, John, 115.
Searls, Jn$^{o}$, 137.
Searls, Salter, 141.
Searls, William, 115.
Sears, Bartholomew, 17.
Sears, Charles, 84.
Sears, Comfort, 29.
Sears, Daniel, 29.
Sears, David, 81.
Sears, Ebenezer, 81.
Sears, Elijah, 17.
Sears, Elisha, 87.
Sears, Elkanah, 81.
Sears, Francis, 101.
Sears, Gershom, 17.
Sears, Hezekiah, 80.
Sears, Isaac, 81.
Sears, John, 72.
Sears, John, 87.
Sears, Knowles, 29.
Sears, Matthew, 81.
Sears, Nathan, 87.
Sears, Peter, 88.
Sears, Remington, 115.
Sears, Richard, 17.
Sears, Stephen. 87.
Sears, Willard, 81.
Sebens, Josiah, 27.
Sebor, Jacob, 85.
Sebor, Jacob, 129.
Sedgwick, Abram, 47.
Sedgwick, John, 57.
Sedgwick, Mary, 61.
Sedgwick, Samuel, 35.
Sedgwick, William, 47.
Sedgwik, John A., 57 .
Sedgwith, Stephen, 41.
Sedgwith, Stephen, Jr., 41.
Seeley, Abner, 72.
Seeley, David, 66
Seeley, Ebenezer, 64.
Seeley, Elizabeth, 59.
Seeley, John, 69.
Seeley, John, 106.
Seeley, Joseph, 72.
Seeley, Nathaniel, 64.
Seelly, Isaac, 100.
Seely, Abijah, 26.
Seely, Abijah, Jun$^{r}$, 26.
Seely, Agar, 29.
Seely, Benjamin, 29.
Seely, Benjamin, 64.
Seely, David, 30.
Seely, Ebenezer, 26.
Seely, Elijah, 30.
Seely, Eliphalet, 26.
Seely, Elnathan, 29.
Seely, Esther (W$^{d}$), 26.
Seely, John, 25.
Seely, Jonas, 26.
Seely, Joseph, 26.
Seely, Justice, 64.
Seely, Nathan, 26.
Seely, Obadiah, 25.
Seely, Samuel, 26.
Seely, Silvanus, 26.
Seely, Silvanus, Jun$^{r}$, 26.
Seely, Wix, 26.
Seers, Stephen, 62.
Segar, Augustus, 44.
Segar, John, 44.
Segar, Joseph, 59.
Seger, Daniel, 10.
Seger, Eli, 11.
Seger, Joseph, 48.
Seger, Michael, 48.
Seit, James, 10.
Seirs, James, 29.
Selbe, Jere$^{h}$, 81.
Selbe, W$^{m}$, 81.
Selby, Abraham, 106.
Selby, Abraham, 2$^{nd}$, 106.
Selby, David M., 36.
Selden, Caleb, 144.
Selden, David, 80.
Selden, Dudley, 122.
Selden, Edward, 83.
Selden, Elias, 84.
Selden, Elisabeth, 122.
Selden, Ely, 122.
Selden, Ezra, 123.
Selden, Joseph, 41.
Selden, Joseph, 83.
Selden, Samuel, 122.
Seldon, Aaron, 80.
Seldon, Charles, 152.
Seldon, Elijah, 122.
Seldon, Joseph, 82.
Seldon, Seephas, 83.
Seldon, Thomas, 80.
Selleck, Daniel, 26.
Selleck, Edward, 26.
Selleck, Gershom, 26.
Selleck, Isaac, 23.
Selleck, Jacob, 23.
Selleck, James, 23.
Selleck, Jesse, 27.
Selleck, Joseph, 15.
Selleck, Mary (W$^{d}$), 26.
Selleck, Nathan, 26.
Selleck, Nathaniel, 22.
Selleck, Peter, 24.
Selleck, Samuel, 26.
Selleck, Seymore, 26.
Selleck, Silvanus, 15.
Selleck, Simeon, 26.
Selleck, Stephen, 24.
Selleck, Stephen, J$^{r}$, 26.
Selleck, Thaddeus, 23.
Selleck, Uriah, 22.
Selleck, Wray, 27.
Sellers, Phillip, 42.
Sellew, John, 42.
Sellick, Jesse, 28.
Sellick, Noah, 67.
Selm, Patience, 53.
Selvey, Ephraim, 62.
Selvey, William, 62.
Seman, Abraham, 19.
Semans, Abel, 139.
Semour, John, 79.
Semour, John, 2$^{d}$, 79.
Semour, Joseph, 79.
Senior, Dan$^{l}$, 62.
Senot, Thomas, 126.
Senter, John, 130.
Sergeants, Isaac, 147.
Sergeants, Isaac, Jn$^{r}$, 147.
Sergeants, Sam$^{l}$, 147.
Servant, James, 64.
Sessions, Amasa, 138.
Sessions, Amasa, 149.
Sessions, Darious, 150.
Sessions, Eben$^{r}$, 138.
Sessions, Jn$^{o}$, 139.
Sessions, John, 143.
Sessions, Joseph, 153.
Sessions, Leonard, 147.
Sessions, Nath$^{l}$, 139.
Sessions, Nath$^{l}$, 139.
Sessions, Sam$^{l}$, 134.
Sessions, Squire, 149.
Sessions, Waller, 139.
Sessons, Abijah, 138.
Sessons, Benj., 137.
Setle, Thomas, 19.
Sevans, David, 21.
Seward, Amos, 110.
Seward, Charles, 48.
Seward, Daniel, 62.
Seward, David, 98.
Seward, David, 2$^{nd}$, 98.
Seward, John, 83.
Seward, Moses, 96.
Seward, Nathan, 57.
Seward, Samuel, 74.
Seward, Samuel, 96.
Seward, Solomon, 74.
Seward, Timothy, 98.
Sexton, Asabel, 40.
Sexton, Betsy, 121.
Sexton, George, 121.
Sexton, Jessey, 81.
Sexton, Joseph, 136.
Sexton, Joseph, 2$^{d}$, 136.
Sexton, Samuel, 81.
Sexton, Simeon, 33.
Sexton, Stephen 136.
Sexton, Thomas, 40.
Seymore, Abijah, 22.
Seymore, Anne (W$^{d}$), 22.
Seymore, Daniel, 24.
Seymore, David, 22.
Seymore, David, 62.
Seymore, Elias, 63.
Seymore, Elijah, 59.
Seymore, Ezra, 22.
Seymore, Hezekiah, 63.
Seymore, James, 22.
Seymore, Jared, 26.
Seymore, John, 22.
Seymore, John, 22.
Seymore, Jonathan, 21.
Seymore, Moses, 65.
Seymore, Noah, 60.
Seymore, Phebe (W$^{d}$), 22.
Seymore, Rebecca (W$^{d}$), 22.
Seymore, Roger, 92.
Seymore, Samuel, 15.
Seymore, Samuel, 22.
Seymore, Samuel, 65.
Seymore, Seth, 22.
Seymore, Stephen, 64.
Seymore, Thomas, 22.
Seymore, Uriah, 63.
Seymore, William, 22.
Seymour, Aaron, 47.
Seymour, Aaron, 47.
Seymour, Allyn, 47.
Seymour, Asa, 46.
Seymour, Asa, 47.
Seymour, Ashbel, 54.
Seymour, Calvin, 47.
Seymour, Charles, 47.
Seymour, Charles, 47.
Seymour, Daniel, 47.
Seymour, Eli, 47.
Seymour, Elias, 54.
Seymour, Elisha, 52.
Seymour, Freeman, 47.
Seymour, George, 47.
Seymour, Hezekiah, 46.
Seymour, John, 47.
Seymour, Jonathan, 33.
Seymour, Joseph, 68.
Seymour, Joseph, 2$^{d}$, 68.
Seymour, Joseph Whiting, 47.
Seymour, Lewis, 33.
Seymour, Matthew, 28.
Seymour, Michael, 47.
Seymour, Moses, 47.
Seymour, Nathaniel, 47.
Seymour, Norman, 47.
Seymour, Richard, 47.
Seymour, Robert, 46.
Seymour, Thankfull, 54.
Seymour, Thomas, 28.
Seymour, Thomas, Esq$^{r}$, 46.
Seymour, Thomas, 2$^{d}$, 28.
Seymour, Thomas Y., 47.
Seymour, Timothy, 47.
Seymour, Uriah, 28.
Seymour, Zebulon, 47.
Shaddock, Joseph, 63.
Shaddock, Moses, 52.
Shadrack (Negro) 120.
Shaler, Aaron, 83.
Shaler, Asa, 83.
Shaler, Bezeleel, 83.
Shaler, Ezra, 83.
Shaler, Hezekiah, 83.
Shaler, Hezekiah, Jun$^{r}$, 83.
Shaler, James, 83.
Shaler, Jeremiah, 83.
Shaler, Nathaniel, 86.
Shaler, Reuben, 83.
Shaler, Samuel, 83.
Shaler, Simon, 83.
Shaler, Thomas, 83.
Shally, Ebenezer, 97.
Shapley, John, 145.
Shapley, Mary, 129.
Sharkweather, Anne, 148.
Sharkweather, Richard, 148.
Sharman, James, 62.
Sharp, Abigail, 149.
Sharp, Asa, 149.
sharp, Caleb, 149.
Sharp, David, 149.
Sharp, Eliakim, 19.
Sharp, Eliakim, 75.
Sharp, Gershom, 149.
Sharp, Gershom, Secn$^{d}$, 149.
Sharp, Jesse, 19.
Sharp, Joab, 74.
Sharp, John, 149.
Sharp, Joseph, 126.
Sharp (Negro), 115.
Sharp, Reubin & co., 144.
Sharp, Robert, 149.
Sharp, Ruth, 149.
Sharp, Solomon, 140.
Sharp, Thomas, 20.
Sharp, William, 75.
Sharp, William, 150.
Sharper (Negroe), 103.
Sharper (Negroe), 109.
Shatdock, William, 60.
Shatlief, Nathaniel, 110.
Shattuck, David, 121.
Shattuck, Randal, 81.
Shattuck, Robart, 121.
Shattuck, Robert, 87.
Shaw, Amos, 116.
Shaw, Benj$^{n}$, 142.
Shaw, Daniel, 127.
Shaw, David, 38.
Shaw, Gid, 139.
Shaw, James, 26.
Shaw, John, 69.
Shaw, Peleg, 117.
Shaw, Thomas, 126.
Shaw, Thomas, 152.
Shaw, Thomas, 2$^{d}$, 126.
Shaw, William, 142.
Shayler, Joseph, 107.
Sheers, Rebecca, 86.
Sheet, Hester, 108.
Sheffield, Achors, 117.
Sheffield, Amos, 118.
Sheffield, George, 117.
Sheffield, Isaac, 118.
Sheffield, Isaac, Jun$^{r}$, 118.
Sheffield, Paul, 14.
Sheffield, Paul, 119.
Sheffield, Robart, Jun$^{r}$, 117.
Sheffield, Sam$^{l}$, 125.
Sheffield, William, 117.
Sheffield, William, 2$^{d}$, 117.
Shelbey, Ebenezer, 29.
Shelden, Ephephsas, 62.
Shelden, Moses, 62.
Shelden, Roger, 63.
Sheldon, Asher, 91.
Sheldon, Benjamin, 50.
Sheldon, Charles, 136.
Sheldon, Daniel, 50.
Sheldon, Daniel, 64.
Sheldon, Ebenezer, 50.
Sheldon, Elijah, 51.
Sheldon, Elisha, 69.
Sheldon, Elisha, 2$^{d}$, 69.
Sheldon, Ely, 69.
Sheldon, Eunice, 148.
Sheldon, Ezra, 62.
Sheldon, George, 61.
Sheldon, Gersham, 50.
Sheldon, Hannah, 101.
Sheldon, Jacob, 50.
Sheldon, James, 46.
Sheldon, John, 46.
Sheldon, John, 51.
Sheldon, John, Jr., 46.
Sheldon, Jonathan, 50.
Sheldon, Jonathan, Jr., 50.
Sheldon, Joseph, 47.
Sheldon, Joseph, Jr., 47.
Sheldon, Josiah, 51.
Sheldon, Martin, 50.
Sheldon, Oliver, 51.
Sheldon, Phineas, 50.
Sheldon, Prince, 47.
Sheldon, Rachel, 50.
Sheldon, Remember, 54.
Sheldon, Roderic, 47.
Sheldon, Selah, 55.
Sheldon, Simeon, 50.
Sheldon, Thomas, 51.
Sheldon, William, 113.
Sheldorn, Sam$^{l}$, 65.
Shelley, Abram, 72.
Shelly, Edmond, 98.
Shelly, Joel, 97.
Shelly, John, 98.
Shelly, Lucy, 98.
Shelly, Medad, 98.
Shelly, Ruben, 98.
Shelly, Ruben, 2$^{nd}$, 98.
Shelly, Shubal, 98.
Shelly, Timothy, 97.
Shelp, Joseph, 25.
Shelton, Abijah, 18.
Shelton, Abijah, 2$^{d}$, 18.
Shelton, Ager, 18.
Shelton, Andrew, 17.
Shelton, Benjamin, 17.
Shelton, Daniel, 17.
Shelton, Daniel, 18.
Shelton, Daniel, 79.
Shelton, Elisha, 18.
Shelton, Eunice, 18.
Shelton, Gershom, 79.
Shelton, Isaac W., 34.
Shelton, James, 18.
Shelton, Jeremiah, 17.
Shelton, Joane, 18.
Shelton, Noah, 18.
Shelton, Philo, 14.
Shelton, Samuel, 17.
Shelton, Sealee, 18.
Shelton, Thaddeus, 18.
Shelton, William, 18.
Shelton, William, 78.
Shelton, Zacheriah, 17.
Shepard, Amos, 40.
Shepard, Ashbel, 46.
Shepard, Ashbel, 47.
Shepard, Benj$^{n}$, 141.
Shepard, Charles, 46.
Shepard, Elisha, 46.
Shepard, Isaiah, 33.
Shepard, Jesse, 40.
Shepard, John, 47.
Shepard, Luther, 40.
Shepard, Mary, 47.
Shepard, Nathaniel, 50.
Shepard, Nath$^{l}$, 151.
Shepard, Noah, 40.
Shepard, Noah, 40.
Shepard, Richard, 46.
Shepard, Samuel, 50.
Shepard, Samuel, Jr., 50.
Shepard, Sarah, 47.
Shepard, Stephen, 47.
Shepard, Stephen, 97.
Shepard, Thomas, 41.
Shepard, Timothy, 46.
Shepard, Uriah, 46.
Shepard, Whitmore, 141.
Shephard, Ebenener, 57.
Shephard, Eldad, 67.
Shephard, Isaac, 136.
Shepherd, Abel, 80.
Shepherd, Abraham, 20.
Shepherd, Amos, 20.
Shepherd, Amos, 80.
Shepherd, Benoni, 138.
Shepherd, Billy, 80.
Shepherd, Daniel, 80.
Shepherd, Daniel, Jun$^{r}$, 80.
Shepherd, David, 20.
Shepherd, Edward, 80.
Shepherd, Edward, Jun$^{r}$, 80.
Shepherd, Elisha, 80.
Shepherd, Elisha, Jun$^{r}$, 80.
Shepherd, Elisha, Jun$^{r}$, 80.
Shepherd, George, 20.
Shepherd, George, 80.
Shepherd, Gideon, 20.
Shepherd, Jacob, 136.
Shepherd, James, 20.
Shepherd, Jered, 88.
Shepherd, John, 20.
Shepherd, John, 80.
Shepherd, John, 128.
Shepherd, John, Jun$^{r}$, 80.
Shepherd, Rev$^{d}$ John, 25.
Shepherd, Joseph, 88.
Shepherd, Merrit, 20.
Shepherd, Moses, 20.
Shepherd, Noah, 80.
Shepherd, Simeon, 21.
Shepherd, Stephen, 20.
Shepherd, Stephen, 68.
Shepherd, Thomas, 80.
Shepherd, Thomas, 81.
Sheppard, Abraham, 149.
Sheppard, Asa, 142.
Sheppard, Daniel, 63.
Sheppard, Isaac, 108.
Sheppard, James, 118.
Sheppard, James, 141.
Sheppard, John, 97.
Sheppard, John, 149.
Sheppard, John, 149.
Sheppard, Joseph, 64.
Sheppard, Joseph, 97.
Sheppard, Joseph, 148.
Sheppard, Josiah, 59.
Sheppard, Lyda, 149.
Sheppard, Moses, 64.
Sheppard, Olver, 62.
Sheppard, Phinehas, 59.
Sheppard, Reubin, 148.
Sheppard, Samuel, 97.
Sheppard, Simon, 148.
Sheppard, Stephen, 60.
Sheppard, Stephen, 149.
Sheppard, Thomas, 97.
Sheppard, William, 154.
Sheppard, Zebulon, 61.
Sheppardson, Jn$^{o}$, 83.
Sheppardson, Will$^{m}$, 83.
Shepperd, Joseph, 66.
Sherborn, Benjamin, 20.
Sheridan, Mary, 122.
Sherman, Amos, 111.
Sherman, Benjamin, 83.
Sherman, Daniel, 72.
Sherman, Daniel, 74.
Sherman, Daniel, 79.
Sherman, Daniel, 2$^{d}$, 79.
Sherman, David, 79.
Sherman, Eli, 72.
Sherman, Elijah, 79.
Sherman, Elisabeth, 113.
Sherman, Ephraim, 19.
Sherman, Ezra, 72.
Sherman, Jabez, 133.
Sherman, James, 128.
Sherman, Jese, 111.
Sherman, Jesse, 19.
Sherman, John, 28.
Sherman, John, 79.
Sherman, John, 104.
Sherman, John, 131.
Sherman, John, 2$^{d}$, 79.
Sherman, Lemuel, 103.
Sherman, Mathew, 79.
Sherman, Molly, 102.
Sherman, Nathanel, 17.
Sherman, Nathanel, Ju$^{r}$, 17.
Sherman, Nathaniel, 38.
Sherman, Peter, 75.
Sherman, Philo, 17.
Sherman, Phineus, 17.
Sherman, Reuben, 79.
Sherman, Roger, 104.
Sherman, Rufus, 10.
Sherman, Samuel, 10.
Sherman, Samuel, 103.
Sherman, Sarah, 89.
Sherman, Solomon, 79.
Sherman, Taylor, 23.
Sherman, Tesna, 59.
Sherman, Vincen, 18.
Sherman, Walker, 17.
Sherman, William, 103.
Sherman, Zadock, 10.
Shermon, Andrew, 31.
Shermon, David, 20.
Shermon, David, 29.
Shermon, Ebenezer, 20.
Shermon, Elijah, 20.
Shermon, Ezra, 20.
Shermon, Filo, 19.
Shermon, Filo, 20.
Shermon, James, 30.
Shermon, John, 20.
Shermon, John, 30.
Shermon, Josiah, 31.
Shermon, Jotham, 20.
Shermon, Lemuel, 20.
Shermon, Lewis, 19.
Shermon, Lymon, 19.
Shermon, Lymon, 20.
Shermon, Matthew, 21.
Shermon, Nathan, 20.
Shermon, Nathan, 30.
Shermon, Sarah, 32.
Shermon, Seth, 20.

# INDEX.

Shermon, Seth, 29.
Sherry, Joseph, 103.
Sherwood, Fanton, 31.
Sherwood, Abel, 14.
Sherwood, Abel, 19.
Sherwood, Albert, 13.
Sherwood, Amos, 31.
Sherwood, Amy, 56.
Sherwood, Asahel, 12.
Sherwood, Benjamin, 14.
Sherwood, Benjamin, 28.
Sherwood, Benjamin, Jnr, 15.
Sherwood, Daniel, 12.
Sherwood, Daniel, 12.
Sherwood, Daniel, 13.
Sherwood, Daniel, 15.
Sherwood, Daniel, 21.
Sherwood, Daniel, 31.
Sherwood, Daniel, 72.
Sherwood, David, 13.
Sherwood, David, 29.
Sherwood, Eben, 21.
Sherwood, Ebenezer, 18.
Sherwood, Ebenezer, 29.
Sherwood, Elihue, 13.
Sherwood, Eliphilet, 13.
Sherwood, Elnathan, 16.
Sherwood, Ephraim, 17.
Sherwood, Gershom, 13.
Sherwood, Gilbert, 16.
Sherwood, Increase, 13.
Sherwood, Isaac, 27.
Sherwood, Jabez, 16.
Sherwood, Jabez, 32.
Sherwood, James, 16.
Sherwood, Jehiel, 13.
Sherwood, John, 13.
Sherwood, John, 27.
Sherwood, John, 31.
Sherwood, John, Jnr, 13.
Sherwood, Jonathan, 28.
Sherwood, Jonathan, 79.
Sherwood, Joseph, 13.
Sherwood, Joseph, 32.
Sherwood, Joseph, 94.
Sherwood, Justin, 13.
Sherwood, Levet, 32.
Sherwood, Mathew, 25.
Sherwood, Matthew, 31.
Sherwood, Moses, 12.
Sherwood, Nathan, 15.
Sherwood, Nathan, 18.
Sherwood, Nathan, 28.
Sherwood, Nehemiah, 28.
Sherwood, Nehemiah, Jr, 16.
Sherwood, Noah, 13.
Sherwood, Oliver, 16.
Sherwood, Ralph, 13.
Sherwood, Reuben, 28.
Sherwood, Reuben, 72.
Sherwood, Reubin, 15.
Sherwood, Samuel, 30.
Sherwood, Samuel, 1st, 13.
Sherwood, Samuel, 2d, 14.
Sherwood, Samuel B., 32.
Sherwood, Sarah, 14.
Sherwood, Sarah, 15.
Sherwood, Seth, 14.
Sherwood, Seymour, 12.
Sherwood, Stephen, 26.
Sherwood, Stephen, 30.
Sherwood, Squire, 13.
Sherwood, Thomas, 31.
Sherwood, Thomas, 31.
Sherwood, Warren, 75.
Sherwood, Zachariah, 15.
Sherwood, Zalmon, 14.
Shether, Saml, 65.
Shewood, Hannah, 57.
Shields, Hannah, 128.
Shields, James, 80.
Shiffields, Nathl, 150.
Shinger, Sarah, 148.
Shipman, Abner, 124.
Shipman, Edwd, 91.
Shipman, Elias, 89.
Shipman, Elias, 104.
Shipman, Israel, 91.
Shipman, James, 89.
Shipman, John, 42.
Shipman, Jno, 89.
Shipman, Jno, 89.
Shipman, Jonathan, 66.
Shipman, Joseph, 91.
Shipman, Michael, 91.
Shipman, Nathl, 89.
Shipman, Nathl, 131.
Shipman, Samuel, 33.
Shipman, Samuel, 89.
Shipman, Stephen, 42.
Shipman, Stephen, Jr., 42.
Shipman, William, 124.
Shirland, Stephen, 90.
Shirtland, Saml, 89.
Shirtland, Saml, 2d, 89.
Shirtland, Wm E., 89.
Shirtliff, Jonathan, 43.
Shoals, Jabez, 125.
Shoals, John, 118.
Shoals, John, 119.
Shoals, Mary, 118.
Shoals, Susanna, 119.
Shoals, Whealer, 119.

Sholes, Miner, 129.
Short, Hannah, 128.
Short, Joseph, 94.
Short, Seth, 144.
Short, Siloam, 144.
Shortman, William, 46.
Shove, Daniel, 11.
Shove, Daniel, Jur, 11.
Shove, Levi, 11.
Shove, Seth, 11.
Shovel, Michael, 61.
Shrinner, Elijah, 133.
Shubel (negroe), 95.
Shumway, Elijah, 149.
Shumway, Joseph, 147.
Shurtliff, Jno, 138.
Shurtlift, Jno, 134.
Shuster, John, 67.
Shute, Richard, 11.
Sibley, Asa, 153.
Sibley, Ezekel, 140.
Sibley, Ezra, 139.
Sibley, Jno, 139.
Sibley, Moses, 139.
Sibley, Richard, 25.
Siely, Abel, 30.
Siely, Abel, 32.
Siely, Betty (Wid.), 30.
Siely, Ebenezer, 31.
Siely, Mable, 30.
Siely, Michael, 30.
Siely, Michael, 31.
Siely, Nathaniel, 31.
Siely, Phebe, 30.
Siely, Seth, 30.
Sikes, Gideon, 51.
Silas (Negroe), 97.
Sileman, John, 59.
Silemon, Hezekiah, 31.
Silik, Benjamin, 11.
Silik, James, 11.
Silik, Nathanel, 11.
Siliman, Christian, 14.
Siliman, David, 31.
Siliman, David, Junr, 31.
Siliman, David, 3d, 31.
Silkrags, Trunans, 110.
Silkrigs, Jonathan G., 65.
Silkrogs, Nicholas, 109.
Sill, David F., 123.
Sill, Elisha, 60.
Sill, Giles, 123.
Sill, Isaac, 124.
Sill, John, 54.
Sill, John, 123.
Sill, Richard, 89.
Sill, Richd L., 54.
Sill, Samuel, 123.
Sill, Samuel, 124.
Sill, Silas, 123.
Sill, William, 123.
Silleck, Peter, Junr, 24.
Sillick, Bethiel, 66.
Sillick, Ezra, 66.
Sillick, Joseph, 66.
Silliman, Data, 17.
Silliman, Ebenezer, 12.
Silliman, Ebenezer, 14.
Silliman, Gould, 14.
Silliman, James, 31.
Silliman, Job, 14.
Silliman, Doctr Joseph, 22.
Silliman, Mary, 14.
Silliman, Samuel, 15.
Silliman, Samuel C., 22.
Silliman, Seth, 15.
Silliman, Thomas, Esq., 90.
Silliman, William, 14.
Silloman, Justus, 31.
Silly, John, 29.
Silsby, John, 142.
Silsby, Jona, 131.
Silsby, Polly, 131.
Silva (Negro), 131.
Silvia (Negro), 128.
Simbo, Prince, 42.
Simeon (Negroe), 102.
Simers, Hezekiah, 32.
Simmon, Abel, Senr, 141.
Simmonds, John, 129.
Simmons, Abel, 140.
Simmons, Benjn, 143.
Simmons, Isaac, 15.
Simmons, Jemimah (Wd), 16.
Simmons, John, 64.
Simmons, Joshua, 106.
Simmons, Perer, 70.
Simmons, Rufus, 64.
Simmons, Sally, 129.
Simmons, Samuel, 87.
Simmons, Sarah, 120.
Simmons, Solomon, 64.
Simmons, Thos, 148.
Simmons, Timothy (negro), 15.
Simms, William, 144.
Simon, Abel, 77.
Simon, Gideon, 77.
Simon (Widow), 134.
Simons, Amos, 77.
Simons, Ann, 126.
Simons, Asael, 154.
Simons, Asahel, 39.
Simons, Benjamin, 39.
Simons, Benjamin, Jr., 39.

Simons, Chapman, 129.
Simons, Darious, 147.
Simons, Elijah, 143.
Simons, Elijah, 143.
Simons, Elipht, 147.
Simons, Francis, 142.
Simons, Israel, 37.
Simons, James, 132.
Simons, Joel, 39.
Simons, John, 37.
Simons, Jonathan, 147.
Simons, Joseph, 37.
Simons, Joseph, 43.
Simons, Joseph, 77.
Simons, Josiah, 77.
Simons, Nathan, 148.
Simons, Nathan, 152.
Simons, Paul G., 39.
Simons, Reuben, 49.
Simons, Richard, 1st, 77.
Simons, Richard, 2d, 77.
Simons, Samuel, 37.
Simons, Samuel, 37.
Simons, Samuel, 77.
Simons, Shubael, 143.
Simons, Silas, 38.
Simons, Thomas, 112.
Simons (Widow), 132.
Simons, Wiliam, 68.
Simons, William, 53.
Singlehuff, John, 77.
Sipeo (Negro), 113.
Sipro (Negro), 122.
Sipro (Negro), 122.
Sirdam, Tunis, 63.
Sisco, Hannah, 14.
Sissen, William, 18.
Sisson, James, 103.
Sisson, James, 120.
Sisson, William, 116.
Sistarre, Gabriel, 127.
Sistarre, Gabriel, 2d, 129.
Sitkuggs, Osi, 77.
Siverana, Nicholas, 94.
Sizer, Abel, 88.
Sizer, Anthony, 86.
Sizer, Daniel, 86.
Sizer, Eli, 87.
Sizer, Lemuel, 87.
Skeel, Asa, 80.
Skeels, Ephraim, 74.
Skeels, Ephraim, 2d, 74.
Skeels, John, 74.
Skelding, James, 24.
Skelding, John, 24.
Skidmore, Abel, 21.
Skidmore, Amos, 21.
Skidmore, Daniel, 21.
Skidmore, Ephraim, 21.
Skidmore, John, 21.
Skieff, Stephen, 59.
Skiff, Joseph, 59.
Skiff, Nathan, 59.
Skiffe, Joseph, 152.
Skift, Benjamin, 67.
Skilton, Avery, 56.
Skilton, David, 77.
Skinner, Abijah, 37.
Skinner, Abraham, 43.
Skinner, Abraham, 154.
Skinner, Abraham, Jr., 43.
Skinner, Ashbel, 58.
Skinner, Augustus, 37.
Skinner, Azariah, 37.
Skinner, Benjamin, 37.
Skinner, Benjamin, 43.
Skinner, Benjn, 135.
Skinner, Daniel, 39.
Skinner, Daniel, 46.
Skinner, Daniel, 46.
Skinner, Daniel, 134.
Skinner, Danl, 134.
Skinner, Daniel, Jr., 46.
Skinner, David, 120.
Skinner, David, 135.
Skinner, Deborah, 43.
Skinner, Ebenezer, 84.
Skinner, Elias, 37.
Skinner, Elias, 37.
Skinner, Elisha, 46.
Skinner, Hezekiah, 44.
Skinner, Ira, 58.
Skinner, Isaac, 55.
Skinner, Isaac, Ju., 55.
Skinner, Israel, 132.
Skinner, Jared, 46.
Skinner, John, 36.
Skinner, John, 46.
Skinner, John, 120.
Skinner, Jno, 133.
Skinner, Jonathan, 37.
Skinner, Jonathan, 47.
Skinner, Jona, 132.
Skinner, Jonath, 152.
Skinner, Joseph, 47.
Skinner, Jo., 137.
Skinner, Mary, 38.
Skinner, Nathaniel, 47.
Skinner, Noah, 121.
Skinner, Noah, Junr, 120.
Skinner, Oliver, 39.
Skinner, Priscilla, 154.

Skinner, Richard, 47.
Skinner, Richard, 84.
Skinner, Richard, 132.
Skinner, Richard, 132.
Skinner, Roswell, 45.
Skinner, Ruben, 132.
Skinner, Samuel, 38.
Skinner, Saml, 121.
Skinner, Saml, 132.
Skinner, Stephen, 47.
Skinner, Stephen, 120.
Skinner, Stephen, 154.
Skinner, Theodore, 46.
Skinner, Thomas, 58.
Skinner, Thomas, 121.
Skinner, Timothy, 64.
Skinner, Uriah, 132.
Skinner, William, 46.
Skinner, William, 128.
Skinner, William, 154.
Skinner, William, Jur, 154.
Skinner, William, 2d, 128.
Slack, Able, 117.
Slack, Amos, 117.
Slack, Joseph, 144.
Slack, William, 117.
Slack, William, 144.
Slade, Jonathan, 149.
Slade, William, 62.
Slane, Charles, 17.
Slason, Abraham, 26.
Slason, Charles, 26.
Slason, David, 26.
Slason, Deliverance, 26.
Slason, Gershom, 26.
Slason, Israel, 26.
Slason, Jacob, 26.
Slason, Jonathan, 26.
Slason, Jonathan, Junr, 26.
Slason, Stephen, 22.
Slason, Thomas, 25.
Slason, Zepheniah, 26.
Slate, Ezekl, 148.
Slate, Ezekl, 136.
Slater, Abraham, Jnr, 144.
Slater, Abraham, Senr, 144.
Slater, Benjamin, 44.
Slater, Benjn, 140.
Slater, Eleazr, 147.
Slater, Francis, 66.
Slater, Jeremlah, 143.
Slater, Saml, 147.
Slater, Shered, 48.
Slater, Zerobabel, 128.
Slawter, Anthony, 134.
Slawter, Moses, 134.
Sleet, Eliphet, 57.
Slevell, James, 60.
Slight, Joseph, 117.
Sloakum, Edward, 131.
Sloan, Mary, 102.
Sloan, Robert, 46.
Sloan, Robert, 46.
Sloan, Thomas, 46.
Sloane, William, 118.
Sloson, Nathan, 59.
Sly, Thomas, 32.
Sly, Thomas, 113.
Smaley, Enoch, 57.
Small, William, 114.
Smally, Jacob, 40.
Smally, John, 33.
Smedley, Ephraim, 65.
Smedley, Gideon, 71.
Smedley, James, 14.
Smedley, Nathan, 59.
Smedley, Samuel, 14.
Smith, Aaron, 75.
Smith, Aaron, 83.
Smith, Abel, 10.
Smith, Abel, 95.
Smith, Abel, 111.
Smith, Abiel, 106.
Smith, Abigail, 24.
Smith, Abijah, 94.
Smith, Abijah, 137.
Smith, Abijah, 141.
Smith, Abijah, 145.
Smith, Abisha, 51.
Smith, Abisha, 83.
Smith, Abner, 88.
Smith, Abner, 94.
Smith, Abner, 129.
Smith, Abraham, 24.
Smith, Abraham, 42.
Smith, Abraham, 72.
Smith, Abraham, 94.
Smith, Abraham, 94.
Smith, Abraham, 100.
Smith, Abraham, 150.
Smith, Adney, 111.
Smith, Allan, 138.
Smith, Allen, 67.
Smith, Allen, 91.
Smith, Allyn, 33.
Smith, Alvin, 47.
Smith, Amasa, 58.
Smith, Ambrose, 96.
Smith, Amos, 10.

Smith, Amos, 25.
Smith, Amos, 35.
Smith, Amos, 79.
Smith, Amos, 123.
Smith, Amos, Jnr, 10.
Smith, Andrew, 94.
Smith, Andrew, 94.
Smith, Andrew, 102.
Smith, Andrew, 105.
Smith, Andrew, 130.
Smith, Anna, 93.
Smith, Anthony, 110.
Smith, Asa, 43.
Smith, Asa, 79.
Smith, Asa, 114.
Smith, Asa, 128.
Smith, Asa, 140.
Smith, Asa, 142.
Smith, Asa, 1st, 58.
Smith, Asa, 2d, 58.
Smith, Asahel, 61.
Smith, Asahel, 129.
Smith, Asaph, 33.
Smith, Asher, 59.
Smith, Austin, 25.
Smith, Austin, 110.
Smith, Austin, 111.
Smith, Austin, Junr, 25.
Smith, Azariah, 68.
Smith, Azor, 28.
Smith, Bathoheba, 42.
Smith, Benajah, 71.
Smith, Benjamin, 13.
Smith, Benjamin, 28.
Smith, Benjamin, 42.
Smith, Benjamin, 66.
Smith, Benjamin, 80.
Smith, Benjamin, 97.
Smith, Benjamin, 102.
Smith, Benjamin, 103.
Smith, Benjamin, 105.
Smith, Benjamin, 118.
Smith, Benjn, 135.
Smith, Benjn, 135.
Smith, Benjn, 142.
Smith, Benjn, 142.
Smith, Benjn, 149.
Smith, Benjn, 153.
Smith, Benjamin, 2nd, 105.
Smith, Bethel, 79.
Smith, Caleb, 97.
Smith, Caleb, 101.
Smith, Chancy, 64.
Smith, Charles, 25.
Smith, Charles, 59.
Smith, Charles, 59.
Smith, Charles, 80.
Smith, Charles, 83.
Smith, Charles, 119.
Smith, Chester, 115.
Smith, Chilleab, 69.
Smith, Christopher, 94.
Smith, Clemence, 28.
Smith, Cooper, 93.
Smith, Cornal, 18.
Smith, Cotten M., 63.
Smith, Daniel, 13.
Smith, Daniel, 22.
Smith, Daniel, 25.
Smith, Daniel, 56.
Smith, Daniel, 74.
Smith, Daniel, 80.
Smith, Daniel, 96.
Smith, Daniel, 107.
Smith, Daniel, 111.
Smith, Daniel, 113.
Smith, Daniel, 126.
Smith, Daniel, 131.
Smith, Danl, 138.
Smith, Danl, 154.
Smith, Daniel, Junr, 83.
Smith, Daniel, 2d, 28.
Smith, Daniel, 2d, 126.
Smith, Daniel, 3d, 28.
Smith, Daniel, 4th, 28.
Smith, Darcus, 105.
Smith, Darius, 113.
Smith, David, 10.
Smith, David, 25.
Smith, David, 28.
Smith, David, 32.
Smith, David, 43.
Smith, David, 49.
Smith, David, 53.
Smith, David, 59.
Smith, David, 59.
Smith, David, 77.
Smith, David, 80.
Smith, David, 80.
Smith, David, 84.
Smith, David, 95.
Smith, David, 102.
Smith, David, 111.
Smith, David, 111.
Smith, David, 113.
Smith, David, 124.
Smith, David, 126.
Smith, David, 137.
Smith, David, 142.
Smith, David, Junr, 25.
Smith, David, Jr., 49.

# INDEX.

Smith, David, 3d, 25.
Smith, Doct' David, 22.
Smith, **Dayton,** 128.
Smith, Denison, 119.
Smith, Dow, 92.
Smith, Dudley, 124.
Smith, Eben, 25.
Smith, Ebenezer, 10.
Smith, Ebenezer, 13.
Smith, Ebenezer, 28.
Smith, Ebenezer, 42.
Smith, Ebenezer, 48.
Smith, Ebenezer, 74.
Smith, Ebenezer, 101.
Smith, Ebenezer, 102.
Smith, Eben', 125.
Smith, Eben', 140.
Smith, Eben', 151.
Smith, Eben', 154.
Smith, Eben', 2d, 125.
Smith, Edmond, 103.
Smith, Edward, 87.
Smith, Edward, 105.
Smith, Edward, 118.
Smith, Edward, 124.
Smith, Elam, 93.
Smith, Eldad, 36.
Smith, Eldad, 51.
Smith, Eleazer, 63.
Smith, Eleazer, 152.
Smith, Eli, 10.
Smith, Eli, 18.
Smith, Eli, 60.
Smith, Eli, 72.
Smith, Eli, 105.
Smith, Eli, 108.
Smith, Eliakim, 22.
Smith, Eliakim, 22.
Smith, Elias, 59.
Smith, Elias, 83.
Smith, Elieaser, 27.
Smith, Elihu, 35.
Smith, Elihu, 42.
Smith, Elihu, 84.
Smith, Elijah, 28.
Smith, Elijah, 33.
Smith, Elijah, 43.
Smith, Elijah, 62.
Smith, Elijah, 74.
Smith, Elijah, 121.
Smith, Elijah, 126.
Smith, Elijah, 145.
Smith, Elijah, 146.
Smith, Eliphlet, 77.
Smith, **Elisha,** 68.
Smith, Elisha, 108.
Smith, Elisha, 124.
Smith, Elisha, 126.
Smith, Elisha, 144.
Smith, Elizabeth, 66.
Smith, Elizabeth, 73.
Smith, Elizabeth, 95.
Smith, Elizabeth, 107.
Smith, Elizabeth, 110.
Smith, Elizer, 67.
Smith, Elkanah, 112.
Smith, Elnathan, 14.
Smith, Elnathan, 33.
Smith, Elnathan, 64.
Smith, Eneas, 94.
Smith, Enoch, 80.
Smith, Enoch, 85.
Smith, Enoch, 94.
Smith, Enoch, Jun', 80.
Smith, Ephraim, 2d, 93.
Smith, **Ephraim,** 66.
Smith, Ephraim, 109.
Smith, Ephraim, 114.
Smith, Ephraim, 129.
Smith, Ephraim, 152.
Smith, **Ephrim,** 93.
Smith, Ephrim 110.
Smith, **Ephrim,** 2d, 93.
Smith, Ethan, 24.
Smith, Eunice (Wd), 24.
Smith, Experience, 134.
Smith, **Ezariah,** 49.
Smith, **Ezekiel,** 24.
Smith, **Ezekiel,** 53.
Smith, **Ezekiel,** 112.
Smith, **Ezekiel,** 126.
Smith, Ezra, 24.
Smith, Ezra, 81.
Smith, Ezra, 140.
Smith, Frances, 47.
Smith, Francis, 151.
Smith, Frederick, 79.
Smith, Frederick, 83.
Smith, Frederick, 145.
Smith, Frien, 64.
Smith, Gabriel, 25.
Smith, George, 46.
Smith, George, 72.
Smith, George, 103.
Smith, George, 105.
Smith, George, 127.
Smith, George, 140.
Smith, George Clark, 72.
Smith, Gideon, 28.
Smith, Gideon, 69.
Smith, Gidian, 60.
Smith, Gilbert, & Son, 119.
Smith, Gould, 25.

Smith, Gould, 105.
Smith, Grace, 134.
Smith, **Grove,** 35.
Smith, Grove, 62.
Smith, Hannah, 42.
Smith, Hannah (Wd), 21.
Smith, Hannah (Wd), 25.
Smith, Harvey, 49.
Smith, Havilah, 61.
Smith, Haziel, 81.
Smith, Heber, 17.
Smith, Heil, 111.
Smith, Heman, 64.
Smith, Heman, 80.
Smith, Henry, 22.
Smith, Henry, 65.
Smith, Henry, 84.
Smith, Henry, 128.
Smith, Henry, 149.
Smith, Hezekiah, 28.
Smith, Hezekiah, 64.
Smith, Hezekiah, 83.
Smith, Hezekiah, 101.
Smith, Hezekiah, 111.
Smith, Hezekiah, 126.
Smith, Heza, 144.
Smith, Hezekiah, 2d, 28.
Smith, **Hubard,** 141.
Smith, **Hubbard,** 83.
Smith, Hugh, 126.
Smith, Huldy, 105.
Smith, Hutton, 21.
Smith, Ichabod, 51.
Smith, Ichabod, 123.
Smith, Ignatious, 83.
Smith, Ira, 97.
Smith, Isaac, 16.
Smith, Isaac, 25.
Smith, Isaac, 43.
Smith, Isaac, 49.
Smith, Isaac, 77.
Smith, Isaac, 81.
Smith, Isaac, 92.
Smith, Isaac, 94.
Smith, Isaac, 101.
Smith, Isaac, 134.
Smith, Isaac, Jun', 81.
Smith, Israel, 52.
Smith, Israel, 70.
Smith, Israel, 84.
Smith, Israel, 93.
Smith, Israel, 104.
Smith, Israel, 111.
Smith, Israel, 150.
Smith, Ithamer, 124.
Smith, Ithomar, 37.
Smith, Jabez, 25.
Smith, Jabez, 28.
Smith, Jabez, 119.
Smith, Jacob, 28.
Smith, Jacob, 59.
Smith, Jacob, 61.
Smith, Jacob, 142.
Smith, Jacob, 145.
Smith, James, 21.
Smith, James, 28.
Smith, James, 43.
Smith, James, 48.
Smith, James, 49.
Smith, James, 51.
Smith, James, 52.
Smith, James, 83.
Smith, James, 87.
Smith, James, 92.
Smith, James, 94.
Smith, James, 106.
Smith, James, 113.
Smith, James, 119.
Smith, James, 128.
Smith, James, 143.
Smith, James, Jun', 119.
Smith, James, 2d, 28.
Smith, James, 3d, 84.
Smith, Jarad, 93.
Smith, Jarus, 142.
Smith, Jeames, 77.
Smith, Jedediah, 42.
Smith, Jeffry, 98.
Smith, Jehiel, 10.
Smith, Jeremiah, 21.
Smith, Jeremiah, 28.
Smith, Jeremiah, 58.
Smith, Jereh, 81.
Smith, Jeremiah, 101.
Smith, Jeremiah, 105.
Smith, Jeremiah, 119.
Smith, Jesse, 24.
Smith, Jesse, 58.
Smith, Jesse, 95.
Smith, Jesse, 105.
Smith, Jesse, 111.
Smith, Jesse, Jun', 24.
Smith, Job, 28.
Smith, Job, 96.
Smith, Job I., 118.
Smith, Joel, 27.
Smith, Joel, 33.
Smith, Joel, 72.
Smith, Joel, 101.
Smith, John, 21.
Smith, John, 24.
Smith, John, 28.

Smith, John, 29.
Smith, John, 31.
Smith, John, 33.
Smith, John, 35.
Smith, John, 35.
Smith, John, 36.
Smith, John, 38.
Smith, John, 42.
Smith, John, 75.
Smith, John, 77.
Smith, John, 83.
Smith, John, 84.
Smith, John, 93.
Smith, John, 94.
Smith, John, 97.
Smith, John, 102.
Smith, John, 104.
Smith, John, 104.
Smith, John, 106.
Smith, John, 110.
Smith, John, 114.
Smith, John, 126.
Smith, John, 127.
Smith, John, 129.
Smith, Jno, 134.
Smith, Jno, 139.
Smith, John, 140.
Smith, John, 140.
Smith, John, 142.
Smith, John, 144.
Smith, John, 151.
Smith, John, Jun', 25.
Smith, John, Jun', 84.
Smith, John, Sen', 144.
Smith, John, 1st, 72.
Smith, John, 2d, 72.
Smith, John, 2d, 75.
Smith, John, 2d, 131.
Smith, John C., 63.
Smith, Jno H., 83.
Smith, John R., 149.
Smith, Jonah, 153.
Smith, Jonaiah, 60.
Smith, Jonathan, 30.
Smith, Jonathan, 42.
Smith, Jonathan, 52.
Smith, Jonathan, 56.
Smith, Jonathan, 79.
Smith, Jonathan, 83.
Smith, Jonathan, 83.
Smith, Jonathan, 112.
Smith, Jonathan, 113.
Smith, Jona, 114.
Smith, Jonathan, 114.
Smith, Jona, 130.
Smith, Jona, 131.
Smith, Jona, 133.
Smith, Jonathan, Jur, 56.
Smith, Jordan, 92.
Smith, Joseph, 10.
Smith, Joseph, 10.
Smith, Joseph, 18.
Smith, Joseph, 18.
Smith, Joseph, 24.
Smith, Joseph, 25.
Smith, Joseph, 33.
Smith, Joseph, 35.
Smith, Joseph, 35.
Smith, Joseph, 36.
Smith, Joseph, 39.
Smith Joseph, 50.
Smith, Joseph, 51.
Smith, Joseph, 52.
Smith, Joseph, 64.
Smith, Joseph, 66.
Smith, Joseph, 84.
Smith, Joseph, 86.
Smith, Joseph, 92.
Smith, Joseph, 96.
Smith, Joseph, 96.
Smith, Joseph, 101.
Smith, Joseph, 102.
Smith, Joseph, 103.
Smith, Joseph, 105.
Smith, Joseph, 105.
Smith, Joseph, 113.
Smith, Joseph, 115.
Smith, Joseph, 123.
Smith, Joseph, 124.
Smith, Joseph, 124.
Smith, Joseph, 125.
Smith, Joseph, 127.
Smith, Joseph, 128.
Smith, Jos., 139.
Smith, Joseph, 144.
Smith, Joseph, Jun', 26.
Smith, Joseph, 2r, 35.
Smith, Joseph, 2nd, 104.
Smith, Joseph, 3d, 10.
Smith, Joseph, 3rd, 103.
Smith, Joseph, 4th, 123.
Smith, Joshua, 25.
Smith, Joshua, 66.
Smith, Joshua, 102.
Smith, Joshua, 118.
Smith, Joshua, 126.
Smith, Joshua, 129.
Smith, Joshua, 2d, 129.
Smith, Joshua, 3d, 130.
Smith, Josiah, 10.
Smith, Josiah, 25.
Smith, Josiah, 30.

Smith, Josiah, 34.
Smith, Josiah, 52.
Smith, Josiah, 61.
Smith, Josiah, 72.
Smith, Josiah, 94.
Smith, Josiah, 124.
Smith, Josiah, 153.
Smith, Josiah, 2d, 93.
Smith, Josiah, 2d, 124.
Smith, Justice, 105.
Smith, Justin, 30.
Smith, King, 126.
Smith, Kinner, 79.
Smith, Lamberton, 112.
Smith, Latham, 123.
Smith, Lemuel, 80.
Smith, Lemuel, 116.
Smith, Levi, 28.
Smith, Levi, 52.
Smith, Levi, 60.
Smith, Levi, 110.
Smith, Lewis, 127.
Smith, Lewis, 84.
Smith, Lidia, 106.
Smith, Louis, 97.
Smith, Lucy, 94.
Smith, Luther, 148.
Smith, Lydia, 40.
Smith, Lydia, 97.
Smith, Mabel, 43.
Smith, Mabel, 97.
Smith, Manoah, 42.
Smith, Manus, 54.
Smith, Martha, 83.
Smith, Martha, 96.
Smith, Martha, 3d, 83.
Smith, Martha (Wd), 24.
Smith, Martha (Wd), 24.
Smith, Martin, 61.
Smith, Martin, 67.
Smith, Mary, 101.
Smith, Mary, 142.
Smith, Mary (Wd), 24.
Smith, Mary (Wd), 25.
Smith, Mathew, 153.
Smith, Matthew, 28.
Smith, Matthew, 70.
Smith, Matthew, 81.
Smith, Matthew, 2d, 81.
Smith, Medad, 51.
Smith, Mercy, 126.
Smith, Michael, Jun', 80.
Smith, Miner, 152.
Smith, Molly (Wd), 25.
Smith, Moses, 36.
Smith, Moses, 47.
Smith, Moses, 59.
Smith, Moses, 75.
Smith, Moses, 120.
Smith, Moses, 134.
Smith, Nathan, 18.
Smith, Nathan, 28.
Smith, Nathan, 94.
Smith, Nathan, 105.
Smith, Nathan, 105.
Smith, Nathan, 111.
Smith, Nathan, 118.
Smith, Nathan, 124.
Smith, Natha, 125.
Smith, Nathan, 2nd, 111.
Smith, Nathanel, 25.
Smith, Nathaniel, 64.
Smith, Nathaniel, 64.
Smith, Nathaniel, 72.
Smith, Nathaniel, 79.
Smith, Nathaniel, 88.
Smith, Nathl, 112.
Smith, Nathl, 122.
Smith, Nathl, 135.
Smith, Nathl, 153.
Smith, Nathel, Jun', 25.
Smith, Nathen, 64.
Smith (Negro), 116.
Smith, Nehamiah, 97.
Smith, Nehamiah, 105.
Smith, Nehemiah, 25.
Smith, Nehemiah, 36.
Smith, Nehemiah, 118.
Smith, Nehemiah, 124.
Smith, Niamiah (Negroe), 112.
Smith, Noah, 22.
Smith, Noah, 22.
Smith, Noah, 80.
Smith, Noah, 1st, 59.
Smith, Noah, 2d, 59.
Smith, Noah Day, 59.
Smith, Nodeah, 62.
Smith, Obadiah, 54.
Smith, Obadiah, 130.
Smith, Oliver, 105.
Smith, Oliver, 117.
Smith, Oliver, 152.
Smith, Patience, 131.
Smith, Paul, 63.
Smith, Paul, 126.
Smith, Paul, 2d, 63.
Smith, Peabody, 74.
Smith, Peter, 13.
Smith, Peter, 23.
Smith, Peter, 24.
Smith, Peter, 80.

Smith, Peter T., 47.
Smith, Phebe, 151.
Smith, Phineas, 35.
Smith, Phineas, 79.
Smith, Phineas, 122.
Smith, Phinehas, 23.
Smith, Phinehas, 28.
Smith, Phinehas, 63.
Smith, Phinehas, 64.
Smith, Phinehas, 84.
Smith, Phlomon, 105.
Smith, Poly Carp, 112.
Smith, Ralp, 80.
Smith, Ralph, 10.
Smith, Ralph, 81.
Smith, Rebecca, 70.
Smith, Reuben, 26.
Smith, Reuben, 61.
Smith, Reuben, 64.
Smith, Reuben, 70.
Smith, Reuben, 77.
Smith, Reuben, 83.
Smith, Reubin, 27.
Smith, Richard, 10.
Smith, Richard, 42.
Smith, Richard, 79.
Smith, Richard, 95.
Smith, Richard, 119.
Smith, Richard, 124.
Smith, Richard, Jun', 119.
Smith, Richard, 2d, 123.
Smith, Robert, 79.
Smith, Robert, 84.
Smith, Roda, 68.
Smith, Roger, 43.
Smith, Roger, 130.
Smith, Roswell, 117.
Smith, Ruama, 64.
Smith, Rufus, 119.
Smith, Russell, 124.
Smith, Sabra, 79.
Smith, Samuel, 11.
Smith, Samuel, 12.
Smith, Samuel, 13.
Smith, Samuel, 23.
Smith, Samuel, 24.
Smith, Samuel, 27.
Smith, Samuel, 33.
Smith, Samuel, 35.
Smith, Samuel, 36.
Smith, Samuel, 38.
Smith, Samuel, 39.
Smith, Samuel, 41.
Smith, Samuel, 43.
Smith, Samuel, 50.
Smith, Samuel, 63.
Smith, Samuel, 63.
Smith, Samuel, 78.
Smith, Samuel, 75.
Smith, Samuel, 79.
Smith, Samuel, 84.
Smith, Samuel, 84.
Smith, Samuel, 95.
Smith, Samuel, 97.
Smith, Samuel, 97.
Smith, Samuel, 98.
Smith, Samuel, 102.
Smith, Samuel, 105.
Smith, Samuel, 113.
Smith, Saml, 118.
Smith, Samuel, 124.
Smith, Samuel, 126.
Smith, Saml, 129.
Smith, Saml, 149.
Smith, Samuel, Jun', 23.
Smith, Samuel, Jr., 35.
Smith, Saml, Jun', 119.
Smith, Samuel, 2d, 42.
Smith, Saml, 2d, 126.
Smith, Saml, 3d, 119.
Smith, Samuel B., 105.
Smith, Sarah, 126.
Smith, Sarah, 130.
Smith, Sarah, 140.
Smith, **Sarah,** 2d, 28.
Smith, **Sarah,** 3d (Ww), 28.
Smith, Sarah (Wd), 21.
Smith, Seth, 32.
Smith, Seth, 51.
Smith, Seth, 61.
Smith, Seth, 67.
Smith, Seth, 68.
Smith, Seth, 115.
Smith, Seth, 124.
Smith, Seymore, 102.
Smith, Sherman, 10.
Smith, Silas, 114.
Smith, Silvanus, 123.
Smith, Simeon, 49.
Smith, Simeon, 120.
Smith, Simeon, 129.
Smith, Simeon, 140.
Smith, Simon, 126.
Smith, Solomon, 25.
Smith, Solomon, 33.
Smith, Solomon, 143.
Smith, Solomon, 148.
Smith, Solomon, Jn', 143.
Smith, Sparrow, 81.
Smith, Stephen, 25.
Smith, Stephen, 28.
Smith, Stephen, 77.
Smith, Stephen, 83.

INDEX. 215

Smith, Stephen, 92.
Smith, Stephen, 97.
Smith, Stephen, 123.
Smith, Stephen, 124.
Smith, Stephen, Junr, 83.
Smith, Susanna, 53.
Smith, Sylvenus, 83.
Smith, Thaddeus, 28.
Smith, Thankfull, 106.
Smith, Theodore, 66.
Smith, Theophelus, 60.
Smith, Theophelus, 2d, 60.
Smith, Thomas, 28.
Smith, Thomas, 41.
Smith, Thomas, 72.
Smith, Thomas, 77.
Smith, Thomas, 79.
Smith, Thos, 81.
Smith, Thomas, 105.
Smith, Thomas, 105.
Smith, Thomas, 106.
Smith, Thomas, 112.
Smith, Thomas, 115.
Smith, Thomas, 124.
Smith, Thomas, 141.
Smith, Thos, 2d, 83.
Smith, Timothy, 80.
Smith, Titus, 93.
Smith, Titus, 105.
Smith, Titus, 111.
Smith, Uriah, 28.
Smith, Uriah, 147.
Smith, Victore, 132.
Smith, Wait, 34.
Smith, Wait, 64.
Smith, Wart, 77.
Smith, Wells, 83.
Smith, Wharam, 105.
Smith, Whitman, 24.
Smith (Widow), 43.
Smith, Willard, 67.
Smith, William, 42.
Smith, William, 50.
Smith, William, 83.
Smith, William, 84.
Smith, William, 93.
Smith, William, 94.
Smith, William, 102.
Smith, William, 107.
Smith, William, 118.
Smith, William, 123.
Smith, Wm, 126.
Smith, William, 141.
Smith, William, 2d, 120.
Smith, Zadock, 124.
Smith, Zalmon, 10.
Smith, Zalmon, 18.
Smith, Zebadiah, 131.
Smith, Zebina, 60.
Smith, Zepheniah, 74.
Smithson, Robert, 96.
Snell, William, 140.
Snell, William, Jnr, 140.
Snow, Abraham, 143.
Snow, Abraham, 145.
Snow, Arunnah, 141.
Snow, Bela, 140.
Snow, Benjn, 140.
Snow, Billarky, 141.
Snow, Ebenezer, 80.
Snow, Ebene, 148.
Snow, Edmond, 90.
Snow, Francis, 146.
Snow, Gideon, 83.
Snow, James, 140.
Snow, John, 84.
Snow, Jonath, 140.
Snow, Joseph, 140.
Snow, Natha, 134.
Snow, Oliver, 140.
Snow, Robert, 141.
Snow, Samuel, 103.
Snow, Saml, Jnr, 140.
Snow, Saml, Senr, 140.
Snow, Simon, 140.
Snow, Stephen, 140.
Snow, Stephen, Jnr, 140.
Snow, Sylvanus, 134.
Snow, Thomas, 153.
Snow, Thomas, 153.
Snow, William, 84.
Snow, William, 140.
Soams, Consider, 150.
Sole, Jonathn, 149.
Solomon (Negro), 117.
Somers, Sylvester, 135.
Sommers, Abel, 2d, 102.
Soper, David, 69.
Soper, Joel, 70.
Soper, John, 127.
Soper, Timothy, 41.
Sorith, Elkany, 50.
Sortune, Mary, 109.
Soughton, Oliver, 77.
Southard, Samuel, 29.
Southard, William, 30.
Southerland, Roger, 16.
Southern, Thomas, 86.
Southland, Beldwin, 60.
Southmayd, Danl, 82.
Southmay'd, Daniel, 96.
Southmayd, Giles, 88.
Southmayd, Jonathan, 86.
Southmayd, Partridge, 88.
Southmayd, Samuel, 77.
Southmayd, William, 85.
Southmayd, William, Junr, 86.
Southward, Andrew, 83.
Southward, Beriah, 145.
Southward, Constant, 147.
Southward, John, 140.
Southward, Joseph, 96.
Southward, Joseph, 147.
Southward, Josiah, 147.
Southward, Nathan, 90.
Southward, Nathan, 2d, 90.
Southward, Nathl, 147.
Southward, Saml, 147.
Southward, William, 153.
Southwell, John, 50.
Southworth, Gideon, 90.
Southworth, Isaac, 90.
Southworth, Martin, 90.
Southworth, Nancy, 90.
Southworth, Willm, 91.
Sowers, Hannah, 95.
Spafford, Abraham, 147.
Spafford, Asa, 152.
Spafford, Eliphalet, 152.
Spafford, Jehiel, 153.
Spafford, Jesse, 147.
Spafford, John, 152.
Spafford, Moses, 152.
Spafford, Nathan, 146.
Spafford, Oliver, 152.
Spafford, Oliver, 153.
Spafford, Pheneas, 152.
Spalden, Barbara, 61.
Spalden, Isaac, 63.
Spalden, Rowland, 14.
Spaldin, Jesse, 148.
Spalding, Abel, 141.
Spalding, Amos, 143.
Spalding, Andrew, 148.
Spalding, Asa, 116.
Spalding, Asa, 131.
Spalding, Asial, 69.
Spalding, Azariah, 148.
Spalding, Benjn, 143.
Spalding, Caleb, 141.
Spalding, Danl, 148.
Spalding, Davis, 143.
Spalding, Ebenr, 141.
Spalding, Ephraim, 141.
Spalding, Ezekiel, 142.
Spalding, Ezra, 148.
Spalding Heza, 148.
Spalding, Jacob, 67.
Spalding, Jacob, 142.
Spalding, James, 153.
Spalding, John, 69.
Spalding, John, 103.
Spalding, Jonas, 79.
Spalding, Jonathn, 148.
Spalding, Joseph, 148.
Spalding, Josiah, 140.
Spalding, Miner, 149.
Spalding, Nathl, 143.
Spalding, Obedh, 144.
Spalding, Oliver, 79.
Spalding, Pearl, 142.
Spalding, Phillip, 148.
Spalding, Reubin, 148.
Spalding, Reubin, 149.
Spalding, Saml, 148.
Spalding, Saml, 151.
Spalding, Silas, 144.
Spalding, Simon, 143.
Spalding, Stephen, 148.
Spalding, Thos, 142.
Spalding, Zadock, 143.
Spaldwin, Edward, 62.
Spargo, Edward, 117.
Sparkes, Jos., 139.
Sparks, Jno, 132.
Sparks, Reuben, 43.
Sparks, Thomas, 43.
Sparrow, Deborah, 82.
Sparrow, Nathl, 82.
Spary, Elijah, 51.
Spearks, Isaiah, 140.
Spearks, John, 144.
Spearks, Lemuel, 143.
Spearks, Saml, 144.
Spears, Asabel, 51.
Spears, Mary, 154.
Spears, Moses, 51.
Spears, Wm, 134.
Spelman, David, 68.
Spelman, Elizabeth, 96.
Spelman, Rohda, 96.
Spence, Deborah, 128.
Spence, Joshua, 151.
Spence, Silas, 143.
Spencer, Abigail, 81.
Spencer, Abigail, 83.
Spencer, Abigail, 84.
Spencer, Abner, 83.
Spencer, Amasah, 82.
Spencer, Ansel, 111.
Spencer, Asahel, 66.
Spencer, Ashbel, 46.
Spencer, Augustus, 51.
Spencer, Benjamin, 46.
Spencer, Caleb, 48.
Spencer, Caleb, 90.
Spencer, Caleb, 118.
Spencer, Calvin, 124.
Spencer, Christopher, 98.
Spencer, Culver, 110.
Spencer, Daniel, 51.
Spencer, Daniel, 84.
Spencer, Daniel, 90.
Spencer, Dan., 91.
Spencer, David, 81.
Spencer, David, 83.
Spencer, David, 143.
Spencer, David, 152.
Spencer, David B., 81.
Spencer, Deborah, 90.
Spencer, Ebenezer, 44.
Spencer, Ebenezer, 82.
Spencer, Ebenr, 138.
Spencer, Eber, 136.
Spencer, Elia, 84.
Spencer, Elihu, 51.
Spencer, Elihu, 84.
Spencer, Eliphalet, 50.
Spencer, Eliphas, 62.
Spencer, Elisha, 51.
Spencer, Elisha, 84.
Spencer, Elizabeth, 86.
Spencer, Elizur, 83.
Spencer, Epaphras, 46.
Spencer, Ephraim, 71.
Spencer, Gideon, 36.
Spencer, Gideon, 81.
Spencer, Gideon, Jr, 36.
Spencer, Hannah, 82.
Spencer, Henry, 109.
Spencer, Hezekiah, 51.
Spencer, Hezekiah, 136.
Spencer, Hez., Jr., 136.
Spencer, Ichabod, 89.
Spencer, Ichabod, 122.
Spencer, Isaac, 82.
Spencer, Isaac, Jur, Esqr, 82.
Spencer, Isrl, 136.
Spencer, Israel, Esqr, 82.
Spencer, Jabez, 100.
Spencer, James, 83.
Spencer, Jared, 35.
Spencer, Jared, Esqr, 82.
Spencer, Jared W., 81.
Spencer, Jeduthan, 152.
Spencer, Job, 62.
Spencer, Job, 2d, 62.
Spencer, Joel, 82.
Spencer, Joel, 94.
Spencer, John, 36.
Spencer, John, 36.
Spencer, John, 51.
Spencer, John, 84.
Spencer, John, 85.
Spencer, John, 96.
Spencer, John, 106.
Spencer, John, 117.
Spencer, John, Jr., 46.
Spencer, Jonathan, 81.
Spencer, Jona, 136.
Spencer, Joseph, 35.
Spencer, Joseph, 84.
Spencer, Joseph, 90.
Spencer, Joseph, 2d, 90.
Spencer, Juda, 81.
Spencer, Lina, 46.
Spencer, Mark, 97.
Spencer, Mary, 81.
Spencer, Matthias, 82.
Spencer, Michael, 46.
Spencer, Michael, 91.
Spencer, Miney, 97.
Spencer, Nathaniel, 102.
Spencer, Obedh, 136.
Spencer, Peter, 90.
Spencer, Peter, 145.
Spencer, Rebeca, 51.
Spencer, Reuben, 51.
Spencer, Reuben, 82.
Spencer, Reuben, 82.
Spencer, Roger, 96.
Spencer, Roswell, 48.
Spencer, Samuel, 18.
Spencer, Samuel, 51.
Spencer, Samuel, 60.
Spencer, Samuel, 88.
Spencer, Samuel, 152.
Spencer, Sarah, 81.
Spencer, Sarah, 83.
Spencer, Seldon, 82.
Spencer, Seldon, 93.
Spencer, Silas, 58.
Spencer, Silas, 81.
Spencer, Simeon, 51.
Spencer, Simeon, 81.
Spencer, Solomon, 81.
Spencer, Stephen, 84.
Spencer, Stephen, 96.
Spencer, Theadore, 46.
Spencer, Thomas, 37.
Spencer, Thomas, 46.
Spencer, Thomas, 68.
Spencer, Thomas, Jr., 37.
Spencer, Timothy, 46.
Spencer, Timo, 82.
Spencer, Timo, 132.
Spencer, Toby, 90.
Spencer, Uriah, 97.
Spencer, William, 60.
Spencer, Wm, 83.
Spencer, William, 84.
Spencer, Willm, 90.
Spencer, Wo, 91.
Spencer, Zachariah, 81.
Spencer, Zacheus, 60.
Spener, George, 151.
Spenscer, Aseph, 68.
Spenser, Ashbel, 70.
Spensor, Abel, 66.
Spensor, Alexander, 63.
Spensor, Elisha, 66.
Spensor, Frederick, 68.
Spensor, Hezekiah, 63.
Spensor, James, 70.
Spensor, Jessee, 61.
Spensor, John, 70.
Spensor, Jonah, 68.
Spensor, Michael, 70.
Spensor, Nathaniel, 70.
Spensor, Samuel, 61.
Spensor, Stephen, 66.
Spensor, Thomas, 62.
Spensor, Thomas, 63.
Spercy, Allen, 68.
Sperry, Alexander, 72.
Sperry, Alexander, 74.
Sperry, Ambrose, 74.
Sperry, Amie, 111.
Sperry, Amie, 112.
Sperry, Amos, 111.
Sperry, Asa, 111.
Sperry, Asa, 111.
Sperry, Benjamin, 12.
Sperry, Benjamin, 93.
Sperry, Caleb, 111.
Sperry, Charles, 61.
Sperry, Darius, 63.
Sperry, David, 111.
Sperry, Demas, 112.
Sperry, Ebeneza, 58.
Sperry, Ebenezer, 111.
Sperry, Eber, 104.
Sperry, Edon, 105.
Sperry, Elam, 112.
Sperry, Eliakim, 111.
Sperry, Elijah, 54.
Sperry, Elizabeth, 112.
Sperry, Ezra, 112.
Sperry, Ezra, 2nd, 112.
Sperry, Hezekiah, 112.
Sperry, Isaac, 111.
Sperry, Jacob, 110.
Sperry, James, 111.
Sperry, Jared, 72.
Sperry, Jesse, 110.
Sperry, Job, 94.
Sperry, Job, 111.
Sperry, Joel, 111.
Sperry, John, 72.
Sperry, John, 100.
Sperry, Jonathan, 95.
Sperry, Joseph, 94.
Sperry, Joseph, 105.
Sperry, Lemuel, 77.
Sperry, Lent, 111.
Sperry, Levi, 105.
Sperry, Lidia, 111.
Sperry, Lois, 111.
Sperry, N., 112.
Sperry, Nathaniel, 111.
Sperry, Richard, 111.
Sperry, Rohda, 94.
Sperry, Ruben, 112.
Sperry, Samuel, 111.
Sperry, Samuel, 111.
Sperry, Simeon, 111.
Sperry, Thomas, 111.
Sperry, William, 105.
Spicer, Able, 115.
Spicer, Amos, 118.
Spicer, Asa, 114.
Spicer, Asher, 99.
Spicer, Daniel, 114.
Spicer, Edward, 118.
Spicer, Edward, Junr, 118.
Spicer, Elderkin, 126.
Spicer, John, 118.
Spicer, Joshua, 131.
Spicer, Oliver, 114.
Spicer, Oliver, 118.
Spicer, Sarah, 118.
Spicer, Silas, 118.
Spicer, William, 120.
Spiner, Elijah, 142.
Spinish, Nathaniel, 98.
Spink, Asa, 125.
Spinks, Richard, 91.
Spony, Elizabeth, 109.
Spooner, Ebenezer, 59.
Spooner, Ebenezer, 74.
Spooner, George, 86.
Spooner, John, 74.
Spooner, Nathaniel, 74.
Spooner, William, 74.
Spooner, William, 2d, 74.
Sprage, Lucy, 128.
Spragg, Joseph, 14.
Sprague, Benjn, 144.
Sprague, Dan., 146.
Sprague, Danl, 143.
Sprague, Elisha, 134.
Sprague, Jame, 139.
Sprague, John, 143.
Sprague, John, 154.
Sprague, Jonathan, 61.
Sprague, Perez, 133.
Sprague, Saml., 134.
Sprague, Saml, Jr., 134.
Sprague, Simeon, 61.
Sprague, Thos., 138.
Sprats, William, 65.
Spring, Ebenezer, 35.
Spring, Samuel, 73.
Spring, Saml, 141.
Spring, Silvester, 44.
Spring, Silvester, 44.
Spring, Thomas, 44.
Spring, Timothy, 34.
Springer, John, 128.
Squeer, Seely, 23.
Squier, John, 128.
Squire, Abiather, 96.
Squire, Abijah, 57.
Squire, Ambrose, 96.
Squire, Amos, 79.
Squire, Arel, 31.
Squire, Asher, 96.
Squire, Benjamin, 14.
Squire, Benjamin, 79.
Squire, Clement, 65.
Squire, Daniel, 14.
Squire, Daniel, 38.
Squire, Daniel, 74.
Squire, Danl, 138.
Squire, David, 14.
Squire, David, 74.
Squire, Ebenezer, 14.
Squire, Ebenezer, 72.
Squire, Ebenezer, 96.
Squire, Elias, 34.
Squire, Ephraim, 140.
Squire, George, 14.
Squire, Jessee, 62.
Squire, John, 14.
Squire, John, 54.
Squire, John, 2d, 74.
Squire, Joseph, 14.
Squire, Joseph, 72.
Squire, Joseph, 74.
Squire, Josiah, 126.
Squire, Justice, 59.
Squire, Nathan, 79.
Squire, Phineas, 96.
Squire, Samuel, 14.
Squire, Samuel, 96.
Squire, Samuel, Jnr, 14.
Squire, Sealy, 32.
Squire, Seth, 12.
Squire, Seth, 27.
Squire, Seth, 31.
Squire, Solomon, 33.
Squire, Stephen, 31.
Squire, Stephen, 74.
Squire, Thadeus, 96.
Squire, Thomas, 32.
Squire, Thomas, 79.
Squire, Thomas, 2d, 79.
Squire, William, 14.
Squire, William, 20.
Squires, Ezekiel, 38.
Squires, Samuel, 50.
Squre, Hulda, 63.
Stacey, Samuel, 64.
Stackhouse, Stacy, 46.
Stacy, Rebecca, 129.
Stafford, Andrew, 115.
Stafford, John, 69.
Stales, Adam, 117.
Stalief, Joseph, 110.
Stalief, Joseph, 2nd, 110.
Stalker, Anne, 11.
Stanard, Abel, 66.
Stanbury, John, 151.
Standish, Amasa, 114.
Standish, Israel, 114.
Standish, Israel, 118.
Standish, James, 53.
Standish, Jeremiah, 43.
Standish, John, 53.
Standish, Levi, 114.
Standish, Nathan, 114.
Standish, Saml, 115.
Standley, Elisha, 70.
Standley, Jessee, 69.
Standley, Joseph, 12.
Standley, Moses, 133.
Standley, Samuel, 41.
Standley, Samuel, Jr., 41.
Standley, Timothy, 60.
Standley, Timothy, 70.
Standley, William, 69.
Staniford, John, 152.
Stanley, Aaron, 68.
Stanley, Abraham, 108.
Stanley, Allyn, 47.
Stanley, Amaziah, 47.
Stanley, Anna (Wid.), 47.
Stanley, Benjamin, 39.
Stanley, Comfort, 60.
Stanley, Comfort, 60.
Stanley, Elijah, 33.
Stanley, Frederic, 46.
Stanley, Fredrick, 152.
Stanley, Gad, 33.
Stanley, George, 52.

216 INDEX.


Stanley, Hannah (Wid.), 47.
Stanley, James, 47.
Stanley, James, 53.
Stanley, Jeremh, 140.
Stanley, John, 33.
Stanley, Jno, 138.
Stanley, Jonathan, 36.
Stanley, Lott, 33.
Stanley, Martha, 33.
Stanley, Nathan, 67.
Stanley, Noadiah, 47.
Stanley, Noah, 33.
Stanley, Oliver, 33.
Stanley, Oliver, 108.
Stanley, Roswell, 46.
Stanley, Rufus, 60.
Stanley, Ruth, 33.
Stanley, Selah, 77.
Stanley, Seth, 33.
Stanley, Seth, 34.
Stanley, Timothy, 33.
Stanley, Whiting, 93.
Stanlif, Jeames, 74.
Stanlif, Saml, 68.
Stanly, Caleb, 133.
Stanly, Theodore, 36.
Stannard, Abner, 90.
Stannard, Elias, 99.
Stannard, Ephraim, 90.
Stannard, Ezra, 67.
Stannard, Jasper, 90.
Stannard, Job, 90.
Stannard, Jno, 90.
Stannard, Jno, 2d, 90.
Stannard, Joseph, 90.
Stannard, Josiah, 90.
Stannard, Nathan, 90.
Stannard, Peter, 90.
Stannard, Samuel, 67.
Stannard, Samuel, 84.
Stannard, Seth, 64.
Stannard, Temperance, 90.
Stannard, Wm, 90.
Stantliff, James, Junr, 80.
Stanton, Adam, 85.
Stanton, Amon, Sr., 142.
Stanton, Azariah, 118.
Stanton, Daniel, 98.
Stanton, Danl, 116.
Stanton, David, 113.
Stanton, David, Junr, 113.
Stanton, Ebenr, 118.
Stanton, Eli, 117.
Stanton, Elijah, 69.
Stanton, Isaac, 118.
Stanton, Jabez, 113.
Stanton, Jabez, 113.
Stanton, Jesse, 117.
Stanton, Job, 117.
Stanton, John, 98.
Stanton, John, 117.
Stanton, John, 120.
Stanton, John, 125.
Stanton, Joseph, 120.
Stanton, Joseph, 151.
Stanton, Joshua, 63.
Stanton, Joshua, 116.
Stanton, Nathan, 113.
Stanton, Nathan, 114.
Stanton, Nathan, 117.
Stanton, Peleg, 117.
Stanton, Prudence, 118.
Stanton, Robart, 113.
Stanton, Robart, 116.
Stanton, Robart, Junr, 113.
Stanton, Robt, 137.
Stanton, Saml, 113.
Stanton, Samuel, 118.
Stanton, Saml, 118.
Stanton, Saml, 139.
Stanton, Saml, 3d, 116.
Stanton, Sarah, 59.
Stanton, Thankfull, 118.
Stanton, Thomas, 117.
Stanton, Thomas, 117.
Stanton, Thomas, 141.
Stanton, Thomas, Junr, 117.
Stanton, Wait, 116.
Stanton, William, 65.
Stanton, William, 113.
Stanton, William, 116.
Stanton, William, 117.
Stanton, William, 117.
Stanton, William, 3d, 117.
Stanton, Zebulun, 118.
Staples, Abel, 141.
Staples, Benjamin, 121.
Staples, Elijah, 121.
Staples, Elijah, Junr, 121.
Staples, John, 13.
Staples, John, 120.
Staples, John, 142.
Staples, Samuel, 31.
Staples, Thomas, 14.
Staples, Thomas, 14.
Staplin, Edward, 127.
Star, Eward, 27.
Stark, Abiel, 145.
Stark, Benjamin, 129.
Stark, Daniel, Junr, 119.
Stark, Samuel, 123.
Stark, Silas, 121.
Stark, Solomon, 119.
Stark, William, 129.
Starkey, Charles, 89.
Starkey, John, 89.
Starkey, Noah, 89.
Starkey, Timothy, Esqr, 90.
Starkey, Willm, 89.
Starks, Daniel, 94.
Starks, Ebenezar, 39.
Starks, Ichabod, 35.
Starks, Ichabod, Jr., 35.
Starkweather, Athur, 115.
Starkweather, Benajah, 39.
Starkweather, Charles, 115.
Starkweather, Elijah, 144.
Starkweather, Ephraim, 113.
Starkweather, Jekey, 148.
Starkweather, Jesse, 114.
Starkweather, John, 115.
Starkweather, Joseph, 113.
Starkweather, Richard, 114.
Starkweather, Robert, 115.
Starkweather, Thomas, 39.
Starlin, Abijah, 29.
Starlin, Ephraim, 30.
Starlin, Jacob, 21.
Starlin, Simon, 82.
Starlin, Stephen, 29.
Starlin, Stephen, Jur, 29.
Starling, Daniel, 21.
Starling, David, 21.
Starling, Elijah, 29.
Starling, John, 69.
Starling, Samuel, 21.
Starling, Samuel, Jr, 21.
Starling, William, 21.
Starling, William, Jr, 21.
Starns, Levi, 39.
Starr, Abigail, 130.
Starr, Anna, 86.
Starr, Calep, 11.
Starr, Cloe, 86.
Starr, Daniel, 65.
Starr, Daniel, 87.
Starr, David, 27.
Starr, David, 87.
Starr, David, Junr, 27.
Starr, Ebenr, 150.
Starr, Eliakam, 12.
Starr, Elihu, Esqr, 85.
Starr, Elijah, 10.
Starr, Ephraim, 70.
Starr, Ethel, 10.
Starr, Ezra, 12.
Starr, George, 85.
Starr, Giddeon, 10.
Starr, Jabes, 11.
Starr, James, 10.
Starr, James, 86.
Starr, Jared, 128.
Starr, Jehosaphat, 87.
Starr, Jehosaphat, Junr, 86.
Starr, Jesse, 119.
Starr, John, 10.
Starr, John, 42.
Starr, John, 98.
Starr, John, 119.
Starr, Jonathan, 12.
Starr, Jonathan, 12.
Starr, Jonathan, 128.
Starr, Jona, 130.
Starr, Jonathan, Junr, 128.
Starr, Joseph, 10.
Starr, Joseph, 12.
Starr, Joseph, 86.
Starr, Joseph, 119.
Starr, Joseph, Jur, 12.
Starr, Joseph, 3d, 86.
Starr, Joshua, 128.
Starr, Josiah, 12.
Starr, Josiah, 72.
Starr, Josiah, 86.
Starr, Levi, 27.
Starr, Lucy, 128.
Starr, Mathew, 12.
Starr, Mijah, 27.
Starr, Nathan, 12.
Starr, Nathan, 86.
Starr, Nathanel, 10.
Starr, Capt Nathanel, 24.
Starr, Peter, 29.
Starr, Peter, 74.
Starr, Platt, 74.
Starr, Rachel, 11.
Starr, Rebekah, 11.
Starr, Robbin, 73.
Starr, Samuel, 12.
Starr, Samuel, 86.
Starr, Samuel, Junr, 86.
Starr, Sarah, 28.
Starr, Thaddeus, 12.
Starr, Thomas, 10.
Starr, Thomas, 27.
Starr, Thomas, 86.
Starr, Thomas, 119.
Starr, Thomas, Jnr, 11.
Starr, Thomas, Junr, 86.
Starr, Timothy, 85.
Starr, Timothy, Junr, 86.
Starr, Vim, 86.
Starr, Vine, 119.
Starr, William, 86.
Starr, William, 98.
Starr, William, 119.
Starr, William, Junr, 86.
Starr, Zadock, 12.
Starr, Zarr, 10.
Starry, Nathan, 106.
Starry, Oliver, 118.
Start, Daniel, 119.
Start, Ebenr, 120.
Starter, James, 47.
State, Thomas, 37.
Stead, John, 57.
Steadman, Benjamin, 120.
Steadman, John, 120.
Steadman, Sarah, 118.
Steark, Joshua, 145.
Steark, Nathan, 145.
Stearkweather, Bilchar, 142.
Stearkweather, Joel, 147.
Stearkweather, Nathan, 145.
Stearkweather, Nathl, 145.
Stearn, Boas, 148.
Stearns, Boaz, 143.
Stearns, Elias, 143.
Stearns, Jos., 138.
Stearns, Roswill, 146.
Stearns, Saml, 143.
Stearns (Widow), 138.
Stebbens, Uriah, 105.
Stebbin, Jonathan, 36.
Stebbins, Ann, 28.
Stebbins, Benjamin, 28.
Stebbins, Ebenezer, 28.
Stebbins, Edward, 124.
Stebbins, Jabez, 124.
Stebbins, John, 127.
Stebbins, John, 2d, 127.
Stebbins, Joseph, 28.
Stebbins, Joseph, 53.
Stebbins, Joseph, 127.
Stebbins, Lucy, 129.
Stebbins, Samuel, 28.
Stebbins, Thomas, 140.
Stebens, Benony, 91.
Stebens, Stephen, 30.
Stebins, Revd Samuel, 48.
Stedman, Charles, Jr., 33.
Stedman, Comfort, 37.
Stedman, Elizabeth, 40.
Stedman, Hannah, 143.
Stedman, Harry, 152.
Stedman, John, 33.
Stedman, Lemuel, 35.
Stedman, Nathan, 37.
Stedman, Sarah, 92.
Stedman, Sarah, 93.
Stedman, Selah, 50.
Stedman, Stephen, 39.
Stedman, Stephen, Jr., 39.
Stedman, Thomas, 33.
Stedman, Thos, 143.
Stedman, Thos, Jnr, 143.
Stedman, Timothy, 37.
Stedwell, Gilbert, 19.
Stedwell, Roger, 19.
Steel, Ashbel, 77.
Steel, Ashbel, 138.
Steel, Bradford, 95.
Steel, Bradford, 2nd, 95.
Steel, Daniel, 56.
Steel, Elezer, 138.
Steel, Elezr, Jr, 138.
Steel, Elijah, 77.
Steel, Elijah, 1st, 57.
Steel, Elijah, 2d, 57.
Steel, Elisha, 56.
Steel, Elisha, 95.
Steel, Isaac, 69.
Steel, James, 55.
Steel, James, 134.
Steel, John, 56.
Steel, Jno, 138.
Steel, John, 2d, 56.
Steel, Mary, 59.
Steel, Mathew M., 57.
Steel, Perez, 138.
Steel, Samuel, 77.
Steel, Stephen, 138.
Steel, William, 67.
Steele, Aaron, 47.
Steele, Allyn, 47.
Steele, David, 34.
Steele, Ebenezer, 33.
Steele, Ebenezer, 33.
Steele, Ebenezer, 47.
Steele, Ebizur, 35.
Steele, Frederic, 47.
Steele, James, 47.
Steele, James, Jr., 47.
Steele, Joel, 47.
Steele, John, 47.
Steele, Jonathan, 47.
Steele, Joseph, 54.
Steele, Josiah, 33.
Steele, Lemuel, 47.
Steele, Moses, 47.
Steele, Rachel (Wid.), 47.
Steele, Selah, 33.
Steele, Thomas, 46.
Steele, Timothy, 47.
Steele, William, 33.
Steephens, David, 105.
Steephens, Jesse, 105.
Step (Negro), 126.
Stephans, Simeon, 63.
Stephen, Benjamin, 66.
Stephen, John, 63.
Stephen, Nathaniel, 57.
Stephen, Nathaniel, 66.
Stephen, Simeon, 67.
Stephen, Zebulon, 66.
Stephens, Aaron, 60.
Stephens, Aaron, 84.
Stephens, Aaron, 149.
Stephens, Abel, 62.
Stephens, Abel, 63.
Stephens, Abijah, 65.
Stephens, Ager, 10.
Stephens, Amos, 19.
Stephens, Amos, 90.
Stephens, Andrew, 66.
Stephens, Ashael, 106.
Stephens, Benjamin, 18.
Stephens, Cypian, 143.
Stephens, Daniel, 10.
Stephens, Daniel, 19.
Stephens, Daniel, 61.
Stephens, Ebenezer, 19.
Stephens, Ebenezer, 64.
Stephens, Eden, 10.
Stephens, Edmond, 44.
Stephens, Eli, 18.
Stephens, Eliakim, 84.
Stephens, Elias, 85.
Stephens, Elijah, 11.
Stephens, Eliphilet, 11.
Stephens, Eliphilet, 18.
Stephens, Ezra, 11.
Stephens, Ezra, Jnr, 11.
Stephens, Forward, 11.
Stephens, Henry, 67.
Stephens, Heny, 134.
Stephens, Hezekiah, 10.
Stephens, Hezekiah, Jur, 10.
Stephens, Israel, 19.
Stephens, James, 11.
Stephens, James, 63.
Stephens, Joel, 64.
Stephens, John, 10.
Stephens, John, 112.
Stephens, John, 141.
Stephens, Jonathan, 11.
Stephens, Joseph, 19.
Stephens, Joshua, 10.
Stephens, Joshua, 35.
Stephens, Joshua, 58.
Stephens, Josiah, 10.
Stephens, Levi, 112.
Stephens, Lois, 84.
Stephens, Moses, 112.
Stephens, Nathan, 67.
Stephens, Nathanl, 149.
Stephens, Oliver, 67.
Stephens, Peter, 84.
Stephens, Phinias, 44.
Stephens, Reubin, 19.
Stephens, Roswell, 63.
Stephens, Roswell, 63.
Stephens, Samuel, 11.
Stephens, Samuel, 60.
Stephens, Saml, 63.
Stephens, Saml, 90.
Stephens, Samuel, Junr, 84.
Stephens, Sarah, 117.
Stephens, Simon, 151.
Stephens, Stafford, 67.
Stephens, Thomas, 44.
Stephens, Thomas, 1st, 11.
Stephens, Thomas, 2d, 11.
Stephens, William, 50.
Stephens, William, 130.
Stephens, Zebulon, 67.
Stephensen, John, 108.
Stephenson, Stephen, 19.
Stephenson, Thomas, 105.
Sterling, Betsy, 123.
Sterling, Elisha, 70.
Sterling, Jacob, 123.
Sterling, John, 123.
Sterling, Samuel, 123.
Sterling, Thaddeus, 22.
Sterling, William, 123.
Stern, Nathl, 148.
Sterns, Daniel, 141.
Stersy, Abigail, 115.
Stersy, Consider, 115.
Stertin, Jeames, 57.
Stevans, John, 105.
Stevans, Leveret, 104.
Stevans, Thomas, Junr, 85.
Stevens, Aaron, 90.
Stevens, Abner, 26.
Stevens, Abraham, 26.
Stevens, Adams, 142.
Stevens, Admer, 26.
Stevens, Amos, 26.
Stevens, Amos Junr, 26.
Stevens, Daniel, 26.
Stevens, Dan., 56.
Stevens, David, 26.
Stevens, Elijah, 42.
Stevens, Elijah, 91.
Stevens, Elijah, 110.
Stevens, Eliphalet, 101.
Stevens, Elnathan, 85.
Stevens, George, 42.
Stevens, Hannah (Wd), 26.
Stevens, Henry, 26.
Stevens, Hepsibah, Sr., 148.
Stevens, Hubbell, 84.
Stevens, Isaac, 26.
Stevens, Isaac, 52.
Stevens, Jacob, 26.
Stevens, James, 25.
Stevens, James, 42.
Stevens, Jane, 85.
Stevens, Jared, 85.
Stevens, Jeduthan, 148.
Stevens, Jeremiah, 85.
Stevens, John, 26.
Stevens, Jonas, 85.
Stevens, Jonathan, 26.
Stevens, Joseph, 26.
Stevens, Joseph, Jr, 26.
Stevens, Josiah, 42.
Stevens, Leml, 149.
Stevens, Nathan, 29.
Stevens, Nathan, 110.
Stevens, Nathaniel, 85.
Stevens, Nathaniel, 99.
Stevens, Nathaniel, 2nd, 99.
Stevens, Obadiah, 26.
Stevens, Oliver, 144.
Stevens, Peter, 42.
Stevens, Phillip, 85.
Stevens, Rebecca, 85.
Stevens, Reuben, 26.
Stevens, Reuben, 85.
Stevens, Robert, 142.
Stevens, Samuel, 84.
Stevens, Samuel, 97.
Stevens, Sarah (Wd), 26.
Stevens, Seth, 26.
Stevens, Solomon, 26.
Stevens, Thomas, 42.
Stevens, Thomas, 85.
Stevens, Thomas, 96.
Stevens, Thomas, 102.
Stevens, Timothy, 42.
Stevens, Timothy, 99.
Stevens, Willard, 92.
Stevens, William, 42.
Stevens, Zachariah, 29.
Stevenson, Jeames, 59.
Steward, Alexander, 10.
Steward, Charles, 32.
Steward, James, 10.
Steward, John, 102.
Steward, Sylvanus, 19.
Stewart, Alexander, 19.
Stewart, Alexander, Jur, 19.
Stewart, Benja, 82.
Stewart, Daniel, 57.
Stewart, Daniel, 80.
Stewart, Elihue, 19.
Stewart, John, 28.
Stewart, John, 57.
Stewart, John, 82.
Stewart, Jno, 135.
Stewart, John, 151.
Stewart, Joseph, 57.
Stewart, Joseph, 82.
Stewart, Michael, 80.
Stewart, Nathan, 70.
Stewart, Nathaniel, 72.
Stewart, Oliver, 57.
Stewart, Robert, 59.
Stewart, Robert, 80.
Stewart, Saml, 82.
Stewart, Saml, 147.
Stewart, Silas, 59.
Stewart, Stephen, 57.
Stewart, Stephen, 72.
Stewart, Thomas, 147.
Stewart, Wm, 82.
Stewart, William, 128.
Stewart, Wm, 2d, 82.
Stibbins, Enos, 37.
Stiles, Aaron, 135.
Stiles, Amos, 151.
Stiles, Asahel, 38.
Stiles, Ashbel, 54.
Stiles, Benjamin, 73.
Stiles, Benjamin, 2d, 73.
Stiles, Benjamin, 145.
Stiles, Benoni, 38.
Stiles, Chauncey, 51.
Stiles, Clarke, 106.
Stiles, Dan., 95.
Stiles, David, 56.
Stiles, David, 73.
Stiles, Ephraim, 73.
Stiles, Revd Ezra, 104.
Stiles, Galo, 139.
Stiles, Isaac, 73.
Stiles, Israel, 38.
Stiles, Job, 54.
Stiles, Jno, 134.
Stiles, Nathan, 73.
Stiles, Noah, 38.
Stiles, Robert, 33.
Stiles, Samuel, 38.
Stiles, Samuel, 54.
Stiles, Saml, 68.
Stiles, Samuel, 73.
Stiles, Stephen, 135.
Stiles, Truman, 73.
Stillman, Allyn, 52.
Stillman, Allyn, Jr., 53.
Stillman, David, 47.
Stillman, George, 84.

INDEX. 217


Stillman, William, 53.
Stillwell, Mary, 104.
Stilman, Amos, 35.
Stilman, Appleton, 64.
Stilman, Ashbel, 102.
Stilman, Benjamin, 102.
Stilman, Charles, 90.
Stilman, Elisha, 52.
Stilman, Joseph, 52.
Stilman, Nathaniel, 53.
Stilman, Natha, Jr., 53.
Stilman, Robert, 64.
Stilman, Roger, 64.
Stilman, Samuel, 52.
Stilman, Saml, 89.
Stilman, Zeporah, 114.
Stilson, Aaron, 21.
Stilson, Abel, 21.
Stilson, Abel, 56.
Stilson, Amos, 77.
Stilson, Bailey, 20.
Stilson, Benjamin, 20.
Stilson, Eli, 75.
Stilson, Elnathan, 21.
Stilson, George, 74.
Stilson, Israel, 20.
Stilson, Jacob, 20.
Stilson, John, 72.
Stilson, Jonathan, 20.
Stilson, Joseph, 56.
Stilson, Josiah, 56.
Stilson, Nathan, 72.
Stilson, Nehemiah, 20.
Stilson, Revinus, 72.
Stilson, Thomas, 21.
Stilson, Truman, 72.
Stilson, Vincent, 21.
Stilwell, Elias, 103.
Stimel, John, 128.
Stimpson, Stephen, 138.
Stimpson, Thos, 138.
Stint, Elizus, 91.
Stiveson, Abner, 51.
Stock, Moses, 91.
Stocker, Mary, 32.
Stocker, Thadeus, 66.
Stockin, John, 33.
Stockin, Luther, 33.
Stocking, Abner, 80.
Stocking, Amasa, 80.
Stocking, Ansel, 42.
Stocking, Benjamin, 80.
Stocking, David, 80.
Stocking, David, 81.
Stocking, Daniel, 87.
Stocking, Elisha, 42.
Stocking, Ellis, 83.
Stocking, John, 80.
Stocking, Jozeb, 87.
Stocking, Marshall, 80.
Stocking, Moses, 80.
Stocking, Reuben, 80.
Stocking, Samuel, 88.
Stocking, Seth, 88.
Stocking, William, 87.
Stockman, Jacob, 128.
Stockwell, Elisabeth, 131.
Stockwell, Israel, 150.
Stockwell, Peter, 150.
Stockwell, Reuben, 39.
Stockwell, Robert, 16.
Stodard, Daniel, 64.
Stodard, Danl, 118.
Stodard, David, 64.
Stodard, Deborah, 118.
Stodard, Elisha, 120.
Stodard, Ichabod, 118.
Stodard, Increase, 120.
Stodard, James, 65.
Stodard, James, 118.
Stodard, James, Junr, 118.
Stodard, Jonathan, 118.
Stodard, Joseph, 54.
Stodard, Margarett, 118.
Stodard, Mark, 118.
Stodard, Mary, 64.
Stodard, Mortimer, 114.
Stodard, Ralph, 119.
Stodard, Ralph, Junr, 118.
Stodard, Robart, 118.
Stodard, Robart, Junr, 118.
Stodard, Silas, 119.
Stodard, Tabitha, 119.
Stodard, Vine, 119.
Stodard, Wait, 119.
Stodard, William, 121.
Stoddard, Briant, 70.
Stoddard, Curtis, 56.
Stoddard, Cyreamus, 74.
Stoddard, Daniel, 79.
Stoddard, David, 54.
Stoddard, David, 79.
Stoddard, David, 2d, 79.
Stoddard, Dorothy, 54.
Stoddard, Ebenezar, 42.
Stoddard, Ebenezer, 53.
Stoddard, Ebenezer, 65.
Stoddard, Ebene, 154.
Stoddard, Elisha, 56.
Stoddard, Elisha, 79.
Stoddard, Epephras, 53.
Stoddard, Eunice, 79.
Stoddard, Giddeon, 56.
Stoddard, Gideon, 79.
Stoddard, Ichabod, 79.
Stoddard, Israel, 79.
Stoddard, Jeames, 75.
Stoddard, John, 56.
Stoddard, John, 71.
Stoddard, John, 77.
Stoddard, Jonathan, 54.
Stoddard, Moses, 59.
Stoddard, Philo, 79.
Stoddard, Sampson, 77.
Stoddard, Seth, 79.
Stoddard, Simeon, 79.
Stoddard, Solomon, 54.
Stoddard, Solomon, 129.
Stoddard, Thaddeus, 79.
Stoddard, Truman, 74.
Stoddard, Wells, 58.
Stoddard, Wills, 77.
Stoddord, Ebenr, 149.
Stoe, Robert, 27.
Stoel, Asa, 139.
Stoel, Elisha, 149.
Stoel, Josiel, 147.
Stoel, Robt, 137.
Stoel, Samuel, 139.
Stokam, Reuben, 16.
Stokes, Richd, 90.
Stone, Abner, 97.
Stone, Abraham, 98.
Stone, Anne, 11.
Stone, Aron, 2nd, 99.
Stone, Asahel, 72.
Stone, Barsom, 150.
Stone, Bela, 98.
Stone, Benajah, 72.
Stone, Benjamin, 72.
Stone, Benjamin, 72.
Stone, Benjamin, 84.
Stone, Benjamin, 98.
Stone, Canfield, 72.
Stone, Christopher, 35.
Stone, Cyrus, 103.
Stone, Dane, 134.
Stone, Daniel, 72.
Stone, David, 72.
Stone, Deodama, 64.
Stone, Eber, 99.
Stone, Edmond, 58.
Stone, Edmond, 98.
Stone, Elihu, 92.
Stone, Elizabeth, 11.
Stone, Elizabeth (Wd), 22.
Stone, Ephraim, 86.
Stone, Ezra, 99.
Stone, Heber, 65.
Stone, Heman, 59.
Stone, Henry & Co., 150.
Stone, Isaac, 99.
Stone, Isaac, 153.
Stone, Ithiel, 72.
Stone, James, 34.
Stone, James, 70.
Stone, James, 97.
Stone, James, 137.
Stone, Jedediah, 84.
Stone, Jedediah, Junr, 84.
Stone, Jerad, 97.
Stone, John, 64.
Stone, John, 74.
Stone, John, 98.
Stone, John, 99.
Stone, John, 100.
Stone, John, 128.
Stone, Jonah, 66.
Stone, Jona, 150.
Stone, Joseph, 35.
Stone, Joseph, 98.
Stone, Jos., 138.
Stone, Julius, 72.
Stone, Leman, 14.
Stone, Levi, 11.
Stone, Levi, 66.
Stone, Levi, 97.
Stone, Levi, 150.
Stone, Luther, 98.
Stone, Mansfield, 74.
Stone, Mary, 64.
Stone, Mary, 98.
Stone, Medad, 98.
Stone, Mercy, 97.
Stone, Miles, 97.
Stone, Natha, 35.
Stone, Nathaniel, 97.
Stone, Nehemiah, 84.
Stone, Noah, 98.
Stone, Oliver, 11.
Stone, Onely, 22.
Stone, Osborne, 100.
Stone, Rachel, 98.
Stone, Reuben, 66.
Stone, Reuben, 72.
Stone, Ruben, 98.
Stone, Samuel, 102.
Stone, Sarah, 93.
Stone, Seth, 98.
Stone, Sibel, 97.
Stone, Silvanus, 66.
Stone, Simon, 150.
Stone, Soloman, 98.
Stone, Solomon, 35.
Stone, Stephen, 59.
Stone, Stephen, 134.
Stone, Thomas, 66.
Stone, Thomas, 98.
Stone, Thomas W., 71.
Stone, Timothy, 98.
Stone, Timothy, 145.
Stone, Trueman, 72.
Stone, William, 58.
Stone, William, 59.
Stone, William, 98.
Stone, William, 98.
Stone, William, 149.
Stone, William, 151.
Stone, William, 2d, 74.
Stone, Willim, 74.
Storer, John, 102.
Storer, Joseph, 102.
Storer, Sarah, 102.
Storms, James, 87.
Storrs, Amariah, 147.
Storrs, Benjn, 147.
Storrs, Cordial, 147.
Storrs, Dan., 147.
Storrs, Experience, 147.
Storrs, Jehiel, 148.
Storrs, John, 146.
Storrs, Josiah, 147.
Storrs, Judah, 146.
Storrs, Lemuel, 85.
Storrs, Mary, 147.
Storrs, Prince, 52.
Storrs, Royal, 147.
Storrs, Saml, 148.
Storrs, Thos, 148.
Story, Ebenr, 114.
Story, Ephraim, 129.
Story, Ephraim, 130.
Story, Henry, 130.
Story, Henry, 2d, 130.
Story, Jabez, 114.
Story, James, 130.
Story, Jonathan, 114.
Story, Mehitable, 114.
Story, Nathaniel, 102.
Story, Saml, 122.
Story, Samuel, 125.
Story, Solomon, 114.
Story, Solomon, 131.
Story, William, 126.
Stoters, Jonathan, 79.
Stoughton, Augustus, 38.
Stoughton, Elijah, 38.
Stoughton, Elisha, 54.
Stoughton, Israel, 54.
Stoughton, John, 39.
Stoughton, Jonathan, 39.
Stoughton, Lemuel, 38.
Stoughton, Oliver, 38.
Stoughton, Russell, 37.
Stoughton, Saml, 55.
Stoughton, Shem, 39.
Stoughton, William, 37.
Stove, Samuel, 12.
Stow, Abraham, 96.
Stow, Amos, 88.
Stow, Daniel, Junr, 80.
Stow, David, 86.
Stow, Ebenezer, 54.
Stow, Ebenezer, 77.
Stow, Elihu, 89.
Stow, Freelove, 101.
Stow, Jedediah, 101.
Stow, John, 86.
Stow, John, 101.
Stow, Jonathan, 88.
Stow, Joseph, 88.
Stow, Joshua, 89.
Stow, Peter, 86.
Stow, Samuel, 101.
Stow, Samuel, 116.
Stow, Solomon, Junr, 86.
Stow, Stephen, 101.
Stow, Thomas, 106.
Stow, Timothy, 96.
Stow, William, 101.
Stow, Zachariah, 88.
Stow, Zebulon, 88.
Stowe, Saml, 67.
Stowel, Amasa, 147.
Stowel, Lemuel, 149.
Stowel, Jonath, 153.
Strakey, Stephen, 89.
Stranaham, James, 148.
Strang, Jared, 16.
Strange, Hannah, 131.
Straten, Hannah, 44.
Stratton, Cornelius, 13.
Stratton, David, 31.
Stratton, John, 14.
Stratton, John, 51.
Stratton, John, 2d, 51.
Stratton, Joseph, 13.
Stratton, Samuel, 14.
Stratton, Samuel, 42.
Stratton, Samuel, Jr., 42.
Stratton, Samuel, 3d, 42.
Stratton, Stephen, 27.
Stratton, Thomas, 31.
Street, Caleb, 107.
Street, David, 27.
Street, Elnathan, 107.
Street, Glover, 108.
Street, James, 51.
Street, James, 119.
Street, John, 103.
Street, Joseph, 26.
Street, Louis, 92.
Street, Nathaniel, 22.
Street, Nicholas, 97.
Street, Samuel, 107.
Street, Samuel, 108.
Street, Samuel, 2nd, 108.
Street, Thankfull, 41.
Stretton, Anna, 30.
Strickland, Abel, 80.
Strickland, Amos, 126.
Strickland, Asahel, 45.
Strickland, Benjamin, 37.
Strickland, Howel, 43.
Strickland, John, 127.
Strickland, Jonas, 132.
Strickland, Joseph, 45.
Strickland, Joseph, Jr., 45.
Strickland, Nathl, 141.
Strickland, Nehemiah, 43.
Strickland, Nehemiah, Jr., 43.
Strickland, Peter, 124.
Strickland, Peter, 126.
Strickland, Peter, Junr, 126.
Strickland, Peter, 3d, 126.
Strickland, Richard, 38.
Strickland, Samuel, 77.
Strickland, Saml, 137.
Strickland, Sarah, 126.
Strickland, Seth, 80.
Strickland, Simeon, 42.
Strickland, Stephen, 43.
Strickland, Stephen, Jr., 42.
Strickland, Stephen, 3d, 43.
Strickland, William, 126.
Strict, Henry, 72.
String, David, 137.
String, Saml, 139.
Stringham, Peter, 10.
Strong, Aaron, 132.
Strong, Abel, 55.
Strong, Adino, 74.
Strong, Adonijah, 62.
Strong, Adonijah, 81.
Strong, Alexander, 139.
Strong, Amasa, 74.
Strong, Ambrus, 121.
Strong, Amos, 43.
Strong, Amos, 120.
Strong, Anna, 71.
Strong, Anna, 71.
Strong, Benajah, 133.
Strong, Benjamin, 73.
Strong, Benjamin, 80.
Strong, Caleb, 80.
Strong, Caverly, 74.
Strong, Charles, 74.
Strong, Charles, 132.
Strong, Revr Cuprian, 80.
Strong, Daniel, 56.
Strong, Daniel, 145.
Strong, Daniel, Jnr, 145.
Strong, David, 120.
Strong, David, 132.
Strong, David, 135.
Strong, David, 146.
Strong, David, Jnr, 146.
Strong, Ebenezer, 73.
Strong, Ebenezer, 121.
Strong, Ebr, 132.
Strong, Eber, 74.
Strong, Elezer, 135.
Strong, Eli, 45.
Strong, Eliakim, 96.
Strong, Elijah, 39.
Strong, Elisha, 41.
Strong, Elisha, 54.
Strong, Elizabeth, 86.
Strong, Elnathan, 44.
Strong, Elnathan, 74.
Strong, Elnathan, 102.
Strong, Elnathan, 138.
Strong, Ephrahim, 102.
Strong, Ephrahim, 102.
Strong, Israel, 39.
Strong, Jacob, 133.
Strong, Joel, 62.
Strong, Joel, 67.
Strong, John, 38.
Strong, John, 38.
Strong, John, 42.
Strong, John, 69.
Strong, John, 79.
Strong, John, 80.
Strong, John, 96.
Strong, John, 101.
Strong, Joseph, 14.
Strong, Joseph, 131.
Strong, Josiah, 63.
Strong, Josiah, 80.
Strong, Josiah, 95.
Strong, Judas, 132.
Strong, Leroy, 132.
Strong, Medad, 96.
Strong, Moses, 105.
Strong, Reve N., 133.
Strong, Revd Nathan, 46.
Strong, Nathan, 86.
Strong, Nathn, 132.
Strong, Nathaniel, 38.
Strong, Nathaniel, Jr., 38.
Strong, Nehemiah, 20.
Strong, Oliver, 145.
Strong, Philip, 74.
Strong, Phenias, 135.
Strong, Phineas, 134.
Strong, Return, 73.
Strong, Samuel, 56.
Strong, Sarah, 54.
Strong, Seth, 96.
Strong, Silah, 73.
Strong, Solomon, 78.
Strong, Thomas, 96.
Strong, Timothy, 38.
Strong, Timothy, 56.
Strong, William, 52.
Strong, Zebulun, 121.
Stroughton, Alexander, 38.
Strowd, Richard, 128.
Stuard, Aaron, 25.
Stuard, Loas, 66.
Stuard, Sarah, 23.
Stuard, Simon, 21.
Stuart, Albert, 21.
Stuart, Benjamin, 24.
Stuart, Elexander, 113.
Stuart, Elisha, 127.
Stuart, Ephraim, 24.
Stuart, Isaac, 23.
Stuart, Jeames, 59.
Stuart, John, 24.
Stuart, Justice, 23.
Stuart, Nathan, 116.
Stuart, Samuel, 21.
Stuart, Saml, 67.
Stuart, Saml, 151.
Stuart, Sarah (Wd), 23.
Stuart, Simeon, 24.
Stuart, Thaddeus, 22.
Stuart, William, 127.
Studivant, Ozar, 41.
Studley, Jos., 138.
Studley, Joshua, 60.
Studwell, Anthony, 15.
Studwell, Deborah (Wd), 15.
Studwell, Gabriel, 16.
Studwell, Henry, 16.
Studwell, Sarah (Wd), 16.
Sturdaphant, James, 63.
Sturdefant, John, 19.
Sturdefant, Jonathan, 19.
Sturdephant, George, 60.
Sturdevant, John, 10.
Sturdevant, Timothy, 10.
Sturdivant, Azor, 41.
Sturdivant, James, 41.
Sturges, Abigail, 14.
Sturges, Abigail, 14.
Sturges, Aquilla, 22.
Sturges, Augustus, 72.
Sturges, Barlow, 14.
Sturges, Benjamin, 14.
Sturges, Benjamin, 27.
Sturges, Daniel, 24.
Sturges, Dimon, 14.
Sturges, Ebenezer, 14.
Sturges, Ebenezer, 27.
Sturges, Elias, 24.
Sturges, Eliphalet, 24.
Sturges, Eward, 14.
Sturges, Ezekiel, 31.
Sturges, Hezekiah, 14.
Sturges, Hezekiah, Jnr, 14.
Sturges, Jabel, 31.
Sturges, James, 32.
Sturges, Jonathan, 14.
Sturges, Joseph, 11.
Sturges, Lewis, 29.
Sturges, Moris S., 11.
Sturges, Moses, 32.
Sturges, Perry, 27.
Sturges, Peter, 32.
Sturges, Seth, 14.
Sturges, Solomon, 14.
Sturges, Stephen, 32.
Sturges, William, 14.
Sturgis, Andrew, 12.
Sturgis, Elnathan, 28.
Sturgis, James, 28.
Sturgis, Nehemiah, 28.
Sturgis, Thaddeus, 28.
Sturgis, Ward, 28.
Sturtevant, John, 72.
Sturtevant, John, 2d, 72.
Sturtevant, Pelg, 74.
Sturtevant, Samuel, 59.
Sturtevant, Zebedee, 59.
Stutson, Anne, 147.
Suaney, John, 123.
Suard, Samuel, 26.
Suard, Revd William, 16.
Sudmore, Joseph, 26.
Sugden, Lidia, 100.
Suitar, John, 46.
Suitleif, Sylvester, 141.
Sulard, Joseph, 146.
Sullard, Jacob, 124.
Sullard, James, 124.
Summers, Aaron, 29.
Summers, Abel, 102.
Summers, Abijah, 29.
Summers, Agnes, 102.
Summers, Andrew, 72.
Summers, Asahel, 61.
Summers, Daniel, 30.

# INDEX.

Summers, David, 29.
Summers, Elijah, 31.
Summers, Elnathan, 29.
Summers, Gershom, 21.
Summers, Henery, 31.
Summers, Henry, 102.
Summers, Isaac, 31.
Summers, Isaac, 102.
Summers, Jabez, 29.
Summers, John, 20.
Summers, Jonah, 74.
Summers, Luke, 18.
Summers, Mark, 10.
Summers, Nathan, 32.
Summers, Oliver, 72.
Summers, Robert, 20.
Summers, Samuel, 29.
Summers, Samuel, 72.
Summers, Stephen, 29.
Summers, Zacheriah S., 17.
Sumnar, Sam¹, 149.
Sumner, Benjⁿ, 141.
Sumner, Dan¹, 151.
Sumner, Eben⁰, 141.
Sumner, Edward, 140.
Sumner, Elizabeth, 87.
Sumner, James F., 141.
Sumner, John, 141.
Sumner, Jonaᵗʰ, 145.
Sumner, Moses, 153.
Sumner, Robert, 141.
Sumner, Ruben, 134.
Sumner, Samuel, 141.
Sumner, Sarah, 153.
Sumner, Susannah, 86.
Sumner, William, 86.
Sumner, Wᵐ, 135.
Surdephant, Abijah, 63.
Susanna (Negro), 121.
Susant, James, 129.
Sutley, David, 68.
Sutlif, Abel, 1ˢᵗ, 77.
Sutliff, Abel, 2ᵈ, 77.
Sutliff, David, 77.
Sutliff, James, 83.
Sutliff, Jannah, 130.
Sutliff, John, 77.
Sutliff, John, 84.
Sutliff, John, 131.
Sutliff, Lucas, 77.
Sutliff, Nathaniel, 84.
Sutliff, Samuel, 77.
Sutlow, Richard, 18.
Suttey, Sam¹, 62.
Sutton, Benjamin, 16.
Sutton, David, 135.
Sutton, Henry, 77.
Sutton, Jn⁰, 135.
Sutton (Negro), 131.
Sutton, William, 16.
Sutton, William, 37.
Sutton, William, 93.
Swaddle, Jemima, 125.
Swaddle, John, 87.
Swaddle, John, 130.
Swaddle, Sam¹, 125.
Swaddle, Sarah, 80.
Swain, Peter, 129.
Swaine, Benjamin, 44.
Swan, Amos, 74.
Swan, Asa, 121.
Swan, Charles, 115.
Swan, David, 115.
Swan, Edward, 115.
Swan, Elias, 120.
Swan, Elisha, 115.
Swan, Elizabeth, 75.
Swan, George, 117.
Swan, Isaac, 74.
Swan, Jabez, 82.
Swan, Jesse, 115.
Swan, John, 116.
Swan, Joseph, 43.
Swan, Joshua, 118.
Swan, Mary, 116.
Swan, Nathan, 66.
Swan, Patience, 115.
Swan, Robart, 115.
Swan, Samuel, 75.
Swan, Thomas, 115.
Swan, Timothy, 50.
Swan, Timothy, 114.
Swan, Timothy, 115.
Swat, Pelix, 66.
Sweatland, Jonah, 146.
Sweet, Benjⁿ, 148.
Sweet, Ebenʳ, 151.
Sweet, Ezekiel, 151.
Sweet, James, 69.
Sweet, Jonathan, 68.
Sweet, Joseph, 68.
Sweet, Palmer, 40.
Sweet, Stephen, 40.
Sweetland, Aaron, 67.
Sweetlove, Elis, 18.
Swetland, Aaron, 135.
Swetland, Azariah, 135.
Swetland, Benjamin, 37.
Swetland, Daniel, 37.
Swetland, Joel, 135.
Swetland, Joseph, 37.
Swetland, Joseph, 59.

Swetland, Levi, 133.
Swetland, Lewis, 74.
Swetland, Luke, 132.
Swetland, Peter, 135.
Swetland, Thoˢ, 136.
Swett, John, 60.
Swif, Rufus, 57.
Swift, Asaph, 59.
Swift, Barzilla, 59.
Swift, Barzillia, 147.
Swift, Charles, 146.
Swift, Daniel, 107.
Swift, Elisha, 57.
Swift, Elisha, 67.
Swift, Heman, 57.
Swift, Jabez, 74.
Swift, James, 107.
Swift, James, 151.
Swift, John, 95.
Swift, John, 147.
Swift, Joseph, 92.
Swift, Nathaniel, 2ᵈ, 74.
Swift, Philoe, 60.
Swift, Rowland, 146.
Swift, Rowland, Jnʳ, 146.
Swift, Thomas, 147.
Swift, Wilard, 61.
Swift, William, 119.
Swift, William, 146.
Swift, Zeph, 152.
Swords, Frances D., 14.
Sykes, David, 51.
Sykes, Jonathan, 51.
Sykes, Lott, 51.
Sykes, Paul, 51.
Sykes, Ruben, 136.
Sykes, Samuel, 51.
Sykes, Victory, 51.
Sykes, Victory, 2ᵈ, 51.
Syllivan, Mott, 72.
Syms, George, 146.
Syphax (Negro), 21.
Syrus (Negroe), 111.

Tabor, Jeremiah, 127.
Tabor, Job, 128.
Tabor, Pardon, 128.
Tabor, Sam¹, 127.
Tabor, Sam¹, Junʳ, 127.
Tabor, Wardon T., 129.
Tainter, Charles, 121.
Tainter, Isaac, 92.
Tainter, John, 120.
Tainter, Joseph, 132.
Tainter, Medad, 92.
Tainter, Michael, 92.
Tainter, Michael, 2ⁿᵈ, 92.
Tainter, Roger, 120.
Taintor, John, 145.
Taintor, Joseph, 64.
Talbert, Benjamin, 144.
Talbert, Jared, 144.
Talcot, Josⁿ, 132.
Talcott, Abraham, 42.
Talcott, Annar, 42.
Talcott, Dan¹, 54.
Talcott, Ebenezer, 52.
Talcott, Elizur, 40.
Talcott, Elizur, 42.
Talcott, Elizur, Jr., 42.
Talcott, George, 42.
Talcott, Hezekiah, 89.
Talcott, Isaac, 43.
Talcott, Jabez, 43.
Talcott, Job, 41.
Talcott, John, 42.
Talcott, Jonathan, 43.
Talcott, Joseph, 46.
Talcott, Mary, 52.
Talcott, Mathew, Esqʳ, 85.
Talcott, Moses, 52.
Talcott, Nathaniel, 42.
Talcott, Nathaniel, Jr., 42.
Talcott, Noah, 96.
Talcott, Oliver, 42.
Talcott, Ruth, 42.
Talcott, Samuel, 46.
Talcott, Samuel, 52.
Talcott, Samuel, Jr., 46.
Tallbard, William, 83.
Tallmadge, Benjamin, 64.
Tallman, Peter, 99.
Talmadge, Ichabod, 50.
Talmage, Alsop, 111.
Talmage, Bethiah (Wᵈ), 26.
Talmage, Ezra, 102.
Talmage, Jacob, 110.
Talmage, James, 26.
Talmage, John, 74.
Talmage, John, 110.
Talmage, Jonathan, 26.
Talmage, Josiah, 93.
Talmage, Samuel, 93.
Talmage, Seymore, 26.
Talmage, Soloman, 92.
Talmage, Timothy, 105.
Talman, Ebenezer, 79.
Talman, Josiah, 79.
Talmap, Hannah, 100.
Talmash, Daniel, 100.
Tammage, Elisha, 119.
Tanner, Considʳ, 57.
Tanner, Ebenezer, 74.

Tanner, Ephraim, 74.
Tanner, Joseph, 115.
Tanner, Trial, 57.
Tanner, William, 57.
Tanner, William, 148.
Tappen, John, 104.
Tappin, Richard, 140.
Tarball, William, 122.
Tarbox, Benjamin, 86.
Tarbox, Caleb, 144.
Tarbox, David, 136.
Tarbox, Godfry, 136.
Tarbox, Jonᵃ, 135.
Tarbox, Solⁿ, 136.
Tarbox, Zenas, 136.
Taulsom, Elias, 30.
Tausket, Mary, 69.
Tausly, Matthews, 62.
Tayler, Abner, 66.
Tayler, Abner, 66.
Tayler, Benjᵃ, 135.
Tayler, David, 70.
Tayler, Hugh, 59.
Tayler, John, 119.
Tayler, Jn⁰, 134.
Tayler, Jn⁰, 136.
Tayler, Paul, 22.
Taylor, Abijah, 23.
Taylor, Abram, 72.
Taylor, Andrew, 10.
Taylor, Anna, 65.
Taylor, Anne, 15.
Taylor, Augustin, 63.
Taylor, Azariah, 42.
Taylor, Baroch, 31.
Taylor, Benajah, 54.
Taylor, Benjamin, 19.
Taylor, Benjamin, 65.
Taylor, Charles, 79.
Taylor, Chiles, 68.
Taylor, Daniel, 72.
Taylor, David, 31.
Taylor, David, 42.
Taylor, David, 74.
Taylor, David, 109.
Taylor, David, 132.
Taylor, Ebenezer, 12.
Taylor, Ebenezer, 20.
Taylor, Ebenezer, 68.
Taylor, Elezer, 11.
Taylor, Elezur, 35.
Taylor, Eli, 12.
Taylor, Eli, 72.
Taylor, Eliad, 12.
Taylor, Eliakam, 12.
Taylor, Elias, 74.
Taylor, Elisha, 65.
Taylor, Elisha, 80.
Taylor, Elisha, 139.
Taylor, Ezra, 121.
Taylor, Gad, 50.
Taylor, Gamaliel, 23.
Taylor, George, 42.
Taylor, George, 148.
Taylor, Gilead, 12.
Taylor, Giles, 36.
Taylor, Henry, 96.
Taylor, Isaac, 82.
Taylor, Jabes, 12.
Taylor, Jabes, Juʳ, 12.
Taylor, James, 47.
Taylor, Jesse, 47.
Taylor, Job, 119.
Taylor, Joel, 65.
Taylor, John, 11.
Taylor, John, 24.
Taylor, John, 36.
Taylor, John, 66.
Taylor, John, 69.
Taylor, John, 129.
Taylor, John, 129.
Taylor, Jn⁰, 132.
Taylor, Jn⁰, 133.
Taylor, John, Juʳ, 12.
Taylor, John E., 49.
Taylor, Jonathan, 11.
Taylor, Jonathan, 12.
Taylor, Jonathan, 24.
Taylor, Jonathan, 32.
Taylor, Jonathan, 42.
Taylor, Jonathan, 46.
Taylor, Jonathan, 86.
Taylor, Joseph, 12.
Taylor, Joseph, 42.
Taylor, Joseph, 62.
Taylor, Joseph, 83.
Taylor, Joseph, 120.
Taylor, Joseph, 120.
Taylor, Joseph, 147.
Taylor, Joseph, 2ᵈ, 74.
Taylor, Joshua, 12.
Taylor, Julus, 39.
Taylor, Lemwell, 12.
Taylor, Levi, 23.
Taylor, Major, 10.
Taylor, Marthy (Wᵈ), 23.
Taylor, Micah, 153.
Taylor, Nathan, 12.
Taylor, Nathan, 113.
Taylor, Nathan, 152.
Taylor, Nath¹, 132.
Taylor, Nathaniel, 1ˢᵗ, 72.
Taylor, Nathaniel, 2ᵈ, 72.
Taylor, Nathaniel, 3ᵈ, 72.

Taylor, Nicholas, 20.
Taylor, Noadiah, 49.
Taylor, Noadiah, 80.
Taylor, Noadiah, 80.
Taylor, Noah, 12.
Taylor, Obadiah, 60.
Taylor, Ozias, 49.
Taylor, Phineus, 12.
Taylor, Phineus, 21.
Taylor, Phineus, Jr., 21.
Taylor, Prince, 68.
Taylor, Roswell, 47.
Taylor, Russell, 44.
Taylor, Ruth (Wid.), 49.
Taylor, Samuel, 12.
Taylor, Samuel, 13.
Taylor, Samuel, 42.
Taylor, Samuel, 80.
Taylor, Sanford, 115.
Taylor, Silas, 12.
Taylor, Simeon, 64.
Taylor, Simeon, 79.
Taylor, Simon, 127.
Taylor, Stephen, 20.
Taylor, Stephen, 65.
Taylor, Stephen, 81.
Taylor, Stephen, 121.
Taylor, Thad., 51.
Taylor, Theodore, 109.
Taylor, Theofelus, 11.
Taylor, Thofelus, 19.
Taylor, Thomas, 12.
Taylor, Thomas, 12.
Taylor, Thoˢ, 138.
Taylor, Thoˢ, 139.
Taylor, Timothy, 12.
Taylor, Timothy, Juʳ, 11.
Taylor, Wait, 35.
Taylor, William, 31.
Taylor, William, 49.
Taylor, William, 70.
Taylor, William, 72.
Taylor, Zalmon, 11.
Taylor, Zebediah, 15.
Teague, Jerusha, 127.
Teal, Benjamin, 99.
Teal, John, 37.
Tebbalds, Abner, 108.
Tebbalds, Arnold, 101.
Tebbalds, James, 101.
Teel, Isaac, 139.
Teel, Joseph, 114.
Teil, Joseph, 35.
Tenant, Calib, 42.
Tennant, John, 121.
Tennant, Moses, 81.
Tenny, Jeremiah, 117.
Tenpany, Michael C., 15.
Tente, Ammon, 52.
Teplay, Ashbel, 60.
Terrett, William, 117.
Terrill, Abel, 59.
Terrill, Daniel, 59.
Terrill, Jonathan, 79.
Terrill, Lee, 79.
Terrill, Nathaniel, 79.
Terrill, Timothy, 79.
Territt, Caleb, 72.
Territt, Caleb, 2ᵈ, 72.
Territt, Enoch, 72.
Territt, Isaac, 72.
Territt, Jared, 72.
Territt, Jeames, 72.
Territt, Jeames, 2ᵈ, 72.
Territt, Joab, 72.
Territt, Joel, 72.
Territt, John, 72.
Territt, Nathan, 72.
Territt, Oliver, 72.
Territt, Stephen, 72.
Terrol, Lettie, 67.
Terry, Aseph, 40.
Terry, Benjamin, 2ⁿᵈ, 39.
Terry, Daniel, 40.
Terry, David, 40.
Terry, Ebenezer, 40.
Terry, Ebenezer, 2ᵈ, 39.
Terry, Elijah, 39.
Terry, Eliphalet, Esqʳ, 39.
Terry, Ephraim, 39.
Terry, Ephraim, 145.
Terry, Hirum, 40.
Terry, Jacob, 39.
Terry, Jacob, Jr., 39.
Terry, John, 40.
Terry, John G., 47.
Terry, Jonathan, 40.
Terry, Joseph, 39.
Terry, Joseph, 66.
Terry, Julus, 39.
Terry, Col⁰ Nathaniel, 39.
Terry, Samuel, 38.
Terry, Samuel, 39.
Terry, Samuel, 47.
Terry, Samuel, 85.
Terry, Selah, 39.
Terry, Selah, Jr., 39.
Terry, Shadrack, 39.
Terry, Solomon, 40.
Terry, Solomon, 48.
Terry, Zeno, 39.
Tewisdel, John, 69.
Thacher, Jacob, 72.

Thainer (Negro), 86.
Thair, Ezekiel, 59.
Thair, Lemuel, 72.
Thallter, Thaddeus B., 21.
Thare, Shadrick, 139.
Tharp, Abner, 106.
Tharp, Abner, 108.
Tharp, Asa, 106.
Tharp, Asher, 66.
Tharp, David, 69.
Tharp, David, 106.
Tharp, David, 2ⁿᵈ, 106.
Tharp, Elnathan, 107.
Tharp, Jerad, 107.
Tharp, Joel, 103.
Tharp, Linus, 35.
Tharp, Mosses, 105.
Tharp, Samuel, 106.
Tharp, Timothy, 106.
Tharp, Titus, 105.
Thatcher, Abigal, 146.
Thatcher, Asa, 153.
Thatcher, Benjᵃ, 146.
Thatcher, John, 103.
Thatcher, John, 132.
Thatcher, Josiah, Juʳ, 23.
Thatcher, Samuel, 104.
Thatcher, Sam¹, 132.
Thatcher, Thomas, 40.
Thayer, Cornelius, 79.
thayer, Ezekiel, 142.
Thayer, Hester, 110.
Thayer, Jonathan, 87.
Thayer, Mebisheth, 154.
Thayer, Nath¹, 150.
Thayer, Oliver, 151.
Thayer, Phillip, 150.
Thayer, Reubin, 150.
Thays, Thomas, 119.
Thillam, Samuel, 112.
Thomas, Aaron, 84.
Thomas, Abigail, 114.
Thomas, Abigail, 120.
Thomas, Abijah, 145.
Thomas, Abram, 79.
Thomas, Amos, 111.
Thomas, Amos, 112.
Thomas, Amos, 145.
Thomas, Amos, Jnʳ, 145.
Thomas, Aron, 105.
Thomas, Asael, 105.
Thomas, Benjamin, 67.
Thomas, Benjamin, 105.
Thomas, Caleb, 101.
Thomas, Charles, 79.
Thomas, Daniel, 105.
Thomas, Daniel, 114.
Thomas, Daniel, 146.
Thomas, David, 48.
Thomas, David, 79.
Thomas, David, 81.
Thomas, David, 112.
Thomas, Ebenezer, 79.
Thomas, Ebenezer, 83.
Thomas, Ebenʳ, 132.
Thomas, Ebenezer, Junʳ, 83.
Thomas, Edward, 105.
Thomas, Elihu, 145.
Thomas, Eliph¹, 146.
Thomas, Elisha, 111.
Thomas, Enoch, 56.
Thomas, Enoch, 92.
Thomas, Enoch, 2ⁿᵈ, 92.
Thomas, Ephraim, 111.
Thomas, Evan, 83.
Thomas, Evan, 88.
Thomas, Friend, 79.
Thomas, Garthom, 112.
Thomas, Gregory, 22.
Thomas, Henry, 83.
Thomas, Hester, 105.
Thomas, Hezekiah, 112.
Thomas, Ira, 79.
Thomas, Isaac, 100.
Thomas, James, 20.
Thomas, James, 83.
Thomas, James, 110.
Thomas, James, 112.
Thomas, James, 181.
Thomas, James, 145.
Thomas, Jeremiah, 79.
Thomas, John, 46.
Thomas, John, 74.
Thomas, John, 79.
Thomas, John, 103.
Thomas, John, 112.
Thomas, John, 129.
Thomas, Jn⁰, 138.
Thomas, John, 2ᵈ, 112.
Thomas, Joseph, 22.
Thomas, Joseph, 64.
Thomas, Joseph, 105.
Thomas, Josiah, 106.
Thomas, Lemuel, 72.
Thomas, Moses, 112.
Thomas (Negro), 132.
Thomas, Noah, 112.
Thomas, Peleg, 145.
Thomas, Recompence, 29.
Thomas, Recompence, 2ᵈ, 29.
Thomas, Rhoda, 105.
Thomas, Roger, 83.
Thomas, Ruben, 111.
Thomas, Samuel, 48.

# INDEX.

Thomas, Samuel, 77.
Thomas, Samuel, 103.
Thomas, Sarah, 105.
Thomas, Simeon, 132.
Thomas, Solomon, 49.
Thomas, Susanah, 105.
Thomas, Thomas L., 132.
Thomas, William, 81.
Thomas, William, 92.
Thomas, Zelpha, 41.
Thompson, Abel, 41.
Thompson, Abel, 94.
Thompson, Abel, 109.
Thompson, Abel, 2nd, 109.
Thompson, Abraham, 17.
Thompson, Abraham, 104.
Thompson, Abraham, 104.
Thompson, Alexander, 38.
Thompson, Wm, 61.
Thompson, Amos, 97.
Thompson, Ardon, 50.
Thompson, Asa, 41.
Thompson, Asa, 93.
Thompson, Asa, 137.
Thompson, Barnabas, 41.
Thompson, Daniel, 41.
Thompson, Daniel, 111.
Thompson, David, 17.
Thompson, David, 30.
Thompson, David, 70.
Thompson, David, 90.
Thompson, David, 99.
Thompson, David, 139.
Thompson, Edmund, 45.
Thompson, Edward, 45.
Thompson, Edward, Jr, 45.
Thompson, Elexander, 115.
Thompson, Elihu, 108.
Thompson, Elihue, 17.
Thompson, Elijah, 66.
Thompson, Elijah, 67.
Thompson, Eliphras, 70.
Thompson, Elisha, 67.
Thompson, Elisha, 70.
Thompson, Elisha, 105.
Thompson, Elizabeth, 97.
Thompson, George, 136.
Thompson, Henry, 100.
Thompson, Henry, 137.
Thompson, Ichabod, 154.
Thompson, Isaac, 104.
Thompson, Isaac, 147.
Thompson, Isaiah, 34.
Thompson, Israel, 134.
Thompson, Jabez, 95.
Thompson, Jacob, 104.
Thompson, Jame, 139.
Thompson, James, 12.
Thompson, James, 38.
Thompson, James, 64.
Thompson, James, 70.
Thompson, James, 101.
Thompson, James, 105.
Thompson, James, 105.
Thompson, James, 115.
Thompson, James, Junr, 115.
Thompson, Jared, 97.
Thompson, Jared, 147.
Thompson, Jemima, 45.
Thompson, Jerad, 104.
Thompson, Jeremiah, 104.
Thompson, Jesse, 93.
Thompson, Joel, 64.
Thompson, Joel, 97.
Thompson, John, 38.
Thompson, John, 41.
Thompson, John, 61.
Thompson, John, 61.
Thompson, John, 109.
Thompson, John, 124.
Thompson, Jno, 139.
Thompson, John, Jr., 38.
Thompson, Jonas, 31.
Thompson, Jonathan, 17.
Thompson, Jona, 133.
Thompson, Jona, 139.
Thompson, Joseph, 104.
Thompson, Justus, 139.
Thompson, Levi, 41.
Thompson, Lott, 41.
Thompson, Luke, 41.
Thompson, Luther, 134.
Thompson, Margeret, 105.
Thompson, Mathew, 40.
Thompson, Mathew, 51.
Thompson, Moses, 97.
Thompson, Moses, 115.
Thompson, Nathan, 17.
Thompson, Nathaniel, 41.
Thompson, Nathl, 125.
Thompson, Phebe, 104.
Thompson, Reuben, 34.
Thompson, Robart, 115.
Thompson, Rockmary, 93.
Thompson, Ruth, 41.
Thompson, Samuel, 17.
Thompson, Samuel, 41.
Thompson, Samuel, 65.
Thompson, Samuel, 66.
Thompson, Samuel, 81.
Thompson, Samuel, 93.
Thompson, Samuel, 97.
Thompson, Samuel, 125.
Thompson, Saml, 134.

Thompson, Saml, 147.
Thompson, Saml, Jr, 147.
Thompson, Sarah, 104.
Thompson, Stephen, 29.
Thompson, Stephen, 65.
Thompson, Stephen, 97.
Thompson, Stephen, 97.
Thompson, Stephen, 105.
Thompson, Thadeus, 111.
Thompson, Thomas, 41.
Thompson, Thos, 134.
Thompson, Thomas, 151.
Thompson, Timothy, 97.
Thompson, Timothy, 102.
Thompson (Wid.), 50.
Thompson, William, 38.
Thompson, William, 103.
Thompson, William, 125.
Thompson, Wm, 134.
Thompson, Zebulon, 69.
Thomson, Aaron, 56.
Thomson, Abijah, 31.
Thomson, Benjamin, 126.
Thomson, Charles, 126.
Thomson, Daniel, 59.
Thomson, David, 30.
Thomson, David, 117.
Thomson, Edward, 65.
Thomson, Elisabeth, 119.
Thomson, Elizur, 59.
Thomson, Esther, 74.
Thomson, George, 74.
Thomson, Henry, 56.
Thomson, Hezekiah, 79.
Thomson, James, 127.
Thomson, Jedediah, 117.
Thomson, John, 24.
Thomson, John, 30.
Thomson, Jonathan, 41.
Thomson, Jonathan, 65.
Thomson, Joseph, 116.
Thomson, Joseph, 147.
Thomson, Ezekl, 140.
Thomson, Levi, 56.
Thomson, Levi, 61.
Thomson, Martha, 57.
Thomson, Nathl, 117.
Thomson, Nehemiah, 31.
Thomson, Robart, 129.
Thomson, Samuel, 56.
Thomson, Saml, 146.
Thomson, Thomas, 56.
Thomson, Timothy, 41.
Thomson, Zacheriah, 56.
Thorn, Abel, 57.
Thorn, William, 66.
Thornton, Ezra, 66.
Thornton, Samuel, 50.
Thorp, Aaron, 145.
Thorp, Amos, 128.
Thorp, David, 32.
Thorp, Earle, 63.
Thorp, Ebenezer, 32.
Thorp, Ebenezer, Junr, 32.
Thorp, Eliphilet, 14.
Thorp, Ezekiel, 128.
Thorp, Gershom, 13.
Thorp, Gershom, 32.
Thorp, Hezekiah, 31.
Thorp, Jabez, 14.
Thorp, Jabez, 32.
Thorp, Jacob, 32.
Thorp, Jehiel, 13.
Thorp, John, 32.
Thorp, Lyman, 27.
Thorp, Nathan, 32.
Thorp, Nathl, 128.
Thorp, Nathl, 2d, 128.
Thorp, Peter, 32.
Thorp, Peter, 75.
Thorp, Ruel, 13.
Thorp, Samuel, 31.
Thorp, Stephen, 13.
Thorp, Thadeus, 32.
Thorp, William, 13.
Thrall, ——, 56.
Thrall, Benjn, 56.
Thrall, Charles, 68.
Thrall, Daniel, 68.
Thrall, David, 54.
Thrall, Eli, 69.
Thrall, Eliza, 54.
Thrall, Friend, 68.
Thrall, Isaac, 55.
Thrall, Jesse, 54.
Thrall, John, 55.
Thrall, John, 56.
Thrall, John, 3d, 56.
Thrall, Levi, 68.
Thrall, Noah, 60.
Thrall, Pardon, 62.
Thrash, John, 50.
Thrash, Oliver, 50.
Thrash, Reuben, 50.
Thrash, Samuel, 50.
Thrasher, Bezaleel, 88.
Thrasher, Christopher, 137.
Thrasher, Eben, 137.
Thrasher, Elnathan, 110.
Thrasher, Josu., 137.
Thrasher, Noah, 137.
Thrasher, Sampson, 137.
Thrawl, Leml, 133.
Throll, Aaron, 68.

Throop, Benjamin, 59.
Throop, Benja, 126.
Throop, Cary, 129.
Throop, John R., 103.
Throop, Joseph, 59.
Throop, Phebe, 82.
Throop, William, 59.
Throop, Wm, 126.
Throope, Benjamin, 145.
Throope, Dan., 145.
Throope, Joseph, 145.
Thurber, Luther, 114.
Thurston, David, 149.
Thurston, Edward, 116.
Thurstone, Saml, 148.
Tibbalds, Arnold, 101.
Tibbalds, Benedick, 101.
Tibbalds, David, 101.
Tibbalds, Ebenezur, 96.
Tibbalds, James, 96.
Tibbalds, Joseph, 96.
Tibbalds, Lemuel, 101.
Tibbalds, Samuel, 101.
Tibbals, Nathan, 75.
Tibbells, Eben, 83.
Tibbells, Stephen, 83.
Tibbels, Elizabeth, 83.
Tibbets, Obediah, 19.
Tibbles, Samuel, 68.
Tibbots, Thomas, 61.
Tibbots, Thomas, 68.
Tickner, Isaac, 146.
Tickner, James, 146.
Tickner, John, 62.
Tiff, John, 115.
Tiff, Joseph, 115.
Tiff, Oliver, 115.
Tiff, Oliver, 116.
Tiff, Solomon, 120.
Tiffany, Ebenr, 122.
Tiffany, Ebenr, Junr, 122.
Tiffany, Mary, 123.
Tiffany, Mary, Junr, 123.
Tiffany, Nathan, 57.
Tiffany, Nathl, 136.
Tiffany, Ol, 133.
Tiffany, Philomon, 122.
Tiffany, Samuel, 66.
Tiffeny, Recompense, 146.
Tiffeny, Timothy, 68.
Tiffery, Humphrey, 48.
Tilden, Daniel, 146.
Tilden, Ebenr, 146.
Tilden, Ithamar, 147.
Tilden, Joshua, 147.
Tilden, Littice, 153.
Tiler, Jonathan, 58.
Tiler, Roger, 55.
Tileston, Thomas, 152.
Tiley, Asa, 52.
Tiley, David, 89.
Tiley, James, 46.
Tiley, Samuel, 46.
Till, Joseph, 48.
Tillerson, John, 124.
Tillet, James, 23.
Tilley, James, 128.
Tilley, John, 128.
Tillotson, Abm, 135.
Tillotson, Abm, Jr., 135.
Tillotson, Ashbel, 41.
Tillotson, Bela, 124.
Tillotson, Daniel, 41.
Tillotson, Daniel, 124.
Tillotson, Danil, 145.
Tillotson, Elezr, 135.
Tillotson, Elezer, 135.
Tillotson, Elias, 41.
Tillotson, George, 124.
Tillotson, Isaac, 124.
Tillotson, Jacob, 124.
Tillotson, Jno, 136.
Tillotson, Mary, 122.
Tillotson, Saml, 126.
Tillotson, Simeon, 122.
Tillotson, Simeon, 124.
Tillotson, Thomas, 72.
Tillotson, William, 124.
Tillotson, Zenas, 48.
Tim (Negroe), 112.
Timons, Elijah, 134.
Tinker, Absolmn, 110.
Tinker, Amos, 102.
Tinker, Amos, 123.
Tinker, Amos, Junr, 123.
Tinker, Benja, 127.
Tinker, Benjamin, 2d, 127.
Tinker, Daniel, 128.
Tinker, Durin, 124.
Tinker, Edward, 128.
Tinker, Ezekiel, 128.
Tinker, Jeremiah, 128.
Tinker, John, 127.
Tinker, John, Junr, 127.
Tinker, Jonathan, 36.
Tinker, Joseph, 123.
Tinker, Joseph, 127.
Tinker, Joshua, 122.
Tinker, Josiah, 128.
Tinker, Nathan, 123.
Tinker, Nathan, 124.
Tinker, Oliver, 111.

Tinker, Perry, 127.
Tinker, Peter, 123.
Tinker, Jerad, 127.
Tinker, Saml, 127.
Tinker, Silvanus, 81.
Tinker, Silvanus, 124.
Tinker, Stephen, 123.
Tinker, Temperance, 81.
Tinker, William, 124.
Tinker, William, 2d, 124.
Tinney, Asa, 130.
Tinney, Mary, 130.
Tinney, Reuben, 130.
Tinsdale, Samuel, 58.
Tisdale, Daniel, 15.
Tisdale, Ebenezr, 145.
Tisdale, Elijah, 145.
Tisdale, Eliphalet, 145.
Tisdale, Thomas, 46.
Tisdale, William, 49.
Tish, Isaac, 49.
Tish, Solomon, 49.
Titus, Amos, 77.
Titus, Comfort, 152.
Titus, Daniel, 15.
Titus (Eatheopian), 78.
Titus, Ebenr, 152.
Titus, Joel, 75.
Titus, John, 28.
Titus, Joseph, 75.
Titus, Moses, 75.
Titus, Noan, 72.
Titus, Onosimus, 75.
Titus, Samuel, 15.
Titus, Simon, 152.
Titus, William, 15.
Tober, Daniel, 69.
Tobey, Elisha, 69.
Tobey, Jonathan, 69.
Tobey, Saml, 138.
Tobin, James, 51.
Tobins, James, 63.
Tobins, John W., 63.
Tobins, Meriah, 66.
Toby, Abraham, 63.
Toby, George, 63.
Toby, Miles, 63.
Toby (Negro), 30.
Toby, Samuel, 23.
Todd, Abner, 100.
Todd, Ambrose, 48.
Todd, Asa, 108.
Todd, Bethuel, 100.
Todd, Bethuel, 106.
Todd, Caleb, 93.
Todd, Caleb, 106.
Todd, Caleb, 107.
Todd, Daniel, 94.
Todd, Daniel, 106.
Todd, Daniel, 2nd, 95.
Todd, David, 51.
Todd, Ebenezer, 68.
Todd, Ebenezer, 68.
Todd, Edmond, 77.
Todd, Elam, 77.
Todd, Eli, 68.
Todd, Eli, 72.
Todd, Enos, 106.
Todd, Etham, 106.
Todd, Ethmah, 106.
Todd, Gideon, 106.
Todd, Anne, 144.
Todd, Heil, 108.
Todd, Hezekiah, 93.
Todd, Hezekiah, 106.
Todd, Isaac, 106.
Todd, James, 106.
Todd, Job, 100.
Todd, Joel, 100.
Todd, Joel, 106.
Todd, John, 25.
Todd, John, 99.
Todd, Jonathan, 99.
Todd, Jonathan, 99.
Todd, Josiah, 111.
Todd, Lidia, 92.
Todd, Lydia, 77.
Todd, Lyman, 106.
Todd, Michael, 103.
Todd, Rachael, 112.
Todd, Samuel, 77.
Todd, Samuel, 106.
Todd, Samuel, 110.
Todd, Seth, 106.
Todd, Soloman, 106.
Todd, Stephen, 108.
Todd, Titus, 106.
Todd, Walter, 110.
Todd, Yale, 106.
Tolcot, Benja, 132.
Tolcot, Benja, 2d, 133.
Tolcot, Caleb, 132.
Tolcot, Elijah, 132.
Tolcot, Gad, 135.
Tolcot, Jno, 132.
Tolcot, Jona, 132.
Tolcot, Jos., 133.
Tolcot, Justus, 132.
Tolcot, Saml, 132.
Tolcot, Seth, 132.
Tolcot, Wm, 135.
Toles, Abraham, 111.
Toles, Bethsheba, 105.
Toles, Hannah, 111.
Toles, Jacob, 58.

Toles, Lazurus, 111.
Tolles, Daniel, 112.
Tolles, Jerad, 112.
Tolles, Lamberton, 112.
Tolmap, Daniel, 2nd, 100.
Tom, 61.
Tom (Negroe), 99.
Tom, Stephen, 80.
Tomkins, David, 110.
Tomkins, Edmond, 77.
Tomkins, Elizabeth, 109.
Tomkins, Feanes, 77.
Tomkins, Joseph, 79.
Tomkins, Oliver, 16.
Tomkins, Philip, 109.
Tomlinson, Abraham, 30.
Tomlinson, Abraham, 101.
Tomlinson, Ager, 18.
Tomlinson, Auger, 18.
Tomlinson, Beach, 18.
Tomlinson, Benjamin, 94.
Tomlinson, Benjamin, 2nd, 94.
Tomlinson, Curtis, 18.
Tomlinson, Daniel, 94.
Tomlinson, David, 95.
Tomlinson, David, 102.
Tomlinson, David, 2d, 94.
Tomlinson, Elizabeth, 94.
Tomlinson, Henery, 19.
Tomlinson, Henry, 94.
Tomlinson, Isaac, 79.
Tomlinson, Isaac, 94.
Tomlinson, Isaac, 102.
Tomlinson, Jabez, 72.
Tomlinson, Jabez N., 31.
Tomlinson, John, 94.
Tomlinson, John, 94.
Tomlinson, Joseph, 10.
Tomlinson, Josiah, 19.
Tomlinson, Levi, 95.
Tomlinson, Nathaniel, 94.
Tomlinson, Noah, 95.
Tomlinson, Noah, 2nd, 95.
Tomlinson, Phebe (Wid.), 29.
Tomlinson, Robert, 106.
Tomlinson, Russell, 94.
Tomlinson, Samuel, 79.
Tomlinson, Sarah, 94.
Tomlinson, Timothy, 79.
Tomlinson, Victory, 77.
Tomlinson, Webb, 94.
Tomlinson, William, 101.
Tompkins, Phillip, 34.
Tompson, Solomon, 70.
Tonkum, Gida, 138.
Tonkum, Peter, 133.
Toocker, Joseph, 46.
Tooley, Lemuel, 41.
Tooley, Nabby, 68.
Tooly, Hannah, 85.
Tooly, William, 85.
Toot, Robert, 49.
Toping, Josiah, 43.
Toping, Josiah, Jr, 43.
Topliff, Calvan, 147.
Topliff, Clement, 139.
Topliff, Jarum. See Peirce, Fred'k, 147.
Torrence, Samuel, 79.
Torrey, Anne, 144.
Torrey, Asa, 146.
Torrey, David, 140.
Torrey, Elisha, 153.
Torrey, Hubard, 144.
Torrey, Joseph, 144.
Torrey, Oliver, 144.
Torrey, Saml, 154.
Torry, Amos, 137.
Torry, Elijah, 134.
Torry, Ezra, 137.
Torry, Jame, Jr., 137.
Torry, James, 137.
Tosbery, John, 116.
Totten, Dorcas, 45.
Totten, Samuel, 81.
Toun, William, 24.
Tousbey, Samuel, 61.
Tousey, Abel, 21.
Tousey, John, 20.
Tousey, Oliver, 20.
Tousey, Rebecka (Wid.), 21.
Touslery, Joseph, 70.
Tousley, John, 70.
Towers, Joshua, 104.
Towles, Ira, 79.
Towles, Nehemiah, 79.
Town, Archelous, 150.
Town, Jonathan, 15.
Town, Joseph, 150.
Town, Joseph, Jnr, 150.
Town, William, 150.
Towner, Abi, 70.
Towner, Abraham, 90.
Towner, Benjamin, 72.
Towner, Dan., 19.
Towner, Daniel, 83.
Towner, Daniel, 84.
Towner, Elijah, 59.
Towner, Ephraim, 59.
Towner, Jacob, 91.
Towner, John, 74.
Towner, Jonathan, 91.
Towner, Joseph, 74.

# INDEX.

Towner, Joseph, 2d, 74.
Towner, Nathanel, 10.
Towner, Reuben, 84.
Towner, Samuel, 84.
Towner, Sarah, 70.
Towner, Timothy, 83.
Towner, Zacheus, 18.
Townes, John, 95.
Townsend, Benja, 137.
Townsend, Caleb, 59.
Townsend, Coles, 15.
Townsend, David, 135.
Townsend, David, Jr., 135.
Townsend, Ebenezer, 103.
Townsend, Elias, 103.
Townsend, Ezra, 79.
Townsend, Gibs, 137.
Townsend, Isaac, 103.
Townsend, Jeremiah, 103.
Townsend, Jeremiah, 104.
Townsend, John, 104.
Townsend, Jno, 137.
Townsend, Jona, 135.
Townsend, Jona, 135.
Townsend, Neeland, 103.
Townsend, Robert, 103.
Townsend, Samuel, 97.
Townsend, Soloman, 102.
Townsend, Timothy, 104.
Townsend, Woodbridge, 103.
Townshend, Nathl, 131.
Townshend, William, 120.
Towrley, Levi, 68.
Towser, Julias, 122.
Towser, Richard, 122.
Towsie, Donald, 20.
Towsie, Filo, 20.
Towsie, Isaac, 20.
Towsie, Zalmon, 20.
Towsie, Zalmon, 20.
Towsley, Arial, 67.
Towsley, Mike, 52.
Towsley, Vistory S., 61.
Tozier, Charles, 152.
Tracy, Andw, 113.
Tracy, Andw, 131.
Tracy, Calvin, 129.
Tracy, Daniel, 121.
Tracy, Daniel, 130.
Tracy, Daniel, 131.
Tracy, David, 130.
Tracy, Dudley, 130.
Tracy, Ebenezer, 86.
Tracy, Ebenezer, 113.
Tracy, Edward, 114.
Tracy, Elijah, 113.
Tracy, Eliphalet, 129.
Tracy, Elisha, 114.
Tracy, Elisha, 129.
Tracy, Elisha, 132.
Tracy, Esanius, 130.
Tracy, Fridrick, 131.
Tracy, Hezekiah, 130.
Tracy, Isaac, 130.
Tracy, Isael, 114.
Tracy, Israel, 147.
Tracy, Jabez, 130.
Tracy, Jabez, Junr, 130.
Tracy, Jared, 132.
Tracy, Jesse, 113.
Tracy, John, 75.
Tracy, John, 114.
Tracy, John, 130.
Tracy, John, Junr, 130.
Tracy, Joseph, 115.
Tracy, Joshua, 130.
Tracy, Josiah, 129.
Tracy, Josiah, Junr, 130.
Tracy, Lucy, 113.
Tracy, Miner, 115.
Tracy, Moses, 115.
Tracy, Moses, 125.
Tracy, Mundator, 131.
Tracy, Naomi, 130.
Tracy, Nathan, 132.
Tracy, Percy, 152.
Tracy, Peres, 132.
Tracy, Peter, 129.
Tracy, Philemon, 132.
Tracy, Prince, 152.
Tracy, Prince, 152.
Tracy, Samuel, 113.
Tracy, Saml, 131.
Tracy, Silas, 75.
Tracy, Susanna, 81.
Tracy, Uriah, 60.
Tracy, Uriah, 132.
Tracy, Zebh, 152.
Tracy, Zurriah, 142.
Trafford, William, 67.
Traicy, Gamaliel R., 81.
Traicy, Nehh, 81.
Trall, Ezekiel, 48.
Trall, Oliver, 85.
Trant, Philo, 101.
Trapp, Caleb, 131.
Trapp, Ephraim, 131.
Trapp, Saml, 131.
Treadaway, David, 146.
Treadaway, William, 146.
Treadway, Abigail, 122.
Treadway, Alpheus, 122.

Treadway, Amos, 86.
Treadway, Amos, Junr, 86.
Treadway, Asa, 121.
Treadway, Charles, 122.
Treadway, David, 122.
Treadway, Elijah, 122.
Treadway, Elijah, Esqr, 86.
Treadway, James, 122.
Treadway, John, 122.
Treadway, Josiah, 86.
Treadway, Phebe, 86.
Treadwell, Agur, 72.
Treadwell, Benjamin, 31.
Treadwell, Daniel, 31.
Treadwell, David, 31.
Treadwell, David, Junr, 31.
Treadwell, Hezekiah, 72.
Treadwell, Humphrey, 84.
Treadwell, John, 41.
Treadwell, Joseph, 32.
Treadwell, Nathan, 32.
Treadwell, Thomas, 32.
Treat, Abijah, 72.
Treat, Bethuel, 74.
Treat, Bulah, 75.
Treat, Charles, 42.
Treat, Charles, 43.
Treat, Charles, 52.
Treat, Damarus, 52.
Treat, Daniel, 102.
Treat, Dorotheus, 42.
Treat, Edmond, 102.
Treat, Elisha, 42.
Treat, Elisha, 52.
Treat, Elisha, 102.
Treat, Francis, 102.
Treat, Gershom, 42.
Treat, Gideon, 72.
Treat, Henry, 37.
Treat, Isaac, 102.
Treat, Isaac, 102.
Treat, John, 52.
Treat, John, 72.
Treat, John, 88.
Treat, John, 102.
Treat, John, 2nd, 102.
Treat, Jonathan, 36.
Treat, Jonathan, 43.
Treat, Jonathan, 102.
Treat, Jonathan, Jr., 43.
Treat, Joseph, 86.
Treat, Joseph, 102.
Treat, Joseph, 2nd, 102.
Treat, Mathias, 36.
Treat, Peter, 42.
Treat, Rebecca, 88.
Treat, Richard, 36.
Treat, Richard, 77.
Treat, Richard, 102.
Treat, Robert, 102.
Treat, Robert, 102.
Treat, Sam Peat, 75.
Treat, Samuel, 37.
Treat, Samuel, 42.
Treat, Samuel, 102.
Treat, Samuel, 114.
Treat, Stephen, 36.
Treat, Stephen, 88.
Treat, Stephen, 102.
Treat, Stephen, Junr, 88.
Treat, Theodore, 36.
Treby, Isaac, 129.
Treby, John, 129.
Tredway, John, 10.
Tredwell, Abel, 14.
Tredwell, Cato, 17.
Tredwell, David, 14.
Tredwell, Samuel, 25.
Tredwell, Sarah, 29.
Tredwell, Sarah, 30.
Tredwell, Timothy, 20.
Treet, George, 68.
Treet, Isaac, 62.
Treet, John, 61.
Trent, Abijah, 111.
Trevana, Richard, 87.
Tribble, James, 90.
Tribe, John, 117.
Trickey, Jerard, 103.
Trimklin, Ic, 138.
Trip, John, 91.
Trip, Willm, 89.
Tripp, James, 117.
Tripp, Nathl, 117.
Triscatt, Dorathy, 147.
Triscot, Joseph, 140.
Trisdal, Darias, 154.
Triseth, William, 85.
Tritten, Elizb, 103.
Trobridge, Daniel, 72.
Trobridge, Ebenezer, 72.
Trobridge, Isaac, 12.
Trobridge, James, 12.
Trobridge, John, 11.
Trobridge, John, 18.
Trobridge, John, 79.
Trobridge, Mary, 149.
Trobridge, Seth, 18.
Trobridge, Stephen, 12.
Trott, Jonathan, 129.
Trowbridge, Caleb, 103.
Trowbridge, Daniel, 103.
Trowbridge, Danl, 149.

Trowbridge, David, 105.
Trowbridge, Ebenezer, 81.
Trowbridge, James, 63.
Trowbridge, James, 149.
Trowbridge, John, 103.
Trowbridge, John, 149.
Trowbridge, John, Junr, 81.
Trowbridge, Jonathan, 81.
Trowbridge, Joseph, 103.
Trowbridge, Joseph, 2nd, 104.
Trowbridge, Joseph E., 103.
Trowbridge, Mabel, 103.
Trowbridge, Newman, 103.
Trowbridge, Rutherford, 103.
Trowbridge, Samuel, 21.
Trowbridge, Samuel, 105.
Trowbridge, Stephen, 103.
Trowbridge, Stephen, 103.
Trowbridge, Stephen, 3rd, 103.
Trowbridge, Thomas, 64.
Trowbridge, William, 103.
Trowbridge, William, 105.
Trubey, Answell, 14.
Truesdall, Asa, 50.
Truitt, Mattha, 77.
Truman, Daniel, 127.
Truman, Jonathan, 114.
Truman, Thaniel, 66.
Trumbal, Ezekiel, 65.
Trumbel, Asa, 135.
Trumble, Elizabeth, 95.
Trumble, Ephraim, 45.
Trumble, John, 46.
Trumbul, Eli, 50.
Trumbull, Benjamin, 106.
Trumbull, Benjn, 132.
Trumbull, David, 38.
Trumbull, David, 145.
Trumbull, John, 132.
Trumbull, John, 150.
Trumbull, Jonathan, 65.
Trumbull, Jonathan, 145.
Trumbull, Levi, 51.
Trumbull, Luther, 51.
Trumbull, Oliver, 51.
Trumbull, Shadrack, 51.
Trumbull, Walter, 147.
Trumbull, William, 147.
Trupper, Thomas, 67.
Truscoat, Solon, 61.
Trusdale, Ebenezur, 92.
Trusdale, Joel, 35.
Trusdell, Jeduthem, 149.
Trussell, Elizabeth, 102.
Tryall, William, 34.
Tryon, Aaron, 37.
Tryon, Aaron, 39.
Tryon, Abel, 87.
Tryon, Abijah, 53.
Tryon, Amos, 87.
Tryon, Asa, 89.
Tryon, Benjamin, 26.
Tryon, Caleb, 87.
Tryon, Charles, 87.
Tryon, David, 66.
Tryon, David, Junr, 87.
Tryon, Edward, 89.
Tryon, Edward, 2d, 89.
Tryon, Elee, 87.
Tryon, Elisha, 87.
Tryon, Elizuh, 42.
Tryon, Ely, 60.
Tryon, George, 43.
Tryon, Isaac, 43.
Tryon, James, 33.
Tryon, Jessy, 87.
Tryon, John, 49.
Tryon, John, 64.
Tryon, Joseph, 43.
Tryon, Joseph, 64.
Tryon, Josiah, 53.
Tryon, Josiah, 87.
Tryon, Lydia (Wid.), 47.
Tryon, Mary, 47.
Tryon, Moses, 52.
Tryon, Noah, 42.
Tryon, Samuel, 25.
Tryon, Stephen, 87.
Tryon, Thomas, 42.
Tryon, Thomas, 87.
Tryon, William, 42.
Tryon, William, 47.
Tryon, William, Jr., 42.
Tthroop, Dan., 59.
Tubbs, Ammon, 40.
Tubbs, Amos, 40.
Tubbs, Elisha, 35.
Tubbs, Elisha, 35.
Tubbs, Ezekiel, 43.
Tubbs, Lemuel, 43.
Tubbs, Lemuel, 81.
Tubbs, Simeon, 59.
Tubs, Ahimus, 124.
Tubs, Daniel, 112.
Tubs, John B., 124.
Tubs, John M., 124.
Tubs, Luman, 65.
Tubs, Peter, 124.
Tuch, Benjamin, 86.
Tuch, Comfort, 86.
Tuch, Enoch, 86.
Tuch, Micajah, 86.

Tuch, Richard, 135.
Tuch, Samuel, 86.
Tucker, Anner, 83.
Tucker, Asa, 51.
Tucker, Benjamin, 43.
Tucker, Daniel, 95.
Tucker, Daniel, 56.
Tucker, Elijah, 132.
Tucker, Em, 132.
Tucker, Ephraim, 63.
Tucker, Ephraim, 113.
Tucker, Ephraim, 149.
Tucker, Ephm, 154.
Tucker, Gideon, 54.
Tucker, Gideon, 95.
Tucker, Isaac, 26.
Tucker, Isaac, 47.
Tucker, James, 89.
Tucker, Jedediah, 63.
Tucker, Job, 124.
Tucker, Jonah, 95.
Tucker, Jona, 133.
Tucker, Joseph, 89.
Tucker, Jos., 132.
Tucker, Noah, 102.
Tucker, Phillup, 123.
Tucker, Reuben, 66.
Tucker, Reuben, 95.
Tucker, Richard, 89.
Tucker, Richard, 144.
Tucker, Rufus, 140.
Tucker, Samuel, 95.
Tucker, Samuel, 95.
Tucker, Stephen, 123.
Tucker, Stephen, 153.
Tucker, Stephen, Senr, 153.
Tucker, Tabor, 89.
Tucker, Thomas, 11.
Tucker, Timothy, 90.
Tucker, Timothy, 144.
Tucker, Uriah, 72.
Tucker, William, 94.
Tucker, William, 113.
Tucker, Zapthali, 96.
Tucker, Zephaniah, 94.
Tucker, Zephh, 153.
Tuckerman, Benjamin, 151.
Tuckerman, Jacob, 148.
Tuday, Huldah, 17.
Tudor, Elihu, 37.
Tudor, Samuel, 37.
Tuffie, Robert, 52.
Tuft, Joshua, 105.
Tufts, Aaron, 141.
Tufts, Peter, 141.
Tuley, Amos, 126.
Tullar, Elijah, Jr., 48.
Tullar, Joel, 48.
Tullar, Samuel, 48.
Tuller, Abel, 48.
Tuller, Amasa, 49.
Tuller, David, 102.
Tuller, Eli, 48.
Tuller, Elijah, 48.
Tuller, Elisha, 48.
Tuller, Isaac, 48.
Tuller, Jacob, 48.
Tuller, James, 48.
Tuller, John, 63.
Tuller, Joseph, 48.
Tuller, Joseph, Jr., 48.
Tuller, Martin, 94.
Tuller, Reuben, 48.
Tuller, Samuel, 48.
Tulley, Wm, 89.
Tully, Elias, 89.
Tully, Saml, Esqr, 89.
Tumey, John, 20.
Tupper, Charles, 19.
Tupper, Jos., 138.
Tupper, Mayo, 81.
Tupper, Saml, 67.
Tupper, Solm, 137.
Tupper, William, 67.
Turner, Abraham, 84.
Turner, Abraham, 100.
Turner, Amos, 87.
Turner, Amos, 134.
Turner, Amos, Junr, 119.
Turner, Barts, 61.
Turner, Bethuel, 77.
Turner, Caleb, 46.
Turner, Caleb, 106.
Turner, Caleb, 106.
Turner, Daniel, 61.
Turner, David, 77.
Turner, Easter, 63.
Turner, Edward, 106.
Turner, Eleazr, 148.
Turner, Elijah, 147.
Turner, Elijah, 148.
Turner, Elisha, 100.
Turner, Elizabeth, 84.
Turner, Enoch, 103.
Turner, Ephraim, 35.
Turner, Ezekiel, 119.
Turner, Gurden, 100.
Turner, Henry, 96.
Turner, Hezekiah, 66.
Turner, Isaac, 85.
Turner, Isaac, 124.
Turner, Isaac, 147.
Turner, Jabez, 100.

Turner, Jacob, 84.
Turner, Jesse, 102.
Turner, Jethro, 134.
Turner, John, 66.
Turner, John, 88.
Turner, John, 131.
Turner, Jonathan, 89.
Turner, Jos., 133.
Turner, Joshua, 125.
Turner, Mary, 145.
Turner, Mathew, 125.
Turner, Peletiah, 47.
Turner, Perigreen, 125.
Turner, Pheneas, 147.
Turner, Phillip, 148.
Turner, Phillup, 132.
Turner, Prince, 147.
Turner, Robt, 133.
Turner, Samuel, 46.
Turner, Saml, 62.
Turner, Saml, 133.
Turner, Saml, 147.
Turner, Sarah, 128.
Turner, Seth, 103.
Turner, Stephen, 77.
Turner, Stephen, 88.
Turner, Stephen, 147.
Turner, Stephen, 148.
Turner, Thomas, 124.
Turner, Thomas, 148.
Turner, Thomas, 2d, 124.
Turner, Timothy, 100.
Turner, Timothy, 147.
Turner, Titus, 66.
Turner (Widow), 134.
Turner, Wm, 90.
Turney, Aaron, 14.
Turney, Abel, 14.
Turney, Abiah, 14.
Turney, Asa, 14.
Turney, Daniel, 29.
Turney, David, 29.
Turney, David, 31.
Turney, Elnathan, 29.
Turney, Ephraim, 29.
Turney, Gershom, 29.
Turney, Isaac, 14.
Turney, John, 29.
Turney, John, 29.
Turney, Nathan, 21.
Turney, Peter, 14.
Turney, Robert, 29.
Turney, Samuel, 29.
Turpin, Henry, 87.
Turrel, Amos, 109.
Turrel, Binjamin, 109.
Turrel, David, 101.
Turrel, Elihu, 111.
Turrel, Enoch, 94.
Turrel, Enoch, 111.
Turrel, Ephrahim, 2nd, 93.
Turrel, Ephrim, 93.
Turrel, George, 21.
Turrel, Icobald, 110.
Turrel, Isaac, 95.
Turrel, Isaac, 110.
Turrel, Isaiah, 110.
Turrel, Israel, 110.
Turrel, Jared, 20.
Turrel, Jerad, 110.
Turrel, Jesse, 112.
Turrel, Josiah, 110.
Turrel, Mary, 102.
Turrel, Olivir, 110.
Turrel, Phineas, 112.
Turrel, Ruben, 21.
Turrel, Samuel, 101.
Turrell, Nathaniel, 23.
Turril, Amos, 21.
Turril, Boger, 21.
Turril, Daniel, 32.
Turril, Stephen, 32.
Turtels, Benjamin, 144.
Turtolot, Barnabas, 150.
Turtolot, Erick, 150.
Turtolot, Isaac, 150.
Turtolot, Israel, 150.
Turtolot, Joshua, 150.
Turtolot, Michl, 150.
Tush, Joseph, 69.
Tuttle, Aaron, 79.
Tuttle, Abigail (Wd), 22.
Tuttle, Abigal, 100.
Tuttle, Abigal, 106.
Tuttle, Abner, 104.
Tuttle, Abraham, 50.
Tuttle, Abraham, 102.
Tuttle, Abraham, 2nd, 103.
Tuttle, Abram, 79.
Tuttle, Aexander, 100.
Tuttle, Amos, 75.
Tuttle, Amos, 101.
Tuttle, Andrew, 79.
Tuttle, Andrew, 101.
Tuttle, Andrew, 2nd, 101.
Tuttle, Annie, 95.
Tuttle, Aron, 100.
Tuttle, Ayers, 79.
Tuttle, Benj, 108.
Tuttle, Bostwick, 79.
Tuttle, Caleb, 112.
Tuttle, Charles, 107.
Tuttle, Christopher, 97.

# INDEX. 221

Tuttle, Clem, 60.
Tuttle, Daniel, 20.
Tuttle, Daniel, 79.
Tuttle, Daniel, 97.
Tuttle, Daniel, 100.
Tuttle, Daniel, 105.
Tuttle, Daniel, 110.
Tuttle, David, 23.
Tuttle, David, 79.
Tuttle, David, 106.
Tuttle, Deborah, 106.
Tuttle, Ebenezer, 22.
Tuttle, Ebenezer, 92.
Tuttle, Edmond, 24.
Tuttle, Edmond, 92.
Tuttle, Eli, 22.
Tuttle, Eli, 75.
Tuttle, Elisha, 70.
Tuttle, Enos, 94.
Tuttle, Enoch, 22.
Tuttle, Enos, 100.
Tuttle, Enos, 100.
Tuttle, Ethmah, 106.
Tuttle, Ephraim, 79.
Tuttle, Ephraim, 92.
Tuttle, Ezekiel, 79.
Tuttle, Ezra, 106.
Tuttle, Gideon, 59.
Tuttle, Hannah, 109.
Tuttle, Hezekiah, 100.
Tuttle, Hezekiah, 104.
Tuttle, Hezekiah, 106.
Tuttle, Hoy, 105.
Tuttle, Isaac, 60.
Tuttle, Isaac, 106.
Tuttle, Isaah, 61.
Tuttle, Jabez, 100.
Tuttle, Jecobed, 92.
Tuttle, Jeremiah, 112.
Tuttle, Jery, 66.
Tuttle, Jesse, 22.
Tuttle, Jesse, 100.
Tuttle, Jesse, 109.
Tuttle, Jetus, 108.
Tuttle, Joathan, 100.
Tuttle, Joel, 57.
Tuttle, Joel, 98.
Tuttle, Joel, 106.
Tuttle, John, 77.
Tuttle, John, 106.
Tuttle, Jonathan, 75.
Tuttle, Jonathan, 106.
Tuttle, Jonathan, 108.
Tuttle, Josepʰ, 96.
Tuttle, Lazerus, 92.
Tuttle, Levi, 22.
Tuttle, Limuel, 106.
Tuttle, Martha, 39.
Tuttle, Moses, 63.
Tuttle, Moses, 92.
Tuttle, Moses, 2ⁿᵈ, 93.
Tuttle, Nathan, 22.
Tuttle, Nathan, Jʳ, 22.
Tuttle, Nathaniel, 74.
Tuttle, Nathaniel, 111.
Tuttle, Newton, 74.
Tuttle, Noah, 65.
Tuttle, Noah, 74.
Tuttle, Noah, 77.
Tuttle, Obediah, 77.
Tuttle, Pelatiah, 125.
Tuttle, Peter, 24.
Tuttle, Richard, 104.
Tuttle, Ruben, 106.
Tuttle, Samuel, 79.
Tuttle, Samuel, 92.
Tuttle, Samuel, 97.
Tuttle, Samuel, 106.
Tuttle, Simeon, 106.
Tuttle, Soloman, 106.
Tuttle, Stephan, 97.
Tuttle, Stephen, 77.
Tuttle, Uriah, 111.
Tuttle, William, 77.
Tuttle, Zenas, 50.
Tweedy, Samuel, 11.
Twichel, David, 95.
Twichet, Benjamin, 95.
Twichet, David, 95.
Twichet, Ebenezer, 95.
Twichet, Elizabeth, 95.
Twichet, Enoch, 95.
Twichet, Joseph, 95.
Twichett, John, 95.
Twicket, Joseph, 110.
Twiner, George, 17.
Twiss, John, 56.
Twiss, Samuel, 75.
Twist, Benjamin, 93.
Twist, David, 139.
Twogood, Samˡ, 144.
Tylar, Caleb, 114.
Tylar, Elisha, 113.
Tylar, James, 113.
Tylar, John, 113.
Tylar, John, Junʳ, 113.
Tylar, Joseph, 113.
Tylar, Joseph, 114.
Tylar, Lemuel, 114.
Tylar, Samuel, 113.
Tylar, Solomon, 119.
Tyler, Abel, 70.
Tyler, Abial, 70.

Tyler, Abraham, 83.
Tyler, Abraham, 110.
Tyler, Adonijah, 57.
Tyler, Amos, 60.
Tyler, Amos, 70.
Tyler, Amos, 94.
Tyler, Asa, 141.
Tyler, Banijah, 61.
Tyler, Benjamin, 91.
Tyler, Broadstreat, 139.
Tyler, Broadᵗ, 2ᵈ, 139.
Tyler, Daniel, 110.
Tyler, Danˡ, 141.
Tyler, Danˡ, 146.
Tyler, Danˡ, Jnʳ, 141.
Tyler, Daniel, 2ᵈ, 110.
Tyler, Ebenezer, 79.
Tyler, Elisha, 70.
Tyler, Isaac, 94.
Tyler, Isaac, 2ⁿᵈ, 94.
Tyler, Isael, 92.
Tyler, Jacob, 49.
Tyler, James, 139.
Tyler, Jason, 108.
Tyler, Jeames, 79.
Tyler, Jeames, 2ᵈ, 79.
Tyler, Jedior, 70.
Tyler, Jerad, 108.
Tyler, Job, 141.
Tyler, John, 97.
Tyler, John, 108.
Tyler, John, 142.
Tyler, Jonathan, 92.
Tyler, Josep, 106.
Tyler, Joseph, 83.
Tyler, Joseph, 91.
Tyler, Joseph, 93.
Tyler, Joseph, 141.
Tyler, Joseph, Junʳ, 83.
Tyler, Josiah, 91.
Tyler, Molly, 100.
Tyler, Nathan, 83.
Tyler, Nathaniel, Junʳ, 83.
Tyler, Nehemiah, 83.
Tyler, Obed, 91.
Tyler, Obed, 91.
Tyler, Oliver, 142.
Tyler, Osias, 77.
Tyler, Patty, 91.
Tyler, Paul, 92.
Tyler, Peter, 91.
Tyler, Peter, 92.
Tyler, Philomen, 91.
Tyler, Roswell, 79.
Tyler, Ruben, 109.
Tyler, Ruth, 93.
Tyler, Samuel, 83.
Tyler, Samuel, 91.
Tyler, Samuel, 91.
Tyler, Samuel, 108.
Tyler, Samˡ, 141.
Tyler, Simon, 83.
Tyler, Soloman, 91.
Tyler, Solomon, 66.
Tyler, Thomas, 83.
Tyler, Timothy, 83.
Tyler, William, 92.
Tyler, Zebulon, 142.
Tyler (Widow), 137.
Tylford, Philathia, 71.
Tyrel, Amos, 17.
Tyrel, John, 17.
Tyrell, Eliakin, 112.
Tyrell, John, 112.
Tyrell, Philomin, 112.

Ufford, Benjamin, 29.
Ufford, Daniel, 29.
Ufford, Ebenezer, 30.
Ufford, Elakim, 80.
Ufford, John, 29.
Ufford, John, 29.
Ufford, John, 80.
Ufford, John, Junʳ, 80.
Ufford, Jonathan, 80.
Ufford, Samuel, 29.
Ufford, Samuel, 30.
Umphrevile, Patty, 18.
Umstead, John, 121.
Underhill, John, 20.
Underwood, John, 112.
Underwood, Josiah, 149.
Underwood, Josiah, 154.
Underwood, Lemuel, 154.
Underwood, Lott, 149.
Underwood, Nehᵇ, 154.
Underwood, Timothy, 149.
Underwood, William, 150.
Upham, Isaac, 150.
Upham, Ivory, 150.
Upham, Jonathⁿ, 150.
Upham, Joseph, 147.
Upham, Luther, 150.
Upham, Noah, 147.
Upsom, Jesse, 105.
Upson, Amos, 50.
Upson, Asa, 34.
Upson, Asa, Jr., 34.
Upson, Ashbel, 110.
Upson, Benjamin, 77.
Upson, Benjamin, 109.
Upson, Benoni, 33.
Upson, Charles, 110.

Upson, Daniel, 110.
Upson, Ezekiel, 110.
Upson, Friman, 34.
Upson, Isaac, 50.
Upson, James, 93.
Upson, John, 50.
Upson, Joseph, 77.
Upson, Josiah, 50.
Upson, Josiah, 50.
Upson, Noah, 77.
Upson, Rusel, 77.
Upson, Samuel, 109.
Upson, Saul, 34.
Upson, Thomas, 50.
Upson, Timothy, 50.
Upton, John, 24.
Upton, Lucy, 143.
Upum, Wate, 21.
Uri, John, 69.
Usher, Hezʰ, 82.
Usher, Oliver, 82.
Usher, Robert, 81.
Utley, Abigal, 140.
Utley, Amos, 143.
Utley, Amos, Jnʳ, 143.
Utley, Asahel, 136.
Utley, Elijah, 116.
Utley, John, 116.
Utley, Jnᵒ, 139.
Utley, Joseph, 38.
Utley, Joseph, 55.
Utley, Oliver, 147.
Utley, Peleg, 115.
Utley, Samˡ, 140.
Utley, Samˡ, 143.
Utley, Stephen, 149.
Utley, Thoˢ, 143.
Utley (Wid͏ᵉ), 149.
Utter, Stephen, 90.
Uttley, Stephen, 134.
Uttley, Timᵒ, 134.
Uvit, John, 19.

Vail, Jonathan, 97.
Vail, Revʳ Joseph, 82.
Vale, Christopher, 131.
Vale, William, 114.
Vallet, Jeremiah, 2ᵈ, 125.
Vallet, Jeremiah, 3ᵈ, 124.
Vandeuerson, William, 86.
Vandoore, Charles, 59.
Van Doosen, John, 11.
Vandooser, Abraham, 69.
Vandusen, Content, 67.
Vanduser, Thomas, 101.
Vanette, James, 107.
Vanevert, Abraham, 16.
Vanorden, John, 105.
Vanorstrain, Aaron, 18.
Vanostran, Aaron, 17.
Vansant, Christopher, 80.
Vanziekland, Minna, 16.
Varnold, John, 29.
Varnum, Wᵐ, 134.
Vates, John, 48.
Vaughn, Danˡ, 151.
Vaughn, Jesse, 151.
Vaughn, Martha, 146.
Vaughn, Philander, 73.
Vaun, William, 61.
Vaune, Benjamin, 18.
Vaune, Olive, 14.
Vaune, William, 18.
Veal, Daniel, 70.
Veal, John, 10.
Veal, Jonathan, 98.
Veal, Joseph, 70.
Veal, Moses, 12.
Veal, Nathaniel, 98.
Veale, Joshua, 98.
Veets, David, 68.
Veits, Abner, 44.
Veits, Benoni, 44.
Veits, James, 44
Veits, Jonathan, 44.
Veits, Luke, 44.
Veits, Seth, 44.
Venterhouse, John, 83.
Venterhouse, John, Junʳ, 83.
Vergoson, Diah, 126.
Vergoson, Jeremiah, 126.
Vergoson, John, 126.
Vibber, Nathˡ, 125.
Vibber, Thomas, 121.
Vibber, William, 125.
Vibbert, David, 37.
Vibbert, Elisha, 46.
Vibbert, James, 37.
Vibbert, James, 37.
Vibbert, Jesse, 36.
Vibbert, John, 36
Videto, Jeames, 72.
Villey, Cornelius, 67.
Vincent, Joseph, 117.
Vincent, William, 116.
Vinen, Josiah, 11.
Viney, Elias, 47.
Vining, Alexander, 38.
Vining, Richard, 44.
Vintin, David, 139.
Vintin, Samˡ, 139.
Vintin, Seth, 139.

Vinton, Timothy, 153.
Vira (Negro), 121.
Virstille, William, 38.
Vislon, Elijah, 133.
Vitelo, John, 64.
Voce, Adam, 94.
Voce, Charles, 108.
Voce, Jesse, 107.
Volph, Anthony, 120.
Volumn, Lenard, 104.
Vorce, Wᵐ, 130.
Vors, Edward, 116.
Vorse, Samuel, 38.
Vosburgh, Jacob, 63.
Vose, Lemˡ, 149.

Wack, Lydea, 120.
Wacket (Freeman), 81.
Waddoms, Solomon, 60.
Waddy, Peter, 28.
Wade, Abraham, 123.
Wade, Dredley, 38.
Wade, Ebenezer, 107.
Wade, Elihu, 123.
Wade, Elisha, 123.
Wade, George, 123.
Wade, Hannah, 122.
Wade, Increse, 77.
Wade, James, 130.
Wade, John, 123.
Wade, John, 2ⁿᵈ, 107.
Wade, Jonᵃ, 130.
Wade, Martin, 124.
Wade, Sarah, 132.
Wade, William, 113.
Wadeling, Esther, 19.
Wadham, Jonathan, 64.
Wadhams, Abraham, 65.
Wadhams, Ingersol, 73.
Wadhams, John, 69.
Wadhams, Moses, 64.
Wadhams, Noah, 73.
Wadhams, Seth, 64.
Wadkins, Abel, 31.
Wadkins, Ephᵐ, 81.
Wadkins, William, 31.
Wadsworth, Abigail, 46.
Wadsworth, Asahel, 40.
Wadsworth, Daniel, 47.
Wadsworth, David, 46.
Wadsworth, Eben, 59.
Wadsworth, Eliphalet, 40.
Wadsworth, Elisha, 46.
Wadsworth, Elisha, Jr., 47.
Wadsworth, Eunice, 40.
Wadsworth, George, 46.
Wadsworth, George, 46.
Wadsworth, Gurdon, 46.
Wadsworth, Henry, 46.
Wadsworth, Hester, 96.
Wadsworth, Hezekiah, 41.
Wadsworth, Icabod, 134.
Wadsworth, James, 46.
Wadsworth, James, 96.
Wadsworth, Jeams, 57.
Wadsworth, Jeremiah, 46.
Wadsworth, Jerusha, 36.
Wadsworth, John, 67.
Wadsworth, John M., 96.
Wadsworth, Joseph, 46.
Wadsworth, Joseph, 57.
Wadsworth, Josiah, 63.
Wadsworth, Luke, 40.
Wadsworth, Rachel (Wid.), 46.
Wadsworth, Reubin, 40.
Wadsworth, Roger, 46.
Wadsworth, Samuel, 36.
Wadsworth, Samuel, 46.
Wadsworth, Samuel, 57.
Wadsworth, Theodore, 49.
Wadsworth, Thomas, 37.
Wadsworth, Thomas, 46.
Wadsworth, Timothy, 44.
Wadsworth, William, 36.
Wadsworth, Wᵐ, 40.
Waggoner, Adam, 74.
Waggoner, David, 74.
Waggoner, Henry, 46.
Waid, Josiah, 62.
Wainwright, Jonathan, 93.
Waistcott, Jeremiah, 23.
Wait, John, 69.
Wait, John, 123.
Wait, Joseph, 123.
Wait, Loen, 123.
Wait, Marvin, 126.
Wait, Remick, 123.
Wait, Richard, 123.
Wait, Richard, Junʳ, 123.
Wait, Thomas G., 124.
Wait, Wᵐ, 55.
Wakefield, Elijah, 137.
Wakefield, Jnᵒ, 137.
Wakefield, John, 150.
Wakefield, Levy, 137.
Wakefield, Partrof, 64.
Wakefield, Ziel, 137.
Wakelee, James, 18.
Wakelee, Josiah S., 18.
Wakeley, Asa, 83.
Wakeley, Henry, 79.
Wakeley, Lemwell, 10.

Wakeley, Platt, 79.
Wakeley, Samuel, Jnʳ, 17.
Wakeley, Solomon, 84.
Wakelin, Abel, 14.
Wakelin, David, 18.
Wakelin, Isaac, 17.
Wakelin, James, 10.
Wakelin, Samuel, 17.
Wakelin, Samuel, 31.
Wakely, Anna, 30.
Wakely, David, 30.
Wakely, David, 110.
Wakely, John, 12.
Wakely, Jonathan, 29.
Wakely, Molly (Wid.), 30.
Wakely, Nehemiah, 30.
Wakely, Thomas, 29.
Wakeman, Aaron, 32.
Wakeman, Abel, 13.
Wakeman, Andrew, 14.
Wakeman, Daniel, 31.
Wakeman, David, 19.
Wakeman, Ebenezer, 13.
Wakeman, Ebenezer, 14.
Wakeman, Eli, 13.
Wakeman, Epaphras, 13.
Wakeman, Gershom, 13.
Wakeman, Giddeon, 13.
Wakeman, Giddeon, 19.
Wakeman, Jabez, 27.
Wakeman, Jeremiah, 19.
Wakeman, John, 3ᵈ, 13.
Wakeman, Joseph, 13.
Wakeman, Liman, 13.
Wakeman, Moses, 13.
Wakeman, Samuel, Junʳ, 31.
Wakeman, Seth, 19.
Wakeman, Thaddeus, 13.
Wakeman, Timothy, 27.
Wakeman, William, 13.
Wakeman, William, 19.
Waker, Mary, 140.
Waker, Samˡ, Jnʳ, 140.
Wakley, Ebenezer, 110.
Wakman, Elijah, 31.
Wakman, Ephraim, 29.
Wakman, Lloyd, 31.
Wakman, Nathan, 31.
Wakman, Samuel, 31.
Walbridge, Amos, 137.
Walbridge, Ebenezer, 130.
Walbridge, Gustavus, 130.
Walbridge, Jnᵒ, 133.
Walbridge, Jonᵃ, 134.
Walbridge, Lemˡ, 133.
Walbridge, Samˡ, 134.
Walbridge, Wᵐ, 137.
Walcott, Abigail, 54.
Walcott, Jabez, 153.
Walcott, John, 64.
Walcott, Moses, 143.
Walcott, Nathˡ, 153.
Walcott, William, 37.
Walden, Elisabeth, 126.
Walden, Eᵐ, 132.
Walden, Jeremiah, 46.
Walden, John, 126.
Walden, Nathaniel, 85.
Waldo, Abigene, 149.
Waldo, Bethuel, 134.
Waldo, Cornelius, 115.
Waldo, Edward, 142.
Waldo, Jesse, 147.
Waldo, Jesse, Senʳ, 147.
Waldo, Joanna, 149.
Waldo, John, 129.
Waldo, John E., 143.
Waldo, Nathan, 133.
Waldo, Roger, 147.
Waldo, Samˡ, 149.
Waldo, Syprean, 61.
Waldo (Widow), 133.
Waldo, Zachᵇ, 142.
Waldo, Zachᵘˢ, 153.
Waldo, Zachᵘˢ, Jnʳ, 153.
Waldon, John, 153.
Waldon, John, Jnʳ, 153.
Waldren, Isaac, 118.
Waldren, Lowis, 117.
Wales, Elijah, 139.
Wales, Horatio, 47.
Wales, Jonathan, 152.
Wales, Nathan, 140.
Wales, Nathaniel, 152.
Wales, Revᵈ Samuel, 104.
Wales, Solˡ, 139.
Wales, William, 152.
Waley, Aaron, 13.
Waley, David, 125.
Waley, Elexander, 125.
Waley, Hezekiah, 13.
Waley, James, 125.
Waley, Jonathan, 125.
Waley, Samuel, 125.
Walker, Abigal, 97.
Walker, Andrew, 150.
Walker, Asael, 153.
Walker, Benjⁿ, 138.
Walker, Benjⁿ, 140.
Walker, Benjⁿ, 2ᵈ, 138.
Walker, David, 75.
Walker, Ebenᵉ, 140.
Walker, Ebenʳ, Jnʳ, 141.

222 INDEX.


Walker, Eben$^{e}$, Sen$^{r}$, 141.
Walker, Eliakim, 29.
Walker, Eph$^{m}$, 141.
Walker, James, 30.
Walker, James, 89.
Walker, James, 140.
Walker, James, Jun$^{r}$, 30.
Walker, John, 20.
Walker, John, 129.
Walker, Jn$^{o}$, 132.
Walker, Jn$^{o}$, 2$^{d}$, 132.
Walker, Joseph, 30.
Walker, Joseph, 30.
Walker, Joseph, 79.
Walker, Joseph, 123.
Walker, Joseph, 2$^{d}$, 79.
Walker, Leonard, 153.
Walker, Peter, 79.
Walker, Phebe (Wid.), 30.
Walker, Pheneas, 153.
Walker, Robert, 29.
Walker, Samuel, 79.
Walker, Sam$^{l}$, 140.
Walker, Stephen, 141.
Walker, Tim$^{o}$, 138.
Walker, Webber, 111.
Walker, William, 97.
Walker, William, 141.
Walkley, Ebenezer, 99.
Walkley, Richard, 84.
Wall, James, 130.
Wall, William, 148.
Wallace, Anna, 65.
Wallace, Richard, 64.
Wallace, William, 28.
Wallace, William, 103.
Wallen, Daniel, 70.
Wallen, James, 67.
Wallen, James, 70.
Wallen, John, 70.
Wallen, Thomas, 70.
Wallen, William, 60.
Waller, Elijah, 59.
Waller, Hannah, 132.
Waller, Joseph, 73.
Waller, Peter, 59.
Waller, Samuel, 59.
Waller, Silas, 132.
Wallice, Ab$^{m}$, 136.
Wallin, Cornelious, 144.
Walling, Ezekiel, 148.
Wallis, Ab$^{m}$, 134.
Wallis, Jacob, 20.
Wallis, James, 36.
Wallis, James, 137.
Wallis, John, 37.
Wallis, William, 37.
Wallis, W$^{m}$, 134.
Wallworth, Daniel, 86.
Wally, John, 129.
Wally, John, 154.
Walmsbey, William, 26.
Walstone, Thomas, 97.
Walter, Clark, 63.
Walter, Jacob, 106.
Walter, John, 67.
Walter, Mahitabel, 106.
Walter, Moses, 63.
Walter, William, 63.
Walter, William, 66.
Walter, William, 103.
Walton, Daniel, 113.
Walton, Francis, 93.
Walton, Joseph, 153.
Walton, Oliver, 113.
Walton, William, 62.
Walworth, Benjamin, 126.
Walworth, Joshua, 119.
Walworth, Sarah, 120.
Wane, Russel, 19.
Wanner, Dav$^{d}$, 132.
Wanright, Thomas, 61.
Wanright, Wiliam, 29.
Wanton (Negro), 113.
Wanzer, Abraham, 18.
Wanzer, Ebenezer, 18.
Wanzer, Eliud, 19.
Wanzer, Husted, 19.
Wanzer, Moses, 18.
Wanzer, Nicholas, 18.
Ward, Abel, 112.
Ward, Abiel, 88.
Ward, Abigail, 87.
Ward, Abijah, 62.
Ward, Amasa, 67.
Ward, Ambros, 103.
Ward, Ambrose, 92.
Ward, Ambrose, J$^{r}$, 103.
Ward, Amie, 108.
Ward, Andrew, 98.
Ward, Bela, 88.
Ward, Bethuel, 74.
Ward, Buley, 98.
Ward, Crittendon, 129.
Ward, Daniel, 42.
Ward, Dan$^{l}$, 64.
Ward, David, 60.
Ward, Edward, 88.
Ward, Elizabeth, 98.
Ward, Henry, 105.
Ward, Ichabod, 85.
Ward, Ichabod, 140.
Ward, Ichabod, 142.
Ward, Jacob, 136.
Ward, James, 64.
Ward, James, 85.
Ward, James, 136.
Ward, James T., 88.
Ward, John, 60.
Ward, John, 87.
Ward, John, 89.
Ward, John, 103.
Ward, John, 105.
Ward, John, 129.
Ward, John, 4$^{th}$, 87.
Ward, John, 5$^{th}$, 87.
Ward, Joseph, 88.
Ward, Joseph, Jun$^{r}$, 88.
Ward, Joshua, 88.
Ward, Josiah, 87.
Ward, Josiah, Jun$^{r}$, 87.
Ward, Levi, 99.
Ward, Macork, 74.
Ward, Obediah, 138.
Ward, Phebe, 141.
Ward, Rufus, 50.
Ward, Samuel, 29.
Ward, Samuel, 87.
Ward, Sam$^{l}$, 141.
Ward, Samuel, Jun$^{r}$, 87.
Ward, Sibel, 105.
Ward, Smith, 90.
Ward, Thelas, 98.
Ward, Thomas, 39.
Ward, Thomas, 88.
Ward, Thomas, 105.
Ward, Timothy, 93.
Ward, Titus, 103.
Ward, William, 71.
Ward, William, 86.
Ward, William, 88.
Ward, William, 89.
Ward, William, 146.
Ward, William, Jun$^{r}$, 89.
Ward, Zenas, 1$^{st}$, 74.
Ward, Zenas, 2$^{d}$, 74.
Warden, William, 29.
Warden, William, Jn$^{r}$, 14.
Wardstark, W$^{m}$, 90.
Warduher, Sarah, 29.
Wardwel, David, 136.
Wardwell, Abigail (W$^{d}$), 27.
Wardwell, Eber, 137.
Wardwell, Jacob, 24.
Wardwell, Nath$^{el}$, 136.
Ware, Daniel, 39.
Ware, John, 70.
Wares, Joseph, 43.
Warin, Martin, 133.
Waring, Deborah (W$^{d}$), 22.
Waring, Eliakim, 22.
Waring, Elizabeth (W$^{d}$), 24.
Waring, Enoch, 23.
Waring, Eunice (W$^{d}$), 22.
Waring, Henry, 15.
Waring, Hezron, 25.
Waring, Jesse, 22.
Waring, Jesse, 25.
Waring, Jonathan, 25.
Waring, Joseph, 23.
Waring, Joseph, 25.
Waring, Joseph, J$^{r}$, 22.
Waring, Linas, 25.
Waring, Major, 19.
Waring, Martha (W$^{d}$), 26.
Waring, Mary (W$^{d}$), 26.
Waring, Nathan, 24.
Waring, Noah, 25.
Waring, Sally (w$^{d}$), 26.
Waring, Samuel, 19.
Waring, Samuel, 26.
Waring, Silvanus, 26.
Waring, Solomon, 22.
Waring, Thaddeus, 24.
Warker, Comfort, 144.
Warley, Mary (W$^{d}$), 23.
Warner, ——, 128.
Warner, Aaron, 52.
Warner, Aaron, 77.
Warner, Abigal, 100.
Warner, Abijah, 109.
Warner, Abijail, 79.
Warner, Ab$^{m}$, 82.
Warner, Abraham, 105.
Warner, Amasy, 63.
Warner, Amos, 100.
Warner, Andrew, 109.
Warner, Asa, 73.
Warner, Austin, 63.
Warner, Benjamin, 79.
Warner, Benjamin, 100.
Warner, Benjamin, 144.
Warner, Chapman, 122.
Warner, Daniel, 33.
Warner, Daniel, 53.
Warner, Dan$^{l}$, 81.
Warner, Daniel, 134.
Warner, David, 77.
Warner, David, 79.
Warner, David, 91.
Warner, David, 100.
Warner, Deliverance, 80.
Warner, Demus, 40.
Warner, Ebenezer, 79.
Warner, Ebenezer, 100.
Warner, Ebenezer, 109.
Warner, Ebenezer, 2$^{d}$, 79.
Warner, Ebenezer, 2$^{nd}$, 100.
Warner, Eleaz$^{r}$, 147.
Warner, Eli, 47.
Warner, Eli, 51.
Warner, Elihu, 122.
Warner, Elijah, 73.
Warner, Elijah, 77.
Warner, Elinor, 109.
Warner, Eliphalet, 39.
Warner, Elisha, 77.
Warner, Elizebeth, 105.
Warner, Elizuer, 73.
Warner, Emm, 79.
Warner, Eneas, 110.
Warner, Enos, 79.
Warner, Ephrahim, 109.
Warner, Ephraim, 109.
Warner, Esther, 79.
Warner, Gideon, 79.
Warner, Hannah, 53.
Warner, Hannah, 81.
Warner, Hannah (W$^{d}$), 39.
Warner, Hezekiah, 100.
Warner, Hope, 86.
Warner, Isaac, 51.
Warner, J. Ichabod, 75.
Warner, Jabez, 81.
Warner, Jabez, 2$^{d}$, 82.
Warner, Jacob, 102.
Warner, James H., 109.
Warner, Jared, 149.
Warner, Jeames, 77.
Warner, Jesse, 100.
Warner, John, 35.
Warner, John, 39.
Warner, John, 51.
Warner, John, 52.
Warner, John, 55.
Warner, John, 73.
Warner, John, 81.
Warner, John, 88.
Warner, John, 104.
Warner, John, 2$^{d}$, 51.
Warner, John, 2$^{d}$, 52.
Warner, John, 2$^{d}$, 73.
Warner, John, 2$^{d}$, 77.
Warner, John, 2$^{d}$, 82.
Warner, John, 3$^{d}$, 52.
Warner, John, 3$^{d}$, 77.
Warner, Jonah, 100.
Warner, Jon$^{a}$, 90.
Warner, Jonathan, 122.
Warner, Joseph, 79.
Warner, Joseph, 81.
Warner, Joseph, 102.
Warner, Joseph, 110.
Warner, Joseph, 2$^{d}$, 82.
Warner, Joseph, 2$^{nd}$, 109.
Warner, Josiah, 109.
Warner, Justice, 109.
Warner, Lemuel, 73.
Warner, Levi, 53.
Warner, Lois, 88.
Warner, Loomis, 55.
Warner, Mark, 109.
Warner, Martin, 10.
Warner, Molly, 20.
Warner, Moses, 51.
Warner, Moses, 137.
Warner, Nath$^{n}$, 35.
Warner, Nathan, 79.
Warner, Nathan, 122.
Warner, Nathaniel, 35.
Warner, Nathaniel, 51.
Warner, Nath$^{l}$, 121.
Warner, Nath$^{l}$, 152.
Warner, Noadiah, 74.
Warner, Noadoc, 20.
Warner, Noah, 77.
Warner, Oliver, 73.
Warner, Oliver, 81.
Warner, Oliver, 122.
Warner, Orange, 73.
Warner, Osias, 77.
Warner, Phillip, 134.
Warner, Phinehas, 91.
Warner, Prudence, 52.
Warner, Reuben, 73.
Warner, Reuben, 2$^{d}$, 73.
Warner, Rhoda, 53.
Warner, Rhoda, 79.
Warner, Richard, 51.
Warner, Robert, 52.
Warner, Robert, 85.
Warner, Ruben, 109.
Warner, Rugles, 10.
Warner, Samuel, 35.
Warner, Samuel, 35.
Warner, Samuel, 51.
Warner, Samuel, 79.
Warner, Sam$^{l}$, 82.
Warner, Samuel, 100.
Warner, Sam$^{l}$, 134.
Warner, Samuel, Jr., 35.
Warner, Saul, 79.
Warner, Selden, 122.
Warner, Seldon, 81.
Warner, Seth, 74.
Warner, Silas, 51.
Warner, Solomon, 10.
Warner, Stephen, 110.
Warner, Thaddeus, 51.
Warner, Thomas, 33.
Warner, Thomas, 52.
Warner, Thomas, 79.
Warner, Thomas, 140.
Warner, Wait, 53.
Warner, William, 52.
Warner, William, 86.
Warner, Will$^{m}$, 91.
Warner, William, 153.
Warren, Abigal, 112.
Warren, Ashbel, 36.
Warren, Daniel, 36.
Warren, Dorus, 47.
Warren, Edward, 36.
Warren, Edward, 112.
Warren, Eleaz$^{r}$, 144.
Warren, Eleaz$^{r}$, Jn$^{r}$, 144.
Warren, Elisha, 36.
Warren, Elizur, 47.
Warren, Ephraim, 143.
Warren, Ephraim, 144.
Warren, Ezra, 148.
Warren, Henery, 43.
Warren, Isaac, 144.
Warren, John, 43.
Warren, Jn$^{o}$, 138.
Warren, John, 140.
Warren, Jonathan, 102.
Warren, Jotham, 148.
Warren, Lemuel, 131.
Warren, Mea, 70.
Warren, Michael, 28.
Warren, Moses, 124.
Warren, Moses, 142.
Warren, Moses, 2$^{d}$, 124.
Warren, Nathan$^{l}$, 60.
Warren, Nath$^{l}$, 152.
Warren, Nathen, 112.
Warren, Samuel, 41.
Warren, Sam$^{l}$, 148.
Warren, Thomas, 119.
Warren, William, 36.
Warrener, Aaron, 38.
Warson, John, 14.
Warson, Robert, 21.
Wartis, Enos, 136.
Wartis, Jn$^{o}$, 136.
Wartis, Jos., 136.
Wartis, Phel$^{n}$, 136.
Wartis (Wid.), 135.
Wartis (Wid.), 136.
Warton, Abel, 95.
Washborn, Josiah, 95.
Washboun, Bowen, 95.
Washbourn, Ebenezer, 86.
Washbourn, Ezra, 137.
Washbourn, Ezra, Jr., 137.
Washbourn, John, 80.
Washbourn, John, 96.
Washbourn, Joseph, 88.
Washbourn, Levi, 135.
Washbourn, Moses, 137.
Washbourn, Nath$^{n}$, 137.
Washbourn, Noah, 46.
Washbourn, Sol$^{n}$, 137.
Washbourn, W$^{m}$, 137.
Washburn, Edman, 11.
Washburn, Eli, 142.
Washburn, Ephraim, 11.
Washburn, Joseph, 10.
Washburn, Neh$^{m}$, 137.
Washburn, Sol$^{n}$, 137.
Washburn, William, 66.
Washburn, W$^{m}$, 137.
Washburn, Zebee, 20.
Wass, Jn$^{o}$, 135.
Waterbury, Benjamin, 27.
Waterbury, Cloe (W$^{d}$), 24.
Waterbury, David, 25.
Waterbury, David, J$^{r}$, 24.
Waterbury, David, 3$^{d}$, 27.
Waterbury, Deodate, 27.
Waterbury, Ebenezer, 26.
Waterbury, Elizabeth, 24.
Waterbury, Enos, 25.
Waterbury, Epenetus, 27.
Waterbury, Hannah (W$^{d}$), 26.
Waterbury, Jacob, 26.
Waterbury, James, 26.
Waterbury, Janus, 24.
Waterbury, Jemimah (W$^{d}$), 24.
Waterbury, John, 26.
Waterbury, John, Jun$^{r}$, 26.
Waterbury, John, 4$^{th}$, 24.
Waterbury, Jonathan, 24.
Waterbury, Joseph, 52.
Waterbury, Martha (W$^{d}$), 26.
Waterbury, Nathaniel, 24.
Waterbury, Nathaniel, 26.
Waterbury, Phinehas, 24.
Waterbury, Rebecca (W$^{d}$), 26.
Waterbury, Thaddeus, 24.
Waterbury, Thankful (W$^{d}$), 26.
Waterbury, W$^{m}$, 26.
Waterbury, W$^{m}$, J$^{r}$, 26.
Waterhouse, Abraham, 90.
Waterhouse, Abr$^{m}$, J$^{r}$, 90.
Waterhouse, Ambrose, 89.
Waterhouse, Amos, 119.
Waterhouse, Andrew, 94.
Waterhouse, Austin, 90.
Waterhouse, Benj$^{a}$, 91.
Waterhouse, Elijah, 90.
Waterhouse, Gideon, 91.
Waterhouse, Isaac, 94.
Waterhouse, Jabez, 120.
Waterhouse, Jn$^{o}$, 89.
Waterhouse, Jn$^{o}$, 90.
Waterhouse, John, 126.
Waterhouse, Josiah, 90.
Waterhouse, Mary, 81.
Waterhouse, Nath$^{l}$, 126.
Waterhouse, Stephen, 90.
Waterhouse, Thomas, 125.
Waterhouse, Timothy, 120.
Waterhouse, Timothy, 2$^{d}$, 120.
Waterhouse, W$^{m}$, 89.
Waterman, Andrew, 145.
Waterman, Arunah, 131.
Waterman, Asahel, 43.
Waterman, Benjamin, 126.
Waterman, David, 70.
Waterman, Eunice, 131.
Waterman, Ezekiel, 130.
Waterman, Ezra, 132.
Waterman, Gideon, 144.
Waterman, Ignatius, 131.
Waterman, John, 126.
Waterman, John, 130.
Waterman, Joseph, 145.
Waterman, Lucy, 131.
Waterman, Nehemiah, 126.
Waterman, Nehemiah, 2$^{d}$, 126.
Waterman, Peter, 130.
Waterman, Robert, 47.
Waterman, Samuel, 80.
Waterman, Simeon, 145.
Waterman, Sylvenus, 80.
Waterman, Timothy, 132.
Waterman, Uriah, 132.
Waterman, William, 131.
Waterman, Zebulun, 122.
Waterous, John, 28.
Waters, Aaron, 145.
Waters, Benjamin, 47.
Waters, Benjamin, Jr., 47.
Waters, Bevil, 55.
Waters, David, 43.
Waters, Elisha, 26.
Waters, Gideon, 43.
Waters, Jacob, 25.
Waters, Jacob, 148.
Waters, Jacob, Jn$^{r}$, 148.
Waters, John, 26.
Waters, John, 67.
Waters, John, sr., 149.
Waters, Joseph, 47.
Waters, Lydia, 113.
Waters, Richard, 96.
Waters, Robert, 21.
Waters, Sam$^{l}$, 122.
Waters, Sarah, 97.
Waters, Temperance, 91.
Waters, Thomas, 46.
Waters, William, 47.
Watkins, Abijah, 17.
Watkins, Amasa, 140.
Watkins, Henekiah, 58.
Watkins, Hezekiah, 17.
Watkins, Jedediah, 140.
Watkins, John, 58.
Watkins, Pheneas, 140.
Watkins, Sarah, 140.
Watkins, Thaddeus, 140.
Watkins, William, 17.
Watkins, William, 140.
Watrous, Jona$^{th}$, 146.
Watrous, Josiah, 85.
Watrous, Nathaniel, 39.
Watrous, Stephen, 128.
Watrus, Benjamin, 127.
Watrus, Easter, 123.
Watrus, Elijah, 127.
Watrus, Gershom, 123.
Watrus, Gideon, 123.
Watrus, Gordon, 2$^{d}$, 124.
Watrus, Gusdon, 124.
Watrus, Henry, 121.
Watrus, John, 121.
Watrus, John R., 120.
Watrus, Joseph, 121.
Watrus, Lazarus, 121.
Watrus, Pheba, 124.
Watrus, Phineas, 123.
Watrus, Samuel, 121.
Watrus, Sarah, 127.
Watrus, Theodore, 120.
Watrus, Timothy, 121.
Watrus, William, 121.
Watson, Abigal, 150.
Watson, David, 38.
Watson, Ebenezar, 38.
Watson, Ebenezer, Jr., 38.
Watson, Hezikah, 67.
Watson, John, 34.
Watson, John, 38.
Watson, John, 46.
Watson, John, 61.
Watson, John, 83.
Watson, John, 128.
Watson, John, Jun$^{r}$, 83.
Watson, Levi, 60.
Watson, Levi, 70.
Watson, Mathew, 150.
Watson, Robert, 38.
Watson, Samuel, 38.

# INDEX.

Watson, Sarah, 38.
Watson, William, 67.
Watson, William, 77.
Watson, Zachariah, 60.
Watter, Daniel, 60.
Watter, Elijah, 61.
Watter, Heman, 61.
Watter, Henry, 60.
Watter, Joel, 61.
Watter, John, 60.
Watter, Pierce, 66.
Watter, Samuel, 64.
Wattles, Belcher, 145.
Wattles, Charles, 145.
Wattles, Daniel, 145.
Wattles, Denison, 145.
Wattles, Elijah, 130.
Wattles, Henry, 131.
Wattles, Joshua, 145.
Wattles, Mason, 145.
Wattles, Oliver, 145.
Wattles, Roswell, 47.
Wattles, Thos, 145.
Waugh, Alexander, 59.
Waugh, John, 59.
Waugh, Robert, 59.
Waugh, Samuel, 59.
Waugh, Thomas, 59.
Way, Abel, 77.
Way, Azariah, 127.
Way, Barsheba, 121.
Way, Daniel, 79.
Way, Daniel, 124.
Way, David, 108.
Way, Durin, 124.
Way, Ebenezer, 128.
Way, Elijah, 68.
Way, Elisha, 124.
Way, George, Junr, 124.
Way, Isaac, 79.
Way, Jerusha, 127.
Way, Job, 105.
Way, John, 122.
Way, John, 128.
Way, Joseph, 35.
Way, Joseph, 124.
Way, Nathl, 128.
Way, Peter, 122.
Way, Philemon, 56.
Way, Reynold, 124.
Way, Roswell, 56.
Way, Samuel, 77.
Way, Thomas, 124.
Way, Thomas, 1st, 77.
Way, Thomas, 2d, 77.
Way, Thomas, 2d, 124.
Way, Timothy, 97.
Wayres, Archibald, 130.
Ways, Abner, 107.
Ways, John, 107.
Ways, John, 121.
Wead, Daniel, 69.
Weare, William, 46.
Weaver, Anna, 141.
Weaver, Constant, 144.
Weaver, John, 141.
Weaver, Rimington, 141.
Weaver, Thos, 151.
Weaver, Timothy, 144.
Weaver, William, 128.
Web, Eliphᵗ, 137.
Webb, Abigail, 37.
Webb, Abner, 152.
Webb, Benjamin, 25.
Webb, Calvin, 90.
Webb, Charles, Esqʳ, 24.
Webb, Christopher, 142.
Webb, Constant, 90.
Webb, Daniel, 110.
Webb, David, 24.
Webb, David, 65.
Webb, David, Junr, 26.
Webb, Ebenezer, 25.
Webb, Ebenezer, 52.
Webb, Ebenezʳ, 153.
Webb, Ebenezer, Jr., 24.
Webb, Elisha, 25.
Webb, Elizabeth (Wd), 24.
Webb, Elizabeth, Jr (Wd), 24.
Webb, Epenetus, 24.
Webb, Epenetus, Junr, 24.
Webb, Epenetus, 3d, 24.
Webb, Ezra, 52.
Webb, Gidn, 91.
Webb, Gideon, 93.
Webb, Isaac, 13.
Webb, Jabez, 140.
Webb, James, 81.
Webb, James, 90.
Webb, Jared, 24.
Webb, Jared, 152.
Webb, John, 107.
Webb, John, 130.
Webb, John, 152.
Webb, Jonah, 92.
Webb, Jonathan, 65.
Webb, Jonathan, 65.
Webb, Jonathan, 112.
Webb, Joseph, 52.
Webb, Joshua, 148.
Webb, Josiah, 74.
Webb, Lebeus, 152.
Webb, Mary, 90.
Webb, Nancy, 110.
Webb, Nathel, 25.
Webb, Nathl, 152.
Webb, Nathaniel, jr, 25.
Webb, Nathaniel, 3d, 25.
Webb, Patience, 90.
Webb, Peter, 152.
Webb, Reynold, 90.
Webb, Samuel, 24.
Webb, Samuel, 152.
Webb, Samuel, Jr, 24.
Webb, Sarah (Wd), 24.
Webb, Seth, 24.
Webb, Stephn, 90.
Webb, Stephen, 153.
Webb, William, 24.
Webb, William, 53.
Webb, Willm, 91.
Webber, Benj., 149.
Webber, John, 103.
Webber, Stephen, 108.
Weber, Jno, 139.
Weber, Thos., 139.
Webster, Aaron, 34.
Webster, Amos, 54.
Webster, Amos, 58.
Webster, Asahel, 132.
Webster, Benjamin, 66.
Webster, Benjamin, 88.
Webster, Charles, 58.
Webster, Charles, 70.
Webster, Charles, Jr, 66.
Webster, Cyprian, 58.
Webster, Cyrenus, 39.
Webster, Daniel, 38.
Webster, Daniel, 47.
Webster, David, 34.
Webster, David, 132.
Webster, David, Jr., 34.
Webster, Eleazer, 37.
Webster, Elijah, 66.
Webster, Elijah, 133.
Webster, Elijah, 134.
Webster, Elisabeth, 121.
Webster, Ephraim, 37.
Webster, Hezh, 55.
Webster, Isaac, 47.
Webster, Isaac, Jr., 47.
Webster, James, 55.
Webster, James, 66.
Webster, James, 71.
Webster, James, 146.
Webster, Joel, 39.
Webster, John, 66.
Webster, John, 151.
Webster, Jonathan, 37.
Webster, Joseph, 55.
Webster, Jos, 132.
Webster, Jos., 137.
Webster, Joshua, 33.
Webster, Joshua, 43.
Webster, Josiah, 145.
Webster, Justus, 35.
Webster, Justus, Jr., 35.
Webster, Levi, 121.
Webster, Lucy, 55.
Webster, Martin, 135.
Webster, Mathew, 47.
Webster, Medad, 47.
Webster, Moses, 147.
Webster, Noah, 47.
Webster, Noah, Jr., 46.
Webster, Obed, 94.
Webster, Philologus, 49.
Webster, Ransford, 133.
Webster, Ruth, 146.
Webster, Samuel, 37.
Webster, Samuel, 38.
Webster, Samuel, 1st, 47.
Webster, Samuel, 2d, 47.
Webster, Stephen, 47.
Webster, Stephen, 66.
Webster, Stephen, 121.
Webster, Stephen, 149.
Webster, Thomas, 22.
Webster, Thos, 132.
Webster, Timo, 138.
Webster, Zurvey, 146.
Wedd, Ebenezer, Junr, 24.
Wedge, Amos, 151.
Wedge, Asahel, 74.
Wedge, David, 131.
Wedge, Isaac, 74.
Wedge, Stephen, 74.
Weeb, Isaac, 63.
Weed, Aaron, 25.
Weed, Aaron, 44.
Weed, Abisha, 25.
Weed, Abraham, 22.
Weed, Abraham, 26.
Weed, Amos, 25.
Weed, Amos, Junr, 25.
Weed, Ananias, 25.
Weed, Asa, 11.
Weed, Asahel, 25.
Weed, Azer, 11.
Weed, Bartholomew, 29.
Weed, Belden, 69.
Weed, Benjamin, 25.
Weed, Benjamin, 44.
Weed, Benjamin, Jr, 25.
Weed, Benjamin, 3d, 26.
Weed, Charles, 26.
Weed, Daniel, 26.
Weed, David, 11.
Weed, David, 15.
Weed, Deborah, 44.
Weed, Deodate, 26.
Weed, Ebenezer, 11.
Weed, Ebenezer, 26.
Weed, Ebenezer P., 25.
Weed, Eliphalet, 24.
Weed, Enos, 25.
Weed, Enos, 26.
Weed, Ephraim, 11.
Weed, Ezra, 26.
Weed, Ezra, 66.
Weed, Gideon, 25.
Weed, Gideon, 26.
Weed, Gideon, Junr, 26.
Weed, Hannah, 26.
Weed, Henry, 26.
Weed, Hezekiah, 24.
Weed, Isaac, 15.
Weed, Israel, 25.
Weed, Israel, Junr, 25.
Weed, Jabez, 25.
Weed, Jacob, 28.
Weed, James, 26.
Weed, James, Junr, 26.
Weed, James, 3d, 24.
Weed, Jesse, 25.
Weed, Jesse, 77.
Weed, Joel, 26.
Weed, John, 11.
Weed, John, 24.
Weed, John, Junr, 26.
Weed, Jonas, 11.
Weed, Jonas, 12.
Weed, Jonas, 26.
Weed, Jonas, 69.
Weed, Jonas, Jur, 12.
Weed, Jonas, Junr, 26.
Weed, Jonas, 3d, 26.
Weed, Jonas, 4th, 26.
Weed, Jonathan, 25.
Weed, Jonathan, Junr, 25.
Weed, Jonathan, 3d, 26.
Weed, Josiah, 26.
Weed, Mary (Wd), 26.
Weed, Mary (Wd), 27.
Weed, Mary, Junr (Wd), 26.
Weed, Mercy (Wd), 25.
Weed, Miles, 25.
Weed, Moses, 44.
Weed, Nathan, 24.
Weed, Nathan, Junr, 24.
Weed, Peter, 25.
Weed, Peter, 26.
Weed, Samuel, 11.
Weed, Samuel, 25.
Weed, Sarah (Wd), 26.
Weed, Scudder, 22.
Weed, Seth, 26.
Weed, Seth, Junr, 25.
Weed, Silvanus, 26.
Weed, Smith, 24.
Weed, Solomon, 12.
Weed, Solomon, 20.
Weed, Stephen, 26.
Weed, Thaddeus, 24.
Weed, Throm, 11.
Weed, Wm, 26.
Weeden, Elijah, 113.
Weeden, Isaac, 128.
Weeks, Ebenr, 141.
Weeks, Henry, 25.
Weeks, Samuel, 73.
Weever, Elijah, 114.
Weever, Jonathan, 115.
Weever, Jonathan, Junr, 117.
Weever, Joshua, 117.
Weever, Lodowick, 115.
Weild, Samuel, 96.
Welch, Charles, 116.
Welch, Constant, 81.
Welch, Danil, 63.
Welch, Daniel, 121.
Welch, Daniel, Junr, 121.
Welch, David, 70.
Welch, Elijah, 66.
Welch, Jeremiah, 153.
Welch, John, 70.
Welch, John, 81.
Welch, John, 123.
Welch, John, 148.
Welch, John, 153.
Welch, John, Jnr, 153.
Welch, Jude, 137.
Welch, Lemuel, 54.
Welch, Moses Cook, 147.
Welch, Paul, 1st, 73.
Welch, Paul, 2d, 73.
Welch, Peter, 153.
Welch, Reuben, 153.
Welch, Solomon, 140.
Welch, William, 81.
Welch, William, 81.
Welcop, John, 131.
Weldeer, Joseph, 68.
Welden, Oliver, 117.
Weldon, Abraham, 63.
Weldon, John, 63.
Welford, John, 91.
Welimar, Thomas, 11.
Well, Abijah, 48.
Well, Benjamin, 29.
Well, Isaac, 29.
Weller, Abel, 73.
Weller, Daniel, 79.
Weller, Samuel, 79.
Weller, Zacheriah, 79.
Welles, Amos, 121.
Welles, Ann, 121.
Welles, Benjn, 132.
Welles, Chaunsey, 121.
Welles, David, 52.
Welles, David, 116.
Welles, Elezer, 132.
Welles, Elijah, 43.
Welles, Elijah, 79.
Welles, Elisha, 52.
Welles, Ephraim, 42.
Welles, Ephraim, 121.
Welles, Israel W., 121.
Welles, Jarred, 132.
Welles, John, 42.
Welles, John, 120.
Welles, Jonathan, 42.
Welles, Joseph, 42.
Welles, Joseph, 83.
Welles, Joshua, 122.
Welles, Lucy, 128.
Welles, Martin, 121.
Welles, Oliver, 121.
Welles, Samuel, 42.
Welles, Samuel, Jr., 42.
Welles, Thomas, 80.
Welles, Thomas, 120.
Welles, Thos, 138.
Welles, Wait, 120.
Wells, Abner, 18.
Wells, Absalom, 54.
Wells, Agar, 29.
Wells, Asahel, 60.
Wells, Ashbel, 47.
Wells, Ashbel, Jr., 46.
Wells, Bateman, 134.
Wells, Bayza, 41.
Wells, Benjamin, 29.
Wells, Benjamin, 67.
Wells, Bille, 52.
Wells, Chester, 53.
Wells, Christopher, 53.
Wells, Daniel, 18.
Wells, David, 30.
Wells, Ebenezer, 47.
Wells, Eli, 53.
Wells, Elias, 30.
Wells, Elijah, 53.
Wells, Elijah, 54.
Wells, Elisha, 41.
Wells, Elisha, 47.
Wells, Elisha, 47.
Wells, Elisha, Jr., 41.
Wells, Esther, 37.
Wells, Gad, 102.
Wells, George, 41.
Wells, Giddeon, 18.
Wells, Gideon, 30.
Wells, Gideon, 53.
Wells, Hanah (Wid.), 30.
Wells, Hezekiah, 38.
Wells, Hezekiah, 53.
Wells, Isaac, 20.
Wells, Isaac, 42.
Wells, Israel, 48.
Wells, James, 30.
Wells, James, 54.
Wells, James A., 46.
Wells, Jamus, 54.
Wells, Jedediah F., 30.
Wells, Joana, 18.
Wells, John, 36.
Wells, John, 46.
Wells, John, 53.
Wells, John, 57.
Wells, Jno, 135.
Wells, Jonathan, 36.
Wells, Jonathan, 52.
Wells, Jonathan, 96.
Wells, Jonth, Jr, 36.
Wells, Joseph, 29.
Wells, Joseph, 33.
Wells, Joseph, 53.
Wells, Joseph, 97.
Wells, Joseph, Jr., 33.
Wells, Joseph, 2nd, 98.
Wells, Joshua, 38.
Wells, Joshua, 38.
Wells, Joshua, Jr., 53.
Wells, Josiah, 53.
Wells, Lampson, 38.
Wells, Legrand, 29.
Wells, Levi, 53.
Wells, Levi, 54.
Wells, Levi, 134.
Wells, Mary, 96.
Wells, Mosses, 38.
Wells, Mosses, 102.
Wells, Nathan, 31.
Wells, Noah, 38.
Wells, Noah, 67.
Wells, Oliver, 83.
Wells, Philip, 31.
Wells, Prudence, 53.
Wells, Robert, 18.
Wells, Robert, 54.
Wells, Robert, Jr., 54.
Wells, Roger, 54.
Wells, Rufus, 134.
Wells, Ruth, 53.
Wells, Samuel, 31.
Wells, Samuel, 31.
Wells, Samuel, 67.
Wells, Samuel, Junr, 31.
Wells, Samuel, 2d, 52.
Wells, Samuel, 2d, 53.
Wells, Shipman, 134.
Wells, Simon, 54.
Wells, Solomon, 53.
Wells, Stephen, 31.
Wells, Sylvester, 33.
Wells, Thaddeus, 43.
Wells, Theodore, 53.
Wells, Thomas, 46.
Wells, Thomas, 73.
Wells, Thomas, 79.
Wells, Thos, 134.
Wells, Thomas, 2d, 52.
Wells, Timothy, 70.
Wells, Timo, 135.
Wells, William, 29.
Wells, William, 30.
Wells, William, 103.
Wells, Zalmon, 18.
Welsh, Martha, 102.
Welsh, Patrick, 109.
Welsh, Thomas, 102.
Welton, Amassa, 109.
Welton, Andrew, 109.
Welton, Benjamin, 41.
Welton, Dan., 77.
Welton, David, 109.
Welton, Ebenezer, 111.
Welton, Eli, 1st, 77.
Welton, Eli, 2d, 77.
Welton, Eliakim, 110.
Welton, Eliakim, 2nd, 110.
Welton, Eliakim, 2nd, 111.
Welton, Hy, 109.
Welton, Jeames, 77.
Welton, Jesse, 77.
Welton, Joel, 40.
Welton, John, 109.
Welton, Josiah, 77.
Welton, Lemuel, 110.
Welton, Levi, 109.
Welton, Martha, 109.
Welton, Oliver, 109.
Welton, Reuben, 77.
Welton, Richard, 109.
Welton, Solomon, 41.
Welton, Stephen, 77.
Welton, Stephen, 109.
Wenslow, Jesse, 81.
Wentworth, Edward, 23.
Wentworth, Elizabeth, 130.
Wentworth, James, 95.
Wentworth, John, 142.
Wentworth, Sion, 54.
Wentworth, William, 142.
Wescots, John, 21.
Wescott, David, 23.
Wescott, Elijah, 22.
Wescott, Elizabeth, 128.
Wesland, Joseph, 55.
Wesland, Robert, 55.
Wesley, Wm, 137.
Wessells, Lawrence, 64.
West, Aaron, 63.
West, Abbe, 137.
West, Abel, 132.
West, Agnes, 91.
West, Amos, 66.
West, Amos, 146.
West, Asael, 126.
West, Daniel, 128.
West, David, 68.
West, David, 138.
West, David, 145.
West, Ebenezʳ, 145.
West, Elias, 126.
West, Hezekiah, 35.
West, Ira, 132.
West, Jabez, 128.
West, Jabez, 138.
West, Jm, 138.
West, Job, 138.
West, Joshua, 125.
West, Josiah, 57.
West, Judy, 60.
West, Lemuel, 81.
West, Levi, 146.
West, Nathan, 126.
West, Ruben, 135.
West, Ruful, 138.
West, Samuel, 73.
West, Saml, 146.
West, Soln, 138.
Westcoat, Amos, 150.
Westcoat, Hukely, 149.
Westcott, William, 127.
Weston, Abraham, 110.
Weston, Abm, 139.
Weston, Amaziah, 131.
Weston, Benjamin, 53.
Weston, Darius, 87.
Weston, James, 139.
Weston, Jona, 139.
Weston, Noah, 48.
Weston, Samuel, 74.

224 INDEX.


Weston (Widow), 138.
Westover, Joseph, 59.
Wetherby, Seth, 37.
Wetherill, David, 33.
Wetmore, Asa, 89.
Wetmore, Charles, 96.
Wetmore, Daniel, 89.
Wetmore, Elizabeth, 77.
Wetmore, Esther, 86.
Wetmore, Hannah, 86.
Wetmore, Hezekiah, 30.
Wetmore, Hezekiah, 103.
Wetmore, Ichabod, 85.
Wetmore, Izrahiah, 131.
Wetmore, James, 19.
Wetmore, John, 86.
Wetmore, John, 109.
Wetmore, Jno, Junr, 86.
Wetmore, John, 2d, 89.
Wetmore, Joseph, 89.
Wetmore, Joseph, 101.
Wetmore, Joseph, 121.
Wetmore, Josiah, 18.
Wetmore, Oliver, 88.
Wetmore, Seth, 88.
Wettlesey, Elisha, 2d, 107.
Wetton, Elijah, 70.
Wever, Benjn, 139.
Wever, David, 139.
Wever (Wid.), 139.
Whaley, Theophilus, 112.
Whaples, Elezur, 33.
Whaples, Eli, 54.
Whaples, Reuben, 54.
Wharton, James, 149.
Wheador, Thomas, 49.
Whealer, Amos, 116.
Whealer, Benjamin, 69.
Whealer, David, 115.
Whealer, Edward, 113.
Whealer, Eliphalet, 31.
Whealer, Elisha, 117.
Whealer, Ephraim, 115.
Whealer, Ephraim, 119.
Whealer, Ephraim, 125.
Whealer, Ephraim, 2d, 125.
Whealer, Guy, 126.
Whealer, Hannah, 116.
Whealer, Hosea, 116.
Whealer, James, 125.
Whealer, Jeremi, 116.
Whealer, John, 113.
Whealer, John, 116.
Whealer, John, Junr, 116.
Whealer, John, 3d, 116.
Whealer, Jonathan, 116.
Whealer, Jonathan, Junr, 116.
Whealer, Joseph, 116.
Whealer, Joshua, 116.
Whealer, Lester, 116.
Whealer, Nathan, 69.
Whealer, Parley, 113.
Whealer, Paul, 116.
Whealer, Peres, 117.
Whealer, Richard, 116.
Whealer, Rufus, 117.
Whealer, Sheppard, 116.
Whealer, Thomas, 116.
Whealer, Thomas, 2d, 116.
Whealer, William, 125.
Whealer, Zachius, 126.
Whealor, Isaac, 66.
Wheat, Benjn, 143.
Wheat, Jonas, 80.
Wheat, Samuel, 128.
Wheat, William, 128.
Wheaton, Esack, 73.
Wheaton, Jacob, 147.
Wheaton, James, 149.
Wheaton, Orange, 75.
Wheaton, Resolved, 144.
Wheaton, Rufus, 99.
Wheaton, Samuel, 25.
Wheaton, Sarah, 77.
Wheaton, Simon, 143.
Wheaton, Sylvester, 75.
Wheelar, Elnathan, 42.
Wheelar, Joseph, 47.
Wheelar, Lazarius, 42.
Wheelar, Silent, 43.
Wheeler, Aaron, 148.
Wheeler, Abel, 95.
Wheeler, Aden, 74.
Wheeler, Agur, 74.
Wheeler, Amos, 10.
Wheeler, Amos, 74.
Wheeler, Ann (Wid.), 20.
Wheeler, Anne, 18.
Wheeler, Asa, 139.
Wheeler, Asa, 1st, 74.
Wheeler, Asa, 2d, 74.
Wheeler, Benjamin, 14.
Wheeler, Bennett, 20.
Wheeler, Calep, 18.
Wheeler, Calvin, 31.
Wheeler, Chancy, 14.
Wheeler, Daniel, 10.
Wheeler, Daniel, 13.
Wheeler, David, 14.
Wheeler, David, 20.
Wheeler, David, 153.
Wheeler, David, 153.
Wheeler, David B., 17.
Wheeler, Deborah, 29.
Wheeler, Dimon, 31.
Wheeler, Dobson, 73.
Wheeler, Ebenezer, 74.
Wheeler, Elene, 17.
Wheeler, Elene, 18.
Wheeler, Eli, 20.
Wheeler, Elisha, 18.
Wheeler, Elnathan, 29.
Wheeler, Elnathan, 31.
Wheeler, Elnathan, Jur, 29.
Wheeler, Enoch, 19.
Wheeler, Enos, 27.
Wheeler, Ephraim, 27.
Wheeler, Ephraim, 29.
Wheeler, Ephraim, 148.
Wheeler, Ezra, 31.
Wheeler, Gideon, 31.
Wheeler, Hezekiah, 14.
Wheeler, Ichabod, 28.
Wheeler, Ichaburd, 14.
Wheeler, Jabez, 31.
Wheeler, James, 19.
Wheeler, James, 112.
Wheeler, James, 154.
Wheeler, Jedediah, 19.
Wheeler, Jedediah, 73.
Wheeler, Jeremiah, 150.
Wheeler, Jerusha (Wid.), 20.
Wheeler, Jesse, 74.
Wheeler, Joab, 74.
Wheeler, Job, 84.
Wheeler, Joel, 111.
Wheeler, John, 18.
Wheeler, John, 27.
Wheeler, John, 29.
Wheeler, John, 31.
Wheeler, John, 74.
Wheeler, John, 95.
Wheeler, John, 142.
Wheeler, John, 149.
Wheeler, Johnson, 74.
Wheeler, Jonas, 148.
Wheeler, Jonathn, 142.
Wheeler, Joseph, 20.
Wheeler, Joseph, 20.
Wheeler, Joseph, 84.
Wheeler, Joseph, 94.
Wheeler, Jos., 139.
Wheeler, Josiah, 70.
Wheeler, Lemuel, 70.
Wheeler, Louis, 95.
Wheeler, Moses, 18.
Wheeler, Moses, 18.
Wheeler, Moses, 95.
Wheeler, Moses, 148.
Wheeler, Nathan, 13.
Wheeler, Nathan, 18.
Wheeler, Nathan, 31.
Wheeler, Nathanel, 29.
Wheeler, Nathaniel, 95.
Wheeler, Nehemiah, 19.
Wheeler, Obediah, 1st, 74.
Wheeler, Obediah, 2d, 74.
Wheeler, Philip, 12.
Wheeler, Rebeckah, 14.
Wheeler, Samuel, 14.
Wheeler, Samuel, 19.
Wheeler, Samuel, 31.
Wheeler, Samuel, 31.
Wheeler, Samuel, 47.
Wheeler, Samuel, 95.
Wheeler, Saml, 149.
Wheeler, Seth, 27.
Wheeler, Simion, 112.
Wheeler, Stephen, 21.
Wheeler, Thomas, 20.
Wheeler, Thomas, 99.
Wheeler, Thomas, Jnr, 13.
Wheeler, Timothy, 14.
Wheeler (Widow), 133.
Wheeler (Widow), 138.
Wheeler, William, 34.
Wheeler, William, 144.
Wheeler, Willson, 14.
Wheeler, Zophas, 74.
Wheelersom, Jos., 138.
Wheelock, Saml, 144.
Wheelor, Elizur, 56.
Wheelor, John, 56.
Wheeton, Chapman, 96.
Wheeton, James, 92.
Wheeton, Mary, 91.
Wheeton, Nathal, 91.
Wheeton, Roswell, 92.
Wheeton, Ruben, 92.
Wheeton, Samuel, 91.
Wheeton, Samuel, 92.
Wheeton, William, 92.
Wheeton, William, 92.
Wheldon, Jno, 134.
Wheldon, Jona, 133.
Whelpley, Abigail, 15.
Whelpley, Amos, 25.
Whelpley, Anne (Wd), 15.
Whelpley, Ebenezer, 15.
Whelpley, Isaac, 16.
Whilford, Robert, 69.
Whipple, Abraham, 38.
Whipple, Amos, 116.
Whipple, Anthony, 127.
Whipple, Elijah, 114.
Whipple, Frederick, 125.
Whipple, Jesse, 144.
Whipple, John, 128.
Whipple, Jonathan, 114.
Whipple, Jonathan, 148.
Whipple, Joseph, 67.
Whipple, Joseph, 114.
Whipple, Joshua, 130.
Whipple, Luther, 114.
Whipple, Rebecka, 112.
Whipple, Saml, 138.
Whipple, Saml, 149.
Whipple, Silas, 125.
Whipple, Thomas, 129.
Whipple, Titus, 126.
Whipple, William, 116.
Whipple, Wm, 131.
Whipple, Zebulon, 148.
Whipple, Zephaniah, 131.
Whipples, John, 127.
Whipples, Joseph, 117.
Whipples, Robart, 117.
Whisler, Zadock, 137.
Whitaker, Samuel, 68.
Whitcomb, Hiram, 49.
White, Aaron, 88.
White, Aaron, 144.
White, Abagail, 87.
White, Adam, 149.
White, Adno, 133.
White, Adonjah, 135.
White, Amos, 81.
White, Amy, 69.
White, Antipass, 149.
White, Asa, 153.
White, Charles, 27.
White, Charles, 96.
White, Christopher, 119.
White, Consider, 46.
White, Cornelious, 153.
White, Daniel, 94.
White, Danl, 134.
White, Daniel, 135.
White, Danl, 149.
White, David, 80.
White, David, 150.
White, Deah, 135.
White, Dudley, 85.
White, Ebenr, 138.
White, Ebenezer, Esqr, 80.
White, Ebenezer R., 11.
White, Elias, 87.
White, Elijah, 132.
White, Elisha, 152.
White, Elizer, 67.
White, Enoch, 145.
White, Ephraim, 81.
White, Ezekiel, 125.
White, Ezekiel, 2d, 125.
White, Ezra, 33.
White, Ezra, 64.
White, Fairchild, 12.
White, Freind, 39.
White, George, 62.
White, George, 80.
White, Hannah, 127.
White, Henery, 39.
White, Herman, 69.
White, Isaac, 49.
White, Isaac, 60.
White, Israhel, 70.
White, Jabez, 132.
White, Jacob, 13.
White, Jacob, 25.
White, Jacob, 66.
White, Jacob, 149.
White, Jacob, 150.
White, Jacob, Junr, 24.
White, James, 135.
White, James, 135.
White, James, 149.
White, Jedediah, 59.
White, Joel, 132.
White, John, 46.
White, John, 47.
White, John, 60.
White, John, 70.
White, John, 88.
White, John, 95.
White, John, 104.
White, John, Jr., 47.
White, Jona, 133.
White, Jonath, 150.
White, Joseph, 80.
White, Joseph, 94.
White, Jos. 135.
White, Joseph M., 10.
White, Josiah, Junr, 80.
White, Lemuel, 36.
White, Mary, 116.
White, Moses, 55.
White, Moses, 81.
White, Nathan, 51.
White, Nathaniel, 58.
White, Nathl, 146.
White, Noadiah, 80.
White, Noadiah, Junr, 80.
White, Oliver, 89.
White, Peregrine, 153.
White, Peter, 22.
White, Phillip, 81.
White, Prince, 153.
White, Right, 14.
White, Samuel, 22.
White, Samuel, 60.
White, Samuel, 74.
White, Saml 133.
White, Sam., 136.
White, Sarah, 106.
White, Stephen, 152.
White, Sylvanus, 145.
White, Thos, 132.
White, Thomas P., 11.
White, Timothy, 88.
White, Timothy, 102.
White, William, 25.
White, William, 61.
White, William, 61.
White, William, 81.
Whitebread, Elizabeth, 86.
Whitehead, David, 13.
Whitehead, Jehiel, 13.
Whitehead, Jeremiah, 13.
Whitehead, Nathaniel, 31.
Whitehead, Sibbely, 21.
Whitehouse, Thomas, 147.
Whiteley, William, 73.
Whitely, John, 145.
Whitford, Asa, 151.
Whitford, David, 142.
Whitford, John, 67.
Whiting, Allyn, 47.
Whiting, Asa, 63.
Whiting, Caleb, 126.
Whiting, Christophar, 66.
Whiting, Cornelius, 143.
Whiting, David, 29.
Whiting, David, 30.
Whiting, Ebenr, 130.
Whiting, Frederick S., 10.
Whiting, Gurdin, 47.
Whiting, Isaac, 42.
Whiting, James, 21.
Whiting, John, 30.
Whiting, John, 68.
Whiting, John, 91.
Whiting, John, 101.
Whiting, Jonathan, 103.
Whiting, Joseph, 29.
Whiting, Joseph, 47.
Whiting, Joseph, 102.
Whiting, Nathan H., 47.
Whiting, Samuel, 15.
Whiting, Samuel, 20.
Whiting, Samuel, 26.
Whiting, Samuel, 30.
Whiting, Samuel, 96.
Whiting, Samuel, 103.
Whiting, Samuel, 107.
Whiting, Sarah, 103.
Whiting, Sarah, 111.
Whiting, William, 47.
Whiting, William, 65.
Whiting, William J., 104.
Whitlesey, Elisha, 11.
Whitlesey, Joseph, 94.
Whitlock, Abel, 21.
Whitlock, Daniel, 22.
Whitlock, Daniel, Jr, 22.
Whitlock, David, 22.
Whitlock, Ebenezer, 12.
Whitlock, Ephraim, 27.
Whitlock, Hezekiah, 12.
Whitlock, Hezekiah, 23.
Whitlock, Joel, 74.
Whitlock, John, 12.
Whitlock, Justus, 27.
Whitlock, Mary (Wd), 21.
Whitlock, Nathan, 27.
Whitlock, Nathaniel, 27.
Whitlock, Nehemiah, 12.
Whitlock, Samuel, 11.
Whitlock, Samuel, 74.
Whitlock, Seth, 12.
Whitlock, Squire, 12.
Whitlock, Thomas, 24.
Whitman, Abigail, 47.
Whitman, Abraham, 126.
Whitman, Amos, 126.
Whitman, Daniel, 126.
Whitman, Elnathan, 41.
Whitman, Isaac, 119.
Whitman, Israel, 126.
Whitman, John, 47.
Whitman, John, 113.
Whitman, John, 126.
Whitman, John, Jr., 47.
Whitman, Jonathan, 50.
Whitman, Samuel, 47.
Whitman, Solomon, 41.
Whitman, Solomon, Jr., 40.
Whitman, Timothy, 119.
Whitman, Timothy, Junr, 119.
Whitman, Volentine, 126.
Whitman, William, 47.
Whitman, William, 145.
Whitman, Zorobable, 126.
Whitmon, John, 150.
Whitmore, Aaron, 147.
Whitmore, Abel, 63.
Whitmore, Benjn, 144.
Whitmore, Beriah, 87.
Whitmore, Caleb, 65.
Whitmore, Clark, 60.
Whitmore, Daniel, 87.
Whitmore, Ebenezer. 86.
Whitmore, Ebenezer ,87.
Whitmore, Francis, 87.
Whitmore, Gordon, 87.
Whitmore, Hezekiah, 53.
Whitmore, Increase, 68.
Whitmore, Jabez, 35.
Whitmore, Jabez, 150.
Whitmore, Jacob, 86.
Whitmore, Jacob, 139.
Whitmore, Jacob, Junr, 86.
Whitmore, Jehiel, 87.
Whitmore, Jessey, 88.
Whitmore, Joel, 62.
Whitmore, John, 65.
Whitmore, John, 151.
Whitmore, Luther, 80.
Whitmore, Pearley, 144.
Whitmore, Samuel, 60.
Whitmore, Saml, 63.
Whitmore, Saml, 65.
Whitmore, Samuel B., 84.
Whitmore, Solomon, 22.
Whitmore, Stephen, 87.
Whitmore, Timothy, 60.
Whitmore, Timothy, 87.
Whitmore, William, 66.
Whitmore, William, 150.
Whitmore, William, Jnr, 150.
Whitney, Abraham, 23.
Whitney, Asa, 144.
Whitney, Charles, 26.
Whitney, Cornelus, 70.
Whitney, Daniel, 24.
Whitney, Daniel, 120.
Whitney, Daniel, Junr, 24.
Whitney, David, 23.
Whitney, Eliasaph, 26.
Whitney, Enos, 108.
Whitney, Ezekiel, 29.
Whitney, Henry, 26.
Whitney, Henry, 28.
Whitney, Henry, 94.
Whitney, Capt Henry, 28.
Whitney, Hezekiah, 75.
Whitney, Isaac, 101.
Whitney, James, 109.
Whitney, John, 68.
Whitney, John, 91.
Whitney, John, 2d, 68.
Whitney, Jonathan, 24.
Whitney, Jona, 144.
Whitney, Joseph, 74.
Whitney, Jos., 134.
Whitney, Joshua, 59.
Whitney, Josiah, 13.
Whitney, Josiah, 94.
Whitney, Josiah, 141.
Whitney, Justice, 24.
Whitney, Lois (Wd), 22.
Whitney, Matthias, 144.
Whitney, Nathan, 11.
Whitney, Peter, 14.
Whitney, Ransford, 77.
Whitney, Samuel, 13.
Whitney, Samuel, 13.
Whitney, Samuel, 79.
Whitney, Saml, 144.
Whitney, Stephen, 59.
Whitney, Stephen, 61.
Whitney, Stephen, 94.
Whitney, Timothy, 23.
Whitney, William, 94.
Whiton, Amos, 152.
Whiton, Caleb, 139.
Whiton, Elijah, 138.
Whiton, Hannah, 140.
Whiton, James, 140.
Whiton, Joseph, 140.
Whiton, Whitfield, 140.
Whittelsey, Ambrose, 89.
Whittelsey, Ambrose, 2d, 89.
Whittelsey, David, 89.
Whittelsey, Hannah, 89.
Whittelsey, Hezekiah, 89.
Whittelsey, Joseph, 90.
Whittelsey, Saml W., 89.
Whittelsey (Wido), 91.
Whittemore, Caleb, 150.
Whittemore, Danl, 144.
Whittemore, Joseph, 148.
Whittemore, Joseph, Jr, 147.
Whittemore, Joshua, 144.
Whittemore, Saml, 129.
Whittemore, Saml, 147.
Whitten, Thomas, 59.
Whittikar, Abm, 137.
Whittikar, Jona, 137.
Whittikar, Jona, 2d, 137.
Whittikar, Stephen, 137.
Whittiker, Saml, 141.
Whittles, Isaac, 116.
Whittles, Isaac, Junr, 116.
Whittlesery, John, 75.
Whittlesey, Abner, 41.
Whittlesey, Azariah, 89.
Whittlesey, Bula, 86.
Whittlesey, Chauncey, Esqr, 85.
Whittlesey, David, 75.
Whittlesey, Elisha, 2nd, 108.
Whittlesey, Joseph, 75.
Whittlesey, Lemuel, 54.
Whittlesey, Martin, 75.
Whittlesey, Patty, 103.
Whittlesey, Saml, 138.

INDEX. 225

Whittock, Justus, 28.
Whittock, Robert, 28.
Whittock, Thaddeus, 28.
Whitty, John, 101.
Whitwell, An, 149.
Wholer, John, 63.
Wholf, Henry, 95.
Wholf, Seth D., 106.
Whore, Ed$^{w}$, 137.
Wiard, Seth, 35.
Wick, Edward, 99.
Wick, John, 99.
Wickham, David, 42.
Wickham, David, 82.
Wickham, Hezekiah, 43.
Wickham, Hezekiah, Jr., 43.
Wicks, Alexander, 14.
Wicks, Joseph, 123.
Wicks, Nathaniel, 13.
Wicks, Rebecka, 128.
Wicks, Zadock, 74.
Wickwin, Nathan, 57.
Wickwin, Richard, 57.
Wickwin, Samuel, 57.
Wickwire, Ichabord, 67.
Wickwire, James, 59.
Wickwire, James, 82.
Wickwire, Jeremiah, 125.
Wickwire, Jonas, 125.
Wickwire, Solomon, 140.
Wickwise, Lucretia, 124.
Widger, And$^{w}$, 118.
Widger, Eli, 119.
Widger, Jno., 90.
Widger, John, 119.
Widger, John, 119.
Widger, Sam$^{l}$, 119.
Wiggins, Arthur, 73.
Wiggins, Josiah, 51.
Wight, John, 114.
Wight, Joseph, 114.
Wightman, Allen, 121.
Wignall, William, 128.
Wilard, Eunice, 68.
Wilbar, Oliver, 151.
Wilbar, William, 148.
Wilbar, William, 154.
Wilbee, Ab$^{m}$, 82.
Wilber, Jeremiah, 131.
Wilbert, Abner, Sr., 148.
Wilbur, Joseph, 113.
Wilch, David, 148.
Wilcock, Roger, 48.
Wilcocks, Aaron, 50.
Wilcocks, Elijah, 48.
Wilcocks, Elijah, Jr., 48.
Wilcocks, Jehiel, 135.
Wilcocks, Ruth, 50.
Wilcox, Aaron, 48.
Wilcox, Abijah, 94.
Wilcox Abraham, 146.
Wilcox Anna (Wid.), 29.
Wilcox, Arnold, 116.
Wilcox, Asa, 40.
Wilcox, Asahel, 65.
Wilcox, Benjamin, 34.
Wilcox, Collins, 115.
Wilcox, Daniel, 115.
Wilcox, David, 116.
Wilcox, Eben$^{r}$, 117.
Wilcox, Edward, 117.
Wilcox, Elijah, 35.
Wilcox, Elisha, 30.
Wilcox, Elisha, 63.
Wilcox, Elisha, 114.
Wilcox, Elnathan, 31.
Wilcox, Ephraim, 31.
Wilcox, Ephraim, 145.
Wilcox, Francis, 115.
Wilcox, Gideon, 31.
Wilcox, Hesana, 61.
Wilcox, Hosea, 62.
Wilcox, Isaiah, 115.
Wilcox, Israel, 34.
Wilcox, Jacob, 34.
Wilcox, Jeremi, 116.
Wilcox, Jeremiah, 61.
Wilcox, Jesse, 40.
Wilcox, Johiel, 65.
Wilcox, John, 34.
Wilcox, John, 35.
Wilcox, John, 95.
Wilcox, John, 117.
Wilcox, Joseph, 114.
Wilcox, Joshua, 118.
Wilcox, Josiah, 34.
Wilcox, Justus, 49.
Wilcox, Mary, 120.
Wilcox, Mosas, 66.
Wilcox, Moses, 1$^{st}$, 58.
Wilcox, Moses, 2$^{d}$, 58.
Wilcox, Nathan, 31.
Wilcox, Nathan, 116.
Wilcox, Oliver, 115.
Wilcox, Philomen, 110.
Wilcox, Robart, 116.
Wilcox, Samuel, 34.
Wilcox, Samuel, 57.
Wilcox, Sarah, 34.
Wilcox, Stephen, 79.
Wilcox, Thomas, 62.
Wilcox, Thomas, 140.
Wilcox, William, 29.
Wilcox, William, 98.
Wilcox, Zadock, 57.
Wild, John, 128.
Wildar, Ephraim, 62.
Wildeer, Gamaliall, 68.
Wildeer, John, 69.
Wildeer, John, 69.
Wilden, Peleg, 43.
Wildman, Benjamin, 74.
Wildman, David, 74.
Wildman, Joseph, 73.
Wildman, Josiah, 73.
Wildman, Mathew, 73.
Wildman, Matthew, 2$^{d}$, 73.
Wileman, Abraham, 11.
Wileman, David, 10.
Wileman, Ezekiel, 10.
Wileman, Isaac, 10.
Wileman, Isaac, Jn$^{r}$, 10.
Wileman, John, 12.
Wileman, Joseph, 11.
Wileman, Lebeus, 10.
Wileman, Noah, 10.
Wileman, Paul, 19.
Wilemsn, Richard, 10.
Wileman, Samuel, 11.
Wileman, Samuel, Ju$^{r}$, 11.
Wileman, Timothy, 10.
Wiles, Jonas, 133.
Wiling, John, 64.
Wilkerson, John, 73.
Wilkerson, Malachi, 123.
Wilkes, Augustus, 26.
Wilkeson, Abel, 73.
Wilkeson, Augustine, 73.
Wilkeson, David, 73.
Wilkeson, Levi, 66.
Wilkeson, Peter, 73.
Wilkinson, Amos, 33.
Wilkinson, George, 115.
Wilkinson, James Y., 151.
Wilkinson, Jessee, 64.
Wilkinson, John, 53.
Wilkinson, John, 96.
Wilkinson, Jonathan, 62.
Wilkinson, Olivei, 45.
Wilkinson, Rhodes, 154.
Wilkinson, William, 151.
Wilkinson, William, Jn$^{r}$, 151.
Wilks, Mathew, 11.
Wilks, Mathew, Jn$^{r}$, 11.
Wilkson, James, 32.
Will, 64.
Will, Jephet, 53.
Will (Negro), 115.
Will (Negro), 117.
Will (Negro), 117.
Will (Negro), 132.
Willamson, John, 70.
Willard, Daniel, 54.
Willard, Dan$^{l}$, 90.
Willard, Daniel, Jr., 54.
Willard, Elias, 99.
Willard, Elisha, 85.
Willard, Hiel, 99.
Willard, Rev. I., 137.
Willard, James, 99.
Willard, Jerad, 99.
Willard, John, 107.
Willard, Joseph, 89.
Willard, Josiah, 52.
Willard, Julius, 99.
Willard, Nath$^{l}$, 89.
Willard, Peleg, 85.
Willard, Simon, 52.
Willard, Stephen, 52.
Willard, Stephen, 99.
Willard, William, 29.
Willcocks, Daniel, 48.
Willcocks, David, 44.
Willcocks, Elisha, 48.
Willcocks, Ezra, 48.
Willcocks, Isaac, 48.
Willcocks, Jedediah, 48.
Willcocks, Robert, 48.
Willcocks, Roswold, 48.
Willcocks, Simeon, 48.
Willcox, Aaron, 80.
Willcox, Abel, 84.
Willcox, Abel, Jun$^{r}$, 84.
Willcox, Abell, 86.
Willcox, Abraham, 84.
Willcox, Adam, 84.
Willcox, Adam, 84.
Willcox, Amos, 48.
Willcox, Asa, 70.
Willcox, Benjamin, 84.
Willcox, Benjamin, 99.
Willcox, Charles, 48.
Willcox, Daniel, 85.
Willcox, David, 18.
Willcox, David, 84.
Willcox, Ebenezer, 85.
Willcox, Edmond, 99.
Willcox, Eleazer, 41.
Willcox, Eli, 88.
Willcox, Elias, 35.
Willcox, Elijah, 85.
Willcox, Elijah, 88.
Willcox, Eliphalett, 88.
Willcox, Elisha, 88.
Willcox, Ezra, 41.
Willcox, Ezra, 99.
Willcox, Ezra, 2$^{d}$, 99.
Willcox, George, 49.
Willcox, Giles, 88.
Willcox, Ira, 48.
Willcox, Isaac, 48.
Willcox, James, 18.
Willcox, James, 40.
Willcox, James, 83.
Willcox, James, 88.
Willcox, Jeremiah, 88.
Willcox, Jesse, 41.
Willcox, Jiles, 36.
Willcox, Joel, 84.
Willcox, John, 18.
Willcox, John, 44.
Willcox, John, 83.
Willcox, John, 85.
Willcox, John, 85.
Willcox, John, 88.
Willcox, John, Jun$^{r}$, 88.
Willcox, John, 2$^{d}$, 85.
Willcox, Jonathan, 98.
Willcox, Joseph, 80.
Willcox, Joseph, 84.
Willcox, Joseph, 88.
Willcox, Joseph, 99.
Willcox, Joseph, 2$^{d}$, 85.
Willcox, Joseph, 2$^{nd}$, 99.
Willcox, Josiah, 41.
Willcox, Lois, 88.
Willcox, Nathan, 84.
Willcox, Nathan, 2$^{d}$, 85.
Willcox, Nathan, 3$^{d}$, 84.
Willcox, Nathaniel, 99.
Willcox, Ozias, 88.
Willcox, Philander, 70.
Willcox, Reuben, 80.
Willcox, Ruben, 96.
Willcox, Sadoss, 45.
Willcox, Samuel, 80.
Willcox, Samuel, 88.
Willcox, Simeon, 85.
Willcox, Stephen, 34.
Willcox, Stephen, 35.
Willcox, Stephen, 85.
Willcox, Timothy, 18.
Willcox, William, 48.
Willcox, William, 83.
Willer, Daniel, 69.
Willer, William, 69.
Willes, Henry, 130.
Willes, Jabez, 130.
Willes, Joshua, 130.
Willes, Sol$^{n}$, 138.
Willes, Tho$^{s}$, Jr., 135.
Willet, Jedediah, 130.
Willet, John, 130.
Willet, John, Jun$^{r}$, 130.
Willet, Joshua, 130.
Willey, Aaron, 82.
Willey, Alford, 82.
Willey, Barzilla, 89.
Willey, Benaiah, 82.
Willey, Cyrus, 82.
Willey, David, 81.
Willey, Eph$^{m}$, 82.
Willey, Eph$^{m}$, Jun$^{r}$, 82.
Willey, Ezra, 82.
Willey, G. Warren, 82.
Willey, Jabez, 82.
Willey, John, 81.
Willey, John, 82.
Willey, Jonathan, 59.
Willey, Jonathan, 81.
Willey, Joseph, 82.
Willey, Josiah, 82.
Willey, Noah, 82.
Willey, Sam$^{l}$, 82.
Willey, Seth, 82.
Willey, Susannah, 82.
Willey, Titus, 82.
Willford, Elizabeth, 91.
William, Benj$^{n}$, Jr., 141.
William, Daniel, 11.
William, David, 154.
William, Eleaz$^{r}$, 143.
William, Ezekiel, 52.
William, Isaac, 70.
William, Isaiah, 142.
William, Israel, 146.
William, John, 149.
William, Joshua, 36.
William (Negro), 119.
William, Stephen, 149.
William, Stephen, 154.
William, William, 59.
William, William, 152.
William, William, Jn$^{r}$, 145.
Williams, 74.
Williams, Aaron, 118.
Williams, Abraham, 36.
Williams, Ab$^{m}$, 83.
Williams, Abraham, 84.
Williams, Amariah, 147.
Williams, Ambrose, 146.
Williams, Amos, 19.
Williams, Amos, 118.
Williams, Aron, 93.
Williams, Asa, 141.
Williams, Ashur, 130.
Williams, Benadam, 116.
Williams, Benjamin, 12.
Williams, Benjamin, 86.
Williams, Benj$^{a}$, 90.
Williams, Benj$^{a}$, 152.
Williams, Benjamin, 2$^{d}$, 90.
Williams, Bennajah, 62.
Williams, Caleb, 120.
Williams, Carey, 118.
Williams, Charles, 82.
Williams, Charles, 89.
Williams, Charles, 121.
Williams, Charles, 145.
Williams, Christopher, 118.
Williams, Daniel, 36.
Williams, Daniel, 53.
Williams, Daniel, 77.
Williams, Daniel, 121.
Williams, Daniel, 127.
Williams, David, 13.
Williams, David, 44.
Williams, David, 68.
Williams, David, 79.
Williams, David, 89.
Williams, David, 153.
Williams, Deavenport, 92.
Williams, Easter, 125.
Williams, Eastes, 61.
Williams, Ebenezer, 89.
Williams, Ebenezer, 116.
Williams, Ebenezer, Jun$^{r}$, 116.
Williams, Edward, 36.
Williams, Eleazer, 116.
Williams, Elias, 53.
Williams, Elijah, 54.
Williams, Elijah, 82.
Williams, Elijah, 121.
Williams, Elijah, 130.
Williams, Elijah, 142.
Williams, Elijah, 154.
Williams, Eliphalet, 36.
Williams, Elisabeth, 125.
Williams, Elisha, 36.
Williams, Elisha, 52.
Williams, Elisha, 116.
Williams, Elisha, 120.
Williams, Elnathan, 32.
Williams, Enos, 122.
Williams, Ephraim, 53.
Williams, Ephraim, 62.
Williams, Ephraim, 116.
Williams, Ezra, 73.
Williams, Ezra, 112.
Williams, Fredrick, 145.
Williams, Freelove, 149.
Williams, George, 126.
Williams, George, 145.
Williams, Gideon, 33.
Williams, Gilbert, 116.
Williams, Harmon, 108.
Williams, Hecter (Negroe), 104.
Williams, Henry, 118.
Williams, Hezekiah, 12.
Williams, Hezekiah, 131.
Williams, Huldah, 13.
Williams, Isaac, 43.
Williams, Isaac, 86.
Williams, Isaac, 116.
Williams, Isaac, 118.
Williams, Isaac, 145.
Williams, Isaac, Jun$^{r}$, 116.
Williams, Isaiah, 145.
Williams, Israel, 53.
Williams, Israel, 62.
Williams, Israel, 66.
Williams, Jabez, 73.
Williams, Jacob, 24.
Williams, Jacob, 36.
Williams, Jacob, 53.
Williams, Jacob, 67.
Williams, James, 62.
Williams, James, 149.
Williams, Jeames, 77.
Williams, Jehiel, 53.
Williams, Jehiel, 88.
Williams, Jehiel, 145.
Williams, Jerusha, 43.
Williams, Jesse, 114.
Williams, Jesse, 147.
Williams, Joatham, 105.
Williams, John, 14.
Williams, John, 20.
Williams, John, 21.
Williams, John, 36.
Williams, John, 52.
Williams, John, 53.
Williams, John, 60.
Williams, John, 77.
Williams, John, 87.
Williams, Jn$^{o}$, 89.
Williams, John, 93.
Williams, John, 112.
Williams, John, 117.
Williams, John, 118.
Williams, John, 122.
Williams, John, 125.
Williams, John, 145.
Williams, John, 146.
Williams, John, Jun$^{r}$, 118.
Williams, John, Jn$^{r}$, 146.
Williams, John, 2$^{d}$, 116.
Williams, John, 3$^{d}$, 117.
Williams, John, 3$^{d}$, 119.
Williams, Jonathan, 84.
Williams, Jonathan, 85.
Williams, Jona$^{th}$, 145.
Williams, Joseph, 36.
Williams, Joseph, 120.
Williams, Joseph, 130.
Williams, Joseph, Jun$^{r}$, 120.
Williams, Joshua, 58.
Williams, Joshua, 117.
Williams, Joshua, 149.
Williams, Levi, 53.
Williams, Lucretia, 146.
Williams, Lydia, 90.
Williams, Margaret, 120.
Williams, Martha, 141.
Williams, Mary, 85.
Williams, Mary, 110.
Williams, Mary, 118.
Williams, Mercy, 117.
Williams, Moses, 53.
Williams, Moses, 114.
Williams, Moses, Jun$^{r}$, 114.
Williams, Rev. N., 138.
Williams, Nathan, 24.
Williams, Nathan, 121.
Williams, Nathan, 143.
Williams, Nath$^{l}$, 116.
Williams, Nath$^{l}$, 125.
Williams, Nehemiah, 116.
Williams, Nehemiah, 149.
Williams, Obed, 110.
Williams, Oliver, 125.
Williams, Park, 116.
Williams, Peleg, 118.
Williams, Peter, 32.
Williams, Peter, 86.
Williams, Peter, 118.
Williams, Peter, 119.
Williams, Phillip, 83.
Williams, Phineas, 36.
Williams, Polley, 70.
Williams, Richard, 89.
Williams, Richard, 118.
Williams, Robart, 117.
Williams, Robart, 118.
Williams, Robinson, 83.
Williams, Robinson, Ju$^{r}$, 83.
Williams, Roger, 120.
Williams, Roger, 141.
Williams, Ruben, 94.
Williams, Ruben, 110.
Williams, Samuel, 33.
Williams, Samuel, 90.
Williams, Samuel, 114.
Williams, Sam$^{l}$, 120.
Williams, Sam$^{l}$, 141.
Williams, Sam$^{l}$, Jun$^{r}$, 120.
Williams, Sam$^{l}$, Jn$^{r}$, 141.
Williams, Sam$^{l}$, 3$^{d}$, 120.
Williams, Samuel W., 52.
Williams, Seth, 118.
Williams, Simeon, 114.
Williams, Simon, 145.
Williams, Solomon, 28.
Williams, Solomon, 36.
Williams, Solomon, 120.
Williams, Solomon, 130.
Williams, Stephen, 92.
Williams, Stephen, 141.
Williams, Thaddeus, 12.
Williams, Theoda, 119.
Williams, Thomas, 58.
Williams, Thomas, 77.
Williams, Thomas, 81.
Williams, Tho$^{s}$, 82.
Williams, Thomas, 116.
Williams, Thomas, 119.
Williams, Thomas, 131.
Williams, Thomas, 145.
Williams, Tho$^{s}$, 148.
Williams, Timothy, 36.
Williams, Timothy, 77.
Williams, Uriah, 116.
Williams, Visalamos, 129.
Williams, Vitch, 145.
Williams, Wait, 63.
Williams, Waram, 91.
Williams, Washam, 116.
Williams, Washam, Jun$^{r}$, 116.
Williams, Weeks, 121.
Williams, Wilks, 138.
Williams, William, 13.
Williams, W$^{m}$, 44.
Williams, William, 52.
Williams, William, 53.
Williams, William, 80.
Williams, William, 108.
Williams, William, 116.
Williams, W$^{m}$, 120.
Williams, W$^{m}$, 138.
Williams, William, Jun$^{r}$, 116.
Williams, William, Ju., 152.
Williams, William, 2$^{d}$, 120.
Williams, William, 3$^{d}$, 145.
Williams, Hon$^{r}$ William, 145.
Williams, Willoby, 108.
Williamson, Caleb, 142.
Williamson, Caleb, Sen$^{r}$, 142.
Williamson, Cornelious, 142.
Williamson, Dorotha, 47.
Williamson, George, 142.

# INDEX.

Williamson, Joseph, 142.
Willington, Noah, 105.
Willis, Eunice, 42.
Willis, Ichabod, 53.
Willis, James, 148.
Willis, James, Jn[r], 148.
Willis, Jamima, 86.
Willis, Jeduthan, 121.
Willis, Joab, 150.
Willis, Joseph, 86.
Willis, Micajah, 148.
Willis, Sarah, 100.
Willis, Seth, 53.
Willis, Will[m], 147.
Willisson, John, 21.
Williston, Consider, 50.
Willman, Zadock, 85.
Willoby, Christopher, 105.
Willoughby, Bliss, 125.
Willoughby, Bridget, 125.
Willoughby, Elijah, 113.
Willoughby, Josiah, 67.
Willoughby, Samuel, 67.
Willoughby, Westil, 67.
Willougheby, Salmon, 57.
Willowbe, Isaac, 154.
Wills, Eleaz[r], 146.
Wills, Gideon, 142.
Wills, Jacob, 152.
Wills, Jonathan, 47.
Wills, Roger, 55.
Wills, Seth, 67.
Wills, Thomas, 116.
Willson, Amos, 15.
Willson, Ann, 15.
Willson, Daniel, 15.
Willson, Elijah, Jun[r], 85.
Willson, Isaac, 14.
Willson, Jesse, 13.
Willson, John, 14.
Willson, John, 84.
Willson, Jonathan, 14.
Willson, Nathanel, Jn[r], 15.
Willson, Robert, 13.
Willson, Silliman, 15.
Willson, Stebbins, 47.
Willson, W[m], 133.
Willson, Zilpah, 37.
Wilman, Jonathan, 85.
Wilmot, Abijah, 109.
Wilmot, Alexander, 74.
Wilmot, Amos, 94.
Wilmot, Asa, 94.
Wilmot, David, 112.
Wilmot, Ebenezer, 105.
Wilmot, Elijah, 94.
Wilmot, Frank, 15.
Wilmot, John, 66.
Wilmot, Jonah, 74.
Wilmot, Joseph, 26.
Wilmot, Samuel, 15.
Wilmot, Samuel, 103.
Wilmot, Silas, 109.
Wilmot, Thomas, 105.
Wilmot, Volantine, 112.
Wilmot, Volantine, 2[nd], 112.
Wilmot, Walter, 112.
Wilmoth, Zopher, 25.
Wilmott, Elijah, 94.
Wilmott, Joel, 94.
Wilmut, Thomas, 35.
Wilson, Abiel, 55.
Wilson, Abijah, 65.
Wilson, Abner, 29.
Wilson, Abner, 58.
Wilson, Abraham, 148.
Wilson, Amos, 16.
Wilson, Amos, 65.
Wilson, Andrew, 143.
Wilson, Benjamin, 15.
Wilson, Benjamin, 93.
Wilson, Calvin, 55.
Wilson, Charles, 24.
Wilson, Daniel, 16.
Wilson, Daniel, 58.
Wilson, David, 16.
Wilson, David, 39.
Wilson, Eben[r], 144.
Wilson, Eli, 58.
Wilson, Elias, 141.
Wilson, Elizabeth (W[d]), 24.
Wilson, Ezekiel, 28.
Wilson, George, 123.
Wilson, Hez[h], 55.
Wilson, Ignatus, 141.
Wilson, Jacob, 138.
Wilson, Jacob, 140.
Wilson, Jacob, Jn[r], 141.
Wilson, James, 150.
Wilson, Jeremiah, 28.
Wilson, Job, 59.
Wilson, Joel, 55.
Wilson, Joel, 55.
Wilson, John, 26.
Wilson, John, 48.
Wilson, John, 60.
Wilson, John, 63.
Wilson, John, 113.
Wilson, Jn[o], 133.
Wilson, John, 150.
Wilson, John, Jn[r], 14.
Wilson, John, 1[st], 58.
Wilson, John, 2[d], 58.
Wilson, Jonathan, 150.
Wilson, Joseph, 16.
Wilson, Joseph, 31.
Wilson, Joseph, 55.
Wilson, Joseph, 62.
Wilson, Jotham, 16.
Wilson, Lucy, 98.
Wilson, Mary (W[d]), 25.
Wilson, Moses, 54.
Wilson, Nathan, 21.
Wilson, Nathaniel, 14.
Wilson, Nath[l], 89.
Wilson, Nehemiah, 16.
Wilson, Nehemiah, Jun[r], 15.
Wilson, Noah, 65.
Wilson, Noah, 65.
Wilson, Peter, 63.
Wilson, Phinehas, 55.
Wilson, Robert, 151.
Wilson, Roger, 68.
Wilson, Rust, 133.
Wilson, Samuel, 13.
Wilson, Sam[l], 150.
Wilson, Sarah, 103.
Wilson, Sharp, 150.
Wilson, Silus, 53.
Wilson, Solomon, 15.
Wilson, Thomas, 28.
Wilson, Thomas, 57.
Wilson, Thomas, 110.
Wilson, Thomas, 129.
Wilson, Uriah, 15.
Wilson, William, 59.
Wilson, William, 66.
Wilson, W[m], 132.
Wilton, Benjamin, 110.
Wilton, Daniel, 69.
Wilton, George, 73.
Wilton, Luther, 34.
Winages, Philip, 67.
Winborne, Prince, 86.
Winchel, Daniel, 69.
Winchel, Daniel, 92.
Winchel, Elihu, 56.
Winchel, Jehiel, 43.
Winchel, Nathaniel, 45.
Winchell, Dan., 49.
Winchell, Elisha, 45.
Winchell, Elisha, Jr, 45.
Winchell, Ezeriah, 92.
Winchell, Grove, 45.
Winchell, Hezekiah, 33.
Winchell, Jehiel, 45.
Winchell, John, 46.
Winchell, Mary, 44.
Winchell, Oliver, 45.
Winchell, Roger, 33.
Winchell, Salmon, 33.
Winchell, Simeon, 44.
Winchell, Solomon, 33.
Winchell, Stephen, 33.
Winchell, William, 33.
Winchester, Amaj[h], 108.
Winchester, Amaziah, 131.
Winchester, Andrew, 142.
Winchester, Andrew, 142.
Winchester, Benj[a], 136.
Winchester, Jabez, 141.
Winchester, Joel, 131.
Winecoop, John, 27.
Winegar, Handriks, 59.
Winegar, Mary, 59.
Winegar, Samuel, 59.
Wing, Charles, 29.
Wing, Lydia, 54.
Wing, Moses, 54.
Wing, Thomas, 19.
Winkley, Henery, 32.
Winshell, John, 46.
Winship, Joseph, 47.
Winship, Philemon, 131.
Winship, Samuel, 46.
Winship, Samuel, 86.
Winslow, Job, 124.
Winslow, Jn[o], 138.
Winslow, William, 114.
Winston, Azariah, 152.
Winston, John, 35.
Winston, John, 107.
Winstone, John, 41.
Winter, Abner, 131.
Winter, Amasa, 151.
Winter, Amos, 114.
Winter, Asa, 142.
Winter, Asa, 151.
Winter, Ebenezer, 114.
Winter, Ephraim, 149.
Winter, Frederick, 114.
Winter, Jacob, 131.
Winter, Jonah, 114.
Winter, Jonathan W., 47.
Winter, Jos., 137.
Winter, Josiah, 141.
Winter, Nathan, 141.
Winter, Nathan, 144.
Winthrop, Ann, 128.
Winthrop, Elisabeth, 129.
Winthrop, Frank, 128.
Winthrop, Mark, 86.
Winton, Abiel, 73.
Winton, Daniel, 20.
Winton, David, 17.
Winton, David, Ju[r], 17.
Winton, Ezra, 31.
Winton, James, 31.
Winton, John, 31.
Winton, Joseph, 31.
Winton, Lockwood, 20.
Winton, Samuel, 17.
Wintor, Weedon, 151.
Wintr, Niolas, 135.
Wintworth, Abigail, 132.
Wintworth, Amos, 114.
Wintworth, Eben[r], 133.
Wintworth, Ezekiel, 133.
Wintworth, Lemuel, 131.
Wintworth, William, 112.
Wire, Aaron, 50.
Wire, Daniel, 50.
Wire, John, 43.
Wire, Nehemiah, 43.
Wire, Thomas, 65.
Wise, John, 104.
Wise, John, Jun[r], 104.
Wise, Rhoda, 104.
Wise, Ruben, 134.
Wise, Samuel, 101.
Wise, Samuel, 104.
Wisland, Amos, Ju., 55.
Wisson, Samuel, 58.
Witbert, Abner, Sr., 148.
Witch, Benjamin, 48.
Witherel, Henry, 81.
Witherell, Jonathan, 80.
Withy, Eunice, 141.
Withy, James, 141.
Witing, Benjamin, 68.
Witmon, Victory, 30.
Witmore, Turrel, 95.
Witter, William, 116.
Witton, Stephen, 59.
Wix, Bartholomew, 25.
Wix, Deborah, 129.
Wix, James, 124.
Wix, John, 16.
Wix, Joseph, 128.
Wix, Rebacah, 63.
Wix, Stephen, 21.
Wllen, David, 70.
Wolcot, Elisha, 105.
Wolcot, Joseph, 112.
Wolcott, Abel, 93.
Wolcott, Albertus, 38.
Wolcott, Benjamin, 37.
Wolcott, Benjamin, 2[d], 39.
Wolcott, Caleb, 54.
Wolcott, Claudeus, 62.
Wolcott, Elezur, 38.
Wolcott, Elisha, 53.
Wolcott, Elisha, J[r] 53.
Wolcott, Epaphras, 38.
Wolcott, Ephraim, 38.
Wolcott, Honererable Erastus, 38.
Wolcott, Erastus, Jr., 38.
Wolcott, George, 54.
Wolcott, Gideon, 38.
Wolcott, Gye, 65.
Wolcott, H., 100.
Wolcott, Henery, 38.
Wolcott, James, 38.
Wolcott, John, 101.
Wolcott, Josiah, 37.
Wolcott, Josiah, 53.
Wolcott, Josiah, 54.
Wolcott, Noah, 100.
Wolcott, Permenis, 37.
Wolcott, Peter, 38.
Wolcott, Roger, 37.
Wolcott, Samuel, 37.
Wolcott, Samuel, 53.
Wolcott, Simon, 39.
Wolcott, Simon, 128.
Wolcott, Solomon, 53.
Wolcott, Solomon, 122.
Wolcott, Theodore, 35.
Wolcott, William, 53.
Wolcutt, Thomas, 106.
Wolf, Christian, 74.
Wolf, Daniel, 60.
Wolford, Jeremiah, 67.
Wollcot, Samuel, 108.
Wollner, Zebulon, 67.
Wooard, John, 77.
Wood, Abner, 137.
Wood, Andrew, 28.
Wood, Augustus, 142.
Wood, Barney, 63.
Wood, Benjamin, 47.
Wood, Benj[n], 146.
Wood, Daniel, 10.
Wood, Dan[l], 136.
Wood, Dan[l], 136.
Wood, Daniel, Jn[r], 10.
Wood, David, 10.
Wood, David, 16.
Wood, David, 122.
Wood, David, 123.
Wood, David, Jun[r], 122.
Wood, Edward, 40.
Wood, Eli, 40.
Wood, Elijah, 12.
Wood, Elijah, 70.
Wood, Elijah, 70.
Wood, Elisabeth, 120.
Wood, Elisha, 152.
Wood, Ephraim A., 150.
Wood, Gophar, 118.
Wood, Harber, 136.
Wood, Isaih, 153.
Wood, James, 10.
Wood, James, 37.
Wood, Jason, 80.
Wood, Joel, 81.
Wood, John, 10.
Wood, John, 11.
Wood, John, 37.
Wood, John, 69.
Wood, John, 119.
Wood, John, 122.
Wood, Jn[o], 136.
Wood, Jn[o], 136.
Wood, John, Jun[r], 119.
Wood, Jonathan, 28.
Wood, Jonathan, 57.
Wood, Joseph, 74.
Wood, Josiah, 136.
Wood, Josiah, 145.
Wood, Lemuel, 16.
Wood, Margarett, 122.
Wood, Mary, 16.
Wood, Mary, 90.
Wood, Mary, 153.
Wood, Miss, 125.
Wood, Nathan, 10.
Wood, Nath[a], 137.
Wood, Nath[a], 137.
Wood, Noah, 148.
Wood, Obadiah, 32.
Wood, Obediah, 37.
Wood, Phinehas, 129.
Wood, Preserve, 10.
Wood, Robert, 37.
Wood, Ruth, 38.
Wood, Samuel, 10.
Wood, Samuel, 12.
Wood, Samuel, 32.
Wood, Samuel, 57.
Wood, Sam[l], 119.
Wood, Sam[l], 147.
Wood, Timothy, 147.
Wood, Timothy, 147.
Wood, William, 119.
Wood, William, Jun[r], 119.
Woodard, Abel, 77.
Woodard, Abisha, 129.
Woodard, Antipas, 77.
Woodard, Asa, 19.
Woodard, Asa, 115.
Woodard, Caleb, 115.
Woodard, Content, 115.
Woodard, David, 59.
Woodard, Edward, 77.
Woodard, Elijah, 77.
Woodard, Israel, 77.
Woodard, John, 129.
Woodard, Lucretia, 119.
Woodard, Moses, 113.
Woodard, Nathan, 77.
Woodard, Park, 115.
Woodard, Ruben, 113.
Woodard, Thomas, 114.
Woodbridge, Ashbel, 39.
Woodbridge, Deodat, 37.
Woodbridge, Howel, 42.
Woodbridge, James, 118.
Woodbridge, Joseph, 47.
Woodbridge, Micha, 119.
Woodbridge, Russell, 36.
Woodbridge, Samuel, 36.
Woodbridge, Samuel, 61.
Woodbridge, Samuel, 131.
Woodbridge, Theodore, 42.
Woodbridge, Theodore, 48.
Woodbridge, Timothy, 121.
Woodbridge, Ward, 36.
Woodbrige, Dudley, 117.
Woodburn, Pruda, 114.
Woodbury, David, 154.
Woodcoalk, W[m], 51.
Woodcock, Israel, 144.
Woodcok, Jonathan, 66.
Woodcok, Sam[l], 66.
Wooden, Amos, 77.
Wooden, Asa, 77.
Wooden, Benjamin, 101.
Wooden, Calvin, 58.
Wooden, Charles, 95.
Wooden, Cyrus, 111.
Wooden, Edmond, 111.
Wooden, Elias, 75.
Wooden, Elizabeth, 111.
Wooden, Eri, 75.
Wooden, Hannah, 101.
Wooden, Hezekiah, 95.
Wooden, Isaac, 101.
Wooden, Jaben, 101.
Wooden, John, 111.
Wooden, Lidia, 100.
Wooden, Millow, 74.
Wooden, Nathaniel, 101.
Wooden, Philo, 74.
Wooden, Stephen, 94.
Wooden, William, 95.
Wooden, William, 2[nd], 95.
Woodford, Amos, 41.
Woodford, Bissel, 33.
Woodford, Charles, 41.
Woodford, Dudley, 41.
Woodford, Elijah, 41.
Woodford, Elijah, 41.
Woodford, Ezekiel, 41.
Woodford, Isaac, 41.
Woodford, John, 35.
Woodford, John, 41.
Woodford, Joseph, 41.
Woodford, Josiah, 35.
Woodford, Levi, 48.
Woodford, Roger, 41.
Woodford, Samuel, 41.
Woodford, Selah, 41.
Woodford, Solomon, 48.
Woodford, W[m], 41.
Woodford, W[m], Jr., 41.
Woodhouse, Abijah, 53.
Woodhouse, Anna, 53.
Woodhouse, John, 53.
Woodhouse, Samuel, 53.
Woodhouse, Samuel, 53.
Woodhouse, William, 53.
Woodhull, Abraham C., 14.
Woodhull, Richard, 104.
Woodhull, Stephen, 29.
Wooding, David, 95.
Woodman, Samuel, 79.
Woodmansee, John, 119.
Woodmansee, Joseph, 119.
Woodrough, Asa, 19.
Woodruf, Gideon, 77.
Woodruf, Jesse, 58.
Woodruf, John, 77.
Woodruf, Samuel, 107.
Woodruff, Aaron, 41.
Woodruff, Aaron, Jr., 41.
Woodruff, Abel, 41.
Woodruff, Amos, 33.
Woodruff, Amos, 50.
Woodruff, Andrew, 59.
Woodruff, Anna, 59.
Woodruff, Appleton, 41.
Woodruff, Asa, 35.
Woodruff, Asa, 49.
Woodruff, Benjamin, 64.
Woodruff, Charles, 59.
Woodruff, D., 83.
Woodruff, Eldad, 41.
Woodruff, Elias, 60.
Woodruff, Elijah, Jr., 41.
Woodruff, Elisha, 41.
Woodruff, Elisha, 49.
Woodruff, Ezekiel, 35.
Woodruff, Ezekiel, Esq[r], 85.
Woodruff, Gad, 33.
Woodruff, Gedar, 41.
Woodruff, Gurdin, 37.
Woodruff, Hezekiah, 60.
Woodruff, Hezekiah, 117.
Woodruff, Isaac, 60.
Woodruff, Isaac, 60.
Woodruff, Jacob, 64.
Woodruff, Jacob, 64.
Woodruff, James, 41.
Woodruff, James, 64.
Woodruff, Jason, 49.
Woodruff, John, 41.
Woodruff, John, 50.
Woodruff, John, 59.
Woodruff, John, 75.
Woodruff, John, Jr., 50.
Woodruff, Jonah, 110.
Woodruff, Jonathan, 49.
Woodruff, Joseph, 41.
Woodruff, Joseph, 41.
Woodruff, Joseph, 102.
Woodruff, Joshua, 41.
Woodruff, Josiah, 69.
Woodruff, Judah, 41.
Woodruff, Lambert, 77.
Woodruff, Levi, 40.
Woodruff, Levi, 65.
Woodruff, Lois, 40.
Woodruff, Lott, 41.
Woodruff, Lydia, 49.
Woodruff, Marten, 62.
Woodruff, Martin, 41.
Woodruff, Mary, 50.
Woodruff, Mather, 102.
Woodruff, Mathew, 102.
Woodruff, Medad, 41.
Woodruff, Micah, 41.
Woodruff, Moses, 41.
Woodruff, Nathaniel, 59.
Woodruff, Nathaniel, 65.
Woodruff, Noah, 41.
Woodruff, Obed, 50.
Woodruff, Oliver, 40.
Woodruff, Oliver, 59.
Woodruff, Phebe, 102.
Woodruff, Philoe, 59.
Woodruff, Phinas, 50.
Woodruff, Reuben, 41.
Woodruff, Robert, 50.
Woodruff, Roswell, 34.
Woodruff, Samuel, 49.
Woodruff, Samuel, 65.
Woodruff, Samuel, 77.
Woodruff, Sarah, 77.
Woodruff, Selah, 34.
Woodruff, Seth, 33.
Woodruff, Seth, 35.
Woodruff, Solomon, 41.
Woodruff, Solomon, 59.

# INDEX.

Woodruff, Solomon, 70.
Woodruff, Thomas, 41.
Woodruff, Timothy, 35.
Woodruff, Timothy, 41.
Woodruff, Timothy, Jr., 35.
Woodruff, W. Right, 64.
Woodruff, W$^m$, 35.
Woodruff, Zebulon, 41.
Woodruk, Barnabas, 101.
Woods, John, 35.
Woods, Ruth, 88.
Woods, Samuell, 102.
Woods, Sarah (W$^d$), 22.
Woods, Stephen, 22.
Woods, Titus, 101.
Woodward, ——, 52.
Woodward, Abner, 139.
Woodward, Abraham, 98.
Woodward, Amos, 138.
Woodward, Caleb, 46.
Woodward, Cathrine, 152.
Woodward, Comfort, 150.
Woodward, Eleaz$^r$, 146.
Woodward, Elias, 148.
Woodward, Elisha, 138.
Woodward, Gaskin, 91.
Woodward, Israel, 146.
Woodward, Israel, Jn$^r$, 146.
Woodward, Jason, 140.
Woodward, John, 64.
Woodward, John, 97.
Woodward, John, 140.
Woodward, John, 150.
Woodward, John, Jun$^r$, 96.
Woodward, Joseph, 140.
Woodward, Moses, 133.
Woodward, Moses H., 86.
Woodward, Nath$^l$, 133.
Woodward, Oliver, 55.
Woodward, Peter, 142.
Woodward, Richard, 102.
Woodward, Rosswell, 98.
Woodward, Samuel, 69.
Woodward, Serenus, 65.
Woodward, Sibbel, 87.
Woodward, Ward, 141.
Woodworth, Arasa, 129.
Woodworth, Amos, 129.
Woodworth, Asa, 126.
Woodworth, Asa, 130.
Woodworth, Asa, Jun$^r$, 130.
Woodworth, Asael, 119.
Woodworth, Benjamin, 126.
Woodworth, Benj$^a$, 2$^d$, 126.
Woodworth, Charles, 137.
Woodworth, Darius, 130.
Woodworth, Ebenez$^r$, 146.
Woodworth, Eliph$^t$, 146.
Woodworth, Jabez, 126.
Woodworth, James, 146.
Woodworth, Jasper, 130.
Woodworth, Jehiel, 146.
Woodworth, Jeremiah, 146.
Woodworth, Jesse, 134.
Woodworth, John, 120.
Woodworth, Joseph, 119.
Woodworth, Joshua, 125.
Woodworth, Jos$^i$, 133.
Woodworth, Lebens, 146.
Woodworth, Oliver, 119.
Woodworth, Peleg, 134.
Woodworth, Sam$^l$, 132.
Woodworth, Simeon, 130.
Woodworth, Swift, 146.
Woodworth, Walter, 145.
Woodworth, Ziba, 126.
Woolcott, Alex$^r$, 54.
Woolcott, Christopher, 55.
Woolcott, George, 55.
Woolcott, Joshua, 80.
Woolcott, Oliver, 65.
Woolcott, Solomon, 55.
Woolcut, Huldah, 53.
Woolf, Samuel, 123.
Woolf, William D., 123.
Wooster, Abel, 95.
Wooster, Abraham, 95.
Wooster, Aurther, 94.
Wooster, Daniel, 94.
Wooster, Daniel, 95.
Wooster, David, 110.
Wooster, Ebenezer, 24.
Wooster, Ebenezer, 95.
Wooster, Ebenezer, 95.
Wooster, Elizabeth, 95.
Wooster, Elizabeth, 110.
Wooster, Ephraim, 17.
Wooster, Eprahim, 94.
Wooster, Henry, 95.
Wooster, Henry, 2$^{nd}$, 95.
Wooster, Isaac, 73.
Wooster, Jabez, 73.
Wooster, Joan, 18.
Wooster, John, 95.
Wooster, John, 2$^{nd}$, 95.
Wooster, Joseph, 95.
Wooster, Joseph L., 18.
Wooster, Marchant, 95.
Wooster, Mary, 102.
Wooster, Mary (W$^d$), 24.
Wooster, Miles, 109.
Wooster, Nathaniel, 94.
Wooster, Samuel, 95.
Wooster, Sylvester, 73.
Wooster, Sylvester, 74.
Wooster, Thomas, 95.
Wooster, Thomas, 102.
Wooster, Walt, 110.
Wooster, Walter, 110.
Wootworth, Timothy, 51.
Worden, Daniel, 115.
Worden, Ebenezer, 62.
Worden, Henry, 118.
Worden, James, 120.
Worden, Joseph, 59.
Worden, Joseph, 120.
Worden, Mary, 117.
Worden, Nath$^l$, 115.
Worden, Roger, 16.
Worden, Sitorster, 115.
Worden, Thomas, 77.
Worden, Walter, 116.
Wordon, Wait, 127.
Work, Alexander, 149.
Work, Josiah, Sen$^r$, 141.
Works, Hen$^y$, 139.
Works, Ingolsby, 141.
Works, John, 140.
Works, Joseph, 140.
Worter, Benjamin, 66.
Worter, Samuel, 66.
Worthey, Benjamin, 62.
Worthington, Abigail, 121.
Worthington, Asa, 120.
Worthington, Dan, 114.
Worthington, Dan, 125.
Worthington, Elias, 81.
Worthington, Elijah, 122.
Worthington, Erastus, 121.
Worthington, Gad, 121.
Worthington, Joel, 122.
Worthington, John, 109.
Worthington, Sarah, 125.
Worthington, W$^m$, 90.
Worthington, William, 122.
Worthinton, Elizabeth, 108.
Woster, Peter, 73.
Woston, John, 74.
Wrathbun, Daniel, 44.
Wright, Aaron, 37.
Wright, Abel, 19.
Wright, Abijah, 54.
Wright, Abraham, 34.
Wright, Amaziah, 148.
Wright, Amos, 77.
Wright, Ann, 33.
Wright, Ashbel, 52.
Wright, Asher, 96.
Wright, Azariah, 121.
Wright, Benjamin, 43.
Wright, Benjamin, 53.
Wright, Benjamin, 85.
Wright, Benjamin, 98.
Wright, Benj$^a$, 90.
Wright, Benj$^n$, 140.
Wright, Charles, 54.
Wright, Charles, 146.
Wright, Chloe, 147.
Wright, Daniel, 43.
Wright, Daniel, 53.
Wright, Daniel, 100.
Wright, David, 52.
Wright, David, 126.
Wright, Dennis, 23.
Wright, Dennis, 26.
Wright, Dudley, 120.
Wright, Ebenezer, 52.
Wright, Eben$^r$, 140.
Wright, Ebenez$^r$, 148.
Wright, Eleaz$^r$, 148.
Wright, Elezur, 40.
Wright, Elijah, 52.
Wright, Elijah, 133.
Wright, Elijah, 2$^d$, 133.
Wright, Elisha, 62.
Wright, Elizur, 53.
Wright, Enos, 93.
Wright, Enos, 135.
Wright, Ephraim, 62.
Wright, Esther, 54.
Wright, Ezekiel, 63.
Wright, Ezekiel, 90.
Wright, Grace, 85.
Wright, Hannah, 86.
Wright, Henry, 24.
Wright, Isaac, 42.
Wright, Jabez, 65.
Wright, Jabez, 146.
Wright, James, 66.
Wright, James, 85.
Wright, Jeremiah, 44.
Wright, Jerem$^h$, 90.
Wright, Jeremiah, N$^o$ 1, 62.
Wright, Jeriah, 146.
Wright, Jiles, 54.
Wright, Job, Esq$^r$, 85.
Wright, Joel, 146.
Wright, John, 44.
Wright, John, 57.
Wright, John, 80.
Wright, John, 121.
Wright, Jonas, 80.
Wright, Jonathan, 60.
Wright, Jonathan, 64.
Wright, Joseph, 33.
Wright, Joseph, 43.
Wright, Joseph, 96.
Wright, Joseph, 2$^{nd}$, 96.
Wright, Joseph Allen, 77.
Wright, Josiah, 52.
Wright, Josiah, 90.
Wright, Josiah, Jr., 52.
Wright, Jude, 135.
Wright, Justus, 51.
Wright, Martin, 90.
Wright, Mehitable, 121.
Wright, Mehitable, 146.
Wright, Moses, 53.
Wright, Moses, 64.
Wright, Mosses, 95.
Wright, Nathan, 85.
Wright, Nathan, 140.
Wright, Nathaniel, 53.
Wright, Nath$^el$, 133.
Wright (Negro), 122.
Wright, Obadiah, 23.
Wright, Reuben, 33.
Wright, Reuben, 85.
Wright, Samuel, 42.
Wright, Sam$^l$, 81.
Wright, Sam$^l$, 90.
Wright, Samuel, 96.
Wright, Samuel, 108.
Wright, Sam$^l$, 135.
Wright, Sam$^l$, 136.
Wright, Sam$^l$, 142.
Wright, Sam$^l$, 143.
Wright, Seth, 69.
Wright, Uring, 45.
Wright, William, 80.
Write, Lucy, 53.
Write, Sam$^l$, 138.
Wyard, Lemuel, 33.
Wyatt, Sarah (W$^d$), 26.
Wyldur, Jonathan, 63.
Wyles, David, 36.
Wyles, David, 122.
Wyles, John, 36.
Wyles, Thomas, 36.
Wyley, John, 151.
Wyley, Joseph, 151.
Wyley, Moses, 151.
Wyllis, William, 128.
Wyllys, George, 47.
Wyllys, John, 37.
Wyllys, Samuel, 46.
Wyman, Ebenezer, 51.
Wyman, Solomon, 47.
Wynkoop, Grisel, 12.
Wynkoop, James, 14.

Yabecomb, Gilbart, 28.
Yale, Amassa, 108.
Yale, Amiton, 107.
Yale, Anna, 107.
Yale, Ashal, 107.
Yale, Daniel, 107.
Yale, Elihu, 108.
Yale, Elisha, 61.
Yale, Elisha, 2$^d$, 61.
Yale, Elsa, 66.
Yale, Hannah, 109.
Yale, James, 62.
Yale, Job, 92.
Yale, Joel, 107.
Yale, Joel, 108.
Yale, John, 106.
Yale, Jonathan, 107.
Yale, Joseph, 131.
Yale, Nathaniel, 107.
Yale, Nathaniel, 107.
Yale, Nathaniel, 107.
Yale, Noah, 107.
Yale, Noah, 107.
Yale, Osiers, 92.
Yale, Samuel, 108.
Yale, Stephen, 107.
Yale, Thomas, 94.
Yate, Abel, 34.
Yate, Ezra, 35.
Yate, Thomas, 34.
Yates, Aaron, 66.
Yates, John, 17.
Yates, Paul, 19.
Yeamons, Elizabeth, 107.
Yemmons, Daniel, 117.
Yemmons, David, 121.
Yemmons, Moses, 117.
Yemmons, Sam$^l$, 113.
Yemmons, Sarah, 121.
Yemmons, Thomas, 115.
Yeoman, John, 107.
Yeomans, Daniel, 145.
Yeomans, Giles, 146.
Yeomans, John, 140.
Yeomans, Joshua, 130.
Yerrington, Abraham, 113.
Yerrington, Ezekiel, 119.
Yerrington, Joseph, 115.
Yerrington, Ruben, 113.
Yongue, Moses, 138.
Yonguer, Eb$^{nr}$, 136.
York, Allen, 116.
York, Bel, 115.
York, Bel, Jun$^r$, 115.
York, Collins, 115.
York, Elisha, 114.
York, James, 115.
York, Jesse, 116.
York, John, 116.
York (Negro), 116.
York (Negro), 123.
York (Negro), 124.
York, Oliver, 116.
Yorke, Henry, 103.
Young, Asaph, 83.
Young, Caleb, 143.
Young, Daniel, 30.
Young, David, 145.
Young, Elijah, 80.
Young, Ezekel, 143.
Young, Happy, 109.
Young, James, 129.
Young, James, 129.
Young, Joel, 144.
Young, John, 131.
Young, Jonah, 152.
Young, Joseph, 85.
Young, Joseph, 128.
Young, Mary (W$^d$), 26.
Young, Nabby, 131.
Young, Nicholas, 115.
Young, Robart, 121.
Young, Robert, 26.
Young, Samuel, 26.
Young, Samuel, 80.
Young, Sam$^l$, 152.
Young, Sylvanus, 87.
Young, Thomas, 131.
Young, Thomas, 140.
Young, William, 57.
Young, William, 152.
Young, William, 152.
Younges, Richard, 22.
Younges, Samuel, 26.
Youngher, John, 66.
Youngs, Abraham, 24.
Youngs, Benjamin, 25.
Youngs, Benjamin, 67.
Youngs, Clemence, 25.
Youngs, Joshua, 41.
Youngs, Othoniel, 143.
Youngs, Samuel, 67.
Youngs, Soloman, 60.
Youngs, William, 60.
Youngslove, Sam$^l$, 66.

Zants, Monsieur, 129.
Zicke, 66.
Zimri (Negro), 12.
Zitaw, Jehon, 59.

——, Nathan, 45.

www.ingramcontent.com/pod-product-compliance
Lightning Source LLC
Chambersburg PA
CBHW042352070526
44585CB00028B/2897